SOCIAL SECURITY LEGISLATION 2024/25

VOLUME I: NON MEANS TESTED BENEFITS

SOCIAL SECURITY LEGISLATION 2024/25

General Editor
Nick Wikeley, M.A. (Cantab)

VOLUME I: NON MEANS TESTED BENEFITS

Commentary By

Ian Hooker, LL.B.
Formerly Lecturer in Law, University of Nottingham,
Formerly Chairman, Social Security Tribunals

John Mesher, B.A., B.C.L. (Oxon), LL.M. (Yale)
Retired Judge of the Upper Tribunal
Emeritus Professor of Law, University of Sheffield

Edward Mitchell, LL.B.
Judge of the Upper Tribunal

Christopher Ward, M.A. (Cantab)
Judge of the Upper Tribunal

Nick Wikeley, M.A. (Cantab)
Judge of the Upper Tribunal,
Emeritus Professor of Law, University of Southampton

Consultant Editor
Child Poverty Action Group

Sweet & Maxwell

Thomson Reuters™

Published in 2024 by Thomson Reuters, trading as Sweet & Maxwell.
Registered in England & Wales, Company No.1679046.
Registered Office and address for service: 5 Canada Square,
Canary Wharf, London, E14 5AQ.

For further information on our products and services, visit
http://www.sweetandmaxwell.co.uk.

Typeset by Cheshire Typesetting Ltd, Cuddington, Cheshire
Printed and bound by CPI Group (UK) Ltd, Croydon, CR0 4YY

FSC
www.fsc.org
MIX
Paper | Supporting
responsible forestry
FSC® C013604

A CIP catalogue record for this book is available from the British Library.

ISBN (print): 978-0-414-12147-8
ISBN (e-book): 978-0-414-12149-2
ISBN (print and e-book): 978-0-414-12148-5

Thomson Reuters, the Thomson Reuters Logo and
Sweet & Maxwell® are trademarks of Thomson Reuters.

CHILD POVERTY ACTION GROUP

The Child Poverty Action Group (CPAG) is a charity, founded in 1965, which campaigns for the relief of poverty in the United Kingdom. It has a particular reputation in the field of welfare benefits law derived from its legal work, publications, training and parliamentary and policy work, and is widely recognised as the leading organisation for taking test cases on social security law.

CPAG is therefore ideally placed to act as Consultant Editor to this 5-volume work—**Social Security Legislation**. CPAG is not responsible for the detail of what is contained in each volume, and the authors' views are not necessarily those of CPAG. The Consultant Editor's role is to act in an advisory capacity on the overall structure, focus and direction of the work.

For more information about CPAG, its rights and policy publications or training courses, its address is 30 Micawber Street, London, N1 7TB (telephone: 020 7837 7979—website: *http://www.cpag.org.uk*).

FOREWORD

These volumes of the *Social Security Legislation* are an indispensable resource for the judiciary of the First-tier Tribunal (Social Entitlement Chamber) and all those involved in social security proceedings. Along with expert commentaries, they provide comprehensive, up-to-date and learned coverage of this vast and complex field of law. Given the scale and complexity of the legislation and the continuing development of the jurisprudence by the Upper Tribunal and appellate courts, the subject matter would be practically inaccessible without these books. As ever, I am grateful to the authors and to Sweet and Maxwell for their continued commitment to producing them each year.

Judge Kate Markus KC
Chamber President of the First-tier Tribunal,
Social Entitlement Chamber

PREFACE

Non-Means Tested Benefits is Volume I of *Social Security Legislation 2024/25*. The companion volumes are Volume II: *Universal Credit, State Pension Credit and the Social Fund;* Volume III: *Administration, Adjudication and the European Dimension;* Volume IV: *HMRC-administered Social Security Benefits and Scotland*; and (from 2021/22) Volume V: *Income Support and the Legacy Benefits*. The "year" in the title of the works relates to the tax/contribution year, and conveys the period the books (and the mid-year Supplement) are designed to cover.

Three years ago we began the process of restructuring the series to reflect the fact that Universal Credit (UC) has now become the default means-tested benefit in the social security system. This has resulted in some re-ordering of material across the Volumes to provide readers with a clear and coherent explanation (at least so far as we can) of the various social security benefits (see further the Note on Restructuring the Social Security Legislation Series at p.xi of last year's edition of this Volume).

Each of the volumes in the series provides the text of benefits legislation in Great Britain, clearly showing the form and date of amendments, and is up to date to April 11, 2024. This year has seen relatively little change to primary legislation. However, this edition includes the usual miscellany of detailed amendments made by secondary legislation to the scope of the benefits system. More generally, so far as developments in the case law since the previous edition are concerned, the burgeoning jurisprudence of the Upper Tribunal continues to provide clarification in respect of the conditions of entitlement to social security benefits, especially for personal independence payment (PIP). The commentary provides extensive and in-depth analysis of such developments. Where possible, the commentary includes references to some later case law since April 11, 2024.

As always, revising and updating the legislative text and commentary has required considerable flexibility on the part of the publisher and a great deal of help from a number of sources, including CPAG as advisory editor to the series. We remain grateful for this assistance in our task of providing an authoritative reflection on the current state of the law. To maximise space for explanatory commentary in books which seem to grow in size year on year, we have provided lists of definitions only where the commentary on the provision is substantial, or where reference to definitions is essential for a proper understanding. Users of the books should always check whether particular words or phrases they are called upon to apply have a particular meaning ascribed to them in legislation. Generally, the first or second regulation in each set of regulations contains definitions of key terms (check the "Arrangement of Regulations" at the beginning of each set for an indication of the subject matter covered by each regulation). There are also definition or "interpretation" sections in primary legislation.

Users of the series, and its predecessor works, have over the years contributed to their effectiveness by providing valuable comments on our commentary, as well as pointing out where the text of some provision has been omitted in error, or become garbled, or not been brought fully up to date. In some cases, this has drawn attention to an error which might otherwise have gone unnoticed. In providing such feedback, users of the work have helped to shape the content and ensure the accuracy of our material. We hope that users of the work will continue to provide such helpful input and feedback. This is all the more important given the major restructuring of the series that has taken place. Please write to the General Editor of the series, Emeritus Professor Nick Wikeley, c/o School of Law, University of Southampton, Highfield, Southampton SO17 1BJ, e-mail njw@soton.ac.uk, and he will pass on any comments received to the appropriate commentator.

Our gratitude also goes to the Chamber President of the Social Entitlement Chamber of the First-tier Tribunal and her colleagues there for continuing the now long tradition of help and encouragement in our endeavours.

Last, but by no means least, we wish to recognise that the 2023/24 main edition of Vol.III in this series was the last for which Mark Rowland had a direct responsibility (although much of what he has written will undoubtedly continue to feature in the book for many editions to come). The current editors of all the volumes would like to take this opportunity to pay tribute to Mark's tremendous contribution to the series as a whole since 1993, when he first produced the volume on *Medical and Disability Appeal Tribunals* that went into three editions before the restructuring of the series in 2000. In that restructuring, he took on joint responsibility with Robin White for Vol.III, *Administration, Adjudication and the European Dimension*. Thus, for more than 20 years Mark has brought his formidable knowledge and experience of social security law and adjudication, from his work as an advocate, as a part-time chair of appeal tribunals and then as a Social Security Commissioner and later Upper Tribunal Judge to bear on the often opaque legislative material on administration, decision-making and appeals. As readers will know, his gift for clarity of exposition enabled his commentary both to bring out matters of principle and to provide practical guidance to tribunals and users with an appreciation of the way problems actually arise. More behind the scenes, Mark's contribution to the way in which the series as a whole has developed, from wise advice about the needs of readers to knowledge of why choices were or were not made over the years, cannot be overstated. The current editors will greatly miss having that wisdom and experience on tap.

August 2024

Ian Hooker
John Mesher
Ed Mitchell
Christopher Ward
Nick Wikeley

CONTENTS

PART I
STATUTES

REGULATIONS

PART II
CONTRIBUTION CREDITS AND HOME RESPONSIBILITIES PROTECTION

PART III
REGULATIONS COMMON TO SEVERAL BENEFITS

PART IV
DISABILITY BENEFITS

PART V
MATERNITY BENEFITS

PART VI
PENSIONS, SURVIVORS' BENEFITS AND GRADUATED RETIREMENT BENEFIT

PART VII
NEW STYLE JOBSEEKER'S ALLOWANCE

PART VIII
NEW STYLE EMPLOYMENT AND SUPPORT ALLOWANCE

PART IX
LIMITED CAPABILTY FOR WORK AND LIMITED CAPABILITY FOR WORK-RELATED ACTIVITY FOR "OLD-STYLE" EMPLOYMENT AND SUPPORT ALLOWANCE

PART X
INDUSTRIAL INJURIES AND PRESCRIBED DISEASES

PART XI
MESOTHELIOMA LUMP SUM PAYMENTS

PART XII
VACCINE DAMAGE PAYMENTS

USING THIS BOOK: AN INTRODUCTION TO LEGISLATION AND CASE LAW

Introduction

This book is not a general introduction to, or general textbook on, the law relating to social security but it is nonetheless concerned with both of the principal sources of social security law—*legislation* (both primary and secondary) and *case law*. It sets out the text of the most important legislation, as currently in force, and then there is added commentary that refers to the relevant case law. Lawyers will be familiar with this style of publication, which inevitably follows the structure of the legislation.

This note is designed primarily to assist readers who are not lawyers to find their way around the legislation and to understand the references to case law, but information it contains about how to find social security case law is intended to be of assistance to lawyers too.

Primary legislation

Primary legislation of the United Kingdom Parliament consists of *Acts of Parliament* (also known as *Statutes*). They will have been introduced to Parliament as *Bills*. There are opportunities for Members of Parliament and peers to debate individual clauses and to vote on amendments before a Bill is passed and becomes an Act (at which point the clauses become sections). No tribunal or court has the power to disapply, or hold to be invalid, an Act of Parliament, although, until December 31, 2020, that could be done if it was inconsistent with European Union law.

An Act is known by its "short title", which incorporates the year in which it was passed (e.g. the Social Security Contributions and Benefits Act 1992), and is given a chapter number (abbreviated as, for instance, "c.4" indicating that the Act was the fourth passed in that year). It is seldom necessary to refer to the chapter number but it appears in the running headers in this book.

Each *section* (abbreviated as "s." or, in the plural, "ss.") of an Act is numbered and may be divided into *subsections* (abbreviated as "subs." and represented by a number in brackets), which in turn may be divided into *paragraphs* (abbreviated as "para." and represented by a lower case letter in brackets) and *subparagraphs* (abbreviated as "subpara." and represented by a small roman numeral in brackets). Subparagraph (ii) of para.(a) of subs. (1) of s.72 will usually be referred to simply as "s.72(1)(a)(ii)". Upper case letters may be used where additional sections or subsections are inserted by amendment and additional lower case letters may be used where new paragraphs and subparagraphs are inserted. This accounts for the rather ungainly s.109B(2A)(aa) of the Social Security Administration Act 1992.

Sections of a large Act may be grouped into a numbered *Part*, which may even be divided into *Chapters*. It is not usual to refer to a Part or a Chapter unless referring to the whole Part or Chapter.

Where a section would otherwise become unwieldy because it is necessary to include a list or complicated technical provisions, the section may simply refer to a *Schedule* at the end of the Act. A Schedule (abbreviated as "Sch.") may be divided into paragraphs and subparagraphs and further divided into heads and subheads. Again, it is usual to refer simply to, say, "para.23(3)(b)(ii) of Sch.3". Whereas it is conventional to speak of a section *of* an Act, it is usual to speak of a Schedule *to* an Act.

Secondary legislation

Secondary legislation (also known as *subordinate legislation* or *delegated legislation*) is made by *statutory instrument* in the form of a set of *Regulations* or a set of *Rules* or an *Order*. The power to make such legislation is conferred on ministers and other persons or bodies by Acts of Parliament. To the extent that a statutory instrument is made beyond the powers (in Latin, *ultra vires*) conferred by primary legislation, it may be held by a tribunal or court to be invalid and ineffective. Secondary legislation must be laid before Parliament. However, most secondary legislation is not debated in Parliament and, even when it is, it cannot be amended although an entire statutory instrument may be rejected.

A set of Regulations or Rules or an Order has a name indicating its scope and the year it was made and also a number, as in the Social Security (Disability Living Allowance) Regulations 1991 (SI 1991/2890) (the 2890th statutory instrument issued in 1991). Because there are over a thousand statutory instruments each year, the number of a particular statutory instrument is important as a means of identification and it should usually be cited the first time reference is made to that statutory instrument.

Sets of Regulations or Rules are made up of individual *regulations* (abbreviated as "reg.") or *rules* (abbreviated as "r." or, in the plural, "rr."). An Order is made up of *articles* (abbreviated as "art."). Regulations, rules and articles may be divided into paragraphs, subparagraphs and heads. As in Acts, a set of Regulations or Rules or an Order may have one or more Schedules attached to it. The style of numbering used in statutory instruments is the same as in sections of, and Schedules to, Acts of Parliament. As in Acts, a large statutory instrument may have regulations or rules grouped into Parts and, occasionally, Chapters. Statutory instruments may be amended in the same sort of way as Acts.

Scottish legislation

Most of the social security legislation passed by the United Kingdom Parliament applies throughout Great Britain, i.e. in England, Wales and Scotland, but a separate Scottish social security system is gradually being developed and relevant legislation is included in Volume IV in this series. Acts of the Scottish Parliament are similar to Acts of the United Kingdom Parliament and Scottish Statutory Instruments are also similar to their United Kingdom counterparts. One minor difference is that "schedule" usually has a lower case "s" and references are to a schedule *of* an Act, rather than *to* an Act.

Northern Ireland legislation

Most of the legislation set out in this series applies only in Great Britain, social security not generally being an excepted or reserved matter in relation to Northern Ireland. However, Northern Irish legislation—both primary legislation, most relevantly in the form of *Orders in Council* (which, although statutory instruments, had the effect of primary legislation in Northern Ireland while there was direct rule from Westminster and still do when made under the Northern Ireland (Welfare Reform) Act 2015) and *Acts of the Northern Ireland Assembly*, and subordinate legislation, in the form of *statutory rules*—largely replicates legislation in Great Britain so that much of the commentary in this book will be applicable to equivalent provisions in Northern Ireland legislation. Although there has latterly been a greater reluctance in Northern Ireland to maintain parity with Great Britain, one example of which led to some delay in enacting legislation equivalent to the Welfare Reform Act 2012, this is usually resolved politically by, for instance, the allocation of funds to allow the effects of some of the changes to be mitigated in Northern Ireland while the broad legislative structure remains similar.

European Union legislation

European Union primary legislation is in the form of the *Treaties* agreed by the Member States. Relevant subordinate legislation is in the form of *Regulations*, adopted to give effect to the provisions of the Treaties, and *Directives*, addressed to Member States and requiring them to incorporate certain provisions into their domestic laws. Directives are relevant because, where a person brings proceedings against an organ of the State, as is invariably the case where social security is concerned, that person may rely on the Directive as having direct effect if the Member State has failed to comply with it. Treaties, Regulations and Directives are divided into *Articles* (abbreviated as "Art.").

While the United Kingdom was a Member State of the European Union, United Kingdom legislation that was inconsistent with European Union legislation had to be disapplied. The United Kingdom ceased to be a Member State on January 31, 2020, but the effect of the European Union (Withdrawal Act) 2018, as amended in 2020, is that, with very limited exceptions, European Union law continued to apply in the United Kingdom during the implementation period ending on December 31, 2020. After that date, European Union law remains relevant only to the extent that United Kingdom legislation so provides. For instance, the 2018 Act, as amended, provides for the enforcement of the Withdrawal Agreement, under which rights acquired by individuals before the end of the implementation period may be retained.

Finding legislation in this book

If you know the name of the piece of legislation for which you are looking, use the list of contents at the beginning of each volume of this series which lists the pieces of legislation contained in the volume. That will give you the paragraph reference to enable you to find the beginning of the piece of legislation. Then, it is easy to find the relevant section, regulation, rule, article or Schedule by using the running headers on the right hand pages. If you do not know the name of the piece of legislation, you will probably need to use the index at the end of the volume in order to find the relevant paragraph number but will then be taken straight to a particular provision.

The legislation is set out as amended, the amendments being indicated by numbered sets of square brackets. The numbers refer to the numbered entries under the heading "AMENDMENTS" at the end of the relevant section, regulation, rule, article or Schedule, which identify the amending statute or statutory instrument. Where an Act has been consolidated, there is a list of "DERIVATIONS" identifying the provisions of earlier legislation from which the section or Schedule has been derived.

As regards the European Union, United Kingdom legislation concerned with the consequences of the United Kingdom's withdrawal is set out in Part V of Volume III in this series, together with relevant extracts from the Withdrawal Agreement and the Social Security Protocol to the Trade and Cooperation Agreement. Following the extracts from the Withdrawal Agreement is up-dating commentary on the European Union legislation that is set out in Part III of the 2020–21 edition of Volume III. Readers are encouraged to retain that volume so as to be able to find the main text of relevant European Union legislation there.

Finding other legislation

United Kingdom legislation and legislation made by the legislatures in Scotland, Wales and Northern Ireland may now be found on *http://www.legislation.gov.uk* in both its original form and (usually) its amended form. Northern Ireland social security legislation may also be found at *https://www.communities-ni.gov.uk/services/law-relating-social-security-northern-ireland-blue-volumes*. European Union legislation may be found at *https://eur-lex.europa.eu/homepage.html*.

Interpreting legislation

Legislation is written in English (or, at least, there is an official English version) and generally means what it says. However, languages being complicated, more than one interpretation is often possible. Most legislation itself contains definitions. Sometimes these are in the particular provision in which a word occurs but, where a word is used in more than one place, any definition will appear with others. In an Act, an interpretation section is usually to be found towards the end of the Act or of the relevant Part of the Act. In a statutory instrument, an interpretation provision usually appears near the beginning of the statutory instrument or the relevant Part of it. In the more important pieces of legislation in this series, there is included after every section, regulation, rule, article or Schedule a list of "DEFINITIONS", showing where definitions of words used in the provision are to be found.

However, not all words are statutorily defined and there is in any event more to interpreting legislation than merely defining its terms (see the note to s.3(1) of the Tribunals, Courts and Enforcement Act 2007 in Part III of Volume III of this series). Decision-makers and tribunals need to know how to apply the law in different types of situations. That is where case law comes in.

Case law and the commentary in this book

In deciding individual cases, courts and tribunals interpret the relevant law and incidentally establish legal principles. Decisions on questions of legal principle of the superior courts and appellate tribunals are said to be binding on decision-makers and the First-tier Tribunal, which means that decision-makers and the First-tier Tribunal must apply those principles. Thus the judicial decisions of the superior courts and appellate tribunals form part of the law. The commentary to the legislation in this series, under the heading "GENERAL NOTE" after a section, regulation, rule, article or Schedule, refers to this *case law*.

Most case law regarding social security benefits is in the form of decisions of the Upper Tribunal (Administrative Appeals Chamber), to which the functions of the former Social Security Commissioners and Child Support Commissioners in Great Britain were transferred on November 3, 2008. However, decisions of those Commissioners remain relevant, as are decisions of the Commissioners who still sit in Northern Ireland.

The commentary in this series is not itself binding on any decision-maker or tribunal because it is merely the opinion of the author. It is what is actually said in the legislation or in the judicial decision that is important. The legislation is set out in this series, but it will generally be necessary to look elsewhere for the precise words used in judicial decisions. The way that decisions are cited in the commentary enables that to be done.

The reporting of decisions of the Upper Tribunal and Commissioners

A few of the most important decisions of the Administrative Appeals Chamber of the Upper Tribunal are selected to be "reported" each year in the Administrative Appeals Chamber Reports (AACR), using the same criteria as were formerly used for reporting Commissioners' decisions in Great Britain. The selection is made by an editorial board of judges and decisions are selected for reporting only if they are of general importance and command the assent of at least a majority of the relevant judges. The term "reported" simply means that they are published in printed form as well as on the Internet (see *Finding case law*, below) with headnotes (i.e. summaries) and indexes, but reported decisions also have a greater precedential status than ordinary decisions (see *Judicial precedent* below).

A handful of Northern Ireland Commissioners' decisions are also selected for reporting in the Administrative Appeals Chamber Reports each year, the selection being made by the Chief Social Security Commissioner in Northern Ireland.

Citing case law

As has been mentioned, much social security case law is still to be found in decisions of Social Security Commissioners and Child Support Commissioners, even though the Commissioners have now effectively been abolished in Great Britain.

Reported decisions of Commissioners were known merely by a number or, more accurately, a series of letters and numbers beginning with an "R". The type of benefit in issue was indicated by letters in brackets (e.g. "IS" was income support, "P" was retirement pension, and so on) and the year in which the decision was selected for reporting or, from 2000, the year in which it was published as a reported decision, was indicated by the last two digits, as in *R(IS) 2/08*. In Northern Ireland there was a similar system until 2009, save that the type of benefit was identified by letters in brackets after the number, as in *R 1/07 (DLA)*.

Unreported decisions of the Commissioners in Great Britain were known simply by their file numbers, which began with a "C", as in *CIS/2287/2008*. The letters following the "C" indicated the type of benefit in issue in the case. Scottish and, at one time, Welsh cases were indicated by a "S" or "W" immediately after the "C", as in *CSIS/467/2007*. The last four digits indicated the calendar year in which the case was registered, rather than the year it was decided. A similar system operated in Northern Ireland until 2009, save that the letters indicating the type of benefit appeared in brackets after the numbers and, from April 1999, the financial year rather than the calendar year was identified, as in *C 10/06-07 (IS)*.

Decisions of the Upper Tribunal, of courts and, since 2010, of the Northern Ireland Commissioners are generally known by the names of the parties (or just two of them in multi-party cases). In social security and some other types of cases, individuals are anonymised through the use of initials in the names of decisions of the Upper Tribunal and the Northern Ireland Commissioners. Anonymity is much rarer in the names of decisions of courts. In this series, the names of official bodies are also abbreviated in the names of decisions of the Upper Tribunal and the Northern Ireland Commissioners (e.g. "SSWP" for the Secretary of State for Work and Pensions, "HMRC" for Her/His Majesty's Revenue and Customs, "CMEC" for the Child Maintenance and Enforcement Commission, "DSD" for the Department for Social Development in Northern Ireland and "DC" for the Department for Communities in Northern Ireland). Since 2010, such decisions have also been given a "flag" in brackets to indicate the subject matter of the decision, which in social security cases indicates the principal benefit in issue in the case. Thus, the name of one universal credit case is *SSWP v AJ (UC)*.

Any decision of the Upper Tribunal, of a court since 2001 or of a Northern Ireland Commissioner since 2010 that has been intended for publication has also given a neutral citation number which enables the decision to be more precisely identified. This indicates, in square brackets, the year the decision was made (although in relation to decisions of the courts it sometimes merely indicates the year the number was issued) and also indicates the court or tribunal that made the decision (e.g. "UKUT" for the Upper Tribunal (which sits in Great Britain for social security purposes but throughout the United Kingdom for some others), "UT" for the separate Upper Tribunal for Scotland, "NICom" for a Northern Ireland Commissioner, "EWCA Civ" for the Civil Division of the Court of Appeal in England and Wales, "NICA" for the Court of Appeal in Northern Ireland, "CSIH" for the Inner House of the Court of Session (in Scotland), "UKSC" for the Supreme Court and so on). A number is added so that the reference is unique and finally, in the case of the Upper Tribunal or the High Court in England and Wales, the relevant chamber of the Upper Tribunal or the relevant division or other part of the High Court is identified (e.g."(AAC)" for the Administrative Appeals Chamber, "(Admin)" for the Administrative Court and so on). Examples of decisions of the Upper

Tribunal and a Northern Ireland Commissioner with their neutral citation numbers are *SSWP v AJ (UC)* [2020] UKUT 48 (AAC) and *AR v DSD (IB)* [2010] NICom 6.

If the case is reported in the Administrative Appeals Chamber Reports or another series of law reports, a reference to the report usually follows the neutral citation number. Conventionally, this includes either the year the case was decided (in round brackets) or the year in which it was reported (in square brackets), followed by the volume number (if any), the name of the series of reports (in abbreviated form, so see the Table of Abbreviations at the beginning of each volume of this series) and either the page number or the case number. However, before 2010, cases reported in the Administrative Appeals Chamber Reports or with Commissioners' decisions were numbered in the same way as reported Commissioners' decisions. *Abdirahman v Secretary of State for Work and Pensions* [2007] EWCA Civ 657; [2008] 1 W.L.R. 254 (also reported as *R(IS) 8/07*) is a Court of Appeal decision, decided in 2007 but reported in 2008 in volume 1 of the Weekly Law Reports at page 254 and also in the 2007 volume of reported Commissioners' decisions. *NT v SSWP* [2009] UKUT 37 (AAC); *R(DLA) 1/09* is an Upper Tribunal case decided in 2009 and reported in the Administrative Appeals Chamber Reports in the same year. *Martin v Secretary of State for Work and Pensions* [2009] EWCA Civ 1289; [2010] AACR 9 is a decision of the Court of Appeal that was decided in 2009 and was the ninth decision reported in the Administrative Appeals Chamber Reports in 2010.

It is usually necessary to include the neutral citation number or a reference to a series of reports only the first time a decision is cited in any document. After that, the name of the case is usually sufficient.

All decisions of the Upper Tribunal that are on their website have neutral citation numbers. If you wish to refer a tribunal or decision-maker to a decision of the Upper Tribunal that does not have a neutral citation number, contact the office of the Administrative Appeals Chamber (*adminappeals@justice.gov.uk*) who will provide a number and add the decision to the website.

Decision-makers and claimants are entitled to assume that judges of both the First-tier Tribunal and the Upper Tribunal have immediate access to reported decisions of Commissioners or the Upper Tribunal and they need not provide copies, although it may sometimes be helpful to do so. However, where either a decision-maker or a claimant intends to rely on an unreported decision, it will be necessary to provide a copy of the decision to the judge and other members of the tribunal. A copy of the decision should also be provided to the other party before the hearing because otherwise it may be necessary for there to be an adjournment to enable that party to take advice on the significance of the decision.

Finding case law

The extensive references described above are used so as to enable people easily to find the full text of a decision. Most decisions of any significance since the late 1990s can be found on the Internet.

Decisions of the Upper Tribunal may be found at *https://www.gov.uk/administrative-appeals-tribunal-decisions*. The link from that page to "decisions made in 2015 or earlier" leads also to decisions of the Commissioners in Great Britain. This includes reported decisions since 1991 and other decisions considered likely to be of interest to tribunals and tribunal users since about 2000, together with a few older decisions. Decisions of Commissioners in Northern Ireland may be found on *https://iaccess.communities-ni.gov.uk/NIDOC*.

The Administrative Appeals Chamber Reports are also published by the Stationery Office in bound volumes which follow on from the bound volumes of Commissioners' decisions published from 1948.

Copies of decisions of the Administrative Appeals Chamber of the Upper Tribunal or of Commissioners that are otherwise unavailable may be obtained from the offices of the Upper Tribunal (Administrative Appeals Chamber) or, in Northern Ireland, from the Office of the Social Security and Child Support Commissioners.

Decisions of a wide variety of courts and tribunals in the United Kingdom may be found on the free website of the British and Irish Legal Information Institute, *http://www.bailii.org*. It includes all decisions of the Supreme Court and provides fairly comprehensive coverage of decisions given since about 1996 by the House of Lords and Privy Council and most of the higher courts in England and Wales, decisions given since 1998 by the Court of Session and decisions given since 2000 by the Court of Appeal and High Court in Northern Ireland. Some earlier decisions have been included, so it is always worth looking and, indeed, those decisions dating from 1873 or earlier and reported in the English Reports may be found through a link to *http://www.commonlii.org/uk/cases/EngR/*. Since 2022, decisions of the Upper Tribunal, the Employment Appeal Tribunal and most courts that sit in England and Wales are also to be found on The National Archives' website at *caselaw.nationalarchives.gov.uk/structured_search*. However, courts and tribunals that sit only in Wales, Scotland or Northern Ireland are not included there. Decisions of the Upper Tribunal for Scotland and of Scottish courts can be found at *https://www.scotcourts.gov.uk*.

Decisions of the Court of Justice of the European Union are all to be found at *https://curia.europa.eu*.

Decisions of the European Court of Human Rights are available at *https://www.echr.coe.int*.

Most decisions of the courts in social security cases, including decisions of the Court of Justice of the European Union on cases referred by United Kingdom courts and tribunals, are reported in the Administrative Appeals Chamber Reports or with the reported decisions of Commissioners and may therefore be found on the same websites and in the same printed series of reported decisions. So, for example, *R(I)1/00* contains Commissioner's decision *CSI/12/1998*, the decision of the Court of Session upholding the Commissioner's decision and the decision of the House of Lords in *Chief Adjudication Officer v Faulds*, reversing the decision of the Court of Session. The most important decisions of the courts can also be found in the various series of law reports familiar to lawyers (in particular, in the *Law Reports*, the *Weekly Law Reports*, the *All England Law Reports*, the *Public and Third Sector Law Reports*, the *Industrial Cases Reports* and the *Family Law Reports*) but these are not widely available outside academic or other law libraries, or subscription-based websites. See the Table of Cases at the beginning of each volume of this series for all the places where a decision mentioned in that volume is reported.

If you know the name or number of a decision and wish to know where in a volume of this series there is a reference to it, use the Table of Cases or the Table of Commissioners' Decisions 1948–2009 in the relevant volume to find the paragraph(s) where the decision is mentioned.

Judicial precedent

As already mentioned, decisions of the Upper Tribunal, the Commissioners and the higher courts in Great Britain become case law because they set binding precedents which must be followed by decision-makers and the First-tier Tribunal in Great Britain. This means that, where the Upper Tribunal, Commissioner or court has decided a point of legal principle, decision-makers and appeal tribunals must make their decisions in conformity with the decision of the Upper Tribunal, Commissioner or court, applying the same principle and accepting the interpretation of the law contained in the decision. So a decision of the Upper Tribunal, a Commissioner or a superior court explaining what a term in a particular regulation means, lays down the definition of that term in much the same way as if the term had been defined in the regulations themselves. The decision may also help in deciding what the same term means when it is used in a different set of regulations, provided that the term appears to have been used in a similar context.

Only decisions on points of law set precedents that are binding and, strictly speaking, only decisions on points of law that were necessary to the overall conclusion reached by the Upper Tribunal, Commissioner or court are binding. Other parts of a decision (which used to be known as obiter dicta) may be regarded as helpful guidance but need not be followed if a decision-maker or the First-tier Tribunal is persuaded that there is a better approach. It is particularly important to bear this in mind in relation to older decisions of Social Security Commissioners because, until 1987, most rights of appeal to a Commissioner were not confined to points of law.

Where there is a conflict between precedents, a decision-maker or the First-tier Tribunal is generally free to choose between decisions of equal status. For these purposes, most decisions of the Upper Tribunal and decisions of Commissioners are of equal status. However, a decision-maker or First-tier Tribunal should generally prefer a reported decision to an unreported one unless the unreported decision was the later decision and the Commissioner or Upper Tribunal expressly decided not to follow the earlier reported decision. This is simply because the fact that a decision has been reported shows that at least half of the relevant judges of the Upper Tribunal or the Commissioners agreed with it at the time. A decision of a Tribunal of Commissioners (i.e. three Commissioners sitting together) or a decision of a three-judge panel of the Upper Tribunal must be preferred to a decision of a single Commissioner or a single judge of the Upper Tribunal.

A single judge of the Upper Tribunal will normally follow a decision of a single Commissioner or another judge of the Upper Tribunal, but is not bound to do so. A three-judge panel of the Upper Tribunal will generally follow a decision of another such panel or of a Tribunal of Commissioners, but similarly is not bound to do so, whereas a single judge of the Upper Tribunal will always follow such a decision.

Strictly speaking, the Northern Ireland Commissioners do not set binding precedent that must be followed in Great Britain but their decisions are relevant, due to the similarity of the legislation in Northern Ireland, and are usually regarded as highly persuasive with the result that, in practice, they are generally given as much weight as decisions of the Great Britain Commissioners. The same approach is taken in Northern Ireland to decisions of the Upper Tribunal on social security matters and to decisions of the Great Britain Commissioners. Similarly, the Upper Tribunal and the Upper Tribunal for Scotland are likely to find each other's decisions persuasive where the issues are the same, or similar.

Decisions of the superior courts in Great Britain and Northern Ireland on questions of legal principle are almost invariably followed by decision-makers, tribunals and the Upper Tribunal, even when they are not strictly binding because the relevant court was in a different part of the United Kingdom or exercised a parallel – but not superior – jurisdiction.

Decisions of the Court of Justice of the European Union come in two parts: the Opinion of the Advocate General and the decision of the Court. It is the decision of the Court which is binding. The Court is assisted by hearing the Opinion of the Advocate General before itself coming to a conclusion on the issue before it. The Court does not always follow its Advocate General. Where it does, the Opinion of the Advocate General often elaborates the arguments in greater detail than the single collegiate judgment of the Court. Within the European Union, courts and tribunals must apply decisions of the Court of Justice of the European Union, where relevant to cases before them, in preference to other authorities binding on them. This is no longer so in the United Kingdom, but it will still be necessary for courts and tribunals in the United Kingdom to take account of such decisions when issues of European Union law are relevant, and they are arguably bound by a decision of the Court of Justice on the interpretation of the Citizens' Rights provisions of the Withdrawal Agreement.

The European Court of Human Rights in Strasbourg is quite separate from the Court of Justice of the European Union in Luxembourg and serves a different purpose: interpreting and applying the European Convention on Human Rights, which is incorporated into United Kingdom law by the Human Rights Act 1998. Since October 2, 2000, public authorities in the United Kingdom, including courts, Commissioners, tribunals and decision-makers have been required to act in accordance with the incorporated provisions of the Convention, unless statute prevents this. They must take into account the Strasbourg case law and are required to interpret domestic legislation, so far as it is possible to do so, to give effect to the incorporated Convention rights. Any court or tribunal may declare secondary legislation incompatible with those rights and, in certain circumstances, invalidate it. Only the higher courts can declare a provision of primary legislation to be incompatible with those rights, but no court, tribunal or Upper Tribunal can invalidate primary legislation. The work of the Strasbourg Court and the impact of the Human Rights Act 1998 on social security are discussed in the commentary in Part IV of Volume III of this series.

See the note to s.3(2) of the Tribunals, Courts and Enforcement Act 2007 in Part III of Volume III of this series for a more detailed and technical consideration of the rules of precedent.

Other sources of information and commentary on social security law

For a comprehensive overview of the social security system in Great Britain, CPAG's *Welfare Benefits and Tax Credits Handbook*, published annually each spring, is unrivalled as a practical introduction from the claimant's viewpoint.

From a different perspective, the Department for Work and Pensions publishes the 14-volume *Decision Makers' Guide* and the newer *Advice for Decision Making*, which covers personal independence payment, universal credit and the "new" versions of Jobseeker's Allowance and Employment and Support Allowance (search for the relevant guide by name at *https://www.gov.uk* under the topic "Welfare"). Similarly, His Majesty's Revenue and Customs publish manuals relating to tax credits, child benefit and guardian's allowance, which they administer, see *https://www.gov.uk/government/collections/hmrc-manuals*. (Note that the *Child Benefit Technical Manual* also covers guardian's allowance.) These guides and manuals are extremely useful but their interpretation of the law is not binding on tribunals and the courts, being merely internal guidance for the use of decision-makers.

There are a number of other sources of valuable information or commentary on social security case law: see in particular publications such as the *Journal of Social Security Law*, CPAG's *Welfare Rights Bulletin*, *Legal Action* and the *Adviser*. As far as online resources go there is little to beat *Rightsnet* (*https://www.rightsnet.org.uk*). This site contains a wealth of resources for people working in the welfare benefits field but of special relevance in this context are Commissioners'/Upper Tribunal Decisions section of the "Toolkit" area and also the "Briefcase" area which contains summaries of the decisions (with links to the full decisions). Sweet and Maxwell's online subscription service *Westlaw* is another valuable source (*https://legalsolutions.thomsonreuters.co.uk/en/products-services/westlaw-uk.html*), as is LexisNexis *Lexis* (*https://www.lexisnexis.co.uk*).

Conclusion

The internet provides a vast resource but a search needs to be focused. Social security schemes are essentially statutory and so in Great Britain the legislation which is set out in this series forms the basic structure of social security law. However, the case law shows how the legislation should be interpreted and applied. The commentary in this series should point the way to the case law relevant to each provision and the Internet can then be used to find it where that is necessary.

CHANGE OF NAME FROM DEPARTMENT OF SOCIAL SECURITY TO DEPARTMENT FOR WORK AND PENSIONS

The Secretaries of State for Education and Skills and for Work and Pensions Order 2002 (SI 2002/1397) makes provision for the change of name from the Department of Social Security to Department for Work and Pensions. Article 9(5) provides:

"(5) Subject to article 12 [which makes specific amendments], any enactment or instrument passed or made before the coming into force of this Order shall have effect, so far as may be necessary for the purposes of or in consequence of the entrusting to the Secretary of State for Work and Pensions of the social security functions, as if any reference to the Secretary of State for Social Security, to the Department of Social Security or to an officer of the Secretary of State for Social Security (including any reference which is to be construed as such as reference) were a reference to the Secretary of State for Work and Pensions, to the Department for Work and Pensions or, as the case may be, to an officer of the Secretary of State for Work and Pensions."

CHANGES IN TERMINOLOGY CONSEQUENT UPON THE ENTRY INTO FORCE OF THE TREATY OF LISBON

The Treaty of Lisbon (Changes in Terminology) Order 2011 (SI 2011/1043) (which came into force on April 22, 2011) makes a number of changes to terminology used in primary and secondary legislation as a consequence of the entry into force of the Treaty of Lisbon on December 1, 2009. The Order accomplishes this by requiring certain terms in primary and secondary legislation to be read in accordance with the requirements of the Order. No substantive changes to the law are involved.

The changes are somewhat complex because of the different ways in which the term "Community" is used, and the abbreviations "EC" or "EEC" are used. References to the "European Community", "European Communities", "European Coal and Steel Communities", "the Community", "the EC", and "the EEC" are generally to be read as references to the "European Union".

The following table shows the more common usages involving the word "Community" in the first column which are now to be read in the form set out in the second column:

Original term	**To be read as**
Community treaties	EU treaties
Community institution	EU institution
Community instrument	EU instrument
Community obligation	EU obligation
Enforceable Community right	Enforceable EU right
Community law, or European Community law	EU law
Community legislation, or European Community legislation	EU legislation
Community provision, or European Community provision	EU provision

Provision is also made for changes to certain legislation relating to Wales in the Welsh language.

Relevant extracts from the Order can be found in Vol.III, *Administration, Adjudication and the European Dimension.*

THE MARRIAGE (SAME SEX COUPLES) ACT 2013

The Marriage (Same Sex Couples) Act 2013 (c.30) provides in s.3 and Schedules 3 and 4 that the terms 'marriage', 'married couple' and being 'married' in existing and future legislation in England and Wales are to be read as references to a marriage between persons of the same sex. The same approach is taken to any legislation about couples living together as if married. This is subject to certain specified exclusions contained in Sch.4, and in any Order providing for a contrary approach to be taken.

Sch.2 to The Marriage (Same Sex Couples) Act 2013 (Consequential and Contrary provisions and Scotland) Order 2014 (SI 2014/560) contains a substantial list of contrary provisions to s.11(1) and (2) and paras 1 to 3 of Sch.3 to the 2013 Act. Most of these relate to specific enactments, but note that Pt 2 of the Schedule provides that s.11(1) and (2) do not apply to "EU instruments". This term is defined in Sch.1 to the European Communities Act 1972 (as amended) as "any instrument issued by an EU institution". It refers mainly to regulations, directives, decisions, recommendations and opinions issued by the institutions.

TABLE OF CASES

A-K v Secretary of State for Work and Pensions (DLA) [2017] UKUT 420 (AAC); [2018] 1 W.L.R. 2657; [2017] 10 WLUK 325 .... 4.35
AA v Secretary of State for Work and Pensions (JSA) [2012] UKUT 100 (AAC); [2012] AACR 42 .... 1.707, 1.708
AA v Secretary of State for Work and Pensions (PIP) [2018] UKUT 339 (AAC) 4.257
AB v Secretary of State for Work and Pensions (DLA) [2015] UKUT 522 (AAC) **1.233**
AB v Secretary of State for Work and Pensions (DLA) [2015] UKUT 89 (AAC) 1.1002
AB v Secretary of State for Work and Pensions (ESA) [2012] UKUT 151 (AAC) **9.110**
AB v Secretary of State for Work and Pensions (ESA) [2016] UKUT 96 (AAC) **9.116**
AB v Secretary of State for Work and Pensions (PIP) [2017] UKUT 217 (AAC) 4.177, 4.253
AC v Secretary of State for Work and Pensions (DLA) [2009] UKUT 83 (AAC) 1.213
AC v Secretary of State for Work and Pensions (PIP) [2021] UKUT 216 (AAC) 4.252
AD v Secretary of State for Work and Pensions (DLA) [2017] UKUT 29 (AAC) 1.239
AD v Secretary of State for Work and Pensions (ESA) [2011] UKUT 307 (AAC) 9.10
AD v Secretary of State for Work and Pensions (II) [2019] UKUT 198 (AAC) 10.162
Adjudication Officer v Bath R(G) 1/00 .... 1.1102
AF v Secretary of State for Work and Pensions (ESA) [2011] UKUT 61 (AAC) 9.99
AG v Secretary of State for Work and Pensions (ESA) [2013] UKUT 77 (AAC) 9.99
AG v Secretary of State for Work and Pensions (ESA) [2017] UKUT 413 (AAC) 9.102
AG v Secretary of State for Work and Pensions (ESA) [2018] UKUT 137 (AAC) 9.105
AH v Secretary of State for Work and Pensions (DLA) [2012] UKUT 387 (AAC) 1.240, 4.94, 4.95, 4.239
AH v Secretary of State for Work and Pensions (ESA) [2011] UKUT 333 (AAC) 9.10, 9.96, 9.111
AH v Secretary of State for Work and Pensions (ESA) [2013] UKUT 118 (AAC); [2013] AACR 32 .... **9.73**, 9.74, 9.77, 9.102, **9.124**
AH v Secretary of State for Work and Pensions (PIP) [2016] UKUT 147 (AAC) 4.252
AH v Secretary of State for Work and Pensions (PIP) [2016] UKUT 276 (AAC) 4.244
AH v Secretary of State for Work and Pensions (PIP) [2016] UKUT 541 (AAC) **4.184**
AH v Secretary of State for Work and Pensions [2016] UKUT 558 (AAC) 1.207
AI v Secretary of State for Work and Pensions (DLA) [2015] UKUT 176 (AAC) 4.240
AI v Secretary of State for Work and Pensions (PIP) [2016] UKUT 322 (AAC) 4.238, **4.240**
AI v Secretary of State for Work and Pensions (PIP) [2019] UKUT 103 (AAC) 4.188
AJ v Secretary of State for Work and Pensions (ESA) [2013] UKUT 279 (AAC) **9.48**
AJ v Secretary of State for Work and Pensions (II) [2012] UKUT 209 (AAC) 1.570
AK v Secretary of State for Work and Pensions (ESA) [2013] UKUT 435 (AAC) 9.74
AK v Secretary of State for Work and Pensions (PIP) [2015] UKUT 620 (AAC) 4.184
AK v Secretary of State for Work and Pensions (PIP) [2016] UKUT 256 (AAC) 4.172, 4.245
Akhter v Khan and the Attorney General. *See* NA v MSK
AL v Secretary of State for Work and Pensions (ESA) [2011] UKUT 512 (AAC) 9.21, 9.27
AM v Secretary of State for Work and Pensions (DLA) [2013] UKUT 94 (AAC) 1.709
AM v Secretary of State for Work and Pensions (ESA) [2013] UKUT 458 (AAC) 9.98
AM v Secretary of State for Work and Pensions (PIP) [2017] UKUT 7 (AAC) 4.252
Amwell View School Governors v Dogherty [2006] 9 WLUK 205; [2007] I.C.R. 135; [2007] I.R.L.R. 198 EAT 4.188
AP v Secretary of State for Work and Pensions (ESA) [2013] UKUT 293 (AAC) **9.118**
AP v Secretary of State for Work and Pensions (ESA) [2013] UKUT 553 (AAC) 9.74
AP v Secretary of State for Work and Pensions (ESA) [2014] UKUT 35 (AAC) 9.74
AP v Secretary of State for Work and Pensions (PIP) [2016] UKUT 416 (AAC) 4.174, 4.186
AP v Secretary of State for Work and Pensions (PIP) [2016] UKUT 501 (AAC) **4.172**, **4.248**, 4.259
Appleby v Chief Adjudication Officer R(I)5/99 .... 10.150

TABLE OF SOCIAL SECURITY COMMISSIONERS' DECISIONS

TABLE OF ABBREVIATIONS USED IN THIS SERIES

1975 Act	Social Security Act 1975
1977 Act	Marriage (Scotland) Act 1977
1979 Act	Pneumoconiosis (Workers' Compensation) Act 1979
1986 Act	Social Security Act 1986
1996 Act	Employment Rights Act 1996
1998 Act	Social Security Act 1998
2002 Act	Tax Credits Act 2002
2004 Act	Gender Recognition Act 2004
2006 Act	Armed Forces Act 2006
2008 Act	Child Maintenance and Other Payments Act 2008
2013 Act	Marriage (Same Sex Couples) Act 2013
2014 Act	Marriage and Civil Partnership (Scotland) Act 2014
A1P1	Art.1 of Protocol 1 to the European Convention on Human Rights
AA	Attendance Allowance
AA 1992	Attendance Allowance Act 1992
AAC	Administrative Appeals Chamber
AACR	Administrative Appeals Chamber Reports
A.C.	Law Reports, Appeal Cases
A.C.D.	Administrative Court Digest
Admin	Administrative Court
Admin L.R.	Administrative Law Reports
Administration Act	Social Security Administration Act 1992
Administration Regulations	Statutory Paternity Pay and Statutory Adoption Pay (Administration) Regulations 2002
AIP	assessed income period
All E.R.	All England Reports
All E.R. (E.C.)	All England Reports (European Cases)
AMA	Adjudicating Medical Authorities
AO	Adjudication Officer
AOG	*Adjudication Officers Guide*
art.	article
Art.	Article
ASD	Autistic Spectrum Disorder
ASPP	Additional Statutory Paternity Pay

ASVG	Allgemeines Sozialversicherungsgesetz (General Social Security Act)
A.T.C.	Annotated Tax Cases
Attendance Allowance Regulations	Social Security (Attendance Allowance) Regulations 1991
AWT	All Work Test
BA	Benefits Agency
Benefits Act	Social Security Contributions and Benefits Act 1992
B.H.R.C.	Butterworths Human Rights Cases
B.L.G.R.	Butterworths Local Government Reports
Blue Books	*The Law Relating to Social Security*, Vols 1–11
B.P.I.R.	Bankruptcy and Personal Insolvency Reports
BSVG	Bauern-Sozialversicherungsgesetz (Social Security Act for Farmers)
B.T.C.	British Tax Cases
BTEC	Business and Technology Education Council
B.V.C.	British Value Added Tax Reporter
B.W.C.C.	Butterworths Workmen's Compensation Cases
c.	chapter
C	Commissioner's decision
C&BA 1992	Social Security Contributions and Benefits Act 1992
CAA 2001	Capital Allowances Act 2001
CAB	Citizens Advice Bureau
CAO	Chief Adjudication Officer
CB	Child Benefit
CBA 1975	Child Benefit Act 1975
CBJSA	Contribution-Based Jobseeker's Allowance
C.C.L. Rep.	Community Care Law Reports
CCM	HMRC *New Tax Credits Claimant Compliance Manual*
C.E.C.	European Community Cases
CERA	cortical evoked response audiogram
CESA	Contribution-based Employment and Support Allowance
CFS	chronic fatigue syndrome
Ch.	Chancery Division Law Reports; Chapter
Citizenship Directive	Directive 2004/38/EC of the European Parliament and of the Council of April 29, 2004
CJEC	Court of Justice of the European Communities
CJEU	Court of Justice of the European Union
Claims and Payments Regulations	Social Security (Claims and Payments) Regulations 1987
Claims and Payments Regulations 1979	Social Security (Claims and Payments) Regulations 1979

Claims and Payments Regulations 2013	Universal Credit, Personal Independence Payment, Jobseeker's Allowance and Employment and Support Allowance (Claims and Payments) Regulations 2013
CM	Case Manager
CMA	Chief Medical Adviser
CMEC	Child Maintenance and Enforcement Commission
C.M.L.R.	Common Market Law Reports
C.O.D.	Crown Office Digest
COLL	*Collective Investment Schemes Sourcebook*
Community, The	European Community
Computation of Earnings Regulations	Social Security Benefit (Computation of Earnings) Regulations 1978
Computation of Earnings Regulations 1996	Social Security Benefit (Computation of Earnings) Regulations 1996
Consequential Provisions Act	Social Security (Consequential Provisions) Act 1992
Contributions and Benefits Act	Social Security Contributions and Benefits Act 1992
Contributions Regulations	Social Security (Contributions) Regulations 2001
COPD	chronic obstructive pulmonary disease
CP	Carer Premium; Chamber President
CPAG	Child Poverty Action Group
CPR	Civil Procedure Rules
Cr. App. R.	Criminal Appeal Reports
CRCA 2005	Commissioners for Revenue and Customs Act 2005
Credits Regulations 1974	Social Security (Credits) Regulations 1974
Credits Regulations 1975	Social Security (Credits) Regulations 1975
Crim. L.R.	Criminal Law Review
CRU	Compensation Recovery Unit
CSA 1995	Children (Scotland) Act 1995
CSIH	Inner House of the Court of Session (Scotland)
CSM	Child Support Maintenance
CS(NI)O 1995	Child Support (Northern Ireland) Order 1995
CSOH	Outer House of the Court of Session (Scotland)
CSPSSA 2000	Child Support, Pensions and Social Security Act 2000
CTA	Common Travel Area
CTA 2009	Corporation Tax Act 2009
CTA 2010	Corporation Tax Act 2010
CTB	Council Tax Benefit
CTC	Child Tax Credit
CTC Regulations	Child Tax Credit Regulations 2002
CTF	child trust fund

CTS	Carpal Tunnel Syndrome
DAC	Directive 2011/16/ EU (Directive on administrative co-operation in the field of taxation)
DAT	Disability Appeal Tribunal
dB	decibels
DCA	Department for Constitutional Affairs
DCP	Disabled Child Premium
Decisions and Appeals Regulations 1999	Social Security Contributions (Decisions and Appeals) Regulations 1999
Dependency Regulations	Social Security Benefit (Dependency) Regulations 1977
DfEE	Department for Education and Employment
DHSS	Department of Health and Social Security
Disability Living Allowance Regulations	Social Security (Disability Living Allowance) Regulations
DIY	do it yourself
DLA	Disability Living Allowance
DLA Regs 1991	Social Security (Disability Living Allowance) Regulations 1991
DLAAB	Disability Living Allowance Advisory Board
DLADWAA 1991	Disability Living Allowance and Disability Working Allowance Act 1991
DM	Decision Maker
DMA	Decision-making and Appeals
DMG	*Decision Makers' Guide*
DMP	Delegated Medical Practitioner
DP	Disability Premium
DPP	Director of Public Prosecutions
DPT	diffuse pleural thickening
DPTC	Disabled Person's Tax Credit
DRO	Debt Relief Order
DSD	Department for Social Development (Northern Ireland)
DSM IV; DSM-5	Diagnostic and Statistical Manual of Mental Disorders of the American Psychiatric Association
DSS	Department of Social Security
DTI	Department of Trade and Industry
DWA	Disability Working Allowance
DWP	Department for Work and Pensions
DWPMS	Department for Work and Pensions Medical Service
EAA	Extrinsic Allergic Alveolitis
EAT	Employment Appeal Tribunal
EC	European Community
ECHR	European Convention on Human Rights

ECJ	European Court of Justice
E.C.R.	European Court Reports
ECSC	European Coal and Steel Community
ECSMA	European Convention on Social and Medical Assistance
EEA	European Economic Area
EEC	European Economic Community
EESSI	Electronic Exchange of Social Security Information
E.G.	Estates Gazette
E.G.L.R.	Estates Gazette Law Reports
EHC plan	education, health and care plan
EHIC	European Health Insurance Card
EHRC	European Human Rights Commission
E.H.R.R.	European Human Rights Reports
EL	employers' liability
E.L.R	Education Law Reports
EMA	Education Maintenance Allowance
EMP	Examining Medical Practitioner
Employment and Support Allowance	Employment and Support Allowance
Regulations	Regulations 2008
EPS	extended period of sickness
Eq. L.R.	Equality Law Reports
ERA	evoked response audiometry
ERA scheme	Employment, Retention and Advancement scheme
ES	Employment Service
ESA	Employment and Support Allowance
ESA Regs 2013	Employment and Support Allowance Regulations 2013
ESA Regulations	Employment and Support Allowance Regulations 2008
ESA WCAt	Employment and Support Allowance Work Capability Assessment
ESC	employer supported childcare
ESE Scheme	Employment, Skills and Enterprise Scheme
ESE Regulations	Jobseeker's Allowance (Employment, Skills and Enterprise Scheme) Regulations 2011
ESES Regulations	Jobseeker's Allowance (Employment, Skills and Enterprise Scheme) Regulations 2011
ETA 1973	Employment and Training Act 1973
ETA(NI) 1950	Employment and Training Act (Northern Ireland) 1950
ETS	European Treaty Series
EU	European Union
Eu.L.R.	European Law Reports

EWCA Civ	Civil Division of the Court of Appeal (England and Wales)
EWHC Admin	Administrative Court Division of the High Court (England and Wales)
FA 1993	Finance Act 1993
FA 1996	Finance Act 1996
FA 2004	Finance Act 2004
Fam. Law	Family Law
FAS	Financial Assistance Scheme
FCDO	Foreign, Commonwealth and Development Office
F.C.R.	Family Court Reporter
FEV	forced expiratory volume
FIS	Family Income Supplement
FISMA 2000	Financial Services and Markets Act 2000
F.L.R.	Family Law Reports
FME	further medical evidence
F(No.2)A 2005	Finance (No.2) Act 2005
FOTRA	Free of Tax to Residents Abroad
FRAA	flat rate accrual amount
FRS Act 2004	Fire and Rescue Services Act 2004
FSCS	Financial Services Compensation Scheme
FTT	First-tier Tribunal
General Benefit Regulations 1982	Social Security (General Benefit) Regulations 1982
General Regulations	Statutory Shared Parental Pay (General) Regulations 2014
GMC	Group Medical Coverage
GMCA	Greater Manchester Combined Authority
GMFRA	Greater Manchester Fire and Rescue Authority
GMP	Guaranteed Minimum Pension
GMWDA	Greater Manchester Waste Disposal Authority
GNVQ	General National Vocational Qualification
GP	General Practitioner
GRA	Gender Recognition Act 2004
GRB	Graduated Retirement Benefit
GRP	Graduated Retirement Pension
GSVG	Gewerbliches Sozialversicherungsgesetz (Federal Act on Social Insurance for Persons engaged in Trade and Commerce)
HB	Housing Benefit
HB (WSP) R (NI) 2017	Housing Benefit (Welfare Social Payment) Regulations (Northern Ireland) 2017
HBRB	Housing Benefit Review Board
HCA	Homes and Communities Agency
HCD	House of Commons Debates

HCP	healthcare professional
HCV	Hepatitis C virus
Health Service Act	National Health Service Act 2006
Health Service (Wales) Act	National Health Service (Wales) Act 2006
HIV	Human Immunodeficiency Virus
HL	House of Lords
H.L.R.	Housing Law Reports
HMIT	His Majesty's Inspector of Taxes
HMRC	His Majesty's Revenue and Customs
HMSO	His Majesty's Stationery Office
Hospital In-Patients Regulations 1975	Social Security (Hospital In-Patients) Regulations 1975
HP	Health Professional
HPP	Higher Pensioner Premium
HRA 1998	Human Rights Act 1998
H.R.L.R.	Human Rights Law Reports
HRP	Home Responsibilities Protection
HSE	Health and Safety Executive
IAC	Immigration and Asylum Chamber
IAP	Intensive Activity Period
IB	Incapacity Benefit
IB PCA	Incapacity Benefit Personal Capability Assessment
IB Regs	Social Security (Incapacity Benefit) Regulations 1994
IB Regulations	Social Security (Incapacity Benefit) Regulations 1994
IB/IS/SDA	Incapacity Benefits Regime
IBJSA	Income-Based Jobseeker's Allowance
IBS	Irritable Bowel Syndrome
ICA	Invalid Care Allowance
I.C.R.	Industrial Cases Reports
ICTA 1988	Income and Corporation Taxes Act 1988
IFW Regulations	Incapacity for Work (General) Regulations 1995
IH	Inner House of the Court of Session
I.I.	Industrial Injuries
IIAC	Industrial Injuries Advisory Council
IIDB	Industrial Injuries Disablement Benefit
ILO	International Labour Organization
Imm. A.R.	Immigration Appeal Reports
Incapacity for Work Regulations	Social Security (Incapacity for Work) (General) Regulations 1995
Income Support General Regulations	Income Support (General) Regulations 1987
IND	Immigration and Nationality Directorate of the Home Office

I.N.L.R.	Immigration and Nationality Law Reports
I.O.	Insurance Officer
IPPR	Institute of Public Policy Research
IRESA	Income-Related Employment and Support Allowance
I.R.L.R.	Industrial Relations Law Reports
IS	Income Support
IS Regs	Income Support Regulations
IS Regulations	Income Support (General) Regulations 1987
ISA	Individual Savings Account
ISBN	International Standard Book Number
ITA 2007	Income Tax Act 2007
ITEPA 2003	Income Tax, Earnings and Pensions Act 2003
I.T.L. Rep.	International Tax Law Reports
I.T.R.	Industrial Tribunals Reports
ITS	Independent Tribunal Service
ITTOIA 2005	Income Tax (Trading and Other Income) Act 2005
IVB	Invalidity Benefit
IW (General) Regs	Social Security (Incapacity for Work) (General) Regulations 1995
IW (Transitional) Regs	Incapacity for Work (Transitional) Regulations
Jobseeker's Allowance Regulations	Jobseeker's Allowance Regulations 1996
Jobseeker's Regulations 1996	Jobseeker's Allowance Regulations 1996
JSA	Jobseeker's Allowance
JSA 1995	Jobseekers Act 1995
JSA (NI) Regulations	Jobseeker's Allowance (Northern Ireland) Regulations 1996
JSA (Transitional) Regulations	Jobseeker's Allowance (Transitional) Regulations 1996
JSA Regs 1996	Jobseeker's Allowance Regulations 1996
JSA Regs 2013	Jobseeker's Allowance Regulations 2013
JS(NI)O 1995	Jobseekers (Northern Ireland) Order 1995
J.S.S.L.	Journal of Social Security Law
J.S.W.L.	Journal of Social Welfare Law
K.B.	Law Reports, King's Bench
L.& T.R.	Landlord and Tenant Reports
LCW	limited capability for work
LCWA	Limited Capability for Work Assessment
LCWRA	limited capability for work-related activity
LDEDC Act 2009	Local Democracy, Economic Development and Construction Act 2009
LEA	local education authority
LEL	Lower Earnings Limit
LET	low earnings threshold
L.G. Rev.	Local Government Review

L.G.L.R.	Local Government Reports
L.J.R.	Law Journal Reports
LRP	liable relative payment
L.S.G.	Law Society Gazette
Luxembourg Court	Court of Justice of the European Union (also referred to as CJEC and ECJ)
MA	Maternity Allowance
MAF	Medical Assessment Framework
Maternity Allowance Regulations	Social Security (Maternity Allowance) Regulations 1987
MDC	Mayoral development corporation
ME	myalgic encephalomyelitis
Medical Evidence Regulations	Social Security (Medical Evidence) Regulations 1976
MEN	Mandatory Employment Notification
Mesher and Wood	*Income Support, the Social Fund and Family Credit: the Legislation* (1996)
M.H.L.R.	Mental Health Law Reports
MHP	mental health problems
MIF	minimum income floor
MIG	minimum income guarantee
Migration Regulations	Employment and Support Allowance (Transitional Provisions, Housing Benefit and Council Tax Benefit (Existing Awards) (No.2) Regulations 2010
MP	Member of Parliament
MRSA	methicillin-resistant Staphylococcus aureus
MS	Medical Services
MWA Regulations	Jobseeker's Allowance (Mandatory Work Activity Scheme) Regulations 2011
MWAS Regulations	Jobseeker's Allowance (Mandatory Work Activity Scheme) Regulations 2011
NCB	National Coal Board
NDPD	Notes on the Diagnosis of Prescribed Diseases
NHS	National Health Service
NI	National Insurance
N.I..	Northern Ireland Law Reports
NICA	Northern Ireland Court of Appeal
NICom	Northern Ireland Commissioner
NICs	National Insurance Contributions
NINO	National Insurance Number
NIRS 2	National Insurance Recording System
N.L.J.	New Law Journal
NMC	Nursing and Midwifery Council
Northern Ireland Contributions and Benefits Act	Social Security Contributions and Benefits (Northern Ireland) Act 1992
N.P.C.	New Property Cases

NRCGT	non-resident capital gains tax
NTC Manual	Clerical procedures manual on tax credits
NUM	National Union of Mineworkers
NUS	National Union of Students
OCD	obsessive compulsive disorder
Ogus, Barendt and Wikeley	A. Ogus, E. Barendt and N. Wikeley, *The Law of Social Security* (1995)
Old Cases Act	Industrial Injuries and Diseases (Old Cases) Act 1975
OPB	One Parent Benefit
O.P.L.R.	Occupational Pensions Law Reports
OPSSAT	Office of the President of Social Security Appeal Tribunals
Overlapping Benefits Regulations	Social Security (Overlapping Benefits) Regulations 1975
P	retirement pension case
P. & C.R.	Property and Compensation Reports
para.	paragraph
Pay Regulations	Statutory Paternity Pay and Statutory Adoption Pay (General) Regulations 2002; Statutory Shared Parental Pay (General) Regulations 2014
PAYE	Pay As You Earn
PC	Privy Council
PCA	Personal Capability Assessment
PCC	Police and Crime Commissioner
PD	Practice Direction; prescribed disease
Pens. L.R.	Pensions Law Reports
Pensions Act	Pension Schemes Act 1993
PEP	Personal Equity Plan
Persons Abroad Regulations	Social Security Benefit (Persons Abroad) Regulations 1975
Persons Residing Together Regulations	Social Security Benefit (Persons Residing Together) Regulations 1977
PIE	Period of Interruption of Employment
PILON	pay in lieu of notice
Pilot Scheme Regulations	Universal Credit (Work-Related Requirements) In Work Pilot Scheme and Amendment Regulations 2015
PIP	Personal Independence Payment
P.I.Q.R.	Personal Injuries and Quantum Reports
Polygamous Marriages Regulations	Social Security and Family Allowances (Polygamous Marriages) Regulations 1975
PPF	Pension Protection Fund
Prescribed Diseases Regulations	Social Security (Industrial Injuries) (Prescribed Diseases) Regulations 1985
PSCS	Pension Service Computer System
Pt	Part

PTA	pure tone audiometry
P.T.S.R.	Public and Third Sector Law Reports
PTWR 2000	Part-time Workers (Prevention of Less Favourable Treatment) Regulations 2000
PVS	private and voluntary sectors
Q.B.	Queen's Bench Law Reports
QBD	Queen's Bench Division
QCS Board	Quality Contract Scheme Board
QEF	qualifying earnings factor
QYP	qualifying young person
r.	rule
R	Reported Decision
R.C.	Rules of the Court of Session
REA	Reduced Earnings Allowance
reg.	regulation
REULRRA	Retained EU Law (Revocation and Reform) Act 2023
RIPA	Regulation of Investigatory Powers Act 2000
RMO	Responsible Medical Officer
rr.	rules
RR	reference rate
RSI	repetitive strain injury
RTI	Real Time Information
R.V.R.	Rating & Valuation Reporter
s.	section
S	Scottish Decision
SAP	Statutory Adoption Pay
SAPOE Regulations	Jobseeker's Allowance (Schemes for Assisting Persons to Obtain Employment) Regulations 2013
SAWS	Seasonal Agricultural Work Scheme
SAYE	Save As You Earn
SB	Supplementary Benefit
SBAT	Supplementary Benefit Appeal Tribunal
SBC	Supplementary Benefits Commission
S.C.	Session Cases
S.C. (H.L.)	Session Cases (House of Lords)
S.C. (P.C.)	Session Cases (Privy Council)
S.C.C.R.	Scottish Criminal Case Reports
S.C.L.R.	Scottish Civil Law Reports
Sch.	Schedule
SDA	Severe Disablement Allowance
SDP	Severe Disability Premium
SEC	Social Entitlement Chamber
SEN	special educational needs

SERPS	State Earnings Related Pension Scheme
ShPP	statutory shared parental pay
ShPP Regulations	Statutory Shared Parental Pay (General) Regulations 2014
SI	Statutory Instrument
SIP	Share Incentive Plan
S.J.	Solicitors Journal
S.J.L.B.	Solicitors Journal Law Brief
SLAN	statement like an award notice
S.L.T.	Scots Law Times
SMP	Statutory Maternity Pay
SMP (General) Regulations 1986	Statutory Maternity Pay (General) Regulations 1986
SPC	State Pension Credit
SPC Regulations	State Pension Credit Regulations 2002
SPCA 2002	State Pension Credit Act 2002
SPL Regulations	Shared Parental Leave Regulations 2014
SPP	Statutory Paternity Pay
ss.	sections
SS (No.2) A 1980	Social Security (No.2) Act 1980
SSA 1975	Social Security Act 1975
SSA 1977	Social Security Act 1977
SSA 1978	Social Security Act 1978
SSA 1979	Social Security Act 1979
SSA 1981	Social Security Act 1981
SSA 1986	Social Security Act 1986
SSA 1988	Social Security Act 1988
SSA 1989	Social Security Act 1989
SSA 1990	Social Security Act 1990
SSA 1998	Social Security Act 1998
SSAA 1992	Social Security Administration Act 1992
SSAC	Social Security Advisory Committee
SSAT	Social Security Appeal Tribunal
SSCBA 1992	Social Security Contributions and Benefits Act 1992
SSCB(NI)A 1992	Social Security Contributions and Benefits (Northern Ireland) Act 1992
SSCPA 1992	Social Security (Consequential Provisions) Act 1992
SSD	Secretary of State for Defence
SSHBA 1982	Social Security and Housing Benefits Act 1982
SSHD	Secretary of State for the Home Department
SSI	Scottish Statutory Instrument
SS(MP)A 1977	Social Security (Miscellaneous Provisions) Act 1977
SSP	Statutory Sick Pay

SSP (General) Regulations	Statutory Sick Pay (General) Regulations 1982
SSPA 1975	Social Security Pensions Act 1975
SSPP	statutory shared parental pay
SSWP	Secretary of State for Work and Pensions
State Pension Credit Regulations	State Pension Credit Regulations 2002
S.T.C.	Simon's Tax Cases
S.T.C. (S.C.D.)	Simon's Tax Cases: Special Commissioners' Decisions
S.T.I.	Simon's Tax Intelligence
STIB	Short-Term Incapacity Benefit
subpara.	subparagraph
subs.	subsection
T	Tribunal of Commissioners' Decision
T.C.	Tax Cases
TCA 1999	Tax Credits Act 1999
TCA 2002	Tax Credits Act 2002
TCC	Technology and Construction Court
TCEA 2007	Tribunals, Courts and Enforcement Act 2007
TCGA 1992	Taxation of Chargeable Gains Act 2002
TCTM	*Tax Credits Technical Manual*
TEC	Treaty Establishing the European Community
TENS	transcutaneous electrical nerve stimulation
TEU	Treaty on European Union
TFC	tax-free childcare
TFEU	Treaty on the Functioning of the European Union
TIOPA 2010	Taxation (International and Other Provisions) Act 2010
TMA 1970	Taxes Management Act 1970
T.R.	Taxation Reports
Transfer of Functions Act	Social Security Contributions (Transfer of Functions etc.) Act 1999
Tribunal Procedure Rules	Tribunal Procedure (First-tier Tribunal)(Social Entitlement Chamber) Rules 2008
UB	Unemployment Benefit
UC	Universal Credit
UC Regs 2013	Universal Credit Regulations 2013
UCITS	Undertakings for Collective Investments in Transferable Securities
UKAIT	UK Asylum and Immigration Tribunal
UKBA	UK Border Agency of the Home Office
UKCC	United Kingdom Central Council for Nursing, Midwifery and Health Visiting
UKFTT	United Kingdom First-tier Tribunal Tax Chamber
UKHL	United Kingdom House of Lords

U.K.H.R.R.	United Kingdom Human Rights Reports
UKSC	United Kingdom Supreme Court
UKUT	United Kingdom Upper Tribunal
UN	United Nations
Universal Credit Regulations	Universal Credit Regulations 2013
URL	uniform resource locator
USI Regs	Social Security (Unemployment, Sickness and Invalidity Benefit) Regulations 1983
USI Regulations	Social Security (Unemployment, Sickness and Invalidity Benefit) Regulations 1983
UT	Upper Tribunal
VAT	Value Added Tax
VCM	vinyl chloride monomer
Vol.	Volume
VWF	Vibration White Finger
W	Welsh Decision
WCA	Work Capability Assessment
WCAt	limited capability for work assessment
WFHRAt	Work-Focused Health-Related Assessment
WFI	work-focused interview
WFTC	Working Families Tax Credit
Wikeley, Annotations	N. Wikeley, "Annotations to Jobseekers Act 1995 (c.18)" in *Current Law Statutes Annotated* (1995)
Wikeley, Ogus and Barendt	Wikeley, Ogus and Barendt, *The Law of Social Security* (2002)
W.L.R.	Weekly Law Reports
WLUK	Westlaw UK
Workmen's Compensation Acts	Workmen's Compensation Acts 1925 to 1945
WP	Widow's Pension
WPS	War Pensions Scheme
WRA 2007	Welfare Reform Act 2007
WRA 2009	Welfare Reform Act 2009
WRA 2012	Welfare Reform Act 2012
W-RA Regulations	Employment and Support Allowance (Work-Related Activity) Regulations 2011
WRAAt	Work-Related Activity Assessment
WRPA 1999	Welfare Reform and Pensions Act 1999
WRP(NI)O 1999	Welfare Reform and Pensions (Northern Ireland) Order 1999
WRWA 2016	Welfare Reform and Work Act 2016
WSP (LCP) R (NI) 2016	Welfare Supplementary Payment (Loss of Carer Payments) Regulations (Northern Ireland) 2016
WSP (LDRP) R (NI) 2016	Welfare Supplementary Payment (Loss of Disability-Related Premiums) Regulations (Northern Ireland) 2016

WSPR (NI) 2016	Welfare Supplementary Payment Regulations (Northern Ireland) 2016
WTC	Working Tax Credit
WTC Regulations	Working Tax Credit (Entitlement and Maximum Rate) Regulations 2002

PART I

STATUTES

Vaccine Damage Payments Act 1979

(1979 C.17)

ARRANGEMENT OF SECTIONS

An Act to provide for payments to be made out of public funds in cases where severe disablement occurs as a result of vaccination against certain diseases or of contact with a person who has been vaccinated against any of those diseases; to make provision in connection with similar payments made before the passing of this Act; and for purposes connected therewith.
[22nd March 1979]

Payments to persons severely disabled by vaccination

1.—(1) If, on consideration of a claim, the Secretary of State is satisfied— **1.2**

(a) that a person is, or was immediately before his death, severely disabled as a result of vaccination against any of the diseases to which this Act applies; and

(b) that the conditions of entitlement which are applicable in accordance with section 2 below are fulfilled,

he shall in accordance with this Act make a payment of [[1]the relevant statutory sum] to or for the benefit of that person or to his personal representatives.

[[1](1A) In subsection (1) above "statutory sum" means £10,000 or such other sum as is specified by the Secretary of State for the purposes of this Act by order made by statutory instrument with the consent of the Treasury; and the relevant statutory sum for the purposes of that subsection is the statutory sum at the time when a claim for payment is first made.]

(2) The diseases to which this Act applies are–

(a) diphtheria,
(b) tetanus,
(c) whooping cough,
(d) poliomyelitis,
(e) measles,
(f) rubella,
(g) tuberculosis,
(h) smallpox, and

(i) any other disease which is specified by the Secretary of State for the purposes of this Act by order made by statutory instrument.

(3) Subject to section 2(3) below, this Act has effect with respect to a person who is severely disabled as a result of a vaccination given to his mother before he was born as if the vaccination had been given directly to him and, in such circumstances as may be prescribed by regulations under this Act, this Act has effect with respect to a person who is severely disabled as a result of contracting a disease through contact with a third person who was vaccinated against it as if the vaccination had been given to him and the disablement resulted from it.

(4) For the purposes of this Act, a person is severely disabled if he suffers disablement to the extent of [[2]60] per cent. or more, assessed as for the purposes of section 57 of the Social Security Act 1975 or the Social Security (Northern Ireland) Act 1975 (disablement gratuity and pension).

[[1](4A) No order shall be made by virtue of subsection (1A) above unless a draft of the order has been laid before Parliament and been approved by a resolution of each House.]

(5) A statutory instrument under subsection (2)(i) above shall be subject to annulment in pursuance of a resolution of either House of Parliament.

AMENDMENTS

1. Social Security Act 1985 s.23.

2. Regulatory Reform (Vaccine Damage Payments Act 1979) Order 2002 (SI 2002/1592) art.2 (June 16, 2002).

GENERAL NOTE

1.3 With effect from November 1, 2021, the Secretary of State for Health and Social Care (DHSC) has been responsible for both the policy and the operational side of the 1979 Act. Before that date, DHSC was responsible for policy (and hence legislation) while DWP was responsible for operational matters in processing claims. DHSC has now directed the National Health Service Business Services Authority (NHSBSA) to operate the Scheme on behalf of DHSC; see also the Transfer of Functions (Vaccine Damage Payments) Order 2021 (SI 2021/1469).

The 1979 Act is subject to detailed analysis in *SSWP v G (VDP)* [2015] UKUT 321 (AAC). The Secretary of State appealed to the Court of Appeal against the Upper Tribunal's decision in *G*. The Court dismissed the appeal. Davis LJ, who gave the principal judgment, said "I would endorse the decision of the [Upper Tribunal Judge] in all respects" (*John (A Minor: Vaccine Damage Payments scheme), Re* ([2017] AACR 20; [2017] EWCA Civ 61; [2017] EWCA Civ 61, [2017] 1 W.L.R. 1956; [2017] W.L.R.(D) 118). A child ("John") had a vaccination against pandemic influenza A (H1N1, or swine flu) when aged 7, and later developed narcolepsy and cataplexy. John's mother made a claim under the 1979 Act. Causation was not in dispute, but the Secretary of State disputed that John met the disablement threshold of 60 per cent. In particular, the Secretary of State argued that future developments should be discounted and John should simply be compared with a boy of the same age in normal health at the date of assessment. The First-tier Tribunal rejected that argument and decided that John's mother was entitled to the statutory award of £120,000, taking into account future disability.

Judge Mitchell noted that s.1(1)(a) essentially set out three fundamental conditions of entitlement, namely:

"(a) causation must be established. A person must be disabled 'as a result of' vaccination; and

(b) a disability threshold must be reached: the disability must be 'severe' and

(c) the vaccination must have been against a disease to which the Act applies" (para.44).

There are then the further conditions set out in s.1(1)(b) and (2) relating to the place and date of vaccination (in the UK after July 5, 1948), the age of the disabled person at vaccination (where relevant) and their age at date of claim (at least 2).

The assessment of disablement is governed by subs.(4), the effect of which is that s.103 of the SSCBA 1992 applies with any necessary modifications (see Judge Mitchell at paras 75-77; thus Sch.6 para.6(2) and (3) of the SSCBA do not apply – see paras 103-104). Having reviewed the principles from the industrial injuries scheme, Judge Mitchell held as follows:

"81. . .In order, therefore, to comply with the requirement in section 1(4) of the VDPA 1979 to assess disablement 'as for the purposes of' section 103, the VDPA 1979 assessment should reflect these elements. This calls for:

(a) identification of an event akin to a relevant accident that has caused personal injury. That is if course the vaccination;
(b) identification of a loss of physical or mental faculty (or both) because of the vaccination;
(c) identification of disability or disabilities incurred as a result of the loss of faculty;
(c) a judgement to be made as to the extent of disablement, expressed as a percentage which represents the sum of the person's disabilities."

This also requires the relevant principles from Schedule 6 of the SSCBA 1992 to be imported:

"86. If this is dissected, it shows:

(a) Schedule 6(1)(a) is about identifying the disabilities to be taken into account in assessing the extent of a person's disablement. Its role in the overall assessment is limited to that;
(b) the assessment is over a particular period (the 'period taken into account by the assessment') although this period is not fixed by paragraph (a);
(c) unless excluded by sub-paragraphs (b) to (d), the disabilities to be taken into account are 'all disabilities so incurred' (as a result of the loss of faculty) to which the individual 'may be expected to be subject during the period taken into account'. This requires, therefore, the assessor to make predictions about what is likely to happen during the period taken into account;
(d) in identifying the disabilities to which the person may be expected to be subject over the period taken into account, regard must be had to the individual's 'physical and mental condition at the date of the assessment';
(e) in identifying the disabilities expected during the period taken into account, a comparison is to be made with 'a person of the same age and sex whose physical and mental condition is normal'."

See also, on the application of reg.11 of the Social Security (General) Benefit) Regulations 1982, Judge Mitchell's decision at paras 106–114.

Based on this careful analysis, Judge Mitchell concluded that the assessment of disablement under the 1979 Act is not a snapshot, restricted to the presenting disablement at the time of the assessment, but rather could take into account future disability (paras 116–121). The Court of Appeal agreed with that conclusion, dismissing the Secretary of State's principal ground of appeal (at paras 34–42); Davis LJ was "in no real doubt that the FTT was justified in looking (as it did) to the future prognosis, on the balance of probabilities, in assessing whether the threshold was crossed for the necessary 60% disablement" (at para.42). In the Upper Tribunal decision Judge Mitchell gave the following general guidance about the assessment of disablement (at para.149):

"(a) the need to identify something akin to an accident. This is straightforward because it is, of course, is the vaccination;

(b) the need to identify a loss of faculty, which is generally taken to mean 'an impairment of the proper functioning of part of the body or mind';

(c) the need to identify the period to be taken into account by the assessment. In many cases, the nature of vaccine damage is that this is the disabled person's lifetime because that will be the period during which the person is expected to suffer from the loss of faculty;

(d) the need to identify the disabilities, resulting from the vaccination, that may be expected during that period. A disability is generally taken to mean 'partial or total failure of power to perform normal bodily or mental processes';

(e) the need to understand how the prescribed scale of disablement functions and the extent to which it is legitimate to rely on it. I think it is clear that vaccine damage would be most unlikely to take the form of an injury on the prescribed scale because prescribed injuries all tend to be various types of physical trauma. Therefore, it will be used for comparative purposes only. A meaningful comparison is only likely to be made between disabilities, rather than injuries. To do that effectively calls for the disabilities associated with the prescribed injury to be compared with those associated with disabilities resulting from vaccination;

(f) the final stage in the process is to express the sum of disabilities in terms of overall disablement, using a percentage. At this stage, I think it is important to note that vaccine damage, tending often to be systemic in nature, may well result in a constellation of disabilities. These should be carefully identified;

(g) it should be remembered that personal factors may not be taken into account, other than age, sex, physical and mental condition. However, evidence about personal activities is perfectly acceptable if it says something relevant about disability or disablement."

Finally, Judge Mitchell was also highly critical of the conduct of the appeal by the Vaccine Damage Unit, in particular with regard to the poor quality of the appeal papers (paras 13, 28–29 and 145) and failure to send a presenting officer to the First-tier Tribunal hearing (para.30). The Court of Appeal subsequently affirmed Judge Mitchell's "observation that *disabilities* themselves are but a stepping-stone towards the assessment of *disablement*" (per Davis LJ at para.46, emphasis in the original).

Subsection (1A)

1.4 The statutory sum was increased to £120,000 by the Vaccine Damage Payments Act 1979 Statutory Sum Order 2007 (SI 2007/1931) with effect from July 12, 2007.

Subsection (2)

1.5 Mumps is added to the lists of diseases by the Vaccine Damage Payments (Specified Disease) Order 1990 (SI 1990/623) and haemophilus influenza type b infection was added by the Vaccine Damage Payments (Specified Disease) Order 1995 (SI 1995/1164).

Meningococcal Group C was added to the list by the Vaccine Damage Payments (Specified Disease) Order 2001 (SI 2001/1652).

With effect from September 4, 2006, pneumococcal infection was added to the list of diseases by the Vaccine Damage Payments (Specified Disease) Order 2006 (SI 2006/2066).

With effect from September 1, 2008, human papillomavirus was added to the list of diseases by the Vaccine Damage Payments (Specified Disease) Order 2008 (SI 2008/2103).

With effect from September 1, 2010, influenza caused by the pandemic influenza A (H1N1) 2009 virus ("swine flu") was removed from the list of diseases to which the Act applies by the Vaccine Damage Payments (Specified Disease) (Revocation and Savings) Order 2010 (SI 2010/1988). Article 4 of the Order ensures, however, that protection under the Act remains applicable to anyone who received the vaccination prior to September 1, 2010.

With effect from February 28, 2015, rotavirus and influenza, other than influenza caused by a pandemic influenza virus, were added to the list of diseases by the Vaccine Damage Payments (Specified Disease) Order 2015 (SI 2015/47). The addition of influenza (other than influenza caused by a pandemic influenza virus) does not, however, affect any entitlement arising under the Vaccine Damage Payments (Specified Disease) Order 2009 (SI 2009/2516), which added pandemic influenza A (H1N1 virus), and references in the 2015 Order to pandemic influenza are to be construed accordingly. With effect from April 29, 2016, Meningococcal Groups B and W were added to the list by the Vaccine Damage Payments (Specified Disease) Order 2016 (SI 2016/454). Most notably, and with effect from December 31, 2020. COVID-19 was specified as a disease to which the Act applies (see the Vaccine Damage Payments (Specified Disease) Order 2020 (SI 2020/1411)).

Subsection (4)

The substitution of 60 per cent for 80 per cent applies to claims made on or after June 16, 2002 (the specified date). There is transitional provision in Art.4 and the Schedule to the Order. Art.4 provides:

"Transitional claims

4. The provisions in the Schedule to this Order shall have effect and are designäted as subordinate provisions for the purposes of section 4(3) of the Regulatory Reform Act 2001."

The Schedule to the Order deals with Transitional Claims (defined in paragraph 3(1) of the Schedule) and provides as follows:

Article 4 SCHEDULE

TRANSITIONAL CLAIMS

1.—A transitional claim may be made in the cases specified in paragraph 3(1). **1.6**

2. In this Schedule—

(a) references to sections are to sections of the Act;

(b) "advised" means—

(i) informed in written form; or

(ii) informed orally where there is a record in written form created by the adviser at the time when, or shortly after the time when, that advice was given;

(c) "in written form" means in a manner which is in, or which is capable of being reproduced in, legible form;

(d) "the amended section 1(4)" means section 1(4) as it is in force on or after the specified date;

(e) "the amended section 3(1)(c)" means section 3(1)(c) as it is in force on or after the specified date;

(f) "the extra-statutory scheme" means the non-statutory scheme of payments referred to in section 7;

(g) "the previous section 1(4)" means section 1(4) as it was in force prior to the specified date;

(h) "the previous section 3(1)(c)" means section 3(1)(c) as it was in force prior to the specified date;

(i) "the specified date" means the date this Order comes into force; and

(j) "transitional claim" has the meaning given in paragraph 4.

3.—(1) Subject to sub-paragraph (2), the specified cases are those where—

(a) a claim for a payment under section 1(1) was made prior to the specified date and—

(i) the Secretary of State refused to consider the application for a claim on the ground that the previous section 3(1)(c) was not satisfied but the amended section 3(1)(c) would have been satisfied had it been in force at the time of that refusal; or

(ii) it was determined that no payment was due under section 1(1) on the basis that the previous section 1(4) was not satisfied;

(b) a claim for a payment was made under the extra-statutory scheme and it was determined that no payment was due on the basis that the disabled person did not suffer disablement to the extent of 80 per cent. or more;

(c) no claim for a payment under section 1(1) was made prior to the specified date and the Secretary of State is satisfied that—

(i) the reason such a claim was not made was that the disabled person, those acting on his behalf or, as the case may be, his personal representatives had been advised prior to the specified date that either the previous section 1(4) or the previous section 3(1)(c) would not be satisfied if such a claim were made; and

(ii) the amended section 3(1)(c) would have been satisfied had it been in force at the date the advice referred to in paragraph (i) was given; or

(d) no claim for a payment under the extra-statutory scheme was made whilst it was in force and the Secretary of State is satisfied that the reason such a claim was not made was that the disabled person, those acting on his behalf or, as the case may be, his personal representatives had been advised whilst the extra-statutory scheme was in force that the requirement in the extra-statutory scheme that the disabled person suffers disablement to the extent of 80 per cent. or more would not be satisfied if such a claim were made.

(2) The Secretary of State shall not be satisfied for the purposes of sub-paragraph (1)(c) or (d) unless there has been produced to him the written form of the advice referred to in those paragraphs or a copy of it.

4.—A "transitional claim" is a claim for a payment under section 1 (1) which is made—

(a) by or on behalf of the disabled person concerned or, as the case may be, by his personal representatives;

(b) in the manner prescribed by regulations under the Act for a claim under section 3; and

(c) within 3 years after the date on which this Order came into force.

5.—(1) Where sub-paragraph (2) or (3) applies, a transitional claim shall be determined on the basis that the disabled person is, or was immediately before his death, disabled as a result of vaccination against any of the diseases to which the Act applies and whether he is, or was, severely disabled shall be determined in accordance with the amended section 1(4).

(2) This sub-paragraph applies where—

(a) a case is a specified case by virtue of paragraph 3(1)(a)(ii); and

(b) at the time of the claim referred to in paragraph 3(1)(a) it was determined that the condition that the person was disabled as a result of vaccination against any of the diseases to which the Act applies was satisfied but the condition that he was severely disabled in accordance with the previous section 1(4) was not satisfied.

(3) This sub-paragraph applies where—

(a) a case is a specified case by virtue of paragraph 3(1)(b); and

(b) at the time of the claim referred to in paragraph 3(1)(b) it was determined that the condition that the person was disabled as a result of vaccination against any of the diseases to which the extra-statutory scheme applied was satisfied but the condition that he suffered disablement to the extent of 80 per cent. or more was not satisfied.

6.—Subject to paragraph 5, a transitional claim shall be treated for the purposes of the Act as a claim which satisfies the conditions in section 3(1).

General Note

1.7 Note that the method of assessing the percentage degree of disablement is the same as that for industrial injuries disablement pension: see further SSCBA 1992 s.103 and commentary thereto.

Conditions of entitlement

1.8 **2.**—(1) Subject to the provisions of this section, the conditions of entitlement referred to in section 1(1)(b) above are—

(a) that the vaccination in question was carried out—

(i) in the United Kingdom or the Isle of Man, and

(ii) on or after 5th July 1948, and

(iii) in the case of vaccination against smallpox, before 1st August 1971;

(b) except in the case of vaccination against poliomyelitis or rubella, that the vaccination was carried out either at a time when the person to whom it was given was under the age of eighteen or at the time of an outbreak within the United Kingdom or the Isle of Man of the disease against which the vaccination was given; and

(c) that the disabled person was over the age of two on the date when the claim was made or, if he died before that date, that he died after 9th May 1978 and was over the age of two when he died.

(2) An order under section 1(2)(i) above specifying a disease for the purposes of this Act may provide that, in relation to vaccination against that disease, the conditions of entitlement specified in subsection (1) above shall have effect subject to such modifications as may be specified in the order.

(3) In a case where this Act has effect by virtue of section 1(3) above, the reference in subsection (1)(b) above to the person to whom a vaccination was given is a reference to the person to whom it was actually given and not to the disabled person.

(4) With respect to claims made after such date as may be specified in the order and relating to vaccination against such disease as may be so specified, the Secretary of State may by order made by statutory instrument—

(a) provide that, in such circumstances as may be specified in the order, one or more of the conditions of entitlement appropriate to vaccination against that disease need not be fulfilled; or

(b) add to the conditions of entitlement which are appropriate to vaccination against that disease, either generally or in such circumstances as may be specified in the order.

(5) Regulations under this Act shall specify the cases in which vaccinations given outside the United Kingdom and the Isle of Man to persons defined in the regulations as serving members of Her Majesty's forces or members of their families are to be treated for the purposes of this Act as carried out in England.

(6) The Secretary of State shall not make an order containing any provision made by virtue of paragraph (b) of subsection (4) above unless a draft of the order has been laid before Parliament and approved by a resolution of each House; and a statutory instrument by which any other order is made under that subsection shall be subject to annulment in pursuance of a resolution of either House of Parliament.

GENERAL NOTE

See generally *SSWP v G (VDP)* [2015] UKUT 321 (AAC) at paras 42–51. **1.9**

Subsection (1)(a)(ii), (2)

This stipulates that the vaccination was carried out on or after July 5, 1948. As regards vaccination against rotavirus, that date is changed to July 1, 2013, while for vaccination against influenza (other than influenza caused by a pandemic influenza virus) the relevant date is September 1, 2013. See Vaccine Damage Payments (Specified Disease) Order 2015 (SI 2015/47) art.3. **1.10**

Subsection (1)(b), (2)

The condition in subs.(1)(b) (age or time at which vaccination was carried out) does not apply to vaccination against the following diseases: **1.11**

- Meningococcal Group C (Vaccine Damage Payments (Specified Disease) Order 2001 (SI 2001/1652) art.3);
- Human papillomavirus (Vaccine Damage Payments (Specified Disease) Order 2008 (SI 2008/2103) art.3);

- Influenza caused by the pandemic influenza A (H1N1) 2009 virus (Vaccine Damage Payments (Specified Disease) Order 2009 (SI 2009/2516) art.3).

Moreover, as regards vaccination against rotavirus or influenza (other than influenza caused by a pandemic influenza virus) subs.(1)(b) as set out in the statutory text above does not apply and is substituted by the Vaccine Damage Payments (Specified Disease) Order 2015 (SI 2015/47) art.3(c) to read as follows:

"(b) that the vaccination was carried out at a time when the person to whom it was given was under the age of eighteen; and".

Determination of claims

1.12 **3.**—(1) Any reference in this Act, other than section 7, to a claim is a reference to a claim for a payment under section 1(1) above which is made—

(a) by or on behalf of the disabled person concerned or, as the case may be, by his personal representatives; and

(b) in the manner prescribed by regulations under this Act; and

[2(c) on or before whichever is the later of—

(i) the date on which the disabled person attains the age of 21, or where he has died, the date on which he would have attained the age of 21; and

(ii) the end of the period of six years beginning with the date of the vaccination to which the claim relates;]

and, in relation to a claim, any reference to the claimant is a reference to the person by whom the claim was made and any reference to the disabled person is a reference to the person in respect of whose disablement a payment under subsection (1) above is claimed to be payable.

(2) As soon as practicable after he has received a claim, the Secretary of State shall give notice in writing to the claimant of his determination whether he is satisfied that a payment is due under section 1(1) above to or for the benefit of the disabled person or to his personal representatives.

(3) If the Secretary of State is not satisfied that a payment is due as mentioned in subsection (2) above, the notice in writing under that subsection shall state the grounds on which he is not so satisfied.

(4) If, in the case of any claim, the Secretary of State—

(a) is satisfied that the conditions of entitlement which are applicable in accordance with section 2 above are fulfilled, but

(b) is not satisfied that the disabled person is or, where he has died, was immediately before his death severely disabled as a result of vaccination against any of the diseases to which this Act applies,

the notice in writing under subsection (2) above shall inform the claimant [1of the right of appeal conferred by section 4 below.]

(5) If in any case a person is severely disabled, the question whether his severe disablement results from vaccination against any of the diseases to which this Act applies shall be determined for the purposes of this Act on the balance of probability.

AMENDMENTS

1. Social Security Act 1998, Sch.7 para.5 (October 18, 1999).

2. Regulatory Reform (Vaccine Damage Payments Act 1979) Order 2002 (SI 2002/1592) art.3 (June 16, 2002).

General Note

Section 3(1) creates a time limit for claiming by defining a claim as being a claim for payment made on or before the later of two dates, being (i) the date on which the disabled person attains 21 and (ii) the end of six years starting with the date of vaccination. As Judge Mitchell noted in *SSWP v G (VDP)* [2015] UKUT 321 (AAC): 1.13

> "54. If a 'claim' is made outside this window, it is not a claim at all. The Secretary of State's duty to make a payment under section 1(1) VDPA 1979 can only arise 'on consideration of a claim'. The duty cannot be triggered, therefore, by a non-claim which is why the definition of 'claim' effectively imposes a time-limit for claiming. In this case, the claim was in-time."

[1 Decisions reversing earlier decisions

3A.—(1) Subject to subsection (2) below, any decision of the Secretary of State under section 3 above or this section, and any decision of [2 a tribunal] under section 4 below, may be reversed by a decision made by the Secretary of State— 1.14

(a) either within the prescribed period or in prescribed cases or circumstances; and

(b) either on an application made for the purpose or on his own initiative.

(2) In making a decision under subsection (1) above, the Secretary of State need not consider any issue that is not raised by the application or, as the case may be, did not cause him to act on his own initiative.

(3) Regulations may prescribe the procedure by which a decision may be made under this section.

(4) Such notice as may be prescribed by regulations shall be given of a decision under this section.

(5) Except as provided by section 5(4) below, no payment under section 1(1) above shall be recoverable by virtue of a decision under this section.

(6) In this section and sections 4 and 8 below "appeal tribunal" means an appeal tribunal constituted under Chapter I of Part I of the Social Security Act 1998.]

Amendments

1. Social Security Act 1998 s.45 (October 18, 1999).

2. Transfer of Tribunal Functions Order 2008 (SI 2008/2833) art.6 and Sch.3 para.31 (November 3, 2008).

General Note

In *SSWP v G (VDP)* [2015] UKUT 321 (AAC), Judge Mitchell explained the position as regards the reversal of previous decisions as follows: 1.15

> "65. Drawing the reversal strings together, the upshot, so far as unsuccessful claimants are concerned, is that, if they go to tribunal and lose, they have a limited period in which to apply for reversal. This is either two years from notification of the tribunal's decision or six years from notification of the original decision of the Secretary of State, whichever is later. But if they keep their powder dry, as it were, and do not appeal, there is no time limit and an application for reversal may be made at any time. However, the Secretary of State's power to reverse on his own initiative expires six years after notification of his original decision (unless he wishes to reverse due to misrepresentation of or failure to disclose a material fact which I imagine means converting a decision to award a payment into a decision to refuse)."

[1Appeals to appeal tribunals

1.16 **4.**—(1) The claimant may appeal to [2the First-tier Tribunal] against any decision of the Secretary of State under section 3 or 3A above.

[3(1B) If the claimant's address is not in Northern Ireland, regulations may provide that, in such cases or circumstances as may be prescribed, there is a right of appeal only if the Secretary of State has considered whether to reverse the decision under section 3A.

(1C) The regulations may in particular provide that that condition is met only where–

(a) the consideration by the Secretary of State was on an application,
(b) the Secretary of State considered issues of a specified description, or
(c) the consideration by the Secretary of State satisfied any other condition specified in the regulations.]

(2) Regulations may make–

(a) provision as to the manner in which, and the time within which, appeals are to be brought;
(b) [2. . .]
[3(c) provision that, where in accordance with regulations under subsection (1B) there is no right of appeal against a decision, any purported appeal may be treated as an application to reverse the decision under section 3A.]

(3) The regulations may in particular make any provision of a kind mentioned in Schedule 5 to the Social Security Act 1998.

(4) In deciding an appeal under this section, [2the First-tier Tribunal] shall consider all the circumstances of the case (including any not obtaining at the time when the decision appealed against was made).]

AMENDMENTS

1. This version of s.4 (October 18, 1999) was substituted by Social Security Act 1998 s.46.
2. Transfer of Tribunal Functions Order 2008 (SI 2008/2833) art.6 and Sch.3 para.32 (November 3, 2008).
3. Welfare Reform Act 2012 s.102(6) and Sch.11 paras 1, 2 (February 25, 2013).

GENERAL NOTE

1.17 Note that there is no time limit for bringing an appeal (*SSWP v G (VDP)* [2015] UKUT 321 (AAC) at para.68). Judge Mitchell also noted that by virtue of s.4(4) the "default position" for social security appeals in s.12(8) of the Social Security Act 1988 does not apply to appeals under the 1979 Act. "Accordingly, all relevant circumstances up to the date of the appeal hearing are to be taken into account. This is consistent with the absence of a time limit for bringing an appeal because, in theory, many years might elapse between decision and appeal hearing" (at para.69).

The non-sequential numbering is to accommodate a new subs. (1A) inserted by the Welfare Reform Act 2007 s.57(2), to affect Northern Ireland only, which has not yet been brought into effect.

Reconsideration of determinations and recovery of payments in certain cases

1.18 **5.**—[1 *Subss. (1)–(3) Repealed.*]

(4) If, whether fraudulently or otherwise, any person misrepresents or fails to disclose any material fact and in consequence of the misrepresentation

or failure a payment is made under section 1(1) above, the person to whom the payment was made shall be liable to repay the amount of that payment to the Secretary of State unless he can show that the misrepresentation or failure occurred without his connivance or consent.

(5) [[1] *Repealed*]

AMENDMENT

1. Social Security Act 1998 Sch.7 para.6 (October 18, 1999).

Payments to or for the benefit of disabled persons

6.—(1) Where a payment under section 1(1) above falls to be made in respect of a disabled person who is over eighteen and capable of managing his own affairs, the payment shall be made to him. 1.19

(2) Where such a payment falls to be made in respect of a disabled person who has died, the payment shall be made to his personal representatives.

(3) Where such a payment falls to be made in respect of any other disabled person, the payment shall be made for his benefit by paying it to such trustees as the Secretary of State may appoint to be held by them upon such trusts or, in Scotland, for such purposes and upon such conditions as may be declared by the Secretary of State.

(4) The making of a claim for, or the receipt of, a payment under section 1(1) above does not prejudice the right of any person to institute or carry on proceedings in respect of disablement suffered as a result of vaccination against any disease to which this Act applies; but in any civil proceedings brought in respect of disablement resulting from vaccination against such a disease, the court shall treat a payment made to or in respect of the disabled person concerned under section 1(1) above as paid on account of any damages which the court awards in respect of such disablement.

GENERAL NOTE

As Judge Mitchell explained in *Secretary of State for Work and Pensions v G* [2015] UKUT 321 (AAC) (at para.72), s.6(4) means that "a payment under the VDPA 1979 does not affect any rights to bring proceedings but, where civil proceedings are brought in respect of disablement, the payment will reduce the damages received by the claimant." 1.20

Payments, claims etc. made prior to the Act

7.—(1) Any reference in this section to an extra-statutory payment is a reference to a payment of £10,000 made by the Secretary of State to or in respect of a disabled person after 9th May 1978 and before the passing of this Act pursuant to a non-statutory scheme of payments for severe vaccine damage. 1.21

(2) No such claim as is referred to in section 3(1) above shall be entertained if an extra-statutory payment has been made to or for the benefit of the disabled person or his personal representatives.

(3) For the purposes of [[1]section 3A above], a determination that an extra-statutory payment should be made shall be treated as a determination that a payment should be made under section 1(1) above [[1] . . .].

(4) [[1] Section 5(4) above] and section 6(4) above shall apply in relation to an extra-statutory payment as they apply in relation to a payment made under section 1(1) above.

(5) For the purposes of this Act (other than this section) regulations under this Act may—

(a) treat claims which were made in connection with the scheme referred to in subsection (1) above and which have not been disposed of at the commencement of this Act as claims falling within section 3(1) above; and

(b) treat information and other evidence furnished and other things done before the commencement of this Act in connection with any such claim as is referred to in paragraph (a) above as furnished or done in connection with a claim falling within section 3(1) above.

AMENDMENT

1. Social Security Act 1998 Sch.7 para.7 (October 18, 1999).

[1 Correction of errors and setting aside of decisions

1.22 **7A.**—(1) Regulations may make provision with respect to—

(a) the correction of accidental errors in any decision or record of a decision under section [2 3 or 3A] of this Act; [2 . . .].

(2) Nothing in subsection (1) shall be construed as derogating from any power to correct errors [2 . . .] which is exercisable apart from regulations made by virtue of that subsection.]

AMENDMENTS

1. Inserted by Social Security Act 1998 s.47 (October 18, 1999).
2. Transfer of Tribunal Functions Order 2008 (SI 2008/2833) art.6 and Sch.3 para.34 (November 3, 2008).

[1Finality of decisions

1.23 **7B.**—(1) Subject to the provisions of this Act [2 and article 4 of, and the Schedule to, the Regulatory Reform (Vaccine Damage Payments Act 1979) Order 2002 (modifications of this Act in relation to transitional claims)], any decision made in accordance with the foregoing provisions of this Act shall be final.

(2) If and to the extent that regulations so provide, any finding of fact or other determination embodied in or necessary to such a decision, or on which such a decision is based, shall be conclusive for the purposes of—

(a) further such decisions;

(b) decisions made in accordance with sections 8 to 16 of the Social Security Act 1998, or with regulations under section 11 of that Act; and

(c) decisions made under the Child Support Act 1991.]

AMENDMENTS

1. Inserted by Social Security Act 1998 Sch.7 para.8 (October 18, 1999).
2. Regulatory Reform (Vaccine Damage Payments Act 1979) Order 2002 (SI 2002/1592) art.5 (June 16, 2002).

GENERAL NOTE

Subsection (1)

1.24 Article 4 of and the Schedule to the Order are reproduced in the annotation to s.1(4), above.

Regulations

8.—(1) Any reference in the preceding provisions of this Act to regulations under this Act is a reference to regulations made by the Secretary of State. 1.25

(2) Any power of the Secretary of State under this Act to make regulations—

(a) shall be exercisable by statutory instrument [2. . .]; and

(b) includes power to make such incidental or supplementary provision as appears to the Secretary of State to be appropriate.

[2(2A) A statutory instrument containing regulations made by the Secretary of State under this Act–

(a) except in the case of an instrument containing regulations under section 4(1B), is subject to annulment in pursuance of a resolution of either House of Parliament;

(b) in the case of an instrument containing regulations under section 4(1B), may not be made unless a draft of the instrument has been laid before and approved by a resolution of each House of Parliament.]

(3) Regulations made by the Secretary of State may contain provision—

(a) with respect to the information and other evidence to be furnished in connection with a claim;

(b) requiring disabled persons to undergo medical examination before their claims are determined or for the purposes of [1a decision under section 3A above];

(c) restricting the disclosure of medical evidence and advice tendered in connection with a claim or [1a decision under section 3A above]; and

(d) conferring functions on [1appeal tribunals] with respect to the matters referred to in paragraphs (a) to (c) above.

[2(5) The power to make regulations under section 4(1B) may be exercised–

(a) in relation to all cases to which it extends, in relation to those cases but subject to specified exceptions or in relation to any specified cases or classes of case;

(b) so as to make, as respects the cases in relation to which it is exercised–

(i) the full provision to which it extends or any lesser provision (whether by way of exception or otherwise);

(ii) the same provision for all cases, different provision for different cases or classes of case or different provision as respects the same case or class of case but for different purposes of this Act;

(iii) provision which is either unconditional or is subject to any specified condition.]

AMENDMENTS

1. Social Security Act 1998 Sch.7 para.9 (March 4, 1999).
2. Welfare Reform Act 2012 s.102(6) and Sch.11 paras 1, 2 (February 25, 2013).

GENERAL NOTE

The non-sequential numbering is to accommodate a new subs. (4) inserted by the Welfare Reform Act 2007 Sch.7 para.1(7), relating only to Northern Ireland, which has not yet been brought into effect. 1.26

Fraudulent statements etc.

1.27 **9.**—(1) Any person who, for the purpose of obtaining any payment under this Act, whether for himself or some other person,—

(a) knowingly makes any false statement or representation, or

(b) produces or furnishes or causes or knowingly allows to be produced or furnished any document or information which he knows to be false in a material particular,

shall be liable on summary conviction to a fine not exceeding [1 level 5 on the standard scale]

(2) In the application of subsection (1) above to the Isle of Man, for the words following "liable" there shall be substituted the words "on summary conviction, within the meaning of the Interpretation Act 1976 (an Act of Tynwald), to a fine of £400 and on conviction on information to a fine".

AMENDMENT

1. Words substituted by virtue of Criminal Justice Act 1982 (c.48) s.46, Criminal Procedure (Scotland) Act 1975 (c.21) s.289G, and for Northern Ireland by SI 1984/703 (NI3) arts 5, 6.

1.28 *Sections 9A, 10 and 11 omitted.*

Financial provisions

1.29 **12.**—(1) [2 *Repealed*].

(2) The Secretary of State shall pay such fees as he considers appropriate to medical practitioners, as defined in [1 section 191 of the Social Security Administration Act 1992] who provide information or other evidence in connection with claims.

(3) The Secretary of State shall pay such travelling and other allowances as he may determine—

(a) to persons required under this Act to undergo medical examinations; [3 . . .] and

(c) in circumstances where he considers it appropriate, to any person who accompanies a disabled person to such a medical examination [3 . . .].

(4) There shall be paid out of moneys provided by Parliament—

(a) any expenditure incurred by the Secretary of State in making payments under section 1(1) above;

(b) any expenditure incurred by the Secretary of State by virtue of subsections (1) to (3) above; and

(c) any increase in the administrative expenses of the Secretary of State attributable to this Act.

(5) Any sums repaid to the Secretary of State by virtue of section 5(4) above shall be paid into the Consolidated Fund.

AMENDMENTS

1. Social Security (Consequential Provisions) Act 1992 Sch.2 para.54 (July 1, 1992).

2. Social Security Act 1998 Sch.7 para.10 (October 18, 1999).

3. Transfer of Tribunal Functions Order 2008 (SI 2008/2833) art.6 and Sch.3 para.36 (November 3, 2008).

Short title and extent

13.—(1) This Act may be cited as the Vaccine Damage Payments Act 1979. 1.30

(2) This Act extends to Northern Ireland and the Isle of Man.

Pneumoconiosis etc. (Workers' Compensation) Act 1979

(1979 C.41)

ARRANGEMENT OF SECTIONS

An Act to make provision for lump sum payments to or in respect of certain persons who are, or were immediately before they died, disabled by pneumoconiosis, byssinosis or diffuse mesothelioma; and for connected purposes.

[4th April 1979]

Dependants

3. — (1) In this Act "dependant", in relation to a person who, immediately before he died, was disabled by a disease to which this Act applies, means— 1.32

(a) if he left a spouse [1 or civil partner] who was residing with him or was receiving or entitled to receive from him periodical payments for her maintenance, that spouse [1 or civil partner];

(b) if paragraph (a) above does not apply but he left a child or children who fall within subsection (2) below, that child or those children;

[1 (c) if neither of the preceding paragraphs applies but he left a person who was residing with him and with whom he was in a qualifying relationship, that person;]

(d) if none of the preceding paragraphs applies, any relative or relatives of his who fall within subsection (2) below and who were, in the opinion of the Secretary of State, wholly or mainly dependent on him at the date of his death.

(2) A person falls within this subsection if, at the relevant date, he was—

(a) under the age of 16;

(b) under the age of 21 and not gainfully employed full-time; or

(c) permanently incapable of self-support;

and in this subsection "relevant date" means the date of the deceased's death or the date of the coming into force of this Act, whichever is the later.

[2(2A) For the purposes of subsection (1)(c) two persons are in a qualifying relationship if they are living together [3 as if they were a married couple or civil partners].]

...

(4) In this section—

"child" includes posthumous child;

"relative" means brother, sister, lineal ancestor or lineal descendant; and for the purposes of this section a relationship shall be established as if any illegitimate child or step-child of a person had been a child born to him in wedlock.

AMENDMENTS

1. Welfare Reform Act 2007 s.59 (July 3, 2007).

2. Marriage (Same Sex Couples) Act 2013 (Consequential and Contrary Provisions and Scotland) Order 2014 (SI 214/560) art.2 and Sch.1 para.18 (March 13, 2014) (as regards England and Wales only) and Marriage and Civil Partnership (Scotland) Act 2014 and Civil Partnership Act 2004 (Consequential Provisions and Modifications) Order 2014 (SI 2014/3229) art.29, Sch.5 para.7(a) (December 16, 2014) (Scotland only).

3. Civil Partnership (Opposite-sex Couples) Regulations 2019 (SI 2019/1458) reg.41(a) and Sch.3, Part 1 para.7 (December 2, 2019).

Short title, construction, commencement and extent

1.33 **10.**—(1) This Act may be cited as the Pneumoconiosis etc (Workers' Compensation) Act 1979.

(2) Except where the context otherwise requires, any expression to which a meaning is assigned by [1 the Social Security Contributions and Benefits Act 1992 or the Social Security Administration Act 1992], or by any regulations made under [1 either of those Acts], has that meaning also for the purposes of this Act.

(3) This Act shall come into force on the expiration of a period of three months beginning with the day on which it is passed.

(4) This Act does not extend to Northern Ireland.

AMENDMENT

1. Social Security (Consequential Provisions) Act 1992 s.4, Sch.2 para.57 (July 1, 1992).

GENERAL NOTE

1.34 The relevant provisions of s.3 of the Pneumoconiosis etc. (Workers' Compensation) Act 1979 have been included in this volume as the definitions therein (e.g. as to who is a "dependant") apply for the purposes of the 2008 Diffuse Mesothelioma Scheme (see Child Maintenance and Other Payments Act 2008 s.46(4)). The definition of "dependant" in s.3 has also been incorporated by the scheme established under the Mesothelioma Act 2014 (see s.18(1)).

Section 10 is included in this volume because of s.10(2). The effect of this is that for the purposes of the 2008 Scheme the (fatal) condition of diffuse mesothelioma is as defined by Prescribed Disease D3 in Sch.1 to the Social Security (Industrial Injuries) (Prescribed Diseases) Regulations 1985 (SI 1985/967) (according to reg.1(2)).

On the scheme of the 1979 Act generally, see the decision by Judge Mitchell in the compensation recovery appeal case, *Aviva Insurance v SSWP* [2015] UKUT 613 (AAC).

Social Security Contributions and Benefits Act 1992

(1992 c.4)

ARRANGEMENT OF SECTIONS

PART I

CONTRIBUTIONS

Preliminary

PART II

CONTRIBUTORY BENEFITS

Preliminary

Unemployment benefit

Incapacity benefit

For the text of these sections, see the 2011/12 edition of this Volume.

Sickness benefit

Invalidity benefits

Child's special allowance

Provisions relating to unemployment benefit, sickness benefit and invalidity benefit

Invalidity benefit-disqualifications etc.

Complete or partial failure to satisfy contribution conditions

Graduated retirement benefit

PART III

NON-CONTRIBUTORY BENEFITS

Attendance allowance

Severe disablement allowance

Invalid care allowance

Disability living allowance

Guardian's allowance

Benefits for the aged

PART IV

INCREASES FOR DEPENDANTS

Child dependants

Adult dependants

Miscellaneous

93. Dependency increases on termination of employment after period of entitlement to disability working allowance.

PART V

BENEFIT FOR INDUSTRIAL INJURIES

General provisions

94. Right to industrial injuries benefit.
95. Relevant employments.
96. Persons treated as employers for certain purposes.
97. Accidents in course of illegal employments.
98. Earner acting in breach of regulations, etc.
99. Earner travelling in employer's transport.
100. Accidents happening while meeting emergency.
101. Accident caused by another's misconduct etc.

Sickness benefit

102. *Repealed.*

Disablement pension

103. Disablement pension.
104. Increase where constant attendance needed.
105. Increase for exceptionally severe disablement.

Other benefits and increases

106. Benefits and increases subject to qualifications as to time.

Successive accidents

107. Adjustments for successive accidents.

Prescribed industrial diseases, etc.

108. Benefit in respect of prescribed industrial diseases, etc.
109. General provisions relating to benefit under section 108.
110. Respiratory diseases.

Old cases

111. Workmen's compensation etc.

PART VI

MISCELLANEOUS PROVISIONS RELATING TO PARTS I TO V

Earnings

112. Certain sums to be earnings.

Disqualification and suspension

113. General provisions as to disqualification and suspension.

Persons maintaining dependants etc.

114. Persons maintaining dependants, etc.

Special cases

115. Crown employment—Parts I to VI.
116. Her Majesty's forces.
117. Mariners, airmen, etc.
118. Married women and widows.
119. Persons outside Great Britain.
120. Employment at sea (continental shelf operations).
121. Treatment of certain marriages.

Interpretation

122. Interpretation of Parts I to VI and supplementary provisions.

PART VII

INCOME-RELATED BENEFITS

Omitted.

See *the 2021–22 edition of Vol. V and the cumulative supplement in this year's Vol. II.*

PART VIII

THE SOCIAL FUND

Omitted.

See *Vol. II: Universal Credit.*

Part IX

Child Benefit

141.–147. *Omitted.* See *Vol IV: HMRC-administered Social Security Benefits and Scotland.*

Part X

Christmas Bonus for Pensioners

148. Entitlement of pensioners to Christmas bonus.
149. Provisions supplementary to section 148.
150. Interpretation of Part X.

Part XI

Statutory Sick Pay

151.–163. *Omitted.*
See Vol IV: HMRC-administered Social Security Benefits and Scotland.

Part XII

Statutory Maternity Pay

164.–171. *Omitted.*
See Vol IV: HMRC-administered Social Security Benefits and Scotland.

Part XIIZA

Statutory Paternity Pay

171ZA.–171ZK. *Omitted.*
See Vol IV: HMRC-administered Social Security Benefits and Scotland.

Part XIIZB

Statutory Adoption Pay

171ZL.–171ZT. *Omitted.*
See Vol IV: HMRC-administered Social Security Benefits and Scotland.

PART XIIZC

STATUTORY SHARED PARENTAL PAY

171ZU.– 171ZZ5. *Omitted.*
See Vol IV: HMRC-administered Social Security Benefits and Scotland.

PART XII ZD

STATUTORY PARENTAL BEREAVEMENT PAY

171ZZ6.– 171ZZ15. *Omitted.*
See Vol IV: HMRC-administered Social Security Benefits and Scotland.

PART XIIA

INCAPACITY FOR WORK

171A.–171G. *Omitted.*
For the text of these sections see the 2011/12 edition of this Volume.

PART XIII

GENERAL

Interpretation

172. Application of Act in relation to territorial waters.
173. Age.
174. References to Acts.

Subordinate legislation

175. Regulations, orders and schemes.
176. Parliamentary control.

Short title, commencement and extent

177. Short title, commencement and extent.

SCHEDULES

Schedule 1—*Omitted.*
Schedule 2—*Omitted.*
Schedule 3—Contribution conditions for entitlement to benefit.

An Act to consolidate certain enactments relating to social security contributions and benefits with amendments to give effect to recommendations of the Law Commission and the Scottish Law Commission.

[13TH FEBRUARY 1992]

PART I

CONTRIBUTIONS

Preliminary

Outline of contributory system

1.—(1) The funds required— 1.36

(a) for paying such benefits under this Act [16 or any other Act] as are payable out of the National Insurance Fund and not out of other public money; and

(b) for the making of payments under section 162 of the Administration Act towards the cost of the National Health Service,

shall be provided by means of contributions payable to the [1 Inland Revenue] by earners, employers and others, together with the additions under subsection (5) below [2 and amounts payable under section 2 of the Social Security Act 1993].

(2) Contributions under this Part of this Act shall be of the following [3[19. . .]] classes—

(a) Class 1, earnings-related, payable under section 6 below, being—

(i) primary Class 1 contributions from employed earners; and

(ii) secondary Class 1 contributions from employers and other persons paying earnings;

(b) Class 1A, payable under section 10 below [4 . . .] by persons liable to pay secondary Class 1 contributions and certain other persons;

[5(bb) Class 1B, payable under section 10A below by persons who are accountable to the Inland Revenue in respect of income tax on [6 general earnings] in accordance with a PAYE settlement agreement;]

(c) Class 2, flat-rate, payable [17. . .] under section 11 below by self-employed earners;

(d) Class 3, payable under section 13 [14 or 13A] below by earners and others voluntarily with a view to providing entitlement to benefit, or making up entitlement; [19. . .]

[19(da) Class 3A, payable by eligible people voluntarily under section 14A with a view to obtaining units of additional pension; and]

(e) Class 4, payable under section 15 below in respect of the profits or gains of a trade, profession or vocation, or under section 18 below in respect of equivalent earnings.

(3) The amounts and rates of contributions in this Part of this Act and the other figures in it which affect the liability of contributions shall—

(a) be subject to regulations under sections 19(4) and 116 to 120 below; and

(b) to the extent provided for by Part IX of the Administration Act be subject to alteration by orders made by the [7 Treasury] from year to year under that Part [8. . .].

(4) Schedule 1 to this Act—

(a) shall have effect with respect to the computation, collection and recovery of contributions of Classes 1, 1A, [9 1B,] 2, 3, [19 and 3A] and otherwise with respect to contributions of those classes; and

(b) shall also, to the extent provided by regulations made under section 18 below, have effect with respect to the computation, collection and recovery of Class 4 contributions, and otherwise with respect to such contributions [10 . . .].

(5) For each financial year there shall, by way of addition to contributions, be paid out of money provided by Parliament, in such manner and at such times as the Treasury may determine, amounts the total of which for any such year is equal to the aggregate of all statutory sick pay [11, statutory maternity pay], [15statutory paternity pay,][11 statutory adoption pay] [,18 statutory shared parental pay and statutory parental bereavement pay] recovered by employers and others in that year, as estimated by the Government Actuary or the Deputy Government Actuary.

(6) No person shall—

(a) be liable to pay Class 1, Class 1A [12, Class 1B] or Class 2 contributions unless he fulfils prescribed conditions as to residence or presence in Great Britain;

(b) be entitled to pay Class 3 contributions unless he fulfils such conditions; or

(c) be entitled to pay Class 1, Class 1A [12, Class 1B] or Class 2 contributions other than those which he is liable to pay, except so far as he is permitted by regulations to pay them.

[13 (7) Regulations under subsection (6) above shall be made by the Treasury.]

AMENDMENTS

1. Social Security Contributions (Transfer of Functions, etc.) Act 1999 Sch.1 para.5(2) (February 25, 1999 for the purpose of enabling the Secretary of State to make subordinate legislation conferring functions on the Commissioners of Inland Revenue; April 1, 1999 otherwise).

2. Social Security Act 1993 s.2(9) (January 29, 1993).

3. Social Security Act 1998 Sch.7 para.56(1) (September 8, 1998 for the purpose of authorising the making of regulations or orders; April 6, 1999 otherwise).

4. Child Support, Pensions and Social Security Act 2000 Sch.9 (Part VIII), para.1 (April 6, 2000: repeal has effect in relation to the tax year beginning April 6, 2000 and subsequent tax years).

5. Social Security Act 1998 Sch.7 para.56(1) (September 8, 1998 for the purpose of authorising the making of regulations or orders; April 6, 1999 otherwise).

6. Income Tax (Earnings and Pensions) Act 2003 Sch.6(2) para.170 (April 6, 2003 subject to transitional provisions and savings specified in 2003 c.1 Sch.7).

7. Social Security Contributions (Transfer of Functions, etc.) Act 1999 Sch.3 para.1(2) (April 1, 1999).

8. Pensions Act 2014 Sch.13 para.49 (April 6, 2016).

9. Social Security Act 1998 Sch.7 para.56(2) (September 8, 1998 for the purpose of authorising the making of regulations or orders; April 6, 1999 otherwise).

10. Social Security Contributions (Transfer of Functions, etc.) Act 1999 Sch.1 para.5(3) (February 25, 1999 for the purpose of enabling the Secretary of State to make subordinate legislation conferring functions on the Commissioners of Inland Revenue; April 1, 1999 otherwise).

11. Employment Act 2002 Pt 1, s.6(3) (December 8, 2002 subject to transitional provisions specified in SI 2002/2866 Sch.3; not yet in force otherwise).

12. Social Security Act 1998 Sch.7, para.56(3) (September 8, 1998 for the purpose of authorising the making of regulations or orders; April 6, 1999 otherwise).

13. Social Security Contributions (Transfer of Functions, etc.) Act 1999 Sch.3, para.1(3) (April 1, 1999).

14. Pensions Act 2008 s.135(3) (April 6, 2009).

15. Children and Families Act 2014 s.126, Sch.7, para.7(a) (April 5, 2015).

16. Pensions Act 2014 Sch.12 para.3 (April 6, 2016).

17. National Insurance Contributions Act 2015 s.2 Sch.1 para.2 (April 6, 2015).

18. Parental Bereavement (Leave and Pay) Act 2018 s.1 and Sch. para.9 (January 18, 2020).

19. Pensions Act 2014 Sch.15(1) para.2 (October 12, 2015).

Categories of earners

2.—(1) In this Part of this Act and Parts II to V below— **1.37**

(a) "employed earner" means a person who is gainfully employed in Great Britain either under a contract of service, or in an office (including elective office) with [2 [3 . . .] earnings]; and

(b) "self-employed earner" means a person who is gainfully employed in Great Britain otherwise than in employed earner's employment (whether or not he is also employed in such employment).

(2) Regulations may provide—

(a) for employment of any prescribed description to be disregarded in relation to liability for contributions otherwise arising from employment of that description;

(b) for a person in employment of any prescribed description to be treated, for the purposes of this Act, as falling within one or other of the categories of earner defined in subsection (1) above, notwithstanding that he would not fall within that category apart from the regulations.

[4(2ZA) Regulations under subsection (2)(b) may make provision treating a person ("P") as falling within one or other of the categories of earner in relation to an employment where arrangements have been entered into the main purpose, or one of the main purposes, of which is to secure—

(a) that P is not treated by other provision in regulations under subsection (2)(b) as falling within that category of earner in relation to the employment, or

(b) that a person is not treated as the secondary contributor in respect of earnings paid to or for the benefit of P in respect of the employment.

(2ZB) In subsection (2ZA) "arrangements" include any scheme, transaction or series of transactions, agreement or understanding, whether or not legally enforceable, and any associated operations.]

[1 (2A) Regulations under subsection (2) above shall be made by the Treasury and, in the case of regulations under paragraph (b) of that subsection, with the concurrence of the Secretary of State.]

(3) Where a person is to be treated by reference to any employment of his as an employed earner, then he is to be so treated for all purposes of this Act; and references throughout this Act to employed earner's employment shall be construed accordingly.

(4) Subsections (1) to (3) above are subject to the provision made by section 95 below as to the employments which are to be treated, for the purposes of industrial injuries benefit, as employed earner's employments.

(5) For the purposes of this Act, a person shall be treated as a self-employed earner as respects any week during any part of which he is such an earner (without prejudice to his being also treated as an employed earner as respects that week by reference to any other employment of his).

AMENDMENTS

1. Welfare Reform and Pensions Act 1999 Sch.11 para.2 (April 6, 2000), replacing an earlier amendment made by the Transfer of Functions Act 1999, Sch.3 para.2 (April 1, 1999).

2. Income Tax (Earnings and Pensions) Act 2003 s.722, Sch.6 paras 169 and 171 (April 6, 2003).

3. National Insurance Contributions Act 2014, s.15(1) (May 13, 2014).

4. National Insurance Contributions Act 2015 s.6(3) (December 12, 2015)

DERIVATION

1.38 SSA 1975 s.2.

DEFINITIONS

"contract of service"—s.122.
"employment"—s.122.
"prescribed"—s.122.

GENERAL NOTE

1.39 The definitions in this section are primarily of importance in determining liability to pay contributions of a particular class, which is a matter for HMRC. Their importance for tribunals is that the definition of "earnings" in s.3 refers back to this section.

The definition of employed earners refers to a person being "gainfully employed". This notion has caused some difficulty but it appears that it refers to cases where there is an obligation by an employer to pay remuneration to an employee for those tasks the employee is bound to perform for the employer under the contract of employment: see Slade J. in *Vandyk v Minister of Pensions and National Insurance* [1955] 1 Q.B. 29 at 38.

"Contract of service"

This is broadly defined by the Act to include any contract of service or apprenticeship, whether written or oral and whether express or implied. The existence of an employer/employee relationship may not always be obvious. The trend of a complex general case law on the issue is that in determining whether a person is self-employed or employed, particular regard will be had to whether the person has risked his or her own capital in the enterprise: *Young and Woods v West* [1980] I.R.L.R. 201 at 209. For a detailed discussion of the question see *Wikeley Ogus & Barendt*, pp.96–109, and see now *Autoclenz Ltd v Belcher* [2011] UKSC 41; [2011] I.C.R. 1157 and *Stringfellow Restaurants Ltd v Quashie* [2012] EWCA Civ 1735; [2013] I.R.L.R. 99; see further *Pimlico Plumbers v Smith* [2018] UKSC 29. 1.40

"Earnings" and "earner"

3.—(1) In this Part of this Act and Parts II to V below— 1.41

(a) "earnings" includes any remuneration or profit derived from an employment; and

(b) "earner" shall be construed accordingly.

(2) For the purposes of this Part of this Act and of Parts II to V below other than those of Schedule 8—

(a) the amount of a person's earnings for any period; or

(b) the amount of his earnings to be treated as comprised in any payment made to him or for his benefit,

shall be calculated or estimated in such manner and on such basis as may be prescribed [1 by regulations made by the Treasury with the concurrence of the Secretary of State.]

[2 (2A) Regulations made for the purposes of subsection (2) above may provide that, where a payment is made or a benefit provided to or for the benefit of two or more earners, a proportion (determined in such manner as may be prescribed) of the amount or value of the payment or benefit shall be attributed to each earner.]

(3) Regulations made for the purposes of subsection (2) above may prescribe that payments of a particular class or description made or falling to be made to or by a person shall, to such extent as may be prescribed, be disregarded or, as the case may be, be deducted from the amount of that person's earnings.

[3 (4) Subsection (5) below applies to regulations made for the purposes of subsection (2) above which make special provision with respect to the earnings periods of directors and former directors of companies.

(5) Regulations to which this subsection applies may make provisions—

(a) for enabling companies, and directors and former directors of companies, to pay on account of any earnings-related contributions that may become payable by them such amounts as would be payable by way of such contributions if the special provision had not been made; and

(b) for requiring any payments made in accordance with the regulations to be treated, for prescribed purposes, as if they were the contributions on account of which they were made.]

AMENDMENTS

1. Transfer of Functions Act 1999 Sch.3 para.3 (April 1, 1999).
2. Social Security Act 1998 s.48 (September 8, 1998).
3. Social Security Act 1998 s.49(1) (September 8, 1998).

DERIVATION

1.42 SSA 1975 s.3(1)–(3).

DEFINITIONS

"employment"—s.122.
"prescribed"—s.122.

GENERAL NOTE

1.43 The computation of earnings is required in connection with a number of benefits:

(1) to calculate reduced earnings allowance;

(2) in disregarding casual or subsidiary work producing small sums in relation to entitlement to benefits based on incapacity for work, unemployment or retirement, and allowance;

(3) to determine entitlement to increases of benefit for children and dependants; and

(4) to determine any reduction of retirement pensions by reason of earnings.

The rules on computation are to be found in the Computation of Earnings Regulations and in Commissioners' decisions. The Computation of Earnings Regulations 1996 take an approach to the calculation of earnings in relation to non-means tested benefits which closely parallels that which has applied for some time to the calculation of earnings for income-related benefits.

Payments treated as remuneration, and earnings

1.44 **4.**—(1) For the purposes of section 3 above there shall be treated as remuneration derived from employed earner's employment—

(a) any sum paid to or for the benefit of a person in satisfaction (whether in whole or in part) of any entitlement of that person to—
  (i) statutory sick pay; or
  (ii) statutory maternity pay;
  [6 (iii) [8 . . .] statutory paternity pay];
  (iv) [9 . . .]
  [6 (v) statutory adoption pay];
  [9 [10. . .](vi) statutory shared parental pay;] [10 or
  (vii) statutory parental bereavement pay;] and]

(b) any sickness payment made—
  (i) to or for the benefit of the employed earner; and
  (ii) in accordance with arrangements under which the person who is the secondary contributor in relation to the employment concerned has made, or remains liable to make, payments towards the provision of that sickness payment.

(2) Where the funds for making sickness payments under arrangements of the kind mentioned in paragraph (b) of subsection (1) above are attributable in part to contributions to those funds made by the employed earner, regulations may make provision for disregarding, for the purposes of that subsection, the prescribed part of any sum paid as a result of the arrangements.

(3) For the purposes of subsections (1) and (2) above "sickness payment" means any payment made in respect of absence from work due to incapacity for work, [[1] . . .].

[[2] (4) For the purposes of section 3 above there shall be treated as remuneration derived from an employed earner's employment—

[[7] (a) the amount of any gain calculated under section 479 or 480 of ITEPA 2003 in respect of which an amount counts as employment income of the earner under section 476 or 477 of that Act (charge on exercise, assignment or release of share option);]

(b) any sum paid (or treated as paid) to or for the benefit of the earner which is chargeable to tax by virtue of [section 225 or 226 of ITEPA 2003] (taxation of consideration for certain restrictive undertakings).]

(5) For the purposes of section 3 above regulations may make provision for treating as remuneration derived from an employed earner's employment any payment made by a body corporate to or for the benefit of any of its directors where that payment would, when made, not be earnings for the purposes of this Act.

[[3] (6) Regulations may make provision for the purposes of this Part—

(a) for treating any amount on which an employed earner is chargeable to income tax under [[7] the employment income Parts of ITEPA 2003] as remuneration derived from the earner's employment; and

(b) for treating any amount which in accordance with regulations under paragraph (a) above constitutes remuneration as an amount of remuneration paid, at such time as may be determined in accordance with the regulations, to or for the benefit of the earner in respect of his employment.]

[[4] (7) Regulations under this section shall be made by the Treasury with the concurrence of the Secretary of State.]

AMENDMENTS

1. Incapacity for Work Act 1994 Sch.1 para.1 (April 13, 1995).
2. Social Security Act 1998 s.50(1) (September 8, 1998).
3. Child Support, Pensions and Social Security Act 2000 s.74(3) (April 6, 2000).
4. Transfer of Functions Act 1999 Sch.3 para.5 (April, 1999).
5. Employment Act 2002 s.53 and Sch.7 paras 2 and 3 (December 8, 2002).
6. Work and Families Act 2006 Sch.1, para. 3 (April 6, 2010).
7. Income Tax (Earnings and Pensions) Act 2003 s.722, Sch.6 paras 169 and 172 (April 5, 2003).
8. Children and Families Act 2014 s.126, Sch.7, para.8(a) (April 5, 2015).
9. Children and Families Act 2014 Sch.7, paras 8(b) & (c) (December 1, 2014).
10. Parental Bereavement (Leave and Pay) Act 2018 s.1 and Sch. para.10 (January 18, 2020).

DERIVATION

SSA 1975 s.3(1A)–(1D) and (4). 1.45

Sections 4A–19 omitted. 1.46

Part II

Contributory Benefits

Preliminary

Descriptions of contributory benefits

1.47 **20.**—(1) Contributory benefits under this Part of this Act are of the following descriptions, namely—

(a) [4 . . .]

[3 (b) incapacity benefit, comprising—

(i) short-term incapacity benefit, and

(ii) long-term incapacity benefit;]

(c) [3 . . .]

(d) maternity allowance [10 . . .];

(e) widow's benefit, comprising—

(i) [5 . . .]

(ii) widowed mother's allowance [8 . . .]

(iii) widow's pension;

[12 (ea) widowed parent's allowance;]

(f) retirement pensions of the following categories—

(i) Category A, payable to a person by virtue of his own contributions (with increase for adult [8. . .] dependants); and

[3(ii) Category B, payable to a person by virtue of the contributions of a spouse [8 . . .] [9or civil partner];]

[6 (fa) shared additional pensions]

(g) for existing beneficiaries only, child's special allowance.

(2) In this Act—

"long-term benefit" means—

[2 (a) long-term incapacity benefit;]

(b) a widowed mother's allowance;

[7 (ba) widowed parent's allowance;

[12 (bb) . . ..]]

(c) a widow's pension; [6 . . ..]

(d) a Category A or Category B retirement pension; and

[12(e) a shared additional pension under section 55A below].

"short-term benefit" means—

(a) [4 . . .]

[2 (b) short-term incapacity benefit; and]

(c) maternity allowance.

(3) The provisions of this Part of this Act are subject to the provisions of [1Chapter II of Part III of the Pensions Act [11 (reduction in benefits for members of schemes that were contracted-out)]].

Amendments

1. Pensions Schemes Act 1993 Sch.8 para.35 (February 7, 1994).
2. Social Security (Incapacity for Work) Act 1994 Sch.1 para.2 (April 13, 1995).
3. Pensions Act 1995 Sch.4 para.21 (July 19, 1995).
4. Jobseekers Act 1995 Sch.3 para.1 (October 7, 1996).
5. Welfare Reform and Pensions Act 1999 Sch.13 para.1 (April 24, 2000).

6. Welfare Reform and Pensions Act 1999 Sch.8 para.3 (December 1, 2000).
7. Welfare Reform and Pensions Act 1999 Sch.8 para.3 (April 9, 2001).
8. Tax Credits Act 2002 Sch.6 para.1 (April 6, 2003).
9. Civil Partnership Act 2004 Sch.24 para.13 (December 5, 2005).
10. Welfare Reform Act 2009 Sch.7 para.1 (April 6, 2010).
11. Pensions Act 2014 Sch.13 para.53 (April 6, 2016).
12. Pensions Act 2014 Sch.16 para.3 (April 6, 2017).

Contribution conditions

21.—(1) Entitlement to any of the benefits specified in section 20(1) above, [1 other than [2 short-term incapacity benefit under subsection (1)(b) of section 30A below] long-term incapacity benefit under [2 subsection (5) of that section] [3 maternity allowance under section 35 [14 or 35B] below] or short-term or long-term incapacity benefit under 40 or 41 below], [4 or a shared additional pension under section 55A [15 or 55AA] below] depends on contribution conditions being satisfied (either by the claimant or by some other person, according to the particular benefit). 1.48

(2) The class or classes of contribution which, for the purposes of subsection (1) above, are relevant in relation to each of those benefits are as follows—

Short-term benefit

[5 . . .]
[1 short-term incapacity benefit under section [6 30A(1)(a)] below. Class 1 or 2
[7 . . .]

Other benefits

[8 [16 . . .]
Widowed mother's allowance Class 1, 2 or 3
[8 Widowed parent's allowance Class 1, 2 or 3
[16 . . .]
Widow's pension Class 1, 2 or 3
Category A retirement pension Class 1, 2 or 3
Category B retirement pension Class 1, 2 or 3
Child's special allowance Class 1, 2 or 3

(3) The relevant contribution conditions in relation to the benefits specified in subsection (2) above are those specified in Part I of Schedule 3 to this Act.

(4) [16 . . .]

(5) In subsection (4) above and Schedule 3 to this Act—

(a) "the contributor concerned" for the purposes of any contribution condition, means the person by whom the condition is to be satisfied.
(b) "a relevant class", in relation to any benefit, means a class of contributions specified in relation to that benefit in subsection (2) above;
(c) "the earnings factor"—
 (i) where the year in question is 1987–88 or any subsequent tax year, means, in relation to a person, the aggregate of his earnings factors derived from [12 so much of his earnings as did not

exceed the upper earnings limit] upon which primary Class 1 contributions have been paid or treated as paid and from his Class 2 and Class 3 contributions; and

(ii) where the year in question is any earlier tax year, means, in relation to a person's contributions of any class or classes, the aggregate of his earnings factors derived from all those contributions;

(d) except in the expression "benefit year", "year" means a tax year.

[9 (5A) Where primary Class 1 contributions have been paid or treated as paid on any part of a person's earnings, the following provisions, namely—

(a) subsection (5)(c) above;

(b) sections 22(1)(a) [10 (2A)] and (3)(a), 23(3)(a), 24(2)(a), [10 44(6) (za) and (a)] [11 . . .] below; and

(c) paragraphs 2(4)(a) and (5)(a), 4(2)(a), 5(2)(b) and 4(a) [13, 5A(3) (a)] and 7(a) of Schedule 3 to this Act,

shall have effect as if such contributions had been paid or treated as paid on so much of the earnings as did not exceed the upper earnings limit.]

(6) In this Part of this Act "benefit year", means a period—

(a) beginning with the first Sunday in January in any calendar year, and

(b) ending with the Saturday immediately preceding the first Sunday in January in the following calendar year;

but for any prescribed purposes of this Part of this Act "benefit year" may by regulations be made to mean such other period (whether or not a period of 12 months) as may be specified in the regulations.

AMENDMENTS

1. Social Security (Incapacity for Work) Act 1994 Sch.1 para.3 (April 13, 1995).
2. Welfare Reform and Pensions Act 1999 s.70 (April 6, 2001).
3. Welfare Reform and Pensions Act 1999 Sch.8 para.31(2) (April 2, 2000).
4. Welfare Reform & Pensions Act 1999 Sch.12 para.15(16) (December 1, 2000).
5. Jobseekers Act 1995 Sch.3 (October 10, 1996).
6. Welfare Reform and Pensions Act 1999 s.88 (April 6, 2001).
7. Welfare Reform and Pensions Act 1999 Sch.8 para.31(3) & (4) (April 2, 2000).
8. Welfare Reform and Pensions Act 1999 s.70 (April 8, 2001).
9. Social Security Act 1998 Sch.7, para.61 (April 6, 1999).
10. Child Support, Pensions and Social Security Act 2000 s.35(2) (April 6, 2002).
11. Tax Credits Act 2002 Sch.6 (April 6, 2003).
12. National Insurance Contributions Act 2002 Sch.1 para.6 (April 6, 2003).
13. Pensions Act 2008 Sch.4 para.2 (January 3, 2012).
14. Social Security (Maternity Allowance) (Participating Wife or Civil Partner of Self-employed Earner) Regulations 2014 Social Security (Maternity Allowance) (Participating Wife or Civil Partner of Self-employed Earner) Regulations 2014 (SI 2014/606) reg.2(1) and (2) (April 1, 2014).
15. Pensions Act 2014 s.15 and Sch.11 paras 2 and 3 (April 6, 2016).
16. Pensions Act 2014 Sch.16 para.4 (April 6, 2017).

Earnings factors

1.49 **22.**—(1) A person shall, for the purposes specified in subsection (2) below, be treated as having annual earnings factors derived—

(a) in the case of 1987–88 or any subsequent tax year, from [3so much of his earnings as did not exceed the upper earnings limit and] upon which primary Class 1 contributions have been paid or treated as paid and from Class 2 and Class 3 contributions; and

(b) in the case of any earlier tax year, from his contributions of any of Classes 1, 2 and 3;

but subject to the following provisions of this section and those of section 23 below.

(2) The purposes referred to in subsection (1) above are those of—

(a) establishing, by reference to the satisfaction of contribution conditions, entitlement to [1a contribution-based jobseeker's allowance [10, to a contributory employment and support allowance] or to] any benefit specified in section 20(1) above, other than maternity allowance; [11...]

(b) calculating the additional pension in the rate of a long-term benefit [11; and]

[11 (c) establishing entitlement to a state pension under Part 1 of the Pensions Act 2014 and, where relevant, calculating the rate of a state pension under that Part [12 and]]

[12 (d) establishing entitlement to bereavement support payment under section 30 of the Pensions Act 2014.]

[3(2A) For the purposes specified in subsection (2)(b) above, in the case of the first appointed year or any subsequent tax year a person's earnings factor shall be treated as derived only from [4so much of his earnings as did not exceed [5the applicable limit] and] on which primary Class 1 contributions have been paid or treated as paid.] [5This subsection does not affect the operation of sections 44A and 44B (deemed earnings factors).]

[5(2B) "The applicable limit" means—

(a) in relation to a tax year before [92009–10], the upper earnings limit;

(b) in relation to [92009–10] or any subsequent tax year, the upper accrual point.]

(3) Separate earnings factors may be derived for 1987–88 and subsequent tax years—

(a) from earnings [4not exceeding the upper earnings limit] upon which primary Class 1 contributions have been paid or treated as paid.

(b) from earnings which have been credited;

(c) from contributions of different classes paid or credited in the same tax year;

(d) by any combination of the methods mentioned in paragraphs (a) to (c) above,

and may be derived for any earlier tax year from contributions of different classes paid or credited in the same tax year, and from contributions which have actually been paid, as opposed to those not paid but credited.

(4) Subject to regulations under section 19(4) to (6) above, no earnings factor shall be derived–

(a) for 1987–88 or any subsequent tax year, from earnings [2 in respect of which] primary Class 1 contributions are paid at the reduced rate, or

(b) for any earlier tax year, from primary Class 1 contributions paid at the reduced rate or from secondary Class 1 contributions.

(5) Regulations may provide for crediting—

(a) for 1987–88 or any subsequent tax year, earnings or Class 2 or Class 3 contributions, or

(b) for any earlier tax year, contributions of any class,

for the purpose of bringing a person's earnings factor for that tax year to a figure which will enable him to satisfy contribution conditions of entitlement to [1a contribution based jobseeker's allowance or to] any prescribed description of benefit (whether his own entitlement or another person's).

[11 (5ZA) Regulations may provide for crediting—

(a) for 1987-88 or any subsequent tax year, earnings or Class 2 or Class 3 contributions, or

(b) for any earlier tax year, contributions of any class,

for the purpose of bringing an earnings factor for that tax year to a figure which will make that year a "qualifying year", "pre-commencement qualifying year" or "post-commencement qualifying year" of a person for the purposes of Part 1 of the Pensions Act 2014 (see sections 2(4) and 4(4) of that Act).

(5ZB) Regulations under subsection (5ZA) must provide for crediting a person with such contributions as may be specified in respect of periods on or after 6 April 1975 during which the person was—

(a) a spouse or civil partner of a member of Her Majesty's forces,

(b) accompanying the member on an assignment outside the United Kingdom, and

(c) not of a description specified in the regulations.]

[7(5A) Section 23A makes provision for the crediting of Class 3 contributions for the purpose of determining entitlement to the benefits to which that section applies.]

(6) Regulations may impose limits with respect to the earnings factors which a person may have or be treated as having in respect of any one tax year.

(7) The power to amend regulations made before 30th March 1977 (the passing of the Social Security (Miscellaneous Provisions) Act 1977) under subsection (5) above may be so exercised as to restrict the circumstances in which and the purposes for which a person is entitled to credits in respect of weeks before the coming into force of the amending regulations; but not so as to affect any benefit for a period before the coming into force of the amending regulations if it was claimed before 18th March 1977.

[10(8) In this section, "contributory employment and support allowance" means a contributory allowance under Part 1 of the Welfare Reform Act 2007 (employment and support allowance).]

[8 (9) References in this Act or any other Act to earnings factors derived from so much of a person's earnings as do not exceed the upper accrual point or the upper earnings limit are to be read, in relation to earners paid otherwise than weekly, as references to earnings factors derived from so much of those earnings as do not exceed the prescribed equivalent.]

AMENDMENTS

1. Jobseekers Act 1995 Sch.2 para.22 (October 7, 1996).
2. Social Security Act 1998 Sch.7 para.61 (April 6, 1999).
3. Child Support, Pensions and Social Security Act 2000 s.30(1) (April 6, 2002).
4. National Insurance Contributions Act 2002 Sch.1 para.7 (April 6, 2002).
5. Pensions Act 2007 s.12 (September 26, 2007).
6. Pensions Act 2007 Sch.1 para.33 (September 26, 2007).
7. Pensions Act 2007 Sch.1 para.9 (September 26, 2007).
8. National Insurance Contributions Act 2008 Sch.1 para.2 (September 22, 2008).
9. National Insurance Contributions Act 2008 s.3(2) (September 22, 2008).
10. Welfare Reform Act 2007 Sch.3 para.9 (October 27, 2008).
11. Pensions Act 2014 s.23 and Sch.12 paras 2 and 6 (April 6, 2016).
12. Pensions Act 2014 Sch.16 para.5 (April 6, 2017).

Section 23 *omitted because the province of HMRC* 1.50

[1 Contributions credits for relevant parents and carers

23A.—(1) This section applies to the following benefits— 1.51

(a) a Category A retirement pension in a case where the contributor concerned attains pensionable age on or after 6th April 2010;
(b) a Category B retirement pension payable by virtue of section 48A [2 or 48AA] below in a case where the contributor concerned attains pensionable age on or after that date;
(c) a Category B retirement pension payable by virtue of section 48B below in a case where the contributor concerned dies on or after that date without having attained pensionable age before that date;
(d) a widowed parent's allowance payable in a case where the contributor concerned dies on or after that date.
(e) [4 . . .]

(2) The contributor concerned in the case of a benefit to which this section applies shall be credited with a Class 3 contribution for each week falling after 6th April 2010 in respect of which the contributor was a relevant carer.

(3) A person is a relevant carer in respect of a week if the person—
(a) is awarded child benefit for any part of that week in respect of a child under the age of 12,
(b) is a foster parent for any part of that week, or
(c) is engaged in caring, within the meaning given by regulations, in that week.

(4) Regulations may make provision for a person's entitlement to be credited with Class 3 contributions by virtue of falling within subsection (3)(b) or (c) above to be conditional on the person—
(a) applying to be so credited in accordance with the prescribed requirements, and
(b) complying with the prescribed requirements as to the provision of information to the Secretary of State.

(5) The contributor concerned in the case of a benefit to which this section applies shall be credited with 52 Class 3 contributions for each tax year ending before 6th April 2010 in which the contributor was precluded from regular employment by responsibilities at home within the meaning of regulations under paragraph 5(7) of Schedule 3.

(6) But the maximum number of tax years for which a person can be credited with contributions under subsection (5) above is—
(a) in the case of a benefit mentioned in subsection (1)(a) to (c) above, 22;
(b) in the case of a benefit mentioned in subsection (1)(d) [4 . . .] above, half the requisite number of years of the person's working life.

(7) The table in paragraph 5(5) of Schedule 3 (requisite number of years of a working life of given duration) applies for the purposes of subsection (6)(b) above as it applies for the purposes of the second condition set out in paragraph 5(3)of that Schedule.

(8) For the purpose of determining entitlement to a benefit to which this section applies, a week that falls partly in one tax year and partly in another is to be treated as falling in the year in which it begins and not in the following year.

[3 (8A) Where this section, or regulations made under it, have the effect that the contributor concerned is credited, on or after 6 April 2016, with contributions for a tax year starting before that date, the contributions are to be treated for the purposes of calculating the rate under paragraph 3 of Schedule 1 to the Pensions Act 2014 as having been credited before 6 April 2016.]

(9) In this section—

"the contributor concerned" has the meaning given in section 21(5)(a) above;

"foster parent" has the meaning given by regulations.]

AMENDMENTS

1. Pensions Act 2007 s.3(1) (September 2, 2007).
2. Pensions Act 2014 Sch.11 para.58 (April 6, 2016).
3. Pensions Act 2014 (Consequential and Supplementary Amendments) Order 2016 (SI 2016/224) art.2(2) (April 6, 2016).
4. Pensions Act 2014 Sch.16 para.6 (April 6, 2017).

DEFINITIONS

"engaged in caring"—see reg.5 Social Security (Contributions Credits for Parents and Carers) Regulations 2010.

"foster parent"—see reg.4, Social Security (Contributions Credits for Parents and Carers) Regulations 2010.

"relevant carer"—see subs.(3).

"the contributor concerned"—see s.21(5)(a).

GENERAL NOTE

1.52 This section introduces weekly National Insurance credits (which replace Home Responsibilities Protection for periods of caring from April 6, 2010) for parents (including foster-parents) and carers in respect of their caring activities.

Although awarding these credits in cases dependent on the award of child benefit has been transferred to HMRC, their administration is done on behalf of the Secretary of State and appeals still lie to the First-tier Tribunal (Social Entitlement Chamber) and the Upper Tribunal (Administrative Appeals Chamber) rather than to the tax tribunals: see the National Insurance Contribution Credits (Transfer of Functions) Order 2009 (SI 2009/1377). The regulations governing the award of these credits are the Social Security (Contributions Credits for Parents and Carers) Regulations 2010 (SI 2010/19): see Pt II of this book.

The section applies to the benefits listed in subs.(1) where the determining event (attainment of pensionable age or death) occurs on or after April 6, 2010. In respect of such benefits, the contributor concerned (see subs.(9) and s.21(5)(a)) is to be credited with a Class 3 contribution for each week falling after April 6, 2010 in respect of which the contributor was a "relevant carer". Subsection (3) stipulates that someone is a "relevant carer" in respect of a week) if he is awarded child benefit for any part of that week in respect of a child under the age of 12, or is a foster parent for any part of that week, or is in that week engaged in caring, within the meaning given by regulations (see reg.5 of the Social Security (Contributions Credits for Parents and Carers) Regulations 2010). Under subs.(5), the contributor concerned is to be credited with 52 Class 3 contributions for each tax year ending before April 6, 2010 in which the contributor was precluded from regular employment by responsibilities at home within the meaning of regulations under para.5(7) of Sch.3 (see further the Social Security Pensions (Home Responsibilities Regulations 1994 in Pt II of this book). But subs.(6) sets maximum limits on the number of tax years in respect of which home responsibilities credits under subs.(5) can be used. The limits are 22 years (Category A or B retirement pensions) or half the requisite number of years of the person's working life (widowed parent's allowance or bereavement allowance).

Section 24 *omitted because the province of HMRC.* 1.53

Unemployment benefit

Unemployment benefit

[1 *Sections 25–30 repealed.*] 1.54

REPEAL

1. Jobseekers Act 1995 Sch.3 (October 7, 1996).

[Incapacity Benefit]

30A.—30E. *Omitted.* 1.55
For the text of and commentary to these sections see the 2011/12 edition of this Volume.

Maternity

State maternity allowance [7 for employed or self-employed earner]

35.—[1 (1) A woman shall be entitled to a maternity allowance [7 under this section], at the appropriate weekly rate determined under section (35A) below if— 1.56

(a) she has become pregnant and has reached, or been confined before reaching, the commencement of the 11th week before the expected week of confinement; and

(b) she has been engaged in employment as an employed or self-employed earner for any part of the week in the case of at least 26 of the 66 weeks immediately preceding the expected week of confinement; and

[6(c) her average weekly earnings (within the meaning of section 35A below) are not less than the maternity allowance threshold for the tax year in which the beginning of the period of 66 weeks mentioned in paragraph (b) above falls;]

(d) she is not entitled to statutory maternity pay for the same week in respect of the same pregnancy].

(2) Subject to the following provisions of this section, a maternity allowance [7under this section] shall be payable for the period ("the maternity allowance period") which, if she were entitled to statutory maternity pay, would be the maternity pay period under section 165 below.

(3) Regulations may provide—

(a) for disqualifying a woman for receiving a maternity allowance [7under this section] if—

[5(i) during the maternity allowance period, except in prescribed cases, she does any work in employment as an employed or self-employed earner;

(ia) during the maternity allowance period she fails without good cause to observe any prescribed rules of behaviour; or]

(ii) at any time before she is confined she fails without good cause to attend for, or submit herself to, any medical examination required in accordance with the regulations;

(b) that this section and [1 Section 35A below] shall have effect subject to prescribed modifications in relation to cases in which a woman has been confined and—

(i) has not made a claim for a maternity allowance [7under this section] in expectation of that confinement (other than a claim which has been disallowed); or

(ii) has made a claim for a maternity allowance [7under this section] in expectation of that confinement (other than a claim which has been disallowed), but she was confined more than 11 weeks before the expected week of confinement.

[2(c) that subsection (2) above shall have effect subject to prescribed modifications in relation to cases in which a woman fails to satisfy the conditions referred to in subsection (1)(b) [1[6 or (c) above]] at the commencement of the 11th week before the expected week of confinement, but subsequently satisfies those conditions at any time before she is confined.]

[8 (3A) Regulations may provide for the duration of the maternity allowance period as it applies to a woman to be reduced, subject to prescribed restrictions and conditions.

(3B) Regulations under subsection (3A) are to secure that the reduced period ends at a time—

(a) after a prescribed period beginning with the day on which the woman is confined, and

(b) when at least a prescribed part of the maternity allowance period remains unexpired.

(3C) Regulations under subsection (3A) may, in particular, prescribe restrictions and conditions relating to—

(a) the end of the woman's entitlement to maternity leave;

(b) the doing of work by the woman;

(c) the taking of prescribed steps by the woman or another person as regards leave under section 75E of the Employment Rights Act 1996 in respect of the child;

(d) the taking of prescribed steps by a person other than the woman as regards statutory shared parental pay in respect of the child.

(3D) Regulations may provide for a reduction in the duration of the maternity allowance period as it applies to a woman to be revoked, or to be treated as revoked, subject to prescribed restrictions and conditions.

(3E) A woman who would, but for the reduction in duration of a maternity pay period by virtue of section 165(3A), be entitled to statutory maternity pay for a week is not entitled to a maternity allowance for that week.]

(4) A woman who has become entitled to a maternity allowance [7under this section] shall cease to be entitled to it if she dies before the beginning

of the maternity allowance period; and if she dies after the beginning, but before the end, of that period, the allowance shall not be payable for any week subsequent to that in which she dies.

(5) Where for any purpose of this Part of this Act or of regulations it is necessary to calculate the daily rate of a maternity allowance [7under this section] [4the amount payable by way of that allowance for any day shall be taken as one seventh of the weekly rate of that allowance.]

(6) In this section "confinement" means—

(a) labour resulting in the issue of a living child, or

(b) labour after [324 weeks] of pregnancy resulting in the issue of a child whether alive or dead,

and "confined" shall be construed accordingly; and where a woman's labour begun on one day results in the issue of a child on another day she shall be taken to be confined on the day of the issue of the child or, if labour results in the issue of twins or a greater number of children, she shall be taken to be confined on the day of the issue of the last of them.

[6 (6A) In this section 'the maternity allowance threshold', in relation to a tax year, means (subject to subsection (6B) below) £30.

(6B) The Secretary of State may, in relation to any tax year after 2001-2002, by order increase the amount for the time being specified in subsection (6A) above to such amount as is specified in the order.

(6C) When deciding whether, and (if so) by how much, to increase the amount so specified the Secretary of State shall have regard to the movement, over such period as he thinks fit, in the general level of prices obtaining in Great Britain (estimated in such manner as he thinks fit).

(6D) The Secretary of State shall in each tax year carry out such a review of the amount for the time being specified in subsection (6A) above as he thinks fit.]

(7) The fact that the mother of a child is being paid maternity allowance [7under this section] shall not be taken into consideration by any court in deciding whether to order payment of expenses incidental to the birth of the child.

AMENDMENTS

1. Welfare Reform and Pensions Act 1999 s.53 (April 2, 2000).
2. Maternity Allowance and Statutory Maternity Pay Regulations 1994 (SI 1994/1230) reg.2 (October 16, 1994).
3. Still Birth (Definition) Act 1992 s.2(1)(a) (October 1, 1992).
4. Social Security Act 1998 s.67 (October 1, 2006).
5. Work and Families Act 2006 Sch.1 para.6 (October 1, 2006).
6. Employment Act 2002 Sch.7 para.4 (April 6, 2003).
7. Social Security (Maternity Allowance) (Participating Wife or Civil Partner of Self-Employed Earner) Regulations 2014 (SI 2014/606) (April 1, 2014).
8. Children and Families Act 2014 s.120 (June 30, 2014).

DERIVATION

SSA 1978 s.22. **1.57**

DEFINITIONS

"Confinement"—see subs.(6).
"Confined"—*ibid.*

General Note

1.58 State Maternity Allowance, MA, is a benefit equivalent to Statutory Maternity Pay. It is paid chiefly to women who have been self-employed. It will also cover women whose service with their current employer does not qualify them for SMP; and women who have been in employment and whose job ended more than 15 weeks before their expected date of confinement and for a reason other than their pregnancy.

From April 2000 this benefit is no longer a contributory benefit. When the claimant's expected week of confinement is on or after April 2, 2000, entitlement will depend upon her showing involvement in work as either an employee or as a self-employed person for a total of 26 weeks out of the preceding 66 weeks. As well, she will have to show a certain level of earnings depending upon which she will qualify for benefit and be paid either standard rate MA, or a lower variable rate MA.

The allowance is payable when the claimant has become pregnant and has been confined, or has reached a stage in her pregnancy, which is the beginning of the 11th week before her expected week of confinement (s.165). There is no definition of pregnancy in the legislation but sufficient proof of that condition will normally follow from the need to prove an expected confinement. Confinement is defined in subs.6 as labour resulting in a living child, or labour after 24 weeks of pregnancy resulting in the issue of a child whether alive or dead. The only dispute that is likely to arise is whether a woman has been pregnant for 24 weeks, or more, before she gives birth to a still-born child. In one case, the Commissioner fixed the date that the pregnancy would be assumed to have commenced by calculating back from the estimated date of confinement for the period of a normal pregnancy *(R(G) 4/56)*. In another, he accepted medical evidence of the duration of the pregnancy from an examination of the foetus (*R(G) 12/59*).

Subsection (2)

1.59 The maternity allowance period is defined by reference to the SMP period. This is defined in s.165 of this Act (and extended by reg.2 of SMP (General) Regulations). Generally it is for a continuous period of 39 weeks beginning not earlier than the 11th week before the expected week of confinement. What is important for this purpose is the correct expected week of confinement rather than the actual week of confinement, even though the confinement may have taken place by the time the decision-maker comes to make a decision (see *R(G) 8/55*). But where regulations alter the allowance period by reference to when a woman is confined it is the date of confinement that applies. Regulation 3 of the Maternity Allowance Regulations permits the shifting of the allowance period where a woman is not entitled at the date of the 11th week before her expected date of confinement, but becomes entitled before she is confined. The allowance period is altered also in the case of a woman who gives birth unexpectedly early. This is because the allowance period is determined by reference to what would have been the Statutory Maternity Pay period had she been entitled to SMP and then by reference to reg.2(3) of the Statutory Maternity Pay Regulations.

Subsection (3)

1.60 Regulations may also provide for the claimant to be disqualified if at any time during the allowance period, she does any work as an employed or self-employed earner. She is not disqualified if she merely does her own housework. Regulations that provided for disqualification of a woman who failed to take care of her health were repealed with effect from 2015, but she may still be disqualified if she fails, without good cause, to attend for a medical examination that has been required on behalf of the Secretary of State. See Maternity Allowance Regulations 1987.

Subsection 3A

1.61 Subsection (3A) was added, with effect from June 30, 2014, by the Children and Families Act 2014. The regulations made in furtherance of it are the Maternity

Allowance (Curtailment) Regulations (SI 2014/3053). These regulations permit a woman to curtail her maternity allowance period so as to allow her partner (which can be either her spouse or the father of her child) to claim statutory shared parental pay and statutory shared parental leave for the balance of the period that remains.

Subsection (5)

With effect from October 1, 2006 s.35(5) was amended by the Social Security Act 1998 (Commencement No. 14) Order 2006 (SI 2006/2376). This brought into force s.67 of Social Security Act 1998 which provides for the daily rate of Maternity Allowance to be calculated at the rate of one-seventh of the weekly rate. This amount will apply to a woman whose date of confinement falls on or after April 1, 2007. A woman whose date of confinement is earlier will be covered by the earlier version of s.35 which provided for a Sunday to be disregarded as a day of entitlement, and any other day to be paid at a rate of one-sixth of the weekly rate. (For the original version of s.35 see earlier editions of the main volume of this work). 1.62

[1 Appropriate weekly rate of maternity allowance [5under section 35]

35A.—[2 (1) For the purposes of section 35(1) above the appropriate weekly rate is (subject to subsection (5A) below) whichever is the lower rate of— 1.63

(a) a weekly rate equivalent to 90 per cent of the woman's average weekly earnings; and

(b) the weekly rate for the time being prescribed under section 166(1)(b) below.]

(2) [. . .]

(3) [. . .]

(4) For the purposes of this section a woman's "average weekly earnings" shall be taken to be the average weekly amount (as determined in accordance with regulations) of specified payments which—

(a) were made to her or for her benefit as an employed earner, or

(b) are (in accordance with regulations) to be treated as made to her or for her benefit as a self-employed earner,

during the specified period.

(5) Regulations may, for the purposes of subsection (4) above, provide—

(a) for the amount of any payments falling within paragraph (a) or (b) of that subsection to be calculated or estimated in such manner and on such basis as may be prescribed;

(b) for a payment made outside the specified period to be treated as made during that period where it was referable to that period or any part of it;

(c) for a woman engaged in employment as a self-employed earner to be treated as having received a payment in respect of a week—

(i) equal to [4 an amount 90 per cent of which is equal to the weekly rate prescribed under section 166(1)(b) below that is] in force on the last day of the week, if she [6 has] paid a Class 2 contribution in respect of the week, or

(ii) equal to the maternity allowance threshold in force on that day, if she [6 could have paid, but has not paid,] such a contribution in respect of the week;

(d) for aggregating payment made or treated as made to or for the benefit of a woman where, either in the same week or in different weeks, she was engaged in two or more employments (whether, in each case, as an employed earner or a self-employed earner).

[2 (5A) Where subsection (5B) below applies the appropriate weekly rate is the weekly rate for the time being prescribed under section 166(1)(b) below.

(5B) This subsection applies where a woman is treated by virtue of regulations under sub-paragraph (i) of paragraph (c) of subsection (5) above as having received a payment in respect of each week in the specified period equal to the amount mentioned in that sub-paragraph.]

[3 (6) In this section "the maternity allowance threshold" has the same meaning as in section 35 above and "specified" means prescribed by or determined in accordance with regulations.]

AMENDMENTS

1. Welfare Reform and Pensions Act 1999 s.53 (April 2, 2000).
2. Employment Act 2002 s.48 (April 6, 2003).
3. Employment Act 2002 Sch.7 (April 6, 2003).
4. Employment Act 2002 s.48(1)(b) (November 24, 2004).
5. Social Security (Maternity Allowance) (Participating Wife or Civil Partner of Self Employed Earner) Regulations 2014 (SI 2014/606) reg.2 (April 1, 2014).
6. National Insurance Contributions Act 2015 s.2 Sch.1 para.6 (April 6, 2015).

GENERAL NOTE

1.64 This section applied when the woman's expected week of confinement began on or after August 20, 2000.

[1 State maternity allowance for participating wife or civil partner of self-employed earner

1.65 **35B.** (1) A woman (W) shall be entitled to a maternity allowance under this section, at the weekly rate given by subsection (3) below, if—

(a) W has become pregnant and has reached, or been confined before reaching, the commencement of the 11th week before the expected week of confinement; and
(b) for any part of the week in the case of at least 26 of the 66 weeks immediately preceding the expected week of confinement, W has worked with a person (S) who at the time of her doing so—
  (i) was her spouse or civil partner, and
  (ii) was engaged in employment as a self-employed earner; and
(c) S [2 has paid] a Class 2 contribution in respect of the 26 weeks referred to in paragraph (1)(b); and
(d) W is not entitled to a maternity allowance under section 35 above, or statutory maternity pay, for the same week in respect of the same pregnancy.

(2) In this section—

(a) a reference to W working with S is a reference to W participating in the activities engaged in by S as a self-employed earner, performing the same tasks or ancillary tasks, without being employed by S or being in partnership with S;
(b) a reference to W ceasing to work with S is a reference to W ceasing to do so either permanently or until after her confinement.

(3) The rate of allowance under this section for any particular week is 90 per cent of the amount of the maternity allowance threshold for the tax year in which the week ends.

(4) Subject to subsections (10) and (11) below, a maternity allowance under this section shall be payable for the period of 14 weeks ("the 14-week

period") beginning as set out in subsection (5), (6), (7) or (8) below (whichever applies).

(5) If W ceases to work with S before the commencement of the 11th week before the expected week of confinement, the 14-week period begins with the commencement of the 11th week before the expected week of confinement.

(6) If W ceases to work with S on a day that falls within the period beginning with the commencement of the 11th week before the expected week of confinement and ending with the end of the fifth week before the expected week of confinement, the 14-week period begins immediately after that day.

(7) If on a day that falls within the period beginning with the commencement of the fourth week before the expected week of confinement and ending with the date of confinement—

(a) W ceases to work with S, or
(b) she refrains from working with S wholly or partly because of her pregnancy or confinement, the 14-week period begins immediately after the day on which she ceases or refrains.

(8) If none of subsections (5) to (7) above applies, the 14-week period begins immediately after the date of confinement.

(9) In relation to maternity allowance under this section, a reference in a provision contained in or made under any enactment to the maternity allowance period shall be read as a reference to the 14-week period.

(10) Subsections (4) to (7) of section 35 above have effect for the purposes of this section as they have effect for the purposes of that section (reading references to the maternity allowance period as references to the 14-week period).

(11) Regulations under section 35 above may make provision for the purposes of this section corresponding or similar to the provision that may be made by virtue of subsection (3)(a), (b) or (c) of that section.]

AMENDMENTS

1. Social Security (Maternity Allowance) (Participating Wife or Civil Partner of Self Employed Earner) Regulations 2014 (SI 2014/606) reg.2 (April 1, 2014).
2. National Insurance Contributions Act 2015 s.2 Sch.1 para.7 (April 6, 2015).

GENERAL NOTE

This section applied when a woman's expected week of confinement began on or after July 27, 2014. **1.66**

Bereavement benefits: deaths before the day on which section 30 of the Pensions Act 2014 comes into force

Bereavement payment

36.—*Repealed.* **1.67**

GENERAL NOTE

This section was repealed with effect from April 6, 2017 by para.8 of Sch.16 to the Pensions Act 2014. Bereavement payments replaced Widow's Payment from April 9, 2001. They have been replaced in turn by Bereavement Support Payment, under **1.68**

Part 5 of the Pensions Act 2014, with effect from April 6, 2017. Claimants whose spouse or partner died before that date will still qualify for this benefit and not for the new benefit. For further comments on this benefit please refer to Vol.I of the edition for 2016/17 of this work.

Cases in which sections 37 to 40 apply

1.69 **36A.**—*Repealed.*

GENERAL NOTE

1.70 This section was repealed with effect from April 6, 2017 by para.8 of Sch.16 to the Pensions Act 2014.

Widowed mother's allowance [7: deaths before 9 April 2001]

1.71 **37.**— [7 (A1) This section applies only in cases where a woman's husband has died before 9 April 2001.]

(1) A woman who has been widowed shall be entitled to a widowed mother's allowance at the rate determined in accordance with section 39 below if her late husband satisfied the contribution conditions for a widowed mother's allowance specified in Schedule 3, Part I, paragraph 5 and either—

(a) the woman is entitled to child benefit in respect of a child [3 or qualifying young person] falling within subsection (2) below; or

(b) the woman is pregnant by her late husband; or

(c) if the woman and her late husband were residing together immediately before the time of his death, the woman is pregnant as the result of being artificially inseminated before that time with the semen of some person other than her husband, or as the result of the placing in her before that time of an embryo, of an egg in the process of fertilisation, or of sperm and eggs.

(2) A child [3 or qualifying young person] falls within this subsection if [4 [5 . . .]] the child [3 or qualifying young person] is either—

(a) a son or daughter of the woman and her late husband; or

(b) a child [3 or qualifying young person] in respect of whom her late husband was immediately before his death entitled to child benefit; or

(c) if the woman and her late husband were residing together immediately before his death, a child [3 or qualifying young person] in respect of whom she was then entitled to child benefit.

(3) The widow shall not be entitled to the allowance for any period after she remarries [2 or forms a civil partnership], but, subject to that, she shall continue to be entitled to it for any period throughout which she satisfies the requirements of subsection (1)(a), (b) or (c) above.

(4) A widowed mother's allowance shall not be payable—

(a) for any period falling before the day on which the widow's entitlement is to be regarded as commencing for that purpose by virtue of section 5(1)(k) of the Administration Act; [2 [6 or

(b) for any period during which she and a person whom she is not married to, or in a civil partnership with, are living together [8 as if they were a married couple or civil partners].]]

AMENDMENTS

1. Tax Credits Act 2003 Sch.3 (April 6, 2003).
2. Civil Partnership Act 2004 Sch.24 (December 5, 2005).

3. Child Benefit Act 2005 Sch.1 (April 10, 2006).
4. Welfare Reform Act 2007 s.50 and art.2(3)(a) of the Welfare Reform Act 2007 (Commencement No.7, Transitional and Savings Provisions) Order 2008 (SI 2008/2101) (October 7, 2008).
5. Welfare Reform Act 2007 s.67 and art.2(b) of the Welfare Reform Act 2007 (Commencement No.10, Transitional and Savings Provisions) Order 2009 (SI 2009/775) (March 27, 2009).
6. Marriage (Same Sex Couples) Act 2013 (Consequential and Contrary Provisions and Scotland) Order 2014 (SI 2014/560) art.2 and Sch.1 (March 13, 2014).
7. Pensions Act 2014 Sch.16 para.10 (April 6, 2017).
8. The Civil Partnership (Opposite-sex Couples) Regulations 2019 (SI 2019/1458) reg.41(a) and Sch.3, Part 1 para.14(2)(a) (December 2, 2019).

DERIVATION

SSA 1975 s.25. **1.72**

DEFINITION

"late husband"—see s.122 below.

GENERAL NOTE

This benefit is payable only to a widow whose husband died before April 9, 2001 and who is the mother of children for whom she is entitled to claim Child Benefit. For further commentary on this section please refer to Vol.I of the edition of this work for 2016/17. **1.73**

Widow's pension [4: deaths before 9 April 2001]

38.— [4 (A1) This section applies only in cases where a woman's husband has died before 9 April 2001.] **1.74**

(1) A woman who has been widowed shall be entitled to a widow's pension at the rate determined in accordance with section 39 below if her late husband satisfied the contribution conditions for a widow's pension specified in Schedule 3, Part I, paragraph 5 and either—

(a) she was, at the husband's death, over the age of 45 but under the age of 65; or
(b) she ceased to be entitled to a widowed mother's allowance at a time when she was over the age of 45 but under the age of 65.

(2) The widow shall not be entitled to the pension for any period after she remarries [1 or forms a civil partnership], but, subject to that, she shall continue to be entitled to it until she attains [2 pensionable age].

(3) A widow's pension shall not be payable—

(a) for any period falling before the day on which the widow's entitlement is to be regarded as commencing for that purpose by virtue of section 5(1)(k) of the Administration Act;
(b) for any period for which she is entitled to a widowed mother's allowance;
[2 [3 or
(c) for any period during which she and a person whom she is not married to, or in a civil partnership with, are living together [5 as if they were a married couple or civil partners].]]

(4) In the case of a widow whose late husband died before 11th April 1988 and who either—

(a) was over the age of 40 but under the age of 55 at the time of her husband's death; or

(b) is over the age of 40 but under the age of 55 at the time when she ceases to be entitled to a widowed mother's allowance,

subsection (1) above shall have effect as if for "45" there were substituted "40".

AMENDMENT

1. Civil Partnership Act 2004 Sch.24 (December 5, 2005).

2. Pension Act 2007 Sch.1 Pt.8 para.40. This amendment was originally not to have effect until April 6, 2024, but now has had effect from April 6, 2018—see Pensions Act 2011 s.1.

3. Marriage (Same Sex Couples) Act 2013 (Consequential and Contrary Provisions and Scotland) Order 2014 (SI 2014/560) art.2 and Sch.1 (March 13, 2014).

4. Pensions Act 2014 Sch.16 para.11 (April 6, 2017).

5. The Civil Partnership (Opposite-sex Couples) Regulations 2019 (SI 2019/1458) reg.41(a) and Sch.3, Part 1 para.14(b) (December 2, 2019).

DERIVATION

1.75 SSA 1975 s.26.

DEFINITION

"late husband"—see s.122.

GENERAL NOTE

1.76 Note: the amendment to subs.(1) and (2) above to "pensionable age" did not have effect until April 6, 2018. Until that time the section should be read as if it retained the words "the age of 65".

This benefit is payable only to a widow whose husband died before April 9, 2001. For further commentary on this section please refer to Vol.I of the edition of this work for 2016/17.

Rate of widowed mother's allowance and widow's pension

1.77 **39.**—(1) The weekly rate of—

(a) a widowed mother's allowance,

(b) a widow's pension,

shall be determined in accordance with the provisions of sections [1 44 to [2 45B]] [3 [5. . .]] below as they apply in the case of a Category A retirement pension, but subject, in particular, to the following provisions of this section and section [7 46] below.

(2) In the application of sections [1 44 to [2 45B]] [3 [5. . .]] below by virtue of subsection (1) above—

(a) where the woman's husband was over pensionable age when he died, references in those sections to the pensioner shall be taken as references to the husband, and

(b) where the husband was under pensionable age when he died, references in those sections to the pensioner and the tax year in which he attained pensionable age shall be taken as references to the husband and the tax year in which he died.

[4 (2A) In its application by virtue of subsection (1) above, section 44(4) below is to be read as if for the first amount specified in that provision there were substituted a reference to the amount prescribed for the purposes of this subsection.]

(3) [6 omitted]

(4) Where a widow's pension is payable to a woman who was under the age of 55 at the time when the applicable qualifying condition was fulfilled, the weekly rate of the pension shall be reduced by 7 per cent. of what it would be apart from this subsection multiplied by the number of years by which her age at that time was less than 55 (any fraction of a year being counted as a year).

(5) For the purposes of subsection (4) above, the time when the applicable qualifying condition was fulfilled is the time when the woman's late husband died or, as the case may be, the time when she ceased to be entitled to a widowed mother's allowance.

(6) In the case of a widow whose late husband died before 11th April 1988 and who either—

(a) was over the age of 40 but under the age of 55 at the time of her husband's death; or

(b) is over the age of 40 but under the age of 55 at the time when she ceases to be entitled to a widowed mother's allowance, subsection (4) above shall have effect as if for "55" there were substituted "50" in both places where it occurs.

AMENDMENTS

1. Pensions Act 1995 s.127(2) where ss.127(3)–(5) of that Act apply.
2. Welfare Reform and Pensions Act 1999 Sch.12 (April 9, 2001).
3. Child Support, Pensions and Social Security Act 2000 s.35 (April 6, 2002).
4. Pensions Act 2007 s.6(5) (July 26, 2007).
5. Pensions Act 2007 Sch.7 Pt 5 (September 26, 2007).
6. Pensions Act 2007 Sch.2 Pt 3 para.3 (September 26, 2007).
7. Pensions Act 2008 Sch.4 para.3 (January 3, 2012).

DERIVATIONS

SSA 1975 s.13 and s.26. 1.78
SSA 1986 s.19 and s.36.

[1 Widowed parent's allowance

39A.—[8 (1) This section applies where— 1.79

(a) a person's [10 spouse, civil partner or cohabiting partner] has died before the day on which section 30 of the Pensions Act 2014 comes into force (but see subsection (1A),

(b) the person has not married or formed a civil partnership [10 or a cohabiting partnership] after the death but before that day, and

(c) the person is under pensionable age on that day.

(1A) This section does not apply in cases where a woman's husband has died before 9 April 2001.]

(2) The surviving [3][10 spouse, civil partner or cohabiting partner] shall be entitled to a widowed parent's allowance at the rate determined in accordance with section 39C below if the deceased [3][10 spouse, civil partner or cohabiting partner] satisfied the contribution conditions for a widowed parent's allowance specified in Schedule 3, Part I, paragraph 5 and—

(a) the surviving [3][10 spouse, civil partner or cohabiting partner] is entitled to child benefit in respect of a child [4 or qualifying young person] falling within subsection (3) below;
(b) the surviving spouse [10 or cohabiting partner] is a woman who either—
(i) is pregnant by her late husband [10 or the deceased cohabiting partner], or
(ii) if she and he were residing together immediately before the time of his death, is pregnant in circumstances falling within section 37(1)(c) above [10 (which is to be read as if the references to her late husband included a reference to the deceased cohabiting partner)] [3 or
(c) the surviving civil partner [10 or cohabiting partner] is a woman who—
(i) was residing together with the deceased civil partner [10 or cohabiting partner] immediately before the time of the death, and
(ii) is pregnant as the result of being artificially inseminated before that time with the semen of some person, or as a result of the placing in her before that time of an embryo, of an egg in the process of fertilisation, or of sperm and eggs].

(3) A child [4 or qualifying young person] falls within this subsection if [5[6. . .]]the child [4 or qualifying young person] is either—
(a) a son or daughter of the surviving [3] [10 spouse, civil partner or cohabiting partner] and the deceased [3] [10 spouse, civil partner or cohabiting partner]; or
(b) a child in respect of whom the deceased [3] [10 spouse, civil partner or cohabiting partner] was immediately before his or her death entitled to child benefit; or
(c) if the surviving spouse and the deceased spouse were residing together immediately before his or her death, a child [4 or qualifying young person] in respect of whom the surviving [3] [10 spouse, civil partner or cohabiting partner] was then entitled to child benefit.

[10 (3A) Only one person is entitled to a widowed parent's allowance in respect of one death.

(3B) Where, apart from subsection (3A), more than one person would be so entitled, entitlement is to be determined in accordance with subsections (3C) and (3D).

(3C) Where only one of those persons is a member of the same household as the deceased, that person is entitled.

(3D) Where there is more than one person who is a member of the same household as the deceased and would (apart from subsection (3A)) be entitled—
(a) if one of those persons is the deceased's spouse or civil partner and is pregnant or entitled to child benefit as described in subsection (2), that person is entitled;
(b) if there is no spouse or civil partner entitled under paragraph (a), the deceased's cohabiting partner who is pregnant or entitled to child benefit as described in subsection (2) is entitled (but this is subject to paragraphs (c) and (d));
(c) if there is more than one cohabiting partner within paragraph (b), the cohabiting partner who has been a member of the same household as the deceased for longest is entitled;

(d) if there is more than one cohabiting partner within paragraph (b) and each partner has been a member of the same household as the deceased for the same length of time, the Secretary of State must determine who is entitled.]

(4) The surviving spouse shall not be entitled to the allowance for any period after she or he remarries [3 or forms a civil partnership [10 or a cohabiting partnership]], but, subject to that, the surviving spouse shall continue to be entitled to it for any period throughout which she or he—

(a) satisfied the requirements for subsection (2)(a) or (b) above; and
(b) is under pensionable age.

[3 (4A) The surviving civil partner shall not be entitled to the allowance for any period after she or he forms a subsequent civil partnership [10 or a cohabiting partnership] or marries, but, subject to that, the surviving civil partner shall continue to be entitled to it for any period throughout which she or he—

(a) satisfies the requirements of subsection (2)(a) or (b) above; and
(b) is under pensionable age].

[10 (4B) The surviving cohabiting partner shall not be entitled to the allowance for any period after she or he forms a subsequent cohabiting partnership or a civil partnership or marries, but, subject to that, the surviving cohabiting partner shall continue to be entitled to it for any period throughout which she or he—

(a) satisfies the requirements of subsection (2)(a), (b) or (c) above; and
(b) is under pensionable age.]

(5) A widowed parent's allowance shall not be payable—

(a) for any period falling before the day on which the surviving [3] [10 spouse's, civil partner's or cohabiting partner's] entitlement is to be regarded as commencing by virtue of section 5(1)(k) of the Administration Act; [3 [7 or
(b) for any period during which the surviving spouse or civil partner and a person whom she or he is not married to, or in a civil partnership with, are living together [9 as if they were a married couple or civil partners].]]

[10 (6) For the purposes of this section, the Secretary of State may by regulations prescribe—

(a) circumstances in which the fact that two persons are married to each other, or are civil partners or cohabiting partners of each other, is to be disregarded;
(b) circumstances in which two persons are to be treated as if they were married to each other or were civil partners or cohabiting partners of each other (or as marrying or forming a civil partnership or a cohabiting partnership);
(c) circumstances in which people are to be treated as being, or as not being, members of the same household.

(7) For the purposes of this section and section 39C, two persons are cohabiting partners if they are not married to, or civil partners of, each other but are living together as if they were married or in a civil partnership (and "cohabiting partnership" is to be read accordingly).

(8) The Secretary of State must issue a statement of the Secretary of State's policy with respect to making determinations under subsection (3D)(d).]

AMENDMENTS

1. Welfare Reform and Pension Act 1999 s.55 (April 9, 2001).
2. Tax Credits Act 2003 Sch.3, (April 6, 2003).
3. Civil Partnership Act 2004 Sch.24 (December 5, 2005).
4. Child Benefit Act 2005 Sch.1 (April 10, 2006).
5. Welfare Reform Act 2007 s.51 and art.2(3)(b) of the Welfare Reform Act 2007 (Commencement No.7, Transitional and Savings Provisions) Order 2008 (SI 2008/2101) (October 7, 2008).
6. Welfare Reform Act 2007 s.67 and art.2(b) of the Welfare Reform Act 2007 (Commencement No. 10, Transitional and Savings Provisions) Order 2009 (SI 2009/775) (March 27, 2009).
7. Marriage (Same Sex Couples) Act 2013 (Consequential and Contrary Provisions and Scotland) Order 2014 (SI 2014/560) art.2 and Sch.1 (March 13, 2014).
8. Pensions Act 2014 Sch.16 para.12 (April 6, 2017).
9. The Civil Partnership (Opposite-sex Couples) Regulations (2019/1458) reg.41(a) and Sch.3, Part 1 para.14(c) (December 2, 2019).
10. Bereavement Benefits (Remedial) Order 2023 (SI 2023/134) art.5 (February 9, 2023).

GENERAL NOTE

1.80 The Bereavement Benefits (Remedial) Order 2023 (SI 2023/134) came into effect on February 9, 2023. It amends this section to allow a claim by the survivor of cohabiting partners and who is either pregnant or is entitled to child benefit. The Order has retrospective effect by allowing claims to be made with effect from August 18, 2018. An extended period for making a claim is provided for in art.3 of the Order. Cohabiting Partners are defined in subs.(7) above as being not married to, or civil partners of each other, but are living together as if they were married or in a civil partnership. For an overview of the effect of the Remedial Order and examples of its operation see Welfare Rights Bulletin No. 293 published by CPAG.

The Order provides that only one person can be entitled in respect of one death, but art.2 (Transitional provisions) allows for the continued entitlement by an existing award even though another claimant may make a retrospective claim and become entitled as a result of these amendments.

The Order envisages that competing claims may be made in respect of this benefit and provides an order of priority for entitlement. Where the deceased was living, at the time of death, in the same household as the claimant, that person will have entitlement to the exclusion of any other. Where the deceased was living at the time of death in more than one household subs.(3D) provides an order of priority for entitlement.

Further discussion of the effect of the Remedial Order may found in the notes to Bereavement Support Payment following s.30 of the Pensions Act 2014 in this volume.

Note that in respect of Widowed Parent's Allowance entitlement is lost if the claimant forms a cohabiting partnership with another person or enters a civil partnership or marries.

Bereavement allowance where no dependent children

1.81 **39B.**—*Repealed.*

GENERAL NOTE

1.82 This section was repealed by the Pensions Act 2014 Sch.16 para.13 with effect from April 6, 2017.

[1 Rate of widowed parent's allowance [9 . . .]

1.83 **39C.**—(1) The weekly rate of a widowed parent's allowance shall be determined in accordance with the provisions of section 44 to [7[8 45AA and Schedules 4A and 4B below as they apply]] in the case of a Category A retirement pension, but subject, in particular, to the following provisions of this section [7 46] below.

[5 (1A) In its application by virtue of subsection (1) above, section 44(4) below is to be read as if for the first amount specified in that provision there were substituted a reference to the amount prescribed for the purposes of this subsection.

(2) [9...]]

(3) In the application of sections 44 to [7[8 45AA and Schedules 4A and 4B below by virtue of subsection (1) above]]

(a) where the deceased [4] [9 spouse, civil partner or cohabiting partner] was over pensionable age at his or her death, references in those [6 provisions] to the pensioner shall be taken as references to the deceased [4] [9 spouse, civil partner or cohabiting partner], and

(b) where the deceased [4] [9 spouse, civil partner or cohabiting partner] was under pensionable age at his or her death, references in those [6 provisions] to the pensioner and the tax year in which he attained pensionable age shall be taken as references to the deceased [4] [9 spouse, civil partner or cohabiting partner] and the tax year in which he or she died.

(4) Where a widowed parent's allowance is payable to a person whose [4] [9 spouse, civil partner or cohabiting partner] dies after 5th April 2000, the additional pension falling to be calculated under sections 44 to [7[8 45AA and Schedules 4A and 4B below]] by virtue of subsection (1) above shall be one half of the amount which it would be apart from this subsection.

(5) [9...]]

AMENDMENTS

1.84 1. Welfare Reform and Pension Act 1999 s.55 (April 9, 2001).
2. Child Support, Pensions and Social Security Acbt 2000 s.35 (April 6, 2002).
3. Tax Credit Act 2002 Sch.3 (April 6, 2003).
4. Civil Partnership Act 2004 Sch.24 (December 5, 2005).
5. Pensions Act 2007 s.6(6) (July 26, 2007).
6. Pensions Act 2007 Sch.2 Pt 3 (July 26, 2007).
7. Pensions Act 2008 Sch.4 para.2 (January 3, 2012) (except in relation to 4C).
8. Pensions Act 2014 Sch.12 para.93 (April 6, 2016).
8. Pensions Act 2014 Sch.16 para.14 (April 6, 2017).

GENERAL NOTE FOR SECTIONS 36–39C.

1.85 For commentary on ss.36-39C please refer to the notes following s.39C in Vol.I of the edition of this work for 2016/17.

Long-term incapacity benefit for widows

1.86 [1 **40.**—(1) Subject to subsection (2) below, this section applies to a woman who—

(a) on her late husband's death is not entitled to a widowed mother's allowance or subsequently ceases to be entitled to such an allowance;

(b) is incapable of work at the time when he dies or when she subsequently ceases to be so entitled;

(c) either—

(i) would have been entitled to a widow's pension if she had been over the age of 45 when her husband died or when she ceased to be entitled to a widowed mother's allowance; or

(ii) is entitled to such a pension with a reduction under section 39(4) above; and

(d) is not entitled to incapacity benefit apart from this section.

(2) This section does not apply to a woman unless—

(a) her husband died after 5th April 1979; or

(b) she ceased to be entitled to a widowed mother's allowance after that date (whenever her husband died).

(3) A woman to whom this section applies is entitled to long-term incapacity benefit under this section for any day of incapacity for work which—

(a) falls in a period of incapacity for work that began before the time when her late husband died or she subsequently ceased to be entitled to a widowed mother's allowance; and

(b) is after that time and after the first 364 days of incapacity for work in that period.

(4) A woman to whom this section applies who is not entitled to long-term incapacity benefit under subsection (3) above, but who is terminally ill, is entitled to short-term incapacity benefit under this section for any day of incapacity for work which—

(a) falls in a period of incapacity for work that began before the time when her late husband died or she subsequently ceased to be entitled to a widowed mother's allowance, and

(b) is after that time and after the first 196 days of incapacity for work in that period

For the purposes of this subsection a woman is terminally ill if she suffers from a progressive disease and her death in consequence of that disease can reasonably be expected within 6 months.

(5) The weekly rate of incapacity benefit payable under this section is—

(a) if the woman is not entitled to a widow's pension, that which would apply if she were entitled to long-term incapacity benefit under section 30A above; and

(b) if she is entitled to a widow's pension with a reduction under section 39(4) above, the difference between the weekly rate of that pension and the weekly rate referred to in paragraph (a) above.

(6) A woman is not entitled to incapacity benefit under this section if she is over pensionable age; but if she has attained pensionable age and the period of incapacity for work mentioned in subsection (3)(a) or (4)(a) above did not terminate before she attained that age—

(a) she shall, if not otherwise entitled to a Category A retirement pension, be entitled to such a pension, and

(b) the weekly rate of the Category A retirement pension to which she is entitled (whether by virtue of paragraph (a) above or otherwise) shall be determined in the prescribed manner.

(7) Where a woman entitled to short-term incapacity benefit under subsection (4) above attains pensionable age and defers her entitlement to a Category A pension or makes an election under section 54(1) below, the days of incapacity for work falling within the period of incapacity for work mentioned in that subsection shall, for the purpose of determining any

subsequent entitlement to incapacity benefit under section 30A above or the rate of that benefit, be treated as if they had been days of entitlement to short-term incapacity benefit.

(8) References to short-term incapacity benefit at the higher rate shall be construed as including short-term incapacity benefit payable under subsection (4) above.]

AMENDMENT

1. Social Security (Incapacity for Work) Act 1994 Sch.1 (April 13, 1995).

DERIVATION

SSA 1975 s.15. 1.87
Substituted by Social Security (Incapacity for Work) Act 1994.

DEFINITIONS

"entitled"—see s.122.
"day of incapacity for work"—see s.57.
"period of interruption of employment"—see s.57.

GENERAL NOTE

This benefit will in appropriate circumstances, be affected by the Gender Recognition Act 2004. A person in receipt of benefit by virtue of this section who obtains a gender recognition certificate will cease to be entitled to benefit (and will lose, as well, the right to transfer to Category A Retirement Pension in due course). This is surprising because s.41 that follows makes an equivalent provision for widowers. See the notes to the Gender Recognition Act in Vol.III of this work. 1.88

Long-term incapacity benefit for widowers

[1 **41.**—(1) This section applies to a man whose wife has died on or after 6th April 1979 and who either— 1.89

(a) was incapable of work at the time when she died, or
(b) becomes incapable of work within the prescribed period after that time,

and is not entitled to incapacity benefit apart from this section.

(2) A man to whom this section applies is entitled to long-term incapacity benefit under this section for any day of incapacity for work which—

(a) falls in a period of incapacity for work that began before the time when his wife died or within the prescribed period after that time, and
(b) is after that time and after the first 364 days of incapacity for work in that period.

(3) A man to whom this section applies who is not entitled to longterm incapacity benefit under subsection (2) above, but who is terminally ill, is entitled to short-term incapacity benefit under this section for any day of incapacity for work which—

(a) falls in a period of incapacity for work that began before the time when his wife died or within the prescribed period after that time, and
(b) is after that time and after the first 196 days of incapacity for work in that period.

For the purposes of this subsection a man is terminally ill if he suffers from a progressive disease and his death in consequence of that disease can reasonably be expected within 6 months.

(4) The weekly rate of incapacity benefit payable under this section is that which would apply if he were entitled to long-term incapacity benefit under section 30A above.

(5) A man is not entitled to incapacity benefit under this section if he is over pensionable age; but if he has attained pensionable age, and the period of incapacity for work mentioned in subsection (2)(a) or (3)(a) above did not terminate before he attained that age—

(a) he shall, if not otherwise entitled to a Category A retirement pension and also not entitled to a Category B retirement pension by virtue of [2 the contributions of his wife] be entitled to Category A retirement pension; and

(b) the weekly rate of the Category A retirement pension to which he is entitled (whether by virtue of paragraph (a) above or otherwise) shall be determined in the prescribed manner.

(6) Where a man entitled to short-term incapacity benefit under subsection (3) above attains pensionable age and defers his entitlement to a Category A pension or makes an election under section 54(1) below, the days of incapacity for work falling within the period of incapacity for work mentioned in that subsection shall, for the purpose of determining any subsequent entitlement to incapacity benefit under section 30A above or the rate of that benefit, be treated as if they had been days of entitlement to short-term incapacity benefit.

(7) References to short-term incapacity benefit at the higher rate shall be construed as including short-term incapacity benefit payable under subsection (3) above.]

AMENDMENTS

1. Social Security (Incapacity for Work) Act 1994 Sch.1 para.9 (April 13, 1995).

2. Pensions Act 1995 Sch.4, para.21(4) (July 19, 1995).

DERIVATIONS

1.90 SSPA 1975 s.16.
SSA 1977 s.4.
SSA 1979 s.5.
SSA 1986 s.19.
SSA 1989 s.7.
SSA 1990 s.4.
Substituted by Social Security (Incapacity for Work) Act 1994.

GENERAL NOTE

1.91 This benefit will in appropriate circumstances, be affected by the Gender Recognition Act 2004. A person in receipt of benefit by virtue of this section who obtains a gender recognition certificate will cease to be entitled to benefit (and will lose, as well, the right to transfer to Category A Retirement Pension in due course). This is surprising because Section 40 above makes an equivalent provision for widows. See the notes to the Gender Recognition Act in Vol.III of this work.

Entitlement under s.40 or 41 after period of employment or training for work

42.—[2(1) Where a person claims incapacity benefit under section 40 or 41 above for a period commencing after he has ceased to be in qualifying remunerative work (within the meaning of Part 1 of the Tax Credits Act 2002) and— 1.92

(a) the day following that on which he so ceased was a day of incapacity for work for him,

(b) he has been entitled to incapacity benefit under that section within the period of two years ending with that day of incapacity for work, and

(c) he satisfied the relevant tax credit conditions on the day before he so ceased,

every day during that period on which he satisfied those conditions is to be treated for the purposes of the claim as a day of incapacity for work for him.

(1A) A person satisfies the relevant tax credit conditions on a day if—

(a) he is entitled for the day to the disability element of working tax credit (on a claim made by him or by him jointly with another) or would be so entitled but for the fact that the relevant income (within the meaning of Part 1 of the Tax Credits Act 2002) in his or their case is such that he is not so entitled, and

(b) either working tax credit or any element of child tax credit other than the family element is paid in respect of the day on such a claim.]

(2) Where—

(a) a person becomes engaged in training for work, and

(b) he was entitled to incapacity benefit under section 40 or 41 above for one or more of the 56 days immediately before he became so engaged, and

(c) the first day after he ceases to be so engaged is for him a day of incapacity for work and falls not later than the end of the period of two years beginning with the last day for which he was entitled to incapacity benefit under that section,

any day since that day in which he was engaged in training for work shall be treated for the purposes of any claim for incapacity benefit under that section for a period commencing after he ceases to be so engaged as having been a day of incapacity for work.

In this subsection "training for work" means training for work in pursuance of arrangements made under section 2(1) of the Employment and Training Act 1973 or section 2(3) of the Enterprise and New Towns (Scotland) Act 1990 or training of such other description as may be prescribed.

(3) For the purposes of this section "week" means any period of 7 days.]

AMENDMENTS

1. Social Security (Incapacity for Work) Act 1994 Sch.1 para.10 (April 13, 1995).

2. Tax Credits Act 2002 Sch.3 para.30 (April 6, 2003).

DERIVATIONS

1.93 SSPA 1975 s.16A.
DLA and DWAA 1991 s.9.
Substituted by Social Security (Incapacity for Work) Act 1994.

GENERAL NOTE

1.94 Note that in respect of someone who claims incapacity benefit on or before April 6, 2005 under s.40 or 41, s.42 has effect as if, after subs.(1A) there were inserted

"(1B) A person also satisfies the relevant tax credit conditions on any day before 7th April 2003 if that day falls within a week for which he is entitled to a disabled person's tax credit."

See Tax Credits Act 2002 (Commencement No.4, Transitional Provisions and Savings) Order SI 2003/962, art.5(3).

Retirement pensions (Categories A and B)

Persons entitled to more than one retirement pension

1.95 **43.**—(1) A person shall not be entitled for the same period to more than one retirement pension under this Part of this Act except as provided by subsection (2) below[4 and section 61ZC below (which deals with unusual cases involving units of additional pension)].

(2) A person who, apart from subsection (1) above, would be entitled for the same period to both—

(a) a Category A or a Category B retirement pension under this Part; and
(b) a Category C or a Category D retirement pension under Part III below,

shall be entitled to both of those pensions for that period, subject to any adjustment of them in pursuance of regulations under section 73 of the Administration Act.

(3) A person who, apart from subsection (1) above, would be entitled—

[2 (a) to both a Category A retirement pension and one or more Category B retirement pensions under this Part for the same period,
(aa) to more than one Category B retirement pension (but not a Category A retirement pension) under this Part for the same period, or]
(b) to both a Category C and a Category D retirement pension under Part III below for the same period,

may from time to time give notice in writing to the Secretary of State specifying which of the pensions referred to in [2 paragraph (a), (aa) or (b) (as the case may be)] he wishes to receive.

(4) If a person gives such a notice, the pension so specified shall be the one to which he is entitled in respect of any week commencing after the date of the notice.

(5) If no such notice is given, the person shall be entitled to whichever of the pensions is from time to time the most favourable to him (whether it is the pension which he claimed or not).

[1 (6) For the purpose of this section a provision under section 55A [3 or 55AA] below is not a retirement pension.]

AMENDMENTS

1. Welfare Reform and Pensions Act 1999 Sch.12 para.18 (April 9, 2001).
2. Pensions Act 2004 s.296 (November 18, 2004).
3. Pensions Act 2014 Sch.11 para. 4 (April 6, 2016).
4. Pensions Act 2014 Sch.15 para.15 (October 12, 2015).

GENERAL NOTE.

Section 43 was the key section for all claims to state retirement pensions for those reaching state pensionable age up to and including April 5, 2016. From April 6, 2016 no new claim can be made under this section and the sections that follow. Claims for those reaching state pensionable age on or after April 6, 2016 must be made for a state pension under the Pensions Act 2014. See the general note to s.1 of that Act below. This and the following provisions of the 1992 Act are preserved both for past cases where pensions are already in payment and in relation to transitional cases preserved by the Pensions Act 2014. **1.96**

The Pensions Act 2014 introduces major changes to the structure of the state pension including the introduction of a single tier pension, the abolition (subject to transitional provisions) of pensions based on a spouse's or partner's contributions (Category B pensions), the abolition of the state second pension or additional pension, and the abolition of Category C pensions. Much of the detailed comment on these sections in previous editions of this work is therefore of no continuing relevance to current and future new claims and is therefore not repeated here. See the 2015/16 edition (or other previous editions) of this work for a full explanation and analysis.

Category A retirement pension

44.—(1) A person shall be entitled to a Category A retirement pension if— **1.97**

[[14] (a) the person attained pensionable age before 6 April 2016,] and
[[10](b) he satisfies the relevant conditions or condition].

and, subject to the provisions of this Act, he shall become so entitled on the day on which he attains pensionable age and his entitlement will continue throughout his life.

[[10](1A) In subsection (1)(b) above "the relevant conditions or condition" means—

(a) in a case where the person attains pensionable age before 6th April 2010, the conditions specified in Schedule 3, Part I, paragraph 5;
(b) in a case where the person attains pensionable age on or after that date, the condition specified in Schedule 3, Part I, paragraph 5A.]

(2) A Category A retirement pension shall not be payable in respect of any period falling before the day on which the pensioner's entitlement is to be regarded as commencing for that purpose by virtue of section 5(1)(k) of the Administration Act.

(3) A Category A retirement pension shall consist of—

(a) a basic pension payable at a weekly rate; and
(b) an additional pension payable where there are one or more surpluses in the pensioner's earnings factors for the relevant years [[15] or where the pensioner has one or more units of additional pension.

For units of additional pension, see section 14A.]

[16 (4) The weekly rate of the basic pension shall be [1 £169.50] except that, so far as the sum is relevant for the purpose of calculating the [2 rate of short-term incapacity benefit under section 30B(3) above] it shall be [1 £133.25].

In this subsection "the lower rate" means the rate payable for the first 196 days of entitlement in any period of incapacity for work]

(5) For the purposes of this section and section 45 below—

(a) there is a surplus in the pensioner's earnings factor for a relevant year if that factor exceeds the qualifying earnings factor for the final relevant year; and

(b) the amount of the surplus is the amount of that excess; and for the purposes of paragraph (a) above the pensioner's earnings factor for any relevant year shall be taken to be that factor as increased by the last order under section 148 of the Administration Act to come into force before the end of the final relevant year.

[3 (5A) For the purposes of this section and section 45 [8 and [11 Schedules 4A and 4B]] below—

(a) there is a surplus in the pensioner's earnings factor for a relevant year if that factor exceeds the qualifying earnings factor for [8that year,

(b) the amount of the surplus is the amount of that excess, and

(c) for the purposes of section 45(1) and (2)(a) and (b) below, the adjusted amount of the surplus] is the amount of that excess, as increased by the last order under section 148 of the Administration Act to come into force before the end of the final relevant year.

(6) [4 [5Subject to subsection (7A) below] any reference in this section or section 45 [8 or [11 Schedule 4A or 4B]] below to the pensioner's earnings factor for any relevant year is a reference—

[7 (za)] where the relevant year is the first appointed year or any subsequent year, to the aggregate of his earnings factors derived from [9 so much of his earnings as did not exceed [12 the applicable limit]] upon which primary Class 1 contributions have been paid or treated as paid in respect of that year;

(a) where the relevant year is 1987–88 or any subsequent tax year [7 before the first appointed year], to the aggregate of—

(i) his earnings factors derived from earnings upon which primary Class 1 contributions were paid or treated as paid in respect of that year, and

(ii) his earnings factors derived from Class 2 and Class 3 contributions actually paid in respect of that year, or, if less, the qualifying earnings factor for that year; and

(b) where the relevant year is an earlier tax year, to the aggregate of—

(i) his earnings factors derived from Class 1 contributions actually paid by him in respect of that year, and

(ii) his earnings factors derived from Class 2 and Class 3 contributions actually paid by him in respect of that year, or, if less, the qualifying earnings factor for that year.]

(7) In this section—

(a) "relevant year" means 1978–79 or any subsequent tax year in the period between—

(i) (inclusive) the tax year in which the pensioner attained the age of 16, and

(ii) (exclusive) the tax year in which he attained pensionable age;
(b) "final relevant year" means the last tax year which is a relevant year in relation to the pensioner.
[10 (c) "the applicable limit" means—
(i) in relation to a tax year before [132009–10] the upper earnings limit;
(ii) in relation to [132009–10] or any subsequent tax year, the upper accrual point.]

[5 (7A) The Secretary of State may prescribe circumstances in which pensioners' earnings factors for any relevant year may be calculated in such manner as may be prescribed.]

(8) For the purposes of this section any order under [6 section 21 of the Social Security Pensions Act 1975] (which made provision corresponding to section 148 of the Administration Act) shall be treated as an order under section 148 (but without prejudice to sections 16 and 17 of the Interpretation Act 1978).

AMENDMENTS

1. The Social Security Benefits Up-rating Order 2024 (SI 2024/242) art.4(2) (April 8, 2024).
2. Social Security (Incapacity for Work) Act 1994 Sch.1 para.11 (April 13, 1995).
3. Pensions Act 1995 s.128(1), subs.(5A) applies in substitution for subs.(5) where ss.128(4)–(6) of that Act apply.
4. Pension Act 1995 s.128. This version of subs.(6) takes effect where the relevant person reaches pensionable age, or dies, after April 5, 2000.
5. Social Security (Consequential Provisions) Act 1992 Sch.4 para.3.
6. Pensions Schemes Act 1993 Sch.8 para.38 (February 7, 1994).
7. Child Support, Pensions and Social Security Act 2000 s.30 (April 6, 2002).
8. Child Support, Pensions and Social Security Act 2000 s.35 (April 6, 2002).
9. National Insurance Contributions Act 2002 Sch.1 para.8 (April 6, 2002).
10. Pensions Act 2007 Sch.1 para.1 (September 26, 2007).
11. Pensions Act 2007 Sch.2 Pt 3, para.5 (September 26, 2007).
12. Pensions Act 2007 s.12 (September 26, 2007).
13. National Insurance Contributions Act 2008 s.3(3) (September 21, 2008).
14. Pensions Act 2014 Sch.12 para.55 (April 6, 2016).
15. Pensions Act 2014 Sch.15 para.6 (October 12, 2015).
16. Social Security Act 1998 s.68 (September 8, 1988).

DEFINITION

"pensionable age"—see s.122.

GENERAL NOTE

The amendment to subs.(1)(a) of this section closes it to those reaching state pensionable age after April 5, 2016. This is because they can now make claims only under the Pensions Act 2014 s.1 and following for a state pension. See the general note to that Act below. 1.98

While this section remains relevant to those already of state pensionable age and claiming a pension by that date and in connection with some transitional cases, no new claims can therefore be made under this section. As noted to s.43 above, much of the detail of the state pension has changed. See the 2015/16 edition (or other previous editions) of this work for a full explanation and analysis of this section as it applies to existing pensioners and transitional cases.

Note that subsection (1)'s declaration that a person retains entitlement to a Category A pension "throughout his life" does not necessarily mean that the person has the right to be paid the pension at the same rate throughout his life. This was illustrated by the Upper Tribunal's decision in *BB v Secretary of State for Work & Pensions* (RP) [2021] UKUT 141 (AAC). Upper Tribunal Judge Wikeley held that a pensioner's 7% enhancement to the rate of his Category A pension, referable to his receipt of New Zealand national superannuation, ceased to be payable once he began to reside outside the EU (he had moved from Malta to Turkey). While the pensioner's entitlement to a 7% enhancement persisted, the enhancement was only payable in accordance with the Social Security (New Zealand) Order 1983 (SI 1983/1894) (as modified by the Social Security (Application of Reciprocal Agreements with Australia, Canada and New Zealand) (EEA States and Switzerland) Regulations 2015 (SI 2015/349)). This reflects the distinction sometimes drawn by the 1992 Act between entitlement to benefit and its payability (*Campbell v Secretary of State for Work and Pensions* [2005] EWCA Civ 989).

Section 44 is modified to the extent necessary to give effect to a Convention on Social Security entered into on February 1, 2019, by the Government of the United Kingdom and the Government of Ireland (Article 2(1) of the Social Security (Ireland) Order 2019 (SI 2019/622). The Convention seeks to maintain, following the UK's withdrawal from the European Union, certain UK social security entitlements of citizens of the Republic of Ireland. This includes mutual recognition of social security contributions for the purposes of UK retirement pension.

Deemed earnings factors

1.99 **44A.** [3 (A1) Subsections (1) to (4) below apply to the first appointed year or any subsequent tax year before 2010–11.]

(1) For the purposes of section 44(6)(za) above, if any of the conditions in subsection (2) below is satisfied for a relevant year [3 to which this subsection applies], a pensioner is deemed to have an earnings factor for that year which—

(a) is derived from [2 so much of his earnings as did not exceed [4 the applicable limit] and] on which primary Class 1 contributions were paid; and

(b) is equal to the amount which, when added to any other earnings factors taken into account under that provision, produces an aggregate of earnings factors equal to the low earnings threshold.

(2) The conditions referred to in subsection (1) above are that—

(a) the pensioner would, apart from this section, have an earnings factor for the year—

 (i) equal to or greater than the qualifying earnings factor for the year; but

 (ii) less than the low earnings threshold for the year;

(b) [1 carer's allowance]—

 (i) was payable to the pensioner throughout the year; or

 (ii) would have been so payable but for the fact that under regulations the amount payable to him was reduced to nil because of his receipt of other benefits;

(c) for the purposes of paragraph 5(7)(b) of Schedule 3, the pensioner is taken to be precluded from regular employment by responsibilities at home throughout the year by virtue of—

 (i) the fact that child benefit was payable to him in respect of a child under the age of six; or

 (ii) his satisfying such other condition as may be prescribed;

(d) the pensioner is a person satisfying the requirement in subsection (3) below to whom long-term incapacity benefit [5 or qualifying employment and support allowance] was payable throughout the year, or would have been so payable but for the fact that—

(i) he did not satisfy the contribution conditions in paragraph 2 of Schedule 3 [5 or, as the case may be, [6 in paragraphs 1 and 2] of Schedule 1 to the Welfare Reform Act [6 2007]].; or

(ii) under regulations the amount payable to him was reduced to nil because of his receipt of other benefits or of payments from an occupational pension scheme or personal pension scheme.

(3) The requirement referred to in subsection (2)(d) above is that—

(a) for one or more relevant years the pensioner has paid, or (apart from this section) is treated as having paid, primary Class 1 contributions on earnings equal to or greater than the qualifying earnings factor; and

(b) the years for which he has such a factor constitute at least one tenth of his working life.

(4) For the purposes of subsection (3)(b) above—

(a) a pensioner's working life shall not include—

(i) any tax year before 1978–79; or

(ii) any year in which he is deemed under subsection (1) above to have an earnings factor by virtue of fulfilling the condition in subsection (2)(b) or (c) above; and

(b) the figure calculated by dividing his working life by ten shall be rounded to the nearest whole year (and any half year shall be rounded down).

[3 (4A) The following do not apply to a pensioner attaining pensionable age on or after 6th April 2010—

(a) the requirement referred to in subsection (2)(d) above, and

(b) subsections (3) and (4) above.]

(5) The low earnings threshold for the first appointed year and subsequent tax years shall be £9,500 (but subject to section 148A of the Administration Act).

[4 (5A) In subsection (1)(a) "the applicable limit" has the same meaning as in section 44.]

(6) In subsection (2)(d)(ii) above, "occupational pension scheme" and "personal pension scheme" have the meanings given by subsection (6) of section 30DD above for the purposes of subsection (5) of that section.]

[5 (7) In subsection (2)(d) "qualifying employment and support allowance" means contributory employment and support allowance where—

(a) that allowance was payable for a continuous period of 52 weeks;

(b) that allowance included the support component under section 2(2) of the Welfare Reform Act [2007]; or

(c) in the case of—

(i) a man born between 6th April 1944 and 5th April 1947; or

(ii) a woman born between 6th April 1949 and 5th April 1951, that allowance was payable for a continuous period of 13 weeks immediately following a period throughout which statutory sick pay was payable.]

AMENDMENTS

1. Regulatory Reform (Carer's Allowance) Order 2002 (SI 2002/1457), art.2 (April 1, 2003).

2. National Insurance Contributions Act 2002 Sch.1 para.11 (April 6, 2003).
3. Pensions Act 2007 Sch.1 para.34 (September 26, 2007).
4. National Insurance Contributions Act 2008 Sch.1 para.4 (September 21, 2008).
5. Employment and Support Allowance (Consequential Provisions) (No. 2) Regulations 2008 (SI 2008/1554) (October 27, 2008).
6. Social Security (Miscellaneous Amendment) (No.3) Regulations 2010 (SI 2010/840) (June 6, 2010).

General Note

1.100 This section introduced what is sometimes known as the second state pension. In *Jayawardhana v Secretary of State for Work and Pensions* [2006] EWCA Civ 1865, it was held that the effect of this and the preceding section could apply only prospectively and not retrospectively. Where, therefore, the claimant had reached retirement age in the tax year 2002/03, (which year could not be counted under s.44(7)(a)(ii)) and the amended version of this section became effective only from April 2002, it could have no application to him.

Regulations made under subsection (2)(c)(ii) specify an additional means by which a pensioner is to be taken as precluded from regular employment throughout the year. See regulation 6 of the Additional Pension and Social Security Pensions (Home Responsibilities) (Amendment) Regulations 2001 (SI 2001/1323).

Subsection (5)

1.101 *Low earnings threshold:* this annual figure currently stands at £15,300, having been raised to that level for 2015/16 and successive tax years (see Social Security Pensions (Low Earnings Threshold) Order 2015 (SI 2015/186) art.2), and has not been increased since.

[1 44B. Deemed earnings factors: 2010–11 onwards

1.102 (1) This section applies to 2010–11 and subsequent tax years.

(2) For the purposes of section 44(6)(za) above, if any of Conditions A to C in subsections (3) to (5) below is satisfied for a relevant year to which this section applies, a pensioner is deemed to have an earnings factor for that year which—

(a) is derived from so much of his earnings as did not exceed [1the upper accrual point] and on which primary Class 1 contributions were paid; and
(b) is equal to the amount which, when added to any other earnings factors taken into account under that provision, produces an aggregate of earnings factors equal to the low earnings threshold.

(3) Condition A is that the pensioner would, apart from this section, have an earnings factor for the year—

(a) equal to or greater than the qualifying earnings factor ("the QEF") for the year, but
(b) less than the low earnings threshold for the year.

(4) Condition B is that the pensioner—

(a) would, apart from this section and section 44C below, have an earnings factor for the year less than the QEF for the year, but
(b) is entitled to an aggregate amount of earnings factor credits for that year under section 44C below equal to the difference between the QEF for the year and the earnings factor mentioned in paragraph (a) above.

(5) Condition C is that the pensioner is entitled to 52 earnings factor credits for that year under section 44C below.

(6) This section has effect in relation to the flat rate introduction year and any subsequent tax year as if—

(a) subsection (2)(b) referred to an aggregate of earnings factors greater than the QEF, but less than the low earnings threshold, for the year (rather than to one equal to that threshold); and

(b) Condition A in subsection (3) (and the reference to it in subsection (2)) were omitted.

(7) In this section—

(a) [2 *Repealed*]

(b) "the low earnings threshold" means the low earnings threshold for the year concerned as specified in section 44A above; and

(c) in subsections (3) and (4), any reference to the pensioner's earnings factor for a relevant year is to be construed in accordance with section 44(6)(za) above.

AMENDMENTS

1. National Insurance Contributions Act 2008 Sch.1 para.5 (September 21, 2008).
2. National Insurance Contributions Act 2008 Sch.2 (September 21, 2008).

MODIFICATION

Section 44B is modified by Sch.2 para.46 of the Employment and Support Allowance (Transitional Provisions, Housing Benefit and Council Tax Benefit) (Existing Awards) (No. 2) Regulations 2010 (SI 2010/1907) (as amended) for the purposes specified in reg.6(1). For details of the modification, see the text of those Regulations below.

44C. Earnings factor credits

(1) This section applies, for the purposes of Conditions B and C in section 44B(4) and (5) above, to 2010–11 and subsequent tax years. **1.103**

(2) In respect of each week—

(a) which falls in a relevant year to which this section applies, and

(b) in respect of which a pensioner is eligible for earnings factor enhancement,

the pensioner is entitled to an earnings factor credit equal to 1/52 of the QEF for that year.

This is subject to subsection (5) below.

(3) A pensioner is eligible for earnings factor enhancement in respect of a week if one or more of the following apply—

(a) he was a relevant carer in respect of that week for the purposes of section 23A above (see section 23A(3));

(b) carer's allowance was payable to him for any part of that week, or would have been so payable but for the fact that under regulations the amount payable to him was reduced to nil because of his receipt of other benefits;

(c) severe disablement allowance was payable to him for any part of that week;

(d) long-term incapacity benefit was payable to him for any part of that week or would have been so payable but for the fact that—

(i) he did not satisfy the contribution conditions in paragraph 2 of Schedule 3, or

(ii) under regulations the amount payable to him was reduced to nil because of his receipt of other benefits or of payments from an occupational pension scheme or personal pension scheme;

(e) he satisfies such other conditions as may be prescribed.

(4) In subsection (3)(d)(ii) above "occupational pension scheme" and "personal pension scheme" have the meanings given by subsection (6) of section 30DD above for the purposes of subsection (5) of that section.

(5) For the purposes of Condition B in section 44B(4) above a person is not entitled to an aggregate amount of earnings factor credits in respect of a year that is greater than the difference referred to in that Condition.

(6) For the purposes of this section a week that falls partly in one tax year and partly in another is to be treated as falling in the year in which it begins and not in the following year.

(7) In section 44B above and this section—

(a) "the QEF" means the qualifying earnings factor, and

(b) any reference to a person being entitled to an earnings factor credit of a particular amount (or to an aggregate amount of earnings factor credits) for a year is a reference to the person being treated as having for that year an earnings factor (within the meaning of section 44(6)(za) above) of the amount in question by virtue of subsection (2) above.]

AMENDMENT

1. Pensions Act 2007 s.9(1) (September 26, 2007).

The additional pension in a Category A retirement pension

1.104 **45.**—(1) The weekly rate of the additional pension in a Category A retirement pension in any case where the pensioner attained pensionable age in a tax year before 6th April 1999 shall be [4 the sum of the following—

(a) in relation to any surpluses in the pensioner's earnings factors, weekly equivalent of 1¼ per cent. of the [1 adjusted] amount of the surpluses mentioned in section 44(3)(b) above; and

(b) if the pensioner has one or more units of additional pension, a specified amount for each of those units.]

(2) The weekly rate of the additional pension in a Category A retirement pension in any case where the pensioner attained pensionable age in a tax year after 5th April 1999 shall be [2 the sum of the following]

(a) in relation to any surpluses in the pensioner's earnings factors for the tax years in the period beginning with 1978–79 and ending with 1987–88, the weekly equivalent of 25/N per cent. of the [1 adjusted] amount of those surpluses; and

(b) in relation to any surpluses in the pensioner's earnings factors in a tax year after 1987–88 [2 but before the first appointed year], the weekly equivalent of the relevant percentage of the [1 adjusted] amount of those surpluses.

[2 (c) in relation to any tax years falling within subsection (3A) below, the weekly equivalent of the amount calculated in accordance with Schedule 4A to this Act.]

[3 and
(d) in relation to the flat rate introduction year and subsequent tax years, the weekly equivalent of the amount calculated in accordance with Schedule 4B to this Act.] [4 ; and
(e) if the pensioner has one or more units of additional pension, a specified amount for each of those units.]

[4 (2A) For the purposes of subsections (1)(b) and (2)(e) the "specified amount" is an amount to be specified by the Secretary of State in regulations.]

(3) In subsection (2)(b) above, "relevant percentage" means—
(a) 20/N per cent., where the pensioner attained pensionable age in 2009–10 or any subsequent tax year;
(b) (20 + X)/N per cent., where the pensioner attained pensionable age in a tax year falling within the period commencing with 1999–2000 and ending with 2008–9.

[2 (3A) The following tax years fall within this subsection—
(a) the first appointed year;
(b) subsequent tax years] [3 before the flat rate introduction year.]

(4) In this section—
(a) X = 0.5 for each tax year by which the tax year in which the pensioner attained pensionable age precedes 2009–10; and
(b) N = the number of tax years in the pensioner's working life which fall after 5th April 1978;

but paragraph (b) above is subject, in particular, to subsection (5) and, where applicable, section 46 below.

(5) Regulations may direct that in prescribed cases or classes of cases any tax year shall be disregarded for the purpose of calculating N under subsection (4)(b) above, if it is a tax year after 5th April 1978 in which the pensioner—
(a) was credited with contributions or earnings under this Act by virtue of regulations under section 22(5) above, or
(b) was precluded from regular employment by responsibilities at home, or
(c) in prescribed circumstances, would have been treated as falling within paragraph (a) or (b) above,

but not so as to reduce the number of years below 20.

(6) For the purposes of subsections (1) and (2) above, the weekly equivalent of [1 any amount] shall be calculated by dividing that amount by 52 and rounding the result to the nearest whole penny, taking any ½p as nearest to the next whole penny.

(7) Where the amount falling to be rounded under subsection (6) above is a sum less than ½p, the amount calculated under that subsection shall be taken to be zero, notwithstanding any other provision of this Act or the Administration Act.

(8) The sums which are the weekly rate of the additional pension in a Category A retirement pension are subject to alteration by orders made by the Secretary of State under section 150 of the Administration Act.

AMENDMENTS

1. Child Support, Pensions and Social Security Act 2000 s.35 (April 6, 2002).
2. Child Support, Pensions and Social Security Act 2000 s.31 (April 6, 2002).
3. Pensions Act 2007 s.11 (September 26, 2007).
4. Pensions Act 2014 Sch.15 para.7 (October 12, 2015).

DERIVATION

SSPA 1975 s.6.

GENERAL NOTE

1.105 The Social Security Class 3A Contributions (Units of Additional Pension) Regulations 2014 (SI 2014/3240) contain the "specified amount" for the purposes of subsections (1b) and (2A). It is £1.

1.106 **[45A.**—[1 *Repealed*]

REPEALS

1. Tax Credits Act 2002 Sch.6 (April 1, 2003).

[1 Effect of working families' tax credit and disabled person's tax credit on earnings factor

1.107 **45AA.**—(1) For the purposes of calculating additional pension under sections 44 and 45 where, in the case of any relevant year, working families' tax credit is paid in respect of any employed earner, or disabled person's tax credit is paid to any employed earner, section 44(6)(a)(i) shall have effect as if—

(a) where that person had earnings of not less than the qualifying earnings factor for that year, being earnings upon which primary class 1 contributions were paid or treated as paid ("qualifying earnings") in respect of that year, the amount of those qualifying earnings were increased by the aggregate amount ("AG") of working families' tax credit, or, as the case may be, disabled person's tax credit paid in respect of that year, and

(b) in any other case, that person had qualifying earnings in respect of that year and the amount of those qualifying earnings were equal to AG plus the qualifying earnings factor for that year.

(2) The reference in subsection (1) to the person in respect of whom working families' tax credit is paid—

(a) where it is paid to one of a couple, is a reference to the prescribed member of the couple, and

(b) in any other case, is a reference to the person to whom it is paid.

(3) A person's qualifying earnings in respect of any year cannot be treated by virtue of subsection (1) as exceeding the upper earnings limit for that year multiplied by 53.

(4) Subsection (1) does not apply to any woman who has made, or is treated as having made, an election under regulations under section 19(4), which has not been revoked, that her liability in respect of primary Class 1 contributions shall be at a reduced rate.

(5) In this section—

"couple" has the same meaning as in Part 7 (see section 137);

"relevant year" has the same meaning as in section 44.]

AMENDMENT

1. Pensions Act 2008 Sch.4 para.5(1) (January 3, 2012).

General Note

The insertion of s.45AA (and consequent amendments are together referred to below as "the relevant provisions") have effect in relation to a pensioner who attains pensionable age after April 5, 1999 and, in relation to widowed mother's allowance and widow's pension, to a widow whose husband dies after that date and, in relation to a claim based on a spouse's contributions, to a claimant whose spouse dies after that date, in accordance with subparas (2), (3), (4), and (5) of para.5 of Sch.4 of Pensions Act 2008 as follows: **1.108**

"(3) Subject to sub-paragraphs (4) and (5), the relevant provisions apply to a person ("the pensioner") who attains pensionable age after 5 April 1999 and, in relation to such a person—

(a) have effect for 1995-96 and subsequent tax years, and

(b) are deemed so to have had effect (with the necessary modifications) during the period—

(i) beginning with 6 April 2003, and

(ii) ending with the coming into force of this paragraph.

(4) Where the pensioner is a woman, the relevant provisions have effect in the case of additional pension falling to be calculated under sections 44 and 45 of the Social Security Contributions and Benefits Act 1992 (c. 4) by virtue of section 39 of that Act (widowed mother's allowance and widow's pension), including Category B retirement pension payable under section 48B(4), if her husband—

(a) dies after 5 April 1999, and

(b) has not attained pensionable age on or before that date.

(5) The relevant provisions have effect, where additional pension falls to be calculated under sections 44 and 45 of the Social Security Contributions and Benefits Act 1992 as applied by section 48A or 48B(2) of that Act (other Category B retirement pension) if—

(a) the pensioner attains pensionable age after 5 April 1999, and

(b) the pensioner's spouse has not attained pensionable age on or before that date."

For claims based upon an earlier period see previous editions of this work.

[1 Reduction of additional pension in Category A retirement pension: pension sharing

45B.—(1) The weekly rate of the additional pension in a Category A retirement pension shall be reduced as follows in any case where— **1.109**

(a) the pensioner has become subject to a state scheme pension debit, and

(b) the debit is to any extent referable to the additional pension.

(2) If the pensioner became subject to the debit in or after the final relevant year, the weekly rate of the additional pension shall be reduced by the appropriate weekly amount.

(3) If the pensioner became subject to the debit before the final relevant year, the weekly rate of the additional pension shall be reduced by the appropriate weekly amount multiplied by the relevant revaluation percentage.

(4) The appropriate weekly amount for the purposes of subsections (2) and (3) above is the weekly rate, expressed in terms of the valuation day, at which the cash equivalent, on that day, of the pension mentioned in subsection (5) below is equal to so much of the debit as is referable to the additional pension.

(5) The pension referred to above is a notional pension for the pensioner by virtue of section 44(3)(b) above which becomes payable on the later of—

(a) his attaining pensionable age, and

(b) the valuation day.

(6) For the purposes of subsection (3) above, the relevant revaluation percentage is the percentage specified, in relation to earnings factors for the tax year in which the pensioner became subject to the debit, by the last order under section 148 of the Administration Act to come into force before the end of the final relevant year.

[[2](7) The Secretary of State may by regulations make provision about the calculation and verification of cash equivalents for the purposes of this section.

(7A) The power conferred by subsection (7) above includes power to provide—

(a) for calculation or verification in such manner as may be approved by or on behalf of the Government Actuary, and

(b) for things done under the regulations to be required to be done in accordance with guidance from time to time prepared by a person prescribed by the regulations.]

(8) In this section—

"final relevant year" means the tax year immediately preceding that in which the pensioner attains pensionable age;

"state scheme pension debit" means a debit under section 49(1)(a) of the Welfare Reform and Pensions Act 1999 (debit for the purposes of this Part of this Act);

"valuation day" means the day on which the pensioner became subject to the state scheme pension debit.]

AMENDMENTS

1. Welfare Reform and Pensions Act 1999 Sch.6 para.2 (December 1, 2001).
2. Child Support, Pensions and Social Security Act s.41(2) (September 29, 2000).

GENERAL NOTE

1.110 The Sharing of State Scheme Rights (Provision of Information and Valuation) (No.2) Regulations 2000 (SI 2000/2914) are made under subsection (7).

Modifications of section 45 for calculating the additional pension in certain benefits

1.111 **46.**—(1) [[8]. . .].

(2) For the purpose of determining the additional pension falling to be calculated under section 45 above by virtue of section 39(1) [[1] or 39C(1)] above or section [[2] [[7]...] [[6] 48B(2)] [[1] . . .]] below in a case where the deceased spouse died under pensionable age [[4] or by virtue of section 39C(1) above or section [[7]...] 48BB(2) below in a case where the deceased civil partner died under pensionable age] [[9] or by virtue of section 39C(1) above in a case where the deceased cohabiting partner died under pensionable age], the following definition shall be substituted for the definition of "N" in section 45(4)(b) above—

[[2] "N" =

(a) the number of tax years which begin after 5th April 1978 and end before the date when the entitlement to the additional pension commences, or

(b) the number of tax years in the period—

(i) beginning with the tax year in which the deceased [[9] spouse, civil partner or cohabiting partner] ("S") attained the age of 16 or if later 1978–79, and

(ii) ending immediately before the tax year in which S would have attained pensionable age if S had not died earlier,

whichever is the smaller number].

[3 (3) For the purpose of determining the additional pension falling to be calculated under section 45 above by virtue of section 48BB below in a case where the deceased spouse [4 or civil partner] died under pensionable age, the following definition shall be substituted for the definition of "N" in section 45(4)(b) above—

" 'N' =

(a) the number of tax years which begin after 5th April 1978 and end before the date when the deceased spouse [4 or civil partner] dies, or

(b) the number of tax years in the period—

(i) beginning with the tax year in which the deceased spouse [4 or civil partner] ('S') attained the age of 16 or, if later, 1978–79, and

(ii) ending immediately before the tax year in which S would have attained pensionable age if S had not died earlier,

whichever is the smaller number."]

[5 (4) For the purpose of determining the additional pension falling to be calculated under section 45 above by virtue of section 39C(1) above in a case where the deceased [9 spouse, civil partner or cohabiting partner] died under pensionable age, section 45 has effect subject to the following additional modifications—

(a) the omission of subsection (2)(d), and

(b) the omission in subsection (3A)(b) of the words "before the flat rate introduction year".]

AMENDMENTS

1. Welfare Reform and Pensions Act 1999 Sch.8 (April 9, 2001).
2. Pensions Act 1995 Sch.4 (July 19, 1995).
3. Child Support, Pensions and Social Security Act 2000 s.32 (April 9, 2001).
4. Civil Partnership Act 2004 Sch.24 (December 5, 2005).
5. Pensions Act 2007 Sch.2 Pt 3, para.46 (September 26, 2007).
6. Pensions Act 2008 Sch.4 para.6(3) (January 3, 2012).
7. Pensions Act 2014 Sch.12 para.59 (April 6, 2016).
8. Social Security (Incapacity for Work) Act 1994 Sch.1 para. 12(a) (April 13, 1995).
9. The Bereavement Benefits (Remedial) Order 2023 (SI 2023/134) art.5(4) (August 30, 2018: the amendment came into force on February 13, 2023 but, by virtue of art.1(3), is treated as having had effect from August 30, 2018).

Increase of Category A retirement pension for incapacity

47.—(1) Subject to section 61 below, the weekly rate of a Category A retirement pension shall be increased if the pensioner was entitled to an [1 age addition to long-term incapacity benefit by virtue of regulations under section 30B(7) above] in respect of— 1.112

(a) any day falling within the period of 8 weeks ending immediately before the day on which he attains pensionable age; or

(b) the last day before the beginning of that period;

and the increase shall, subject to subsection (2) below, be of an amount equal to the appropriate weekly rate of the [1 age addition to long-term incapacity benefit by virtue of regulations under section 30B(7) above on that day.]

(2) Where for any period the weekly rate of a Category A retirement pension includes an additional pension, for that period the relevant amount shall be deducted from the amount that would otherwise be the increase under subsection (1) above and the pensioner shall be entitled to an increase under that subsection only if there is a balance remaining after that deduction and, if there is such a balance, of an amount equal to it.

(3) In subsection (2) above the "relevant amount" means an amount equal to the additional pension, reduced by the amount of any reduction in the weekly rate of the Category A retirement pension made by virtue of [2 section 46] of the Pensions Act.

[3 (3A) In subsections (2) and (3) above references to additional pension do not include any amount of additional pension attributable to units of additional pension.

(3B) For units of additional pension, see section 14A.]

(4) In this section any reference to an additional pension is a reference to that pension after any increase under section 52(3) below but without any increase under paragraphs 1 and 2 of Schedule 5 to this Act.

(5) In ascertaining for the purposes of subsection (1) above the rate of a pensioner's [1 age addition to long-term incapacity benefit by virtue of regulations under section 30B(7) above] regard shall be had to the rates in force from time to time.

(6) Regulations may provide that subsection (1) above shall have effect as if for the reference to 8 weeks there were substituted a reference to a larger number of weeks specified in the regulations.

AMENDMENTS

1. Social Security (Incapacity for Work) Act 1994 Sch.1 (April 13, 1995).
2. Pensions Schemes Act 1993 Sch.8 (February 7, 1994).
3. Pensions Act (Consequential Amendments)(Unit of Additional Pensions) Order 2014 (SI 2014/3213) art.2 (October 12, 2015).

GENERAL NOTE

1.113 Note that under s.46 of the Pensions Schemes Act 1993, the amount of any retirement pension is reduced by the guaranteed minimum pension to which the claimant may be entitled. See notes to that section.

Regulation 23 of the Social Security (Incapacity Benefit) (Transitional) Regulations 1995 (SI 1995/310) is made under subsection (6). It provides:

> **"23. Increase of Category A retirement pension for incapacity**
> (1) Where a person has been entitled to invalidity allowance or transitional invalidity allowance at any time during a period of 57 days before attaining pensionable age, sections 47 and 61 of the 1992 Act shall continue to have effect as though section 11 of, and paragraph 13 of Schedule 1 to, the 1994 Act had not come into force and as though any reference to invalidity allowance in section 47 were a reference to transitional invalidity allowance or invalidity allowance.
> (2) In the case of a person who is a welfare to work beneficiary in accordance with regulation 13A of the Social Security (Incapacity for Work) (General) Regulations 1995, the reference in paragraph (1) to a period of 57 days shall be treated as a reference to a period of 104 weeks."

Use of former spouse's contributions

1.114 **48.**—(1) Where a person [3 who attained pensionable age before 6 April 2016]—

(a) has been [1 in a relevant relationship], and
(b) in respect of the tax year in which the [1 relationship] terminated or any previous tax year, does not with his own contributions satisfy the contribution conditions for a Category A retirement pension,

then, for the purpose of enabling him to satisfy those conditions (but only in respect of any claim for a Category A retirement pension), the contributions of his former spouse may to the prescribed extent be treated as if they were his own contributions.

(2) Subsection (1) above shall not apply in relation to any person who attained pensionable age before 6th April 1979 if the termination of his [1 relevant relationship] also occurred before that date.

[3 (2A) Regulations under subsection (1) may not provide for contributions of a person in respect of times on or after 6 April 2016 to be treated as contributions of another person.]

(3) [1 (3) Where a person has been in a relevant relationship more than once, this section applies only to the last relevant relationship and the references to his relevant relationship and his former spouse or civil partner shall be construed accordingly.

(4) In this section, "relevant relationship" means a marriage or civil partnership].

[2 (5) For the purposes of this section, a civil partnership is not to be treated as having terminated by reason of its having been—

(a) converted into a marriage under section 9 of the Marriage (Same Sex Couples) Act 2013 [4 or Part 3 of the Marriage and Civil Partnership (Northern Ireland) (No 2) Regulations 2020 or Part 3 or 4 of the Marriage of Same Sex Couples (Conversion of Civil Partnership) Regulations 2014];
(b) changed into a marriage under the Marriage (Scotland) Act 1977;
(c) changed into a marriage in accordance with provision made under section 10 of the Marriage and Civil Partnership (Scotland) Act 2014; or
(d) changed into a marriage under Part 5 of the Marriage and Civil Partnership (Scotland) Act 2014 and Civil Partnership Act 2004 (Consequential Provisions and Modifications) Order 2014.]

[4 (6) For the purposes of this section, a marriage is not to be treated as having terminated by reason of its having been converted into a civil partnership under Part 3, 4 or 5 of the Marriage and Civil Partnership (Northern Ireland) (No 2) Regulations 2020.]

AMENDMENTS

1. Civil Partnership Act 2004 Sch.24 (December 5, 2005).
2. Marriage and Civil Partnership (Scotland) Act 2014 and Civil Partnership Act 2004 (Consequential Provisions and Modifications) Order 2014 (SI 2014/3229) Sch.4 para.2 (December 12, 2014).
3. Pensions Act 2014 Sch.12 para. 56 (April 6, 2016).
4. Marriage and Civil Partnership (Northern Ireland) (No.2) Regulations 2020 (SI 2020/1143) reg.38 (December 7, 2020).

DERIVATIONS

SSPA 1975 s.20. 1.115
SSA 1979 s.5.

General Note

1.116 The principle of forfeiture will apply in a case where the death of the former spouse is the result of homicide committed by the claimant. An example of its application and the exercise of discretion by the Commissioner is *CFP/4349/2004*. There the claimant had pleaded guilty to the manslaughter of her husband on the grounds of diminished responsibility and was sentenced to a term of probation. She made no claim to widows' benefits for the next 13 years, but then claimed retirement pension relying, in part, on her husband's contribution record. It was held that the forfeiture rule applied, but that relief should be granted with effect from the time of the claim for retirement pension.

The amendment in 2016 made by the Pensions Act 2014 ensures that the section does not apply to any contributions made after the introduction of the single state pension (see the note to s.44 above). This follows the decision to abolish Category B pensions from that date save for existing pensioners and transitional cases.

[1 Category B retirement pension for married person or civil partner

1.117 **48A.**–(1) A married person is entitled to a Category B retirement pension by virtue of the contributions of his or her spouse if—

(a) the person attained pensionable age before 6 April 2016, and

(b) the spouse—

(i) has attained pensionable age, and

(ii) satisfies the relevant contribution condition.

(2) But subsection (1) does not confer a right to a Category B retirement pension on—

(a) a man whose spouse was born before 6 April 1950, or

(b) a woman whose wife was born before 6 April 1950.

(3) A person who is a civil partner is entitled to a Category B retirement pension by virtue of the contributions of his or her civil partner ("the contributing civil partner") if—

(a) the person attained pensionable age before 6 April 2016, and

(b) the contributing civil partner—

(i) was born on or after 6 April 1950,

(ii) has attained pensionable age, and

(iii) satisfies the condition in paragraph 5A of Schedule 3.

(4) A Category B retirement pension payable under this section is payable at the weekly rate specified in paragraph 5 of Part 1 of Schedule 4.

(5) A person ceases to be entitled to a Category B retirement pension under this section if—

(a) the person's spouse or civil partner dies (but see sections 48B and 51), or

(b) the person otherwise ceases to be married or in the civil partnership (but see section 48AA).

(6) In subsection (1)(b)(ii) "the relevant contribution condition" means—

(a) in a case where the spouse was born before 6 April 1945, the conditions in paragraph 5 of Schedule 3;

(b) in any other case, the condition in paragraph 5A of Schedule 3.

[2 (6A) For the purposes of subsection (5)(b), a person is not to be treated as having ceased to be in a civil partnership by reason of its having been converted into a marriage under --

(a) Part 3 of the Marriage and Civil Partnership (Northern Ireland) (No 2) Regulations 2020, or

(b) Part 3 or 4 of the Marriage of Same Sex Couples (Conversion of Civil Partnership) Regulations 2014 where the civil partnership is a convertible Northern Ireland civil partnership as defined by regulation 2 of those Regulations.

(6B) For the purposes of subsection (5)(b), a person is not to be treated as having ceased to be married by reason of the person's marriage having been converted into a civil partnership under Part 3, 4 or 5 of the Marriage and Civil Partnership (Northern Ireland) (No 2) Regulations 2020.]

(7) For the purposes of any provision of this Act as it applies in relation to this section, no account is to be taken of any earnings factors of the spouse or contributing civil partner for the tax year beginning with 6 April 2016 or any later tax year.]

AMENDMENTS

1. Pensions Act 2014 Sch.12 para 60 (April 6, 2016).
2. Marriage and Civil Partnership (Northern Ireland) (No.2) Regulations 2020 (SI 2020/1143) reg.38 (December 7, 2020).

GENERAL NOTE

The new ss.48A and 48AA replace the previous s.48A in consequence of the general changes introduced by Pensions Act 2016. The new sections prevent anyone who reaches state pensionable age on or after April 6, 2016 from claiming entitlement to a Category B pension in respect of any marriage or civil partnership. The rights of those who reach that age before that date are, however, protected subject to the provisions of the sections. For a fuller analysis of the previous provisions under which protected claims could be made see the commentary to the previous s.48A in previous editions of this volume. 1.118

An attempted challenge to s.48A's general exclusion of those who attained pensionable age on or after April 6, 2016 was made in *FY v Secretary of State for Work & Pensions* (RP) [2018] UKUT 146 (AAC). The appellant attained pensionable age on April 21, 2016 and his wife, for whom the appellant wished to secure a category B pension, would attain pensionable age on January 11, 2021. The condition in s.48A(1)(a) was not met because the wife had not attained pensionable age by April 6, 2016. While the wife's entitlement to a Category B pension was in issue, the proceedings were brought by the husband and followed the Secretary of State's decision on his own claim for retirement pension. Upper Tribunal Judge Wikeley held that no decision had been made about the wife's entitlement to a category B pension. In the absence of such a decision, there was nothing to be challenged before the First-tier Tribunal and, in turn, the Upper Tribunal. The Upper Tribunal could not, therefore, consider the Appellant's substantive arguments.

In *FY*, the Appellant husband did, in fact, apply without success to the First-tier Tribunal for his wife to be made a party to the proceedings. Judge Wikeley rejected the husband's challenge to the First-tier Tribunal's refusal to make his wife a party to the proceedings. In the absence of a decision as to her entitlement to a Category B pension, the First-tier Tribunal rightly refused to make the wife to a party to the proceedings. Judge Wikeley went on to observe that, in advance of a decision as to the wife's entitlement to a Category B pension, which could not possibly be given before 2021 when she attained pensionable age, the only potential means of challenging what the Appellant described as the 'abolition' of Category B pensions was a claim for judicial review in the High Court.

In certain cases, no claim is required in order for a person to be entitled to a Category B retirement provision. See regulation 3 of the Social Security (Claims and Payments) Regulations 1987 (volume III of this work) and the note to section 51A of this Act.

[1 Category B retirement pension for divorcee or former civil partner

1.119 **48BAA.**–(1) A person who has been in a marriage that has been dissolved is entitled to a Category B retirement pension by virtue of the contributions of his or her former spouse if—

(a) the person attained pensionable age—
 (i) before 6 April 2016, and
 (ii) before the marriage was dissolved, and
(b) the former spouse—
 (i) attained pensionable age before the marriage was dissolved, and
 (ii) satisfied the relevant contribution condition.

(2) But subsection (1) does not confer a right to a Category B retirement pension on—

(a) a man whose former spouse was born before 6 April 1950, or
(b) a woman whose former wife was born before 6 April 1950.

(3) A person who has been in a civil partnership that has been dissolved is entitled to a Category B retirement pension by virtue of the contributions of his or her former civil partner if—

(a) the person attained pensionable age—
 (i) before 6 April 2016, and
 (ii) before the civil partnership was dissolved, and
(b) the former civil partner—
 (i) was born on or after 6 April 1950,
 (ii) attained pensionable age before the civil partnership was dissolved, and
 (iii) satisfied the condition in paragraph 5A of Schedule 3.

(4) During any period when the person's former spouse or civil partner is alive, a Category B retirement pension payable under this section is payable at the weekly rate specified in paragraph 5 of Part 1 of Schedule 4.

(5) During any period after the person's former spouse or civil partner is dead, a Category B retirement pension payable under this section is payable at the weekly rate of the basic pension specified in section 44(4).

(6) In subsection (1)(b)(ii) "the relevant contribution condition" means—

(a) in a case where the former spouse was born before 6 April 1945, the conditions in paragraph 5 of Schedule 3;
(b) in any other case, the condition in paragraph 5A of Schedule 3.

(7) For the purposes of any provision of this Act as it applies in relation to this section, no account is to be taken of any earnings factors of the former spouse or civil partner for the tax year beginning with 6 April 2016 or any later tax year.

(8) A voidable marriage or civil partnership which has been annulled is to be treated for the purposes of this section as if it had been a valid marriage or civil partnership which was dissolved at the date of annulment.

(9) Section 51ZA contains special rules for cases involving changes in gender.]

AMENDMENT

1. Pensions Act 2014 Sch.12 para.60 (April 6, 2016).

GENERAL NOTE

1.120 See General Note to s.48A.

Category B retirement pension for widows and widowers

[1 **48B.**—[10 (1) A person ("the pensioner") whose spouse died while they were married is entitled to a Category B retirement pension by virtue of the contributions of his or her spouse if— 1.121

(a) the pensioner attained pensionable age—

(i) before 6 April 2016, and

(ii) before the spouse died, and

(b) the spouse satisfied the relevant contribution condition.

(1ZA) But subsection (1) does not confer a right to a Category B retirement pension on—

(a) a man who attained pensionable age before 6 April 2010, or

(b) a woman who attained pensionable age before 6 April 2010 and whose spouse was a woman.

(1ZB) In subsection (1)(b) "the relevant contribution condition" means—

(a) in a case where the spouse—

(i) died before 6 April 2010, or

(ii) died on or after that date having attained pensionable age before that date,

the conditions in paragraph 5 of Schedule 3, and

(b) in any other case, the condition in paragraph 5A of Schedule 3.

(1A) A person ("the pensioner") whose civil partner died while they were civil partners of each other is entitled to a Category B retirement pension by virtue of the contributions of his or her civil partner if—

(a) the pensioner attained pensionable age—

(i) on or after 6 April 2010 but before 6 April 2016, and

(ii) before the civil partner died, and

(b) the civil partner satisfied the relevant contribution condition.

(1B) In subsection (1A)(b) "the relevant contribution condition" means—

(a) in a case where the deceased civil partner attained pensionable age before 6 April 2010, the conditions in paragraph 5 of Schedule 3, and

(b) in any other case, the condition in paragraph 5A of Schedule 3.]

(2) A Category B retirement pension payable by virtue of subsection (1) [5 or (1A)] above shall be payable at a weekly rate corresponding to—

(a) the weekly rate of the basic pension, plus

(b) half of the weekly rate of the additional pension,

determined in accordance with the provisions of sections 44 to [2 45B] [3 and [6 Schedules 4A and 4B below] above as they apply in relation to a Category A retirement pension, but subject to section [8 46 . . .] above and the modifications in subsection (3) below and section 48C(4) below.

(3) Where the spouse [5 or civil partner] died under pensionable age, references in the provisions of sections 44 to [3 45B] [2 and Schedule 4A below] above as applied by subsection (2) above to the tax year in which the pensioner attained pensionable age shall be taken as references to the tax year in which the spouse [5 or civil partner] died.

[10 (3A) For the purposes of any provision of this Act as it applies in relation to this section, no account is to be taken of any earnings factors of the deceased for the tax year beginning with 6 April 2016 or any later tax year.]

[10(4) A woman ("the pensioner") whose husband died before she attained pensionable age is entitled to a Category B retirement pension by virtue of the contributions of her husband if—

(a) she attained pensionable age before 6 April 2016, and
(b) the condition in subsection (5) is satisfied.

(4A) A man ("the pensioner") whose wife died before he attained pensionable age is entitled to a Category B retirement pension by virtue of the contributions of his wife if—

(a) he attained pensionable age on or after 6 April 2010 but before 6 April 2016, and
(b) the condition in subsection (5) would have been satisfied on the assumption mentioned in subsection (7).]

(5) The condition is that the pensioner—

(a) is entitled (or is treated by regulations as entitled) to a widow's pension by virtue of section 38 above, and
(b) became entitled to that pension in consequence of the spouse's death.

(6) A Category B retirement pension payable by virtue of subsection (4) [10 or (4A)] above shall be payable—

(a) where the pensioner is a woman, at the same weekly rate as her widow's pension, and
(b) where the pensioner is a man, at the same weekly rate as that of the pension to which he would have been entitled by virtue of section 38 above on the assumption mentioned in subsection (7) below.

(7) The assumption referred to in subsections [10(4A)] and (6) above is that a man is entitled to a pension by virtue of section 38 above on the same terms and conditions, and at the same rate, as a woman.]

[4 (8) Nothing in subsections (4) to (7) above applies in a case where the spouse dies on or after [12 9 April 2001],]

[10 (9) Section 51ZA contains special rules for cases involving changes in gender.]

[11 (10) Subsection (11) applies in the case of a pensioner entitled to a Category B retirement pension by virtue of subsection (1) or (1A) whose spouse or civil partner—

(a) attained pensionable age on or after 6 April 2016, and
(b) died after attaining pensionable age.

(11) Where this subsection applies, the amount determined in accordance with subsection (2) as the weekly rate of the additional pension payable to the pensioner must be increased by such percentage as equals the overall percentage by which, had the pension been in payment as from the date when the spouse or civil partner reached pensionable age until the spouse's or civil partner's death, that weekly rate would have increased during that period by virtue of orders under section 150 of the Administration Act (annual uprating of benefits).]

AMENDMENTS

1. Pensions Act 1995 Sch.4 (July 19, 1995).
2. Welfare Reform and Pensions Act 1999 Sch.12 para.00 (April 9, 2001).
3. Child Support, Pensions and Social Security Act 2000 s.35 (April 6, 2002).
4. Welfare Reform and Pensions Act 1999 Sch.8 para.00 (April 9, 2001).
5. Civil Partnership Act 2004 Sch.24 (December 5, 2005).
6. Pensions Act 2007 Sch.1 (September 26, 2007).
7. Pensions Act 2007 Sch.2 Pt 3, para.8 (September 26, 2007).
8. Pensions Act 2014 Sch.4 para.96 repealing amendments made by Pensions Act 2008 (October 1, 2014).

9. Marriage (Same Sex Couples) Act 2013 Sch.4 Pt.5, para.12(3) (March 13, 2014). (Provisions that relate to a claim based on a gender recognition certificate will come into force at a later date-see Marriage (Same Sex Couples) Act 2013 (Commencement No.2 and Transitional Provisions Order 2014 (SI 2014/93) art.3.See also Marriage and Civil Partnership (Scotland) Act 2014 and Civil Partnership Act 2004 (Consequential Provisions and Modifications) Order 2014 (SI 2014/3229) Sch.4 para.2 (with effect from December 12, 2014).

10. Pensions Act 2014 Sch.12 para.61 (April 6, 2016).

11. Pensions Act 2014 (Consequential and Supplementary Amendments) Order 2016 (SI 2016/44) art.2(3) (April 6, 2016).

12. Pensions Act 2014 Sch.16 para.15 (April 6, 2017).

General Note

The amendments to this section made by and under the Pensions Act 2016 follow through the policy of that Act by closing entitlement to Category B pensions to anyone reaching state pensionable age on or after April 6, 2016. See subs. (1), (1A),(4) and (4A). Existing rights for those reaching pensionable age before that date are protected by the amended legislation. For a comment on those rights see the note to s.48B in previous editions of this work. 1.122

Regulation 7A of the Social Security (Widow's Benefit and Retirement Pensions) Regulations 1979 (SI 1979/643) sets out when a person is to be treated as entitled to a widow's pension for the purposes of subsection (5)(a).

[1 Category B retirement pension: entitlement by reference to benefits under section 39A or 39B

48BB.—(1) Subsection (2) below applies where a person ("the pensioner") [8 who attained pensionable age before 6 April 2016]— 1.123

(a) was, immediately before attaining that age, entitled to a widowed parent's allowance in consequence of the death of his or her spouse [5 or civil partner]; and

(b) has not [5 following the death, married or formed a civil partnership].

(2) The pensioner shall be entitled to a Category B retirement pension by virtue of the contributions of the spouse [5 or civil partner], which shall be payable at the same weekly rate as the widowed parent's allowance.

(3) Subsections (4) to (10) below apply where a person ("the pensioner") [8 who attained pensionable age before 6 April 2016]—

(a) was in consequence of the death of his or her spouse [5 or civil partner] either—

(i) entitled to a bereavement allowance [9 under section 39B (before that section was repealed)] at any time prior to attaining that age, or

(ii) entitled to a widowed parent's allowance at any time when over the age of 45 (but not immediately before attaining pensionable age); and

(b) has not [5 following the death, married or formed a civil partnership].

(4) The pensioner shall be entitled to a Category B retirement pension by virtue of the contributions of the spouse [5 or civil partner].

(5) A Category B retirement pension payable by virtue of subsection (4) above shall be payable at a weekly rate corresponding to the weekly rate of the additional pension determined in accordance with the provisions of sections 44 to [7 45] above [2 and [6 Schedules 4A [7 and 4B]] below] as they apply in relation to a Category A retirement pension, but [6 subject to

section [7 46] above and to the following provisions of this section and the modification in section 48C(4) below.]

(6) Where the spouse [5 or civil partner] died under pensionable age, references in the provisions of sections 44 to [7 45AA and 45B] above [2 and Schedule 4A below], as applied by subsection (5) above, to the tax year in which the pensioner attained pensionable age shall be taken as references to the tax year in which the spouse [5 or civil partner] died.

(7) Where the spouse [5 or civil partner] dies after [10 5th October 2002], the pension payable by virtue of subsection (4) above shall (before making any reduction required by subsection (8) below) be one half of the amount which it would be apart from this subsection.

(8) Where the pensioner was under the age of 55 at the relevant time, the weekly rate of the pension shall be reduced by 7 per cent. of what it would be apart from this subsection multiplied—

(a) by the number of years by which the pensioner's age at that time was less than 55 (any fraction of a year being counted as a year), or

(b) by ten, if that number exceeds ten.

(9) In subsection (8) above "the relevant time" means—

(a) where the pensioner became entitled to a widowed parent's allowance in consequence of the death of the spouse [5 or civil partner], the time when the pensioner's entitlement to that allowance ended; and

(b) otherwise, the time of the spouse's [5 or civil partner's] death.

(10) The amount determined in accordance with subsections (5) to (9) above as the weekly rate of the pension payable to the pensioner by virtue of subsection (4) above shall be increased by such percentage as equals the overall percentage by which, had the pension been in payment as from the date of the spouse's [5 or civil partner's] death until the date when the pensioner attained pensionable age, that weekly rate would have been increased during that period by virtue of any orders under section 150 of the Administration Act (annual up-rating of benefits).]

AMENDMENTS

1. Welfare Reform and Pensions Act 1999 s.56 (April 9, 2001).
2. Child Support Pensions and Social Security Act 2000 s.35 (April 6, 2002).
3. Child Support Pensions and Social Security Act 2000 s.32(2) (April 9, 2001).
4. Tax Credit Act 2002 Sch.3 (April 6, 2003).
5. Civil Partnership Act 2004 Sch.24 (December 5, 2005).
6. Pensions Act 2007 Sch.2, Pt 3, para.9 (September 26, 2007).
7. Pensions Act 2014 Sch.14, para.96 repealing amendments earlier made by the Pensions Act 2008 (October 1, 2014).
8. Pensions Act 2014 Sch.12 para.62 (April 6, 2016).
9. Pensions Act 2014 Sch.16 para.16 (April 6, 2017).
10. Child Support, Pensions and Social Security Act 2000 s.39, which provides that this amendment has retrospective effect.

GENERAL NOTE

1.124 The amendments made by Pensions Act 2014 close entitlement to include only those who reached state pensionable age on or before April 5, 2016. See the note to s.48B above.

Category B retirement pension: general

1.125 [1 **48C.**—(1) Subject to the provisions of this Act, a person's entitlement to a Category B retirement pension shall begin on the day on which the conditions of entitlement become satisfied and shall continue for life.

(2) In any case where—

(a) a person would, apart from section 43(1) above, be entitled both to a Category A and to a Category B retirement pension, and

(b) section 47(1) above would apply for the increase of the Category A retirement pension,

section 47(1) above shall be taken as applying also for the increase of the Category B retirement pension, subject to reduction or extinguishment of the increase by the application of section 47(2) above or section 46(5) of the Pensions Act.

(3) In the case of a pensioner whose spouse died on or before [9 5th October 2002], [8 section] 48B(2)(b) above shall have effect with the omission of the words "half of".

(4) In the application of the provisions of sections 44 to [2 45B] [3 and [5 Schedules 4A [6 and 4B]] below] above by virtue of sections [8...] 48B(2) [4 or 48BB(5) above, references in those provisions to the pensioner shall be taken as references to the spouse [7 or civil partner].]

AMENDMENTS

1. Pensions Act 1995 Sch.4 (July 19, 1995).
2. Welfare Reform and Pensions Act 1999 Sch.12 (April 9, 2001).
3. Child Support Pensions and Social Security Act 2000 s.35 (April 6, 2002).
4. Welfare Reform and Pensions Act 1999 Sch.8 (April 9, 2001).
5. Pensions Act 2007 Sch.2 Pt 3, para.10 (September 26, 2007).
6. Pensions Act 2014 Sch.14 para.96 repealing amendments earlier made by the Pensions Act 2008 (October 1, 2014).
7. Civil Partnership (Pensions and Benefits Payments) (Consequential, etc. Provisions) Order 2005 (SI 2005/2053) (December 5, 2005).
8. Pensions Act 2014 Sch.12 para.63 (April 6, 2016).
9. Child Support, Pensions and Social Security Act 2000 s.39, which provides that this amendment has retrospective effect.

GENERAL NOTE 1.126

Section 48C is modified to the extent necessary to give effect to a Convention on Social Security entered into on February 1, 2019, by the Government of the United Kingdom and the Government of Ireland (Article 2(1) of the Social Security (Ireland) Order 2019 (SI 2019/622). The Convention seeks to maintain, following the UK's withdrawal from the European Union, certain UK social security entitlements of citizens of the Republic of Ireland. This includes rules for mutual recognition of social security contributions for the purposes of UK retirement pension.

Sections 49 and 50 repealed.

[1 Category B retirement pension for widows, widowers and surviving civil partners who attained pensionable age before 6 April 2010

51.–(1) A person ("the pensioner") whose spouse died while they were married is entitled to a Category B retirement pension if— 1.127

(a) they were both over pensionable age at the time of the death,

(b) the pensioner attained pensionable age before 6 April 2010,

and

(c) the spouse satisfied the relevant contribution condition.

(2) But subsection (1) does not confer a right to a Category B retirement pension on—

(a) a woman whose husband has died, or

(b) a man whose wife died before 6 April 1979.

(3) In subsection (1)(c) "the relevant contribution condition" means—

(a) in a case where the spouse attained pensionable age before 6 April 2010, the conditions in paragraph 5 of Schedule 3, and

(b) in a case where the spouse attained pensionable age on or after 6 April 2010, the condition in paragraph 5A of Schedule 3.

(4) A person ("the pensioner") whose civil partner died while they were civil partners of each other is entitled to a Category B retirement pension if—

(a) they were both over pensionable age at the time of the death,

(b) the pensioner attained pensionable age before 6 April 2010, and

(c) the deceased civil partner satisfied the relevant contribution condition.

(5) In subsection (4)(c) "the relevant contribution condition" means—

(a) in a case where the deceased civil partner attained pensionable age before 6 April 2010, the conditions in paragraph 5 of Schedule 3, and

(b) in a case where the deceased civil partner attained pensionable age on or after 6 April 2010, the condition in paragraph 5A of Schedule 3.

(6) The weekly rate of a person's Category B retirement pension under this section is to be determined in accordance with sections 44 to 45AA and [2 Schedule 4A and 4B] as they apply in the case of a Category A retirement pension taking references in those sections to the pensioner as references to the spouse or deceased civil partner.

(7) But in the case of—

(a) a man whose wife dies after 5 October 2002,

(b) a surviving party to a marriage of a same sex couple, or

(c) a surviving civil partner,

any amount of additional pension falling to be calculated under subsection (6) is to be halved.

(8) For the purposes of any provision of this Act as it applies in relation to this section, no account is to be taken of any earnings factors of the spouse or deceased civil partner for the tax year beginning with 6 April 2016 or any later tax year.

(9) Subject to the provisions of this Act, a person becomes entitled to a Category B retirement pension under this section on the day on which the conditions of entitlement become satisfied and the entitlement continues throughout the person's life.

(10) Section 51ZA contains special rules for cases involving changes in gender.]

[2(11) Subsection (12) applies in the case of a pensioner whose spouse or civil partner—

(a) attained pensionable age on or after 6 April 2016, and

(b) died after attaining pensionable age.

(12) Where this subsection applies, the amount determined in accordance with this section as the weekly rate of the additional pension payable to the pensioner must be increased by such percentage as equals the overall percentage by which, had the pension been in payment as from the date

when the spouse or civil partner reached pensionable age until the spouse's or civil partner's death, that weekly rate would have increased during that period by virtue of orders under section 150 of the Administration Act (annual uprating of benefits).]

AMENDMENTS

1. Pensions Act 2014 Sch.12 para.64 (April 6, 2016).
2. Pensions Act 2014 (Consequential and Supplementary Amendments) Order 2016 (SI 2016/224) art. 2(4) (April 6, 2016).

DEFINITION

"pensionable age"—see s.122.

GENERAL NOTE

This section and s.51ZA below tidy up the existing legislation providing for Category B pensions, while at the same time following the policy of the Pensions Act 2014 in preventing anyone reaching state pensionable age on or after April 6, 2016 from claiming a Category B pension (save in transitional cases). In those cases the section again confirms the policy of the Act in excluding from any such claim any contributions paid after the Pensions Act 2014 took effect. **1.128**

Section 51 is modified to the extent necessary to give effect to a Convention on Social Security entered into on February 1, 2019, by the Government of the United Kingdom and the Government of Ireland (Article 2(1) of the Social Security (Ireland) Order 2019 (SI 2019/622). The Convention seeks to maintain, following the UK's withdrawal from the European Union, certain UK social security entitlements of citizens of the Republic of Ireland. This includes rules for mutual recognition of social security contributions for the purposes of UK retirement pension.

[[1] Special provision for married person whose spouse changed gender

51ZA.–(1) Section 48A(2)(b) does not prevent a woman from being entitled to a Category B retirement pension under that section in a case where— **1.129**

(a) her spouse is a woman by virtue of a full gender recognition certificate having been issued under the Gender Recognition Act 2004, and
(b) the marriage subsisted before the time when that certificate was issued.

(2) Section 48AA(2)(b) does not prevent a woman from being entitled to a Category B retirement pension under that section in a case where—

(a) her former spouse was, at the time the marriage was dissolved, a woman by virtue of a full gender recognition certificate having been issued under the Gender Recognition Act 2004, and
(b) the marriage subsisted before the time when that certificate was issued.

(3) Section 48B(1ZA)(b) does not prevent a woman from being entitled to a Category B retirement pension under that section in a case where—

(a) her dead spouse was, at the time of death, a woman by virtue of a full gender recognition certificate having been issued under the Gender Recognition Act 2004, and
(b) the marriage subsisted before the time when that certificate was issued,

and in such a case the reference in section 48B(1ZB)(a)(ii) to the spouse having attained pensionable age before 6 April 2010 is to be read as a reference to the spouse having been born before 6 April 1945.

(4) Section 51(1) does not confer a right to a Category B retirement pension on a woman if—

(a) her dead spouse was, at the time of death, a woman by virtue of a full gender recognition certificate having been issued under the Gender Recognition Act 2004, and

(b) the marriage subsisted before the time when that certificate was issued.]

AMENDMENT

1. Pensions Act 2014 Sch.12 para.65 (April 6, 2016).

Special provision for married people

1.130 [1 **51A.**—This section has effect where, apart from section 43(1) above, a married person [2 or civil partner] would be entitled both—

(a) to a Category A retirement pension, and

(b) to a Category B retirement pension by virtue of the contributions of the other party to the marriage [2 or civil partnership].

(2) If by reason of a deficiency of contributions the basic pension in the Category A retirement pension falls short of the weekly rate specified in Schedule 4, Part I, paragraph 5, that basic pension shall be increased by the lesser of—

(a) the amount of the shortfall, or

(b) the amount of the weekly rate of the Category B retirement pension.

(3) This section does not apply in any case where both parties to the marriage [2 or civil partnership] attained pensionable age before 6th April 1979].

AMENDMENTS

1. Pensions Act 1995 Sch.4, para.21(6) (July 19, 1995).
2. Civil Partnership Act 2004 Sch.4 (December 5, 2005).

GENERAL NOTE

In *GM v Secretary of State for Work & Pensions* (RP) [2022] UKUT 85 (AAC), Upper Tribunal Judge Wikeley considered that section 51A's purpose was accurately described as follows in Wikeley and Ogus' *The Law of Social Security* (Butterworths 2002, 5th edn.) at pp.604-5:

> "A married woman who has reached pensionable age may be entitled to a Category A pension on the basis of her own contributions in the same way as a man. Alternatively, she may be entitled to a Category B pension on her husband's contributions. She cannot claim both but she may be able to use her Category B entitlement to enhance the value of her Category A pension. In such a case the Category A pension entitlement can be increased by either the whole of the Category B pension derived from the husband's contributions or as much of it as is necessary to raise the Category A basic pension to the level of the lower-rate Category B pension, whichever is less. The resulting 'composite' pension is the claimant's Category A pension, even if most of it is payable by virtue of the husband's contributions."

GM concerned the general rule, provided for by section 1(1) of the Social Security Administration Act 1992 (see volume III of this work), that no person shall be entitled to any benefit unless the person makes a claim for it. The general rule does not apply to exceptions prescribed by reg.3 of the Social Security (Claims and Payments) Regulations 1987 (see volume III). With effect from 17 March 2008, regulation was amended by inserting reg.3(1)(cb). This enacted, in relation to a Category B retirement pension, an exception to the general rule that, without a claim, there can be no entitlement. So far as relevant in *GM*, the exception described a claimant "entitled to a category A retirement pension. . .and (i) the spouse. . .of the [claimant] becomes entitled to a Category A pension. . .". Since the Appellant in *GM* was already entitled to a Category A pension, her additional entitlement to a Category B pension relied on section 51A (an exception to the general rule that a person may not be entitled to more than one Category of retirement pension).

The Appellant in *GM* was a woman and it is therefore convenient to describe the decision in terms of husbands and wives. The issue was whether the removal of the requirement to claim a Category B retirement pension applied only to those wives whose husbands became entitled to a Category A pension on or after the amendment to reg.3(1)(cb) took effect on 17 March 2008 (the narrower interpretation, as advanced by the Secretary of State). The alternative interpretation was that reg.3(1)(cb) also applied to any wife whose husband became entitled to a Category A pension before 17 March 2008 (the broader interpretation, advanced by the Appellant). The Appellant's husband became entitled to a Category A pension before 17 March 2008. Under the narrower interpretation, her entitlement to a Category B pension would be dependent on a claim being made (many years after 2008, and many years after she could have first made a claim).

Judge Wikeley agreed with the narrower interpretation of reg.3(1)(cb) advanced by the Secretary of State. Judge Wikeley found that the statutory language used in reg.3(1)(cb) supported the narrower interpretation. The provision refers to a spouse who "becomes entitled to a Category A retirement pension". The key word used was 'becomes' whose natural meaning, within reg.3(1)(cb), connotes something happening on or after a provision comes into force, namely a spouse's entitlement to a Category A pension. That the natural meaning of the statutory language reflected the legislative intention was reinforced by witness statement evidence that reg.3(1)(cb)'s enactment was linked to upgrades to DWP IT systems which meant that, by 2008, claims for Category B pensions could be dispensed with for married women whose husbands subsequently claimed a Category A pension (see paragraphs 55 to 60 of the decision).

Judge Wikeley rejected the Appellant's arguments that the narrower interpretation constituted discrimination contrary to Article 14 of the European Convention on Human Rights. The Appellants' reliance on *Thlimmenos v Greece* (2001) EHRR 15 was not made out. *Thlimmenos* discrimination concerns state failure, without objective and reasonable justification, to treat differently those whose situations are significantly different. The Appellant, however, had not been placed at a disadvantage nor was there relevantly similar treatment. She could not argue that she was at a disadvantage as compared to a person claiming a Category A pension for the first time (she already had a Category A pension). In any event, this aspect of the Appellants' case was, in substance, a challenge to the general rule in section 1 of the Social Security Administration Act 1992 that entitlement to benefit is dependent on a claim. But the Upper Tribunal has no power to make a declaration that primary legislation is incompatible with Convention rights (see section 4 of the Human Rights Act 1998). Judge Wikeley also rejected the Appellant's argument of indirect discrimination. While the judge accepted that a woman whose entitlement to a Category B pension remained dependent on a claim being made had an 'other status' for the purposes of Article 14, any difference of treatment as compared to those without that status was shown by the Secretary of State to be justified. The 2008 amendment to the Claims and Payments Regulations was introduced to make it easier for a cohort of women to receive Category B pensions, without making a claim, in circumstances where the DWP could reasonably assume that those women wished to receive a Category B pension. In the light of its purpose, the amendment was neither unfair, inefficient nor disproportionate.

Judge Wikeley's decision was given after full oral argument. It is suggested that it should be preferred to the contrary decision of Deputy Upper Tribunal Judge Sir Crispin Agnew of Lochnaw Bt QC in *CP/345/2011* which Sir Crispin himself declined to follow in *CSP/5/2013*.

1.131 The effect of *Secretary of State for Work and Pensions v Nelligan, R(P)2/03* is extended to include s.51A in *CP/271/2005*. The claimant's wife had, like that in *Nelligan*, qualified for a Category A pension of her own on reaching age 60, but at a reduced rate. Subsequently, her husband qualified for his pension at the full rate at which point the claimant could have qualified for an increased pension on the basis of s.51A. Unfortunately the claimant did not discover this until some two years later and when she then claimed, she was allowed backdating for only the usual three month period.

The claimant argued that *Nelligan* did not apply to s.51A, and that if it did, then *Nelligan* was decided per incuriam since no reference there had been made to s.51A. That section, it was argued, should be read as creating entitlement without the need for a claim to be made. It was contended, on her behalf, that her increased entitlement arose under s.51A as a result of a decision to supersede her existing award of Category A pension and without a fresh claim being made.

This argument failed, however, because, as the Commissioner points out, the supersession takes effect only from the date of a relevant change of circumstances which, for the purpose of s.51A, could only be by her becoming entitled to a Category B pension, and as *Nelligan* had held, that entitlement depended upon a claim having been made.

Special provision for surviving spouses

1.132 **52.**—(1) This section has effect where, apart from section 43(1) above, a person would be entitled both—

(a) to a Category A retirement pension; and

[1 (b) to a Category B retirement pension by virtue of the contributions of a spouse [2 or civil partner] who has died]

(2) If by reason of a deficiency of contributions the basic pension in the Category A retirement pension falls short of the full amount, that basic pension shall be increased by the lesser of—

(a) the amount of the shortfall, or

(b) the amount of the basic pension in the rate of the Category B retirement pension,

"full amount" meaning for this purpose the sum specified in section 44(4) above as the weekly rate of the basic pension in a Category A retirement pension.

(3) If the additional pension in the Category A retirement pension falls short of the [3 maximum amount specified in regulations], that additional pension shall be increased by the lesser of—

(a) the amount of the shortfall, or

(b) the amount of the additional pension in the Category B retirement pension.

[4 (3A) In subsection (3) the references to additional pension in a Category A or Category B retirement pension do not include any amount of additional pension attributable to units of additional pension.

(3B) If an amount of additional pension in the Category B retirement pension is attributable to units of additional pension, the additional pension in the Category A retirement pension is increased by that amount (in addition to any increase under subsection (3)).]

(4) This section does not apply in any case where the death of the wife or husband, as the case may be, occurred before 6th April 1979 and the surviving spouse had attained pensionable age before that date.

AMENDMENTS

1. Pensions Act 1995 Sch.4, para.21(7) (July 19, 1995).
2. Civil Partnership Act 2004 Sch.24 (December 5, 2005).
3. Pensions Act 2014 Sch.12 para.66 (April 6, 2016).
4. Pensions Act 2014 Sch.15 para.8 (October 12, 2015).

GENERAL NOTE

As with the sections above, this section now only applies to those who reached state pensionable age before April 6, 2016 or have a transitional entitlement after that date. For a comment on this section see the previous (2015/16) edition of this volume. 1.133

Section 53 repealed. 1.134

Category A and Category B retirement pensions: supplemental provisions

54. – (1) Regulations may provide that in the case of a person of any prescribed description who— 1.135
(a) has become entitled to a Category A or Category B retirement pension; and
(b) elects in such manner and in accordance with such conditions as may be prescribed that the regulations shall apply in his case,
this Part of this Act shall have effect as if that person had not become entitled to such a retirement pension [1 or to a shared additional pension].

(2) Regulations under subsection (1) above may make such modifications of the provisions of this Part of this Act, or of those of [2 Chapter II of Part I of the Social Security Act 1998] as those provisions apply in a case where a person makes an election under the regulations, as may appear to the Secretary of State necessary or expedient.

GENERAL NOTE

This section authorises regulations that set out the procedure to be followed and conditions to be met in order for a person to defer entitlement to a Category A or B retirement pension. The regulations are the Social Security (Deferral of Retirement Pensions) Regulations 2005 (SI 2005/453, see below in this volume). 1.136

In relation to the new state pension under the Pensions Act 2014, which came into effect on April 6, 2016, entitlement may be deferred through a pensioner suspending or postponing their pension. This is governed by the State Pension Regulations 2015 (see below in this volume). However, deferral of Category A or B retirement pensions under the Social Security (Deferral of Retirement Pensions) Regulations 2005 may remain of ongoing relevance in some cases. For example, if there is a dispute as to whether a Category A or B retirement pension was duly deferred or where a person claims to be entitled to a survivor's pension based on inheritance of deferred old state pension under s.9 of the Pensions Act 2014.

AMENDMENTS

1. Welfare Reform and Pensions Act 1999 Sch.12 Pt I paras 14 & 22 (December 1, 2000).
2. Social Security Act 1998 Sch.7 para.62 (December 6, 1999).

[2 Pension increase or lump sum where entitlement to retirement pension is deferred

1.137 **55.**—(1) Where a person's entitlement to a Category A or Category B retirement pension is deferred, Schedule 5 to this Act has effect.

(2) In that Schedule—

paragraph A1 makes provision enabling an election to be made where the pensioner's entitlement is deferred

paragraphs 1 to 3 make provision about increasing pension where the pensioner's entitlement is deferred

paragraphs 3A and 3B make provision about lump sum payments where the pensioner's entitlement is deferred

paragraph 3C makes provision enabling an election to be made where the pensioner's deceased spouse [4 or civil partner] has deferred entitlement

paragraphs 4 to 7 make provision about increasing pension where the pensioner's deceased spouse [4 or civil partner] has deferred entitlement

paragraphs 7A and 7B make provision about lump sum payments where the pensioner's deceased spouse [4 or civil partner] has deferred entitlement

paragraphs 7C to 9 make supplementary provision.

(3) For the purposes of this Act a person's entitlement to a Category A or Category B retirement pension is deferred if and so long as that person—

[3 (a) does not become entitled to that pension by reason only of not satisfying the conditions of section 1 of the Administration Act (entitlement to benefit dependent on claim), or]

(b) in consequence of an election under section 54(1), falls to be treated as not having become entitled to that pension,

and, in relation to any such pension, "period of deferment" shall be construed accordingly.]

AMENDMENTS

1. Pensions Act 1995 s.134(3) (July 19, 1995).
2. Pensions Act 2004 s.297 (April 6, 2005, subs.(3) from November 18, 2004).
3. Pensions Act 2007 Sch.1 para.7 (September 26, 2007).
4 Civil Partnership (Pensions and Benefits Payments) (Consequential, etc. Provisions) Order 2005 art.2, Sch. para.3 (SI 2005/2053) (December 5, 2005).

DERIVATIONS

1.138 SSPA 1975 s.12.
SSA 1989 s.7.

GENERAL NOTE

1.139 Note that the increase in pension does not depend upon the claimant having decided to defer his claim. As subs.(2)(a)(i) makes clear, it applies equally to a person making a late claim for pension where the delay is the result of ignorance of entitlement, or otherwise. In *CP/14276/1996* the claimant had been resident in China and made her claim five years after she reached pensionable age. Although her claim could be backdated only one year (see SSAA 1992, s.1), it was paid at an enhanced rate to reflect the effective period of delay—four years.

In *KH v SSWP* [2014] UKUT 138 (AAC) Judge Wikeley held that the calculation of the increase in pension entitlement occurred only once when a decision on the claim to a pension was made; thereafter payment of the pension was made, with that increase, and adjusted by the annual up-rating procedure. The claimant had argued that because of the words used in a departmental booklet, that he was entitled to have his pension calculated afresh each year and then have the percentage increase that had been earned by deferment applied to that new annual total. The judge found that whatever the booklet might have suggested (and he did not find that it was necessarily misleading) that the meaning of the provisions in Sch.5 to this act that govern the calculation could admit of only one meaning—the claim was determined at the outset and the percentage increase then applied to the pension; the percentage increase so earned then remained as a part of his pension for life. The provisions for calculating the amount of the increase are found in Sch.5 to this Act and any increases provided for in the annual up-rating of Benefits Order. Note that from April 2005, benefit that is deferred for a year or more may be taken in the form of a lump sum.

This section may be affected, in appropriate cases, by the operation of the Gender Recognition Act 2004.

[1 Shared additional pension [4 because of an old state scheme pension credit]

55A. [4 (1) A person is entitled to a shared additional pension under this section if— 1.140

(a) the person attained pensionable age before 6 April 2016, and

(b) the person is entitled to an old state scheme pension credit.]

(2) A person's entitlement to a shared additional pension [4 under this section] shall continue throughout his life.

(3) The weekly rate of a shared additional pension [4 under this section] shall be the appropriate weekly amount, unless the pensioner's entitlement to the [4 old] state scheme pension credit arose before the final relevant year, in which case it shall be that amount multiplied by the relevant revaluation percentage.

(4) The appropriate weekly amount for the purposes of subsection (3) above is the weekly rate, expressed in terms of the valuation day, at which the cash equivalent, on that day, of the pensioner's entitlement, or prospective entitlement, to the shared additional pension is equal to the [4 old] state scheme pension credit.

(5) The relevant revaluation percentage for the purposes of that subsection is the percentage specified, in relation to earnings factors for the tax year in which the entitlement to the [4 old] state scheme pension credit arose, by the last order under section 148 of the Administration Act to come into force before the end of the final relevant year.

[2 (6) The Secretary of State may by regulations make provision about the calculation and verification of cash equivalents for the purposes of this section.

(6A) The power conferred by subsection (6) above includes power to provide—

(a) for calculation or verification in such manner as may be approved by or on behalf of the Government Actuary, and

(b) for things done under the regulations to be required to be done in accordance with guidance from time to time prepared by a person prescribed by the regulations.]

(7) In this section—

"final relevant year" means the tax year immediately preceding that in which the pensioner attains pensionable age;

"[4 old] state scheme pension credit" means a credit under section 49(1)(b) of the Welfare Reform and Pensions Act 1999 (credit for the purposes of this Part of this Act);

"valuation day" means the day on which the pensioner becomes entitled to the state scheme pension credit.]

AMENDMENTS

1. Welfare Reform and Pensions Act 1999 Sch.6 para.3 (April 9, 2001).
2. Child Support, Pensions and Social Security Act 2000 s.41 (September 29, 2000).
3. Pensions Act 2007 Sch.1 para.7 (September 26, 2007).
4. Pensions Act 2014 Sch.11 para.5 (April 6, 2016).

GENERAL NOTE

1.141 Note the special provisions made for persons claiming a shared additional pension between April 6, 2005 and April 5, 2006 in reg.10 of the Shared Additional Pensions (Miscellaneous Amendments) Regulations 2005 (S1 2005/ 1551).

The sums which are shared additional pensions under this section were increased, with effect from April 8, 2024, by 6.7 per cent: see art.4(4) of the Social Security Benefits Up-rating Order 2024 (SI 2024/242). For previous years' increases, see previous editions of this work.

[1 Shared additional pension because of a new state scheme pension credit

1.142 **55AA** .–(1) A person is entitled to a shared additional pension under this section if—

(a) the person reached pensionable age before 6 April 2016, and

(b) the person is entitled to a new state scheme pension credit.

(2) A person's entitlement to a shared additional pension under this section continues throughout his or her life.

(3) The weekly rate of a shared additional pension under this section is equal to the amount of the new state scheme pension credit.

(4) In this section "new state scheme pension credit" means a credit under section 49A(2)(b) of the Welfare Reform and Pensions Act 1999.]

AMENDMENTS

1. Pensions Act 2014 Sch.11 para.6 (April 6, 2016).

GENERAL NOTE

1.143 The sums which are shared additional pensions under this section were increased, with effect from April 8, 2024, by 6.7 per cent: see art.4(4) of the Social Security Benefits Up-rating Order 2024 (SI 2024/242). For previous years' increases, see previous editions of this work.

[1 Reduction of shared additional pension: pension sharing

1.144 **55B.**—(1) The weekly rate of a shared additional pension shall be reduced as follows in any case where—

(a) the pensioner has become subject to [3 an old] state scheme pension debit, and

(b) the debit is to any extent referable to the pension.

(2) If the pensioner became subject to the debit in or after the final relevant year, the weekly rate of the pension shall be reduced by the appropriate weekly amount.

(3) If the pensioner became subject to the debit before the final relevant year, the weekly rate of the additional pension shall be reduced by the appropriate weekly amount multiplied by the relevant revaluation percentage.

(4) The appropriate weekly amount for the purposes of subsections (2) and (3) above is the weekly rate, expressed in terms of the valuation day, at which the cash equivalent, on that day, of the pension mentioned in subsection (5) below is equal to so much of the debit as is referable to the shared additional pension.

(5) The pension referred to above is a notional pension for the pensioner by virtue of section [3 55A or 55AA (as the case may be)] which becomes payable on the later of—

(a) his attaining pensionable age, and

(b) the valuation day.

(6) For the purposes of subsection (3) above, the relevant revaluation percentage is the percentage specified, in relation to earnings factors for the tax year in which the pensioner became subject to the debit, by the last order under section 148 of the Administration Act to come into force before the end of the final relevant year.

[2 (7) The Secretary of State may by regulations make provision about the calculation and verification of cash equivalents for the purposes of this section.

(7A) The power conferred by subsection (7) above includes power to provide—

(a) for calculation or verification in such manner as may be approved by or on behalf of the Government Actuary, and

(b) for things done under the regulations to be required to be done in accordance with guidance from time to time prepared by a person prescribed by the regulations.]

(8) In this section—

"final relevant year" means the tax year immediately preceding that in which the pensioner attains pensionable age;

"[3 old] state scheme pension debit" means a debit under section 49(1)(a) of the Welfare Reform and Pensions Act 1999 (debit for the purposes of this Part of this Act);

"valuation day" means the day on which the pensioner became subject to the state scheme pension debit.]

AMENDMENTS

1. Welfare Reform and Pensions Act 1999 Sch.6 para.3 (April 9, 2001).

2. Child Support, Pensions and Social Security Act 2000 s.41 (September 29, 2000).

3. Pensions Act 2014 Sch.11 para.7 (April 6, 2016).

[1 Pension increase or lump sum where entitlement to shared additional pension is deferred

55C.—(1) Where a person's entitlement to a shared additional pension is deferred, Schedule 5A to this Act has effect. **1.145**

(2) In that Schedule—

paragraph 1 makes provision enabling an election to be made where the person's entitlement is deferred

paragraphs 2 and 3 make provision about increasing pension where the person's entitlement is deferred

paragraphs 4 and 5 make provision about lump sum payments where the person's entitlement is deferred.

(3) For the purposes of this Act, a person's entitlement to a shared additional pension is deferred—

(a) where he would be entitled to a Category A or Category B retirement pension but for the fact that his entitlement is deferred, if and so long as his entitlement to such a pension is deferred, and

(b) otherwise, if and so long as he does not become entitled to the shared additional pension by reason only of not satisfying the conditions of section 1 of the Administration Act (entitlement to benefit dependent on claim),

and, in relation to a shared additional pension, "period of deferment" shall be construed accordingly.]

AMENDMENTS

1. Pensions Act 2004 s.297 (April 6, 2005).

Child's special allowance

Child's special allowance—existing beneficiaries

1.146 **56.**—*Omitted.*

1.147 *Sections 57 to 59 repealed.*

Complete or partial failure to satisfy contribution conditions

1.148 **60.** – (1) Subject to the provisions of this section, regulations may provide for persons to be entitled to any of the following benefits, namely—

(a) a widowed mother's allowance,

[1 (aa) a widowed parent's allowance,]

(b) a widow's pension,

(c) a Category A retirement pension,

(d) a Category B retirement pension,

in cases where the first contribution condition specified in relation to that benefit in paragraph 5 of Schedule 3 to this Act is satisfied and the second contribution condition so specified is not.

(2) Subject to subsection (8) below, in any case where—

(a) an employed earner who is married [2 or a civil partner] dies as a result of—

(i) a personal injury of a kind mentioned in section 94(1) below, or

(ii) a disease or injury such as is mentioned in section 108(1) below, and

(b) the contribution conditions are not wholly satisfied in respect of [3 the employed earner], those conditions shall be taken to be satisfied for the purposes of [3 the entitlement of the employed earner's [2 widow, widower or surviving civil partner]] to any of the benefits specified in subsection (3) below.

(3) The benefits referred to in subsection (2) above are the following—

[4 (a) ...]

(b) a widowed mother's allowance;

[1 (ba) a widowed parent's allowance;]

(c) a widow's pension;

[3 (d) a Category B retirement pension payable by virtue of section 48B [1 or 48BB] above].

(4) Subject to [6 subsection (7)] below, regulations under subsection (1) above shall provide for benefit payable by virtue of any such regulations to be payable at a rate, or to be of an amount, less than that which would be applicable under this Part of this Act had both of the relevant contribution conditions been fully satisfied.

(5) Subject to [5 subsection (7)] below, the rate or amount prescribed by regulations under subsection (1) above may vary with the extent to which the relevant contribution conditions are satisfied (and may be nil).

[6 (6)...]

(7) Regulations may provide that where—

(a) a person is entitled by virtue of subsection (1) above to a Category A or Category B retirement pension consisting only of the additional pension with no basic pension, and

(b) that retirement pension, and any graduated retirement benefit to which he may be entitled, together amount to less than the prescribed rate,

that person's entitlement as respects that retirement pension shall be satisfied either altogether or for a prescribed period by the making of a single payment of the prescribed amount.

(8) Subsection (2) above only has effect where the employed earner's death occurred on or after 11th April 1988.

[7 (9) References in this section to a Category A or Category B retirement pension do not include one to which Schedule 3, Part I, paragraph 5A applies.]

DERIVATION

Subsection (1) and (4) to (6): SSA 1975 s.33(1) to (3). **1.149**
Subsections (2) & (3): SSA 1986 s.39.
Subsection (7): SSPA 1975 s.19(5).
Subsection (8): SSA 1988 s.2.

AMENDMENTS

1. Welfare Reform and Pensions Act 1999 Sch.8, para.8 (April 9, 2001).
2. Civil Partnership Act 2004 Sch.24, para.31 (December 5, 2005).
3. Pensions Act 1995 Sch.4, para.21 (July 19, 1995).
4. Pensions Act 2014 Sch.16, para.17 (April 6, 2017).
5. Tax Credits Act 2002 Sch.3, para.33 (April 6, 2003).
6. Tax Credits Act 2002 Sch.6, para.1 (April 6, 2003).
7. Pensions Act 2007 Sch.1, para.4 (September 26, 2007).

GENERAL NOTE

This section provides, in two types of case, for a person to be entitled to certain contributory benefits despite partial satisfaction of the relevant contribution conditions. **1.150**

The first type of case applies where, in relation to the benefits specified in subsection (1), the first contribution condition for that benefit specified in Sch.3(5) to the Act is satisfied but the second contribution condition is not. Subsection (1) authorises regulations to provide that a person, despite the second condition being unsatisfied, is entitled to benefit albeit at a reduced rate. Such regulations have been made: see reg.6 of the Social Security (Widow's Benefit and Retirement Pensions) Regulations 1979 below in this volume.

The second case, provided for on the face of s.60 rather than in regulations, is intended to benefit a surviving spouse or civil partner of an employed earner who dies as a result of an industrial injury or an industrial disease. Where the contribution conditions for the benefits specified in subsection (3) are not wholly satisfied in relation to the deceased employed earner, subsection (2) deems the contribution conditions to be satisfied.

[1 Failure to satisfy contribution condition in paragraph 5A of Schedule 3

1.151 **60A.** – (1) Subsection (2) below applies if the contribution condition in Schedule 3, Part I, paragraph 5A is not satisfied in relation to a benefit to which that paragraph applies.

(2) A person who would have been entitled to the benefit had the condition been satisfied shall nevertheless be entitled to a prescribed proportion of that benefit in respect of each of the years of the contributor's working life that falls within subsection (3) below.

(3) A year of the contributor's working life falls within this subsection if it is a year in relation to which the requirements in paragraph 5A(2)(a) and (b) of Part I of Schedule 3 are satisfied.

(4) "The contributor" means the person by whom the condition is to be satisfied.

(5) In any case where—

(a) an employed earner who is married or a civil partner dies on or after 6th April 2010 as a result of—

(i) a personal injury of a kind mentioned in section 94(1) below, or

(ii) a disease or injury such as is mentioned in section 108(1) below, and

(b) the contribution condition specified in Schedule 3, Part I, paragraph 5A is not satisfied in respect of the employed earner,

that condition shall be taken to be satisfied for the purposes of the entitlement of the employed earner's widow, widower or surviving civil partner to a Category B retirement pension payable by virtue of section 48B.

(6) In subsections (1) to (3) any reference—

(a) to the contribution condition in Schedule 3, Part I, paragraph 5A, or

(b) to the requirements of paragraph 5A(2)(a) and (b),

includes a reference to that condition or those requirements as modified by virtue of paragraph 5A(4).]

AMENDMENT

1. Pensions Act 2007 Sch.1, para.5 (September 26, 2007).

GENERAL NOTE

1.152 This section relates to the single contribution condition for a Category A retirement pension and, in turn, a Category B pension, set out in para.5A of Sch.3 to the Act (that condition only applies to a person who reaches state pension age on or after

6 April 2010). The single contribution condition requires contribution and earnings factor criteria to be met for at least 30 years of a contributor's working life. Subsections (2) and (3) provide for a reduced Category A or B pension entitlement where a contributor has a shortfall in qualifying years. Regulations set out the prescribed portion of the full pension for such cases: see regulation 6A of the Social Security (Widow's Benefit and Retirement Pensions0 Regulations 1979 below in this volume.

Subsection (5) makes similar provision, in relation to employed earners who die after April 6, 2010, to that made by s.60(2) in relation to earners not subject to the single contribution condition: see the note to s.60.

Exclusion of increase of benefit for failure to satisfy contribution condition

61. – (1) A Category A or Category B retirement pension which is payable by virtue of section 60(1) above and a widowed mother's allowance [1 or widowed parent's allowance] which is so payable shall not be increased under section 47(1) above or under Part IV below if the pension or allowance contains no basic pension in consequence of a failure to satisfy a contribution condition. 1.153

[2 (2) Where a person is entitled to short-term incapacity benefit at a rate determined under section 30B(3) above and the retirement pension by reference to which the rate of the benefit is determined—

(a) would have been payable only by virtue of section 60 above, and
(b) would, in consequence of a failure to satisfy a contribution condition, have contained no basic pension,

the benefit shall not be increased under section 47(1) above or under Part IV below.]

DERIVATION

SS(MP)A 1977 s.8(1), (2). 1.154

AMENDMENTS

1. Welfare Reform and Pensions Act 1999 Sch.8, para.9 (April 9, 2001).
2. Jobseekers Act 1995 Sch.2, para.23 (October 7, 1996).

[1 Shortfall in contributions: people with units of additional pension]

61ZA. – (1) This section applies to a person who has one or more units of additional pension if the person— 1.155

(a) is not entitled to a Category A retirement pension, but
(b) would be entitled to a Category A retirement pension if the relevant contribution conditions were satisfied.

(2) The relevant contribution conditions are to be taken to be satisfied for the purposes of the person's entitlement to a Category A retirement pension.

(3) But where a person is entitled to a Category A retirement pension because of this section, the only element of that pension to which the person is so entitled is the additional pension attributable to the units of additional pension.

(4) For units of additional pension, see section 14A.]

AMENDMENT

1. Pensions Act 2014 Sch.15, para.9 (October 12, 2015).

General Note

1.156 The additional pension secured through payment of Class 3A contributions forms part of a pensioner's Category A retirement pension. This section ensures that pensioners who have attained one or more units of additional pension through payment of Class 3A contributions but who do not have an entitlement to a Category A retirement pension nevertheless receive payments of additional pension. It does this by deeming the pensioner to be entitled to a Category A pension but that entitlement relates only to the pensioner's units of additional pension.

[1 Shortfall in contributions: people whose dead spouse had units of additional pension

1.157 **61ZB.** – (1) This section applies to a person whose spouse or civil partner died with one or more units of additional pension if the person—

(a) is not entitled to a Category B retirement pension as a result of the death, but

(b) would be entitled to a Category B retirement pension as a result of the death if the relevant contribution conditions were satisfied.

(2) The relevant contribution conditions are to be taken to be satisfied for the purposes of the person's entitlement to that Category B retirement pension.

(3) But where a person is entitled to a Category B retirement pension because of this section, the only element of that pension to which the person is so entitled is the additional pension attributable to the units of additional pension.

(4) For units of additional pension, see section 14A.]

Amendment

1. Pensions Act 2014 Sch.15, para.9 (October 12, 2015).

General Note

1.158 A surviving spouse's additional pension secured through payment of Class 3A contributions by the deceased spouse forms part of the survivor's Category B retirement pension. This section ensures that survivors who have attained one or more units of additional pension through payment of Class 3A contributions but who do not have an entitlement to a Category B retirement pension nevertheless receive payments of additional pension. It does this by deeming the survivor to be entitled to a Category B pension but that entitlement relates only to the survivor's units of additional pension.

[1 Entitlement to more than one pension: sections 61ZA and 61ZB

1.159 **61ZC.** –(1) Section 43 does not prevent a person from being entitled for the same period to both—

(a) a Category A retirement pension because of section 61ZA, and

(b) one Category B retirement pension.

(2) Section 43 does not prevent a person from being entitled for the same period to both—

(a) a Category A retirement pension, and

(b) one Category B retirement pension because of section 61ZB (or, if there is more than one such Category B retirement pension, the most favourable of them).

(3) Accordingly—

(a) in section 43(2)(a) the reference to "a Category A or a Category B retirement pension", in a case in which subsection (1) or (2) of this section applies, includes "a Category A and a Category B retirement pension",
(b) in sections 43(3)(a) and (aa), 51A and 52 "Category A retirement pension" does not include a pension to which a person is entitled because of section 61ZA, and
(c) in sections 43(3)(a) and 52 "Category B retirement pension" does not include a pension to which a person is entitled because of section 61ZB.]

AMENDMENT

1. Pensions Act 2004 Sch.15, para.9 (October 12, 2015).

[1 Contributions paid in error

61A. –(1) This section applies in the case of any individual if— **1.160**
(a) the individual has paid amounts by way of primary Class 1 contributions which, because the individual was not an employed earner, were paid in error, and
(b) prescribed conditions are satisfied.
(2) Regulations may, where—
(a) this section applies in the case of any individual, and
(b) the [2 Inland Revenue are] of the opinion that it is appropriate for the regulations to apply to the individual,

provide for entitlement to, and the amount of, additional pension to be determined as if the individual had been an employed earner and, accordingly, those contributions had been properly paid.

(3) The reference in subsection (2) above to additional pension is to additional pension for the individual or the individual's spouse [3 or civil partner] falling to be calculated under section 45 above for the purposes of—
(a) Category A retirement pension,
(b) Category B retirement pension for [3 widows, widowers or surviving civil partners] [4 (payable by virtue of section 48B or 48BB above)],
(c) widowed mother's allowance and widow's pension, [5 and]
[4 (ca) widowed parent's allowance,] and
(d) incapacity benefit (except in transitional cases).
(4) Regulations may, where—
(a) this section applies in the case of any individual, and
(b) the [2 Inland Revenue are] of the opinion that it is appropriate for regulations made by virtue of section 4(8) of the Social Security (Incapacity for Work) Act 1994 (provision during transition from invalidity benefit to incapacity benefit for incapacity benefit to include the additional pension element of invalidity pension) to have the following effect in the case of the individual,

provide for the regulations made by virtue of that section to have effect as if, in relation to the provisions in force before the commencement of that section with respect to that additional pension element, the individual had been an employed earner and, accordingly, the contributions had been properly paid.

(5) Where such provision made by regulations as is mentioned in subsection (2) or (4) above applies in respect of any individual, regulations under paragraph 8(1)(m) of Schedule 1 to this Act may not require the amounts paid by way of primary Class 1 contributions to be repaid.

(6) Regulations may provide, where—

(a) such provision made by regulations as is mentioned in subsection (2) or (4) above applies in respect of any individual,

(b) prescribed conditions are satisfied, and

(c) any amount calculated by reference to the contributions in question has been paid in respect of that individual by way of minimum contributions under section 43 of the Pension Schemes Act 1993 (contributions to personal pension schemes),

for that individual to be treated for the purposes of that Act as if that individual had been an employed earner and, accordingly, the amount had been properly paid.]

AMENDMENTS

1. Pensions Act 1995 s.133 (July 19, 1995).
2. Social Security Contributions (Transfer of Functions, etc) Act 1999 Sch.1 para.8 (February 25, 1999).
3. Civil Partnership Act 2004 Sch.24, para.32 (December 5, 2005).
4. Welfare Reform and Pensions Act 1999 Sch.8, para.10 (April 9, 2001).
5. Welfare Reform Act 2007 Sch.3, para.9 (October 27, 2008)

GENERAL NOTE

1.161 Note that entitlement to additional pension due to primary Class 1 contributions made in error is dependent, even where prescribed conditions are met, on the exercise of a statutory discretion vested in HMRC (see subsection (2)(b)).

The Social Security (Additional Pension) (Contributions Paid in Error) Regulations 1996 (SI 1996/1245) are made under this section, see below in this volume.

Graduated retirement benefit

1.162 **62.**—(1) So long as sections 36 and 37 of the National Insurance Act 1965 (graduated retirement benefit) continue in force by virtue of regulations made under Schedule 3 to the Social Security (Consequential Provisions) Act 1975 or under Schedule 3 to the Consequential Provisions Act, regulations may make provision—

(a) for [1 amending section 36(2) of the National Insurance Act 1965 (value of unit of graduated contributions) so that the value is the same for women as it is for men and for replacing section 36(4) of that Act] (increase of graduated retirement benefit in cases of deferred retirement) with provisions corresponding to those of paragraphs [6 A1 to 3B and 7C] of Schedule 5 to this Act;

[2 (aa) for amending section 36(7) of that Act (persons to be treated as receiving nominal retirement pension) so that where a person has claimed a Category A or Category B retirement pension but—

(i) because of an election under section 54(1) above, or

(ii) because he has withdrawn his claim for the pension,

he is not entitled to such a pension, he is not to be treated for the purposes of the preceding provisions of that section as receiving such a pension at a nominal weekly rate;]

[5 (ab) for extending section 37 of that Act (increase of woman's retirement pension by reference to her late husband's graduated retirement benefit) to civil partners [7 and their late civil partners] and for that section (except subsection (5)) so to apply as it applies to women and their late husbands;]

[4 (ac) for extending section 37 of that Act (increase of woman's retirement pension by reference to her late husband's graduated retirement benefit) to civil partners and their late civil partners who attain pensionable age before 6th April 2010 and for that section (except subsection (5)) so to apply as it applies to men and their late wives;]

[8 (ad) for extending section 37 of that Act (increase of woman's retirement pension by reference to her late husband's graduated retirement benefit) to—

(i) men and their late husbands, and

(ii) women and their late wives,

and for that section (except subsection (5)) so to apply as it applies to women and their late husbands;

(ae) for extending section 37 of that Act (increase of woman's retirement pension by reference to her late husband's graduated retirement benefit) to—

(i) men and their late husbands, and

(ii) women and their late wives,

who attained pensionable age before 6th April 2010 and for that section (except subsection (5)) so to apply as it applies to men and their late wives;]

(b) for extending section 37 of that Act (increase of woman's retirement pension by reference to her late husband's graduated retirement benefit) to men and their late wives [3 and for that section (except subsection (5)) so to apply as it applies to women and their late husbands].

[6 (c) for amending that section in order to make provisions corresponding to those of paragraphs 3C, 4(1) and (1A) and 7A to 7C of Schedule 5 to this Act enabling a widowed person [7 or surviving civil partner] to elect to receive a lump sum, rather than an increase in the weekly rate of retirement pension, in respect of the graduated retirement benefit of his or her deceased spouse [7 or civil partner].]

(2) This section is without prejudice to any power to modify the said sections 36 and 37 conferred by Schedule 3 to the Consequential Provisions Act.

[8 (3) In relevant gender change cases, women and their late wives are to be treated for the purposes of sections 36 and 37 of the National Insurance Act 1965 in the same way as women and their late husbands.

(4) For that purpose "relevant gender change case", in relation to a woman ("the pensioner") and her late wife, means a case where—

(a) the late wife was, at the time of her death, a woman by virtue of a full gender recognition certificate having been issued under the Gender Recognition Act 2004, and

(b) the marriage of the pensioner and her late wife subsisted before the time when the certificate was issued.]

AMENDMENTS

1. Pensions Act 1995 Sch.4 para.7(a). (July 19, 1995).
2. Pensions Act 1995 s.131(1) (July 19, 1995).
3. Pensions Act 1995 Sch.4 para.7(b) (July 19, 1995).
4. Civil Partnership (Miscellaneous and Consequential Provisions) Order 2005 (SI 2005/3029) Sch.1, (October 29, 2005).

5. Civil Partnership Act 2004 Sch.24 (December 5, 2005).
6. Pensions Act 2004 Sch.11 (April 4, 2005).
7. Civil Partnership (Pensions and Benefits Payments) (Consequential, etc. Provisions) Order 2005 (SI 2005/2053) (December 5, 2005).
8. Marriage (Same Sex Couples) Act 2013 Sch.4 Pt. 5 para.14. See also the Marriage and Civil Partnership (Scotland) Act 2014 and Civil Partnership Act 2004 (Consequential Provisions and Modifications) Order 2014 (SI 2014/3229) Sch.4 para.2 (with effect from December 12, 2014).

DERIVATION

1.163 SSPA 1975 s.24.

GENERAL NOTE

1.164 *R(P) 1/08* Commissioner Williams demonstrated the complexity that arises in relation to claims for GRB and to appeals from those decisions. Unlike other contributory benefits no part of the functions of the Secretary of State for Work and Pensions has been transferred to His Majesty's Revenue and Customs. Yet HMRC are still responsible for recording and providing any information necessary in relation to a claimant's contribution record. This means that officers of HMRC must do so as agents acting on behalf of the SSWP, and any decision made by them becomes one for which the SSWP is legally responsible. This means, in turn, that all such decisions are appealable to the tribunal system. This decision also contains useful guidance for tribunals on the correct approach to questions that arise from the contribution record.

A Convention on Social Security, entered into on February 1, 2019, by the Government of the United Kingdom and the Government of Ireland (given effect in UK law by art.2(1) of the Social Security (Ireland) Order 2019 (SI 2019/622)), generally seeks to maintain, following the UK's withdrawal from the European Union, certain UK social security entitlements of citizens of the Republic of Ireland. The Convention includes rules for mutual recognition of social security contributions for the purposes of UK pension benefits. However, these rules do not apply for the purposes of graduated retirement benefit payable by virtue of any graduated contributions paid before 6 April 1975 (art.29 of the Convention).

PART III

NON-CONTRIBUTORY BENEFITS

Descriptions of non-contributory benefits

1.165 **63.**—Non-contributory benefits under this Part of this Act are of the following descriptions, namely—

(a) attendance allowance;
(b) [4...];
(c) [1 carer's allowance] [5 [2...]];
(d) disability living allowance;
(e) guardian's allowance;
(f) retirement pensions of the following categories—
  (i) Category C, [3 payable in certain cases to a widow whose husband was over pensionable age on 5 July 1948 or to a woman whose marriage to a husband who was over pensionable age on that date was terminated otherwise than by his death] (with increase for adult [2 . . .] dependants), and
  (ii) Category D, payable to persons over the age of 80;

(g) age addition payable, in the case of persons over the age of 80, by way of increase of a retirement pension of any category [3 under this Act] or of some other pension or allowance from the Secretary of State.

AMENDMENTS

1. Regulatory Reform (Carer's Allowance) Order 2002 (SI 2002/1457) art.2 (April 1, 2003).
2. Tax Credits Act 2002 Sch.6 (April 6, 2003).
3. Pensions Act 2014 Sch.12 paras.79 and 85 (April 6, 2016).
4. Welfare Reform and Pensions Act 1999 Sch.13 Pt 4 (April 6, 2001).
5. Welfare Reform Act 2009 Sch.7 Pt 2 (April 6, 2010).

DERIVATION

SSA 1975 s.34. **1.166**

GENERAL NOTE

Note that para.(f)(i) retains an entitlement for adult dependants of claimants covered by that subparagraph. Such increases were abolished in general from 2010 (see Pensions Act 2007) but no provision has been made removing these words. **1.167**

Attendance allowance

Entitlement

64.—(1) A person shall be entitled to an attendance allowance if he [2 has attained pensionable age], he is not entitled to [3 an allowance within subsection (1A)] and he satisfies either— **1.168**

(a) the condition specified in subsection (2) below ("the day attendance condition"), or
(b) the condition specified in subsection (3) below ("the night attendance condition"),

and prescribed conditions as to residence and presence in Great Britain.

[3 (1A) The following allowances are within this subsection—

(a) personal independence payment;
[4 (aa) adult disability payment;]
(b) the care component of a disability living allowance.]

(2) A person satisfies the day attendance condition if he is so severely disabled physically or mentally that, by day, he requires from another person either—

(a) frequent attention throughout the day in connection with his bodily functions, or
(b) continual supervision throughout the day in order to avoid substantial danger to himself or others.

(3) A person satisfies the night attendance condition if he is so severely disabled physically or mentally that, at night,—

(a) he requires from another person prolonged or repeated attention in connection with his bodily functions, or
(b) in order to avoid substantial danger to himself or others he requires another person to be awake for a prolonged period or at frequent intervals for the purpose of watching over him.

[1 (4) Circumstances may be prescribed in which a person is to be taken to satisfy or not to satisfy such of the conditions mentioned in subsections (2) and (3) above as may be prescribed.]

AMENDMENT

1. Welfare Reform and Pensions Act 1999 s.66 (January 12, 2000).

2. Pensions Act 2007 Sch.1 Pt 8 para.41. This amendment was orginally not to have effect until April 6, 2024, but now has had effect from April 6, 2018—see Pensions Act 2011 s.1.

3. Welfare Law Reform 2012 Sch.9 (April 8, 2013).

4. Scotland Act 2016 (Social Security) (Adult Disability Payment and Child Disability Payment) (Amendment) Regulations 2022 (SI 2022/335) reg.2 (March 21, 2022).

DERIVATION

1.169 SSA 1975 s.35(1).

GENERAL NOTE

1.170 Note: the amendment to subs.(1) above to "pensionable age" did not have effect until April 6, 2018. Until that time the section should be read as if it retained the words "is aged 65 or over".

Attendance Allowance is a weekly benefit paid to those who are disabled so as to need a sufficient level of care and attention from someone else. The benefit is usually paid to the claimant rather than to the carer. It is not necessary that the claimant is actually paying for the care (or, in theory, even that he is receiving the care). What is necessary is that he should *need* the care.

See the discussion of this point in relation to DLA where the wording is the same. In *KK v SSWP* [2012] UKUT 356 (AAC) Judge Jacobs held that there was an error of law where the FTT failed to explain to the claimant that he may be entitled to benefit even though he chose not spend it on acquiring care; he had said that he would not want a carer entering his home and intruding on his privacy. The FTT treated this as withdrawing his claim for the care component. The UT affirms that the question to be decided is whether the claimant *needs* care (though not obtaining care may be some evidence that it is not required) and the FTT has a duty, in its inquisitorial role, to explain that to the claimant.

Attendance Allowance was originally introduced in 1970 and was then payable at just one rate to those who needed attention or supervision both day and night. In 1972, the lower rate was introduced for those who required attention or supervision by day or at night but not both.

Attendance Allowance is payable to those persons who become disabled after they attain pensionable age or who first claim this allowance after that age even though they may have been disabled earlier. The allowance is not payable to anyone who is in receipt of the care component of Disability Living Allowance and who turned 65 before April 2013. Nor is it payable to someone in receipt of Personal Independence Payment. Attendance Allowance is less generous than the care component of Disability Living Allowance in two respects. First, it has a six-month qualifying period (s.65(1)(b)) as opposed to the three-month period for the care component (s.72(2)(a)) although neither qualifying period applies in the case of a person who is terminally ill. Secondly, there are only two rates of Attendance Allowance, which are the same as the highest and middle rate of the care component. There is no equivalent to the lowest rate of the care component.

The lack of an equivalent lowest rate of benefit in Attendance Allowance was attacked by the claimant in *CS v SSWP* [2009] UKUT 257 (AAC). He was aged 71 and, therefore, excluded from making a claim for DLA. He argued that the absence of benefit at the lowest rate was discrimination on the ground of age contrary to the Human Rights Act. Judge Lane rejected that argument, though she accepted that his right to a social security benefit was within art.1 of Protocol 1 and that the difference in treatment was discrimination on the ground of age. She held that this discrimination was justified because in her view it was rational and proportionate, she said, to distinguish those who were affected by disability at a younger age and whose earning capacity was thus reduced. Retirement pension, she said, was there to make provision, at least in part, for those over retiring age. (cf. *NT v SSWP* [2009] UKUT 37 (AAC); *R(DLA) 1/09*, in relation to the mobility component of DLA).

The limitations that these conditions impose are shown by the decision in *CA/2574/2007*. The claimant was a widow who was agoraphobic, anorexic and depressed, and had lived as a recluse since the death of her husband. She was visited daily by her daughter who supplied all her physical needs and remained each day for a period of several hours to stimulate and encourage her mother. A report by a consultant psychiatrist suggested that the claimant was being kept alive by the services and the visits of her daughter. This much was accepted as true by the Commissioner, but still could not qualify her for AA. The services such as shopping and housekeeping supplied by the daughter could not qualify as they were not sufficiently "personal" (see notes that follow s.72) and, although the Commissioner was prepared to accept that the time spent stimulating her mother might qualify as attention in connection with the bodily functioning of the brain, it was neither "frequent" nor "continual" throughout the day so as to satisfy the conditions of subs.(2). Had the claimant been able to claim DLA (she could not because of her age) she might have succeeded in a claim for the lowest rate of that benefit on the basis that the attention was for a "significant portion of the day".

Note that although Attendance Allowance has no equivalent to the mobility component provided under DLA, or as in PIP, it is possible for a claimant who requires assistance in moving about to include that help in the assessment of their need for attention in connection with their bodily functions—in this case, the bodily function of mobilising whether within doors, or out of doors. Thus, for someone in a wheelchair who requires another person to push them about, that assistance can count towards the frequency and extent of the assistance that they require: see *JB v SSWP* [2015] UKUT 361 (AAC).

Subsection (1)

For the circumstances in which a person over 65 is entitled to the care component 1.171
of a disability living allowance, see s.75 and also reg.3 of and Sch.1 to the Disability Living Allowance Regulations. For prescribed conditions as to residence and presence, see reg.2 of the Social Security (Attendance Allowance) Regulations 1991.

Subsections (2) and (3)

Subs.(3) contains two alternative "day" conditions and subs.(3) contains two 1.172
alternative "night" conditions. Subject to the waiting period imposed by s.65(1)(b), attendance allowance is paid at the higher rate if both a "day" and a "night" condition are satisfied and at the lower rate if the conditions are satisfied only for the day or the night (s.65(3)).

The attendance conditions in subss.(2) and (3) are the same as those in paras (b) and (c) of s.72(1) and reference should be made to the notes to that subsection.

Note that both conditions may be deemed to be satisfied in the case of a person who is terminally ill and can reasonably be expected to die within six months (s.66).

Note also that reg.5 of the Attendance Allowance Regulations provides that certain people undergoing renal dialysis are deemed to satisfy either the day or the night attention condition so as to qualify them for attendance allowance at the lower rate. There is no reason why they should not satisfy another condition for other reasons and so qualify for the higher rate.

Before March 15, 1988, the night condition was different. Under the earlier version it was possible for supervision to be provided by someone who was "on call", though not necessarily awake, so as to be ready to render assistance as necessary (*Moran v Secretary of State for Social Services* reported as appendix to *R(A) 1/88*). After that date it has been necessary for the carer to be awake and watching over the claimant.

Since May 5, 2005 Attendance Allowance can be claimed by those who have gone to live in another European Union country. This is because the decision of the European Court in Case C-299/05, *Commission v European Parliament and Council*

[2007] ECR I-8695 held that this benefit, together with Carer's Allowance and the care component of Disability Living Allowance, were not properly excluded from entitlement and could be claimed as a form of sickness benefits.

And note too the decision in *SSWP v LT* [2012] UKUT 282 (AAC). This is a decision of a three judge panel which holds that the care component of DLA is exportable even when the claimant had ceased all employment or self-employment before she left the UK. It was sufficient that she had been employed and had preserved benefits in the form of an entitlement to a retirement pension when she reached retirement age.

That decision was appealed but has ultimately been confirmed by the answers to questions put to the EUECJ by the Supreme Court: see *SSWP v Tolley* [2017] EUECJ C-430/15). They confirm that the care component is a "sickness benefit" and that the claimant's past contribution record made her an "employed person" and therefore within the protection of the regulation. This case is concerned with the old Regulation 1408/71 but it is likely that the same result would follow under the current Regulation 883/04.

Period and rate of allowance

1.173 **65.**—(1) Subject to the following provisions of this Act, the period for which a person is entitled to an attendance allowance shall be—

(a) a period throughout which he has satisfied or is likely to satisfy the day or the night attendance condition or both; and

(b) a period preceded immediately, or within such period as may be prescribed, by one of not less than six months throughout which he satisfied, or is likely to satisfy, one or both of those conditions.

(2) For the purposes of subsection (1) above a person who suffers from renal failure and is undergoing such form of treatment as may be prescribed shall, in such circumstances as may be prescribed, be deemed to satisfy or to be likely to satisfy the day or the night attendance condition or both.

(3) The weekly rate of the attendance allowance payable to a person for any period shall be the higher rate specified in Schedule 4, Part III, paragraph 1, if both as regards that period and as regards the period of six months mentioned in subsection (1)(b) above he has satisfied or is likely to satisfy both the day and the night attendance conditions, and shall be the lower rate in any other case.

(4) A person shall not be entitled to an attendance allowance for any period preceding the date on which he makes or is treated as making a claim for it.

(5) Notwithstanding anything in subsection (4) above, provision may be made by regulations for a person to be entitled to an attendance allowance for a period preceding the date on which he makes or is treated as making a claim for it if such an allowance has previously been paid to or in respect of him.

(6) Except in so far as regulations otherwise provide and subject to section 66(1) below—

(a) a claim for an attendance allowance may be made during the period of six months immediately preceding the period for which the person to whom the claim relates is entitled to the allowance; and

(b) an award may be made in pursuance of a claim so made, subject to the condition that, throughout that period of six months, that person satisfies—

(i) both the day and the night attendance conditions, or

(ii) if the award is at the lower rate, one of those conditions.

[[1] (7) A person to whom either Regulation (EC) No 1408/71 or Regulation/(EC) No 883/2004 applies shall not be entitled to an attendance allowance for a period unless during that period the UK is competent for payment of sickness benefits in cash to the person for the purposes of Chapter 1 of Title III of the Regulation in question.]

DERIVATION

SSA 1975 ss.35(2), (2A), (3), (4) and (4A). 1.174

AMENDMENTS

1. Social Security (Disability Living Allowance, Attendance Allowance and Carer's Allowance) (Miscellaneous Amendments) Regulations 2011, reg.5(3). (SI 2011/2426) (October 31, 2011).

GENERAL NOTE

Subsection (1)

Paragraph (a) has the effect that an award of attendance allowance should be for the period for which the claimant has satisfied or is *likely* to satisfy one or both of the attendance conditions. An award may be for life or for a specified period. There is no minimum period specified but it will seldom be appropriate to make an award for less than six months which is the minimum period for an award of the care component of a disability living allowance (see s.72(2)(b)). In this case, "likely" can be read as "more likely than not" since the subsection is concerned with the continued satisfaction of the conditions of entitlement. If the prognosis is uncertain, the award should be limited in time. 1.175

It is not necessary that the conditions are likely to be satisfied in respect of every day. *R(A) 2/74* concerned a claimant who had to undergo renal dialysis for 10 hours on three nights a week, at a time before any specific provision was made for such claimants (see now reg.5 of the Social Security (Attendance Allowance) Regulations 1991). The Commissioner held that it was wrong to take a purely arithmetical approach and that the claimant was not, as a matter of law, excluded from entitlement. Variations in a claimant's condition present greater problems because they are irregular and difficult to predict. "These are matters for the good sense and judgment of the [decision-maker]."

Both attendance conditions are deemed to be satisfied for the remainder of the life of a person suffering from a progressive disease and likely to die within six months (s.66(1)(a)(i)).

Paragraph (b) provides for the six-month qualifying period. A person is not entitled to attendance allowance until he or she has satisfied an attendance condition for six months. The combined effect of this subsection and subs.(3) is that, if a person has been receiving the lower rate because he or she satisfies only, say, the day attendance condition and then his or her condition deteriorates so that he or she also satisfies the night condition, he or she does not become entitled to the higher rate until six months have elapsed. This six-month qualifying period is waived in the case of a person who is suffering from a progressive disease and likely to die within six months (s.66(1)(a)(ii)). Other claimants may make their claims during the qualifying period so that a decision can be made straightaway and payment can start as soon as the qualifying period has been completed (subs.(4)(a)).

Usually the six-month qualifying period immediately precedes the period of entitlement but it may fall within such other period as may be prescribed. Reg.3 of the Social Security (Attendance Allowance) Regulations 1991 prescribes the period of two years.

Subsection (2)

This enables regulations to be made so that a person who undergoes renal dialysis is deemed to satisfy either or both of the day and the night attendance conditions. Reg.5 of the Social Security (Attendance Allowance) Regulations 1991 allows a person having such treatment at least twice a week to be deemed, in some circumstances, to satisfy one, but not both, of the attendance conditions. Any question 1.176

whether a person suffers renal failure is determined by an appeal tribunal which includes a medically qualified member and one with a disability qualification on appeal from the Secretary of State.

Subsections (4) and (5)

1.177 Awards of attendance allowance cannot usually be made in respect of a period before the date of claim. For details affecting the date a claim is treated as made see reg.6 of Claims and Payments Regulations in Vol.I of this work.

Regulation 4 of the Social Security (Attendance Allowance) Regulations 1991, treated as made under subs.(5), allowed an award to be made from the end of a previous period of entitlement if the renewal claim was made within six months but that regulation was revoked from September 1, 1997.

Subsection (6)

1.178 A claim may be made in advance during the six-month waiting period. The award is, of course, conditional on the claimant continuing to satisfy the attendance conditions. In *CA/1474/97*, the Commissioner held that a tribunal who found that the attendance conditions had been satisfied for a period of less than six months could make a prospective award. However, they were not bound to do so and could decline to reach any firm conclusion as to whether the attendance conditions had been satisfied for that period although, if they took that course, they were obliged to tell the claimant that he or she could make another claim so as to have the question determined. Since the coming into force of para.3(2) of Sch.6 to the Social Security Act 1998 on May 21, 1998, it is possible to make a prospective award only if the attendance conditions were satisfied at the date of the decision-maker's decision so that the decision-maker could have made a prospective award.

Subsection (7)

1.179 Subsection (7) was held to be valid in *IG v SSWP* [2016] UKUT 176 (AAC); [2016] AACR 41. Judge Jacobs held that attendance allowance was a sickness benefit and that the UK was entitled under Regulation (EC) 883/2004 to make this regulation which had the effect of denying benefit where a foreign state was the competent state in respect of sickness benefits.

Attendance allowance for the terminally ill

1.180 **66.**—(1) If a terminally ill person makes a claim expressly on the ground that he is such a person then—

(a) he shall be taken—

(i) to satisfy, or to be likely to satisfy, both the day attendance condition and the night attendance condition [1 for so much of the period for which he is terminally ill as does not fall before the date of claim;] and

(ii) to have satisfied those conditions for the period of [2 12] months immediately preceding [1 the date of the claim or, if later, the first date on which he is terminally ill] (so however that no allowance shall be payable by virtue of this sub-paragraph for any period preceding that date); and

(b) the period for which he is entitled to attendance allowance shall be [1 so much of the period for which he is terminally ill as does not fall before the date of the claim].

(2) For the purposes of subsection (1) above—

(a) a person is "terminally ill" at any time if at that time he suffers from a progressive disease and his death in consequence of that disease can reasonably be expected within [2 12] months; and

(b) where a person purports to make a claim for an attendance allowance by virtue of that subsection on behalf of another, that other shall be regarded as making the claim, notwithstanding that it is made without his knowledge or authority.

AMENDMENTS

1. Welfare Reform and Pensions Act 1999 s.66 (January 12, 2000).
2. Social Security (Special Rules for End of Life) Act 2022 s.1 (April 3, 2023).

DERIVATION

SSA 1975 ss.35(2B), (2C). 1.181

GENERAL NOTE

Terminally ill patients are deemed to satisfy both attendance conditions and therefore qualify for benefit at the higher rate. Furthermore, in order to meet the criticism that such patients sometimes died before they could complete what was the normal six-month qualifying period, the benefit is paid under this section from the date of claim. (The claimant is deemed to satisfy the conditions for the remainder of his life and to have done so in the six months preceding his claim.) Nor is it necessary for the claimant to show that he requires attention, etc.; this is assumed to be the case for those who are terminally ill. 1.182

Subs.(2)(a) provides the definition of when a person is "terminally ill". A person is terminally ill when he suffers from a progressive disease and his death from the cause can "reasonably be expected within 12 months". Previously this test required death to be expected within six months. A decision of the High Court in Northern Ireland, *Cox (re an application for judicial review)* [2020] NIQB 53, had found this requirement to be discriminatory in the case of a claimant whose consultant could not say that death was to be expected within six months and given that many successful claimants did survive longer than six months. Advances in medical treatment mean that such an outcome is now not unlikely. The increase to a period of 12 months may help to resolve that difficulty.

This phrase, though potentially of uncertain meaning, does not seem to have given rise to difficulty. It is fairly clear that someone whose death is more likely than not is "reasonably expected" to die. Equally, where the doctor says that his patient is likely to survive beyond 12 months it would seem true to say his death is not "expected" within that period. But what of those cases where the outcome is simply very uncertain? Could death be "reasonably expected" when it is "quite possible", though not yet "probable"? Note that some of this difficulty will be obviated by the need to show that death is expected from a "progressive disease". This will include conditions such as cancer but in most cases will not cover other common causes of death such as heart attacks.

It is important to note that the question to be considered by the decision-maker, and a tribunal on appeal, is prospective in the sense that what must be determined is whether death is reasonably to be expected within 12 months of the date of claim. Medical evidence in the form of the doctor's opinion must relate to that question regardless of what may have transpired since the claim was made. In *R(A) 1/94* a claim had been made for a baby born with brain damage. The award was made from a date six months after the baby's birth. The baby's mother applied for review of the award to run from the date of birth and a consultant was asked to answer the question as above. However, by the time he came to answer the baby had already survived for more than a year and he felt unable to answer, given what was now known. The AO decided that death was not to be expected, etc. The Commissioner allowed an appeal, holding that the survival of the baby was irrelevant to the question that had to be answered, *viz.* what was reasonably to be expected at the date the review was requested, and he allowed the appeal. This did not avail the mother, however, as this claim was made under the old legislation for attendance allowance. Those provisions required a claimant to have been present in Great Britain for six months. In the case of a baby the Commissioner held that this meant an award could not begin until six months after its birth. In the case of disability living allowance, for which a claim of this sort would now be made, this requirement is expressly removed (reg.2(4) of the Disability Living Allowance Regulations) and benefit would be paid from birth, or from the time the baby left an NHS hospital.

In any event, death must be expected as a result of a progressive disease, rather than some other cause. This may be a significant qualification for a few very elderly people. A question whether a person is terminally ill is decided by the Secretary of State with appeal to an appeal tribunal which includes a medically qualified member and one with a disability qualification. Although a claim must be made expressly on the ground that the claimant is terminally ill, the Secretary of State may accept any notification that a person is terminally ill as being sufficient to amount to a claim (reg.4 of the Social Security (Claims and Payments) Regulations 1987). Presumably, in the case of a claimant with an existing award of attendance allowance at the lower rate, an application for a review on this ground counts as a claim for the purposes of s.66. In any case this decision will now be made by the Secretary of State. Subs.(2)(b) allows someone else to make a claim on this basis on behalf of the claimant, which enables a claim to be made in a case where the claimant's prognosis is being kept from him or her.

Exclusions by regulation

1.183 **67.**—(1) Regulations may provide that, in such circumstances, and for such purposes as may be prescribed, a person who is, or is treated under the regulations as, undergoing treatment for renal failure in a hospital or other similar institution otherwise than as an in-patient shall be deemed not to satisfy or to be unlikely to satisfy the day attendance condition or the night attendance condition or both of them.

[3 (2) Regulations may provide that an attendance allowance shall not be payable in respect of a person for a period when he is a resident of a care home in circumstances in which any of the costs of any qualifying services provided for him are borne out of public or local funds under a specified enactment.

(3) The reference in subsection (2) to a care home is to an establishment that provides accommodation together with nursing or personal care.

(4) The following are qualifying services for the purposes of subsection (2)—

(a) accommodation,

(b) board, and

(c) personal care.

(5) The reference in subsection (2) to a specified enactment is to an enactment which is, or is of a description, specified for the purposes of that subsection by regulations.

(6) The power to specify an enactment for the purposes of subsection (2) includes power to specify it only in relation to its application for a particular purpose.

(7) In this section, "enactment" includes an enactment comprised in, or in an instrument made under, an Act of the Scottish Parliament.]

AMENDMENTS

1. Mental Health (Care and Treatment) (Scotland) Act 2003 (Consequential Provisions) Order (SI 2005/2078) Sch.1 para.4 (October 5, 2005).

2. National Health Service (Consequential Provisions) Act 2006 Sch.1 para.143 (March 1, 2007).

3. Welfare Reform Act 2007 s.60(1) (October 29, 2007).

DERIVATION

SSA 1975 ss.35(5A), (6). 1.184

GENERAL NOTE

Subsection (1)

See reg.5(3) and 5(4) of the Social Security (Attendance Allowance) Regulations 1991. 1.185

Subsection (2)

See regs 6–8 of the Social Security (Attendance Allowance) Regulations 1991. 1.186

Severe disablement allowance

[The entry into force on April 6, 2001 of s.65 of the Welfare Reform and Pensions Act means that ss.68 and 69 ceased to have effect on that date. However, certain existing entitlements continue under a transitional provision in art.4 of the Welfare Reform and Pensions Act 1999 (Commencement No. 9, and Transitional and Savings Provisions) Order 2000 (SI 2000/2958) in respect of any entitlement to SDA for a day of incapacity on or after April 6, 2001 forming part of a period of incapacity beginning before April 6, 2001. Art.4 of the Order provides: 1.187

"Saving for existing severe disablement allowance beneficiaries

4.—Notwithstanding the commencement of the provisions referred to in article 2(3)(d), (f) and (g) and (6)(b) ("severe disablement allowance provisions"), the provisions referred to in paragraphs 26 *[SSCBA 1992, s. 90]* and 27 of Schedule 8 and Part IV of Schedule 13 *[SSCBA 1992, ss. 68, 69]* shall continue to have effect, in the period of incapacity for work beginning before 6th April 2001 which would have continued, whether or not by virtue of section 30C or 68(10) or (10A) of the Contributions and Benefits Act or regulations made thereunder, on or after that date but for the commencement of the severe disablement allowance provisions, as if those provisions had not been commenced— 1.188

(a) in relation to a person, to whom paragraph (b) does not apply, who is entitled to severe disablement allowance under section 68 or 69 of the Contributions and Benefits Act on any day of incapacity for work in that period of incapacity for work; or

(b) until the beginning of 6th April 2002, in relation to a person who —

  (i) was under the age of 20 years on 6th April 2001, and

  (ii) is entitled to severe disablement allowance under section 68(1) of the Contributions and Benefits Act on any day of incapacity for work in that period of incapacity for work." (Provisions in italics added by commentator.)

Accordingly, ss.68 and 69 can be found in the 2005 edition of this volume for the purposes of those continued entitlements, which cover those over 20 on April 6, 2001 until SDA entitlement ceases under the preserved SDA rules. Those under 20 on April 6, 2001 who remain entitled to, or are receiving, SDA in that period of incapacity until on or immediately before April 5, 2002, will on April 6, 2002, if still incapable of work, be transferred to long-term incapacity benefit without having to satisfy the contribution conditions, and without that entitlement being subject to reduction for pension payments under s.30DD. So will those aged under 20 on April 6, 2001, then entitled to SDA, whose period of incapacity for work covers the period on or immediately after April 5, 2002. See SSCBA s.30A(1)(b), (2A), and IB Regs, Pt IV, reg.19.

Entitlement and rate

1.189 **68.**—*Section 68 omitted*

1.190 **69.**—*Section 69 omitted*

Invalid Care Allowance

1.191 **70.**—(1) A person shall be entitled to [2 a carer's allowance] for any day on which he is engaged in caring for a severely disabled person if—

(a) he is regularly and substantially engaged in caring for that person;

(b) he is not gainfully employed; and

(c) the severely disabled person is either such relative of his as may be prescribed or a person of any such other description as may be prescribed.

[2 (1A) A person who was entitled to an allowance under this section immediately before the death of the severely disabled person referred to in subsection (1) shall continue to be entitled to it, even though he is no longer engaged in caring for a severely disabled person (and the requirements of subsection (1)(a) and (c) are not satisfied), until—

(a) the end of the week in which he ceases to satisfy any other requirement as to entitlement to the allowance; or

(b) the expiry of the period of eight weeks beginning with the Sunday following the death (or beginning with the date of the death if the death occurred on a Sunday), whichever occurs first].

(2) In this section, "severely disabled person" means a person in respect of whom there is payable either an attendance allowance or a disability living allowance by virtue of entitlement to the care component at the highest or middle rate [5 or personal independence payment by virtue of entitlement to the daily living component at the standard or enhanced rate] [8 [9 adult disability payment by virtue of entitlement to the daily living component at the standard or enhanced rate or child disability payment by virtue of entitlement to the care component at the middle or highest rate]] [6 or armed forces independence payment under the Armed Forces and Reserve Forces (Compensation Scheme) Order 2011] or such other payment out of public funds on account of his need for attendance as may be prescribed.

(3) A person shall not be entitled to an allowance under this section if he is under the age of 16 or receiving full-time education.

(4) A person shall not be entitled to an allowance under this section unless he satisfies prescribed conditions as to residence or presence in Great Britain.

[4 (4A) A person to whom either Regulation (EC) No 1408/71 or Regulation (EC) No 883/2004 applies shall not be entitled to an allowance under this section for a period unless during that period the UK is competent for payment of sickness benefits in cash to the person for the purposes of Chapter 1 of Title III of the Regulation in question.]

(5) [2 . . .]

(6) [2 . . .]

[10 (7) No person shall be entitled for the same day to—

(a) more than one allowance under this section; or

(b) both an allowance under this section and carer support payment.

(7ZA) Where, apart from this subsection, two or more persons would have a relevant entitlement for the same day in respect of the same severely disabled person, one of them only shall have that entitlement and that shall be such one of them—

(a) as they may jointly elect in the prescribed manner; or

(b) as may, in default of such an election, be determined by the Secretary of State in the Secretary of State's discretion.

(7ZB) Subsection (7ZC) applies where a person (A)—

(a) (disregarding the effect of regulation 5(3) of the Carer's Assistance (Carer Support Payment) (Scotland) Regulations 2023) has, or would have, an entitlement to carer support payment; or

(b) has, or would have, an entitlement to carer's allowance in respect of which the Scottish Ministers have the power to make decisions, for a day in respect of a severely disabled person.

(7ZC) Another person (B) shall not have a relevant entitlement for the same day in respect of the same severely disabled person unless—

(a) A and B jointly elect in the prescribed manner that B shall have the relevant entitlement (and that A shall not have an entitlement mentioned in subsection (7ZB)) for that day in respect of that severely disabled person; or

(b) in default of such an election, the Secretary of State is satisfied, following consultation with the Scottish Ministers, that—

(i) the Scottish Ministers have decided, or will decide, that A shall not have an entitlement mentioned in subsection (7ZB); and

(ii) B shall have the relevant entitlement, for that day in respect of that severely disabled person.]

[7 (7A) For the purposes of [10 subsections (7ZA) and (7ZC)] a person has a "relevant entitlement" if—

(a) the person is entitled to a carer's allowance [10 in respect of which the Secretary of State has the power to make decisions], or

(b) the person is entitled under section 12 of the Welfare Reform Act 2012 to the inclusion in an award of universal credit of an amount in respect of the fact that the person has regular and substantial caring responsibilities for a severely disabled person.]

[10 (7B) In subsections (7) and (7ZB), "carer support payment" means carer's assistance given in accordance with the Carer's Assistance (Carer Support Payment) (Scotland) Regulations 2023.]

Note the version of subsections (7) to (7B) above applies to England and Wales only. The version below applies only to Scotland.

[11 (7) No person shall be entitled for the same day to—

(a) more than one allowance under this section; or

(b) both an allowance under this section and carer support payment.

(7ZA) Where, apart from this subsection, two or more persons would have an entitlement to carer's allowance for the same day in respect of the same severely disabled person, one of them only shall have that entitlement and that shall be such one of them—

(a) as they may jointly elect in the prescribed manner; or

(b) as may, in default of such an election, be determined by the Scottish Ministers.

(7ZB) Subsection (7ZC) applies where a person (A)—

(a) (disregarding the effect of regulation 5(3) of the Carer's Assistance (Carer Support Payment) (Scotland) Regulations 2023) has, or would have, an entitlement to carer support payment; or

(b) has, or would have, an entitlement to carer's allowance in respect of which the Secretary of State has the power to make decisions,

for a day in respect of a severely disabled person.

(7ZC) Another person (B) shall not have an entitlement to carer's allowance for the same day in respect of the same severely disabled person unless—

(a) A and B jointly elect in the prescribed manner that B shall have an entitlement to carer's allowance (and that A shall not have an entitlement mentioned in subsection (7ZB)) for that day in respect of that severely disabled person; or

(b) in default of such an election, the Scottish Ministers are satisfied—

(i) that either—

(aa) A shall not have an entitlement mentioned in subsection (7ZB)(a); or

(bb) the Secretary of State has decided, or will decide, that A shall not have an entitlement mentioned in subsection (7ZB)(b); and

(ii) that B shall have an entitlement to carer's allowance,

for that day in respect of that severely disabled person.

(7ZD) Subsection (7ZE) applies where (but for regulation 29 of the Universal Credit Regulations 2013 preventing entitlement by different persons to the carer element and to carer's allowance) a person (A) has, or would have, an entitlement to universal credit carer element for a day in respect of a severely disabled person.

(7ZE) Another person (B) shall not have an entitlement to carer's allowance for the same day in respect of the same severely disabled person unless—

(a) A and B jointly elect in the prescribed manner that B shall have an entitlement to carer's allowance (and that A shall not have an entitlement to universal credit carer element) for that day in respect of that severely disabled person; or

(b) in default of such an election, the Scottish Ministers are satisfied that—

(i) the Secretary of State has decided, or will decide, that A shall not have an entitlement to universal credit carer element; and

(ii) B shall have an entitlement to carer's allowance,

for that day in respect of that severely disabled person.

(7A) For the purposes of subsections (7ZD) and (7ZE), "universal credit carer element" means the inclusion in an award of universal credit of an amount in respect of the fact that the person has regular and substantial caring responsibilities for a severely disabled person under section 12 of the Welfare Reform Act 2012.

(7B) In subsections (7) and (7ZB), "carer support payment" means carer's assistance given in accordance with the Carer's Assistance (Carer Support Payment) (Scotland) Regulations 2023.]

(8) Regulations may prescribe the circumstances in which a person is or is not to be treated for the purposes of this section as engaged, or regularly and substantially engaged, in caring for a severely disabled person, as gainfully employed or as receiving full-time education.

(9) [[3] A carer's allowance] shall be payable at the weekly rate specified in Schedule 4, Part III, paragraph 4.

(10)[[1] . . .]

AMENDMENTS

1. Social Security (Severe Disablement Allowance and Invalid Care Allowance) Amendment Regulations 1994 (SI 1994/2556) reg.2(3) (October 28, 1994).
2. Regulatory Reform (Carer's Allowance) Order 2002 (SI 2002/1457) art.3 (April 1, 2003).
3. Regulatory Reform (Carer's Allowance) Order 2002 (SI 2002/1457) art.2 (October 28, 2002).
4. Social Security (Disability Living Allowance, Attendance Allowance and Carer's Allowance) (Miscellaneous Amendments) Regulations 2011 reg.5(3) (SI 2011/2426) (October 31, 2011).
5. Personal Independence Payment (Supplementary, Provisional and Consequential) Regulations 2013 Sch., para.5 (SI 2013/388) April 8, 2013.
6. Armed Forces and Reserve Forces (Compensation Scheme) (Consequential Provisions: Primary Legislation) Order 2013 art.2 (SI 2013/796) (April 8, 2013).
7. Universal Credit and Miscellaneous Amendment Regulations 2015 (SI 2015/1754) reg.11, (November 5, 2015).
8. Disability Assistance for Children and Young People (Scotland) Regulations 2021 (SSI 2021/174) reg.43 (July 26, 2021).
9. Social Security (Scotland) Act 2018 (Disability Assistance and Information-Sharing) (Consequential Provision and Modifications) Order 2022 (SI 2022/332) art.13 (March 21, 2022).
10. Carer's Assistance (Carer Support Payment) (Scotland) Regulations 2023 (Consequential Modifications) Order 2023 (SI 2023/1214) art.2 (November 19, 2023).
11. Carer's Assistance (Carer Support Payment) (Scotland) Regulations 2023 (Consequential Modifications) Order 2023 (SI 2023/1214) art.3 (November 19, 2023).

DERIVATION

SSA 1975 s.37. **1.192**

GENERAL NOTE

Until April 2003 Carer's Allowance (CA) was known as Invalid Care Allowance (ICA). The side-note to s.70 remains unchanged, but for all other purposes ICA has become CA and will be so referred to in this note. Note too, that the regulations that were made for ICA have also never been renamed and therefore references to the regulations that cover CA remain as references to the Invalid Care Allowance Regulations.

Carer's Allowance is a weekly benefit payable to those who spend at least 35 hours per week caring for another person who is in receipt of a relevant benefit. Those benefits that qualify for this purpose are: attendance allowance, the care component of disability allowance at the middle or the higher rate, personal independence payment by virtue of the daily living component at the standard or enhanced rate, constant attendance allowance under the industrial injuries or the war disablement schemes and armed forces independence payment under the Armed Forces and Reserve Forces scheme. To this list must now be added also adult disability payment by virtue of the daily living component at the standard or enhanced rate or child disability payment by virtue of entitlement to the care component at the middle or highest rate. These benefits are provided for in Scottish legislation but may still be payable if the claimant moves to England or Wales. A new Scottish benefit that is the equivalent of Carer's Allowance (CA) was introduced with effect from November 19, 2023. It is known as Carer Support Payment and is paid to those who care for a severely disabled person where the claimant is normally resident in Scotland and on similar terms to those that would qualify for Carer's Allowance in England and Wales. The new benefit will be rolled out geographically across Scotland. That process is expected to be complete by October 2024.

Various amendments to this section and to the Invalid Care Allowance Regulations have been necessary to accommodate claimants who might move between Scotland and another part of the United Kingdom and vice versa.

Note that there is nothing in s.70 that requires a claimant, when they make a claim, to have the consent of the disabled person for whom they are caring. This may be important because the fact that someone is in receipt of CA may affect the entitlement to other benefits of the person who is cared for. It is possibly for this reason that the CA claim form makes provision for a signature of that person. See *SSWP v GK (ESA)* [2023] UKUT 273 (AAC).

Where the person who is being cared for dies so that the claimant is no longer caring, subs.(1A) now provides that the carer's entitlement will continue for a period of 8 weeks following the death, but only so long as the claimant satisfies the remaining conditions of entitlement. When first enacted, s.37 of the Social Security Act 1975 excluded married or cohabiting women from entitlement. In Case 150/85 *Drake v Chief Adjudication Officer* [1987] Q.B. 166 that exclusion was held to be contrary to Council Directive 79/7 so the offending words were removed from subs. (3) retrospectively by the Social Security Act 1986.

Note that there is nothing in the rules defining entitlement to CA, or in those defining entitlement to the benefit of the person who is cared for, that prevents a claimant receiving both CA and also one of those benefits in respect of their own disablement. It is simply a question of the claimant's ability to perform the tasks of caring while being disabled themselves and that will turn upon the facts of each case (see *MC v SSWP* UKUT [2012] 337 (AAC)).

Subsection (1)(a)

1.193 Neither this section nor the Regulations define what is meant by "caring". Given the degree of disablement that has to be shown in the patient, it is likely that the statutory authorities have accepted any period in which the claimant is present for the purpose of company and supervision, as well as actual assistance, as qualifying.

Two unreported Commissioners' decisions throw some light on the meaning of caring. In the first, a starred decision, *CG/012/91*, the claimant received CA in respect of her brother who was tetraplegic. Notwithstanding his condition he went abroad on holiday with friends for four months. The claimant remained in the UK and continued to draw CA. When the absence became known to the DSS they sought to recover the CA paid beyond the usual four-week period of absence (see ICA Regulations). The claimant resisted recovery using two arguments: first, that in respect of the whole period she continued to care for her brother because she had to be ready on "stand-by" to fly immediately to his aid. His condition was such that he could very quickly suffer major problems in the hands of inexperienced nurses or assistants. Secondly, that in respect of at least the final month of absence she was engaged for long hours each week (in excess of 35) in trying to arrange sufficient nursing care for her brother upon his return. The Commissioner rejected both arguments. He points to the connection between CA of the claimant and AA (or DLA) of the patient. This connection, he says, supports the view that caring presupposes the more or less continuous presence of the person cared for. Some degree of absence might be acceptable, for example shopping for the patient, or the patient's absence for treatment, and dealing with the affairs of the patient might be seen as caring. But the claimant could not be caring, he said, when the patient was not "from day to day available to be cared for". Even the month spent in making arrangements therefore, did not count as caring.

This contrasts, though is not necessarily inconsistent with the other decision, *CG/006/1990*. This case arose through the question of whether the claimant could satisfy the 35 hours per week which is defined by regulation as "regularly and substantially caring". The claimant's son was normally resident in a special school for severely disabled patients. He returned to the claimant's home every other weekend, Friday evening to Monday morning—approximately 60 hours. The claimant said she spent at least five hours of the Friday preparing for his visit in shopping, cooking and other matters that related solely to his visit. She also spent at least another five hours cleaning up and washing on the Monday after his visit. When aggregated this gave at least 35 hours of caring in each week. The Commissioner accepted that all of this time qualifies as time spent in caring.

The difference between the cases is one of degree. A month spent in preparation and making arrangements cannot be seen as caring "on a day to day basis" as required in the starred decision, while preparation (and cleaning up) on the day of presence can.

The meaning of "regularly and substantially engaged" in caring is provided for in reg.4 of the ICA Regulations.

Subsection (1)(b)

What amounts to gainful employment is defined in reg.8 of the ICA Regulations. 1.194
This fixes a limit on earnings, but higher sums may be earned in weeks while the claimant is on holiday.

Several unreported Commissioners' decisions have highlighted the problem of claimants who have been paid a "salary" usually from a firm owned by their husband or in which they are partners, with little or nothing having been required from them by way of work. In such circumstances they have claimed CA not realising that the sum received may disqualify them on the grounds that they are "gainfully employed" and claims to recover substantial overpayments have resulted.

In such a case it is important to ascertain that the claimant is in fact employed by that employer, or working as a self-employed person. As decision *CG/068/1993* makes clear it is not enough that the claimant's name appears on the company's books as receiving a salary, if, as was claimed in this case, she does not realise that she is being paid as an employee. The claimant, whose husband was a solicitor, was, at first, paid a personal cheque each month for housekeeping. Later, when he became a partner in the firm, she was paid by a cheque drawn on the firm's account and appeared in the books as an employee, but she claimed to know nothing of her new status. The Commissioner held that she could not become an employee without her knowledge and consent, and directed that the appeal be re-heard to make further findings of fact. Earlier cases such as *R(P) 4/67* have referred to the undesirability of allowing claimants to "blow hot and cold" in their dealings with different departments of state (namely the HM Revenue and Customs). But that does not answer the question as to which of the inconsistent statements is inaccurate. In any case, the claimant here could not be treated as adopting the role of employee unless she herself had assented to it in a tax return, rather than a return made by her husband or his firm.

The difficulties presented by the definition of "gainful employment" (reg.8) are 1.195
highlighted by a further unreported Commissioner's decision. In *CG/058/92*, the claimant who looked after her disabled daughter had, with her husband, purchased a seaside hotel. Annual accounts submitted to the Inland Revenue disclosed the business to be run as a partnership and in four out of the five relevant years, the claimant's share of profits had clearly exceeded the limit prescribed by reg.8. The tribunal which had heard her appeal accepted that the claimant did not work to any appreciable extent in the business and that she did not draw any share of the profits at all. Nevertheless because of the width of the definition in reg.8 the claimant was disqualified from receiving CA and an overpayment was recoverable from her.

Regulation 8 refers to "earnings" which in turn is defined in s.3. The essence of earnings is that it is reward from employment or self-employment but not income from investment (see General Note to s.3). In this case, the Commissioner holds that the tribunal was correct to find that the claimant was a partner in the hotel business, that she was entitled to a half share of the profits, and that she was, therefore, not entitled to CA. But what of the true "sleeping partner". Someone whose only interest is to put capital into a business and to draw on income in the form of a share of profit, if there is any, should be regarded as receiving an investment income. It would be unfortunate if entitlement to CA, (and liability to repay an overpayment) were to turn upon the precise legal forms used by an investor as to whether he is partner or a creditor or a shareholder.

It should also be noted that Statutory Sick Pay or Statutory Maternity Pay qualify as "earnings" (see Contributions and Benefits Act, s.4) and therefore, under reg. 8 of the ICA Regulations, mean that a person is in gainful employment for the purposes of the section.

Subsection (1)(c)

1.196 This creates no limit on the persons who may claim because reg.6 of the ICA Regulations prescribes for this purpose, all persons who are in fact caring for a severely disabled person.

Subsection (1A)

1.197 A person entitled to a CA will continue to receive the benefit for a period of eight weeks if they cease caring because their patient has died. If they cease to care because they are no longer providing care for 35 hours per week then (unless that is because the patient has entered hospital) the entitlement will end forthwith.

Subsection (2)

1.198 The person cared for is classed as "severely disabled" under this subsection if they are in receipt of one of the qualifying benefits. These are:

(i) Attendance Allowance;
(ii) Disability Living Allowance at either the middle or the highest rate;
(iii) Personal Independence Payment of the care component at either the standard or the enhanced rate;
(iv) Armed Forces Independence Payment; or
(v) Constant Attendance Allowance under either the industrial injuries or war pensions disablement schemes (see reg.3 of the CA regulations).

In the past problems have arisen in relation to overpayments that occurred when people in receipt over DLA had their entitlement reduced to the lowest level. For discussion of these cases see an earlier edition of this work.

Subsection (3)

1.199 A claimant must be at least 16 years of age and not receiving full-time education. For the meaning of full-time education in this context see reg.5 of the ICA Regulations and the notes to that regulation.

The meaning to be given to the words "under the age of 16" in this subsection, has been examined by Judge Scolding KC in *SSWP v BC (CA)* [2023] UKUT 10 (AAC). When s.70 was enacted the age of 16 was the school leaving age, but following the enactment of the Education Act 1996 the school leaving age was redefined to mean, effectively, the end of the academic year following the child's 16th birthday. The claimant in this case was not attending a school; she was said to be being home schooled by her parents but was not in fact receiving any education that could be recognised as amounting to "efficient full-time education" as required by the Education Act. (Her parents had been served with a notice preliminary to taking proceedings against them, but that was not acted upon.) The claimant was already caring for her brother for more than the requisite time when she turned 16 in January and made a claim for benefit. The claim was refused, but her appeal was allowed by the FTT. In allowing this further appeal to the UT Judge Scolding has adopted what might be described as a constructive approach to statutory interpretation by combining the policy objective of the 1992 Act, which was to limit entitlement to those over compulsory school leaving age, with the policy objective of the 1996 Act which was to move the compulsory school leaving age to the end of the academic year so as to enable all school leavers to have been able to complete their course and gain qualifications. The Judge therefore determines that being "over 16" in this context, requires that the claimant be "over compulsory school age" or, to put it in the words of the statute, being under the age of 16 means under compulsory school age.

An extension to cover this period has been provided for in relation to Child Benefit and for the means-tested benefits but seems to have been overlooked in relation to Carer's Allowance; Judge Scolding has provided for that omission. In doing so she recognises that this will serve justice because otherwise a claimant whose parents were failing in their duty to provide education would be rewarded by gaining benefit, whereas a claimant whose parents fulfilled that duty, would not.

Subsection (4)

Benefit is payable only if the claimant is present and ordinarily resident in Great Britain but regulations provide for some absences (reg.9 of the ICA Regulations). **1.200**

Since May 5, 2005 it has been possible for a claimant who has moved to another European Union country to continue claiming Carer's Allowance. This is because the decision of the European Court in Case C-299/05, *Commission v European Parliament and Council* [2007] E.C.R. I-8695 held that this benefit, together with Attendance Allowance and the care component of Disability Living Allowance, were not properly excludable from payment and could be claimed as a form of sickness benefits.

For questions that involve persons either coming from or going to another country that is a part of the European Union reference should be made to the relevant sections of Vol.III of this Work.

Subsection (4A)

The effect of this provision has been considered by Judge Jacobs in a series of cases, two of which apply to CA (*JG v SSWP (CA)* [2019] UKUT 83 (AAC) and at *GK v SSWP (CA)* [2019] UKUT 87 (AAC)). The claimant in both cases had become habitually resident in France and while there commenced caring for another who was in receipt of a qualifying benefit (AA) that they had exported when they had moved to France. Judge Jacobs holds that although CA and the qualifying benefit are closely related, they are separate benefits and that entitlement must depend upon determining which is the competent state in respect of the claim to CA. In both cases he holds that must be France. For a more detailed account of these issues, please refers to Vol III of this work. **1.201**

Paragraph (7) of subs.(4A) was held to be valid in *IG v SSWP* [2016] UKUT 176 (AAC); [2016] AACR 41. Judge Jacobs held that attendance allowance was a sickness benefit and that the UK was entitled under Regulation (EC) 883/2004 to make this regulation which had the effect of denying benefit where a foreign state was the competent state in respect of a sickness benefit. Carer's allowance is also a classed as a sickness benefit.

Subsections (5) and (6)

These subsections were repealed with effect from October 28, 2002 so that a claim may now be made by a person over 65. The effect of this change will be strictly limited because CA is covered by the Overlapping Benefits Regulations so that it will overlap with Retirement Pensions. It seems likely that most claimants will be entitled to one or other category of RP and if that is paid at a higher rate than CA then only the higher benefit will be paid. **1.202**

Under the previous regulations a person could not claim over the age of 65, but if they were already in receipt of benefit when they reached that age their entitlement continued for life even if they ceased to care for their patient—e.g. if their patient died. This will no longer be the case. A claimant whose patient dies loses entitlement after six weeks. See subs.(1A) above. There is, however, a saving for claimants who were over 65 on October 28, 2002 under art.4 of Regulatory Reform (Carer's Allowance) Order 2002 (2002/1457).

Prior to October 1994, CA was not payable to a claimant over pensionable age. This meant a cut-off age for women of 60 years and for men of 65 years. That discrimination was held to be unlawful under the Equal Treatment Directive (79/7) in *Secretary of State v Thomas* [1993] Q.B. 747 and *R(G) 2/94*. The UK law should have been amended to provide equality from 1984, when the Equal Treatment Directive should have been implemented. The United Kingdom law was so amended, but not until October 1994. In the meantime many women had been refused benefit, or discouraged from making a claim for benefit, because of the continued insistence on differential ages. Art.4(1) of Directive 79/7 (which imposes the requirement of equal treatment) has been held to be sufficiently clear and precise for those rights to be directly enforceable within the Member States by those persons entitled to rely upon them. A Commissioner's decision, *CG/5425/95*, has helped to clarify a number of points that may arise in such claims.

The claimant had cared for her invalid mother for a number of years but attendance allowance and hence entitlement to CA became payable in respect of her mother only from a time about six months after the claimant's 60th birthday. She became aware that she may have had a valid claim under European law only in 1989 (when she did make a claim), by which time she was already over 65 years. At about that time, too, her mother died, but under subs.(6) the claimant would have remained entitled to CA for the rest of her life.

Clearly, under UK law the claimant became entitled by virtue of reg.10A of the ICA Regulations, but only from October 1994. Could she use her rights under European law to claim from some other earlier point in time?

In the case of this particular claimant, the Commissioner decided that she could not. But that was because she did not form a part of the "working population" to whom the rights under art.4 are confined. The claimant had last worked in 1949 when she left work to commence a family. She had never re-entered the workforce or sought paid employment and she could not therefore claim under European law. However, the Commissioner did go on to consider what the position would have been had she been so qualified. The Department argued that because she did not claim until after she was 65, she could not now be entitled (as neither would a man) even under European law. The Commissioner held that her failure to claim before reaching 65 years of age was because the legislation, the department's publications and its officers all then said that she could not do so. To accept its argument would be to perpetuate their own failure to implement the Directive. In his view the claimant would have been entitled to benefit from when it was claimed (1989) and back-dated for 12 months from that date (*i.e.* 1988). Further back-dating would be prevented by the SS(A) Act s.1. Such limitation is not a breach of Directive 79/7: *Johnson v CAO (No.2) (R(S) 1/95)*. Before leaving the case the Commissioner made one further observation. Since the claimant had plainly been deprived of benefit since at least 1988 by the United Kingdom Government's failure to implement equal treatment, he suggested that the minister might consider an *ex gratia* payment of an equivalent amount rather than put the claimant and her legal advisers to the trouble and expense of pursuing a claim under the principle of *Francovich v Republic of Italy* [1991] E.C.R. 5357—though whether the *Francovich* claim should start at 1988 rather than 1984 is another matter.

A different approach on the question of late claims made by women past retirement age has been taken in decision *CSG/6/95*. The Commissioner there rejects the robust approach adopted, *obiter*, in *CG/5425/95*, but reaches a similar conclusion, at least on the facts of the new case, by another route. The claimant had given up work in 1979 in order to care for her husband. She reached the retirement age for women (60) in December 1982, but under Directive 79/7 (which came into force in December 1984) would have remained entitled to claim until December 1987. In the meantime (September 1985) the UK law had been changed to require a claim to be made for entitlement to benefit to begin. The claimant eventually made her claim in November 1993 well past her 65th birthday. The Commissioner rejected the argument that had found favour in *CG/5425/95*, namely that the requirement to claim before that age could be ignored because of the continued non-compliance of UK domestic law. Instead, he held that the claimant had, in 1984, become "entitled" to benefit in accordance with *I.O. v McCaffrey* [1985] 1 All E.R. 5 and that entitlement had not been removed by the introduction of the need for a claim to be made in 1985. It followed that the claimant could satisfy the conditions for entitlement in accordance with reg.10 of the CA Regulation prior to her 65th birthday and was accordingly entitled to payment of that benefit from the time that she did claim (1993) though back-dating was limited to one year.

Subsection (7)

This makes it clear that a claimant can receive only one payment of CA no matter **1.203**
how many patients he may be caring for, and that each patient can provide the basis for payment to only one carer at a time. Furthermore, reg.4 of the ICA Regulations has been amended to ensure that a claimant must qualify for the benefit by looking after a single patient for the requisite number of hours each week and cannot aggregate the hours spent looking after two or more patients. It should be noted as well that CA overlaps with several other benefits. (See reg.4 of the Overlapping Benefits Regulations.)

In *R(S)2/89* a widow who gave up work to care for her invalid daughter was refused CA (then ICA) because she was already in receipt of a widow's pension. She argued that this was discriminatory, contrary to Art.4 of European Community Directive 79/7, in that a man would not be refused CA. The Commissioner rejected that argument on the ground that the difference in treatment did not arise from discrimination in relation to that benefit, but because a man could not qualify for widow's pension at all; the regulations were therefore not discriminatory in terms of the European Community Directive.

Disability living allowance

Disability living allowance

71.—(1) Disability living allowance shall consist of a care component and **1.204**
a mobility component.

(2) A person's entitlement to a disability living allowance may be an entitlement to either component or to both of them.

(3) A person may be awarded either component for a fixed period or [1 for an indefinite period], but if his award of a disability living allowance consists of both components, he may not be awarded the components for different fixed periods.

(4) The weekly rate of a person's disability living allowance for a week for which he has only been awarded one component is the appropriate weekly rate for that component as determined in accordance with this Act or regulations under it.

(5) The weekly rate of a person's disability living allowance for a week for which he has been awarded both components is the aggregate of the appropriate weekly rates for the two components as so determined.

(6) A person shall not be entitled to a disability living allowance unless he satisfies prescribed conditions as to residence and presence in Great Britain.

[2(7) A person shall not be entitled to a disability living allowance while they are entitled to [3 adult disability payment or child disability payment].

AMENDMENTS

1. Welfare Reform and Pensions Act 1999 s.67(1) (January 12, 2000).

2. Scotland Act 2016 (Social Security) (Consequential Provision) (Miscellaneous Amendment) Regulations 2021 (SI 2021/804) reg.2 (July 26, 2021).

3. Scotland Act 2016 (Social Security) (Adult Disability Payment and Child Disability Payment) (Amendment) Regulations 2022 (SI 2022/335) reg.2 (March 21, 2022).

DERIVATION

1.205 SSA 1975 s.37ZA.

GENERAL NOTE

1.206 Disability Living Allowance (DLA) is a non-contributory benefit paid to those who are so disabled as to need assistance in leading a normal life or so disabled as to be unable to walk properly. From April 8, 2013 it has been replaced for persons of working age by Personal Independence Payment (PIP). This means that DLA is now a benefit that is available only to children up to the age of 16 and to those who were in receipt of that benefit and were aged 65 or over on April 8, 2013 (i.e., were born before April 8, 1948). Appeals may come before FTT involving these mainly retired claimants in respect of claims for renewal or revision, but on new claims appeals will be in respect of those brought on behalf of children. Claimants over the age of 16 may remain in receipt of DLA until they are transferred to PIP by the DWP. Any change in their DLA entitlement is likely to be treated by DWP as an occasion for transfer to PIP.

This means that some of the commentary that has appeared in the past following these sections in this book will no longer be appropriate to those appeals and the commentary has been modified accordingly. Users of this work who require access to that text are referred to previous editions of this work.

DLA consists of two components. The care component (s.72) is similar to attendance allowance but includes a third lower rate of payment for those requiring a lesser degree of care. The mobility component (s.73) is paid at two rates. For both components there is a qualifying period of three months, rather than the six months for attendance allowance, and the disability must be one which is likely to continue for at least six months.

Subsections (2)–(5)

1.207 Although a person may be awarded either just one component or both, the components are not entirely separate benefits. In *R(DLA) 2/97*, it was held:

> "Where a claim under appeal relates only to one component and there is no award of the other component and no evidence of substance relating to that other component, a tribunal may safely accept, record and proceed upon a restriction of the appeal to the component claimed."

Although DLA consists of two components it is paid as only a single allowance. It is not uncommon, however, for decisions on the two components to be taken separately. It should be noted that where the separate components are each awarded for a fixed period, that must be for the same period. In other words, the issue of "limping" awards can arise only where one component has been awarded for an indefinite period and the other for a fixed period.

There is now (under the Social Security Act 1998) no special protection for awards for life. (For discussion of the problems that did arise under the older system of review & revision of awards in the SSAA 1992, see earlier editions of this work.) In *CDLA/1000/2001*, the Commissioner held that an appeal under s.12 of the SSA 1998 raised anything that was covered by the substance of the information provided by the appellant and was not confined to the specific point against which he had appealed. This means that where the claimant appeals against an award of benefit at, say, the lower or middle rate on the ground that it is too low, it is open to a tribunal to find, on the contrary, that it is too high, and reduce the award accordingly. But where a tribunal is minded to do this it may do so only deliberately and consciously and, furthermore, it can do so only after giving a clear warning to the claimant that such may be the outcome of the appeal so that the claimant has a chance then to abandon the appeal. See *CDLA/2084/2007*.

Where the claimant is appealing against a refusal or a reduction of benefit on a renewal award the tribunal should be provided with a copy of the paperwork in respect of the previous claim—see r.24 of the Tribunal Procedure (First-tier Tribunal) (Social Entitlement Chamber) Rules 2008. Where that has not been done the FTT should consider whether to adjourn and call for the documentation to be provided. They will not be compelled always to do so, but should be cautious about proceeding without doing so: see *AH v Secretary of State for Work and Pensions* [2016] UKUT 558 (AAC).

If a person is awarded both components, there is one award of DLA at a rate calculated by aggregating the appropriate rates of the components and the award, if for a fixed period, must be for one common period and not different periods for the different components. It follows that, if one component has been awarded and the claimant appeals against refusal of the other, the tribunal must be informed of the period of the award (*CDLA/52/94*).

In determining whether a claimant qualifies for these benefits, a tribunal, must reach its conclusion in accordance with the restrictions imposed upon it by s.20(3) of the SSA 1998. This section prevents the tribunal from making a physical examination of the claimant and it precludes a physical test for the purposes of the mobility component of DLA. It does not, however, prevent the tribunal from reaching a conclusion based upon their observation of the claimant's physical abilities, or based upon his response to questions that test what he is capable of doing and, except in relation to mobility, it does not prevent the tribunal asking the claimant to carry out a simple physical task e.g. to pick an object up from the floor. The claimant may refuse, but in that case the tribunal may draw an inference from his refusal provided that in doing so they make due allowance for any reason he may give for that refusal. (See *R(DLA)5/03* and commentary to s.20 in *Vol.III: Administration, Adjudication and the European Dimension*.

In case *CDLA/433/99* the Commissioner holds that a tribunal which has, contrary to s.55(2)(a) of AA 1992, conducted an examination of the claimant does not make an error of law that requires the decision to be set aside unless the evidence obtained by that examination has influenced the tribunal's decision. In this case he held that it did not. The claimant had appealed against the disallowance of DLA care component in respect of ecezma on her hands. The note of evidence recorded that the medical member had "examined" her hands, but the decisions, and the reasons for decision, made clear that the tribunal had not regarded the condition as viewed on the day, as being indicative of her condition generally, which was said to vary from time to time. The Commissioner also suggested that a distinction could be drawn between an "examination" and a general observation as, for example, when the claimant might show her hands to the tribunal.

Decision makers and tribunals are frequently faced with a conflict of opinion as to the extent of a claimant's disablement. This is often between information provided by the claimant, and sometimes their own medical adviser, and the EMP who has been appointed by the department to examine the claimant.. Where there is such a conflict in the evidence brought before a FTT there is a duty to consider all of the evidence without giving any particular preference given to the evidence of the

EMP for the reason, for example, that it is "independent" or "unbiased"—see *MW v SSWP* [2013] UKUT 158 (AAC).

In *NK v SSWP (PIP)* [2020] UKUT 14 (AAC) Judge Church has made clear that the FTT must make findings of fact before it can dismiss an appeal. The claimant had appealed by his appointee against a refusal of benefit. The appeal was scheduled to be heard before the FTT on several occasions, on each of which the appointee had failed to appear or to provide any evidence other than her own statement of the difficulties experienced by the claimant. The DM had called for her to provide a note from her son's GP, but none was forthcoming. The FTT had dismissed the appeal giving as their reasons that the mother's evidence was not corroborated and that without that, they could make no finding of fact regarding the claimant's disability. Judge Church finds that it was an error of law to require corroboration of the mother's statement and it was also an error of law to dismiss the appeal without making some finding of fact as to the claimant's condition. The case was remitted to a fresh tribunal.

Subsection (6)

1.208 See reg.2 of the DLA Regulations.

While the UK remained a member of the EU an award of the care component of DLA was exportable to another member state -see *SSWP v Tolley* [2017] AACR 40 (CJEU only). Since the UK ceased to be a member of the EU and the transition period ended (December 31, 2020) claimants may still be entitled if they live in an EEA state or in Switzerland -see reg.2B of the DLA Regulations.

The mobility component was not exportable -see *Bartlett, Ramos and Taylor v SSWP* [2012] UKUT 26 (AAC).

Three cases concern the export of DLA to other EU member countries. All are decisions by Judge Jacobs. In the first, *SSWP v MC (DLA)* [2019] UKUT 84 (AAC), the claimant while in receipt of the benefit had moved to Germany where he took up employment. In those circumstances the judge held that Germany had become the competent state for the payment of sickness benefits and hence the claimant had not been entitled to the payment of DLA while he worked there. In the second, *KR v SSWP (DLA)* [2019] UKUT 85 (AAC); [2019] AACR 22, the claimant had moved to Finland and became habitually resident there but not employed. In this case it was held that she retained her right to export the benefit as the UK remained the competent state for sickness benefits.

In a third case, *SSWP v TG (DLA)* [2019] UKUT 86 (AAC), where the claimant had become habitually resident (though not employed) in Cyprus before making his claim for DLA, the judge held that Cyprus had become the competent state in respect of sickness benefits and therefore the claimant was not entitled.

For more detail of these and other cases involving a European dimension, please see the relevant material in Vol III of this work.

The care component

1.209 **72.**—(1) Subject to the provisions of this Act, a person shall be entitled to the care component of a disability living allowance for any period throughout which—

(a) he is so severely disabled physically or mentally that—

(i) he requires in connection with his bodily functions attention from another person for a significant portion of the day (whether during a single period or a number of periods); or

(ii) he cannot prepare a cooked main meal for himself if he has the ingredients; or

(b) he is so severely disabled physically or mentally that, by day, he requires from another person—

(i) frequent attention throughout the day in connection with his bodily functions; or

(ii) continual supervision throughout the day in order to avoid substantial danger to himself or others; or

(c) he is so severely disabled physically or mentally that, at night,—

(i) he requires from another person prolonged or repeated attention in connection with his bodily functions; or

(ii) in order to avoid substantial danger to himself or others he requires another person to be awake for a prolonged period or at frequent intervals for the purpose of watching over him.

[[4] (1A) In its application to a person in relation to so much of a period as falls before the day on which he reaches the age of 16, subsection (1) has effect subject to the following modifications—

(a) the condition mentioned in subsection (1)(a)(ii) shall not apply, and

(b) none of the other conditions mentioned in subsection (1) shall be taken to be satisfied unless—

(i) he has requirements of a description mentioned in the condition substantially in excess of the normal requirements of persons of his age, or

(ii) he has substantial requirements of such a description which younger persons in normal physical and mental health may also have but which persons of his age and in normal physical and mental health would not have.]

(2) Subject to the following provisions of this section, a person shall not be entitled to the care component of a disability living allowance unless—

(a) throughout—

(i) the period of three months immediately preceding the date on which the award of that component would begin; or

(ii) such other period of three months as may be prescribed,

he has satisfied or is likely to satisfy one or other of the conditions mentioned in subsection (1)(a) to (c) above; and

(b) he is likely to continue to satisfy one or other of those conditions throughout—

(i) the period of six months beginning with that date; or

(ii) (if his death is expected within the period of six months beginning with that date) the period so beginning and ending with his death.

[[4] (2A) The modifications mentioned in subsection (1A) shall have effect in relation to the application of subsection (1) for the purposes of subsection (2), but only—

(a) in the case of a person who is under the age of 16 on the date on which the award of the care component would begin, and

(b) in relation to so much of any period mentioned in subsection (2) as falls before the day on which he reaches the age of 16.]

(3) Three weekly rates of the care component shall be prescribed.

(4) The weekly rate of the care component payable to a person for each week in the period for which he is awarded that component shall be—

(a) the highest rate, if he falls within subsection (2) above by virtue of having satisfied or being likely to satisfy both the conditions mentioned in subsection (1)(b) and (c) above throughout both the period mentioned in paragraph (a) of subsection (2) above and that mentioned in paragraph (b) of that subsection;

(b) the middle rate, if he falls within that subsection by virtue of having satisfied or being likely to satisfy one or other of those conditions throughout both those periods; and

(c) the lowest rate in any other case.

(5) For the purposes of this section, a person who is terminally ill, as defined in section 66(2) above, and makes a claim expressly on the ground that he is such a person, shall [[4] (notwithstanding subsection (1A)(b))] be taken—

(a) to have satisfied the conditions mentioned in subsection (1)(b) and (c) above for the period of three months immediately preceding the date of the claim, or, if later, the first date on which he is terminally ill (so however that the care component shall not be payable by virtue of this paragraph for any period preceding that date); and

(b) to satisfy or to be likely to satisfy those conditions [[1] for so much of the period for which he is terminally ill as does not fall before the date of the claim.]

(6) [[5] *repealed*]

(7) Subject to [[4] subsection (5)] above, circumstances may be prescribed in which a person is to be taken to satisfy or not to satisfy such of the conditions mentioned in subsection (1)(a) to (c) above as may be prescribed.

[[4] (7A) Subsection (1A) has effect subject to regulations made under subsection (7) (except as otherwise prescribed).]

[[7] (7B) A person to whom either Regulation (EC) No 1408/71 or Regulation (EC) No 883/2004 applies shall not be entitled to the care component of a disability living allowance for a period unless during that period the United Kingdom is competent for payment of sickness benefits in cash to the person for the purposes of Chapter 1 of Title III of the Regulation in question.]

[[6] (8) Regulations may provide that no amount in respect of a disability living allowance which is attributable to entitlement to the care component shall be payable in respect of a person for a period when he is a resident of a care home in circumstances in which any of the costs of any qualifying services provided for him are borne out of public or local funds under a specified enactment.

(9) The reference in subsection (8) to a care home is to an establishment that provides accommodation together with nursing or personal care.

(10) The following are qualifying services for the purposes of subsection (8)—

(a) accommodation,

(b) board, and

(c) personal care.

(11) The reference in subsection (8) to a specified enactment is to an enactment which is, or is of a description, specified for the purposes of that subsection by regulations.

(12) The power to specify an enactment for the purposes of subsection (8) includes power to specify it only in relation to its application for a particular purpose.

(13) In this section, "enactment" includes an enactment comprised in, or in an instrument made under, an Act of the Scottish Parliament.]

AMENDMENTS

1. Welfare Reform and Pension Act 1999 s.67(2) (January 12, 2000).
2. Mental Health (Care and Treatment) (Scotland) Act 2003 (Consequential Provisions) Order 2005 (SI 2005/2078) Sch.1 para.4 (October 5, 2005).
3. National Health Service (Consequential Provisions) Act 2006 Sch.1 para.144 (March 1, 2007).
4. Welfare Reform Act 2007 s.52 (October 1, 2007).
5. Welfare Reform Act 2007 Sch.8 (October 1, 2007).
6. Welfare Reform Act 2007 s.60(2) (October 29, 2007).
7. Social Security (Disability Living Allowance, Attendance Allowance and Carer's Allowance)(Miscellaneous Amendments) Regulations 2011 reg.5(5). (SI 2011/2426) (October 31, 2011).

DERIVATION

SSA 1975 s.37ZB. 1.210

GENERAL NOTE

This section defines the conditions for the care component of DLA. Subsection (1) provides for three levels of benefit according to different requirements for care. 1.211

Para.(a) specifies two conditions, one of attention that is needed and the other of an inability to cook a meal, but the latter ("the cooking test") is not available on a claim made for a child.

Para.(b) specifies one condition of attention and one alternative condition for supervision, both during the day.

Para.(c) has one condition for attention and an alternative one for supervision, both by night.

Neither "attention" nor "supervision" is defined in the statute, and there may be some overlap between care that is given as attention and that which is supervision. In general, attention might involve some active intervention, while supervision might be entirely passive.

Benefit is paid at the lowest rate if the patient satisfies only para.(a); at the middle rate if they satisfy either para (b) or (c); and at the highest rate if they satisfy both (b) and (c). There is no increase if the claimant satisfies (a) and another paragraph.

Note that reg.7 of the DLA Regulations deems certain people undergoing renal dialysis to satisfy either the day or the night attention condition and so qualify for the middle rate of the care component.

Note also that, under subs.(5), terminally ill claimants may be deemed to satisfy both the day and night conditions and so qualify for the highest rate of the care component for the rest of their lives.

Certain phrases in this section will apply to all claims:

For any period throughout which: These words require some consistency in the claimant's need for attendance over the whole period of an award but they do not require that the conditions should be satisfied on every day. The former Attendance Allowance Board's *Handbook for Delegated Medical Practitioners* suggested that a man satisfies the night attention condition if he "invariably requires prolonged or repeated attention on more nights of the week than he does not". Although DLA is a weekly benefit, there does not seem to be any particular reason for requiring that it should *invariably* be the case that a person should satisfy the statutory criteria in the majority of the days of a week. In *R(A) 2/74*, the Commissioner said: 1.212

> "I think that the delegate should take a broad view of the matter, asking himself some such question as whether in the whole circumstances the words of the statute do or do not as a matter of the ordinary usage of the English language cover or apply to the facts. These are matters for the good sense and judgment of the delegate."

Thus, it may be appropriate in some cases to make an award covering a substantial period notwithstanding that there may be expected to be periods of remission in the claimant's condition lasting longer than a week. Both the length of the periods of remission and their frequency are likely to be relevant considerations as, perhaps, is the severity of the disablement during other periods. If the disability is one from which a substantial period of remission is quite likely, an award for a short period may be appropriate. If at the end of that period the claimant no longer satisfies the conditions for an award, or an award at the same rate, but the period of remission lasts less than two years, reg.6 of the DLA Regulations enables the claimant to qualify again without having to wait the usual three months (or six months if the claimant is over 65).

1.213 *So severely disabled mentally or physically:* There has been a difference of opinion between Commissioners on the significance of these words. On the one hand the view has sometimes been taken that they act as a prerequisite by which a claimant must show a disability in a medical sense that is recognised and labelled as such by a doctor; on the other hand the words are regarded simply as a complement to the need for care so that if it is shown that the claimant requires care and that it is something to do with their mental or physical condition they succeed.

This issue has been resolved by a decision of a Tribunal of Commissioners in *R(DLA)3/06*. They held that the words do not require the finding of a specific disease or medical condition that is identifiable as the cause of the claimant's disability. All that is necessary is to identify some functional lack of ability that can be traced to a physical or mental cause in the claimant. This means that a medical condition will often be a relevant piece of evidence to support the claim (see e.g. *CDLA/4475/2004*), but it is not an essential prerequisite. For example, where the claimant is a child, as in the present case, behavioural difficulties may cause a need for care, so as to satisfy the conditions necessary for the care component, and for the mobility component too if the child may not be trusted to walk out alone. In that case the child may need the care etc. to compensate for a functional inability, without having to prescribe a medical condition. But this conclusion still requires two matters to be satisfied: first, does the inability have some physical or mental cause? This would be satisfied where the child suffers from arrested development or from a very low I.Q., or where they do suffer from some diagnosable medical condition, but not where their conduct is simply wilful or irresponsible misbehaviour, and cases, like those in the past where that may have been the cause of the claimant's inability, would still fail. (See, for example *R(A)2/92*, where the Commissioners suggest that the correct approach would have been to ask whether the claimant could desist from his aggressive and irresponsible behaviour.)

Apart from the element of volition, however, the Commissioners otherwise found it difficult to envisage a situation in which a disability that expressed a need for care etc. was not the result of some physical or mental cause. Those words, they thought, were intended to be inclusive rather than exclusive so as to include any psychological as well as physical cause. But they do confirm the decision in *CA/137/1984*. That was the case in which the claimant, a Muslim child who had a disabled right hand, had claimed on the basis that he needed assistance in eating. In his religion all food must be handled only with the right hand because the left is used for washing after defecating. The claim failed because the Commissioner took the view that his need arose from his culture rather than his disability. The Tribunal here confirm that decision, though they do not explain how it is to be reconciled with the decision in *Fairey* (see below) where the emphasis is on allowing the claimant to lead a normal life which should presumably mean normal in his own culture.

The second requirement of this phrase is that the disability must be "severe". Here the tribunal of Commissioners confirms that the test of severity does not condition the degree of disability other than by reference to the scale of requirements that the section provides for. The words of the section, they point out, are "so severely disabled . . . that." In other words the test of severity is satisfied by the claimant proving the requisite level of need according to the particular claim he has made, (adopting the approach used in *R(DLA) 10/02*). The commissioners therefore conclude:

> "in our view, section 72 raises two issues. (i) Does the claimant have a disability, i.e. does he have a functional deficiency, physical or mental? (ii) If so, do the care needs to which the functional deficiency give rise satisfy any of paragraphs (i) or (ii) of section 72 (1)(a) to (c),and if so which? Section 73 (1)(d) gives rise to similar questions in relation to mobility".

Although this question appeared to have been resolved in *R (DLA) 3/06,* the matter has been opened again, at least in relation to a very young child, by Judge May. The case concerned a three-year-old child who was described as exhibiting behavioural difficulties, but in respect of whom there was no medical diagnosis of any mental condition or abnormality. The judge makes clear his disagreement with the decision in *R (DLA) 3/06,* but accepts that he must follow it. In doing so, however, he distinguishes the case of a very young child, as here— (the child in *R(DLA)3/06* was aged 12). In the case of a very young child he says there must still be a medical diagnosis because behaviour (for which read misbehaviour) alone, cannot be a disability.

That much was accepted by the Tribunal of commissioners in *R(DLA)3/06,* but they go on to say that behaviour may be evidence of a mental deficiency of some sort such that the claimant was incapable of controlling his behaviour, and that could be a disability. The trouble with this, says Judge May in *AC v SSWP* [2009] UKUT 83 (AAC), is that young children generally are incapable of controlling their behaviour by the standards of adult society and that is what they all learn to do, as a process of maturing by growing up. He upheld the decision of the First-tier Tribunal to refuse benefit.

It is not clear that it was necessary for him to go so far as to distinguish *R(DLA) 3/06* in order to do so; the absence of any medical diagnosis could certainly be taken account of as a part of the totality of the evidence before the tribunal and without it, there was very little else to support a finding of disability.

In relation to the problem of bed wetting which has also caused a divergence of **1.214** decisions among Commissioners it will no longer (in accordance with *R(DLA)3/06)* be necessary to find some medical reason for the incontinence. However, it will still remain necessary to establish that the claimant is suffering from a disability. This means that the incontinence must at least, be something that is not normal for a person of his age, and, in the case of a young child, that he has requirements that are substantially in excess of what is normal for a child of that age. (See subs.(1A) discussed below.)

Similar reasoning will now apply to cases of chronic fatigue syndrome and psychosomatic pain. The only question should be whether the claimant suffers the fatigue or pain, genuinely and is thereby disabled so as to need the care, without any need to provide a medical diagnosis.

In many cases the claimant's disablement will be defined by the extent to which they can do things without experiencing pain or discomfort to an unacceptable extent. Detailed advice for tribunals on the matter of pain is given by Commissioner Jacobs in *CDLA/0902/2004*.

Tribunals sometimes have a difficult task in determining whether a claim of **1.215** disablement involving pain or discomfort is genuine. Medical examiners sometimes remark upon inappropriate responses made by patients during examination that might tend to suggest that they are exaggerating their condition—the so-called "Waddell signs" (named after Prof. Waddell). In *CDLA/2747/2006* the tribunal had dismissed an appeal on the grounds that the claimant had displayed those signs and his claim could then be taken, for that reason, to be unjustified. The Commissioner allowed an appeal. It was an error of law he said, to reach such a conclusion on the basis ofWaddell signs alone. That evidence, he says, might be indicative of exaggeration, but could equally indicate that the claimant has both physical and mental components in his disablement. The correct approach, he says, is to look at that evidence within the context of the evidence as a whole that is before the tribunal, and reach a conclusion on the whole of the evidence.

The information upon which a tribunal will rely when hearing an appeal will generally be derived from three sources: the claimant themselves (including that provided on the claim form) or in the case of a child, that of the claimant's appointee (usually their parent); the claimant's GP; and an examining health practitioner (when a report has been requested by the DWP). The approach to be adopted to information from each of these sources has been considered in *HL v Secretary for State for Work and Pensions* [2011] UKUT 183 (AAC) where Judge Jacobs remarks:

> "All too often, judges present the tribunal's reasons as if the tribunal had a choice between accepting the evidence of the GP or of the examining medical practitioner. There may be cases where that is so, but in many cases the reports each have their strengths and each their limitations as an assessment of the claimant's disablement. In those cases, what a proper analysis usually requires is for the tribunal to show a balance between the value that can be distilled from each report and its limitations."

In *MW v SSWP* [2013] UKUT 158 (AAC) Judge Bano has reminded FTT that they should not regard a conflict of medical evidence as a contest between the claimant's own advisers and the EMP and in particular should not simply prefer that of the EMP on the ground that it was "independent". The evidence, he says, must be looked at as a whole and such evidence as was relevant taken from each.

1.216 *Requires:* This means reasonably requires not medically requires (see *Mallinson*). In *CA/96/84* it was suggested that an eight-year-old girl who suffered from enuresis would suffer no harm if left in her wet bedding for the rest of the night. The Commissioner held that attention was reasonably required simply to make her comfortable again and added that otherwise a person unable to dress themselves could be said to have no need for attention because they could stay in a dressing gown all day.

The section provides that care must be required; it does not have to be shown that care is in fact provided. But if care, whether by attention or supervision, is in fact provided, that may be strong evidence that the care is required. As one Commissioner put it "mothers would be unlikely to exhaust themselves by providing it for years" (*R(A) 1/73*). On the other hand if the claimant chooses to do without care, that may be a clear indication that care is not required (*CDLA/899/1994*). Tribunals should consider why the claimant does not use the care and whether their life can be considered normal without it (see below).

In *KK v Secretary of State for Work and Pensions* [2012] UKUT 356 (AAC) Judge Jacobs held that a First-tier Tribunal had made an error of law when they failed to explain to the claimant that he could be entitled to the benefit even though he might choose not to spend the benefit by acquiring any assistance. The claimant had claimed both the mobility and the care components, but said that he would not want anyone coming into his home and invading his privacy. The FTT treated that as abandonment of any claim for the care component. The judge examines the obligation of a tribunal to explore the inquisitorial aspect of its jurisdiction by making it clear to the claimant that his entitlement depended upon his need and not upon how he chose to spend the benefit. In the case of a child this point would mean that there is no need for the parent to show that they spent the money by acquiring further help.

Where care is provided there has been some difference of opinion about the source of that care. In two cases, *CSDLA/427/2006* and *CSDLA/2349/2010* (now [2012] UKUT 222 (AAC)) Judge May had decided that the care provided, in the first case, by teachers at school and in the other, by a district nurse, could not be included in the claim for DLA because both forms of care were provided through publicly funded arrangements and to include it in the claim would mean "double funding" at public expense. This argument has been disapproved by a tribunal of judges in *KM v SSWP (DLA)* [2013] UKUT 159 (AAC); [2014] AACR 2. The judges there decide that there is no reason to read the words of the statute with such a gloss put upon them. Indeed, they argue that the provisions of the DLA Regulations suggest that there could have been no such intention when the statute was passed because regs 8 and 9 remove the payability of benefit when the claimant is in publicly funded accommodation thereby implying that otherwise he is entitled. An alternative argument advanced by Judge May, that care provided by medical staff could not qualify was also not approved, though because that point did not arise on the facts of the case before them they confined themselves to general comments. What they say, however, is consistent with the view they expressed above—that there is no reason to limit the words of the statute in this way. It could also be argued that reg.7 of the DLA Regulations (which qualifies a renal patient for DLA) supports that conclusion because it specifically excludes a claimant who has dialysis in an NHS hospital unless no member of the staff is assisting him; the specific exclusion in this instance suggests that it is not applicable in other circumstances.

The question of whether a claimant "requires" attention will be affected by whether some aid or device might assist the claimant so as to eliminate the need for attention. This matter was considered by Judge Ward in the case of *SF v SSWP* [2010] UKUT 78 (AAC). There, the claim had been refused by the First-tier Tribunal on the ground that the claimant's need for assistance in bathing could be obviated by the provision of a bath-board, or by the fitting of a bath with showering facilities. Judge Ward followed an earlier decision in *CDLA/304/07* in holding that it must be found to be reasonable for the claimant to obtain such devices. He remitted the case to a new tribunal for further findings to be made as to the availability of such measures and consideration of the timing, as well as the cost, with which they might be accomplished within the six-month qualifying period of that claim. In the instant case it was argued that major alterations might not have been reasonable because the claimant was moving house at that time. In *CA/3943/2006*, the Deputy Commissioner held that it would be difficult ever to conclude that the use of a bucket in the kitchen, as a substitute for a lavatory, could be regarded as acceptable so as to render assistance that was needed to climb the stairs, no longer "reasonably required". The question of whether the use of a commode downstairs, if that were available, would be acceptable, she decided, should be left to a subsequent tribunal. And see also *JF v SSWP* [2012] UKUT 335 (AAC) where Judge Rowland considered the size of the claimant's kitchen in relation to the use of a high stool to assist her when preparing food. 1.217

Though in *CDLA/2495/2004* the Commissioner held that the claimant, who had mental health problems and required prompting by his mother before he would do anything more than get out of bed, did not qualify for benefit at the middle rate—frequent attention—because some of the tasks for which he needed to be prompted, such as shaving, were performed only every four days, and the Commissioner suggested that as the claimant rarely went out, even help with dressing did not necessarily require her attention every day.

It is sometimes suggested, particularly in relation to supervision, that the claimant could avoid the need for care by adapting their lifestyle to avoid that risk. The scope for this suggestion now seems strictly limited. 1.218

In *R(A) 3/89* the Commissioner ridiculed the suggestion by asking whether the claimant was expected to remain chairbound to avoid the risk of falling and in *R(A) 5/90* a Tribunal of Commissioners said that any tribunal adopting the argument that the claimant could avoid a danger should identify the precautions to be taken and explain how they were compatible with normal domestic arrangements. The leading case on this point must now be *Secretary of State v Fairey* [1997] 1 W.L.R. 799 (reported as *R(A) 2/98*) in which the House of Lords held that the claimant who was profoundly deaf was entitled to care on the basis that she needed the assistance of an interpreter by way of sign language to assist her in travelling and carrying out other social activities. Lord Slynn of Hadley said at 815:

> "In my opinion the yardstick of a 'normal life' is important; it is a better approach than adopting the test as to whether something is 'essential' or 'desirable.' Social life in the sense of mixing with others, taking part in activities with others, undertaking recreation and cultural activities can be part of normal life. It is not in any way unreasonable that the severely disabled person should wish to be involved in them despite his disability. What is reasonable will depend on the age, sex, interests of the applicant and other circumstances. To take part in such activities sight and hearing are normally necessary and if they are impaired attention is required in connection with the bodily functions of seeing and hearing to enable the person to overcome his disability. As Swinton Thomas L.J. in the Court of Appeal said: 'Attention given to a profoundly deaf person to enable that person to carry on, so far as possible in the circumstances, an ordinary life is capable of being attention that is reasonably required.'
>
> How much attention is reasonably required and how frequently it is required are questions of fact for the adjudication officer."

But it may not yet be possible to say that the claimant should be put in exactly the same position as if they had no disability. In *CDLA/267/94* it was suggested that a claimant who was blind and needed assistance to find anything he had lost, might reasonably be expected to wait for periods of attention by finding. This would affect the issue of whether his need was "frequent" (see below).

1.219 *Attention and Supervision:* The difference between these terms has been explored in *CA/6/72 (approved in R(A) 3/74)*. Attention was taken to involve personal service of an active nature, such as bathing or feeding, while supervision was more passive, such as being present to warn or give guidance and to intervene when necessary. This distinction was accepted by the Court of Appeal in *Moran v Secretary of State for Social Services* (reported as appendix *R(A) 1/88*) and approved in *Mallinson v Secretary of State for Social Security* [1994] 1 W.L.R. 630, also reported as appendix to *R(A) 3/94* where the point was made that the concepts were not necessarily mutually exclusive—a person might be supervising a blind person while at the same time providing attention by way of guidance.

1.220 *Attention in connection with bodily functions:* From the start it has been recognised that these words hold the key to qualification for most claimants. In *R. v National Insurance Commissioner Ex. p. the Secretary of State for Social Services* (*Packer's case*) [1981] 1 W.L.R. 1017 Lord Denning M.R. said bodily functions:

> "include breathing, hearing, seeing, eating, drinking, walking, sitting, sleeping, getting out of bed, dressing, undressing, eliminating waste products—and the like—all of which an ordinary person—who is not suffering from any disability—does for himself. But they do not include cooking, shopping or other things which a wife or daughter does as part of her domestic duties: or generally which one member of the household normally does for the rest of the family".

Although he accepted that cooking could be said to be "connected with" the function of eating, it was, he thought, too remote. In subsequent cases (*R. v Woodling* [1984] 1 W.L.R. 348; *Cockburn* (reported as *R(A) 2/98*): and *Fairey*) this distinction between activities that are close and intimate to the claimant and those which are not has been sustained. It has, however, created a complex and often conflicting path between Commissioners' decisions.

The concept of "bodily functions" has been examined by a tribunal of Commissioners in *R(DLA) 1/07*. The case concerned a child claimant whose mother described her as having behavioural problems, memory loss, difficulty concentrating and other problems, as well as being hyperactive. It was clear that at school she required special attention to motivate her and to aid in integrating with her peers, while at home her mother said she had to be with her all the time to control her behaviour and to ensure her safety. While there was no medical diagnosis of the condition a report by a paediatric neuropsychologist described her as "having significant learning difficulties with prominent language processing disorder and associated behavioural problems". The claimant's need for attention could probably be summed up as requiring help with motivation, communication and social integration. Her claim for the mobility component of DLA at the lower rate, and for care component at the middle rate, was refused and her appeal to a tribunal dismissed on the ground that the assistance she needed was not help in relation to her bodily functions.

The Tribunal of Commissioners allowed an appeal. They begin their reasons by facing the issue squarely and deciding: "Firstly, the functions of the brain are included within the term 'bodily functions'. They found authority for that proposition in a series of cases including *Packer's Case, Mallinson, Cockburn*, and *Fairey*.

In accepting that cognitive functioning (thinking) can be a bodily function they expressly overrule a line of cases (*CSDLA/867/1997, CSDLA/832/1999* and *CSDLA/860/2000)* asserting that it was not. The Commissioners also refer to *R(DLA) 3/03*, which had been relied on by the appeal tribunal, but they distinguished it as deciding only that the claimant there did not need the assistance for which he was claiming—the evidence suggested that he was able to communicate adequately without assistance—and did not decide that communication could never be a bodily function. **1.221**

The Commissioners in the present case made no reference to *CDLA/2974/2004*, a decision of Mr Commissioner Rowland, in which he accepted that the defective cognitive processes of a 16-year-old autistic boy could amount to a defective bodily function.

The problem that the Commissioners then faced in their decision was to make any distinction between what has been known as activities and bodily functions. Here they break new ground by suggesting that what may be regarded as activities should be broken down into the parts that are contributed by individual organs of the body. If such organs are defective so as to need assistance then that may be help in connection with a bodily function for the purposes of a claim to DLA. The Tribunal express their reasons for this as follows:

> "33. As identified by Dunn LJ in *Packer's Case*, a 'bodily function' primarily refers to the normal action of any organ of the body. For example, the function or a function of the lower jaw is to move up and down, i.e. its normal action. By way of extension, we consider it quite appropriate to extend this reference to the organ's immediate purpose: in our example, the purpose of the lower jaw moving up and down is to masticate food, and we do not consider it would be incorrect to refer to such mastication as a 'bodily function', i.e. a function of the lower jaw. It appears to us that the term is sufficiently wide to cover this extension.
>
> 34. Such functions might be voluntarily controlled (e.g. the lower jaw, as in our example), or involuntary (e.g. it is the function of the kidneys to filter waste products from the blood, which it does without any voluntary instigating action).
>
> 35. Furthermore, as Dunn LJ indicated in *Packer's Case* (see paragraph 30 above), 'bodily functions' includes not only the action of one organ of the body, but also those of any set of such organs in concert. Therefore, when the lower jaw is looked at with the mouth and various internal organs including the stomach and alimentary tract, it can properly be said of that set of organs of which the jaw is a part that the bodily function (in the sense of purpose as described above) is eating. We see no inconsistency between the proposition that it is a function of the lower jaw to move up and down and masticate food, and, as part of a set of organs, its function is also eating. Indeed, far from there being a strict dichotomy between 'microfunctions' and 'macrofunctions'—and to be fair to Mr Collins he did not submit that there was such a clear and absolute dichotomy—in terms of the organs of the body, there is complex web of functionality that requires acknowledgment.

36. However, of course, there are limits. Not every activity performed by the body is a 'bodily function', because it cannot properly be said that that activity is either a normal action or purpose of that organ or set of organs. Shopping is one example which falls clearly on the wrong side of the line: whilst no doubt involving various functions of the body, shopping could not properly be said itself to be a function (in terms of either simple actions or purpose) of any organ or set of organs of the body. Similarly, it was not suggested by any of the judges in *Packer's Case* that cooking could itself be a 'bodily function'. There may be difficult, borderline cases; but, like Lord Slynn (and with respect to Lord Denning's obiter dicta in *Packer's Case* and those of subsequent judges, to which we have referred: see paragraph 31 above), we do not consider that getting in and out of bed, or dressing and undressing, are 'bodily functions', because (in our respectful view) it cannot properly be said that it is the normal action or purpose of any organ or sets of organs to perform these exercises. These are not functions of organs of the body, but merely things which a body can do if the relevant bodily functions (e.g. movement of the limbs) are working normally.

37. However, given that activities such as shopping, dressing and undressing, getting in and out of bed necessarily involve bodily functions of one sort or another (which can be specifically identified, if necessary), why does the relevant 'bodily function' matter in any specific case? The answer to this lies in looking at the wording of the statutory provisions as a whole, as has been urged by the House of Lords (see paragraph 16 above) and in the approach to those provisions of Lord Woolf in *Mallinson* and the tribunal of Commissioners in *R(DLA) 3/06*. As already indicated (paragraphs 8–11), the focus of these provisions is on the disablement (i.e. functional deficiency) of the claimant. Even where such a disablement is shown, the relevant attention is that *reasonably required* by virtue of that functional deficiency. On the issue of relevant attention, it may therefore be necessary to focus upon the functional deficiency with some particularity. It may not be crucial whether the bodily function impaired in someone who cannot move his legs and consequently walk is looked at as (i) movement of the legs, or (ii) walking. We consider both have equal validity for the reasons we give above. However the function is viewed, the necessary attention to address the claimant's reasonable care requirements will be the same. But in other cases it may be of importance, because it will be necessary to identify the bodily function that is impaired with some precision so that the attention reasonably required to address the impairment can be properly identified and assessed.

38. For example, Mr Mallinson was blind, and was consequently unable to walk in unfamiliar surroundings because (as Lord Woolf put it, at page 639H) he did not know where to walk or (e.g. when crossing the road) when to walk. As Lord Woolf pointed out (at page 639G), to say whether the attention he received in the form of being guided was 'in connection with his bodily functions' (i.e. reasonably necessary as the result of an impairment to those functions), it was necessary to identify the bodily function or functions to which the attention relates. We consider that in substance this is no more than ensuring that the relevant attention is reasonably necessary—because, as indicated above (paragraphs 8–9), the severity of the functional disablement is in fact defined by that attention. Therefore, although in one sense it could be said that Mr Mallinson's ability to walk was impaired (in the ways identified by Lord Woolf), in considering this question, as Mr Mallinson's legs were working normally—but his eyesight was not—of the interwoven bodily functions involved, 'it is preferable to focus on that function [i.e. his deficient ability to see]' (per Lord Woolf at page 641A). The relevant 'bodily function' that is impaired (i.e. the disablement) must therefore be identified with sufficient particularity so that the assistance reasonably required can be identified and assessed; and this is why 'bodily function' cannot be given a definition so wide as to include all human activity or indeed any particularly complex activity. This is therefore another reflection of the close relationship

> between functional disablement and the assistance reasonably required to cope with that disablement referred to in paragraph 9 above of identifying the relevant bodily functions given above.
>
> 39. However, even where an activity is such that it cannot itself properly be described as a bodily function, that will not be the end of the matter—because recourse will then have to be had to the discrete bodily functions which are involved in the activity and the extent to which they are impaired, and particularly as to whether the functions or any of them are so impaired that assistance to the level of any of the provisions of section 72 is required in respect of the disablement. In these circumstances, the relevant discrete bodily functions will have to be identified and 'unbundled', considered and assessed. Indeed, given the purpose 36–37), in functionally complex activities which may be borderline, we regard this 'unbundling' exercise as the correct approach in any event, and warn against the temptation of considering in very fine detail whether the complex activity can truly be described as a single bodily function or not. We consider the potential dangers of such an arid exercise are well illustrated in this very case. As the various House of Lords opinions referred to above (but notably that of Lord Slynn in *Cockburn*) make clear, in borderline cases it cannot be incorrect to unbundle functions in this way, and it is likely to be helpful in approaching the issue of assistance reasonably required."

The Commissioners then go on to point out that just identifying a bodily function that is deficient so as to need assistance, is not a sufficient condition to qualify for DLA. It will remain necessary, as well, to show that the assistance has the requisite degree of intimacy, and also that it satisfies one of the tests as to frequency, constancy, etc.

Applying all this to the facts of the present case the Commissioners found it to be an error of law to say that communication was not a bodily function. It was necessary, they say, to "unbundle" that word and examine what the claimant's difficulty in communicating was caused by. Clearly elements such as hearing, seeing and speaking can qualify for assistance and now we can say also, in the light of their decision above, comprehending, thinking and concentrating. Cases that have held to the contrary were disapproved. Similarly, social integration needed to be unbundled so as to analyse the parts with which the claimant required assistance. Where these could be identified as requiring assistance in the form of close personal care and attention to particular mental processes the claimant may be regarded as requiring assistance with bodily functions. The case was referred to a fresh tribunal for further consideration of the evidence. **1.222**

The cases that were overruled in *R(DLA) 1/07* concerned claimants who were described as having Asperger's syndrome. It seems now that that condition may qualify for benefit if the assistance given can be identified as relating to a bodily function when communicating and social integration are appropriately unbundled and if that assistance otherwise satisfies the statutory requirements. Decision *R(DLA) 3/03*, in which an Asperger's claimant had also been refused, was distinguished on the ground that there the claimant was capable of communicating without assistance and the fact that he did so in a manner that might be different, did not qualify the assistance given as being assistance in connection with a bodily function.

A three judge court of the UT has resolved the differences that had arisen in cases concerning claimants who suffered from dyslexia. In several cases such claims had succeeded while in others they were rejected. In some of the successful cases the bodily function for which attention was necessary was said to be "seeing" while in others it was held to be a malfunction of the brain. Those claims which had failed, did so on the ground either, that the attention given was for education rather than assistance with any disability, or that it was attention that was provided already out of public funds and could not, therefore, have been intended by parliament to qualify for an award of DLA. All of these points have been dealt with by the UT in *KM v SSWP (DLA)* [2013] UKUT 159 (AAC); [2014] AACR 2. The claimant was a child who was dyslexic, but also suffered from a syndrome that causes difficulty in dealing with fine visual tasks.

The UT quote extensively from the earlier decisions and give detailed advice to the FTT to whom the case would be returned, but in essence they confirm that there is no need to distinguish between the function of seeing and other brain functions—the important point is to determine whether the claimant requires the requisite level of attention because of some mental or physical disability whatever the label that might be attached to it. They reject the argument that attention given in helping the claimant to learn to read cannot qualify for DLA. It will all depend upon the basis of facts that are found by the FTT. It may be necessary to distinguish between the claimant and a slow learner, but that will depend upon finding the necessary disability in the functioning of his seeing/brain processes as well as making a comparison with help that may be required by children of a similar age but without that disability.

The UT rejects the suggestion that care provided by publicly funded bodies cannot be included in the DLA claim. They refer to regs 8 and 9 of the DLA Regulations (which remove the *payability* of benefit when the claimant is in a publicly funded care-home or a hospital) as demonstrating that he otherwise is *entitled*. They point out that much of the care that is received by claimants must come from care workers provided by the social services departments of local authorities because not all claimants will have family and friends able and willing to provide necessary help.

In *BM v SSWP (DLA)* [2015] UKUT 18 (AAC); [2015] AACR 29 (discussed more fully below—see *Subs 1A*) Judge Markus has made clear that the decision in *KM* is applicable in all cases of learning disability. In the case of *BM* the FTT had declined to consider the extra attention required by a child in learning at school because, they said, it was not a case of dyslexia as *KM* had been. Judge Markus explains that the reasoning of that case must apply in any case where the child's deficiency can be said to be associated with a bodily function. In *KM* it was the function of the brain in learning to read; in *BM*, where the child had difficulties with speech, it was the bodily function of speaking or, again, the function of the brain.

KM and *BM* emphasise the care that must be taken by DM and tribunals in finding the facts that are relevant before proceeding to the task of measuring them against the criteria for awarding DLA of either component and at any of the rates. The importance of getting the terminology right, and of establishing what it is that claimants, representatives and expert witness statements mean by the terms that they use has been emphasised by Judge Jacobs in *PW v SSWP (PIP)* [2023] UKUT 121 (AAC). This was a PIP case, but it arose on the transfer of the claimant from his award of DLA onto PIP and the evidence and the processes involved are essentially the same. The decision of the FTT was expressed in terms that referred to both learning difficulty and learning disability while his mother, in the appeal application, had referred to cognitive impairment. The Judge undertook internet research before granting leave to appeal to the UT but found no consistent or authoritative statement of whether the terms used were interchangeable, or if different, what those meanings might be. Judge Jacobs holds that it was an error of law for the FTT not to have determined what the mother meant when she referred to her son having a disability so as to understand the points that she was making and for them not to identify what those terms meant in the documentary evidence submitted in support of the claim.

The UT in *KM* deals also with an associated argument that had been advanced by Judge May in *KG v SSWP* [2012] UKUT 222 (AAC). There he suggested that attention given by a medically qualified person could not be included in a claim for DLA. In that case the claimant had ulcers on his legs which were dressed daily by the district nurse. The UT in *KM* dealt with this argument only in general terms because it was not relevant to the case of the dyslexic child, but they do say that they see no reason in applying the words of the statute to make this distinction. Rather, they say, the matter should be determined by a careful consideration of the facts and the application then of the DLA criteria. Thus in the case of *KG* it appeared that the need for care arose because the ulcers required attention by a medically skilled person. There was no evidence that the claimant could not reach the ulcers himself (though he did need help with socks and shoes) and it followed that his need for care of the ulcers did not arise from his disability, but from lack of medical skill.

The activity of the brain as a bodily function was considered by Commissioner Mesher in *CA/2574/*2007. The claimant was an elderly widow who suffered from agoraphobia, anorexia and depression and had lived as a recluse since the death of her husband three years earlier. She was visited daily by her daughter who, in addition to taking care of all her mother's physical needs by way of shopping, housekeeping etc., also spent several hours each day providing stimulation and encouragement to her mother. The Commissioner allowed an appeal against the decision of a tribunal, who had failed to consider the latter involvement as attention in connection with the bodily function of brain activity, though he then went on to reject the claim in entering his own decision on the ground that she could not satisfy the more restricted requirements for AA. A claim for DLA at lowest rate (had she been younger) might have been successful.

After *Mallinson* and *Fairey* it is clear that a sense of physical intimacy will suffice **1.223**
and that physical contact is not necessary. Thus in the case of a blind man, guidance by words is sufficient and interpreting by sign language is sufficient for the deaf. In the case of *Cockburn* (reported as *R(A) 2/98*) it was accepted that some attention might even be given without the claimant being present so long as it was a continuance of attention that began in person (though this will now be limited by reg.10c of the DLA Regulations). In that case the claimant was both incontinent and arthritic. Help that was given in changing her bedclothes and wringing out wet sheets was all a part of the attention to her bodily functions, though this did not extend to doing her laundry for her the next day. Many services such as shopping, cooking and cleaning done for another would not count as attention, being too remote, but if these same activities are attempted by the claimant in person, with the carer providing assistance to them, for example reading labels to a blind claimant, or reaching items on the shelf for a physically disabled one, then they should qualify as attention in connecting with seeing and lifting respectively (*CDLA/3711/95* and *CDLA/12381/96* though there are conflicting Commissioners' decisions in *CSDLA/281/1996* and *CSDLA/314/1997*).

It needs to be borne in mind that there is still a distinction between attention in the sense of any assistance that is given to a disabled person to enable them to lead a normal life and "attention in connection with a bodily function". It is only that help which has the sufficient degree of closeness and intimacy with the claimant's person that will qualify. A useful examination of the criteria was made in *CDLA/8167/95*. There the claimant was a blind woman who was in receipt of the care component at the lowest rate. She applied for a review of her entitlement claiming the middle rate. In order to demonstrate the frequency with which she needed help from others she listed at least 17 occasions daily when she needed such assistance. These included checking that the food in her kitchen was fit to eat, that her appearance was acceptable and that her clothing was appropriate, as well as help with public transport, shopping, dealing with correspondence, domestic chores, gardening and, finally, cleaning up after her guide dog. The commissioner, allowing an appeal, rejected her claim on the basis that many of these actions were not sufficiently closely related to her bodily function of seeing. As he put it;

> "If you have to tell another person they have gravy on their chin this is not an act of close personal contact or intimacy, whether they are sighted and have forgotten to look in the mirror or are blind and unable to do so. The required closeness of contact or intimacy only comes if the degree and nature of the disability means that you also have to do something like guiding their arm or standing over them to help with the applying of a wet cloth to their face, without which they could not reasonably cope with such a personal thing for themselves. Steering a blind person across the road or on to a bus or helping them to read their own correspondence all count, as these actions have been accepted by the House of Lords to involve the required degree of contact or intimacy beyond what is ordinary between adult

human beings apart from the disability. So has enabling a deaf person to conduct a conversation with someone else by taking part in it for them as an interpreter. Again the help involves what would ordinarily be an intrusion into the personal space and privacy of the individual. On the other hand merely telling a blind person about their appearance, helping them choose matching clothes to put on, helping them locate things they have put down somewhere, telling them whether the carpet is hovered properly, a picture hung straight or the windows smeary, all things readily acceptable as reasonably required to help deal with their disability in the course of leading a normal life, are not things that appear to me self-evidently to have the special character of personal contact or intimacy which the House of Lords has expressly confirmed is essential for 'attention'."

The distinction is not, he says, between household duties and other tasks—even help with domestic duties may qualify—but what is important, in his words, is that the attention should be given to the blind person so as to enable them to do the housework, rather than that housework is done for them. But the importance of a close enough connection between the claimant's disability and the assistance needed has been reasserted by the Court of Appeal in *Secretary of State for Work and Pensions v Batty* [2005] EWCA Civ 1746 *R(A) 1/06*. The claimant, who was severely restricted by arthritis, could not carry a drink of any kind from a place where it was prepared to a place where it might conveniently be consumed. She therefore needed someone's assistance every time she wished to have a drink both at home and at work, where she was able to work at her desk. The Commissioner who had found in her favour did so on the basis that, short of standing at the sink every time she needed a drink, she could not live a reasonably normal life without such assistance. The Court of Appeal, however, returned to the basics of earlier decisions such as Packer and decided that while helping a claimant to drink was clearly attention in connection with a bodily function, bringing a drink to them was not. And see too *CSA/694/2007* where it was held that assistance given to a blind claimant with her correspondence could qualify whereas assistance in driving her to social and other events would not.

A more recent attempt to extend the scope of assistance to include any support that might enable the claimant to lead a normal life was rejected in *CDLA/3376/2005*, but the decision still demonstrates the breadth of activities for which assistance may be required and can qualify the claimant for the care component. It also demonstrates the correct approach to be adopted to the question by tribunals. The claimant, who was blind from birth, had been allowed mobility component at the lower rate and care component at the lowest rate. She appealed against a refusal to grant the care component at a higher rate. The appeal tribunal, who rejected that appeal, did so by approaching the list of activities for which she claimed she needed assistance as falling into a category of domestic activities for which no assistance could qualify. The decision of Commissioner Jacobs demonstrates the error in this approach. The decisions of the House of Lords in *Cockburn* (reported as *R(A) 2/98)* and the Court of Appeal in *Ramsden (R(DLA) 2/03*) make clear that the only limiting device on the range of activities to be considered is whether it is reasonable for the claimant to experience that as part of a normal family and community life. (Together with the fact that the assistance given must be sufficiently intimate and personal to qualify.) In this case the Commissioner accepted that help given to the claimant to assist her in doing her own shopping, laundry and housework could all qualify for the benefit. This decision was made before the decision in *R(DLA) 1/07T*, and it may be useful to counter the impression that could be given by that decision that shopping, dressing etc could not be considered as the subject of assistance (see paras36 and 37 above). What is said there is that shopping, for example, should not itself be regarded as a bodily function for which assistance is given. Quite so, but the bodily function, in this case, would be seeing, for which assistance is given in connection with the reasonable activity of shopping.

In the case of the claimants who are mentally disabled the appropriate "bodily function" is of course, thinking; this is confirmed in *CDLA/2974/2004*.

The Court of Appeal gave further consideration to this phrase in *Ramsden v Secretary of State for Work and Pensions* [2003] EWCA Civ 32, R(DLA) 2/03. The claimant, aged twelve, was faecally incontinent as a result of spina bifida, but for psychological reasons did not wear incontinence pads. He soiled himself once or twice a day and required attention from his mother in cleaning him up in a bath and shower, and also cleaning up the clothes, towels, bedding, carpets, furniture and other surfaces that had been fouled. On a renewal claim the AO refused to renew and that decision was upheld by a tribunal. The tribunal took into account the washing of the claimant, and the rinsing of his soiled clothing, bedding, etc, but specifically excluded any time spent in laundering the clothing etc as required, in their view, by the decision in *Cockburn*. The tribunal made no overt reference to the time spent cleaning carpets, furniture, and other surfaces, though, in the proceedings that followed, it was assumed that that time, too, was excluded on the basis that it was not sufficiently closely connected with the child's bodily function. A Commissioner upheld the tribunal decision. 1.224

The Court of Appeal, in allowing the appeal, reviewed thoroughly the speeches in *Cockburn*. That case, they concluded, recognised that certain acts of attendance performed by way of cleaning-up after an incident of incontinence could qualify as acts of attendance for the purpose of this benefit. Potter L.J., giving the first judgment continued (at para.37):

> "Within the constraints of the requirement that such cleaning-up should take place in the presence or the vicinity of the applicant, I consider that steps taken for the *immediate* removal of soiling from clothes, towels or bed linen or adjacent surfaces are apt to qualify under this head. In a case of faecal incontinence which results in the soiling of clothes, towels or bed linen, or the dropping or smearing of faeces on carpets or furniture, it is at the very least in the interests of hygiene that such occurrences be rectified immediately as a part and parcel of the cleaning-up operation necessary following the incident of incontinence giving rise to such soiling. If that is done, then, even if the operation concerned is one of thorough washing rather than merely 'rinsing', the criteria of immediacy and intimacy are sufficiently satisfied and the time spent in cleaning-up should be taken into account when assessing whether or not the attention given amounts to a significant portion of the day".

The court returned the case to a fresh tribunal to consider whether the attention amounted to "a significant portion of the day". On that point, too, they take a flexible view of what is meant by "significant". (See below.) That this approach is correct has been affirmed by Judge Wikeley in *KH v SSWP (DLA)* [2022] UKUT 303 (AAC). *Ramsden* was a case of faecal incontinence, but the Judge confirms that the same test will apply to urinary incontinence. 1.225

Giving support and encouragement to someone who is severely disabled by phobias, depression and paranoid illnesses has now been held to be attention in connection with bodily functions. With that support the claimant was able to get up from bed, to cook, to eat properly, and generally to take care of herself so as to create a reasonable quality of life (*CDLA/1148/97*). This was a re-hearing of the case after an appeal to the Court of Appeal. The other point held by the Commissioner in this case, that such care could be provided over the telephone, has been short lived. Its effect was reversed by reg.10c of DLA regulations (and reg.8BA of the AA regulations). But see *CDLA/4333/2004* noted after that regulation. Support and encouragement has also been held to qualify as attention when it is given to a person suffering from obsessive compulsive disorder (OCD), to encourage him to desist from his behaviour. In *CDLA/618/2006* the claimant had been awarded the lowest rate of care component because his obsessive need to wash and clean himself, or his equipment, effectively prevented him from accomplishing the task of cooking a meal. But the Commissioner considered that, as well, he might qualify for care component at the middle rate, if he could show that encouragement for the purpose of dissuading him from his compulsive behaviour was necessary. On the facts of this case, however, he held that there was no evidence that such encouragement would have assisted him.

Attention in soothing a person to sleep (at least in the case of a child) has been held to be attention in connection with a bodily function so long as the difficulty in sleeping is connected with a physical or mental disability (*CSDLA/567/2005*).

There are conflicting decisions on whether the preparation of meals that involve a special diet with careful control of the ingredients for illnesses such as pheylketonuria, or even diabetes, could qualify as attention in connection with a bodily function. In *R(A) 1/87* the Commissioner held that the extra care and attention required over and above that of normal cooking made a difference, but in *CSDLA/160/95* that decision was disapproved of on the ground that it had not referred to the concept of intimacy as required in *Woodling*.

With regard to the attention that is given to a deaf person by someone using sign language when the *Fairey* case was before Commissioner Sanders (*CA/780/91*) he drew a distinction between someone communicating with a claimant who is deaf by the use of sign language when they are acting as an interpreter to a third party, and when they are not. In the former, the interpreter is clearly providing attention to the claimant in connection with the bodily function of hearing and speaking; in the latter he may be merely holding a conversation with the claimant in the language in which they are both comfortable. The Commissioner seems to have been saying that merely because the signing might be slower or involve more effort than oral communication for both of them, it could not, for that reason alone, be regarded as "attention". Thus a conversation between the claimant and his wife using sign language about ordinary domestic matters would not be "attention" but his wife communicating those matters to a visitor would be. What subsequently emerged in the Court of Appeal, and was not criticised in the House of Lords, was that this did not preclude the possibility that an attendant who had to use physical contact to make the claimant aware, or "if the person giving the attention . . . has to do extra work, or take extra time, away from the attendant's ordinary duties to help the disabled person that may, as a question of fact, qualify as attention". This much seems clear from two decisions of Commissioner Sanders, himself (*CDLA/17189/96* and *CDLA/15884/96*), where he draws these conclusions from what was said in the Court of Appeal. The same formulation has been approved by another Commissioner in *CDLA/16668/96* and again, after a very full consideration, in *R(DLA) 1/02*. In a similar case (*R(DLA) 2/02*) Commissioner Levenson, after careful consideration of all the authorities, has suggested the following propositions as representing the current law:

- the operation of the senses is a bodily function and a defect in the senses leads to disability in connection with which attention might be required;
- the test is whether the attention is reasonably required to enable the severely disabled person as far as reasonably possible to live a normal life;
- the aggregate of attention that is reasonably required includes such attention as may enable the claimant to carry out a reasonable level of social activity;
- what is reasonable will depend on the age, sex, interests of the applicant and other circumstances;
- how much attention is reasonably required and how frequently it is required are questions of fact;
- attention in connection with bodily functions includes unusual efforts reasonably required to attract the attention of the deaf person in order to communicate with her. Unusual in this context means steps that are not or would not be required in respect of attracting the attention of a person in the same environment who is not deaf;
- a person is not providing attention when communicating with a deaf claimant by means of reasonably fluent signing unless communication is particularly slow and difficult;
- if communicating through an interpreter is significantly more efficient or effective than communicating through writing, or trying to converse with a

person who has to shout loudly, then it might well be that the services of an interpreter are reasonably required even if initiating the communication or conducting a two-way conversation does not itself constitute attention;

- help required to undertake activities other than those "concerned with the relatively mundane everyday activities of functioning as a human being in ordinary life" does not count as attention for these purposes;
- although, in order to count as attention, any service provided must be of a close and intimate nature involving personal contact carried out in the presence of a disabled person, in the case of a deaf person this includes communication between that person and an interpreter;
- for these purposes there is no significant difference between the interpretation of the written word and the interpretation of speech.

With the possible proviso that a decision-maker must remember that "communicating with" is not the same thing as "interpreting for" (which will always be attention) these points seem unexceptionable. **1.226**

Two Commissioners' decisions return to the question of the extra effort required to communicate with a deaf person, and the extra effort that may be required to initiate communication with them. In *R(DLA) 3/02*, Commissioner Fellner had to consider the case of a pre-lingually deaf person, now of middle age, who had completed City & Guilds qualifications, and worked as a foreman joiner on building sites and other places. She allowed an appeal against a decision awarding only lowest rate care component (on the grounds of inadequate facts and reasons) but substituted her own decision also at the lowest rate.

In doing so she accepted the law developed in the decisions cited above, including, generally, the points made by Commissioner Levenson, but with the *caveat* that the extra effort involved both in effecting two-person communication, and in attracting the attention of a person for that communication must be something more than de minimis. It must also be more than would be required to communicate with a hearing person in like circumstances. While she emphasises that these matters must always be ones for the decision-maker on the basis of the particular facts found by them, she suggests that tapping the shoulder, stamping a foot, flashing a light or throwing a paper ball, might all be regarded as so minimal as not to count on this basis. Similarly, though the claimant probably required people to go to him to communicate in the workplace, the same would be true of a hearing person doing that job because of the general level of noise on a building site. The Commissioner suggests the same may be true of many instances of initiating communication in the home—even hearing-able people may need to be contacted by going to them when they are cooking, watching television or doing DIY. The Commissioner suggested that the fact-finding stage of the decision process should begin with the claimant's need for attention in relation to his current level of activity, and then go on to explore further needs for attention based upon the "wish list" suggested by the claimant. But in doing so the decision-maker must approach the claimant's declared aspirations with a robust sense of what would be feasible, realistic and practicable as well as the established (but not very helpful) test of what is reasonable.

In this case, for example, she thought it would not be feasible for the claimant to have someone read the newspaper and magazines to him, given the time that it would take and the pattern of his existing daily life. Again, she thought it would be unrealistic to suggest that the claimant might accept the presence of an interpreter in the home, every evening, to help him watch television programmes without subtitles, and impractical to suggest that an interpreter could assist at the cinema (because of darkness) or on a building site (because of danger and unfamiliarity). She did not accept that an interpreter could attend work site meetings and that his services would be justified to replace the extra time and effort that was currently spent in communicating with the claimant. This is a useful case for decision-makers because it goes a long way to explore some of the practical application of the legal principles.

In the other case, *R(A) 1/03*, Commissioner Parker allowed an appeal against refusal of the lower rate of Attendance Allowance. (The claimant was over 65 at the date of his first claim although he was pre-lingually deaf, probably from birth.) The appeal was allowed for more than one reason, one of them being that the tribunal had discounted the assistance that the claimant already received from a centre for sensory impaired people. Commissioner Parker follows both the decision of Commissioner Levenson, *CDLA/3433/1999*, and that of Commissioner Fellner, *CDLA/1534/00*, above. In doing so she accepts the latter's constraint that the extra effort involved either in communication or attracting attention must be more than *de minimus*, but she reconciles this to some extent with Commissioner Levenson by drawing attention to his point that the extra effort in communicating, once it is significant, may justify a need for an interpreter which then will qualify as attention.

In *EG* v *SSWP* [2009] UKUT 112 (AAC) Judge Ward upheld the appeal of a deaf claimant who could lip-read, but only in Polish, and who therefore required the services of a translator in order to communicate. The First-tier Tribunal had rejected her appeal on the ground that her need arose from a language difficulty rather than from her hearing difficulty. The judge held that this was wrong; her inability to communicate arose at least for a reasonable period, from her inability to hear. Until such time as she might reasonably be expected to develop the skill of lip-reading in English, she would need the services of a translator. (The judge recognises that there might be a real difficulty in learning to associate the movements of the mouth with the meaning of words in English.)

It is also clear from *Mallinson* that a claimant may receive attention in connection with a bodily function even though that bodily function is completely inoperative. A person who is totally blind, for example, receives attention in connection with the bodily function of sight when his guide provides a substitute method of seeing and assistance given to a person by pushing them in a manual wheelchair when they are unable to walk or to move the wheelchair by themselves, is attention given in connection with the function of walking—see *SJ v SSWP* [2014] UKUT 222 (AAC).

In *CDLA/2333/2005* Commissioner Mesher holds that care in the form of supervision for the purpose of walking outside (mobility component) counts also for the purpose of attention or supervision of the bodily function of walking in the care components. This is not surprising because it is simply the converse of *R(DLA) 4/01*, but is a point that deserves to be noted.

And see too the decision in *DN v SSWP (DLA)* [2016] 233 (AAC), where the claimant's age of only four years precluded attention given to him when walking outside qualifying in respect of the lower rate of the mobility component, but should nevertheless have been taken into account when considering his entitlement to the care component.

Lowest Rate Entitlement

1.227 In order to claim benefit at the lowest rate the claimant must show that he satisfies one or other, or both, of the conditions in subs.(1)(a).

1.228 *Attention for a significant portion of the day:* To qualify under para.(a)(i) the claimant must show that he requires attention in connection with his bodily functions for a *significant portion of the day*. In *CDLA/205/2005* it appeared to the Commissioner that the tribunal had before it evidence of how long it took the claimant to do things for himself, but not how long it might have taken, were assistance to be given. The Commissioner points out that it is the latter which is relevant to the question of whether attention is for a significant portion of the day. How long things took for the claimant to do for himself might, however, be relevant to the question of whether he required assistance in the first place. This phrase has now been considered by the Court of Appeal in *Ramsden v Secretary of State for Work and Pensions* [2003] EWCA Civ 32 reported as *R(DLA) 2/03*. This case determines that the meaning of the word "day" is to be consistent with the time remaining as a residue of 24 hours when the "night" has been accounted for as in *R. v National Insurance Commissioner Ex p. Secretary of State for Social Services* [1974] 1 W.L.R. 1290; in other words it is the period between the time when the household becomes active in the morning and when its members finally retire to bed at night. The earlier suggestion in *CDLA/1463/99* that "day" should mean the whole 24 hour period is thus overruled. While this undoubtedly is the better interpretation of the section it does seem to work unjustly in the case of a claimant who requires some, though not significant, attention, during the day and one, far more disruptive, event at night, because, unless the night time attention is prolonged or repeated, it appears that that attention cannot be accounted for at all. On the other hand, of course, by limiting the time period of day it does become easier for the claimant to show that his day time attention is significant as a proportion of that period.

The Court of Appeal also considers what should be regarded as a "significant portion" of a day and they endorse the view that the phrase should be interpreted so as to make a "broad determination" of the question. Lord Justice Potter, giving the leading judgment, accepts that the task for the tribunal is principally a mathematical exercise involving comparison of the aggregate of time spent in giving attention, with the day as a whole. But he continues,

> "However it is also likely to be affected by the total time available in the day, by the extent to which the relevant tasks become a matter of routine, and the concentration and intensity of the activity comprised in those tasks. Thus while in broad terms it seems to me that a period of one hour, made up of two half-hour periods [of] concentrated activity, would reasonably be regarded as a significant portion of a day, in different circumstances there may well be room for a different view".

This passage is followed by one in which Potter L.J. expressly approves the reasoning in *CSDLA/29/94* in which Commissioner Walker puts forward the view that the day, and the "significant portion" of it, must be assessed from the position of the attender. In that case the Commissioner had held that even a lesser period than an hour might be significant if it consisted of many short periods that so broke up the day of the attender that for *them* the total, represented a greater inconvenience that the arithmetic sum of time might suggest. He also suggested that the tribunal should take a broad determination to record the total portion or percentage of the normal day that was involved for this household. Combining this with the decision of the Court of Appeal it would seem now possible to argue that, for an attender with an especially long and busy day, the time spent attending does become significant when it might not be for someone who was otherwise largely idle. For the busy attender, the time spent attending is significant because without it their day might seem already full, or, again, if the tasks required are arduous and physically or mentally demanding the time spent becomes significant because the effect of those tasks may be to exhaust the attender. For him or her their "day" (in the sense of what is achievable) would be largely used up. On the other hand if the tasks become routine and can be fitted in to the attender's regular daily pattern of life they will offer less inconvenience and may become a less than significant part of their "day".

As to the "one-hour" rule of thumb used by many tribunals and referred to in the Parlimentary debates, this case makes clear that there is no such minimum period–*CDLA/58/93* must to that extent be overruled. While, no doubt, tribunals may still choose to centre their thinking around a total time period of an hour, it is now clear that they must reach their decision on the basis of their own common sense and judgment of what is significant and explain that in their reasoning. In *SO v SSWP (DLA)* [2019] UKUT 272 (AAC) Judge Wright allowed an appeal against the decision of an FTT that attention given to a 13 year old autistic child for "more than one and a half hours per day" did not amount to attention for a significant portion of the day. He held that in the light of the views expressed in *Ramsden* (to which the FTT had referred) their reasons for the decision they had made failed to explain why the claim should not succeed. The decision was set aside and referred to a fresh tribunal.

The Cooking Test

1.229 The condition provided for in subs.(a)(ii) is not available to a claimant under the age of 16–see subs.(1A) (a). Discussion of the cooking test can be found in earlier editions of this work.

MIDDLE RATE ENTITLEMENT

1.230 In order to qualify for benefit at the middle rate a claimant must show that he qualifies under one or both of the conditions in subs.(1)(b) (the day conditions) **or,** one or both of the conditions under subs.(1)(c) (the night conditions) Where the claimant satisfies both of the day conditions or both of the night conditions there is no increase in the amount of benefit that is paid.

HIGHEST RATE ENTITLEMENT

1.231 In order to qualify for benefit at the highest rate a claimant must show that he qualifies under at least one of the conditions in subs.(1)(b) (the day conditions) **and**, at least one of the conditions under subs.(1)(c) (the night conditions).

THE DAY CONDITIONS

1.232 *Frequent attention throughout the day*: To satisfy para.(b)(i) the claimant must be shown to require "frequent attention throughout the day."

The meaning of "day" has been determined by the Court of Appeal in *Ramsden v SSWP* [2003] EWCA Civ 32 to mean that part of a period of 24 hours as is remaining after the "night" has been accounted for in relation to subs.(1)(c) below in accordance with *R v National Insurance Commissioner Ex p. Secretary of State for Social Services* [1974] 1 W.L.R. 1290. In other words "day" means that period between the time that the household becomes active in the morning and when its members retire to bed at night.

Frequent attention has been said to be "several times—not once or twice" (*per* Lord Denning M.R., *R. v National Insurance Commissioner Ex. p. the Secretary of State for Social Services*) and in *CA/281/89* the Commissioner held that the need should be "at intervals spread over the day".

In *CA/147/84* a child who required attention on four occasions spread approximately equally across the day was held not to qualify, but in *CA/1140/85* the Chief Commissioner stressed that even a person whose main attention was required at the beginning and end of each day could qualify so long as there were other events that required some brief attention during the day. The claimant was blind, and help in making tea, eating meals, putting on his coat and outdoor shoes qualified him even though he was largely self reliant once he had been got up and dressed each morning.

Commissioner's decision *CSDLA/590/00* considers the relationship between frequency of attention and the duration of that attention. It holds (as had *CDLA/12150/1996*) that the proper approach to frequency takes no account of the duration of attention, either in aggregate, or separately—except to exclude the instance of attention that is *de minimis* in the latter respect.

In this case the claimant was a five-year-old child with talipes of one foot. This caused him to fall between 5 and 10 times each day. In addition his mother had to manipulate his foot "several times" each day. The tribunal had rejected the claim on the basis that the need for attention did not amount to frequent attention throughout the day because it would amount to only, approximately, one hour in total during the day. Both representatives and the Commissioner thought this wrong. But the representative of the Secretary of State drew on *CSDLA/24/98* to suggest that the aggregate of attention time could be considered a factor in determining frequency. This seems to be a misinterpretation of that case where it seems the Commissioner was willing to uphold the decision because the tribunal had given its attention specifically to frequency as a separate issue in holding that four or five attendances were not frequent (although other cases have held that they can be).

In the present case the Commissioner accepts that entitlement depends solely upon pattern and frequency and not the total duration. It may be that the thinking of the tribunal in this case, and in *CSDLA/24/1998*, was inspired by the thought that if attention amounting to no more than one hour per day could not qualify a claimant for the lowest rate of care component, it might seem odd that it should, nevertheless, qualify him for the middle rate if it were spread in small periods frequently throughout the day. This point is answered effectively in *CDLA/12150/1996* (and quoted again in this decision). In the first place it is the inevitable outcome of giving the different words their natural meaning and secondly it would be supported as a rational outcome if the cost of providing numerous instances of attention spread over the whole day were greater than fewer points at either end of it, as would seem likely to be the case.

But all this must now be considered in the light of *R(DLA) 5/05*. Judge G. R. Hickinbottom, the Chief Commissioner, has carried the approach to interpretation that was set by the House of Lords in *Moyna* across to the rest of the criteria for qualification for DLA care component in s.72(1). This means, he says, that decision makers and tribunals must take a broad view of the matter, reading the words of the section in their context so as to identify the correct legal test and then deciding each case as a question of fact according to whether it falls on one side of that line of the other. Thereafter, an appeal on points of law could only interfere with their decision if either they have identified the wrong legal line or if they have reached a conclusion which is "outside the bounds of reasonable judgment", *i.e.* irrational.

Judge Hickinbottom goes on to point out that the oft quoted guidance taken **1.233** from the judgment of Lord Denning in *R. v National Insurance Commissioner, Ex p. Secretary of State for Social Services* [1981] 1 W.L.R. 1017, on the meaning of these phrases, was not only obiter, but was only a limited attempt to identify some fairly obvious characteristics of the words used, and must not be regarded as providing anything like definitions—as he suggests commentators appear to have done. He also takes to task certain Commissioners for attempting to paraphrase the sections in alternative words to explain their meaning.

The test of "frequently throughout the day", he suggests, is not to be approached in two stages—how often and over what period—but is to be treated as a single composite impression. Again, frequency is not just a question of number, but may be affected by the nature and duration of the occurrences, thus disagreeing with Commissioner Parker in *CSDLA/590/2000*. By way of example he contrasts the meaning of frequent when used in relation to an ice age with its use in relation to a train timetable; or again, a long distance train service every hour might be regarded as frequent when an hourly local service was not. As well, he points out that, although the scheme of s.72(1) is not necessarily one of gradation, in as much as the qualifying conditions in each of the three paragraphs are quite distinct and different, the context requires a recognition that Parliament can hardly have intended that a claimant should qualify for the middle-rate benefit on a lesser requirement for care than was necessary to gain the lowest rate of benefit.

All of this makes good sense. But it may make things difficult for tribunals for two reasons. First, tribunals must give reasons to support their decision. Often, an attempt to explain a decision will consist of rephrasing the statute to explain the line the tribunal is taking. If tribunals are not to rephrase the section to explain what they take to be its meaning, will it suffice for a tribunal to say, e.g. "we find this to be frequent attention because we think it is"? Secondly, decisions that are treated as findings of fact and appealable to a Commissioner only when they are grossly unreasonable may result in inequitable chaos. For example, in one of the cases that was considered in this appeal the Judge concluded, as had the tribunal, that an epileptic claimant who regularly required attention, at night, once or twice a week for up to 20 minutes on each occasion, did not satisfy the test of requiring "prolonged attention" throughout the period of his claim. Taking a broad view of the matter, and in particular the length of the fits and the pattern on an unpredictable but regular basis, he concluded that the claimant's need did not constitute prolonged attention throughout the relevant period. But what if a more generously inclined tribunal on a similar case were to conclude that it did? Would that be so unreasonable as to be appealable? (It could not be said to be out of line with the treatment of a lowest-rate claimant because the drafting of the section envisages that night-time care will be treated differently.) But if it is not appealable, then will it not be inequitable for the first claimant?

But note it is still possible to find an example where an error of law has occurred by the application of the wrong legal test to the facts found by the FTT. In *AB v SSWP* [2015] UKUT 522 (AAC) the claimant was a person who required stimulation to her mental processes at several points during the day on about half of the days each week, although the claimant did not require someone to be with her all of the day and could safely be left on her own for part of each day. The FTT held on the facts as found by them that this qualified her for benefit at only the lower rate—attention needed for a significant portion of the day. They held that that she did not qualify at the middle rate because, it seemed, they required the attention to have been necessary not only frequently, but also throughout the day—meaning that she might require someone to be with her all day. Judge Gray held that this was a mistake in the law as explained by Judge Hickinbottom, and that on the facts found by the FTT she was able to make the award at the middle rate without requiring a rehearing.

1.234 *Continual supervision—in order to avoid danger:* To satisfy para.(b)(ii) the claimant must show that he requires "continual supervision . . . in order to avoid danger to himself or others". Note the point made by Commissioner May (as he then was) in *CSDLA/867/97* that supervision by the teachers at school to protect the claimant from bullying could not qualify because it served to prevent danger to the claimant from others, whereas, in his view, the subsection envisages protection of the claimant (and others) from himself. This decision has been disapproved on other grounds but without reference to this point.

Supervision may be of two kinds. It can be precautionary or anticipatory, as when a carer watches over his patient ready to intervene when necessary; or, it may be ancillary to a series of acts of attention, as when the carer accompanies a blind person on a walk and offers guidance both physical and verbal. (In either case where the intervention becomes frequent the claimant may qualify anyway under para.(b)(i).)

Supervision is more passive than attention, but even supervision of the precautionary kind must be something more than mere presence (*CDLA/42/94*). It requires a degree of monitoring by the carer so that they do more than merely respond to a call from the claimant. Even so, it has been held in *Moran v Secretary of State for Social Services* (*The Times*, March 14, 1987, CA) that a supervisor could be in another room and even may be asleep, if they are so attuned to the needs of their patient that they would respond immediately by sensing the onset of, in that case, a fit.

In order to be *substantial* the danger must be "considerable, solid or big" (*R(A) 1/73*) but it need not be life threatening. In *R(A) 11/83* a Tribunal of Commissioners felt that the risk of a claimant biting his tongue in an epileptic fit was a substantial danger to him and in *CSA/68/89* the risk of impulsive suicide was a substantial danger even though it was not determined and was unlikely to succeed.

The danger is also substantial if the risk of harm is high. Although the language used by Commissioners in a number of decisions is sometimes inconsistent it is clear that risk is a factor of both the degree of harm that is possible, and the likelihood of a harmful event occurring. Thus although the likelihood of a house catching fire might be low, the consequence to a tetraplegic who was caught within it, would be fatal and the danger to him would therefore be substantial (see *R(A) 2/89*). Likewise in *R(A) 1/81* and *R(A) 5/81* the point is made that it only takes a child to run out into traffic once to present a substantial danger to himself and others.

In *R(A) 1/73* the Commissioner said that the word "continual" was not synonymous with continuous. This means that supervision may be continual notwithstanding some short breaks. In order to "avoid" substantial danger it is not necessary to eliminate the risk altogether; it is enough to effect a real reduction in the risk. In *R(A) 3/92* the Commissioner accepted that no amount of supervision could prevent a determined suicide but it could substantially reduce the risk that it would succeed.

Many cases on supervision involve the risk of falling. In *R(A) 3/89* a Commissioner proposed that in such cases the following questions should be determined. **1.235**

"(i) Are the situations in which the claimant may fall predictable or unpredictable? That is to say, does the claimant have a liability to fall anywhere at any time? Or does he fall only in certain circumstances or situations? This is, of course, a matter of medical opinion: but the opinion must be based on evidence.

(ii) If the falling is predictable, can the claimant reasonably be expected to avoid the risk of falling or to place himself at such risk only when adequately supervised? That again is a matter of medical opinion. If the claimant cannot reasonably be expected either to avoid the risk or to place himself at risk only when adequately supervised, the DMP should treat the case as one in which the falling was unpredictable.

(iii) If the falling is unpredictable, will the falling give rise to substantial danger to himself? This is again, of course, a matter of medical opinion. Nevertheless it must be borne in mind that a person, particularly a disabled person, may when falling hit his head on the corner of a cupboard or on a fire kerb or radiator; and whether or not he is injured in the course of falling, he may by reason of his disability be unable to rise or be unable to summon help. Or he may be of such an age that a fall will be likely to have serious consequences. Clearly such matters ought in an appropriate case to be taken into account.

(iv) Is the substantial danger too remote? In the present case, the DMP stated that in his medical opinion the risk of substantial danger arising from a fall 'is so remote a possibility that it ought to be reasonably disregarded.' But he has failed to give any indication why he reached that conclusion or to indicate on what evidence he relied to support that conclusion. Although, as I have said, those questions are matters of medical opinion, it is incumbent upon a DMP to consider all the evidence, including the evidence of the claimant, to make the relevant findings of fact and to give adequate reasons for the conclusions which he reaches upon those findings of fact so that the claimant 'looking at the decision should be able to discern on the face of it the reasons why' the evidence failed to satisfy the DMP: *R(A) 1/72* at paragraph 8. In my judgment the DMP has failed to do so in the present case."

In *R(A) 5/90* a Tribunal of Commissioners cautioned against treating these questions as a statutory requirement and said that it was not an error of law if the DMP failed to answer them. But they also said that his failure to do so might well reflect an insufficiency of reasons for his decision. A single instance of falling does not show a propensity to fall (*CA/233/95*) and even where there is a propensity to fall it does not follow that there is a need for continual supervision to avoid danger. In *CDLA/899/94* the Commissioner said:

"10. . . . This is not a case of a person who is so unsteady that he requires to be supported whenever he stands, which may have been the case in *R(A) 3/89*. It is always possible that a person who falls may suffer some injury. However, that is far more likely in the case of a person who falls due to a fit or loss of consciousness and therefore cannot take any steps to mitigate the effects of the fall. In the present case, the risk of falling at home is slight and the risk of serious injury when falling at home is even slighter. This is not the case of an elderly person who is particularly frail. It really cannot be said that the claimant reasonably requires someone to be so close to him the whole time as to be able to catch him should he fall.

> 11. It is of course theoretically possible that a person falls and the effects of the fall are made worse by the lack of immediate response. Supervision may be required in some case in order to avoid the risk of danger arising after a fall. However, one must have regard to the relative frequency of falls and the likelihood of serious injury, *of a type that might be avoided if there were supervision*, arising from them."

But it is not necessary that the supervision should be able to prevent the fall—it is enough that supervision will reduce the risk of serious harm as a consequence of falling (*R(A) 2/92*).

Where the need for supervision is based upon the claimant's mental disablement some medical evidence may be necessary (*CA/147/84*), though it is possible that a history of previous suicide attempts may suffice. In *R(A) 2/91* the Commissioner held that a view expressed by the consultant psychiatrist that "the claimant was at times significantly depressed and potentially at risk to herself" was sufficient to justify supervision.

THE NIGHT CONDITIONS

1.236 In order to qualify for benefit at the highest rate a claimant must show that they satisfy at least one of the conditions in subs.(1)(c) (the night conditions) and, at least one, of the conditions in subs.(1)(b) (the day conditions)—see above.

Subs.(1)(c) provides two conditions either of which must be satisfied "at night".

Night was defined in *R. v National Insurance Commissioner Ex p. Secretary of State for Social Services* [1974] 1 W.L.R. 1290, Appendix to *R(A) 4/74*, as being:

> "that period of inactivity or that principal period of inactivity through which each household goes in the dark hours and to measure the beginning of the night from the time at which the household as it were, closed down for the night".

This case has probably been credited with deciding more than it did. The Court of Appeal were considering an appeal from a Commissioner who had himself allowed an appeal from an Attendance Allowance Board. Then, as now, the Commissioner was limited to allowing an appeal on a point of law. The decision of the Court was simply that in their view no error of law could be seen in the decision of the Board and that the Commissioner had therefore been wrong in allowing an appeal. Any definition that they gave was strictly speaking *obiter*, but in any case they expressly eschew any attempt to provide any general definition. Nevertheless they did adopt the formulae that had been agreed by counsel which formed the test above and which has since been adopted and applied elsewhere (see e.g. *Ramsden R(DLA) 2/03*). But that is not the end of the matter. The definition of night which the Court of Appeal commended was no different from that of the Commissioner in that case, nor so far as can be seen, from the Board. Where they differed was in the application of that test to the facts. The particular point of contention was whether assistance given to the claimant, (a paraplegic) in undressing and getting into bed, and in getting up and dressing in the morning, should be regarded as assistance rendered by night. The Board had regarded both as being given by day. The Commissioner thought that at least the process of getting to bed should be part of his night attention-in his view, applying the words of the test, getting undressed and into bed is a part of the process of "closing down" for the night. All that the Court of Appeal decided was that there was no error of law in the decision of the Board that undressing etc was accomplished as a part of the day, but they make equally clear that the decision on the point, in their view, was one of fact to be decided in accordance with the common sense of the Board and, it follows, that were the Board, (or a tribunal now) to decide that going to bed was part of what one does at night, there would be, equally, nothing wrong with that decision.

For the past thirty years, however, tribunals have accepted that night begins only when the claimant has got into bed and ends when he climbs out. It may be too late for such a revolutionary change.

While this definition seems to address itself to the habits of the particular household there should be room to take account of a more objective, typical household. Thus if one (possibly the only other) member of the household remains up late to undertake what is a regular attention need that should be regarded as a night time need because otherwise the household would, as a whole, have been retired to bed. Conversely, when children have gone to bed, but their parents have not, any attention prior to the parents normal bed time will be attention by day, and any attention to the child before the parents' usual time of rising will be attention at night. The first part of this approach was confirmed in *R(A) 1/78* (rejecting another part of Lord Widgery's judgment in the case above).

In *CDLA/997/2003*, the child who, because of his disabilities, had to be attended to whenever he was awake, woke regularly every morning at about 5.00 am. His mother had to rise then to give continual supervision. Had the child not woken at that time she would not have risen until 7.00 am. The Commissioner accepted the argument that the night of the household should be defined by what the household would normally do. In this case the household as a whole would not have risen before 7.00 am and therefore the period of supervision between 5.00 am and 7.00 am should count as being given at night.

Again, in *R(A) 1/04*, the claimant frequently got up at 4.30 am and then went for a walk. The Commissioner held that a tribunal was wrong to fix the end of the night by reference to what that particular claimant did; the distinction should have a more objective element to reflect what ordinary households did. In this case it would probably be fair to say that the ordinary use of language would be to describe the claimant as going out for a walk in the night. The Commissioner suggests that a normal period of night, as identified in accordance with the test above, would be something like the hours between 11.00 pm and 7.00 am. 1.237

This approach has been confirmed again in *LB v SSWP (DLA)* [2018] UKUT 445 (AAC), where Judge Hemingway, in giving guidance to the FTT to whom the case was returned, said it should take account of time when the claimant's mother stayed up later than she might otherwise have done, even when just remaining awake beside the child could be regarded as time spent caring for the claimant at night.

Prolonged or repeated attention: In order to satisfy para.(c)(i) the claimant must show that he requires, by night, "prolonged or repeated attention". 1.238

"Prolonged", seems to be accepted by decision-makers to mean 20 minutes or more. In *R. v National Insurance Commissioners Ex p. Secretary of State for Social Services*, [1981], W.L.R. 1017, CA, *R(A) 2/80*, Lord Denning said "repeated means more than once at any rate". Since the decision of the Court was that the Attendance Allowance Board had been correct in finding that the claimant satisfied only the day conditions it would seem that anything said as to the meaning of the night conditions was obiter, but as a minimum, it must mean at least twice.. It is therefore open to a tribunal to require more than two acts of attention during the night, but current experience suggests that generally twice per night has sufficed.

It is not necessary that the care is needed every night. If the need is there on most nights the claim should succeed and in *R(A) 2/74* the Commissioner suggested that decision-makers should take a broad view of the matter and consider whether, in all of the circumstances, their good sense indicates that the words of the statute are satisfied. This might suggest care that is needed several times a week without focusing on counting nights every week.

In *DJ v SSWP* [2016] UKUT 169 (AAC) Judge Hemingway dealt with the case of a five-year-old child whose medical condition caused him to require attention when he woke at night suffering acute pain. The evidence recorded by the FTT showed typically that on three nights of the week he would wake several times for an hour or more at a time, and on the other four nights he would wake only once, usually for between 30 and 60 minutes. The FTT had refused an appeal on the ground that on most nights he did not require prolonged or repeated attention. This conclusion seems to have been reached by conflating the requirements 1.239

of s.72(1) with those of s.72(1A)—see below. The judge had little difficulty in concluding that, looked at broadly and not arithmetically, the claimant could be described as requiring prolonged attention most of the time. And see too the decision of Judge Brunner QC in *AD v SSWP (DLA)* [2017] UKUT 29 (AAC), a case on similar facts.

1.240 *Awake for a prolonged period or at frequent intervals for the purpose of watching over:* In order to satisfy para.(c)(ii) the claimant must show that, by night, he requires someone to be "awake for a prolonged period or at frequent intervals for the purpose of watching over him" in order to avoid substantial danger to himself or others.

For the meaning of "prolonged", see above under para.(c)(i). For the meaning of "frequent", see above under para.(b)(i)—though it is possible that fewer occurrences should be spread throughout the night (cf. the wording of para.(b)(i)).

Under this paragraph it is no longer possible for the carer to be asleep "on call". They must be awake and watching over the claimant. It is suggested that, as with supervision, the carer might be watching over, without actually looking at, the claimant at the time, e.g. they could be watching television in a room nearby. But as to the requirement of being awake there can be no compromise.

There has been some consideration of the use of CCTV and baby-minder devices as a means of watching over in *JH v SSWP* [2010] UKUT 456, but that case was a decision on para.(6) of reg.12 of the Disability Living Allowance Regulations and that provision requires that the carer is "present" when watching over the claimant.

This point has been considered again in *AH v Secretary of State for Work and Pensions* [2012] UKUT 387, another case on reg.12, where the judge suggests that use of CCTV may be a suitable way of watching over. He observes also that a person may be "watching over" without having the patient in view all of the time. It is significant, he suggests, that the expression, in both contexts, is "watching over" and not "looking at".

Subsection (1A)

1.241 A child (being for this purpose someone under 16) cannot qualify under the cooking test (subs.(1A)(a)), but otherwise there is no lower age limit for the care component. However, since all young children need a certain amount of attention and supervision, a disabled child qualifies for the care component only if he or she requires more attention or supervision than children of the same age who are not disabled. Note that the child is the claimant although an adult will be appointed to act on his or her behalf. In *CSDLA/567/2005* Commissioner Parker held that even attention given in soothing a child back to sleep could be attention in connection with their bodily function provided that the sleeplessness was linked to a disability and, under this subsection, would qualify only if it were substantially in excess of that which would be normal for a child of that age. This has been followed by Judge Wikeley in *ES (by his appointee CS) v SSWP (DLA)* [2020] UKUT 10 (AAC). There, one of the child's disabilities, at the age of 25 months, was delay in language development. It was argued that this disability extended considerably the time taken to sooth him back to sleep after frequent periods awake through the night. The Judge found that the FTT had erred in looking for a causal connection between the child's condition and his inability to sleep for longer periods or his ability to get back to sleep after waking; they should, he said, have asked themselves simply whether he required "from another person prolonged or repeated attention with his bodily functions." On the additional child test under this subsection he found that the bodily function in question was that of communicating not of sleeping and that, as well, the test applied by the FTT in comparing the claimant with a "1 or 2 year old" child was too loose when the statute requires comparison with a child of the *same* age. The case was remitted for rehearing. In *DJ v SSWP* [2016] UKUT 169 (AAC) the FTT had remarked of a child who needed attention at night for 30–60 minutes on four nights of the week that "This would not be unusual for some five year olds". In allowing an appeal, Judge Hemingway doubted the correctness of that statement, but in any case was able to point out that the test is one of comparison with "normal" children of that age, which must relate to children generally and would not be satisfied only if some children required that attention.

In *CDLA/3737/2002* the Commissioner held that attention provided to a partially sighted child by her teachers at school to assist her in the bodily function of seeing and so learning could qualify her for the middle rate of care component. The amount of attention she required was considerably in excess of that which was required by a normally sighted child. There is nothing in the legislation to suggest that this sort of care should not be taken into account even if it is provided by a publicly funded institution.

This point has now been confirmed in the decision of a tribunal of judges—see *KM v SSWP (DLA)* [2013] UKUT 159 (AAC); [2014] AACR 2.

Where a claim is made on behalf of a child, and it is based on the care and attention necessary to clean and wash as a result of the child not having developed control over their bowel or bladder, it may seem that the most obvious question is whether the child satisfies the requirement set in this subsection namely, is that attention substantially in excess of the normal requirements for a child of his age. But, as has been pointed out in *CSDLA/552/01*, and now again in *R(DLA)1/05*, there is another question that needs to be decided first—is there evidence that the child's condition is the result of any physical or mental disability? The fact that a child is late in developing control of the bowels, etc. is not, in itself, evidence of disability, and nocturnal enuresis may continue in a normal child for several years. In this case a claim for a child of six failed because the evidence did not necessarily show a disability even though she wet and sometimes fouled herself on most nights of the week. But the Commissioner did add that as she grew older a continuing failure to develop control might become some evidence of disability that might then be supported by medical evidence, though the need to find a medical condition will no longer apply since the decision in *R(DLA)2/06*. **1.242**

Paragraph (a) provides that a claim for the lowest rate cannot be based on a child's inability to prepare a main meal, even if the child is 15.

Paragraph (b) defines the extra requirement that must be shown for a child claimant to succeed. This is either, under sub-para.(i) that they have care requirements of the kind defined in subs.(1) which are substantially in excess of the requirements of a normal child of that age; or, under sub-para.(ii) that they have extra such care requirements that would be common to younger children, but which children of their age would normally have grown out of. Obviously the younger a child is the more difficult it will be to show these conditions have been satisfied.

In *CA/92/92* the Deputy Commissioner made the following points: **1.243**

> "5. In the case of a child, it is to be noted that the attention or supervision required must be 'substantially in excess of that normally required by a child of the same age and sex.' Attention or supervision may be required 'substantially in excess of that normally required' either by virtue of the time over which it is required or by virtue of the quality or degree of attention or supervision which is required.
>
> 6. The idea of a greater quality or degree of attention can be illustrated by considering meal times. A young child may require attention in connection with eating because he or she requires the food to be cut up. A disabled child of the same age may require attention in excess of that normally required by a child of the same age because he or she not only requires the food to be cut up but also requires it to be spooned into the mouth. The fact that the child will be supervised anyway is irrelevant: there is still an additional requirement for attention. Whether such additional attention, taken with any other additional attention requirements, is 'substantial' and 'frequent . . . throughout the day' are matters of judgement to be determined in each case where the condition in section [72(1)(b)(i)] is being considered. Those may be significant limiting factors.
>
> 7. When considering the condition in section [72(1)(b)(ii)], the additional condition that the supervision required must be substantially in excess of that normally required by a child of the same age is indeed 'stringent' as it was described in *CA/21/88*. Because young children normally require continual supervision

throughout the day in order to avoid substantial danger to themselves, the focus will be on the quality or degree of supervision. Thus a very young immobile baby or an older child might normally be regarded as being adequately supervised by a person who was getting on with his or her own chores in a different part of the home. On the other hand, a disabled child of the same age may need much closer supervision amounting, perhaps, to being watched over. That would be supervision in excess of that normally required. Again, it is necessary to consider whether such additional supervision is 'substantial' and 'continual . . . throughout the day' and those may be significant limiting factors.

8. Similar considerations apply to the night conditions in section [72(1)(c)], although it may in practice be more difficult for claimants to qualify on the basis of the additional quality or degree of attention or watching over rather than on the basis of the additional frequency or length of time for which attention or watching over is required.

9. The other general question raised by this appeal is how one judges what attention of supervision is normally required by a child of the same age and sex. Children vary considerably in their requirements for attention and supervision, particularly when they are young. At any age, there is a range of requirements for attention or supervision. It is significant that the legislation does not speak of attention or supervision substantially in excess of that which would be required by the particular child being considered were he not physically or mentally disabled. So that, if it were possible to ascribe tantrums to frustration arising out of a disability, that would not be enough for the child to qualify unless the attention or supervision was substantially in excess of that normally required by a child of the same age and sex. It seems to me that the legislation contemplates a yardstick of an average child, neither particularly bright or well behaved nor particularly dull or badly behaved, and then the attention or supervision required by the child whose case is being considered must be judged to decide whether it is 'substantially' more than would normally be required by the average child. That, I think, comes to much the same thing as saying that the attention or supervision required must be substantially more than that normally required by *most* children, which is the way the delegated medical practitioner put it in paragraph 4 of his decision in this case. Attention or supervision is not to be regarded as 'substantially' in excess of that normally required unless it is outside the whole range of attention or supervision that would normally be required by the average child. However, it need not necessarily be substantially in excess of that which would be required by a particularly dull or badly behaved, but not physically or mentally disabled, child. I appreciate that all this is pitched at a fairly theoretical level and that there may be significant evidential problems and problems of judgement in individual cases, but it seems desirable to provide some sort of theoretical framework within which the present case can be considered."

The distinction between the tests posed by subpara.(i) and that of subpara.(ii) has been considered in *BM v SSWP (DLA)* [2015] UKUT 18 (AAC); [2015] AACR 29. The child in this case suffered from several conditions all of which contributed to his developmental delay. The FTT that heard an appeal brought on his behalf for both the care component and the mobility component held that he did not satisfy the requirements of subpara. (i) – they gave no consideration to subpara.(ii). In the UT it was at first argued on behalf of the Secretary of State that there was effectively no difference in practice between the two tests, though subsequently it was accepted that the two tests were different. Judge Markus concedes that the difference in practice is not easy to see, but she explains that in subpara.(i) the focus is upon the question whether the claimant requires more attention though of the same kind as that which a non-disabled child of the same age might need; whereas subpara.(ii) is focused on the need for attention that is different from that required by children of the same age, though it might be the same as that required by children of a younger age. On this basis a claim might succeed so long as the different attention required is "substantial", but would not necessarily have to be overall "substantially in excess" of that required by a child of the same age. She puts it thus:

> "34. Once it has been determined that a claimant has requirements falling within section 72(1) (which I have assumed to be the case in the above hypothetical examples), the issues which arise for determination under section 72(1A)(b)(i) are: (a) what the relevant requirements are of normally healthy children of the same age; and (b) whether the claimant's requirements are substantially in excess of those in (a). Under section 72(1A)(b)(ii) the issues which arise are: (a) whether the claimant's requirements are substantial; (b) whether the claimant's requirements are different from those of children of the claimant's age in normal physical and mental health; (c) whether younger children in normal physical and mental health would have those requirements."

An example of how *subs.(1A)* is to be applied in the case of a very young child (there a matter of six months) is provided by *CDLA/3525/2004*. The child required a special diet and careful supervision. The majority of the tribunal found this extra care did not amount to care substantially in excess of what would be required for such a young child anyway. The Commissioner held that the tribunal had applied the right test and the conclusion they reached, essentially a finding of fact, could not be said to show any error of law.

The care needs of a very young child were considered in *CDLA/4100/2004*. The claimant was a child of 17 months who was profoundly deaf. She was provided with hearing aids which gave limited hearing ability, but it was claimed still required considerably more attention and supervision than a normal child of that age. Commissioner Rowland allowed her appeal and awarded the middle rate care component on the basis of the written evidence before him.

Further consideration of a child's claim is given by Commissioner Parker in **1.244** *CDLA/829/2004* where she extends to three stages the test she suggested earlier in *CSDLA/552/01*. In these cases it is necessary, she suggests, to decide first; whether the claimant has a mental or physical disability (as now explained in *CDLA/1721/2004*), secondly whether they satisfy one or more of the care requirements, and then thirdly whether that amount of care substantially exceeds that required for a normal child of that age. For the question of what is normal, she adopts the approach of Commissioner Rowland in *R(DLA) 1/05* as being a matter of quality as well as quantity, frequency, duration etc. A useful resume of these cases can be found again in *CSDLA/535/2007*, another decision of Commissioner Parker.

In *CDLA/3779/2004* the Commissioner points out that evidence from the school of supervision, or rather, lack of any extra supervision that is required for the claimant, may be misleading because the school may find it necessary to supervise all the children together, and that supervision may suffice for the claimant. But that is not to say that at other times, and away from school, that the claimant does not need supervision in circumstances (e.g. playing on his own) when a normal child would not.

A child who is terminally ill is taken to satisfy para.(b) and (c) of subs.(1) by virtue of subs.(5). Subsection (6)(b) has no application in such a case (*R(DLA) 1/99*).

Subsection (2)

Paragraph (a) imposes the three-month qualifying period but this is deemed to be **1.245** satisfied in the case of a person who is terminally ill (see subs.(5)). If a person's condition deteriorates so that he or she satisfies a further condition and would qualify for a higher rate of the care component, the effect of subs.(4) is that the claimant must still wait three months before qualifying for the higher rate unless terminally ill. See *KH v SSWP* [2009] UKUT 54 (AAC) where the claimant had applied for her benefit to be increased from a certain date, but the increased rate could be paid only from a date three months later because there was no evidence that the claimant had qualified for the higher rate before the application for supersession was received. Under s.76(1), an award cannot usually be made before the date of claim but this does not prevent the three-month qualifying period imposed by s.72(2)(a) from being satisfied as at the date of claim if the conditions were met during the three months before the date of claim. The date of claim is determined in accordance with Reg.6 of the Social Security (Claims and Payments) Regulations—see Vol. III of this work. Reg.6 of the DLA Regulations prescribes, for the purpose of para. (a)(ii), a period of three months ending on the day on which the claimant was last entitled to the component or to attendance allowance if that was not more than two years before the current period of entitlement would otherwise begin. This has the practical effect in most cases that the three-month qualifying period is deemed to be satisfied if the current claim is within two years of a previous period of entitlement at the relevant rate.

Under paras 3(2) and 7(2) of Sch.1 to the DLA Regulations, a period of six months is substituted for the period of three months in subs.(2) in the case of a person over the age of 65 who makes a renewal claim for DLA or whose entitlement is to be revised on review.

Paragraph (b) requires that a person should be expected to satisfy the conditions for the component for six months, unless he or she is expected to die sooner. In *CDLA/3461/2006*, it was held that this requirement applies equally to a renewal claim as much as to a new claim. Thus where, on the medical evidence provided, it was reasonable to expect that the claimant would be recovered within the next six months, even though he may not have recovered yet, the claim was properly refused.

Although this means that six months will normally be the minimum period for which an award will be made this section does not prevent an award for a lesser period when that is appropriate. In *R(DLA) 11/02* the claimant had applied unsuccessfully and then appealed. Before that appeal could be heard her condition had deteriorated and she made a fresh claim that was allowed. The Commissioner held that an award of less than six months could be made to fill the gap between the date when she was now regarded as qualifying and the date when the existing award commenced even though that was less than six months. This period of six months begins as the three-month (or six-month for those over 65) qualifying period ends and both conditions are intended to ensure that only the chronically disabled are entitled to DLA.

As the need for assistance may also depend upon the facilities and adaptations that are available to the claimant it will be necessary for the DM to decide what it is reasonable for a claimant to acquire and how quickly he may be expected to do that. In *SF v SSWP* [2010] UKUT 78 (AAC) a tribunal was directed to make enquiries as to the fitting of a shower for the claimant which matter would itself require information about the claimant's accommodation and his resources. If it was reasonable for him to have the shower within six months, that might preclude the basis of a claim.

On an appeal the claimant's disability must be judged on the basis of his condition at the time of claim and up to the time of the DM decision. Information that only becomes available after that time is still admissible before a tribunal provided that it relates to the claimant's condition within that period–see *R(DLA) 2/01*. Where, however the question relates to the claimant's prospective condition it must be evidence as to what might then have been expected to happen, rather than what has in fact happened by the time of the tribunal determination.

This was the conclusion reached in *CDLA/2878/2000*. The claimant (who was a nurse) developed a condition of her back as a result of which she became unable to care for herself and suffered restricted mobility. She claimed both components of DLA, but less than three months later, and, according to her, quite unexpectedly she was operated on successfully and had recovered sufficiently to return to work within six months of her date of claim. The tribunal, which heard an appeal several weeks after that, held that she could not be entitled because events had proved the condition not to have lasted the requisite period. The Commissioner allowed her appeal for the reasons stated above after making a full review of authorities across a wide range of ex post facto situations. He drew a distinction between those cases where the subsequent event is relevant to establish a fact that might be shown to have pre-existed, and those cases, such as this (and the situation in *R(A) 1/94*), where the decision-maker must decide what was then a likely outcome.

Subsection (2A)

This subsection defines the period for the operation of subs.(1A) above. **1.246**

Subsections (3) and (4)

Regulation 4(1) of the DLA Regulations provides for three rates of benefit. **1.247**

Despite the strange use of the words "in any other case" in subs.(4)(c) it is plain that it is intended that the lowest rate is applicable only if a claimant satisfies the condition mentioned in subs.(1)(a) without also satisfying the condition in either subs.(1)(b) or (1)(c) If he or she were to satisfy the conditions in, say, both subs.(1)(a) and (1)(c), the middle rate would be applicable. see *CDLA/2495/2004*.

Subsection (5)

Under s.66(2), a person is "terminally ill" if "he suffers from a progressive disease and his death in consequence of that disease can reasonably be expected within six months". See the notes to that section. Note also that someone may make a claim on this ground on behalf of the claimant without the claimant's knowledge or authority (s.76(3)). **1.248**

The effect of this subsection is that a terminally ill person is deemed to satisfy the three-month (or six-month in the case of a person over 65) qualifying period and is entitled to an award of the highest rate of the care component for the remainder of his or her life, subject only to satisfying presence and residence conditions and the rules about people in hospital and other accommodation. Even those are relaxed. Reg.2(4) of the DLA Regulations relaxes the presence conditions for terminally ill claimants so that it is not necessary for them to have been in Great Britain before the day in respect of which the claim is made. Reg.9(3) also enables such claimants to receive the care component even though they are in accommodation where the cost could be, but is not, borne wholly or partly out of public or local funds.

Subsection (7)

Regulation 7 of the DLA Regulations deems people undergoing renal dialysis to satisfy the condition of either subs.(1)(b) or (1)(c). **1.249**

Subsection (8)

See regs 8–10 of the DLA Regulations. **1.250**

The mobility component

73.—(1) Subject to the provisions of this Act, a person shall be entitled to the mobility component of a disability living allowance for any period in which he is over [[1] the relevant age] and throughout which— **1.251**

(a) he is suffering from physical disablement such that he is either unable to walk or virtually unable to do so; or

[[6] (ab) he falls within subsection (1AB) below; or

(b) he does not fall within that subsection but does fall within subsection (2) below; or]

(c) he falls within subsection (3) below; or

(d) he is able to walk but is so severely disabled physically or mentally that, disregarding any ability he may have to use routes which are familiar to him on his own, he cannot take advantage of the faculty out of doors without guidance or supervision from another person most of the time.

[[1] (1A) In subsection (1) above "the relevant age" means—

(a) in relation to the conditions mentioned in paragraph (a), [[6](ab),] (b) or (c) of that subsection, the age of 3;
(b) in relation to the conditions mentioned in paragraph (d) of that subsection, the age of 5.]

[[6](1AB) A person falls within this subsection if—
(a) he has such severe visual impairment as may be prescribed; and
(b) he satisfies such other conditions as may be prescribed.]

(2) A person falls within this subsection if—
(a) he is both blind and deaf; and
(b) he satisfies such other conditions as may be prescribed.

(3) A person falls within this subsection if—
(a) he is severely mentally impaired; and
(b) he displays severe behavioural problems; and
(c) he satisfies both the conditions mentioned in section 72(1)(b) and (c) above.

[[3] (4A) In its application to a person in relation to so much of a period as falls before the day on which he reaches the age of 16, subsection (1) has effect subject to the modification that the condition mentioned in paragraph (d) shall not be taken to be satisfied unless—
(a) he requires substantially more guidance or supervision from another person than persons of his age in normal physical and mental health would require, or
(b) persons of his age in normal physical and mental health would not require such guidance or supervision

(5) [[4] . . .], circumstances may be prescribed in which a person is to be taken to satisfy or not to satisfy a condition mentioned in subsection (1)(a) or (d) or subsection (2)(a) above.

[[3] (5A) Subsection (4A) has effect subject to regulations made under subsection (5) (except as otherwise prescribed).]

(6) Regulations shall specify the cases which fall within subsection (3)(a) and (b) above.

(7) A person who is to be taken for the purposes of section 72 above to satisfy or not to satisfy a condition mentioned in subsection (1)(b) or (c)of that section is to be taken to satisfy or not to satisfy it for the purposes of subsection (3)(c) above.

(8) A person shall not be entitled to the mobility component for a period unless during most of that period his condition will be such as permits him from time to time to benefit from enhanced facilities for locomotion.

(9) A person shall not be entitled to the mobility component of a disability living allowance unless—
(a) throughout—
  (i) the period of three months immediately preceding the date on which the award of that component would begin; or
  (ii) such other period of three months as may be prescribed, he has satisfied or is likely to satisfy one or other of the conditions mentioned in subsection (1) [[5] (a) to (d)] above; and
(b) he is likely to continue to satisfy one or other of those conditions throughout—
  (i) the period of six months beginning with that date; or
  (ii) (if his death is expected within the period of six months beginning with that date) the period so beginning and ending with his death.

[3 (9A) The modifications mentioned in subsection (4A) shall have effect in relation to the application of subsection (1) for the purposes of subsection (9), but only—

(a) in the case of a person who is under the age of 16 on the date on which the award of the mobility component would begin, and

(b) in relation to so much of any period mentioned in subsection (9) as falls before the day on which he reaches the age of 16.]

(10) Two weekly rates of the mobility component shall be prescribed.

(11) The weekly rate of the mobility component payable to a person for each week in the period for which he is awarded that component shall be—

(a) the higher rate, if he falls within subsection (9) above by virtue of having satisfied or being likely to satisfy one or other of the conditions mentioned in subsection (1)(a), [6 (ab),] (b) and (c) above throughout both the period mentioned in paragraph (a) of subsection (9) above and that mentioned in paragraph (b) of that subsection; and

(b) the lower rate in any other case.

(12) For the purposes of this section in its application to a person who is terminally ill, as defined in section 66(2) above, and who makes a claim expressly on the ground that he is such a person—

(a) subsection (9)(a) above shall be omitted; and

(b) subsection (11)(a) above shall have effect as if for the words from "both" to "subsection", in the fourth place where it occurs, there were substituted the words "the period mentioned in subsection (9)(b) above".

(13) Regulations may prescribe cases in which a person who has the use—

(a) of an invalid carriage or other vehicle provided by [2the Welsh Ministers under paragraph 9 of Schedule 1 to the National Health Service (Wales) Act 2006, or the Secretary of State under paragraph 9 of Schedule 1 to the National Health Service Act 2006] or under section 46 of the National Health Service (Scotland) Act 1978 or provided under Article 30(1) of the Health and Personal Social Services (Northern Ireland) Order 1972; or

(b) of any prescribed description of appliance supplied under the enactments relating to the National Health Service being such an appliance as is primarily designed to afford a means of personal and independent locomotion out of doors,

is not to be paid any amount attributable to entitlement to the mobility component or is to be paid disability living allowance at a reduced rate in so far as it is attributable to that component.

(14) A payment to or in respect of any person which is attributable to his entitlement to the mobility component, and the right to receive such a payment, shall (except in prescribed circumstances and for prescribed purposes) be disregarded in applying any enactment or instrument under which regard is to be had to a person's means.

AMENDMENTS

1. Welfare Reform and Pensions Act 1999 s.67 (April 9, 2001).

2. National Health Service (Consequential Provisions) Act 2006 Sch.1 para.145 (March 1, 2007).

3. Welfare Reform Act 2007 s.53(2) (October 1, 2007).

4. Welfare Reform Act 2007 Sch.8 (October 1, 2007).
5. Welfare Reform Act 2007 Sch.7 para.2(2) (October 1, 2007).
6. Welfare Reform Act 2009 s.14 (October 15, 2010).

DERIVATION

1.252 SSA 1975 s.37ZC.

GENERAL NOTE

Subsection (1)

1.253 The mobility component of DLA is a benefit paid to claimants who experience difficulty, to the requisite extent, in getting about on foot. It is paid at two levels. From April 2001 a claimant may qualify for benefit at the higher level from the age of three, but for the lower level only from the age of five. In respect of the lower rate infant claimants have to satisfy an extra requirement test until they reach the age of 16. An attempt to have the lower age restriction declared to be in breach of Convention Rights failed in *SM v Advocate General for Scotland* [2010] CSOH 15. S.75 imposes an upper limit of 65, though claimants who have been entitled before reaching that age can continue to be entitled for the remainder of their life. It is no longer possible for a person to first claim for benefit over the age of 65 except in the case of someone moving from a previous entitlement under the invalid carriage scheme (DLA Regulations, Sch.2).

Note that the inability to walk or virtual inability to walk must exist throughout the period on which the claim is based. This has been interpreted, in *CDLA/496/2008*, as having the same meaning as the same words in s.72 have been given in *Secretary of State for Work and Pensions v Moyna* [2003] UKHL 44; [2003] 1 W.L.R. 1929; and *R(DLA) 7/03*. There, it was explained as being a matter of judgment, rather than arithmetical calculation, whether a person could fairly be described as being unable to cook themselves a main meal throughout the period in question, and the same will be said of their ability to walk. In this case the claimant suffered from epilepsy and sometimes had seizures when she was out walking. Commissioner Rowland held that her walking ability needed to be considered in three phases; one when she was out walking normally (for which she was entitled to mobility component at the lower rate because she needed to be supervised in case she had a seizure); another when she was unable to walk immediately after a seizure and when she could benefit from facilities for enhanced locomotion by being transported home in a car; and thirdly when she needed to sleep for a period of hours and sometimes days, to recover after the seizure. During this third period he felt she could not benefit from enhanced locomotion because she needed to remain resting and usually asleep (see subs.(8)). On this basis it was only the relatively short period during which she was travelling home that could qualify for benefit at the higher rate (unable to walk), and this, even if repeated, was insufficient to constitute an inability to walk throughout the period.

Paragraph (a)

1.254 This was the original basis upon which a mobility benefit was paid and still forms the basis of most claims. Note that claims under this paragraph are limited to ones in which the claimant has a *physical* disability; claims based on a mental disability may be considered under para.(d), or under subs.(3) below. For a detailed consideration of this distinction see the notes to reg.12 of the DLA regulations below. The circumstances in which a person can be taken to be "unable to walk or virtually unable to do so" are set out in reg.12 of the DLA regulations made under subs.(5) of this section. For a detailed discussion of those circumstances and the meaning of "physical disablement", see the notes to that Regulation.

Paragraph (ab)

1.255 The claimant will qualify under this paragraph if they satisfy the conditions prescribed in reg.12(1A) of the DLA regulations.

Regulation 12(1A) was held to be ultra vires, though not a nullity, by Judge Agnew in *YR v SSWP* [2014] UKUT 80 (AAC). That decision was appealed to the Court of Session (*SSWP v Robertson* [2015] CSIH 82), but the court found the appeal to be incompetent, presumably on the ground that the judge's finding had been unnecessary to his decision and therefore an *obiter dictum*. The consequence has been that the Secretary of State has continued to apply the regulation as drafted.

Paragraph (b)

The claimant qualifies under this paragraph if he satisfies the conditions of subs. (2)—see below. **1.256**

Paragraph (c)

The claimant qualifies under this paragraph if he satisfies the conditions of subs. (3)—see below. **1.257**

Paragraph (d)

The phrase "so severely disabled physically or mentally" is to be treated in the same way as the identical phrase in s.72. It does not require the claimant to show that they suffer from some medically prescribed condition and that it is severe, but only that they have a disability, mental or physical, that severely affects their ability in relation to walking. (See *CDLA/3831/2004* and *R(DLA) 3/06*.) **1.258**

This paragraph which qualifies a claimant for benefit at the lower rate only, is designed to help those who do not qualify under the paragraphs above, yet still need assistance to enable them to walk normally out of doors. It was passed in consequence of the decision of the House of Lords in *Lees v Secretary of State for Social Services* [1985] 1 A.C. 930, also reported as appendix to *R(M) 1/84*. In that case the claimant was blind but suffered as well from a severe impairment of her capacity for spatial orientation. This meant that she could walk outside only with someone to guide her—otherwise she had no idea in which direction to move. An argument that this meant she was virtually unable to walk was not accepted. Under this paragraph, however, she would clearly qualify on the grounds that she needed guidance from another most of the time. The paragraph applies in cases of mental disability as well as physical disability in cases where mere supervision is required in order for the claimant to take advantage of the ability to walk. Thus a mentally handicapped adult who requires supervision before he or she can safely be allowed to walk near traffic would appear to qualify. This approach is reinforced by subs.(4) which makes it an additional condition in the case of a child under 16 that he or she should require substantially more guidance or supervision than a child of the same age in normal health. That makes it clear that the sort of supervision normally required by children may well be sufficient to enable an adult to qualify. Note that ability to use familiar routes is to be ignored so that the fact that a claimant can get to and from a local shop may not be a bar to entitlement. But, although the ability to use familiar routes is to be ignored in applying this test, such ability may still be relevant in an evidential sense in determining whether the claimant has shown at least some aspects of an inability when using unfamiliar routes. That is the approach suggested by Commissioner Parker in *R (DLA) 2/08* as follows:

> "11. In *CSDLA/12/03*, cited by the representative, at paragraph 28 I gave the two usual questions relevant to entitlement to lower mobility:
>
> '(a) First of all, [a tribunal] must determine whether, through disablement, the appellant is unable to walk on familiar routes without guidance or supervision, in which case he satisfies;
>
> (b) However, if the appellant does not qualify in this way, the tribunal must then ask if it is different if the routes are unfamiliar viz. is the appellant unable to walk on such routes without guidance or supervision? If he is not so able, he satisfies.'

12. If a claimant is unable to walk even on familiar routes without guidance or supervision, then it logically follows that he will also be unable to do so on unfamiliar ones; but the converse does not apply. It will depend upon the nature of the claimant's condition. If the complaint is of a bad left knee causing falls, then the difficulties are likely to be the same whether the route is familiar or unfamiliar; however if, for example, a claimant has genuine anxiety and panic, then what he is able to do on a familiar route does not necessarily govern his capacity on an unfamiliar one.

13. The present tribunal, in effect, ran together the two stage process; however, that is not a problem provided the relevant issues are in substance addressed, and the tribunal did so. It first of all explained (when rejecting entitlement to the higher rate of the mobility component) why it refused to accept the claimed physical difficulties in the present case (particularly the asserted collapses of the appellant's left knee), which were in the circumstances relevant also to an ability both on familiar and unfamiliar routes. It then turned to the assertion about anxiety and panic attacks, which had greater significance with respect to unfamiliar routes. For reasons it fully explained, the tribunal refused to accept that any of these claims were other than exaggerated. No error is demonstrated in the way the tribunal weighed the evidence and it was entitled to rely, if it wished, on the EMP's report.

14. In consideration of the *legal* criteria for entitlement to lower mobility, there must be ignored any ability to use familiar routes, albeit not an inability. However, when considering whether the claimant is unable to walk on unfamiliar routes without guidance or supervision, it may be *evidentially* relevant to that question as a matter of fact what, if any, are his difficulties with familiar routes. When a claimant does not differentiate between problems on familiar and unfamiliar routes, and there is nothing inherent in his condition to suggest a relevant distinction, then if he is unable to satisfy a tribunal that he has the required difficulty on familiar routes, in a context where the onus of proof on all matters lies on him, a tribunal may legitimately infer that he therefore would not need guidance or supervision on unfamiliar routes either. It is not that an adjudicating authority is requiring as a matter of law that he has difficulties on familiar routes before it will accept entitlement to lower mobility but rather that, from all the evidence, when considering his capacity on unfamiliar routes, it makes deductions from the information about his ability on familiar ones. A tribunal usually has to so reason because a claimant often says that he never walks on unfamiliar routes, which is entirely understandable.

15. In the present case, the tribunal correctly considered that, if the claimant genuinely suffered from anxiety and panic, this could make a material difference to his capacity on unfamiliar routes when compared with familiar ones. This is the clear implication of its reasoning. However, the tribunal was not satisfied of the genuine nature of his alleged problems, whether physical or mental; it neither applied the wrong legal approach nor, having regard to the evidence, drew any irrational conclusions and its explanation of which evidence was accepted, and which rejected, and why, was impeccable. It is apparent from the tribunal's whole reasoning that it answered 'no' to both the sequential questions posed in my paragraph 11 above."

Evidence as to whether a claimant has need of guidance or supervision can be derived in a number of ways. In *R 1/07(DLA)* the commissioner in Northern Ireland held that evidence of the claimant's ability to drive a motor car, was properly accepted as showing the claimant's "clear headedness and competency" which could be relevant to that aspect of her ability to walk on an unfamiliar route without the need for guidance or supervision.

The decision in *R1/07(DLA)* using the claimant's ability to drive as evidence of his ability to go out on foot without guidance or supervision has been approved in two more recent UT decisions, though with a word of caution. The caution has been to remind first-tier tribunals that such information is evidence of that ability, but is not necessarily decisive. It is suggested, for example, that the claimant's disability may be in the nature of anxiety about being outside-something that might not affect him when in his own motor car, but still be overpowering when on foot. See *JW v Secretary of State for Work and Pensions* [2012] UKUT 336 (AAC).

In *RR v SSWP* [2009] UKUT 272 (AAC) Judge Levenson considered the case of a claimant who, because of his mental state, frequently found himself in strange places not knowing how he came to be there. The fact that he could then get himself back home safely by asking for assistance and by using his mobile phone was not relevant, said the judge, because the test was whether he needed supervision to avoid getting into strange places to begin with.

The meaning of "guidance" and "supervision" in this context was considered in *CDLA/42/94* in which the Commissioner summarised his conclusions as follows: **1.259**

"(i) The meaning of guidance or supervision must be considered within the context of action which is aimed at enabling the claimant to take advantage of the faculty of walking despite the limits imposed by her physical or mental condition. It is not a condition that guidance or supervision should be necessary to avoid a risk of danger to the claimant or others.

(j) Guidance means the action of directing or leading. It may, for example, be constituted by physically directing or leading the claimant or by oral direction, persuasion or suggestion.

(k) Supervision, in the context of section 73(1)(d), means accompanying the claimant and at the least monitoring the claimant or the circumstances for signs of a need to intervene so as to prevent the claimant's ability to take advantage of the faculty of walking being compromised. Other, more active, measures may also amount to supervision. The monitoring does not cease to fall within the meaning of supervision by reason only that intervention by the person accompanying the claimant has not in the past actually been necessary.

(l) The fact that the claimant derives reassurance from the presence of the other person does not prevent action which would otherwise fall within point (j) or (k) from being guidance or supervision."

In *R(DLA) 3/04* Commissioner Rowland considered the case of a claimant who, because of her state of anxiety and depression, suffered severe panic attacks if she tried to walk out on her own. She could only walk for any significant distance if she was accompanied by one of her family who would provide continuous reassurance and encouragement. The Commissioner held that this level of support could constitute guidance and supervision. He went on to hold that her claim was not precluded by reg.12(7) of the Disability Living Allowance Regulations because her state of anxiety was a symptom of a mental disability provided for under reg.12(8).

In *SSWP v PA* [2010] UKUT 401 (AAC) Judge Mark upheld a decision in favour of a claimant for lower rate mobility component who suffered severely from Crohn's Disease which made him unexpectedly and urgently incontinent. The judge held, that on the evidence that had been before the tribunal and before the Upper Tribunal, that the claimant had shown a sufficient need for supervision in assisting him to find a public toilet and assisting him in cleaning himself.

In *CDLA/52/94* the claimant suffered from epilepsy and the Commissioner said: **1.260**

"7. Where a person has only occasional fits, the expression 'most of the time' focuses attention on the needs of the claimant between fits, rather than during or immediately after them. Therefore, so far as epilepsy is concerned, guidance may be of little relevance. The question then arises whether a person who is accompanying the claimant is thereby exercising 'supervision'. . . .

8. It is likely that a claimant who, due to epilepsy, satisfies the condition of section 72(1)(b)(ii) and is entitled to the care component of disability living allowance on

the ground that he or she 'requires from another person . . . continual supervision throughout the day in order to avoid substantial danger to himself or others' will also satisfy the condition of section 73(i)(d). What is less clear is whether a person who fails to satisfy the condition of section 72(1)(b)(ii), because he or she merely needs a person to be nearby, will also fail to satisfy the condition of section 73(1)(d), because all that can be shown is a need to be accompanied when walking. Is a person accompanying such a claimant out walking in any different position from that of a person 'who keeps himself available to be called' while the claimant is at home?

9. It is, I think, important to bear in mind that Nicholls L.J. [in *Moran*—see note to s.72(1), above] did not exclude the possibility that a person 'who keeps himself available to be called' *might* be exercising supervision. 'It will all depend on the facts of the case.' In my view, the most significant factor is that a person who is keeping himself available while the claimant is at home (or at work) is likely to be able to get on with his or her own activities, whereas having to accompany a claimant is likely to preclude that and, unless he or she wishes to go on the same journey anyway, there is inevitably an element of service involved. It is that element of service that is significant. In my view, the use of the word 'monitoring' by the Commissioner in *CDLA/42/94* reflects the facts of the case before the Commissioner and the need for there to be some element of service rather than mere presence. In a case where a claimant can give warning to a person who is accompanying him or her, I do not think that it can reasonably be said that the accompanying person is 'monitoring' the claimant. However, even though there may be an absence of monitoring, I take the view that a need to be accompanied when walking may amount to a need for supervision. In practice, where epilepsy is concerned, the focus is likely to be on the reasonableness of the claim that there is a *need* to be accompanied when walking a modest distance. Relevant issues will be the likelihood of a fit occurring when the claimant is out walking and the risk of substantial danger if one does occur then. There may well be a greater risk of danger when the claimant has a fit out in the street than when he or she is at home."

1.261 In other cases, however, it had been suggested that if supervision were of a kind that might have qualified the claimant under s.72(1)(b) for the care component, it could not at the same time be used as part of a claim under this section. That difference of opinion was put to rest by the decision of a Tribunal of Commissioners in four joined appeals reported as *R(DLA) 4/01*.

The Tribunal finds nothing in the law to prevent the same type of assistance enabling the claimant to qualify for both parts of the benefit. On the other hand the Commissioners reject the suggestion that a claimant who qualifies for the care condition should be passported automatically to the other. While they accept that many such claimants are likely to succeed to both components, they emphasise that the test applicable to each component must be considered separately and applied by the decision-maker to the facts found in respect of each claim.

The decision will enable many claimants who are mentally ill, or epileptic, or deaf or blind to qualify for the mobility component. Three of the cases joined in this appeal, and several of those in which Commissioners had previously disagreed dealt with deaf claimants. In this decision the Commissioners dealt specifically with the problems of pre-lingually deaf claimants. In such cases, they thought, it would be quite appropriate to find that the claimant required guidance (or possibly supervision) all of the time he was walking over unfamiliar routes because without that company he would not attempt that route for fear of becoming lost and being unable to communicate effectively with anyone. They accept that supervision must require something more than just keeping another company, but they hold that a person who is present to lend assistance whenever that may become necessary is supervising in the sense of being ancillary to an episode of attention. In any case where the claimant is unable to communicate and is undertaking unfamiliar routes such attention may be frequent enough to be guidance. The Commissioners emphasise that such cases depend upon clear findings of fact as to the claimant's ability to communicate by writing, or lip reading and to his ability to read maps and other directions.

The Tribunal in *R(DLA) 4/01* also took the opportunity of considering whether the words "cannot take advantage of" should be read as conditioned by some word such as "reasonably" so that a claimant need not show that, without assistance, he is totally unable to take advantage of outdoor walking. The Commissioners held it is unnecessary to read in any such words because the paragraph as a whole makes it apparent that some outside walking ability is assumed, for example, the claimant's inability need apply only to unfamiliar routes, and to most of the time. The Tribunal felt that it could safely be left to the good sense of decision-makers to decide when a claimant might otherwise require assistance over unfamiliar routes.

This does not however resolve the difference between Commissioners over **1.262** whether it must be shown that the claimant is capable of walking out of doors when given the benefit of guidance and supervision. Commissioners have differed as to whether guidance or supervision will only be relevant if it will enable the claimant to overcome his or her inability to make use of the faculty of walking. In *CDLA/42/94* the Commissioner said that "it would be absurd if a claimant whose disablement was so severe that she was not able to take advantage of the faculty of walking on unfamiliar routes out of doors even with guidance or supervision was excluded from s.73(1)(d). Because of the negative formulation of the provision, a claimant does not necessarily have to show an ability to take advantage of that faculty with guidance or supervision." However, in *CDLA/2364/95* (followed in *CSDLA/12/2003*), the Commissioner rejected that approach and decided that a person who suffered from claustrophobia and agoraphobia and who could not be persuaded to walk outdoors would not be entitled to the lower rate of the mobility component. These latter decisions have been upheld by the Court of Appeal in NI in *Mongan v Department of Social Development* [2005] NICA 16. That court holds that a claimant must show that the guidance or supervision will enhance the claimant's walking ability. But a person can qualify for mobility component at the lower rate under paragraph (d) even though they may never undertake to walk on unfamiliar routes. The test is hypothetical in the sense that the claimant is entitled if they could not walk that route without guidance or supervision — it matters not that they would not walk there anyway. In *R(DLA) 6/03* the tribunal had found that the claimant (to whom they had already refused mobility allowance at the higher rate) would not have gone walking on unfamiliar routes (or seemingly on familar routes) because of the danger of falling. It seems that the claimant must have said that the provision of supervision would have made no difference to her because the chairman went on to remark "There is no point in making an award if its purpose is frustrated". The Commissioner allowed the appeal remarking that the element of an award being frustrated is provided for in subs.(8), but that provision requires that the claimant be *unable to* benefit from locomotion not merely that he chooses not to. Notice that in this case the claimant *could* have walked on unfamiliar routes with supervision—it was simply that she chose not to, whereas in *CDLA/2364/95* the claimant was unable to walk outside because their medical condition prevented them from doing so even with supervision.

The decision in *CDLA/2364/95* has been followed and that in *Mongan v Department of Social Development* applied in *KH v SSWP (DLA)* [2015] UKUT 8 (AAC). This was another case where the claimant had for many years refused to leave her home. Evidence suggested that no amount of persuasion would encourage her to do so. Although the decision of the FTT seemed to swing between an approach based on *para. (d)* and one based on *subs. (8)* (claimant able to benefit from facilities for enhanced locomotion) Judge Hemingway holds that their decision was correctly decided on the basis that a claimant should succeed under *para. (d)* only if it can be shown that with guidance or supervision they would be able to walk out of doors. Note, however that this is exactly the sort of claim which may now succeed under the Personal Independence Payment provisions. (See descriptor (e) in the Mobility Activities in Sch.1 of those regulations).

In *CDLA/835/97*, the Commissioner directed that, in considering entitlement to the lower rate of the mobility component under s.73(1)(d), the tribunal to whom he was referring the case should exclude any supervision required to stop the claimant from "going off and getting into trouble shoplifting and the like." He held that supervision to prevent a claimant getting himself into criminal activity or moral danger was outside the scope of the subsection. This part of the decision was, however, set aside (by consent) by the Court of Appeal in *V (a child) v Secretary of State for Social Security* (February 23, 2001), and *CDLA/3781/2003* holds that this has the effect of rendering all of *CDLA/835/97* of no legal effect.

In *AR v SSWP* [2013] UKUT 463 (AAC) the claimant suffered from hyperacusis—an extreme intolerance to noise. In his claim form he said that exposure to noise made him anxious and aggressive. He had been arrested on several occasions as a result of confrontational behaviour resulting from this medical condition. He claimed mobility component on the ground that he needed someone to accompany him to provide reassurance and supervision when walking outside most of the time. The FTT that heard his appeal against refusal of benefit held, in a carefully reasoned decision, that a person accompanying him would not be providing "guidance or supervision" and that any guidance or supervision that was available would, in any case, make no difference to him. In the UT Judge Wikeley expressed his sympathy with the FTT in dealing with a difficult and novel case only on the paper record before them, however, he held that on both these points there was an error of law and directed that the case be reheard before a fresh tribunal. The representative of the Secretary of State had supported the appeal on both grounds, though she argued too, that mobility allowance could not be awarded if the purpose of supervision were to prevent or dissuade the claimant from engaging in criminal activity. Judge Wikeley says this proposition must be approached with caution in the light of cases referred to above. It is possible that benefit might be available, he suggests, if the supervision is needed to prevent a person with a psychiatric condition engaging in criminal or at least anti-social behaviour.

In *C19/98(DLA)*, the Northern Ireland Commissioner holds that the use of suitable aids and appliances can be taken into account when considering s.73(1)(d) even though there is no specific provision to that effect.

Subsection (1A)

1.263 This means that a child can qualify for the higher rate of mobility component from the age of three years, but for the lower rate only from the age of five years.

Subsection (1AB)

1.264 The level of visual impairment is specified in subs.(1A) of reg.12 of the DLA regulations.

Subsection (2)

1.265 Regulation 12(2) of the DLA Regulations 1991, made under subs.(5), defines blindness and deafness for the purposes of para.(a). It is not necessary for the claimant to have total loss of vision and hearing (see the note to that regulation). Reg.12(3), made under para.(b), makes it a further condition of entitlement that the combined effects of the claimant's blindness and deafness should make him unable, without the assistance of another, to walk to any intended or required destination while out of doors.

Subsection (3)

1.266 This provision is intended to reduce the immense difficulties caused in mobility allowance cases by the fact that only virtual inability to walk due to *physical* disablement could be taken into account. Some of those who would qualify under this subsection would also qualify under subs.(1)(a) but adjudication in such cases is made much simpler by this new provision. The conditions imposed by this subsection are quite stringent but those who fail to qualify may be able to qualify under subs.(1)

(a) for the higher rate (if they can show physical disablement) or under subs.(1)(d) for the lower rate.

Regulations 12(5) and 12(6) of the DLA Regulations 1991, made under subs.(6), specify who falls within paras (a) and (b) as suffering from mental impairment and displaying severe behavioural problems. A person falls within para.(a) if "he suffers from a state of arrested development or incomplete physical development of the brain, which results in severe impairment of intelligence and social functioning". In *M (A child) v Chief Adjudication Officer*, reported as *R(DLA) 1/00*, the Court of Appeal held that an I.Q. test of the claimant was not conclusive of whether the claimant satisfied this test. It has been usual to look for a score of less than 55 as indicative of a severe impairment of intelligence. In this case the claimant was autistic and had an I.Q. score considerably above that level. The Court of Appeal hold that the claimant's I.Q. is only one of several factors that are relevant. It is a useful starting point, but a full evaluation of intelligence and social functioning should include other elements of social interaction, "sagacity" and "insight". A person falls within para. (b) if the disruptive behaviour "(a) is extreme, (b) regularly requires another person to intervene and physically restrain him in order to prevent him causing physical injury to himself or another, or damage to property, and (c) is so unpredicable that he requires another person to be present and watching over him whenever he is awake." In *CSDLA/202/2007*, a claim for higher rate mobility component made on behalf of a child of 3, who was autistic, was returned for consideration by a new tribunal because the first appeal tribunal had failed to consider both of the possible routes by which such a claim might succeed; *viz.* either under s.73(1)(a) (temporary paralysis as to walking resulting from the autism), or, by s.73(1)(c) (severely mentally impaired and severe behavioural problems, etc.). In doing so, Commissioner Parker adopts both *R(DLA)1/00* and *R(DLA)7/02*. Both of these routes now have age limitations in respect of a child—see subs.(1A) above.

Under para.(c), it is also necessary for the claimant to satisfy the conditions for the highest rate of the care component. It is not clear why entitlement to an allowance in respect of mobility outdoors should require satisfaction of the night attendance condition for the care component, and this may be a major obstacle for some claimants. Subs.(7) has the effect that those who are deemed to satisfy one or both of the attendance conditions for the care component because they undergo renal dialysis or are terminally ill may rely on the same provisions for the purpose of satisfying para.(c)

Subsection (4A)

Subsection (4A) imposes similar conditions on a claim made under s.73(1)(d) 1.267
in respect of a child, to those that are provided in s.72(1A). A recent decision of Commissioner Parker (*CSDLA/91/2003*) applies the same reasoning to the conditions for mobility as that adopted for the care component. When guidance and supervision is required it must be substantially more than would be required for a child of that age of normal physical and mental development. In judging what is substantially more, account must be taken of both the quality and the quantity of the supervision. Thus where all children might need to be accompanied on a certain route, a disabled child who required support, or restraint, or encouragement, or even constant surveillance should qualify. This has been confirmed by the decision in *KC-MS v SSWP* [2015] UKUT 284 (AAC). The FTT had rejected an appeal by the mother of a six-year-old child in respect of the middle rate of benefit. In doing so they observed that no six-year-old would be permitted to go out on unfamiliar routes without supervision. Judge Gray allowed an appeal pointing out that the test was not whether all such children would require supervision, but whether this disabled child required substantially more supervision, or a different kind of supervision, than that required by a normal child of that age.

Note too, the decision in *BM v SSWP* (CDLA) [2014] UKUT 18 (AAC); [2015] AACR 29 where Judge Markus has given a careful analysis of the provisions in s.72 (1A). Although the wording is not identical the approach adopted should be the same.

Subsections (5) and (6)

1.268 See regs 12 to 12c of the DLA Regulations, 1991.

Subsection (8)

1.269 This is in the same terms as s.37A(2)(b) of the Social Security Act 1975 relating to mobility allowance which was considered by a Commissioner in *R(M) 2/83*. He approved a passage in the second edition of Ogus and Barendt, *The Law of Social Security*, in which they said:

> "This obviously excludes human vegetables and those whom it is unsafe to move, but it is arguable that of the remainder there will be few who will not receive some benefit from the occasional sortie, and it is not easy to draw a line between the deserving and the undeserving except on some arbitrary basis."

The Commissioner pointed out that the word "benefit" was a wide one and that the provision contained the words "from time to time" but he added a further category of excluded persons, "that is persons so severely mentally deranged that a high degree of supervision and restraint would be required to prevent them either injuring themselves or others."

Although the claimant need show only that he will benefit from locomotion "from time to time" during "most" of the period in respect of which his claim is made it is necessary, as well, to satisfy *subs (1)* of this section that the claimant can be said to be unable to walk "throughout" that period.

This has been given a meaning consistent with the approach adopted in *Secretary of State v Moyna* [2003] UKHL 44, (that it is a matter of judgement rather than arithmetical calculation), but unless the need for help is more than brief and more frequent than occasional, it will not satisfy this test- see the decision of Judge Rowland in *CDLA/496/2008* noted above in relation to *subs (1)*. Whereas the words in these two subsections might appear to be inconsistent they should not be so if proper regard is given to their respective purposes. *Subs (1)* sets the standard to qualify for the benefit; *subs (8)* deprives an otherwise qualified claimant of his benefit if he cannot make sufficient use of it.

The expression "from time to time" conditions the claimant's ability to benefit in the sense that he might enjoy even just an occasional outing, though his need for assistance to achieve locomotion might be constant. But even if the claimant's need for assistance does apply throughout the period his claim would still fail if his ability to benefit from locomotion is only on rare occasions because then he would not be able to do so "most" of the time.

In *CDLA/2142/2005* the Commissioner agrees with the decision in *CSDLA/12/2003* that the claimant, who was agoraphobic, must be willing to make use of the assistance by walking out of doors so as to show that she would benefit from enhanced locomotion. But he returned the case to a new tribunal with the suggestion to consider whether walking within the confines of the claimant's own back garden, which was all that she could be persuaded to do, could satisfy that test if it were beneficial to the health, both mental and physical, of the claimant.

This matter has been considered again by Judge Wikeley in the Upper Tribunal. See *BP v SSWP* [2009] UKUT 90 (AAC). The claimant was a middle-aged man who suffered from chronic fatigue syndrome and ME. He described himself in the claim papers as "bedridden and housebound" and had not in fact been further than his bedroom and the bathroom on the upper floor of his home for several years. He had been in receipt of the mobility component at the higher rate, but on a renewal claim the DM took the view that subs.(8) applied and refused the claim. This decision was upheld by the First-tier Tribunal. Judge Wikeley allowed an appeal. He draws attention to the lack of any evidence that the claimant was prevented from leaving his house (or going downstairs) because of any mental state that prevented him from doing so. The limitation on the claimant's going out seemed to stem from the weakness of his legs and consequent inability to get down stairs; indeed, his wife gave evidence that if there were a man to carry him down to a wheelchair, she could certainly take him out in the car with her. The judge reiterated the point that the operation of this subsection should be limited to those claimants for whom it would be impossible to be taken out and those for whom it would present a danger to their health. On that basis the cases of patients suffering from agoraphobia would be explicable either on the basis that their refusal to leave the home was an instance of impossibility, (they could hardly be forced to leave even if for their own good), or, of creating a danger to their mental health, again, if they were forced to leave.

The Judge deals with two other points. First, that the argument presented on behalf of the claimant that because he lived in a country location he needed his car so that his wife could collect medicines for him was not sufficient for him to show that he would benefit by "enhanced facilities for locomotion." Judge Wikeley holds that the enhanced facility must refer to the claimant's own locomotion to be of benefit to him. 1.270

Secondly, the Judge draws attention also to the caveat that Commissioner Morcom had added to his decision in *R (M) 2/83*. The commissioner had suggested that there might be a further category of excluded claimants—those who were so mentally deranged that they would require a high degree of supervision and security to avoid danger to themselves and others. Judge Wikeley suggests that this qualification might need to be reconsidered in light of the fact that mobility component, (as distinct from the old Mobility Benefit that was in force at the time of the earlier case) extends now to those who are "severely mentally impaired" and those who display "severe behavioural problems".

This case is useful also in demonstrating the importance of the difference between a decision that records the evidence, and one that makes findings of fact. An extensive, even verbatim, record of the evidence is no substitute for a statement of the facts as found by the tribunal.

In *CDLA/1639/2006* the Commissioner held that a tribunal which allowed a claim for higher rate mobility component in respect of a claimant suffering from severe attacks of migraine had erred in law by overlooking the effects of s.73(8). As the commissioner pointed out the only time that the claimant would have had any need for attention was during the time he was suffering a migraine attack; at that same time however, on his own evidence, he was compelled to sit or to lie down, so no amount of assistance could aid his mobility.

And see too *CDLA/496/2008* noted above in relation to *subs. (1)*, where it was held that the period for which the claimant required to be resting and usually asleep, could not be included as part of the time in which she could benefit from facilities for enhanced locomotion.

Subsection (9)

Paragraph (a) imposes the three-month qualifying period but this is deemed to be satisfied in the case of a person who is terminally ill (see subs.(12)). If a person is entitled to the lower rate of the mobility component by virtue of satisfying the condition in subs.(1)(d) and his or her condition deteriorates so that he or she would satisfy one or other of the conditions in subs.(1)(a), (b) or (c) the effect of subs.(11)(a) is that the claimant must still wait three months before qualifying for the higher rate unless terminally ill. Under s.76(1), an award cannot usually be made before the date of claim which is determined in accordance with reg.6(1) and (5) of the Social Security (Claims and Payments) Regulations 1987 (see Vol.III of this work). Reg.11 of the DLA Regulations prescribes, for the purpose of para.(a)(ii) a period of three months ending on the day on which the claimant was last entitled to the component if that was not more than two years before the current period of entitlement would otherwise begin. This has the practical effect in most cases that the three-month qualifying period is deemed to be satisfied if the current claim is within two years of a previous period of entitlement at the relevant rate. 1.271

Under para.4(2) of Sch.1 to the DLA Regulations, a period of six months is substituted for the period of three months in para.(a) in the case of a person over the age of 65 who makes a claim for the mobility component and is entitled to do so because he or she was formerly entitled to a car or other assistance under an invalid vehicle scheme.

Paragraph (b) requires that a person should be expected to satisfy the conditions for the component for six months, unless he or she is expected to die sooner.

Although this means that six months will normally be the minimum period for which an award will be made, this section does not prevent an award for a lesser period when that is appropriate. In *R(DLA) 11/02* the claimant had applied unsuccessfully and then appealed. Before that appeal could be heard her condition had deteriorated and she made a fresh claim that was allowed. The Commissioner held that an award of less than six months could be made to fill the gap between the date when she was now regarded as qualifying and the date when the existing award commenced even though that was less than six months. This period of six months begins as the three-month (or six-month for those over 65) qualifying period ends and both conditions are intended to ensure that only the chronically disabled are entitled to DLA.

Note that since the condition is prospective the matter must be determined on the basis of the information available and the prognosis at the time of the claim. For the effect of this, see note to s.72(2)(b) above.

Subsections (10) and (11)

1.272 The higher rate is payable if one or other of the conditions in subs. (a), (ab), (b), or (c) is satisfied and the lower rate is payable in any other case. In *KS v SSWP* [2013] UKUT 390 (AAC) it was argued that the limitation of the higher rate of the mobility component to conditions having a physical cause was overruled by the provisions of the Equality Act 2010 as being discriminatory on the grounds of mental disablement. The argument failed because the terms of that act specify that nothing is unlawful if that action is required by the terms of legislation (see Sch.22, para.(1) of that Act). To be entitled at the higher rate, it is not necessary that the *same* condition should have been satisfied throughout the qualifying period and the period of the award.

Subsection (12)

1.273 Under s.66(2), a person is "terminally ill" if "he suffers from a progressive disease and his death in consequence of that disease can reasonably be expected within 12 months". See the notes to that section.

The effect of this subsection is that a terminally ill person is deemed to satisfy the three-month qualifying period (or the six-month period in the case of a person over 65 formerly entitled to an invalid vehicle). Note also that reg.2(4) of the DLA Regulations relaxes the presence conditions for terminally ill claimants so that it is not necessary for them to have been in Great Britain before the day in respect of which the claim is made. However, while terminally ill claimants are deemed to satisfy the conditions for the highest rate of the care component, they are not deemed to satisfy any of the conditions for the mobility component except subs.(3)(c) (see subs.(7)). This is confirmed in *R(DLA) 7/06.*

Subsection (13)

1.274 Sch.2 to the DLA Regulations makes provision allowing former invalid vehicle scheme beneficiaries to be deemed to satisfy the conditions for the higher rate of the mobility component and Sch.1, para.4 permits them to claim the mobility component even if they are aged over 65.

Subsection (14)

1.275 There is specific provision in the legislation governing disability working allowance which ensures that disability living allowance is not to be treated as income

(Sch.3, para.4 to the Disability Working Allowance (General) Regulations 1991). But *quaere* whether para.8(a) of Sch.4 to those Regulations (which allows arrears of disability living allowance to be disregarded as capital only for 52 weeks and so implies it should be taken into account after that) is overridden by this subsection so that the arrears may continue to be disregarded for longer. The power to make regulations under this subsection is not referred to in the preamble to those Regulations. This provision also applies to any local authority scheme applying a means test where there is a statutory power to make charges for services, e.g. charges for home helps under para.3 of Sch.8 to the National Health Service Act 1977.

Mobility component for certain persons eligible for invalid carriages

74.—(1) Regulations may provide for the issue, variation and cancellation of certificates in respect of prescribed categories of persons to whom this section applies; and a person in respect of whom such a certificate is issued shall, during any period while the certificate is in force, be deemed for the purposes of section 73 above to satisfy the condition mentioned in subsection (1)(a) of that section and to fall within paragraphs (a) and (b) of subsection (9) by virtue of having satisfied or being likely to satisfy that condition throughout both the periods mentioned in those paragraphs. 1.276

(2) This section applies to any person whom the Secretary of State considers—

(a) was on 1st January 1976 in possession of an invalid carriage or other vehicle provided in pursuance of section 33 of the Health Services and Public Health Act 1968 (which related to vehicles for persons suffering from physical defect or disability) or receiving payments in pursuance of subsection (3) of that section; or

(b) had at that date, or at a later date specified by the Secretary of State, made an application which the Secretary of State approved for such a carriage or vehicle or for such payments; or

(c) was, both at some time during a prescribed period before that date and at some time during a prescribed period after that date, in possession of such a carriage or vehicle or receiving such payments; or

(d) would have been, by virtue of any of the preceding paragraphs, a person to whom this section applies but for some error or delay for which in the opinion of the Secretary of State the person was not responsible and which was brought to the attention of the Secretary of State within the period of one year beginning with 30th March 1977 (the date of the passing of the Social Security (Miscellaneous Provisions) Act 1977, section 13 of which made provisions corresponding to the provision made by this section).

DERIVATION

SS(MP)A 1977 s.13. 1.277

GENERAL NOTE

For regulations, see reg.13 of, and Sch.2 to, the Social Security (Disability Living Allowance) Regulations 1991, which are treated by s.2(2) of the Social Security (Consequential Provisions) Act 1992 as having been made under this section. 1.278

Mobility allowance (which was introduced by s.22 of the Social Security Pensions Act 1975 and was later replaced by the higher rate of the mobility component of disability living allowance) was intended to replace the provision of invalid vehicles and the alternative system of paying for vehicles. Those who were already entitled to vehicles or payments under the Health Services and Public Health Act 1968 on January 1, 1976, have retained the right to them but may at any time exchange them for the higher rate of the mobility component of disability living allowance, even if they are over the usual maximum age of 65.

[1 Persons who have attained pensionable age]

1.279 **75.**—(1) Except to the extent to which regulations provide otherwise, no person shall be entitled to either component of a disability living allowance for any period after he attains [1 pensionable age] otherwise than by virtue of an award made before he attains that age.

(2) Regulations may provide in relation to persons who are entitled to a component of a disability living allowance by virtue of subsection (1) above that any provisions of this Act which relates to disability living allowance, other than section 74 above, so far as it so relates, and any provision of the Administration Act which is relevant to disability living allowance—

(a) shall have effect subject to modifications, additions or amendments; or

(b) shall not have effect.

Amendment

1. Pensions Act 2007 Sch.1 Pt 8 para.42. This amendment was originally not to have effect until April 6, 2024, but now has had effect from April 6, 2018—see Pensions Act 2011 s.1.

Derivation

1.280 SSA 1975 s.37ZD

General Note

1.281 Note: the amendment to subs.(1) above to "pensionable age" did not have effect until April 6, 2018. Until that time the section should be read as if it retained the words "the age of 65".

The general rule established by this subsection is that a person is not entitled to DLA for any period after reaching the age of 65 unless entitled by virtue of an award made before he or she reaches that age. Reg.3 of, Sch.1 to, the DLA Regulations are made under this section.

Note that the age of 65 is to be replaced by the phrase "pensionable age" by Pensions Act 2007 s.13, but the effect of this amendment was postponed until April 2024. That date is now due to be brought forward to December 6, 2018. (Pensions Act 2011 Sch.1).

An attempt was made in *NT v SSWP* [2009] UKUT 37(AAC); *R(DLA) 1/09* to show that the denial of mobility component to those over pensionable age was unlawful as a denial of the claimant's human rights by reason of discriminating on the ground of age. The judge of the Upper Tribunal, Judge Levenson, found that a claim to mobility component did engage the rights of the claimant under Article 1 of the First Protocol, and her rights under Article 8. He found, as well, that a distinction based upon age was capable of being discrimination under Article 14, but even so, the judge disallowed the appeal. He accepted that the

DWP had demonstrated a rational and proportionate justification for the difference in treatment because the mobility component of DLA had always been intended to benefit those of working age who found that their earning capacity, as well as their life style, was affected adversely by their disability. When the claimant reached an age at which earning could be assumed to be replaced by entitlement to other benefits, such as retirement pension, the reason for mobility component had largely ceased.

And note too *GS v SSWP* (DLA) [2015] UKUT 687 (AAC). The claimant had previously been in receipt of a mobility component when he lived in this country, but that entitlement ceased when he emigrated to another EU country. He returned to live here after he had attained the age of 65 and his claim was refused. His argument in the UT that refusal on the ground of his age was a denial of the freedom of movement was rejected.

Regulation 3 originally provided for two exceptions to the general rule. First, a person who would have qualified at the age of 65 could be awarded DLA provided a claim was made before he or she reached the age of 66. That provision was revoked from October 6, 1997. Secondly, if a claimant reaches the age of 65 during the three-month qualifiying period for either component, having claimed before reaching that age, then the claimant is not prejudiced by the fact that the award is not made, or effective, until after his or her 65th birthday. There is a further exception under para.4 of Sch.1 of the DLA Regulations allowing a former invalid vehicle scheme beneficiary to qualify for the mobility component. Sch.1 to the DLA Regulations also enables further awards to be made to those people who have established entitlement to DLA beyond the age of 65, although there are some restrictions.

Where the claimant's entitlement to DLA is revised after reaching the age of 65 and it is concluded that he is no longer entitled to the care component at the higher or middle rate, or the mobility component at the higher rate, it is not possible for him to qualify then for the lowest rate of the care component, nor for the lower rate of mobility component, if the review is based upon a change of circumstances occurring after he has reached the age of 65 (see *R(DLA) 5/02*). Where, however, the revision is based upon a change of circumstances that occurred before he reached that age (or is based upon a mistake of law or fact made at the initial award, or a subsequent renewal, before that age), the claimant may be entitled to an award at the lowest rate for care and for the lower rate of mobility where his condition would justify such an award from the appropriate date before the age of 65. See reg.3 and Sch.1 the Disability Living Allowance Regulations 1991 and the decision of Commissioner Parker, *CSDLA/388/2000* and see too *CDLA/754/2000* where the Commissioner draws attention, for the benefit of a new tribunal, to the effect of paras 3 and 5 of Sch.1 which is that in an appropriate case a claimant whose entitlement to the DLA components ceases even when he is over the age of 65 may have those entitlements restored if his condition then deteriorates again. See also the decisions in *CDLA/301/05* noted after Sch.1, in which the Commissioner also holds that a claim for the lowest rate of DLA may succeed even if the need for that care developed after the age of 65, so long as the basis of the review was something that occurred before that age.

People over 65 who are not entitled to DLA may instead qualify for attendance allowance under s.64. Note that although attendance allowance has no equivalent to the mobility component provided under DLA it is possible for a claimant who requires assistance in moving about to include that help in the assessment of their need for attention in connection with their bodily functions—in that case the bodily function of mobilising, whether within doors or out of doors. Thus, for someone in a wheelchair who requires another person to push them about, that assistance can count towards the frequency and extent of the assistance that they require: see *JB v SSWP* [2015] UKUT 361 (AAC).

Disability living allowance—supplementary

1.282 **76.**—(1) Subject to subsection (2) below, a person shall not be entitled to a disability living allowance for any period preceding the date on which a claim for it is made or treated as made by him or on his behalf.

(2) Notwithstanding anything in subsection (1) above, provision may be made by regulations for a person to be entitled to a component of a disability living allowance for a period preceding the date on which a claim for such an allowance is made or treated as made by him or on his behalf if he has previously been entitled to that component.

(3) For the purposes of sections 72(5) and 73(12) above where—

(a) a person purports to make a claim for a disability living allowance on behalf of another; and

(b) the claim is made expressly on the ground that the person on whose behalf it purports to be made is terminally ill,

that person shall be regarded as making the claim notwithstanding that it is made without his knowledge or authority.

DERIVATION

1.283 SSA 1975 s.37ZE.

GENERAL NOTE

1.284 This section makes provision for claims to DLA.

Subsections (1) and (2)

1.285 This states the general rule that claims for DLA cannot be backdated to cover a period before the date on which a claim is made or *is treated as made*. The general rule has been criticised as unduly severe. Claims for most other social security benefits can be backdated, including benefits in respect of incapacity for work which suggests that the gathering of medical evidence in respect of past periods is not an insuperable problem. It should, however, be noted that the three-month qualifying period (six months for people over 65) is normally before the date of claim, so to that extent, claims can be regarded as being backdated over that period. There is also some further flexibility. Reg.6(1)(a) of the Claims and Payments Regulations 1987 provides that a claim shall be treated as made on the date it is received in an appropriate office of the Department of Social Security. Reg.4(1) requires a claim to be made in writing either on a claim form or in such other manner as the Secretary of State may accept as suffcient. If the Secretary of State does not accept a document as a claim, he may ask the claimant to complete a proper claim form or simply to give further information. If that is done within a reasonable period, the claim is then treated as having been made when the original document was received (regs 4(7) and 6(1)(b)). More specific provision is made in respect of DLA and attendance allowance in reg.6(8) under which a claim is treated as having been made when a request for a claim form is received by the Department, provided that the claimant duly completes and returns the claim form within six weeks or such longer period as the Secretary of State considers reasonable. Leaflets widely available to claimants include requests for claim forms rather than claim forms themselves which are bulky documents. If a claim is delayed in the post owing to industrial action, it is treated as having been made on the date it would have arrived in the ordinary course of post (reg.6(7)). Until October 6, 1997, reg.5 of the DLA Regulations, made under subs.(2), allowed a claim to be backdated to the end of a previous period of entitlement to the same component of DLA, provided that the renewal claim was made within six months of the end of that period of entitlement and the claimant satisfied the conditions of entitlement throughout the intervening period. For these purposes, a previous period of entitlement to attendance allowance was treated as a period of entitlement to the care component and a previous period of entitlement to mobility allowance was treated as a period of entitlement to the mobility component.

Subsection (3)

This is necessary to enable a person to make a claim for DLA on behalf of someone who is terminally ill in a case when the claimant is not to be told of the prognosis in his case. 1.286

Guardian's allowance

Guardian's allowance

77. *Omitted.* See *Vol.IV: HMRC-administered Social Security Benefits and Scotland.* 1.287

Benefits for the aged

Category C and Category D retirement pensions and other benefits for the aged

78.—(1) [3...] 1.288

(2) [3...]

(3) A person who is over the age of 80 [3 , who reached pensionable age before 6 April 2016 and who satisfies] such conditions as may be prescribed shall be entitled to a Category D retirement pension at the appropriate weekly rate if—

(a) he is not entitled to a Category A, Category B or Category C retirement pension; or

(b) he is entitled to such a pension, but it is payable at a weekly rate which, disregarding those elements specified in subsection (4) below, is less than the appropriate weekly rate.

(4) The elements referred to in subsection (3)(b) above are—

(a) any additional pension;

(b) any increase so far as attributable to—

(i) any additional pension, or

(ii) any increase in a guaranteed minimum pension;

(c) any graduated retirement benefit; and

(d) [2 . . .]

(5) [3...]

(6) The appropriate weekly rate of a Category D retirement pension shall be that specified in Schedule 4, Part III, paragraph 7.

(7) Entitlement to a [3...] Category D retirement pension shall continue throughout the pensioner's life.

(8) A [3...] Category D retirement pension shall not be payable for any period falling before the day on which the pensioner's entitlement is to be regarded as commencing for that purpose by virtue of section 5(1)(k) of the Administration Act.

(9) Regulations may provide for the payment—

(a) to a widow whose husband was over pensionable age on 5th July 1948; or
(b) to a woman whose marriage to a husband who was over pensionable age on that date was terminated otherwise than by his death.

of a Category C retirement pension or of benefit corresponding to a widow's pension or a widowed mother's allowance; and any such retirement pension or any such benefit shall be at the prescribed rate.

AMENDMENTS

1. Tax Credits Act 2002 Sch.6 (April 6, 2003).
2. Pensions Act 2007 Sch.1 para.13 (September 26, 2007).
3. Pensions Act 2014 Sch.12 para.84 (April 6, 2016)

GENERAL NOTE

1.289 The repeal of subss.(1), (2) and (5) remove entitlement to Category C pensions generally, following the policy of the Pensions Act 2014, leaving only existing pensions and transitional cases to be dealt with under that legislation. The amendments also close off Category D pensions to those reaching state pensionable age on or after April 6, 2016.

In *Secretary of State for Work and Pensions v JG (RP)* [2013] UKUT 300 (AAC) Judge White of the Upper Tribunal discussed the application of the section to a claim for a category D pension in the context of a claimant who spent considerable periods of his life outside the United Kingdom in various countries including Gibraltar and the Isle of Man. That decision was over-ruled by the Court of Appeal as *Secretary of State for Work and Pensions v Garland* [2014] EWCA Civ 1550.

Age addition

1.290 **79.**—(1) A person who is over the age of 80 and entitled to a retirement pension of any category [1 under this Act] shall be entitled to an increase of the pension, to be known as "age addition".

(2) Where a person is in receipt of a pension or allowance payable by the Secretary of State by virtue of any prescribed enactment or instrument (whether passed or made before or after this Act) and—
(a) he is over the age of 80; and
(b) he fulfils such other conditions as may be prescribed, he shall be entitled to an increase of that pension or allowance, also known as age addition.

(3) Age addition shall be payable for the life of the person entitled, at the weekly rate specified in Schedule 4, Part III, paragraph 8.

AMENDMENT

1.291 1. Pensions Act 2014 Sch.12 para.85 (April 6, 2016).

GENERAL NOTE

1.292 The amendment to this section by the Pensions Act 2014 restricts entitlement to pensions awarded or claimed under this Act and excludes any pension entitlement under the 2014 Act.

PART IV

INCREASES FOR DEPENDANTS

Child dependants

Beneficiary's dependent children

80. [1 . . .] 1.293

AMENDMENT

1. Repealed by the Tax Credits Act 2002 s.60 and Sch.6 (April 6, 2003).

SAVING

Child dependency increases pursuant to art.3 of the Tax Credits Act 2002 (Commencement No. 3 and Transitional Provisions and Savings) Order 2003 (SI 2003/938) (see previous editions for details) have now run their course.

Restrictions on increase—child not living with beneficiary etc.

81. [1 . . .] 1.294

AMENDMENT

1. Repealed by the Tax Credits Act 2002 s.60 and Sch.6 (April 6, 2003).

SAVING

Child dependency increases pursuant to art.3 of the Tax Credits Act 2002 (Commencement No. 3 and Transitional Provisions and Savings) Order 2003 (SI 2003/938) (see previous editions for details) have now run their course.

Adult dependants

Short-term benefit: increase for adult dependants

82. [1 . . .] 1.295

AMENDMENT

1. Repealed by the Welfare Reform Act 2009 s.15 (April 6, 2010).

SAVING

Section 15(2)(a) of the Welfare Reform Act 2009 provides: 1.296

"(2) Nothing in subsection (1) or Part 2 of Schedule 7 applies in relation to—

(a) the amount of a maternity allowance payable for a maternity allowance period (within the meaning of section 35(2) of the Benefits Act) which begins before 6 April 2010 but ends on or after that date, ..."

Pension increase (wife)

1.297 **83.**—[. . .]

General Note

1.298 This section ceased to have effect on April 6, 2010 under s.4 of the Pensions Act 2007.

Saving

1.299 Section 4(5)–(8) of the Pensions Act 2007 provides:

"(5) Nothing in–

(a) the repeals in subsection (1),
(b) the amendments in Part 4 of Schedule 1, or
(c) the repeals in Part 2 of Schedule 7,

applies in relation to a qualifying person at any time falling on or after 6th April 2010 but before the appropriate date.

(6) In subsection (5) a "qualifying person" means a person who–

(a) has, before 6th April 2010, made a claim for a relevant increase in accordance with section 1 of the Administration Act; and
(b) immediately before that date is either–

(i) entitled to the increase claimed, or
(ii) a beneficiary to whom section 92 of the SSCBA (continuation of awards where fluctuating earnings) applies in respect of that increase.

(7) In subsection (5) "the appropriate date" means the earlier (or earliest) of–

(a) 6th April 2020;
(b) the date when the qualifying person ceases to be either entitled to the relevant increase or a beneficiary to whom section 92 of the SSCBA applies in respect of it;
(c) where the relevant increase is payable to the qualifying person under section 83 of that Act, the date on which his wife attains pensionable age.

(8) In this section "relevant increase" means an increase in a Category A or Category C retirement pension under section 83, 84 or 85 of the SSCBA."

General Note

1.300 Note that s.83, where applicable, does not cease to apply because of a change of gender and accordingly references to a man or to his wife are to be construed accordingly. (Marriage (Same Sex Couples) Act 2013 Sch.4 Pt 5, para.15(1)).

With effect from December 16, 2014 art.11(1) of the Marriage and Civil Partnership (Scotland) Act 2014 and Civil Partnership Act 2004 (Consequential Provisions and Modifications Order 2001 (SI 2014/3229) provides:

"In a case where a full gender recognition certificate is issued to a person under the 2004 Act—

(a) section 83 of the 1992 Act (pension increase (wife)) does not cease to apply by virtue of the change of gender; and
(b) in the continued application of section 83 in such a case, references to a pension payable to a man, or references to his wife, are to be construed accordingly."

Pension increase (husband)

1.301 **84.**—[. . .]

General note

This section ceased to have effect on April 6, 2010 under s.4, Pensions Act 2007. The saving referred to in the annotations to s.83 also applies to this section. 1.302

Note also that in relation to cases under s.84 where that section is still applicable it does not cease to apply because of a change of gender and references in that case to a woman and to her husband are to be construed accordingly. (Marriage (Same Sex Couples) Act 2013 Sch.4 Pt 5, para.15(2)).

With effect from December 16, 2014 art.11(2) of the Marriage and Civil Partnership (Scotland) Act 2014 and Civil Partnership Act 2004 (Consequential Provisions and Modifications Order 2001 (SI 2014/3229) provides: 1.303

> "In a case where a full gender recognition certificate is issued to a person under the 2004 Act—
>
> (a) section 84 of the 1992 Act (pension increase (husband)) does not cease to apply by virtue of the change of gender; and
> (b) in the continued application of section 83 in such a case, references to a pension payable to a woman, or references to her husband, are to be construed accordingly."

Pension increase (person with care of children [1 or qualifying young person])

85.—[. . .] 1.304

General note

This section ceased to have effect on April 6, 2010 under s.4 of the Pensions Act 2007. The saving referred to in the annotations to s.83 also applies to this section. 1.305

Incapacity benefit—increases for adult dependants

[1 **86A.**—(1) The weekly rates of short-term and long-term incapacity benefit shall, in such circumstances as may be prescribed, be increased for adult dependants by the appropriate amounts specified in relation to benefit of that description in Schedule 4, Part IV, column (3). 1.306

(2) Regulations may provide that where the person in respect of whom an increase of benefit is claimed has earnings in excess of such amount as may be prescribed there shall be no increase in benefit under this section.]

Amendment

1. Social Security (Incapacity for Work) Act 1994 s.2(5) (November 18, 1994 for regulation-making purposes; April 13, 1995 for other purposes).

Rate of increase where associated retirement pension is attributable to reduced contributions

87.—(1) Where a person— 1.307

[1 (a) is entitled to a short-term incapacity benefit under section 30A(2)(b); and]

(b) would have been entitled only by virtue of section 60(1) above to the retirement pension by reference to which the rate of that benefit [2 . . .] is determined,

the amount of any increase of the benefit attributable to sections 82 to [3 85] above shall be determined in accordance with regulations under this section.

(2) The regulations shall not provide for any such increase in a case where the retirement pension by reference to which the rate of the said benefit [2 . . .] or invalidity pension is determined—

(a) would have been payable only by virtue of section 60 above; and
(b) would, in consequence of a failure to satisfy a contribution condition, have contained no basic pension.

AMENDMENTS

1. Jobseekers Act 1995 Sch.2 para.26 (October 7, 1996).
2. Social Security (Incapacity for Work) Act 1994 Sch.1, para.24(3) and Sch.2 (April 13, 1995).
3. Welfare Reform Act 2007 s.28 and Sch.3 para.9(7) (October 27, 2008).

DERIVATION

1.308 SSA 1975 s.47A as amended.

GENERAL NOTE

1.309 See reg.13 of the Dependency Regulations.

Increases to be in respect of only one adult dependant

1.310 [1 **88.** A person shall not [2 by virtue of section 86A] above be entitled for the same period to an increase of benefit in respect of more than one person.]

AMENDMENTS

1. Social Security (Incapacity for Work) Act 1994 Sch.1 para.25 (April 13, 1995).
2. Pensions Act 2007 Sch.1 para.14 (September 26, 2007).

DERIVATION

1.311 SSA 1975 s.48.

Miscellaneous

Earnings to include occupational and personal pensions [3 etc.] for purposes of provisions relating to increases of benefits in respect of [1. . .] adult dependants

1.312 **89.**—(1) Except as may be prescribed, in [1 . . .] [2 [4 sections 82 and 86A]] above, any reference to earnings includes a reference to payments by way of occupational or personal pension.

[3 (1A) Except as may be prescribed, in [4 sections 82 and 86A] above, and in regulations under section 86A above, any reference to earnings includes a reference to payments by way of PPF periodic payments.]

(2) For the purposes of the provisions mentioned in [3 subsections (1) and (1A) above], the Secretary of State may by regulations provide, in relation to cases where payments by way of occupational or personal pension [3 or PPF periodic payments] are made otherwise than weekly, that any necessary apportionment of the payments shall be made in such manner and on such basis as may be prescribed.

[3 (3) In this section "PPF periodic payments" means—

(a) any periodic compensation payments made in relation to a person, payable under the pension compensation provisions as specified in section 162(2) of the Pensions Act 2004 or Article 146(2) of the Pensions (Northern Ireland) order 2005 (the pension compensation provisions); or

(b) any periodic payments made in relation to a person, payable under section 166 of the Pensions Act 2004 or Article 150 of the Pensions (Northern Ireland) Order 2005 (duty to pay scheme benefits unpaid at assessment date etc.),

other than payments made to a surviving dependant of a person entitled to such compensation.]

AMENDMENTS

1. Tax Credits Act 2002 s.60 and Sch.6 (April 6, 2003).
2. Social Security (Incapacity for Work) Act 1994 Sch.1 para.26 (April 13, 1995).
3. The Pensions Act 2004 (PPF Payments and FAS Payments) (Consequential Provisions) Order 2006 (SI 2006/343) (February 14, 2006).
4. Pensions Act 2007 Sch.1 para.15 (September 26, 2007).
5. Welfare Reform Act 2007 s.28 and Sch.3 para.9(8) (October 27, 2008).

DERIVATION

SSA 1975 s.47B as amended. 1.313

GENERAL NOTE

In *R(U) 1/89* it was held that payments under a Civil Service pension have sufficient cognate features with payments under ordinary occupational pensions to bring them within the ambit of the term "payments by way of occupational pension" in s.5 of the SS (No.2) A 1980. By analogy they will fall to be treated as payments by way of occupational pension under the provisions of this Part of this Act. 1.314

Beneficiaries under sections 68 and 70

90 [1 . . .] 1.315

AMENDMENT

1. Repealed by the Welfare Reform Act 2009 s.15 (April 6, 2010).

SAVING

Section 15(2)(b) of the Welfare Reform Act 2009 provides: 1.316

"(2) Nothing in subsection (1) or Part 2 of Schedule 7 applies in relation to—

(a) . . .
(b) the amount of a carer's allowance payable to a qualifying person at any time on or after 6 April 2010 but before the appropriate date."

Section 15(3) of the same Act defines the relevant terms as follows: 1.317

"“a qualifying person” means a person who—

(a) has, before 6 April 2010, made a claim for an increase in a carer's allowance under section 90 of the Benefits Act; and
(b) immediately before that date is either entitled to the increase claimed or a beneficiary to whom section 92 of the Benefits Act applies in respect of that increase (continuation of awards where fluctuating earnings);

"the appropriate date" means whichever is the earlier of—

(a) 6 April 2020; and
(b) the date when the qualifying person ceases to be either entitled to that increase or a beneficiary to whom section 92 of the Benefits Act applies in respect of that increase."

Effect of trade disputes on entitlement to increases

1.318 **91.**—(1) A beneficiary shall not be entitled—
(a) to an increase in any benefit [1 under or by virtue of sections 82 to 88 above]; or
(b) to an increase in benefit [2 . . .] by virtue of regulations under section 90 above,

if the person in respect of whom he would be entitled to the increase falls within subsection (2) below.

[3(2) A person falls within this subsection if—
(a) he is prevented from being entitled to a jobseeker's allowance by section 14 of the Jobseekers Act 1995 (trade disputes); or
(b) he would be so prevented if he were otherwise entitled to that benefit.]

AMENDMENTS

1. Social Security (Incapacity for Work) Act 1994 Sch.1 para.27 (April 13, 1995).
2. Tax Credits Act 2002 s.60 and Sch.6.
3. Jobseekers Act 1995 Sch.2 para.27 (October 7, 1996).

DERIVATION

1.319 SSA 1975 s.49A as amended.

GENERAL NOTE

1.320 This section provides that no increases of benefit are payable in respect of any person caught by the disqualification for receiving jobseeker's allowance under s.14 of the Jobseekers Act 1995 or who would be so disqualified if otherwise entitled to that benefit.

See annotations to s.14 of the Jobseekers Act 1995 in the 2021–22 edition of *Vol. V: Income Support and the Legacy Benefits* and the cumulative Supplement in this year's Vol. II.

SAVING

In relation to the deletion of the words "for an adult dependant" in subs.(1)(b), there is a saving provided in art.3 of The Tax Credits Act 2002 (Commencement No. 3 and Transitional Provisions and Savings) Order 2003 (SI 2003/938) which provides:

"Saving provision

1.321 **3.**—(1) Notwithstanding the coming into force of the specified provisions, the Contributions and Benefits Act and the Administration Act shall, in cases to which paragraph (2) applies, subject to paragraph (3), continue to have effect from the commencement date as if those provisions had not come into force.

(2) This paragraph applies where a person—
(a) is entitled to a relevant increase on the day before the commencement date; or
(b) claims a relevant increase on or after the commencement date and it is subsequently determined that he is entitled to a relevant increase in respect of a period which includes the day before the commencement date.

(3) The provisions saved by paragraph (1) shall continue to have effect until—

(a) subject to sub-paragraph (c), where a relevant increase ceases to be payable to a person to whom paragraph (2) applies for a period greater than 58 days beginning with the day on which it was last payable, on the day 59 days after the day on which it was last payable; or

(b) in any other case, subject to sub-paragraph (c), on the date on which entitlement to a relevant increase ceases;

(c) where regulation 6(19) or (23) of the Social Security (Claims and Payments) Regulations 1987[4]] applies to a further claim for a relevant increase, on the date on which entitlement to that relevant increase ceases.

(4) In this article—

"the commencement date" means 6th April 2003;

"a relevant increase" means an increase under section 80 or 90 of the Contributions and Benefits Act;

"the specified provisions" means the provisions of the 2002 Act which are brought into force by article 2."

Dependency increases: continuation of awards in cases of fluctuating earnings

92.—(1) Where a beneficiary— 1.322

(a) has been awarded an increase of benefit under this Part of this Act, but

(b) ceases to be entitled to the increase by reason only that the weekly earnings of some other person ("the relevant earner") exceed the amount of the increase or, as the case may be, some specified amount,

then, if and so long as the beneficiary would have continued to be entitled to the increase, disregarding any such excess of earnings, the award shall continue in force but the increase shall not be payable for any week if the earnings relevant to that week exceed the amount of the increase or, as the case may be, the specified amount.

(2) In this section the earnings which are relevant to any week are those earnings of the relevant earner which, apart from this section, would be taken into account in determining whether the beneficiary is entitled to the increase in question for that week.

Derivation

SSA 1975 s.84A as amended. 1.323

General Note

The meaning of this section is obscure. Nor is its relationship with reg.8(3) of the Computation of Earnings Regulations entirely clear. The difficulty arises because of the use of the term "fluctuating earnings" in the title of the section and the reference to fluctuating earnings in reg.8(3). Correspondence with the Department for Work and Pensions has revealed that its operation in practice is very different from that set out in the commentary in earlier editions. The Department's view is that the notion of fluctuating earnings in s.92 is different from the notion of earnings which fluctuate in reg.8(3). The view of the Department is that s.92 is intended to cover the situation where an award of a dependency increase is made where the dependent person is either not earning or is earning under the earnings limit for the award, and on a later date becomes an earner with earnings over the earnings limit. This is what is intended by the reference in the title to the section to fluctuating. In such a situation entitlement continues but payment will cease for 1.324

the period in which the earnings limit is exceeded, but can be resurrected when the earnings fall below the limit (presumably without the need for a fresh claim).

The practice of the Department is described in the correspondence as follows.

> "In terms of section 92 . . . we have always operated on the basis that, for dependency benefit purposes, entitlement, once established, always exists and it is only the payment which is disqualified for the weeks following any periods during which the dependant's earnings exceeds the specified amount. In this event any change in earnings which takes the earnings over the limit or reduces them to under the limit will be grounds to review (supersede) the award to either disqualify or reinstate payment. The date of change will be that determined under the [Computation of Earnings] Regulations. In cases of actual fluctuating earnings there can be no continuation of payment until a permanent change can be established. The weekly rate of earnings are established under the provisions of regulation 8 of the above Regulations and the date on which a particular payment of earnings is due determines the date on which a disqualification of payment of dependency increase is imposed or removed."

Dependency increases on termination of employment after period of entitlement to disability working allowance

1.325 **93.**—Where—

(a) [1 a person becomes entitled—
    (i) to the higher rate of short-term incapacity benefit, or to long-term incapacity benefit, by virtue of section 30C(5) or (6) or section 42 above,] [2 . . .]

(b) when he was last entitled to that [3 benefit] [2 . . .], it was increased in respect of a dependant by virtue of—
    (i) regulation 8(6) of the Social Security Benefit (Dependency) Regulations 1977;
    (ii) regulation 2 of the Social Security (Savings for Existing Beneficiaries) Regulations 1984;
    (iii) regulation 3 of the Social Security Benefit (Dependency) Amendment Regulations 1984; or
    (iv) regulation 4 of the Social Security Benefit (Dependency and Computation of Earnings) Amendment Regulations 1989,

for the purpose of determining whether his [3 benefit] [2 . . .] should be increased by virtue of that regulation for any period beginning with the day on which he again becomes entitled to his [3 benefit] [2 . . .] the increase in respect of that dependant shall be treated as having been payable to him on each day between the last day on which his [3 benefit] [2 . . .] was previously payable and the day on which he again becomes entitled to it.

AMENDMENTS

1. Social Security (Incapacity for Work) Act 1994 Sch.1 para.28(a) (April 13, 1995).
2. Welfare Reform and Pensions Act 1999 Sch.13 Pt IV (April 6, 2001).
3. Social Security (Incapacity for Work) Act 1994 Sch.1 para.28(b) (April 13, 1995).

DERIVATION

1.326 DLADWAA 1991 s.9(5).

General Note

Disability working allowance (subsequently disabled person's tax credit) was a benefit modelled on family credit designed to top up low pay received by people who are disabled. In order to encourage those who are disabled to engage in work, a special rule concerning requalification for a benefit connected with the disability is provided in s.42 if they leave that work within a two-year period. They become immediately qualified to receive the benefit they were receiving before becoming in receipt of disability working allowance. 1.327

The rule in this section simply allows such persons to receive any increases of the benefit in respect of dependants.

The section has not yet been amended on the introduction of disabled person's tax credit to replace disability working allowance, nor on its replacement by the disability component of working tax credit.

Part V

Benefit for Industrial Injuries

General provisions

Right to industrial injuries benefit

94.—(1) Industrial injuries benefit shall be payable where an employed earner suffers personal injury caused [1 . . .] by accident arising out of and in the course of his employment, being employed earner's employment. 1.328

(2) Industrial injuries benefit consists of the following benefits—

(a) disablement benefit payable in accordance with sections 103 to 105 below, paragraphs 2 and 3 of Schedule 7 below and Parts II and III of that Schedule;

(b) reduced earnings allowance payable in accordance with Part IV;

(c) retirement allowance payable in accordance with Part V; and

(d) industrial death benefit, payable in accordance with Part VI.

(3) For the purposes of industrial injuries benefit an accident arising in the course of an employed earner's employment shall be taken, in the absence of evidence to the contrary, also to have arisen out of that employment.

(4) Regulations may make provision as to the day which, in the case of night workers and other special cases, is to be treated for the purposes of industrial injuries benefit as the day of the accident.

(5) Subject to sections 117, 119 and 120 below, industrial injuries benefit shall not be payable in respect of an accident happening while the earner is outside Great Britain.

(6) In the following provisions of this Part of this Act "work" in the contexts "incapable of work" and "incapacity for work" means work which the person in question can be reasonably expected to do.

Amendment

1. Welfare Reform Act 2012 s.64 (December 5, 2012).

Derivation

1.329 SSA 1975 s.50 as amended.

Definitions

"employed earner"—see s.2(1)(a), above.
"employed earner's employment"—see s.95, below.
"work"—see subs.(6).

General Note

1.330 This section contains the basic elements of the industrial injuries scheme. The scheme has undergone significant change. Injury benefit was abolished in 1982; death benefit was abolished (in respect of deaths occurring on or after April 11, 1988) in April 1988; title to disablement benefit was substantially diminished by provisions in the SSA 1986 which are dealt with below.

The system for decision-making and appeals for claims to industrial injuries benefits has undergone several reforms over the years. However, one constant throughout this period of change is that the question of whether a claimant is an employed or self-employed earner, and whether a specific employment is, or is not, employed earner's employment, is to be decided not by the Secretary of State, but by officers of HMRC (Social Security Contributions (Transfer of Functions, etc.) Act 1999 s.8(1)). Accordingly, such decisions are not matters of appeal for the FTT Social Entitlement Chamber but rather for appeal to the FTT Tax Chamber. Such decisions and appeals are regulated by the Social Security Contributions (Decisions and Appeals) Regs 1999 (SI 1999/1027).

Historically, for all other industrial injuries matters, there was a distinction between medical issues (the disablement questions), decided by the medical adjudicating authorities, including on appeal the former MAT, and non-medical issues, decided by insurance officers (and later adjudication officers), with appeals to the former SSAT (or its predecessor). However, on July 5, 1999, the functions of adjudication officers with respect to industrial injuries benefits and the making of industrial accident declarations were transferred to the Secretary of State (SSA 1998, ss.1, 8 and Commencement Order No.8). He or she may, however, refer certain issues for report to a medical practitioner (now a health care professional) who has experience of the issues. The issues so referable are: (a) the extent of a personal injury for the purposes of s.94; (b) whether the claimant has a prescribed industrial disease and the extent of the resulting disablement; and (c) whether, for disablement benefit purposes, the claimant has a disablement and its extent (Decisions and Appeals Regs 1999 reg.12(1)).

1.331 After 1999 decisions by the Secretary of State on industrial injuries benefits, including those on prescribed industrial diseases, and on the matter of an industrial accident declaration, were appealable to the so-called "unified" appeal tribunal, composed of a legally qualified member and up to two medically qualified members (SSA 1998 ss.4, 12, Schs 2 and 3). Like the Secretary of State, that tribunal was competent to deal with the both the medical and non-medical aspect of industrial injuries matters. Since November 3, 2008, and as a result of the Tribunals, Courts and Enforcement Act 2007, the FTT Social Entitlement Chamber has assumed these appellate functions.

The key point from all this for industrial injuries matters is that the historic distinction between medical issues and non-medical issues is no longer relevant. Consequently both the FTT and the Upper Tribunal now have jurisdiction over both medical and non-medical matters. So, an Upper Tribunal judge, allowing an appeal on a point of law, can now take his or her own decision on the facts rather than remitting it to another tribunal. Commissioner Williams did so in *CI/1307/1999* giving a staged assessment of disablement in respect of post-traumatic stress disorder. The decision considers the medical aspects of the claimant's case found to be an industrial accident in *CI/15589/ 1996*, noted below. In paras 15–17, Commissioner Williams distinguished 'diagnosis' and 'disablement' decisions. The former is essentially "a question of medical expertise". A "disablement" decision in contrast is not dissimilar to the tasks performed by judges in assessing common law damages or in applying the tariff of the Criminal Injuries Compensation Authority. In assessing disablement for industrial injuries benefits, however, that Criminal Injuries tariff is not an appropriate yardstick. Instead, supplementing SSCBA 1992 s.103 and Sch.6, regard should be had also to reg.11 and Sch.2 to the General Benefit Regulations, below. Nonetheless, the import of para.37 of the decision is that exercise of the Commissioner's (and now the Upper Tribunal's) power to decide on the facts available, rather than remitting to another tribunal, may well be rare. Even so, the decision contrasts markedly with the traditional view of such matters as ones for medical rather than legal judgment (see, for example, Commissioner Howell in *CI/636/93*). Note that the suitability of cross-reference to Sch.2 was also advocated in *R(I) 5/95*, where Commissioner Rowland stated that "assessment of disablement should be brought into line with those prescribed in the Schedule", with assessment also reflecting any intermittent or episodic character of the disablement (para.16).

Subsection (1)

Whilst it is possible to divide this subsection conveniently for explanation, there is some overlap between the various conditions of entitlement and the temptation to categorise issues *too* rigidly should be avoided. To qualify for benefit: (i) the claimant must be an employed earner . . . [in] employed earner's employment; (ii) the claimant must suffer personal injury caused by accident; (iii) [the accident] must be arising out of and in the course of his [employed earner's] employment. **1.332**

"Employed earner . . . employed earner's employment"

The definition of employed earner in s.2(1)(a), above, applies. Power is given to the Secretary of State to make regulations providing that certain employment shall (or shall not) be treated as employed earner's employment (see note to s.95, below). Whether a specific employment is, or is not, employed earner's employment is determined solely by the Commissioners for His Majesty's Revenue and Customs. **1.333**

The employment that the accident occurs in must be employed earner's employment.

"Suffers personal injury caused by accident"

Suffers personal injury: The injury must be to the living body of a human being. Damage to some artificial appendage of the body (spectacles, false teeth, etc.) is not enough (*R(I) 7/56, R(I) 1/82*), unless the appendage is so intimately linked with the body so as to form a part of it (*R(I) 5/81*—damage to artificial hip joint held to be personal injury). Damage to an artificial limb *may* constitute personal injury depending on the circumstances. (How should damage to a heart pacemaker be treated?) This situation is less likely to be significant given the abolition of injury benefit because of the short-term nature of damage of this kind. However, the question may arise where the damage causes incapacity for work which lasts longer than 15 weeks (is there entitlement to disablement benefit?), or where the claimant does not meet the contribution conditions for sickness benefit (is the incapacity for work the result of a personal injury?). Despite the demise of sickness benefit on April 13, 1995, the matter retains importance for those who transferred from it or from invalidity benefit to the replacement incapacity benefit, and who are covered by the IW (Transitional) Regulations, below. **1.334**

The injury must be sufficiently severe to constitute a discernible physiological change for the worse so that a "strain" or an "increase of pain" will not constitute injury unless there is such a change (*R(I) 19/60, R(I) 1/76*). If incapacity is caused by increased or aggravated pain, or the gradual worsening of an existing condition it is also relevant to consider whether the claimant has suffered an accident (see *R(I) 1/76* and notes on "accident" below).

1.335 *By accident:* Leaving the question of causation to the last, the claimant must show that his injury resulted from an identifiable *accident*. Problems arise in defining "accident"; in distinguishing between accident and process; and in cases where suffering the injury is alleged to constitute the accident.

The usual definition of accident is that of Lord MacNaughten in *Fenton v Thorley* [1903] A.C. 443, ". . . an unlooked-for mishap or an untoward event which is neither expected or designed". "Designed" means planned by the claimant and does not exclude him from benefit where the accident has been planned by others (*Trim Joint District School Board v Kelly* [1914] A.C. 667). In *CI/365/89*, Commissioner Skinner, upholding the SSAT's decision that the incidents and events in that case did not constitute an "accident", stated:

> "The question of the existence of the personal injury and of its cause or causes is one of fact, but the question as to whether such cause or causes amounts to an accident within the meaning of the [legislation] is a question of law; *Fenton v. Thorley* . . . so decided in relation to the Workmen's Compensation Act and in my judgment that principle is equally applicable to the question which was before the tribunal." (para.6).

The width and imprecision of the principles on "accident" in *Fenton v Thorley* (above) and *Trim Joint District Schoolboard v Kelly* (above) are apt to cause problems if not approached with a commonsense understanding of the natural everyday sense of the word "accident" (*per* Commissioner Rice in *CI/5249/95*). Hence in *CI/5249/95*, Commissioner Rice rejected the claim that someone, suffering a nervous breakdown on being suspended from work by his employer, had suffered injury through "accident". While the suspension may have been "unexpected" (from the point of view of the claimant), it would fly in the face of the ordinary use of the English language and be regarded as absurd by the man in the street to regard it as an "accident" in the sense used in s.94.

1.336 Focusing on the "untoward" aspect of *Trim* and its deployment in respect of vaccinations in *R(I) 15/61*, Commissioner Mesher in *CI/732/2007* was of the opinion that a vaccination, administered in the course of employment, to which the claimant had consented, was not an "accident" for the purposes of this section (see paras 14–17). Since she could also not show a personal injury (which might have constituted the accident) flowing from the vaccination, her claim for an industrial accident declaration was rightly rejected by the appeal tribunal.

The "not expected" or "unforeseen" aspect has given some difficulties, in so far as there are some occupations where the risk of some injury might be said to be foreseeable, for example, prison officer, fireman or policeman. The matter has been considered recently in two cases: in *CI/15589/96*, a decision of Commissioner Goodman; and in *CAO v Faulds*, in which the issue was pronounced on both by the Inner House of the Scottish Court of Session and, on appeal, by the House of Lords. Both courts emphatically rejected the notion that the nature of such employments precludes incidents being regarded as accidents. In approaching the matter the emphasis needs to be on the perspective of the "victim"; the incident must not have been wanted or intended by him. But the focus must be on the identifiable incident said to rank as the "accident"; it is not enough that the injury was an unexpected untoward event. As noted below, following *Faulds* and *SSWP v Scullion* [2010] EWCA Civ 310, in which the Court of Appeal found erroneous in law the decision of Commissioner Bano in *CI/2842/2006* conflating injury and accident, although the injury and accident can overlap, they cannot merge indistinguishably.

In *CAO v Faulds* 1998 S.L.T. 1203, 1998 S.C.L.R. 719 (judgments included in *R(I) 1/00*), the Inner House of the Scottish Court of Session (the equivalent of the Court of Appeal in England and Wales) affirmed Commissioner Walker's decision in *CSI/26/96* reported as part of *R(I) 1/00*, that a fireman who suffered post-traumatic stress disorder after having attended a series of horrific fatalities in the course of his employment had suffered "accidents". The Inner House rejected the argument that, given his special training and the nature of his job, these horrific events did not constitute "accidents".

The Secretary of State appealed to the House of Lords. In *CAO v Faulds* [2000] 2 All E.R. 961, reported as *R(I) 1/00*, their Lordships held (Lord Hutton dissenting) that the Inner House had erred in law by not identifying the precise incidents that ranked as accidents. Rather harshly perhaps, the majority considered the Inner House to have erroneously based their decision on the notion that the post-traumatic stress disorder had arisen "accidentally". In essence they referred the case back down the line for evidential findings which would enable resolution of the accident/process issue. But their Lordships all stressed that something which happens as an ordinary element in, or an incident of, an employment can still be an "accident". Lord Hope expressly approved that part of the judgment of the Inner House, in which it rejected the CAO's argument "that an injury could not be said to have been sustained 'by accident' where the event or events causing it were foreseeable . . . the sustaining of an *unexpected* personal injury by an *expected* event or incident may itself amount to an accident" ([2000] 2 All E.R. 961 at 969). Lord Clyde (with whose opinion Lords Browne-Wilkinson, Mackay and Hope concurred), referring to Lord Macnaghten's definition and the *Trim* case, said: 1.337

> "The decision in the *Trim* case is important not only in stressing that Lord Macnaghten's formulation is to be taken as descriptive and not definitive, but also in pointing out that the question whether there has been an accident requires particular consideration to be paid to the victim. At least the accident cannot be something he intended to happen. Where his injury came about through the operation of some external force, that operation must have been something that he did not intend to happen. Where his injury has followed on some action or activity of his own, then the consequences of his doing what he did cannot have been intended by him. The mischance or the mishap was something which was not in any way wanted or intended. It was not meant to happen. . . . Indeed even where it may be foreseen that a person may possibly suffer physical injury in the ordinary course of his work when the incident occurs and injury is sustained it is still proper to recognise that event as an accident. Lord Shaw of Dunfermline gave the examples in this context of prison warders, lunatic asylum attendants and gamekeepers, and the same may hold true of their modern equivalents" ([2000] 2 All E.R. 961 at 978–979).

Lord Hutton, supporting the decision of the Inner House, stated that "the authorities establish that an accident may happen in the ordinary course of the employee's work" ([2000] 2 All E.R. 961, at 983).

This need for a definition of "accident" and the overall requirement that the accident should be identifiable as something distinct from the injury to which it gives rise (*Faulds,* above; *SSWP v Scullion* [2010] EWCA Civ 310, below) both reflect the crucial importance (for purposes of establishing title to benefit) of distinguishing between:

- Injury caused by "accident" (within s.94(1)) and injury caused by "process" (outside s.94(1)); and
- Injury caused by accident happening *because of* the claimant's work (within the scheme) and injury merely happening *at* work but brought about by some non-work-related cause (e.g. a stress disorder because of acute problems in a marital or other close relationship; a cardiac arrest suffered at work but the

> pure product of a congenital defect such that the arrest might have happened anywhere, at any time) (outside the scheme).

Title to industrial injuries benefits through s.94 will depend on decision-makers, tribunals and judges grappling with some difficult distinctions and problems of causation (*Scullion*).

1.338 While most diseases will tend to arise by process rather than accident—and thus be covered under the scheme only if a prescribed industrial disease—this will not invariably be the case. So where a workman was burnt on the lip by a splash of hot metal and the burn became cancerous, that cancer would arise "by accident". Similarly, a stress-related illness can be the product of an industrial accident. Distinguishing *CI/5249/95* on the facts, Commissioner Williams in *CI/2414/98* was not prepared to say that an SSAT had no basis for finding that a claimant who had suffered extreme post-traumatic stress after a particular conversation with a senior colleague had suffered an industrial accident for the purposes of the scheme. The conversation related to a situation which had brought about a period of post-traumatic stress and depression. That situation concerned an industrial dispute during which the claimant, a team leader and deputy manager at an office of the Employment Service, had been given the job of manning the office entrance from early morning to ensure the well-being of non-striking staff crossing the picket-line to come into work. She suffered a high level of abuse from those on the picket-line and was worried by their aggressive behaviour. When she returned to work after her illness she transferred to another job at another office. In the conversation found to be an "accident" she was told by the senior colleague, wrongly as it turned out, that no disciplinary action was to be taken against those abusive and aggressive former colleagues. Commissioner Williams considered the argument that words cannot be, or cause, an industrial accident, with *CI/7/71* being cited in support of the proposition that the phrase "suffers personal injury by accident" cannot cover the use of language alone. Commissioner Williams commented that:

> "while that observation may apply to most situations, I do not agree with those views as applied to all forms of personal injury in all circumstances. Given that 'accident' includes deliberate actions, and that words can constitute assault or other crimes to the person, the statement in *CI/7/71* is too general. For example verbal sexual harassment at work might be such in extreme cases as to amount to an accident or series of accidents, as might misinformation designed to shock or causing shock. I note that in the recent decision of *CI/4642/97* and linked cases, the Commissioner reaches the same conclusion. Any claim that words cause an accident must also be taken in context. This conversation reopened an issue that had clearly traumatised the claimant. That is relevant in considering its effect on her. It was not just the words by themselves that must be considered, but the context of those words and what the words concerned" (para.8).

Commissioner Williams pointed out that the incident alleged to constitute an "accident" need not be the sole or main cause of all injury suffered (para.12). Nor was the stressful nature of the claimant's job a relevant factor. This was an unusual case. An appeal to the Court of Appeal by the adjudication officer was not pursued. See also *CI/554/1992*, noted later in this annotation.

1.339 In *CI/105/1998*, Commissioner Rowland considered the case of a senior member of the teaching staff of a further education college who suffered from depression following what the tribunal found to be three aggressive and bullying interviews with the principal and vice-principal over a six-month period. The Commissioner declined to find erroneous in law the tribunal's finding that the injury arose through accident rather than process. Accepting *CI/7/71* (on file as *CI/789/70*) as correctly decided on its facts, he, like Commissioner Williams in *CI/2414/98*, disagreed with its broader *obiter* propositions. Given that a physical assault during an interview would rank as personal injury caused by accident, Commissioner Rowland found:

> "it very difficult to see why a person who suffers psychological injury having been caused, by words from a superior, to apprehend immediate and unlawful violence, should not be said to have suffered personal injury caused by accident. Such a person would have been the victim of an unlawful assault at common law by the superior and it seems obvious that he or she should be covered by the industrial injuries scheme just as the schoolmaster was covered by the Workmen's Compensation Acts in *Trim* . . . But coverage by the scheme does not depend on someone having done something unlawful; it is enough that the conversation was an untoward event. I agree with the view expressed in *CI/5249/95* that a perfectly proper conversation cannot itself constitute an accident because it seems to me that it may be an event but it cannot be an untoward event. However, I do not agree with the suggestion in *CI/7/71* that use of language alone can never *constitute* an accident. In my view the tribunal in the present case were quite entitled to regard the three material interviews as being sufficient to amount to accidental causes of any injury that flowed from them. On the tribunal's findings, those interviews were quite untoward" (para.17).

However, it is the conversation itself, rather than suspension, dismissal or criticism, which must cause the injury; one looks to the *manner* of dismissal rather than dismissal itself (para.18); or, in the context of a claim in respect of the effects of an unexpected interview, said to have brought on the claimant's depression and chronic anxiety, to the manner and context of the interview (*CI/142/2006*). So the less outrageous the employer's behaviour, the more difficult will be the claimant's task. Injury arising from a series of events can rank as 'accident' rather than 'process'; the tribunal's conclusion that it so ranked here was not such that no tribunal, acting judicially and properly instructed as to the law, could have reached on the material before it (paras 22, 23). As Commissioner Fellner noted in *CI/3511/2002*, on balance, stress illnesses are more likely to arise through process rather than accident (para.14). Stress illnesses are not currently listed as Prescribed Industrial Diseases, and, in a paper published in 2004—Position Paper no.13, *Stress at Work* [found at URL *http://www.iiac.org.uk/papers/13.pdf*]—the Industrial Injuries Advisory Council considered itself unable to recommend extending the schedule of prescription to include adverse health outcomes ascribed to stress at work, but is to keep the area under review (para.56). However, as Commissioner Howell made clear in *CI/4708/2001*, work related stress can arise through accident where one can identify an event which produced a pathological change for the worse in the claimant's condition. Referring the tribunal to which he remitted the case to *CI/105/1998* noted above, he further emphasised that

> "in the light of present more up-to-date knowledge about the way people can suffer breakdowns and stress reactions to particular events, it should no longer be taken to be the law, if ever it was, that words alone can never give rise to an 'accident' for this purpose" (para.11).

As *CAO v Faulds* (above) makes clear, however, there must be something describable as an accident. In *CI/3696/2005*, Commissioner Levenson, summarising and applying the principles in *Faulds* (see para.11) upheld a tribunal decision that the claimant, suffering from stress as a result of allegations made against him of false expenses claims, had not suffered an accident: neither being suspended nor receiving the letter of suspension could properly be regarded as an accident in the ordinary sense of the word (paras 12, 13).

Where the injury appears to result from a general deterioration of the claimant's **1.340** condition over a period of time it may not be possible to identify a precise moment when there was a discernible physiological change for the worse, nor to identify a particular incident which occasioned the deterioration. In these circumstances, the claimant may have difficulty in establishing personal injury (see above) and/or in proving that there was an accident. Describing the distinction between accident and process, Lord Porter said,

"... two types of case have not always been sufficiently differentiated. In one type there is to be found a simple accident followed by a resultant injury ... or a series of specific and ascertainable accidents followed by an injury which may be the consequence of any or all of them ... In the other type of case there is a continuous process going on substantially from day to day though not necessarily from hour to hour, which gradually and over a period of years produces incapacity. In the first of these types of cases the resulting incapacity is held to be injury by accident; in the second it is not ... There must come a time when the indefinite number of so-called accidents and the length of time over which they occur take away the element of accident and substitute that of process." (*Roberts v Dorothea Slate Quarries Ltd* [1948] 2 All E.R. 201).

Although an accident denotes a moment at which an injury occurred, so long as such a moment can be identified, uncertainty (years after the event) as to the precise date, does not prevent a finding of accident (*CI/278/1993*). In *CI/1714/2002* Commissioner Rowland stressed that it is not necessary for the claimant to identify when the accident took place more precisely than necessary for the determination of the claim, so that there "the summer of 1978" sufficed (para.10). The key point is rather that the tribunal should be satisfied that an accident occurred, and on this aspect it is important to note that the law does not require corroboration of the claimant's evidence if the tribunal believe that evidence (para.11).

Whether the injury is caused by accident(s) or process is an important question of fact for the decision-maker or tribunal. A number of Commissioners decisions have given guidance on the principles to be applied in reaching a decision but the facts of each case will be crucial. Modern authority has directed attention away from the length of the period over which the injury developed as the most significant factor (as Lord Porter seemed to suggest) and emphasised that it is a question of fact and degree in each case (see *R(I) 11/74* and Appendix). Attention must be given to the nature of the injury, the nature of the work, and the nature of the incidents which are alleged to constitute the accident when reaching a decision. As always where fine distinctions need to be made, it is not easy to reconcile all the cases. As Commissioner Howell put it in *CI/4708/2001*, it is a difficult and invidious line for decision-makers and tribunals to have to draw (paras 6, 11).

1.341 An examination of the accident/process distinction was undertaken by Commissioner Goodman in *CI/72/1987*. In that case, an oboeist in a world famous orchestra sought a declaration that he had suffered an industrial accident in the course of playing the oboe which had caused hernia of the throat. The Commissioner observed that the question of accident or process is one of fact and laid emphasis on medical evidence which referred to a series of incidents causing the conditions. He held that there had by a specific date (the date on which the condition had been diagnosed) been an accident or accidents which would have occurred on a distinct occasion or occasions. The decision of the adjudication officer and the unanimous decision of the local tribunal was reversed. *R(I) 6/91* affirms that usually harm suffered (e.g. asthma, bronchial complaints) because of "passive smoking" (the inhalation of the smoke from other people's smoking) will not be attributable to accident but to process. However, in the particular circumstances of that case, where the claimant was able to point to six separate and isolated incidents involving her being moved into smoky environments, the Commissioner granted her six accident declarations under SSA 1975 s.107 (now SSA 1998 s.29, formerly AA 1992 s.44). In *CI/156/1993* the claimant was unsuccessful in her claim for an accident declaration in respect of harm suffered through passive smoking, thus indicating the exceptional nature of the decision in *R(I) 6/91*. Nor had her claim in respect of prescribed disease D7 (occupational asthma) been successful. In most cases, a claimant suffering mental or physical injury because of stress at work would rightly be regarded as having suffered it through process, rather than through accident, putting the matter outside s.94. Although Commissioner Goodman was careful to characterise his decision as dependent on its "highly individual facts and on the detailed nature of the medical evidence given in the High Court action [against his employer for damages]", and while he was anxious to deny that his decision constituted a precedent "for any other case where it may be asserted that stress at work has caused a claimant mental or physical injury" (para.16), nonetheless his decision in *CI/554/1992*, granting the claimant an accident declaration, is a welcome reminder that, in circumstances which may well be rare, mental injury through stress can arise through accident. Tribunals should thus take great care in any such case with the evidence, and not assume that any case of injury through stress inevitably *must* be through process. In *CI/554/1992*, Commissioner Goodman noted *R(I) 43/55* (explosions leading to psychoneurotic disorder, an identifiable series of accidents) and decided that the medical evidence showed that the claimant was "more or less all right at one moment and severely ill the next" and that the stressful situation at work in September/October 1974 was an industrial "accident" which tipped him over the edge into depression. The fact that he was abnormally sensitive to stress did not prevent this finding: the "egg shell skull" principle noted in para.11 of *R(I) 6/91* (the passive smoking case) applied. See also *CI/2414/98*, noted earlier.

CI/737/1994 and *CI/1195/1995*, two decisions of Commissioner Henty, both apply *R(I) 6/91* (the "passive smoking" case) and contain useful reviews of the major authorities on the difficult accident/process distinction. In *CI/737/1994*, the Commissioner made a declaration that on each occasion between 1973 and 1983 when the claimant suffered temporary deafness/tinnitus after a shooting practice session as part of his police firearms training, he suffered an accident. Although not as well documented as in *R(I) 6/91*, the evidence was clear that there were such occasions (para.14). Furthermore, despite the fact that the permanent condition only manifested itself some four years after the claimant fired his last shot, the Commissioner declared also that the permanent injury was caused by accident (para.15). In *CI/3600/2004*, Commissioner Fellner considered the case of a school care assistant, who had to give up work, suffering from a major depressive disorder, post-traumatic stress disorder and a number of physical or somatic manifestations. It was argued that this had arisen through process, since she had become increasingly concerned at the nature of physical restraint applied by school staff, and the tribunal had so decided. There was, indeed, that backdrop, but Commissioner Fellner, taking account of *Mullen* noted below, considered that the evidence established that the "trigger" incident was one some three weeks before she left, when she witnessed a pupil being inappropriately restrained by another teacher, and granted an industrial accident declaration (see esp. paras 14–18). In contrast, in *CI/1195/1995*, Commissioner Henty could point to no particular incidents triggering off the claimant's heart attack; it came about as a result of a cumulative process (para.9).

The following situations are only illustrative—the tribunal must decide each case upon its facts: **1.342**

(i) The period of development may be too short to indicate process:

R(I) 18/54	(two months, but there was also an identifiable point at which the injury was first noticed)
R(I) 43/61	(less than three days' use of scissors causing digital neuritis—but compare *R(I) 19/56*)
R(I) 4/62	(about two weeks' welding causing ganglion)

(ii) There may be an identifiable series of individual accidents:

R(I) 77/51	(repeated operation of stiff levers)
R(I) 24/54	(repeated burns and pricks on hands)

R(I) 43/55	(explosions leading to psychoneurotic disorder) (see note above)
CI/71/1987	(oboe playing and rehearsal leading to laryngoceles) (see note above)
CI/737/1994	(shooting practice leading to temporary deafness/tinnitus) (see note above)
CAO v Faulds	1998 S.L.T. 1203 (remitted for further evidence by the House of Lords (see [2000] 2 All E.R. 961))
CI/3370/1999	(the case of a teacher who claimed that her injury (nodules on her bilateral vocal chords) had resulted from a series of interacting incidents, constituting "accident", at school. The decision-maker had already given an accident declaration in respect of one such incident when she was trapped in a stock cupboard by a pupil and had to shout before escaping. Commissioner remitted to tribunal for further consideration but implying support for the "accident" view')
Mullen v Secretary of State for Work and Pensions, 2002 S.L.T. 149	(the Court of Session Second Division in a Scottish case held that a former assistant care officer incapacitated by back pain brought about through lifting patients had suffereda series of accidents over a seven year period, and had thus suffered injury caused by accident, even though it was not possible to identify the date of each of the accidents or to state which of them, if not all, caused or contributed to the back condition.)

(iii) There may be a process:

CI/257/49	(development of "Raynaud's phenomenon" as a result of operating a grinding machine for five years)
CI/83/50	(doctor developing tuberculosis after two years of treating persons suffering from it)
R(I) 42/51	(strained chest muscles over two-month period)
R(I) 19/56	(osteoarthritis of the fingers was the "cumulative result" of three days of leather stitching and had come on gradually during that period)
R(I) 7/66	(prolonged exposure to nitro-glycerine resulting in death)
R(I) 11/74	(condition of left elbow developing over five months' work with heavy electrical boring machine)
CI/1195/1995	(cumulative process leading to heart attack) (see note above)
CAO v Faulds	[2000] 2 All E.R. 961, reported as *R(I) 1/00* (post-traumatic stress disorder remitted by House of Lords to Court of Session for further evidence on the issue).
CSI/371/2001	(not available on the Commissioners' website) placed on the process side of the line a case where a civil servant had suffered stress and anxiety because of excessive workload and a number of incidents of friction with his line manager, whom he saw as unreasonable. The tribunal had not there been prepared to find that the claimant's appreciation of excessive workload was the sort of triggering event that had enabled success in *CI/554/1992*, noted above, one of the rare cases where mental injury through stress resulted from accident)
CI/3511/2002	(Commissioner Fellner considered the case of an ambulance technician incapacitated because of work-related stress. The

single person tribunal erred in law by holding that the claimant was entitled to an industrial accident declaration because this was a case of accident by process. Commissioner Fellner held that the case fell on the 'process' side of the line—there was no identifiable accident or series of accidents).

The claimant who develops a disease or other condition as a result of his work may be entitled to benefit notwithstanding that there is no accident so long as the disease or condition is one which is "prescribed" for his employment (see s.108, below).

Decision-makers, tribunals and judges will also have to make a difficult decision where the claimant, in common-parlance terms, alleges that the personal injury suffered at work constitutes the "accident" for the purposes of the section. The supermarket shelf-stacker who strains his back muscles when picking up a case of baked beans is likely to say that he has had an "accident" at work. But since he was doing nothing other than he was accustomed to, he is thus likely to see the "injury" as the "accident".

Legally speaking, the leading authorities (*Faulds*, above; *Scullion*, below) decide that **1.343** the wording of s.94(1) requires that the two be clearly distinguished. The wording is "personal injury caused by accident" rather than the Workmen's Compensation Acts' formula, "personal injury by accident", so that broad statements in House of Lords' authorities on those Acts need to be approached very cautiously to avoid falling into the error of applying the industrial injuries benefits scheme too widely to take in any "accidental injury". "Injury" and "accident" cannot legally merge indistinguishably, so that a cardiac arrest suffered at work cannot be both the injury and the accident. It constitutes the requisite "injury", but to be brought within the scheme there must be identified some incident or small series of incidents (the "accident") which caused the cardiac arrest, and that this occurred both at and through work ("arising out of and in the course of employment"). Thus the authorities suggest that s.94(1) covers the standard case where the accident and injury are clearly distinct (the forklift truck drives over and breaks the employee's legs) and the more difficult case where, on a common-parlance approach, there is a degree of overlap between the accident and the injury (the supermarket shelf-stacker straining his back because of lifting the case of baked beans). This more difficult class of case will be within the section so long as there is an internal physiological change for the worse (e.g. the strained muscles; a cardiac arrest; post traumatic stress disorder) which is partly caused by the work activity which the claimant is performing at the time (e.g. lifting the case of baked beans or heavy papers; wrestling with a jammed filing cabinet drawer) or by the act of another, performed at and connected with the claimant's work (e.g. a teacher's heart attack at school caused by being threatened or struck there by an irate pupil or parent).

In *Jones v Secretary of State for Social Services* [1972] A.C. 944, the claimant suffered a heart attack some days after he had been doing heavy lifting at work. A tribunal held that the heart attack had been brought on by the heavy work and the House of Lords decided that there had been an accident within the terms of the section. Lord Diplock said that he would call a perfectly ordinary part of a man's work (here the heavy lifting) an accident if it had the effect of causing injury. It would appear that the only injuries excluded will be those which would have happened whether the claimant was at work or not. Such injuries are not attributable to the work done but are risks of everyday activity.

The law was stated thus in *R(I) 11/80* (where the claimant sustained a head injury by banging his head after an unexplained fall):

> "where (in what is sometimes called an internal accident) a physiological or pathological change for the worse occurs while a person is at work, such as a fit or a heart attack or a dislocation, that change for the worse is, if caused by the work that is being done itself, injury by accident for the purposes of the section; but that, on the other hand, where one of these happens while a person is at work but not because of his work the change is not itself injury by accident . . . But in

> any case if the internal accident causes the person concerned to fall and injure himself that injury may be injury by accident arising out of and in the course of employment even if the change itself was not."

1.344 This statement was approved in *R(I) 6/82* where the claimant had broken his ankle while carrying out his duties as a maintenance engineer in a bakery. In holding that the claimant had not had an accident, the Commissioner said,

> "walking, standing, sitting etc. are all part of everyday human activity and unless they represent a special danger to a claimant because of some inherent, idiopathic, characteristic of the individual claimant, accidents happening during those activities, even in the course of employment cannot be said to arise out of the employment unless there is the additional factor of an injury by contact with the employer's premises etc. There is no distinction in my view between a heart attack suffered by a sedentary employee and an unexplained bone fracture or dislocation suffered by a walking employee. Neither will constitute an industrial accident unless some aspect of the employment caused the heart attack, the fracture or the dislocation or they were caused by the employee coming into contact with the employer's plant, premises, or machinery."

In *CAO v Faulds* 1998 S.L.T. 1203, 1998 S.C.L.R. 719, reported with *R(I) 1/00*, the Inner House of the Scottish Court of Session (the equivalent of the Court of Appeal in England and Wales) affirmed Commissioner Walker's decision in *CSI/26/96* (reported as part of *R(I) 1/00*), that a fireman who suffered post-traumatic stress disorder after having attended a series of horrific fatalities in the course of his employment had suffered "accidents" (a series of "accidents", not a "process") (see above). Lord McCluskey said in giving the opinion of the court:

> "in a case like the present just as in *R(I)22/59*, *CI/15589/1996* and *R(I)43/55*, also quoted to us, the accidental cause is found in the exposure of the employee on one or several—or even many—occasions to shocking sights or other such phenomena, resulting in his suffering a severe—and unintended— nervous reaction. We do not consider that the wording of the Act requires that there be found a separable 'accident' in the form of a distinct event separate from the injury and preceding it in point of time. In circumstances in which the horror of the exposure triggers a response which takes the form of nervous trauma, the injury and its cause may merge indistinguishably, but the injury may still be properly said to be caused by accident" (1998 S.L.T. 1203 at 1210).

In *CAO v Faulds* [2000] 2 All E.R. 961, reported as *R(I) 1/00* the majority of the House of Lords (Lord Hutton dissenting) rather harshly read this passage as failing sufficiently to identify, as was necessary, particular incidents, constituting accidents, which produced the injury (the post-traumatic stress disorder) and as erroneously tending to suggest that it sufficed for purposes of the industrial injuries scheme that the injury had arisen "accidentally" (see Lord Hope at 969, Lord Clyde at 973). In short, their Lordships considered that there was insufficient evidence for SSAT, Commissioner and the Inner House to find "accident" rather than "process" and remitted the matter back to the Inner House (doubtless to pass on to the Commissioner and to a differently constituted appeal tribunal) for further consideration. Lord Hutton took the view that the Inner House had identified a series of incidents producing and aggravating the post-traumatic stress disorder and was entitled to find as it did. The House of Lords, while unhappy with its precise application in the particular case of psychological injury before them in *Faulds*, approved a line of cases involving physical injury held to be within the scheme in which the distinction between "accident" and "injury" becomes blurred: *Fenton v Thorley* [1903] A.C. 443 (rupture when turning an unexpectedly resistant wheel); *Welsh v Glasgow Coal* 1916 S.C. (HL)

141 (workman immersed in water developed rheumatism); *Clover, Clayton & Co. Ltd v Hughes* [1910] A.C. 242 (death from burst aneurism when tightening a nut with a spanner); *Falmouth Docks and Engineering Co. Ltd v Treloar* [1933] A.C. 481 (man suffering from heart disease dropped dead when lifting his hand, holding a hook, above his head) (see Lord Clyde [2000] 2 All E.R. 961 at 976–977). The key point is the need to identify some causative event or small series of events, remembering, in Lord Hope's words, "that the sustaining of an *unexpected* personal injury caused by an *expected* event or incident may itself amount to an accident" ([2000] 2 All E.R. 961 at 969). In the context of injury through shock or stress, there is still need to:

> "identify the accident of which notice would require to be given, and the injury which was caused by it. The principle established in the cases of physical injury should in that respect be applicable to cases of psychological injury. In cases of shock and stress the activity which triggers the accident may only consist of the claimant confronting an horrific spectacle. It may involve some additional activity, such as the handling or the close examination of something particularly gruesome or distressing. But in every case, although the concepts may overlap, it should be possible to identify an accident as well as the consequent injury. But the identification of the accident and the establishment of a causal connection between the incident and the injury may well call for a very careful investigation of the circumstances of the case and the nature of the condition" ([2000] 2 All E.R. 961 at 979, *per* Lord Clyde).

Commissioner Parker, sitting as a Deputy Commissioner in Northern Ireland, in broader context, encapsulated the matter well: **1.345**

> "although the majority of the House of Lords recognises that there are cases where the elements of accident and injury overlap, it is nevertheless stressed that there is a distinction between the two which must be observed. A physiological or psychological change for the worse can only constitute an accident if it is, at least partly, caused by the work which the claimant is doing at the time; if there is no causal link to the relevant work and the injury would have happened whether the claimant was at work or not then the internal accident does not count as amounting to accidental injury in the sense of the statute. A claimant must identify some causative event or events which produced the physiological or pathological change for the worse, such as turning a wheel or a screw or lifting his hand, and that such trigger was *because* of his ordinary work not merely *at* his work. That in such case it is hardly possible to distinguish in time between "accident" and "injury" does not negate the distinction. The reasoning of the House of Lords stressed the essential requirement of identifying an incident which brought about the physiological injury which constitutes, in effect, the required accident/injury. It is only when there is a triggering work event for an injury that it can be accepted that the very injury suffered constitutes the necessary accident for the purposes of the section" (*C1/06-07(II)*, para.30).

Accordingly, accepting this, Commissioner Bano in *CI/2842/2006*, held that, since his cardiologist accepted that the claimant's work conditions might have contributed to his condition, it was more likely than not that the exceptional work pressures, to which he was subject immediately prior to his suffering a cardiac arrest at work, contributed to that cardiac arrest and that this was properly to be regarded as an accident, "even though it occurred in the normal course of the claimant's duties and was not preceded by any [separate] abnormal event" (paras 13, 16).

The Court of Appeal, however, unanimously allowed the Secretary of State's appeal against Commissioner Bano's decision (*SSWP* v *Scullion* [2010] EWCA Civ 310; [2010] AACR 29). The Court undertook a thorough review of the authorities on Workmen's Compensation and the post-1948 industrial injuries scheme, but particularly *Faulds*. In the light of that, it held that Commissioner Bano had erred in law in treating the "injury" (the cardiac arrest")—being improbable, sudden and an unlooked for mishap or untoward event—as also constituting the "accident", so that the only issue for him was the "out of employment" aspect, the "necessary causal connection with his work" (the stressful situation). Having dealt with step one (identifying the "injury") he ought also to have dealt with step two (specifying the identifiable "accident") and considered:

> "what external event or series of events (allied or not to some action by the claimant) had some physiological or psychological effect on the claimant .. [T]he plain fact here is that there is no evidence that any external event, even if allied to some action by Mr Scullion, such as lifting a very heavy pile of papers, opening a file drawer which had stuck, or even lifting an arm to get heavy papers from a shelf, caused the cardiac arrest. Therefore, the claimant failed to prove that his personal injury, viz. the cardiac arrest and all that followed from it, was "caused by accident" within the meaning of section 94(1) of the 1992 Act" (paras 53, 54, per Aikens L.J.).

As Pill L.J. stressed, "the statements of principle [in *Faulds*] are inconsistent with the assertion that the cardiac arrest was itself an accident within the meaning of [s. 94(1)]" (para.20). In such cases, decision-makers, tribunal and judges need to identify the precipitating external event(s). On that basis, the fact that a work environment or a mode of work may be stressful and produce a deleterious effect (the "injury") such as a mental disorder, a breakdown or a cardiac arrest will not suffice; a precipitating cause within the notion "accident" must also be present, as, for example, in cases such as *Jones* or *CI/4708/2001* or *CI/105/1998*, noted earlier in this annotation; otherwise the injury (as perhaps in most cases of stress illness: see *CI/3511/2002*) appears rather as the result of "process".

1.346 *Caused by accident:* The meaning of "accident" has been discussed above.

The injury must be *caused* by the accident. Three situations should be noted: (i) where the claimant is predisposed to the injury suffered because of disease or constitutional weakness; (ii) where the injury suffered renders the claimant susceptible to other forms of injury; (iii) where the injury suffered is aggravated by a further non-industrial accident.

If the claimant is predisposed to injury it will still be proper to say that the accident caused the injury if it would not have happened but for the accident (*R(I) 12/52*—a bus conductor with abnormally fragile bones; *R(I) 14/51*—a miner with an existing heart condition; *R(I) 73/51*—a labourer suffering from Paget's disease). Note that there must still be something which can be termed an accident occurring as a result of the particular duties of the employment (see above).

1.347 Where the claimant can show that the original industrial injury was an effective cause of the eventual non-industrial injury he will also succeed in his claim. In *R(I) 3/56*, a Tribunal of Commissioners allowed a claim by a man who had been injured in a fall on the way to work as a result of a previous accident at work. The Tribunal said,

> ". . . if the immediate cause of his incapacity is an injury by non-industrial accident the claimant will be entitled to injury benefit if he can prove that a previous injury by industrial accident was an effective cause of the injury by non-industrial accident which was the immediate cause of his incapacity."

Similar successful claims may be found in *CI/129/49* and *R(I) 59/51*.

The same principle is relevant to determine cases where the non-industrial injury is an aggravation of the industrial injury but is not related to it. Illness following upon an injury or a completely unrelated non-industrial accident which incapacitates the claimant will not be taken into account except in so far as the industrial injury continues to be an effective cause of the claimant's incapacity.

Provision is made for taking into account a combination of industrial and non-industrial accidents in assessing the extent of disablement for the purposes of disablement benefit. See ss.103, 107, and General Benefit Regs below.

"arising out of and in the course of employment"

This phrase first appeared in the Workmen's Compensation Act 1897 to limit compensation paid under the original scheme to injuries which were suffered through work and not merely at work. 1.348

The two tests, "in the course of" and "out of", look to different things. The former embraces time, place and activity. The latter requires a causal nexus between the injury and the employment. The separateness of the two tests is affirmed by the statutory presumption in s.94(3), readily defeasible if there is any evidence to the contrary, that an accident "in the course of" also arises "out of" the employment (*Chief Adjudication Officer v Rhodes,* reported as *R(I) 1/99*). The distinct nature of the two tests is also manifest in the deeming provision in s.101 (an accident arising "in the course of" employment will be deemed to arise "out of" it in a bewildering range of situations whose only common factor consists of their being situations which courts or commissioners had ruled as not arising out of the employment applying general principles). A person may satisfy one test but not secure benefit because failing to meet the other. So, in *Rhodes*, above, in the case of the civil servant assaulted on her drive by a neighbour because of her work (she had reported him as claiming benefit whilst working), the work nexus satisfied the "out of" test, but her claim failed. While all the other requisites of s.94(1) were met, she was not "in the course of" her employment because when assaulted she was at home on sick leave, returning from a visit to her doctor, and not engaged at the material time in performing any work tasks.

Arising out of . . . employment: The first part of the phrase confines the industrial injuries scheme to those injuries which are work-related and seeks to exclude those which result from the ordinary risks which affect everybody. To give two examples, in *R(I) 62/53* a lorry driver suffered a corneal abrasion when something went into his eye whilst he was driving. The Commissioner held that he was not entitled to benefit because the accident did not arise out of the employment—the risk was general and not particular to his employment. By contrast, a policeman on motor-bike patrol duty who was similarly injured *was* entitled to benefit because the risk of eye injury whilst riding a motor-bike on duty was greater than normal (*R(I) 67/53*). 1.349

There is a further interesting comparison between *R(I) 22/59* and unreported decision *CI/387/1988*. In the former case, a miner suffered nervous debility resulting from the shock of hearing of his son's death in an accident at the same mine; in the latter case, a worker suffered anxietal depression after seeing a colleague in the terminal stages of angiosarcoma of the liver, a disease to which his own work exposed him.

In *R(I) 22/59*, the accident (hearing of the death) was held not to have arisen out of employment; in *CI/387/1988*, the accident (sighting the colleague) was held to have arisen out of the employment. The distinction taken was that the father could have been shocked at the son's death wherever he worked; the latter claimant would not have suffered shock unless he had been working at the particular place where industrial conditions created the hazard which threatened him. *CI/387/1988* was distinguished by Commissioner Goodman in *CI/289/1994* when he upheld the decision of an SSAT (which applied *R(I) 22/59* and *R(I) 62/53*) that the post-traumatic stress disorder suffered by a lorry driver when he learned over the radio in his cab of the Zeebrugge ferry disaster did not arise out of his employment:

> "In [*CI/387/1988*], the claimant himself had worked for many years with vinyl chloride monomer and therefore was at potential risk of developing cancer of the liver . . . But that is not the same as the facts of the present case. Admittedly the claimant had had to use the same ferry crossing but he had successfully made the trips. Any danger that there might have been from the ferry sailing [which had been on a different vessel] had gone as soon as the claimant had driven off the ferry. There was no continuing risk such as the continuing risk of cancer [in *CI/387/1988*] nor was there necessarily any such risk in the future, particularly as

the claimant could reasonably assume that the occurrence of the disaster would cause further safety precautions to be taken" (para.10).

1.350 It is thus crucial for the "out of" employment issue properly to analyse the nature of the risk in the case. *CSI/154/89*, a decision of Commissioner Walker shows the difficulties of drawing a line between injuries resulting from the ordinary risks to which everyone is exposed, whether employed or not (not arising out of employment) and those injuries resulting from risks created by the employment (which do arise out of the employment as being work-related). The case takes a more generous approach than some other decisions (e.g. *R(I) 62/53* and *R(I) 52/54*). Indeed the case is strikingly similar on its facts to *R(I) 52/54*, but it is an approach which draws on leading authorities on the interpretation of the same phraseology in the Workmen's Compensation legislation (*White v W & T Avery*, 1916 S.C. 209, *McNeice v Singer Sewing Machine Co Ltd* 1911 S.C. 12 and the House of Lords' decision, *Dennis v AJ White & Co.* [1917] A.C. 479). In *Dennis*, Lord Finlay L.C. said:

> "If a servant in the course of his master's business has to pass along the public street, whether it be on foot or on a bicycle, or on an omnibus or car, and he sustains an accident by reason of the risks incidental to the street, the accident arises out of as well as in the course of his employment. The frequency or infrequency of the occasions on which the risk is incurred has nothing to do with the question whether an accident resulting from that risk arose out of the employment . . . but as soon as it is established that the work itself involves exposure to the perils of the streets the workmen can recover for any injury so occasioned.
>
> Where the risk is one shared by all men, whether in or out of employment, it must be established that special exposure to it is involved. But when a workman is sent into the street on his master's business, whether it be occasionally or habitually, his employment necessarily involves exposure to the risks of the streets, and injury from such a cause arises out of his employment." (cited in para.17).

Further, Commissioner Walker recalls Lord Denning's exhortation in *Vandyke v Fender* [1970] 2 Q.B. 292 that this phraseology be given the same interpretation whether used in industrial injuries legislation, road traffic legislation or employer's liability policies. One can here note that something like that approach is inherent in the way Commissioners, dealing with "travelling cases" under the industrial injuries scheme, have drawn on the tests in the House of Lords' decision in *Smith v Stages* [1989] 1 All E.R. 833, dealing with similar issues in the law of torts. Commissioner Walker then noted, looking to *Smith v Stages*, that what is incidental to the employment appears to be relevant to the issue "out of" as well as that of "in the course of" with which that case dealt. The court decisions he had cited persuaded him that the SSAT had adopted an incorrect analysis of the claimant's situation, and was thus erroneous in law:

> "The question which they should have asked themselves was whether the claimant was exposed to the risk by the job or whether the risk was one that could have affected her whether or not in the employment at that time. That raises the question as to what was the risk. In this case I conclude that it was the risk of falling, as evidenced by the finding of fact that she fell on the pavement. That is a normal risk of the streets but it was a risk to which she became exposed only because her employment put her in the relevant place at the relevant time. And so I come at last to the question whether the fact that Mrs Falconer was reacting there and then to an emergency [trying to save a child who had run into the road] yet takes her out of the scope and/or course of her employment.
>
> I approach these two questions separately. 'In the course of' is simple. The Commissioner in *R(I) 52/54* would have taken it for granted. The claimant was where she was at the time of the accident because so required or at least permitted by her employment. She had not deviated nor gone deliberately out of her way.

> The employment was not interrupted. So I hold that Mrs Falconer's accident occurred in the course of her employment. As to whether it arose 'out of ' that employment I am persuaded by the language quoted above from *White v Avery, McNeice* and *Dennis v AJ White & Co.* that it is the risk that has to be considered rather than what brought it to pass. How it came to pass might affect liability in a damages claim but not for present purposes—*cf.* the potato picker's case [*R(I) 17/63*]. It was not outwith the nature and type of risk that might befall a messenger. That seems to me to be enough. I think that the word 'emergency' is misleading in, and inappropriate to this case. I have therefore to add that I am unable to agree with the decision *R(I) 52/54*. So I hold that the accident here arose 'out of ' the claimant's employment as well." (paras 19 and 20; words in brackets added by commentator).

In *CI/1654/2008* Commissioner Jacobs considered the case of an employee who slipped and was injured while showering at a hotel before attending a training session there. He held that the accident befell her when in the course of her employment; her actions in making herself presentable were reasonably incidental to her duties and she was where she was because of her work. But it did not arise "out" of the employment: 1.351

> "The risk was not created by her employment. It was inherent in the nature of a shower. It was a risk that anyone would run who took a shower. Indeed, it was not limited to the shower. There was a similar risk in the bathroom outside the shower. The claimant's employment did not expose her to any hazard that was additional to, or exceptional when compared with, the risk that anyone else would run who was taking a shower or using a hotel bathroom" (paras 36, 37).

Nor did SSCBA 1992 s.101 operate so as to treat this accident arising in the course of employment as also arising out of it; there was "no evidence that the accident was caused by someone else's misconduct, skylarking or negligence" (para.28).

Note the relationship between this concept and the question of whether an accident has occurred, in circumstances where the claimant merely suffers injury at work which might have happened anywhere, e.g. a heart attack, a fit or a dislocation. In *R(I) 6/82* (above), the Commissioner held that there was no accident, but, even if there had been, it would not have arisen out of the course of employment unless there had been an injury caused by contact with the employer's plant, premises or machinery or unless some aspect of the employment caused the injury.

The claimant is assisted by the provision in subs.(3) of this section (noted below) that an accident which occurs in the course of employment shall be deemed to have arisen out of the employment unless there is evidence to the contrary. Note also, for cases of any doubt, the role of s.101 (deemed "out of").

Arising . . . in the course of employment: This looks to matters of time, place and activity. As Lord Loreburn put it in *Moore v Manchester Liners Ltd* [1910] A.C. 498 at 500–501: 1.352

> "An accident befalls a man 'in the course of' his employment if it occurs while he is doing what a man so employed may reasonably do within a time during which he is employed, and at a place where he may reasonably be during that time to do that thing".

The test requires a focus on what the claimant is doing rather than on what was done to the claimant. This principle is demonstrated well by *EJMcC v Department for Social Communities (II)* [2021] NICom 12, in which a worker suffered catastrophic head injuries when using a machine after hours in his workplace to polish a letter-box for his own private purposes. As the Commissioner observed (at para.37), dismissing the claimant's challenge to the appeal tribunal's decision:

> "The appellant was not performing an employment duty under his contract of employment. He was outside his working hours. He was in his place of work, but in a part normally locked and inaccessible to him, and to which he had borrowed a key. The task that he was undertaking was entirely of a personal nature. The only factor connecting the circumstances to the appellant's employment was that he was using a piece of machinery which was owned by his employer."

Moreover, "even if the employer directly authorised the appellant to carry out a "homer" on his own time, I do not consider that such permission could transform his actions into something reasonably incidental to his contract of employment" (para.40).

In *Chief Adjudication Officer v Rhodes*, reported as *R(I) 1/99*), Schiemann L.J. (with whose judgment Roch L.J. concurred to give the majority in the case) approved Hoffmann L.J.'s statement in *Faulkner v Chief Adjudication Officer* [1994] P.I.Q.R. 244 at 256; *The Times*, April 8, 1994 (one citing as authority *Smith v Stages* [1989] A.C. 928) reported as *R(I) 8/94* and adapted it so as to read (adaptation in square brackets):

> "An office or employment involves a legal relationship: it entails the existence of specific duties on the part of the employee. An act or event happens 'in the course of employment' if [what the employee is doing] constitutes the discharge of one of those duties or is reasonably incidental thereto".

One must first ascertain what the employee is employed to do and then consider whether what the employee was doing at the material time constitutes the discharge of one of those duties or something reasonably incidental thereto.

This "back to basics" approach in *Rhodes* is firmly located within the structure of this statutory regime and within the mass of authority since the tests were first included in the Workmen's Compensation Act 1897 (see R. Lewis, *Compensation for Industrial Injury* (1987), p.51). So, for example, the approach meshes with the general formulation found in the headnote to an earlier Court of Appeal decision, *R. v Industrial Injuries Commissioner Ex p. A.E.U. (No. 2)* [1966] 2 Q.B. 31 (*Culverwell's* case):

> "The test whether a man is acting 'in the course of his employment' is not the strict test of whether he is at the relevant time performing a duty for his employer, for he may be 'in the course of his employment' when he acts casually, negligently or even disobediently, so long as it is something reasonably incidental to his contract of employment".

With respect to the dissenting Swinton Thomas L.J. in *Rhodes*, above, matters of time and place are important: those injured away from the employer's premises during a lunch break, unless performing tasks for their employer, are not "in the course of employment". The system has always been predicated on there being a difference between injuries suffered at work during working hours and those suffered while resting at home or when travelling to or from a fixed point of work. Were that not so, the justifications for a separate system of compensation for work injuries would be further called into question. Crucial lines drawn by a raft of previous authority (e.g. on travelling to and from a fixed place of work generally being outside the scheme [*Lewis*, pp.76, 77] and, by implication, the deeming provision in s.99 (passengers travelling in employer provided transport)) would respectively be rendered nugatory and unnecessary.

1.353 The matter of the proper approach to "in the course of employment" had been thrown into some disarray by the Court of Appeal decision in *Nancollas v Insurance Officer* [1985] 1 All E.R. 833. That case dealt with the issue of whether two claimants injured in motor accidents were injured in the course of employment. In the case, Lord Donaldson M.R. went so far as to suggest that there were no legal rules (other than the plain statutory language) for courts or tribunals to follow, merely factors pointing one way or the other. Hence the proper approach was for tribunals to look at the factual picture as a whole, rejecting any approach based on the fallacious concept that any one factor is conclusive. The Court of Appeal decision in *Rhodes*, above, is a firm affirmation of the trend (see *Smith v Stages* [1989] A.C. 928, especially Lord Lowry at 948, 955–956, and the Court of Appeal in *Faulkner v Chief Adjudication Officer* [1994] P.I.Q.R. 244 reported as *R(I) 8/94*), of effectively relegating the *Nancollas* impressionistic "factor" approach to the secondary issue of the characterisation of particular acts once the central questions have been posed: what was the claimant employed to do and was s/he doing it, or something reasonably incidental to it, when the accident occured. This is both right in principle and, by more clearly establishing parameters, enables an expert body of Commissioners more closely to scrutinise decisions of appeals tribunals, the better to ensure a degree of "horizontal equity between claimants" (see Wikeley, Ogus and Barendt, *The Law of Social Security*, p.728), since it is submitted that the "back to basics" approach in *Rhodes* offers a framework of analysis relatively more certain and consistent than the impressionist, artistic brushwork of Lord Donaldson M.R. in *Nancollas*. Whilst part of his judgment in *Nancollas* was approved by Lord Goff in *Smith v Stages*, it is clear that the House of Lords did not approve the proposition that there are no rules. Indeed, Lord Lowry set out six propositions designed to assist with the question whether a person travelling could be regarded as being in the course of employment (see annotations to s.99, below, "Introduction"). Although *Smith v Stages* was not concerned with a social security question, but rather with the matter of an employer's vicarious liability for the acts of his employee in the law of torts, the same phrase, "acting in the course of employment" was under consideration. Moreover, their Lordships reverted to older authorities for guidance, relying particularly on *St Helens Colliery Limited v Hewitson* [1924] A.C. 59, and stated that *Vandyke v Fender* [1970] 2 Q.B. 292 is still good law. Indeed in *R(I) 1/88* (see further the annotations to s.99, below, "Introduction"), the Commissioner held that *Nancollas* did not remove the well-accepted distinction betwen acts done under an obligation to an employer and acts merely done with his permission: in the former case it almost necessarily follows that the employee was acting in the course of his employment, but this does not equally necessarily follow from the fact that the employee was doing what was authorised by the employer.

Rightly, however, given the immense variety of the world of work, the post-*Nancollas* reappraisal culminating in *Rhodes* nonetheless requires the application of broad principle to the facts of individual cases rather than proceeding on the basis that a similar fact case *dictates* the result. Tribunals should not rely too heavily on previous decisions without relating them to a detailed consideration of the facts of the particular case *(R(I) 1/93; CI 110/98)*. In *R(I) 1/93*, Commissioner Johnson set aside an SSAT decision as erroneous in law because it failed to look at the factual picture as a whole:

> "the tribunal clearly relied on apparently similar cases [Commissioners' decisions] in reaching their decisions, whereas they should have given primary consideration to the particular facts of the case before them" (para.6).

In the particular case the claimant was injured when she tripped and fell during a site meeting, held on her employer's premises, but not at her usual workplace. The purpose of the meeting was to discuss the pending actions brought against the company by the claimant and others with respect to repetitive strain injury (RSI). The factor which tipped the balance for the Commissioner, who held that the accident befell her out of and in the course of her employment, was "the company's interest in her attending the site meeting" which might well save time and costs in the litigation even if it did not secure a settlement of the claims (paras 10, 11).

1.354 "In the course of employment" and the tests noted above have a good degree of elasticity. That, as held in *Rhodes* above (see further below, "(iv) Flexible working and employees on sick leave"), those incapable of work, and thus not as such "in the course of their employment", can still be protected if injured while performing one of their work tasks (the performance bringing them back within the course of their employment) amply illustrates the flexibility of application inherent in the central tests, adherence to which is essential in a compensation system for accidents suffered at or during work and because of it.

There are four statutory "extensions" in ss.98–101 bringing certain accidents, which would otherwise not arise in the course of [ss.98–100], or out of [s.101], employment, within the scope of the scheme. Travelling accidents, a continual problem, are dealt with in the note to s.99. Three other common types of claim illustrate the difficulty of determining the course of employment when applying s.94.

(i) Beginnings and endings

1.355 When does the course of employment start and finish on the normal working day? Clocking in and out? Getting into and out of working clothes? Getting onto and off the employer's premises? The terms of employment may be part of the answer but all the facts must be considered and weighed, perhaps with a view to asking whether at the point at which the accident happened the employee was exposed to the risks of the workplace or merely those risks which he would run as a member of the general public. By way of example of successful claims:

NE v SSWP (II) [2021] UKUT 240 (AAC) (claimant having accident while showering before contracted working hours when living on-site)

R. v N.I. Commissioner Ex p. East [1976] I.C.R. 206 (accident suffered by claimant in works canteen prior to clocking-on)

R(I) 3/62 (employee habitually arriving very early at work to avoid rush-hour travel)

R(I) 22/56 (miner suffering accident on colliery road after visiting colliery canteen at the end of work to avoid the rush for the first bus)

R(I) 72/54 (miner suffering accident on way to collect replacement for bootlace broken whilst changing into working clothes)

CI/105/1990 (employee injured while getting into taxi to have her injury checked and, if necessary, treated, in hospital: see below).

Unsuccessful claims:

R(I) 22/53 (railwayman injured on his way from home to work—on railway land but half a mile from the depot where he worked)

R(I) 11/54 (miner visiting canteen before his shift to buy sandwiches to eat during shift—injured on canteen steps)

R(I) 14/61 (part-time clerk completing work at 1.00pm then taking lunch in the canteen and suffering injury on leaving)

CI/114/1987 (employee going in to work on day off for sole purpose of collecting pay and suffering injury outside the wages office).

(ii) Taking a break

1.356 Is the course of employment interrupted where the claimant takes a break in the working day? Again, a matter of fact for the decision-maker or tribunal, but it may be useful to discover whether the break was imposed by the employer, permitted, condoned, provided for in the terms of employment, or proscribed. Were any particular activities required (or prohibited) during the break? Was the claimant still on duty, or on call during the break? *R. v Industrial Injuries Commissioner Ex p. A.E.U. (No.2)* [1996] 2 Q.B. 31 (*Culverwell's* case) concerned an accident happening during a break. The claimant was only permitted to smoke in a designated booth. Throughout a permitted break the booth was occupied and the claimant was injured by a fork-lift truck as he waited outside the booth after the end of the permitted break. The Court of Appeal held that he was not in the course of employment because he had overstayed the permitted break and was doing something for his own purposes quite unconnected with his employment.

As examples of successful claims:

R(I) 21/53, *R(I) 11/55*, *R(I) 20/61* and *R(I) 4/67* (all concern bus drivers or conductors injured during a break from duty and observing the instructions or permission of their employer about the way the break should be spent)

R(I) 7/80 (police sergeant in charge of station permitted to take meal break at home whilst remaining on call—injured on journey back to station).

Unsuccessful claims:

R(I) 6/53 and *R(I) 4/79* (bus crews)

R(I) 6/76 (interruption of work due to bomb scare)

R(I) 5/81 (fire officer travelling from office to home to begin on-call period)

R(I) 10/81 (merchant seaman going ashore for his own purposes during an official break).

(iii) Recreational activity

Some employments have recreational activity as a part of the work; some offer facilities for recreation; some offer periods of inactivity during which employees may take recreation. Whether an accident occurring during recreational activity has arisen in the course of employment must be a question of mixed fact and law, but whereas one type of claim has generally been successful, two other types have not. This may indicate the important questions to ask in such a case. **1.357**

The successful claims have been in cases where the employee is required to take part in the activity:

CI/228/50 (apprentice injured during compulsory physical training as part of day class he was required to attend—see also *R(I) 4/51*, *R(I) 31/53*)

R(I) 13/51 (male nurse at mental hospital injured whilst playing football with patients—see also *R(I) 3/57*)

R(I) 68/51 (fireman injured playing volleyball during compulsory fitness training period—see also *R(I) 13/66*)

R(I) 3/81 (police cadet injured whilst travelling back from National Swimming Championships in which she had been detailed to take part).

The unsuccessful claims have been in cases where the recreational activity is merely encouraged (even strongly encouraged) rather than compulsory (*R . v N.I. Commissioners Ex p. Michael* [1977] 1 W.L.R. 109, Appendix to *R(I) 5/75*); or where the employee takes recreation during an off-duty period or during an enforced break in employment:

R(I) 2/69 (laboratory technician playing football during the lunch-hour)

R(I) 2/80 (fireman attending residential college injured playing football in the evening)

R(I) 4/81 (airline stewardess injured playing tennis during a stop-over between flights).

R. v N.I. Commissioners Ex p. Michael has been followed by the Court of Appeal, in preference to *Nancollas*, in *Faulkner v Chief Adjudication Officer*, *The Times*, April 8, 1994 reported as *R(I) 8/94*. In *Faulkner*, the claimant policeman sustained personal injury while playing football for his police football team. The SSAT held this to have arisen in the course of his employment but their decision was set aside as erroneous in law on September 30, 1990 by Commissioner Johnson. The Court of Appeal upheld the Commissioner's decision; there was no evidence before the SSAT which could justify such a conclusion. Following *Michael*, the question was whether the claimant was doing his job when injured and not whether he was doing something reasonably incidental to it. The court considered that the implication of a contractual term was not to be made because it seemed sensible or reasonable that such a term should be implied or because the chief police officer, the Police Federation representative, or the claimant regarded community policing as a good and useful policy, but in accordance with the ordinary legal principle that an obligation could be read into a contract if it was such as the nature of the contract itself implicitly required. The claimant had sought to rely on *Nancollas* to argue that *Michael* should be reconsidered in the light of changing social circumstances. The Court decided that *Nancollas* gave no basis for distinguishing *Michael.*

(iv) Flexible working and employees on sick leave

1.358 In *R(I) 1/99*, Commissioner Goodman held that "in the course of employment" embraced the employee, a Benefits Agency clerical officer at home on sick leave, incapable of work and, by rights, doing none, who was assaulted in her drive by her neighbour for reasons clearly connected with and the product of her employment (she had reported the neighbour to the appropriate Benefits Agency authorities for claiming benefits whilst working). While the injury undoubtedly arose out of the employment, it is difficult, applying factors of time, place and activity, to regard such a claimant as properly being in the course of her employment (see further D. Bonner, "Compensation for Assault: an Unusual Dimension to the Industrial Injuries System" (1998) 5 J.S.S.L. 68). The Court of Appeal, by majority (Schiemann and Roch L.JJ., Swinton Thomas L.J. dissenting), upheld the appeal against Commissioner Goodman's decision: *Chief Adjudication Officer v Rhodes*, reported as *R(I) 1/99*; see further Bonner (1999) 6 J.S.S.L. 33). Commissioner Goodman had erred in law. While Mrs Rhodes at the time of the assault was clearly still employed as an employed earner, and while the work-connected reason for the assault undoubtedly rendered this "accident" one arising "out of" of the employment, the reason for the assault could not of itself bring her within "the course of employment". "Out of" and "in the course of" are distinct conditions *both* of which must be satisifed to render the accident an industrial one. "In the course of" requires a focus on what the claimant was doing rather than on what was done to her. There was no basis for saying that at the material time Mrs Rhodes was doing something she was employed to do or something reasonably incidental thereto, that being the established test (see above). Commissioner Goodman had instead concentrated in effect (though not in form) on whether or not she was an employed earner. Undoubtedly she was, even when on sick leave. But so too would be a claimant injured when on a skiing holiday. Merely being still an employed earner does not render one in the course of employment. Roch L.J. rejected Commissioner Goodman's view that, being still employed and on sick leave, she was thus at home only with the consent and authority of her employer, in so far as that view misleadingly suggested that the employer required her to be at home. Hence, merely being on permitted sick leave does not bring a claimant within the course of employment. Roch L.J. saw the Commissioner's decision and the points made in support of Mrs Rhodes (and by implication Swinton Thomas L.J.'s dissent?) as foundering "on the ground that they elide the two requirements into a single requirement, namely has the accident arisen out of the claimant's employment". The two are separate, something affirmed as Parliament's intention by the presumption in s.94(3) that accidents in the course of also arise out of employment in the absence of any evidence to the contrary. "In the course of" requires examination of *the activity of* the claimant, not of *what is being done to* the claimant. Schiemann L.J. considered, however, (and Roch L.J. agreed with his reasoning) that someone on sick leave can still be in the course of employment if performing duties required of him (and similar propositions must apply to those working at home under flexible working arrangements). For example someone in hospital with a broken leg in traction but whose mental faculties are unimpaired could be given files to read and would be in the course of employment when doing that. Similarly if Mrs Rhodes had actually been working on material from the office. If, when off sick, she had been assaulted while using a mobile phone to report a fraudulent claimant, that, for Schiemann L.J., would be something reasonably incidental to what she was employed to do. He might also have so held, though he saw lesser force in this situation, if the assault had occurred just after she had ended the telephone conversation. But none of this could avail

Mrs Rhodes whose information was given days, if not weeks, before. Although she sometimes did work at home under the Agency's flexi-time system, there was no material before the Commissioner for him to find as a fact that at the relevant time Mrs Rhodes was working at home. The matters the claimant drew to the court's attention—the fact that she was sometimes sent material to help her to keep up to date with the law and practice in the field in which she was employed:

> "did not suggest that on that particular day she was actually doing anything, although she could have been required to do something . . . simply as a matter of construction of the relevant section [SSCBA, s.94(1)], the twin test is not satisfied.
>
> One of the pillars is fulfilled, the accident did arise out of the employment, but it does not seem to me that it arose in the course of the employment. To say that something was causally linked to something which has been done in the course of employment does not seem to me to be good enough".

However, had Mrs Rhodes been assaulted on her drive while giving advice in her official capacity to her neighbour on benefit matters, one might surely agree with the dissenting Swinton Thomas L.J. that such an accident arose not only "out of" but also "in the course of" her employment.

In *CI/1098/2004*, Commissioner Howell was faced with an application for an accident declaration from a hospital staff nurse, who argued that he had suffered psychological damage because of what he was told in the course of a telephone conversation he made to his Directorate Manager when at home on sick leave, having earlier been telephoned from work and asked to call his Directorate Manager. Commissioner Howell directed the tribunal to which he remitted the application for an accident declaration that for that purpose the telephone conversation was one made in the course of and out of the applicant's employment 1.359

> "but that it is for the claimant to establish to the satisfaction of the tribunal that he did in fact suffer something in the course of or as the immediate consequence of that conversation which is identifiable as an 'accident' before he can be granted the declaration he seeks. This is something the tribunal must determine for itself, the apparent departmental acceptance that he has suffered some form of personal injury being insufficient" (para.2).

It cannot be emphasised too strongly that the whole of this note on the course of employment should be read in the light of the comments in the *Nancollas* case, *Smith v Stages, Faulkner v Chief Adjudication Officer* and *CAO v Rhodes* (above) about the proper approach to determining the question of whether a claimant is, or is not, in the course of his employment. In starred decision *CI/105/1990*, Commissioner Goodman considered how one should approach the case in which several accidents (in this instance two on the same day) are each said to be industrial accidents:

> "[I]n deciding whether or not first, second or subsequent accidents are of themselves industrial accidents, each must be looked at in isolation, though what happened in one accident may have some bearing on whether or not when a subsequent accident occurred the claimant was still within the course of employment. *But* it must still be established independently that the second accident did arise out of and in the course of employment, as that is required imperatively by section 50(1) of the Social Security Act 1975 [now s.94(1)]" (para.13).

In *CI/105/1990*, the claimant home carer (home help) slipped on an icy pavement on her way to her first visit of the day, incurring what was later established to be a hairline fracture of the fibula. She nevertheless continued work and undertook a number of tasks at and in relation to her first call. Being still in pain, she informed her supervisor that she was going to hospital to have her leg checked and, if necessary, treated. "It was either expressed or implied that if all was well she would be carrying on with her schedule of visits for the day." Unfortunately, she slipped on the icy pavement when the taxi came, suffering a "potts fracture" of the right ankle, so severe that she had not at the time of the Commissioner's hearing been able to resume work as a home carer. The SSAT upheld her appeal against the AO's refusal to grant any declaration of industrial accident, but only in relation to the first incident. On appeal by the claimant from the SSAT, Commissioner Goodman considered the proper course was to regard there as having been two separate decisions by the SSAT, so that he was only concerned with the second incident. He considered that when it occurred, the claimant was still in the course of her employment, acting as an employee would if there was continued pain in the leg, namely to obtain some medical investigation of it, in her case in the only way open to a peripatetic worker, that is, by going to hospital. In this case, dependent on this point entirely on its own facts, the line dividing the course of employment and its cessation for that day was to be drawn only when it was clear that the claimant would not be coming back to work that day, something which only became clear when investigations took place in the hospital (see paras 10 and 11).

Subsection (2)

1.360 Industrial death benefit is no longer payable except in respect of deaths occurring before April 11, 1988. On reduced earnings allowance and retirement allowance, see commentary to Sch.7, Pts IV and V.

Subsection (3)

1.361 This provision has been referred to in the note on subs.(1) above. The so-called presumption created by this subsection has no operation where all the facts are known—it can only help the claimant where there is some doubt about the circumstances of the accident.

In *R. v N.I. (Industrial Injuries) Commissioner Ex p. Richardson* [1958] 1 W.L.R. 851 (Appendix to *R(I) 21/58*), the Divisional Court considered the equivalent provision in an earlier statute:

> "if . . . there is no other evidence except that [the claimant] suffered an accident in the course of his employment, then it is to be deemed, it is taken to be proved, that it arose out of the employment. But if there is evidence to the contrary by whoever it is given, that is to say, the facts which are before the Commissioner can amount to evidence to the contrary, then the presumption or the deeming disappears, and if once that deeming disappears it is then for [the claimant] to prove that the accident did arise not only in the course of but also out of his employment."

In *R(I) 16/61*, a Tribunal of Commissioners said that, ". . . as the facts are known and it is a question of applying the law to them it seems to us that there is no room for the application of [the presumption]."

In *R(I) 1/64*, the Commissioner suggested that "evidence to the contrary" in the subsection meant something more than speculative inference, but something less than proof. All the authorities were considered in *R(I) 6/82* (maintenance engineer in bakery suffering unexplained fracture to ankle whilst walking round a milling machine) where the subsection was held to be inapplicable because all the circumstances of the accident were known.

The presumption was considered again recently in *CI/207/1987*, where Commissioner Hoolahan considered the nature of the evidence required to rebut the presumption. He rejected the proposition that an inference could amount to evidence, since an inference may only be drawn from an established fact. If no clear inference can be drawn from the established facts, there is no evidence "to the contrary" for the purposes of this section.

Subsection (5)

Except for the special groups of workers referred to, industrial injuries benefit is not payable in respect of accidents happening outside Great Britain, notwithstanding that the victim may be carrying out his job abroad. This apparent anomaly was rectified by an amendment to the Persons Abroad Regulations which permits a claim for benefit in respect of accidents happening abroad to an employed earner, with effect from October 1, 1986. 1.362

Subsection (6)

For "incapable of work" and "incapacity for work" see the notes to s.57 (pp.180–182, and 187–194 of Bonner, Hooker and White, *Non Means Tested Benefits: The Legislation* (1994)). The new tests of incapacity in Pt XIIA do not apply for the purposes of industrial injuries benefits (s.171G(1)(a), below). 1.363

Relevant employments

95.—(1) In section 94 above, this section and sections 98 and 109 below "employed earner's employment" shall be taken to include any employment by virtue of which a person is, or is treated by regulations as being for the purposes of industrial injuries benefit, an employed earner. 1.364

(2) Regulations may provide that any prescribed employment shall not be treated for the purposes of industrial injuries benefit as employed earner's employment notwithstanding that it would be so treated apart from the regulations.

(3) For the purposes of the provisions of this Act mentioned in subsection (1) above an employment shall be an employed earner's employment in relation to an accident if (and only if) it is, or is treated by regulations as being, such an employment when the accident occurs.

(4) Any reference in the industrial injuries and diseases provisions to an "employed earner" or "employed earner's employment" is to be construed, in relation to any time before 6th April 1975, as a reference respectively to an "insured person" or "insurable employment" within the meaning of the provisions relating to industrial injuries and diseases which were in force at that time.

(5) In subsection (4) above "the industrial injuries and diseases provisions" means—

(a) this section and sections 96 to 110 below;
(b) any other provisions of this Act so far as they relate to those sections; and
(c) [1 any provisions of the Administration Act, Chapter II of Part I of the Social Security Act 1998 or Part II of the Social Security Contributions (Transfer of Functions, etc.) Act 1999, so far as they so relate.]

AMENDMENT

1. Social Security Act 1998 Sch.7 para.64 and Social Security Contributions (Transfer of Functions, etc.) Act 1999 Sch.7 para.4 (July 5, 1999).

DERIVATION

SSA 1975 s.51 as amended; SS(MP)A 1977 s.17(3). 1.365

General Note

1.366 The regulations referred to in this section are the Social Security (Employed Earner's Employments for Industrial Injuries Purposes) Regulations 1975 (SI 1975/467) (as amended). Decisions on whether a person is, or was, employed in employed earner's employment so as to bring him within the scheme were until April 1, 1999 solely for the Secretary of State (SSAA 1992 s.17). From April 1, 1999, such decisions became matters for officers of the Board of Revenue and Customs (see Social Security Contributions (Transfer of Functions, etc.) Act 1999 s.8(1)(b), below) and are now the province of the Commissioners for His Majesty's Revenue and Customs (see Commissioners for Revenue and Customs Act 2005 s.5(2)).

[[1]Employment training schemes etc

1.367 **95A.**—(1) In the industrial injuries and diseases provisions any reference to employed earner's employment shall be taken to include participation in an employment training scheme or employment training course of a prescribed description (and "employed earner" shall be construed accordingly).

(2) In those provisions, a reference to an employer, in relation to any such participation, shall be taken to be a prescribed person.

(3) In this section "industrial injuries and diseases provisions" has the same meaning as in s.95(4) above.]

Amendment

1.368 1. Welfare Reform Act 2012 s.66 (October 31, 2013).

General Note

1.369 As part of the simplification of benefits schemes, this applies the industrial injuries scheme to cover accidents and prescribed diseases resulting from participation in an employment training scheme or employment training course of a prescribed description, rather than, as previously, having participants covered under the Analogous Industrial Injuries Scheme (AIIS). Such participation is treated as employed earner's employment, participants as employed earner's (for II purposes) and "a prescribed person" is treated as the employer of such participants. See the Industrial Injuries Benefit (Employment Training Schemes and Courses) Regulations 2013 (SI 2013/2540). The "employers" for industrial injuries benefit purposes are persons providing an employment training scheme or employment training course of a description prescribed in reg.2 of those Regulations (reg.3).

Persons treated as employers for certain purposes

1.370 **96.**—In relation to—

(a) a person who is an employed earner for the purposes of this Part of this Act otherwise than by virtue of a contract of service or apprenticeship; or

(b) any other employed earner—

(i) who is employed for the purpose of any game or recreation and is engaged or paid through a club; or

(ii) in whose case it appears to the Secretary of State there is special difficulty in the application of all or any of the provisions of this Part of this Act relating to employers, regulations may provide for a prescribed person to be treated in respect of industrial injuries benefit and its administration as the earner's employer.

Accidents in course of illegal employments

97.—(1) Subsection (2) below has effect in any case where— 1.371

(a) a claim is made for industrial injuries benefit in respect of an accident, or of a prescribed disease or injury; or

(b) [1 an application is made under section 29 of the Social Security Act 1998 for a declaration that an accident was an industrial accident, or for a corresponding declaration as to a prescribed disease or injury.]

(2) The Secretary of State may direct that the relevant employment shall, in relation to that accident, disease or injury, be treated as having been employed earner's employment notwithstanding that by reason of a contravention of, or non-compliance with, some provision contained in or having effect under an enactment passed for the protection of employed persons or any class of employed persons, either—

(a) the contract purporting to govern the employment was void; or

(b) the employed person was not lawfully employed in the relevant employment at the time when, or in the place where, the accident happened or the disease or injury was contracted or received.

(3) In subsection (2) above "relevant employment" means—

(a) in relation to an accident, the employment out of and in the course of which the accident arises, and

(b) in relation to a prescribed disease or injury, the employment to the nature of which the disease or injury is due.

AMENDMENT

1. Social Security Act 1998 Sch.7 para.64 (July 5, 1999).

Earner acting in breach of regulations, etc.

98.—An accident shall be taken to arise out of and in the course of an employed earner's employment, notwithstanding that he is at the time of the accident acting in contravention of any statutory or other regulations applicable to his employment, or of any orders given by or on behalf of his employer, or that he is acting without instructions from his employer, if— 1.372

(a) the accident would have been taken so to have arisen had the act not been done in contravention of any such regulations or orders, or without such instructions, as the case may be; and

(b) the act is done for the purposes of and in connection with the employer's trade or business.

DERIVATION

SSA 1975 s.52. 1.373

GENERAL NOTE

This is the first of four successive sections which extend the scheme to situations in which, on general principle, the accident would not be regarded as arising out of, or in the course of, employment. For three of the four sections it is still necessary to consider the question of whether, on a given hypothesis, the accident happened 1.374

in the course of employment and reference must, therefore, be made to the general discussion in the note to s.94(1) above.

If an accident happens to an employee who is acting contrary to regulations, or without the permission of or contrary to the instructions of his employer it would not be difficult to conclude that he had taken himself out of the course of employment by virtue of his acts. This section *deems* the accident to have arisen out of and in the course of employment provided two conditions are fulfilled. In *CI/210/50*, where a miner had (contrary to the Coal Mines Act 1911) jumped on a tram to ride back to the shaft bottom and was injured when it was derailed, the Commissioner formulated the following approach to the application of the equivalent section of the National Insurance (Industrial Injuries) Act 1946:

(a) looking at the facts as a whole, including any regulations or orders affecting the claimant, was the accident one which arose out of and in the course of employment?

(b) if the answer to the first question is "no"—is that because the claimant was acting in contravention of some regulation or order?

(c) if the answer to the second question is "yes"—was the claimant's act done for the purposes of and in connection with the employer's business?

Following through the reasoning, if the answer to the first question is "yes", the claimant will have proved that part of his case without recourse to the section. The approach recommended by the Commissioner demonstrates that it is still necessary to determine whether the accident arose in the course of employment, either taking account of or ignoring the breach of regulation or instruction. That question must be answered on general principles.

Particular difficulty has been encountered in cases where the claimant has done something unauthorised which was outside his normal duties. In *R(I) 12/61*, a repairer in a colliery was injured in an explosion occurring as he illegally connected up detonators—a job reserved for shotfirers, and in *R(I) 1/66*, a dock labourer was killed when, to expedite the loading of a ship, he attempted to use a fork-lift truck which he drove off the dock—driving being a job reserved for authorised fork-lift drivers. Both claims for benefit failed because the Commissioner held that the victim had been doing something which was not part of his job and, therefore, was not in the course of his employment. The victim was not doing his job in an unauthorised way—he was not doing *his* job. This restrictive approach was relaxed somewhat in *R(I) 1/70* where a wider view was taken of what amounted to the claimant's "job".

Earner travelling in employer's transport

1.375 **99.**—(1) An accident happening while an employed earner is, with the express or implied permission of his employer, travelling as a passenger by any vehicle to or from his place of work shall, notwithstanding that he is under no obligation to his employer to travel by that vehicle, be taken to arise out of and in the course of his employment if—

(a) the accident would have been taken so to have arisen had he been under such an obligation; and

(b) at the time of the accident, the vehicle—

(i) is being operated by or on behalf of his employer or some other person by whom it is provided in pursuance of arrangements made with his employer; and

(ii) is not being operated in the ordinary course of a public transport service.

(2) In this section references to a vehicle include a ship, vessel, hovercraft or aircraft.

DERIVATION

SSA 1975, s.53. 1.376

GENERAL NOTE

(1) Introduction: looking at "travelling" accidents within the general principles set out in s.94 1.377

Accidents occurring in the course of travel cause many problems. A person whose work requires travel (the sales representative, the fireman, the lorry driver, etc.) should be able to show that an accident happening during such travelling arose in the course of his employment, although there may be the same uncertainty about when the course of employment begins and ends as in other jobs. Equally, a person who is merely travelling to his work is unlikely to be able to show that the course of his employment has begun until, at least, he has reached work.

There are a mass of decisions on travelling accidents which attempt to distinguish significant features to place the accident inside or outside the course of employment. Some of them are considered in *Nancollas v Insurance Officer* [1985] 1 All E.R. 833 and others in the later House of Lords decision *Smith v Stages* [1989] 1 All E.R. 833, considered further, below. The *Nancollas* decision deals with two appeals from the Commissioner *(R(I) 14/81* and *R(I) 7/85)* which had both been decided against the claimant concerned. In the former, N was in a job (disablement resettlement officer) based at Worthing which required him to call in at other centres and to make home visits throughout Sussex and Surrey. He did not work fixed hours and determined his own itinerary. On the day in question he had to visit Aldershot and set out to travel there direct from home without first going into the office at Worthing. He was injured in a motor accident. In the other appeal, B was a police finger-print expert living, and normally working, at Wakefield. He was also a sailing instructor and, as part of his police duties, gave sailing courses to police cadets at a reservoir 40 miles from Wakefield. He was injured in an accident whilst travelling on his motorcycle to the reservoir to give a course. In both cases the Commissioner held that the accident did not arise in the course of employment, but the Court of Appeal allowed both appeals. The impressionistic, total factor, no rules, no binding precedents approach in *Nancollas* has been considered in the annotations to "arising in the course of employment" in s.94. Subsequent decisions seem to have relegated it to the secondary characterisation of particular acts once the principal questions have been posed: what was the claimant employed to do and was s/he doing it, or something reasonably incidental to it, when the accident occurred. But in *R(I) 1/88* (decided before this reappraisal), the Commissioner had in any event held that *Nancollas* did not remove the well-accepted distinction between acts done under an obligation to an employer and acts merely done with his permission: in the former case it almost necessarily follows that the employee was acting in the course of his employment, but this does not equally necessarily follow from the fact that the employee was doing what was authorised by the employer. So that in *R(I) 1/88*, a British Telecom employee, who usually travelled by train, was given the use of a company vehicle to enable him to work overtime on a specific project, and was given specific permission, subject to strict rules, to use the vehicle to return home when the job was completed later than expected. The Commissioner held that the accident suffered on the journey home arose in the course of the man's employment.

The House of Lords decision in *Smith v Stages* was not concerned specifically with s.99, nor even with the industrial injuries legislation generally, but it is instructive to set out the propositions formulated by Lord Lowry since they have general application to the interpretation of the phrase "arising in the course of employment" and specific application to travelling.

In *Smith v Stages* there had been a motor accident causing injury which had occurred whilst the employees were on their way home from a job away from their normal place of work. There were, of course, specific circumstances which led to the particular decision, but Lord Lowry attempted a more general analysis. He said (at [1989] 1 All E.R. at 851):

> "It is impossible to provide for every eventuality and foolish, without the benefit of argument, to make the attempt, but some prima facie propositions may be stated with reasonable confidence. (1) An employee travelling from his ordinary residence to his regular place of work, whatever the means of transport and even if it is provided by his employer, is not on duty and is not acting in the course of his employment, but, if he is obliged by his contract of service to use the employer's transport, he will normally, in the absence of an express condition to the contrary, be regarded as acting in the course of his employment while doing so. (2) Travelling in the employer's time between workplaces (one of which may be the regular workplace) or in the course of a peripatetic occupation whether accompanied by goods or tools or simply in order to reach a succession of workplaces (as an inspector of gas meters might do), will be in the course of employment. (3) Receipt of wages (though not receipt of a travelling allowance) will indicate that the employee is travelling in the employer's time and for his benefit and is acting in the course of his employment, and in such a case the fact that the employee may have discretion as to the mode and time of travelling will not take the journey out of the course of his employment. (4) An employee travelling *in the employer's time* from his ordinary residence to a work-place other than his regular workplace or in the course of a peripatetic occupation or to the scene of an emergency (such as a fire, an accident or a mechanical breakdown of plant) will be acting in the course of his employment. (5) A deviation from or interruption of a journey undertaken in the course of employment (unless the deviation or interruption is merely incidental to the journey) will for the time being (which may include an overnight interruption) take the employee out of the course of his employment. (6) Return journeys are to be treated on the same footing as outward journeys."

These remarks were said expressly not to refer to salaried employees and there are, of course, some observations which are not entirely appropriate to a social security context. Nonetheless, the case was quickly referred to with approval in two unreported decisions, *CI/110/1988* and *CI/163/1988*. In *R(I)1/91*, Commissioner Rice considered the above quoted statement of Lord Lowry in *Smith v Stages* in upholding the tribunal's decision that the claimant, severely injured in a motor accident 10 minutes after finishing work, was not still in the course of his employment when the accident occurred. On the facts, the Commissioner rejected the view that the claimant was being paid by the employer to travel to and from the place of work, but went on to say that, even if he had been, "it did not necessarily follow that this in itself meant that he was in the course of his employment" (para.9). Here the Commissioner cited Lord Goff in *Smith v Stages* [1989] 2 W.L.R. 529 at 534:

> ". . . the fact that a man is being paid by his employer in respect of the relevant period of time is often important, but cannot of itself be decisive. A man is usually paid nowadays during his holidays; and it often happens that an employer may allow a man to take the afternoon off, or even a whole day off, without affecting his wages. In such circumstances, he would ordinarily, not be acting in the course of his employment despite the fact that he is being paid. Indeed, any rule that payment at the relevant time is decisive would be very difficult to apply in the case of a salaried man. Let me however give an example concerned with travelling to work. Suppose that a man is applying for a job, and it turns out that he would have a pretty arduous journey between his home and his new place of work, lasting about an hour each way, which is deterring him from taking the job. His prospective employer may want to employ him, and may entice him by offering an extra hour's pay at each end of the day—say 10 hours' pay instead of eight. In those circumstances he would not I think, be acting in the course of his employment when travelling to or from work. This is because he would not be employed

to make the journey: the extra pay would simply be given to him in recognition of the fact that his journey to and from work was an arduous one."

(2) The effect of s.99

The provisions of this section extend the course of employment to include an accident occurring on transport provided by the employer for the benefit of his workers, but which is not obligatory. (If use of the transport *is* obligatory, as with building contractors taking employees to a site by lorry from an arranged pick-up point, then the course of employment is likely to begin when the employee boards the transport.) **1.378**

Subsection (1)

The extension is limited by the conditions which are attached by the section. **1.379**

(a) The claimant must be travelling with the express or implied permission of his employer. Implied permission is sufficient (*R(I) 8/62*—bus conductress on her way to work picked up by empty bus returning to depot, a practice condoned by the employer), but must normally be given in advance. If permission is given retrospectively it must be express (*R(I) 5/80*—no permission given by employer for bus journey to be continued in the private car of the bus driver);

(b) The accident would have been in the course of employment if the claimant had been under an obligation to use the transport.

This again involves a consideration of the general principles in the note to s.94(1) and "Introduction", above. The nature of the accident and its relationship to the claimant's employment and his presence on the transport will be relevant.

(c) The transport is operated by or on behalf of the employer, *or* is operated as a result of arrangements made by the employer. These are alternative conditions. It should not be difficult to ascertain whether the transport is provided by the employer or on his behalf—so long as there is some measure of control exercised by the employer over the transport that should be enough (*R(I) 42/56*). The meaning of "arrangements" is less clear, but a similar concept of control has been used to determine what sort of transport service should fall within the section. It is not necessary that there should be a contract between the employer and the person who provides the transport, but there must be something more than a mere request or suggestion from the employer.

In *R(I) 67/51*, the Commissioner said,

> "The 'arrangements' would normally be made by contract between the employer and the provider of the vehicle but in the absence of a contract one would expect to find at least some definite ascertainable engagement between the employer and the provider of the service whereby the employer 'arranged' for it to be provided. One would expect to find also that the employer had the exclusive use of the vehicle and that members of the public travelling as ordinary fare-paying passengers would not be carried."

Acquiescence in a scheme made by another employer is sufficient (*R(I) 49/53*), but a purely private agreement under which an employee was given the use of a company car to get to work whilst his own was under repair is not, even though he was in the habit of bringing other employees to work in his own car (*R(I) 5/60*).

(d) The transport is not being operated in the ordinary course of a public transport service.

This condition may already have been taken into account in deciding whether the employer had sufficient control over the provision of the transport for it to be said that it was provided under an arrangement with him, but it is a separate statutory requirement. In *R(I) 15/57* it was regarded as significant that the bus bore no destination indicator, did not stop to pick up members of the public, did not appear on published timetables, did not run during factory closures, and finished the journey on a private road to the factory. It was suggested in *R(I) 3/59* that once members of the public were permitted to ride on the bus it would lose its "private" status, but this may be too restrictive given the words "operated in the ordinary course of . . .".

Subsection (2)

1.380 Special provision is made for mariners and airmen by SI 1975/470 and SI 1975/469 respectively.

Accidents happening while meeting emergency

1.381 **100.**—An accident happening to an employed earner in or about any premises at which he is for the time being employed for the purposes of his employer's trade or business shall be taken to arise out of and in the course of his employment if it happens while he is taking steps, on an actual or supposed emergency at those premises, to rescue, succour or protect persons who are, or are thought to be or possibly to be, injured or imperilled, or to avert or minimise serious damage to property.

DERIVATION

1.382 SSA 1975 s.54.

GENERAL NOTE

1.383 Prior to 1946, when the forerunner of this section first appeared in the National Insurance (Industrial Injuries) Act, the courts had decided that accidents sustained in responding to an "emergency" could be regarded as "arising out of and in the course of employment" so long as the response was broadly incidental to the employee's duties. Since 1946, the Commissioners have taken the same line and this section need only be considered when, on general principle, the accident has not arisen in the course of employment (*CI/280/49*).

Emergencies under general principle (i.e. within s.94)

1.384 Once the Court of Appeal had decided that a ship's baker, injured on remonstrating with an Egyptian who had used foul language to two lady passengers, had suffered an accident arising out of and in the course of his employment (*Culpeck v Orient Steam Navigation Co. Ltd* (1922) B.W.C.C. 187), the way was clear for a reasonable response to any unexpected occurrence to be within the course of employment so long as the acts done were within the general nature of the claimant's employment. Hence, an employee assisting a fellow employee in difficulties (*CI/280/49*); a lorry driver assisting a stranded motorist (*R(I) 11/51*); a security guard assisting a policeman to investigate suspicious circumstances in another building (*R(I) 62/51*); a delivery driver assisting in moving an obstructing concrete mixer (*R(I) 11/56*); and an Admiralty policeman stopping an inhabited runaway push-chair (*R(I) 46/60*), were all acting in the course of their employment.

There seem to have been relatively few unsuccessful claims on this ground. In *R(I) 32/54*, the response of climbing through a first-floor window to enter a locked factory rather than waiting for the key was held to be unreasonable, and in *R(I) 52/54*, a civil servant was held not to be in the course of his employment when rescuing a child on a runaway tricycle on his way to make an interview visit to a private house. For a different approach to a similar situation to *R(I) 52/54* see *CSI/54/89*, noted above in the annotation to s.94(1) ("arising out of the employment").

Emergencies under the section

The section has only been considered extensively in *R(I) 6/63*. It is clear from that decision that the section can operate where the acts done were no part of the general duties of the employee, nor done for the employer's purposes. However, some of the phrases in the section may be restrictive. 1.385

"in or about premises"—does not include the highway generally (*R(I) 52/54*), but does include the road adjacent to particular premises (*R(I) 46/60*).

"rescue, succour or protect"—should be wide enough to cover most circumstances where there is actual or supposed danger to the person, but note that if steps are taken to protect property the damage to be averted or minimised must be "serious".

Note that the "emergency" must be "*at* these premises".

Accident caused by another's misconduct, etc.

101.—An accident happening after 19th December 1961 shall be treated for the purposes of industrial injuries benefit, where it would not apart from this section be so treated, as arising out of an employed earner's employment if— 1.386

(a) the accident arises in the course of the employment; and

(b) the accident either is caused—

  (i) by another person's misconduct, skylarking or negligence, or

  (ii) by steps taken in consequence of any such misconduct, skylarking or negligence, or

  (iii) by the behaviour or presence of an animal (including a bird, fish or insect), or is caused by or consists in the employed earner being struck by any object or by lightning; and

(c) the employed earner did not directly or indirectly induce or contribute to the happening of the accident by his conduct outside the employment or by any act not incidental to the employment.

Derivation

SSA 1975 s.55. 1.387

General Note

This deeming provision brings within the scheme some accidents which happen *at* work, rather than *through* work. It was a response to some apparent injustices in the operation of the scheme and was first introduced in 1961. For a rare case where this was considered, see *CI/1654/2008*, noted in the commentary to s.94, above ("out of . . . the employment"). It did not there assist the claimant. 1.388

Subsection 1(a)

The accident must still arise in the course of employment (see note to s.94(1), above). The "deeming" effect of the section applies only to the "out of employment" aspect. 1.389

Subsection 1(b)

R(I) 3/67 seems to be the only reported decision on this section and it concerned "skylarking" and its aftermath. The claimant, whilst having a permitted smoking break in the appointed place, was hit by a snowball thrown by a fellow-employee. He followed the snowballer towards the cloak-room to remonstrate. As he reached the cloakroom, the door was slammed on him and his hand went through it. Was he still in the course of his employment? The Commissioner held that remonstration was reasonably incidental to his employment. 1.390

Subsection 1(c)

1.391 *R(I) 3/67* (above) also considered whether the claimant had fallen foul of this subsection, but the Commissioner held that whereas remonstration was incidental to employment, retaliation would not have been. Note also that conduct outside employment which induces or contributes to the happening of the accident may debar the claimant.

Sickness benefit

1.392 *Section 102 repealed from April 13, 1995 by the Social Security (Incapacity for Work) Act 1994 Sch.1, para.29.*

Disablement pension

Disablement pension

1.393 **103.**—(1) Subject to the provisions of this section, an employed earner shall be entitled to disablement pension if he suffers as the result of the relevant accident from loss of physical or mental faculty such that the assessed extent of the resulting disablement amounts to not less than 14 per cent. or, on a claim made before 1st October 1986, 20 per cent.

(2) In the determination of the extent of an employed earner's disablement for the purposes of this section there may be added to the percentage of the disablement resulting from the relevant accident the assessed percentage of any present disablement of his—

(a) which resulted from any other accident [1 . .] arising out of and in the course of his employment, being employed earner's employment, and

(b) in respect of which a disablement gratuity was not paid to him after a final assessment of his disablement,

(as well as any percentage which may be so added in accordance with regulations under subsection (2) of section 109 below made by virtue of subsection (4)(b) of that section).

(3) Subject to subsection (4) below, where the assessment of disablement is a percentage between 20 and 100 which is not a multiple of 10, it shall be treated—

(a) if it is a multiple of 5, as being the next higher percentage which is a multiple of 10, and

(b) if it is not a multiple of 5, as being the nearest percentage which is a multiple of 10,

and where the assessment of disablement on a claim made on or after 1st October 1986 is less than 20 per cent., but not less than 14 per cent., it shall be treated as 20 per cent.

(4) Where subsection (2) above applies, subsection (3) above shall have effect in relation to the aggregate percentage and not in relation to any percentage forming part of the aggregate.

(5) In this Part of this Act "assessed", in relation to the extent of any disablement, means assessed in accordance with Schedule 6 to this Act; and for the purposes of that Schedule there shall be taken to be no relevant loss of faculty when the extent of the resulting disablement, if so assessed, would not amount to 1 per cent.

(6) A person shall not be entitled to a disablement pension until after the expiry of the period of 90 days (disregarding Sundays) beginning with the day of the relevant accident.

(7) Subject to subsection (8) below, where disablement pension is payable for a period, it shall be paid at the appropriate weekly rate specified in Schedule 4, Part V, paragraph 1.

(8) Where the period referred to in subsection (7) above is limited by reference to a definite date, the pension shall cease on the death of the beneficiary before that date.

AMENDMENT

1. Welfare Reform Act 2012 s.64 (December 5, 2012).

DERIVATION

SSA 1975 s.57 as amended. **1.394**

DEFINITIONS

"employed earner"—s.2(1)(a), above.
"relevant accident"—s.122(1).
"loss of physical faculty"—*ibid.*

GENERAL NOTE

Subsection (1)

Disablement benefit is payable in respect of disablement even if the claimant's capacity for work is unimpaired. The practice of the Department has been to require a separate claim for disablement benefit in respect of each industrial accident. However, in *CI/6872/95*, following the approach he had taken in *CI/420/94*, the Commissioner held that, where disablement benefit had been claimed in respect of one accident but had not been finally determined, a further claim in respect of another accident was not required. If disablement benefit is already in payment in respect of one accident, a further "claim" in respect of another accident is really an application for review. Equally, if there is in existence an assessment of disablement but disablement benefit is not payable because the assessment is below 14 per cent, an application for review of the assessment must be treated as a claim for disablement benefit if benefit is to be paid. **1.395**

A useful checklist of questions

In *CI/2930/2005*, Commissioner Williams applied a key statement (definitions and cautions) of Lord Simon in *Jones v Secretary of State for Social Services* [1972] A.C. 944 at p.1019: **1.396**

> "although in particular cases the concepts may overlap, the statute envisages them as separate — in order for 'disablement' benefit to be payable, the 'accident' must result in 'injury', which must result in 'loss of faculty', which must result in 'disability' . . . my understanding of the terminology is as follows: . . . 'injury' is hurt to body or mind . . . 'loss of faculty' is impairment of the proper functioning of part of the body or mind . . . 'disability' is partial or total failure of power to perform normal bodily or mental processes . . . 'disablement' is the sum of disabilities which, by contrast with the powers of a normal person, can be expressed as a percentage."

He then set out in para.36 a useful framework of questions to be answered and the order of the rules to be applied under s.103:

"Reading that vocabulary into the statutory issues that I must consider, the questions to be answered are:

(a) Did the claimant 'suffer personal injury ['hurt to body or mind'] caused' by the relevant accident?
Social Security Contributions and Benefits Act 1992 ('1992 Act'), section 94(1)

(b) If so, did the claimant 'suffer as a result of the relevant accident from loss of physical or mental faculty' ['impairment of the proper functioning of part of the body or mind'] during the period relevant to this assessment?
1992 Act, section 103(1)

(c) If so, what were 'the disabilities ['the partial or total failure of power to perform normal bodily or mental functions'] incurred by the claimant as a result of the relevant loss of faculty ['impairment of the proper functioning']'?
1992 Act, Schedule 6, paragraph 1. Paragraph 1(a) requires that 'the disabilities to be taken into account shall be all disabilities so incurred (whether or not involving loss of earning power or additional expense) to which the claimant may be expected, having regard to his physical and mental condition at the date of the assessment, to be subject during the period taken into account by the assessment as compared with a person of the same age and sex whose physical and mental condition is normal'

(d) Do those disabilities ['failure of power to perform . . .'] take into account 'disabilities which, though resulting from the relevant loss of faculty ['impairment of the proper functioning . . .'], also result, or without the relevant accident might be expected to result, from a cause other than the relevant accident', if there are any?
This is required by 1992 Act, Schedule 6, paragraph 1(b) and Social Security (General Benefit) Regulations 1982 (SI 1982 No 1408 as amended)("1982 Regulations"), regulation 11.

(e) What is the total percentage of the 'assessed extent of the resulting disablement' ['the sum of disabilities', or of 'failure of power to perform . . .'] —

(i) by reference to those disabilities ['failure of power to perform . . .'] without reference to the particular circumstances of the claimant other than age, sex and physical and mental condition, and

(ii) adding 'to the percentage of the disablement ['the sum of disabilities . . .'] . . . the assessed percentage of any present disablement" of the claimant resulting from any other industrial accident or any prescribed disease?

1992 Act, section 103(1), (2), and Schedule 6, paragraph 1(c)

(f) If the answers to (d) and (e) include disabilities ['failure of power to perform. . .'] resulting from the loss of faculty ['impairment of the proper functioning. . .'] both from the relevant accident and from any effective cause other than the relevant accident (whether congenital defect, injury or disease) that predate the accident, then what is the extent of disablement ['the sum of disabilities'] 'to which the claimant would have been subject . . . if the relevant accident had not occurred'?
1992 Act, Schedule 6, paragraph 1(c) and 1982 Regulations, regulation 11(3). Regulation 11(5)requires that where there are two or more industrial accidents (or disease) then the disablement resulting from both or all "shall only be taken into account in assessing the extent of disablement resulting from . . . the one which occurred or developed last in point of time".

(g) If the answers to (d) and (e) include disabilities ['failure of power to perform . . .'] resulting from the loss of faculty ['impairment of the proper functioning . . .'] both from the relevant accident and from any effective cause that postdates the accident and are not directly attributable to it, then what is the extent of disablement if that other effective cause had not arisen? *1982 Regulations, regulation 11(4). That requires that if the answer to (g) is not less than 11 per cent, then the answer to (e) 'shall also take account of any disablement to which the claimant may be subject as a result of that other effective cause except to the extent to which the claimant would have been subject thereto in the relevant accident had not occurred'. See also regulation 11(5) noted to question (f)*".

Employed earner: See the note to s.94. **1.397**

Accident: See the note to s.94. S.108 has the effect that disablement benefit is also payable in respect of prescribed diseases and prescribed personal injuries not caused by accident.

Loss of physical or mental faculty as a result of the relevant accident: "Loss of faculty" means "an impairment of the proper functioning of part of the body or mind" (*Jones v Secretary of State for Social Services* [1972] A.C. 944 at 1009 also reported as an appendix to *R(I) 3/69*). Thus a loss of a kidney by a claimant, which necessarily results in a loss of useful function, must, as a matter of law, mean he or she has suffered a loss of faculty even if the claimant can live normally in every way (*R(I) 14/66*). It was pointed out in *R(I) 14/66* that it does not follow that there is any resulting disablement. Nevertheless, adjudicating medical authorities have been advised to assess a "loss of reserve function" which in the case of a kidney is usually put at between 5 and 10 per cent. It is doubtful whether that is correct since that seems to be an assessment of loss of faculty rather than an assessment of disablement. The Deputy Commissioner in *R(I) 14/66* expressed concern that a claimant's assessment of disablement could not be increased if he or she lost the other kidney owing to a non-industrial disease or accident. Although *R(I) 11/66*, to which he referred, was overturned in the Court of Appeal (*R. v Medical Appeal Tribunal Ex p. Cable*, appendix to *R(I) 11/66*), reg.11(4) of the Social Security (General Benefit) Regulations 1982 appears to limit the effect of *Cable* to cases where the assessment of disablement before the loss of the second kidney has been assessed at not less than 11 per cent. **1.398**

In *JL and DO* v *SSWP (II)* [2011] UKUT 294 (AAC); [2012] AACR 15, in the context of PD A14 (osteoarthritis of the knee), Judge Ward considered whether it made any difference where a claimant's osteoarthritis resulted in knee replacement surgery. He held that, where the original loss of faculty was osteoarthritis of the knee, the knee replacement surgery did not break the chain of causation so as to substitute a new cause of ongoing loss of faculty. The relevance of the knee replacement surgery went rather to the stage of assessment of the degree of disablement.

The definition of "loss of physical faculty" in s.122(1) makes special provision so hat it includes disfigurement whether or not accompanied by any actual loss of faculty.

Dealing with differences of expert medical opinion: Where medical experts differ on whether there is loss of faculty or whether it was the result of the relevant industrial accident(s), the First-tier Tribunal must give sufficient reasons for preferring the view of one expert and rejecting that of the other(s). See Judge Wikeley in *DB v SSWP (II)* [2010] UKUT 144 (AAC), paras 40–51, citing statements by different three judge panels of the Upper Tribunal in *Hampshire CC v JP* [2009] UKUT 239 (AAC) (now reported as [2010] AACR 15) and *BB v South London & Maudsley NHS Trust and Ministry of Justice* [2009] UKUT 157 (AAC). The relevant factors for a tribunal to consider are set out in Judge Edward Jacobs's *Tribunal Practice and Procedure* (4th edn., 2016), at paras.11.120-11.131. They relate to "the expert(s), the area of expertise and the evidence" (para.44). As respects the experts, matters to consider are each expert's qualifications, expertise and experience on the issue **1.399** material to the appeal. On expertise, the tribunal must "bear in mind the limits to which the doctors' areas of expertise can actually provide answers to the issue in the appeal" (para.46). On the expert evidence itself, it is a question of examining the "factual basis and soundness of the experts' respective reasoned opinions" (para.47). This may be difficult where, as in this case, there was a clash between the "majority view" of the "medical establishment" and the "minority view" provided by one of the experts. As Judge Wikeley noted, experience in hindsight of changes in medical opinion indicates that the fact that an expert is in the minority does not mean that his/her opinion is thereby necessarily wrong. Lacking hindsight, the tribunal, drawing on the expertise of its medical members in full compliance with the rules of natural justice and fairness, "will have to form its own best judgment today on the soundness of the science and reasons underpinning [the minority expert's evidence] in this appeal" (para.50).

1.400 *Resulting disablement amounts to not less than 14 per cent*: It is disablement which must be assessed and not loss of faculty. In *R(I) 3/76*, it was held that:

> " 'disability' means inability to do something which persons of the same age and sex and normal physical and mental powers can do; 'disablement' means a collection of disabilities, that is to say the sum total of all the relevant disabilities found present in a given case."

"14 per cent" was substituted for "one per cent" in s.57(1) of the Social Security Act 1975 from October 1, 1986 (SSA 1986, Sch.3, para.3). Before that date, disablement benefit was paid in the form of a gratuity if the assessment was less than 20 per cent and in the form of a pension if the assessment was 20 per cent or more. That remains the case where a claim was made before that date (Social Security (Industrial Injuries and Diseases) Miscellaneous Provisions Regulations 1986 reg.14). Any pension is payable under this section and any gratuity is payable under Sch.7, para.9. This remains important where, on a claim made before October 1, 1986, there have been a series of provisional assessments. If a claim is made after October 1, 1986 in respect of a period before that date, the new legislation applies (*R(I) 1/90, R(I)/3/96*).

Disablement benefit is also payable where the assessment is less than 14 per cent, but at least one per cent, if it is due to pneumoconiosis, byssinosis or diffuse mesothelioma (Prescribed Diseases Regulations reg.20(1)).

The provisions for aggregating assessments of disablement have been considered in *R(I) 3/00*. The claimant had received a disablement gratuity in respect of prescribed disease A11 giving rise to disablement assessed at 7 per cent from April 1, 1985 for life. In May 1992, he claimed disablement benefit in respect of prescribed disease D4 and the disablement owing to that disease was assessed at 8 per cent from January 1, 1960 for life. He then applied for a review of the assessment of disablement in respect of prescribed disease A11 on the ground of unforeseen aggravation and the consequent disablement was assessed at 8 per cent from May 3, 1995 for life.

The Commissioner considered the way in which disablement gratuities were calculated and, in particular, the way further gratuities payable following reviews had been calculated under reg.85 of the Social Security (Adjudication) Regulations 1984. He concluded that disablement in respect of which a gratuity had been awarded did not fall to be aggregated under s.103 for the first seven years of the period of the assessment but did thereafter and that, following a review on the ground of unforeseen aggravation, the whole of the new assessment fell to be aggregated and not just the difference between the old and the new assessments. Accordingly, no disablement pension was payable to the claimant in respect of the period before April 1, 1992 (because only the 8 per cent in respect of prescribed disease D4 could be taken into account) but disablement pension was payable to the claimant thereafter on the basis that his aggregated disablement was 15 per cent from April 1, 1992 and 16 per cent from May 3, 1995.

Following *R(I)4/03*, Commissioner Rowland in *CI/954/2006* agreed that aggregation is a mere alternative to a separate award of disablement pension (para.16). It can be set in motion by an application for supersession. See also *ED v SSWP* [2009] UKUT 206 (AAC) and *DD v SSWP* (II) [2020] UKUT 302 (AAC), discussed in the commentary to SSA 1998, s.10. See further *MH v SSWP* (II) [2020] UKUT 297 (AAC).

Subsection (5)

There is deemed to be no loss of faculty if the resulting disablement is assessed at less than 1 per cent. In *R(I) 6/61*, the Commissioner held that it was desirable that a medical appeal tribunal should indicate whether they have concluded that there is *no* loss of faculty or whether they have concluded that there *is* a loss of faculty, but that the resulting disablement does not amount to 1 per cent. Note that, under s.110(3), a person suffering from pneumoconiosis *shall* be treated as suffering from a loss of faculty such that the assessed extent of disablement amounts to not less than 1 per cent. **1.401**

For notes on the assessment of disablement, see the annotations to Sch.6 to the Act and to reg.11 of the General Benefit Regulations 1982.

Both the unified tribunal and the Commissioners now have jurisdiction over medical and non-medical matters. A Commissioner, allowing an appeal on a point of law, can now take his or her own decision on the facts available rather than remitting it to another tribunal. Commissioner Williams did so in *CI/1307/1999* giving a staged assessment of disablement in respect of post-traumatic stress disorder. The decision considers the medical aspects of the claimant's case found to be an industrial accident in *CI/15589/1996*, noted in the annotation to "accident" in respect of SSCBA 1992 s.94. In paras 15–17, Commissioner Williams distinguished "diagnosis" and "disablement" decisions. The former is essentially "a question of medical expertise". A "disablement" decision in contrast is not dissimilar to the tasks performed by judges in assessing common law damages or in applying the tariff of the Criminal Injuries Compensation Authority. In assessing disablement for industrial injuries benefits, however, that Criminal Injuries tariff is not an appropriate yardstick. Instead, supplementing SSCBA 1992 s.103 and Sch.6, regard should be had also to reg.11 and Sch.2 to the General Benefit Regulations below. Nonetheless, the import of para.37 of the decision is that exercise of the Commissioner's power to decide on the facts, rather than remitting to another tribunal, may well be rare. Even so, the decision contrasts markedly with the traditional view of such matters as ones for medical rather than legal judgment (see, for example, Commissioner Howell in *CI/636/93*). Note that the suitability of cross-reference to Sch.2 was also advocated in *R(I) 5/95*, where Commissioner Rowland stated that "assessment of disablement should be brought into line with those prescribed in the Schedule", with assessment also reflecting any intermittent or episodic character of the disablement (para.16).

Subsection (6)

This does not apply where a person is awarded disablement benefit in respect of occupational deafness (reg.28 of the Prescribed Diseases Regulations) or where a claim is made in respect of diffuse mesothelioma, see *ibid.* reg.20(4). **1.402**

Subsection (7)

Under Sch.4, the amount of the pension depends on whether the claimant is over 18 and on the extent of disablement. A person over 18 whose disablement is assessed at 100 per cent receives £182.00 per week. The amount paid to people with lower assessments is proportionately less. **1.403**

Increase where constant attendance needed

104.—(1) Where a disablement pension is payable in respect of an assessment of 100 per cent, then, if as the result of the relevant loss of faculty the **1.404**

beneficiary requires constant attendance, the weekly rate of the pension shall be increased by an amount, not exceeding the appropriate amount specified in Schedule 4, Part V, paragraph 2 determined in accordance with regulations by reference to the extent and nature of the attendance required by the beneficiary.

(2) An increase of pension under this section shall be payable for such period as may be determined at the time it is granted, but may be renewed from time to time.

(3) The Secretary of State may by regulations direct that any provision of sections 64 to 67 above shall have effect, with or without modifications, in relation to increases of pension under this section.

(4) In subsection (3) above, "modifications" includes additions and omissions.

DERIVATION

1.405 SSA 1975 s.61.

DEFINITIONS

"beneficiary" and "relevant loss of faculty"—see s.122(1).
"modifications"—see subs.(4).

GENERAL NOTE

1.406 See regs 19–21 of the Social Security (General Benefit) Regulations 1982 for further provisions relating to constant attendance allowance. Note that, under para.5 of Sch.1 to the Overlapping Benefits Regulations, constant attendance allowance overlaps with attendance allowance under s.35 and the care component of disability living allowance.

The Secretary of State's decision on constant attendance allowance is not appealable (Decisions and Appeals Regulations 1999 Sch.2, para.14(a)).

Increase for exceptionally severe disablement

1.407 **105.**—(1) Where a disablement pension is payable to a person—

(a) who is or, but for having received medical or other treatment as an in patient in a hospital or similar institution, would be entitled to an increase of the weekly rate of the pension under section 104 above, and the weekly rate of the increase exceeds the amount specified in Schedule 4, Part V, paragraph 2(a); and

(b) his need for constant attendance of an extent and nature qualifying him for such an increase at a weekly rate in excess of that amount is likely to be permanent,

the weekly rate of the pension shall, in addition to any increase under section 104 above, be further increased by the amount specified in Schedule 4, Part V, paragraph 3.

(2) An increase under this section shall be payable for such period as may be determined at the time it is granted, but may be renewed from time to time.

DERIVATION

1.408 SSA 1975 s.63.

DEFINITIONS

"medical treatment"—see s.122(1).

GENERAL NOTE

The Secretary of State's decision on exceptionally severe disablement allowance is not appealable (Decisions and Appeals Regulations 1999 Sch.2 para.14(b)). **1.409**

Other benefits and increases

Benefits and increases subject to qualifications as to time

106.—Schedule 7 to this Act shall have effect in relation— **1.410**
(a) to unemployability supplement;
(b) to disablement gratuity;
(c) to increases of disablement pension during hospital treatment;
(d) to reduced earnings allowance;
(e) to retirement allowance; and
(f) to industrial death benefit,
for all of which the qualifications include special qualifications as to time.

Successive accidents

Adjustments for successive accidents

107.—(1) Where a person suffers two or more successive accidents arising out of and in the course of his employed earner's employment— **1.411**
(a) he shall not for the same period be entitled (apart from any increase of benefit mentioned in subsection (2) below) to receive industrial injuries benefit by way of two or more disablement pensions at an aggregate weekly rate exceeding the appropriate amount specified in Schedule 4, Part V, paragraph 4; and
(b) regulations may provide for adjusting—
(i) disablement benefit, or the conditions for the receipt of that benefit, in any case where he has received or may be entitled to a disablement gratuity;
(ii) any increase of benefit mentioned in subsection (2) below, or the conditions for its receipt.

(2) The increases of benefit referred to in subsection (1) above are those under the following provisions of this Act—
section 104,
section 105,
paragraph 2, 4 or 6 of Schedule 7.

DERIVATION

SSA 1975 s.91. **1.412**

DEFINITIONS

"employed earner"—see ss.2 and 95(4).

"employed earner's employment"—see ss.95 and 97.
"entitled", "employment" and "industrial injuries benefit"—see s.122(1).

GENERAL NOTE

1.413 In *CI/402/1994*, the Commissioner stated that the 1986 amendments to the industrial injuries scheme "stopped the making of separate awards" so from then on there could only ever be one award of disablement benefit in respect of any period. On that view, it appeared that this section was only of relevance where the last claim was made before October 1, 1986. Commissioner Howell in *R(I)4/03* makes it clear that this is not in fact so:

> " . . . unfortunately the continued provision in the post-1986 legislation for a person to have two or more disablement pensions for successive accidents (section 107(1)(a) above, and its predecessor section 91 Social Security Act 1975), was not drawn to the Commissioner's attention in that case. Moreover the later decision in *CI/12311/1996* above plainly holds otherwise, and a similar line of reasoning on separate claims for reduced earnings allowance has since been overruled by the Court of Appeal, in *Hagan v. Secretary of State* [2001] EWCA Civ 1452, 30 July 2001. I do not therefore think what was said in *CI/420/1994* should be taken as a ground for depriving claimants of the benefit of the normal prescribed time for claiming a new entitlement in the way that happened here" (para.34).

See also *ED v SSWP* [2009] UKUT 206 (AAC) and *DD v SSWP (II)* [2020] UKUT 302 (AAC), discussed in the commentary to SSA 1998, s.10, both cases in which the claimant had suffered an industrial injury or had contracted an industrial disease and it had been found that, after some years of not suffering any loss of faculty in respect of that injury or disease, the claimant was now suffering such a loss of faculty. See further *MH v SSWP (II)* [2020] UKUT 297 (AAC).

Regulations 38 and 39 of the General Benefit Regulations 1982 are treated as made under this section (SSCBA 1992 s.2(2)).

Prescribed industrial diseases, etc.

Benefit in respect of prescribed industrial diseases, etc

1.414 **108.**—(1) Industrial injuries benefits shall, in respect of a person who has been in employed earner's employment, be payable in accordance with this section and sections 109 and 110 below in respect of—

(a) any prescribed disease, or
(b) any prescribed personal injury (other than an injury caused by accident arising out of and in the course of his employment),

which is a disease or injury due to the nature of that employment [1 . . .].

(2) A disease or injury may be prescribed in relation to any employed earners if the Secretary of State is satisfied that—

(a) it ought to be treated, having regard to its causes and incidence and any other relevant considerations, as a risk of their occupations and not as a risk common to all persons; and
(b) it is such that, in the absence of special circumstances, the attribution of particular cases to the nature of the employment can be established or presumed with reasonable certainty.

(3) Regulations prescribing any disease or injury for those purposes may provide that a person who developed the disease or injury on or at

any time after a date specified in the regulations (being a date before the regulations come into force [1 . . .]) shall be treated, subject to any prescribed modifications of this section or section 109 or 110 below, as if the regulations had been in force when he developed the disease or injury.

(4) Provision may be made by regulations for determining—

(a) the time at which a person is to be treated as having developed any prescribed disease or injury; and

(b) the circumstances in which such a disease or injury is, where the person in question has previously suffered from it, to be treated as having recrudesced or as having been contracted or received afresh.

(5) Notwithstanding any other provision of this Act, the power conferred by subsection (4)(a) above includes power to provide that the time at which a person shall be treated as having developed a prescribed disease or injury shall be the date on which he first makes a claim which results in the payment of benefit by virtue of this section or section 110 below in respect of that disease or injury.

(6) Nothing in this section or in section 109 or 110 below affects the right of any person to benefit in respect of a disease which is a personal injury by accident within the meaning of this Part of this Act, except that a person shall not be entitled to benefit in respect of a disease as being an injury by accident arising out of and in the course of any employment if at the time of the accident the disease is in relation to him a prescribed disease by virtue of the occupation in which he is engaged in that employment.

AMENDMENT

1. Welfare Reform Act 2012 s.64 (December 5, 2012).

DERIVATION

SSA 1975 s.76. **1.415**

DEFINITIONS

"employed earner"—see ss.2 and 95(4).
"employed earner's employment"—see ss.95 and 97.
"entitled", "employment", "industrial injuries benefit" and "prescribe"—see s.122(1).

GENERAL NOTE

This section makes general provision for payment of industrial injuries benefits to employed earners who are suffering from a disease or personal injury which was *not* caused by accident and so could not give rise to entitlement under s.94. S.109 makes more detailed provision. For the prescribed diseases, see col.1 of Sch.1 to the Social Security (Industrial Injuries) (Prescribed Diseases) Regulations 1985. Each disease is prescribed in relation to a fairly narrowly defined occupation. **1.416**

Subsection (3)

See reg.43 of, and Sch.4 to, the Prescribed Diseases Regulations 1985. **1.417**

Subsections (4) and (5)

See regs 6 and 7 of the Prescribed Diseases Regulations 1985. **1.418**

Subsection (6)

1.419 This makes it clear that a person who develops, as the result of an accident, a disease which *is not* prescribed in relation to him or her remains entitled to benefit under s.94. On the other hand, if the disease *is* prescribed in relation to the claimant, he or she must rely on the provisions relating to prescribed diseases and cannot claim benefit in respect of it under s.94.

General provisions relating to benefit under section 108

1.420 **109.**—(1) Subject to the power to make different provision by regulations, and to the following provisions of this section and section 110 below—

(a) the benefit payable under section 108 above in respect of a prescribed disease or injury, and

(b) the conditions for receipt of benefit,

shall be the same as in the case of personal injury by accident arising out of and in the course of employment.

[1 (2) In relation to prescribed diseases and injuries, regulations may provide—

(a) for modifying any provisions contained in this Act, the Administration Act or Chapter II of Part I of the Social Security Act 1998 which relate to disablement benefit or reduced earnings allowance or their administration; and

(b) for adapting references in this Act, that Act and that Chapter to accidents,

and for the purposes of this subsection the provisions of that Act and that Chapter which relate to the administration of disablement benefit or reduced earnings allowance, shall be taken to include section 1 of that Act and any provision which relates to the administration of both the benefit in question and other benefits.]

(3) Without prejudice to the generality of subsection (2) above, regulations under that subsection may in particular include provision—

(a) for presuming any prescribed disease or injury—

(i) to be due, unless the contrary is proved, to the nature of a person's employment where he was employed in any prescribed occupation at the time when, or within a prescribed period or for a prescribed length of time (whether continuous or not) before, he developed the disease or injury,

(ii) not to be due to the nature of person's employment unless he was employed in some prescribed occupation at the time when, or within a prescribed period or for a prescribed length of time (whether continuous or not) before, he developed the disease or injury;

(b) for such matters as appear to the Secretary of State to be incidental to or consequential on provisions included in the regulations by virtue of subsection (2) and paragraph (a) above.

(4) Regulations under subsection (2) above may also provide—

(a) that, in the determination of the extent of an employed earner's disablement resulting from a prescribed disease or injury, the appropriate percentage may be added to the percentage of that disablement; and

(b) that, in the determination of the extent of an employed earner's disablement for the purposes of section 103 above, the appropriate percentage may be added to the percentage of disablement resulting from the relevant accident.

(5) In subsection (4)(a) above "the appropriate percentage" means the assessed percentage of any present disablement of the earner which resulted—

(a) from any accident [2 . . .] arising out of and in the course of his employment, being employed earner's employment, or

(b) from any other prescribed disease or injury due to the nature of that employment [2 . . .],

and in respect of which a disablement gratuity was not paid to him after a final assessment of his disablement.

(6) In subsection (4)(b) above "the appropriate percentage" means the assessed percentage of any present disablement of the earner—

(a) which resulted from any prescribed disease or injury due to the nature of his employment [2 . . .], and

(b) in respect of which a disablement gratuity was not paid to him after a final assessment of his disablement.

(7) Where regulations under subsection (2) above—

(a) make provision such as is mentioned in subsection (4) above, and

(b) also make provision corresponding to that in section 103(3) above,

they may also make provision to the effect that those corresponding provisions shall have effect in relation to the aggregate percentage and not in relation to any percentage forming part of the aggregate.

AMENDMENT

1. Social Security Act 1998 Sch.7 para.65 (July 5, 1999).
2. Welfare Reform Act 2012 s.64 (December 5, 2012).

DERIVATION

SSA 1975 s.77. **1.421**

DEFINITIONS

"employed earner"—see ss.2 and 95(4).
"employed earner's employment"—see ss.95 and 97.
"assessed"—see s.103(5).
"employment", "employed", "prescribe" and "relevant accident"—see s.122(1).

GENERAL NOTE

In general the same benefits are payable in respect of prescribed diseases as are payable in respect of injuries caused by accident. For regulations, see the Prescribed Diseases Regulations 1985. The practice of the Department has been to require a separate claim for disablement benefit in respect of each disease. However, in *CI/420/94*, it was held that, where disablement benefit was in payment in respect of one disease, a "claim" in respect of another disease was really an application for review. The concluding words of subs.(2) were added to s.77(2) of the Social Security Act 1975 in order to reverse the effect of *McKiernon v Secretary of State for Social Security, The Times*, November 1, 1989 in which reg.25 of the 1985 Regulations had been held to be ultra vires. In *Chatterton v Chief Adjudication Officer, McKiernon v Chief Adjudication Officer* (reported in *R(I) 1/94*), the Court of Appeal held that the amendment did have the intended effect. **1.422**

Respiratory diseases

110.—(1) As respects pneumoconiosis, regulations may further provide that, where a person is found to be suffering from pneumoconiosis **1.423**

accompanied by tuberculosis, the effects of the tuberculosis shall be treated for the purposes of this section and sections 108 and 109 above as if they were effects of the pneumoconiosis.

(2) Subsection (1) above shall have effect as if after "tuberculosis" (in both places) there were inserted "emphysema or chronic bronchitis", but only in relation to a person the extent of whose disablement resulting from pneumoconiosis, or from pneumoconiosis accompanied by tuberculosis, would (if his physical condition were otherwise normal) be assessed at not less than 50 per cent.

(3) A person found to be suffering from pneumoconiosis shall be treated for the purposes of this Act as suffering from a loss of faculty such that the assessed extent of the resulting disablement amounts to not less than 1 per cent.

(4) In respect of byssinosis, a person shall not (unless regulations otherwise provide) be entitled to disablement benefit unless he is found to be suffering, as the result of byssinosis, from loss of faculty which is likely to be permanent.

DERIVATION

1.424 SSA 1975 s.78.

DEFINITIONS

"assessed"—see s.103(5).
"pneumoconiosis"—see s.122(1).

GENERAL NOTE

Subsections (1) and (2)

1.425 See regs 21 and 22 of the Prescribed Diseases Regulations 1985.

Subsection (3)

1.426 This requires that a person suffering from pneumoconiosis *shall* be treated as being disabled to the extent of at least 1 per cent, even if the disablement is in fact negligible. Under reg.20(1) of the Prescribed Diseases Regulations 1985 a person suffering from pneumoconiosis is entitled to disablement benefit if the resulting disablement is at least 1 per cent.

Subsection (4)

1.427 This subsection is disapplied by reg.20(2) of the Prescribed Diseases Regulations 1985.

1.428 *Section 111 repealed by Welfare Reform Act 2012 s.64 (December 5, 2012).*

PART VI

MISCELLANEOUS PROVISIONS RELATING TO PARTS I TO V

Earnings

Certain sums to be earnings

1.429 **112.**—(1) [1 The Treasury may by regulations made with the concurrence of the Secretary of State] provide—

(a) that any employment protection entitlement shall be deemed for the purposes of this Act and the Administration Act to be earnings payable by and to such persons as are prescribed and to be so payable in respect of such periods as are prescribed; and
(b) that those periods shall, so far as they are not periods of employment, be deemed for those purposes to be periods of employment.

(2) In subsection (1) above "employment protection entitlement" means—
(a) any sum, or a prescribed part of any sum, mentioned in subsection (3) below; and
(b) prescribed amounts which the regulations provide are to be treated as related to any of those sums.

[[1](2A) Regulations under subsection (2) above shall be made by the Treasury with the concurrence of the Secretary of State.]

(3) The sums referred to in subsection (2) above are the following—
(a) a sum payable in respect of arrears of pay in pursuance of an order for reinstatement or re-engagement under [[2] the Employment Rights Act 1996],
(b) a sum payable by way of pay in pursuance of an order under that Act [[3] or the Trade Union and Labour Relations (Consolidation) Act 1992] for the continuation of a contract of employment,
(c) a sum payable by way of remuneration in pursuance of a protective award under [[4] the Trade Union and Labour Relations (Consolidation) Act 1992].

AMENDMENTS

1. Transfer of Functions Act 1999 Sch.3 para.21 (April 1, 1999). 1.430
2. Employment Rights Act 1996 Sch.1 para.51(4)(a) (August 22, 1996).
3. Employment Rights Act 1996 Sch.1 para.51(4)(b) (August 22, 1996).
4. Employment Rights Act 1996 Sch.1 para.51(4)(c) (August 22, 1996).

DERIVATION

SS(MP)A 1977 s.18. 1.431

Disqualification and suspension

General provisions as to disqualification and suspension

113.—(1) Except where regulations otherwise provide, a person shall be disqualified for receiving any benefit under Parts II to V of this Act, and an increase of such benefit shall not be payable in respect of any person as the beneficiary's [[2] wife, husband or civil partner], for any period during which the person— 1.432
(a) is absent from Great Britain; or
(b) is undergoing imprisonment or detention in legal custody.

(2) Regulations may provide for suspending payment of such benefit to a person during any period in which he is undergoing medical or other treatment as an in-patient in a hospital or similar institution.

(3) Regulations may provide for a person who would be entitled to any such benefit but for the operation of any provision of this Act [1, the Administration Act or Chapter II of Part I of the Social Security Act 1998] to be treated as if entitled to it for the purposes of any rights or obligations (whether his own or another's) which depend on his entitlement, other than the right to payment of the benefit.

AMENDMENTS

1. Social Security Act 1998 Sch.7 para.66 (July 5, 1999).
2. Civil Partnership Act 2004 s.254 and Sch.24 para.38 (December 5, 2005).

DERIVATION

1.433 SSA 1975 s.82(5)–(6) and s.83 as amended.

DEFINITION

"Great Britain"—by art.1 of the Union with Scotland Act 1706, this means England, Scotland and Wales and see s.172.

GENERAL NOTE

1.434 Subs.(1) states two general disqualifications for receiving benefit: absence from Great Britain and undergoing imprisonment or detention in legal custody.

A Tribunal of Commissioners has clarified that this provision stops the payment of benefit rather than entitlement: *CIB/3645/2002*.

Absence from Great Britain

1.435 Absence means "not physically present" in England, Scotland or Wales; it does not necessitate the presence of the person in the past in England, Scotland or Wales: *R(U) 18/60* and *R(U) 16/62*. To be absent from Great Britain, a person must be absent throughout a whole day: *R(S) 1/66*. For the impact of absence from Great Britain on particular benefits, see the Persons Abroad Regulations, which are largely concerned with displacing the disqualification either permanently or temporarily. Very broadly speaking, the disqualification is displaced where the benefit is not related to the ability to work; some temporary relief is given where the benefit arises by reason of incapacity or confinement; and no relief at all is given where the benefit arises by reason of unemployment.

Undergoing imprisonment or detention in legal custody

1.436 Although the wording of subs.(1)(b) makes no reference to imprisonment being connected with criminal proceedings, there is now authority for reading in such a requirement. The history of the controversy is well summarised by the Commissioner in *R(S) 8/79* where the Commissioner concludes,

> "I am bound by these decisions to hold that a person is not disqualified under section 82(5)(b) of the Social Security Act 1975 by reason of undergoing detention in legal custody which has nothing to do with a criminal offence" (para.5). "The decisions that I am following are all based on the proposition that imprisonment in the section means imprisonment imposed by a court exercising criminal jurisdiction . . ." (para.8).

So imprisonment for non-payment of maintenance did not disqualify the claimant from receiving invalidity benefit.

See also regs 2 and 3 of the General Benefit Regulations.

In *R(P) 1/02* the Commissioner upholds a decision to disqualify the claimant while in prison from entitlement to any part of his retirement pension. In particular, he holds that the disqualification extends to additional pension under SERPS and to graduated retirement pension. The disqualification is also held to be compatible with the requirements of the Human Rights Act 1998.

For a decision of the Administrative Court on the eligibility of post-tariff life prisoners to income support on transfer from prison to a mental health hospital, see *R. (RD and PM)* v *Secretary of State for Work and Pensions* [2008] EWHC 2635 (Admin), which confirmed that there was no such entitlement.

Reciprocal agreements

Following the withdrawal of the United Kingdom from the European Union, the landscape has significantly altered for nationals of EU countries. Some may benefit from the Citizens' Rights provisions in the Withdrawal Agreement; others from the Protocol on Social Security Co-ordination forming part of the Trade and Co-operation Agreement entered into on December 24, 2020. These in many respects operate as an overarching reciprocal agreement. Separate agreements have been concluded with the Economic Area countries (Iceland, Liechtenstein and Norway) for nationals of those countries and with Switzerland. Further detail may be found in Vol III: *Administration, Adjudication and the European Dimension*. **1.437**

Following EU exit, the UK is no longer covered by the EU's international agreements. This includes so-called 'mixed bilateral' international agreements between the EU and its member States on the one hand, and a third country on the other hand, such as the Association or Co-operation Agreements between the EU and a number of countries bordering the Mediterranean in the Middle East and North Africa which extend entitlement to social security benefits to nationals of those countries. For a decision on the EU–Morocco agreement, see *R(S) 1/00* and *HMRC v HEH and SSWP (TC and CHB)* [2018] UKUT 237 (AAC).

The UK has sought to reproduce the effects of some of the international agreements that previously applied to it, including a number of agreements with Euro-Mediterranean partners. This is done largely on the basis of applying the Euro-Mediterranean Agreements *mutatis mutandis*, except where contrary provision is made. A list of the UK's trade agreements (as the Foreign and Commonwealth Office considers them) with non-EU countries (and their status) can be found here: *https://www.gov.uk/guidance/uk-trade-agreements-in-effect* (accessed April 25, 2024).

By way of example, the UK/Morocco Association Agreement is currently being provisionally applied on such a basis. The modifications to the text of the EU's Euro-Mediterranean Agreement do not fundamentally affect art.65, the key article for social security purposes. However, questions of enforceability may now present themselves, given that the arrangements now in force are matters of international law.

There may also be a reciprocal agreement which may smooth the way to benefit entitlement for a particular claimant.

Though Ireland is an EU member State and the Citizens' Rights provisions of the Withdrawal Agreement and the Protocol on Social Security Co-ordination are in principle relevant, there is also a Convention on Social Security between the UK and Ireland, likely to be of considerable practical importance in view of the close links between the countries, reflected in the Common Travel Area. Effect was given to the Convention in domestic law by the Social Security (Ireland) Order 2019 SI 2019/622 and the Convention itself appears in the Schedule. The text of the Order and Convention can be found in the 2022-23 edition of volume III or at *www.gov.uk/government/publications/ukireland-convention-on-social-security-ts-no62021*.

There remain some reciprocal agreements with other EEA countries, which may assist in limited circumstances where the Brexit settlement does not, though most of these have in practice been superseded.

There are also reciprocal agreements with Barbados, Bermuda, Canada, Guernsey, Isle of Man, Israel, Jamaica, Japan, Jersey, Mauritius, New Zealand, Philippines, Republics of former Yugoslavia (the Republics of Bosnia-Herzegovina, North Macedonia, Serbia, Montenegro and Kosovo), Turkey and USA.

There are further reciprocal agreements with Chile, Japan and South Korea, but they only extend to contributions, not benefits.

Reciprocal agreements also exist with Northern Ireland, which although part of the United Kingdom has its own, largely parallel, social security system.

For a decision that explores the GB/Jamaica agreement, and the lack of appeal rights in respect of Secretary of State decisions made thereunder, see *CIB/3645/2002*.

R(S) 1/93 illustrates the need to take care to look at the definitions contained in each set of relevant regulations requiring to be considered in determining a question arising on appeal and to distinguish between points of legal principle and distinctions of fact. In this case the tribunal had correctly concluded that a claimant who had been resident in Malta for nearly seven years, because he found relief in the warm climate for the symptoms of his multiple sclerosis, was not temporarily absent from Great Britain under reg.2 of the Persons Abroad Regulations. The tribunal nevertheless went on to hold that the claimant was "temporarily" in Malta under Art.9A of the Order establishing reciprocal arrangements with Malta, because it felt bound by the decision in *CS/02/1976* in which the immigration status of the claimant, described in that case as being that of a "temporary visitor", was regarded as powerful evidence for consideration even though the claimant had been in Malta for two years with no foreseeable prospect of leaving unless required to do so by the immigration authorities. The fact remained that for immigration purposes the claimant's presence was "on sufferance without a right of permanent residence".

Commissioner Johnson held that *CS/02/1976* turned on a question of fact and degree and that the conclusion in *CS/02/1976* was not binding upon the tribunal. Commissioner Johnson says the facts of the two cases are "plainly distinguishable" whereas the tribunal had described them as "virtually indistinguishable". The outcome was that the expressed inclination (as distinct from the decision) of the tribunal that the claimant was not temporarily in Malta was correct.

The result is that there are now two decisions of Commissioners which place differing emphasis on the immigration status of the individual. *CS/02/1976* suggests that it is powerful evidence of status, whereas *R(S) 1/93* (paras 13–15) suggests that it is just one factor which can be displaced by other facts present in the case.

1.438 The Social Security (Reciprocal Agreements) Order 1995 (SI 1995/767) amends the reciprocal agreements listed in Sch.2 to the Order (which includes all the agreements mentioned in these annotations) by deeming references to sickness and invalidity benefits to include references to incapacity benefit. References to the calculation of benefit under the law of the UK are to be read so as to apply to short-term and long-term incapacity benefit: see further SI 2012/360 (below).

The Social Security (Reciprocal Agreements) Order 1996 (SI 1996/1928) provides for certain reciprocal agreements listed in its Sch.2 to be modified to take account of changes made by the Jobseekers Act 1995.

The Social Security (Reciprocal Agreements) Order 2001 (SI 2001/407) entering into force on April 9, 2001, provided for social security legislation to be modified or adapted in the reciprocal agreements listed in the Order to accommodate changes made by the Welfare Reform and Pensions Act 1999 in introducing new bereavement benefits; see further SI 2007/159 (below).

1.439 Note that the Social Security (Reciprocal Agreements) Order 2005 (SI 2005/2765) makes provision for the Social Security Contributions and Benefits Act 1992 and the Social Security Administration Act 1992 to be modified to reflect changes made to the benefit entitlement of spouses and civil partners by the Welfare Reform and Pensions Act 1999 and the Civil Partnership Act 2004 in relation to the Orders in Council referred to in Sch.2 to the Order.

The Social Security (Reciprocal Agreements) Order 2012 (SI 2012/360), which entered into force on February 22, 2012, makes provision for the Social Security Contributions and Benefits Act 1992, the Social Security Administration Act 1992, and Pt I of the Welfare Reform Act 2007 to be modified to reflect the transition from incapacity benefit to employment and support allowance in relation to the Orders in Council specified in Sch.2 to the Order.

The Social Security (Reciprocal Agreements) Order 2017 (SI 2017/159) makes provision for the Social Security Administration Act 1992, the Social Security Contributions and Benefits Act 1992 and Part 5 (bereavement support payment) of the Pensions Act 2014 and regulations made under those Acts or section 30 of the Pensions Act 2014 to be modified to reflect the replacement of various bereavement benefits by bereavement support payment.

Persons maintaining dependants, etc.

Persons maintaining dependants, etc.

114.—(1) Regulations may provide for determining the circumstances in which a person is or is not to be taken, for the purposes of Parts II to V of this Act— 1.440

(a) to be wholly or mainly, or to a substantial extent, maintaining, or to be contributing at any weekly rate to the maintenance of, another person; or

(b) to be, or have been, contributing at any weekly rate to the cost of providing for a child [2 or qualifying young person].

(2) Regulations under this section may provide, for the purposes of the provisions relating to an increase of benefit under Parts II to V of this Act in respect of a [1 wife, civil partner] or other adult dependant, that where—

(a) a person is partly maintained by each of two or more beneficiaries, each of whom would be entitled to such an increase in respect of that person if he were wholly or mainly maintaining that person, and

(b) the contributions made by those two or more beneficiaries towards the maintenance of that person amount in the aggregate to sums which would, if they had been contributed by one of those beneficiaries, have been sufficient to satisfy the requirements of regulations under this section.

that person shall be taken to be wholly or mainly maintained by such of those beneficiaries as may be prescribed.

(3) Regulations may provide for any sum or sums paid by a person by way of contribution towards either or both the following, that is to say—

(a) the maintenance of his or her spouse [1 or civil partner], and

(b) the cost of providing for one or more children [2 or qualifying persons], to be treated for the purposes of any of the provisions of this Act specified in subsection (4) below as such contributions, of such respective amounts equal in the aggregate to the said sum or sums, in respect of such persons, as may be determined in accordance with the regulations so as to secure as large a payment as possible by way of benefit in respect of the dependants.

(4) The provisions in question are [3 sections 56, 86 and paragraphs 5 and 6 of Schedule 7] to this Act.

AMENDMENTS

1. Civil Partnership Act 2004 s.254 and Sch.24 para.39 (December 5, 2005).
2. Child Benefit Act 2005 Sch.1 para.7 (April 10, 2006).
3. Welfare Reform Act 2009 Sch.7(2) para.1 (April 6, 2010).

Derivation

1.441 SSA 1975 s.84 as amended.

Special cases

Crown employment—Parts I to VI

1.442 **115.**—(1) Subject to the provisions of this section, Parts I to V and this Part of this Act apply to persons employed by or under the Crown in like manner as if they were employed by a private person.

(2) Subsection (1) above does not apply to persons serving as members of Her Majesty's forces in their capacity as such.

(3) Employment as a member of His Majesty's forces and any other prescribed employment under the Crown are not, and are not to be treated as, employed earner's employment for any of the purposes of Part V of this Act.

(4) The references to Parts I to V of this Act in this section and sections 116, 117, 119, 120 and 121 below do not include references to section 111 above.

Derivation

1.443 SSA 1975 s.127.

General Note

1.444 In *CI/7507/1999*, the Commissioner notes that s.115(1) is designed to reverse the common law rule that persons serving the Crown in whatever capacity are not "in a master and servant" relationship with the Crown (para.13). But the reversal of the common law rule in s.115(1) is made subject to exceptions in subs.(2) and (3) in relation to persons serving as members of His Majesty's forces in their capacity as such. So, during a period of service in the Royal Air Force, a person is not treated as being employed by the Crown for the purpose of being in employed earner's employment for industrial injuries purposes.

The preclusion covers service in the Territorial Army (see subs.(3) and Social Security (Contribution) Regulation 2001 Sch.6 Pt I item 6). Exemptions in the Social Security (Benefit) (Members of the Forces) Regulations, reg.2, do not embrace industrial injuries benefits. Accordingly, in *CI/0293/2005*, Commissioner Fellner held that a Territorial Army cook, injured through slipping when cooking, was not entitled to those benefits. In *MH v SSWP (II)* [2020] UKUT 297 (AAC) at [68] Judge Rowland points out that a person precluded by this provision may nonetheless have an entitlement to a service disablement pension under Part II of the Naval, Military and Air Forces Etc. (Disablement and Death) Service Pensions Order 2006 (SI 2006/606).

Her Majesty's forces

1.445 **116.**—(1) Subject to section 115(2) and (3) above and to this section, a person who is serving as a member of Her Majesty's forces shall, while he is so serving, be treated as an employed earner, in respect of his membership of those forces, for the purposes—

(a) of Parts I to V and this Part of this Act; and
(b) of any provision of the Administration Act in its application to him as an employed earner.

(2) [1 The Treasury may with the concurrence of the Secretary of State] make regulations modifying Parts I to V and this Part of this Act, [2 and Part

II of the Social Security Contributions (Transfer of Functions, etc.) Act 1999] and any [3 provisions of Chapter II of Part I of the Social Security Act 1998 which correspond to] provisions of Part III of the 1975 Act, in such matter as [1 the Treasury think] proper, in their application to persons who are or have been members of Her Majesty's forces; and regulations under this section may in particular provide [4, in the case of persons who are employed earners in respect of their membership of those forces, for reducing the rate of the contributions payable in respect of their employment and determining—

(a) the amounts payable on account of those contributions by the Secretary of State and the time and manner of payment, and

(b) the deduction (if any) to be made on account of those contributions from the pay of those persons;]

(3) For the purposes of Parts I to V and this Part of this Act, Her Majesty's forces shall be taken to consist of such establishments and organisation as may be prescribed, [1 by regulations made by the Treasury with the concurrence of the Secretary of State] being establishments and organisations in which persons serve under the control of the Defence Council.

AMENDMENTS

1. Transfer of Functions Act 1999 Sch.3 para.22 (April 1, 1999).
2. Transfer of Functions Act 1999 Sch.7 paras 5–6 (April 1, 1999).
3. Social Security Act 1998 Sch.7 paras 67–68 (July 5, 1999).
4. Jobseekers Act 1995 Sch.2 para.28

DERIVATION

SSA 1975 s.128. **1.446**

GENERAL NOTE

In *CI/7507/1999*, the Commissioner notes that s.116 is "dealing largely with the question of the payment of contributions" (para.13) and so there is no real contradiction between the wording of ss.115 and 116. **1.447**

Mariners, airmen, etc.

117.—[1 (1) The Treasury may with the concurrence of the Secretary of State] make regulations modifying provisions of Parts I to V and this Part of this Act, [2 and Part II of the Social Security Contributions (Transfer of Functions, etc.) Act 1999] and any [3 provisions of Chapter II of Part I of the Social Security Act 1998 which correspond to] provisions of Part III of the 1975 Act, in such manner as [1 the Treasury think] proper, in their application to persons who are or have been, or are to be, employed on board any ship, vessel, hovercraft or aircraft. **1.448**

(2) Regulations under subsection (1) above may in particular provide—

(a) for any such provision to apply to such persons, notwithstanding that it would not otherwise apply;

(b) for excepting such persons from the application of any such provision where they neither are domiciled nor have a place of residence in any part of Great Britain;

(c) for requiring the payment of secondary Class 1 contributions in respect of such persons, whether or not they are (within the meaning of Part I of this Act) employed earners;

(d) for the taking of evidence, for the purposes of any claim to benefit, in a country or territory outside Great Britain, by a British consular official or such other person as may be prescribed;
(e) for enabling persons who are or have been so employed to authorise the payment of the whole or any part of any benefit to which they are or may become entitled to such of their dependants as may be prescribed.

AMENDMENTS

1. Transfer of Functions Act 1999 Sch.3 para.23 (April 1, 1999).
2. Transfer of Functions Act 1999 Sch.7 paras 5–6 (April 1, 1999).
3. Social Security Act 1998 ss.116–17 (July 5, 1999).

DERIVATION

1.449 SSA 1975 s.129.

Married women and widows

1.450 **118.** [1 The Treasury may with the concurrence of the Secretary of State] make regulations modifying any of the following provisions of this Act, namely—
(a) Part I;
(b) Part II (except section 60); and
(c) Parts III and IV,
in such manner as [1 the Treasury think] proper, in their application to women who are or have been married.

AMENDMENT

1. Transfer of Functions Act 1999 Sch.3 para.24 (April 1, 1999).

DERIVATION

1.451 SSA 1975 s.130.

Persons outside Great Britain

1.452 **119.**—[1 The Treasury may with the concurrence of the Secretary of State] make regulations modifying Parts I to V of this Act [2 and Part II of the Social Security Contributions (Transfer of Functions, etc.) Act 1999] and any [3 provisions of Chapter II of Part I of the Social Security Act 1998 which corresponds to] provisions of Part III of the 1975 Act, in such manner as [1 the Treasury think] proper, in their application to persons who are or have been outside Great Britain at any prescribed time or in any prescribed circumstances.

AMENDMENTS

1. Transfer of Functions Act 1999 Sch.3 para.25 (April 1, 1999).
2. Transfer of Functions Act 1999 Sch.7 paras 7–8 (April 1, 1999).
3. Social Security Act 1998 Sch.7 paras 69–70.

DERIVATION

1.453 SSA 1975 s.131.

Employment at sea (continental shelf operations)

120.—(1) [1 The Treasury may with the concurrence of the Secretary of State] make regulations modifying Parts I to V and this Part of this Act [2 and Part II of the Social Security Contributions (Transfer of Functions, etc.) Act 1999], and any [3 provisions of Chapter II of Part I of the Social Security Act 1998 which corresponds to] provisions of Part III of the 1975 Act, in such manner as [1 the Treasury think] proper, in their application to persons in any prescribed employment (whether under a contract of service or not) in connection with continental shelf operations. 1.454

(2) "Continental shelf operations" means any activities which, if paragraphs (a) and (d) of [4 subsection 18) of section 11 of the Petroleum Act 1998] (application of civil law to certain offshore activities) were omitted, would nevertheless fall within subsection (2) of that section.

(3) In particular (but without prejudice to the generality of subsection (1) above), the regulations may provide for any prescribed provision of Parts I to V and this Part of this Act to apply to any such person notwithstanding that he does not fall within the description of an employed or self-employed earner, or does not fulfil the conditions prescribed under section 1(6) above as to residence or presence in Great Britain.

[5 (4) The Treasury may also, by regulations, make provision for, and in connection with, the issue by Her Majesty's Revenue and Customs of certificates to prescribed persons who are, by virtue of regulations under subsection (1), to be treated as the secondary contributor in relation to the payment of earnings to or for the benefit of one or more continental shelf workers—

(a) confirming that the prescribed person's liabilities to pay contributions in respect of the continental shelf workers specified or described in the certificate are being met by another person, and
(b) discharging the prescribed person, while the certificate is in force, from liability to make any payments in respect of the contributions, in the event that the other person fails to pay them in full.

(5) Regulations under subsection (4) may, in particular, make provision about—

(a) applying for a certificate;
(b) the circumstances in which a certificate may, or must, be issued or cancelled;
(c) the form and content of a certificate;
(d) the effect of a certificate (including provision modifying the effect mentioned in subsection (4)(b) or specifying further effects;
(e) the effect of cancelling a certificate.]

AMENDMENTS

1. Transfer of Functions Act 1999 Sch.3 para.26 (April 1, 1999).
2. Transfer of Functions Act 1999 Sch.7 paras 7–8 (April 1, 1999).
3. Social Security Act 1998 Sch.7 paras 69–70.
4. Petroleum Act 1998 Sch.4 para.30 (February 15, 1999).
5. National Insurance Contributions Act 2014 s.12(4) (March 13, 2014).

DERIVATION

SSA 1975 s.132 as amended. 1.455

Treatment of certain marriages

121.—(1) Regulations [1 made by the Treasury with the concurrence of the Secretary of State] may provide— 1.456

(a) for a voidable marriage which has been annulled, whether before or after the date when the regulations come into force, to be treated for the purposes of the provisions to which this subsection applies as if it had been a valid marriage which was terminated by divorce at the date of annulment;

[3 (aa) for a voidable civil partnership which has been annulled, whether before or after the date when the regulations come into force, to be treated for the purposes of the provisions to which this subsection applies as if it had been a valid civil partnership which was dissolved at the date of annulment;]

(b) as to the circumstances in which, for the purposes of the enactments to which this section [2 applies, a marriage during the subsistence of which a party to it is at any time married to more than one person is to be treated as having, or as not having, the same consequences as any other marriage.]

(2) Subsection (1) above applies—

(a) to any enactment contained in Parts I to V or this Part of this Act; and

(b) to regulations under any such enactment.

AMENDMENTS

1. Transfer of Functions Act 1999 Sch.3 para.27 (April 1, 1999).

2. Private International Law (Miscellaneous Provisions) Act 1995 Sch. para.4(2) (January 8, 1996).

3. Civil Partnership Act 2004 s.254 and Sch.24 para.40 (December 5, 2005).

DERIVATION

1.457 SSA 1975 s.162.

Interpretation

Interpretation of Parts I to VI and supplementary provisions

1.458 **122.**—(1) In Parts I to V above and this Part of this Act, unless the context otherwise requires—

[1 "additional Class 4 percentage" is to be construed in accordance with section 15(3ZA)(b) above;

"additional primary percentage" is to be construed in accordance with section 8(2)(b) above;]

[35 "adult disability payment" means disability assistance given in accordance with the Disability Assistance for Working Age People (Scotland) Regulations 2022;]

[30 "age-related secondary percentage" is to be construed in accordance with section 9A(2) above;]

[19 "Bank of England base rate" means—

(a) the rate announced from time to time by the Monetary Policy Committee of the Bank of England as the official dealing rate, being the rate at which the Bank is willing to enter into transactions for providing short term liquidity in the money markets, or

(b) where an order under section 19 of the Bank of England Act 1998 is in force, any equivalent rate determined by the Treasury under that section;]

"beneficiary", in relation to any benefit, means the person entitled to that benefit;

"benefit" means—

(a) benefit under Parts II to V of this Act other than Old Cases payments;

(b) as respects any period before 1st July 1992 but not before 6th April 1975, benefit under Part II of the 1975 Act; or

(c) as respects any period before 6th April 1975, benefit under—

(i) the National Insurance Act 1946 or 1965; or

(ii) The National Insurance (Industrial Injuries) Act 1946 or 1965;

[[29] (For the meaning of "benefit" in Part 1, see also section 19B);]

[[12] "the benefits code" has the meaning given by section 63(1) of ITEPA 2003;]

[[15] "child" has the same meaning as in Part 9 of this Act;]

[[35][[36] "child disability payment" means disability assistance given in accordance with the Disability Assistance for Children and Young People (Scotland) Regulations 2021;]]

"claim" is to be construed in accordance with "claimant";

"claimant", in relation to benefit other than industrial injuries benefit, means a person who has claimed benefit;

"claimant", in relation to industrial injuries benefit, means a person who has claimed industrial injuries benefit;

"contract of service" means any contract of service or apprenticeship whether written or oral and whether express or implied;

[[2] "contribution-based jobseeker's allowance" has the same meaning as in the Jobseeker's Act 1995];

"current", in relation to the lower and upper earnings limits [[3] and primary and secondary thresholds] under section 5(1) above, means for the time being in force;

[[4] "day of interruption of employment" has the meaning given by section 25A(1)(c) above];

[[33]"deferred" and "period of deferment" --

(a) in relation to a Category A or Category B retirement pension, have the meanings given by section 55(3), and

(b) in relation to a shared additional pension, have the meanings given by section 55C(3);]

"earner" and "earnings" are to be construed in accordance with sections 3, 4 and 112 above;

"employed earner" has the meaning assigned to it by section 2 above;

"employment" includes any trade, business, profession, office or vocation and "employed" has a corresponding meaning;

[[20] "the employment income parts of ITEPA 2003" means [[34]Parts 2 to 7A] of that Act;]

"entitled", in relation to any benefit, is to be construed in accordance with—

(a) the provisions specifically relating to that benefit;

(b) in the case of a benefit specified in section 20(1) above, section 21 above; and

(c) sections 1 to 3 of the Administration Act [[5] and section 27 of the Social Security Act 1998];

[[12] . . .]

[6 "first appointed year" means such tax year, no earlier than 2002–03, as may be appointed by order, and "second appointed year" means such subsequent tax year as may be so appointed;]

[21 "the flat rate introduction year" means such tax year as may be designated by order;]

[12 "general earnings" has the meaning given by section 7 of ITEPA 2003 and accordingly sections 3 and 112 of this Act do not apply in relation to the word "earnings" when used in the expression "general earnings"]

"industrial injuries benefit" means benefit under Part V of this Act, other than under Schedule 8;

[7 . . .]

"the Inland Revenue" means the Commissioners of Inland Revenue;

[12 "ITEPA 2003" means the Income Tax (Earnings and Pensions) Act 2003;]

"late husband", in relation to a woman who has been more than once married, means her last husband;

"long-term benefit" has the meaning assigned to it by section 20(2) and section 20(3) above;

"loss of physical faculty" includes disfigurement whether or not accompanied by any loss of physical faculty;

[8 "lower earnings limit" and "upper earnings limit" [3 . . .] [3 "primary threshold" and "secondary threshold"] are to be construed in accordance with subsection (1) of section 5 above, and references to the lower or upper earnings limit, or to [3 . . .] [3 the primary or secondary] threshold, of a tax year are to whatever is (or was) for that year the limit or threshold in force under that subsection;]

[7 . . .]

[31"lower-paid employment as a minister of religion" has the meaning given by section 290D of ITEPA 2003;]

[1 "main Class 4 percentage" is to be construed in accordance with section 15(3ZA) above;

"main primary percentage" is to be construed in accordance with section 8(2) above;]

"medical examination" includes bacteriological and radiographical tests and similar investigations, and "medically examined" has a corresponding meaning;

"medical treatment" means medical, surgical or rehabilitative treatment (including any course or diet or other regimen), and references to a person receiving or submitting himself to medical treatment are to be construed accordingly;

"the Northern Ireland Department" means the Department of Health and Social Services for Northern Ireland;

"Old Cases payments" means payments under Part I or II of Schedule 8 to this Act;

[2 "PAYE settlement agreement" has the same meaning as in [12 Chapter 5 of Part 11 of ITEPA 2003];]

"payments by way of occupational or personal pension" means, in relation to a person, periodical payments which, in connection with the coming to an end of an employment of his, fall to be made to him—

(a) out of money provided wholly or partly by the employer or under arrangements made by the employer; or

(b) out of money provided under an enactment or instrument having the force of law in any part of the United Kingdom or elsewhere; or

(c) under a personal pension scheme as defined in section 84(1) of the 1986 Act; or

[[22] (d) under a pension scheme registered under section 153 of the Finance Act 2004;]

and such other payments as are prescribed.

[[4] "pensionable age" has the meaning given by the rules in paragraph 1 to Schedule 4 to the Pensions Act 1995];

[[16] "PPF periodic payments" means—

(a) any periodic compensation payments made in relation to a person, payable under the pension compensation provisions as specified in section 162(2) of the Pensions Act 2004 or Article 146(2) of the Pensions (Northern Ireland) Order 2005 (the pension compensation provisions); or

(b) any periodic payments made in relation to a person, payable under section 166 of the Pensions Act 2004 or Article 150 of the Pensions (Northern Ireland) Order 2005 (duty to pay scheme benefits unpaid at assessment date etc.);

"pneumoconiosis" means fibrosis of the lungs due to silica dust, asbestos dust, or other dust, and includes the condition of the lungs known as dust-reticulation;

"prescribe" means prescribe by regulations;

[. . .]

"qualifying earnings factor" means an earnings factor equal to the lower earnings limit for the tax year in question multiplied by 52;

[[15] "qualifying young person" has the same meaning as in Part 9 of this Act;]

[[25] "Regulation (EC) No 1408/71" means Council Regulation (EC) No 1408/71 of 14 June 1971 [[32] as amended from time to time] on the application of social security schemes to employed persons, to self-employed persons and to members of their families moving within the Community;

"Regulation (EC) No 883/2004" means Regulation (EC) No 883/2004 of the European Parliament and of the Council of 29 April 2004 [[32] as amended from time to time] on the coordination of social security systems;]

"relative" includes a person who is a relative by marriage [[14] or civil partnership];

"relevant accident" means the accident in respect of which industrial injuries benefit is claimed or payable;

"relevant injury" means the injury in respect of which industrial injuries benefit is claimed or payable;

"relevant loss of faculty" means—

[[9] . . .]

(b) in relation to industrial injuries benefit, the loss of faculty resulting from the relevant injury;

[[1] "secondary percentage" is to be construed in accordance with section 9(2) above;]

"self-employed earner" has the meaning assigned to it by section 2 above;

"short-term benefit" has the meaning assigned to it by section 20(2) above;

"tax week" means one of the successive periods in a tax year beginning with the first day of that year and every seventh day thereafter, the last day of a tax year (or, in the case of a tax year ending in a leap year, the last two days) to be treated accordingly as a separate tax week;

"tax year" means the 12 months beginning with 6th April in any year, the expression "1978–79" meaning the tax year beginning with 6th April 1978, and any correspondingly framed reference to a pair of successive years being construed as a reference to the tax year beginning with 6th April in the earlier of them;

"trade or business" includes, in relation to a public or local authority, the exercise and performance of the powers and duties of that authority;

"trade union" means an association of employed earners;

[28 "unit of additional pension" means a unit of additional pension for which a person has paid a Class 3A contribution under section 14A;]

[18 "[24 the upper accrual point" is £770;]]

"week", [13 . . .], means a period of 7 days beginning with Sunday.

[2 "working life" has the meaning given by paragraph 5(8) of Schedule 3 to this Act].

[1A] . . . [26,27]

(2) Regulations [11 made by the Treasury with the concurrence of the Secretary of State] may make provision modifying the meaning of "employment" for the purposes of any provision of Parts I to V and this Part of this Act.

(3) Provision may be made [11 by the Treasury by regulations made with the concurrence of the Secretary of State] as to the circumstances in which a person is to be treated as residing or not residing with another person for any of the purposes of Parts I to V and this Part of this Act and as to the circumstances in which persons are to be treated for any of those purposes as residing or not residing together.

(4) A person who is residing with his spouse shall be treated for the purposes of Parts I to V and this Part of this Act as entitled to any child benefit to which his spouse is entitled.

(5) Regulations may, for the purposes of any provision of those Parts under which the right to any benefit or increase of benefit depends on a person being or having been entitled to child benefit, make provision whereby a person is to be treated as if he were or had been so entitled or as if he were not or had not been so entitled.

(6) For the purposes of Parts I to V and this Part of this Act a person is "permanently incapable of self-support" if (but only if) he is incapable of supporting himself by reason of physical or mental infirmity and is likely to remain so incapable for the remainder of his life.

[23 (6A) The Treasury may by regulations prescribe an equivalent of the upper accrual point in relation to earners paid otherwise than weekly (and references in this or any other Act to "the prescribed equivalent", in the context of the upper accrual point, are to the equivalent prescribed under this subsection in relation to such earners).

(6B) The power conferred by subsection (6A) includes power to prescribe an amount which exceeds by not more than £1 the amount which is the arithmetical equivalent of the upper accrual point.]

[23. . .]

AMENDMENTS

1. National Insurance Contributions Act 2002 s.6 and Sch.1 para.12 (has effect in relation to the tax year beginning April 6, 2003 and subsequent tax years: see National Insurance Contributions Act 2002, s.8(2)).
2. Jobseekers Act 1995 Sch.2 para.29 (October 7, 1996).
3. Welfare Reform and Pensions Act 1999 Sch.12 para.77 (April 6, 2000).
4. Social Security (Incapacity for Work) Act 1994 Sch.1 para.30 (April 13, 1995).
5. Social Security Act 1998 Sch.7 para.71(a) (July 5, 1999).
6. Child Support, Pensions and Social Security Act 2000 s.35 (January 8, 2001).
7. Social Security Act 1998 Sch.7 para.71(b) (July 5, 1999).
8. Social Security Act 1998 Sch.7 para.71(c) (July 5, 1999).
9. Welfare Reform and Pensions Act 1999 Sch.13 Pt IV (April 6, 2001).
10. Tax Credits Act 1999 Sch.1 para.2 (October 5, 1999).
11. Transfer of Functions Act 1999 Sch.3 para.28 (April 1, 1999).
12. Finance Act 2015 c.11 Sch.1(2) para.23(4)(a) (March 26, 2015).
13. Tax Credits Act 2002 Sch.6 (April 6, 2003).
14. Civil Partnership Act 2004 s.254 and Sch.24 para.41 (December 5, 2005).
15. Child Benefit Act 2005 c.6 Sch.1 Part, para.8 (April 10, 2006).
16. The Pensions 2004 (PPF Payments and FAS Payments)(Consequential Provisions) Order 2006 (SI 2006/343) (February 14, 2006).
17. Pensions Act 2007 s.11 (September 26, 2007).
18. Pensions Act 2007 s.12 (September 26, 2007).
19. Pensions Act 2004 Sch.11(2) para.18(a) (November 18, 2004 for enabling the making of regulations; April 6, 2005 otherwise).
20. Income Tax (Earnings and Pensions) Act 2003 Sch.6(2) para.178(2) (April 6, 2003 subject to transitional provisions and savings specified in 2003 c.1 Sch.7).
21. Pensions Act 2007 Pt 1, s.11(4) (September 26, 2007).
22. Taxation of Pension Schemes (Consequential Amendments) Order 2006 (SI 2006/745) Pt 1 art.4(3) (April 6, 2006).
23. National Insurance Contributions Act 2008 Sch.2 para.1 (September 22, 2008 for purposes specified in 2008 c.16 s.6(1); shall come into force on the commencement of 2007 c.22, Sch.4 para.45(2) otherwise).
24. National Insurance Contributions Act 2008 s.3(4) (September 21, 2008).
25. The Social Security (Disability Living Allowance, Attendance Allowance and Carer's Allowance) (Miscellaneous Amendments) Regulations 2011 (SI 2011/2426) (October 31, 2011).
26. The Marriage (Same Sex Couples) Act 2013 (Consequential and Contrary Provisions and Scotland) Order 2014 (SI 2014/560) art.22(7) (March 13, 2014).
27. The Marriage and Civil Partnership (Scotland) Act 2014 and Civil Partnership Act 2004 (Consequential Provisions and Modifications) Order 2014 (SI 2014/3229) Sch.4 para.2(12) (December 12, 2014).
28. Pensions Act 2014 Sch.15 para.10 (October 12, 2015).
29. Pensions Act 2014 Sch.12 para.7 (April 6, 2016).
30. National Insurance Contributions Act 2014 s.9(4) (April 6, 2015).
31. Finance Act 2015 c.11 Sch.1(2) para.23(4)(b) (March 26, 2015).
32. Social Security (Updating of EU References) (Amendment) Regulations 2018 (SI 2018/1084) reg.2 (November 15, 2018).
33. Pensions Act 2004 Sch.11(2) para.18(b) (November 18, 2004 for enabling the making of regulations; April 6, 2005 otherwise).
34. Finance Act 2011 Sch.2 para.50(a) (July 19, 2011).
35. Scotland Act 2016 (Social Security) (Consequential Provision) (Miscellaneous Amendment) Regulations 2021 (SI 2021/804) reg.2 (July 26, 2021).
36. Scotland Act 2016 (Social Security) (Adult Disability Payment and Child Disability Payment) (Amendment) Regulations 2022 (SI 2022/335) reg.2 (March 21, 2022).

General Note

1.459 On the meaning of "dust-reticulation" in the definition of pneumoconiosis see *S (on behalf of S, deceased) v SSWP* [2016] UKUT 485 (AAC); see further the annotation to Sch.1 of the Social Security (Industrial Injuries) (Prescribed Diseases) Regulations 1985 (SI 1985/967).

1.460 *For Pt VII see the 2021–22 edition of Vol.V and the cumulative supplement in this year's Vol.II and for Pt VIII see Vol.II.*

Part IX

Child Benefit

Child benefit

1.461 **141.—147.** *Omitted.* See *Vol IV: HMRC-administered Social Security Benefits and Scotland.*

Part X

Christmas bonus for pensioners

Entitlement of Pensioners to Christmas Bonus

1.462 **148.**—(1) Any person who in any year—

(a) is present or ordinarily resident in the United Kingdom [5, an EEA state or Switzerland] at any time during the relevant week; and

(b) is entitled to a payment of a qualifying benefit in respect of a period which includes a day in that week or is to be treated as entitled to a payment of a qualifying benefit in respect of such a period,

shall, subject to the following provisions of this Part of this Act and to section 1 of the Administration Act, be entitled to payment under this subsection in respect of that year.

(2) Subject to the following provisions of this Part of this Act, any person who is a member of a couple and is entitled to a payment under subsection (1) above in respect of a year shall also be entitled to payment under this subsection in respect of that year if—

(a) both members have attained pensionable age not later than the end of the relevant week; and

(b) the other member satisifies the condition mentioned in subsection (1)(a) above; and

(c) either—

(i) he is entitled or treated as entitled, in respect of the other member, to an increase in the payment of the qualifying benefit; or

(ii) the only qualifying benefit to which he is entitled is [2 state pension credit].

[4 (2ZA) In a case where a person is entitled to a payment of armed forces independence payment, the reference in subsection (1) to section 1 of the Administration Act is to be read as a reference to article 43 of the

Armed Forces and Reserve Forces (Compensation Scheme) Order 2011 (SI 2011/517)].

[2 (2A) In a case falling within paragraph (c)(ii) of subsection (2) above, paragraph (a) of that subsection has effect with the substitution of "qualifying age for state pension credit" for "pensionable age".]

(3) A payment under subsection (1) and (2) above—

(a) is to be made by the Secretary of State; and

(b) is to be of [3 £ 10]or such larger sum as the Secretary of State may by order specify.

[2 . . .]

(4) [2 . . .]

(5) Only one sum shall be payable in respect of any person.

AMENDMENTS

1. Pensions Act 1995 Sch.4 (July 19, 1995).

2. State Pension Credit Act 2002 Sch.2(1) para.5(2) (July 2, 2002 for the purposes of exercising powers to make regulations or orders; October 6, 2003 otherwise).

3. Christmas Bonus (Specified Sum) Order 2008 (SI 2008/3255) para.2 (December 19, 2008).

4. The Armed Forces and Reserve Forces (Compensation Scheme) (Consequential Provisions: Primary Legislation) Order 2013 (SI 2013/796) art.3 (April 8, 2013).

5. Social Security (Amendment) Regulations 2021 (SI 2021/1152) reg.2 (December 3, 2021).

GENERAL NOTE

A decision whether a person is entitled to payment of a Christmas Bonus is a decision against which no appeal lies to the First-tier Tribunal: Social Security Act 1998 s.12(1), Sch.2 para.2. 1.463

Provisions supplementary to section 148

149.— (1) For the purposes of section 148 above the Channel Islands, the Isle of Man and Gibraltar shall be treated as though they were part of the United Kingdom. 1.464

(2) A person shall be treated for the purposes of section 148(1)(b) above as entitled to a payment of a qualifying benefit if he would be so entitled—

(a) in the case of a qualifying benefit [2 other than state pension credit], but for the fact that he or, if he is a member of a couple, the other member is entitled to receive some other payment out of public funds;

(b) in the case of [2 state pension credit], but for the fact that his income or, if he is a member of a couple, the income of the other member was exceptionally of an amount which resulted in his having ceased to be entitled to [2 state pension credit]

(3) A person shall be treated for the purpose of section 148(2)(c)(i) above as entitled in respect of the other member of the couple to an increase in a payment of a qualifying benefit if he would be so entitled—

(a) but for the fact that he or the other member is entitled to receive some other payment out of public funds;

(b) but for the operation of any provision of [1 . . .] paragraph 6(4) of Schedule 7 to this Act or any regulations made under paragraph 6(3) of that Schedule whereby entitlement to benefit is affected by the amount of a person's earnings in a given period.

(4) For the purposes of section 148 above a person shall be taken not to be entitled to a payment of a war disablement pension unless not later than the end of the relevant week he has attained [3[4 pensionable age]].

(5) A sum payable under section 148 above shall not be treated as benefit for the purposes of any enactment or instrument under which entitlement to the relevant qualifying benefit arises or is to be treated as arising.

(6) A payment and the right to receive a payment—

(a) under section 148 above or any enactment corresponding to it in Northern Ireland; or

(b) under regulations relating to widows which are made by the Secretary of State under any enactment relating to police and which contain a statement that the regulations provide for payments corresponding to payments under that section,

shall be disregarded for all purposes of income tax and for the purposes of any enactment or instrument under which regard is had to a person's means.

AMENDMENTS

1. Pensions Act 2007 Sch.1 para.17 (September 26, 2007).
2. State Pension Credit Act 2002 Sch.2(1) para.6(2) (July 2, 2002 for the purposes of exercising powers to make regulations or orders; October 6, 2003 otherwise).
3. Pensions Act 1995 Sch.4(II) para.8 (July 19, 1995).
4. Pensions Act 2007 Sch.1 para. 43 (April 6, 2018).

Interpretation of Part X

1.465 **150.**—(1) In this Part of this Act "qualifying benefit" means—

(a) a retirement pension;
[1 (b) long-term incapacity benefit;]
[2 (ba) a qualifying employment and support allowance;]
[3 (bb) personal independence payment;]
[13 (bc) armed forces independence payment;]
[15 (bd) adult disability payment;]
(c) a widowed mother's allowance [4 , widowed parent's allowance] or widow's pension;
(d) [5 . . .]
(e) [6 a carer's allowance;]
[17 (ea) carer support payment;]
(f) industrial death benefit;
(g) an attendance allowance;
(h) an unemployability supplement or allowance;
(i) a war disablement pension;
(j) a war widow's pension;
(k) [7 state pension credit;]
[8 (l) a mobility supplement].

(2) in this Part of this Act—

[15 "adult disability payment" means disability assistance given in accordance with the Disability Assistance for Working Age People (Scotland) Regulations 2022] (SI 2022/54);

[13 "armed forces independence payment" means armed forces independence payment under the Armed Forces and Reserve Forces (Compensation Scheme) Order 2011 (SI 2011/517)];

"attendance allowance" means—

(a) an attendance allowance;

(b) a disability living allowance;
(c) an increase of disablement pension under section 104 or 105 above;
(d) a payment under regulations made in exercise of the powers in section 159(3)(b) of the 1975 Act or paragraph 7(2) of Schedule 8 to this Act;
(e) an increase of allowance under article 8 of the Pneumoconiosis, Byssionosis and Miscellaneous Diseases Benefit Scheme 1983 (constant attendance allowance for certain persons to whom that scheme applies) or under the corresponding provision of any Scheme which may replace that Scheme;
(f) an allowance in respect of constant attendance on account of disablement for which a person is in receipt of a war disablement pension, including an allowance in respect of exceptionally severe disablement;
[[16] (g) a child disability payment given in accordance with regulations made under section 31 of the Social Security (Scotland) Act;]

[[17] "carer support payment" means carer's assistance given in accordance with the Carer's Assistance (Carer's Support Payment) (Scotland) Regulations 2023;]

[[8] "mobility supplement" means a supplement awarded in respect of disablement which affects a person's ability to walk and for which the person is in receipt of a war disablement pension;]

[[9] "pensionable age" has the meaning given by the rules in paragraph 1 of Schedule 4 to the Pensions Act 1995];

[[7] "the qualifying age for state pension credit" is (in accordance with section 1(2)(b) and (6) of the State Pension Credit Act 2002)—
(a) in the case of a woman, pensionable age; or
(b) in the case of a man, the age which is pensionable age in the case of a woman born on the same day as a man;]

[[2] "qualifying employment and support allowance" means [[10] a contributory allowance] under Part 1 of the Welfare Reform Act 2007 the calculation of the amount of which includes an addition in respect of the support component or the work-related activity component.]

[[14] "retirement pension" means—
(a) a state pension under Part 1 of the Pensions Act 2014,
(b) a retirement pension under this Act, or
(c) graduated retirement benefit.] [[8] . . .];

[[7] "state pension credit" means state pension credit under the State Pension Credit Act 2002;]

"unemployability supplement or allowance" means—
(a) an unemployability supplement payable under Part 1 of Schedule 7 to this Act; or
(b) any corresponding allowance payable—
  (i) by virtue of paragraph 6(4)(a) of Schedule 8 to this Act[6];
  (ii) by way of supplement to retired pay or pension exempt from income tax under [[11] section 641 of the Income Tax (Earnings and Pensions) Act 2003;]
  (iii) under the Personal Injuries (Emergency Provisions) Act 1939; [[8] . . .]
  (iv) by way of supplement to retired pay or pension under the Polish Resettlement Act 1947;
  (v) [[11] . . .];

"war disablement pension" means—

(a) any retired pay, pension or allowance granted in respect of disablement under powers conferred by or under the Air Force (Contribution) Act 1917, the Personal Injuries (Emergency Provisions) Act 1939; the Pensions (Navy, Army, Air Force and Mercantile Marine Act 1939, the Polish Resettlement Act 1947, or Part VII or section 151 of the Reserve Forces Act 1980;

(b) without prejudice to paragraph (a) of this definition, any retired pay or pension to which [11 any of paragraphs (a) to (f) of section 641(1) of the Income Tax (Earnings and Pensions) Act 2003] applies;

"war widow's pension" means any widow's [12 or surviving civil partner's] pension or allowance granted in respect of a death due to service or war injury and payable by virtue of any enactment mentioned in paragraph (a) of the preceding definition or a pension or allowance for a widow [12 or surviving civil partner] granted under any scheme mentioned in [11 section 641(1)(e) or (f) of the Income Tax (Earnings and Pensions) Act 2003];

and each of the following expressions, namely "attendance allowance", "unemployability supplement or allowance", "war disablement pension" and "war widow's pension", includes any payment which the Secretary of State accepts as being analogous to it.

[12 (3) In this Part of this Act, "couple" has the meaning given by section 137(1) above].

(4) In this Part of this Act "the relevant week", in relation to any year, means the week beginning with the first Monday in December or such other week as may be specified in an order made by the Secretary of State.

AMENDMENTS

1. Social Security (Incapacity for Work) Act 1994 Sch.1 para.33 (April 13, 1995).
2. Welfare Reform Act 2007 Sch.3 para.9(11) (October 27, 2008).
3. Welfare Reform Act 2012 Sch.9 para.6 (April 8, 2013).
4. Welfare Reform and Pensions Act 1999 s.70 (April 9, 2001).
5. Welfare Reform and Pensions Act 1999 s.88 (April 6, 2001).
6. Regulatory Reform (Carer's Allowance) Order 2002 (SI 2002/1457) Sch.1 para.2(e) (September 1, 2002).
7. State Pension Credit Act 2002 Sch.2 para.7 (July 2, 2002).
8. Pensions Act 1995 s.132 (July 19, 1995).
9. Pensions Act 1995 Sch.4 para.13 (July 19, 1995).
10. Welfare Reform Act 2007 s.37(3) (November 12, 2009).
11. Income Tax (Earnings and Pensions) Act 2003 Sch.6 para.180 (April 6, 2003).
12. Civil Partnership Act 2004 Sch.24 para.49 (December 5, 2005).
13. Armed Forces and Reserve Forces (Compensation Scheme) (Consequential Provisions: Primary Legislation) Order 2013 (SI 2013/796) art.3 (April 8, 2013).
14. Pensions Act 2014 Sch.12 para.86. (April 6, 2016).
15. Social Security (Scotland) Act 2018 (Disability Assistance and Information-Sharing) (Consequential Provision and Modifications) Order 2022 (SI 2022/332) Pt 4 art.14(2)(b) (March 21, 2022).
16. Social Security (Scotland) Act 2018 (Disability Assistance for Children and Young People) Consequential Modifications) (No2) Order (SI 2021/1301) art.3 (November 17, 2021).
17. Carer's Assistance (Carer Support Payment) (Scotland) Regulations 2023 (Consequential Modifications) Order 2023 (SI 2023/1214) art.4(2) (November 16, 2023).

Part XI

Statutory Sick Pay

Omitted as the province of the Board of Inland Revenue. See Vol.IV. **1.466**

Part XII

Statutory Maternity Pay

164.–171. *Omitted.*
See Vol IV: HMRC-administered Social Security Benefits and Scotland

Part XIIZA

Statutory Paternity Pay

171ZA.–171ZK. *Omitted.*
See Vol IV: HMRC-administered Social Security Benefits and Scotland

Part XIIZB

Statutory Adoption Pay

171ZL.–171ZT. *Omitted.*
See Vol IV: HMRC-administered Social Security Benefits and Scotland

Part XIIZC

Statutory Shared Parental Pay

171ZU.–171ZZ5. *Omitted.*
See Vol IV: HMRC-administered Social Security Benefits and Scotland

Part XIIZD

Statutory Parental Bereavement Pay

171ZzB.–171ZZ15. Omitted.
See Vol IV: HMRC-administered Social Security Benefits and Scotland

PART XIIA

INCAPACITY FOR WORK

1.467 171A.–171G. *Omitted.*
For the text of and commentary to these sections see the 2011/12 edition of this Volume.

PART XIIZD

STATUTORY PARENTAL BEREAVEMENT PAY

171ZZ6.-171ZZ15. *Omitted*
See *Vol. IV: HMRC-Administered Social Security Benefits and Scotland*

PART XIII

GENERAL

Interpretation

Application of Act in relation to territorial waters

1.468 **172.**—In this Act—

(a) any reference to Great Britain includes a reference to the territorial waters of the United Kingdom adjacent to Great Britain;
(b) any reference to the United Kingdom includes a reference to the territorial waters of the United Kingdom.

DERIVATION

1.469 SSHBA 1982 s.26 as amended.

Age

1.470 **173.**—For the purposes of this Act a person—

(a) is over or under a particular age if he has or, as the case may be, has not attained that age; and
(b) is between two particular ages if he has attained the first but not the second;

and in Scotland (as in England and Wales) the time at which a person attains a particular age expressed in years is the commencement of the relevant anniversary of the date of his birth.

DERIVATION

1.471 SSA 1975 s.168(1) and Sch.20 as amended.

References to Acts

1.472 **174.**—In this Act—

"the 1975 Act" means the Social Security Act 1975;
"the 1986 Act" means the Social Security Act 1986;

"the Administration Act" means the Social Security Administration Act 1992;
"the Consequential Provisions Act" means the Social Security (Consequential Provisions) Act 1992;
"the Northern Ireland Contributions and Benefits Act" means the Social Security Contributions and Benefits (Northern Ireland) Act 1992;
"the Old Cases Act" means the Industrial Injuries and Diseases (Old Cases) Act 1975; and
"the Pensions Act" means the [1 Pension Schemes Act 1993].

AMENDMENT

1. Pension Schemes Act 1993 Sch.8 para.41 (February 7, 1994).

Subordinate legislation

Regulations, orders and schemes

175.—(1) Subject to [1 subsection (1A) below] regulations and orders under this Act shall be made by the Secretary of State. **1.473**

[1 (1A) Subsection (1) above has effect subject to—

(a) any provision [4 . . .] providing for regulations or an order to be made by the Treasury or by the Commissioners of Inland Revenue,

(b) [4 . . .]]

(2) Powers under this Act to make regulations, orders or schemes shall be exercisable by statutory instrument.

(3) Except in the case of an order under section 145(3) above and in so far as this Act otherwise provides, any power under this Act to make regulations or an order may be exercised—

(a) either in relation to all cases to which the power extends, or in relation to those cases subject to specified exceptions, or in relation to any specified cases or classes of case;

(b) so as to make, as respects the cases in relation to which it is exercised—

(i) the full provision to which the power extends or any less provision (whether by way of exception or otherwise),

(ii) the same provision for all cases in relation to which the power is exercised, or different provision for different cases or different classes of case or different provision as respects the same case or class for different purposes of this Act,

(iii) any such provision either unconditionally or subject to any specified condition;

and where such a power is expressed to be exercisable for alternative purposes it may be exercised in relation to the same case for any or all of those purposes; and powers to make regulations or an order for the purposes of any one provision of this Act are without prejudice to powers to make regulations or an order for the purposes of any other provision.

(4) Without prejudice to any specific provision in this Act, any power conferred by this Act to make regulations or an order (other than the power conferred in section 145(3) above) includes power to make thereby such incidental, supplementary, consequential or transitional provision as

appears to the [1 person making the regulations or order] to be expedient for the purposes of the regulations or order.

(5) Without prejudice to any specific provisions in this Act, a power conferred by any provision of this Act except—

(a) sections 30, 47(6), [2 25B(2)(a)] and 145(3) above and paragraph 3(9) of Schedule 7 to this Act;

(b) section 122(1) above in relation to the definition of "payments by way of occupational or personal pension"; and

(c) Part XI,

to make regulations or an order includes power to provide for a person to exercise a discretion in dealing with any matter.

[6(5A) . . .]

(6) [5 . . .]

(7) Any power of the Secretary of State under any provision of this Act, except the provisions mentioned in subsection (5)(a) and (b) above and Part IX, to make any regulations or order, where the power is not expressed to be exercisable with the consent of the Treasury, shall if the Treasury so direct be exercisable only in conjunction with them.

(8) Any power under any of sections 116 to 120 above to modify provisions of this Act or the Administration Act extends also to modifying so much of any other provision of this Act or that Act as re-enacts provisions of the 1975 Act which replace provisions of the National Insurance (Industrial Injuries) Act 1965 to 1974.

(9) A power to make regulations under any of sections 116 to 120 above shall be exercisable in relation to any enactment passed after this Act which is directed to be construed as one with this Act; but this subsection applies only so far as a contrary intention is not expressed in the enactment so passed, and is without prejudice to the generality of any such direction.

(10) Any reference in this section or section 176 below to an order or regulations under this Act includes a reference to an order or regulations made under any provision of an enactment passed after this Act and directed to be construed as one with this Act; but this subsection applies only so far as a contrary intention is not expressed in the enactment so passed, and without prejudice to the generality of any such direction.

AMENDMENTS

1. Transfer of Functions Act 1999 Sch.3 para.29 (April 1, 1999).
2. Social Security (Incapacity for Work) Act 1994 Sch.1 para.36 (April 13, 1995).
3. Local Government Finance Act 1992 Sch.9 para.10 (March 6, 1992).
4. Tax Credits Act 2002 Sch.6 (April 1, 2003).
5. Welfare Reform Act 2012 Sch.14(1) para.1 (April 1, 2013, subject to certain transitional provisions and savings in SI 2013/358).
6. Coronavirus Act 2020 s.89 (March 25, 2022).

DERIVATION

1.474 SSA 1975 ss.162, 166 and 168 as amended.

GENERAL NOTE

1.475 By virtue of Sch.2 Pt V para.20 and with effect from October 5, 1999, s.175 is to be construed, in relation to tax credit, as if references to the Secretary of State were references to the Treasury or, as the case may be, the Board of the Inland Revenue now His Majesty's Revenue and Customs.

Coronavirus Act 2020 s.41, which provided that s.175 "has effect as if" subsection (5A) were inserted, has now expired.

Parliamentary control

176.—(1) Subject to the provisions of this section, a statutory instrument containing (whether alone or with other provisions)— 1.476

[1 (za) regulations under section 5 specifying the lower earnings limit for the tax year following the designated tax year (see section 5(4) of the Pensions Act 2007) or any subsequent tax year;]

[2 (zb) regulations under section 5 specifying the upper earnings limit;]

(a) regulations made by virtue of—

[3 section 4B(2);
section 4C;]
[27 section 9A(7)]
[28 section 9B(4), (8) or (10)]
[4 section 10ZC;]
[29 section 11(8) or (9)]
[26 section 14A]
section 18;
[30 section 18A;]
section 19(4) to (6);
section 28(3);
[5 section 30DD(5)(b) or (c);]
[26 section 45(2A)]
[6 . . .]
section 104(3);
section 117;
section 118;
[7 . . .]
section 145;
[8 section 171ZE(1)];
[24 . . .]
[30 . . .]
[31 any of sections 171ZU to 171ZY;]
[33 any of sections 171ZZ6 to 171ZZ9;]
[9 . . .]
[10 (aa) the first regulations made by virtue of section 23A(3)(c);]
[25 (ab) the first regulations made by virtue of section 130A(5) or (6);]

(b) regulations prescribing payments for the purposes of the definition of "payments by way of occupational or personal pension" in section 122(1) above;

[11 (bb) regulations prescribing a percentage rate for the purposes of–
(i) paragraph 3B(3) or 7B(3) of Schedule 5, or
(ii) paragraph 5(3) of Schedule 5A;]

(c) an order under—

[12 section 25B(1);]
section 28(2);
[13 section 35A(7);]

[14 . . .]
[15 . . .]
[6 . . .]
section 148(3)(b);
section 157(2);
[16. . .]
[17 section 159A(1),]

shall not be made unless a draft of the instrument has been laid before Parliament and been approved by a resolution of each House.

(2) Subsection (1) above does not apply to a statutory instrument by reason only that it contains—

(a) regulations under section 117 which the instrument states are made for the purpose of making provision consequential on the making of an order under section 141, 143, 145, 146 or 162 of the Administration Act;

(b) regulations under powers conferred by any provision mentioned in paragraph (a) of that subsection [18 . . .] which are to be made for the purpose of consolidating regulations to be revoked in the instrument;

(c) regulations which, in so far as they are made under powers conferred by any provision mentioned in paragraph (a) of that subsection (other than [19 section 145]), only replace provisions of previous regulations with new provisions to the same effect.

[20 (2A) In the case of a statutory instrument containing (whether alone or with other provisions) regulations made by virtue of section 4B(2) to which subsection (1) above applies, the draft of the instrument must be laid before Parliament before the end of the period of 12 months beginning with the appropriate date.

(2B) For the purposes of subsection (2A), the "appropriate date" means–

(a) where the corresponding retrospective tax provision was passed or made before the day on which the National Insurance Contributions Act 2006 was passed, the date upon which that Act was passed, and

(b) in any other case, the date upon which the corresponding retrospective tax provision was passed or made.

(2C) For the purposes of subsection (2B), "the corresponding retrospective tax provision" in relation to the regulations means–

(a) the retrospective tax provision mentioned in subsection (1) of section 4B in relation to which the regulations are to be made by virtue of subsection (2) of that section, or

(b) where there is more than one such tax provision, whichever of those provisions was the first to be passed or made.]

(3) A statutory instrument—

(a) which contains (whether alone or with other provisions) any order, regulations or scheme made under this Act by the Secretary of State, [21 the Treasury or the Commissioners of Inland Revenue] other than an order under section 145(3) above; and

(b) which is not subject to any requirement that a draft of the instrument shall be laid before and approved by a resolution of each House of Parliament,

shall be subject to annulment in pursuance of a resolution of either House of Parliament.

[32 (4) Subsection (3) above does not apply to a statutory instrument by reason only that it contains an order appointing the first or second appointed year [23 or designating the flat rate introduction year] (within the meanings given by section 122(1) above).]

AMENDMENTS

1. Pensions Act 2007 Pt 1 s.7(5) (September 26, 2007).
2. National Insurance Contributions Act 2008 s.1(2) (September 22, 2008: insertion has effect in relation to regulations specifying the upper earnings limit for 2009-10 or any subsequent tax year).
3. National Insurance Contributions Act 2006 s.1(2)(a) (March 30, 2006).
4. National Insurance Contributions Act 2006 s.3(2) (March 30, 2006).
5. Welfare Reform and Pensions Act 1999 Sch.8(II) para.25 (November 3, 2000).
6. Social Security (Incapacity for Work) Act 1994 Sch.2 para.1 (April 13, 1995).
7. Welfare Reform Act 2007 Pt 2, s.31(3).
8. Employment Act 2002 Sch.7 para.7 (December 8, 2002).
9. Statutory Sick Pay Percentage Threshold Order 1995 (SI 1995/512), art.6(1)(a)(i) (April 6, 1995).
10. Pensions Act 2007 Sch.1(3) para.10 (September 26, 2007).
11. Pensions Act 2004 Sch.11(2) para.19 (November 18, 2004 for enabling the making of regulations; April 6, 2005 otherwise).
12. Social Security (Incapacity for Work) Act 1994 Sch.1(I) para.37(b) (April 13, 1995).
13. Welfare Reform and Pensions Act 1999 Sch.8(VI) para.32 (January 12, 2000 for the purpose of making regulations; April 2, 2000 otherwise).
14. National Insurance Contributions Act 2008 Sch.2 para.1 (September 22, 2008 for purposes specified in 2008 c.16, s.6(1); shall come into force on the commencement of 2007 c.22, Sch.4 para.45(2) otherwise).
15. Welfare Reform Act 2007 Pt 2, s.31(3).
16. Statutory Sick Pay Percentage Threshold Order 1995 (SI 1995/512) art.6(1)(a)(ii) (April 6, 1995).
17. Statutory Sick Pay Act 1994 s.3(2) (February 10, 1994).
18. Statutory Sick Pay Percentage Threshold Order 1995 (SI 1995/512) art.6(1)(a)(iii) (April 6, 1995).
19. Statutory Sick Pay Percentage Threshold Order 1995 (SI 1995/512) art.6(1)(a)(iv) (April 6, 1995).
20. National Insurance Contributions Act 2006 s.1(2)(b) (March 30, 2006).
21. Social Security Contributions (Transfer of Functions, etc.) Act 1999 Sch.3 para.30 (April 1, 1999).
22. Child Support, Pensions and Social Security Act 2000 s.35(15) (April 6, 2002).
23. Pensions Act 2007 Sch.1 Pt 7 para.35(b) (September 26, 2007).
24. Children and Families Act 2014 Sch.7, para.22 (April 5, 2015)
25. Welfare Reform Act 2012 s.69(4) (January 1, 2013).
26. Pensions Act 2014 s.15 and Sch.15 para.11 (October 13, 2014).
27. National Insurance Contributions Act 2014 s.9(5) (May 13, 2014).
28. National Insurance Contributions Act 2015 s.1(5) (April 6, 2016).
29. National Insurance Contributions Act 2015 s.2 and Sch.1, para.8 (April 6, 2015).
30. Children and Families Act 2014 s.124(2) (April 5, 2015).
31. Children and Families Act 2014 s.119(2) (June 30, 2014).
32. Child Support, Pensions and Social Security Act 2000 s.35(15) (January 8, 2001 for regulation and order-making purposes, January 25, 2001 for certain other purposes–see SI 2001/153, art.2(a)(i)–and April 6, 2002 for all other purposes).
33. Parental Bereavement (Leave and Pay) Act 2018 Sch.1(2), para.6 (January 18, 2020).

DERIVATION

SSA 1975 s.167 as amended. **1.477**

GENERAL NOTE

1.478 By virtue of Sch.2 Pt V, para.20 and with effect from October 5, 1999, s.176(3) is to be construed, in relation to tax credit, as if references to the Secretary of State were references to the Treasury or, as the case may be, the Board of the Revenue and Customs.

Short title, commencement and extent

1.479 **177.**—(1) This Act may be cited as the Social Security Contributions and Benefits Act 1992.

(2) This Act is to be read, where appropriate, with the Administration Act and the Consequential Provisions Act.

(3) The enactments consolidated by this Act are repealed, in consequence of the consolidation, by the Consequential Provisions Act.

(4) Except as provided in Schedule 4 to the Consequential Provisions Act, this Act shall come into force on 1st July 1992.

(5) The following provisions extend to Northern Ireland—

section 16 and Schedule 2;

section 116(2); and this section.

(6) Except as provided by this section, this Act does not extend to Northern Ireland.

SCHEDULES

Schedules 1 and 2 *Omitted because the province of the Board of Inland Revenue.*

SCHEDULE 3

CONTRIBUTION CONDITIONS FOR ENTITLEMENT TO BENEFIT

PART I

THE CONDITIONS

[1 Unemployment benefit

1.480 **1.**—[. . .]

[2 Short-term incapacity benefit]

1.481 **2.**—(1) The contribution conditions for [2 short-term incapacity benefit] are the following.

(2) The first condition is that—

[3

(a) the claimant must have actually paid contributions of a relevant class in respect of one of the last three complete years before the beginning of the relevant benefit year, and those contributions must have been paid before the relevant time; and]

(b) the earnings factor derived as mentioned in sub-paragraph (4) below

must be not less than that year's lower earnings limit multiplied by 25.

(3) The second condition is that—

(a) the claimant must in respect of the last two complete years before the beginning of the relevant benefit year have either paid or been credited with contributions of a relevant class or been credited (in the case of 1987–88 or any subsequent year) with earnings; and

(b) the earnings factor derived as mentioned in sub-paragraph (5) below must be not less in each of those years than the year's lower earnings limit multiplied by 50.

(4) The earnings factor referred to in paragraph (b) of sub-paragraph (2) above is that which is derived—

(a) if the year in question is 1987–88 or any subsequent year—

(i) from [18 so much of the claimant's earnings as did not exceed the upper earnings limit and] upon which primary Class 1 contributions have been paid or treated as paid; or
(ii) from Class 2 contributions; and
(b) if the year in question is an earlier year, from the contributions paid as mentioned in paragraph (a) of that sub-paragraph.

(5) The earnings factor referred to in paragraph (b) of sub-paragraph (3) above is that which is derived—
(a) if the year in question is 1987–88 or any subsequent year—
(i) from [18 so much of the claimant's earnings as did not exceed the upper earnings limit and] upon which primary Class 1 contributions have been paid or treated as paid or from earnings credited; or
(ii) from Class 2 contributions; and
(b) if the year in question is an earlier year, from the contributions referred to in paragraph (a) of that sub-paragraph.

(6) For the purposes of these conditions—
(a) "the relevant time" is the day in respect of which benefit is claimed;
(b) "the relevant benefit year" is the benefit year in which there falls the beginning of the [4 period of incapacity for work] which includes the relevant time.

[5 (7) Where a person makes a claim for incapacity benefit and does not satisfy [6 the first contribution condition (specified in sub-paragraph (2) above) or, as the case may be,] the second contribution condition (specified in sub-paragraph (3) above) and, in a later benefit year in which he would satisfy that condition had no such claim been made, he makes a further claim for incapacity benefit, the previous claim shall be disregarded.]

[6 (8) Regulations may—
(a) provide for the first contribution condition (specified in sub-paragraph (2) above) to be taken to be satisfied in the case of persons who have been entitled to any prescribed description of benefit during any prescribed period or at any prescribed time;
(b) with a view to securing any relaxation of the requirements of that condition (as so specified) in relation to persons who have been so entitled, provide for that condition to apply in relation to them subject to prescribed modifications.

(9) In sub-paragraph (8)—
"benefit" includes (in addition to any benefit under Parts II to V of this Act)—
(a) any benefit under Parts VII to XII of this Act, and
(b) credits under regulations under section 22(5) above;
"modifications" includes additions, omissions and amendments.]

Maternity Allowance

3.—[7 . . .] **1.482**

[8 [22. . .]]

4.—[22. . .] **1.483**

Widowed mother's allowance [9, widowed parent's allowance, bereavement allowance,] and widow's pension; retirement pensions (Categories A and B)

5.—[21 (1) This paragraph sets out the contribution conditions for– **1.484**
(a) a widowed mother's allowance, a widowed parent's allowance or a widow's pension;
(b) a Category A retirement pension (other than one in relation to which paragraph 5A applies);
(c) a Category B retirement pension in the cases provided for by any of sections 48A to 51ZA.]

(2) The first condition is that—
(a) the contributor concerned must in respect of any one relevant year have actually paid contributions of a relevant class; and
(b) the earnings factor derived—
(i) if that year is 1987–88 or any subsequent year, from [18 so much of the claimant's earnings as did not exceed the upper earnings limit and] upon which such of those contributions as are primary Class 1 contributions were paid or treated as paid and any Class 2 or Class 3 contributions, or
(ii) if that year is an earlier year, from the contributions referred to in paragraph (a) above,

must be not less than the qualifying earnings factor of that year.

(3) The second condition is that—

(a) the contributor concerned must, in respect of each of not less than the requisite number of years of his working life, have paid or been credited with contributions of a relevant class [10 or been credited (in the case of 1987–88 or any subsequent year) with earnings]; and

(b) in the case of each of those years, the earnings factor derived as mentioned in sub-paragraph (4) below must be not less than the qualifying earnings factor for that year.

(4) For the purposes of paragraph (b) of sub-paragraph (3) above, the earnings factor—

(a) in the case of 1987–88 or any subsequent year, is that which is derived from—

(i) [18 so much of the claimant's earnings as did not exceed the upper earnings limit and] upon which such of the contributions mentioned in paragraph (a) of that sub-paragraph as are primary Class 1 contributions were paid or treated as paid or earnings credited; and

(ii) any Class 2 or Class 3 contributions for the year; or

(b) in the case of any earlier year, is that which is derived from the contributions mentioned in paragraph (a) of that sub-paragraph.

(5) For the purposes of the first condition, a relevant year is any year ending before that in which the contributor concerned attained pensionable age or died under that age; and the following table shows the requisite number of years for the purpose of the second condition, by reference to a working life of a given duration—

Duration of working life	*Requisite number of years*
10 years or less	*The number of years of the working life, minus 1.*
20 years or less (but more than 10)	*The number of years of the working life, minus 2.*
30 years or less (but more than 20)	*The number of years of the working life, minus 3.*
40 years or less (but more than 30)	*The number of years of the working life, minus 4.*
More than 40 years	*The number of years of the working life, minus 5.*

(6) The first condition shall be taken to be satisfied if the contributor concerned was entitled to [11 long-term incapacity benefit] at any time during—

(a) the year in which he attained pensionable age or died under that age, or

(b) the year immediately preceding that year.

[20 (6A) The first condition shall be taken to be satisfied if the contributor concerned was entitled to main phase employment and support allowance at any time during–

(a) the year in which he attained pensionable age or died under that age, or

(b) the year immediately preceding that year.

(6B) The reference in sub-paragraph (6A) to main phase employment and support allowance is to an employment and support allowance in the case of which the calculation of the amount payable in respect of the claimant includes an addition under section 2(1)(b) or 4(2)(b) of the Welfare Reform Act 2007 (addition where conditions of entitlement to support component or work-related activity component satisfied).]

(7) The second condition shall be taken to be satisfied notwithstanding that paragraphs (a) and (b) of sub-paragraph (3) above are not complied with as respects each of the requisite number of years if—

(a) those paragraphs are complied with as respects at least half that number of years [12 *(or at least 20 of them, if that is less than half)*]; and

(b) in each of the other years the contributor concerned was, within the meaning of regulations, precluded from regular employment by responsibilities at home.

[23 But nothing in this sub-paragraph applies in relation to any benefit to which section 23A above applies.]

[13 (7A) Regulations may provide that a person is not to be taken for the purposes of sub-paragraph (7)(b) above as precluded from regular employment by responsibilities at home unless he meets the prescribed requirements as to the provision of information to the Secretary of State.]

(8) For the purposes of [14 Parts I to VI of this Act] a person's working life is the period between—

(a) (inclusive) the tax year in which he attained the age of 16; and

(b) (exclusive) the tax year in which he attained pensionable age or died under that age.

1.485 **[19 5A**—(1) This paragraph applies to—

(a) a Category A retirement pension in a case where the contributor concerned attains pensionable age on or after 6th April 2010;

[21 (b) a Category B retirement pension in the cases provided for by any of sections 48A to 51ZA.]

(2) The contribution condition for a Category A or Category B retirement pension in relation to which this paragraph applies is that—

(a) the contributor concerned must, in respect of each of not less than 30 years of his working life, have paid or been credited with contributions of a relevant class or been credited (in the case of 1987–88 or any subsequent year) with earnings; and

(b) in the case of each of those years, the earnings factor derived as mentioned in sub-paragraph (3) below must be not less than the qualifying earnings factor for that year.

(3) For the purposes of paragraph (b) of sub-paragraph (2) above, the earnings factor—

(a) in the case of 1987–88 or any subsequent year, is that which is derived from—

(i) so much of the contributor's earnings as did not exceed the upper earnings limit and upon which such of the contributions mentioned in paragraph (a) of that sub-paragraph as are primary Class 1 contributions were paid or treated as paid or earnings credited; and

(ii) any Class 2 or Class 3 contributions for the year; or

(b) in the case of any earlier year, is that which is derived from the contributions mentioned in paragraph (a) of that sub-paragraph.

(4) Regulations may modify sub-paragraphs (2) and (3) above for the purposes of their application in a case where—

(a) the contributor concerned has paid, or been credited with, contributions, or

(b) contributions have been deemed to be, or treated as, paid by or credited to him, under the National Insurance Act 1946 or the National Insurance Act 1965.]

Child's special allowance

6.—(1) The contribution condition for a child's special allowance is that— **1.486**

(a) the contributor concerned must in respect of any one relevant year have actually paid contributions of a relevant class; and

(b) the earnings factor derived from those contributions must be not less than that year's lower earnings limit multiplied by 50.

(2) For the purposes of this condition, a relevant year is any year ending before the date on which the contributor concerned attained pensionable age or died under that age.

PART II

SATISFACTION OF CONDITIONS IN EARLY YEARS OF CONTRIBUTION

7.—[22. . .] **1.487**

8. Where a person claims [16 short-term incapacity benefit], he shall be taken to satisfy the first contribution condition for the benefit if on a previous claim for any short-term benefit he has satisfied the first contribution condition for that benefit, by virtue of paragraph 8 of Schedule 3 to the 1975 Act, with contributions of a class relevant to [16 short-term incapacity benefit].

9. [22. . .]

REPEALS AND AMENDMENTS

1. Repealed by Jobseekers Act 1995 Sch.3 para.1 (October 10, 1996).
2. Social Security (Incapacity for Work) Act 1994 s.1(2) (April 13, 1995).
3. Welfare Reform and Pensions Act 1999 s.62(2) (April 6, 2001).
4. Social Security (Incapacity for Work) Act 1994 Sch.1 para.38(2) (April 13, 1995).
5. Social Security (Incapacity for Work) Act 1994 s.3(2) (April 13, 1995).
6. Welfare Reform and Pensions Act 1999 ss.62(3), (4) (April 6, 2001).
7. Welfare Reform and Pensions Act 1999 Sch.13 Pt V (April 2, 2000).
8. Welfare Reform and Pensions Act 1999 Sch.8 Pt I, para.13(2) (April 9, 2001).
9. Welfare Reform and Pensions Act 1999 Sch.8 Pt I, para.13(3) (April 9, 2001).
10. Pensions Act 1995 s.129 (July 19, 1995).
11. Social Security (Incapacity for Work) Act 1994 Sch.1 para.38(3) (April 13, 1995).

12. These words are deleted as regards any person reaching pensionable age after April 5, 2010, by the Pensions Act 1995 Sch.4 para.4 and Sch.7 Pt II.
13. Child Support, Pensions and Social Security Act 2000 s.40 (January 8, 2001).
14. Pensions Act 1995 s.134(5) (July 19, 1995).
15. Welfare Reform and Pensions Act 1999 Sch.8 Pt I, para.13(4) (April 24, 2000).
16. Social Security (Incapacity for Work) Act 1994 Sch.1 para.38(4) (April 13, 1995).
17. Welfare Reform and Pensions Act 1999 Sch.8 Pt I, para.13(5)(b) (April 24, 2000).
18. National Insurance Contributions Act 2002 Sch.1 para.14 (April 6, 2003).
19. Pensions Act 2007 s.1 (September 26, 2007).
20. Welfare Reform Act 2007 s.40 and Sch.5 para.9(13) (October 27, 2008).
21. Pensions Act 2014 s.23 and Sch.12 paras 57 and 67 (April 6, 2016).
22. Pensions Act 2014 Sch.16 para.18 (April 6, 2017).
23. Pensions Act 2007 s.3(2) (September 26, 2007).

DERIVATIONS

1.488 SSA 1975 Sch.3.
SSPA 1975 Sch.1.

DEFINITIONS

"benefit" (in para.2(8))—see para.2(9).
"benefit"—see s.122(1).
"benefit year"—see s.21(6).
"claimant"—see s.122(1).
"contributor concerned"—see s.21(5)(a).
"earnings"—see s.122(1).
"earnings factor"—see s.21(5)(c).
"lower earnings limit"—see s.122(1).
"modifications" (in para.2(8))—see para.2(9).
"period of incapacity for work"—see s.30C(1).
"qualifying earnings factor"—see s.122(1).
"relevant benefit year"—see para.2(6)(b).
"relevant class"—see s.21(5)(a).
"relevant time"—see para.2(6)(a).
"relevant year" (in para.6)—see para.6(2).
"short-term benefit"—see ss.122(1), 20(2).
"working life"—see para.5(8).
"year"—see s.21(5)(d).

GENERAL NOTE

What the Schedule covers

1.489 By their nature, certain "contributory benefits" require, as a precondition of entitlement, that the claimant, or in certain cases, the claimant's husband or, sometimes, spouse, have a valid contribution record in terms of national insurance contributions. Pt I of this Schedule sets out the contribution conditions which must be met for entitlement to certain "contributory benefits":

- short-term incapacity benefit (s.30A);
- bereavement payment (s.36);
- widowed mothers allowance (s.37);
- widowed parent's allowance (s.39A);
- bereavement allowance (s.39B);

- widow's pension (s.38);
- categories A and B retirement pensions (ss.43–54);
- child's special allowance (s.59).

Pt II of the Schedule, deals with the matter of satisfaction of conditions in early years of contribution in respect of bereavement payment and of short-term incapacity benefit.

Contributions matters: a division of responsibility

Since the coming into force of the SSA 1998, contribution conditions are more directly relevant to appeals tribunals and the Commissioners, although cases raising them are likely relatively to be rare. The position is also complicated because some relevant matters are ones for HM Revenue and Customs (not appealable to appeals tribunals or social security commissioners) while others are ones for the Secretary of State and are appealable to unified appeals tribunals and to the social security commissioners (now the First-tier Tribunal and the Upper Tribunal respectively). **1.490**

Prior to the implementation of the decision-making and appeals changes in that Act, whether the contribution conditions were satisfied or not was a "Secretary of State's question" rather than a matter of decision for the AO. It was, accordingly, not as such appealable to an SSAT (SSAA 1992 s.17(1)(b), (2), set out with commentary in Bonner, Hooker and White, *Non Means Tested Benefits: Legislation 1999*, pp.16–19). It was thought at one time that the terms of section 17 were, however, to be narrowly construed, so that while a tribunal could not properly deal with whether the claimant should have been credited with contributions (*R(U) 6/89*), the "statutory authorities" (AO, SSAT and Commissioner) were the ones with jurisdiction over certain phrases in the contribution conditions: over establishing the date of claim ("the relevant time"), over identifying the pertinent benefit year (the one in which there falls the first day of the period of incapacity for work of which the day of claim forms part) and thus over identifying the appropriate past tax/contribution years to be considered with regard to the question (determinable by the Secretary of State and not appealable to an SSAT) of whether in the relevant tax years the requisite level of paid contributions (the first contribution condition) or paid and/or credited contributions (the second contribution condition) had been reached (see *R(G) 1/82(T)*). But the approach in *R(G) 1/82(T)* was rejected by the Court of Appeal in *Secretary of State v Scully* (reported as *R(S) 5/93)*. The section (then SSA 1975 s.93) was to be read according to its "plain and natural meaning" and left it to the Secretary of State to make all determinations relevant to the contribution conditions.

After the implementation of the SSA 1998 changes, as regards all contributory benefits, whether someone satisfies the contribution conditions for the benefit is a decision of the Secretary of State and now appealable to a tribunal, and onwards to the Commissioners, as a decision on a claim or award of benefit not otherwise rendered non-appealable (SSA 1998 s.12 and Sch.2; Decisions and Appeals Regs, reg.27 and Sch.2). See further *Vol.III: Administration, Adjudication and the European Dimension.* In *R(IB) 1/09*, Commissioner Williams held that disputes about the interpretation of the Earnings factor regulations lay within the jurisdiction of the Secretary of State, rather than HMRC, and that appeal about that interpretation lay to the social security (now First-tier) tribunal. See para.7 for his summary of the proper procedure.

Some contributions matters are ones, however, for officers of HM Revenue and Customs, and appealable through a different system (Social Security Contributions (Transfer of Functions) Act 1999 ss.8(1)(a)–(e), 11, 12). The matters in question are those of the categorisation of earners, which class of contributions a person is liable or entitled to pay, and whether they have been paid (or should be treated as having been paid: see *R(JSA) 8/02*) in respect of any period. Decisions on such matters will impact to some degree on the Secretary of State's (and thus **1.491** an appeal tribunal's or a Commissioner's) decisions on whether the contribution conditions for a benefit are met. There is a special procedure for the Secretary of State or the appeal tribunal to refer relevant questions to HM Revenue and Customs (SSA 1998, ss.10A, 24A; Decisions and Appeals Regs, regs.11A, 38A). Note that under s.8(1)(m) of that Transfer of Functions Act, regulations can transfer further issues relating to contributions. So the decision-maker on particular issues could change (see further *Vol.III: Administration, Adjudication and the European Dimension*).

The administrative process on the matter of referring to HM Revenue and Customs [formerly Board of Inland Revenue] questions on whether contributions have been paid has been subjected to scathing criticism by two Commissioners. In *CIB/1602/2006*, Commissioner Williams, like Commissioner Rowland in interim decision *CIB/3327/2004*, criticised the process as set out in the DMG guidance (Vol.3, ch.3, paras 03230–03233). Reading it with the more accurate guidance in Vol.1, ch.1, he thought the guidance to be:

> "internally inconsistent. Compare 01055 and 01056 with 56014. And it also guides administrators to make assumptions about contribution issues rather than decide them. See 01055 and 03231. And it does not tell the administrators to make it clear that their decisions depend on assumptions about a claimant's NI record rather than decisions about it. In my view the instruction to officials to make undisclosed assumptions about contribution issues combined with the failure to make it clear that there has been no decision on a contribution question have contributed to the systems failure to which Commissioner Rowland draws attention. In particular, there is a recurring failure to make a clear appealable decision on a question of credited earnings and a system in place that enables administrators to avoid the need to make the required decisions. This may explain why, even in this case where there was a decision, it has been assumed that there was no decision." (Para.19.)

He also considered DMG, paras 56014 and 56015 to "contain errors of law" (para.16).

In *CIB/1602/2006*, the matter in dispute was whether the claimant had sufficient credited earnings in tax/contribution year 2002–2003 to meet the second contribution condition. This turned on a much neglected area: in this case the complicated provisions of the Credits Regulations 1974 regs 3 and 8A. Commissioner Williams' decision on that is noted in the commentary to those regs, below. In *R(IB) 1/09*, he set out the proper procedure for determining issues in a dispute about the application of the Social Security (Earnings Factor) Regulations 1979 to a claim for incapacity benefit:

> "(a) It is for the National Insurance Contributions Office of Her Majesty's Revenue and Customs to decide any question about the contribution record of a claimant for incapacity benefit.
>
> (b) Any challenge to that decision on either an issue of fact or a question of law goes to a tax tribunal, not a social security tribunal. If an appeal involving a question about a claimant's contributions comes before a social security tribunal, then the social security tribunal must apply regulation 38A of the Social Security and Child Support (Decisions and Appeals) Regulations 1999. This requires it to adjourn the appeal and refer the matter to the Secretary of State for onward reference to Her Majesty's Revenue and Customs for decision. The tribunal may decide the appeal only after a decision has been received from Her Majesty's Revenue and Customs.
>
> (c) It is for the Secretary of State for Work and Pensions to decide any question about the interpretation and application of the Social Security (Earnings Factor) Regulations 1979 to the individual contribution record of any claimant for incapacity benefit.

(d) If a claimant disputes the decision of the Secretary of State on any issue of fact or law arising under the 1979 Regulations, then that dispute is to be decided by a social security tribunal. This includes any dispute about calculating the earnings factor attributable to a claimant under those regulations. If necessary, it is the task of the tribunal itself to check any disputed calculations" (para.7).

For further consideration of some of the difficulties arising where records have been destroyed as part of normal administrative processes and for the text of the regulations on unemployment credits covering 1977-89, see Commissioner Williams' decision in *CP/1792/2007*. **1.492**

Commissioner Rowland's interim decision in *CIB/3327/2004* delineated the effect on a claimant's claim and appeals of the confusion generated by changes in jurisdiction on contributions matters (paras 2–4) and on the matter of awarding credits for spells of unemployment, a situation in which she was passed from pillar to post, a process during which Commissioner Rowland considered that there had been no actual decision on the award of credits for those spells, but only on non-entitlement to JSA (paras 19–21). This resulted in part from the changes on decision-making, appeals and jurisdictions wrought by the 1998 and 1999 legislation. But Commissioner Rowland rightly drew to attention for remedial action "some more fundamental flaws in the way in which the Department functions" in respect of these matters. Essentially, the key flaw was that no system had been put in place for informing the claimant that credits for unemployment had not been awarded. In the Commissioner's view, what was needed, "above all" was the establishment of:

> "a system . . . to ensure that challenges to refusals of credits result in formal decisions that comply with regulation 28 of the [Decisions and Appeals Regs] and inform the contributor of his or her right of appeal. That is so whether credits decisions are to be made during the relevant contribution year or after it has ended" (para.29).

Commissioner Williams considered in *CIB/1602/2006* that he had to reiterate that call for action:

> "That decision was made a year ago. It was an interim decision. I understand that as a result of later proceedings in the appeal the matter has now ceased to be an active appeal and that therefore the Commissioner will not be issuing a final decision. I have also seen no offcial response to that decision beyond the specific case. I therefore consider that I should adopt and repeat some of that analysis as it applies to this case in order to make clear why I entirely agree with him that the existing situation does not accord with the law. I depart from the approach of Commissioner Rowland in taking the view that in this case there is an appealable decision. But his criticisms of the lack of system are clearly part of the explanation for the confusion on the part of the secretary of state's representatives and the tribunal in this case" (para.14).

To that, this commentator can only add his support. This is a crucial area for contribution-based benefits and claimants and tribunals are entitled to expect at least as much decision-making clarity here as elsewhere in the benefits system. So far it is conspicuously lacking.

Some problems, of course, have arisen because of the mismatch in data on credits in the respective departments' computer and recording systems: the DWP's Pension Service Computer System (PSCS) and the National Insurance Recording System (NIRS 2) system. Work is in hand to reconcile the latter with the former. It appears that up to 30,000 people may have been underpaid and about 90,000 may have been overpaid as a result of incorrect records. Overpayments are dealt with in amendments to the Credits Regulations 1975. Underpayments are to be **1.493** made good by administrative action. See further the Explanatory Memorandum to the amending regulations (SI 2007/2582) at *http://www.opsi.gov.uk/si/si200725.htm.*

Whether a person's contributions record should be *credited* with contributions/earnings remains, however, one for the Secretary of State and is now appealable to an appeal tribunal (SSA 1998 Sch.3, para.17; *CIB/2338/00, CG2309/2002, CIB/2161/2000*). So does the question whether a person was (within the meaning of regulations) precluded from regular employment by responsibilities at home (SSA 1998 Sch.3, para.16). On when contributions may be credited, see s.22, above, and the Social Security (Credits) Regulations 1975, below. On entitlement to home responsibilities protection, see para.5(7) of this Schedule and the Social Security Pensions (Home Responsibilities) Regulations 1994.

On difficulties arising where the periods to be considered predate the abolition of sickness benefit and unemployment benefit and the re-allocation of functions and jurisdictions, see the decision of Commissioner Williams in *CIB/3734/2002*. On the complexities split jurisdiction can produce in pensions' entitlement cases, see his decision in *CP/4205/2006*.

With that division of responsibilities in mind, it is useful to give a brief outline of the contributory system as regards payments and credits, the better to understand the contributions conditions for entitlement to a contributory benefit.

An outline of the contributory system: payments, credits and the earnings factor (the amount added to the contribution record)

1.494 The contributory system embraces distinct classes of contribution: Class 1 (primary and secondary), Class 1A, Class 1B, Class 2, Class 3, Class 3A and Class 4. This last category—a levy on the profits of the self-employed—is irrelevant in respect of title to benefit. So are secondary Class 1 contributions and Class 1A and 1B contributions.

1.495 *Class 1 contributions*—capable of establishing entitlement to all the contributory benefits listed in s.21(2) and to bereavement support payment—are paid by employed earners (see s.2(1)(a)), that is by persons employed under a contract of service (employees) and by certain office holders (e.g. constables, MPs). They are earnings-related, and are paid on weekly/ monthly earnings between a lower and an upper earnings limit. Those limits change for each tax (contribution) year. Where earnings fall below the relevant lower limit for the tax (contribution) year, there is no liability or ability to pay— for the period in question the contribution record will be blank in terms of Class 1. Primary Class 1 contributions are also the only class of contribution relevant for title to contribution-based jobseeker's allowance (see Jobseekers Act 1995 s.2 and commentary in *Vol.II: Income Support, Jobseeker's Allowance, State Pension Credit and the Social Fund*). Secondary Class 1 contributions and Class IA or 1B contributions are paid by the primary contributor's employer and are not relevant to title to benefit.

Basically, each primary Class 1 contribution paid generates an earnings factor, that is puts into the person's contribution record for the year an amount equivalent to the weekly/monthly earnings (but only up to the relevant upper earnings limit for that year) in respect of which it is paid. So in each week in tax (contribution) year 1999/2000, a weekly paid person earning £300 per week would each week have that amount added to his record.

1.496 *Class 2 contributions*—also capable of establishing entitlement to all the contributory benefits listed in s.21(2) and bereavement support payment—are paid by self-employed earners (see s.2(1)(b)), basically those employed under a contract for services. A Class 2 contribution generates an *earnings factor*, that is puts into the person's contribution record for the year a weekly amount equivalent to the lower earnings limit for that year for Class 1 contributions' liability. Even where a person is not liable to pay them, s/he can pay voluntarily so as to maintain their contribution record.

Class 3 contributions cannot generate title to incapacity benefit, but can in respect of the other contributory benefits listed in s.21(2): bereavement payment; widowed mother's allowance, widowed parent's allowance, bereavement allowance, widow's pension, category A and B retirement pensions. There is no liability, only an ability, to pay—they are always voluntary, paid to remedy deficiencies in the contribution record for particular years. Each Class 3 contribution paid generates an earnings factor, that is puts into the person's contribution record for the year a weekly amount equivalent to the lower earnings limit for that year for Class 1 contributions' liability. 1.497

Certain married women and widows could before April 5, 1977 elect to pay Class 1 contributions at a *reduced rate*, or not to pay a Class 2 contribution. Non-payment of the latter means no earnings factor, no amount added to the contribution record. Payment of Class 1 at the reduced rate generates no earnings factor, produces no amount to add to the contribution record (see s.22(4)).

The scheme recognises that in certain situations, for socially valid reasons someone may not be able to pay contributions, and protects that person's contribution record by crediting a certain amount to the person's contribution account (see s.22(5), Social Security (Credits) Regulations 1975). The weekly amount generated (the earnings factor) is one equivalent to the lower earnings limit for purposes of Class 1 contributions' liability. Where someone is precluded from working because of responsibilities at home, the scheme gives protection by a different route; it provides a degree of home responsibilities protection for the contribution record by, in certain circumstances, treating the second contribution condition (the one that can be satisfied by paid and/ or credited contributions) as fulfilled in any year in which the person "was, within the meaning of regulations, precluded from regular employment by responsibilities at home" (Sch.3, para.5(7); Social Security Pensions (Home Responsibilities) Regulations 1994). This applies only in respect of bereavement payment (s.36); widowed mothers allowance (s.37); widowed parent's allowance (s.39A); bereavement allowance (s.39B); widow's pension (s.38); and categories A and B retirement pensions (ss. 43–54).

Class 3A contributions: Between October 2015 and April 5, 2017, it was possible for people with entitlement to a State Pension, and who had reached their state pension age before April 6, 2016, to pay voluntary Class 3A contributions to purchase additional State Pension. 1.498

With that outline in mind, the particular contribution conditions for each of the benefits listed in s.21 can now be examined in more detail.

PART I

THE CONDITIONS

Paragraph 2 read with s.30A(2)(a): short-term incapacity benefit for claimants under pensionable age

Unless he is a person incapacitated in youth (before 20 or sometimes 25) (see s.30A(1)(b), (2A)) a claimant must fulfil the requirements of this paragraph. There are two contribution conditions. The first can be met only by *paid* contributions of the relevant class (primary Class 1 or Class 2) reaching the requisite level in a tax year. The second can be satisfied by *paid and/or credited* contributions in a tax year. 1.499

This aspect of title to short-term incapacity benefit has been rendered more complex in that the first condition was altered substantially from April 6, 2001 to require for those under pensionable age a more recent connection with the world of work in terms of paid contributions than had previously been the case, whether with incapacity benefit or its predecessors, sickness and invalidity benefits.

However, the rigour of the new rule is relaxed in certain situations (para.2(8), (9), IB Regulations, Pt IA, reg.2B) and by the fact that the change is not retrospective so that those whose continuing period of incapacity began before April 6, 2001 remain subject to the previous contribution condition first until that period of incapacity ends.

In order to appreciate the requirements of para.2, and the terms and operation of the contribution conditions, take first, as an illustrative example, the position of someone claiming incapacity benefit for the very first time in May 2001 (that is, with no link back to any previous period of incapacity for work) and never having claimed or received any other benefit. He must meet *both of the two contribution conditions* set out in para.2. The first step is to identify the relevant benefit year, the one which includes the first day of the period of incapacity of which his claim is part (para.2(6)). This identification of the relevant benefit year is the real substantive matter for the Secretary of State or the appeal tribunal to focus on, since that determines the tax/contribution years in which the requisite record must be fulfilled. His first day of claim—the relevant time (para.2(6))—in May 2001 falls in benefit year 2001–2002 (the relevant benefit year: see s.21(6)). "Year", standing alone, means tax/contribution year (s.21(5)(d). The tax/contribution years in *one of which* the first contribution condition (sub-para.(2)) must be fulfilled are the last three tax/contribution years (April 6–April 5) complete before the start of the relevant benefit year (early January 2001). The tax/contribution years to which to have regard are thus 1999/2000, 1998/1999, and 1997/1998. The contribution record in tax/ contribution year 2000/2001 cannot be taken into account because it was not complete at the start of the relevant benefit year (early January 2001). The first contribution condition (sub-para.(2)) can only be met with paid contributions of the relevant class—Class 1 (employed earners) or Class 2 (self-employed earners)—reaching the requisite level (an earnings factor of 25 times the lower earnings limit (LEL) for Class 1 contributions purposes for the tax year in question—remember that each Class 2 contribution generates an earnings factor equal to the LEL pertinent to the tax/contribution year in question, while the amount of earnings on which Class 1 contributions are paid generates the earnings factor for an employed earner claimant. See further, s.21, and the "outline of the contributory system" earlier in this annotation.

1.500 The second contribution condition (sub-para.(3)) requires examination of the last two tax years complete before the start of the relevant benefit year (early January 2001), that is 1999/2000 and 1998/1999. The claimant's contribution record in each of those tax/contribution years must attain 50 times the lower earnings limit for the year. But the condition can be met through paid and/or credited contributions (a Class 1 credit can be received, for example, for each week of unemployment; see further Social Security (Credits) Regulations 1975). On difficulties arising where the periods to be considered predate the abolition of sickness benefit and unemployment benefit and the re-allocation of functions and jurisdictions, see the decision of Commissioner Williams in *CIB/3734/2002*.

From May 5, 2003, the definition of "relevant benefit year" is different in the case of someone discharged from Her Majesty's forces and in respect of whom days of sickness absence from duty recorded by the Secretary of State for Defence are, under s.30D, included in calculating the number of days for which he has been entitled to short-term incapacity benefit. In such a case, the "relevant benefit year" is that in which there falls the beginning of the period to which the claim for incapacity benefit relates. See reg.4 of the Social Security Contributions and Benefits Act 1992 (Modifications for Her Majesty's Forces and Incapacity Benefit) Regulations 2003, below. See also annotations to s.30A(3) and s.30D.

Note that sub-para.(8) enables regulations to relax the rules set out above which apply to all claims in a period of incapacity for work commencing on or after April 6, 2001. So a claim in principle subject to these rules, is not just the first ever claim for incapacity benefit as used in the illustrative example, above. A "new" claim subject to those rules, could, for instance, just as well come from someone on incapacity benefit during 2000 whose "period of incapacity" came to an end in December 2000. If such a person claims again in, say, August 2001, he would, in principle, be subject to those rules, because his two spells of incapacity do not "link" to form one under the "linking rule" in s.30C. Note that the relaxation afforded applies not just to benefits under Pts II–V and VII–XII of the SSCBA 1992 but also to contributions credits (sub-paras(8), (9)). The "relaxation" rules are contained in IB Regulations, Pt 1A, reg.2B, and are annotated there.

Various groups will have difficulty meeting these contribution conditions:

(a) *those who have never been employed*: The requirement in the first contribution condition for payment of contributions effectively excludes those who, whether through unemployment, incapacity or disability, have been unable to build a contribution record in terms of paid contributions.

(b) *some of the long-term unemployed* (last employed in a tax year earlier than the first of the three on which the first contribution condition focuses).

(c) *very low-paid, probably part-time, employees*: those whose weekly or monthly earnings fall below the lower earnings limit for the whole or main part of the relevant tax years will not satisfy the contribution conditions since there is no liability or ability to pay Class 1 contributions where earnings fall below that limit, and, because they are in work, no Class 1 credits are generated from unemployment.

(d) *certain married women and widows paying reduced rate contributions*: these do not generate any earnings factor (and so do not count) for incapacity benefit purposes (s.22(4)).

Severe Disablement Allowance (SDA) was introduced in 1984 to cater for those who were incapacitated below the age of 20, or, if incapacitated later, were also assessed as 80 per cent disabled (see ss.68, 69). SDA was abolished on April 2, 2001 for new claims. Of course, some of the above, if incapacitated in youth (before 20 or sometimes 25) (s.30A(1)(b), (2A); IB Regulations, Pt IV, regs14–19), will be able to take advantage of the intended counter-balancing measure for those more likely than others to have been unable to build up a contribution record—the non-contributory route into incapacity benefit (see commentary to subs.(2A)). Those incapacitated, even through severe disability, later in life, will have to look to income support, with all its disability premiums, to underwrite their incapacity for work. While they may well be eligible for various components of disability living allowance, that is a benefit designed to provide for the extra costs that disability, as opposed to incapacity for work, brings with it. The transitional provisions protect existing recipients and those whose period of incapacity (without receipt of SDA) spans April 6, 2001. See further the prefatory commentary to ss.68 and 69, preserved in force for those individuals.

Paragraph 3: maternity allowance

There are now no contribution conditions in respect of maternity allowance. See s.35. **1.501**

Paragraph 5: widowed mother's allowance, widowed parent's allowance, bereavement allowance, widow's pension, category A and B retirement pensions

These long-term benefits (where available) all require satisfaction of the same contribution conditions. Like the short-term benefits there are two conditions to be satisfied. The first requires actual payment of contributions; the second may be satisfied by payments or by credits. **1.502**

The person whose contribution record is to be tested will depend upon the benefit claimed. For a Category A Retirement Pension it will be the claimant's own record. For a Category B Retirement Pension it will be the record of the claimant's spouse. For a Widowed Parent's Allowance and a Bereavement Allowance it is the late spouse's contribution record; and for a Widowed Mother's Allowance or Widow's Pension her late husband's record. (For the various widow's and bereavement benefits the condition may also be satisfied if the contributor has died as a result of an industrial injury or disease.)

The first condition for these benefits requires that the contributor has actually paid contributions (either Class 1, Class 2 or Class 3) in any one year to produce an earnings factor of at least 52 times the lower earnings limit for that year (the "qualifying earnings factor": see s.122(1)). The year can be any year that ends before the year in which that person retires or dies. The condition is also deemed to be satisfied if that person was in receipt of long-term incapacity benefit in the year in which they reached retirement age or died, or if they were in receipt of that benefit in the preceding year. Before 1975, Class 1 contributions were paid as a flat rate "stamp" each week. This condition will also be satisfied by 50 flat rate contributions in any year.

1.503 The second condition must be fulfilled in each of what may be a much longer period of years. The requisite period is defined by reference to the length of the person's working life (the years between that in which they reach the age of 16 and the last complete tax year before they reach retirement age or die under that age), but subject to a reduction in the total number of years according to the scale that appears in App.3, para.5, sub-para.5 above. Once the "requisite number of years" has been defined the contributor must be shown to have paid, or been credited with, payments that produce an earnings factor equal to at least 52 times the lower earnings limit for each of those years. (For years before 1975 the number of satisfied years is calculated by counting all the weekly payments made over those years and dividing by 50. The answer is rounded up to the next whole number.)

The requisite number of years may also be reduced by years of home responsibility as explained above. Such years are deducted from the working life and may reduce the requisite number of years to 20 or to half of what they would otherwise have been, whichever is the lower.

Where the second condition is satisfied the long-term benefits will be paid at their full rate. Where the condition is only partially satisfied, benefit will be paid at a percentage of that rate corresponding to the percentage of satisfied years, so long as at least 25 per cent of those years are so satisfied.

Paragraph 5A: Category A retirement pensions where the contributor attains pensionable age on or after April 6, 2010 and certain Category B retirement pensions

1.504 For people reaching state pension age (a term interchangeable with 'pensionable age') from April 6, 2010, the previous contribution conditions for Category A and B pensions were replaced with a single contribution condition. The same condition applies to the spouse or civil partner of a claimant of a Category B pension (within sections 48A to 51ZA) where the spouse or civil partner reaches state pension age on or after April 6, 2010 (or dies on or after that date without having reached that age).

For those reaching state pension age from April 6, 2010, the number of years needed to qualify for a full Category A or B pension was reduced from 44 years for a man and 39 years for a woman to 30 qualifying years for men and women alike. A person who has less than 30 qualifying years is entitled to a proportion of the full basic state pension for each qualifying year they have built up.

The position must however now be considered in the light of the changes made by the Pensions Act 2014.

Paragraph 6: child's special allowance

1.505 This has only one contribution condition (sub-para(1)), satisfiable only by contributions of the relevant class—(Class 1, 2 or 3, separately or combined (s.21(2))—paid by the contributor concerned in respect of any one relevant tax (contribution) year to a level not less than 50 times that year's lower earnings limit. A "relevant year" is any one ending before the date on which the contributor concerned attained pensionable age or died under that age (sub-para.(2)). The claimant for child's special allowance is a woman whose marriage has been terminated by divorce, and the "contributor concerned" is the deceased husband of that marriage who was contributing to the cost of providing for the child or from whom she was entitled to receive, under a court order, a trust or agreement, maintenance for the child (s.56).

PART II

SATISFACTION OF CONDITIONS IN EARLY YEARS OF CONTRIBUTION

Paragraph 8

This applies only to short-term incapacity benefit, and seems to protect previous recipients of the contributory maternity allowance. It enables a claimant for short-term incapacity benefit to be treated as satisfying its first contribution condition (see para. 2(2)) if on a previous claim for any short-term benefit (defined in s.20(2) to cover short-term incapacity benefit and maternity allowance) he satisfied the first contribution condition for that shortterm benefit by virtue of SSA 1975, Sched. 3, para. 8, with contributions of the class relevant to short-term incapacity benefit (Class 1 or 2 and their predecessors). Paragraph 8 in the 1975 Act dealt with aggregation of contributions as regards early years of contribution in a similar way to para. 7 of this Schedule and bereavement payment. 1.506

SCHEDULE 4

RATES OF BENEFIT ETC.

PART I

CONTRIBUTORY PERIODICAL BENEFITS

1.507

Description of benefit		*Weekly rate*	
2.	Short-term incapacity benefit.	(a) lower rate	£104.85
		(b) higher rate	£124.00
2A.	Long-term incapacity benefit.		£138.90
5.	Category B retirement pension where section 48A(4) or 48AA(4) applies.		£101.55

PART II

BEREAVEMENT PAYMENT

[5. . .] 1.508

PART III

NON-CONTRIBUTORY PERIODICAL BENEFITS

1.509

Description of benefit		*Weekly rate*	
1.	Attendance allowance.	(a) higher rate	£108.55
		(b) lower rate	£72.65

Description of benefit		*Weekly rate*	
		(the appropriate rate being determined in accordance with section 65(3)).	
2.	Severe disablement allowance.		£98.40
3.	Age related addition.	(a) higher rate	£14.70
		(b) middle rate	£8.15
		(c) lower rate	£8.15
		(the appropriate rate being determined in accordance with section 69(1)).	
4.	Carer's allowance.		£81.90
5.	Guardian's allowance.		[2 £21.75]
7.	Category D retirement pension.		£101.55
8.	Age addition (to a pension of any category, and otherwise under section 79).		£0.25.

PART IV

INCREASES FOR DEPENDANTS

1.510

Benefit to which increase applies (1)			*Increase for adult dependant (3)*
			£
1A.	Short-term incapacity benefit—		
	(a)	where the beneficiary is under pensionable age;	62.85
	(b)	where the beneficiary is over pensionable age.	77.70
2.	Long-term incapacity benefit.		80.70
8.	Severe disablement allowance.		48.40

PART V

RATES OF INDUSTRIAL INJURIES BENEFIT

1.511

Description of benefit, etc.	*Rate*		
1. Disablement pension (weekly rates).	For the several degrees of disablement set out in column (1) of the following Table, the respective amounts in column (2) of that Table.		
	Degree of Disablement	*Amount*	
	(1)	*(2)*	
	Per cent.	*£*	
	100	221.50	
	90	199.35	
	80	177.20	
	70	155.05	
	60	132.90	
	50	110.75	
	40	88.60	
	30	66.45	
	20	44.30	
2. Maximum increase of weekly rate of disablement pension where constant attendance needed.	(a)	except in cases of exceptionally severe disablement	£88.70;
	(b)	in any case	£177.40.
3. Increase of weekly rate of disablement pension (exceptionally severe disablement).			£88.70.
4. Maximum of aggregate of weekly benefit payable for successive accidents.			£221.50.
5. Unemployability supplement under paragraph 2 of Schedule 7.			£137.00.
6. Increase under paragraph 3 of Schedule 7 of weekly rate of unemployability supplement.	(a)	if on the qualifying date the beneficiary was under the age of 35 or if that date fell before 5th July 1948	£28.40

Description of benefit, etc.	*Rate*		
	(b)	if head (a) above does not apply and on the qualifying date the beneficiary was under the age of 40 and he had not attained pensionable age before 6th April 1979	£28.40
	(c)	if heads (a) and (b) above do not apply and on the qualifying date the beneficiary was under the age of 45	£18.20
	(d)	if heads (a), (b) and (c) above do not apply and on the qualifying date the beneficiary was under the age of 50 and had not attained pensionable age before 6th April 1979	£18.20
	(e)	in any other case	£9.10.
7. Increase under paragraph 4 of Schedule 7 of weekly rate of disablement pension.			£11.35.
8. Increase under paragraph 6 of Schedule 7 of weekly rate of disablement pension.			£81.90.
9. Maximum disablement gratuity under paragraph 9 of Schedule 7.			£14,700.00
10. Widow's pension (weekly rates).	(b)	higher permanent rate	£169.50;
	(c)	lower permanent rate 30 per cent of the first sum specified in section 44(4) (Category A basic retirement pension) (the appropriate rate being determined in accordance with paragraph 16 of Schedule 7)	
11. Widower's pension (weekly rate).			£169.50.

Description of benefit, etc.	Rate	
12. Weekly rate of allowance in respect of children and qualifying young persons under paragraph 18 of Schedule 7.	In respect of each child or qualifying young person	£11.35.

AMENDMENTS

1. The whole Schedule was substituted by the Social Security Benefits Up-rating Order 2024 (SI 2024/242) art.3 and Sch.1 to take effect on April 8, 2024. Where relevant, parallel amendments for Scotland were made by the Social Security Up-rating (Scotland) Order 2024 (SSI 2024/106).

2. Tax Credits, Child Benefit and Guardian's Allowance Regulations 2024 (SI 2024/247) reg.6 (April 8, 2024).

3. Pensions Act 2014 s.23 and Sch.12 paras 57 and 68 (April 6, 2016).

4. Pensions Act 2014 Sch.16 para.19 (April 6, 2017).

[1 SCHEDULE 4A

[2 ADDITIONAL PENSION ACCRUAL RATES FOR PURPOSES OF SECTION 45 (2)(C)]

PART I

THE AMOUNT

1.—(1) The amount referred to in section 45(2)(c) above is to be calculated as follows— 1.512

(a) take for each tax year concerned the amount for the year which is found under the following provisions of this Schedule;
(b) add the amounts together;
(c) divide the sum of the amounts by the number of relevant years;
(d) the resulting amount is the amount referred to in section 45(2)(c) above, except that if the resulting amount is a negative one the amount so referred to is nil.

(2) For the purpose of applying sub-paragraph (1) above in the determination of the rate of any additional pension by virtue of section [2 . . .], 39C(1)[5. . .] or 48B(2) above, in a case where the deceased spouse died under pensionable age, [3 or by virtue of section 39C(1) [5 . . .] or 48B(2) above, in a case where the deceased civil partner died under pensionable age,] [6 or by virtue of section 39C(1) above, in a case where the deceased cohabiting partner died under pensionable age,] the divisor used for the purposes of sub-paragraph (1)(c) above shall be whichever is the smaller of the alternative numbers referred to below (instead of the number of relevant years).

(3) The first alternative number is the number of tax years which begin after 5th April 1978 and end before the date when the entitlement to the additional pension commences.

(4) The second alternative number is the number of tax years in the period—

(a) beginning with the tax year in which the deceased [3 [6 spouse, civil partner or cohabiting partner]] attained the age of 16 or, if later, 1978–79; and
(b) ending immediately before the tax year in which the deceased [3 [6 spouse, civil partner or cohabiting partner]] would have attained pensionable age if he had not died earlier.

(5) For the purpose of applying sub-paragraph (1) above in the determination of the rate of any additional pension by virtue of section 48BB(5) above, in a case where the deceased spouse [3 or civil partner] died under pensionable age, the divisor used for the purposes of sub-paragraph (1)(c) above shall be whichever is the smaller of the alternative numbers referred to below (instead of the number of relevant years).

(6) The first alternative number is the number of tax years which begin after 5th April

1978 and end before the date when the deceased spouse [3 or civil partner] dies.

(7) The second alternative number is the number of tax years in the period—

(a) beginning with the tax year in which the deceased spouse [3 or civil partner] attained the age of 16 or, if later, 1978–79; and

(b) ending immediately before the tax year in which the deceased spouse [3 or civil partner] would have attained pensionable age if he had not died earlier.

(8) In this paragraph "relevant year" has the same meaning as in section 44 above.

PART II

SURPLUS EARNINGS FACTOR

1.513 **2.**—(1) This Part of this Schedule applies if for the tax year concerned there is a surplus in the pensioner's earnings factor.

(2) The amount for the year is to be found as follows—

(a) calculate the part of the surplus for that year falling into each of the bands specified in the appropriate table below;

(b) multiply the amount of each such part in accordance with the last order under section 148 of the Administration Act to come into force before the end of the final relevant year;

(c) multiply each amount found under paragraph (b) above by the percentage specified in the appropriate table in relation to the appropriate band;

(d) add together the amounts calculated under paragraph (c) above

(3) The appropriate table for persons attaining pensionable age after the end of the first appointed year but before 6th April 2009 is as follows—

1.514 **TABLE 1**

Amount of surplus	*Percentage*
Band 1. Not exceeding LET	40 + 2N
Band 2. Exceeding LET but not exceeding 3LET–2QEF	10 + N/2
Band 3. Exceeding 3LET–2QEF	20 + N

(4) The appropriate table for persons attaining pensionable age on or after April 6th 2009 [2 where the tax year concerned falls before 2010–11] is as follows—

1.515 **TABLE 2**

Amount of surplus	*Percentage*
Band 1. Not exceeding LET	40
Band 2. Exceeding LET but not exceeding 3LET–2QEF	10
Band 3. Exceeding 3LET–2QEF	20

[2 (4A) The appropriate table for persons attaining pensionable age on or after 6th April 2009 where the tax year concerned is 2010–11 or a subsequent tax year is as follows—

1.516 **TABLE 2A**

Amount of surplus	*Percentage*
Band 1. Not exceeding LET	40
Band 2. Exceeding LET [4 . . .]	10]

(5) Regulations may provide, in relation to persons attaining pensionable age after such date as may be prescribed, that the amount found under this Part of this Schedule for the second appointed year or any subsequent tax year is to be calculated using only so much of the surplus in the pensioner's earnings factor for that year as falls into Band 1 in the table in sub-paragraph (4) above.

(6) For the purposes of the tables in this paragraph—

(a) the value of N is 0.5 for each tax year by which the tax year in which the pensioner attained pensionable age precedes 2009–10;

(b) "LET" means the low earnings threshold for that year as specified in section 44A above;

(c) "QEF" means the qualifying earnings factor for the tax year concerned.

[2 [4 . . .]]

(7) In the calculation of "2QEF" the amount produced by doubling QEF shall be rounded to the nearest whole £100 (taking any amount of £50 as nearest to the previous whole £100).

(8) In this paragraph "final relevant year" has the same meaning as in section 44 above.

PART III

Contracted-Out Employment

Introduction

3.—(1) This Part of this Schedule applies if the following condition is satisfied in relation to each tax week in the tax year concerned. 1.517

(2) The condition is that any earnings paid to or for the benefit of the pensioner in the tax week in respect of employment were in respect of employment qualifying him for a pension provided by a salary related contracted-out scheme or by a money purchase contracted-out scheme or by an appropriate personal pension scheme.

(3) If the condition is satisfied in relation to one or more tax weeks in the tax year concerned, Part II of this Schedule does not apply in relation to the year.

The amount

4.—The amount for the year is amount C where— 1.518

(a) amount C is equal to amount A minus amount B, and
(b) amounts A and B are calculated as follows.

Amount A

5.—(1) Amount A is to be calculated as follows. 1.519

(2) If there is an assumed surplus in the pensioner's earnings factor for the year—

(a) calculate the part of the surplus for that year falling into each of the bands specified in the appropriate table below;
(b) multiply the amount of each such part in accordance with the last order under section 148 of the Administration Act to come into force before the end of the final relevant year;
(c) multiply each amount found under paragraph (b) above by the percentage specified in the appropriate table in relation to the appropriate band;
(d) add together the amounts calculated under paragraph (c) above

(3) The appropriate table for persons attaining pensionable age after the end of the first appointed year but before 6th April 2009 is as follows—

TABLE 3 1.520

Amount of surplus	*Percentage*
Band 1. Not exceeding LET	40 + 2N
Band 2. Exceeding LET but not exceeding 3LET–2QEF	10 + N/2
Band 3. Exceeding 3LET–2QEF	20 + N

(4) The appropriate table for persons attaining pensionable age on or after 6th April 2009 [2 where the tax year concerned falls before 2010–11] is as follows—

TABLE 4 1.521

Amount of surplus	*Percentage*
Band 1. Not exceeding LET	40
Band 2. Exceeding LET but not exceeding 3LET–2QEF	10
Band 3. Exceeding 3LET–2QEF	20

[2 (4A) The appropriate table for persons attaining pensionable age on or after 6th April 2009 where the tax year concerned is 2010–11 or a subsequent tax year is as follows—

TABLE 4A 1.522

Amount of surplus	*Percentage*
Band 1. Not exceeding LET	40
Band 2. Exceeding LET [4 . . .]	10]

Amount B (first case)

6.—(1) Amount B is to be calculated in accordance with this paragraph if the pensioner's employment was entirely employment qualifying him for a pension provided by a salary related contracted-out scheme or by a money purchase contracted-out scheme. 1.523

(2) If there is an assumed surplus in the pensioner's earnings factor for the year—

(a) multiply the amount of the assumed surplus in accordance with the last order under section 148 of the Administration Act to come into force before the end of the final relevant year;

(b) multiply the amount found under paragraph (a) above by the percentage specified in sub-paragraph (3) below.

(3) The percentage is—

(a) 20 + N if the person attained pensionable age after the end of the first appointed year but before 6th April 2009;

(b) 20 if the person attained pensionable age on or after 6th April 2009.

Amount B (second case)

1.524 **7.**—(1) Amount B is to be calculated in accordance with this paragraph if the pensioner's employment was entirely employment qualifying him for a pension provided by an appropriate personal pension scheme.

(2) If there is an assumed surplus in the pensioner's earnings factor for the year—

(a) calculate the part of the surplus for that year falling into each of the bands specified in the appropriate table below;

(b) multiply the amount of each such part in accordance with the last order under section 148 of the Administration Act to come into force before the end of the final relevant year;

(c) multiply each amount found under paragraph (b) above by the percentage specified in the appropriate table in relation to the appropriate band;

(d) add together the amounts calculated under paragraph (c) above.

(3) The appropriate table for persons attaining pensionable age after the end of the first appointed year but before April 6th 2009 is as follows—

1.525 **TABLE 5**

Amount of surplus	*Percentage*
Band 1. Not exceeding LET	40 + 2N
Band 2. Exceeding LET but not exceeding 3LET–2QEF	10 + N/2
Band 3. Exceeding 3LET–2QEF	20 + N

(4) The appropriate table for persons attaining pensionable age on or after April 6th 2009 [2 where the tax year concerned falls before 2010–11] is as follows—

1.526 **TABLE 6**

Amount of surplus	*Percentage*
Band 1. Not exceeding LET	40
Band 2. Exceeding LET but not exceeding 3LET–2QEF	10
Band 3. Exceeding 3LET–2QEF	20

[2 (4A) The appropriate table for persons attaining pensionable age on or after 6th April 2009 where the tax year concerned is 2010–11 or a subsequent tax year is as follows—

1.527 **TABLE 6A**

Amount of surplus	*Percentage*
Band 1. Not exceeding LET	40
Band 2. Exceeding LET [4 . . .]	10.]

Interpretation

1.528 **8.**—(1) In this Part of this Schedule "salary related contracted-out scheme", "money purchase contracted-out scheme" and "appropriate personal pension scheme" have the same meanings as in the Pension Schemes Act 1993.

(2) For the purposes of this Part of this Schedule the assumed surplus in the pensioner's earnings factor for the year is the surplus there would be in that factor for the year if section 48A(1) of the Pension Schemes Act 1993 (no primary Class 1 contributions deemed to be paid) did not apply in relation to any tax week falling in the year.

(3) Section 44A above shall be ignored in applying 44(6) above for the purpose of calculating amount B.

(4) For the purposes of this Part of this Schedule—

(a) the value of N is 0.5 for each tax year by which the tax year in which the pensioner attained pensionable age precedes 2009–10;

(b) "LET" means the low earnings threshold for that year as specified in section 44A above;

(c) "QEF" is the qualifying earnings factor for the tax year concerned.

[2 [4 . . .]]

(5) In the calculation of "2QEF" the amount produced by doubling QEF shall be rounded to the nearest whole £100 (taking any amount of £50 as nearest to the previous whole £100).

(6) In this Part of this Schedule "final relevant year" has the same meaning as in section 44 above.

PART IV

OTHER CASES

9.—The Secretary of State may make regulations containing provisions for finding the amount for a tax year in— 1.529

(a) cases where the circumstances relating to the pensioner change in the course of the year;
(b) such other cases as the Secretary of State thinks fit.]

AMENDMENTS

1. Sch.4A inserted by Child Support, Pensions and Social Security Act 2000 s.31 and Sch.4 (April 6, 2002).
2. Pensions Act 2007 s.10 and Sch.7 Pt 5 (September 26, 2007).
3. Civil Partnership Act 2004 s 254(1) Sch.24 Pt 3 para.51 (December 5, 2005).
4. National Insurance Contributions Act 2008 Sch.2 (September 21, 2008).
5. Pensions Act 2014 Sch.12 para.69 (April 6, 2016).
6. The Bereavement Benefits (Remedial) Order 2023 (SI 2023/134) art.5(5) (August 30, 2018: the amendment came into force on February 13, 2023 but, by virtue of art.1(3), is treated as having had effect from August 30, 2018).

GENERAL NOTE

The Additional Pension and Social Security Pensions (Home Responsibilities) (Amendment) Regulations 2001 (SI 2001/1323) are made under para.9. 1.530

[1 SCHEDULE 4B

ADDITIONAL PENSION: ACCRUAL RATES FOR PURPOSES OF SECTION 45(2)(D)

PART I

AMOUNT FOR PURPOSES OF SECTION 45(2)(D)

1 (1) The amount referred to in section 45(2)(d) is to be calculated as follows— 1.531

(a) calculate the appropriate amount for each of the relevant years within section 45(2)(d) to which Part 2 of this Schedule applies;
(b) calculate the appropriate amount for each of the relevant years within section 45(2)(d) to which Part 3 of this Schedule applies; and
(c) add those amounts together.

(2) But if the resulting amount is a negative one, the amount referred to in section 45(2)(d) is nil.

PART II

NORMAL RULES: EMPLOYMENT NOT CONTRACTED-OUT

Application

2 This Part applies to a relevant year if [3— 1.532

(a)] the contracted-out condition is not satisfied in respect of any tax week in the year [3 and
(b) there is a surplus in the pensioner's earnings factor for the year.]

Appropriate amount for year

3 The appropriate amount for the year for the purposes of paragraph 1 is either— 1.533

(a) the flat rate amount for the year (if [3 the pensioner's earnings factor for the year] does not exceed the LET), or

(b) the sum of the flat rate amount and the earnings-related amount for the year (if [3 that earnings factor] exceeds the LET).

4 [4 (1) Where the final relevant year is 2015–16 or an earlier tax year,] the flat rate amount for the year is calculated by multiplying the FRAA in accordance with the last order under section 148AA of the Administration Act to come into force before the end of the final relevant year.

[4 (2) Otherwise, the flat rate amount is calculated by increasing the FRAA by the percentage by which earnings factors for 2015-16 are directed to be increased by the last order under section 148 of the Administration Act to come into force before the end of the final relevant year.]

5 The earnings-related amount for the year is calculated as follows—

(a) take the part of the [3 earnings factor] for the year which exceeds the LET [2*repealed*]
(b) multiply that amount in accordance with the last order under section 148 of the Administration Act to come into force before the end of the final relevant year;
(c) multiply the amount found under paragraph (b) by 10%;
(d) divide the amount found under paragraph (c) by 44.

Part III

Contracted-out Employment

Application

1.534 6 This Part applies to a relevant year if [3—

(a)] the contracted-out condition is satisfied in respect of each tax week in the year[3 and
(b) there would be a surplus in the pensioner's earnings factor for the year if section 48A of the Pensions Schemes Act 1993 did not apply in relation to any tax week falling in the year.]

Appropriate amount for year

1.535 7 The appropriate amount for the year for the purposes of paragraph 1 is calculated as follows—

(a) calculate amounts A and B in accordance with paragraphs 8 to 10;
(b) subtract amount B from amount A.

Amount A: assumed [3 earnings factor] not exceeding LET

1.536 8 (1) Amount A is calculated in accordance with this paragraph if [3 the pensioner's assumed earnings factor for the year] does not exceed the LET.

(2) In such a case, amount A is the flat rate amount for the year.

(3) [4 Where the final relevant year is 2015–16 or an earlier tax year,] the flat rate amount for the year is calculated by multiplying the FRAA in accordance with the last order under section 148AA of the Administration Act to come into force before the end of the final relevant year.

[4 (4) Otherwise, the flat rate amount is calculated by increasing the FRAA by the percentage by which earnings factors for 2015–16 are directed to be increased by the last order under section 148 of the Administration Act to come into force before the end of the final relevant year.]

Amount A: assumed [3 earnings factor] exceeding LET

1.537 9 (1) Amount A is calculated in accordance with this paragraph if [3 the pensioner's assumed earnings factor for the year] exceeds the LET.

(2) In such a case, amount A is calculated as follows—

(a) take the part of the [3 assumed earnings factor] for the year which exceeds the LET [2*repealed*]
(b) multiply that amount in accordance with the last order under section 148 of the Administration Act to come into force before the end of the final relevant year;
(c) multiply the amount found under paragraph (b) by 10%;
(d) divide the amount found under paragraph (c) by 44;
(e) add the amount found under paragraph (d) to the flat rate amount for the year.

(3) [4 Where the final relevant year is 2015–16 or an earlier tax year,] the flat rate amount for the year is calculated by multiplying the FRAA in accordance with the last order under section 148AA of the Administration Act to come into force before the end of the final relevant year.

[4 (4) Otherwise, the flat rate amount is calculated by increasing the FRAA by the percentage by which earnings factors for 2015–16 are directed to be increased by the last order under section 148 of the Administration Act to come into force before the end of the final relevant year.]

Amount B

10 (1) Amount B is calculated as follows— **1.538**

(a) take the part of the [3 pensioner's assumed earnings factor] for the year which exceeds the QEF [2*repealed*];

(b) multiply that amount in accordance with the last order under section 148 of the Administration Act to come into force before the end of the final relevant year;

(c) multiply the amount found under paragraph (b) by 20%;

(d) divide the amount found under paragraph (c) by the number of relevant years in the pensioner's working life.

(2) Section 44B is to be ignored in applying section 44(6) for the purposes of this paragraph.

PART IV

OTHER CASES

11 The Secretary of State may make regulations containing provision for finding for a tax year the amount referred to in section 45(2)(d)— **1.539**

(a) in cases where the circumstances relating to the pensioner change in the course of the year, and

(b) in such other cases as the Secretary of State thinks fit.

PART 5

INTERPRETATION

12 In this Schedule— **1.540**

- [3 *omitted*]
- "the contracted-out condition", in relation to a tax week, means the condition that any earnings paid to or for the benefit of the pensioner in that week in respect of employment were in respect of employment qualifying him for a pension provided by a salary related contracted-out scheme (within the meaning of the Pension Schemes Act 1993);
- "the FRAA" has the meaning given by paragraph 13;
- "the LET", in relation to a tax year, means the low earnings threshold for the year as specified in section 44A above;
- "the QEF", in relation to a tax year, means the qualifying earnings factor for the year;
- [3 "the pensioner's assumed earnings factor", in relation to a year, means the earnings factor that the pensioner would have for the year if section 48A(1) of the Pension Schemes Act 1993 did not apply in relation to any tax week falling in the year;];
- "relevant year" and "final relevant year" have the same meanings as in section 44 above;
- [2*repealed*]

13 (1) "The FRAA" means the flat rate accrual amount.

(2) [4 Where the final relevant year is 2015–16 or an earlier tax year,] that amount is £72.80 for the flat rate introduction year and subsequent tax years (but subject to section 148AA of the Administration Act).]

[4 (3) Otherwise, that amount is £93.60 for the flat rate introduction year and subsequent tax years.]

AMENDMENTS

1. Schedule 4B was added by Sch.2 of the Pensions Act 2007 (September 26, 2007).
2. National Insurance Contributions Act 2008 Sch.3 (September 21, 2008).
3. Pensions Act 2008 Sch.4, para.12 (January 3, 2012).
4. Pensions Act 2014 (Consequential and Supplementary Amendments) Order 2016 (SI 2016/224) art.2(5)–(8) (April 6, 2016).

General Note

1.541 The flat rate accrual rate was raised to £93.60 for the 2015/16 tax year and subsequent years (see Social Security Pensions (Flat Rate Accrual Amount) Order 2015 (SI 2015/185)) and has not been increased since.

SCHEDULE 5

[5 Pension Increase or Lump Sum Where Entitlement to Retirement Pension is Deferred]

[5 Choice between increase of pension and lump sum where pensioner's entitlement is deferred

1.542 **A1.**—(1) Where a person's entitlement to a Category A or Category B retirement pension is deferred and the period of deferment is at least 12 months, the person shall, on claiming his pension or within a prescribed period after claiming it, elect in the prescribed manner either—

(a) that paragraph 1 (entitlement to increase of pension) is to apply in relation to the period of deferment, or

(b) that paragraph 3A (entitlement to lump sum) is to apply in relation to the period of deferment.

(2) If no election under sub-paragraph (1) is made within the period prescribed under that sub-paragraph, the person is to be treated as having made an election under sub-paragraph (1)(b).

(3) Regulations—

(a) may enable a person who has made an election under sub-paragraph (1) (including one that the person is treated by sub-paragraph (2) as having made) to change the election within a prescribed period and in a prescribed manner, if prescribed conditions are satisfied, and

(b) if they enable a person to make an election under sub-paragraph (1)(b) in respect of a period of deferment after receiving any increase of pension under paragraph 1 by reference to that period, may for the purpose of avoiding duplication of payment—

(i) enable an amount determined in accordance with the regulations to be recovered from the person in a prescribed manner and within a prescribed period, or

(ii) provide for an amount determined in accordance with the regulations to be treated as having been paid on account of the amount to which the person is entitled under paragraph 3A.

(4) Where the Category A or Category B retirement pension includes any increase under [6 paragraphs 5 to 6A], no election under sub-paragraph (1) applies to so much of the pension as consists of that increase (an entitlement to an increase of pension in respect of such an increase after a period of deferment being conferred either by paragraphs 1 and 2 or by paragraph 2A).]

Increase of pension where pension entitlement is deferred.

1.543 [5 **1.**— (1) This paragraph applies where a person's entitlement to a Category A or Category B retirement pension is deferred and one of the following conditions is met—

(a) the period of deferment is less than 12 months, or

(b) the person has made an election under paragraph A1(1)(a) in relation to the period of deferment.

(2) The rate of the person's Category A or Category B retirement pension shall be increased by an amount equal to the aggregate of the increments to which he is entitled under paragraph 2, but only if that amount is enough to increase the rate of the pension by at least 1 per cent.]

2.—(1) Subject to paragraph 3 below, a person is entitled to an increment under this paragraph for each complete incremental period in his period of enhancement.

(2) In this Schedule—

"incremental period" means any period of six days which are treated by regulations as days of increment for the purposes of this Schedule in relation to the person and the pension in question: and

"the period of enhancement", in relation to that person and that pension, means the period which—

(a) begins on the same day as the period of deferment in question; and

(b) ends on the same day as that period or, if earlier, on the day before the 5th anniversary of the beginning of that period.

(3) Subject to paragraph 3 below, the amount of the increment for any such incremental period shall be 1/7 per cent. of the weekly rate of the Category A or Category B retirement pension to which that person would have been entitled for the period if his entitlement had not been deferred.

(4) Where an amount is required to be calculated in accordance with the provisions of sub-paragraph (3) above

(a) the amount so calculated shall be rounded to the nearest penny, taking any 1/2p as nearest to the next whole penny above; and

(b) where the amount so calculated would, apart from this sub-paragraph, be a sum less than 1/2p, that amount shall be taken to be zero, notwithstanding any other provision of this Act, the Pensions Act or the Administration Act.

(5) For the purposes of sub-paragraph (3) above the weekly rate of pension for any period shall be taken—

(a) to include any increase under section 47(1) above and any increase under [6 paragraphs 4, 5, 5A, 6 or 6A] below, but

(b) not to include any increase under section [1 . . .], [5 83A or] 85 above or any graduated retirement benefit.

(6) The reference in sub-paragraph (5) above to any increase under subsection (1) of section 47 above shall be taken as a reference to any increase that would take place under that subsection if subsection (2) of that section and [4 section 46(5)] of the Pensions Act were disregarded.

(7) Where one or more orders have come into force under section 150 [7 or 150A] of the Administration Act during the period of enhancement, the rate for any incremental period shall be determined as if the order or orders had come into force before the beginning of the period of enhancement.

(8) Where a pension's rights premium is paid in respect of a person who is, or if his entitlement had not been deferred would be, entitled to a Category A or Category B retirement pension, then, in calculating any increment under this paragraph which falls to be paid to him in respect of such a pension after the date on which the premium is paid there shall be disregarded any guaranteed minimum pension to which the pensioner was entitled in connection with the employment to which the premium relates.

[5 **2A.**—(1) This paragraph applies where—

(a) a person's entitlement to a Category A or Category B retirement pension is deferred,

(b) the pension includes an increase under [6 paragraphs 5 to 6A], and

(c) the person has made (or is treated as having made) an election under paragraph A1(1)(b) in relation to the period of deferment.

(2) The rate of the person's Category A or Category B retirement pension shall be increased by an amount equal to the aggregate of the increments to which he is entitled under sub-paragraph (3).

(3) For each complete incremental period in the person's period of deferment, the amount of the increment shall be 1/5th per cent. of the weekly rate of the increase to which the person would have been entitled under [6 paragraphs 5 to 6A] for the period if his entitlement to the Category A or Category B retirement pension had not been deferred.]

3.—(1) Regulations may provide that sub-paragraphs (1) to (3) of paragraph 2 above shall have effect with such additions, omissions and amendments as are prescribed in relation to a person during whose period of enhancement there has been a change, other than a change made by such an order as is mentioned in sub-paragraph (7) of that paragraph, in the rate of the Category A or Category B retirement pension to which he would have been entitled if his entitlement to the pension had commenced on attaining pensionable age.

(2) Any regulations under this paragraph may make such consequential additions, omissions and amendments in paragraph 8(3) below as the Secretary of State considers are appropriate in consequence of any changes made by virtue of this paragraph in paragraph 2 above.

Note: For incremental periods after April 6, 2005 the words in para.1 above "period of enhancement" will be read as "period of deferment" and the definition of period of enhancement in para.(2) is repealed. Also the fraction of 1/7 in para.(3) will be read as 1/5. See Pensions Act 1995 Sch.4 para.6.

[5 Lump sum where pensioner's entitlement is deferred

3A.—(1) This paragraph applies where— 1.544

(a) a person's entitlement to a Category A or Category B retirement pension is deferred, and

(b) the person has made (or is treated as having made) an election under paragraph A1(1)(b) in relation to the period of deferment.

(2) The person is entitled to an amount calculated in accordance with paragraph 3B (a "lump sum").

Calculation of lump sum

1.545 **3B.**—(1) The lump sum is the accrued amount for the last accrual period beginning during the period of deferment.

(2) In this paragraph—

"accrued amount" means the amount calculated in accordance with sub-paragraph (3);

"accrual period" means any period of seven days beginning with a prescribed day of the week, where that day falls within the period of deferment.

(3) The accrued amount for an accrual period for a person is—

$$(A + P) \times \sqrt[52]{\left(1 + \frac{R}{100}\right)}$$

where—

A is the accrued amount for the previous accrual period (or, in the case of the first accrual period beginning during the period of deferment, zero);

P is the amount of the Category A or Category B retirement pension to which the person would have been entitled for the accrual period if his entitlement had not been deferred;

R is—

(a) a percentage rate two per cent. higher than the Bank of England base rate, or

(b) if regulations so provide, such higher rate as may be prescribed.

(4) For the purposes of sub-paragraph (3), any change in the Bank of England base rate is to be treated as taking effect—

(a) at the beginning of the accrual period immediately following the accrual period during which the change took effect, or

(b) if regulations so provide, at such other time as may be prescribed.

(5) For the purposes of the calculation of the lump sum, the amount of Category A or Category B retirement pension to which the person would have been entitled for an accrual period—

(a) includes any increase under section 47(1) and any increase under paragraph 4 of this Schedule, but

(b) does not include—

(i) any increase under section 83A or 85 or [6 paragraphs 5 to 6A] of this Schedule,

(ii) any graduated retirement benefit, or

(iii) in prescribed circumstances, such other amount of Category A or Category B retirement pension as may be prescribed.

(6) The reference in sub-paragraph (5)(a) to any increase under subsection (1) of section 47 shall be taken as a reference to any increase that would take place under that subsection if subsection (2) of that section and section 46(5) of the Pensions Act were disregarded.]

Choice between increase of pension and lump sum where pensioner's deceased spouse [6 or civil partner] has deferred entitlement

1.546 **3C.**—(1) Subject to paragraph 8, this paragraph applies where—

(a) [6 widow, widower or surviving civil partner] ("W") is entitled to a Category A or Category B retirement pension,

(b) W was married to [6 or was the civil partner of] the other party to the marriage [6 or civil partnership] ("S") when S died,

(c) S's entitlement to a Category A or Category B retirement pension was deferred when S died, and

(d) S's entitlement had been deferred throughout the period of 12 months ending with the day before S's death.

(2) We shall within the prescribed period elect in the prescribed manner either—

(a) that paragraph 4 (entitlement to increase of pension) is to apply in relation to S's period of deferment, or

(b) that paragraph 7A (entitlement to lump sum) is to apply in relation to S's period of deferment.

(3) If no election under sub-paragraph (2) is made within the period prescribed under that sub-paragraph, W is to be treated as having made an election under sub-paragraph (2)(b).

(4) Regulations—

(a) may enable a person who has made an election under sub-paragraph (2) (including one that the person is treated by sub-paragraph (3) as having made) to change the election within a prescribed period and in a prescribed manner, if prescribed conditions are satisfied, and

(b) if they enable a person to make an election under sub-paragraph (2)(b) in respect of a period of deferment after receiving any increase of pension under paragraph 4 by reference to that period, may for the purpose of avoiding duplication of payment—

(i) enable an amount determined in accordance with the regulations to be recovered from the person in a prescribed manner and within a prescribed period, or

(ii) provide for an amount determined in accordance with the regulations to be treated as having been paid on account of the amount to which the person is entitled under paragraph 7A.

(5) The making of an election under sub-paragraph (2)(b) does not affect the application of [[6] paragraphs 5 to 6A] (which relate to an increase in pension where the pensioner's deceased spouse [[6] or civil partner] had deferred an entitlement to a guaranteed minimum pension).]

Increase of pension where pensioner's deceased spouse [[6] or civil partner] has deferred entitlement

4.[[5] (1) Subject to paragraph 8, this paragraph applies where a [[6] widow, widower or surviving civil partner] ("W") is entitled to a Category A or Category B retirement pension and was married to [[6] or was the civil partner of] the other party to the marriage [[6] or civil partnership] ("S") when S died and one of the following conditions is met— 1.547

(a) S was entitled to a Category A or Category B retirement pension with an increase under this Schedule,

(b) W is a [[6] widow, widower or surviving civil partner] to whom paragraph 3C applies and has made an election under paragraph 3C(2)(a), or

(c) paragraph 3C would apply to W but for the fact that the condition in sub-paragraph (1)(d) of that paragraph is not met.

(1A) Subject to sub-paragraph (3), the rate of W's pension shall be increased—

(a) in a case falling within sub-paragraph (1)(a), by an amount equal to the increase to which S was entitled under this Schedule, apart from [[6] paragraphs 5 to 6A] [[9] [[11] . . .]],

(b) in a case falling within sub-paragraph (1)(b), by an amount equal to the increase to which S would have been entitled under this Schedule, apart from [[6] paragraphs 5 to 6A] [[9] [[11] . . .]], if the period of deferment had ended immediately before S's death and S had then made an election under paragraph A1(1)(a), or

(c) in a case falling within sub-paragraph (1)(c), by an amount equal to the increase to which S would have been entitled under this Schedule, apart from [[6] paragraphs 5 to 6A] [[11] . . .], if the period of deferment had ended immediately before S's death.]

(2) [[2] . . .]

(3) If a married person dies after [[12] 5th October 2002] [[6] or civil partner dies on or after 5 December, 2005] the rate of the retirement pension for that person's [[6] widow, widower or surviving civil partner] shall be increased by an amount equivalent to the sum of—

(a) the increase in the basic pension to which the deceased spouse [[6] or civil partner] was entitled; and

(b) one-half of the increase in the additional pension.

(4) In any case where—

(a) there is a period between the death of the former spouse [[6] or civil partner] and the date on which the surviving spouse [[6] or civil partner] becomes entitled to a Category A or Category B retirement pension, and

(b) one or more orders have come into force under section 150 of the Administration act during that period,

the amount of the increase to which the surviving spouse [[6] or civil partner] is entitled under this paragraph shall be determined as if the order or orders had come into force before the beginning of that period.

(5) This paragraph does not apply in any case where the deceased spouse died before 6th April, 1979 and the widow or widower attained pensionable age before that date.

[3 **5.**—(1) Where—

(a) a [6 widow, widower or civil partner] (call that person 'W') is entitled to a Category A or Category B retirement pension and was married to [6 or was the civil partner of] the other party to the marriage [6 or civil partnership] (call that person 'S') when S died, and

(b) S either—

(i) was entitled to a guaranteed minimum pension with an increase under section 15(1) of the Pensions Act, or

(ii) would have been so entitled if S had retired on the date of S's death,

the rate of W's pension shall be increased by the following amount.

(2) The amount is—

[10 (a) where W is a woman—

(i) whose deceased spouse was a man; or

(ii) who falls within paragraph 7(3) below,

an amount equal to the sum of the amounts set out in paragraph 5A(2) or (3) below (as the case may be),],

(b) where W is a [10 man whose deceased spouse was a woman], an amount equal to the sum of the amounts set out in paragraph 6(2), (3) or (4) below (as the case may be). [6 , and

[10 (c) where W is—

(i) a woman who does not fall within paragraph 7(3) below and whose deceased spouse was a woman;

(ii) a man whose deceased spouse was a man; or

(iii) a surviving civil partner,

an amount equal to the sum of the amounts set out in paragraph (6A)(2) below.]

1.548 **5A.**—[10 (1) This paragraph applies where W (referred to in paragraph 5 above) is a woman—

(a) whose deceased spouse was a man; or

(b) who falls within paragraph 7(3) below.]

(2) Where the [10 spouse] dies before [12 6th October 2002], the amounts referred to in paragraph 5(2)(a) above are the following—

(a) an amount equal to one-half of the increase mentioned in paragraph 5(1)(b) above,

(b) [9 *repealed*]

(c) an amount equal to any increase to which the [10 spouse] had been entitled under paragraph 5 above.

(3) Where [13 the apouse] dies after [12 6th October 2002], the amounts referred to in paragraph 5(2)(a) above are the following—

(a) [9 repealed]

(b) one-half of any increase to which [13 the apouse] had been entitled under paragraph 5 above.

6.—(1) This paragraph applies where W (referred to in paragraph 5 above) is a [10 man whose deceased spouse was a woman]

(2) Where the wife dies before 6th April, 1989, the amounts referred to in paragraph 5(2)(b) above are the following—

(a) an amount equal to the increase mentioned in paragraph 5(1)(b) above,

(b) [9 repealed]

(c) an amount equal to any increase to which the wife had been entitled under paragraph 5 above.

(3) Where the wife dies after 5th April, 1989 but before [12 6th October 2002], the amounts referred to in paragraph 5(2) above are the following—

(a) the increase mentioned in paragraph 5(1)(b) above, so far as attributable to employment before 6th April, 1988,

(b) one-half of that increase, so far as attributable to employment after 5th April, 1988,

(c) [9 repealed]

(d) any increase to which the wife had been entitled under paragraph 5 above.

(4) Where the wife dies after [12 6th October 2002], the amounts referred to in paragraph 5(2)(b) above are the following—

(a) one-half of the increase mentioned in paragraph 5(1)(b) above, so far as attributable to employment before 6th April, 1988,

(b) [9 repealed]

(c) one-half of any increase to which the wife had been entitled under paragraph 5 above].

1.549 [6 **6A.**—[10 (1) This paragraph applies where W (referred to in paragraph 5 above) is—

(a) a woman who does not fall within paragraph 7(3) below and whose deceased spouse was a woman;
(b) a man whose deceased spouse was a man; or
(c) a surviving civil partner.]

(2) The amounts referred to in paragraph 5(2)(c) above are the following—
(a) one-half of the increase mentioned in paragraph 5(1)(b) above, so far as attributable to employment before 6th April 1988,
(b) [9 repealed]
(c) one-half of any increase to which the deceased [10 spouse or] civil partner had been entitled under paragraph 5 above.]

7.—(1) [9 *repealed*]

(2) Where an amount is required to be calculated in accordance with the provisions of [6 paragraphs 5, 5A, 6 or 6A] or sub-paragraph (1) above—
(a) the amount so calculated shall be rounded to the nearest penny, taking any 1/2p as nearest to the next whole penny above; and
(b) where the amount so calculated would, apart from this sub-paragraph, be a sum less than 1/2p, that amount shall be taken to be zero, notwithstanding any other provision of this Act, the Pensions Act or the Administration Act.

[10 (3) For the purposes of paragraphs 5, 5A and 6A above, a woman falls within this sub-paragraph if—
(a) she was married to another woman who, at the time of her death, was a woman by virtue of a full gender recognition certificate having been issued under the Gender Recognition Act 2004; and
(b) that marriage subsisted before the time when that certificate was issued.].

[11 **7ZA**.–(1) This paragraph modifies paragraphs 5A to 6A in cases where— **1.550**
(a) W became entitled to a Category A or Category B retirement pension before 6 April 2012, and
(b) S died before 6 April 2012.

("W" and "S" have the same meaning as in paragraph 5.)

(2) Paragraph 5A applies as if—
(a) in sub-paragraph (2), after paragraph (a), there were inserted—
"(b) the appropriate amount; and";
(b) in sub-paragraph (3), after "following—", there were inserted—
"(a) one half of the appropriate amount; and".

(3) Paragraph 6 applies as if—
(a) in sub-paragraph (2), after paragraph (a), there were inserted—
"(b) the appropriate amount; and";
(b) in sub-paragraph (3), after paragraph (b), there were inserted—
"(c) the appropriate amount reduced by the amount of any increases under section 109 of the Pensions Act; and";
(c) in sub-paragraph (4), after paragraph (a), there were inserted—
"(b) one half of the appropriate amount; and".

(4) Paragraph 6A applies as if in sub-paragraph (2), after paragraph (a), there were inserted—
"(b) one half of the appropriate amount; and".

(5) In paragraphs 5A to 6A as modified by this paragraph, the "appropriate amount" means the greater of—
(a) the amount by which the deceased person's Category A or Category B retirement pension had been increased under section 150(1)(e) of the Administration Act; or
(b) the amount by which his or her Category A or Category B retirement pension would have been so increased had he or she died immediately before the surviving spouse or civil partner became entitled to a Category A or Category B retirement pension.

(6) In sub-paragraph (1)(a) the reference to becoming entitled to a pension before 6 April 2012 includes a reference to becoming entitled on or after that day to the payment of a pension in respect of a period before that day.]

[5 Entitlement to lump sum where pensioner's deceased spouse [6 or civil partner] has deferred entitlement

7A.—(1) This paragraph applies where a person to whom paragraph 3C applies ("W") has made (or is treated as having made) an election under paragraph 3C(2)(b). **1.551**

(2) W is entitled to an amount calculated in accordance with paragraph 7B (a "widowed person's [6 or surviving civil partner's] lump sum").

Calculation of widowed person's [6 or surviving civil partner's] lump sum

1.552 **7B.**—(1) The widowed person's [6 or surviving civil partner's] lump sum is the accrued amount for the last accrual period beginning during the period which—

(a) began at the beginning of S's period of deferment, and
(b) ended on the day before S's death.

(2) In this paragraph—

"S" means the other party to the marriage; [6 or civil partnership]
"accrued amount" means the amount calculated in accordance with sub-paragraph (3);
"accrual period" means any period of seven days beginning with a prescribed day of the week, where that day falls within S's period of deferment.

(3) The accrued amount for an accrual period for W is—

$$(A + P) \times \sqrt[52]{\left(1 + \frac{R}{100}\right)}$$

where—

A is the accrued amount for the previous accrual period (or, in the case of the first accrual period beginning during the period mentioned in sub-paragraph (1), zero);

P is—

(a) the basic pension, and
(b) half of the additional pension, to which S would have been entitled for the accrual period if his entitlement had not been deferred during the period mentioned in sub-paragraph (1);

R is—

(a) a percentage rate two per cent. higher than the Bank of England base rate, or
(b) if regulations so provide, such higher rate as may be prescribed.

(4) For the purposes of sub-paragraph (3), any change in the Bank of England base rate is to be treated as taking effect—

(a) at the beginning of the accrual period immediately following the accrual period during which the change took effect, or
(b) if regulations so provide, at such other time as may be prescribed.

(5) For the purposes of the calculation of the widowed person's lump sum, the amount of Category A or Category B retirement pension to which S would have been entitled for an accrual period—

(a) includes any increase under section 47(1) and any increase under paragraph 4 of this Schedule, but
(b) does not include—
  (i) any increase under section 83A or 85 or [6 paragraphs 5 to 6A] of this Schedule [9 [11 . . .]],
  (ii) any graduated retirement benefit, or
  (iii) in prescribed circumstances, such other amount of Category A or Category B retirement pension as may be prescribed.

(6) The reference in sub-paragraph (5)(a) to any increase under subsection (1) of section 47 shall be taken as a reference to any increase that would take place under that subsection if subsection (2) of that section and section 46(5) of the Pensions Act were disregarded.

(7) In any case where—

(a) there is a period between the death of S and the date on which W becomes entitled to a Category A or Category B retirement pension, and
(b) one or more orders have come into force under section 150 of the Administration Act during that period,

the amount of the lump sum shall be increased in accordance with that order or those orders.]

[5 Supplementary

1.553 **7C.**—(1) Any lump sum calculated under paragraph 3B or 7B must be rounded to the nearest penny, taking any 1/2p as nearest to the next whole penny above.

(2) In prescribing a percentage rate for the purposes of paragraphs 3B and 7B, the Secretary of State must have regard to—

(a) the national economic situation, and
(b) any other matters which he considers relevant.]

[5 Married Couples [6 and civil partners]]

[2 **8.**—(1) [2 . . .] 1.554
(2) [8 . . .]]
[2 (3) [8 . . .]
[5(4) The conditions in paragraph 3C(1)(c) and 4(1)(a) are not satisfied by a Category B retirement pension to which S was or would have been entitled by virtue of W's contributions.

(5) Where the Category A retirement pension to which S was or would have been entitled includes an increase under section 51A(2) attributable to W's contributions, the increase or lump sum to which W is entitled under paragraph 4(1A) or 7A(2) is to be calculated as if there had been no increase under that section.

(6) In sub-paragraphs (4) and (5), "W" and "S" have the same meaning as in paragraph 3C, 4 or 7A, as the case requires.]

Uprating

9.—The sums which are the increases in the rates of retirement pension under this Schedule are subject to alteration by order made by the Secretary of State under section 150 of the Administration Act. 1.555

AMENDMENTS

1. Tax Credits Act 2002 Sch.6 (April 6, 2003).
2. Pensions Act 1995 Sch.4 (July 19, 1995) and Sch.7 (April 6, 2005).
3. Social Security (Incapacity for Work) Act 1994 Sch.1 para.40 (April 13, 1995).
4. Pensions Schemes Act 1993 Sch.8 (Feb. 7, 1994).
5. Pensions Act 2004 Sch.11 (April 6, 2005).
6. Civil Partnership (Pensions and Benefit Payments) (Consequential Provisions) Order 2005 (SI 2005/2053) (December 5, 2005).
7. Pensions Act 2007 Sch.1 para.19 (July 26, 2007).
8. Pensions Act 2007 Sch.7 (September 26, 2007 and April 6, 2010).
9. Pensions Act 2011 s.2(5) and (6) and Sch.2 (April 6, 2012).
10. Marriage and Civil Partnership (Scotland) Act 2014 and Civil Partnership Act 2004 (Consequential Provisions and Modifications) Order 2014 (SI 2014/3229) Sch.4 para.2 (December 14, 2014)
11. Pensions Act 2014 Sch.12 para. 94 (April 6, 2016).
12. Child Support, Pensions and Social Security Act 2000 s.39, which provides that the amendments have retrospective effect.
13. SI 2014/3168, in relation to England and Wales (December 10, 2014); SI 2014/3229, in relation to Scotland (December 16, 2014).

GENERAL NOTE

Under para.4(1) above a man reaching pensionable age before April 6, 2010 is also required to have been over pensionable age when his wife (S) died. (See Pensions Act 1995 Sch.4 para.21 (14) and (16).) 1.556

In relation to any incremental period and accrual period beginning before April 6, 2010 references in para.2 (5)(b), 3B (5)(b) and 7B (5)(b) to section 83A of the principal Act are to be taken as references to s.83 or 84 of that Act—see Sch.11 of Pensions Act 2004.

The changes made by s.2 of the Pensions Act 2011 to this schedule do not apply if W became entitled to either a Category A or B retirement pension before those changes came into force and S died before that day. See s.2(7) and (8) of that Act.

The sums which are increases in the rates of retirement pensions under Sch.5 were increased by 6.7 per cent with effect from April 8, 2024: see the Social Security Benefits Up-rating Order 2024 (SI 2024/242) art.4(3). And the sums which are lump sums to which surviving spouses or civil partners will become entitled under para.7A of the Schedule on becoming entitled to a Category A or Category B retirement pension were also increased by 6.7 per cent from April 8, 2024 (see art.4(3) of the 2024 Order). For previous years' increases, see previous editions of this work.

In *KH v Secretary of State for Work and Pensions* [2014] UKUT 138 (AAC) Judge Wikeley refused permission to appeal to a claimant because there was no arguable error of law in the decision by the First-tier Tribunal in refusing a claim about deferral put forward by a claimant. The Upper Tribunal reported the decision because the claimant had argued his case on the specific wording of the Departmental leaflet *Your Guide to State Pension deferral (SPD1)*. The leaflet was wrong and did not accurately reflect the law, which the First-tier Tribunal had rightly applied.

[1 SCHEDULE 5A

Pension Increase or Lump Sum Where Entitlement to Shared Additional Pension is Deferred

Choice between pension increase and lump sum where entitlement to shared additional pension is deferred

1.557 **1.**—(1) Where a person's entitlement to a shared additional pension is deferred and the period of deferment is at least 12 months, the person shall, on claiming his pension or within a prescribed period after claiming it, elect in the prescribed manner either—

(a) that paragraph 2 (entitlement to increase of pension) is to apply in relation to the period of deferment, or

(b) that paragraph 4 (entitlement to lump sum) is to apply in relation to the period of deferment.

(2) If no election under sub-paragraph (1) is made within the period prescribed under that sub-paragraph, the person is to be treated as having made an election under sub-paragraph (1)(b).

(3) Regulations—

(a) may enable a person who has made an election under sub-paragraph (1) (including one that the person is treated by sub-paragraph (2) as having made) to change the election within a prescribed period and in a prescribed manner, if prescribed conditions are satisfied, and

(b) if they enable a person to make an election under sub-paragraph (1)(b) in respect of a period of deferment after receiving any increase of pension under paragraph 2 by reference to that period, may for the purpose of avoiding duplication of payment—

(i) enable an amount determined in accordance with the regulations to be recovered from the person in a prescribed manner and within a prescribed period, or

(ii) provide for an amount determined in accordance with the regulations to be treated as having been paid on account of the amount to which the person is entitled under paragraph 4.

Increase of pension where entitlement deferred

1.558 **2.**—(1) This paragraph applies where a person's entitlement to a shared additional pension is deferred and either—

(a) the period of deferment is less than 12 months, or

(b) the person has made an election under paragraph 1(1)(a) in relation to the period of deferment.

(2) The rate of the person's shared additional pension shall be increased by an amount equal to the aggregate of the increments to which he is entitled under paragraph 3, but only if that amount is enough to increase the rate of the pension by at least 1 per cent.

Calculation of increment

1.559 **3.**—(1) A person is entitled to an increment under this paragraph for each complete incremental period in his period of deferment.

(2) The amount of the increment for an incremental period shall be 1/5th per cent. of the weekly rate of the shared additional pension to which the person would have been entitled for the period if his entitlement had not been deferred.

(3) Amounts under sub-paragraph (2) shall be rounded to the nearest penny, taking any 1/2p as nearest to the next whole penny.

(4) Where an amount under sub-paragraph (2) would, apart from this sub-paragraph, be a sum less than 1/2p, the amount shall be taken to be zero, notwithstanding any other provision of this Act, the Pensions Act or the Administration Act.

(5) In this paragraph "incremental period" means any period of six days which are treated by regulations as days of increment for the purposes of this paragraph in relation to the person and pension in question.

(6) Where one or more orders have come into force under section 150 of the Administration Act during the period of deferment, the rate for any incremental period shall be determined as if the order or orders had come into force before the beginning of the period of deferment.

(7) The sums which are the increases in the rates of shared additional pension under this paragraph are subject to alteration by order made by the Secretary of State under section 150 of the Administration Act.

Lump sum where entitlement to shared additional pension is deferred

4.—(1) This paragraph applies where— 1.560

(a) a person's entitlement to a shared additional pension is deferred, and

(b) the person has made (or is treated as having made) an election under paragraph 1(1)(b) in relation to the period of deferment.

(2) The person is entitled to an amount calculated in accordance with paragraph 5 (a "lump sum").

Calculation of lump sum

5.—(1) The lump sum is the accrued amount for the last accrual period beginning during the period of deferment. 1.561

(2) In this paragraph—

'accrued amount' means the amount calculated in accordance with sub-paragraph (3);

'accrual period' means any period of seven days beginning with a prescribed day of the week, where that day falls within the period of deferment.

(3) The accrued amount for an accrual period for a person is—

$$(A + P) \times \sqrt[52]{\left(1 + \frac{R}{100}\right)}$$

where—

A is the accrued amount for the previous accrual period (or, in the case of the first accrual period beginning during the period of deferment, zero);

P is the amount of the shared additional pension to which the person would have been entitled for the accrual period if his entitlement had not been deferred;

R is—

(a) a percentage rate two per cent. higher than the Bank of England base rate, or

(b) if a higher rate is prescribed for the purposes of paragraphs 3B and 7B of Schedule 5, that higher rate.

(4) For the purposes of sub-paragraph (3), any change in the Bank of England base rate is to be treated as taking effect—

(a) at the beginning of the accrual period immediately following the accrual period during which the change took effect, or

(b) if regulations so provide, at such other time as may be prescribed.

(5) For the purpose of the calculation of the lump sum, the amount of the shared additional pension to which the person would have been entitled for an accrual period does not include, in prescribed circumstances, such amount as may be prescribed.

(6) The lump sum must be rounded to the nearest penny, taking any 1/2p as nearest to the next whole penny.]

AMENDMENT

1. Pensions Act 2004 Sch.11 (April 6, 2005).

GENERAL NOTE

The sums which, under para.2 of Sch5A are increases in the rates of shared additional pensions, were increased by 10.1 per cent with effect from April 10, 2023: see Social Security Benefits Up-rating Order 2022 (SI 2023/316) art.4(4). For previous years' increases, see previous editions of this work. 1.562

SCHEDULE 6

Assessment of Extent of Disablement

General provisions as to method of assessment

1.563 **1.**—For the purposes of [1 section 103] above and Part II of Schedule 7 to this Act, the extent of disablement shall be assessed, by reference to the disabilities incurred by the claimant as a result of the relevant loss of faculty in accordance with the following general principles—

(a) except as provided in paragraphs (b) to (d) below, the disabilities to be taken into account shall be all disabilities so incurred (whether or not involving loss of earning power or additional expense) to which the claimant may be expected, having regard to his physical and mental condition at the date of the assessment, to be subject during the period taken into account by the assessment as compared with a person of the same age and sex whose physical and mental condition is normal;

(b) [1 . . .] regulations may make provision as to the extent (if any) to which any disabilities are to be taken into account where they are disabilities which, though resulting from the relevant loss of faculty, also result, or without the relevant accident might have been expected to result, from a cause other than the relevant accident;

(c) the assessment shall be made without reference to the particular circumstances of the claimant other than age, sex, and physical and mental condition;

(d) the disabilities resulting from such loss of faculty as may be prescribed shall be taken as amounting to 100 per cent. disablement and other disabilities shall be assessed accordingly.

2.—Provisions may be made by regulations for further defining the principles on which the extent of disablement is to be assessed and such regulations may in particular direct that a prescribed loss of faculty shall be treated as resulting in a prescribed degree of disablement; and, in connection with any such direction, nothing in paragraph 1(c) above prevents the making of different provision, in the case of loss of faculty in or affecting hand or arm, for right-handed and for left-handed persons.

3.—Regulations under paragraph 1(d) or 2 above may include provision—

(a) for adjusting or reviewing an assessment made before the date of the coming into force of those regulations;

(b) for any resulting alteration of that assessment to have effect as from that date; so however that no assessment shall be reduced by virtue of this paragraph.

Severe disablement allowance

1.564 **4.**— [1 . . .]

5.— [1 . . .]

Disablement benefit

1.565 **6.**—(1) Subject to sub-paragraphs (2) and (3) below, the period to be taken into account by an assessment for the purposes of section 103 above and Part II of Schedule 7 to this Act of the extent of a claimant's disablement shall be the period (beginning not earlier than the end of the period of 90 days referred to in section 103(6) above and in paragraph 9(3) of that Schedule and limited by reference either to the claimant's life or to a definite date) during which the claimant has suffered and may be expected to continue to suffer from the relevant loss of faculty.

(2) If on any assessment the condition of the claimant is not such, having regard to the possibility of changes in that condition (whether predictable or not), as to allow of a final assessment being made up to the end of the period provided by sub-paragraph (1) above, then, subject to sub-paragraph (3) below—

(a) a provisional assessment shall be made, taking into account such shorter period only as seems reasonable having regard to his condition and that possibility; and

(b) on the next assessment the period to be taken into account shall begin with the end of the period taken into account by the provisional assessment.

(3) Where the assessed extent of a claimant's disablement amounts to less than 14 per cent., then, subject to sub-paragraphs (4) and (5) below, that assessment shall be a final assessment and the period to be taken into account by it shall not end before the earliest date on which it seems likely that the extent of the disablement will be less than 1 per cent.

(4) Sub-paragraph (3) above does not apply in any case where it seems likely that—

(a) the assessed extent of the disablement will be aggregated with the assessed extent of any present disablement, and

(b) that aggregate will amount to 14 per cent. or more.

(5) Where the extent of the claimant's disablement is assessed at different percentages for different parts of the period taken into account by the assessment, then—

(a) sub-paragraph (3) above does not apply in relation to the assessment unless the percentage assessed for the latest part of that period is less than 14 per cent., and

(b) in any such case that sub-paragraph shall apply only in relation to that part of that period (and subject to sub-paragraph (4) above).

7.—An assessment for the purposes of section 103 above and Part II of Schedule 7 to this Act shall—

(a) state the degree of disablement in the form of a percentage;

(b) specify the period taken into account by the assessment; and

(c) where that period is limited by reference to a definite date, specify whether the assessment is provisional or final;

but the percentage and the period shall not be specified more particularly than is necessary for the purpose of determining in accordance with section 103 above and Parts II and IV of Schedule 7 to this Act the claimant's rights as to disablement pension or gratuity and reduced earnings allowance (whether or not a claim has been made).

Special provision as to entitlement to constant attendance allowance, etc.

8.—(1) For the purpose of determining whether a person is entitled— **1.566**

(a) to an increase of a disablement pension under section 104 above; or

(b) to a corresponding increase of any other benefit by virtue of paragraph 6(4)(b) or 7(2)(b) of Schedule 8 to this Act,

regulations may provide for the extent of the person's disablement resulting from the relevant injury or disease to be determined in such manner as may be provided for by the regulations by reference to all disabilities to which that person is subject which result either from the relevant injury or disease or from any other injury or disease in respect of which there fall to be made to the person payments of any of the descriptions listed in sub-paragraph (2) below.

(2) Those payments are—

(a) payments by way of disablement pension;

(b) payments by way of benefit under paragraph 4 or 7(1) of Schedule 8 to this Act; or

(c) payments in such circumstances as may be prescribed by way of such other benefit as may be prescribed (being benefit in connection with any hostilities or with service as a member of Her Majesty's forces or of such other organisation as may be specified in the regulations).

AMENDMENT

1. Welfare Reform and Pensions Act 1999 Sch.13(IV) para.1 (April 6, 2001).

DERIVATION

SSA 1975 Sch.8. **1.567**

GENERAL NOTE

Regulation 11 of the Social Security (General Benefit) Regulations 1982 is treated (by s.2(2) of the SSCPA 1992) as having been made under this Schedule to further define the principles on which the extent of disablement is to be assessed. **1.568**

In the case of some prescribed diseases, special provision is made by the Prescribed Diseases Regulations and this Schedule and reg.11 of the General Benefit Regulations must be read as subject to that.

Paragraph 1

Sub-paras (a) and (c) make it plain that disablement is to be assessed by comparing the claimant with a person of the same age and sex whose physical and mental condition is normal *without* taking into account loss of earning power, additional expense or other circumstances peculiar to the claimant (e.g. the distance from home to public transport or other facilities) other than, of course, age, sex **1.569** and physical and mental condition. This cannot be too strongly emphasised. As Commissioner Fellner rightly noted in a deafness case, *CI/5092/2002*

> "It must not be forgotten that the comparison under Schedule 6 is simply with another person of the same age and sex, and that individual hobbies and preferences are not to be taken into account. Thus, this claimant's complaints of loss of pleasure in particular kinds of music and in birdsong, and having to have the TV volume high, are relevant only in so far as other men of his age might be able to have, or not to be burdened with, these things. His being a radio ham, as he told the tribunal, would not be relevant" (para.17).

The one exception is allowed by sub-para.(b) which permits the taking into account of disabilities which are due not only to the relevant accident or disease but also to another cause (see reg.11(2)–(4) of the General Benefit Regulations).

Sub-para.(d) enables regulations to prescribe disabilities amounting to 100 per cent. Other disabilities must be assessed accordingly (see reg.11(7) of, and Sch.2 to, the General Benefit Regulations). In *R(I) 30/61*, it was made clear that "a man entitled to an assessment of 100 per cent is not necessarily totally disabled, and that any scale of values which a member of an assessing body has in the back of his mind should take account of that fact".

While there are certain prescribed degrees of disablement in respect of certain injuries in Sch.2 to the General Benefit Regulations (e.g. loss of the sight in one eye [30 per cent]), these can be departed from, whether by way of increase or decrease, as may be reasonable in the case if that prescribed degree of disablement does not provide a reasonable assessment of the extent of disablement resulting from the relevant loss of faculty (reg.11(6) of the General Benefit Regulations).

Coming to a decision, within those parameters, on the appropriate percentage assessment of disablement flowing from the relevant loss of faculty is a difficult matter of judgment, the matter of guidance on which has been considered in many Commissioners' decisions (e.g. *CI/499/2000, CI/1802/2001, CI/2553/2001, CI/3758 and 3759/2003*). It has most recently been considered by a Tribunal of Commissioners in *R(I) 2/06*. In most respects, since it found no relevant error of law in the approach and decision of the tribunals appealed from, the comments are ultimately *obiter*.

1.570 That Tribunal of Commissioners, dealt specifically with two appeal tribunal decisions awarding 7 per cent and 4 per cent respectively in respect of claimants suffering from PD A11 (Vibration White Finger) as a result of their work with percussive tools as coal miners. While making it clear that it was not possible to produce a template for assessment decisions, the Tribunal hoped that its comments would assist advisers, decision-makers, and tribunals by identifying the correct approach to such decisions and indicating matters which should be taken into account, matters which should not be taken into account, and matters which need not be taken into account (para.78). The scheme leaves considerable discretion to decision-makers and tribunals. (*ibid.*). Commissioners and courts can only interfere if the decision appealed exhibits an error of law (on which see: paras 28-31, citing *R(A)1/72* and *R. (Iran)* v *Secretary of State for the Home Department* [2005] EWCA Civ 982, paras 9–10 per Brooke L.J.; and Vol III of this series). The Tribunal of Commissioners rightly stressed that the matter of assessment of the percentage of functional disablement in any given case is essentially a factual and medical assessment for the tribunal hearing and seeing the evidence in the case to make. A disputed judgement of degree on a question of fact is not an error of law in the sense set out in those cases. It is not for an appellate body whose jurisdiction is limited to points of law to offer or impose its substituted view (para.31). That said, however,

> "Commissioners have always regarded it as part of their function to give guidance where needed for the assistance of tribunals and departmental decision makers on the relevant principles of law to be applied in this specialised jurisdiction: this is an area where certainty and consistency of approach and an orderly

development of the law are of particular importance given the complex nature of the legislation and the very large number of individual cases potentially involved. However it is a function to be exercised cautiously, particularly in an instance such as the present where the questions of assessment of an individual's percentage level of functional disablement are not primarily matters of legal interpretation at all, but of factual judgment – including judgment on medical matters – entrusted by the legislation to the specialist tribunals best qualified to decide them. There is a danger in misinterpreting the observations of individual Commissioners on the facts of such cases as laying down additional rules of law where only helpful guidance on the fact-finding process was intended. There was some evidence of that in the way the notices of appeal before us were formulated. What matters is not whether express reference is made to some such guidance, but whether the substance of the tribunal's decision, and its statement of the factors taken into account in reaching it, demonstrates any error of law" (para. 68).

Following *R(I) 2/06(T)*, Judge Wikeley held in *AJ v SSWP (II)* [2012] UKUT 209 (AAC) that the simple fact that the claimant's own doctors disagreed with the first-tier tribunal's assessment of disablement did not mean that the tribunal had erred in law (paras 17–19).

One species of error of law, of course, is a failure of an appeal tribunal to give adequate reasons for its decision. Thus in *CI/499/2000*, Commissioner Jacobs held erroneous in law a tribunal assessment of disablement because it focused purely on impaired manual dexterity resulting from the claimant's laceration to his finger. It should also have considered any mental effect, the effect of pain preventing or hindering the performance of an activity, and disfigurement (a scar had been left). The Tribunal should have made clear why it did not believe the claimant to be as disabled as he claimed. Nor had it properly explained its assessment of 8 per cent. Such explanation is required and an assessment could be explained in several ways. A Tribunal could give a general indication of why it made an assessment at a particular level (e.g. the effects were intermittent). It might properly explain its assessment by reference to the prescribed degrees of disablement in Sch.2 to the General Benefit Regulations. It might explain the significance of its clinical findings in terms of function (e.g. findings on the movement of joints might be explained in terms of how much useful grip was retained by the claimant). On this matter of giving adequate reasons, the Tribunal of Commissioners expressly approved, in para.45 of its decision, Deputy Commissioner Warren's statements in *CI/1802/2001* on what was required of tribunals assessing the degree of disablement. The Deputy Commissioner there stated: **1.571**

"7. Vibration white finger is not one of those conditions for which there is a prescribed degree of disablement in Schedule 2 of the General Benefit Regulations. Those Regulations therefore state only that the tribunal 'may have such regard as may be appropriate to the prescribed degrees of disablement' when making its assessment. This indicates the very broad discretion which individual tribunals have in this type of case. In many cases it is simply not possible for a tribunal to give precise reasons for the conclusion which it has reached.

8. In my judgment, however, as a minimum, the claimant and the Secretary of State are entitled to know the factual basis upon which the assessment has been made; in other words what disabilities were taken into account by the tribunal in concluding that a particular percentage disablement was appropriate.

9. This can often be simply expressed. In many cases it will be enough to say that the evidence given by the claimant about the effect of a particular accident or disease on his or her daily life has been accepted. In some cases, where the claimant's evidence is for some reason found to be unreliable, it may be that

the tribunal will state that it felt able to accept only those disabilities which in its expert opinion were likely to flow from problems disclosed on clinical examination. Other cases may need more detail. But if it is not possible to discern the material on which the assessment is based, then the tribunal's statement of reasons is likely to be inadequate."

1.572 Commissioners had, of course, proffered guidance for tribunals approaching the task of assessment of the degree of disablement. Both Deputy Commissioner Warren and Commissioner Jacobs in their decisions referred with caveats to the role of Sch.2 of the General Benefit Regulations (and see also approval of such cross-referral in *R(I) 5/95*). The Tribunal of Commissioners had taken on board at their oral hearing a debate on whether the degrees of disablement there prescribed for hand and finger conditions could offer assistance to tribunals dealing with disablement from vibration white finger (VWF). It considered that the assistance to be derived from them to be "relatively small" (para.72). The Schedule might well inform to an extent an appropriate percentage for a particular VWF case but was of "very limited value in assessing percentages for such conditions" (para.73).

In three decisions (*CI/2553/2001, CI/3758 and 3759/2003*), Commissioner Williams had drawn the attention of tribunals to judicial guidelines on assessing damages in civil personal injury claims in tort, but had stressed the need to approach this with caution. As the Tribunal of Commissioners saw it, Commissioner Williams has stressed that he drew nothing from the bands of damages set out in those guidelines. Rather, as the Tribunal of Commissioners put it, he "merely directed the tribunal to take into account certain specific criteria referred to in those guidelines, namely the length and severity of the claimant's attacks and symptoms, the extent and/or severity and/or rapidity of deterioration of his condition, and his age and prognosis" (para.57). To that degree, the guidelines may provide a useful list of entirely unexceptional matters for a tribunal to take into account in its assessment of functional disablement (*ibid.*). Those guidelines were drawn up for an entirely different purpose (see Diplock L.J., as he then was, in *R. v Medical Appeal Tribunal Ex p Cable* reported as an Appendix to *R(I) 11/66*, quoted in full in para.75 of the Tribunal of Commissioners' decision). His caution there against cross-referencing across schemes would extend to proposed comparison with any other system, such as the Criminal Injuries Compensation Scheme (para.75).

Both Commissioner Jacobs in *CI/499/2000* and Commissioner Williams in *CI/2553/2001* offered guidance on the proper role of Departmental guidance such as the MAF (Medical Assessment Framework) used by examining doctors for disablement benefit and severe disablement allowance. Both had counseled extreme caution in referring to this "rough guide". The Tribunal of Commissioners made no specific comment on the MAF other than noting with approval that Dr Reed, the doctor giving evidence on behalf of the Secretary of State, had stressed the emphasis given to all medical staff that nothing in MAF (the current version of which needed review) was to fetter their own individual judgment on a particular case (para.77). The Tribunal of Commissioners confirmed that it was no part of a tribunal's function to apply, or even necessarily to take into account, such internal guidance which, while properly aiming at clarity and consistency of approach, sets out merely the view of one of the parties to an appeal (the Government) on what was required by the law and by good practice. Such guidance was in no way binding on tribunals. A tribunal wanting to take such guidance into account had to bear all those caveats and cautions in mind (*ibid.*).

Paragraph 2

1.573 Regulation 11 of the General Benefit Regulations is made under this paragraph. There is no specific provision for compensating for the loss of the "dominant hand" but, even in a case where the injury is one specified in Sch.2 to the Regulations, reg.11(6) permits "such increase or reduction in [the prescribed] degree of disablement as may be reasonable in the circumstances in the case".

Paragraph 6

This looks back as well as forward: the period of assessment is to be that during which the claimant has suffered and may be expected to continue to suffer from the relevant loss of faculty resulting in disablement of at least one per cent. 1.574

As regards looking back, where a prescribed disease was only prescribed after the claimant had begun (due to his work) to suffer from it, however, it is not necessary to specify more particularly the period other than to say that it began at a date before prescription and then to assess the degree of disablement from the date of prescription. In *JR v SSWP (II)* [2011] UKUT 450 (AAC), Judge Ward, drawing on observations (albeit not made following argument on the point) of an experienced Commissioner in *CI/3521/1999*, preferred this construction of the legislation because a claimant cannot have any right to disablement benefit or REA before the date of prescription (see especially paras 33–35).

As regards looking to the future, if the prognosis is uncertain and the assessment is at least 14 per cent a provisional assessment should be made so that the extent of the claimant's disability is reassessed at the end of the period of the provisional assessment. A final assessment which is for a definite period rather than "life" implies *either* that the claimant will be suffering from no loss of faculty *or* the resulting disablement will be less than 1 per cent from the end of the period of assessment *or* that any disablement from which the claimant may be expected to be suffering at the end of the period of assessment would have been present even if the relevant accident had not occurred. If the claimant is still disabled at the end of the period, he or she may apply for revision under s.9 of the SSA 1998. There is no reason why the claimant's disablement should not be assessed at different percentages for different parts of the period; nor why those parts should be lengthy. In *R(I) 30/61*, the medical appeal tribunal assessed disablement from January 11 to March 25, 1960, at 30 per cent; March 26 to June 24, 1960, at 100 per cent; June 25 to July 24, 1960, at 40 per cent; and from June 25, 1960 to January 24, 1961, at 30 per cent. That was a provisional assessment and reflected the fact that the claimant had been in hospital from March to June and was then recuperating. Although an appeal was allowed on the ground of inadequate reasons, the tribunal's general approach was not criticised and the Commissioner said,

> "the disabilities resulting from the relevant loss of faculty must be related to the period covered by the assessment, and . . . the assessing body must not be misled by the fact that a very serious disability is expected not to last long. The answer to that situation is a high assessment for a short period."

Since disablement benefit is calculated on a weekly basis, it might be slightly more convenient for decision-makers if short periods were calculated in weeks rather than months if the evidence permits it.

Sub-paras (3)–(5) normally prevent a provisional assessment if the assessment, at least for the last part of the period, is less than 14 per cent. If the extent of the claimant's disablement resulting from the relevant loss of faculty is likely to become less over time, the adjudicating medical authority is then bound to determine a date from which the claimant's extent of disablement may be expected to be less than 1 per cent. If the extent of disablement is expected to become greater but the adjudicating medical authority cannot tell when and so is unable to include an assessment of at least 14 per cent within the period of assessment, a life assessment should be made and the burden rests upon the claimant to make an application for revision under s.9 of the SSA 1998 when the extent of disablement does become at least 14 per cent. An exception is made by sub-para.(4) if the assessment of the extent of disablement may be aggregated with another assessment and the aggregate may amount to 14 per cent or more. In such a case, a provisional assessment may be made if the prognosis is uncertain. 1.575

Regulation 20(3) of the Prescribed Diseases Regulations provides that the minimum period of assessment in a case of byssinosis shall be one year. Reg.29 provides that the initial assessment in a case of occupational deafness shall always be provisional and for a period of five years and that all subsequent assessments shall be for a period of at least five years.

Paragraph 6

1.576 Where a claim is made in respect of diffuse mesothelioma, see reg.20(4) of the Prescribed Diseases Regulations.

Paragraph 7

1.577 An assessment shall not specify the percentage or period more particularly than is necessary for the purpose of determining entitlement to industrial injuries benefits. This means that, where the assessment is under 14 per cent but not under 1 per cent, it is not necessary for the adjudicating medical authority to go into greater detail unless either the assessment may be aggregated with another and the aggregate might be more than 14 per cent or else the claimant is suffering from pneumoconiosis, byssinosis or diffuse mesothelioma in which case it matters whether the assessment is greater than 10 per cent or not for the purpose of determining the amount of disablement benefit payable (reg.20 of the Prescribed Diseases Regulations).

Paragraph 8

1.578 See reg.20 of the General Benefit Regulations.

SCHEDULE 7

Industrial Injuries Benefits

Part I

Unemployability Supplement

Availability

1.579 **1.**—This Part of this Schedule applies only in relation to persons who were beneficiaries in receipt of unemployability supplement under section 58 of the 1975 Act immediately before 6th April 1987.

Rate and duration

1.580 **2.**—(1) The weekly rate of a disablement pension shall, if as the result of the relevant loss of faculty the beneficiary is incapable of work and likely to remain so permanently, be increased by the amount specified in Schedule 4, Part V, paragraph 5.

(2) An increase of pension under this paragraph is referred to in this Act as an "unemployability supplement".

(3) For the purposes of this paragraph a person may be treated as being incapable of work and likely to remain so permanently, notwithstanding that the loss of faculty is not such as to prevent him being capable of work, if it is likely to prevent his earnings in a year exceeding a prescribed amount not less than £104.

(4) An unemployability supplement shall be payable for such period as may be determined at the time it is granted, but may be renewed from time to time.

Increase of unemployability supplement

1.581 **3.**—(1) Subject to the following provisions of this paragraph, if on the qualifying date the beneficiary was—

(a) a man under the age of 60, or
(b) a woman under the age of 55,

the weekly rate of unemployability supplement shall be increased by the appropriate amount specified in Schedule 4, Part V, paragraph 6.

(2) Where for any period the beneficiary is entitled to a Category A or Category B retirement pension [1 . . .] and the weekly rate of the pension includes an additional pension such as is mentioned in section 44(3)(b) above, for that period the relevant amount shall be deducted from the amount that would otherwise be the increase under this paragraph and the beneficiary shall be entitled to an increase only if there is a balance after that deduction and, if there is such a balance, only to an amount equal to it.

(3) In this paragraph "the relevant amount" means an amount equal to the additional pension reduced by the amount of any reduction in the weekly rate of the retirement pension [1 . . .] made by virtue of [2 section 46] [10 or 46A] of the Pensions Act.

[12 (3A) In sub-paragraphs (2) and (3) above references to additional pension do not include any amount of additional pension attributable to units of additional pension.

(3B) For units of additional pension, see section 14A.]

(4) In this paragraph references to an additional pension are references to that pension after any increase under section 52(3) above but without any increase under paragraphs 1 and 2 of Schedule 5 to this Act.

(5) In this paragraph "the qualifying date" means, subject to sub-paragraphs (6) and (7) below, the beginning of the first week for which the beneficiary qualified for unemployability supplement.

(6) If the incapacity for work in respect of which unemployability supplement is payable forms part of a period of interruption of employment which has continued from a date earlier than the date fixed under sub-paragraph (5) above, the qualifying date means the first day in that period which is a day of incapacity for work, or such earlier day as may be prescribed.

(7) Subject to sub-paragraph (6) above, if there have been two or more periods for which the beneficiary was entitled to unemployability supplement, the qualifying date shall be, in relation to unemployability supplement for a day in any one of those periods, the beginning of the first week of that period.

(8) for the purposes of sub-paragraph (7) above—

(a) a break of more than 8 weeks in entitlement to unemployability supplement means that the periods before and after the break are two different periods; and

(b) a break of 8 weeks or less is to be disregarded.

(9) The Secretary of State may by regulations provide that sub-paragraph (8) above shall have effect as if for the references to 8 weeks there were substituted references to a larger number of weeks specified in the regulations.

(10) In this paragraph "period of interruption of employment" has the same meaning as [3 a jobseeking period and any period linked to such a period has for the purposes of the Jobseekers Act 1995].

(11) The provisions of this paragraph are subject to [2 section 46(6) and (7) (entitlement to guaranteed minimum pensions and increases of unemployability supplement).]

Increase for beneficiary's dependent children [8 and qualifying young persons]

4.—(1) Subject to the provisions of this paragraph and paragraph 5 below, the weekly rate of a disablement pension where the beneficiary is entitled to an unemployability supplement shall be increased for any period during which the beneficiary is entitled to child benefit in respect of [8 one or more children or qualifying young persons]. **1.582**

(2) The amount of the increase shall be as specified in Schedule 4, Part V, paragraph 7.

(3) In any case where—

[7 (a) a beneficiary is one of two persons who are --

(i) spouses or civil partners residing together, [11 or]]

[11 (ii) two people who are not married to, or civil partners of, each other but are living together [13 as if they were a married couple or civil partners], and]

(b) the other person had earnings in any week,

the beneficiary's right to payment of increases for the following week under this paragraph shall be determined in accordance with sub-paragraph (4) below.

(4) No such increase shall be payable—

(a) in respect of the first child [8 or qualifying young person] where the earnings were [9 £215] or more; and

(b) in respect of a further child [8 or qualifying young person] for each complete [4 £28] by which the earnings exceeded [9 £215].

(5) The Secretary of State may by order substitute larger amounts for the amounts for the time being specified in sub-paragraph (4) above.

(6) In this paragraph "week" means such period of 7 days as may be prescribed by regulations made for the purposes of this paragraph.

Additional provisions as to increase under paragraph 4

1.583 5.—(1) An increase under paragraph 4 above of any amount in respect of a particular child [8 or qualifying young person] shall for any period be payable only if during that period one or other of the following conditions is satisfied with respect to the child [8 or qualifying young person]

(a) the beneficiary would be treated for the purposes of Part IX of this Act as having the child [8 or qualifying young person] living with him; or
(b) the requisite contributions are being made to the cost of providing for the child [8 or qualifying young person].

(2) The condition specified in paragraph (b) of sub-paragraph (1) above is to be treated as satisfied if, and only if—

(a) such contributions are being made at a weekly rate not less than the amount referred to in that sub-paragraph—
  (i) by the beneficiary, or
  (ii) where the beneficiary is one of two spouses [7 or civil partners] residing together, by them together; and
(b) except in prescribed cases, the contributions are over and above those required for the purposes of satisfying section 143(1)(b) above.

Increase for adult dependants

1.584 6.—(1) The weekly rate of a disablement pension where the beneficiary is entitled to an unemployability supplement shall be increased under this paragraph for any period during which—

(a) the beneficiary is—
  (i) residing with his spouse [7 or civil partner], or
  (ii) contributing to the maintenance of his spouse [7 or civil partner] at the requisite rate; or
(b) a person—
  (i) who is neither the spouse [7 or civil partner] of the beneficiary nor a child [8 or qualifying young person], and
  (ii) in relation to whom such further conditions as may be prescribed are fulfilled,

has the care of [8 one or more children or qualifying young persons] in respect of whom the beneficiary is entitled to child benefit.

(2) The amount of the increase under this paragraph shall be that specified in Schedule 4, Part V, paragraph 8 and the requisite rate for the purposes of sub-paragraph (1)(a) above is a weekly rate not less than that amount.

(3) Regulations may provide that, for any period during which—

(a) the beneficiary is contributing to the maintenance of his or her spouse [7 or civil partner] at the requisite rate, and
(b) the weekly earnings of the spouse [7 or civil partner] exceed such amount as may be prescribed

there shall be no increase of benefit under this paragraph.

(4) Regulations may provide that, for any period during which the beneficiary is residing with his or her spouse [7 or civil partner] and the spouse [7 or civil partner] has earnings—

(a) the increase of benefit under this paragraph shall be subject to a reduction in respect of the spouse's [7 or civil partner's] earnings; or
(b) there shall be no increase of benefit under this paragraph.

(5) Regulations may, in a case within sub-paragraph (1)(b) above in which the person there referred to is residing with the beneficiary and fulfils such further conditions as may be prescribed, authorise an increase of benefit under this paragraph, but subject, taking account of the earnings of the person residing with the beneficiary, other than such of that person's earnings from employment by the beneficiary as may be prescribed, to provisions comparable to those that may be made by virtue of sub-paragraph (4) above.

(6) Regulations under this paragraph may, in connection with any reduction or extinguishment of an increase in benefit in respect of earnings, prescribe the method of calculating or estimating the earnings.

(7) A beneficiary shall not be entitled to an increase of benefit under this paragraph in respect of more than one person for the same period.

Earnings to include occupational and personal pensions for purposes of disablement pension

7.—(1) Except as may be prescribed, any reference to earnings in paragraph 4 or 6 above includes a reference to payments by way of occupational or personal pension. 1.585

(2) For the purposes of those paragraphs, the Secretary of State may by regulations provide, in relation to cases where payments by way of occupational or personal pension are made otherwise than weekly, that any necessary apportionment of the payments shall be made in such manner and on such basis as may be prescribed.

Dependency increases: continuation of awards in cases of fluctuating earnings

8.—(1) Where a beneficiary— 1.586

(a) has been awarded an increase of benefit under paragraph 4 or 6 above, but
(b) ceases to be entitled to the increase by reason only that the weekly earnings of some other person ("the relevant earner") exceed the amount of the increase or, as the case may be, some specified amount,

then, if and so long as the beneficiary would have continued to be entitled to the increase, disregarding any such excess of earnings, the award shall continue in force but the increase shall not be payable for any week if the earnings relevant to that week exceed the amount of the increase or, as the case may be, the specified amount.

(2) In this paragraph the earnings which are relevant to any week are those earnings of the relevant earner which, apart from this paragraph, would be taken into account in determining whether the beneficiary is entitled to the increase in question for that week.

Part II

Disablement Gratuity

9.—(1) An employed earner shall be entitled to a disablement gratuity, if— 1.587

(a) he made a claim for disablement benefit before 1st October, 1986;
(b) he suffered as the result of the relevant accident from loss of physical or mental faculty such that the extent of the resulting disablement assessed in accordance with Schedule 6 to this Act amounts to not less than 1 per cent.; and
(c) the extent of the disablement is assessed for the period taken into account as amounting to less than 20 per cent.

(2) A disablement gratuity shall be—

(a) of an amount fixed, in accordance with the length of the period and the degree of the disablement, by a prescribed scale, but not in any case exceeding the amount specified in Schedule 4, Part V, paragraph 9; and
(b) payable, if and in such cases as regulations so provide, by instalments.

(3) A person shall not be entitled to disablement gratuity until after the expiry of the period of 90 days (disregarding Sundays) beginning with the day of the relevant accident.

Part III

Increase of Disablement Pension During Hospital Treatment

10.—(1) This Part of this Schedule has effect in relation to a period during which a person is receiving medical treatment as an in-patient in a hospital or similar institution and which— 1.588

(a) commenced before 6th April 1987; or
(b) commenced after that date but within a period of 28 days from the end of the period during which he last received an increase of benefit under section 62 of the 1975 Act or this paragraph in respect of such treatment for the relevant injury or loss of faculty.

(2) Where a person is awarded disablement benefit, but the extent of his disablement is assessed for the period taken into account by the assessment at less than 100 per cent., it shall be treated as assessed at 100 per cent. for any part of that period, whether before or after the making of the assessment or the award of benefit, during which he receives, as an in-patient in a hospital or similar institution, medical treatment for the relevant injury or loss of faculty.

(3) Where the extent of the disablement is assessed for that period at less than 20 per cent., sub-paragraph (2) above shall not affect the assessment; but in the case of a disablement pension payable by virtue of this paragraph to a person awarded a disablement gratuity wholly or partly in respect of the same period, the weekly rate of the pension (after allowing for any increase under Part V of this Act) shall be reduced by the amount prescribed as being the weekly value of his gratuity.

PART IV

REDUCED EARNINGS ALLOWANCE

1.589 **11.**—(1) Subject to the provisions of this paragraph, an employed earner shall be entitled to reduced earnings allowance if—

(a) he is entitled to a disablement pension or would be so entitled if that pension were payable where disablement is assessed at not less than 1 per cent.; and

(b) as a result of the relevant loss of faculty, he is either—

(i) incapable, and likely to remain permanently incapable, of following his regular occupation; and

(ii) incapable of following employment of an equivalent standard which is suitable in his case,

or is, and has at all times since the end of the period of 90 days referred to in section 103(6) above been, incapable of following that occupation or any such employment;

but a person shall not be entitled to reduced earnings allowance to the extent that the relevant loss of faculty results from an accident happening on or after 1st October 1990 (the day on which section 3 of the Social Security Act 1990 came into force) [5 and a person shall not be entitled to reduced earnings allowance—

(i) in relation to a disease prescribed on or after 10th October 1994 under section 108(2) above; or

(ii) in relation to a disease prescribed before 10th October 1994 whose prescription is extended on or after that date under section 108(2) above but only in so far as the prescription has been so extended].

(2) A person—

(a) who immediately before that date is entitled to reduced earnings allowance in consequence of the relevant accident; but

(b) who subsequently ceases to be entitled to that allowance for one or more days,

shall not again be entitled to reduced earnings allowance in consequence of that accident; but this sub-paragraph does not prevent the making at any time of a claim for, or an award of, reduced earnings allowance in consequence of that accident for a period which commences not later than the day after that on which the claimant was last entitled to that allowance in consequence of that accident.

(3) For the purposes of sub-paragraph (2) above—

(a) a person who, apart from section 103(6) above, would have been entitled to reduced earnings allowance immediately before 1st October 1990 shall be treated as entitled to that allowance on any day (including a Sunday) on which he would have been entitled to it apart from that provision;

(b) regulations may prescribe other circumstances in which a person is to be treated as entitled, or as having been entitled, to reduced earnings allowance on any prescribed day.

(4) The Secretary of State may by regulations provide that in prescribed circumstances employed earner's employment in which a claimant was engaged when the relevant accident took place but which was not his regular occupation is to be treated as if it had been his regular occupation.

(5) In sub-paragraph (1) above—

(a) references to a person's regular occupation are to be taken as not including any subsidiary occupation, except to the extent that they fall to be treated as including such an occupation by virtue of regulations under sub-paragraph (4) above; and

(b) employment of an equivalent standard is to be taken as not including employment other than employed earner's employment;

and in assessing the standard of remuneration in any employment, including a person's regular occupation, regard is to be had to his reasonable prospect of advancement.

(6) For the purposes of this Part of this Schedule a person's regular occupation is to be treated as extending to and including employment in the capacities to which the persons in that occupation (or a class or description of them to which he belonged at the time of the relevant accident) are in the normal course advanced, and to which, if he had continued to follow that occupation without having suffered the relevant loss of faculty, he would have had at least the normal prospects of advancement; and so long as he is, as a result of the relevant loss of faculty, deprived in whole or in part of those prospects, he is to be treated as incapable of following that occupation.

(7) Regulations may for the purposes of this Part of this Schedule provide that a person is not to be treated as capable of following an occupation or employment merely because of his working thereat during a period of trial or for purposes of rehabilitation or training or in other prescribed circumstances.

(8) Reduced earnings allowance shall be awarded—

(a) for such period as may be determined at the time of the award; and

(b) if at the end of that period the beneficiary submits a fresh claim for the allowance, for such further period, commencing as mentioned in sub-paragraph (2) above, as may be determined.

(9) The award may not be for a period longer than the period to be taken into account under paragraph 4 or 6 of Schedule 6 to this Act.

(10) Reduced earnings allowance shall be payable at a rate determined by reference to the beneficiary's probable standard of remuneration during the period for which it is granted in any employed earner's employments which are suitable in his case and which he is likely to be capable of following as compared with that in the relevant occupation, but in no case at a rate higher than 40 per cent of the maximum rate of a disablement pension or at a rate such that the aggregate of disablement pension (not including increases in disablement pension under any provision of this Act) and reduced earnings allowance awarded to the beneficiary exceeds 140 per cent. of the maximum rate of a disablement pension.

(11) Sub-paragraph (10) above shall have effect in the case of a person who retired from regular employment before 6th April 1987 with the substitution for "140 per cent." of "100 per cent.".

(12) In sub-paragraph (10) above "the relevant occupation" means—

(a) in relation to a person who is entitled to reduced earnings allowance by virtue of regulations under sub-paragraph (4) above, the occupation in which he was engaged when the relevant accident took place; and

(b) in relation to any other person who is entitled to reduced earnings allowance, his regular occupation within the meaning of sub-paragraph (1) above.

[[6] (12A) The reference in sub-paragraph (11) above to a person who has retired from regular employment includes a reference—

(a) to a person who under subsection (3) of section 27 of the 1975 Act was treated for the purposes of that Act as having retired from regular employment; and

(b) to a person who under subsection (5) of that section was deemed for those purposes to have retired from it.]

(13) On any award except the first the probable standard of his remuneration shall be determined in such manner as may be prescribed; and, without prejudice to the generality of this sub-paragraph, regulations may provide in prescribed circumstances for the probable standard of remuneration to be determined by reference—

(a) to the standard determined at the time of the last previous award of reduced earnings allowance; and

(b) to scales or indices of earnings in a particular industry or description of industries or any other data relating to such earnings.

(14) In this paragraph "maximum rate of a disablement pension" means the rate specified in the first entry in column (2) of Schedule 4, Part V, paragraph 1 and does not include increases in disablement pension under any provision of this Act.

Supplementary

12.—(1) A person who on 10th April 1988 or 9th April 1989 satisfies the conditions— **1.590**

(a) that he has attained pensionable age;

(b) that he has retired from regular employment; and

(c) that he is entitled to reduced earnings allowance,

shall be entitled to that allowance for life.

(2) In the case of any beneficiary who is entitled to reduced earnings allowance by virtue of sub-paragraph (1) above, the allowance shall be payable, subject to any enactment contained in Part V or VI of this Act or in the Administration Act and to any regulations made under any

such enactment, at the weekly rate at which it was payable to the beneficiary on the relevant date or would have been payable to him on that date but for any such enactment or regulations.

(3) For the purpose of determining under sub-paragraph (2) above the weekly rate of reduced earnings allowance payable in the case of a qualifying beneficiary, it shall be assumed that the weekly rate at which the allowance was payable to him on the relevant date was—

(a) £25.84, where that date is 10th April 1988, or
(b) £26.96, where that date is 9th April 1989.

(4) In sub-paragraph (3) above "qualifying beneficiary" means a person entitled to reduced earnings allowance by virtue of sub-paragraph (1) above who—

(a) did not attain pensionable age before 6th April 1987, or
(b) did not retire from regular employment before that date,

and who, on the relevant date, was entitled to the allowance at a rate which was restricted under paragraph 11(10) above by reference to 40 per cent. of the maximum rate of disablement pension.

(5) For a beneficiary who is entitled to reduced earnings allowance by virtue of satisfying the conditions in sub-paragraph (1) above on 10th April 1988 the relevant date is that date.

(6) For a beneficiary who is entitled to it by virtue only of satisfying those conditions on 9th April 1989 the relevant date is that date.

[[6] (7) The reference in sub-paragraph (1) above to a person who has retired from regular employment includes a reference—

(a) to a person who under subsection (3) of section 27 of the 1975 Act was treated for the purposes of that Act as having retired from regular employment; and
(b) to a person who under subsection (5) of that section was deemed for those purposes to have retired from it.]

Part V

Retirement Allowance

1.591 **13.**—(1) Subject to the provisions of this Part of this Schedule, a person who—

(a) has attained pensionable age; and
(b) gives up regular employment on or after 10th April 1989; and
(c) was entitled to reduced earnings allowance (by virtue either of one award or of a number of awards) on the day immediately before he gave up such employment,

shall cease to be entitled to reduced earnings allowance as from the day on which he gives up regular employment.

(2) If the day before a person ceases under sub-paragraph (1) above to be entitled to reduced earnings allowance he is entitled to the allowance (by virtue either of one award or of a number of awards) at a weekly rate or aggregate weekly rate of not less than £2.00, he shall be entitled to a benefit, to be known as "retirement allowance".

(3) Retirement allowance shall be payable to him (subject to any enactment contained in Part V or VI of this Act or in the Administration Act and to any regulations made under any such enactment) for life.

(4) Subject to sub-paragraph (6) below, the weekly rate of a beneficiary's retirement allowance shall be—

(a) 25 per cent of the weekly rate at which he was last entitled to reduced earnings allowance; or
(b) 10 per cent of the maximum rate of a disablement pension, whichever is the less.

(5) For the purpose of determining under sub-paragraph (4) above the weekly rate of retirement allowance in the case of a beneficiary who—

(a) retires or is deemed to have retired on 10th April 1989, and
(b) on 9th April 1989 was entitled to reduced earnings allowance at a rate which was restricted under paragraph 11(10) above by reference to 40 per cent. of the maximum rate of disablement pension,

it shall be assumed that the weekly rate of reduced earnings allowance to which he was entitled on 9th April 1989 was £26.96.

(6) If the weekly rate of the beneficiary's retirement allowance—

(a) would not be a whole number of pence; and
(b) would exceed the whole number of pence next below it by ½p or more,

the beneficiary shall be entitled to retirement allowance at a rate equal to the next higher whole number of pence.

(7) The sums falling to be calculated under sub-paragraph (4) above are subject to alteration by orders made by the Secretary of State under section 150 of the Administration Act.

(8) Regulations may—

(a) make provision with respect to the meaning of "regular employment" for the purposes of this paragraph; and

(b) prescribe circumstances in which, and periods for which, a person is or is not to be regarded for those purposes as having given up such employment.

(9) Regulations under sub-paragraph (8) above may, in particular—

(a) provide for a person to be regarded—

(i) as having given up regular employment, notwithstanding that he is or intends to be an earner; or

(ii) as not having given up regular employment, notwithstanding that he has or may have one or more days of interruption of employment; and

(b) prescribe circumstances in which a person is or is not to be regarded as having given up regular employment by reference to—

(i) the level or frequency of his earnings during a prescribed period; or

(ii) the number of hours for which he works during a prescribed period calculated in a prescribed manner.

[[3] (10) "Day of interruption of employment" means a day which forms part of—

(a) a jobseeking period (as defined by the Jobseekers Act 1995), or

(b) a linked period (as defined by that Act).]

(11) In this paragraph "maximum rate of a disablement pension" means the rate specified in the first entry in column (2) of Schedule 4, Part V, paragraph 1 and does not include increases in disablement pension under any provision of this Act.

GENERAL NOTE

The sums falling to be calculated under para.13(4) above are to be increased by 6.7 per cent with effect from April 8, 2024: see Social Security Benefits Up-rating Order 2024 (SI 2024/242) art.4(1). 1.592

PART VI

INDUSTRIAL DEATH BENEFIT

Introductory

Paras 14.–21. *Omitted. With effect from December 5, 2012, s.67 of the Welfare Reform Act 2012 amended para.14 so that no claim for industrial death benefit can be made on or after that date. Since claims had already been restricted to deaths occurring before April 10, 1988 it is unlikely that any new claims will be forthcoming (none have been made for many years), but any that do will instead be dealt with under the bereavement benefit legislation.* 1.593

AMENDMENTS

1. Social Security (Incapacity for Work) Act 1994 Sch.1 para.41 (April 13, 1995).
2. Pensions Schemes Act 1993 Sch.8 para.43 (February 7, 1994).
3. Jobseekers Act 1995 Sch.2 para.36 (October 14, 1994).
4. Social Security (Industrial Injuries) (Dependency) (Permitted Earnings Limits) Order 2012 (SI 2012/823) art.2 (April 11, 2012).
5. Social Security (Industrial Injuries) (Prescribed Diseases) Regulations 1985 reg.14A (October 10, 1994).
6. Social Security (Consequential Provisions) Act 1992 Sch.4 paras.10 and 11 (transitorily).
7. Civil Partnership Act 2004 s.254 and Sch.24 Pt 3, para.52 (December 5, 2005).
8. Child Benefit Act 2005 ss.1 and 2, Sch.1 para.16 (April 10, 2006).
9. Social Security (Industrial Injuries) (Dependency) (Permitted Earnings Limits) Order 2012 (SI 2012/823) art.2 (April 11, 2012).
10. Pensions Act 2008 Sch.4 para.13 (January 3, 2012).

11. Marriage (Same Sex Couples) Act 2013 (Consequential and Contrary Provisions and Scotland) Order 2014 art.2, Sch.1 para.22 (March 13, 2014). (England and Wales only) and Marriage and Civil Partnership (Scotland) Act 2014 and Civil Partnership Act 2004 (Consequential Provisions and Modifications) Order 2014 (SI 2014/3229) art.5(3) Sch.4 para.2(1) and (20) (December 16, 2014) (Scotland only).

12. Pensions Act 2014 (Consequential Amendments) (Units of Additional Pension) Order 2014 (SI 2016/3213) art.3 (October 12, 2015).

13. Civil Partnership (Opposite-sex Couples) Regulations 2019 (SI 2019/1458) reg.41(a) and Sch.3, Pt 1, para.14(2)(e) (December 2, 2019).

Derivations

1.594 SSA 1975 ss.57–59B, 62, 64–64A and 84A; SS (No. 2)A, s.3(4); SSA 1986 s.39 and Sch.3; SSA 1988 s.2.

General Note

1.595 This Schedule preserves for certain claimants entitlement to industrial injuries benefits that have been abolished. Pt I preserves unemployability supplement, which was an increase of disablement pension for those incapable of work owing to an industrial accident or prescribed disease, but only for those who were entitled to it immediately before April 6, 1987. Pt II preserves disablement gratuities, which were lump sums paid instead of disablement pension for those whose disablement was assessed at between 1 per cent and 19 per cent. It applies where the claim was made before October 1, 1986 and still has relevance where there has been a series of provisional assessments since then. Pt III preserves hospital treatment allowance for those who have been more or less continuously entitled to it since April 6, 1987. Parts IV and V preserve reduced earnings allowance and retirement allowance for those whose earning capacity has been reduced by an industrial accident occurring before, or an industrial disease the onset of which was before, October 1, 1990 (see *CI/3178/2003*).

No entitlement to REA (and therefore also retirement allowance) can arise in respect of a disease prescribed on or after October 10, 1994, nor in respect of the extension aspect of a disease prescribed prior to that date, but extended on or after October 10, 1994. Those who were entitled to reduced earnings allowance before April 10, 1989 and had retired before that date, remain entitled to the allowance for life at a frozen rate. Otherwise, people who have reached pensionable age are no longer entitled to reduced earnings allowance and become entitled to retirement allowance instead, unless they remain in regular employment for at least 10 hours a week (see the Social Security (Industrial Injuries) (Regular Employment) Regulations 1990 (SI 1990/256) as amended and *R(I) 2/99* in which the tortuous history of this legislation is examined).

As Commissioner Howell put it in *CI/5138/2002*,

> "a person must *either* have a contract of service whose terms include the minimum 10-hour average requirement in (a), *or* be actually undertaking work, e.g. on his or her own account as a self-employed person or as a casual employee, which when one looks at the amount and duration of work actually done meets the alternative 10-hour average condition in (b). If there is any break, however short, in the continuity of meeting those conditions, then the person concerned is regarded for good as having given up regular employment from the start of the first week in which the conditions are no longer met, and can never thereafter regain the right to reduced earnings allowance" (para.7).

Whether activities carried on by the claimant amount to "gainful employment" is a matter of fact and degree for the tribunal seeing and hearing the evidence to determine (*ibid*, para.12). Pt VI, which is omitted, provides for industrial death benefit in relation to deaths before April 11, 1988.

Sch. Pt IV: Reduced Earnings Allowance

(1) Reduced Earnings Allowance: its creation and slow demise **1.596**

The precursor of this Part (SSA 1975 s.59A) was inserted by SSA 1986 Sch.3, para.5(1) with effect from October 1, 1986, and was further amended with effect from October 1, 1990, so as to provide for the gradual phasing out of the benefit, as is explained below.

Reduced Earnings Allowance (REA) replaced the misnamed Special Hardship Allowance and is a benefit in its own right, rather than a mere supplement to disablement benefit. The benefits remain linked and a claimant cannot be entitled to REA without making a claim to disablement benefit (*Whalley* v *Secretary of State for Work and Pensions* [2001] EWCA Civ 166, reported as *R(I) 2/03*, disapproving Commissioner Williams on this point in *CI 6207/1999*). The conditions of entitlement are, however, similar to those that applied to Special Hardship Allowance, so that decisions on the meaning of the same statutory phrases in the context of that allowance remain authoritative. REA can continue in payment after retirement, but only for those entitled to it at retirement, who retired on or before April 9, 1989. For those retiring after that date, and entitled to REA immediately before retirement, retirement allowance (see Pt V, below) is available as a replacement for REA during retirement, and is payable for life.

In *Chief Adjudication Officer v Maguire* (reported as *R(I) 3/99*), the Court of Appeal held that it is still possible to claim special hardship allowance which was the predecessor of reduced earnings allowance. However, the Secretary of State does not issue claim forms for special hardship allowance and so must be persuaded to accept some other document as a claim although it is arguable that the fact that he does not issue proper claim forms may limit the extent to which he can properly decide not to accept other documents as valid claims.

The October 1990 changes implemented the Government's policy of preventing arising new entitlements to reduced earnings allowance, while preserving existing entitlements until they otherwise cease, so that ensuing phased reductions in expenditure on this benefit (estimated £1m in 1990–91, £15m in 1991–82 and £40m in 1992–93—see *Hansard*, HC Vol.165, col.630, *per* the Secretary of State for Social Security) could be deployed to help finance a package of new benefits to improve the position of disabled people as a whole during the 1990s. It was considered that payment of reduced earnings allowance was in many cases unnecessarily duplicative, since many non-working recipients of it also received invalidity benefit.

Note that in general, references to the date of an accident are to be construed, in the case of prescribed diseases, as references to the date of onset of the disease (see ss.108 and 109, Prescribed Diseases Regs, regs.11 and 12; (*CI/3178/2003*).

The wording of para.11(1) ("but a person shall not be entitled . . . from an accident happening on or after the appointed day") prevents arising any new entitlement, or the enhancement through increased incapacity of an existing entitlement, in respect of a loss of faculty resulting from an accident which happens on or after October 1, 1990 (that being the date s.3 of the SSA 1990 came into force.) In *JR v Secretary of State for Work and Pensions (II)* [2013] UKUT 317 (AAC), Judge Mesher considered the effect of the October 1994 amendment to para.11(1):

> "and a person shall not be entitled to reduced earnings allowance—
>
> . . .
>
> (ii) in relation to a disease prescribed before 10th October 1994 whose prescription is extended on or after that date under section 108(2) above but only in so far as the prescription has been so extended]."

He held that since the

> "prescription process under section 108 can only be regarded as covering the definition of both diseases and occupational groups. [there was] nothing in the

> fact that the reference in paragraph 11(1) of Schedule 7 is to section 108(2) to suggest that extension of the prescription is limited to the definition of occupational groups covered. . . . the identification of those groups of employed earners for whom a disease ought to be treated as a risk of their occupation is directed just as much (if not more so in the light of paragraph (b)) at the identification and definition of the disease concerned as at the identification of the appropriate occupational groups" (para. 20)

1.597 A decision by a tribunal determining the date of onset for a PD, whether given in respect of disablement benefit or REA, as the case may be, binds a later tribunal considering the issue for either benefit. Where there was a refusal by a tribunal of a claim for disablement benefit on the ground that the claimant did not have PD A11 at the date of the decision, a later decision-maker, faced with a new claim for that benefit or for REA, cannot specify a date of onset for the disease which is prior to the refusal of the first claim. See also *CI/2531/2001*, para.15:

> "if a person makes a claim or successive claims for disablement benefit (and, by the same token, reduced earnings allowance, which depend on establishing the same loss of faculty) in respect of occupational deafness, the 'date of onset' can never be earlier than that of the *first* such claim which results in the actual payment of benefit; and the date so determined is also, by regulation 6(1), to be treated as the date of onset for the purposes of each subsequent claim" (*per* Commissioner Howell).

See further *CI/4249/2003*, another decision of Commissioner Howell. But note that two Commissioners take the view that *Whalley* is not wholly applicable in respect of decisions made under the DMA regime post SSA 1998. Commissioner Rowland in *R(I) 2/04* considered the remarks in *Whalley* to have been *obiter*. Moreover, the reasoning applied on the basis of the decision-making processes prior to the SSA 1998, so that the demise of the earlier provisions on finality of an MAT's decision, means that the binding nature of a decision on a date of onset of a PD for disablement benefit purposes flows from the terms of Prescribed Diseases Regs, reg.6(para.14), a view endorsed by Commissioner Howell in *R(I) 5/04* (paras 16–18). See further the commentary to that regulation, below.

As modified from October 10, 1994, para. 11(1) also precludes entitlement to REA in respect of a disease prescribed on or after that date, and prevents entitlement to the allowance in respect of the extension aspect of a disease prescribed prior to that date, but extended on or after October 10, 1994 (see reg.3 of the Social Security (Industrial Injuries) (Prescribed Diseases) Amendment Regulations 1994 (SI 1994/2343), inserting Social Security (Industrial Injuries) (Prescribed Diseases) Regulations 1985 (SI 1985/967), reg.14A).

Sub-paras (2) and (3) set out the circumstances in which entitlement to reduced earnings allowance is protected. In effect entitlement is here a wider than normal notion since the provisions protect both those who were beneficiaries immediately before October 1, 1990, and those whose accident or onset of a prescribed industrial disease occurred before that date and who would have been beneficiaries but for the fact that the 90-day waiting period set by s.103(6) had not expired. Moreover, regulations can extend the categories of persons entitled (sub-para.(3)(b)). A single day's gap in entitlement on or after October 1, 1990, brings the preserved entitlement to an end; to remain, preserved entitlement must exist on and be continuous after October 1, 1990. Entitlement, of course, depends on the making of a valid claim (SSAA 1992, s.1). So, no doubt to prevent loss of title for example because a renewal claim is not made on the day following the lapse of the previous award, and to cater for late claims and the consequence of revision or appeal of a decision, sub-para.(2) specifically provides, to allay any doubts, that its preclusive rule does not prevent the making at any time of a claim for, or an award of, reduced earnings allowance in consequence of an accident which occurred before October 1, 1990, for a period providing complete continuity with the previous period of entitlement in respect of that accident.

On the application of para.(2) to seasonal workers who lose entitlement to REA during their off-season because there is then no reduction in earning power, see *CI/4940/01* applying *R(I) 56/53*.

(2) Reduced Earnings Allowance: conditions of entitlement 1.598

For those not precluded from REA by the provisions noted above, the key conditions of entitlement are set out in para.11.

The structure of the paragraph is as follows:

Sub-para.(1) Conditions of entitlement—basic concepts of "the relevant loss of faculty", "regular occupation", "suitable employment of an equivalent standard", "incapacity".

Sub-para.(4) Regular occupation—deeming regulations.

Sub-para.(5) Regular occupation; equivalent standard; standard of remuneration—partial definitions.

Sub-para.(6) Regular occupation—effect of prospects of advancement.

Sub-para.(7) Incapacity—trial period and rehabilitative work.

Sub-para.(8) Length of award—general.

Sub-para.(9) Length of award—limitation to period of assessment.

Sub-paras (10), (11) Amount of award—method of calculation.

Sub-para.(12) Relevant occupation—definition.

In *CI/4478/1999* (reported as part of *R(I)2/02*), Commissioner Rowland held that 1.599
where someone had a cumulative loss of earnings due to a number of industrial accidents *each of which made him incapable of following a different "regular occupation"*, he can have only one award of REA, subject to the statutory maximum, in respect of all the accidents. In *Hagan v Secretary of State for Social Security* (neutral citation EWCA Civ 1452—reported as part of *R(I) 2/02*), the Court of Appeal on July 30, 2001 set this aside as erroneous in law. The Court of Appeal accepted the Secretary of State's argument, summarised as follows:

> "(1) there can be multiple claims for awards of REA in circumstances where there are successive industrial injuries each of which causes a change from the previous regular occupation; (2) on each claim the maximum amount of REA payable is 40 per cent of the maximum disablement pension; but (3) this 40 per cent limit applies only to each claim separately and if there are multiple claims then the maximum amount payable is not 40 per cent but the 140 per cent referred to in the last part of paragraph 11(10).

The Secretary of State put before the court the following example. In 1986 a mining foreman suffers an injury in the mine and loses his hearing such that he can no longer be a foreman and has to be 'demoted' to a miner. The assessment of disability by reason of the loss of hearing is 20 per cent and the reduction in earnings is significantly in excess of 40 per cent of the disablement pension. On a claim for REA and disablement pension immediately after this accident he would have been awarded 20 per cent of the maximum disablement pension as disablement pension, and 40 per cent of the maximum disablement pension as REA. Two years later he lost the use of an arm by reason of an explosion in the mine, as a result of which he could no longer work down the mine and had to be further 'demoted' to a 'winchman'. His assessment of disability in relation to this accident (loss of use of arm) is 30 per cent, leading to an aggregated disablement pension award under section 103(2) of 50 per cent. His loss of earnings is again substantially in excess of 40 per cent of the maximum disablement pension and so on the basis of his second accident and the second change of regular occupation, he would again be entitled to 40 per cent of REA. The cumulative effect is 80 per cent of the maximum disablement pension by way of REA and 50 per cent by way of disability pension. This is less than the maximum in the final part of para.11(10) and therefore total benefit amounting to 130 per cent of the maximum amount of disablement pension is payable by reason of the two accidents under the separate benefits.

On the analysis of the Social Security Commissioner on the same facts, the miner would be entitled to 50 per cent disablement pension because of the aggregated effect of the injuries pursuant to section 103(2) but would only be entitled to make one REA claim giving rise to a maximum entitlement of 40 per cent of REA and thus an overall total of 90 per cent of the maximum disability pension. That example illustrates why it is that I said at the beginning of this judgment that the Secretary of State is in the relatively unusual position of arguing for a more generous interpretation of the law.' (paras 28–30).

1.600 In *CI/1052/2001*, Commissioner Rowland distinguished *Hagan*, which

> "was concerned with a case where the claimant claimed to have lost earnings due to becoming incapable of following one occupation as a result of one accident and then to have lost further earnings due to becoming incapable of following another regular occupation as a result of another accident. In the present case, it is the Secretary of State's case that the claimant's regular occupation at the onset of his vibration white finger was the same as his regular occupation at the time of his 1985 accident" (para.7).

In the situation before him in the present case, citing *R(I) 2/56*, the Commissioner considered that

> "only one award of reduced earnings allowance, which might equally well have been made in respect of either the 1985 accident or the vibration white finger, may be made. As an award had already been made at the maximum rate in respect of the 1985 accident, the tribunal's decision in respect of the vibration white finger was not erroneous in point of law" (para.9).

1.601 *Sub-paragraph (1)(a):* For entitlement to disablement pension see s.103 and notes, above. The allowance may be paid where the assessment of disablement is at least 1 per cent, and one of the other two conditions in sub-para.1(b), below, is satisfied. Note that the allowance is still linked with disablement pension—the claimant must actually be entitled to disablement pension, or entitled but for the level of assessment. The allowance will not, therefore, be payable until the 15-week waiting period (see s.103(6), above) has elapsed.

1.602 *Sub-paragraph (1)(b):* The claimant must show that he is (as a result of the relevant loss of faculty) incapable of following his regular occupation or suitable employment of an equivalent standard. In addition, he must show *either* that he is likely to remain permanently incapable of following his regular occupation (the "permanent" condition), *or* that he has been incapable of following his regular occupation or employment of an equivalent standard at all times since the end of the 15 week waiting period (the "continuous" condition). Incapacity for the regular occupation must be caused by the relevant loss of faculty. Thus, the claim for REA failed in *IE v SSWP (II)* [2011] UKUT 383 (AAC) where the claimant's incapacity for his regular occupation instead resulted solely from degenerative disease and not in any material degree from loss of faculty due to his industrial accident.

In *CI/3379/2002*, Commissioner Howell reminded us that

> "[as] was held by the Commissioner in reported decision *R(I) 7/53* . . ., the question of whether a claimant is likely to remain permanently incapable of following his regular occupation for the purposes of reduced earnings allowance is one to be assessed by the tribunal, on the probabilities of the case, and having regard to the evidence before them. As the Commissioner says in paragraph 10, the burden of proving that he is likely to remain permanently incapable rests on the claimant; or

as I would for my part prefer to put it in an inquisitorial jurisdiction, the tribunal must be affirmatively satisfied on the evidence before them that he *is* so incapable, on one test or the other, before they can hold him entitled to the benefit (para.14).

While PD A11 (Vibration white finger) is degenerative and will not improve once contracted, no rule of law can be deduced from *R(I) 2/81, CI 15803/1996* or AOG, para.85738 to the effect that a tribunal must necessarily assume, regardless of the full evidence, that a claimant suffering from vibration white finger cannot continue with his regular occupation. This may be so in many cases, and be a sensible medical and administrative assumption. But a tribunal must consider the matter in the light of all the evidence. Future injury and risk are relevant factors to consider, but no more than that. Nor can the claimant rely on statements in the AOG (now DMG) as creating a legitimate expectation, since neither Guide is binding on tribunals. Commissioner Williams so held in *CI/3038/2000*.

See also *SSWP v RD (II)* [2018] UKUT 481 (AAC); [2019] AACR 2, where Judge Rowland held that *R(I) 2/81* could not simply be read to mean that a person suffering from occupational deafness cannot continue with his regular employment, regardless of the evidence and facts. Judge Rowland also accepted that the claimant's return to his regular occupation demonstrated that he was capable of following that occupation; moreover, this will normally preclude entitlement to REA on the basis of satisfying the 'continuous' conditions. However, Judge Rowland further held that different considerations apply if REA is claimed in respect of a period *after* the claimant has given up their regular occupation, with reliance being placed on the 'permanent' conditions (applying *R(I) 15/74*).

Regular occupation: The claimant's regular occupation is to be determined as a matter of fact taking into account the provisions of sub-paras (4), (5) and (6) and decided cases. Sub-para.(4) gives the Secretary of State power to make "deeming" regulations (see the note to the sub-para., below). **1.603**

The normal case of the claimant who has worked in one job for a number of years presents no problem nor, probably, does the case of the claimant who changes jobs very frequently for it will be easy to regard him as "acquiring" a regular occupation very quickly—and in this context, regular occupation means a *type* of job not limited by reference to a particular area or a particular employer (*R. v Deputy I.I. Commissioner Ex p. Humphreys* [1966] 2 W.L.R. 63). But what of claimants with a new job, more than one job, in training for a job, or with prospects of promotion from the job they were doing at the time of the accident?

The normal approach seems to be to consider that the job which caused the loss of earning capacity should be regarded as the regular occupation (*R(I) 5/52*) (even if it was a new job) unless there is evidence that the claimant did not so regard it, or he had been in it an exceptionally short time (*R(I) 18/60*), or he had been in a previous job for a long period (*R(I) 22/52, R(I) 65/54*).

Sub-paragraph (5): excludes subsidiary occupations from consideration but that does not prevent the decision-maker or tribunal from finding that more than one job makes up the claimant's regular occupation if neither, or none, of them can be said to be truly subsidiary to the other(s). If the claimant does more than one job for the same employer, then it is probably right to regard them together as his regular occupation unless one or more of them is abnormal and irregular (*R(I) 42/52, R(I) 24/55* and *R(I) 10/65*): but such claims are not always successful (*R(I) 58/54* and *R(I) 13/62*). Where the jobs are done for different employers the question is the same—can one (or more) of the jobs be regarded as subsidiary to the other(s)?—but the claimant may have more difficulty in establishing that his regular occupation consists of the totality of the jobs (*R(I) 33/58* and *R(I) 2/70*). There is no easy test emerging from the decisions as to what will constitute subsidiary as against regular occupation, although in settling this question of fact, the number of employers, the relative remuneration in each job, and the amount of time spent on them will be significant factors. **1.604**

The difficulty of ascertaining the regular occupation of a claimant in training is eased by the provision of sub-para.(7) (below) if it is reasonably clear what job the training is directed towards. Otherwise, the decision-maker or tribunal will have to speculate about future job prospects and then use the subsection (as in *R(I) 6/75*), or categorise training as the regular occupation (as in *R(I) 4/60*) with the likely disadvantages for the claimant of a low standard of remuneration in the regular occupation when it comes to determining title to benefit and, ultimately, the amount of the award.

1.605 *Sub-paragraph (6):* extends the ambit of regular occupation to jobs to which the claimant would have been promoted but for the loss of faculty, although the wording has been interpreted to mean that promotions must be almost automatic rather than selective. In *R(I) 8/67*, the claimant contended that, as a result of contracting a prescribed disease, he had been prevented from progressing from shipwright grade B to grade A. The Commissioner formulated the appropriate questions thus:

(1) In general, are persons in the claimant's position normally promoted or advanced to a higher grade or level?

(2) Would the claimant himself have had the normal prospects of advancement if he had continued in his regular occupation without loss of faculty?

(3) Was the claimant deprived in part or in whole of those prospects by the industrial injury?

R(I) 8/73 placed the emphasis in those questions on the word "normal". The Commissioner said:

> "I doubt whether (the subsection) will, as a rule, assist a claimant unless the occupation which he follows is a broad-based one in which some degree of advancement is regarded as almost automatic. Where the predominant factor in a claimant's occupation or profession is that of selectivity the claimant will rarely, I think, be able successfully to invoke [the subsection]." (See also *R(I) 8/80*.)

A sideways move to a better paid job in the same basic grade was not, in *R(I) 12/81*, evidence of prospects of advancement. In determining that the new job, which the claimant actually did before ill-health forced him to abandon it, did not constitute a job of a higher grade or level, the Commissioner found that the skill and training involved was largely the same as in the former job (the regular occupation) and that the enhanced pay was merely to compensate for other unattractive features of the new job.

1.606 *Employment of an equivalent standard . . . suitable in his case:* Reduced earnings allowance compensates the claimant for loss of earning capacity, so that it is logical to require him to show not only that he cannot do his regular job, but also that he cannot do another suitable job which will bring him just as much money.

The word "standard" appears here and in sub-para.(10), below, where it has a slightly different meaning. Here, "employment of an equivalent standard" is determined by considering the normal earnings in a job of which the claimant is capable with the normal earnings in the claimant's regular occupation. If the earnings in the alternative job are at least equal to those in the regular occupation, the alternative job is of an equivalent standard:

> "[T]he comparison of the standard of remuneration afforded by the two employments, the regular employment and the prospective new employment, is one which in this subsection is unaffected by any consideration personal to the beneficiary and has to be treated objectively. The standard of remuneration in each case must, I think, be taken to be the standard of remuneration which an employee of normal efficiency and industriousness, where efficiency and industriousness are relevant considerations, will be likely to earn working in that employment for such number of hours in a week or other period which can be regarded

as normal for persons employed in that employment, having regard to the conditions of the employment and the circumstances of the trade or industry in the appropriate geographical area under consideration." (*R. v N.I. Commissioner Ex p. Mellors* [1971] 2 W.L.R. 593. See also *R(I) 1/72, R(I) 1/76.*)

A payment designed to cover expenses is not remuneration for the purposes of deciding whether one employment is of an equivalent standard to another (*R(I) 1/54*). So in *CO v SSWP (II)* [2011] UKUT 105 (AAC), Judge Rowland held that a £175.03 pw non-taxable subsistence payment for living in digs near a construction site and away from home had to be ignored since the evidence showed that the allowance was paid only where expense was incurred and was only made when the claimant worked away from home. This meant that his remuneration was below that of his regular employment so that the job being done was not of an equivalent standard to that employment. Judge Rowland also distinguished *R(I) 24/59*: there a "subsistence allowance" counted as remuneration because on the facts of the case it was properly seen as a "perquisite annexed to his wages", since it was paid regardless of whether the employee worked away from home or not.

An element of subjectivity is introduced into the test by the requirement that employment of equivalent standard should be suitable for the claimant. Once it can be shown that jobs which the claimant can do (for the test of incapacity, see next paragraph) pay as much or more than his regular occupation, the claim will fail unless the alternative job is unsuitable. The department will normally produce a list of jobs for the tribunal which are said to be suitable (see the comments of the Commissioner in *R(S) 7/85*) and each must be examined in the light of all evidence. "Suitability refers to such matters as education, experience or training and has to be judged by reference to the claimant's past industrial history" (*R(I) 22/61*). Employments which are so exceptional that they ought not to be considered as proper comparisons may be excluded (*R(I) 6/77*, employment in sheltered work offered by Remploy Ltd—see also *R(I) 42/52, R(I) 73/52, R(I) 7/58*). In *R(I) 1/74* the Commissioner pointed up an important distinction between unsuitability and incapacity—unsuitability may result from *any* of the claimant's personal characteristics (see also *R(I) 29/52*).

Incapable: See also the discussion of incapacity for work in relation to sickness **1.607**
and invalidity benefit in the annotation to SSCBA 1992, s.57 as in force prior to April 13, 1995 (the introduction of incapacity benefit), which can be found in Bonner, Hooker and White, *Non-Means Tested Benefits: Legislation 1994*, pp.187–194. Just as with those benefits, so for reduced earnings allowance it is relevant to look beyond the claimant's state of health (important though that is) to his age, education and other personal factors.

The statutory rubric requires that the claimant demonstrates that, as a result of the relevant loss of faculty, he is incapable of following his regular occupation or suitable employment of an equivalent standard. "Regular occupation", it will be recalled, means a *type* of job not limited by reference to a particular area or a particular employer (*R. v Deputy I.I. Commissioner Ex p. Humphreys* [1966] 2 W.L.R. 63). This matter of incapacity in respect of his regular occupation or of suitable employment of an equivalent standard, is more complicated when the claimant has returned to work after the accident, and even more so if he has returned to his regular occupation. Returning to his regular occupation is, of course, good evidence that he is indeed capable of it. But such a claimant may, in some cases, be able to derive assistance from regulations which leave out of account periods of rehabilitative work (see annotation to sub-para.(7), below). Assistance in such a case may also be derived from a range of Commissioner's decisions which require that one ascertain the degree to which he is actually capable of fulfilling the normal requirements of the type of job in issue, and the basis on which he has been employed to do that job. In *CI/443/50(KL) (reported)*, a Tribunal of Commissioners laid down the relevant broad test and illustrated its application:

> "If a person cannot obtain employment in his regular field of labour because (as a result of the relevant loss of faculty) he is unable to fulfil all the ordinary requirements of employers in that field of labour, he is incapable of following his regular occupation . . .
>
> The matter may be illustrated thus. If a person obtains employment in his old job only through charity or because he has an exceptional employer, he should be regarded as incapable of following his regular occupation. On the other hand if a person is able to do his old job except that as a result of the relevant loss of faculty he cannot work overtime, he should not be regarded as incapable of following his regular occupation, unless as a result of this inability he cannot comply with the ordinary requirements of employers in his regular field of labour" (paras 11, 12).

In that particular case a tool-room fitter, temporarily unable to do overtime was held capable of following his regular occupation. But ultimately the precise application of this broad test depends on the facts of the instant case with decided cases illustrating matters constituting some of the relevant factors, rather than invariably being decisive considerations (*CI/1589/1998*, paras 14, 19). It is important also to recall that in pre-1987 cases Commissioners were able to reconsider all the issues (factual or legal) arising in the case and, since Commissioner's decisions are only binding in so far as they decide points of law, "it is necessary to disentangle statements of law from the Commissioner's analysis of the facts and the application of the law to those facts" (*ibid.*, para.12). Finally, note carefully that it is not a matter of whether the claimant is doing the same job as before, nor is the test one of what is acceptable to the claimant's employer, but rather is to be related to the normal requirements of "employers in that field of labour" (*ibid.*, para.19; and see *R(I) 10/59*, para.13). So, if the claimant has to be helped by workmates (*R(I) 29/52*, *R(I) 39/52*), or if he cannot meet the normal requirements of that type of job (*R(I) 39/55*), or if he has to pay other workers to carry out some of his duties (*R(I) 5/58*), or if the employer retains him only out of sympathy (*CI/445/50(KL) (reported)*), these will all be relevant factors in deciding in the context of the case as a whole whether he is incapable of performing his regular occupation. In the five cases just mentioned, the claimants were held incapable of their regular occupation. But it does depend on the particular circumstances and on the reference point of "the ordinary requirements of employers in his regular field of labour". So, in *CI 446/50(KL) (reported),* while the claimant farm-worker was unable to do piecework, he did remain capable of a wide range of farm work and so was held capable of his regular occupation (see para.6). Application of the test is particularly difficult where the claimant has returned to the same occupation as before the accident but, as a result of the loss of faculty, "follows it more slowly, or for fewer hours, or less productively, or omits some parts of the occupation he used to perform" (*CI 443/50(KL) (reported)*, para.9). If the hours he can work are substantially reduced by comparison with the period prior to the loss of faculty, this may point to his being incapable of following his regular occupation. A reduction from five days to three and a half had that effect in *CI/444/50(KL) (reported)* (although there was also some element of having to have others do some lifting and carrying, that the claimant had previously managed herself), as did a drop from 44 hours to 31 hours in *R(I) 6/66*. A reduction in output or speed must be to such a degree as to prevent the claimant satisfying the ordinary requirements of employers in his regular field of labour (*CI/447/50(KL)*, *CI/448/50(KL) (both reported)*). Jobs involving piecework pose obvious difficulties here. In *R(I) 4/77*, the Commissioner warned against applying the language of the test in *CI/443/50(KL) (reported)* as if it were a statute and of the danger of isolating statements of law from the factual context of the case in which they were laid down and applied (a point re-emphasised in *CI/1589/1998*). The Commissioner in *R(I) 4/77* saw the claimant's remuneration as an important factor. He referred to the significance of remuneration in determining whether employment was of an equivalent standard and held that in determining incapacity in the case of a pieceworker it was proper to ask whether as a result of the relevant loss of faculty the claimant can attain the same level of remuneration in his regular occupation as he did before that loss of faculty.

As a result of the relevant loss of faculty: The incapacity must be caused by the loss of faculty. Causation is a matter of fact for the Secretary of State or tribunal. See note to s.94(1), above, on causation. **1.608**

Sub-paragraph (4): Refer to note on regular occupation above. The regulation made under this section is reg.2 of the Social Security (Industrial Injuries and Diseases) Miscellaneous Provisions Regulations 1986 (SI 1986/1561). **1.609**

Sub-paragraph (5): This subsection is discussed in the notes on sub-para.(1), above. **1.610**

Sub-paragraph (6): See note on "regular occupation" in sub-para.(1), above. **1.611**

Sub-paragraph (7): The regulations referred to are the General Benefit Regulations, reg.17. **1.612**

Sub-paragraph (9): The period referred to in the section is the period for which disablement is assessed in accordance with the provisions of the Act. **1.613**

Sub-paragraphs (10) and (11): The phrase "standard of remuneration" used in sub-para.(1), above, to determine entitlement to the allowance is also used in this subsection to determine the amount of the award, but it bears a different meaning. In quantifying the award, the right approach is to determine the normal earnings of the claimant in the occupation which he is capable of following without any regard to the number of hours worked, the rate paid, or the working conditions in the new job. It is a crude comparison between the money the claimant would have got in his old job, and the money he gets in his new job (see the *Mellors* case, above, and *R(I) 6/68, R(I) 1/72*). **1.614**

The amount of the allowance is eventually determined by the difference between the two figures, subject to the 40 per cent maximum. It is important to note that the 140 per cent figure in this subsection is modified to 100 per cent in respect of persons who retired from regular employment before April 6, 1987 (sub-para.(11)). Note that it is possible to show entitlement to the allowance by meeting the conditions in sub-para.(1), but discover that the amount is nil on applying the test in this subsection.

The "relevant occupation" for the purposes of comparison is defined in sub-para.(12).

Sub-paragraph (13): The difficulties of calculating the probable standard of remuneration in individual cases, often many years after the accident, have been alleviated by the provisions of this subsection. The regulations referred to are the Social Security (Industrial Injuries) (Reduced Earnings Allowance and Transitional) Regulations 1987, below. This section and the regulations apply to any award of the allowance except the first subject to specific situations covered by the regulations. See further the notes to the regulations. **1.615**

Sub-paragraph (14): The predecessor of this sub-paragraph was inserted by SSA 1988, s.16(1), with effect from March 15, 1988. **1.616**

(3) Reduced Earnings Allowance: the rate for those retired persons entitled to it

Paragraph 12(1) preserves entitlement to REA for those who are of pensionable age and have retired from regular employment either on April 10, 1988, or on April 9, 1989. Although entitlement is preserved for life, the rate of REA is frozen: see sub-paras (2)–(6). **1.617**

Sch.7, Pt V: Retirement Allowance

1.618 It was the intention of the Government that the new benefit which replaced Special Hardship Allowance (Reduced Earnings Allowance) should only subsist during the working life of the claimant up to pensionable age. A further new benefit was introduced to compensate, in retirement, the claimant who, as a result of an industrial accident or disease, may find that an earnings-related pension has been diminished by reduced earnings during his working life. This new benefit, retirement allowance, was created by the Social Security Act 1988 and introduced by way of an insertion of a new section (s.59B) into the Social Security Act 1975.

1.619 *Sub-paragraph (1):* terminates entitlement to reduced earnings allowance on retirement on or after attainment of pensionable age. It ceases from the day on which regular employment is given up. It also precludes a person being entitled to REA for a period falling after the attainment of pensionable age and the giving up of regular employment in circumstances in which that person had another award of REA prior to those dates (*TA v SSWP (II)* [2014] UKUT 127 (AAC), paras 70-79). In *TA*, however, Judge Wright declined to decide whether (as the Secretary of State accepted) REA can still be awarded *for the first time* on a backdated claim made after the claimant has given up regular employment and reached pensionable age with such award continuing, in effect, for life (para.63), a strange situation given that post retirement and giving up employment it is difficult to see how a remuneration comparison can meaningfully be made (paras 64-70).

The words "gives up regular employment" are not used in an unusual sense. They are to be construed in their natural and ordinary meaning, so that they did not catch the particular claimant who was dismissed from his job at a newsagents shop (*R(I) 2/93*, paras 20 and 21). This does not mean, however, that all dismissals fall outwith the phrase. Citing instances where a dismissed claimant has nevertheless been held to have voluntarily left his employment for disqualification purposes under SSCBA 1992, s.28(1)(a) (*R(U) 16/52, R(U) 2/74*) (see now Jobseekers Act, s.19), the Commissioner in *R(I) 2/93* said:

> "A claimant may act in such a way as to force his employer to dismiss him and it will be a question of fact in each case whether or not the claimant had by his conduct evinced an intention to give up regular employment (para.13).

In any event, to be caught by sub-para.(1), the claimant must have given up regular employment *on or after April 10, 1989*, so that those in receipt of REA when they gave up such employment before that date, are not thereby disentitled to it by virtue of para.13 of Sch.7 (see *R(I) 3/93, CI/11015/1995* and decision *CI/209/1991*).

Note, however, that with effect from March 24, 1996, regulations dictate a broader approach to "gives up regular employment" than that taken in *R(I) 2/93*. With effect from that date, reg.3 of the Social Security (Industrial Injuries) (Regular Employment) Regulations 1990 (inserted by reg.6(3) of the Social Security (Industrial Injuries and Diseases) (Miscellaneous Amendment) Regulations 1996 (SI 1996/425) provides that a person who has attained pensionable age must be regarded as having given up regular employment at the start of the first week in which *he is not in regular employment* after the later of the week during which the regulation came into force or the week in which he attained pensionable age. But this does not apply if the person is entitled to REA for life by virtue of para.12(1), above. It is submitted that the "week during which this regulation comes into force" (reg.3(a)) must be the week including March 24, 1996, the date the amendment took effect, and not that including April 1, 1990, the date set out in reg.1(1) of the 1990 Regs, which merely sets out the date the original set of regulations, not including reg.3, came into operation. Had the intention been to make the reg.3, retrospective, one would have expected clear words to that effect.

"gives up regular employment": the effect of the new reg.3.

R(I) 2/99 is very useful in charting the bumpy and twisting path of attempts to make entitlement to REA cease on retirement, and the decisions reported there make clear that reg.3 is *intra vires* the rule-making power in SSCBA 1992, Sch.7, para.13(8). **1.620**

In *Hepple v CAO* (Case C–196/98, judgment of May 23, 2000 reported as *R(I) 2/00*), the ECJ held that the discriminatory cut-off conditions introduced by the UK from 1986 onwards for REA claimants over state pension age were not invalid under the Equal Treatment Directive 79/7 as they were within the permitted exclusion in Art.7 for the determination of state pension age and "the possible consequences for other benefits". The court rejected the Advocate-General's opinion. It rejected the argument that Art.7 did not permit Member States to introduce fresh heads of discrimination in non-pension benefits by linking them to the pension age long after the Directive itself was in full effect. The court held that since "the principal aim of the legislative amendments . . . was to discontinue payment of REA . . . to persons no longer of working age by imposing conditions based on the statutory retirement age", then "maintenance of the rules at issue . . . is objectively necessary to preserve . . . coherence" between REA and the state pension. In consequence, the discrimination was held "objectively and necessarily linked to the difference between the retirement age for men and that for women". It was, therefore, permitted by Art.7.

The end result is that reg.3 has now been conclusively upheld as valid in both UK national and EU law.

A person cannot be in employment under a contract which has ceased to exist, and is thus to be treated as having given up regular employment on its cessation—on the harsh operation of the rule in the case of seasonal and casual workers, see *SSWP* v *NH (II)* [2010] UKUT 84 (AAC). See also *AR v SSWP (II)* [2021] UKUT 279 (AAC), which was concerned with how the reduced earnings allowance legislation drafted in 1990 applies today to zero hours contracts. See further the annotation to reg.2 (Meaning of "regular employment") of the Social Security (Industrial Injuries) Regulations 1990 (SI 1990/256).

Sub-paragraph (2): transfers a claimant to retirement allowance if, on the day before he ceases to be entitled to reduced earnings allowance under subs.(1), he was entitled to reduced earnings allowance at a weekly rate of not less than £2. There is some potential difficulty in the subsection since the use of the word "entitled" might suggest that the decision-maker or tribunal could investigate entitlement even if there had been no claim. However, the qualifying words in brackets, "by virtue either of one award or of a number of awards", suggest that the benefit must actually have been awarded at the relevant time. However many awards of REA the claimant was receiving, there can only be entitlement to one award of retirement allowance (*TA* v *SSWP (II)* [2010] UKUT 101 (AAC)). **1.621**

Sub-paragraph (3)–(7): stipulate that entitlement to retirement allowance is for life, and fix the rate at which benefit will be paid. Consistent with the freezing of reduced earnings allowance for those retired people over pensionable age in receipt of that benefit (see para.12 noted above), retirement allowance will be paid at a rate fixed by reference to the date of retirement. Note, however, that the sums falling to be calculated under sub-para.(4) are subject to alteration by up-rating orders (sub-para. (7)). **1.622**

The whole of s.59B was amended and subss.(7) and (8) added by SSA 1989 to take account of the abolition of the earnings rules and the substitution of the text of "giving up regular employment" for the text of retirement or deemed retirement.

The meaning of "regular employment" for the purposes of the section is defined by the Social Security (Industrial Injuries) (Regular Employment) Regulations 1990 (SI 1990/256) which are included in the regulations on individual injuries set out at the end of the volume.

1.623 *Sub-paragraph (10):* Note the link to "jobseeking period" and "linked period" as defined in the Jobseekers Act 1995. These terms are in fact given real definition in JSA Regs1996, regs 47–49. See *Vol. V: Income Support and the Legacy Benefits.*

1.624 **Schedule 8.** *Repealed by Welfare Reform Act 2012, s.64 (December 5, 2012).*

1.625 **Schedules 9–11:** *Omitted.* See *Vol.IV: HMRC-administered Social Security Benefits and Scotland.*

SCHEDULE 12

Relationship of Statutory Sick Pay with Benefits and Other Payments, etc.

The general principle

1.626 **1.**—Any day which—

(a) is a day of incapacity for work in relation to any contract of service; and

(b) falls within a period of entitlement (whether or not it is also a qualifying day), shall not be treated for the purposes of this Act as a day of incapacity for work for the purposes of determining whether a period is [1] [2 a period of incapacity for work for the purposes of incapacity benefit.]

Contractual remuneration

1.627 **2.**—(1) Subject to sub-paragraphs (2) and (3) below, any entitlement to statutory sick pay shall not affect any right of any employee in relation to remuneration under any contract of service ("contractual remuneration").

(2) Subject to sub-paragraph (3) below—

(a) any contractual remuneration paid to any employee by an employer of his in respect of a day of incapacity for work shall go towards discharging any liability for that employer to pay statutory sick pay to that employee in respect of that day; and

(b) any statutory sick pay paid by an employer to an employee of his in respect of a day of incapacity for work shall go towards discharging any liability of that employer to pay contractual remuneration to that employee in respect of that day.

(3) Regulations may make provision as to payments which are, and those which are not, to be treated as contractual remuneration for the purposes of sub-paragraph (1) or (2) above.

[2 Incapacity benefit

1.628 **3.**—(1) This paragraph and paragraph 4 below have effect to exclude, where a period of entitlement as between an employee and an employer of his comes to an end, the provisions by virtue of which short-term incapacity benefit is not paid for the first three days.

(2) If the first day immediately following the day on which the period of entitlement came to an end—

(a) is a day of incapacity for work in relation to that employee, and

(b) is not a day in relation to which paragraph 1 above applies by reason of any entitlement as between the employee and another employer,

that day shall, except in prescribed cases, be or form part of a period of incapacity for work notwithstanding section 30C(1)(b) above (by virtue of which a period of incapacity for work must be at least 4 days long).

(3) Where each of the first two consecutive days, or the first three consecutive days, following the day on which the period of entitlement came to an end is a day to which paragraphs (a) and (b) of sub-paragraph (2) above apply, that sub-paragraph has effect in relation to the second day or, as the case may be, in relation to the second and third days, as it has effect in relation to the first.

4.—(1) Where a period of entitlement as between an employee and an employer of his comes to an end, section 30A(3) above (exclusion of benefit for first 3 days of period) does not apply in relation to any day which—

(a) is or forms part of a period of incapacity for work (whether by virtue of paragraph 3 above or otherwise), and

(b) falls within the period of 57 days immediately following the day on which the period of entitlement came to an end.

(2) Where sub-paragraph (1) above applies in relation to a day, section 30A(3) above does not apply in relation to any later day in the same period of incapacity for work.]

[2 Incapacity benefit for widows and widowers

5.—Paragraph 1 above does not apply for the purpose of determining whether the conditions specified in section 40(3) or (4) or section 41(2) or (3) above are satisfied.] **1.629**

Unemployability supplement

6.—Paragraph 1 above does not apply in relation to paragraph 3 of Schedule 7 to this Act and accordingly the references in paragraph 3 of that Schedule to a period of interruption of employment shall be construed as if the provisions re-enacted in this Part of this Act had not been enacted. **1.630**

AMENDMENTS

1. Jobseekers Act 1995 Sch.3 para.1. (October 7, 1996).
2. Social Security (Incapacity for Work) Act 1994 Sch.1 para.44 (April 13, 1995).

DERIVATION

SSHBA 1982 Sch.2. **1.631**

GENERAL NOTE

Paragraph 1

No day of incapacity (whether or not a qualifying day) within a period of entitlement can count as part of a period of interruption of employment. Thus such a day cannot give entitlement to, say, incapacity benefit. **1.632**

Paragraphs 3 and 4

These assist certain persons not caught by para.1, who have days of incapacity subsequent to the end of a period of entitlement, to qualify for State benefits by not applying the normal rules on period of interruption of employment and waiting days. See also with respect to para.3., reg.12 of the SSP (Gen.) Regulations. **1.633**

SCHEDULE 13

RELATIONSHIP OF STATUTORY MATERNITY PAY WITH BENEFITS AND OTHER PAYMENTS, ETC.

The general principle

[1 **1.**—Except as may be prescribed, a day which falls within the maternity pay period shall not be treated as a day of incapacity for work for the purposes of determining, for this Act, whether it forms part of a period of incapacity for work for the purposes of incapacity benefit.] **1.634**

[2 Incapacity benefit

2.—(1) Regulations may provide that in prescribed circumstances a day which falls within the maternity pay period shall be treated as a day of incapacity for work for the purpose of determining entitlement to the higher rate of short-term incapacity benefit or to long-term incapacity benefit. **1.635**

(2) Regulations may provide that an amount equal to a woman's statutory maternity pay for a period shall be deducted from any such benefit in respect of the same period and a woman shall be entitled to such benefit only if there is a balance after the deduction and, if there is such a balance, at a weekly rate equal to it.]

Contractual remuneration

1.636 **3.**—(1) Subject to sub-paragraphs (2) and (3) below, any entitlement to statutory maternity pay shall not affect any right of a woman in relation to remuneration under any contract of service ("contractual remuneration").

(2) Subject to sub-paragraph (3) below—

(a) any contractual remuneration paid to a woman by an employer of hers in respect of a week in the maternity pay period shall go towards discharging any liability of that employer to pay statutory maternity pay to her in respect of that week; and

(b) any statutory maternity pay paid by an employer to a woman who is an employee of his in respect of a week in the maternity pay period shall go towards discharging any liability of that employer to pay contractual remuneration to her in respect of that week.

[[3] (2A) In sub-paragraph (2) "week" means a period of seven days beginning with the day of the week on which the maternity pay period begins.]

(3) Regulations may make provision as to payments which are, and those which are not, to be treated as contractual remuneration for the purposes of sub-paragraphs (1) and (2) above.

AMENDMENTS

1. Jobseekers Act 1995 Sch.2 para.37 (October 7, 1996).
2. Social Security (Incapacity for Work) Act 1994 Sch.1 para.45 (April 13, 1995).
3. Work and Families Act 2006 Sch.1 para.23 (October 1, 2006).

Social Security (Consequential Provisions) Act 1992

(1992 C.6)

1.637 *For the text and commentary on this Act, see Vol I of the 2015/16 edition of this series.*

Pension Schemes Act 1993

(1993 C.48)

SECTIONS REPRODUCED

PART III

CERTIFICATION OF PENSION SCHEMES AND EFFECTS ON MEMBERS' STATE SCHEME RIGHTS AND DUTIES

Preliminary

CHAPTER II

REDUCTION IN STATE SCHEME CONTRIBUTIONS AND SOCIAL SECURITY BENEFITS FOR MEMBERS OF CERTIFIED SCHEMES

SECTION

GENERAL NOTE

The main scope of Part III of the Pension Schemes Act 1993 was to provide the legislative authority for the introduction of the state second pension or additional pension in place of its predecessor SERPS or the state earnings related pension scheme. 1.639

The Pensions Act 2014 abolished all aspects of the state second pension with effect from April 6, 2016 for anyone reaching state pensionable age on or after that date. Until that date employees could join occupational schemes that provided them with second pensions in place of the state second pension. They would normally be required to pay pension contributions for the second pension but in exchange could be entitled to pay reduced rates of Class 1 National Insurance contributions if the pension scheme was registered for contracted-out employment.

April 6, 2016 is the second stage of abolition of the state second pension. From that date there is no status of contracted-out employment and no reduced rate of Class 1 contributions. The first stage, which took place with effect from April 6, 2012, was the abolition of contracted-out status for defined contribution schemes and the availability of reduced rates for such schemes. From April 6, 2016 those reaching state pensionable age can claim only the single rate state pension. Any occupational pensions are for arrangement between employers and employees and do not involve the National Insurance contribution or state pension systems.

To give effect to this, the Pensions Act 2014 abolishes contracted-out status for salary-related schemes and repeals the relevant provisions in the Pension Schemes Act 1993—see s.24 of, and Sch.13 to, that Act. These came into effect on April 6, 2016: s.56 of that Act.

However, the Pensions Act 2014 (Savings) Order 2015 (SI 2015/1502) keeps some of those provisions in effect for the purpose of ensuring continuity of entitlement to those already drawing pensions under such schemes. Both the scope of that Order and most of the remaining provisions of the 1993 Act are beyond the scope of this work. A few sections remain in force and of relevance to those who have reached state pensionable age before April 6, 2016 and also have entitlements to a second pension. These sections are set out in this volume. However, the lengthy explanation and analysis of these sections is now only of relevance to such transitional cases. It has therefore been edited down for the purposes of this volume. Anyone wishing to read a fuller analysis is referred to the 2015/16 edition of this volume (or its annual predecessors).

Effect of entitlement to guaranteed minimum pensions on payment of social security benefits

46.—(1) Where for any period a person is entitled both— 1.640

(a) to a Category A or Category B retirement pension, a widowed mother's allowance [1, a widowed parent's allowance] [2 or a widow's pension] under the Social Security Contributions and Benefits Act 1992; and

(b) to one or more guaranteed minimum pensions

the weekly rate of the benefit mentioned in paragraph (a) shall for that period be reduced by an amount equal—

[3 (i) to that part of its additional pension which is attributable to earnings factors for any tax years ending before the principal appointed day], or

(ii) to the weekly rate of the pension mentioned in paragraph (b) (or, if there is more than one such pension, their aggregate weekly rates), whichever is the less.

(2) [[2] . . .]

[[2] (3) Where for any period—

(a) a person is entitled to one or more guaranteed minimum pensions; and

(b) he is also entitled to long-term incapacity benefit under section 30A of the Social Security Contributions and Benefits Act 1992,

for that period an amount equal to the weekly rate or aggregate weekly rates of the guaranteed minimum pension or pensions shall be deducted from any increase payable under regulations under section 30B(7) of that Act and he shall be entitled to such an increase only if there is a balance after the deduction and, if there is such a balance, at a weekly rate equal to it.]

(4) Where for any period—

(a) a person is entitled to one or more guaranteed minimum pensions;

(b) he is also entitled to a Category A retirement pension under section 44 of the Social Security Contributions and Benefits Act 1992; and

(c) the weekly rate of his pension includes an additional pension such as is mentioned in section 44(3)(b) of that Act,

for that period section 47 of that Act shall have effect as if the following subsection were substituted for subsection (3)—

> "(3) In subsection (2) above 'the relevant amount' means an amount equal to the aggregate of—
>
> (a) the additional pension; and
>
> (b) the weekly rate or aggregate weekly rates of the guaranteed minimum pension or pensions,
>
> reduced by the amount of any reduction in the weekly rate of the Category A retirement pension made by virtue of section 46(1) of the Pension Schemes Act 1993.".

(5) Where for any period—

(a) a person is entitled to one or more guaranteed minimum pensions;

(b) he is also entitled to a Category A retirement pension under section 44 of the Social Security Contributions and Benefits Act 1992; and

(c) the weekly rate of his Category A retirement pension does not include an additional pension such as is mentioned in subsection (3)(b) of that section,

for that period the relevant amount shall be deducted from the amount that would otherwise be the increase under section 47(1) of that Act and the pensioner shall be entitled to an increase under that section only if there is a balance remaining after that deduction and, if there is such a balance, of an amount equal to it.

(6) Where for any period—

(a) a person is entitled to one or more guaranteed minimum pensions;

(b) he is also entitled—

(i) [[2] . . .]

(ii) to a Category A retirement pension under section 44 of that Act; or

(iii) to a Category B retirement pension under [4 section [5 . . .] [1, 48B or 48BB] of that Act; and

(c) the weekly rate of the pension includes an additional pension such as is mentioned in section 44(3)(b) of that Act,

for that period paragraph 3 of Schedule 7 to that Act shall have effect as if the following sub-paragraph were substituted for sub-paragraph (3)—

"(3) In this paragraph 'the relevant amount' means an amount equal to the aggregate of—

(a) the additional pension; and

(b) the weekly rate or aggregate weekly rates of the guaranteed minimum pension or pensions,

reduced by the amount of any reduction in the weekly rate of the pension made by virtue of section 46(1) of the Pension Schemes Act 1993.".

(7) Where for any period—

(a) a person is entitled to one or more guaranteed minimum pensions;

(b) he is also entitled to any of the pensions under the Social Security Contributions and Benefits Act 1992 mentioned in subsection (6)(b); and

(c) the weekly rate of the pension does not include an additional pension such as is mentioned in section 44(3)(b) of that Act,

for that period the relevant amount shall be deducted from the amount that would otherwise be the increase under paragraph 3 of Schedule 7 to that Act and the beneficiary shall be entitled to an increase only if there is a balance after that deduction and, if there is a balance, only to an amount equal to it.

(8) In this section "the relevant amount" means an amount equal to the weekly rate or aggregate weekly rates of the guaranteed minimum pension or pensions—

(a) [2 . . .]

(b) in the case of subsection (5), reduced by the amount of any reduction in the weekly rate of the Category A retirement pension made by virtue of subsection (1);

and references in this section to the weekly rate of a guaranteed minimum pension are references to that rate without any increase under section 15(1).

(9) [2 . . .]

[6 (10) In this section a reference to "additional pension" does not include any amount of additional pension attributable to units of additional pension.

(11) For units of additional pension, see section 14A of the Social Security Contributions and Benefits Act 1992.]

AMENDMENTS AND REPEALS

1. Welfare Reform and Pensions Act 1999 s.70 (April 9, 2001).
2. Social Security (Incapacity for Work) Act 1994 Sch.1 (April 13, 1995).
3. Pensions Act 1995 Sch.5 para.44, (April 6, 1997).
4. Pensions Act 1995 Sch.4 para.22 (July 19, 1995).
5. Pensions Act 2014 Sch.12 para.71.
6. Pensions Act (Consequential Amendments)(Units of Additional Pension) Order 2014 (SI 2014/3213) art.4 (October 12, 2015).

General Note

1.641 This section provides the mechanism to offset any claim for the former state second pension or SERPS by reference to any entitlement to pensions payable under contracted-out schemes (for which the pensioner will have paid reduced Class 1 contributions). As noted in the general note to the Act, contracted-out schemes all closed with effect from April 6, 2016 so this problem no longer arises in respect of those reaching state pensionable age on or after April 6, 2016 save in transitional cases. Readers are referred to previous editions of this work for a detailed discussion of the section to which should be added the Court of Appeal's decision in *Robins v Secretary of State for Work and Pensions* [2023] EWCA Civ 890. *Robins* concerned a widow entitled to a GMP by virtue of her late husband's membership of an occupational pension scheme. The court accepted the Secretary of State's argument that the weekly rate of her Category A pension was to be reduced by an amount equal to the weekly rate of her GMP (the amount specified under s.46(1)(ii), since in her case this was less than the amount under s.46(1)(i)).

Further provisions concerning entitlement to guaranteed minimum pensions for the purposes of section 46

1.642 **47.**—(1) The reference in section 46(1) to a person entitled to a guaranteed minimum pension shall be construed as including a reference to a person so entitled by virtue of being the widower [[11], surviving same sex spouse] [[7] or surviving civil partner] of an earner [[5] in any case where he is entitled to a benefit other than a widowed parent's allowance] [[1] . . .] only if—

[[5] (a) he is also entitled to a Category B retirement pension by virtue of the earner's contributions (or would be so entitled but for section 43(1) of the Social Security Contributions and Benefits Act 1992); or]

(b) he is also entitled to a Category A retirement pension by virtue of [[5] section 41(5)] of [[5] that Act].

(2) For the purposes of [[9] [[12] section 46]] a person shall be treated as entitled to any guaranteed minimum pension to which he would have been entitled—

(a) if its commencement had not been postponed, as mentioned in section 13(4); or

(b) if there had not been made a transfer payment or transfer under regulations made by virtue of section 20 as a result of which—

(i) he is no longer entitled to guaranteed minimum pensions under the scheme by which the transfer payment or transfer was made, and

(ii) he has not become entitled to guaranteed minimum pensions under the scheme to which the transfer payment or transfer was made.

(3) Where—

(a) guaranteed minimum pensions provided for a member or the member's [[7] widow, widower or surviving civil partner] under a contracted-out scheme have been wholly or partly secured as mentioned in subsection (3) of section 19; and

(b) either—

(i) the transaction wholly or partly securing them was carried out before 1st January 1986 and discharged the trustees or managers of the scheme as mentioned in subsection (1) of that section; or

(ii) it was carried out on or after that date without any of the requirements specified in subsection (5)(a) to (c) of that section being satisfied in relation to it and the scheme has been wound up; and

(c) any company with which any relevant policy of insurance or annuity contract was taken out or entered into is unable to meet the liabilities under policies issued or securities given by it; and

(d) the combined proceeds of—

(i) any relevant policies and annuity contracts, and

(ii) any cash sums paid or alternative arrangements made under the [4 Financial Services Compensation Scheme],

the member and the member's [7 widow, widower or surviving civil partner] shall be treated for the purposes of [9[12 section 46]] as only entitled to such part (if any) of the member's or, as the case may be, the member's [7widow's, widower's or surviving partner's] guaranteed minimum pension as is provided by the proceeds mentioned in paragraph (d).

(4) A policy or annuity is relevant for the purposes of subsection (3) if taking it out or entering into it constituted the transaction to which section 19 applies.

(5) For the purposes of [9[12 section 46]] a person shall be treated as entitled to any guaranteed minimum pension to which he would have been entitled—

(a) if a lump sum had not been paid instead of that pension under provisions included in a scheme by virtue of section 21(1); or

(b) if that pension had not been forfeited under provisions included in a scheme by virtue of section 21(2).

[2 (6) For the purposes of [9[12 section 46]], a person shall be treated as entitled to any guaranteed minimum pension to which he would have been entitled but for any reduction under section 15A.]

[3 (7) For the purposes of [9[12 section 46]], a person shall be treated as entitled to any guaranteed minimum pension to which he would have been entitled but for any order under section 32A of the Insolvency Act 1986 (recovery of excessive pension contributions) or under [13 s.101 of the Bankruptcy (Scotland) Act 2016].]

[6 (8) For the purposes of [9[12 section 46]], a person shall be treated as entitled to a guaranteed minimum pension to which he would have been entitled but for the fact that the trustees or managers were discharged from their liability to provide that pension on the Board of the Pension Protection Fund assuming responsibility for the scheme.]

[8(9) For the purposes of [9[12 section 46]], a person shall be treated as entitled to a guaranteed minimum pension to which, in the opinion of the Commissioners for Her Majesty's Revenue and Customs, he would have been entitled but for the amendment of a scheme so that it no longer contains the guaranteed minimum pension rules.

(10) Where the earner's accrued rights have been transferred after the amendment of the scheme, in making the calculation under subsection (9) the Commissioners shall assume the application of section 16(1) after the transfer.

(11) In making the calculation under subsection (9) the Commissioners shall ignore any effect of the scheme being wound up.]

AMENDMENTS

1. Social Security (Incapacity for Work Act) 1994 Sch.1 para.57 and Sch.2 (April 13, 1995).

2. Welfare Reform and Pensions Act 1999 s.32(4) (December 1, 2000).

3. Welfare Reform and Pensions Act 1999 s.18 and Sch.2 para.6 (April 6, 2002).
4. Financial Services and Markets Act 2000 (Consequential Amendments and Repeals) Order 2001 (SI 2001/3649) reg.120 (December 1, 2001).
5. State Pension Credit Act 2002 s.18 (March 19, 2002).
6. Pensions Act 2004 s.165(3) (April 6, 2006).
7. Civil Partnership (Contracted-out Occupational and Appropriate Personal Pension Schemes) (Surviving Civil Partners) Order 2005 (SI 2005/2050) Sch.1 para.14 (December 5, 2005).
8. Pensions Act 2007 s.14(5), (April 6, 2009).
9. Pensions Act 2008 Sch.4 para.17 (January 3, 2012).
10. Marriage (Same Sex Couples) Act 2013 Sch.4 Pt.5 para.24. (March 13, 2014).
11. Civil Partnership Act 2004 (Consequential Provisions and Modifications) Order 2014 (SI 2014/3229) Sch.5 para.11 (December 12, 2014).
12. Pensions Act 2014 Sch.12 para.72 (April 6, 2016).
13. The Bankruptcy (Scotland) Act 2016 (Consequential Provisions and Modifications) Order 2016 (SI 2016/1034) Sch.1 para.11 (November 30, 2016).

Reduced benefits where minimum payment or minimum contributions paid

1.643 **48.**—(1) Subject to subsection (3), this subsection applies where for any period—

(a) minimum payments have been made in respect of an earner to an occupational pension scheme which is a money purchase contracted-out scheme in relation to the earner's employment, or
(b) minimum contributions have been paid in respect of an earner under section 43.

(2) Where subsection (1) applies then, for the purposes of [4 sections 46 and 46A]—

(a) the earner shall be treated, as from the date on which he reaches pensionable age, as entitled to a guaranteed minimum pension at a prescribed weekly rate arising from that period in that employment;
(b) [2 . . .], and
(c) in prescribed circumstances [2 . . .] any [3 widow, widower or surviving civil partner] or the earner shall be treated as entitled to a guaranteed minimum pension at a prescribed weekly rate arising from that period;

and where subsection (1)(b) applies paragraphs (a) to (c) of this subsection apply also for the purposes of [1 section] 47(2) of the Social Security Contributions and Benefits Act 1992] and paragraph 3(2) of Schedule 7 to that Act, but with the omission from paragraph (a) of the words "in that employment".

(3) Where the earner is a married woman or widow, subsection (1) shall not have effect by virtue of paragraph (a) of that subsection in relation to any period during which there is operative an election that her liability in respect of primary Class 1 contributions shall be a liability to contribute at a reduced rate.

(4) The power to prescribe a rate conferred by subsection (2)(a) includes power to prescribe a nil rate.

Amendments and Repeals

1. Social Security (Incapacity for Work) Act 1994 Sch.1 (April 13, 1995).
2. Pensions Act 1995 s.140(2) (April 6, 1996).
3. Civil Partnership (Contracted-out Occupational and Appropriate Personal Pension Schemes) (Surviving Civil Partners) Order 2005 (SI 2005/2050) Sch.1, para.14 (December 5, 2005).
4. Pensions Act 2008 Sch.4 para.18 (January 3, 2012).

General Note

Section 48 ceases to have effect for minimum payments and minimum contributions from April 6, 1997 (Pensions Act 1995 s.140(3)). 1.644

In *Secretary of State for Work and Pensions v MH* [2014] UKUT 113 (AAC) Judge Jacobs found himself unable to read modifications to the pensionable age of women made by subsequent legislation into section 48 of the Pension Schemes Act 1993. He records that the Department for Work and Pensions accepted that this was an error in drafting the legislation but he was unable to interpret the provision to remove the error. Nor, as a judge of the Upper Tribunal, was he able to consider any incompatibility with human rights legislation.

Note, however, that in the subsequent case of *SSWP v GS (WB)* [2015] UKUT 33 (AAC), the Secretary of State argued that no such concession by the DWP had been made in *MH*. In *GS* Judge Mark held, contrary to the finding in *MH*, that for the purposes of the calculations under s.46 up to the date the claimant qualified for the state pension, then "the Secretary of State ought to have determined how much, if any, of the Respondent's GMP was attributable to payments before 6 April 1997 which fell within section 48 of the 1993 Act, and to have excluded that part of the pension in calculating how much should be deducted from the additional element of the widow's pension" (at para.(16i)). Permission to appeal to the Court of Appeal was granted in *GS* but the case was subsequently settled between the parties (*Swan v SSWP* C3/2016/0431).

[1 Effect of reduced contributions and rebates on social security benefits

48A.—(1) [4 In relation to— 1.645

(a) any tax week falling before the first abolition date where the amount of a Class 1 contribution attributable to section 8(1)(a) of the Social Security Contributions and Benefits Act 1992 in respect of the earnings paid to or for the benefit of an earner in that week was reduced under section 42A of this Act (as it then had effect),

(b) any tax week falling before the second abolition date where the amount of a Class 1 contribution attributable to section 8(1)(a) of the Social Security Contributions and Benefits Act 1992 in respect of the earnings paid to or for the benefit of an earner in that week was reduced under section 41 of this Act (as it then had effect), or

(c) any tax week falling before the first abolition date where an amount was paid under section 45(1) of this Act (as it then had effect) in respect of the earnings paid to or for the benefit of an earner,]

section 44(6) of the Social Security Contributions and Benefits Act 1992 (earnings factors for additional pension) shall have effect, except in prescribed circumstances, as if no [2 such] primary Class 1 contributions had been paid or treated as paid upon those earnings for that week and section 45A of that Act did not apply (where it would, apart from this subsection, apply).

(2) Where the whole or part of a contributions equivalent premium has been paid or treated as paid in respect of the earner, the Secretary of State may make a determination reducing or eliminating the application of subsection (1).

(3) Subsection (1) is subject to regulations under paragraph 5(3A) to (3E) of Schedule 2.

(4) Regulations may, so far as is required for the purpose of providing entitlement to additional pension (such as is mentioned in section 44(3)(b) of

the Social Security Contributions and Benefits Act 1992) but to the extent only that the amount of additional pension is attributable to provision made by regulations under section 45(5) of that Act, disapply subsection (1).

(5) In relation to earners where, by virtue of subsection (1), section 44(6) of the Social Security Contributions and Benefits Act 1992 has effect, in any tax year, as mentioned in that subsection in relation to some but not all of their earnings, regulations may modify the application of section 44(5) [5 or (5A)] of that Act.]

AMENDMENTS

1. Pensions Act 1995 s.140(1) (April 6, 1997).
2. National Insurance Contributions Act 2002 Sch.1 para.39 (April 6, 2003).
3. Pensions Act 2007 Sch.4 para.23 (September 26, 2007).
4. Pensions Act 2014 Sch.13 para.31 (April 6, 2016).
5. Child Support, Pensions and Social Security Act 2000 s.38(1) (July 28, 2000).

[1 Women, married women and widows

1.646 **49.** [*repealed*]

AMENDMENTS

1. Pensions Act 2014 s.24 Sch.13 para.32 (April 6, 2016).

Social Security (Incapacity for Work) Act 1994

(1994 c.18)

1.647 *For the text of and commentary to relevant sections of this Act, see the 2011/12 edition of this Volume.*

New Style Jobseekers Act 1995

(1995 c.18)

SECTIONS REPRODUCED

AS AMENDED BY THE WELFARE REFORM ACT 2012

PART I

THE JOBSEEKER'S ALLOWANCE

Entitlement

SCHEDULES

Schedule 1 — Supplementary Provisions.

An Act to provide for a jobseeker's allowance and to make other provision to promote the employment of the unemployed and the assistance of persons without a settled way of life. [June 28, 1995]

GENERAL NOTE

1.649 The form of the Act set out below (described in this volume as the new style Jobseekers Act 1995) is as amended in cases in which universal credit has come into operation, so that IBJSA has been abolished, and any new claim for JSA can only be for new style JSA under the Act as amended. The circumstance that brings about the abolition of IBJSA under s.33(1)(a) of the WRA 2012 and the coming into force of the amendments to the 1995 Act under later provisions is the making of a new claim for JSA (or for other benefits including universal credit and ESA) in an area where "full service" universal credit has been rolled out and where the particular claimant is legally able to make a claim for universal credit (see arts 4(1) and (2) of the Welfare Reform Act 2012 (Commencement No.9 and Transitional and Transitory Provisions and Commencement No.8 and Savings and Transitional Provisions (Amendment) Order 2013 (SI 2013/983) as further applied in later Commencement Orders). The Orders are now set out so far as still relevant in Vol.V of this series, 2021/22 edition as updated in Cumulative Supplements included in Vol.II of this series and in mid-year Supplements. The position was reached in December 2018 when the universal credit rollout had extended to the whole of Great Britain. Some prohibitions on claiming universal credit remained, in particular the so-called SDP gateway, where a claimant who was entitled to an income-related benefit including the severe disability premium was prohibited from claiming universal credit (reg.4A of the Universal Credit (Transitional Provisions) Regulations 2014 (SI 2014/1230)). That prohibition was removed by the revocation of reg.4A with effect from January 27, 2021. The two further remaining prohibitions have now also been removed. The former exception for "frontier workers" was removed with effect from March 30, 2022 by SI 2022/302 and the discretion given to the Secretary of State under reg.4 of the Transitional Provisions Regulations 2014 to determine (for the safeguarding of efficient administration or ensuring the efficient testing of administrative systems) that no claims for universal credit were to be accepted in an area or category of case was removed with effect from July 25, 2022 by reg.2 of the Universal Credit (Transitional Provisions) Amendment Regulations 2022 (SI 2022/752). There is thus now no exception, however remote, to the proposition that any new claim for JSA can only be for new style JSA.

Entitlement to old style JSA can only now exist as part of a continuing award made earlier (see now in Vol.V of this series, 2021/22 edition as updated in Cumulative Supplements included in Vol.II of this series and in mid-year Supplements). Since entitlement to contribution-based benefit in old style JSA is limited to 182 days in any jobseeking period (s.5 of the old style Jobseekers Act 1995), no award made at a time when a new claim for old style JSA was still generally possible could survive long after April 2021. In practice continuing awards will overwhelmingly be awards of income-based old style JSA.

To save space and complication, the only amendments identified below are those made in and under the Welfare Reform Act 2012, and subsequent amendments to this form of the Act. Previous amendments are not identified, but can be traced in the previous editions of what was then Vol.II of this series. In addition, provisions that have been completely revoked under the WRA 2012 to produce the structure of new style JSA have simply been omitted from the text without any remaining reference.

PART I

THE JOBSEEKER'S ALLOWANCE

Entitlement

The jobseeker's allowance

1.—(1) An allowance, to be known as a jobseeker's allowance, shall be payable in accordance with the provisions of this Act. 1.650

(2) Subject to the provisions of this Act, a claimant is entitled to a jobseeker's allowance if he–

(a) [1 . . .];
(b) has [2 accepted a claimant commitment];
(c) [1 . . .];
(d) satisfies the conditions set out in section 2;
(e) is not engaged in remunerative work;
(f) does not have limited capability for work;
(g) is not receiving relevant education;
(h) is under pensionable age; and
(i) is in Great Britain.

(2A) – (2D) [3 . . .].

(3) A jobseeker's allowance is payable in respect of a week.

(4) [3 . . .].

AMENDMENTS

1. Welfare Reform Act 2012 s.49(2) (trigger date on or after April 29, 2013).
2. Welfare Reform Act 2012 s.44(2) (trigger date on or after April 29, 2013).
3. Welfare Reform Act 2012 Sch.14 Pt 1 (trigger date on or after April 29, 2013).

DEFINITIONS

"claimant"—see s.35(1).
"claimant commitment"—see s.6A.
"Great Britain"—see s.35(1)
"limited capability for work"—see s.35(2) and Sch.1.
"pensionable age"—see s.35(1) and reg.2(1) of the JSA Regulations 2013 and SSCBA 1992 s.122(1).
"relevant education"—see s.35(2) and Sch.1.
"remunerative work"—*ibid.*, and JSA Regulations 2013, reg.42(1).
"week"—see s.35(1).

GENERAL NOTE

Subsection (2) sets out the basic conditions of entitlement to new style JSA. 1.651
It is merely a framework, amplified by other sections of and Schedules to the Act ("Subject to the provisions of this Act") and in the detail of the Jobseeker's Allowance Regulations 2013 (the JSA Regulations 2013). All seven basic conditions must be satisfied for there to be entitlement, but they are applicable to the individual claimant only. The circumstances of any partner or other member of the family are irrelevant. There is no power to make regulations allowing entitlement without satisfaction of all the basic conditions (apart from subs.(2)(i): para.11 of Sch.1), but Sch.1 allows regulations to treat some (but not all) of the conditions as

satisfied or not satisfied in prescribed circumstances. Similarly, there is no provision for any payment to be made while the satisfaction of the basic conditions is being investigated, but there can be some deeming of such satisfaction at the start of a claim and of course, if satisfied from the outset, new style JSA can be awarded from the beginning of the period of claim. In addition, universal credit may be payable, in arrears, on the basis of the income actually received or not received from sources such as new style JSA.

There will nearly always be very good reasons for a person who is entitled to universal credit also, if qualified, to claim new style JSA, even though the amount of JSA payable reduces the amount of universal credit pound for pound. The entitlement to new style JSA can continue even if the claimant temporarily acquires capital or other income such as to exclude universal credit entitlement and the crucial, but commonly overlooked, reg.5 of the JSA Regulations 2013 secures that during dual entitlement new style JSA work-related and connected requirements, with the associated sanctions provisions, do not apply.

Readers familiar with old style JSA must remember that neither being available for employment nor actively seeking employment is a condition of entitlement to new style JSA. Such matters are the possible subject of work-related requirements under ss.6D and 6E, backed up by sanctions for failure without good reason to comply.

1.652 *Section 2 conditions (subs.(2)(d))*

Taking the subs.(2) conditions slightly out of the statutory order, in some ways the most basic is that in s.1(2)(d), that the conditions set out in s.2 are satisfied. Section 2 imposes the contribution conditions for the benefit, and the rule excluding entitlement if the claimant's earnings exceed a prescribed level. See the notes to s.2 for the details. The contribution conditions require the claimant to have undertaken relatively recent employment as an employed earner and paid at least some Class 1 national insurance contributions. Although there is no minimum age for entitlement specified in s.1 or elsewhere, the contribution conditions have the practical effect of excluding the under-18s. Earnings of the claimant exclude entitlement completely if after taking account of any disregards they exceed the age-related applicable amount under s.4(1)(a) and reg.49 of the JSA Regulations 2013 (reg.48). Earnings below that prescribed level can affect the amount of new style JSA payable (see s.4(1)(b) and reg.50)

1.653 *Has accepted a claimant commitment (subs.(2)(b))*

The concept of a claimant commitment as a condition of receiving benefit is an important part of the underlying policy behind the Government's social security benefit reforms, adopted for both universal credit and new style JSA. See the notes to s.6A below for extensive discussion. Note that the condition is met merely by having accepted the most up-to-date version of the claimant commitment. A failure to comply with the terms of the claimant commitment does not entail any breach of subs.(2)(b), nor is that in itself any ground for a sanction, although sanctions may be imposed for failures to comply with work-related and connected requirements that are recorded in the claimant commitment and other legal consequences may follow from failures to carry out other obligations.

In contrast to the position in the universal credit legislation, there is nothing in s.1 or s.6A or Sch.1 specifically to allow regulations to permit entitlement where a claimant has not accepted a claimant commitment or to treat a commitment as having been accepted in any prescribed circumstances. Section 6A(5) provides that a commitment can only be accepted if a claimant accepts the most up-to-date version "in such manner as may be prescribed". See the notes to s.6A for further discussion. There must therefore be grave doubt whether reg.8 of the JSA Regulations 2013, prescribing two circumstances in which there can be entitlement without having accepted a claimant commitment, was validly made (see previous editions of this volume for the apparent importance of reg.8 to the operation of new style JSA during the coronavirus pandemic). There must also be doubt about the validity of reg.7(1) and (2) in prescribing when a claimant is to be treated as having accepted a commitment on a date earlier than that of actual acceptance. That seems to go beyond "manner" in s.6A(5). However, presumably no-one will object to the DWP applying the beneficial relaxations in regs.7 and 8 even if not authorised by primary legislation. See the notes to reg.7 for how the system is meant to work both at the beginning of a claim and when a review of an existing commitment is being considered, plus discussion of when a sanction, rather than denial of entitlement, might follow from a failure by the claimant to participate in the process.

Is not engaged in remunerative work (subs.(2)(e)) 1.654

See further s.21 and Sch.1 para.1, which together enabled the making of the amplificatory provisions in regs 42 to 44 of the JSA Regulations 2013. It may seem obvious that those who have a job cannot be said to be unemployed. But previous regimes have always catered for partial unemployment, and it is inevitably a matter of controversy at what point a line is to be drawn beyond which claimants are working to such an extent that they cannot properly be said to be unemployed and need state support. The remunerative work rules draw that line for new style JSA in the same place as for old style JSA. Regulation 42 sets the threshold for the claimant (work by a partner or other member of the family being irrelevant) at 16 hours per week, with provision for averaging, and defines "remunerative work" as work for which payment is made or which is done in expectation of payment. There is some guidance on hours that are not to count. These rules apply regardless of the amount paid for the work, but there are exceptions for volunteering and some other sorts of work in reg.44.

Regulation 43 of the JSA Regulations 2013 deals with those who are to be treated as engaged in remunerative work, notwithstanding that they may not at the time at issue be doing any work at all, and thus be excluded from entitlement. Regulation 43(1) covers those who are without good cause or by reason of holiday absent from what constitutes remunerative work under reg.42 (those on maternity leave, paternity leave, shared parental leave or parental bereavement or adoption leave or absent from work through illness are protected). Regulation 43(2) covers those who have received holiday pay within four weeks of the termination or interruption of employment (reg.58(1)(c)). Receipt of final earnings or of a payment in lieu of notice or of compensation for breach of the contract of employment does not trigger the operation of reg.43(2).

Regulation 44 protects a range of claimants who are working by treating them as not engaged in remunerative work, mainly charity or voluntary workers paid only expenses and those carrying out various worthy activities (see the notes to reg.44 for the details).

Does not have limited capability for work (subs.(2)(f)) 1.655

This condition represents, as in the past, a demarcation line between benefits for those able to work but unable to find employment and benefits for those incapable of work (now new style ESA). However, complications inevitably occurred when claimants had to transfer from one type of benefit to the other, particularly in respect of periods of short-term incapacity, with dangers of undue administrative burdens and of claimants falling between both stools. Hence the demarcation is no longer as strict as in the past. Regulations 46 and 46A of the JSA Regulations 2013 allow someone to remain in receipt of new style JSA whilst unable to work on account of some specific disease or disablement for up to two weeks (reg.46) or up to 13 weeks (reg.46A). No more than two reg.46 periods are permitted in any jobseeking period of less than 12 months and no more than one reg.46A period. The regulations operate by treating the claimant, where the necessary conditions (which include satisfying the conditions in s.1(2) apart from (f)) are satisfied, as not having limited capability for work.

Unfortunately, para.2 of Sch.1 to the Act dealing with limited capability for work merely provides that the question whether a person has or does not have limited capability for work for the purposes of new style JSA is to be determined in accordance with the test for new style ESA or universal credit, requiring the respective legislative provisions to have effect for this purpose also. That contains no express power to make regulations treating a claimant who actually has limited capability for work as not having that limited capability or allowing there to be entitlement to new style JSA despite not satisfying the condition in s.1(2)(f). However, para.1(a) of Sch.2 to the Welfare Reform Act 2007 does empower the making of regulations treating a claimant in prescribed circumstances as having or as not having limited capability for work. Section 37(6) of the Welfare Rights Act 2012 does the same in relation to universal credit. Since para.2(2) and (3) of Sch.1 to the new style Jobseekers Act 1995 gives those provisions effect for its purposes, they can be regarded as authorising regs 46 and 46A. It is unfortunate that such a circuitous route has to be found to reach that result.

1.656 *Is not receiving relevant education (subs.(2)(g))*

Regulation 45 of the JSA Regulations 2013, made under s.21 and Sch.1 para.14, defines when a claimant is to be treated as receiving relevant education. See the notes to reg.45 for the details. The meaning generally covers those who are "qualifying young persons", i.e. aged 16 or more but less than 20 and enrolled for full-time non-advanced education (reg.45(1)(a), (7) and (8)) or others undertaking a full-time course of advanced education or a course for which a student loan or grant is available (reg.45(1)(b), (2), (4), (5) and (6)). Anyone aged under 16 would not be caught by those categories, but would in practice be excluded from entitlement under para.(d) by being unable to satisfy the contribution conditions. In any event, any claimant not caught by the above provisions (including in theory under-16s) undertaking a course of study or training that is not compatible with any work-related requirement that has been imposed is deemed by reg.45(3) to be receiving relevant education.

1.657 *Is under pensionable age (subs.(2)(h))*

New style JSA, like old style JSA, is a working-age benefit. "Pensionable age" is defined as in the SSCBA 1992 s.122(1) (see s.35(1) below and reg.2(1) of the JSA Regulations 2013), which in turn refers on to the rules in Sch.4 to the Pensions Act 1995, as amended, where detailed tables are set out. The age has now, from November 2018, been equalised for all. From December 2018 it rose by one month every two months, reaching 66 in October 2020. It remains at 66 for anyone born before April 6, 1960 and is scheduled to reach 67 for those born from that date on in a staged process beginning in 2026 and ending in 2028, as confirmed in the State Pension age Review 2023 presented to Parliament in March 2023.

1.658 *Is in Great Britain (subs.(2)(i))*

Note that the condition of entitlement is not habitual residence, ordinary residence or even residence. It is merely presence in Great Britain, including its territorial waters (s.35(1)). That means England, Wales and Scotland, but not Northern Ireland. Section 21 and para.11 of Sch.1 enabled the making of reg.41 of the JSA Regulations 2013, which treats temporary absences for certain specified purposes (e.g. to attend an employment interview) as presence in Great Britain. See reg.11 of the Persons Abroad Regulations 1975 on the Continental Shelf.

The provision in subs.(3) that JSA is payable in respect of a week has some significant consequences, including that a failure to satisfy one of the basic conditions of entitlement on any one day of a week leads to disentitlement for the entire week. Paragraph 5 of Sch.1 enables the making of regulations to permit payment of new style JSA for a period of less than a week. The circumstances in which this may be done are contained in regs 64 – 66 of the JSA Regulations 2013.

Temporary Coronavirus Provisions

1.659 The effect of the temporary coronavirus provisions relevant to new style JSA has expired. See previous editions of this volume for the details.

The contribution-based conditions

2.—(1) The conditions referred to in section 1(2)(d) are that the claimant— 1.660

(a) has actually paid Class 1 contributions [3 or Class 2 contributions under Case G of Part 9 of the Social Security (Contributions) Regulations 2001] in respect of one ("the base year") of the last two complete years before the beginning of the relevant benefit year and satisfies the additional conditions set out in subsection (2);

(b) has, in respect of the last two complete years before the beginning of the relevant benefit year, either paid Class 1 contributions [3 or Class 2 contributions under Case G of Part 9 of the Social Security (Contributions) Regulations 2001] or been credited with earnings and satisfies the additional condition set out in subsection (3);

(c) does not have earnings in excess of the prescribed amount; [1. . .]

(d) [1 . . .].

(2) The additional conditions mentioned in subsection (1)(a) are that—

(a) the contributions have been paid before the week for which the jobseeker's allowance is claimed;

(b) the claimant's relevant earnings for the base year upon which primary Class 1 contributions [3 or Class 2 contributions under Case G of Part 9 of the Social Security (Contributions) Regulations 2001] have been paid or treated as paid are not less than the base year's lower earnings limit multiplied by 26.

(2A) Regulations may make provision for the purposes of subsection (2)(b) for determining the claimant's relevant earnings for the base year.

(2B) Regulations under subsection (2A) may, in particular, make provision—

(a) for making that determination by reference to the amount of a person's earnings for periods comprised in the base year;

(b) for determining the amount of a person's earnings for any such period by—

  (i) first determining the amount of the earnings for the period in accordance with regulations made for the purposes of section 3(2) of the Benefits Act, and

  (ii) then disregarding so much of the amount found in accordance with sub- paragraph (i) as exceeded the base year's lower earnings limit (or the prescribed equivalent.

(3) The additional condition mentioned in subsection (1)(b) is that the earnings factor derived from so much of the claimant's earnings as did not exceed the upper earnings limit and upon which primary Class 1 contributions [3 or Class 2 contributions under Case G of Part 9 of the Social Security (Contributions) Regulations 2001] have been paid or treated as paid or from earnings credited is not less, in each of the two complete years, than the lower earnings limit for the year multiplied by 50.

(3A) Where primary Class 1 contributions [3 or Class 2 contributions under Case G of Part 9 of the Social Security (Contributions) Regulations 2001] have been paid or treated as paid on any part of a person's earnings, subsection (3) above shall have effect as if such contributions had been paid or treated as paid on so much of the earnings as did not exceed the upper earnings limit.

(3B) Regulations may—

(a) provide for the first set of conditions to be taken to be satisfied in the case of persons—

(i) who have been entitled to any prescribed description of benefit during any prescribed period or at any prescribed time, or

(ii) who satisfy other prescribed conditions;

(3C) In subsection (3B)—

"the first set of conditions" means the condition set out in subsection (1)(a) and the additional conditions set out in subsection (2);

"benefit" means—

[2 (za) universal credit,]

(a) any benefit within the meaning of section 122(1) of the Benefits Act,

(b) any benefit under Parts 7 to 12 of the Benefits Act,

(c) credits under regulations under section 22(5) of the Benefits Act,

(d) a [1 . . .] jobseeker's allowance, [1 . . .]

(e) [1 . . .].

(4) For the purposes of this section—

(a) "benefit year" means a period which is a benefit year for the purposes of Part II of the Benefits Act or such other period as may be prescribed for the purposes of this section;

(b) "the relevant benefit year" is the benefit year which includes—

(i) the beginning of the jobseeking period which includes the week for which a jobseeker's allowance is claimed, or

(ii) (if earlier) the beginning of any linked period; and

(c) other expressions which are used in this section and the Benefits Act have the same meaning in this section as they have in that Act.

AMENDMENTS

1. Welfare Reform Act 2012 Sch.14 Pt 1 (trigger date on or after April 29, 2013).

2. Welfare Reform Act 2012 Sch.2 para.35 (April 29, 2013).

3. JSA Regulations 2013 reg.75 (trigger date on or after April 29, 2013).

DEFINITIONS

"the Benefits Act"—see s.35(1).
"claimant"—*ibid.*
"earnings"—see s.35(3) and Sch.1 and reg.2(2) of the JSA Regulations 2013.
"earnings factor"—see sub.(4)(c) and SSCBA 1992 ss.22 and 23.
"jobseeking period"—see s.35(1) and regs 2(1) and 47 of the JSA Regulations 2013.
"linked period"—see s.35(2) and Sch.1 para.3 and reg.39 of the JSA Regulations 2013.
"lower earnings limit"—see subs.(4)(c) and SSCBA 1992 s.5(1)(a).
"prescribed"—see s.35(1).
"primary Class 1 contributions"—see subs.(4)(c) and SSCBA 1992 ss.6 and 8.
"upper earnings limit"—see subs.(4)(c) and SSCBA 1992 ss.122(1) and 5(1).
"week"—see s.35(1).
"year"—*ibid.*

GENERAL NOTE

This provision fills out the basic condition of entitlement in s.1(2)(d) by specifying the contribution conditions for new style JSA and imposing the condition that the claimant's earnings do not exceed a prescribed limit (subs.(1)(c)). 1.661

The contribution conditions 1.662

As to be expected in an insurance or contribution-based benefit, the claimant must satisfy conditions as to past contributions in terms of a specified mixture of paid and credited Class 1 social security contributions (those paid by employed earners) in specified recent years (subs.(1) (a) and (b)). The years specified are either of two complete years (tax years: s.35(1)) ending before the beginning of the relevant benefit year, i.e. the benefit year including the start of the jobseeking period, including linked periods, of which the week of potential entitlement is part.

The first step in applying the contribution conditions is to identify the relevant benefit year. A benefit year runs generally from the first Sunday in January in one calendar year to the first Saturday in January in the next calendar year. By virtue of subs.(4)(b), the relevant year is that including the beginning of the jobseeking period containing the week in question or, importantly, any earlier linked period. See regs 37–40 of the JSA Regulations 2013 for these concepts in detail, but the essence is that a jobseeking period is a period during which the conditions of entitlement in s.1(2) were met and for which a claim for JSA was made. Separate such periods may be linked into one jobseeking period if separated by less than 12 weeks or by a "linked period". If a linked period precedes a jobseeking period as strictly defined, with no more than a 12-week gap, the relevant benefit year is that including the beginning of the linked period. Linked periods are periods during which the claimant is entitled to carer's allowance or maternity allowance, has or is treated as having limited capability for work, is or is treated as incapable of work or is undergoing training attracting a training allowance. Those rules may enable qualification for new style JSA to be assessed by reference to employment and contributions many years in the past. So, to take the simplest example not involving any linking, if someone's first ever claim for any benefit was for JSA in October 2020, the relevant benefit year is January 2020–January 2021.

The second step is to ascertain the two contribution/tax years (April 6 in one calendar year to April 5 in the next) in which the requisite level of contributions must be met: the last two complete such years before the start of the relevant benefit year. So if the relevant benefit year is 2020–2021 (January–January), the tax/contribution years are 2017–2018 and 2018–2019 (April–April), since tax/contribution year 2019–2020 was not complete at the start of the relevant benefit year.

The final steps are to determine whether in one of those tax/ contribution years (the "base year") the requisite level of actually paid contributions has been met (the first contribution condition) (subss.(1)(a) and (2)(b)) and, if so, whether the requisite level of paid and/or credited contributions has also been met in respect of each of the two tax years (the second contribution condition) (subss.(1)(b) and (3)). Paid (or treated as paid) means paid (or treated as paid) on so much of the earnings in the relevant years as did not exceed the upper earnings limit for contributions payment purposes (subs.(3A)). See further commentary to SSCBA 1992 Sch.3. For the first contribution condition the contributions actually paid over the base year must have been generated by earnings ("relevant earnings") of at least 26 times the lower earnings limit for making contributions (LEL). Although in the past it was possible for higher earners to reach that level after not very many weeks of employment, that is now prevented by reg.34 of the JSA Regulations 2013, which provides that a claimant's earnings above the LEL are to be disregarded for this purpose. For the second contribution condition, the contributions paid or credited in each of the relevant tax years must have been generated by actual or credited earnings of at least 50 times the LEL.

NH v SSWP (JSA) [2021] UKUT 227 (AAC) contains a detailed and helpful description of the working of the two contribution conditions in s.2(1) and in particular of how it may be the case that a claimant satisfies the second condition, but not the first, which can only be satisfied by Class 1 contributions that have actually been paid and has more restrictive rules about the calculation of relevant earnings that can go towards satisfying the condition. In *NH*, the claim for new style JSA was made on April 6, 2020, so that the "base years" in which the contribution conditions had to be satisfied were the tax years 2017/18 and 2018/19. The claimant accepted that she did not satisfy the first contribution condition in 2018/19, but disagreed with the DWP's view that she did not satisfy it in 2017/18. In that tax year she was only employed until June 6, 2017, when she was made redundant. She had received four weeks' wages (on which Class 1 contributions were paid) on each of April 14 and May 15 and three weeks' on June 9. But on that date she was also paid 13 weeks' wages in lieu of notice and two and a half weeks' holiday pay. She argued that she had been paid for 26 and a half weeks at a rate that worked out above the weekly LEL in force at the time. Judge Wikeley upheld the First-tier Tribunal's rejection of that argument. Liability to Class 1 contributions under the SSCBA 1992 arises on the amounts received in particular weeks, not on a cumulative aggregation of earnings over a year. The claimant could therefore only rely on the contributions that had actually been made, not on contributions that would notionally have been made if the payment in lieu and notice and holiday pay was disaggregated and notionally regarded as paid for the future weeks involved. Although the earnings-related contribution due in the last week of employment would have been greatly increased by the inclusion of those payments in the claimant's earnings, reg.34 of the JSA Regulations 2013 prevented putting any earnings in that week above the amount of the LEL towards the amount of "relevant earnings" to be taken into account in applying the test in s.2(2)(b) (relevant earnings 26 times the LEL).

Although the claimant may have been mistaken in describing her situation on dismissal as effectively being on gardening leave (as she was no longer in employment, and so not "on leave"), it appears that the result would have been the same if her employment had not terminated until the expiry of her 13 weeks' notice and the employer had chosen to pay the 13 weeks' pay in advance in a lump sum. It would have been different if she had been paid as normal during the notice period, but that would not have allowed the weeks of holiday pay to be counted, so probably not different enough to affect the outcome.

As with all contributory benefits, whether someone satisfies the contribution conditions for the benefit is a decision for the Secretary of State and now appealable to the Social Entitlement Chamber of the First-tier Tribunal as a decision on a claim for or award of benefit not otherwise rendered non-appealable (SSA 1998, s.12 and Sch.2; Decisions and Appeals Regulations 2013 reg.50 and Sch.3). From April 1, 1999, that has to some extent been affected by the entry into force of the Social Security (Transfer of Functions, etc.) Act 1999 (Vol.III) which transfers certain functions from the Secretary of State to the Board of Inland Revenue, whose functions were transferred to what is now His Majesty's Revenue and Customs (HMRC) by s.5(2) of the Commissioners for Revenue and Customs Act 2005. Certain matters as to categorisation of earners, which class of contributions a person is liable or entitled to pay, and whether they have been paid in respect of any period become decisions for HMRC, thus impacting to some degree on the Secretary of State's decision as to whether the conditions specific to benefit entitlement are met. Appeals on such decisions would go to the Tax Chamber rather than the Social Entitlement Chamber. It remains the position that decisions on whether the contribution conditions for benefit are satisfied, including, say, what tax/contribution years are relevant, are for the Secretary of State, while the decisions on what contributions of what Class were actually paid in any year are for HMRC. See the notes to s.8 of the Transfer of Functions Act in Vol.III.

The effect of the contribution conditions is inevitably to exclude some categories of potential claimants from entitlement or to disadvantage them in qualifying. Sometimes that is inherent in the notion of a contributory benefit, with the consequence that one has to have paid in, at least to some extent, before one can draw out benefit. So those who have never worked in the past, for whatever reason, plainly cannot satisfy the conditions. Nor can those who have been employed in the relevant tax/contribution years, but whose earnings were below the LEL or above it for insufficient weeks. Similarly, the exclusion of those who have been solely or mainly self-employed in the relevant years, although they may have contributed for many years in the past or more recently as employees can find justification on the basis that the self-employed do not pay social security contributions designed to fund benefits such as new style JSA. One consequence of the most straightforward exclusion is to apply an effective minimum age of qualification for new style JSA through the basic condition of entitlement in s.1(2)(d). No-one under the age of 16 is liable (or therefore able) to make Class 1 contributions or can have contributions credited. Accordingly, at least two tax/contribution years with the earliest containing the sixteenth birthday must build up before there can be a possibility of satisfying the contribution conditions in a subsequent benefit year.

Some other exclusions, though, begin to look a bit more arbitrary and unlinked to the merits of particular cases. For instance, the structure of relevant benefit years and contribution years can throw up inconsistent results depending on what could be regarded as accidents of the calendar. If a claimant makes a first claim in the December of a year, the test is applied by reference to contributions made more than 19 or 20 months ago, with more recent contributions being irrelevant. However, the reference for a claim that is made in February can take account of contributions made as recently as 10 months ago. On the other hand, the linking rules enable contributions sometimes very many years in the past to be taken into account in generally deserving cases, but not every such case. *LE v SSWP* [2009] UKUT 166 (AAC) holds that the omission of taking a career break to care for young children from the provision for linked periods, while indirectly discriminatory against women, was justified, so as not to infringe art.14 of the ECHR.

The Social Security Advisory Committee's paper on *The future of working age benefits for those not in paid work* (Occasional Paper No.26, dated July 2022, but not added to the website until October 28, 2022) details at p.48 some ways in which it considers the current operation of the contribution conditions to be inequitable, e.g. the arbitrariness in when recent contributions come into play depending on the accident of when in the year the jobseeking period begins and the exclusion of claimants who have paid in for maybe 30 years and then are excluded by an insufficiency of contributions in two recent years. The government's response, published on September 12, 2023, rejected the making of any changes to the contribution requirements, at least until after the complete migration of legacy benefit cases to universal credit.

Note that claimants in receipt of JSA are automatically credited with contributions under reg.8A(2)(a) of the Social Security (Credits) Regulations 1975, but unemployed people not so in receipt must make a claim within a reasonable time (reg.8A(2)(b) – (d) and (3)). See *SM v SSWP (JSA)* [2021] UKUT 179 (AAC) and *KL v SSWP (JSA)* [2022] UKUT 270.

The earnings condition 1.663

From the beginning of the whole JSA scheme in 1996 the rules for contribution-based benefit have contained the condition that the claimant's earnings do not exceed the contribution-based allowance that they would otherwise receive. One way of looking at that condition (and to some extent reconciling the rule with conceptions of new style JSA as a benefit paid irrespective of means) might be to regard it as a statement that those earning in excess of the prescribed amount cannot in reality be said to be unemployed but are, in effect, deemed to be "employed". The rule could thus be said to play a parallel role to that of the "remunerative work" condition in s.1(2)(e) which rules out claimants working 16 or more hours per week (see reg.42 of the JSA Regulations 2013), regardless of the amount earned. Both rules deal with the perennially troublesome area of partial unemployment. Another way of looking at this condition, however, especially when also considering the rules contained in s.4(1) on reduction or abatement of new style JSA because of earnings and pension payments, is to see it as a further intrusion of elements of means-testing into contributory benefits, something that had been increasing stealthily since 1980. But the position is still far from fully-fledged means-testing, with no tests of other income or capital and no aggregation of the income or capital of other members of the family.

The condition is a simple cliff-edged one. If earnings exceed the prescribed amount by the smallest amount there can be no entitlement. If earnings equal that amount, or are lower, the basic condition of entitlement in s.1(2)(d) is satisfied if the contribution conditions under s.2 are also satisfied. The fact that the rule precludes entitlement, rather than merely affects the amount payable, means that weeks covered by it do not eat into a claimant's maximum 182 days of entitlement to new style JSA (see s.5).

The prescribed amount is not the same for everyone, but is determined for a particular claimant in accordance with the formula set out in reg.48 of the JSA Regulations 2013: a level equal to the claimant's personal age-related amount of new style JSA (determined in accordance with s.4(1)(a) and reg.49(1) of the JSA Regulations 2013) plus the appropriate disregards from their earnings, minus one penny. Only the claimant's earnings are taken into account.

On what constitutes "earnings" and their calculation, see s.35(3), which requires the term to be construed in accordance with SSCBA 1992 s.3 (earnings includes any remuneration or profit derived from an employment and to be calculated in accordance with regulations), but subject to any regulations made for the purposes of s.35(3). In contrast to the position for old style JSA, the definition of "earnings" in reg.2(1) of the JSA Regulations 2013 is expressly for those purposes and refers to the meanings in regs 58 and 60, thus expressly including earnings from self-employment (reg.60) as well as earnings from employment as an employed earner (reg.58). That definition in itself seems not enough to exclude the operation of the Computation of Earnings Regulations (see Pt III of this volume) made under s.3 of the SSCBA 1992, in calculating or estimating the amount of earnings as defined in regs 58 and 60 (see the notes to s.35(3)). But reg.48 of the JSA Regulations 2013, authorised by s.2(1)(c), provides that in calculating the prescribed amount of earnings that must not be exceeded the amount of any applicable disregard in the Schedule to the Regulations must be added in. That bridges one difference between the Computation of Earnings Regulations provisions and those in Pt 7 of the JSA Regulations 2013.

Section 2 is modified in relation to its application to share fishermen by reg.69 of the JSA Regulations 2013. Since the modification applies only in those restricted cases it is not included in the text above. By contrast, the modification in reg.75 (covering volunteer development workers who have taken up the option of paying Class 2 contributions while abroad) is made general and is included.

Amount payable by way of jobseeker's allowance

1.664 **4.**—(1) In the case of a [1 . . .] jobseeker's allowance, the amount payable in respect of a claimant ("his personal rate") shall be calculated by—

(a) determining the age-related amount applicable to him; and

(b) making prescribed deductions in respect of earnings, pension payments, PPF payments and FAS payments.

(2) The age-related amount applicable to a claimant, for the purposes of subsection (1)(a), shall be determined in accordance with regulations.

(3) and (3A) [1 . . .].

(4) Except in prescribed circumstances, a jobseeker's allowance shall not be payable where the amount otherwise payable would be less than a prescribed minimum.

(5) The applicable amount shall be such amount or the aggregate of such amounts as may be determined in accordance with regulations.

(6) – (11A) [1. . .].

AMENDMENT

1. Welfare Reform Act 2012 Sch.14 Pt 1 (trigger date on or after April 29, 2013).

DEFINITIONS

"claimant"—see s.35(1).
"earnings"—see s.35(3).
"FAS payments"—see s.35(1).
"pension payments"—*ibid.*
"PPF payments"—*ibid.*
"prescribed"—*ibid.*
"regulations"—*ibid.*

GENERAL NOTE

If the claimant is entitled to new style JSA, the amount payable ("his personal rate") is calculated by deducting from the appropriate age-related amount (see reg.49 of the JSA Regulations 2013: a higher rate for those aged 25 or over, a lower rate for under-25s) any earnings that they have, subject to deductions and disregards (see reg.50), and pension, PPF (pension protection fund) and FAS (financial assistance scheme) payments (reg.51), in so far as the aggregate of reg.51 payments exceeds £50 a week. The rate of benefit is therefore not related to the level of previous earnings or to household responsibilities and is not generous. The April 2024 25+ rate is £90.50 per week and the under-25 rate £71.70. In *R. (on the application of Carson and Reynolds* [2005] UKHL, [2006] 1 A.C. 173, the House of Lords dismissed an appeal against the Court of Appeal's decision in *Reynolds* that the differential treatment of the under-25s was not discriminatory contrary to the Human Rights Act 1998 and art.14 of the ECHR. Lord Hoffmann considered that the circumstances of JSA (then old style JSA) and income support claimants aged up to and over 25 were relevantly different. Those under 25 were likely to have lower living expenses, e.g. from living with parents or otherwise not in an independent household, and to have lower earnings expectations. Also a line had to be drawn somewhere, so that there would have been justification if it had been concluded that similar circumstances had been treated differently. It is not clear how far that reasoning applies to new style JSA if a claimant under 25 has satisfied the contribution conditions. 1.665

In the Institute for Government and the SSAC's 2021 joint report *Jobs and benefits: The Covid-19 challenge* it was recommended that contributory JSA should be strengthened to provide a more generous short-term buffer against the immediate drop in income on losing employment and that its rates should not be below those provided by the standard allowance in universal credit (pp.20-1 and 34). That recommendation was merely noted in the Government's response of March 22, 2022, with the comment that the benefit system is not intended to replicate the income that a claimant was receiving prior to making a claim.

Only the claimant's own earnings and occupational or personal pension payments are relevant. On what constitutes "earnings" and their calculation, see s.35(3), which requires the term to be construed in accordance with SSCBA 1992 s.3 (earnings includes any remuneration or profit derived from an employment) and accordingly to be calculated or estimated in accordance with the Computation of Earnings Regulations made under s.3, but subject to any regulations made for the purposes of s.35(3). In contrast to the position for old style JSA, the definition of "earnings" in reg.2(1) of the JSA Regulations 2013 is expressly for those purposes and refers to the meanings in regs 58 and 60, thus expressly including earnings from self-employment (reg.60) as well as earnings from employment as an employed earner (reg.58). That definition in itself seems not enough to exclude the operation of the Computation of Earnings Regulations (Pt III of this volume) in calculating or estimating the amount of earnings (see the notes to s.35(3)). However, reg.50 of the JSA Regulations 2013 provides that the amount to be deducted under s.4(1)(b) is to be the amount of earnings calculated in accordance with Pt. 7 of the Regulations (i.e. regs 53-63 and the Schedule). That specific provision, authorised by s.4(1)(b), would seem to indicate an intention contrary to the general effect of s.35(3), even though it does not expressly mention s.35(3). Note that Pt 7 produces a calculation of earnings net of income tax, national insurance contributions and half of pensions contributions and that the exclusions for employed earners in reg.58(2) and the disregards in the Schedule to the Regulations, in particular the general £5 disregard under para.5, are to be applied before the deduction for earnings under reg.50 is made.

For the nature of relevant pension and cognate payments, see the notes to reg.51 of the JSA Regulations 2013, which provision brings only the amount by which the aggregate of such payments exceeds £50 per week into the s.4(1)(b) calculation. The £50 figure has not altered since the very start of the JSA scheme in 1996. The state pension is not relevant, as anyone in receipt of it will be excluded from entitlement under s.1(2)(h), and anyway it would fall outside the meaning of pension payments.

Note that the definition of "pension payments" in s.35(1) is in terms of periodical payments. Thus, the receipt of a lump sum under the scheme in question does not give rise to any amount to be deducted under s.4(1)(b). Since there is no "deprivation" rule in new style JSA, claimants who could have received higher periodical payments if they had opted to receive a smaller lump sum cannot be treated as receiving anything more than the actual amount of the periodical payments. And of course the amount of a claimant's capital is irrelevant. The definitions of "PPF payments" and "FAS payments" are not specifically restricted to periodical payments, but it is submitted that the overall context of reg.51 is clearly to restrict its application to payments in respect of a period and not to extend it to capital payments.

The deduction of net earnings pound for pound after disregards may, as discussed in the notes to s.2 in relation to subs.(2)(c), be seen as a reflection of a view that claimants are not unemployed to the extent that their activities generate earnings and an attempt to deal with the problem of partial unemployment when being unemployed is not as such a condition of entitlement. Then the taking account of pension and cognate payments might be said to reflect the same view in the context of pensions representing deferred earnings, but with the £50 allowance (unaltered since 1996) in recognition of the contributions that the workers concerned will have made towards the funding of those payments. However, it is hard to avoid a conclusion that the deductions also represent a creeping incursion of means-testing into contributory benefits.

The Social Security Advisory Committee's paper on *The future of working age benefits for those not in paid work* (Occasional Paper No.26, dated July 2022, but not added to the website until October 28, 2022) at pp.58-9 takes the view that the means-testing of a contributory benefit against pension income sits oddly in a world where the majority of private sector pension schemes are defined-contribution and members are free to draw flexibly from the funds through retirement. Nor was it clear why only that form of non-earned income should be identified for means-testing. It recommends that the test should be reviewed and consideration given to removing it. It may also be relevant to that view that the pension freedoms kick in at age 55 and the taking of benefits may not be an indication of withdrawal (or complete withdrawal) from the labour market. The government's response, published on September 12, 2023, rejected any review of the means-testing of the amount of new style JSA against pension income, saying that it "is unreasonable to pay full New Style JSA or ESA to people who had retired from their regular occupation with a significant occupational pension before reaching state pension age". Many in such circumstances are still in the labour market and £50 per week, a sum unchanged since 1996, is scarcely significant, except perhaps by comparison with the measly level of new style JSA.

The end result may be that such deductions for earnings and pension payments result in no amount being payable, despite an underlying entitlement. Further, it would appear that even where the personal rate payable is nil because of such abatement, nevertheless, because there remains an underlying entitlement, weeks subject to that abatement still count towards the maximum period of entitlement to new style JSA (182 days in any period for which the person's entitlement is established by reference (under s.2(1)(b)) to the same two years—see s.5(1)). This contrasts with the position under s.2(1)(c) where the weekly earnings (on their own) exceed the prescribed amount. In that situation there is no entitlement (the person in effect is treated as if employed) and the periods covered do not eat into the 182 days' maximum entitlement.

Subsection (5) does not appear to have any practical application for new style JSA purposes.

Duration of a [1. . .] jobseeker's allowance

5.—(1) The period for which a person is entitled to a [1. . .] jobseeker's allowance shall not exceed, in the aggregate, 182 days in any period for which his entitlement is established by reference (under section 2(1)(b)) to the same two years. **1.666**

(2) The fact that a person's entitlement to a [1. . .] jobseeker's allowance ("his previous entitlement") has ceased as a result of subsection (1), does not prevent his being entitled to a further [1 . . .] jobseeker's allowance if—

(a) he satisfies the contribution-based conditions; and

(b) the two years by reference to which he satisfies those conditions includes at least one year which is later than the second of the two years by reference to which his previous entitlement was established.

(3) Regulations may provide that a person who would be entitled to a [1. . .] jobseeker's allowance but for the operation of prescribed provisions of, or made under, this Act shall be treated as if entitled to the allowance for the purposes of this section.

AMENDMENT

1. Welfare Reform Act 2012 Sch.14 Pt 1 (trigger date on or after April 29, 2013).

DEFINITIONS

"contribution-based conditions"—see s.35(1).
"entitled"—*ibid.*
"prescribed"—*ibid.*
"regulations"—*ibid.*
"year"—*ibid.*

GENERAL NOTE

The maximum duration of entitlement to new style JSA within any one jobseeking period is 182 days. A claimant can re-qualify under subs.(2) following the expiry of the 182 days, but on conditions which on the face of it would have led to the start of a new limit under subs.(1) anyway. Tribunals will need more knowledge of contributions than in the past (if only to understand the Secretary of State's decision communicated to them), since both the "exhaustion rule" (subs.(1)) and the "requalification rule" (subs.(2)) refer to the contribution-based conditions in s.2, the central ones for requalification purposes being those dealing with the claimant's contribution record. See further the annotations to that section. **1.667**

In the Institute for Government and the SSAC's 2021 joint report *Jobs and benefits: The Covid-19 challenge* it was recommended that contributory JSA should be strengthened to provide a more generous short-term buffer against the immediate drop in income on losing employment and that it should run for a year rather than six months, in line with ESA (pp.20-1 and 34). That recommendation was merely noted in the Government's response of March 22, 2022.

In *PL v SSWP (JSA)* [2016] UKUT 177 (AAC), Judge Markus gave the opinion that, in the light of the assistance that the claimant had received from her specialist disability employment adviser and specialist Work Choice provider, she had not been discriminated against under art.14 of the ECHR by the limit on the duration of old style contribution-based JSA and the accepted evidence that those with disabilities take longer to find work than those without. Even if there had been discrimination, the judge had no doubt that it was justified, both in the initial introduction of the rule in 1996 and in its continuing application. The opinion was not a necessary part of the decision because, as the Upper Tribunal has no power to give a declaration of incompatibility of primary legislation under s.4 of the Human Rights Act 1998, the judge had no alternative to dismissing the claimant's appeal against the disallowance of benefit on the expiry of the 182-day limit.

1.668 *Subsection (1): the exhaustion rule*

This stipulates that the period for which a person can be entitled to new style JSA cannot exceed in total 182 days in any period for which their entitlement is established by reference (under s.2(1)(b): the second contribution condition) to the same two tax/contribution years.

In the simplest case of continuous unemployment, this effectively means that after serving the seven "waiting days" (JSA Regulations 2013 reg.36) the exhaustion point is reached after 26 weeks, since new style JSA operates on a full week basis.

However, more complicated cases can arise. Some people suffer intermittent unemployment, with spells of unemployment being interspersed with a variety of other spells: periods of incapacity for work, perioss of employment, periods of training, periods caring for an invalid, periods of pregnancy. How is one to ascertain whether the days in an initial spell of unemployment are to be aggregated with ones in a later spell for purposes of this exhaustion rule? The answer lies in the rubric: "182 days in any period for which his entitlement is established by reference" (under s.2(1) (b): the second contribution condition) to the same two tax/contribution years. Translating and applying this requires some understanding of the concepts, "jobseeking period" (see further, reg.37 of the JSA Regulations 2013) "linking" (see further reg.39(1)) and "linked period" (see further, reg.39(2)). It also requires some understanding of the contribution-record conditions in s.2.See the notes to s.2 for an outline of those concepts and the notes to the JSA Regulations 2013 for more detail.

Although s.5 does not refer to "jobseeking period" or to "linked period" but deliberately to "any period for which his entitlement is established by reference (under s.2(1) (b)) to the same two [tax/contribution] years, identifying the beginning of the jobseeking period identifies the relevant benefit year and thus the two relevant tax/contribution years. Those are the last two complete tax/contribution years (April-April) before the start of the relevant benefit year (first Sunday in calendar year to last Saturday in next). So days of entitlement to new style JSA (or old style JSA under the provisions noted below) in apparently separate jobseeking periods can still be aggregated for purposes of the exhaustion rule provided that entitlement to new style JSA in each is determined by reference to the same two tax/contribution years. Which takes one to the essentials of the contribution-record conditions (see further the annotations to s.2).

Interpreting and applying the rubric "any period for which a person is entitled to a contribution-based jobseeker's allowance" requires making and maintaining the important distinction between "entitled" and "payable". While an allowance cannot be payable without entitlement, a person can be entitled to an allowance but, nevertheless, it may not be payable. So, if weekly earnings exceed the prescribed amount, there is no entitlement (s.2(1)(c)). If, in contrast, a combination of earnings and pension payments merely reduce the amount otherwise payable to nil under the abatement provisions of s.4, there is entitlement, but no payable amount. Similarly, a claimant caught by the trade dispute provision in s.14 is not entitled to an allowance, whereas in contrast the effect of a sanction under s.6J or 6K merely reduces the amount payable, usually to nil (see further in the notes to subs.(3) below on the power to treat a claimant as entitled). Days of entitlement to new style JSA, even if nothing is payable, count towards the 182-day limit. Days of non-entitlement do not.

Subsection (2): the requalification rule 1.669

Requalification here does not mean that the person will necessarily be entitled to benefit or that it will in fact be payable even if requalification is triggered. Actual entitlement will depend on fulfilling the conditions of entitlement set out in s.1, while the amount payable depends as normal on the principles in s.4. Requalification essentially means getting back on track for reconsideration of possible entitlement to new style JSA.

In order to requalify for consideration, the claimant must satisfy the ordinary contribution-record conditions in s.2. Further, however, the two tax/contribution years by reference to which the contribution-record conditions are satisfied must include at least one tax/contribution year which is later than the second tax/contribution year by reference to which "his previous entitlement" to new style JSA (now exhausted applying subs.(1)) was established. So someone who remains continuously unemployed after exhausting title, or whose spells of intermittent unemployment are not separated by periods that break the link, cannot requalify. Yet, in contrast, a claimant who breaks the link back to the previous period (for example by working for 16 or more hours per week for a continuous period of at least 13 weeks) can requalify if thereafter without work, or working less than 16 hours per week, provided that the new claim, starting a new jobseeking period, is in a later relevant benefit year. The claimant would also of course have to satisfy the contribution conditions in the new set of two tax/contribution years and satisfy the other conditions of entitlement actually to receive an award. The link would also be broken by not claiming new style JSA for a continuous 13-week period, since a period of no claim cannot be a jobseeking period (reg.37(2)(a) of the JSA Regulations 2013), but that apparent ability to move a new claim into a benefit year more favourable for requalification purposes is not one open to those without work who need an income from the state in the form of new style JSA (e.g. because of possessing too much capital to qualify for universal credit).

Paragraph (3) 1.670

Regulation 37(3) of the JSA Regulations 2013 is apparently made under subs.(3). It provides that a day within a jobseeking period counts against the 182-day limit if the claimant satisfies the purely contribution conditions in s.2 and the amount of benefit payable has been reduced to nil following a sanction under s.6J or 6K or a fraud sanction. However, in those circumstances the provision appears to be unnecessary (and possibly ultra vires) because the effect of a reduction in the amount of benefit payable under s.6J or 6K to nil is not to remove entitlement. Similarly, the Social Security Fraud Act 2001 imposes restrictions on payability of benefit and does not remove entitlement.

The transition from old style JSA

In subss.(1) and (2) (the first reference), the references to jobseeker's allowance are, 1.671
where art.12(1) and (2) of the Welfare Reform Act 2012 (Commencement No.9 and Transitional and Transitory Provisions and Commencement No.8 and Savings and Transitional Provisions (Amendment)) Order 2013 (as amended and set out in Vol.V of this series, 2021/22 edition as updated in Cumulative Supplements included in Vol. II of this series and in mid-year Supplements) applies, to be read as if they included a reference to an old style contribution-based JSA award (art.12(4) of that Order).

[1 *Work-related requirements*

Work-related requirements

6.—(1) The following provisions of this Act provide for the Secretary of State to impose work-related requirements with which claimants must comply for the purposes of this Act. 1.672

(2) In this Act "work-related requirement" means—
(a) a work-focused interview requirement (see section 6B);
(b) a work preparation requirement (see section 6C);
(c) a work search requirement (see section 6D);
(d) a work availability requirement (see section 6E).]

AMENDMENT

1. Welfare Reform Act 2012 s.49(3) (trigger date on or after April 29, 2013).

DEFINITION

"claimant"—see s.35(1).

GENERAL NOTE

1.673 Sections 6–6L replace ss.6–10 of the old style Jobseekers Act 1995 on jobseeking. They in the main set out what sort of work-related requirements can be imposed on which new style claimants, as well as the system for imposing sanctions (reductions in benefit) on claimants for failure to comply with those requirements and for other failures. The provisions are very similar to those in ss.13–28 of the Welfare Reform Act 2012 on universal credit (see Vol.II of this series, *Universal Credit etc.*), except that as in general all new style JSA claimants are subject to the work-related requirements regime, there is no need for the complicated provisions about what sort of requirements can be imposed on what sort of universal credit claimants. That is subject to the important qualification in reg.5 of the JSA Regulations 2013 (made under ss.6F(1) and 6H(1)(a)) that if a person is entitled both to new style JSA and to universal credit the work-related requirements under this Act do not apply, although a claimant commitment under s.6A below must still be accepted. Thus the control of conditionality and the imposition of sanctions appears to be restricted to universal credit, which could have bizarre results (see the annotations to reg.5). There is also a general exemption for recent victims of domestic violence (s.6H(5)–(6) and reg.15 of the JSA Regulations 2013) and for miscellaneous categories of deserving claimants specified in regs 16 and 16A.

Although s.6 refers only to work-related requirements as defined in ss.6B–6E, s.6G allows the Secretary of State to require claimants to participate in an interview for various related purposes, to provide information and evidence and to report specified changes in their circumstances. A failure for no good reason to comply with a requirement under s.6G can lead to a sanction and reduction of benefit under s.6K(2)(b). A failure for no good reason to comply with a work-related requirement can lead to a sanction and reduction of benefit under s.6K(2)(a), unless the circumstances fall within s.6J (higher-level sanctions).

Section 6A contains rules about the "claimant commitment", acceptance of which is a condition of entitlement under s.1(2)(b).

It was noted in paras 17 and 18 of *S v SSWP (UC)* [2017] UKUT 477 (AAC) that the universal credit equivalent of s.6(1) means that a work-related requirement can only come into being when it has been *imposed* by the Secretary of State (under the duty in s.6F). See the discussion in the notes to s.6A for the important implications for the effect in law of the standard terms of claimant commitments.

[1 Claimant commitment

1.674 **6A.**—(1) A claimant commitment is a record of a claimant's responsibilities in relation to an award of a jobseeker's allowance.

(2) A claimant commitment is to be prepared by the Secretary of State and may be reviewed and updated as the Secretary of State thinks fit.

(3) A claimant commitment is to be in such form as the Secretary of State thinks fit.

(4) A claimant commitment is to include—

(a) a record of the requirements that the claimant must comply with under this Act (or such of them as the Secretary of State considers it appropriate to include),
(b) any prescribed information, and
(c) any other information the Secretary of State considers it appropriate to include.

(5) For the purposes of this Act a claimant accepts a claimant commitment if, and only if, the claimant accepts the most up-to-date version of it in such manner as may be prescribed.]

AMENDMENT

1. Welfare Reform Act 2012 s.49(3) (trigger date on or after April 29, 2013).

DEFINITIONS

"claimant"—see s.35(1).
"prescribed"—*ibid.*

GENERAL NOTE

Under s.1(2)(b) it is one of the conditions of entitlement to new style JSA, as it is for universal credit, that the claimant has accepted a claimant commitment. See the notes to s.1 in previous editions for the continuance of this condition during the 2020 coronavirus outbreak, subject to the apparent operation of the exception in reg.8(b) of the JSA Regulations 2013, and its reintroduction as capacity allowed from July 1, 2020. Section 6A defines the nature of a claimant commitment and there are further provisions in regs 7 and 8 of the JSA Regulations 2013 about methods of acceptance and exceptions from the condition. **1.675**

Note that when the important reg.5 of the JSA Regulations 2013 applies, because a new style JSA beneficiary is also entitled to universal credit, so that the work-related requirements in ss.6B–6I do not apply, s.6A is left untouched. But there is then a question what could be included in a JSA claimant commitment.

Subsections (1) and (2) define a claimant commitment as a record prepared by the Secretary of State (in such form as he thinks fit: subs.(3)) of a claimant's responsibilities in relation to an award of new style JSA. In particular, by subs.(4)(a), the record is to include the requirements that the particular claimant must comply with under the Act, in the main work-related and connected requirements (see ss.6B–6G). Those requirements can sometimes be to take specific action (e.g. to participate in a particular interview under s.6B or to take particular action to improve prospects of paid work under s.6C or to obtain paid work under s.6D), although often the specification of such action by the Secretary of State will take place outside the claimant commitment (see the discussion in *JB v SSWP (UC)* [2018] UKUT 360 (AAC), below and the notes to s.6B). Nonetheless, the document may need to be fairly detailed and subject to frequent change, although there is a discretion in subs.(4)(a) to omit requirements if appropriate. The process of review and updating under subs.(2) appears to be completely informal, in stark contrast to the process for variation of a jobseeker's agreement under s.10 of the old style Jobseekers Act 1995, so can accommodate that. Each updating will trigger a new requirement to accept the most up-to-date version. Subsection (4)(b) allows the record to contain any prescribed information. Regulations have not as yet prescribed any such information. Subsection (4)(c) allows the record to contain any other information (note, information, not a further requirement) that the Secretary of State considers appropriate. For the claimant commitment to serve the basic purpose discussed below, that information must at least include information about the potential consequences under the Act of receiving a sanction for failure to carry out a requirement.

Note that, since subs.(4) is not an exhaustive statement of what a claimant commitment can contain, merely a statement of elements that it must contain, there is no reason why other responsibilities in relation to an award of new style JSA cannot also be recorded, along with any appropriate accompanying information, although the perceived need to include subs.(4)(c) could be argued to cast doubt on that conclusion. For instance, the general obligations under regs 38 and 44 of the Claims and Payments Regulations 2013 to supply information and evidence in connection with an award and to notify changes of circumstances should probably be recorded, as it is in the example mentioned in para.1.680 below.

Exceptions from the application of the basic condition in s.1(2)(b) are set out in reg.8 of the JSA Regulations 2013, although see the notes to s.1(2)(b) and to regs 7 and 8 for the doubtful validity of those regulations, there being no power in the Act for regulations to prescribe circumstances in which there can be entitlement without satisfying all the conditions in s.1(2) (apart from para.(i)). The Act does not seek to define what is meant by acceptance of a claimant commitment beyond the provision in s.6A(5) that it must be the most up-to-date version that has been accepted in such manner as prescribed in regulations. Regulation 7 of the JSA Regulations 2013 provides for the time within which and the manner in which the claimant commitment must be accepted, but says nothing about what accepting the commitment entails in substance. See the further discussion of the point at which a claimant is to be regarded as having not accepted the most up-to-date version of the claimant commitment, and so as not satisfying the basic condition in s.1(2)(b), in the notes to reg.7.

Since the commitment is the record of the particular claimant's responsibilities, it does not seem that acceptance can mean much more than an acknowledgement of its receipt or possibly also that the claimant understands the implications of the requirements set out. There can be no question of a claimant having to express any agreement with the justice or reasonableness of the requirements, let alone of the policy behind the imposition of "conditionality" in JSA and universal credit. Nor does acceptance seem to involve any personal commitment to carrying out the stated requirements. The obligation to comply with any requirements imposed under the new style Jobseekers Act 1995 does not rest on any contractual or consensual basis. It rests on the terms of the legislation. Further, a failure to comply with any requirement imposed by the Secretary of State is a matter for a potential sanction under s.6J or 6K, not for a conclusion that the basic condition of entitlement in s.1(2)(b) is no longer met. There is no direct sanction for a failure to comply with a requirement just because it is included in the claimant commitment, nor does such a failure show that the claimant commitment has ceased to be accepted in the sense suggested above. However, as inclusion in the claimant commitment is an acceptable means of notifying a claimant of a work-related or connected requirement (s.6H(4)), the absence of a direct sanction for not complying with a claimant commitment may be of limited practical significance.

Despite the incontrovertible nature of the legal framework, official sources continue to describe an essential feature of the claimant commitment as being that it and its conditionality requirements have been agreed by the claimant. See the DWP's statement of the aim of conditionality and sanctions set out in para.10 of the House of Commons Work and Pensions Committee's report of November 6, 2018 on *Benefit Sanctions* (HC 995 2017–19) and the Committee's own description of the claimant commitment as recording "the actions a [. . .] claimant has agreed to undertake as a condition of receiving their benefit". Even the Social Security Advisory Committee's March 19, 2019 call for evidence on the operation of the claimant commitment in universal credit for those subject to all work-related requirements talked of the commitment setting out what a claimant has agreed to do to prepare for work, or to increase their earnings if they are already working, and what will happen if a claimant fails to meet the agreed responsibilities. It might not matter much if such terminology is restricted to policy discussions. No doubt, for the sort of reasons mentioned below, it will always be better if the requirements set out in the claimant commitment have been worked out after a full and co-operative discussion with the work coach and the claimant agrees that the requirements are realistic and achievable. But there is evidence that the approach has infected the standard terms of claimant commitments, with consequent problems in ascertaining whether the legal requirements for the imposition of sanctions have been made out (see the discussion below of the standard terms and of the decision in *JB v SSWP (UC)* [2018] UKUT 360 (AAC)).

Work requirements are supposed to be set through a one-to-one relationship between work coach and claimant, enabling the development of a good understanding of the claimant's circumstances, so that the work coach can best help the claimant find work (see the DWP's evidence to the Work and Pensions Committee, para.87 of the report above). However, the Committee received evidence that many claimant commitments were "generic" in nature, failing to take account of individual circumstances, and that "easements" (i.e. circumstances in which in accordance with regulations the requirement in question could be lifted) were insufficiently used. Taking the view that it was unrealistic for claimants to know the rules about when easements could apply or for them to pour out the details of their personal lives at each meeting, the Committee recommended that the DWP develop a standard set of questions that work coaches routinely ask claimants when developing their claimant commitments, as well as improve the information available to claimants on easements. The DWP's response (House of Commons Work and Pensions Committee, *Benefit Sanctions: Government Response* (HC 1949 2017–19, February 11, 2019, paras 55–65)) was that current training, guidance and monitoring of work coaches involved standard key questions to identify things like caring responsibilities, health conditions and other complex circumstances that could impact ability to meet requirements. Additional easements were said to be more specific and sensitive, so should not be presented as if they would apply to the majority of claimants. Instead, a new information package on easements to be provided at the start of the claim was to become available in Spring 2019.

The SSAC's September 2019 study on *The effectiveness of the claimant commitment in Universal Credit* (Occasional Paper No.21), which is also relevant to new style JSA, contains much interesting information on policy and practical operation of the claimant commitment, without addressing the mismatch suggested above with the legal framework. It puts forward, within the overarching principle that the process of developing a commitment for a particular claimant should be reasonable and based on evidence of what works to help people move into sustained employment, five principles for the effectiveness of a commitment for a claimant in the intensive work search regime. It should be accessible, clear, tailored to the needs of each claimant, accepted by both parties and the claimant should have the right information. The SSAC identified many examples of good practice by work coaches, but also examples of failure to meet those principles, especially on the tailoring to individual needs and circumstances. **1.676**

The Parliamentary answer (WQ 62431) of July 1, 2020 by the Under-Secretary of State, Mims Davies, stressed that claimant commitments agreed or reviewed from that date would have to be reasonable for the "new normal" after the coronavirus pandemic and acknowledge the reality of a person's local jobs market and personal circumstances.

The notion of the claimant commitment is in many ways at the heart of what "conditionality" is meant to achieve under new style JSA and universal credit. It looks on its face to be an expression of what Charles Reich in his classic essay *The New Property* 73 Yale Law Journal 733 (1964) called "the New Feudalism". The claimant not only has, as the price of securing entitlement to the benefit, to accept a defined status that involves the giving up of some rights normally enjoyed by ordinary citizens, but appears to have to undertake some kind of oath of fealty by accepting a commitment to the feudal duties of that status. However, in reality the claimant commitment is a much more prosaic, and more sensible, thing. In its interesting paper *Universal Credit and Conditionality* (Social Security Advisory Committee Occasional Paper No.9, 2012) the SSAC reported research findings that many claimants of current benefits subject to a sanctions regime did not understand what conduct could lead to a sanction, how the sanctions system worked (some not even realising that they had been sanctioned) and in particular what the consequences of a sanction would be on current and future entitlement. Paragraph 3.12 of the paper states:

"The lessons to be learned from the research ought to be relatively straightforward to implement, although providing the appropriate training for a large number of Personal Advisers may present a considerable challenge:

- claimants need to have the link between conditionality and the application of sanctions fully explained at the start of any claim
- clear and unambiguous communication about the sanctions regime between advisers and claimants is vital at the start of any claim and must form a key element in the Claimant Commitment
- claimants need to know when they are in danger of receiving a sanction and to be told when a sanction has been imposed, the amount and the duration
- claimants need to know what actions they have to take to reverse a sanction – the process and consequences of re-compliance."

If one of the main aims of conditionality, of encouraging claimants to avoid behaviour that would impede a possible return to or entry into work and thus reducing the incidence of the imposition of sanctions or of more severe sanctions, is to be furthered, it therefore makes sense to build into the system a requirement to set out each claimant's responsibilities and the consequences of not meeting them in understandable terms. However, as the SSAC suggests, the nature of the personal interaction between personal advisers (now known as work coaches) and claimants may be much more important than a formal written document in getting over the realities of the situation and in encouraging claimants to take steps to avoid or reduce dependence on benefit.

A similar line of thought seems to be behind what was set out in paras 65 and 66 of the joint judgment of Lords Neuberger and Toulson in *R. (on the application of Reilly and Wilson) v SSWP* [2013] UKSC 68; [2014] 1 A.C. 453 in relation to the old style JSA regime, after noting the serious consequence of imposing a requirement to engage in unpaid work on a claimant on pain of discontinuance of benefits:

"65. Fairness therefore requires that a claimant should have access to such information about the scheme as he or she may need in order to make informed and meaningful representations to the decision-maker before a decision is made. Such claimants are likely to vary considerably in their levels of education and ability to express themselves in an interview at a Jobcentre at a time when they may be under considerable stress. The principle does not depend on the categorisation of the Secretary of State's decision to introduce a particular scheme under statutory powers as a policy: it arises as a matter of fairness from the Secretary of State's proposal to invoke a statutory power in a way which will or may involve a requirement to perform work and which may have serious consequences on a claimant's ability to meet his or her living needs.

66. Properly informed claimants, with knowledge not merely of the schemes available, but also of the criteria for being placed on such schemes, should be able to explain what would, in their view, be the most reasonable and appropriate scheme for them, in a way which would be unlikely to be possible without such information. Some claimants may have access to information downloadable from a government website, if they knew what to look for, but many will not. For many of those dependent on benefits, voluntary agencies such as Citizens Advice Bureaus play an important role in informing and assisting them in relation to benefits to which they may be entitled, how they should apply, and what matters they should draw to the attention of their Jobcentre adviser."

However, how such principles might impact on the new style JSA and universal credit will have to be worked out in particular legislative contexts. See further in the notes to s.6K and in the notes to reg.7 of the JSA Regulations 2013 for discussion of the potential application of the prior information duty to the process of drawing up and reviewing claimant commitments, including the problems illustrated in *FO v SSWP (UC)* [2022] UKUT 56 (AAC).

A probably now rather out-dated sample claimant commitment for universal credit purposes has been produced by the DWP in response to a freedom of information request (available at: *https://www.gov.uk/government/publications/foi-query-universal-credit-claimant-commitment-example*) [Accessed May 26, 2014], or through a link in the universal credit part of the discussion forum on the Rightsnet website). The document puts things in terms of what the claimant says he or she will do. It is suggested above that that is not quite what the legislation requires, but there is obviously a tension with an attempt to use everyday and simple language. Nevertheless, the document is long and complicated. In the sample, there is no attempt to specify the precise length of the sanction that would be imposed for a failure for no good reason (the document says "without good reason") to comply with a requirement, but the maximum possible duration is included, plus the words "up to". It is arguable that this information is insufficiently precise.

No more recent sample claimant commitment has become publicly available. **1.677** However, universal credit examples that have emerged in tribunal documents display the same fundamental defects and, it is submitted, a misunderstanding of the DWP's own legislation. There is also a Child Poverty Action Group mock-up of an automated universal credit claimant commitment at pp.58–59 of R. Mears and S. Howes, *You Reap What You Code: Universal credit, digitalisation and the rule of law* (Child Poverty Action Group, June 2023). There is no reason to think that new style JSA claimant commitments do not take the same form. The emphasis is on what claimants commit themselves to doing, in terms of finding and taking work and the actions and activities involved, rather than making any record of the requirements imposed on them under the legislation. Examples would be "I will be available to attend a job interview immediately [and to] start work immediately", "I will normally spend 35 hours per week looking and preparing for work" and "I will also attend and take part in appointments with my adviser when required". Thus, it appears that claimant commitments in that form may fail to carry out the duty in s.6A(4)(a) to record "the requirements that the claimant must comply with" under the new style Jobseekers Act 1995. As noted in paras 17 and 28 of *S v SSWP (UC)* [2017] UKUT 477 (AAC) (see the introductory part of the note to s.6J), s.13(1) of the WRA 2012 (the equivalent of s.6(1)) means that a work-related requirement only comes into being when imposed by the Secretary of State and s.22(2) of the WRA 2012 (the equivalent of s.6F(1)) requires the Secretary of State to impose a work search requirement and a work availability requirement on claimants who are not exempted from those requirements (with a discretion to impose a work-focused interview requirement and/or a work preparation requirement on non-exempt claimants). Requirements must be *imposed*, with notification required by s.6H(4), not merely undertaken by claimants.

In *JB v SSWP (UC)* [2018] UKUT 360 (AAC) the claimant was made subject to a sanction under s.27(2)(a) of the WRA 2012, the equivalent of s.6K(2)(a), for failing for no good reason to comply with a work-related requirement under s.15 (work-focused interview requirement), the equivalent of s.6B. He had failed to attend an appointment with an adviser on January 12, 2017, saying later that he had thought that the appointment was for the next day and later still that he did not attend because of health issues.

The First-tier Tribunal found that the claimant had signed and agreed a claimant commitment on October 27, 2016 that included a requirement to attend and take part in appointments with advisers when required and had been notified at a previous appointment of the requirement to attend on January 12, 2017. In fact the provision before the tribunal was "I will attend and take part in appointments with my adviser when required". The tribunal rejected his argument that he had had good reason for failing to attend. However, the claimant commitment supplied in evidence by the SSWP was not signed or dated and contained a provision for action to be taken by September 20, 2016. It was therefore improbable that the document in the papers had been notified to the claimant on October 27, 2016 and the SSWP had not supplied any other evidence of what claimant commitment had been accepted and what requirements might have been notified in it. Accordingly, although the unrepresented claimant had not raised the issue of whether he had been properly notified of the requirement to attend the particular appointment, the tribunal went wrong in law by proceeding on the basis that a claimant commitment agreed by the claimant on October 27, 2016 imposed a work-related requirement to attend a work-focused interview. Nor had the SSWP put forward coherent evidence of what had been said at an earlier appointment. The written submission relied on an attendance on June 1, 2016, which did not work because the universal credit claim began on September 7, 2016. The appointment history showed a "work-focused review" on December 21, 2016, but there was no evidence of any notification then of a future appointment. There could be no reliance on any presumption of regularity because there was no evidence of a general practice or "script" of what claimants are told at appointments about the need to attend work-focused interviews. Although it was implicit in the claimant's position that he knew of the appointment on January 12, 2017, a sanction could only be imposed if there had been proper notification of the requirement in question and the SSWP had failed to show that. The case was remitted to a new tribunal for rehearing, as it was fair (the issue not having been raised until the Upper Tribunal judge gave permission to appeal), to allow the SSWP an opportunity to produce further evidence.

Judge Poole QC therefore did not need to decide whether the terms of the claimant commitment in the papers were capable of constituting a notification of a requirement to participate in work-focused interviews when notified of appointments. However, she did make interesting observations on that and other wider issues. The SSWP had submitted that the standard terms of claimant commitments were prepared so that claimants could understand them, but were clear and imperative, and that in the context of a system including sanctions claimants and advisers knew that when they were requested to attend interviews it was obligatory to turn up. Judge Poole did not in so many words either accept or reject that submission, but her observations indicate that it could only be accepted subject to heavy qualifications.

In her introductory discussion of the legal principles, which are equally relevant to new style JSA, the judge stressed that while the universal credit legislation gave the SSWP considerable flexibility, the flip side of that was that in sanctions cases the SSWP had to be able to evidence the imposition of the requirement in question. The more informal the means of communication to a claimant the more efficient its recording systems will have to be, so that copies can be produced in cases of appeal. Her opinions on the wider issues were set out as follows in para.29:

> "29.1 The UC legislation is deliberately drafted to leave a degree of flexibility for the SSWP, and permits multiple methods of communication to claimants (paragraphs 16 and 17 above). There is a flexibility in the manner and means of notification. Given this legislative intention, it would be inappropriate for the Upper Tribunal to set out particular requirements for wording of notifications, or the means by which this is done.
>
> 29.2 In cases where the issue arises, the key matter for tribunals to consider is whether fair notice has been given, having regard to all the communications between the SSWP and the claimant (paragraphs 18–20 above). What tribunals need to do is look at the evidence produced by the SSWP, in the context in which it arises, together with any evidence taken from the claimant, and ask the question: does the evidence show that the substance of the relevant requirement and consequences of non-compliance were notified to the claimant? The answer to this question will turn on the particular circumstances of a case.
>
> 29.3 There is a virtue in plain English, and in couching notifications about what a claimant has to do in terms that claimants can readily understand. The Upper Tribunal Judge who granted permission raised the issue of whether requirements should be spelled out expressly and not left to implication. In my view

it is not necessary that there is reproduction of statutory wording or reference to particular section or regulation numbers, or indeed any prescribed form of wording. *What is important is the substance. In this case the question was whether it could fairly be said, on the totality of the evidence, that the claimant had been notified of an obligation to attend a work-focused interview and the consequences of non-compliance.* [emphasis added by editor]

29.4 Unless the only evidence bearing on the imposition of a requirement in a sanctions case is the claimant commitment, it is artificial to focus on the sufficiency of the precise terms of the claimant commitment. This is because requirements can be imposed in various ways, including by a combination of documents (paragraph 20 above). Indeed, in this case the SSWP does not maintain that the wording in the claimant commitment of itself imposed a work-related requirement to attend a work-focused interview on 12 January 2017. Where a claimant commitment is part of the evidence, general reference to 'appointments' in the claimant commitment seems to me to be a sensible shorthand way of conveying a need to attend meetings but leaving flexibility to impose requirements at a later stage under either Section 15 or Section 23 of the 2012 Act. I also consider the passages set out in paragraph 26 above about sanctions for not meeting requirements, giving detail of how payments are cut, and sanctions for not meeting requirements. So where the claimant commitment has been notified, then those requirements have to be considered in conjunction with other evidence before the tribunal bearing on communication to the claimant of requirements and consequences of non-compliance. This can include, for example, later appointment cards, texts about appointments, and verbal communications at interview. It seems to me that when considering the efficacy of verbal communication, although the SSWP's record keeping will be key, it is permissible to take into account a regular pattern of interviews. For example, a claimant may have been asked at interview to come back for the same sort of interview two weeks later. The claimant's experience from earlier interviews may be relevant to whether they have been informed of the substance of a requirement and consequences of non-compliance. Further, while intimation of date, time and place of appointment is a necessary component of intimation, that will be insufficient of itself unless linked in some way to notification to a claimant of a requirement to attend and consequences of non-compliance. The overall point is that tribunals have to consider not only the wording of the claimant commitment, but of all the evidence bearing on whether the substance of the relevant requirement and consequences of non-compliance were notified to the claimant.

29.5 [Deals with some of the consequences of the differences between the powers in s.15 and s.23 of the WRA 2012]."

That overall approach may not be too difficult to apply if the DWP takes on board at all levels the lessons of *JB* and routinely maintains and provides to tribunals clear and consistent records of the requirements imposed on claimants. However, if the familiar lazy assumptions exemplified in *JB* continue (or appear in older cases from before a hoped-for change of practice), a sharper focus may be necessary on how to resolve the tensions between some of the principles canvassed in para.29 in the circumstances of individual cases. For instance, at a broad level it might continue wrongly to be assumed that, if what is done (e.g. in the drafting of the standard form of terms in claimant commitments) is sensible in policy terms, the actual terms of the relevant legislation have been complied with. At a more grassroots level, there might well continue to be a failure to realise the need to provide tribunals with copies of all the evidence beyond the claimant commitment necessary to show the imposition of the requirement in question and the consequences of non-compliance. In either case, it might become necessary to address directly the effect of the standard form of terms in the claimant commitment. As well as the provision about appointments in issue in *JB*, drafted in terms of what the claimant said he would do rather than in terms of the imposition of a requirement, other standard provisions take the same form (see the examples given above from the sample claimant commitment). It is submitted that the principle expressed at the end of para.29.3 (and in earlier paragraphs) of *JB* that the test is whether the evidence shows that the claimant has been notified of an obligation becomes primary and that there is a fundamental difference between a commitment being undertaken by a claimant and a requirement being imposed by the SSWP.

1.678 In para.34 of *JB*, Judge Poole mentions two documents produced to the Upper Tribunal by the SSWP, of potential relevance in the rehearing. One was a computer printout recording the signing, acceptance and issue of a claimant commitment on September 13, 2016, together with something called a "claimant pack". The other was a standard form document headed "Your meeting plan" with spaces for entering dates, times and contacts of next meeting, with a warning on the back that missing meetings without rearranging in advance risks a sanction. According to the SSWP, the meeting plan document is issued with the "commitment pack", which the judge noted might or might not be the same thing as the "claimant pack". Such documents, in particular a complete copy of the claimant or commitment pack, might well be relevant in future cases, but only if properly put into evidence before tribunals.

Quite rigorous guidance was issued to decision-makers in the universal credit context in Memo ADM 5/19, that should be equally relevant to new style JSA. It in general emphasises the necessity for the SSWP to be able, in order to show that any failure to comply with a requirement is sanctionable, to evidence that the requirement has been imposed and that the claimant has been properly been informed of the substance of the requirement and the consequences of non-compliance. The memo accepts that evidence other than the claimant commitment will be crucial and that copies of all relevant communications will need to be included in any appeal papers to found a notification by a combination of means. Paragraph 7 states that:

> "it is expected that the SSWP will produce to a tribunal, as a minimum, copies of
> 1. the claimant commitment
> 2. any appointment letters ((for example, standard notification letters used for referring to employment programmes such as sbwa [sector based work academy], WHP [Work and Health Programme] etc)
> 3. records of telephone or electronic communications (for example, a copy of the relevant 'to-do' or journal notes)
> 4. internal electronic records (for example, a copy of the sanctions information screen)
> 5. any other relevant documents (for example a copy of the relevant ALP [Action List Prompt])
> that shows the imposition of any work-related requirement and the consequences of non-compliance to the claimant."

It is not known whether all of those forms of communication are relevant to the administration of new style JSA. Paragraph 14 says rather oddly that the ordinary meaning of "substance" is "to specify the intended purpose or subject matter". The meaning surely is not so restricted, but the Memo emphasises that where interviews are concerned the claimant must be told the purpose of the interview and the reason for it. There is now more comprehensive guidance in the section on "Public Law Principles of Fairness" in Ch.K1 of the *ADM*.

In para.29 of *S v SSWP (UC)* [2017] UKUT 477 (AAC), the judge accepted that, if the Secretary of State failed to carry out the equivalent of the s.6F(1) duty, the claimant should not bear the consequences of that (which must entail that the requirement(s) in question had not been imposed and there could be no sanction for failing to comply).

In *S*, it was said that the imposition of the work search requirement was not in issue, but the evidence to support that conclusion was not spelled out. The decision should not therefore be taken as any endorsement of a view that terms of a claimant commitment like that in *S* would be sufficient in themselves to impose work-related requirements on a claimant.

There is some difficulty in working out what remedies a claimant would have who disagrees with the imposition of a requirement included in the claimant commitment. If the claimant declines to accept the Secretary of State's form of the record, at the outset of the claim or as later reviewed and up-dated, then any initial disallowance of the claim or subsequent supersession of an awarding decision would be appealable. However, it is not clear whether such an appeal could succeed on the basis that a requirement in fact included in the claimant commitment should not have been imposed. If the requirement was one whose imposition was prohibited by the legislation and the claimant was prepared to accept everything else, it is submitted that it could properly be concluded that the condition in s.1(2)(b) had been satisfied from the outset (compare the approach of Judge Rowland in *CJSA/1080/2002* and *GM v SSWP (JSA)* [2014] UKUT 57 (AAC) in holding that a claimant was to be accepted as satisfying a condition of attendance at a Jobcentre when he had in fact not attended after being informed that he was not entitled to JSA so that attendance was pointless: see the annotations to reg.23 of the JSA Regulations 1996 in Vol.V of this series, 2021/22 edition as updated in Cumulative Supplements included in Vol.II of this series and in mid-year Supplements. If it was a matter of the Secretary of State's discretion under s.6F(2), the result might be different. A claimant who accepts a claimant commitment under protest about some requirement may no doubt request the Secretary of State not to impose the challenged requirement and in consequence to review the claimant commitment, as mentioned in reg.7(2) of the JSA Regulations 2013. However, it appears that the claimant cannot appeal directly against either imposition of the requirement or the content of the claimant commitment or a refusal by the Secretary of State to remove a requirement and to review the claimant commitment. See the discussion in the note to s.6F below, which would apply equally to any of the kinds of decision mentioned. None of them are "outcome" decisions.

[1 Work-focused interview requirement

6B.—(1) In this Act a "work-focused interview requirement" is a requirement that a claimant participate in one or more work-focused interviews as specified by the Secretary of State. **1.679**

(2) A work-focused interview is an interview for prescribed purposes relating to work or work preparation.

(3) The purposes which may be prescribed under subsection (2) include in particular that of making it more likely in the opinion of the Secretary of State that the claimant will obtain paid work (or more paid work or better-paid work).

(4) The Secretary of State may specify how, when and where a work-focused interview is to take place.]

Amendment

1. Welfare Reform Act 2012 s.49(3) (trigger date on or after April 29, 2013).

Definitions

"claimant"—see s.35(1).
"prescribed"—*ibid.*

General Note

This section defines what a "work-focused interview" is and makes the related requirement "participation" in the interview. By virtue of s.6F(2)(a) below the Secretary of State has a discretion whether or not to impose the work-focused interview requirement, the exemptions from the imposition of work-related requirements in regs 16 and 16A of the JSA Regulations 2013 not applying to the work-focused interview requirement , although reg.15 (domestic violence) does apply. **1.680**

Under subss.(2) and (3) regulations must prescribe the purposes, relating to work or, importantly, work preparation, for which an interview may be required. The prescription, in very wide terms, is in reg.10 of the JSA Regulations 2013. Note that those purposes do not as such include the drawing up or review of a claimant commitment, but discussion of work may be relevant to what requirements should or should not be included in the commitment.

Regulation 10 like s.6B, uses the word "work", not "paid work". The Secretary of State is allowed under subss.(1) and (4) to specify how, when and where the interview is to take place, so that there is no straightforward limit on the number or frequency of the interviews that may be specified, or on the persons who may conduct the interview. The interviews must of course properly be for one of the purposes prescribed in reg.10. The requirement to participate in interviews cannot be used for punitive purposes or simply as a means of control of a claimant. No doubt it is also to be implied that only rational requirements may be imposed, so that a specification of two interviews in different places at the same time or so that they could not practically be co-ordinated could be disregarded as invalid (see the approach of Judge Rowland in *GM v SSWP (JSA)* [2014] UKUT 57 (AAC): notes to s.6A above). Rationality would also require that what was specified should not be incompatible with other requirements, in particular the work search and work availability requirements where there is no discretion under s.6F about their imposition. Thus, a claimant could not validly be required to attend so many interviews that it made it impossible to take work search actions for the hours specified under s.6D, unless there was a corresponding reduction in the s.6D requirements. These are rather extreme examples, which it is hoped would not arise in practice. Because, as discussed in the notes to s.6H, there is no right of appeal against an imposition of a work-related or connected requirement as such, the issues will normally arise in the course of appeals against reductions of benefit following a sanction for non-compliance under s.6K(2)(a). The question of the reasonableness or otherwise of the requirement imposed will then usually be dealt with in the consideration of whether the claimant had a good reason for not complying with the requirement in question.

However, there may also often be questions whether a requirement has in fact been imposed. There appear to be two stages. The Secretary of State may indicate in general that a claimant will be required to participate in interviews (although see the notes to s.6A for serious doubts whether the current standard form of claimant commitment achieves that result). But the requirement under subs.(1) appears not to arise, in the sense of a requirement that the claimant can comply with or fail to comply with for sanctions purposes, until the Secretary of State has specified the particular interview or interviews under subs.(4) and probably (although subs.(1) is not entirely clear) that the claimant participate. Specification must necessarily imply communication to the claimant in time to attend the interview. See the notes to s.6A for extensive discussion of the decision in *JB v SSWP (UC)* [2018] UKUT 360 (AAC) on the evidence that the SSWP needs to produce to show that a requirement to participate in a s.6B interview has been imposed and the guidance given to decision-makers in the universal credit context in Memo ADM 5/19. Paragraph 6 of *JB* states that it is a condition precedent of imposing any sanction under the equivalent of s.6K(2)(a) that the claimant was subject to the work-related requirement in issue, thus confirming the approach in para.29 of *S v SSWP (UC)* [2017] UKUT 477 (AAC) that if a specific requirement has not been imposed by the SSWP, no sanction can follow.

JB was endorsed and applied in *KG v SSWP (UC)* [2020] UKUT 307 (AAC). Before the Upper Tribunal the Secretary of State accepted that the available evidence did not show that the claimant had been properly notified of the requirement to take part in the particular telephone interview with his work coach, so that no sanction could be applied under the equivalent of s.6K. The documents were ambiguous as to whether the interview was under the equivalent of s.6B or the equivalent of s.6G (connected requirements) and what issues the claimant was told were to be investigated, and left it unclear whether he had been adequately informed of the consequences of non-compliance.

There is no requirement that the specification under subs.(4) of how, when and where a work-focused interview is to take place should be in writing or in other permanent form. However, good practice, plus the potential need for acceptable evidence of the existence and terms of the specification in the light of the principle that the claimant should in sanctions cases be given the benefit of any doubt that might reasonably arise (*DL v SSWP (JSA)* [2013] UKUT 295 (AAC)), must surely point to the need for written or computer records to be kept and to be available to the claimant for reference. That is confirmed by Memo ADM 5/19 (above). Arguably, the "prior information duty" (see the notes to ss.6A and 6K for detailed discussion) would require that information about the purpose of the particular interview be given in the specification. Arguably also, in accordance with the approach in *SSWP v DC (JSA)* [2017] UKUT 464 (AAC), reported as [2018] AACR 16, and *PO'R v DFC (JSA)* [2018] NI Com 1 (see the notes to s.6K), a copy of the appointment letter should be included in the Secretary of State's submission on any appeal against a sanction for failing to comply with a requirement to participate in the interview.

Note that the requirement, as for universal credit and now old style JSA, is not attendance at an interview at the specified time and date, but participation in it. This would appear to mean that a claimant can be required to participate in an interview over the telephone, providing that that manner of conducting it has been specified under subs.(4). However, in an ambiguous Parliamentary answer on November 24, 2015 (UIN 17005), the Minister of State, Priti Patel, said:

> "Under JSA, claimants are not sanctioned for failing to answer their telephone. In Universal Credit, claimants who have a prearranged telephone interview with their Work Coach, and who fail to participate without good reason, can be referred for a sanction decision."

There is no further provision about what participating in a work-focused interview entails. It must at least entail turning up at the place and time specified, although the decision of Judge Knowles in *SA v SSWP (JSA)* [2015] UKUT 454 (AAC) (see the notes to s.6K for full discussion) would indicate that tribunals should consider, in cases where the claimant arrives not very late, whether it is proportionate to the nature of all the circumstances to regard that as a failure to participate in an interview. There were all sorts of mitigating circumstances in *SA*, that may well not be present in other cases. See *SN v SSWP (JSA)* [2018] UKUT 279 (AAC), detailed in the notes s.6K, for discussion of what might amount to a failure to participate (in that case in a mandatory work activity scheme and involving conduct before the scheme started) and the expression in para.45 of some doubt about the result in *SA*. The requirement to participate must also extend to making some meaningful contribution to the interview, but the limits will probably not be established until there have been some more sanctions appeals that reach the Upper Tribunal. Behaviour that leads to the premature termination of the interview may well amount to a failure to participate (see the facts of *DM v SSWP (JSA)* [2015] UKUT 67 (AAC) in the notes to s.6K). There may, though, in cases of uncooperative claimants or heavy-handed officials or a combination, be difficult questions about when an interview has ceased to exist, so that subsequent behaviour cannot be relevant to whether there has been a failure to participate (see *PH v SSWP (ESA)* [2016] UKUT 119 (AAC) on failing to submit to a medical examination).

It was recognised in *CS v SSWP (JSA)* [2019] UKUT 218 (AAC), detailed in the notes to s.6K, that it was legitimate for a scheme provider to require an attender to verify their identity before starting a scheme, so that a refusal to do so would usually amount to a failure to participate in the scheme. The same principle could apply to an interview, but the particular issues that arose in *CS*, to do with a scheme provider external to the DWP, are unlikely to arise if it is an interview with an employment officer that has been notified.

A failure for no good reason to comply with any work-related requirement is sanctionable under s.6K(2)(a). That is the context in which what amounts to a failure to comply will be identified, as well as what might amount to a good reason for non-compliance. For instance, there are no provisions prescribing the length of notice of an interview to be given or how far a claimant can be required to travel, but there could plainly be a good reason for failing to comply with unreasonable requirements, especially if the claimant had attempted in advance to draw any problem with attendance to the Secretary of State's attention. If a specific requirement has not been imposed, then no sanction could follow (*S v SSWP (UC)* [2017] UKUT 477 (AAC) para.29).

Note that under s.6G(1) the Secretary of State is empowered to require a claimant to participate in an interview relating to the imposition of a work-related requirement on the claimant or assisting the claimant to comply with a requirement. Under s.6G(3) he can require the provision of information and evidence for the purpose of verifying compliance with a work-related requirement and that the claimant confirm compliance in any manner. A failure for no good reason to comply with any of those connected requirements is also sanctionable under s.6K(2)(b).

[1 Work preparation requirement

1.681 **6C.**—(1) In this Act a "work preparation requirement" is a requirement that a claimant take particular action specified by the Secretary of State for the purpose of making it more likely in the opinion of the Secretary of State that the claimant will obtain paid work (or more paid work or better-paid work).

(2) The Secretary of State may under subsection (1) specify the time to be devoted to any particular action.

(3) Action which may be specified under subsection (1) includes in particular—

(a) attending a skills assessment;
(b) improving personal presentation;
(c) participating in training;
(d) participating in an employment programme;
(e) undertaking work experience or a work placement;
(f) developing a business plan;
(g) any action prescribed for the purpose in subsection (1).]

AMENDMENT

1. Welfare Reform Act 2012 s.49(3) (trigger date on or after April 29, 2013).

DEFINITION

"claimant"—see s.35(1).

GENERAL NOTE

1.682 This section defines "work preparation requirement". The requirement is to take particular action specified by the Secretary of State for the purpose of making it more likely that the claimant will obtain paid work or obtain more or better-paid such work. It appears that the requirement therefore cannot arise until the Secretary of State has specified the particular action, so that general statements in a claimant commitment about normally spending 35 hours a week looking and preparing for work (even if they could be regarded as *imposed* by the Secretary of State: see the notes to s.6A) would not be enough in themselves. Subsection (3) gives a non-exhaustive list of actions that may be specified, including under para.(g) any action prescribed in regulations. No such regulations have as yet been made. The list is in fairly broad terms, not further defined in the legislation, even "employment programme". The sorts of activities required do not themselves have to be paid, so long as they can legitimately be related to the purpose of improving prospects of obtaining paid work or more or better paid work (see below). So unpaid work experience or placements (e.g. as an intern) or voluntary work can be made mandatory. See the notes to s.6B above for the need for the co-ordination with the practical application of other work-related or connected requirements for the specification of any particular work preparation requirement to be rational.

The Secretary of State may under subs.(2) specify the time to be devoted to any particular action, but in practice this is likely to be less controversial than the similar power in s.6D(2) in relation to a work search requirement. Subsections (4) and (5) allow the making of regulations requiring limitations to be attached to the kind of work in relation to which the claimant has to take action. See reg.14 of the JSA Regulations 2013. By virtue of s.6F(2)(a) below the Secretary of State has a discretion whether or not to impose the work preparation requirement, the exemptions from the imposition of work-related requirements in regs 16 and 16A of the JSA Regulations 2013 not applying to the work preparation requirement, although reg.15 (domestic violence) does apply.

There is no requirement that the specification under subss.(1) and (2) of particular action to be taken by the claimant and the time to be devoted to it should be in writing or in other permanent form. However, good practice, plus the potential need for acceptable evidence of the existence and terms of the specification in the light of the principle that the claimant should in sanctions cases be given the benefit of any doubt that might reasonably arise (*DL v SSWP (JSA)* [2013] UKUT 295 (AAC)), must surely point to the need for written or computer records to be kept and to be available to the claimant for reference.

A failure for no good reason to comply with a requirement under this heading to undertake a work placement of a prescribed description is sanctionable under s.6J(2)(a) (higher-level sanctions), but the only prescribed placement has ceased to operate. Outside that limited category, failure for no good reason to comply with any work-related requirement is sanctionable under s.6K(2)(a). That is the context in which there will be exploration of what action can be said to make it more likely that the claimant will obtain paid work or more or better-paid work, since the addition of the Secretary of State's opinion in subs.(1) will not be allowed to take away the power of tribunals to reach their own conclusions on that matter. What amounts to a failure to comply will also be identified, as well as what might amount to a good reason for non-compliance. *JS v SSWP (ESA)* [2013] UKUT 635 (AAC), at para.15 suggests that if a claimant is patently not going to be able to obtain work at any stage or is already in an appropriate apprenticeship or placement no action could make it more likely that work or more work would be obtained, so that no action could legitimately be specified. However, in the present context it has to be considered whether prospects of obtaining paid or better paid work could be improved.

Note that under s.6G(1) the Secretary of State is empowered to require a claimant to participate in an interview relating to the imposition of a work-related requirement on the claimant or assisting the claimant to comply with a requirement. Under s.6G(3) he can require the provision of information and evidence for the purpose of verifying compliance with a work-related requirement and that the claimant confirm compliance in any manner. A failure for no good reason to comply with any of those connected requirements is also sanctionable under s.6K(2)(b).

[1 Work search requirement

6D.—(1) In this Part a "work search requirement" is a requirement that a claimant take— 1.683

(a) all reasonable action, and

(b) any particular action specified by the Secretary of State,

for the purpose of obtaining paid work (or more paid work or better-paid work).

(2) The Secretary of State may under subsection (1)(b) specify the time to be devoted to any particular action.

(3) Action which may be specified under subsection (1)(b) includes in particular—

(a) carrying out work searches;
(b) making applications;
(c) creating and maintaining an online profile;
(d) registering with an employment agency;
(e) seeking references;
(f) any other action prescribed for the purpose in subsection (1).

(4) Regulations may impose limitations on a work search requirement by reference to the work to which it relates; and the Secretary of State may in any particular case specify further such limitations on such a requirement.

(5) A limitation under subsection (4) may in particular be by reference to—

(a) work of a particular nature,
(b) work with a particular level of remuneration,
(c) work in particular locations, or
(d) work available for a certain number of hours per week or at particular times,

and may be indefinite or for a particular period.]

AMENDMENT

1. Welfare Reform Act 2012 s.49(3) (trigger date on or after April 29, 2013).

DEFINITIONS

"claimant"—see s.35(1).
"regulations"—*ibid.*

GENERAL NOTE

Temporary Coronavirus Provisions

1.684 The effect of the temporary coronavirus provisions relevant to the work search requirement in new style JSA expired at the end of November 12, 2020. See previous editions of this volume for the details.

This section defines "work search requirement", which is one of the requirements that, by virtue of s.6F(1)(a), the Secretary of State must impose on all new style JSA claimants, unless exempted by regulations. See the notes to s.6A for discussion of whether the current standard terms of claimant commitments are sufficient in themselves to *impose* such a requirement. It is a requirement that a claimant take both all reasonable action (subs.(1)(a)) and any particular action specified by the Secretary of State (subs.(1)(b)) for the purpose of obtaining paid work or more or better-paid work. "Paid work" is not defined in the Act, nor is it defined in regulations for the specific purpose of s.6D. However, under the power in s.6I, regs 11 and 12 of the JSA Regulations 2013 deem the work search requirement not to have been complied with in certain circumstances and make references to "obtaining paid work". For those purposes, the extension in reg.3(7) to cover obtaining more or better paid work will apply, but this appears to add nothing of substance to the terms of s.6D itself. There is no further definition of what amounts to paid work. Thus it appears that both self-employment and employment can be considered under the ordinary meaning of the phrase "paid work" and that voluntary work or unpaid internship or work placements are excluded. However, according to the then Minister of State Esther McVey (House of Commons written answers April 2, 2014 and September 1, 2014), guidance to Jobcentre Plus staff is that JSA claimants (in contrast to universal credit claimants) are not to be mandated to apply for vacancies for zero hours contracts, apparently whether there is an exclusivity clause (made unenforceable from May 26, 2015 by the new s.27A of the Employment Rights Act 1996) or not. Thus no sanction under s.6J(2)(b) should arise from a failure to apply for such a vacancy.

It is notable, by contrast with the position in old style JSA for actively seeking employment, that complying with a work search requirement is not a condition of entitlement to new style JSA, failure to satisfy which means that there can be no entitlement to benefit at all, although it is a condition of entitlement under s.1(2)(b) to accept a claimant commitment that should record the requirement. Instead, a failure to comply with a work search requirement, if the claimant is not exempted from it, is merely a potential basis for a sanction under s.6J or 6K. Under s.6J(2)(b) a higher-level sanction can be imposed if a claimant fails for no good reason to comply with a requirement to apply for a particular vacancy for paid work. Section 6K(2)(a) requires the imposition of a lower level sanction for a failure for no good reason to comply with any work-related requirement.

Subsections (4) and (5) allow regulations to impose limitations on the kind of work search which can be required and also allow the Secretary of State to specify further limitations. Regulation 14 of the JSA Regulations 2013 contains the prescribed limitations, in terms of hours of work for carers and those with a disability, of the maximum time for travel to and from work and of the type of work recently undertaken. See the notes to reg.14 for further details, particularly on the controversial February 2022 amendment to reg.14(3) on the period for which a claimant is permitted to restrict work search and availability to work of the nature or level of remuneration previously carried out. Only reg.14(5) appears to allow any limitation in terms of the weekly hours of work that the claimant is prepared to contemplate, for the particular categories covered (some carers and anyone with a physical or mental impairment). Note also that reg.16 exempts claimants carrying out a variety of categories of worthwhile activity from the imposition or continued application of a work search requirement and that reg.15 exempts victims of domestic violence for a fixed period. Regulation 16A exempts claimants falling within the new reg.46A (extended period of sickness). See the annotations to those regulations.

What is all reasonable action under subs.(1)(a) for the purpose of obtaining paid work within any applicable limitations is obviously in general a matter of judgment. That includes a judgment about what counts as "action". The actions mentioned in subs.(3) might be a starting point, but other things could plainly count, such as carrying out research into the job market or potential for self-employment. No doubt just sitting and thinking falls the other side of the line, but can often form an essential element of the hours devoted to some more active action. But reg.12 of the JSA Regulations 2013 deems a claimant not to have complied with that requirement unless quite stringent conditions about the weekly hours devoted to work search are satisfied. See the annotations to reg.12 and remember that the sanction in s.6K(2)(a) can only be imposed when there was no good reason for the failure to comply. Paragraph 15 of *JS v SSWP (ESA)* [2013] UKUT 635 (AAC) suggests that if a claimant is patently not going to be able to obtain work at any stage or is already in an appropriate apprenticeship or placement no action could make it more likely that work or more work would be obtained, so that it could not be reasonable to take any further action. However, in the present context it has to be considered whether prospects obtaining paid or better paid work could be improved.

The particular action that can be specified by Secretary of State under subs.(1)(b) can, by subs.(3), include a number of actions, including under para.(g) those prescribed in regulations. No such regulation has yet been made. Where a claimant has been required to apply for a particular vacancy (which it seems can only fall under subs.(1)(b) rather than (1)(a)), reg.11 of the JSA Regulations 2013 deems the work search requirement not to have been complied with where the claimant fails to participate in an interview offered in connection with the vacancy. The specific sanction in s.6J(2)(b) for failing to comply with a requirement to apply for a particular vacancy can only be imposed when there was no good reason for the failure to comply.

Could the Secretary of State be allowed to specify under subss.(1)(b) and (2) **1.685**
time in excess of the "expected hours" minus relevant deductions under reg.12 of the JSA Regulations 2013 and subs.(1)(a)? In the notes to reg.12 it is submitted that satisfaction of the condition specified there in substance leads to a conclusion that

a claimant has taken all reasonable action for the purpose of obtaining paid work. In that light, it is certainly arguable that rationality and the demands of fairness and consistency require that when acting under subs.(1)(b) the Secretary of State should not impose a more time-consuming burden than under subs.(1)(a). That would involve taking account of the "relevant deductions" specified in reg.12(2) as well as the expected number of hours under reg.9. The same principles would require that no action may be specified under para.(1)(b) that would not be reasonable in accordance with para.(1)(a).

There is no requirement that the specification under subss.(1)(b), (2) and (3) of the particular actions to be taken and the time to be devoted to them should be in writing or in other permanent form. However, good practice, plus the potential need for acceptable evidence of the existence and terms of the specification in the light of the principle that the claimant should in sanctions cases be given the benefit of any doubt that might reasonably arise (*DL v SSWP (JSA)* [2013] UKUT 295 (AAC)), must surely point to the need for written or computer records to be kept and to be available to the claimant for reference.

Note that under s.6G(1) the Secretary of State is empowered to require a claimant to participate in an interview relating to the imposition of a work-related requirement on the claimant or assisting the claimant to comply with a requirement. Under s.6G(3) he can require the provision of information and evidence for the purpose of verifying compliance with a work-related requirement and that the claimant confirm compliance in any manner. A failure for no good reason to comply with any of those connected requirements is also sanctionable under s.6K(2)(b).

[1 Work availability requirement

1.686 **6E.**—(1) In this Act a "work availability requirement" is a requirement that a claimant be available for work.

(2) For the purposes of this section "available for work" means able and willing immediately to take up paid work (or more paid work or better-paid work).

(3) Regulations may impose limitations on a work availability requirement by reference to the work to which it relates; and the Secretary of State may in any particular case specify further such limitations on such a requirement.

(4) A limitation under subsection (3) may in particular be by reference to—

(a) work of a particular nature,

(b) work with a particular level of remuneration,

(c) work in particular locations, or

(d) work available for a certain number of hours per week or at particular times,

and may be indefinite or for a particular period.

(5) Regulations may for the purposes of subsection (2) define what is meant by able and willing immediately to take up work.]

AMENDMENT

1. Welfare Reform Act 2012 s.49(3) (trigger date on or after April 29, 2013).

DEFINITIONS

"claimant"—see s.35(1).

"regulations"—*ibid.*

GENERAL NOTE

Temporary Coronavirus Provisions

1.687 The effect of the temporary coronavirus provisions relevant to the work availability requirement in new style JSA expired at the end of November 12, 2020. See previous editions of this volume for the details.

This section defines "work availability requirement", which is one of the requirements that, by virtue of s.6F(1)(a), the Secretary of State must impose on all new style JSA claimants, unless exempted by regulations (see in particular reg.15 of the JSA Regulations 2013 (domestic violence)). See the notes to s.6A for discussion of whether the current standard terms of claimant commitments are sufficient in themselves to *impose* such a requirement. It imposes the apparently extremely stringent requirement that a claimant be able and willing immediately to take up paid work, or more or better-paid work. "Paid work" is not defined in the Act, nor is it defined in regulations for the specific purpose of s6E. However, under the power in s.6I, reg.13 of the JSA Regulations 2013 deems the work availability requirement not to have been complied with in certain circumstances and to have been satisfied in other circumstances and makes references to "paid work". For those purposes, the extension in reg.3(7) to cover obtaining more or better paid will apply, but this appears to add nothing of substance to the terms of s.6E itself. There is no further definition of what amounts to paid work. Thus it appears that both self-employment and employment can be considered under the ordinary meaning of the phrase "paid work" and that voluntary work or unpaid internship or work placements are excluded (but see s.6C on work preparation).

It is notable, by contrast with the position that will be familiar to many readers from old style JSA and, before it, unemployment benefit, that being available for work is not a condition of entitlement to new style JSA, failure to satisfy which means that there can be no entitlement to benefit at all, although it is a condition of entitlement under s.1(2)(b) to accept a claimant commitment that should record the requirement. Instead, a failure to comply with the work availability requirement, if the claimant is not exempted from it, is merely a potential basis for a sanction under s.6J or 6K. Under s.6J(2)(c) a higher-level sanction can be imposed if a claimant fails for no good reason to comply by not taking up an offer of paid work. Section 6K(2)(a) requires the imposition of a lower level sanction for a failure for no good reason to comply with any work-related requirement.

Note that reg.11 in effect extends the requirement to be able and willing immediately to take up paid work to ability and willingness immediately to attend an interview in connection with obtaining paid work. There is no specification of who the interview can be with.

The general formulation of the obligation under s.6E is in many ways the same as that imposed statutorily for old style JSA (on which see Vol.V of this series, 2021/22 edition as up-dated in Cumulative Supplements included in this volume and in mid-year Supplements) and developed in the case law on unemployment benefit. However, the structure of the new style JSA legislation is not the same. In some ways what was apparently intended as simplification has left holes that make the route to a coherent or even rational position troublesome. ADM para. R4112 continues to rely on *R(U) 5/80* for the proposition that availability implies being available in an active, positive sense and taking steps to draw attention to that availability. However, as convincingly demonstrated by Judge Lane in paras 22–25 of *RL v SSWP (JSA)* [2018] UKUT 177 (AAC), the separate existence for old style JSA of the actively seeking employment condition meant that that proposition was no longer relevant. The same must apply for new style JSA and questions of whether claimants are taking sufficient active steps should be considered under s.6D on the work search requirement.

The rest of this note first sets out how the JSA Regulations 2013, made under subss (3) – (5) and ss 6H and 6I, provide some specific rules that avoid the need to grapple with the implications of the general s.6E obligation and then discusses some problem areas relevant to that obligation. The relevant provisions are regs 13, 14, 16 and 16A. Note also that reg.15 prevents the imposition of any work-related requirement on recent victims of domestic violence.

Regulation 13. Section 6I(a) allows regulations to specify circumstances in which a claimant is to be treated as having complied or not complied with a requirement.

Regulation 13(2) provides that a claimant is to be treated as having complied with a work availability requirement, despite not being able immediately to take up employment (or presumably, by necessary implication, not being willing), where para.(3), (4) or (5) applies. Paragraph (3) applies to responsible carers or relevant carers who need a longer period of up to a month to take up work or 48 hours to attend an interview and are able and willing to take up the work or attend the interview on being given notice of the period. Under reg.4(1), a responsible carer is a single person or the nominated member of a couple who is responsible for a child (under 16) as determined under reg.4. A relevant carer is anyone else who has caring responsibilities (not further defined) for the child or for someone who has a physical or mental impairment that makes the caring necessary. That is therefore an important protection from the "immediately" test. Paragraph (4) provides an equivalent rule for claimants carrying out voluntary work and para.(5) for claimants employed under a contract of service who have to give notice to terminate the contract.

Regulation 14. Subsections (3) and (4) allow regulations to impose limitations on the kind of work for which a claimant can be required to be available and also allow the Secretary of State to specify further limitations. Regulation 14 contains the prescribed limitations, in terms of hours of work for responsible and relevant carers and those with a physical or mental impairment (to be limited to the "expected hours" under reg.9(2)), of the maximum time for travel to and from work and of the nature of and remuneration for work, either recently undertaken or within the ability of claimants with a physical or mental impairment. See the notes to reg.14 for detailed discussion. Presumably as well as some claimants not being required to be willing to take up work that involves more than the expected hours, they are not to be expected to take up work immediately at a time affected by circumstances relevant to reg.14. There appears to be no specific limitation on the number of hours a week that work could involve while still falling for consideration or the times in the week at which a claimant was expected to take up work, apart from in the cases of the particular categories of claimant identified in reg.14, but the Secretary of State could use their power in subs.(3) to specify further limitations in particular cases. See the further discussion below under *Type of work* and *Immediately*. Where a limitation under reg.14 or s.6E(3) applies, there may also be a deemed compliance under reg.13 or a further qualification to the meaning of the availability requirement under reg.16.

Regulation 16. Subsection (5) allows regulations to define what is meant in subs.(2) by being able and willing immediately to take up work. It is that power that reg.16, so far as it concerns availability, exercises. Thus, the effect if any of the prescribed circumstances exists is similar to the effect of reg.13, but through a different mechanism. Regulation 16(1)(b) provides in relation to the work availability requirement that claimants in any of the circumstances set out in para.(3), (4), (5) or (5B) are regarded as being available for work if able and willing to take up paid work or attend an interview immediately after the relevant circumstance ceases to apply. Paragraph (3) applies to a variety of circumstances where the claimant is prevented from being available by something outside their control or is subject to some particularly testing experience, usually of a temporary nature. Paragraph (4) applies, oddly, where it is unreasonable to require the claimant to comply with a work search requirement because of temporary child care responsibilities, temporary circumstances, carrying out a public duty or, importantly, carrying out work preparation. Paragraph (5), with an exception under (5A) and (5B), applies where the claimant is unfit for work for up to 14 days.

Regulation 16A. This regulation has a similar effect to reg.16(5) where the claimant is unable to work because of some specific disease or disablement for more than two weeks but less than thirteen and meets the other conditions in reg.46A, provided it is unreasonable to expect the claimant to comply with a work availability requirement.

Able and willing

There was a body of case law under the old unemployment benefit regime on inability to take up employment that may possibly be relevant to new style JSA, although many particular issues have now been overtaken by specific rules. Examples are where immigration law precludes the claimant working (*Shaukat Ali v CAO*, Appendix to *R(U)1/85*), but now see s.115 of the Immigration and Asylum Act 1999 and Part V of Vol.II of this series; where the claimant is about to go abroad (*R(U)2/90*—dealing with the position of wives of servicemen about to join their husbands for a posting abroad); or is contractually bound to another employer (*R(U)11/51*), for example, to be on call each working day, but now see reg.13(5). Thus, it would seem that a person subject to a zero hours contract who is given no hours of work could be available for work. Even if the contract contained an exclusivity clause (not made ineffective until the coming into force of s.153 of the Small Business, Enterprise and Employment Act 2015 on May 26, 2015), the claimant might be deemed to have complied with the availability requirement if all the conditions of reg.13(5) are met. By the same token, it is arguable that a person "furloughed" under the Coronavirus Job Retention Scheme, which by its initial terms only prohibited employment by the furloughing employer, was available for alternative employment unless the contract of employment prohibited that. The issue of possible inability to take up work while away on holiday is discussed under *Immediately* below.

What claimants are willing and not willing to do can, of course, most obviously be judged from their professions of willingness in interviews that then form the basis for the content of a work search requirement. But it can also be inferred from conduct (see *R(U)4/53*). There the claimant had shown by his long practice of not taking up the option of working voluntary shifts on Saturdays that he was not available for work on Saturdays. See *Type of work* below for how far claimants can restrict the kind of work they are willing to do.

Type of work

Section 6E(3) with subs.(4)(a) and (d) allows regulations to impose limitations on the work availability requirement by reference to work of a particular nature and to work available for a certain number of hours per week or at particular times. That power has only been exercised in reg.14(3) and (4), to now quite a limited effect where a claimant has previously carried out work of a particular nature and level of remuneration, and in reg.14(5), where the claimant has a physical or mental impairment, in relation to the nature and location of employment. Otherwise, there is nothing specific in the legislation about how far claimants can restrict the types of work or the hours of work they are willing to undertake and still meet the work availability requirement. The rule is not in terms of being available for suitable work. However, reg.14 applies both to the work search requirement under s.6D and the work availability requirement. It appears that, for consistency, the question of the nature of work or number of hours or level of remuneration that a claimant is prepared to accept must be assessed primarily by reference to the content of the s.6D requirement, since s.6E contains no further conditions on those matters. Since the fundamental requirement in s.6D is to take all reasonable action for the purpose of obtaining paid work or more or better-paid work, with the requirement to take any particular action specified by the Secretary of State necessarily restricted to actions that are reasonable, the same standard must be applied in so far as s.6E involves asking what kind of work and/or hours and what level of remuneration the claimant can be required to be prepared to accept. That seems to be acknowledged in the current DWP universal credit guidance document on availability for work deposited in the House of Commons Library (collected in the Resources section of the Rightsnet website), where it is said that "any agreed restriction on hours of availability will determine a claimant's 'expected hours' of work search". The reverse would seem to be equally valid. The guidance also contains a general section about the tailoring of work search requirements to individual claimants. The Child Poverty Action Group mock-up of a tailored claimant commitment in Mears & Howes, *You reap what you code: Universal credit, digitalisation and the rule of law* (CPAG June 2023), lumps work search and availability together under a heading of "Work I can do" and restricts the contents of the "My availability" box to the issue of immediate availability for interviews or to take up work. Such tailoring of the work availability requirement must rest on the use of the power in s.6E(3) for the Secretary of State to specify further limitations than those provided by reg.14.

There may well be scope for differences of opinion between claimants and work coaches about how far it is reasonable for them to restrict their work search and availability to their usual kind of work or the kind of work for which they are particularly suited or trained, rather than merely excluding the kind of work of which are simply not capable. A current impetus, as exemplified in the justification for the February 2022 amendment to reg.14(3) (permitted period reduced to four weeks), is towards encouraging claimants into any work that they can do, as more beneficial to them and to the economy, rather than waiting around for the ideal opportunity. Claimants might legitimately argue for more time before expanding their search, especially if their particular prospects of finding work of a particular kind are good, but no doubt policy arguments about the general economic good are outside the remit of work coaches. However any arguments are resolved, there should be clarity in the requirement that is in the end imposed on behalf of the Secretary of State about the scope of work the claimant must be willing and able to take up.

Claimants may have religious or other conscientious objections to particular kinds of work, such as vegetarians or vegans to working in a meat pie or sausage factory, even perhaps in the office. Readers can no doubt think of many other examples. Such restrictions can be accommodated by work coaches specifying a suitable limitation under s.6E(3). If such a limitation is not accepted, then if a case gets to the stage of a sanction being imposed for failure to comply with the availability for work requirement, the question of whether the claimant had no good reason for the failure would come to the fore.

So far as hours of work are concerned, the default position, outside the cases specifically dealt with by reg.14, appears to be that claimants should be able and willing to take up full-time work or additional work to take the weekly hours up to the reg.9 expected hours (starting point, 35 hours). Thus, where those expected hours are reduced from 35, affecting in particular responsible carers and relevant carers of children and claimants with a physical or mental impairment, there is a knock-on effect on the availability for work requirement. The default position would also be that the hours could be distributed over any days of the week. However, as specifically recognised in the DWP guidance document deposited in the House of Commons Library, the effect of sincerely held religious beliefs against working on repeated days (like Saturdays or Sundays) or on specific festival days should be accepted. The same document notes that a pattern of availability may be agreed with a claimant so long as they have reasonable prospects of finding work within that pattern. It is submitted that it would in general not be reasonable to require claimants to be willing to work seven days a week. Especially for those with any caring responsibilities for school age children and young persons working at weekends might be problematic.

Immediately

The condition of being able and willing immediately to take up paid work or attend an interview is on its face an oppressive one. It apparently requires a claimant to be willing immediately, on a moment's notice, to take up an offer of work in the middle of the night, seven days a week (say, for shelf-stacking in a supermarket). Although the general formulation of the rule can be traced back at least as far as the 1930s, under unemployment benefit there was arguably some restriction to opportunities brought to the claimant's notice during normal business hours and under old style JSA there was an explicit link between the "immediate" obligation and a statutorily recognised pattern of availability (see *R(JSA) 2/07*). Modern conditions, with an extension of the 24-hour economy, have made the issues more pointed.

The dangers for claimants, along with some suggestions as to a common sense approach to "immediately", in the specific context of reg.7 of the JSA Regulations 1996 on old style JSA, were pointed out by Simon Brown LJ in *Secretary of State for Social Security v David*, reported in R(JSA) 3/01, at paras 25 and 26:

> "That 'immediately' means within a very short space of time indeed is clear not only from the word itself but also from regulation 5 which provides for exceptions to this requirement in the case of those with caring responsibilities or engaged in voluntary work (who need only be willing and able to take up employment on 48 hours' notice) and certain others engaged in providing a service (who get 24 hours' notice). No doubt the requirement for immediate availability allows the claimant time to wash, dress and have his breakfast, but strictly it would seem inconsistent with, say, a claimant's stay overnight with a friend or relative, or attendance at a weekend cricket match, or even an evening at the cinema (unless perhaps he had left a contact number and had not travelled far).
>
> 26. In these circumstances, claimants ought clearly to be wary of entering into an agreement which offers unrestricted availability throughout the entire week, day and night, weekdays and weekends."

Some claimants will escape the full rigour of the "immediate" requirement through reg.13 or 16 or by way of limitations under s.6E(3). It must also be the case that, if a pattern of availability has been accepted, that will also control the days on which the claimant is required to be willing immediately to take up employment. Thus, it would seem always to be in the interests of a claimant to get such a pattern into the claimant commitment. The DWP universal credit guidance document deposited in the House of Commons Library says that claimants must be as ready and flexible as possible to attend interviews and start work and that if they have regular commitments they must consider how they can be rearranged so they can take up interviews or start work. That seems in itself an unobjectionable approach and it may be that, from the absence of examples of oppressive requirements, some sensible flexibility is allowed in practice. Nevertheless, the formula apparently used in claimant commitments without a pattern of availability is in peremptory terms ("I will be available to attend a job interview immediately. I will be available to start work immediately", repeated in essence in the CPAG mock-up mentioned above). If it were just a matter of that wording in the claimant commitment, it could perhaps be rejected as so unduly oppressive as to be irrational. But if all the documents and information made available to the claimant, including the claimant commitment, are sufficient to impose the availability for work requirement (on which see the notes to s.6A), then it is the requirement as defined in s.6E(2) that is imposed, including the reference to being able and willing immediately to take up paid work (or attend an interview: reg.11). Can that be interpreted in a non-oppressive way without some express basis in the legislation for doing so? It seems wrong that a claimant commitment should contain a requirement in terms that no-one could be expected actually to follow, even if there would almost automatically be good reason for any failure to comply in the context of a middle of the night summons to a job if a case got to the stage of a sanction.

Note that under s.6G(1) the Secretary of State is empowered to require a claimant to participate in an interview relating to the imposition of a work-related requirement on the claimant or assisting the claimant to comply with a requirement. Under s.6G(3) they can require the provision of information and evidence for the purpose of verifying compliance with a work-related requirement and that the claimant confirm compliance in any manner. Under s.6G(4) they can require the reporting of any changes in the claimant's circumstances. A failure for no good reason to comply with any of those connected requirements is also sanctionable under s.6K(2)(b).

[[1] Imposition of work-related requirements

1.688 **6F.**—(1) The Secretary of State must, except in prescribed circumstances, impose on a claimant—

(a) a work search requirement, and

(b) a work availability requirement.

(2) The Secretary of State may, subject to this Act, impose either or both of the following on a claimant—

(a) a work-focused interview requirement;

(b) a work preparation requirement.]

AMENDMENT

1. Welfare Reform Act 2012 s.49(3) (trigger date on or after April 29, 2013).

DEFINITIONS

"claimant"—see s.35(1).
"work availability requirement"—see ss.35(1) and 6E(1).
"work preparation requirement"—see ss.35(1) and 6C(1).
"work search requirement"—see ss.35(1) and 6D(1).
"work-focused interview requirement"—see ss.35(1) and 6B(1).
"work-related requirement"—see ss.35(1) and 6(2).

GENERAL NOTE

1.689 This section sets out the default position that any claimant of new style JSA is, unless exempted under reg.15, 16 or 16A of the JSA Regulations 2013, to be subject to the work search and work availability requirements. The imposition of the work-focused interview and the work preparation requirement is, subject only to a possible exemption under reg.15 (domestic violence), a matter for the discretion of the Secretary of State under subs.(2). The content of the requirements is set out in ss.6B–6E and associated regulations. Under s.6G(1) the Secretary of State is empowered to require a claimant to participate in an interview relating to the imposition of a work-related requirement or assisting the claimant to comply with a requirement. Under s.6G(3) he can require the provision of information and evidence for the purpose of verifying compliance with a work-related requirement, that the claimant confirm compliance in any manner and that the claimant report specified changes in circumstances.

See s.6H for the process of imposing a requirement.

See the notes to s.6A for discussion of *JB v SSWP (UC)* [2018] UKUT 360 (AAC) and the question whether the current standard terms of claimant commitments (e.g. in the form of provisions like "I will also attend and take part in appointments with my adviser when required", "I will be available to attend a job interview immediately [and to] start work immediately" or "I will normally spend 35 hours per week looking and preparing for work") are sufficient in themselves to carry out the duty in the equivalent of s.6F(1) and the power in the equivalent of s.6F(2) to impose the specified work-related requirements. The judge considered that that question would rarely arise in practice and that what was important was whether consideration of all the evidence produced by the SSWP of communications to the claimant showed that the substance of the requirement in issue and the consequences of non-compliance had been properly notified to the claimant. In para.29 of *S v SSWP (UC)* [2017] UKUT 477 (AAC), the judge accepted that, if the SSWP failed to carry out the equivalent of the s.6F(1) duty, the claimant should not bear the consequences of that (which must entail that the requirement(s) in question had not been imposed and there could be no sanction for failing to comply). That approach has in effect been confirmed in para.6 of *JB*, where it was said to be a condition precedent of the imposition of a sanction under the equivalent of s.6K(2)(a) that the claimant was subject to the work-related requirement in question. See also the notes to ss.6 and 6H.

JB was endorsed and applied in *KG v SSWP (UC)* [2020] UKUT 307 (AAC). Before the Upper Tribunal the Secretary of State accepted that the available evidence did not show that the claimant had been properly notified of the requirement to take part in the particular telephone interview with his work coach, so that no sanction could be applied under the equivalent of s.6K. The documents were ambiguous as to whether the interview was under the equivalent of s.6B (work-focused interview requirement) or the equivalent of s.6G (connected requirements) and what issues the claimant was told were to be investigated, and left it unclear whether he had been adequately informed of the consequences of non-compliance.

Note the important reg.5 of the JSA Regulations 2013, under which, if a claimant is concurrently entitled to new style JSA and to universal credit, no work-related requirements under ss.6B–6I can be imposed, nor can any sanctions under s.6J or 6K operate.

[1 Connected requirements

6G.—(1) The Secretary of State may require a claimant to participate in an interview for any purpose relating to— 1.690

(a) the imposition of a work-related requirement on the claimant;
(b) verifying the claimant's compliance with a work-related requirement;
(c) assisting the claimant to comply with a work-related requirement.

(2) The Secretary of State may specify how, when and where such an interview is to take place.

(3) The Secretary of State may, for the purpose of verifying the claimant's compliance with a work-related requirement, require a claimant to—

(a) provide to the Secretary of State information and evidence specified by the Secretary of State in a manner so specified;
(b) confirm compliance in a manner so specified.

(4) The Secretary of State may require a claimant to report to the Secretary of State any specified changes in their circumstances which are relevant to—

(a) the imposition of work-related requirements on the claimant;
(b) the claimant's compliance with a work-related requirement.]

AMENDMENT

1. Welfare Reform Act 2012 s.49(3) (trigger date on or after April 29, 2013).

DEFINITIONS

"claimant"—see s.35(1).
"work-related requirement"—see ss.35(1) and 6(2).

GENERAL NOTE

This section gives the Secretary of State power to require a claimant to do various things related to the imposition of work-related requirements, verifying compliance and assisting claimants to comply: to participate in an interview (subss.(1) and (2)); for the purpose of verifying compliance, to provide specified information and evidence or to confirm compliance (subs.(3)); or to report specified changes of circumstances relevant to the imposition of or compliance with requirements. Note that the permitted purposes of an interview under subs.(1) do not include discussion of the drawing up or review of a claimant commitment as such. However, discussion of 1.691

whether a work-related requirement should be imposed and what its content should be, which would then be recorded in a claimant commitment, would be included.

The requirements under s.6G do not fall within the meaning of "work-related requirement", but there is a separate ground of sanction under s.6K(2)(b) for failing for no good reason to comply. The Secretary of State is allowed under subs.(2) to specify how, when and where any interview under subs.(1) is to take place, so that the requirement to participate must at least entail turning up at the place and time specified, although the decision of Judge Knowles in *SA v SSWP (JSA)* [2015] UKUT 454 (AAC) (see the notes to s.6K for full discussion) would indicate that tribunals should consider, in cases where the claimant arrives not very late, whether it is proportionate to the nature of all the circumstances to regard that as a failure to participate in an interview. There were all sorts of mitigating circumstances in *SA*, that may well not be present in other cases. See *SN v SSWP (JSA)* [2018] UKUT 279 (AAC), detailed in the notes to s.6K, for discussion of what might amount to a failure to participate (in that case in a mandatory work activity scheme) and the expression in para.45 of some doubt about the result in *SA*. The requirement to participate must also extend to making some meaningful contribution to the interview, but the limits will probably not be established until some more sanctions appeals have reached the Upper Tribunal. Behaviour that leads to the premature termination of the interview may well amount to a failure to participate (see the facts of *DM v SSWP (JSA)* [2015] UKUT 67 (AAC) in the notes to s.6K). There may, though, in cases of unco-operative claimants or heavy-handed officials or a combination, be difficult questions about when an interview has ceased to exist, so that subsequent behaviour cannot be relevant to whether there has been a failure to participate (see *PH v SSWP (ESA)* [2016] UKUT 119 (AAC) on failing to submit to a medical examination). The compulsory imposition of a sanction for a failure for no good reason to report specified changes in circumstances, to provide specified information or evidence or to confirm compliance with a work-related requirement is a new departure.

JB v SSWP (UC) [2018] UKUT 360 (AAC) (see the notes to ss.6A and 6B) was endorsed and applied in *KG v SSWP (UC)* [2020] UKUT 307 (AAC). Before the Upper Tribunal the Secretary of State accepted that the available evidence did not show that the claimant had been properly notified of the requirement to take part in the particular telephone interview with his work coach, so that no sanction could be applied under the equivalent of s.6K. The documents were ambiguous as to whether the interview was under the equivalent of s.6B (work-focused interview requirement) or the equivalent of s.6G (connected requirements) and what issues the claimant was told were to be investigated, and left it unclear whether he had been adequately informed of the consequences of non-compliance.

It was recognised in *CS v SSWP (JSA)* [2019] UKUT 218 (AAC), detailed in the notes to s.6K, that it was legitimate for a scheme provider to require an attender to verify their identity before starting a scheme, so that a refusal to do so would usually amount to a failure to participate in the scheme. The same principle could apply to an interview, but the particular issues that arose in *CS*, to do with a scheme provider external to the DWP, are unlikely to arise if it is an interview with an employment officer that has been notified.

See s.6H for the process of imposing a requirement.

[1 Imposition of work-related and connected requirements: supplementary

1.692 **6H.**—(1) Regulations may make provision—

(a) where the Secretary of State may impose a requirement under the preceding provisions of this Act, as to when the requirement must or must not be imposed;

(b) where the Secretary of State may specify any action to be taken in relation to a requirement under the preceding provisions of this Act, as to what action must or must not be specified;

(c) where the Secretary of State may specify any other matter in relation to a such requirement, as to what must or must not be specified in respect of that matter.

(2) Where the Secretary of State may impose a work-focused interview requirement, or specify a particular action under section 6C(1) or 6D(1)(b), the Secretary of State must have regard to such matters as may be prescribed.

(3) Where the Secretary of State may impose a requirement under the preceding provisions of this Act, or specify any action to be taken in relation to such a requirement, the Secretary of State may revoke or change what has been imposed or specified.

(4) Notification of a requirement imposed under the preceding provisions of this Act (or any change to or revocation of such a requirement) is, if not included in the claimant commitment, to be in such manner as the Secretary of State may determine.

(5) Regulations must make provision to secure that, in prescribed circumstances, where a claimant has recently been a victim of domestic violence—

(a) a requirement imposed on the claimant under the preceding provisions of this Act ceases to have effect for a period of 13 weeks, and

(b) the Secretary of State may not impose any other requirement on the claimant during that period.

(6) For the purposes of subsection (5)—

(a) "domestic violence" has such meaning as may be prescribed;

(b) "victim of domestic violence" means a person on or against whom domestic violence is inflicted or threatened (and regulations under subsection (5) may prescribe circumstances in which a person is to be treated as being or not being a victim of domestic violence);

(c) a person has recently been a victim of domestic violence if a prescribed period has not expired since the violence was inflicted or threatened.]

AMENDMENT

1. Welfare Reform Act 2012 s.49(3) (trigger date on or after April 29, 2013).

DEFINITIONS

"claimant commitment"—see s.6A(1).
"prescribed"—see s.35(1).
"regulations"—*ibid.*
"work-focused interview requirement"—see ss.35(1) and 6B(1).
"work-related requirement"—see ss.35(1) and 6(2).

GENERAL NOTE

This section contains a variety of powers and duties in relation to the imposition by the Secretary of State of either a work-related requirement or a connected requirement under s.6G. It makes the imposition of a requirement and the notification to the claimant a moderately formal process, which raises the question of whether the decision of the Secretary of State to impose a requirement is a decision that is appealable to a First-tier Tribunal under s.12(1) of the SSA 1998, either as a decision on a claim or award or one which falls to be made under the WRA 2012 as a "relevant enactment" (s.8(1)(a) and (c) of the SSA 1998). However, if it is a decision not made on a claim or award, it is not covered in Sch.3 to the SSA 1998 (or in Sch.2 to the **1.693**

Decisions and Appeals Regulations 2013 (see Vol.III of this series)), so is not appealable under that heading. The discussion in the note to s.12(1) of the SSA 1998 in Vol. III would indicate that, since the imposition of a requirement is not an "outcome" decision determining entitlement to or payability of new style JSA or the amount payable, it is not appealable under s.12(1)(a) as a decision on a claim or award.

Thus, it appears that a direct challenge to the imposition of any particular requirement, including any element specified by the Secretary of State and/or its inclusion in a claimant commitment under s.6 of this Act, can only be made by way of judicial review in the High Court, with the possibility of a discretionary transfer to the Upper Tribunal. Otherwise, a challenge by way of appeal appears not be possible unless and until a reduction of benefit for a sanctionable failure is imposed on the claimant for a failure to comply with a requirement. It must therefore be the case that in any such appeal the claimant can challenge whether the conditions for the imposition of the requirement in question were met, with the result that, if that challenge is successful, the sanction must be removed. That appears to have been the assumption of the Supreme Court in *R. (on the application of Reilly and Wilson) v SSWP* [2013] UKSC 68; [2014] 1 A.C. 453. At para.29 of their joint judgment, Lords Neuberger and Toulson mentioned without any adverse comment Foskett J's holding at first instance that a consequence of a breach of a regulation requiring a claimant to be given notice of a requirement to participate in a scheme was that no sanction could lawfully be imposed on the claimant for failure to participate in the scheme. In para.29 of *S v SSWP (UC)* [2017] UKUT 477 (AAC), the judge accepted that, if the SSWP failed to carry out the equivalent of the s.6F(1) duty, the claimant should not bear the consequences of that (which must entail that the requirement(s) in question had not been imposed and there could be no sanction for failing to comply). That approach has in effect been confirmed in para.6 of *JB v SSWP (UC)* [2018] UKUT 360 (AAC), where it was said to be a condition precedent of the imposition of a sanction under the equivalent of s.6K(2)(a) that the claimant was subject to the work-related requirement in question.

There is serious doubt whether the standard terms currently used in new style JSA claimant commitments are sufficient in themselves to impose any work-related requirements (see the notes to s.6A). If they are not, the necessity for notification by some other means (it being necessarily implied in subs.(4) in conjunction with ss.6(1) and 6F that a claimant is not subject to a work-related requirement if the Secretary of State has not notified them of its imposition: see para.29 of *S v SSWP (UC)* [2017] UKUT 477 (AAC)), as allowed by subs.(4), becomes more important. Careful consideration will need to be given by tribunals to what evidence of imposition by the Secretary of State and notification to the claimant has been put before them. Now see the decision in *JB* (above), discussed in detail in the notes to s.6A. There the judge considered that the question of the sufficiency of the terms of the claimant commitment alone would rarely arise in practice and that what was important was whether consideration of all the evidence produced by the SSWP of communications to the claimant showed that the substance of the requirement in issue and the consequences of non-compliance had been properly notified to the claimant. There is reference there to many kinds of communication that might be relevant. Rigorous guidance has been given to decision-makers in the universal credit context (which must be equally applicable to new style JSA) in Memo ADM 5/19.

It is plainly arguable that no work-related or connected requirement can be imposed unless the claimant has received sufficient information about the requirement to enable them to make meaningful representations about whether the requirement should be imposed or not (the "prior information duty"). That duty stems from principles stated by the Supreme Court in *Reilly* and *Wilson* (above) and elaborated by the *Court of Appeal in Secretary of State for Work and Pensions v Reilly and Hewstone* and *Secretary of State for Work and Pensions v Jeffrey and Bevan* [2016] EWCA Civ 413; [2017] Q.B. 657; [2017] AACR 14. See the discussion in the notes to s.6K and the notes to s.6J at 1.707 for points about when any breach of the duty might be material and when issues about the duty arise on appeals. If the process for the production of claimant commitments as described in the notes to s.6A is followed, there should be ample opportunity for the giving of sufficient information, although what happened in practice in individual cases will be what matters.

It is also arguable that if an initial or revised claimant commitment was put to a claimant for formal acceptance in breach of the duties described above a failure to accept that commitment should not lead to the conclusion that the basic condition of entitlement in s.1(2)(b) (has accepted a claimant commitment) was not satisfied. See the notes to reg.7 of the JSA Regulations 2013 for further discussion.

Subsection (1)

Regulations 16 and 16A of the JSA Regulations 2013 are made under para.(a), reg.15 on domestic violence falling more specifically under subss.(5) and (6). No regulations appear to have been made under paras (b) or (c) of subs.(1). **1.694**

Subsection (2)

No regulations appear to have been made under this provision. **1.695**

Subsection (3)

The inclusion of this express power to revoke or change any requirement, or any specification of action, is an indication of the formality entailed in the imposition of a requirement. However, there appears to be no restriction on the circumstances in which the Secretary of State may carry out such a revocation or change, subject of course to the legislative conditions being met for whatever the new position is. A mere change of mind without any change in circumstances or mistake or error as to the existing circumstances will do. **1.696**

Subsection (4)

This provision allows the Secretary of State to notify the claimant of the imposition of any requirement, if not included in a claimant commitment under s.6A, in any manner. Thus, it may be done orally (or presumably even through the medium of mime), but it is a necessary implication that a requirement must be notified to the claimant. That in turn implies that, whatever the manner of notification, the content must be such as is reasonably capable of being understood by the particular claimant with the characteristics known to the officer of the Secretary of State (so perhaps the medium of mime will not do after all). Less flippantly, this principle may be important for claimants with sensory problems, e.g. hearing or vision difficulties. The expectation of course is that the requirements imposed under the Act will be included in the claimant commitment, one of whose aims is to ensure that claimants know and understand what is being required of them and the potential consequences of failing to comply. That expectation may not in practice have been fulfilled. However, it is clear in law that the validity of a requirement is not dependent on inclusion in the claimant commitment. There is no such express condition and under s.6A(4)(a) the Secretary of State is only under a duty to record in the claimant commitment such of the requirements under the Act as they consider it appropriate to include. And often a specification by the Secretary of State of a precise manifestation of a general requirement will be done outside the claimant commitment (see the notes to ss.6B–6D). It may be that the fact that a requirement is not recorded in the claimant commitment could be put forward as part of an argument for there having been a good reason for failing to comply with the requirement. **1.697**

Subsections (5) and (6)

The duty to make regulations providing that no work-related requirement or connected requirement under s.6G may be imposed for a period of 13 weeks on a claimant who has recently been a victim of domestic violence is carried out in reg.15 of the JSA Regulations 2013. Most of the meat is in the regulation, including the definition of "domestic violence", which has been amended since April 2013. See **1.698** the annotations to reg.15 for the details. However, subs.(6)(b) does define "victim" to include not just those on whom domestic violence is inflicted but also those against whom it is threatened.

[1 Compliance with work-related and connected requirements

1.699 **6I.**—Regulations may make provision as to circumstances in which a claimant is to be treated as having—

(a) complied with or not complied with any requirement imposed under the preceding provisions of this Act or any aspect of such a requirement, or

(b) taken or not taken any particular action specified by the Secretary of State in relation to such a requirement.]

AMENDMENT

1. Welfare Reform Act 2012 s.49(3) (trigger date on or after April 29, 2013).

DEFINITIONS

"claimant"—see s.35(1).
"regulations"—*ibid.*
"work-related requirement"—see ss.35(1) and 6(1).

GENERAL NOTE

1.700 Under subs.(a) regulations may deem a claimant either to have or not to have complied with any work-related requirement or connected requirement under s.6G in particular circumstances. Regulations 11–13 of the JSA Regulations 2013 make use of this power, mainly in treating claimants as not having complied. No regulations appear to have been made as yet under subs.(b).

[1 Higher-level sanctions

1.701 **6J.**—(1) The amount of an award of jobseeker's allowance is to be reduced in accordance with this section in the event of a failure by a claimant which is sanctionable under this section.

(2) It is a failure sanctionable under this section if a claimant—

(a) fails for no good reason to comply with a requirement imposed by the Secretary of State under a work preparation requirement to undertake a work placement of a prescribed description;

(b) fails for no good reason to comply with a requirement imposed by the Secretary of State under a work search requirement to apply for a particular vacancy for paid work;

(c) fails for no good reason to comply with a work availability requirement by not taking up an offer of paid work;

(d) by reason of misconduct, or voluntarily and for no good reason, ceases paid work or loses pay.

(3) It is a failure sanctionable under this section if, at any time before making the claim by reference to which the award is made, the claimant—

(a) for no good reason failed to take up an offer of paid work, or

(b) by reason of misconduct, or voluntarily and for no good reason, ceased paid work or lost pay.

(4) For the purposes of subsections (2) and (3) regulations may provide—

(a) for circumstances in which ceasing to work or losing pay is to be treated as occurring or not occurring by reason of misconduct or voluntarily;

(b) for loss of pay below a prescribed level to be disregarded.

(5) Regulations are to specify—

(a) the amount of a reduction under this section;

(b) the period for which such a reduction has effect, not exceeding three years in relation to any failure sanctionable under this section.

(6) Regulations under subsection (5)(b) may in particular provide for the period of a reduction to depend on either or both of the following—

(a) the number of failures by the claimant sanctionable under this section;

(b) the period between such failures.

(7) Regulations may provide—

(a) for cases in which no reduction is to be made under this section;

(b) for a reduction under this section made in relation to an award that is terminated to be applied to any new award made within a prescribed period of the termination;

(c) for the termination or suspension of a reduction under this section.]

AMENDMENT

1. Welfare Reform Act 2012 s.49(3) (trigger date on or after April 29, 2013).

DEFINITIONS

"claimant"—see s.35(1).
"prescribed"—*ibid.*
"regulations"—*ibid.*
"work availability requirement"—see ss.35(1) and 6E(1).
"work preparation requirement"—see ss.35(1) and 6C(1).
"work search requirement"—see ss.35(1) and 6D(1).
"work-related requirement"—see ss.35(1) and 6(2).

GENERAL NOTE

Sections 6J and 6K set up a very similar structure of sanctions leading to reductions in the amount of JSA payable to that already imposed in the universal credit scheme by ss.26 and 27 of the WRA 2012. The main difference for new style JSA, apart from the omission of elements specifically linked to the particular nature of universal credit as a general income maintenance benefit, covering people in quite substantial work as well as those out of work for various reasons, is that "other" sanctions apart from higher-level sanctions are divided into only two levels (medium and low), rather than three. There are also similarities to the new ss.19–20 of the old style Jobseekers Act 1995 in operation from October 22, 2012 (see Vol.V of this series, 2021/22 edition as updated in Cumulative Supplements included in Vol.II of this series and in mid-year Supplements). The similarity there is in the creation of higher-level sanctions, here under s.6J, and of a lower level of other sanctions, here under s.6K, and in the stringency of the fixed periods and the amount of reductions to be imposed, in particular for higher-level sanctions. Section 6J also takes over a number of concepts that are very familiar from the history of unemployment benefit and JSA and on which a wealth of case-law authority has built up, much of which remains relevant to new style JSA. There are, however, some potentially significant differences in the wording of otherwise similar provisions as between the old style and the new style Jobseekers Act 1995, which will be noted below. 1.702

Note, however, the extraordinary claim made by DWP officials at a meeting of the Social Security Advisory Committee (SSAC) on September 8, 2021, relating to the proposal to make regulations amending reg.18 of the JSA Regulations 2013 to correct a drafting error from November 1, 2021 onwards (see the notes to reg.18 for details), that no sanctions had previously been imposed on any new style JSA or

ESA claimant, apparently since 2013, the focus instead having been on engagement and encouragement by work coaches (para.2.2(b) of the SSAC minutes). Such a claim is hard to accept in the light of the DWP's own regular issues of benefit sanctions statistics (and, if true, would be regarded by many as a dereliction of duty to the public). For instance, the January 2020 issue records 5,000 JSA sanction decisions as having been made in 2019. The statistics do not distinguish between old style and new style JSA, but some at least of the 5,000 must (even taking account of the effect of reg.5 of the JSA Regulations 2013) have been in new style JSA. What the statistics do show is a steady and heavy decline from 2013 in the number of JSA sanctions decisions. Could the officials have been referring only to sanctions particularly linked to "conditionality" in the sense of new style work-related requirements, rather than the "traditional" grounds like misconduct or leaving voluntarily for no good reason?

Some further, but not conclusive, information was eventually given in the Social Security Advisory Committee's paper on *The future of working age benefits for those not in paid work* (Occasional Paper No.26, dated July 2022, but not added to the website until October 28, 2022). There is a specific reference on p.37 to the non-application of sanctions in new style JSA in the period prior to November 1, 2021 where claimants did not uphold their responsibilities under their claimant commitment, but on p.70 it is said that there was an operational impediment in that the JSAPS computer payment system would not allow the application of reductions of benefit for sanctions. That impediment would seem to have applied to all forms of sanction, whether specifically related to conditionality or not, so that the claim described above as extraordinary may well have been correct, but none the less extraordinary.

The central concept under these provisions is of a "sanctionable failure", which under s.6J(1) (subject to reg.28 of the JSA Regulations 2013) and s.6K(1), is to lead to a reduction in the amount of an award of new style JSA. For higher-level sanctions under s.6J, the reduction initially was in brief of 100 per cent of the claimant's entitlement under reg.49 for 91 days for a first higher-level failure, 182 days for a second such failure (or universal credit failure) within a year, and 1095 days for a third or subsequent such failure within a year. However, an amendment with effect from November 27, 2019 changed the period in the third category to 182 days. That was in fulfilment of the undertaking by the then Secretary of State (Amber Rudd) in her written statement to Parliament on May 9, 2019 (HCWS 1545) to remove three-year sanctions for third and subsequent failures and to reduce the maximum sanction length to six months by the end of the year. Regulation 5(2) of the amending Regulations (see Part III of this volume) makes the transitional provision that, where an award of new style JSA was subject to a 1095-day reduction under s.6J as at November 27, 2019, that reduction is to be terminated where the award had been reduced for at least 182 days.

It must, though, be noted that there has been no amendment to reg.18(3) of the JSA Regulations 2013, which imposes a 1095-day limit on the total outstanding reduction period that is allowed. Because by virtue of reg.18(2) reduction periods under new style JSA (as for universal credit, but not old style JSA) run consecutively, the result is still that a claimant subject to a series of higher-level sanctions, each individually limited to 182 days, may be subject to a continuous reduction of benefit for up to 1095 days. The precise words of Amber Rudd's pledge set out above may thus have been carried out, but the effect is not as comprehensive as may have been thought.

There remains doubt whether, following an amendment to reg.18 with effect from July 25, 2016, the legislation allowed the "escalation" of the sanction period for second or subsequent sanctionable failures within a year. The reasons for that doubt, with a suggestion that a principle of statutory interpretation required the words of that amendment to be corrected as plainly mistaken, are set out in the notes to reg.18. That doubt has been removed with effect from November 1, 2021 by further amendment. As noted above, the DWP apparently considers the resolution of the doubt in relation to the period from July 25, 2016 to October 31, 2021 to be unnecessary on the unlikely basis that no new style JSA sanctions were imposed in that period.

For other sanctions under s.6K the reduction is of the same amount, but generally for limited periods. As noted below, regulations set out the amount and period of the reduction.

There is no discretion under either s.6J or 6K as to whether or not to apply a reduction if the conditions are met and no discretion under the regulations as to the amount and period of the reduction as calculated under the complicated formulae there. Regulation 28 of the JSA Regulations 2013, made under s.6J(7)(a), sets out limited circumstances in which no reduction is to be made for a sanctionable failure under s.6J. Those circumstances are not relevant to the sanctionable failures covered by s.6K.

See the notes to regs 18–21 of the JSA Regulations 2013 for the position where there has been a transition from old style JSA to new style JSA, either in the form of some unexpired period of reduction of old style JSA or the existence of a previous sanctionable failure under that legislation.

Sight must also never be lost of the important provision in reg.5(3) of the JSA Regulations 2013, made under s.6J(7)(a) and s.6K(9)(a), that where a person is entitled to both universal credit and new style JSA, reductions of an award of JSA under ss.6J or 6K and the relevant part of the JSA Regulations 2013 do not apply. That appears to mean that, if such a claimant who has income from new style JSA topped up by universal credit commits a sanctionable failure, the amount of the JSA award cannot be reduced and only the amount of the universal credit top-up can be available for reduction under the universal credit sanctions provisions. See further the annotations to reg.5. 1.703

As a matter of principle, a claimant has to be able, in any appeal against a reduction in benefit on the imposition of a sanction, to challenge whether the conditions for the imposition of the requirement in question were met. That is stated in terms in para.6 of *JB v SSWP (UC)* [2018] UKUT 360 (AAC) and see further in the note to s.6H.

It has recently been stated that the Secretary of State need not in all sanctions cases provide evidence in the appeal bundle to support the satisfaction of all the preconditions to imposing a sanction, but that principle must be properly understood in context. In *SSWP v CN (JSA)* [2020] UKUT 26 (AAC), the claimant's sole ground of appeal against a sanction for failing to participate in the Work Programme by not attending an appointment was that she had never failed to keep an appointment (i.e. implicitly that she could not have received the notice of the appointment and/or had good cause under the regulations then in force). The tribunal allowed her appeal on the ground that the bundle did not contain a copy of the notice referring her to the Work Programme (i.e. the WP05) so that it was not satisfied that she had properly been notified of the requirement to participate. The tribunal appeared to think that that issue was one "raised by the appeal" within s.12(8)(a) of the SSA 1998, which it manifestly was not as the Secretary of State's submission in the bundle that there was no dispute that the claimant was referred to the Work Programme had not been challenged. Nor did it give any explanation, if it had exercised its discretion under s.12(8)(a) to consider the issue, of why it did so and how the issue was clearly apparent from the evidence so as to be capable of being dealt with under that discretion. Even if those hurdles had been overcome, the Secretary of State had not been given a fair opportunity to deal with the point. What evidence it was necessary for the Secretary of State to provide in the appeal bundle depended on what issues have been put in dispute in the appeal. Having therefore set the tribunal's decision aside, Judge Wright substituted a decision finding on the evidence that the claimant had received the letter notifying her of the appointment in question.

The same approach was applied in *SSWP v SD (JSA)* [2020] UKUT 39 (AAC). There, the tribunal had raised and sought evidence on its own initiative on the issue whether the "prior information duty" (on which see the notes to ss.6A and 6K) had been satisfied at the stage of initial referral to the Work Programme, which the claimant had never challenged. As well as the s.12(8)(a) problem, the tribunal had failed to explain why, even if there was a breach of the duty at that stage, the breach was material. In substituting a decision the judge rejected any unfairness in the referral to the Work Programme and rejected on the evidence the claimant's contention about the appointment.

That view of what evidence must be provided in the appeal bundle as to satisfaction of the preconditions to imposing a sanction must be read in the light of the approach in *SSWP v DC (JSA)* [2017] UKUT 464 (AAC), reported as [2018] AACR 16, and *PO'R v DFC (JSA)* [2018] NI Com 1. There it was said that the Secretary of State should in all cases involving a failure to participate in some scheme or interview where notice of certain details of the scheme etc was required to be given, as well as notice of date, time and place, include in the appeal bundle a copy of the appointment letter, whether the claimant had raised any issue as to the terms of the letter or not. That was on the basis that unrepresented claimants could not be expected to identify technical issues about the validity of notices and it could not be predicted what particular issues might arise in the course of an appeal. If the letter was not included in the initial bundle, the decisions approved the action of tribunals in directing its production as a proper exercise of their inquisitorial jurisdiction. That exercise must rest on a use of the discretion in s.12(8)(a) to consider issues not raised by the appeal. The resolution of the approaches is no doubt that whenever a tribunal exercises that discretion it must do so consciously and explain why it has done so in any statement of reasons, and give the Secretary of State a fair opportunity to produce the document(s). It may be that an adequate explanation of a tribunal's approach is to be found more readily when it is a notice of a specific appointment that is in issue rather than an initial reference to a scheme.

Another important common concept is that of a "good reason" for the conduct or failure to comply with a requirement under either form of the Jobseekers Act 1995 or the Welfare Reform Act 2012. Most of the definitions of sanctionable failures in ss.6J and 6K incorporate the condition that the failure was "for no good reason". Paragraph 14AA of Sch.1 to the new style Jobseekers Act 1995 allows regulations to prescribe circumstances in which a claimant is to be treated as having or as not having a good reason for an act or omission and to prescribe matters that are or are not to be taken into account in determining whether a claimant has a good reason. No regulations have been made under this power. There is no equivalent to reg.72 of the JSA Regulations 1996 (but the problem dealt with there is covered by the allowance of limitations on work search and work availability requirements in new style JSA).

The House of Commons Work and Pensions Committee (report of November 6, 2018 on *Benefit Sanctions* (HC 995 2017–19), para.111) has recommended that regulations be introduced containing a non-exhaustive list of circumstances that could constitute good reason. The DWP (House of Commons Work and Pensions Committee, *Benefit Sanctions: Government Response* (HC 1949 2017–19, February 11, 2019), paras 66–69) rejected that recommendation as undermining flexibility, while noting that a list of good reasons is available in the *DMG* and on GOV.uk (the link provided in the response is to chapter K2 of the *ADM* for universal credit).

Thus, the concept of "good reason" remains an open-ended one, no doubt requiring consideration of all relevant circumstances but also containing a large element of judgment according to the individual facts of particular cases. The amount and quality of information provided to the claimant in the claimant commitment or otherwise about responsibilities under the new style Jobseekers Act 1995 and the consequences of a failure to comply will no doubt be relevant, especially in the light of the approach of the Supreme Court in paras 65 and 66 of *R. (on the application of Reilly and Wilson) v SSWP* [2013] UKSC 68; [2014] 1 A.C. 453 and of the Court of Appeal in *SSWP v Reilly and Hewstone and SSWP v Jeffrey and Bevan* [2016] EWCA Civ 413; [2017] Q.B. 657; [2017] AACR 14 on the prior information requirement or duty (see the notes to ss.6A and 6K). Probably, in addition, as in the previously familiar concept of "just cause", a balancing is required between the interests of the claimant and those of the community of those whose contributions and taxes finance the benefit in question. See the extended discussion under the heading of "Without a good reason" in the note to subs.(3) below.

However, there is a potentially significant difference in wording. In ss.6J and 6K the condition is that the claimant fails "for no good reason", not that the claimant acts or omits to act "without a good reason" (as in ss.19 and 19A of the old style Jobseekers Act 1995). It may eventually be established that these two phrases have the same meaning, but in the ordinary use of language the phrase "for no good reason" carries a suggestion that something has been done or not done capriciously or arbitrarily, without any real thought or application of reason. It could therefore be argued that it is easier for claimants to show that they did not act for no good reason and on that basis that the balancing of interests referred to above could not be applicable. It would be enough that the claimant acted or failed to act rationally in the light of his or her own interests. It can of course be objected that such an argument fails to give the proper weight to the identification of what is a *good* reason and that it would seem contrary to the overall policy of the legislation if it was much easier to escape a new style JSA (or universal credit) sanction than an old style JSA sanction. On the other hand, it can be asked why Parliament chose to use a different phrase for the purposes of new style JSA and universal credit sanctions than "without a good reason" when the latter phrase could have fitted happily into s.6J and 6K. It is to be hoped that the ambiguity will will eventually be finally resolved by decisions of the Upper Tribunal.

One of the points raised when permission to appeal to the Upper Tribunal was given in *S v SSWP (UC)* [2017] UKUT 477 (AAC) was whether "for no good reason" has any different meaning from "without a good reason". In para.54 Judge Mitchell expresses the view that there is no material difference and that both phrases refer to the absence of a good reason. However, the point made in the previous paragraph about a possible difference in meaning may not yet have been conclusively rejected, as it is not clear that in the particular circumstances of *S* it would have mattered which was adopted.

The case actually decides only a relatively short point about the meaning of "for no good reason" in ss.26 and 27 of the WRA 2012 (the equivalent of ss.6J and 6K). The First-tier Tribunal had said that the claimant's professed ignorance of the effect of work (including part-time work) on his universal credit entitlement could not amount to a good reason for failing to undertake all reasonable work search action because ignorance of the law was no defence. On the claimant's appeal to the Upper Tribunal the Secretary of State accepted that, by analogy with the well-established case law on good cause for a delay in claiming, ignorance of the law was capable of constituting a good reason. The judge agreed that the tribunal had erred in law, but concluded that the error was not material because the only proper conclusion on the evidence was that the claimant could reasonably have been expected to raise with his work coach or other DWP official any concerns or confusions over the financial implications on his universal credit award of taking any of the sorts of work he had agreed to search for. Thus, even on the correct approach the claimant did not have a good reason for what the tribunal had concluded was a failure under s.27(2)(a) of the WRA 2012 (the equivalent of s.6K(2)(a)).

It may be that the analogy with good cause (indeed in para.57 the judge said that "good reason" expressed the same concept as "good cause" but in more modern language) is misleading or at least incomplete. That is because when considering good cause for a delay in claiming there is no difficulty in adopting the general meaning approved in *R(SB) 6/83* of some fact that, having regard to all the circumstances (including a claimant's state of health and the information that he had or might have obtained), would probably have caused a reasonable person of the same age and experience to act or fail to act as the claimant had done. It was in that context that the principle that a reasonable ignorance or mistaken belief as to rights could constitute good cause was established. But the question there is what a reasonable person could be expected to do to secure an advantage to them in the form of the benefit claimed late. In the context of universal credit and new style JSA sanctions, the notion of reasonableness carries a distinctly different force. So where the work search requirement under s.6D(1)(a) to take all reasonable action to obtain paid work is concerned, reasonableness must be based on what level of activity the community that funds new style JSA is entitled to expect from a claimant as a condition of receipt of the benefit. Similar, although not necessarily identical, factors are present in relation to the other work-related requirements and the sanctions for voluntarily and for no good reason ceasing paid work or losing pay. Although all personal circumstances are relevant, the notion of a balance between those circumstances and the claimant's proper responsibilities is not captured by the traditional concept of "good cause". The better analogy would seem to be with "just cause" as used in unemployment benefit and in old style JSA before the 2012 amendments. The adoption of the "good cause" approach in relation to claimed ignorance of rights in *S* cannot be taken as excluding such an approach. The full meaning of "for no good reason" remains to be worked out.

Subsections (2) and (3) set out what can be a sanctionable failure for the purposes of s.6J and higher-level sanctions. Subsections (4)–(7) give regulation-making powers. These provisions are substantially identical to s.26 of the Welfare Reform Act 2012 on universal credit with the omission of subs.(3) which is relevant only to the special case of a person being entitled to universal credit while in substantial work.

Subsection (2)

1.704 (a) It is a higher-level sanctionable failure for a claimant to fail for no good reason (on which see the note above) to comply with a work preparation requirement under s.6C to undertake a work placement of a description prescribed in regulations. Regulation 29(1) of the JSA Regulations 2013 prescribes Mandatory Work Activity as a work placement for the purposes of this provision. Regulation 29(2) as substituted with effect from April 29, 2013 provides a description of the nature of that scheme that is probably sufficient for the scheme to be validly prescribed for the purposes of subs.(2)(a) in accordance with the principles adopted by the Supreme Court in *R. (on the application of Reilly and Wilson) v SSWP* [2013] UKSC 68; [2014] 1 A.C. 453. See also the decision of the Court of Appeal in *Smith v SSWP* [2015] EWCA Civ 229. Note that the scheme has ceased to operate after April 2016.

Before undertaking a Mandatory Work Activity scheme could have become a work preparation requirement it must have been specified for the claimant in question by or on behalf of the Secretary of State. As the particular scheme and the potential application of subs.(2)(a) has been defunct for some years, cases on such specification and what amounts to a failure to participate in a scheme are discussed in the notes to s.6K(2)(a) on failure for no good reason to comply with any work-related requirement.

(b) It is a higher-level sanctionable failure for a claimant to fail for no good reason (on which see the note above) to comply with a work search requirement under s.6D to apply for a particular vacancy for paid work. It would seem that for there to have been a requirement to apply for a particular vacancy the taking of that action must have been specified by or on behalf of the Secretary of State under s.6D(1)(b). It appears that scheme providers can be authorised persons under s.6L to act on behalf of the Secretary of State to "mandate" claimants to apply for a particular vacancy or to accept it if offered (see note 3 to ADM para. K3051, on the assumption that that applies to new style JSA as well as to universal credit). See the note to s.6D for discussion of the meaning of "paid work" and of the guidance to Jobcentre Plus staff that claimants should not be required to apply for a vacancy involving a zero hours contract. Thus no sanction should arise under the present provision for failing to apply for such a vacancy, although if such a requirement was in fact imposed, it would be arguable that the nature of the contract, especially if prior to May 26, 2015 (Employment Rights Act 1996, s.27A) it contained an enforceable exclusivity clause, constituted a good reason for failing to apply. Regulation 28(1)(a) of the JSA Regulations 2013 prevents any reduction in benefit being made when the vacancy was because of a strike arising from a trade dispute.

It appears in the nature of the word "vacancy" that it is for employment as an employed earner, or possibly some form of self-employment that is closely analogous to such employment, e.g. through an agency. In *MT v SSWP (JSA)* [2016] UKUT 72 (AAC) doubts were expressed whether failure to register with an employment agency could fall within s.19(2)(c) of the old style Jobseekers Act 1995 on refusing to apply for a vacancy, at least without evidence of some specific vacancy. It is not entirely clear whether a vacancy has actually to exist at the time that the Secretary of State specifies that the claimant is to apply for it or whether it is enough that a vacancy is about to arise at that point (compare the terms of s.19(2)(c)). It may be that it is enough that the requirement is conditional on the post becoming open for applications before the next official meeting, but the "failure" cannot take place until applications are possible. And the claimant must have been given sufficient information about the vacancy in order to have been able to make meaningful representations at the time about whether the requirement should be imposed (see notes to ss.6A and 6K for discussion of the "prior information duty"). Some doubt was expressed in *CJSA/4179/1997* whether the offer of a "trial" as a part-time car washer properly fell within s.19(2)(c). It was suggested that if it did not, the case should have been considered under s.19(2)(d) (neglect to avail oneself of a reasonable opportunity of employment), to which there is no direct equivalent in the new style JSA legislation (see the notes to para.(c) below). But if applying for or accepting the offer of the trial had been specified by the Secretary of State as a work search action under s.6D, failure to comply for no good reason would be a sanctionable failure under s.6K(2)(a), as would a failure to register with an agency, if so specified.

There is no express provision that the vacancy is for work that is suitable for the claimant in question. However, plainly the question of suitability would be relevant to the issue of whether a claimant had no good reason for failing to apply for the vacancy. In the case law on the old style JSA provision there had been a general intertwining of issues of what was then suitability and "good cause" (for the details see previous editions of what was then Vol.II of this series). Now, in *PL v DSD (JSA)* [2015] NI Com 72 (followed and applied in *PO'R v DFC (JSA)* [2018] NI Com 1), the Chief Commissioner for Northern Ireland has approved and applied the obiter suggestion of Judge Ward in *PL v SSWP (JSA)* [2013] UKUT 227 (AAC) (on the pre-October 2012 form of the Great Britain legislation) that, in deciding whether claimants have good cause for failing to avail themselves of a reasonable opportunity of a place on a training scheme or employment programme, a tribunal erred in law, where the circumstances raised the issue, in failing to consider the appropriateness of the particular scheme or programme to the particular claimant in the light of their skills and experience and previous attendance on any placements. Judge Ward's suggestion had been that the test was whether the claimant had reasonably considered that what was provided would not help him. It seems likely that a similar general approach will be taken to the issue of "good reason" under s.6J(2)(b) and the appropriateness of the situation in question, as also suggested in *MT* (above). It may though still need to be sorted out how far the issue turns on the claimant's subjective view, within the bounds of reasonableness, in the light of the information provided at the time, as against a tribunal's view of the appropriateness of the situation in employment. The Chief Commissioner made no comment in *PL* on the treatment of the claimant's refusal to complete and sign forms with information about criminal convictions and health, that the First-tier Tribunal had found were reasonably required by the training provider as part of its application process for the scheme, as a failure by the claimant to avail himself of a reasonable opportunity of a place on the training scheme (see further below).

Failure to apply for a vacancy no doubt encompasses an outright refusal to apply or, say, forgetting about the matter or negligently failing to note a closing date and also behaviour that is "tantamount to inviting a refusal by the employer to engage [the claimant]" (*R(U) 28/55* para.7). In that case the claimant had presented himself for an interview for a job as a parcel porter in what the employer had described as a dirty and unshaven state, as a result of which he was not engaged. The Commissioner accepted that on the employer's evidence the claimant had neglected to avail himself of a reasonable opportunity of suitable employment. There is no reason why that general approach should not also apply in the present context.

It has long been accepted that a refusal or failure to complete an unobjectionable application form can amount to a failure to apply (see *R(U) 32/52* and *CJSA/2692/1999*). As Commissioner Howell noted in para.5 of *CJSA/4665/2001* there will be cases:

> "where the way a claimant completes or spoils a job application will be unsatisfactory and unfit to put in front of any employer so as to prevent it counting as a genuine application at all, so that he or she will have 'failed to apply': it is all a question of fact."

In *CJSA/4665/2001* itself, though, the Employment Service had refused to pass on otherwise properly completed application forms because the claimant had included criticisms of the Service and of government training initiatives. The Commissioner held that in the absence of any evidence that employers had been or would have been put off from considering the claimant by his comments or of any evidence of an intention to spoil his chances it had not been shown that he had failed to apply for the vacancies. A similar approach was taken by Commissioner Rowland in a case in which the claimant disputed the necessity of including a photograph with the application form (*CJSA/2082/2002* and *CJSA/5415/2002*). As the employment officer did not have clear information from the employer contrary to the claimant's contention and had not tested the matter by submitting a form without a photograph, the sanction should not have been applied.

See the notes to para.(a) above for further discussion of good reason. Apart from the suitability and location of the work, personal, domestic and financial circumstances might be relevant. No doubt, as in the past, conscientious or religious objections would need particularly careful consideration. For instance, in *R(U) 2/77* (on neglect to avail) the claimant's sincerely held objection on what he described as moral grounds to joining a trade union were held to make to make an opportunity of employment unsuitable and unreasonable (and see *R(U) 5/71* for a case where a more intellectual conviction against joining a teachers' registration scheme did not have that effect). In contrast to the position for universal credit (see reg.97 of the Universal Credit Regulations) there is nothing to impose a maximum travel time to a location before a work search requirement can be imposed. That matter comes under the general head of suitability in the claimant's particular circumstances.

In *KB v SSWP* (UC) [2019] UKUT 408 (AAC) the claimant failed to apply for a vacancy (as a barista) as she had agreed with her work coach to do. She said that she had later concluded that there was no point in applying, as she was temperamentally unsuited to the employer's requirements (she did not have "a passion for coffee" and was an introvert). The judge suggests that, in the absence of any further consultation with the work coach about the matter, there could not be a good reason for the failure. Although there was a misguided emphasis by the Secretary of State and the First-tier Tribunal on what the claimant agreed to do in her claimant commitment, there was no dispute that the Secretary of State had, through the work coach, "required" her to take the specified action of applying for the vacancy by, after discussion, saving the details to her Universal Jobmatch account.

For a further example on its own facts (and no more than that) of a potential good reason for not applying for a vacancy, see *GR v SSWP* (JSA) [2013] UKUT 645 (AAC), where it was held that a claimant with a genuine fear that prevented him going to the town where a course was to take place had good cause (under reg.7 of the Jobseeker's Allowance (Employment, Skills and Enterprise Scheme) Regulations 2011 (SI 2011/917) for failing to participate in the scheme.

Regulation 11 of the JSA Regulations 2013 deems a claimant not to have complied with a requirement to apply for a particular vacancy for paid work where the claimant fails to participate in an interview offered in connection with the vacancy. Participation must at least entail turning up at the place and time for the interview, although the decision of Judge Knowles in *SA v SSWP (JSA)* [2015] UKUT 454 (AAC) (see the notes to s.6K for full discussion) would indicate that tribunals should consider, in cases where the claimant arrives not very late, whether it is proportionate to the nature of all the circumstances to regard that as a failure to participate in an interview. There were all sorts of mitigating circumstances in *SA*, that may well not be present in other cases. Participation must also extend to making some meaningful contribution to the interview, but the limits will probably not be established until there have been some more sanctions appeals to the Upper Tribunal. Behaviour that leads to the premature termination of the interview may well amount to a failure to participate (see the facts of *DM v SSWP (JSA)* [2015] UKUT 67 (AAC), although there the direction to participate in the course was found to be unreasonable). There may, though, in cases of uncooperative claimants or heavy-handed officials or a combination, be difficult questions about when an interview has ceased to exist, so that subsequent behaviour cannot be relevant to whether there has been a failure to participate (see *PH v SSWP (ESA)* [2016] UKUT 119 (AAC) on failing to submit to a medical examination). 1.705

It was recognised in *CS v SSWP (JSA)* [2019] UKUT 218 (AAC), that it was legitimate for a scheme provider to require an attender to verify their identity before starting a scheme, so that a refusal to do so would usually amount to a failure to participate in the scheme. The same principle could apply to an interview with a prospective employer. In *CS* the claimant had refused to verify various items of information about him on the scheme provider's computer screen, partly because of concerns about the security of information held by scheme providers. It was held that the tribunal had gone wrong in law in concluding that the claimant had refused to verify his identity, and thereby had failed to participate in the course, without making findings about whether he had been given the opportunity to do so by other means, e.g. by producing a passport or driving licence in addition to the appointment letter that he had already produced. It might in other cases be necessary to consider what the appointment letter or other documents say about verifying identity.

See also *SN v SSWP (JSA)* [2018] UKUT 279 (AAC), detailed in the notes to s.6K(2)(a), which indicates that conduct before the start of a course (as in that case, but the same would apply to an interview) can be relevant to a failure to participate where the claimant has physically turned up at the right time and place.

(c) It is a higher-level sanctionable failure for a claimant to fail for no good reason (on which see the note above) to comply with a work availability requirement under s.6E by not taking up an offer of paid work. See the note to s.6D for discussion of the meaning of "paid work" and for the approach to zero hours contracts. Since the requirement under s.6E is in the very general terms of being able and willing immediately to take up paid work, the relevance of not taking up an offer can only be in revealing an absence of such ability or willingness. There is no power in s.6E to require or "mandate" that a claimant take up any particular offer of paid work. It is just possible that that could be specified by or on behalf of the Secretary of State under s.6D(1)(b), but then any sanction for failing to comply could only fall under s.6K(2)(b).

Both any limitations under reg.14 of the JSA Regulations 2013 on the kinds of paid work that a claimant must be able and willing to take up immediately and the provisions of reg.13(2)–(5) on when a claimant is deemed to have complied with the requirement despite not being able to satisfy the "immediately" condition must be taken into account in determining whether a claimant has failed to comply with the requirement. There is case law on what might amount to refusing or failing to accept a situation in employment that is vacant or about to become vacant (under s.19(2)(c) of the old style Jobseekers Act 1995) that may still be relevant, subject to possible differences between that test and not taking up an offer of paid work. Accepting an offer but then telling lies which caused the employer to withdraw it was treated as refusal in a Northern Ireland decision *(R 6/50 (UB))*. In *CSU/7/1995* the claimant accepted the offer of a job of a lampshade maker at a wage of £79 per week, having been informed of the vacancy by the Employment Service. But she changed her mind and did not start the job because the wage was too low to meet her commitments. The tribunal decided that since she did accept the offer of employment, the equivalent of s.19(2)(c) did not operate to disqualify her from receiving unemployment benefit. However, the Commissioner held that although, normally, acceptance of an offer of a situation would be tantamount to accepting the situation it could not have been intended that it would be possible to defeat the operation of the legislation by an acceptance in theory but a repudiation in practice. The claimant had not "accepted the situation" within the meaning of the legislation.

See also *CJSA/4179/1997* in which the claimant was offered a "trial" as a part-time car washer. The tribunal dealt with the case under s.19(2)(c) of the old style Jobseekers Act 1995, but the Commissioner expressed doubt as to whether the "trial" was an offer of a "situation in any employment". The tribunal should have investigated what the trial involved. If that provision did not apply, s.19(2)(d) (neglect to avail oneself of a reasonable opportunity of employment) should then have been considered. There is no equivalent of s.19(2)(d) in s.6J. However, it may be that even a "trial", if remunerated, is an offer of paid work.

Note also reg.28(1)(a) of the JSA Regulations 2013 excluding consideration of vacancies due to strikes arising from trade disputes. On what might be a good reason for not taking up an offer see *GR v SSWP (JSA)* [2013] UKUT 645 (AAC) and *KB v SSWP (UC)* [2019] UKUT 408 (AAC) mentioned at the end of the note to subs.(2)(b).

(d) It is a higher-level sanctionable failure for a claimant to cease paid work or lose pay by reason of misconduct or voluntarily and for no good reason (on which see the note above). Subsection (3)(b) below covers such circumstances occurring before the claim for new style JSA is made, but this provision can apply while a claimant is in receipt of benefit and working at a level not sufficient to amount to "remunerative work" under s.1(2)(e). See the note to s.6D for discussion of the meaning of "paid work". See the note to subs.(3) below for discussion of the meanings of "misconduct" and "voluntarily and for no good reason", as well as of the implications of fixed and severe sanctions for losing pay apparently no matter what the amount of loss, subject to the possible application of exceptions in reg.28(1) of the JSA Regulations 2013. See reg.28(1)(b) (trial periods in work where the claimant attempts hours additional to a limitation under ss.6D(4) or 16E(3)); (d) (voluntarily ceasing paid work or losing pay because of a strike); (e) (voluntarily ceasing paid work or losing pay as a member of the regular or reserve forces); and (f) (volunteering for redundancy or lay-off or short-time). According to the then Minister of State Esther McVey (House of Commons written answers April 2, 2014), guidance to Jobcentre Plus staff is that if a JSA claimant leaves a zero hours contract there should be no sanction for misconduct or voluntarily ceasing work.

Subsection (3)

1.706 It is a higher-level sanctionable failure if before making the claim relevant to the award the claimant for no good reason failed to take up an offer of paid work (para.(a)) or by reason of misconduct or voluntarily and for no good reason ceased paid work or lost pay (para.(b)). A practical limit to how far back before the date of claim such action or inaction can be to lead to a reduction of benefit is set by regs 19(3) and 28(1)(c) of the JSA Regulations 2013. If the gap between the action or inaction and the date of claim is longer than or equal to the period of the reduction that would otherwise be imposed, there is to be no reduction. Thus a lot depends on whether it is a first, second or subsequent "offence" within a year. These two grounds of sanction are the most similar to the familiar unemployment benefit and old style JSA grounds now in s.19(2)(a), (b) and (c) of the old style Jobseekers Act 1995.

Under subs.(3)(a), see the discussion in the note to subs.(2)(c), but note that this sanction applies to any offer of paid work. Therefore, all questions of whether the work is suitable for the claimant and whether or not it was reasonable for the claimant not to take it up will have to be considered under the "no good reason" condition. See the introductory part of the note to this section for the meaning of that phrase as compared with "without a good reason".

Under para.(b), it would appear that misconduct and voluntarily ceasing paid work will have the same general meaning as losing employment through misconduct and leaving employment voluntarily for the purposes of old style JSA and, before it, unemployment benefit. See the extensive discussion below of that established authority. The scope of the sanction has to be slightly wider to take account of the possibility of becoming entitled to new style JSA while still working part-time. Ceasing paid work certainly has a significantly wider meaning than losing employment as an employed earner if it encompasses self-employment in addition, as suggested in the note to s.6D. The notion of ceasing paid work seems in itself wider than that of losing employment and to avoid difficulties over whether suspension from work without dismissal and particular ways of bringing a contract of employment to an end are covered. But remember that under reg.28(1)(f) of the JSA Regulations 2013 a reduction cannot be applied on the ground of voluntarily ceasing paid work where the claimant has volunteered for redundancy or has claimed a redundancy payment after being subject to lay-off or short-time working, although the action remains a sanctionable failure. See also the exceptions for voluntarily ceasing paid work or losing pay because of a strike arising from a trade dispute or as a member of the regular or reserve forces (reg.28(1)(d) and (e)). According to the then Minister of State Esther McVey (House of Commons written answers April 2, 2014), guidance to Jobcentre Plus staff is that if a JSA claimant leaves a zero hours contract there should be no sanction for misconduct or voluntarily ceasing work. However, it is hard to see the legal basis for such guidance. If a claimant did have employment (even though under a zero hours contract) and committed an act of misconduct that led to its loss, that would appear to be a sanctionable failure requiring a reduction of benefit in the absence of any legislative exemption. Similarly, ceasing such employment would appear to bring the legislation into play but the terms of the contract might contribute to a good reason for ceasing the employment.

The other particularly significant widening of the scope of the sanction as compared with those in old style JSA is in the application of this and the similar sanctions under previous subsections to losing pay as well as to ceasing paid work. This is necessary, both in relation to circumstances before the date of claim and later, because it is possible for a claimant to be entitled to new style JSA while still in some paid work.

Any degree of loss of pay triggers the sanction if it was voluntary (subject to good reason) or by reason of misconduct. In the light of the absence of any discretion as to the imposition of a reduction of benefit or as to the amount and period of the reduction, if the statutory conditions are met, it must be arguable that trivial or disproportionate losses of pay are to be ignored (compare *SA v SSWP (JSA)* [2015] UKUT 454 (AAC) on turning up late for a course).

Old style JSA authority on losing employment through misconduct and new style JSA **1.707**

As explained above, the authority built up in unemployment benefit and old style JSA remains highly relevant to the new style JSA sanctions for ceasing paid work or losing pay by reason of misconduct. Possible points of difference will be noted below.

"*Loses employment as an employed earner*". This concept was not confined to dismissal, but could also embrace persons claiming benefit while suspended from work for misconduct *(R(U)10/71)* and the person who accepts the chance to resign rather than be dismissed as a result of his misconduct *(R(U) 3/76*, where the claimant used a company car without permission to give driving lessons and was found at home in the bath when he should have been out selling). In *CU/56/1989*, Commissioner Heggs, dealing with a situation in which the claimant had been allowed to resign rather than be dismissed, noted in para.7:

> "In Decision *R(U) 17/64* it was held that 'loss of employment' is a more comprehensive phrase than 'leaving voluntarily' because loss of employment may result either from voluntarily leaving or from dismissal. In considering whether employment has been lost through misconduct, therefore, it is not always necessary to determine categorically whether the claimant left voluntarily or was dismissed. In the present case the tribunal, in my view, correctly concluded that the claimant lost his employment through misconduct"

The claimant had been allowed to resign rather than be dismissed after he had been caught eating company products (pies) at his workplace in violation of a general prohibition on eating company products in the production area. He had previously violated this rule and been warned about his conduct. He had also received a final written warning that future misconduct would result in his summary dismissal. Unfortunately, the SSAT decision was erroneous in law because it contained no explanation of why the claimant's admitted conduct constituted misconduct.

The notion of ceasing paid work in s.6J cannot be any narrower than that of losing employment, if not wider in encompassing any route to ceasing work, quite apart from the addition of the category of losing pay as a result of misconduct. That seems to open up the possibility of a sanction for someone in part-time work who remains in that employment, but is disciplined and subjected to deductions from earnings or given reduced hours of work by reason of misconduct. There is definitely a wider application through the use of the term "paid work", which would apply to self-employment as well as employment and avoids some of the other problems about the meaning of "employment" in old style JSA (see the notes to s.19(2)(a) of the old style Jobseekers Act 1995 in Vol.V of this series, 2021/22 edition as updated in Cumulative Supplements included in Vol.II of this series and in mid-year Supplements).

"*Through misconduct*". The term in s.6J is "by reason of", but there is nothing to indicate that any difference of substance was intended. The old style JSA principle was that the loss of employment must be brought about because of the claimant's misconduct, not anyone else's. Any contrary reading would be absurd and unjust and contrary to the aim of penalising "voluntary unemployment".

Where there were several reasons for the loss of employment, the claimant's misconduct did not need to be the sole cause of the loss of employment so long as it was a contributory cause, a necessary element in bringing about the loss (*R(U) 1/57*; *R(U) 14/57*; *CU/34/92*). Suggestions that it had to be the main cause in order to ground disqualification read too much into *R(U) 20/59*, where the Commissioner's statement that misconduct (trouble with the police) was there the main cause seems to be no more than a finding of fact in that particular case in which the multiple cause point was not really an issue.

The meaning and scope of misconduct. "Misconduct" has never been statutorily defined. Case law offers such definition as there is. The term has to be interpreted in a common-sense manner and applied with due regard to the circumstances of each case (*R(U) 24/56*; *R(U) 8/57*, para.6). It is narrower than unsatisfactory conduct (*R 124/51 (UB)*). Misconduct is "conduct which is causally but not necessarily directly connected with the employment, and having regard to the relationship of employer and employee and the rights and duties of both, can fairly be described as blameworthy, reprehensible and wrong" (*R(U) 2/77*, para.15). The Commissioner, in para.6, saw nothing wrong with a tribunal's description of it as an indictment of the claimant's character as an employee. A useful test, particularly where the conduct in question occurred away from work, would be: was the claimant's blameworthy, reprehensible and wrong conduct such as would cause a reasonable employer to dispense with their services on the ground that, having regard to this conduct they were not a fit person to hold that appointment (*R(U) 7/57*, para.6).

The act or omission alleged to constitute misconduct need not have been deliberate or intentional, although such might often be the case. Misconduct can consist in carelessness or negligence, but there it is necessary to discriminate between that type and degree of carelessness which may have to be put up with in human affairs, and the more deliberate or serious type of carelessness which justifies withholding benefit because the claimant has lost their employment through their own avoidable fault. In *R(U) 8/57* the claimant, a manager of a branch pharmacy, was dismissed for "negligence in the discharge of responsible duties" when a number of cash shortages were discovered over a period of weeks. Serious carelessness could legitimately be inferred and his disqualification was upheld, notwithstanding his acquittal on a charge of embezzlement arising out of the same situation. A claimant who acts on a genuine misunderstanding cannot properly be said to be guilty of misconduct; the behaviour cannot there be described as "blameworthy, reprehensible and wrong" (*CU/122/92*, para.6, citing *R(U) 14/56*).

Where the conduct grounding the loss of employment might be regarded as whistleblowing (public interest disclosure) the public interest disclosure provisions in the Employment Rights Act 1996 (ss.43A–43L, 47B and 103) should be considered, since the question of whether the disclosure was a protected one is relevant to the question of whether the conduct was blameworthy, reprehensible and wrong. Judge Mesher so held in *AA v SSWP (JSA)* [2012] UKUT 100 (AAC), reported as [2012] AACR 42 (see especially paras 10–15). There it had been appropriate for the claimant School Manager to refer concerns about the head teacher's expenses claim to the appropriate LEA officer and probably to the school governors. However, the misconduct found by the disciplinary panel and grounding the dismissal (the "loss of employment") was his disclosure to several other employees to whom, under the legislation, it was not reasonable to disclose the matter. So that, while the tribunal had erred in law by not considering the public interest disclosure provisions, that error was not material. Note that with effect from June 25, 2013 s.43B(1) of the Employment Rights Act has been amended to add the specific condition that the disclosure is made in the public interest (see *Chesterton Global Ltd v Nurmohamed* [2017] EWCA Civ 979; [2018] I.C.R. 731). In *Kilraine v London Borough of Wandsworth* [2018] EWCA Civ 1436, [2018] I.C.R. 1850 it is clarified that, to qualify, a disclosure must in its context have sufficient factual content to count as a disclosure of "information".

Misconduct which occurred before the claimant took up the employment, the loss of which by reason of the misconduct is under consideration, cannot ground a sanction: see *R(U) 26/56*, where an accountant was dismissed when his employers learned of a conviction for fraud which occurred before he commenced employment with them. There, both the conduct and its consequences (the criminal conviction) occurred before the employment was taken up. *R(U) 1/58* applied the same principle where the conduct occurred before the taking-up of the employment, but the consequences came after its commencement. There a civil engineer and buyer was awaiting trial for certain acts committed before he entered the employment. By agreement with his employer he ceased work pending the result of the trial. On conviction, he simply did not return to the employment. Nor, however, was he pressed to do so. The Commissioner held that "acts or omissions occurring before the commencement of the employment do not constitute 'misconduct'" (at para.4), citing *R(U) 26/56*, so the only matter remaining was the issue of voluntary leaving without just cause. The leaving was not voluntary: "he merely anticipated a decision by his employers to dispense with his services; he was not altogether a free agent when deciding or agreeing not to attend further at his place of business" (at paras 5 and 6). So, to refer to a case of interest notified to the authors, an SSAT was correct in holding that a van driver, dismissed after conviction of a drink-driving offence and disqualification from driving, could not be disqualified from benefit because the conduct constituting the offence had taken place before he took up the employment in question, even though the conviction came after he had done so.

It may perhaps be arguable that the authority discussed in the previous paragraph depended to an extent on an adoption (whether explicit or implicit) of the "causal theory" of unemployment benefit disqualifications, that the primary object was not to penalise the claimant, but more to discourage avoidable claims against the fund from which benefit was paid. As it was put in *R(U) 20/64*, the "basic purpose of unemployment benefit is to provide against the misfortune of unemployment happening against a person's will." Thus there was a responsibility on a claimant to do what was reasonable to avoid becoming a burden on the fund that could only arise once the claimant became employed. The causal theory was in the past bolstered by the limitation of the period of disqualification to a maximum of six weeks, after which time it was said that the primary cause of continued unemployment was the state of the labour market, rather than the claimant's act of misconduct or leaving employment voluntarily or whatever. Now that the sanctions regime gives every appearance of imposing penalties, with more extensive periods of exclusion from benefit possible (even though now reduced from their peak), it might be argued that it is irrelevant to whether such penalties are deserved or not that the misconduct occurred before the claimant started the paid work that later ceased. However, it is submitted that to constitute misconduct an act still has to be "blameworthy" in the context of the employment relationship and that there cannot be blameworthiness in that sense if the person has not yet taken up the employment in question.

Note, however, that instances of dishonesty during employment or in the application or appointment process about matters occurring before the employment starts can properly be regarded as misconduct. Examples might be knowingly answering inaccurately questions on an application form about previous convictions or matters that might embarrass the prospective employer. There might even be some special categories of office or employment where there can be said to be an ongoing duty to disclose information, so that merely continuing to keep quiet about a matter, even though not specifically asked about it, would be misconduct during the office or employment (see *R. (on the application of the Chief Constable of Thames Valley Police) v A Legally Qualified Chair* [2024] EWHC 1454 (Admin) in the very particular police context).

The causal connection with the employment need not be direct (*R(U) 2/77*, para.15), though there the refusal to join a union in a closed shop was found not to be misconduct. The conduct need not have taken place at work or in working hours, though cases where it did will be common. In *R(U) 1/71* the Chief Commissioner upheld the disqualification of a local authority parks' gardener dismissed for an act of gross indecency with another man, away from work and out of working hours (although apparently not in private within the meaning of s.1 of the Sexual Offences Act 1967), but reduced the period of disqualification to one week (an option not available under the current legislation). The Commissioner said in para.10:

> "If a person loses his employment by reason of misconduct which has a sufficient connection with the employment it may not matter that it was committed outside the employment. Common examples are those of the man employed as a motor vehicle driver who loses his licence as a result of his driving outside his employment and is disqualified from driving: there is an obvious link between the misconduct and the work. [See, e.g. *R(U) 7/57* and *R(U) 24/64*.] Similarly a person who commits offences of dishonesty outside his work may be disqualified [. . .], since most employers regard a thief as unsuitable to have about their premises. [See, e.g. *R(U) 10/53*.]" (Case references added by annotator.)

Sexual offences outside the employment were said by the Commissioner in para.11 to present considerable difficulty but could rank as misconduct in special circumstances where they could be said to have something to do with the employment:

> "The commercial traveller's case [*CU/381/51*] is a good instance. The employers may well have thought that there was a real danger that when visiting houses trying to sell ribbons, probably to women who might often be alone in the house, the claimant might attempt some sort of liberties. Further, there are some employments where the employer has a legitimate interest in the conduct of employees even outside the employment. One example may be that of a person who holds a special position, e.g. a school teacher. Another may be that of an employee of a government department or a local authority, who rightly feel that their employees should maintain a high standard of conduct at all times."

In *R(U) 1/71* itself, even though the claimant did not work in public parks, the Commissioner, in a case he thought close to the line, was not prepared to overturn the tribunal's view that the claimant had lost his employment through misconduct, though substantially reducing the period of disqualification. Modern sensibilities might make the assessment of such circumstances more complex. On the one hand there is a widespread feeling that no opprobrium should attach to the acts involved in the offence concerned. On the other, there is perhaps a more widespread feeling than in the past that actions and opinions outside employment are relevant to whether that employment should continue.

Examples of misconduct. Apart from those already noted, instances have been: **1.708**
persistent absenteeism without permission (*R(U) 22/52*, *R(U) 8/61*); unauthorised absence through ill health and/or domestic circumstances when coupled with failure to notify the employer (*R(U) 23/58*; *R(U) 11/59*); repeated unauthorised absence to seek work more suited to the claimant's state of health in circumstances in which the claimant gave the employer no reasons for his absences and he had received previous warnings about his conduct (*R(U) 8/61*); overstaying a holiday without permission (*R(U) 2/74*; *R(U) 11/59*). Theft from fellow workers at a works' social function has been held to be misconduct (*R(U) 10/53*). So has offensive behaviour to fellow employees, consisting of obscene language and an element of what would now be termed sexual harassment (suggestive remarks to and, in their presence, about female colleagues) (*R(U) 12/56*). By analogy, one would today expect many other types of abuse and discrimination to be capable of constituting misconduct. Recklessly or knowingly making false allegations about superiors or colleagues can be misconduct, and where a false criminal charge is so laid it would plainly be misconduct (*R(U) 24/55*, para.13), but it was not enough to prove misconduct to show that the employee's charge of assault by his supervisor had been dismissed in the magistrates' court (*ibid.*). Refusal to obey a reasonable instruction in line with the claimant's contract of employment (e.g. a refusal to work overtime) has been held to be misconduct (*R(U) 38/58*), even where obeying the instruction would conflict with trade union policies (*R(U) 41/53*). However, disobedience of such an order due to a genuine misunderstanding has been held not to constitute misconduct (*R(U) 14/56*), and not every breach of every trivial rule would suffice (*R(U) 24/56*). And, of course, the claimant can legitimately refuse to obey instructions not contractually stipulated for without its constituting misconduct (*R(U) 9/59*; *R 9/60 (UB)*). Where an employee was dismissed for refusing to join a trade union as part of a closed-shop arrangement negotiated after his employment commenced, he did not lose his job through misconduct *(R(U) 2/77)*.

Establishing misconduct, matters of proof and the duties of the statutory authorities; decision-makers, First-tier Tribunals and the Upper Tribunal. The Secretary of State (decision-maker) bears the onus of proof of establishing misconduct, and it must be clearly proved by the best available evidence. As a general rule, of course, hearsay evidence can be accepted by the statutory authorities, but particularly where a claimant is charged with misconduct and disputes the facts that are alleged to constitute it, "it is desirable that the most direct evidence of those facts should be adduced, so that the allegations may be properly tested" (*R(U) 2/60*, para.7).

Officers of the Secretary of State now have extensive powers to require employers to provide information (see e.g. ss.109A and 109B of the SSAA 1992) and First-tier Tribunals have power to summons witnesses and/or require them to produce documents and answer questions (reg.16 of the Tribunal Procedure (First-tier Tribunal) (Social Entitlement Chamber) Rules 2008: Vol.III of this series). Nevertheless, the use of such powers is often considered out of proportion if, say, an employer is reluctant to supply much detail on request and it may be difficult to get to the truth of the matter. In some cases the statutory authorities may be able to have regard to what has happened in other legal or disciplinary proceedings arising out of the same situation now said to show misconduct. Where such proceedings are pending one option in difficult cases where the available evidence about the relevant conduct conflicts would be to postpone a decision on the "sanctionable failure" issue until the outcome of such proceedings as are pending is known. There is no obligation to await their outcome (*R(U) 10/54* and see *AA v SSWP (JSA)* [2011] AACR 42, above), and one must always keep in view the relationship between those proceedings and the precise issues before new style JSA tribunals.

Another option would be to try to resolve the matter by weighing and comparing the evidence available (e.g. does the tribunal believe the direct evidence given by a claimant it has seen and questioned and how does that compare with the indirect and/or hearsay evidence in any written material from the employer or others which is relied on by the decision-maker) and ultimately, where doubts persist, allow the matter to be settled by application of the rules on onus of proof. It would presumably be open to the decision-maker to revise or supersede the tribunal's decision if new material facts came to light in the course of those other proceedings. The other legal proceedings could be criminal proceedings, court proceedings for breach of contract, or complaints of unfair dismissal heard in employment tribunals. Disciplinary proceedings may take place before a much wider variety of bodies. An important issue is what is the relationship to the decision-making task of the JSA decision-makers and tribunals, of decisions given by these other bodies on a matter relevant to the claimant's case?

While in varying degrees decisions given by such bodies certainly can constitute relevant evidence for the statutory authorities, they are not, legally speaking, conclusive of the outcome before the JSA authorities, who are duty bound to make up their own minds as to what constitutes misconduct grounding reduction of benefit, irrespective of the conclusions reached by employers, the courts or other tribunals or disciplinary bodies (*R(U) 10/54*, para.6; *R(U) 2/74*, para.15). The other proceedings do not deal with the exact issue dealt with by the JSA decision-makers and tribunals. For example, a motoring conviction as a private motorist which did not attract a ban from driving would not necessarily constitute misconduct warranting the disqualification of a lorry-driver who had been sacked by his employer as a result. It would depend on the nature of the conduct constituting the offence: the claimant might be able to show that notwithstanding the conviction his conduct was not "blameworthy" (*R(U) 22/64*, para.6). It must be remembered too that the standard of proof of guilt in criminal cases is proof beyond reasonable doubt, a higher standard than that applicable here—proof on the balance of probabilities. So an acquittal on a criminal charge arising out of the conduct now said to constitute misconduct does not necessarily preclude a finding of misconduct. Thus in *R(U) 8/57*, where the manager of the branch pharmacy was acquitted of embezzlement in relation to the cash shortages, he nonetheless lost his employment through misconduct since his inadequate supervision of staff amounted to serious carelessness.

Similarly, there are important differences between proceedings before First-tier Tribunals on the one hand, and unfair dismissal proceedings in the employment tribunal on the other. In unfair dismissal, while the employee's conduct is relevant, the main issue before the employment tribunal concerns the employer's behaviour in consequence. Before the tribunals dealing with JSA, in contrast, the emphasis is more on the employee's conduct, although that of the employer is also relevant. The issues of losing employment through misconduct and of ceasing paid work by reason of misconduct entail consideration of what is fair between claimant and the other contributors to the insurance fund and not simply what is fair as between employer and employee. Commissioners stressed that social security tribunals when dealing with misconduct cases should not express their decisions in such terms as fair or unfair dismissal or proper or improper dismissal. The onus of proof in employment tribunal proceedings may not be the same on issues relevant to the JSA tribunals' task as it is in proceedings before those JSA tribunals. Equally, while the issue before the JSA tribunals is one of substance, the employment tribunal can find a dismissal unfair on procedural grounds. Hence, while the decision of the employment tribunal is conclusive of the matters it had to decide, it does not conclude anything in proceedings before the JSA decision-makers and tribunals authorities, and its findings of fact are not binding on them, even where some of the facts before the employment tribunals are identical with facts relevant to the JSA proceedings:

> "There will, therefore, be cases where a claimant succeeds before an [employment] tribunal on the unfair dismissal question, but the relevant adjudicating authority has decided that disqualification [from benefit] must be imposed by reason of misconduct, and vice versa" (per Commissioner Rice in *CU/90/1988*, para.4).

The findings of fact in the employment tribunal are, however, cogent evidence on which JSA decision-makers and tribunals can act (*CU/17/1993*), since it may well be that with both employer and employee present and examined by the employment tribunal, a judicial authority presided over by a lawyer, reaching its deliberate findings of fact after due inquiry, it is better placed than the JSA decision-makers and tribunals to fully investigate the facts of the matter. But the JSA decision-makers and tribunals are not bound to decide the facts in the same way as the employment tribunal (*R(U) 2/74*, paras 14 and 15 and see generally on the relationship between the two sets of proceedings: *R(U) 4/78* and *R(U) 3/79*). **1.709**

For similar reasons of ability to obtain and to probe evidence, decisions of the criminal courts on matters relevant to the case before the JSA decision-makers and tribunals are entitled to great respect. Thus, where it is clear that a criminal court has decided the identical issue which the claimant needs to reopen before the judicial authorities (First-tier or Upper Tribunal) in order to succeed in their appeal, the decision of that court is likely in practice to have considerable weight before those authorities. The approach in *R(U) 24/55* that in such circumstances the benefit authorities must, save in exceptional cases, treat a conviction by a criminal court as conclusive proof that the act or omission constituting the offence did occur seems now to have been generally rejected. Even that approach would not have prevented a claimant from seeking to explain or give further information on the circumstances of the offence and, in any event allowed for a more direct challenge in exceptional cases. Nor would it prevent argument on the legal inferences to be drawn in the misconduct context from the fact of the criminal act or omission. A more flexible approach was taken in *R(S) 2/80*, where the Commissioner held that the fact of a conviction would have a bearing in benefit appeals, once it had been shown to be relevant to the benefit issue in question, because of the burden of proof in criminal cases, but that the burden would then in the benefit appeal shift to the claimant to show that they were nonetheless entitled to the benefit in question. In *AM v SSWP (DLA)* [2013] UKUT 94 (AAC) Judge Mark considered that *R(S) 2/80* was wrongly decided if it was intended to refer to the legal burden of proof rather than the evidential burden. In that case, as well as in *Newcastle City Council v LW (HB)* [2013] UKUT 123 (AAC) and *KL v SSWP (DLA)* [2015] UKUT 222 (AAC), the same Judge appears to endorse even more flexibility. The criminal conviction is not conclusive as res judicata before the benefit authorities. Then it would depend on whether it was an abuse of process for the claimant to attempt to reargue an issue of fact that was a necessary part of the criminal conviction. But in sanctions appeal cases claimants would not be caught by the principle that it is an abuse of process for a person to use civil proceedings to attack a criminal conviction, because they are not in a position analogous to a plaintiff, but are defending themselves against the imposition of a penalty by the Secretary of State. Then in considering whether the administration of justice would be brought into disrepute it would all depend on the circumstances, including if new or convincing evidence has come to light, whether the claimant pleaded guilty in the criminal proceedings (and if so, why) and whether the particular expertise of the specialist tribunal leads to a re-evaluation of the legal findings and inferences. See para.1.96 of Vol.III of this series and Buchanan-Smith, *Bound or Unrestrained: Social Security Tribunals, Res Judicata and Abuse of Process* (2022) 29 J.S.S.L. 129, where it is suggested, with some justice, that this area is ripe for some authoritative resolution by the Upper Tribunal of the confusing case law.

It has always been for the person relying on it to prove the fact of a conviction, and it is preferably done through official certification (*R(U) 24/64*).

Where the decisions of disciplinary bodies (which may well examine a wide range of witnesses) are concerned, it appears that although never binding on the JSA decision-makers and tribunals, they are entitled to an increasing degree of respect the more their proceedings approximate to proceedings in a court of law. Thus a finding by a chief constable after police disciplinary proceedings was cogent evidence that the claimant had committed particular acts (*R(U) 10/63*), but a decision by a hospital management committee, the precise reasons for which were not disclosed to the Commissioner, was not so regarded (*R(U) 7/61*).

Whether the concern is with decisions of the courts, of employment tribunals or disciplinary proceedings, it is submitted that crucial questions for the JSA decision-makers and tribunals will be: what was the decision; by what sort of body, how, by what process, and on what sort(s) of evidence was the decision made; and how closely does the matter involved in that decision relate to that before the JSA decision-makers and tribunals? But where the other decision is from a prima facie cogent source and is properly proved by one party, a tribunal need not go behind that decision unless the other party comes forward with sufficient evidential or legal argument. See also the discussion in the notes to s.3 of the Tribunals, Courts and Enforcement Act 2007 under the heading Relying on decisions of other bodies in Vol.III of this series.

1.710 *Old style JSA authority on leaving voluntarily without just cause and new style JSA*

As explained above, the authority built up in unemployment benefit and old style JSA remains highly relevant to the new style JSA sanctions for voluntarily and for no good reason ceasing paid work or losing pay. Possible points of difference will be noted below.

Note at the outset the protections given by reg.28 of the JSA Regulations 2013 (made under s.6J(7)(a)) from reductions in benefit when there has been a sanctionable failure under s.6J. Those particularly relevant to voluntarily and for no good reason ceasing paid work or losing pay are as follows. Regulation 28(1)(b) protects current claimants whose work search and availability requirements are limited to a certain number of weekly hours and who take up paid work for extra hours for a trial period. There is to be no reduction of benefit if they voluntarily cease that paid work or lose pay. There is no protection when such ceasing is a pre-claim failure, but there might always be, as also in cases covered by reg.28, good reason for ending a trial period of employment so that there is not in fact a sanctionable failure (see further below). Regulation 28(1)(d) protects anyone voluntarily ceasing paid work or losing pay because of a strike arising from a trade dispute. Regulation 28(1)(e) protects anyone voluntarily ceasing work as a member of the regular or reserve forces. Regulation 28(1)(f) protects anyone who has voluntarily ceased paid work either (i) by reason of redundancy after volunteering or agreeing to be dismissed or (ii) on an agreed date without being dismissed following an agreement on voluntary redundancy or under this head or (iii) when laid off or kept on short time. See the notes to reg.28 for more details.

Section 6J(2)(d) and (3)(b) refers to voluntarily ceasing any paid work, so that there is now no need to consider the possible limitations in the meaning of "employment" in s.19(2)(b) of the old style Jobseekers Act 1995. It would appear that self-employment as well as any form of employment is covered. According to the then Minister of State Esther McVey (House of Commons written answers April 2, 2014), guidance to Jobcentre Plus staff is that if a JSA claimant leaves a zero hours contract there should be no sanction for misconduct or voluntarily ceasing work. However, it is hard to see the legal basis for such guidance. Ceasing such employment would appear to bring the legislation into play, although the terms of the contract might contribute to a good reason for ceasing the work.

In *CJSA/3304/1999*, Commissioner Levenson considered the case of someone who had left employment A for unspecified reasons, then found employment with employer B, from which he was dismissed, and only then claimed JSA. The tribunal allowed the claimant's appeal against preclusion of payment founded on his having voluntarily left employment A without just cause. The Commissioner upheld the tribunal, saying that payment could only be precluded where a claim for benefit had been made and only "in respect of the employment immediately preceding the claim" (at para.16). Insofar as *R(U) 13/64* might be thought to say otherwise, the Commissioner, drawing support from Commissioner Goodman in para.9 of *CU/64/1994*, declined to follow it. The issue does not really arise under s.6J(2)(d), but in relation to s.6J(3)(b) on pre-claim failures it may be arguable that the reference to "at any time before making the claim" reverses the effect of *CJSA/3304/1999*. However, as noted above, regs 19(3) and 28(1)(c) of the JSA Regulations 2013 set a practical limit to how far back a voluntary ceasing of work can be relevant.

The extension of the sanction to voluntarily losing pay, mirroring the universal credit legislation where the extension is necessary because of the possibility of entitlement while doing a substantial amount of paid work, theoretically opens a wide range of potential sanctions. The extension applies equally to potential pre-claim circumstances as to those arising during the course of an award. There will be a great many situations in which a claimant (pre-claim or during an award) loses pay in a way that could be regarded as voluntary (e.g. a person on a zero hours contract opting for fewer hours of work in one week than previously). The power in s.6J(4)(b) to make regulations providing for the disregard of loss of pay below a prescribed level has not been exercised. Nor is there any discretion to shorten the prescribed periods for reduction of benefit (minimum, 91 days) in proportion to the gravity of the "offence" if the conditions for application of a s.6J higher-level sanction are met. In those circumstances, it must be arguable that trivial or disproportionately small losses of pay are to be ignored (compare *SA v SSWP (JSA)* [2015] UKUT 454 (AAC) on turning up late for a course). Even so, a great deal of weight will be put on what is a "good reason" for losing pay and also on common sense in not referring trivial situations to a decision-maker for determination.

In the discussion below references to ceasing paid work should be taken to include losing pay unless there is some specific point of difference that needs to be identified.

Onus of proof. Those who assert that the claimant left employment or ceased paid work and did so voluntarily must prove it. Once done, it was clear that under the "without just cause" test the onus passed to the claimant to prove on the balance of probabilities that they had just cause for so leaving (*R(U) 20/64(T)*). The use of the formula "voluntarily and for no good reason" could be argued to make showing the absence of good reason part of what the Secretary of State has to prove. However, there is no evidence of an intention to make such a radical change. And it would be contrary to the approach in principle demanded by *Kerr v Department for Social Development* [2004] UKHL 23; [2004] 1 W.L.R. 1372; *R 1/04 (SF)*, putting emphasis on who is in a better position to supply information on any particular issue in a co-operative process, rather than formal concepts of onus of proof. The claimant will in the great majority of cases be the person best placed to come forward with an explanation of their reasons for ceasing paid work. It is assumed below that the onus of showing, on the balance of probabilities, that they had a good reason lies on the claimant. See the detailed discussion of good reason below.

1.711 "*Voluntarily leaves*": The commonest case of voluntarily leaving was when the claimant of their own accord handed in their notice or otherwise terminated their contract of employment. Indeed, in many cases there would be no dispute about this aspect of the case; the real issue was that of "just cause" or "good reason". The same will apply to voluntarily ceasing paid work. But voluntarily leaving also embraced other means by which employment was lost. So the actors who threatened to leave unless certain demands were met and were then treated by their employers as having given notice left voluntarily (*R(U) 33/51*). It was still voluntarily leaving where the employment ended because the employer refused to accept the claimant's withdrawal of notice (*R(U) 27/59*). It could also embrace in limited instances cases where the loss of employment took the form of a dismissal brought about by conduct of the claimant which would inevitably lead to termination of the employment (*R(U) 16/52*; *R(U) 2/54*, *R(U) 9/59*, *R(U) 7/74*), but such situations had to be looked at with caution and restraint (*R(U) 2/77*). Thus, in *R(U) 16/52* the claimant's appointment was conditional on her completing a satisfactory medical. She refused to undergo X-ray examination and was given notice. The Commissioner stated as a general rule of unemployment insurance law that if a person deliberately and knowingly acts in a way that makes it necessary for his employer to dismiss him, he may be regarded as having left his employment voluntarily. But another Commissioner later made clear in *R(U) 7/74* that "this would normally require a finding that the employee had acted, or was threatening to act, in a manner involving a deliberate repudiation of his contract of employment". So in that case an employee whose written terms of employment made no reference to a requirement to work overtime, did not leave voluntarily when he was dismissed for refusing to work overtime (cf. *R(U) 9/59*). Similarly, dismissal of an existing employee for refusal to join a trade union when a closed shop agreement was negotiated was not voluntary leaving (*R(U) 2/77*). Nor was dismissal for refusing for good reason to pay a trade union subscription (*R(U) 4/51*). Leaving was not voluntary where the claimant who departed had no effective choice but to quit, e.g. because dismissal appeared inevitable (*R(U) 1/58*: cf. *R(U) 2/76*). That appears to be in line with the employment law principle of "constructive dismissal", though perhaps with a wider scope because of the focus on the voluntariness of the ceasing of work rather than on whether the claimant was dismissed or not. It is submitted that the "general rule of unemployment insurance law" invoked in *R(U) 16/52* should be taken, with the qualifications mentioned above, to apply to the question of whether a claimant has voluntarily ceased paid work even when it was the employer who terminated the contract of employment.

In *R(U) 1/96*, Commissioner Goodman considered the case of a female nursery assistant who gave her employer four weeks' notice, was prepared to work out those weeks, but whose employer, after an unsuccessful attempt to persuade her to stay on, told her to leave after two days. The Commissioner considered and applied *CU/155/50* and *R(U) 2/54* so as to reject the argument that the claimant had not left voluntarily but had been dismissed (and could therefore only be disqualified if misconduct could be proved). He regarded *British Midland Airways v Lewis* [1978] I.C.R. 782 (a decision of the Employment Appeal Tribunal in the context of dismissal under labour legislation) as not laying down "any categorical proposition of law" but as merely being a decision on the facts of that case, and continued:

> "In my view the ruling in *CU/155/50* and *R(U) 2/54* that there is a voluntary leaving applies equally, whether it is a case of an employer not allowing an employee to work out his or her notice or whether it is a case of actual notice to leave given first by the employee, followed by a notice of termination given during the currency of the employee's notice by the employer. In the latter case, once the employee has given in his notice to leave it is a unilateral termination of the employment

contract and cannot be withdrawn without the consent of the employer (*Riordan v War Office* [1959] 1 W.L.R. 1046). It follows that in the present case, when the claimant gave her four weeks notice in on Wednesday December 9, 1992 she had herself terminated the employment and thereby left it voluntarily. Even if what the employer did on Friday December 11, 1992 can be construed as giving in a counter-notice requiring her to leave on that day and not to work out her four weeks notice, that does not, in my view, alter the fact that the effective termination of the employment was a voluntary leaving by the claimant." (At para.12.)

Taking early retirement could constitute voluntarily leaving (*R(U) 26/51*, *R(U) 20/64*, *R(U) 4/70*, *R(U) 1/81*). Even where a schoolteacher retired three years early in response to the generalised encouragement to take early retirement offered to teachers in his position by his local education authority, which further certified that his retirement was in the interests of the efficient discharge of the education authority's functions, it was still voluntarily leaving (*Crewe v Social Security Commissioner* [1982] 2 All E.R. 745 CA, appendix to *R(U) 3/81*). However, in *R(U) 1/83* the Commissioner distinguished *Crewe* and held that a civil servant who acceded to his employer's specific request that he retire early should not be regarded as having left his employment voluntarily. Now, for new style JSA (in contrast to the position for old style JSA), reg.28(1)(f) prevents there being any reduction in benefit whenever a claimant is dismissed for redundancy after volunteering or agreeing to be dismissed or ceases work on an agreed date in pursuance of a voluntary redundancy agreement. That would appear to exempt claimants on the *Crewe* side of the line. The voluntary ceasing of work, if for no good reason, would remain a sanctionable failure, but, importantly for purposes of calculating the period of reduction for future sanctionable failures, not a "sanctionable failure giving rise to a higher-level sanction" (reg.19(4)(a) of the JSA Regulations 2013). For early retirement cases not saved by reg.28, the fine distinction between the *Crewe* type of case and those of the type considered in *R(U) 1/83* may still be important. In *CSU/22/94*, Commissioner Mitchell applied *R(U) 1/83* in favour of a claimant (a principal teacher) who had been pressured by his employers to accept an early retirement package, in a context in which his only alternative was to accept a lower status position (albeit one without loss of income) (being placed on a long-term supply teacher basis). That alternative was one which "a teacher of the claimant's experience and standing could not reasonably be expected to accept" (at para.5). The decision thus stresses the need for tribunals carefully to consider whether the claimant can be said to have left voluntarily before moving on to the "for no good reason" aspect.

"*For no good reason*". There is no definition of "good reason" in the new style Jobseekers Act 1995, just as there was none of "just cause" or "good cause" in previous legislation dealing with disqualification from benefit or preclusion of payment of JSA and none of "good reason" in the old style JSA amendments to put the test in terms of "without a good reason" from October 2012. When those amendments were introduced there was some expression of an intention that "good reason" would be applied in the same way as the predecessor terms. See the beginning of this note on s.6J as a whole for discussion of the possible (just) difference between "without a good reason" and "for no good reason", of whether, despite the views expressed in *S v SSWP UC)* [2017] UKUT 477 (AAC), the proper analogy in the context of voluntarily ceasing work is with "just cause" as explained below, rather than with "good cause", and for the government's rejection of proposals for regulations to set out a non-exhaustive list of circumstances that could constitute good reasons. It is therefore still necessary to examine the case law authority on "just cause" when that was the test for unemployment benefit and old style JSA before considering the "no good reason" test. 1.712

That case law avoided laying down hard and fast rules for all circumstances, but most significantly "just cause" was regarded as requiring a balancing of the interests of the claimant with those of the community of fellow contributors to the National

Insurance Fund. It was not a matter simply of what was in the best interests of the claimant, or of what was just as between employee and employer, or of what was in the public interest generally. To establish that they did not leave without just cause (that phraseology giving the proper emphasis) claimants had to show that in leaving they acted reasonably in circumstances that made it just that the burden of their unemployment should be cast on the National Insurance Fund (*Crewe v Social Security Commissioner* [1982] 2 All E.R. 745, per Slade LJ, at 752; per Donaldson LJ, at 750–751, explaining *R(U) 20/64(T)*, para.8; per Lord Denning MR, at 749). Was what the claimant did right and reasonable in the context of the risk of unemployment? Was the voluntary leaving such as to create an unreasonable risk of unemployment, bearing in mind that there may be circumstances that leave a person no reasonable alternative but to leave employment (per Donaldson LJ, at 750)? Establishing just cause may well be a heavier burden than showing "good cause" (per Slade LJ, at 751). In *R(U) 4/87*, Commissioner Monroe stated that "the analogy with insurance seems now the paramount criterion of just cause" (para.8). His examination of decisions on the matter led him "to think that in general it is only where circumstances are such that a person has virtually no alternative to leaving voluntarily that he will be found to have had just cause for doing so, rather as a person who throws his baggage overboard to make room in the lifeboat can claim on his baggage insurance" (para.9).

There is therefore a faint suggestion in the earlier authority that there may be some difference in the ordinary use of language between "good cause" and "just cause". It may also be arguable that the formula "with no good reason" shifts the focus away from the notion of a balance between the interests of the claimant and those of the community of contributors to the fund from which benefit is paid towards more emphasis on the interests of the claimant. That would make it easier for a claimant to avoid the imposition of a sanction. In *SA v SSWP (JSA)* [2015] UKUT 454 (AAC), a decision on s.19A(2)(c) of the old style Jobseekers Act 1995 and failing to carry out a jobseeker's direction, Judge Knowles accepted the Secretary of State's submission that in determining whether a good reason had been shown for the failure all the circumstances should be considered and that the question was whether those circumstances would have caused a reasonable person (with the characteristics of the claimant in question) to act as the claimant did. Expressing the approach in such terms tends to point away from the notion of a balance.

In *S v SSWP (UC)* [2017] UKUT 477 (AAC), however, a similar approach was taken. The First-tier Tribunal had said that the claimant's professed ignorance of the effect of work (including part-time work) on his universal credit entitlement could not amount to a good reason for failing to undertake all reasonable work search action (thus leading to a sanction under s.27(2)(a) of the WRA 2012, the equivalent of s.6K(2)(a)) because ignorance of the law was no defence. On the claimant's appeal to the Upper Tribunal the Secretary of State accepted that, by analogy with the well-established case law on good cause for a delay in claiming, ignorance of the law was capable of constituting a good reason. There was reference to the general meaning approved in *R(SB) 6/83* of some fact that, having regard to all the circumstances (including a claimant's state of health and the information that he had or might have obtained), would probably have caused a reasonable person of the same age and experience to act or fail to act as the claimant had done. Judge Mitchell agreed that the tribunal had erred in law, but concluded that the error was not material because the only proper conclusion on the evidence was that the claimant could reasonably have been expected to raise with his work coach or other DWP official any concerns or confusions over the financial implications on his universal credit award of taking any of the sorts of work he had agreed to search for. Thus, even on the correct approach the claimant did not have a good reason for what the tribunal had concluded was a failure under s.27(2)(a). The statements discussed below about the analogy of "good reason" with "good cause" were thus not necessary to the decision.

It is submitted that the analogy with good cause in *S* and in *SA* (indeed in para.57 of *S* the judge said that "good reason" expressed the same concept as "good cause" but in more modern language) is misleading in the present context or at least incomplete. That is because when considering good cause for a delay in claiming there is no difficulty in adopting the general meaning approved in *R(SB) 6/83*. It was in that context that the principle that a reasonable ignorance or mistaken belief as to rights could constitute good cause was established. But the question there is what a reasonable person could be expected to do to secure an advantage to them in the form of the benefit claimed late. In the context of universal credit and JSA sanctions, the notion of reasonableness carries a distinctly different force. So when considering what circumstances could justify a voluntary ceasing of work, it is submitted that the notion of a good reason must still be based on whether it is reasonable to place the burden of the claimant's unemployment on the community that funds new style JSA. Although many personal circumstances will be relevant, the notion of a balance between those circumstances and the claimant's proper responsibilities is not captured by the traditional concept of "good cause" in the context of delay in claiming. The better analogy would seem to be with "just cause" as used in unemployment benefit and in old style JSA before the 2012 amendments (or with "good cause" as used in some of those provisions). The adoption of the "good cause" approach in relation to claimed ignorance of rights in S cannot be taken as excluding such an approach to s.6J(2) (d) and (3)(b). The full meaning of "for no good reason" in this context remains to be worked out.

Accordingly, reference to authority based on the notion of a balance and reasonableness in the sense adopted above remains valuable.

Whether the claimant succeeds in discharging the burden of showing a good reason depends essentially on all the circumstances of the case, including the reasons for leaving and such matters as whether they had another job to go to, whether before they left they had made reasonable inquiries about other work or its prospects, or whether there were in their case good prospects of finding other work. Such elements should not be considered in water-tight compartments (*R(U) 20/64(T)*), para.9). The previous claims record is not directly relevant (*R(U) 20/64(T)*) para.18). In *R(U) 4/87* Commissioner Monroe, following para.10 of *R(U) 3/81* (approved in *Crewe*), ruled as remote from and irrelevant to the just cause issue long-term considerations prayed in aid by the claimant who had "urged that his leaving had in the long run actually benefited the national insurance fund, in that he had made available a vacancy for someone who would otherwise have continued unemployed, and that he was now earning more so that he was paying higher contributions" (at para.10). Such factors had nothing to do with the issue of being forced to leave.

In *CU/048/90*, Commissioner Sanders considered the appeal of a claimant who had, as a result of his employer's attitude, become dissatisfied with his employment and had sought alternative employment by circulating his curriculum vitae to 30 companies. During interviews with Barclays Bank he was given the impression that his application for a particular post would be successful, and he resigned from his employment. In the event he was not offered the post. Commissioner Sanders considered the correct approach to "just cause" to be that set out in *R(U) 4/87* (para.9). He thought that the "circumstances have to be very demanding before a claimant can establish just cause for leaving" (para.3). It seemed to the Commissioner "that in the circumstances of the case the claimant had reason to leave because he thought he was not progressing in his career" but took the view "that the circumstances were not so pressing as to justify his leaving, from an unemployment benefit point of view, before he had secured the job with Barclays Bank even though he had been led to believe that his application for that job would be successful". He agreed with the SSAT that the claimant did not have just cause for leaving voluntarily and had to be disqualified.

In some cases, probably rare in practice, an actual promise of immediate suitable new employment (which then falls through after the employment was left or the start of which is delayed) might afford just cause in the absence of other justificatory circumstances (*R(U) 20/64(T)*, para.17; *Crewe*, per Donaldson LJ, para.750). However, there was no rule of law saying that just cause cannot be established where the claimant leaves without another job to go to. Indeed, in *R(U) 20/64(T)* a Tribunal of Commissioners suggested that there could be circumstances in the claimant's personal or domestic life which become so pressing that they justify leaving employment "without regard to the question of other employment" (para.12) and they cited as illustrations *R(U) 14/52*, *R(U) 19/52* and *R(U) 31/59*, all noted below. Equally, it was clearly established that some feature of the claimant's existing employment may justify leaving it immediately without any regard to the question of other employment (para.11) and here the Commissioners quoted as instances *CU 248/49*, *R(U) 15/53*, *R(U) 38/53* and *R(U) 18/57*, also considered below. But there had to be some urgency in the matter and, as regards the latter class of case, the circumstances had to be so pressing that it would not be reasonable to expect the claimant to take such steps before leaving as were open to them to resolve the grievance connected with work through the proper channels of existing grievance procedures. *CU/106/1987* made it clear that a tribunal could not merely rely on the Secretary of State's (decision-maker's) suggestion that there would be such a grievance procedure in the circumstances of the claimant's employment. It was wrong in law to take account of a suggested grievance procedure to reject the claimant's appeal without having proper findings of fact as to its existence. One would equally have thought that a tribunal should also consider whether any procedure found to exist could cover the claimant's complaint and whether it was reasonable in the circumstances to expect the claimant to have resort to it.

1.713 A simple desire to change jobs was not usually enough to warrant putting the burden of one's unemployment on the Fund. Nor did moving house without more constitute just cause; it depended on the reasons for the move (*R(U) 20/64(T)*, para.15). Rather than approaching the just cause issue from the angle of considering it necessary for the claimant to be assured of suitable alternative employment, unless there were circumstances justifying them in leaving without it (the approach in *R(U) 14/52*), the Commissioners in *R(U) 20/64(T)* preferred a different perspective. They preferred to look: (1) at whether the reasons for leaving themselves amounted to just cause (i.e. leaving aside the matter of alternative employment or its prospects); and (2) where the reasons did not of themselves establish just cause to then consider whether the "promises or prospects of other employment may be effective as an additional factor which may help the claimant establish just cause. For example, where a man almost establishes just cause [in relation to, e.g. pressing personal or domestic circumstances] the fact that he has a promise or prospects of other employment may serve to tip the scale in his favour . . . In considering these matters of course the strength of his chances of employment and the gap, if any, likely to occur between the two employments must be taken into account" (para.17). The Commissioners stated:

> "that it is impossible to lay down any period of time representing a gap between employments, or any degree of probability of fresh employment which will give an automatic answer to the question whether the claimant has shown just cause for leaving. We think that there is a distinction between on the one hand, having suitable employment to go to, as where there is an actual promise of employment, and having only prospects of employment on the other. It may be reasonable to expect a claimant who has only prospects to take some steps before leaving, such as communicating with the employment exchange to see whether his prospects cannot be made more certain."

A number of cases concerning, on the one hand, grievances about existing employment and, on the other, personal or domestic circumstances, can usefully be quoted as instances in which just cause was established, and it may be useful to note in contrast a number of examples in each category where it was not, subject to the importance of looking to the precise circumstances of each and every case and not regarding factual decisions as legal precedents.

(i) Grievances about work. In *R(U) 15/53* a piece-worker who lost his job when he refused to accept a substantial reduction in earnings thrust on him by his employer had just cause for leaving. In *R(U) 38/53* the claimant left after subjection to pressure to join a trade union and was able to establish just cause; it would have been

intolerable if he had to remain. In *R(U) 18/57* an apprentice ordered to do work clearly outside the scope of his apprenticeship had only the options of doing as he was told or leaving immediately. In choosing the latter he had just cause. It may be now that working under a zero-hours contract, especially when it was still legally possible for an exclusivity clause to be enforceable, could contribute towards a good reason for ceasing the employment (and see the guidance mentioned above under "such employment"). But mere failure to get on with colleagues (*R(U) 17/54*) or strained relations with one's employer (*R(U) 8/74*) has been held not enough. Not feeling oneself capable of the work, where one's employer was satisfied, was unlikely to be enough without clear medical evidence of that fact (*R(U) 13/52*), but leaving employment during a probationary period because the claimant considered himself unsuited to the work and that it was unfair to his employer to continue training him was more generously treated in *R(U) 3/73*.

Indeed, in *CU/43/87* Commissioner Davenport said that "a person who is experimenting in trying a new line of work should not lightly be penalised if that experiment fails". People should be encouraged to try new types of employment where work in their usual field is not available:

> "It must be recognised that in such circumstances a person may find that he cannot stay in his employment and it may be that he is reasonable in leaving that employment, whereas a person who had more experience in the field in question would not be held to have acted reasonably if he gave up the employment. Not everyone finds that new and unfamiliar employment is such that she or he can reasonably stay in it". (At para.7.)

CU/90/91 further illustrates that claimants who left employment as unsuitable after a trial period could have just cause for doing so and be protected from preclusion of payment without having to rely on the time-limited "trial period" concept found in the old style JSA legislation. Commissioner Hallett stated:

> "It is clear from the evidence, which I accept, that the claimant took the job with Fords (which would have been permanent) on trial, conditionally on his being able to obtain accommodation in the area. It is well-settled in social security unemployment law that claimants should be encouraged to take jobs on trial and that if, after trial, the job proves unsuitable, they do have just cause for leaving. It is in the interests of the national insurance fund, and of public policy, to encourage persons to obtain employment and not penalise them if, after fair trial, the job proves unsuitable". (At para.10.)

The claimant had just cause for leaving. There is no such well-settled principle applying to leaving a job taken, not on trial, but as a "stop-gap" pending something better turning up (*R(U) 40/53*; *CJSA/63/2007*, para.15).

(ii) Personal or domestic circumstances. In *R(U) 14/52* the claimant had just cause for leaving his job in order to be with his elderly and sick wife who lived alone. It was not possible for her to move to live with him so as to be near enough to his work. He also thought his chances of employment would be good in his wife's area, but there was little evidence in the case of searching inquiries about those prospects. In *R(U) 19/52* the claimant, who left her job to move with her service-man husband to a new posting, likely to be more than short-term, had just cause. Had the posting been short-term, however, she would have had to make inquiries about job prospects in the new area before leaving. See further *R(U) 4/87* and *CU/110/1987*. In *CU/110/1987* the claimant's service-man husband received telephone notice of posting to Germany on February 14, 1986. He went there on March 1, 1986. On February 14, the claimant gave the one week's notice required under her contract of employment and ceased work on February 21, claiming benefit the next day. She had to be available to vacate the married quarters in Aldershot from March 1. However, she did not join her husband in Germany until March 25, since repairs were needed to the married quarters there. Commissioner Monroe held that in those circumstances she had just cause for leaving when she did, rather than later. That, rather than whether

she should have left at all, was the real issue in the case, since in the Commissioner's view it could hardly be said that she did not have just cause to leave (whenever she could) to join her husband in Germany. She was not to be disqualified from benefit. Actual entitlement to benefit, however, would turn on the unresolved matter of her availability for work. On the issue of availability in that context, see *R(U) 2/90(T)*. In *R(U) 31/59* the reason for leaving was the move to a new home, too far from the job, because the existing home (two small attic rooms) was wholly unsuitable for the claimant's family. By contrast, in *R(U) 6/53* the 21-year-old woman who left her job to move with her rather strict parents to a new area did not have just cause; it was reasonable to expect her to live alone, at least until she could find work in the new area. In *CJSA/2507/2005*, Commissioner Williams applied Commissioner Monroe's statement at para.9 of *R(U) 4/87*, quoted in para.1.712 above, to dismiss the 28-year-old claimant's appeal against a tribunal-imposed three week disqualification for voluntary leaving (the decision-maker had imposed eight weeks). He had left to join his fiancée and get married, but had no job to go to. The three-week disqualification represented the period up to the marriage. The Commissioner also noted the need to treat with some caution decisions on this area which are 50 years' old, reflecting a very different job market and attitudes to married women, and given when appeal to the Commissioners covered fact and law.

Leaving for a financial advantage, e.g. to draw a marriage gratuity only payable on resignation (*R(U) 14/55*), or to take early retirement, even where this was encouraged by the employer and might be said to be in the public interest in terms of opening the way for younger teachers and promoting the efficiency of the education service, has been held not to rank as just cause (*Crewe v Social Security Commissioner* [1982] 2 All E.R. 745; *R(U) 26/51*; *R(U) 23/59*; *R(U) 20/64(T)*; *R(U) 4/70*; *R(U) 1/81*). However, if "good reason" has different nuances of meaning from "just cause", as discussed above, that might justify more emphasis on what was reasonable in the claimant's own interests. Further, it may be that a different approach is justified where a claimant leaves a job to avoid hardship rather than to pursue extra money (as suggested in *CJSA/1737/2014*, where one of the claimant's arguments was that the cost of travel to and from work was prohibitive).

Note the significant assistance, discussed above, that may be provided by reg.28(1)(f) of the JSA Regulations 2013 in cases of voluntary redundancy, although that provision only prevents a reduction in benefit rather than making the voluntary ceasing of paid work not a sanctionable failure.

Subsection (4)

1.714 Regulations may deem ceasing work or losing pay not to be by reason of misconduct or voluntarily in certain circumstances and may provide that loss of pay below a prescribed level is to be disregarded. No such regulations have been made. Regulation 28 of the JSA Regulations 2013 is made under the powers in subs.(7)(a) and only affects whether a reduction in benefit is to be imposed, not whether there is or is not a sanctionable failure.

Subsections (5) and (6)

1.715 See regs 18 and 19 and 22–27 of the JSA Regulations 2013 for the amount and period of the reduction in benefit under a higher-level sanction. The three-year-limit is imposed in subs.(5)(b) and cannot be extended in regulations.

Subsection (7)

1.716 Under para.(a), see reg.28 of the JSA Regulations 2013. Under para.(b), see reg.23. Under para.(c), see regs 24 and 25.

[1 Other sanctions

1.717 **6K.**—(1) The amount of an award of a jobseeker's allowance is to be reduced in accordance with this section in the event of a failure by a claimant which is sanctionable under this section.

(2) It is a failure sanctionable under this section if a claimant—

(a) fails for no good reason to comply with a work-related requirement;

(b) fails for no good reason to comply with a requirement under section 6G.

(3) But a failure by a claimant is not sanctionable under this section if it is also a failure sanctionable under section 6J.

(4) Regulations must specify—

(a) the amount of a reduction under this section;

(b) the period for which such a reduction has effect.

(5) Regulations under subsection (4)(b) may provide that a reduction under this section in relation to any failure is to have effect for—

(a) a period continuing until the claimant meets a compliance condition specified by the Secretary of State,

(b) a fixed period not exceeding 26 weeks which is—

(i) specified in the regulations, or

(ii) determined in any case by the Secretary of State, or

(c) a combination of both.

(6) In subsection (5)(a) "compliance condition" means—

(a) a condition that the failure ceases, or

(b) a condition relating to future compliance with a work-related requirement or a requirement under section 6G.

(7) A compliance condition specified under subsection (5)(a) may be—

(a) revoked or varied by the Secretary of State;

(b) notified to the claimant in such manner as the Secretary of State may determine.

(8) A period fixed under subsection (5)(b) may in particular depend on either or both the following—

(a) the number of failures by the claimant sanctionable under this section;

(b) the period between such failures.

(9) Regulations may provide—

(a) for cases in which no reduction is to be made under this section;

(b) for a reduction under this section made in relation to an award that is terminated to be applied to any new award made within a prescribed period of the termination;

(c) for the termination or suspension of a reduction under this section.]

Amendment

1. Welfare Reform Act 2012 s.49(3) (trigger date on or after April 29, 2013).

Definitions

"claimant"—see s.35(1).
"regulations"—*ibid.*
"work-related requirement"—see ss.35(1) and 6(2).

General Note

See the introductory part of the annotations to s.6J for the general nature of the new style JSA sanctions regime under ss.6J and 6K and for discussion of the meaning of "for no good reason". Section 6K(1) and (2) requires there to be a reduction, of the amount and period set out in regulations, wherever the claimant has failed for no good reason to comply with any work-related requirement or a connected requirement under s.6G. There is no general discretion whether or not to apply the prescribed deduction, but that is subject to the rule in subs.(3) that if **1.718** a failure is sanctionable under s.6J (and therefore potentially subject to the higher-level regime) it is not to be sanctionable under s.6K. Note also the important effect of reg.5 of the JSA Regulations 2013 (discussed in the note to s.6J) where a claimant is also entitled to universal credit.

While the duty and power under subs.(4) for regulations to provide for the amount and period of the reduction to be imposed is in fact more open-ended than that in s.6J(5), because it does not have the three-year limit, subss.(5)–(7) introduce the specific power (that did not of course have to be used) for regulations to provide for the period of the reduction for a particular sanctionable failure to continue until the claimant meets a "compliance condition" (subs.(6)) or for a fixed period not exceeding 26 weeks specified in regulations or determined by the Secretary of State or a combination of both. The 26-week limit in subs.(5)(b) appears not to have any decisive effect because a longer period could always be prescribed under subs.(4)(b), unless "may" in subs.(5) is to be construed as meaning "may only". In practice, the powers have been used in the JSA Regulations 2013 to set up a structure of medium-level (regs 17 and 20) and low-level (regs 17 and 21) sanctions. See the annotations to those regulations for the details.

The medium-level sanction, by virtue of the definition in reg.17, applies only to failures to comply with a work search requirement under s.6D(1)(a) to take all reasonable action to obtain paid work etc or to comply with a work availability requirement under s.6E(1). A failure to comply with a work search requirement under s.6D(1)(b) to apply for a particular vacancy attracts a higher-level sanction under s.6J(2)(b). The reduction period under reg.20 is 28 days for a first "offence" and 91 days for a second "offence" or subsequent offence within a year of the previous failure (which also includes medium-level universal credit sanctions).

The low-level sanction, by virtue of the definition in reg.17, applies where the claimant fails to comply with a work-focused interview requirement under s.6B(1), a work preparation requirement under s.6C(1), a work search requirement under s.6D(1)(b) to take any specified action specified by the Secretary of State or a connected requirement in s.6G. The reduction period under reg.20 lasts until the claimant complies with the requirement in question or the award of JSA terminates, plus seven days for a first "offence", 14 days for a second "offence" within a year of the previous failure and 28 days for a third or subsequent "offence" within a year (which also includes a low-level universal credit or employment and support allowance sanction).

For the purposes of reg.21, "compliance condition" is defined in subs.(6) to mean either a condition that the failure to comply ceases or a condition relating to future compliance. A compliance condition may be revoked or varied by the Secretary of State, apparently at will, and may be (not must be) notified to the claimant in such manner as the Secretary of State may determine (subs.(7)). But under reg.21 a compliance condition has to be "specified" by the Secretary of State. On the one hand, it is difficult to envisage it being decided that the Secretary of State can specify such a condition to himself, rather than to the claimant. On the other hand, it is difficult to envisage it being decided that a claimant who has in fact complied with a requirement has not met a compliance condition merely because the Secretary of State failed to give proper notice of the condition. It appears that during the 2020 COVID-19 outbreak, if the same approach is taken as for universal credit, any contact by the claimant with the DWP is treated as compliance with any condition, thus bringing that part of the reduction period to an end.

One of the most common grounds of sanction under s.6K(2)(a), given the demise of the Mandatory Work Activity Scheme covered by s.6J(2)(a), is the failure to comply with a work-related requirement to participate in an interview under s.6B (work-focused interview requirement) or s.6D and reg.11 of the JSA Regulations 2013 (work search requirement: applying for particular vacancies and interviews). There is a separate power in s.6G to require a claimant to participate in an interview for any purpose relating to the imposition of a work-related requirement on a claimant, verification of compliance with work-related requirements or assisting a claimant to comply. Failure to comply attracts a sanction under s.6K(2)(b).

Many work preparation requirements (s.6C) and other work-related requirements involve attendance and/or participation in various courses, assessments, training programmes etc, often provided by third parties contracted to the DWP. All of those areas raise similar questions about whether the requirement and the specification of what the claimant is to do has been properly notified, about what is involved in "participation" and about what could amount to a good reason for failure to comply. Similar issues were raised in relation to requirements to participate in various schemes under s.17A of the old style Jobseekers Act 1995.

For a sanction to be applied, the relevant work requirement must have been imposed in accordance with the legislation and been made enforceable where necessary by specification of a particular appointment and an obligation to attend and participate. See the notes to s.6A for the general principles, in particular the general guidance and application to the specific facts in *JB v SSWP (UC)* [2018] UKUT 360 (AAC), and to s.6B for other points on interviews. This will often involve a two-stage process, although in the case of s.6B or 6G (connected requirements) interviews, it would appear, as pointed out by Judge Jacobs in *SP v SSWP (UC)* [2018] UKUT 227 (AAC), that even if a general obligation to attend interviews is mentioned in the claimant commitment the requirement does not become enforceable until a particular interview has been specified. Thus in *JB*, the evidence that the DWP produced to the First-tier Tribunal did not show notification of the specific interview in which it was said that the claimant had failed to participate. But Judge Poole QC stressed in para.29 the flexibility given by the legislation in permitting multiple methods of communication with claimants, such that it would be inappropriate for the Upper Tribunal to set out particular requirements for the wording of notifications or for methods used. She stated in para.29.3:

> "What is important is the substance. In this case the question was whether it could fairly be said, on the totality of the evidence, that the claimant had been notified of an obligation to attend a work-focused interview and the consequences of non-compliance."

In *SP* Judge Jacobs also suggested that it is inherent in the nature of notification that it cannot be effective unless and until it is received. However, he did not have to rely on that proposition in dealing with a case where the claimant's evidence was that an appointment letter was not delivered until after the time of the appointment. That was because, even if notification were regarded as having been given, there was necessarily a good reason for not participating in an interview when the claimant was not aware of the appointment.

Sometimes the question of satisfaction of those legislative requirements becomes entangled with the question of whether the public law duty of fairness, often described as the "prior information duty" in the current context, has been fulfilled. Thus, in *KG v SSWP (UC)* [2020] UKUT 360 (AAC) not only did the documents in evidence fail to show whether the interview in question was required under the equivalent of s.6B or the equivalent of s.6G, but they failed to show that the claimant had been informed what issues were to be investigated in the interview and of the consequences of non-compliance. And in *JB* the importance of notifying the claimant of the consequences of non-compliance seemed to stem from the duty of fairness rather than from the legislative obligation to go beyond mere notification of date, time and place of appointment to communicate an requirement to attend and participate. The prior information duty is considered separately below.

The necessity for a sufficiently specific requirement to have been imposed does not necessarily mean that the DWP in the case of an appeal must, either in the response to the appeal in the bundle of documents or at a hearing, produce a full paper-trail. It all depends on what issues have been raised by the appeal or have been legitimately raised by the tribunal.

In *SSWP v CN (JSA)* [2020] UKUT 26 (AAC), the claimant's sole ground of appeal against a sanction for failing to participate in the Work Programme by not attending an appointment was that she had never failed to keep an appointment (i.e. implicitly that she could not have received the notice of the appointment and/or had good cause under the regulations then in force). The tribunal allowed her appeal on the ground that the bundle did not contain a copy of the notice referring her to the Work Programme (i.e. the WP05) so that it was not satisfied that she had properly been notified of the requirement to participate. The tribunal appeared to think that that issue was one raised by the appeal within s.12(8)(a) of the SSA 1998, which it manifestly was not as the Secretary of State's submission in the bundle, unchallenged by the claimant, was that there was no dispute that the claimant was referred to the Work Programme. Nor did it give any explanation, if it had exercised its discretion under s.12(8)(a) to consider the issue, of why it did so and how it was clearly apparent from the evidence so as to be capable of being dealt with under that discretion. Even if those hurdles had been overcome, the Secretary of State had not been given a fair opportunity to deal with the point. It is not necessary for the Secretary of State in all sanctions cases to provide evidence in the appeal bundle that all preconditions for the imposition of the sanction are satisfied. It depends what issues have been put in dispute in the appeal. Having therefore set the tribunal's decision aside, Judge Wright substituted a decision finding on the evidence that the claimant had received the letter notifying her of the appointment in question.

The judge's statement that the Secretary of State need not in all sanctions cases provide evidence in the appeal bundle to support the satisfaction of all the preconditions to imposing a sanction must, though, be read in the light of the approach in *SSWP v DC (JSA)* [2017] UKUT 464 (AAC), reported as [2018] AACR 16, and *PO'R v DFC (JSA)* [2018] NI Com 1.There it was said that the Secretary of State should in all cases involving a failure to participate in some scheme or interview where notice of certain details of the scheme etc. was required to be given, as well as notice of date, time and place, include in the appeal bundle a copy of the appointment letter, whether the claimant had raised any issue as to the terms of the letter or not. That was on the basis that unrepresented claimants could not be expected to identify technical issues about the validity of notices and it could not be predicted what particular issues might arise in the course of an appeal. If the letter was not included in the initial bundle, the decisions approved the action of tribunals in directing its production as a proper exercise of their inquisitorial jurisdiction. That exercise must rest on a use of the discretion in s.12(8)(a) to consider issues not raised by the appeal. The resolution of the approaches is no doubt that whenever a tribunal exercises that discretion it must do so consciously and explain why it has done so in any statement of reasons, and give the Secretary of State a fair opportunity to produce the document(s). It may be that an adequate explanation is to be found more readily when it is a notice of a specific appointment that is in issue rather than an initial reference to a scheme.

DC concerned two sanctions imposed in August 2013 for failures, without good cause, to participate in a Scheme as required under reg.4 of the Jobseekers Allowance (Employment, Skills and Enterprise Schemes) Regulations 2011 (SI 2011/917) in June and August 2012. By August 2013 the Regulations had been revoked, but continued to apply in relation to failures to participate that occurred while they were in force. For the same reason, the sanctions provisions in reg.8 (revoked with effect from October 22, 2012) applied in *DC*, rather than s.19A of the old style Jobseekers Act 1995.

1.719 The first appeal (in relation to August 2012) raised the issue of the effect of the Secretary of State's being unable to provide to the First-tier Tribunal, as directed, a copy of the appointment letter known as a Mandatory Activity Notification (MAN) sent or handed to the claimant in respect of the appointment that he failed to attend. The tribunal had allowed the claimant's appeal on the basis that the Secretary of State had failed to show that the claimant had been properly notified in accordance with the conditions in reg.4(2). In concluding that there was no error of law in that, Judge Rowland held that this was not a matter of the drawing of adverse inferences, but of the Secretary of State simply having failed to come forward with evidence on a matter on which the burden of proof was on him. Although there was evidence before the tribunal that the claimant had been given an appointment letter, that evidence did not go beyond showing the date and time of the appointment. It did not show where the claimant was to attend or what other information was provided and how it was expressed. The judge rejected the Secretary of State's submission relying on the presumption of regularity and the "inherent probabilities". Although the tribunal could, using its specialist experience, properly have concluded that the letter had contained enough information to make it effective, it was not bound to do so, given that it is not unknown for documents to be issued in an unapproved form or to use language that is not intelligible to an uninitiated recipient. The judge agreed with the tribunal that a copy of the appointment letter should have been in the tribunal bundle: a decision-maker might be able to rely on the presumption of regularity, but on an appeal (where it is not known what issues may eventually emerge) a copy of the letter should be provided. Much the same approach was taken by the Chief Commissioner in Northern Ireland in *PO'R*, where it was said that the tribunal there should not have decided against the claimant without having adjourned to obtain a copy of the appointment letter.

If a copy of the appointment letter was not in the bundle, then Judge Rowland's view was that a tribunal could, using its inquisitorial jurisdiction in an area where unrepresented claimants in particular could not be expected to identify such technical points, properly exercise its discretion under s.12(8)(a) of the SSA 1998 to direct that a copy be provided. It would not be fair to decide the case against the Secretary of State without giving that opportunity to provide the evidence. But where, as in *DC*, the evidence directed was not provided, the tribunal could properly conclude that the Secretary of State had failed to come forward with evidence on a matter on which the burden of proof was on him. There is therefore no formal incompatibility with the decision of Judge Wright in *CN*, although there was less emphasis there on the inquisitorial role of the tribunal. If there were any incompatibility, the fact that *DC* is a reported decision would point to its being preferred.

Judge Rowland accepted that the tribunal in *DC* had erred in law in deciding against the Secretary of State on the authorisation point (discussed below) without giving him an opportunity to provide relevant evidence, but that error was not material as, even if there was evidence that the provider was authorised to issue reg.4 notices, the tribunal would have been entitled to allow the claimant's appeal on the basis of the lack of necessary evidence that an effective notice had been given.

The second appeal (in relation to June 2012) raised the issue of whether the tribunal had been entitled to conclude that the Secretary of State had not shown that the Scheme provider in question had been authorised under reg.18 of the ESES Regulations to give reg.4 notices when he was unable to produce a copy of a letter of authorisation. Judge Rowland held that the tribunal had gone wrong in law. Regulation 18 did not specify the form in which authorisation had to be given (nor does s.6L of the new style Jobseekers Act 1995 on delegation and contracting out), so that it was a matter of fact and degree. Authority could be found to exist in evidence as to the conduct of those concerned, including what they have said and written over a period. The tribunal did not consider that possibility, raised by the provider acting as though authorised and the Secretary of State asserting that authority had been given. The judge went on to re-make the decision on the appeal. It had emerged that, by an administrative mistake, no formal letter of authority had ever been issued, but the existence of a contract between the Secretary of State and the main contractor for the sub-contractor to act in the area in question and a draft authorisation letter was sufficient to satisfy reg.18. He found that the claimant had been properly notified and had not shown good cause for his failure to participate, so that a sanction was to be imposed. On close analysis of reg.8 the sanction was to be for four weeks, rather than the 26 that had originally been imposed.

Even though the literal legislative requirements of notification have been satisfied, it may be that the claimant has not been "properly" notified because of a material breach of the public law duty of fairness or more specifically the prior information duty. That principle in the present context stems from paras 65 and 66 of the joint judgment of Lords Neuberger and Toulson in *R. (on the application of Reilly and Wilson) v Secretary of State for Work and Pensions* [2013] UKSC 68; [2014] 1 A.C. 453, in relation to a "back to work" scheme under the old style JSA regime. After noting the serious consequence of imposing a requirement to engage in unpaid work on a claimant on pain of discontinuance of benefits, the judges continued:

> "65. Fairness therefore requires that a claimant should have access to such information about the scheme as he or she may need in order to make informed and meaningful representations to the decision-maker before a decision is made. Such claimants are likely to vary considerably in their levels of education and ability to express themselves in an interview at a Jobcentre at a time when they may be under considerable stress. The principle does not depend on the categorisation of the Secretary of State's decision to introduce a particular scheme under statutory powers as a policy: it arises as a matter of fairness from the Secretary of State's proposal to invoke a statutory power in a way which will or may involve a requirement to perform work and which may have serious consequences on a claimant's ability to meet his or her living needs.
>
> 66. Properly informed claimants, with knowledge not merely of the schemes available, but also of the criteria for being placed on such schemes, should be able to explain what would, in their view, be the most reasonable and appropriate scheme for them, in a way which would be unlikely to be possible without such information. Some claimants may have access to information downloadable from a government website, if they know what to look for, but many will not. For many of those dependent on benefits, voluntary agencies such as Citizens Advice Bureaux play an important role in informing and assisting them in relation to benefits to which they may be entitled, how they should apply, and what matters they should draw to the attention of their Jobcentre adviser."

1.720 Those principles were discussed by the Court of Appeal in *SSWP v Reilly and Hewstone and SSWP v Jeffrey and Bevan* [2016] EWCA Civ 413; [2017] Q.B. 657; [2017] AACR 14 in relation to Mr Bevan's cross-appeal against the decision of the three-judge panel of the Upper Tribunal in *SSWP v TJ (JSA)* [2015] UKUT 56 (AAC). There was a detailed description and discussion of the decision in *TJ* in the 2015/16 edition of Vol.II of this series, which need not be repeated here in the light of the Court of Appeal's decision. The Upper Tribunal had concluded, in the terms of its own summary in para.13(vi), that in the case of schemes which were mandatory both at the stages of referral onto them and once on them, no basis could be identified on which meaningful representations could be made prior to the decision to refer, in the sense of those representations being able to affect the decision to refer. In the 2015/16 edition of Vol.II there was some criticism of the Upper Tribunal's use of the word "mandatory" in this context.

The Court of Appeal first held that the Upper Tribunal had been right on the particular facts of Mr Bevan's case (where his complaint was that he could not afford the bus fare to attend the appointment given, so needed payment in advance rather than a refund) to find that it would have made no difference to what he would have said to the provider about the fares if he had known about what The Work Programme Provider Guidance issued by the DWP said about ability to use transportation.

So far as the Upper Tribunal's general guidance is concerned, the Court said this in para.172 about the submission that the Upper Tribunal had erred in saying that there was no scope for making representations in connection with a decision to refer a claimant to the Work Programme since referral was mandatory:

> "We do not believe that that is a fair reading of what the Tribunal said; and if it is properly understood there does not seem to be any dispute of principle between the parties. The Tribunal was not laying down any absolute rule. The Secretary of State's policy, embodied in the guidance, is that referral to the Programme should be automatic (ignoring the specified exceptions) if the criteria are met. All that

the Tribunal was doing was to point out that, that being so, any representations would have to address the question why he should depart from the policy; and that it was not easy to see what such representations might be. That seems to us an obvious common sense observation, particularly since referral to the Work Programme does not as such involve any specific obligation: see para.151 above. But it does not mean that there could never be such cases, and indeed para.224 is expressly addressed to that possibility. The Tribunal did not depart from anything that the Supreme Court said in [Reilly and Wilson]. It was simply considering its application in the particular circumstances of referral to the Work Programme."

The Court considered that in the real world application of the prior information duty was unlikely to be important at the point of initial referral to the Work Programme under the old style JSA legislation, as claimants were unlikely to object at that stage, before any specific requirements were imposed. Problems were likely to emerge when particular requirements were imposed on claimants that they considered unreasonable or inappropriate. The Upper Tribunal had appeared to say in para.249 of its decision that there was little or no scope for the operation of the duty at that stage. The Court of Appeal says this in paras 177 and 178:

"177. Mr de la Mare [counsel for Mr Bevan] submitted that that is wrong. If it is indeed what the Tribunal meant, we agree. So also does Ms Leventhal [counsel for the Secretary of State], who explicitly accepted in her written submissions that 'the requirements of fairness continue to apply after referral'. In principle, JSA claimants who are required, or who it is proposed should be required, under the Work Programme to participate in a particular activity should have sufficient information to enable them to make meaningful representations about the requirement – for example, that the activity in question is unsuitable for them or that there are practical obstacles to their participation. The fact that participation is mandatory if the requirement is made is beside the point: the whole purpose of the representations, and thus of the claimant having the relevant information to be able to make them, is so that the provider may be persuaded that the requirement should not be made, or should be withdrawn or modified.

178. However we should emphasise that the foregoing is concerned with the position in principle. It is quite another matter whether the Work Programme as operated in fact fails to give claimants such information. The Secretary of State's evidence before the Tribunal was that the relevant guidance in fact provides for them to be very fully informed. We have already referred to the Tribunal's findings about the information given at the referral interview. But it was also the evidence that at the initial interview with the provider post-referral, which is designed to find out how the claimant can be best supported, and in the subsequent inter-actions between claimant and provider claimants are supposed to be given both information and the opportunity to make representations. Whether in any particular case there has nevertheless been a failure to give information necessary to enable the claimant to make meaningful representations will have to be judged on the facts of the particular case. Tribunals will no doubt bear in mind the point made in [*Reilly and Wilson*] that it is important not to be prescriptive about how any necessary information is provided: see para.74 of the judgment of Lord Neuberger and Lord Toulson."

In relation to new style JSA, there might well be scope therefore for the application of the general principle of fairness at the stage of the application of a work-related or connected requirement and at the stage of specification of particular actions or activities. However, the process of discussion leading to the drawing up of a claimant commitment and its notification of the requirements imposed, as described in the notes to s.6A, certainly, if properly followed, gives full opportunity for the provision of sufficient information to enable claimants to make meaningful representations about the content of the claimant commitment and to decide whether or not to accept initially and to make meaningful representations and decisions about taking particular specified actions further down the line. But the crucial questions in any appeals will most likely be, as suggested in para.178 of *Jeffrey and Bevan*, how the process was actually carried out in the particular case in question.

In *NM v SSWP (JSA)* [2016] UKUT 351 (AAC) Judge Wright held, as eventually conceded by the Secretary of State, that the inability to show that relevant DWP guidance had been considered before the claimant was given notice to participate in a Mandatory Work Activity scheme meant either that the claimant should not have been referred to the scheme (because the officer either would have followed the guidance or could have been persuaded to do so on representations from the claimant) or that he had good reason for not participating in the scheme. The appeal related to a sanction for failing to participate, through behaviour on the scheme. The guidance, in something called Mandatory Work Activity Guidance or Operational Instructions– Procedural Guidance–Mandatory Work Activity–January 2012, was relevant because at the time it instructed that claimants should not be considered for referral to Mandatory Work Activity if, among other circumstances, they were currently working (paid or voluntary). The claimant had been volunteering in a Sue Ryder shop, which he had to give up to attend the required scheme as a volunteer in a Salvation Army shop. The Secretary of State submitted that the guidance had since been changed to introduce an element of discretion about referral of claimants doing voluntary work. Judge Wright held that this would not excuse a failure by an officer of the Secretary of State to consider his own guidance or, on any appeal, a failure to provide the guidance to a First-tier Tribunal in accordance with the principles of natural justice.

Judge Wright has since emphasised some important elements of the application of the prior information duty, that should serve to rein in an over-enthusiastic use of the principle in some First-tier Tribunals, but only when properly placed in context. In *SSWP v SD (JSA)* [2020] UKUT 39 (AAC) he stressed, by reference both to the Supreme Court in *Reilly and Wilson* and the Court of Appeal in *Reilly and Hewstone* and *Jeffrey and Bevan*, that even if there had been a breach of the duty at the stage of initial referral to the Work Programme the notice of referral would only be invalidated if the breach was material. In the particular case, the claimant had never objected to his referral and his appeal against a sanction for failing to participate by non-attendance at a notified appointment was solely based on the ground that he had previously been told not to attend by his work coach. The tribunal, which had raised and sought evidence on the prior information duty point on its own initiative, failed to explain why it considered any breach of the duty material. In substituting a decision the judge rejected any unfairness in the referral to the Work Programme and rejected on the evidence the claimant's contention about the appointment.

Many of the requirements that can give rise to sanctions under s.6K involve undertaking or participating in interviews, courses, assessments, programmes etc that that have a specified start time. Participation must in general involve at least turning up at the right time and place and also making some meaningful contribution to whatever is involved. Behaviour that leads to the premature termination of the interview or course may well amount to a failure to participate (see the facts of *DM v SSWP (JSA)* [2015] UKUT 67 (AAC) where the claimant was asked to leave a session that he was said to be disrupting by asking questions and heckling (but see the discussion below about good reasons for failing to comply with requirements and the suitability of courses etc). There may, though, in cases of uncooperative claimants or heavy-handed officials or a combination, be difficult questions an interview or course has ceased to exist. Behaviour after the interview or course has ceased to exist cannot be evidence of a failure to participate, in contrast to behaviour before it starts (see below).

1.721 In *SA v SSWP (JSA)* [2015] UKUT 454 (AAC) the claimant, who had hearing difficulties and wore a hearing aid in one ear, was directed by an employment officer to attend and complete a CV writing course with Learn Direct two days later from 11.15 a.m. to 12.15 p.m. He was given a letter to confirm the time and date. The claimant arrived at 11.25 a.m. and was told that he was too late and so had been deemed to have missed his appointment. He immediately went to the Jobcentre Plus office to rebook an appointment for the course and explained that he had misheard the time for the appointment as 11.50, the time that he normally signed on. A fixed four-week sanction for failing, without a good reason, to carry out a reasonable jobseeker's direction was imposed. On appeal the claimant said that at the meeting with the employment officer he had not been wearing his hearing aid and that he had not thought to check the time of the appointment on the letter as he genuinely thought that it was the same as his two previous appointments. The First-tier Tribunal regarded it as clear that the direction had been reasonable and that the claimant had failed to comply with it, so that the sole question was whether he had had a good reason for the failure. On that question, the tribunal concluded that, although the error was genuine, that did not in itself give him a good reason and that he had failed to take reasonable steps to confirm the time of the appointment and dismissed his appeal.

In setting aside the tribunal's decision and substituting her own decision reversing the imposition of the sanction (as had been suggested by the Secretary of State), Judge Knowles held that the tribunal had erred in law by failing to consider the question of whether the claimant had failed to comply with the direction. In the substituted decision, she concluded that, the claimant not having refused to carry out the direction and taking into account that his error was genuine and that he took immediate steps to rebook, it was disproportionate to treat his late arrival in isolation as amounting to a failure to comply with the direction. That can only be regarded as a determination on the particular facts that does not constitute any sort of precedent to be applied as a matter of law in other cases. The outcome may have reflected an understandable desire in a deserving case to get around the absence of any scope for varying the fixed period of four weeks for a sanction under s.19A of the old style Jobseekers Act 1995 for a "first offence". However, there could have been nothing unreasonable about a conclusion that arriving 10 minutes after the beginning of a course that only lasted for an hour amounted to a failure to comply with a direction to attend and complete the course, no matter how genuine the error that led to the late arrival.

SN v SSWP (JSA) [2018] UKUT 279 (AAC) discusses, from para.42 onwards, what can amount to a failure to participate in a scheme (at a time when the consequent sanction was under reg.8 of the Jobseeker's Allowance (Mandatory Work Activity Scheme) Regulations 2011 (SI 2011/688), rather than s.19(2)(e) of the old style Jobseekers Act 1995). It confirms that conduct of the claimant related to the ordinary requirements of the work activity in question leading to the termination of their placement can amount to a failure to participate. In particular, it was held in paras 59-62 that actions before the start of the scheme can be relevant. In *SN* the claimant was required to work for four weeks as a retail assistant in a charity shop. As found by Judge Wright in substituting a decision on the appeal, the claimant visited the shop about a week before the placement was due to start, to find out what would be entailed. During the visit he used offensive language to one member of staff and about the nature of the work involved, that was unreasonable in any work setting. He attended at the shop at the specified time for the start of the placement, but, as the representative of the programme provider was not to arrive for about 20 minutes, retired to a changing cubicle to sit down, took off his shoes and appeared to go to sleep. When the representative arrived, the deputy manager of the shop told him that the claimant would not be allowed to work there in view of his earlier offensive conduct. The judge concluded that the combination of the claimant's behaviour on the earlier visit and his attitude of antagonism and lack of interest on the first day of the placement meant that he had failed to meet the notified requirements for participation in the scheme. There was no good cause for the failure to participate. Some doubt is expressed in para.45 about the result in *SA*.

In *CS v SSWP (JSA)* [2019] UKUT 218 (AAC) Judge Hemingway accepted that it was legitimate for a scheme provider to require someone attending to verify their identity before starting the scheme, so that a refusal to do so would usually amount to a failure to participate in the scheme. However, in the particular case the claimant had declined to verify various items of information about him appearing on a computer screen, largely because of misguided views about the effect of the Data Protection Act 1998, but also because of concerns about the security of social security information held by scheme providers. The judge held that the tribunal had erred in law by failing to make findings of fact about whether the claimant had been offered the opportunity to verify his identity by other means, e.g. by producing a passport or driving licence or other document in addition to the appointment letter that he had already produced. In the absence of such findings the tribunal had not been entitled to conclude that the claimant had refused to confirm his identity rather than merely refused to confirm it by the method initially put forward by the scheme provider. It might in other cases be relevant to enquire what the appointment letter or other documents do or do not say about confirming identity.

Claimants who are found not in fact to have been aware of an interview must have a good reason for failing to comply, whether or not the requirement is said to have been imposed in such circumstances (*SP v SSWP (UC)* [2018] UKUT 227 (AAC)).

See the notes to s.6J for general discussion of what might be a good reason and in particular for the suggestion that in the present context, if any analogy is to be drawn with previous authority, it should not be with the concept of "good cause" for a late claim, but with "just cause" for leaving employment voluntarily or with "good cause" under the pre-2012 form of s.19 of the old style Jobseekers Act 1995. It would seem that on any appeal, if the Secretary of State has proved on the balance of probabilities that there had been a failure to comply with a work-related or connected requirement, the practical burden would fall on the claimant of showing on the balance of probabilities that they have a good reason for the failure. That would be in accord with the principle demanded by *Kerr v Department for Social Development* [2004] UKHL 23; [2004] 1 W.L.R. 1372; *R 1/04 (SF)*, putting emphasis on who is in a better position to supply information on any particular issue in a co-operative process, rather than formal concepts of onus of proof. The claimant will in the great majority of cases be the person best placed to come forward with an explanation of their reasons for failing to comply with the requirement in question.

1.722 It appears to be accepted that the suitability of whatever it is that the claimant has been required to do is relevant to whether there is a good reason for not complying with the requirement. In *PL v DSD (JSA)* [2015] NI Com 72 (followed and applied in *PO'R v DFC (JSA)* [2018] NI Com 1), the Chief Commissioner for Northern Ireland has approved and applied the obiter suggestion of Judge Ward in *PL v SSWP (JSA)* [2013] UKUT 227 (AAC) (on the pre-October 2012 form of the Great Britain legislation) that, in deciding whether claimants have good cause for failing to avail themselves of a reasonable opportunity of a place on a training scheme or employment programme, a tribunal erred in law, where the circumstances raised the issue, in failing to consider the appropriateness of the particular scheme or programme to the particular claimant in the light of their skills and experience and previous attendance on any placements. Judge Ward's suggestion had been that the test was whether the claimant had reasonably considered that what was provided would not help him. It seems likely that a similar general approach will be taken to the issue of "good reason" under s.6K(2)(b) and the appropriateness of the activity in question. It may though still need to be sorted out how far the issue turns on the claimant's subjective view, within the bounds of reasonableness, in the light of the information provided at the time, as against a tribunal's view of the appropriateness of the activity. There may also be difficult questions in circumstances where what has been required seems quite reasonable and suitable and fairly imposed, but what is provided when the claimant attends turns out to be something different and of no assistance in the claimant's particular case, as in *DM v SSWP (JSA)* [2015] UKUT 67 (AAC) below. In such circumstances, does the claimant have a good reason for not participating in the activity at all, perhaps after raising queries with the provider, or are they, to escape sanction, obliged to sit through to the end?

DM was a case on jobseekers directions under s.19A(2)(c) of the old style Jobseekers Act 1995, but with insights relevant to new style JSA. The claimant was directed to attend and participate in a group information session for work programme returnees that it was said would enable him to improve his chances of employment in several ways. Judge Rowley apparently accepted the claimant's evidence that the course turned out to be about the sanctions regime. After he was asked to leave before the end because he was said to be disrupting the course by asking questions and heckling, he was sanctioned for failing to carry out a reasonable jobseeker's direction by not fully participating in the session. The judge was able to dispose of the case on the basis that the direction was not reasonable in the absence of any evidence of how the group information session would have assisted the particular claimant to find employment or have improved his prospects of becoming employed and in the absence of evidence that the administrative guidance that directions should be personalised and appropriate to the individual claimant had been applied. Thus she did not have to grapple with the question of whether the claimant had had a good reason for failing to comply with the direction. That question may well arise in cases where the imposition of the requirement in question and a failure to comply cannot be challenged.

In *DH v SSWP (JSA)* [2016] UKUT 355 (AAC), a case about the Jobseeker's Allowance (Schemes for Assisting Persons to Obtain Employment) Regulations 2013 SI 2013/3196 (see Vol.V of this series, 2021/22 edition as updated in Cumulative Supplements included in Vol.II of this series and in mid-year Supplements), it was held that the First-tier Tribunal erred in law in apparently dismissing the claimant's objections to attending a Work Programme run by a particular provider (on the grounds that staff of the company concerned had lied in a police statement and in court about whether travel expenses had been refunded to him and had bullied him) as, even if true, irrelevant to whether he had a good reason for failing to comply with requirements to participate. The tribunal had said that the claimant's remedies were to contact the police and to use appropriate complaints procedures, not to refuse to attend interviews or courses. The judge asked the rhetorical question in para.20 of what could amount to good reason if such matters did not. The circumstances are to be distinguished from those in *R(JSA) 7/03*, not mentioned in *DH*, where the claimant's objection was a generalised, though principled, one to the involvement of private companies in the provision of such schemes, rather than to specific aspects of the particular provider. The Commissioner held that that was not a "conscientious" objection under special provisions then in reg.73 of the JSA Regulations 1996 and did not amount to good cause for failing to carry out a direction to enroll in a Jobplan workshop, because his state of mind did not exist as a fact independently of his refusal to attend the workshop. It was not like having a particular fear of carrying out some activity that would be involved in the course or being in the location involved (on which see *GR v SSWP (JSA)* [2013] UKUT 645 (AAC) in the notes to s.6J).

Note that reg.28 of the JSA Regulations 2013, prescribing circumstances in which no reduction is to be made for a sanctionable failure, does not apply to s.6K, only to s.6J.

Under para.(b) of subs.(9), see reg.23. Under para.(c), see regs 24 and 25.

[1 Delegation and contracting out

6L.—(1) The functions of the Secretary of State under sections 6 to 6I may be exercised by, or by the employees of, such person as the Secretary of State may authorise for the purpose (an "authorised person"). 1.723

(2) An authorisation given by virtue of this section may authorise the exercise of a function—

(a) wholly or to a limited extent;
(b) generally or in particular cases or areas;
(c) unconditionally or subject to conditions.

(3) An authorisation under this section—

(a) may specify its duration;
(b) may be varied or revoked at any time by the Secretary of State;
(c) does not prevent the Secretary of State or another person from exercising the function to which the authorisation relates.

(4) Anything done or omitted to be done by or in relation to an authorised person (or an employee of that person) in, or in connection with, the exercise or purported exercise of the function concerned is to be treated for all purposes as done or omitted to be done by or in relation to the Secretary of State or (as the case may be) an officer of the Secretary of State.

(5) Subsection (4) does not apply—

(a) for the purposes of so much of any contract made between the authorised person and the Secretary of State as relates to the exercise of the function, or
(b) for the purposes of any criminal proceedings brought in respect of anything done or omitted to be done by the authorised person (or an employee of that person).

(6) Where—

(a) the authorisation of an authorised person is revoked, and
(b) at the time of the revocation so much of any contract made between the authorised person and the Secretary of State as relates to the exercise of the function is subsisting, the authorised person is entitled to treat the contract as repudiated by the Secretary of State (and not as frustrated by reason of the revocation).]

AMENDMENT

1. Welfare Reform Act 2012 s.49(3) (trigger date on or after April 29, 2013).

DEFINITION

"person"—see Interpretation Act 1978 Sch.1.

GENERAL NOTE

1.724 This section allows the Secretary of State to authorise other persons (which word in accordance with the Interpretation Act 1978 includes corporate and unincorporated associations, such as companies) and their employees to carry out any of his functions under s.6–6I. Any such authorisation will not in practice cover the making of regulations, but may well (depending on the extent of the authorisations given) extend to specifying various matters under those sections. The involvement of private sector organisations, operating for profit, in running various schemes within the scope of the benefit system is something that claimants sometimes object to. Such a generalised objection, even if on principled grounds, is unlikely to amount in itself to a good reason for failing to engage with a scheme in question (although see the discussion in the note to s.6J on whether "for no good reason" has a restricted meaning). An objection based on previous experience with the organisation concerned or the nature of the course may raise more difficult issues. See also the discussion in *R(JSA) 7/03* plus *CJSA/495/2007* and *CJSA/505/2007*.

In *DH v SSWP (JSA)* [2016] UKUT 355 (AAC), a case about the SAPOE Regulations, it was held that the First-tier Tribunal erred in law in apparently dismissing the claimant's objections to attending a Work Programme run by a particular provider (on the grounds that staff of the company concerned had lied in a police statement and in court about whether travel expenses had been refunded to him and had bullied him) as, even if true, irrelevant to whether he had a good reason for failing to comply with requirements to attend. The tribunal had said that the claimant's remedies were to contact the police and to use appropriate complaints procedures, not to refuse to attend interviews or courses. The judge asked the rhetorical question in para.20 what could amount to good reason if such matters did not. The circumstances are to be distinguished from those in *R(JSA) 7/03*, not mentioned in *DH*, where the claimant's objection was a generalised one to the involvement of private companies in the provision of such schemes.

Jobseeker's agreement: reviews and appeals

11.—[*Repealed.*] 1.725

Income and capital

Income and capital: general

12.—(1) In relation to a claim for a jobseeker's allowance, the income and capital of a person shall be calculated or estimated in such manner as may be prescribed. 1.726

(2) A person's income in respect of a week shall be calculated in accordance with prescribed rules.

(3) The rules may provide for the calculation to be made by reference to an average over a period (which need not include the week concerned).

(4) Circumstances may be prescribed in which–

(a) a person is treated as possessing capital or income which he does not possess;

(b) capital or income which a person does possess is to be disregarded;

(c) income is to be treated as capital;

(d) capital is to be treated as income.

DEFINITIONS 1.727

"prescribed"—see s.35(1).
"week"—*ibid.*

Trade disputes

Trade disputes

14.—(1) Where— 1.728

(a) there is a stoppage of work which causes a person not to be employed on any day, and

(b) the stoppage is due to a trade dispute at his place of work,

that person is not entitled to a jobseeker's allowance for the week which includes that day unless he proves that he is not directly interested in the dispute.

(2) A person who withdraws his labour on any day in furtherance of a trade dispute, but to whom subsection (1) does not apply, is not entitled to a jobseeker's allowance for the week which includes that day.

(3) If a person who is prevented by subsection (1) from being entitled to a jobseeker's allowance proves that during the stoppage—

(a) he became bona fide employed elsewhere;
(b) his employment was terminated by reason of redundancy within the meaning of section 139(1) of the Employment Rights Act 1996, or
(c) the bona fide resumed employment with his employer but subsequently left for a reason other than the trade dispute,

subsection (1) shall be taken to have ceased to apply to him on the occurrence of the event referred to in paragraph (a) or (b) or (as the case may be) the first event referred to in paragraph (c).

(4) In this section "place of work", in relation to any person, means the premises or place at which he was employed.

(5) Where separate branches of work which are commonly carried on as separate businesses in separate premises or at separate places are in any case carried on in separate departments on the same premises or at the same place, each of those departments shall, for the purposes of subsection (4), be deemed to be separate premises or (as the case may be) a separate place.

DEFINITIONS

"employment"—see s.35(1) and reg.2(1) of the JSA Regulations 2013.
"entitled"—se s.35(1).
"trade dispute"—*ibid.*
"week"—*ibid.*

GENERAL NOTE

1.729 This section denies entitlement to new style JSA (in identical terms to those for old style JSA) to certain persons affected by or involved in trade disputes in two situations. First, where a stoppage of work due to a trade dispute at the claimant's place of work causes them not to be employed on any day, they will not be entitled to new style JSA for the week which includes that day, unless either they can establish that they are not directly interested in the dispute or they can invoke one of the escape routes provided by subs.(3) (subs.(1)). The second situation where entitlement is denied throughout a week is where in furtherance of a trade dispute the claimant withdraws their labour on any day in that week, but not in such a way as to be caught by subs.(1) (the first situation of denial of entitlement) (subs.(2)).

Note that this provision is not replicated in the universal credit legislation. There is no mention of trade disputes in the WRA 2012. Instead, reg.56 of the Universal Credit Regulations 2013 deems someone who has employed earnings and has withdrawn their labour in furtherance of a trade dispute (differently defined) to have employed earnings at the level that they would have had were it not for the trade dispute, unless their contract of employment has been terminated. There are problems of interpretation of that provision, discussed in the notes to reg.56 in Vol. II of this series. The deeming thus applies in roughly the cases covered by s.14(2), with slight adjustments. But outside the scope of that deeming, a claimant may be disentitled to new style JSA by reason of a trade dispute, but able to make up the loss of that benefit by entitlement to a correspondingly increased amount of universal credit. That depends of course on not having too much capital and satisfying other conditions of entitlement.

In many respects the section replicates the trade dispute disqualification from unemployment benefit in s.27 of SSCBA 1992 and, as noted below, case law interpreting that and its precursor provisions will still be relevant in interpreting this new style JSA provision. There is some difference of terminology without apparent difference of meaning (e.g. "place of work" rather than "place of employment"). That one day affected bars title for the whole week rather than just for the day, as would have been the case with unemployment benefit, is unsurprising; it reflects the change from a daily benefit (UB) to a weekly benefit (JSA).

Note that this provision denies entitlement. Hence weeks ruled out do not form part of a jobseeking period (JSA Regulations 2013 reg.37(2)(d)), but nor do they erode the 182-day maximum period of entitlement to new style JSA founded on a contribution record in a single set of two tax/contribution years (see further notes to ss.2 and 5). This is in marked contrast to the double penalty suffered by those who, for example, lose their job through misconduct, precluded from payment of new style JSA by s.6J(3)(b), who not only are denied payment but have the 182-day period eroded by the period of preclusion imposed under that section (see further notes to ss.5 and 6J). This differential can to some degree be rationalised on the basis that the role of ss.6J and 6K is to preclude payment to those who are in some way responsible for their own unemployment, whereas, as shown below, the trade dispute preclusion can catch the innocent, and in part is said to manifest state neutrality in the dispute, the merits of which should not concern the benefit system.

Subsection (1) 1.730

To bring the trade dispute preclusion in subs.(1) into operation, subject to the escape routes discussed at the end of this note, the Secretary of State (decision-maker) must prove on the balance of probabilities that:

(1) there was a *trade dispute*;
(2) at the claimant's *place of work*;
(3) which resulted in a *stoppage of work*; and
(4) that stoppage caused the claimant not to be employed on a day.

That adapts for this section the approach to the unemployment benefit trade dispute disqualification set out in *R(U) 17/52(T)*. Each of those conditions contains terms (highlighted above) whose interpretation is vital to the correct application of the section's denial of entitlement to new style JSA.

Trade dispute 1.731

Determining the existence of a trade dispute seems logically the first task of the adjudicating authorities, because in the absence of a trade dispute the other conditions cannot apply. The basic definition, in very broad terms, is in s.35(1). It differs from the employment law definition adopted for universal credit purposes. The definition clearly includes strikes, whether official or unofficial (*R(U) 5/59*), lockouts (*R(U) 17/52*) and demarcation disputes (*R(U) 14/64*). There is no requirement that the claimant be a party to the trade dispute (*R(U) 3/69* below). It has been held that there can be a trade dispute between an employer and employees of another employer who picket the employer's premises and persuade its employees to strike (*R(U) 1/74*). There is a requirement in the definition that the dispute concern employment or non-employment of persons or conditions or terms of employment. Disputes outside these parameters are not trade disputes for the purpose of this section. It is now clearly established that a dispute about safety procedures is within the definition (*R(U) 3/71*, *R(U) 5/77* and *R. v National Insurance Commissioner, Ex p. Thompson* (1977), appendix to *R(U) 5/77*). In *R(U) 5/87* Commissioner Rice held that the words "any dispute . . . which is connected with the employment . . . of any person" are wide enough to include any dispute connected with the manner in which the employment is carried out, and in that case covered the dispute over the employees' "go slow". In most cases establishing the existence of a trade dispute is unlikely to be problematic. But note that in para.6 of *R(U) 21/59* the Commissioner indicated that a dispute between an employer and an employee must have reached "a certain stage of contention before it may properly be termed a [trade] dispute".

The Commissioner was clearly satisfied that evidence that the workforce had met to consider their response to their employer's rejection of their claims concerning their terms of employment amounted to a trade dispute and suggested that one may well have existed some time before the meeting took place.

Note that in determining the existence of a trade dispute it is no part of the adjudicating authorities' task to make any assessment of the merits of the dispute (*Ex p. Thompson* (above) and *R(SSP) 1/86*). It may be necessary to make findings of fact about when the trade dispute started and ended, but it should be remembered that the more important dates relate to when the stoppage of work started and ended. That is discussed below. There is a clear distinction to be drawn between a trade dispute and a stoppage of work under the section.

1.732 *Place of work*

The trade dispute must be at the claimant's place of work as defined in subs.(4). Read with subs.(5) this allows some separation of departments within a range of employment operated by a single employer. It will usually be a straightforward task to identify the premises or place at which the claimant is employed. Obviously each case must be determined on its own facts. How broadly or narrowly the place will be defined will vary according to the circumstances of each case. In *R(U) 4/58* the place of employment of an employee loading ships was held to be the whole of the docks.

Where the decision-maker shows on the balance of probabilities a place of work, it will be for the claimant to prove on the balance of probabilities that there are separate branches of work under subs.(5) and that the trade dispute is not at their place of work so construed (para.14 of *R(U) 1/70*). The escape route in accord with the terms of subss.(4) and (5) is complex because the claimant, who may not be best placed to do so, must adduce evidence to show that:

(a) there are separate branches of work; claimants are unlikely to succeed unless they can show that the branch is engaged in work that is not part of an integrated process of production (para.7 of *R(U) 4/62*);

(b) the separate branches of work are commonly carried on as separate businesses in separate premises or at separate places; this necessarily involves adducing evidence as to patterns in other similar businesses: *(R(U) 4/62* and para.17 of *R(U) 1/70)*; and

(c) at their place of employment the branches of work are in fact carried out in separate departments at the same premises or place.

In cases involving such arguments, clear findings of fact are obviously vital. *CU/66/1986(T)* affords an illustration. There the claimant successfully appealed her trade dispute disqualification to a Tribunal of Commissioners. She was a canteen worker at Frickley Colliery, laid off during the miner's strike in 1984–1985. The Commissioners held that there was carried on in the canteen a separate branch of work, and one which is commonly carried on as a separate business in separate premises or at a separate place. But was the canteen a separate department? The evidence of the NUM Branch Secretary at the colliery was that the canteen was inside the colliery gates and had been attached to or added to the pit-head baths that had been built in 1937. The manageress was appointed by and answerable to the NCB Catering Manager at Doncaster. While applications for jobs at the canteen would be made to the colliery's personnel manager, the area canteen manager would be responsible for making the appointment. As regards disciplinary matters with respect to canteen workers, again, the area manager would be involved but the colliery manager would also have to be informed. Profits and losses in the canteen did not appear to feature in figures about the profitability of the colliery. The Commissioners, in the light of this evidence, decided that the work carried on in the canteen was a separate branch of work carried on in a separate department on the same premises or at the same place as the colliery. Accordingly, since the trade dispute that caused the stoppage of work was not at the claimant's place of employment she would not be disqualified from benefit. The Commissioners also referred to an Umpire's decision (*Case 2185/29*, Umpires Decisions, Vol.VIII, p.88) under the equivalent provision in s.8(1) of the Unemployment Insurance Act 1920. There, a blacksmith employed in the blacksmiths' department at a colliery, which department did both wagon repairing and general colliery work, was able to rely on the escape route, notwithstanding that only some work in that department was carried on as a separate department from coal-mining.

Stoppage of work 1.733

Generally defining a stoppage of work is relatively easy. But defining when it begins may be more problematic and a useful approach may be to adopt the reverse of the principles laid down in the decisions on the ending of stoppages of work discussed below. The starting point will always be to consider the definition given by the Tribunal of Commissioners in *R(U) 17/52(T)*:

> "A stoppage of work must be in the nature of a strike or lockout, that is to say it must be a move in a contest between an employer and his employees, the object of which is that employment shall be resumed on certain conditions."

In *R(U) 7/58* it was held that a stoppage of work occurred when 38 production workers out of a total of 90 withdrew their labour. In *R(U) 1/87* Commissioner Skinner said that "stoppage of work" means "a situation in which operations are being stopped or hindered otherwise than to a negligible extent" (para.7). There the closure of the furriers' fleshing shop on May 2, 1984, causing a 60 per cent loss of production, resulted in a stoppage from that date. In *R(U) 1/65*, following a long line of Commissioners' decisions, it was held that where there was a trade dispute and subsequently the employer indicated that he would never re-employ the strikers, the stoppage of work continued to be due to the trade dispute despite the high improbability that the strikers would be re-employed and despite their acceptance of that position. In effect the disqualification could only end when they became bona fide employed elsewhere or when the stoppage ended. In *R(U) 25/57*, the Commissioner adopted the approach taken by the Umpire in 1926 as establishing the principles to be applied in determining when the end of a stoppage of work occurred:

> "A stoppage of work may come to an end without any settlement of the dispute, by the workers returning to work in a body, or by driblets, or by their places being taken by other men. In such cases the stoppage of work comes to an end when the employers have got all the workers they require, that is, when work is no longer being stopped or hindered by the refusal of workers to work on the employer's terms or the refusal of employers to employ the workers on the workers' terms . . . When work is again proceeding normally and is not being held up, either by the men holding back or by circumstances directly resulting from the stoppage of work, the stoppage of work is at an end." (para.6)

That approach was cited with approval in *R(U) 1/65*. It is consistent with that approach that, where a dispute had ended but work was needed to industrial plant to carry out repairs necessitated by the stoppage, a lay-off while those repairs were carried out was a part of the stoppage due to the trade dispute (*R. v National Insurance Commissioner Ex p. Dawber*, appendix to *R(U) 9/80*).

The stoppage causes the claimant not to be employed on a day 1.734

If the stoppage causes the claimant not to be employed on any day, entitlement to new style JSA is lost for the week including that day (unless one of the escape routes can be invoked).

It has already been noted that the claimant need not be a party to the trade dispute to be caught by the disqualification. Claimants are caught if the stoppage is the effective cause of their not working. So, if enough people stay away from work for a stoppage to occur, all those losing days of employment, whether by their own choice or by force of circumstances, such as picketing or being laid off by the employer, are to be regarded as having lost their employment by reason of the stoppage.

1.735 *Escape routes*

There are four escape routes for avoiding the preclusive effect of subs.(1): the proviso in the subsection itself and the three exceptions set out in subs.(3).

(1) The proviso: Claimants can avoid the disqualification by proving that they have no direct interest in the trade dispute. In determining what constitutes a direct interest, it is necessary to look no further than the decision of the House of Lords in *Presho v Insurance Officer* [1984] 1 All E.R. 97, appendix 2 to *R(U) 1/84*), followed by the Court of Appeal in *Cartlidge v Chief Adjudication Officer* [1986] 2 All E.R. 1, appendix to *R(U) 5/86*. In *Presho* Lord Brandon said that the words should be given their natural and ordinary meaning and continued:

> "Where different groups of workers, belonging to different unions, are employed by the same employers at the same place of work and there is a trade dispute between the common employers and one of the unions to which one of the groups of workers belong, those in the other groups of workers belonging to other unions are directly, and not merely indirectly, interested in that trade dispute provided that two conditions are fulfilled. The first condition is that, whatever may be the outcome of the trade dispute, it will be applied by the common employers not only to the group of workers belonging to the one union participating in the dispute, but also to the other groups of workers belonging to the other unions concerned. The second condition is that the application of the outcome of the dispute 'across the board' . . . should come about automatically as a result of one or other of three things: first, a collective agreement which is legally binding; or, second, a collective agreement which is not legally binding; or, third, established industrial custom and practice at the place of work concerned. [These issues involve] a question of fact of a kind which insurance officers, local tribunals and the commissioner, are by reason of their wide knowledge and experience of matters pertaining to industrial relations, exceptionally well qualified to answer." (At 101–102.)

In *Cartlidge*, the Commissioners had found that the miners' dispute concerned both pay and pit closures, so that Mr Cartlidge, the amount of whose redundancy payment on his impending leaving could thereby be affected, was directly interested in the trade dispute. It follows that it will be extremely difficult for claimants to take advantage of this escape route. However, the fact that the claimant was at one time directly interested in the trade dispute (and thus then unable to invoke the proviso) does not preclude them from successfully invoking it later during the stoppage should they cease to have a direct interest. The proviso is not invocable once and once only during a stoppage (para.9 of *R(U) 1/87*, relying on paras 15-28 of *R(U) 5/86(T)*, where a Tribunal of Commissioners disapproved statements to the contrary in *R(U) 4/79(T)* because a line of Commissioners' authority running contrary to that relied on in *R(U) 4/79(T)* had not been cited or considered. A claimant initially directly interested in the trade dispute (and therefore rightly denied benefit) can cease to be so interested, and thus claim the benefit of the proviso to conclude the period of denial, where their dismissal by their employer genuinely indicates the employer's intention to sever all relations with them and is not just a tactical manoeuvre in the dispute. In *R(U) 1/87* the hindsight available to the Commissioner showed that the claimant's dismissal on the first day of the stoppage was part of plans to trim the size of the workforce and thus a genuine severance of all relations with the claimant rather than a tactical move in the dispute. Accordingly, the claimant was not subject to disqualification after that first day. Of course, were that case being decided now, with respect to new style JSA, the whole week in which that day occurred would be ruled out by subs.(1).

(2) Bona fide employed elsewhere (subs.(3)(a)): If someone caught by the subs. (1) preclusion proves that during the stoppage they became bona fide employed elsewhere, subs.(1) is to be taken to cease to apply to them from the point at which they became so employed elsewhere.

The burden of proof is on the claimant to establish the bona fide nature of the employment. Bona fide means that the employment must not merely be a device to avoid the disqualification; both the employment and the reason for taking it must be genuine (*R(U) 6/74*). There is no objection to the taking of temporary employment so long as it is genuine. It will usually be necessary to show that the relationship with the former employer with whom there was a trade dispute has been permanently severed. So a former boiler-maker who obtained intermittent work in his usual occupation in a different port, but returned to his former employer on the ending of the dispute was held not to have established that he was bona fide employed elsewhere (*R(U) 39/56*).

(3) Employment terminated by reason of redundancy (subs.(3)(b)): If someone caught by the subs.(1) preclusion proves that during the stoppage their employment was terminated by reason of redundancy within the meaning of s.139(1) of the Employment Rights Act 1996, subs.(1) is to be taken to have ceased to apply to them from the point of such termination. As to "by reason of redundancy within the meaning of section 139(1)", termination will be by reason of redundancy if it is attributable wholly or mainly to: (a) the fact that the employer has ceased, or intends to cease, to carry on that business in the place where the employee [the claimant] was employed, or (b) the fact that the requirements of that business for employees to carry out work of a particular kind, or for employees to carry out work of a particular kind in the place where [the claimant] was employed, have ceased or diminished or are expected to cease or diminish.

The precursor of this provision was inserted into the unemployment benefit trade dispute disqualification scheme to remove the injustice perceived to exist in the *Cartlidge* case. Mr Cartlidge had volunteered for redundancy prior to the start of the miners' dispute in 1984. Between receiving his notice of redundancy and its taking effect, a stoppage due to a trade dispute at his place of work caused him to not to be employed on some days. He had tried to work and had done so for much of the period but had lost some days' work because of the picketing of his pit. The Court of Appeal reluctantly held that the trade dispute disqualification extended beyond the termination of his employment because the stoppage of work was still continuing (the relevant provision then disqualified "for any day during the stoppage"). The effect of this provision is that subs.(1) can have no preclusive effect beyond the point of termination of employment by reason of redundancy.

(4) Bona fide resumption of employment and subsequent leaving for another reason (subs.(3)(c)): If someone caught by the subs.(1) preclusion proves that during the stoppage they bona fide resumed employment with their employer, subs.(1) is to be taken to have ceased to apply to them from the point at which they bona fide resumed their employment.

This is an escape route for claimants who have lost employment, subsequently **1.736** returned to work, but then left it for a reason unconnected with the trade dispute. The reason will usually be something other than leaving their job to take another: subs.(3)(a) would there afford an easier escape route. Bona fide is to be interpreted as in subs.(3)(a). But otherwise it is not easy to see how this provision will work in practice. Does resumption mean that the employment was terminated and re-employment offered, or merely that the claimant returned to work during the trade dispute, or both? There appears to be no case law on the precursor of this provision, so many points await interpretation.

Subsection (2) **1.737**

This subsection makes it clear that anyone not falling within subs.(1) who with- draws their labour on any day in furtherance of a trade dispute is not entitled to new style JSA for the week which includes that day. It fills a gap in the test in subs.(1)(a) because it does not require any stoppage of work to have occurred. Nor does it require the trade dispute to be at the claimant's place of work. As long as the withdrawal of labour is in furtherance of a trade dispute, the preclusion operates. It could require the authorities to draw a distinction between a "withdrawal of labour" and a "lock-out" (*Ogus, Barendt and Wikeley, The Law of Social Security*, p.141), risking an opinion on the merits of the dispute.

The rule can only be applied to claimants who have withdrawn their labour. That would cover straightforward strikes or refusals to carry out some significant part of contractual duties, even if the latter led to the employer sending the employees home completely. On the other hand, refusals to work voluntary overtime or works-to-rule would not be covered. And if an employer has initiated a lock-out before the occurrence of anything that would otherwise count as a withdrawal of labour it would seem that the employees could not be regarded as a having withdrawn their labour. A withdrawal must involve a voluntary choice not to work. Much more troublesome would be cases where employees decline to cross picket lines. Being physically prevented from entering work premises or being subjected to threats of violence against self or others would no doubt negate the necessary element of voluntary choice. At the other end of the spectrum, agreeing to polite and reasoned requests not to cross a picket line would also no doubt be regarded as a withdrawal of labour. But there will be many circumstances in the middle where the question will be very difficult to answer. If there are many pickets, with shouted insults and imprecations or more, when do spirited attempts at persuasion turn into intimidation?

The rule also requires that the individual's withdrawal of labour is in furtherance of a trade dispute as defined in s.35(1) (see the discussion above). There is no requirement that the dispute has led to any stoppages of work or similar, nor that the claimant potentially caught by subs.(2) has any material interest in the outcome of the dispute. Presumably a trade dispute has to be in existence before a withdrawal of labour can be in furtherance of it. In para.6 of *R(U) 21/59* the Commissioner indicated that a dispute between an employer and an employee must have reached "a certain stage of contention before it may properly be termed a [trade] dispute". He was clearly satisfied that evidence that the workforce had met to consider their response to their employer's rejection of their claims concerning their terms of employment amounted to a trade dispute and suggested that one may well have existed some time before the meeting took place.

"Furtherance" presumably points towards whatever subjective intention behind the withdrawal of labour can properly be attributed to the claimant, rather than whether the withdrawal is likely to have any practical influence on the outcome of the trade dispute. That would be consistent with the inherent principle that a solo withdrawal of labour can trigger the application of subs.(2). It is not necessary for the claimant to have acted in concert with others, provided that the withdrawal of labour was in furtherance of a trade dispute.

Some assistance might possibly be gained from the case law about the meaning of "furtherance" in the context of the legality of industrial action (see most recently *Warrington BC v Unite the Union* [2023] EWHC 3039 (KB); [2024] I.C.R. 599). It is accepted in that context, where the actions of unions are in issue, that the union need not be acting exclusively in furtherance of a trade dispute.

Note that, in contrast to the position under reg.56 of the Universal Credit Regulations the application of the rule does not automatically cease on the termination of the claimant's contract of employment. But its continued application can only be justified if the claimant can be said still to be withdrawing their labour. If the employer has terminated the contract of employment it must be arguable that the claimant no longer has anything to withdraw their labour from.

Miscellaneous

Supplementary provisions

21.—Further provisions in relation to jobseeker's allowance are set out in Schedule 1. 1.738

Members of the forces

22.—(1) Regulations may modify any provision of this Act, in such manner as the Secretary of State thinks proper, in its application to persons who are or have been members of Her Majesty's forces. 1.739

(2) [[1] ...].

(3) For the purposes of this section, Her Majesty's forces shall be taken to consist of such establishments and organisations in which persons serve under the control of the Defence Council as may be prescribed.

AMENDMENT

1. Welfare Reform Act 2012 Sch.14 Pt 4 (trigger date on or after April 29, 2013).

DEFINITIONS

"prescribed"—see s.35(1).
"regulations"—*ibid.*

PART II

BACK TO WORK SCHEMES

Pilot schemes

29.—(1) Any regulations to which this subsection applies may be made so as to have effect for a specified period not exceeding 36 months. 1.740

(2) Any regulations which, by virtue of subsection (1), are to have effect for a limited period are referred to in this section as "a pilot scheme".

(3) A pilot scheme may provide that its provisions are to apply only in relation to—

(a) one or more specified areas or localities;
(b) one or more specified classes of person;
(c) persons selected—
  (i) by reference to prescribed criteria; or
  (ii) on a sampling basis.

(4) A pilot scheme may make consequential or transitional provision with respect to the cessation of the scheme on the expiry of the specified period.

(5) A pilot scheme ("the previous scheme") may be replaced by a further pilot scheme making the same, or similar, provision (apart from the specified period) to that made by the previous scheme.

(6) Subject to subsection (8), subsection (1) applies to—

(a) regulations made under this Act, other than—
  (i) regulations made under section 4(2) or (5) which have the effect of reducing any age-related amount or applicable amount; or
  (ii) regulations made under section 27;

(b) regulations made under the Administration Act, so far as they relate to a jobseeker's allowance;
(c) regulations made under Part VII of the Benefits Act (income-related benefits), other than any mentioned in subsection (7); and
(d) regulations made under the Administration Act, so far as they relate to income- related benefits payable under Part VII of the Benefits Act.

(7) The regulations referred to in subsection (6)(c) are—
(a) [*repealed*];
(b) [*repealed*];
(c) regulations under section 130(4) of that Act which have the effect of reducing the appropriate maximum housing benefit;
(d) regulations under section 131(10)(a) of that Act which have the effect of reducing the appropriate maximum council tax benefit; and
(e) regulations reducing any of the sums prescribed under section 135(1) of that Act.

(8) Subsection (1) applies only if the regulations are made with a view to [1testing the extent to which the provision made by the regulations is likely to promote—
(a) people remaining in work, or
(b) people obtaining or being able to obtain work (or more work or better-paid work).]

AMENDMENT

1. Welfare Reform Act 2012 s.49(4) (trigger date on or after April 29, 2013).

DEFINITIONS

1.741 "the Administration Act"—see s.35(1).
"the Benefits Act"—*ibid.*
"regulations"—*ibid.*

PART III

MISCELLANEOUS AND SUPPLEMENTAL

Interpretation

1.742 **35.**—(1) In this Act—
"the Administration Act" means the Social Security Administration Act 1992;
"applicable amount" means the applicable amount determined in accordance with regulations under section 4;
"benefit year" has the meaning given by section 2(4);
"the Benefits Act" means the Social Security Contributions and Benefits Act 1992;
"child" means a person under the age of 16;
"claimant" means a person who claims a jobseeker's allowance [2. . .];
"continental shelf operations" has the same meaning as in section 120 of the Benefits Act;

"contribution-based conditions" means the conditions set out in section 2;

[2. . .];

[4 "couple" means—

(a) two people who are married to, or civil partners of, each other and are members of the same household; or

(b) two people who are not married, or civil partners of, each other but are living together as a [5as if they were a married couple or civil partners] otherwise than in prescribed circumstances

"employed earner" has the meaning prescribed for the circumstances of this Act;

"employment", [3. . .], has the meaning prescribed for the purposes of this Act;

[3. . .];

"entitled", in relation to a jobseeker's allowance, is to be construed in accordance with—

(a) the provisions of this Act relating to entitlement; and

(b) sections 1 of the Administration Act and section 27 of the Social Security Act 1998.

"family" means—

(a) a couple;

(b) a couple and a member of the same household for whom one of them is, or both are, responsible and who is a child or a person of a prescribed description;

(c) except in prescribed circumstances, a person who is not a member of a couple and a member of the same household for whom that person is responsible and who is a child or a person of a prescribed description;

"FAS payments" means payments made under the Financial Assistance Scheme Regulations 2005;

"Great Britain" includes the territorial waters of the United Kingdom adjacent to Great Britain;

[2. . .];

[3. . .];

"jobseeking period" has the meaning prescribed for the purposes of this Act;

[3. . .];

[2. . .];

"occupational pension scheme" has the same meaning as it has in the Pension Schemes Act 1993 by virtue of section 1 of that Act;

"pensionable age" has the meaning prescribed for the purposes of this Act;

"pension payments" means—

(a) periodical payments made in relation to a person, under a personal pension scheme or, in connection with the coming to an end of an employment of his, under an occupational pension scheme or a public service pension scheme; and

(b) such other payments as may be prescribed;

"personal pension scheme" means—

(a) a personal pension scheme as defined by section 1 of the Pension Schemes Act 1993;

(b) an annuity contract or trust scheme approved under section 620 or 621 of the Income and Corporation Taxes Act 1988 or a substituted contract within the meaning of section 622(3) of that Act which is treated as having become a registered pension scheme by virtue of paragraph 1(1)(f) of Schedule 36 to the Finance Act 2004; and

(c) a personal pension scheme approved under Chapter 4 of Part 14 of the Income and Corporation Taxes Act 1988 which is treated as having become a registered pension scheme by virtue of paragraph 1(1)(g) of Schedule 36 to the Finance Act 2004;]

"PPF payments" means any payments made in relation to a person—

(a) payable under the pension compensation provisions as specified in section 162(2) of the Pensions Act 2004 or Article 146(2) of the Pensions (Northern Ireland) Order 2005 (the pension compensation provisions); or

(b) payable under section 166 of the Pensions Act 2004 or Article 150 of the Pensions (Northern Ireland) Order 2005 (duty to pay scheme benefits unpaid at assessment date etc.);

"prescribed", except in section 27 (and in section 36 so far as relating to regulations under section 27), means specified in or determined in accordance with regulations;

"public service pension scheme" has the same meaning as it has in the Pension Schemes Act 1993 by virtue of section 1 of that Act;

"regulations" means regulations made by the Secretary of State;

"tax year", except in section 27 (and in section 36 so far relating to regulations under section 27), means the 12 months beginning with 6th April in any year;

[[3]. . .];

"week" means a period of 7 days beginning with a Sunday or such other period of 7 days as may be prescribed;

"work" has the meaning prescribed for the purposes of this Act;

[[1]"work availability requirement" has the meaning given by section 6E;

"work preparation requirement" has the meaning given by section 6C;

"work search requirement" has the meaning given by section 6D;

"work-focused interview requirement" has the meaning given by section 6B;

"work-related requirement" has the meaning given by section 6;]

"year", except in the expression "benefit year", means a tax year.

(1A) [[4] . . .]

(2) The expressions "limited capability for work", "linked period", "relevant education" and "remunerative work" are to be read with paragraphs 2, 3, 14 and 1 of Schedule 1.

(3) Subject to any regulations made for the purposes of this subsection, "earnings" is to be construed for the purposes of this Act in accordance with section 3 of the Benefits Act and paragraph 6 of Schedule 1 to this Act.

AMENDMENTS

1. Welfare Reform Act 2012 s.49(5) (trigger date on or after April 29, 2013).
2. Welfare Reform Act 2012 Sch.14 Pt 1 (trigger date on or after April 29, 2013).
3. Welfare Reform Act 2012 Sch.14 Pt 4 (trigger date on or after April 29, 2013).

4. Marriage (Same Sex Couples) Act 2013 (Consequential and Contrary Provisions and Scotland) Order 2014 (SI 2014/516) art.2 and Sch.1 para.26 (March 13, 2014 in relation to England and Wales); Marriage and Civil Partnership (Scotland) Act 2014 and Civil Partnership Act 2004 (Consequential Provisions and Modifications) Order 2014 (SI 2014/3229) art.29 and Sch.5 para.12 (December 16, 2014 in relation to Scotland).

5. Civil Partnership (Opposite-sex Couples) Regulations 2019 (SI 2019/1458) reg.41(a) and Sch.3 para.18 (December 2, 2019).

DEFINITION

"civil partner"—see Interpretation Act 1978 Sch.1.

GENERAL NOTE

This section defines certain terms used in the legislation, but leaves some to be construed in accordance with specified paragraphs of Sch.1 and others to be defined through regulations, some of which definitions relate to the whole of the JSA Regulations 2013 (see reg.2(1) and (2)) and some of which only apply to specified Parts. 1.743

"Child". The restriction to a person under 16 gives rise to the need to define "young person" in reg.2(2) of the JSA Regulations 2013 to cater for the over-15s, referring on to the definition of "qualifying young person" in s.142 of the SSCBA 1992 for child benefit purposes (see the notes to reg.2(2)).

"Couple". The 2014 definition of "couple" (including civil partners for the first time) was significantly amended with effect from December 2, 2019 by the Civil Partnership (Opposite-sex Couples) Regulations 2019 (SI 2019/1458), the same date on which the amendment to the definition of "civil partnership" in the Civil Partnerships Act 2014 and Sch.1 to the Interpretation Act 1978 came into force. Those amendments extended the definition to include partners of the opposite sex. They make it easier for persons to come within para.(a) of the definition of couple, providing that the people who are married or members of a civil partnership are members of the same household. They perhaps make the application of para.(b) on living together as if a married couple or civil partners slightly more problematic. No circumstances appear to have been prescribed for the purposes of para.(b) where the meaning therein is not be applied.

The so-called cohabitation rule in para.(b) and the issue of being members of the same household in para.(a) are unlikely to cause frequent problems in new style JSA. Accordingly, readers are referred to the notes to reg.2(1) of the Income Support Regulations in Vol.V of this series on those matters.

"Employed earner". See reg.2(1) of the JSA Regulations 2013, referring on to s.2(1)(a) of the SSCBA 1992.

"Employment". See reg.2(1) of the JSA Regulations 2013, which expressly includes any trade, business, profession, office or vocation, except in relation to s.14 (trade disputes) where it means employed earner's employment for the purposes of the SSCBA 1992.

"Family". The definition effectively covers couples with or without children and single claimants with children (under 16) or a qualifying young person (16–19 in full-time non-advanced education) in the household. The single claimant or one of the couple must be "responsible" for the child or qualifying young person for them to count as part of the family. Regulation 3(3) of the JSA Regulations 2013 makes "a person of a prescribed description" a "young person", which reg.2(2) then defines as someone within the definition of "qualifying young person" for child benefit purposes in s.142 of the SSCBA 1992 (see the notes to reg.2(2)). Regulation 3(1) extends the meaning of family to cover polygamous marriages.

On the general test of membership of the household and children, see *England v Secretary of State for Social Services* [1982] 3 F.L.R. 222; *R(FIS) 4/83* and *R(SB) 14/87*.

"FAS payments". "PPF payments" (see below) are not available in respect of pension schemes that wound up before April 6, 2005. Payments under the Financial Assistance Scheme Regulations 2005 are intended to cover defined benefit occupational pension schemes that wound up between January 1997 and April 2005 because of employer insolvency.

"Occupational pension scheme". Section 1(1) of the Pension Schemes Act 1993 (as amended by s.239 of the Pensions Act 2004 with effect from September 22, 2005 in the case of an occupational pension scheme that has its main administration in the UK and with effect from April 6, 2006 in all other cases (see art.2(7) of the Pensions Act 2004 (Commencement No.6, Transitional Provisions and Savings) Order 2005 (SI 2005/1720), and as further amended with effect from November 26, 2007 by reg.2(b) of the Occupational Pension Schemes (EEA States) Regulations 2007 (SI 2007/3014)) defines an "occupational pension scheme" as:

"a pension scheme—

(a) that—
  (i) for the purpose of providing benefits to, or in respect of, people with service in employments of a description, or
  (ii) for that purpose and also for the purpose of providing benefits to, or in respect of, other people,

  is established by, or by persons who include, a person to whom subsection (2) applies when the scheme is established or (as the case may be) to whom that subsection would have applied when the scheme was established had that subsection then been in force, and

(b) that has its main administration in the United Kingdom or outside the EEA states,

or a pension scheme that is prescribed or is of a prescribed description."

Section 1(2)–(5) provides:

"(2) This subsection applies—

(a) where people in employments of the description concerned are employed by someone, to a person who employs such people,
(b) to a person in an employment of that description, and
(c) to a person representing interests of a description framed so as to include—
  (i) interests of persons who employ people in employments of the description mentioned in paragraph (a), or
  (ii) interests of people in employments of that description.

(3) For the purposes of subsection (2), if a person is in an employment of the description concerned by reason of holding an office (including an elective office) and is entitled to remuneration for holding it, the person responsible

  for paying the remuneration shall be taken to employ the office-holder.

(4) In the definition in subsection (1) of "occupational pension scheme", the reference to a description includes a description framed by reference to an employment being of any of two or more kinds.

(5) In subsection (1) "pension scheme" (except in the phrases "occupational pension scheme", "personal pension scheme" and "public service pension scheme") means a scheme or other arrangements, comprised in one or more instruments or agreements, having or capable of having effect so as to provide benefits to or in respect of people—
  (a) on retirement,
  (b) on having reached a particular age, or
  (c) on termination of service in an employment."

1.744 *Chief Constable of Derbyshire Constabulary v Clark* [2023] EAT 135; [2024] I.C.R. 239 contains a lengthy discussion of the legal background in answering the question whether a police disablement gratuity under reg.12 of the Police Injury

Benefit Regulations 2006 fell within the definition of "occupational pension scheme" in s.1 of the Pension Schemes Act 1993, as amended. The gratuity was payable to officers injured in the execution of their duty who had ceased to be a member of a police force and who became totally and permanently disabled as a result of the injury, within 12 months of the injury. The two claimants were refused gratuities because more than 12 months had elapsed between the injury and the disablement. They wished to challenge that ground of refusal in an employment tribunal (ET) as demonstrating disability discrimination. It was thought that the ET would only have jurisdiction if the gratuity formed part of an occupational pension scheme. The scheme of injury benefits was separated from the arrangements for police pensions. The President of the Employment Appeal Tribunal, Eady J, held that the gratuity did not fall within the Pension Schemes Act definition because, although it was a condition of payment that the officer had ceased to be a member of a police force, entitlement could only be established at the point where the officer was deemed to be totally and permanently disabled. The regulation did not require any causative link between the ceasing of employment and the injury or disablement. Thus, the benefit was not provided on retirement or termination of service. On the claimants' appeal, the Court of Appeal confirmed that analysis, while ruling that the ET had jurisdiction for another reason (*Clark v Chief Constable of Derbyshire* [2024] EWCA Civ 676).

"Pensionable age". The prescribed meaning is in reg.2(1) of the JSA Regulations 2013, i.e. the same meaning as under s.122(1) of the SSCBA 1992, which in turn refers on to the rules in para.1 of Sch.4 to the Pensions Act 1995. The rules are now the same for men and women. For anyone born after October 5, 1954 but before April 6, 1960, pensionable age is 66. For anyone born after April 5, 1960 but before March 6, 1961, the pensionable age increases by one month for each month after the first date. For anyone born after March 5, 1961 but before April 6, 1977, pensionable age is 67. 1.745

"Personal pension scheme". The meaning in s.1(1) of the Pension Schemes Act 1993 (as amended by s.239 of the Pensions Act 2004 with effect from April 6, 2006 (see art.2(7) of the Pensions Act 2004 (Commencement No.6, Transitional Provisions and Savings) Order 2005 (SI 2005/1720), and as further amended with effect from April 6, 2007 by the Finance Act 2007 Sch.27 Pt 3(2) para.1) is:

> "a pension scheme that—
> (a) is not an occupational pension scheme, and
> (b) is established by a person within section 154(1) of the Finance Act 2004."

See the notes on "occupational pension scheme" (above) for the further definition of "pension scheme" in s.1(5)

"PPF payments". The Pension Protection Fund ("PPF") was set up under the Pensions Act 2004 in order to provide protection for members of defined benefit (i.e. normally final salary) occupational pension schemes and in relation to the defined elements of hybrid pension schemes in the event of the employer's insolvency. For the complex provisions see Pt 2 of the Pensions Act 2004.

"Public service pension scheme". A "public service pension scheme" is defined in s.1(1) of the Pensions Schemes Act 1993 as:

> "an occupational pension scheme [as defined above] established by or under an enactment or the Royal prerogative or a Royal charter, being a scheme
> (a) all the particulars of which are set out in, or in a legislative instrument made under, an enactment, Royal warrant or charter, or
> (b) which cannot come into force, or be amended, without the scheme or amendment being approved by a Minister of the Crown or government department or by the Scottish Ministers."

The term includes:

> "any occupational pension scheme established, with the concurrence of the Treasury, by or with the approval of any Minister of the Crown or established

by or with the approval of the Scottish Ministers and any occupational pension scheme prescribed by regulations made by the Secretary of State and the Treasury jointly as being a scheme which ought in their opinion to be treated as a public service pension scheme for the purposes of this Act."

1.746 *Subsection (3)*

Section 35(3) provides that, subject to any regulations made for this specific purpose, the term "earnings" is to be construed in accordance with s.3 of the SSCBA and para.6 of Sch.1. Under new style JSA, the amount of any earnings is only relevant to the condition of entitlement in s.2(1)(c) (that earnings must not exceed the amount of the applicable age-related allowance) and to potential deductions from the amount payable under s.4(1)(b). Section 3 of the SSCBA 1992 provides that "earnings "includes any remuneration or profit derived from employment and that their amount is to be calculated or estimated in the way prescribed by regulations, so that s.35(3) appears to extend to the method of calculation or estimation of earnings. The regulations made under s.3 of the SSCBA 1992 are the Computation of Earnings Regulations (see Pt III of this volume). The definition of "earnings" in reg.2(1) of the JSA Regulations 2013, expressly for the purposes of s.35(3), provides that the term is to have the meaning in reg.58 for employed earners and in reg.60 for self-employed earners. However, those regulations are only concerned with what sort of payments or receipts count as earnings for those purposes. The calculation of the amount of earnings, including any disregards and deductions for income tax and social security and pension contribution, to be attributed to any week is the subject of other regulations. There is therefore an argument that that process is to be carried out under the Computation of Earnings Regulations, which would produce similar but not by any means identical results. It is to be noted that in *CJSA/3928/2003* and *CJSA/3931/2003* Commissioner Howell applied the Computation of Earnings Regulations in relation to s.2(1)(c) of the old style Jobseekers Act 1995. However, the problems may be more apparent than real. In relation to s.4(1)(b) and the deduction of earnings, reg.50 of the JSA Regulations 2013 provides that the deduction is to be the amount as calculated in accordance with the whole of Pt 7 (i.e. regs 53-63). That specific provision under the power in s.4(1)(b) presumably indicates an intention contrary to any general inconsistent effect under s.35(3) even though reg.50 does not expressly mention s.35(3). In relation to s.2(1)(c), reg.48 of the JSA Regulations 2013 provides that in calculating the prescribed amount of earnings that cannot be exceeded the disregards in the Schedule to the Regulations are to be applied. That provision would not be necessary (indeed would be problematic) if those disregards under Pt 7 were to be applied in calculating the amount of the claimant's earnings. The existence of the specifically targeted new style JSA disregards is the major difference between the Computation of Earnings Regulations calculations and those under Pt 7 of the JSA Regulations 2013.

Regulations and orders

1.747 **36.**—(1) Any power under this Act to make regulations or orders, other than an order under section 8(3), 9(13, 16(4) or 19(10)(a), shall be exercisable by statutory instrument.

(1A) [1. . .]

(2) Any such power may be exercised—

(a) either in relation to all cases to which it extends, or in relation to those cases subject to specified exceptions, or in relation to any specified cases or classes of case;

(b) so as to make, as respects the cases in relation to which it is exercised—

(i) the full provision to which the power extends or any less provision (whether by way of exception or otherwise),

(ii) the same provision for all cases in relation to which it is exercised, or different provision for different cases or different classes of case or different provision as respects the same case or class of case for different purposes of this Act,

(iii) any such provision either unconditionally or subject to any specified condition.

(3) Where any such power is expressed to be exercisable for alternative purposes it may be exercised in relation to the same case for any or all of those purposes.

(4) Any such power includes power—

(a) to make such incidental, supplemental, consequential or transitional provision as appears to the Secretary of State, or (in the case of regulations made by the Treasury) to the Treasury, to be expedient; and

(b) to provide for a person to exercise a discretion in dealing with any matter.

(4A) [1. . .].

(5) Any power to make regulations or an order for the purposes of any provision of this Act is without prejudice to any power to make regulations or an order for the purposes of any other provision.

AMENDMENT

1. Welfare Reform Act 2012 Sch.14 Pt 4 (trigger date on or after April 29, 2013).

DEFINITION

"regulations"—see s.35(1).

Parliamentary control

37.—(1) Subsection (2) applies in relation to the following regulations (whether made alone or with other regulations)— **1.748**

(a) regulations made under, or by virtue of, any provision of this Act other than—

(i) section [4. . .], 26, 29 or 40,

(ii) paragraph (b) of the definition of "pension payments" in section 35(1), or

(iii) paragraph 17 of Schedule 1,

before the date on which jobseeker's allowances first become payable;

[3(aa) the first regulations to be made under section 6J or 6K;]

(ab) [4. . .];

(b) the first regulations to be made under section 26;

(c) regulations made under section [1. . .], 29, paragraph (b) of the definition of "pension payments" in section 35(1) [2. . .] or paragraph 8B or 17 of Schedule 1.

(2) No regulations to which this subsection applies shall be made unless a draft of the statutory instrument containing the regulations has been laid before Parliament and approved by a resolution of each House.

(3) Any other statutory instrument made under this Act, other than one made under section 41(2), shall be subject to annulment in pursuance of a resolution of either House of Parliament.

AMENDMENTS

1. Welfare Reform Act 2012 s.47 (March 20, 2012).
2. Welfare Reform Act 2012 Sch.14 Pt 6 (May 8, 2012).
3. Welfare Reform Act 2012 s.49(6) (February 25, 2013).
4. Welfare Reform Act 2012 Sch.14 Pt 4 (trigger date on or after April 29, 2013).

DEFINITION

"regulations"—see s.35(1).

General financial arrangements

1.749 **38.** [*Omitted as not relevant*]

Provision for Northern Ireland

1.750 **39.** [*Omitted as not relevant*]

Transitional provisions

1.751 **40.**—(1) The Secretary of State may by regulations make such transitional provision, consequential provision or savings as he considers necessary or expedient for the purposes of or in connection with—

(a) the coming into force of any provision of this Act; or
(b) the operation of any enactment repealed or amended by any such provision during any period when the repeal or amendment is not wholly in force.

(2) Regulations under this section may in particular make provision—

(a) for the termination or cancellation of awards of unemployment benefit or income support;
(b) for a person whose award of unemployment benefit or income support has been terminated or cancelled under regulations made by virtue of paragraph (a) to be treated as having been awarded a jobseeker's allowance (a "transitional allowance")—
 (i) of such a kind,
 (ii) for such period,
 (iii) of such an amount, and
 (iv) subject to such conditions,

 as may be determined in accordance with the regulations;
(c) for a person's continuing entitlement to a transitional allowance to be determined by reference to such provision as may be made by the regulations;
(d) for the termination of an award of a transitional allowance;
(e) for the review of an award of a transitional allowance;
(f) for a contribution-based jobseeker's allowance not to be payable for a prescribed period where a person is disqualified for receiving unemployment benefit;
(g) that days which were days of unemployment for the purposes of entitlement to unemployment benefit, and such other days as may be prescribed, are to be treated as having been days during which a person was, or would have been, entitled to a jobseeker's allowance;
(h) that days which were days of entitlement to unemployment benefit, and such other days as may be prescribed, are to be treated as

having been days of entitlement to a contribution-based jobseeker's allowance;

(i) that the rate of a contribution-based transitional allowance is to be calculated by reference to the rate of unemployment benefit paid or payable.

DEFINITIONS

"entitled"—see s.35(1).
"regulations"—*ibid.*

GENERAL NOTE

Although the repeal of this provision was included in Pt 1 of Sch.14 to the Welfare Reform Act 2012 it was not brought into operation with rest of Pt 1 by the Commencement No.9 Order (SI 2013/983). So far as can be ascertained, the repeal has not been brought into operation by any subsequent Commencement Order, although the section appears to be redundant in the context of new style JSA. 1.752

Short title, commencement, extent, etc.

41.—(1) This Act may be cited as the Jobseekers Act 1995. 1.753

(2) Section 39 and this section (apart from subsections (4) and (5)) come into force on the passing of this Act, but otherwise the provisions of this Act come into force on such day as the Secretary of State may by order appoint.

(3) Different days may be appointed for different purposes.

(4) Schedule 2 makes consequential amendments.

(5) The repeals set out in Schedule 3 shall have effect.

(6) Apart from this section, section 39 and paragraphs 11 to 16, 28, 67 and 68 of Schedule 2, this Act does not extend to Northern Ireland.

SCHEDULE A1

[Repealed by the Welfare Reform Act 2012, s.60(1), with effect from May 8, 2012] 1.754

SCHEDULE 1

SUPPLEMENTARY PROVISIONS

Remunerative work

1.—(1) For the purposes of this Act, "remunerative work" has such meaning as may be prescribed. 1.755

(2) Regulations may prescribe circumstances in which, for the purposes of this Act—

(a) a person who is not engaged in remunerative work is to be treated as engaged in remunerative work; or

(b) a person who is engaged in remunerative work is to be treated as not engaged in remunerative work.

Limited capability for work

2.—(1) The question whether a person has, or does not have, limited capability for work shall be determined, for the purposes of this Act, in accordance with the provisions of Part 1 of the Welfare Reform Act 2007 (employment and support allowance) [[3]or Part 1 of the Welfare Reform Act 2012 (universal credit) as the Secretary of State considers appropriate in the person's case]. 1.756

(2) References in Part 1 of the Welfare Reform Act 2007 to the purposes of that Part shall be construed, where the provisions of that Part have effect for the purposes of this Act, as references to the purposes of this Act.

[3(3) References in Part 1 of the Welfare Reform Act 2012 to the purposes of that Part are to be construed, where the provisions of that Part have effect for the purposes of this Act, as references to the purposes of this Act.]

Linking periods

1.757 **3.**—Regulations may provide—

(a) for jobseeking periods which are separated by not more than a prescribed number of weeks to be treated, for purposes of this Act, as one jobseeking period;

(b) for prescribed periods ("linked periods") to be linked, for purposes of this Act, to any jobseeking period.

Waiting days

1.758 **4.**—Except in prescribed circumstances, a person is not entitled to a jobseeker's allowance in respect of a prescribed number of days at the beginning of a jobseeking period.

Periods of less than a week

1.759 **5.**—Regulations may make provision in relation to—

(a) entitlement to a jobseeker's allowance, or

(b) the amount payable by way of such an allowance,

in respect of any period of less than a week.

Employment protection sums

1.760 **6.**—(1) In relation to any [3. . .] jobseeker's allowance, regulations may make provision—

(a) for any employment protection sum to be treated as earnings payable by such person, to such person and for such period as may be determined in accordance with the regulations; and

(b) for any such period so far as it is not a period of employment, to be treated as a period of employment.

(2) In this paragraph "employment protection sum" means—

(a) any sum, or a prescribed part of any sum—

(i) payable, in respect of arrears of pay, under an order for reinstatement or re-engagement made under the Employment Rights Act 1996;

(ii) payable, by way of pay, under an order made under that Act for the continuation of a contract of employment;

(iii) payable, by way of remuneration, under a protection award made under section 189 of the Trade Union and Labour Relations (Consolidation) Act 1992; and

(b) any prescribed sum which the regulations provide is to be treated as related to any sum within paragraph (a).

Pension payments

1.761 **7.**—Regulations may make provision, for the purposes of any provision of, or made under, this Act—

(a) for such sums by way of pension payments to be disregarded for prescribed purposes;

(b) as to the week in which any pension payments are to be treated as having begun;

(c) for treating, in a case where—

(i) a lump sum is paid to a person in connection with a former employment of his or arrangement are made for a lump sum to be so paid; or

(ii) benefits of any description are made available to a person in connection with a former employment of his or arrangements are made for them to be made so available; or

(iii) pension payments to a person are assigned, reduced or postponed or are made otherwise than weekly,

such payments as being made to a person by way of weekly pension payments as are specified in or determined under the regulations;

(d) for the method of determining whether pension payments are made to a person for any week and their amount.

Exemptions

8.—[4. . .]. 1.762
8A.—[4. . .].
8B.—[5. . .].
9.—[4. . .].

Continuity of claims and awards: persons ceasing to be a joint-claim couple

9A.—[4. . .].

Continuity of claims and awards: persons again becoming a joint-claim couple

9B.—[4. . .].

Continuity of claims and awards: couple becoming to be a joint-claim couple

9C.—[4. . .].

Paragraphs 9A to 9C: supplementary

9D.—[4. . .]. 1.763

Claims yet to be determined and suspended payments

10.—[4. . .].

Presence in and absence from Great Britain

11.—(1) Regulations may provide that in prescribed circumstances a claimant who is not in Great Britain may nevertheless be entitled to a [4. . .] jobseeker's allowance.

(2) Regulations may make provision for the purposes of this Act as to the circumstances in which a person is to be treated as being or not being in Great Britain.

Households

12.—Regulations may make provision for the purposes of this Act as to the circumstances in which persons are to be treated as being or not being members of the same household. 1.764

Responsibility for another person

13.—Regulations may make provision for the purposes of this Act as to the circumstances in which one person is to be treated as responsible or not responsible for another.

Relevant education

14.—Regulations may make provision for the purposes of this Act— 1.765

(a) as to what is or not be treated as relevant education; and
(b) as to the circumstances in which a person is or is not to be treated as receiving relevant education.

[2**14AA.**—For any purposes of this Act regulations may provide for—

(a) circumstances in which a person is to be treated as having or not having a good reason for an act or omission;
(b) matters which are or are not to be taken into account in determining whether a person has a good reason for an act or omission.]

Calculation of periods

15.—Regulations may make provisions for calculating periods for any purposes of this Act.

Employment on ships etc.

16.—(1) Regulations may modify any provision of this Act in its application to any person who is, has been, or is to be— 1.766

(a) employed on board any ship, vessel, hovercraft or aircraft,
(b) outside Great Britain at any prescribed time or in any prescribed circumstances, or
(c) in prescribed employment in connection with continental shelf operations, so far as that provision relates to a [4. . .] jobseeker's allowance.

(2) The regulations may in particular provide—
(a) for any such provision to apply even though it would not otherwise apply;
(b) for any such provision not to apply even though it would otherwise apply;
(c) for the taking of evidence, in a country or territory outside Great Britain, by a British consular official or other prescribed person;
(d) for enabling payment of the whole, or any part of a [4. . .] jobseeker's allowance to be paid to such of the claimant's dependants as may be prescribed.

Additional conditions

17.—Regulations may require additional conditions to be satisfied with respect to the payment of a jobseeker's allowance to any person who is, has been, or is to be, in employment which falls within a prescribed description.

Benefits Act purposes

1.767 **18.**—Regulations may provide for—
(a) a jobseeker's allowance;
(b) [4. . .];
(c) [4. . .],
to be treated, for prescribed purposes of the Benefits Act, as a benefit, or a benefit of a prescribed description.

Treatment of information supplied as information relating to Social Security

19.—Information supplied in pursuance of any provision made by or under this Act [1. . .] shall be taken for all purposes to be information relating to social security.

AMENDMENTS

1. Welfare Reform Act 2012 Sch.14 Pt 6 (May 8, 2012).
2. Welfare Reform Act 2012 s.46(3)(b) (June 10, 2012, for purposes of making regulations; October 22, 2012).
3. Universal Credit (Consequential, Supplementary, Incidental and Miscellaneous Provisions Regulations 2013 (SI 2013/630) reg.10 (April 29, 2013).
4. Welfare Reform Act 2012 Sch.14 Pt 1 (trigger date on or after April 29, 2013).
5. Welfare Reform Act 2012 Sch.14 Pt 4 (trigger date on or after April 29, 2013).

DEFINITIONS

"the Benefits Act"—see s.35(1).
"employment"—see s.35(1) and JSA Regulations 2013 reg.2(1).
"Great Britain"—see s.35(1).
"jobseeking period"—*ibid.*
"pension payments"—*ibid.*
"regulations"—*ibid.*
"prescribed"—*ibid.*
"week"—*ibid.*

GENERAL NOTE

1.768 Schedule 1 supplies a variety of regulation-making powers. See the notes to the regulations identified below for further discussion.

On para.1, see regs 42–45. On para.3, see regs 37–40 for jobseeking periods, linked periods and linking. On para.4, see reg.36 on waiting days. On para.5, see regs 64–65 on part-weeks. On para.6, see reg.58(1)(f)–(h) on treatment as earnings. The power in para.6(1)(b) has not been exercised. Under para.7, see reg.51 on pension payments. On para.11(2), see reg.41. The power in para.11(1) appears not to have been exercised in relation to new style JSA. The powers in paras 12 and 13 appear not to have been exercised in relation to new style JSA. On para.14, see reg.45 and note that this covers students of any age in full-time advanced education as well as 16–19 year-olds who count as "qualifying young persons" and anyone else on a course or training that is not compatible with a work-related requirement imposed on them. The powers in 14AA appear not to have been exercised in relation to new style JSA, consistently with the approach in universal credit. The power in para.16 appears not to have been exercised in relation to new style JSA. On para.17, see regs 67–75.

As well as inserting para.14AA, s.46(3) of the Welfare Reform Act 2012 also, in paras (a) and (c), purported to amend para.14B of Sch.1 and a heading preceding para.14B (and maybe thus preceding para.14AA). But s.30(1) of the Welfare Reform Act 2009 inserting para.14B and the heading appears never to have been brought into operation. Therefore (subject to correction in the future) those provisions have been omitted.

Pensions Act 1995

(1995 c.26)

Sections Reproduced

Part II

State Pensions

126. Equalisation of pensionable age and of entitlement to certain benefits. **1.769**
127. [*Repeated*].
128. Additional pension: calculation of surpluses.

Schedules

Schedule 4—Equalisation.
Part I—Pensionable ages for men and women.
Part II—Entitlement to certain pension and other benefits. Part III—Consequential amendments.

Part II

State Pensions

Equalisation of pension age and of entitlement to certain benefits [1 and increase in pensionable age] **1.770**

126.—Schedule 4 to this Act, of which—

(a) Part I has effect to equalise pensionable age for men and women [1 [2 and then to increase it.]],
(b) Part II makes provision for bringing equality for men and women to certain pension and other benefits, and
(c) Part III makes consequential amendments of enactments,

shall have effect.

Amendment

1. Pensions Act 2007 Sch.3 paras 1 and 2 (September 26, 2007).
2. Pensions Act 2011 Sch.1 (January 3, 2012).

General Note

In *R (Delve & Anor) v The Secretary of State for Work and Pensions* [2020] EWCA Civ 1199, the Court of Appeal rejected a challenge brought against the equalisation of state pension ages for men and women, as provided for by section 126 (as amended) and connected subordinate legislation, which involves raising the state pension age for women born after 5 April 1950. The case was brought by two women who, at the date of the Court's decision, had state pension ages of 66 in common with any man or woman born between 6 October 1954 and 5 April 1960. The claimants' challenge had been rejected by the High Court (Divisional Court) and the case went on appeal to the Court of Appeal.

The first ground of challenge was that the claimants had been subjected to discrimination, contrary to Article 14 of the European Convention on Human Rights, taken with Article 1 of Protocol 1 to the Convention. Article 1 provides that every person is entitled to the peaceful enjoyment of her possessions, and that no one is to be deprived of her possessions except in the public interest and subject to conditions provided for by law and the general principles of international law. The claimants drew attention to the staggered equalisation of state pension age, which divides the female (and male) population into cohorts by reference to date of birth, and argued that they were subject to a difference of treatment as compared with the cohorts for older women namely for those born between April 6, 1950 and October 5, 1954 (pensionable age falling between 60 and 66) and for women born before April 6, 1950 pensionable age of 60). On the basis that the claimants had established a difference of treatment, the issue under Article 14 was whether the difference was justified. The Court of Appeal held that there was no basis for impugning the High Court's conclusion that the legislation which equalised (and then raised) state pension age was justified. The legislation was operating in a field of macro-economic policy where "the decision-making power of Parliament is very great". The evidence of the UK Government, accepted by the High Court, was that there had been an urgent economic need for pensions reform and that, in formulating pensions policy, the Government had recognised the difficulties that women still face in building up adequate pension entitlement. The Court of Appeal agreed with the High Court's assessment that the Government's decision to strike the balance it did between various age groups, as expressed in the framing of equalisation cohorts, could not be described as manifestly without reasonable foundation. It was not therefore discriminatory contrary to Article 14 of the Convention.

The Court of Appeal also rejected the claimants' argument that the equalisation legislation was indirectly discriminatory on the ground of sex. The claimants had relied on Article 4 of the Social Security Directive which prohibits discrimination on the ground of sex, directly or indirectly, regarding, amongst other things, calculation of benefits and conditions governing the duration and retention of entitlement to benefits. The Court, however, accepted the UK Government's argument that Article 7 of the Directive applied, which provides that the Directive is without prejudice to the right of Member States to exclude from its scope "the determination of pensionable age for the purposes of granting old age and retirement benefits". In particular, the claimants' argument that Article 7 does not permit progressive adaptation towards equalisation as opposed to temporary retention of differential pension ages, was rejected.

Finally, the Court of Appeal rejected the claimants' challenges to the High Court's findings that the steps taken by the UK Government to notify the claimants of changes to their pension entitlements were neither inadequate nor unreasonable. The High Court's finding was properly supported by the evidence before it of various measures taken by the UK Government to publicise changes to state pension age.

Enhancement of additional pension, etc., where family credit or disability working allowance paid

1.771 **127.**—[1 . . .]

AMENDMENT

1. Tax Credits Act 2002 Sch.6 para.1 (April 6, 2003).

Additional Pension: calculation of surplus

1.772 **128.**—*[Subsections (1) and (2) amend section 44 of the Social Security Contributions and Benefits Act 1992].*

(3) Section 148 of the Social Security Administration Act 1992 (revaluation of earnings factors) shall have effect in relation to surpluses in a person's earnings factors under section 44(5A) of the Social Security Contributions and Benefits Act 1992 [1 for the purposes of section 45(1) and (2)(a) and (b) of that Act] as it has effect in relation to earnings factors.

(4) Subject to subsections (5) [2, (5A)] and (6) below, this section has effect in relation to a person ("the pensioner") who attains pensionable age after 5th April, 2000.

(5) Where the pensioner is a woman, this section has effect in the case of additional pension falling to be calculated under sections 44 and 45 of the Social Security Contributions and Benefits Act 1992 by virtue of section 39 of that Act (widowed mother's allowance and widow's pension), including Category B retirement pension payable under section 48B(4), if her husband—

(a) dies after 5th April, 2000, and

(b) has not attained pensionable age on or before that date.

[2 (5A) This section has effect in the case of additional pension falling to be calculated under sections 44 and 45 of the Social Security Contributions and Benefits Act 1992 by virtue of section 39C(1) of that Act (widowed parent's allowance), including Category B retirement pension payable under section 48BB(2), if the pensioner's spouse—

(a) dies after 5th April, 2000; and

(b) has not attained pensionable age on or before that date.]

(6) This section has effect where additional pension falls to be calculated under sections 44 and 45 of the Social Security Contributions and Benefits Act 1992 as applied by section [3 . . .] [2, 48B(2) or 48BB(5)] of that Act (other Category B retirement pension) if—

(a) the pensioner attains pensionable age after 5th April, 2000, and

(b) the pensioner's spouse has not attained pensionable age on or before that date.

AMENDMENTS

1. Child Support, Pensions and Social Security Act 2000 s.33 (January 25, 2001).
2. Welfare Reform and Pensions Act 1999 s.70 (April 9, 2001).
3. Pensions Act 2014 Sch.12 para.72 (April 6, 2016).

SCHEDULE 4

[3 EQUALISATION OF AND INCREASE IN PENSIONABLE AGE FOR MEN AND WOMEN]

PART I

PENSIONABLE AGES FOR MEN AND WOMEN

1.—The following rules apply for the purposes of the enactments relating to social security, that is, the following Acts and the instruments made, or having effect as if made, under them: the Social Security Contributions and Benefits Act 1992, the Social Security Administration Act 1992 [1 the Pension Schemes Act 1993][5, the State Pension Credit Act 2002][9, Part 1 of the Welfare Reform Act 2007 and the Pensions Act 2014.] **1.773**

Rules

(1) A man [3 born before [4 December 6, 1953]] attains pensionable age when he attains the age of 65 years. **1.774**

(2) A woman born before 6th April 1950 attains pensionable age when she attains the age of 60.

(3) A woman born on any day in a period mentioned in column 1 of [3 table 1] attains pensionable age at the commencement of the day shown against that period in column 2.

[3 (4) [4*omitted*].]

1.775 [[2] Table 1]

(1) *Period within which woman's birthday falls*	(2) *Day pensionable age attained*
6th April 1950 to 5th May 1950	6th May 2010
6th May 1950 to 5th June 1950	6th July 2010
6th June 1950 to 5th July 1950	6th September 2010
6th July 1950 to 5th August 1950	6th November 2010
6th August 1950 to 5th September 1950	6th January 2011
6th September 1950 to 5th October 1950	6th March 2011
6th October 1950 to 5th November 1950	6th May 2011
6th November 1950 to 5th December 1950	6th July 2011
6th December 1950 to 5th January 1951	6th September 2011
6th January 1951 to 5th February 1951	6th November 2011
6th February 1951 to 5th March 1951	6th January 2012
6th March 1951 to 5th April 1951	6th March 2012
6th April 1951 to 5th May 1951	6th May 2012
6th May 1951 to 5th June 1951	6th July 2012
6th June 1951 to 5th July 1951	6th September 2012
6th July 1951 to 5th August 1951	6th November 2012
6th August 1951 to 5th September 1951	6th January 2013
6th September 1951 to 5th October 1951	6th March 2013
6th October 1951 to 5th November 1951	6th May 2013
6th November 1951 to 5th December 1951	6th July 2013
6th December 1951 to 5th January 1952	6th September 2013
6th January 1952 to 5th February 1952	6th November 2013
6th February 1952 to 5th March 1952	6th January 2014
6th March 1952 to 5th April 1952	6th March 2014
6th April 1952 to 5th May 1952	6th May 2014
6th May 1952 to 5th June 1952	6th July 2014
6th June 1952 to 5th July 1952	6th September 2014
6th July 1952 to 5th August 1952	6th November 2014
6th August 1952 to 5th September 1952	6th January 2015
6th September 1952 to 5th October 1952	6th March 2015
6th October 1952 to 5th November 1952	6th May 2015
6th November 1952 to 5th December 1952	6th July 2015
6th December 1952 to 5th January 1953	6th September 2015
6th January 1953 to 5th February 1953	6th November 2015
6th February 1953 to 5th March 1953	6th January 2016
6th March 1953 to 5th April 1953	6th March 2016
[6th April 1953 to 5th May 1953	6th July 2016
6th May 1953 to 5th June 1953	6th November 2016
6th June 1953 to 5th July 1953	6th March 2017
6th July 1953 to 5th August 1953	6th July 2017
6th August 1953 to 5th September 1953	6th November 2017
6th September 1953 to 5th October 1953	6th March 2018
6th October 1953 to 5th November 1953	6th July 2018
6th November 1953 to 5th December 1953	6th November 2018]

[[2] (5) A person born on any day in a period mentioned in column 1 of table 2 attains pensionable age at the commencement of the day shown against that period in column 2.

1.776 [[10]Table 2

(1) *Period within which birthday falls*	(2) *Day pensionable age attained*
6th December 1953 to 5th January 1954	6th March 2019
6th January 1954 to 5th February 1954	6th May 2019

[10 TABLE 2

(1) Period within which birthday falls	(2) Day pensionable age attained
6th February 1954 to 5th March 1954	6th July 2019
6th March 1954 to 5th April 1954	6th September 2019
6th April 1954 to 5th May 1954	6th November 2019
6th May 1954 to 5th June 1954	6th January 2020
6th June 1954 to 5th July 1954	6th March 2020
6th July 1954 to 5th August 1954	6th May 2020
6th August 1954 to 5th September 1954	6th July 2020
6th September 1954 to 5th October 1954	6th September 2020]

(6) A person born after 5th October 1954 but before [5 6th April 1960] attains pensionable age when the person attains the age of 66.

[5 (7) A person born on any day in a period mentioned in column 1 of table 3 attains pensionable age when the person attains the age shown against that period in column 2.

TABLE 3 **1.777**

(1) Period within which birthday falls	(2) Day pensionable age attained
6th April 1960 to 5th May 1960	66 years and 1 month
6th May 1960 to 5th June 1960	66 years and 2 months
6th June 1960 to 5th July 1960	66 years and 3 months
6th July 1960 to 5th August 1960	66 years and 4 months
6th August 1960 to 5th September 1960	66 years and 5 months
6th September 1960 to 5th October 1960	66 years and 6 months
6th October 1960 to 5th November 1960	66 years and 7 months
6th November 1960 to 5th December 1960	66 years and 8 months
6th December 1960 to 5th January 1961	66 years and 9 months
6th January 1961 to 5th February 1961	66 years and 10 months
6th February 1961 to 5th March 1961	66 years and 11 months

(7A) For the purposes of table 3— **1.778**

(a) a person born on 31st July 1960 is to be taken to attain the age of 66 years and 4 months at the commencement of 30th November 2026;

(b) a person born on 31st December 1960 is to be taken to attain the age of 66 years and 9 months at the commencement of 30th September 2027;

(c) a person born on 31st January 1961 is to be taken to attain the age of 66 years and 10 months at the commencement of 30th November 2027.

(8) A person born after [7 5th March 1961] but before 6th April 1977 attains pensionable age when the person attains the age of 67.

(9) A person born on any day in a period mentioned in column 1 of table 4 attains pensionable age at the commencement of the day shown against that period in column 2.

TABLE 4 **1.779**

(1) Period within which birthday falls	(2) Day pensionable age attained
6th April 1977 to 5th May 1977	6th May 2044
6th May 1977 to 5th June 1977	6th July 2044
6th June 1977 to 5th July 1977	6th September 2044
6th July 1977 to 5th August 1977	6th November 2044
6th August 1977 to 5th September 1977	6th January 2045
6th September 1977 to 5th October 1977	6th March 2045
6th October 1977 to 5th November 1977	6th May 2045
6th November 1977 to 5th December 1977	6th July 2045
6th December 1977 to 5th January 1978	6th September 2045

TABLE 4

(1) *Period within which birthday falls*	(2) *Day pensionable age attained*
6th January 1978 to 5th February 1978	6th November 2045
6th February 1978 to 5th March 1978	6th January 2046
6th March 1978 to 5th April 1978	6th March 2046

(10) A person born after 5th April 1978 attains pensionable age when the person attains the age of 68.]

PART II

ENTITLEMENT TO CERTAIN PENSIONS AND OTHER BENEFITS

Pension increases for dependent spouses

1.780 **2.**— [4 . . .]

Category B retirement pensions

1.781 **3.**—(1) *Omitted.*
(2) [10 . . .]
(3) [10 . . .]

Home responsibilities protection

1.782 **4.**—(1) In paragraph 5 of Schedule 3 to the Social Security Contributions and Benefits Act 1992 (contribution conditions for entitlement to retirement pension), in sub-paragraph (7)(a) (condition that contributor must have paid or been credited with contributions of the relevant class for not less than the requisite number of years modified in the case of those precluded from regular employment by responsibilities at home), "(or at least 20 of them, if that is less than half)" is omitted.

(2) This paragraph shall have effect in relation to any person attaining pensionable age on or after 6th April 2010.

5.—*Omitted.*

Increments

1.783 **6.**—(1) In section 54(1) of the Social Security Contributions and Benefits Act 1992 (election to defer right to pension), in paragraph (a), the words from "but" to "70" are omitted.

(2) In Schedule 5 to that Act—

(a) in paragraph 2(2), the definition of "period of enhancement" (and the preceding "and") are omitted, and
(b) for "period of enhancement" (in every other place in paragraphs 2 and 3 where it appears) there is substituted "period of deferment".

(3) In paragraph 2(3) of that Schedule, for "1/7th per cent." there is substituted "1/5th per cent."

(4) In paragraph 8 of that Schedule, sub-paragraphs (1) and (2) are omitted.

[2(5) The preceding sub-paragraphs shall come into force as follows—

(a) sub-paragraphs (1) and (4) shall come into force on 6th April 2005;
(b) sub-paragraphs (2) and (3) shall have effect in relation to incremental periods (within the meaning of Schedule 5 to the Social Security Contributions and Benefits Act 1992 (c. 4)) beginning on or after that date.]

Graduated retirement benefit

1.784 **7.**—*Omitted.*

Christmas bonus for pensioners

1.785 **8.**—*Omitted.*

PART III

CONSEQUENTIAL AMENDMENTS

Category B retirement pensions

21.—(1)–(14) *Omitted.* 1.786
(15) *Amends Schedule 5 to the Social Security Contributions and Benefits Act 1992.*
(16) Paragraph 5(1) of that Schedule (inserted by sub-paragraph (15) above) shall have effect, where W is a man who attained pensionable age before 6th April, 2010, as if paragraph (a) also required him to have been over pensionable age when S died.
(17) and (18) *Omitted.*

AMENDMENTS

1. State Pension Credit Act 2002 s.14 Sch.2 Pt.3 para.39 (October 6, 2003).
2. Pensions Act 2004 s.297 (April 6, 2005).
3. Pensions Act 2007 Sch.3 para.3 (September 26, 2007).
4. Pensions Act 2007 Sch.7 Pt 2 (September 26, 2007).
5. Welfare Reform Act 2007 s.28(1) Sch.3 para.13 (October 27, 2008).
6. Pensions Act 2011 s.1 (subs.2–6) (January 3, 2012).
7. Pensions Act 2014 s.26 (July 14, 2014).
8. Pensions Act 2014 s.23 Sch.12 Pt.1 para.30 (April 6, 2016).
9. Pensions Act 2014 Sch.12 para.73 (April 6, 2016).
10. Pensions Act 2011 s.1 (January 3, 2012).

Welfare Reform and Pensions Act 1999

(1999 c.30)

SECTIONS REPRODUCED

PART IV

PENSION SHARING

CHAPTER II

SHARING OF STATE SCHEME RIGHTS

CHAPTER II

SHARING OF STATE SCHEME RIGHTS

Shareable State Scheme rights

1.788 **47.**—(1) Pension sharing is available under this Chapter in relation to a person's shareable state scheme rights.

[1 (1A) For the purposes of this Chapter, a person's shareable state scheme rights are—

(a) the person's shareable old state scheme rights;

(b) the person's shareable new state scheme rights.]

(2) For the purposes of this Chapter, a person's shareable [1 old] state scheme rights are—

(a) his entitlement, or prospective entitlement, to a Category A retirement pension by virtue of section 44(3)(b) of the Contributions and Benefits Act ([2 . . .] additional pension), and

(b) his entitlement, or prospective entitlement, to a pension under section 55A [1 or 55AA] of that Act (shared additional pension).

[1 (3) For the purposes of this Chapter, a person's shareable new state scheme rights are the person's entitlement, or prospective entitlement, to the excess amount in a state pension under section 4 of the Pensions Act 2014.

(4) "The excess amount", in relation to a state pension under section 4 of the Pensions Act 2014, means any amount by which the rate of the pension exceeds the full rate of the state pension (see section 3 of that Act).

(5) In determining the rate of a state pension under section 4 of the Pensions Act 2014 for the purposes of this Chapter, ignore Schedule 6 to that Act (reduced rate elections: effect on rate of section 4 pension).]

AMENDMENTS

1. Pensions Act 2014 Sch.11 para.10 (April 6, 2016).
2. Pensions Act 2014 Sch.15 para. 14 (October 12, 2015).

Activation of Benefit Sharing

1.789 **48.**—(1) [2 Section 49 or 49A applies where any of the following has taken effect in relation to a person's shareable state scheme rights]—

(a) a pension sharing order under the Matrimonial Causes Act 1973,

[1 (aa) a pensions sharing order under Schedule 5 to the Civil Partnership Act 2004,]

(b) [3 . . .]

(c) [3 . . .]

(d) an order under Part III of the Matrimonial and Family Proceedings Act 1984 (financial relief in England and Wales in relation to overseas divorce etc.) corresponding to such an order as is mentioned in paragraph (a),

[4 (da) an order under Schedule 7 to the 2004 Act (financial relief in England and Wales after overseas dissolution etc of a civil partnership) corresponding to such an order as is mentioned in paragraph (aa),]

(e) a pension sharing order under the Family Law (Scotland) Act 1985,

(f) provision which corresponds to the provision which may be made by such an order and which—

(i) is contained in a qualifying agreement between the parties to a marriage [4 or between persons who are civil partners of each other],

(ii) is in such form as the Secretary of State may prescribe by regulations, and

(iii) takes effect on the grant, in relation to the marriage, of decree of divorce under the Divorce (Scotland) Act 1976 or of declarator of nullity [4 or (as the case may be) on the grant, in relation to the civil partnership, of decree of dissolution or of declarator of nullity],

(g) an order under Part IV of the Matrimonial and Family Proceedings Act 1984 (financial relief in Scotland in relation to overseas divorce etc.) [4 [or under Schedule 11 to the 2004 Act (financial provision in Scotland after overseas proceedings)]] corresponding to such an order as is mentioned in paragraph (e),

(h) a pension sharing order under [4 the Matrimonial Causes (Northern Ireland) Order 1978 (SI 1978/1045 (NI 15)),], and

(i) an order under Part IV of the Matrimonial and Family Proceedings (Northern Ireland) Order 1989 (financial relief in Northern Ireland in relation to overseas divorce etc.) corresponding to such an order as is mentioned in paragraph (h).

[4 (j) a pension sharing order under Schedule 15 to the 2004 Act, and

(k) an order under Schedule 17 to the 2004 Act (financial relief in Northern Ireland after overseas dissolution etc of a civil partnership) corresponding to such an order as is mentioned in paragraph (j)].

(2) [3...]

(3) [3...]

(4) [3...]

(5) [3...]

(6) For the purposes of this section, an order or provision falling within subsection (1)(e), (f) or (g) shall be deemed never to have taken effect if the Secretary of State does not receive before the end of the period of 2 months beginning with the relevant date—

(a) copies of the relevant [1 . . .] documents, and

(b) such information relating to the transferor and transferee as the Secretary of State may prescribe by regulations under section 34(1)(b)(ii).

(7) The relevant date for the purposes of subsection (6) is—

(a) in the case of an order or provision falling within subsection (1)(e) or (f), the date of the extract of the decree or declarator responsible for the divorce [4, dissolution] or annulment to which the order or provision relates, and

(b) in the cases of an order falling within subsection (1)(g), the date of disposal of the application under section 28 of the Matrimonial and Family Proceedings Act 1984 [4 or, where the order is under Schedule 11 to the 2004 Act, the date of disposal of the application under paragraph 2 of that Schedule].

(8) The reference in subsection (6)(a) to the relevant [1 . . .] documents is—

(a) in the case of an order falling within subsection (1)(e) or (g), to copies of the order and the order, decree or declarator responsible for the divorce or annulment to which it relates, and
(b) in the case of provision falling within subsection (1)(f), to—
  (i) copies of the provision and the order, decree or declarator responsible for the divorce [4, dissolution] or annulment to which it relates, and
  (ii) documentary evidence that the agreement containing the provision is one to which subsection (3)(a) applies.

(9) [5 The Court of Session or the sheriff] may, on the application of any person having an interest, make an order—
(a) extending the period of two months referred to in subsection (6), and
(b) if that period has already expired, providing that, if the Secretary of State receives the documents and information concerned before the end of the period specified in the order, subsection (6) is to be treated as never having applied.

AMENDMENTS

1. Civil Partnership Act 2004 Sch.24 (December 5, 2005).
2. Pensions Act 2014 Sch.11 para.11 (April 6, 2016).
3. Children and Families Act 2014 s.18(3) (May 13, 2014).
4. Civil Partnership Act 2004 Sch.27 (December 5, 2005).
5. Pensions Act 2008 s.128 (26 January, 2009).

Creation of State Scheme pension debits and credits [2: transferor in old state pension system or pension sharing activated before 6 April 2016]

1.790 **49.**—[2 (A1) This section applies if—
(a) the transferor is in the old state pension system, or
(b) the transferor is in the new state pension system but the transfer day was before 6 April 2016.

(1) Where this section applies because of a relevant order or provision—
(a) the transferor is subject, for the purposes of the relevant state pension legislation, to a debit of the appropriate amount, and
(b) the transferee is entitled, for the purposes of the relevant state pension legislation, to a credit of that amount.]

(2) Where the relevant order or provision specifies a percentage value to be transferred, the appropriate amount for the purposes of subsection (1) is the specified percentage of the cash equivalent on the transfer day of the transferor's shareable [2 old] state scheme rights immediately before that day.

(3) Where the relevant order or provision specifies an amount to be transferred, the appropriate amount for the purposes of subsection (1) is the lesser of—
(a) the specified amount, and
(b) the cash equivalent on the transfer day of the transferor's [2 shareable old] state scheme rights immediately before that day.

[1 (4) The Secretary of State may by regulations make provision about the calculation and verification of cash equivalents for the purposes of this section.

(4A) The power conferred by subsection (4) above includes power to provide–

(a) for calculation or verification in such manner as may be approved by or on behalf of the Government Actuary, and
(b) for things done under the regulations to be required to be done in accordance with guidance from time to time prepared by a person prescribed by the regulations.]

(5) In determining prospective entitlement to a Category A retirement pension for the purposes of this section, only tax years before that in which the transfer day falls shall be taken into account.

[[2] (5A) The fact that a person who reaches pensionable age on or after 6 April 2016 is not entitled to a pension of the kind mentioned in section 47(2)(a) or (b) does not affect the calculation under this section of the appropriate amount by reference to the transferor's prospective entitlement, immediately before the transfer day, to a pension of that kind.]

(6) In this section—

"relevant order or provision" means the order or provision by virtue of which this section applies;

[[2] "the relevant state pension legislation"—
(a) in relation to a transferor or transferee in the old state pension system, means Part 2 of the Contributions and Benefits Act, and
(b) in relation to a transferor or transferee in the new state pension system, means Part 1 of the Pensions Act 2014.]

"transfer day" means the day on which the relevant order or provision takes effect;

"transferor" means the person to whose rights the relevant order or provision relates;

"transferee" means the person for whose benefit the relevant order or provision is made.

AMENDMENTS

1. Child Support, Pensions and Social Security Act 2000 s.41(1) (September 29, 2000).
2. Pensions Act 2014 Sch.11 para.12 (April 6, 2016).

[[1] Creation of debits and credits: transferor in new state pension system and sharing activated on or after 6 April 2016

49A.–(1) This section applies if— 1.791
(a) the transferor is in the new state pension system, and
(b) the transfer day is 6 April 2016 or any later date.

(2) Where this section applies because of a relevant order or provision—
(a) the transferor is subject, for the purposes of section 14 of the Pensions Act 2014, to a debit of the shared weekly amount, and
(b) the transferee is entitled, for the purposes of the relevant state pension legislation, to a credit of the shared weekly amount.

(3) The shared weekly amount is the specified percentage of the excess amount of the transferor's state pension under section 4 of the Pensions Act 2014 as at the transfer day.

(4) For the purposes of calculating the shared weekly amount—
(a) a transferor who is under pensionable age on the transfer day is to be treated as having reached pensionable age and to have become entitled to the state pension under section 4 of the Pensions Act 2014 on the transfer day;

(b) a transferor who has reached pensionable age on the transfer day but who has not yet become entitled to the state pension under section 4 of the Pensions Act 2014 is to be treated as having become entitled to the pension on that day.

(5) In this section—

"the excess amount" has the meaning given by section 47(4);

"relevant order or provision" means the order or provision by virtue of which this section applies (see section 48);

"the relevant state pension legislation"—

(a) in relation to a transferee in the old state pension system, means Part 2 of the Contributions and Benefits Act, and

(b) in relation to a transferee in the new state pension system, means Part 1 of the Pensions Act 2014;

"specified percentage" means the percentage specified in the relevant order or provision for the purposes of subsection (3);

"transfer day" means the day on which the relevant order or provision takes effect;

"transferor" means the person to whose rights the relevant order or provision relates;

"transferee" means the person for whose benefit the relevant order or provision is made.]"

AMENDMENTS

1. Pensions Act 2014 Sch.11 para.13 (April 6, 2016).

Interpretation of Chapter II

1.792 **51.**—(1) In this Chapter—

[1 "shareable state scheme rights", and related expressions, have the meaning given by section 47;] and

"tax year" has the meaning given by section 122(1) of the Contributions and Benefits Act.

[1 (2) For the purposes of this Chapter—

(a) a person is in the old state pension system if the person reached pensionable age before 6 April 2016 (or would have done so if the person had lived until pensionable age), and

(b) a person is in the new state pension system if the person reached pensionable age on or after 6 April 2016 (or will do so if the person lives until pensionable age).]

AMENDMENTS

1. Pensions Act 2014 Sch.11 para.14 (April 6, 2016).

Gender Recognition Act 2004

(2004 c.7)

ARRANGEMENT OF SECTIONS

SCHEDULES

Schedules 1–4—*Omitted.* 1.794
Schedule 5—Benefits and pensions.
Schedule 6—*Omitted.*

COMMENCEMENT

Certain formalities provisions entered into force on Royal Assent, but the whole Act entered into force on April 4, 2005: The Gender Recognition Act 2004 (Commencement) Order 2005 (SI 2005/54).

GENERAL NOTE

This Act makes provision, for the first time, for recognition of a change of gender identity for a transsexual. It follows judgments of the European Court of Human Rights against the United Kingdom finding violations of Convention rights in *Goodwin v United Kingdom* (App. 28957/95), Judgment of July 11, 2002, (2002) 35 E.H.R.R. 18, and *I v United Kingdom* (App. 25680/94), Judgment of July 11, 2002, (2003) 36 E.H.R.R. 53. 1.795

The scheme introduced by the Act is essentially a system of recognition of gender identity through the issue of a gender recognition certificate. The qualifying conditions for such a certificate are that the applicant (1) has or has had gender dysphoria; (2) has lived in the acquired gender for at least two years; and (3) intends to continue to live in the acquired gender until death. There is no requirement that an applicant has undergone gender reassignment surgery. Provision is made for recognition of a change of gender identity under the law of another country. Where the Act refers to "gender" it refers to male or to female gender. It does not permit recognition of a person's gender as non-binary: *R. (on the application of Castellucci) v Gender Recognition Panel* [2024] EWHC 54 (Admin).

Provision is made for two types of certificate: an interim certificate and a full certificate. Unmarried applicants can only receive full certificates, whereas prior to the coming into force of the Marriage (Same Sex Couples) Act 2013 married applicants could only receive interim certificates. Matrimonial law was amended so that the issue of an interim certificate constitutes a ground for a marriage to be declared a nullity provided that proceedings are begun within six months of issue of the certificate. A court declaring a marriage a nullity under this ground must also issue a full gender recognition certificate. Since the 2013 Act came into force, the Gender Recognition Panel is obliged to issue a full certificate to a married applicant if the appliciant's spouse consents.

In *C-451/16 MB v SSWP* the requirement (in a pre-2013 Act case) for a person claiming retirement pension in their acquired gender who was married to have had that marriage annulled was held by the CJEU to constitute unlawful direct discrimination contrary to Council Directive 79/7/EEC.

The effect of the full certificate is to be found in s.9 which provides that a person's gender becomes for all purposes the acquired gender, although it does not affect things done or events occurring before the certificate is issued. This general principle is made subject to the express provisions of this Act and any other enactment. It is destined to become known as the "section 9 principle".

A challenge to the DWP's policies for retention and processing of historic gender data on the grounds inter alia that they contravened ss.9 and 22 of the Act failed in *R(C) v SSWP* [2017] UKSC 72.

The Act contains a range of provisions seeking to work out the practical implications of the issue of a gender recognition certificate. Section 13 and Sch.5 concern social security benefits and pensions. These provisions are concerned only with old age and survivors benefits. The operation of the provisions of the section 9 principle will apply in relation to applications for any social security benefit not covered in this part of the Act, and that should be the starting point for any determination of an application for such benefit by the holder of a full gender recognition certificate. With effect from December 2, 2019, Part 5 of the Civil Partnership (Opposite-sex Couples) Regulations 2019 (SI 2019/1458) made amendments to the Act consequential upon the extension of civil partnerships to couples of the opposite sex.

Following the UK Government's review of the Act during 2018 and subsequent consultation, in a written statement to Parliament (September 22, 2020), the Minister (Liz Truss MP) indicated the Government's view was that the balance struck by the Act was correct.

The Gender Reform (Scotland) Bill was passed by the Scottish Parliament in December 2022 but at the time of writing its progress into law is blocked by the UK Government under Scotland Act 1998, s.35.

Social security benefits and pensions

1.796 **13.** Schedule 5 (entitlement to benefits and pensions) has effect.

GENERAL NOTE

1.797 The provisions of the Schedule constitute a set of free-standing rules rather than amendments to the Contributions and Benefits Act (and its counterparts elsewhere in the United Kingdom). They apply where a person holds a full gender recognition certificate. Perhaps unsurprisingly where the change of gender identity is from female to male, the rules applicable to men apply. These are, of course, generally less favourable in the field of old age and survivors benefits because of the age discrimination still operative in this area of social security. However, where the change of identity is from male to female, the position is less straightforward. Provision is made for entitlement to a retirement pension at age 60, but generally in relation to entitlement to benefits based on a spouse's national insurance contributions, there is no automatic passport to these.

Commissioners have decided that provisions of the Gender Recognition Act 2004 are not compatible with the prohibition of discrimination in art.4(1) of Directive 79/7/EEC. Note, in particular, *CIB/2248/2006* and the decisions of a Tribunal of Commissioners in *R(P) 1/09* and *R(P) 2/09*. These, and other cases, are discussed in more detail in the annotations to art.4 of Directive 79/7/EEC in editions of Vol.III up to the 2020–21 edition.

Note also *Timbrell v SSWP* [2010] EWCA Civ 701, which concerned entitlement to a retirement pension by a male-to-female transsexual under the legal regime applicable *prior to* the entry into force of the Gender Recognition Act. This case is also discussed in the annotations to art.4 of Directive 79/7 in Vol.III up to the 2020–21 edition.

SP v SSWP (RP) [2013] UKUT 156 considers the effect of the *Timbrell* judgment on R(P) 1/09 and R(P) 2/09. It finds that claims for backdated payments of retirement pension will only be possible where, as in the *Timbrell* case, there is an earlier claim upon which no decision has been made. In the absence of such a claim, the most that can be done is payment of arrears of deferred pension from April 27, 2006 (the date of the *Richards* judgment). The decision contains a useful summary of *R(P) 1/09, R(P) 2/09* and the *Timbrell* judgment.

SSWP v HY and LO (RP) [2017] UKUT 303 (AAC) concerned a claim by two male-to-female persons that precluding their being able to receive retirement pensions in respect of periods before they acquired gender recognition certificates constituted discrimination in breach of art.4 of Directive 79/7/EEC. The first claimant underwent gender reassignment surgery in 1986, but did not obtain a gender recognition certificate until February 2015. This had been prompted by refusal to award a retirement pension from July 2014 when she reached pensionable age for a woman. The second claimant underwent gender reassignment surgery in 1988. She obtained a gender recognition certificate in February 2014 by which time she was already aged 65. She claimed a retirement pension from May 2008 when she had reached the age of 60. Judge Rowland reviews both the relevant legislative and case law history. He concludes that the circumstances of the two claimants were distinguishable from those which had arisen in the *Richards* and *Timbrell* cases. Those cases had been concerned with entitlements in respect of periods in the absence of a national scheme for recognition of a changed gender identity. In the instant cases, there had been delay in obtaining a gender recognition certificate after the scheme in the Gender Recognition Act 2004 had come into force. On the facts, both claimants could have sought gender recognition certificates in a timely manner to enable claims to be successful from the relevant pensionable ages for a woman. The claimants argued that there was nonetheless unfavourable treatment when they compared themselves to persons who had been registered as women from birth. Judge Rowland concluded that the Directive did not require the United Kingdom to establish a scheme which permitted the retrospective award of gender recognition certificates, and the United Kingdom had chosen to make them prospective only. There was accordingly no discrimination which fell foul of the prohibition in art.4 of Directive 79/7/EEC. Any difference in treatment could be objectively justified.

In *C-451/16 MB v SSWP* the requirement (in a pre-2013 Act case) for a person claiming retirement pension in their acquired gender who was married to have had that marriage annulled was held by the CJEU to constitute unlawful direct discrimination contrary to Council Directive 79/7/EEC.

Interpretation

25. In this Act— **1.798**

"the acquired gender" is to be construed in accordance with s.1(2),

"approved country or territory" has the meaning given by s.2(4),

"the appointed day" means the day appointed by order under s.26,

[2 . . .]

"enactment" includes an enactment contained in an Act of the Scottish Parliament or in any Northern Ireland legislation,

"full gender recognition certificate" and "interim gender recognition certificate" mean the certificates issued as such under [1 section 4, 5 or 5A] and "gender recognition certificate" means either of those sorts of certificate,

"gender dysphoria" means the disorder variously referred to as gender dysphoria, gender identity disorder and transsexualism,

"Gender Recognition Panel" (and "Panel") is to be construed in accordance with Schedule 1,

[3"protected civil partnership" means

(a) a civil partnership under the law of England and Wales [6or under the law of Northern Ireland], or

(b) an overseas relationship that is treated as a civil partnership by virtue of Chapter 2 of Part 5 of the Civil Partnership Act 2004,

and "protected overseas relationship" means a protected civil partnership within paragraph (b),]

[4 "protected marriage" means—

(a) a marriage under the law of England and Wales [6 or under the law of Northern Ireland], or

(b) a marriage under the law of a country or territory outside the United Kingdom,]

[7"protected Scottish civil partnership" means a civil partnership registered in Scotland,

"protected Scottish marriage" means a marriage solemnised in Scotland,]

[2 "registered psychologist" means a person registered in the part of the register maintained under the the [5 Health Professions Order 2001] which relates to practitioner psychologists,]

[4 "statutory declaration of consent" has the meaning given by section 3(6B)(a),]

"subordinate legislation" means an Order in Council, an order, rules, regulations, a scheme, a warrant, bye-laws or any other instrument made under an enactment, and

"UK birth register entry" has the meaning given by s.10(2).

AMENDMENTS

1. Civil Partnership Act 2004 Pt 7 s.250(7) (December 5, 2005).

2. Health Care and Associated Professions (Miscellaneous Amendments and Practitioner Psychologists) Order 2009 (SI 2009/1182) Sch.5(1) para.8 (July 1, 2009).

3. Civil Partnership (Opposite-sex Couples) Regulations 2019/1458 Pt 5 reg.33 (December 2, 2019).

4. The Marriage (Same Sex Couples) Act 2013 Sch.5(1) para.14 (December 10, 2014); insertion has effect as subject to transitional and transitory provision: SI 2014/3169.

5. Children and Social Work Act 2017 Sch.5(2) para.48(d) (December 2, 2019).

6. Marriage (Same-sex Couples) and Civil Partnership (Opposite-sex Couples) (Northern Ireland) Regulations 2019 (SI 2019/1154) reg.47 (January 13, 2020).

7. The Civil Partnership (Scotland) Act 2020 and Marriage and Civil Partnership (Scotland) Act 2014 (Consequential Modifications) Order 2022 (SI 2022/74) Sch.1 para.1(5) (January 27, 2022).

SCHEDULE 5

BENEFITS AND PENSIONS

PART I

INTRODUCTORY

1.799 1. This Schedule applies where a full gender recognition certificate is issued to a person.

PART II

STATE BENEFITS

Introductory

1.800 2.—(1) In this Part of this Schedule "the 1992 Act" means—

(a) in England and Wales and Scotland, the Social Security Contributions and Benefits Act 1992 (c. 4), and

(b) in Northern Ireland, the Social Security Contributions and Benefits (Northern Ireland) Act 1992 (c. 7).

(2) In this Part of this Schedule "the Administration Act" means—

(a) in England and Wales and Scotland, the Social Security Administration Act 1992 (c. 5), and

(b) in Northern Ireland, the Social Security Administration (Northern Ireland) Act 1992 (c. 8).

(3) Expressions used in this Part of this Schedule and in Part 2 of the 1992 Act have the same meaning in this Part of this Schedule as in Part 2 of the 1992 Act.

Widowed mother's allowance

3.—(1) If (immediately before the certificate is issued) the person is, or but for section 1 of the Administration Act would be, entitled to a widowed mother's allowance under section 37 of the 1992 Act (allowance for woman whose husband died before 9th April 2001)— **1.801**

(a) the person is not entitled to that allowance afterwards, but

(b) (instead) subsections (2) to (5) of section 39A of the 1992 Act (widowed parent's allowance) apply in relation to the person.

(2) If (immediately before the certificate is issued) the person is (actually) entitled to a widowed mother's allowance, the entitlement to widowed parent's allowance conferred by sub-paragraph (1) is not subject to section 1 of the Administration Act.

GENERAL NOTE

This paragraph applies in the case of a female to male transsexual. If, immediately prior to the issue of the certificate, the person was (or would be but for having made a claim) entitled to widowed mother's allowance, entitlement to that benefit ceases on issue of the certificate, but the man becomes entitled to claim a widowed parent's allowance under the specified provisions of the Contributions and Benefits Act. If, however, widowed mother's allowance has been claimed and awarded, then the benefit converts to widowed parent's allowance without the need for a claim. **1.802**

Widow's pension

4. If (immediately before the certificate is issued) the person is entitled to a widow's pension under section 38 of the 1992 Act (pension for woman whose husband died before 9th April 2001), the person is not entitled to that pension afterwards. **1.803**

GENERAL NOTE

This paragraph applies in the case of a female to male transsexual. Since there is no equivalent pension under the bereavement benefits scheme (a widower's pension), the entitlement to the widow's pension ceases on issue of the certificate. **1.804**

Widowed parent's allowance

5. If (immediately before the certificate is issued) the person is, or but for section 1 of the Administration Act would be, entitled to a widowed parent's allowance by virtue of subsection (1)(b) of section 39A of the 1992 Act (allowance for man whose wife died before 9th April 2001), subsections (2) to (5) of that section continue to apply in relation to the person afterwards. **1.805**

GENERAL NOTE

Widowed parent's allowance is predominantly a gender neutral benefit, and the provision here is simply for entitlement to widowed parent's allowance to continue where a man has claimed in respect of a bereavement before April 2001. However, women in receipt of widowed mother's allowance have the potential right to move on to widow's pension, but no provision is made for transfer in a relevant case from widowed parent's allowance to widowed mother's allowance. **1.806**

Long-term incapacity benefit etc.

6. If (immediately before the certificate is issued) the person is entitled to incapacity benefit, or a Category A retirement pension, under— **1.807**

(a) section 40 of the 1992 Act (long-term incapacity benefit etc. for woman whose husband died before 9th April 2001), or

(b) section 41 of the 1992 Act (long-term incapacity benefit etc. for man whose wife died before that date),

the person is not so entitled afterwards.

General Note

1.808 The effect of these provisions is at first surprising. Sections 40 and 41 make provision respectively for widow and widowers which enabled a person incapable of work at the time of the bereavement to claim incapacity benefit even though the contribution conditions were not satisfied. On reaching pensionable age, the incapacity benefit would convert into a Category A retirement pension if the person was not otherwise entitled to retirement pension. For both male to female, and female to male, transsexuals, the entitlement to incapacity benefit on this basis ceases. This would appear to be because the principle adopted throughout the Schedule would seem to be to treat all those holding a gender recognition certificate as if they had been bereaved *after* April 2001. Sections 40 and 41 apply only where the person was bereaved before April 2001.

[1 Pension under Part 1 of the Pensions Act 2014

1.809 **6A.**–(1) Any question—
(a) whether the person is entitled to a state pension under Part 1 of the Pensions Act 2014 for any period after the certificate is issued, and
(b) (if so) the rate at which the person is so entitled for the period,
is to be decided as if the person's gender were the acquired gender.
(2) Accordingly, if (immediately before the certificate is issued) the person—
(a) is a woman entitled to a state pension under Part 1 of the Pensions Act 2014, but
(b) has not attained the age of 65,
the person ceases to be so entitled when it is issued.
(3) And, conversely, if (immediately before the certificate is issued) the person—
(a) is a man who has attained the age at which a woman of the same age attains pensionable age, but
(b) has not attained the age of 65, the person is to be treated for the purposes of Part 1 of the Pensions Act 2014 as attaining pensionable age when it is issued.
(4) But sub-paragraph (1) does not apply if and to the extent that the decision of any question to which it refers is affected by the payment or crediting of contributions, or the crediting of earnings, in respect of a period ending before the certificate is issued.
(5) If the person's acquired gender is the male gender, sections 11 and 12 of, and Schedules 6 and 7 to, the Pensions Act 2014 (effect of reduced rate elections) apply in relation to the person as they apply in relation to a woman (but only once the person has reached pensionable age for a man).
(6) Paragraph 10 makes provision about deferment of state pensions under Part 1 of the Pensions Act 2014.]

Pension under Part 1 of the Pensions Act (Northern Ireland) 2015

[8**6B.**—(1) Any question —
(a) whether the person is entitled to a state pension under Part 1 of the Pensions Act (Northern Ireland) 2015 for any period after the certificate is issued, and
(b) (if so) the rate at which the person is so entitled for the period,
is to be decided as if the person's gender were the acquired gender.
(2) Accordingly, if (immediately before the certificate is issued) the person --
(a) is a woman entitled to a state pension under Part 1 of the Pensions Act (Northern Ireland) 2015, but
(b) has not attained the age of 65,
the person ceases to be so entitled when it is issued.
(3) And, conversely, if (immediately before the certificate is issued) the person --
(a) is a man who has attained the age at which a woman of the same age attains pensionable age, but
(b) has not attained the age of 65,
the person is to be treated for the purposes of Part 1 of the Pensions Act (Northern Ireland) 2015 as attaining pensionable age when it is issued.
(4) But sub-paragraph (1) does not apply if and to the extent that the decision of any question to which it refers is affected by the payment or crediting of contributions, or the crediting of earnings, in respect of a period ending before the certificate is issued.
(5) If the person's acquired gender is the male gender, sections 11 and 12 of, and Schedules 6 and 7 to, the Pensions Act (Northern Ireland) 2015 (effect of reduced rate elections) apply

in relation to the person as they apply in relation to a woman (but only once the person has reached pensionable age for a man).

(6) Paragraph 10 makes provision about deferment of state pensions under Part 1 of the Pensions Act (Northern Ireland) 2015.]

Category A retirement pension

7.—(1) Any question— 1.810

(a) whether the person is entitled to a Category A retirement pension (under section 44 of the 1992 Act) for any period after the certificate is issued, and

(b) (if so) the rate at which the person is so entitled for the period,

is to be decided as if the person's gender had always been the acquired gender [[2] (but this is subject to sub-paragraph (3))].

(2) Accordingly, if (immediately before the certificate is issued) the person—

(a) is a woman entitled to a Category A retirement pension, but

(b) has not attained the age of 65,

the person ceases to be so entitled when it is issued.

(3) And, conversely, if (immediately before the certificate is issued) the person—

(a) is a man who has attained the age at which a woman of the same age attains pensionable age, but

(b) has not attained the age of 65,

the person is to be treated for the purposes of section 44 of the 1992 Act as attaining pensionable age when it is issued.

(4) But sub-paragraph (1) does not apply if and to the extent that the decision of any question to which it refers is affected by—

(a) the payment or crediting of contributions, or the crediting of earnings, in respect of a period ending before the certificate is issued, or

(b) preclusion from regular employment by responsibilities at home for such a period.

(5) Paragraph 10 makes provision about deferment of Category A retirement pensions.

GENERAL NOTE

The general principle in sub-paragraph (1) is an exception to the section 9 principle, because for these purposes the person's acquired gender is treated as though it has always been the person's gender. So a female to male transsexual who changes gender between the ages of 60 and 65 ceases to be entitled to any Category A retirement pension awarded, whereas a male to female transsexual who changes gender between the ages of 60 and 65 is treated for the purposes of determining entitlement to a Category A retirement pension as though she attained pensionable age on the date of issue of the certificate, but not before. There is no retrospectivity of entitlement. 1.811

Note that, although art.7(1) provides that any question of entitlement, and, if so, the rate of entitlement, is to be decided as if the person's acquired gender had always been their gender, this is subject to an exception in para.(4) that covers the payment and crediting of contributions, and the treatment of earnings that have been made before the change of gender. In *CP/98/2007*, the claimant was over 65 at the time she changed her gender from male to female. The decision maker decided that the contributions she had made between the ages of 60 and 65, when she was a man, should not be included in calculating her additional state pension, but the Commissioner allowed her appeal on the basis of the exception provided in para.(4).

Category B retirement pension etc.

8.—(1) Any question whether the person is entitled to— 1.812

(a) a Category B retirement pension (under [[3] section 48A, 48AA, 48B, 48BB or 51] of the 1992 Act), or

(b) an increase in a Category A retirement pension under section 51A or 52 of the 1992 Act (increase in Category A retirement pension by reference to amount of Category B retirement pension),

for any period after the certificate is issued is (in accordance with section 9(1)) to be decided as if the person's gender were the acquired gender (but subject to sub-paragraph (4)).

(2) Accordingly, if (immediately before the certificate is issued) the person is a woman entitled to—

(a) a Category B retirement pension, or

(b) an increase in a Category A retirement pension under section 51A or 52 of the 1992 Act,

the person may cease to be so entitled when it is issued.

(3) And, conversely, if (immediately before the certificate is issued) the person—

(a) is a man who has attained the age at which a woman of the same age attains pensionable age, but

(b) has not attained the age of 65,

the person is to be treated for the purposes of [3 sections 48A, 48AA, 48B and 48BB] of the 1992 Act as attaining pensionable age when it is issued.

(4) But a person who is a man (immediately before the certificate is issued) is not entitled to a Category B retirement pension under section 48B of the 1992 Act for any period after it is issued if the person—

(a) attains (or has attained) the age of 65 before 6th April 2010, and

(b) would not have been entitled to a Category B retirement pension under section 51 of the 1992 Act for that period if still a man.

(5) Paragraph 10 makes provision about deferment of Category B retirement pensions.

GENERAL NOTE

1.813 These rather complex provisions reflect the four different routes to entitlement to a Category B retirement pension coupled with the change which came into effect in 2010 under which men began to acquire entitlement to Category B retirement pension. The general principle adopted in relation to acquisition of entitlement to a Category B retirement pension is that any question of entitlement after the issue of a gender recognition certificate is to be determined by applying the rules applicable to persons of the acquired gender. That means that if the acquired gender is that of a woman, the rules applicable to women are applied to the claimant, and, if the acquired gender is that of a man, the rules applicable to men are applied to the claimant. In both cases no concessions to the change of gender identity are made. The exception is sub-paragraph (4) which limits the ability of a male to female transsexual acquiring entitlement under s.48B of the Contributions and Benefits Act.

Shared additional pension

1.814 **9.**—(1) Any question—

(a) whether the person is entitled to a shared additional pension (under section 55A [4 or 55AA] of the 1992 Act) for any period after the certificate is issued, and

(b) (if so) the rate at which the person is so entitled for the period,

is to be decided on the basis of the person attaining pensionable age on the same date as someone of the acquired gender (and the same age).

(2) Accordingly, if (immediately before the certificate is issued) the person—

(a) is a woman entitled to a shared additional pension, but

(b) has not attained the age of 65,

the person ceases to be so entitled when it is issued.

(3) And, conversely, if (immediately before the certificate is issued) the person—

(a) is a man who has attained the age at which a woman of the same age attains pensionable age, but

(b) has not attained the age of 65,

the person is to be treated for the purposes of section 55A [4 or 55AA] of the 1992 Act as attaining pensionable age when it is issued.

(4) Paragraph 10 makes provision about deferment of shared additional pensions.

Deferment of pensions

1.815 **10.**—(1) The person's entitlement to—

[5 (za) a state pension under Part 1 of the Pensions Act 2014,]

[7(zb) a state pension under Part 1 of the Pensions Act (Northern Ireland) 2015,]

(a) a Category A retirement pension,

(b) a Category B retirement pension, or

(c) a shared additional pension,

is not to be taken to have been deferred for any period ending before the certificate is issued unless the condition in sub-paragraph (2) is satisfied.

(2) The condition is that the entitlement both—

(a) was actually deferred during the period, and

(b) would have been capable of being so deferred had the person's gender been the acquired gender.

GENERAL NOTE

The principle applied here is that there can be no notional deferment of pension on recognition of a change of gender identity. **1.816**

Category C retirement pension for widows

11. [6 . . .] **1.817**

GENERAL NOTE

It would be surprising if this provision proves problematic in operation, since it relates (a) to persons who attained pensionable age before July 5, 1948, and (b) to the wives and widows of such persons. A change of gender identity from woman to man results in the loss of the entitlement. **1.818**

Graduated retirement benefit: Great Britain

12.—(1) The provision that may be made by regulations under paragraph 15 of Schedule 3 to the Social Security (Consequential Provisions) Act 1992 (c. 6) (power to retain provisions repealed by Social Security Act 1973 (c. 38), with or without modification, for transitional purposes) includes provision modifying the preserved graduated retirement benefit provisions in consequence of this Act. **1.819**

(2) "The preserved graduated retirement benefit provisions" are the provisions of the National Insurance Act 1965 (c. 51) relating to graduated retirement benefit continued in force, with or without modification, by regulations having effect as if made under that paragraph.

Graduated retirement benefit: Northern Ireland

13.—(1) The provision that may be made by regulations under paragraph 15 of Schedule 3 to the Social Security (Consequential Provisions) (Northern Ireland) Act 1992 (c. 9) (corresponding power for Northern Ireland) includes provision modifying the Northern Ireland preserved graduated retirement benefit provisions in consequence of this Act. **1.820**

(2) "The Northern Ireland preserved graduated retirement benefit provisions" are the provisions of the National Insurance Act (Northern Ireland) 1966 (c. 6 (N.I.)) relating to graduated retirement benefit continued in force, with or without modification, by regulations having effect as if made under that paragraph.

PART 3

OCCUPATIONAL PENSION SCHEMES

GENERAL NOTE

The Schedule does not make any rules about occupational pension schemes, but it does have to deal with the provisions guaranteeing those in receipt of occupational pensions the guaranteed minimum pension, and preserved equivalent pension benefits. **1.821**

Guaranteed minimum pensions etc.: Great Britain

1.822 **14.**—(1) In this paragraph "the 1993 Act" means the Pension Schemes Act 1993 (c. 48); and expressions used in this paragraph and in that Act have the same meaning in this paragraph as in that Act.

(2) The fact that the person's gender has become the acquired gender does not affect the operation of section 14 of the 1993 Act (guaranteed minimum) in relation to the person, except to the extent that its operation depends on section 16 of the 1993 Act (revaluation); and sub-paragraphs (3) and (5) have effect subject to that.

(3) If (immediately before the certificate is issued) the person is a woman who is entitled to a guaranteed minimum pension but has not attained the age of 65—

(a) the person is for the purposes of section 13 of the 1993 Act and the guaranteed minimum pension provisions to be treated after it is issued as not having attained pensionable age (so that the entitlement ceases) but as attaining pensionable age on subsequently attaining the age of 65, and

(b) in a case where the person's guaranteed minimum pension has commenced before the certificate is issued, it is to be treated for the purposes of Chapter 3 of Part 4 of the 1993 Act (anti-franking) as if it had not.

(4) But sub-paragraph (3)(a) does not—

(a) affect any pension previously paid to the person, or

(b) prevent section 15 of the 1993 Act (increase of guaranteed minimum where commencement of guaranteed minimum pension postponed) operating to increase the person's guaranteed minimum by reason of a postponement of the commencement of the person's guaranteed minimum pension for a period ending before the certificate is issued.

(5) If (immediately before the certificate is issued) the person is a man who—

(a) has attained the age of 60, but

(b) has not attained the age of 65,

the person is to be treated for the purposes of section 13 of the 1993 Act and the guaranteed minimum pension provisions as attaining pensionable age when it is issued.

(6) If at that time the person has attained the age of 65, the fact that the person's gender has become the acquired gender does not affect the person's pensionable age for those purposes.

(7) The fact that the person's gender has become the acquired gender does not affect any guaranteed minimum pension to which the person is entitled as a widow or widower immediately before the certificate is issued (except in consequence of the operation of the previous provisions of this Schedule).

(8) If a transaction to which section 19 of the 1993 Act applies which is carried out before the certificate is issued discharges a liability to provide a guaranteed minimum pension for or in respect of the person, it continues to do so afterwards.

(9) "The guaranteed minimum pension provision" means so much of the 1993 Act (apart from section 13) and of any other enactment as relates to guaranteed minimum pensions.

Guaranteed minimum pensions etc.: Northern Ireland

1.823 **15.**—(1) In this paragraph "the 1993 Act" means the Pension Schemes (Northern Ireland) Act 1993 (c. 49); and expressions used in this paragraph and in that Act have the same meaning in this paragraph as in that Act.

(2) The fact that the person's gender has become the acquired gender does not affect the operation of section 10 of the 1993 Act (guaranteed minimum) in relation to the person, except to the extent that its operation depends on section 12 of the 1993 Act (revaluation); and sub-paragraphs (3) and (5) have effect subject to that.

(3) If (immediately before the certificate is issued) the person is a woman who is entitled to a guaranteed minimum pension but has not attained the age of 65—

(a) the person is for the purposes of section 9 of the 1993 Act and the guaranteed minimum pension provisions to be treated after it is issued as not having attained pensionable age (so that the entitlement ceases) but as attaining pensionable age on subsequently attaining the age of 65, and

(b) in a case where the person's guaranteed minimum pension has commenced before the certificate is issued, it is to be treated for the purposes of Chapter 3 of Part 4 of the 1993 Act (anti-franking) as if it had not.

(4) But sub-paragraph (3)(a) does not—

(a) affect any pension previously paid to the person, or

(b) prevent section 11 of the 1993 Act (increase of guaranteed minimum where commencement of guaranteed minimum pension postponed) operating to increase the person's guaranteed minimum by reason of a postponement of the commencement of the person's guaranteed minimum pension for a period ending before the certificate is issued.

(5) If (immediately before the certificate is issued) the person is a man who—

(a) has attained the age of 60, but

(b) has not attained the age of 65,

the person is to be treated for the purposes of section 9 of the 1993 Act and the guaranteed minimum pension provisions as attaining pensionable age when it is issued.

(6) If at that time the person has attained the age of 65, the fact that the person's gender has become the acquired gender does not affect the person's pensionable age for those purposes.

(7) The fact that the person's gender has become the acquired gender does not affect any guaranteed minimum pension to which the person is entitled as a widow or widower [[9] or surviving civil partner] immediately before the certificate is issued (except in consequence of the operation of the previous provisions of this Schedule).

(8) If a transaction to which section 15 of the 1993 Act applies which is carried out before the certificate is issued discharges a liability to provide a guaranteed minimum pension for or in respect of the person, it continues to do so afterwards.

(9) "The guaranteed minimum pension provision" means so much of the 1993 Act (apart from section 9) and of any other enactment as relates to guaranteed minimum pensions.

Equivalent pension benefits: Great Britain

16.—(1) The provision that may be made by regulations under paragraph 15 of Schedule 3 to the Social Security (Consequential Provisions) Act 1992 (c. 6) (power to retain provisions repealed by Social Security Act 1973 (c. 38), with or without modification, for transitional purposes) includes provision modifying the preserved equivalent pension benefits provisions in consequence of this Act. **1.824**

(2) "The preserved equivalent pension benefits provisions" are the provisions of the National Insurance Act 1965 (c. 51) relating to equivalent pension benefits continued in force, with or without modification, by regulations having effect as if made under that paragraph.

Equivalent pension benefits: Northern Ireland

17.—(1) The provision that may be made by regulations under paragraph 15 of Schedule 3 to the Social Security (Consequential Provisions) (Northern Ireland) Act 1992 (c. 9) (corresponding power for Northern Ireland) includes provision modifying the Northern Ireland preserved equivalent pension benefits provisions in consequence of this Act. **1.825**

(2) "The Northern Ireland preserved equivalent pension benefits provisions" are the provisions of the National Insurance Act (Northern Ireland) 1966 (c. 6 (N.I.)) relating to equivalent pension benefits continued in force, with or without modification, by regulations having effect as if made under that paragraph.

AMENDMENTS

1. Added by Pensions Act 2014 Sch.12(1) para.48(2) (April 6, 2016).
2. Pensions Act 2014 Sch.12(1) para.48(3) (April 6, 2016).
3. Pensions Act 2014 Sch.12(2) para.76 (April 6, 2016).
4. Pensions Act 2014 Sch.11 para.16 (April 6, 2016).
5. Pensions Act 2014 Sch.12(1) para.48(4) (April 6, 2016).
6. Pensions Act 2014 Sch.12(2) para.83 (April 6, 2016).
7. Pensions Act (Northern Ireland) 2015 Sch.12(1) para.43(3) (April 6, 2016).
8. Pensions Act (Northern Ireland) 2015 Sch.12(1) para.43(2) (April 6, 2016).
9. The Marriage and Civil Partnership (Northern Ireland) (No.2) Regulations 2020 (SI 2020/1143) reg.43 (December 7, 2020).

'New Style' Welfare Reform Act 2007

(2007 c.5) (As Amended)

Arrangement of Sections

PART 1

EMPLOYMENT AND SUPPORT ALLOWANCE

Entitlement

Assessments relating to entitlement

Work-related requirements

Miscellaneous

An Act to make provision about social security; to amend the Vaccine Damage Payments Act 1979; and for connected purposes. [3rd May 2007]

GENERAL NOTE

1.826 The form of the Act set out below (described in this volume as the new style Welfare Reform Act 2007) is as amended in cases in which universal credit has come into operation, so that IRESA has been abolished, and any new claim for ESA can only be for new style ESA under the Act as amended. The circumstance that brings about the abolition of IRESA under s.33(1)(b) of the WRA 2012 and the coming into force of the amendments to the 2007 Act under later provisions is the making of a new claim for ESA (or for other benefits including universal credit and JSA) in an area where "full service" universal credit has been rolled out and where the particular claimant is legally able to make a claim for universal credit (see arts 4(1) and (2) of the Welfare Reform Act 2012 (Commencement No.9 and Transitional and Transitory Provisions and Commencement No.8 and Savings and Transitional Provisions (Amendment) Order 2013 (SI 2013/983) as further applied in later Commencement Orders). The Orders are now set out so far as still relevant in Vol.V of this series.

The position was reached in December 2018 when the universal credit rollout had extended to the whole of Great Britain. Some prohibitions on claiming universal credit remained for a while at least, in particular the so-called SDP gateway, where a claimant who was entitled to an income-related benefit including the severe disability premium was prohibited from claiming universal credit (reg.4A of the Universal Credit (Transitional Provisions) Regulations 2014 (SI 2014/1230)). That prohibition was removed by the revocation of reg.4A with effect from January 27, 2021. The former exception for "frontier workers" was removed with effect from March 30, 2022 by SI 2022/302. Finally, the only remaining prohibition – the emergency discretion under reg.4 of the Transitional Provisions Regulations 2014 to stop accepting claims for operational reasons – was revoked as from July 25, 2022 by SI 2022/752.

It follows that entitlement to old style ESA can only now exist as part of a continuing award made earlier (see now in Vol.V of this series). In practice continuing awards will overwhelmingly be awards of income-based old style ESA (see Vol.V of this series). To save space and complication, the only amendments identified below are those made in and under the Welfare Reform Act 2012, and subsequent amendments to this form of the Act. Previous amendments are not identified, but can be traced in the previous editions of what was then Vol.II of this series. In addition provisions that have been completely revoked under the WRA 2012 to produce the structure of new style JSA have simply been omitted from the text without any remaining reference.

PART 1

EMPLOYMENT AND SUPPORT ALLOWANCE

Entitlement

Employment and support allowance 1.827

1.—(1) An allowance, to be known as an employment and support allowance, shall be payable in accordance with the provisions of this Part.

(2) Subject to the provisions of this Part, a claimant is entitled to an employment and support allowance if he satisfies the basic conditions and

[3. . .]—

(a) the first and the second conditions set out in [3. . .] Schedule 1 (conditions relating to national insurance) or the third condition set out in [3. . .] that Schedule (condition relating to youth), [3. . .]

[3. . .].

(3) The basic conditions are that the claimant—

(a) has limited capability for work,

[2(aa) has accepted a claimant commitment,]

(b) is at least 16 years old,

(c) has not reached pensionable age,

(d) is in Great Britain, [[3]and]
(e) is not entitled to income support, and
(f) is not entitled to a jobseeker's allowance [[3]. . .].

[[1](3A) After the coming into force of this subsection no claim may be made for an employment and support allowance by virtue of the third condition set out in [[3]. . .] Schedule 1 (youth).]

(4) For the purposes of this Part, a person has limited capability for work if—

(a) his capability for work is limited by his physical or mental condition, and

(b) the limitation is such that it is not reasonable to require him to work.

(5) An employment and support allowance is payable in respect of a week.

(6) In subsection (3)—

[[3]. . .];

"pensionable age" has the meaning given by the rules in paragraph 1 of Schedule 4 to the Pensions Act 1995.

[[3]. . .].

(6A) [[3]. . .].

(7) [[3]. . .]

AMENDMENTS

1. Welfare Reform Act 2012 s.53 (May 1, 2012).
2. Welfare Reform Act 2012 s.54(1), (2) (various dates on or after April 29, 2013).
3. Welfare Reform Act 2012 s.33(3), Sch.3 para.23, s.147 and Sch.14 Pt 1 (various dates on or after April 29, 2013).

DEFINITIONS

"claimant"—see s.24(1).
"pensionable age" —see subs.(6).

GENERAL NOTE

Subsections (1) and (2)

1.828 This section establishes "new style" Employment and Support Allowance (ESA), which is payable in accordance with the terms set out in the remainder of Part I of the Act, a framework clothed with the detail of the Employment and Support Allowance Regulations 2013 (SI 2013/379). "New style" ESA is a contributory incapacity benefit which was introduced in universal credit areas following the abolition (at least for new claimants) of "old style" ESA, which had both a contributory and means-tested form (see further the Employment and Support Allowance Regulations 2008 (SI 2008/794)). Thus at the outset ESA, like JSA, was a single benefit with two forms: contributory ESA (CESA) and income-related ESA (IRESA). A claimant could be entitled to one or the other or, in some cases, both. See further *LH v SSWP* (ESA) [2014] UKUT 480 (AAC); [2015] AACR 14. For a contextual overview of the development of ESA and its policy aims see the commentary to the original s.1 of this Act (now in Vol.V of this series) and *RS v SSWP* (ESA) [2021] UKUT 112 (AAC).

Since ESA was first introduced in October 2008, there have been a series of amendments to the secondary legislation governing the descriptors that apply for the purposes of the work capability assessment (WCA). These changes are discussed in the commentary to Sch.2 and Sch.3 to the Employment and Support Allowance Regulations 2008 (SI 2008/794). There have also been two major changes since the 2007 Act to the framework in the primary legislation. The first has been the gradual introduction of universal credit under the Welfare Reform Act 2012, which replaced income-related ESA for new claimants in affected areas. The second has been the abolition of the work-related activity component in ESA for (broadly speaking) claims made on or after April 3, 2017.

ESA can be claimed by persons with an employer (after SSP is exhausted) (see s.20(1)), the self-employed, and those without employment. It is payable in respect of a week to provide support to those clearly unable to work, through a "support component" paid in addition to their basic allowance, and to require those capable of work-related activity to engage in it in return (at least for claims made before April 3, 2017) for a "work-related activity component" on top of their basic allowance, the hope being that they will eventually return to the labour force. ESA is a benefit with similarities to JSA (even "new style" ESA, despite being a contributory benefit, can be reduced on account of certain other income). Moreover, initially ESA had no time limit on either its contributory or income related forms, save that entitlement ceased on reaching pensionable age (s.1(3)(c)). However, for those not in the support group, both CESA and "new style" ESA have from May 1, 2012 been time-limited to 365 days (counting days of entitlement before, on and after that date) (see: ss.1A and 1B).

Eligibility for "new style" ESA depends on fulfilment of contribution conditions showing a recent connection with the world of work (see Sch.1, Pt 1). Initially, persons incapacitated in youth (before 20 or in some cases 25) could have access to CESA without meeting the contribution conditions. This route was barred to new claimants claiming on or after May 1, 2012 (see subs.(3A)) so that route is unlikely to cover many "new style" ESA claimants at all.

Assuming the contributions conditions are satisfied, the basic conditions of entitlement are that the claimant is at least 16; has not reached pensionable age; is in Great Britain; is not entitled to IS; is not entitled to JSA; has accepted a claimant commitment and has limited capability for work (see subs.(3)). A "claimant commitment" is a record of the responsibilities of a claimant entitled to "new style" ESA (see further s.11A, below). The matter of capacity is either assessed by a work-related capability assessment (a functional test involving a medical examination) or is deemed to exist for a much reduced set of "exempt" groups. Generally, three "waiting days" of non-entitlement have to be served (s.22, Sch.2 para.4; ESA Regs 2013 reg.85). During the (generally 13-week) assessment period, only basic allowance ESA is payable. Additional components (support or, where still available, work-related activity) depend on the claimant being assessed or treated as having limited capability for work/work-related activity respectively. The personal allowance aspect of the ESA basic allowance (a lower rate for those under 25) is based on the personal allowances in JSA (single person, lone parent or couple). After the assessment period ends (when the claimant has been assessed or treated as having limited capacity for work), claimants become eligible for one (but not both) of two additional components: the support component; or the work-related activity component. However, the work-related activity component is not payable on (broadly speaking) new claims made on or after April 3, 2017. To be eligible for the support component, claimants must have limited capability for work-related activity (capacity for that must be limited by their physical or mental condition to such an extent that it is not reasonable to require them to undertake such activity). If they do not have limited capacity for work-related activity (i.e. capability for work-related activity is not limited by physical or mental condition or, if it is, the limitations are not such as to render it unreasonable to undertake such activity), they will be eligible for the work-related activity component on top of the basic allowance (but only for claims made before April 3, 2017), provided they meet prescribed conditions on work-related activity. Should they not do so, they can be sanctioned by progressive reduction (ultimately removal) of the amount of that component to which they would otherwise be entitled.

As with the legacy benefits, claimants entitled to "new style" ESA can be disqualified from it where their conduct conduces to their incapacity (e.g. because of misconduct in bringing it about or in refusing treatment which would alleviate it) or their failure to adhere to prescribed rules of behaviour (s.18; ESA Regs 2013 regs 93, 95). "Persons in hardship" cannot be disqualified but receive a reduced rate of personal allowance (ESA Regs 2013 regs. 63 and 94). Absences from Great Britain (other than certain temporary absences) preclude entitlement to ESA (s.18(4), Sch.2 paras 5, 6, 8; ESA Regs 2013 regs 88-92). Imprisonment or detention in legal custody each disqualify from "new style" ESA and, if longer than six weeks, results in the person being treated as not having limited capability for work, thus impacting on ability to link spells of limited capability for work (s.18(4); ESA Regs 2013 regs 95-97).

Subsection (3)

1.829 This stipulates the "basic conditions" which must be satisfied where the claimant claims "new style" ESA. The claimant must:

- be at least 16
  this is the current school-leaving age and so this lower limit is apt for a benefit that is an earnings replacement one;
- be under pensionable age
  "pensionable age" is here defined according to the rules in Pensions Act 2004, Sch.4, para.1 (see subs.(6)). It thus links to the sliding scale of pensionable ages found there as the pensions system moves steadily towards equal pension ages for men and women;
- be in Great Britain
  absences from Great Britain (other than certain temporary absences) preclude entitlement to ESA. See further s.18(4), Sch.2 paras 5, 6, 8; ESA Regs 2012 regs 88–92. Essentially this is a presence rather than a residence test;
- not be entitled to IS (under SSCBA 1992, s.124)
  this establishes the mutual exclusivity of "new style" ESA and IS;
- not be entitled to JSA (under JSA 1995)
  this establishes the mutual exclusivity of "new style" ESA and JSA;
- have limited capability for work
  the basic test for this is set out in subs.(4): claimants will have limited capability for work where their capability for work is limited by their physical or mental condition and that limitation is such that it is not reasonable to require them to work. ESA Regs 2013 reg.15(1) elaborates that this is to be determined on the basis of a limited capability for work assessment. This is:

  > "an assessment of the extent to which a claimant who has some specific disease or bodily or mental disablement is capable of performing the activities prescribed in Schedule 2 [to the ESA Regs] or is incapable by reason of such disease or bodily or mental disablement of performing those activities" (ESA Regs reg.15(2)).

  The claimant is to be matched, in the light of all the evidence, by the decision-maker or tribunal against a range of activities and descriptors, and an appropriate "score" awarded. The threshold "score" for entitlement is 15 points, but as regards its computation see further the commentary to s.8 and to ESA Regs 2013 Pt 4 (regs 15–29) and Sch.2.
- have accepted a claimant commitment
  This condition, inserted by s.54(2) of the WRA 2012, initially applied only to "new style" ESA in universal credit areas. It was then implemented more widely as from the summer of 2017. It replaces the conditionality requirement in the original version of the WRA 2007.

Subsection (4)

This sets out the basic definition of "limited capability for work". See commentary to subs.(3), s.8 and to ESA Regs 2013 Pt 4 (regs 15–29) and Sch.2. 1.830

Subsection (5)

Emulating JSA, "new style" ESA is a weekly benefit, one paid in respect of a week. For cases of part-week entitlement see s.22, Sch.2 para.3 and ESA Regs 2013 Pt 13 (regs 98–102). 1.831

Subsection (6)

This defines "pensionable age" by reference to other legislation. 1.832

[1Duration of [2. . .] allowance

1A.—(1) The period for which a person is entitled to [2an employment and support allowance] by virtue of the first and second conditions set out in [2. . .] Schedule 1 shall not exceed, in the aggregate, the relevant maximum number of days in any period for which his entitlement is established by reference (under the second condition set out in [2. . .] Schedule 1) to the same two tax years. 1.833

(2) In subsection (1) the "relevant maximum number of days" is—

(a) 365 days, or

(b) if the Secretary of State by order specifies a greater number of days, that number of days.

(3) The fact that a person's entitlement to [2an employment and support allowance] has ceased as a result of subsection (1) does not prevent his being entitled to a further such allowance if—

(a) he satisfies the first and second conditions set out in [2. . .] Schedule 1, and

(b) the two tax years by reference to which he satisfies the second condition include at least one year which is later than the second of the two years by reference to which (under the second condition) his previous entitlement was established.

(4) The period for which a person is entitled to [2an employment and support allowance] by virtue of the third condition set out in [2. . .] Schedule 1 (youth) shall not exceed—

(a) 365 days, or

(b) if the Secretary of State by order specifies a greater number of days, that number of days.

(5) In calculating for the purposes of subsection (1) or (4) the length of the period for which a person is entitled to [2an employment and support allowance], the following are not to be counted—

(a) days in which the person is a member of the support group,

(b) days not falling within paragraph (a) in respect of which the person is entitled to the support component referred to in section 2(1)(b), and

(c) days in the assessment phase, where the days immediately following that phase fall within paragraph (a) or (b).

(6) In calculating for the purposes of subsection (1) or (4) the length of the period for which a person is entitled to [2an employment and support allowance], days occurring before the coming into force of this section are to be counted (as well as those occurring afterwards).]

AMENDMENTS

1. Welfare Reform Act 2012 s.51 (May 1, 2012).
2. Welfare Reform Act 2012 s.33(3) and Sch.3 para.26(a), s.147 and Sch.14 Pt 1 (various dates on or after April 29, 2013).

DEFINITIONS

"relevant maximum number of days"— see subs.(2).

GENERAL NOTE

1.834 As noted in the annotation to WRA 2007 s.1, this section has the effect that, for those not in the support group, "new style" ESA—whether obtained by the contributory route (subss.(1) and (2)) or as a person incapacitated in youth (subs.(4))—is time-limited to 365 days (counting days of entitlement before, on and after that date), even if the period of limited capability for work exceeds this period. This time limit has applied since May 1, 2012. Termination on this ground is appealable, and in any such appeal termination can be contested on the basis that the claimant at the point of termination, although not regarded by the Secretary of State as being in the support group, ought to have been because the claimant at that point in fact had limited capability for work-related activity (or was to be treated as such) (*MC and JH v SSWP* (ESA) [2014] UKUT 125 (AAC)). Note that the Secretary of State can by order increase the time-limit (subss.(2)(b) and (4)(b)). To requalify for a further period of entitlement to "new style" ESA, the conditions in subs.(3) must be met with the second contribution condition being met in at least one tax year later than the second of the two tax years by reference to which (under the second contribution condition) the claimant's previous period of entitlement to "new style" ESA had been based. Since someone may move from the support group to the work-related activity group and back again, calculating when the maximum period of entitlement to "new style" ESA is reached can be more complicated than simply counting 365 days of entitlement. Hence, the days stipulated in subs.(5) do not count in calculating the maximum period of entitlement.

[1Further entitlement after time-limiting

1.835 **1B.**—(1) Where a person's entitlement to [2an employment and support allowance] has ceased as a result of section 1A(1) or (4) but—

(a) the person has not at any subsequent time ceased to have (or to be treated as having) limited capability for work,
(b) the person satisfies the basic conditions, and
(c) the person has (or is treated as having) limited capability for work related activity,

the claimant is entitled to an employment and support allowance by virtue of this section.]

(2) [3 . . .]

AMENDMENTS

1. Welfare Reform Act 2012 s.51 (May 1, 2012).
2. Welfare Reform Act 2012 s.33(3) and Sch.3 para.26(b) (various dates on or after April 29, 2013).
3. Welfare Reform Act 2012 s.147 and Sch.14 Pt 1 (various dates on or after April 29, 2013).

DEFINITIONS

"basic conditions"—see s.1(3), above.

General Note

This section has the effect that where a person's "new style" ESA ceased under s.1A as a result of time limiting, but their health condition has deteriorated so that they are later placed in the support group, they will be able to re-qualify for an award of "new style" ESA if the three conditions in subs.(1) are satisfied: 1.836

- the person has not ceased to have (or be treated as having) limited capability for work;
- the person satisfies the basic conditions (see WRA 2007 s.1(3)); and
- the person has (or is treated as having) limited capability for work-related activity.

Entitlement to the award only subsists for as long as the person has (or is treated as having) limited capability for work-related activity (and so falls into the support group). If a subsequent work capability assessment places the recipient in the work related activity group, then entitlement to an award arising by virtue of this section ceases.

Amount of [1 . . .] allowance

2.—(1) [1The amount payable by way of an employment and support allowance] in respect of a claimant shall be calculated by— 1.837

(a) taking such amount as may be prescribed;

(b) if in his case the conditions of entitlement to the support component [2 . . .] are satisfied, adding the amount of that component; and

(c) making prescribed deductions in respect of any payments to which section 3 applies.

(2) The conditions of entitlement to the support component are—

(a) that the assessment phase has ended;

(b) that the claimant has limited capability for work-related activity; and

(c) that such other conditions as may be prescribed are satisfied.

(3) [2 . . .]

(4) Regulations may—

(a) prescribe circumstances in which paragraph (a) of subsection (2) [2 . . .] is not to apply;

(b) prescribe circumstances in which entitlement under subsection (2) [2 . . .] is to be backdated;

(c) make provision about the amount of the component under subsection (2) [2 . . .].

(5) For the purposes of this Part, a person has limited capability for work related activity if—

(a) his capability for work-related activity is limited by his physical or mental condition; and

(b) the limitation is such that it is not reasonable to require him to undertake such activity.

Amendments

1. Welfare Reform Act 2012 s.33(3) and Sch.3 para.26(a), s.147 and Sch.14 Pt 1 (various dates on or after April 29, 2013).

2. Welfare Reform and Work Act 2016 s.15(2) (April 3, 2017).

Definitions

"assessment phase"—see s.24(2), (3).

"claimant"—see s.24(1).
"limited capability for work-related activity"—see subs.(5).
"prescribed"—see s.24(1).
"regulations"—see s.24(1).
"work-related activity"—see ss.24(1), 13(7), below.

GENERAL NOTE

1.838 This section deals with the calculation of amount of "new style" ESA to which a particular claimant can be entitled, both during the "assessment phase" and after it has ended (subss.(1)–(2)). It provides rule-making powers to modify some of the conditions, to set amounts and to enable backdating of entitlement (subs.(4)). Finally it defines when someone has "limited capability for work-related activity" (subs.(5)).

Subsection (1)

1.839 This sets out the elements making up "new style" ESA and the basic arithmetic for determining the amount of "new style" ESA to which the claimant is entitled. The basic arithmetic during the "assessment phase" is the prescribed (age-related) amount minus any s.3 deductions. After the "assessment phase", it changes to single prescribed amount plus the appropriate component (support or, but only for claims predating April 3, 2017, work related activity) minus any s.3 deductions. Since entitlement varies as between the period of the "assessment phase" and after it has ended, it is useful to begin with analysis of that concept.

The "assessment phase" starts on the first day of the period for which the claimant is entitled to ESA (the day after service of the three waiting days of non-entitlement (see s.22, Sch.2 para.2, and ESA Regs 2013 reg.85)). It ends on whichever is the later of either 13 weeks from that first day of entitlement or the date of determination of limited capability for work (either of actual limited capability or of "deemed" limited capability (treated as having limited capability) (see s.24(2), ESA Regs 2013 reg.5). The ESA scheme deals with intermittent incapacity through "linking" rules. These impact on identification of the end of the "assessment phase". Under ESA Regs 2013 reg.86, periods of limited capability for work "link" and are treated as one single period (to which further ones may be added if the linking rules are met). Periods not separated by more than 12 weeks' "link" in this way (see ESA Regs 2013 reg.86). Where the assessment phase had not ended in the first such period, it ends at the appropriate point (the later of 13 weeks or the date of the limited capability of work determination) in the linked period(s). There can only be one assessment period in any single period of limited capability for work. So where another spell of such limited capability arises and is forged into one with an earlier period by the appropriate 12 week linking rule, and the "assessment phase" had ended in the earlier period, the claimant's entitlement in this second (or subsequent "spell") will be to prescribed amount plus appropriate component minus any s.3 deductions (s.2(4)(a); ESA Regs 2013 reg.7(1)(b)). If the linking rule does not operate so as to forge the two spells into one, the second "spell" constitutes a new period of incapacity, in respect of which the three "waiting days" will again have to be served and a new "assessment phase" will begin again on the first day of entitlement after service of those waiting days and end according to the rules considered above.

Note finally that appealing against a determination that the claimant does not have limited capability for work extends the "assessment phase" until the appeal is determined by an appeal tribunal (s.24(2)(b); ESA Regs 2013, regs 7(4)).

The first element of "new style" ESA is the prescribed amount of "basic allowance". Although this is not a term used in the Act or the Regulations, its use is standard in the literature, policy and explanatory documents on ESA, and accordingly is also deployed here. It is normally the only element of "new style" ESA to which a claimant (other than one terminally ill) can be entitled during the "assessment phase". During that phase, the amount of "new style" ESA (subject to any s.3

deductions) to which the claimant can be entitled varies according to age. If under 25, a lower weekly rate is prescribed. The rates are equivalent to those applicable for CBJSA.

During the assessment phase (whether ending after 13 weeks or a later date of determination of limited capability for work), it will have been determined whether the claimant has limited capability for work (actual limited capability) or should be treated as having it (deemed limited capability). It will also have been determined whether the claimant has limited capability for work related activity or should be treated as having it. If the claimant does have (or is treated as having) such limited capacity, this grounds entitlement to "support component", subject to other conditions set out in regulations, but generally only once the assessment phase has ended (subs.(2)) (see below for an exception in respect of the terminally ill). For claims before April 3, 2017, if the claimant does not have (or is treated as not having) such limited capacity, entitlement (subject to conditionality) can only be to the work-related activity component (see subs.(3), now repealed). For claims made on or after April 3, 2017, the only additional element available is the support component, following the abolition of the work-related activity component. So the basic picture after the assessment period is the prescribed amount plus the appropriate component minus any s.3 deductions.

Once the assessment phase is ended there is a single prescribed weekly amount, regardless of age (see ESA Regs 2013 reg.62, Sch.4, para.1(1)(b)). To this will be added, as appropriate, either the support component (see para.(b); ESA Regs 2013 reg.62(2), Sch.4 Pt 4, para.13) or, at least for claims predating April 3, 2017, the lower value work-related activity component. The amount of "new style" ESA actually payable, however, is subject to reduction in accordance with s.3.

For those who are "terminally ill" (subs.(4)(a); ESA Regs 2013 regs 2(1), 7(1)(a)), entitlement to the components (support or, where appropriate, work-related activity) is not conditioned on the assessment phase having ended. So throughout their period of limited capability for work, entitlement will be to "new style" ESA composed of the basic allowance plus any appropriate component minus any s.3 deductions.

Subsection (2)

This sets out the conditions of entitlement to the support component in "new style" ESA. Entitlement can generally only arise after the assessment phase has ended. An exception to this is in the case of the terminally ill (subs.(4)(a); ESA Regs 2013 reg.7(1)(a)). The claimant must be assessed as having, or be treated by regulations as having, limited capability for work-related activity. Entitlement also depends on other prescribed conditions (i.e. ones set out in regulations). **1.840**

Subsection (3)

This sub-section, now repealed, previously stipulated the conditions of entitlement to the work-related activity component of ESA. Entitlement generally only arose after the assessment phase had ended (see the former subs.(3)(a)). An exception to this was in the case of the terminally ill (subs.(4)(a); ESA Regs 2013 reg.7(1)(a)). The claimant must also have been assessed as not having, or be treated by regulations as not having, limited capability for work-related activity (former subs.(3)(b)). Entitlement also depended on other prescribed conditions (i.e. ones set out in regulations; former subs.(3(c))). **1.841**

However, subs.(3) was repealed by s.15(2) of the Welfare Reform and Work Act 2016 with effect from April 3, 2017 (see reg.3(a) of the Pensions Act 2014 (Commencement No. 9) and the Welfare Reform and Work Act 2016 (Commencement No. 4) Regulations 2017 (SI 2017/111)). This implemented an announcement first made in the Summer 2015 Budget, namely that the work-related activity component paid to those in the work-related activity group would be abolished for new ESA claims as from April 3, 2017. A parallel amendment was made to the legislation governing universal credit. The policy justification for the change was said to be the need to remove the financial incentives in the benefits system that could otherwise discourage claimants from taking steps back into work. The practical effect of the reform was a cut of £29.05 a week (at 2017/18 rates), so aligning the rate of ESA for this group with the rate of benefit paid to JSA claimants. This was anticipated to save £450 million a year by 2020/21 (Budget 2016 estimate).

In broad terms, the abolition of the work-related activity component applied only to new claims as from April 3, 2017. Those claimants already in receipt of that component continue to receive it, providing they remain on ESA. The transitional rules are in Sch.2 to the Employment and Support Allowance and Universal Credit (Miscellaneous Amendments and Transitional and Savings Provisions) Regulations 2017 (SI 2017/207). These cover the following circumstances:

- where an ESA claim was made before April 3, 2017 and that claim results in an award after that date;
- where an ESA claim was made on or after April 3, 2017 but the claimant had previously been entitled to ESA and their period of limited capability for work started before April 3, 2017 with a linking period of less than 12 weeks;
- where an existing incapacity benefit claimant who, as part of the conversion process to ESA, is subsequently found to have limited capability for work after April 3, 2017;
- where an ESA claim was made on or after April 3, 2017 but ESA is deemed payable from before April 3, 2017;
- where an ESA claim was made on or after April 3, 2017 but the claimant's assessment phase is deemed to have started before April 3, 2017;
- where a claimant (who was previously entitled to ESA as part of a claim made before April 3, 2017) having been in receipt of a maternity allowance makes a new claim for ESA within 12 weeks of the date that their maternity allowance ended (and where their maternity allowance terminated their award to contributory ESA).

Applying Subsections (2) or (3) after a break in entitlement

1.842 It is submitted that the approach of Judge Mesher in *SSWP v PT* (ESA) [2011] UKUT 317 (AAC) to breaks of entitlement are equally applicable as regards the component of the allowance returned to after a comparable break in entitlement. See further commentary to WRA 2007 s.4, below.

Subsection (5)

1.843 This defines "limited capability for work-related activity" (LCWRA). Whether the claimant has it or not is crucial for identifying which group of ESA (support or work related activity) is applicable in the case. Claimants have LCWRA where their capability for work-related activity is limited by their physical or mental condition such that it is not reasonable to require them to undertake such activity. "Work-related activity" is defined as activity which makes it more likely that the person whose capability is being tested will obtain or remain in work or be able to do so (ss.24(1), 13(7)).

Deductions from [1. . .] allowance: supplementary

1.844 **3.**—(1) This section applies to payments of the following kinds which are payable to the claimant—

(a) pension payments,
(b) PPF periodic payments, and

(c) payments of a prescribed description made to a person who is a member of, or has been appointed to, a prescribed body carrying out public or local functions.

(2) Regulations may—

(a) disapply section 2(1)(c), so far as relating to pension payments or PPF periodic payments, in relation to persons of a prescribed description;

(b) provide for pension payments or PPF periodic payments of a prescribed description to be treated for the purposes of that provision as not being payments to which this section applies;

(c) provide for sums of a prescribed description to be treated for the purposes of this section as payable to persons as pension payments or PPF periodic payments (including, in particular, sums in relation to which there is a deferred right of receipt);

(d) make provision for the method of determining how payments to which this section applies are, for the purposes of section 2, to be related to periods for which a person is entitled to [2an employment and support allowance].

(3) In this section—

"pension payment" means—

(a) a periodical payment made in relation to a person under a personal pension scheme or, in connection with the coming to an end of an employment of his, under an occupational pension scheme or a public service pension scheme,

(b) a payment of a prescribed description made under an insurance policy providing benefits in connection with physical or mental illness or disability, and (c) such other payments as may be prescribed;

"PPF periodic payment" means—

(a) any periodic compensation payment made in relation to a person, payable under the pension compensation provisions as specified in section 162(2) of the Pensions Act 2004 (c.35) or Article 146(2) of the Pensions (Northern Ireland) Order 2005 (S.I. 2005/255) (NI 1) (the pension compensation provisions), and

(b) any periodic payment made in relation to a person, payable under section 166 of the Pensions Act 2004 or Article 150 of the Pensions (Northern Ireland) Order 2005 (duty to pay scheme benefits unpaid at assessment date etc.).

(4) For the purposes of subsection (3), "occupational pension scheme", "personal pension scheme" and "public service pension scheme" each have the meaning given by section 1 of the Pension Schemes Act 1993 (c.48), except that "personal pension scheme" includes—

(a) an annuity contract or trust scheme approved under section 620 or 621 of the Income and Corporation Taxes Act 1988 (c.1), and

(b) a substituted contract within the meaning of section 622(3) of that Act, which is treated as having become a registered pension scheme by virtue of paragraph 1(1)(f) of Schedule 36 to the Finance Act 2004 (c.12).

AMENDMENTS

1. Welfare Reform Act 2012 s.147 and Sch.14 Pt 1 (various dates on or after April 29, 2013).

2. Welfare Reform Act 2012 s.33(3) and Sch.3 para.26 (c) (various dates on or after April 29, 2013).

DEFINITIONS

"claimant"—see s.24(1), below.
"occupational pension scheme"—see subs.(4).
"pension payment"—see subs.(3).
"personal pension scheme"—see subs.(4).
"PPF periodic payment"—see subs.(3).
"prescribed"—see s.24(1), below.

GENERAL NOTE

1.845 Under s.2 above, the amount of "new style" ESA to which the claimant is otherwise entitled will normally (see subs.(2)(a) of this section) be reduced as set out in regulations (ESA Regs 2013 regs 64–72) by the payments set out in this section which are payable to the claimant. This section and ESA Regs 2013, regs 64–72 thus bring into ESA the concept of the abatement of a contributory benefit. This is familiar from jobseeker's allowance (see JSA 1995 s.21, Sch.1 para.7; JSA Regs regs 80, 81 in Vol.I) and the former incapacity benefit (see SSCBA 1992 ss.30DD and 30E; IB Regs regs 20–26) and unemployment benefit (see SSCBA 1992 s.30 and the former USI Regs 23–28). While not making them fully income-related benefits along the lines of e.g. income support or income-related jobseeker's allowance, such abatement of "new style" ESA nonetheless continues the practice of bringing into a contributory benefit an element of means testing. Given the provenance of these provisions, when interpreting this section and its associated regulations some cross-reference to case law under those JSA and IB schemes will be appropriate insofar as the definitions are identical or analogous.

Subsection (1)

1.846 This stipulates that this section covers pension payments (para.(a)—defined in subss.(3), (4)), PPF periodic payments (para.(b)—defined in subs.(3)) and "payments of a prescribed description made to a person who is a member of, or has been appointed to, a prescribed body carrying out public or local functions" (para. (c)). For the rules on taking pension payments and PPF payments into account, see ESA Regs 2013 reg.67. Currently, under para.(c), ESA Regs 2013 reg.66 prescribes only "councillor's allowance" in respect of those councils referred to in the definition of "councillor" in ESA Regs 2013 reg.2(1). For the rules on taking "councillor's allowance" into account, see ESA Regs 2013 reg.69. On the meaning of "payable to", see *R(IB) 1/04* and *R(IB) 1/05*.

Subsection (2)

1.847 Under para.(b), see ESA Regs 2013 reg.68.
Under para.(d), see ESA Regs 2013 regs.70-72.

Subsection (3)

1.848 Under para.(b) of the definition of pension payment, see ESA Regs 2013 reg.64 whereby "pension payment" includes a "permanent health insurance payment" as defined in that regulation.

Amount of income-related allowance

1.849 **4.** [1. . .].

AMENDMENT

1. Repealed by Welfare Reform Act 2012 s.147 and Sch.14 Pt 1 (various dates on or after April 29, 2013).

Advance award of income-related allowance

5. [1. . .]. 1.850

AMENDMENT

1. Repealed by Welfare Reform Act 2012 s.147 and Sch.14 Pt 1 ((various dates on or after April 29, 2013).

Amount payable where claimant entitled to both forms of allowance

6. [1. . .]. 1.851

AMENDMENT

1. Repealed by Welfare Reform Act 2012 s.147 and Sch.14 Pt 1 (various dates on or after April 29, 2013).

Exclusion of payments below prescribed minimum

7.—Except in such circumstances as regulations may provide, an employment and support allowance shall not be payable where the amount otherwise payable would be less than a prescribed minimum. 1.852

DEFINITIONS

"prescribed"—see s.24(1).
"regulations"—see s.24(1).

GENERAL NOTE

ESA is not payable where it falls below the minimum amount prescribed in regulations. This amount is set at 10p in the Claims and Payments Regs 1987 reg.26C(6). Compare JSA Regs reg.87A. 1.853

Assessments relating to entitlement

Limited capability for work

8.—(1) For the purposes of this Part, whether a person's capability for work is limited by his physical or mental condition and, if it is, whether the limitation is such that it is not reasonable to require him to work shall be determined in accordance with regulations. 1.854

(2) Regulations under subsection (1) shall—

(a) provide for determination on the basis of an assessment of the person concerned;
(b) define the assessment by reference to the extent to which a person who has some specific disease or bodily or mental disablement is capable or incapable of performing such activities as may be prescribed;
(c) make provision as to the manner of carrying out the assessment.

(3) Regulations under subsection (1) may, in particular, make provision—

(a) as to the information or evidence required for the purpose of determining the matters mentioned in that subsection;

(b) as to the manner in which that information or evidence is to be provided;

(c) for a person in relation to whom it falls to be determined whether he has limited capability for work to be called to attend for such medical examination as the regulations may require.

(4) Regulations under subsection (1) may include provision—

(a) for a person to be treated as not having limited capability for work if he fails without good cause—

(i) to provide information or evidence which he is required under such regulations to provide,

(ii) to provide information or evidence in the manner in which he is required under such regulations to provide it, or

(iii) to attend for, or submit himself to, a medical examination for which he is called under such regulations to attend;

(b) as to matters which are, or are not, to be taken into account in determining for the purposes of any provision made by virtue of paragraph (a) whether a person has good cause for any act or omission;

(c) as to circumstances in which a person is, or is not, to be regarded for the purposes of any such provision as having good cause for any act or omission.

(5) Regulations may provide that, in prescribed circumstances, a person in relation to whom it falls to be determined whether he has limited capability for work, shall, if prescribed conditions are met, be treated as having limited capability for work until such time as—

(a) it has been determined whether he has limited capability for work, or

(b) he falls in accordance with regulations under this section to be treated as not having limited capability for work.

(6) The prescribed conditions referred to in subsection (5) may include the condition that it has not previously been determined, within such period as may be prescribed, that the person in question does not have, or is to be treated as not having, limited capability for work.

DEFINITIONS

"limited capability for work"—see s.1(4).
"medical examination"—
"prescribed"—see s.24(1).
"regulations"—see s.24(1)

GENERAL NOTE

Subsections (1), (2)

1.855 A key condition of entitlement to ESA is that the claimant has limited capability for work (LCW), namely that their capability for work is limited by their physical or mental condition such that it is not reasonable to require them to work (s.1(3)(a), (4)). This section provides that whether this is so is to be determined in accordance with regulations made under subss.(2)–(6) of this section. The regulations are Pt 4 of the ESA Regs 2013, regs 15–29. These embody the Work Capability

Assessment (WCA), governing entitlement to ESA, the successor to the former Personal Capability Assessment (PCA) in the previous incapacity benefits' regime. The assessment also determines whether or not a claimant has limited capability for work-related activity (LCWRA). If so, the claimant will be placed in the support group as eligible for the support component. Claimants who do not have limited capability for work-related activity will be placed in the work-related activity group and subject to the work-related requirements regime (see ss.11–11K). Note that payment of the separate work-related activity component has not been available for new claims to ESA since April 3, 2017 (subject to transitional provisions): see the annotation to the former s.2(3) above (and see further section 15(2) and (3) of the Welfare Reform and Work Act 2016 and reg.3(a) of the Pensions Act 2014 (Commencement No. 9) and the Welfare Reform and Work Act 2016 (Commencement No. 4) Regulations 2017 (SI 2017/111)).

Subsections (3), (4)

Note that whether the claimant has good cause for failure to comply with the information-gathering and examination aspects of that assessment is to some extent structured by regulations in that ESA Regs 2013, reg.20 provides a non-exhaustive list of matters to be taken into account in determining that good cause issue. No regulations have yet been made under para.(4)(c) to determine what does, or does not, rank as good cause. **1.856**

Limited capability for work-related activity

9.—(1) For the purposes of this Part, whether a person's capability for work-related activity is limited by his physical or mental condition and, if it is, whether the limitation is such that it is not reasonable to require him to undertake such activity shall be determined in accordance with regulations. **1.857**

(2) Regulations under subsection (1) shall—

(a) provide for determination on the basis of an assessment of the person concerned;

(b) define the assessment by reference to such matters as the regulations may provide;

(c) make provision as to the manner of carrying out the assessment.

(3) Regulations under subsection (1) may, in particular, make provision—

(a) as to the information or evidence required for the purpose of determining the matters mentioned in that subsection;

(b) as to the manner in which that information or evidence is to be provided;

(c) for a person in relation to whom it falls to be determined whether he has limited capability for work-related activity to be called to attend for such medical examination as the regulations may require.

(4) Regulations under subsection (1) may include provision—

(a) for a person to be treated as not having limited capability for work-related activity if he fails without good cause—

(i) to provide information or evidence which he is required under such regulations to provide,

(ii) to provide information or evidence in the manner in which he is required under such regulations to provide it, or

(iii) to attend for, or submit himself to, a medical examination for which he is called under such regulations to attend;

(b) as to matters which are, or are not, to be taken into account in determining for the purposes of any provision made by virtue of paragraph (a) whether a person has good cause for any act or omission;
(c) as to circumstances in which a person is, or is not, to be regarded for the purposes of any such provision as having good cause for any act or omission.

DEFINITIONS

"regulations"—see s.24(1).
"work-related activity"—see ss.24(1), 13(7)

GENERAL NOTE

Subsections (1), (2)

1.858 Whether ESA claimants are entitled to the more generous support component or, at least for claims predating April 3, 2017, the less generous work-related activity component in addition to their basic allowance turns on whether they do (support component) or do not (work-related activity component) have limited capability for work-related activity (s.2(2), (3)). A person has "limited capability for work-related activity" (LCWRA) where their capability for such activity is limited by their physical or mental condition such that it is not reasonable to require them to undertake it (s.2(5)). "Work-related activity" is activity which makes it more likely that they will obtain or remain in work or be able to do so (ss.24(1), 13(7)). This section provides that whether or not a person has such limited capability is to be determined in accordance with regulations under subss.(2), (4) of this section. The regulations in question are ESA Regs 2013, Pt 5, regs 30–36, which flesh out the nature of the work related activity assessment.

Subsections (3), (4)

1.859 Note that whether the claimant has good cause for failure to comply with the information-gathering and examination aspects of that assessment is to some extent structured by regulations in that ESA Regs 2013, reg.36 provides a non-exhaustive list of matters to be taken into account in determining that good cause issue. No regulations have yet been made under para.(4)(c) to determine what does, or does not, rank as good cause.

Report

1.860 **10.**—The Secretary of State shall lay before Parliament an independent report on the operation of the assessments under sections 8 and 9 annually for the first five years after those sections come into force.

GENERAL NOTE

1.861 This provision–requiring an independent annual report on the operation of work capability assessments to be laid before Parliament by the Secretary of State – is now otiose, as the requirement was only for the first five years after commencement. See further the commentary on Schedule 2 of the ESA Regulations 2013.

[1 Work-related requirements

Work-related requirements

11. — (1) The following provisions of this Part provide for the Secretary of State to impose work-related requirements with which persons entitled to an employment and support allowance must comply for the purposes of this Part. 1.862

(2) In this Part "work-related requirement" means—

(a) a work-focused interview requirement (see section 11B);

(b) a work preparation requirement (see section 11C).

(3) The work-related requirements which may be imposed on a person depend on which of the following groups the person falls into—

(a) persons subject to no work-related requirements (see section 11D);

(b) persons subject to work-focused interview requirement only (see section 11E);

(c) persons subject to work-focused interview and work preparation requirements (see section 11F).]

AMENDMENT

1. Welfare Reform Act 2012 s.57(1), (2) (various dates on or after April 29, 2013).

DEFINITIONS

"work-focused interview requirement"—see s.11B(1).
"work-related requirement"—see subs.(2).
"work preparation requirement"—see s.11C(1).

GENERAL NOTE

For "new style" ESA, the imposition of "work-related requirements" by the Secretary of State replaces the "conditionality" applicable to "old style" ESA. The idea behind both is to provide deterrents to ensure that benefit recipients meet specified responsibilities, which vary according to the group into which the person falls (see subs.(3)), but are designed to enhance ability ultimately to return to the labour market. Unless completely exempt (see s.11D), a person entitled to "new style" ESA must comply with the requirements validly imposed. Failure for no good reason to comply is punishable by a sanction in the form of a reduction of ESA for a period (see ss.11I and 11J). 1.863

"Work-related requirements" consist of a work interview requirement (see s.11B) and/or one a number of work preparation requirements (see s.11C). Some claimants cannot be subject to any work-related requirements (see s.11D). Others may be subject only to a work interview requirement (see s.11E). The remainder can be subject to both a work interview requirement and work preparation requirements (see s.11F). All those entitled to ESA can be required to meet the "connected requirement" of participation in an interview for a purpose(s) related to the imposition of a work-related requirement, verification of compliance with any imposed or assisting the subject of the requirement to comply with it (see s.11G).

[1Claimant commitment

11A. — (1) A claimant commitment is a record of the responsibilities of a person entitled to an employment and support allowance in relation to the award of the allowance. 1.864

(2) A claimant commitment is to be prepared by the Secretary of State and may be reviewed and updated as the Secretary of State thinks fit.

(3) A claimant commitment is to be in such form as the Secretary of State thinks fit.

(4) A claimant commitment is to include—

(a) a record of the requirements that the person must comply with under this Part (or such of them as the Secretary of State considers it appropriate to include),

(b) any prescribed information, and

(c) any other information the Secretary of State considers it appropriate to include.

(5) For the purposes of this Part a person accepts a claimant commitment if, and only if, the claimant accepts the most up-to-date version of it in such manner as may be prescribed.]

AMENDMENT

1. Welfare Reform Act 2012 s.57(1), (2) (various dates on or after April 29, 2013).

DEFINITIONS

"prescribed"—see s.24(1).

GENERAL NOTE

1.865 The "claimant commitment" is a feature of "new style" ESA, "new style" JSA and UC. On the background to it, its nature and how (if at all) a claimant may challenge it, see further the annotations to Welfare Reform Act 2012 s.14 in Vol.II. As regards "new style" JSA, this section defines the "claimant commitment" and is amplified by ESA Regs 2013 regs 44 (date and method of acceptance) and 45 (exceptions).

A "claimant commitment" is thus a record of the responsibilities of someone entitled to "new style" ESA in relation to an award in such form as the Secretary of State thinks fit, drawn up by her/him and reviewed and updated as s/he thinks fit. It must include such of the claimant's commitments as the Secretary of State thinks appropriate, any information prescribed by regulations, and such further information as the Secretary of State thinks appropriate. It is thus in some ways reminiscent of the jobseeker's agreement in "old style" JSA in that (in practice) it is something imposed by the Secretary of State rather than something into which a claimant enters voluntarily.

[[1]Work-focused interview requirement

1.866 **11B.** — (1) In this Part a "work-focused interview requirement" is a requirement that a person participate in one or more work-focused interviews as specified by the Secretary of State.

(2) A work-focused interview is an interview for prescribed purposes relating to work or work preparation.

(3) The purposes which may be prescribed under subsection (2) include in particular that of making it more likely in the opinion of the Secretary of State that the person will obtain paid work (or more paid work or better-paid work).

(4) The Secretary of State may specify how, when and where a work-focused interview is to take place.]

AMENDMENT

1. Welfare Reform Act 2012 s.57(1), (2) (various dates on or after April 29, 2013).

DEFINITION

"prescribed"—see s.24(1).
"work-focused interview requirement"—see subs.(1).

GENERAL NOTE

This section must be read with s.11D and ESA Regs 2013 reg.46, which specify those persons subject to no work-related requirements, who thus cannot be subjects of a work-focused interview requirement with which this section deals. This section is further amplified by ESA Regs 2013 reg.46 (purposes of a work-focused interview). **1.867**

Imposition of a work-focused interview requirement means that its subject must participate in such number of work-focused interviews as the Secretary of State requires (subs.(1)). Such interviews are ones for prescribed purposes relating to work or work preparation, the central purpose is one of enhancing the likelihood of the claimant obtaining paid work, more paid work or better paid work (subss. (2), (3)). On the purposes of such an interview, see ESA Regs 2013 reg.46. The Secretary of State stipulates how, when and where a work-focused interview is to take place (subs.(4))

[[1]Work preparation requirement

11C. — (1) In this Part a "work preparation requirement" is a requirement that a person take particular action specified by the Secretary of State for the purpose of making it more likely in the opinion of the Secretary of State that the person will obtain paid work (or more paid work or betterpaid work). **1.868**

(2) The Secretary of State may under subsection (1) specify the time to be devoted to any particular action.

(3) Action which may be specified under subsection (1) includes in particular—

(a) attending a skills assessment;
(b) improving personal presentation;
(c) participating in training;
(d) participating in an employment programme;
(e) undertaking work experience or a work placement;
(f) developing a business plan;
(g) any action prescribed for the purpose in subsection (1).

(4) The action which may be specified under subsection (1) includes taking part in a work-focused health-related assessment.

(5) In subsection (4) "work-focused health-related assessment" means an assessment by a health care professional approved by the Secretary of State which is carried out for the purpose of assessing—

(a) the extent to which the person's capability for work may be improved by taking steps in relation to their physical or mental condition, and
(b) such other matters relating to their physical or mental condition and the likelihood of their obtaining or remaining in work or being able to do so as may be prescribed.

(6) In subsection (5) "health care professional" means—
(a) a registered medical practitioner,
(b) a registered nurse,
(c) an occupational therapist or physiotherapist registered with a regulatory body established by an Order in Council under section 60 of the Health Act 1999, or (d) a member of such other profession regulated by a body mentioned in section 25(3) of the National Health Service Reform and Health Care Professions Act 2002 as may be prescribed.]

AMENDMENT

1. Welfare Reform Act 2012 s.57(1), (2) (various dates on or after April 29, 2013).

DEFINITONS

"health care professional"—see subs.(6).
"prescribed"—see s.24(1).
"work-focused health-related assessment"—see subs.(5).
"work preparation requirement"—see subs.(1).

GENERAL NOTE

1.869 This section must be read with s.11D and ESA Regs 2013 reg.47, which together set out those persons who cannot be subject to any work-related requirement at all, and with ESA Regs 2013 reg.48 which, in stipulating which persons can be subject only to a work-focused interview requirement, exempt those persons from the work-preparation requirements with which this section deals.

Work-preparation requirements require their subject to take particular actions specified by the Secretary of State as in her/his opinion are likely to enhance the likelihood of that claimant obtaining paid work, more paid work or better paid work (subs.(1)). An inclusive (i.e. not exhaustive) list of such actions is set out in subs. (3) and (4) and there is power to set out further ones in regulations (subs. (3)(g), although as yet this power has not been exercised. The time to be spent on each action will also be stipulated by the Secretary of State (subs.(2)). Although s.11H(2) provides that in considering whether to impose a work-focused interview requirement the Secretary of State must have regard to such matters as may be prescribed, as yet it appears that none have been prescribed.

[1Persons subject to no work-related requirements

1.870 **11D.**—(1) The Secretary of State may not impose any work-related requirement on a person falling within this section.

(2) A person falls within this section if—
(a) the person has limited capability for work and work-related activity,
(b) the person has regular and substantial caring responsibilities for a severely disabled person,
(c) the person is a single person responsible for a child under the age of 1,
(d) the person is of a prescribed description.

(3) Where a person falls within this section, any work-related requirement previously applying to the person ceases to have effect.

(4) In this section—

"regular and substantial caring responsibilities" has such meaning as may be prescribed;

"severely disabled" has such meaning as may be prescribed.]

AMENDMENT

1. Welfare Reform Act 2012 s.57(1), (2) (various dates on or after April 29, 2013).

DEFINITONS

"limited capability for work"—see ss.24(1), 1(4).
"limited capability for work-related activity"—see ss.24(1), 2(5).
"prescribed"—see s.24(1).
"regular and substantial caring responsibilities"—see subs.(4); ESA Regs 2013 reg.47(2), (3).
"severely disabled"—see subs.(4); ESA Regs 2013 reg.47(5).

GENERAL NOTE

This section, together with ESA Regs 2013 reg.47, sets out those who are exempt from the imposition of any work-related requirement (subs.(1), (2)). 1.871

Some claimants will fall permanently within one of the exempt groups and thus never be subject to such requirements. Others, as their condition improves or relevant circumstances change (e.g. the single parent as their child gets older) may move out of the exempt group and can then be subject to such requirements. Others, subject to such requirements because not in an exempt category, may find that their condition worsens or relevant circumstances change (e.g. a child is born to a single parent or the claimant has taken on regular and substantial caring responsibilities for a severely disabled person) so that they then fall into an exempt category, in which case any work-related requirement previously applying to them ceases to have effect (subs.(3)).

Subs.(2) sets out four exempt categories. Firstly, it exempts persons falling within the "support" group as having limited capability both for work and work-related activity (para. (a)). Secondly, it protects from imposition of work-related requirements those having regular and substantial caring responsibilities for a severely disabled person (para. (b)), those key terms being defined in ESA Regs 2013 reg.47(2), (3) (regular and substantial caring responsibilities) and 47(5) (severely disabled). Thirdly, it exempts single parents having responsibility for a child under the age of one (para.(c)). Finally, it exempts those of a "prescribed description", currently those groups listed in ESA Regs 2013 reg.47(1).

[1Persons subject to work-focused interview requirement only

11E. —(1) A person falls within this section if— 1.872

(a) the person is a single person responsible for a child who is aged at least 1 and is under a prescribed age (which may not be less than 3), or
(b) the person is of a prescribed description.

(2) The Secretary of State may, subject to this Part, impose a work-focused interview requirement on a person entitled to an employment and support allowance who falls within this section.

(3) The Secretary of State may not impose a work preparation requirement on a person falling within this section (and, where a person falls within this section, a work preparation requirement previously applying to the person ceases to have effect).]

AMENDMENT

1. Welfare Reform Act 2012 s.57(1), (2) (various dates on or after April 29, 2013).

DEFINITONS

1.873 "prescribed"—see s.24(1).
"work-focused interview requirement"—see s.11B(1).
"work preparation requirement"—see s.11C(1).

GENERAL NOTE

1.874 This section, together with ESA Regs 2013 reg.48, sets out those who, while not exempt from the imposition of all work-related requirements under s.11D, can be subject only to the work-focused interview requirement, thus affording such person exemption from the imposition of any work-preparation requirement. Since someone might not at the outset of the "new style" ESA award have been in one of the categories protected by this section and have thus been the subject of a work-preparation requirement, any such requirement will cease to have effect if later in the currency of the award that person falls into one or more of the protected categories.

Subs.(1) stipulates two protected categories. First, it protects a single person responsible for a child who is aged at least one and below three (the prescribed age set in ESA Regs 2013 reg.48(1)). Secondly, it exempts from work preparation requirements anyone of a prescribed description, currently those listed in ESA Regs 2013 reg.47(1). Although s.11H(2) provides that in considering whether to impose a work-focused interview requirement the Secretary of State must have regard to such matters as may be prescribed, as yet it appears that none have been prescribed.

[1Persons subject to work preparation and work-focused interview requirement

1.875 **11F.**— (1) A person who does not fall within section 11D or 11E falls within this section.

(2) The Secretary of State may, subject to this Part, impose a work preparation requirement or work-focused interview requirement on a person entitled to an employment and support allowance who falls within this section.]

AMENDMENT

1. Welfare Reform Act 2012 s.57(1), (2) (various dates on or after April 29, 2013).

DEFINITONS

"work-focused interview requirement"—see s.11B(1).
"work preparation requirement"—see s.11C(1).

GENERAL NOTE

1.876 This section stipulates that anyone entitled to "new style" ESA and who is not protected by ss.11D or 11E, above, can be subject to a work-focused interview requirement, to a work-preparation requirement or to both such requirements.

[1Connected requirements

1.877 **11G.** —(1) The Secretary of State may require a person entitled to an employment and support allowance to participate in an interview for any purpose relating to—

(a) the imposition of a work-related requirement on the person;

(b) verifying the person's compliance with a work-related requirement;
(c) assisting the person to comply with a work-related requirement.

(2) The Secretary of State may specify how, when and where such an interview is to take place.

(3) The Secretary of State may, for the purpose of verifying a person's compliance with a work-related requirement, require the person to—
(a) provide to the Secretary of State information and evidence specified by the Secretary of State in a manner so specified;
(b) confirm compliance in a manner so specified.

(4) The Secretary of State may require a person to report to the Secretary of State any specified changes in their circumstances which are relevant to—
(a) the imposition of work-related requirements on the person;
(b) the person's compliance with a work-related requirement.]

AMENDMENT

1. Welfare Reform Act 2012 s.57(1), (2) (various dates on or after April 29, 2013).

DEFINITION

"work-related requirement"—see s.11(2).

GENERAL NOTE

This section deals with the processes surrounding the imposition of work-related requirements, with monitoring compliance with them and with assisting those subject to them with compliance with them. The processes can involve participation in an interview with respect to such matters (subs.(1), (2)), providing specified information and evidence or simply confirmation of compliance as part of verification of compliance (subs.(3)), and reporting specified changes of relevant circumstances (subs.(4)). 1.878

[1 Imposition of requirements

11H.—(1) Regulations may make provision— 1.879

(a) Where the Secretary of State may impose a requirement under this Part, as to when the requirement must or must not be imposed;

(b) where the Secretary of State may specify any action to be taken in relation to a requirement under this Part, as to what action must or must not be specified;

(c) where the Secretary of State may specify any other matter in relation to a requirement under this Part, as to what must or must not be specified in respect of that matter.

(2) Where the Secretary of State may impose a work-focused interview requirement, or specify a particular action under section 11C(1), the Secretary of State must have regard to such matters as may be prescribed.

(3) Where the Secretary of State may impose a requirement under this Part, or specify any action to be taken in relation to such a requirement, the Secretary of State may revoke or change what has been imposed or specified.

(4) Notification of a requirement imposed under this Part (or any change to or revocation of such a requirement) is, if not included in the claimant commitment, to be in such manner as the Secretary of State may determine.

(5) Regulations must make provision to secure that, in prescribed circumstances, where a person has recently been a victim of domestic violence—

(a) a requirement imposed on that person under this Part ceases to have effect for a period of 13 weeks, and
(b) the Secretary of State may not impose any other requirement on that person during that period.

(6) For the purposes of subsection (5)—
(a) "domestic violence" has such meaning as may be prescribed;
(b) "victim of domestic violence" means a person on or against whom domestic violence is inflicted or threatened (and regulations under subsection (5) may prescribe circumstances in which a person is to be treated as being or not being a victim of domestic violence);
(c) a person has recently been a victim of domestic violence if a prescribed period has not expired since the violence was inflicted or threatened.]

AMENDMENT

1. Welfare Reform Act 2012 s.57(1), (2) (various dates on or after April 29, 2013).

DEFINITONS

1.880 "domestic violence"—see subs.(6)(a); ESA Regs 2013 reg.49(5).
"prescribed"—see s.24(1).
"regulations"—see s.24(1).
"victim of domestic violence"—see subs.(6)(b).
"week"—see s.24(1).
"work-focused interview requirement"—see s.11B(1).

GENERAL NOTE

1.881 Subs.(1) and (5) enable regulations to be made on a variety of matters concerned with the imposition of work-related requirements on those who can be subject to them. To date, the only one made appears to be ESA Regs 2013 reg.48—made pursuant to subs.(5)— dealing with the respite period afforded recent victims of domestic violence. Although subs.(2) provides that in considering whether to impose a work-focused interview requirement the Secretary of State must have regard to such matters as may be prescribed, as yet it appears that none have been prescribed. Work-related requirements imposed or particular action specified can be revoked or changed (subs.(3)). If not embodied in the claimant commitment (see s.11A), the imposition of requirements or their revocation or alteration is to be made in such manner as the Secretary of State determines (subs.(4)).

[[1]Compliance with requirements

1.882 **11I.** — Regulations may make provision as to circumstances in which a person is to be treated as having—
(a) complied with or not complied with any requirement imposed under this Part or any aspect of such a requirement, or
(b) taken or not taken any particular action specified by the Secretary of State in relation to such a requirement.]

AMENDMENT

1. Welfare Reform Act 2012 s.57(1), (2) (various dates on or after April 29, 2013).

DEFINITONS

"regulations"—see s.24(1).

GENERAL NOTE

This is comparable to WRA 2012, s.25, as regards UC, and Jobseekers Act 1995 s.6I, as regards "new style" JSA. The comparator provisions have resulted in UC Regs 2013 regs 94–97 and JSA Regs 2013 regs 11–13. In contrast, this section has produced no amplifying regulations. 1.883

[[1]Sanctions

11J.—(1) The amount of an award of an employment and support allowance is to be reduced in accordance with this section in the event of a failure by a person which is sanctionable under this section. 1.884

(2) It is a failure sanctionable under this section if a person—

(a) fails for no good reason to comply with a work-related requirement;

(b) fails for no good reason to comply with a requirement under section 11G.

(3) Regulations are to specify—

(a) the amount of a reduction under this section, and

(b) the period for which such a reduction has effect.

(4) Regulations under subsection (3)(b) may provide that a reduction under this section in relation to any failure is to have effect for—

(a) a period continuing until the person meets a compliance condition specified by the Secretary of State,

(b) a fixed period not exceeding 26 weeks which is—

(i) specified in the regulations, or

(ii) determined in any case by the Secretary of State, or

(c) a combination of both.

(5) In subsection (4)(a) "compliance condition" means—

(a) a condition that the failure ceases, or

(b) a condition relating to future compliance with a work-related requirement or a requirement under section 11G.

(6) A compliance condition specified under subsection (4) (a) may be—

(a) revoked or varied by the Secretary of State;

(b) notified to the person in such manner as the Secretary of State may determine.

(7) A period fixed under subsection (4) (b) may in particular depend on either or both the following—

(a) the number of failures by the person sanctionable under this section;

(b) the period between such failures.

(8) Regulations may provide—

(a) for cases in which no reduction is to be made under this section;

(b) for a reduction under this section made in relation to an award that is terminated to be applied to any new award made within a prescribed period of the termination;

(c) for the termination or suspension of a reduction under this section.]

AMENDMENT

1. Welfare Reform Act 2012 s.57(1), (2) (various dates on or after April 29, 2013).

DEFINITONS

"compliance condition"—see subs.(5).
"prescribed"—see s.24(1).
"regulations"—see s.24(1).
"week"—see s.24(1).
"work-related requirement"—see s.11(2).

GENERAL NOTE

1.885 There is no direct sanction for failing to comply with a claimant commitment (see s.11A). Instead failure "for no good reason" to comply with a work-related requirement or with a connected requirement under s.11G is sanctionable under this section (subss.(1), (2)).

Exactly what is meant by the phrase "fails for no good reason" remains to be fully clarified through appeals against sanctions. This term is used both here and as regards UC (WRA 2012 ss.26, 27, see Vol.II) and "new style" JSA (see Jobseekers Act 1995 ss.6J, 6K in this Part of this volume). In contrast, "old style" JSA deploys the term "without a good reason" while "new style" ESA in the ESA Regs 2013 refers to "without good cause" as regards failures to provide information or attend for or participate in a medical examinations, as do the comparable provisions with respect to "old style" ESA in the ESA Regs 2008. Despite the variations in terminology, the common idea behind each is that in certain circumstances failures are to be "excused", namely not to be punished with a sanction. It may be that, despite the differences in wording, there will be a commonalty of interpretation, with decision-makers and tribunals seeing their application as requiring consideration of all relevant circumstances but also containing a large element of judgement according to the individual facts of particular cases. There is certainly authority to the effect there is no difference in meaning between "for no good reason" and without a good reason": see *S v SSWP* (UC) [2017] UKUT 477 (AAC) at para.4 and see further the analysis of WRA 2012 s.26 in Vol II of this series.

The sanction itself consists of reduction of an ESA award for a period, the amount and the period being determined by regulations (subs.(3)). As regards the period, such regulations may provide that a reduction under this section in relation to any failure is to have effect (i) for a period continuing until the person meets a compliance condition specified by the Secretary of State or (ii) for a fixed period of not more than 26 weeks set by regulations, or determined in any case by the Secretary of State, or (iii) for a period combining (i) and (ii) (subs.(4)). The length of period (ii) (the fixed period) can depend on the number of failures by the person sanctionable under this section, the period between them, or both (subs.(7)). As regards period (i), a compliance condition is one requiring that the failure cease and/or one relating to future compliance with a work-related requirement or with a connected requirement under s.11G (subs.(5), (6)). The regulations in question are ESA Regs 2013 regs 50–53, 58–60, on which see the detailed commentary in Part VIII of this volume.

Under subs.(8)(c), regulations can provide for the termination or suspension of a reduction. On its termination see ESA Regs 2013 reg.57. On its suspension see ESA Regs 2013 reg.56. Subs.(8)(b) empowers regulations to enable the unexpired reduction period in respect of an award of ESA that is terminated to be applied to a subsequent award of ESA within a prescribed period. The product is ESA Regs 2013 reg.55.

Although subs.(8)(a) empowers regulations to specify cases in which no reduction is to be made, this power has not yet been exercised as regards "new style" ESA, although the comparator powers as regards UC and "new style" JSA have been.

[1Delegation and contracting out

11K.—(1) The functions of the Secretary of State under sections 11 to 11I may be exercised by, or by the employees of, such person as the Secretary of State may authorise for the purpose (an "authorised person"). 1.886

(2) An authorisation given by virtue of this section may authorise the exercise of a function—

(a) wholly or to a limited extent;
(b) generally or in particular cases or areas;
(c) unconditionally or subject to conditions.

(3) An authorisation under this section—

(a) may specify its duration;
(b) may be varied or revoked at any time by the Secretary of State;
(c) does not prevent the Secretary of State or another person from exercising the function to which the authorisation relates.

(4) Anything done or omitted to be done by or in relation to an authorised person (or an employee of that person) in, or in connection with, the exercise or purported exercise of the function concerned is to be treated for all purposes as done or omitted to be done by or in relation to the Secretary of State or (as the case may be) an officer of the Secretary of State.

(5) Subsection (4) does not apply—

(a) for the purposes of so much of any contract made between the authorised person and the Secretary of State as relates to the exercise of the function, or
(b) for the purposes of any criminal proceedings brought in respect of anything done or omitted to be done by the authorised person (or an employee of that person).

(6) Where—

(a) the authorisation of an authorised person is revoked, and
(b) at the time of the revocation so much of any contract made between the authorised person and the Secretary of State as relates to the exercise of the function is subsisting, the authorised person is entitled to treat the contract as repudiated by the Secretary of State (and not as frustrated by reason of the revocation).]

AMENDMENT

1. Welfare Reform Act 2012 s.57(1), (2) (various dates on or after April 29, 2013).

DEFINITONS

"authorised person"—see subs.(1).

GENERAL NOTE

This section gives the Secretary of State wide powers to delegate the exercise of certain of the minister's functions to others and to contract them out to public or private sector providers. The functions, however, are only those listed in ss.11 to 11I, and so by definition do not embrace the imposition of sanctions covered by s.11J. 1.887

Work-focussed interviews

12. [1. . .] 1.888

AMENDMENT

1. Note that ss.11-11K (as set out above) were substituted for the original ss.11-16 by Welfare Reform Act 2012 s.57(2) (various dates on or after April 29, 2013).

Work-related activity

1.889 **13.** [1...]

AMENDMENT

1. Note that ss.11-11K (as set out above) were substituted for the original ss. 11-16 by Welfare Reform Act 2012 s.57(2) (various dates on or after April 29, 2013).

Action plans in connection with work-focussed interviews

1.890 **14.** [1...]

AMENDMENT

1. Note that ss.11-11K (as set out above) were substituted for the original ss.11-16 by Welfare Reform Act 2012 s.57(2) (various dates on or after April 29, 2013).

Directions about work-related activity

1.891 **15.** [1...]

AMENDMENT

1. Note that ss.11-11K (as set out above) were substituted for the original ss.11-16 by Welfare Reform Act 2012 s.57(2) (various dates on or after April 29, 2013).

Persons dependent upon drugs etc.

1.892 **15A.** [1...]

AMENDMENT

1. Note that ss.11-11K (as set out above) were substituted for the original ss. 11-16 by Welfare Reform Act 2012 s.57(2) (various dates on or after April 29, 2013).

Contracting out

1.893 **16.** [1...]

AMENDMENT

1. Note that ss.11-11K (as set out above) were substituted for the original ss.11-16 by Welfare Reform Act 2012 s.57(2) (various dates on or after April 29, 2013).

Hardship payments

1.894 **16A.** [1...]

AMENDMENT

1. Repealed by Welfare Reform Act 2012 s.147 and Sch.14 Pt 5 (various dates on or after April 29, 2013).

Miscellaneous

Income and capital: general

17.—(1) In relation to a claim for an employment and support allowance, the income and capital of a person shall be calculated or estimated in such manner as may be prescribed. **1.895**

(2) A person's income in respect of a week shall be calculated in accordance with prescribed rules, which may provide for the calculation to be made by reference to an average over a period (which need not include the week concerned).

(3) Circumstances may be prescribed in which—

(a) a person is to be treated as possessing capital or income which he does not possess;

(b) capital or income which a person does possess is to be disregarded;

(c) income is to be treated as capital;

(d) capital is to be treated as income.

(4) Regulations may provide that a person's capital shall be deemed for the purposes of this Part to yield him an income at a prescribed rate.

DEFINITONS

"prescribed"—see s.24(1).
"regulations"—ibid.
"week"—ibid.

GENERAL NOTE

This section is very similar to s.136(3)–(5) of the Contributions and Benefits Act and s.12 of the old style Jobseekers Act 1995 (see Vol.V). It enables the Secretary of State to introduce detailed regulations governing the treatment of income and capital, principally for the purposes of old style ESA. See Pt 10 of and Schs 7, 8 and 9 to the ESA Regulations 2008. **1.896**

Disqualification

18.—(1) Regulations may provide for a person to be disqualified for receiving an employment and support allowance, or treated for such purposes as the regulations may provide as not having limited capability for work, if— **1.897**

(a) he has become someone who has limited capability for work through his own misconduct,

(b) he remains someone who has limited capability for work through his failure without good cause to follow medical advice, or

(c) he fails without good cause to observe any prescribed rules of behaviour.

(2) Regulations under subsection (1) shall provide for any such disqualification, or treatment, to be for such period not exceeding 6 weeks as may be determined in accordance with Chapter 2 of Part 1 of the Social Security Act 1998 (c. 14).

(3) Regulations may prescribe for the purposes of subsection (1)—

(a) matters which are, or are not, to be taken into account in determining whether a person has good cause for any act or omission;

(b) circumstances in which a person is, or is not, to be regarded as having good cause for any act or omission.

(4) Except where regulations otherwise provide, a person shall be disqualified for receiving [[1]an employment and support allowance] for any period during which he is—

(a) absent from Great Britain, or
(b) undergoing imprisonment or detention in legal custody.

AMENDMENT

1. Welfare Reform Act 2012 s.33(3) and Sch.3 para.26 (d) (various dates on or after April 29, 2013).

DEFINITONS

"limited capability for work"—see s.1(4).
"prescribed"—see s.24(1).
"regulations"—see s.24(1).
"week"—see s.24(1).

GENERAL NOTE

Subsections (1)-(3)

1.898 ESA embodies disqualification from benefit, or treating someone as not having limited capability for work, for a period not exceeding six weeks as sanctions in respect of conduct which conduces to a person's limited capability for work either by bringing it about through misconduct (subs.(1)(a)) or by remaining someone with limited capacity by failing without good cause to follow medical advice (subs.(1)(b)) or by failing without good cause to adhere to prescribed rules of behaviour (subs.(1)(c)). These subsections provide rule-making power for the regime of disqualification. The relevant regulation for "new style" ESA is ESA Regs 2013 reg.93, which has the same effect as ESA Regs 2008 reg.157. Note the protection from disqualification for a "person in hardship" and someone disqualified from receiving ESA because of regulations made pursuant to s.7 of the Social Security Fraud Act 2001 (reg.93(3); for that section and the consequent Social Security (Loss of Benefit) Regs 2001, see Vol.III in this series). Although subs.(3) enables regs to be made dealing with aspects of the "good cause" issue (matters to take into or leave out of account; things which do or do not rank as "good cause"), no such regulations have yet been made. "Good cause" thus remains a matter for the decision-maker or tribunal, circumscribed by case law on analogous provisions.

Subsection (4)

1.899 This mandates disqualification from "new style" ESA in respect of periods of absence from GB or of imprisonment or detention in legal custody. Exceptions from disqualification can be afforded by regs ESA Regs 2013 regs 88–92, which have the same effect as ESA Regs 2008 regs 151–155.

Pilot schemes

1.900 **19.**—(1) Any regulations to which this subsection applies may be made so as to have effect for a specified period not exceeding [136 months].

(2) Subject to subsection (3), subsection (1) applies to—

(a) regulations which are made under any provision of this Part, other than sections 3, 8 and 9;

(b) regulations which are made under the Administration Act, so far as they relate to an employment and support allowance.

(3) Subsection (1) only applies to regulations if they are made with a view to ascertaining whether their provisions will or will be likely to—

(a) encourage persons to obtain or remain in work, or

(b) make it more likely that persons will obtain or remain in work or be able to do so.

(4) Regulations which, by virtue of subsection (1), are to have effect for a limited period are referred to in this section as a "pilot scheme".

(5) A pilot scheme may provide that its provisions are to apply only in relation to—

(a) one or more specified areas;

(b) one or more specified classes of person;

(c) persons selected—

(i) by reference to prescribed criteria, or

(ii) on a sampling basis.

(6) A pilot scheme may make consequential or transitional provision with respect to the cessation of the scheme on the expiry of the specified period.

(7) A pilot scheme may be replaced by a further pilot scheme making the same or similar provision.

AMENDMENT

1. Welfare Reform Act 2009 s.28(2) (November 12, 2009).

DEFINITONS

"Administration Act"—see. s.65.
"prescribed"—see. s.24(1).
"regulations"—ibid.

GENERAL NOTE

This is similar to s.29 of the old style Jobseekers Act 1995 (see Vol.V in this series). From November 12, 2009 the initial period for which a pilot scheme can run was extended to three years; in addition such a scheme can be repeated (see subs.(7)). Any regulations under Pt 1 of the Act or associated rules under the SSAA 1992 may be piloted, other than regulations concerning deductions from "new style" ESA (s.3), limited capability for work (s.8) and limited capability for work-related activity (s.9). Regulations made under this section are subject to the affirmative resolution procedure (s.26(1)(c)). 1.901

Relationship with statutory payments

20.—(1) A person is not entitled to an employment and support allowance in respect of a day if, for the purposes of statutory sick pay, that day– 1.902

(a) is a day of incapacity for work in relation to a contract of service, and

(b) falls within a period of entitlement (whether or not it is a qualifying day).

(2) Except as regulations may provide, a woman who is entitled to statutory maternity pay is not entitled to [1an employment and support allowance] in respect of a day that falls within the maternity pay period.

(3) Regulations may provide that–

(a) an amount equal to a woman's statutory maternity pay for a period shall be deducted from [1an employment and support allowance] in respect of the same period,
(b) a woman shall only be entitled to [1an employment and support allowance] if there is a balance after the deduction, and
(c) if there is such a balance, a woman shall be entitled to [1an employment and support allowance] at a weekly rate equal to it.

(4) Except as regulations may provide, a person who is entitled to statutory adoption pay is not entitled to [1an employment and support allowance] in respect of a day that falls within the adoption pay period.

(5) Regulations may provide that–
(a) an amount equal to a person's statutory adoption pay for a period shall be deducted from [1an employment and support allowance] in respect of the same period,
(b) a person shall only be entitled to [1an employment and support allowance] if there is a balance after the deduction, and
(c) if there is such a balance, a person shall be entitled to [1an employment and support allowance] at a weekly rate equal to it.

(6) Except as regulations may provide, a person who is entitled to [2 statutory shared parental pay] is not entitled to [1 an employment and support allowance] in respect of [2 a day that falls within a period in respect of which statutory shared parental pay is payable].

(7) Regulations may provide that–
(a) an amount equal to a person's [2 statutory shared parental pay for a period] shall be deducted from [1an employment and support allowance] in respect of the same period,
(b) a person shall only be entitled to [1an employment and support allowance] if there is a balance after the deduction, and
(c) if there is such a balance, a person shall be entitled to [1an employment and support allowance] at a weekly rate equal to it.

(8) In this section–

[3 . . .]

"the adoption pay period" has the meaning given in section 171ZN(2) of that Act;

"the maternity pay period" has the meaning given in section 165(1) of that Act.

AMENDMENTS

1. Welfare Reform Act 2012 s.33 and Sch.3 para.26(e) (various dates on or after April 29, 2013).

2. Children and Families Act 2014 c. 6 Sch.7 para.73(2) and (3) (June 30, 2014)

3. Children and Families Act 2014 c. 6 Sch.7 para.73(4) (April 5, 2015).

DEFINITONS

"the additional paternity pay period"—see subs.(8).
"the adoption pay period"—see subs.(8).
"Contributions and Benefits Act"—see s.65.
"entitled"—see s.24(1).
"the maternity pay period"—see subs.(8).

GENERAL NOTE

This section deals with the relationship between "new style" ESA and certain other "employer paid" statutory payments, the overall responsibility for them lying with HMRC. The payments covered by this section are statutory sick pay (SSP), statutory maternity pay (SMP), statutory adoption pay (SAP) and statutory shared parental pay (SShPP). They are dealt with in Vol.IV: Tax Credits and HMRC-administered Social Security Benefits. The relationships are not all of a piece. ESA cannot be paid in respect of days for which there is SSP entitlement (subs.(1)). As regards SMP, SAP and SShPP, the general rule is that "new style" ESA cannot be payable at the same time as any of these other payments, but exceptions can be made by regulations (subss.(2)–(7)). The relevant regs are the ESA Regs 2013, regs 73 (SMP), 74 (SAP) and 75A (SShPP). Where they operate to enable ESA to be paid, however, the amount of "new style" ESA payable is reduced by the amount of the relevant statutory payment, and only any balance of ESA remaining is payable. **1.903**

Deemed entitlement for other purposes

21.—Regulations may provide for a person who would be entitled to an employment and support allowance but for the operation of any provision of, or made under, this Part, the Administration Act or Chapter 2 of Part 1 of the Social Security Act 1998 (c. 14) (social security decisions and appeals) to be treated as if entitled to the allowance for the purposes of any rights or obligations (whether his own or another's) which depend on his entitlement, other than the right to payment of it. **1.904**

DEFINITONS

"Administration Act"—see s.65.
"regulations"—see s.24(1).

GENERAL NOTE

This section is identical to SSCBA 1992 s.113(3). It enables regulations to be made enabling someone to be treated as still entitled to "new style" ESA, though not to payment of it, even though provisions of or made under this Part of the WRA 2007, the SSAA 1992 or SSA 1998, Pt I Ch.2 operate to disentitle that person. Claimants will only be treated as entitled in this way to enable them or someone else to retain rights and obligations under social security law more generally. **1.905**

Supplementary provisions

22.—Schedule 2 (which contains further provisions in relation to an employment and support allowance) has effect. **1.906**

GENERAL NOTE

This provides the basis for giving effect to the detailed provisions on ESA set out in Sch.2. These concern rule-making in respect of: treating someone as having or not having limited capability for work/work-related activity (as the case may be), waiting days, linking periods, payments of benefit for less than a week, presence in GB, entitlement to "new style" ESA by persons not in GB, modifying entitlement to "new style" ESA in respect of employment on ships, vessels, aircraft or hovercraft, the effect of work, treating ESA as "benefit", ESA information to be treated as social security information, the making of advance claims, and modifying provisions in respect of ESA as regards Members of His Majesty's forces. **1.907**

Recovery of sums in respect of maintenance

1.908 **23.** [1 . . .]

AMENDMENT

1. Repealed by Welfare Reform Act 2012 s.147 and Sch.14 Pt 1 (various dates on or after April 29, 2013)

General

Interpretation of Part 1

1.909 **24.**—(1) In this Part—

[1"child" means a person under the age of 16];

"claimant" means a person who has claimed an employment and support allowance;

[2. . .];

"employment" and "employed" have the meanings prescribed for the purposes of this Part;

"entitled", in relation to an employment and support allowance, is to be construed in accordance with—

(a) the provisions of this Act,

(b) section 1 of the Administration Act (entitlement dependent on making of claim), and

(c) section 27 of the Social Security Act 1998 (c. 14) (restrictions on entitlement in certain cases of error);

[2. . .];

[2. . .];

"income support" means income support under section 124 of the Contributions and Benefits Act;

"limited capability for work" shall be construed in accordance with section 1(4);

"limited capability for work-related activity" shall be construed in accordance with section 2(5);

"period of limited capability for work" has the meaning prescribed for the purposes of this Part;

"prescribed" means specified in, or determined in accordance with, regulations;

[1"single person" means an individual who is not a member of a couple (within the meaning of Part 1 of the Welfare Reform Act 2012);]

"regulations" means regulations made by the Secretary of State;

[1 "work" has such meaning as may be prescribed;

"work-focused interview requirement" has the meaning given by section 11B;

"work preparation requirement" has the meaning given by section 11C;]

"week" means a period of 7 days beginning with a Sunday or such other period of 7 days as may be prescribed;

[1 "work-related requirement" has the meaning given by section 11;]

"work-related activity" has the meaning given by section 13(7).

(2) For the purposes of this Part, the assessment phase, in relation to a claimant, is the period—

(a) beginning, subject to subsection (3), with the first day of the period for which he is entitled to an employment and support allowance, and

(b) ending with such day as may be prescribed.

(3) Regulations may prescribe circumstances in which the assessment phase is to begin with such day as may be prescribed.

(3A) [3...]

(3B) [3...]

(4) For the purposes of this Part, a person is a member of the support group if he is a person in respect of whom it is determined that he has, or is to be treated as having, limited capability for work-related activity.

AMENDMENTS

1. Welfare Reform Act 2012 s.57(4) (various dates on or after April 29, 2013).
2. Repealed by Welfare Reform Act 2012 s.147 and Sch.14 Pt 1 (various dates on or after April 29, 2013).
3. Repealed by Welfare Reform Act 2012 s.147 and Sch.14 Pt 5 ((various dates on or after April 29, 2013).

DEFINITONS

"Administration Act"—see s.65.
"Contributions and Benefits Act"—see s.65

GENERAL NOTE

This defines, sometimes by referring the reader to other provisions or leaving the meaning to be set out in regulations, a number of key terms in respect of "new style" ESA. Note in particular that the "assessment phase", during which there can generally only be entitlement to basic allowance ESA, is generally to begin on the first such day of entitlement and to end in accordance with regulations (subss.(2), (3)). See on this ESA Regs 2013 regs 5–7. Note also that membership of the support group, and thus eligibility for the "support component" in addition to basic allowance ESA, is dependent on a determination that the person has, or is to be treated as having, limited capability for work-related activity (subs.(4)). The various repealing amendments relate to definitions which are relevant to IRESA but not "new style" ESA. 1.910

Regulations [1 and orders]

25.—(1) Any power under this Part to make regulations [1 or an order] shall be exercisable by statutory instrument. 1.911

(2) Any such power may be exercised—

(a) in relation to all cases to which it extends,

(b) in relation to those cases subject to specified exceptions, or

(c) in relation to any specified cases or classes of case.

(3) Any such power may be exercised so as to make, as respects the cases in relation to which it is exercised—

(a) the full provision to which the power extends or any less provision (whether by way of exception or otherwise);

(b) the same provision for all cases in relation to which it is exercised, or different provision for different cases or different classes of case or different provision as respects the same case or class of case for different purposes of this Part;

(c) any such provision either unconditionally or subject to any specified condition.

(4) Where any such power is expressed to be exercisable for alternative purposes, it may be exercised in relation to the same case for all or any of those purposes.

(5) Any such power includes power—

(a) to make such incidental, supplementary, consequential or transitional provision or savings as appear to the Secretary of State to be expedient;

(b) to provide for a person to exercise a discretion in dealing with any matter.

(6) Without prejudice to the generality of the provisions of this section, regulations under any of [3sections 11 to 11J] [2...] may make provision which applies only in relation to an area or areas specified in the regulations.

(7) The fact that a power to make regulations is conferred by this Part is not to be taken to prejudice the extent of any other power to make regulations so conferred.

AMENDMENTS

1. Welfare Reform Act 2012 s.51(2) (March 20, 2012 (regulation-making purposes); May 1, 2012 (all other purposes)).

2. Welfare Reform Act 2012 s.147 and Sch.14 Pt 6 para.1 (May 8, 2012).

3. Welfare Reform Act 2012 s.57(5) (April 29, 2013).

GENERAL NOTE

1.912 This section is similar to s.175 of the Contributions and Benefits Act and s.36 of the Jobseekers Act.

Parliamentary control

1.913 **26.**—(1) None of the following regulations shall be made unless a draft of the statutory instrument containing them has been laid before, and approved by a resolution of, each House of Parliament—

(a) regulations under section 2(2)(c) or (3)(c)[5 ...];

[4 (aa) the first regulations under section 11D(2)(d)or 11J;]

[6 (b) ...];

(c) regulations which by virtue of section 19(1) are to have effect for a limited period.

[1, 3 ...]

(2) A statutory instrument that—

(a) contains regulations made under this Part, and

(b) is not subject to a requirement that a draft of the instrument be laid before, and approved by a resolution of, each House of Parliament, shall be subject to annulment in pursuance of a resolution of either House of Parliament.

[2(3) A statutory instrument containing an order under section 1A shall be subject to annulment in pursuance of a resolution of either House of Parliament.]

AMENDMENTS

1. Welfare Reform Act 2009 s.11 and Sch.3 para.8(4) (November 12, 2009).

2. Welfare Reform Act 2012 s.51(3) (March 20, 2012 (regulation-making purposes); May 1, 2012 (all other purposes)).

3. Welfare Reform Act 2012 s.147 and Sch.14 Pt 6 para.1 (May 8, 2012).

4. Welfare Reform Act 2012 s.57(6) (February 25, 2013).

5. Welfare Reform Act 2012 s.147 and Sch.14 Pt 1 (various dates on or after April 29, 2013).

6. Welfare Reform Act 2012 s.147 and Sch.14 Pt 5 (various dates on or after April 29, 2013)

GENERAL NOTE

This section is similar to s.176 of the Contributions and Benefits Act and s.37 of the Jobseekers Act.

Financial provisions relating to Part 1

27.—(1) There shall be paid out of the National Insurance Fund [1 any sums payable by way of employment and support allowance]. 1.914

(2) There shall be paid out of money provided by Parliament—

(a) [2 . . .]

(b) any administrative expenses of the Secretary of State or the Commissioners for Her Majesty's Revenue and Customs in carrying this Part into effect.

(3) The Secretary of State shall pay into the National Insurance Fund sums estimated by him to be equivalent in amount to sums recovered by him in connection with payments of [1employment and support] allowance.

(4) [2 . . .].

AMENDMENTS

1. Welfare Reform Act 2012 s.33 and Sch.3 para.25 (various dates on or after April 29, 2013).

2. Welfare Reform Act 2012 s.147 and Sch.14 Pt 1 (various dates on or after April 29, 2013).

GENERAL NOTE

This section is similar to s.163 of the Administration Act, s.38 of the Jobseekers Act and s.20 of the State Pension Credit Act 2002. 1.915

Consequential amendments relating to Part 1

28.—(1) Schedule 3 (which makes amendments consequential on this Part) has effect. 1.916

(2) Regulations may make provision consequential on this Part amending, repealing or revoking any provision of—

(a) an Act passed on or before the last day of the Session in which this Act is passed, or

(b) an instrument made under an Act before the passing of this Act.

(3) In subsection (2), "Act" includes an Act of the Scottish Parliament.

DEFINITONS

"Act"—see subs.(3).
"regulations"—see s.24(1).

GENERAL NOTE

Subsection (1)

This gives effect to a range of consequential amendments of other Acts of Parliament set out in Sch.3 incorporated elsewhere in this book. 1.917

Subsection (2)

This enables the making of consequential regulations amending Acts (including ones of the Scottish Parliament) passed on or before the last day of the 2006–07 Westminster parliamentary session (the one in which the WRA 2007 was passed) (para.(a), subs.(3)). It also enables consequential regulations to amend subordinate 1.918

legislation, already made before the passing of the WRA 2007, under Acts (including those of the Scottish Parliament) (para.(b), subs.(3)).

Transition relating to Part 1

1.919 **29.** Schedule 4 (which makes provision with respect to transition in relation to this Part) has effect.

1.920 *Sections 30–63 Omitted*

PART 5

GENERAL

Northern Ireland

1.921 **64.**—(1) This section applies to an Order in Council under paragraph 1(1) of the Schedule to the Northern Ireland Act 2000 (c. 1) (legislation for Northern Ireland during suspension of devolved government) which contains a statement that it is made only for purposes corresponding to those of this Act.

(2) Such an Order—

(a) is not subject to paragraph 2 of that Schedule (affirmative resolution of both Houses of Parliament), but

(b) is subject to annulment in pursuance of a resolution of either House of Parliament.

GENERAL NOTE

1.922 Part I of the WRA 2007 dealing with "new style" ESA applies only to Great Britain (i.e. England, Wales and Scotland). This is true of the social security system generally. But comparable provision in respect of social security for Northern Ireland is always made by Order in Council under its devolution Act. This section deals with parliamentary scrutiny and control over such an Order. It provides that any such Order, stated to be made only for purposes corresponding to those of the WRA 2007, is to be subject to annulment by either House of Parliament rather than to the affirmative resolution procedure that would otherwise be applicable.

General interpretation

1.923 **65.**—In this Act—

"Administration Act" means the Social Security Administration Act 1992 (c. 5);

"Contributions and Benefits Act" means the Social Security Contributions and Benefits Act 1992 (c. 4).

Financial provisions: general

1.924 66.—(1) There shall be paid out of money provided by Parliament—

(a) any expenditure incurred by the Secretary of State in consequence of Parts 2 to 4 of this Act, and

(b) any increase attributable to this Act in the sums payable out of money so provided under any other enactment.

(2) There shall be paid into the Consolidated Fund any increase attributable to this Act in the sums payable into that Fund under any other enactment.

Repeals

67.—The enactments specified in Schedule 8 are hereby repealed to the extent specified. 1.925

Section 68 omitted 1.926

Extent

69.—(1) Subject to the following provisions, this Act extends to England and Wales and Scotland only. 1.927

(2) The following provisions extend to England and Wales only—

(a) [1 . . .]

(b) paragraphs 6, 11(2) and 16 of Schedule 3.

(3) Paragraphs 1, 2, 4, 11(3), 14 and 22 of Schedule 3 extend to Scotland only.

(4) The following provisions also extend to Northern Ireland—

(a) sections 33(7), 49, 56, 57, 61, 64, 65, 68, this section and sections 70 and 71,

(b) paragraph 15 of Schedule 2, and sections 22 and 24 to 26 so far as relating thereto,

(c) paragraphs 5, 10(1) and (28), 17(1) and (2), 19, 23(1) to (3) and (6) to (8) and 24 of Schedule 3, and section 28 so far as relating thereto,

(d) paragraph 1 of Schedule 7, and section 63 so far as relating thereto, and (e) Schedule 8, so far as relating to the Vaccine Damage Payments Act 1979 (c. 17), the Income and Corporation Taxes Act 1988 (c. 1), the Disability (Grants) Act 1993 (c. 14), section 2 of the Social Security Act 1998 (c. 14) and the Income Tax (Earnings and Pensions) Act 2003 (c. 1), and section 67 so far as relating thereto.

(5) The following provisions extend to Northern Ireland only—

(a) section 45, and

(b) Schedule 8, so far as relating to the Social Security Administration (Northern Ireland) Act 1992 (c. 8), and section 67 so far as relating thereto.

(6) The following provisions also extend to the Isle of Man—

(a) sections 56 and 57, section 68, this section and sections 70 and 71,

(b) paragraph 1 of Schedule 7, and section 63 so far as relating thereto, and

(c) Schedule 8, so far as relating to the Vaccine Damage Payments Act 1979, and section 67 so far as relating thereto.

Amendments

1. Welfare Reform Act 2012 s.133(6)(b) (July 2, 2012).

General Note

Only subs.(1) directly concerns ESA. It means that the ESA scheme under Pt I of the Act applies only to England, Wales and Scotland. Comparable provision can be made for Northern Ireland through Order in Council under the devolution legislation (s.64). The devolution arrangements and the complicated political background in Northern Ireland may, however, mean that relevant legislation may have to be enacted by the Northern Ireland Assembly. 1.928

Commencement

1.929 **70.**—(1) The following provisions shall come into force at the end of the period of 2 months beginning with the day on which this Act is passed—

(a) sections 41(2) and (3), 44, 45, 54, 55, 59, 61(1)(b) and (2) to (6) and 62,
(b) paragraphs 1 to 4, 10, 11 and 14 of Schedule 5, and section 40 so far as relating thereto,
(c) paragraphs 2(1) and (3), 3 and 4 of Schedule 7, and section 63 so far as relating thereto, and
(d) Schedule 8, so far as relating to—
  (i) section 3(5) of the Pneumoconiosis etc. (Workers' Compensation) Act 1979 (c. 41)
  (ii) section 140(1A) of the Contributions and Benefits Act,
  (iii) sections 71(5), 71ZA(2), 134(8)(a) and 168(3)(d) of the Administration Act,
  (iv) section 69(5) of the Social Security Administration (Northern Ireland) Act 1992,
  (v) Schedule 13 to the Local Government etc. (Scotland) Act 1994 (c. 39),
  (vi) section 38(7)(a) of, and paragraph 81(2) of Schedule 7 to, the Social Security Act 1998 (c. 14), and
  (vii) paragraph 65 of Schedule 24 to the Civil Partnership Act 2004 (c. 33), and section 67 so far as relating thereto.

(2) The remaining provisions of this Act, except—

(a) this section,
(b) sections 64, 65, 66, 68, 69 and 71, and
(c) paragraph 8 of Schedule 5, and section 40 so far as relating thereto,

shall come into force on such day as the Secretary of State may by order made by statutory instrument appoint, and different days may be so appointed for different purposes.

General Note

1.930 The key operative date for the ESA regime is October 27, 2008.

Short title

1.931 **71.**—This Act may be cited as the Welfare Reform Act 2007.

SCHEDULES

SCHEDULE 1 **section 1**

Employment and support allowance: additional conditions

Part 1

[4 . . .]

Conditions relating to national insurance

1.932 **1.**—(1) The first condition is that—

(a) the claimant has actually paid Class 1 or Class 2 contributions in respect of one of the last [2two] complete tax years ("the base tax year") before the beginning of the relevant benefit year,
(b) those contributions must have been paid before the relevant benefit week, and
[2(c) the claimant's earnings determined in accordance with sub-paragraph (2) must be not less than the base tax year's lower earnings limit multiplied by 26.]
[2(2) The earnings referred to in sub-paragraph (1)(c) are the aggregate of—
(a) the claimant's relevant earnings for the base tax year upon which primary Class 1 contributions have been paid or treated as paid, and
(b) the claimant's earnings factors derived from Class 2 contributions.
(3) Regulations may make provision for the purposes of sub-paragraph (2)(a) for determining the claimant's relevant earnings for the base tax year.
(3A) Regulations under sub-paragraph (3) may, in particular, make provision—
(a) for making that determination by reference to the amount of a person's earnings for periods comprised in the base tax year;
(b) for determining the amount of a person's earnings for any such period by—
(i) first determining the amount of the earnings for the period in accordance with regulations made for the purposes of section 3(2) of the Contributions and Benefits Act, and
(ii) then disregarding so much of the amount found in accordance with sub-paragraph (i) as exceeded the base tax year's lower earnings limit (or the prescribed equivalent).]
(4) Regulations may—
(a) provide for the condition set out in sub-paragraph (1) to be taken to be satisfied in the case of [3persons—
(i) who] have been entitled to any prescribed description of benefit during any prescribed period or at any prescribed time [3or
(ii) who satisfy other prescribed conditions]
(b) with a view to securing any relaxation of the requirements of that condition in relation to persons who have been [3entitled as mentioned in paragraph (a)(i)], provide for that condition to apply in relation to them subject to prescribed modifications.
(5) In sub-paragraph (4), "benefit" means—
[6(za) universal credit;]
(a) any benefit within the meaning of section 122(1) of the Contributions and Benefits Act,
(b) any benefit under Parts 7 to 12 of that Act,
(c) credits under regulations under section 22(5) of that Act,
[1(ca) credits under section 23A of that Act,]
(d) [5an employment and support allowance], and
(e) working tax credit.
2.—(1) The second condition is that—
(a) the claimant has in respect of the last two complete tax years before the beginning of the relevant benefit year either paid or been credited with Class 1 or Class 2 contributions or been credited with earnings, and
(b) the earnings factor derived as mentioned in sub-paragraph (2) must be not less in each of those years than the year's lower earnings limit multiplied by 50.
(2) The earnings factor referred to in sub-paragraph (1)(b) is the aggregate of the claimant's earnings factors derived—
(a) from so much of his earnings as did not exceed the upper earnings limit for the year and upon which primary Class 1 contributions have been paid or treated as paid or from earnings credited, and
(b) from Class 2 contributions.
(3) Where primary Class 1 contributions have been paid or treated as paid on any part of a person's earnings, sub-paragraph (2)(a) shall have effect as if such contributions had been paid or treated as paid on so much of the earnings as did not exceed the upper earnings limit for the year.
3.—(1) For the purposes of paragraphs 1 and 2—
(a) "benefit year" means a period which is a benefit year for the purposes of Part 2 of the Contributions and Benefits Act or such other period as may be prescribed for the purposes of this Part of this Schedule;
(b) "Class 1 contributions", "Class 2 contributions" and "primary Class 1 contributions" have the same meaning as in the Contributions and Benefits Act (see section 1 of that Act);

(c) "earnings" shall be construed in accordance with sections 3, 4 and 112 of that Act;
(d) "earnings factor" shall be construed in accordance with sections 22 and 23 of that Act;
(e) "lower earnings limit" and "upper earnings limit" shall be construed in accordance with section 5 of that Act and references to the lower or upper earnings limit of a tax year are to whatever is (or was) the limit in force for that year under that section;
(f) "relevant benefit year" is the benefit year which includes the beginning of the period of limited capability for work which includes the relevant benefit week;
(g) "tax year" means the 12 months beginning with 6th April in any year.

(2) Regulations may provide for sub-paragraph (1)(f) to have effect in prescribed circumstances with prescribed modifications in the case of—

(a) a person who has previously ceased to be entitled to [5an employment and support allowance];
(b) a person who has made a claim for an employment and support allowance in connection with which he failed to satisfy one or both of the conditions in paragraphs 1 and 2.

Condition relating to youth

1.933 4.—(1) The third condition is that—

(a) the claimant was under 20 or, in prescribed cases, 25 when the relevant period of limited capability for work began,
(b) he is not receiving full-time education,
(c) he satisfies such conditions as may be prescribed with respect to residence or presence in Great Britain (or both), and
(d) there has been a day in the relevant period of limited capability for work—
(i) which was a day on which he was aged at least 16, and
(ii) which was preceded by a period of 196 consecutive days throughout which he had limited capability for work.

(2) In sub-paragraph (1), "relevant period of limited capability for work" means the period of limited capability for work which includes the relevant benefit week.

(3) Regulations may prescribe circumstances in which sub-paragraph (1)(a) does not apply in the case of a person who has previously ceased to be entitled to an employment and support allowance to which he was entitled by virtue of satisfying the condition set out in sub-paragraph (1).

(4) Regulations may make provision about when, for the purposes of sub-paragraph (1)(b), a person is, or is not, to be treated as receiving full-time education.

"Relevant benefit week"

1.934 5.—In this Part of this Schedule, "relevant benefit week" means the week in relation to which the question of entitlement to an employment and support allowance is being considered.

AMENDMENTS

1. Pensions Act 2007 Sch.1 para.11 (September 27, 2007).
2. Welfare Reform Act 2009 s.13 (November 1, 2010).
3. Welfare Reform Act 2009 s.13(5) (November 29, 2011).
4. Welfare Reform Act 2012 s.147 and Sch.14 Pt 1 (various dates on or after April 29, 2013).
5. Welfare Reform Act 2012 s.33(3) and Sch.3 para.26 (f) (various dates on or after April 29, 2013).
6. Welfare Reform Act 2012 s.31 and Sch.2 para.65 (April 29, 2013).

DEFINITONS

"the base tax year"—see para.1(1) (a).
"benefit"—see para.1(5).
"benefit year"—see para.3(1) (a) .
"Class 1 contributions"—see para.3(1) (b).
"Class 2 contributions"—see para.3(1) (b).
"Contributions and Benefits Act"—see s.65.
"earnings"—see para.3(1) €.
"earnings factor"—see para.3(1) (d).

"entitled"—see s.24(1).
"limited capability for work"—see s.1(4).
"lower earnings limit"—see para.3(1) €.
"primary Class 1 contributions"—see para.3(1) (b).
"regulations"—see s.24(1).
"relevant benefit week"—see para.5.
"relevant benefit year"—see para.3(1)(f).
"relevant period of limited capability for work"—see para.4(2).
"tax year"—see para.3(1) (g).
"upper earnings limit"—see para.3(1)€.
"week"—see s.24(1)

GENERAL NOTE

Paragraphs (1)–(3)

"New style" ESA is principally a contributory or national insurance benefit. Entitlement generally requires the claimant to have an adequate contribution record. S/he must satisfy the first and second conditions set out in paras 1 and 2 (s.1(2)(a)), with respect to which paras 3 and 5 provide key definitions. Paragraph 3 also enables modifications to be effected by regulations. This annotation should be read in the light of those parts of the commentary to SSCBA 1992 Sch.3 dealing with "Contributions matters: a division of responsibility" and "an outline of the contributory system: payments, credits and the earnings generated (the amount of earnings added to the contribution record)". 1.935

The changes effected from November 1, 2010 (by s.13 of the Welfare Reform Act 2009) significantly tightened the conditions for the contributory form of ESA by requiring a more recent and stronger connection with the world of work than was previously the case, whether under ESA or IB. The changes do so in that the first condition can from then only be satisfied in one of the last two (rather than the last three) tax years (April 6–April 5) complete before the start of the relevant benefit year (early January) (as with JSA); and by raising the requisite level of earnings in the tax year relied on to 26 (rather than 25) times that year's lower earnings limit. Moreover, the conditions now only count earnings at that lower earnings limit (ignoring earnings in excess of it) so that new claimants will have to have worked for at least 26 weeks in one of the last two tax years. Prior to these amendments, when the level was 25 times the LEL and the scheme looked also to earnings between the lower and upper earnings limits, a high-earner could qualify on less than four weeks' work in the tax year and someone at the national minimum wage could qualify in about 12 weeks.

The national insurance conditions: a claimant must satisfy both of the contribution conditions elaborated in paras 1 and 2 (unless they are a person who was incapacitated in youth (before 20 or sometimes 25) and claimed before May 1, 2012). The first (para.1) can be met only by paid contributions of the relevant class (primary Class 1 or Class 2) reaching the requisite level in a specific tax year. The second can be satisfied by paid and/or credited contributions in both of two specific tax years. The conditions thus require a more recent connection with the world of work in terms of paid contributions than had previously been the case. However, the rigour of the first condition is relaxed in certain situations (paras 1(4), 3(2), ESA Regs 2013, reg.9).

In order to appreciate the requirements of paras 1 and 2, and the terms and operation of the contribution conditions, take first, as an illustrative example, the position of someone claiming "new style" ESA for the very first time in August 2020 (that is, with no link back to any previous period of incapacity for work) and never having claimed or received any other benefit. The person must meet both of the two contribution conditions set out in paras 1 and 2. The first step is to identify the relevant benefit year, the one which includes the first day of the period of limited capability for work of which his claim is part (para.3(1)(f)). This identification of the relevant benefit year is the real substantive matter for the Secretary of State or the tribunal to focus on, since that determines the tax years in which the requisite record must be fulfilled. The claimant's first day of claim in the relevant benefit week (para.5) in August 2020 falls in benefit year 2020/2021 (the relevant benefit year: defined to refer to SSCBA 1992 s.21(6) and any modifying regulations made for the purposes of this Part of this Schedule (see para.3(1)(a))). The tax years in one of which the first contribution condition (sub-para.(2)) must be fulfilled are the last two tax years (April 6–April 5) (para.3(1)(g)) complete before the start of the relevant benefit year (early January 2020). The tax years to which to have regard are thus 2017/2018 and 2018/2019. The contribution record in tax year 2019/2020 cannot be taken into account because it was not complete at the start of the relevant benefit year (early January 2020). The first contribution condition (para.1(1)) can only be met with paid contributions of the relevant class—Class 1 (employed earners) or Class 2 (self-employed earners)—reaching the requisite level (26 times the lower earnings limit (LEL) for Class 1 contributions purposes) for the tax year in question—remember that each Class 2 contribution generates earnings equal to the LEL pertinent to the tax/contribution year in question, while the amount of earnings on which Class 1 contributions are paid generates the earnings for an employed earner claimant. Note here also, as explained above, that the November 2010 changes now only count earnings at that lower earnings limit (ignoring earnings in excess of it) so that new claimants will have to have worked for at least 26 weeks in one of the last two tax years.

The second contribution condition (para.1(2)) requires examination of the last two tax years complete before the start of the relevant benefit year (early January 2020), that is 2017/2018 and 2018/2019. The claimant's contribution record in each of those tax/contribution years must attain 50 times the lower earnings limit for the year. But the condition can be met through paid and/or credited contributions (a Class 1 credit can be received, for example, for each week of unemployment; see further Social Security (Credits) Regulations 1975). Note that para.1(4) enables regulations to provide for the first condition to be taken to be satisfied by certain benefit recipients and provide for it to apply in modified form. The relevant "relaxation" regulation is ESA Regs 2013 reg.9. Note also that para.3(2) enables regulations to relax the rules on relevant benefit year. The product is ESA Regs 2013 reg.14.

Various groups will have difficulty meeting the contribution conditions:

(a) those who have never been employed: The requirement in the first contribution condition for payment of contributions effectively excludes those who, whether through unemployment, incapacity or disability, have been unable to build a contribution record in terms of paid contributions.
(b) some of the long-term unemployed: i.e. those last employed in a tax year earlier than the first of the two years on which the first contribution condition focuses.
(c) very low-paid, probably part-time, employees: those whose weekly or monthly earnings fall below the lower earnings limit for the whole or main part of the relevant tax years will not satisfy the contribution conditions since there is no liability or ability to pay Class 1 contributions where earnings fall below that limit, and, because they are in work, no Class 1 credits are generated from unemployment.
(d) certain married women and widows paying reduced rate contributions: these do not generate any earnings factor (and so do not count) for ESA purposes (para.3(d); SSCBA 1992 s.22(4)).

Paragraph 4

1.936 Severe Disablement Allowance (SDA) was introduced in 1984 to cater for those who were incapacitated below the age of 20, or, if incapacitated later, were also assessed as 80 per cent disabled (see SSCBA 1992 ss.68, 69). SDA was abolished on April 6, 2001 for new claims, but non-contributory access was afforded to IB for persons incapacitated in youth (before 20 or sometimes 25). The same facility was made available in respect of contributory ESA. However, this route was barred to new claimants claiming contributory ESA on or after May 1, 2012 (see: Welfare Reform Act 2012 s.53, inserting a new subs.(3A) into s.1 of this Act). See further the commentary on para. 4 in the 2020/21 edition of this Volume.

PART 2

[1 . . .] 1.937

AMENDMENT

1. Welfare Reform Act 2012 s.147 and Sch.14 Pt 1 with effect from various dates on or after April 29, 2013.

[1 SCHEDULE 1A **Section 15A**

PERSONS DEPENDENT ON DRUGS ETC.

[2 . . .] 1.938

AMENDMENT

1. Welfare Reform Act 2009 s.11 and Sch.3 para.7 (November 12, 2009).
2. Welfare Reform Act 2012 ss.60(2), 150(2) (b) (May 8, 2012).

SCHEDULE 2 **Section 22**

EMPLOYMENT AND SUPPORT ALLOWANCE: SUPPLEMENTARY PROVISIONS

Limited capability for work

1.—Regulations may make provision— 1.939
(a) for a person to be treated in prescribed circumstances as having, or as not having, limited capability for work;
(b) for the question of whether a person has limited capability for work to be determined notwithstanding that he is for the time being treated by virtue of regulations under sub-paragraph (a) as having limited capability for work;
(c) for the question of whether a person has limited capability for work to be determined afresh in prescribed circumstances.

Waiting days

2.—Except in prescribed circumstances, a person is not entitled to an employment and support allowance in respect of a prescribed number of days at the beginning of a period of limited capability for work

Periods of less than a week

3.—Regulations may make provision in relation to—
(a) entitlement to an employment and support allowance, or
(b) the amount payable by way of such an allowance, in respect of any period of less than a week.

Linking periods

4.—(1) Regulations may provide for circumstances in which a period of limited capability for work which is separated from another period of limited capability for work by not more than a prescribed length of time is to be treated for the purposes of this Part as a continuation of the earlier period.

(2) Regulations may provide, in relation to periods which are linked by virtue of regulations under sub-paragraph (1), that a condition which was satisfied in relation to the earlier period is to be treated for the purposes of this Part as satisfied in relation to the later period.

[2 Exemption

1.940 **4A.** Regulations may prescribe circumstances in which a person may be entitled to employment and support allowance without having accepted a claimant commitment.]

Presence in Great Britain

5.—Regulations may make provision for the purposes of this Part as to the circumstances in which a person is to be treated as being, or not being, in Great Britain.

[3. . .] Entitlement in case of absence from Great Britain

6.—Regulations may provide that in prescribed circumstances a claimant who is not in Great Britain may nevertheless be entitled to [4 an employment and support allowance].

[3. . .] Modification in relation to employment on ships etc.

7.—(1) Regulations may modify any provision of this Part, so far as relating to [4 an employment and support allowance], in its application to any person who is, has been, or is to be—

(a) employed on board any ship, vessel, hovercraft or aircraft,
(b) outside Great Britain at any prescribed time or in any prescribed circumstances, or
(c) in prescribed employment in connection with continental shelf operations.

(2) Regulations under this paragraph may, in particular, provide—

(a) for any provision of this Part to apply even though it would not otherwise apply;
(b) for any such provision not to apply even though it would otherwise apply;
(c) for the taking of evidence, in a country or territory outside Great Britain, by a consular official or other prescribed person;
(d) for enabling the whole, or any part, of [4 an employment and support allowance] to be paid to such of the claimant's dependants as may be prescribed.

(3) In this paragraph, "continental shelf operations" has the same meaning as in section 120 of the Contributions and Benefits Act.

Income-related allowance: entitlement in case of absence from Great Britain

1.941 **8.** [3 . . .].

Limited capability for work-related activity

9.—Regulations may make provision—

(a) for a person to be treated in prescribed circumstances as having, or as not having, limited capability for work-related activity;
(b) for the question of whether a person has limited capability for work-related activity to be determined notwithstanding that he is for the time being treated by virtue of regulations under sub-paragraph (a) as having limited capability for work-related activity;
(c) for the question of whether a person has limited capability for work-related activity to be determined afresh in prescribed circumstances

Effect of work

10.—Regulations may prescribe circumstances in which a person is to be treated as not entitled to an employment and support allowance because of his doing work.

Treatment of allowance as "benefit"

11.—Regulations may provide for—

(a) an employment and support allowance,
(b) [3 . . .],
(c) [3 . . .], to be treated, for prescribed purposes of the Contributions and Benefits Act, as a benefit, or a benefit of a prescribed description.

Attribution of reductions in cases where allowance taken to consist of two elements

12. [3 . . .].

Treatment of information supplied as information relating to social security

13.—Information supplied in pursuance of regulations under any of sections 8, 9 and 11 to [6 11K] [1 [5...]] shall be taken for all purposes to be information relating to social security. **1.942**

Advance claims

14.—This Part shall have effect with prescribed modifications in relation to cases where a claim to an employment and support allowance is by virtue of regulations under section 5(1)(c) of the Administration Act (advance claims) made, or treated as if made, for a period wholly or partly after the date on which it is made.

Members of the forces

15.—(1) Regulations may modify—

(a) any provision of this Part, or

(b) any corresponding provision made for Northern Ireland, in its application to persons who are or have been members of Her Majesty's forces.

(2) For the purposes of this paragraph, Her Majesty's forces shall be taken to consist of prescribed establishments and organisations in which persons serve under the control of the Defence Council.

AMENDMENTS

1. Welfare Reform Act 2009 s.11 and Sch.3 para.8(5) (November 12, 2009).
2. Welfare Reform Act 2012 s.54(6) (February 25, 2013).
3. Welfare Reform Act 2012 s.147 and Sch.14 Pt 1 (various dates on or after April 29, 2013).
4. Welfare Reform Act 2012 s.33(3) and Sch.3 para.26(g) (various dates on or after April 29, 2013).
5. Welfare Reform Act 2012 Sch.14 Pt 6 (May 8, 2012).
6. Welfare Reform Act 2012 s.57(9) (various dates on or after April 29, 2013).

DEFINITONS

"Administration Act"—see s.65.
"continental shelf operations"—see para.7(3).
"Contributions and Benefits Act"—see s.65.
"employed"—see s.24(1).
"employment"—see s.24(1).
"entitled"—see s.24(1).
"Her Majesty's forces"—see para.15(2).
"limited capability for work-related activity"—see s.2(5).
"period of limited capability for work"—see s.24(1).
"prescribed"—see s.24(1).
"regulations"—see s.24(1)

GENERAL NOTE

Para. (2) (waiting days)

The general rule, as with the former contributory incapacity benefit regimes, is that there is no entitlement to ESA in respect of a number of "waiting days" at the beginning of a period of limited capability for work. The general rule has a number of exceptions set out in ESA Regs 2013 reg.85(2). In addition, the general rule is, of course, affected by the "linking rules" (on which see reg.86) in a case of intermittent incapacity where those rules fuse into one ostensibly separate spells of limited **1.943** capability for work: the "waiting days" only have to be served once in a period of limited capability for work. Regulation 85 originally set the number of these days of non-entitlement ("waiting days") at three. From October 27, 2014 that was increased to seven with respect to a new claim in respect of a waiting period starting on or after that date.

Para. (3) (periods of less than a week)

1.944 ESA, like JSA, is a weekly benefit, paid in respect of a week of limited capability for work. It is paid fortnightly in arrears, and the day of the week on which payment is to be made is determined by reference to the last two digits of the claimant's national insurance number (Claims and Payments Regs, reg.26C (see Vol.III). This para of Sch.2 enables regs to make provision for payment in respect of periods of less than a week: see ESA Regs 2013 regs 98–102.

Para. (4) (linking periods)

1.945 The linking rules are crucial for those suffering from intermittent incapacity. They impact, to the claimant's benefit, as regards "waiting days"; those days of non-entitlement (see para. (2)) only have to be served once in any period of limited capability for work. They are also relevant to determining the relevant benefit year and hence the appropriate tax years to which to have regard with respect to the application of the national insurance contribution conditions (see further the commentary to Sch.1 Pt 1 paras 1–3). The linking rule works on the basis that two ostensibly separate spells of limited capability for work will be fused into one where the separation period between the spells is not more than 12 weeks. This fusing does not, however, mean that days in the separation period thereby become ones of limited capability for work (*Chief Adjudication Officer v Astle* (Court of Appeal, judgment of March 17, 1999, available on LEXIS and noted in [1999] 6 J.S.S.L. 203). A period of limited capability for work can only be formed of days of actual limited capability for work and/or ones which the legislative scheme treats as ones of limited capability for work. See further ESA Regs 2013 reg.86.

Para. (5) (presence in Great Britain)

1.946 Entitlement to ESA generally requires presence in Great Britain (s.1(3)(d)). This paragraph enables regulations to treat someone, whatever the actual reality in terms of presence or absence, as being or not being in Great Britain; see ESA Regs 2013 reg.12 (condition relating to youth—residence or presence).

Para. (6) (entitlement when absent from Great Britain)

1.947 Entitlement to "new style" ESA generally requires presence in Great Britain (s.1(3)(d)). This paragraph enables regulations to give entitlement where the claimant is not in Great Britain. See ESA Regs 2013 regs 88–92.

Para. (7) (modification of ESA for those employed on ships etc)

1.948 This enables regulations to modify the rules on entitlement to "new style" ESA as regards those who are, have been or are to be, employed on any ship, vessel, hovercraft or aircraft; outside Great Britain; or in prescribed employment in connection with continental shelf operations.

Para. (10) (effect of work)

1.949 Unsurprisingly, in a benefits regime founded on limited capability for work, the general rule in respect of "new style" ESA is that the doing of any work negatives limited capability: see ESA Regs 2013, reg.37, precluding entitlement to ESA in any week in which a claimant does work. But like the previous incapacity benefit regime, the general preclusive rule is modified to permit engagement in a range of work without loss of benefit. This recognizes that work can assist recovery or help the claimant into thinking about work and a possibility to return to work, or merely not wanting to exclude the sick and disabled from participation in civic office or a range of voluntary or charitable work. See further ESA Regs 2013 regs 37–40.

Para.(14) (advance claims)

See Universal Credit, Personal Independence Payment, Jobseeker's Allowance and Employment and Support Allowance (Claims and Payments) Regulations 2013 (SI 2013/380) reg.34 in Vol.II in this series. **1.950**

Para.(15) (members of Her Majesty's forces)

ESA Regs 2013 reg.92 and Sch.1. **1.951**

SCHEDULE 3 **Section 28**

CONSEQUENTIAL AMENDMENTS RELATING TO PART 1

Insofar as the provisions in this Schedule amend legislation contained in the main volumes and have themselves been further amended or repealed, these amendments and repeals have been taken into account in preparing the legislative text. **1.952**

[[1]SCHEDULE 4 **Section 29** **1.953**

TRANSITION RELATING TO PART 1]

General power to provide for transition relating to Part 1

1.(1) Regulations may make such provision as the Secretary of State considers necessary or expedient—

(a) in connection with the coming into force of any provision of, or repeal relating to, this Part, or

(b) otherwise for the purposes of, or in connection with, the transition to employment and support allowance.

(2) The following provisions of this Schedule are not to be taken as prejudicing the generality of sub-paragraph (1).

Pre-commencement claims

2. Regulations may—

(a) make provision for a claim for incapacity benefit, income support or severe disablement allowance which is made before the appointed day to be treated wholly or partly as a claim for an employment and support allowance;

(b) make provision for the purpose of enabling claims for an employment and support allowance to be made before the appointed day for a period beginning on or after that day.

3. Regulations may–

(a) make provision excluding the making of a claim for incapacity benefit or severe disablement allowance on or after the appointed day;

(b) make provision for a claim for incapacity benefit, income support or severe disablement allowance which is made on or after the appointed day to be treated in prescribed circumstances as a claim for an employment and support allowance;

(c) make provision for a claim for an employment and support allowance to be treated wholly or partly as a claim for incapacity benefit, income support or severe disablement allowance;

(d) make provision excluding the making of a claim for an employment and support allowance by a person who is entitled to an existing award.

4. *(not yet in force)*.

5. *(not yet in force)*.

6. *(not yet in force)*.

Treatment of existing awards

7(1) Regulations may—

(a) make provision for converting existing awards into awards of an employment and support allowance, and with respect to the terms of conversion;

(b) make provision for the termination of existing awards in prescribed circumstances.

(2) Regulations under sub-paragraph

(1)(a) may, in particular—

(a) make provision for conversion of an existing award—
  (i) on application, in accordance with the regulations, by the person entitled to the award, or
  (ii) without application;

(b) make provision about the conditions to be satisfied in relation to an application for conversion;

(c) make provision about the timing of conversion;

(d) provide for an existing award to have effect after conversion as an award of an employment and support allowance—
  (i) of such a kind,
  (ii) for such period,
  (iii) of such an amount, and
  (iv) subject to such conditions,
  as the regulations may provide;

(e) make provision for determining in connection with conversion of an existing award whether a person has limited capability for work-related activity.

(f) make provision modifying the application of section 1A in relation to awards of an employment and support allowance to persons previously entitled to existing awards.

(3) Regulations under sub-paragraph (1)(a) may, in relation to existing awards which have been the subject of conversion under this paragraph, include provision about revision under section 9 of the Social Security Act 1998 (c. 14), or supersession under section 10 of that Act in respect of the period before conversion.

Transitional allowances

8. (1) Regulations may—

(a) make provision for a person's continuing entitlement to an employment and support allowance awarded by virtue of regulations under paragraph 7 (a "transitional allowance") to be determined by reference to such provision as may be made by the regulations;

(b) make provision for the review of an award of a transitional allowance;

(c) make provision for the termination of an award of a transitional allowance;

(d) make provision for this Part, or any other enactment relating to social security, to have effect with prescribed modifications in relation to a person with a transitional allowance;

(e) make provision for the purpose of enabling a transitional allowance to be revised under section 9 of the Social Security Act 1998 or superseded under section 10 of that Act.

(2) In this paragraph "enactment" includes an enactment contained in subordinate legislation (within the meaning of the Interpretation Act 1978).

9. *(not yet in force).*

Post-commencement up-rating of incapacity benefit and severe disablement allowance

10. Regulations may provide for section 150 of the Administration Act (annual up-rating of benefits), so far as relating to—

(a) incapacity benefit under section 30A of the Contributions and Benefits Act, or

(b) severe disablement allowance,

to have effect with prescribed modifications in relation to tax years beginning on or after the appointed day.

Interpretation

11. In this Schedule—

"appointed day" means the day appointed for the coming into force of section 1;

"existing award" means—

(a) an award of incapacity benefit,

(b) an award of severe disablement allowance, and

(c) an award of income support made to a person to whom regulation 6(4)(a) or 13(2)(b) or (bb) of, or paragraph 7(a) or (b), 10, 12 or 13 of Schedule 1B to, the Income Support (General) Regulations 1987 (S.I. 1987/1967) (persons incapable of work or disabled) applies;

"incapacity benefit" (except in paragraph 10(a)) means—

(a) incapacity benefit under section 30A, 40 or 41 of the Contributions and Benefits Act,

(b) long-term incapacity benefit under regulation 11(4) of the Social Security (Incapacity Benefit) (Transitional) Regulations 1995 (S.I. 1995/310) (former sickness benefit), and

(c) invalidity benefit which has effect by virtue of regulation 17(1) of those regulations as if it were long-term incapacity benefit;

"severe disablement allowance" means severe disablement allowance under section 68 of that Act (as it has effect by virtue of article 4 of the Welfare Reform and Pensions Act 1999 (Commencement No. 9, and Transitional and Savings Provisions) Order 2000 (S.I. 2000/2958))

"transitional allowance" has the meaning given by paragraph 8(1)(a).

Child Maintenance and Other Payments Act 2008

(2008 c.6)

ARRANGEMENT OF SECTIONS

PART 4

LUMP SUM PAYMENTS: MESOTHELIOMA ETC.

Mesothelioma lump sum payments

GENERAL NOTE

1.955 Part 4 of the Child Maintenance and Other Payments Act 2008 establishes a new no-fault compensation scheme for victims of mesothelioma, an asbestos-related cancer that is invariably fatal. Known as the 2008 Diffuse Mesothelioma Scheme, the new arrangements are modelled on, but also extend the scope of, the provisions of the Pneumoconiosis etc. (Workers' Compensation) Act 1979 (on which see *Ballantine v Newalls Insulation Co Ltd* [2001] ICR 25). Most mesothelioma victims are middle-aged or elderly men who were employed in industries where heavy exposure to asbestos dust was commonplace until better controls were gradually introduced from the 1970s onwards. There are currently about 2,000 mesothelioma deaths in Great Britain each year, a figure which is expected to rise to about 2,400 a year by 2013, before the total begins to fall away to an expected annual toll of 500 in 2050. Mesothelioma, unlike asbestosis and asbestos-related lung cancer, can be caused by relatively low levels of exposure and so can also occur outside the workplace (see generally N.J. Wikeley, *Compensation for Industrial Disease*, (Aldershot: Dartmouth Publishing Group, 1993)).

Before these reforms, mesothelioma sufferers had three main routes to claiming compensation: (1) a civil claim for damages against their former employer; (2) where no such potential defendant remained in existence, a claim under the Pneumoconiosis etc. (Workers' Compensation) Act 1979; and (3) a claim for industrial disablement benefit on the basis of having a prescribed disease (subject to the recovery rules under the Social Security (Recovery of Benefits) Act 1997). However, three groups of mesothelioma victims found it difficult or impossible to bring a claim under any of these arrangements (see further N.J. Wikeley, "The New Mesothelioma Compensation Scheme" (2009) 16 J.S.S.L. 30, on the background to the 2008 Scheme).

The first group were self-employed workers, who by definition had no employer to sue for damages in tort. As they were not "employed earners", they also did not qualify for industrial disablement benefit (or under the 1979 Act). Self-employment has always been common in the construction industry, one of the occupations in which exposure levels to asbestos dust were at their highest in the four decades or so after the Second World War, leaving large numbers of victims with no effective means of redress.

The second category comprised para-occupational mesothelioma victims (or cases of "household exposure"), e.g. family members who were exposed to asbestos dust at home because of close contact with an asbestos worker's overalls, such as by shaking and washing overalls. Household victims may in theory have a claim in tort, but in many cases the difficulties of establishing the requisite date of knowledge on the employer's part for the purposes of establishing a duty of care will be fatal (see e.g. *Maguire v Harland and Wolff plc* [2005] EWCA Civ 1). Family members who contract mesothelioma indirectly through household exposure are not themselves "employed earners", and so have no claim under the industrial disablement scheme or the 1979 Act.

The third (and probably smallest) group comprises environmental cases, where victims have been exposed to asbestos dust in the vicinity of their home. In extreme cases they may be able to recover in tort (see e.g. *Margereson and Hancock v J. W. Roberts Ltd* [1996] EWCA Civ 1316) but again they have no claim under the industrial disablement scheme or 1979 Act because of the absence of a personal occupational link.

The new scheme under Part 4 is designed to provide early assistance to all such mesothelioma victims, irrespective of their previous employment status. The Government anticipates that up to 600 mesothelioma victims who previously received no state support will receive an average payment of £6,000 during the first year of the scheme's operation. The scheme is to be funded from recoveries from subsequent compensation payments made by defendants and insurers. The Government anticipates that payments will be brought up to the levels under the 1979 Act by the third year of the new scheme, as compensation recoveries begin to accrue. The Child Maintenance and Other Payments Act 2008 (Commencement) Order 2008 (SI 2008/1476 (C.67)) brought Part 4 into force with effect from October 1, 2008.

PART 4

LUMP SUM PAYMENTS: MESOTHELIOMA ETC.

Mesothelioma lump sum payments

Lump sum payments

46.—(1) A claim for a payment under this Part may be made by— 1.956

(a) a person with diffuse mesothelioma, or

(b) a dependant of a person who, immediately before death, had diffuse mesothelioma.

(2) The Secretary of State must make the payment to the claimant if satisfied that the conditions of entitlement in section 47 are fulfilled.

(3) Regulations—

(a) may prescribe the amount of any payment;

(b) may prescribe different amounts for different cases or classes of cases or for different circumstances.

(4) In this Part—

"dependant" has the meaning given by section 3 of the Pneumoconiosis etc. (Workers' Compensation) Act 1979 (c. 41) ("the 1979 Act");

"diffuse mesothelioma" has the same meaning as in the 1979 Act.

(5) Where, because of section 3(1)(b) or (d) of the 1979 Act (children, siblings etc.), a payment may be claimed by two or more persons, the payment is to be made to one of them or divided between some or all of them as the Secretary of State thinks fit.

DEFINITIONS

"dependant"—subs.(4).
"diffuse mesothelioma"—*ibid.*

GENERAL NOTE

1.957 This section provides for the Secretary of State to make lump sum payments to persons with diffuse mesothelioma, or to their dependants, if the person in question has died (subs.(1); if the payment is to a dependent minor, see s.52). Indeed, if the criteria set out in s.47 are satisfied the Secretary of State *must* make such a lump sum payment (subs.(2)). Regulations may prescribe the amounts in question, which may be different for different cases or classes of cases and circumstances (subs.(3); see further reg.5 and the Schedule to the Mesothelioma Lump Sum Payments (Conditions and Amounts) Regulations 2008 (SI 2008/1963). These regulations, like the Pneumoconiosis etc. (Workers' Compensation) Act 1979, set payments at different levels by age and according to whether they are made to a sufferer or a dependant. The terms "dependant" and "diffuse mesothelioma" both carry the same meaning as in the 1979 Act (subs.(4); note that the definition of "dependant" in the 1979 Act was amended and updated by s.59 of the Welfare Reform Act 2007). If there are two or more dependants eligible to claim, the payment may be apportioned (or not) according to the discretion of the Secretary of State (subs (5)).

Conditions of entitlement

1.958 **47.**—(1) In the case of a person who has diffuse mesothelioma, the conditions of entitlement are—
(a) that no payment within subsection (3) has been made in consequence of the disease;
(b) that the person is not eligible for any payment in consequence of the disease that is of a description prescribed by regulations;
(c) that such requirement, if any, as may be prescribed by regulations as to the person's connection with the United Kingdom is satisfied.

(2) In the case of a dependant of a person who, immediately before death, had diffuse mesothelioma, the conditions of entitlement are—
(a) that no payment within subsection (3) has been made in consequence of the disease to that or another dependant or to the deceased or the deceased's personal representatives;
(b) that the dependant is not, and the deceased was not, eligible for any payment in consequence of the disease that is of a description prescribed by regulations;
(c) that such requirement, if any, as may be prescribed by regulations as to the deceased's connection with the United Kingdom is satisfied.

(3) The payments referred to in subsections (1)(a) and (2)(a) are—
(a) a payment under this Part or under corresponding provision made for Northern Ireland;
(b) a payment under the 1979 Act or under corresponding provision made for Northern Ireland;
[[1] (ba) a payment under the Diffuse Mesothelioma Payment Scheme (for the scheme, see the Mesothelioma Act 2014);]

(c) an extra-statutory payment;
(d) damages or a payment in settlement of a claim for damages;
(e) a payment of a description prescribed by regulations.

(4) A payment is to be disregarded for the purposes of subsection (1)(a) or (2)(a) if it has been, or is liable to be, repaid—

(a) under section 49 of this Act or under corresponding provision made for Northern Ireland;
(b) under section 5 of the 1979 Act or under corresponding provision made for Northern Ireland;
(c) under the terms of an extra-statutory payment;
(d) in circumstances prescribed for the purposes of this section by regulations.

(5) In this section "extra-statutory payment" has the meaning given by section 1A(5)(d) of the Social Security (Recovery of Benefits) Act 1997.

AMENDMENT

1. Mesothelioma Act 2014 Sch.2 para.2 (March 31, 2014).

DEFINITIONS

"extra-statutory payment"—subs.(5).

GENERAL NOTE

This section sets out the conditions of entitlement for a lump sum payment. The relevant conditions for a mesothelioma sufferer are in subs.(1) and for a dependant of a mesothelioma sufferer in subs.(2). In both instances there are three criteria, each of which must be met. **1.959**

First, there must have been no payment already in consequence of the disease, as defined by subs.(3) (and subject to the disregards in subs.(4)). Such payments include a payment of damages or settlement of a claim for damages, as well as payments under this Part, payments under the 1979 Act, extra-statutory payments and payments of a prescribed nature. The definition of "extra-statutory payment" is the same as for recoupment purposes, namely one made where a claim has been rejected under the 1979 Act (subs.(5) and see s.54, inserting a new s.1A(5) into the Social Security (Recovery of Benefits) Act 1997). The category of prescribed payments includes payments by government departments (including the Ministry of Defence) and payments by various public sector and other employers which are exempt from employers' liability compulsory insurance (see Employers' Liability (Compulsory Insurance) Regulations 1998 (SI 1998/2573) Sch.2, paras 1-13 and see the Mesothelioma Lump Sum Payments (Conditions and Amounts) Regulations 2008 (SI 2008/1963) reg.2(1)). Note that where a lump sum payment is made under s.46 and there is a later award of damages or settlement in a civil case, the Secretary of State may recoup part or all of the cost of the earlier payment from that figure (see s.54 and the new s.1A of the Social Security (Recovery of Benefits) Act 1997).

Second, there must be no eligibility for any payment of a description as prescribed by regulations. This category includes payments under the Ministry of Defence's War Pensions Scheme or Armed Forces Compensation Scheme: see the Mesothelioma Lump Sum Payments (Conditions and Amounts) Regulations 2008 (SI 2008/1963) reg.2(2).

Third, the mesothelioma victim must have satisfied the prescribed "connection with the United Kingdom" test. The Government's concern is to protect the scheme against (the probably fairly remote) risk of "benefit tourism" by persons who contracted mesothelioma while living abroad and who then travel to the United Kingdom to take advantage of the compensation arrangements. See further the Mesothelioma Lump Sum Payments (Conditions and Amounts) Regulations 2008 (SI 2008/1963) reg.4.

In this context it should be noted that there is no freestanding express statutory requirement that the victim contracted mesothelioma *as a result of* asbestos exposure. In practice, of course, asbestos is the only known cause of mesothelioma. However, a minority of victims have no known exposure to asbestos (this may be because they were in fact exposed, but there is no record of such exposure, or because there are indeed some instances of cryptogenic mesothelioma unrelated to asbestos exposure). The statute simply requires that the person has "diffuse mesothelioma", as defined by s.10(2) of the 1979 Act (see s.46(4)), which in turn refers to the social security definition for the purposes of the industrial injuries scheme. Regulation 1(2) of the Social Security (Industrial Injuries) (Prescribed Diseases) Regulations 1985 (SI 1985/967) defines "diffuse mesothelioma" as the disease numbered P.D. D3 in the Schedule to those Regulations. This refers (under the column headed "Prescribed disease or injury") to "primary neoplasm of the mesothelium of the pleura or of the pericardium or of the peritoneum". It is arguable that this is the limit of the definition, and that it does not include the occupational test in the next column of the Schedule, which refers specifically to asbestos exposure. If that is right, it is arguable that the terms of reg.4 of the Mesothelioma Lump Sum Payments (Conditions and Amounts) Regulations 2008 may be ultra vires, as that provision requires that the person concerned "was in the United Kingdom at a time when and place where" that person "*was exposed to asbestos*" (emphasis added).

Determination of claims

1.960 **48.**—(1) A claim under section 46 must be made in the manner and within the period prescribed by regulations.

(2) Regulations may prescribe different periods for different cases or classes of cases or for different circumstances.

(3) Regulations may in particular provide that no claim may be made in cases where the prescribed period expired before the commencement of section 46 (or would have done but for any discretion to extend it).

(4) The Secretary of State may, before determining any claim under section 46, appoint a person to inquire into any question arising on the claim, or any matters arising in connection with it, and to report on the question, or on those matters, to the Secretary of State.

General Note

Subsections (1) and (2)

1.961 This section deals with the determination of claims made under s.46. Claims must be made in the prescribed manner and within time limits: see further the Mesothelioma Lump Sum Payments (Claims and Reconsiderations) Regulations 2008 (SI 2008/1595) regs 2 and 3. The general time limit for claims is 12 months from the diagnosis of mesothelioma (or, in the case of a dependant, 12 months from the death of the person with mesothelioma), as under s.4(1) of the Pneumoconiosis etc. (Workers' Compensation) Act 1979. As under the 1979 Act, this time limit is subject to extension for good cause.

Subsection (3)

1.962 There is an initial absolute time limit on backdating of 12 months prior to the regulations coming into force, to avoid the possibility of claims by dependants going back as far as 1948: see Mesothelioma Lump Sum Payments (Claims and Reconsiderations) Regulations 2008 (SI 2008/1595) reg.3(1).

Subsection (4)

This provision is modelled on the now repealed s.17(4) of the Social Security Administration Act 1992, although that referred to an appointment to a person "to hold an inquiry" rather than merely "to inquire" (see also to similar effect s.4(2) of the Pneumoconiosis etc. (Workers' Compensation) Act 1979). 1.963

Reconsideration

49.—(1) Subject to subsection (2), the Secretary of State— 1.964

(a) may reconsider a determination that a payment should not be made under this Part, on the ground that there has been a material change of circumstances since the determination was made; and

(b) may reconsider a determination either that a payment should or that a payment should not be made under this Part, on the ground that the determination was made in ignorance of, or was based on a mistake as to, a material fact.

(2) Regulations must prescribe the manner in which and [1 may prescribe] the period within which—

(a) an application may be made to the Secretary of State for reconsideration of a determination; or

(b) the Secretary of State may institute such a reconsideration without an application.

(3) Section 48(4) applies in relation to any reconsideration of a determination under this section as it applies in relation to the determination of a claim.

(4) Subsection (5) applies if—

(a) whether fraudulently or otherwise, any person misrepresents or fails to disclose any material fact, and

(b) in consequence of the misrepresentation or failure, a payment is made under this Part.

(5) The person to whom the payment was made is liable to repay the amount of that payment to the Secretary of State unless that person can show that the misrepresentation or failure occurred without that person's connivance or consent.

(6) Except as provided by subsection (5), no payment under this Part is recoverable by virtue of a reconsideration of a determination under this section.

(7) Any sums repaid to the Secretary of State by virtue of subsection (5) are to be paid into the Consolidated Fund.

AMENDMENT

1. Welfare Reform Act 2012 s.102(6) and Sch.11 paras 15 &16 (February 25, 2013).

GENERAL NOTE

This section makes provision for the Secretary of State to carry out a reconsideration of a determination made under s.48. 1.965

Subsection (1)

Reconsiderations are possible where there has been a material change in circumstances or the original determination was made in ignorance of or based on a mistake as to a material fact (subs.(1)). These grounds have been borrowed from the 1.966

social security jurisdiction. This section also broadly follows the model of s.5 of the Pneumoconiosis etc. (Workers' Compensation) Act 1979.

Subsections (2) and (3)

1.967 See the Mesothelioma Lump Sum Payments (Claims and Reconsiderations) Regulations 2008 (SI 2008/1595) regs 4 and 5. The Secretary of State has the same power as when dealing with an initial determination to appoint a person to inquire into matters arising (see s.48(4)).

Subsections (4) and (5)

1.968 The Secretary of State may recover payments under the scheme where they have been caused by misrepresentation or failure to disclose; again, these concepts are borrowed from social security law—see Social Security Administration Act 1992 s.71. However the potential defence under subs.(5) that the misrepresentation or failure to disclose "occurred without that person's connivance or consent" does not appear in social security law (except in the context of s.5(4) of the Vaccine Damages Act 1979).

Appeal to [1 First-tier Tribunal]

1.969 **50.**—(1) A person who has made a claim under section 46 may appeal against a determination made by the Secretary of State—

(a) on the claim, or

(b) on reconsideration under section 49 of a determination made on the claim.

[2 (1A) Regulations may provide that, in such cases or circumstances as may be prescribed, a person may appeal against a determination made on a claim only if the Secretary of State has decided whether to reconsider the determination under section 49.

(1B) The regulations may in particular provide that that condition is met only where—

(a) the decision of the Secretary of State was on an application,

(b) the Secretary of State considered issues of a specified description, or

(c) the decision of the Secretary of State satisfied any other condition specified in the regulations.]

(2) Subject to regulations under subsection (4)(c), the Secretary of State must refer any appeal to [1 the First-tier Tribunal].

(3) On an appeal the tribunal may substitute for the determination concerned any determination which could have been made in accordance with this Part.

(4) Regulations may make provision—

(a) as to the manner in which, and the time within which, an appeal may be made;

(b) [1. . .];

(c) for the purpose of enabling an appeal under subsection (1)(a) [2 (or, where in accordance with regulations under subsection (1A) there is no right of appeal, any purported appeal)] to be treated as an application for reconsideration under section 49 of the determination made on the claim.

Amendments

1. Transfer of Tribunal Functions Order 2008 (SI 2008/2833) art.6, Sch.3 para.226 (November 3, 2008).

2. Welfare Reform Act 2012 s.102(6) and Sch.11 paras 15 &17(1)-(3) (February 25, 2013).

General note

A person making a claim under s.46 has a right of appeal to the First-tier Tribunal against the Secretary of State's determination on the claim under s.48 or reconsideration under s.49. There is a further right of appeal (on a point of law and with permission) from the First-tier Tribunal to the Upper Tribunal (Tribunals, Courts and Enforcement Act 2007 s.11). 1.970

Note that the right of appeal is under the 2008 Act; there is no right of appeal to a tribunal in respect of decisions made under the 1979 Act, although there is a reconsideration process under that legislation.

Appeal to Social Security Commissioner

51.—[1. . .] 1.971

Amendment

1. Transfer of Tribunal Functions Order 2008 (SI 2008/2833) art.6, Sch.3 para.227 (November 3, 2008).

General note

As originally enacted, there was a further right of appeal from the decision of an appeal tribunal (now the First-tier Tribunal) under s.50 to the Social Security Commissioner. The jurisdiction of the Commissioner has now been assumed by the Upper Tribunal under the Tribunals, Courts and Enforcement Act 2007. The bringing into force of s.11 of that Act, which provides for a right of appeal, subject to permission being granted, from the First-tier Tribunal to the Upper Tribunal on a point of law swiftly made s.51 redundant. 1.972

Minors and people who lack capacity

52.—(1) This section applies where a payment under this Part falls to be made to— 1.973

(a) a person aged under 18, or
(b) a person who lacks capacity within the meaning of the Mental Capacity Act 2005 (or, in Scotland, who is incapable within the meaning of the Adults with Incapacity (Scotland) Act 2000 (asp 4)) in relation to financial matters.

(2) Subject to section 46(5) the payment is to be made for that person's benefit by paying it to such trustees as the Secretary of State may appoint.

(3) The trustees are to hold the payment on such trusts or, in Scotland, for such purposes and on such conditions as the Secretary of State may declare.

General note

This section makes special provision for cases in which a payment is due to be made to a child or to a person who lacks capacity; in such cases payments are to be made to trustees. This provision is similar to s.6 of the Pneumoconiosis etc. (Workers' Compensation) Act 1979. 1.974

Regulations: Part 4

1.975 **53.**—(1) A reference in this Part to regulations is a reference to regulations made by the Secretary of State.

(2) The power to make regulations under this Part—

(a) is exercisable by statutory instrument;

(b) includes power to make such incidental, supplementary or transitional provision as the Secretary of State thinks fit;

(c) may be exercised so as to provide for a person to exercise a discretion in dealing with any matter.

[1 (2A) The power to make regulations under section 50(1A) may be exercised—

(a) in relation to all cases to which it extends, in relation to those cases but subject to specified exceptions or in relation to any specified cases or classes of case;

(b) so as to make, as respects the cases in relation to which it is exercised—

(i) the full provision to which it extends or any lesser provision (whether by way of exception or otherwise);

(ii) the same provision for all cases, different provision for different cases or classes of case or different provision as respects the same case or class of case but for different purposes of this Act;

(iii) provision which is either unconditional or is subject to any specified condition.]

(3) No regulations may be made under section 46 [1or 50(1A)] unless a draft of the statutory instrument containing the regulations has been laid before, and approved by a resolution of, each House of Parliament.

(4) No regulations may be made under any provision of section 47 if they are the first regulations to be made under that section, unless a draft of the statutory instrument containing the regulations has been laid before, and approved by a resolution of, each House of Parliament.

(5) A statutory instrument that—

(a) contains regulations under this Part, and

(b) is not subject to a requirement that a draft of the instrument be laid before, and approved by a resolution of, each House of Parliament,

shall be subject to annulment in pursuance of a resolution of either House of Parliament.

AMENDMENT

1. Welfare Reform Act 2012, s.102(6) and Sch.11 paras.15 &18(1)-(3) (February 25, 2013).

GENERAL NOTE

1.976 Regulations made under s.46 which make provision for lump sum payments in respect of mesothelioma are subject to the affirmative procedure (subs.(3)); all other regulations under this Part are subject to the negative procedure (subs.(4)).

Recovery of mesothelioma and other lump sum payments

Amendment of Social Security (Recovery of Benefits) Act 1997

54—(*omitted:* see Vol.III). **1.977**

GENERAL NOTE

This section inserts a new s.1A into the Social Security (Recovery of Benefits) Act 1997. The 1997 Act applies wherever a person makes a payment "to or in respect of any other person in consequence of any accident, injury or disease suffered by the other" and where as a result certain prescribed benefits have been (or are likely) to be paid to or for the other person during the relevant period. The new s.1A allows the Secretary of State to make regulations providing for the recovery of lump sum payments in analogous circumstances: see further the Social Security (Recovery of Benefits) (Lump Sum Payments) Regulations 2008 (SI 2008/1596). These regulations establish a freestanding compensation recovery scheme to recoup lump sum mesothelioma payments under Part 4 of the present Act as well as those under the Pneumoconiosis etc. (Workers' Compensation) Act 1979 and certain extra-statutory payments. The intention is to recover such payments from any civil compensation award paid to the person in respect of the same disease (or diseases) for which the lump sum payment was made. The underlying principle is that a person should not be compensated twice for the same loss. **1.978**

Welfare Reform Act 2009

(2009 c.24)

SECTIONS REPRODUCED

PART 1

SOCIAL SECURITY

"Work for your benefit" schemes etc.

An Act to amend the law relating to social security; to make provision enabling disabled people to be given greater control over the way in which certain public services are provided for them; to amend the law relating to child support; to make provision about the registration of births; and for connected purposes. [12th November 2009]

Parliamentary procedure: regulations imposing work-related activity requirements on lone parents of children under 7

1.980 **8.** [[1] *Repealed.*]

AMENDMENT

1. Welfare Reform Act 2012 Sch.14(5) para.1 (April 29, 2013).

Jobseeker's allowance and employment and support allowance: drugs

Claimants dependent on drugs etc.

1.981 **11.** [[1] *Repealed.*]

AMENDMENT

1. Welfare Reform Act 2012 ss.60(3), 150(2)(b) (May 8, 2012).

Contributory jobseeker's allowance and employment and support allowance

Conditions for contributory employment and support allowance

13.—(1) Paragraph 1 of Schedule 1 to the Welfare Reform Act 2007 (c. 5) (employment and support allowance: conditions relating to national insurance) is amended as follows. 1.982

(2)–(5) *amendments made by these subsections have been embodied in the current text of Sch. 1 to the WRA 2007*

GENERAL NOTE

The changes effected from November 1, 2010 by this section and the regulations made under it, significantly tighten the contribution conditions for CESA by requiring a more recent and stronger connection with the world of work. It does so in that the first condition can from then only be satisfied in one of the last *two* (rather than three) tax years (April 6–April 5) complete before the start of the relevant benefit year (early January) (as with JSA); and by raising the requisite level of earnings in the tax year relied on to 26 (rather than 25) times that year's lower earnings limit. Moreover, since the conditions now only count earnings at that lower earnings limit (ignoring earnings in excess of it) new claimants will have to have worked for at least 26 weeks in one of the last two tax years (in effect each week's work at or above the LEL generates in essence one "contribution" (a virtual equivalent of the old regime of NI stamps) towards the target of 26 contributions, and has redolence with the earliest years of the National Insurance scheme operative from 1913 which worked on "flat-rate" contributions. Prior to these amendments, when the level was 25 times the LEL and the scheme looked also to earnings between the lower and upper earnings limits, a high-earner could qualify on less than four weeks work in the tax year and someone at the national minimum wage could qualify in about 12 weeks. The relevant regulations made under subss.(3) and (3A) are the Social Security (Contribution Conditions for Jobseeker's Allowance and Employment and Support Allowance) Regulations 2010 (SI 2010/2446), and amendments effected by them have been taken into account in producing the current text of the ESA Regulations. 1.983

Abolition of adult dependency increases

Maternity allowance and carer's allowance

15.—(1) The following provisions of the Social Security Contributions and Benefits Act 1992 (c. 4) ("the Benefits Act") are omitted on 6 April 2010— 1.984

(a) section 82 (maternity allowance: increase for adult dependants); and
(b) section 90 (carer's allowance: increase for adult dependants).

(2) Nothing in subsection (1) or Part 2 of Schedule 7 applies in relation to—

(a) the amount of a maternity allowance payable for a maternity allowance period (within the meaning of section 35(2) of the Benefits Act) which begins before 6 April 2010 but ends on or after that date, or
(b) the amount of a carer's allowance payable to a qualifying person at any time on or after 6 April 2010 but before the appropriate date.

(3) In subsection (2)(b)—

"a qualifying person" means a person who—

(a) has, before 6 April 2010, made a claim for an increase in a carer's allowance under section 90 of the Benefits Act; and

(b) immediately before that date is either entitled to the increase claimed or a beneficiary to whom section 92 of the Benefits Act applies in respect of that increase (continuation of awards where fluctuating earnings);

"the appropriate date" means whichever is the earlier of—

(a) 6 April 2020; and

(b) the date when the qualifying person ceases to be either entitled to that increase or a beneficiary to whom section 92 of the Benefits Act applies in respect of that increase.

Miscellaneous

37. Minor amendments

1.985 (1) Sections 80 and 81 of the Benefits Act (which continue to have effect in certain cases despite their repeal by the Tax Credits Act 2002 (c.21)) are to have effect as if the references in those sections to a child or children included references to a qualifying young person or persons.

(2) "Qualifying young person" has the same meaning as in Part 9 of the Benefits Act.

(3)—*amendments made by this subsection have been taken into account in Vol. III*

(4) Despite the provision made by the Welfare Reform Act 2007 (Commencement No. 6 and Consequential Provisions) Order 2008 (S.I. 2008/ 787), paragraph 9(7) and (8) of Schedule 3 to the Welfare Reform Act 2007 (c.5) (which amend sections 88 and 89 of the Benefits Act) are deemed not to be in force by virtue of the provision made by that order at any time after the passing of this Act.

(5) In this section "the Benefits Act" means the Social Security Contributions and Benefits Act 1992 (c.4).

PART 5

GENERAL

Consequential amendments of subordinate legislation

1.986 **57.—**(1) The Secretary of State may by regulations made by statutory instrument make such provision amending or revoking any instrument made under any other Act before the passing of this Act as appears to the Secretary of State to be appropriate in consequence of any provision of this Act, other than a provision contained in Part 2.

(2) Regulations under this section may include—

(a) transitional provisions or savings, and

(b) provision conferring a discretion on any person.

(3) A statutory instrument containing regulations under this section is subject to annulment in pursuance of a resolution of either House of Parliament.

Repeals and revocations

1.987 **58.**—(1) Schedule 7 contains repeals and revocations.

(2) *Lists repeals and revocations in Pt 2 of that Schedule (made in consequence of s.15(1)) which have effect on April 6, 2010. They have been incorporated in the text of the legislation in the appropriate Volume in this series*

(3) The repeal in that Part of paragraph 9 of Part 4 of Schedule 4 to the Social Security Contributions and Benefits Act 1992 is not to be taken as affecting the operation of article 3 of the Tax Credits Act 2002 (Commencement No. 3 and Transitional Provisions and Savings) Order 2003 (S.I. 2003/ 938) (savings in relation to the abolition of child dependency increases).

Financial provisions

59.—(1) There is to be paid out of money provided by Parliament— **1.988**

(a) any expenditure incurred in consequence of this Act by a Minister of the Crown, a government department or the Registrar General for England and Wales, and

(b) any increase attributable to this Act in the sums payable under any other Act out of money so provided.

(2) There is to be paid into the Consolidated Fund any increase attributable to this Act in the sums payable into that Fund under any other Act.

Extent

60.—(1) The following provisions of this Act extend to England and Wales, Scotland and Northern Ireland— **1.989**

section 24 and Schedule 4 (loss of benefit provisions);
section 36 (power to rename council tax benefit); and
this section and sections 61 and 62.

(2) Section 56 and Schedule 6 (birth registration) extend to England and Wales only.

(3) Subject to subsection (4), the other provisions of this Act extend to England and Wales and Scotland only.

(4) Any amendment, repeal or revocation made by this Act has the same extent as the enactment to which it relates.

(5) Subsection (4) is subject to paragraph 20(2) of Schedule 6.

Commencement

61.—(1) The following provisions of this Act come into force on the day on which this Act is passed— **1.990**

sections 1 and 2;
section 8;
section 11;
section 23;
sections 27 and 28;
section 37;
section 57;
sections 59 and 60;
this section;
section 62; and
Schedule 3.

(2) The following provisions of this Act come into force at the end of the period of 2 months beginning with the day on which this Act is passed—

section 15;
section 34;
Part 2;
section 58(2) and (3); and
Part 2 of Schedule 7 so far as relating to the repeals and revocation mentioned in section 58(2).

(3) The other provisions of this Act come into force on such day as the Secretary of State may by order made by statutory instrument appoint.

(4) An order under subsection (3) may—

(a) appoint different days for different purposes and in relation to different areas;

(b) make such provision as the Secretary of State considers necessary or expedient for transitory, transitional or saving purposes in connection with the coming into force of any provision falling within that subsection.

(5) Before making an order under subsection (3) in relation to any provision of Part 1 of Schedule 6 (birth registration), the Secretary of State must consult the Registrar General for England and Wales.

Short title

1.991 **62.**—This Act may be cited as the Welfare Reform Act 2009

SCHEDULE 3

CLAIMANTS DEPENDENT ON DRUGS ETC.

1.992 [[1] *Repealed.*]

REPEALS

1. Welfare Reform Act 2012 ss.60(3), 150(2)(b) (May 8, 2012).

Welfare Reform Act 2012

(2012 c. 5)

Sections Reproduced

Part 3

Other benefit changes

Industrial Injuries

Part 4

Personal independence payment

Personal independence payment

Entitlement and payability: further provision

Supplementary

General

PART 3

OTHER BENEFIT CHANGES

Industrial Injuries

Injuries arising before 5 July 1948

1.998 **64.**—(1) and (2): *amendments made by these subsections have been taken into account in updating the legislative text in this Volume.*

(3) The Secretary of State may make regulations—

(a) for, and in relation to, the payment of industrial injuries benefit to persons to whom, before the commencement of this section, compensation or benefits were payable under section 111 of, and Schedule 8 to, the Social Security Contributions and Benefits Act 1992;

(b) for claims for the payment of such compensation or benefit to be treated as claims for industrial injuries benefit.

(4) In subsection (3) "industrial injuries benefit" has the meaning given by section 122(1) of the Social Security Contributions and Benefits Act 1992.

(5) Regulations under this section are to be made by statutory instrument.

(6) A statutory instrument containing regulations under this section is subject to annulment in pursuance of a resolution of either House of Parliament.

GENERAL NOTE

1.999 This entered into force on October 30, 2012 for the purpose of making regulations and for all other purposes (the amendments effected by subss.(1) and (2)) on December 5, 2012.

From July 1948 until December 5, 2012 there was separate provision for State compensation to be paid for accidents and diseases at work occurring before July 5, 1948 through the "pre-1948 schemes: the Workmen's Compensation (Supplementation) Scheme 1982 and the Pneumoconiosis Byssinosis and Miscellaneous Diseases Benefit Scheme 1983. These two schemes are known collectively as the "pre-1948 schemes". This section repeals the legislation that maintains the existence of two separate schemes for providing State compensation for work injuries occurring before 1948.

This means that on or after December 5, 2012 all claims for State "no-fault" compensation for work injuries will be dealt with as claims under the main Industrial Injuries Disablement Benefit (IIDB) scheme regardless of when the disease or accident occurred. The Industrial Injuries Benefit (Injuries arising before July 5, 1948) Regulations 2012 (SI 2012/2743) (as amended) give further effect to this so that all claims for industrial injured will be made, decided and appealed in the same way regardless of the date of the accident or onset of the prescribed disease.

Trainees

66.—(1) *This inserted the new s.95A into SSCBA 1992 with effect from October 31, 2013.* 1.1000

(2) *Omitted.*

(3) The Secretary of State may make regulations—

(a) for, and in relation to, the payment of industrial injuries benefit to persons to whom, before the commencement of this section, payments were payable under section 11(3) of the Employment and Training Act 1973;

(b) for claims for such payments to be treated as claims for industrial injuries benefit.

(4) In subsection (3) "industrial injuries benefit" has the meaning given by section 122(1) of the Social Security Contributions and Benefits Act 1992.

(5) Regulations under this section are to be made by statutory instrument.

(6) A statutory instrument containing regulations under this section is subject to annulment in pursuance of a resolution of either House of Parliament.

PART 4

PERSONAL INDEPENDENCE PAYMENT

Personal independence payment

Personal independence payment

77.—(1) An allowance known as personal independence payment is payable in accordance with this Part. 1.1001

(2) A person's entitlement to personal independence payment may be an entitlement to—

(a) the daily living component (see section 78);

(b) the mobility component (see section 79); or

(c) both those components.

(3) A person is not entitled to personal independence payment unless the person meets prescribed conditions relating to residence and presence in Great Britain.

[[1] (4) A person is not entitled to personal independence payment while they are entitled to [[2] adult disability payment or child disability payment].

AMENDMENTS

1. Scotland Act 2016 (Social Security) (Consequential Provision) (Miscellaneous Amendment) Regulations 2021 (SI 2021/804) reg.3 (July 26, 2021).

2. Scotland Act 2016 (Social Security) (Adult Disability Payment and Child Disability Payment) (Amendment) Regulations 2022 (SI 2022/335) reg.3 (March 21, 2022).

GENERAL NOTE

Personal independence payments replace Disability Living Allowance for claimants of working age. Like DLA this benefit is a non-contributory benefit for persons who are so disabled, mentally or physically, as to require assistance to lead a normal 1.1002 life or so disabled as not to be able to walk properly or to walk without guidance and support. Like DLA, it too, is composed of two components, a living component and a mobility component. PIP will not be payable to claimants under 16. Nor will it be payable to claimants over pensionable age. DLA will continue as the disability benefit for those claimants aged less than 16. Attendance Allowance will be available for new claimants aged over pensionable age. Those who are in receipt of PIP when they reach pensionable age will be able to continue in receipt of PIP so long as they continue otherwise to qualify.

A person may be entitled to PIP whether they are in or out of work; the qualifying condition is that they are so disabled in some respect that they require assistance to the requisite extent to enable them to live a normal life. Similarly a claimant for PIP may be in receipt of other benefits. Most commonly that will be Employment and Support Allowance which is awarded following an assessment of disability in relation to the claimant's ability to work. The test to be applied in relation to PIP is not the same as that for ESA, but where a claimant has claimed for both, the evidence used in relation to one may be relevant to the other. Similarly, a claimant for PIP may be in receipt of Carer's Allowance – the fact that they are able to care for another is relevant only in respect of the fact finding to be undertaken by a tribunal in determining whether the evidence before them, of the claimant's disability, is consistent with the care that he is providing, in just the same way that the evidence of disability must be consistent with the work done by a claimant who is in work. See *PB v SSWP (PIP)* [2017] UKUT 493 (AAC).

PIP was introduced for new claims during 2013. Claimants who are of working age and in receipt of DLA are being transferred to PIP by stages from 2013.

PIP is intended to achieve broadly the same or a similar coverage of disability as that provided by DLA though some of the standards to be applied may be stricter. In a few cases a claim may succeed for PIP when it would fail for DLA. The chief difference will be in the way that an assessment of that disability is made and in the fact that almost all awards are intended to be for a fixed period and subject to review, rather than an award for life as was usual for DLA. Some of the words and phrases used to define entitlement to PIP are the same or similar to those used for DLA. To that extent, decisions that have been made in relation to DLA may be relevant to PIP.

The importance of getting the terminology right, and of establishing what it is that claimants, representatives and expert witness statements mean by the terms that they use has been emphasised by Judge Jacobs in *PW v SSWP (PIP)* [2023] UKUT 121 (AAC). This was a PIP case, but it arose on the transfer of the claimant from his award of DLA onto PIP and the evidence and the processes involved are essentially the same. The decision of the FTT was expressed in terms that referred to both learning difficulty and learning disability while his mother, in the appeal application, had referred to cognitive impairment. The Judge undertook internet research before granting leave to appeal to the UT but found no consistent or authoritative statement of whether the terms used were interchangeable, or if different, what those meanings might be. Judge Jacobs holds that it was an error law for the FTT not to have determined what the mother meant when she referred to her son having a disability so as to understand the points she was making and for them not to identify what those terms meant in the documentary evidence submitted in support of the claim.

In *BTC v SSWP* [2015] UKUT 155 (AAC) the tribunals hearing appeals in relation to claims for PIP are advised that some of the procedural principles that have developed in relation to claims for DLA are likely to be applicable also to PIP appeals. For example in the instant case the tribunal had reduced the claimant's entitlement in a case where she had appealed for an increase in the award. The argument adopted by the FTT had not been raised by the respondent at all. Judge Bano, in the UT, makes the point that such a course of action should be taken with caution and possibly only after an adjournment to enable the parties to prepare fully for that argument. In this case the tribunal had proceeded after warning that her appeal might result in a loss of benefit, but the claimant had declined to withdraw. And note too *MS v SSWP (DLA and PIP)* [2021] UKUT 41 (AAC), where the FTT gave a warning to an unrepresented claimant appealing against the recovery of a substantial overpayment that they might find it appropriate to revise his entitlement from an even earlier date than that pursued by the Secretary of State. They allowed the claimant to leave the room in order to consult with members of his family, but then resumed the hearing at his request after a delay of only 4 minutes.

Judge Wikeley, in the UT, found this to be a breach of the claimant's right to natural justice. Another principle that is likely to be adopted in PIP cases is that which has been applied to renewal claims (or even fresh claims that follow a recent award) in which the tribunal is minded to reduce or to remove entitlement to benefit. In those cases it has been held that the tribunal has a duty to make clear the reasons why that has been the result of the appeal. (See *R(M)* 1/96 and cases following it including most recently *AB v SSWP* [2015] UKUT 89 (AAC)). This situation may be expected to arise more frequently in relation to PIP awards because, although DWP have now accepted that some awards should be made for an indefinite period, most will still be of limited duration. And note *BB v SSWP (PIP)* [2017] UKUT 506 (AAC), where the tribunal had failed to explain its reasons for a reduced award on a renewal claim.

The correct approach to be followed in such cases where the claimant may be in receipt of, or at least claiming, both parts of PIP is considered again in *ET v SSWP (PIP)* [2017] UKUT 478 (AAC). Judge Wright suggests, following that earlier case law and *Hooper v SSWP* [2007] EWCA Civ 495 in the Court of Appeal, that the correct approach is to determine first, if an issue is raised on the appeal; if it is, then the tribunal must give its attention to it, but if it is not raised the tribunal may still consider it, but in doing so must act consciously and judicially and must give adequate warning and explanation to the claimant of their reasons for doing so. On a related matter Judge Hemingway has pointed out in *KKL v SSWP (PIP)* [2018] UKUT 17 (AAC) that where a concession is made by a claimant that matter no longer remains as an issue in the appeal, but, for that reason where the concession is made by an unrepresented claimant the tribunal must take care to ensure that the claimant does so having properly understood the consequences of their action.

In *KM v SSWP (PIP)* [2018] UKUT 296 (AAC) Judge Rowland adopted a novel approach to the problem that arises where the claimant has appealed to the UT on a decision where they have been successful in claiming one component of PIP and is appealing only against refusal of the other. If the judge in the UT upholds that appeal, but directs that there should be a rehearing of the matter before a fresh tribunal, the claimant may lose their income from the part to which they are entitled pending the outcome of the whole appeal. He observes that the ability of DWP to make payment on account of benefit is more limited in relation to PIP. In this case he agreed, unusually, to set aside only that part of the decision which he found to be wrong in law and return that part to an FTT to, in effect, complete the decision. Note, however, that he does warn that this course will be appropriate only in certain cases because it does risk decisions as to entitlement being made at different times and possibly on inconsistent views of the facts.

Subsection (3)

Conditions as to residence and presence are prescribed in Pt 4 of the Social Security (Personal Independence Payments) Regulations 2013. **1.1003**

Daily living component

78.—(1) A person is entitled to the daily living component at the standard rate if— **1.1004**

(a) the person's ability to carry out daily living activities is limited by the person's physical or mental condition; and

(b) the person meets the required period condition.

(2) A person is entitled to the daily living component at the enhanced rate if—

(a) the person's ability to carry out daily living activities is severely limited by the person's physical or mental condition; and
(b) the person meets the required period condition.

(3) In this section, in relation to the daily living component—
(a) "the standard rate" means such weekly rate as may be prescribed;
(b) "the enhanced rate" means such weekly rate as may be prescribed.

(4) In this Part "daily living activities" means such activities as may be prescribed for the purposes of this section.

(5) See sections 80 and 81 for provision about determining—
(a) whether the requirements of subsection (1)(a) or (2)(a) above are met;
(b) whether a person meets "the required period condition" for the purposes of subsection (1)(b) or (2)(b) above.

(6) This section is subject to the provisions of this Part, or regulations under it, relating to entitlement to the daily living component (see in particular sections 82 (persons who are terminally ill) and 83 (persons of pensionable age)).

GENERAL NOTE

1.1005 The daily living component will be paid at one of two rates; at a standard rate if the claimant's ability to accomplish daily living activities is limited to the requisite extent and at an enhanced rate if their ability to do so is limited severely. Daily living activities are defined by regulation—see the Personal Independence Payment Regulations 2013 Sch.1, part. 2.

The claimant must be disabled "physically or mentally". These words have been the subject of decisions in relation to DLA—see *R(DLA)3/06.*There it was decided that it was not necessary for the claimant to have a diagnosis of a specific disease or medical condition, but only to show that his limited ability had some cause that was either physical or mental. Physical, in this context, will mean anything connected with the claimant's body including experiencing sensation such as pain or dizziness, while mental, includes any mental health condition or intellectual or cognitive impairment. But the cause must be some "condition" and that will mean something more than just a defect of character or irresponsible behaviour. The line that has been drawn in relation to DLA for claims based on alcoholism is between those where the claimant can be said to be able to desist in his behaviour and those where he is compelled by an addiction that he cannot reasonably be expected to control. (Though even where alcoholism is an addiction, care should be taken in examining how much of the time the claimant is so affected as to need assistance etc.).

The extent to which the claimant is limited in doing those activities will be measured by their ability to achieve the tasks listed in the PIP Regulations. This will be assessed from the information provided by the claimant (see reg.8 of the PIP Regs) and, where the claimant is called upon to attend what is referred to in the regulations as a consultation, (see reg.9 of the PIP Regs) by the results observed in that consultation.

For the purposes of administering PIP the decision makers will be known as Case Managers (CM). The consultation will be undertaken with a Health Professional (HP) engaged by one of the companies that will work under a contract made with DWP.

Each of the activities prescribed in Pt 2 of the schedule to the PIP Regs has a range of descriptors. Each descriptor has a point score and the points for each activity are aggregated to measure the claimant's degree of disability. A "score" of eight points qualifies the claimant for PIP at the standard rate and a total of 12 for the enhanced rate.

Subsection (1)(b)

1.1006 "the required period condition" is defined by reg.12 of the PIP Regs made in accordance with s.81 below.

Mobility component

79.—(1) A person is entitled to the mobility component at the standard rate if— 1.1007
(a) the person is of or over the age prescribed for the purposes of this subsection;
(b) the person's ability to carry out mobility activities is limited by the person's physical or mental condition; and
(c) the person meets the required period condition.
(2) A person is entitled to the mobility component at the enhanced rate if—
(a) the person is of or over the age prescribed for the purposes of this subsection;
(b) the person's ability to carry out mobility activities is severely limited by the person's physical or mental condition; and
(c) the person meets the required period condition.
(3) In this section, in relation to the mobility component—
(a) "the standard rate" means such weekly rate as may be prescribed;
(b) "the enhanced rate" means such weekly rate as may be prescribed.
(4) In this Part "mobility activities" means such activities as may be prescribed for the purposes of this section.
(5) See sections 80 and 81 for provision about determining—
(a) whether the requirements of subsections (1)(b) or (2)(b) above are met;
(b) whether a person meets "the required period condition" for the purposes of subsections (1)(c) or (2)(c) above.
(6) This section is subject to the provisions of this Part, or regulations under it, relating to entitlement to the mobility component (see in particular sections 82 and 83).
(7) Regulations may provide that a person is not entitled to the mobility component for a period (even though the requirements in subsections (1) or (2) are met) in prescribed circumstances where the person's condition is such that during all or most of the period the person is unlikely to benefit from enhanced mobility.

General Note

The mobility component will be paid at one of two rates; at the standard rate if a person's mobility activity is limited to the requisite extent and at an enhanced rate if it is limited severely. Mobility activities are defined by regulation—see Personal Independence Payment Regulations 2013 Sch.1 Pt 3. 1.1008

The extent to which the claimant is limited in doing those activities will be measured by their ability to achieve the tasks listed there and this will be assessed by the CM from the information provided by the claimant—see reg.8 of the PIP Regs). Where the claimant is called upon to attend what is referred to in the regulations as a consultation (see reg.9 of the PIP Regs) by the results observed in that consultation.

Each of the activities prescribed in Pt 3 of the schedule to the PIP Regs has a range of descriptors. Each descriptor has a point score and the points for each activity are aggregated to measure the claimant's degree of disability. A score of eight points qualifies the claimant for the mobility component at the standard rate and a total of 12 for the enhanced rate.

The claimant's limitation must be by reason of their "mental or physical condition"—(see the note to s.78 above for the meaning of this phrase). The mobility component of DLA is limited in most cases to the claimant's physical disability. For PIP a mental disability will suffice so long as the claimant satisfies the assessment procedure; so an agoraphobic should now qualify at the standard rate. (See Sch.1 Activity 1 Descriptor e). But see too, the possibility that such a claimant might qualify at the higher rate following the decision in *MH v SSWP (PIP)* [2016] UKUT 531 (AAC); [2018] AACR 22 discussed in the General Note to the Mobility Component–Activities and Descriptors, later in this book.

Subsection (1) (a)

1.1009 PIP is presently limited to claimants of 16 years and over. This provision seems to have been included in anticipation of extending PIP, eventually, to include children.

Subsection (1)(c)

1.1010 "the required period condition" is defined by reg.12 of the PIP Regs made in accordance with s.81 below.

Subsection (7)

1.1011 Regulations may be made to provide that entitlement could be withheld where a claimant is unlikely to benefit from enhanced mobility during all or most of the period. (cf. reg.12(8) of the Disability Living Allowance Regulations).

Ability to carry out daily living activities or mobility activities

1.1012 **80.**—(1) For the purposes of this Part, the following questions are to be determined in accordance with regulations—

(a) whether a person's ability to carry out daily living activities is limited by the person's physical or mental condition;
(b) whether a person's ability to carry out daily living activities is severely limited by the person's physical or mental condition;
(c) whether a person's ability to carry out mobility activities is limited by the person's physical or mental condition;
(d) whether a person's ability to carry out mobility activities is severely limited by the person's physical or mental condition.

(2) Regulations must make provision for determining, for the purposes of each of sections 78(1) and (2) and 79(1) and (2), whether a person meets "the required period condition" (see further section 81).

(3) Regulations under this section—

(a) must provide for the questions mentioned in subsections (1) and (2) to be determined, except in prescribed circumstances, on the basis of an assessment (or repeated assessments) of the person;
(b) must provide for the way in which an assessment is to be carried out;
(c) may make provision about matters which are, or are not, to be taken into account in assessing a person.

(4) The regulations may, in particular, make provision—

(a) about the information or evidence required for the purpose of determining the questions mentioned in subsections (1) and (2);
(b) about the way in which that information or evidence is to be provided;
(c) requiring a person to participate in such a consultation, with a person approved by the Secretary of State, as may be determined under the regulations (and to attend for the consultation at a place, date and time determined under the regulations).

(5) The regulations may include provision—

(a) for a negative determination to be treated as made if a person fails without a good reason to comply with a requirement imposed under subsection (4);
(b) about what does or does not constitute a good reason for such a failure;
(c) about matters which are, or are not, to be taken into account in determining whether a person has a good reason for such a failure.

(6) In subsection (5)(a) a "negative determination" means a determination that a person does not meet the requirements of—
(a) section 78(1)(a) and (b) or (2)(a) and (b) (daily living component);
(b) section 79(1)(a) to (c) or (2)(a) to (c) (mobility component).

GENERAL NOTE

Regulations made under this section are the Personal Independence Payment Regulations 2013 (SI 2013/377). 1.1013

Required period condition: further provision

81.—(1) Regulations under section 80(2) must provide for the question of whether a person meets "the required period condition" for the purposes of section 78(1) or (2) or 79(1) or (2) to be determined by reference to— 1.1014
(a) whether, as respects every time in the previous three months, it is likely that if the relevant ability had been assessed at that time that ability would have been determined to be limited or (as the case may be) severely limited by the person's physical or mental condition; and
(b) whether, as respects every time in the next nine months, it is likely that if the relevant ability were to be assessed at that time that ability would be determined to be limited or (as the case may be) severely limited by the person's physical or mental condition.

(2) In subsection (1) "the relevant ability" means—
(a) in relation to section 78(1) or (2), the person's ability to carry out daily living activities;
(b) in relation to section 79(1) or (2), the person's ability to carry out mobility activities.

(3) In subsection (1)—
(a) "assessed" means assessed in accordance with regulations under section 80;
(b) "the previous 3 months" means the three months ending with the prescribed date;
(c) "the next 9 months" means the nine months beginning with the day after that date.

(4) Regulations under section 80(2) may provide that in prescribed cases the question of whether a person meets "the required period condition" for the purposes of sections 78(1) or (2) or 79(1) or (2)—
(a) is not to be determined in accordance with the provision made by virtue of subsections (1) to (3) above;
(b) is to be determined in accordance with provision made in relation to those cases by the regulations.

GENERAL NOTE

Regulations made under this section are regs 12 and 13 of the Personal Independence Payment Regulations 2013 (SI 2013/377). 1.1015

To qualify for either component under these regulations the claimant must be able to show that he would have fulfilled the requirements of an assessment (at which ever rate of benefit is appropriate) for the whole of a past period of three months and that he may be expected to continue to satisfy that requirement for a further nine months.

Entitlement and payability: further provision

Terminal illness

1.1016 **82.**—(1) This section applies to a person who—

(a) is terminally ill; and

(b) has made a claim for personal independence payment expressly on the ground of terminal illness.

(2) A person to whom this section applies is entitled to the daily living component at the enhanced rate (and accordingly section 78(1) and (2) do not apply to such a person).

(3) Section 79(1)(c) and (2)(c) (required period condition for mobility component) do not apply to a person to whom this section applies.

(4) For the purposes of this section a person is "terminally ill" at any time if at that time the person suffers from a progressive disease and the person's death in consequence of that disease can reasonably be expected within [[1] 12] months.

(5) For the purposes of this section, where—

(a) a person purports to make a claim for personal independence payment on behalf of another, and

(b) the claim is made expressly on the ground that the person on whose behalf it purports to be made is terminally ill,

that person is to be regarded as making the claim despite its being made without that person's knowledge or authority.

(6) In subsection (2) "the enhanced rate" has the meaning given by section 78(3).

AMENDMENT

1. Social Security (Special Rules for End of Life) Act 2022 s.1 (April 3, 2023).

GENERAL NOTE

1.1017 A claimant will qualify automatically for the daily living component of PIP, at the enhanced rate, if their claim is made expressly on the ground that they are suffering from a terminal illness. A person is terminally ill if they are suffering from a progressive disease and their death from that disease can be reasonably expected within 12 months.

Previously this test required death to be expected within six months. A decision of the High Court in Northern Ireland, *Cox (re an application for judicial review)* [2020] NIQB 53, had found this requirement to be discriminatory in the case of a claimant whose consultant could not say that death was to be expected within six months and given that many successful claimants did survive longer than six months. Advances in medical treatment mean that such an outcome is now not unlikely. The increase to a period of 12 months may help to resolve that difficulty.

A claim for benefit on the ground that the claimant is terminally ill is made by a special, fast-track procedure. Whether or not a claimant is terminally ill will be determined by the CM, but only after the claim and the information received, has been referred to the HP for a report. This report should be returned to the CM within 48 hours.

Guidance issued to the HP requires that they must find, on the balance of probabilities, that it is "more likely than not" that the claimant will die within 12 months. This seems a more stringent test than that which has applied in relation to DLA where the same words are used. For DLA it seems that a claim would succeed so long as death within 12 months was not unlikely. A reasonable expectation (which is what the section requires) should not necessarily require a finding of probability. Where medical opinion is that the claimant's death within 12 months "is quite possible, though they might live longer", it seems correct, as a matter of ordinary language to say that their death within 12 months "can reasonably be expected". Decisions on this matter are likely to turn on the way in which the question has been put to the claimant's consultant and by any further inquiry made by the HP.

It is not necessary for such a claimant to fulfil a qualifying period so that their claim, if successful, is paid from the time that it is made.

A decision of the High Court in Northern Ireland in *Cox (re an application for judicial review)* [2020] NIQB 53 has found that the requirement for death to be reasonably expected within 6 months is unlawful as being in breach of the claimant's human rights (Art. 14 read with Art. 8 and Art.1 of Protocol 1- ECHR). In this case the claimant had been diagnosed with Motor Neurone Disease, but, though her condition was known to be terminal, her consultant was unable to say that her death could be expected within 6 months. The court held that this requirement was discriminatory when comparison was made with a claimant whose death could be so predicted, but who survived beyond that time, yet remained entitled to benefit at the enhanced rate. Although such discrimination may be justified, the judge found also that there was "no evidence, justification or rationale" for the difference in treatment and hence that it was "manifestly without reasonable foundation".

Yet it must remain necessary for a claimant to show that their illness is terminal. This must mean that there is no known cure, that the claimant can be expected to die because of that illness, and probably, that there is no ameliorative treatment that will prolong life for an extensive period. In the present case the claimant was given a life expectancy of 2 to 5 years, but there must remain some doubt about the point at which the condition of a claimant can be said to be terminal.

In Northern Ireland, the 6-month requirement is contained in secondary legislation and so it would have been possible for the judge to read down the regulation (under s.3 of the HRA 1998) without the words specifying the 6-month limitation. He did not do so because he thought that to do so would be to usurp the role of the legislature, and in any case, the claimant had already been awarded *ex gratia* payments.

This decision is of persuasive authority only in the rest of the UK and the requirement there is in the primary legislation; there would need to be a similar decision in the High Court (or Court of Session) and a declaration of incompatibility.

Although it remains necessary for a claimant to show that they are present and habitually resident in Great Britain it will not be necessary for them to show that they have been present for a period amounting to 104 weeks out of the preceding three years. (See regs 16 and 21 of the Personal Independence Regulations 2013 (SI 2013/377)).

A terminally ill claimant does not qualify automatically for the mobility component; they must satisfy the assessment criteria in the usual way, but, if successful, they will be exempted from the need to fulfil a qualifying period for that component too.

A claim on the ground of terminal illness can be made by another person without the consent, or even the knowledge, of the person on whose behalf it is made—see subs.(5) above.

Persons of pensionable age

83.—(1) A person is not entitled to the daily living component or the mobility component for any period after the person reaches the relevant age. **1.1018**

(2) In subsection (1) "the relevant age" means—

(a) pensionable age (within the meaning given by the rules in paragraph 1 of Schedule 4 to the Pensions Act 1995); or

(b) if higher, 65.

(3) Subsection (1) is subject to such exceptions as may be provided by regulations.

General note

1.1019 Entitlement to PIP by virtue of a new claim will generally cease when a claimant reaches pensionable age.

Claimants who have an existing award of either or both components of PIP when they reach the relevant age will continue to be entitled in accordance with regs 25–27 of the Personal Independence Payment Regulations (SI 2013/377).

No entitlement to daily living component where UK is not competent state

1.1020 **84.**—(1) A person to whom a relevant EU Regulation applies is not entitled to the daily living component for a period unless during that period the United Kingdom is competent for payment of sickness benefits in cash to the person for the purposes of Chapter 1 of Title III of the Regulation in question.

(2) Each of the following is a "relevant EU Regulation" for the purposes of this section—

(a) Council Regulation (EC) No.1408/71 of 14 June 1971 [[1], as amended from time to time,] on the application of social security schemes to employed persons, to self-employed persons and to members of their families moving within the Community;

(b) Regulation (EC) No.883/2004 of the European Parliament and of the Council of 29 April 2004 [[1], as amended from time to time,] on the coordination of social security systems.

Amendments

1. Social Security (Updating of EU References) (Amendment) Regulations (SI 2018/1084) reg. 3 (November 15, 2018).

Care home residents

1.1021 **85.**—(1) Regulations may provide that no amount in respect of personal independence payment which is attributable to entitlement to the daily living component is payable in respect of a person for a period when the person meets the condition in subsection (2).

(2) The condition is that the person is a resident of a care home in circumstances in which any of the costs of any qualifying services provided for the person are borne out of public or local funds by virtue of a specified enactment.

(3) In this section "care home" means an establishment that provides accommodation together with nursing or personal care.

(4) The following are "qualifying services" for the purposes of subsection (2)—

(a) accommodation;

(b) board;

(c) personal care;

(d) such other services as may be prescribed.

(5) The reference in subsection (2) to a "specified enactment" is to an enactment which is specified for the purposes of that subsection by regulations or is of a description so specified.

(6) The power to specify an enactment for the purposes of subsection (2) includes power to specify it only in relation to its application for a particular purpose.

(7) In this section "enactment" includes an enactment comprised in an Act of the Scottish Parliament or in an instrument made under such an Act.

GENERAL NOTE

The regulations made under this section are regs 28, 30 and 32 of the Personal Independence Payment Regulations 2013 (SI 2013/377). 1.1022

Hospital in-patients

86.—(1) Regulations may provide as mentioned in either or both of the following paragraphs— 1.1023

(a) that no amount in respect of personal independence payment which is attributable to entitlement to the daily living component is payable in respect of a person for a period when the person meets the condition in subsection (2);

(b) that no amount in respect of personal independence payment which is attributable to entitlement to the mobility component is payable in respect of a person for a period when the person meets the condition in subsection (2).

(2) The condition is that the person is undergoing medical or other treatment as an in-patient at a hospital or similar institution in circumstances in which any of the costs of the treatment, accommodation and any related services provided for the person are borne out of public funds.

(3) For the purposes of subsection (2) the question of whether any of the costs of medical or other treatment, accommodation and related services provided for a person are borne out of public funds is to be determined in accordance with the regulations.

GENERAL NOTE

The regulations made under this section are regs 29, 30 and 32 of the Personal Independence Payment Regulations 2013 (SI 2013/377). This section (and regulation 29 made under it) were held not to discriminate unjustifiably by the withholding of the mobility component so as to be in breach of art.14 of the European Convention on Human Rights (and hence of the Human Rights Act 1998) in *MH v SSWP (PIP)* [2017] UKUT 424 (AAC; [2018] AACR 15. The claimant was resident in a Neurodisability centre which, it was agreed, was similar to a publicly funded hospital. Judge Lane held that neither disabled claimants living at home, nor those living in a care home, were sufficiently similar to constitute valid comparators for the claimant, but, even if the latter group were to be considered as comparators, she also held that the difference in treatment under this section and regulation 29 would be justified on the ground that payment of the mobility component of PIP would amount to double provision from public funds. 1.1024

Prisoners and detainees

87.—Except to the extent that regulations provide otherwise, no amount in respect of personal independence payment is payable in respect of a person for a period during which the person is undergoing imprisonment or detention in legal custody. 1.1025

General note

1.1026 The regulations made under this section are regs 31 and 32 of the Personal Independence Payments Regulations 2013 (SI 2013/377).

Under these regulations a claimant who is in receipt of PIP at the time he enters prison will remain entitled for the first 28 days of that imprisonment. Note that the words that are used in this section are the same as those in s.113 of the SSCBA. That section has been interpreted to mean that disqualification applies only where the claimant is in detention or legal custody in consequence of criminal proceedings and not where imprisonment is the result of a civil contempt. See *R(S) 8/79* and *JC v SSWP (ESA)* [2024] UKUT 13 (AAC).

Supplementary

Claims, awards and information

1.1027 **88.**—(1) A person is not entitled to personal independence payment for any period before the date on which a claim for it is made or treated as made by that person or on that person's behalf.

(2) An award of personal independence payment is to be for a fixed term except where the person making the award considers that a fixed term award would be inappropriate.

(3) In deciding whether a fixed term award would be inappropriate, that person must have regard to guidance issued by the Secretary of State.

(4) Information supplied under this Part is to be taken for all purposes to be information relating to social security.

General note

1.1028 PIP, like DLA, is not payable in respect of any period before a claim for it is made, though the period of three months before the date of claim can count as the qualifying period.

Subsection (2) provides that payment of benefit is to be for a fixed term unless the DM considers that a fixed term is inappropriate. In *RS v SSWP* [2016] UKUT 85 (AAC) Judge Mitchell decided that this decision by a DM is appealable. The claimant, who had been in receipt of DLA, considered that his condition had worsened and informed the DWP of a change of circumstances. He was invited to apply for PIP under the transitional provisions. That claim succeeded and he was awarded benefit at a rate that was higher than his previous entitlement—in fact at the highest possible rate. But his DLA award had been indefinite and new award was for a fixed term of three years. The claimant appealed against the decision to award only for a fixed term (the appeal was also against the date at which his increased entitlement commenced, but that part of the decision was upheld). The FTT had struck out his appeal against the length of his award, but Judge Mitchell held that the decision to make that award and the exercise of the discretion in subs.(2) which requires the DM to consider whether the fixed term award might be "inappropriate" were appealable and that reasons should be produced to the FTT to justify that decision. The judge observed that the permanence or otherwise of the claimant's condition and the relative ease with which an application for review could be taken were factors to which the FTT might have regard. He observed also that the FTT should have regard to the guidance provided for under subs.(3), but with the caveat that it was only guidance and not the law.

This decision was affirmed by Judge Hemingway in *GT v SSWP (PIP)* [2019] UKUT 30 (AAC). The judge thought that more emphasis need be given to the possibility that an appeal might be made solely on the basis that an award had been made for a fixed term. The DWP has since modified their practice and accepted that on-going awards may be more appropriate in some cases.

Report to Parliament

89.—[*omitted*] 1.1029

General

Abolition of disability living allowance

90.—Sections 71 to 76 of the Social Security Contributions and Benefits Act 1992 (Disability Living Allowance) are repealed. 1.1030

GENERAL NOTE

This provision is not yet in force and, presumably, will not be brought into force until all claims to DLA are replaced by this or another benefit. 1.1031

Amendments

91.—[*omitted*]. 1.1032

Power to make supplementary and consequential provision

92.—(1) Regulations may make such consequential, supplementary or incidental provision in relation to any provision of this Part as the Secretary of State considers appropriate. 1.1033

(2) Regulations under this section may—

(a) amend, repeal or revoke any primary or secondary legislation passed or made before the day on which this Act is passed, or

(b) amend or repeal any provision of an Act passed on or after that day but in the same session of Parliament.

(3) In this section—

(a) "primary legislation" means an Act or Act of the Scottish Parliament;

(b) "secondary legislation" means any instrument made under primary legislation.

Transitional

93.—(1) Regulations may make such provision as the Secretary of State considers necessary or expedient in connection with the coming into force of any provision of this Part. 1.1034

(2) Schedule 10 (transitional provision for introduction of personal independence payment) has effect.

GENERAL NOTE

The regulations made under this section and in accordance with Sch.10, are the Personal Independence Payment (Transitional Provisions) Regulations 2013 (SI 2013/387). 1.1035

Regulations

94.—(1) Regulations under this Part are to be made by the Secretary of State. 1.1036

(2) A power to make regulations under this Part may be exercised—

(a) so as to make different provision for different cases or purposes;

(b) in relation to all or only some of the cases or purposes for which it may be exercised.

(3) Such a power includes—

(a) power to make incidental, supplementary, consequential or transitional provision or savings;

(b) power to provide for a person to exercise a discretion in dealing with any matter.

(4) The power under subsection (2)(a) includes, in particular, power to make different provision for persons of different ages.

(5) Regulations under this Part are to be made by statutory instrument.

(6) A statutory instrument containing (whether alone or with other provision) any of the following—

(a) the first regulations under sections 78(4) or 79(4);

(b) the first regulations under section 80;

(c) the first regulations under that section containing provision about assessment of persons under the age of 16, may not be made unless a draft of the instrument has been laid before, and approved by a resolution of, each House of Parliament.

(7) Any other statutory instrument containing regulations under this Part is subject to annulment in pursuance of a resolution of either House of Parliament.

GENERAL NOTE

1.1037 The regulations made under this section are the Social Security (Personal Independence Payment) Regulations (SI 2013/377).

Interpretation of Part 4

1.1038 **95.**—In this Part—

[2 "adult disability payment" means disability assistance given in accordance with the Disability Assistance for Working Age People (Scotland) Regulations 2022;]

[1 [2 "child disability payment" means disability assistance given in accordance with the Disability Assistance for Children and Young People (Scotland) Regulations 2021 (SSI 2021/174);]

"daily living activities" has the meaning given by section 78(4);

"daily living component" means the daily living component of personal independence payment;

"mobility activities" has the meaning given by section 79(4);

"mobility component" means the mobility component of personal independence payment;

"prescribed" means prescribed by regulations.

AMENDMENTS

1. Scotland Act 2016 (Social Security) (Consequential Provision) (Miscellaneous Amendment) Regulations 2021 (SI 2021/804) reg.3 (July 26, 2021).

2. Scotland Act 2016 (Social Security) (Adult Disability Payment and Child Disability Payment) (Amendment) Regulations 2022 (SI 2022/335) reg.3 (March 21, 2022).

Mesothelioma Act 2014

(2014 c.1)

Arrangement Of Sections

Diffuse Mesothelioma Payment Scheme **1.1039**

Eligibility

Payments and procedure

Scheme administration

Recovery of payments etc.

Relationship with other legislation

Levy on insurers

Insurance disputes

General

An Act to establish a Diffuse Mesothelioma Payment Scheme and make related provision; and to make provision about the resolution of certain insurance disputes.

[30th January 2014]

GENERAL NOTE

1.1040 The Mesothelioma Act 2014 paves the way for the Diffuse Mesothelioma Payment Scheme 2014, which is the third statutory scheme to provide a degree of compensation for victims of the asbestos-related cancer mesothelioma, outside the normal arrangements for personal injuries claims in the law of torts. The 2014 Act thus follows in the footsteps of the Pneumoconiosis etc. (Workers' Compensation) Act 1979 and, more recently, the Diffuse Mesothelioma Scheme 2008, established by the Child Maintenance and Other Payments Act 2008. As Judge Markus QC observed in *DP v Topmark Claims Management Ltd* [2020] UKUT 106 (AAC), "the Mesothelioma Act does not provide an alternative to a civil remedy where that is available. It was common ground in these proceedings that it creates a scheme of last resort. If a claim cannot be made because the employer or insurer cannot be found, no longer exist or for any other reason … the Scheme provides a remedy because the civil justice system cannot be used to obtain compensation."

The Mesothelioma Act 2014 is essentially a State-driven but privately-funded measure which seeks to correct a significant market failure in the employers' liability (EL) insurance industry. It establishes a limited scheme of last resort to pay eligible applicants in mesothelioma cases who are unable either to find their employer or to trace their employer's EL insurer. Most employers carrying on business in Great Britain have been required, since January 1, 1972, to insure their liability to their employees for bodily injury or disease sustained in the course of their employment, as a result of the Employers' Liability (Compulsory Insurance) Act 1969, although EL insurance was also widespread, if not actually compulsory, before the 1969 Act. For many years now, proving that their employer acted in breach of their duty of care in negligence has been the least of the difficulties facing employees who have contracted mesothelioma. Thus, in practice, establishing liability is usually relatively straightforward for those who were exposed to asbestos in the workplace and who bring a civil claim. However, mesothelioma has a long latency period (typically 30-40 years) and by the time the worker is diagnosed with the disease, many years later, the relevant insurance records may have already been lost or destroyed. Thus a victim may be unable actually to recover compensation because no solvent employer remains to be sued, and the employee's solicitors may be unable to trace any insurer who was providing EL insurance cover to their employer at the material time. All this happens at a time that the victim is, literally, living on borrowed time—the average life expectancy from date of diagnosis is in the order of 9–12 months.

In February 2010, under the then Labour government, the DWP published a consultation document, seeking stakeholders' views on proposals for improving the process for tracing employment and insurance records and for providing access to compensation (DWP, *Accessing Compensation—Supporting people who need to trace Employers' Liability Insurance*). The Coalition Government's response to the consultation exercise was eventually published in July 2012 (DWP, *Accessing Compensation – Supporting people who need to trace Employers' Liability Insurance: Government response to consultation*). In that response the Government announced (p.8):

> "we propose setting up a support scheme for those people with mesothelioma who were exposed to asbestos through their employer's negligence and who remain unable to trace a liable insurer or employer.
> The proposed scheme will be funded by a levy on insurers currently writing EL policies. Payments from the scheme will be at a level set such that the overall amount received by the claimant will be somewhere between that offered by state benefits and average payouts from civil action. This will ensure that those who are able to trace an insurer remain incentivised to do so in order to claim full compensation."

The Mesothelioma Bill, which emerged from this consultation process, was introduced in the House of Lords on May 9, 2013 and received the Royal Assent on January 30, 2014. It is a UK-wide measure (s.20(1)). The long title declares that its purpose is "to establish a Diffuse Mesothelioma Payment Scheme and make related provision; and to make provision about the resolution of certain insurance disputes". The Act itself is essentially an enabling measure, which provides no hard-edged detail about the 2014 Scheme (see s.1(1)). However, the Act makes provision for both mandatory and optional elements in such a scheme (see s.1(2)). The mandatory elements of the scheme include both the right to request a review of a decision taken under the scheme (s.6(1)(a)) and a right of appeal to the First-tier Tribunal against a decision taken on a review (s.6(3)). Sections 2 and 3 of the Act set out the core eligibility criteria for the two categories of claimants, namely "eligible people with diffuse mesothelioma" and "eligible dependants" respectively. The remaining provisions of the Act deal with payments and procedure (ss.4-6), scheme administration (ss.7-9), recovery of payments (ss.10 and 11), relationship with other legislation (s.12), the levy on insurers (ss.13 and 14) and insurance disputes (ss.15 and 16), along with various general provisions (ss.17-21). Further and more detailed provision for the new scheme is contained in the Diffuse Mesothelioma Payment Scheme Regulations 2014 (SI 2014/916). For details of the levy imposed on EL insurers, see now the Diffuse Mesothelioma Payment Scheme (Levy) Regulations 2014 (SI 2014/2904).

It should be noted that the Mesothelioma Act 2014, unlike the 1979 and 2008 Acts, does *not* establish a no-fault scheme. Thus it is a condition of entitlement that "a relevant employer has negligently or in breach of statutory duty caused or permitted the person to be exposed to asbestos" (s.2(1)(a)). Similarly, the scheme administrator must "in considering an application, apply the normal civil standard of proof (the balance of probability) when deciding all matters of fact which require evidence to establish them" (Diffuse Mesothelioma Payment Scheme Regulations 2014, reg.5(3)(a)). The fact that the new scheme is to be paid for by a levy on existing EL insurers means that it is necessarily a compromise measure. Three aspects of the scheme proved to be particularly controversial during the debates in Parliament. The first was the "cut-off", namely the fact that the new scheme is only available to those victims who were first diagnosed *after* July 25, 2012 (s.2(1)(b); this was the date of the publication of the Government response, whereas many argued that the relevant date should have been the issue of the original consultation document in 2010). The second concerned the levels of compensation, which were originally set at a ceiling representing 80 per cent of average civil compensation awards (but were subsequently increased to 100 per cent of such an average; see further the commentary to the Diffuse Mesothelioma Payment Scheme Regulations 2014 reg.19). The third was the decision to focus this scheme of last resort on mesothelioma, so excluding other asbestos-related cancers (notably asbestos-related lung cancer), let alone other long-tail occupational diseases where there are similar problems in locating a former employer and/or their EL insurer. For further analysis, see N. Wikeley, "Diffuse Mesothelioma Payment Scheme 2014" (2014) 21 J.S.S.L. 61–78.

Diffuse Mesothelioma Payment Scheme

Power to establish the scheme

1.1041 **1.**—(1) The Secretary of State may by regulations establish a scheme called the Diffuse Mesothelioma Payment Scheme for making payments to—

(a) eligible people with diffuse mesothelioma, and
(b) eligible dependants of those who have died with diffuse mesothelioma.

(2) Later sections of this Act set out things that must be included in the scheme and some of the things that may be included.

Eligibility

Eligible people with diffuse mesothelioma

1.1042 **2.**—(1) A person diagnosed with diffuse mesothelioma is eligible for a payment under the scheme if—

(a) a relevant employer has negligently or in breach of statutory duty caused or permitted the person to be exposed to asbestos,
(b) the person was first diagnosed with the disease on or after 25 July 2012,
(c) the person has not brought an action for damages in respect of the disease against the relevant employer or any insurer with whom the employer maintained employers' liability insurance at the time of the person's exposure to asbestos,
(d) the person is unable to bring an action for damages in respect of the disease against any employer of the person or any insurer with whom such an employer maintained employers' liability insurance (because they cannot be found or no longer exist or for any other reason), and
(e) the person has not received damages or a specified payment in respect of the disease and is not eligible to receive a specified payment.

(2) In this section—

"first diagnosed" has the meaning to be given to it by the scheme;

"relevant employer" means an employer who, at the time of the person's exposure to asbestos—

(a) was required by the compulsory insurance legislation to maintain insurance covering any liability arising because of the exposure to asbestos, or
(b) would have been required by the compulsory insurance legislation to maintain insurance covering any liability arising because of the exposure to asbestos if the legislation had been in force at that time;

"specified payment" has the meaning to be given to it by the scheme.

Eligible dependants

1.1043 **3.**—(1) A dependant of a person who has died with diffuse mesothelioma is eligible for a payment under the scheme if—

(a) the person with the disease was eligible for a payment under the scheme (see section 2) but did not make an application in accordance with the scheme,

(b) no one has brought an action for damages in respect of the disease under the fatal accidents legislation, or on behalf of the estate of the person with the disease, against the relevant employer or any insurer with whom the employer maintained employers' liability insurance at the time of that person's exposure to asbestos,

(c) no one is able to bring an action for damages in respect of the disease under the fatal accidents legislation, or on behalf of the estate of the person with the disease, against any employer of that person or any insurer with whom such an employer maintained employers' liability insurance (because they cannot be found or no longer exist or for any other reason), and

(d) no one has received damages or a specified payment in respect of the disease or is eligible to receive a specified payment.

(2) Where a person who has died with diffuse mesothelioma is first diagnosed with the disease following his or her death and would have been eligible for a payment under the scheme if the diagnosis had been made immediately before the death, assume for the purposes of subsection (1)(a) that the person was eligible for a payment under the scheme.

(3) A person ceases to be an eligible dependant if the person gives notice in accordance with the scheme that he or she does not want a payment (and this may increase a payment for other dependants - see section 4(2)(b)).

(4) Where a person with diffuse mesothelioma died on or after 25 July 2012 but before this Act came into force, assume for the purposes of subsections (1)(a) and (2) that this Act has been in force since immediately before the death.

(5) In this section—

"first diagnosed" has the meaning to be given to it by the scheme;

"specified payment" has the meaning to be given to it by the scheme.

GENERAL NOTE

The meaning of s.3(1)(c) was at issue in *DP v Topmark Claims Management Ltd* [2020] UKUT 106 (AAC), where Judge Markus rejected the appellant's submission that once the limitation period for a civil claim had expired, the appellant was not "able to bring an action for damages...for any other reason" within s.3(1)(c). The Judge found that reg.7 of the 2014 Scheme prescribes circumstances which constitute "any other reason" within s.3(1)(c) and that s.18(3) of the Act does not add a further category to those in s.3(1)(c) (at para.34). Further, as the Judge concluded (at para.43), the legislative history indicated that: 1.1044

> "... the general words were inserted in order to guard against an unforeseen omission or to enable clarification, but not to extend the application of section 3(1)(c) to circumstances of a wholly different kind to the two specified reasons. The meaning of the phrase "any other reason" takes its colour from the first two circumstances specified in the brackets at the end of section 3(1)(c). Section 3(1)(c) is concerned with the circumstances of the putative defendant ... not of an applicant. The words "any other reason" are to be construed accordingly."

It followed that the expiry of the limitation period for a civil claim was not "any other reason" for the purposes of s.3(1)(c).

Note that HMRC may disclose information held by them to a person who applies for a payment under the Diffuse Mesothelioma Payment Scheme, on the basis that he or she is eligible for such a payment under s.3, for use in connection with the application (Deregulation Act 2015 s.85(1)(c)). Further note that in addition, and with effect from July 31, 2017, s.77 of the Digital Economy Act 2017 enables HMRC to share the name and address of an employer and associated reference numbers with the Employer Liability Tracing Office (ELTO) for the purpose of assisting with such claims. ELTO is a non-profit making company that maintains a database of insurance policies to enable employees to trace former or current employers and their insurers in order to obtain compensation for workplace injuries. It is anticipated that access to this information will help to improve the quality of the ELTO databases.

Payments and procedure

Payments

1.1045 **4.**—(1) The amount of a payment under the scheme is to be determined in accordance with the scheme.

(2) The scheme—

(a) may provide for the amount of the payment to depend on the age of the person with diffuse mesothelioma, and

(b) must ensure that where there are two or more eligible dependants, the amount for each of them is the amount for a single eligible dependant divided by the number of eligible dependants in the case in question.

(3) The scheme may—

(a) make provision for payments to be made subject to conditions (including conditions as to how a payment may be used), and

(b) in particular, give the scheme administrator power to decide when to impose conditions or what conditions to impose.

(4) The scheme may make provision for payments to be repaid (in whole or in part) in specified circumstances.

(5) An amount that falls to be repaid under subsection (4) is recoverable by the scheme administrator as a debt.

(6) The scheme must provide that where an eligible person has made an application in accordance with the scheme and has died before the payment is made, the payment must be made to his or her personal representatives.

Applications and procedure

1.1046 **5.**—(1) The scheme may deal with the procedure for the making and deciding of applications and, in particular, may—

(a) impose time limits for making an application or taking other steps;

(b) enable the scheme administrator to require a person to produce documents;

(c) make other provision about evidence.

(2) The scheme may enable a court to order a person to comply with a requirement to produce documents.

Reviews and appeals

1.1047 **6.**—(1) The scheme—

(a) must give an applicant the right to request a review of a decision taken under the scheme, and

(b) may require or allow reviews in other circumstances.

(2) The scheme may contain provision about initiating and deciding reviews (including provision imposing time limits).

(3) The scheme must confer a right of appeal to the First-tier Tribunal against a decision taken on a review.

(4) In a case where a person makes an application and then dies, the reference in subsection (1)(a) to an applicant is to be read as a reference to his or her personal representatives.

General Note

Judge Markus QC held in *DP v Topmark Claims Management Ltd* [2020] UKUT 106 (AAC) that the FTT conducts a full merits review appeal and is not restricted to considering the position as at the date of the Scheme review (in other words, s.12(8) of SSA 1998 does not apply). The FTT in that case had considered the position as it was at the date of the Scheme administrator's decision. At that date, the limitation period for bringing a claim had not expired and so the FTT found the appellant was not "unable" to bring an action for damages against the employer. Judge Markus concluded the FTT "should have approached the appeal on the basis of the circumstances as they were at that time" (para.27), i.e. at the time of the FTT hearing (when in fact the limitation period had expired). However, in the event the FTT's error as to the date for consideration was immaterial and so the appeal was dismissed. According to the Judge, 1.1048

> "21. On appeal the First-tier Tribunal is concerned with whether the decision appealed against was right or wrong. In effect the First-tier Tribunal stands in the shoes of the administrator on review. As there is no contrary indication in the legislation, the tribunal should approach the appeal in the same way that the administrator did on review and so is not limited to considering eligibility as it was at a particular date. Just as the administrator must do on review, the First-tier Tribunal should take into account all relevant evidence and determine eligibility in the light of the circumstances as at the date of its determination."

Scheme administration

Scheme administration

7.—(1) The Secretary of State may— 1.1049
(a) administer the scheme, or
(b) make arrangements for a body to administer the scheme.
(2) Arrangements under subsection (1)(b)—
(a) may include provision for payments by the Secretary of State;
(b) may allow the body to arrange for someone else to administer the scheme or any part of the scheme on behalf of the body;
(c) may include provision about bringing the arrangements to an end.
(3) Arrangements under subsection (1)(b) may be made with—
(a) a company formed by the Secretary of State under the Companies Act 2006 for that purpose,
(b) a body corporate established by the Secretary of State by regulations under this paragraph for that purpose, or
(c) any other body.

(4) A body administering the scheme in accordance with arrangements under subsection (1)(b) is not to be regarded as exercising functions of the Secretary of State or as acting on behalf of the Secretary of State.

(5) The Secretary of State may by regulations make transitional provision for when there is a change in the scheme administrator (including provision modifying the application of any enactment).

(6) For the purposes of this Act, a reference to administering the scheme includes carrying out any functions conferred by or under any enactment on the scheme administrator.

1.1050 *Sections 8 and 9 omitted.*

Recovery of payments etc

Power of scheme administrator to help people bring proceedings

1.1051 **10.—**(1) Where a payment is made under the scheme, the scheme administrator may help a person to bring relevant proceedings (for example by conducting proceedings or by giving advice or financial help).

(2) "Relevant proceedings" means—

(a) proceedings by the person with diffuse mesothelioma against—

(i) an employer for the negligence or breach of statutory duty mentioned in section 2(1)(a), or

(ii) an insurer with whom the employer maintained insurance covering that liability,

(b) proceedings by any other person against the employer or insurer for damages under the fatal accidents legislation in respect of the death of the person with diffuse mesothelioma, or

(c) any appeal arising out of proceedings within paragraph (a) or (b).

(3) In subsection (2) a reference to a person includes a reference to his or her personal representatives.

(4) The scheme may include provision about the scheme administrator's functions under this section, including provision as to the circumstances in which the scheme administrator may help a person to bring proceedings.

(5) The Secretary of State may by regulations amend subsection (2) to include other proceedings (which may be proceedings against someone other than an employer or insurer).

Recovery of benefits etc from payments and recovery of payments

1.1052 **11.—**Schedule 1 contains amendments to other legislation. Broadly—

Part 1 allows benefits and other sums to be recovered from scheme payments,

Part 2 allows scheme payments to be recovered from compensation, and

Part 3 contains related amendments to do with information sharing.

Relationship with other legislation

Exclusion of payments under other legislation

1.1053 **12.—**Schedule 2 contains amendments to other legislation to ensure that where an application is made under the scheme a person does not receive certain other payments.

1.1054 *Sections 13–17 omitted.*

Defined terms used in more than one section of this Act

1.1055 **18.—**(1) In this Act—

"application" means an application for a payment under the scheme;

"active insurer" has the meaning given by section 13;

"the compulsory insurance legislation" means—

(a) the Employers' Liability (Compulsory Insurance) Act 1969, or
(b) the Employer's Liability (Defective Equipment and Compulsory Insurance) (Northern Ireland) Order 1972 (S.I. 1972/963 (N.I. 6));

"damages" includes a payment in settlement of a claim for damages;

"dependant", in relation to a person who has died with diffuse mesothelioma, has the meaning given by section 3(1) of the Pneumoconiosis etc (Workers' Compensation) Act 1979 (reading the reference to the Secretary of State as a reference to the scheme administrator);

"employers' liability insurance", in relation to an employer and a particular time, means insurance that the employer—
(a) was required by the compulsory insurance legislation to maintain at that time, or
(b) would have been required by the compulsory insurance legislation to maintain if that legislation had been in force at that time;

"the fatal accidents legislation" means—
(a) the Fatal Accidents Act 1976,
(b) the Fatal Accidents (Northern Ireland) Order 1977 (S.I. 1977/1251 (N.I. 18)), or
(c) section 4 of the Damages (Scotland) Act 2011;

"levy" means a levy under section 13;

"relevant employer" has the meaning given by section 2;

"the scheme" means the Diffuse Mesothelioma Payment Scheme;

"scheme administrator" means the person for the time being administering the scheme (see section 7);

"the Technical Committee" means a committee established in accordance with arrangements under section 15.

(2) In determining for the purposes of this Act whether an employer would have been required to maintain insurance if the compulsory insurance legislation had been in force at any given time, assume that any exemption that has at any time applied under the following provisions applied at the time in question—
(a) section 3(1)(a) to (c) of the Employers' Liability (Compulsory Insurance) Act 1969, and
(b) Article 7(a) to (c) of the Employer's Liability (Defective Equipment and Compulsory Insurance) (Northern Ireland) Order 1972.

(3) The scheme may specify circumstances in which a person is, or is not, to be treated as able to bring an action for the purposes of section 2(1)(d) or 3(1)(c).

GENERAL NOTE

The meaning of s.18(3) was at issue in *DP v Topmark Claims Management Ltd* [2020] UKUT 106 (AAC), where Judge Markus held that reg.7 of the 2014 Scheme prescribes circumstances which constitute "any other reason" within s.3(1)(c) and that s.18(3) does not add a further category to those in s.3(1)(c) (at para.34). Moreover s.18(3) "creates a power not a duty to specify circumstances" (at para.36) and the background legislative material (see paras 11 and 12 of the decision) "makes it clear that the purpose of section 18(3) was to clarify that circumstances which had not been foreseen at the time of drafting were included within section 3(1)(c), but that it was not intended to limit the generality of the main test" (at para.37). 1.1056

Commencement

1.1057 **19.—**(1) This Act comes into force on such day or days as the Secretary of State may by order appoint, subject as follows.

(2) This section and sections 20 and 21 come into force on the day on which this Act is passed.

(3) The Secretary of State may by order make transitional, transitory or saving provision in connection with the coming into force of any provision of this Act.

(4) An order under subsection (1) may appoint different days for different purposes.

(5) An order under this section is to be made by statutory instrument.

Extent

1.1058 **20.—**(1) This Act extends to—

(a) England and Wales,

(b) Scotland, and

(c) Northern Ireland.

(2) Any amendment or repeal made by this Act has the same extent as the enactment to which it relates.

Short title

1.1059 **21.—**This Act may be cited as the Mesothelioma Act 2014.

Pensions Act 2014

(2014 c.19)

ARRANGEMENT OF SECTIONS

PART 1

STATE PENSION

Introduction

PART 3

PENSIONABLE AGE

PART 5

BEREAVEMENT SUPPORT PAYMENT

PART 7

FINAL PROVISIONS

SCHEDULES

Part 1

State pension

Introduction

State pension

1.—(1) This Part creates a benefit called state pension. 1.1061

(2) A person who reaches pensionable age before 6 April 2016 is not entitled to benefits under this Part (but may be entitled to similar benefits under Part 2 of the Contributions and Benefits Act).

General note

Part 1 of the Pensions Act 2014 and the associated Schedules (1 to 14) entered fully into effect on April 6, 2016: Pensions Act 2014, s.56(4). Subject to transitional provisions noted below, the Act abolishes the pension that used to be called state retirement pension and replaces it with the "state pension". In the consultative and explanatory literature issued before the Act it was described as a "single tier pension", but the Act has gone for the simplest name. In doing so it removes from the statute book most continuing mentions of the old title of "state retirement pension" or "retirement pension". Pensions payable under legislation in effect before April 6, 2016 are labelled "old state pensions". 1.1062

The provisions strip away much of the potential complication of the old state pensions save for transitional cases. While, as with all pension law, it will be many years before all transitional provisions have expired, it is important to note that in principle anyone reaching state pensionable age on or after April 6, 2016 is now covered **exclusively** by the state pension and has no claim under the previous law.

State pensionable age for men as at April 6, 2016 is the 65th birthday and therefore applied to all men born on or after April 6, 1951. State pensionable age for women is increasing under the terms of the Pension Act 2011. Under that Act any woman born on or before April 5, 1953 reached state pensionable age on March 6, 2016. Those born on or after April 6, 1953 reach state pensionable age on July 6, 2016.

The Government consulted widely on the new pension and issued several papers detailing the proposals, as well as the Bill and the usual explanatory notes. These documents are all accessible on the GOV.UK website. The key policy paper was issued under the title *The single-tier pension: a simple foundation for saving* in January 2013. A formal White Paper was issued as CM 8528. These are included, together with a useful executive summary, on the website.

State pension at the full or reduced rate

Entitlement to state pension at full or reduced rate

2.—(1) A person is entitled to a state pension payable at the full rate if— 1.1063

(a) the person has reached pensionable age, and
(b) the person has 35 or more qualifying years.

(2) A person is entitled to a state pension payable at the reduced rate if—

(a) the person has reached pensionable age, and
(b) the person has at leat the minimum number of qualifying years but fewer than 35 qualifying years.

(3) The minimum number of qualifying years for a state pension payable at the reduced rate is to be specified in regulations and may not be more than 10.

(4) In this Part "qualifying year" means a tax year, during a person's working life, in which the person's earnings factor (or the sum of the person's earnings factors) is equal to or greater than the qualifying earnings factor for the year.

(5) For earnings factors, see sections 22 and 23 of the Contributions and Benefits Act.

(6) For transitional cases in which a person may be entitled to a different state pension (instead of a state pension under this section), see sections 4 and 12.

(7) There are provisions elsewhere that affect a person's entitlement to a state pension under this section or the rate at which it is payable.

GENERAL NOTE

1.1064 This section sets the two key rules for the new state pension. To receive a full pension the pensioner must have completed 35 years during each of which adequate levels of National Insurance contribution are paid or credited. This is the same rule for both women and men, and is a reduction on a requirement based on the traditional full working life (from 16 to 65 for men) required for many years under the National Insurance Acts.

This emphasises that the state pension remains a contributory pension and that anyone claiming a pension must satisfy the contribution conditions. As with state retirement pension, the issues about payment of contributions and a claimant's contribution record are matters for decision by the National Insurance Contributions Office of His Majesty's Revenue and Customs (HMRC) with any appeals going to the First-tier Tribunal Tax Chamber and so are beyond the scope of this work.

In the jargon of the policy documents, to obtain a full pension the pensioner must have a "foundation amount" equal to 35 years. To obtain any pension, the pensioner must have a foundation amount that meets the requirements of s.2(3). The minimum number of years for s.2(3) is set at 10 by reg.13 of the State Pension Regulations 2015 (below).

The policy documents identify four groups of pensioners for whom provision must be made. The first group is those whose records show that they have completed the necessary contribution requirements to have obtained a full foundation amount.

The three other groups are: those who have not reached the full 35 year level and/or have been in contracted-out employment for part of that period; those whose contribution records (in particular those before April 6, 2016) exceed the total; and those with an inadequate record (or none at all) so that they are outside the Act.

The section also flags up ss.4 and 12 which provide for the second and third groups of pensioners. Those with no state pension entitlement may have entitlement to state pension credit, and are not otherwise considered in this Act.

Section 2 is modified to the extent necessary to give effect to a Convention on Social Security entered into on February 1, 2019, by the Government of the United Kingdom and the Government of Ireland (Article 2(1) of the Social Security (Ireland) Order 2019 (SI 2019/622). The Convention seeks to maintain, following the UK's departure from the European Union, certain UK social security entitlements of citizens of the Republic of Ireland. This includes rules for mutual recognition of social security contributions for the purposes of state pension under the 2014 Act.

Full and reduced rates of state pension

1.1065 **3.**—(1) The full rate of the state pension is the weekly rate for the time being specified in regulations.

(2) The reduced rate of the state pension for a person is the following proportion of the full rate—

1/35 × the person's number of qualifying years

(3) Once the full rate has been specified, the power to make regulations under subsection (1) may not be re-exercised so as to reduce the rate.

GENERAL NOTE

The full rate of state pension is set by reg.1A of the State Pension Regulations 2015, see para.6.169. 1.1066

State pension at the transitional rate

Entitlement to state pension at transitional rate

4.—(1) A person is entitled to a state pension payable at the transitional rate if— 1.1067

(a) the person has reached pensionable age,
(b) the person has at least the minimum number of qualifying years, and
(c) the person has at least one pre-commencement qualifying year.

(2) The minimum number of qualifying years for a state pension payable at the transitional rate is to be specified in regulations and may not be more than 10.

(3) A person entitled to a state pension payable at the transitional rate is not entitled to a state pension under section 2.

(4) In this Part—

"post-commencement qualifying year" means a qualifying year beginning on or after 6 April 2016;

"pre-commencement qualifying year" means—

(a) a qualifying year beginning on or after 6 April 1978 and ending before 6 April 2016, or
(b) a reckonable year that would have been treated under regulation 13(1) of the Social Security (Widow's Benefit, Retirement Pensions and Other Benefits) (Transitional) Regulations 1979 as a qualifying year for the purposes of determining the person's entitlement to an old state pension that is a Category A retirement pension.

(5) A reckonable year mentioned in paragraph (b) of the definition of "precommencement qualifying year" counts towards the minimum number of qualifying years required by subsection (1)(b) (even though it does not come within the definition of "qualifying year" for the purposes of this Part).

(6) For earnings factors, see sections 22 and 23 of the Contributions and Benefits Act.

(7) There are provisions elsewhere that affect a person's entitlement to a state pension under this section or the rate at which it is payable.

GENERAL NOTE

This section together with s.5 and Sch.1 provide for the main group of those entitled to a transitional award under the new state pension scheme rather than receiving the state pension without more. These are those who, on reaching state pensionable age on or after April 6, 2016, have not received the full foundation amount of 35 contribution years but have received more than the minimum amount. That amount, set under the terms of subs.(2) above is 10 years, 1.1068 the same lower limit a for s.2. See reg.13 of the State Pension Regulations 2015 (below).

The detailed calculations to be made to find out the foundation amount for these claimants are set out in Sch.1. The most important aspect of that schedule is that it requires HMRC to calculate both the "new" and the "old" levels of contribution payment or credit, and to base the calculation entitlement on which ever of the two is the larger. See steps 1, 2 and 3 of the calculation in Part 2 of Sch.1. As noted above, that remains within the remit of HMRC so is not part of the formal determination of a pension by DWP.

Transitional rate of state pension

1.1069 **5.**—(1) The transitional rate of the state pension for a person is a weekly rate equal to—

(a) the sum of the amounts calculated under Schedule 1 for the person's pre-commencement and post-commencement qualifying years capped at the full rate of the state pension on the day on which the person reaches pensionable age, or

(b) if higher, the amount for the person's pre-commencement qualifying years alone.

(2) The transitional rate of the state pension for a person is to be increased from time to time in accordance with the applicable paragraph of Schedule 2.

(3) Section 6 requires the transitional rate of the state pension for a person to be recalculated in certain circumstances.

(4) There are special rules about the transitional rate for certain women: see section 11 (reduced rate elections).

Recalculation and backdating of transitional rate in special cases

1.1070 **6.**—(1) This section modifies the transitional rate of the state pension for a person if, after the person has reached pensionable age, a determination is made under section 48A(2) of the Pension Schemes Act 1993 (contracting-out: reinstatement in state scheme following payment of contributions equivalent premium).

(2) The person's transitional rate is to be recalculated (taking the determination into account under paragraph 3(8) of Schedule 1).

(3) The recalculated rate has effect as from the day on which the person reached pensionable age (and the other provisions of this Part apply accordingly).

Transitional entitlement based on contributions of others

Survivor's pension based on inheritance of additional old state pension

1.1071 **7.**—(1) A person is entitled to a state pension under this section if—

(a) the person has reached pensionable age,

(b) the person's spouse died while they were married or the person's civil partner died while they were civil partners of each other, and

(c) the person is entitled to an inherited amount under Schedule 3.

(2) A state pension under this section is payable at a weekly rate equal to the inherited amount.

(3) The rate of the state pension for a person under this section is to be increased from time to time in accordance with the applicable paragraph of Schedule 4.

(4) Regulations may provide that if at any time the sum of the relevant state pensions for a person exceeds an amount provided for by regulations, the rate of any state pension payable to the person under this section is to be reduced by the amount of the excess.

(5) The "sum of the relevant state pensions" for a person is the sum of—

(a) the rate of any state pension payable to the person under this section (ignoring any reduction under subsection (4)), and

(b) the rate of any state pension payable to the person under section 2, 4 or 12.

(6) In subsections (4) and (5) a reference to the rate of a person's state pension is to the rate—

(a) taking into account any reduction under section 14 (in the case of a state pension under section 4), but

(b) ignoring any increase under section 17.

(7) There are provisions elsewhere that affect a person's entitlement to a state pension under this section or the rate at which it is payable.

GENERAL NOTE

This section, together with ss.8 and 9 and Schs.3 to 5 deal with the transitional provisions dealing with pensioners seeking to claim in whole or part on the basis of the contributions paid by a spouse or partner during their joint lives. These measures are necessary because there are no derived or inherited rights to a new state pension under s.2 and amendments have removed any entitlement for anyone to rely on the National Insurance contributions of any other person with effect from April 6, 2016. This effectively stops any new rights to a Category B (or Category AB) pension, to use the old language. However, the transitional right to have the benefit of past contributions taken into account includes, through these provisions, the right to continue to rely on derived and inherited contributions made before April 6, 2016. 1.1072

Choice of lump sum or survivor's pension under section 9 in certain cases

8.—(1) A person is entitled to a choice under this section if— 1.1073

(a) the person has reached pensionable age,

(b) the person's spouse died while they were married or the person's civil partner died while they were civil partners of each other,

(c) the spouse or civil partner's entitlement to an old state pension was deferred at the time of death and throughout the period of 12 months ending with the day before the death,

(d) either:

(i) the person was under pensionable age when the spouse or civil partner died and did not marry or form a civil partnership after the death and before reaching pensionable age, or

(ii) the person was over pensionable age when the spouse or civil partner died, and

(e) the person would, on reaching pensionable age or on the death of the spouse or civil partner, have been entitled to an old state pension if in the relevant provisions of the Contributions and Benefits Act:

(i) the words "before 6 April 2016" were omitted, and

(ii) any reference to a bereavement allowance included a reference to bereavement support payment under section 30 of this Act.

(2) The person may choose—

(a) to be paid a lump sum under this section, or

(b) to be paid a state pension under section 9.

(3) Regulations are to set out the manner in which, and the period within which, that choice is to be made.

(4) A person who chooses to be paid a lump sum under this section, or who fails to choose within that period, is entitled to a "widowed person's or surviving civil partner's lump sum" calculated under paragraph 7B of Schedule 5 to the Contributions and Benefits Act.

(5) In that paragraph as it applies for the purposes of this section—

(a) read the references to "W" as references to the person,

(b) read sub-paragraph (5) as if it required increases under paragraph 4 of the Schedule to be excluded, and

(c) read the reference in sub-paragraph (7)(a) to the date on which W becomes entitled to a Category A or Category B retirement pension as a reference to the date on which the person becomes entitled to make a choice under this section.

(6) There are provisions elsewhere that affect a person's entitlement to a lump sum under this section.

(7) Regulations may allow a person, in specified circumstances—

(a) to alter his or her choice under this section;

(b) to make a late choice.

(8) Regulations under subsection (7) may, for the purpose of avoiding the duplication of payment—

(a) enable recovery of an amount paid to the person, or

(b)reduce the amount of a lump sum to be paid to the person.

(9) For the purposes of this section—

(a) "deferred" has the meaning given by section 55(3) of the Contributions and Benefits Act,

(b) "the relevant provisions" of the Contributions and Benefits Act are—

section 44(1)(a);

section 48(1);

section 48A(1) and (3);

section 48B(1), (1A), (4) and (4A);

section 48BB(1) and (3), and

(c) in determining whether a person would have been entitled to an old state pension as mentioned in subsection (1)(e) ignore any requirement to make a claim.

Survivor's pension based on inheritance of deferred old state pension

1.1074 **9.—**(1) A person is entitled to a state pension under this section if—

(a) the person has reached pensionable age,

(b) the person's spouse died while they were married or the person's civil partner died while they were civil partners of each other,

(c) either:

(i) the person was under pensionable age when the spouse or civil partner died and did not marry or form a civil partnership after the death and before reaching pensionable age, or

(ii) the person was over pensionable age when the spouse or civil partner died,

(d) the person is entitled to an inherited deferral amount under Schedule 5, and

(e) in the case of a person entitled to a choice under section 8, the person has chosen to be paid a state pension under this section.

(2) A state pension under this section is payable at a weekly rate equal to the inherited deferral amount.

(3) But if at any time an order under section 151A of the Administration Act comes into force, the rate of the person's state pension under this section is increased (at that time) by the percentage specified in the order.

(4) A person may be entitled to more than one state pension under this section.

(5) There are provisions elsewhere that affect a person's entitlement to a state pension under this section or the rate at which it is payable.

GENERAL NOTE

The sums which, under this section, are survivors' pensions based on inheritance of deferred old state pensions, were increased, with effect from April 8, 2024, by 6.7 per cent: see art.6(3)(a) of the Social Security Benefits Up-rating Order 2024 (SI 2024/242). For the meaning of "old state pension", see s.21. For previous years' increases, see previous editions of this work. 1.1075

Inheritance of graduated retirement benefit

10.—(1) Regulations may make provision corresponding or similar to any provision of sections 7 to 9 and Schedules 3 to 5 for the purpose of conferring benefits on a person whose dead spouse or civil partner paid graduated contributions as an insured person. 1.1076

(2) The regulations may—

(a) include provision corresponding or similar to any provision that may be made by regulations under section 7 or 8;

(b) amend or otherwise modify this Act or any other enactment (whenever passed or made).

(3) In this section "graduated contributions" and "insured person" have the meanings given by section 36(8) of the National Insurance Act 1965.

GENERAL NOTE

For the provisions giving effect to this section see regs.15-20 of the State Pension Regulations 2015 below. Together the provisions protect a transitional claim drawing on contributions made under the former graduated retirement benefit scheme. 1.1077

Transition: women who have had a reduced rate election

Reduced rate elections: effect on section 4 pensions

11.—(1) Section 4(1)(b) (minimum number of qualifying years for state pension at the transitional rate) does not apply to a woman if a reduced rate election was in force in respect of her at the beginning of the relevant 35-year period. 1.1078

(2) Schedule 6 modifies the rules about the transitional rate of the state pension for a woman if a reduced rate election was in force in respect of her at the beginning of the relevant 35-year period.

(3) In this section—

"reduced rate election" means an election made, or treated as having been made, under regulations under section 19(4) of the Contributions and Benefits Act;

"relevant 35-year period" means the 35-year period ending with the tax year before the one in which the woman reached pensionable age.

GENERAL NOTE

1.1079 This section, together with s.12 and Schs. 6 and 7, deal with transitional cases involving another of the major changes made by the Pensions Act 2014, namely the abolition of the right of a woman to pay National Insurance contributions at a reduced rate. At the same time, provisions are required to prevent a woman who paid only the reduced rate contributions from being treated as if those reduced rate contributions had not been paid.

These provisions contain the necessary provisions to adjust the foundation amount or alternative contribution record of anyone within this group of pensioners to ensure that pension is not overpaid.

Reduced rate elections: pension for women with no section 4 pension

1.1080 **12.**—(1) A woman is entitled to a state pension under this section if—

(a) she has reached pensionable age,

(b) a reduced rate election was in force in respect of her at the beginning of the relevant 35-year period,

(c) she does not have any pre-commencement qualifying years, and

(d) she is entitled to a basic amount under Schedule 7.

(2) A state pension under this section is payable at a weekly rate equal to the basic amount.

(3) But if at any time the full rate of the state pension is increased, the rate of the woman's state pension under this section is increased (at that time) by the same percentage as the increase in the full rate.

(4) In subsection (3) the reference to the rate of the woman's state pension is to the

rate ignoring any increase under section 17.

(5) A woman is not entitled to a state pension under this section and section 2 at the same time: she is only entitled to the one with the higher rate.

(6) There are provisions elsewhere that affect a woman's entitlement to a state pension under this section or the rate at which it is payable.

(7) In this section—

"reduced rate election" means an election made, or treated as having been made, under regulations under section 19(4) of the Contributions and Benefits Act;

"relevant 35-year period" means the 35-year period ending with the tax year before the one in which the woman reached pensionable age.

Transition: pension sharing on divorce etc

Shared state pension on divorce etc

1.1081 **13.**—(1) A person is entitled to a state pension under this section if—

(a) the person has reached pensionable age, and

(b) the person is entitled to a state scheme pension credit.

(2) A state pension under this section is payable at the appropriate weekly rate set out in Schedule 8.

(3) The rate of the state pension for a person under this section is to be increased from time to time in accordance with the applicable paragraph of Schedule 9.

(4) A person may be entitled to more than one state pension under this section.

(5) There are provisions elsewhere that affect a person's entitlement to a state pension under this section or the rate at which it is payable.

(6) In this Part—

"state scheme pension credit" means—

(a) a new state scheme pension credit, or

(b) an old state scheme pension credit;

"new state scheme pension credit" means a credit under section 49A(2)(b) of the Welfare Reform and Pensions Act 1999;

"old state scheme pension credit" means a credit under section 49(1)(b) of that Act.

GENERAL NOTE

This section, together with s.14 and Schs.8 to 10 deal with the need to continue the shareable state scheme rights created under the Welfare Reform and Pensions Act 1999 (see above in this volume). Section 15 incorporates Sch.11 which sets out amendments to that Act and related provisions. These are included in the relevant provisions above. 1.1082

Pension sharing: reduction in the sharer's section 4 pension

14.—(1) The rate of a person's state pension under section 4 is reduced under this section if the person is subject to a state scheme pension debit. 1.1083

(2) The amount by which the rate is reduced is the amount of the appropriate weekly reduction set out in Schedule 10.

(3) A person's state pension may be reduced more than once under this section.

(4) In this Part—

"state scheme pension debit" means—

(a) a new state scheme pension debit, or

(b) an old state scheme pension debit.

"new state scheme pension debit" means a debit under section 49A(2)(a) of the Welfare Reform and Pensions Act 1999;

"old state scheme pension debit" means a debit under section 49(1)(a) of that Act.

Pension sharing: amendments

15.—Schedule 11 contains amendments to do with pension sharing. 1.1084

Postponing or suspending state pension

Pensioner's option to suspend state pension

16.—(1) A person who has become entitled to a state pension under this Part may opt to suspend his or her entitlement in accordance with regulations. 1.1085

(2) A person is not entitled to any state pension under this Part for the period for which the person has opted to suspend his or her entitlement.

(3) For other effects of a person exercising the option, see section 17.

(4) A person may not opt to suspend his or her entitlement to a state pension under this Part on more than one occasion.

(5) Regulations may specify other circumstances in which a person may not opt to suspend his or her entitlement to a state pension under this Part.

(6) Regulations may allow a person who has opted to suspend his or her entitlement to a state pension under this Part to cancel the exercise of that option (in whole or in part) in relation to a past period.

Effect of pensioner postponing or suspending state pension

1.1086 **17.**—(1) If a person's entitlement to a state pension under this Part has been deferred for a period, the weekly rate of the person's state pension is increased by an amount equal to the sum of the increments to which the person is entitled.

(2) But the weekly rate is not to be increased under subsection (1) if the increase would be less than 1% of the persons weekly rate ignoring that subsection.

(3) A person is entitled to one increment for each whole week in the period during which the person's entitlement to a state pension was deferred.

(4) The amount of an increment is equal to a specified percentage of the weekly rate of the state pension to which the person would have been entitled immediately before the end of that period if the person's entitlement had not been deferred.

(5) In subsection (4) "specified" means specified in regulations.

(6) The amount of an increase under this section is itself to be increased from time to time in accordance with any order made under section 150 of the Administration Act (annual up-rating of benefits).

(7) For the purposes of this section and section 18 a person's entitlement to a state pension under this Part is deferred for a period if the person has opted under section 16 to suspend his or her entitlement for that period.

(8) For the purposes of this section and section 18 a person's entitlement to a state pension under this Part is also deferred for a period if the person is not entitled to it for that period by reason only of—

(a) not satisfying the conditions in section 1 of the Administration Act (entitlement dependent on claim etc), or

(b) subsection (9) below.

(9) A person is not entitled to a state pension under this Part for any period during which his or her entitlement to any other state pension under this Part is deferred.

General Note

1.1087 The sums which are increases under this section in the rates of state pensions under Pt 1 of this Act were increased, with effect from April 8, 2024, by 6.7 per cent: see art.6(2) of the Social Security Benefits Up-rating Order 2024 (SI 2024/242). For previous years' increases, see previous editions of this work.

Section 17 supplementary: calculating weeks, overseas residents, etc

18.—(1) Regulations may— 1.1088

(a) provide for circumstances in which a part of a week is to be treated for the purposes of section 17(3) as a whole week, and

(b) provide for circumstances in which a day does not count in determining a number of whole weeks for the purposes of section 17(3) (for example if the person is receiving other benefits).

(2) Regulations may modify section 17(4) in cases where, at any time in the period during which a person's entitlement to a state pension is deferred, the rate for the person would have changed otherwise than because of an up-rating increase.

(3) Regulations may modify section 17(4) in relation to a person who has been an overseas resident during any part of the period for which the person's entitlement to a state pension has been deferred.

(4) In subsection (3) "overseas resident" means a person who is not ordinarily resident in Great Britain or any other territory specified in the regulations.

(5) Regulations may amend the percentage specified in section 17(2).

Prisoners and overseas residents

Prisoners

19.—(1) Regulations may provide that a person is not to be paid a state pension under this Part for any period during which the person is a prisoner. 1.1089

(2) "Prisoner" means a person (in Great Britain or elsewhere) who is—

(a) imprisoned or detained in legal custody, or

(b) unlawfully at large.

(3) In the case of a person remanded in custody for an offence, regulations under subsection (1) may be made so as to apply only if a sentence of a specified description is later imposed on the person for the offence.

GENERAL NOTE

There was some lack of clarity in previous law about the extent to which the fact that someone was or should have been a prisoner affected entitlement to a state pension. This section, read with regs.2 and 3 of the State Pension Regulations 2015 (below) seeks to remove any ambiguity and to prevent pension awards to those who are in custody either here or elsewhere with a few clearly defined limits. 1.1090

Overseas residents

20.—(1) Regulations may provide that an overseas resident who is entitled to a state pension under this Part is not entitled to up-rating increases. 1.1091

(2) In this section "overseas resident" means a person who is not ordinarily resident in Great Britain or any territory specified in the regulations.

(3) Regulations under this section do not affect the rate of an overseas resident's state pension for any period during which he or she is in Great Britain or a territory specified in the regulations (but once the overseas resident ceases to be in Great Britain or a specified territory the rate reverts to what it would have been had he or she not been in Great Britain or a specified territory).

(4) Regulations under this section do not affect the rate of a person's state pension once the person stops being an overseas resident.

GENERAL NOTE

1.1092 Regulations to give effect to this section are in regs.21 to 23 of the State Pension Regulations 2015 below.

Definitions

"Old state pension"

1.1093 **21.**—(1) In this Part "old state pension" means a Category A retirement pension or a Category B retirement pension.

(2) A reference in this Part to the rate of an old state pension (however expressed) does not include—

(a) graduated retirement benefit under the National Insurance Act 1965, or

(b) any increase in the rate because of Schedule 5 to the Contributions and Benefits Act (deferral increases).

General definitions etc

1.1094 **22.**—(1) In this Part—

"the Administration Act" means the Social Security Administration Act 1992;

"Category A retirement pension" means a Category A retirement pension under Part 2 of the Contributions and Benefits Act;

"Category B retirement pension" means a Category B retirement pension under Part 2 of the Contributions and Benefits Act;

"the Contributions and Benefits Act" means the Social Security Contributions and Benefits Act 1992;

"enactment" includes an enactment contained in subordinate legislation within the meaning of the Interpretation Act 1978;

"full rate" means the rate mentioned in section 3(1);

"old state pension" has the meaning given by section 21 (and references to the rate of an old state pension are to be read in accordance with that section);

"pensionable age" has the meaning given by section 122(1) of the Contributions and Benefits Act; and a person is "over" pensionable age if the person has reached that age (and is otherwise "under" that age);

"post-commencement qualifying year" has the meaning given by section 4(4);

"pre-commencement qualifying year" is to be read in accordance with section 4(4) and (5);

"qualifying earnings factor" has "qualifying earnings factor" has the meaning given by section 122(1) of the Contributions and Benefits Act;

"qualifying year" has the meaning given by section 2(4);

"reduced rate" means the rate mentioned in section 3(2);

"regulations" means regulations made by the Secretary of State;

"state scheme pension credit", and related expressions, have the meaning given by section 13;

"state scheme pension debit", and related expressions, have the meaning given by section 14;

"tax year" has the meaning given by section 122(1) of the Contributions and Benefits Act;
"transitional rate" means the rate mentioned in section 5;
"up-rating increase", in relation to a state pension under this Part, means—
(a) an increase in the rate of the state pension because of an increase in the amount specified in regulations under section 3(1),[1 ...]
(b) an increase in the rate of the state pension because of section 9(3), 12(3) or 17(6) or Schedule 2, 4 or 9; [1 or
(c) an increase in the rate of the state pension because of regulations under section 10 which make provision corresponding or similar to section 9(3) or Schedule 4;]
"working life" has the meaning given by section 122(1) of the Contributions and Benefits Act.

(2) For the purposes of any other provision of this Part two people are to be treated as if they are not married to each other in relation to times when either of them is married to a third person.

Consequential and other amendments

Amendments

23.—In Schedule 12— 1.1095
Part 1 contains amendments to do with state pensions under this Part;
Part 2 contains key amendments to do with the old state pension system;
Part 3 contains amendments to do with state pension credit;
Part 4 contains other amendments to do with this Part.

Abolition of contracting-out for salary related schemes etc

24.—(1) Schedule 13 contains amendments to abolish contracting-out for salary related schemes. 1.1096

(2) An employer may amend an occupational pension scheme in relation to some or all of its members to take account of increases in the employer's national insurance contributions in respect of some or all of the members to whom the amendments apply because of the repeal of section 41 of the Pension Schemes Act 1993 (by Schedule 13 to this Act).

(3) The power may be used to make amendments that will apply in relation to future members and correspond to the amendments being made in relation to current members.

(4) The power may not be used—

(a) to make amendments that apply to a member who is a protected person in relation to a scheme, or

(b) to amend a public service pension scheme or a scheme of a description specified in regulations under this paragraph.

(5) Regulations must define what is meant by a protected person in relation to a scheme for the purposes of subsection (4)(a).

(6) Schedule 14 contains more detail about the power.

(7) In this section and Schedule 14—

"current member", in relation to a scheme, means a person who is a member of the scheme at the time that the power is used (and "future member" is to be read accordingly);

"employer", in relation to a scheme, means the employer of persons in the description of employment to which the scheme relates;

"member" has the meaning given by section 124(1) of the Pensions Act 1995;

"national insurance contributions", in relation to an employer, means secondary Class 1 national insurance contributions payable by the employer;

"occupational pension scheme" has the meaning given by section 1 of the Pension Schemes Act 1993;

"public service pension scheme" has the meaning given by that section.

(8) Subsections (2) to (7) and Schedule 14 are repealed at the end of the period of 5 years beginning with 6 April 2016.

(9) The Secretary of State may by order amend subsection (8) to extend the period for the time being mentioned there.

PART 2

OPTION TO BOOST OLD RETIREMENT PENSIONS

Option to boost old retirement pensions

1.1097 **25.**—In Schedule 15—

Part 1 contains amendments to allow certain people to pay additional contributions to boost their retirement pensions;

Part 2 contains amendments to allow corresponding legislation to be put in place for Northern Ireland.

PART 3

PENSIONABLE AGE

Increase in pensionable age to 67

1.1098 **26.** *This amends Sch.4 to the Pensions Act 1995, and the amendments are set out there.*

Periodic review of rules about pensionable age

1.1099 **27.**—(1) The Secretary of State must from time to time—

(a) review whether the rules about pensionable age are appropriate, having regard to life expectancy and other factors that the Secretary of State considers relevant, and

(b) prepare and publish a report on the outcome of the review.

(2) The first report must be published before 7 May 2017.

(3) Each subsequent report must be published before the end of the period of 6 years beginning with the day on which the previous report was published.

(4) For the purposes of each review, the Secretary of State must require the Government Actuary or Deputy Government Actuary to prepare a report for the Secretary of State on—

(a) whether the rules about pensionable age mean that, on average, a person who reaches pensionable age within a specified period can be expected to spend a specified proportion of his or her adult life in retirement, and

(b) if not, ways in which the rules might be changed with a view to achieving that result.

(5) The Secretary of State must, for the purposes of a review, appoint a person or persons to prepare a report for the Secretary of State on other specified factors relevant to the review.

(6) The Secretary of State must lay before Parliament any report prepared under this section.

(7) For the purposes of subsection (4)—

(a) a person's adult life is the part of the person's life after he or she reaches the specified age;

(b) the proportion of a person's adult life spent in retirement is the proportion of his or her adult life spent after reaching pensionable age.

(8) In this section—

"pensionable age" has the meaning given by the rules in paragraph 1 of Schedule 4 to the Pensions Act 1995 (and "the rules about pensionable age" means those rules);

"specified" means specified by the Secretary of State.

PART 5

BEREAVEMENT SUPPORT PAYMENT

Bereavement support payment

30—(1) A person is entitled to a benefit called bereavement support payment if— **1.1100**

(a) the person's [1 spouse, civil partner or cohabiting partner] dies,

[1 (aa) in the case of a person whose cohabiting partner dies, the person is pregnant or entitled to child benefit in circumstances specified under subsection (4) or, where no such circumstances are specified, in such circumstances as the Secretary of State may specify by regulations,]

(b) the person is under pensionable age when the [1 spouse, civil partner or cohabiting partner] dies,

(c) the person is ordinarily resident in Great Britain, or a specified territory, when the [1 spouse, civil partner or cohabiting partner] dies, and

(d) the contribution condition is met (see section 31).

[1 (1A) Only one person is entitled to bereavement support payment in respect of one death.

(1B) Where, apart from subsection (1A), more than one person would be so entitled, entitlement is to be determined in accordance with subsections (1C) and (1D).

(1C) Where only one of those persons is a member of the same household as the deceased, that person is entitled.

(1D) Where there is more than one person who is a member of the same household as the deceased and would (apart from subsection (1A)) be entitled—

(a) if one of those persons is the deceased's spouse or civil partner and is pregnant or entitled to child benefit in circumstances specified under subsection (1)(aa) or (4), that person is entitled;
(b) if there is no spouse or civil partner entitled under paragraph (a), the deceased's cohabiting partner who is pregnant or entitled to child benefit in circumstances specified under subsection (1)(aa) or (4) is entitled (but this is subject to paragraphs (c) and (d));
(c) if there is more than one cohabiting partner within paragraph (b), the cohabiting partner who has been a member of the same household as the deceased for longest is entitled;
(d) if there is more than one cohabiting partner within paragraph (b) and each partner has been a member of the same household as the deceased for the same length of time, the Secretary of State must determine who is entitled.]

(2) The Secretary of State must by regulations specify—
(a) the rate of the benefit, and
(b) the period for which it is payable.

(3) The regulations may specify different rates for different periods.

(4) In the case of a person who is pregnant or entitled to child benefit in specified circumstances, the regulations may—
(a) specify a higher rate;
(b) provide for the allowance to be payable for a longer period.

(5) A person is not entitled to bereavement support payment for periods after the person has reached pensionable age.

(6) A person is not entitled to bereavement support payment if the death occurred before this section came fully into force.

[1 (6A) For the purposes of this section, the Secretary of State may by regulations specify—
(a) circumstances in which the fact that two persons are married to each other, or are civil partners or cohabiting partners of each other, is to be disregarded;
(b) circumstances in which two persons are to be treated as if they were married to each other or were civil partners or cohabiting partners of each other;
(c) circumstances in which people are to be treated as being, or as not being, members of the same household.

(6B) For the purposes of this section, two persons are cohabiting partners if they are not married to, or civil partners of, each other but are living together as if they were married or civil partners.

(6C) The Secretary of State must issue a statement of the Secretary of State's policy with respect to making determinations under subsection (1D)(d).]

(7) In this section—

"pensionable age" has the meaning given by the rules in paragraph 1 of Schedule 4 to the Pensions Act 1995;

"specified territory" means a territory specified in regulations made by the Secretary of State.

AMENDMENT

1. Bereavement Benefits (Remedial) Order 2023 (SI 2023/134) art.4 (the amendment came into force on February 13, 2023 but, by virtue of art.1(3), is treated as having had effect from August 30, 2018).

General Note

Bereavement Support Payment replaced all previous forms of bereavement benefits for new claims made after April 6, 2017. Existing entitlement to the earlier benefits remained. Initially claims could be made only by persons who were either married to or had a civil partnership with the deceased. With effect from August 30, 2018 the Bereavement Benefits (Remedial) Order 2023 (SI 2023/134) has extended entitlement to a claimant who was living as a cohabiting partner with the deceased at the time of death and the claimant is, at that time, either pregnant or entitled to child benefit in circumstances as may be specified by regulations made under subs. (4) of this section. Those circumstances are to be found in reg.4 (Persons entitled to a higher rate of bereavement support payment) of the Bereavement Support Payment Regulations 2017 (BSP). Paragraphs (2)–(4) of that regulation specify the circumstances in which a claimant will be entitled to the higher rate of payment of BSP. Although para.(aa) of s.30(1) refers only to the claimant being entitled to child benefit, para.(4) of the regulation referred to above will cover the case of a claimant where it was the deceased who was entitled to child benefit (note the effect of the rules of priority under Sch.10 to the Contributions and Benefits Act) at the time of death, but the claimant becomes entitled following the death. Note that under that paragraph the child or young person must have been living with the claimant or the deceased at the time of death and the claimant can only have been a cohabitant if they were also living with the deceased at that time. **1.1101**

This amendment to the legislation was in consequence of the cases of *McLaughlin, Re Judicial Review (Northern Ireland)* [2018] UKSC 48 and *R (Jackson and Others) v SSWP* [2020] EWHC 183 where the courts had held that the rejection of claims from cohabiting partners with children in the family was in breach of their Human Rights and a declaration of incompatibility was made. The Remedial Order limits the amendment made to that situation.

An attempt to have the exclusion of a claim by the survivor of a childless cohabiting couple declared to be incompatible with their Human Rights was rejected in *HM v SSWP (BB); MK v SSWP (BB):* [2023] UKUT 15 (AAC). The claimant in each case was the survivor of a different-sex couple who had for various reasons not married, and who could not enter a civil partnership because, at that time, civil partnership was limited to same-sex couples. Judge Ward in the UT held, following the decision of CA in *SSWP v Akhtar* [2021] EWCA Civ 1353, that cohabiting couples were not in an analogous position to spouses and civil partners and therefore to treat them differently was not discriminatory. Even if that view were wrong, he would have found different treatment to be justified.

The term cohabiting partners is defined in subs.(6B) as being where two persons who are not married to, or civil partners of, each other but are living together as if they were married or civil partners. This concept (formerly known as cohabitation) of people living together as if they were a married couple or in a civil partnership has a long and recurring history in the Social Security system. (See previous editions of this work in relation to Widow's Pension, Supplementary Benefit, Income Support and now Universal Credit). Generally, the concept has had the effect of disqualifying a claimant from receiving benefit at all, or from receiving benefit as a single claimant. Over the years, an extensive jurisprudence has grown up around this concept. It will be interesting to see if the factors applied and the evidence relied upon will be any different here, where the concept becomes a qualifying condition. Currently the Guidance offered to DM is to be found in Volume 3 Chapter 11, of the DMG. This guidance, though dated 2017, gives a fair representation of the body of jurisprudence at that date and is likely to be relied upon now by DM when considering entitlement to Bereavement Support for cohabitees. Note however, that for the purposes of disqualifying from benefit a couple must be both living in the same household and doing so as if they were a married couple or in a civil partnership, whereas, in the amended form of s. 30 qualification for BSP may involve each of those concepts being considered separately and that may lead to complications.

Subs.(1A) provides that only one person can be entitled in respect of one death. (But see below in relation to Transitional Provisions).

Where more than one person may otherwise be entitled subs.(1C) and subs.(1D) provide for an order of priority.

Subs.(1C) provides that where only one potential claimant was living in the same household as the deceased, that person takes priority.

Subs.(1D) accepts that more than one claimant could be living in the same household as the deceased. What is not clear is whether that means two claimants sharing one household with the deceased, or whether the deceased might have been living in two households with one claimant in each. Past decisions in relation to other benefits have held that a person can be living in only one household (see *R (SB) 8/85*) or, at any rate, one household at one time (see *CIS/11304/1995*), but this is a point where a new approach might be invited. More recent economic and social habits have resulted in more people living in one place during the working week and another at weekends. It seems possible for the deceased to have been living as a member of the household in both places. What might be more difficult will be for a claimant to show that they were living with the deceased as if married or in a civil partnership because those relationships envisage a state of monogamy. Where the claimant is aware that the deceased had a continuing relationship with another partner it may be hard to succeed, but where each partner was unaware of the other's existence, or of the nature of that relationship, very difficult decisions may arise. If the deceased had been living with his childless wife at weekends and with a pregnant cohabitee during the week it might not be too difficult for the cohabitee to show that he was living with her as a married couple or civil partners and that he was living in her household to the exclusion of his wife's because he will be there more days of the week (though that might not be regarded as the only determinative factor). But, if the roles were reversed, for example, he works away only at weekends, the cohabitee could succeed only if she could show first, that she was living with him as a married couple or civil partner, and then in order to have priority over the spouse she would have to show that he was living in her household to the exclusion of the wife's household (which might seem less likely) or, that he was living in both households at the same time. It would be unfortunate if living in only one household at a time meant that entitlement might turn on which house the deceased happened to be at, when he died.

In cases where both claimants are pregnant or entitled to child benefit subs.(1D)(a) gives priority to the spouse or civil partner. A suggestion by the Joint Committee on Human Rights that the BSP be split was not adopted.

In cases where both claimants are qualifying cohabitees and both are living in the same household as the deceased subs.(1D)(c) gives priority to the one who has been a member of the household the longest and where those periods are equal (1D)(d) leaves it to the Secretary of State to decide.

Where the deceased has separated from a spouse or civil partner and at the time of death is living only with a cohabiting partner who is pregnant or in receipt of child benefit, only the cohabiting partner can claim even though the parties might have agreed that a claim should be made by a deserted spouse who may still have responsibility for the children of the marriage. Subsection (1A) prescribes that "only one person is entitled" and (1C) provides that where the deceased was living in the same household as one of those who might otherwise be entitled that person "is entitled". The consequence must be that the spouse is not entitled and cannot make a claim. (Here, priority is determined by entitlement and not by payability - *cf.* child benefit where there may be competing entitlements).

The Remedial Order provides that only one person can be entitled in respect of one death, but art.2 of the Remedial Order (Transitional Provisions) allows for the continued entitlement of an existing award even though another claimant may make a retrospective claim and become entitled as a result of these amendments. For an overview of the effect of the Remedial Order and examples of its operation see Welfare Rights Bulletin No. 293 published by CPAG.

Bereavement support payments are a contributory benefit the requirement for which is defined in s.31. As with the benefits that it replaces both Class 1 and Class 2 contributions will qualify and the extent of the contribution required is the "lighter" test that demonstrates involvement in the labour force at some time in the deceased's working life; there are special provisions in respect of a person who dies in an industrial accident or as a result of an industrial disease. But see the case of *O'Donnell v Department for Communities* [2020] NICA 36, and that of *R. (Jwanczuk) v SSWP* [2022] EWHC 2298 (Admin). Both these cases are discussed in the note following s.31 below.

In other respects, the essential requirements of a claim are similar to those of the benefits that preceded Bereavement Support Payment. The claimant must be under pensionable age at the time their spouse, civil partner or cohabiting partner dies, and they must be within the UK or a specified territory defined by regulations. It remains necessary to prove the fact of death, and the rule of forfeiture will apply. But in respect of this benefit there is no disqualification if a claimant remarries, or lives with another person as if in a marriage or civil partnership. This will be so even if the claimant is living with another partner at the time of the death, though, in this case, a cohabitee may struggle to succeed if they have left the deceased and gone to form a relationship with another person; they would have become a former cohabitee no longer living with the deceased as if they were a married couple or civil partners, because both those relationships envisage a state of monogamy.

Most claims to Bereavement Support payment will continue to be made based on a marriage or civil partnership because such formal arrangements are still more common than cohabitation, and proof of the necessary relationship will still be easier. Proof of a cohabiting partnership may require detailed examination of the claimant's living arrangement with the deceased.

In one other respect a marriage or civil partnership will still hold an advantage over cohabitation. Subsection (6B) defines cohabiting partners in the present tense ("are living together") so if the parties have separated a former cohabitee will have no entitlement, whereas a surviving spouse or civil partner will.

For those reasons proof of a valid marriage or civil partnership will still be important and the notes that follow are still important.

Marriage will include same sex marriage, and civil partnership includes different sex civil partnership. Either relationship can be contracted with a transsexual where that person has a full gender recognition certificate in accordance with the Gender Recognition Act 2013.

Proof of a valid marriage

As to whether a marriage is valid the matter is determined by the general law including those rules of law concerning the recognition of foreign marriages and divorces. A marriage celebrated in England and Wales must satisfy the formalities of the law as to notice and ceremony, civil or religious, and is usually proved by production of a copy of the marriage certificate. If the certificate is not available, other evidence of the ceremony coupled with subsequent cohabitation will raise a presumption that there was a valid marriage. That presumption can be rebutted by evidence that the marriage was invalid, but it will probably require proof beyond reasonable doubt that it was invalid (*R(G) 2/70*). It should be noted that in this instance the presumption of marriage is supported by the evidence of cohabitation but only when there is also evidence that the appropriate ceremony took place. In *R(G) 2/70* the parties went through what was apparently a bogus ceremony (though it was thought by the claimant to be genuine) followed by many years of cohabitation. It was held that no marriage could be presumed. This case must now be viewed as doubtful. Although it was distinguished by the Court of Appeal in *Adjudication Officer v Bath* reported as *R(G) 1/00* Lord Justice Evans, giving the leading judgment, says that the basis of the argument used in *R(G) 2/70* is not correct. The decision in *R(G) 1/00* would suggest that the presumption should have also availed the claimant in **1.1102** the earlier case. In *R(G) 1/00* the partners were "married" in a religious ceremony in a Sikh Temple in West London (1956). They lived together thereafter for 37 years, bringing up a family, until the "husband" died in 1994. The Sikh Temple was not at that time a registered building for marriages under the Marriage Act 1949. (It was so registered in 1983 but such registration is not retrospective.)

There was no evidence, and it was not suggested by the claimant, that there had been any other civil ceremony of marriage at a Registry Office. It appears that the claimant believed herself to have been validly married in the religious ceremony and made her claim to widow's benefits accordingly.

The AO rejected that claim on the basis that no marriage, valid in accordance with the Marriage Act 1949, had been shown. That decision was upheld by the SSAT, with an expression of sympathy for the claimant's situation. The Commissioner allowed an appeal after recourse to the presumption outlined above as stated in *Halsbury's Laws of England*, paras 992 and 993 (4th edn, Vol.22).

The second of these paragraphs is headed "Presumption from cohabitation after Ceremony" and would appear to be the more appropriate. That paragraph makes clear, however, that the presumption is only that all essentials of the ceremony will be presumed valid *unless the contrary is proved*. Here, it would seem the evidence rebutted the validity of the ceremony because the Temple was not a registered building. However, the footnotes in *Halsbury* include the case of *Re Shephard, George v Thyer* (1904) in which the presumption was applied although the only ceremony alleged was a marriage in France that was agreed to be invalid. The Commissioner took the view that he could follow this case as an earlier High Court precedent. In doing so he rejects the conclusion of the Commissioner in *R(G) 2/70* who had himself refused to follow *Re Shephard*. In any case, Commissioner Goodman suggests that *R(G) 2/70* might be distinguished on the narrow ground that the ceremony relied upon there had been in a bogus Registry Office (although believed to be genuine by the claimant), whereas the ceremony in this case had been in a genuine religious Temple.

The Commissioner also found the claim to be supportable under the first paragraph cited. This paragraph is headed "Presumption from Cohabitation without Ceremony". This presumption should apply after long cohabitation even in the absence of evidence of a marriage ceremony. The Commissioner's reasoning here seems to be that someone who has gone through what they believed to be a valid ceremony should not be worse off than someone who believed themselves to be married without any ceremony at all.

The Commissioner seems to have created a marriage very similar to the Scottish marriage "by habit and repute". There is, however, this difference. In Scotland, marriage can be presumed by long cohabitation with a willingness (and ability) to marry. In the English case it would seem to be necessary to prove a *belief* that the parties were married. That is just as well for otherwise we would have invented a true common law marriage that depended only on the parties long monogamous cohabitation.

The Court of Appeal's decision confirms the reasoning of the Commissioner, though they did also doubt whether the evidence available was sufficient to prove that the Sikh Temple was not a registered building in 1956. The sympathy of the judges was apparent for the widow of a man who had duly paid his income tax and national insurance contributions throughout his working life only for her to be told, when it was already too late, that she had never been married at all, but the key to their reasoning seems to be that nothing in the Marriage Act 1949 invalidates such a marriage unless the parties "knowingly and wilfully" intermarry without compliance with that Act. There was no evidence in this case that the parties were acting otherwise than in the honest belief that their marriage was validly celebrated, and in the absence of any statutory disqualification they were entitled to the benefit of the presumption outlined above.

The CA has allowed an appeal against the decision reached in the Family Court in the case of *Akhter v Khan and the Attorney General* [2018] EWFC 54. That was the case in which Williams J. had found that a Muslim religious marriage (a Nikah) could be regarded as a void marriage so as to give the claimant access to relief under the Matrimonial Causes Act. The CA, in allowing the appeal (reported as *Attorney General v Akhter and Khan* [2020] EWCA Civ 122), held that such a purported marriage was not a void marriage and could only ever be regarded as a "non-qualifying ceremony", which was the term that they preferred for what has formerly been described as a non-marriage. The court also held that neither the ECHR nor the HRA would lead to them adopting a more flexible approach to the interpretation of the Matrimonial Causes Act as the court below had done.

In *NA v SSWP (BB)* [2019] UKUT 144 (AAC) Judge Wikeley had used the ECHR and the HRA to aid in the interpretation of the Polygamous Marriages Regulations 1975 so as to allow an appeal for a claimant who had married in Pakistan a man who was already married to a wife in the UK. He divorced that wife after their return to the UK and thereafter they lived here together monogamously. The Court of Appeal in *SSWP v Akhtar* [2021] EWCA Civ 1353 has allowed a further appeal against that decision holding that the Polygamous Marriages Regulations cannot be applied to a marriage which is void – in this case, the marriage being bigamous meant that the deceased, at the time of the marriage, lacked the capacity to marry. Nor did they think that the ECHR and HRA could be applied in this situation.

Until 2006 it was possible as well, in Scotland, to prove a marriage "by cohabitation with habit and repute". This rule has been abolished with effect from May 4, 2006. (Family Law (Scotland) Act 2006 s.3). That abolition is, however, prospective only; couples whose living arrangements began before that date may still be able to take advantage of the rule—see s.3(2) of the Act. In *SSWP v AB (BB)* [2022] UKUT 83 (AAC) Judge Ward allowed an appeal against an award of Bereavement Benefit that had been made by an FTT. The parties had been living together since 2000 and the male partner died in 2019, but the deceased had not divorced his wife until 2016. This meant that until then he lacked the capacity to marry. An earlier case, *Vosilius v Vosilius* 2000 SCLR 679, had established that whilst either of the parties lacked capacity to marry the necessary period of cohabitation by habit and repute could not commence. In the present case Judge Ward decided that this rule meant that the claimant could not take advantage of the exemption because it meant that her cohabitation, as a matter of law rather than of fact, began only after 2006. But his decision was made without argument. Although the claimant had asked for a hearing (which the judge held was not justified in this case) her advisers put forward no argument in rebuttal of the point made above even though they were invited to do so. This is a pity because although (as the Judge points out) the claimant might have had a difficult case to make, it might have been argued that the words "cohabitation with habit and repute" as used in s.3(2) referred to the factual situation as it existed before 2006. The claimant would then have had only 3 years of living together to rely upon, but the character of those years might have been viewed in the light of the longer period.

In the special case of widow or a widower whose marriage was celebrated outside the United Kingdom and has subsequently been discovered to have been invalid, the rule may still be applied even if the cohabitation with habit and repute began after May 2006. But this will only apply where the surviving party became aware of the invalidity of the marriage after the spouse's death—see s.3 (3) and s.3 (4).

In its modern form, proof of marriage by cohabitation with habit and repute, required that the parties prove that they were free to marry, that they were, or had been, cohabiting in Scotland as husband and wife (there appears to have been no suggestion that this might extend to civil partnerships) and that they had done so for a sufficient period of time- generally this meant a long time. More problematically, they must have been reputed to be husband and wife; this meant not merely that they lived as if they were married to each other, but that people generally believed that they were so married. Given modern attitudes to cohabitation it seems unlikely that the rule would have had much scope for application. For more detailed information about this form of marriage see earlier editions of this book.

Foreign marriages, and divorces, raise difficult and often obscure points of law that may depend upon proof of foreign law. It is impossible to deal fully with these points in this note. Tribunals which require assistance on matters of foreign law should identify the party raising the issue that required proof of foreign law and require that party to obtain suitable evidence. Note that the foreign law as found by a Commissioner is a finding of fact. When the Commissioner applies that law it does not thereby become a part of the social security law being used by the Commissioner. This means that a subsequent tribunal is not bound to accept the same conclusion as to the foreign law as has been accepted in a previous Commissioner's decision. In the absence of a contrary expert opinion a tribunal will doubtless accept the view adopted in an earlier decision when that is provided to them, but where there is conflicting expert evidence available, the tribunal must consider all of the evidence and choose that which is most persuasive to them.

This was the course adopted in *R(G) 2/00*. The issue there was the validity of a foreign marriage which itself depended upon the recognition of the previous divorce of one of the parties. The divorce was by talaq in Bangladesh in 1973. Earlier Commissioners' decisions had accepted that a talaq divorce would be recognised only when the formalities had included its notification to the Chairman of the Union Council. In the present case, new expert evidence was given to the effect that, at the time when Bangladesh was only very recently created as a state, there was no such official. In any case, further evidence suggested that more recently talaq divorces were accepted in Bangladesh as valid without notification and might therefore be recognised in English law also. In this case, the Commissioner upheld the decision of a tribunal which had accepted the validity of the divorce and subsequent marriage (and therefore awarded a widow's pension) notwithstanding the contrary conclusion in earlier cases. Other cases involving foreign law include *R(G) 4/93* (marriage celebrated in Bangladesh) and *R(G) 1/94* (talaq divorce). Note that a talaq divorce, even if valid by the law of domicile of the parties, cannot be effective if it is proclaimed in this country. This is because s.16 of the Domicile and Matrimonial Proceedings Act 1973, provides that no proceedings in this country shall be regarded as validly dissolving marriage unless those proceedings are instituted in a court of law.

The capacity of a person to marry is determined by that person's domicile (see below) at the time of the marriage, but the formalities of a marriage (sometimes referred to as the formal validity of that marriage) are determined by the law of the place that the marriage takes place (often referred to as the *lex loci celebrationus*). Thus, an Englishman can effect a valid marriage in Las Vegas, or on the beach in the Bahamas, provided that the ceremony is in accordance with the law of that place. Further complications arise, however, where the place that the marriage occurs is unclear. That was the problem in *SB v SSWP* [2014] UKUT 495 (AAC), [2015] AACR 15. The claimant was the widow of a man originally from Pakistan. She married him in Pakistan and had had three children by him. Her claim for bereavement benefits had been refused because there was evidence that the deceased had been married already at the time of the claimant's marriage and there was no evidence that that marriage had been dissolved, or that his first wife had predeceased him. The factual background was confused, but by the time the case came before the Upper Tribunal it had become clear that the earlier marriage had been conducted by telephone at a time that the deceased was in the UK and the putative wife was in Pakistan. The question was, therefore, by what law the ceremony of marriage should be governed when the parties were in different places; or to put it another way—what is the place of a marriage transacted on the telephone? The decision of Judge West in the UT is unequivocal—to be valid the marriage must be valid by the laws of both places. As a telephone marriage is not valid in the UK it followed that the first marriage of the deceased had been void and that the claimant's marriage was, therefore, good and her claim succeeded. This appears to be the first time that the validity of a telephonic marriage has been determined in English law. The decision of Judge West was in accordance with the revised opinion expressed on behalf of the Secretary of State and represented the considered views of other departments of state (e.g. the Border Agency) to whom these are matters of great concern.

Even proving the existence of a marriage that is claimed to have been celebrated in a foreign country may be difficult where there is, or was at the time, little formality in connection with the ceremony and no reliable records of marriages are maintained The difficulties associated with proof of some marriages have been demonstrated in *CP/4062/2004* and again in *CP/891/2008*. In both these cases the parties had been married in Yemen from where no formal record of the marriage was available. Both parties to the marriage made statements about the celebration of the marriage and the wife, who had remained at all times in Yemen, was interviewed there through an interpreter. Some of the information that was given about the marriage appeared to be contradictory. For that reason, and others, the claim for a Category B pension was refused. The interest in both of these cases lies in the approach taken by Commissioner Jacobs, and adopted in the later case by Deputy Commissioner Wikeley, to the absence of reliable documentary evidence of the marriage. In both cases the DM and the appeal tribunal had relied upon that absence, at least in part, as the reason for their decision that no marriage had been shown to exist. The commissioners find this to be a wrong approach. In the words of Commissioner Jacobs the absence of contemporary documentary evidence

> "is a neutral factor. The decision maker and the tribunal have to decide if the claimant is genuine or dishonest. It is wrong to approach that task by taking the lack of contemporaneous evidence as a factor against the claimant. To do so would be to assume what has to be decided."

This point has been reiterated in *AR v SSWP* [2012] UKUT 467 (AAC). There the question was whether it could be proved that the claimant's late husband had been divorced from his first wife at the time of his marriage to the claimant. Both marriages and the alleged divorce had taken place in the Yemen where there was no official record kept. In the UT, Judge Wikeley, was able to allow the appeal and substitute his own decision largely because a retirement pension, awarded on the basis of her husband's contribution record, had already been in payment to the claimant for more than 13 years. Payment was stopped when the department received a claim from another woman in the Yemen also claiming to be a widow of the deceased husband. This was his first wife whom the claimant said had been divorced before her own marriage. The FTT had approached the question on the basis that the claimant would have to prove the validity of that divorce in order to succeed in her claim. Judge Wikeley points out that this was an error of law. As the pension was already in payment the onus of proof rested with the department to prove that her husband had not been divorced so that the claimant's marriage was polygamous—as to which see below. On the evidence before him the judge was able to find that they had not done so. 1.1103

Further consideration of the way in which evidence as to the existence of a marriage should be approached has been given in *SA v SSWP* [2013] 436 (AAC). The claim for bereavement benefits had been rejected for various reasons, but by the time the matter came before Judge Wikeley in the UT it was settled that the issue concerned a possible earlier marriage of the deceased to a wife who had remained in Bangladesh and by whom he had claimed, some years earlier, to have had four children. Evidence of this claim (and therefore the marriage) was contained in a statutory declaration that the deceased had made to the tax authority in this country. In the FTT the claim for bereavement benefit made by the woman now claiming to have been his wife was refused. They found that a claimed talaq divorce from his alleged first wife was invalid because by the time of the divorce he was already domiciled in the UK (see below) and consequently his marriage to the claimant was bigamous and invalid. But the question remained-was he ever in fact married in Bangladesh? The FTT held that the evidence provided by the statutory declaration was decisive; they said that there would need to be "the strongest possible evidence" to rebut the conclusion that the deceased had been married. Judge Wikeley found this to be an error of law. (The representative of the SSWP had supported that view). The judge found that while a statutory declaration is more "than a statement written down" so as to reflect the formality and solemnity with which it is made, it still needs to be examined within the context of all the other evidence presented with it. In this case there was a considerable amount of contrary evidence. In particular the claimant's representative had suggested that the deceased's declaration had probably been made untruthfully to gain some advantage in relation to his tax coding. The judge found that on the totality of the evidence before him it was probable that the deceased had not been married in Bangladesh and he adds an appendix that refers to some research of his own that would give credence to the explanation offered by the representative.

Polygamous marriages raise special problems of their own. As the law stands, a marriage which is actually polygamous will not be recognised as a valid marriage at all—even when only one wife is in this country. However, where the marriage is only potentially polygamous or was previously polygamous, but is no longer so, it will be treated as a valid marriage for any period in which it is in fact monogamous (See reg.2 of the Social Security and Family Allowances (Polygamous Marriages) Regulations 1975 (SI 1975/561)). But the marriage must be valid according to the foreign law in question, and a person domiciled in England at the time cannot contract a valid polygamous marriage. See s.11(d) of the Matrimonial Causes Act 1973). There have been several recent Commissioners' decisions on this point. All of them involve parties from the Indian subcontinent who have married there, then come to live in the UK (or at least the husband has) and then returned to India for a period during which the husband has contracted a second marriage. This second marriage is valid by the law of, say, Bangladesh, but will not be valid in English law if the husband at the time of that marriage had acquired a domicile of choice in the UK. If he was then domiciled in the UK the second marriage is void and his first marriage remains legally monogamous. In the event of his death the first wife may then claim a widow's pension whether she is resident in the UK or not (*R(G) 1/95*).

1.1104 Note the importance of identifying the time at which the domicile of the parties, or one of them, must be determined. See the decision of Judge Wikeley in *SB v SSWP* [2010] UKUT 219 (AAC) where the critical point was the domicile of the husband at the time of his marriage to the claimant. If he were then domiciled in England that marriage was polygamous and so invalid, but if he were then domiciled in Bangladesh, it was a valid polygamous marriage by the law of that country and his other wife having predeceased him, the claimant was now his only surviving widow, and entitled to the benefit.

The capacity of a person to marry (or divorce) is determined by that person's domicile at that time. Domicile is a technical status and often poses a complex question of law. In *R(G) 1/93*, the Commissioner relied upon the principle set out in the standard work, Dicey and Morris, *Conflict of Laws*. He puts it as follows:

> "Under English law every person receives a domicile of origin at birth and, throughout his life, cannot ever be without a domicile and, further, at any one time, can only have one domicile. However, a person can acquire a domicile of choice by residing in a country, other than that of his domicile of origin, with the intention of staying there either permanently or indefinitely. All surrounding circumstances must be taken into account when determining whether a person has acquired a domicile of choice, including his motive for taking up residence initially and whether or not that residence was precarious. A person may abandon a domicile of choice only if he both ceases to reside and ceases to intend to reside there; it is not, for example, necessary to show a positive intention not to return, it suffices to prove an absence of intention to continue to reside. When a person abandons a domicile of choice he either acquires a new domicile of choice or his domicile of origin revives."

In the present case the Commissioner substituted his own decision for that of the tribunal. He found that the husband had a domicile of origin in what is now Bangladesh; had acquired a domicile of choice by many years of residence in the UK, but that he had abandoned that domicile of choice when he returned to Bangladesh for a period of two years and tried to set up business there. It was at that time that he married a second wife. Subsequently, he returned to England and to his first wife who had remained here all along. At the time of his death in England he may well have re-acquired his domicile of choice here but that was not important.

What mattered was his domicile at the time of the second marriage. Since that was in Bangladesh the marriage was valid and since both wives survived him they were both polygamous marriages. Neither wife could therefore claim a widow's pension.

The importance of determining the deceased's domicile at the time of marriage has been reiterated in another case before Judge Wikeley in *SSWP v MN (BB)* [2018] UKUT 68 (AAC). In his case the first wife had predeceased her husband, but there were insufficient facts found by the FTT from which to determine his domicile at the time of his second marriage; if at that time he had already acquired a domicile of choice in England and Wales his marriage to the claimant was invalid under the Matrimonial Causes Act 1973 which meant that she was not married to him at all and hence could not be a surviving spouse for the purposes of a claim for Bereavement Benefit.

Even where no issue of domicile arises it will still be necessary for the claimant to show that her marriage was in fact monogamous at the time of her husband's death. Where the marriage has been polygamous at some earlier time that may require proof either that all other wives have predeceased their husband or that the earlier marriage has been dissolved by a valid decree of divorce as well as proof that the claimant's own marriage was valid. All of these issues arose in *CG/1822/1998*. Deputy Commissioner Gamble gave extensive instructions to the legally qualified member of the tribunal, to whom the decision was returned, which other tribunals may find of assistance.

The complications of qualifying for a widow's benefit and the difficulties that can arise in determining the validity of the claimant's foreign marriage when that in turn depends upon a foreign divorce, are graphically illustrated in *CP/3108/2004*.

The divorce and marriage had taken place in Pakistan in 1961 so this required consideration of no fewer than three recognition statutes, and two versions of the common law. Perhaps the most interesting feature of this case is, however, that the claimant was the second widow to claim a pension on the basis of marriage to the same husband; both claims have gone before a Commissioner and both have been successful! There are, therefore, conflicting decisions as to the validity of the same divorce. Commissioner Edward Jacobs points out that at the moment there is no way effectively to avoid the possibility of this happening. He suggests that there should be a power for the Secretary of State to refer decisions to be considered together by a Tribunal or by a Commissioner. An appeal to the Court of Appeal might be expected, but the decision in respect of the first widow is now probably out of time.

The effect of the Human Rights Act on the treatment of polygamous marriages has been considered by a Tribunal of Commissioners considering appeals in three cases. (*R(P)2/06*).

In all of them both marriages had taken place in Bangladesh and all the partners **1.1105**
had been domiciled there at the time of those marriages. Both marriages would therefore be regarded by English Law as valid marriages for most purposes. However, it was accepted that for widow's benefits the Court Appeal had decided in *(Fuljuan) Bibi v CAO* [1998] 1 F.L.R. 375 that where a man was survived by two polygamously married wives neither of them could qualify as his "widow" for the purpose of claiming benefits. The question was, therefore, whether this treatment amounted to an improper interpretation of the legislation in the light of the Human Rights Act. It was conceded, at least before the commissioners, that the claim engaged their rights under Art.8 (right to family life) and it was argued that disqualifying a polygamous wife was unlawful discrimination under Art.14. All of the tribunal held that it was not. A majority (Chief Commissioner Hickinbottom and Commissioner Howell) held that to treat a person who was polygamously married at the relevant time, differently from one who was monogamously (even if potentially polygamously) married, was not discrimination within any of the grounds of Art.14. In their view it was a difference of treatment based upon a factual difference that was rational and in accordance with the accepted norms of our society, and therefore, not discrimination.

Perhaps more convincingly, Commissioner Levenson held that it was discrimination on the grounds of "status", but that it was justified and proportional for the same reasons.

A marriage lasts until it is dissolved by a decree of divorce or of annulment. In either case the marriage persists until the decree absolute is granted. Foreign divorces raise the same problems as foreign marriages. Recognition is provided for under s.46 of the Family Law Act 1986. Foreign divorces will be recognised where they are valid by the law of the country in which they are obtained and if, at that time, either party to the marriage was habitually resident in that country, or was domiciled there, or was a national of that country. Where a marriage is void, for example, because it is bigamous, it has no legal effect whatsoever, and no benefits can be claimed on the basis of it. Where, however, a marriage is annulled for a reason that makes it only voidable, for example because of non-consummation, it is now clear that the marriage is to be regarded as valid and subsisting up to the date of annulment (see Nullity of Marriage Act 1975 s.5 and *R(G) 1/85*).

Proof of death

1.1106 The death of the claimant's spouse is usually proved by production of the death certificate. Difficulties can arise, however, where no certificate is issued because the spouse has simply disappeared. Since October 1, 2014 it has been possible in England and Wales to apply to the High Court for a declaration of presumption of death. (The same has been possible in Scotland since 1977). The application may be made where the court is satisfied that a person has died, or where that cannot be established that they have not been known to be alive for a period of at least 7 years. Any person may make the application, but the person who is missing must have been domiciled in this country or to have been resident here for at least one year when they were last known to be alive and where the applicant is the spouse or civil partner of the missing person they too, must be either domiciled in this country or to have been resident here for a year at the date the application is made. Where the application is made by a person who is not a spouse, civil partner or a close relative the court must refuse to make the declaration if they consider that the application does not have a sufficient interest in that decision. Where the court is satisfied that the person has died the declaration will include a finding as to the date and time of death; where that is uncertain it will be at the end of the period after which the court is satisfied that they have died. Where the court cannot be satisfied that the person is dead, but is satisfied that they have been missing and not known to have been alive for at least seven years, the finding will be that they have died at the end of the seven years after they were last known to have been alive. Although this jurisdiction applies only to the High Court the act does not abolish the power of any other court or tribunal to make a decision based upon the common law presumption of death. Thus it appears possible for social security tribunals to continue to consider an application for bereavement benefits on that basis. In doing so it appears to have been accepted that the decision can be based on either a finding that the missing person has died (where on the evidence it is appropriate to do so) or, on the basis that death can be presumed because the person has been missing and not known to have been alive for at least seven years. (See the High Court decision in *Chard v Chard* [1956] P. 259) That this is the correct approach seems to be confirmed by s.16 of the Presumption of Death Act because that section requires any other court or tribunal making such a determination to include the requirements of s.2 as to date and time of death. Note, however, that the Act does not require that a spouse or civil partner who is seeking that finding before a tribunal to be domiciled or resident in this country, so it would appear to be possible still for a widow living overseas to make a claim based on that presumption.

Special provision is now made in ss.3 and 4 of the Administration Act for late claims to be made in respect of a death which is only recently discovered or presumed so that such spouses can claim back-payment of benefit in respect of a period of more than the usual one year. Note, however, that in the case of a widow who had only just discovered the fact of her husband's death, though that may have occurred several years earlier, the effect of s.3 is only to permit a claim for back-payment of benefit for up to 24 months at most (see *CG/75/96*).

There is one situation in which a spouse will forfeit all their rights to bereavement benefit though it is not mentioned in the legislation at all. This is where the claimant has been guilty of the homicide of the spouse (see *R. v Chief N.I. Commissioner Ex p. Connor* [1981] 1 Q.B. 758). The rule is one of public policy, based upon the principle that no one should profit by their own wrongdoing and applies generally to all interests deriving from the death of the deceased.

At common law the consequence of the forfeiture rule was that the spouse lost the pension rights entirely, but since the introduction of the Forfeiture Act 1982, it has been possible for a Commissioner (now a judge of the Upper Tribunal) to modify the effect of the rule. Under the Forfeiture Act 1982, the question whether a spouse's right to any benefit is to be forfeited must be determined at first instance by the UT. The matter can no longer come before an appeal tribunal though where the UT has determined that the right to benefit is not to be forfeited, any other issues as to entitlement should be determined by a decision-maker in the usual way, unless the claimant has consented to the UT deciding the matter (*R(G) 3/84*).

Not all homicides will result in forfeiture. Even before 1982 the courts had developed some exceptions to the rule, e.g. in motor manslaughter cases and, later, in cases of diminished responsibility where the level of culpability was non-existent. Now, however, the Court of Appeal has suggested (in *Dunbar v Plant* [1997] 4 All E.R. 289) that the better approach is to regard the forfeiture rule as applicable to all homicides and to leave any relief against the rule to be achieved using the Forfeiture Act. In *Dunbar v Plant* the rule was applied to the property rights of the survivor of a suicide pact, though the majority of that court thought that she should then be relieved from any forfeiture at all, so that she took both the title to joint property by survivorship, and the proceeds of an insurance policy on the life of her partner. In that case also the Court of Appeal settles a point previously the subject of dispute; it is now clear that the Forfeiture Act permits the court (the UT) to remove the effect of forfeiture entirely where it is appropriate to do so.

In *CFP/2688/2004* (to be reported as *R(FP) 1/05*) Commissioner Rowland confirms that the effect of *Dunbar v Plant* is that the forfeiture rule should normally apply in all cases where the UT is satisfied that the claimant is guilty of manslaughter. That applies even where the claimant may have been acquitted of manslaughter in the Crown Court, as in *Gray v Barr* [1971] 2 Q.B. 554.

Commissioner Rowland does leave open the possibility, however, that the UT could find a conviction of manslaughter on the ground of diminished responsibility to be inappropriate, and conclude that the claimant should be regarded instead, as not guilty of homicide by reason of insanity. This could happen, for example, where the claimant has pleaded guilty to manslaughter on the ground of diminished responsibility and a hospital order has been imposed, rather than to have stood trial and pleaded not guilty to murder by reason of insanity. In such a case, if the UT finds that a claimant should have been found not guilty by reason of insanity, the rule of forfeiture would not apply at all. It is likely, however, that it will be more usual for the forfeiture rule to be applied and the UT then grant full, or partial, relief against that forfeiture. In the present case no relief was allowed because the sum involved was only 47p per week and the commissioner felt its loss reflected the role of the claimant in causing the death of his wife.

The Act, however, does not permit any relief where the party claiming has committed murder. A spouse convicted of murder, therefore, must lose all bereavement benefits—see *R(G) 1/90*. In *R(FG) 1/04* the claimant had been convicted of soliciting her husband's murder (an offence under the Offences Against the Person Act, 1861). She claimed a widow's pension after her release from prison. The Commissioner held that the forfeiture rule applied to her claim because she had "unlawfully counselled" her husband's death within s.1(2) of the Forfeiture Act 1982, but that it was not caught by s.5 of that Act which proscribed any relief where the claimant was convicted of murder. This meant that it was open to the Commissioner to modify the effect of forfeiture. On the facts of this case however, he held that no modification was appropriate because she had been closely and directly involved in the murder. Where the spouse has been convicted only of manslaughter the matter will depend upon all the circumstances of the case, in particular upon the degree of culpability inherent in the act (compare *R(G) 1/83 and R(G) 3/84*) and upon whether the killing was the result of provocation—see *R(G) 1/98* where the Commissioner restored benefits from the date of his decision, some seven years after the death, and limited, to 50 per cent, the widow's future entitlement to a Category B pension. *BC v SSWP* [2014] UKUT 237 (AAC) is a further example of the claimant's being relieved entirely of the effect of the forfeiture rule. The claimant had been convicted of the manslaughter of her husband after pleading guilty at trial. The death resulted from a drunken brawl after many years in a violent marriage. The trial judge imposed only a 3 year period of probation as her sentence. The Upper Tribunal Judge took account of the leniency of the sentence in deciding that the relief against forfeiture should be given in full- thus the claimant was able to rely upon her deceased husband's contribution record in now making a claim for retirement pension. Although the claimant had delayed making her claim for many years (and the rules against back-dating a claim would apply) the relief was granted, with effect from the date of her conviction, so that she was able to take advantage of the enhancement by deferment that had occurred. In *CFG 4622/03* the claimant had been convicted of manslaughter of his wife on his own admission (the jury having been directed to find him not guilty of murder because of his wife's provocation). The Commissioner, taking account of the comments made by the judge in passing sentence, applied the rule of forfeiture to the bereavement payment, but relieved him of forfeiture in all other respects so that he was entitled to Widowed Parent's Allowance in respect of 2 children for whom he was responsible, and for any potential pension entitlement that he might have as a result of his wife's contributions. And note the decision of Judge Wikeley in *ES (deceased) (FRP)* [2022] UKUT 48 (AAC), where entitlement to an underpayment of Retirement Pension was reduced because, although the deceased had been convicted only of manslaughter by reason of diminished responsibility (she had a severe depressive illness) the trial judge had found there to be a "measure of deliberation" about her crime. Judge Wikeley thought that this should be reflected by a reduction of 25% to the significant sum that was due to her estate.

Note that it is not necessary that the spouse should have been convicted of the homicide; it is enough that they have committed it. Accordingly, when bereavement benefits have been paid between the death and the conviction (or more usually apprehension) there will be an overpayment that is almost certainly recoverable. Note as well, that although forfeiture is mandatory following a conviction for murder, there is no principle under which there must necessarily be relief when the claimant is convicted of manslaughter. In *R(G) 1/91* the claimant's conviction of murder was quashed, because some evidence was admitted that was technically hearsay, but a sentence of life imprisonment was imposed and the Commissioner held that there should be no relief of the forfeiture rule.

Bereavement support payment: contribution condition and amendments

1.1107 **31**—(1) For the purposes of section 30(1)(d) the contribution condition is that, for at least one tax year during the deceased's working life—

(a) he or she actually paid Class 1 or Class 2 national insurance contributions, and

(b) those contributions give rise to an earnings factor (or total earnings factors) equal to or greater than 25 times the lower earnings limit for the tax year.

(2) For earnings factors, see sections 22 and 23 of the Social Security Contributions and Benefits Act 1992.

(3) For the purposes of section 30(1)(d) the contribution condition is to be treated as met if the deceased was an employed earner and died as a result of—

(a) a personal injury of the kind mentioned in section 94(1) of the Social Security Contributions and Benefits Act 1992, or
(b) a disease or personal injury of the kind mentioned in section 108(1) of that Act.

(4) In this section the following expressions have the meaning given by section 122(1) of the Social Security Contributions and Benefits Act 1992—

"employed earner",
"lower earnings limit",
"tax year", and
"working life".

(5) Schedule 16 contains amendments to do with bereavement support payment.

General Note

The condition specified in this section - that the deceased person must have "actually paid" NI contributions to the requisite (albeit modest) extent - has been found to be discriminatory in two cases. The first, *O'Donnell v Department for Communities* [2020] NICA 36 was a decision of the CA in Northern Ireland. The second, *R. (Jwanczuk)* [2022] EWHC 2298, is a decision of the High Court in England & Wales. In both cases the deceased person was disabled so that they had been unable to undertake any form of employment throughout their life. In the first case the court found that the section treated the deceased in the same way as it would a person who had chosen not to undertake any form of employment and was therefore discriminatory in the *Thlimmenos* sense (treating cases in a like manner when their circumstances are different) and refusal of benefit was a breach of the claimant's Human Rights. In the second case Kerr J did not regard himself as bound by the earlier decision, but having found that the cases were "on all fours" factually, and that both the conclusions reached and the reasons for doing so in that decision were correct, he chose to follow the earlier decision. He also adopted the same remedy that had been applied in that case. The CA in NI having observed that s.31(3) already provided that the contribution condition should be treated as being met where the deceased had died as a result of industrial injury or disease, they felt able to read into that subsection a third exception in the case of a person "unable to comply with s.30(1) throughout her working life due to disability". The decision in *R. (on the application of Jwanczuk) v SSWP* [2022] EWHC 2298 (Admin), has been upheld in the Court of Appeal—see *R. (on the application of Jwanczuk) v SSWP* [2023] EWCA Civ 1156; [2024] 2 W.L.R. 795. 1.1108

Bereavement support payment: prisoners

32—(1) The Secretary of State may by regulations provide that a person is not to be paid bereavement support payment for any period during which the person is a prisoner. 1.1109

(2) "Prisoner" means a person (in Great Britain or elsewhere) who is—

(a) imprisoned or detained in legal custody, or
(b) unlawfully at large.

(3) In the case of a person remanded in custody for an offence, regulations under subsection (1) may be made so as to apply only if a sentence of a specified description is later imposed on the person for the offence.

PART 7

FINAL PROVISIONS

Power to make consequential amendments etc

1.1110 **53.**—(1) The Secretary of State or the Treasury may by order make consequential, incidental or supplementary provision in connection with any provision made by this Act.

(2) An order under this section may amend, repeal, revoke or otherwise modify any enactment (whenever passed or made).

(3) "Enactment" includes an enactment contained in subordinate legislation within the meaning of the Interpretation Act 1978.

Regulations and orders

1.1111 **54.**—(1) Regulations and orders under this Act are to be made by statutory instrument.

(2) A statutory instrument containing (whether alone or with other provisions)—

(a) regulations under section 3, 17, 18(3) or (5), 19, 20, 30, 32 or 34,
(b) the first regulations under section 10,
(c) an order under section 53 that amends or repeals a provision of an Act,
(d) regulations under Schedule 17,
(e) regulations under paragraph 2 of Schedule 18 or regulations under paragraph 7 of that Schedule that amend a provision of an Act,
(f) the first regulations under paragraph 1 or 3 of that Schedule, [[1] or
(g) the first regulations under paragraph 1 or 3 of that Schedule that make provision in relation to collective money purchase schemes within the meaning of Part 1 of the Pension Schemes Act 2021 (see section 1 of that Act)],

may not be made unless a draft of the instrument has been laid before and approved by a resolution of each House of Parliament.

(3) Any other statutory instrument containing regulations or an order under this Act is subject to annulment in pursuance of a resolution of either House of Parliament.

(4) Subsection (3) does not apply to a statutory instrument containing an order under section 56(1), (6) or (8) only.

(5) A power to make regulations or an order under this Act may be used—

(a) to make different provision for different purposes;
(b) in relation to all or only some of the purposes for which it may be used.

(6) Regulations or orders under this Act may include incidental, supplementary, consequential, transitional, transitory or saving provision.

AMENDMENTS

1. Pensions Schemes Act 2021 s.48 and Sch.3 para.24(3) (December 13, 2021).

Extent

1.1112 **55.**—(1) This Act extends to England and Wales and Scotland only, subject to the following provisions of this section.

(2) Any amendment or repeal made by this Act has the same extent as the enactment to which it relates.

(3) This Part extends also to Northern Ireland.

Commencement

56.—(1) This Act comes into force on such day or days as the Secretary of State may by order appoint, subject as follows. **1.1113**

(2) The following come into force on the day on which this Act is passed—

(a) section 29;

(b) section 51;

(c) this Part.

(3) The following come into force at the end of the period of 2 months beginning with the day on which this Act is passed—

(a) Part 3;

(b) sections 34 and 35;

(c) section 41;

(d) sections 47 and 48;

(e) paragraph 30(2) of Schedule 13.

(4) Part 1 comes into force on 6 April 2016, so far as not brought into force earlier by an order under subsection (1).

(5) The Secretary of State may by order—

(a) amend subsection (4) so as to replace the reference to 6 April 2016 with a later date, and

(b) make corresponding amendments in Part 1 or any enactment amended by it.

(6) Section 52 comes into force on such day or days as the Treasury may by order appoint.

(7) An order under subsection (1) or (6) may appoint different days for different purposes.

(8) The Secretary of State may by order make transitional, transitory or saving provision in connection with the coming into force of any provision of this Act.

GENERAL NOTE

All the provisions relevant to the new state pension came into effect on or before April 6, 2016 (the earlier introduction of some provisions being to allow regulations to be made). The power in subs. (5) was not used. That being so, this volume does not include the various commencement regulations under which provisions were introduced before April 6, 2016. If reference need to be made to a particular date, then this can be seen most conveniently in the schedule to the last of the eight commencement orders used to introduce the provisions of the Act. See Pensions Act (Commencement No.8) Order 2016 (SI 2016/203) made on February 22, 2016, where the other commencement orders are also detailed. **1.1114**

Short title

57.—This Act may be cited as the Pensions Act 2014. **1.1115**

SCHEDULE 1

TRANSITIONAL RATE OF STATE PENSION: CALCULATING THE AMOUNT

PART 1

INTRODUCTION

1.1116 1 (1) This Schedule sets out how to calculate the amounts used to work out the transitional rate of a person's state pension.

(2) Part 2 of the Schedule sets out how to calculate the amount for a person's pre-commencement qualifying years.

(3) Part 3 of the Schedule sets out how to calculate the amount for a person's post-commencement qualifying years (if any).

PART 2

AMOUNT FOR PRE-COMMENCEMENT QUALIFYING YEARS

How to calculate the amount for pre-commencement qualifying years

1.1117 2 A person's amount for pre-commencement qualifying years is calculated as follows.

Step 1 - calculate the person's pension under the old system

Calculate the weekly rate based on the old state pension and graduated retirement benefit (see paragraph 3 for more about this).

Step 2 - calculate a pension based on the new system

Calculate the weekly rate based on the new state pension (see paragraph 4 for more about this).

Step 3 - take whichever rate is higher (the foundation amount)

Take whichever of the rates found under Steps 1 and 2 is higher.

Step 4 - revalue to date when the person reached pensionable age

Revalue the amount of that rate in accordance with paragraph 6.

The amount for the person's pre-commencement qualifying years is the amount as revalued under Step 4.

Step 1: calculation of the person's pension under the old system

3 (1) For the purposes of Step 1 of the calculation in paragraph 2, the weekly rate based on the old state pension and graduated retirement benefit is

(a) the rate of any Category A retirement pension and graduated retirement benefit to which the person would have been entitled if the person had reached pensionable age on 6 April 2016, or

(b) the rate of any graduated retirement benefit to which the person would have been entitled under section 36(7) of the National Insurance Act 1965 (persons not entitled to retirement pension) if the person had reached pensionable age on that date.

(2) The following rules apply for the purposes of calculating that rate.

(3) Calculate the rate that would have had effect on 6 April 2016 (but see subparagraph (6)).

(4) Ignore—

(a) the amendments made by paragraphs 53 and 55 of Schedule 12 (which limit Category A retirement pensions and graduated retirement benefit to people who reach pensionable age before 6 April 2016);

(b) any requirement to make a claim;

(c) any provision suspending payment of, or disqualifying a person from receiving, any amount;

(d) section 45B of the Contributions and Benefits Act (reduction of additional pension because of pension sharing);

(e) section 37 of the National Insurance Act 1965 (graduated retirement benefit for widows etc).

(5) Read the reference in section 45(4)(b) of the Contributions and Benefits Act (additional pension) to a person's working life as a reference to the period—

(a) beginning with the tax year in which the person reached 16, and

(b) ending with the tax year before the one in which the person actually reached pensionable age.

(6) If an order under section 150 or 150A of the Administration Act (up-rating) is made before 6 April 2016 and it provides for an increase to come into force after that date, it is to be treated for the purposes of calculating the rate under this paragraph as having already come into force.

(7) Where regulations under section 22(5ZA) of the Contributions and Benefits Act have the effect that a person is credited, on or after 6 April 2016, with earnings or contributions for a tax year starting before that date, the earnings or contributions are to be treated for the purposes of calculating the rate under this paragraph as having been credited before 6 April 2016.

(8) A determination under section 48A(2) of the Pension Schemes Act 1993 (contracting-out: reinstatement in state scheme following payment of contributions equivalent premium) made on or after 6 April 2016 is to be treated for the purposes of calculating the rate under this paragraph as having been made before 6 April 2016.

Step 2: calculation of a pension based on the new system

4 (1) For the purposes of Step 2 of the calculation in paragraph 2, the weekly rate based on the new state pension is as follows.

(2) If the person has 35 or more pre-commencement qualifying years, the rate is equal to—

(a) the full rate of the state pension on 6 April 2016, less

(b) any amount to reflect contracting out under the old system (see paragraph 5).

(3) If the person has fewer than 35 pre-commencement qualifying years, the rate is equal to—

(a) the appropriate proportion of the full rate of the state pension on 6 April 2016, less

(b) any amount to reflect contracting out under the old system (see paragraph 5).

(4) The "appropriate proportion", in relation to a person, is—

5 (1) In paragraph 4(2) and (3) references to an "amount to reflect contracting out under the old system" are to an amount equal to any difference between—

(a) the amount of any additional pension included in the Category A retirement pension calculated for the purposes of Step 1 of the calculation in paragraph 2, and

(b) the amount of any additional pension that would have been included if—

(i) sections 46 and 48A of the Pension Schemes Act 1993 were ignored, and

(ii) for the purposes of calculating the amounts referred to in section 45(2)(c) and (d) of the Contributions and Benefits Act any earnings paid to or for the benefit of the person in respect of contracted-out employment were treated as if they were not in respect of contracted-out employment.

(2) "Contracted-out employment" means employment qualifying a person for a pension provided by a salary related contracted-out scheme, a money purchase contracted-out scheme or an appropriate personal pension scheme (and expressions used in this definition have the same meaning as in the Pension Schemes Act 1993).

Step 4: revaluation

6 (1) This paragraph determines how the amount mentioned in Step 4 of the calculation in paragraph 2 is to be revalued for the purposes of that Step.

(2) If the amount is equal to or less than the full rate of the state pension on 6 April 2016, the amount is to be revalued in accordance with increases in the full rate of the state pension (see sub-paragraph (4)).

(3) If the amount is greater than the full rate of the state pension on 6 April 2016—

(a) so much of the amount as is equal to the full rate of the state pension on 6 April 2016 is to be revalued in accordance with increases in the full rate of the state pension (see sub-paragraph (4)), and

(b) so much of the amount as exceeds the full rate of the state pension on that date is to be revalued in accordance with increases in the general level of prices (see sub-paragraph (5)).

(4) For the purposes of sub-paragraphs (2) and (3)(a), an amount is revalued in accordance with increases in the full rate of the state pension by increasing it by the same percentage as any increase in the full rate of the state pension in the period—

(a) beginning with 6 April 2016, and

(b) ending with the day on which the person reached pensionable age.

(5) For the purposes of sub-paragraph (3)(b), an amount is revalued in accordance with increases in the general level of prices by adding—

(a) the amount, and

(b) the amount multiplied by the revaluing percentage specified in the last order under section 148AC(3) of the Administration Act to come into force before the person reached pensionable age.

PART 3

AMOUNT FOR POST-COMMENCEMENT QUALIFYING YEARS

1.1118 7 (1) A person's amount for post-commencement qualifying years (if any) is calculated as follows.

(2) If the person has 35 or more post-commencement qualifying years, the amount is equal to the full rate of the state pension on the day on which the person reached pensionable age.

(3) If the person has fewer than 35 post-commencement qualifying years, the amount is equal to the following proportion of the full rate of the state pension on the day on which the person reached pensionable age—

1/35 x number of person's post commencement qualifying years

GENERAL NOTE

Paragraph 4

1.1119 In *FE v Secretary of State for Work & Pensions* (RP) [2019] UKUT 61 (AAC) Upper Tribunal Judge Wikeley held that (a) pre-March 2001 periods of Australian residency were to be taken into account for the purposes of Step 1, but (b) to be ignored for the purposes of Step 2. The reason for (a) is that, until March 2001, a Reciprocal Social Security Agreement between the UK and Australia had effect and the recognition of Australian periods of residency provided for by the Agreement are preserved in relation to the benefits mentioned in s.299 of the Pensions Act 2004, which includes retirement pension. Step 1 is concerned with how a claimant's retirement pension (as opposed to the new state pension) would have been calculated. The reason for (b) is that the effect of the former Reciprocal Agreement has not been preserved by s.299 for the purposes of the new state pension. Accordingly, periods of Australian residency cannot be relied upon in calculating entitlement to the new state pension and Step 2 operates by reference to the entitlement rules for the new state pension.

FE was followed by Upper Tribunal Judge Church in *DB v Secretary of State for Work & Pensions* [2023] UKUT 144 (AAC). Judge Church also rejected the argument that the failure to take into account the claimant's Australian residence was contrary to art.14 of the European Convention on Human Rights (ECHR) (rights under the Convention to be enjoyed without discrimination on any ground) taken with art.8 (right to respect for private and family life, home and correspondence). The claimant argued that residents of New Zealand and Canada were able to rely on their residence in those countries for the purposes of Step 2 in the calculation of the amount of state pension referable to pre-commencement qualifying years and that his inability to rely on his Australian residence was discriminatory contrary to art.14. Judge Church rejected the submission that the claimant's situation fell within the ambit of art.8, for art.14 purposes, because he was unable to spend a reasonable amount of time with his family on account of pension-related financial limitations. This "purely financial consideration" had "too tenuous a link with his private and family life to bring his situation within Article 8". But, if the judge was wrong regarding "ambit", the claimant failed to satisfy the other three elements necessary for a successful art.14 claim identified by Lady Black in *R. (on the application of Stott) v Secretary of State for Justice* [2020] A.C. 51 (UKSC); [2018] 3 W.L.R. 1831. Firstly, Judge Church doubted whether the difference of treatment was based on country of residence, as the claimant argued, rather than the absence of an applicable reciprocal agreement between the UK and Australia. Secondly, the claimant was not in a relevantly similar position to his chosen comparators (that argument was precluded by the European Court of Human Rights' decision in *Carson v United Kingdom* (2010) 51 E.H.R.R. 13; 29 B.H.R.C. 22). Finally, the UK, in not affording the same advantages to Australian residents as those enjoyed by Canadians and New Zealanders, could not be characterised as acting in a way which was manifestly without reasonable foundation.

SCHEDULE 2 **Section 5**

TRANSITIONAL RATE OF STATE PENSION: UP-RATING

1 This Schedule sets out how to up-rate the transitional rate of a person's state pension. **1.1120**

2 In this Schedule a reference to the transitional rate of a person's state pension is to the rate—

(a) taking into account any reduction under section 14, but

(b) ignoring any increase under section 17.

3 (1) The transitional rate of a person's state pension is to be increased under this paragraph if it is equal to or less than the full rate.

(2) If at any time the full rate of the state pension is increased, the person's transitional rate is increased (at that time) by the same percentage as the increase in the full rate.

4 (1) The transitional rate of a person's state pension is to be increased under this paragraph if it exceeds the full rate.

(2) If at any time the full rate of the state pension is increased, the person's transitional rate is increased (at that time) by the same amount as the amount by which the full rate is increased.

(3) If at any time an order under section 151A of the Administration Act comes into force, the person's transitional rate is increased (at that time) by an amount equal to the appropriate percentage of the excess.

(4) In sub-paragraph (3)—

"the appropriate percentage" means the percentage specified in the order, and

"the excess" means the amount by which the transitional rate exceeded the full rate immediately before the order came into force.

GENERAL NOTE

The sums which, under para.4(3) of Sch.2, are the amounts of state pensions under Pt 1 of this Act as the transitional rate which exceed the full rate were increased, with effect from April 8, 2024, by 6.7 per cent: see art.6(3)(b) of the Social Security Benefits Up-rating Order 2024 (SI 2024/242). For previous years' increases, see previous editions of this work. **1.1121**

SCHEDULE 3 **Section 7**

SURVIVOR'S PENSION UNDER SECTION 7: INHERITED AMOUNT

Introduction

1 This Schedule— **1.1122**

(a) sets out the circumstances in which a person (the "pensioner") is entitled to an inherited amount for the purpose of section 7, and
(b) determines that amount.

Dead spouse or civil partner in old state pension system etc

2 (1) A pensioner whose spouse or civil partner has died is entitled to an inherited amount under this paragraph if— **1.1123**

(a) the marriage took place or the civil partnership was formed before 6 April 2016,
(b) the spouse or civil partner died before 6 April 2016,
(c) the pensioner was under pensionable age when the spouse or civil partner died, and
(d) the pensioner would, on reaching pensionable age, have been entitled to a Category B retirement pension under section 48B(4) or (4A) or 48BB of the Contributions and Benefits Act if the words "before 6 April 2016" were omitted.

(2) The inherited amount is equal to the weekly rate at which that Category B retirement pension would have been payable on the day on which the pensioner reached pensionable age if any element of the rate attributable to the basic pension were ignored.

3 (1) A pensioner whose spouse or civil partner has died is entitled to an inherited amount under this paragraph if—

(a) the marriage took place or the civil partnership was formed before 6 April 2016,
(b) the spouse or civil partner reached pensionable age before 6 April 2016 but died on or after that date,
(c) the pensioner was under pensionable age when the spouse or civil partner died, and

(d) the pensioner would, on reaching pensionable age, have been entitled to a Category B retirement pension under section 48BB of the Contributions and Benefits Act if in subsection (3) of that section:
 (i) the words "before 6 April 2016" were omitted, and
 (ii) the reference to a bereavement allowance were a reference to bereavement support payment under section 30 of this Act.

(2) The inherited amount is equal to the weekly rate at which that Category B retirement pension would have been payable on the day on which the pensioner reached pensionable age if section 48BB(8) and (9) of the Contributions and Benefits Act were ignored.

4 (1) A pensioner whose spouse or civil partner has died is entitled to an inherited amount under this paragraph if—
(a) the marriage took place or the civil partnership was formed before 6 April 2016,
(b) the spouse or civil partner reached pensionable age before 6 April 2016 but died on or after that date,
(c) the pensioner was over pensionable age when the spouse or civil partner died, and
(d) the pensioner would, when the spouse or civil partner died, have been entitled to a Category B retirement pension under section 48B(1) or (1A) of the Contributions and Benefits Act if the words "before 6 April 2016" were omitted.

(2) The inherited amount is equal to the weekly rate at which that Category B retirement pension would have been payable on the day on which the spouse or civil partner died if any element of the rate attributable to the basic pension were ignored.

Dead spouse or civil partner in new state pension system

1.1124 5 (1) A pensioner whose spouse or civil partner has died is entitled to an inherited amount under this paragraph if—
(a) the marriage took place or the civil partnership was formed before 6 April 2016,
(b) the pensioner was over pensionable age when the spouse or civil partner died,
(c) the spouse or civil partner was, immediately before his or her death, entitled to a state pension payable at the transitional rate, and
(d) that transitional rate exceeded the full rate of the state pension.

(2) The inherited amount is half of the amount by which the transitional rate of the state pension for the spouse or civil partner exceeded the full rate of the state pension immediately before the death.

6 (1) A pensioner whose spouse or civil partner has died is entitled to an inherited amount under this paragraph if—
(a) the marriage took place or the civil partnership was formed before 6 April 2016,
(b) the pensioner was under pensionable age when the spouse or civil partner died,
(c) the spouse or civil partner was, immediately before his or her death, entitled to a state pension payable at the transitional rate,
(d) that transitional rate exceeded the full rate of the state pension, and
(e) the pensioner did not marry or form a civil partnership after the death and before reaching pensionable age.

(2) The inherited amount is half of the amount by which the transitional rate of the state pension for the spouse or civil partner would have exceeded the full rate of the state pension if he or she had been alive on the day on which the pensioner reached pensionable age.

7 (1) A pensioner whose spouse or civil partner has died is entitled to an inherited amount under this paragraph if—
(a) the marriage took place or the civil partnership was formed before 6 April 2016,
(b) the pensioner was over pensionable age when the spouse or civil partner died,
(c) the spouse or civil partner was under pensionable age when he or she died but would have been entitled to a state pension payable at the transitional rate if he or she had reached pensionable age on the day of the death, and
(d) that transitional rate would have exceeded the full rate of the state pension.

(2) The inherited amount is half of the amount by which the transitional rate of the state pension for the spouse or civil partner would have exceeded the full rate of the state pension if he or she had reached pensionable age on the day of the death.

8 (1) A pensioner whose spouse or civil partner has died is entitled to an inherited amount under this paragraph if—
(a) the marriage took place or the civil partnership was formed before 6 April 2016,
(b) the pensioner was under pensionable age when the spouse or civil partner died,
(c) the spouse or civil partner died on or after 6 April 2016,
(d) the spouse or civil partner was under pensionable age when he or she died,

(e) the spouse or civil partner would have been entitled to a state pension payable at the transitional rate if he or she had reached pensionable age on the same day as the pensioner,

(f) that transitional rate would have exceeded the full rate of the state pension, and

(g) the pensioner did not marry or form a civil partnership after the death and before reaching pensionable age.

(2) The inherited amount is half of the amount by which the transitional rate of the state pension for the spouse or civil partner would have exceeded the full rate of the state pension if he or she had reached pensionable age on the same day as the pensioner.

Supplementary

9 When determining entitlement to, or calculating, an inherited amount under this Schedule based on entitlement to an old state pension or a state pension under this Part of this Act ignore— **1.1125**

(a) any requirement to make a claim for that pension;

(b) any provision suspending payment of, or disqualifying a person from receiving, any amount of that pension.

SCHEDULE 4 — **Section 7**

SURVIVOR'S PENSION UNDER SECTION 7: UP-RATING

Introduction

1 This Schedule sets out how to up-rate the rate of a person's state pension under section 7. **1.1126**

2 In this Schedule a reference to the rate of a person's state pension is to the rate—

(a) ignoring any reduction under section 7(4) (in the case of a state pension under section 7),

(b) taking into account any reduction under section 14 (in the case of a state pension under section 4), and

(c) ignoring any increase under section 17.

3 In this Schedule a reference to "the amount of any state pension that has priority" means the rate of any state pension to which the person is entitled under section 2, 4 or 12.

Rate of section 7 pension, when added to any priority pension, is less than the full rate

4 (1) The rate of the person's state pension under section 7 is to be increased under this paragraph if, when added to the amount of any state pension that has priority, it is equal to or less than the full rate of the state pension.

(2) If at any time the full rate is increased, the rate of the person's state pension under section 7 is increased (at that time) by the same percentage as the increase in the full rate.

Rate of section 7 pension, when added to any priority pension, straddles the full rate

5 (1) The rate of the person's state pension under section 7 is to be increased under this paragraph if— **1.1127**

(a) the amount of any state pension that has priority is less than the full rate of the state pension, but

(b) the rate of the state pension under section 7, when added to the amount of any state pension that has priority, exceeds the full rate.

(2) If at any time the full rate of the state pension is increased, the rate of the person's state pension under section 7 is increased (at that time) by an amount equal to the appropriate percentage of the shortfall immediately before that time.

(3) If at any time an order under section 151A of the Administration Act comes into force, the rate of the person's state pension under section 7 is increased (at that time) by an amount equal to the appropriate percentage of the excess immediately before the order comes into force.

(4) In this paragraph—

"the appropriate percentage"—

(a) in sub-paragraph (2), means the percentage by which the full rate is increased;

(b) in sub-paragraph (3), means the percentage specified in the order;

"the excess" means the amount by which the rate of the state pension under section 7, when added to the amount of any state pension that has priority, exceeds the full rate;

"the shortfall" means the amount by which the amount of any state pension that has priority is less than the full rate.

Priority pension alone is equal to or higher than the full rate

6 (1) The rate of the person's state pension under section 7 is to be increased under this paragraph if the amount of any state pension that has priority is equal to or higher than the full rate of the state pension.

(2) If at any time an order under section 151A of the Administration Act comes into force, the rate of the person's state pension under section 7 is increased (at that time) by the percentage specified in the order.

GENERAL NOTE

1.1128 The amounts which, under paras 5(3) and 6 of Sch.4, are the amounts of survivors' pensions which either alone or in combination with one or more other pension/s under Pt 1 of this Act exceed the full rate were increased, with effect from April 8, 2024, by 6.7 per cent: see art.6(3)(c) of the Social Security Benefits Up-rating Order 2024 (SI 2024/242). For previous years' increases, see previous editions of this work.

SCHEDULE 5 **Section 9**

SURVIVOR'S PENSION UNDER SECTION 9: INHERITED DEFERRAL AMOUNT

Introduction

1.1129 1 This Schedule—

(a) sets out the circumstances in which a person (the "pensioner") is entitled to an inherited deferral amount for the purpose of section 9, and

(b) determines that amount.

Dead spouse or civil partner entitled to old state pension with deferral increase

2 (1) A pensioner whose spouse or civil partner has died is entitled to an inherited deferral amount under this paragraph if—

(a) the spouse or civil partner was entitled to an old state pension with an increase under paragraph 1 or 2A of Schedule 5 to the Contributions and Benefits Act, and

(b) the pensioner would, on reaching pensionable age or on the death of the spouse or civil partner, have been entitled to an old state pension if in the relevant provisions of the Contributions and Benefits Act:

(i) the words "before 6 April 2016" were omitted, and

(ii) any reference to a bereavement allowance included a reference to bereavement support payment under section 30 of this Act.

(2) The inherited deferral amount is equal to the amount by which the weekly rate of the old state pension for the pensioner would have been increased under paragraph 4 of Schedule 5 to the Contributions and Benefits Act on the day on which the pensioner became entitled to the inherited deferral amount.

(3) For the purposes of calculating the amount of that increase, paragraph 4(1A) of Schedule 5 to the Contributions and Benefits Act has effect as if after the words "apart from" (in each place) there were inserted "this paragraph and".

Dead spouse or civil partner's entitlement to old state pension deferred at time of death

1.1130 3 (1) A pensioner whose spouse or civil partner has died is entitled to an inherited deferral amount under this paragraph if—

(a) the spouse or civil partner's entitlement to an old state pension was deferred when he or she died, and

(b) the pensioner would, on reaching pensionable age or on the death of the spouse or civil partner, have been entitled to an old state pension if in the relevant provisions of the Contributions and Benefits Act:

(i) the words "before 6 April 2016" were omitted, and
(ii) any reference to a bereavement allowance included a reference to bereavement support payment under section 30 of this Act.

(2) The inherited deferral amount is equal to the amount by which the weekly rate of the old state pension for the pensioner would have been increased under paragraph 4 of Schedule 5 to the Contributions and Benefits Act on the day on which the pensioner became entitled to the inherited deferral amount.

(3) For the purposes of calculating the amount of that increase—
(a) a pensioner who is not entitled to a choice under section 8 is to be treated as having met the condition in paragraph 4(1)(c) of Schedule 5 to the Contributions and Benefits Act,
(b) a pensioner who has chosen under section 8 to be paid a state pension under section 9 is to be treated as having met the condition in paragraph 4(1)(b) of Schedule 5 to the Contributions and Benefits Act, and
(c) paragraph 4(1A) of Schedule 5 to the Contributions and Benefits Act has effect as if after the words "apart from" (in each place) there were inserted "this paragraph and".

(4) In this paragraph "deferred" has the meaning given by section 55(3) of the Contributions and Benefits Act.

"The relevant provisions" of the Contributions and Benefits Act

4 For the purposes of this Schedule "the relevant provisions" of the Contributions and Benefits Act are those mentioned in section 8(9)(b).

Supplementary

5 When determining entitlement to, or calculating, an inherited deferral amount under this Schedule based on entitlement to an old state pension ignore—
(a) any requirement to make a claim for that pension;
(b) any provision suspending payment of, or disqualifying a person from receiving, any amount of that pension.

SCHEDULE 6 — **Section 11**

REDUCED RATE ELECTIONS: EFFECT ON RATE OF SECTION 4 PENSION

Introduction

1 This Schedule modifies the rules about the transitional rate of the state pension for a woman **1.1131**
if a reduced rate election was in force in respect of her at the beginning of the relevant 35-year period (and expressions used in this paragraph have the same meaning as in section 11).

Increased transitional rate for woman married to person over pensionable age etc

2 (1) This paragraph applies to the woman if on reaching pensionable age—
(a) she is married to a person who has reached pensionable age, or
(b) she is in a civil partnership with a person who has reached that age.

(2) The transitional rate of the state pension for the woman is—
(a) the rate determined for her under section 5, or
(b) if higher, a weekly rate equal to the modified amount for her precommencement qualifying years alone.

(3) The modified amount for the woman's pre-commencement qualifying years alone is the amount that would be calculated under Schedule 1 for her precommencement qualifying years alone if the basic pension in any Category A retirement pension calculated for her for the purposes of paragraph 3 of that Schedule were equal to the basic Category B amount.

(4) "The basic Category B amount" is the amount specified in paragraph 5 of Part 1 of Schedule 4 to the Contributions and Benefits Act on 6 April 2016.

(5) To find out what happens if the marriage or civil partnership comes to an end, see paragraph 4.

Increased transitional rate for widows or divorcees etc

3 (1) This paragraph applies to the woman if on reaching pensionable age she is **1.1132**
not married or in a civil partnership but she has been married or in a civil partnership before.

(2) The transitional rate of the state pension for the woman is—

(a) the rate determined for her under section 5, or

(b) if higher, a weekly rate equal to the modified amount for her precommencement qualifying years alone.

(3) The modified amount for the woman's pre-commencement qualifying years alone is the amount that would be calculated under Schedule 1 for her precommencement qualifying years alone if the basic pension in any Category A retirement pension calculated for her for the purposes of paragraph 3 of that Schedule were equal to the full amount of the basic pension.

(4) "The full amount of the basic pension" is the amount of the basic pension specified in section 44(4) of the Contributions and Benefits Act on 6 April 2016.

Recalculation of transitional rate where circumstances change

4[[1](1)] If the woman is married or in a civil partnership on reaching pensionable age but the marriage or civil partnership comes to an end (because of the death of her spouse or civil partner or otherwise)—

(a) her transitional rate is to be recalculated applying paragraph 3(2), and

(b) Schedule 2 (up-rating) applies as if the recalculated rate had been the woman's transitional rate on the day on which she reached pensionable age.

[[1](2) For the purposes of this paragraph --

(a) a civil partnership is not to be treated as having come to an end by reason of its having been converted into a marriage under Part 3 of the Marriage and Civil Partnership (Northern Ireland) (No 2) Regulations 2020;

(b) a civil partnership is not to be treated as having come to an end by reason of its having been converted into a marriage under Part 3 or 4 of the Marriage of Same Sex Couples (Conversion of Civil Partnership) Regulations 2014 where it is a convertible Northern Ireland civil partnership as defined by regulation 2 of those Regulations.

(3) For the purposes of this paragraph, a marriage is not to be treated as having come to an end by reason of its having been converted into a civil partnership under Part 3, 4 or 5 of the Marriage and Civil Partnership (Northern Ireland) (No 2) Regulations 2020.]

5 (1) If neither of paragraphs 2 and 3 apply to the woman but she subsequently comes within paragraph (a) or (b) of paragraph 2(1)—

(a) her transitional rate is to be recalculated applying paragraph 2(2), and

(b) Schedule 2 (up-rating) applies as if the recalculated rate had been the woman's transitional rate on the day on which she reached pensionable age.

(2) But the woman's rate is not to be recalculated under sub-paragraph (1) if it has already been recalculated under paragraph 4.

6 Nothing in paragraph 4 or 5 affects—

(a) the amount of state pension to which a woman is entitled for periods before that paragraph applies to her, or

(b) the amount of any increase under section 17 in a case where the period for which the woman's state pension is deferred has ended before that paragraph applies to her.

AMENDMENT

1. Marriage and Civil Partnership (Northern Ireland) (No. 2) Regulations 2020 (SI 2020/1143), reg. 47 (December 7, 2020).

SCHEDULE 7 **Section 12**

REDUCED RATE ELECTIONS: BASIC AMOUNT OF STATE PENSION UNDER SECTION 12

1.1133 1 This Schedule—

(a) sets out the circumstances in which a woman is entitled to a basic amount for the purpose of section 12, and

(b) determines that basic amount.

2 (1) A woman is entitled to a basic amount under this paragraph if she has reached pensionable age and—

(a) she is married to a person who has reached pensionable age, or

(b) she is in a civil partnership with a person who has reached that age.

(2) The basic amount is the amount specified in paragraph 5 of Part 1 of Schedule 4 to the Contributions and Benefits Act on the day on which the woman became entitled under this paragraph.

3 (1) A woman is entitled to a basic amount under this paragraph if—

(a) on reaching pensionable age she is not married or in a civil partnership but she has been married or in a civil partnership before, or

(b) on reaching pensionable age she was married or in a civil partnership and the marriage or civil partnership has come to an end (because of the death of her spouse or civil partner or otherwise).

(2) The basic amount is the amount of the basic pension specified in section 44(4) of the Contributions and Benefits Act on the day on which the woman became entitled under this paragraph.

4 A woman who is entitled to a basic amount under paragraph 3 is not entitled to a basic amount under paragraph 2.

SCHEDULE 8 **Section 13**

PENSION SHARING: APPROPRIATE WEEKLY RATE UNDER SECTION 13

Introduction

1 This Schedule sets out the appropriate weekly rate of a person's state pension under section 13. **1.1134**

Appropriate weekly rate for pensioner with old state scheme pension credit

2 (1) This paragraph sets out the appropriate weekly rate if the person is entitled to a state pension under section 13 because of an old state scheme pension credit.

(2) If the person became entitled to the old state scheme pension credit in or after the final relevant year, the appropriate weekly rate is a weekly rate equal to the person's notional rate.

(3) If the person became entitled to the old state scheme pension credit before the final relevant year, the appropriate weekly rate is a weekly rate equal to the person's notional rate multiplied by the appropriate revaluation percentage.

(4) For the purposes of sub-paragraphs (2) and (3), a person's "notional rate" is the weekly rate of a notional pension under section 13 the cash equivalent of which would, on the valuation day, have been equal to the amount of the old state scheme pension credit.

(5) For the purposes of sub-paragraph (4) assume that the notional pension becomes payable on the later of—

(a) the day on which the person reaches pensionable age, and

(b) the valuation day.

(6) The "appropriate revaluation percentage" is the percentage specified, in relation to earnings factors for the tax year in which the person became entitled to the old state scheme pension credit, by the last order under section 148 of the Administration Act to come into force before the end of the final relevant year.

(7) In this paragraph—

"final relevant year" means the tax year immediately before that in which the person reaches pensionable age;

"valuation day" means the day on which the person became entitled to the old state scheme pension credit.

Appropriate weekly rate for pensioner with new state scheme pension credit

3 (1) This paragraph sets out the appropriate weekly rate if the person is entitled to a state pension under section 13 because of a new state scheme pension credit. **1.1135**

(2) If the person was over pensionable age when he or she became entitled to the new state scheme pension credit, the appropriate weekly rate is a weekly rate equal to the amount of the credit.

(3) If the person was under pensionable age when he or she became entitled to the new state scheme pension credit, the appropriate weekly rate is a weekly rate equal to the amount of the credit multiplied by the appropriate revaluation percentage.

(4) The "appropriate revaluation percentage" is the percentage specified, in relation to the tax year in which the person became entitled to the new state scheme pension credit, by the

last order under section 148AD of the Administration Act to come into force before the person reached pensionable age.

Supplementary

4 (1) Regulations may make provision about the calculation and verification of notional rates under paragraph 2.

(2) The regulations may, in particular, provide—

(a) for calculation or verification in such manner as may be approved by or on behalf of the Government Actuary, or

(b) for things done under the regulations to be required to be done in accordance with guidance from time to time prepared by a person specified in the regulations.

SCHEDULE 9 **Section 13**

PENSION SHARING: UP-RATING STATE PENSION UNDER SECTION 13

Introduction

1.1136 1 This Schedule sets out how to up-rate the rate of a person's state pension under section 13.

2 In this Schedule a reference to the rate of a person's state pension is to the rate—

(a) ignoring any reduction under section 7(4) (in the case of a state pension under section 7),

(b) taking into account any reduction under section 14 (in the case of a state pension under section 4), and

(c) ignoring any increase under section 17.

3 (1) In this Schedule "the total amount of any state pension that has priority", in relation to a person's state pension under section 13, means the sum of—

(a) the rate of any state pension to which the person is entitled under section 2, 4 or 12,

(b) the rate of any state pension to which the person is entitled under section 7, [1 ...

(ba) the rate of any state pension to which the person is entitled under regulations made under section 10 which make provision corresponding or similar to section 7 and Schedules 3 and 4, and]

(c) the rate of any earlier state pension to which the person is entitled under section 13 (see sub-paragraph (2)).

(2) Where a person is entitled to two or more state pensions under section 13 because he or she has become entitled to two or more state scheme pension credits, a pension arising because of an earlier credit is an "earlier" state pension for the purposes of sub-paragraph (1)(c).

Rate of section 13 pension, when added to any priority pension, is less than the full rate

4 (1) The rate of the person's state pension under section 13 is to be increased under this paragraph if, when added to the total amount of any state pension that has priority, it is equal to or less than the full rate of the state pension.

(2) If at any time the full rate is increased, the rate of the person's state pension under section 13 is increased (at that time) by the same percentage as the increase in the full rate.

Rate of section 13 pension, when added to any priority pension, straddles the full rate

5 (1) The rate of the person's state pension under section 13 is to be increased under this paragraph if—

(a) the total amount of any state pension that has priority is less than the full rate of the state pension, but

(b) the rate of the state pension under section 13, when added to the total amount of any state pension that has priority, exceeds the full rate.

(2) If at any time the full rate of the state pension is increased, the rate of the person's state pension under section 13 is increased (at that time) by an amount equal to the appropriate percentage of the shortfall immediately before that time.

(3) If at any time an order under section 151A of the Administration Act comes into force, the rate of the person's state pension under section 13 is increased (at that time) by an amount equal to the appropriate percentage of the excess immediately before the order comes into force.

(4) In this paragraph—
"the appropriate percentage"—
(a) in sub-paragraph (2), means the percentage by which the full rate is increased;
(b) in sub-paragraph (3), means the percentage specified in the order;
"the excess" means the amount by which the rate of the state pension under section 13, when added to the total amount of any state pension that has priority, exceeds the full rate;
"the shortfall" means the amount by which the total amount of any state pension that has priority is less than the full rate.

Priority pension alone is equal to or higher than the full rate

6 (1) The rate of the person's state pension under section 13 is to be increased under this paragraph if the total amount of any state pension that has priority is equal to or higher than the full rate of the state pension.

(2) If at any time an order under section 151A of the Administration Act comes into force, the rate of the person's state pension under section 13 is increased (at that time) by the percentage specified in the order.

AMENDMENT

1. State Pension and Occupational Pension Schemes (Miscellaneous Amendments) Regulations 2016 (SI 2016/169) reg.5 (April 6, 2016).

GENERAL NOTE

The amounts which, under paras 5(3) and 6 of Sch.9, are the amounts of shared state pensions under Pt 1 of this Act which either alone or in combination with one or more other pensions under Pt 1 exceed the full rate were increased, with effect from April 8, 2024, by 6.7 per cent: see art.6(3)(d) of the Social Security Benefits Up-rating Order 2024 (SI 2024/242). For previous years' increases, see previous editions of this work. **1.1137**

SCHEDULE 10 **Section 14**

PENSION SHARING: APPROPRIATE WEEKLY REDUCTION UNDER SECTION 14

Introduction

1 This Schedule sets out the appropriate weekly reduction in the rate of a person's state pension for the purposes of section 14. **1.1138**

Appropriate weekly reduction for person subject to old state scheme pension debit

2 (1) This paragraph sets out the appropriate weekly reduction if the person is subject to an old state scheme pension debit.

(2) If the person became subject to the old state scheme pension debit in or after the final relevant year, the appropriate weekly reduction is an amount equal to the person's notional rate.

(3) If the person became subject to the old state scheme pension debit before the final relevant year, the appropriate weekly reduction is an amount equal to the person's notional rate multiplied by the appropriate revaluation percentage.

(4) For the purposes of sub-paragraphs (2) and (3), a person's "notional rate" is the weekly rate of a notional pension under section 4 the cash equivalent of which would, on the valuation day, have been equal to the amount of the old state scheme pension debit.

(5) For the purposes of sub-paragraph (4) assume that the notional pension becomes payable on the later of—
(a) the day on which the person reaches pensionable age, and
(b) the valuation day.

(6) The "appropriate revaluation percentage" is the percentage specified, in relation to earnings factors for the tax year in which the person became subject to the old state scheme pension debit, by the last order under section 148 of the Administration Act to come into force before the end of the final relevant year.

(7) In this paragraph—

"final relevant year" means the tax year immediately before that in which the person reaches pensionable age;

"valuation day" means the day on which the person became subject to the old state scheme pension debit.

1.1139 *Appropriate weekly reduction for person subject to new state scheme pension debit*

3 (1) This paragraph sets out the appropriate weekly reduction if the person is subject to a new state scheme pension debit.

(2) If the person was over pensionable age when he or she became subject to the new state scheme pension debit, the appropriate weekly reduction is an amount equal to the amount of the debit.

(3) If the person was under pensionable age when he or she became subject to the new state scheme pension debit, the appropriate weekly reduction is an amount equal to the amount of the debit multiplied by the appropriate revaluation percentage.

(4) The "appropriate revaluation percentage" is the percentage specified, in relation to the tax year in which the person became subject to the new state scheme pension debit, by the last order under section 148AD of the Administration Act to come into force before the person reached pensionable age.

Supplementary

4 (1) Regulations may make provision about the calculation and verification of notional rates under paragraph 2.

(2) The regulations may, in particular, provide—

(a) for calculation or verification in such manner as may be approved by or on behalf of the Government Actuary, or

(b) for things done under the regulations to be required to be done in accordance with guidance from time to time prepared by a person specified in the regulations.

SCHEDULE 11 **Section 15**

PENSION SHARING: AMENDMENTS

1.1140 *The amendments relevant to this volume are included in the appropriate provisions above.*

SCHEDULE 12 **Section 23**

STATE PENSION: AMENDMENTS

1.1141 *The amendments relevant to this volume are included in the appropriate provisions above.*

SCHEDULE 13 **Section 24**

ABOLITION OF CONTRACTING-OUT FOR SALARY RELATED SCHEMES

1.1142 *The amendments relevant to this volume are included in the appropriate provisions above.*

SCHEDULE 14 **Section 24**

POWER TO AMEND SCHEMES TO REFLECT ABOLITION OF CONTRACTING-OUT

1.1143 *Not included in this work as the provisions relate only to former salary related contracted-out pension schemes now closed by the provisions in Schedule 13.*

SCHEDULE 15 **Section 25**

OPTION TO BOOST OLD RETIREMENT PENSIONS

Not included in this volume. See the note to s.25 of the Act above. **1.1144**

Welfare Reform and Work Act 2016

(2016 c.7)

SECTIONS REPRODUCED

15. Employment and support allowance: work-related activity component **1.1145**

An Act to make provision about reports on progress towards full employment and the apprenticeships target; to make provision about reports on the effect of certain support for troubled families; to make provision about life chances; to make provision about the benefit cap; to make provision about social security and tax credits; to make provision for loans for mortgage interest and other liabilities; and to make provision about social housing rents.

[16th March 2016]

Employment and support allowance: work-related activity component

15.—(1) Part 1 of the Welfare Reform Act 2007 (employment and support allowance) is amended as follows.

(2) In section 2 (amount of contributory allowance)—

(a) in subsection (1)(b), omit "or the work-related activity component";
(b) omit subsection (3);
(c) in subsection (4), in each of paragraphs (a), (b) and (c), omit "or (3)".

(3) In section 4 (amount of income-related allowance) (so far as it remains in force)—

(a) in subsection (2)(b), omit "or the work-related activity component";
(b) omit subsection (5);
(c) in subsection (6), in each of paragraphs (a), (b) and (c), omit "or (5)".

(4) The Secretary of State may by regulations make such transitional or transitory provision or savings as the Secretary of State considers necessary or expedient in connection with the coming into force of subsections (1) to (3).

(5) Regulations under subsection (4) may in particular make provision about including a work-related activity component in an award of employment and support allowance that is converted under paragraph 7 of Schedule 4 to the Welfare Reform Act 2007 from an award of incapacity benefit, severe disablement allowance or income support after the coming into force of subsections (1) to (3).

(6) Regulations under this section must be made by statutory instrument.

(7) A statutory instrument containing regulations under this section is subject to annulment in pursuance of a resolution of either House of Parliament.

GENERAL NOTE

1.1146 For discussion of the significant effects of the important amendments made by subs.(2) and (3), see the commentary to ss.2 and 4 of the WRA 2007 above.

REGULATIONS

Preliminary Note: change of name from Department of Social Security to Department for Work and Pensions

1.1147 The Secretaries of State for Education and Skills and for Work and Pensions Order 2002 (SI 2002/1397) make provision for the change of name from the Department of Social Security to Department for Work and Pensions. Article 9(5) provides:

> "(5) Subject to article 12 [which makes specific amendments], any enactment or instrument passed or made before the coming into force of this Order shall have effect, so far as may be necessary for the purposes of or in consequence of the entrusting to the Secretary of State for Work and Pensions of the social security functions, as if any reference to the Secretary of State for Social Security, to the Department of Social Security or to an officer of the Secretary of State for Social Security (including any reference which is to be construed as such a reference) were a reference to the Secretary of State for Work and Pensions, to the Department for Work and Pensions or, as the case may be, to an officer of the Secretary of State for Work and Pensions."

PART II

CONTRIBUTION CREDITS AND HOME RESPONSIBILITIES PROTECTION

The Social Security (Credits) Regulations 1975

(SI 1975/556) (*as amended*)

ARRANGEMENT OF REGULATIONS

The Secretary of State for Social Services in exercise of the powers conferred upon her by section 13(4) of the Social Security Act 1975 and section 2(1) of, and paragraph 3 of Schedule 3 to, the Social Security (Consequential Provisions) Act 1975 and of all other powers enabling her in that behalf, without having referred any proposals on the matter to the National Insurance Advisory Committee since it appears to her that by reason of urgency it is inexpedient to do so, hereby makes the following regulations:

Citation and commencement

1.—These regulations may be cited as the Social Security (Credits) Regulations 1975 and shall come into operation on 6th April 1975. 2.2

Interpretation

2.—(1) In these regulations, unless the context otherwise requires,— 2.3
"the Act" means the Social Security Act 1975;

[11"the 2012 Act" means the Welfare Reform Act 2012;]
[12 "benefit"—
(a) includes—
(i) a contribution-based jobseeker's allowance;
(ii) a contributory employment and support allowance;
(b) does not include—
(i) an income-based jobseeker's allowance;
(ii) an income-related employment and support allowance;
(iii) a state pension under Part 1 of the Pensions Act 2014;]
[2 [13 . . .];
[13 . . .]
[1 . . .]
[11"contribution-based jobseeker's allowance" means an allowance under the Jobseekers Act 1995 as amended by the provisions of Part 1 of Schedule 14 to the 2012 Act that remove references to an income-based allowance, and a contribution-based allowance under the Jobseekers Act 1995 as that Act has effect apart from those provisions;]
[11"contributory employment and support allowance" means an allowance under Part 1 of the Welfare Reform Act as amended by the provisions of Schedule 3, and Part 1 of Schedule 14, to the 2012 Act that remove references to an income-related allowance, and a contributory allowance under Part 1 of the Welfare Reform Act as that Part has effect apart from those provisions;]
[3 "the Contributions and Benefits Act" means the Social Security Contributions and Benefits Act 1992;]
"credits" and "a credit" shall be construed in accordance with regulation 3;
[4 . . .];
[1 . . .];
[1 "income-based jobseeker's allowance" has the same meaning as in the Jobseekers Act 1995;
"jobseeker's allowance" means an allowance payable under Part I of the Jobseekers Act 1995;]
[10 "income-related employment and support allowance" means an income-related allowance under Part 1 of the Welfare Reform Act (employment and support allowance);
[1 . . .];
[9 "reckonable year" means a year for which the relevant earnings factor of the contributor concerned was sufficient to satisfy—
(a) in relation to short-term incapacity benefit, widowed mother's allowance, [widowed parent's allowance, [13 . . .]] widow's pension or Category A or Category B retirement pension, paragraph (b) of the second contribution condition specified in relation to that benefit in Schedule 3 to the Contributions and Benefits Act; [10 . . .]
(b) in relation to contribution-based jobseeker's allowance, the additional condition specified in section 2(3) of the Jobseekers Act 1995;] [10 or
(c) in relation to a contributory employment and support allowance, the condition specified in paragraph 2(1) of Schedule 1 to the Welfare Reform Act (conditions relating to national insurance);]

"relevant benefit year" [1 has the same meaning as it has—

(a) in relation to short-term incapacity benefit, in paragraph 2(6)(b) of Schedule 3 to the Contributions and Benefits Act; and

(b) in relation to contribution-based jobseeker's allowance, the additional condition specified in section 2(4)(b) of the Jobseekers Act 1995;]

"relevant earnings factor" [5 in relation to any benefit, means—

(a) [1 if the benefit is a contribution-based jobseeker's allowance or if the contributions relevant to the benefit under section 21 of the Contributions and Benefits Act] are Class 1 contributions, the earnings factor derived from earnings [6 in respect of which] primary Class 1 contributions have been paid or treated as paid, or credited earnings;

(b) if the contributions relevant to that benefit under that section are Class 1 and Class 2 contributions, the earnings factor or the aggregate of the earnings factors derived from—

(i) earnings [6 in respect of] which primary Class 1 contributions have been paid or treated as paid, or credited earnings, and

(ii) Class 2 contributions;

(c) if the contributions relevant to that benefit under [6 that section] are Class 1, Class 2 and Class 3 contributions, the earnings factor or the aggregate of the earnings factors derived from—

(i) earnings [6 in respect of which] primary contributions have been paid or treated as paid, or credited earnings,

(ii) Class 2 contributions, and

(iii) Class 3 contributions paid or credited];

[7 "relevant past year" means the last complete year before the beginning of the relevant benefit year;]

[11"universal credit" means universal credit under Part 1 of the 2012 Act;]

[10 "the Welfare Reform Act" means the Welfare Reform Act 2007;

[2 "widowed parent's allowance" means an allowance referred to in section 39A of the Contributions and Benefits Act;]

[4 "working tax credit" means a working tax credit under section 10 of the Tax Credits Act 2002];

[8 "year" means tax year;]

and other expressions have the same meanings as in the Act.

(2) The rules for the construction of Acts of Parliament contained in the Interpretation Act 1889 shall apply for the purposes of the interpretation of these regulations as they apply for the purposes of the interpretation of an Act of Parliament.

(3) Unless the context otherwise requires, any reference in these regulations—

(a) to a numbered section is a reference to the section of the Act bearing that number;

(b) to a numbered regulation is a reference to the regulation bearing that number in these regulations, and any reference in a regulation to a numbered paragraph is a reference to the paragraph of that regulation bearing that number;

(c) to any provision made by or contained in any enactment or instrument shall be construed as a reference to that provision as amended or extended by any enactment or instrument and as including a reference to any provision which it re-enacts or replaces or which may re-enact or replace it with or without modification.

(4) Nothing in these regulations shall be construed as entitling any person to be credited with contributions for the purposes of any benefit for a day, period or event occurring before 6th April 1975.

AMENDMENTS

1. Social Security (Credits and Contributions) (Jobseeker's Allowance Consequential and Miscellaneous Amendments) Regulations 1996 (SI 1996/2367) reg.2(2) (October 7, 1996).

2. Social Security (Benefits for Widows and Widowers) (Consequential Amendments) Regulations 2000 (SI 2000/1483) reg.3(2).

3. Social Security (Incapacity Benefit) (Consequential and Transitional Amendments and Savings) Regulations 1995 (SI 1995/829) reg.6(2) (April 13, 1995).

4. Social Security (Working Tax Credit and Child Tax Credit) (Consequential Amendments) Regulations 2003 (SI 2003/455) reg.6 and Sch.4 para.1 (April 7, 2003).

5. Social Security (Credits) Amendment Regulations 1987 (SI 1987/414) reg.2 (April 6, 1987).

6. Social Security (Contributions and Credits) (Miscellaneous Amendments) Regulations 1999 (SI 1999/568) reg.20(a) (April 6, 1999).

7. Social Security (Credits) Amendment (No. 4) Regulations 1988 (SI 1988/1545) reg.2(2) (October 2, 1988).

8. Social Security (Credits) Amendment (No. 2) Regulations 1988 (SI 1988/1230) reg.2(2) (October 2, 1988).

9. Social Security (Miscellaneous Amendments) (No.3) Regulations 2007 (SI 2007/1749) reg.8(2) (July 16, 2007).

10. Employment and Support Allowance (Consequential Provisions) (No.2) Regulations 2008 (SI 2008/1554) reg.48(2) (October 27, 2008).

11. Universal Credit (Consequential, Supplementary, Incidental and Miscellaneous Provisions) Regulations 2013 (SI 2013/630) reg.70(1), (2) (April 29, 2013).

12. Pensions Act 2014 (Consequential, Supplementary and Incidental Amendments) Order 2015 (SI 2015/1985) art.2 (April 6, 2016)

13. Pensions Act 2014 (Consequential, Supplementary and Incidental Amendments) Order 2017 (SI 2017/422) art.4(2) (April 6, 2017).

General provisions relating to the crediting of contributions [1 and earnings]

2.4 **3.**—[2(1) Any contributions or earnings credited in accordance with these Regulations shall be only for the purpose of enabling the person concerned to satisfy—

[4(aa) in relation to short-term incapacity benefit, the second contribution condition specified in paragraph 2(3) of Schedule 3 (contribution conditions for entitlement to benefit) to the Contributions and Benefits Act;

(ab) in relation to—

(i) widowed mother's allowance;

(ii) widowed parent's allowance;

(iii) [5 . . .]

(iv) widow's pension,

the second contribution condition specified in paragraph 5(3) of Schedule 3 to the Contributions and Benefits Act;

(ac) in relation to a Category A or Category B retirement pension—
(i) in the case of a retirement pension to which paragraph 5 of Schedule 3 to the Contributions and Benefits Act applies, the second contribution condition specified in paragraph 5(3); and
(ii) otherwise, the contribution condition specified in paragraph 5A(2) of Schedule 3 to that Act;]
(b) in relation to contribution-based jobseeker's allowance, the condition specified in section 2(1)(b) of the Jobseekers Act 1995; [3or
(c) in relation to a contributory employment and support allowance, the condition specified in paragraph 2(1) of Schedule 1 to the Welfare Reform Act,]

and accordingly, where under any of the provisions of these Regulations a person would, but for this paragraph, be entitled to be credited with any contributions or earnings for a year, or in respect of any week in a year, he shall be so entitled for the purposes of any benefit only if and to no greater extent than that by which his relevant earnings factor for that year falls short of the level required to make that year a reckonable year.]

(2) Where under these regulations a person is entitled for the purposes of any benefit to—
(a) be credited [1 with earnings] for a year, he is to be credited with such amount of [1earnings] as may be required to bring his relevant earnings factor to the level required to make that year a reckonable year
(b) [1 ...];

(3) Where under these regulations a person is entitled to be credited [1with earnings] or a contribution in respect of a week which is partly in one tax year and partly in another, he shall be entitled to [1 be credited with those earnings or that contribution] for the tax year in which that week began and not for the following year.

AMENDMENTS

1. Social Security (Credits) Amendment Regulations 1987 (SI 1987/414) reg.3 (April 6, 1987).
2. Social Security (Credits and Contributions) (Jobseeker's Allowance Consequential and Miscellaneous Amendments) Regulations 1996 (SI 1996/2367) reg.2(3) (October 7, 1996).
3. Employment and Support Allowance (Consequential Provisions) (No. 2) Regulations 2008 (SI 2008/1554) reg.48(3) (October 27, 2008).
4. Social Security (State Pension and National Insurance Credits) Regulations 2009 (SI 2009/2206) reg.29 (April 6, 2010).
5. Pensions Act 2014 (Consequential, Supplementary and Incidental Amendments) Order 2017 (SI 2017/422) art.4(3) (April 6, 2017).

DEFINITIONS

"benefit"—see reg.2(1).
"reckonable year"—see reg.2(1).
"relevant earnings factor"—see reg.2(1).
"tax year"—see SSCBA 1992 s.122(1).
"year": see reg.2(1).

GENERAL NOTE

This provides that credits can only be awarded under these regulations to enable the person to satisfy the second contribution condition for particular benefits (paras (1) and (2) read with reg.2(1)): 2.5

- short-term incapacity benefit (SSCBA 1992 s.30A);
- widowed mother's allowance (SSCBA 1992 s.37);
- widowed parent's allowance (SSCBA 1992 s.39A);
- widow's pension (SSCBA 1992 s.38);
- Category A or B retirement pension (SSCBA 1992 ss.43–54);
- contribution-based jobseeker's allowance (Jobseekers Act 1995 s.2—see *this Volume*.
- contributory employment and support allowance

Moreover, they can only be awarded to the extent necessary to make up the shortfall between the actual record in paid contributions in the relevant tax year and the level needed to satisfy the particular second condition (50 times the lower earnings limit for Class 1 contributions liability purposes in that year—52 times for retirement pension), that is, to make that year a "reckonable year" (para.(2)).

Paragraph (3) deals with the situation where the week in which someone is entitled to be credited spans two tax years, and provides that the tax year to be credited is the one in which the week began.

The role and importance of reg.3 is generally overlooked. It is, however, crucial in determining whether "credits" (crediting earnings and earnings factors to a claimant's contribution account) for which the claimant is eligible under other provisions of these regulations can actually be awarded in respect of the specified benefits. It is as if it had to be read as an integral part of each of those other regulations. It is, moreover, a provision that causes particular problems in respect on its interaction with the provision on credits for unemployment in reg.8A. Commissioner Williams sets out the law on crediting contributions in *CIB/1602/2006*:

"24. Provision is made to allow credited earnings under section 22(5) of the 1992 Act. This provides, as relevant to this appeal:

'Regulations may provide for crediting—

(a) for 1987–88 or any subsequent year, earnings . . .
for the purpose of bringing a person's earnings factor for that tax year to a figure which will enable him to satisfy contribution conditions of entitlement to . . . any prescribed description of benefit . . .'"

This applies to D's claim for incapacity benefit. It makes clear that credited earnings can only apply when the individual has not paid enough actual contributions for the year. This, equally clearly, can only be decided after the end of the tax year, which occurs in April each calendar year. (For employed earners this will be in practice after the time limit in the following May or June when all employers are required to make a return of total contributions collected for their employees during the year ending in April. See Sch.4 para.22 to the Social Security (Contributions) Regulations 2001 (SI 2001 No 1004)).

25. The regulations allowing credited earnings for periods of unemployment are regulations 3 (general provisions relating to the crediting of contributions and earnings) and 8A (credits for unemployment) of the Social Security (Credits) Regulations 1975 ("the Credits Regulations") (SI 1975 No 556). These are complicated and much amended regulations. Little attention has been paid for years past to the structure of the Credits Regulations and the way that they are empowered by, and link to, section 22(5) of the 1992 Act and its predecessors back to section 13 of the Social Security Act 1975. The Regulations follow the usual pattern of stating the commencement provisions in regulation 1 and definitions in regulation 2. Regulation 3 then lays down general provisions relating to the crediting of contributions and earnings. Regulations 4 to 9F follow with provisions for specific forms of credit or credited earnings in specific situations. It is abundantly clear from this that, reflecting the authority granted in section 22(5), regulation 3 is to be applied in each case along with the specific regulation. That has not happened here. As

Commissioner Rowland commented in CIB 3327 2004, regulation 3 is rarely mentioned in connection with the award of credited earnings. It is not the subject, so far as I can see, of any comment in the *DMG*. Nor has it been mentioned in this appeal.
2-6. The Credits Regulations have been amended many times since first being written. The most important of the amendments—only partially executed—take account of the abolition of contribution credits on 6 04 1987. From that date (the start of the tax year 1987–88) the previous system of awarding weekly credits was abolished. It was replaced by a system of crediting earnings and earnings factors to a claimant only when necessary at the end of a tax year. Commissioner Rowland explores these concepts in CIB 3327 2004, and I do not repeat that. The difficulties in cases such as this are because the fundamental change in the nature of contribution "credits" does not appear yet to have been absorbed into the relevant administrative processes for identifying and awarding credited earnings. That failure is in part hidden because of a failure fully to amend the Credits Regulations themselves to reflect the changes made in 1987".

The problem this generates with claims for credits for unemployment were then considered by Commissioner Williams (and a solution found). The matter is considered in the update to the commentary to reg.8A, below. For further consideration of some of the difficulties arising where records have been destroyed as part of normal administrative processes and for the text of the regulations on unemployment credits covering 1977-89, see Commissioner Williams' decision in *CP/1792/2007*.

Starting credits for the purposes of a retirement pension, a widowed mother's allowance, a widowed parent's allowance [4 . . .] and a widow's pension

4.—(1) [3 Subject to paragraph (1A),] for the purposes of entitlement to a Category A or a Category B retirement pension, a widowed mother's allowance [1, a widowed parent's allowance [4 . . .]] or a widow's pension [2 by virtue of a person's earnings or contributions], he shall be credited with such number of Class 3 contributions as may be required to bring his relevant earnings factor in respect of the tax year in which he attained the age of 16 and for each of the two following tax years to the level required to make those years reckonable years; so however, subject to paragraph (2), no contribution shall be credited under this regulation in respect of any tax year commencing before 6th April 1975. 2.6

[3(1A) For the purposes of entitlement to a Category A or a Category B retirement pension, no contribution shall be credited under this regulation—

(a) in respect of any tax year commencing on or after 6th April 2010;
(b) in respect of any other tax year, where an application under regulation 9 (application for allocation of national insurance number) of the Social Security (Crediting and Treatment of Contributions, and National Insurance Numbers) Regulations 2001 is made on or after 6th April 2010.]

(2) Where a person was in Great Britain on 6th April 1975 and had attained the age of 16 but was not an insured person under the National Insurance Act 1965, he shall be credited with contributions under paragraph (1) in respect of the tax year commencing on 6th April 1974.

AMENDMENTS

1. Social Security (Benefits for Widows and Widowers) (Consequential Amendments) Regulations 2000 (SI 2000/1483) reg.3(4) (April 9, 2001).

2. Social Security (Credits) Amendment (No. 4) Regulations 1988 (SI 1988/1545) reg.2(5) (October 2, 1988).

3. National Insurance Contributions Credits (Miscellaneous Amendments) Regulations 2011 (SI 2011/709) reg.2 (April 5, 2011).

4. Pensions Act 2014 (Consequential, Supplementary and Incidental Amendments) Order 2017 (SI 2017/422) art.4(4) (April 6, 2017).

DEFINITIONS

"reckonable year"—see reg.2(1).
"relevant earnings factor"—see reg.2(1).
"tax year"—see SSCBA 1992 s.122(1).

GENERAL NOTE

2.7 As with all of the Regulations making claimants eligible for the award of credits, this must be read with reg.3 (*CIB/1602/2006*; *CIB/3327/2004*). One can only have them insofar as they are necessary to bring one's record up to the level required for satisfying the second contribution condition for the relevant benefit (see para.(1), reg.3 and reg.2(1) ("reckonable year")).

This applies only for the purposes of a retirement pension, a widowed mother's allowance, a widowed parent's allowance, a bereavement allowance and a widow's pension. It awards someone sufficient Class 3 credits to bring his contribution record in a particular tax year up to the requisite level for the second contribution condition (to make the year a "reckonable year"). The tax years in question are the one in which he reached 16 and the two tax years following that year. No credits are awardable prior to April 6, 1975, save that tax year 1974–75 can be credited as respects someone 16 or over, who was in Great Britain on that date but was not an insured person under the National Insurance Act 1965.

As regards Category A or B pensions, note that para.(1A) precludes contribution credits ("starting credits") for any tax year later than 2009/10 or in respect of any tax year where applications for a national insurance number are made after April 6, 2010. The governmental view was that the reduction in the number of qualifying years needed for a full basic State Pension to 30 years, effected in April 2010, meant that few people who have spent most of their working lives in the UK will need starting credits for this purpose.

Starting credits for the purposes of unemployment benefit, sickness benefit and maternity allowance

2.8 **5.**—[1 . . .]

REVOCATION

1. Social Security (Credits) Amendment (No. 2) Regulations 1988 (SI 1988/1230) reg.3(1).

Starting credits for the purposes of a maternity grant

2.9 **6.**—[1 . . .]

REVOCATION

1. Social Security (Credits) Amendment Regulations 1988 (SI 1988/516), reg.3(1).

Credits for approved training

2.10 **7.**—(1) For the purposes of entitlement to any benefit [1 by virtue of a person's earnings or contributions] he shall, subject to [5 paragraphs (2) to (4)], be entitled to [2 be credited with earnings equal to the lower earnings limit then in force], in respect of each week in any part of which he was undergoing (otherwise than in pursuance of his employment as an employed earner) a course of [3 . . .] training approved by the Secretary of State for the purposes of this regulation.

[3 (2) Paragraph (1) shall apply to a person only if—

(a) the course is—

(i) a course of full-time training; or

(ii) a course of training which he attends for not less than 15 hours in the week in question and he is a disabled person within the meaning of the Disabled Persons (Employment) Act 1944; or

(iii) a course of training introductory to a course to which paragraph (i) or (ii) above applies; and

(b) when the course began it was not intended to continue for more than 12 months or, if he was a disabled person within the meaning of the Disabled Persons (Employment) Act 1944 and the training was provided under the Employment and Training Act 1973 [4 or the Enterprise and New Towns (Scotland) Act 1990], for such longer period as is reasonable in the circumstances of his case; and

(c) he had attained the age of 18 before the beginning of the tax year in which the week in question began.]

(3) Paragraph (1) shall not apply to a woman in respect of any week in any part of which she was a married woman in respect of whom an election made by her under regulations made under section 3(2) of the Social Security Pensions Act 1975 had effect.

[5(4) Paragraph (1) shall not apply to a person in respect of any week in any part of which that person was entitled to universal credit.]

AMENDMENTS

1. Social Security (Credits) Amendment (No. 4) Regulations 1988 (SI 1988/1545) reg.2(5) (October 2, 1988).

2. Social Security (Credits) Amendment Regulations 1987 (SI 1987/414) reg.5 (April 6, 1987).

3. Social Security (Credits) Amendment (No. 3) Regulations 1988 (SI 1988/1439) reg.2 (September 4, 1988).

4. Enterprise (Scotland) Consequential Amendments Order 1991 (SI 1991/387) art.3(a) (April 1, 1991).

5. Universal Credit (Consequential, Supplementary, Incidental and Miscellaneous Provisions) Regulations 2013 (SI 2013/630) reg.70(1), (3) (April 29, 2013).

DEFINITIONS

"benefit"—see reg.2(1).
"employed earner"—see SSCBA 1992 s.2(1)(a).
"lower earnings limit"—see SSCBA 1992 s.122(1).
"tax year"—see SSCBA 1992 s.122(1).

GENERAL NOTE

As with all of the Regulations making claimants eligible for the award of credits, this must be read with reg.3 (*CIB/1602/2006*; *CIB/3327/2004*). One can only have them insofar as they are necessary to bring one's record up to the level required for satisfying the second contribution condition for the relevant benefit (see para.(1), reg.3 and reg.2(1) ("reckonable year")). **2.11**

It enables credits to be awarded to a person for each week in which he was undergoing an approved course of training, otherwise than in pursuance of his employed earner's employment. Approved means approved by the Secretary of State for the purposes of this regulation. The conditions in para.(2) must be met. The course must be full time or, where someone is disabled within the meaning of the Disabled Persons (Employment) Act 1944, one attended for at least 15 hours in the week for which the credit is sought, or it must be a course of training introductory to such a course (para.(2)(a). In addition the person must have been 18 before the beginning of the tax year containing the week sought to be credited (para.(2)(c)). Furthermore, when commenced the course must not have been intended to last more than 12 months, or, where the person is disabled within the meaning of that 1944 Act and the training was provided under specified legislation, for such longer period as is reasonable in his case (para.(2)(b)).

A woman cannot gain a credit under this provision in respect of any week in any part of which as a married woman a certificate of election to pay contributions at reduced rate applied to her (para.(3)). Nor can a person obtain a credit under this provision in respect of a week in any part of which that person was entitled to universal credit (para.(4)).

[1 Credits for [2 carer's allowance] [10 or carer support payment]

2.12 **7A.**—(1) For the purposes of entitlement to any benefit [3 by virtue of a person's earnings or contributions] he shall, subject to paragraph (2), be entitled to [4 be credited with earnings equal to the lower earnings limit then in force], in respect of each week for any part of which [2 a carer's allowance] [10 or carer support payment] is paid to him, [5 or would be paid to him but for a restriction under section [8 6B or] 7 of the Social Security Fraud Act 2001 (loss of benefit provisions)] or in the case of [7 widow, widower or surviving civil partner] would have been so payable but for [10 regulation 16 of the Carer's Assistance (Carer Support Payment) (Scotland) Regulations 2023 or] the provisions of the Social Security (Overlapping Benefits) Regulations 1975, as amended by the Social Security (Invalid Care Allowance) Regulations 1976, requiring adjustment of [2 a carer's allowance] [10 or carer support payment] against widow's benefit, [9 widowed parent's allowance] or benefit by virtue of section 39(4) corresponding to a widowed mother's allowance or a widow's pension.

(2) Paragraph (1) shall not apply—

(a) to a person in respect of any week where he is entitled to [4 be credited with earnings] under [6 regulation 8A or 8B] in respect of the same week; or

(b) to a woman in respect of any week in any part of which she was a married woman in respect of whom an election made by her under regulations made under section 3(2) of the Social Security Pensions Act 1975 had effect.]

[10 (3) In this regulation "carer support payment" means carer's assistance given in accordance with the Carer's Assistance (Carer Support Payment) (Scotland) Regulations 2023.]

AMENDMENTS

1. Social Security (Invalid Care Allowance) Regulations 1976 (SI 1976/409) reg.19 (April 12, 1976).

2. Social Security Amendment (Carer's Allowance) Regulations 2002 (SI 2002/2497) reg.3 and Sch.2 (April 1, 2003).

3. Social Security (Credits) Amendment (No. 4) Regulations 1988 (SI 1988/1545) reg.2(5) (October 2, 1988).

4. Social Security (Credits) Amendment Regulations 1987 (SI 1987/414) reg.6 (April 6, 1987).
5. Social Security (Loss of Benefit) (Consequential Amendments) Regulations (SI 2002/490) reg.3(a) (April 1, 2002).
6. Social Security (Credits and Contributions) (Jobseeker's Allowance Conseq uential and Miscellaneous Amendments) Regulations 1996 (SI 1996/2367) reg.2 (October 7, 1996).
7. Civil Partnership (Pensions, Social Security and Child Support) (Consequential, etc. Provisions) Order 2005 (SI 2005/2877) art.2(3) and Sch.3, para.4(2) (December 5, 2005).
8. Social Security (Loss of Benefit) Amendment Regulations 2010 (SI 2010/1160) reg.13 (April 1, 2010).
9. Pensions Act 2014 (Consequential, Supplementary and Incidental Amendments) Order 2017 (SI 2017/422) art.4(5) (April 6, 2017).
10. Carer's Assistance (Carer Support Payment) (Scotland) Regulations 2023 (Consequential Amendments) Order 2023 (SI 2023/1218) art.3 (November 19, 2023).

DEFINITIONS

"benefit"—see reg.2(1).
"lower earnings limit"—see SSCBA 1992 s.122(1).

GENERAL NOTE

As with all of the Regulations making claimants eligible for the award of credits, this must be read with reg.3 (*CIB/1602/2006*; *CIB/3327/2004*). One can only have them insofar as they are necessary to bring one's record up to the level required for satisfying the second contribution condition for the relevant benefit (see para.(1), reg.3 and reg.2(1) ("reckonable year")). 2.13

It enables a credit equal to that tax year's lower earnings limit to be awarded for each week in respect of part of which someone has a carer's allowance paid to him; or where it would have been paid to him but for the loss of benefit provision in the Social Security Fraud Act 2001 s.7; or where, as a widow or widower it is not because of the adjustment provisions in the Overlapping Benefit Regulations. In *CG/2902/2003*, Deputy Commissioner Mark considered when it could be said that invalid care allowance (now care allowance) was "paid" to someone for the purposes of this regulation. He concluded that it is not "paid" in the required sense:

> "where it has been decided subsequent to payment that the claimant was not entitled to such an allowance for that period. Accordingly, the secretary of state was correct not to award credits in respect of that period and the tribunal was correct to dismiss the claimant's appeal" (para.22).

He expressed no view as to the effect on an existing award of credits where the award of invalid care allowance is revised or superseded.

Note that a woman cannot gain a credit under this provision in respect of any week in any part of which as a married woman a certificate of election to pay contributions at reduced rate applied to her (para.(2)(b)). Nor can a credit be awarded under this provision if a credit entitlement for the week arises under reg.8A (unemployment) or 8B (incapacity for work) (para.(2)(a)).

[1 Credits for [2 disability element of working tax credit]

7B.—(1) For the purposes of entitlement to any benefit by virtue of a person's earnings or contributions he shall, subject to paragraphs (2) and (3), be credited with earnings equal to the lower earnings limit then in force in respect of each week for any part of which [2 the disability element or the severe disability element of working tax credit as specified in regulation 20(1)(b) and (f) of the Working Tax Credit (Entitlement and Maximum Rate) Regulations 2002 is included in an award of working tax credit which] is paid to him. 2.14

(2) Paragraph (1) shall apply to a person only if he is—

(a) an employed earner; [4 . . .]

[4 (b) a self-employed earner whose profits for the year are below the small profits threshold specified in [5section 11(4)(b)] of the Contributions and Benefits Act, who would otherwise [6 ... [5 ...]] be treated as having actually paid,] a Class 2 contribution; or

(c) excepted from [6 being treated as having actually paid] a Class 2 contribution by virtue of regulation 43 of the Social Security (Contributions) Regulations 2001.]

(3) Paragraph (1) shall not apply—

(a) to a person in respect of any week where he is entitled to be credited with earnings under [3 regulation 8A or 8B] in respect of the same week; or

(b) to a woman in respect of any week in any part of which she was a married woman in respect of whom an election made by her under regulations made under section 3(2) of the Social Security Pension Act 1975 had effect.]

AMENDMENTS

1. Social Security (Credits) Amendment Regulations 1991 (SI 1991/2772) reg.3 (April 6, 1992).

2. Social Security (Working Tax Credit and Child Tax Credit) (Consequential Amendments) Regulations 2003 (SI 2003/455) reg.6 and Sch.4 para.1 (April 7, 2003).

3. Social Security (Credits and Contributions) (Jobseeker's Allowance Conseq uential and Miscellaneous Amendments) Regulations 1996 (SI 1996/2367) reg.2 (October 7, 1996).

4. Social Security (Credits, and Crediting and Treatment of Contributions) (Consequential and Miscellaneous Amendments) Regulations 2016 (SI 2016/1145) reg.3(2) (January 1, 2017).

5. Social Security (Class 2 National Insurance Contributions Increase of Threshold) Regulations 2022 (SI 2022/1329) reg.6(1)(a) (in force December 14, 2022, with effect from April 6, 2022).

6. Social Security (Class 2 National Insurance Contributions) (Consequential Amendments and Savings) Regulations 2024 (SI 2024/377) reg.8(1)(a) (April 6, 2024).

DEFINITIONS

"employed earner"—see SSCBA 1992 s.2(1)(a).
"lower earnings limit"—see SSCBA 1992 s.122(1).
"self-employed earner"—see SSCBA 1992 s.2(1)(b).
"working tax credit"—see reg.2(1).

GENERAL NOTE

2.15 As with all of the Regulations making claimants eligible for the award of credits, this must be read with reg.3 (*CIB/1602/2006*; *CIB/3327/2004*). One can only have them insofar as they are necessary to bring one's record up to the level required for satisfying the second contribution condition for the relevant benefit (see para.(1), reg.3 and reg.2(1) ("reckonable year")).

It enables a credit equal to that tax year's lower earnings limit to be awarded for each week in respect of part of which someone has a working tax credit inclusive of the disability or severe disability element paid to him (para.(1)). He must either be an employed earner, or a self-employed earner exempt from paying Class 2 contributions because of the "small earnings" exception (para.(2)). Note that a woman cannot gain a credit under this provision in respect of any week in any part of which as a married woman a certificate of election to pay contributions at reduced rate applied to her (para.(3)(b)). Nor can a credit be awarded under this provision if a credit entitlement for the week arises under reg.8A (unemployment) or 8B (incapacity for work) (para.(3)(a)).

[1 Credits for [2 working tax credit]

7C.—(1) [2 Subject to regulation 7B], for the purposes of entitlement to a Category A or a Category B retirement pension, a widowed mother's allowance, a widowed parent's allowance [7 . . .] or a widow's pension by virtue of a person's earnings or contributions, where [2 working tax credit] is paid for any week in respect of— 2.16

(a) an employed earner; [6 . . .]

[6 (b) a self-employed earner—

(i) whose profits for the year are below the small profits threshold specified in [5section 11(4)(b)] of the Contributions and Benefits Act, who would otherwise [9 ... [5 ...]] be treated as having actually paid,] a Class 2 contribution; or

(ii) who is excepted from [9 being treated as having actually paid] a Class 2 contribution by virtue of regulation 43 of the Social Security (Contributions) Regulations 2001,]

that person shall, subject to paragraphs (4) and (5), be credited with earnings equal to the lower earnings limit then in force in respect of that week.

(2) The reference in paragraph (1) to the person in respect of whom [2 working tax credit] is paid—

(a) where it is paid to one of [5 a couple], is a reference to the member of that couple specified in paragraph (3); and

(b) in any other case, is a reference to the person to whom it is paid.

(3) the member of [5 a couple] specified for the purposes of paragraph (2)(a) is—

(a) where only one member is assessed for the purposes of the award of [2 working tax credit] as having income consisting of earnings, that member; or

(b) [2 . . .]

(c) where the earnings of each member are assessed [2 . . .], the member to whom the [2 working tax credit] is paid.

(4) Paragraph (1) shall not apply—

(a) to a person in respect of any week he is entitled to be credited with earnings under regulation 8A or 8B in respect of the same week; or

(b) to a woman in respect of any week in any part of which she is a married woman in respect of whom an election made by her under regulations made under section 19(4) of the Contributions and Benefits Act has effect.

(5) [2 . . .].

(6) In this regulation [5 couple has] the same meaning as in Part VII of the Contributions and Benefits Act.]

AMENDMENTS

1. Social Security (Credits) Amendment Regulations 1995 (SI 1995/2558) reg.2 (November 1, 1995).

2. Social Security (Working Tax Credit and Child Tax Credit) (Consequential Amendments) Regulations 2003 (SI 2003/455) reg.6 and Sch.4 para.1 (April 7, 2003).

3. Social Security (Credits and Contributions) (Jobseeker's Allowance Consequential and Miscellaneous Amendments) Regulations 1996 (SI 1996/2367) reg.2 (October 7, 1996).

4. Social Security (Benefits for Widows and Widowers) (Consequential Amendments) Regulations 2000 (SI 2000/1483) reg.3(6).

5. Civil Partnership (Pensions, Social Security and Child Support) (Consequential, etc. Provisions) Order 2005 (SI 2005/2877) art.2(3) and Sch.3 para.4(3) (December 5, 2005).
6. Social Security (Credits, and Crediting and Treatment of Contributions) (Consequential and Miscellaneous Amendments) Regulations 2016 (SI 2016/1145) reg.3(3) (January 1, 2017).
7. Pensions Act 2014 (Consequential, Supplementary and Incidental Amendments) Order 2017 (SI 2017/422) art.4(6) (April 6, 2017).
8. Social Security (Class 2 National Insurance Contributions Increase of Threshold) Regulations 2022 (SI 2022/1329) reg.6(1)(b) (in force December 14, 2022, with effect from April 6, 2022).
9. Social Security (Class 2 National Insurance Contributions) (Consequential Amendments and Savings) Regulations 2024 (SI 2024/377) reg.8(1)(b) (April 6, 2024).

DEFINITIONS

"employed earner"—see SSCBA 1992 s.2(1)(a).
"married couple"—see para.(6); SSCBA 1992 s.137(1).
"pensionable age"—see SSCBA 1992 s.122(1).
"self-employed earner"—see SSCBA 1992 s.2(1)(b).
"unmarried couple"—see para.(6); SSCBA 1992 s.137(1).
"working families' tax credit"—see reg.2(1); SSCBA 1992 s.128.

GENERAL NOTE

2.17 As with all of the Regulations making claimants eligible for the award of credits, this must be read with reg.3 (*CIB/1602/2006*; *CIB/3327/2004*). One can only have them insofar as they are necessary to bring one's record up to the level required for satisfying the second contribution condition for the relevant benefit (see para.(1), reg.3 and reg.2(1) ("reckonable year")).

It covers an employed earner, or a self-employed earner exempt from paying Class 2 contributions because of the "small earnings" exception, to whom working tax credit is paid for any week, and enables a credit equal to that tax year's lower earnings limit to be awarded for each such week. Where the person is one of a married or unmarried couple, note the rules in para.(3) stipulating who gets the award of the credit: the sole assessed earner; or, where both are assessed, the partner to whom working tax credit is paid.

The credit is only awardable to those attaining or due to attain pensionable age after April 5, 1999 and only with respect to weeks falling wholly or partly in tax year 1995–96 or subsequent tax years (para.(5)).

Note that a woman cannot gain a credit under this provision in respect of any week in any part of which as a married woman a certificate of election to pay contributions at reduced rate applied to her (para.(4)(b)). Nor can a credit be awarded under this provision if a credit entitlement for the week arises under reg.8A (unemployment) or 8B (incapacity for work) (para.(4)(a)).

Credits on termination of full-time education, training or apprenticeship

2.18 **8.**—[1 (1) For the purposes of his entitlement to [2 a contribution based jobseeker's allowance] [3 short-term incapacity benefit or a contributory employment and support allowance] a person shall be entitled to be credited with earnings equal to the lower earnings limit then in force for either one of the last two complete years before the beginning of the relevant benefit year if—

(a) during any part of that year he was—
(i) undergoing a course of full-time education; or
(ii) undergoing—

(a) a course of training which was full-time and which was arranged under section 2(1) of the Employment and Training Act 1973 or [4 section 2(3) of the Enterprise and New Towns (Scotland) Act 1990]; or
(b) any other full-time course the sole or main purpose of which was the acquisition of occupational or vocational skills; or
(c) if he is a disabled person within the meaning of the Disabled Persons (Employment) Act 1944 a part-time course attended for at least 15 hours a week which, if it was full-time, would fall within either of heads (a) or (b) above; or

(iii) an apprentice; and

(b) the other year is, in his case, a reckonable year; and
(c) that course or, as the case may be, his apprenticeship has terminated.]

(2) Paragraph (1) shall not apply—

(a) where the course of education or training or the apprenticeship commenced after the person had attained the age of 21;
(b) to a woman in respect of any tax year immediately before the end of which she was a married woman and an election made by her under regulations made [5 under section 3(2) of the Social Security Pensions Act 1975] had effect[6;
(c) to a person in respect of any tax year before that in which he attains the age of 18.]

AMENDMENTS

1. Social Security (Credits) Amendment Regulations 1989 (SI 1989/1627) reg.3 (October 1, 1989).
2. Social Security (Credits and Contributions) (Jobseeker's Allowance Consequential and Miscellaneous Amendments) Regulations 1996 reg.2(5) (SI 1996/2367).
3. Employment and Support Allowance (Consequential Provisions) (No. 2) Regulations 2008 (SI 2008/1554) reg.48(4) (October 27, 2008).
4. Enterprise (Scotland) Consequential Amendments Order 1991 (SI 1991/387) art.3 (April 1, 1991).
5. Social Security (Credits) Amendment and (Earnings Factor) Transitional Regulations 1978 (SI 1978/409) reg.2(2) (April 6, 1978).
6. Social Security (Credits) Amendment (No. 2) Regulations 1988 (SI 1988/1230) reg.2(3) (October 2, 1988).

DEFINITIONS

"lower earnings limit"—see SSCBA 1992 s.122(1).
"relevant benefit year"—see reg.2(1).
"tax year"—see SSCBA 1992 s.122(1).
"year"—see reg.2(1).

GENERAL NOTE

As with all of the Regulations making claimants eligible for the award of credits, this must be read with reg.3 (*CIB/1602/2006*; *CIB/3327/2004*). One can only have them insofar as they are necessary to bring one's record up to the level required for satisfying the second contribution condition for the relevant benefit (see para.(1), reg.3 and reg.2(1) ("reckonable year")). 2.19

This applies only for purposes of entitlement to contribution-based jobseeker's allowance (CBJSA), short-term incapacity benefit (STIB) or a contributory employment and support allowance (CESA). For both these benefits, the second contribution condition requires that the contribution record in terms of paid and/or credited contributions reaches the requisite level (50 times the tax year's lower earnings limit) in respect of *each* of the last two tax years complete before the beginning of the relevant benefit year (the year in which there falls the first day of the jobseeking period or linked period [CBJSA: see Jobseekers Act 1995, s.2(1)(b)] or period of incapacity for work [STIB: see SSCBA 1992, Sch.3, para.2] or period of limited capability for work [CESA, see WRA 2007, Sch.1, para.2] of which the claim for benefit is part). It enables credits to be awarded, where in one of those tax years the second condition is met (it is a "reckonable year"), in order to make the record in the other tax year up to the requisite level (to make it also a "reckonable year"). The provision applies where during any part of the relevant benefit year, he was an apprentice, or was someone undergoing a course of full-time education, or a course of full-time training under specified legislation, or a full-time course the sole or main purpose of which was the acquisition of occupational or vocational skills (para.(1)(a)). Where he is disabled within the meaning of the Disabled Persons (Employment) Act 1944, it suffices that such a course was part-time (attended for at least 15 hours a week) (para.(1)(a)(ii)(c)). The final condition for the award of the credit is that the apprenticeship or course must have terminated (para.(1)(c)).

No award can be made where the apprenticeship or course commenced after the person attained the age of 21 (para.(2)(a)) or in respect of any tax year prior to that in which he became 18 (para.(2)(c)). Note finally that a woman cannot gain a credit under this provision in respect of any tax year immediately before the end of which she was a married woman and a certificate of election to pay contributions at reduced rate had effect in relation to her (para.(2)(b)).

2.20 **[[1]Credits for unemployment**

8A.—(1) For the purposes of entitlement to any benefit by virtue of a person's earnings or contributions, he shall be entitled to be credited with earnings equal to the lower earnings limit then in force, in respect of each week to which this regulation applies.

(2) Subject to paragraph (5) this regulation applies to a week which, in relation to the person concerned, is—

(a) a week for the whole of which he was paid a jobseeker's allowance; or

[[11](b) a week for the whole of which the person in relation to old style JSA—

(i) satisfied or was treated as having satisfied the conditions set out in paragraphs (a), (c) and (e) to (h) of section 1(2) of the Jobseekers Act 1995 (conditions for entitlement to a jobseeker's allowance); and

(ii) satisfied the further condition specified in paragraph (3) below; or

(ba) a week for the whole of which the person in relation to new style JSA—

(i) satisfied or was treated as having satisfied the conditions set out in paragraphs (e) to (h) of section 1(2) of the Jobseekers Act 1995 (conditions for entitlement to a jobseeker's allowance);

(ii) satisfied or was treated as having satisfied the work-related requirements under section 6D and 6E of the Jobseekers Act 1995 (work search and work availability requirements); and

(iii) satisfied the further condition specified in paragraph (3) below; or]

(c) a week which would have been a week described in sub-paragraph (b) [[11]or (ba)] but for the fact that he was incapable of work [[5]or had limited capability for work] for part of it, or

[3(d) a week in respect of which he would have been paid a jobseeker's allowance but for a restriction imposed pursuant to [6 . . .] [2section [76B,] 7, 8 or 9 of the Social Security Fraud Act 2001 (loss of benefit provisions)]].

(3) The further condition referred to in paragraph (2)(b) [11and (ba)] is that the person concerned—

(a) furnished to the Secretary of State notice in writing of the grounds on which he claims to be entitled to be credited with earnings—

(i) on the first day of the period for which he claims to be so entitled in which the week in question fell; or

(ii) within such further time as may be reasonable in the circumstances of the case; and

(b) has provided any evidence required by the Secretary of State that the conditions referred to in paragraph (2)(b) [11or the conditions and requirements in paragraph (2)(ba)] are satisfied.

(4) [10*Omitted.*]

(5) This regulation shall not apply to—

(a) a week in respect of which the person concerned was not entitled to a jobseeker's allowance (or would not have been if he had claimed it) because of section 14 of the Jobseekers Act 1995 (trade disputes); or

(b) a week in respect of which, in relation to the person concerned, there was in force a direction under section 16 of that Act (which relates to persons who have reached the age of 16 but not the age of 18 and who are in severe hard ship); or

[11(c) a week in respect of which, in relation to the person concerned—

(i) an old style JSA was reduced in accordance with section 19 or 19A, or regulations made under section 19B, of the Jobseekers Act 1995; or

(ii) a new style JSA was reduced in accordance with section 6J or 6K of the Jobseekers Act 1995; or]

(d) a week in respect of which a jobseeker's allowance was payable to the person concerned only by virtue of regulation 141 of the Jobseeker's Allowance Regulations 1996 (circumstances in which an income-based jobseeker's allowance is payable to a person in hard ship); or

[4(dd) a week in respect of which a joint-claim jobseeker's allowance was payable in respect of a joint-claim couple of which the person is a member only by virtue of regulation 146C of the Jobseeker's Allowance Regulations 1996 (circumstances in which a joint –claim jobseeker's allowance is payable where a joint-claim couple is a couple in hard ship);

[11(de)a week where paragraph (2)(b), (ba) or (c) apply and the person concerned was entitled to universal credit for any part of that week; or]

(e) where the person concerned is a married woman, a week in respect of any part of which an election made by her under regulations made under section 19(4) of the Contributions and Benefits Act had effect.]

[11(6) In this regulation—

"new style JSA" means a jobseeker's allowance under the Jobseekers Act 1995 as amended by the provisions of Part 1 of Schedule 14 to the 2012 Act that remove references to an income-based allowance;

"old style JSA" means a jobseeker's allowance under the Jobseekers Act 1995 as it has effect apart from the amendments made by Part 1 of

Schedule 14 to the 2012 Act that remove references to an income-based allowance.]

AMENDMENTS

1. Social Security (Credits and Contributions) (Jobseeker's Allowance Consequential and Miscellaneous Amendments) Regulations 1996 (SI 1996/2367) reg.2(6) (October 7, 1996).
2. Social Security (Loss of Benefit) (Consequential Amendments) Regulations 2002 (SI 2002/490) reg.3 (April 1, 2002).
3. Social Security (Breach of Community Order) (Consequential Amendments) Regulations 2001 (SI 2001/1711) reg.2(5) (October 15, 2001).
4. Social Security Amendment (Joint Claims) Regulations 2001 (SI 2001/518) reg.3 (March 19, 2001).
5. Employment and Support Allowance (Consequential Provisions) (No. 2) Regulations 2008 (SI 2008/1554) reg.48(5) (October 27, 2008).
6. Welfare Reform Act 2009 (Section 26) (Consequential Amendments) Regulations 2010 (SI 2010/424) reg.2 (April 2, 2010).
7. Social Security (Loss of Benefit) Amendment Regulations 2010 (SI 2010/1160) reg.13 (April 1, 2010).
8. Jobseeker's Allowance (Sanctions for Failure to Attend) Regulations 2010 (SI 2010/509) reg.4(5) (April 6, 2010).
9. Jobseeker's Allowance (Sanctions) (Amendment) Regulations 2012 (SI 2012/2568) reg.9 (October 22, 2012).
10. Social Security (Miscellaneous Amendments)(No.3) Regulations 2013 (SI 2013/2536) reg.3 (October 29, 2013).
11. Universal Credit (Consequential, Supplementary, Incidental and Miscellaneous Provisions) Regulations 2013 (SI 2013/630) reg.70(1), (4) (April 29, 2013).

DEFINITIONS

"benefit"—see reg.2(1).
"jobseeker's allowance"—see reg.2(1).
"lower earnings limit"—see SSCBA 1992 s.122(1).

GENERAL NOTE

2.21 As with all of the Regulations making claimants eligible for the award of credits, this must be read with reg.3 (*CIB/1602/2006*; *CIB/3327/2004*). One can only have them insofar as they are necessary to bring one's record up to the level required for satisfying the second contribution condition for the relevant benefit (see para.(1), reg.3 and reg.2(1) ("reckonable year")).

It enables a credit equal to that tax year's lower earnings limit to be awarded for each week in respect of which one of the situations in para.(1) pertains.

The position is that it cannot be known whether a claimant is entitled to claim credits (credited with earnings) until some time after the end of the tax year for which the claim for them is made. The difficulties that can be caused by this complex interaction of Credits Regulations with those applicable to Jobseeker's Allowance, in a context in which there appear to be decision-making problems as a result of responsibilities divided between the DWP and HMRC, are explored in *CIB/1602/2006.*

Regulation 8A(3)(a)(i) stipulates that to be eligible for unemployment credits, in respect of a period of non-payment of JSA under para.(2)(b), a person must give notice in writing of the grounds on which he claims to be entitled to be credited with earnings

> "(i) on the first day of the period for which he claims to be entitled in which the week in question fell; or (ii) within such further time as may be reasonable in the circumstances of the case".

2.22 In reality it is the second (fallback) option which will have to apply. This means that in a case such as that in *CIB/1602/2006*, where the claimant on a claim for incapacity benefit was arguing that he should have been awarded credits for a period of unemployment several years earlier in which he was not entitled to payment of JSA, that

> "the Secretary of State can do no more than require that a claimant makes a claim in writing, setting out the grounds for it, within a reasonable time of becoming entitled. That is a question of fact. It will take into account the guidance given to a claimant (all of which is set out above, unless something is added orally).
>
> Noting the guidance and correspondence put in evidence to the tribunal in this appeal, I have little difficulty in finding on the facts that D's correspondence with the Jobcentre and with the Member of Parliament and the Minister did raise the matter adequately in writing and within a reasonable time" (paras 33, 34).

The decision on whether earnings should be credited is not a HMRC decision, but one for the Secretary of State and appealable to the appeals tribunal, the Commissioner and the courts. In *CIB/1602/2006*, it was whether reg.8A(2)(b) applied in the claimant's case. The claimant needed two weeks' credited earnings to bring his record to the requisite level (50 times the lower earnings limit), having already been credited with 48 times that limit. Here, the Commissioner found from the correspondence that a decision had been made to refuse to credit the claimant with earnings for the period at issue because during the time at issue he was out of the United Kingdom. The Commissioner found that, although on holiday, he had satisfied the availability condition because he had informed the Jobcentre of his holiday with his children (and could thus have returned on request with the 48 hour notice period allowed). In terms of actively seeking work he could also take advantage of the "deemed actively seeking work" for two weeks of properly notified holiday (Jobseeker's Regulations 1996, reg.19(1)(p)). Absence from Great Britain precludes entitlement to JSA. But it does not as such preclude entitlement to unemployment credits for the period of absence, since reg.8A(2)(b) while linking back to specifically enumerated conditions in Jobseekers Act 1995, s.1(2), does not include the "present in Great Britain" condition. Accordingly, Commissioner Williams concluded that the claimant met the second contribution condition for entitlement to incapacity benefit.

No credit, however, can be awarded as regards a week in respect of which one of the situations in para.(5) exists.

For confirmation that reg.8A can apply to unemployed people who are not claiming JSA, see *KL v SSWP (JSA)* [2022] UKUT 270 (AAC). The decision also confirms that whether the claim was made "within such further time as may be reasonable in the circumstances of the case" (within reg.8A(3)) is ultimately a question of fact (see *CIB/2445/2006*, decided under reg.8B).

[1 Credits for incapacity for work [4 or limited capability for work]

8B.—(1) [2 For] the purposes of entitlement to any benefit by virtue of a person's earnings or contributions, he shall be entitled to be credited with earnings equal to the lower earnings limit then in force, in respect of each week to which this regulation applies. 2.23

(2) Subject to paragraphs [7 (2A),] (3) and (4) this regulation applies to—

[5(a) a week in which, in relation to the person concerned, each of the days—

(i) was a day of incapacity for work under section 30C of the Contributions and Benefits Act (incapacity benefit: days and periods of incapacity for work); or

(ii) would have been such a day had the person concerned claimed short-term incapacity benefit or maternity allowance within the prescribed time; or

(iii) was a day of incapacity for work for the purposes of statutory sick pay under section 151 of the Contributions and Benefits

Act and fell within a period of entitlement under section 153 of that Act; or

(iv) was a day of limited capability for work for the purposes of Part 1 of the Welfare Reform Act (limited capability for work) or would have been such a day had the person concerned been entitled to an employment and support allowance by virtue of section 1(2)(a) of the Welfare Reform Act; or

[6(iva) would have been a day of limited capability for work for the purposes of Part 1 of the Welfare Reform Act (limited capability for work) where the person concerned would have been entitled to an employment and support allowance but for the application of section 1A of that Act; or]

(v) would have been a day of limited capability for work for the purposes of Part 1 of the Welfare Reform Act (limited capability for work) had that person claimed an employment and support allowance or maternity allowance within the prescribed time;]

[5 (aa) . . .];

[3(b) a week for any part of which an unemployability supplement or allowance was payable by virtue of—

(i) Schedule 7 to the Contributions and Benefits Act;

[5 (ii) Article 12 of the Naval, Military and Air Forces Etc. (Disablement and Death) Service Pensions Order 2006;] or

(iii) Article 18 of the Personal Injuries (Civilians) Scheme 1983.]

[7(2A) This regulation shall not apply to a week where—

(a) under paragraph (2)(a)(i) the person concerned was not entitled to incapacity benefit, severe disablement allowance or maternity allowance;

(b) paragraph (2)(a)(ii), (iva) or (v) apply; or

(c) under paragraph (2)(a)(iv) the person concerned was not entitled to an employment and support allowance by virtue of section 1(2)(a) of the Welfare Reform Act,

and the person concerned was entitled to universal credit for any part of that week.

(3) Where the person concerned is a married woman, this regulation shall not apply to a week in respect of any part of which an election made by her under regulations made under section 19(4) of the Contributions and Benefits Act had effect.

(4) A day shall not be a day to which paragraph (2)(a) applies unless the person concerned has—

(a) before the end of the benefit year immediately following the year in which that day fell; or

(b) within such further time as may be reasonable in the circumstances of the case,

furnished to the Secretary of State notice in writing of the grounds on which he claims to be entitled to be credited with earnings.]

AMENDMENTS

1. Social Security (Credits and Contributions) (Jobseeker's Allowance Consequential and Miscellaneous Amendments) Regulations 1996 (SI 1996/2367) reg.2(6) (October 7, 1996).

2. Social Security (Incapacity Benefit) Miscellaneous Amendments Regulations 2000 (SI 2000/3120) reg.4(b) (April 6, 2001).

3. Social Security (Miscellaneous Amendments) (No.3) Regulations 2007 (SI 2007/1749) reg.8(3) (July 16, 2007).
4. Employment and Support Allowance (Consequential Provisions) (No.2) Regulations 2008 (SI 2008/1554) reg.48(6) (October 27, 2008).
5. Social Security (Credits)(Amendment) Regulations 2010 (SI 2010/385) reg.2(2) (April 6, 2010).
6. Employment and Support Allowance (Duration of Contributory Allowance) (Consequential Amendments) Regulations 2012 (SI 2012/913) reg.2 (May 1, 2012).
7. Universal Credit (Consequential, Supplementary, Incidental and Miscellaneous Provisions) Regulations 2013 (SI 2013/630) reg.70(1), (5) (April 29, 2013).

DEFINITIONS

"benefit"—see reg.2(1).
"benefit year"—see SSCBA 1992 s.21(6).
"lower earnings limit"—see SSCBA 1992 s.122(1).
"year"—see reg.2(1).

GENERAL NOTE

As with all of the Regulations making claimants eligible for the award of credits, this must be read with reg.3 (*CIB/1602/2006*; *CIB/3327/2004*). One can only have them insofar as they are necessary to bring one's record up to the level required for satisfying the second contribution condition for the relevant benefit (see para.(1), reg.3 and reg.2(1) ("reckonable year")). 2.24

It enables a credit equal to that tax year's lower earnings limit to be awarded for each week in respect of which one of the following situations pertains (para.(1)):

- each of its days was one of incapacity for work under SSCBA 1992 s.30C (or would have been had s/he claimed in time for short-term incapacity benefit or maternity allowance or been entitled to incapacity benefit under s.30A)—provided that the written notification and statement of grounds conditions in para.(4) are met (para.(2)(a)(i), (ii));
- each of its days was one of incapacity for work within a period of entitlement for SSP purposes (SSCBA 1992 ss.151 and 153)—provided that the written notification and statement of grounds conditions in para.(4) are met (para.2(a)(iii));
- each of its days was one of limited capability for work for the purposes of Pt I of the WRA 2007 or would have been had s/he claimed in time for ESA or maternity allowance or had been entitled to ESA under WRA 2007 s.1(2)(a)—provided that the written notification and statement of grounds conditions in para.(4) are met (para.(2)(a) (iv), (v);
- each of its days was one of continuing limited capability for work where entitlement to CESA has ceased only because the time-limit (currently 365 days for those not in the support group) set by the WRA 2007 s.1A has been reached.
- unemployability supplement was payable for part of it (see SSCBA 1992 Sch.7 Pt I) (para.(2)(b)).

Commissioner Mesher considered this phrase in *CIB/2445/2006* when concluding that the appeal tribunal was within its permitted area of judgment when concluding that what would have been a reasonable time for claiming credits for any of the years 1989/90 to 2000/01 had expired by the time the claimant claimed them on May 13, 2005 (para.27). As the Commissioner pointed out, the test in reg.8B(4) is not one of "good cause" for a late claim but

> "the more general test of what is a reasonable time in the circumstances for a claim to be made. Therefore . . . the length of the time after the period for which credits are claimed is a factor, along with all the other circumstances. When entitlement to credits rests on proof of incapacity for work, the assessment of the evidence

and the making of a proper decision becomes more difficult the further away from the period in question one gets. As a general proposition it can be accepted that the longer the gap from the tax year in question the more compelling the other circumstances must be for it to be concluded that the time for claiming, outside the following benefit year, is reasonable" (para.29).

Even with respect to the most recent tax years in respect of which credits were claimed (2000/01), the range of communications indicating a shortfall in his contributions record were such that the tribunal was entitled to conclude that the time for claiming credits was, by May 2005, no longer reasonable.

Note that a woman cannot gain a credit under this provision in respect of any week in any part of which as a married woman a certificate of election to pay contributions at reduced rate applied to her (para.(3)). Nor can one be given where any of the situations in para.(2A) exists, involving entitlement to universal credit.

For a case involving the operation of reg.8B, and the potential linkage to a claim for universal credit, see *JW v SSWP (UC)* [2022] UKUT 117 (AAC).

Credits on termination of bereavement benefits

2.25 **[[1] 8C.**—(1) This regulation applies for the purpose only of enabling a person who previously received a bereavement benefit ("the recipient") to satisfy, as the case may be, the condition referred to in—

(a) paragraph 2(3)(b) of Schedule 3 to the Contributions and Benefits Act in relation to short-term incapacity benefit; [[3] . . .]

(b) section 2(1)(b) of the Jobseekers Act 1995 in relation to contribution-based jobseeker's allowance. [;[3] or

(c) paragraph 2(1) of Schedule 1 to the Welfare Reform Act in relation to a contributory employment and support allowance.]

[[1](2) For every year up to and including that in which the recipient ceased to be entitled to a bereavement benefit otherwise than by reason of remarriage [[2], forming a civil partnership], or living together with [[4]another person [[6] as if they were a married couple or civil partners]], the recipient shall be credited with such earnings as may be required to enable the condition referred to above to be satisfied.]

[[5] (3) In this regulation, "bereavement benefit" means—

(a) a bereavement payment referred to in section 36 of the Contributions and Benefits Act as in force immediately before it was repealed by paragraph 8 of Schedule 16 to the Pensions Act 2014;

(b) a bereavement allowance referred to in section 39B of the Contributions and Benefits Act as in force immediately before it was repealed by paragraph 13 of Schedule 16 to the Pensions Act 2014; and

(c) widowed parent's allowance.]

Revocation and Amendments

1. Social Security (Benefits for Widows and Widowers) (Consequential Amendments) Regulations 2000 (SI 2000/1483) reg.3(7) (April 9, 2001).

2. Civil Partnership (Pensions, Social Security and Child Support) (Consequential, etc. Provisions) Order 2005 (SI 2005/2877) art.2(3) and Sch.3 para.4(4) (December 5, 2005).

3. Employment and Support Allowance (Consequential Provisions) (No. 2) Regulations 2008 (SI 2008/1554) reg.48(7) (October 27, 2008).

4. Marriage (Same Sex Couples) Act 2013 and Marriage and Civil Partnership (Scotland) Act 2014 (Consequential Provisions) Order 2014 (SI 2014/3061) art.2 and Sch.1 para,4(1), (2) (December 10, 2014 (England and Wales) and December 16, 2014 (Scotland) (see art.1).

5. Pensions Act 2014 (Consequential, Supplementary and Incidental Amendments) Order 2017 (SI 2017/422) art.4(7) (April 6, 2017).
6. Civil Partnership (Opposite-sex Couples) Regulations 2019 (SI 2019/1458) reg.41(b) and Sch.3 Part 2 para.37(2) (December 2, 2019).

DEFINITIONS

"bereavement benefit"—para.(3); SSCBA 1992 s.20(1)(ea).
"the recipient"—para.(1).

GENERAL NOTE

As with all of the Regulations making claimants eligible for the award of credits, this must be read with reg.3 (*CIB/1602/2006*; *CIB/3327/2004*). One can only have them insofar as they are necessary to bring one's record up to the level required for satisfying the second contribution condition for the relevant benefit (see para.(1), reg.3 and reg.2(1) ("reckonable year")). 2.26

Regulation 8C applies only in respect of awarding sufficient credits to satisfy the second contribution condition for contribution-based jobseeker's allowance [CBJSA], short-term incapacity benefit [STIB] or contributory employment and support allowance [ESA]. For these benefits, the second contribution condition requires that the contribution record in terms of paid and/or credited contributions reaches the requisite level (50 times the tax year's lower earnings limit) in respect of *each* of the last two tax years complete before the beginning of the relevant benefit year (the year in which there falls the first day of the jobseeking period or linked period [CBJSA: see Jobseekers Act 1995 s.2(1)(b); *Vol.I: Non Means Tested Benefits*], period of incapacity for work [STIB: see SSCBA 1992 Sch.3, para.2] or period of limited capability for work [CESA, see WRA 2007 Sch.1, para.2] of which the claim for benefit is part). It enables the award of sufficient credits to someone who previously received a "bereavement benefit". Those credits can be awarded for every tax year up to and including the one in which the person ceased to be entitled to the bereavement benefit, provided that entitlement was not lost by reason of remarriage or cohabitation as husband and wife with someone of the opposite sex. "Bereavement benefit" has the same meaning as in SSCBA 1992 s.20(1)(ea), above (reg.2(1)).

[1 Credits for the purposes of entitlement to incapacity benefit following official error

8D.—(1) This regulation applies for the purpose only of enabling a person who was previously entitled to incapacity benefit to satisfy the condition referred to in paragraph 2(3)(a) of Schedule 3 to the Contributions and Benefits Act in respect of a subsequent claim for incapacity benefit where his period of incapacity for work is, together with a previous period of incapacity for work, to be treated as one period of incapacity for work under section 30C of that Act. 2.27

(2) Where—

(a) a person was previously entitled to incapacity benefit;
(b) the award of incapacity benefit was as a result of satisfying the condition referred to in paragraph (1) by virtue of being credited with earnings for incapacity for work or approved training in the tax years from 1993–94 to 2007–08;
(c) some or all of those credits were credited by virtue of official error derived from the failure to transpose correctly information relating to those credits from the Department for Work and Pensions' Pension Strategy Computer System to Her Majesty's Revenue and Customs' computer system (NIRS2) or from related clerical procedures;

(d) that person makes a further claim for incapacity benefit; and
(e) his period of incapacity for work is, together with the period of incapacity for work to which his previous entitlement referred to in sub-paragraph (a) related, to be treated as one period of incapacity for work under section 30C of the Contributions and Benefits Act,

that person shall be credited with such earnings as may be required to enable the condition referred to in paragraph (1) to be satisfied.

(3) In this regulation and in regulations 8E and 8F, "official error" means an error made by—

(a) an officer of the Department for Work and Pensions or an officer of Revenue and Customs acting as such which no person outside the Department or Her Majesty's Revenue and Customs caused or to which no person outside the Department for Work and Pensions or Her Majesty's Revenue and Customs materially contributed; or
(b) a person employed by a service provider and to which no person who was not so employed materially contributed,

but excludes any error of law which is shown to have been an error by virtue of a subsequent decision of a Commissioner or the court.

(4) In paragraph (3)—

"Commissioner" means the Chief Social Security Commissioner or any other Social Security Commissioner and includes a tribunal of three or more Commissioners constituted under section 16(7) of the Social Security Act 1998;

"service provider" means a person providing services to the Secretary of State for Work and Pensions or to Her Majesty's Revenue and Customs.]

AMENDMENT

1. Social Security (National Insurance Credits) Amendment Regulations 2007 (SI 2007/2582) reg.2 (October 1, 2007).

Credits for the purposes of entitlement to retirement pension following official error

2.28 **8E.**—(1) This regulation applies for the purpose only of enabling the condition referred to in paragraph 5(3)(a) of Schedule 3 to the Contributions and Benefits Act to be satisfied in respect of a claim for retirement pension made by a person ("the claimant")—

(a) who would attain pensionable age no later than 31st May 2008;
(b) not falling within sub-paragraph (a) but based on the satisfaction of that condition by another person—
 (i) who would attain, or would have attained, pensionable age no later than 31st May 2008; or
 (ii) in respect of whose death the claimant received a bereavement benefit.

(2) Where—

(a) a person claims retirement pension;
(b) the satisfaction of the condition referred to in paragraph (1) would be based on earnings credited for incapacity for work or approved training in the tax years from 1993–94 to 2007–08; and
(c) some or all of those credits were credited by virtue of official error derived from the failure to transpose correctly information relating to those credits from the Department for Work and Pensions' Pension

Strategy Computer System to Her Majesty's Revenue and Customs' computer system (NIRS2) or from related clerical procedures,

those earnings shall be credited.

(3) In this regulation, "bereavement benefit" means a bereavement allowance [2 referred to in section 39B of the Contributions and Benefits Act as in force immediately before it was repealed by paragraph 13 of Schedule 16 to the Pensions Act 2014], a widowed mother's allowance, a widowed parent's allowance or a widow's pension.

AMENDMENTS

1. Social Security (National Insurance Credits) Amendment Regulations 2007 (SI 2007/2582) reg.2 (October 1, 2007).

2. Pensions Act 2014 (Consequential, Supplementary and Incidental Amendments) Order 2017 (SI 2017/422) art.4(8) (April 6, 2017).

[1 Credits for the purposes of entitlement to contribution-based jobseeker's allowance following official error

8F.—(1) This regulation applies for the purpose only of enabling a person to satisfy the condition referred to in section 2(1)(b) of the Jobseekers Act 1995. 2.29

(2) Where—

(a) a person claims a jobseeker's allowance;

(b) the satisfaction of the condition referred to in paragraph (1) would be based on earnings credited for incapacity for work or approved training in the tax years from 1993–94 to 2007–08; and

(c) some or all of those credits were credited by virtue of official error derived from the failure to transpose correctly information relating to those credits from the Department for Work and Pensions' Pension Strategy Computer System to Her Majesty's Revenue and Customs' computer system (NIRS2) or from related clerical procedures,

that person shall be credited with those earnings.]

AMENDMENT

1. Social Security (National Insurance Credits) Amendment Regulations 2007 (SI 2007/2582) reg.2 (October 1, 2007).

[1Credits for persons entitled to universal credit

8G.—(1) For the purposes of entitlement to a benefit to which this regulation applies, a person shall be credited with a Class 3 contribution in respect of a week if that person is entitled to universal credit under Part 1 of the Welfare Reform Act 2012 for any part of that week. 2.30

(2) This regulation applies to—

(a) a Category A retirement pension;

(b) a Category B retirement pension;

(c) a widowed parent's allowance;

(d) [2 . . .]

AMENDMENTS

1. Universal Credit (Consequential, Supplementary, Incidental and Miscellaneous Provisions) Regulations 2013 (SI 2013/630) reg.70(1), (6) (April 29, 2013).

2. Pensions Act 2014 (Consequential, Supplementary and Incidental Amendments) Order 2017 (SI 2017/422) art.4(9) (April 6, 2017).

Crediting of earnings for the purposes of entitlement to short-term incapacity benefit—further conditions

2.31 **9.**—[1 . . .]

REVOCATION

1. Social Security (Incapacity Benefit) Miscellaneous Amendments Regulations 2000 (SI 2000/3120) reg.4(c) (April 16, 2001).

[1 Credits for persons approaching pensionable age

2.32 **9A.**—(1) For the purposes of entitlement to any benefit by virtue of a person's earnings or contributions [3 a person to whom this regulation applies] shall, subject to the following paragraphs, be credited with such earnings as may be required to bring his relevant earnings factor in respect of a tax year to which this regulation applies to the level required to make that year a reckonable year.

[3 (1A) This regulation applies to a man born before 6th October 1954 but who has not attained the age of 65.]

[3 (2) This regulation shall apply to—

(a) the tax year in which a man attains the age which is pensionable age in the case of a woman born on the same day as that man; and

(b) to any succeeding tax year,

but not including the tax year in which he attains the age of 65 or any subsequent tax year.]

(3) Paragraph (1) shall apply, in the case of a self-employed earner, only if he is—

(a) liable to pay a Class 2 contribution in respect of any week in a tax year to which this regulation applies; or

(b) excepted from liability to pay Class 2 contributions in respect of any week in a tax year to which this regulation applies by virtue of his earnings being less than, or being treated by regulations as less than, the amount specified in section 11(4) of the Social Security Contributions and Benefits Act 1992 (exception from liability for Class 2 contributions on account of small earnings),

so that he shall be credited with earnings equal to the lower earnings limit then in force in respect of each week for which he is not so liable.

(4) [2 . . .]

(5) Where in any tax year to which this regulation applies a person is absent from Great Britain for more than 182 days, he shall not by virtue of this regulation be credited with any earnings or contributions in that tax year.]

AMENDMENTS

1. Social Security (Credits) Amendment Regulations 1994 (SI 1994/1837) reg.3 (August 8, 1994).

2. Social Security (Credits and Contributions) (Jobseeker's Allowance Consequential and Miscellaneous Amendments) Regulations 1996 (SI 1996/2367) reg.2(8) (October 7, 1996).

3. Social Security (State Pension and National Insurance Credits) Regulations 2009 (SI 2009/2206) reg.30 (April 6, 2010).

DEFINITIONS

"benefit"—see reg.2(1).
"pensionable age"—see SSCBA 1992 s.122(1).
"reckonable year"—see reg.2(1).
"relevant earnings factor"—see reg.2(1).
"self-employed earner"—see SSCBA 1992 s.2(1)(b).
"tax year"—see SSCBA 1992 s.122(1).
"year"—see reg.2(1).

GENERAL NOTE

As with all of the Regulations making claimants eligible for the award of credits, this must be read with reg.3 (*CIB/1602/2006*; *CIB/3327/2004*). One can only have them insofar as they are necessary to bring one's record up to the level required for satisfying the second contribution condition for the relevant benefit (see para.(1), reg.3 and reg.2(1) ("reckonable year")). 2.33

It is applicable only to the tax year in which the person attained 60 and to each of the four succeeding tax years (para.(2)). It enables the award of sufficient credits to give the requisite record for the purposes of the second contribution condition (to make that year a "reckonable year") (para.(1)). As respects a self-employed earner, it can only do so if he is exempt from paying Class 2 contributions because of the "small earnings" exception (para.(3)). It cannot do so in respect of any tax year to which this regulation applies, if in that year the person is absent from Great Britain for more than 182 days (para.(4)).

[1 Credits for jury service

9B.—(1) Subject to paragraphs (2) and (3), for the purposes of entitlement to any benefit [2 by virtue of a person's earnings or contributions] he shall be entitled to be credited with earnings equal to the lower earnings limit then in force, in respect of each week for any part of which he attended at Court for jury service. 2.34

(2) A person shall be entitled to be credited with earnings in respect of a week by virtue of the provisions of this regulation only if—

(a) his earnings in respect of that week from any employment of his as an employed earner are below the lower earnings limit then in force; and
(b) he furnished to the Secretary of State notice in writing of his claim to be entitled to be credited with earnings and did so before the end of the benefit year immediately following the tax year in which that week or part of that week fell or within such further time as may be reasonable in the circumstances of his case.

(3) Paragraph (1) shall not apply—

(a) to a woman in respect of any week in any part of which she was a married woman in respect of whom an election made by her under Regulations made under section 3(2) of the Social Security Pensions Act 1975 had effect; or
(b) in respect of any week falling wholly or partly within a year commencing before 6th April 1988[3, or
(c) to a person in respect of any week in any part of which he is a self-employed earner.]]

AMENDMENTS

1. Social Security (Credits) Amendment Regulations 1988 (SI 1988/516) reg.2(3) (April 6, 1988).

2. Social Security (Credits) Amendment (No. 4) Regulations 1988 (SI 1988/1545) reg.2(5) (October 2, 1988).

3. Social Security (Credits) Amendment Regulations 1994 (SI 1994/1837) reg.4.

DEFINITIONS

"benefit"—see reg.2(1).
"benefit year"—see SSCBA 1992 s.21(6).
"employed earner"—see SSCBA 1992 s.2(1)(a).
"lower earnings limit"—see SSCBA 1992 s.122(1).
"self-employed earner"—see SSCBA 1992 s.2(1)(b).
"tax year"—see SSCBA 1992 s.122(1).

GENERAL NOTE

2.35 As with all of the Regulations making claimants eligible for the award of credits, this must be read with reg.3 (*CIB/1602/2006*; *CIB/3327/2004*). One can only have them insofar as they are necessary to bring one's record up to the level required for satisfying the second contribution condition for the relevant benefit (see para.(1), reg.3 and reg.2(1) ("reckonable year")).

It enables the award of a credit equal to the lower earnings limit for the tax year in question only to an employed earner as regards a week for any part of which he attended at Court for jury service, provided that his earnings in respect of that week from his employment fall below the then applicable lower earnings limit. He must claim in time and in writing (para.(2)(b)).

No award is possible in respect of a week falling wholly or partly in a tax year before April 6, 1988 (para.(3)(b)). Nor can one be made to someone in any week in part of which he is a self-employed earner (thus ruling out the person who in that week is both employed and self-employed, or who changes from one category to another during that week) (para.(3)(c)).

Note, finally, that a woman cannot gain a credit under this provision in respect of any week in any part of which as a married woman a certificate of election to pay contributions at reduced rate applied to her (para.(3)).

[2Credits for adoption pay period, [3 shared parental pay period,] [4 parental bereavement pay period,] additional paternity pay period and maternity pay period]

2.36 [1**9C.**—(1) For the purposes of entitlement to any benefit by virtue of—

(a) in the case of a person referred to in paragraph (2)(a) [4, (aa) or (d)], that person's earnings or contributions;

(b) in the case of a woman referred to in paragraph (2)(b), her earnings or contributions, [3; or]

[3 (c) the shared parental pay period in respect of which statutory shared parental pay is paid to a person.]

that person or that woman, as the case may be, shall be entitled to be credited with earnings equal to the lower earnings limit then in force in respect of each week to which this regulation applies.

(2) Subject to paragraphs (3) and (4), this regulation applies to each week during—

(a) the adoption pay period in respect of which statutory adoption pay was paid to a person; or

[2(aa) the additional paternity pay period in respect of which additional statutory paternity pay was paid to a person; or]

(b) the maternity pay period in respect of which statutory maternity pay was paid to a woman [3; or

(c) the shared parental pay period in respect of which statutory shared parental pay is paid to a person] [4; or

(d) the parental bereavement pay period in respect of which statutory parental bereavement pay is paid to a person].

(3) A person or woman referred to above shall be entitled to be credited with earnings in respect of a week by virtue of this regulation only if he or she—

(a) furnished to the Secretary of State notice in writing of his or her claim to be entitled to be credited with earnings; and

(b) did so—

(i) before the end of the benefit year immediately following the tax year in which that week began, or

(ii) within such further time as may be reasonable in the circumstances of his or her case.

(4) This regulation shall not apply to a woman in respect of any week in any part of which she was a married woman in respect of whom an election made by her under regulations made under section 19(4) of the Contributions and Benefits Act had effect.

(5) In this regulation

(a) "adoption pay period", [2"additional paternity pay period",] "maternity pay period", "statutory adoption pay", [2"additional statutory paternity pay"] and "statutory maternity pay" have the same meaning as in the Contributions and Benefits Act.]

[(b) "statutory shared parental pay" means statutory shared parental pay payable in accordance with Part 12ZC of that Act and "shared parental pay period" means the weeks in respect of which statutory shared parental pay is payable to a person under section 171ZY(2) of that Act] [4; or

(c) "statutory parental bereavement pay" means statutory parental bereavement pay payable in accordance with Part 12ZD of that Act and "parental bereavement pay period" means the weeks in respect of which statutory parental bereavement pay is payable to a person under section 171ZZ9(2) of that Act].

AMENDMENTS

1. Social Security (Credits) Amendment Regulations 2003 (SI 2003/521) reg.2(3) (April 6, 2003).

2. Social Security (Credits) (Amendment) Regulations 2012 (SI 2012/766) reg.2 (April 5, 2012).

3. Shared Parental Leave and Statutory Shared Parental Pay (Consequential Amendments to Subordinate Legislation) Order 2014 (SI 2014/3255) art.2 (April 5, 2015).

4. Parental Bereavement Leave and Pay (Consequential Amendments to Subordinate Legislation) Regulations 2020 (SI 2020/354) reg.2 (April 6, 2020).

DEFINITIONS

"additional paternity pay period"—para.(5); SSCBA 1992 s.171ZEE(2);
"additional statutory paternity pay"—para.(5); SSCBA 1992 ss.171ZEA(1), 171ZEB(1);
"adoption pay period"—para.(5); SSCBA 1992 ss.171ZN(2), 171ZS(1).
"benefit"—see reg.2(1).
"benefit year"—see SSCBA 1992 s.21(6).

"lower earnings limit"—see SSCBA 1992 s.122(1).
"maternity pay period"—see para.(5); SSCBA 1992 s.165(1).
"statutory adoption pay"—see para.(5); SSCBA 1992 s.171ZL(1).
"statutory maternity pay"—see para.(5); SSCBA 1992 s.164(1).
"tax year"—see SSCBA 1992 s.122(1).

General Note

2.37 As with all of the Regulations making claimants eligible for the award of credits, this must be read with reg.3 (*CIB/1602/2006*; *CIB/3327/2004*). One can only have them insofar as they are necessary to bring one's record up to the level required for satisfying the second contribution condition for the relevant benefit (see para.(1), reg.3 and reg.2(1) ("reckonable year")).

It enables the award of a credit equal to the lower earnings limit for the tax year in question in respect of each week (for a woman) a maternity pay period, (for a man) an additional paternity pay period or (for any person) an adoption pay period in respect of which, as the case may be, statutory maternity pay, additional statutory paternity pay or statutory adoption pay was paid to the person. This regulation does not apply to a woman who has elected to pay contributions at a reduced rate (para.(4)).

[1 Credits for certain periods of imprisonment or detention in legal custody

2.38 **9D.**—(1) Subject to paragraphs (2) and (4), for the purposes of entitlement to any benefit by virtue of a person's earnings or contributions, where—

(a) a person is imprisoned or otherwise detained in legal custody by reason of his conviction of an offence or convictions in respect of two or more offences;

(b) that conviction or, as the case may be, each of those convictions is subsequently quashed by the Crown Court, the Court of Appeal or the High Court of Justiciary; and

(c) he is released from that imprisonment or detention, whether prior, or pursuant, to the quashing of that conviction or, as the case may be, each of those convictions,

that person shall, if he has made an application in writing to the Secretary of State for the purpose, be entitled to be credited with earnings or, in the case of any year earlier than 1987–88, contributions, in accordance with paragraph (3).

(2) Paragraph (1) shall not apply in respect of any period during which the person was also imprisoned or otherwise detained in legal custody for reasons unconnected with the conviction or convictions referred to in that paragraph.

(3) The earnings or, as the case may be, the contributions referred to in paragraph (1) are, in respect of any week in any part of which the person was—

(a) detained in legal custody—

(i) prior to the conviction or convictions referred to in that paragraph, but,

(ii) for the purposes of any proceedings in relation to any offence referred to in sub-paragraph (a) of that paragraph; or

(b) imprisoned or otherwise detained in legal custody by reason of that conviction or those convictions, those necessary for the purpose of bringing his earnings factor, for the year in which such a week falls, to the level required to make that year a reckonable year.

(4) Subject to paragraph (5), paragraph (1) shall not apply to a woman in respect of any week referred to in paragraph (3) in any part of which she was a married woman in respect of whom an election made by her under regulations made under section 19(4) of the Contributions and Benefits Act had effect.

(5) Paragraph (4) shall not apply to any woman—

(a) who was imprisoned or otherwise detained in legal custody as referred to in paragraph (3) for a continuous period which included 2 complete years; and

(b) whose election ceased to have effect in accordance with regulation 101(1)(c) of the Social Security (Contributions) Regulations 1979 (which provides for an election to cease to have effect at the end of 2 consecutive years which began on or after 6th April 1978 during which the woman is not liable for primary Class 1 or Class 2 contributions).

(6) An application referred to in paragraph (1) may be transmitted by electronic means.]

AMENDMENT

1. Social Security (Credits and Incapacity Benefit) Amendment Regulations 2001 (SI 2001/573) reg.2 (March 26, 2001).

DEFINITIONS

"benefit"—see reg.2(1).
"reckonable year"—see reg.2(1).
"year"—see reg.2(1).

GENERAL NOTE

As with all of the Regulations making claimants eligible for the award of credits, this must be read with reg.3 (*CIB/1602/2006*; *CIB/3327/2004*). One can only have them insofar as they are necessary to bring one's record up to the level required for satisfying the second contribution condition for the relevant benefit (see para.(1), reg.3 and reg.2(1) ("reckonable year")). **2.39**

It enables the award of a credit equal to the relevant lower earnings limit for each week for part of which the person was imprisoned or detained in legal custody because of a conviction of an offence, where the conviction that alone grounded that imprisonment or detention (whether prior to or *post* conviction) is quashed by a specified court. Credits can be so awarded to meet the amount by which the record for the tax year containing the weeks of imprisonment or detention falls short of the requisite level for the second condition for the benefit in question (paras (1)–(3)). The person must claim in time and in the proper manner, which can include e-mail (paras (1), (6)).

Note, finally, that a woman cannot gain a credit under this provision in respect of any week in any part of which as a married woman a certificate of election to pay contributions at reduced rate applied to her, unless the relevant period of imprisonment included two complete tax years so that the election ceased to have effect under Social Security (Contributions) Regulations 1979, reg.101(1)(c) (paras (4), (5)). See now Social Security (Contributions) Regulations 2001 (SI 2001/1004), reg.128(1)(c).

[[1]Credits for certain spouses and civil partners of members of Her Majesty's forces

2.40 **9E.**—(1) For the purposes of entitlement to any benefit by virtue of a person's earnings or contributions, that person shall, subject to the following paragraphs, be entitled to be credited with earnings equal to the lower earnings limit then in force, in respect of each week to which paragraph (2) applies.

(2) This paragraph applies to each week for any part of which the person is—

(a) the spouse or civil partner of a member of Her Majesty's forces or treated as such by the Secretary of State for the purposes of occupying accommodation, and

(b) accompanying the member of Her Majesty's forces on an assignment outside the United Kingdom or treated as such by the Secretary of State.

(3) A person referred to in paragraph (2) shall be entitled to be credited with earnings in respect of a week by virtue of this regulation only if that person has made an application to the Secretary of State for the purpose.

(4) An application under paragraph (3) must—

(a) be properly completed and on a form approved by the Secretary of State, or in such manner as the Secretary of State accepts as sufficient in the particular circumstances, and

(b) include—

(i) a statement confirming that the conditions referred to in paragraph (2) are met and signed by or on behalf of the Defence Council or a person authorised by them, and

(ii) such other information as the Secretary of State may require.

(5) An application under paragraph (3) is to be made—

(a) once the end date of the assignment referred to in paragraph (2) has been confirmed, or

(b) at such earlier time as the Secretary of State is prepared to accept in the particular circumstances of the case.

(6) An application made in accordance with paragraph (5)(a) must be made before the end of the tax year immediately following the tax year in which the assignment referred to in paragraph (2) ended, or within such further time as may be reasonable in the circumstances of the case.

(7) Where the Secretary of State accepts an application in accordance with paragraph (5)(b), this regulation entitles the person referred to in paragraph (2) to be credited with earnings in respect of any week subsequent to that application only if that person has made a further application to the Secretary of State in accordance with paragraphs (3) to (6).

(8) This regulation shall not apply—

(a) to a person in respect of any week where the person is entitled to be credited with earnings under regulation 7A, 8A or 8B in respect of the same week;

(b) to a woman in respect of any week in any part of which she was a married woman in respect of whom an election made by her under regulations made under section 19(4) of the Contributions and Benefits Act had effect; or

(c) in respect of any week commencing before 6th April 2010.]

AMENDMENT

1. Inserted by Social Security (Credits) (Amendment) Regulations 2010 (SI 2010/385) reg.2(3) (April 6, 2010).

DEFINITIONS

"benefit"—see reg.2(1).
"reckonable year"—see reg.2(1).
"year"—see reg.2(1).

GENERAL NOTE

As with all of the Regulations making claimants eligible for the award of credits, this must be read with reg.3 (*CIB/1602/2006*; *CIB/3327/2004*). One can only have them insofar as they are necessary to bring one's record up to the level required for satisfying the second contribution condition for the relevant benefit (see para. (1), reg.3 and reg.2(1) ("reckonable year")). From April 6, 2010, this regulation provides for a credit of earnings equal to the relevant lower earnings limit to the accompanying spouse or civil partner of a member of His Majesty's forces who is on an assignment outside the United Kingdom. It cannot apply in respect of any week prior to April 6, 2010 (para.(8)(c)), and will not apply where the person is entitled to be credited for the same week under regs 7A, 8A or 8B (para.8(a)). Nor can it provide credits where the married woman concerned has made a reduced rate contributions election (para.(8)(b)). 2.41

[1Credits for persons providing care for a child under the age of 12

9F.—(1) Subject to paragraphs (2), (5) and (6), the contributor concerned in the case of a benefit listed in paragraph (3) shall be credited with a Class 3 contribution for each week ("the relevant week") falling after 6th April 2011 during which that contributor satisfied the conditions in paragraph (4). 2.42

(2) Contributions shall only be credited in so far as is necessary to enable the contributor concerned to satisfy—

(a) in relation to a Category A or Category B retirement pension, the contribution condition specified in paragraph 5A(2) of Schedule 3 to the Contributions and Benefits Act;

(b) in relation to a widowed parent's allowance [3. . .], the second contribution condition specified in paragraph 5(3) of Schedule 3 to the Contributions and Benefits Act.

(3) This regulation applies to the following benefits—

(a) a Category A retirement pension in a case where the contributor concerned attains pensionable age on or after 6th April 2012;

(b) a Category B retirement pension payable by virtue of section 48A of the Contributions and Benefits Act in a case where the contributor concerned attains pensionable age on or after that date;

(c) a Category B retirement pension payable by virtue of section 48B of that Act in a case where the contributor concerned dies on or after that date without having attained pensionable age before that date;

(d) a widowed parent's allowance payable in a case where the contributor concerned dies on or after that date;

(e) [3. . .].

(4) The conditions are that in the relevant week the contributor concerned—

(a) provided care in respect of a child under the age of 12;

(b) is, in relation to that child, a person specified in the Schedule (other than a person who is a relevant carer for the purposes of section 23A of the Contributions and Benefits Act); and
(c) was ordinarily resident in Great Britain.

(5) Only one contributor may be credited with Class 3 contributions under this Regulation in respect of any relevant week.

(6) The contributor concerned shall not be credited with Class 3 contributions by virtue of paragraph (1) unless—
(a) a person other than that contributor satisfies the conditions in paragraph (7); and
(b) an application to the Secretary of State to be so credited is made in accordance with paragraph (8).

(7) The conditions are that—
(a) child benefit was awarded to that other person in relation to the child for whom, and in respect of the week in which, child care was provided by the contributor concerned; and
(b) the aggregate of that other person's earnings factors, [2 other than where those earnings factors are derived from Class 3 contributions credited by virtue of section 23A(2) and (3)(a) of the Contributions and Benefits Act (crediting of contributions for a person awarded child benefit in respect of a child under 12)], exceed the qualifying earnings factor for the year in which the relevant week falls.

(8) An application under paragraph (6)(b) must—
(a) include the name and date of birth of the child cared for;
(b) where requested by the Secretary of State or the Commissioners for Her Majesty's Revenue and Customs, include a declaration by the person awarded child benefit in respect of that child that the conditions in paragraph (4) are satisfied;
(c) specify the relevant week or weeks in which the child was cared for; and
(d) be received after the end of the tax year in which a week, which is the subject of the application, falls.

(9) In this regulation, "the contributor concerned" has the meaning given in section 21(5)(a) of the Contributions and Benefits Act.]

AMENDMENTS

1. National Insurance Contributions Credits (Miscellaneous Amendments) Regulations 2011 (SI 2011/709) reg.2(3) (April 5, 2011).

2. Social Security (Credits) (Amendment) (No. 2) Regulations 2012 (SI 2012/2680) reg.2 (December 1, 2012).

3. Pensions Act 2014 (Consequential, Supplementary and Incidental Amendments) Order 2017 (SI 2017/422) art.4(10) (April 6, 2017).

GENERAL NOTE

2.43 This new regulation provides for the award of Class 3 National Insurance contribution credits, for a tax year commencing on or after April 6, 2011, in respect of a claim for a basic state pension or bereavement benefits for specified adults who provide care for children under 12. The specified adults are listed in the new Sch. to these Regulations. The provision reflects concern over the position of grandparents and other adult relatives undertaking familial child care to enable the child's parent(s) to work.

Transitional provisions

10.—[1 . . .]. 2.44

REVOCATION

1. Social Security (Credits) Amendment Regulations 1987 (SI 1987/414) reg.10 (April 6, 1987).

[1SCHEDULE

Persons who may qualify as carers for a child under the age of 12

1.—(1) Parent. 2.45
(2) Grandparent.
(3) Great-grandparent.
(4) Great-great-grandparent.
(5) Sibling.
(6) Parent's sibling.
(7) Spouse or former spouse of any of the persons listed in sub-paragraphs (1) to (6).
(8) Civil partner or former civil partner of any of the persons listed in sub-paragraphs (1) to (6).
(9) Partner or former partner of any of the persons listed in sub-paragraphs (1) to (8).
(10) Son or daughter of persons listed in sub-paragraphs (5) to (9).
(11) In respect of the son or daughter of a person listed in sub-paragraph (6), that person's—
(a) spouse or former spouse;
(b) civil partner or former civil partner; or
(c) partner or former partner.

2. For the purposes of paragraph 1(5) and (6), a sibling includes a sibling of the half blood, a step sibling and an adopted sibling.

3. For the purposes of paragraph 1(9) and (11)(c), a partner is the other member of a couple consisting of [1 two people who are not married to or civil partners of each other but are living together [6 as if they were a married couple or civil partners]]. 2.46

AMENDMENT

1. Marriage (Same Sex Couples) Act 2013 and Marriage and Civil Partnership (Scotland) Act 2014 (Consequential Provisions) Order 2014 (SI 2014/3061) art.2 and Sch.1 para.4(1), (3) (December 10, 2014 (England and Wales) and December 16, 2014 (Scotland) (see art.1)).

2. Civil Partnership (Opposite-sex Couples) Regulations 2019 (SI 2019/1458) reg.41(b) and Sch.3, Part 2 para.37(3) (December 2, 2019).

The Social Security Pensions (Home Responsibilities) Regulations 1994

(SI 1994/704) (*AS AMENDED*)

ARRANGEMENT OF REGULATIONS

The Secretary of State for Social Security, in exercise of the powers conferred on him by sections 21(3) and 175(1) to (5) of, and paragraph 5(7)(b) of Schedule 3 to, the Social Security Contributions and Benefits Act 1992 and of all other powers enabling him in that behalf, after agreement by the Social Security Advisory Committee that proposals to make these Regulations should not be referred to it, hereby makes the following Regulations:

Citation, commencement and interpretation

2.48 **1.**—(1) These Regulations may be cited as the Social Security Pensions (Home Responsibilities) Regulations 1994, and shall come into force on 6th April 1994.

(2) In these Regulations, unless the context otherwise requires—

"the Act" means the Social Security Contributions and Benefits Act 1992;

"child benefit" means child benefit within the meaning of section 141 of the Act;

[1 "foster parent" means a person approved as—

(a) a foster parent in accordance with the provisions of Part IV of the Fostering Services Regulations 2002 (approval of foster parents); or

(b) a foster carer in accordance with the provisions of Part II of the Fostering of Children (Scotland) Regulations 1996(approval of foster carers);]

[2 "the General Regulations" means the Child Benefit (General) Regulations 2003;]

"Personal Injuries Scheme", "Pneumoconiosis and Byssinosis Benefit Scheme", "Service Pensions Instrument" and "1914–1918 War Injuries Scheme" have the same meaning as assigned to them in regulation 2 of the Social Security (Overlapping Benefits) Regulations 1979;

"year" means tax year.

AMENDMENTS

1. Social Security Pensions (Home Responsibilities) Amendment Regulations 2003 (SI 2003/1767) reg.2(2) (September 1, 2003).

2. Social Security Pensions (Home Responsibilities) (Amendment) Regulations 2005 (SI 2005/48) reg.2(2) (February 9, 2005).

DEFINITION

"tax year"—see SSCBA 1992, s.122(1).

Preclusion from regular employment for the purpose of paragraph 5(7)(b) of Schedule 3 to the Act

2.49 **2.**—(1) For the purpose of paragraph 5(7)(b) of Schedule 3 to the Act a person shall, subject to paragraph (5) below, be taken to be precluded from regular employment by responsibilities at home in any year—

(a) throughout which he satisfies any of the conditions specified in paragraph (2) below;

(b) throughout which he satisfies the conditions specified in paragraph (3) below; or

(c) in which he satisfies, for part of the year, any of the conditions specified in paragraph (2) below and for the remainder of the year, the condition specified in paragraph (3)(a) below.

(2) The conditions specified in this paragraph are—

(a) that child benefit awarded to him was payable in respect of a child under the age of 16;

[6 (aa) that child benefit awarded to his partner was payable in respect of a child under the age of 16;]

(b) that—

(i) [6 he is a person to whom paragraphs 4 to 6 of Schedule 1B to the Income Support (General) Regulations 1987 apply,and]

(ii) income support is payable to him;

[3 (c) that he was a foster parent] [6 throughout the year 2003–2004 or any subsequent year].

(3) The conditions specified in this paragraph are—

(a) that he was regularly engaged, for at least 35 hours per week, in caring for a person in respect of whom there was payable any of the benefits specified in paragraph (4) below;

(b) that those benefits were payable to that person for at least 48 weeks in that year.

(4) The benefits referred to in paragraph (3) above are an attendance allowance under section 64 of the Act, the care component of disability living allowance at the highest or middle rate prescribed in accordance with section 72 of the Act, a constant attendance allowance under any Service Pensions Instrument, Personal Injuries Scheme or 1914–1918 War Injuries Scheme, an increase of disablement pension under section 104 of the Act in respect of constant attendance and any benefit corresponding to such an increase under a Pneumoconiosis and Byssinosis Benefit Scheme or under Regulations under paragraph 7(2) of Schedule 8 to the Act.

[1 (4A) For the purposes of paragraph (2)(a) above, where—

(a) child benefit first becomes payable to a person in respect of a child on the first Monday in a year; and

(b) child benefit would, but for the provisions of section 147(2) of the Act, have been payable to that person in respect of that child for the part of that year falling before that Monday,

that person shall be treated as if he were entitled to child benefit and, accordingly, as if child benefit were payable to him for that part of that year.]

[5 (4B) For the purposes of paragraph (2)(a) above, in respect of the year 2004–2005 or any subsequent year, where—

(a) a notice is given under regulation 15(1) of the General Regulations (modification of priority between persons entitled to child benefit) by the person who is entitled to child benefit;

(b) that notice becomes effective in relation to any week falling in the first three months of a year;

(c) as a result of that notice, child benefit becomes payable to another person ("the new payee") in priority to anyone else;

(d) for each week of that year prior to that notice becoming effective, child benefit would, but for the provisions of regulation 15(2)(b) of those Regulations, have been payable to the new payee; and

(e) no other notice under regulation 15(1) of those Regulations was given in respect of the same child which became effective during any week referred to in sub-paragraph (d);

the new payee shall be treated as if he were entitled to child benefit and, accordingly, as if child benefit were payable to him for each week of the year prior to the notice becoming effective.]

[6 (4C) In paragraph (2)(aa), "partner" means the person with whom he was both residing and sharing responsibility for the child throughout that year.]

(5) Except where paragraph (6) below applies, paragraph (1) above shall not apply in relation to any year—

(a) if the person in question is a woman who has made or is treated as having made an election in accordance with regulations having effect under section 19(4) of the Act and that election had effect at the beginning of that year; or

[6 (aza) in the case of a person who satisfies the condition in paragraph (2)(aa) above—

(i) such information is not furnished as the Secretary of State may from time to time require which is relevant to the question of whether in that year he was precluded from regular employment by responsibilities at home within the meaning of these Regulations;

(ii) he attained pensionable age on or before 5th April 2008 or, in relation to a claim for a bereavement benefit in respect of his death, he died on or before that date; or

(iii) the aggregate of his partner's earnings factors—

(aa) in respect of any year preceding 2002–2003;

(bb) in respect of the year 2002–2003 or any subsequent year, where those earnings factors are derived from so much of his earnings as do not exceed the upper earnings limit and upon which primary Class 1 contributions have been paid or treated as paid,

is less than the qualifying earnings factor for the year in question.]

[4(aa) in the case of a person who satisfies the condition in paragraph (2)(c) above in respect of the year 2003–04 or any subsequent year, if he does not furnish such information as the Secretary of State may from time to time require which is relevant to the question of whether in that year he was precluded from regular employment by responsibilities at home within the meaning of these Regulations; or]

[2(b) in the case of a person who satisfies the conditions in paragraph (3) above in respect of any year preceding 2002–2003, if he does not furnish such information as the Secretary of State may from time to time require which is relevant to the question of whether in that year he was precluded from regular employment by responsibilities at home within the meaning of these Regulations; or

(c) in the case of a person who satisfies the conditions in paragraph (3) above in respect of the year 2002–2003 or any subsequent year, if he does not, within the period of three years immediately following the end of that year, furnish such information as the Secretary of State may from time to time require which is relevant to the question of whether, in that year, he was precluded from regular employment by responsibilities at home within the meaning of these Regulations.]

(6) This paragraph applies to a woman who throughout the period beginning on 6th April 1975 and ending on 5th April 1980—

(a) had no earnings in respect of which primary Class 1 contributions were payable; and

(b) was not at any time a self-employed earner.

AMENDMENTS

1. Social Security Pensions (Home Responsibilities) (Amendment) Regulations 2001 (SI 2001/1265) reg.2 (April 6, 2002).

2. Additional Pension and Social Security Pensions (Home Responsibilities) (Amendment) Regulations 2001 (SI 2001/1323) reg.7 (April 6, 2002).

3. Social Security Pensions (Home Responsibilities) Amendment Regulations 2003 (SI 2003/1767) reg.2(3) (September 1, 2003).

4. Social Security Pensions (Home Responsibilities) Amendment Regulations 2003 (SI 2003/1767) reg.2(4) (September 1, 2003).

5. Social Security Pensions (Home Responsibilities) (Amendment) Regulations 2005 (SI 2005/48) reg.2(3) (February 9, 2005).

6. Social Security Pensions (Home Responsibilities) Amendment Regulations 2008 (SI 2008/498) reg.2 (April 6, 2008).

DEFINITIONS

"child benefit"—see reg.1(2); SSCBA 1992 s.141.
"the General Regulations"—see reg.1(2).
"year"—see reg.1(2).

GENERAL NOTE

This deals with home responsibilities protection, which provides help in satisfying the second contribution condition for the range of long-term benefits in SSCBA 1992, Sch.3 para.5: 2.50

- widowed mother's allowance (SSCBA 1992 s.37);
- widowed parent's allowance (SSCBA 1992 s.39A);
- widow's pension (SSCBA 1992 s.38);
- Category A or B retirement pension (SSCBA 1992 ss.43–54).

It helps by stipulating when a year is one of home responsibilities protection. Such years are then deducted from the number of years in which the person would otherwise have to satisfy the contribution conditions, but the reduction effected can only halve the requisite number of years or reduce them to 20 whichever is the lower (SSCBA 1992, Sch.3, para.5(a)).

Note that home responsibilities protection was abolished on 6 April 2010 and replaced with national insurance credits for certain parents and carers.

A tax year is one of home responsibilities protection in the following situations:

- throughout it the person received child benefit for a child under 16 (paras (1)(a), (2)(a), (4A)) (see *CG/173/2002*) and note the aid afforded by para.(4B) in satisfying the "throughout" element; but see further, below, the note on *SF v SSWP and HMRC (HRP)* [2013] UKUT 175 (AAC) with respect to the position of a UK national, exercising free movement rights under EU law, who had received the equivalent of child benefit in another Member State.
- throughout it the person received income support as someone looking after a disabled person (paras (1)(a), (2)(b));
- throughout it the person was an approved foster parent (this applies in respect of the year 2003–04 and any subsequent year);
- for 48 weeks of the tax year the person spent 35 hours a week looking after someone receiving attendance allowance, constant attendance allowance under the industrial injuries or war pensions schemes, or the higher or middle rate components of disability living allowance (paras (1)(b), (3), (4));
- a tax year which is a mix of such periods (para.(1)(c)).

A person must claim in time and in the proper manner (para.5(aa)(b), (c)).

In *SF v SSWP and HMRC (HRP)* [2013] UKUT 175 (AAC), Judge Wikeley considered the position as regards HRP of a woman who had received one year of child benefit and HRP in the UK before moving to Belgium where she received several years of the Belgian equivalent of child benefit, *allocation familiales*. He held that, as regards HRP, HMRC makes decisions as an agent of the Secretary of State so that its decisions on HRP are decisions on social security benefits and properly within the jurisdiction of the First-tier Tribunal (Social Entitlement Chamber) (paras 9, 10). He also decided that art.21 TFEU and reg.1408/71 required the Secretary of State, for the purposes of awarding a UK state retirement pension, to take account of the claimant's child-raising period in Belgium as if that period had been completed in the UK and her pre-existing award of child benefit had continued without interruption, thus treating her periods of receipt of *allocations familiales* as if they were periods of receipt of UK child benefit. This was because the "receipt of child benefit" requirement for HRP, linked as it was to the presence or residence in the UK test as regards child benefit, acts as a restriction on the right of free movement in the EU which is not objectively justified (paras 28–52). From May 1, 2010, reg.1408/71 was replaced by reg.883/2004. While art.5 thereof corresponds to the claimant's position, it could not aid her in these proceedings since it entered into force after the date of the HMRC decision on HRP (paras 53–57).

See further *FH v HMRC and SSWP (HRP)* [2015] UKUT 672 (AAC), emphasising that years which are qualifying years in any event cannot qualify for HRP. See also *JM v SSWP and HMRC* [2018] UKUT 2 (AAC), where the claimant and her husband had lived in the Netherlands from 1982 to 1984 and received Dutch family benefits. The claimant qualified for a UK state pension in 2002, at age 60, and a Dutch state pension, based on the 2-year child-raising period, in 2007, when she was aged 65. Judge Wikeley held that neither EU nor domestic law required the claimant to receive HRP for the 1982-84 period, which would effectively amount to double recovery given the receipt of the Dutch pension (even though it was paid later).

Although home responsibilities protection can be claimed by both sexes, substantially more women than men are covered by it. Although it affords less help when compared to an equivalent period of unemployment for which credits are awarded, deputy Commissioner Gamble held in *CP/4017/2006* that this differentiation did not constitute indirect discrimination contrary to art.14 ECHR. *McAuslane v Secretary of State for Work and Pensions*, the appeal against this decision, is pending before the Court of Appeal, but has been removed from the list pending resolution of a costs issue.

Note finally that a woman with an election to pay reduced rate contributions, which was in effect at the beginning of the tax year, cannot have that year treated as one of home responsibilities protection, unless throughout the period April 6, 1975 to April 5, 1980, she is not a self-employed earner and had no earnings in respect of which primary Class 1 contributions were payable (paras (5)(a), (6)).

REVOCATIONS

3.—*Omitted* as not relevant.

Schedule. *Omitted* as not relevant.

The Social Security (Benefit) (Married Women and Widows Special Provisions) Regulations 1974

(SI 1974/2010) (*AS AMENDED*)

REGULATION REPRODUCED

Modifications, in relation to widows, of provisions with respect to [1short-term incapacity benefit] [3 ...][2employment and support allowance], maternity allowance, and Category A retirement pension

3.—(1) Subject to the following provisions of this regulation, where, otherwise than by reason of remarriage or cohabitation with a man as his wife, a woman ceases to be entitled either to a widow's allowance or to a widowed mother's allowance— 2.52

(a) she shall be deemed to have satisfied the first contribution condition for [1 . . .] [1 short-term incapacity benefit] or [1 . . .] maternity allowance [1 . . .] referred to in paragraph 1 [1 or] 3 [1 . . .], as the case may be, of Schedule 3 to the Act [2 or, in relation to [3 ...] employment and support allowance, she shall be deemed to have satisfied the first condition referred to in paragraph 1(1) of Schedule 1 to the Welfare Reform Act;

(b) for the purpose only of enabling her to satisfy the second contribution condition for unemployment and [1short-term incapacity benefit] or maternity allowance referred to in paragraph 1 or 3, as the case may be, of Schedule 3 to the Act, [2 or, in relation to [3 ...] employment and support allowance, she shall be deemed to have satisfied the second condition referred to in paragraph 2(1) of Schedule 1 to the Welfare Reform Act], there shall be credited to her such Class 1 contributions (if any) for every year up to and including that in which she ceased to be entitled as aforesaid as are required to enable her to satisfy that condition; and

(c) [1 . . .]

(2)–(10) *omitted as not relevant and/or revoked.*

AMENDMENTS

1. Social Security (Incapacity Benefit) (Consequential and Transitional Amendments and Savings) Regulations 1995 (SI 1995/829) reg.2(a) (April 13, 1995).

2. Employment and Support Allowance (Consequential Provisions) (No. 2) Regulations 2008 (SI 2008/1554) reg.64(3) (October 27, 2008).

3. Universal Credit (Consequential, Supplementary, Incidental and Miscellaneous Provisions) Regulations 2013 (SI 2013/630) reg.20(1), (3) (April 29, 2013).

GENERAL NOTE

2.53 Taken together with Social Security (Credits) Regulations 1975, reg.8C, above, the effect of para.(1)(a) appears effectively to waive altogether the contributions conditions for short-term incapacity benefit or employment and support allowance for certain widows.

The Social Security (Crediting and Treatment of Contributions, and National Insurance Numbers) Regulations 2001

(SI 2001/769) (*AS AMENDED*)

REGULATIONS REPRODUCED

The Secretary of State for Social Security, with the concurrence of the Inland Revenue in so far as required, in exercise of powers conferred by sections 13(3), 22(5), 122(1) and 175(1) to (4) of, and paragraphs 8(1)(d) and (1A) and 10 of Schedule 1 to, the Social Security Contributions and Benefits Act 1992 and sections 182C and 189(1) and (3) to (6) of the Social Security Administration Act 1992 and of all other powers enabling him in that behalf and for the purpose only of consolidating other regulations hereby revoked, hereby makes the following Regulations:

Citation, commencement and interpretation

2.55 **1.**—(1) These Regulations may be cited as the Social Security (Crediting and Treatment of Contributions, and National Insurance

Numbers) Regulations 2001 and shall come into force on 6th April 2001.

(2) In these Regulations, including this regulation—

"the Act" means the Social Security Contributions and Benefits Act 1992;

"the Contributions Regulations" means the Social Security (Contributions) Regulations [[5] 2001];

"contribution week" means a period of seven days beginning with midnight between Saturday and Sunday;

[[4]"contribution-based jobseeker's allowance" means an allowance under the Jobseekers Act 1995 as amended by the provisions of Part 1 of Schedule 14 to the Welfare Reform Act 2012 that remove references to an income-based allowance, and a contribution-based allowance under the Jobseekers Act 1995 as that Act has effect apart from those provisions;]

"contributory benefit" includes a contribution-based jobseeker's allowance but not an income-based jobseeker's allowance; [[2] and includes a contributory employment and support allowance but not an income-related employment and support allowance]

[[4]"contributory employment and support allowance" means an allowance under Part 1 of the Welfare Reform Act as amended by the provisions of Schedule 3, and Part 1 of Schedule 14, to the Welfare Reform Act 2012 that remove references to an income-related allowance, and a contributory allowance under Part 1 of the Welfare Reform Act as that Part has effect apart from those provisions;]

[[5] "due date" (subject to regulation 4(11)) means, in relation to—

(a) any Class 1 contribution, the date by which payment falls to be made;

(b) any Class 2 contribution which a person is [[6] ...] entitled to pay, the 31st January following the end of the year in respect of which it is payable;

(c) any Class 3 contribution, the date 42 days after the end of the year in respect of which it is paid;]

"earnings factor" has the meaning assigned to it in section 21(5)(c) of the Act;

[[4]"income-based jobseeker's allowance" has the same meaning as in the Jobseekers Act 1995;]

[[2] "income-related employment and support allowance" means an income-related allowance under Part 1 of the Welfare Reform Act (employment and support allowance);]

"relevant benefit year" has the meaning assigned to it in—

(a) section 2(4)(b) of the Jobseekers Act 1995, in relation to a contribution-based jobseeker's allowance;

(b) paragraph 2(6)(b) of Schedule 3 to the Act (contribution conditions for entitlement to short-term incapacity benefit), in relation to short-term incapacity benefit;

[[2] (c) paragraph 3(1)(f) of Schedule 1 to the Welfare Reform Act (conditions relating to national insurance), in relation to a contributory employment and support allowance.]

"relevant time", in relation to short-term incapacity benefit, has the meaning assigned to it in paragraph 2(6)(a) of Schedule 3 to the Act;

[[2] "the Welfare Reform Act" means the Welfare Reform Act 2007;]

"year" means tax year.

[1 (3) In these Regulations, "official error" means an error made by—

(a) an officer of the Department for Work and Pensions or an officer of Revenue and Customs acting as such which no person outside the Department or Her Majesty's Revenue and Customs caused or to which no person outside the Department or Her Majesty's Revenue and Customs materially contributed; or

(b) a person employed by a service provider and to which no person who was not so employed materially contributed,

but excludes any error of law which is shown to have been an error by virtue of a subsequent decision of [3 the Upper Tribunal] or the court.

(4) In paragraph (3)—

[3. . .]

"service provider" means a person providing services to the Secretary of State for Work and Pensions or to Her Majesty's Revenue and Customs.]

AMENDMENTS

1. Social Security (National Insurance Credits) Amendment Regulations 2007 (SI 2007/2582) reg.3 (October 1, 2007).

2. Employment and Support Allowance (Consequential Provisions) (No. 2) Regulations 2008 (SI 2008/1554) reg.49(2) (October 27, 2008).

3. Tribunals, Courts and Enforcement Act 2007 (Transitional and Consequential Provisions) Order 2008 (SI 2008/2683) art.6(1) and Sch.1 para.147 (November 3, 2008).

4. Universal Credit (Consequential, Supplementary, Incidental and Miscellaneous Provisions) Regulations 2013 (SI 2013/630) reg.71 (April 29, 2013).

5. Social Security (Credits, and Crediting and Treatment of Contributions) (Consequential and Miscellaneous Amendments) Regulations 2016 (SOI 2016/1145) reg. 5(2) (January 1, 2017).

6. Social Security (Class 2 National Insurance Contributions) (Consequential Amendments and Savings) Regulations 2024 (SI 2024/377) reg.8(9)(a) (April 6, 2024).

Appropriation of Class 3 contributions

2.56 **2.**—Any person paying Class 3 contributions in one year may appropriate such contributions to the earnings factor of another year if such contributions are payable in respect of that other year or, in the absence of any such appropriation, the Inland Revenue may, with the consent of the contributor, make such appropriation.

Crediting of Class 3 contributions

2.57 **3.**—Where, for any year, a contributor's earnings factor derived from—

(a) earnings upon which primary Class 1 contributions have been paid or treated as paid;

(b) credited earnings;

(c) Class 2 or Class 3 contributions paid by or credited to him; or

(d) any or all of such earnings and contributions,

falls short of a figure which is 52 times that year's lower earnings limit for Class 1 contributions by an amount which is equal to, or less than, half that year's lower earnings limit, that contributor shall be credited with a Class 3 contribution for that year.

Treatment for the purpose of any contributory benefit of late paid contributions

4.—(1) Subject to the provisions of regulations 5 [1 to 6C] below and regulation [6 61] of the Contributions Regulations (voluntary Class 2 contributions not paid within permitted period), for the purpose of entitlement to any contributory benefit, [5 paragraphs (1B)] to (9) below shall apply to contributions ("relevant contributions")— 2.58

(a) paid after the due date; or

(b) treated as paid after the due date under regulation 7(2) below.

[2 (1A) Any relevant contribution which is paid—

(a) by virtue of an official error; and

(b) more than six years after the end of the year in which the contributor was first advised of that error,

shall be treated as not paid.]

[5(1B) Where contributions are paid in accordance with regulation 63A of the Social Security (Contributions) Regulations 2001 (collection of unpaid Class 2 contributions through PAYE code), any relevant contributions are to be treated as paid on 5th April of the tax year in which they are paid.]

(2) Subject to the provisions of paragraph (4) below, any relevant contribution other than one referred to in paragraph (3) below–

(a) if paid [6 after the end of the second year]—

(i) [6 . . .] following the year in which liability for that contribution arises, [6 or]

[6 (ii) following the year in respect of which a person is entitled, but not liable, to pay the contribution,]

shall be treated as not paid;

(b) if paid before the end of the said second year, shall, subject to paragraphs (7) and (8) below, be treated as paid on the date on which payment of the contribution is made.

(3) Subject to the provisions of paragraph (4) below, any relevant Class 2 contribution payable in respect of a contribution week after 5th April 1983 or any relevant Class 3 contribution payable in respect of a year after 5th April 1982—

(a) if paid [6 after the end of the sixth year]—

(i) [6 . . .] following the year in which liability for that contribution arises, [6 or]

[6 (ii) following the year in respect of which a person is entitled, but not liable, to pay the contribution,]

shall be treated as not paid;

(b) if paid before the end of the said sixth year, shall, subject to paragraphs (7) [6 or] (8) below, be treated as paid on the date on which payment of the contribution is made.

(4) A Class 3 contribution payable by a person to whom regulation [6 48(3)(b)(ii) or (iii)] of the Contributions Regulations (which specify the conditions to be complied with before a person may pay a Class 3 contribution) applies in respect of a year which includes a period of education, apprenticeship, training, imprisonment or detention in legal custody such as is specified in that regulation—

(a) if paid after the end of the sixth year specified in that regulation, shall be treated as not paid;

(b) if paid before the end of the said sixth year shall, subject to the provisions of paragraphs (7) and (8) below, be treated as paid on the date on which payment of the contribution is made.

(5) Notwithstanding the provisions of paragraph (4) above, for the purpose of entitlement to any contributory benefit, where—

(a) a Class 3 contribution other than one referred to in sub-paragraph (b) below which is payable in respect of a year specified in that sub-paragraph, is paid after—
  (i) the due date, and
  (ii) the end of the second year following the year preceding that in which occurred the relevant time or, as the case may be, the relevant event,

that contribution shall be treated as not paid;

(b) in respect of a year after 5th April 1982, a Class 3 contribution which is payable in respect of a year specified in paragraph (4) above, is paid after—
  (i) the due date, and
  (ii) the end of the sixth year following the year preceding that in which occurred the relevant time or, as the case may be, the relevant event,

that contribution shall be treated as not paid.

(6) For the purposes of paragraph (5) above, "relevant event" means the date on which the person concerned attained pensionable age or, as the case may be, died under that age.

(7) Notwithstanding the provisions of paragraphs (2), (3) and (4) above, in determining whether the relevant contribution conditions are satisfied in whole or in part for the purpose of entitlement to any contributory benefit, any relevant contribution which is paid within the time specified in paragraph (2)(b), (3)(b) or, as the case may be, (4)(b) above shall be treated—

(a) for the purpose of entitlement in respect of any period before the date on which the payment of the contribution is made, as not paid; and

(b) subject to the provisions of paragraph (8) below, for the purpose of entitlement in respect of any other period, as paid on the date on which the payment of the contribution is made.

[[5](7A) In determining whether the relevant contribution conditions are satisfied in whole or in part for the purpose of entitlement to any contributory benefit, any relevant contribution which is treated as paid on the date specified in paragraph (1B) shall be treated—

(a) for the purpose of entitlement in respect of any period before the date on which payment of the contribution is treated as paid, as not paid; and

(b) subject to the provisions of paragraph (8) below, for the purpose of entitlement in respect of any other period, as paid on the date specified in paragraph (1B).]

[[6] (8) For the purpose of determining whether the second contribution condition for entitlement to a contribution-based jobseeker's allowance or a contributory employment and support allowance is satisfied in whole or in part a relevant contribution is to be treated—

(a) if a Class 1 contribution paid before the beginning of the relevant benefit year, as paid on the due date;

(b) if, subject to paragraph (2)(a), a Class 1 contribution paid after the end of the benefit year immediately preceding the relevant benefit year or, subject to paragraph (3)(a), a Class 2 contribution—
  (i) as not paid in relation to the benefit claimed in respect of any day before the expiry of a period of 42 days (including Sundays) commencing with the date on which the payment of that contribution is made; and
  (ii) as paid at the expiry of that period in relation to entitlement to such benefit in respect of any other period.]

(9) For the purposes of paragraph (8) above, "second contribution condition" in relation to—
(a) a contribution-based jobseeker's allowance is a reference to the condition specified in section 2(1)(b) of the Jobseekers Act 1995;
(b) short-term incapacity benefit is a reference to the condition specified in paragraph 2(3) of Schedule 3 to the Act;
[4 (c) a contributory employment and support allowance is a reference to the condition specified in paragraph 2(1) of Schedule 1 to the Welfare Reform Act.]

(10) This regulation shall not apply to Class 4 contributions.

[3 (11) Where an amount is retrospectively treated as earnings ("retrospective earnings") by regulations made by virtue of section 4B(2) of the Act, the "due date" for earnings-related contributions in respect of those earnings is the date given by paragraph 11A of Schedule 4 to the Social Security (Contributions) Regulations 2001, for the purposes of this regulation and regulations 5 and 5A.]

AMENDMENTS

1. Social Security (Additional Class 3 National Insurance Contributions) Amendment Regulations 2009 (SI 2009/659) reg.3(2) (April 6, 2009).
2. Social Security (National Insurance Credits) Amendment Regulations 2007 (SI 2007/2582) reg.4(3)(b) (October 1, 2007).
3. Social Security, Occupational Pension Schemes and Statutory Payments (Consequential Provisions) Regulations 2007 (SI 2007/1154) reg.2(2) (April 6, 2007).
4. Employment and Support Allowance (Consequential Provisions) (No.2) Regulations 2008 (SI 2008/1554) reg.49(3) (October 27, 2008).
5. Social Security (Crediting and Treatment of Contributions, and National Insurance Numbers) (Amendment) Regulations 2013 (SI 2013/3165) reg. 2 (April 6, 2014).
6. Social Security (Credits, and Crediting and Treatment of Contributions) (Consequential and Miscellaneous Amendments) Regulations 2016 (SOI 2016/1145) reg. 5(3) (January 1, 2017).

Treatment for the purpose of any contributory benefit of late paid primary Class 1 contributions where there was no consent, connivance or negligence by the primary contributor

5.—(1) This regulation applies where a primary Class 1 contribution which is payable on a primary contributor's behalf by a secondary contributor— 2.59
(a) is paid after the due date; or
(b) in relation to any claim for—
  (i) a contribution-based jobseeker's allowance, is not paid before the beginning of the relevant benefit year,

(ii) short-term incapacity benefit, is not paid before the relevant time,[2 or

(iii) a contributory employment and support allowance, is not paid before the beginning of the relevant benefit year,]

and the delay in making payment is shown to the satisfaction of [1an officer of] the Inland Revenue not to have been with the consent or connivance of, or attributable to any negligence on the part of, the primary contributor.

(2) Where paragraph (1) above applies, the primary Class 1 contribution shall be treated—

(a) for the purpose of the first contribution condition of entitlement to a contribution-based jobseeker's allowance [2, short-term incapacity benefit or a contributory employment and support allowance], as paid on the day on which payment is made of the earnings in respect of which the contribution is payable; and

(b) for any other purpose relating to entitlement to any contributory benefit, as paid on the due date.

(3) For the purposes of this regulation—

(a) "first contribution condition" in relation to—

(i) a contribution-based jobseeker's allowance is a reference to the condition specified in section 2(1)(a) of the Jobseekers Act 1995,

(ii) short-term incapacity benefit is a reference to the condition specified in paragraph 2(2) of Schedule 3 to the Act;

[2 "(iii) a contributory employment and support allowance is a reference to the condition specified in paragraph 1(1) of Schedule 1 to the Welfare Reform Act;]

(b) "primary contributor" means the person liable to pay a primary Class 1 contribution in accordance with section 6(4)(a) of the Act (liability for Class 1 contributions);

(c) "secondary contributor" means the person who, in respect of earnings from employed earner's employment, is liable to pay a secondary Class 1 contribution in accordance with section 6(4)(b) of the Act.

AMENDMENTS

1. Social Security, Occupational Pension Schemes and Statutory Payments (Consequential Provisions) Regulations 2007 (SI 2007/1154) reg.2(2) (April 6, 2007).

2. Employment and Support Allowance (Consequential Provisions) (No.2) Regulations 2008 (SI 2008/1554) reg.49(4) (October 27, 2008).

[1 Treatment for the purpose of any contributory benefit of duly paid primary Class 1 contributions in respect of retrospective earnings

2.60 **5A.**—Where a primary Class 1 contribution payable in respect of retrospective earnings is paid by the due date, it shall be treated—

(a) for the purposes of the first contribution condition of entitlement to a contribution-based jobseeker's allowance [2, short-term incapacity benefit or a contributory employment and support allowance], as paid on the day on which payment is made of the retrospective earnings in respect of which the contribution is payable; and

(b) for any other purpose relating to entitlement to any contributory benefit, as paid on the due date.]

AMENDMENTS

1. Social Security, Occupational Pension Schemes and Statutory Payments (Consequential Provisions) Regulations 2007 (SI 2007/1154) reg.2(2) (April 6, 2007).
2. Employment and Support Allowance (Consequential Provisions) (No.2) Regulations 2008 (SI 2008/1554) reg.49(5) (October 27, 2008).

Treatment for the purpose of any contributory benefit of contributions under the Act paid late through ignorance or error

6.—(1) In the case of a contribution paid by or in respect of a person after the due date, where— 2.61

(a) the contribution is paid after the time when it would, under regulation 4 or 5 above, have been treated as paid for the purpose of entitlement to contributory benefit; and
(b) it is shown to the satisfaction of [1 an officer of] the Inland Revenue that the failure to pay the contribution before that time is attributable to ignorance or error on the part of that person or the person making the payment and that that ignorance or error was not due to any failure on the part of such person to exercise due care and diligence,

[1 an officer of the Inland Revenue may direct], for the purposes of those regulations, the contribution shall be treated as paid on such earlier day as [1 the officer considers] appropriate in the circumstances, and those regulations shall have effect subject to any such direction.

(2) This regulation shall not apply to a Class 4 contribution.

[1 Treatment for the purposes of any contributory benefit of certain Class 3 contributions

6A.—(1) For the purposes of entitlement to any contributory benefit, this regulation applies in the case of a Class 3 contribution paid after the due date— 2.62

(a) which would otherwise under regulation 4—
    (i) have been treated as paid on a day other than on the day on which it was actually paid; or
    (ii) have been treated as not paid; and
(b) which is paid in respect of a year after 5th April 1996 but before 6th April 2002.

(2) A contribution referred to in paragraph (1), where it is paid on or before 5th April 2009 by or in respect of a person who attains pensionable age on or after 6th April 2008, shall be treated as paid on the day on which it is paid.

(3) A contribution referred to in paragraph (1), where it is paid on or before 5th April 2009 by or in respect of a person who attains pensionable age on or after 24th October 2004 but before 6th April 2008, shall be treated as paid on—

(a) the day on which it is paid; or
(b) the date on which the person attained pensionable age,

whichever is the earlier.

(4) A contribution referred to in paragraph (1), where it is paid on or before 5th April 2010 by or in respect of a person who attains pensionable

age on or after 6th April 1998 but before 24th October 2004, shall be treated as paid on—

(a) 1st October 1998; or

(b) the date on which the person attained pensionable age,

whichever is the later.]

AMENDMENT

1. Social Security (Crediting and Treatment of Contributions, and National Insurance Numbers) Amendment Regulations 2004 (SI 2004/1361) reg.2(b) (May 17, 2004).

[1 Treatment for the purpose of any contributory benefit of certain Class 2 or Class 3 contributions

2.63 **6B.**—For the purpose of entitlement to any contributory benefit, a Class 2 or a Class 3 contribution paid after the due date—

(a) which would otherwise under regulation 4 (apart from paragraph (1A) of that regulation)—

(i) have been treated as paid on a day other than the day on which it was actually paid; or

(ii) have been treated as not paid; and

(b) which was paid after the due date by virtue of an official error,

shall be treated as paid on the day on which it is paid.]

AMENDMENT

1. Social Security (National Insurance Credits) Amendment Regulations 2007 (SI 2007/2582) reg.4(4) (October 1, 2007).

[1Treatment of Class 3 contributions paid under section 13A of the Act

2.64 **6C.**—(1) This regulation applies to a Class 3 contribution paid by an eligible person under section 13A (right to pay additional Class 3 contributions in certain cases) of the Act.

(2) A contribution paid after 5th April 2009 but before 6th April 2011 shall be treated as paid on—

(a) the day on which it is paid; or

(b) the date on which the person attained pensionable age,

whichever is the earlier.

(3) A contribution paid after 5th April 2011 shall be treated as paid on the day on which it is paid.]

AMENDMENT

1. Social Security (Additional Class 3 National Insurance Contributions) Amendment Regulations 2009 (SI 2009/659) reg.3(3) (April 6, 2009).

[1 Treatment for the purpose of any contributory benefit of contributions paid under certain provisions relating to the payment and collection of contributions]

2.65 **7.**—[1 (1) Subject to the provisions of paragraph (2), for the purpose of entitlement to any contributory benefit except a contribution-based jobseeker's allowance or a contributory employment and support allowance, where—

(a) a person pays a Class 2 contribution under [3 section 11] of the Act, or a Class 3 contribution in accordance with regulation 89, 89A, 90 or 148C of the Contributions Regulations (provisions relating to the method of, and time for, payment of Class 2 and Class 3 contributions etc.); and

(b) the due date for payment of that contribution [2or (in the case of a contribution treated as paid as a result of section 11(5B) of the Act) the first day on which the contribution would otherwise be treated as having been paid,] is a date after the relevant day,

that contribution is treated as paid by the relevant day.]

(2) Where, in respect of any part of a late notification period, a person pays a Class 2 contribution which he is [3. . .][1 entitled] to pay, that contribution shall be treated as paid after the due date, whether or not it was paid by the due date.

(3) For the purposes of this regulation—

(a) "late notification period" means the period beginning with the day a person [3. . .][1 entitled] to pay a Class 2 contribution was first required to notify the Inland Revenue in accordance with the provisions of regulation [1 87, 87A or 87AA] of the Contributions Regulations (notification of commencement or cessation of payment of Class 2 or Class 3 contributions) and ending on the [1 day on] which he gives that notification;

(b) "relevant day" means the first day in respect of which a person would have been entitled to receive the contributory benefit in question if any contribution condition relevant to that benefit had already been satisfied.

(c) [1 . . .]

Amendments

1. Social Security (Credits, and Crediting and Treatment of Contributions) (Consequential and Miscellaneous Amendments) Regulations 2016 (SOI 2016/1145) reg. 5(4) (January 1, 2017).

2. Social Security (Class 2 National Insurance Contributions Increase of Threshold) Regulations 2022 (SI 2022/1329) reg.8(3) (in force December 14, 2022, with effect from April 6, 2022).

3. Social Security (Class 2 National Insurance Contributions) (Consequential Amendments and Savings) Regulations 2024 (SI 2024/377) reg.8(9)(b) (April 6, 2024).

[1 Treatment for the purpose of a contribution-based jobseeker's allowance or a contributory employment and support allowance of Class 2 contributions paid in accordance with the Act

7A.—(1) For the purpose of entitlement to a contribution-based job- **2.66**
seeker's allowance or a contributory employment and support allowance, a Class 2 contribution is to be treated as paid as set out in paragraph (2) if the contribution is paid—

(a) in relation to—

(i) a contribution-based jobseeker's allowance, on or after the first day of the week for which the jobseeker's allowance is claimed; or

(ii) a contributory employment and support allowance, on or after the first day of the relevant benefit week; and

(b) by the due date.

(2) The contribution is treated as paid—

(a) in relation to a contribution-based jobseeker's allowance, before the week for which the jobseeker's allowance is claimed; or

(b) in relation to a contributory employment and support allowance, before the relevant benefit week.

(3) "Relevant benefit week" has the meaning given in paragraph 5 of Schedule 1 to the Welfare Reform Act.]

AMENDMENT

1. Social Security (Credits, and Crediting and Treatment of Contributions) (Consequential and Miscellaneous Amendments) Regulations 2016 (SOI 2016/1145) reg. 5(5) (January 1, 2017).

Treatment for the purpose of any contributory benefit of contributions paid under an arrangement

2.67 **8.** For the purposes of regulations 4 to [1 7A] above and regulation [1 61] of the Contributions Regulations (voluntary Class 2 contributions not paid within permitted period)—

(a) where a contribution is paid under an arrangement to which regulations [1 68 and 84] or, as the case may be, regulation [1 90] of the Contributions Regulations (other methods of collection and recovery of earnings-related contributions; special provisions relating to primary Class 1 contributions and arrangements approved by the Inland Revenue for method of, and time for, payment of Class 2 and Class 3 contributions respectively) apply, the date by which, but for the said regulations 4 to [1 7A] and [1 61], the contribution would have fallen due to be paid shall, in relation to that contribution, be the due date;

(b) any payment made of, or as on account of, a contribution in accordance with any such arrangement shall, on and after the due date, be treated as a contribution paid on the due date.

AMENDMENT

1. Social Security (Credits, and Crediting and Treatment of Contributions) (Consequential and Miscellaneous Amendments) Regulations 2016 (SOI 2016/1145) reg. 5(6) (January 1, 2017).

Application for allocation of national insurance number

2.68 **9.**—(1) Subject to the provisions of [4 paragraphs (2) and (2A)] below, every person, who is over the age of 16 and satisfies the conditions specified in regulation 87 or 119 of the Contributions Regulations(conditions of domicile or residence and conditions as to residence or presence in Great Britain respectively), shall, unless he has already been allocated a national insurance number under the Act, the Social Security Act 1975 or the National Insurance Act 1965, apply either to the Secretary of State or to [the Commissioners for Her Majesty's Revenue and Customs] for the allocation of a national insurance number and shall make such application at such time and in such manner as the Secretary of State shall direct.

[1 (1A) An application under paragraph (1) shall be accompanied by a document of a description specified [3 in Schedule 1].]

(2) As respects any person who is neither an employed earner nor a self-employed earner the provisions of paragraph (1) above shall not apply unless and until that person wishes to pay a Class 3 or 3A contribution.

[4 (2A) The provisions of paragraph (1) shall not apply to a person in respect of whom the Secretary of State or the Commissioners for Her Majesty's Revenue and Customs are notified that a biometric immigration document is to be issued pursuant to regulation 13 [5 or 13A] of the Immigration (Biometric Registration) Regulations 2008.]

(3) The Secretary of State may authorise arrangements for the allocation of a national insurance number to any person during the 12 months before that person reaches the age of 16, and in particular may direct that a person who will attain the age of 16 within 12 months after such direction shall apply for the allocation of a national insurance number before attaining the age of 16, and any such person shall accordingly comply with such direction.

[2 (4) Where a person–

(a) qualifies for a loan made in accordance with regulations made under section 22 of the Teaching and Higher Education Act 1998 (new arrangements For giving financial support to students) or sections 73 to 74(1) of the Education (Scotland) Act 1980 in connection with an academic year beginning on or after 1st September 2007; and

(b) has been required as a condition of entitlement to payment of the loan to provide his national insurance number, he shall, unless he has already been allocated a national insurance number, apply to the Secretary of State or the Commissioners for Her Majesty's Revenue and Customs for one to be allocated to him, and the Secretary of State or, as the case may be, the Commissioners may direct how the application is to be made.]

AMENDMENTS

1. Social Security (National Insurance Numbers) Amendment Regulations 2006 (SI 2006/2897) reg.2(a) (December 11, 2006).

2. Social Security (National Insurance Numbers) Amendment Regulations 2006 (SI 2006/2897) reg.2(b) (March 1, 2007).

3. Social Security (National Insurance Numbers) Amendment Regulations 2008 (SI 2008/223) reg.2(2) (February 29, 2008).

4. Social Security (Miscellaneous Amendments) Regulations 2015 (SI 2015/67) reg.5 (February 23, 2015).

5. Social Security (Crediting and Treatment of Contributions, and National Insurance Numbers) (Amendment) Regulations 2015 (SI 2015/1828) reg.2 (November 30, 2015).

Regs 10 to 12 and Schedule are omitted as within responsibility of HMRC and not the Secretary of State or beyond the scope of this work. 2.69

The Social Security (Contributions Credits for Parents and Carers) Regulations 2010

(SI 2010/19)

ARRANGEMENT OF REGULATIONS

PART 1

GENERAL PROVISIONS

PART 2

MEANING OF "FOSTER PARENT" AND "ENGAGED IN CARING"

PART 3

APPLICATIONS

The Secretary of State makes the following Regulations in exercise of the powers conferred by section 23A(3)(c), (4) and (9) and section 175(1), (4) and (5) of the Social Security Contributions and Benefits Act 1992.

A draft of this instrument was laid before and approved by a resolution of each House of Parliament in accordance with section 176(1)(aa) of that Act.

The Social Security Advisory Committee has agreed that proposals in respect of these Regulations should not be referred to it.

PART 1

GENERAL PROVISIONS

Citation and commencement

1.—These Regulations may be cited as the Social Security (Contributions Credits for Parents and Carers) Regulations 2010 and shall come into force on 6th April 2010. 2.71

GENERAL NOTE

SSCBA 1992 s.23A introduces weekly National Insurance credits (which replace Home Responsibilities Protection for periods of caring from April 6, 2010) for parents (including foster-parents) and carers in respect of their caring activities. 2.72

Although the task of awarding these credits in cases despendent on the award of child benefit has been transferred to HMRC, their administration is done on behalf of the Secretary of State and appeals lie to the First-tier Tribunal (Social Entitlement Chamber) and the Upper Tribunal (Administrative Appeals Chamber) rather than to the tax commissioners (see the National Insurance Contribution Credits (Transfer of Functions) Order 2009 (SI 2009/1377)). These regulations govern the award of these parents and carers credits. Generally, application for credits has to be made to HMRC (regs 9, 12: where the person is a carer because of the award of child benefit) or the Secretary of State (regs 10–12: persons engaged in caring because of the award of a relevant benefit), and generally before the end of the tax year in which the week(s) of engagement in caring fall (reg.12).

Section 23A applies to the benefits listed in subs.(1) where the determining event (attainment of pensionable age or death) occurs on or after April 6, 2010. The benefits are: Category A retirement pension; Category B retirement pension (under s.48A or 48B; widowed parent's allowance; and bereavement allowance. In respect of such benefits, the contributor concerned (see subs.(9) and s.21(5)(a)) is to be credited with a Class 3 contribution for each week falling after April 6, 2010 in respect of which the contributor was a "relevant carer". Subsection (3) stipulates that someone is a "relevant carer" in respect of a week) if he is awarded child benefit for any part of that week in respect of a child under the age of 12, or is a foster parent for any part of that week, or is in that week engaged in caring, within the meaning given by these regulations.

Interpretation

2.—(1) In these Regulations— 2.73

"partner" means the person with whom another person—

(a) resides; and

(b) shares responsibility for a child under the age of 12;

"relevant benefit" means—

(a) attendance allowance in accordance with section 64 (entitlement);

(b) the care component of disability living allowance in accordance with section 72 (the care component), at the middle or highest rate prescribed in accordance with subsection (3) of that section;

(c) an increase in the rate of disablement pension in accordance with section 104 (increase where constant attendance needed);

(d) any benefit by virtue of—

(i) the Pneumoconiosis, Byssinosis and Miscellaneous Diseases Benefit Scheme 1983; or

(ii) regulations made under paragraph 7(2) in Part 2 (regulations providing for benefit) of Schedule 8 (industrial injuries and diseases (old cases)),

which is payable as if the injury or disease were one in respect of which a disablement pension were for the time being payable in respect of an assessment of 100 per cent.;

(e) a constant attendance allowance payable by virtue of—

(i) article 8 (constant attendance allowance) of the Naval, Military and Air Forces etc. (Disablement and Death) Service Pensions Order 2006; or

(ii) article 14 (constant attendance allowance) of the Personal Injuries (Civilians) Scheme 1983.

[[1](f) the daily living component of personal independence payment in accordance with section 78 of the Welfare Reform Act 2012;

[[2](g) armed forces independence payment in accordance with the Armed Forces and Reserve Forces (Compensation Scheme) Order 2011.]

(2) In these Regulations, a reference to a section or Schedule by number alone is a reference to the section or Schedule so numbered in the Social Security Contributions and Benefits Act 1992.

AMENDMENTS

1. Personal Independence Payment (Supplementary Provisions and Consequential Amendments) Regulations 2013 (SI 2013/388) reg.8 and Sch. para.46 (April 8, 2013).

2. Armed Forces and Reserve Forces Compensation Scheme (Consequential Provisions: Subordinate Legislation) Order 2013 (SI 2013/591) art.7, Sch. para.44 (April 8, 2013).

Transitional provision

2.74 **3.**—For the period of 12 weeks from the date on which these Regulations come into force, regulation 7(1)(a) has effect as if the reference in regulation 7(1) to 12 weeks were a reference to the number of complete weeks since these Regulations came into force.

PART 2

MEANING OF "FOSTER PARENT" AND "ENGAGED IN CARING"

Meaning of "foster parent"

2.75 4.—(1) For the purposes of subsection (3)(b) of section 23A (contributions credits for relevant parents and carers), a foster parent is a person approved as—

(a) a foster parent in accordance with Part 4 (approval of foster parents) of the Fostering Services Regulations 2002; [[1] . . .

(aa) a kinship carer in accordance with Part 5 (kinship care) of the Looked After Children (Scotland) Regulations 2009;]

(b) a foster carer in accordance with Part 7 (fostering) of the Looked After Children (Scotland) Regulations 2009. [[1]; or

(c) a foster parent in accordance with Part 2 (approvals and placements) of the Foster Placement (Children) Regulations (Northern Ireland) 1996.]

(2) Paragraph (1) is subject to regulation 8.

AMENDMENT

1. National Insurance Contributions Credits (Miscellaneous Amendments) Regulations 2011 (SI 2011/709) reg.3 (April 5, 2011).

GENERAL NOTE

This regulation—subject to reg.8, below—defines "foster parent" for the purposes of SSCBA 1992 s.23(3)(b) by reference to the definitions in the stipulated legislation. Regulation 8 provides that a foster-parent ceases to be such when not ordinarily resident in Great Britain or when undergoing a period of imprisonment or detention in legal custody. 2.76

Meaning of "engaged in caring"

5.—(1) For the purposes of subsection (3)(c) of section 23A, a person is engaged in caring in a week— 2.77

(a) if that person is the partner of a person who is awarded child benefit for any part of that week in respect of a child under the age of 12;

(b) if that person is caring for another person or persons for a total of 20 or more hours in that week and—

(i) that other person is, or each of the persons cared for are, entitled to a relevant benefit for that week; or

(ii) the Secretary of State considers that level of care to be appropriate;

(c) if that person is one to whom any of paragraphs 4 to 6 (persons caring for another person) of Schedule 1B (prescribed categories of person) to the Income Support (General) Regulations 1987 applies.

(2) Paragraph (1) is subject to regulations 6 to 8.

DEFINITIONS

"partner"—see reg.2(1).
"relevant benefit"—see reg.2(1).

GENERAL NOTE

Paragraph (1) of this regulation sets out when, for the purposes of s.23A(3)(c), a person is "engaged in caring". The three alternatives set out in para.(1) are, however, all subject to regs 6–8, below (para.(2)) 2.78

Limit on the period in respect of partners of persons awarded child benefit

6.—(1) Regulation 5(1)(a) does not apply to any week which falls within a tax year in respect of which the person awarded child benefit satisfies the following condition. 2.79

(2) The condition is that that person's earnings factor for the purposes of section 45 (additional pension in a Category A retirement pension) does not exceed the qualifying earnings factor for that year.

(3) In calculating a person's earnings factor for the purposes of paragraph (2), no account is to be taken of any earnings factor derived from contributions credited by virtue of that person being a relevant carer due to an award of child benefit.

GENERAL NOTE

2.80 Regulation 5(1)(a) specifies that someone is engaged in caring in any week where they are the partner of a person awarded for any part of that week child benefit in respect of a child under 12. This regulation provides that this shall not be the case in any week in a tax year where the person awarded child benefit has an earnings factor less than that year's qualifying earnings factor for purposes of the additional pension in Category A retirement pension. In calculating that earnings factor no account is to be taken of contributions credited by virtue of that person being a relevant carer because of a child benefit award.

Additional period in respect of entitlement to carer's allowance [1 or carer support payment] and relevant benefits

2.81 **7.**—(1) A person is engaged in caring for a period of 12 weeks—

(a) prior to the date on which that person becomes entitled to carer's allowance by virtue of subsection (1) of section 70 (carer's allowance) [1 or carer support payment under the Carer's Assistance (Carer Support Payment) (Scotland) Regulations 2023];

(b) subject to paragraph (2), following the end of the week in which that person ceases to be entitled to carer's allowance by virtue of that subsection [1 or carer support payment by virtue of those Regulations];

(c) following the end of a week in which regulation 5(1)(b) ceases to be satisfied.

(2) For the purposes of paragraph (1)(b), a person is not engaged in caring in a week in respect of which that person is entitled, under regulations made under subsection (5) of section 22 (earnings factors), to be credited with contributions by virtue of being entitled to an allowance under section 70 [1 or a payment under the Carer's Assistance (Carer Support Payment) (Scotland) Regulations 2023].

AMENDMENT

1. Carer's Assistance (Carer Support Payment) (Scotland) Regulations 2023 (Consequential Amendments) Order 2023 (SI 2023/1218) art.20(2) (November 19, 2023).

Disqualification due to residence or imprisonment

2.82 **8.**—A person is not a foster parent or engaged in caring for the purposes of section 23A during any period in respect of which that person is—

(a) not ordinarily resident in Great Britain; or

(b) undergoing imprisonment or detention in legal custody.

GENERAL NOTE

2.83 On "undergoing imprisonment or detention in legal custody" see the commentary to SSCBA 1992 s.113(1)(b) and WRA 2009 s.18(4)(b).

PART 3

APPLICATIONS

Applications: foster parents and partners of persons awarded child benefit

2.84 **9.**—A person shall not be entitled to be credited with Class 3 contributions under—

(a) subsection (3)(b) (foster parent) of section 23A; or
(b) subsection (3)(c) (person engaged in caring) of section 23A by virtue of regulation 5(1)(a),

unless an application to be so credited is received by the Commissioners for Her Majesty's Revenue and Customs.

Applications: carers for 20 or more hours per week

10.—(1) A person shall not be entitled to be credited with Class 3 contributions under subsection (3)(c) of section 23A by virtue of regulation 5(1)(b) unless an application to be so credited is received by the Secretary of State. **2.85**

(2) Paragraph (1) does not apply where that person—

(a) [[1] . . .]
(b) is a married woman who is not entitled to be credited with contributions under paragraph (1) of regulation 7A (credits for carer's allowance) of the Social Security (Credits) Regulations 1975 by virtue of paragraph (2)(b) (reduced contribution rate election under regulations under section 19(4)) of that regulation.

Provision of information: carers for 20 or more hours per week

11.—(1) With respect to an application to which regulation 10(1) applies, the application must include— **2.86**

(a) a declaration by the applicant that the applicant cares for a person or persons for 20 or more hours per week;
(b) the name and, where known, the national insurance number of each person cared for;
(c) where applicable, which relevant benefit each person cared for is entitled to; and
(d) where requested by the Secretary of State, a declaration signed by an appropriate person as to the level of care which is required for each person cared for.

(2) For the purposes of paragraph (1)(d), an appropriate person is a person who is—

(a) involved in the health care or social care of the person cared for; and
(b) considered by the Secretary of State as appropriate to make a declaration as to the level of care required.

Time limit for applications

12.—An application under regulation 9 or 10 must be received— **2.87**

(a) before the end of the tax year following the tax year in which a week, which is the subject of the application, falls; or
(b) within such further time as the Secretary of State or the Commissioners for Her Majesty's Revenue and Customs, as the case may be, consider reasonable in the circumstances.

AMENDMENT

1. Social Security (Credits) (Amendment) Regulations 2010 (SI 2010/385) reg.3 (April 6, 2010).

PART III

REGULATIONS COMMON TO SEVERAL BENEFITS

The Social Security Benefit (Computation of Earnings) Regulations 1996

(SI 1996/2745) (*as amended*)

ARRANGEMENT OF REGULATIONS

PART I

GENERAL

PART II

EMPLOYED EARNERS

PART III

SELF-EMPLOYED EARNERS

PART IV

TRANSITIONAL PROVISIONS, CONSEQUENTIAL AMENDMENTS AND REVOCATIONS

SCHEDULES

The Secretary of State for Social Security, in exercise of the powers conferred by sections 3(2) and (3), 80(7), 89, 112, 119 and 175(1), (3) and (4) of, and paragraph 4(6) of Schedule 7 to, the Social Security Contributions and Benefits Act 1992, sections 5(1)(n) and (r), 71(7), 189(4) and (5) and 191 of the Social Security Administration Act 1992 and of all other powers enabling him in that behalf, after agreement by the Social Security Advisory Committee that the proposals to make these Regulations should not be referred to it hereby makes the following Regulations:

PART I

GENERAL

Citation and commencement

3.2 **1.**—These Regulations may be cited as the Social Security Benefit (Computation of Earnings) Regulations 1996 and shall come into force on 25th November 1996.

GENERAL NOTE

3.3 These regulations replaced the Computation of Earnings Regulations 1978 (SI 1978/1698). They contain in a more detailed manner the rules for determining earnings and include provision for determining notional earnings.

Interpretation

3.4 **2.**—(1) In these Regulations, unless the context otherwise requires—

[[1] . . .]

[[6] "basic rate" means the rate of income tax of that name in pursuance of section 6(2) of the Income Tax Act 2007;]

"benefit week" means—

(a) any period of 7 days corresponding to the week in respect of which the relevant social security benefit is due to be paid, and, where appropriate in respect of payments due to be paid before that week,

(b) the period of 7 days ending on the day before the first day of the first such week following the date of claim or any one of the consecutive periods of seven days prior to that period;

"board and lodging accommodation" means—

(a) accommodation provided to a person or, if he is a member of a family, to him or any other member of his family, for a charge which is inclusive of the provision of that accommodation and at least some cooked or prepared meals which both are cooked or prepared (by a person other than the person to whom the accommodation is provided or a member of his family) and are consumed in that accommodation or associated premises; or

(b) accommodation provided to a person in a hotel, guest house, lodging house or some similar establishment,

except accommodation provided by a close relative of his or of any other member of his family, or other than on a commercial basis;

"claim" means a claim for a benefit, pension or allowance under Parts II to V of the Contributions and Benefits Act;

"claimant" means a person claiming a benefit, pension or allowance under Parts II to V of the Contributions and Benefits Act and includes a claimant's spouse or partner and any adult in respect of whom a claim for an increase in benefit is made under Part IV of that Act;

[4 ...]

"close relative" means a parent, parent-in-law, son, son-in-law, daughter, daughter-in-law, step-parent, step-son, step-daughter, brother, sister, [3 or if any of the preceding persons is one member of a couple, the other member of that couple;]

"the Contributions and Benefits Act" means the Social Security Contributions and Benefits Act 1992;

[5 "couple" means

(a) two people who are married to, or civil partners of, each other and are members of the same household; or

(b) two people who are not married to, or civil partners of, each other but are living together [7 as if they were a married couple or civil partners];

"Crown property" means property held by Her Majesty in right of the Crown or by a government department or which is held in trust for Her Majesty for the purposes of a government department, except (in the case of an interest held by Her Majesty in right of the Crown) where the interest is under the management of the Crown Estate Commissioners;

"date of claim" means the date on which the claimant makes, or is treated as making, a claim for a benefit, pension or allowance for the purposes of regulation 6 of the Social Security (Claims and Payments) Regulations 1987;

"dwelling occupied as the home" means the dwelling together with any garage, garden and outbuildings, normally occupied by the claimant as his home including any premises not so occupied which it is impracticable or unreasonable to sell separately, in particular, in Scotland, any croft land on which the dwelling is situated;

"earnings" has the meaning prescribed in regulation 9 or, as the case may be, 12, and for the purposes only of sections 80, 82 to 86A and 89 of, and paragraphs 4, 6 and 7 of Schedule 7 to, the Contributions and Benefits Act includes payments by way of occupational or personal pension within the meaning of section 122 of the Contributions and Benefits Act (interpretation);

"employed earner" means a person who is in gainful employment in Great Britain under a contract of service, or in an office (including elective office) with emoluments chargeable to income tax under Schedule E and includes—

(a) a person in any employment which would be such employment if it were in Great Britain, and

(b) a person in any such employment which, in accordance with the provisions of the Contributions and Benefits Act and of any regulations made thereunder, is to be disregarded in relation to liability for contributions;

"employment" includes any trade, business, profession, office or vocation;

[4"integrated care board" means an integrated care board established under Chapter A3 of Part 2 of the National Health Service Act 2006;]

"invalid carriage or other vehicle" means a vehicle propelled by petrol engine or by electric power supplied for use on the road and to be controlled by the occupant;

"lone parent" means a person who has no partner and who is responsible for, and a member of the same household as, a child within the meaning of section 142 of the Contributions and Benefits Act (meaning of "child");

[6 . . .]

[2 . . .];

"net earnings" means such earnings as are calculated in accordance with regulation 10(4);

"net profit" means such profit as is calculated in accordance with regulation 13(4);

"occupational pension scheme" has the same meaning as in section 1 of the Pension Schemes Act 1993;

"partner" means where a claimant—

(a) is a member of a [3 . . .] couple, the other member of that couple;

(b) is married polygamously to two or more members of his household, any such member;

"payment" includes a part of a payment;

"pay period" means the period in respect of which a claimant is, or expects to be, normally paid by his employer, being a week, a fortnight, four weeks, a month or other shorter or longer period as the case may be;

"personal pension scheme" has the same meaning as in section 1 of the Pension Schemes Act 1993 and, in the case of a self-employed earner, includes a scheme approved by the Inland Revenue under Chapter IV of Part XIV of the Income and Corporation Taxes Act 1988;

"polygamous marriage" means any marriage during the subsistence of which a party to it is married to more than one person and the ceremony of marriage took place under the law of a country which permits polygamy;

"relevant earnings limit" means the amount of a claimant's earnings in excess of which the benefit, supplement, allowance, pension or increase in question is not payable;

"retirement annuity contract" means a contract or trust scheme approved under Chapter III of Part XIV of the Income and Corporation Taxes Act 1988;

[6 "Scottish basic rate" means the rate of income tax of that name calculated in accordance with section 6A of the Income Tax Act 2007;]

[6 "Scottish taxpayer" has the same meaning as in Chapter 2 of Part 4A of the Scotland Act 1998;]

"self-employed earner" means a person who is in gainful employment in Great Britain otherwise than as an employed earner and includes—

(a) a person in any employment which would be such employment if it were in Great Britain, and

(b) a person in any such employment which, in accordance with the provisions of the Contributions and Benefits Act and of any regulations made thereunder, is to be disregarded in relation to liability for contributions;

"voluntary organisation" means a body, other than a public or local authority, the activities of which are carried on otherwise than for profit;

"week" means a period of 7 days and for the purposes of section 80 of, and paragraph 4(6) of Schedule 7 to, the Contributions and Benefits Act, a period of 7 days being the relevant benefit week;

"year of assessment" has the meaning prescribed in section 832(1) of the Income and Corporation Taxes Act 1988.

(2) In these Regulations, unless the context otherwise requires, a reference—

(a) to a numbered regulation or Schedule is to the regulation in or Schedule to these Regulations bearing that number;

(b) in a regulation or Schedule to a numbered paragraph is to the paragraph in that regulation or Schedule bearing that number;

(c) in a paragraph to a lettered or numbered sub-paragraph is to the sub-paragraph in that paragraph bearing that letter or number.

AMENDMENTS

1. The Social Security Act 1998 (Commencement No. 9 and Savings and Consequential and Transitional Provisions) Order 1999 (SI 1999/2422) Sch.13 para.2 (September 6, 1999).

2. The Social Security Benefit (Computation of Earnings) (Amendment) Regulations 2002 (SI 2002/2823) reg.2 (April 1, 2003).

3. The Civil Partnership Act 2004 (Tax Credits, etc.) (Consequential Amendments) Order 2005 (SI 2005/2919) (December 5, 2005).

4. Health and Care Act 2022 (Consequential and Related Amendments and Transitional Provisions) Regulations 2022 (SI 2022/634) Pt 2 reg.12 (July 1, 2022).

5. The Marriage (Same Sex Couples) Act 2013 (Consequential Provisions) Order 2014 (SI 2014/107) reg.20 (March 13, 2014).

6. The Social Security Benefit (Computation of Earnings) (Amendment) Regulations 2016 (SI 2016/267) reg.2 (April 6, 2016).

7. The Civil Partnership (Opposite-sex Couples) Regulations 2019 (SI 2019/1458) reg.41(b) and Sch.3 Pt2, para.49 (December 2, 2019).

GENERAL NOTE

With effect from December 5, 2005, art.3 of the Civil Partnership Act 2004 (Relationships Arising Through Civil Partnership) Order 2005 (SI 2005/3137) applies the provisions of s.246 of the Civil Partnership Act 2004 which deals, in the civil partnership context, with the interpretation of statutory references to step-children, to the definition of "close relative" in reg.2(1). 3.5

For a decision which is of significance in drawing the dividing line between employer earners and self-employed earners, which arose in the context of computing the earnings of a GCSE examiner, see *CG/4139/2006.* The Commissioner concludes his decision with the words:

> "12. . . . . I also hope that the Secretary of State takes steps to ensure that the guidance given to officers dealing with carer's allowance and other benefits to which the Computation of Earnings Regulations are relevant takes account of the

deeming in regulation 2(3) and paragraph 6 of Schedule 1 to the Categorisation of Earners Regulations."

With effect from December 16, 2014, art.29 and Sch.6 para.14 of the Marriage and Civil Partnership (Scotland) Act 2014 and Civil Partnership Act 2004 (Consequential Provisions and Modifications Order 2001 (SI 2014/3229) amended the definition of "couple" by substituting a definition in the same terms as the existing definition. However, the existing definition applied only to England and Wales; the new definition applies to England, Wales, Scotland and Northern Ireland.

Calculation of earnings

3.6 **3.**—(1) For the purposes of Parts II to V (other than those of Schedule 8) of the Contributions and Benefits Act (a) and of any regulations made thereunder which relate to benefit under those Parts of that Act or regulations, the earnings of a claimant shall be calculated by determining in accordance with these Regulations the weekly amount of his earnings.

(2) The amount of a claimant's earnings for any period shall be the whole of those earnings (including any earnings which he is treated as possessing under regulation 4 (notional earnings)) except in so far as regulations 10 and 13 provide that certain sums shall be disregarded or deducted as appropriate.

General Note

3.7 The calculation of earnings is to be carried out in accordance with the rules contained in the Regulations. The whole of earnings after making the deductions and allowing the disregards provided for by the Regulations is to be taken into account. The provisions for estimating earnings are replaced by the notional earnings rules set out in reg.4. The rules apply to all benefits listed in Pts II to V of the Contributions and Benefits Act: incapacity benefit, sickness and invalidity benefits (so far as still relevant), maternity benefits, bereavement benefits, retirement pensions, child's special allowance, attendance allowance, disability living allowance, guardian's allowance, and increases for dependants, as well as benefits for industrial injuries.

Some of the broad areas of discretion previously available under the former Regulations are replaced by regulation-based rules for determining earnings.

In *Secretary of State for Work and Pensions v Doyle* [2006] EWCA Civ 466, reported as *R(IB) 1/06*, the Court of Appeal ruled that these regulations apply to the computation of earnings for the purposes of entitlement to incapacity benefit where a person is working "on the advice of a doctor". The essential grounding of entitlement of incapacity benefit in Pt II of the Act was sufficient for reg.3 to apply even though Pt XIIA lays down the detailed scheme.

Notional earnings

3.8 **4.**—(1) Where a claimant's earnings are not ascertainable at the date [1 on which a decision falls to be made by the Secretary of State under Chapter II of Part I of the Social Security Act 1998 or regulations made thereunder the claimant shall be treated] as possessing such earnings as is reasonable in the circumstances of the case having regard to the number of hours worked and the earnings paid for comparable employment in the area.

(2) [2 . . .]

(3) Where a claimant is treated as possessing any earnings under paragraph (1) [2 . . .] these Regulations shall apply for the purposes of calculating the amount of those earnings as if a payment had actually been made and as if they were actual earnings which he does possess except that paragraph

(4) of regulation 10 (calculation of net earnings of employed earners) shall not apply and his net earnings shall be calculated by taking into account the earnings which he is treated as possessing, less—

(a) an amount in respect of income tax equivalent to an amount calculated by applying to those earnings the [5 basic rate, or in the case of a Scottish taxpayer, the Scottish basic rate,] of tax in the year of assessment less only the [5 personal reliefs to which the claimant is entitled under Chapters 2, 3 and 3A of Part 3 of the Income Tax Act 2007 as are] appropriate to his circumstances; but, if the period over which those earnings are to be taken into account is less than a year, the earnings to which the [5 basic rate, or the Scottish basic rate,] of tax is to be applied and the amount of the personal [5 reliefs] deductible under this paragraph shall be calculated on a pro rata basis;

(b) where the weekly amount of those earnings equals or exceeds the lower earnings limit, an amount representing primary Class 1 contributions under the Contributions and Benefits Act, calculated by applying to those earnings the initial and main primary percentages in accordance with section 8(1)(a) and (b) of that Act; and

(c) one half of any sum payable by the claimant in respect of a pay period by way of a contribution towards an occupational or personal pension scheme.

AMENDMENTS

1. The Social Security Act 1998 (Commencement No. 11 and Transitional Provisions) Order 1999 (SI 1999/2860) Sch.15, para.3(a) (October 18, 1999).

2. The Social Security Benefit (Computation of Earnings) (Amendment) Regulations 2016 (SI 2016/267) reg.2(3) (April 6, 2016).

GENERAL NOTE

The provisions on notional earnings are new in relation to the benefits covered by these regulations. **3.9**

Earnings not ascertainable (paragraph (1))

The first question for the decision-maker will be to determine whether the earnings (which may be from employment or self-employment) are ascertainable. That is not the same as saying that they have not yet been ascertained. Whether the earnings are ascertainable will be for the judgment of the decision-maker. In these cases, the claimant is treated as possessing such earnings as he or she might reasonably be paid for comparable employment in the area. It is not clear who has the burden of proof. But the decision-maker is likely to be in a better position than the claimant to present the evidence needed to form the conclusions required by the regulation. Furthermore, in many cases the earnings will serve to disentitle the person from a benefit, and there is an argument that in those cases the burden should be on the decision-maker. In practice the burden is likely to be "neutral" in that both parties can be expected to come to the decision-maker with as much information as possible from which a conclusion can be drawn. **3.10**

Though the terms used in para.(1) apply to both employment and self-employment, the remainder of the regulation requires that the calculation of notional earnings should be made on the basis that the person is a notional employed earner. This is presumably because there are no valid comparators in the case of self-employment. So a self-employed painter whose earnings are not ascertainable will be treated as possessing the earnings paid for comparable employment as a painter.

Paragraph (3)

3.11 Paragraph (3) provides the mechanism for determining notional earnings, which will need to be added to any actual earnings.

Rounding of fractions

3.12 **5.**—Where any calculation under these Regulations results in a fraction of a penny that fraction shall, if it would be to the claimant's advantage, be treated as a penny, otherwise it shall be disregarded.

PART II

EMPLOYED EARNERS

GENERAL NOTE

3.13 Regulations 6 to 10 are replete with difficulty. In *DC v SSWP* [2008] UKUT 23 (AAC) the Judge said:

> ". . . I have been trying to understand the operation of regulations 6 to 9 of the Social Security (Computation of Earnings) Regulations 1996. In the end, I have decided that was too ambitious a task. The way that those provisions operate is not entirely clear and they would benefit from being reconsidered, if not redrafted" (para.1).

It is perhaps trite to say that the purpose of the regulations is to identify what counts as earnings, to attribute earnings to particular weeks, and to provide a means for converting them to weekly amounts. The starting point is perhaps reg.9 which defines what constitute earnings of employed earners, and reg.10 which concerns net earnings. Regulation 6 provides the means for calculating the earnings of employed earners in terms of weeks. Regulation 7 treats earnings as paid on a particular date which means that the weeks to which they are attributable can be determined. Finally reg.8 provides the methods of converting earnings to weekly amounts. Particular difficulties seem to arise in relation to certain payments when employment comes to an end. The Commissioner in *CG/4172/2001* and the Judge in *DC v SSWP* [2008] UKUT 23 (AAC) both accepted that such payments are attributable to a future period, since the money received is available for future expenditure. But the judge in the latter case also concluded:

> ". . . the regulations do not necessarily produce an income that is in any way tied to the reality of the period for which payments are made or over which they are likely to be spent" (para.29).

The appeal against the Judge's decision was dismissed in *Cotton v SSWP*, [2009] EWCA Civ 1333, [2010] AACR 17, where Goldring L.J. said:

> "30. As it seems to me (as Mr. Forsdick submitted) the function of the 1996 Regulations is firstly to identify what counts as earnings. Regulation 9 does that. Secondly, they attribute those earnings to a particular week or weeks. Regulation 7 determines the date on which the earnings are treated as paid. Regulation 6 determines the period over which they are to be attributed. Thirdly, regulation 8 converts the earnings into weekly amounts in order to determine whether the earnings threshold (laid down in regulation 8(1) of the 1976 Regulations) has been exceeded.
>
> 31. The range of possible earnings in regulation 9 is wide. Many different kinds of periodic earnings are encompassed. Some may be paid at regular intervals. Some may be one off (as in the present case). The regulations have to provide a

workable means of assessing and attributing this wide range of periodic earnings to the many different circumstances which can arise as simply as possible.
32. An assessment of the beginning of the period is straightforward. The same cannot be said of the assessment of the end. To ascertain that would in many cases be difficult or impossible. That is why, as I conclude, a deeming provision was necessary. It results in a scheme which imposes a general rule under which all regulation 9 earnings payable in respect of a period are treated as payable for a period starting with the first day of the benefit week in which they are paid and ending on the day before the next payment of ordinary earnings (the next pay day). That deemed end date is not tied to the actual length of the period in respect of which any particular payment was made."

Calculation of earnings of employed earners

6.—(1) Earnings derived from employment as an employed earner shall be calculated or estimated over a period determined in accordance with the following paragraphs and at a weekly amount determined in accordance with regulation 8 (calculation of weekly amount of earnings). 3.14

(2) Subject to paragraphs (3) and (5) to (8), the period over which a payment is to be taken into account—

(a) in a case where it is payable in respect of a period, shall be a period equal to a benefit week or such number of benefit weeks as comprise the period commencing on the date on which earnings are treated as paid under regulation 7 (date on which earnings are treated as paid) and ending on the day before the date on which earnings of the same kind (excluding earnings of the kind mentioned at regulation 9(1)(a) to (j)) and from the same source would, or would if the employment was continuing, next be treated as paid under that regulation;

(b) in any other case, shall be a period equal to such number of weeks as is equal to the number (less any fraction of a whole number) calculated in accordance with the formula—

$$\frac{P}{Q + R}$$

where—

P is the net earnings;

Q is the amount of the relevant earnings limit plus one penny; and

R is the total of the sums which would fall to be disregarded or deducted as appropriate under regulation 10(2) or (3) (calculation of net earnings of employed earners),

and that period shall begin on the date on which the payment is treated as paid under regulation 7 (date on which earnings are treated as paid).

(3) Where earnings not of the same kind are derived from the same source and the periods in respect of which those earnings would, but for this paragraph, fall to be taken into account overlap, wholly or partly, those earnings shall be taken into account over a period—

(a) equal to the aggregate length of those periods, and

(b) beginning with the earliest date on which any part of those earnings would otherwise be treated as paid under regulation 7 (date on which earnings are treated as paid).

(4) In a case to which paragraph (3) applies, earnings under regulation 9 (earnings of employed earners) shall be taken into account in the following order of priority—

(a) earnings normally derived from the employment;

(b) any payment to which paragraph (1)(b) or (c) of that regulation applies;

(c) any payment to which paragraph (1)(i) of that regulation applies;

(d) any payment to which paragraph (1)(d) of that regulation applies.

(5) Where earnings to which regulation 9(1)(b) to (d) (earnings of employed earners) applies are paid in respect of part of a day, those earnings shall be taken into account over a period equal to a week.

(6) Where earnings to which regulations 9(1)(i)(i) (earnings of employed earners) applies are paid in respect of or on the termination of any employment which is not part-time employment, the period over which they are to be taken into account shall be—

(a) a period equal to such number of weeks as is equal to the number (less any fraction of a whole number) obtained by dividing the net earnings by the maximum weekly amount which, on the date on which the payment of earnings is made, is specified in section 227(1) of the Employment Rights Act 1996; or

(b) a period equal to the length of the specified period,

whichever is the shorter, and that period shall begin on the date on which the payment is treated as paid under regulation 7 (date on which earnings are treated as paid).

(7) Any earnings to which regulation 9(1)(i)(ii) applies which are paid in respect of or on the termination of part-time employment, shall be taken into account over a period equal to one week.

(8) In this regulation—

"part-time employment" means—

(a) subject to the provisions of sub-paragraphs (b) to (d) of this definition, employment in which a person is engaged, or, where his hours of work fluctuate, he is engaged on average, for less than 16 hours a week being work for which payment is made or which is done in expectation of payment;

(b) subject to sub-paragraph (c) of this definition, the number of hours for which a person is engaged in work shall be determined—

(i) where no recognisable cycle has been established in respect of a person's work, by reference to the number of hours or, where those hours are likely to fluctuate, the average of the hours, which he is expected to work in a week;

(ii) where the number of hours for which he is engaged fluctuate, by reference to the average of hours worked over—

(aa) if there is a recognisable cycle of work, the period of one complete cycle (including, where the cycle involves periods in which the person does not work, those periods but disregarding any other absences);

(bb) in any other case, the period of five weeks immediately before the date of claim or the date [[1]on which a revision or supersession of a decision falls to be made], or such other length of time as may, in the particular case, enable the person's average hours of work to be determined more accurately;

(c) where for the purpose of sub-paragraph (b)(ii)(aa) of this definition, a person's recognisable cycle of work at a school, other educational establishment or other place of employment is one year and includes periods of school holidays or similar vacations during which he does not work, those periods and any other periods not forming part of such holidays or vacations during which he is not required to work shall be disregarded in establishing the average hours for which he is engaged in work;

(d) for the purposes of sub-paragraphs (a) and (b) of this definition, in determining the number of hours for which a person is engaged in work, that number shall include any time allowed to that person by his employer for a meal or for refreshment, but only where that person is, or expects to be, paid earnings in respect of that time;

"specified period" means a period equal to—

(a) a week or such number of weeks (less any fraction of a whole number) as comprise the period of notice which is applicable to a person, or would have been applicable if it had not been waived; less

(b) any part of that period during which the person has continued to work in the employment in question or in respect of which he has received a payment to which regulation 9(1)(c) applies,

and for the purposes of this definition "period of notice" means the period of notice of termination of employment to which a person is entitled by statute or by contract, whichever is the longer, or, if he is not entitled to such notice, the period of notice which is customary in the employment in question.

AMENDMENT

1. The Social Security Act 1998 (Commencement No.9 and Savings and Consequental and Transitional Provisions) Order 1999 (SI 1999/2422) Sch.13 para.4 (September 6, 1999).

GENERAL NOTE

There are similarities between provisions of this regulation and reg.29 of the Income Support (General) Regulations 1987: see references to the annotations in the 2021–22 edition of Vol.V and the cumulative supplement in this year's Vol.II. **3.15**

Earnings are always related to a week or number of weeks. Those paid weekly or fortnightly (or other multiples of weeks) are likely to be easiest to deal with. In other cases (for example, monthly paid employees) the formula set out in the regulation will need to be applied.

Special rules apply to termination payments, which frequently causes difficulty, particularly where claimants have not fully appreciated their impact on benefit claims.

Paragraph (2)

In *CG/4172/2001,* the appellant received two final payments in respect of the termination of his employment on July 3, 2000. One was paid on June 25, 2000 representing his last full month's salary from his employment. Regulations 6(2)(a) and 7(b) could readily be applied to this payment. The second was paid on July 25, 2000 and consisted of a payment of £278.35 gross in respect of salary for the final working weeks and £1,031.13 gross representing 14 days accrued holiday pay up to his termination date in respect of holiday which had not been taken. The application of the same regulations enabled the salary payment to be taken into account: the start date was July 24, 2000 (the first day of the benefit week in which it was due to be paid) and the end date was August 20, 2000 (the day before the first day **3.16** of the benefit week in which the next salary payment would have been made if the employment continued): para.9.

The holiday pay was much more problematic. Regulation 6(2)(a) only applies if the holiday pay was payable "in respect of a period". If it was not, then reg.6(2)(b) applied. The Commissioner concludes (following earlier decisions) that it was paid "in respect of a period". The Commissioner also concludes that the holiday pay was due on the termination of the employment. This should be interpreted in accordance with its ordinary meaning: the employment terminated on July 3, 2000 and so this was the start date for attributing this period. Determining the end date was considerably less straightforward. Regulation 6(2)(a) could not easily be applied to payments such as holiday pay. Regulation 6(2)(a) refers to "earnings of the same kind"; and reg.9 lists types of payments which are included within the concept of "earnings". This includes "holiday pay". The Commissioner concludes that the only sensible meaning of the words in reg.9 is that holiday pay and ordinary earnings both constitute earnings of the same kind.

That conclusion, according to the Commissioner, left a problem with the interpretation of paragraphs (3) and (4) of regulation 6: see para.14 of the decision. The Commissioner felt compelled to conclude that the words "earnings of the same kind" have a different meaning in reg.6(2)(a) from that in reg.6(3) and (4). As a result the end date for the holiday pay was July 23, 2000. But the effect of the overlapping provisions in paragraphs (3) and (4) is that holiday pay (as having a lower order of priority is deemed to run for the period of three weeks from July 24, 2000. So the final conclusion was as follows:

- First salary payment attributable to June 19 to July 23, 2000,
- Second salary payment attributable to July 24, to August 20, 2000,
- Holiday pay attributable to July 24 to August 13, 2000.

3.17 The judge in *DC v SSWP* [2008] UKUT 23 (AAC) has followed the Commissioner's decision. In doing so, the judge observes:

> 44. Left entirely to my own devices, I would have been tempted to decide that, within the meaning of regulation 6(2), accrued holiday pay was not paid in respect of a period. That would mean that regulation 6(2)(b) would apply.
>
> 45. I have not taken that course for three reasons. First, in *Chief Supplementary Benefit Officer v Cunningham* [1985] ICR 660, Waller LJ (at page 665) said that one day accrued holiday pay was paid for a period. Second, neither party argued that regulation 6(2)(b) applied. Third, regulation 6(2)(b) operates to attribute a payment to the maximum number of weeks over which the claimant can be excluded from benefit. Mr Richards argued that the claimant had an entitlement under section 70 to a carer's allowance and that a provision that deprived him of it should be interpreted restrictively. I do not accept that argument. Section 70 does not confer an entitlement. It sets out the basic conditions and provides for more detailed provisions to be made by regulations. Regulation 6 is one of those regulations. However, given that the provision does operate harshly on claimant and the Secretary of State has not argued that it applies, I do not consider it appropriate to apply regulation 6(2)(b).

In dismissing the appeal against this decision in *Cotton v SSWP*, [2009] EWCA Civ 1333, [2010] AACR 17, Goldring L.J., giving the lead judgment, had this to say on the interpretation of reg.6:

> "38. While it may be unfortunate that the words "*earnings not of the same kind*" may bear a different meaning for the purposes of regulation 6(3) than "*earnings of the same kind*" in regulation 6(2)(a), the context in which the words are used in each regulation is somewhat different. The words in parenthesis in regulation 6(2)(a) are absent in regulation 6(3). Moreover, the words as used in regulation 6(2)(a) are performing an essentially different function from those in regulation 6(3) (taken in conjunction with regulation 6(4)).

39. While any statutory scheme should be understood as a whole, this cannot lead to the immutable rule that the same words used in the same legislation necessarily have the same meaning.
40. In short, in spite of the opacity of the language, I have come to the view that this is a deeming provision which seeks to make relatively simple the assessment of the end date when a periodic payment is made which does not consist of ordinary pay."

Wilson L.J. also dismissed the appeal but for reasons different from those of Goldring L.J. and Laws L.J.

Date on which earnings are treated as paid

7.—Earnings to which regulation 6 (calculation of earnings of employed earners) or 11(2) (calculation of earnings of self-employed earners) applies shall be treated as paid— **3.18**

(a) (i) in the case of a payment in respect of an adult dependant of an increase of maternity allowance payable under section 82(2) of the Contributions and Benefits Act or an increase of [[1] carer's allowance] payable under paragraph 7 of Schedule 2 to the Social Security Benefit (Dependency) Regulations 1977; or

(ii) in the case of a payment in respect of an adult dependant who is not residing with the claimant of an increase of Category A or Category C retirement pension payable under section 83(2)(b) or 84(1) and 84(2)(b) of the Contributions and Benefits Act or a disablement pension where the claimant is entitled to an unemployability supplement payable under paragraph 6(1)(a)(ii) of Schedule 7 to the Contributions and Benefits Act,

on the first day of the benefit week following the benefit week in which the payment is due to be paid;

(b) in any other case, on the first day of the benefit week in which the payment is due to be paid.

Amendment

1. The Social Security Benefit (Computation of Earnings) (Amendment) Regulations 2002 (SI 2002/2823) reg.2 (April 1, 2003).

Calculation of weekly amount of earnings

8.—(1) For the purposes of regulation 6 (calculation of earnings of employed earners), subject to paragraphs (2) to (4), where the period in respect of which a payment is made— **3.19**

(a) does not exceed a week, the weekly amount shall be the amount of that payment;

(b) exceeds a week, the weekly amount shall be determined—

(i) in a case where that period is a month, by multiplying the amount of that payment by 12 and dividing the product by 52;

(ii) in a case where that period is three months, by multiplying the amount of the payment by 4 and dividing the product by 52;

(iii) in a case where that period is a year, by dividing the amount of the payment by 52;

(iv) in any other case, by multiplying the amount of the payment by 7 and dividing the product by the number equal to the number of days in the period in respect of which it is made.

(2) Where a payment of earnings from a particular source is or has been paid regularly and that payment falls to be taken into account in the same benefit week as a payment of the same kind and from the same source, the amount of those earnings to be taken into account in any one benefit week shall not exceed the weekly amount determined under paragraph (1)(a) or (b), as the case may be, of the payment which under regulation 7 (date on which earnings are treated as paid) is treated as paid first.

(3) Where the amount of the claimant's net earnings fluctuates and has changed more than once, or a claimant's regular pattern of work is such that he does not work every week, the application of the foregoing paragraphs may be modified so that the weekly amount of his earnings is determined by reference to his average weekly earnings—

(a) if there is a recognisable cycle of work, over the period of one complete cycle (including, where the cycle involves periods in which the claimant does no work, those periods but disregarding any other absences);

(b) if any other case, over a period of five weeks or such other period as may, in the particular case, enable the claimant's average weekly earnings to be determined more accurately.

(4) Where any payment of earnings is taken into account under paragraph (7) of regulation 6 (calculation of earnings of employed earners), over the period specified in that paragraph, the amount to be taken into account shall be equal to the amount of the payment.

General Note

3.20 *CG/4941/2003* concerned an overpayment of invalid care allowance (now carer's allowance) which had arisen when fluctuations in the claimant's earnings took her out of entitlement to the benefit for certain weeks. The Commissioner provides useful guidance on the interpretation of reg.8 in the decision:

> 18. Thus in simple terms, for a person both working and paid on a regular weekly basis, say on Fridays, the earnings for each benefit week starting on Monday will be the amount of the payment he or she receives on the Friday of the same week, and the normal rule is that if those earnings are over the weekly limit in force on the last day of that week, he or she will be "gainfully employed" for ICA purposes throughout the next benefit week starting on the following Monday. For a person paid on a regular monthly basis on the last working day of each calendar month, as this claimant was from 1 July 2001 onwards, the monthly earnings are treated as paid on the Monday of the benefit week that contains the actual monthly pay day, and that payment is treated as giving the claimant "earnings" for each of the (four or five) benefit weeks starting with that one and ending with the one before the week that will contain the next regular monthly pay day; the weekly amount of the earnings in each of those weeks being taken as the most recent monthly payment multiplied by 12 and divided by 52. For persons such as the claimant having fluctuating earnings (but, as is agreed, no recognisable "cycle" of work and non-work to bring into play the separate provision in regulation 8(3)(a) for such cases) the weekly or monthly payments received *may* instead be averaged under regulation 8(3)(b), so as to substitute a different weekly figure for the "earnings" attributable to the claimant, though still over the period of benefit weeks which each actual payment of earnings is treated as having to cover for the purposes of regulations 6 and 7.
>
> 19. As the very helpful and detailed written submission of Mr Cahill on behalf of the Secretary of State points out, regulation 8(3)(b) gives the Secretary of State a discretion to be applied rationally on a case by case basis, but is

limited in its purpose to the use of a five-week or other period in place of the actual weekly, monthly or other calculation under regulation 8(1) to **"enable the claimant's average weekly earnings to be determined more accurately"**; and this is less clear that it might be since strictly the *accuracy* of an average is simply a matter of doing the arithmetic correctly, irrespective of the periods you happen to select for the calculation. Regulation 8(3) must I think be taken as intended less literally (or mathematically), to mean that the Secretary of State is to have the power of substituting an alternative averaging calculation to produce a standardised weekly figure for the week or month, etc., identified in regulation 8(1) as the one in respect of which a given payment is actually made *where he is satisfied this would more accurately reflect the true rate of the claimant's weekly earnings* current at the period for which a week by week figure for those earnings has to be identified, in order to determine some question of entitlement: such as the one here, of whether or at what point the claimant had crossed the line of having weekly earnings over the limit to make her count as "gainfully employed" for invalid care allowance purposes in each day of the following benefit week.

20. It has to be borne in mind that the overriding purpose of the exercise, in the context of a weekly benefit such as invalid care allowance which is there to provide assistance with current weekly living expenses for people without sufficient weekly earnings of their own, is the relatively short term one of producing a working week by week figure so as to know as quickly as possible whether benefit is payable or not. Mr Cahill is I think right in saying that the application of regulation 8(3) in this context may often have to be more a matter of judgment than of science, and there may be no necessarily "right" answer: it has to be a matter of dealing reasonably with the evidence of actual earnings for the current payment periods as disclosed (or as it should be disclosed) by the claimant to the Secretary of State week by week or month by month. It cannot in my judgment be said that the existence of the discretionary power in regulation 8(3)(b) requires the Secretary of State in a case such as this to "wait and see" over a very extended period, and then juggle and aggregate a whole succession of payments that were each in fact made in respect of specific weekly and monthly periods either side of a significant change in the rate of working and earning, so as to treat them as in effect equivalent to one lumped-together payment for work spread evenly throughout. There are no grounds on which it could be described as "more accurate" to ignore a step-change in the rate of working and earning such as shown here in the late summer of 2001, and pretend that the claimant's work and earnings had carried on at one uniform rate all year.

CG/0607/2008 concerned the calculation of earnings in relation to the earnings limit for entitlement to a carer's allowance. This lengthy decision contains much useful comment and guidance on such cases, which seem to be a problematic area (perhaps because there is no taper—if a person's earnings are one penny over the limit, then entitlement to the carer's allowance ceases completely). The context was one in which an informal employment contract was intended to provide the appellant with earnings at, but not above, the earnings limit for entitlement to a carer's allowance. The appeal turned on the proper calculation of the appellant's weekly earnings. The Commissioner counsels care in looking at the definition provision in the regulations, and goes on to comment: **3.21**

36. The Regulations have the primary purpose of identifying the weekly amount of a claimant's earnings. They provide answers to the questions necessary for the conversion of actual earnings of an employee into weekly amounts of earnings by which to test those earnings against the earnings limit. They are the same essential questions that must be asked in any exercise of assessing

earnings for the application of any social security or tax rate or limit. There must be defined periods with defined start and end dates and defined rules for attributing actual earnings to those periods. The key questions are:

(1) Are earnings included when received, or when entitlement arises, or on some other basis?
(2) When are specific earnings received or earned?
(3) How are specific earnings linked to specific periods of assessment or benefit?

The use of deeming provisions in the Regulations means that the answers provided to those questions for carer's allowance purposes are not findings of fact about what happened, but are questions of law about how the deeming provisions in the Regulations are to be applied to those facts.

CG/0607/2008 has been considered and distinguished in *KJ v SSWP (CA)* [2011] AACR 7. The case concerned a full-time employee who reduced his hours in order to be able to care for his sick mother and to enable him to claim carer's allowance. For the month of March 2008, the employee was paid the pro-rata equivalent of his full-time salary for two days and the reduced amount for the remaining days in the month, but he also received a tax rebate. The question which arose was how this monthly pay should be used for the purpose of determining his earnings in relation to his claim for carer's allowance. The Upper Tribunal Judge concluded that this was not a case in which earnings fluctuated such that the more flexible provisions in reg.8(3) applied; that paragraph contemplated a situation in which the amount "has changed more than once". There was no basis for separating out the March salary into two payments: one attributable to the first two days of the month and so attributable to only one week. The "normal" calculation in converting the monthly pay into weekly earnings applied.

Earnings of employed earners

3.22 **9.**—(1) Subject to paragraphs (2) and (3), "earnings", in the case of employment as an employed earner, means any remuneration or profit derived from that employment and includes—

(a) any bonus or commission;
(b) any payment in lieu of remuneration except any periodic sum paid to a claimant on account of the termination of his employment by reason of redundancy;
(c) any payment in lieu of notice;
(d) any holiday pay except any payable more than four weeks after the termination or interruption of employment;
(e) any payment by way of a retainer;
(f) any payment made by the claimant's employer in respect of expenses not wholly, exclusively and necessarily incurred in the performance of the duties of the employment, including any payment made by the claimant's employer in respect of—
    (i) travelling expenses incurred by the claimant between his home and place of employment;
    (ii) expenses incurred by the claimant under arrangements made for the care of a member of his family owing to the claimant's absence from home;
(g) any award of compensation made under section 112(4) or 117(3)(a) of the Employment Rights Act 1996 (remedies and compensation);
(h) any such sum as is referred to in section 112(3) of the Contributions and Benefits Act (certain sums to be earnings for social security purposes);

(i) where—

(i) a payment of compensation is made in respect of employment which is not part-time employment and that payment is not less than the maximum weekly amount, the amount of the compensation less the deductible remainder, where that is applicable;

(ii) a payment of compensation is made in respect of employment which is part-time employment, the amount of the compensation;

[[1] (j) any remuneration paid by or on behalf of an employer to the claimant in respect of a period througho`ut which the claimant is—

(i) on maternity leave;

(ii) on paternity leave;

(iii) on adoption leave; or

(iv) absent from work because he is ill.]

(2) For the purposes of paragraph (1)(i)(i) the "deductible remainder"—

(a) applies in cases where dividing the amount of the compensation by the maximum weekly amount produces a whole number plus a fraction; and

(b) is equal to the difference between—

(i) the amount of the compensation; and

(ii) the product of the maximum weekly amount multiplied by the whole number.

[[2](3)"Earnings" shall not include any payment in respect of expenses—

(a) wholly, exclusively and necessarily incurred in the performance of the duties of the employment; or

(b) arising out of the [[4] claimant participating as a service user].

[[4] (3A) The reference in paragraph (3)(b) to a claimant participating as a service user is to—

(a) a person who is being consulted by or on behalf of—

(i) a body which has a statutory duty to provide services in the field of health, social care or social housing; or

(ii) a body which conducts research or undertakes monitoring for the purpose of planning or improving such services,

in their capacity as a user, potential user, carer of a user or person otherwise affected by the provision of those services;

(b) a person who is being consulted by or on behalf of—

(i) the Secretary of State in relation to any of his functions in the field of social security or child support or under section 2 of the Employment and Training Act 1973; or

(ii a body which conducts research or undertakes monitoring for the purpose of planning or improving such functions,

in their capacity as a person affected or potentially affected by the exercise of those functions or the carer of such a person; or

(c) the carer of a person consulted under sub-paragraphs (a) or (b).]

(4) In this regulation—

[[1] "adoption leave" means a period of absence from work on ordinary or additional adoption leave under section 75A or 75B of the Employment Rights Act 1996;]

"compensation" means any payment made in respect of or on the termination of employment in a case where a person has not received or received only part of a payment in lieu of notice due or which would have been due to him had he not waived his right to receive it, other than—

(a) any payment specified in paragraph (1)(a) to (h);
(b) any payment specified in paragraph (3);
(c) any redundancy payment within the meaning of section 135 of the Employment Rights Act 1996;
(d) any refund of contributions to which that person was entitled under an occupational pension scheme;
(e) any compensation payable by virtue of section 173 or section 178(3) or (4) of the Education Reform Act 1988;

[2 "enactment" includes an enactment comprised in, or an instrument made under, an Act of the Scottish Parliament;]

[1 "maternity leave" means a period during which a woman is absent from work because she is pregnant or has given birth to a child, and at the end of which she has a right to return to work either under the terms of her contract of employment or under Part 8 of the Employment Rights Act 1996;]

"maximum weekly amount" means the maximum weekly amount which, on the date on which the payment of compensation is made, is specified in section 227(1) of the Employment Rights Act 1996;

"part-time employment" has the same meaning as in regulation 6(8) (calculation of earnings of employed earners);

[1 "paternity leave" means a period of absence from work on leave under section 80A or 80B of the Employment Rights Act 1996.]

[2 "public authority" includes any person certain of whose functions are functions of a public nature;]

[2 [4 ...]]

AMENDMENTS

1. The Social Security Benefit (Computation of Earnings) (Amendment) Regulations 2002 (SI 2002/2823) reg.2 (April 1, 2003).

2. The Social Security Benefit (Computation of Earnings) (Amendment) Regulations 2009 (SI 2009/2678) reg.2 (October 26, 2009).

3. The Housing and Regeneration Act 2008 (Consequential Provisions) (No. 2) Order 2010 (SI 2010/671) art.4 and Sch.1 (April 1, 2010).

4. The Social Security Benefit (Computation of Earnings) (Amendment) Regulations 2015 (SI 2015/784) reg.2 (July 1, 2015).

GENERAL NOTE

3.23 This regulation mirrors reg.35 of the Income Support (General) Regulations 1987 and reference to the annotations in the 2021–22 edition of Vol.V and the cumulative Supplement in this year's Vol. II is advised since a number of the provisions of reg.35 have been the subject of consideration by the Commissioners.

The claimant in *CP/3017/2004* had made an advance claim for an increase of his retirement pension in respect of his wife. She had earnings and the decision maker had determined that these were in excess of the specified figure with the result that the claimant had no entitlement to the increase. The appeal tribunal confirmed the decision, but the Commissioner found that they had erred in law and substituted his own decision awarding the increase. The claimant's wife worked as a sales promoter of a variety of goods in supermarkets. She made the planning arrangements for promotional visits to the supermarkets from home and attended at supermarkets in the region to ensure the successful operation of the promotion. She received expenses relating to travel (including travel from home), maintenance of her car and car parking. The Commissioner concluded that, in the particular circumstances of this case, the expenses were to be excluded from the calculation of the earnings of the claimant's wife under reg.9(3), which trumped the provisions in reg.9(1)(f)(i).

CG/0645/2008 raised, among other things, the question of the proper computation of a person's weekly earnings in relation to the earnings limit for entitlement to a carer's allowance. The tribunal made its decision without reference to the regulations, which are described as "a comprehensive code" (para.54). The facts were complex since the appellant argued that part of what she received was on behalf of a third party. The Deputy Commissioner says:

> 57. In my view there is a common thread running through the definitions in section 3 of SSCBA 1992 and the 1996 Regulations. That is, however expansively one defines "earnings", the earnings in question must still be the earnings of the individual in question. Thus "any remuneration or profit derived from employment" must mean derived from the claimant's employment, not from someone else's employment.

The Deputy Commissioner agrees that what are to be taken into account are payments actually received, not entitlement which has not resulted in payments, that is, payments actually received for service rendered under that person's own contract of employment.

SSWP v KM [2009] UKUT 85 (AAC) is a further appeal from the First-tier Tribunal following the remission of the appeal for a re-hearing in *CG/0645/2008*. The appeal had again to be remitted since the tribunal had not found all the facts necessary to determine all the issues identified in the earlier decision. The Upper Tribunal Judge strongly criticises the Secretary of State for failing to comply with a direction on the earlier appeal that the Secretary of State should be represented in a case with the complexity of issues presented by this appeal.

Calculation of net earnings of employed earners

10.—(1) For the purposes of regulations 3 (calculation of earnings) and 6 (calculation of earnings of employed earners) the earnings of a claimant derived from employment as an employed earner to be taken into account shall, subject to paragraphs (2) and (3), be his net earnings. 3.24

(2) Except in a case to which paragraph (3) applies, there shall be disregarded or deducted as appropriate from a claimant's net earnings—

(a) any sum, where applicable, specified in Schedule 1; and

(b) any relevant child care charges to which Schedule 2 applies up to a maximum deduction in respect of any claimant of £60 per week.

(3) In the case of entitlement to [1 carer's allowance] under section 70 of the Contributions and Benefits Act there shall be disregarded or deducted as appropriate from a claimant's net earnings—

(a) any sum, where applicable, specified in Schedule 1; and

(b) any care charges to which Schedule 3 applies up to a maximum deduction, in respect of such care charges incurred by any claimant, of 50% of his net earnings less those sums, if any, specified in Schedule 1 which are disregarded.

(4) For the purposes of paragraph (1) net earnings shall be calculated by taking into account the gross earnings of the claimant from that employment less—

(a) any amount deducted from those earnings by way of—

(i) income tax;

(ii) primary Class 1 contributions under the Contributions and Benefits Act; and

(b) one half of any sum paid by the claimant in respect of a pay period by way of a contribution towards an occupation or personal pension scheme.

AMENDMENT

1. The Social Security Benefit (Computation of Earnings) (Amendment) Regulations 2002 (SI 2002/2823) reg.2 (April 1, 2003).

GENERAL NOTE

3.25 This regulation follows, with modification, reg.36 of the Income Support (General) Regulations 1987. Child care costs are to be disregarded if Sch.2 applies provided they do not exceed £60 per week. Where entitlement to carer's allowance (formerly invalid care allowance) is the relevant benefit, care charges are to be disregarded if Sch.3 applies provided they do not exceed the maximum calculated in accordance with reg.10(3)(b).

Paragraph (3)

3.26 In *CG/4024/2001* the Commissioner had to consider whether the cost of the rental for a careline telephone link constituted a "care charge" under reg.10(3). The claimant paid a small rental for the telephone line, which allowed her daughter (who suffered from epilepsy) to press a button held on a cord around her neck. This sounded a warning with the monitoring station and established a telephone link; the claimant could then attend to provide care, or arrange for someone else to do so. Both the tribunal and the Commissioner decided that the cost of the rental was not a care charge. The Commissioner says,

> "16. It is not necessary for me to define the word 'care'. It is sufficient to say that in the context it is not appropriate to cover the link. The natural interpretation of the arrangement is that the monitoring arrangement exists to allow someone to be called who can care for the claimant's daughter. It does not itself provide that care. Nor does the person who monitors alarms at the station.
>
> 17. The tribunal came to the correct conclusion and the only one that was open to it as a reasonable tribunal familiar with the use of language. I direct the tribunal at the rehearing that the cost of the line rental is not deductible."

PART III

SELF-EMPLOYED EARNERS

Calculation of earnings of self-employed earners

3.27 **11.**—(1) Except where paragraph (2) applies, where a claimant's earnings consist of earnings from employment as a self-employed earner the weekly amount of his earnings shall be determined by reference to his average weekly earnings from that employment

(a) over a period of one year; or
(b) where the claimant has recently become engaged in that employment or there has been a change which is likely to affect the normal pattern of business, over such other period as may, in any particular case, enable the weekly amount of his earnings to be determined more accurately.

(2) Where the claimant's earnings consist of [1 any items to which paragraph (2A) applies] those earnings shall be taken into account over

a period equal to such number of weeks as is equal to the number (less any fraction of the whole number) calculated in accordance with the formula—

$$\frac{S}{T + U}$$

where—

S is the earnings

T is the relevant earnings limit plus one penny; and

U is the total of the sums which would fall to be disregarded or deducted as appropriate under regulation 13(2) or (3) (calculation of net profit of self-employed earners).

[1 (2A) This paragraph applies to—

(a) royalties or other sums paid as a consideration for the use of, or the right to use, any copyright, design, patent or trade mark; or

(b) any payment in respect of any—

(i) book registered under the Public Lending Right Scheme 1982, or

(ii) work made under any international public lending right scheme that is analogous to the Public Lending Rights Scheme 1982,

where the claimant is the first owner of the copyright, design, patent or trade mark, or any original contributor to the book or work concerned.]

(3) The period mentioned in paragraph (2) shall begin on the date on which the payment is treated as paid under regulation 7 (date on which earnings are treated as paid).

AMENDMENT

1. The Social Security Benefit (Computation of Earnings) (Amendment) Regulations 2009 (SI 2009/2678) reg.2 (October 26, 2009).

Earnings of self-employed earners

12.—(1) [1 . . .] "Earnings", in the case of employment as a self-employed earner, means the gross receipts of the employment and shall include any allowance paid under section 2 of the Employment and Training Act 1973 or section 2 of the Enterprise and New Towns (Scotland) Act 1990 to the claimant for the purpose of assisting him in carrying on his business. 3.28

[1 . . .]

AMENDMENT

1. The Social Security Benefit (Computation of Earnings) (Amendment) Regulations 2007 (SI 2007/2613) (October 1, 2007).

Calculation of net profit of self-employed earners

13.—(1) For the purposes of regulations 3 (calculation of earnings) and 11 (calculation of earnings of self-employed earners), the earnings of a claimant to be taken into account shall be— 3.29

(a) in the case of a self-employed earner who is engaged in employment on his own account, the net profit derived from that employment;

(b) in the case of a self-employed earner whose employment is carried on in partnership or is that of a share fisherman his share of the net profit derived from that employment less—

(i) an amount in respect of income tax and of social security contributions payable under the Contributions and Benefits Act calculated in accordance with regulation 14 (deduction of tax and contributions for self-employed earners); and

(ii) one half of any premium paid in the period that is relevant under regulation 11 in respect of a retirement annuity contract or a personal pension scheme;

(c) in paragraph (b) "share fisherman" means any person who—

(i) is ordinarily employed in the fishing industry otherwise than under a contract of service, as a master or member of the crew of any fishing boat manned by more than one person, and is remunerated in respect of that employment in whole or in part by a share of profits or gross earnings of the fishing boat; or

(ii) has ordinarily been so employed, but who by reason of age or infirmity permanently ceases to be so employed and becomes ordinarily engaged in employment ashore in Great Britain, otherwise than under a contract of service, making or mending any gear appurtenant to a fishing boat or performing other services ancillary to or in connection with that boat and is remunerated in respect of that employment in whole or in part by a share of the profits or gross earnings of that boat and has not ceased to be ordinarily engaged in such employment.

(2) Except in a case to which paragraph (3) applies, there shall be disregarded or deducted as appropriate from a claimant's net profit—

(a) any sum, where applicable, specified in Schedule 1; and

(b) any relevant child care charges to which Schedule 2 applies up to a maximum deduction in respect of any claimant of £60 per week.

(3) In the case of entitlement to [1 carer's allowance] under section 70 of the Contributions and Benefits Act there shall be disregarded or deducted as appropriate from a claimant's net profit—

(a) any sum where applicable, specified in Schedule 1; and

(b) any care charges to which Schedule 3 applies up to a maximum deduction, in respect of such care charges incurred by any claimant, of 50% of his net profit less those sums, if any, specified in Schedule 1 which are disregarded.

(4) For the purposes of paragraph (1)(a), the net profit of the employment shall, except where paragraph (10) applies, be calculated by taking into account the earnings of the employment over the period determined under regulation 11 (calculation of earnings of self-employed earners) less—

(a) subject to paragraphs (6) to (8), any expenses wholly and exclusively defrayed in that period for the purposes of that employment;

(b) an amount in respect of—

(i) income tax; and

(ii) social security contributions payable under the Contributions and Benefits Act, calculated in accordance with regulation 14 (deduction of tax and contributions for self-employed earners); and

(c) one half of any premium paid in the period that is relevant under regulation 11 in respect of a retirement annuity contract or a personal pension scheme.

(5) For the purposes of paragraph (1)(b), the net profit of the employment shall be calculated by taking into account the earnings of the

employment over the period determined under regulation 11 less, subject to paragraphs (6) to (8), any expenses wholly and exclusively defrayed in that period for the purposes of that employment.

(6) Subject to paragraph (7), no deduction shall be made under paragraph (4)(a) or (5) in respect of—

(a) any capital expenditure;
(b) the depreciation of any capital asset;
(c) any sum employed or intended to be employed in the setting up or expansion of the employment;
(d) any loss incurred before the beginning of the period determined under regulation 11 (calculation of earnings of self-employed earners);
(e) the repayment of capital on any loan taken out for the purposes of the employment;
(f) any expenses incurred in providing business entertainment.
[4 (g) where the claimant provides accommodation to another person in the dwelling the claimant occupies as his home, any expenses defrayed by the claimant in providing the accommodation to that person (including any defrayed in providing board as well as lodging).]

(7) A deduction shall be made under paragraph (4)(a) or (5) in respect of the repayment of capital on any loan used for—

(a) the replacement in the course of business of equipment or machinery; and
(b) the repair of an existing business asset except to the extent that any sum is payable under an insurance policy for its repair.

(8) [2 A deduction shall not be made] in respect of any expenses under paragraph (4)(a) or (5) where [3 the Secretary of State] is not satisfied that the expense has been defrayed or, having regard to the nature of the expense and its amount, that it has been reasonably incurred.

(9) For the avoidance of doubt—

(a) a deduction shall not be made under paragraph (4)(a) or (5) in respect of any sum unless it has been expended for the purposes of the business;
(b) a deduction shall be made thereunder in respect of—
    (i) the excess of any VAT paid over VAT received in the period determined under regulation 11 (calculation of earnings of self-employed earners);
    (ii) any income expended in the repair of an existing asset except to the extent that any sum is payable under an insurance policy for its repair;
    (iii) any payment of interest on a loan taken out for the purposes of the employment.

(10) Where a claimant is engaged in employment as a child minder the net profit of the employment shall be one-third of the earnings of that employment, less—

(a) an amount in respect of—
    (i) income tax;
    (ii) social security contributions payable under the Contributions and Benefits Act, calculated in accordance with regulation 14 (deduction of tax and contributions for self-employed earners); and
(b) one half of any premium paid in respect of a retirement annuity contract or a personal pension scheme.

(11) Notwithstanding regulation 11 (calculation of earnings of self-employed earners) and the foregoing paragraphs, [3 the Secretary of State] may assess any item of a claimant's earnings or expenditure over a period other than that determined under regulation 11 as may, in the particular case, enable the weekly amount of that item of earnings or expenditure to be determined more accurately.

(12) For the avoidance of doubt where a claimant is engaged in employment as a self-employed earner and he is engaged in one or more other employments as a self-employed or employed earner any loss incurred in any one of his employments shall not be offset against his earnings in any other of his employments.

AMENDMENTS

1. The Social Security Benefit (Computation of Earnings) (Amendment) Regulations 2002 (SI 2002/2823) reg.2 (April 1, 2003).

2. The Social Security Act 1998 (Commencement No.9 and Savings and Consequential and Transitional Provisions) Order 1999 (SI 1999/2422) Sch.13 para.5 (September 6, 1999).

3. The Social Security Act 1998 (Commencement No.9 and Savings and Consequential and Transitional Provisions) Order 1999 (SI 1999/2422) Sch.13 para.1 (September 6, 1999).

4. The Social Security Benefit (Computation of Earnings) (Amendment) Regulations 2007 (SI 2007/2613) (October 1, 2007).

GENERAL NOTE

3.30 This regulation largely mirrors reg.38 of the Income Support (General) Regulations 1987. See annotations to that provision in the 2021–22 edition of Vol.V and the cumulative Supplement in this year's Vol. II.

SSWP v SK [2014] UKUT 12 (AAC) considers the significance of the use of the word 'defrayed' in reg.13(5) and concludes, after a review of the authorities, that a reduction in the value of stock at the end of the accounting period compared with the beginning of the accounting period cannot be taken into account in determining weekly earnings from self employment.

In *Secretary of State v Doyle*, reported as *R(IB) 1/06*, the Court of Appeal ruled that the Computations of Earnings Regulations apply for the purpose of the calculation of entitlement to entitlement to incapacity benefit. *R(IB)3/07* is the Commissioner's consideration of the application of the Computation of Earnings Regulations to the circumstances of the case on remission of the appeal for consideration by the Commissioner. The decision also includes as appendices the earlier decision and the decision of the Court of Appeal.

The Commissioner had to consider whether the deduction provided for in reg.13(2) and para.3 to Sch.1 for a fixed-rate deduction to be made from earnings from board and lodging accommodation is in addition to the disregard provided for in reg.13(4)(a). The Commissioner concluded that the regulations did provide for both to be applied to a claimant's case (though in the particular circumstances presented by the claimant that was not necessary to bring him within the earnings limit for incapacity benefit).

Note the effect of the amendment to reg.13(6) by the addition of a new sub-paragraph (f). The explanatory memorandum to the amending regulations says:

> "A Social Security Commissioner recently decided that due to way the regulations were drafted, when the accommodation is provided in the customer's home, the formula disregard is to be applied twice, together with a further disregard of any other allowable business expenses. This provides for the provision of 3 separate disregards. The amended regulations will ensure that only one disregard of £20 and then 50% of the balance will be applied to any income from boarders, and restore the original policy intent."

Deduction of tax and contributions for self-employed earners

14.—(1) The amount to be deducted in respect of income tax under regulation 13(1)(b)(i), (4)(b)(i) or (10)(a)(i) (calculation of net profit of self-employed earners) shall be calculated on the basis of the amount of chargeable income and as if that income were assessable to income tax at the [3 basic rate, or in the case of a Scottish taxpayer, the Scottish basic rate, of tax less only the personal reliefs to which the claimant is entitled under Chapters 2, 3 and 3A of Part 3 of the Income Tax Act 2007 as are] appropriate to his circumstances; but, if the period determined under regulation 11 (calculation of earnings of self-employed earners) is less than a year, the earnings to which the [3 basic rate, or the Scottish basic rate,] of tax is to be applied and the amount of the personal [3 reliefs] deductible under this paragraph shall be calculated on a pro rata basis. **3.31**

(2) The amount to be deducted in respect of social security contributions under regulation 13(1)(b)(i), (4)(b)(ii) or (10)(a)(ii) shall be the total of—

(a) [5 ...]

(b) the amount of Class 4 contributions (if any) which would be payable under section 15 of that Act (Class 4 contributions recoverable under the Income Tax Acts) at the percentage rate applicable at the date [1 on which a decision is made by the Secretary of State under Chapter II of Part I of the Social Security Act 1998 or regulations made thereunder] on so much of the chargeable income as exceeds the lower limit but does not exceed the upper limit of profits and gains applicable for the tax year in which that date falls; but if the assessment period is less than a year, those limits shall be reduced pro rata.

(3) In this regulation "chargeable income" means—

(a) except where sub-paragraph (b) applies, the earnings derived from the employment less any expenses deducted under paragraph (4)(a) or, as the case may be, (5) of regulation 13;

(b) in the case of employment as a child minder, one-third of the earnings of that employment.

AMENDMENTS

1. The Social Security Act 1998 (Commencement No.9 and Savings and Consequential and Transitional Provisions) Order 1999 (SI 1999/2422) Sch.13 para.6 (September 6, 1999).

2. The Social Security (Miscellaneous Amendments No. 2) Regulations 2015 (SI 2015/478) reg.30 (April 6, 2015).

3. The Social Security Benefit (Computation of Earnings) (Amendment) Regulations 2016 (SI 2016/267) reg.2(4) (April 6, 2016).

4. The Social Security (Class 2 National Insurance Contributions Increase of Threshold) Regulations 2022 (SI 2022/1329) reg.5 (in force December 14, 2022 but (by reg.1) having effect from April 6, 2022).

5. The Social Security (Class 2 National Insurance Contributions) (Consequential Amendments and Savings) Regulations 2024 (SI 2024/377) reg.8(7) (April 6, 2024).

Part IV

Transitional Provisions, Consequential Amendments and Revocations

3.32 *Regulations 15–18 omitted.*

SCHEDULE 1 **Regulations 10(2) and 13(2)**

Sums to be Disregarded in the Calculation of Earnings

3.33 **1.**—Any payment made to the claimant by a person who normally resides with the claimant, which is a contribution towards that person's living and accommodation costs, except where that person is residing with the claimant in circumstances to which paragraph 2 or 3 refers.

2.—Where the claimant occupies a dwelling as his home and the dwelling is also occupied by another person and there is a contractual liability to make payments to the claimant in respect of the occupation of the dwelling by that person or a member of his family—

[3 (a) where the aggregate of any payments made in respect of any one week in respect of the occupation of that dwelling by that person or a member of his family, or by that person and a member of his family, is less than £20, the whole of that amount; or

(b) where the aggregate of any such payments in £20 or more per week, £20.]

3.—Where the claimant occupies a dwelling as his home and he provides in that dwelling board and lodging accommodation, an amount, in respect of each person for whom such accommodation is provided for the whole or any part of a week, equal to—

(a) where the aggregate of any payments made in respect of any one week in respect of such accommodation provided to such person does not exceed £20.00, 100% of such payments; or

(b) where the aggregate of any such payments exceeds £20.00, £20.00 and 50% of the excess over £20.00.

4.—Except in the case of a claimant who is absent from Great Britain and not disqualified for receiving any benefit, pension, allowance or supplement, by virtue of the Social Security Benefit (Persons Abroad) Regulations 1975—

(a) any earnings derived from employment which are payable in a country outside the United Kingdom for such period during which there is a prohibition against the transfer to the United Kingdom of those earnings;

(b) where a payment of earnings is made in a currency other than sterling, any banking charge or commission payable in converting that payment into sterling.

5.—Any earnings which are due to be paid before the date of claim and which would otherwise fall to be taken into account in the same benefit week as a payment of the same kind and from the same source.

6.—Any payment made by a local authority to the claimant with whom a person is accommodated by virtue of arrangements made under section 23(2)(a) of the Children Act 1989 (provision of accommodation and maintenance for a child whom they are looking after) [8 , section 81 of the Social Services and Well-being (Wales) Act 2014, or] section 21 of the Social Work (Scotland) Act 1968 or by a voluntary organisation under section 59(1)(a) of the 1989 Act (provision of accommodation by voluntary organisations) or by a care authority under regulation 9 of the Boarding-out and Fostering of Children (Scotland) Regulations 1985 (provision of accommodation and maintenance for children in care).

7.—Any payment made by a health authority, [6 [9 an integrated care board], [10 NHS England], a local authority or a voluntary organization] to the claimant in respect of a person who is not normally a member of the claimant's household but is temporarily in his care.

8.—In respect of regulation 16 of the Social Security (General Benefit) Regulations 1982 any earnings not earned during the period of the award.

9.—Any bounty paid at intervals of at least one year and derived from employments as—

[7 (a) a part-time fire-fighter employed by a fire and rescue authority under the Fire and Rescue Services Act 2004 or by the Scottish Fire and Rescue Service established under section 1A of the Fire (Scotland) Act 2005;]

[7 (aa) ...]

[7 (ab) ...]

(b) an auxiliary coastguard in respect of coastal rescue activities;

(c) a person engaged part-time in the manning or launching of a lifeboat;
(d) a member of any territorial or reserve force prescribed in Part I of Schedule 3 to the Social Security (Contributions) Regulations 1979.

10.—Any amount by way of refund of income tax deducted from profits or emoluments chargeable to income tax under Schedule D or E.

11.—In the case of employment as an employed earner, any advance of earnings or any loan made by the claimant's employer.

[2 **12.**—(1) Any earnings, other than items to which sub-paragraph (2) applies, paid or due to be paid from the claimant's employment as an employed earner which ended before the day in respect of which the claimant first satisfies the conditions for entitlement to the benefit, pension or allowance to which the claim relates.

(2) This sub-paragraph applies to—
(a) any payment by way of occupational or personal pension; and
(b) except in a case where the claimant's employment terminated by reason of retirement at a time when he had attained pensionable age (within the meaning given by rules in paragraph 1 of Schedule 4 to the Pensions Act 1995)—
(i) any payment or remuneration of the nature described in regulation 9(1)(e) or (j), and
(ii) any award or sum of the nature described in regulation 9(1)(g) or (h) (including any payment made following the settlement of a complaint to an employment tribunal or of court proceedings).

(3) Sub-paragraph (1) is subject to the following provisions.

(4) Sub-paragraph (1) does not apply in relation to a claim for, or an award of, incapacity benefit (within the meaning given by paragraph 11 of Schedule 4 to the Welfare Reform Act 2007) or severe disablement allowance (also within the meaning given by that paragraph).

(5) Sub-paragraph (1) applies in relation to a claim for an increase in benefit under Part IV of the Contributions and Benefits Act (increases in respect of dependants) only in a case where—
(a) the spouse or partner or other adult in respect of whom that claim is made was in employment as an employed earner, but
(b) that employment ended before the day referred to in sub-paragraph (1).]

AMENDMENTS

1. The Fire and Rescue Services Act 2004 (Consequential Amendments) (England) Order 2004 (SI 2004/3168) art.39 (December 30, 2004) (in relation to England only). The Fire and Rescue Services Act 2004 (Consequential Amendments) (Wales) Order 2005 (SI 2005/2929) (October 25, 2005) (in relation to Wales only).
2. The Social Security Benefit (Computation of Earnings) (Amendment) Regulations 2007 (SI 2007/2613) (October 1, 2007).
3. The Social Security Benefit (Computation of Earnings) (Amendment) Regulations 2007 (SI 2007/2613) (April 7, 2008).
4. The Fire (Scotland) Act 2005 (Consequential Provisions and Modifications) Order 2005 (SI 2005/2060) art.3 (August 2, 2005)
5. The Police and Fire Reform (Scotland) Act 2012 (Consequential Provisions and Modifications) Order 2013 (SI 2013/602) Sch.2 para.75 (April 1, 2013).
6. The National Treatment Agency (Abolition) and the Health and Social Care Act 2012 (Consequential, Transitional and Savings Provisions) Order 2013 (SI 2013/235) art.11 and para.32(3) of Pt 1 of Sch.2 (April 1, 2013).
7. The Social Security (Miscellaneous Amendments) (No. 3) Regulations 2013 (SI 2013/2536) reg.7 (October 29, 2013).
8. The Social Security Benefit (Computation of Earnings) (Amendment) Regulations 2016 (SI 2016/267) reg.2(5) (April 6, 2016).
9. The Health and Care Act 2022 (Consequential and Related Amendments and Transitional Provisions) Regulations 2022 (SI 2022/634) Sch.1 para.1(1) (July 1, 2022).
10. The Health and Care Act 2022 (Further Consequential Amendments) (No.2) Regulations 2023 (SI 2023/1071) reg.107 and Sch. para.1 (November 6, 2023).

GENERAL NOTE

Pt I of Sch.3 to the Social Security (Contributions) Regulations 1979 (SI 1979/591, as amended) reads: **3.34**

"*Prescribed establishments and organisations for purposes of section 128(3) of the Act*

1. Any of the regular navy, military or air forces of the Crown.
2. Retired and Emergency Lists of Officers of the Royal Navy.
3. Royal Naval Reserves (including Women's Royal Naval Reserve and Queen Alexandra's Royal Naval Nursing Service Reserve).
4. Royal Marines Reserve.
5. Army Reserves (including Regular Army Reserve of Officers, Regular Reserves, Long Term Reserve and Army Pensioners).
6. Territorial and Army Volunteer Reserve.
7. Royal Air Force Reserves (including Royal Air Force Reserve of Officers, Women's Royal Air Force Reserve of Officers, Royal Air Force Volunteer Reserve, Women's Royal Air Force Volunteer Reserve, Class E Reserve of Airmen, Princess Mary's Royal Air Force Nursing Service Reserve, Officers on the Retired List of the Royal Air Force and Royal Air Force Pensioners).
8. Royal Auxiliary Air Force (including Women's Royal Auxiliary Air Force).
9. The Royal Irish Regiment, to the extent that its members are not members of any force falling within paragraph 1 of this Part of this Schedule."

In *CG/1752/2006*, the Commissioner considered the proper interpretation of the word "temporarily" in para.7. Following *CIS/17020/1996* (which was about a paragraph in the same terms in the Income Support General Regulations), the Commissioner concluded that "an arrangement which is not permanent is not necessarily temporary." In defining the term "temporarily" as meaning "not permanent", the tribunal had erred in law. For an illustration of the evidential issues which may arise in applying para.12(1) see (in relation to the relevant Northern Ireland Legislation) *MC v Department for Communities* (CA) [2021] NiCom 19.

SCHEDULE 2 **Regulations 10(2) and 13(2)**

CHILD CARE CHARGES TO BE DEDUCTED IN THE CALCULATION OF EARNINGS

3.35 **1.**—This Schedule applies where a claimant is incurring relevant child care charges and—

(a) is a lone parent;
(b) is a member of a couple both of whom are engaged in employment; or
(c) is a member of a couple where one member is engaged in employment and the other member is incapacitated.

2.—In this Schedule—

"relevant child care charges" means the charges paid by the claimant for care provided for any child of the claimant's family who is under the age of 11 years, other than charges paid in respect of the child's compulsory education or charges paid by a claimant to a partner or by a partner to a claimant in respect of any child for whom either or any of them is responsible in accordance with section 143 of the Contributions and Benefits Act (circumstances in which a person is to be treated as responsible or not responsible for another), where the care is provided—

(a) by persons registered under section 71 of the Children Act 1989 (registration of child minders and persons providing day care for young children); or
(b) for children aged 8 and over but under 11, out of school hours, by a school on school premises or by a local authority; or
(c) by a child care scheme operating on Crown property where registration under section 71 of the Children Act 1989 is not required; or
(d) in schools or establishments which are exempted from registration under section 71 of the Children Act 1989 by virtue of section 71(16) of, and paragraph 3 or 4 of Schedule 9 to, that Act,
[1 or
(e) by persons registered under Part XA of the Children Act 1989; or
(f) in schools or establishments which are exempted from registration under Part XA of the Children Act 1989 by virtue of paragraph 1 of Schedule 9A to that Act; or
[3 (g) by—
(i) persons registered under section 59(1) of the Public Services Reform (Scotland) Act 2010; or

(ii) local authorities registered under section 83(1) of that Act,

where the care provided is child minding or day care of children within the meaning of that Act,]

and shall be calculated on a weekly basis in accordance with paragraphs 4 to 7;

"school term-time" means the school term-time applicable to the child for whom care is provided.

3.—The age of a child referred to in paragraph 2 shall be determined by reference to the age of the child at the date on which the benefit week began.

4.—Subject to paragraphs 5 to 7, relevant child care charges shall be calculated in accordance with the formula—

$$\frac{X + Y}{52}$$

where—

X is the average weekly charge paid for child care in the most recent 4 complete weeks which fall in school term-time in respect of the child or children concerned, multiplied by 39; and

Y is the average weekly charge paid for child care in the most recent 2 complete weeks which fall out of school term-time in respect of that child or those children, multiplied by 13.

5.—Subject to paragraph 6, where child care charges are being incurred in respect of a child who does not yet attend school, the relevant child care charges shall mean the average weekly charge paid for care provided in respect of that child in the most recent 4 complete weeks.

6.—Where in any case the charges in respect of child care are paid monthly, the average weekly charge for the purposes of paragraph 4 shall be established—

(a) where the charges are for a fixed monthly amount, by multiplying that amount by 12 and dividing the product by 52;

(b) where the charges are for variable monthly amounts, by aggregating the charges for the previous 12 months and dividing the total by 52.

7.—In a case where there is no information or insufficient information for establishing the average weekly charge paid for child care in accordance with paragraphs 4 to 6, the average weekly charge for care shall be estimated by reference to information provided by the child minder or person providing the care or, if such information is not available, by reference to information provided by the claimant.

8.—For the purposes of paragraph 1(c) the other member of a couple is incapacitated where—

(a) [5 . . .] housing benefit is payable under Part VII of the Contributions and Benefits Act to the other member or his partner and the applicable amount of the person entitled to the benefit includes—

(i) a disability premium; or

[2 (ii) a higher pensioner premium by virtue of the satisfaction of—

[5 (aa) . . .]

(bb) in the case of housing benefit, paragraph 11(2)(b) of Schedule 3 to the Housing Benefit Regulations 2006;

on account of the other member's incapacity or [5 . . .] regulation 28(1)C of the Housing Benefit Regulations 2006 (treatment of child care charges) applies in that person's case;]

(b) there is payable in respect of him one or more of the following pensions [4, payments] or allowances—

(i) long-term incapacity benefit under section 30A, 40 or 41 of the Contributions and Benefits Act;

(ii) attendance allowance under section 64 of that Act;

(iii) severe disablement allowance under section 68 of that Act;

(iv) disability living allowance under section 71 of that Act;

(v) an increase of disablement pension under section 104 of that Act;

(vi) a pension increase under a war pension scheme or an industrial injuries scheme which is analogous to an allowance or increase of disablement pension under head (ii), (iv) or (v) above;

[4 (vii) personal independence payment under Part 4 of the Welfare Reform Act 2012;]

[6 (viii) armed forces independence payment under the Armed Forces and Reserve Forces (Compensation Scheme) Order 2011]

(c) a pension [4 , payment] or allowance to which head (ii), (iv), (v) [4 , (vi) or (vii)] of sub-paragraph (b) refers, was payable on account of his incapacity but has ceased to be payable—

[4 (i)] in consequence of his becoming a patient (other than a person who is serving a sentence imposed by a court in a prison or youth custody institution) who is regarded as receiving free in-patient treatment within the meaning of the Social Security (Hospital In-Patients) Regulations 1975; [4 or]

[4 (ii) in accordance with regulations made [under] section 86(1) (hospital in-patients) of the Welfare Reform Act 2012;]

(d) sub-paragraph (b) or (c) would apply to him if the legislative provisions referred to in those sub-paragraphs were provisions under any corresponding enactment having effect in Northern Ireland; or

(e) he has an invalid carriage or other vehicle provided to him by the Secretary of State under section 5(2)(a) of, and Schedule 2 to, the National Health Service Act 1977 or under section 46 of the National Health Service (Scotland) Act 1978 or provided by the Department of Health and Social Services for Northern Ireland under article 30(1) of the Health and Personal Social Services (Northern Ireland) Order 1972.

AMENDMENTS

1. The Social Security Benefit (Computation of Earnings) (Child Care Charges) Regulations 2002 (SI 2002/842) (April 1, 2002).

2. The Housing Benefit and Council Tax Benefit (Consequential Provisions) Regulations 2006 (SI 2006/217) (March 6, 2006).

3. Public Services Reform (Scotland) Act 2010 (Consequential Modifications of Enactments) Order 2011 (SI 2011/2581) Sch.2 para.23 (October 28, 2011).

4. The Personal Independence Payments (Supplementary Provisions and Consequential Amendments) Regulations 2013 (SI 2013/388) reg.8 and Sch. para.17 (April 8, 2013).

5. The Council Tax Benefit Abolition (Consequential Provision) Regulations 2013 (SI 2013/458) reg.3 (April 1, 2013).

6. The Armed Forces and Reserve Forces Compensation Scheme (Consequential Provisions: Subordinate Legislation) Order 2013 (SI 2013/591) reg.7 and Sch. para.12 (April 8, 2013).

SCHEDULE 3 **Regulations 10(3) and 13(3)**

CARE CHARGES TO BE DEDUCTED IN THE CALCULATION OF EARNINGS FOR ENTITLEMENT TO [1 CARER'S ALLOWANCE]

3.36 **1.**— This Schedule applies where a claimant is—

(a) entitled to [1 carer's allowance] under section 70 of the Contributions and Benefits Act; and

(b) incurring relevant care charges.

2.—In this Schedule—

"close relative" means a parent, son, daughter, brother, sister or partner;

"relevant care charges" means the charges paid by the claimant for care which is provided by a person, who is not a close relative of either the severely disabled person or the claimant, for—

(a) the severely disabled person; or

(b) any child aged under 16 on the date on which the benefit week begins in respect of whom the claimant or his partner is entitled to child benefit under section 141 of the Contributions and Benefits Act because the claimant is unable to care for any of those persons because he is carrying out duties in connection with his employment;

"severely disabled person" means the severely disabled person in respect of whom entitlement to *invalid care allowance* arises.

AMENDMENT

1. The Social Security Benefit (Computation of Earnings) (Amendment) Regulations 2002 (SI 2002/2823) reg.2 (April 1, 2003).

GENERAL NOTE

3.37 The italicised words must now be taken as referring to carer's allowance.

3.38 *Schedule 4 omitted.*

The Social Security Benefit (Dependency) Regulations 1977

(SI 1977/343) (*AS AMENDED*)

ARRANGEMENT OF REGULATIONS

PART I

GENERAL

PART II

CHILD DEPENDANTS

PART III

ADULT DEPENDANTS

PART IV

MISCELLANEOUS

The Secretary of State for Social Services, in exercise of the powers conferred upon him by sections 33(2), 44, 46, 47, 49, 66 and 84 of, and Schedule 20 to, the Social Security Act 1975, as amended in the case of the said sections 44, 46 and 66 and Schedule 20 by section 21(1) of, and Schedule 4 to, the Child Benefit Act 1975 and section 20(1) of the Child Benefit Act 1975 and all other powers enabling him in that behalf, hereby makes the following regulations for the purpose only of consolidating regulations hereby revoked:

PART I

GENERAL

Citation, commencement and interpretation

3.40 **1.**—(1) These regulations may be cited as the Social Security Benefit (Dependency) Regulations 1977 and shall come into operation on April 4, 1977, immediately after the coming into operation of the Social Security (Child Benefit Consequential) Regulations 1977.

(2) In these regulations, unless the context otherwise requires—

"the Act" means the Social Security Act 1975;

"the Child Benefit Act" means the Child Benefit Act 1975;

[[1] "the Contributions and Benefits Act" means the Social Security Contributions and Benefits Act 1992];

[[2] "the determining authority" means, as the case may require, the Secretary of State, [[7] the First-tier Tribunal or the Upper Tribunal]];

"entitled to child benefit" includes treated as so entitled;

"parent" has the meaning assigned to it by section 24(3) of the Child Benefit Act;

"the standard rate of increase" means the amount specified in Part IV or Part V of Schedule 4 to the Act as the amount of an increase for an adult dependant of the benefit in question,

and other expressions have the same meanings as in the Act.

[[3] (3) Regulations 2(2) and (3), 4 and 5(1) shall, with any necessary modifications, apply to [[4] carer's allowance] as they apply to retirement pension.]

[5 (3A) Nothing in these Regulations applies for the purposes of incapacity benefit under section 30A of the Contributions and Benefits Act.]

(4) Unless the context otherwise requires, any reference in these regulations to—

(a) a numbered section is to the section of the Act bearing that number;

(b) a numbered regulation is a reference to the regulation bearing that number in these regulations and any reference in a regulation to a numbered paragraph is a reference to the paragraph of that regulation bearing that number;

(c) any provision made by or contained in any enactment or instrument shall be construed as a reference to that provision as amended or extended by any enactment or instrument and as including a reference to any provision which may re-enact or replace it, with or without modification.

(5) The rules for the construction of Acts of Parliament contained in the Interpretation Act 1889 shall apply in relation to this instrument and in relation to any revocation effected by it as if this instrument, the regulations revoked by it and any regulations revoked by the regulations so revoked were Acts of Parliament, and as if each revocation were a repeal.

AMENDMENTS

1. The Social Security Benefit (Dependency) Amendment Regulations 1992 (SI 1992/3041) reg.2 (December 5, 1992).

2. The Social Security Act 1998 (Commencement No. 12 and Consequential and Transitional Provisions) Order 1999 (SI 1999/3178) Sch.2 (November 29, 1999).

3. The Social Security (Incapacity—Increases for Dependants) Regulations 1994 (SI 1994/2945) reg.15(2)(a) (April 13, 1995).

4. The Social Security Amendment (Carer's Allowance) Regulations 2002 (SI 2002/2497) reg.3 and Sch.2 (April 1, 2003).

5. The Social Security (Incapacity—Increases for Dependants) Regulations 1994 (SI 1994/2945) reg.15(2)(b) (April 13, 1995).

6. The Social Security Act 1998 (Commencement No. 9 and Savings and Consequential and Transitional Provisions) Order 1999 (SI 1992/2422), Sch.2, and The Social Security Act 1998 (Commencement No. 11 and Transitional Provisions) Order 1999 (SI 1999/2860) Sch.2 (October 18, 1999).

7. The Tribunals, Courts and Enforcement Act 2007 (Transitional and Consequential Provisions) Order 2008 (SI 2008/2683) reg.7 (November 3, 2008).

GENERAL NOTE

Interpretation Act 1889

By s.25(2) of the Interpretation Act 1978, this reference is to be treated as a reference to the 1978 Act. **3.41**

Provisions as to maintenance for the purposes of increase of benefit in respect of dependants

2.—(1) Subject to paragraph (2), a beneficiary shall not for the purposes of the Act be deemed to be wholly or mainly maintaining another person unless the beneficiary— **3.42**

(a) when [1 . . .] incapable of work, or, as the case may be, [2 entitled to a Category A or Category B retirement pension], contributes towards the maintenance of that person an amount not less than the amount of increase of benefit received in respect of that person; and

(b) when in employment, or not incapable of work, or, as the case may be, not so [2 entitled] (except in a case where the dependency did not arise until after that time) contributed more than half of the actual cost of maintenance of that person.

(2) In a case where—

(a) a person is partly maintained by each of 2 or more other persons each of whom could be entitled to an increase of benefit under the Act in respect of that person if he were wholly or mainly maintaining that person, and

(b) the contributions made by those other persons towards the maintenance of that person amount in the aggregate to sums which, if they were contributed by one of them, would be sufficient to satisfy the foregoing requirements of this regulation,

that person shall for the purposes of the Act be deemed to be wholly or mainly maintained by that one of the said other persons who—

(i) makes the larger or largest contributions to the maintenance of that person, or

(ii) in a case where no person makes the larger or largest contributions as aforesaid, is the elder or eldest of the said other persons, or

(iii) in any case, is a person designated in that behalf by a notice in writing signed by a majority of the said other persons and addressed to the Secretary of State,

so long as that one of the said other persons continues to be entitled to benefit under the Act and to satisfy the condition contained in paragraph (1)(a) of this regulation.

(3) A notice and the designation contained therein given under the foregoing paragraph may be revoked at any time by a fresh notice signed by a majority of such persons and another one of their number may be designated.

AMENDMENTS

1. The Social and Child Support (Jobseeker's Allowance) (Consequential Amendments) Regulations 1996 (SI 1996/1345) reg.12(2) (October 7, 1996).

2. The Social Security (Abolition of Earnings Rule) (Consequential) Regulations 1989 (SI 1989/1642) reg.4 (October 1, 1989).

DEFINITIONS

"the Act"—para.(1).
"beneficiary"—SSCBA 1992 s.122.

GENERAL NOTE

3.43 The primary rule in reg.2(1) requires two conditions to be satisfied:

(1) when incapable of work, the claimant must contribute to the maintenance of the other person an amount equal to or exceeding the amount of the increase of benefit, *and*

(2) when not incapable of work, the claimant must contribute towards the maintenance of the other person an amount exceeding half the *actual* cost of maintaining that other person.

The test under (1) is largely mathematical, but the test under (2) requires a judgment as to what amounts to the actual cost of maintaining a person. It is also arguable that maintenance may be in kind. There are certainly some old Commissioner's decisions which regard payment in kind of items the cost of which would normally be expenditure on day to day living as payment of maintenance: *R(I) 10/51*. Examples would be provision of food, clothes or coal. The principle may also be applicable to the transfer of property to a spouse: *R(U) 3/66*; or even to the transfer of a business share: *R(I) 37/54*.

The secondary rule in para.(2) deals with those rare cases where a dependant is being maintained by more than one person and establishes the order of priority between them in relation to entitlement to an increase of benefit. Note that the preferred beneficiary must also satisfy the condition in para.(1)(a). This is consistent with the principle that increases of benefit are not a means of benefiting the claimant, but to help meet the cost of supporting dependants.

The Family Fund Test

Where a number of people live in the same household, it will often be difficult to determine who supports whom and to what extent. An elaborate test known as the "family fund test" or "method" has been devised over many decades as a means of determining the actual cost of maintaining dependants in such cases and so of determining the amount of contribution required to qualify for an increase of benefit. The applicability of the test was re-affirmed by Tribunals of Commissioners in *R(I) 1/57*, *R(I) 20/60*, and *CS/130/1987*, a starred decision of a Tribunal of Commissioners. In *R(I) 20/60* the Tribunal of Commissioners confirmed that the family fund basis of calculation should be adopted unless it can be shown that it would produce a result which is clearly at variance with the evidence as to the family circumstances. More recently in *R(S) 12/83* the test has been approved and guidance given as to its application. The Commissioner said, "[T]he method should be applied where the maintainer and the person maintained are living in the same household unless there are wholly exceptional circumstances." (para.6). The Commissioner went on to spell out the test as it applies to a claimant. This may be summarised as follows: 3.44

(1) The members of the household are identified.

(2) The weekly income of the household (including its source) is calculated. Income here includes earnings, social security payments including supplementary benefit and family income supplement (now income support and working families' tax credit), and maintenance payments. From these will be deducted reasonable expenses, such as tax and national insurance contributions. The crucial date for determination is the period immediately prior to the incident which gives rise to the claim for an increase for a dependant (for example, immediately before the claimant became incapable of work or unemployed): *CS/130/1987*.

(3) The net weekly income is the family fund which is assumed to be the aggregate cost of maintaining the whole household. Each member of the household aged 14 or over counts as one unit and each member aged 13 or less counts as one-half a unit. The total number of units in the household enables the "unit cost" of each member of the household to be calculated by sharing the family fund in proportion to the units in the household. In *R(S) 7/89*, para.12, the Commissioners note that the time may now be ripe to reconsider the allocation of units and half units "to take account of social conditions at the end of the twentieth century." This point is repeated in *CS/299/1988*.

(4) The net earnings of each member of the household are treated as contributed to the family fund by that member of the household. Occupational pensions are treated as contributed by the member entitled to them (*CS/58/49*) and contributory benefits are regarded as provided by the person on whose national insurance contributions they are paid. Supplementary benefit (and presumably now income support) is *not* attributed to its recipient: *R(S) 7/89(T)* approving para.21 of *R(I) 1/57(T)* and disapproving para.7 of *R(S) 2/85*. It would seem to follow that family income supplement (and now working families' tax credit) is not treated as attributed to its recipient.

(5) Child benefit is not treated as earmarked for the child or children in respect of whom it is paid (see below), though the Commissioner leaves open the question of whether it is contributed by "outsiders" or by the member of the family to whom it is actually paid. The Commissioner's preference in *R(S) 12/83* appears to be that child benefit is contributed by "outsiders". The rationale for the view that child benefit is not earmarked for the child in respect of whom it is payable is that in practice child benefit simply augments the family fund rather than provides resources solely for the child.

(6) The contributions to the family fund are then divided into three groups: (a) those derived from the claimant: (b) those derived from other members of the household; and (c) those derived from "outsiders". The claimant's contribution is first used up against his or her own unit cost. Only if the contribution exceeds the unit cost will there be any surplus available which can be used to contribute to the cost of maintaining others. The same principle is applied to other members of the household. The result is that each member of the household ends up with a surplus or a deficit.

(7) Contributions from outsiders are classified into those which are earmarked for particular members of the household and those which are not. Earmarked contributions are set on one side for the moment, but other contributions are applied rateably to reduce any deficits of members of the household.

(8) Earmarked contributions to the family fund by "outsiders" (for example, additions for dependants, payments of maintenance for children) are applied to reduce any deficit of the member of the household for whom they are earmarked.

(9) Where the amount of a claimant's surplus applied rateably towards meeting the deficits of members of the household amounts to more than one-half of the net unit cost of any member, the claimant is wholly or mainly maintaining that person. If it is less, the claimant is not.

3.45 An example based on figures as at January 1988 for the facts of *R(S) 12/83* will help unravel this complex provision. Suppose a household consists of an unmarried couple, M and W. There are four children, all aged under 11. M is the father of one of them, but not of the other three. Immediately before he becomes incapable of work M's net earnings are £65.00 per week. The family also receives child benefit of £29.00 and FIS of £35.70. The total net income per week is £129.70.

The family consists of four units. M and W are each one unit and each child is one-half unit. The unit cost of M and W is therefore £32.43 (£129.70 divided by four) and of each of the children is £16.21 (£129.70 divided by eight).

The only contributor to the family's income other than outsiders is M who contributes his net wages less his own unit costs: £32.57 (£65.00 less £32.43). M has a surplus of £32.57. By contrast W and each of the children have deficits of £32.43 and £16.21 respectively because they have no income of their own to contribute.

Child benefit and FIS, as contributions from "outsiders" to the family fund, are applied rateably to reduce the deficits of W and the children. So £21.57 is deducted from W's deficit leaving a deficit of £10.86 and £10.79 is deducted from the deficits of each child leaving each with a deficit of £5.42.

It is now the time to consider how M's surplus of £32.57 is to be distributed in order to determine whether he is wholly or mainly maintaining W and the children. In order to be wholly or mainly maintaining them M must contribute more than half of their unit costs out of his surplus. So M must contribute £16.21 to W's maintenance and £8.10 to the maintenance of each child in order to qualify as wholly or mainly maintaining them. Since the remaining deficits are less than these sums, M cannot be said to be wholly or mainly maintaining them. To put it another way M's contribution would need to be £48.61 before he would be deemed on the application of the family fund test to contribute sufficient to meet the test. His contribution is his surplus of £32.57.

In *CS/229/1988* the Commissioner held, distinguishing the treatment of constant attendance allowance in *R(I) 1/57*, that attendance allowance for a child is not to be taken as a contribution to the family fund by either the child or the child's mother as the person with legal entitlement. The Commissioner says that the attendance allowance must be "disregarded altogether".

CU/108/1993 provides a helpful example of the application of the family fund test to modern day circumstances. It clarifies one or two points. Child benefit should be treated as a contribution by the recipient, that is, the parent who receives it (para.5). Maintenance paid for a child should always be earmarked for the child in respect of whom it is paid (para.6). School fees are treated no differently than other payments for the maintenance of the child (para.7). Absence of a child at boarding school does not affect the unit costs for that child (para.8). Loans are disregarded (para.9). Gifts can be distinguished from payments in kind, such as the regular supply of coal to a miner, and should be disregarded (para.9).

Allocation of contributions for [1 . . .] [2 . . .] [10 spouse or civil partner.]

3.—(1) Subject to the provisions of this regulation, any sum or sums paid by a person by way of contribution towards either or both of the following, that is to say the maintenance of his [1 spouse] [10 or civil partner] and the cost of providing for one or more children to which this regulation refers, shall be treated for the purposes of section 31(c)(i), [2 . . .], [3 . . .], [4 44(3)(a),] 45(2)(b), [4 45A(2)(b), [5 . . .]] 65(1), 66(1)(a), or [6 70(2)] (conditions as to maintenance) as such contributions of such respective amounts equal in the aggregate to the said sum or sums, in respect of such of the persons hereinafter mentioned, that is to say, his [7 spouse] [10 or civil partner] or any child or children to which this regulation refers, as may be determined by the determining authority so as to secure as large a payment as possible by way of benefit in respect of dependants. 3.46

(2) A sum paid by way of contribution towards the maintenance of a [8 spouse] [10 or civil partner] shall not be treated by virtue of this regulation as a sum paid by way of contribution towards the cost of providing for a child or children, and a sum paid by way of contribution towards the cost of providing for a child or children shall not be so treated as a sum paid by way of contribution towards the maintenance of a [8 spouse], [10 or civil partner] unless in either case the [8 spouse] [10 or civil partner] is entitled to child benefit in respect of the child or children.

(3) Except for the purposes of [section 56(1)(c) of the Social Security Contributions and Benefits Act 1992] (child's special allowance), the children to whom this regulation refers are any children in respect of whom, in the period for which the sum in question is paid by the person, that person is entitled to child benefit or could have been so entitled by virtue of regulations had he contributed to the cost of providing for the child at a sufficient weekly rate.

(4) For the purposes of [section 56(1)(c)]—

(a) the children to whom this regulation refers are any such children to whom [section 56(1)(b)] applies;

(b) a determination made under paragraph (1) in order to ascertain the weekly rate at which the husband had before his death been contributing to the cost of providing for a child may be [9 superseded] from time to time by the [9 Secretary of State] so often as may be necessary to secure as large a payment as possible by way of the child's special allowance, so however that no such [9 supersession] shall affect entitlement in respect of any period before the date of the [9 supersession]; and

(c) the condition in paragraph (2) shall be deemed to be satisfied if it would have been satisfied but for the fact that the child was not then in Great Britain.

[1 (5) In the heading to this regulation and in paragraphs (1) and (2) the word "spouse" includes both husband and wife except in relation to maintenance contributions for the purposes of [sections 82(1)(b), 82(3), of the Social Security Contributions and Benefits Act 1992] where it means wife only, and in relation to maintenance contributions for the purposes of [sections 83(2)(b) and 84(2)(b) of the Social Security Contributions and Benefits Act 1992] where it means husband only].

AMENDMENTS

1. The Social Security Benefit (Dependency) Amendment Regulations 1983 (SI 1983/1001) reg.2(2) and (3) (November 21, 1983).

2. The Social Security (Working Tax Credit and Child Tax Credit) (Consequential Amendments) (No.2) Regulations 2003 (SI 2003/937) reg.2 (April 6, 2003).

3. The Social Security and Child Support (Jobseeker's Allowance) (Consequential Amendments) Regulations 1996 (SI 1996/1345) reg.12(3)(a) (October 7, 1996).

4. The Social Security Benefit (Dependency) Amendment (No. 2) Regulations 1985 (SI 1985/1305) reg.2(2) (September 16, 1985).

5. The Social Security (Incapacity—Increases for Dependants) Regulations 1994 (SI 1994/2945) reg.15(3)(a) (April 13, 1995).

6. The Social Security Benefit (Dependency, Claims and Payments and Hospital In-Patients) Amendment Regulations 1984 (SI 1984/1699) reg.3(a) (November 28, 1984).

7. The Social Security Benefit (Dependency) Amendment (No. 2) Regulations 1985 (SI 1985/1305), reg.2(3) (September 16, 1985) and The Social Security and Child Support (Jobseeker's Allowance) (Consequential Amendments) Regulations 1996 (SI 1996/1345) reg.12(3)(b) (October 7, 1996).

8. The Social Security Benefit (Dependency) Amendment Regulations 1983 (SI 1983/1001) reg.2(3) and (4) (November 21, 1983).

9. The Social Security Act 1998 (Commencement No. 12 and Consequential and Transitional Provisions) Order 1999 (SI 1999/3178) Sch.2 (November 29, 1999).

10. Civil Partnership (Pensions, Social Security and Child Support) (Consequential, etc. Provisions) Order 2005 (SI 2005/2877) (December 5, 2005).

GENERAL NOTE

3.47 This regulation contains a principle of allocation which is designed to assist claimants. Regardless of the designation of payments by the payer, maintenance payments are to be apportioned by determining authorities in such a way as to entitle the claimant to the largest payment by way of an increase of benefit. The approach to be taken is to aggregate all maintenance payments and to allocate as the first slice the prescribed amount of maintenance for an adult dependant, as the second slice the prescribed amount for the maintenance of a child, and so on, although there can be no unapportioned residue. There is no possibility of carrying forward any surplus unless, of course, the payment is intended to cover more than one week: *R(S) 3/74*.

[1 Deeming benefit under the Act abated under [section 74(3) of the Social Security Administration Act 1992] to be a contribution for the maintenance of children or adult dependants]

4.—Where for any period a person (in this regulation referred to as A) is entitled to, or to an increase in the amount of, any benefit prescribed pursuant to [section 74(3)(a) of the Social Security Contributions and Benefits Act 1992] (prevention of duplication of payments) in respect of another person (in this regulation referred to as B) and the amount of, or of the increase in, any such benefit is abated under [section 74(3) of the Social Security Contributions and Benefits Act 1992] then in determining for the purpose of the Act whether A is wholly or mainly maintaining or is contributing at any weekly rate to the maintenance of, or is or has been contributing at any weekly rate to the cost of providing for, B, the amount by which such benefit for any week has been so abated shall be deemed to be a contribution of that amount for that week made by A for the maintenance of B.] **3.48**

AMENDMENT

1. The Social Security Benefit (Dependency) Amendment Regulations 1988 (SI 1988/554) reg.2 (April 11, 1988).

GENERAL NOTE

Most payments of most social security benefits, training allowances and social security benefits paid by Member States of the European Union are prescribed under s.74 of the Administration Act. Section 74(3) provides that where a prescribed benefit, such as child benefit, can be claimed by a person (called A) on the basis of making contributions to the maintenance of another person (called B), then if income support has been paid to B because the contribution was not in fact made, the additional benefit paid to B as a consequence may be deducted from the prescribed benefit paid to A. This regulation contains a corresponding rule to the effect that such deductions count as contributions made by A to the maintenance of B if an issue arises as to whether A is wholly or mainly maintaining B. **3.49**

Secretary of State for Work and Pensions v Adams [2003] EWCA Civ 796, Judgment of June 18, 2003, reported as *R(G) 1/03* concerned the question of whether the decision to resume payment of invalid care allowance (now carer's allowance) following the application of reg.4 was a supersession decision under s.10 SSA 1998 or a decision under s.8 SSA 1998 either on a claim for a benefit or under or by virtue of a relevant enactment.

The claimant had for a number of years being caring for his severely disabled partner and had become entitled to an invalid care allowance. He subsequently became entitled to, and in receipt of, an incapacity benefit which overlapped with his invalid care allowance. In accordance with reg.4 the contributory benefit (incapacity benefit) was deducted from the non-contributory benefit (invalid care allowance). The result was that invalid care allowance ceased to be payable. The claimant's incapacity benefit subsequently terminated and the effect was to revive his entitlement to an invalid care allowance. The Court of Appeal concludes that the decision to resume payments is a decision under s.8. The court describes reg.4 as an "accounting provision designed to ensure that parallel payments do not result in excessive payment." (para.20). Were the decision allocated to s.10 the claimant would be deprived of the possibility of backdating the decision.

Circumstances in which a person who is not entitled to child benefit is to be treated as if he were so entitled

3.50 **4A.**—(1) For the purposes of [section 77 of the Social Security Contributions and Benefits Act 1992] (guardian's allowance) or [sections [1 . . .] 82(4), 85(2) and 90 of the Social Security Contributions and Benefits Act 1992] (increase of benefit in respect of dependent children, and [2 . . .] persons having care of dependent children) a person shall be treated as if he were entitled to child benefit in respect of a child for any period throughout which—

(a) child benefit has been awarded to a parent of that child with whom that child is living and with whom that person is residing and either—

(i) the child is being wholly or mainly maintained by that person; or

(ii) that person is also a parent of the child; or

(b) he, or his spouse [6 or civil partner] with whom he is residing, would have been entitled to child benefit in respect of that child had the child been born at the end of the week immediately preceding the week in which birth occurred.

(2) [2 . . .]

(3) For the purpose of determining whether a person is entitled to a guardian's allowance under [section 77], where in respect of a child that allowance is payable to a person for a continuous period of 7 days and would have been payable to that person for the immediately preceding 7 days had he been entitled to child benefit in respect of that child for an earlier week, he shall be treated as if he were entitled to child benefit in respect of that child for that earlier week.

(4) If for any period a person who is in Great Britain could have been entitled to receive payment of an amount by way of a benefit or allowance or an increase of a benefit or an allowance under the Act in respect of a child or [4 . . .] person who has the care of a child but for the fact that in pursuance of any agreement with the government of a country outside the United Kingdom he, or his [5 spouse] [6 or civil partner] who is residing with him, is entitled in respect of the child in question to the family benefits of that country and is not entitled to child benefit, he shall for the purposes of entitlement to the said payment be treated as if he were entitled to child benefit for the period in question.

(5) The expression "earlier week" in paragraph (3) means the week immediately preceding the first week for which the person referred to in that paragraph was entitled to child benefit in respect of the child referred to in that paragraph.

(6) For the purposes of paragraph (1) the word "week" has the meaning assigned to it by [section 147(1) of the Social Security Contributions and Benefits Act 1992]; and for the purposes of paragraphs (1) and (2) a child shall not be regarded as living with a person unless he can be so regarded for the purposes of [section 143 of the Social Security Contributions and Benefits Act 1992] (meaning of "person responsible for child") of the said Act.

AMENDMENTS

Regulation 4A was inserted by The Social Security Benefit (Dependency) Amendment Regulations 1980 (SI 1980/585) reg.2 (June 2, 1980).

1. The Social Security (Working Tax Credit and Child Tax Credit) (Consequential Amendments) (No. 2) Regulations 2003 (SI 2003/937) reg.2 (April 6, 2003).

2. The Social Security Benefit (Dependency) Amendment Regulations 1989 (SI 1989/523) reg.2 (April 11, 1989).

3. The Social Security Benefit (Dependency) Amendment Regulations 1984 (SI 1984/1698) reg.2(13) (November 26, 1984) subject to savings contained in SI 1984/1698 reg.3.

4. The Social Security Benefit (Dependency) Amendment Regulations 1984 (SI 1984/1968) reg.2(3) (November 26, 1984).

5. The Social Security Benefit (Dependency) Amendment Regulations 1984 (SI 1984/1968) reg.2(3) (November 26, 1984).

6. Civil Partnership (Pensions, Social Security and Child Support) (Consequential, etc. Provisions) Order 2005 (SI 2005/2877) (December 5, 2005).

GENERAL NOTE

This is a deeming rule. If the conditions are satisfied, a person is to be treated as if he or she is entitled to child benefit even though not in fact entitled to the benefit. **3.51**

On "residing together" see the Persons Residing Together Regulations.

The family fund test will be important in determining whether the child is being wholly or mainly maintained under para.(1)(a)(i). See *R(S) 12/83* and notes to reg.2.

[1 Circumstances in which a person entitled to child benefit is to be treated as if he were not so entitled

4B.—(1) For the purposes of— **3.52**

(a) section 56 (child's special allowance);
(b) section 77 (guardian's allowance);
(c) [2 . . .];
(d) section 82(4) (short-term benefits—increase for adult dependants);
(e) [2 . . .];
(f) section 90 (increase in benefits for beneficiaries under sections 68 and 70), of the Contributions and Benefits Act, and
(g) paragraphs 4(1) (unemployability supplement: increase for beneficiary's dependent children) and 6(1) (unemployability supplement: increase for dependent adults) of Schedule 7 to,

that Act, a person who is entitled to child benefit in respect of a child shall be treated as if he were not so entitled for the periods referred to in paragraph (2) below.

(2) The periods referred to in paragraph (1) above are—

(a) any period throughout which—
  (i) the person referred to in that paragraph, not being a parent of the child, does not fall to be treated as responsible for the child under section 143(1)(a) of the Contributions and Benefits Act, and
  (ii) a parent of that child falls to be treated as responsible for the child under the said section 143(1)(a); or
(b) any period throughout which—
  (i) that person, not being a parent of that child, falls to be treated as responsible for the child under section 143(1)(a) of the Contributions and Benefits Act, and

(ii) a parent of that child also falls to be treated as responsible for the child under the said section 143(1)(a); or

(c) any day following that day on which that child died.

(3) Sub-paragraph (b) of paragraph (2) shall not apply in the case of a person who is wholly or mainly maintaining the child referred to in that sub-paragraph.

(4) For the purposes of—

(a) section 37(1) (entitlement to a widowed mother's allowance);
(b) section 39A(2) (entitlement to a widowed parent's allowance);
(c) section 56(1)(b);
(d) section 77(1);
(e) section 80;
(f) section 82(4);
(g) section 85(2);
(h) section 90;

of the Contributions and Benefits Act, and

(i) paragraphs 4(1), 6(1) and 18(1)(a)(ii) of Schedule 7 (industrial death benefit: child of deceased's family) to,

that Act, a person who is entitled to child benefit in respect of a child shall be treated as if he were not so entitled for any period for which that benefit is not payable by virtue of any of the provisions referred to in paragraph (5) below.

(5) The provisions referred to in paragraph (4) above are—

(a) regulation 7 (circumstances in which a person who has ceased to receive full-time education is to continue to be treated as a child);
(b) regulation 7A (exclusion from benefit of children aged 16 but under the age of 19 who are receiving advanced education);
(c) regulation 7B (child receiving training under the youth training scheme); or
(d) regulation 7C (child receiving income support),

of the Child Benefit (General) Regulations 1976 or any provision contained in regulations made under section 144(1) of the Contributions and Benefits Act in so far as those regulations provide that child benefit is not to be payable by virtue of section 142(1)(b) of that Act and regulations made thereunder.]

AMENDMENTS

1. The Social Security (Benefits for Widows and Widowers) (Consequential Amendments) Regulations 2000 reg.5 (SI 2000/1483) (April 9, 2001).

2. The Social Security (Working Tax Credit and Child Tax Credit) (Consequential Amendments) (No. 2) Regulations 2003 (SI 2003/937) reg.2 (April 6, 2003).

GENERAL NOTE

3.53 This regulation contains a corresponding deeming rule to that contained in reg.4A. It deems a person entitled to child benefit not to be so entitled if the conditions of the regulation are satisfied.

PART II

CHILD DEPENDANTS

Contributions towards cost of providing for child

5.—(1) Where, apart from [section 81(1) and (2) of the Social Security Contributions and Benefits Act 1992], a person is entitled to receive, in respect of a particular child, payment under the Act of an amount by way of a child's special allowance ([section 56]), or a guardian's allowance ([section 77]) or of an increase under any of the provisions of [section 80 of the Social Security Contributions and Benefits Act 1992] of any benefit, or payment of an increase or allowance of any amount under section 64 or section 70, for any period, and neither of the conditions set out in the following paragraphs is satisfied, that person shall nevertheless for the purposes of the said [section 81(1) or (2) of the Social Security Contributions and Benefits Act 1992] be deemed as respects that period to be making the contributions so required at a weekly rate not less than that required by the said section [81(1) or (2)] if— 3.54

(a) he gives an undertaking in writing to make such contributions; and
(b) on receiving the amount of the allowance or increase in question, he in fact makes such contributions.

(2) The conditions referred to in paragraph (1) are—

(a) the person would be treated for the purposes of [Part IX of the Social Security Contributions and Benefits Act 1992] as having the child living with him; or
(b) contributions are being made to the cost of providing for the child at a rate equal to the amount of the relevant increase of benefit.

(3) Where, in respect of any period, the person referred to in this regulation fails to make the contributions which he has undertaken to make in accordance with the first paragraph of this regulation, the decision awarding the increase or allowance in question for that period in respect of the child shall be revised.

(4) [1 . . .]

[2 (5) Except in a case to which regulation 15 (preservation of entitlement to benefit in payment before April 4, 1977 for a child dependant) or regulation 13A of the Social Security Benefit (Persons Abroad) Regulations 1975, as amended (modification of the Act in relation to title to benefit for beneficiary's child dependants) applies, paragraph (b) of [section 81(3) of the Social Security Contributions and Benefits Act 1992] (contributions mentioned in those paragraphs to be over and above those required for the purposes of [section 143(1)(b) of the Social Security Contributions and Benefits Act 1992]) shall not apply in a case where neither the beneficiary nor his spouse [3 or, as the case may be, his civil partner] (or if he has a spouse [3 or civil partner] and his spouse [3 or civil partner] is residing with him) is in fact entitled to child benefit in respect of the child in question.]

AMENDMENTS

1. The Social Security Benefit (Miscellaneous Amendments) Regulations 1978 (SI 1978/433) reg.7 (April 3, 1978).

2. The Social Security Benefit (Dependency) Amendment Regulations 1977 (SI 1977/620) reg.2 (April 4, 1977).

3. The Civil Partnership (Pensions, Social Security and Child Support) (Consequential, etc. Provisions) Order 2005 (SI 2005/2877) (December 5, 2005).

GENERAL NOTE

3.55 This useful regulation allows a claimant who fails to satisfy the requirements of para.(2) to give an undertaking in writing to make contributions for the maintenance of a child of an amount equal to the benefit or increase of benefit in order to qualify for one of the benefits mentioned in the regulation. Failure to make the promised payments results in revision of entitlement (para.(3)). Care must be taken that the claimant increases the payments to the level of any benefit increases: *R(S) 3/74*. The undertaking cannot operate retrospectively for more than a week; *R(U) 3/78*, but a later undertaking may be regarded as merely confirming an earlier undertaking even though there has been a break in the payments made under the earlier undertaking: *R(U)6/79*.

3.56 *Regulation 6 revoked by The Social Security (Computation of Earnings) Regulations 1996 (SI 1996/2745), Sch.4 (November 25, 1996).*

3.57 *Regulation 7 revoked by The Social Security Benefit (Dependency) Amendment Regulations 1980 (SI 1980/585), reg.3 (June 2, 1980).*

PART III

ADULT DEPENDANTS

Earnings rules for increases for adult dependants

3.58 **8.**—(1) This paragraph applies in cases where an increase of benefit is claimed [1 . . .] in respect of a spouse who is residing with the beneficiary and the increase is claimed under any of the following provisions of the Contributions and Benefits Act—

(a) section 83(2) (increase of Category A or Category C retirement pension in respect of a wife); [4 or]

(b) section 84(1) (increase of Category A retirement pension in respect of a husband); [4 . . .]

(c) [4 . . .]

[4 (1A)This paragraph applies in cases where an increase of benefit is claimed in respect of a spouse or a civil partner who, in either case, is residing with the beneficiary and the increase is claimed under paragraph 6(1)(a)(i) of Schedule 7 to the Contributions and Benefits Act (increase of disablement pension in respect of a spouse or civil partner where beneficiary entitled to unemployability supplement).]

(2) Where paragraph (1) [4 or (1A)] applies, there shall be no increase of benefit for any period during which the beneficiary is residing with his spouse [4 or civil partner] and his spouse [4 or civil partner] has earnings if the earnings of the spouse [4 or civil partner] in the week in that period which falls immediately before the week in which the beneficiary is entitled to benefit under any provision specified in paragraph (1) exceed [2 the amount for the time being

specified in regulation 79(1)C of the Jobseeker's Allowance regulations 1996 (age related amount for a claimant who has attained the age of 25).]

(3) Where the person referred to in section 85(2) of the Contributions and Benefits Act ("the dependant") is residing with the pensioner, the weekly rate of a pension to which section 85 of that Act applies shall be increased by the amount specified in relation to that pension in column 3 of Part IV of Schedule 4 to that Act but there shall be no increase of pension for any period—

(a) during which the pensioner is residing with the dependant; and

(b) the dependant has earnings,

if the earnings of the dependant in the week in that period which falls immediately before the week in which the pensioner is entitled to the pension exceed [2 the amount as for the time being specified in regulation 79(1)(c) of the Jobseeker's Allowance Regulations 1996 (age related amount for a claimant who has attained the age of 25).]

(4) Where the person referred to in paragraph 6(1)(b) of Schedule 7 to the Contributions and Benefits Act ("the dependant") is residing with the beneficiary, the weekly rate of the disablement pension to which that paragraph applies shall be increased by the amount referred to in paragraph 8 of Part V of Schedule 4 to that Act but there shall be no increase of disablement pension for any period—

(a) during which the beneficiary is residing with the dependant; and

(b) the dependant has earnings,

if the earnings of the dependant in the week in that period which falls immediately before the week in which the beneficiary is entitled to a disablement pension [2 exceed the amount as for the time being specified in regulation 79(1)(c) of the Jobseeker's Allowance Regulations 1996 (age related amount for a claimant who has attained the age of 25).]

(5) In determining the earnings of a dependant for the purposes of paragraphs (3) and (4), no account shall be taken of any earnings of that person from employment by the pensioner or the beneficiary as the case may be in caring for a child or children in respect of whom the pensioner or the beneficiary is entitled to child benefit.

(6) Where an increase of benefit is claimed in respect of a spouse [4 or civil partner] who is not residing with the beneficiary and the increase is claimed under paragraph 6(1)(a)(ii) of Schedule 7 to the Contributions and Benefits Act there shall be no increase of benefit for any period during which the beneficiary is contributing to the maintenance of the spouse at a rate less than the standard rate of the increase and the weekly earnings of the spouse [4 or civil partner] exceed that rate.

(7) In this regulation—

(a) "week" means—

(i) in relation to Category A or Category C retirement pension the period of 7 days beginning with the day on which in accordance with the provisions of regulation 22 of and paragraph 5 of Schedule 6 to the Social Security (Claims and Payments) Regulations 1987(a) is the day for payment of the retirement pension in question; and

(ii) in relation to any other benefit [3 any period of 7 days corresponding to the week in respect of which the relevant social security benefit is due to be paid or ending on the day before the first day of the first such week following the date of claim]; and

(b) any reference to earnings includes a reference to payments by way of occupational or personal pension.

Amendments

This regulation was substituted by the Social Security (Dependency) Amendment Regulations 1992 (SI 1992/3041) reg.3 (December 5, 1992).

1. The Social Security (Incapacity—Increases for Dependants) Regulations 1994 (SI 1992/2945) reg.15(4) (April 13, 1995).

2. The Social Security and Child Support (Jobseeker's Allowance) (Consequential Amendments) Regulations 1996 (SI 1996/1345) reg.12(4) (October 7, 1996).

3. The Social Security (Computation of Earnings) Regulations 1996 (SI 1996/2745) reg.17(a) (November 25, 1996).

4. The Civil Partnership (Pensions, Social Security and Child Support) (Consequential, etc. Provisions) Order 2005 (SI 2005/2877) (December 5, 2005).

General Note

3.59 On "having the care of a child" see annotations to s.82 of the C & BA 1992. The revised text of reg.8 set out above was inserted with effect from December 5, 1992, by the Social Security Benefit (Dependency) Amendment Regulations 1992 (SI 1992/3041). There is an important transitional provision in reg.4 of the Amendment Regulations preserving entitlement under the earlier text for those in receipt of an increase of benefit on December 4, 1992.

Two relevant unreported decisions on reg.8(6) as previously enacted are *CP/068/1989* (printed as Appendix to *R(P) 3/93*) and *R(P) 3/93*. The latter decision holds that increases of invalidity benefit and of retirement pension are different increases even though the amounts at the material time were the same. So a claimant moving from increase of invalidity benefit to increase of retirement pension on attaining the age of 70 lost the protection of reg.8(6).

In *CP/3017/2004* the Commissioner said,

> "6. Before going on to mention the legislative provisions that set out rules for calculating earnings for the purposes of benefits including retirement pension, there is one oddity arising from regulation 8(2) of the Dependency Regulations to be examined. Regulation 8(2) lays down a test to be applied week by week for each week of payment of retirement pension (see the definition in regulation 8(7)(a)), which test depends on the spouse's earnings in the previous week. The application of a week by week test seems to be reinforced by section 92 of the Social Security Contributions and Benefits Act 1992, which applies where an award of an increase has been made and causes the award to continue in force even though entitlement is interrupted by a week or weeks in which the spouse's earnings exceed the limit. In the present case, the first week of payment of retirement pension to the claimant would have been that beginning on Monday 31 May 2004. It might be said that at the date of the decision in question there could have been absolutely no evidence of what the wife's earnings would be in the week commencing Monday 24 May 2004 or in any subsequent week. How therefore could a decision be given disallowing an increase?
> 7. The main answer stems from regulation 15(1) of the Claims and Payments Regulations and the decision of the Tribunal of Commissioners in *CDLA/2751/2003* and others, about advance renewal claims for disability living allowance (DLA). It was held there that the legislative power to make an award of DLA in advance of the start date of the period of the award carried with it the power to disallow the claim in advance. The same must also apply to regulation 15(1), so that there is a power to disallow a claim for an increase of retirement pension for a wife up to four months before a claimant might become entitled to the pension. Then, in accordance with section 8(2) of the Social Security Act 1998 as explained by the Tribunal of Commissioners, in making such a decision

the Secretary of State would be prohibited from taking into account any changes of circumstances anticipated to occur after the date of the decision. Equally, on appeal, an appeal tribunal would be prohibited from taking into account any actual changes of circumstances after that date (Social Security Act 1998, section 12(8)(b)). The Tribunal of Commissioners seems to have thought that if there was change of circumstances in favour of a claimant between the date of the decision and the date from which the disallowance of the claim took effect, there could be a supersession on the ground of relevant change of circumstances (Social Security and Child Support (Decisions and Appeals) Regulations 1999, regulation 6(2)(a)(i)). However, there is a problem with that view because regulation 6(2)(a)(i), as amended with effect from 5 May 2003, allows supersession only where there has been a relevant change of circumstances since the decision to be superseded "had effect". That seems to rule out a supersession for a change occurring between the date of an advance decision and its effective date. A claimant would thus be restricted to making a fresh claim, on the basis of the changed circumstances, from some date after the effective date of the disallowing decision.

8. In paragraph 24 of *CDLA/2751/2003* and others, the Tribunal of Commissioners did suggest that, in some cases where there was likely to be a significant change of circumstances before the start date of the period covered by a claim, it might well be good practice to defer making a decision until it was known whether that change had actually materialised. It seems to me that the present case is one where that course should have been taken. It was plain from the evidence provided that the claimant's wife's earnings fluctuated a great deal from one pay period to another. And the nature of the case is different from that of a person suffering some potentially disabling or incapacitating condition, where in most cases there can be a sensible prediction about how the condition might progress in the future. It was simply unknown on 3 March 2004 what the claimant's wife's earnings might be in the week prior to 31 May 2004. Quite apart from the doubts that I explain below about the averaging process carried out by the officer, it would have been better to have waited until close to 28 May 2004 and then considered the current evidence about the wife's earnings. I do not think that there would have been any difficulty in making an advance decision on the claimant's own retirement pension entitlement, but deferring the decision on the increase. However, that did not happen. A decision disallowing the increase was made on 3 March 2004 and I must deal with the consequences."

In para.21 of his decision, the Commissioner concluded, **3.60**

"21. If I adopt the same method as the officer who made the decision of 3 March 2004 and take an average of the seven payslips, counting only the taxable pay, the result is £32.59 per week. With the addition of the weekly amount of the wife's occupational pension, the total earnings are well below the limit in regulation 8(2) of the Dependency Regulations. I have doubts about the use of averaging under regulation 8(3) of the Computation of Earnings Regulations. That provision allows averaging over a recognisable cycle of work or some other period that will allow average weekly earnings to be identified more accurately. But, for the reasons given in paragraph 6 above, the Dependency Regulations may properly work on the amount of actual earnings received week by week (with payments received at other intervals spread according to the rules in regulation 8(1) and (2) of the Computation of Earnings Regulations). If so, the use of an average figure might not be appropriate at all. But I do not have to decide the issue. I have already shown that the result of averaging under regulation 8(3) is in favour of the claimant. If I do not apply regulation 8(3), the circumstances as at 3 March 2004 were that, for six of the payments in evidence, the weekly equivalent of the earnings received was below the limit, usually well below. It was only in respect of the payment received on 14 December 2003 that the weekly equivalent (£98) was over the limit. There might well have been unusual circumstances in the run-up to Christmas. Looking at that evidence, and not knowing what earnings had been received immediately before 3 March 2004, I have no difficulty in concluding that the level of the wife's earnings to be taken into account in respect of the period from 28 May 2004 onwards is below the limit in regulation 8(2) of the Dependency Regulations. Thus, on either approach, the claimant's appeal succeeds and he is to be awarded the increase of retirement pension."

There has been no reg.9 since September 16, 1985 when the former regs 8 and 9 were replaced by a revised reg.8.

Apportionment of payments by way of occupational [1 or personal] pension made otherwise than weekly

3.61 **9A.**—[2 For the purposes of section 89(1) of, and paragraph 7(1) of Schedule 7 to, the Contributions and Benefits Act, where payment by way of occupational or personal pension, or for the purposes of section 89(1A) of that Act by way of PPF periodic payment,] is for any period made otherwise than weekly, the amount of any such payment for any week in that period shall be determined—

(a) where payment is made for a year, by dividing the total by 52;
(b) where payment is made for three months, by dividing the total by 13;
(c) where payment is made for a month, by multiplying the total by 12 and dividing the result by 52;
(d) where payment is made for two or more months, otherwise than for a year or for three months, by dividing the total by the number of months, multiplying the result by 12 and dividing the result of that multiplication by 52; or
(e) in any other case, by dividing the amount of the payment by the number of days in the period for which it is made and multiplying the result by 7.

AMENDMENTS

Regulation 9A was inserted by The Social Security Benefit (Dependency) Amendment Regulations 1989 (SI 1989/523) reg.5 (April 11, 1989).

1. The Social Security (Miscellaneous Provisions) Amendment Regulations 1992 (SI 1992/247) reg.4(2) (March 9, 1992). This amendment is superseded by the amendment listed below.

2. The Social Security (PPF Payments and FAS Payments) (Consequential Amendments) Regulations 2006 (SI 2006/1069) reg.2 (May 5, 2006).

Increase of benefit for [1 . . .] person having care of child [14 or qualifying young person]

3.62 **10.**—(1) Subject to the provisions of [section 82 of the Social Security Contributions and Benefits Act 1992] (increase [2 . . .] of a maternity allowance), [section 85 of the Social Security Contributions and Benefits Act 1992] (increase of a Category A or Category C retirement pension [3 . . .]), or section 66 (increase [2 . . .] of a disablement pension where the beneficiary is entitled to an unemployability supplement), this regulation shall apply for the purpose of determining whether a beneficiary is entitled to an increase of benefit under [section 82(3) and 85(2) of the Social Security Contributions and Benefits Act 1992] in respect of a [4 . . .] person who has the care of a child or children [14 or a qualifying young person or persons] in respect of whom the beneficiary is entitled to child benefit.

(2) A beneficiary shall not be entitled to an increase under the said [section 82(3) and 85(2)] unless the [4 . . .] person referred to in those sections—

(a) has the care of such a child [14 or qualifying young person] as is referred to in those sections [5 . . .]; and

(b) either—

(i) is residing with the beneficiary, or

(ii) is employed by him in an employment in respect of which the weekly expenses incurred by the beneficiary are not less than the standard rate of increase and was so employed by him before he became [6 . . .] incapable of work or [7 entitled to a Category A or Category B retirement pension], as the case may be, subject to the qualification that the condition of employment before that event shall not apply in a case where the necessity for [8 the] employment first arose thereafter; or

(iii) is a person to whose maintenance the beneficiary is contributing at a weekly rate not less than the standard rate of increase; and

(c) subject to paragraph (3), is not absent from Great Britain; and

(d) is not undergoing imprisonment or detention in legal custody; and

[9 (e) either—

(i) has no earnings or has earnings but they do not exceed the standard rate of increase (there being disregarded for this purpose any earnings derived from employment by the beneficiary in caring for a child or children [14 or a qualifying young person or persons] in respect of whom the beneficiary is entitled to child benefit), or

(ii) is employed by the beneficiary in caring for such child or children [14 or a qualifying young person or persons] and is not residing with him;]

(f) [10 . . .]

(3) In the case of [11 . . .] any pension to which this regulation applies, the condition referred to in sub-paragraph (c) of paragraph (2) shall not apply as respects any period during which the said [11 . . .] person is residing with the beneficiary outside Great Britain and for which by virtue of the provisions of any regulations made under section 82(5) (disqualification) or 131 (persons outside Great Britain) the beneficiary is not disqualified for receiving that benefit.

(4) [12 . . .].

(5) [13 . . .].

AMENDMENTS

1. The Social Security Benefit (Dependency) Amendment Regulations 1984 (SI 1984/1698) reg.10 (November 26, 1984).

2. The Social Security and Child Support (Jobseeker's Allowance) (Consequential Amendments) Regulations 1996 (SI 1996/1345) reg.12(7)(a) (October 7, 1996).

3. The Social Security (Incapacity—Increases for Dependants) Regulations 1994 (SI 1994/2945) reg.15(5)(a) (April 13, 1995).

4. The Social Security (Abolition of Injury Benefit) (Consequential) Regulations 1983 (SI 1983/186) reg.7(3) (April 6, 1983).

5. The Social Security Benefit (Dependency, Claims and Payments and Hospital In-Patients) Amendments Regulations 1984 (SI 1984/1699) reg.3(b) (November 26, 1984).

6. The Social Security and Child Support (Jobseeker's Allowance) (Consequential Amendments) Regulations 1996 (SI 1996/1345) reg.12(7)(b) (October 7, 1996).

7. The Social Security (Abolition of Earnings Rule) (Consequential) Regulations 1989 (SI 1989/1642) reg.4 (October 1, 1989).

8. The Social Security Benefit (Dependency) Amendment Regulations 1984 (SI 1984/1698) reg.2(6) (November 26, 1984).

9. The Social Security Benefit (Dependency) Amendment Regulations 1989 (SI 1989/523) reg.6 (April 11, 1989).

10. The Social Security Benefit (Dependency) Amendment Regulations 1989 (SI 1989/523) reg.7 (April 11, 1989).

11. The Social Security Benefit (Dependency) Amendment Regulations 1984 (SI 1984/1698) reg.2(9) (November 26, 1984).

12. The Social Security Benefit (Dependency) Amendment Regulations 1985 (SI 1985/1190) reg.5 (September 16, 1985).

13. The Social Security Benefit (Dependency) Amendment Regulations 1984 (SI 1984/1698) reg.8 (January 1, 1979).

14. The Social Security (Provisions relating to Qualifying Young Persons) (Amendment) Regulations 2006 (SI 2006/692) (April 10, 2006).

General Note

3.63 On "residing together," see the Persons Residing Together Regulations.

On "having the care of a child," see annotations to s.82 of the SSCBA 1992.

Contribution to maintenance of adult dependant

3.64 **11.**—(1) Subject to paragraphs (2) and (3), for the purposes of [section 82(1) and (3), 83(2), 84 of the Social Security Contributions and Benefits Act 1992] (increase of a Category A or Category C retirement pension or benefit to which section 66 applies in respect of a spouse) or of regulation 10(2)(b)(iii) (increase of a Category A or Category C retirement pension or benefit to which section 66 applies in respect of a person having the care of a child [or qualifying young person])—

(a) a beneficiary shall not be deemed to satisfy the requirement contained in the said sections or the said regulation that he is contributing to the maintenance of the spouse or the person having the care of a child [or qualifying young person], as the case may be, at a weekly rate of not less than the standard rate of increase unless when in employment, or not incapable of work, or not entitled to a Category A or Category B retirement pension, as the case may be (except in a case where the dependency did not arise until later), he contributed to that spouse's or person's maintenance at a weekly rate of not less than the standard rate of increase;

(b) in a case where an increase of benefit is, apart from the said requirement, payable at a weekly rate less than the standard rate of increase, a beneficiary shall, subject to sub-paragraph (a) above, be deemed to satisfy the said requirement if he is contributing to the maintenance of the spouse or person having the care of a child [or qualifying young person], as the case may be, at a weekly rate of not less than that of the increase.

[(1A) Subject to paragraphs (2) and (3), for the purposes of section 82 of, and paragraph 6(1)(a)(i) of Schedule 7 to, the Contributions and Benefits

Act (increase of maternity allowance and increase of disablement pension where beneficiary entitled to unemployability supplement) a beneficiary shall not be deemed to satisfy the requirement contained in those provisions (that he is contributing to the maintenance of his civil partner at a weekly rate of not less than the standard rate of increase) unless when in employment, or not incapable of work, or not entitled to a Category A or a Category B retirement pension, as the case may be (except in a case where the dependency did not arise until later), he contributed to his civil partner's maintenance at a weekly rate not less than the standard rate of increase.]

(2) Where, within one month of having been entitled to an increase of unemployment benefit under [section 82(1) of the Social Security Contributions and Benefits Act 1992] or under [section 82(3)(c) of the Social Security Contributions and Benefits Act 1992] by virtue of having satisfied the requirement in head (iii) of sub-paragraph (b) of regulation 10(2) (but no other requirement in that sub-paragraph), or of having been entitled to an increase of short-term incapacity benefit by virtue of having satisfied the requirements of regulation 9(1)(b) or (3)(b) of the Social Security (Incapacity Benefit—Increases for Dependents) Regulations 1994, a person becomes entitled to a benefit which attracts a standard rate of increase higher than that of the benefit to which he had been entitled, he shall be deemed to satisfy the condition in paragraph (1)(a) if he satisfies it in relation to the benefit to which he had been entitled; and in this paragraph "entitled" includes deemed to have been entitled.

(2A) Where, within one month of having been entitled to an increase of unemployment benefit under [section 82(3)(a) of the Social Security Contributions and Benefits Act 1992] by virtue of contributing to the maintenance of her husband at a weekly rate not less than the standard rate of the increase, or of having been entitled to an increase of shortterm incapacity benefit by virtue of having satisfied the requirements of regulation 9(1)(b) or (3)(b) of the Social Security (Incapacity Benefit—Increases for Dependents) Regulations 1994, a woman becomes entitled to a benefit which attracts a standard rate of increase higher than that of the benefit to which she had been entitled, she shall be deemed to satisfy the condition in paragraph (1)(a) if she satisfies it in relation to the benefit to which she had been entitled, and in this paragraph "entitled" includes deemed to have been entitled.

(3) For the purposes of paragraphs (2) and (2A) a person shall be deemed to have been entitled to an increase of unemployment benefit at a lower standard rate of increase if (assuming satisfaction of the relevant contribution conditions) he would have been so entitled but for the provisions of [section 82(1)(b) of the Social Security Contributions and Benefits Act 1992] or, as the case may be, regulation 10(2)(e) or the condition of [section 82(3)(a) of the Social Security Contributions and Benefits Act 1992] that her husband is not engaged in any one or more employments from which his weekly earnings exceed the standard rate of increase.

(4) Where a person is entitled to an addition to a contribution-based jobseeker's allowance under regulation 9(4) of the Jobseeker's Allowance (Transitional Provisions) Regulations 1995 by virtue of having satisfied the requirements for an increase of unemployment benefit referred to in paragraphs (2), (2A) or (3), he shall be treated for the purposes of those paragraphs as if he had been entitled to an increase of unemployment benefit.

AMENDMENTS

There have been multiple small amendments to the text of reg.11, none of which appear to be time sensitive. Accordingly the text of the regulation is printed above without multiple annotations.

Paragraph (1) has been amended by:

The Social Security Benefit (Dependency) Amendment Regulations 1983 (SI 1983/1001); The Social Security Benefit (Dependency) Amendment Regulations 1984 (SI 1984/1698);

The Social Security (Abolition of Earnings Rule) (Consequential) Regulations 1989 (SI 1989/1642);

The Social Security (Incapacity—Increases for Dependants) Regulations 1994 (SI 1994/2945); and

The Social Security and Child Support (Jobseeker's Allowance) (Consequential Amendments) Regulations 1996 (SI 1996/1345).

Paragraph (1A) was inserted by the Civil Partnership (Pensions, Social Security and Child Support) (Consequential, etc. Provisions) Order 2005 (SI 2005/2877) (December 5, 2005).

The Social Security (Provisions relating to Qualifying Young Persons) (Amendment) Regulations 2006 (SI 2006/692) (April 10, 2006).

Paragraph (2) has been amended by:

The Social Security Benefit (Amendment) Regulations 1987 (SI 1987/355);

The Social Security (Incapacity—Increases for Dependants) Regulations 1994 (SI 1994/2945).

Paragraph (2A) was inserted by The Social Security Benefit (Amendment) Regulations 1987 (SI 1987/355) and has been amended by The Social Security (Incapacity—Increases for Dependants) Regulations 1994 (SI 1994/2945).

Paragraph (3) has been amended by The Social Security (Incapacity—Increases for Dependants) Regulations 1994 (SI 1994/2945).

Paragraph (4) was added by The Social Security and Child Support (Jobseeker's Allowance) (Consequential Amendments) Regulations 1996 (SI 1996/1345).

GENERAL NOTE

3.65 On "having the care of a child," see annotations to s.82 of the SSCBA 1992.

PART IV

MISCELLANEOUS

Prescribed circumstances for the purposes of section 90 of the Social Security Contributions and Benefits Act

3.66 **12.**—(1) The provisions of Part IV of the Contributions and Benefits Act (increases for dependants) and of the Social Security (Incapacity Benefit—Increases for Dependants) Regulations 1994 shall apply in relation to increases of severe disablement allowance for child or adult dependants under section 90 of the Contributions and Benefits Act as they apply to increases of long-term incapacity benefit for child or adult dependants.

(2) For the purposes of increases of [1 carer's allowance] for child or adult dependants under section 90 of the Contributions and Benefits Act, the prescribed circumstances in which a beneficiary is entitled to such an increase shall be as set out in Schedule 2 to these Regulations.

AMENDMENTS

Regulation 12 substituted by The Social Security (Incapacity—Increases for Dependants) Regulations 1994 (SI 1994/2945) reg.15(7) (April 13, 1995).

1. The Social Security Amendment (Carer's Allowance) Regulations 2002 (SI 2002/2497) reg.3 and Sch.2 (April 1, 2003).

Regulation 13 revoked by The Social Security and Child Support (Jobseeker's Allowance) (Consequential Amendments) Regulations 1996 (SI 1996/1345) from October 7, 1996. 3.67

Regulation 14 ceased to have effect from October 5, 1986. 3.68

PART V

TRANSITIONAL PROVISION AND REVOCATIONS

Preservation of entitlement to benefit in payment before 4th April, 1977 for a child dependant

15.—Where— 3.69

(a) immediately before 4th April, 1977 a person is absent from Great Britain other than temporarily; and

(b) as respects a period before and including 3rd April, 1977 he satisfies the conditions then in force for, and is entitled to receive, payment of an amount by way of a benefit or allowance or an increase of a benefit or an allowance under the Act in respect of a child who is ordinarily resident in Great Britain; and

(c) would cease, as from 4th April, 1977, to be entitled to that payment by reason of the fact that he does not satisfy one of the conditions for receiving such a payment, namely, that he is entitled to child benefit in respect of that child,

that person shall, for any period beginning not earlier than 4th April, 1977 during which he would, or could had he made an appropriate claim, be entitled to child benefit in respect of that child were he not absent from Great Britain, be treated as so entitled while he continues to satisfy all other conditions applicable to such a payment (including making contributions to the cost of providing for that child over and above those that would have been required for the purpose of satisfying subsection (1)(b) of section 3 of the Child Benefit Act) unless subsequent to 4th April, 1977 he becomes ordinarily resident in Great Britain.

Regulation 15A revoked by The Social Security Benefit (Dependency) Amendment Regulations 1984 (SI 1984/1698) as from November 26, 1984. 3.70

Regulation 16 omitted. 3.71

SCHEDULE 2 **Regulation 12(2)**

PRESCRIBED CIRCUMSTANCES FOR INCREASE OF [4 A CARER'S ALLOWANCE]

PART I

Increase of [4 carer's allowance] for child dependants

3.72 **1.**—For the purposes of increases of [4 carer's allowance] for child dependants under [section 90 of the Contributions and Benefits Act 1992], the prescribed circumstances in which a beneficiary is entitled to such an increase for any period shall be as set out in the following paragraphs.

2.—The weekly rate of [4 a carer's allowance] for any period for which the beneficiary is entitled to child benefit in respect of a child or children [*12 (Scotland) or a qualifying young person or persons*] shall be increased in respect of that child [*12 (Scotland) or qualifying young person*], or each respectively of those children [*12 (Scotland) or qualifying young persons*], by the appropriate amount specified in relation to that allowance in column (2) of Part IV of Schedule 4 to the Act.

[1 **2A.**—Where—

[6 (a) a beneficiary is a member of a couple; and]

(b) the other [6 member of a couple] has earnings in any week,

the beneficiary's right to payment of increases for the following week under paragraph 2 above shall be determined in accordance with paragraph 2B below.]

[1**2B.**—No such increase shall be payable—

(a) in respect of the first child [*12 (Scotland) or qualifying young person*] where the earnings were [5 £280] or more; and

(b) in respect of a further child [*12 (Scotland) or qualifying young person*] for each complete [5 £37] by which the earnings exceeded [5 £280].]

[2 **2BB.**—The provisions of paragraphs 2A and 2B above shall not apply so as to affect entitlement to an increase of [4 carer's allowance] in respect of a child in any case where the beneficiary—

(a) was entitled to receive such an increase immediately before 26th November, 1984; and

(b) throughout the period from and including that date to the date of coming into operation of this paragraph was, or but for the operation of those paragraphs would have been, continuously so entitled,

until such time as he would otherwise first cease to be so entitled.]

[1 **2C.**—In this Part of this Schedule—

[6 . . .]

[12 "child" includes a qualifying young person and "children" includes qualifying young persons;]

[10 "couple" means—

(a) two people who are married to, or civil partners of, each other and are members of the same household; or

(b) two people who are not married to, or civil partners of, each other but are living together [11 as if they were a married couple or civil partners]];

[3 "week" means any period of 7 days corresponding to the week in respect of which the relevant social security benefit is due to be paid or ending on the day before the first day of the first such week following the date of claim.]]

3.—Where a person is entitled to receive payment of an amount by way of an increase of [4 a carer's allowance] under paragraph 2 above, that increase shall not be payable unless one of the following conditions is satisfied—

(a) that the beneficiary would be treated for the purposes of [Part IX of the Contributions and Benefits Act 1992] as having the child [*12 (Scotland) or qualifying young person*] living with him; or

(b) that the requisite contributions are being made to the cost of providing for the child [*12 (Scotland) or qualifying young person*].

4.—The condition specified in paragraph 3(b) above is to be treated as satisfied if, but only if—

(a) such contributions are being made at a weekly rate not less than the amount referred to in paragraph 2 above—

(i) by the beneficiary, or

(ii) where the beneficiary is one of two spouses [6 or civil partners] residing together, by them together; and

(b) the contributions are over and above those required for the purposes of satisfying [section 143(1)(b) of the Social Security Contributions and Benefits Act 1992].

5.—Any sum or sums paid by a person by way of contribution towards the cost of providing for two or more children [12 (Scotland) *or qualifying young persons*] being children [12 (Scotland) *or qualifying young persons*] in respect of whom, in the period for which the sum in question is paid by the person, he is entitled to child benefit shall be treated as such contributions, of such respective amounts equal in the aggregate to the said sum or sums, in respect of those children [12 (Scotland) *or qualifying young persons*] so as to secure as large a payment as possible by way of [1 carer's allowance] in respect of them.

PART II

Increase of [4 carer's allowance] for adult dependants

6.—For the purposes of increases of [4 carer's allowance] for adult dependants under [9 section 90 of the Social Security Contributions and Benefits Act], the prescribed circumstances in which a beneficiary is entitled to such an increase for any period shall be as set out in paragraph 7 below. **3.73**

7.—The weekly rate of an [4 carer's allowance] shall be increased by the amount specified in relation to that allowance in column (3) of Part IV of Schedule 4 to [9 the Contributions and Benefits Act] for any period during which the beneficiary is residing with—

(a) a spouse [6 or civil partner] whose weekly earnings do not exceed that amount; or
(b) some person (not being a child [7 or qualifying young person]) who—
  (i) has the care of a child or children [7 or a qualifying young person or persons] in respect of whom the beneficiary is entitled to child benefit [2 . . .];
  (ii) is not undergoing imprisonment or detention in legal custody;
  (iii) if he has earnings, does not have weekly earnings exceeding that amount and for this purpose there shall be disregarded any weekly earnings derived from employment by the beneficiary in caring for a child or children [7 or a qualifying young person or persons] in respect of whom the beneficiary is entitled to child benefit;
  (iv) is not absent from Great Britain, except for any period during which the person is residing with the beneficiary outside Great Britain and for which the beneficiary is entitled to an [4 carer's allowance].

8.—A person who is entitled to an increase of [4 a carer's allowance] under paragraph 7(a) above shall not be entitled to an increase of that benefit under paragraph 7(b) above.

[2**9.**—(1) Subject to sub-paragraph (2) below in this Schedule any reference to earnings includes a reference to payments by way of occupational or personal pension [8 or PPF periodical payment.].

(2) Sub-paragraph (1) above shall not apply so as to affect entitlement to an increase of [4 carer's allowance] in respect of a child or adult dependant in any case where the beneficiary—

(a) was entitled to receive such an increase immediately before this paragraph came into operation; and
(b) but for the operation of sub-paragraph (1) above would continue to be so entitled, until such time as he would first otherwise cease to be so entitled.]

AMENDMENTS

1. The Social Security Benefit (Dependency, Claims and Payments and Hospital In-Patients) Amendment Regulations 1984 (SI 1984/1699) reg.3 (November 26, 1984).
2. The Social Security Benefit (Dependency) Amendment Regulations 1987 (SI 1987/355) reg.5 (April 6, 1987).
3. The Social Security Benefit (Computation of Earnings) Regulations 1996 (SI 1996/2745) reg.17 (November 26, 1996).
4. The Social Security Amendment (Carer's Allowance) Regulations 2002 (SI 2002/2497) reg.3 (April 1, 2003).
5. The Social Security Benefits Up-rating Regulations 2023 (SI 2023/340) reg.5 (April 10, 2023).
6. The Civil Partnership (Pensions, Social Security and Child Support) (Consequential, etc. Provisions) Order 2005 (SI 2005/2877) (December 5, 2005).
7. The Social Security (Provisions relating to Qualifying Young Persons) (Amendment) Regulations 2006 (SI 2006/692) (April 10, 2006).
8. The Social Security (PPF Payments and FAS Payments) (Consequential Amendments) Regulations 2006 (SI 2006/1069) (May 5, 2006).

9. The Social Security (Miscellaneous Amendments) (No. 3) Regulations 2011 (SI 2011/2425) reg.5 (October 31, 2011).
10. The Marriage and Civil Partnership Act (Scotland) Act 2014 and Civil Partnership Act 2004 (Consequential Provisions and Modifications) Order 2014 (SI 2014/3229) art.29 and Sch.6 para.2 (December 16, 2014).
11. The Civil Partnership (Opposite-sex Couples) Regulations 2019 (SI 2019/1458) reg.41(b) and Sch.3 Pt.2 para.38 (December 2, 2019).
12. Social Security (Up-rating) (Miscellaneous Amendment) (Scotland) Regulations 2021 (SI 2021/170) reg.6 (April 1, 2021, effective only in Scotland).

The Social Security (Hospital In-Patients) Regulations 2005

(SI 2005/3360) (*AS AMENDED)*

ARRANGEMENT OF REGULATIONS

The Secretary of State for Work and Pensions makes the following regulations in exercise of the powers conferred upon him by sections 113(1)(b), 123(1)(a), (d) and (e), 124(5), 130(4), 131(10), 135(1), 136(3), 137(1), 138(2) and (4) and 175(1), (3) and (4) of the Social Security Contributions and Benefits Act 1992, sections 5(1)(p), 73(1)(b) and 189(1), (4) and (5) of the Social Security Administration Act 1992, sections 4(5) and 36(1), (2) and (4)(a) of the Jobseekers Act 1995 and sections 2(3), (6) and (9), 3(8), 17(1) and 19(1) of the State Pension Credit Act 2002.

The Social Security Advisory Committee has agreed that the proposals to make these Regulations should not be referred to it.

GENERAL NOTE

3.75 Very broadly, these regulations mark the end of the era of what has come to be known as "hospital downrating" under which benefits are reduced following lengthy periods in hospital. But some aspects of the abolished system are retained.

A challenge relating to the exclusion from benefits of prisoners transferred to mental hospital under these regulations as being in breach of Article 14 of the European Convention when read with Article 1 of Protocol No. 1 has failed with one exception: see *R. (on the application of M)* v *Secretary of State for Work and Pensions,* [2009] EWHC 454 (Admin). The excepted class is a small group (there were 45 such persons in detention when the case was decided) of what are described as "technical lifers", namely those, although sentenced to life imprisonment, are treated by the Secretary of State after transfer to hospital as though they had been made the subject of a hospital order under s.37 of the Mental Health Act 1983 and to a restriction order under s.41 of that Act. The trial judge said that:

> "The reality is that the 45 technical lifers are the unintended victims of a policy that had different objects in its sight. The technical lifer cannot be returned to prison and is treated for all other purposes as if he was subject to a section 37 order with a section 41 restriction. The arguments advanced by the Secretary of State in support of the policy barely touched this group of patient." (para.40)

Citation and commencement

1. These Regulations may be cited as the Social Security (Hospital In-Patients) Regulations 2005 and shall come into force for the purposes of— 3.76

(a) this regulation and regulations 2, 5, 7 and 8, on 10th April 2006,
(b) regulation 3—
  (i) in so far as it relates to a particular beneficiary other than a beneficiary in receipt of incapacity benefit or severe disablement allowance, on 10th April 2006 if it is his day for payment or, if not, on his day for payment next following 10th April 2006 ("day for payment" has the same meaning as in regulation 22(3) of, and Schedule 6 to, the Social Security (Claims and Payments) Regulations 1987),
  (ii) in so far as it relates to a particular beneficiary in receipt of incapacity benefit or severe disablement allowance, on 10th April 2006,
(c) regulation 4, in so far as it relates to a particular beneficiary, on the first day of the first benefit week to commence for that beneficiary on or after 10th April 2006 ("benefit week" has the same meaning as in the Income Support (General) Regulations 1987),
(d) regulation 6, in so far as it relates to a particular beneficiary, on the first day of the first benefit week to commence for that beneficiary on or after 10th April 2006 ("benefit week" has the same meaning as in the Jobseeker's Allowance Regulations 1996), and
(e) regulation 9—
  (i) in so far as it relates to a beneficiary specified in paragraphs (b) to (d), on the dates specified in those paragraphs for that beneficiary, and
  (ii) otherwise, on 10th April 2006.

Hospital in-patients entitled to an increase in benefit for a dependant

2.—(1) Paragraphs (2) and (3) apply where a beneficiary is entitled to an increase in benefit for an adult or child dependant under Part IV of the Social Security Contributions and Benefits Act 1992. 3.77

(2) Where the beneficiary has received free in-patient treatment for a period of not less than 52 weeks, the increase shall not be payable unless the beneficiary applies to the Secretary of State to pay the increase on behalf of the beneficiary to—

(a) the dependant, or

(b) some other person who is approved by the Secretary of State and who satisfies the Secretary of State that he will apply the increase for the benefit of the dependant.

(3) Where both the beneficiary and the dependant are in-patients and each has received free inpatient treatment for a period of not less than 52 weeks, the increase shall not be payable unless the beneficiary applies to the Secretary of State to pay the increase on behalf of the beneficiary to—

(a) the dependant, or

(b) some other person who is approved by the Secretary of State and who satisfies the Secretary of State that he will apply the increase for the benefit of a child [[1] of the beneficiary.]

(4) For the purposes of this regulation, a person shall be regarded as receiving or having received free in-patient treatment for any period for which he is or has been maintained free of charge while undergoing medical or other treatment as an in-patient—

(a) in a hospital or similar institution under the National Health Service Act 1977, the National Health Service (Scotland) Act 1978 or the National Health Service and Community Care Act 1990, or

(b) in a hospital or similar institution maintained or administered by the Defence Council,

and such a person shall for the purposes of sub-paragraph (a) be regarded as being maintained free of charge in a hospital or similar institution unless his accommodation and services are provided under section 65 of the National Health Service Act 1977, section 57 of the National Health Service (Scotland) Act 1978 or paragraph 14 of Schedule 2 to the National Health Service and Community Care Act 1990.

(5) For the purposes of paragraph (4), a period during which a person is regarded as receiving or having received free in-patient treatment shall be deemed to begin on the day after the day on which he enters a hospital or similar institution referred to in that paragraph and to end on the day on which he leaves such a hospital or similar institution.

(6) For the purposes of this regulation—

(a) where an increase in a person's benefit is payable in respect of an adult or child dependant the increase shall be treated as a separate benefit, and

(b) where a beneficiary's spouse or civil partner ("dependant") is temporarily absent from Great Britain for the purpose of being treated for incapacity which commenced before he left Great Britain the absence shall be disregarded for the purpose of determining whether the beneficiary is residing with the dependant and is entitled to an increase in benefit for him.

AMENDMENT

1. The Social Security (Miscellaneous Amendments) Regulations 2006 (SI 2006/588) (March 10, 2006).

GENERAL NOTE

3.78 Provision is made for continued payment of an increase in benefit for a dependant after 52 weeks on application to the Secretary of State. This is the only remaining free-standing provision on payments in relation to hospital in-patients. All other aspects of payments are incorporated into the specific benefit rules by the amendments made by regs 3 to 8 of these Regulations. Note that there are no linking rules in relation to these provisions. The regulation is drafted such that the only reading possible is that the beneficiary must have been in hospital for a continuous period of at least 52 weeks. Separate periods in hospital cannot be linked to form the 52 week qualifying period.

The question of whether a person is in a "hospital or similar institution" is nowadays determined not so much by the inherent nature of the accommodation but by whether the person's assessed needs for care is such that the National Health Service is under a duty to fund the accommodation free of charge. In the less straightforward cases, tribunals will need to take evidence and consider who is actually funding the accommodation. *R(DLA) 2/06* is instructive of the complexities which can arise.

Revocation of the Social Security (Hospital In-Patients) Regulations 1975 and other regulations

9.—(1) The Social Security (Hospital In-Patients) Regulations 1975 shall be revoked. **3.79**

(2) The provisions in the subordinate legislation set out in the Schedule shall be revoked.

The Social Security (Overlapping Benefits) Regulations 1979

(SI 1979/597) (*as amended*)

ARRANGEMENT OF REGULATIONS

SCHEDULES

Schedule 1—Personal benefits which are required to be adjusted by reference to benefits not under Chapters I and II of Part II of the Act.
Schedule 2—*Omitted.*

The Secretary of State for Social Services, in exercise of powers conferred by sections 83(1) and 85 of the Social Security Act 1975 and of all other powers enabling him in that behalf hereby makes the following regulations which only consolidate the regulations herein revoked and which accordingly by virtue of paragraph 20 of Schedule 15 to the Social Security Act 1975, are not subject to the requirement of section 139(1) of that Act for prior reference to the National Insurance Advisory Committee:

Citation and commencement

3.81 **1.**—These regulations may be cited as the Social Security (Overlapping Benefits) Regulations 1979 and shall come into operation on 29th June, 1979.

Interpretation

3.82 **2.**—(1) In these regulations, unless the context otherwise requires—

[[15] "the 2012 Act" means the Welfare Reform Act 2012;]

"the Act" means the Social Security Act 1975;

[[16] "armed forces independence payment" means a payment under Article 24A of the Armed Forces and Reserve Forces (Compensation Scheme) Order 2011;]

[[1] "the Contributions and Benefits Act" means the Social Security Contributions and Benefits Act 1992];

"the Pensions Act" means the Social Security Pensions Act 1975;

"benefit under Chapters I and II of Part II of the Act" includes benefit treated as included in Chapter I of Part II of the Act by virtue of section 66(2)(b) of the Pensions Act;

[[20]. . .]

"the Child Benefit Act" means the Child Benefit Act 1975;

"child benefit" means benefit under Part I of the Child Benefit Act;

[[17] "contribution-based jobseeker's allowance" means an allowance under the Jobseekers Act as amended by the provisions of Part 1 of Schedule 14 to the 2012 Act that remove references to an income-based allowance, and a contribution-based allowance under the Jobseekers Act as that Act has effect apart from those provisions;]

[[3] "contributory benefit" means any benefit payable under Part II of the Contributions and Benefits Act, [[12] a contribution-based jobseeker's allowance and a contributory employment and support allowance];

[[17] "contributory employment and support allowance" means an allowance under Part 1 of the Welfare Reform Act as amended by the provisions of Schedule 3, and Part 1 of Schedule 14, to the 2012 Act that remove references to an income-related allowance, and a contributory allowance under Part 1 of the Welfare Reform Act as that Part has effect apart from those provisions;]

[[15] "the daily living component of personal independence payment" means a payment in accordance with section 78 of the 2012 Act;]

"death benefit" means any benefit, pension or allowance which, apart from these regulations, is payable (whether under the Act or otherwise) in respect of the death of any person;

"the deceased" means, in relation to any death benefit, the person in respect of whose death that benefit, apart from these regulations, is payable;

"dependency benefit" means that benefit, pension or allowance which, apart from these regulations, is payable (whether under the Act or otherwise) to a person in respect of another person who is a child or an adult dependant, it includes child's special allowance and any personal benefit by way of pension payable to a child under any Personal Injuries Scheme, Service Pensions Instrument or 1914–1918 War Injuries Scheme but does not include benefit under section 73 of the Act (allowances to a woman who has care of children of person who died as a result of an industrial accident) [[4] or child tax credit under the Tax Credits Act 2002];

"disablement pension" includes a disablement payment on a pension basis and retired pay or pension in respect of any disablement, wound, injury or disease;

[[16] "the enhanced rate" in relation to the daily living component of personal independence payment means the rate prescribed in regulation 24(1)(b) of the Social Security (Personal Independence Payment) Regulations 2013;]

[[17] "income-based jobseeker's allowance" means an income-based allowance under the Jobseekers Act;

"income-related employment and support allowance" means an income-related allowance under Part 1 of the Welfare Reform Act;]

[[5] "the Jobseekers Act" means the Jobseekers Act 1995];

"personal benefit" means any benefit, pension or allowance [[11] , except a shared additional pension] [[6] (whether under the Act or otherwise)] which is not a dependency benefit [[17] or universal credit under Part 1 of the Welfare Reform Act] [[6] and includes [[12] a contributory employment and support allowance but not an income-related employment and support allowance and includes] a contribution-based jobseeker's allowance but not an income-based jobseeker's allowance] and which [[6] apart from these regulations,] is payable to any person;

[[15] "personal independence payment" means personal independence payment under Part 4 of the 2012 Act;]

"Personal Injuries Scheme" means any scheme made under the Personal Injuries (Emergency Provisions) Act 1939 or under the Pensions (Navy, Army, Air Force and Mercantile Marine) Act 1939;

"Pneumoconiosis and Byssinosis Benefit Scheme" means any scheme made under section 5 of the Industrial Injuries and Diseases (Old Cases) Act 1975;

[[7] "Service Pensions Instrument" means any instrument described in sub-paragraphs (a) or (b) below in so far, but only in so far, as the pensions or other benefits provided by that instrument are not calculated or determined by reference to length of service, namely:—

(a) any instrument made in exercise of powers—

(i) referred to in section 12(1) of the Social Security (Miscellaneous Provisions) Act 1977 (pensions or other benefits for disablement or death due to service in the armed forces of the Crown); or

(ii) under section 1 of the Polish Resettlement Act 1947 (pensions and other benefits for disablement or death due to service in certain Polish forces); or

(b) any instrument under which a pension or other benefit may be paid to a person (not being a member of the armed forces of the Crown) out of public funds in respect of death or disablement, wound, injury, or disease due to service in any nursing service or other auxiliary service of any of the armed forces of the Crown, or in any other organisation established under the control of the Defence Council or formerly established under the control of the Admiralty, the Army Council or the Air Council.]

[[11] "shared additional pension" means a shared additional pension under section 55A [[19] or 55AA] of the Contributions and Benefits Act;]

"training allowance" means an allowance (whether by way of periodical grants or otherwise) payable out of public funds by a Government department or by or on behalf of [[8] Scottish Enterprise, Highlands and Islands Enterprise] [[14]. . .] [[13] [[19] the Secretary of State]] [[10], the National Assembly for Wales] or the Secretary of State to a person for his maintenance, or in respect of any dependant of his, for the period, or part of the period, during which he is following a course of training or instruction provided by that department in relation to him or so provided by or on behalf of [[8] Scottish Enterprise, Highlands and Islands Enterprise] [[10] , the National Assembly for Wales] or the Secretary of State; but it does not include—

(a) an allowance paid by any Government department to or in respect of a person by reason of the fact that he is following a course of full-time education or is in training as a teacher; or

(b) a payment made by or on behalf of [[8] Scottish Enterprise, Highlands and Islands Enterprise] or the Secretary of State to any person by way of training premium or training bonus in consequence of that person's use of facilities for training provided in pursuance of arrangements made under section 2 of the Employment and Training Act 1973 or [[8] section 8 of the Enterprise and New Towns (Scotland) Act 1990.]

"treatment allowance" means an allowance payable under a Personal Injuries Scheme, Service Pensions Instrument or 1914–1918 War Injuries Scheme only to a person undergoing a course of medical, surgical or rehabilitative treatment in consequence of a disablement in respect of which a pension may be or has been paid, or an allowance payable to any such person pending the determination of the question whether he is entitled to receive such a pension;

"unemployment supplement" includes an increase on account of unemployability under—

(a) any Pneumoconiosis and Byssinosis Benefit Scheme; and

(b) any Personal Injuries Scheme, Service Pensions Instrument or 1914–1918 War Injuries Scheme;

"war pension death benefit" means a death benefit by way of pension or allowance under any Personal Injuries Scheme, Service Pensions Instrument or 1914–1918 War Injuries Scheme, but does not include a rent allowance or a grant payable by reason of the beneficiary being in receipt of a pension and being a specific age which is not less than 65 or a pension or an allowance calculated by reference to the necessities of the beneficiary;

[12 "the Welfare Reform Act" means the Welfare Reform Act 2007].

[19 "widowed mother's allowance" means an allowance referred to in section 37 of the Contributions and Benefits Act (widowed mother's allowance);]

[2 "widowed parent's allowance" means an allowance referred to in section 39A of the Contributions and Benefits Act;]

[19 "widow's pension" means a pension referred to in section 38 of the Contributions and Benefits Act (widow's pension);]

"1914–1918 War Injuries Scheme" means any scheme made under the Injuries in War (Compensation) Act 1914 or under the Injuries in War Compensation Act 1914 (Session 2) or any Government scheme for compensation in respect of persons injured in any merchant ship or fishing vessel as the result of hostilities during the 1914–1918 War.

(2) For the purposes of these regulations, unless otherwise specified, [9 additional pension] payable by virtue of the Act or the Pensions Act shall be deemed to include any increase so far as attributable to any additional pension or to any increase by virtue of section 126A of the Act or paragraph 4A of Schedule 1 to the Pensions Act or to any increase of graduated retirement benefit and shall be treated as a separate personal benefit included in Chapter I of Part II of the Act.

AMENDMENTS

1. The Social Security (Overlapping Benefits) Amendment (No. 2) Regulations 1992 (SI 1992/3194) reg.2 (January 13, 1993).

2. The Social Security (Benefits for Widows and Widowers) (Consequential Amendments) Regulations 2000 (SI 2000/1483) reg.6 (April 9, 2001).

3. The Social Security and Child Support (Jobseeker's Allowance) (Consequential Amendments) Regulations 1996 (SI 1996/1345) reg.22(2)(a) (October 7, 1996).

4. The Social Security (Working Tax Credit and Child Tax Credit) (Consequential Amendments) (No. 2) Regulations 2003 (SI 2003/937) reg.2 (April 6, 2003).

5. The Social Security and Child Support (Jobseeker's Allowance) (Consequential Amendments) Regulations 1996 (SI 1996/1345) reg.22(2)(b) (October 7, 1996).

6. The Social Security and Child Support (Jobseeker's Allowance) (Consequential Amendments) Reglations 1996 (SI 1996/1345) reg.22(2)(c) (October 7, 1996).

7. The Social Security (Overlapping Benefits) Amendments Regulations 1980 (SI 1980/1927) reg.2(b) (January 5, 1981).

8. The Enterprise (Scotland) Consequential Amendments Order 1991 (SI 1991/387) reg.2(1) (April 4, 1991).

9. Social Security Act 1986 s.18(1) (April 6, 1987).

10. The Social Security, Child Support and Tax Credits (Miscellaneous Amendments) Regulations 2005 (SI 2005/337) reg.11 (March 18, 2005).

11. The Social Security (Shared Additional Pension) (Miscellaneous Amendments) Regulations 2005 (SI 2005/1551) (July 6, 2005).

12. The Employment and Support Allowance (Consequential Provisions) (No. 2) Regulations 2008 (SI 2008/1554) reg.51 (October 27, 2008).

13. The Apprenticeship, Skills, Children and Learning Act 2009 (Consequential Amendments to Subordinate Legislation) (England) Order 2010 (SI 2010/1941) reg.2 (September 1, 2010).

14. The Young People's Learning Agency Abolition (Consequential Amendments to Subordinate Legislation) (England) Order 2012 (SI 2012/956) reg.2 (May 1, 2012).

15. The Personal Independence Payments (Supplementary Provisions and Consequential Amendments) Regulations 2013 (SI 2013/388) reg.8 and Sch. para.10 (April 8, 2013).

16. The Armed Forces and Reserve Forces Compensation Scheme (Consequential Provisions: Subordinate Legislation) Order 2013 (SI 2013/591) reg.7 and Sch. para.3 (April 8, 2013).

17. The Universal Credit (Consequential Supplementary, Incidental and Miscellaneous Provisions) Regulations 2013 (SI 2013/630) reg.25 (April 29, 2013).

18. Deregulation Act 2015 (Consequential Amendments) Order 2015 (SI 2015/971) art.2 and Sch.3 para.1 (May 26, 2015).

19. The Pensions Act 2014 (Consequential, Supplementary and Incidental Amendments) Order 2015 (SI 2015/1985) art.4(2) (April 6, 2016).

20. Pensions Act 2014 (Consequential, Supplementary and Incidental Amendments) Order 2017 (SI 2017/422) art.6 (April 6, 2017).

3.83 *Regulation 3 revoked by The Social Security (Incapacity Benefit) Consequential and Transitional Amendments and Savings) Regulations 1995 (SI 1995/829), reg.14(2) (April 13, 1995) subject to the savings set out below.*

TRANSITIONAL PROTECTION

3.84 Regulation 3 is revoked with effect from April 13, 1995, but reg.14(9) of the Social Security (Incapacity Benefit)(Consequential and Transitional Amendments and Savings) Regulations 1995 (SI 1995/829) provides as follows:

"(9) Where before the appointed day regulation 3 of the Overlapping Benefits Regulations (special provisions for widow's benefit and invalidity pension) applied to a widow; and

(a) on or after that day she remains entitled to either a widowed mother's allowance or a widow's pension; and
(b) she is either a transitional case for the purposes of Part IV of the Social Security (Incapacity Benefit) (Transitional) Regulations 1995 or, has an award of long-term incapacity benefit by virtue of regulation 19 or 20 of the Social Security (Incapacity Benefit) (Transitional) Regulations 1995; and
(c) she is under pensionable age,

regulation 3 of the Overlapping Benefits Regulations shall continue to apply to her as if the revocation made by paragraph (2) above had not been made subject to the modification made in paragraph (10) below."

3.85 Regulation 14(10) of the Social Security (Incapacity Benefit)(Consequential and Transitional Amendments and Savings) Regulations 1995 (SI 1995/829) modifes revoked reg.3 so that it reads as follows in its application to those covered by the saving in Regulation 14(9) above.

"**3.**—(1) This regulation applies where, apart from these regulations, there is payable for the same period to a person under pensionable age both—

(a) a long-term incapacity benefit; and
(b) a widowed mother's allowance or widow's pension (hereafter referred to in this regulation as "the widow's benefit").

(2) The total amount payable in respect of these benefits under this regulation shall be—

(a) an amount equal to either the basic rate of long-term incapacity benefit referred to in regulation 18(1)(a) of the Social Security (Incapacity Benefit)

(Transitional) Regulations 1995 paid in a transitional case or an award of widow's basic pension calculated by reference to section 44(1) of the Contributions and Benefits Act or an amount equal to the greater of them; and

(b) the sum of the incapacity benefit payable at the additional rate in accordance with regulation 18(1)(b) of the Social Security (Incapacity Benefit) (Transitional) Regulations 1995 and widow's pension determined in accordance with section 44(3) of the Contributions and Benefits Act.

(3) Subject to paragraph (4)—

(a) where the beneficiary has made application, before the payment is made, that the total amount should be treated as being made up of the rate of the long-term incapacity benefit, any balance being the widow's benefit, it shall be so treated;

(b) in any other case, that amount shall be treated as being made up of the rate of the widow's benefit, any balance being the long-term incapacity benefit.

(4) For the purposes of the remainder of these regulations (other than regulation 6(5)), which shall apply after adjustment has been made under this regulation, the total amount payable under this regulation shall be treated as a single long-term benefit payable on a weekly basis."

Adjustment of personal benefit under Parts II and III of the Contributions and Benefits Act where other personal benefit under those Parts or graduated retirement benefit is payable

4.—[1 (1) Subject to paragraphs (2), (3) and (4) and regulation 12, an adjustment shall be made in accordance with paragraph (5) where either— 3.86

(a) two or more personal benefits (whether of the same or a different description) are, or but for this regulation would be, payable under Parts II and III of the Contributions and Benefits Act (which relate to benefits other than industrial injuries benefits) [9 Part 1 of the Welfare Reform Act] [10 , Part 1 of the Pensions Act 2014] [2 or under the Jobseekers Act] for any period; or

(b) graduated retirement benefit is payable under sections 36 and 37 of the National Insurance Act 1965 together with one or more personal benefits (whether of the same or a different description) which are, or but for this regulation would be, payable under Parts II and III of the Contributions and Benefits Act for any period].

(2) Paragraph (1) shall not require the adjustment of, or by reference to—

(a) a death grant;

(b) a maternity grant;

(c) any other sum paid otherwise than in respect of a period;

(d) an earnings-related supplement or earnings-related addition to any benefit (except as provided by regulation 5 and in the case of [3 severe disablement allowance] or [8carer's allowance]);

(e) an attendance allowance;

(f) [4 additional pension] or graduated retirement benefit (except as provided by paragraph (4) [10 and (4A)]);

(g) [5disability living allowance]

[6 (2A) Paragraph (1) shall not require an adjustment of widow's pension reduced in accordance with section 39(4) of the Contributions and Benefits Act only by reference to long-term incapacity benefit in accordance with section 40(5)(b) of that Act].

(3) Paragraph (1) shall require an adjustment of age addition only by reference to another age addition.

(4) [10 Except where paragraph (4A) applies,] where there are payable two or more personal benefits to which this regulation applies with which [4 additional pension] or graduated retirement benefit is payable as part of the rate of benefit or as an increase of benefit, or, in a case where the person entitled to receive the benefits is over pensionable age and one or more of the benefits includes either additional pension or graduated retirement benefit while another of the benefits is payable at the rate referred to in [section 31(6) or 33(4) of the Social Security Contributions and Benefits Act 1992], then the following provisions shall apply—

(a) for the purposes of adjustment falling to be made under paragraph (5) that [4 additional pension] or graduated retirement benefit shall be treated as part of the personal benefit with which it is so payable;

(b) the provisions of sub-paragraph (a) shall apply before any further adjustment under these regulations; and

(c) for the purpose of any such further adjustment, the beneficiary shall be treated as having a single long-term benefit inclusive of whichever before adjustment under sub-paragraph (a) is the highest of the following amounts—

(i) the highest additional pension payable, or

(ii) the highest graduated retirement benefit payable, or

(iii) the highest total of additional pension and graduated retirement benefit payable together as part of the rate of and as an increase of any of those personal benefits.

[10 (4A) Where the person is entitled to additional pension, a state pension under Part 1 of the Pensions Act 2014 and either widow's pension or widowed mother's allowance, paragraph (1) shall require adjustment of additional pension.]

(5) Where an adjustment falls to be made in accordance with this paragraph and—

(a) one of the benefits is a contributory benefit and one is a noncontributory benefit, the non-contributory benefit shall be adjusted by deducting from it the amount of the contributory benefit and only the balance, if any, shall be payable;

(b) sub-paragraph (a) above does not apply, if one of the benefits is payable on a weekly basis—

(i) where the beneficiary has made application, before the payment is made, to have the benefit payable on a weekly basis adjusted, it shall be adjusted by deducting from it the amount of the other benefit and only the balance of it, if any, shall be payable,

(ii) in any other case, the benefit not payable on a weekly basis shall be adjusted by deducting from it the amount of the other benefit and only the balance of it, if any, shall be payable;

(c) sub-paragraphs (a) and (b) above do not apply, the amount payable in respect of the benefits in question shall be an amount equal to that which would but for this provision be payable in respect of—

(i) one of them, if they would have been payable at the same rate, or

(ii) the higher or highest of them, if they would have been payable at different rates, so however that in a case where more than 2 benefits would be payable then the total amount payable shall not exceed the amount which would be ascertained under sub-paragraph (c).

[[7] (6) For the purposes of this regulation—

"additional pension" means a pension payable with a personal benefit under Part II of the Contribution and Benefits Act or an additional rate; and

"additional rate" means an additional amount equal to the rate paid or payable as an additional pension with invalidity benefit immediately before 13 April 1995 which is payable after that date pursuant to regulation 18 of the Social Security (Incapacity Benefit) (Transitional) Regulations 1995.]

AMENDMENTS

1. The Social Security (Overlapping Benefits) Amendment (No. 2) Regulations 1992 (SI 1992/3194) reg.3(2) (January 13, 1993).

2. The Social Security and Child Support (Jobseeker's Allowance) (Consequential Amendments) Regulations 1996 (SI 1996/1345) reg.22(3) (October 7, 1996).

3. The Social Security (Severe Disablement Allowance) Reglations 1984 (SI 1984/1303) reg.11 (November 29, 1984).

4. Social Security Act 1986 s.18(1) (April 6, 1987).

5. The Disability Living Allowance and Disability Working Allowance (Consequential Provisions) Regulations 1991 (SI 1991/2742) reg.5(2) (April 6, 1992).

6. The Social Security (Incapacity Benefit) Consequential and Transitional Amendments and Savings) Regulations 1995 (SI 1995/829) reg.14(3) (April 13, 1995).

7. The Social Security (Incapacity for Work and Miscellaneous Amendments) Regulations 1996 (SI 1996/3207) reg.4 (January 6, 1997).

8. The Social Security (Carer's Allowance) Regulations 2002 (SI 2002/2497) Sch.2 (April 1, 2003).

9. The Employment and Support Allowance (Consequential Provisions) (No. 2) Regulations 2008 (SI 2008/1554) reg.51 (October 27, 2008).

10. The Pensions Act 2014 (Consequential, Supplementary and Incidental Amendments) Order 2015 (SI 2015/1985) art.4(3) (April 6, 2016).

DEFINITIONS

"benefit under Chapters I and II of Part II of the Act"—reg.2.

"personal benefit"—reg.2.

GENERAL NOTE

This complex regulation states in para.(5) the basic general rules on overlapping benefits (though no adjustment is needed for any of the benefits specified in para. (2)). **3.87**

Unless reg.3 applies, only the highest of the following benefits is payable: carer's allowance, invalidity pension, maternity allowance, non contributory widow's benefit, retirement pension, severe disablement allowance, sickness benefit, unemployment benefit, widowed mother's allowance, widow's pension, employment and support allowance and jobseeker's allowance.

There are a number of points to note in relation to additions to benefits. An age addition only overlaps with another age addition (para.(3)). Paragraph (4) contains special rules where additional pensions under SERPS or graduated retirement pension is payable.

Special provision for earnings-related supplements and earnings-related addition to widow's allowance

3.88 **5.**—(1) Where two or more earnings-related supplements to any benefits under the Act would apart from this regulation be payable for the same period, for the purposes of regulation 4(1) each such supplement shall be treated as part of the benefit it supplements.

(2) Where an earnings-related addition to widow's allowance would apart from this regulation be payable for the same period as any other benefit under the Act which is calculated whether wholly or in part by reference to the contributions of a husband who has died, that other benefit shall be adjusted by deducting from it the amount of the earnings-related addition, provided that where the widow is also entitled for the same period to graduated retirement benefit or [1 additional pension], or both of them, by virtue of her own contributions and the contributions of the husband who has died, the graduated retirement benefit or [1 additional pension] to be adjusted shall be only that part which is payable by virtue of the contributions of the husband who has died.

(3) Paragraph (1) shall not apply where apart from this regulation a widow's allowance would be payable for the same period as 2 or more other benefits under the Act; in such a case the earnings-related supplement to any of those other benefits shall be adjusted so that only the higher or highest of them is payable.

(4) For the purposes of paragraph (2), [1 additional pension] or graduated retirement benefit, where it is, or but for this regulation would be, payable as part of the rate of or as an increase of another personal benefit, shall be treated as part of the personal benefit with which it is so payable.

AMENDMENT

1. Social Security Act 1986 s.18(1) (April 6, 1987).

Adjustments of personal benefit under Chapters I and II of Part II of the Act by reference to industrial injuries benefits and benefits not under the Act, and adjustments of industrial injuries benefits

3.89 **6.**—(1) Subject to paragraph (5) and regulation 12, where a personal benefit which is specified in column (1) of Schedule 1 to these regulations ("the column (1) benefit") is, or but for this regulation would be payable to a person for the same period as a personal benefit which is specified in the corresponding paragraph of column (2) of that Schedule ("the column (2) benefit") the column (1) benefit shall be adjusted by deducting from it the amount of the column (2) benefit and, subject to any further adjustment under regulation 4, only the balance, if any, shall be payable.

(2) Any reference in paragraph (1), or in Schedule 1 to these regulations, to a benefit, other than a training allowance, does not include an earnings-related supplement or earnings-related addition to it.

[6 (3) Paragraph (1) and Schedule 1 have effect in relation to—

(a) the following allowances and payments—

(i) an attendance allowance;

(ii) the care component of disability living allowance; and

(iii) the daily living component of personal independence payment; [7 . . .]

[7 (iv) armed forces independence payment up to the value of the daily living component of personal independence payment at the enhanced rate; and]

(b) any benefit by reference to which an allowance or payment under paragraph (a) above is to be adjusted;

as requiring adjustment where both that allowance or payment and the benefit are payable in respect of the same person (whether or not one or both of them are payable to that person).]

(4) Paragraph (1) and Schedule 1 to these regulations shall not require the adjustment of, or by reference to, [2 additional pension] or graduated retirement benefit.

(5) Where—

(a) the column (2) benefit is industrial death benefit or war pension death benefit in either case payable to the beneficiary as the surviving spouse [5 or civil partner], and

(b) the column (1) benefit is Category A retirement pension [3 . . .] which

(i) [4 . . .]

(ii) has a [2 basic pension] by virtue of the beneficiary's own contributions (but not by virtue of those of a former spouse [5 or civil partner]) which consists of either the rate specified in [section 44(3)(a) and (4) of the Social Security Contributions and Benefits Act 1992] or some percentage of that rate prescribed by regulations made under [section 60(1) of the Social Security Contributions and Benefits Act 1992],

the adjustment under paragraph (1) shall not reduce that Column (1) benefit to less than the appropriate rate in sub-paragraph (b)(ii), together with, if any, increments payable under paragraph 2 of [Schedule 5 of the Social Security Contributions and Benefits Act 1992] and increase under [section 47(1) of the Social Security Contributions and Benefits Act 1992].

AMENDMENTS

1. The Disability Living Allowance and Disability Working Allowance (Consequential Provisions) Regulations 1991 (SI 1991/2742) reg.5(3) (April 6, 1992).

2. Social Security Act 1986 s.18(1) (April 6, 1987).

3. The Social Security (Incapacity Benefit) (Consequential and Transitional Amendments and Savings) Regulations 1995 (SI 1995/829) reg.14(4)(a) (April 13, 1995).

4. The Social Security (Incapacity Benefit) Consequential and Transitional Amendments and Savings) Regulations 1995 (SI 1995/829) reg.14(4)(b) (April 13, 1995).

5. The Civil Partnership (Pensions, Social Security and Child Support) (Consequential, etc. Provisions) Order 2005 (SI 2005/2877) (December 5, 2005).

6. The Personal Independence Payments (Supplementary Provisions and Consequential Amendments) Regulations 2013 (SI 2013/388) reg.8 and Sch. para.10(3) (April 8, 2013).

7. The Armed Forces and Reserve Forces Compensation Scheme (Consequential Provisions: Subordinate Legislation) Order 2013 (SI 2013/591) reg.7 and Sch. para.3 (April 8, 2013).

GENERAL NOTE

Regulation 14(4) of the Social Security (Incapacity Benefit) (Consequential and Transitional Amendments and Savings) Regulations 1995 (SI 1995/829) amends this regulation with effect from April 13, 1995 by revoking the reference to invalidity 3.90

benefit in para.(5)(b) and omitting para.(5)(b)(i), but reg.14(11) contains a saving provision as follows:

"(11) Notwithstanding the amendment made by paragraph (4) above, where in a transitional case long-term incapacity benefit falls to be adjusted by reference to a benefit within column (2) of Schedule 1 to the Overlapping Benefits Regulations, that benefit shall be adjusted on or after the appointed day as if the words 'or invalidity benefit' had not been omitted from regulation 6 of those Regulations."

Adjustment of dependency benefit in respect of a child where other dependency benefit is payable for that child

3.91 7.—(1) Subject to regulation 12, where dependency benefit under the Act is payable, or but for this regulation would be payable, to any person in respect of a child and any other dependency benefit specified in paragraph (2) is payable to that or any other person in respect of that child for the same period, an adjustment shall be made in accordance with regulation 4(5) so however that where one of the dependency benefits is death benefit under [paras. 18 and 19 of Schedule 7 to the Social Security Contributions and Benefits Act 1992] by way of an allowance, or is a guardian's allowance under [section 77 of the Social Security Contributions and Benefits Act 1992] (the other dependency benefit not being benefit under either the said [section 77 or paragraphs 18 and 19 to Schedule 7 of the Social Security Contributions and Benefits Act 1992]) the adjustment shall be made in accordance with paragraph (4) of this regulation.

(2) Subject to paragraph (3), the other dependency benefit referred to in paragraph (1) is any dependency benefit under—

(a) the Act;
(b) any Personal Injuries Scheme, Service Pensions Instrument or 1914–1918 War Injuries Scheme;
(c) any Pneumoconiosis and Byssinosis Benefit Scheme;
(d) any scheme, being a benefit by way of training allowance.

(3) Sub-paragraph (b) of paragraph (2) does not include an allowance payable or the purpose of the child's education and for the purposes of that sub-paragraph—

(a) any personal benefit by way of a pension payable to a child shall be treated as a dependency benefit payable to another person in respect of that child;
(b) any dependency benefit payable as part of a disablement pension shall be disregarded unless it is payable as an increase of an unemployability supplement.

(4) Where one of the dependency benefits is death benefit under section 70 by way of an allowance or is a guardian's allowance, except in a case to which paragraph (5) applies, the other dependency benefit shall be adjusted by deducting from it the amount of that death benefit or, as the case may be, guardian's allowance, and only the balance, if any, shall be payable.

(5) Where a death benefit by way of an allowance under section 70 or a guardian's allowance is payable to a person in respect of a child and any other dependency benefit specified in sub-paragraph (b) or (d) of paragraph (2) is payable to that or any other person in respect of that child for the same period, the death benefit or, as the case may be, the guardian's allowance shall be adjusted by deducting from it the other benefit and only the balance, if any, shall be payable.

Child benefit

8.—(1) Subject to the following provisions of this regulation, where any benefit, or increase of a benefit, under the Act is payable to a beneficiary, the weekly rate of that benefit or increase shall not be adjusted by reference to child benefit. **3.92**

(2) Where child benefit is payable to a beneficiary at the rate for the time being specified in regulation 2(1)(a)(ii) of the Child Benefit and Social Security (Fixing and Adjustment of Rates) Regulations 1976 (in this regulation referred to as the "Child Benefit Rates Regulations") (weekly rate for only, elder or eldest child of a lone parent) and for the same period, in respect of the same child, any benefit or increase in benefit under the Contributions and Benefits Act [1 except where that benefit is guardian's allowance payable to any person under section 77 of that Act,] the weekly rate of that benefit or increase thereof shall be reduced by—

(a) [2 . . .];

(b) [2 . . .] an amount equal to the amount, less [3 £3.65], by which the rate specified in regulation 2(1)(a)(ii) of the Child Benefit Rates Regulations exceeds the rate specified in regulation 2(1)(b) of those Regulations.

(3) Subject to paragraph (6) of this regulation, where child benefit is payable to a beneficiary at the rate for the time being specified in regulation 2(1)(a)(i) of the Child Benefit Rates Regulations (weekly rate for only, elder or eldest child) and for the same period, in respect of the same child, any benefit or increase in benefit under the Contributions and Benefits Act [1 except where that benefit is guardian's allowance payable to any person under section 77 of that Act,] the weekly rate of that benefit or the increase thereof shall be reduced by an amount equal to the amount, less [3 £3.65], by which the rate specified in regulation 2(1)(a)(i) of the Child Benefit Rates Regulations exceeds the rate specified in regulation 2(1)(b) of those Regulations.

(4) [1 . . .]

(5) [1 . . .]

(6) Where the weekly rate of any benefit or increase of benefit under the Act or the weekly rate of child benefit or both are increased in consequence of an order under section 63(2) of the Social Security Act 1986 and as a result the amount by which the benefit being adjusted under paragraph (3) changes, the weekly rate of benefit or increase shall not be reduced by the increased amount until the date on which the change in that benefit or increase of benefit has effect.

(7) [1 . . .]]

AMENDMENTS

Regulation 8 was substituted by The Social Security (Overlapping Benefits) Amendment Regulations 1991 (SI 1991/547) reg.2 (April 8, 1991). Paragraphs (2) and (3) were substituted by The Child Benefit, Child Support and Social Security (Miscellaneous Amendments) Regulations 1996 (SI 1996/1803) reg.47(a) (April 7, 1997), and para.(6) was substituted by The Social Security (Overlapping Benefits) Amendment Regulations 1992 (SI 1992/589) reg.2(c) (April 6, 1992).

1. The Child Benefit, Child Support and Social Security (Miscellaneous Amendments) Regulations 1996 (SI 1996/1803) reg.47(b) (April 7, 1997).

2. The Social Security (Overlapping Benefits) Amendment Regulations 2003 (SI 2003/136) reg.2 (April 7, 2003).

3. The Social Security (Miscellaneous Amendments) Regulations 2004, SI 2004/565 reg.8, (April 12, 2004).

Adjustment of dependency benefit in respect of an adult dependant where other dependency benefit is payable

3.93 **9.**—(1) Subject to paragraph (3) and regulation 12, where for any period any dependency benefit under the Act is, or but for this regulation would be, payable to any person in respect of an adult dependant and any other dependency benefit specified in paragraph (2) is payable for that period to—

(a) that person in respect of that or any other adult dependant; or
(b) any other person in respect of that dependant,

an adjustment shall be made in accordance with regulation 4(5).

(2) The other dependency benefit referred to in paragraph (1) is any dependency benefit under—

(a) the Act;
(b) any Personal Injuries Scheme, Service Pensions Instrument or 1914–1918 War Injuries Scheme;
(c) any Pneumoconiosis and Byssinosis Benefit Scheme;
(d) any scheme being a benefit by way of training allowance.

(3) Paragraph (1) shall not require an adjustment to be made where one of the dependency benefits in question is an increase of benefit under [section 82(4) or 85(2) of the Social Security Contributions and Benefits Act 1992] in respect of a person who is employed by the beneficiary but is not residing with him and the other such benefit is payable to a person other than the beneficiary [[1] or to a person entitled to an increase of incapacity benefit under regulation 9(1)(d) of the Social Security (Incapacity Benefit—Increases for Dependants) Regulations 1994 who satisfies the requirements of paragraph (3)(a) of that regulation.]

(4) For the purposes of paragraph (2)(b) any dependency benefit which is payable with a disablement pension shall be disregarded unless it is payable as an increase of an unemployability supplement.

AMENDMENT

1. The Social Security (Incapacity Benefit) (Consequential and Transitional Amendments and Savings) Regulations 1995 (SI 1995/829) reg.14(5) (April 14, 1995).

Adjustment of dependency benefit where certain personal benefit is payable

3.94 **10.**—(1) Subject to the following provisions of this regulation, where a dependency benefit under the Act is payable for the same period as one or more of the following personal benefits is, or but for the provisions of these regulations would be, payable to the dependant—

(a) a personal benefit under Chapter I or II of Part II of the Act (other than a benefit specified in regulation 4(2)(a)(b)(c)(e) or (g));
(b) an unemployability supplement;
(c) [[1] . . .];
(d) industrial death benefit;
(e) war pension death benefit;

(f) a training allowance,
[2 (g) a temporary allowance under the provisions of section 1 of the Job Release Act 1977];
[3 (h) a weekly allowance pursuant to arrangements made by the Manpower Services Commission under section 2 of the Employment and Training Act 1973 or section 2 of the Enterprise and New Towns (Scotland) Act 1990 for the purpose of the Enterprise Allowance Scheme];
[4 (i) graduated retirement benefit];
[5 (j) a contribution-based jobseeker's allowance].
[8 (k) a contributory employment and support allowance;]

the dependency benefit shall be adjusted in accordance with paragraph (2).

(2) Where the weekly rate of the personal benefit (or, if more than one, the aggregate weekly rate payable after any adjustment made by virtue of regulations 4(1) or 6(1)—

(a) is equal to or exceeds the weekly rate of the dependency benefit, the dependency benefit shall not be paid;
(b) in any other case, the weekly rate of the dependency benefit payable shall be adjusted, if necessary, so that it does not exceed the difference between the weekly rate of the personal benefit and that of the unadjusted dependency benefit.

(3) Paragraph (1) does not apply to an increase of benefit under [section 82(4) or 85(2) of the Social Security Contributions and Benefits Act 1992] in respect of a person who is employed by, but is not residing with, the beneficiary [6 or to a person entitled to an increase of incapacity benefit under regulation 9(1)(d) of the Social Security (Incapacity Benefit—Increases for Dependants) Regulations 1994 who satisfies the requirements of paragraph (3)(a) of that regulation.]

(4) Where the personal benefit to which paragraph (1) applies is sickness benefit [7 but not incapacity benefit] payable to a married woman which falls to be adjusted by virtue of regulations under [section 73(1)(b) of the Social Security Administration Act 1992] (hospital in-patients) and the dependency benefit would be payable to her husband, the rate of sickness benefit to be taken into account for the purposes of paragraph (1) shall be the rate after it has been so adjusted.

AMENDMENTS

1. The Social Security (Abolition of Injury Benefit) (Consequential) Regulations 1983 (SI 1983/186) reg.10(2) (April 6, 1983).

2. The Social Security (Overlapping Benefits) Amendment Regulations 1980 (SI 1980/1927) reg.2 (January 5, 1981).

3. The Social Security (Overlapping Benefits) Amendment Regulations 1982 (SI 1982/1173) reg.2 (September 14, 1982).

4. The Social Security (Overlapping Benefits) Amendment (No. 2) Regulations 1992 (SI 1992/3194) reg.4 (January 13, 1993).

5. The Social Security and Child Support (Jobseeker's Allowance) (Consequential Amendments) Regulations 1996 (SI 1996/1345) reg.22(4) (October 7, 1996).

6. The Social Security (Incapacity Benefit) (Consequential and Transitional Amendments and Savings) Regulations 1995 (SI 1995/829) reg.14(6)(a) (April 13, 1995).

7. The Social Security (Incapacity Benefit) (Consequential and Transitional Amendments and Savings) Regulations 1995 (SI 1995/829) reg.14(6)(b) (April 13, 1995).

8. The Employment and Support Allowance (Consequential Provisions) (No. 2) Regulations 2008 (SI 2008/1554) reg.51 (October 27, 2008).

General Note

3.95 In *Jones v Chief Adjudication Officer* [1990] I.R.L.R. 533, *R(G) 2/91*, the Court of Appeal held that reg.10 is not discriminatory on grounds of sex contrary to Art.4 of EEC Directive 79/7 on the Progressive Implementation of the Principle of Equal Treatment of Men and Women in Matters of Social Security.

The facts arising in *R(S) 5/94* were that the claimant received an increase of invalidity benefit in respect of his wife. She had retired and received a pension consisting of three components: the basic pension, an additional pension, and a graduated retirement pension. The question was the extent to which the pension benefits received by the wife should be taken into account as overlapping with the increase of invalidity benefit. No one doubted that reg.10 applied, nor that the basic component of the retirement pension was a personal benefit to be taken into account. The argument concerned the graduated retirement pension and the additional pension. The Commissioner held, first, that the graduated retirement pension was not to be taken into account. This had been established in *Pearse v Chief Adjudication Officer and Secretary of State for Social Security*, CA (Civ Div), Judgment of June 12, 1992, *The Times*, June 18, 1992. The additional pension and the basic pension are aggregated for the purposes of the application of reg.10 and the total must be deducted from the increase of invalidity benefit.

Dependency benefit under the Act not to be payable if a training allowance is payable

3.96 **11.**—Dependency benefit under the Act shall not be payable to any person for any period in respect of which any personal benefit by way of training allowance is payable to him so however that this regulation shall not apply where such personal benefit has itself been adjusted by reference to any benefit under the Act.

Special provision relating to the adjustment of [1 severe disablement allowance] and [2 carer's allowance]

3.97 **12.**—In any case where personal benefit or dependency benefit by way of a severe disablement allowance or [2 a carer's allowance] would, in accordance with the provision of regulations 4, 6, 7 or 9, fall to be adjusted by reference to any other personal benefit (other than [3 additional pension] or graduated retirement benefit) or dependency benefit, it shall be reduced by the amount which is, or but for these regulations would be, payable by way of that other benefit both as personal benefit and as dependency benefit, so however that the amount payable by way of a [1 severe disablement allowance] or [2 a carer's allowance] and that other benefit shall in no case be less than the sum of the amounts which, but for any adjustment, would have been payable by way of a [1 severe disablement allowance] or [2 a carer's allowance] as personal benefit and dependency benefit.

Amendments

1. The Social Security (Severe Disablement Allowance) Regulations 1984 (SI 1984/1303) reg.11 (November 29, 1984).
2. The Social Security Amendment (Carer's Allowance) Regulations 2002 (SI 2002/2497) reg.3 and Sch.2 (April 1, 2003).
3. Social Security Act 1986 s.18(1) (April 6, 1987).

Increases in respect of more than one dependant to be treated as separate dependency benefits

13.—For the purposes of these regulations, where dependency benefit by way of an increase is payable in respect of more than one person (whether a child or adult dependant), each such increase shall be treated as a separate dependency benefit. 3.98

Provisions for adjusting benefit for part of a week

[2 **14.**—(1) Where an adjustment falls to be made under these regulations for part of a week, benefit (whether under the Contributions and Benefits Act or otherwise) shall be deemed to be payable at a rate equal to one-seventh of the appropriate weekly rate for each day of the week in respect of any such benefit.] 3.99

(2) [1 . . .]

(3) In paragraph (1) "appropriate weekly rate" means the weekly rate at which the benefit in question would be payable but for these regulations.

AMENDMENTS

1. The Social Security and Child Support (Jobseeker's Allowance) (Consequential Amendments) Regulations 1996 (SI 1996/1345) reg.14(2) (October 7, 1996).

2. The Statutory Maternity Pay, Social Security (Maternity Allowance) and Social Security (Overlapping Benefits) (Amendment) Regulations 2006 (SI 2006/2379) (October 1, 2006).

Priority between persons entitled to increase of benefit

15.—(1) Subject to paragraphs (5) and (6), the following provisions shall apply for the purpose of determining priority as between two persons entitled to an increase of benefit under the Act in respect of a third person. 3.100

(2) Where, but for the provisions of this paragraph, a man and his wife would both be entitled to an increase of retirement pension (being an increase of Category A or Category C retirement pension in his case and a Category B or Category C retirement pension in hers) in respect of the same child or children, that man shall, and his wife shall not, be entitled to the increase; and he shall be treated as so entitled for the purposes of this paragraph during any period for which he would be entitled but for the operation of any provision of the Act, with the exception of [section 113(1)(b) of the Social Security Contributions and Benefits Act 1992] (disqualification while undergoing imprisonment or detention), disqualifying him for the receipt of benefit.

(3) Subject to paragraphs (2), (5) and (6), where, but for the provisions of this paragraph, more than one person would be entitled to an increase of benefit in respect of the same child for the same period—

(a) in a case where one of those persons has been awarded child benefit in respect of the child for that period, that one of them shall be entitled to the said increase;

(b) in the case where sub-paragraph (a) does not apply but where one of those persons is entitled otherwise than by virtue of regulations made under Schedule 20 to the Act to child benefit in respect of the child for that period, that one of them shall be entitled to the said increase;

(c) in a case where neither sub-paragraph (a) nor sub-paragraph (b) applies but where the child is living with one and no other of those persons for that period, that one of them with whom the child is living shall be entitled to the said increase;
(d) in a case where none of the preceding sub-paragraphs applies but where one of those persons is a parent of the child, that one of them shall be entitled to the said increase.

(4) Subject to paragraphs (5) and (6), where, but for the provisions of this paragraph, more than one person would be entitled to an increase of benefit in respect of an adult dependant for the same period—
(a) in a case where one of those persons is the spouse [1 or civil partner] of the adult dependant that one of them shall be entitled to the said increase;
(b) in a case where sub-paragraph (a) above does not apply that one of them with whom the adult dependant is residing shall be entitled to the said increase.

(5) Nothing in paragraphs (3) and (4) shall prevent a written notice signed by one or, as the case may be, a majority of the said persons designating another of them as the person to be entitled to the increase, being sent to the Secretary of State; so however that such notice shall not be effective to confer entitlement to an increase in respect of any period for which such increase has already been paid to someone other than the person so designated.

(6) Nothing in paragraphs (3) and (4) shall prevent a person who, in accordance with any of those paragraphs, is not entitled to an increase from being paid an amount equivalent to the amount, if any, by which the increase which would otherwise have been paid to such person exceeds the increase payable to the person entitled by virtue of any of the said paragraphs.

AMENDMENT

1. The Civil Partnership (Pensions, Social Security and Child Support) (Consequential, etc. Provisions) Order 2005 (SI 2005/2877) (December 5, 2005).

Persons to be treated as entitled to benefit for certain purposes

3.101 **16.** Any person who would be entitled to any benefit under the Act [2, Part 1 of the Welfare Reform Act] [3 , under Part 4 of the 2012 Act] [4 or under the Jobseekers Act, or entitled to armed forces independence payment] but for these regulations shall be treated as if he were entitled thereto for the purpose of any rights or obligations under the Act and the regulations made under it [2 , Part 1 of the Welfare Reform Act and regulations made under it] [4 or under the Jobseekers Act and regulations made under it, or entitled to armed forces independence payment] [3 , Part 4 of the 2012 Act and regulations made under it] (whether of himself or some other person) which depend on his being so entitled, other than for the purposes of the right to payment of that benefit.

AMENDMENTS

1. The Social Security and Child Support (Jobseeker's Allowance) (Consequential Amendments) Regulations 1996 (SI 1996/1345) reg.22(6)(a) and (b) (October 7, 1996).

2. The Employment and Support Allowance (Consequential Provisions) (No. 2) Regulations 2008 (SI 2008/1554) reg.51 (October 27, 2008).

3. The Personal Independence Payments (Supplementary Provisions and Consequential Amendments) Regulations 2013 (SI 2013/388) reg.8 and Sch. para.10(4) (April 8, 2013).

4. The Armed Forces and Reserve Forces Compensation Scheme (Consequential Provisions: Subordinate Legislation) Order 2013 (SI 2013/591) reg.7 and Sch. para.3 (April 8, 2013).

Prevention of double adjustments

17.—No adjustment shall be made under regulations 6 to 10 to any benefit under the Act [1 . . .] [2 the Jobseekers Act [3 , Part 1 of the Welfare Reform Act or Part 4 of the 2012 Act]] by reference to any other benefit, whether under the Act [1 . . .] [2 the Jobseekers Act or Part 1 of the Welfare Reform Act] or otherwise, where the latter benefit has itself been adjusted by reference to the former benefit. 3.102

AMENDMENTS

1. The Social Security and Child Support (Jobseeker's Allowance) (Consequential Amendments) Regulations 1996 (SI 1996/1345) reg.22(7) (October 7, 1996).

2. The Employment and Support Allowance (Consequential Provisions) (No. 2) Regulations 2008 (SI 2008/1554) reg.51 (October 27, 2008).

3. The Personal Independence Payments (Supplementary Provisions and Consequential Amendments) Regulations 2013 (SI 2013/388) reg.8 and Sch. para.10(5) (April 8, 2013).

Regulation 18 omitted. 3.103

SCHEDULE 1 **Regulation 6**

PERSONAL BENEFITS WHICH ARE REQUIRED TO BE ADJUSTED BY REFERENCE TO BENEFITS NOT UNDER CHAPTERS I AND II OF PART II OF THE ACT 3.104

Column (1) *Personal benefit*	*Column (2)* *Other personal benefit by reference to which the benefit in column (1) is to be adjusted*
1. A contribution-based jobseeker's allowance or short-term incapacity benefit.	1. Unemployability supplement and training allowance.
2. Maternity allowance.	2. Training allowance.
3. Widow's benefit, [[1 . . .] widowed parent's allowance] and benefit by virtue of [section 78(9) of the Contributions and Benefits Act] corresponding to widowed mother's allowance or widow's pension.	3. Unemployability supplement, industrial death benefit or war pension death benefit in either case payable to a woman as widow of the deceased and (except where the benefit in column (1) is widow's allowance) training allowance.
4. Retirement pension of any category (except any age addition) or incapacity benefit, severe disablement allowance, contributory employment and support allowance or carer's allowance.	4. Unemployability supplement, industrial death benefit or war pension death benefit in either case payable to that person as the surviving spouse or civil partner, and training allowance.
4A. State pension under Part 1 of the Pensions Act 2014	4A. Unemployability supplement and training allowance.
5. Attendance allowance, the care component of disability living allowance, the daily living component of personal independence payment or armed forces independence payment up to the value of the daily living component of personal independence payment at the enhanced rate;	5. Any benefit based on need for attendance under section 61 or under any Pneumoconiosis and Byssinosis Benefit Scheme, Personal Injuries Scheme, Service Pensions Instruments or 1914–1918 War Injuries Scheme.

Column (1) *Personal benefit*	*Column (2)* *Other personal benefit by reference to which the benefit in column (1) is to be adjusted*
5a. Personal independence payment, attendance allowance or disability living allowance.	5a. Armed forces independence payment
6. Invalidity allowance or an increase in the rate of incapacity benefit in accordance with regulation 10(1) of the Social Security (Incapacity Benefit) Regulation 1994.	6. An increase under section 59(1) of an unemployability supplement and an additional allowance payable only to a beneficiary who is entitled to an unemployability supplement under any Personal Injuries Scheme, Service Pensions Instrument or 1914–1918 War Injuries Scheme.
7. [. . .]	7. [. . .]
8. Unemployability supplement.	8. Any other unemployability supplement.
9. Increase of disablement pension during hospital treatment.	9. Treatment allowance.

AMENDMENTS

For the sake of clarity of the text of the Schedule, it is reproduced without indication of the amendments up to April 2021. The Schedule has been amended by:

The Social Security (Abolition of Injury Benefit) (Consequential) Regulations 1983 (SI 1983/186) (April, 1983).

The Social Security (Severe Disablement Allowance) Regulations 1984 (SI 1984/1303) (November 29, 1984).

The Disability Living Allowance and Disability Working Allowance (Consequential Provisions) Regulations 1991 (SI 1991/2742) (April 6, 1992).

The Social Security (Incapacity Benefit) (Consequential and Transitional Amendments and Savings) Regulations 1995 (SI 1995/829) (April 13, 1995). The Social Security and Child Support (Jobseeker's Allowance) (Consequential Amendments) Regulations 1996 (SI 1996/1345) (October 7, 1996).

The Social Security (Benefits for Widows and Widowers) (Consequential Amendments) Regulations 2000 (SI 2000/1483), reg.6 (April 9, 2001).

Social Security Amendment (Carer's Allowance) Regulations 2002/2497 reg.3 and Sch.2 (April 1, 2003).

The Civil Partnership (Pensions, Social Security and Child Support) (Consequential, etc. Provisions) Order 2005 (SI 2005/2877) (December 5, 2005).

The Employment and Support Allowance (Consequential Provisions) (No. 2) Regulations 2008 (SI 2008/1554), reg.51 (October 27, 2008).

The Personal Independence Payment (Supplementary Provisions and Consequential Amendments) Regulations 2013 (SI 2013/388), reg.8 and Sch. para.10(6) (April 8, 2013).

The Armed Forces and Reserve Forces Compensation Scheme (Consequential Provisions: Subordinate Legislation) Order 2013 (SI 2013/591), reg.7 and Sch. para.3 (April 8, 2013).

The Pensions Act 2014 (Consequential, Supplementary and Incidental Amendments) Order 2015 (SI 2015/1985) art.4(4) (April 6, 2016).

The Pensions Act 2014 (Consequential, Supplementary and Incidental Amendments) Order 2017 (SI 2017/422) art.6 (April 6, 2017).

3.105 *Schedule 2 omitted.*

The Social Security Benefit (Persons Abroad) Regulations 1975

(SI 1975/563) (*as amended*)

ARRANGEMENT OF REGULATIONS

The Secretary of State for Social Services, in exercise of powers conferred upon her by sections 21(3), 30(3), 32(5), 114(1), 131 and 132 of the Social Security Act 1975 and of all other powers enabling her in that behalf, without having referred any proposals on the matter to the National Insurance Advisory Committee or the Industrial Injuries Advisory Council since it appears to her that by reasons of urgency it is inexpedient to do so, hereby makes the following regulations:

Citation, commencement and interpretation

1.—(1) These regulations may be cited as the Social Security Benefit (Persons Abroad) Regulations 1975 and shall come into operation on April 6, 1975. 3.107

(2) In these regulations, unless the context otherwise requires—

"the Act" means the Social Security Act 1975;

[12 . . .]

[3 "child benefit" means benefit under Part I of the Child Benefit Act;]

[4 "the Child Benefit Act" means the Child Benefit Act 1975];

[5 "the Contributions and Benefits Act" means the Social Security Contributions and Benefits Act 1992];

"the Contributions Regulations" means the Social Security (Contributions) Regulations [3 1979];

[3 "entitled to child benefit" includes treated as so entitled;]

"the former Death Grant Regulations" means the National Insurance (Death Grant) Regulations 1973;

"the former Principal Act" means the National Insurance Act 1965;

"the former Widow's Benefit and Retirement Pensions Regulations" means the National Insurance (Widow's Benefit and Retirement Pensions) Regulations 1972;

[6 "guaranteed minimum pension" has the meaning given to it in section 26(2) of the Social Security Pensions Act 1975 as construed in accordance with section 9 of the Social Security Act 1986];

[10 . . .]

"the Industrial Injuries Employment Regulations" means the Social Security (Employed Earners' Employments for Industrial Injuries Purposes) Regulations 1975;

[11 "jobseeker's allowance" means an allowance under the Jobseekers Act 1995 as amended by the provisions of Part 1 of Schedule 14 to the Welfare Reform Act 2012 that remove references to an income-based allowance, and a contribution-based allowance under the Jobseekers Act 1995 as that Act has effect apart from those provisions;]

["the other party" in the case of a person who has been married or been in a civil partnership more than once, refers to the person by virtue of whose contributions that person is entitled to the benefit in question;]

"the Overlapping Benefits Regulations" means the National Insurance (Overlapping Benefit) Regulations 1975;

"the former Old Persons' Pensions Regulations" means the National Insurance (Old Persons' Pensions) Regulations 1970;

"retired" means retired from regular employment;

[7 "serving member of the forces" has the meaning given to it in regulation 1(2) of the Contributions Regulations];"

[9 "shared additional pension" means a shared additional pension under section 55A or the Contributions and Benefits Act;]

"the Special Provisions Regulations" means the Social Security (Benefit) (Married Women and Widows Special Provisions) Regulations 1974;

"the Widow's Benefit and Retirement Pensions Regulations" means the Social Security (Widow's Benefit and Retirement Pensions) Regulations 1974;

"widow's benefit" and "widow's pension" include benefit under section 39(4) of the Act corresponding to a widow's pension or a widowed mother's allowance;

[1 "widowed parent's allowance" means an allowance referred to in section 39A of the Social Security Contributions and Benefits Act 1992;]

and other expressions have the same meanings as in the Act.

(3) Any reference in these regulations to any provision made by or contained in any enactment or instrument shall, except in so far as the

context otherwise requires, be construed as a reference to that provision as amended or extended by any enactment or instrument, and as including a reference to any provision which it re-enacts or replaces, or which may re-enact or replace it, with or without modification.

(4) The rules for the construction of Acts of Parliament contained in the Interpretation Act 1889 shall apply for the purposes of the interpretation of these regulations as they apply for the purposes of the interpretation of an Act of Parliament.

AMENDMENTS

1. The Welfare Reform and Pensions (Persons Abroad: Benefits for Widows and Widowers) (Consequential Amendments) Regulations 2000 (SI 2000/2876) reg.2 (April 9, 2001).
2. The Welfare Reform and Pensions (Persons Abroad: Benefits for Widows and Widowers) (Consequential Amendments) Regulations 2001 (SI 2001/2618) reg.2(2) (August 20, 2001).
3. The Social Security (Child Benefit) (Consequential) Regulations 1977 (SI 1977/342) reg.13(2) (April 4, 1977).
4. The Social Security (Child Benefit) (Consequential) Regulations 1977 (SI 1977/342) reg.13(2) (April 4, 1977).
5. The Social Security (Maternity Grant) Amendment Regulations 1981 (SI 1981/1157) reg.3(2) (April 1, 1982).
6. The Social Security Benefit (Persons Abroad) Amendment (No. 2) Regulations 1990 (SI 1990/621) reg.2(2) (April 6, 1990).
7. The Social Security Benefit (Persons Abroad) Amendment Regulations 1990 (SI 1990/40) reg.2(2) (February 8, 1990).
8. The Social Security (Miscellaneous Provisions) Amendment (No. 2) Regulations 1992 (SI 1992/2595) reg.9 (November 16, 1992).
9. The Social Security (Shared Additional Pension) (Miscellaneous Amendments) Regulations 2005 (SI 2005/1551) (July 6, 2005).
10. The Social Security Benefit (Persons Abroad) (Amendment) Regulations 2010 (SI 2010/788) reg.3 (April 6, 2010).
11. The Universal Credit (Consequential Supplementary, Incidental and Miscellaneous Provisions) Regulations 2013 (SI 2013/630) reg.23(2) (April 29, 2013).
12. The Pensions Act 2014 (Consequential, Supplementary and Incidental Amendments) Order 2017 (SI 2017/422) art.5 (April 6, 2017).

GENERAL NOTE

Interpretation Act 1889

By s.25(2) of the Interpretation Act 1978, the reference to the Interpretation Act 1889 is to be treated as a reference to the 1978 Act. **3.108**

Regulation 1(2) refers to the definition of "serving member of the forces" in the Social Security (Contributions) Regulations 1979 (SI 1979/591). There the item is defined as follows:

> "'serving member of the forces' means a person (not being a person mentioned in Part II of Schedule 3 to these regulations) who, being over the age of 16, is a member of any establishment or organisation in Part I of Schedule 3 to these regulations (being a member who gives full pay service) but does not include any such person while absent on desertion."

Part I of Sch.3 of these Regulations is reproduced in the annotations to reg.3 of the Computation of Earnings Regulations.

Part II of Sch.3 reads as follows:

"By virtue of regulation 113 of these regulations, Her Majesty's forces shall not be taken to consist of any of the establishments or organisations specified in Part I of this Schedule by virtue only of the employment in such establishment of the following persons—

(a) any person who is serving as a member of any naval force of Her Majesty's forces and who (not having been an insured person under the former principal Act or, as the case may be, the National Insurance Act (Northern Ireland) 1966 and not being a contributor under the Act) locally entered that force at an overseas base;

(b) any person who is serving as a member of any military force of Her Majesty's forces and who entered that force, or was recruited for that force outside the United Kingdom, and the depot of whose unit is situated outside the United Kingdom;

(c) any person who is serving as a member of any air force of Her Majesty's forces and who entered that force, or was recruited for that force, outside the United Kingdom, and is liable under the terms of his engagement to serve only in a specified part of the world outside the United Kingdom."

Modification of the Act in relation to [1 incapacity benefit], severe disablement allowance, unemployability supplement and maternity allowance

3.109 **2.**—(1) [2 Except as provided by paragraph (1A) or (1B) below, a] [person shall not be disqualified for receiving [2 any benefit in respect of incapacity]] by reason of being temporarily absent from Great Britain for any day [3 falling within the first 26 weeks beginning with the day following the day on which he left Great Britain] if—

[4 (a) the Secretary of State has certified that it is consistent with the proper administration of the Act that, subject to the satisfaction of one of the conditions in sub-paragraphs (b), (bb) and (c) below, the disqualification under [section 113(1)(a) of the Social Security Contributions and Benefits Act 1992] should not apply, and]

(b) the absence is for the specific purpose of being treated for incapacity which commenced before he left Great Britain, or

[5 (bb) in the case of incapacity benefit, the incapacity for work is the result of a personal injury of a kind mentioned in [section 94(1) of the Social Security Contributions and Benefits Act 1992], and the absence is for the specific purpose of receiving treatment which is appropriate to that injury, or]

[6 (c) on the day on which the absence began he was, and had for the past 6 months continuously been, incapable of work and on the day for which benefit is claimed he has remained continuously so incapable since the absence began]

(d) [7 . . .]

[8 (1A) Subject to paragraph (1B), a person who is in receipt of attendance allowance [14 , disability living allowance [15 , armed forces independence payment under the Armed Forces and Reserve Forces (Compensation Scheme) Order 2011] or personal independence payment under Part 4 of the Welfare Reform Act 2012] shall not by reason of being temporarily absent from Great Britain be disqualified for receiving any benefit in respect of incapacity if—

(a) the absence is for the specific purpose of being treated for incapacity which commenced before he left Great Britain; or

(b) in the case of [2 incapacity benefit] the incapacity for work is the result of a personal injury of a kind mentioned in section 94(1) of the Social Security Contributions and Benefits Act 1992 and the absence is for the specific purpose of receiving treatment which is appropriate to that injury; or

(c) on the day on which the absence began he was, and had for the past 6 months continuously been, incapable of work and on the day for which benefit is claimed he has remained continuously so incapable since the absence began.

(1B) A person who is a member of the family of a serving member of the forces and temporarily absent from Great Britain by reason only of the fact that he is living with that member shall not by reason of being temporarily absent be disqualified—

(a) for receiving any benefit in respect of incapacity except severe disablement allowance if—

(i) the absence is for the specific purpose of being treated for incapacity which began before he left Great Britain, or

(ii) in the case of [1 incapacity benefit] the incapacity for work is the result of a personal injury of the kind mentioned in section 94(1) of the Social Security Contributions and Benefits Act 1992 and the absence is for the specific purpose of receiving treatment which is appropriate to that injury, or

(iii) on the day on which the absence began he was, and had for the past 6 months continuously been, incapable of work and on the day for which benefit is claimed he has remained continuously so incapable since the absence began; or

(b) for the receipt of severe disablement allowance.]

(2) [9 . . .]

(3) [10 . . .]

(4) [10 . . .]

[11 (5) In this regulation—

(a) "benefit in respect of incapacity" means [1 incapacity benefit], severe disablement allowance, an unemployability supplement or a maternity allowance;

(b) "member of the family of a serving member of the forces" means the spouse, [13 civil partner,] son, daughter, step-son, step-daughter, father, father-in-law, step-father, mother, mother-in-law or step-mother of such a member; and

(c) "week" means any period of seven days.]

AMENDMENTS

1. The Social Security (Incapacity Benefit) (Consequential and Transitional Amendments and Savings) Regulations 1995 (SI 1995/829) reg.7 (April 13, 1995).

2. The Social Security Benefit (Persons Abroad) Amendment Regulations 1994 (SI 1994/268) reg.2(2)(a) (March 8, 1994).

3. The Social Security Benefit (Persons Abroad) Amendment Regulations 1994 (SI 1994/268) reg.2(2)(c) (March 8, 1994).

4. The Social Security (Persons Abroad) Amendment Regulations 1977 (SI 1977/1679) reg.2(2) (November 14, 1977); The Social Security (Abolition of Injury Benefit) (Consequential) Regulations 1983 (SI 1983/186) reg.5(2) (April 6, 1983); The

Social Security Benefit (Persons Abroad) Amendment Regulations 1990 (SI 1990/40) reg.2(3)(a)(ii) (February 8, 1990); and The Social Security Benefit (Persons Abroad) Amendment Regulations 1994 (and SI 1994/268) reg.2(2)(d) (March 8, 1994).

5. The Social Security (Abolition of Injury Benefit) (Consequential) Regulatins 1983 (SI 1983/186) reg.5(2) (April 4, 1983); The Social Security Benefit (Persons Abroad) Amendment (No.2) Regulations 1986 (SI 1986/1545) reg.2 (October 1, 1986); and The Social Security (Incapacity Benefit) (Consequential and Transitional Amendments and Savings) Regulations 1995 (SI 1995/829) reg.7(b) (April 13, 1995).

6. The Social Security Benefit (Persons Abroad) Amendment Regulations 1990 (SI 1990/40) reg.2(3)(b) (February 8, 1990); and The Social Security Benefit (Persons Abroad) Amendment Regulations 1994 (SI 1994/268) reg.2(2)(e) (March 8, 1994).

7. The Social Security Benefit (Persons Abroad) Amendment Regulations 1994 (SI 1994/268) reg.2(2)(e) (March 8, 1994).

8. Reg. 2(1A) and (1B) inserted by The Social Security Benefit (Persons Abroad) Amendment Regulations 1994 (SI 1994/268) reg.2(3) (March 8, 1994).

9. The Social Security Benefit (Persons Abroad) Amendment Regulations 1977 (SI 1977/1679) reg.2(4) (November 14, 1977).

10. The Social Security (Incapacity Benefit) (Consequential and Transitional Amendment and Savings) Regulations 1995 (SI 1995/829) reg 7(e) (April 13, 1995).

11. The Social Security Benefit (Persons Abroad) Amendment Regulations 1994 (SI 1994/268) reg.2(4) (March 8, 1994).

12. The Social Security (Severe Disablement Allowance) Regulations 1984 (SI 1984/1303) reg.16 (November 28, 1984).

13. The Civil Partnership (Pensions, Social Security and Child Support) (Consequential, etc. Provisions) Order 2005 (SI 2005/2877) (December 5, 2005).

14. The Personal Independence Payments (Supplementary Provisions and Consequential Amendments) Regulations 2013 (SI 2013/388) reg.8 and Sch. para.8 (April 8, 2013).

15. The Armed Forces and Reserve Forces Compensation Scheme (Consequential Provisions: Subordinate Legislation) Order 2013 (SI 2013/591) reg.7 and Sch. para.1 (April 8, 2013).

DEFINITIONS

"the Act"—reg.1.

"the former Principal Act"—reg.1.

"Great Britain"—by art.1 of the Union with Scotland Act 1706, this means England, Scotland and Wales.

GENERAL NOTE

3.110 This regulation applies to the specified benefits for incapacity. Three conditions must be satisfied for the disqualification in s.113 of the Contributions and Benefits Act to be avoided for the first 26 weeks:

(a) The absence from Great Britain must be temporary.
(b) The Secretary of State must certify that it is consistent with the proper administration of the Act that the disqualification should not apply.
(c) The claimant must establish that either
  (i) the absence is for the specific purpose of being treated for incapacity that existed before he or she left Great Britain; or
  (ii) in the case of incapacity benefit, the incapacity is the result of an industrial injury and the absence is for the specific purpose of receiving treatment appropriate to that injury; or
  (iii) on the day the absence began, the claimant was, and had for six months continuously been, incapable of work and the claimant has been continuously incapable of work since leaving Great Britain.

Paragraph (1A) exempts from the limitation to 26 weeks of the continuation of benefit those in receipt of attendance allowance or disability living allowance who meet the three conditions set out in that paragraph.

Paragraph (1B) makes a similar exemption for someone who is a member of the family of a serving member of the forces temporarily absent from Great Britain as a consequence of that status who meets the conditions set out in the paragraph.

Civil Partnership Act 2004

With effect from December 5, 2005, art.3 of the Civil Partnership Act 2004 (Relations Arising Through Civil Partnership) Order 2005 (SI 2005/3137) applies the provisions of s.246 of the Civil Partnership Act 2004 to the definition of "member of the family of a serving member of the forces" in reg.2(5)(b). Section 246 explains how references to "step" and "in-law" relationships are to be interpreted in the context of civil partnerships. **3.111**

Temporary absence

What amounts to temporary absence is not defined and so is a matter for the exercise of judgment by the adjudicating authorities, though considerable guidance is now available from Commissioners' decisions. In *R(S) 1/85*, Commissioner Edwards-Jones offered the following guidance: **3.112**

> "There is, in my judgment, no universal period by reference to which the issue as to an absence being, or not being, temporary falls to be determined: the particular circumstances of the case are crucial." (para.19).
>
> "The phrase 'temporarily absent from Great Britain' . . . is to be construed as to give rise to the position that whilst demonstration that an absence is 'permanent' will preclude it counting as 'temporary,' demonstration that it is not necessarily 'permanent' does not of itself establish that it is 'temporary.' In particular, an absence may though intended as 'temporary' at its outset cease to count as such if by force of circumstances no certain time (and I do not by a 'certain time' mean necessarily a precise date or hour, but something broader) can be set as to when it will terminate. It is not a 'temporary' absence if it is indefinite." (para.20).

Relevant factors will be all the surrounding circumstances (including in the case of determination by tribunals events subsequent to the adjudication officer's decision: *R(S) 10/83*), which include the claimant's intentions though these will not be decisive: *R(S) 10/83*. As a general rule absences of more than 12 months are not temporary unless there are exceptional circumstances: *R(U) 16/62*. Serious doubts were cast in *R(S) 1/85* on the correctness of *R(S) 9/55* in which it was held that absence of three years and nine months undergoing treatment for tuberculosis in Switzerland was temporary, but the Commissioner in *R(S) 9/55* regarded the case in any event as restricted to its own rather special facts and notes that absences of more than a year will not normally be temporary.

In *CS/207/1990* the claimant suffered from multiple sclerosis and had been resident in Malta for almost seven years because the climate provided relief for his symptoms. He had, nevertheless, expressed a wish to return to Great Britain if and when his health improved sufficiently. Commissioner Johnson upheld the decision of the tribunal that the claimant could not be regarded as temporarily absent from Great Britain.

The Court of Appeal has considered the meaning of the word "temporarily" in this Regulation in *Chief Adjudication Officer v Belmer and Ahmed*, CA, March 16, 1994, *Guardian*, April 18, 1994 reported as *R(S)1/96*. Neill L.J. giving judgment said that it was wrong to construe "temporarily" as being synonymous with "not permanent". Though it would be exceptional to show that an absence lasting for some years remained temporary, the proper approach was to consider whether the absence could be considered as temporary in the light of all the circumstances. The quality of the absence could change with the passage of time.

What began as a temporary absence could change to one of permanent absence. Equally the fact that there was no fixed return date could not be taken as showing that the absence was necessarily not temporary. The claimant's expressed intention would be relevant but not decisive, so there is an element of objectivity in the determination.

CDLA/2089/2004 concerned the interpretation of differently worded reg.2(2)(d) and (e) of the Disability Living Allowance Regulations on temporary absence from Great Britain, but the point the Commissioner makes may well have relevance when the provisions of this regulation are considered. The Commissioner rules that the continuation of benefit payment is based on two facts: first, that the absence from Great Britain must be for a temporary purpose, and secondly, that the absence has not lasted for more than 26 weeks. The period of 26 weeks does not define the word "temporary"; it merely limits to a maximum of 26 weeks the period during which benefit can remain in payment if the absence is temporary (provided that any other conditions set out in the regulations are satisfied).

Secretary of State's certificate

3.113 The certificate condition was introduced in 1975 to limit some of the problems inherent in the test. The regulation introducing it was held to be ultra vires by a Commissioner in *CS/5/76* and the regulation was replaced in 1977 in its current form. This formulation has been held to be lawful: *R(S) 8/83*.

Paragraph (1)(b) and (bb)

3.114 In *R(S) 2/86* a Tribunal of Commissioners reviewed the effect of para.(1)(b) in the light of a sizeable case law and in a majority decision explained that the requirements of para.(1)(b) were threefold:

(1) the claimant must show that immediately prior to the departure from Great Britain, he or she was incapacitated for work by reason of some specific disease or bodily or mental disablement (so pregnancy will not suffice: *R(S) 1/75*); and

(2) the going abroad is for the purpose of having treatment for the condition; and

(3) the condition giving rise to the incapacity abroad is capable of being identified with the condition giving rise to the incapacity subsisting at the date of departure abroad.

The majority specifically left open the question whether or not the incapacity for work arising during absence abroad must have continued unbroken between the start of the absence abroad and the day or days for which the claim is made. Their view was, however, that the period of incapacity need not be continuous. Commissioner Penny, the dissenting Commissioner, doubted the correctness of this view.

In *R(S) 2/86* a number of earlier decisions were qualified. In particular the presumption suggested in *R(S) 6/61* that the specific purpose of going abroad is for treatment where treatment for an incapacity is received abroad was rejected. Statements in *R(S) 1/75* were qualified by making it clear that it remained to be settled to what extent absence abroad could be for the specific purpose of receiving treatment where the initial absence was for some other reason, for example, where a person suffering an incapacity goes abroad for a holiday but subsequently extends the period abroad in order to receive treatment for the incapacity.

Treatment means "some activity by someone other than the claimant": *R(S) 10/51*. So trips abroad for convalescence, for a change of environment or for relaxation will not qualify: *R(S) 1/69*, *R. v National Insurance Commissioner Ex p. McMenemey* (Appendix to *R(S) 2/69*), *R(S) 4/80* and *R(S) 6/81*. Whether treatment involves some specific medical supervision or care is uncertain: *R(S) 2/51* and *R(S) 10/51* seem to assume that it does not, while *R(S) 16/51*, *R(S) 5/61*, *R(S) 10/62* and *R(S) 2/69* seem to assume that it does. Indeed it seems that being under a doctor's professional care may not be conclusive particularly if the incapacity is mental illness: *R(S) 5/61*, though treatment here may include non-medical treatment: *R(S) 1/65*.

Some Commissioners' decisions on absence for the specific purpose of receiving treatment under paras (1)(b) and (bb) have stressed that specific medical supervision is required to bring a claimant within the ambit of the provisions. **3.115**

In *CS/061/1992* Commissioner Morcom adds to the list of such authorities by concluding that treatment by a herbalist in Sri Lanka who "derived his occupation partly by family tradition and partly by experience . . . does not represent the qualified skill or service required to justify the decision that the claimant's absence from Great Britain was for the specific purpose of being treated for his incapacity." (para.5). The more modern authorities requiring specific medical supervision now considerably outnumber the earlier authorities which seem to suggest that treatment need not involve such a regime.

So decision-makers are left with a confusing body of authority on the meaning of treatment from which it is difficult to draw any clear guidance. In such circumstances, tribunals should take great care to make findings of facts as to the precise nature of the incapacity and the treatment proposed for it, including findings as to the personnel who will administer it. Once this has been done, whether it constitutes "treatment" within para.(1)(b) is essentially a matter for the judgment of the tribunal in the light of all the circumstances of the case.

R(S) 1/90 is an important decision of a Tribunal of Commissioners. It contains a comprehensive review of the requirements of reg.2(1)(b) and (bb) on the intention of the claimant in going abroad. The nub of the decision is to be found in paras 29–30: **3.116**

> "**29.** If we were required to approach the problem afresh, we would without hesitation take the view that for paragraph (b) to apply the purpose or intention to be treated (or to receive treatment under paragragh (bb)) must have been formed before the claimant's departure from Great Britain. There is great force in the observations of the Tribunal of Commissioners in *R(S) 2/86* at paragraph 12 . . . and we agree with them that 'it is a necessary and basic requirement for success in invoking regulation 2(1)(b)' that the claimant, in addition to the other requirements 'went abroad for the purpose of having treatment.'
>
> **30.** In our view, the decisions which favour the claimant in the present case—namely, that a claimant will avoid disqualification if, while abroad, he obtains or receives treatment although he had no such purpose or intention at the time of departure—are an over-liberal and erroneous interpretation of paragraph (b). The decisions to which we have referred span a period of 40 years. Overseas travelling facilities have in that period of time been radically changed and a re-appraisal of those earlier decisions is overdue. It falls to this tribunal to make that re-appraisal. We accept the strict construction adopted by the Tribunal of Commissioners in *R(S) 2/86* at paragraph 12, and have reached the decision set out in paragraph 29 above."

The effect of this decision is that the interpretation of the regulation in the following cases is no longer good law: *CS/317/1949(KL)*, *CSS/71/1949*, *R(S) 6/61*, *CS/01/1971*, *R(S) 1/75* and *R(S) 1/77*.

CIB/1956/2001 concerned a claimant who suffered from, among other ailments, eczema of both hands and feet. He had retired from work as a labourer on medical grounds. He received sickness benefit, followed by invalidity benefit which converted to incapacity benefit on its introduction. The principal point in the appeal concerned his absence in India for what was described by the claimant as a holiday but during which he consulted a hakim about his eczema. It was accepted that *R(S) 6/61* remained good authority for the proposition that the claimant's absence abroad must be for the specific purpose of being treated, but need not be for the sole purpose of being treated. The Commissioner goes further and indicates that medical treatment need not be the main purpose of the trip abroad, although an intention to secure treatment must have been in mind before the absence started. Just because a person has treatment abroad, it should not, however, be assumed that this was in mind before the trip began. In this case, there was enough evidence to meet that requirement. The Commissioner says,

> "I have no doubt that the trip was also a holiday and, like the tribunal, I incline to the view that that was the main purpose of the journey. I therefore do not find it surprising that the claimant referred to it as a holiday. However, I accept that the claimant's eczema, which was one cause of his retirement and was obviously defeating Western medical science, was so irritating for the claimant that finding a cure for it added to his desire to go to India, even though he had no high hopes of success. That, in my view, is enough to make "being treated" in India a "specific purpose" of the absence." (para.8).

Paragraph (1)(c)

3.117 This condition is designed to assist the long-term incapacitated. For this group the absence, though temporary, need not be for the specific purpose of receiving treatment.

In *CS/143/1993* the claimant had been awarded sickness benefit followed by invalidity benefit from January 3, 1989 to September 20, 1990. There was then a break in the payment of invalidity benefit until July 8, 1991, because she had been on an employment training course and received an allowance from the Secretary of State. In August 1991 she went on an extended holiday to Australia returning to Great Britain in February 1992. A question arose as to her continued entitlement to invalidity benefit when outside Great Britain. The claimant sought to rely on the provisions of reg.2(1)(c) to sustain her claim to receive the benefit while abroad. The adjudication officer argued that she could not establish the necessary six months' incapacity for work because reg.7(1)(f) of the USI Regulations provides that a day is not to be *treated* as a day of incapacity for work if on that day a person is attending a training course provided by or on behalf of the Secretary of State.

Commissioner Heggs concludes that the adjudication officer's case is misconceived and that provisions included in one set of regulations are not, without clear indication that they are intended to be, to be incorporated into other sets of regulations. The test in reg.2(1)(c) is a *factual* test contained in regulations made for a different purpose than the USI Regulations.

The 1994 amendments

3.118 The Persons Abroad Amendment Regulations 1994 (SI 1994/268) made changes to this regulation with effect from March 8, 1994 which, subject to exceptions, restricted the availability of benefits to a 26 week period.

There is a transitional provision in reg.3 of the amending regulations preserving entitlement to those who already had it in the following terms:

> "**3.**—(1) In this regulation "the former regulation 2" means regulation 2 of the principal Regulations as in force immediately before these Regulations came into force.
>
> (2) Where immediately before the coming into force of these Regulations, a person was absent from Great Britain but by virtue of the former regulation 2 was not disqualified for receiving any benefit, allowance or supplement referred to in paragraph (1) of the former regulation 2, that person shall continue not to be disqualified in respect of any day, if he—
>
> (a) has been continuously absent from Great Britain since these Regulations came into force; and
> (b) would, had the former regulation 2 been in force on that day, have satisfied the provisions of that regulation in respect of that benefit, allowance or supplement."

(SI 1975/563 reg.3) (as amended)

Regulation 3 revoked by The Social Security Benefit (Persons Abroad) Amendment Regulations 1990 (SI 1990/40), reg.3 (February 8, 1990). 3.119

Modification of the Act in relation to widow's benefit, [12 widowed parent's allowance] child's special allowance, guardian's allowance and retirement pension

4.—(1) Subject to the provisions of this regulation and of regulation 5 below, a person shall not be disqualified for receiving widow's benefit, [12 widowed parent's allowance]] child's special allowance, a guardian's allowance [2, a retirement pension of any category [9, a shared additional pension] or graduated retirement benefit] by reason of being absent from Great Britain. 3.120

(2) In the case of a widow's allowance paragraph (1) above shall apply only where either—

(a) the woman or her late husband was in Great Britain at the time of his death; or

(b) the contribution conditions for widowed mother's allowance and widow's pension set out in paragraph 5 of Schedule 3 to [11 the Contributions and Benefits Act] or in regulation [3 6 of the Social Security (Widow's Benefit and Retirement Pensions) Regulations 1979] are satisfied in relation to the woman.

[3 (2A) In the case of a widow's payment, paragraph (1) above shall apply only where—

(a) the woman or her late husband was in Great Britain at the time of his death; or

(b) sub-paragraph (a) above does not apply but the woman returned to Great Britain within 4 weeks of her husband's death; or

(c) the contribution conditions for widowed mother's allowance and widow's pension set out in paragraph 5 of Schedule 3 to [11 the Contributions and Benefits Act] or in regulation 6 of the Social Security (Widow's Benefit and Retirement Pensions) Regulations 1979 are satisfied in relation to the woman.]

(2B) [12 . . .]

[5 (3) In the case of a Category A retirement pension the [6 basic pension] of which falls to be increased under the provisions of [11 section 51A(2) or 52(2) of the Contributions and Benefits Act (special provision for married people and for surviving spouses)], the amount of the increase shall not exceed the sum which would be required to raise the [6 basic pension] of that Category A retirement pension to the sum specified in [11 section 44(4) of the Contributions and Benefits Act] (rate of [6 basic pension] of Category A retirement pension) or the weekly rate of Category B retirement pension specified in [11 paragraph 5 of Part 1 of Schedule 4 to the Contributions and Benefits Act], as the case may be, current at—

[7 (a) the date on which the person whose pension falls to be increased first became entitled to that pension; or]

(b) the date on which that person was last ordinarily resident in Great Britain; whichever is the later.

(4) Where, in the case of Category A retirement pension the [6 additional pension] of which falls to be increased under the provisions of [11 section 52(3) of the Contributions and Benefits Act], the surviving spouse [10 or surviving civil partner] whose pension falls to be so increased, being over

pensionable age at the date of the death of the former spouse [10 or former civil partner], is not ordinarily resident in Great Britain, the amount of the increase shall not exceed the sum which would be required to raise the additional pension of that Category A retirement pension to the maximum prescribed by [11 regulation 3 of the Social Security (Maximum Additional Pension) Regulations 2010] which would have been appropriate had the former spouse [10 or former civil partner] died on—

(a) the date on which the surviving spouse was last ordinarily resident in Great Britain; or

(b) 6th April 1979;

whichever is the later.]

AMENDMENTS

1. The Welfare Reform and Pensions (Persons Abroad: Benefits for Widows and Widowers) (Consequential Amendments) Regulations 2000 (SI 2000/2876) reg.2 (April 9, 2001).

2. The Social Security Benefit (Persons Abroad) Amendment Regulations 1992 (SI 1992/1700) reg.2 (August 5, 1992).

3. The Social Security Benefit (Persons Abroad) Amendment Regulations 1988 (SI 1988/435) reg.2 (April 11, 1988).

4. The Welfare Reform and Pensions (Persons Abroad: Benefits for Widows and Widowers) (Consequential Amendments) Regulations 2001 (SI 2001/2618) reg.2(3) (August 20, 2001).

5. The Social Security Benefit (Persons Abroad) Amendment (No.2) Regulations 1979 (SI 1979/1432) reg.2(b) (November 10, 1979).

6. Social Security Act 1986 s.18(1) (April 6, 1987).

7. The Social Security (Abolition of Earnings Rule) (Consequential) Regulations 1989 (SI 1989/1642) reg.4(3) (October 1, 1989).

8. The Social Security Benefit (Persons Abroad) Amendment (No. 2) Regulations 1979 (SI 1979/1432) reg.2(a) (November 10, 1979).

9. The Social Security (Shared Additional Pension) (Miscellaneous Amendments) Regulations 2005 (SI 2005/1551) (July 6, 2005).

10. The Civil Partnership (Pensions, Social Security and Child Support) (Consequential, etc. Provisions) Order 2005 (SI 2005/2877) (December 5, 2005).

11. The Social Security Benefit (Persons Abroad) (Amendment) Regulations 2010 (SI 2010/788) reg.4 (April 6, 2010).

12. The Pensions Act 2014 (Consequential, Supplementary and Incidental Amendments) Order 2017 (SI 2017/422) art.5 (April 6, 2017).

GENERAL NOTE

3.121 The broad effect of this regulation taken together with regs 5 and 6 is that for the specified benefits, absence abroad is not a disqualifying condition. The reason is that the benefits are contributory, are not related to capacity to work and so require less supervision. Up-rating of benefit applies automatically only to those "ordinarily resident" in Great Britain (see notes to reg.5). A claimant cannot defer retirement if not ordinarily resident in Great Britain (reg.6).

In the case of widow's benefit, the woman or her late husband must additionally have been in Great Britain at the date of his death and the specified contribution conditions have to be met.

Application of disqualification in respect of up-rating of benefits

3.122 **5.**—(1) Where regulations made in consequence of an order under [19 section 150 (annual up-rating of benefits) or 150A (annual uprating of basic pension etc and standard minimum guarantee) of the Social Security

Administration Act 1992] provide for the application of this regulation to any additional benefit becoming payable by virtue of that order, the following provisions of this regulation shall, subject to regulation 12 below and the provisions of those regulations, have effect in relation to the entitlement to that benefit of persons absent from Great Britain.

(2) In this regulation [2 and in regulation 5A]—

(a) references to additional benefit of any description are to be construed as referring to additional benefit of that description which is, or but for this regulation would be, payable by virtue (either directly or indirectly) of the said order; and

(b) "the appointed date" means the date appointed for the coming into force of the said order.

(3) [3 Subject to paragraph (8) and the Schedule below,] where a person is not ordinarily resident in Great Britain immediately before the appointed date the provisions of these regulations (except this regulation) shall not, unless and until he becomes ordinarily resident in Great Britain, affect his disqualification while he is absent from Great Britain for receiving—

(a) in the case of a [19 person] who immediately before the appointed date was a [19 married person or civil partner] and [4 was not entitled to a Category B retirement pension], any additional Category B retirement pension, if immediately before that date [19 the other party to the marriage or civil partnership] [4 was entitled to a Category A retirement pension] and was not ordinarily resident in Great Britain;

[5 (aa) in the case of a married person or civil partner], any additional Category B retirement pension if immediately before the appointed day [19 the other party to the marriage or civil partnership] was entitled to a Category A retirement pension and was not ordinarily resident in Great Britain (whether or not [19 they were married to each other or were partners of the other] immediately before that date);]

[6 (b) in the case of a person who immediately before the appointed date is [18 a widow, a widower or a surviving civil partner], any additional Category B retirement pensions, if the former spouse [18 or former civil partner] had died before the appointed day.]

[19 (ba) in the case of a married person or civil partner entitled to a Category B retirement pension under section 48A of the Contributions and Benefits Act (Category B retirement pension for a married person or a civil partner), other than a case that falls within sub-paragraphs (a) to (b), any additional Category B retirement pension where immediately before the appointed date that person's spouse or civil partner was not ordinarily resident in Great Britain;]

[7 (c) in any other case, any additional retirement pension of any category [17, any additional shared additional pension] or any additional graduated retirement benefit, if that person had become entitled to a retirement pension [17, a shared additional pension] or to graduated retirement benefit before the appointed date;]

(d) any additional widow's benefit [8 or [20 widowed parent's allowance] if the deceased spouse] [18 or deceased civil partner] [9 had become entitled to a Category A retirement pension or had] die before the appointed date;

(e) any additional child's special allowance if her former husband had died before the appointed date;

[10 (f) any additional guardian's allowance in respect of a child if he were entitled to that allowance in respect of that child before the appointed date.]

(4) [11 . . .]

(5) The provisions of these regulations shall not affect the disqualification while absent from Great Britain of a widow who—

(a) is not ordinarily resident in Great Britain immediately before the appointed date, and was entitled to widow's benefit immediately before attaining pensionable age, or would, but for any provision of the Act disqualifying her for the receipt of such benefit, have been so entitled; and

(b) is or becomes entitled to a Category A retirement pension the right to which is determined by taking into account under [12 regulation 8 of the Social Security (Widow's Benefit and Retirement Pensions) Regulations 1979] her husband's contributions;

for receiving any additional Category A retirement pension the right to which is so determined unless and until she becomes ordinarily resident in Great Britain if—

(i) before the appointed date her husband [13 was entitled to a Category A retirement pension] and was not ordinarily resident in Great Britain; or

(ii) he died before the appointed date.

[14 (6) Subject to paragraph (8) and the Schedule below, the provisions of these regulations shall not affect the disqualification while absent from Great Britain of a person referred to in regulation 8 of the Social Security (Widow's Benefit and Retirement Pensions) Regulations 1979, being any such person other than a widow, who—

(a) is not ordinarily resident in Great Britain immediately before the appointed date; and

(b) is or becomes entitled to a Category A retirement pension the right to which is determined by taking into account under regulation 8 of the Social Security (Widow's Benefit and Retirement Pensions) Regulations 1979 the contribution of that person's former spouse [18 or former civil partner];

for receiving any additional Category A retirement pension the right to which is so determined unless and until that person becomes ordinarily resident in Great Britain if—

(i) before the appointed date the former spouse [18 or former civil partner] was entitled to a Category A retirement pension and was not ordinarily resident in Great Britain; or

(ii) the former spouse [18 or former civil partner] died before the appointed date.]

[15 (7) Paragraph (3)(c) of this regulations shall not apply to a person in relation to a Category B retirement pension if that person's spouse [18 or civil partner] was not entitled to a Category A retirement pension before the appointed date and either that person and that person's spouse [18 or civil partner]—

(i) were husband and wife [18 or were civil partners] immediately before that date; or

(ii) became husband and wife [18 or formed a civil partnership] on or after that date.]

[15 (8) The Schedule below shall have effect in relation to disqualifications for receiving additional benefit in the circumstances specified in that

Schedule (being certain cases in which a person was awarded a widow's benefit or a retirement pension or a higher rate of retirement pension between 1st September 1985 and 7th August 1991).]

AMENDMENTS

1. The Social Security Benefit (Persons Abroad) Amendment Regulations 1988 (SI 1988/435) reg.3 (April 11, 1988).
2. The Social Security Benefit (Persons Abroad) Amendment (No. 2) Regulations 1990 (SI 1990/621) reg.2(3) (April 6, 1990).
3. The Social Security Benefit (Persons Abroad) Amendment (No. 2) Regulations 1994 (SI 1994/1832) reg.2(2) (August 6, 1994).
4. The Social Security (Abolition of Earnings Rule) (Consequential) Regulations 1989 (SI 1989/1642) reg.8(3)(a)(i) (October 1, 1989).
5. The Social Security Benefit (Persons Abroad) Amendment (No. 2) Regulations 1994 (SI 1994/1832) reg.2(3) (August 6, 1994).
6. The Social Security Benefit (Persons Abroad) Amendment (No. 2) Regulations 1979 (SI 1979/1432) reg.3(3) (November 11, 1979).
7. The Social Security (Abolition of Earnings Rule) (Consequential) Regulations 1989 (SI 1989/1642) reg.8(3)(a)(ii) (October 1, 1989); and The Social Security Benefit (Persons Abroad) Amendment Regulations 1992 (SI 1992/1700) reg.3 (August 5, 1992).
8. The Welfare Reform and Pensions (Persons Abroad: Benefits for Widows and Widowers) (Consequential Amendments) Regulations 2000 (SI 2000/2876) reg.2 (April 9, 2001).
9. The Social Security (Abolition of Earnings Rule) (Consequential) Regulations 1989 (SI 1989/1642) reg.8(3)(a)(iii) (October 1, 1989).
10. The Social Security (Child Benefit) (Consequential) Regulations 1977 (SI 1977/342) reg.13(3) (April 4, 1977).
11. The Social Security (Child Benefit) (Consequential) Regulations 1977 (SI 1977/342) reg.13(3)(b) (April 4, 1977).
12. The Social Security Benefit (Person Abroad) Amendment (No. 2) Regulations 1979 (SI 1979/1432) reg.3(4) (November 10, 1979).
13. The Social Security (Abolition of Earnings Rule) (Consequential) Regulations 1989 (SI 1989/1642) reg.3(5) (October 1, 1989).
14. The Social Security Benefit (Person Abroad) Amendment (No. 2) Regulations 1979 (SI 1979/1432) reg.3(5) (November 10, 1979); The Social Security (Abolition of Earnings Rule) (Consequential) Regulations 1989 (SI 1989/1642) reg.8(3)(c) (October 1, 1989); and The Social Security Benefit (Persons Abroad) Amendment (No. 2) Regulations 1994 (SI 1994/1832) reg.2(2) (August 6, 1994).
15. The Social Security Benefit (Persons Abroad) Amendment (No. 2) Regulations 1979 (SI 1979/1432) reg.3(6) (November 10, 1979); and The Social Security (Abolition of Earnings Rule) (Consequential) Regulations 1989 (SI 1989/1642) reg.8(3)(d) (October 1, 1989).
16. The Social Security Benefit (Persons Abroad) Amendment (No. 2) Regulations 1994 (SI 1994/1832) reg.2(4) (August 6, 1994).
17. The Social Security (Shared Additional Pension) (Miscellaneous Amendments) Regulations 2005 (SI 2005/1551) (July 6, 2005).
18. The Civil Partnership (Pensions, Social Security and Child Support) (Consequential, etc. Provisions) Order 2005 (SI 2005/2877) (December 5, 2005).
19. The Social Security Benefit (Persons Abroad) (Amendment) Regulations 2010 (SI 2010/788) reg.5 (April 6, 2010).
20. The Pensions Act 2014 (Consequential, Supplementary and Incidental Amendments) Order 2017 (SI 2017/422) art.5 (April 6, 2017).

GENERAL NOTE

3.123 See annotations to reg.4.

Reg.3 of the annual Social Security Benefits Up-rating Regulations provides for this regulation to apply.

"ordinarily resident"

3.124 These words are used rather less frequently in the social security regulations than simple "residence" and must mean something different from "resident". Guidance as to the meaning of ordinary residence was given in *R(P) 1/78*. It imports more than residence (on which see guidance in *R(P)2/67*). In *R(P) 1/78* the Commissioner said "ordinary residence . . . connotes residence in a place with some degree of continuity and apart from accidental and temporary absences." He went on to say that the words are used with the intention of "seeking to exclude from entitlement to an increase persons . . . who live mostly abroad, and come to reside here intermittently without the intention of settling indefinitely." Such persons cannot be said to be ordinarily resident here. Such an approach is consistent with the general law. In *R. v London Borough of Barnet Ex p. Shah* [1983] 2 W.L.R. 16, the House of Lords considered the meaning of ordinary residence as used in regulations made under the Education Act 1962. In the absence of a statutory definition the words are to be given their natural and ordinary meaning. The House of Lords unanimously concluded that ordinary residence referred to a person's "abode in a particular place or country which he has adopted voluntarily and for settled purposes as part of the regular order of his life for the time being, whether of short or long duration." This could not apply to residence which was unlawful, for example because it was in breach of immigration laws. The reasoning of the House of Lords was adopted by the Commissioner in *R(M) 1/85*.

The authorities were reviewed by Newey LJ in *Arthur v HMRC* [2017] EWCA Civ 1756, who helpfully summarised the relevant legal principles as follows:

> "16. Guidance on the meaning of "ordinarily resident" can be found in three decisions of the House of Lords: *Levene v Inland Revenue Commissioners* [1928] AC 217, *Inland Revenue Commissioners v Lysaght* [1928] AC 234 and *R (Shah) v Barnet LBC* [1983] 2 AC 309. Those cases provide authority for the following propositions:
>
> i) The expression "ordinary residence" "connotes residence in a place with some degree of continuity and apart from accidental or temporary absences" (*Levene*, at 225, per Viscount Cave LC);
>
> ii) "[T]he converse to 'ordinarily' is 'extraordinarily' and ... part of the regular order of a man's life, adopted voluntarily and for settled purposes, is not 'extraordinary'" (*Lysaght*, at 243, per Viscount Sumner). Consistently with this, "ordinarily resident" "refers to a man's abode in a particular place or country which he has adopted voluntarily and for settled purposes as part of the regular order of his life for the time being, whether of short or long duration" (*Shah*, at 343, per Lord Scarman);
>
> iii) "Ordinary residence" differs little from "residence" (*Levene*, at 222, per Viscount Cave LC). "Ordinarily resident" means "no more than that the residence is not casual and uncertain but that the person held to reside does so in the ordinary course of his life" (*Lysaght*, at 248, per Lord Buckmaster);
>
> iv) A person can be resident in a place even though "from time to time he leaves it for the purpose of business or pleasure" and, conversely, "a person who has his home abroad and visits the United Kingdom from time to time for temporary purposes without setting up an establishment in this country is not considered to be resident here" (*Levene*, at 222-223, per Viscount Cave LC);
>
> v) A person can also be resident in a place even though he would prefer to be elsewhere. In *Lysaght*, Lord Buckmaster said (at 248):

"A man might well be compelled to reside here completely against his will; the exigencies of business often forbid the choice of residence, and though a man may make his home elsewhere and stay in this country only because business compels him, yet none the less, if the periods for which and the conditions under which he stays are such that they may be regarded as constituting residence, as in my opinion they were in this case, it is open to the Commissioners to find that in fact he does so reside";

vi) A person may reside in more than one place (*Levene*, at 223, per Viscount Cave LC);

vii) "Ordinary residence" is not synonymous with "domicile" or "permanent home" (*Shah*, at 342-343 and 345, per Lord Scarman);

viii) "Immigration status" "may or may not be a guide to a person's intention in establishing a residence in this country" (*Shah*, 348, per Lord Scarman); and

ix) "There are two, and no more than two, respects in which the mind of the 'propositus' is important in determining ordinary residence": "[t]he residence must be voluntarily adopted" and "there must be a degree of settled purpose", which could potentially be "a specific limited purpose" (*Shah*, at 344 and 348, per Lord Scarman). Lord Scarman explained in *Shah* (at 344):

"The purpose may be one; or there may be several. It may be specific or general. All that the law requires is that there is a settled purpose. This is not to say that the 'propositus' intends to stay where he is indefinitely; indeed his purpose, while settled, may be for a limited period. Education, business or profession, employment, health, family, or merely love of the place spring to mind as common reasons for a choice of regular abode. and there may well be many others. All that is necessary is that the purpose of living where one does has a sufficient degree of continuity to be properly described as settled.""

CP/3638/2006 was a complex case which concerned the question of the up-rating of a wife's benefit following the death of her husband. The claim in issue was initially by a wife, but later by a widow (the appellant). Her husband had become entitled to a Category A retirement pension in March 1976. When he emigrated to Canada the amount of that pension ceased to be up-rated; it was frozen at the November 1975 rate. In September 2001 the appellant married him. She then became entitled to a Category B retirement pension based upon his contributions. That pension was fixed at the November 1975 rate rather than the higher September 2001 rate. The husband died in May 2002 and the appellant's claim was converted to one on widowhood. The Commissioner ruled that there had been a change of status, the effect of which was that the restriction on up-rating applied only from the new award which should be made at the rate effective at the time of that award.

The decision has been reversed on appeal as *SSWP v Yates* [2009] EWCA Civ 479. Carnwath L.J., delivering the judgment of the Court reversed the Commissioner essentially on the application of the policy behind the restriction on up-rating. He says:

"37. I have not found this an easy question to resolve. I see the force of the Commissioner's interpretation, on a strict reading of the wording of the regulation. However, it makes no sense in practical terms. The general statutory policy (under section 113) is to deprive those absent from the country from any entitlement to such benefits, but to restore it only to the extent that Regulations provided. It is hard to see any reason for restoring the benefit for husbands at rates frozen by reference to the time when they left the country, while allowing a more generous rate for their wives, whose entitlement is equally dependent on their husbands' contributions. There is therefore a strong incentive to read any ambiguity in the Regulations so as to accord with the evident policy intention."

AY v SSWP (RP) [2011] UKUT 324 (AAC) is the decision of the Upper Tribunal on the remission of the case to the Upper Tribunal following the judgment of the Court of Appeal in *SSWP v Yates* [2009] EWCA Civ 479. The Judge addresses two remaining issues: (1) whether reg.5 is ultra vires; and (2) whether there has been discrimination in breach of the European Convention on Human Rights.

On the first issue, the judge finds that reg.5 is not ultra vires, though it is poorly drafted. On the second issue, the judge finds, on a concession by the Secretary of State, that there has been a breach of art.14 ECHR when read with art.1 of Protocol 1. The judge also concludes that the situation falls within the ambit of art.8 ECHR, but that the outcome would be exactly the same.

[1 Rate of guaranteed minimum pension for the purposes of section 29 of the Pensions Act

3.125 **5A.**—Where a person is absent from Great Britain and disqualified for receiving additional Category A or Category B retirement pension, additional widowed mother's allowance [2, [3 . . .] widowed parent's allowance] or additional widow's pension then—

(a) the rate of guaranteed minimum pension shall for the purposes only of section 29(1) of the Pensions Act be determined in his case as if any Order under section 37A of the Pensions Act which came into force while he was disqualified had instead come into force on the first day on which he ceased to be disqualified, and

(b) so long as the person is disqualified, section 37A(7) shall apply to him as if the reference to section 29(1) were omitted.]

AMENDMENTS

1. The Social Security Benefit (Persons Abroad) Amendment (No. 2) Regulations 1990 (SI 1990/621) reg.2(4) (April 6, 1990).

2. The Welfare Reform and Pensions (Persons Abroad: Benefits for Widows and Widowers) (Consequential Amendments) Regulations 2000 (SI 2000/2876) reg.2 (April 9, 2001).

3. The Pensions Act 2014 (Consequential, Supplementary and Incidental Amendments) Order 2017 (SI 2017/422) art.5 (April 6, 2017).

Modification of right to elect to be treated as not having retired

3.126 **6.**—Notwithstanding the provisions of regulation 2 of the Widow's Benefit and Retirement Pensions Regulations [1 . . .] a person who is not ordinarily resident in Great Britain shall not be entitled to elect that that regulation shall apply in his case.

AMENDMENT

1. The Social Security (Abolition of Earnings Rule) (Consequential) Regulations 1989 (SI 1989/1642) reg.8(4) (October 1, 1989).

GENERAL NOTE

3.127 See annotations to reg.4.

3.128 *Regulation 7 revoked by The Social Security Benefit (Persons Abroad) Amendment Regulations 1990 (SI 1990/40) reg.3 (February 8, 1990).*

Modification of the Act in relation to age addition

8.—(1) A person shall not be disqualified for receiving age addition by reason of being absent from Great Britain if— 3.129

(a) he is ordinarily resident in Great Britain; or

(b) he was ordinarily resident in Great Britain and was entitled to age addition before he ceased to be ordinarily so resident; or

(c) in the case of a person who ceased to be ordinarily resident in Great Britain before September 20, 1971, he is entitled to a retirement pension of any category and, by virtue of an Order in Council made under section 143 of the Act or under section 105 of the former Principal Act, he is not disqualified for receiving that pension at a higher rate than was applicable in his case when he was last ordinarily resident in Great Britain; or

(d) in the case of a person who ceased to be ordinarily resident in Great Britain on or after September 20, 1971, he is entitled to a retirement pension of any category, and had he ceased to be ordinarily resident in Great Britain before that date, by virtue of an Order in Council made under section 143 of the Act or under section 105 of the former Principal Act, he would not have been disqualified for receiving that pension at a higher rate after that date than before it.

(2) Where a person is entitled to a retirement pension of any category at a rate which is calculated by reference to any period completed by that person in some territory outside Great Britain, any age addition to which he may be entitled shall be calculated as if it were an increase in that pension.

General Note

On the meaning of "ordinarily resident" see annotations to reg.5. 3.130

Modification of the Act in relation to title to [1 . . .] disablement benefit and industrial death benefit

9.—(1) [2 . . .] 3.131

(2) [3 . . .]

(3) A person shall not be disqualified for receiving [4 disablement benefit (other than any increase thereof under sections 58, 59, 61, 62, 63 or 66 of the Act)] by reason of being absent from Great Britain.

(4) A person shall not be disqualified for receiving an increase of disablement pension in respect of the need for constant attendance under section 61, or under regulations made under section 159(3), or in respect of exceptionally severe disablement under section 63, of the Act, by reason of being temporarily absent from Great Britain during the period of 6 months from the date on which such absence commences or during such longer period as the Secretary of State may, having regard to the purpose of the absence and any other factors which appear to him to be relevant, allow.

(5) A person shall not be disqualified for receiving [5 reduced earnings allowance under section 59A of the Act,] by reason of being temporarily absent from Great Britain during the period of 3 months from the date on which such absence commences or during such longer period as the Secretary of State may, having regard to the purpose of the absence and

any other factors which appear to him to be relevant, allow, so however that—

(a) such absence or any part thereof is not for the purpose of or in connection with any employment, trade or business;
(b) a claim as a result of which a decision is given awarding such allowance in respect of such period of absence or part thereof was made before the commencement of such absence; and
(c) the period taken into account by the award of such allowance to that person either includes the day of commencement of such absence or follows a period so taken into account which includes that day without there being a break in entitlement by that person to such increase from that day.

(6) A person shall not be disqualified for receiving industrial death benefit by reason of being absent from Great Britain.

[[6] (7) A person shall not be disqualified for receiving retirement allowance under paragraph 13 of Schedule 7 to the Contributions and Benefits Act by reason of being absent from Great Britain.]

AMENDMENTS

1. The Social Security (Abolition of Injury Benefit) (Consequential) Regulations 1983 (SI 1983/186) reg.5(3) (April 6, 1983).

2. The Social Security (Abolition of Injury Benefit) (Consequential) Regulations 1983 (SI 1983/186) reg.5(4) (April 6, 1983).

3. The Social Security (Persons Abroad) Amendment Regulations 1977 (SI 1977/1679) reg.2(4) (November 14, 1977).

4. The Social Security (Industrial Injuries and Diseases) (Miscellaneous Provisions) Regulations 1986 (SI 1986/1561) reg.4(a) (October 1, 1986).

5. The Social Security (Industrial Injuries and Diseases) (Miscellaneous Provisions) Regulations 1986 (SI 1986/1561) reg.4(b) (October 1, 1986).

6. The Social Security (Miscellaenous Provisions) Amendment (No.2) Regulations 1992 (SI 1992/2595) reg.10 (November 16, 1992).

Modification of the Act in relation to attendance allowance

3.132 **10.**—A person shall not be disqualified for receiving attendance allowance [[1] or disability living allowance] by reason of being absent from Great Britain.

AMENDMENT

1. The Disability Living Allowance and Disability Working Allowance (Consequential Provisions) Regulations 1991 (SI 1991/2742) reg.2(2) (April 6, 1992).

3.133 *Regulation 10A revoked by The Disability Living Allowance and Disability Working Allowance (Consequential Provisions) Regulations 1991 (SI 1991/2742) reg.2(3) (April 6, 1992).*

Modification of the Act in relation to [[2] carer's allowance]

3.134 [[1] **10B.**—A person shall not be disqualified for receiving [[2] a carer's allowance] by reason of being absent from Great Britain.]

AMENDMENTS

1. The Social Security (Invalid Care Allowance) Regulations 1976 (SI 1976/409) reg.20 (April 12, 1976).

2. The Social Security Amendment (Carer's Allowance) Regulations 2002 (SI 2002/2497) reg.3 and Sch.2 (April 1, 2003).

Modification of Parts II and III of the Act in relation to accidents happening or prescribed diseases contracted outside Great Britain

10C.—(1) In this regulation— 3.135

"prescribed area" means an area over which Norway or any member State [4 ...] exercises sovereign rights for the purpose of exploring the seabed and subsoil and exploiting their natural resources, being an area outside the territorial seas of Norway or such member State;

"prescribed disease" means a disease or injury prescribed for the purposes of Chapter V of Part II of the Act; and

"prescribed employment" means employment in a prescribed area in connection with the exploration of the seabed and subsoil and the exploitation of the natural resources of that area, or prescribed employment as defined in regulation 11 of these regulations (modification of the Act in relation to the United Kingdom continental shelf).

(2) Where on or after 30th November 1964 a person sustains or has sustained an accident or contracts or has contracted a prescribed disease while outside Great Britain, for the purposes of Chapter IV or V of Part II of the Act (benefit for industrial injuries and diseases) [section 94(5) of the Social Security Contributions and Benefits Act 1992] or regulation 14 of the Social Security (Industrial Injuries) (Prescribed Diseases) Regulations 1975 shall not operate to make benefit not payable in respect of that accident or prescribed disease if that person—

(a) in connection with prescribed employment has sustained the accident or contracted the prescribed disease in a prescribed area, or while travelling between one prescribed area and another, or while travelling between a designated area (as defined in regulation 11 of these regulations) and a prescribed area, or while travelling between Norway [4, a member State or the United Kingdom] and a prescribed area; or

(b) has sustained the accident or contracted the prescribed disease while in the territory of a member State [4 ...].

[1 (2A) Where a person sustains an accident or contracts a prescribed disease while outside Great Britain in circumstances to which paragraph (2)(a) applies and the employment of that person would, but for the employment being outside of Great Britain, have been employed earner's employment, that employment shall for the purposes of Chapter IV or V of Part II of the Act (benefit for industrial injuries and diseases) be treated as employed earner's employment if:—

(a) that person is ordinarily resident in Great Britain and immediately before the commencement of the employment was resident therein, and

(b) the employer of that person has a place of business in Great Britain.]

(3) Where, before the date on which this regulation comes into operation, a decision has been given disallowing a claim for industrial injuries benefit in respect of an accident sustained or a prescribed disease contracted on or after 30th November 1964, then notwithstanding the provisions of section 107(6)(b) of the Act (decision that an accident not an industrial accident not reviewable) that decision may be reviewed by an insurance officer under [section 25(1)(b) of the Social Security Administration Act 1992] (review

on ground of relevant change of circumstances) if he is satisfied that had paragraphs (1) and (2) of this regulation been in force when that decision was given those paragraphs would have applied, but a decision on review under this paragraph shall not make industrial injuries benefit payable for any period before the date on which this regulation comes into operation.

(4) Paragraph (3) of this regulation shall apply to a decision refusing a declaration that an accident was an industrial accident as it applies to a decision disallowing a claim for industrial injuries benefit.

[2 (5) Where on or after October 1, 1986 a person to whom this paragraph applies sustains an accident arising out of, and in the course of, his employment, or contracts a prescribed disease due to the nature of his employment, such employment shall for the purposes of Chapters IV and V of Part II of the Act (benefit for industrial injuries and diseases) be treated as employed earner's employment notwithstanding that he is employed outside Great Britain, and any benefit which would be payable under those chapters but for the provisions of [section 94(5) of the Social Security Contributions and Benefits Act 1992] and regulation 14 of the Social Security (Industrial Injuries) (Prescribed Diseases) Regulations 1985 shall be payable from the date of his return to Great Britain notwithstanding that the accident happened or the disease was contracted while he was outside it.

(6) Paragraph (5) applies to any person in respect of whom Class 1 contributions are payable by virtue of regulation 120 of the Social Security (Contributions) Regulations 1979 or who is paying Class 2 (volunteer development workers) contributions under Case G of those regulations.]

AMENDMENTS

1. The Social Security Benefit (Persons Abroad) Amendment Regulations 1979 (SI 1982/388) reg.2 (April 14, 1982).

2. Paragraphs (5) and (6) added by the Social Security Benefit (Persons Abroad) Amendment (No. 2) Regulations 1986 (SI 1986/1545) reg.3 (October 1, 1986).

3. The Social Security Benefit (Persons Abroad) Amendment Regulations 1979 (SI 1979/463) reg.2 (April 17, 1979).

4. The Social Security (Amendment) (EU Exit) Regulations 2019 (SI 2019/128) reg.4 and Schedule (as applied by European Union (Withdrawal Agreement) Act 2020 Sch.5 para.1(1)) (December 31, 2020).

Modification of the Act in relation to employment on the Continental Shelf

3.136 **11.**—(1) In this regulation—

"the Continental Shelf Act" means the Continental Shelf Act 1964;

"designated area" means any area which may from time to time be designated by Order in Council under the Continental Shelf Act as an area within which the rights of the United Kingdom with respect to the seabed and subsoil and their natural resources may be exercised;

"prescribed disease" means a disease or injury prescribed for the purposes of [sections 108–110 of the Social Security Contributions and Benefits Act 1992]; and

[1 "prescribed employment" means any employment (whether under a contract of service or not) in any designated area or prescribed area, being employment in connection with any activity mentioned in section 23(2) of the Oil and Gas (Enterprise) Act 1982 in any designated area or in any prescribed area]; and

[1 "prescribed area" means any area over which Norway or any member State [4 . . .] exercises sovereign rights for the purpose of exploring the seabed and subsoil and exploiting their natural resources, being an area outside the territorial seas of Norway or such member State, or any other area which is from time to time specified under section 22(5) of the Oil and Gas (Enterprise) Act 1982.]

[3 (1A) Where a claimant would be entitled to a [5 . . .] jobseeker's allowance but for section 1(2)(i) of the Jobseekers Act 1995 (conditions of entitlement to a jobseeker's allowance: requirement to be in Great Britain), he shall be entitled to a [5 . . .] jobseeker's allowance notwithstanding his absence from Great Britain if—

(a) the absence from Great Britain is due to his being or having been in prescribed employment in a designated area; or

(b) subject to paragraph (2B), he is, in connection with prescribed employment—

(i) in a prescribed area; or

(ii) travelling between one prescribed area and another; or

(iii) travelling between a designated area and a prescribed area; or

(iv) travelling between Norway [6, a member State or the United Kingdom] and a prescribed area.]

(2) Where benefit under Part II of the Act would, but for the provisions of [section 113(1)(a) of the Social Security Contributions and Benefits Act 1992] (absence from Great Britain), be payable to a person in a designated area, that benefit shall be payable notwithstanding the absence of that person from Great Britain, if the absence is due to his being or having been in prescribed employment in [1 a designated area].

[3 (2A) Subject to paragraph (2B) where benefit under Part II of the Act would be payable to a person were that person in Great Britain, that person shall not be disqualified for receiving such benefit by reason only of the fact that he is, in connection with prescribed employment:—

(a) in a prescribed area; or

(b) travelling between one prescribed area and another; or

(c) travelling between a designated area and a prescribed area; or

(d) travelling between Norway [6, a member State or the United Kingdom] and a prescribed area.

(2B) Paragraphs (1A) and (2A) shall not apply where, under the legislation administered by Norway or any member State [6. . .] benefit is payable in respect of a person for the same contingency and for the same period for which benefit is claimed under the Act.]

(3) Where benefit under Chapter IV or V of Part II of the Act would, but for the provisions of [section 94(5) of the Social Security Contributions and Benefits Act 1992], be payable to a person in respect of an accident arising out of and in the course of, or a prescribed disease due to the nature of, any employment by virtue of which any person is treated as an employed earner under paragraph 7 of Part I of Schedule 1 to the Industrial Injuries Employments Regulations, that benefit shall be payable notwithstanding that the accident happens or the disease is contracted while such person is outside Great Britain, if at the time that the accident happens or the disease is contracted the person is either in a designated area or travelling from one designated area to another or from or to Great Britain to or from a designated area.

(4) The provisions of the Act and of the regulations and orders made thereunder[3, and the Jobseekers Act 1995 and regulations made

thereunder] shall, so far as they are not inconsistent with the provisions of this regulation, apply in relation to persons in prescribed employment with this modification, that where such a person is, on account of his being outside Great Britain by reason of his employment, being prescribed employment, unable to perform any act required to be done either forthwith or on the happening of a certain event or within a specified time, he shall be deemed to have complied with that requirement if he performs the act as soon as is reasonably practicable, although after the happening of the event or the expiration of the specified time.

AMENDMENTS

1. The Social Security and Statutory Sick Pay (Oil and Gas (Enterprise) Act 1982) (Consequential) Regulations (SI 1982/1738) reg.2 (December 31, 1982).
2. Paras (2A) and (2B) added by The Social Security and Statutory Sick Pay (Oil and Gas (Enterprise) Act 1982) (Consequential) Regulations 1982 (SI 1982/1738), reg.2 (December 31, 1982). Word added to para.(2B) by The Jobseeker's Allowance Regulations 1996 (SI 1996/207) reg.165(3) (October 7, 1996).
3. The Jobseeker's Allowance Regulations 1996 (SI 1996/207) reg.165(4) (October 7, 1996).
4. The Jobseeker's Allowance Regulations 1996 (SI 1996/207) reg 165(2) (October 7, 1996).
5. The Universal Credit (Consequential, Supplementary, Incidental and Miscellaneous Provisions) Regulations 2013 (SI 2013/630) reg.23(3) (April 29, 2013).
6. The Social Security (Amendment) (EU Exit) Regulations 2019 SI 2019/128, reg.4 and Schedule (as applied by European Union (Withdrawal Agreement) Act 2020 Sch.5 para.1(1)) (December 31, 2020).

Modification of the Act in relation to the Channel Islands

3.137 **12.**—(1) Notwithstanding any provisions of the Act or of these regulations a person shall not—

(a) be disqualified for receiving any benefit under the Act by reason of absence from Great Britain [1 . . .];
(b) be disentitled to a maternity grant in respect of a confinement outside Great Britain; or
(c) be disqualified for receiving a death grant in respect of a death occurring outside Great Britain,

if that person is, or, as the case may be, that confinement or that death occurred, in a part of the Channel Islands which is not subject to an order made under section 143 of the Act or section 105 of the former Principal Act.

(2) A person who—

(a)
  (i) is in any part of the Channel Islands which is not the subject of an order made under section 143 of the Act or section 84 of the National Insurance (Industrial Injuries) Act 1965, or
  (ii) is going from (or to) Great Britain to (or from) such a part of the Channel Islands; and who
(b) suffers an industrial accident in the course of his employment (being employed earner's employment by virtue of regulation 94 of the Contributions Regulations),

shall, subject to the provisions of [section 95 of the Social Security Contributions and Benefits Act 1992], be treated as if the employment were employed earner's employment for the purposes of industrial injuries and as if the accident occurred in Great Britain.

AMENDMENT

1. The Social Security and Child Support (Jobseeker's Allowance) (Consequential Amendments) Regulations 1996 (SI 1996/1345) reg.15(2) (October 7, 1996).

Modification of the Act in relation to a dependant

13.—A husband or wife [1 or civil partner] shall not be disqualified for receiving any increase (where payable) of benefit in respect of his or her spouse [1 or civil partner] by reason of the spouse's [1 or civil partner's] being absent from Great Britain provided that the spouse [1 or civil partner] is resident with [1 the husband, wife or civil partner], as the case may be. 3.138

AMENDMENT

1. The Civil Partnership (Pensions, Social Security and Child Support) (Consequential, etc. Provisions) Order 2005 (SI 2005/2877) (December 5, 2005).

GENERAL NOTE

See annotations to reg.2 of the Persons Residing Together Regulations. 3.139

[1Modification of the Act in relation to title to benefit for beneficiary's child dependants

13A.—(1) By reason only of the fact that he is not entitled to child benefit in respect of a child, a person shall not be disentitled from receiving a benefit or an allowance or an increase of a benefit or an allowance under the Act in respect of a child (hereafter in this regulation referred to as "child dependency benefit") in respect of that child for any period during which he and the child are, or the child is, absent from Great Britain in a country in circumstances in which he would, in pursuance of any agreement with the government of a country outside the United Kingdom, be entitled to receive child dependency benefit in respect of the child were he entitled to child benefit in respect of the child if— 3.140

(a) he would, or could, had he made an appropriate claim, have been entitled to child benefit in respect of the child had all the requirements of [section 146(2) and (3) of the Social Security Contributions and Benefits Act 1992] (requirements as to presence in Great Britain) been satisfied; and

(b) in a case where he would not be treated for the purposes of [Part IX of the Social Security Contributions and Benefits Act 1992] as having the child living with him, he is contributing to the cost of providing for the child, in addition to any contribution he may be required to make under the Act, at a weekly rate not less than that of the child benefit which would be payable to him in respect of the child were child benefit so payable to him; and

(c) no other person is entitled to child benefit in respect of the child.

(2) For any period during which a person who is absent from Great Britain would satisfy the requirements of paragraph (1) in relation to a child but for the fact that that child is present in Great Britain that child shall, for the purposes of that paragraph, be treated as being present in the country in which that person is.

(3) By reason only of the fact that he is not entitled to child benefit in respect of a child, a person shall not be disentitled from receiving child dependency benefit in respect of that child for any period during which he or the child is, or both of them are, absent from Great Britain in circumstances in which, otherwise than in pursuance of such an agreement as is referred to in paragraph (1) or of regulations made under section 142 of the Act (co-ordination with Northern Ireland) were he entitled to child benefit in respect of the child he would be entitled to receive child dependency benefit in respect of the child if—

(a) he would, or could had he made an appropriate claim, have been entitled to child benefit in respect of the child had all the requirements of [section 146(2) and (3) of the Social Security Contributions and Benefits Act 1992] (requirements as to presence in Great Britain) been satisfied; and

(b) in a case where he would not be treated for the purposes of [Part IX of the Social Security Contributions and Benefits Act 1992] as having the child living with him, he is contributing to the cost of providing for the child, in addition to any contribution he may be required to make under the Act, at a weekly rate not less than that of the child benefit which would be payable to him in respect of the child were child benefit so payable to him; and

(c) he establishes that any absence from Great Britain of himself or the child was, when it began, intended to be temporary and has throughout continued to be temporary; and

(d) no other person is entitled to child benefit in respect of the child.

(4) For the purpose of paragraph (1), such a person or child as is there referred to may be treated as being absent from Great Britain notwithstanding that he has not previously been present in Great Britain; and for the purposes of paragraph (3), a child born during the absence from Great Britain of his mother shall, if she was pregnant of that child at a time when she was present in Great Britain, be treated as having been present in Great Britain on the date on which his mother was last present in Great Britain before the child was born.

(5) Where a person—

(a) immediately before returning to Great Britain was entitled to receive child dependency benefit in respect of a child; and

(b) would on his return to Great Britain have continued to be entitled to receive child dependency benefit in respect of that child were he entitled to child benefit in respect of the child,

he shall not be disentitled from receiving child dependency benefit in respect of the child by reason only of the fact that he is not entitled to child benefit in respect of the child if—

(i) he would, or could had he made an appropriate claim, have been entitled to child benefit in respect of the child had all the requirements of [section 146(2) and (3) of the Social Security Contributions and Benefits Act 1992] (requirements as to presence in Great Britain) been satisfied; and

(ii) in a case where he would not be treated for the purposes of [Part IX of the Social Security Contributions and Benefits Act 1992] as having the child living with him, he is contributing to the cost of providing for the child, in addition to any contribution he may be required to make under the Act, at a weekly rate not less than that of the child benefit which would be payable to him in respect of the child were child benefit so payable to him; and

(iii) no other person is entitled to child benefit in respect of the child.

(6) Where a person who was absent from Great Britain immediately before April 4, 1977, (the date on which child benefit first becomes payable) or a subsequent date on which the rate or any of the rates of child benefit is or are increased—

(a) is entitled to receive child dependency benefit in respect of a child for a continuous period beginning before and continuing after that date; and

(b) no other person is entitled to child benefit in respect of that child for that period,

any provision made pursuant to section 17(1) or (4) of the Child Benefit Act whereby, having regard to the introduction of child benefit or to an increase in the rate or any of the rates of child benefit, the weekly rate of child dependency benefit payable in respect of that child would be subject to a reduction shall not have effect so as (by reason only of that reduction) to reduce the total weekly rate of benefit (including benefit (if any) which is not child dependency benefit payable in respect of that child) payable to that person below the total weekly rate of such benefit payable to him immediately before that date.]

AMENDMENT

1. The Social Security (Child Benefit) (Consequential) Regulations 1977 (SI 1977/342) reg.13(5) (April 4, 1977).

GENERAL NOTE

The effect of this regulation is that if the claimant's child dependant is abroad, the claimant remains entitled to an increase for the child if the claimant is entitled to child benefit for the child. See Child Benefit (Residence and Persons Abroad) Regulations 1976 (SI 1976/963). **3.141**

If the claimant is not entitled to child benefit but would be if in Great Britain, the claimant will receive the increase if there is no one else entitled to child benefit for the child.

Regulation 13B revoked by The Social Security and Child Support (Jobseeker's Allowance) (Consequential Amendments) Regulations 1996 (SI 1996/1345), Sch. (October 7, 1996). **3.142**

Administrative arrangements about payment of benefits

14.—Where the right to benefit arises by virtue of these regulations the benefit shall be payable subject to the furnishing of such information and evidence as the Secretary of State may from time to time require; and the Secretary of State shall make arrangements as to the time and manner of payment which shall have effect in place of the provisions as to time and manner of payment which would have been applicable by virtue of other regulations made under the Act [[1], or in connection with jobseeker's allowance,] if the person concerned had not been absent from Great Britain. **3.143**

AMENDMENT

1. The Social Security and Child Support (Jobseeker's Allowance) (Consequential Amendments) Regulations 1996 (SI 1996/1345) reg.15(3) (October 7, 1996).

3.144 *Regulation 15 omitted.*

[1 SCHEDULE **Regulation 5(8)**

UP-RATING IN RESPECT OF CERTAIN AWARDS MADE BETWEEN 1ST SEPTEMBER 1985 AND 7TH AUGUST 1991

3.145 **1.**—A person referred to in a case set out in column (1) shall not be disqualified by reason of being absent from Great Britain for receiving any additional widow's benefit or retirement pension which became payable by virtue of an up-rating order which came into force on or before the date referred to in column (3) if—

(a) the award referred to in column (1) was made during the period specified in column (2); and

(b) immediately before 6th August 1994 that person was being paid a widow's benefit or a retirement pension (as the case may be) at the rate current at the date referred to in column (3).

(1) Case	(2) Period in which award was made	(3) Date after which disqualification to take effect
1. A woman who was awarded a widow's benefit	after 30th May 1988 but not later than 19th February 1990	the date on which she became entitled to a widow's benefit
2. A woman who had been receiving a Category B retirement pension and was awarded that pension at a higher rate after her husband's death	after 13th September 1988 but not later than 6th August 1991	the date of her husband's death
3. A woman who was first awarded a Category B retirement pension on the death of her husband after she attained the age of 60	after 31st January 1990 but not later than 6th August 1991	the date on which she became entitled to a Category B retirement pension
4. A man who had been receiving a Category A retirement pension and was awarded a Category B retirement pension after his wife's death	after 16th November 1986 but not later than 6th August 1991	the date on which he became entitled to a Category B retirement pension
5. A woman who had been receiving a Category B retirement pension and was awarded a Category A retirement pension	after 1st September 1985 but not later than 6th August 1991	the date on which she became entitled to a Category A retirement pension
6. A person who was awarded a Category A retirement pension determined by taking into account the contributions of his or her former spouse under regulation 8 of the Social Security (Widow's Benefit and Retirement Pensions) Regulations 1979	after 16th November 1986 but not later than 6th August 1991	the date on which that person first became entitled to a Category A retirement pension

2.—In paragraph 1 "up-rating order" means an order which was made under section 124 of the Act or section 63 of the Social Security Act 1986.]

AMENDMENT

1. Schedule added by The Social Security Benefit (Persons Abroad) Amendment (No. 2) Regulations 1994 (SI 1994/1832) reg.3 (August 6, 1994).

The Social Security Benefit (Persons Residing Together) Regulations 1977

(SI 1977/956) (*as amended*)

ARRANGEMENT OF REGULATIONS

The Secretary of State for Social Services, in exercise of the powers conferred upon him by section 22(1) of the Social Security (Miscellaneous Provisions) Act 1977 and of all other powers enabling him in that behalf hereby makes the following regulations:

Citation, commencement and interpretation

1.—(1) These regulations may be cited as the Social Security Benefit (Persons Residing Together) Regulations 1977 and shall come into operation on June 27, 1977. 3.147

(2) In these regulations "the Act" means the Social Security Act 1975 and other expressions have the same meanings as in the Act.

(3) Any reference in these regulations to any provision made or contained in any enactment or instrument shall be construed as a reference to that provision as amended or extended by any enactment or instrument and as including a reference to any provision which may re-enact or replace it, with or without modification.

(4) The rules for the construction of Acts of Parliament contained in the Interpretation Act 1889 shall apply in relation to this instrument and in relation to any revocation effected by it as if this instrument, the regulations revoked by it and any regulations revoked by the regulations so revoked were Acts of Parliament, and as if each revocation were a repeal.

GENERAL NOTE

Interpretation Act 1889 3.148

By s.25(2) of the Interpretation Act 1978, this reference is to be treated as a reference to the 1978 Act.

Circumstances in which a person is to be treated as residing or not residing with another person or in which persons are to be treated as residing or not residing together

2.—(1) As respects any requirement of the Act, or contained in any provision made for the purposes thereof, any question as to whether— 3.149

(a) a person is or was residing with another person; or
(b) persons are residing together,

shall be determined in accordance with the following provisions of this regulation.

(2) In relation to—

(a) an increase in respect of an adult dependant under section 44 [4 (short-term benefits: increase for adult dependants)], 45 (increase of Category A or Category C retirement pension [3 ...]), 49 (increase of [2 severe disablement allowance] or invalid care allowance) or 66 (increase [1 ...] of a disablement pension where the beneficiary is entitled to unemployability supplement) [3 or section 86A of the Social Security Contributions and Benefits Act 1992 (incapacity benefit: increases for adult dependants)]; or
(b) an adjustment of benefit under section 85(1)(b) (hospital in-patients)

two spouses [5 or civil partners] shall not be treated as having ceased to reside together by reason only of the fact that either of them is, or they both are, undergoing medical or other treatment as an in-patient in a hospital or similar institution, whether such absence is temporary or not.

(3) In the case of a woman who has been widowed, she shall not be treated as having ceased to reside together with a child or person under the age of 19 by reason of any absence the one from theh other which is not likely to be permanent.

(4) Subject to the foregoing provisions of this regulation, two persons shall not be treated as having ceased to reside together by reason of any temporary absence the one from the other.

AMENDMENTS

1. The Social Security (Abolition of Injury Benefit) (Consequential) Regulations 1983 (SI 1983/186) reg.8 (April 6, 1983).

2. The Social Security (Severe Disablement Allowance) Regulations 1984 (SI 1984/1303) reg.11 (November 29, 1984).

3. The Social Security (Incapacity Benefit) (Consequential and Transitional Amendments and Savings) Regulations 1995 (SI 1995/829) reg.10 (April 13, 1995)

4. The Social Security and Child Support (Jobseeker's Allowance) (Consequential Amendments) Regulations 1996 (SI 1996/1345) reg.16 (October 7, 1996).

5. The Civil Partnership (Pensions, Social Security and Child Support) (Consequential, etc. Provisions) Order 2005 (SI 2005/2877) (December 5, 2005).

DEFINITIONS

"the Act"—reg.1.
"medical treatment"—SSCBA 1992 s.122.

GENERAL NOTE

3.150 Compare reg.11 of the Child Benefit (General) Regulations. As in those regulations, "residing with" does not mean the same as "living with": *R(I) 10/51*; *R(U) 11/62* and *R(F) 2/79*. It is somewhat broader requiring only an element of continuity and permanence, which is to be assessed in the light of all the relevant circumstances of particular cases.

The general rule is that only permanent separation of two people constitutes not residing together. But the regulation sets out two specific rules.

First, if it is the sole cause of the absence of a spouse, periods by one or both spouses as in-patients in a hospital or similar institution are to be treated as periods residing together whether or not the absence is likely to be permanent. This presumably covers situations such as where a spouse is admitted to hospital for terminal care. Difficulties have arisen as to when a patient is an "inpatient". The approach consistently adopted has been that the patient must be "housed overnight" at the hospital or similar institution: *CS/65/49*, *R(S) 8/51* and *R(I) 14/56*.

Secondly, a widow and her child are treated as residing together if their absence from one another can be regarded as temporary, but they are to be treated as residing apart if their absence from one another is likely to be permanent. This appears to add little to the general rule and may owe its origins to particular difficulties over widow's benefit where persons under 19 are away from home for the purposes of full-time education and training. Such persons are presumed to be residing with the widow unless the absence can be said to be permanent.

It is clear that what constitutes a permanent residing together or parting will be **3.151** a matter of judgment for adjudication officers, tribunals and Commissioners in the light of all the facts of particular cases.

The facts of *CSS/18/88* illustrate the importance of determining each case on its own facts and of avoiding an *a priori* approach to cases. In that case a couple had been married for over 40 years. In April 1978 the wife went to Canada to visit relatives. During that visit her brother-in-law was seriously injured in a road traffic accident. The wife remained in Canada to provide care for him. He subsequently died, but the wife's sister was diagnosed as suffering from cancer and the wife again remained in Canada to nurse her. Meanwhile the husband had sought permission to emigrate to Canada. This was obtained, but his own ill health prevented his travelling. The couple remained in touch and the wife returned to Scotland for visits home. This situation lasted until 1987, when the issue of the husband's receipt of an increase of benefit for his wife came before a tribunal.

The tribunal concluded that the absence of the wife in Canada could not be regarded as temporary. The Commissioner disagreed, though he noted the unusual circumstances of the case. The couple had not ceased to reside together permanently. The tribunal had erred by focusing on the nature of the absence *from the United Kingdom*, rather than by focusing on whether they were temporarily absent *from one another*. Provided the husband and wife are residing together, the absence of one spouse abroad is not a disqualifying factor (see reg.13 of the Persons Abroad Regulations).

In *R(P) 1/90* Commissioner Skinner advised: **3.152**

> "Whether or not there is a temporary absence is a question of fact for the tribunal, but the Commissioners have evolved a series of tests over the years which assists the members in dealing with such question. In the earlier cases the purpose of the absence of the husband was considered to be of great importance, but in the later decisions more importance was attached to the duration of the absence. In *C(P)84/50* it was said that a period of absence which has lasted for more than a year, and of which there is no reasonable prospect of its coming to an end, cannot be spoken of as 'temporary.' If a man left home, and if it was ascertained after more than a year had elapsed that there was still no prospect of his return, he would not be said to be temporarily absent. In *R(P) 7/53* it was held that this was the established test for deciding whether absence had ceased to be temporary. It was pointed out that it was not a hard and fast rule, for there may be cases where it can be said long before the year is up the absence is not going to be temporary. It was pointed out that the reasonable prospect [sic] of return are not limited to the prospects within any particular period. In my judgment while the duration of the absence must be part of the test to be applied

by the tribunal, the purpose of the absence and the intention of the parties are also of relevance. Indeed that is recognised in *R(P) 7/53* where the absence [of] more than a year was only fatal to the claimant where there was no reasonable prospect of the absence coming to an end. I do not think it is practicable to lay down any hard and fast rules by which the question can be determined, but the intention of the claimant, the purpose of the absence and its duration are all relevant." (para.8).

In *CS/202/1991*, the Deputy Commissioner adopted the conclusion in *R(P) 1/90* that reg.2(4) modifies reg.13 of the Persons Abroad Regulations, but suggests that the approach to the determination of the temporary nature of any absence in that reported decision may be too stringent in the light of the decision in *Ex p. Akbar* (1992) 4 Admin. L.R. 602 (see annotations to reg.2 of the Persons Abroad Regulations).

3.153 *Regulation 3 omitted.*

The Social Security and Family Allowances (Polygamous Marriages) Regulations 1975

(SI 1975/561) *(as amended)*

3.154

The Secretary of State for Social Services, in exercise of powers conferred upon her under section 162(b) of the Social Security Act 1975 and section 12(2) of the Family Allowance Act 1965, as substituted by paragraph 18 of Schedule 2 to the Social Security (Consequential Provisions) Act 1975, hereby makes the following regulations:

Citation, commencement and interpretation

3.155 **1.**—(1) These regulations may be cited as the Social Security and Family Allowances (Polygamous Marriages) Regulations 1975 and shall come into operation on 6th April 1975.

(2) In these regulations, unless the context otherwise requires—

"the Social Security Act" means the [1 Social Security Contributions and Benefits Act 1992]

[2 "the Family Allowances Act" means the Family Allowances Act 1965;]

"polygamous marriage" means a marriage celebrated under a law which, as it applies to the particular ceremony and to the parties thereto, permits polygamy;

"monogamous marriage" means a marriage celebrated under a law which does not permit polygamy, and "in fact monogamous" is to be construed in accordance with regulation 2(2) below;

and other expressions shall, as appropriate, have the same meanings as in the Social Security Act and the Family Allowances Act.

(3) Any reference in these regulations to any provision made by or contained in any enactment or instrument shall, except in so far as the context otherwise requires, be construed as a reference to that provision as amended or extended by any enactment or instrument and as including a reference to any provision which it re-enacts or replaces, or which may re-enact or replace it, with or without modification.

(4) The rules for the construction of Acts of Parliament contained in the Interpretation Act 1889 shall apply for the purposes of the interpretation of these regulations as they apply for the purposes of the interpretation of an Act of Parliament.

General rule as to the consequences of a polygamous marriage for the purpose of the Social Security Act and the Family Allowances Act

2.—(1) Subject to the following provisions of these regulations, a polygamous marriage shall, for the purpose of the Social Security Act [2 and the Family Allowances Act] and any enactment construed as one with those Acts, be treated as having the same consequences as a monogamous marriage for any day, but only for any day, throughout which the polygamous marriage is in fact monogamous. 3.156

(2) In this and the next following regulation—

(a) a polygamous marriage is referred to as being in fact monogamous when neither party to it has any spouse additional to the other; and

(b) the day on which a polygamous marriage is contracted, or on which it terminates for any reason, shall be treated as a day throughout which that marriage was in fact monogamous if at all times on that day after it was contracted, or as the case may be, before it terminated, it was in fact monogamous.

GENERAL NOTE

In *CG/2611/2003* the Commissioner was determining an appeal in relation to a claim for widow's benefit in respect of a man who married three times. It seems that that the husband, a Bangladeshi, entered into his first marriage in Bangladesh in the early 1960s. In 1968 he married the claimant in Bangladesh in accordance with Muslim law. Some time in the 1970s the husband took a third wife in Bangladesh. At the time of the husband's death, there was some uncertainty about the status of the first marriage, but the second and third marriages were still subsisting. The second wife claimed widow's benefit. The Secretary of State's argument was that the claim to the widow's benefit must be disallowed because the husband had contracted polygamous marriages, at least two of which subsisted at his death, and the claimant was not the husband's only wife at the date he died. Under the Polygamous Marriages Regulations, the claim could only succeed if, at the material time, the marriage was, in fact, monogamous. 3.157

The tribunal had concluded that at the time of marriage to the claimant, the husband was domiciled in the United Kingdom. The Commissioner casts doubt on the correctness of that conclusion but refers the matter back to a fresh tribunal for determination. Were it to be correct, then the marriage contracted with the claimant would have been void by the law of the law of the husband's domicile.

The decision highlights the need for the most careful (and consistent) findings of fact in these complex cases. Subject to what is said below in this note, the place of domicile of the husband at the dates of each of the marriages he contracts will be of fundamental importance in determining the validity of those marriages and consequently the application of the Polygamous Marriages Regulations to any claim for benefit.

SSWP v MN (BB) [2018] UKUT 68 (AAC) demonstrates that the question of the husband's domicile–and hence whether or not he is legally able to enter into a polygamous marriage at all–logically comes before consideration of reg.2. As Judge Wikeley put it, the regulation

> "does not have the effect of converting a void marriage into a valid one simply by virtue of the parties being in practice monogamously married immediately prior to one party's death. Instead, it means that a valid polygamous marriage can be treated as "a monogamous marriage for any day ... throughout which the polygamous marriage is in fact monogamous".

However, existing lines of authority must now be read in the light of the Court of Appeal's decision in *Secretary of State for Work and Pensions v Akhtar* [2021] EWCA Civ 1353, reversing the Upper Tribunal's decision in *NA v SSWP (BB)* [2019] UKUT 144 (AAC).

The claimant had entered into a marriage under Islamic law with Mr A in 2008. At that time, while the claimant was domiciled in Pakistan, Mr A was domiciled in the United Kingdom. Mr A had previously married a Ms B at a time when both he and Ms B were domiciled in Pakistan. The marriage to Ms B was valid under the law of England and Wales. Mr A became domiciled in the UK with the consequence that when in 2001 he pronounced a *talaq* in respect of his marriage with Ms B, it was invalid to terminate that marriage under English law. Consequently, when in 2008 the claimant and Mr A married in Pakistan, their marriage was polygamous and, because of Mr A's domicile at the time, void under English law. Mr A's marriage to Ms B was only terminated under English law by decree absolute in 2009. Ms B died in 2011. The claimant moved to the UK in 2010, had a child with Mr A in 2012 but in 2016 Mr A died. At no point did Mr A live with both the claimant and Ms B.

The Court of Appeal undertook a detailed review of the treatment of polygamous marriages for social security purposes. The Court held that the Regulations applied only to polygamous marriages that were valid under English law and did not make sense if they applied to marriages that were void under English law, as was the respondent's marriage. The expression "in fact monogamous" in reg.2 had to mean that there were, as a matter of law, no other marriages. A polygamous marriage would only be "in fact monogamous" when both parties were spouses and neither had any spouse additional to the other. Neither the primary legislation in relation to bereavement payment and widowed parent's allowance could assist the claimant, as she was not validly married under the law of England and Wales, nor for the reasons above could the Polygamous Marriages Regulations. Her human rights case was no stronger than had already been decided by the Supreme Court in *Re McLaughlin's Application for Judicial Review* [2018] UKSC 48 (as to which, see Vol.3); in particular, in relation to bereavement payment, people who have contracted a marriage which is valid under English law and those who have not were not in an analogous position, alternatively the difference in treatment created by the legislation was justified.

Special rules for retirement pension for women

3.158 **3.**—(1) Subject to the provisions of paragraphs (2) and (3) of this regulation, where on or after the date on which she attained pensionable age a woman was a married woman by virtue of a polygamous marriage and either—

(a) throughout a day, falling on or after the date on which both she and her spouse have attained pensionable age [3 and in respect of which neither of them has an entitlement to a Category A or Category B retirement pension which is deferred,] that marriage was in fact monogamous, or

(b) throughout the day on which her spouse died that marriage was in fact monogamous,

that marriage, whether or not it has at all times been or continues to be in fact monogamous, shall, for the purposes of determining her right to and the rate of a retirement pension of any category under the Social Security Act be treated as having the same consequences as a monogamous marriage from and including the date on which she attained pensionable age or, if the marriage was contracted after that date, from and including the date of the marriage.

(2) Paragraph (1) of this regulation shall not operate so as to entitle a woman to a retirement pension for any period before the first such day as is referred to in sub-paragraph (a) of that paragraph or, in a case where that sub-paragraph does not apply, the day referred to in sub-paragraph (b) of that paragraph.

(3) Where the marriage of a woman is a polygamous marriage which was contracted—

(a) before she attained pensionable age and—
 (i) was not in fact monogamous when she attained that age, but
 (ii) became in fact monogamous on a date after she attained that age; or

(b) on or after the day on which she attained pensionable age and—
 (i) was not in fact monogamous when it was contracted, but
 (ii) became in fact monogamous on a date after it was contracted;

that marriage shall be treated as having the same consequences as a monogamous marriage for the purposes of section 29(10) of the Social Security Act (increase of Category B retirement pension in certain circumstances) only with effect from the date referred to in sub-paragraph (a)(ii) or, as the case may be, sub-paragraph (b)(ii) of this paragraph.

(4) In a case where section 28(3) of and Schedule 7 to the Social Security Act (retirement pension for widows who were widowed before attaining pensionable age) or regulation 4 of the Social Security (Benefit) (Married Women and Widows Special Provisions) Regulations 1974 (retirement pension for women whose marriages have been dissolved) applies to a woman and the relevant marriage for the purposes of that section and Schedule or that regulation was a polygamous marriage and throughout the day on which either—

(a) her marriage was dissolved, or

(b) her spouse died,

that marriage was in fact monogamous, that polygamous marriage shall, for those purposes, notwithstanding that it has not at all times been in fact monogamous, be treated as having the same consequences as if it had been a monogamous marriage.

(5) Where a woman is a married woman by virtue of a polygamous marriage which is in fact monogamous on the date from which she becomes entitled to a Category D retirement pension under section 39(1)(c) of the Social Security Act (retirement pensions for persons over age 80), that marriage, notwithstanding that it ceases to be in fact monogamous, shall, for the purpose of determining the rate of her Category D retirement pension, be treated as having the same consequences as a monogamous marriage.

AMENDMENTS

1. Substituted by Social Security (Consequential Provisions) Act 1992 s.2(4).
2. This provision (or reference) has lapsed with the repeal of the Family Allowances Act.
3. Words substituted by the Social Security (Abolition of Earnings Rule) (Consequential) Regulations 1989 (SI 1989/1642) (October 1, 1989).

PART IV

DISABILITY BENEFITS

The Social Security (Attendance Allowance) Regulations 1991

(SI 1991/2740) (*as amended*)

ARRANGEMENT OF REGULATIONS

SCHEDULE

The Secretary of State for Social Security, in exercise of the powers conferred upon him by sections 35(1), (2)(b), (2A), (4A) and (6), 85(1)(b) and 166(2) and (3) of, and Schedule 20 to, the Social Security Act 1975 and of all other powers enabling him in that behalf, by this instrument, which contains regulations which relate to matters which, in accordance with section 140 of that Act, have been referred to the Attendance Allowance Board, hereby makes the following Regulations:

Citation, commencement and interpretation

1.—(1) These Regulations may be cited as the Social Security (Attendance Allowance) Regulations 1991 and shall come into force on 6th April 1992. 4.2

(2) In these Regulations—

"the Act" means the Social Security Act 1975;

"the NHS Act of 1978" means the National Health Service (Scotland) Act 1978;

[[1] "the NHS Act of 2006" means the National Health Service Act 2006 and "the NHS (Wales) Act of 2006" means the National Health Service (Wales) Act 2006];

"terminally ill" shall be construed in accordance with section 35(2C) of the Act.

(3) Unless the context otherwise requires, any reference in these Regulations to a numbered regulation is a reference to the regulation bearing that number in these Regulations and any reference in a regulation to a numbered paragraph is a reference to the paragraph of that regulation bearing that number.

AMENDMENTS

1. Social Security (Attendance Allowance, Disability living Allowance and Carer's Allowance) (Amendment) Regulations 2013 (SI 2013/389) reg.3 (April 8, 2013).

[[1] Disapplication of section 1(1A) of the Administration Act

4.3 **1A.**—Section 1(1A) of the Administration Act (requirement to state national insurance number) shall not apply to any claim for attendance allowance made or treated as made before 9th February, 1998.]

AMENDMENT

1. Social Security (National Insurance Information: Exemption) Regulations 1997 (SI 1997/2676) (December 1, 1997).

Conditions as to residence and presence in Great Britain

4.4 **2.**—(1) Subject to the following provisions of this regulation [[5] and regulations [[6]2A, 2B and 2C]], the prescribed conditions for the purposes of section 35(1) of the Act as to residence and presence in Great Britain in relation to any person on any day shall be that—

(a) on that day—

(i) he is [[5]habitually] resident in [[5]the United Kingdom, the Republic of Ireland, the Isle of Man or the Channel Islands], and

[[1] (ib) he is not a person subject to immigration control within the meaning of section 115(9) of the Immigration and Asylum Act 1999 or section 115 of that Act does not apply to him for the purposes of entitlement to attendance allowance by virtue of regulation 2 of the Social Security (Immigration and Asylum) Consequential Amendments Regulations 2000,

(ii) he is present in Great Britain, and

(iii) he has been present in Great Britain for a period of, or for periods amounting in the aggregate to, not less than [[5]104] weeks in the [[5] 156] weeks immediately preceding that day;

(b) [[4] . . .]

[[7] (1ZA) A person to whom regulation 53(1) of the Disability Assistance for Working Age People (Scotland) Regulations 2022 applies shall be treated for the period set out in that regulation as though he does not satisfy the condition in paragraph (1)(a)(i) of this regulation.]

[[2] (1A)—[[1] *Omitted*]].

(2) For the purposes of paragraph (1)(a)(ii) and (iii), notwithstanding that on any day a person is absent from Great Britain, he shall be treated as though he were present in Great Britain if his absence is by reason only of the fact that on that day—

(a) he is abroad in his capacity as—

(i) a serving member of the forces,

(ii) an airman or mariner within the meaning of regulations [[5]111 and 115] respectively of the Social Security (Contributions) Regulations [[5]2001], and for the purpose of this provision, the expression "serving members of the forces" has the same meaning as in regulation 1(2) of the Regulations of [[5]2001]; or

(b) he is in employment prescribed for the purposes of section 132 of the Act in connection with continental shelf operations; or

(c) he is living with a person mentioned in sub-paragraph (a)(i) and is the spouse, [[3] civil partner,] son, daughter, step-son, step-daughter, father, father-in-law, step-father, mother, mother-in-law or step-mother of that person; or

[[5] (d) he is temporarily absent from Great Britain and that absence has not lasted for a continuous period exceeding 13 weeks.]

(e) [[5] *omitted*]

(3) Where a person is terminally ill and makes a claim for attendance allowance expressly on the ground that he is such a person, paragraph (1) shall apply to him as if head (iii) of sub-paragraph (a) was omitted.

[[5] (3A) A person shall be treated as habitually resident in Great Britain for the purpose of paragraph (1)(a)(i) where—

(a) he is resident outside Great Britain in his capacity as a serving member of the forces and for this purpose "serving member of the forces" has the meaning given in regulation 1(2) of the Social Security (Contributions) Regulations 2001; or

(b) he is living with a person mentioned in para.(a) and is the spouse, civil partner, son, daughter, step-son, step-daughter, father, father-in-law, step-father, mother, mother-in-law or step-mother of that person.";

[[5] (3B) Where a person is temporarily absent from Great Britain, he is treated as present in Great Britain for the purposes of paragraph (1)(a)(ii) and (iii) for the first 26 weeks of that absence, where—

(a) this absence is solely in connection with arrangements made for the medical treatment of him for a disease or bodily or mental disablement which commenced before he left Great Britain; and

(b) the arrangements referred to in sub-paragraph (a) relate to medical treatment–

(i) outside Great Britain,

(ii) during the period whilst he is temporarily absent from Great Britain, and

(iii) by, or under the supervision of, a person appropriately qualified to carry out that treatment, and

"medical treatment" means medical, surgical or rehabilitative treatment (including any course or diet or regimen), and references to a person receiving or submitting to medical treatment are to be construed accordingly.";

[[5] (3C) For the purpose of paragraph (2)(d) and (3B) a person is "temporarily absent" if, at the beginning of the period of absence, that absence is unlikely to exceed 52 weeks.]

(4) [[4]. . .]

AMENDMENTS

1. Social Security (Immigration and Asylum) Consequential Amendments Regulations 2000 (SI 2000/636), reg.10 (April 3, 2000).

2. Social Security (Persons From Abroad) Miscellaneous Amendments Regulations 1996 (SI 1996/30) reg.2 (February 5, 1996), subject to a saving under reg.12(3).

3. Civil Partnership Act 2004, Sch.24 (December 5, 2005).

4. Social Security (Miscellaneous Amendments) (No.4) Regulations 2006 (SI 2006/2378) reg.7 (October 1, 2006).

5. Social Security (Attendance Allowance, Disability Living Allowance and Carer's Allowance) (Amendment) Regulations 2013 (SI 2013/389) reg.3 (April 8, 2013).

6. Social Security (Miscellaneous Amendment No.4) Regulations (SI 2017/1015) reg.6(2) (November 16, 2017).

7. Scotland Act 2016 (Social Security) (Adult Disability Payment and Child Disability Payment)(Amendment) Regulations 2022 (SI 2022/335) reg.5 (March 21,2022).

GENERAL NOTE

4.5 Section 35(1) of the 1975 Act has now been replaced by s.64(1) of the Social Security Contributions and Benefits Act 1992.

Until April 8, 2013 a claimant need only have shown that they were "ordinarily resident" and there is a saving for existing claims made on that basis. Neither "ordinary" nor "habitual" residence is defined in the statute or regulations. Ordinary residence has usually been taken to mean that you have a settled intention to live in the country (technically now the "common travel area") as your home, but, not necessarily, permanently. Habitual residence, which is intended to be a more stringent test, requires as well that that the claimant has been in the country already for an extended period. How long, will depend upon the circumstances of the claimant; a former resident returning from a period abroad may satisfy this test almost immediately, while a new immigrant may be required to demonstrate a considerable period of residence. The meaning of "habitual residence" has been the subject of extensive case law in relation to claims for means-tested benefits where it has applied for some time. Readers are referred to the notes to relevant sections of Vol.II of this Work. In *MM and SI v SSWP (DLA)* [2016] UKUT 149 (AAC) Judge Markus QC has held that reg.2 (1)(a)(iii) (the past presence test or PPT) must be disapplied in respect of claims made on behalf of applicants who were family members of persons granted refugee status in the UK. She held that the PPT was indirectly discriminatory and could not be justified (when compared to the treatment of UK nationals) under art.28 of the EU Directive 2004/8 3/EC (which gives protection to refugees) and which she held had direct effect in the UK. For the same reason she held that PPT was in breach of the claimant's rights under art.14 of the ECHR. At the time the claims were made, the applicants satisfied the other conditions of reg.2 which meant that their claims should proceed accordingly. This was a decision on a claim for DLA but the ruling applies equally to attendance allowance.

For questions that involve persons either coming from or going to a country that is part of the European Economic Area reference should be made to the relevant sections of Vol.III of this Work.

Subsection (2)(e) which provided for a person to be absent with a certificate issued by the Secretary of State has been abolished with effect from April 8, 2013, but there is a saving provision for those persons who were abroad on that basis at that time—see reg.5 of SI 2013/389.

[1 Persons residing in Great Britain to whom a relevant EU Regulation applies

4.6 **2A.**—(1) Regulation 2(1)(a)(iii) shall not apply where on any day—

(a) the person is habitually resident in Great Britain;

(b) a relevant EU Regulation applies; and

(c) the person can demonstrate a genuine and sufficient link to the United Kingdom social security system.

(2) For the purposes of paragraph (1)(b) and regulation 2B, "relevant EU Regulation" has the meaning given by section 84(2) of the Welfare Reform Act 2012.]

AMENDMENT

1. Social Security (Attendance Allowance, Disability living Allowance and Carer's Allowance) (Amendment) Regulations 2013 (SI 2013/389) reg.3 (April 8, 2013).

GENERAL NOTE

The relevant regulations referred to are (EC) No.1408/71 and (EC) No.883/2004. For detailed discussion see Vol.III of this Work. 4.7

The operation of this subsection has been considered by the CA in *Kavanagh and Mohamed v SSWP* [2019] EWCA Civ 272; [2019] AACR 21 (UT and CA). Both cases had been before Judge Jacobs in the UT where, while it was accepted that each claimant was now habitually resident in the UK, he held that neither was able to establish that they had a genuine and sufficient link to the UK. Judge Jacobs took the view that their reason for coming to the UK could not contribute to establishing that link. The CA have held that the reason for coming here could be relevant. In the case of *MM* the claimant was a 65 year old German national who was claiming AA. She had come to the UK because she needed the care and support of her daughter who was resident here. The CA held that this reason, together with her actual presence here, was enough to establish that link. In the UT Judge Jacobs had observed that the requirement in subs. (2A)(c) that the link be to the UK social security system was unlawful; the CA proceeded on the basis that that was correct and therefore the last three words of that paragraph are to be ignored.

[[1]Persons residing in an EEA state [[2]...] or in Switzerland to whom a relevant EU Regulation applies

2B.—Regulation 2(1)(a)(i) to (iii) shall not apply where on any day— 4.8

(a) the person is habitually resident in—

(i) an EEA state [[2]...]; or

(ii) Switzerland;

(b) a relevant EU Regulation applies; and

(c) the person can demonstrate a genuine and sufficient link to the United Kingdom social security system.]

AMENDMENTS

1. Social Security (Attendance Allowance, Disability Living Allowance and Carer's Allowance) (Amendment) Regulations 2013 (SI 2013/389) reg.3 (April 8, 2013).

2. Social Security (Amendment) (EU Exit) Regulations 2019 (SI 2019/128) reg.4 and Sch. para.6 (January 31, 2020).

[[1][[2] Refugees and certain persons with leave to enter or remain in the United Kingdom]

2C.—(1) Regulation 2(1)(a)(iii) shall not apply where the person has— 4.9

(a) been granted refugee status or humanitarian protection under the immigration rules; [[2]...]

(b) leave to enter or to remain in the United Kingdom as the dependant of a person granted refugee status or humanitarian protection under the immigration rules;

[[2] (c) leave to enter or remain in the United Kingdom granted under the immigration rules by virtue of—

(i) the Afghan Relocations and Assistance Policy; or

(ii) the previous scheme for locally-employed staff in Afghanistan (sometimes referred to as the ex-gratia scheme);

(d) been granted discretionary leave outside the immigration rules as a dependant of a person referred to in sub-paragraph (c);

(e) leave granted under the Afghan Citizens Resettlement Scheme] [3[4[5 ...]]]

(f) leave to enter or remain in the United Kingdom granted under or outside the immigration rules [4, a right] of abode in the United Kingdom within the meaning given in section 2 of the Immigration Act 1971 [4 or does not require leave to enter or remain in the United Kingdom in accordance with section 3ZA of that Act,] where the person—

(i) was residing in Ukraine immediately before 1st January 2022; and

(ii) left Ukraine in connection with the Russian invasion which took place on 24th February 2022; [5[6 ...]]

(g) leave to enter or remain in the United Kingdom granted under or outside the immigration rules, a right of abode in the United Kingdom within the meaning given in section 2 of the Immigration Act 1971 or does not require leave to enter or remain in the United Kingdom in accordance with section 3ZA of that Act, where the person—

(i) was residing in Sudan before 15th April 2023; and

(ii) left Sudan in connection with the violence which rapidly escalated on 15th April 2023] [6, or

(h) leave to enter or remain in the United Kingdom granted under or outside the immigration rules, a right of abode in the United Kingdom within the meaning given in section 2 of the Immigration Act 1971 or does not require leave to enter or remain in the United Kingdom in accordance with section 3ZA of that Act, where the person—

(i) was residing in Israel, the West Bank, the Gaza Strip, East Jerusalem, the Golan Heights or Lebanon immediately before 7th October 2023; and

(ii) left Israel, the West Bank, the Gaza Strip, East Jerusalem, the Golan Heights or Lebanon in connection with the Hamas terrorist attack in Israel on 7th October 2023 or the violence which rapidly escalated in the region following the attack.]

[2 (1A) Regulation 2(1)(a)(i) shall not apply where [3 any sub-paragraph in paragraph (1)] applies to the person.]

(2) For the purposes of this regulation "immigration rules" means the rules laid before Parliament under section 3(2) of the Immigration Act 1971.]

AMENDMENTS

1. Social Security (Miscellaneous Amendments No.4) Regulations 2017 (SI 2017/1015) reg.6(3) (November 16, 2017).

2. Social Security (Habitual Residence and Past Presence) (Amendment) Regulations 2021 (SI 2021/1034) reg.4 (September 15, 2021). The amendments made by these regulations apply in respect of England and Wales only. The same amendments are made with effect from the same date in respect of Scotland only by reg.2 of the Social Security (Residence Requirements) (Afghanistan) (Scotland) Regulations 2021 (SI 2021/320) but in addition that regulation also substitutes for paragraph (2) of reg.2C the following—

"(2) For the purposes of this regulation—

(a) "immigration rules" means the rules laid before Parliament under section 3(2) of the Immigration Act 1971,

(b) "the Afghan Citizens Resettlement Scheme" means the scheme announced by the United Kingdom Government on 18 August 2021."

3. Social Security (Habitual Residence and Past Presence) (Amendment) Regulations 2022 (SI 2022/344) reg.4 (March 22, 2022). Note: this regulation applies only to England and Wales. Identical provision is made for Scotland, with effect from the same date, by the Social Security (Residence Requirements) (Ukraine) (Scotland) Regulations 2022 (SSI 2022/108).

4. Social Security (Habitual Residence and Past Presence (Amendment) (No.2) Regulations 2022 (SI 2022/990) reg.3 (October 18, 2022). Note: this regulation applies only to England and Wales. Identical provision is made for Scotland by the Social Security (Miscellaneous Amendment and Transitional Provision) (Scotland) Regulations 2022 (SI 2022/336) reg.6 (November 28, 2022).

5. Social Security (Habitual Residence and Past Presence) (Amendment) Regulations (SI 2023/532) reg.4 (May 15, 2023). Note: this regulation applies only to England and Wales. Identical provision is made for Scotland with effect from May 17, 2023, by reg.2 of the Social Security (Residence Requirements) (Sudan) (Scotland) Regulations (SSI 2023/149).

6. Social Security (Habitual Residence and Past Presence, and Capital Disregards) Regulations 2023 (SI 2023/1144) reg.10 (October 27, 2023). Note: This amendment applies only to England and Wales. Identical provision is made for Scotland with effect from October 26, 2023, by the Social Security (Residence and Presence Requirements) (Israel, West Bank, the Gaza Strip, East Jerusalem, the Golan Heights and Lebanon) (Scotland) Regulations 2023 (SSI 2023/309).

Extension of qualifying period

3.—The period prescribed for the purposes of section 35(2)(b) of the Act (claimant to satisfy one or both of the conditions in section 35(1) of the Act for 6 months immediately preceeding the date from which attendance allowance is to be awarded) shall be 2 years. 4.10

General Note

Section 35(2)(b) of the 1975 Act has now been replaced by s.65(1)(b) of the Social Security Contributions and Benefits Act 1992. 4.11

Allowance payable before the date of claim in renewal cases

4.—*Revoked by Social Security (Miscellaneous Amendments) (No. 2) Regulations 1997 (SI 1997/793) reg.19(b) with effect from September 1, 1997.* 4.12

General Note

This regulation had allowed a renewal claim made within six months of the date of termination of an earlier award to be backdated to that date. 4.13

Renal dialysis

5.—(1) Subject to paragraph (3), a person who suffers from renal failure and who is undergoing the treatment specified in paragraph (2) shall be deemed to satisfy the conditions— 4.14

(a) in section 35(1)(a) of the Act (severe physical and mental disability) if he undergoes renal dialysis by day;

(b) in section 35(1)(b) of the Act if he undergoes renal dialysis by night;

(c) in either paragraph (a) or paragraph (b) of section 35(1) of the Act, but not both, if he undergoes renal dialysis by day and by night.

(2) The treatment referred to in paragraph (1) is the undergoing of renal dialysis—

(a) two or more times a week; and

(b) which either—

(i) is of a type which normally requires the attendance of or supervision by another person during the period of dialysis, or

(ii) which, because of the particular circumstances of his case, in fact requires another person, during the period of dialysis, to attend in connection with the bodily functions of the person undergoing renal dialysis or to supervise that person in order that he avoids substantial danger to himself.

(3) Except as provided in paragraph (4), paragraph (1) does not apply to a person undergoing the treatment specified in paragraph (2) where the treatment—

(a) is provided under [1 the NHS Act of 1978, the NHS Act of 2006 or the NHS (Wales) Act of 2006];

(b) is in a hospital or similar institution;

(c) is out-patient treatment; and

(d) takes place with the assistance or supervision of any member of staff of the hospital or similar institution.

(4) Paragraph (3) does not apply for the purposes of determining whether a person is to be taken to satisfy either of the conditions specified in paragraph (1) during the period of 6 months referred to in section 35(2)(b) of the 1975 Act (qualifying period for attendance allowance).

AMENDMENTS

1. Social Security (Attendance Allowance, Disability living Allowance and Carer's Allowance) (Amendment) Regulations 2013 (SI 2013/389) reg.3 (April 8, 2013).

GENERAL NOTE

4.15 Under this regulation, a person undergoing renal dialysis at least twice a week may be deemed to satisfy *either* the day *or* the night attendance condition, but not both. Some degree of attention or supervision must be required. This regulation is in slightly different terms from regs 5B and 5C of the Social Security (Attendance Allowance) (No. 2) Regulations 1975 which governed entitlement before April 6, 1992.

Paragraph (1)

4.16 The conditions previously to be found in s.35(1)(a) and (b) of the 1975 Act are now to be found in s.64(2) and (3) of the Social Security Contributions and Benefits Act 1992.

Paragraph (2)(b)

4.17 The dialysis must be *either* of a type which *normally* requires the attendance of or supervision by another person (in which case the actual purpose of the attention or supervision is irrelevant) *or* the dialysis must *in the particular case* require the attention or supervision of the claimant (for the purpose specified in para.(2)(b)(ii)).

Paragraph (3)

4.18 This excludes from the scope of the regulation claimants whose treatment satisfies all four conditions in sub-paras (a)–(d). It is not entirely clear what assistance or supervision actually falls within sub-para.(d) but presumably it is the attention or supervision falling within para.(2)(b) so that only assistance and supervision *during the period of dialysis* is relevant and not any assistance at the beginning or end of the treatment. By virtue of para.(4), para.(3) does not apply in respect of the six-month qualifying period for attendance allowance. This means that a person previously excluded under para.(3) can qualify for attendance allowance under this reg.as soon as one of the excluding conditions of para.(3) ceases to be satisfied. S.35(2)(b) of the 1975 Act has been replaced by s.65(1)(b) of the Social Security Contributions and Benefits Act 1992.

Hospitalisation

6.—[1 (1) Subject to regulation 8, it shall be a condition for the receipt of an attendance allowance for any period in respect of any person that during that period he is not maintained free of charge while undergoing medical or other treatment as an in-patient— 4.19

(a) in a hospital or similar institution under [4 the NHS Act of 1978, the NHS Act of 2006 or the NHS (Wales) Act of 2006]; or

(b) in a hospital or similar institution maintained or administered by the Defence Council.]

(2) For the purposes of [1 paragraph (1)(a)], a person shall only be regarded as not being maintained free of charge in a hospital or similar institution for any period where his accommodation and services are provided under

[4 (a) section 57 of, and paragraph 14 of Schedule 7A to, the NHS Act of 1978;

(b) section 13 of, and paragraph 15 of Schedule 2 to, the NHS Act of 2006;

(c) section 28 of, and paragraph 11 of Schedule 6 to, the NHS Act of 2006;

(d) section 44(6) of, and paragraph 19(1) of Schedule 4 to, the NHS Act of 2006;

(e) section 11 of, and paragraph 15 of Schedule 2 to, the NHS (Wales) Act of 2006;

(f) section 18 of, and paragraph 19(1) of Schedule 3 to, the NHS (Wales) Act of 2006; or

(g) section 22 of, and paragraph 11 of Schedule 5 to, the NHS (Wales) Act of 2006.]

[2 (2A) For the purpose of paragraph (1), a period during which a person is maintained free of charge while undergoing medical or other treatment as an in-patient shall be deemed to begin on the day after the day on which he enters a hospital or similar institution referred to in that paragraph and to end on the day [3 before the day] on which he leaves such a hospital or similar institution.]

(3) [1 . . .].

AMENDMENTS

1. Social Security (Disability Living Allowance and Attendance Allowance) (Amendment) Regulation 1992 (SI 1992/2869) reg.2 (December 15, 1992).

2. Social Security (Hospital In-Patients, Attendance Allowance and Disability Living Allowance) (Amendment) Regulations 1999 (SI 1999/1326) (June 7, 1999).

3. Social Security (Attendance Allowance and Disability Living Allowance) (Amendment) Regulations 2000, (SI 2000/1401) reg.2 (June 19, 2000).

4. Social Security (Attendance Allowance, Disability Living Allowance and Carer's Allowance) (Amendment) Regulations 2013 (SI 2013/389) reg.3 (April 8, 2013).

GENERAL NOTE

By virtue of reg.8, this regulation applies only after a person has been in hospital (or in accommodation to which reg.7 applies) for 28 days although periods separated by intervals not exceeding 28 days may be linked. 4.20

If a person is receiving treatment as an in-patient in one of the hospitals or institutions specified in para.(1), he or she is deemed to be being maintained free of charge unless a private patient (in which case para.(2) will apply). Although the wording of this regulation is different from that considered in *R(S) 4/84*, the overall conclusion reached by the Commissioner appears to be relevant here. The claimant was able to attend college during the day but received treatment from the hospital at night. The Commissioner held that she was not receiving free in-patient treatment because "any period" and "period" must relate to a period of not less than one day.

In *CDLA/11099/95*, the Commissioner decided that the equivalent provision in reg.8 of the Social Security (Disability Living Allowance) Regulations 1991 applied so as to make it a condition of entitlement to benefit only for "complete calendar (i.e. midnight-to-midnight) days throughout which the claimant is not undergoing medical or other treatment as an in-patient" but that the state of affairs existing at the beginning of a day was presumed to continue until the end. However, in *CSS/617/97*, where the claimant of severe disablement allowance went home from hospital from a Friday morning to a Monday evening, the Commissioner construed reg.2(2) of the Social Security (Hospital In-Patients) Regulations 1975 so as to find the claimant entitled to the full rate of benefit for the Friday as well as the Saturday to Monday. The explanation for the different approaches may lie in the slightly different form of the statutory provisions under consideration, in which case the approach taken in *CDLA/11099/95* must be preferred in attendance allowance cases.

In *Chief Adjudication Officer v White* (*R(IS)18/94*), a health authority had made arrangements for patients in a hospital to be moved to a nursing home. It was held by the Court of Appeal that they were receiving treatment in hospital or similar institution under the National Health Service Act 1977. In *CDLA/7980/95*, the claimant was discharged from hospital and the tribunal found that she had gone to live in a house where she was one of six tenants who were all cared for by health authority staff. The tribunal found that the house was not a "hospital or similar institution". The adjudication officer appealed but the Commissioner held that the tribunal had not erred in law in reaching the conclusion they did. He distinguished *White* on the basis that it had not been disputed in that case that the nursing home was an institution. He also rejected submissions that the tribunal ought to have investigated the arrangements further, observing that the adjudication officer had failed to challenge the evidence before the tribunal. The Chief Adjudication Officer was given leave to appeal by the Commissioner but he did not lodge the appeal within time and was refused an extension by the Court of Appeal.

[1 Persons in care homes

4.21 7.—(1) Subject to regulation 8, a person shall not be paid any amount in respect of an attendance allowance for any period where throughout that period he is a resident in a care home in circumstances where any of the costs of any qualifying services provided for him are borne out of public or local funds under a specified enactment.

(2) The specified enactments for the purposes of paragraph (1) are—

(a)

(i) Part III of the National Assistance Act 1948

(ii) [2 sections 59 and 59A] of the Social Work (Scotland) Act 1968,

(iii) the Mental Health (Care and Treatment) (Scotland) Act 2003,

(iv) the Community Care and Health (Scotland) Act 2002,

(v) the Mental Health Act 1983,

[3 (vi) section 57 of the Health and Social Care Act 2001,]

[4 (vii) Part 1 of the Care Act 2014 (care and support),]

[5 (viii) Part 4 of the Social Services and Well-being (Wales) Act 2014 (meeting needs), or]

(b) any other enactment relating to persons under disability.

(3) In this regulation, and in regulation 8, references to the costs of any qualifying services shall not include the cost of—

(a) domiciliary services, including personal care, provided in respect of a person in a private dwelling; or

(b) improvements made to, or furniture or equipment provided for, a private dwelling on account of the needs of a person under disability; or

(c) improvements made to, or furniture or equipment provided for, a care home in respect of which a grant or payment has been made out of public or local funds except where the grant or payment is of a regular or repeated nature; or

(d) social and recreational activities provided outside the care home in respect of which grants or payments are made out of public or local funds; or

(e) the purchase or running of a motor vehicle to be used in connection with any qualifying service provided in a care home in respect of which grants or payments are made out of public or local funds; or

(f) [2 *omitted*]

(4) For the purposes of paragraph (1), a period during which a person is a resident in a care home in the circumstances set out in that paragraph shall, subject to paragraphs (5) and (6), be deemed—

(a) to begin on the day after the day on which he enters a care home, and

(b) to end on the day before the day on which he leaves a care home.

(5) Where a person enters a care home from a hospital or similar institution in circumstances in which paragraph (1) of regulation 6 applies, the period during which he is a resident in the care home shall be deemed to begin on the day he enters that care home.

(6) Where a person leaves a care home and enters a hospital or similar institution in circumstances in which paragraph (1) of regulation 6 applies, the period during which he is a resident in the care home shall be deemed to end on the day he leaves that care home.]

AMENDMENTS

1. Attendance Allowance and Disability Living Allowance (Amendment) Regulations 2007 (SI 2007/2875) (October 29, 2007).

2. Social Security (Attendance Allowance, Disability Living Allowance and Carer's Allowance) (Amendment) Regulations 2013 (SI 2013/389) reg.3 (April 8, 2013).

3. Community Care, Services for Carers and Children's Services (Direct Payments) (England) (Amendment) Regulations (SI 2013/2270) reg.5 (November 1, 2013).

4. Care Act 2014 (Consequential Amendments) (Secondary Legislation) Order 2015 (SI 2015/643) art.6 (April 1, 2015).

5. Social Services and Well-being (Wales) Act 2014 and the Regulation and Inspection of Social Care (Wales) Act 2016 (Consequential Amendments) Order 2017 (SI 2017/901) art.3 (November 3, 2017).

GENERAL NOTE

There is a transitional and saving provision in reg.4 of the Amendment regulations to the effect that this amendment shall not prevent any day before the coming into force of the amended regulations from counting towards the first 28 day period specified in reg.8. 4.22

This is a new version of reg.7, but the commentary that follows remains relevant.

By virtue of reg.8, this regulation applies only after a person has been in the relevant accommodation or in hospital for 28 days although periods separated by intervals not exceeding 28 days may be linked.

The former paragraph (c), now repealed, also provided for disqualification where the cost of accommodation could have been met from public funds even if it was not. Now the regulation applies only where the cost is being met. A question may still arise where costs are being met temporarily while a claimant waits to release funds from which they can meet the costs themselves, by the sale of their former home. In such cases it is usual for the claimant to undertake to reimburse the local authority when their own funds become available.

The effect of the decision in *CAO v Creighton* [2000] N.I. 222 for Northern Ireland, and its adoption in England and Wales in *R(A) 1/02* is that such arrangements do not involve the local authority in meeting the cost of accommodation because the claimant does meet and always has met that cost by virtue of the agreement to reimburse any sums advanced. It follows that the claimant then does have the resources to provide his own accommodation, and the local authority has no power to provide for his accommodation under Pt III—reg.7 does not therefore apply. The position is more doubtful in Scotland. In *CSA/469/2005* (and in *CSA/164/2004* which preceded it), the Commissioner holds that the cost of accommodation in a private nursing home that is met by a payment made to the claimant for personal care allowances under the Community Care and Health (Scotland) Act 2002 is a payment that disqualifies the claimant from entitlement to Attendance Allowance under reg.7. This is so even though the same payment made to a claimant who was living in their own home would not disqualify them. The Commissioner finds that to be the inevitable outcome of legislation that has been enacted only for Scotland and without any amendment to the legislation for Attendance Allowance.

The matters of entitlement to Attendance Allowance and the recovery of nursing home costs by a local authority have been considered again by Judge Mesher in *MP v SSWP* [2010] UKUT 231 (AAC). In this case, when the local authority began to meet the nursing home fees under Pt III of the 1948 act they determined to recover them, eventually, from the claimant and created a charge against the interest that the claimant had in her former home. They were unable to register that charge because the title to the home was shared with the claimant's daughter and at that time the daughter (who held a power of attorney for the claimant), and other members of the family, refused to agree to repayment of the fees, or to registration of the charge. Judge Mesher concluded that agreement to repay was not a necessary part of recovery of the fees because the local authority could create an enforceable charge against the property without their agreement and that charge would be enforceable whether registered or not. This meant that following the *Creighton* case the claimant was still meeting her accommodation costs and should, therefore, have been entitled to the allowance. The case was referred back for further possible findings of fact. The case is useful also for the judge's reference to other legislation that is relevant in this area.

The question of repayment of fees has been considered further in *Secretary of State for Work and Pensions v JL* [2011] UKUT 293; [2012] AACR 14. This was a decision by a three-judge panel of the Appeal Chamber. The case was on DLA but the provisions are the same for AA. The primary point in contention was whether it was necessary for there to have been a prior agreement for the repayment of the nursing home fees. The panel concluded that there is no necessity for a prior agreement. This is in accordance with both *Creighton* and the subsequent case of *R(A) 1/02*. The judges note also that the DMG may be misleading in this regard. But further, this decision considers the effect of several amendments to the regulations, the difference between entitlement to DLA and payability of DLA and whether the effect of the amendment to reg.7 in 2007 should have retrospective effect so as to deprive the claimant of benefit while he was residing in a nursing home. The tribunal held that it did not.

The treatment of a claimant for whom the cost of accommodation is being met by a Local Authority on a temporary basis and subject to repayment by the claimant, was also considered in *CDLA/5106/2001*. In this case the cost of the accommodation was met initially by the Local Authority, but first a contribution was required, and then an obligation to repay in full under s.22 of the 1948 Act. By the time of the hearing, full repayment had been made. Commissioner Turnbull, nevertheless, held that she was disqualified from receiving benefit because her accommodation was provided in accordance with reg.7(1)(a) and the claimant was not exempted by reg.8(6)(b) until she ceased to be entitled to Income Support because she was not, until then, meeting the whole of the cost of accommodation from her own resources. Although the Commissioner makes no reference to *R(A) 1/02*, his decision accords with that case because there, too, the claimant was disqualified for part of the period in question because she was then in receipt of Income Support. It does not appear that in either case an argument was made that the claimant's entitlement to Income Support should be regarded as a part of her own resources.

This has all been carried a stage further by the decision in *CA/3800/2006*. There the claimant had been in receipt of benefit because she was funding the care home fees from her own resources. Eventually, it became necessary to sell her former home and the proceeds were invested to continue that funding. The investments failed and for a time the claimant became dependant upon the local authority for continued payment of fees. The claimant's daughter, acting under a power of attorney, complained to the Financial Services Ombudsman about the investment advice given to her mother and that complaint was upheld, resulting in a compensation payment to her mother. The claimant resumed payment of fees herself and the local authority required repayment of the fees which they had advanced. The question before the Commissioner was whether the claimant should now be entitled to benefit for the period covered by the local authority. The Commissioner held that she was. The decision taken to cancel her benefit when the local authority first assumed responsibility for payment, should have been a decision to suspend payment rather than a decision to supercede. That it was not, was an official error – that being so, the appeal tribunal should have substituted its own decision to suspend and that would mean the claimant would have remained "entitled" to benefit throughout the period, though not entitled to payment during the period of suspension.

This reasoning has now been applied by Judge Mesher in *SSWP v DA* [2009] UKUT 214 (AAC). The case involved the more usual instance of a claimant whose nursing home fees were paid by the local authority for an interim period while the house that had been her home was sold. The difficulties that are presented by the current provisions for revising and for superseding decisions (provisions that have come into existence since the decision in *Creighton* and the other decisions following it) were explained, but effectively overcome by finding that the superseding decision should have been to the effect that the claimant became entitled to benefit (under reg.8(6) below), though payment was suspended, from the time that the arrangements for repayment to the local authority were made known to the department.

Persons to whom regulations 7 and 8 apply with modifications

7A.—[1 . . .] 4.23

REPEAL

1. Social Security Amendment (Residential Care and Nursing Homes) Regulations 2001 (SI 2001/3767) reg.3 (April 8, 2002).

Exemption from regulations 6 and 7

8.—[1 (1) Regulation 6, or as the case may be, regulation 7, shall not, [2 subject to the following provisions of this regulation], apply to a person in respect of the first 28 days of any period during which he— 4.24

(a) is undergoing medical or other treatment in a hospital or other institution in any of the circumstances mentioned in regulation 6; or

(b) would, but for this regulation, be prevented from receiving an attendance allowance by reason of regulation 7(1).]

(2) For the purposes of paragraph (1)—

(a) two or more distinct periods separated by an interval not exceeding 28 days, or by two or more such intervals, shall be treated as a continuous period equal in duration to the total of such distinct periods and ending on the last day of the later or last such period;

(b) any period or periods to which either regulation 6 or regulation 7 refers shall be taken into account and aggregated with any period to which the other of them refers.

(3) Where, on the day a person's entitlement to an attendance allowance commences, he is in accommodation in the circumstances mentioned in regulation 6 or regulation 7, paragraph (1) shall not apply to him for any period of consecutive days, beginning with that day, on which he remains in that accommodation.

[2 (4) Regulation 6 or, as the case may be, regulation 7 shall not apply [3 [4 . . .] in the case of a person who is residing in a hospice and is terminally ill where the Secretary of State has been informed that he is terminally ill—

(a) on a claim for attendance allowance,

(b) on an application for a [5 revision under section 9 of the Social Security Act 1998 or supersession under section 10 of that Act] of an award of attendance allowance, or

(c) in writing in connection with an award of, or a claim for, or an application for a [5 revision under section 9 of the Social Security Act 1998 or supersession under section 10 of that Act] of an award of, attendance allowance.

(5) In paragraph (4) "hospice" means a hospital or other institution [4 whose primary function is to provide palliative care for persons resident there who are suffering from a progressive disease in its final stages] other than—

(a) [7 *omitted*]

(b) a health service hospital (within the meaning of section 108(1) of the NHS Act of 1978) in Scotland;

[7 (ba) a health service hospital (within the meaning of section 275 of the NHS Act of 2006) in England;

(bb) a hospital in Wales vested in—

(i) an NHS Trust;

(ii) a Local Health Board; or

(iii) the Welsh Ministers, for the purpose of functions under the NHS (Wales) Act of 2006;]

(c) a hospital maintained or administered by the Defence Council; or

(d) an institution similar to a hospital mentioned in any of the preceding sub-paragraphs of this paragraph.

[6 (6) Regulation 7 shall not apply in any particular case for any period during which the whole costs of all of the qualifying services are met—

(a) out of the resources of the person for whom the qualifying services are provided, or partly out of his own resources and partly with assistance from another person or a charity, or

(b) on his behalf by another person or a charity.]

[7 (6A) For the purpose of paragraph (5)(bb)—

(a) "NHS Trust" means a body established under section 18 of the NHS (Wales) Act of 2006; and

(b) "Local Health Board" means a body established under section 11 of the NHS (Wales) Act of 2006.]

(7)[3 [4 . . .]]

AMENDMENTS

1. Social Security (Attendance Allowance) Amendment Regulations 1992 (SI 1992/703) reg.5 (April 6, 1992).

2. Social Security Benefits (Amendments Consequential Upon the Introduction of Community Care) Regulations 1992 (SI 1992/3147) reg.8 (April 1, 1993 with saving).

3. Social Security (Attendance Allowance and Disability Living Allowance) (Amendment) Regulations 2000, (2000/1401) reg.2(4) (June 19, 2000).

4. Social Security Benefits (Miscellaneous Amendments) Regulations 1993 (SI 1993/518) reg.2(3) (April 1, 1993).

5. Social Security Act 1998 (Commencement No.11, and savings and consequential and Transitional Provisions) Order 1999 (SI 1999/2860) Sch.8 (October 18, 1999).

6. Attendance Allowance and Disability Living Allowance (Amendment) Regulations 2007 (SI 2007/2875) (October 29, 2007).

7. Social Security (Attendance Allowance, Disability Living Allowance and Carer's Allowance) (Amendment) Regulations 2013 (SI 2013/389) reg.3 (April 8, 2013).

GENERAL NOTE

See notes above to reg.7. 4.25

[1 Adjustment of allowance where medical expenses are paid from public funds under war pensions instruments

8A.—(1) In this regulation— 4.26

"article 25B" means article 25B of the Personal Injuries (Civilians) Scheme 1983 (medical expenses) and includes that article as applied by article 48B of that Scheme; "article [2 21]" means article [2 21] of the Naval, Military and Air Forces etc. (Disablement and Death) Service Pensions Order [2 2006] (medical expenses);

and in this regulation and regulation 8B "relevant accommodation" means accommodation provided as a necessary ancillary to nursing care where the medical expenses involved are wholly borne by the Secretary of State pursuant to article 25B or article [2 21].

(2) This regulation applies where a person is provided with relevant accommodation.

(3) Subject to regulation 8B, where this regulation applies and there are payable in respect of a person both a payment under either article 25B or article 26 and an attendance allowance, the allowance shall be adjusted by deducting from it the amount of the payment under article 25B or article [2 21], as the case may be, and only the balance shall be payable.]

AMENDMENTS

1. Social Security (Attendance Allowance and Disability Living Allowance) (Amendment) Regulations 1994 (SI 1994/1779) reg.2(4) (August 1, 1994).

2. Social Security (Attendance Allowance, Disability Living Allowance and Carer's Allowance) (Amendment) Regulations 2013 (SI 2013/389) reg.3 (April 8, 2013).

[1 Exemption from regulation 8A

4.27 **8B.**—(1) Regulation 8A shall not, subject to the following provisions of this regulation, apply to a person in respect of the first 28 days of any period during which the amount of any attendance allowance would be liable to be adjusted by virtue of regulation 8A(3).

(2) For the purposes of paragraph (1) two or more distinct periods separated by an interval not exceeding 28 days, or by two or more such intervals, shall be treated as a continuous period equal in duration to the aggregate of such distinct periods and ending on the last day of the later or last such period.

(3) For the purposes of this paragraph a day is a relevant day in relation to a person if it fell not earlier than 28 days before the first day on which he was provided with relevant accommodation; and either—

(a) was a day when he was undergoing medical treatment in a hospital or similar institution in any of the circumstances mentioned in regulation 6; or

(b) was a day when he was, or would but for regulation 8 have been, prevented from receiving an attendance allowance by virtue of regulation 7(1);

and where there is in relation to a person a relevant day, paragraph (1) shall have effect as if for "28 days" there were substituted such lesser number of days as is produced by subtracting from 28 the number of relevant days in his case.]

AMENDMENT

1. Social Security (Attendance Allowance and Disability Living Allowance) (Amendment) Regulations 1994 (SI 1994/1779) reg.2(4) (August 1, 1994).

[1 Prescribed circumstances for entitlement

4.28 **8BA.**—For the purposes of section 64(4) of the Social Security Contributions and Benefits Act 1992 (prescribed circumstances in which a person is to be taken to satisfy or not to satisfy the conditions mentioned in section 64(2) and (3) of that Act), a person shall not be taken to satisfy (2)(a) (day attention) or (3)(a) (night attention) unless the attention the severely disabled person requires from another person is required to be given in the physical presence of the severely disabled person.]

AMENDMENT

1. Social Security (Attendance Allowance and Disability Living Allowance) (Amendment) (No. 2) Regulations 2000 (2000/1401) reg.2 (September 25, 2000).

4.29 *Regulations 8C, 8D and 8E have been revoked by Social Security Act 1998 (Commencement No.11, and Savings and Consequential and Transitional Provisions) Order 1999 (SI 1999/2860) Sch.8, with effect from October 18, 1999.*

Regulation 9 omitted.

[1 SCHEDULE **Regulation 7A(1)**

4.30 [1 . . .]

REPEAL

1. Social Security Amendment (Residential Care and Nursing Homes) Regulations 2001 (SI 2001/3767) reg.3 (April 8, 2002).

The Social Security (Disability Living Allowance) Regulations 1991

(SI 1991/2890) (*as amended*)

ARRANGEMENT OF REGULATIONS

PART I

INTRODUCTION

PART II

GENERAL

PART III

CARE COMPONENT

PART IV

MOBILITY COMPONENT

SCHEDULES

Whereas a draft of this instrument was laid before Parliament in accordance with section 12(1) of the Disability Living Allowance and Disability Working Allowance Act 1991 and approved by resolution of each House of Parliament; now therefore the Secretary of State for Social Security, in exercise of the powers conferred by sections 37ZA(6), 37ZB(2), (3), (7) and (8), 37ZC, 37ZD, 37ZE(2), 85(1), 114(1) and 166(2) to (3A) of and Schedule 20 to the Social Security Act 1975, section 13 of the Social Security (Miscellaneous Provisions) Act 1977 and section 5(1) of the Disability Living Allowance and Disability Working Allowance Act 1991, and of all other powers enabling him in that behalf, by this instrument, which contains only regulations made consequential upon section 1 of the Disability Living Allowance and Disability Working Allowance Act 1991, hereby makes the following Regulations:

PART I

INTRODUCTION

Citation, commencement and interpretation

4.32 **1.**—(1) These Regulations may be cited as the Social Security (Disability Living Allowance) Regulations 1991 and shall come into force on 6th April 1992.

(2) In these Regulations—

[1 "the Act" means the Social Security Contributions and Benefits Act 1992;

"the Administration Act" means the Social Security Administration Act 1992];

[2 "the 1998 Act" means the Social Security Act 1998]

[4 *omitted*];

"the NHS Act of 1978" means the National Health Service (Scotland) Act 1978;

[4 "the NHS Act of 2006" means the National Health Service Act 2006; and

"the NHS (Wales) Act of 2006" means the National Health Service (Wales) Act 2006;]

[4 *omitted*];

[2 "adjudicating authority" means, as the case may require, the Secretary of State, [3 the First-tier Tribunal or the Upper Tribunal];]

"care component" means the care component of a disability living allowance;

[5 "child disability payment" has the meaning given in regulation 2 of the Disability Assistance for Children and Young People (Scotland) Regulations 2021;]

[6 "the Claims and Payments Regulations" means the Social Security (Claims and Payments) Regulations 1987;]

"mobility component" means the mobility component of a disability living allowance;

[6 "the residence change date", in relation to a person, means the date on which the person becomes permanently resident in Scotland (whether or not the Secretary of State is notified of the move and whether or not any such notification takes place before or after the person moves to Scotland);

"the run-on period" has the meaning given in paragraph (6);]

"terminally ill" shall be construed in accordance with [1 section 66(2) of the Act].

(3) Unless the context otherwise requires, any reference in these Regulations to a numbered regulation or Schedule is a reference to the regulation or Schedule bearing that number in these Regulations and any reference in a regulation or Schedule to a numbered paragraph is a reference to the paragraph of that regulation or Schedule bearing that number.

[4(4) With effect from 6th December 2018, any reference in these Regulations to—

(a) "age 65 or over", "the age of 65 years", "the age of 65", "65" and "age 65 and over" shall be construed as a reference to "pensionable age";

(b) "aged 65 or over" and "aged 65 and over" shall be construed as a reference to "of pensionable age"; and

(c) "his 65th birthday" shall be construed as a reference to "the day on which he attained pensionable age".

(5) For the purpose of paragraph (4), "pensionable age" has the meaning given by the rules in paragraph 1 of Schedule 4 to the Pensions Act 1995.]

[6 (6) "The run-on period", in relation to a person, is the period—

(a) beginning with the residence change date, and

(b) ending at the end of the day preceding the pay day which falls immediately after the end of the relevant period.

(7) For the purposes of paragraph (6)—

(a) "pay day" means the day on which a payment of disability living allowance is made in accordance with regulation 25 (1) of the Claims and Payments Regulations;

(b) "the relevant period" means the period of 13 weeks beginning with the residence change date.]

AMENDMENTS

1. Social Security (Disability Living Allowance) (Amendment) Regulations 1993 (SI 1993/1939) reg.2(2) (August 26, 1993).

2. Social Security Act 1998 (Commencement No.11 and Savings and Consequential and Transitional Provisions) Order 1999 (SI 1999/2860) (October 18, 1999).

3. Tribunals, Courts and Enforcement Act 2007 Sch.1 (November 3, 2008).

4. Social Security (Attendance Allowance, Disability Living Allowance and Carer's Allowance) (Amendment) Regulations 2013 (SI 2013/389) reg.4 (April 8, 2013).
5. Social Security (Disability Assistance for Working Age People) (Consequential Amendments) Order 2022 (SI 2022/177) art.4 (March 21, 2022).
6. Scotland Act 2016 (Social Security) (Disability Living Allowance) (Amendment) Regulations 2023 (SI 2023/664) reg.2 (July 7, 2023).

[1 Regulations 2 and 2ZA: the status condition and the award condition

1ZA.—(1) For the purposes of regulations 2 and 2ZA, a person satisfies the status condition if—

(a) they were, on the day on which they reached the age of 16, terminally ill and either—
 (i) they are terminally ill, or
 (ii) following a change in their prognosis, they are a person to whom the Secretary of State is required by regulation 3 (5) of the PIP Transitional Regulations to send a PIP notification but to whom such a notification has not yet been sent,
(b) they are an exempt person,
(c) they have ceased to be an exempt person and are a person—
 (i) to whom the Secretary of State is required by regulation 3 (3) or (5) of the PIP Transitional Regulations to send a PIP notification, but
 (ii) to whom such a notification has not yet been sent,
(d) no disability living allowance is payable to them only by virtue of regulation 8, 9 or 12A,
(e) they are a notified person but not a transfer claimant, or
(f) they are a transfer claimant and no assessment determination has been made on their claim for personal independence payment.

(2) For the purposes of regulations 2 and 2ZA, a person satisfies the award condition if they have an award of disability living allowance for the under 16 age group (whether the award is as originally made, as revised in accordance with section 9 of the 1998 Act or follows a supersession in accordance with section 10 of the 1998 Act).

(3) In this regulation—

(a) "PIP notification" means a notification under regulation 3(1) of the PIP Transitional Regulations;
(b) "the PIP Transitional Regulations" means the Personal Independence Payment (Transitional Provisions) Regulations 2013;
(c) "assessment determination", "exempt person", "notified person" and "transfer claimant" have the meanings given in regulation 2(1) of the PIP Transitional Regulations.]

AMENDMENT

1. Scotland Act 2016 (Social Security) (Disability Living Allowance) (Amendment) Regulations 2023 (SI 2023/664) reg.2 (July 7, 2023).

PART II

GENERAL

[1 Disapplication of section 1(1A) of the Administration Act

1A.—Section 1(1A) of the Administration Act (requirement to state national insurance number) shall not apply— 4.33
(a) to a person under the age of 16;
(b) to any claim for disability living allowance made or treated as made before 9th February, 1998.]

AMENDMENT

1. Social Security (National Insurance Information: Exemption) Regulations (SI 1997/2676) (December 1, 1997).

Conditions as to residence and presence in Great Britain

2.—(1) Subject to the following provisions of this regulation [6 and [7 [10 regulations 2ZA, 2ZB, 2A]]], 2B and 2C]], the prescribed conditions for the purposes of [1 section 71](6) of the Act as to residence and presence in Great Britain in relation to any person on any day shall be that— 4.34
(a) on that day—
(i) he is [6 habitually] resident in [6 the United Kingdom, the Republic of Ireland, the Isle of Man or the Channel Islands]; and
[2 (ib) he is not a person subject to immigration control within the meaning of section 115(9) of the Immigration and Asylum Act 1999 or section 115 of that Act does not apply to him for the purposes of entitlement to disability living allowance by virtue of regulation 2 of the Social Security (Immigration and Asylum) Consequential Amendments Regulations 2000, and]
(ii) he is present in [10 the relevant place]; and
(iii) he has been present in Great Britain for a period of, or for periods amounting in the aggregate to, not less than [6 104] weeks in the [6 156] weeks immediately preceding that day;
(b) [5 . . .]

[10 (1ZZA) For the purposes of this regulation, the relevant place is—
(a) if the person is either under the age of 16 or satisfies both the status condition and the award condition, England and Wales;
(b) otherwise, Great Britain.]

[8 (1ZA) A person to whom regulation 36(1) of the Disability Assistance for Children and Young People (Scotland) Regulations 2021 applies shall be treated for the period set out in that regulation as though he does not satisfy the condition in paragraph (1)(a)(i) of this regulation.]

[9 (1ZB) A person to whom regulation 53(1) of the Disability Assistance for Working Age People (Scotland) Regulations 2022 applies shall be treated for the period set out in that regulation as though he does not satisfy the condition in paragraph (1)(a)(i) of this regulation.]

(1A) [2 *omitted*]]

(2) For the purposes of paragraph (1)(a)(ii) and (iii), notwithstanding that on any day a person is absent from Great Britain, he shall be treated as though he was present in [10 the relevant area if his absence from Great Britain] is by reason only of the fact that on that day—

(a) he is abroad in his capacity as—
  (i) a serving member of the forces,
  (ii) an airman or mariner within the meaning of regulations [6 111 and 115] respectively of the Social Security (Contributions) Regulations [6 2001], and for the purpose of this provision, the expression "serving members of the forces" has the same meaning as in regulation 1(2) of the Regulations of [6 2001]; or
(b) he is in employment prescribed for the purposes of [1 section 120] of the Act in connection with continental shelf operations; or
(c) he is living with a person mentioned in sub-paragraph (a)(i) and is the spouse, [4 civil partner] son, daughter, step-son, step-daughter, father, father-in-law, step-father, mother, mother-in-law or step-mother of that person; or
[6 (d) he is temporarily absent from Great Britain and that absence has not lasted for a continuous period exceeding 13 weeks.]
(e) [6 *omitted*]

[10 (2A) Where a person ("P") is required for the purposes of paragraph (1)(a)(ii) to be present in England and Wales, even though P is absent from England and Wales on any day, P is to be treated as though P were present in England and Wales on that day if—
(a) P's absence on that day is by reason only of the fact that P is temporarily absent from England and Wales; and
(b) P is present in Scotland.]

(3) [5 . . .]

[6 (3A) A person shall be treated as habitually resident in Great Britain for the purpose of paragraph (1)(a)(i) where—
(a) he is resident outside Great Britain in his capacity as a serving member of the forces and for this purpose "serving member of the forces" has the meaning given in regulation 1(2) of the Social Security (Contributions) Regulations 2001; or
(b) he is living with a person mentioned in paragraph (a) and is the spouse, civil partner, son, daughter, step-son, step-daughter, father, father-in-law, step-father, mother, mother-in-law or step-mother of that person.

[6 (3B) Where a person is temporarily absent from Great Britain, he is treated as present in [10 the relevant area] for the purposes of paragraph (1)(a)(ii) and (iii) for the first 26 weeks of that absence, where—
(a) this absence is solely in connection with arrangements made for the medical treatment of him for a disease or bodily or mental disablement which commenced before he left Great Britain; and
(b) the arrangements referred to in sub-paragraph (a) relate to medical treatment—
  (i) outside Great Britain,
  (ii) during the period whilst he is temporarily absent from Great Britain, and
  (iii) by, or under the supervision of, a person appropriately qualified to carry out that treatment, and

"medical treatment" means medical, surgical or rehabilitative treatment (including any course or diet or regimen), and references to a person receiving or submitting to medical treatment are to be construed accordingly.

[10 (3BA) In paragraphs (2) and (3B), "the relevant area" means—
(a) for the purposes of paragraph (1)(a)(ii), the relevant place;
(b) for the purposes of paragraph (1)(a)(iii), Great Britain.]

[6 (3C) For the purpose of paragraph (2)(d) and (3B) a person is "temporarily absent" [10 only if], at the beginning of the period of absence, that absence is unlikely to exceed 52 weeks.]

(4) Where a person is terminally ill and—

(a) makes a claim for disability allowance; or

(b) an application is made for a [3 revision under section 9 of the 1998 Act or supersession under section 10 of that Act] of his award of disability living allowance, expressly on the ground that he is such a person, paragraph (1) shall apply to him as if head (iii) of sub-paragraph (a) was omitted.

(5) Paragraph (1) shall apply in the case of a child under the age of 6 months as if in head (iii) of sub-paragraph (a) for the reference to [6 104] weeks there was substituted a reference to 13 weeks.

(6) Where in any particular case a child has by virtue of paragraph (5), entitlement to the care component immediately before the day he attains the age of 6 months, then until the child attains the age of 12 months, head (iii) of sub-paragraph (a) of paragraph (1) shall continue to apply in his case as if for the reference to [6 104] weeks there was substituted a reference to 13 weeks.

[6 (7) Paragraph (1) shall apply in the case of a child who is over the age of six months but who has not exceeded the age of 36 months as if in head (iii) of sub-paragraph (a) for the reference to 104 weeks there was substituted a reference to 26 weeks.]

AMENDMENTS

1. Social Security (Disability Living Allowance) (Amendment) Regulations 1993 (SI 1993/1939) reg.2 (August 26, 1993).

2. Social Security (Immigration and Asylum) Consequential Amendments Regulations 2000 (SI 2000/636) reg.11 (April 3, 2000).

3. Social Security Act 1998 (Commencement No. 11, and savings and consequential and Transitional Provisions) Order 1999 (SI 1999/2860) Sch.7 (October 18, 1999).

4. Civil Partnership (Pensions, Social Security and Child Support) (Consequential, etc. Provisions) Order 2005 (SI 2005/2877) (December 5, 2005).

5. Social Security (Miscellaneous Amendments) (No.4) Regulations 2006 (SI 2006/2378) reg.8 (October 1, 2006).

6. Social Security (Attendance Allowance, Disability Living Allowance and Carer's Allowance) (Amendment) Regulations 2013 (SI 2013/389) reg.4 (April 8, 2013).

7. Social Security (Miscellaneous Amendment No.4) Regulations 2017 (SI 2017/1015) reg.6(2) (November 16, 2017).

8. Scotland Act 2016 (Social Security) (Consequential Provision) (Miscellaneous Amendment) Regulations 2021 (SI 2021/804) reg.5, (July 26, 2021).

9. Scotland Act 2016 (Social Security) (Adult Disability Payment and Child Disability Payment)(Amendment) Regulations 2022 (SI 2022/335) reg.6, (March 21,2022).

10. Scotland Act 2016 (Social Security) (Disability Living Allowance) (Amendment) Regulations 2023 (SI 2023/664) reg.2(4) (July 7, 2023).

GENERAL NOTE

Regulation 2 has been amended since 1996 to require the claimant to be without any restriction on their permission to be in the UK. That restriction was subject to a saving in respect of claimants already entitled to benefit at the time it came into force. A series of decisions culminating in an appeal to the House of Lords has established that the saving is effective only in respect of an award in force at February 5, 1996, 4.35

and not for a renewal of that award. Where the award was for life it remains effective until reviewed. This decision has now been reported as *R(DLA) 7/01*.

In *MS v SSWP (DLA)* [2016] UKUT 42 (AAC) the claimant was a child born in Israel to an Israeli father. He had been brought to the UK by his mother, who was a UK citizen, on a six month visitor visa and by the time of the application for DLA was an over-stayer. Judge Hemingway applied the view expressed (obiter) by Lord Scarman in *R. v London Borough Council Ex parte Shah* [1983] 2 W.L.R. 16, that the child could not be ordinarily resident in the UK because he was not lawfully present in the UK, even though his mother was.

Until April 8, 2013 a claimant need only have shown that they were "ordinarily resident" and there is a saving for existing claims made on that basis. Neither "ordinary" nor "habitual" residence is defined in the statute or regulations. Ordinary residence has usually been taken to mean that you have a settled intention to live in the country (technically now the "common travel area") as your home, but, not necessarily, permanently. Habitual residence, which is intended to be a more stringent test, requires as well that that the claimant has been in the country already for an extended period. How long, will depend upon the circumstances of the claimant; a former resident returning from a period abroad may satisfy this test almost immediately, while a new immigrant may be required to demonstrate a considerable period of residence. The meaning of "habitual residence" has been the subject of extensive case law in relation to claims for means-tested benefits where it has applied for some time. Readers are referred to the notes to relevant sections of Vol.II of this Work.

In *MM and SI v SSWP (DLA)* [2016] UKUT 149 (AAC); [2016] AACR 38 Judge Markus QC has held that regulation 2(1)(a)(iii) (the past presence test or PPT) must be disapplied in respect of claims made on behalf of applicants who were family members of persons granted refugee status in the UK. She held that the PPT was indirectly discriminatory and could not be justified (when compared to the treatment of UK nationals) under art.28 of the EU Directive 2004/83/EC (which gives protection to refugees) and which she held had direct effect in the UK. For the same reason she held that PPT was in breach of the claimant's rights under art.14 of the ECHR. At the time the claims were made the applicants satisfied the other conditions of regulation 2 which meant that their claims should proceed accordingly.

In *FM v SSWP (DLA)* [2017] UKUT 380 (AAC); [2019] AACR 8 Judge Jacobs has held that the past presence test when applied in the case of a child is not discriminatory so as to be a breach of the claimant's rights under the European Convention on Human Rights and the Human Rights Act 1998. The judge doubted that the claimant's residence before coming to this country could be regarded as a status, but that in any case the difference in treatment between a child who had been resident in this country, and the claimant, was justified. He held also that no breach had been shown of the public sector equality duty under the Equality Act 2010 and that the action of the Department was in accordance with the United Nations Convention on the Rights of the Child 1989. The validity of the amendments made to the past presence test in 2013 has been considered again in the UT by Judge Ward in *TS v SSWP (DLA); EK v SSWP (DLA)* [2020] UKUT 284 (AAC); [2021] AACR 4. He finds that the amending regulations were made in breach of the claimant's human rights and has disapplied those regulations. In reaching this conclusion, Judge Ward finds that the claimant's position as a child returning to the UK after a period spent abroad was a matter affecting their status; he reaches a contrary conclusion to that of Judge Jacobs in the case of *FM v SSWP (DLA)* [2017] UKUT 380 (AAC); [2019] AACR 8 because he finds that in the intervening time since that earlier decision was made the concept of status has been widened. He finds also that the difference in treatment between a child suffering from disablement, who has remained resident in this country, and one brought back from abroad (in one case from New Zealand, in the other from Australia) could not be justified by the reasons given for that difference in treatment by the Secretary of State. The reason given was to effect savings in the social security budget. While the judge accepted that cost-saving was a legitimate aim of the Government, he found that as carried out it was manifestly without reasonable justification. As the case had been argued on the basis that it was the 2013 amending regulations that breached the claimant's human rights and those regulations that could not be justified, Judge Ward held that it was open to him to disapply only the amending regulations thereby reinstating the earlier, less onerous, past presence test. In addition, the judge considered whether it was competent for him to consider the validity of the past presence test in its amended form under the requirements of s.149 of the Equality Act 2010—the Public Sector Equality Duty. He finds, after a full consideration of earlier authorities, as had Judge Wright in *A-K v SSWP (DLA)* [2017] UKUT 420 (AAC), that the UT has no jurisdiction in relation to breaches of the PSED, but in view of the fact that his decision might be appealed further, he went on to examine whether, if he had such jurisdiction, he would have found there to have been such a breach. In his view there was. This was contrary to the conclusion reached by Judge Jacobs in the *FM* case, but Judge Ward was provided with a great deal of further evidence regarding the preparation of the 2013 amending regulations alongside the Personal Independence Regulations that were being made at the same time. From this, it had become clear that no Equality Assessment had been prepared for the amending regulations and even the draft assessment that had been prepared for the PIP regulations was never in fact completed and was never submitted to the Minister for consideration.

For questions that involve persons either coming from or going to a country that is part of the European Economic Area reference should be made to the relevant sections of Vol.III of this Work.

Subsection (2)(e) which provided for a person to be absent with a certificate issued by the Secretary of State has been abolished with effect from April 8, 2013, but there is a saving provision for those persons who were abroad on that basis at that time—see reg.5 of SI 2013/389.

[1 Persons who are entitled to disability living allowance: effect of move to Scotland

2ZA.—(1) This regulation applies where a relevant DLA entitled person becomes permanently resident in Scotland on or after 7th July 2023. 4.36

(2) In this regulation "relevant DLA entitled person" means a person who, at the end of the day preceding the residence change date—

(a) is entitled to disability living allowance

(b) is, or in accordance with regulation 2(2), (2A) or (3B) is treated for the purposes of regulation 2(1)(a)(ii) as, present in England and Wales, and

(c) is under the age of 16 or satisfies both the status condition and the award condition.

(3) The relevant DLA entitled person is to be treated as satisfying the condition in regulation 2(1)(a)(ii) for the duration of the run-on period.

(4) If—

(a) the relevant DLA entitled person has an award of any component of disability living allowance which is for a fixed term period, and

(b) the fixed term period is due to expire before the end of the run-on period, the fixed term period is extended so that it expires at the end of the run-on period.

Persons with an ongoing claim for disability living allowance: effect of move to Scotland

2ZB.—(1) This regulation applies where a new DLA claimant has an ongoing claim for disability living allowance on the residence change date.

(2) For the purposes of this regulation—

(a) "new DLA claimant" means a person who—

(i) does not have an award of disability living allowance,

(ii) makes a claim for disability living allowance and is under the age of 16 on the date on which they make that claim ("the claim date"),

(iii) is, or in accordance with regulation 2(2), (2A) or (3B) is treated for the purposes of regulation 2(1)(a)(ii) as, present in England and Wales on the claim date,

(iv) becomes permanently resident in Scotland after the claim date and on or after 7th July 2023, and

(v) is, or in accordance with regulation 2(2), (2A) or (3B) is treated for the purposes of regulation 2(1)(a)(ii) as, present in England and Wales at the end of the day preceding the residence change date;

(b) a new DLA claimant has an ongoing claim for disability living allowance on the residence change date if their claim for disability living allowance has not—

(i) been decided by the Secretary of State under section 8 of the 1998 Act before that date,

(ii) been withdrawn in accordance with regulation 5(2) of the Claims and Payments Regulations before that date, or

(iii) otherwise ceased, before that date, to be under consideration before being decided by the Secretary of State under section 8 of the 1998 Act.

(3) The Secretary of State must make a decision under section 8 of the 1998 Act on the new DLA claimant's claim for disability living allowance, unless the new DLA claimant withdraws the claim in accordance with regulation 5(2) of the Claims and Payments Regulations.

(4) For the purposes of the Secretary of State making such a decision, regulation 2 applies as if the amendments made to that regulation by the Scotland Act 2016 (Social Security) (Disability Living Allowance) (Amendment) Regulations 2023 had not been made.

(5) If the Secretary of State determines that the new DLA claimant is entitled to disability living allowance—

(a) the new DLA claimant is to be treated as satisfying the condition in regulation 2(1)(a)(ii) until the end of the transfer day, and

(b) if—

(i) the new DLA claimant has an award of any component of disability living allowance which is for a fixed term period, and

(ii) the fixed term period is due to expire before the end of the transfer day, the fixed term period is extended so that it expires at the end of the transfer day.

(6) In this regulation—

(a) "the transfer day", in relation to a person, means—

(i) the final day of the run-on period, or

(ii) if earlier, the day preceding the day on which the person's entitlement to Child Disability Payment begins in accordance with regulation 24 of the Disability Assistance for Children and Young People (Scotland) Regulations 2021;

(b) any reference to the date on which a person makes a claim for Disability Living Allowance (however expressed) is to be construed in accordance with regulation 6 of the Claims and Payments Regulations.]

AMENDMENT

1. Scotland Act 2016 (Social Security) (Disability Living Allowance) (Amendment) Regulations 2023 (SI 2023/664) reg.2(4) (July 7, 2023).

[[1]Persons residing in Great Britain to whom a relevant EU Regulation applies

2A.—(1) Regulation 2(1)(a)(iii) shall not apply where on any day— 4.37

(a) the person is habitually resident in Great Britain;

(b) a relevant EU Regulation applies; and

(c) the person can demonstrate a genuine and sufficient link to the United Kingdom social security system.

(2) For the purpose of paragraph (1)(b) and regulation 2B, "relevant EU Regulation" has the meaning given by section 84(2) of the Welfare Reform Act 2012.]

AMENDMENT

1. Social Security (Attendance Allowance, Disability Living Allowance and Carer's Allowance) (Amendment) Regulations 2013 (SI 2013/389) reg.4 (April 8, 2013).

GENERAL NOTE

The relevant regulations referred to are (EC) No.1408/71 and (EC) No.883/2004. For detailed discussion see Vol.III of this Work. 4.38

The operation of this provision was considered by Judge Wright in *PB v SSWP (DLA)* [2016] UKUT 280 (AAC). In this case the applicant was a disabled child of 13 years who was brought by his mother from the Czech Republic to live with his sister in this country. The sister had by this time been living in Great Britain for at least five years, was in full time employment, and had been awarded both Child Tax Credits and Working Tax Credits in respect of the applicant. The FTT had rejected his appeal against refusal of a claim for DLA on the ground that he did not satisfy the past presence test under reg.2 above. His appeal was allowed on the ground that he was a person to whom reg.2A applied. It was accepted that he was now habitually resident in the UK and that EU Regulation 883/2004 applied to him. It was not necessary that he should fall within the definition of a "family member" under that regulation; all that was required was that he show a "genuine and sufficient link" to the UK social security system and that he could do, as he was now living with, and being cared for by, his sister who had a record of at least five years' employment in this country.

The operation of this subsection has been considered by the CA in *Kavanagh and Mohamed v SSWP* [2019] EWCA Civ 272; [2019] AACR 21 (UT and CA). Both cases had been before Judge Jacobs in the UT where, while it was accepted that each claimant was now habitually resident in the UK, he held that neither was able to establish that they had a genuine and sufficient link to the UK. Judge Jacobs took the view that their reason for coming to the UK could not contribute to establishing that link. The CA, however, held that the reason for coming here could be relevant. In the case of *BK* the claimant was a child for whom a claim of DLA had been made by his mother. The mother was a UK national who had lived most of her life in Ireland, but had come to the UK to escape domestic violence and receive the support that she needed with the claimant and two other children from her mother, grandmother and brothers, all of whom were resident here. The CA held that this reason, together with her actual presence here, was enough to establish that link. In the UT Judge Jacobs had observed that the requirement in subs. (2A)(c) that the link be to the UK social security system was unlawful; the CA proceeded on the basis that that was correct and therefore the last three words of that paragraph are to be ignored.

[[1]Persons residing in an EEA state [[2]...] or in Switzerland to whom a relevant EU Regulation applies

4.39 **2B.**—Regulation 2(1)(a)(i) to (iii) shall not apply in relation to the care component where on any day—

(a) the person is habitually resident in—

(i) an EEA state [[2]...]; or

(ii) Switzerland;

(b) a relevant EU Regulation applies; and

(c) the person can demonstrate a genuine and sufficient link to the UK social security system.]

AMENDMENTS

1. Social Security (Attendance Allowance, Disability living Allowance and Carer's Allowance) (Amendment) Regulations 2013 (SI 2013/389) reg.4 (April 8, 2013).

2. Social Security (Amendment) (EU Exit) Regulations 2019 (SI 2019/128) reg.4 and Sch. para. 7 (January 31, 2020).

[[1][[2] Refugees and certain persons with leave to enter or remain in the United Kingdom]

4.40 **2C.**—(1) Regulation 2(1)(a)(iii) shall not apply where the person has—

(a) been granted refugee status or humanitarian protection under the immigration rules; [[2] ...]

(b) leave to enter or to remain in the United Kingdom as the dependant of a person granted refugee status or humanitarian protection under the immigration rules;

[[2](c) leave to enter or remain in the United Kingdom granted under the immigration rules by virtue of—

(i) the Afghan Relocations and Assistance Policy; or

(ii) the previous scheme for locally-employed staff in Afghanistan (sometimes referred to as the ex-gratia scheme);

(d) been granted discretionary leave outside the immigration rules as a dependant of a person referred to in sub-paragraph (c);

(e) leave granted under the Afghan Citizens Resettlement Scheme] [[3] [[4] [[5]...]]]

(f) leave to enter or remain in the United Kingdom granted under or outside the immigration rules [[4], a right] of abode in the United Kingdom within the meaning given in section 2 of the Immigration Act 1971 [[4] or does not require leave to enter or remain in the United Kingdom in accordance with section 3ZA of that Act,] where the person—

(i) was residing in Ukraine immediately before 1st January 2022; and

(ii) left Ukraine in connection with the Russian invasion which took place on 24th February 2022;]

[[5] (g) leave to enter or remain in the United Kingdom granted under or outside the immigration rules, a right of abode in the United Kingdom within the meaning given in section 2 of the Immigration Act 1971 or does not require leave to enter or remain in the United

Kingdom in accordance with section 3ZA of that Act, where the person—
(i) was residing in Sudan before 15th April 2023; and
(ii) left Sudan in connection with the violence which rapidly escalated on 15th April 2023 in Khartoum and across Sudan] [[6], or
(h) leave to enter or remain in the United Kingdom granted under or outside the immigration rules, a right of abode in the United Kingdom within the meaning given in section 2 of the Immigration Act 1971 or does not require leave to enter or remain in the United Kingdom in accordance with section 3ZA of that Act, where the person—
(i) was residing in Israel, the West Bank, the Gaza Strip, East Jerusalem, the Golan Heights or Lebanon immediately before 7th October 2023; and
(ii) left Israel, the West Bank, the Gaza Strip, East Jerusalem, the Golan Heights or Lebanon in connection with the Hamas terrorist attack in Israel on 7th October 2023 or the violence which rapidly escalated in the region following the attack.]

[[2] (1A) Regulation 2(1)(a)(i) shall not apply where [[3] any sub-paragraph in paragraph (1)] applies to the person.]

(2) For the purposes of this regulation "immigration rules" means the rules laid before Parliament under section 3(2) of the Immigration Act 1971.]

AMENDMENTS

1. Social Security (Miscellaneous Amendments No.4) Regulations 2017 (SI 2017/1015) reg.7(3) (November 16, 2017).

2. Social Security (Habitual Residence and Past Presence) (Amendment) Regulations 2021 (SI 2021/1034) reg.4 (September 15, 2021). The amendments made by these regulations apply in respect of England and Wales only. The same amendments are made with effect from the same date in respect of Scotland only by reg.2 of the Social Security (Residence Requirements) (Afghanistan) (Scotland) Regulations 2021 (SI 2021/320) but in addition that regulation also substitutes for paragraph (2) of reg.2C the following—

"(2) For the purposes of this regulation—

(a) "immigration rules" means the rules laid before Parliament under section 3(2) of the Immigration Act 1971,

(b) "the Afghan Citizens Resettlement Scheme" means the scheme announced by the United Kingdom Government on 18 August 2021."

3. Social Security (Habitual Residence and Past Presence) (Amendment) Regulations 2022 (SI 2022/344) reg.4 (March 22, 2022). Note: this regulation applies only to England and Wales. Identical provision is made for Scotland, with effect from the same date, by the Social Security (Residence Requirements) (Ukraine) (Scotland) Regulations 2022 (SSI 2022/108).

4. Social Security (Habitual Residence and Past Presence) (Amendment) (No.2) Regulations 2022 (SI 2022/990) reg.3 (October 18, 2022). Note: this regulation applies only to England and Wales. Identical provision is made for Scotland by the Social Security (Miscellaneous Amendment and Transitional Provision) (Scotland) Regulations 2022 (SI 2022/336) reg.6 (November 28, 2022).

5. Social Security (Habitual Residence and Past Presence) (Amendment) Regulations 2023 (SI 2023/532) reg.4 (May 15, 2023). Note: this regulation applies only to England and Wales. Identical provision is made for Scotland with effect from May 17, 2023, by reg.2 of the Social Security (Residence Requirements) (Sudan) (Scotland) Regulations 2023 (SSI 2023/149).

6. Social Security (Habitual Residence and Past Presence, and Capital Disregards) (Amendment) Regulations 2023 (SI 2023/1144) reg.10 (October 27, 2023).

Note: This amendment applies only to England and Wales. Identical provision is made for Scotland with effect from October 26, 2023, by the Social Security (Residence and Presence Requirements) (Israel, West Bank, the Gaza Strip, East Jerusalem, the Golan Heights and Lebanon) (Scotland) Regulations 2023 (SSI 2023/309).

Age 65 or over

4.41 **3.**—(1) A person shall not be precluded from entitlement to either component of disability living allowance by reason only that he has attained the age of 65 years [1 if he is a person to whom paragraphs (2) and (3) apply].

(2) Paragraph (3) applies to a person who—

(a) made a claim for disability living allowance before he attained the age of 65, which was not determined before he attained that age, and

(b) did not at the time he made the claim have an award of disability living allowance for a period ending on or after the day he attained the age of 65.

(3) In determining the claim of a person to whom this paragraph applies, where the person otherwise satisfies the conditions of entitlement to either or both components of disability living allowance for a period commencing before his 65th birthday (other than the requirements of [2 section 72](2)(a), or, as the case may be, [2 section 73](9)(a) of the Act (3 months qualifying period)), the determination shall be made without regard to the fact that he is aged 65 or over at the time the claim is determined.

[3(3A) A person shall not be precluded from entitlement to the care component of disability living allowance by reason only that he has attained the age of 65 years if the claim is treated as made on 18th October 2007 in accordance with regulation 6(35) of the Social Security (Claims and Payments) Regulations 1987 (date of claim).]

(4) Schedule 1, which makes further provision for persons aged 65 or over shall have effect.

AMENDMENTS

1. Social Security (Disability Living Allowance) Amendments Regulations 1997 (SI 1997/349) reg.2 (October 6, 1997).

2. Social Security (Disability Living Allowance) (Amendment) Regulations 1993 (SI 1993/1939) reg.2 (August 26, 1993).

3. Social Security (Disability Living Allowance, Attendance and Carer's Allowance) (Miscellaneous Amendments) Regulations 2011 (SI 2011/2426) reg.4 (October 31, 2011).

GENERAL NOTE

Paragraph (1)

4.42 Section 75(1) of the Social Security Contributions and Benefits Act 1992 has the effect that normally a person cannot be entitled to disability living allowance after he or she has attained the age of 65 unless awarded it before that age. Before its amendment, this paragraph enabled a person who would have satisfied the conditions of entitlement continuously since the age of 65 to qualify provided he or she made a claim before reaching the age of 66. The amendment means that it is now necessary for the claimant to have made a claim before reaching the age of 65. An earlier unsuccessful claim is irrelevant (*R(M) 4/86*). Where a claim has been determined in the claimant's favour before his or her 65th birthday, para.(4) and

Sch.1 apply and make provision for reviews and renewal claims. Where a claim has not been determined before the claimant's 65th birthday, paras (2) and (3) apply. Those who are too old to be entitled to disability living allowance but who would otherwise qualify for the highest or middle rate of the care component will be entitled to attendance allowance instead, subject to satisfying the longer six-month qualifying condition.

Paragraphs (2) and (3)

Section 75(1) of the 1992 Act specifically provides that a claimant cannot be entitled to disability living allowance unless the *award* has been made before his or her 65th birthday. These paragraphs make provision for a person whose *claim* was made before the 65th birthday and who is not making an advance claim to follow an existing award ending on or after that birthday. In such a case, provided that the conditions of entitlement are satisfied for a period commencing before the claimant's 65th birthday, entitlement is to be determined without regard to the fact that he or she is aged 65 or over at the time of the determination. Note that it is not necessary for the three-month qualifying condition to be satisfied before the claimant reaches the age of 65. Thus a person who becomes seriously disabled, say, a month before his or her birthday, can become entitled to disability living allowance two months after the birthday. **4.43**

Paragraph (3A)

This amendment preserves the entitlement of claimants over 65 who have moved to live in another part of the European Economic Area or to Switzerland. This is achieved by the effect of reg.6(35) of the Claims and Payments regulations which gives effect to the judgment of the European Court of Justice in case C-299/05, *Commission of the European Communities v European Parliament and European Union.* **4.44**

Paragraph 4

See the notes to Sch.1 which deals with the determination of reviews and renewal claims after a person's 65th birthday and with the position of former beneficiaries under the invalid vehicle scheme. **4.45**

Rate of benefit

4.—(1) The three weekly rates of the care component are— **4.46**

(a) the highest rate, payable in accordance with [1 section 72](4)(a) of the Act, [2£108.55];

(b) the middle rate, payable in accordance with [1section 72](4)(b) of the Act, [2£72.65];

(c) the lowest rate, payable in accordance with [1 section 72](4)(c) of the Act, [2£28.70].

(2) The two weekly rates of the mobility component are—

(a) the higher rate, payable in accordance with [1 section 73] (11)(a) of the Act, [2£75.75]; and

(b) the lower rate, payable in accordance with [1 section 73] (11)(b) of the Act, [2£28.70].

AMENDMENTS

1. Social Security (Disability Living Allowance) (Amendment) Regulations 1993 (SI 1993/1939) reg.2 (August 26, 1993).

2. Social Security Benefits (Up-rating) Order 2024 (SI 2024/242) art.14 (April 8, 2024). This Order applies only to England and Wales. For Scotland, the Social Security Up-rating (Scotland) Order 2021 (SSI 2024/106) art.7 makes the same amendments with effect from the same date.

Late claim by a person previously entitled

4.47 **5.**—[1 . . .]

5A.—[2[3 . . .]]

5B.—[2[3 . . .]]

5C.—[2[3 . . .]]

AMENDMENTS

1. Repealed by Social Security (Miscellaneous Amendments) (No. 2) Regulations 1997 (SI 1997/793) reg.19 (September 1, 1997).

2. Social Security (Attendance Allowance and Disability Living Allowance) (Miscellaneous Amendments) Regulations 1997 (SI 1997/1839) reg.3 (August 25, 1997).

3. Social Security Act 1998 (Commencement No. 11, and Savings and Consequential and Transitional Provisions) Order 1999 (SI 1999/2860) Sch.7 para.3 (October 18, 1999).

PART III

CARE COMPONENT

Qualifying period for care component after an interval

4.48 **6.**—(1) The period prescribed for the purposes of [1 section 72] (2)(a)(ii) of the Act is a period of 3 months ending on the day on which the person was last entitled to the care component [2 of disability living allowance, or the care component of child disability payment] or to attendance allowance where that day falls not more than 2 years before the date on which entitlement to the care component [2 of disability living allowance, or the care component of child disability payment] would begin, or would have begun but for any regulations made under [1 section 5(1)(k) of the Administration Act] (which enables regulations to provide for the day on which entitlement to benefit is to begin or end).

(2) Except in a case to which paragraph (3) applies, this regulation shall apply to a person to whom paragraph 3 or 7 of Schedule 1 refers as if for the reference to 3 months there was substituted a reference to 6 months.

(3) Paragraph (1) and not paragraph (2), shall apply to those persons referred to in paragraph (2) who, on the day before they attained the age of 65, had already completed the period of three months referred to in paragraph (1).

(4) For the purposes of paragraph (3), the modification made in Schedule 1—

(a) in paragraph 3 (2) and 7(2), to [1 section 72] (2)(a) of the Act, and

(b) in paragraph 5 (2), to [1 section 73] (9)(a) of the Act,

shall be treated as not having been made.

AMENDMENTS

1. Social Security (Disability Living Allowance) (Amendment) Regulations 1993 (SI 1993/1939), reg.2 (August 26, 1993).

2. Social Security (Disability Assistance for Working Age People) (Consequential Amendments) Order 2022 (SI 2022/177) art.4 (March 21, 2022).

GENERAL NOTE

4.49 The general effect of this provision is that the three-month qualifying period (six months for people aged 65 or over) for the care component is deemed to be satisfied if the new claim is within two years of a previous period of entitlement to the care component (or attendance allowance) at the relevant rate.

Renal Dialysis

7.—(1) A person who suffers from renal failure and falls within the provisions in paragraph (2) shall be taken to satisfy— **4.50**

(a) where he undergoes renal dialysis by day, the conditions in paragraph (b) of subsection (1) of [1 section 72] of the Act (severe physical or mental disability);

(b) where he undergoes renal dialysis by night, the conditions in paragraph (c) of that subsection; or

(c) where he undergoes renal dialysis by day and by night, the conditions in either paragraph (b) or paragraph (c) of subsection (1), but not both.

(2) Subject to paragraph (3), a person falls within this paragraph—

(a) if—

(i) he undergoes renal dialysis two or more times a week; and

(ii) the renal dialysis he undergoes is of a type which normally requires the attendance or supervision of another person during the period of the dialysis; or

(iii) because of the particular circumstances of his case he in fact requires another person, during the period of the dialysis, to attend in connection with his bodily functions or to supervise him in order to avoid substantial danger to himself; and

(b) if, where he undergoes dialysis as an out-patient in a hospital or similar institution, being treatment provided under [2 the NHS Act of 1978, the NHS Act of 2006 or the NHS (Wales) Act of 2006], no member of the staff of the hospital or institution assists with or supervises the dialysis.

[1 (3) Paragraph (2)(b) does not apply for the purpose of determining whether a person is to be taken to satisfy any of the conditions mentioned, in paragraph (1) during the periods mentioned in section 72(2)(a)(i) and (b)(i) of the Act.]

(4) Except to the extent that provision is made in paragraph (2)(b), a person who undergoes treatment by way of renal dialysis as an outpatient in a hospital or similar institution, being treatment provided under [2 the NHS Act of 1978, the NHS Act of 2006 or the NHS (Wales) Act of 2006], shall not be taken solely by reason of the fact that he undergoes such dialysis, as satisfying any of the conditions mentioned in subsection (1)(a) to (c) of [1 section 72] of the Act.

AMENDMENT

1. Social Security (Disability Living Allowance) (Amendment) Regulations 1993 (SI 1993/1939) reg.2 (August 26, 1993).

2. Social Security (Attendance Allowance, Disability Living Allowance and Carer's Allowance) (Amendment) Regulations 2013 (SI 2013/389) reg.4 (April 8, 2013).

GENERAL NOTE

Under this regulation, a person undergoing renal dialysis at least twice a week may be deemed to satisfy *either* the "day" *or* the "night" attendance conditions of s.72(1)(b) and (c) of the Social Security Contributions and Benefits Act 1992, but not both. Some degree of attention or supervision must be required. This **4.51** regulation is in slightly different terms from reg.5 of the Social Security (Attendance Allowance) Regulations 1991.

Paragraph (2)(a)

4.52 The dialysis must be *either* of a type which *normally* requires the attendance of or supervision by another person (in which case the actual purpose of the attention or supervision is irrelevant) *or* the dialysis must *in the particular case* require the attention or supervision of the claimant (for the purpose specified in para.(2)(a)(iii)).

Paragraphs (2)(b), (3) and (4).

4.53 Under paras (2)(b) and (4), a person receiving treatment under the National Health Service cannot qualify for the care component under this regulation if he or she receives assistance or supervision during the dialysis from a member of staff of the hospital or other relevant institution, although there is nothing in para.(4) to prevent the need for any such assistance or supervision from being taken into account when considering whether the ordinary "day" or "night" conditions are satisfied. Para.(3) has the effect that, where a person has been undergoing dialysis falling within para.(2)(a) but para.(2)(b) was not satisfied because, say, supervision was provided in a National Health Service hospital, he or she can qualify under this regulation as soon as that supervision ceases, as long as he or she had been undergoing the dialysis for the usual three-month qualifying period. Presumably para.(3) applies equally to the six-month qualifying period substituted under para.3 of Sch.1 for claimants aged 65 or over.

[5 Hospitalisation of persons aged 18 or over]

4.54 **8.**—[1 (1) Subject to [5 paragraph (2B) and] regulation 10, it shall be a condition for the receipt of a disability living allowance which is attributable to entitlement to the care component for any period in respect of any person that during that period he is not maintained free of charge while undergoing medical or other treatment as an in-patient—

(a) in a hospital or similar institution under [4 the NHS Act of 1978, the NHS Act of 2006 or the NHS (Wales) Act of 2006]; or

(b) in a hospital or other similar institution maintained or administered by the Defence Council.]

(2) For the purposes of [1 paragraph (1)(a)] a person shall only be regarded as not being maintained free of charge in a hospital or similar institution during any period when his accommodation and services are provided under[—]

[4 (a) section 57 of, and paragraph 14 of Schedule 7A to, the NHS Act of 1978;

(b) section 13 of, and paragraph 15 of Schedule 2 to, the NHS Act of 2006;

(c) section 28 of, and paragraph 11 of Schedule 6 to, the NHS Act of 2006;

(d) section 44(6) of, and paragraph 19(1) of Schedule 4 to, the NHS Act of 2006;

(e) section 11 of, and paragraph 15 of Schedule 2 to, the NHS (Wales) Act of 2006;

(f) section 18 of, and paragraph 19(1) of Schedule 3 to, the NHS (Wales) Act of 2006; or

(g) section 22 of, and paragraph 11 of Schedule 5 to, the NHS (Wales) Act of 2006.]

[2 (2A) For the purposes of paragraph (1), a period during which a person is maintained free of charge while undergoing medical or other treatment as an in-patient shall be deemed to begin on the day after the day on which he enters a hospital or similar institution referred to in that paragraph and to end on the day [3 before the day] on which he leaves such a hospital or similar institution].

[5(2B) This regulation does not apply to a person who was under the age of 18 on the day on which he entered the hospital or other similar institution referred to in paragraph (1) to begin his current period as an in-patient.]

(3) [1 . . .].

AMENDMENTS

1. Social Security (Disability Living Allowance and Attendance Allowance) (Amendment) Regulations 1992 (SI 1992/2869) reg.4 (December 15, 1992).

2. Social Security (Hospital In-Patients, Attendance Allowance and Disability Living Allowance) (Amendment) Regulations 1999 (SI 1999/1326) (June 7, 1999).

3. Social Security (Attendance Allowance and Disability Living Allowance) (Amendment) Regulations 2000, (SI 2000/1401) reg.3 (June 19, 2000).

4. Social Security (Attendance Allowance, Disability Living Allowance and Carer's Allowance) (Amendment) Regulations 2013 (SI 2013/389) reg.4 (April 8, 2013).

5. Social Security (Disability Living Allowance and Personal Independence Payment) (Amendment) Regulations 2016 (SI 2016/556) regulation 2 (June 29, 2016).

GENERAL NOTE

Note that this regulation has been amended in response to the decision of the Supreme Court in *Cameron Mathieson v SSWP* [2015] UKSC 47. That decision concerned a claim made on behalf of an infant claimant. The SC held that the previous version of this regulation breached the claimant's rights under the Human Rights Act 1998 and under the European Convention on Human Rights. Accordingly this regulation now applies only to claimants who are aged 18 years or over. **4.55**

An attempt to apply the same argument in the case of an adult claimant has failed in *MOC (by MG v SSWP (DLA)* [2020] UKUT 134 (AAC). The claimant, who was severely disabled with Down's Syndrome and was, as well, both blind and deaf, had been admitted to hospital. After the period of 28 days allowed for in reg.10 below, the DM had removed payability of both the care component and mobility component. In the UT Judge Ward found that even if the claimant's condition could be said to constitute a status for the purpose of the discrimination alleged, which he doubted, any discrimination that might then be said to exist was justified by the policy behind this regulation (and reg.12A below), which was the avoidance of double provision from public funds for the same contingency. The judge found that the case of an adult was distinguishable from that of a child (as in *Mathieson*) because there was no evidence that the claimant would require significant care and attention that went beyond that which was provided in the NHS hospital to which he had been admitted.

See the annotations to reg.6 of the Social Security (Attendance Allowance) Regulations 1991 which is in identical terms.

Note that, by virtue of reg.10, a person may remain entitled to the care component for up to 28 days in hospital but that separate periods in hospital or such accommodation are aggregated unless they are more than 28 days apart.

This regulation disqualifies a claimant who is being treated in a publicly financed hospital. In decision *CDLA/11099/1995* the Commissioner had to decide if it applied to a patient who spent each night in such a hospital but was at home through the day. He held that it did; because the claimant spent a part of each day in a publicly funded hospital he could not qualify for benefit on any day.

Note that a similar issue has arisen in relation to reg.2(2) of the Hospital In-Patients Regulation 1975, where there has been a conflict in Commissioners' decisions. This decision is in accordance with the more recent of those decisions.

In decision *CSDLA/1282/01* the Commissioner holds that a claimant is being maintained free of charge in hospital notwithstanding that the claimant may continue to receive care and support from their family. In this case the claimant was fed and bathed, etc. by her family because she refused to allow nursing staff to provide those services.

In *CDLA/7980/95* the Commissioner had to decide if this provision could cover the case of a claimant formerly accomodated in a hospital, but now living in a privately rented house with full-time care provided by the local Health Service Trust, under the Care in the Community policy. He held that it did not. A privately rented home which the claimant shared with six others, and in which they paid not only the rent, but also for their own food, etc. did not become either a "hospital" or a "similar institution" simply because they were cared for there at public expense. Equally, the Commissioner could have found that while they were living there they were not "maintained free of charge" because they were paying their own rent and other outgoings—presumably being maintained includes the provision of housing, food, etc. as well as care.

It should be noted that there may be some overlap between this regulation and reg.9 because in *CAO v White* (reported as *R(IS) 18/94*) (referred to in *CDLA/7980/95*) it was held that a registered nursing home (which could fall within reg.9) also fell within the description of a "hospital or similar institution" for the purposes of the Hospital In-Patients Regulations 1975 which uses the same expression.

The complex issue of whether care has been provided for in a "hospital or similar institution" so as to be disqualified from benefit under this regulation, or whether instead it was provided under arrangements made by the local authority so as to be disqualified under reg.9, has been examined by a Tribunal of Commissioners in *R(DLA) 2/06*. Put thus, it might seem to matter little to the claimant under which regulation the claim for care must fail, but for claimants entitled also to a mobility component which is covered by transitional protection, and for claimants who are able to claim Income Support, the distinction will be significant because there is no equivalent to reg.9 disqualification for those other benefits. Indeed, in this case it was also argued that neither reg.8 or reg.9 should apply, though then any resulting benefit entitlement would be paid to the local authority for them to pay to the nursing home as had been happening in these cases.

The cases involved claimants who were formerly patients in a mental hospital and who, under the changes made in the early 1990's, were moved into private nursing homes where they still continued to receive the high level of care and nursing services consistent with their condition. No formal assessment of their needs was made, but it was clear from the charges levied for each of them that the service provided was for far more than accommodation with incidental nursing care. The Commissioners concluded therefore that the nursing home fell within the description of an institution similar to a hospital and the disqualification applied. (See *CAO v White R(1S) 18/94*)

4.56 The real protagonists in this case were the local health authority and the DWP. This was because, if the claimants' needs really were those of a hospital patient, then the health authority was liable to supply those needs under the National Health Service Act 1997. But under the ill constructed and poorly evidenced arrangements that the health authority and the local authority had tried to make in this case, they purported to make the claimants into self funding residents of the care homes so that all their benefit entitlements would be available as a contribution to their fees, the balance of which was then made up by the health authority, though paid through the local authority.

The argument put forward by the DWP was that either they were still in a "hospital" and therefore caught by reg.8, or they were being accommodated by the local authority under Pt III of the National Assistance Act and then caught by reg.9. Either way the DWP should not have been paying to the extent of the care component of DLA. In deciding that the arrangements necessary for these claimants amounted to hospital care the commissioners were also saying that the claimants could not be accommodated under Pt III because that power does not extend to accommodating persons who need full hospital care—the whole of such costs, therefore, should have been met by the health authority. The net effect was that some patients (those not qualifying for IS) had been charged considerable sums for which they should not have been liable. None of this was in issue before the Commissioners and was relevant only as being a necessary step in reaching the decisions that they did, but the Commissioners conclude by referring to the ill standards of public administration that this revealed.

The further complications involved in administering this provision (and regs 8 and 12A) are demonstrated in *SSWP v TR (DLA)* [2013] UKUT 622 (AAC). The claimant was accommodated in a home for which the health authority and the local authority had agreed to share the costs on a 50/50 basis. The claimant was subjected to a statutory charge which he paid to the local authority. In the home, 31 per cent of the staff were qualified nurses, there was as well a "physio team", and the home was registered to provide care with nursing and rehabilitation services. The question to be determined was whether the claimant, in these circumstances, was being "maintained free of charge while undergoing medical or other treatment as an in-patient in a hospital or similar institution". The judge in the UT, Judge Fordham, found that he was not. He would have found that the home was a "hospital or similar institution" and he would have found too, that the claimant was "receiving medical treatment as an in-patient" there, but he did not find that the claimant was being "maintained free of charge" in the home. This was not because the claimant was paying a contribution towards his costs- that would have been the effect of giving this phrase its natural and ordinary meaning, but the phrase has a restricted meaning in reg.8(2) (and in reg.12A(2)). The effect of that definition is that a claimant can only be said to be not being maintained in the hospital free of charge if they are there entirely as a private patient; thus for someone in the claimant's position although he was being charged a contribution, he could still be regarded as being there "free of charge"! The judge's decision turns upon what is meant by being "maintained" and the interpretation given to that word in the earlier cases of *R (DLA) 2/06* and *CDLA/509/2009* which followed it. Those cases establish that a claimant is to be regarded as maintained in the hospital or other institution only as long as the health authority has a duty to do so under the relevant National Health Service Act. Correspondingly he cannot be maintained by the local authority while that is so, and he can be maintained by the local authority only when they have a duty to so under Pt III of the National Assistance Act 1948.

In this case it appeared that the local authority took the view that they were obliged to maintain under Pt III and it followed that the health authority were not, therefore "maintaining" him.

This meant that the claimant was entitled to be paid DLA under both reg.8 and reg.12A. But he was not entitled to payment of the care component of DLA because under reg.9 (see below) at least some part of the cost of his accommodation and care was met from public funds.

This a complex area of law that seems to be encumbered by provisions derived from past practices and badly in need of updating.

The meanings of the phrases, "medical or other treatment" and "hospital or similar institution", have been considered at length by Judge Turnbull in *AS v SSWP* [2010] UKUT 482 (AAC). The claimant was living in a private care home that specialised in providing accommodation for autistic people. None of the staff in the home was medically qualified, but the whole of the cost was paid by the health authority. While he had been living at home the claimant had been in receipt of care component of DLA at the highest rate and of mobility component at the higher rate. When he moved to the care home both components were stopped (the care component under reg.8 and the mobility component under reg.12A (see below)) on the basis that he was now "maintained free of charge while undergoing medical or other treatment as an in-patient . . . in a hospital or similar institution". His parents appealed on the basis that, though he might not be entitled to the care component, he should still be receiving the mobility component, as would be the case if his disqualification were made under reg.9 (see below), where disqualification applies only to the care component. However, on 4.57

closer examination the judge pointed out that reg.9 could not apply in this case, as the fees were being paid by the health authority; reg.9 applies only where fees are being met by a local authority. Thus, unless the care home could be classed as a "hospital or similar institution" the claimant would be entitled to both components despite the fact that all of his living expenses (though arguably not his mobility) were being met from public funds. The judge referred to the case of *Minister of Health v House for Incurables at Leamington Spa* [1954] 1 Ch. 530 (CA), a case arising from the creation of the National Health Service, as well as two cases where the same phrases occur in relation to other benefits; *CAO v White R(IS) 18/94* and *Botchett v CAO R(IS) 10/96.* He felt that these cases, together with the interrelated meaning of "medical or other treatment" compelled him to conclude that the care home could not be a hospital or similar institution unless the care that was provided there was delivered by medically qualified staff. In the cases referred to above all of the institutions had qualified nurses on the staff. While he stops short of holding that it is essential to have a nursing staff he does suggest that there should at least be persons who could be described as health-care professionals who are regularly providing services on the premises to those accommodated there. This decision has now been upheld by the Court of Appeal and reported as *Secretary of State for Work and Pensions v Slavin* [2011] EWCA Civ 1515. [2012] AACR 30 The court rejected an argument put on behalf of the Secretary of State that regs 8 (care component) and 12A (mobility component) should be read so as to achieve a broad policy objective of avoiding the payment of benefit for needs that were provided from public funds in some other way. The court denied that any such broad policy objective could be read into those regulations. The court also confirmed that, although nursing practice may have moved on considerably since the time of the *Leamington* decision, the test of whether the claimant was in receipt of "medical or other treatment" should remain that of whether such services were provided by medically qualified staff, which meant at least a nursing qualification or training. Furthermore, they confirmed that such treatment must take place in the institution where the claimant was accommodated. The court did not decide whether the place of accommodation could be regarded as a "hospital or similar institution" in which the claimant received "medical or other treatment" if the treatment were provided by professionally qualified persons at that place, but not by persons employed by the institution. This question was left open because the case had been referred to the court on the basis that the information necessary for a determination of that question had not been obtained from the parties. A further decision may therefore be necessary to determine this point, but such arrangements would presumably have to go beyond the treatment that might normally be available to a patient in their own home.

This case concerned only the claimant's entitlement to the mobility component (It appears that the decision in respect of the care component had not been appealed at the First-tier Tribunal in the mistaken belief that entitlement was removed under reg.9), but the court accepts that the interpretation they apply in relation to reg.12A must apply equally to reg.8.

The meaning of the phrases "undergoing medical or other treatment as an in-patient" and "in a hospital or similar institution" has been considered again by Judge Turnbull in *JP v SSWP* [2013] UKUT 524 (AAC). There the claimant was a young man who suffered from a serious form of epilepsy. Until 2007 he had lived at home with his parents, but then it had been necessary to move him from his home to a place run by a charity that provided accommodation and specialist services for persons with conditions of that kind. The premises extended over a campus like arrangement that included accommodation units, medical and other services and a GP surgery. The claimant lived in an accommodation unit that was staffed only by non-medically qualified persons, but the charity had engaged a number of other medically qualified staff including nurses, a doctor (other than the GP), psychologists and consultants who came to the campus to provide their services. On behalf of the claimant it was argued that where he lived was staffed only by care staff and that the medical services that he received were no more than would have been available from a local hospital etc had he been living still at his parents' home. Judge Turnbull, however, decided that the charity's premises should be regarded as a collective unit that, although clearly not a hospital, could fall within the description of a "similar institution". Furthermore, in his view, the treatment that the claimant received on the premises (though not that from the GP surgery) constituted "medical or other treatment as an in patient". Consequently the appeal against refusal of both the living component (under reg.8) and the mobility component (under reg.12A) was dismissed.

[1 Persons in care homes

9.—(1) Except in the cases specified in paragraphs (3) to (5), and subject to regulation 10, a person shall not be paid any amount in respect of a disability living allowance which is attributable to entitlement to the care component for any period where throughout that period he is a resident in a care home in circumstances where any of the costs of any qualifying services provided for him are borne out of public or local funds under a specified enactment. 4.58

(2) The specified enactments for the purposes of paragraph (1) are—

(a)

(i) Part III of the National Assistance Act 1948,

(ii) [3 sections 59 and 59A] of the Social Work (Scotland) Act 1968,

(iii) the Mental Health (Care and Treatment) (Scotland) Act 2003,

(iv) the Community Care and Health (Scotland) Act 2002,

(v) the Mental Health Act 1983;

[4 (vi) section 57 of the Health and Social Care Act 2001,]

[5 (vii) Part 1 of the Care Act 2014 (care and support),]

[6 (viii) Part 4 of the Social Services and Well-being (Wales) Act 2014 (meeting needs), or]

(b) any other enactment relating to persons under disability or to young persons or to education or training.

(3) Paragraph (2)(b) shall not apply in circumstances where any of the costs of the qualifying services provided for him are borne wholly or partly out of public or local funds by virtue of—

(a) section 485 of the Education Act 1996, section 14 of the Education Act 2002 or section 73 of the Education (Scotland) Act 1980 (which relate to grants in aid of educational services);

(b) [3 *omitted*] sections 49 or 73 of the Education (Scotland) Act 1980 (which relate respectively to the power of education authorities to assist persons to take advantage of educational facilities and the powers of the Secretary of State to make grants to education authorities and others);

(c) section 65 of the Further and Higher Education Act 1992 [7, sections 39 or 40 of the Higher Education and Research Act 2017] or sections 4 or 11 of the Further and Higher Education (Scotland) Act 2005 (which relate respectively to the funding of further education and the administration of funds);

(d) [3 *omitted*]

(e) section 22 of the Teaching and Higher Education Act 1998.

(4) Subject to paragraph (5), paragraphs (1) and (2) shall not apply in the case of a child [6 . . .]—

(a) [6 who] has not attained the age of 16 and is being looked after by a local authority; or

(b) [6 who] has not attained the age of 18 and to whom—
   (i) section 17(10)(b) of the Children Act 1989 or section 93(4)(a)(ii) of the Children (Scotland) Act 1995 (impairment of health and development) applies because his health is likely to be significantly impaired, or further impaired, without the provision of services for him, or
   (ii) section 17(10)(c) of the Children Act 1989 (disability) or section 93(4)(a)(iii) of the Children (Scotland) Act 1995 (disability) applies; or

[6 (ba) to whom section 37, 38 or 42 of the Social Services and Wellbeing (Wales) Act 2014 applies; or]

(c) who is accommodated outside the United Kingdom and the costs of any qualifying services are borne wholly or partly by a local authority pursuant to their powers under section 320 of the Education Act 1996 or section 25 of the Education (Additional Support for Learning) (Scotland) Act 2004.

(5) Sub-paragraphs [6 (a) (b) and (ba)] of paragraph (4) shall only apply during any period which the local authority looking after the child place him in a private dwelling with a family, or a relative of his, or some other suitable person.

(6) In this regulation and in regulation 10, references to the costs of any qualifying services shall not include the cost of—

(a) domiciliary services, including personal care, provided in respect of a person in a private dwelling; or
(b) improvements made to, or furniture or equipment provided for, a private dwelling on account of the needs of a person under disability; or
(c) improvements made to, or furniture or equipment provided for, a care home in respect of which a grant or payment has been made out of public or local funds except where the grant or payment is of a regular or repeated nature; or
(d) social and recreational activities provided outside the care home in respect of which grants or payments are made out of public or local funds; or
(e) the purchase or running of a motor vehicle to be used in connection with any qualifying service provided in a care home in respect of which grants or payments are made out of public or local funds; or
(f) [3 *omitted*]

(7) For the purposes of paragraph (1), a period during which a person is a resident in a care home in the circumstances set out in that paragraph shall, subject to paragraphs (8) and (9), be deemed—

(a) to begin on the day after the day on which he enters a care home, and
(b) to end on the day before the day on which he leaves a care home.

(8) Where a person enters a care home from a hospital or similar institution in circumstances in which paragraph (1) of regulation 6 applies, the period during which he is a resident in the care home shall be deemed to begin on the day he enters that care home.

(9) Where a person leaves a care home and enters a hospital or similar institution in circumstances in which paragraph (1) of regulation 6 applies, the period during which he is a resident in the care home shall be deemed to end on the day he leaves that care home.]

AMENDMENTS

1. Attendance Allowance and Disability Living Allowance (Amendment) Regulations 2007 (SI 2007/2875) (October 29, 2007).

2. Local Education Authorities (Integration of Functions) (Local and Subordinate Legislation) Order 2010 (SI 2010/1172) art.4 and Sch.3 (May 5, 2010).

3. Social Security (Attendance Allowance, Disability Living Allowance and Carer's Allowance) (Amendment) Regulations 2013 (SI 2013/389) reg.4 (April 8, 2013).

4. Community Care, Services for Carers and Children's Services (Direct Payments) (England) (Amendment) Regulations (SI 2013/2270) reg.6 (November 1, 2013).

5. Care Act 2014 (Consequential Amendments) (Secondary Legislation) Order 2015 (SI 2015/643) art.7 (April 1, 2015).

6. Social Services and Well-being (Wales) Act 2014 and the Regulation and Inspection of Social Care (Wales) Act 2016 (Consequential Amendments) Order 2017 (SI 2017/901) art.4 (November 3, 2017).

7. Higher Education and Research Act 2017 (Further Implementation etc.) Regulations 2019 (SI 2019/1027) reg.17 (August 1, 2019).

GENERAL NOTE

There is a transitional and saving provision in reg.4 of the Amendment regulations to the effect that this amendment shall not prevent any day before the coming into force of the amended regulation from counting towards the 28 day and 84 day periods specified in reg.10. **4.59**

Paragraphs (1) and (3)–(6) are in identical terms to reg.7(1)–(5) of the Social Security (Attendance Allowance) Regs 1991. For further annotations, see those Regulations. Note in particular the development of the law with regard to claimants who have moved from their own home into a publicly-funded nursing home and where the claimant subsequently repays the public body for the costs incurred. The decision of a panel of three judges in *Secretary of State for Work and Pensions v JL* [2011] UKUT 293; [2012] AACR 14 has made clear that there is no need for a prior agreement with the local authority for the fees to be paid. The decision also explores the distinction between entitlement to benefit and payability of benefit and the difference between revision, supersession and suspension of benefit. For further comment see the annotation to reg.7 of Attendance Allowance Regulations. Whether or not a claimant is being accommodated in a "hospital or similar institution" has been examined in *R(DLA)2/06*. For comment on that decision see the notes to reg.8, above.

Note that, by virtue of reg.10, a person may remain entitled to the care component for up to 28 days in accommodation covered by reg.9 or in a hospital, but that separate periods in such accommodation or hospital are aggregated unless they are more than 28 days apart.

Paragraphs (3) to (5) make provisions that enable certain children to qualify for the care component even though they might otherwise fall within the provisions of paras (1) and (2). **4.60**

This regulation has been considered in the UT in *ML v SSWP (DLA)* [2016] UKUT 323 (AAC); [2017] AACR 2. The appellant argued that the disqualification provided for here should not apply in the case of his 21-year-old disabled son who had been accommodated in a care home, because the care provided was so inadequate that he had found it necessary to remove his son from that home. The period in question was that while the son was so accommodated there. Judge Markus QC held that the quality of the care provided was not determinative of whether the regulation applied. That was because the regulation made under s.72 of the SSCBA 1992 applied while the claimant was accommodated in a "care home", defined there as "an establishment that provides accommodation together with nursing or personal care". Although evidence had been accepted on the claimant's behalf that his parents were attending to his needs for 90 hours per week, the judge was satisfied that during the rest of the time the home must been providing attention of that kind. She held further that it was inconceivable that the DWP and the tribunal system could have been expected to assess the quality of care provided in order to determine whether the disqualification should apply when there was a special statutory procedure provided under the Health and Social Care Act 2008 by registration with the Care Quality Commission to make that very assessment. More significantly perhaps, the judge also held that regulation 9 is not discriminatory under art.14 of the ECHR. The appellant had argued that, following *Cameron Mathieson v SSWP* [2015] UKSC 47 in the SC, the same reasoning should apply to the claimant and to reg.9 in this case. Judge Markus considered whether the claimant's residence and needs might amount to a "status" so as to come within art.14, but found it unnecessary to reach a conclusion because she felt it was clear that, in this case, any difference in treatment between a person in a care home with those needs, and that of a person who was not so accommodated, was justified.

In *CDLA/1465/98*, the claimant was living in accommodation rented from a county council. The tribunal found that the accommodation was not provided under Pt III of the National Assistance Act 1948. The adjudication officer appealed on the ground that the county council had had no power to enter into the arrangements with the claimant save under Pt III of the 1948 Act. The appeal was dismissed because the Commissioner was not satisfied that the county council could not have acted as they did outside Pt III of the 1948 Act and he was not satisfied that the tribunal had erred in law in their approach, given the way the adjudication officer had argued the case before them. However, he suggested that the claimant's evidence as to the extent to which he could live without assistance called into question the award of the highest rate of the care component, although that was not a matter within the jurisdiction of the tribunal (which was a social security appeal tribunal and not a disability appeal tribunal). In *CA/2985/97*, it was held that provisions identical to reg.9(1)(b) and (c) had ceased to have any effect in England and Wales following amendments made to the National Assistance Act 1948 by the National Health Service and Community Care Act 1990.

In *R(DLA) 6/04* the claimant was accommodated on week days in residential accommodation run by the local authority. This accommodation was provided under the Mental Health Act 1983. The Commissioner holds that the situation is covered by sub-para.(b) of reg.9(1). The Mental Health Act 1983 is not mentioned specifically in sub-para.(a), nor is it listed in the DM guidance, but s.117 of that Act requires the local authority in exercise of its social services function to provide after- care for persons who are under supervision. The question to be answered therefore was whether persons released from hospital, but still receiving after-care under supervision, are persons under a disability within the meaning of reg.9. The Commissioner had no doubt that they were.

[1 Persons to whom regulations 9 and 10 apply with modifications

4.61 **9A.**—[1 . . .]

REPEAL

1. Social Security Amendment (Residential Care and Nursing Homes) Regulations 2001 (SI 2001/3767) reg.4 (April 8, 2002).

Exemption from regulation 8 and 9

4.62 **10.**—(1) Regulation 8, or as the case may be, regulation 9, shall not, [1 subject to the following provisions of this regulation], apply to a person for the first 28 days of any period throughout which he is someone to whom paragraph (4) applies.

(2) [12 . . .]

(3) Where on the day the person's entitlement to the care component commenced, he is a person to whom paragraph (4) refers, then paragraph (1) [12 . . .] shall not apply to him for any period of consecutive days, beginning with that day, in which he continues to be a person to whom paragraph (4) refers.

(4) This paragraph refers to a person who—

(a) is undergoing medical or other treatment in a hospital or other institution in any of the circumstances mentioned in regulation 8; or

[2 (b) would, but for this regulation, be prevented from receiving the care component of a disability working allowance by reason of regulation 9.]

(5) For the purposes of [12 paragraph (1)]—

(a) 2 or more distinct periods separated by an interval not exceeding 28 days, or by 2 or more such intervals shall be treated as a continuous period equal in duration to the total of such distinct periods and ending on the last day of the later or last such period;

(b) any period or periods to which regulations 8(1) or 9(1) refers shall be taken into account and aggregated with any period to which the other of them refers.

[1 (6) Regulation 8 or as the case may be regulation 9 shall not apply [3 . . .] in the case of a person who is residing in a hospice and is terminally ill where the Secretary of State has been informed that he is terminally ill—

(a) on a claim for the care component,

(b) on an application for a [4revision under section 9 of the 1998 Act or supersession under section 10 of that Act] of an award of disability living allowance, or

(c) in writing in connection withan award of, or a claim for, or an application for a [4 revision under section 9 of the 1998 Act or supersession under section 10 of that Act] of an award of, disability living allowance.

(7) In paragraph (6) "hospice" means a hospital or other institution [5 whose primary function is to provide palliative care for persons resident there who are suffering from a progressive disease in its final stages] other than—

(a) [11 *omitted*]

(b) a health service hospital (within the meaning of section 108(1) of the NHS Act of 1978) in Scotland;

[11 (ba) a health service hospital (within the meaning of section 275 of the NHS Act of 2006) in England;

(bb) a hospital in Wales vested in—

(i) an NHS Trust;

(ii) a Local Health Board; or

(iii) the Welsh Ministers, for the purpose of functions under the NHS (Wales) Act of 2006;]

(c) a hospital maintained or administered by the Defence Council; or

(d) an institution similar to a hospital mentioned in any of the preceding sub-paragraphs of this paragraph.

[10 (8) Regulation 9 shall not apply in any particular case for any period during which the whole costs of all of the qualifying services are met—

(a) out of the resources of the person for whom the qualifying services are provided, or partly out of his own resources and partly with the assistance from another person or a charity, or

(b) on his behalf by another person or a charity.]

[11 (8A) For the purpose of paragraph (7)(bb)—

(a) "NHS Trust" means a body established under section 18 of the NHS (Wales) Act of 2006; and

(b) "Local Health Board" means a body established under section 11 of the NHS (Wales) Act of 2006.]

[5 (9) 3 . . .]

AMENDMENTS

1. Social Security Benefits (Amendments Consequential Upon the Introduction of Community Care) Regulations 1992 (SI 1992/3147) reg.7 (April 1, 1993).

2. Social Security (Disability Living Allowance) Amendment Regulations 1992 (SI 1992/633) (April 6, 1992).

3. Social Security (Attendance Allowance) (Amendment) Regulations 2000 (SI 2000/1401) reg.3 (June 19, 2000).

4. Social Security Act 1998 (Commencement No. 11, and Savings and Consequential and Transitional Provisions) Order 1999 (SI 1999/2860) Sch.7 (October 18, 1999).

5. Social Security Benefits (Miscellaneous Amendments) Regulations 1993 (SI 1993/518) reg.3(3) (April 1, 1993).

6. State Pension Credit (Consequential, Transitional and Miscellaneous Provisions) Regulations 2002 (SI 2002/3019) reg.28 (April 1, 2003).

7. Social Security and Child Support (Jobseeker's Allowance) (Consequential Amendments) Regulations 1996 (SI 1996/1345) reg. 17 (October 7, 1996).

8. Social Security (Attendance Allowance and Disability Living Allowance) (Amendment) Regulations 2002, (SI 2002/208) reg.3 (March 1, 2002).

9. Social Security (Attendance Allowance and Disability Allowance) (Amendment) Regulations 2003 (SI 2003/2259) reg.3 (October 6, 2003).

10. Attendance Allowance and Disability Living Allowance (Amendment) Regulations 2007 (SI 2007/2875) (October 29, 2007).

11. Social Security (Attendance Allowance, Disability Living Allowance and Carer's Allowance) (Amendment) Regulations 2013 (SI 2013/389) reg.4 (April 8, 2013).

12. Social Security (Disability Living Allowance and Personal Independence Payment) (Amendment) Regulations 2016 (SI 2016/556) reg.2 (June 29, 2016).

GENERAL NOTE

4.63 A person may remain entitled to the care component for up to 28 days or, in the case of a child, 84 days (see subs.(2)) in a hospital covered by reg.8 or accommodation covered by reg.9. However, separate periods in such a hospital or such accommodation are aggregated unless they are more than 28 days apart. Furthermore, under para.(3), a person cannot first qualify for the care component while in hospital or the relevant accommodation.

In *CM (by appointee Mr CM) v SSWP (DLA)* [2013] 27 (AAC) the claimant was a child aged three who had to enter hospital for a protracted period. While he was there his parents continued to provide care and attention 24 hours of the day by one of them staying in accommodation provided at the hospital by a charity. In doing so they continued to incur considerable expenses in living costs and in travelling costs. They appealed against a decision to suspend his payment of DLA, under reg.(10)(2), after 84 days, on the ground that to do so was a breach of his human rights. Judge Ward held, reluctantly, that it was not.

Although *CM* subsequently died in hospital, these proceedings were continued by his father on his behalf. In the Supreme Court (*CM (dec'd) by his father CM* [2015] UKSC 47; [2015] AACR 19) his argument succeeded. The court held that the child's need for care and attention from his parents was at least as great while in hospital as it had been when at home and that, as there was no requirement in primary legislation for entitlement to the benefit to be withdrawn, it followed that to do so had been unlawful. The court declined, however, to hold that reg.10 in its application to children should be regarded as invalid—in their view there might be cases where the exercise of a discretion to withdraw benefit might not breach a claimant's human rights and that it should be left to the Secretary of State to see whether, with appropriate adjustment, reg.10(2) might still be applied.

[1 Adjustment of allowance where medical expenses are paid from public funds under war pensions instruments

10A.—(1) In this regulation— 4.64

"article 25B" means article 25B of the Personal Injuries (Civilians) Scheme 1983 (medical expenses) and includes that article as applied by article 48B of that Scheme;

"article [2 21]" means article [2 21] of the Naval, Military and Air Forces etc. (Disablement and Death) Service Pensions Order [2 2006] (medical expenses);

and in this regulation and regulation 10B "relevant accommodation" means accommodation provided as a necessary ancillary to nursing care where the medical expenses involved are wholly borne by the Secretary of State pursuant to article 25B or article [2 21].

(2) This regulation applies where a person is provided with relevant accommodation.

(3) Subject to regulation 10B where this regulation applies and there are payable in respect of a person both a payment under article 25B or article [2 21] and a disability living allowance which is attributable to the care component, the allowance, in so far as it is so attributable, shall be adjusted by deducting from it the amount of the payment under article 25B or article [2 21], as the case may be, and only the balance shall be payable.]

AMENDMENTS

1. Social Security (Attendance Allowance and Disability Living Allowance) (Amendment) Regulations 1994 (SI 1994/1779) reg.3(4) (August 1, 1994).

2. Social Security (Attendance Allowance, Disability Living Allowance and Carer's Allowance) (Amendment) Regulations 2013 (SI 2013/389) reg.4 (April 8, 2013).

[1 Exemption from regulation 10A

10B.—(1) Regulation 10A shall not, subject to the following provisions of this regulation, apply to a person in respect of the first 28 days of any period during which the amount of any disability living allowance attributable to the care component would be liable to be adjusted by virtue of regulation 10A(3). 4.65

(2) For the purposes of paragraph (1) two or more distinct periods separated by an interval not exceeding 28 days, or by two or more such intervals, shall be treated as a continuous period equal in duration to the aggregate of such distinct periods and ending on the last day of the later or last such period.

(3) For the purposes of this paragraph a day is a relevant day in relation to a person if it fell not earlier than 28 days before the first day on which he was provided with relevant accommodation; and either—

(a) was a day when he was undergoing medical treatment in a hospital or similar institution in any of the circumstances mentioned in regulation 8; or

(b) was a day when he was, or would but for regulation 10 have been, prevented from receiving a disability living allowance attributable to the care component by virtue of regulation 9(1);

and where there is in relation to a person a relevant day, paragraph (1) shall have effect as if for "28 days" there were substituted such lesser number of days as is produced by subtracting from 28 the number of relevant days in his case.]

AMENDMENT

1. Social Security (Attendance Allowance and Disability Living Allowance) (Amendment) Regulations 1994 (SI 1994/1779) reg.3(4) (August 1, 1994).

[[1] Prescribed circumstance for entitlement to the care component

4.66 **10C.**—For the purposes of section 72(7) of the Act (prescribed circumstances in which a person is to be taken to satisfy or not to satisfy the conditions mentioned in section 72(1)(a) to (c) of that Act), a person shall not be taken to satisfy subsection (1)(a)(i) or (b)(i) (day attention) or (c)(i) (night attention) unless the attention the severely disabled person requires from another person is required to be given in the physical presence of the severely disabled person].

AMENDMENT

1. Social Security (Attendance Allowance and Disability Living Allowance) (Amendment) (No.2) Regulations 2000 (SI 2000/2313) reg.3 (September 25, 2000).

GENERAL NOTE

4.67 An interesting point on the effect of this regulation was made in *CDLA/4333/2004*. The claimant suffered from depression and required support and attention during the day. Some of this was provided by regular telephone calls from her mother. The mother was herself in poor health and unable to visit her daughter. Clearly the telephone calls could not themselves count as attention because of reg.10C, but it was argued that they were evidence of the claimant's need for attention, that would have been provided by a visit, were the mother able to do so. In this particular case the argument failed because the tribunal appeared to have taken account of the telephone calls as if they were "attention", presumably having overlooked reg.10C. But could this situation breathe new life into the concept that attention must be "required"? Would the claimant need to show that her needs were not sufficiently met, or not as effectively met, by the telephone calls in order to succeed? If the mother did in fact visit in person it would be a harsh decision that held such visits were not necessary and that a telephone call would do, but where, as here, the attention is given by telephone, and if it suffices, it may be reasonable to argue that attendance in person is not required.

There is an interesting example of the application of this argument shown in *HP v SSWP* [2013] UKUT 248 (AAC). There the claimant was suffering from depressive mental illness. Although she was living on her own she was able to function to a reasonable extent in managing her own daily care, but only if she received frequent attention in the form of encouragement and reminders from members of her family. At first this was provided chiefly by her sister who did that in person, but her sister moved to live in the USA. Thereafter, the attention was provided by means of a visual telephonic communication system ("Skype"). Evidence was given by the claimant that, without that support, she would not be able to function normally at all. Unfortunately, the FTT that heard her appeal against a refusal of benefit did not refer to this evidence at all; nor did they refer to reg.10C. They simply found that the claimant was self caring and therefore refused the appeal. In the UT Judge Fordham QC found that the decision was deficient in providing reasons for reaching the conclusion that they did. He holds that the only question is whether the claimant needs (requires) such attention and that evidence of attention given in the manner above can be evidence of such need. The reasons given by the FTT did not explain whether they rejected that evidence as untrue, or as irrelevant, or whether they had failed to notice it at all. Judge Fordham suggests, as an example of where telephonic assistance might succeed in showing such need, the case of a carer who formerly assisted in person, but who is prevented, by breaking their leg, from attending in person. He suggests that evidence of telephonic assistance will always be of limited weight and that it is likely to succeed only where the non-presence is involuntary, the claimant and the assistant would unhesitatingly say that actual presence would be preferable and that the telephone assistance is, at best, "fragile or not wholly successful". It remains the case then, that if the telephoned assistance is reliable and is sufficient for the claimant to achieve a reasonably normal level of daily activity it will not have been shown that anything more (i.e. actual assistance in person) is required. The case was returned to a new FTT for rehearing.

Part IV

Mobility Component

Qualifying period for mobility component after an interval

11.—The period prescribed for the purposes of [1 section 73](9)(a)(ii) of the Act is a period of 3 months ending on the day which the person was last entitled to the mobility component [2 of disability living allowance, or the mobility component of child disability payment] or to mobility allowance, where that day falls not more than 2 years before the date on which entitlement to the mobility component [2 of disability living allowance, or the mobility component of child disability payment] would begin or would have begun but for any regulations made under [1 section 5(1)(k) of the Administration Act] (which enables regulations to provide for the day on which entitlement to benefit is to begin or end). 4.68

Amendments

1. Social Security (Disability Living Allowance) (Amendment) Regulations 1993 (SI 1993/1939) reg.2 (August 26, 1993).
2. Social Security (Disability Assistance for Working Age People) (Consequential Amendments) Order 2022 (SI 2022/177) art.4 (March 21, 2022).

General Note

The general effect of this provision is that the three-month qualifying period for the mobility component is deemed to be satisfied if the new claim is within two years of a previous period of entitlement to the mobility component (or mobility allowance) at the relevant rate. 4.69

Entitlement to the mobility component

12.—(1) A person is to be taken to satisfy the conditions mentioned in [1 section 73](1)(a) of the Act (unable or virtually unable to walk) only in the following circumstances— 4.70

(a) his physical condition as a whole is such that, without having regard to circumstances peculiar to that person as to the place of residence or as to place of, or nature of, employment—
   (i) he is unable to walk; or
   (ii) his ability to walk out of doors is so limited, as regards the distance over which or the speed at which or the length of time for which or the manner in which he can make progress on foot without severe discomfort, that he is virtually unable to walk; or
   (iii) the exertion required to walk would constitute a danger to his life or would be likely to lead to a serious deterioration in his health; or

(b) he has both legs amputated at levels which are either through or above the ankle, or he has one leg so amputated and is without the other leg, or is without both legs to the same extent as if it, or they, had been so amputated.

[4(1A) (a) For the purposes of section 73(1AB)(a) of the Act (mobility component for the severely visually impaired) a person is to be taken to satisfy the condition that he has a severe visual impairment if—
   (i) he has visual acuity, with appropriate corrective lenses if necessary, of less than 3/60; or
   (ii) he has visual acuity of 3/60 or more, but less than 6/60, with appropriate corrective lenses if necessary, a complete loss of peripheral visual field and a central visual field of no more than 10° in total.

(b) For the purposes of section 73(1AB)(b), the conditions are that he has been certified as severely sight impaired or blind by a consultant ophthalmologist.

(c) In this paragraph—
   (i) references to visual acuity are to be read as references to the combined visual acuity of both eyes in cases where a person has both eyes;
   (ii) references to measurements of visual acuity are references to visual acuity measured on the Snellen Scale;
   (iii) references to visual field are to be read as references to the combined visual field of both eyes in cases where a person has both eyes.]

(2) For the purposes of [1 section 73](2)(a) of the Act (mobility component for the blind and deaf) a person is to be taken to satisfy—

(a) the condition that he is blind only where the degree of disablement resulting from the loss of vision amounts to 100 per cent; and

(b) the condition that he is deaf only where the degree of disablement resulting from loss of hearing [2 when using any artificial aid which he habitually uses or which is suitable in his case] amounts to not less than 80 per cent on a scale where 100 per cent represents absolute deafness.

(3) For the purposes of [1 section 73](2)(b) of the Act, the conditions are that by reason of the combined effects of the person's blindness and deafness, he is unable, without the assistance of another person, to walk to any intended or required destination while out of doors.

(4) Except in a case to which paragraph (1)(b) applies, a person is to be taken not to satisfy the conditions mentioned in [1 section 73](1)(a) of the Act if he—

(a) is not unable or virtually unable to walk with a prosthesis or artificial aid which he habitually wears or uses, or
(b) would not be unable or virtually unable to walk if he wore or used a prosthesis or an artificial aid which is suitable in his case.

(5) A person falls within subsection (3)(a) of [1 section 73] of the Act (severely mentally impaired) if he suffers from a state of arrested development or incomplete physical development of the brain, which results in severe impairment of intelligence and social functioning.

(6) A person falls within subsection (3)(b) of [1 section 73] of the Act (severe behavioural problems) if he exhibits disruptive behaviour which—
(a) is extreme,
(b) regularly requires another person to intervene and physically restrain him in order to prevent him causing physical injury to himself or another, or damage to property, and
(c) is so unpredictable that he requires another person to be present and watching over him whenever he is awake.

[3 (7) For the purposes of section 73(1)(d) of the Act, a person who is able to walk is to be taken not to satisfy the condition of being so severely disabled physically or mentally that he cannot take advantage of the faculty out of doors without guidance or supervision from another person most of the time if he does not take advantage of the faculty in such circumstances because of fear or anxiety.

(8) Paragraph (7) shall not apply where the fear or anxiety is:
(a) a symptom of a mental disability; and
(b) so severe as to prevent the person from taking advantage of the faculty in such circumstances.]

AMENDMENTS

1. Social Security (Disability Living Allowance) (Amendment) Regulations 1993 (SI 1993/1939) reg.2 (August 26, 1993).
2. Social Security (Attendance Allowance and Disability Living Allowance) (Amendment) Regulations 1994 (SI 1994/1779) reg.3(5)(August 1, 1994).
3. Social Security (Disability Living Allowance) (Amendment) Regulations 2002 (SI 2002/648) reg.2 (April 8, 2002).
4. Social Security (Disability Living Allowance) (Amendment) Regulations 2010 (SI 2010/1651) reg.2 (November 15, 2010 and April 11, 2011).

GENERAL NOTE

Sub-paragraph (1)(a)

This re-enacts reg.3(1)(a) of the Mobility Allowance Regulations 1975 and some of the words and phrases used have been considered by the Commissioners. 4.71

"physical disablement" "physical condition"

It seems fairly clear that the use of the word "physical" is intended to be limiting so that the scope of s.73(1)(a) of the Social Security Contributions and Benefits Act 1992 does not extend to those suffering from purely psychiatric conditions although such people may qualify under s.73(1)(c) or (d). 4.72

In *KS v SSWP (DLA)* [2013] UKUT 390 (AAC) it was argued that the limitation of the higher rate of the mobility component mainly to conditions having a physical cause was overruled by the provisions of the Equality Act 2010 as being discriminatory on the grounds of mental disablement. The argument failed because the terms of that act specify that nothing is unlawful if that action is required by the terms of legislation (see Sch.22 para.(1) of that Act).

Whether or not a person is suffering from "physical" disablement is regarded as primarily a medical question although, in principle, the process of reasoning used by a disability appeal tribunal to reach the conclusion is challengeable on the ground that it is erroneous in point of law. In a fairly uncontroversial case, a medical appeal tribunal did not err in law in holding that, because agoraphobia was not a physical condition, the claimant could not succeed (*R(M) 1/80*). More famously, in *R(M) 2/78*, a Commissioner held that a medical appeal tribunal had not erred in law in deciding that a child (Robert) suffering from Down's syndrome was suffering from a physical condition. The tribunal had said:

> "We agree that the boy is suffering from mongolism, a condition which is due to faulty genetic inheritance and can therefore be classified as a physical disorder. We accept the evidence that while he walks for some yards he is liable to run, stop, lie down and refuse to go further; this reaction which severely impairs mobility is directly due to the physical condition of mongolism".

In refusing leave to appeal, the Chairman added:

> "The submission of the Secretary of State seeks to separate the claimant's mental state from the physical condition to which that mental state is directly due. This cannot be accepted because the mental state is the direct consequence of the physical malformation of a particular chromosome (No. 21)."

The Chief Commissioner said:

> "I think it is plain that the medical appeal tribunal regarded Robert's physical condition as a whole as being a disabling condition, preventing him from doing the particular action of walking. The weight to be attached to physical and mental disablement in cases where both factors may be present is for the medical authorities to decide, and the answer to the question whether the one or the other is, or both are responsible for an inability or virtual inability to walk is for their decision as a medical question. I do not consider that the medical appeal tribunal misapprehended what physical disablement means, or that it can be said that they were wrong in law in concluding from their findings that it was physical disablement which was responsible for his virtual inability to walk."

He stressed that not all Down's cases would have the same result, although it is not entirely clear whether that was because he thought that different conclusions might be reached as to whether the condition was a physical one or whether it was because not all people suffering from Down's syndrome are disabled to the same extent. The Mobility Allowance Regulations 1975 were amended in 1979 following *R(M) 2/78* but, in *R(M) 1/83*, a Tribunal of Commissioners held that the amendments did not affect the reasoning of the Commissioner in *R(M) 2/78. R(M) 3/86* concerned a child who had suffered brain damage at birth leading to severe mental subnormality. While capable of the physical movements of walking, his behaviour while doing so was erratic and unpredictable. In setting aside the decision of a medical appeal tribunal who had disregarded the behavioural problems, the Tribunal of Commissioners held that *R(M) 2/78* is still good law despite what was said in *Lees v Secretary of State for Social Services* (see below) and that behavioural problems arising out of a physical disability were relevant. It should be noted that in *Harrison v Secretary of State for Social Services*, reported as an appendix to *R(M) 1/88*, Lloyd L.J. suggested that *R(M) 2/78* should be regarded with caution in the light of *Lees*, but it is not clear which part of the Commissioner's decision he had in mind.

Furthermore it is not sufficient that the claimant shows that he is unable to walk out of doors because of a physical condition. It is necessary to go further and show the inability to be the result of the physical act of walking. In *Hewitt v Chief*

Adjudication Officer, and *Diment v Chief Adjudication Officer* reported as *R(DLA) 6/99* the Court of Appeal held that claimants who suffered from severe porphyria, a condition of the skin that meant they could spend very little time out of doors, were not entitled to mobility component. The Court said the claimants could walk physically and that their inability to walk out of doors had nothing to do with the physical process of walking. In *CDLA/1639/2006* the claimant gave evidence that he suffered from severe attacks of migraine that caused pain, dizziness, and lack of vision. At such times—at least 80 hours a week—he could do nothing more than sit down or lie down. A tribunal, by a majority allowed his appeal, but the Commissioner held that in doing so their decision demonstrated an error of law. They had failed to examine sufficiently the way in which his headaches affected his ability to walk. The loss of vision, he said, is not relevant to a claim for higher rate mobility component because that relates only to the direction of walking and not to the ability to walk itself. Pain, too, would not count as that had nothing to do with the physical process of walking though it might clearly make the claimant disinclined to walk outside. Dizziness, or loss of balance, however, was relevant because it affects the manner of walking or even the ability to walk at all. The appeal was allowed and returned to a new tribunal to consider the extent of the element of dizziness and its effect. As well, they were asked to consider whether the claimant should qualify for mobility at the lower rate, on the basis of his need for supervision in case of a sudden onset of a migraine attack.

In *R(M) 1/88,* the claimant had injured his back in an accident in 1979. He was awarded mobility allowance up to 1983 but, on a renewal claim, a medical appeal tribunal held that his inability to walk was not due to a physical cause but was hysterical in origin. In the course of his decision, the Commissioner said: 4.73

> "It may be that in the last analysis all mental disablement may be ascribed to physical causes. But, if so, it is obvious that the Act on drawing the distinction between physical and mental disablement did not mean this last analysis to be resorted to."

He held that the question what was and what was not a physical inability to walk was a medical question for the tribunal to determine but he added:

> "This does not mean that in every case of hysteria the medical authorities are bound to hold that a claimant's hysteria is not a manifestation of his physical condition as a whole; but it does mean that if they do so find it will be impossible to disturb their decision on the ground that they ought to have found it to be a manifestation of the claimant's physical condition."

An appeal to the Court of Appeal was dismissed (*Harrison v Secretary of State for Social Services*, reported as an appendix to *R(M) 1/88*). The Court effectively adopted the Commissioner's reasoning. Stocker L.J. said: "Hysteria is not itself a physical condition, since physical and hysterical conditions are often used in contrasting terms, and in my view correctly so." The Commissioner points out, however, that where hysteria is itself a consequence of a physical condition, it is open to a Tribunal or medical board, as a matter of medical opinion, to find that where hysteria is caused by a physical condition, for example due to pain owing to some spinal condition, the inability to walk may itself be caused by that same physical condition. He drew attention, without apparent criticism, to the fact that the claimant has since been awarded mobility allowance on a further claim.

This question has now been considered, at length, by a Tribunal of Commissioners in *R(DLA) 4/06.* Were it not for the Court of Appeal's decision in *Harrison* the Tribunal would have accepted that the phrases "physical disability" (in s.73) and "physical condition as a whole" (in reg.12) should be interpreted to include any claimant whose condition manifested an inability to walk out of doors in the form of physical symptoms of a medical condition, whether that medical condition was physical or mental. (The Tribunal refer to these physical symptoms as being those of a medical condition though they do, as well, affirm the decision reached in *R(DLA) 3/06* so that perhaps their emphasis should have been rather on whether the claimants inability to walk was manifested by physical symptoms whether the cause of those symptoms was physical or mental.) Thus, on the view the Tribunal would prefer to have taken, the agoraphobic would still fail, but a claimant whose psychosomatic condition made it difficult or painful to walk would succeed, effectively adopting the views expressed in cases such as *CDLA/3323/2003*. However, the Tribunal held that they were bound by the decision in *Harrison*. This meant that they affirmed the view that in order to succeed, the claimant must show that his inability to walk outside has some physical cause. Pain, dizziness and fatigue that are purely psychosomatic or mental, are therefore not sufficient to qualify for the higher rate of mobility component, and cases such as *CSDLA/265/97*, *CDLA/948/2000* and *CDLA/3323/2003* should, therefore, no longer be followed.

4.74 But the Tribunal goes on to consider in some detail the difficulties and problems that decision makers will face in determining what is a physical cause. It is accepted that once it is shown that a disability involving some mental element has either a physical origin (e.g. brain damage), or a physical consequence (e.g. muscle wasting from lack of use when a claimant is depressed), that this will suffice to support the claim. The test of causation they suggest, should be one of "material contribution", so that once it is shown that the claimant's inability to walk derives to an extent that is more than trivial, from some physical factor he should succeed even though his disability is caused in part by psychological factors. A majority of the Tribunal held because of the use of the present tense in both s.73 and reg.12 that it was necessary for the physical factor to be still a current operating cause of the claimant's condition. A psychosomatic condition that derived from a past physical cause that is now corrected, would not suffice.

In applying all this to the facts of the two cases that were before them the Tribunal obtained much assistance from expert evidence given on behalf of the Department of Work and Pensions Corporate Medical group. This evidence is reproduced at para.108 of the decision and again, in relation particularly to back pain, at para.145, and for dizziness, at para.162. On the basis of this evidence the Tribunal allowed both appeals and returned the cases for a new Tribunal to consider whether there was any physical element (that was more than minimal) in the cause of the claimant's disability.

In both cases the Tribunal observes "that it may well be that in the past Tribunals have been too ready to conclude that the fact that no specific and precisely identified organic cause for [the particular disability] has been found means that there is not in fact a physical cause".

4.75 Finally the Tribunal was careful to point out that the cases before them involved only back pain, and dizziness. They say that conditions such as autism, Down's Syndrome, learning disabilities, and the extent to which mental disorders such as depression may be the result of genetics or chemical changes in the brain, and therefore also a physical condition was not before them and they refrain from expressing an opinion on these matters. However, to the extent that some of these matters have already been the subject of Commissioner's decisions it is not suggested that they are anything other than still good law. A view which has been confirmed, at least in regard to Down's Syndrome, by the directions given by Judge Levenson in *SC v SSWP (DLA)* [2010] UKUT 76 (AAC). In *CDLA/1525/2008* Judge May has considered the case of a claimant suffering from anorexia nervosa. In his view the claimant could qualify (though the case was returned to another tribunal) because her condition manifested clear physical disablement that affected her ability to walk. It was not necessary, in his view, to consider how those physical conditions might have been caused.

The question of whether a claimant could qualify for mobility component, at the higher rate, on the basis of being "virtually unable to walk" under reg.12(1)(a)(ii) when, because of Alzheimer's disease, she could not progress effectively on her own was considered in *CSDLA/399/2005*. The Commissioner concludes that no error of law had been shown in the decision of a tribunal that had dismissed the claimant's appeal against a refusal of benefit, but she does so on the ground that the appellant had failed at the original hearing to make out a sufficient factual basis for her claim. On the question of whether an Alzheimer's patient could be said to be suffering from a "physical disability", the Commissioner adopted the view expressed in *CDLA/156/1994* which was in favour of such a conclusion, but felt that the claimant may still need to produce evidence in the form of medical opinion to support that view – the time had not yet come, she thought, when a tribunal could take judicial notice of the aetiology of the condition. In the present case the report of the doctor had described the claimant's condition as "100% mental due to Alzheimer's disease" and while this statement could have contained some ambiguity it did mean that there was no evidence before the tribunal to suggest a physical disability.

CDLA/3420/2005 is an example of the application of this to a claimant suffering from Marfan's disease. The risk of aortic aneurysm, which that condition causes, by the exertion of walking had caused anxiety and depression in the claimant. That, combined with his physical condition, made him reluctant to walk. His case was referred to a fresh tribunal for reconsideration on the basis that the physical contribution may have been more than minimal.

Diagnoses of chronic fatigue syndrome raise difficult questions. In *CSDLA/265/97*, the Commissioner said that, if the claimant's muscle pains and other physical problems were not mental, illusory or imaginary, they could be regarded as physical disabilities.

> "The need to determine anything more, such as whether they are in turn caused by a physical condition, such as a virus, a lesion or a malfunction, may matter little for the purposes of section 73 of the Act."

In *CDLA/5183/97*, another case involving chronic fatigue syndrome, the Deputy Commissioner said:

> "This is a controversial and sensitive issue. Accordingly, it is important to be clear about how the Commissioner and tribunals approach this question when it arises. It is not for the Commissioner to rule on whether or not chronic fatigue syndrome has a physical cause. It is not a question of law. Nor is it for the DAT to have some kind of general rule or policy on this matter. What the DAT must do in each individual case, is to examine the evidence before it and reach a conclusion on whether the walking difficulties which an individual appellant experiences arise from 'physical disablement', in order to satisfy the statute; and the individual appellant's 'physical condition as a whole' in order to satisfy the regulation. This evaluation of the evidence is a question of fact for the DAT. See *R(M) 2/78*."

In that case, the Deputy Commissioner found that the tribunal had not erred in law and had reached a decision they were entitled to reach on the evidence before them. "In particular, they have regarded the advice of the DLAAB not as binding on them in any way but simply as a factor to be taken into account."

Further support for the acceptance of chronic fatigue syndrome as the basis of a claim is found in *CDLA/4486/2000*. That case accepts that the condition may not have a clinical explanation but emphasises that it is the effect of the conditions on the claimant's physical ability that matters, not the cause. Note also the discussion of psychosomatic disability in the notes following s.72 above.

"without having regard to circumstances peculiar to that person as to place of residence or as to place of, or nature of, employment"

Note that it is simply the claimant's physical condition which is relevant. The distance to his or her local shops is not relevant although it is often helpful for a tribunal to know whether, and if so how, a claimant manages to get to the local shops and then, having ascertained how far that is, to consider ability to walk in the light of that evidence. **4.76** *"unable to walk"*

4.77 In *R(M) 3/78*, the Commissioner said:

> "The word 'walk' is an ordinary English word in common usage and, in the context of regulation 3 [now reg.12(1) of these regulations]], means to move by means of a person's legs and feet or a combination of them."

In *R(M) 1/83*, no definition was attempted but the Tribunal of Commissioners said:

> "We consider that a person who can walk at all ought not to be regarded as unable to walk, though he may well be regarded as virtually unable to walk. This does not of course preclude the medical authorities from finding that a claimant's method of moving about does not amount to walking at all."

In the course of the litigation in *Lees* (see below) O'Connor L.J., in the Court of Appeal, said:

> "A person is unable to walk if he cannot use his legs for walking, so a person who is bedridden, a person who is a paraplegic and indeed a person who has a leg amputated is unable to walk. The last category can be enabled to walk by artificial aids such as a false limb or crutches and for that reason we find regulation 3(2) [now regulation 12(4)] applies" (see the appendix to *R(M) 1/84*).

In *R(M) 2/89*, it was made clear that a person with only one foot cannot "walk" in the absence of an artificial limb. Where a person uses crutches, it is necessary to consider the way in which they are used. Unless they are used so that the claimant can walk, as opposed to simply swinging through the crutches, the claimant will satisfy the condition of reg.12(1)(a)(i) even if the distance he or she can travel is such that reg.12(1)(a)(ii) would not be satisfied.

The case of *R(M) 2/89* was approved by the court of appeal in *Sandhu v Secretary of State for Work and Pensions* [2010] EWCA Civ 962. They also approved of the reasoning in *CDLA/97/2001*, which, like *Sandhu*, was a case of a claimant with two legs, but only one of which could be used to bear any weight. In *CDLA/97/2001* the claim succeeded because the commissioner accepted that a person who could carry his weight only upon one leg could not be said to be walking, any more than might a person who had only one leg and this was so even though the claimant might make progress with crutches by moving alternate legs. The test was whether the claimant did, or could, rest any weight upon alternate legs. In the *Sandhu* case the court declined an invitation to attempt any further or better definition of walking, though the matter was remitted to another tribunal for further findings of fact.

"virtually unable to walk"

4.78 In *R(M) 1/91* the Commissioner said that "the base point is total inability to walk, which is extended [by reg.12(1)(a)(ii)] to take in people who can technically walk but only to an insignificant extent". There is clearly some scope for disagreement as to what is meant by "virtually" or "insignificant".

It is to be noted that the virtual inability to walk must be a virtual inability to do so "out of doors". A First-tier tribunal may observe the claimant walking indoors and may infer from that that the claimant is not virtually unable to walk out of doors although they should indicate that they have addressed their minds to the different conditions pertaining out of doors. In *R(M) 1/91*, the Commissioner held that the test envisaged walking on the kind of pavement or road which one would normally expect to find in the course of walking out of doors, any unusual hazards peculiar to the claimant's situation being ignored. He also pointed out that some degree of incline must be contemplated but that the question is not whether the claimant is unable or virtually unable to *climb* and any inability to surmount hills or mountains is irrelevant.

The tribunal should have regard to whether what they observe is generally true of the claimant's walking ability and the claimant should be given the opportunity to comment on the inferences that the tribunal intend to draw.

In *R(DLA) 4/02* the Commissioner held that notes made after covert observation of the claimant's walking ability, and a videotape of her walking, were admissible as evidence before a tribunal. None of this evidence, all of which related to the claimant's behaviour in a public place, could be regarded as having been obtained in breach of her human rights, and all of it was admissible without breach of her right to a fair trial.

The assessment of evidence generally on Disability Living Allowance claims, but in particular in relation to walking ability has been considered by Judge Jacobs in *DC* v *SSWP* [2009] UKUT 45 (AAC). He reminds First-tier Tribunals that their assessment of the evidence must be not only rational but also reasoned and that those reasons must be clearly expressed. In relation to the "walking test" he says specifically:

> "22. In order to apply that test, the tribunal has to make findings of fact on the relevant factors. That involves analysing the evidence as a whole to the extent that it can properly be subjected to analysis. The findings of fact can be made with no greater precision than the law requires and the evidence allows. If that means that the findings cannot be expressed in terms of metres per minute or any other precise terms, so be it. All that is necessary is that the findings should be sufficient to support the tribunal's decision whether or not the claimant is virtually unable to walk. It is my view that the findings may have to be expressed more generally than is the current practice of the First-tier Tribunal and that the Upper Tribunal should accept that this is all that is attainable, given the nature of the test and the evidence available to the tribunal. This is not an excuse for poor quality analysis and fact-finding. It is, in fact, more demanding, because it does not allow tribunals to rely on illusory precision to find differences of opinion where they do not exist on a more rigorous analysis of the substance of the evidence."

A good example of a tribunal leaping too readily to a conclusion that the claimant was not virtually unable to walk can be found in *JT v SSWP (DLA)* [2013] UKUT 221 (AAC). There, evidence had been given that the claimant had recently been on holiday to Greece and that in doing so he had been able to walk to and from the aircraft at the airports on either end of his journeys. The FTT accepted this as showing that he was not "virtually unable to walk". The UT allowed an appeal on several grounds. First, the holiday in Greece was at a time after the decision against which he had appealed was made and no reason was given to show that, as evidence, it could be related to the earlier time (though to do so may not have been difficult). Secondly, no attempt had been made to examine the distance over which, the time in which, or the manner in which the claimant had accomplished this walk. Thirdly, it was likely that most, if not all, of the airport walking was done indoors—no attention had been given to the possible differences that might relate to walking out of doors. It is easy to see why the FTT might have been tempted to seize on what looked like clear evidence of walking ability, but it remains essential that the evidence is tested rationally and careful reasons given for the conclusions that are drawn.

Evidence provided by the claimant, as well as that of medical advisers, will be crucial in determining the claimant's ability to walk. But even this evidence must be considered carefully by tribunals to ascertain its reliability. In *CDLA/2423/2007* the claimant was a child whose mother said that on a "good day" her daughter could walk as far as 3 miles in 30 to 40 minutes. This was accepted by the tribunal as clear evidence that she was not "virtually unable to walk". But as the Commissioner pointed out this would suggest a walking speed of between 4.5 and 6 miles per hour; a speed that even a fit adult would find difficult, if not impossible, to achieve.

distance, speed and time

The distance a person can walk is important but it should not be considered without reference to the other relevant factors of speed, length of time and manner of walking. In *R(M) 1/78*, it was held that a medical appeal tribunal had erred in law in holding that a claimant was virtually unable to walk when she could walk **4.79** a mile. However, whether the distance a person can walk means that he or she is virtually unable to walk is generally regarded as a matter of judgment for a tribunal and Commissioners have shown no inclination to interfere. Thus, medical appeal tribunals have not been held to have erred *in law* in holding that claimants were not virtually unable to walk where their walking ability has been very limited. In *CM/39/84*, the claimant could manage 100 yards at 2 mph and, in *CM/47/86*, the claimant could manage only 50 yards. On the other hand, in *R(M) 5/86*, it seems to have been accepted that a claimant who could walk only 50 yards should qualify. Apart from speed, a tribunal should probably consider how long it takes a person to recover after walking a short distance. A claimant who can walk a substantial distance provided that he or she stands still for a couple of minutes every hundred yards has a greater ability to walk than a person who has to rest for an hour after walking a hundred yards. In *CDLA/805/94* the Commissioner suggested that this factor should be taken into account when considering "the length of time for which" the claimant could walk. He pointed out that, as speed is a function of time and distance, consideration of the length of time for which the claimant can walk must involve consideration of something beyond the mere time it necessarily takes the claimant to walk the distance he can manage at the speed he can manage.

In *CDLA/717/98*, the Commissioner considered *CM 145/88* in which a Commissioner said that an ability to walk 90 yards in five minutes was "arguably" tantamount to being "virtually unable to walk". In the later case, the tribunal had found that the claimant was able to cover 100 yards in five to six minutes, including stops, and concluded that the claimant was not "virtually unable to walk". The Commissioner held that

> "it is not for a Commissioner to attempt to lay down a precise formula for determining whether or not a claimant is unable to walk when the legislation does not do so. The legislation allows adjudication officers and tribunals a margin of appreciation."

He declined to interfere with the tribunal's decision, although he said that a tribunal that had reached the opposite conclusion on those facts would also have been entitled to do so. Guidance was also given in *CDLA/608/94*:

> "It is impossible to lay down *a priori* rules for such questions as the distance a person must be found to walk without severe discomfort before he ceases to count as 'virtually unable' to walk, since so much depends on the circumstances and physical state of each particular claimant. However, it has been said that what 'virtually unable to walk' means is a question of law (*R(M) 1/78* para.11), and some general guidance can be gleaned from the reported decisions. In the absence of any special indications from the other three factors, if a claimant is unable to cover more than 25 or 30 yards without suffering severe discomfort, his ability to walk is not 'appreciable' or 'significant'; while if the distance is more than 80 or 100 yards, he is unlikely to count as 'virtually unable to walk' as those words have generally been interpreted in section 73 and regulation 12. In the difficult ground in between, I for my part find helpful the approach of the Commissioner in case *CM 78/89* at para.13, where he said that mobility allowance (as it then was) was never designed to—and does not—embrace those who can walk 60 or 70 yards without severe discomfort. In such a case, therefore, there would have to be some other factor such as extreme slowness or difficulty because of the manner of moving forward on foot before a claimant would count as 'virtually unable'."

The importance of not considering the distance a claimant can walk in isolation from other factors was again emphasised in *CDLA/1389/97* at para.31 but the Commissioner also said, at para.35, that a tribunal did not necessarily err in not referring to all four factors mentioned in reg.12(1)(a)(ii). It depended whether the other factors arose as issues in the circumstances of the case. This issue has been considered again by the Commissioner Rowland in *CDLA/4388/1999*. There a tribunal had held that the claimant was not entitled when the evidence showed that he could walk, with a limp for 50 metres in about 4 minutes. The Commissioner emphasised that the question of whether this should be regarded as being "virtually unable to walk" was a question of fact to be determined by the tribunal and that unless it was a decision that no tribunal, properly directed on the points of law, could have reached, it was unassailable on appeal. At the same time he expressly disagreed with the statement of another Commissioner in *CSDLA/252/94*, that someone who could limp slowly for 50 yards could not "as a matter of law" be virtually unable to walk. In either case the question is one of fact for a tribunal and whichever way they decide could, *in law*, be correct. In the instant case, however, the appeal was allowed and returned for a re-hearing before a different tribunal because the tribunal had not considered what the claimant's condition and walking ability would be after going 50 metres. Would he need to rest? And if so for how long and in what way before he could go further? In *CDLA 2195/2008* Judge Williams was given evidence of the newly introduced guidelines on walking speed that will be used by DM and by medical examiners to assess walking ability. But he reiterated the importance of treating the test as one of overall impression of the claimant's walking ability:

> "Before leaving this topic, I endorse the more general submission by the Secretary of State on this appeal. Whether or not someone is virtually unable to walk is essentially a question of fact that must take into account all the matters referred to in the legislation. In one sense "speed" is central to this because regard must be had to "the distance over which or the speed at which or the length of time for which. . ." the claimant makes progress on foot (regulation 12 of the Social Security (Disability Living Allowance) Regulations 1991). And, of course, speed is distance covered divided by time taken. But those who are virtually unable to walk often do not walk at a consistent speed. It is therefore the whole way in which progress on foot takes place before or with discomfort that must, in fact, be determined. There are no easy ways of turning that into an arithmetical calculation."

the manner in which

Consideration of the manner of walking involves consideration of behaviour while walking as well as the steadiness of the claimant's gait. However, a need for supervision or attendance while walking is not, of itself, relevant under this regulation; it is, of course, relevant under s.73(1)(d). In *R(M) 1/78*, it was not material that the claimant was always accompanied because she suffered from fits. Thus a person who suffers from fits only occasionally is unlikely to qualify on that ground alone but, in *CM/125/1983*, a Commissioner held that the fact that a claimant was liable to suffer from three fits in half a mile might lead to the conclusion that the quality of walking was so poor as to amount to a virtual inability to walk. Similarly, a "propensity to trip . . . would have to be extremely marked before it became relevant to the manner of a claimant's walking" (*CM/364/92*). 4.80

While in *R(M) 1/83* it was pointed out that the need for attendance and supervision was met through the social security system by entitlement to attendance allowance (see now the care component of disability living allowance and also the lower rate of the mobility component), the Tribunal of Commissioners did consider that the need for such assistance was a facet of the manner in which a person can make progress on foot and was to be taken into account by the medical authorities in conjunction with any other matters in determining whether the person concerned was virtually unable to walk. They said: 4.81

> "The main question in each case will be whether the child is so incapable inasmuch as his ability to walk out of doors is so limited as regards the manner in which he is able to make progress on foot, since behavioural limitations on a person's walking generally affect the manner of walking. It is possible also that speed of walking from place to place may enter into it. It will clearly be relevant that tantrums or refusals to walk are of frequent occurrence or not. We accept the submission made to us that the reference in reg.3(1)(b) [now reg.12(1)(a)(ii)] to

> the making of progress on foot means that it is proper to take account of the fact that a major purpose of walking is to get to a designated place. It follows that if a person can be caused to move himself to a designated place only with the benefit of guidance and supervision and possibly after much cajoling *the point may be reached at which he may be found to be virtually unable to walk*. There may be other factors such as blindness and deafness . . . to be taken into account in addition."

That passage needs to be treated with some caution in the light of the decision of the House of Lords in *Lees v Secretary of State for Social Services* (reported as an appendix to *R(M) 1/84*) but it is not inconsistent with it. Christine Lees was blind and suffered from hydrocephalus with symptoms including some impairment of balance and marked impairment of capacity for spatial orientation. She needed an intelligent adult as a "pilot". Lord Scarman rejected the argument that she was virtually unable to walk because the legislation points to consideration of the physical ability to get about on foot. In effect, he said that her position was no different from that of any other blind person who would need a guide of some sort. He also said that some Commissioners' decisions cited to the House and which differ must be regarded as erroneous in law. But it is not clear from his speech which decisions he had in mind or to what extent they are erroneous.

As already noted, in *Harrison*, Lloyd L.J. suggested that *R(M) 2/78* must be treated with caution but in *R(M) 3/86* a Tribunal of Commissioners said that it was correctly stating the law in that a claimant's behavioural problems, including a failure on occasion to exercise his walking powers (stemming from a physical disability) were necessarily relevant. "What is relevant is whether or not they suffer from temporary paralysis (as far as walking is concerned) and, if so, to what extent." In *CM/186/1985*, the Commissioner, relying on *R(M) 3/86*, drew a distinction between, on one hand, a child who suffered from

> "temperamental refusal episodes, these episodes occurring at distances varying between 20 and several hundred yards and on occasion [made] progress impossible by sitting down"

as a result of his physical condition (autism) and, on the other hand, the hypothetical "case of a child who is open to coaxing". Thus once it is established that, due to physical disablement, a person cannot be persuaded to walk in a desired direction, that person may be regarded as virtually unable to walk and so be entitled to the higher rate of the mobility component of disability living allowance and not just to the lower rate under s.73(1)(d) of the Social Security Contributions and Benefits Act 1992.

The distinction that was drawn by the Tribunal of Commissioners in *R(M) 3/86* between a claimant (in most cases of this sort, a child) who *could* not walk and a claimant who *would* not walk was based upon the simple question of whether such a person could be made to move by coaxing or by bribery. The Commissioners' conclusion was that if the child could be persuaded to move, it followed that the disablement was a matter of volition and could not then be the result of his physical condition.

4.82 A series of subsequent cases have questioned this conclusion. They are summarised, and the counter-argument put most powerfully, in *CDLA/4565/2003* by Deputy Commissioner McGavin. There a child suffered from Williams syndrome, a rare condition that caused both learning difficulties and behavioural problems as well as some physical symptoms. But like some claimants suffering from Down's Syndrome, autism and brain damage, though she could walk in a physical sense, she might then sit or lie down, and might become aggressive if her wishes were thwarted.

The Commissioner points out that in the case of claimants such as these, to describe their behaviour as simply that of a naughty child (as the can't walk/won't walk test would seem to compel him to do) flies in the face of all the medical evidence provided and of the combined experience of the claimants' carers. As the Commissioner in *CM/98/1989* (a case concerning the claim of an 18-year-old man with brain damage) put the matter:

> "If . . . the relevant behavioural problems have nothing to do with physical damage what do they derive from? In the case of this 18-year-old are the tribunal suggesting that his behaviour was that of a naughty child who just would not walk when required? And, if they were, is not the fact that a brain damaged 18-year-old behaves like a child something to do with the brain damage?"

In the present case the Commissioner suggests that a tribunal should not conclude that a claimant who can be persuaded to move must be regarded as capable of walking, but instead should look at the medical evidence from which they might conclude that the refusal to walk was still a consequence of the malfunctioning of the brain, rather than simply wilful naughtiness. If so, then a refusal to walk that was frequent, sustained and not easily overcome could still constitute an inability to walk. The can't walk/won't walk distinction has been considered again by Commissioner Jacobs in *CDLA/3839/2007*. The Commissioner concludes that the distinction apparently drawn in *R(M) 3/86* between a deliberate election not to walk and physical disablement; is no such thing. In his view (and that of others he cites), this was simply a disposal of the facts as presented in that particular case, and did not lay down any principle of law to be applied in others. In this case, the claimant was a child suffering from autism (a physical condition) who generally required two adults holding him firmly when taken on any public route to avoid the danger that would be caused to himself and others by his running off uncontrollably. The case was returned to a tribunal for them to consider, and give clear reasons, as to whether, on the evidence presented, the claimant should be regarded as virtually unable to walk.

R(M) 2/81 concerned a blind person who could get around perfectly well with a guide dog until some scaffolding fell on his head and caused a physical injury. The medical appeal tribunal found:

> "The claimant's legs are capable of making the movements required in the activity of walking but he is blind and has a physical disablement in his balance mechanism and sense of direction which makes it impossible for him to control the direction in which he wishes to move . . . With human guidance he can be steered and can with much help progress in a straight line in a desired direction."

In *R(M) 3/86* it was held that that case did not survive *Lees* but it is interesting that the Court of Appeal in *Lees* would have distinguished it on the facts. O'Connor L.J. said:

> "I repeat it is a medical question as to whether physical disablement including a disturbance of directional mechanism, if the doctors decide that that is a physical disablement, renders a person unable to walk or virtually unable to walk."

The House of Lords suggested that they were not disagreeing with the Court of Appeal at all. The extent to which assistance can be of use would appear to be relevant but some of the sweeping *dicta* in *R(M) 2/81* clearly go.

The distance over which, the speed at which, the length of time for which and the manner in which the claimants can make progress are all relevant. However, the need to make findings on each of the factors only applies where the factors are all in issue (*CDLA/8462/95*). Whether a tribunal errs in law in failing to deal with some factors depends very much on the evidence in the particular case.

without severe discomfort

Any ability to make progress on foot must, to be relevant, be without severe discomfort. In *R(M) 1/81*, it was held that a tribunal must ignore any walking which can be managed only with severe discomfort. The most obvious form of discomfort to be suffered by a claimant is pain. The assessment of pain is a frequent and difficult issue before tribunals. Guidance on a proper approach to the issue of pain has been given by Commissioner Jacobs in *CDLA/0902/2004*. **4.83**

In *Cassinelli v Secretary of State for Social Services (R(M) 2/92)*, the Court of Appeal held that a medical appeal tribunal had erred in law when holding that a person was not virtually unable to walk because the exertion of walking did not cause "severe pain or distress". Glidewell L.J. said that that phrase seemed,

> "to be drawing a distinction between the factor of pain, of which discomfort is a lesser concomitant, and the factor of distress which may arise for other reasons than pain; distress may result of course from pain or discomfort, but may also result from breathlessness, which is another matter to which the tribunal referred."

He rejected the argument put on behalf of the Secretary of State that the tribunal had, inferentially at least, applied the right test and answered the right question. It is difficult to follow the logic of the decision but it is clear that tribunals depart from the statutory language at their peril.

Note that the test to be applied is of "severe discomfort" not pain, or severe pain, and the evidence relied upon must be as to that test; or, at least explain the relationship with that test. In *CDLA/3292/2007* the Commissioner allowed the appeal of a claimant whose claim had been denied by a tribunal that relied, in part, on the evidence of her GP that she could walk only 50–100 yards "without being in severe pain". While this might have been consistent with the rest of the evidence relied upon, it could not be said that it was necessarily so, and the tribunal had failed to advert to the difference stated between "severe pain" and "severe discomfort".

In *CDLA/1389/97*, the Commissioner considered the relationship between pain and discomfort and he warned, at para.41, that a tribunal failing to use the statutory term "severe discomfort" was at risk of being held to have applied the wrong test. He suggested that there might be an escalating scale of severity from pain through severe discomfort to severe pain but it was unnecessary for him to decide the point. This issue was considered in greater detail in *R(DLA) 4/98* where the Commissioner said:

> "The fact that someone suffers pain as a result of walking, or walks 'in pain', does not automatically mean that he or she is walking with severe discomfort. The pain may be mild, moderate or severe, short-lived or chronic. The tribunal must decide for itself whether there is severe discomfort considering all the evidence, and perhaps taking into account other factors causing discomfort in addition to the pain."

In *R(DLA) 4/03* Commissioner Parker gave further consideration to the relationship between walking ability and severe discomfort. The appellant had appealed against refusal of benefit arguing that his walking ability should be assessed only up to the point when he began to experience severe discomfort. In *CSDLA/ 678/99* a Commissioner had said that severe discomfort—

> "may onset and then be relieved by rest so that a further distance can be walked before further onset. In such a case the test stops at the first onset."

Commissioner Parker rejects this view as making an unwarranted gloss upon the statutory definition. "Without severe discomfort" is not the same, she argues, as before the onset of severe discomfort. To apply the test in that way would be to devalue the test of overall walking ability contained in the distance-time-speed formula provided by the regulation. The phrase "without discomfort" means that the claimant is not to be assessed with the inclusion of any progress that he makes only while suffering that discomfort, but so long as the rest time taken to avoid or relieve discomfort is included in the overall time taken for a journey then the con sequent calculation of speed will reflect the degree of disablement he suffers. A person who can progress with short, and infrequent periods of rest will probably be able to walk for this purpose; someone who requires frequent or prolonged stops probably will not. The judgment of distance, time and speed is then a matter of fact for the tribunal.

4.84 The possibility of reducing the level of discomfort by taking medication may be taken into account, provided the tribunal explains why taking the medication would be "a reasonable, safe and appropriate thing to do" (*CDLA/3925/97*).

Pain that is suffered after walking, as well as while walking, yet still as a result of walking, should also be taken into account in deciding whether the claimant cannot walk without severe discomfort (*CDLA/3896/2006*).

In *R(DLA) 4/04*, Commissioner Bano held that a claimant who suffered pain all of the time, and whose pain was not made worse by attempting to walk, could still qualify if it was the pain that made it impossible or difficult for the claimant to walk.

Discomfort may take forms other than pain. Breathlessness may result in severe discomfort and other conditions have also been accepted. But the severe discomfort must be some thing that is caused by the act of walking. In *Diment v Chief Adjudication Officer* and *Hewitt v Chief Adjudication Officer* reported as *R(DLA) 6/99*, the claimants suffered from porphyria, a condition that meant they could not expose their skin to the sun, but otherwise were capable of normal perambulation.

In *CDLA/1361/99*, the evidence was that, when walking a very short distance, the claimant suffered pain and then lost control of her bowels. The Commissioner held that the claimant was virtually unable to walk. He said:

> "The discomfort in this case comprises not only the pain but also the physical sensation of having soiled oneself in the ways described in the papers (which would certainly be discomfort in the ordinary sense of the word, though possibly not 'severe'), the embarrassment of knowing that one has soiled oneself (which would again cause discomfort), and the distress caused. Looking at all these elements together they are in my view of such a magnitude in this case that I conclude that walking to any extent causes the claimant severe discomfort after the walking, if not during it (and often both)."

Further support for the view that acute diarrhoea might contribute to severe discomfort so as to qualify the claimant for the higher award of benefit can be found in *MMF v Secretary of State for Work and Pensions* [2012] UKUT 312 (AAC). There, the claimant was an eight-year-old girl who suffered from ulcerative colitis, Judge Lane took the view that her consequent chronic diarrhoea could contribute to her condition as a whole so as to make her virtually unable to walk. The case was remitted for rehearing.

In *CDLA/313/2005* the claimant, who was a teenage girl, was disabled in one leg and as a result, was likely to fall. This could be avoided with the use of a walking stick but the claimant said she was too embarrassed to use the stick. It was argued that her embarrassment was a form of discomfort under reg.12(1)(a)(ii) and that she should be regarded as unable or virtually unable to walk within the meaning prescribed. Commissioner May rejects this argument. Her discomfort, he says, must be of a kind that was part of her "physical condition as a whole" (reg.12(1)(a)), and could not, therefore, include her embarrassment. In doing so he disapproves of the reasoning adopted by the Commissioner in *CDLA/1361/1999* though there it could be suggested that the embarrassment had more to do with physical condition of the claimant than just embarrassment at the use of a device.

An attempt to extend the reasoning of *R(DLA) 1/04* to the case of a blind man suffering from depression was made in *CDLA/3898/2006*. The claimant's depression was said to derive from his blindness and that it caused the claimant to suffer anxiety to the point of severe discomfort so that he was virtually unable to walk outside. He would thus qualify for the higher rate of benefit. This claim was refused and his appeal was rejected by Commissioner Mesher. The Commissioner held that the appeal must fail because the appeal tribunal had found, as a fact, that the claimant did not suffer discomfort from anxiety so long as he had guidance and support from someone to accompany him. The claimant argued that this finding was unjustified because his anxiety would continue unless the particular person he had for company was someone with whom he had a particular relationship of trust, and in whom he could then be confident. But no evidence of this was before the appeal tribunal, and the Commissioner held, therefore, that there could be no error **4.85** of law in the conclusion they had reached. But the Commissioner comments more generally upon the argument that had been put to him. It is important, he says, in a field such as this, which is so complex as to be sometimes almost unjusticiable, (in the sense that it may appear difficult to distinguish clearly and consistently between those cases which succeed and those which fail) that one should return to the basics as explained in *Lees*, and having done so he says:

> "I doubt in the light of *Lees*, and of the decision of the Tribunal of Commissioners in *R (M) 3/86*, whether 'mere' mental distress, turmoil or anxiety (as opposed to physical manifestations like breathlessness, palpitations, dizziness, chest pain or nausea) can amount to severe discomfort even where a physical disorder contributes to the effect to more than a minimal extent. There would also, if such things could count, be difficulty in distinguishing a perfectly rational heightening of caution, vigilance and concentration which presumably could not be regarded as severe discomfort on any basis."

exertion and danger to life or serious risk to health

4.86 In *R(M) 3/78*, the claimant needed oxygen to be available in case of a drop attack (which might also have occurred while she was asleep). The Commissioner held that what is now reg.12(1)(a)(iii)

> "does not extend to conditions or symptoms which might intervene during the course of walking without there being any connection or relationship to or with walking or being precipitated by the exertion of walking."

Although the word "exertion" might suggest the sort of condition associated with pulmonary and cardiac deficiency there are several decisions that have extended it to include any sufficient deterioration in health effected by the act of walking. Thus, in *CDLA/5494/1997*, Commissioner Levenson accepted that a claimant who had been warned that to continue walking would endanger the spine could succeed, and in *CDLA/2973/1999* Commissioner Fellner has held that a claimant whose diabetes had led to neuropathy in his legs and feet could qualify because walking was likely to lead to ulceration of the claimant's feet and a consequent risk of amputation. The meaning of this phrase has been further considered in *CDLA/3941/2005*. The Commissioner allowed an appeal by a claimant who suffered from cartilage damage and arthritis in her knee. The effect of walking for extensive distances, which she had to do in taking her children to and from school, was said to be likely to result in more frequent arthroscopies (wash-out of the knee joint) and eventually would hasten the need for a knee replacement. This, the Commissioner thought should satisfy the test in reg.(12)(1)(a)(iii). He gave his own decision that she was entitled to benefit. The decision in *CDLA/3941/2005* has been disagreed with by Judge Turnbull in *IP v SSWP* [2013] UKUT 235 (AAC). This is an important decision because it suggests a much more restricted interpretation of the subparagraph. In the earlier case Mr Commissioner Angus had suggested that the test to be applied was whether, without endangering life or health, the claimant could walk a distance that would be normal for a healthy person of her age. Judge Turnbull rejects this construction because it might be far too generous. It could result in claimants succeeding when they could walk far beyond, and in a far better manner, than claimants who failed the test under subparagraph (ii). It would mean that a claimant who could point to a serious endangerment to health would succeed, when someone whose walking was limited by pain would not, even though the former might walk much better. In his view this could not have been the intention that the legislation sought to express. This is to adopt a fairly extreme instance of purposive interpretation, but it may well be right.

Judge Turnbull points out that the subparagraphs in reg.12 (1) are made (under s.73(5) of the C&B Act) to define the circumstances specified in s.73(1)(a) of that act-*viz* "unable to walk or virtually unable to do so". Subpara.(i) simply repeats the phrase unable to walk; subparas. (ii) and (iii) should therefore both be seen as expanding the meaning of "virtually unable to do so". This construction would mean that both of those subparagraphs were conditioned by the claimant being rendered virtually unable to walk by reason of his disability. In the present case the claimant could walk for 10 or 12 minutes at a slow pace, even on a bad day, before her heart condition caused her to rest as a result of breathlessness. In the judge's view she was certainly not "virtually unable to walk" and her appeal failed. Judge Turnbull also thought the result of adopting this construction would necessarily mean that the claimant in the case above should have failed—if she could walk 3 miles, even at risk to her knees, she was not virtually unable to walk. But need this be so. If the idea of virtual ability to walk were to include an element of what it was reasonable for the claimant to do, (as earlier cases under this subparagraph have done), rather than a standard of what a person in good health might do, then it could be argued that the 3 miles a day that would have to be walked by the claimant in *CDLA/3941/2005* to get her children to and from school was a justifiable target, whereas more than a 10 minute walk by a middle aged woman was not. But this seems to take decision makers and tribunals into difficult territory and an area of social judgment best avoided.

The deterioration in health need not be permanent or last for any great length of time (*CM/23/1985*) but it must be serious. In *CM/158/94*, the tribunal had found that, although exertion left the claimant exhausted, "it did not result in a serious deterioration in his health since, having rested, he would improve." The Commissioner dismissed the claimant's appeal and suggested that a serious deterioration in a claimant's health would only be shown where:

"(a) there was a worsening of his condition from which he never recovered, or
(b) there was a worsening from which he only recovered after a significant period of time, e.g. 12 months, or
(c) there was a worsening from which recovery could only be effected by some form of medical intervention."

Sub-paragraph (1)(b)

Double amputees may qualify under this provision even if they have recovered sufficiently to have artificial limbs fitted and are no longer either unable to walk or virtually unable to walk. **4.87**

Paragraph (1A)

Regulation 12(1A) has been held to be ultra vires by Judge Sir Crispin Agnew in *YR v SSWP* [2014] UKUT 80 (AAC). This was a case in which the claimant, who was registered blind, suffered from retinitis pigmontosa. This meant that her eyesight was significantly better indoors with ambient light, but virtually non-existent when she was in either reduced light or in bright light, as she would be when out of doors. The test stated in reg.12(1A) is solely by reference to the Snellen test—a test by reading letters from a board conducted under ambient lighting indoors. This meant that she could not satisfy the requirement to qualify for the higher rate of the mobility component. In the FTT it had been held that the claimant could succeed on the basis that the tribunal found her degree of disability out of doors, was equal to that of a person who failed the Snellen test when indoors. In the Upper Tribunal Sir Crispin Agnew held that the invention of an equivalent test by the tribunal below went beyond any power of legitimate interpretation of the regulations and therefore allowed the Secretary of State's appeal. But he went on from there to hold that the regulation was discriminatory in the sense of the *Thlimmenos* type of discrimination (see *Thlimmenos v Greece* (2001) 31 EHRR 411). This applies when a rule fails to treat differently persons whose situations are significantly different (yet remain similarly affected by a disability). **4.88**

A similar case of visual disability had been considered by Judge Bano in *SSWP v MS (DLA)* [2013] UKUT 267 (AAC). There (as here) it was held that the claim must fail because the only test provided under reg.12(1A) was by the Snellen test and no other measurement of the claimant's visual ability could be applied. It does not appear that in that case the discrimination argument had been advanced. In this case counsel for the Secretary of State argued that even if the test were discriminatory, it was indirectly discriminatory and could be justified on the ground that the policy that the regulation sought to achieve was to apply a "bright line" test that would be simple and effective in determining entitlement.

Judge Sir Crispin Agnew rejects that argument; for entitlement to a benefit that was aimed at providing for people to get about independently out of doors, the failure to set a different test for those whose visual acuity was significantly worse when out of doors, was not justified, even allowing for an appropriate "margin of appreciation". But that did not mean that the claimant succeeded. The judge held that although the regulation was ultra vires it was not for that reason a nullity. This meant that the regulation remains in force as the only means by which entitlement to this part of the benefit can be achieved. Indeed, had the judge found that the regulation was a nullity, it would have served the claimant no better, for that would mean that neither she, nor any other visually impaired claimants (even those who would succeed under the Snellen test), could be entitled.

The case was appealed by the Secretary of State to the Court of Session under the title of *SSWP v Robertson* [2015] CSIH 82. It appears that the Secretary of State took the view that the regulation could not be relied upon unless the judge's finding was reversed. However, the Court of Session decided that the appeal was incompetent as the finding of ultra vires had not formed a part of the decision. Although the representative of the Secretary of State had indicated to the court that the DWP would feel bound by the judge's decision, it is understood now that they have decided to continue to apply the regulation without amendment (this is confirmed in DMG 18/15). This may be, in part at least, because it would appear that in such a case a successful claim might be made for Personal Independence Payment—see Descriptor (f) of Activity 1 of Mobility Activities.

The validity of this regulation has been considered again in *JA-K v SSWP (DLA)* [2017] UKUT 420 (AAC). In this case the issue arose not from the method of determining what amounted to severe visual impairment, but from the fact that under s.75 of the Contributions and Benefits Act it could not be awarded to a claimant who was over the age of 65 years at the time the claim was made. The claimant was undoubtedly visually impaired to the requisite extent, but by the time the regulations were made that enabled the higher rate of the mobility component to become available by this route, in 2011, the claimant was already aged 71. She argued that to deny the benefit to her when it was available to a claimant aged less than 65, was a clear case of age discrimination. Judge Wright considered first whether the regulation might be considered to be invalid as being in breach of the public sector equality duty under the Equality Act 2010. He concluded that it could not be because the regulation was made in June 2010, but the Equality Act only came into force in April 2011. The same applied, he thought, to the decisions taken by the SSWP in not superseding the claimant's award of the mobility component to include the higher rate. As well, he pointed out that the discrimination, if there were any, resulted from s.75 of the Contributions and Benefits Act, not from reg.12(1A), and the UT was not competent to make any declaration in respect of an Act of Parliament. More importantly, however, Judge Wright considered the issue of whether the UT is competent to make a decision as to the validity of regulations in relation to the Equality Act 2010. This is a matter on which UT judges have given differing views though in some cases the matter was not put in dispute before them. Judge Wright's view was that, in consequence of s.113 of that Act, the UT was not competent to make a determination of invalidity except in the exercise of its jurisdiction in judicial review; to do that would require the claimant to commence proceedings in the High Court from where the matter might be referred to the UT. The judge would also have held that the SSWP did have due regard to the equality duty when making the regulation. The judge considered, too, an argument based on the Human Rights Act 1998. He rejected that argument also in following *NT v SSWP (DLA)* [2009] UKUT 37 (AAC) (also reported as *R(DLA)* 1/09)—see discussion in note following s.75 of the C&BA 1992.

For the purposes of determining entitlement to benefit under this provision an optometrist or an orthoptist who is registered with their appropriate professional Council is a healthcare professional for the purposes of s.39 of the Social Security Act 1998.

The meaning of the phrase "with appropriate corrective lenses" has been considered in *NC v* SSWP *(DLA)* [2012] UKUT 384 (AAC). There, the claimant's eyesight would qualify automatically for the benefit without her contact lenses, but not if she wore the lenses. (The claimant was unable to wear glasses.) She said that her eyes had become intolerant to wearing contact lenses and that she could use them for only a limited amount of time each week. The judge held that lenses that could be worn only with severe discomfort could not be regarded as "appropriate" for the claimant and remitted the case for rehearing.

Paragraph (2)

There is no indication given as to how the degree of disablement is to be assessed. However, Sch.2 to the Social Security (General Benefit) Regulations 1982 provides that 100 per cent disablement is appropriate for "loss of sight to such an extent as to render the claimant unable to perform any work for which eyesight is essential". Schedule 3 to the Social Security (Industrial Injuries) (Prescribed Diseases) Regulations 1985 sets out a test for establishing an assessment of 80 per cent for occupational deafness. In *R(DLA) 3/95* the Commissioner said that these tests should be used for the purposes of reg.12(2). When the 1982 Regulations are being applied in industrial accident cases, an assessment of 100 per cent for loss of vision is regarded as appropriate where the vision is found to be less than 6/60, using both eyes whilst glasses are used; or where finger counting is not possible beyond one foot. Before *R(DLA) 3/95* was decided, an assessment of 80 per cent for deafness was regarded as appropriate where the claimant was unable to hear a shout beyond one metre using both ears (with aids). This was tested by shouting an instruction or question from just beyond one metre behind the claimant. *CDLA/7090/1999* rejects the use of that test. It emphasises the need for controlled testing and suggests that this should be in an outdoor environment. **4.89**

The test for blindness under para.(2) has been examined extensively by Judge Wright in *GB v SSWP (DLA)* [2016] UKUT 566 (AAC). The judge examines parliamentary material going back as far as 1917, in the form of a white paper preparatory to the Blind Persons Act 1920, from which the wording in para.(2)(a) would seem to have been inherited. He concludes that the "degree of disablement resulting from the loss of vision [amounting] to 100%" is correctly determined in accordance with the approach adopted in *R)DLA) 3/95,* by reference to the claimant's ability to perform work for which eyesight is essential, and not by reference to any numerical score on an eye test. The score on an eye test can be only evidence from which the claimant's working ability might be inferred, but it is not determinative of the result. This demonstrates the difference that there must be between the test in regulation 12(1A)(a), where the test is determined by a numerical score, and under regulation 12(2)(a) which concerns a person who is both blind and deaf. The task of a decision maker and hence a tribunal should be to infer the claimant's ability to undertake tasks that might be involved in paid employment or work for a profit. In this case the FTT had attempted to do that, but they erred in relying on the claimant's manual dexterity and ability to undertake tasks in an educational or social environment drawing inferences from that rather than considering his ability in a work place environment where speed, reliability and possibly a degree of adaptability would be required.

Paragraph (3)

Note that it is only an inability to walk in the right direction due to the *combined* effects of blindness and deafness which can be relevant. **4.90**

Paragraph (4)

4.91 An ability to wear an artificial prosthesis or to use an artificial aid (such as a pair of crutches) must be taken into account and the claimant's ability to get about must usually be assessed on the basis that a prosthesis or aid is used. However, if the claimant does not in fact habitually wear or use such a prosthesis or aid, it is necessary to consider whether one would be suitable for him or her (*R(M) 2/89*). If a prosthesis is habitually, or could be, worn but any walking is, or would be, achieved only with severe discomfort, such ability to walk would not fall within para.(1)(a)(ii) anyway. But a prosthesis might not be suitable even if the discomfort were not severe. It is arguable that a prosthesis or aid cannot be "suitable" until it is actually available to the claimant. Reg.12(4) cannot be read as requiring a person to undergo surgery to improve his or her medical condition (*R(M) 1/95*).

In *MH v SSWP* [2009] UKUT 94 (AAC) the claimant was a woman who habitually used a shopping trolley to support her whenever she walked outside. This was not only when going to the shops and doing the shopping, but also when she was out for any other reason, for instance walking with her grandchildren. Judge Lane upheld the decision of a First-tier Tribunal that had refused benefit on the ground that she was not unable to walk when she was using an artificial aid. The judge confirms that the word "artificial" has no technical meaning in the regulation; if the claimant chooses to use a shopping trolley as her form of walking aid there is no reason why the ordinary meaning of the words "artificial aid" should not include that trolley. Alternatively, she said, it was clear that the claimant was able to make progress on foot with some form of support and if the shopping trolley were not to be regarded as being within the meaning of the regulation, then para.(b) would apply on the basis that she could be expected to walk with the aid of a wheeled walking frame.

Paragraph (5)

4.92 Only those suffering from a state of arrested development or incomplete physical development of the brain can qualify under those provisions. The significance of this construction has been pointed out by Judge Levenson in the context of a Down's Syndrome child in *SC v SSWP* [2010] UKUT 76 (AAC). The First-tier Tribunal had refused to find that the child suffered from "arrested or incomplete development of the mind", but the judge points out that this ellipsis of the words in the section may diminish the correct meaning of the full phrase. He says:

> "28. The meaning of severely mentally impaired is found in regulation 12(5), which is set out above. The First-tier Tribunal found that there was no evidence of "arrested or incomplete development of the brain". However, this is a common but mistaken paraphrase of regulation 12(5), which refers to "arrested development" or "incomplete physical development of the brain". There are two aspects to this error. One is that a distinction is drawn between arrested development generally (not limited to the brain, although there must still be a physical cause) and incomplete physical development of the brain. The other is that "arrested development" does not mean arrested *physical* development (otherwise the regulation would say so, as it says "incomplete *physical* development"). Thus, regulation 12(5) can apply to a person who has arrested emotional or functional development which has a physical cause even if that cause is not related to the development of the brain."

If someone becomes disabled as a result of an injury after the brain has reached full development, he or she will probably have to rely on para.(1)(a) instead. In *R(DLA) 2/96*, the Commissioner, having heard expert medical evidence, held that sufferers from Alzheimer's disease do not satisfy the condition mentioned in reg.12(5). He found that the disease resulted in a deterioration of a developed brain rather than an arrest of development, rejecting the idea that the brain develops throughout life which, he pointed out, would render otiose the restriction implied by reg.12(5). In that case, the expert evidence suggested that the brain had reached maturity by the time a person was aged 30. In *CDLA/393/94*, the claimant was in her early 20s when she became ill and it was held to be arguable that her brain had not fully developed and that she suffered from a state of arrested development or incomplete physical development. The burden of proof rested on the claimant. In *R(DLA) 3/98*, the Commissioner heard evidence in respect of a claimant suffering from schizophrenia and concluded that she suffered from arrested development of the brain but that that did not result in severe impairment of intelligence in her case.

In *NMcM v SSWP (DLA)* [2014] UKUT 312 (AAC) Judge Wikeley has decided two important points about para. (5). First, the so called "age 30 cut off" rule in *R (DLA) 2/96* is disapproved and secondly the novel construction of the paragraph that had been suggested by Judge Levenson in *SC v SSWP* [2010] UKUT 76 referred to at the beginning of this note is also disapproved. As to the first, Judge Wikeley finds that the basis upon which the rule was adopted, namely the state of medical knowledge then held about the development of the brain, was no longer sustainable. In the light of more recent medical research, and especially the benefits of MRI imaging, it was no longer possible to assert that the brain could be regarded as fully developed by that age. Judge Wikeley had before him a report agreed by both the parties, which showed that in one sense the brain continues to develop at least into the third decade of life and possibly in some persons into their forties. In another sense, the brain continues to develop when acquiring new skills that can be reflected in physical changes in the brain, throughout life. The present case, which involved a claimant who had suffered brain damage in a road accident at the age of 32, had been rejected on that ground without further consideration at the FTT. The case has now been referred back for further matters to be considered. First among them will be the question of whether the claimant can be said to be suffering from a state of arrested development or incomplete development of the brain. In doing so they will follow the other part of the Judge's decision which is that each of these phrases is to be read as referring to "the brain". Thus, what must be found is "arrested development of the brain" or, alternatively, "incomplete physical development of the brain". It might be thought that this would present a difficulty, given that the claimant's problems were palpably caused by what we would popularly refer to as "brain damage", but, as the judge points out, the test here is not one of causation; it is, at this stage, just one of medical fact and given the way in which the terms above are now used to describe the medical situation, he thought it possible that the FTT might find accordingly.

A further claim in respect of a woman suffering from schizophrenia has been considered in *DM v SSWP (DLA)* [2015] UKUT 87 (AAC). In this case the claimant had first been diagnosed as suffering from the condition at age 21. The FTT was held to have made an error of law in accepting without further enquiry the opinion of the claimant's medical consultant that she was not suffering from any arrested development or incomplete physical development of the brain. The FTT had made this finding of fact based only on the opinion expressed in the consultant's letter and for which he gave no supporting reasons. It appeared to have been made, in part at least, on the basis that there had been no brain scan ever made of the patient. The case was returned to a fresh tribunal to enquire further as to evidence on this point. The claimant, on whom the burden of proof will lie may find difficulty in doing so. A brain scan will not necessarily form a part of any treatment plan for her condition. Without that being so the cost of an MRI scan is likely to be prohibitive. In the earlier case of *NMcM v SSWP* (above) the department had been able to provide a detailed report on recent medical researches that had been agreed by both parties; without a similar intervention it is likely that the strict conditions imposed by *para.(5)* will again defeat the claim. However Judge Wikeley has pointed out in his judgement that this is one instance where the rules of entitlement to Personal Independence Payment may be more generous than for the mobility component. (See descriptor (f) of the Mobility Activities in Sch.1 of those regulations). This decision also considers whether *para.(5)* might be discriminatory and in breach of the claimant's human rights. In the judge's view this was unlikely to be so, but that a decision on this point was unnecessary to dispose of the present appeal.

In *CDLA/1678/97*, the Commissioner heard expert evidence in a case where the claimant suffered from autism. He concluded that autism arises out of a state of arrested or incomplete development of the brain but he was not satisfied that the claimant's intelligence was severely impaired. The expert evidence was to the effect that only those with an I.Q. of 55 or below were regarded as having *severely* impaired intelligence and that fewer than 10 per cent of those suffering from autism fell within that category. The Commissioner found, on the basis of medical reports and other evdence, that the particular claimant before him was not one of those 10 per cent. In *M (a child) v Chief Adjudication Officer* reported as *R (DLA) 1/00*, the Court of Appeal has held that an intelligence test should not be regarded as a definitive measure of whether a child has a severe impairment of intelligence. In that case the child, who was autistic, had an intelligence quotient well above the quotient of 55 that had been suggested by the medical experts as consistent with a rating of severe impairment. The Court of Appeal held that an intelligence test result is a useful starting point but should not be conclusive. They suggest a full assessment of intelligence should include factors such as "insight and sagacity". It is worth noting that subs.(5) includes the words "social functioning" as well as "intelligence". Although they are linked by the word "and" which suggests that they should be read as cumulative rather than as alternatives, it may be possible to argue that social functioning should be regarded as lending colour in the interpretation of intelligence to support the wider view. This seems to be the position taken in *CD v SSWP (DLA)* [2013] UKUT 68 where the appeal was allowed by Judge Bano because the FTT had failed to take sufficient account of the claimant's lack of awareness of danger. The claimant in this case was another autistic child. The judge held that the FTT had made an error of law also by comparing the behaviour of the claimant with that of a child of similar age who was not disabled. It seems likely that in doing so the FTT were importing the requirements of s.73 (4A), but that subsection applies only to a claim made under s.73 (1)(d); the claim in the present case was made under s.73 (3).It is possible, however, that such comparison might be relevant to assessing the claimant's social functioning.

The approach that treats intelligence and social functioning as parts of a combined test of the claimant's ability to function in "real life situations" has been approved in *MP v SSWP (DLA)* [2014] UKUT 426 (AAC). Judge G. Knowles QC, directed the FTT to whom the case was returned that they should regard *R (DLA) 1/00* as

> "authority for the proposition that evidence about a person's insight and sagacity can satisfy both the test of severe impairment of intelligence **and** severe impairment of social functioning required by regulation 12(5)."

This case was another involving a child (four years old) with autistic spectrum disorder. An appeal was allowed largely because insufficient regard had been given to the communication difficulties that the child was experiencing. As the judge put it,

> "The emphasis in *R (DLA) 1/00* [. . .] on *"the ability to function in real life situations"* or *"useful intelligence"* invites active consideration of a person's language difficulties when considering their social functioning for the purposes of regulation 12(5)."

The judge directed also that when rehearing the case regard must be had to the child's ability to function in less structured situations rather than just his abilities within the home and at school. Furthermore, she thought it necessary that account should be taken of the child's ability to function in relation to strangers and not just those who were familiar to him. She rejected the suggestion made on behalf of the Secretary of State that it would be difficult to assess a child's ability to interact with strangers because many young children are shy with strangers. To do so, she thought, would be to introduce a comparison with a child of that age who was not disabled; a test she points out that is applied specifically only in para.4A. However, it is likely that some reference to the generality of youthful shyness is inevitable because it will still be necessary for there to be a finding that the child's condition has resulted in "impairment".

Regulation 12(5) was considered in *CDLA/5153/97* where the claimant suffered from attention deficit hyperactivity disorder. The Commissioner had detailed medical evidence before him as to the causes of the condition and he was not satisfied that, in the present state of medical knowledge, it was possible to attribute the claimant's condition to "a state of arrested development or incomplete physical development of the brain" as is required to satisfy the condition of reg.12(5). Such a finding by a Commissioner on a question of fact is not binding on tribunals and the Commissioner himself acknowledged that different evidence might become available.

> "It may become possible to make such an attribution for ADHD in the future, with the advances in scanning techniques and genetic knowledge for which Professor Barkley hopes: but it is not so now."

Nonetheless, the decision provides helpful guidance and unless a claimant has technically detailed evidence in support of his or her case, tribunals are likely to adopt the Commissioner's finding.

Paragraph (6)

Physical restraint must be *regularly* required and the behaviour must be *disruptive* and *unpredictable*. Indeed, since "extreme" conditions "disruptive behaviour", it is probably right to say that the behaviour must be extremely disruptive. A person who satisfies the conditions of sub-paras (b) and (c) but who does not exhibit extremely disruptive behaviour may qualify for the mobility component at the lower rate (under s.73(1)(d) of the 1992 Act). **4.93**

Regulation 12(6) was examined in *CDLA/2054/98*. The Deputy Commissioner held that in applying sub-para.(a), it was the claimant's behaviour when taking advantage of the faculty of mobility that had to be considered. But this view has been rejected in the reported decision *R(DLA) 7/02*, by Commissioner (as he then was) Turnbull. He accepted that the rational for this benefit was the claimant's mobility, but in his view the words of the regulation are too plain—the claimant must satisfy the condition in para.(c) "whenever he is awake", and thus must include his behaviour both indoors and outside. This has been followed in a string of decisions (see *CDLA 2470/2006, CSDLA 202/2007, CDLA 2167/2010*) and now in *SSWP v MG (DLA)* [2012] UKUT 429 (AAC) by Judge Wikeley. That much about reg.12 (6) can be regarded as established.

Judge Wikeley goes on in this judgment to give guidance on several of the other points that arise in applying para.(6). These points are reproduced here as a useful source of guidance to tribunals dealing with such cases. The case concerned a claim for higher rate mobility made on behalf of an autistic child. (In the UT the claimant was represented by Mr. Stagg and the secretary of state by Mr. Heath).

> *"What does 'extreme' signify in the context of regulation 12(6)(a)?*
>
> 22. Mr Deputy Commissioner Bano described the word 'extreme' as 'an ordinary English word, connoting behaviour which is wholly out of the ordinary' (CDLA/2054/1998 at paragraph 7a). Although the rest of that passage, which concerned the 'indoors/out of doors' point has been disapproved in R(DLA) 7/02, I am not sure that this definition of 'extreme' can be usefully **4.94**

improved upon very much. However, as Mr Commissioner Rowland observed in CDLA/2470/2006, reading the sub-conditions cumulatively, 'extreme' behaviour is 'of a type that regularly requires a substantial degree of intervention and physical restraint' (at paragraph 13). In other words, the behaviour must be extremely disruptive. Furthermore, the disruptive behaviour must result from the severe mental impairment: 'insofar as such problems are primarily a manifestation of a claimant's age rather than of such mental impairment, they are irrelevant to entitlement' (CSDLA/202/2007 at paragraph 11). This is ultimately a question of fact for the tribunal, involving 'a large element of judgment' (CDLA/2167/2010 at paragraph 8).

What does 'regularly' mean in the context of regulation 12(6)(b)?

23. The claimant' extreme behaviour need not occur constantly, continuously or all the time. That would be to set the threshold for eligibility too high. Rather, it must be such that it 'regularly requires another person to intervene and physically restrain him in order to prevent him causing physical injury to himself or another, or damage to property'. The word 'regularly' is a protean one, so taking its meaning from its context. The Commissioner in CDLA/2470/2006 commented that 'such a degree of intervention and restraint is likely to be required on a significant proportion of occasions when the claimant walks moderate distances outdoors'. I agree with that observation as far as it goes.

24. I do not agree with Mr Stagg's further submission that this means that regularity under regulation 12(6)(b) can be met by such incidents occurring just outdoors. Such an analysis seems to me to be inconsistent with R(DLA) 7/02. Rather, that sort of intervention to deal with extreme disruptive behaviour will also need to be required sufficiently often indoors as well such that, taken overall, one can say that it is required 'regularly' or 'in the ordinary course of events' (see CDLA/2054/1998 at paragraph 7d). When the claimant is outdoors, the need for intervention in the proximity of traffic is the obvious example. The indoors intervention may take any number of different forms: in *MMcG v Department for Social Development (DLA)* the claimant had to be stopped from jumping off the top step of the household stairs. Other examples—and they are no more than that—might be the need for physical restraint to stop the claimant trying to put his fingers in electrical sockets or to stop him damaging internal doors, walls or household furniture when frustrated. As Mr Deputy Commissioner (now Judge) Warren noted in CDLA/17611/1996, the requirements of regulation 12(6) 'fall to be answered in respect of the claimant's condition generally and not with any special emphasis on behaviour when walking out of doors' (at paragraph 11). However, I also agree with Judge Mark's helpful formulation that 'interventions may be regular if they are frequent in one context but infrequent, or even rare, in another context provided that looked at overall there is a regular requirement to intervene and physically restrain the claimant' (*Secretary of State for Work and Pensions v DM (DLA)* [2010] UKUT 318 (AAC) at paragraph 9).

What does 'physically restrain' signify in the context of regulation 12(6)(b)?

25. The 'regularity' requirement under regulation 12(6)(b) is for 'another person to intervene and physically restrain' the claimant. In CDLA/2470/2006 Mr Commissioner Rowland qualified that expression by the comment 'i.e. something much more than merely taking the person by the arm'. I note that the facts of that case concerned a young man with Down's Syndrome who was aged 16 at the date of the tribunal hearing. However, more recently Judge Mesher expressed the view that the Commissioner in CDLA/2470/2006 was not intending 'to lay down any hard and fast rule of general application' (CDLA/2167/2010 at paragraph 15). Judge Mesher found that on the facts of that case the tribunal was entitled to conclude that 'what was needed

was a very firm grip to stop U from rushing off towards whatever caught his attention and that that constituted physical restraint to prevent injury' (also at paragraph 15). In CDLA/2617/2010 the boy U was aged 11 at the date of the FTT hearing.

26. I agree with Mr Stagg's further submission that the nature of the intervention and physical restraint required to satisfy regulation 12(6)(c) will be fact- and context-specific. Obviously a strapping 16-year-old may require a considerably higher level of physical restraint than a slight 5-year-old. A firm grip on the arm of such a 5-year-old may well be sufficient to avert danger, whereas it may have no effect at all on a 16-year-old who may have the strength of an adult. I therefore agree with Judge Mesher in CDLA/2617/2010 that Mr Commissioner Rowland should not be read as imposing some categorical rule by way of the illustration given on the facts of that case.

What does 'watching over' mean in the context of regulation 12(6)(c)?

27. The new tribunal should bear in mind the guidance in the leading case of R(DLA) 9/02. As Mr Commissioner (now Judge) May noted there, the test is 'specifically restrictive' and the carer must be both 'present' and 'watching over': 'It does not seem to me these conditions can be fulfilled when the claimant's bedroom door is closed and he is on one side of it and the carer on the other' (at paragraph 12). Both Mr Heath and Mr Stagg agreed, as I do, that this proposition is subject to a *de minimis* rider, so that for example 'very short intervals without watching over' e.g. for a carer's 'comfort break' (but not, for example, a leisurely cup of tea and a prolonged respite break in the garden whilst the claimant is inside) can be ignored for this purpose (see CDLA/2714/2009 at paragraph 10, cited in *JH v Secretary of State for Work and Pensions (DLA)* [2010] UKUT 456 (AAC) at paragraph 11).

28. Since the oral hearing of this appeal, Judge Mark has issued his decision in *AH v Secretary of State for Work and Pensions (DLA)* [2012] UKUT 387 (AAC). Judge Mark held that 'requires' in regulation 12(6)(c) means 'reasonably requires' (at paragraph 16). That seems to be uncontroversial. Judge Mark also expressed the view that if the carer is present close enough to hear what the claimant is doing and so to intervene if necessary, and is either looking in with sufficient regularity or (conceivably) observing the claimant on CCTV, then the fact that the claimant's bedroom door is shut does not inevitably mean that the carer is not present and watching over the claimant whenever he is awake (at paragraphs 14 and 19). This is at the very least a significant gloss on the Commissioner's ruling in R(DLA) 9/02, although Judge Mark sought support from the observations in CDLA/2167/2010 (at paragraph 13). I considered whether to seek further submissions from both representatives on this issue in the light of the newly available decision. I decided not to, given that the question was not central to this appeal and the case has gone on long enough already.

29. I simply make the following observation. It seems to me that there is some force in Judge Mark's qualification. Obviously the statutory language must take its ordinary meaning from its context, in the absence of any indication to the contrary. 'Watching' means observing, being on the lookout, keeping someone or something in sight, or keeping vigil. However, 'watching over' may carry a slightly different nuance in meaning, of exercising protective care over someone or something. After all, regulation 12(6)(b) does say 'watching over' and not 'looking at'. It is arguable that the Commissioner in R(DLA) 9/02 may have elided the meanings of 'watching over' and 'watching' (see e.g. at paragraph 12). That is not to say that the meaning of 'watching over' can be stretched like a piece of elastic, not least as it is coupled with the restrictive requirement that the carer be 'present'. That, of course, is ultimately a question of fact for the first instance tribunal.

What is the significance of a 'structured environment' in the context of regulation 12(6) (c)?

30. As noted at paragraph 18 above, the submissions of Mr Heath and Mr Stagg were principally concerned with the significance of the claimant's behaviour within a 'structured environment' for the purpose of the regulation 12(6) conditions. Both advocates recognised that there appeared to be a divergence of opinion in the case law on this issue.

31. Mr Heath's argument was that if the claimant was subject to a 'structured environment', whether e.g. at home or at school, such that he did not become extremely disruptive, then by definition regulation 12(6) was not satisfied. He relied in particular on the following passage of Mr Commissioner Turnbull's reported decision in R(DLA) 2/07:

> '14. The first finding of importance for this purpose was that 'he is not disruptive at school, where it is structured and safe.' That finding clearly came from the evidence given by the claimant's mother to that effect before the Tribunal (p.166 of the case papers). The claimant's mother has since confirmed its correctness (see p.195: 'He is well behaved at school due to the extreme structure and teacher/children ratio').
>
> 4.95 15. Now it is no doubt the case that while the claimant is at school there is always an adult 'watching over' him. It may be (although this is unclear) that it is the presence and active interest of a teacher which results in the claimant not being disruptive at school—i.e. that he would become disruptive if left alone there or if left unsupervised with other children. But that is in my judgment not sufficient to satisfy Reg. 12(6)(c). Limb (c) of Reg. 12(6) is in my judgment only satisfied if the constant presence of an adult is necessary in order to intervene and deal with the claimant *if and when he starts actually to become disruptive*. Giving a fair reading to Reg. 12(6)(c) in the context of Reg. 12(6) as a whole, I think the clear meaning is that the 'watching over' must be necessary in order that the person watching (or, I suppose, someone who can be summoned immediately by the person watching) can intervene when the claimant actually does become disruptive. If the structured regime of the school is of itself sufficient to prevent the claimant becoming disruptive, Reg. 12(6)(c) is in my judgment not satisfied. I reach that conclusion for three main reasons. First, that is simply how the provision strikes me. Secondly, the presence of limb (b), referring to physical restraint, before limb (c), leads naturally to the meaning that the presence must be necessary in order actually to deal with unpredictable disruptive behaviour, and not merely (by presence short of physical restraint) to avoid it. Thirdly, Reg. 12(6) can only apply if the claimant does in fact regularly require physical restraint. That means that if a particular claimant were, by supervision short of physical restraint, prevented from ever being disruptive, or from being disruptive on a regular basis, Reg. 12(6) would plainly not be satisfied.
>
> 16. The same consequence in my judgment flows from the Tribunal's findings that at home he only becomes disruptive if his mother leaves the room, or her attention is diverted away from him, or he does not get his own way. (The correctness of that finding has in my view again since been confirmed by the long letter from the claimant's mother at pages 195 to 197 of the case papers). Reg.12(6)(c), again read in the context of Reg.12(6) as a whole, requires that the claimant's disruptive behaviour is so unpredictable that another person is required to be present at all times *in order to deal with the claimant should he become disruptive*. It is not sufficient that the presence and active interest of the claimant's mother at home is sufficient to prevent disruptive behaviour occurring at all.'

32. Mr Stagg, in contrast, relied on Judge Levenson's unreported decision in *LM v Secretary of State for Work and Pensions* [2008] UKUT 24 (AAC) (also known

as CDLA/2955/2006). Referring to Mr Commissioner Turnbull's discussion, in paragraph 15 of R(DLA) 7/02, of regulation 12(6)(c), Judge Levenson stated as follows (at paragraph 10):

> '. . . The Commissioner held that it is not enough if the presence of an adult prevents the claimant from becoming disruptive. In my opinion this is to confuse 12(6)(b) and 12(6)(c). The point about (c) is the unpredictability, not the intervention. If there is no actual requirement to intervene then (b) is not satisfied. Thus, if a claimant is sometimes in an environment that is so well controlled that intervention is unnecessary, but at other times is in an environment where intervention is regularly required, it is still possible for the claimant to fall within section 73(3).'

33. In *Secretary of State for Work and Pensions v DM (DLA)* [2010] UKUT 318 (AAC) Judge Mark then sought to square that circle by both following paragraph 15 of R(DLA) 7/02 and recognising Judge Levenson's point in *LM v Secretary of State for Work and Pensions* that one must not confuse the requirements of regulation 12(6)(b) with those of regulation 12(6)(c). Judge Mark concluded as follows (at paragraph 10):

> '10. If, however, the structured environment is such that there is no real risk of unpredictable violence or not such a risk as to make it reasonable for somebody to be present and watching over him whenever he is awake, then he cannot be said to need another person to be present and watching over him because of his unpredictable disruptive behaviour. If, in practice, he is regularly left alone in his room for lengthy periods while awake, or is not watched over at school because of his unpredictable disruptive behaviour, then that would suggest that his behaviour is not unpredictable, or at least is not unpredictable to such an extent as to require another person to be present and watching over him whenever he is awake.'

34. In *JH v Secretary of State for Work and Pensions (DLA)* [2010] UKUT 456 (AAC) Judge May QC nailed his colours firmly to the mast of R(DLA) 2/07 in preference to *LM v Secretary of State for Work and Pensions* (at paragraph 14). Similarly, in CDLA/1498/2011 Judge Turnbull, remitting an appeal for rehearing, directed the new tribunal in the following uncompromising terms (at paragraph 10):

> '10. I refer the new tribunal to what I said in paras. 15 and 16 of R(DLA) 7/02. I held that reg. 12(6)(c) is only satisfied if the constant presence of an adult is necessary in order to intervene and deal with the claimant if and when he actually starts to become disruptive, and therefore that if the structured regime of the school is of itself sufficient to prevent the claimant becoming disruptive, reg. 12(6)(c) is not satisfied. In so far as Judge Levenson departed from that in CDLA/2955/2008, I direct the new tribunal not to follow Judge Levenson's decision.'

35. However, Judge Levenson's observations in *LM v Secretary of State for Work and Pensions* received support from Judge Mesher in CDLA/2167/2010 at paragraph 13:

> '. . . Although the report confirmed that U had dangerous tendencies or behaviour problems, the problems were stated mainly in terms of wandering off indoors or outdoors and eating inappropriate items, leading to a need for supervision. It was arguable that in that environment U did not require the quality of close watching over necessary to satisfy regulation 12(6)(c). That is so even if (as I tend to think is right) the approach of paragraph 10 of decision

CDLA/2955/2008 (Mr Commissioner Levenson) is preferred to that in paragraph 15 of R(DLA) 7/02 (Mr Commissioner Turnbull) that if 'the structured regime of the school is of itself sufficient to prevent the claimant becoming disruptive, [regulation 12(6)(c)] is in my judgment not satisfied'. Judge Levenson's view was that that was to confuse the conditions in sub-paragraphs (b) and (c), which should be kept separate, as seems also to have been the view of Judge Mark in *Secretary of State for Work and Pensions v DM (DLA)* [2010] UKUT 318 (AAC).'

36. In sum, the case law undoubtedly reveals a divergence of views. Despite Judge Mark's valiant effort in *Secretary of State for Work and Pensions v DM (DLA)* I am not sure those authorities can be satisfactorily reconciled. This is demonstrated by the fact that in CDLA/1498/2011 (at paragraph 10) Judge Turnbull regarded Judge Mark as having adopted the same approach to regulation 12(6)(c) as he had done in R(DLA) 7/02, while in CDLA/2167/2010 Judge Mesher found support in Judge Mark's decision for the view expressed by Judge Levenson in *LM v Secretary of State for Work and Pensions*. Certainly in his recent decision in *AH v Secretary of State for Work and Pensions (DLA)* Judge Mark regarded himself as following Judge Levenson's approach (at paragraph 9).

37. Which view should the new First-tier Tribunal prefer? The principles governing precedent in the former Commissioners' jurisdiction were laid down in R(I) 12/75 (at paragraphs 19-21) and have been adapted for the new tribunal regime in *Dorset Healthcare NHS Foundation Trust v MH* [2009] UKUT 4 (AAC) (at paragraphs 36 & 37). As a general rule a First-tier Tribunal should follow a reported decision of the Upper Tribunal (or previously of the Commissioners) in preference to an unreported decision, if only because a reported decision is one that necessarily commands the general assent of the majority of relevant judges. However, that presumption does not apply if the reported decision has been carefully considered in a later unreported decision but not followed (see R 1/00 (FC)).

38. For myself I prefer what I understand to be the approach of Judges Levenson, Mesher and Mark. In my view an undue focus on labels such as 'structured regimes' or 'structured environments' runs the risk of losing sight of the plain statutory language. It also obscures the need for the tribunal's careful fact-finding. In practice there is a diverse range of 'structured environments' in both mainstream and special needs schools. What the tribunal must do in applying regulation 12(6)(c) is to start by establishing the predictability or otherwise of the extreme disruptive behaviour. At one extreme, is it solely triggered by readily identifiable factors (e.g. traffic, sudden noise or being denied access to a particular activity)? If so, it may be predictable. Or, at the other extreme, is the behaviour typically random, such that, as it was put in CDLA/2470/2006, the carers are 'in a permanent state of apprehension as to what he will do whenever he is out of sight' (at paragraph 11). If so, it may be unpredictable. This will then require consideration of both what happens and what is reasonably required on a regular basis, and whether that amounts to requiring 'another person to be present and watching over him whenever he is awake.' Thus the nature, degree and intensity of the supervision involved all need to be examined.

39. It may be significant that on the facts of R(DLA) 7/02 the child in question attended a specialist autistic unit attached to a mainstream school. It may well be that on those facts it was always going to be difficult to meet the necessary statutory criteria. However, for the most severely disabled and vulnerable young people in some special needs schools, I would not agree with the observation in R(DLA) 7/02 that regulation 12(6)(c) is not satisfied if 'the structured regime of the school is of itself sufficient to prevent the claimant becoming disruptive' (at paragraph 15). It all depends on the nature of the type of supervision that is reasonably required."

It is clear that the question of "structured environment" will continue to give trouble to DM and to tribunals until some resolution might be made by a three judge court, but it should be arguable that if it is the very presence of a teacher or other authority figure, there, ready to intervene when necessary, that creates that structured environment then the claimant would seem to succeed in satisfying para.(6). Where the presence of another (e.g. a parent) placates the claimant without the potential for intervention then he would not.

The operation of paras (5) and (6) of this regulation and therefore also of s.73(3) of the Act has been considered again by Judge Gray in *EC (by SC) v SSWP (DLA)* [2017] UKUT 391 (AAC). The judge held that the FTT had erred in their application of para.(6)(b) because they said that the claimant should be shown to require restraint "for the majority of the time". Judge Gray said that this was not in keeping with the interpretation of Judge Wikeley in *SSWP v MG (DLA)* [2012] UKUT 429 (AAC), where he had held that "regularly" should be interpreted more generally to mean on a significant number of occasions. The judge also observed that the FTT appeared to have treated the evidence of a medical consultant as relevant to the matter of impairment of intelligence and the evidence of the claimant's teacher as relevant to social functioning. She refers to other cases (cited in the notes to this regulation) as showing that all of the evidence was relevant to both these criteria. Judge Gray found that, on the written evidence that was before her, she was able to decide the case in the claimant's favour.

The correct approach to the conditions prescribed in para.(6) is considered in *XTC v SSWP (DLA)* [2020] UKUT 342 (AAC). The claimant was a 10-year-old boy on the autistic spectrum who had been denied mobility component at the higher rate. It was accepted that he met the conditions in s.73(3)(a) of the Contributions and Benefits Act (both the day and the night conditions) and that he also satisfied para.(5) of reg.12 (arrested development etc. affecting intelligence and social functioning), but the FTT that heard his appeal did not accept that his behaviour satisfied the conditions of para.(6). The FTT heard evidence from the boy's father that he had played with his penis in public at the supermarket, at school and in front of a neighbour's child. The tribunal found that this did not amount to "extremely disruptive behaviour", did not involve a risk of physical injury or of damage, and did not require intervention to be made regularly. Judge Church, in the UT took the view that, applying the test of extremely disruptive behaviour as explained in earlier cases, this behaviour was so far "wholly out of the ordinary" and would be so disruptive that it could not be regarded as other than "extreme". He remitted the case on this and other grounds. While it might have been open for the FTT to have found on the evidence before it that there was no risk of physical injury or damage, emphasis seems to have been put by the representative of the Secretary of State on the fact that the child was described by his parents as "not a violent or disruptive child". Judge Church points out that there is no need for the behaviour that might lead to injury or damage to be violent. Clearly that is the case when intervention is necessary to prevent accidental injury. It is likely also that the evidence given by his parents meant that he was not deliberately disruptive whereas, his behaviour might disrupt the activities of others, including his parents, whenever intervention was required.

Judge Church gives further guidance on the matter of the regularity with which intervention is required. It is necessary in his view for the tribunal to ascertain the number and frequency with which incidents occur that satisfy all three conditions prescribed by the paragraph and then to determine if intervention is required regularly according to the ordinary meaning of that word.

This case is interesting also because reference is made to the introduction of video evidence to the FTT hearing. The claimant's father had wished to do that in order to show how large and powerful his son was and how much he had to be restrained. The record of proceedings had no reference to this matter at all. Judge Church points out that such evidence was competent under the Tribunal Rules (as to which see Vol III of this work) and that the record should have shown that the request had been made (he accepted the father's evidence to that effect) and that it should have recorded reasons why the tribunal had decided not to receive such evidence if that were the case. Equally, had they decided to receive the evidence reasons should have been recorded for doing so.

Paragraphs (7) and (8) (fear and anxiety)

4.96 These paras have been inserted despite the opposition of the Social Security Advisory Committee. Their purpose is to negative the effect of certain words used, in passing, in the decision of the Tribunal of Commissioners *R(DLA) 4/01*.

That decision was chiefly concerned with the question of whether attention or supervision which qualified the claimant for care component could equally qualify him for lower rate mobility component when it consisted of supervision of outdoor walking.

The Tribunal of Commissioners held that it could, but in doing so remarked also that when a claimant had some disability (e.g. prelingual deafness) which inhibited his ability to go out alone through fear of getting lost and being unable to seek assistance, that this "fear and anxiety" should provide the causal link between that physical disability and his inability to take advantage of outdoor mobility. In his statement to Parliament the Secretary of State explains that the purpose of this amendment is to prevent that phrase from being used too widely to extend to anyone with a disability who then expresses a fear of going out alone because of that disability. Regrettably the Secretary of State did not respond to the request of SSAC for specific examples to be given to illustrate the intended operation and limits of these new paragraphs. While it is understandable that the department might wish to stem the possible flood of claims from, say, those suffering from a heart condition who might be afraid to walk out alone, it could be argued that fear and anxiety about onset of a heart condition is no less limiting than fear and anxiety of becoming lost for the prelingually deaf; and if not the deaf then what of the blind. It is generally accepted that the lower rate of mobility component was introduced to provide some benefit to claimants such as *Mallinson* who could not undertake routes unfamiliar to them because of blindness. Yet what was Mr. Mallinson's inability to walk unfamiliar routes based upon other than a fear that, if he did so, he might injure himself? To carry the effect of this amendment so far would be absurd, and the Secretary of State's statement to Parliament says clearly that there is no dispute with the conclusion reached in *R(DLA) 4/01* which did accord entitlement to three prelingually deaf claimants.

4.97 Paragraph (8) also provides a saving for those whose fear and anxiety is a symptom of mental disability and is so severe as to prevent the person from walking alone. The statement recognises that there will be difficulty in defining a line at which fear and anxiety become a severe mental disability. It seems likely that a clear medical diagnosis will be necessary.

The operation of these paragraphs has been considered in *R(DLA) 3/04* where the claimant was unable to walk outside for any distance unless she was accompanied by a member of her family who could, by giving her reassurance and encouragement, prevent her from having panic attacks. These attacks were a symptom of a severe state of anxiety and depression from which she was suffering. Commissioner Rowland allowed her appeal, finding that although her inability to walk outside clearly arose from fear and anxiety it was equally clear that, in her case, that anxiety was a symptom of her mental illness. The wording of para.(8) did not require that the mental disability should be some illness other than the anxiety itself.

These paragraphs were also considered in *CSDLA/430/2004*. There, the claimant suffered from asthma and also a chronic anxiety state that made him reluctant to walk outside alone for fear of suffering an asthma attack. Commissioner Parker, in allowing an appeal, points out that in this case there are really two separate questions to be answered. The first, (referring to para.(8)) is whether the anxiety attack was a symptom of mental illness and whether it was so severe as to prevent him walking unaccompanied. The second, and wholly separate question, (in accordance with s.73(1)(d)) was whether real asthma attacks did occur that disabled him, so as to make it necessary for him to be accompanied for the purpose of supervision for most of the time.

The decision in *SSWP v DC (DLA)* [2011] UKUT (AAC) 235 does provide an example of where these provisions have been applied. There the claimant suffered from urinary incontinence. He said that he was embarrassed by incidents that occurred when he was out so that he required his wife always to accompany him and to assist him. The judge rejected his appeal because his need for assistance arose only from "fear and anxiety" on his part.

[1 Hospitalisation [5 of persons aged 18 or over] in mobility component cases

12A.—(1) Subject to [5 paragraph (3) and] regulation 12B (exemption), it shall be a condition for the receipt of a disability living allowance which is attributable to entitlement to the mobility component for any period in respect of any person that during that period he is not maintained free of charge while undergoing medical or other treatment as an in-patient— **4.98**

(a) in a hospital or similar institution under [4 the NHS Act of 1978, the NHS Act of 2006 or the NHS (Wales) Act of 2006]; or

(b) in a hospital or other similar institution maintained or administered by the Defence Council.

(2) For the purposes of paragraph (1)(a) a person shall only be regarded as not being maintained free of charge in a hospital or similar institution during any period when his accommodation and services are provided under[—]

[4 (a) section 57 of, and paragraph 14 of Schedule 7A to, the NHS Act of 1978;

(b) section 13 of, and paragraph 15 of Schedule 2 to, the NHS Act of 2006;

(c) section 28 of, and paragraph 11 of Schedule 6 to, the NHS Act of 2006;

(d) section 44(6) of, and paragraph 19(1) of Schedule 4 to, the NHS Act of 2006;

(e) section 11 of, and paragraph 15 of Schedule 2 to, the NHS (Wales) Act of 2006;

(f) section 18 of, and paragraph 19(1) of Schedule 3 to, the NHS (Wales) Act of 2006; or

(g) section 22 of, and paragraph 11 of Schedule 5 to, the NHS (Wales) Act of 2006.]

[2 (2A) For the purposes of paragraph (1), a period during which a person is maintained free of charge while undergoing medical or other treatment as an in-patient shall be deemed to begin on the day after the day on which he enters a hospital or similar institution referred to in that paragraph and to end on the day [3 before the day] on which he leaves such a hospital or similar institution.]

[5 (3) This regulation does not apply to a person who was under the age of 18 on the day on which he entered the hospital or other similar institution referred to in paragraph (1) to begin his current period as an in-patient.]

AMENDMENTS

1. Social Security (Disability Living Allowance and Claims and Payments) Amendment Regulations 1996 (SI 1996/1436) reg.2 (July 31, 1996).

2. Social Security (Hospital In-Patients, Attendance Allowance and Disability Living Allowance) (Amendment) Regulations 1999 (SI 1999/1326) (June 7, 1999).
3. Social Security (Attendance Allowance and Disability Living Allowance) (Amendment) Regulations 2000, (SI 2000/1401) reg.3 (June 19, 2000).
4. Social Security (Attendance Allowance, Disability Living Allowance and Carer's Allowance) (Amendment) Regulations 2013 (SI 2013/389) reg.4 (April 8, 2013).
5. Social Security (Disability Living Allowance and Personal Independence Payment) (Amendment) Regulations 2016 (SI 2016/556) reg. 2 (June 29, 2016).

General Note

4.99 Until this regulation was introduced in 1996, the mobility component of disability living allowance, like mobility allowance before it, was payable however long the claimant was in hospital. It was only if a claimant ceased to be able to benefit at all from enhanced facilities for locomotion (see s.73(8) of the Social Security Contributions and Benefits Act 1992) that he might lose entitlement. Regs 12B and 12C set out a large number of exemptions and adjustments to the basic rule.

Note that this regulation has been amended in response to the decision of the Supreme Court in *Cameron Mathieson v SSWP* [2015] UKSC 47. That decision concerned a claim made on behalf of an infant claimant. The Supreme Court held that the previous version of this regulation breached the claimant's rights under the Human Rights Act 1998 and under the ECHR. Accordingly, this regulation now applies only to claimants who are aged 18 years or over. An attempt to apply the same argument in the case of an adult claimant has failed in the case of *MOC (by MG) v SSWP (DLA)* [2020] UKUT 134 (AAC) (see the discussion of this case in the Note to regulation 8 above).

An argument that this regulation was ultra vires was rejected in *R. v Secretary of State for Social Security Ex p. Perry and Ex p. McGillivray* (CA, June 30, 1998). In *CDLA/1338/02* a further attack based on the argument that the regulation was contrary to the Human Rights Act 1998 was also rejected. The Commissioner held that he would not regard the right to a non-contributory benefit as a "possession" to be protected by Art.1. Neither did he think that the withdrawal of the benefit for those in a publicly funded hospital could be regarded as discriminatory under Art.14 because decisions based upon the source of funding could not be regarded as unjustified or irrational.

The phrase "medical or other treatment as an in-patient ... in a hospital or similar institution" is used also in reg.8. Decisions relating to the meaning of those words are discussed in the notes following that regulation.

[1 Exemption from regulation 12A

4.100 **12B.**—(1) Subject to paragraph (2), regulation 12A shall not apply to a person—

(a) for the first 28 days; [6 . . .]

(b) [6 . . .]

of any period throughout which he is a person to whom paragraph (10) applies.

(2) Where, on the day on which a person's entitlement to the mobility component commences, he is a person to whom paragraph (10) applies, paragraph (1) shall not apply to him for any period of consecutive days, beginning with that day, in which he continues to be a person to whom paragraph (10) applies.

(3) For the purposes of paragraphs [5 (1), (4), (7), (8) and (8A)], two or more distinct periods separated by an interval not exceeding 28 days, or by two or more such intervals, shall be treated as a continuous period equal in

duration to the total of such distinct periods and ending on the last day of the later such period.

(4) Subject to paragraph (5) and regulation 12C, where—

(a) immediately before 31st July 1996, a person has, for a continuous period of not less than 365 days, been a person to whom paragraph (10) applies and in receipt of the mobility component and on 31st July 1996 is a person to whom that paragraph applies; or

(b) on a day not more than 28 days prior to 31st July 1996, a person has, for a continuous period of not less than 365 days, been a person to whom paragraph (10) applies and in receipt of the mobility component, and on or after 31st July 1996 and not more than 28 days after the last day of the previous distinct period during which that paragraph applies, becomes a person to whom that paragraph again applies,

regulation 12A shall not apply until such time as paragraph (10) first ceases to apply to him for more than 28 consecutive days.

(5) Paragraph (4) shall not apply where on 31st July 1996 a person is detained under Part II or III of the Mental Health Act 1983 or [4 Part 5, 6 or 7 or section 136 of the Mental Health (Care and Treatment) (Scotland) Act 2003 or section 52D or 52M of the Criminal Procedure (Scotland) Act 1995].

(6) Where, on a day after 31st July 1996, a person—

(a) becomes detained under Part II or III of the Mental Health Act 1983 or [4 Part 5, 6 or 7 or section 136 of the Mental Health (Care and Treatment) (Scotland) Act 2003 or section 52D or 52M of the Criminal Procedure (Scotland) Act 1995].; or

(b) ceases to be entitled to the mobility component,

paragraph (4) shall cease to be applicable to that person and shall not again become applicable to him.]

[5 (7) Subject to regulation 12C, where on 8th April 2013, paragraph (10) applies to a person and a Motability agreement entered into by or on behalf of that person is in force, regulation 12A shall, for the period following that referred to in paragraph (1)(a) [6 . . .], continue not to apply to that person for the period that terminates in accordance with paragraph (8).]

[5 (8) The period referred to in paragraph (7) terminates—

(a) on the first day after 8th April 2013 on which paragraph (10) first ceases to apply to the person for more than 28 consecutive days;

(b) in accordance with paragraph (8A); or

(c) on 8th April 2016; whichever is the earliest.]

[5 (8A) The period referred to in paragraph (8)(b) terminates—

(a) in the case of the hire of a vehicle—

(i) where the vehicle is returned to the owner before the expiration of the current term of hire, on the date that the vehicle is returned to the owner;

(ii) where the vehicle is returned to the owner at the expiration of the current term of hire, on expiry of the current term of hire;

(iii) where the vehicle is retained with the owner's consent by or on behalf of the person after the expiration of the current term of hire, on expiry of the current term of hire;

(iv) where the vehicle is retained otherwise than with the owner's consent by or on behalf of the person after the expiration of the current term of hire, on expiry of the current term of hire; or
(v) where the vehicle is retained otherwise than with the owner's consent by or on behalf of the person after the date of an early termination of the current term of hire, on the date of that early termination; and
(b) in the case of a hire-purchase agreement—
(i) on the purchase of the vehicle;
(ii) where the vehicle is returned to the owner under the terms of the agreement before the completion of the purchase, on the date that the vehicle is returned to the owner; or
(iii) where the vehicle is repossessed by the owner under the terms of the agreement before the completion of the purchase, on the date of repossession.]

[[5] (8B) In paragraph (8A)(a) the "current term of hire" means the last term of hire that was agreed on or before 8th April 2013 but does not include any extension of that last term of hire after 8th April 2013.]

(9) [[5] *omitted*]

[[2] (9A) Regulation 12A shall not apply in the case of a person who is residing in a hospice and is terminally ill where the Secretary has been informed that he is terminally ill—
(a) on a claim for disability living allowance;
(b) on an application for a [[3] revision under section 9 of the 1998 Act or supersession under section 10 of that Act] of an award of disability living allowance; or
(c) in writing in connection withan award of, or a claim for, or an application for [[3] revision under section 9 of the 1998 Act or supersession under section 10 of that Act] of an award of, disability living allowance.]

(10) This paragraph refers to a person who is undergoing medical or other treatment in a hospital or other institution in any of the circumstances referred to in regulation 12A.

(11) For the purposes of paragraph (4), receipt of mobility allowance prior to 6th April 1992 shall be treated as receipt of the mobility component.

(12) In this regulation—
[[2] (za) "hospice" has the same meaning as that given in paragraph (7) of regulation 10;]
(a) "motability agreement" means an agreement such as is referred to in regulation 44(1) of the Social Security (Claims and Payments) Regulations 1987 (payment of disability living allowance on behalf of a beneficiary in settlement of liability for payments under an agreement for the hire or hire-purchase of a vehicle);
(b) "Motability" means the company, set up under that name as a charity and originally incorporated under the Companies Act 1985 and subsequently incorporated by Royal Charter.]

AMENDMENTS

1. Social Security (Disability Living Allowance and Claims, and Payments) Amendment Regulations 1996 (SI 1996/1436) reg.2 (July 31, 1996).

2. Social Security (Disability Living Allowance) Amendment Regulations 1996 (SI 1996/1767) reg.2 (July 31, 1996).
3. Social Security Act 1998 (Commencement No. 11, and Savings and Consequential and Transitional Provisions) Order 1999 (SI 1999/2860) Sch.7 (October 18, 1999).
4. Mental Health (Care and Treatment) (Scotland) Act 2003 (Consequential Provisions) Order 2005 (SI 2005/2078) Sch.2, para.13 (October 5, 2005).
5. Social Security (Attendance Allowance, Disability Living Allowance and Carer's Allowance) (Amendment) Regulations 2013 (SI 2013/389) reg.4 (April 8, 2013).
6. Social Security (Disability Living Allowance and Personal Independence Payment) (Amendment) Regulations 2016 (SI 2016/556) reg. 2 (June 29, 2016).

[1 Adjustment of benefit to certain persons exempted from regulation 12A

12C.—(1) Subject to paragraph (3), where a person is a person to whom regulation 12B(4) applies and the mobility component would otherwise be payable at the higher rate prescribed by regulation 4(2)(a), the benefit shall be adjusted so that it is payable at the lower rate prescribed by regulation 4(2)(b). **4.101**

(2) Subject to paragraph (3), where regulation 12B(7) applies, the benefit shall be adjusted so that it is payable at a rate equal to the weekly amount payable under the relevant agreement for the period referred to in that regulation.

(3) Where paragraphs (4) and (7) of regulation 12B both apply, the benefit shall be adjusted so that it is payable either at the lower rate prescribed by regulation 4(2)(b) or at a rate equal to the weekly amount payable under the relevant agreement referred to in regulation 12B(7), whichever is the greater.]

AMENDMENT

1. Social Security (Disability Living Allowance and Claims and Payments) Amendment Regulations 1996 (SI 1996/1436) reg.2 (July 31, 1996).

Invalid Vehicle Scheme

13.—Schedule 2, which relates to the entitlement to mobility component of certain persons eligible for invalid carriages shall have effect. **4.102**

SCHEDULES

SCHEDULE 1 — **Regulation 3(4)**

PERSONS AGED 65 AND OVER

[1 Revision or Supersession] of an award made before person attained 65

1.—(1) This paragraph applies where— **4.103**

(a) a person is aged 65 or over;
(b) the person has an award of disability living allowance made before he attained the age of 65;
(c) an application [1 is made in accordance with section 9 of the 1998 Act or section 10 of that Act for that award to be revised or superseded.]

(d) an adjudicating authority is satisfied that the decision awarding disability living allowance ought to be [1 revised or superseded].

(2) Where paragraph (1) applies, the person to whom the award relates shall not, subject to paragraph (3), be precluded from entitlement to either component of disability living allowance solely by reason of the fact that he is aged 65 or over when the [1 revision or supersession] is made.

(3) Where the adjudicating authority determining the application is satisfied that the decision ought to be [1 superseded] on the ground that there has been a relevant change of circumstances since the decision was given, paragraph (2) shall apply only where the relevant change of circumstances occurred before the person attained the age of 65.

[1 Revision or Superssesion of an award other than a review to which paragraph 1 refers

4.104 **2.**—References in the following paragraphs of this Schedule to a [1 revision or supersession] of an award refer only to those [1revisions or supersessions] where the awards which are being [1 revised or superseded] were made—

(a) on or after the date the person to whom the award relates attained the age of 65; or

(b) before the person to whom the award relates attained the age of 65 where the award is [1 superseded] by reference to a change in the person's circumstances which occurred on or after the day he attained the age of 65.

Age 65 and over and entitled to the care component

4.105 **3.**—(1) This paragraph applies where a person on or after attaining the age of 65—

(a) is entitled to the care component and an adjudicating authority is satisfied that the decision awarding it ought to be [1 revised under section 9 of the 1998 Act or superseded under section 10 of that Act]; or

(b) makes a renewal claim for disability living allowance.

(2) Where a person was entitled on the previous award or on the award [1 being revised or superseded] to the care component payable—

(a) at the lowest rate, that person shall not be precluded, solely by reason of the fact that he is aged 65 or over, from entitlement to the care component; or

(b) at the middle or highest rate, that person shall not be precluded, solely by reason of the fact that he has attained the age of 65, from entitlement to the care component payable at the middle or highest rate,

but in determining that person's entitlement, [2 section 72] of the Act shall have effect as if in paragraph (a) of subsection (2) of that section for the reference to 3 months there was substituted a reference to 6 months and paragraph (b) of that subsection was omitted.

(3) In this paragraph, a renewal claim is a claim made for a disability living allowance where the person making the claim had—

(a) within the period of 12 months immediately preceding the date the claim was made, been entitled under an earlier award to the care component or to attendance allowance (referred to in this paragraph as "the previous award"); and

(b) attained the age of 65 before that entitlement ended.

Invalid Vehicle Scheme

4.106 **4.**—(1) Where—

(a) a certificate issued in respect of a person under section 13(1) of the Social Security (Miscellaneous Provisions) Act 1977 is in force, or

(b) an invalid carriage or other vehicle is or was on or after January 1, 1976 made available to a person by the Secretary of State under [3 section 46(1) of the NHS Act of 1978 or paragraph 9 of Schedule 1 to the NHS Act of 2006 or paragraph 9 of Schedule 1 to the NHS (Wales) Act of 2006], being a carriage or other vehicle which is—

(i) propelled by a petrol engine or an electric motor;

(ii) provided for use on a public road; and

(iii) controlled by the occupant,

that person shall not be precluded from entitlement to mobility component payable at the higher rate specified in regulation 4(2)(a), or a care component payable at the highest or middle rate specified in regulation 4(1)(a) or (b) by reason only that he has attained the age of 65.

(2) In determining a person's entitlement where paragraph (1) applies, [2 section 72] of the Act shall have effect as if in paragraph (a) of subsection (2) of that section for the reference to 3 months there was substituted a reference to 6 months and paragraph (b) of that subsection was omitted.

Age 65 or over and entitled to mobility component

5.—(1) This paragraph applies where a person on or after attaining the age of 65 is entitled to the mobility component payable at the higher rate specified in regulation 4(2)(a), and— 4.107

(a) an adjudicating authority is satisfied that the decision giving effect to that entitlement ought to be [1 revised under section 9 of the 1998 Act or superseded under section 10 of that Act], or

(b) the person makes a renewal claim for disability living allowance.

(2) A person to whom this paragraph applies shall not be precluded, solely by reason of the fact that he has attained the age of 65, from entitlement to the mobility component by virtue of having satisfied or being likely to satisfy one or other of the conditions mentioned in subsection (1)(a), (b) or (c) of [2 section 73] of the Act.

(3) In this paragraph and paragraph 6 and 7 a renewal claim is a claim made for a disability living allowance where the person making the claim had—

(a) within the period of 12 months immediately preceding the date the claim was made been entitled under an earlier award to the mobility component (referred to in these paragraphs as "the previous award"); and

(b) attained the age of 65 before that entitlement ended.

Aged 65 or over and award of lower rate mobility component

6.—(1) This paragraph applies where a person on or after attaining the age of 65 is entitled to the mobility component payable at the lower rate specified in regulation 4(2) and— 4.108

(a) an adjudicating authority is satisfied that the decision giving effect to that entitlement ought to be [1 revised under section 9 of the 1998 Act or superseded under section 10 of that Act], or

(b) the person makes a renewal claim for disability living allowance.

(2) A person to whom this paragraph applies shall not be precluded, solely by reason of the fact that he has attained the age of 65, from entitlement to the mobility component, but in determining the person's entitlement to that component [2 section 73](11) of the Act shall have effect in his case as if paragraph (a), and the words "in any other case" in paragraph (b), were omitted.

Award of care component where person entitled to mobility component

7.—(1) This paragraph applies where a person on or after attaining the age of 65 is entitled to the mobility component and— 4.109

(a) an adjudicating authority is satisfied that the decision giving effect to that entitlement ought to be [1 revised under section 9 of the 1998 Act or superseded under section 10 of that Act], or

(b) the person makes a renewal claim for disability living allowance.

(2) A person to whom this paragraph applies shall not be precluded solely by reason of the fact that he has attained the age of 65 from entitlement under [2 section 72](1) of the Act by virtue of having satisfied either the conditions mentioned in subsection (1)(b) or in subsection (1)(c), or in both those subsections, but in determining a person's entitlement, [2 section 72] of the Act shall have effect as if in paragraph (a) of subsection (2) of that section, for the reference to 3 months there was substituted a reference to 6 months and paragraph (b) of that subsection were omitted.

AMENDMENTS

1. Social Security Act 1998 (Commencement No.11, and Savings and Consequential and Transitional Provisions) Order 1999 (SI 1999/2860) Sch.7 (October 18, 1999).

2. Social Security (Disability Living Allowance) (Amendment) Regulations 1993 (SI 1993/1939) reg.2(2) (August 26, 1993).

3. Social Security (Attendance Allowance, Disability Living Allowance and Carer's Allowance) (Amendment) Regulations 2013 (SI 2013/389) reg.4 (April 8, 2013).

GENERAL NOTE

Paragraph 1

4.110 This is concerned with reviews (now revisions or supersessions) of awards which partly cover a period before the claimant's 65th birthday and partly cover a later period. On a review, entitlement in respect of the latter period is to be determined as though the claimant was under the age of 65 unless the review is on the ground of a change of circumstances which occurred on or after the claimant's 65th birthday (in which case see *para.2*). See *CSDLA/388/2000* noted after s.75 above.

The operation of para.1 of Sch.1. Is considered in some detail in *CDLA/301/05*. The claimant had been in receipt of the middle rate of DLA since before she attained the age of 65. Nine years later, and now over that age, she responded to a routine enquiry form sent out by the Secretary of State in consequence of which it was decided that her award should be superseded on the ground that it had been made under a mistake of fact; namely that she had not ever needed any care at night. The claimant appealed against this decision, but added, as well, that in the event of that appeal failing she should be entitled to, at least, the lowest rate of DLA. At her present age the claimant could not, of course, succeed on the basis of a new claim. She could succeed only if the provisions of para.1 covered her case. (The rest of that schedule being appropriate only to cases where the award that was being reviewed had been made after the age of 65.) Paragraph 1 presented two difficulties. First, the opening words of para.(1)(c), "an application is made" seem to limit the operation of the paragraph to cases where the claimant has made an application for review, and in this case the claimant had not done so. Commissioner Mesher rejected the suggestion that the enquiry form should be treated as an application. He held instead, that the words above could not be read as limiting the paragraph in the way suggested. He did this after referring to the history of the legislation, which, prior to its amendment in 1999, would not have been so limited. The amendments that were then made were expressed to be only for giving effect to the new terminology introduced by the 1998 Act, and, therefore, he reasoned, could not have been intended to make a substantive change to the claimant's rights.

The second difficulty arose because there was some doubt as to whether this claimant's need for assistance in preparing a meal (which had been accepted by the appeal tribunal) had existed before she reached the age of 65, or had developed only later.

The Secretary of State, and the appeal tribunal contended that it was only in the former case that an award could now be made under para.1. Commissioner Mesher disagreed. In his view all the elements of para.1(1) were satisfied, and para.1(3) also was satisfied, because the change of circumstances on which the review was based, was the mistake of fact made on the original application before she reached the age of 65. This left para.1(2) to operate simply as it stated i.e. that her claim should not be precluded on the ground only that she was now over the age of 65. The whole case was returned to a new tribunal for reconsideration.

Paragraph 2

4.111 This is concerned with revisions or supersessions of awards relating solely to a period no earlier than the claimant's 65th birthday or to an award beginning before that birthday but reviewed on the ground of a change of circumstances which occurred on or after that birthday. In such cases, paras 3–7 have the effect that the conditions of entitlement may be different from those applying to younger claimants and are the same as those governing certain renewal claims made at or after the age of 65.

Paragraph 3

4.112 On a revision or supersession (within para.2) or a renewal claim (within sub-para. (3)), a person of or over 65 can continue to be entitled to the care component at the same rate as before or at a higher rate. A person who was previously entitled to the highest rate but no longer satisfies both the "day" and "night" conditions can also become entitled at the middle rate. However, a person previously entitled to either the highest or the middle rate and who no longer satisfies either of the "day" or "night" conditions cannot become entitled to the component at the lowest rate and so will cease to be entitled to any care component. Furthermore, the qualifying period required of those hoping for entitlement to the component at a higher rate than before, is six months rather than three months as it would be for younger claimants. The overall effect of this paragraph is to make the conditions for entitlement to the care component the same as those for entitlement to attendance allowance under s.64 of the Social Security Contributions and Benefits Act 1992 which is the benefit which a person would be required to claim if the claim were an entirely fresh one or a repeat claim too late to be included as a renewal claim within sub-para.(3).

Paragraph 4

Former vehicle scheme beneficiaries who have attained the age of 65 are eligible for the middle or highest rates of the care component or the higher rate of the mobility component. The three-month qualifying period is increased to six months in respect of the care component but is removed altogether in the case of the mobility component. This effectively re-creates the position as it was before disability living allowance replaced attendance allowance and mobility allowance on April 6, 1992. Under s.74(1) of the Social Security Contributions and Benefits Act 1992, a person issued with a certificate under Sch.2 to these Regulations is deemed to satisfy the conditions for the mobility component at the higher rate. **4.113**

Paragraph 5

On a revision or supersession (within para.2) or a renewal claim (within sub-para. (3)), a person of or over 65 previously entitled to the higher rate of the mobility component can continue to be entitled to the higher rate even if the ground of entitlement is different. However, if he or she no longer satisfies one of the conditions for entitlement to the higher rate, he or she cannot qualify for the lower rate instead. See *CDLA/754/2000* noted after s.75 above. **4.114**

Paragraph 6

On a revision or supersession (within para.2) or a renewal claim (within para.5(3)), a person of or over 65 previously entitled to the lower rate of the mobility component can still be awarded the lower rate but cannot qualify for the higher rate. However, if he or she does not qualify for the lower rate on the usual ground (by satisfying the condition of s.73(1)(d) of the Social Security Contributions and Benefits Act 1992), the claimant may qualify for the lower rate by satisfying one of the conditions of s.73(1)(a), (b) or (c) which are usually the grounds for qualifying for the higher rate. **4.115**

The operation of para.6 of this Schedule has been considered in *DB v SSWP (DLA)* [2016] UKUT 205 (AAC). The claimant had qualified for the care component at the middle rate and for the mobility component at the lower rate before he reached his 65th birthday. On two subsequent occasions after he had reached that age, the awards of benefit were reviewed, but the award for mobility component remained the same. The claimant had applied again for an increase in the mobility component arguing that the original award had been made under a mistake of fact because he was, even when the original award was made, unable or virtually unable to walk. The FTT had approached the case as if it were to be determined under para.1 of this Schedule. They dismissed the appeal on the ground that they were not satisfied that the claimant's condition then could be shown to have been such as to qualify. In the UT Judge Gray explains that this was in error; para.1 of the Schedule applies only to the revision or supersession of an award made before the claimant's 65th birthday. In this case two further awards had been made after that date and the present application was for supersession of the later of those awards. In this case para.1 did not apply; only para.6 could do so, and under para.6(2) an award, on whatever grounds he qualified, could only ever be made at the lower rate.

Paragraph 7

4.116 On a revision or supersession (within para.2) or a renewal claim (within para.5(3)), a person of or over 65 previously entitled to the mobility component can be awarded the care component at the higher or middle rates but the qualifying period for the care component is six months rather than the usual three months for younger claimants. Effectively, the conditions are then the same as for attendance allowance which is what a claimant of that age would claim if he or she were not entitled to the mobility component.

SCHEDULE 2 **Regulation 13**

INVALID VEHICLE SCHEME

Interpretation

4.117 **1.**— In this Schedule, unless the context otherwise requires,—

"the 1977 Act" means the Social Security (Miscellaneous Provisions) Act 1977;

"vehicle scheme beneficiary" means any person of a class specified in section 13(3)(a), (c) or (d) of the 1977 Act or any person of the class specified in section 13(3)(b) of the 1977 Act whose application was approved on or after 1st January 1976 and, where an invalid carriage or other vehicle was provided or as the case may be applied for, is a person of any such class in respect of whom the invalid carriage or other vehicle provided or applied for was a vehicle—

(a) propelled by a petrol engine or by an electric motor,
(b) supplied for use on a public road, and
(c) to be controlled by the occupant;

"certificate" means a certificate issued in accordance with paragraph 3.

Prescribed periods for purposes of section 13(3)(c) of the 1977 Act

4.118 **2.**—For the purposes of section 13(3)(c) of the 1977 Act—

(a) the prescribed period before 1 January 1976 shall be that commencing with 31st January 1970 and ending with 31st December 1975; and
(b) the prescribed period after 1st January 1976 shall be that commencing with 2nd January 1976 and ending with 31st March 1978.

Issue of certificates

4.119 **3.**—(1) The Secretary of State shall issue a certificate in the form approved by him in respect of any person—

(a) who has made an application for a certificate in the form approved by the Secretary of State; and
(b) whom the Secretary of State considers satisfies the conditions specified in subparagraph (2).

(2) The conditions specified in this sub-paragraph are that—

(a) the person is a vehicle scheme beneficiary; and
(b) his physical condition has not improved to such an extent that he no longer satisfies the conditions which it was necessary for him to satisfy in order to become a vehicle scheme beneficiary.

Duration and cancellation of certificates

4.120 **4.**—(1) Subject to sub-paragraph (2) the period during which a certificate is in force shall commence on the day specified in the certificate as being the date on which it comes into force and shall continue for the life of the person concerned.

(2) If in any case the Secretary of State determines that the condition specified in paragraph 3(2)(b) is not satisfied, the certificate shall cease to be in force from the date of such non-satisfaction as determined by the Secretary of State (or such later date as appears to the Secretary of State to be reasonable in the circumstances).

Application of these Regulations in relation to vehicle scheme beneficiaries

4.121 **5.**—In relation to a person in respect of whom a certificate is in force these Regulations shall have effect as though regulation 2(1)(a)(iii) were omitted.

General Note

These provisions replace the Mobility Allowance (Vehicle Scheme Beneficiaries) Regulations 1977 (SI 1977/1229). A person issued with a certificate under this Schedule is deemed, by s.74(1) of the Social Security Contributions and Benefits Act 1992, to satisfy the condition of s.73(1)(a) so that he or she can qualify for the mobility component at the higher rate. He or she is also deemed to have satisfied that condition during the three-month qualifying period. Paragraph 1 of Sch.1 to these Regulations entitles such a person to the mobility component notwithstanding that he or she has attained the age of 65. Note that, under reg.7 of the 1977 Regulations, a person could be entitled to mobility allowance for a period *before* the date of claim for the allowance as long as it was after the certificate came into force. No equivalent provision appears in respect of the mobility component of disability living allowance. **4.122**

[1 Schedule 3 **Regulation 9A(1)**

Persons to Whom Regulations 9 and 10 Apply With Modifications **4.123**

[1 . . .]

Repeal

1. Social Security Amendment (Residential Care and Nursing Homes) Regulations 2001 (SI 2001/3767) reg.4 (April 8, 2002).

The Social Security (Invalid Care Allowance) Regulations 1976

(SI 1976/409) (*as amended*)

Arrangement of Regulations

Part I

General

Part II

Miscellaneous Provisions Relating to Invalid Care Allowance

The Secretary of State for Social Services, in exercise of the powers conferred upon her by sections 13(4), 37, 40(2), 49, 79(1), 80, 81(1), (2) and (6), 82(1), (5) and (6), 84(1) and (2), 85(1), 86(5) and 119(3) of the Social Security Act 1975, section 36(7) of the National Insurance Act 1965, as continued in force by regulation 2(2) of the Social Security (Graduated Retirement Benefit) Regulations 1975, and of all other powers enabling her in that behalf, and after reference to the National Insurance Advisory Committee, hereby makes the following regulations:

GENERAL NOTE

4.125 Until 2003 what is now known as Carer's Allowance under s.70 of the Contributions and Benefits Act 1992, was known as Invalid Care Allowance. Despite all references to that benefit being then changed the title of these regulations (and the heading to s.70) have remained unchanged. (See Regulatory Reform (Carer's Allowance) Order (SI 2002/1457) art.2 (April 1, 2003).

PART I

GENERAL

Citation and commencement

4.126 **1.**—These regulations may be cited as the Social Security (Invalid Care Allowance) Regulations 1976 and shall come into operation on 12th April 1976.

Interpretation

4.127 **2.**—[1 (1) In these Regulations, "the Contributions and Benefits Act" means the Social Security Contributions and Benefits Act 1992].

(2) Any reference in these regulations to any provision made by or contained in any enactment or instrument shall, except in so far as the context otherwise requires, be construed as a reference to that provision as amended or extended by any enactment or instrument and as including a reference to any provision whichmay re-enact or replace it, withor without modification.

(3) The rules for the construction of Acts of Parliament contained in the Interpretation Act 1889 shall apply for the purposes of the interpretation of these regulations as they apply for the purposes of the interpretation of an Act of Parliament.

AMENDMENT

1. Social Security (Invalid Care Allowance) Amendment Regulations 1996 (SI 1996/2744) reg.2 (November 25, 1996).

[1 Disapplication of section 1(1A) of the Administration Act

2A.—Section 1(1A) of the Administration Act (requirement to state national insurance number) shall not apply— 4.128

(a) [2 *omitted*];
(b) to any claim for [3 carer's allowance] made or treated as made before 9th February, 1998;
(c) to an adult dependant in respect of whom a claim for an increase of [3 carer's allowance] is made or treated as made before 5th October, 1998.]

[4 (d) to an adult dependant who—
(i) is a person in respect of whom a claim for an increase of carer's allowance is made;
(ii) is subject to immigration control within the meaning of section 115(9)(a) of the Immigration and Asylum Act 1999; and
(iii) has not previously been allocated a national insurance number.]

AMENDMENTS

1. Social Security (National Insurance Information: Exemption) Regulations (SI 1997/2676) (December 1, 1997).
2. Social Security (Working Tax Credit and Child Tax Credit) (Consequential Amendments) (No. 2) Regulations 2003 (SI 2003/937) reg.2 (April 6, 2003).
3. Social Security Amendment (Carer's Allowance) Regulations 2002 (SI 2002/2497) reg.3 (April 1, 2003).
4. Social Security (National Insurance Number Information: Exemption) Regulations 2009 (SI 2009/471) reg.2 (April 6, 2009).

PART II

MISCELLANEOUS PROVISIONS RELATING TO INVALID CARE ALLOWANCE

Prescribed payments out of public funds which constitute the persons in respect of whom they are payable as severely disabled persons

3.—(1) For the purposes of [1 Section 70 of the Contributions and Benefits Act] [2 carer's allowance] the prescribed payments out of public funds which constitute the persons in respect of whom they are payable as severely disabled persons are— 4.129

(a) a payment under [1 section 104 of the Contributions and Benefits Act] (increase of disablement pension where constant attendance needed);
(b) a payment suchas is referred to in section 7(3)(b) of the Industrial Injuries and Diseases (Old Cases) Act 1975 (increase of an allowance under that Act where the person in respect of whom that allowance is payable requires constant attendance as a result of his disablement);

(c) a payment under regulation 44 of the Social Security (Industrial Injuries) (Benefit) Regulations 1975 in respect of the need of constant attendance;

(d) a payment by way of an allowance in respect of constant attendance on account of disablement for which a person is in receipt of a war disablement pension,

being a payment the weekly rate of which is not less than the amount specified in [1 paragraph 7(a) of Part V of Schedule 4 to the Contributions and Benefits Act].

(2) For the purposes of paragraph (1)(d) of this regulation "war disablement pension" means—

(a) retired pay, pension or allowance granted in respect of disablement under powers conferred by or under the Ministry of Pensions Act 1916, the Air Force (Constitution) Act 1917, the Personal Injuries (Emergency Provisions) Act 1939, the Pensions (Navy, Army, Air Force and Mercantile Marine) Act 1939, the Polish Resettlement Act 1947, the Home Guard Act 1951 or the Ulster Defence Regiment Act 1969,

(b) any retired pay or pension to which section 365(1) of the Income and Corporation Taxes Act 1970 applies, not being retired pay, pension or allowance to which sub-paragraph (a) of this paragraph-applies; or

(c) any payment which the Secretary of State has certified can be accepted as being analogous to any suchretired pay, pension or allowance as is referred to in sub-paragraph (a) or (b) of this paragraph.

AMENDMENTS

1. Social Security (Invalid Care Allowance) Amendment Regulations 1996 (SI 1996/2744) reg.2 (November 25, 1996).

2. Social Security Amendment (Carer's Allowance) Regulations 2002 (SI 2002/2497) reg.3 (April 1, 2003).

Circumstances in which persons are or are not to be treated as engaged or regularly and substantially engaged in caring for severely disabled persons

4.130 **4.**—(1) [1 Subject to paragraph (1A) of this regulation,] a person shall be treated as engaged and as regularly and substantially engaged in caring, for a severely disabled person on every day in a week if, and shall not be treated as engaged or regularly and substantially engaged in caring for a severely disabled person on any day in a week unless, as at that week he is, or is likely to be, engaged and regularly engaged for at least 35 hours a week in caring for that severely disabled person.

[1 (1A) A person who is caring for two or more severely disabled persons in a week shall be treated as engaged and regularly and substantially engaged in caring for a severely disabled person only where he is engaged and regularly engaged for at least 35 hours in that week in caring for any one severely disabled person, considered without reference to any other severely disabled person for whom he is caring.]

(2) A week in respect of which a person fails to satisfy the requirements of paragraph (1) of this regulation shall be treated as a week in respect of which that person satisfies those requirements if he establishes—

(a) that he has only temporarily ceased to satisfy them; and

(b) that (disregarding the provisions of this sub-paragraph) he has satisfied them for at least 14 weeks in the period of 26 weeks ending with that week and would have satisfied them for at least 22 weeks in that period but for the fact that either he or the severely disabled person for whom he has been caring was undergoing medical or other treatment as an inpatient in a hospital or similar institution.

AMENDMENT

1. Social Security (Invalid Care Allowance) Amendment (No.2) Regulations 1993 (SI 1993/1851) reg.2 (August 17, 1993).

MODIFICATIONS

With effect from March 30, 2020 the Social Security (Coronavirus) (Further Measures) Regulations 2020 (SI 2020/371) apply to reg.4(2) above. This modification will apply from March 30, 2020 (the date of commencement of these Regulations) until November 12, 2020 (a period of 8 months from March 13, provided for under reg.10 of these Regulations). This period was then extended, first by SI 2020/1201 and then by SI 2021/476. The latter extension and therefore the final expiry of this provision was on August 31, 2021.

The terms "coronavirus", "coronavirus disease", and "isolation" are defined in reg.1 of the Regulations. Regulation 9 of those regulations provides as follows:

(1) This regulation applies where a person in receipt of carer's allowance ("A") is temporarily unable to care for the severely disabled person ("B") in respect of whom the carer's allowance is paid by reason of isolation due to, or infection or contamination with, coronavirus disease of either A or B.

(2) Regulation 4(2) of the Social Security (Invalid Care Allowance) Regulations 1976 is to be read as if the words starting with "and" at the end of sub-paragraph (a) to the end of sub-paragraph (b) were omitted.

(3) In this regulation—

(a) "carer's allowance" means the allowance paid under section 70 of the Social Security Contributions and Benefits Act 1992; and

(b) "severely disabled person" has the meaning given in section 70(2) of that Act.

(4) This regulation extends only to England and Wales.

Note that this provision was effective for England and Wales only but similar provision was made for Scotland by Carer's Allowance (Coronavirus) (Breaks in Care) (Scotland) Regulations 2020 (SI 2020/117).

GENERAL NOTE

Paragraph (1)

A person is entitled to benefit in respect of "any day" on which he is caring, etc. for his patient (see s.70(1) SSCBA 1992). This regulation, however, has the effect of shifting the entitlement to the basis of a week by providing that every day in the week will qualify where the 35-hour test is satisfied, and that no day in the week will qualify where it is not (except under para.(2) below). This is much more administratively convenient. **4.131**

The decision in *R(G) 3/91* confirms that the hours must be counted in respect of each week and cannot be averaged over a period of weeks to satisfy the 35 hour rule.

Note that for Carer's Allowance a week is defined in s.122 as a period from Sunday to Saturday—this may affect a claimant who cares only on alternate week-ends.

A person qualifies for benefit where "he is, or is likely to be, engaged and regularly engaged" in caring for a patient for at least 35 hours per week. There are several difficulties in this phrase but none of them seem to have caused problems. It may be easy to determine that a person "is engaged . . . in caring," but it is not clear what is meant by "is likely to be . . . engaged". The words are probably intended to be prospective so that the benefit can be awarded for a forward period, but they might extend to cover an unexpected temporary absence by the claimant. If the absence is short and no more in total than four weeks in six months the matter would be covered by para.(2) below, but if those weeks have already been consumed or allocated to a "holiday" period, there may be an argument for saying that an unexpected absence due to, say, illness, continues to satisfy para.(1) as being a week in which the claimant had been "likely to be" caring.

Nor does the definition tell us anything about what is meant by "regularly engaged". It is probably sufficient if the care arrangement is intended to be for a reasonable period. It might preclude, for example, someone who is on unpaid holiday from his job, or a student in his vacation.

The activities of the claimant that can be regarded as caring and consequently can satisfy the 35-hour test of caring are considered in two unreported Commissioners' decisions: *CG/012/1991* and *CG/006/1990*. See the discussion of these decisions at s.70 of the Act.

Paragraph (1A)

4.132 This amendment reverses (from August 1993) the effect of an unreported Commissioners' decision that permitted a claimant to aggregate the hours spent in looking after more than one patient to satisfy the total of 35 hours per week. In that case the claimant was the mother of two severely disabled sons neither of whom could stay at home for a full week, but the claimant could look after each of them separately, for part of the week—in some weeks their combined time at home amounted to more than 35 hours per week. This paragraph now precludes such an arrangement. The only scheme now possible would involve each son staying at home for 35 hours (if that were possible) in alternate weeks. A system of care every other week, if consistent, should still be regarded as "regular".

Paragraph (2)

4.133 Note the modification made to this paragraph by the Social Security (Coronavirus) (Further Measures) Regulations 2020 noted under the heading MODIFICATIONS above.

A break in the provision of care is disregarded so long as the break is temporary and so long as it has lasted, or a series of breaks has totalled, no more than four weeks in the past 26 weeks (or 12 weeks in the past 26 if the patient or the claimant has spent at least eight of those weeks in hospital for treatment). In effect the claimant can enjoy a break or "holiday" from his caring of up to four weeks in every six months. Benefit will continue to be payable for the weeks of holiday, but if the claimant continues to receive the benefit himself, it cannot be paid as well to any person who provides substitute care during that period. (See s.70(7) of the Act.)

The decision in *Secretary of State for Work and Pensions v Pridding*, [2002] EWCA Civ 306, CA, reported as *R(G)1/02* limits the effect of this regulation. It does not extend entitlement where the person cared for, has entered hospital beyond the four week period for which that person will be entitled to their own benefits.

Circumstances in which persons are to be regarded as receiving full-time education

4.134 [1 **5.**—(1) For the purposes of [2 section 70(3) of the Contributions and Benefits Act] a person shall be treated as receiving full-time education for any period during which he attends a course of education at a university, college, school or other educational establishment for twenty-one hours or more a week.

(2) In calculating the hours of attendance under paragraph (1) of this regulation—

(a) there shall be included the time spent receiving instruction or tuition, undertaking supervised study, examination or practical work or taking part in any exercise, experiment or project for which provision is made in the curriculum of the course; and

(b) there shall be excluded any time occupied by meal breaks or spent on unsupervised study, whether undertaken on or off the premises of the educational establishment.

(3) In determining the duration of a period of full-time education under paragraph (1) of this regulation, a person who has started on a course of education shall be treated as attending it for the usual number of hours per week throughout any vacation or any temporary interruption of his attendance until the end of the course or such earlier date as he abandons it or is dismissed from it.]

AMENDMENTS

1. Social Security (Invalid Care Allowance) Amendment Regulations 1992 (SI 1992/470).

2. Social Security (Invalid Care Allowance) Amendment Regulations 1996 (SI 1996/2744) reg.2 (November 25, 1996).

GENERAL NOTE

The meaning of "full-time education" has been thoroughly explored by the Court of Appeal in *Secretary of State for Work and Pensions v Deane* [2010] EWCA Civ 699, (AAC), [2010] AACR 42. The court began by holding that the definition of full-time education in reg.5 is not an exhaustive one. This approach had been suggested by Judge Mesher, but was one not open to him, he felt, by reason of earlier precedents in the Court of Appeal. In this case however, the court held that they were not bound by those earlier decisions—that of *Wright-Turner* (CA of NI) [2002] CARC 3567, because the point appeared to have been conceded and in any case did not then form a part of the narrower basis of that decision, and that of *Flemming v Secretary of State for Work and Pensions* [2002] EWCA Civ 641, because, even if it had been accepted, it did not form a part of the decision. The court in the present case contrasted the wording of regs 4 and 8, in both of which the regulation expressly defines what is, and what is not, to be regarded as a part of that definition, with the wording of reg.5 which refers only to what is to be regarded as "full-time education". What this means is that the definition of full-time education by reference to attending a course for 21 or more hours per week is only a partial definition; there may be also be courses of a lesser period which are full-time education. This would have been enough to dispose of the case, because in the view of all the judges who have been involved in these cases, a normal three-year undergraduate degree course (which is what the claimant had been enrolled on) should be full-time education for the purposes of a claim to Carer's Allowance. However, they went on to hold, as well, that the proper approach to the assessment of hours of attendance was by reference to the expectation of the educational establishment rather than the actual hours worked by the student. **4.135**

This should resolve most difficulties in relation to university courses, though the court did accept that there may still be difficult cases in relation to colleges and in cases where exemptions from course requirements have been made.

The case of an atypical student who had been granted exemption from parts of the course was considered in *CG/3189/2004*. There the case was referred to a fresh tribunal for re-consideration of the information provided by the university (and perhaps provided again more exactly for that particular student).

4.136 The *Deane* case has already been applied in *SSWP v PW* [2011] UKUT 3 (AAC). There the claimant was a 17-year-old carer who was taking a course provided as a preparation for employment. She attended classes for 18 hours per week, which was confirmed by the course provider upon enquiry by the DWP, but the provider also asserted that the course was a full-time course. Judge Ward held that the First-tier Tribunal were perfectly entitled to find on the basis of the evidence before them that the course was a part-time course; the assertion of the provider was not conclusive (and *Deane*'s case did not suggest that it should be), but must be considered as a part of all the evidence before the tribunal. In this case the provider also asserted that the course included periods of placement in work. On the evidence it appeared unlikely that the placements were properly to be regarded as a part of the course, but even if they had been, they would not have increased the attendance hours beyond 21 taking the time spent on placements as spread across the whole period of the course. Nor should the course, taken as a whole, be regarded as full-time applying the reasoning in *Deane* that a course might be full-time under s.70 without reference to the partial definition in reg.5. This was a very different case from that of a normal undergraduate course at a university (as in *Deane*) where a tribunal might properly take judicial notice that a claimant was on a full-time course.

The same judge considered such a case in *SSWP v ZC* [2011] UKUT 2 (AAC); [2011] AACR 28. The claimant had completed studies for a BTEC qualification and then commenced a degree course in a related field. She argued that because of her prior courses and the grades that she had obtained in them, she could undertake the degree course by devoting fewer hours to study than the university said that it would require. The First-tier Tribunal had allowed her appeal against refusal of benefit by applying the test in reg.5. They accepted her evidence that she needed to study only 20 hours per week to pass the course. Judge Ward allowed an appeal. Applying what, by this time, had become the correct approach in *Deane,* he concluded that in this case the description given by the university of what they regarded as a full-time course must also lead to that conclusion under the words of s.70(3). The judgment is notable also for the examination of the way in which reg.5 should be applied although, in reaching his decision, the judge does so under s.70.

In *SM v SSWP (CA)* [2016] UKUT 406 (AAC) Judge Mitchell had to decide if a student who had entered upon a course of study, but then had a one year deferral of the course by agreement with the university that she was attending, should be regarded as undertaking a "temporary interruption" of the course within the meaning of para.(3) of this regulation. The year of deferral was taken in order to care for her disabled son. Before the UT the Department's representative accepted that the year of deferral was not within the meaning of the phrase "temporary interruption" as used here and the Judge agreed. In doing so he refers to an equivalent provision (though worded differently) in the rules relating to means tested benefits where the Court of Appeal had held that a student on an intercalated year would qualify for benefit. Treating this deferred year in a similar way was possible if the word "temporary" was given the colloquial meaning of relatively short, rather than the more literal meaning of not permanent. On that basis a break in the course of a whole year was not temporary.

Severely disabled persons prescribed for the purposes of [2 section 70(1)(c) of the Contributions and Benefits Act]

4.137 [1 **6.**—For the purposes of [2 section 70(1)(c) of the Contributions and Benefits Act] (condition of entitlement to [3 a carer's allowance] that the severely disabled person is either such relative of the person caring for him as may be prescribed or a person of any such other description as may be prescribed) where a severely disabled person is being cared for by another person, that disabled person shall be a prescribed person for the purposes of that section, whether he is related to the person caring for him or not.]

AMENDMENTS

1. Social Security (Invalid Care Allowance) Amendment Regulations 1981 (SI 1981/655).
2. Social Security (Invalid Care Allowance) Amendment Regulations 1996 (SI 1996/2744) reg.2 (November 25, 1996).
3. Social Security Amendment (Carer's Allowance) Regulations 2002 (SI 2002/2497) reg.3 (April 1, 2003).

[4 [5 Manner of electing the person entitled to a carer's allowance in respect of a severely disabled person for the purposes of section 70 of the Contributions and Benefits Act]

7.—(1) For the purposes of the provision in [2 [4 [5 section 70(7ZA)]] of the Contributions and Benefits Act] which provides that where, apart from that section, two or more persons would [3 have a relevant entitlement for the same day] in respect of the same severely disabled person one of them only [3 shall have that entitlement], being such one of them as they may jointly elect in the prescribed manner, an election shall be made by giving the Secretary of State a notice in writing signed by the persons who but for the said provision would [3 have a relevant entitlement] in respect of the same severely disabled person specifying one of them as the person [3 to have that entitlement]. 4.138

[4 (1A) For the purposes of section 70(7ZC) of the Contributions and Benefits Act which provides that where, apart from that section, one person (A) would have an entitlement mentioned in subsection (7ZB) and another person (B) would have an entitlement to carer's allowance for the same day in respect of the same severely disabled person, A and B may jointly elect in the prescribed manner which of them shall have such entitlement, an election shall be made by giving the Scottish Ministers a notice in writing signed by both A and B specifying that B shall have entitlement to carer's allowance and A shall not have an entitlement mentioned in subsection (7ZB).

(1B) For the purposes of section 70(7ZE) of the Contributions and Benefits Act which provides that where, apart from that section, one person (A) has, or would have an entitlement to universal credit carer element and another person (B) would have an entitlement to carer's allowance for the same day in respect of the same severely disabled person, A and B may jointly elect in the prescribed manner which of them shall have such entitlement, an election shall be made by giving the Scottish Ministers a notice in writing signed by both A and B specifying that B shall have an entitlement to carer's allowance and A shall not have entitlement to universal credit carer element.]

[5 (1C) For the purposes of section 70(7ZB) and (7ZC) of the Contributions and Benefits Act, which provides that where, apart from those subsections, one person (A) would have an entitlement mentioned in subsection (7ZB) and another person (B) would have a relevant entitlement for the same day in respect of the same severely disabled person, persons A and B may jointly elect in the prescribed manner that B shall have the relevant entitlement and that A shall not have an entitlement mentioned in subsection (7ZB), an election shall be made by giving the Secretary of State a notice in writing signed by both A and B specifying that B shall have the relevant entitlement and A shall not have an entitlement mentioned in subsection (7ZB).]

(2) An election under [4 [5 paragraph (1) or (1C)], (1A) or (1B)] of this regulation shall not be effective to confer [3 a relevant entitlement] either for the day on which the election is made or for any earlier day if such day is one for which [3 a carer's allowance [5, carer support payment] or the care element of universal credit] has been paid in respect of the severely disabled person in question and has not been repaid or recovered.

[3 (3) In paragraph (2) "the carer element of universal credit" means an amount included in an award of universal credit in respect of the fact that a person has regular and substantial caring responsibilities for a severely disabled person.]

[4 (4) In paragraph (2), "carer support payment" means a payment made under the Carer's Assistance (Carer Support Payment) (Scotland) Regulations 2023.]

[5 (5) In paragraph (2), "carer support payment" means carer's assistance given in accordance with the Carer's Assistance (Carer Support Payment) (Scotland) Regulations 2023.]

AMENDMENTS

1. Social Security Amendment (Carer's Allowance) Regulations 2002 (SI 2002/2497) reg.3 (April 1, 2003).

2. Social Security (Invalid Care Allowance) Amendment Regulations 1996 (SI 1996/2744), reg.2 (November 25, 1996).

3. Universal Credit and Miscellaneous Amendment Regulations (SI 2015/1754) reg.12 (November 5, 2015).

4. Carer's Assistance (Carer Support Payment) (Consequential and Miscellaneous Amendments and Transitional Provision) (Scotland) Regulations 2023 (SSI 2023/258) reg.2 (November 19, 2023).

5. Carer's Assistance (Care Support Payment) (Scotland) Regulations 2023 (Consequential Amendments) Order 2023 (SI 2023/1218) art.2 (November 19, 2023).

Circumstances in which a person is or is not to be treated as gainfully employed

4.139 **8.**—(1) For the purposes of [3 section 70(1)(b) of the Contributions and Benefits Act] (condition of a person being entitled to [2 a carer's allowance] for any day that he is not gainfully employed) a person shall not be treated as gainfully employed on any day in a week unless his earnings in the immediately preceding week have exceeded [4 [5 £151]] and, subject to paragraph (2) of this regulation, shall be treated as gainfully employed on every day in a week if his earnings in the immediately preceding week have exceeded [5 £151].

(2) There shall be disregarded for the purposes of paragraph (1) above a person's earnings—

(a) for any week which under paragraph (2) of regulation 4 of these regulations is treated as a week in which that person satisfies the requirements of paragraph (1) of that regulation;

(b) [3 . . .]

(c) [1 . . .]

(3) *Revoked.*

Amendments

1. Social Security (Invalid Care Allowance) Amendment Regulations 1996 (SI 1996/2744) reg.2 (November 25, 1996 with saving under reg.3).
2. Social Security Amendment (Carer's Allowance) Regulations 2002 (SI 2002/2497) reg.3 (April 1, 2003).
3. Social Security (Invalid Care Allowance) Amendment Regulations 1995 (SI 1995/2935) reg.2 (December 12, 1995 with saving under reg.3).
4. Social Security (Invalid Care Allowance) (Amendment) Regulations 2018 (SI 2018/280) reg.2 (April 9, 2018).
5. Social Security Benefits Up-Rating Regulations 2024 (SI 2024/386) reg.4 (April 8, 2024). This regulation extends only to England and Wales. For Scotland the same amendment effective from April 1, 2024 is made by Social Security (Up-rating) (Miscellaneous Amendments) (Scotland) Regulations 2024 (SSI 2024/105).

General Note

Paragraph (1)

Earnings include remuneration or profit from either employment or self-employment. See s.3 of the Act and definition of "employment" in s.122. **4.140**

For the method of calculating earnings see Computation of Earnings Regulations.

In *CG/734/2003*, and again in *CG/4018/2005* it has been confirmed that those regulations do properly apply to the calculation of earnings for the purpose of the benefit, despite the doubts that had been expressed earlier in *CG/6329/1997*, on which see the 2005 edition of this work. Note too, that where a person's earnings fluctuate more than once, or where a person regularly has periods in which they do not work, earnings may be averaged by the application of reg.8(3) of the Computation of Earnings Regulations (see Part III of this book) and for an example of the operation of that regulation see the decision of Judge Wright in *KR v SSWP* (CA) [2023] UKUT 202 (AAC).

Note the observations of the Commissioner in *CG/607/2008*. Whereas most social security benefits (and most taxes) provide for a taper in respect of earnings that exceed an earnings limit, there is no such thing for Carer's Allowance; earnings that are a penny over the limit result in the total loss of benefit. In this case the claimant had taken part-time work for a charity working with the disabled. She was employed for 10 hours per week at an hourly rate calculated so that her earnings would exactly match the earnings limit currently in force. Such a carefully constructed and informed work plan should not have resulted in difficulties, but a complication arose from the fact that although the wages had been expressed to be a weekly sum, for the convenience of the employer, they were, in fact, paid monthly. Because the regulations define benefit weeks for Carer's Allowance as being each week beginning on a Monday, and because some calendar months contain five Mondays rather than four, this meant that in those months her earnings, if spread over a calendar month, exceeded the weekly earnings limit. As this was discovered only after five years it meant that the claimant was faced with a substantial claim for overpayment. The complexity of the Computation of Earnings Regulations resulted in four different decisions, and four different overpayment claims, by the DM, together with a different calculation by the appeal tribunal (which had allowed her appeal) and yet another by her representative before the commissioner. The Commissioner came to the rescue of all of them. He suggested going back to basics. This meant examining the definitions of the concepts that are used in the regulations. From this it emerged that earnings should be the sums payable under the claimant's contract of employment. Although the contract was oral, it was clear both from the parties' intentions, and from their consistent pattern of behaviour over almost all of the five years, that her wages were to be earned weekly even though they may have been paid monthly. This meant that the correct attribution of earnings was on a weekly basis, not monthly. There were a few weeks early in the arrangement when the claimant had worked extra **4.141** hours and therefore had exceeded the earnings limit, but for the most part she had remained within that limit and, therefore, her overpayment was minimal.

Another example of the all-or-nothing character of Carer's Allowance is *SJ v SSWP* (CA) [2009] UKUT 23 (AAC); *R(G) 1/09* where Judge Bano had to consider the effect of PAYE income tax liability on the claimant's earnings. The claimant was not liable to pay tax on her earnings, which were just above the earnings limit for the allowance, but, had she been in receipt of the allowance, she would then have been liable for income tax and that liability, if collected through PAYE, would have reduced her earnings to below the earnings limit, and she would then have been entitled to the allowance. This looks like a classic "Catch 22". But the refusal of benefit was correct. It is clear that Carer's Allowance is a taxable benefit (see Table A of the Income Tax (Earnings and Pensions) Act 1992) and it is also clear that the tax could, and normally would, be collected through the PAYE system, but to qualify for benefit, in the first place, the claimant must have earnings below the earnings limit, and that must be determined before the benefit is paid, not afterwards.

Paragraph (2)

4.142 This exempts from the earnings limit any week in which the claimant is on "holiday" from his patient. Para.(b) which exempted an employee absent from work with the consent of his employer was revoked with effect from December 12, 1995. Para.(c) which exempted earnings from the week preceding the first week of claim was revoked with effect from November 25, 1996. In bothcases there is a saving provision in respect of continuous claims commencing before those dates.

Conditions relating to residence and presence in Great Britain

4.143 **9.**—(1) Subject to the following provisions of this regulation[[9] and regulations [[10] 9A, 9B and 9C]], the prescribed conditions for the purposes of [[1] section 70(4) of the Contributions and Benefits Act] (person not to be entitled to [[2] a carer's allowance] unless he satisfies prescribed conditions as to residence or presence in Great Britain) in relation to any person in respect of any day shall be—

(a) that he is [[9] habitually] resident in [[9] the United Kingdom, the Republic of Ireland, the Isle of Man or the Channel Islands]; and

[[3] (ia) he is not a person subject to immigration control within the meaning of section 115(9) of the Immigration and Asylum Act 1999 or section 115 of that Act does not apply to him for the purposes of entitlement to [[2] a carer's allowance] by virtue of regulation 2 of the Social Security (Immigration and Asylum) Consequential Amendments Regulations 2000, and]

(b) that he is present in Great Britain; and

(c) that he has been present in Great Britain for a period of, or periods amounting in the aggregate to, not less than [[9] 104] weeks in the [[9] 156 weeks] immediately preceding that day.

[[4] (1A) [[3] *omitted*]]

(2) For the purposes of paragraph (1)(b) and (c) of this regulation, a person who is absent from Great Britain on any day shall be treated as being present in Great Britain—

(a) if his absence is, and when it began was, for a temporary purpose and has not lasted for a continuous period exceeding 4 weeks; or

[[9] (b) if his absence is temporary and for the specific purpose of caring for the severely disabled person who is also absent from Great Britain and where any of the following is payable in respect of that disabled person for that day—

(i) attendance allowance;
(ii) the care component of disability living allowance at the highest or middle rate prescribed in accordance with section 72(3) of the Contributions and Benefits Act;
(iii) the daily living component of personal independence payment at the standard or enhanced rate prescribed in accordance with section 78(3) of the Welfare Reform Act 2012; [11 ...
(iiia) armed forces independence payment under the Armed Forces and Reserve Forces (Compensation Scheme) Order 2011;]
(iv) a payment specified in regulation 3(1) of these Regulations;]
[12 (v) the care component of child disability payment at the middle or highest rate in accordance with regulation 11 of the Disability Assistance for Children and Young People (Scotland) Regulations 2021, or
(vi) the daily living component of adult disability payment at the standard or enhanced rate in accordance with regulation 5 of the Disability Assistance for Working Age People (Scotland) Regulations 2022.]

[9 (3) Notwithstanding that on any day a person is absent from Great Britain, he shall be treated as though he were—

(a) habitually resident and present in Great Britain for the purposes of paragraphs (1)(a) to (c) if—
(i) his absence is by reason only of the fact that on that day he is abroad in his capacity as a serving member of the forces and for this purpose "serving member of the forces" has the meaning given in regulation 1(2) of the Social Security (Contributions) Regulations 2001 ("the 2001 Regulations"); or
(ii) he is living with a person mentioned in sub-paragraph (a)(i) and is the spouse, civil partner, son, daughter, step-son, step-daughter, father, father-in-law, step-father, mother, mother-in-law or step-mother of that person; and

(b) present in Great Britain for the purposes of paragraph (1)(b) and (c) if his absence is by reason only of the fact that on that day he is—
(i) abroad in his capacity as an airman within the meaning of regulation 111 of the 2001 Regulations or a mariner within the meaning of regulation 115 of those Regulations; or
(ii) in prescribed employment in connection with continental shelf operations within the meaning of regulation 114(1) of those Regulations.]

AMENDMENTS

1. Social Security (Invalid Care Allowance) Amendment Regulations 1996 (SI 1996/2744) reg.2 (November 25, 1996).

2. Social Security Amendment (Carer's Allowance) Regulations 2002 (SI 2002/2497) reg.4 (April 1, 2003).

3. Social Security (Miscellaneous Amendments) Regulations 1998 (SI 1998/563) reg.18(1) (April 6, 1998).

4. Social Security (Persons From Abroad) Miscellaneous Amendments Regulations 1996 (SI 1996/30) reg.9 (February 5, 1996, subject to a saving under reg.12(3)).

5. Disability Living Allowance and Disability Working Allowance Regulations 1991 (SI 1991/2742) reg.3 (April 6, 1992).

6. Social Security (Child Benefit Consequential) Regulations 1977 (SI 1977/342) reg.18 (April 4, 1977).

7. Civil Partnership (Pensions, Social Security and Child Support) (Consequential, etc. Provisions) Order 2005 (SI 2005/2877) (December 5, 2005).

8. Personal Independence Payment (Supplementary and Consequential Amendments) Regulations 2013 (SI 2013/388) Sch.1 para.9 (April 8, 2013).

9. Social Security (Attendance Allowance, Disability Living Allowance and Carer's Allowance) (Amendment) Regulations 2013 (SI 2013/389) reg.2 (April 8, 2013).

10. Social Security (Miscellaneous Amendment No.4) Regulations 2017 (SI 2017/1015) reg.2(3) (November 16, 2017).

11. Armed Forces and Reserve Forces Compensation Scheme (Consequential Provisions: Subordinate Legislation) Order 2013 (SI 2013/591) art.2(2) and Sch. (April 8, 2013).

12. Disability Assistance (Miscellaneous Amendment) (Scotland) Regulations 2023 (SSI 2023/346) reg.2 (November 20, 2023).

General Note

4.144 Until April 8, 2013 a claimant need only have shown that they were "ordinarily resident" and there is a saving for existing claims made on that basis. Neither "ordinary" nor "habitual" residence is defined in the statute or regulations. Ordinary residence has usually been taken to mean that you have a settled intention to live in the country (technically now the "common travel area") as your home, but, not necessarily, permanently. Habitual residence, which is intended to be a more stringent test, requires as well that that the claimant has been in the country already for an extended period. How long, will depend upon the circumstances of the claimant; a former resident returning from a period abroad may satisfy this test almost immediately, while a new immigrant may be required to demonstrate a considerable period of residence. The meaning of "habitual residence" has been the subject of extensive case law in relation to claims for means-tested benefits where it has applied for some time. Readers are referred to the notes to relevant sections of Vol. II of this Work.

In *MM and SI v SSWP (DLA)* [2016] UKUT 149 (AAC) Judge Markus QC has held that reg.2(1)(a)(iii) of the DLA regulations, the equivalent of reg.9(1)(c) of these regulations (the past presence test or PPT) must be disapplied in respect of claims made on behalf of applicants who were family members of persons granted refugee status in the UK. She held that the PPT was indirectly discriminatory and could not be justified (when compared to the treatment of UK nationals) under art.28 of the EU Directive 2004/8 3/EC (which gives protection to refugees) and which she held had direct effect in the UK. For the same reason she held that PPT was in breach of the claimant's rights under art.14 of the ECHR. At the time the claims were made the applicants satisfied the other conditions of reg.2 which meant that their claims should proceed accordingly. That was a decision in respect of a claim to DLA but the ruling will apply equally to a claim for carer's allowance.

For questions that involve persons either coming from or going to country that is a part of the European Union (or to Switzerland) reference should be made to the relevant sections of Vol.III of this Work.

Paragraph (2)

4.145 A person is regarded as being still present in Great Britain for up to four weeks of temporary absence, or for longer periods if he is abroad caring for his patient who continues to receive the attendance benefit. The four-week period ties in with the period for a break in caring under reg.4 above.

Paragraph (3)

4.146 A person is also regarded as present in Great Britain if his absence is for one of the specified reasons, though if the absence is for more than four weeks it would be necessary for the claimant to continue caring for his patient. Note that service personnel, as defined in para.(3)(a)(i) and their families, as listed in para.(3)(a)(ii) are regarded as both habitually resident and present in Great Britain whilst they are serving abroad.

[1Persons residing in Great Britain to whom a relevant EU Regulation applies

9A.—(1) Regulation 9(1)(c) shall not apply where on any day— 4.147

(a) the person is habitually resident in Great Britain;

(b) a relevant EU Regulation applies; and

(c) the person can demonstrate a genuine and sufficient link to the United Kingdom social security system.

(2) For the purposes of paragraph (1)(b) and regulation 9B, "relevant EU Regulation" has the meaning given by section 84(2) of the Welfare Reform Act 2012.]

AMENDMENT

1. Social Security (Attendance Allowance, Disability Living Allowance and Carer's Allowance) (Amendment) Regulations 2013 (SI 2013/389) reg.2 (April 8, 2013).

GENERAL NOTE

The relevant regulations referred to are (EC) No.1408/71 and (EC) No.883/2004. For detailed discussion see Vol.III of this Work. 4.148

[1Persons residing in an EEA state [2...] or in Switzerland to whom a relevant EU Regulation applies

9B.—Regulation 9(1)(a) to (c) shall not apply where on any day— 4.149

(a) the person is habitually resident in—

(i) an EEA state [2...]; or

(ii) Switzerland;

(b) a relevant EU Regulation applies; and

(c) the person can demonstrate a genuine and sufficient link to the UK social security system]

AMENDMENTS

1. Social Security (Attendance Allowance, Disability Living Allowance and Carer's Allowance) (Amendment) Regulations 2013 (SI 2013/389) reg.2 (April 8, 2013).

2. Social Security (Amendment) (EU Exit) Regulations 2019 (SI 2019/128) Sch.1 para.2(2) (December 31, 2020).

GENERAL NOTE

The relevant regulations referred to are (EC) No.1408/71 and (EC) No.883/2004. 4.150

For detailed discussion see Vol.III of this Work. The aggregation of periods of residence in another EU country has been considered by Judge Jacobs in *BK v SSWP and SSWP v MM* [2016] UKUT 547 (AAC). Relying on the case of *Stewart v SSWP* (C-503/09) the Judge held that mere residence in this country was not sufficient to aggregate that time with time spent in another EU country, but neither was it necessary to show a link with this country's social security system. This decision may be subject to appeal. For further detail see Vol.III of this work.

[1[2 Refugees and certain persons with leave to enter or remain in the United Kingdom]

4.151 **9C.**—(1) Regulation 9(1)(c) shall not apply where the person has—

(a) been granted refugee status or humanitarian protection under the immigration rules; [2...]

(b) leave to enter or to remain in the United Kingdom as the dependant of a person granted refugee status or humanitarian protection under the immigration rules;

[2(c) leave to enter or remain in the United Kingdom granted under the immigration rules by virtue of—

(i) the Afghan Relocations and Assistance Policy; or

(ii) the previous scheme for locally-employed staff in Afghanistan (sometimes referred to as the ex-gratia scheme);

(d) been granted discretionary leave outside the immigration rules as a dependant of a person referred to in sub-paragraph (c);

(e) leave granted under the Afghan Citizens Resettlement Scheme] [3 [4 [5...]]]

(f) leave to enter or remain in the United Kingdom granted under or outside the immigration rules [4, a right] of abode in the United Kingdom within the meaning given in section 2 of the Immigration Act 1971 [4 or does not require leave to enter or remain in the United Kingdom in accordance with section 3ZA of that Act,] where the person—

(i) was residing in Ukraine immediately before 1st January 2022; and

(ii) left Ukraine in connection with the Russian invasion which took place on 24th February 2022;]

[5 or

(g) leave to enter or remain in the United Kingdom granted under or outside the immigration rules, a right of abode in the United Kingdom within the meaning given in section 2 of the Immigration Act 1971 or does not require leave to enter or remain in the United Kingdom in accordance with section 3ZA of that Act, where the person—

(i) was residing in Sudan before 15th April 2023; and

(ii) left Sudan in connection with the violence which rapidly escalated on 15th April 2023 in Khartoum and across Sudan;] [6, or

(h) leave to enter or remain in the United Kingdom granted under or outside the immigration rules, a right of abode in the United Kingdom within the meaning given in section 2 of the Immigration Act 1971 or does not require leave to enter or remain in the United Kingdom in accordance with section 3ZA of that Act, where the person—

(i) was residing in Israel, the West Bank, the Gaza Strip, East Jerusalem, the Golan Heights or Lebanon immediately before 7th October 2023; and

(ii) left Israel, the West Bank, the Gaza Strip, East Jerusalem, the Golan Heights or Lebanon in connection with the Hamas terrorist attack in Israel on 7th October 2023 or the violence which rapidly escalated in the region following the attack.]

[2(1A) Regulation 9(1)(a) shall not apply where [3 any sub-paragraph in paragraph (1)] applies to the person.]

(2) For the purposes of this regulation "immigration rules" means the rules laid before Parliament under section 3(2) of the Immigration Act 1971.]

AMENDMENTS

1. Social Security (Miscellaneous Amendments No.4) Regulations 2017 (SI 2017/1015) reg.2(3) (November 16, 2017).

2. Social Security (Habitual Residence and Past Presence) (Amendment) Regulations 2021 (SI 2021/1034) reg.4 (September 15, 2021). The amendments made by these regulations apply in respect of England and Wales only. The same amendments are made with effect from the same date in respect of Scotland only by reg.2 of the Social Security (Residence Requirements) (Afghanistan) (Scotland) Regulations 2021 (SI 2021/320) but in addition that regulation also substitutes for paragraph (2) of reg.2C the following—

"(2) For the purposes of this regulation—

(a) "immigration rules" means the rules laid before Parliament under section 3(2) of the Immigration Act 1971,

(b) "the Afghan Citizens Resettlement Scheme" means the scheme announced by the United Kingdom Government on 18 August 2021."

3. Social Security (Habitual Residence and Past Presence) (Amendment) Regulations 2022 (SI 2022/344) reg.4 (March 22,2022). Note: this regulation applies only to England and Wales. Identical provision is made for Scotland, with effect from the same date, by the Social Security (Residence Requirements) (Ukraine) (Scotland) Regulations 2022 (SSI 2022/108).

4. Social Security (Habitual Residence and Past Presence) (Amendment) (No.2) Regulations 2022 (SI 2022/990) reg.3, (October18, 2022). Note: this regulation applies only to England and Wales. Identical provision is made for Scotland by the Social Security (Miscellaneous Amendment and Transitional Provision) (Scotland) Regulations 2022 (SI 2022/336) reg.6 (November 28, 2022).

5. Social Security (Habitual Residence and Past Presence) (Amendment) Regulations 2023 (SI 2023/532) reg.4 (May 15, 2023). Note: this regulation applies only to England and Wales. Identical provision is made for Scotland with effect from May 17, 2023, by reg.2 of the Social Security (Residence Requirements) (Sudan) (Scotland) Regulations 2023 (SSI 2023/149).

6. Social Security (Habitual Residence and Past Presence, and Capital Disregards) (Amendment) Regulations 2023 (SI 2023/1144) reg.10 (October 27, 2023). Note: This amendment applies only to England and Wales. Identical provision is made for Scotland with effect from October 26, 2023, by the Social Security (Residence and Presence Requirements) (Israel, West Bank, the Gaza Strip, East Jerusalem, the Golan Heights and Lebanon) (Scotland) Regulations 2023 (SSI 2023/309).

Circumstances in which a person over [1 the age of 65] is to be treated as having been entitled to invalid care allowance immediately before attaining that age

10.—[1 *Revoked.*] 4.152

AMENDMENT

1. Social Security Amendment (Carer's Allowance) Regulations 2002 (SI 2002/2497) reg.3 (October 28, 2002).

[1Women aged 65 before 28th October 1994

10A.—A woman shall be entitled to [2 a carer's allowance] if— 4.153

(a) she attained the age of 65 before 28th October 1994;

(b) immediately before attaining the age of 65 she would have satisfied the requirements for entitlement to [2 a carer's allowance], whether or not she made a claim, but for the condition, which applied prior to 28th October 1994, in section 70(5) of the Contributions and Benefits Act (exclusion of persons who had attained pensionable age and had not been entitled to that allowance immediately before attaining that age); and

(c) she satisfies the requirements for entitlement to [2 a carer's allowance] apart from the conditions in section 70(1)(a) and (b) [3 . . .] of the Contributions and Benefits Act.]

AMENDMENTS

1. Social Security (Severe Disablement Allowance and Invalid Care Allowance) Amendment Regulations 1994 (SI 1994/2556) reg.5 (October 28, 1994).

2. Social Security Amendment (Carer's Allowance) Regulations 2002 (SI 2002/2497) reg.3 (April 1, 2003).

3. Social Security Amendment (Carer's Allowance) Regulations 2002 (SI 2002/2497) reg.3 (October 28, 2002).

Invalid care allowance for persons over [1the age of 65]

4.154 **11.**—[*Revoked.*]

AMENDMENT

1. Social Security Amendment (Carer's Allowance) Regulations 2002 (SI 2002/2497) reg.3 (October 28, 2002).

[1Men aged 65 before 28th October 1994

4.155 **11A.**—A man who—

(a) attained the age of 65 before 28th October 1994; and

(b) was entitled to [2 a carer's allowance] immediately before he attained that age,

shall be entitled to that allowance notwithstanding that, after he attained that age, he was not caring for a severely disabled person or no longer satisfied the requirements of section 70(1)(a) or (b) of the Contributions and Benefits Act, if he satisfies the other requirements for entitlement to that allowance.]

AMENDMENTS

1. Social Security (Severe Disablement Allowance and Invalid Care Allowance) Amendment Regulations 1994 (SI 1994/2556), reg.5 (October 28, 1994).

2. Social Security Amendment (Carer's Allowance) Regulations 2002 (SI 2002/2497) reg.3 (April 1, 2003).

4.156 *Regulations 12 and 13 revoked.*

Application of the Social Security (General Benefit) Regulations 1982 to [1 carer's allowance]

4.157 **14.**—The provisions of the Social Security (General Benefit) Regulations 1982, specified in column (1) of Schedule 1 to these regulations, the subject matter of which is described in column (2) of that Sch., shall, with any necessary modifications, apply to [1 carer's allowance] as they apply to incapacity benefit.

AMENDMENT

1. Social Security Amendment (Carer's Allowance) Regulations 2002 (SI 2002/2497) reg.3 (April 1, 2003).

4.158 *Regulations 15–20 omitted.*

4.159 *Regulation 21 revoked.*

(SI 1976/409 Sch. 1) (as amended)

SCHEDULE 1 **Regulation 14**

PROVISIONS OF THE SOCIAL SECURITY (GENERAL BENEFIT) REGULATIONS 1982 APPLIED TO [1 CARER'S ALLOWANCE]

4.160

Regulation applied (1)	Subject matter (2)
2	Exceptions from disqualification for imprisonment, etc.
3	Suspension of payment of benefit during imprisonment, etc.
4	Interim payments by way of benefit under the Act
9	Payment of benefit and suspension of payments pending a decision on appeals or references, arrears and repayments.

AMENDMENT

1. Social Security Amendment (Carer's Allowance) Regulations 2002 (SI 2002/2497) reg.3 (April 1, 2003).

The Social Security (Severe Disablement Allowance) Regulations 1984

(SI 1984/1303) *(as amended)*

For text of, and commentary on, these Regulations, see the 2005 edition of this volume. **4.161**

The Social Security (Personal Independence Payment) Regulations 2013

(SI 2013/377) (*as amended*)

PART 1

GENERAL

PART 2

PERSONAL INDEPENDENCE PAYMENT ASSESSMENT

PART 3

REQUIRED PERIOD CONDITION

PART 4

Residence and presence conditions

PART 5

RATE OF PERSONAL INDEPENDENCE PAYMENT

PART 6

PROVISIONS RELATING TO AGE

PART 7

PAYABILITY WHEN PERSON IS RESIDING IN CERTAIN ACCOMMODATION OR IS DETAINED IN CUSTODY

The Secretary of State for Work and Pensions, in exercise of the powers conferred by sections 77(3), 78(3) and (4), 79(3) and (4), 80(1), (2), (3), (4) and (5)(a) and (c), 81(1), (3)(b) and (4), 83(3), 85(1), (5) and (6), 86(1) and (3), 87, 92(1) and 94(1), (2), (3)(a) and (4) of the Welfare Reform Act 2012, makes the following Regulations.

A draft of this instrument has been laid before, and approved by a resolution of, each House of Parliament pursuant to section 94(6) of that Act.

These Regulations are made under the provisions of that Act and are made before the end of a period of six months beginning with the coming into force of those provisions.

PART 1

GENERAL

Citation and commencement

1.—(1) These Regulations may be cited as the Social Security (Personal Independence Payment) Regulations 2013. 4.170

(2) These Regulations come into force in relation to a particular case on the day on which Part 4 of the Act comes into force in relation to that case.

Interpretation

2. In these Regulations— 4.171

"the 1998 Act" means the Social Security Act 1998

"the Act" means the Welfare Reform Act 2012;

[1 "adult disability payment" has the meaning given in regulation 2 of the Disability Assistance for Working Age People (Scotland) Regulations 2022]

"aid or appliance"—

(a) means any device which improves, provides or replaces C's impaired physical or mental function; and

(b) includes a prosthesis;

"assessment" means the assessment referred to in regulation 4;

"C" means a person who has made a claim for or, as the case may be, is entitled to personal independence payment;

[1 "child disability payment" has the meaning given in regulation 2 of the Disability Assistance for Children and Young People (Scotland) Regulations 2021]

"component" means the daily living component or, as the case may be, the mobility component of personal independence payment;

"descriptor" means a descriptor in column 2 of the tables in Parts 2 and 3 of Schedule 1;

"disability living allowance" means disability living allowance under section 71 of the Social Security Contributions and Benefits Act 1992;

"medical treatment" means medical, surgical or rehabilitative treatment (including any course or diet or other regimen), and references to a person receiving or submitting to medical treatment are to be construed accordingly;

"prescribed date" means the date prescribed by regulation [114, 15 or 15A];

"previous award" means an award of either or both components to which C has ceased to be entitled;

"revised" means revised under section 9 of the 1998 Act, and "revision" is to be construed accordingly;

"superseded" means superseded under section 10 of the 1998 Act, and "supersession" is to be construed accordingly; and

terms defined for the purposes of a provision of Part 4 of the Act have the same meaning in these Regulations.

AMENDMENT

1. Social Security (Disability Assistance for Working Age People) (Consequential Amendments) Order 2022 (SI 2022/177) art.14 (March 21, 2022).

GENERAL NOTE

4.172 "Aids and appliances" are defined as any device that "improves, provides or replaces the claimant's impaired function". A fundamental point about this definition has been demonstrated by the decision of Judge Brunner in *DA v SSWP (PIP)* [2019] UKUT 320 (AAC). The claimant suffered, amongst other things, from chronic bladder infections. As a means of reducing that condition she adopted the use of sterilised water that she carried in a bottle and sterile wipes to clean herself after both urinating and defecating. The question was whether these items could be an "aid or appliance" that she used in carrying out Activity 5 – Managing toilet needs or incontinence. Both items could be a "device" but was that an item that was used to improve an impaired function that related to her ability to manage her toilet needs? Both the FTT and Judge Brunner in the UT, held that it was not. Toilet needs include the business of "cleaning oneself afterwards" but that was not a function for which the claimant's ability was impaired either physically or mentally – she could clean herself without any difficulty. For a claimant to succeed in relation to this part of the Activity, they would need to show that they lacked the strength or dexterity to accomplish the task and so used some device that enhanced their ability to do so. The function that was impaired could only be the claimant's ability to resist infection, in which case if anything, the use of the water bottle and wipes might be regarded as a form of therapy (Activity 3) that was adopted to manage her medical condition, but the actions required by this claimant do not fit any of the Descriptors in that Activity either. Note that the reasoning used by Judge Brunner adopts the same requirements explained by Judge Jacobs in *CW v SSWP (PIP)* [2016] UKUT 197 (AAC); [2016] AACR 44 discussed below and now accepted in several other cases.

The definition goes on to add "including a prosthesis". In *MR v SSWP (PIP)* [2017] UKUT 86 (AAC) Judge Gray has considered how this definition might relate to devices that have been implanted in the claimant's body. The claimant had a retinal implant in one eye. The question was whether this should be regarded as an aid or appliance for the purpose of his PIP assessment. In the event the judge found it unnecessary to decide that question, but offers some advice nevertheless. She accepts that this, and any other implanted device, would seem to fulfil the literal interpretation of the definition in regulation 2. But to do that would mean, as the argument put forward on behalf of the DWP showed, that someone with a pace-maker or an artificial heart valve would score points on every daily living Activity and qualify for benefit because, in doing any Activity he would do so using an aid or appliance, yet would have no apparent functional disability at all. Judge Gray thought that this absurdity would justify her in examining the legislative preparatory material in accordance with the rule in *Pepper v Hart.* Doing so revealed that the legislative intent had been to benefit those with the greatest functional disablement and that meant that an implant that effected what was almost total (or in the case of eyesight, sufficient) and permanent restoration of the claimant's function should not be regarded as an aid, etc. This did leave the question of whether an implanted device should be regarded as a prosthesis. Again, a literal interpretation might well include any such device. The judge thought that the reference to prosthesis should be confined to replacement limbs and had been included in an excess of caution to ensure that amputees were covered. The result seems to be that permanently implanted devices such as artificial joints, heart valves, stents and retinas will not be an aid or appliance, though detachable ones may be. Hearing aids are accepted as aids (spectacles are specifically excluded) though Judge Gray leaves open the matter of cochlear implants. What then of removable false teeth? Perhaps they should be regarded as being of no evidence of disability in accordance with the approach applied in the *CW* case discussed below.

The use of a dosette box as being an aid in managing medication has been accepted in *AK v SSWP (CSPIP)* [2016] UKUT 256 (AAC) and a commode has been accepted in *KW v SSWP (PIP)* [2017] UKUT 54 (AAC), where its use was made necessary because the claimant had difficulty climbing the stairs to the lavatory. In *YW v SSWP (PIP)* [2017] UKUT 42 (AAC) Judge Wikeley suggests, though not as part of the decision, that light weight pans are not an aid or appliance when used by the claimant in the kitchen. This is despite the fact that they are given as an example of an aid etc in the *PIP Assessment Guide*. The judge justified his view first, by reference to the status of the *Guide* as advice within the DWP and not determinative of the law and, secondly, by reference to the test suggested by Judge Jacobs in the case of *CW* discussed below – in effect, if light weight pans are in such common everyday use by non-disabled people then they are not indicative of any disability.

In *KR v SSWP* [2015] UKUT 547 (AAC) Judge Rowley considered the meaning of "aid or appliance" in relation to the mobility component. The FTT had found that the claimant could move a distance of at least 50 metres and they upheld a decision to award the claimant four points for the mobility component under Descriptor 2b. Before the UT, the claimant's representative contended that in order to achieve that distance the claimant would require to take a puff on an inhaler and argued that this qualified him under Descriptor 2c: "can … move unaided … no more than 50 metres". The question, therefore, (that had not been before the FTT) was whether the inhaler should be regarded as an aid or appliance. Superficially, it certainly appears to satisfy that definition as a "device which improves … [a claimant's] physical … function", but Judge Rowley rejects that conclusion. A distinction must be made, she says, between an aid that assists the claimant's function and a device that delivers medication that assists that function. So, as was conceded by the claimant's representative, the teaspoon that delivers a liquid analgesic could not be regarded as a device that aided the claimant's function and neither, in this case, could the inhaler. This is consistent with the advice given to the HCP in the *PIP Assessment Guide* where it is suggested (in relation to Activity 3 of the daily living component) that "needles, glucose meters and inhalers are not aids" whereas "pill boxes, dosette boxes, blister packs, and alarms" that help to manage medication apparently are. No explanation is given for this distinction, though elsewhere an inhaler is described as being "medication" while a nebuliser is "therapy". The need for an aid or appliance to relate to the activity in question has been affirmed in *RB v SSWP (PIP)* [2016] UKUT 556 (AAC). Judge Jacobs refers to his earlier decision in *CW v SSWP* (discussed below) in which he had said

> "*Aid or appliance* is defined by reference to whether it improves, provides or replaces the claimant's impaired *function*, which for convenience I describe as assisting in overcoming the consequences of a function being impaired. Putting all that together, an aid must help to overcome consequences of a function being impaired that is involved in carrying out an activity and is limited by the claimant's condition. To satisfy an aid or appliance descriptor, the claimant must need an aid to assist in respect of a function involved in the activity that is impaired."

In the present case, the question was whether a nebuliser (which the claimant could manage himself) might be regarded as an aid in relation to Activity 3 (b) (i)– to be able to manage medication. As in the previous case, the nebuliser was the means of delivering the medication; it was an aid to his breathing, but that was not the activity in question. It was agreed that someone who uses an inhaler to ease his breathing was not using an aid (see *KR v SSWP (PIP)* [2015] UKUT 547 (AAC)), but the judge leaves open the question whether, in an appropriate case, the nebuliser might be an aid because it delivered medication in the form of a fine mist that would assist a claimant when the inhaler would not. That might mean the claimant needed help in "managing" his medication, but on the facts of this case that question did not arise. While it is possible to see that this might apply to an *extra* device that is used by someone who lacks the dexterity to manage his own medication, e.g. when using a syringe, it is less easy to see why the means of delivering the medication should become a device just because the form in which the medication is delivered is different.

Several other decisions noted in connection with both the daily living Activities and mobility Activities (see below) have accepted various devices as aids or appliances, some of which might be used by a non-disabled person. These have included a chair to assist in dressing, a stool when cooking and a lever arm tap in the kitchen. It has been pointed out that the criterion is not whether other people might equally choose to use that device, but whether a disabled claimant finds it necessary to do so and whether then, it improves his physical function.

But doubt has been thrown on this principle in a series of cases that have addressed the question of the circumstances in which ordinary items of household furniture and equipment might be regarded as an aid or appliance when used in a particular way to assist a claimant achieve a task that might otherwise be beyond them. In the first, *NA v SSWP (PIP)* [2015] UKUT 572 (AAC), Judge Mark had suggested that it mattered not that the item in question might equally be used by an able person; he thought the question was whether the claimant was unable to accomplish the task without that item. However, a more restrictive approach has emerged. In *CW v SSWP (PIP)* [2016] UKUT 197 (AAC); [2016] AACR 44 Judge Jacobs held that the claimant's use of her bed to sit on, whilst she put her jeans on and when she took them off, was not the use of an aid in connection with the activity of dressing and undressing. As he puts it:

> "The question is this: would this 'aid' usually or normally be used by someone without any limitation in carrying out this particular aspect of the activity? If it would, the 'aid' is not assisting to overcome the consequences of an impaired function that is involved in the activity and its descriptors."

In effect the judge is saying that because sitting on a bed (or chair) is a practice so commonly adopted by non-disabled people the need to do so, even if required all the time, does not indicate a disability; i.e. the claimant is not disabled in relation to that element of dressing and undressing. This reasoning is approved by Judge Markus QC in *AP v SSWP (PIP)* [2016] UKUT 501 (AAC). This was another case involving the use of a bed to assist in dressing by sitting while putting garments on the lower body. As was pointed out in this case, the reasoning in *CW v SSWP* calls in question whether the use of a number of other household items might similarly now be in doubt. The representative of the Secretary of State indicated that use of lever arm taps that had been accepted as an aid in *GB v SSWP (PIP)* [2015] UKUT 546 (and was suggested in the original version of the *PIP Assessment Guide*) was now thought to be wrong. The *Guide* has now been rewritten (Part 2 para.2.1.21) to suggest that where a device might be used in the same way by a non-disabled person it is "unlikely to be considered an aid or appliance". The same reasoning has been adopted in *JM v SSWP (PIP)* [2016] UKUT 542 (AAC) where it was said that a claimant who could manage only slip-on shoes is not to be regarded as using an aid or appliance in dressing. But the question should remain - is the use of the device by this person, in the way that they use it, evidence of a disability?

The reasoning adopted by Judge Jacobs in *CW v SSWP (PIP)* [2016] UKUT 197 (AAC); [2016] AACR 44 has been applied too in *DR v SSWP (PIP)* [2018] UKUT 209 (AAC). There, the claimant had been awarded 2 points by the FTT for needing a "perching stool" to use while preparing a meal (Descriptor 1b). On appeal Judge Lane found that this was an error. On the facts before her she found that the claimant had no greater need to sit while preparing food and cooking a meal than might any person without a disability. Consequently, she said, applying the reasoning of the *CW* case, his need to sit from time to time was no evidence of a need to use an aid or appliance; it was, in effect, no evidence of any disability. Note that much the same result will be achieved if emphasis is placed on the claimant having to show that they *need* to use the aid or appliance to achieve a particular task; it would not be sufficient to show merely that the claimant chooses to use that device, or that their house happens to be equipped in a certain way. What is necessary is to show that without the aid their disability prevents them from performing that Descriptor.

There is a danger that, in focussing on the normality of behaviour in using devices, the point of the PIP Activities and Descriptors may be lost. The point of these Descriptors is to serve as a measure of the claimant's disablement by reference to a number of ordinary daily living actions, but if the test were worded instead as "Can the claimant stand on one leg for more than 3 seconds without support" the actions of other people in putting on their trousers would be irrelevant. Similarly, a test that said "Can the claimant turn on and off a standard bathroom tap" would serve as a measure of his manual strength and dexterity with relevance to a whole host of daily living actions and then reference to lever arm taps as an aid or appliance can be seen as a distraction from the real purpose of these tests. Similarly whether or not a person can tie a bow in their shoe laces is not just about their ability to dress – it is indicative of the extent to which a person afflicted with arthritic hands will require help in other ways. Perhaps the "trouser test", as treated in *CW* above, does produce the right result because the ability to stand on one leg has little relevance in assessing a claimant's abilities to undertake daily living activities, but the use of other devices may have such relevance.

PART 2

PERSONAL INDEPENDENCE PAYMENT ASSESSMENT

Daily living activities and mobility activities

3.—(1) For the purposes of section 78(4) of the Act and these Regulations, daily living activities are the activities set out in column 1 of the table in Part 2 of Schedule 1. 4.173

(2) For the purposes of section 79(4) of the Act and these Regulations, mobility activities are the activities set out in column 1 of the table in Part 3 of Schedule 1.

GENERAL NOTE

4.174 PIP is a benefit that is aimed at broadly the same target group of claimants (of working age) as DLA. The chief difference between the benefits is the method of identifying those who will qualify for benefit. DLA was administered largely on the basis of self declared information about the help that a claimant required to cope with day to day living and mobility supported, where necessary, by evidence from the claimant's health professional advisers. PIP, by contrast, approaches the matter by asking what the claimant can do for themselves. This will be based on the claimant's own response (on a questionnaire), but introduces, as well, an assessment report to be made by an independent Health Professional (HP) engaged to make a detailed report on the basis of the activities and descriptors prescribed in the schedule below. The Health Professional (HP) is equivalent to the Health Care Professional (HCP) that is engaged in Employment and Support Allowance decisions. Because the members of tribunals and UT judges have grown familiar with that terminology the abbreviation HCP will be used also in these notes.

Guidance is given to the HCP in conducting these assessments in the *PIP Assessment Guide* (sometimes referred to as PIPAG) that is available on the DWP website. The *Guide* has been referred by many UT judges in their decisions though always with the warning that the views expressed there are those of the Secretary of State and are not necessarily determinative of the law.

This method of assessment is not dissimilar to that adopted in relation to Employment Support Allowance (ESA). (Though there, unfitness is measured on a descending scale of descriptors; for PIP there is an ascending scale of disability). Advice given by the DWP says that the results of an assessment for ESA will not be used for the purposes of deciding a claim for PIP and *vice versa*. (Though, where there is a claim for PIP on the basis of terminal illness, information contained in the ESA record will be used). In administering claims for PIP the DWP has directed that those taking decisions should be referred to as Case Managers (CM). However, because tribunal members and UT judges are familiar with the more usual nomenclature of Decision Maker (DM) we will use that terminology in these notes.

To the extent that PIP and DLA have a similar objective it is not surprising that some of the same words and phrases are common to both benefits. Where that is the case it will be not unreasonable to suppose that the same meaning should be given to those words as they have been given for the purposes of DLA.

Details of the procedure that will be followed in administering PIP can be found on the DWP website. The process to be followed in dealing with a claim for PIP is explained there in some detail. In *HB v SSWP* [2015] UKUT 346 (AAC) it appears that a further stage may be involved in, at least, some cases. The claimant had been seen at a face-to-face interview by an HCP as a part of the normal process of assessment. She was scored at nine points for the daily living component and would have succeeded on her claim for benefit. But it then appears that, before a decision on her claim was made, the assessment was referred to another HCP for review. That assessment, conducted only as a desk assessment, reduced the score on three descriptors and in consequence the claim failed. The claimant's appeal to an FTT was refused. In the UT, Judge Wikeley allowed the appeal because the FTT had failed to explain why they had accepted the score recorded on review, rather than that made at the face-to-face interview. No explanation seems to have been offered to either tribunal for the desk reassessment. It may be that it was a part of the "reworking" procedure that is provided as a part of the Quality Audit procedure, but if that were the case some explanation ought to have been forthcoming. The FTT should have involved its inquisitorial role to elicit that information and its reasons might then have been able to satisfy both the claimant and the UT.

Another innovation to the procedure that is followed within the DWP has been the introduction of a further reconsideration of entitlement following the making of an appeal by the claimant. Where the Secretary of State is minded to increase the award of points on that assessment the practice has developed of making an "offer" to the claimant but without the Secretary of State actually revising the decision. Where that offer would increase the claimant's entitlement, if accepted, the effect would be for the appeal to lapse. Initially it seems that such offers were made conditional on the claimant abandoning the appeal. Following judicial review proceedings in 2021 that condition was removed and such offers are now made with a statement telling the claimant that, although the current appeal would lapse, there will be a right to appeal against the new decision. The purpose of this process is obviously to avoid the need to continue with appeals in which the Secretary of State is likely to concede that there is a right to further entitlement. The reluctance of the Secretary of State to make a revision is possibly explained by not wishing to deprive the claimant of his appeal when the claimant may wish to argue for an even greater award and may not wish to lose time by having to enter a new appeal.

This was effectively the situation that arose in *DO v SSWP (PIP)* [2021] UKUT 161 (AAC) (though, in that case, it seems that the claimant, who was autistic, may not have understood his right to make a new appeal and simply wanted to have a chance to explain to the tribunal how his condition affected him). The question that arises in these cases is how the FTT should approach the information given to them about the Secretary of State's reconsidered view of the claimant's entitlement. In this case the FTT, having heard that view, nevertheless awarded a lesser amount than the Secretary of State would have been willing to concede (though a greater amount than the original award of benefit). Judge Wright held that it was an error of law to do so, though he does so for what may be two different reasons. On one hand, he takes the view (paras. 45 and 46) that the FTT did not have before it any issue relating to the claimant's entitlement to benefit at the rate for which the Secretary of State had conceded entitlement, and hence had no jurisdiction to decide on that matter. On the other, he went on (para. 47) to observe that if the FTT considered that there was an issue as to the claimant's entitlement to benefit even at the rate that had been conceded and bearing in mind that the claimant was unrepresented and was autistic, fairness would require that the FTT should have at least given a warning, and possibly adjourned the proceedings for the claimant to be able to take advice. Perhaps the answer is that where (as the judge thought in this case) that the Secretary of State has taken an unequivocal and conclusive view of the claimant's entitlement (see para.42) then the former will be the correct course for the FTT to take (though it seems that it would still be necessary to exercise their jurisdiction to make that decision), but if the Secretary of State is thought to be offering a tentative view that is more of an evidential nature to the FTT, then the latter course should be followed. In this case then, Judge Wright allowed the appeal and made an award of benefit in accordance with the SSWP concession.

The same point has been considered by Judge Church in *LH v SSWP (PIP)* [2022] UKUT 32 (AAC). There the Secretary of State had said "that it would be reasonable to suggest" the award of 10 points on a claim for the mobility component and that "Therefore I recommend the tribunal to award" those points. Judge Church does not take up the point made by Judge Wright in the case above that a clear concession by the SSWP would deprive the tribunal of jurisdiction because there remained no issue before them. (Though he does (in para 33) say that the upshot of the SSWP submission "is that entitlement to the mobility component at the standard rate was not in issue between the parties"). Instead, Judge Church continues with the approach that he had indicated when giving leave to appeal to the UT. In his view the concession by the SSWP is not determinative of the issue; it was no more than a further evidential item that came before the tribunal, and it remained their inquisitorial duty to determine that issue. Having failed in their reasons to refer to the concession at all, it followed that either they had not considered the matter, in which case their failure to do so was an error of law, or, if they had considered it but rejected that evidence, they had failed in their duty to give adequate reasons for their decision. This difference of approach needs to be resolved because Judge Church thought that further facts had to be found and in consequence the case had to be remitted for rehearing.

The correct procedure to be followed by the FTT in a case of supersession has been explained by Judge Jacobs in *P v SSWP (PIP)* [2019] UKUT 82 (AAC). The tribunal had decided that a reassessment by the HCP in which it was found that the claimant was not entitled to the benefit was a ground for supersession. The judge holds that this was an error of law; the correct sequence, he says, is for the tribunal first to assess the evidence, then to make findings of fact, and on the basis of those findings decide whether there was a ground for supersession, before finally deciding what the claimant's entitlement should be. In this case neither the DM nor the FTT had made findings of fact as to the claimant's condition; they had simply referred to the conclusion that had been reached by the HCP.

In *LS v SSWP* [2019] UKUT 3 (AAC) Judge Bano affirms that new medical evidence can always be a ground for supersession provided that the FTT explains why they have decided to depart from the earlier award. In doing that to accord with what Judge Jacobs said in the case above they will have necessarily made new findings of fact. Judge Bano has also pointed out that an FTT is not limited in their supersession decision to an award of benefit for the same period as that which they are superseding. In this case the new decision removed entitlement to the mobility component from the date of supersession, but awarded benefit to the care component for a further period which the judge said, if the original award had been for a period that had already expired, could be for a new period beyond the end of that award.

Where an appeal to the FTT is in respect of a transition decision (i.e. moving the claimant from DLA to PIP) and a claimant who was previously awarded DLA is denied any entitlement to PIP at all, Judge Hemingway has decided, in *SM v SSWP (PIP)* [2021] UKUT 140 (AAC), that if the FTT is to dismiss that appeal, it must give reasons explaining why entitlement to benefit has stopped; failure to do so is an error of law. The judge suggests also, though not as part of his decision, that where the tribunal finds contradictions in the evidence before it, those contradictions should be put to the claimant if they are to be relied upon as a part of their decision. Further, he suggests too (though again not as a part of his decision) that there would be few statements of reasons for a decision that are adequate unless some reference is made to regulation 4(2A) in such a way as to demonstrate that the criteria set out there, have been applied in practice, even if not referred to specifically.

The decision of Judge Wikeley in *SF v SSWP (PIP)* [2016] UKUT 481 (AAC) reaffirms that the principle that was established in relation to claims for DLA and AA that, where a previous award of benefit was revised to the detriment of the claimant, clear reasons should be given by a tribunal to explain that revision – see e.g. *R(M)1/96* and *R(A)2/83.* This case applies the same principle where an award of personal independence payment has been superseded. The claimant had received 16 points awarded by the DM upon his initial application for PIP. The award was made for a period of three years (some of which was paid in arrears), but 12 months after the award was made the claimant was invited to complete a new PIP form in what was a planned review of his claim. Following a second examination by an HCP, the claimant scored zero points and his award was withdrawn forthwith. The claimant's appeal was refused, but the FTT made no reference to the earlier award, no reference to the basis upon which that award had been made, and hence no explanation of why they were now upholding such a dramatically different conclusion. Judge Wikeley reiterates the point that simply in the interests of justice such an outcome must demand an explanation.

The case makes another point about the application of the Universal Credit, Personal Independence Payment, Jobseeker's Allowance and Employment Support Allowance (Decisions and Appeals) Regulations 2013 in cases of supersession. Under those regulations supersession might arise either on a change of circumstances—(under reg.23) or upon receipt of a further medical evidence—usually a further report from a HCP—(under reg.26). Where reg.23 is used the tribunal is required to identify the ground on which supersession takes place and also the date from which it is to have effect, or will adopt the default date under s.10(5) of the Social Security Act 1998 (i.e. the date on which the decision is made). Where reg.26 is in issue the grounds will be self-evident and the effective date will be the default date under s.10.

For that reason the representative for the Secretary of State accepted that the regulations should be considered by a tribunal in that order; in other words, reg.23 should be considered first and reg.26 should be a last resort. Judge Wikeley explains that there is a very good reason why this should be so because the supersession following a review might equally have the effect of increasing the claimant's award and adopting this sequence will ensure that he has the advantage of that award being back-dated to the change of circumstances where it is appropriate to do so. This view was not shared by Judge Mesher in the subsequent case of *DS v SSWP (PIP)* [2016] UKUT 538 (AAC); [2017] AACR 19. In a case raising essentially the same points as *SF*, Judge Mesher found no need to adopt the sequential approach to the application of regs 23 and 26; in his view it was open to the DM to adopt either of these provisions and to choose an effective date that reflected the evidence upon which the supersession was made.

Where the DM chose to act upon a fresh report of a HCP or other medical evidence, but chose not to explore the question of whether the claimant should have been aware of his condition so as to put him under an obligation to report a change in his circumstances, that was a course that was open to him and a tribunal that heard an appeal against that decision would be under no obligation to consider whether or not reg.23 should have been applied first. If, however, evidence before the FTT (possibly not available to the DM) raised the possibility that an earlier date was relevant, there was no reason for the FTT not to follow that course under s.12(8)(a) of the Social Security Act 1998. The need for a decision of supersession has been further considered in a series of cases *DS v SSWP (PIP)* [2016] UKUT 538 (AAC), *KB v SSWP (PIP)* [2016] UKUT 537 (AAC), *PM v SSWP (PIP)* [2017] UKUT 37 (AAC) and *TH v SSWP (PIP)* [2017] UKUT 231 (AAC) in the last of which Judge Wikeley confirms his acceptance of the approach that had been adopted by Judge Mesher above in this note.

On the related question of whether, in case like this where the claimant has been in receipt of benefit that is now withdrawn, the report of the HCP that had previously been relied upon should be made available in evidence, Judge Mesher refers to the decision in *FN v SSWP (ESA)* [2015] UKUT 670 (AAC) now reported as [2016] AACR 24. He suggests, by analogy to that decision, that there is no rule of law that requires a tribunal to enquire as to the evidence in the previous claim, but where there is such relevant evidence of which the tribunal is aware the issue should be pursued. In this case the claimant had put the earlier medical condition in issue by asserting that his condition now was the same, or possibly worse, than before and, in the judge's view, that required the FTT to decide if an earlier medical report was relevant, and if it was not, to explain why not, and what they made of the contention that he was now as bad, or possibly worse. Finally, Judge Mesher agrees with the decision of Judge Wikeley in *SF* that the principle applied in *R(M) 1/96*, requiring an FTT to explain the reason for the difference in result, should apply in PIP cases like this. The circumstances in which it might be relevant for an FTT to call for medical evidence that could be available from an earlier award of DLA or of ESA has been considered in a number of cases—see *AP v SSWP (PIP)* [2016] UKUT 416 (AAC), *MA v SSWP (PIP)* [2017] UKUT 351 (AAC) and *GD v SSWP (PIP)* [2017] UKUT 415 (AAC). For a discussion of these cases see the notes following reg.8 of these regulations. The most frequent occasion on which it may be relevant for a tribunal to consider the medical evidence and the basis of an earlier award of benefit is likely to be when a claimant is transitioned from an award of DLA to a claim for PIP. When subsequently there is an appeal against the PIP decision the DWP has argued that evidence from the DLA award is not relevant and need not to be produced on that appeal because it is not an award of the same benefit and the qualifying conditions are not the same for both benefits. This argument is rejected by Judge Ward in *YM v SSWP (PIP)* [2018] UKUT 16 (AAC). Applying the reasoning of Judge Howell in the *R(M) 1/96* he suggests that where the conditions on which a previous benefit has been awarded are reasonably capable of being material to the subsequent benefit the principle established in that case should be applied so as to offer the claimant an explanation for what would otherwise appear to be an inconsistency. The giving of adequate reasons for the appeal decision requires no less. And note too, that where the claim for PIP has been preceded by an earlier award of PIP the tribunal is not necessarily relieved of the need to enquire as to the relevance of earlier medical evidence and the basis of that earlier award merely because the present claim is presented as a new claim, rather than a supersession of the old one–see *BB v SSWP (PIP)* [2017] UKUT 506 (AAC).

The circumstances in which an FTT is obliged to consider evidence that may have been relevant to an earlier claim for benefit, usually on entitlement to DLA, when they are considering an appeal for PIP have been reviewed by Judge Markus QC in two cases heard together, *CH and KN v SSWP (PIP)* [2018] UKUT 330 (AAC); [2019] AACR 11. These were both cases arising on the transfer of former DLA claimants to PIP, but similar issues can arise where the claimant seeks to involve as evidence on the claim for PIP evidence from earlier or contemporaneous claims for ESA, and even from claims for industrial injuries benefit. Judge Markus found that she was required to answer two questions. First, in what circumstances should an FTT obtain evidence of an earlier award of DLA, and secondly, when will the FTT be required to give reasons that explain a difference that arises when the claimant's award of PIP is less beneficial than their previous award of DLA.

In answering the first question the Judge offers detailed advice on when the evidence from the earlier claim will be relevant followed by advice on the circumstances in which an FTT should call for evidence from an earlier claim. This advice can be found in paragraphs 45 to 66 of her judgment. (Judge Markus had been given details of the improved procedures that should now be followed by DWP so that the evidence should already be before the FTT on transfer cases, such as these, if the claimant has requested it.)

In answering the second question Judge Markus supports the remarks that had been made by Judge Ward in *YM v SSWP (PIP)* [2018] UKUT 16 (AAC). She says that she supports Judge Ward's approach in saying that there is no rule of law that requires a difference of outcome to be explained and that it is for the tribunal to determine in the circumstances of a particular case whether there is such an apparent inconsistency that reasons for it, are called for.

On the facts of these two cases she found that, in the first case, the Secretary of State had failed to include medical evidence in the file, even though it had been requested (at the FTT the claimant had not complained of its absence), but Judge Markus thought the evidence before the FTT was so complete, and given that the DLA evidence would have been 12 years old, that there was no error of law in failing to adjourn for that evidence. Nor in those circumstances was there any need for the FTT to explain the reasons for the difference between the claimant's awards. The reason that he did not succeed on the PIP claim was clear, though she does suggest that a brief single sentence to explain why the FTT had preferred the evidence on the current claim might have been desirable. In the second case the judge found that there was sufficient overlap between what was probably the basis of the DLA claim and hence the evidence on which that was based, and the current evidence of panic attacks suffered by the claimant and affecting her ability to go out alone, that the FTT had made an error of law in failing to call for the DLA evidence. The case was remitted for reconsideration by a new tribunal. This matter has been considered again by Judge Markus QC in *NW v SSWP (PIP)* [2019] 150 UKUT (AAC) and further guidance provided for FTT. First, she reiterates that there is no rule that requires an FTT to request the DLA evidence; every case will depend upon its circumstances. In this case it was suggested by the claimant that the latest DLA award included a medical report that could have been relevant to his claim for PIP. The judge also explains how a tribunal should proceed when the DWP say that the required documents cannot be found. Further assurance was given to the judge on the understanding of DWP as to their duty to respond to requests from the tribunal system.

In *AW v SSWP (PIP)* [2018] UKUT 76 (AAC) Judge Wright has considered another case where the evidence on which an award of DLA had been made was not available to the FTT. In that case, however, he felt able on the basis of what could be inferred from the claimant's condition (which counsel for the Secretary of State agreed was unlikely to have changed) to decide the case himself and award the mobility component at the standard rate.

Two further cases deal with these issues. Both are decisions of Judge May QC. In the first, *AR v SSWP (PIP)* [2018] UKUT 313 (AAC) the judge decided that even applying what was said by Judge Ward in the *YM* case that the appeal failed because, as Judge Ward had expressed it in the *YM* case, the evidence from the one claim would need to be "reasonably capable of being material" to the other. In this case the claimant suffered from epilepsy, but the FTT found no evidence that he was at risk of a seizure when he was out. Judge May thought that the DLA claim must have been based on him being "unable or virtually unable to walk" for it to have awarded at the higher rate and could have no relevance to his PIP claim. Again, in *SM v SSWP (PIP)* [2018] UKUT 314 (AAC) Judge May observes that the requirement to explain the award of PIP when it differs from an earlier award of DLA as set out by Judge Ward in *YM v SSWP (PIP)* [2018] UKUT 16 (AAC) was obiter, but, in any case, he finds that the principle should not apply in this appeal because the reasons for which the earlier benefit were awarded (unable or virtually unable to walk) were not relevant to the criteria that the FTT had applied in the present case. The claimant, who suffered from arthritis, was found to satisfy Descriptor 2(d) of the Mobility Activities. It does not appear that she disputed this conclusion; her appeal was based on the fact that she had an abdominal stoma which made it impossible, she said, to use public transport. There was no evidence to suggest that she could walk only 20 metres so as to satisfy Descriptor 2(e) and qualify for the higher rate of mobility.

The need for an FTT to adjourn and call for evidence that formed the basis of an earlier award of DLA has been considered again in *BH v SSWP (PIP)* [2020] UKUT 338 (AAC) by Judge Hemingway. This was a case where the claimant had been awarded the highest rate of the care component and the higher rate of the mobility component for DLA but had scored no points on being transferred to PIP. The FTT that heard his appeal awarded five points for the daily living component and none for mobility and hence dismissed his appeal. They gave as their reasons for not adjourning to obtain the DLA evidence that such evidence would have been five years old and that, in any case, the claimant had not requested that the evidence be produced when that question had been put to him when he made his appeal. Judge Hemingway concluded (though narrowly) that, in the circumstances of this case, those reasons were not a sufficient explanation of the decision not to adjourn. He points out that the nature of the claimant's disability (arthritis in his back and legs) was unlikely to have improved which meant that the five-year-old evidence might still be relevant. Though the waiver of his opportunity to request the medical evidence might be taken into account, it should not regarded as conclusive of whether the FTT should decide to adjourn; but nor did the judge think that the FTT had done that in this case.

Judge Hemingway observed too, that the decision on the DLA claim to award the higher rate of mobility must have meant that the DM then found him to be "virtually unable to walk", a conclusion that could have a direct correlation to the Descriptors to be applied for the mobility component of PIP. The FTT had said that they found the claimant's description of his condition both in writing and before the tribunal to have been "exaggerated". Judge Hemingway thought that although this "came close", it did not succeed as a sufficient explanation of the inconsistency between the awards. It could have been that the FTT thought that the claimant's condition had improved (though, as he had said, that seems unlikely) or that the earlier award had been generous. The case was remitted for a rehearing.

A different aspect of this matter is considered by Judge Wikeley in *FJ v SSWP (PIP)* [2019] UKUT 27 (AAC). This case concerned not the evidence that might be provided by reports from claims for other benefits, but evidence of the claimant's earlier record in relation to this benefit. A claim for PIP had been refused and the claimant had appealed, but after her appeal to the FTT had been refused she made a fresh claim for PIP because she thought that might produce results more quickly than by making a further appeal to the UT. Her representative, in correspondence to the DWP, referred to evidence from the earlier proceedings but the DWP declined to make any refence on the ground that this was a new claim. The claimant appealed again to the FTT and then to the UT. Judge Wikeley took the view that in order to satisfy Rule 24 of the Tribunal Procedure Rules the DWP should have provided a copy of documents relating to the earlier claim.

Further guidance on the procedure to be followed when a claimant has appealed against only one component of a PIP award has been given in *MW v SSWP (PIP)* [2016] UKUT 540 (AAC). Provided that the tribunal is satisfied that the claimant has understood that both components of an award are "at risk" in the appeal, there is no need for an adjournment to be offered. This is certainly the case where the claimant is represented at the hearing because the tribunal is entitled to assume that the representative is competent; it may be otherwise where there is no representative. On the question of whether an adjournment should be considered where the claimant is appealing against only one component of a combined award see also the more considered approach adopted by Judge Markus QC in *GA v SSWP (PIP)* [2017] UKUT 416 (AAC), although there the appeal was allowed because the FTT did not seem to have appreciated that they were making a supersession and had not given the ground upon which the supersession was made.

In *JC v SSWP (PIP)* [2016] UKUT 533 (AAC) representatives were reminded of the dangers of submitting a complete medical record where some of the record had not been read. In this case the very long record (350 pages) included material that was confidential and highly sensitive.

Assessment of ability to carry out activities

4.175 **4.**—(1) For the purposes of section 77(2) and section 78 or 79, as the case may be, of the Act, whether C has limited or severely limited ability to carry out daily living or mobility activities, as a result of C's physical or mental condition, is to be determined on the basis of an assessment.

(2) C's ability to carry out an activity is to be assessed—

(a) on the basis of C's ability whilst wearing or using any aid or appliance which C normally wears or uses; or

(b) as if C were wearing or using any aid or appliance which C could reasonably be expected to wear or use.

[1(2A) Where C's ability to carry out an activity is assessed, C is to be assessed as satisfying a descriptor only if C can do so—

(a) safely;

(b) to an acceptable standard;

(c) repeatedly; and

(d) within a reasonable time period.

(3) Where C has been assessed as having severely limited ability to carry out activities, C is not to be treated as also having limited ability in relation to the same activities.

[1(4) In this regulation—

(a) "safely" means in a manner unlikely to cause harm to C or to another person, either during or after completion of the activity;

(b) "repeatedly" means as often as the activity being assessed is reasonably required to be completed; and

(c) "reasonable time period" means no more than twice as long as the maximum period that a person without a physical or mental condition which limits that person's ability to carry out the activity in question would normally take to complete that activity.]

AMENDMENTS

1. Social Security (Personal Independence Payment) (Amendment) Regulations 2013 (SI 2013/455) reg.2 (April 8, 2013).

DEFINITIONS

"aid or appliance"—see reg.2. **4.176**

GENERAL NOTE

4.177 A more detailed discussion of how the assessment procedure should be carried out can be found in the notes following Pts 1 and 2 of the Schedule to these regulations.

Note that the Personal Independence Payment Regulations 2013 were amended with effect from March 16, 2017 by the Personal Independence Payment (Amendment) Regulations 2017 (SI 2017/194). In *RF v SSWP* [2017] EWHC 3375 (Admin); [2018] AACR 13 Mostyn J. held that para. 2(4) of the amending regulations (SI 2017/194) was in breach of Art.14 of the ECHR and that it was *ultra vires* the regulation making power in Part 4 of the Welfare Reform Act 2012 under which it purported to have been made. The DWP have accepted that that decision is correct. This means that the amendment effected by that part of the regulation is of no effect and the text of original version in Part 3 of Schedule 1 (Mobility Activity, Planning and following journeys) is restored. The law stated in this work is as at April 9, 2018 which means that it is the amended version, apart from Part 3 of Schedule 1, that appears here; for full original version of the regulations the reader is referred to the 2016/17 edition of this work.

Note that although the decision of the High Court in *RF v SSWP* was in respect of the law relating only to Great Britain a Tribunal of Commissioners in Northern Ireland has decided that the same effect should be given when decisions are made under the identical regulations in Northern Ireland – see *HH v Department for Communities (PIP)* [2024] NI Com 8. This decision applies the dictum of Baroness Hale in *RR v SSWP* [2019] UKSC 52 in which she said at para.27:

'There is nothing unconstitutional about a public authority, court or tribunal disapplying a provision of subordinate legislation which would otherwise result in their acting incompatibly with a Convention right, where this is necessary in order to comply with the Human Rights Act. Subordinate legislation is subordinate to the requirements of an Act of Parliament. The Human Rights Act is an Act of Parliament, and its requirements are clear.'

The Commissioners in Northern Ireland took the view that a decision of the High Court in another part of the UK was sufficient authority for a tribunal to disapply the regulation.

These amendments were made in consequence of two decisions in the UT. The first, *SSWP v LB (PIP)* [2016] UKUT 530 (AAC) concerned the definitions of therapy and of managing therapy, managing medication and of monitoring a health condition, together with amendments to Activity 3 in Part 2 of Schedule 1. These amendments remain in force, but because these changes are substantive rather than procedural they affect decisions that were made only after the date that they came into effect (March 16, 2017). This is confirmed in *RS-G v SSWP (PIP)* [2017] UKUT 152 (AAC). This means that for appeals that are brought now, to the FTT or the UT, in respect of decisions made before March 16, 2017, the law to be applied (at least in the FTT) will that in the *LB* decision above.

The second, a decision of a three judge panel, *MH v SSWP (PIP)* [2016] UKUT 531 (AAC); [2018] AACR 12 concerned the application of Activity 1 in Part 3 of the Schedule; it is that part of the amending regulation that has been found to be of no effect and an appeal against the *MH* decision has been withdrawn. This means that all decisions coming before an FTT or the UT now, should be decided in accordance with that decision.

An assessment will be made taking into account the claimant's ability when wearing or using any aid or appliance that he normally wears or, where he does not wear or use such aid etc., taking account of any aid etc. that he could reasonably be expected to wear or use. Whether someone can reasonably be expected to use such a device may depend upon many factors—e.g. whether the claimant already possesses that device, or, where he does not the cost and availability of the item, whether persons suffering from the same condition as the claimant commonly use that item, whether they are commonly advised by health professionals to do so and other factors such as the size and the storage facilities that that might be necessary for the claimant.

An "aid or appliance" is defined in reg.2 above. It will include any device that improves the claimant's ability to accomplish any activity including, most obviously, a wheelchair. Previously this note has suggested that a wheelchair might have to be excluded from the definition of an appliance in order to make sense of Descriptors in Activity 2 relating to the mobility component. However, the better view may be that a wheelchair is an appliance, and a more complex interpretation needs to be given to those Descriptors—see the note to Descriptor f.

The correct approach to be adopted by an FTT in making an assessment of the claimant's ability to perform the tasks required in the Activities and Descriptors is explained in two respects in the decision of Judge Gray in *PM v SSWP (PIP)* [2017] UKUT 154 (AAC). The FTT had concluded that the claimant should not score certain points because they felt (no doubt with the advantage of advice from the medical member of the tribunal) that with an appropriate adjustment of her pain relief medication that she would be able to achieve the tasks required satisfactorily. The Judge said that, while it was the role of the tribunal to be inquisitorial, an assumption about the claimants' treatment should be made only with extreme caution; in this case such an assumption was certainly inappropriate because the claimant's notes stated that a variation of the medication had been tried, but was unsuitable for the claimant. The second point was made in relation to the claim for a mobility component, but the general point is applicable across both components. The FTT had concluded that the claimant should be able to walk up to 50 metres as often as was "reasonably required". To the extent that this seemed to suggest an objective standard that might be set by the tribunal, the Judge thought it to be wrong. While the claimant would not be able to set herself an "extreme regime" of walking so as to generate a higher score, the test should focus more upon what the claimant might wish to do and especially how often she might want to do so. The test, she says, drawing on the words of Lord Slynn of Hadley in *Secretary of State v Fairey* (R(A) 2/98) (a case that involved a claim for Attendance Allowance) should be a comparison with a "normal life," and that should include an element that reflects the life-style of the claimant.

The claimant can be said to accomplish one of the tasks set in the activities prescribed only if he can do so "safely". This is defined in subs.(4) to mean that harm to himself or another person is "unlikely" This is a narrower definition of safety than is commonly used. Safety is usually defined in terms of risk and risk is taken to include the degree of harm that may be caused, as well as the likelihood of that harm happening. The definition above would not regard something as unsafe, even though it might be fatal, if it were unlikely to happen.

This was the meaning adopted, reluctantly, by the judge in *CE v SSWP (PIP)* [2015] UKUT 643 (AAC) and followed in several other cases. But there has now been a contrary conclusion reached by a panel of three judges in *RJ and others v SSWP (PIP)* [2017] UKUT 105 (AAC); [2017] AACR 32. These cases all concerned claimants whose disability put them at considerable risk if a certain event were to occur, but that event occurred only infrequently; they included claimants who suffered from epilepsy and others who were deaf. All these claimants needed to be accompanied or supervised in carrying out certain of the PIP Activities, but the need for intervention from another person at any particular time was "unlikely". The panel decision relies on two earlier decisions in other contexts, one in the House of Lords in *In re H (Minors) (Sexual Abuse): (Standards of Proof)* [1996] AC 563 and the other *Wallis v Bristol Water plc* [2010] PTSR 1986. In the first it was necessary for the local authority to be able to show that harm to a child was "likely" to occur – the court held that this did not require it to be shown that harm was more probable than not; it was sufficient if there was a real likelihood that harm might occur. Similarly, in the second case the water authority was required to show that an improper method of attaching fittings to the water system made it "likely" that contamination would be caused. Again, it was sufficient to show a real possibility of the harm occurring because, were it to do so, the damage could be catastrophic – as that court put it "a possibility that cannot sensibly be ignored having regard to the nature and gravity of the feared harm". Applying this reasoning to the word "unlikely" that is used here means that the claimant cannot be found to accomplish a PIP Activity safely if the risk involved is one that cannot sensibly be ignored. The UT in this case also drew support from the consultation material that was produced when the PIP scheme was developed. From that it became clear that those designing the scheme had intended risk to be treated in the same way as had been done with DLA; there the degree of harm as well as the likelihood of harm was accounted for. See *Moran v Secretary of State for Social Services (The Times March 14, 1987, CA)* where the Court said:

> "the relative frequency or infrequency of the attacks is immaterial so long as the risk of 'substantial' danger is not so remote a possibility that it ought reasonably to be disregarded."

Note too, that this meaning of safely means that there is no longer any need to make any distinction between the word as used in regulation 4(2A) and the definition of "supervision" (presence of another person required to ensure C's safety) in Sch.1.

In *SH v SSWP (PIP)* [2018] UKUT 251 (AAC) Judge Hemingway has made some observations about the functioning of the test for a claimant being able to accomplish an activity safely. The claimant was a profoundly deaf young woman. She had been fitted with cochlear implants that gave a good degree of hearing when she was wearing the external part of the appliance, but those had to be removed when she was bathing or taking a shower. It was argued that she could not bathe or shower safely without some supervision because, in the event of a fire or other catastrophe, she would not be able to hear any alarm or other warning sound. Her circumstances were the same as those of one of the claimants in the *RJ* case. In that case the three-judge tribunal had observed: "On our analysis of regulation 4 and 'supervision', these facts would indicate that she needed supervision to bathe". It seemed that, initially, counsel for the present claimant had argued before the UT that this meant that her client was entitled to succeed in respect of Activity 4b (need for supervision when washing and bathing) but subsequently accepted that a determination on the facts of the case was still required. Judge Hemingway agreed with that position and noted that even in the *RJ* case itself the matter had been remitted to a new tribunal for determination. In the present case he thought that the FTT had applied the correct test in relation to the risk apparent and that their conclusion rejecting the claim was one that they were entitled to reach, except in one respect; in deciding that the claimant could bathe safely without the need for supervision they had suggested that she could reduce the risk of harm occurring by limiting the time spent in the bath or in a shower. This, he decided they were not entitled to do. He refers to *EG v SSWP (PIP)* [2017] UKUT 101 (AAC) in which it was held that the claimant should be assessed in accordance with what they would choose to do and not circumscribe their activities. Doubtless there are limits to a claimant's choice of behaviour but this accords with the approach taken in *Secretary of State v Fairey* [1997] 1 W.L.R. 799 for DLA.

Note too, that the harm risked must be to a person; a risk of damage to property, even if significant, will not suffice; though then the claimant could hardly be said to accomplish the task "to an acceptable standard"—see para.(2A)(b). The harm may be either to the claimant or to another person. This was the point relied upon by the appellant in *JT v SSWP (PIP)* [2018] UKUT 101 (AAC). The claimant suffered from uncontrolled epilepsy; he had about two grand mal fits each week and several petit mal fits. It was argued that this made it too dangerous for him to prepare a meal because of the risk that he might injure himself either when using a knife or when handling hot items. Furthermore, when having a grand mal fit he thrashed about in a manner that might endanger anyone who was there to assist him. For this reason, it was argued, he could not prepare and cook a meal safely at all. Judge Hemingway allowed an appeal on the ground that the FTT had failed to give adequate reasons for their decision refusing benefit. The case was remitted for rehearing and see too, below, the meaning of supervision as might apply to these facts.

Whether the claimant can do something "repeatedly" is only likely to become an issue where the activity requires some degree of exertion- most obviously, perhaps, in relation to mobility (moving). This will bring into question the claimant's need for rest periods as to both frequency and duration and will then link with whether the claimant can be said to be achieving movement to "an acceptable standard".

CE v SSWP (PIP) [2015] UKUT 643 (AAC) also explores new ground in relation to the meaning of the word "repeatedly" in para.(4)(b). The judge in the UT returned the case for rehearing before a new tribunal and gave some guidance for that tribunal. The evidence before the FTT suggested that the claimant's inability to cope with some daily living activities arose from the fact that after an epileptic episode she needed to sleep until late in the morning and even then, when she awoke, she was lethargic and felt dizzy, sick, weak and tired so that she was unable to do very much at all until late morning or midday. The appeal by the Secretary of State had been allowed on the ground that the FTT had failed to explain sufficiently, why they were awarding some of the points that they did. In offering guidance to the new tribunal the judge suggests that they should take a comprehensive account of the times that the claimant was so affected and then, having referred to reg.4(2A), should consider whether the claimant could do those things repeatedly, as defined there, and to a satisfactory standard. As he put it:

> "It seems to me it makes no sense to say a person is able to perform an activity as often as reasonably required if they cannot do so for a part of the day in which they would otherwise reasonably wish or need to do so."

The judge refers also to his own decision in *TR v SSWP (PIP)* [2015] UKUT 626 (AAC); [2016] AACR 23 in which he had adopted the advice given in the *PIP Assessment Guide* that if a descriptor was satisfied for any part of a day (after allowing for the *de minimis* rule) it should be regarded as applying on that day. It seems that he is suggesting that a claimant, whose daily routine was so affected that they could not conform to normal hours for meals, work etc., could be regarded as satisfying some of the Descriptors. The difficulty with this may be to apply that approach to the words of the Descriptors. There is nothing in Descriptor 1, for example, that relates to the time at which the claimant should be capable of preparing a meal, and the reference in para.(2A)(d) to a reasonable time period is only to the speed with which the claimant can accomplish a task – see the definition in para.(4)(c). It would be odd to describe a claimant who took their breakfast at midday as being unable to prepare a meal though note, it would not mean that every person who lies abed until late, could make a claim because for any claim to succeed it would have to be the result of that claimant's mental or physical disability and, even then, not a matter of choice on their part. It is clear that a person with this claimant's degree of disability has a life that is seriously affected by their disability, but unless they can be seen to need supervision for their own safety and that of others, it is difficult to see how their claim can succeed.

The effect on the score of a claimant who takes an unreasonable time (defined in this regulation as more than twice as long as an able-bodied person) to complete daily living activities is demonstrated in a decision of Judge Gray in *SSWP v GP (PIP)* [2016] UKUT 444 (AAC). The claimant was a young man who suffered considerably from Obsessive Compulsive Disorder (OCD). On his claim for PIP the DM had allowed four points for daily living activities – two points for each of Activities 1 and 6. The FTT to whom he had appealed allowed a further eight points under Activity 4 (washing and bathing). The evidence before the FTT was that because of his OCD it took the claimant more than twice as long as is normal for him to eat, wash and dress. They allowed the extra points on the ground that this meant that the claimant could not effectively wash or bathe at all, and was therefore entitled to the maximum points allowable under that activity; they did not alter the points already awarded at all. The Secretary of State appealed on the ground that it was inconsistent, and therefore revealed some error of law, for the FTT to award eight points in relation to Activity 6 while retaining only two points for each of the other activities. Judge Gray held that there was no error of law; there was no compulsion for the FTT to reconsider the points awarded if the claimant had already reached the maximum score required. It was reasonable for the FTT to adopt this practice as a time saving measure in what was usually a busy schedule, though she did observe that where a tribunal does this, it may be as well to add a note to the effect that that is their reason for doing so, to avoid confusion and misunderstanding as in the present case.

What this case does highlight, however, is the inappropriate conclusions to which the fact-finders may be forced as a consequence of the operation of reg.4(2A). In this case, having found that the claimant would take more than twice as long as another person to wash and bathe, the tribunal were required to conclude that he could not wash etc at all— but descriptor 6(g) reads that the claimant "cannot wash at all and needs another person to wash their entire body". It is unlikely that such a measure could ever be adopted with an OCD young man. Further, if the FTT had tried to carry through their reasoning in relation to eating a meal they would have to find that he could not convey food to his mouth and required another person to feed him–another unlikely scenario.

A solution to this conundrum is suggested by the decision of Judge Ovey in *AB v SSWP (PIP)* [2017] UKUT 217 (AAC). This was a case in which the claimant's evidence suggested that he suffered distress when he tried to engage socially with others (Activity 9). Judge Ovey suggests that the requirements of reg.4(2A) should apply only to those Descriptors which test what the claimant can do, and are not applicable to those descriptors that describe what the claimant cannot do. In her view the structure of PIP Activities ranges from a Descriptor at one end that specifies a claimant who can accomplish the activity described without any need for assistance at all, to another at the other extreme where the claimant cannot accomplish that activity at all. By way of illustration she refers to Activity 6—dressing and undressing; that ranges from "can dress and undress unaided"" to "cannot dress or undress at all". It makes sense to test, in accordance with reg.4(2A), whether a claimant can dress (with or without aid) to a satisfactory extent, safely and in a reasonable time, but it does not, she says, make sense to ask whether someone who cannot dress at all does so satisfactorily, safely and timeously.

The inference is that reg.4(2A) was not intended to apply to the "cannot-do" descriptors. Regulation 4(2A) was a late addition to the regulations (as can be seen from the numbering) and in this, as well as other respects, the regulations as a whole, and the Descriptors in particular, have evolved somewhat piecemeal. For those Activities that are worded in the appropriate way this may provide a solution. Some Activities are worded in terms of the claimant's needs (e.g. Activity 3—Managing therapy etc) where the same problem may not arise, but for those in which the cannot-do at all Descriptor is used and is then conditioned by a further phrase, as in the case of Activity 4—washing and bathing, where the descriptor is "cannot wash at all and needs another to wash their entire body", there remains the difficulty of having to ignore the final element.

The effect of a slow walking pace has been considered in *KL v SSWP (PIP)* [2016] UKUT 545 (AAC). There the claimant walked slowly, but did not exceed the time limit prescribed in para.(4)(c). The UT judge held that it was not relevant then to consider the slowness of pace again in relation to whether the claimant could accomplish the Activity to an "an acceptable standard" under para.(2A)(b).

Scoring for daily living activities

4.178 5.—(1) The score C obtains in relation to daily living activities is determined by adding together the number of points (if any) awarded for each activity listed in column 1 of the table in Part 2 of Schedule 1 ("the daily living activities table").

(2) For the purpose of paragraph (1), the number of points awarded to C for each activity listed in column 1 of the daily living activities table is the number shown in column 3 of the table against whichever of the descriptors set out in column 2 of the table for the activity applies to C under regulation 7.

(3) Where C has undergone an assessment, C has—

(a) limited ability to carry out daily living activities where C obtains a score of at least eight points in relation to daily living activities; and

(b) severely limited ability to carry out daily living activities where C obtains a score of at least 12 points in relation to daily living activities.

General Note

4.179 For the daily living component there are 10 activities each of which contains a number of descriptors.

Note that the claimant scores the points for only one descriptor (the higher or highest where he satisfies more than one) in each activity; the aggregate of the scores from all activities is then the measure of the claimant's disability.

Scoring for mobility activities

4.180 6.—(1) The score C obtains in relation to mobility activities is determined by adding together the number of points (if any) awarded for each activity listed in column 1 of the table in Part 3 of Schedule 1 ("the mobility activities table").

(2) For the purpose of paragraph (1), the number of points awarded to C for each activity listed in column 1 of the mobility activities table is the number shown in column 3 of the table against whichever of the descriptors set out in column 2 of the table for the activity applies to C under regulation 7.

(3) Where C has undergone an assessment, C has—

(a) limited ability to carry out mobility activities where C obtains a score of at least eight points in relation to mobility activities; and

(b) severely limited ability to carry out mobility activities where C obtains a score of at least 12 points in relation to mobility activities.

General Note

4.181 For the mobility component there are two activities each of which contains a number of descriptors.

Note that the claimant scores the points for only one descriptor (the higher or highest where he satisfies more than one) in each activity; the aggregate of the scores from all activities is then the measure of the claimant's disability

An application by way of judicial review for a declaration that the Personal Independence Payments Regulations were invalid failed in *R (Sumpter) v SSWP* [2015] EWCA Civ 1033. The applicant had argued that the consultation process that preceded the making of the regulations was unfair and therefore unlawful. In particular he argued that the threshold at which a claimant might be awarded the enhanced rate of benefit in respect of their ability to move about had been changed at a late stage of the process. The early versions of the proposed criteria had appeared to adopt the standard that had been accepted, in practice, in relation to claims for DLA as an ability to move unaided no more than 50 metres, whereas the standard adopted in the draft regulations became effectively no more than 20 metres. The Secretary of State had then undertaken a further period of consultation relating specifically to that point. In the High Court Hickinbottom J. had held that, whatever might have been said about the fairness of the initial consultation, this later extension of consultation made the process, as a whole, fair: *R. (Sumpter) v Secretary of State for Work and Pensions* [2014] EWHC 2434 (Admin). The Court of Appeal upheld that decision.

Scoring: further provision

7.—(1) The descriptor which applies to C in relation to each activity in the tables referred to in regulations 5 and 6 is— **4.182**

(a) where one descriptor is satisfied on over 50% of the days of the required period, that descriptor;

(b) where two or more descriptors are each satisfied on over 50% of the days of the required period, the descriptor which scores the higher or highest number of points; and

(c) where no descriptor is satisfied on over 50% of the days of the required period but two or more descriptors (other than a descriptor which scores 0 points) are satisfied for periods which, when added together, amount to over 50% of the days of the required period—

(i) the descriptor which is satisfied for the greater or greatest proportion of days of the required period; or,

(ii) where both or all descriptors are satisfied for the same proportion, the descriptor which scores the higher or highest number of points.

(2) For the purposes of paragraph (1), a descriptor is satisfied on a day in the required period if it is likely that, if C had been assessed on that day, C would have satisfied that descriptor.

(3) In paragraphs (1) and (2), "required period" means—

(a) in the case where entitlement to personal independence payment falls to be determined, the period of 3 months ending with the prescribed date together with–

(i) in relation to a claim after an interval for the purpose of regulation 15[[1] or 15A], the period of 9 months beginning with the date on which that claim is made;

(ii) in relation to any other claim, the period of 9 months beginning with the day after the prescribed date.

(b) in the case where personal independence payment has been awarded to C—

(i) during the period of 3 months following a determination of entitlement under a claim for the purpose of regulation 15[[1] or 15A], the period of 3 months ending with the prescribed date together with, for each day of the award, the period of 9 months beginning with the day after that date;

(ii) in any other case, for each day of the award, the period of 3 months ending with that date together with the period of 9 months beginning with the day after that date.

AMENDMENT

1. Social Security (Disability Assistance for Working Age People) (Consequential Amendments) Order 2022 (SI 2022/177) art.14 (March 21, 2022).

DEFINITIONS

4.183 "prescribed date"—see reg.14 or 15
"required period"—see para.(3)

GENERAL NOTE

4.184 The required period over which the claimant is assessed is a period of three months that must precede the claim together with a period of nine months that follows. This means that a claimant will ordinarily have to satisfy a descriptor on a majority of the days over a year long period. This does not mean, of course, that the claimant must attempt to undertake the task every other day (e.g. make budgetary decisions), but only that, were he to do so, he would satisfy that Descriptor. Where the activity is measured by hours spent on it in a week (e.g. managing therapy) he might also undertake that Activity on fewer than half the days in a year.

The view expressed above has been confirmed in *DO v SSWP (PIP)* [2017] UKUT 115 (AAC). The claimant there was a cancer patient who, following surgery was incapacitated to a considerable extent but who had made a significant recovery after about six months following the surgery. In the FTT it was found that the claimant scored more than the qualifying points in a period that was more than 50% of the weeks in the required period as defined by regulation 7. But when reference is also made to the required period as defined in regulation 12, it was clear that he could not satisfy the prospective period in regulation 12(1)(b) because he would not have a qualifying score if he were "assessed at every time" in that period as that regulation requires. The question was which "required period" was determinative. Judge Mitchell has held that priority must be given to regulation 12. To do otherwise would mean that regulation 12 was otiose and it was clear that the legislative intention in the WRA was to require the claimant to qualify throughout the 12 month period. Another decision on the effect of regulation 7 and regulation 12 and the required period condition is in *AH v SSWP (PIP)* [2016] UKUT 541 (AAC). In this case Judge Jacobs affirms the rule that a tribunal must judge the case on the information available to it down to the date of the decision that is appealed against. A prospective claim under regulation 33 of the Claims and Payment Regulations can be made only if the tribunal can infer that, using the information available at the date of the decision appealed against, the claimant can be expected to satisfy conditions within the next three months.

Note that, where the claimant is undertaking an Activity that takes place overnight (e.g. renal dialysis or therapeutic feeding) provided some part of the process for which points are scored takes place before midnight and another afterwards, the claimant will satisfy the Descriptor on each of two days–see *SSWP v KS (PIP)* [2018] UKUT 102 (AAC). Judge Mesher held that a claimant who required assistance with a therapeutic source on three nights each week both in the evening when setting it up and again next morning when taking down, satisfied the 50% rule because she required that assistance on six days each week.

The decision of the three judge panel in *RJ v SSWP (PIP)* [2017] UKUT 105 (AAC); [2017] AACR 32 regarding the meaning of the word "safely" in regulation 4 has also resolved the question that had arisen with regard to the relationship between that definition and regulation 7. The UT in that case decides that there can be a need for supervision to ensure that the claimant accomplishes an Activity safely, even though an intervention is required much less frequently than every other day – it is the supervision that is required, perhaps on a daily basis, and not the intervention. The decision in *RJ v SSWP (PIP)* [2017] UKUT 105 (AAC); [2017] AACR 32 has been applied by Judge Mesher in *SSWP v NH (PIP)* [2017] UKUT 258 (AAC). There the claimant wore continence pads every day, though a leakage into them occurred, on average, only two days in the week. The judge held that such precautionary use was reasonably necessary every day and therefore the appropriate descriptor was satisfied on more than 50 percent of the days each week.

Where the claimant's condition varies the process defined by Regulation 7 must be followed to the exclusion of any more general approach that was previously used in relation to DLA. See *JC v SSWP* [2015] UKUT 144 where the appeal was allowed because the FTT had substituted their own assessment in relation to Daily Living Activities by adopting the approach suggested in *Moyna v SSWP* [2003] UKHL44. In this case the UT made clear that for PIP claims the tribunal must follow the 50% rules prescribed by reg.7.

The role that an FTT must play in establishing the facts to satisfy the 50% rule is examined by Judge Church in *AW v SSWP (PIP)* [2022] UKUT 316 (AAC). The claimant had completed the PIP questionnaire that initiated his claim, by ticking the box marked "sometimes" in relation to several of the questions about his need to use an aid or have assistance when doing several of the daily living activities. The FTT had used those answers to conclude that he could perform those activities without an aid or assistance more than 50% of the time. The Judge held this was an error of law when the claimant had added more detailed information in the boxes provided, but the tribunal had failed to consider that evidence or, had they done so, then failed to explain why they reached that conclusion. As he remarked, ""Sometimes" could mean many things to a claimant: it may mean "occasionally", or it may mean "most, but not all of the time", or it may very well mean something in between." The FTT must, therefore make further enquiry and make findings as to the claimant's difficulties.

The problem that arises when a claimant's ability to perform a task varies at different times within a single day has been dealt with in a decision of Judge Hemingway, *TR v SSWP* [2015] UKUT 626 AAC; [2016] AACR 23. The claimant there had restricted eyesight such that she had difficulty in seeing in low light conditions. She had been provided with what she described as her "special lamp" to assist her in reading and she used that also when preparing meals, though her husband still needed to assist her by checking things such as whether the gas was alight, or whether things were boiling on the stove. Her restricted eyesight also limited her ability to go out at night and she would use a taxi if she needed to go to unfamiliar places. Her claim had been refused and an appeal to the FTT failed. The FTT apparently took the view that if she could perform these tasks satisfactorily "the majority of the time" her claim would fail. This may have been an application by the tribunal of the approach that has applied in claims for DLA, or, it may have been that the tribunal thought they should be applying the 50% rule applicable to the case of daily variation as required by reg.7. In the UT counsel for the Secretary of State helpfully referred the judge to the Government's response to consultation on these regulations. There, it was clearly stated that if a Descriptor applied at any time within a period of 24 hours it should be regarded as applying on that day. Furthermore she referred also to the DWP Guidance to the HCP assessors which contained the same criterion in two associated paragraphs to accomplish a task "repeatedly" meaning as often as reasonably required. If it were reasonable for the claimant to go out at night, for example, she should be able to do that without adopting special measures to do so. But the judge approved also two limitations suggested by counsel for the Secretary of State on this approach. First, that the inability to perform a task should be the direct result of the claimant's disability; so that, for example, where the claimant chose not to go out at night for some other reason, that day would not count, and secondly, that any inability to perform a task would be subject to a *de minimis* rule. If, therefore, the claimant's inability could properly be described as fleeting, or even just brief, this would not qualify. In particular this might cover the case of a claimant whose inability arose only until he had taken his usual medication; if the medication acted quickly and enabled the claimant then to manage tasks such as washing and dressing, they would not qualify, whereas, if the medication took so long to be effective as to mean there was an unacceptable delay in the claimant's daily business, that would qualify as an inability to perform that Descriptor.

The provisions of this regulation will provide guidance in some cases where the claimant's condition fluctuates between "good days" and "bad days".

The case of *AK v SSWP (PIP)* [2015] UKUT 620 AAC poses another question in applying reg.7. The claimant suffered from two independent medical conditions each of which affected his living abilities on certain days of the week. One was chronic obstructive pulmonary disease (COPD) and the other was rheumatoid arthritis. Neither disease was causatively linked to the other, but neither were they mutually exclusive- in other words on some days the claimant might be inhibited by one or other of these diseases, on some days it might be by both, and on yet others he might not be inhibited at all by either. The evidence accepted by the FTT supported a finding that the claimant was affected by COPD on average for three days per week and by arthritis for two or three days of the week. Each of these conditions affected his ability to perform various descriptors in four of the daily living activities and one of the mobility activities. The tribunal in this case appears to have assumed that the medical conditions both occurred simultaneously so that the claimant failed the 50% test (required by reg.7) on each descriptor. But would the claimant have failed the 50% rule if the medical conditions did not occur simultaneously? The FTT had made no findings that related each medical condition to the separate descriptors and the case was remitted to a fresh tribunal for that to be done.

Assuming that each medical condition, or both together, might affect the claimant's ability to perform each of the relevant descriptors it would still then be necessary to determine on how many days he was so affected. One way to do this would be for the claimant to have kept a diary of his medical conditions and how they affected him each day, but that had not been done in this case and might not be done in other cases coming before tribunals. More likely, the claimant will report, as here, an estimate of the days in each week that they are affected. Evidence on a weekly basis does not accord with the "required period" as defined in reg.7(3) which refers to the period of three months before (and the nine months after) the date of claim, but it seems likely that tribunals (and others involved in this decision making) will extrapolate from the estimates that claimants can make on a weekly basis, because that is the timescale on which most claimants will think. This point was not referred to in the present case.

Assuming that the tribunal is faced with the situation, as here, where the only information available is that on some days the claimant may be affected by only one of two conditions and on other days by both conditions together, it will be necessary for the tribunal to calculate the probability that they would be affected by one, or other, or by both. This may seem a daunting task, but the method of calculating probability was supplied in this case by the Secretary of State. Using that method, the probability that the claimant might be incapacitated by one or other or both of his conditions was, in the case of rheumatism on three days of the week and COPD also on three days, a probability of 4.7 days, and if rheumatism occurred on only two days of the week and COPD on three days a probability of 4.1 days. This assumes that the each medical condition dealt with separately would affect the claimant's ability on the relevant descriptor to the same extent and both together would do the same. In that case, then the claimant would have satisfied that descriptor on more than 50% of the days in that week. If only one of the medical conditions affected a particular descriptor while the other did not (though it might have affected a lesser descriptor) then the calculation becomes much more complicated and the outcome will depend upon the extent to which each condition affects the claimant's ability in relation to each descriptor and his ability when both conditions occur simultaneously, and as well, as in this case, upon whether the rheumatism affects him on two or on three days of a week! What this does emphasise is the importance of detailed fact finding in relation to each condition, each activity and each descriptor by the FTT.

Judge Ward, in this case, has attached the Secretary of State's method of calculating probabilities as a schedule to his decision. Tribunals that are called upon to perform this exercise can read it there. That calculation produced the number of days on which the claimant was affected by one or other or both of his medical conditions. Readers of this note may find the process easier to understand if they focus, instead, on the number of days in the week that the claimant might be expected to be free of any disabling condition. If we assume that the claimant suffers from condition A on three days of the week, and from an unconnected condition B also for three days of the week, then, the chances of him being free of condition A within the week are 4/7 of the week. His chance then of not having condition B *either* in that week, are only 4/7 of those days on which he does not have A. Represented mathematically this is $4/7 \times 4/7 = 16/49$ of a week, or $16/49 \times 7 = 2.3$. The claimant would be expected to have 2.3 days in a week on which he suffered no disability and, therefore 4.7 days on which he did.

One further point should be noted. In order to satisfy the 50% rule prescribed in reg.7 the probability (expectation value) shown by this calculation will have to be greater than 3.5—reg. 7 requires "over 50% of the days", but what if the result is more than three though less than 3.5. Can the claimant then argue that by applying the "any part of a day" rule exemplified above, he should then have the days' of disablement rounded up to four? The answer is—No. To do that would amount to "double counting" because the part-day rule will have already been employed in identifying the days on which the claimant is affected by each of his conditions. The calculation of the probabilities is then purely an exercise in statistics.

The assessment report made by the HCP will contain advice on the claimant's abilities over both the past three months (the qualifying period) and the likely ability over the next nine months (the prospective period). Most awards of benefit will be made for a fixed period (seldom more than three years—see s.88 (2) WRA 2012 above and the notes that follow it), but the assessment report will also contain advice as to how long the claimant should be left before a review is made of his ability even within that period. In some cases this will be to a claimant's advantage as he will then be picked up automatically when a condition has worsened; in others benefit will be reduced or will end when his condition has improved. Where the claimant's condition is expected to improve within the nine month period (e.g. he is scheduled for corrective surgery in the near future) the claimant will not qualify for benefit, but DWP guidance suggests that he may still be scheduled for review in case the surgery is postponed or unsuccessful.

Information or evidence required for determining limited or severely limited ability to carry out activities

8.—(1) The Secretary of State may require C to provide any information or evidence required to determine whether C has limited ability or severely limited ability to carry out daily living activities or mobility activities. 4.185

(2) Where information or evidence is requested under paragraph (1), C must provide the information or evidence to the Secretary of State within one month from the date of the request being made or within such longer period as the Secretary of State may consider reasonable in the circumstances of the particular case.

(3) Where C fails without good reason to comply with the request referred to in paragraph (1), a negative determination in relation to the component to which the failure related must be made.

GENERAL NOTE

The procedure to be followed on a claim for PIP is described in detail on the DWP website. In brief it is envisaged that most PIP claims will commence with a telephone call or by an online application. For claimants who do not have access to the DWP website, or to a telephone, or who are uncomfortable using one, a paper route is available. When a claim has been received it should contain sufficient information for the DM to decide if the "lay" conditions of entitlement are satisfied. These are the conditions as to residence and presence— see regs 16-23 below. 4.186

Provided those are satisfied the DM will issue a claimant questionnaire to gather information about the claimant's condition. The claimant will be invited at the same time to provide any supporting information and details of his health care professional and others who may be able to help determine his condition. The DM refers the file to the HCP provider. The HCP can then decide whether further evidence is necessary, (which may be obtained by telephone), whether he can then (or with any further evidence obtained) make a report on the basis of the "paperwork" (in fact an e-file) that is available to him, or whether there should be a face-to-face interview with the claimant. In most cases there will be an interview with the claimant. This assessment interview can be at the provider's premises, some other location or, if necessary, in the claimant's home. In claims based upon terminal illness there is a special fast-track procedure that will not involve a face-to-face interview.

The question of whether medical reports and evidence that supported a previous award of DLA should be available to a tribunal when the claimant has appealed following transition from DLA to PIP has been considered in several cases. In *GD v SSWP (PIP)* [2017] UKUT 415 (AAC) it emerged that in all transition cases when the claimant is first interviewed by an officer of the DWP on the PIP claim, the claimant will always be asked if they wish evidence that was used for the DLA award to be considered in relation to their claim for PIP. This question does not appear on the PIP claim form. The SSWP also confirmed that where that information has been asked for by the claimant and used in making a decision it should subsequently appear as part of that claimant's file and be available on an appeal. Judge Markus QC returned the case for a rehearing, but in the light of this information and the fact that although the criteria for DLA and for PIP are different it was, in this case, likely that the information that had supported the award of DLA would have been relevant in assessing the report of the HCP, the judge directed that the SSWP provide that evidence to the new FTT if it were available. (She had also been provided with information from the DWP as to how long such evidence was retained in certain circumstances; that information appears in the judgment).

The information that claimants who are to be transitioned are asked this question will probably come as a surprise to a number of judges who have decided similar cases in the past. In *AP v SSWP (PIP)* [2016] UKUT 416 (AAC) Judge Hemingway decided just such a case. There, the representative of the SSWP had accepted that there was a duty to provide a copy of all documents in the DM's possession that were relevant to the claim, but argued that because the criteria for DLA and for PIP were different and because any medical evidence or other report would necessarily relate to a different time, that such evidence would rarely be required. Judge Hemingway decided this case on the basis that the FTT had erred in law in failing to give sufficient weight to medical evidence with which they had been provided, but he gave as his opinion, as well, that in a case like this, where the claimant had alleged that there was copious evidence relating to the DLA award, that the SSWP should provide at least a list of that evidence, and that the FTT should consider asking for that evidence to be produced where, as here, there was a marked disparity in the decision that had been reached on the award of DLA and that for PIP. He suggests that it might be so too, where there was reason to think that the HCP report might be unreliable; given the frequency with which that is said to be the case by PIP claimants this might turn out to be quite frequent. Judge Hemingway noted that a different conclusion had been reached in *DC v SSWP (PIP)* [2016] UKUT 117 (AAC) but there the DLA evidence related to the claimant's condition eight years before, as well as to the differing criteria. The same point is made by Judge Gray in *MA v SSWP (PIP)* [2017] UKUT 351 (AAC). She directs that the new FTT to whom the case was remitted should be provided with both the relevant DLA award evidence and also evidence from an ESA examination.

It appears that the directions now given to DM preparing cases for appeal to a tribunal may be different from those that applied in earlier cases. That emerges from the information that is contained in the decision of Judge Markus QC in *CH and KN v SSWP (PIP)* [2018] UKUT 330 (AAC). That case, and others, is discussed in the General Note following reg.4 above. Members of FTT will find the guidance offered by Judge Markus and the information provided by the Secretary of State regarding the current process used in transfer cases very helpful.

Claimant may be called for a consultation to determine whether the claimant has limited or severely limited ability to carry out activities

9.—(1) Where it falls to be determined whether C has limited ability or severely limited ability to carry out daily living activities or mobility activities, C may be required to do either or both of the following— 4.187

(a) attend for and participate in a consultation in person;

(b) participate in a consultation by telephone [[1] or by video.]

(2) Subject to paragraph (3), where C fails without good reason to attend for or participate in a consultation referred to in paragraph (1), a negative determination must be made.

(3) Paragraph (2) does not apply unless—

(a) written notice of the date, time and, where applicable, place for, the consultation is sent to C at least 7 days in advance; or

(b) C agrees, whether in writing or otherwise, to accept a shorter period of notice of those matters.

(4) In paragraph (3), reference to written notice includes notice sent by electronic communication where C has agreed to accept correspondence in that way and "electronic communication" has the meaning given in section 15(1) of the Electronic Communications Act 2000.

(5) In this regulation, a reference to consultation is to a consultation with a person approved by the Secretary of State.

AMENDMENT

1. Social Security (Claims and Payments, Employment and Support Allowance, Personal Independence Payment and Universal Credit) (Telephone and Video Assessment) (Amendment) Regulations 2021 (SI 2021/230) reg.5 (March 25, 2021). This regulation applies only to England and Wales. For Scotland, the Social Security (Industrial Injuries Benefit and Personal Independence Payment) (Telephone and Video Assessment) (Miscellaneous Amendments) (Scotland) Regulations 2021 (SI 2021/97 reg.3 makes the same amendment with effect from the same date.

GENERAL NOTE

See notes to reg.8 above. Where the consultation is by telephone a written record of the conversation must be made and must be read back to the claimant. Where there is a face-to-face consultation the claimant may be permitted to record the interview, but only an aural recording, only on certain equipment and only if that then permits him to provide a full and accurate copy of the recording immediately the interview ends. 4.188

The use of a covert recording of the claimant's consultation with an HCP has been considered by Judge Wikeley in *JB v SSWP (PIP)* [2019] UKUT 179 (AAC). The claimant had made an audio-recording of his interview with the HCP in the light, as he put it, of previous experiences with the ATOS (now IAS) system. Although there was no clear assertion that this recording had been made covertly, it appeared from the appeal file that it was almost certainly so, and Judge Wikeley assumed, for the purposes of this appeal, that it was made covertly. The claimant said that he had made the recording on a Dictaphone and later transferred that information to a standard cassette tape format on which he had supplied copies to the DWP, IAS and the tribunal service. He had later supplied also, a handwritten transcript of the tape. The FTT before whom his appeal was heard effectively avoided the question of what use might properly be made of the tape by making no direct reference to either the HCP report or to the tape; the reasons for decision said simply that they had considered all the evidence before them. Permission to appeal had been given on the question whether it was an error of law not to deal directly with the admissibility of the tape-recorded evidence. Judge Wikeley held that it was, because the crux of the claimant's appeal turned on the difference between the account of their interview given by the HCP and that asserted by the claimant. The judge refers to r.15 of the Tribunal Procedure (First-tier Tribunal) (Social Entitlement Chamber) Rules 2008 (SI 2008/2685). The evidence on the tape-recording was clearly relevant and under r.15(2)(a)(i) could be admitted; the question then came down to whether it would be "unfair" to admit that evidence-see r.15(2)(b)(iii). In finding that it would not be "unfair" to admit the recorded evidence Judge Wikeley refers to a decision of the Employment Appeal Tribunal in *Chairman and Governors of Amwell View School v Dogherty* [2007] ICR 135 where it was held that evidence recorded covertly in a disciplinary hearing was admissible. Although the context in which the recordings were made are very different, the judge thought that in both, a party faced with what they regarded as a much more powerful opponent had resorted to the means of covert recording and in both it was not unfair to admit that evidence.

Two other cases have been decided on the operation of this regulation. The regulation calls for a claimant to co-operate by attending for assessment with a HCP or by taking part in a telephone conversation to assist in determining their claim. Where a claimant fails to do so, without good reason, para.(2) provides that a "negative determination must be made". Matters to be taken into account in determining "good reason" are defined in reg.10; they include the claimant's state of health and the nature of any disability.

In the first case, *SY v SSWP (PIP)* [2017] UKUT 363 (AAC) Judge Wikeley allowed the claimant's appeal against a decision that she had failed without good reason to attend or participate in a consultation to which she had been called in accordance with reg.9. This case reveals the problems that can arise in consequence of confusion about the roles of the DWP and of the provider of the independent assessment (in this case ATOS). The claimant, who had several mental health conditions, had made telephone calls to both the DWP and to ATOS. Before the UT the representative of the SSWP accepted that, as a result of these calls, the claimant had been told, and reasonably believed, that she was not required to attend for an assessment provided that she filed further medical evidence, which she had done. Indeed, before the UT a letter was produced that had been sent by ATOS clearly stating that she should not attend as the appointment was cancelled; this letter was not before the FTT. In the light of this, as well as other evidence, the judge was able to allow the appeal and directed that the claim be allowed to proceed for decision by the DM on the evidence that was available to him. What this case does highlight is the lack of any evidence provided to the FTT in support of the negative determination. The papers before the FTT and the UT simply recited that the claimant had failed to attend on four occasions when appointments had been made for her; no evidence was available in the form of appointment letters, other correspondence, records of telephone calls or otherwise, in support of these allegations. Judge Wikeley thought that, at the very least, such information should be provided. Judge Wikeley has dealt with this issue again, twice in respect of the same claimant, the second appeal being *TC v SSWP (No.2) (PIP)* [2018] UKUT 286 (AAC). On both occasions he emphasises the importance of FTT examining thoroughly the evidence on which the decision to reach a negative determination has been made. Yet another consideration of the complications that have arisen from confusion in the DWP and in the FTT are illustrated by another decision of Judge Wikeley in *AI v SSWP (PIP)* [2019] UKUT 103 (AAC). In this case the claimant had failed both to return a medical enquiry form under reg. 8, and to attend an assessment under reg.9. An appeal made originally against the reg. 8 decision but subsequently treated as an appeal against the striking out of his claim after he had eventually attended an assessment and been awarded 0 points was allowed by Judge Wikeley because it did not appear that at any time the DM had taken a decision to refuse benefit!

The second case, a decision of Judge Mesher in *OM v SSWP (PIP)* [2017] UKUT 458 (AAC), has the added complication that the claimant had an appointee in respect of his dealings with the DWP. The construction of reg.9 does not sit comfortably with that situation. In this case too, the judge was able to allow the appeal and reinstate the claim. But here, the decision to discontinue the PIP claim had meant also the termination of the claimant's DLA claim, so that claim was also reinstated. This case again illustrates the confusion that arises from communication being between the appointee (this time with assistance also from a representative some of the time) and both DWP and the healthcare assessment provider (ATOS). The appointee had requested that the claimant be seen at a home visit; at some stage this was approved by the DWP, but was refused by ATOS on the ground of past incidents of aggression by the claimant. Judge Mesher allowed the appeal, ultimately, on the ground that the FTT had not taken a broad enough view of the factors to be considered in relation to the rejection of the element of good reason in reaching a decision of negative determination. Reg.10 "includes" the two reasons given above, but in the judge's view (applying an approach similar to that which has applied to jobseeker's allowance and formerly to unemployment benefit) regard should be had also to the suitability for that claimant of the arrangements that had been made for assessment. As well, he thought that the claimant should be entitled to include in his reasons the likelihood of that assessment producing any evidence that was not to be obtained already from his medical reports and possibly from evidence on his DLA award if that were relevant. The judge suggests also that where the FTT gave as the crux of their decision that the claimant had, in the end, made a conscious choice not to attend the appointment, they had failed to deal sufficiently, or at any rate failed to record their reasons for not doing so, with the fact that the claimant had an appointee whose very existence suggests that the DWP accepted that he was not capable of organising his own affairs when dealing with a claim. He observed also that the language they had used in this part of their decision—that the claimant had not shown that he was "incapable" of attending and that he was not "prevented" from attending, might indicate that they were applying a higher standard than the words of the regulation—having "good reason" not to attend. Judge Mesher outlines a number of other concerns raised by this appeal without reaching final conclusions on them.

Some of these questions, at least, have been resolved by two further decisions of the UT. The first, another decision of Judge Mesher, is *MB v SSWP (PIP)* [2018] UKUT 213 (AAC). In this case no copy of the letter requiring the claimant's attendance for a consultation was included in the appeal papers, nor was there a copy of the standard letter in use at the time. Instead, the appeal papers referred only to the claimant having been "invited" to attend. Judge Mesher in this case applied the words that he had expressed as a provisional view in the *OM* case above. These were, that the FTT must have before it, either a copy of the actual letter that was sent to the claimant, or at least a copy of the standard form letter in use at that time and that the letter must use language from which it was clear that the request to attend was a *requirement* and not merely a request. In that case, and the current decision, it was not enough to prove just that a letter had been sent to the claimant giving the date, time and place of an appointment. Judge Mesher observes that in the grounds giving permission to appeal in the current case specific reference had been made to his decision in the *OM* case and the observation there made, but no submission on the matter had been received on behalf of the Secretary of State. He took this to mean that the view he had expressed in that case could now be regarded as settled. He found support for this also in the decision of Judge Rowland in *SSWP v DC (JSA)* [2017] UKUT 464 (AAC), a case on the imposition of a sanction but raising a similar point.

This position was also accepted in *IR v SSWP (PIP)* [2019] UKUT 374 (AAC) by Judge Wikeley. He goes on as well to consider whether the HCP standard letter used in that case by ATOS did impose a *requirement* to attend. In the Judge's view it did not. Despite the letter using the phrases "It is important that you attend this appointment" and "if you fail to attend without good reason the [DWP] is likely to disallow your claim", Judge Wikeley held that this was not sufficient to make the letter one that "required" the claimant to attend, which was the form of words used in both s.80 of the Welfare Reform Act 2012 (the section that empowered the making of this provision) and in reg.9 itself. On behalf of the Secretary of State it was argued that the words used were an acceptable compromise between compulsion and not wanting to frighten a claimant into fear of attending when it was in their interest to do so. Even so, Judge Wikeley thought that the words used must fail the test- the first phrase made clear that attendance was desirable or highly recommended, but not that it was mandatory; the second was also inaccurate because the effect of reg.9 is not just that the claim is likely to be refused, but that it *must* be refused in the absence of the claimant showing good reason for non-attendance. Judge Wikeley thought there was no reason not to say, "You must attend this appointment" and "If you fail to do so without good reason the [DWP] will disallow your claim". In his view that is what is required by the decisions of the Court of Appeal in *Hooper v SSWP* [2007] EWCA Civ 495 and of the Supreme Court in *R (Reilly and Wilson) v SSWP* [2013] UKSC 68; [2014] AACR 9. Note however, that as this appeal had been resolved on different grounds his observations were not strictly a part of the decision on the case.

The same conclusion has been reached by Judge Poynter in a strongly worded decision regarding the parallel provisions that apply in a claim for Employment Support Allowance- see *PPE v SSWP (ESA)* [2020] UKUT 59 (AAC). The judge held that a letter requiring attendance at a Work Capability Assessment must use "the language of clear and unambiguous mandatory requirement". He held that the letter sent, in this case by Medical Services, was only an invitation to attend and therefore the claimant could not have "failed" to attend as the regulations required. He confirms too, that the appeal file must contain either a copy of the letter sent or, at least a copy of the standard form in use at that time and evidence that a letter in that form had been generated by the computer system and dispatched. He concludes that in the absence of such evidence the proper course of action for an FTT to take in such cases, is to allow the appeal and to reinstate the claim.

Matters to be taken into account in determining good reason in relation to regulations 8 and 9

4.189 **10.** The matters to be taken into account in determining whether C has good reason under regulation 8(3) or 9(2) include—

(a) C's state of health at the relevant time; and

(b) the nature of any disability that C has.

General Note

4.190 Where the claimant fails to return a questionnaire within one month, (see reg.8 above) or if he fails to attend an interview, or to respond to a telephone consultation the DM may make a negative determination (refuse the claim) after having due regard to the matters above i.e. the claimant's state of health and their disabling condition—e.g. a claimant suffering from depression so as not to be able to manage his affairs effectively.

The claimant will have the right to appeal against that determination, but in most cases it will be as well to commence a new claim unless there has been a long delay before the appeal is commenced.

Re-determination of ability to carry out activities

4.191 **11.** Where it has been determined that C has limited ability or severely limited ability to carry out either or both daily living activities or mobility activities, the Secretary of State may, for any reason and at any time, determine afresh in accordance with regulation 4 whether C continues to have such limited ability or severely limited ability.

General Note

This regulation appears to mean that PIP, unlike DLA can be reviewed and superseded by the Secretary of State at any time and for any reason; there would be no need to identify a change of circumstances as has been necessary in respect of other benefits. However, there may be reason to question that conclusion. The literal interpretation that the regulation invites seems to be inconsistent with the provisions made in the relevant Decisions and Appeals regulations (Universal Credit, Personal Independence Payment, Jobseeker's Allowance and Employment Support Allowance (Decisions and Appeals) Regulations 2013 (SI 2013/381). In which case it may be more correct to interpret this regulation merely as authorising a reassessment, in accordance with reg.4, of the claimant's capability at any time, though it would still remain necessary to show that there is a ground for revision or supersession in accordance with the Decisions and Appeals regulations. This, more limited interpretation, of the regulation has been adopted by Judge Mesher in *KB v SSWP (PIP)* [2016] UKUT 537 (AAC). He concludes, though only provisionally because in the event it was not necessary for him to decide the point, that regulation 11 only creates the opportunity for the Secretary of State to re-determine the issue of the claimant's abilities in relation to the prescribed activities and that it remains necessary thereafter for the normal decision process of supersession to be followed under the Decisions and Appeals Regulations. That this interpretation of the regulation is correct is now affirmed in a series of UT decisions— see *DS v SSWP (PIP)* [2016] UKUT 538 (AAC); [2017] AACR 19, *KB v SSWP (PIP)* [2016] UKUT 537 (AAC), *PM v SSWP (PIP)* [2017] UKUT 37 (AAC) and *TH v SSWP (PIP)* [2017] UKUT 231 (AAC). A full analysis of the provisions and the procedure to be followed is provided in the decision of Judge Wright in the *PM* case. And see too, the decision in *BD v SSWP (PIP)* [2020] UKUT 178 (AAC), where these decisions are confirmed again by Judge Jacobs. 4.192

Part 3

Required period condition

Required period condition: daily living component

12.—(1) C meets the required period condition for the purposes of section 78(1) of the Act (daily living component at standard rate) where— 4.193

(a) if C had been assessed at every time in the period of 3 months ending with the prescribed date, it is likely that the Secretary of State would have determined at that time that C had limited ability to carry out daily living activities; and

(b) if C were to be assessed at every time in the period of 9 months beginning with the day after the prescribed date, it is likely that the Secretary of State would determine at that time that C had limited ability to carry out daily living activities.

(2) C meets the required period condition for the purposes of section 78(2) of the Act (daily living component at enhanced rate) where—

(a) if C had been assessed at every time in the period of 3 months ending with the prescribed date, it is likely that the Secretary of State would have determined at that time that C had severely limited ability to carry out daily living activities; and

(b) if C were to be assessed at every time in the period of 9 months beginning with the day after the prescribed date, it is likely that the Secretary of State would determine at that time that C had severely limited ability to carry out daily living activities.

General Note

4.194 See above the notes to reg.7.

Required period condition: mobility component

4.195 **13.**—(1) C meets the required period condition for the purposes of section 79(1) of the Act (mobility component at standard rate) where—

(a) if C had been assessed at every time in the period of 3 months ending with the prescribed date, it is likely that the Secretary of State would have determined at that time that C had limited ability to carry out mobility activities; and

(b) if C were to be assessed at every time in the period of 9 months beginning with the day after the prescribed date, it is likely that the Secretary of State would determine at that time that C had limited ability to carry out mobility activities.

(2) C meets the required period condition for the purposes of section 79(2) of the Act (mobility component at enhanced rate) where—

(a) if C had been assessed at every time in the period of 3 months ending with the prescribed date, it is likely that the Secretary of State would have determined at that time that C had severely limited ability to carry out mobility activities; and

(b) if C were to be assessed at every time in the period of 9 months beginning with the day after the prescribed date, it is likely that the Secretary of State would determine at that time that C had severely limited ability to carry out mobility activities.

General Note

4.196 See above the notes to reg.7.

The prescribed date

4.197 **14.** Except where paragraph (2) or (3) of regulation 15 [1 or paragraph (2) or (3) of regulation 15A] applies, the prescribed date is—

(a) where C has made a claim for personal independence payment which has not been determined, the date of that claim or, if later, the earliest date in relation to which, if C had been assessed in relation to C's ability to carry out daily living activities or, as the case may be, mobility activities, at every time in the previous 3 months, it is likely that the Secretary of State would have determined at that time that C had limited ability or, as the case may be, severely limited ability to carry out those activities; and

(b) where C has an award of either or both components, each day of that award.

Amendment

1. Social Security (Disability Assistance for Working Age People) (Consequential Amendments) Order 2022 (SI 2022/177) art.14 (March 21, 2022).

General Note

4.198 This means that the prescribed date (the date at which both the qualifying period and, a day later, the prospective period will run) will normally be the date of claim. But it may be a later date where the DM can determine that although the claimant would not have satisfied the assessment requirements at that date he has done so at some later time.

Where the claimant has an existing award of benefit para.(b) means that he must always be able to show that his condition can be expected to continue for the next nine months. This may create some difficulty where the claimant reports that he is expecting, within that period, to receive surgery or treatment that will greatly alleviate his condition.

This situation arose in *BM v SSWP (PIP)* [2017] UKUT 486 (AAC). The claimant had a recurring condition that was alleviated by periodic injections of cortisone, but the effect of those injections wore off and there was then a delay before he could get another injection. The claimant was in receipt of the Daily Living component and had claimed previously, unsuccessfully for the Mobility component. He notified the DWP of a deterioration in his condition and completed a new claim form. This claim was to be treated as a supersession of his existing award. The question that then arose was, what was to be treated as the relevant time period (both the past and the prospective period) for the purposes of s.81 of the Welfare Reform Act 2012. That was to be determined in accordance with para. (b) above, but Judge Bano decided that the words "each day of that award" did not mean every day of the award; to do that he thought would make nonsense of the provision because it would mean that the period would be elongated to the full term of the award. The words must mean instead any day of the award that was chosen by the FTT as the prescribed date—in this case the day on which the claimant had reported his deterioration. This Judge Bano held was correct, though he allowed the appeal on another ground.

The prescribed date: claims for personal independence payment after an interval

15.—(1) Paragraphs (2) and (3) apply where— 4.199

(a) C makes a claim for personal independence payment ("the new claim");

(b) C had a previous award [1 for personal independence payment or adult disability payment] which ended not more than 2 years before the date on which the new claim is made;

(c) the previous award referred to in sub-paragraph (b) [1, where that award was in respect of personal independence payment or adult disability payment,] consisted of the same component as the one to which C is entitled (or would be entitled if C met the required period condition) under the new claim; and

(d) the Secretary of State determines that the entitlement under the new claim results from—

(i) substantially the same physical or mental condition or conditions for which the previous award was made; or

(ii) a new physical or mental condition which developed as a result of a condition for which the previous award was made.

(2) In relation to determination of entitlement under the new claim—

(a) the prescribed date for the purposes of regulations 12(1)(a) and (2)(a) and 13(1)(a) and (2)(a) is the date on which the previous award ended [1, where that award was in respect of personal independence payment or adult disability payment,]; and

(b) regulations 12(1)(b) and (2)(b) and 13(1)(b) and (2)(b) have effect in relation to the new claim as if, for the words "the prescribed date" there were substituted "the date on which the new claim for personal independence payment is made".

(3) Where C is awarded either or both components under the new claim, in relation to continued entitlement to that component or, as the case may

be, those components, for the period of 3 months following the date of the new claim—

(a) the prescribed date for the purposes of regulations 12(1)(a) and (2)(a) and 13(1)(a) and (2)(a) is the date on which the previous award ended [[1], where that award was in respect of personal independence payment or adult disability payment,]; and

(b) regulations 12(1)(b) and (2)(b) and 13(1)(b) and (2)(b) have effect in relation to that award as if, for the words "the prescribed date" there were substituted "each day of the award".

(4) This regulation is subject to regulation 26.

AMENDMENT

1. Social Security (Disability Assistance for Working Age People) (Consequential Amendments) Order 2022 (SI 2022/177) art.14 (March 21, 2022).

GENERAL NOTE

4.200 This regulation assists claimants who have a condition that fluctuates in the sense that they may experience protracted periods of remission and then a further onset of the condition. Provided that the episodes of disability occur at intervals not greater than two years the claimant can re-qualify for benefit immediately (no qualifying period) so long as the award will be for the same component of PIP and so long as the new disability results from the same disabling condition, or another condition that is derived from the earlier one.

[[1] The prescribed date: claims for personal independence payment after award of Child Disability Payment

4.201 **15A.**—(1) Paragraphs (2), (3) and (4) apply where—

(a) C makes a claim for personal independence payment ("the new claim");

(b) C had a previous award of child disability payment which ended not more than 2 years before the date on which the new claim is made; and

(c) C is aged 16 years or over at the date of the new claim.

(2) In relation to determination of entitlement under the new claim—

(a) the prescribed date for the purposes of regulations 12(1)(a) and (2)(a) and 13(1)(a) and (2)(a) is the date on which the previous award ended where that award was in respect of child disability payment; and

(b) regulations 12(1)(b) and (2)(b) and 13(1)(b) and (2)(b) have effect in relation to the new claim as if, for the words "the prescribed date" there were substituted "the date on which the new claim for personal independence payment is made".

(3) Where C is awarded either or both components under the new claim, in relation to entitlement to that component or, as the case may be, those components, for the period of 3 months following the date of the new claim—

(a) the prescribed date for the purposes of regulations 12(1)(a) and (2)(a) and 13(1)(a) and (2)(a) is the date on which the previous award ended where that award was in respect of child disability payment; and

(b) regulations 12(1)(b) and (2)(b) and 13(1)(b) and (2)(b) have effect in relation to that award as if, for the words "the prescribed date" there were substituted "each day of the award".

(4) C is to be regarded as meeting such of the conditions contained in the following provisions of these Regulations (as modified by paragraphs (2)

and (3) above) as are relevant to C's new claim, regardless of whether those conditions have been met—

(a) in regulation 12 (required period condition: daily living component), paragraph (1)(a) or (2)(a);

(b) in regulation 13 (required period condition: mobility component), paragraph (1)(a) or (2)(a).]

AMENDMENT

1. Social Security (Disability Assistance for Working Age People) (Consequential Amendments) Order 2022 (SI 2022/177) art.14 (March 21, 2022).

PART 4

RESIDENCE AND PRESENCE CONDITIONS

Conditions relating to residence and presence in Great Britain

16. Subject to the following provisions of this Part, the prescribed conditions for the purposes of section 77(3) of the Act as to residence and presence in Great Britain are that on any day for which C claims personal independence payment C— 4.202

(a) is present in Great Britain;

(b) has been present in Great Britain for a period of, or periods amounting in aggregate to, not less than 104 weeks out of the 156 weeks immediately preceding that day;

(c) is habitually resident in the United Kingdom, the Republic of Ireland, the Isle of Man or the Channel Islands; and

(d) is a person—

  (i) who is not subject to immigration control within the meaning of section 115(9) of the Immigration and Asylum Act 1999; or

  (ii) to whom, by virtue of regulation 2 of the Social Security (Immigration and Asylum) Consequential Amendments Regulations 2000, section 115 of that Act does not apply for the purpose of personal independence payment.

GENERAL NOTE

A claimant must show that he is both present in Great Britain and habitually resident in what is commonly referred to as the common travel area (UK, Republic of Ireland, Channel Islands and the Isle of Man). 4.203

Presence is simply a matter of being physically present and is subject to exceptions in regs 17–23A below. Two cases demonstrate the effect of this regulation and the limitations of the exceptions provided.

In the first, *HRA v SSWP (PIP)* [2023] UKUT 109 (AAC) the claimant was a person with dual Afghan and British nationality. He had returned to Afghanistan to arrange visas for remaining members of his family to travel to Britain, but while there he was arrested and imprisoned for more than four years on what he said were entirely false charges. On his eventual return to Britain, he made a claim for PIP. That claim was refused under reg.16(b). Following an unsuccessful appeal to an FTT, he applied for leave to appeal to the UT. Judge Wikeley refused permission because no error of law in the decision of the FTT was shown. None of the exceptions provided for in regs 17–21 applied to his case and there is no general exception that could exempt a person who was unavoidably and blamelessly detained. Neither could Judge Wikeley see any basis for this regulation to be held to be invalid on the grounds of discrimination, or as being in breach of the claimant's human rights, following the decision of Judge Jacobs in *FM v SSWP (DLA)* [2017] UKUT 380 (AAC); [2019] AACR 9.

In the second case, *AT v SSWP (PIP)* [2023] UKUT 186 (AAC), the claimant was a British citizen who had been living in South Africa. She decided to return to Britain but was then prevented by a serious brain injury suffered after a fall. Although she wished still to return to Britain, the doctors treating her in South Africa refused to allow her to travel. She was detained in hospital and a nursing home for some three years. When she was eventually able to return to Britain she made an immediate application for PIP. Her claim was refused under reg.16(b) and, following an unsuccessful appeal to an FTT, she applied for leave to appeal to the UT. Her application was refused by Judge Wikeley for all the same reasons as above.

Habitual residence is more complicated. It is not defined in any statutory form, but it has been the subject of extensive case law, mainly in relation to means-tested benefits. (Details and discussion of these cases may be found in the notes to the relevant sections of Vol.II of this Work).

In brief, habitual residence requires that you have a settled intention to live in this country as your home, but not necessarily to live here permanently. As well, it requires that that the claimant has been in the country already for an extended period. How long he must have been here, will depend upon the circumstances of the claimant; a former resident returning from a period abroad may satisfy this test almost immediately, while a new immigrant may be required to demonstrate a considerable period of residence.

In *MM and SI v SSWP (DLA)* [2016] UKUT 149 (AAC) Judge Markus QC has held that reg.2(1)(a)(iii) of the DLA regulations, the equivalent of reg.16(b) of these regulations (the past presence test or PPT) must be disapplied in respect of claims made on behalf of applicants who were family members of persons granted refugee status in the UK. She held that the PPT was indirectly discriminatory and could not be justified (when compared to the treatment of UK nationals) under art.28 of the EU Directive 2004/83/EC (which gives protection to refugees) and which she held had direct effect in the UK. For the same reason she held that PPT was in breach of the claimant's rights under art.14 of the ECHR. At the time the claims were made, the applicants satisfied the other conditions of reg.2 which meant that their claims should proceed accordingly. That decision was in respect of a claim for DLA, but the ruling applies equally to a claim for personal independence payment.

Absence from Great Britain

4.204 **17.**—(1) Where C is temporarily absent from Great Britain, C is treated as present in Great Britain for the purposes of regulation 16(a) and (b) for the first 13 weeks of absence.

(2) C is temporarily absent if, at the beginning of the period of absence, C's absence is unlikely to exceed 52 weeks.

Absence from Great Britain to receive medical treatment

4.205 **18.**—(1) Where C is temporarily absent from Great Britain, C is treated as present in Great Britain for the purposes of regulation 16(a) and (b) for the first 26 weeks of that absence, where—

(a) C's absence is solely in connection with arrangements made for the medical treatment of C for a disease or bodily or mental disablement which commenced before C left Great Britain; and
(b) the arrangements referred to in paragraph (1)(a) relate to medical treatment—
  (i) outside Great Britain;
  (ii) during the period whilst C is temporarily absent from Great Britain; and

(iii) by, or under the supervision of, a person appropriately qualified to carry out that treatment.

(2) In this regulation, "temporarily absent" has the same meaning as in regulation 17(2).

DEFINITIONS

"medical treatment" – see reg.2

Absence from Great Britain in special cases

19.—(1) Where C is absent from Great Britain, C is treated as present in Great Britain for the purposes of regulation 16(a) and (b), where— **4.206**

(a) C is abroad in the capacity of—
  (i) a member of Her Majesty's forces;
  (ii) an aircraft worker; or
  (iii) a mariner; or
(b) C is in employment prescribed for the purposes of section 120 (employment at sea (continental shelf operations)) of the Social Security Contributions and Benefits Act 1992 in connection with continental shelf operations; or
(c) C is living with a person mentioned in paragraph (a)(i) and is the spouse, civil partner, son, daughter, step-son, step-daughter, father, father-in-law, step-father, mother, mother-in-law or step-mother of that person.

(2) In this regulation and in regulation 20, "a member of Her Majesty's forces" means a member of "the regular forces" or "the reserve forces" as defined in section 374 of the Armed Forces Act 2006, other than a person who is specified in Schedule 2, who is—

(a) over the age of 16; and
(b) not absent on desertion.

(3) In this regulation—

"aircraft worker" means a person who is employed under a contract of service either as a pilot, commander, navigator or other member of the crew of any aircraft, or in any other capacity on board any aircraft where—

(a) the employment in that other capacity is for the purposes of the aircraft or its crew or of any passengers or cargo or mail carried on that aircraft; and
(b) the contract is entered into in the United Kingdom with a view to its performance (in whole or in part) while the aircraft is in flight, but does not include a person who is in employment as a member of Her Majesty's forces;

"mariner" means a person who is in employment under a contract of service either as a master or member of the crew of any ship or vessel, or in any other capacity on board any ship or vessel where—

(a) the employment in that other capacity is for the purposes of that ship or vessel or the crew or any passengers or cargo or mail carried by the ship or vessel; and
(b) the contract is entered into in the United Kingdom with a view to its performance (in whole or in part) while the ship or vessel is on voyage, but does not include a person who is in employment as a member of Her Majesty's forces.

Serving members of Her Majesty's forces and their family members—further provision

4.207 **20.** C is treated as habitually resident in Great Britain for the purposes of regulation 16(c) where—

(a) C is resident outside Great Britain in the capacity of a member of Her Majesty's forces; or

(b) C is living with a person mentioned in paragraph (a) and is the spouse, civil partner, son, daughter, step-son, step-daughter, father, father-in-law, step-father, mother, mother-in-law or step-mother of that person.

Terminal illness

4.208 **21.** Where C is terminally ill and makes a claim for personal independence payment expressly on that ground, regulation 16 applies as if paragraph (b) were omitted.

GENERAL NOTE

4.209 The claimant must still be present in Great Britain (or treated as present—see regs 17, 18 and 19 above) but if the claim is made on the basis of terminal illness it will not be necessary to show that they have been in the country for two out of the past three years.

The claimant must still be habitually resident in the common travel area and not subject to immigration control etc.

Persons residing in Great Britain to whom a relevant EU Regulation applies

4.210 **22.** Regulation 16(b) does not apply in relation to a claim for personal independence payment where on any day—

(a) C is habitually resident in Great Britain;

(b) a relevant EU Regulation applies; and

(c) C can demonstrate a genuine and sufficient link to the United Kingdom social security system.

GENERAL NOTE

4.211 The relevant EU regulations are those specified in s.84 of the WRA 2012.

If the claimant is an EU national he will still need to be present in Great Britain though not necessarily for 104 weeks out of the past 156 weeks. He will also need to be habitually resident in Great Britain and to demonstrate a sufficient link to the UK social security system.

The aggregation of periods of residence in another EU country has been considered by Judge Jacobs in *BK v SSWP and SSWP v MM* [2016] UKUT 547 (AAC). Relying on the case of *Stewart v SSWP* (C-503/09), the Judge held that mere residence in this country was not sufficient to aggregate that time with time spent in another EU country. The judge also held that the part of the regulation that required the claimant to show a link to the social security system of the United Kingdom (as distinct from just a link to the UK) was void. This case was appealed to the CA, where it is reported as *Kavanagh & Mohamed v SSWP* [2019] EWCA Civ 272; [2019] AACR 21 (UT and CA). There, the Secretary of State did not challenge Judge Jacobs' view that that part of the regulation was invalid. The Court of Appeal effectively adopted his ruling, though, on the facts of the case, they found that the claimant had shown a sufficient link. For a more detailed account see Vol.III of this work.

Persons residing in an EEA state [1…] or in Switzerland to whom a relevant EU Regulation applies

23. Regulation 16(a) to (c) does not apply in relation to entitlement to the daily living component of personal independence payment where on any day— 4.212

(a) C is habitually resident in—

(i) an EEA state [1…]; or

(ii) Switzerland;

(b) a relevant EU Regulation applies; and

(c) C can demonstrate a genuine and sufficient link to the United Kingdom social security system.

AMENDMENT

1. Social Security (Amendment) (EU Exit) Regulations 2019 (SI 2019/128) reg.4 and Sch. para.10 (January 31, 2020).

GENERAL NOTE

The relevant EU regulations are those specified in s.84 of the WRA 2012. 4.213

A claimant who satisfies those regulations and is living abroad will be entitled to PIP (daily living component) if they are habitually resident in an EEA country not being the UK or Switzerland, and if they can demonstrate a sufficient link to the UK social security system. In *SSWP v LT* [2012] UKUT 282 (AAC) it was held, in relation to a claim for DLA (care component), that the claimant had a sufficient connection to the social security system when she had a past record of contributions and an expectation of Retirement Pension in the future.

This decision, and therefore that of the UT, has been upheld by the answers provided by the EUECJ. (See *SSWP v Tolley* [2017] EUECJ C-430/15). They confirm that the care component is a "sickness benefit" and that the claimant's past contribution record made her an "employed person" and therefore within the protection of the regulation. This case is concerned with the old Regulation 1408/71 but it is likely that the same result would follow under the current Regulation 883/04.

[1 Persons in receipt of an equivalent Scottish benefit who move from Scotland to England or Wales

[2 **23ZA.** (1)] Where regulation 36(1) of the Disability Assistance for Children and Young People (Scotland) Regulations 2021 applies to C, regulation 16(c) of these Regulations is treated as not satisfied for the period set out in regulation 36(1) of those Regulations.]

[2 (2) Where regulation 53(1) of the Disability Assistance for Working Age People (Scotland) Regulations 2022 applies to C, regulation 16(c) of these Regulations is treated as not satisfied for the period set out in regulation 53(1) of those Regulations.]

AMENDMENTS

1. Scotland Act 2016 (Social Security) (Consequential Provision) (Miscellaneous Amendment) Regulations 2021 (SI 2021/804) reg.6 (July 26, 2021).

2. Scotland Act 2016 (Social Security) (Adult Disability Payment and Child Disability Payment) (Amendment) Regulations 2022 (SI 2022/335) reg.7 (March 21, 2022).

[1[2 Refugees and certain persons with leave to enter or remain in the United Kingdom]

4.214 **23A.** (1)—Regulation 16(b) does not apply in relation to a claim for personal independence payment where C has—

(a) been granted refugee status or humanitarian protection under the immigration rules; [2 ...]

(b) leave to enter or to remain in the United Kingdom as the dependant of a person granted refugee status or humanitarian protection under the immigration rules;

[2 (c) leave to enter or remain in the United Kingdom granted under the immigration rules by virtue of—

(i) the Afghan Relocations and Assistance Policy; or

(ii) the previous scheme for locally-employed staff in Afghanistan (sometimes referred to as the ex-gratia scheme);

(d) been granted discretionary leave outside the immigration rules as a dependant of a person referred to in sub-paragraph (c);

(e) leave granted under the Afghan Citizens Resettlement Scheme] [3 [4 [5 ...]]]

(f) leave to enter or remain in the United Kingdom granted under or outside the immigration rules [4, a right] of abode in the United Kingdom within the meaning given in section 2 of the Immigration Act 1971 [4 or does not require leave to enter or remain in the United Kingdom in accordance with section 3ZA of that Act,]where the person—

(i) was residing in Ukraine immediately before 1st January 2022; and

(ii) left Ukraine in connection with the Russian invasion which took place on 24th February 2022; [5 or

(g) leave to enter or remain in the United Kingdom granted under or outside the immigration rules, a right of abode in the United Kingdom within the meaning given in section 2 of the Immigration Act 1971 or does not require leave to enter or remain in the United Kingdom in accordance with section 3ZA of that Act, where the person—

(i) was residing in Sudan before 15th April 2023; and

(ii) left Sudan in connection with the violence which rapidly escalated on 15th April 2023 in Khartoum and across Sudan;] [6, or

(h) leave to enter or remain in the United Kingdom granted under or outside the immigration rules, a right of abode in the United Kingdom within the meaning given in section 2 of the Immigration Act 1971 or does not require leave to enter or remain in the United Kingdom in accordance with section 3ZA of that Act, where the person—

(i) was residing in Israel, the West Bank, the Gaza Strip, East Jerusalem, the Golan Heights or Lebanon immediately before 7th October 2023; and

(ii) left Israel, the West Bank, the Gaza Strip, East Jerusalem, the Golan Heights or Lebanon in connection with the Hamas terrorist attack in Israel on 7th October 2023 or the violence which rapidly escalated in the region following the attack.]

[2 (1A) Regulation 16(c) shall not apply where [3 any sub-paragraph in paragraph (1)] applies to the person.]

(2) For the purposes of this regulation "immigration rules" means the rules laid before Parliament under section 3(2) of the Immigration Act 1971.]

AMENDMENTS

1. Social Security (Miscellaneous Amendments No.4) Regulations 2017 (SI 2017/1015) reg.14 (November 16, 2017).

2. Social Security (Habitual Residence and Past Presence) (Amendment) Regulations 2021 (SI 2021/1034) reg.4 (September 15, 2021). The amendments made by these regulations apply in respect of England and Wales only. The same amendments are made with effect from the same date in respect of Scotland only by reg.2 of the Social Security (Residence Requirements) (Afghanistan) (Scotland) Regulations 2021 (SI 2021/320) but in addition that regulation also substitutes for paragraph (2) of reg.2C the following—

"(2) For the purposes of this regulation—

(a) "immigration rules" means the rules laid before Parliament under section 3(2) of the Immigration Act 1971,

(b) "the Afghan Citizens Resettlement Scheme" means the scheme announced by the United Kingdom Government on 18 August 2021."

3. Social Security (Habitual Residence and Past Presence) (Amendment) Regulations 2022 (SI 2022/344) reg.4 (March 22, 2022). Note: this regulation applies only to England and Wales. Identical provision is made for Scotland, with effect from the same date, by the Social Security (Residence Requirements) (Ukraine) (Scotland) Regulations 2022 (SSI 2022/108).

4. Social Security (Habitual Residence and Past Presence (Amendment) (No. 2) Regulations 2022 (SI 2022/990) reg.3 (October 18, 2022). Note: this regulation applies only to England and Wales. Identical provision is made for Scotland by the Social Security (Miscellaneous Amendment and Transitional Provision) (Scotland) Regulations 2022 (SI 2022/336) reg.6 (November 28, 2022).

5. Social Security (Habitual Residence and Past Presence) (Amendment) Regulations 2023 (SI 2023/532) reg.4 (May 15, 2023). Note: this regulation applies only to England and Wales. Identical provision is made for Scotland with effect from May 17, 2023, by reg.2 of the Social Security (Residence Requirements) (Sudan) (Scotland) Regulations 2023 (SSI 2023/149).

6. Social Security (Habitual Residence and Past Presence, and Capital Disregards) (Amendment) Regulations 2023 (SI 2023/1144) reg.10 (October 27, 2023). Note: this amendment applies only to England and Wales. Identical provision is made for Scotland with effect from October 26, 2023, by the Social Security (Residence and Presence Requirements) (Israel, West Bank, the Gaza Strip, East Jerusalem, the Golan Heights and Lebanon) (Scotland) Regulations 2023 (SSI 2023/309).

PART 5

RATE OF PERSONAL INDEPENDENCE PAYMENT

Rate of personal independence payment

24.—(1) The prescribed weekly rates of the daily living component for the purposes of section 78(3) of the Act are— 4.215

(a) the standard rate, [1 £72.65]; and

(b) the enhanced rate, [1 £108.55].

(2) The prescribed weekly rates of the mobility component for the purposes of section 79(3) of the Act are—

(a) the standard rate, [1 £28.70]; and

(b) the enhanced rate, [1 £75.75].

AMENDMENT

1. Social Security Benefits Up-rating Order 2024 (SI 2024/242) art.15 (April 8, 2024). This Order applies only to England and Wales. For Scotland, the Social Security Up-rating (Scotland) Order 2024 (SSI 2024/106) art.8 makes the same amendments with effect from the same date.

PART 6

PROVISIONS RELATING TO AGE

Exceptions to section 83 where entitlement exists or claim made before relevant age

4.216 **25.** Section 83(1) of the Act (persons of pensionable age) does not apply where C has reached the relevant age if C—

(a) was entitled to an award of either or both components on the day preceding the day on which C reached the relevant age; or

(b) made a claim for personal independence payment before reaching the relevant age and that claim was not determined before C reached that age but an award of either or both components would be made in respect of C but for section 83(1) of the Act.

GENERAL NOTE

4.217 No new claim for PIP can normally be made beyond the "relevant age"—this means pensionable age.

Persons who have an award of PIP at the time they reach the relevant age will be able to continue entitlement to PIP so long as they continue to satisfy the other conditions of entitlement. Given that by 2017 all awards of DLA for persons of working age should have been converted to PIP it does mean that DLA for the elderly will disappear eventually.

Persons who have made a claim for PIP before reaching the relevant age will also be entitled to continue that entitlement if their claim is successful.

Claim for personal independence payment after an interval and after reaching the relevant age

4.218 **26.**—(1) Where C has reached the relevant age and makes a new claim in the circumstances set out in regulation 15 the following exceptions apply.

(2) The exceptions referred to in paragraph (1) are—

(a) section 83(1) of the Act (persons of pensionable age) does not apply;

(b) the reference to "2 years" in regulation 15(1)(b) is to be read as "1 year";

(c) where C is assessed as having severely limited ability to carry out mobility activities for the purposes of the new claim—

(i) C is entitled to the enhanced rate of the mobility component only if C was entitled to that rate of that component under the previous award [1 of personal independence payment or adult disability payment]; and

(ii) where C is not entitled to the enhanced rate of that component because of paragraph (i), C is entitled to the standard rate of that component provided that C was entitled to that rate of that component under the previous award [1 of personal independence payment or adult disability payment]; and

(d) where C is assessed as having limited ability to carry out mobility activities for the purposes of the new claim, C is entitled to the standard rate of the mobility component only if C was entitled to that component, at either rate, under the previous award [1 of personal independence payment or adult disability payment].

AMENDMENT

1. Social Security (Disability Assistance for Working Age People) (Consequential Amendments) Order 2022 (SI 2022/177) art.14 (March 21, 2022).

GENERAL NOTE

A person who is over pensionable age may make a new claim for either component of PIP, subject to the same conditions that apply under reg.15, but only if the previous award referred to there ended no more than one year before the new claim is made. Where the new claim is in respect of a mobility component further restrictions apply. The award can only be for the enhanced rate where that rate was in payment in the previous claim; otherwise the award must be at the standard rate whatever the claimant's condition is now. (And the claimant must have been in receipt of the mobility component, presumably at that rate, in the previous award in order to satisfy reg.15). Where the claimant's condition now would justify only an award at the standard rate they can qualify for that rate if they were entitled to either rate in the previous award. 4.219

Revision and supersession of an award after the person has reached the relevant age

27.—(1) Subject to paragraph (2), section 83(1) of the Act (persons of pensionable age) does not apply where— 4.220

(a) C has reached the relevant age and is entitled to an award ("the original award") of either or both components pursuant to an exception in regulation 25 or 26; and

(b) that award falls to be revised or superseded.

[1(2) Where the original award includes an award of the mobility component and is superseded—

(a) pursuant to regulation 23 of the Decisions and Appeals Regulations for a relevant change of circumstance which occurred after C reached the relevant age; or

(b) pursuant to regulation 26(1)(a) of the Decisions and Appeals Regulations, where—

(i) the application for supersession was made by C after C reached the relevant age, or

(ii) the supersession proceedings were initiated by the Secretary of State after C reached the relevant age,

the restrictions in paragraph (3) apply in relation to the supersession.

(2A) In paragraph (2), "the Decisions and Appeals Regulations" means the Universal Credit, Personal Independence Payment, Jobseeker's Allowance and Employment and Support Allowance (Decisions and Appeals) Regulations 2013.]

(3) The restrictions referred to in paragraph (2) are—

(a) where the original mobility component award is for the standard rate then, regardless of whether the award would otherwise have been for the enhanced rate, the Secretary of State—

(i) may only make an award for the standard rate of that component; and
(ii) may only make such an award where entitlement results from substantially the same condition or conditions for which the mobility component in the original award was made.

(b) where the original mobility component award is for the enhanced rate, the Secretary of State may only award that rate of that component where entitlement results from substantially the same condition or conditions for which the mobility award was made.

(4) Where the original award does not include an award of the mobility component but C had a previous award of that component, for the purpose of this regulation entitlement under that previous award is to be treated as if it were under the original award provided that the entitlement under the previous award ceased no more than 1 year prior to the date on which the supersession takes or would take effect.

AMENDMENT

1. Social Security (Personal Independence Payment) (Amendment) Regulations 2020 (SI 2020/1235) reg.2(1) (November 30, 2020). Note the amendments made by these regulations apply only to England and Wales. For Scotland the same amendments, coming into force at the same time have been made by the Social Security (Personal Independence Payment) Amendment (Scotland) Regulations 2020 (SI 2020/340).

GENERAL NOTE

4.221 Where a claimant is over pensionable age and an existing award (referred to in this regulation as the "original award") of either component of PIP is to be revised or superseded there are further restrictions that apply in relation to the mobility component. If the revision and supersession is on the ground of a change of circumstances then, where the existing award is for the standard rate the new award can only be at that rate regardless of the claimant's condition now. Where the existing award is for the enhanced rate the new award can only be at that rate if the current condition results from substantially the same conditions as did the existing award. Where the existing award does not contain the mobility component it is possible for a person over retirement age, exceptionally, to renew a previous award (i.e. an award that was previous to the award that is to be reviewed), at either rate, but only if the claimant had an entitlement to that rate in the previous award and that award ended no more than one year before the new revision and supersession will take effect. Note that the amendment to this regulation has the effect of extending the restrictions imposed by paragraph (3) of the regulation so that it applies not only following supersession for a change of circumstances that occurred after the claimant reached the relevant age, but also applies to a supersession made at the request of the claimant or following intervention by the Secretary of State (usually by the receipt of evidence from an HCP) and where the application for supersession began after the claimant reached the relevant age.

The operation of this regulation has been examined in detail by Judge Wikeley in *SC v SSWP (PIP)* [2022] 97 (AAC). The claimant had been in receipt of both components of DLA. She was transferred to PIP shortly after her 65th birthday with an award of both mobility and daily living components at the standard rate. But following a review, the mobility component was withdrawn. The HCP who examined her then took the view that her mobility had improved following a knee replacement operation. Two years later in the course of another review it was accepted that the claimant's condition had worsened and that, but for her age, she would have qualified for the mobility component at the standard rate. No award could be made, however, because none of the exceptions provided for in regs 25, 26, or 27 applied and in particular, reg.27(4) could not apply because more than a year had elapsed since she had last been entitled to that component. Judge Wikeley clarifies the meaning to be given to the words "original award" as used in this regulation. He finds that, to make sense of para.(4), the words must refer to the current award on which the revision is based and not to a previous award in which the claimant was entitled to mobility component.

An attempt to extend the exceptions to s.83 of Welfare Reform Act 2012 that are provided by this regulation failed *in GH (deceased) (by his wife as his appointee/ attorney) v SSWP (PIP)* [2023] UKUT 104 (AAC). The appellant had transferred from DLA and was in receipt of PIP at the standard rate for both components after he reached retirement age. He then became terminally ill and his daily living award was increased to the higher rate. Section 83 of WRA, however prevents an increase in respect of the mobility component and regulations 25 to 27 make no exception in respect of the terminally ill. The appellant appealed, arguing that this was a breach of his human rights by discriminating between him and a younger terminally person. Judge Wright rejected the appeal. He did so on the ground that whatever the merits of the argument advanced by the appellant, there could be no effective remedy available even if they were to succeed. The disqualification in s.83 for the higher rate was made by statute. Even the High Court could have done no more than make a declaration of incompatibility; the most a tribunal could do would be to disapply the regulations, but that would leave the appellant without any relief because it is the regulations that grant exceptional entitlement in certain cases. Without them, the claimant is simply disqualified. Nor did the Judge think it was possible to read into the regulations a further exception to cover the terminally ill; to do so would be contrary to what he saw in the regulations as the intention of Parliament and therefore, a usurpation of the function of Parliament.

PART 7

PAYABILITY WHEN PERSON IS RESIDING IN CERTAIN ACCOMMODATION OR IS DETAINED IN CUSTODY

Care home residents

28.—(1) Subject to paragraph (3) and regulation 30, no amount of personal independence payment which is attributable to the daily living component is payable in respect of C for any period during which C meets the condition in section 85(2) of the Act (care home residents: costs of qualifying services borne out of public or local funds). 4.222

(2) For the purpose of section 85(2) of the Act the specified enactments are—

(a) Part 3 of the National Assistance Act 1948 (Local Authority Services);
(b) Sections 59 and 59A of the Social Work (Scotland) Act 1968 (provision of residential and other establishments by local authorities and maximum period for repayment of sums borrowed for such provision and grants in respect of secure accommodation for children respectively);
(c) the Mental Health Act 1983
(d) the Community Care and Health (Scotland) Act 2002);
(e) the Mental Health (Care and Treatment) (Scotland) Act 2003;

[1 (ee) section 57 of the Health and Social Care Act 2001;]
[2 (eea) Part 1 of the Care Act 2014 (care and support);]
[3 (eeb) Part 4 of the Social Services and Well-being (Wales) Act 2014 (meeting needs), or]
(f) any other enactment relating to persons under a disability or to young persons or to education or training except—
(i) section 485 of the Education Act 1996 (grants in aid of educational services or research);
(ii) section 14 of the Education Act 2002 (power of Secretary of State or National Assembly for Wales to give financial assistance for purposes related to education or children etc.);
(iii) section 49 of the Education (Scotland) Act 1980 (power of education authorities to assist persons to take advantage of educational facilities) or section 73 of that Act (power of Scottish Ministers to make grants to education authorities and others);
(iv) section 65 of the Further and Higher Education Act 1992 (administration of funds by [4 HEFCW]);
(v) section 4 of the Further and Higher Education (Scotland) Act 2005 (general duty of Scottish Ministers to provide support for funding of higher education) or section 11 of that Act (administration of funds); and
(vi) section 22 of the Teaching and Higher Education Act 1998 (new arrangements for giving financial support to students);
[4(vii) section 39 of the Higher Education and Research Act 2017 (financial support for registered higher education providers) or section 40 of that Act (financial support for certain institutions)].

(3) Subject to paragraph (4), paragraph (1) does not apply in the case of C, where C is a person—
(a) who has not reached the age of 18 and to whom—
(i) section 17(10)(b) of the Children Act 1989 (provision of services for children in need: impaired health and development) or section 93(4)(a)(ii) of the Children (Scotland) Act 1995 (interpretation: children in need of care and attention due to impaired health and development) applies because C's health is likely to be significantly impaired, or further impaired, without the provision of services for C; or
(ii) section 17(10)(c) of the Children Act 1989 (provision of services for children in need: disability) or section 93(4)(a)(iii) of the Children (Scotland) Act 1995 (interpretation: children in need of care and attention due to disability) applies; or
[3 (aa) to whom section 37, 38 or 42 of the Social Services and Well-being (Wales) Act 2014 applies; or]
(b) who is accommodated outside the United Kingdom if the costs of any qualifying services are borne wholly or partly by a local authority pursuant to their powers under section 320 of the Education Act 1996 (provision outside England and Wales for certain children) or section 25 of the Education (Additional Support for Learning) (Scotland) Act 2004 (attendance at establishments outwith the United Kingdom).

(4) [3 Paragraphs (3)(a) and (aa) only apply] during any period in which the local authority looking after C places C in a private dwelling with a family, or with a relative of C, or with some other suitable person.

AMENDMENTS

1. Community Care, Services for Carers and Children's Services (Direct Payments) (England) (Amendment) Regulations (SI 2013/2270) reg.7 (November 1, 2013).
2. Care Act 2014 (Consequential Amendments) (Secondary Legislation) Order 2015 (SI 2015/643) art.40 (April 1, 2015).
3. Social Services and Well-being (Wales) Act 2014 and the Regulation and Inspection of Social Care (Wales) Act 2016 (Consequential Amendments) Order 2017 (SI 2017/901) art.16 (November 3, 2017).
4. Higher Education and Research Act 2017 (Further Implementation etc.) Regulations 2019 (SI 2019/1027) reg.36 (August 1, 2019).

GENERAL NOTE

This regulation will have the same effect as reg.7 of the Attendance Allowance Regulations and reg.9 of the Disability Living Allowance Regulations. It removes payability only in respect of the daily living component. Because it is payability, not entitlement, that is removed a claimant will be able to resume payment of the benefit immediately on leaving the care home and does not need to re-qualify for benefit The meaning of such expressions as "borne out of public or local funds" should be the same as those words as used in those regulations. The treatment accorded to arrangements under which claimants, or their representatives, agree to refund fees paid by a local authority when, for example, the claimant's home has been sold, should apply here too. For discussion of cases detailing these points see the notes following those regulations elsewhere in this book. 4.223

[1 Hospital in-patients aged 18 or over]

29.—(1) Subject to [1 paragraph (3) and] regulation 30, no amount of personal independence payment which is attributable to either component is payable in respect of C for any period during which C meets the condition in section 86(2) of the Act (in-patient treatment: costs of treatment, accommodation and related services borne out of public funds). 4.224

(2) For the purposes of section 86(3) of the Act, the costs of treatment, accommodation or any related services are borne out of public funds if C is undergoing medical or other treatment as an in-patient in—

(a) a hospital or similar institution under—
 (i) the National Health Service Act 2006;
 (ii) the National Health Service (Wales) Act 2006; or
 (iii) the National Health Service (Scotland) Act 1978; or
(b) a hospital or similar institution maintained or administered by the Defence Council.

[1 (3) This regulation does not apply if C was under the age of 18 on the day on which C entered the hospital or similar institution referred to in section 86(2) of the Act to begin C's current period as an in-patient.]

AMENDMENT

1. Social Security (Disability Living Allowance and Personal Independence Payment) (Amendment) Regulations 2016 (SI 2016/556) reg.3 (June 29, 2016).

GENERAL NOTE

Note that this regulation removes payability for both components of PIP. Because it is payability rather than entitlement that is removed, a claimant will be able to 4.225

resume payment of the benefits immediately on leaving hospital and does not have to requalify for benefit. Unlike DLA however, no benefit is payable if the costs are shared between a local authority and the NHS, or even if the claimant pays in part himself. (See for DLA the decision in *SSWP v TR (DLA)* [2013] UKUT 622 (AAC)). This is because whereas reg.8 of the DLA regulations refers to the cost of "maintenance" which is defined in that regulation, reg.29 of these regulations refers instead to the provisions of s.86(2) of the Welfare Reform Act 2012, which provides that the withdrawal of benefit will apply if *any* of the costs of treatment, accommodation and any related services provided for the person are borne out of public funds.

The meaning of terms such as "medical or other treatment as an in-patient in a hospital or other institution" should be the same as those words as used in those other regulations. In particular the meaning of "medical treatment" and "hospital" has been considered in a number of cases that are discussed in the notes that follow those regulations elsewhere in this book.

This regulation has been amended to accord with the decision of the Supreme Court in *Cameron Mathieson v SSWP* [2015] UKSC 47. That decision held that the previous version of this regulation breached the child claimant's rights under the Human Rights Act 1998 and under the European Convention on Human Rights.

An attempt to show that suspension of benefit under this regulation was unlawfully discriminatory as being in breach of the claimant's rights under art.14 of the ECHR failed in *MH v SSWP (PIP)* [2017] UKUT 424 (AAC); [2018] AACR 15. The claimant was permanently resident in accommodation similar to a hospital and maintained out of public funds. Judge Lane held that his status as a hospital in-patient was not analogous to a similarly disabled person living at home and was only weakly analogous to a patient living in a care home (for whom only the daily living component would be removed under reg.28 above). But even if the latter case were sufficiently comparable, the judge found that the difference in treatment by withholding the mobility component as well was justified.

Payability exceptions: care homes and hospitals

4.226 **30.**—(1) Subject to the following paragraphs, regulation 28(1) or, as the case may be, regulation 29(1) does not apply to C in respect of the first 28 days of any period during which C is someone to whom that regulation applies.

(2) Where, on the day on which C's entitlement to personal independence payment commences, C meets the condition in section 85(2) of the Act (care home residents: costs of qualifying services borne out of public or local funds) or section 86(2) of the Act (in-patient treatment: costs of treatment, accommodation and related services borne out of public funds), paragraph (1) does not apply to C in respect of any period of consecutive days, beginning with that day, on which C continues to satisfy that condition.

(3) Regulation 28 or, as the case may be, regulation 29 does not apply where C is residing in a hospice and is terminally ill, and the Secretary of State has been informed that C is terminally ill—

(a) on a claim for personal independence payment;

(b) on an application for a revision or a supersession of an award of personal independence payment; or

(c) in writing in connection with an award of, or a claim for, or an application for a revision or a supersession of an award of, personal independence payment.

(4) In paragraph (3), "hospice" means a hospital or other institution whose primary function is to provide palliative care for persons resident there who are suffering from a progressive disease in its final stages, other than—

(a) a health service hospital in England (within the meaning of section 275 of the National Health Service Act 2006);
(b) a hospital in Wales vested in—
(i) an NHS trust;
(ii) a Local Health Board; or
(iii) the Welsh Ministers,
for the purpose of functions under the National Health Service (Wales) Act 2006;
(c) a health service hospital in Scotland (within the meaning of section 108(1) of the National Health Service (Scotland) Act 1978);
(d) a hospital maintained by the Defence Council; or
(e) an institution similar to a hospital mentioned in any of the preceding sub-paragraphs of this paragraph.

(5) Regulation 28(1) does not apply to a case where, during any period the total cost of the qualifying services are met—
(a) out of the resources of the person for whom the qualifying services are provided, or partly out of that person's own resources and partly with assistance from another person or a charity; or
(b) on that person's behalf by another person or a charity.

(6) In this regulation—
"NHS trust" means a body established under section 18 of the National Health Service (Wales) Act 2006; and
"Local Health Board" means a body established under section 11 of that Act.

(7) In the application of these Regulations to Scotland, "charity" is to be construed as if these Regulations were an enactment to which section 7 of the Charities Act 2011 (application in relation to Scotland) applied.

GENERAL NOTE

The disqualifications under regs 28 and 29 do not apply for the first 28 days that the claimant is in the care home or the hospital, but when the claimant is in such accommodation already, when the award of benefit commences, the disqualification will still apply. Nor does disqualification apply if the claimant is in a hospice and is terminally ill. For the meaning of "hospice" see above para.(4) and for the meaning of "terminally ill" see s.82 of the WRA 2012. The disqualification does not apply where (even if the claimant is in an NHS hospital) all of the "qualifying services" are paid for privately or by a charity. For the meaning of "qualifying services" see s.85(4) of the WRA 2012. **4.227**

Prisoners and detainees

31.—(1) Subject to paragraph (2), section 87 of the Act (prisoners and detainees) does not apply in respect of the first 28 days of any period during which C is a person to whom that section would otherwise apply. **4.228**

(2) Where, on the day on which C's entitlement to personal independence payment commences, C is a person to whom that section applies, paragraph (1) does not apply to C in respect of any period of consecutive days, beginning with that day, on which C continues to be a person to whom that section applies.

(3) Section 87 of the Act does not apply to C in respect of any period after the conclusion of criminal proceedings as a result of which C is detained in a hospital or similar institution in Great Britain as a person

suffering from mental disorder unless C satisfies either of the conditions set out in paragraph (4).

(4) The conditions referred to in paragraph (3) are—

(a) C is—

(i) detained under section 45A of the Mental Health Act 1983 (power of higher courts to direct hospital admission) or section 47 of that Act (removal to hospital of persons serving sentences of imprisonment, etc); and

(ii) being detained on or before the day which the Secretary of State has certified to be C's release date within the meaning of section 50(3) of that Act; or

(b) C is being detained under—

(i) section 59A of the Criminal Procedure (Scotland) Act 1995 (hospital direction); or

(ii) section 136 of the Mental Health (Care and Treatment) (Scotland) Act 2003 (transfer of prisoners for treatment of mental disorder).

(5) For the purposes of this regulation—

(a) "hospital or similar institution" means any place (not being a prison, a detention centre, a young offenders institution or remand centre and not being at or in any such place) in which persons suffering from mental disorder are or may be received for care or treatment;

(b) criminal proceedings against any person are deemed to be concluded upon that person being found insane in those proceedings with the effect that that person cannot be tried or the trial of that person cannot proceed.

(6) Section 87 of the Act does not apply to C where—

(a) C is undergoing imprisonment or detention in legal custody outside Great Britain; and

(b) in similar circumstances in Great Britain, C would have been excepted from the application of that section by virtue of the operation of any provision of this regulation.

GENERAL NOTE

4.229 The disqualification of prisoners and detainees does not apply for the first 28 days of imprisonment. This is a more generous rule than that applies to AA and DLA where disqualification is immediate. In another sense, however, this regulation is less generous because there seems to be no provision for benefit to be only suspended while the prisoner is on remand and does not subsequently receive a sentence of imprisonment. (See Social Security (General Benefit) Regulations 1982 reg.2).

Disqualification ends when the prisoner is released from detention. It ends, under this regulation, also when a prisoner continues to be detained on the grounds of mental disorder after his sentence is completed. In that case, however, the claimant may then be disqualified under s.85 (care homes) or s.86 (hospitals) of the WRA 2012. Note that the words that are used in s.87 are the same as those in s.113 of the SSCBA. That section has been interpreted to mean that disqualification applies only where the claimant is in detention or legal custody in consequence of criminal proceedings and not where imprisonment is the result of a civil contempt. See *R(S) 8/79* and *JC v SSWP (ESA)* [2024] UKUT 13 (AAC).

Periods of residence

32.—(1) In these Regulations, a "period of residence" is a period during which C— 4.230

(a) meets the condition in section 85(2) of the Act (care home residents);

(b) meets the condition in section 86(2) of the Act (hospital in-patients); or

(c) is a person who is undergoing imprisonment or detention in legal custody.

(2) Subject to paragraph (3), for the purposes of section 87 of the Act and regulations 28 and 29, a period of residence—

(a) begins on the day after the day on which C enters a care home, hospital or similar institution or commences a period of imprisonment or detention in legal custody; and

(b) ends on the day before the day on which C leaves a care home, hospital or similar institution or on which a period of imprisonment or detention in legal custody ends.

(3) Where, immediately following a period of residence for the purpose of sub-paragraph (a), (b) or (c) of paragraph (1), C commences another period of residence for the purpose of any of those sub-paragraphs, the earlier period of residence is deemed to end on the day on which C leaves the care home, hospital or similar institution or, as the case may be, on which the period of imprisonment or detention ends.

(4) Subject to paragraph (5), for the purposes of regulations 30(1) and 31(1),—

(a) two or more distinct periods of residence separated by an interval not exceeding 28 days, or by two or more such intervals, are to be treated as a continuous period equal in duration to the total duration of such distinct periods and ending on the last day of the later or last such period; and

(b) any period or periods to which those regulations refer are to be taken into account and aggregated with any other period referred to in those regulations.

(5) Paragraph (4) is, where the periods referred to in sub-paragraph (a) of that paragraph are both or all periods to which section 87 applies, to have effect as if—

(a) the words "subject to paragraph (5)" and "regulation 30(1) and" were omitted;

(b) the reference to "28 days" in sub-paragraph (a) of that paragraph read "one year"; and

(c) the references to "those regulations" in sub-paragraph (b) read "that regulation" and the reference to "refer" read "refers".

General Note

This regulation provides for the linking together of two or more periods spent in one or more of the accommodations referred to in regs 28, 29 and 31. Thus, where a claimant has spent time in a care home, a hospital, or undergoing imprisonment or detention, two or more such periods will be linked together to form a single period when they are separated by no more than 28 days—and the claimant will not enjoy another period of entitlement under reg.30(1) or reg.31(1). Where, however, both (or several) periods were ones of imprisonment or detention, those periods are linked if they occur within one year of each other. 4.231

SCHEDULE 1

PERSONAL INDEPENDENCE PAYMENT ASSESSMENT

PART 1

INTERPRETATION

4.232 1. In this Schedule—

"aided" means with—

(a) the use of an aid or appliance; or

(b) supervision, prompting or assistance;

"assistance" means physical intervention by another person and does not include speech;

"assistance dog" means a dog trained to guide or assist a person with a sensory impairment;

"basic verbal information" means information in C's native language conveyed verbally in a simple sentence;

"basic written information" means signs, symbols and dates written or printed standard size text in C's native language;

"bathe" includes get into or out of an unadapted bath or shower;

"communication support" means support from a person trained or experienced in communicating with people with specific communication needs, including interpreting verbal information into a non-verbal form and vice versa;

"complex budgeting decisions" means decisions involving—

(a) calculating household and personal budgets;

(b) managing and paying bills; and

(c) planning future purchases;

"complex verbal information" means information in C's native language conveyed verbally in either more than one sentence or one complicated sentence;

"complex written information" means more than one sentence of written or printed standard size text in C's native language;

"cook" means heat food at or above waist height;

"dress and undress" includes put on and take off socks and shoes;

"engage socially" means—

(a) interact with others in a contextually and socially appropriate manner;

(b) understand body language; and

(c) establish relationships;

"manage incontinence" means manage involuntary evacuation of the bowel or bladder, including use a collecting device or self-catheterisation, and clean oneself afterwards;

"manage medication [1 . . .]" means take medication [1 . . .], where a failure to do so is likely to result in a deterioration in C's health;

[1 "manage therapy" means undertake therapy, where a failure to do so is likely to result in a deterioration in C's health;]

"medication" means medication to be taken at home which is prescribed or recommended by a registered—

(a) doctor;

(b) nurse; or

(c) pharmacist;

[1 "monitor a health condition"] means—
(a) detect significant changes in C's health condition which are likely to lead to a deterioration in C's health; and
(b) take action advised by a—
(i) registered doctor;
(ii) registered nurse; or
(iii) health professional who is regulated by the Health Professions Council,
without which C's health is likely to deteriorate;
"orientation aid" means a specialist aid designed to assist disabled people to follow a route safely;
"prepare", in the context of food, means make food ready for cooking or eating;
"prompting" means reminding, encouraging or explaining by another person;
"psychological distress" means distress related to an enduring mental health condition or an intellectual or cognitive impairment;
"read" includes read signs, symbols and words but does not include read Braille;
"simple budgeting decisions" means decisions involving—
(a) calculating the cost of goods; and
(b) calculating change required after a purchase;
"simple meal" means a cooked one-course meal for one using fresh ingredients;
"social support" means support from a person trained or experienced in assisting people to engage in social situations;
"stand" means stand upright with at least one biological foot on the ground;
"supervision" means the continuous presence of another person for the purpose of ensuring C's safety;
"take nutrition" means—
(a) cut food into pieces, convey food and drink to one's mouth and chew and swallow food or drink; or
(b) take nutrition by using a therapeutic source;
"therapeutic source" means parenteral or enteral tube feeding, using a rate-limiting device such as a delivery system or feed pump;
"therapy" means therapy to be undertaken at home which is prescribed or recommended by a—
(a) registered—
(i) doctor;
(ii) nurse; or
(iii) pharmacist; or
(b) health professional regulated by the Health Professions Council;
[1 but does not include taking or applying, or otherwise receiving or administering, medication (whether orally, topically or by any other means), or any action which, in C's case, falls within the definition of "monitor a health condition;]
"toilet needs" means—
(a) getting on and off an unadapted toilet;
(b) evacuating the bladder and bowel; and
(c) cleaning oneself afterwards; and
"unaided" means without—
(a) the use of an aid or appliance; or
(b) supervision, prompting or assistance.

General Note

4.233 Part 1 of this Schedule, together with regulation 2 above, provides the definitions of words used in the assessment of a claim for PIP. Some of these definitions have been changed with effect from March 16, 2017. This book is up to date with effect as at April 10, 2017. Hence only the amended version of the regulations appears here. In so far as it may be necessary for tribunals to have access to the earlier version of the Schedule they should have recourse to an earlier version of this work. This may be necessary because these amendments were made to reverse the effect of the UT decision in *SSWP v LB (PIP)* [2016] UKUT 530 (AAC). The Secretary of State has withdrawn the appeal against the decision in *SSWP v LB (PIP)* [2016] UKUT 530 (AAC). This means that appeals to a FTT, or to the UT, from decisions made on the original version of these regulations should be determined in accordance with that decision. At the same time two appeals on the same matters that were to have been heard before a three-judge panel of the UT were also withdrawn. In *KM v SSWP (PIP)* [2018] UKUT 296 (AAC) Judge Rowland has given helpful guidance to tribunals applying the original version of the Schedule in accordance with the decision of Judge Mesher in *SSWP v LB (PIP)* [2016] UKUT 530 (AAC).

Part 2

Daily living activities

4.234

Column 1 *Activity*	*Column 2* *Descriptors*	*Column 3* *Points*
1. Preparing food.	a. Can prepare and cook a simple meal unaided.	0
	b. Needs to use an aid or appliance to be able to either prepare or cook a simple meal.	2
	c. Cannot cook a simple meal using a conventional cooker but is able to do so using a microwave.	2
	d. Needs prompting to be able to either prepare or cook a simple meal.	2
	e. Needs supervision or assistance to either prepare or cook a simple meal.	4
	f. Cannot prepare and cook food.	8
2. Taking nutrition.	a. Can take nutrition unaided.	0
	b. Needs—	2
	(i) to use an aid or appliance to be able to take nutrition; or	
	(ii) supervision to be able to take nutrition; or	
	(iii) assistance to be able to cut up food.	
	c. Needs a therapeutic source to be able to take nutrition.	2
	d. Needs prompting to be able to take nutrition.	4

Column 1 *Activity*	*Column 2* *Descriptors*	*Column 3* *Points*
	e. Needs assistance to be able to manage a therapeutic source to take nutrition.	6
	f. Cannot convey food and drink to their mouth and needs another person to do so.	10
3. Managing therapy or monitoring a health condition.	a. Either—	0
	(i) does not receive medication or therapy or need to monitor a health condition; or	
	(ii) can manage medication or therapy or monitor a health condition unaided.	
	b. Needs [1 any one or more of the following]—	1
	(i) to use an aid or appliance to be able to manage medication; [1 . . .]	
	(ii) supervision, prompting or assistance to be able to manage medication [1 . . .].	
	[1 (iii) supervision, prompting or assistance to be able to monitor a health condition.]	
	c. Needs supervision, prompting or assistance to be able to manage therapy that takes no more than 3.5 hours a week.	2
	d. Needs supervision, prompting or assistance to be able to manage therapy that takes more than 3.5 but no more than 7 hours a week.	4
	e. Needs supervision, prompting or assistance to be able to manage therapy that takes more than 7 but no more than 14 hours a week.	6
	f. Needs supervision, prompting or assistance to be able to manage therapy that takes more than 14 hours a week.	8
4. Washing and bathing.	a. Can wash and bathe unaided.	0
	b. Needs to use an aid or appliance to be able to wash or bathe.	2
	c. Needs supervision or prompting to be able to wash or bathe.	2
	d. Needs assistance to be able to wash either their hair or body below the waist.	2
	e. Needs assistance to be able to get in or out of a bath or shower.	3
	f. Needs assistance to be able to wash their body between the shoulders and waist.	4
	g. Cannot wash and bathe at all and needs another person to wash their entire body.	8

Column 1 *Activity*	*Column 2* *Descriptors*	*Column 3* *Points*
5. Managing toilet needs or incontinence.	a. Can manage toilet needs or incontinence unaided.	0
	b. Needs to use an aid or appliance to be able to manage toilet needs or incontinence.	2
	c. Needs supervision or prompting to be able to manage toilet needs.	2
	d. Needs assistance to be able to manage toilet needs.	4
	e. Needs assistance to be able to manage incontinence of either bladder or bowel.	6
	f. Needs assistance to be able to manage incontinence of both bladder and bowel.	8
6. Dressing and undressing.	a. Can dress and undress unaided.	0
	b. Needs to use an aid or appliance to be able to dress or undress.	2
	c. Needs either—	2
	(i) prompting to be able to dress, undress or determine appropriate circumstances for remaining clothed; or	
	(ii) prompting or assistance to be able to select appropriate clothing.	
	d. Needs assistance to be able to dress or undress their lower body.	2
	e. Needs assistance to be able to dress or undress their upper body.	4
	f. Cannot dress or undress at all.	8
7. Communicating verbally.	a. Can express and understand verbal information unaided.	0
	b. Needs to use an aid or appliance to be able to speak or hear.	2
	c. Needs communication support to be able to express or understand complex verbal information.	4
	d. Needs communication support to be able to express or understand basic verbal information.	8
	e. Cannot express or understand verbal information at all even with communication support.	12

Column 1 *Activity*	*Column 2* *Descriptors*	*Column 3* *Points*
8. Reading and understanding signs, symbols and words.	a. Can read and understand basic and complex written information either unaided or using spectacles or contact lenses.	0
	b. Needs to use an aid or appliance, other than spectacles or contact lenses, to be able to read or understand either basic or complex written information.	2
	c. Needs prompting to be able to read or understand complex written information.	2
	d. Needs prompting to be able to read or understand basic written information.	4
	e. Cannot read or understand signs, symbols or words at all.	8
9. Engaging with other people face to face.	a. Can engage with other people unaided.	0
	b. Needs prompting to be able to engage with other people.	2
	c. Needs social support to be able to engage with other people.	4
	d. Cannot engage with other people due to such engagement causing either—	8
	(i) overwhelming psychological distress to the claimant; or	
	(ii) the claimant to exhibit behaviour which would result in a substantial risk of harm to the claimant or another person.	
10. Making budgeting decisions.	a. Can manage complex budgeting decisions unaided.	0
	b. Needs prompting or assistance to be able to make complex budgeting decisions.	2
	c. Needs prompting or assistance to be able to make simple budgeting decisions.	4
	d. Cannot make any budgeting decisions at all.	6

Part 3

Mobility activities

4.235

Column 1 Activity	Column 2 Descriptors	Column 3 Points
1. Planning and following journeys.	a. Can plan and follow the route of a journey unaided.	0
	b. Needs prompting to be able to undertake any journey to avoid overwhelming psychological distress to the claimant.	4
	c. Cannot plan the route of a journey.	8
	d. Cannot follow the route of an unfamiliar journey without another person, assistance dog or orientation aid.	10
	e. Cannot undertake any journey because it would cause overwhelming psychological distress to the claimant.	10
	f. Cannot follow the route of a familiar journey without another person, an assistance dog or an orientation aid.	12
2. Moving around.	a. Can stand and then move more than 200 metres, either aided or unaided.	0
	b. Can stand and then move more than 50 metres but no more than 200 metres, either aided or unaided	4
	c. Can stand and then move unaided more than 20 metres but no more than 50 metres.	8
	d. Can stand and then move using an aid or appliance more than 20 metres but no more than 50 metres.	10
	e. Can stand and then move more than 1 metre but no more than 20 metres, either aided or unaided.	12
	f. Cannot, either aided or unaided, – (i) stand; or (ii) move more than 1 metre.	12

Amendments

1. Social Security (Personal Independence Payment) (Amendment) Regulations 2017 (SI 2017/194) reg.2 (March 16, 2017).

General Note

4.236 This Schedule was amended with effect from March 16, 2017 by the Social Security (Personal Independence Payment) (Amendment) Regulations 2017 (SI 2017/194). But in December 2017, Mostyn J. held, in *RF v SSWP* [2017] EWHC 3375 [2018] AACR 13, that para.2(4) of those regulation was *ultra vires* the rule making power in Part 4 of the Welfare Reform Act 2012. That decision was then accepted as correct by the DWP. This meant that amendments made in that paragraph to Activity 1 of the Mobility Activities were of no effect and never had been of any effect. The text of the Descriptors c, d and f in Activity 1 of Part 3 of the Schedule has accordingly been restored to its original wording in this volume; otherwise the text shown in this volume is the text as amended by those regulations. However, for some time it will be necessary for advisers and for tribunals to have access to the text of the schedule as it was before these amendments. That is because in determining appeals from decisions of a DM made before that date, the law to be applied will be the law as it was before that date. (See the observations of Judge Gray on this point in *PM v SSWP (PIP)* [2017] UKUT 154 (AAC)).

An attempt to have the rest of the amendments made to these regulations by reg.2(2) and (3) of the amending regulations (those affecting Activity 3—Managing therapy or monitoring a health condition) to be found to be invalid failed in *CK v SSWP (PIP); JM v SSWP (PIP)* [2022] UKUT 122 (AAC). Judge Ward was asked to find those amendments invalid on the grounds that they were either made without consultation, or that they were ultra vires, or that they were discriminatory. He rejected the argument on all three grounds.

This Schedule contains the criteria by which an assessment for PIP will be measured. This is the crux of the difference between this benefit and AA and DLA. Whereas the qualification for those benefits focused on the care and attention that the claimant needs, this test focuses on the things that the claimant can, and cannot, do for themselves. But broadly speaking both tests are aimed at the same target- to identify those who need help, to the requisite extent, to cope with the demands of living a normal everyday life. Although it is expected that qualification for PIP might involve a more rigorous standard, some of these new criteria will accept conditions that were not provided for before.

The tables in Pts 2 and 3 of the schedule each contain a list of "Activities" and of "Descriptors".

Part 2 relates to the Daily Living Component and Pt 3 relates to the Mobility Component.

Each Activity covers some aspect of normal everyday living, or of mobility and each is then divided into a number of Descriptors. The Descriptors pose a series of criteria by which the ability, and thus the disability, of the claimant is measured. Each set of Descriptors begins with a benchmarking criterion (for which the score is zero), that sets the standard for an able person. The subsequent Descriptors describe an ascending scale of disablement.

These criteria, most of which can be thought of as tasks, are designed to measure both physical and mental disability. Any lack of ability to accomplish the task set by a Descriptor must derive from some physical or mental cause; a mere lack of skill, knowledge or training will not suffice unless that has itself some origin in a physical or mental deficiency—see *R(DLA) 3/06* where there was said to be a need to "unbundle" the functional deficiency that the claimant exhibited, in order to see if it might have some physical or mental cause. It is not necessary that the physical or mental cause is a specific disease or condition for which there is a medical diagnosis, but only to show that the limited ability has some cause that was either physical or mental. Physical, in this context, will mean anything connected with the claimant's bodily function including experiencing sensation such as pain, breathlessness or dizziness, while mental, includes any mental health condition or intellectual or cognitive impairment.This approach is confirmed by Judge Gray in *MR v SSWP (PIP)* [2017] UKUT 86 (AAC).

That this will include a psychosomatic condition is confirmed in *NK v SSWP* [2016] UKUT 146 (AAC). The claimant suffered a mental health condition that included experiencing pain for which no physical cause could be found. In the UT Judge Rowley confirmed the decision of the FTT refusing her claim for the mobility component (the evidence showed that she could walk more than 200 metres without difficulty), but she confirmed that the origin of any pain experienced was irrelevant; the question was whether the claimant did experience pain whatever might be its origin.

But the cause must be some "condition" and that will mean something more than just a defect of character or irresponsible behaviour. The line that has been drawn in relation to DLA for claims based on alcoholism, is between those where the claimant can be said to be able to desist in his behaviour and those where he is compelled by an addiction that he cannot reasonably be expected to control. (Though even where alcoholism is an addiction, care should be taken in examining how much of the time the claimant is so affected as to need assistance etc.).

More recent cases relevant to this question are *JG v SSWP* [2013] UKUT 37 (AAC) and *SD v SSWP* [2016] UKUT 100 (AAC); [2016] AACR 35 both cases of a claim for ESA, but where the principles applicable in DLA and now, presumably, PIP may be assumed to be the same. These cases explain the relevance of evidence given by reference to the Diagnostic and Statistical Manual of Mental Disorders of the American Psychiatric Association, DSM-IV and DSM-5. Both cases are more fully discussed in the notes that follow the relevant sections relating to ESA elsewhere in this volume.

The approach to alcohol dependency in relation to benefits that was adopted in the ESA cases was that which had been developed for DLA in *R(DLA) 6/06*. That same approach has now been applied to PIP by Judge Hemingway in *SD v SSWP (PIP)* [2017] UKUT 310 (AAC). The judge affirms that alcohol dependency may be a mental condition for the purposes of this benefit and that an FTT must, therefore, assess and record the extent to which the claimant's ability to achieve the various Activities is affected by their condition. In this case, although the tribunal appeared to accept that the claimant's alcoholism was a mental condition, they failed to make any findings regarding the extent to which that affected his abilities. The judge points out that the degree to which a claimant's ability is affected will vary greatly and will require careful fact finding by the tribunal and that the extent to which they are affected may differ throughout the day, so that the time at which the claimant is required to perform any particular activity will also be relevant.

The effect of an addiction to alcohol in a claimant has been considered again, at length, in *DE v SSWP (PIP)* [2021] UKUT 226 (AAC). The claimant was what was described as a functioning alcoholic who had made a succession of claims for PIP none of which had succeeded. In this latest claim the HCP had accepted that he was entitled to 2 points because he required an aid, in the form of a stool, to support him when cooking a meal. The claimant suffered from a number of physical conditions, as well as depression, all of which, he said, were "alcohol related". The FTT had rejected his appeal; they said that his disability was the result of a "lifestyle choice". In the UT Judge Clough allowed his appeal and returned the case for rehearing before a fresh tribunal. In doing so she gives extensive guidance to the new tribunal as to the correct approach for a tribunal dealing with addiction cases, advice which will be of benefit to all tribunals dealing with such issues. She begins by explaining the nature of addiction that will amount to an identifiable medical condition according to the latest Diagnostic and Statistical Manual of Mental Disorders of the American Psychiatric Association (DSM-5) which now uses the term Alcohol Use Disorder (AUD). As the judge explains AUD is: "a discrete illness, characterised predominantly by a loss of self-control over alcohol use, typically rendering a person incapable of refraining from alcohol consumption despite any impacts it may be having on their health and ability to function (see *R(DLA) 6/06*, and the updated DSM-5)." But that is not to say that the claimant must be totally incapable of exercising self-control. As the judge herself points out, the decision in R (DLA) 6/06 shows that the condition need not be uncontrollable in the sense that it is absolutely impossible for a person to control the condition, it is a matter of degree. Where the evidence before the tribunal includes a diagnosis of AUD (or of its predecessor, Alcohol Dependency Syndrome (ADS)) the way is clear for the tribunal to move to assessing its effect upon the claimant's ability to satisfy daily living activities, but there need not be such a diagnosis if the tribunal can satisfy themselves that, on the evidence before them, the claimant does indeed suffer from AUD—see *R (DLA) 3/06*). Thereafter the task of the FTT will be to make a careful, usually detailed, account of how the claimant's condition affects his ability to satisfy the PIP activities. That may vary according to the time of day and the extent to which the claimant has or has not consumed alcohol, because, especially in the case of a functioning alcoholic, the consumption of alcohol may improve that claimant's ability. The question is not whether the claimant is to be tested before or after he has consumed alcohol, but rather it is to establish the claimant's normal pattern of daily behaviour and to test his ability in the state that he then may be. Having done that the judge explains, in some detail, how the tribunal should then proceed to check that ability against all four of the criteria contained in reg.4(2A)—safely, to a reasonable standard, repeatedly and in a timely manner. Especially with regard to safety, careful fact finding and estimation of risk may be necessary. Finally, after all that the claimant's behaviour must be measured against the requirements of reg.7—the 50% rule. Any tribunal faced with one of these cases would do well to read the whole of this judgment.

Note that in applying the schedules only one Descriptor (the one with the higher or highest points) will count in relation to each Activity; the sum of the points for each Activity is then the claimant's score.

Note too, that where a claimant is able to achieve the task required of a Descriptor on some days, but not on others, then reg.7 prescribes the basis on which those Descriptors will be scored.

In relation to each component of PIP a score of eight points will entitle the claimant to benefit at the standard rate; a score of 12 points will entitle him to the enhanced rate. (See regs 5 and 6 above).

Note that where the claimant is assessed as being entitled to the enhanced rate he cannot at the same time be entitled to the standard rate of that same component—(see reg.4(3)).

Although all but one of the Activities will qualify a claimant, at the standard rate at least, if he is disabled to the greatest extent measured in that Activity, for most claimants it is likely that a qualifying score will be compiled from the aggregate points scored in more than one Activity in respect of each component.

To the extent that most Activities and Descriptors involve similar demands to those that have featured in claims for AA or DLA, it is reasonable to expect that some of the decisions that have been reached in relation to those benefits will be relied upon as giving guidance in relation to decisions for PIP. In other respects we may find that the new benefit is taken as an opportunity for a fresh start. The notes that follow are an attempt to draw some of that earlier experience to bear and also to note where it may be of less relevance.

There are a number of terms that occur frequently throughout the tables of Descriptors that are defined in Pt 1 of the Schedule. Those used most often are:

"*aided*" means either with the use of an "aid or appliance" or with "supervision, prompting or assistance".

An "aid or appliance" is defined, not in the schedule, but in reg.2, as any device which improves, provides or replaces the claimant's impaired physical or mental function including a prosthesis. A fundamental point about this definition has been demonstrated by the decision of Judge Brunner in *DA v SSWP (PIP)* [2019] UKUT 320 (AAC) –the device in question must be used to improve, provide or replace the function that is deficient. For a full description of this case see the Notes that follow reg.2 above. The device need not be something that is designed exclusively for use by a person who is disabled; it may include any device that is used more commonly, but assists the claimant in a particular way. Examples will include an electric tin opener and a slow cooker, as well as a microwave that is mentioned specifically in the Descriptors.

The meaning of "aid or appliance" has been considered by Judge Mark in *NA v SSWP (PIP)* [2015] UKUT 572 (AAC). There, the claimant had been found to require the use of a perching stool when preparing a meal and of a chair when taking a shower or bath, but the FTT had not allowed any points in relation to Activity 6, dressing and undressing. The claimant had said that she could dress and undress by sitting on a chair; the FTT evidently took the view that using a chair when dressing and undressing was not the use of an aid or appliance. Judge Mark held that it could be and the fact that a chair might have some other primary purpose, did not mean that it could not be a "device which improves" the claimant's physical function in accordance with the definition of an aid in reg.2. The fact that able people might also use a **4.237** chair in that manner was not the point; the question to be answered was whether the claimant could dress safely etc and in accordance with reg.4(2A) without using such a chair.

However, a different conclusion on similar facts has been reached by Judge Jacobs in *CW v SSWP* [2016] UKUT 197 (AAC); [2016] AACR 44. There the claimant said that she had to sit on her bed in order to dress herself. The judge held that a bed, which might equally be used by a non-disabled person should not, in these circumstances be regarded as an aid to dressing. While he begins by agreeing with the decision of Judge Mark that an ordinary object may become an aid to a disabled person if that person cannot accomplish the task without it, he goes on to say that the need for assistance must relate to the particular function in question- what might be necessary as an aid in washing and toileting will not necessarily be an aid in dressing. The use of the aid must then be related to the function:

"The question is this: would this 'aid' usually or normally be used by someone without any limitation in carrying out this particular aspect of the activity? If it would, the 'aid' is not assisting to overcome the consequences of an impaired function that is involved in the activity and its descriptors".

On this basis he concludes that while the claimant needed to sit whilst she took her jeans on and off it was just as normal for able persons to do the same— in effect the claimant was not disabled in respect of the function of dressing and undressing because that is commonly the way that dressing etc is done. Note that the use of a perching stool as an aid when preparing food in Activity 1 has been questioned in the decision of Judge Lane in *DR v SSWP (PIP)* [2018] UKUT 209 (AAC). The decision does not deny that a stool might be an aid in some appropriate cases, but it does affect how often that will be so. Judge Lane adopts the reasoning used by Judge Jacobs in *CW v SSWP (PIP)* [2016] UKUT 197 (AAC); [2016] AACR 44. She found that on the facts of this case the claimant had not shown that he needed to sit more often than might be the case for any other person and hence he did not need the stool as an aid in relation to that activity.

In December 2015 the DWP issued a discussion paper entitled *Personal Independence Payment: aids and appliances descriptors*. This resulted in a proposal that certain of the point scores in the daily living Activities should be reduced, but that proposal was subsequently withdrawn.

An appliance will include, most obviously, a wheelchair. However, in relation to the mobility component the claimant's ability to move (activity 2) must be regarded as his ability to do so without the use of a wheelchair; otherwise very few claimants would succeed on that activity in a claim for the mobility component. This is accepted by the DWP in the *PIP Assessment Guide*, though there it is explained on the basis that Descriptor requires the claimant to be unable to stand and then move. In the case of a claimant who can stand, but who cannot then move even one metre, there will need to be another justification. See the notes that follow Activity 2 of the mobility component. Note that a wheelchair may be taken account of as an appliance in relation to other Activities such as the ability to cook and to wash and use a shower.

Note that under reg.4(2), where the claimant normally wears or uses an aid or appliance, he is to be assessed with that aid or appliance. Furthermore, even if the claimant does not wear or use such an aid or appliance, but he could reasonably be expected to do so, he will be assessed as if he were wearing or using the aid or appliance. See the note to reg.4 for discussion of the factors to be taken into account in making such a determination.

"*unaided*" obviously carries the converse meaning to "aided". It means that the claimant can achieve that task without any aid, appliance, assistance, prompting or supervision. If the claimant requires even just one of these forms of help he is not accomplishing the task "unaided", though whether he can then score on any subsequent Descriptor will depend upon whether that form of help is prescribed by that Descriptor.

4.238 "*assistance*" requires physical intervention and is not satisfied by mere speech. The meaning of assistance has been explored by Judge Jacobs in *SSWP v GM*

(PIP) [2017] UKUT 268 (AAC). He points out that the definition in Part I of the schedule is exhaustive—it means "physical intervention by another person". In his view this requires that the person giving assistance is inserting their help into something that is being done by the claimant, and not merely doing the whole of a task for the claimant. In this case the claimant suffered from depression and did not cook himself any meals; instead he lived on snacks. The only time that he ate a whole meal was when his neighbour cooked one for him. In *AI v SSWP (PIP)* [2016] UKUT 322 (AAC) Judge Mesher had suggested that at some future time it might be necessary to decide whether the doing of an entire task for the claimant could amount to assistance- Judge Jacobs decides that it does not. While it is clear that preparing and cooking a whole meal cannot be assistance in relation to Activity 1, there remains the possibility that the Activity might be regarded as a single task, in which case help given in respect of just one part of that task might amount to intervention and hence assistance (e.g. if someone does all the knife work and then hands over to the claimant to complete the meal). This conclusion is supported in the decision of Judge Hemingway in *CP v SSWP (PIP)* [2018] UKUT 5 (AAC). There, the claimant suffered from narcolepsy and cataplexy. At various times while she was preparing and cooking a meal it might be necessary for another person to intervene to prevent the claimant injuring herself or burning the meal. The judge suggested (though as an obiter comment) that such intervention in taking over a part of the process could amount to assistance in relation to Activity 1.

In *JT v SSWP (PIP)* [2018] UKUT 101 (AAC) it is suggested that there may be two sorts of assistance – assistance that supplements the claimant's deficiency by helping him to do something that he is already engaged upon or possibly intervening to prevent harm to the claimant as he is doing a task, and precautionary assistance that would avoid the risk of harm to the claimant by taking over some part of the task for him. The claimant suffered from uncontrolled epilepsy; he had about two grand mal fits each week and several petit mal fits. It was argued that this made it too dangerous for him to prepare a meal because of the risk that he might injure himself either when using a knife or when handling hot items. Furthermore, when having a grand mal fit he thrashed about in a manner that might endanger anyone who was there to assist him. Judge Hemingway suggests that while assistance only of the first sort might mean that the claimant could not cook a meal at all without endangering either himself or the assistant, assistance that was precautionary by taking over the dangerous parts of the process might mean that the claimant was capable of preparing and cooking a meal with assistance. He does concede that if the parts taken over amounted to almost all of the task it could mean that the claimant could not do that task at all.

"*prompting*" means reminding, encouraging or explaining by another person. This does not require the actual presence of the person who is prompting as some of the other definitions do; this means that a telephone call, made for that purpose, should be sufficient to be prompting (cf. reg.10C of the DLA Regulations which was made specifically to prevent a telephone call sufficing for the purposes of DLA). Whether written reminders, left for the claimant, could suffice is doubtful— "prompting" might be thought to convey a sense of immediacy that would be missing in a written note.

In *GG v SSWP (PIP)* [2016] UKUT 194 (AAC) Judge Hemingway considers the circumstances in which the claimant might demonstrate a need for prompting. He begins by accepting that what he had said in the earlier case of *MB v SSWP (PIP)* [2016] UKUT 250 (AAC) was correct—i.e. that a need is not demonstrated merely because the claimant does in fact get prompted, and nor is it shown that there is no need if the claimant is not prompted. The problem in this case was that the claimant, an alcoholic, did motivate himself satisfactorily on those occasions when he had a specific impetus to act, such as an appointment to keep. The evidence given on his behalf showed, however, that when such impetus was lacking he might need prompting to carry out a number of the daily living activities such as washing and dressing as well as preparing food. The FTT had taken the view that he did not need prompting on the majority of days because when there was some impetus to act he was capable of doing so. Judge Hemingway took the view that this was not determinative of the matter. He says:

> "That seems to me to be too simplistic an approach. The mere fact that a claimant might be sufficiently motivated to perform a task when there is specific or unusual impetus to do so does not, of itself, inform as to the overall position and the generality of the situation. So it is not appropriate to limit the scope of the enquiry to such days. True an ability to perform a task without prompting when there is particular pressure to do so might be indicative of a claimant simply exercising a choice not to perform such a task on impetus absent days but that will not necessarily follow. What has to be undertaken is a more general and all-encompassing consideration. So, there needs to be an assessment, in such cases, of why it is that, on days when a claimant does not perform certain tasks, he/she does not do so. If it is because, without any specific impetus, he/she is not motivated to do so as a result of health difficulties and that such days exist for more than 50% of the time in the relevant assessment period, then absent other pertinent considerations, the relevant descriptor or descriptors will apply. That was not this tribunal's approach and I conclude that, in consequence, it did err in law. Of course, though, and obviously, mere indolence will not lead to a genuine need for prompting being established."

This has been confirmed by Judge Markus QC in *PM v SSWP (PIP)* [2017] UKUT 502 (AAC) in giving advice to a tribunal to whom the case was remitted. The claimant suffered from depression; he was the father of two children who stayed with him three and four nights each week alternatively. When his children were with him the claimant was motivated to care for himself properly, but when they were absent he would not dress or wash etc. The judge observes that prompting requires some active steps by another person – mere passive presence would not be enough. In her view though, the presence of the children and what they did with the claimant might have amounted to prompting even if they were not consciously doing so. But the matter did not end there because, in her view, an alternative approach could be that the presence of the children demonstrated that the claimant had a need for prompting even if he did not receive prompting when he needed it. If the need arose on a majority of the days so as to satisfy reg.7 then the prompting descriptor might be satisfied. But it will still be necessary to show that prompting is necessary because the claimant's inability results from his disability - in this case his depression. In *EH v Department for Communities (PIP)* [2018] NI Com 55 the claimant suffered from depression. He admitted that he had never learned to cook and now that he lived apart from his family he ate only sandwiches and takeaway meals. He said he did not know how to turn a cooker on and did not use the kettle. On appeal it had been contended that this meant that he required prompting to prepare a meal. The Commissioner found that the FTT had been correct in concluding that the claimant was capable of cooking a meal; his failure to do so was the result of a cultural or behavioural choice when he had lived as part of a family and his meals were prepared by his mother and then by his wife. Because he had never learned to cook, there was no evidence before the FTT of a connection between his mental health and his ability to cook.

4.239 "*supervision*" means the continuous presence of another person, there to ensure the safety of the claimant. Whether presence will require actual line-of-sight presence will need to be established. A line of cases decided in relation to reg.12(6)(c) of the DLA Regulations suggests that it might not—see for example *AH v SSWP* [2012] UKUT 387 (AAC). It is possible that the type of "presence" required, might vary with the function that is being supervised.

The meaning of supervision has been considered by Judge Wright in *LB v SSWP (PIP)* [2017] UKUT 436 (AAC). The claimant usually cooked a meal at school in a group of eight students who were watched over by two teachers. The FTT had found that this did not amount to "supervision'", apparently because this was not a one-to-one relationship. Judge Wright held that there was no reason to limit the words in Part 1 of the Schedule in this way; those words required only the continuous presence of another person for the purpose of ensuring the claimant's safety. In his view that could be achieved by someone watching over a group of others.

Note that "supervision" must relate to the safety of the claimant. This is more restricted than the definition of "safely" in reg.4 which requires that the claimant accomplish tasks without endangering himself or other people. It would seem that if supervision is required to ensure the safety of others then, without it, the claimant could not be said to accomplish the activity "safely" (e.g. Activity 9, engaging with other people). Though where the presence of another person can be avoided this argument may not apply—see the decision of Judge Gray in *SC v SSWP (PIP)* [2017] 317 (AAC) discussed below. Again, if supervision is required to prevent the claimant causing damage to property, it could be argued that, without it, the claimant cannot accomplish a task "to an acceptable standard"—see reg.4(2A)(b), but there may be some difficulty in identifying the Activity to which the claimant's behaviour can be related.

Other forms of supervision may only amount to "prompting" and, as these terms often occur in separate Descriptors, the difference may be critical.

Note that since the decision in *RJ v SSWP (PIP)* [2017] UKUT 105 (AAC); [2017] AACR 32 relating to the meaning of "safely" in reg.4(2A), it is no longer necessary to distinguish between the need for supervision of the claimant in order to ensure his safety and the test of whether he can perform a task safely – cf. the decision of Judge Bano in *SB v SSWP (PIP)* [2016] UKUT 219 (AAC).

Other terms also defined in Pt 1 are referred to in the discussion of each of the Activities and the Descriptors below.

The Daily Living Component—Activities and Descriptors

Activity 1—Preparing food

Like the so called "cooking test" for DLA it is safe to assume that a claimant's inability to cook must be attributed to a disability of some kind. It will not be sufficient that the claimant is unable to prepare and cook a simple meal because of a lack of experience, or training, or even of the inclination to cook. (See *R v SS for Social Security Ex p. Armstrong* (1996) 8 Admin. LR. 626 CA). This activity is a measure of the claimant's personal ability and not the circumstances in which they are required to perform it. This has been affirmed in *SC v SSWP (PIP)* [2017] UKUT 317 (AAC). There, Judge Gray had to consider the case of a claimant who, it was said, could not prepare a meal because of the presence of her son who suffered from ADHD and was autistic. She said that it was dangerous for her to cook while he was in the kitchen and that he required constant attention. The judge allowed an appeal, but returned the case to a fresh tribunal with a direction that the test to be applied was of the claimant's physical and mental ability to cook without regard to the presence or otherwise of her son. **4.240**

"prepare"," cook" and "simple meal" are all defined in Pt 1 of the schedule above.

"prepare" means making food ready to cook or to eat and will include the opening of packages peeling and cutting with knives and probably the ability to check the age and condition of the raw materials.

"cook" means to heat food at or above waist height- so the ability to bend and to use an oven, will not be required. This has been confirmed in *RH v SSWP (PIP)* [2015] UKUT 281 (AAC) where an appeal by the Secretary of State was allowed, when the FTT had awarded two points under this Descriptor because the claimant could not bend down to use the oven. It appears that the FTT had overlooked the definition of "cook" in art.1 of the Schedule, meaning to heat food at or above waist height. Given that most claimants' "conventional cooker" will provide only a low level oven this means that cooking a meal may have to be accomplished without the use of an oven. The judge does anticipate problems in identifying what is meant by a conventional cooker (compare with DLA where the term used was a traditional cooker). In practice this is likely to be taken as the cooker that is currently available to the claimant. If that cooker is for some reason unusable by them (e.g. the claimant is allergic to gas, or has a phobia about the use of gas) the only issue that could arise would be whether it was reasonable to expect the claimant to replace that cooker with another one—possibly a microwave.

"waist height" in this context presumably means the claimant's own waist height so that, where the claimant is disabled by a condition that causes him to be abnormally short, he will still be able to cook by the use of a "Baby Belling" type cooker and this is likely to come within the term "conventional cooker" used in Descriptor c. (cf. *CDLA/4351/2006*).

"simple meal" means a meal of one course sufficient for one person- so just for the claimant himself. This means that it should be unnecessary to handle large quantities and heavy utensils. (cf. *CDLA/2267/95*).

The simple meal must be a "cooked" meal—a diet of salads will not suffice and it must be prepared from "fresh" ingredients. By fresh it may be taken to mean raw ingredients, so that reheating ready cooked meals will not suffice, and being able to "prepare" the ingredients will exclude frozen and other pot-ready ingredients and note the decision in *AI v SSWP* [2015] UKUT 176 (AAC) (a DLA decision) where it was held that a "cooked main meal" should not take account of ethnic or religious dietary differences. The definition of a "simple meal" makes no reference to this point and cooking a meal "to an acceptable standard" must be essentially an objective test, yet it might seem reasonable to take some account of ethnic and religious differences if they could be shown to be relevant.

Two recent cases relate to the question of cultural or other special dietary requirements. In the first, *ZI v SSWP (PIP)* [2016] UKUT 572 (AAC); [2018] AACR 1 Judge Levenson has followed the line adopted in the DLA decision in holding that a simple meal must be the same for all claimants. The case concerned a claimant who ate an Asian diet that was prepared for him by his wife. The FTT had concluded that, with the aid of a perching-stool he would be able to cook for himself a meal that included the items of an Asian diet if that were required, but the claimant was given leave to appeal. It was argued that the FTT had given insufficient attention to the difficulty that he might have in cooking chapattis. The judge held that it could not have been the intention of Parliament, in making these regulations, that people from different cultural, religious or ethnic backgrounds with the same level of disability, would have a different entitlement to benefit on the basis of their community affiliation.

The second, *SSWP v KJ (PIP)* [2017] UKUT 358 (AAC) was an appeal by the Secretary of State against a decision awarding benefit to a 16 year old boy following his transition from DLA to PIP. The claimant was diabetic. It appears that his mother prepared meals for him, but it was argued that he would need supervision when cooking for himself to ensure that he got quantities and ingredients correct and that, left to himself, he would not eat the "right" sort of food. Judge Wright held that, although the need for a special diet arose from his medical condition, there had been no evidence that showed that the claimant could not prepare a simple meal for himself in the manner required by the descriptors and he allowed the appeal. The case does illustrate the different criteria that apply as between DLA and PIP. A DLA claim could have succeeded when the boy was under 16 because the issue would be how much care and attention he required from his mother; the issue now was simply how much could he do for himself.

In *SSWP v DT (PIP)* [2017] UKUT 272 (AAC) Judge Hemingway has considered the extent to which a claimant's inability to read or to tell the time might affect his ability to prepare a simple meal. The FTT had awarded this claimant, who was dyslexic, 4 points under descriptor 1(e) on the ground that he needed his wife's assistance to read recipes, instructions on packages and to set a timer or to tell the time. Without that help they had accepted that he would not be able to cook a meal to a satisfactory standard. The Secretary of State argued that none of these actions were necessary to satisfy this Activity because cooking a simple meal could be achieved "as a sensory and instinctive act"—in other words that it is unnecessary to read a recipe and that a person can tell when food is cooked by looking at it and testing it with a fork. Judge Hemingway took neither view. In his view the effect of an inability to read and tell the time may vary according to the limitations that it imposes on the particular individual; in such case the tribunal will be required to make careful and detailed findings of fact as to the effect on the claimant. In this case the FTT had made no such findings. The case was returned for rehearing.

Further complexity in applying the Descriptors in this Activity is revealed in *AI v SSWP (PIP)* [2016] UKUT 322 (AAC). There, Judge Mesher has considered the case of a claimant, who had a degree of mental disability and whose evidence, accepted by the HCP and it seems by the FTT, was that he could not prepare a meal himself; all that he ever did was to buy ready prepared meals that he heated in a microwave. The DM had awarded him two points under para.(1)(c)— apparently accepting that he could not cook a simple meal using a conventional oven, but was able to do so using a microwave. The FTT had for an unexplained reason awarded two points but under para.1(b)— needs an aid or appliance to be able to prepare or cook a simple meal. Judge Mesher points out that there is an important difference between para.1(c) and the other paragraphs in the Activity; while all the others refer to both preparing and cooking this paragraph refers only to an ability to cook. That seems to raise the possibility, he suggests, that a claimant might fail to satisfy para.1(c) if he could take fresh ingredients that had been prepared by another person and cook them himself in a microwave oven. However, this does not seem problematical because in that case the enquiry should proceed to consider why the claimant cannot prepare the meal himself. If his mental condition means that he is, at best, able to do so only with prompting he will score two points under para.1(d), while if his physical condition requires that he use aids and appliances then he will again score two points under para.1(b). (It may be that the FTT thought that he should score under para.1(b) treating the use of the microwave as an "aid or appliance". Judge Mesher held that would not be appropriate given the definition of aid or appliance in regulation 2— "any device that improves . . . the claimant's impaired . . . function." It could hardly be said that the microwave does that.) The Judge upheld the appeal on the ground that the FTT had not gone on to consider whether either of the other (higher) scoring descriptors might have applied to the claimant and he returned the case to a fresh FTT for rehearing.

A similar conclusion has been reached by Judge Hemingway in *GG v SSWP (PIP)* [2016] UKUT 194 (AAC). There, the claimant, an alcoholic, who was said to be lacking in motivation, was found by the FTT to be able to cook himself a meal by putting a ready-prepared meal in a microwave— he could cook, they said, when he was hungry enough. Judge Hemingway points out that in relation to prompting (Descriptor 1(d)) it was necessary that the claimant both prepare a meal from fresh ingredients and cook it. Even to cook a simple meal in a microwave requires that the meal is prepared from fresh ingredients, so to heat a ready prepared meal in a microwave would not satisfy Descriptor 1(c) if that meal has been bought from a shop. Judge Hemingway does not consider the possibility of a meal prepared for the claimant by someone else which he then cooks, as suggested by Judge Mesher. Given that even a shop-bought ready meal will have been prepared by someone, at some time, from fresh ingredients, this idea must also require some sort of more personal service to the claimant if it is to have any effect at all.

Decisions under the DLA test have envisaged an ability to achieve a reasonably varied and healthy diet. The DWP guidance to HCP says that menu planning to achieve a varied and healthy diet is not a part of this descriptor which is confined to the simple practical test of preparing and cooking a meal. It might be argued that being limited to a very restricted range of dishes was not to achieve the Descriptor to "an acceptable standard" (see reg.4), and in cases of severe depression and where the claimant has limited intellectual capacity, this could be important; in other cases **4.241** a very limited diet might be more the result of a want of inclination than the result of a disability.

The use of a microwave oven is now expressly provided for in Descriptor c, but it should be noted that what is allowed for is the ability to cook fresh food in that oven and not simply reheating food that has been prepared by others. This has been confirmed in *LC v SSWP (PIP)* [2016] UKUT 150 (AAC). There, an appeal was allowed because the claimant, who had been injured in a motor accident, had lost the use of one arm and hand. The FTT had rejected her appeal because she was able to heat meals in a microwave. Judge Gray, in allowing an appeal, pointed out that they must have overlooked the fact that she was required as well to be able to prepare the meal from fresh ingredients and that the FTT must be assumed to have treated her as capable by cooking ready prepared meals.

As with DLA it is safe to assume that the claimant will be expected to use the appliances that he possesses though not to use ones that he does not possess; the claimant could hardly be said to be able to cook a meal using a microwave (for descriptor c.) if he does not possess a microwave. Although reg.4(2)(b) requires a claimant to be assessed as if using an appliance that he could reasonably be expected to use, in some cases it will not be reasonable to expect the claimant to acquire a microwave oven- though, query, he might well be expected to possess a conventional cooker and the usual utensils.

For the factors that might be taken into account in determining what the claimant might reasonably be expected to possess and what to acquire see the notes to reg.4 above.

For the purpose of Descriptor b. an aid or appliance will include tools that are ergonomically designed to assist people whose ability to grip is reduced, as well as devices that are commonly used by people who are not disabled, but without which the claimant would not be able to achieve a particular task—an electric tin opener and a slow cooker are items that have featured in relation to claims for DLA.

The use of a chair or stool (a so-called perching stool) in the kitchen to assist a claimant whose condition restricted the amount of time for which they could stand, has long been accepted in relation to claims for DLA—so too then, for PIP, it has been accepted in *EG v SSWP (PIP)* [2015] UKUT 275 (AAC) and was referred to specifically in the original version of the *PIP Assessment Guide*. The current version suggests that where a device is in common use by persons who are not disabled the item is unlikely to be regarded as an "aid or appliance." The *EG* case went further because Judge Wright accepts, though without the benefit of full argument, that the same might be said of a walking stick, if that were used by the claimant to improve their steadiness in the kitchen. This might be especially so (with regard to reg.4(2A)) where, without a stick, the claimant would be in danger of falling. Note that the use of a perching stool as an aid when preparing food in Activity 1 has been questioned in the decision of Judge Lane in *DR v SSWP (PIP)* [2018] UKUT 209 (AAC). The decision does not deny that a stool might be an aid in some appropriate cases, but it does affect how often that will be so. Judge Lane adopts the reasoning used by Judge Jacobs in *CW v SSWP (PIP)* [2016] UKUT 197 (AAC); [2016] AACR 44. She found that on the facts of this case the claimant had not shown that he needed to sit more often than might be the case of any person without a disability and hence he did not need the stool as an aid in that activity. Given that she observes that most food preparation and cooking can be accomplished with relatively little time spent standing, and that most people sit at frequent stages while cooking, it seems that the need to use a stool as an appliance might seldom be shown.

It has been held, in *GB v SSWP (PIP)* [2015] UKUT 546 (AAC), that a lever-arm type tap fitted in the claimant's kitchen was an aid or appliance used in preparing food. The judge held that cooking and preparing food were separate processes, but the use of such a tap in connection with the preparation of food alone would suffice to for the purpose of this Descriptor. This point might be unimportant in this case as one could hardly cook certain foods without adding water, but there will be other devices whose use applies only in preparation and not in cooking. The FTT had rejected this part of the claim though it is not clear whether that was because they found that the tap could not be an aid or appliance, or whether they thought that this claimant did not need the aid. The case was returned for rehearing on this and other points. It might be noted, as did the judge, that use of lever type taps is specified as an aid or appliance in the *PIP Assessment Guide*. Presumably if the claimant needs such taps in the kitchen he could equally be shown to have a similar need in the bathroom. And see the discussion of these and other points in the notes to reg.2 above.

In *SSWP v AM* [2015] UKUT 215 (AAC) Judge Mark dealt with a case concerning a claimant who suffered from Asperger's Syndrome and from OCD (obsessive compulsive disorder). When following a recipe those conditions compelled him to cook each ingredient separately with the effect that any meal he prepared became inedible. The FTT had awarded him four points under Descriptor 1e on the ground that he needed someone to assist him in cooking the meal. The Secretary of State had appealed against this finding on the ground that only an award under Descriptor 1d would be appropriate, because what seemed to be called for was prompting, rather than assistance. Judge Mark said the FTT had failed to explain the reason for preferring the higher score, but in the event this error did not matter because the claim succeeded on other grounds.

The vexed question of variable conditions that affect a claimant on some days more than others is likely still to cause difficulty. Regulation 4(2A) requires that the claimant's ability should be assessed so that he satisfies a descriptor only if he can achieve that action "repeatedly". In relation to complex daily tasks like meal preparation, however, more regard is likely to be given to reg.7 where standards are set by reference to the number of days in which a Descriptor can be achieved over the required period.

Regulation 4(2A) also requires that a Descriptor is fulfilled "safely". This may benefit a claimant who can prepare a meal only at some risk to himself—cf. *R(DLA) 1/97* in which a haemophiliac was regarded as capable of cooking and *CDLA/1471/2004* in which a self-harmer was not- in either case it might be argued that the claimant satisfies descriptor e. which refers to needing supervision to prepare a meal. Note the points made in relation to preparing and cooking a meal safely and the effect of assistance or supervision in *JT v SSWP (PIP)* [2018] UKUT 101 (AAC) discussed above.

It is usual for a disabled person to take considerably longer over preparing food because of their disability. Regulation 4(2A) also requires that a Descriptor is satisfied within "a reasonable time period". This is further defined in reg.4(2A)(4)(c).being no more than twice as long as would be taken by an able-bodied person.

See the case of *GP v SSWP (PIP)* [2016] UKUT 444 (AAC) discussed in the notes to reg.4 above where the claimant was a young man who suffered from OCD and for whom preparing and eating a meal took more than twice as long. The FTT was able to find that he should then be treated as being unable to prepare a meal at all.

Activity 2—Taking nutrition

"take nutrition" is defined as cutting up food, conveying food to the mouth, chewing and swallowing food and drink, or taking nutrition by means of a therapeutic source—see below. **4.242**

In *CW v SSWP (PIP)* [2022] UKUT 281 (AAC) Judge Hemingway has decided that each of the elements of the definition of "taking nutrition" should be taken separately and not cumulatively when considering a claimant's entitlement under Descriptor 2.b.(i). The claimant had suffered an injury to his hand that resulted in the amputation of one finger and in consequence of which he needed to use specially adapted cutlery to cut up food. The claimant had been awarded 2 points under Activity 2 but, on appeal, the FTT decided that the claimant could qualify for those points only if he were able to show that he required an aid to accomplish each of the elements specified in "taking nutrition". In other words, he would need to show that he needed an aid not only to cut up food, but also to move it to his mouth, and then an aid to chew it, and again an aid to swallow it. The FTT observed that the elements of the definition were separated only by commas and should therefore be read cumulatively. As well, they thought that to give a purposive interpretation to the Descriptor meant that they should read it so as to restrict entitlement in accordance with the Government's intention expressed when enacting the PIP legislation. Judge Hemingway disagreed. He thought that to give a purposive interpretation required that the elements be treated separately. In his view a claimant who would require an aid or appliance (or even a series of separate items) to accomplish each of these elements would be so rare as to be almost non-existent. If so, it would mean that Descriptor 2.b.(i) had been stripped of any meaningful function at all. (And note that the Secretary of State had conceded that this was the correct interpretation and that the *PIP Assessment Guidance* for HCP provides for the award of points in these circumstances).

The same point had been made in the earlier case of *PA v SSWP (PIP)* [2019] UKUT 270 (AAC) where Judge Church had suggested that a definition of "taking nutrition" that required four elements to be satisfied could hardly be taken to be satisfied when the claimant could achieve only one of those elements.

This was much the same point on which Judge Hemingway had expressed a non-binding (obiter) opinion in *CB v SSWP (PIP)* [2022] UKUT 100 (AAC). There, the claimant suffered from an ulcerated throat so that she was able to swallow food only after it had been processed by a liquidiser or similar machine. It seemed to be accepted that this meant she needed to use an aid to swallow, though not to chew. The definition of "take nutrition" required that an aid was needed to "chew and swallow". In that case the Judge expressed the opinion that each word should be taken separately and in doing so he observes that to read the definition as if it were cumulative would envisage "an aid or appliance of considerable and quite probably unrealistic versatility" such that the only sensible interpretation was to treat each element separately. But the point of real contention in this case was whether artificial dentures could be regarded as an aid or appliance. The claimant had argued that her false teeth were an aid that she needed to chew her food.

Judge Hemingway declined the invitation to comment on this point, but the separation of each element of the definition means that such an argument could be raised. It seems likely that an award of points will be refused on the basis that the use of false teeth is so widespread in the general population that it cannot be regarded as any indication of disablement—see *CW v SSWP (PIP)* [2016] UKUT 197 (AAC) discussed in notes following reg.2 above.

"aid or appliance" in this context it will obviously include specially shaped cutlery, plates and cups.

In *DF v SSWP (CSPIP)* [2017] UKUT 160 (AAC) Judge May QC has held that plastic cutlery cannot be an aid or appliance for the purpose of this Activity. The claimant was a young man whose OCD caused him distress when he had to use objects with reflective surfaces. He could eat his meals, but only when he used plastic cutlery because the reflections in steel or silver cutlery upset him. The Judge refused to accept that plastic cutlery could be an aid or appliance. He says that merely to make the item of a different material does not mean that it becomes a "device" within the definition in regulation 2. Nor does he think that being made of plastic can be said to "improve, provide or replace C's impaired physical or mental condition" as the rest of that definition requires; the fact that it "obviates the claimant's asserted anxiety in using metal cutlery" is, in his view, incidental. But, could it not be argued that, by being made of plastic, the cutlery does improve C's physical (and mental) function in cutting up and eating food, because he would not be able to do so with metal cutlery?

"Therapeutic source" is defined as being feeding through a tube that is either enteral (i.e. into the gastric system) or parenteral (i.e. intravenously) and that uses a rate limiting device and pump. In *SSWP v KS (PIP)* [2018] UKUT 102 (AAC) Judge Mesher was able to award 6 points under Descriptor e on the basis that the claimant needed assistance to set up and take down the therapeutic equipment (a feeding line) each time that she used it overnight. This was on the basis of facts found by the FTT that the strict standards of hygiene and sterile equipment necessitated that help. (Rather confusingly the FTT appeared also to have held that she did not need help in managing the procedure, but it seems that there, they may have been referring to the process throughout the night rather than the set up and taking down of the equipment). Before the UT it had been argued that because the process was followed on only 3 nights of the week that the claimant did not satisfy the 50% rule under reg.7, but Judge Mesher points out that the process being overnight meant that the claimant did need the assistance in respect of two days on each occasion the equipment was used and hence needed assistance on 6 days each week.

In *SA v SSWP (PIP)* [2015] UKUT 512 (AAC) Judge Mark has considered the case of a woman who had a loss of appetite and lacked motivation to either prepare food or to eat it. She stayed with her daughter four days of the week where she could share the meal cooked by her daughter, though still then only with encouragement; the rest of the week she lived on soup and coffee and sometimes a sandwich. The FTT had found that although she lacked motivation to prepare food, that when it was provided for her, she could take food without assistance and refused to award any points. The UT reinstated the four points that had been awarded by the HCP. The judge observed that no attention had been given by the tribunal to the number of days on which the claimant needed assistance, and that the FTT appeared to have confused her lack of motivation to prepare food with her reluctance to eat. On the evidence found by the FTT it required encouragement from her daughter to do so even on the days when a meal had been prepared for her. As this was more than 50 per cent of the days in a week that alone was sufficient to qualify under Descriptor 2b, but the judge seems to suggest also, that the diet followed on the other three days, of soup and coffee etc, was not to be regarded as a satisfactory diet. "Nutrition" is not defined in the regulation, but this suggests that there might be some minimal level of food value necessary to constitute nutrition.

The suggestion that taking nutrition might involve eating a satisfactory diet in the sense that it was healthy and nutritious has been rejected by Judge Wright in two cases that were brought before him together— *MM and BJ v SSWP (PIP)* [2016] UKUT 490 (AAC); [2017] AACR 17. In the first, the claimant had reported that although she could feed herself, she sometimes felt sick or bloated and could eat only cereal or soup. In the second the claimant was depressed and diabetic and reported that he could manage to make himself only a sandwich. In both cases it had been argued that the claimants should score points under this activity on the ground that they needed either supervision or prompting to be able to take nutrition and that without that help, their diet could not be said to satisfy regulation 4(2A) because they would not be taking nutrition to an acceptable standard. Judge Wright rejects that argument. The flaw in it, he points out, is the activity of taking nutrition is defined in Part 1 of Sch.1 to mean (so far as applies in these appeals) to "cut food to pieces, convey food to one's mouth and chew and swallow food or drink". It is that process, and only that process, which must be accomplished to an acceptable standard so the quality of that which is ingested is not relevant to the questions that must be answered. The Judge concedes that where a claimant can, for reasons arising from their physical or mental condition, consume only a liquid diet it might be said that they were not capable of taking nutrition as defined; alternatively he says, a person's diet might be so eccentric that it did not amount to taking food at all, but that would be a truly extreme case. He accepts the decision of Judge Mark in *SA v SSWP (PIP)* [2015] UKUT 512 (AAC) would be correct if it is understood to be decided on the ground that the claimant needed to be prompted to eat, even when meals had been prepared for her by her daughter; the further comments regarding her diet at other times, he suggests, should be regarded as *obiter*. Judge Wright declined to refer to the *PIP Assessment Guide* or to the Government's response to consultation; he did not see how either source could be justified in relation the question of interpretation that was before him. In fact neither source would have helped the argument of the claimants.

However, in *TK v SSWP (PIP)* [2020] UKUT 22 (AAC) Judge Markus QC has made a distinction between the nutritional quality of what is to be eaten and the quantity. The claimant was a young man with cystic fibrosis and several other conditions. He was required to maintain a high level of nutrition in his diet. His mother prepared most of his meals to satisfy that diet, but without encouragement the claimant would often stop eating before he had consumed enough. Judge Markus refers to the decision of Judge Wright in the *MM and BJ* cases but finds a difference between the poor quality of the food taken there and an insufficiency of food as eaten here. In doing so she accepts that it is relevant to refer to the *PIP Assessment Guide* which accepts that a claimant might need prompting to eat or need prompting about portion size. She thought that prompting in relation to this claimant, especially having regard to taking nutrition "repeatedly" in order to satisfy regulation 4(2A) might be properly regarded by the FTT to which the appeal was referred.

The problem of whether neglecting to eat or even a reluctance to eat so as to require prompting by another person can satisfy Descriptor 2d has been referred to by Judge Hemingway in *JW v SSWP (PIP)* [2018] UKUT 169 (AAC). The claimant was autistic. He was currently studying at university for a degree in Game Design. The evidence given to the FTT suggested that he became so engrossed in his work that he would neglect to eat or drink for long periods unless he was prompted by another person to do so. The FTT did not award points in this respect, but they did so on the basis that he had said that he ate when he was hungry and they observed that he appeared well nourished. They concluded that he did not need prompting to take nutrition. Judge Hemingway, however, thought that the FTT had also accepted that sometimes the claimant might neglect to eat for so long as to become weak with hunger, and that sometimes he was distracted from eating even when the pains of hunger might tell him to do so. He felt that no clear finding had been made on that matter and returned the case on that, and other grounds, for reconsideration by a fresh tribunal. In doing so he does remark that if the meaning of this Activity is to be confined by the strict definition as suggested in the *MM* and *BJ* cases, it may be difficult to see how neglect or disinclination to eat can lead to a need for prompting to take nutrition since that involves only the process of getting food to the mouth, chewing and swallowing it. But he did accept that those earlier cases were concerned with the quality of the food taken and did not involve the issue when the claimant might fail to eat at all.

The converse situation has been considered by Judge Grey KC in *SO v SSWP (PIP)* [2023] UKUT 56 (ACC). The claimant suffered from PTSD following army service abroad which at one stage had involved having no food for a period of days. As a result, he now over ate compulsively, and his wife had to intervene to control his diet. His weight had increased significantly since leaving the army. It was agreed by the parties that his difficulty was the result of a "mental or physical health condition". Judge Grey makes a careful examination on the cases that involved undereating and concludes that there is no reason why the same conclusion should not apply to a claimant who needed assistance to avoid overeating.

The need for a person to receive assistance in feeding themselves should involve the cultural requirements of the claimant. In *CA/137/1984* (approved in *R(DLA)3/06*) a claim for DLA was rejected for a Muslim child whose disabled right hand prevented him eating in a manner consistent with the family's religious beliefs. (In Islam all eating must be done with the right hand because the left is used for toileting purposes). This case has been difficult to reconcile with other decisions where emphasis has been on enabling the claimant to lead a normal life, and in relation to PIP the guidance given by DWP to HCP has referred in general (though not in this specific example) to taking account of cultural requirements.

Activity 3 – Managing therapy or monitoring a health condition

This Activity is one of those affected by the *Personal Independence Payment Amendment Regulations* 2017 which came into effect on March 16, 2017. Those regulations have amended the definitions, in Part 1 of the schedule, that are to be used in applying this Activity. In doing so they have reversed the effect of Judge Mesher's decision in *SSWP v LB (PIP)* [2016] UKUT 530 (AAC).The Secretary of State has withdrawn the appeal against that decision so any appeal to an FTT, or to the UT, where the original decision was made prior to March 16, 2017 should be determined in accordance with that decision. In that decision Judge Mesher has tried to make sense of what was an ill drafted and confusing set of Descriptors. In his view they could best be made sense of, and justice be done, if Descriptor 3.b.(ii) were read as applying only when the claimant needed help either with medication, or to manage a health condition; if the claimant needed help in both respects, then they should be treated instead (and assuming that it was possible to do so) as needing help with therapy under one or other of paras c–f as appropriate. He did so because, in his opinion the Activity should not be read as meaning that a claimant (as in the current case) who needed help in both monitoring her condition and managing medication, several times each day, and for significant periods of time, would only ever score one point, while someone who needed help with therapy could score between two and eight points depending upon the time involved. In *KM v SSWP (PIP)* [2018] UKUT 296 (AAC) Judge Rowland has given helpful guidance to tribunals applying the original version of the Schedule in accordance with the decision of Judge Mesher in *SSWP v LB (PIP)* [2016] UKUT 530 (AAC). 4.243

The new definitions in Part I of the Schedule make clear that each concept of managing medication and monitoring a health condition is separate and that therapy cannot include the taking of medication (however that might be administered) nor any part of monitoring a health condition. The result is that someone who needs to use an aid or appliance to manage medication, or needs help (in any of the ways prescribed- supervision, prompting or assistance), or needs help with monitoring a health condition, cannot ever score more than one point even if they need that assistance in more than one, or even in all three, ways. Only the claimant who needs help with therapy, as now defined to exclude medication and monitoring, will score more points.

"Manage medication" means take medication where not doing so is likely to result in a deterioration in the claimant's health. The meaning of "manage medication" might appear to be narrow. This point has emerged in *EH v Department for Communities (PIP)* [2018] NI Com 55, a decision of the Commissioner in Northern Ireland. The Commissioner observed that the definition in Part 1 of the Schedule applied only to a "failure" to take medication "so as to result in a deterioration in the claimant's health". He thought that this might mean that where a claimant requires supervision so as to prevent them overdosing, the definition would not apply. Even if the phrase "deterioration in C's health" could be read, broadly, to include an attempted suicide, the words "failure to [take]" would be difficult to apply to an overdose. Only if "take medication" could be read as meaning, implicitly, taking it correctly, could taking an excess be regarded as a failure to take.

"medication" means something (a medication) taken at home on the prescription or the recommendation of a registered doctor, nurse or pharmacist. Presumably the word medication itself will require that the substance has some curative or therapeutic effect, but it should include pain relief and may extend to health foods and other remedies, so long as they are taken on the recommendation of the registered person described.

"Manage therapy" is now defined as undertaking therapy where failure to do so is likely to result in a deterioration in the claimant's health. Provided that "health" is given a broad interpretation so as to include comfort, it can be assumed that the decision in *RH v SSWP (PIP)* [2015] UKUT 281 (AAC) will still be followed. There, the claimant used a TENS machine every day to relieve his pain and required help in the morning to attach the machine and in the evening to remove it. The machine would probably not have had any therapeutive effect on the condition from which he was suffering so as to avoid any deterioration in his health, but it is probably fair to say that the relief of pain made him more comfortable and in that sense his health was made better.

4.244 It is a pity that the opportunity was not taken in these amending regulations to resolve the ambiguity that is inherent in the words of Descriptors c–f as discussed in both the *RH* case and in *HH v SSWP (PIP)* [2015] UKUT 558. The issue in both cases was whether the time referred to in those Descriptors was the time taken for the assistance, or the time taken for the therapy. In both cases the Judge took the view that it was the former. As this regulation has been amended and no reference made to that interpretation it could be argued that this amounts to parliamentary affirmation of that interpretation. It is also the position taken in the *PIP Assessment Guide*.

Therapy has now been defined to make clear that it does not include the administration of medication however that might be done. It now seems unlikely that the use of an epipen as in *SSWP v IM (PIP)* [2015] UKUT 680 (AAC) could be anything other than the delivery of medication, but doubts remain over the administration of an emollient cream whether it is "medicated" (as it may be popularly described) or not. In *PC v SSWP (PIP)* [2015] UKUT 622 (AAC) it was thought to be a question of fact for the FTT to decide upon. The question has been raised again in the case of *CM v SSWP* (PIP) [2020] UKUT 259 (AAC) where the issue was whether a foot balm product used by diabetics (amongst others) to soften skin on their feet, should be regarded as "medication" or as "therapy". The question was not answered because, before Judge Perez, the claimant abandoned that part of his appeal. The point was not without significance because, in his case, were the product to be regarded as medication it would score one point under Descriptor 3b(ii), but if it were therapy it could score two points under Descriptor 3c and that would have made the difference, for him, between benefit at the standard rate and benefit at the enhanced rate. Judge Perez thought no criticism should attach to either the claimant or his advisers because they were faced with an argument, and 199 pages of supporting evidence, from the Secretary of State in favour of its being medication. But the point remains open now for decision at an FTT. But difficulties remain in distinguishing between medication and therapy because apart from requiring that medication or therapy must be prescribed or at least recommended by a health professional the definition does not help in determining what else each word might mean. The meaning of each word is otherwise left to the tribunal, no doubt with the help of a dictionary and the advice of the medical member.

The meaning to be given to the word "therapy" and the distinction between that and other forms of care and support that might be given to a claimant has arisen in several cases. To begin with the judges are agreed that the word "therapy", in the absence of any more helpful statutory definition, must be given its ordinary dictionary meaning which is "the medical treatment of disease; curative medical or psychiatric treatment" (Oxford English Dictionary). In the first of these cases, *DC v SSWP (PIP)* [2016] UKUT 11 (AAC), Judge Jacobs decides that therapy must involve something more than keeping an eye on the claimant and giving support to general living activities. Nor, he suggests would providing employment for the claimant amount to therapy; it might be described as being therapeutic for him but would not be therapy in this sense. In *KM v SSWP (PIP)* [2018] UKUT 296 (AAC) Judge Rowland agrees with that conclusion though on the case before him he returned the matter to a fresh tribunal to take evidence as to the forms of support that the family provided. In *AH v SSWP (PIP)* [2016] UKUT 276 (AAC) the emphasis was on the need for therapy to have occurred on the advice of a health care professional and "at home". In that case, the encouragement of friends to give up smoking and the attendance at keep-fit classes in a gym, failed for one or both of those reasons. The judge found also that, even if the action had been taken on the advice of her GP, it would not be therapy unless there was a direct correlation to a disease or condition for which it was curative treatment. In *KM*, Judge Rowland adds a gloss to this by saying that he thought the requirement that the activity be "at home" was intended to exclude things done at a hospital or other specialist venues as had been the case in *AH*, rather than to confine activity to being in the house. In other words, support that was given by family members on the advice of a medical professional that took place out of doors, such as walking for exercise in the park might also qualify if it could be shown to be a part of a curative treatment programme.

In *KM v SSWP (PIP)* [2018] UKUT 296 (AAC) Judge Rowland also gives useful advice in relation to the way that attention given to the claimant in relation to more than one PIP Activity and hence, therefore, suggest the possibility of double counting, must be approached. He summarises the effect of these and other cases as follows:

> "20. The overall effect of the case law as it applies for the purposes of this case is therefore that a need for "prompting . . . to be able to manage therapy" must be a need for something more than, or different from, ordinary interactions within a household and also more than, or different from, a need for supervision, prompting or assistance such as would score points either under descriptor 3(b)(ii) as construed in LB or under any of the other daily living or mobility activities.
>
> 21. Subject to that qualification, it seems to me that, insofar as engaging with other people may be therapeutic for a claimant and is in a form recommended by a relevant health professional, engagement by those other people with the claimant may amount to prompting the claimant to undertake therapy for the purposes of descriptors 3(c) to 3(f)"

A wide meaning to the terms "manage therapy" and within that "health" has been suggested by Judge Hemingway in *MM v SSWP (PIP)* [2018] UKUT 193 (AAC). The claimant was a young person who was profoundly deaf. She had been fitted with cochlear implants that improved her ability to hear, but on the advice of her audiologist she undertook exercises, with which her mother assisted, to train her brain so as to take full advantage of the implants. It was contended that this assistance should score under Activity 3 c or d depending on the time taken each week. The judge did not make a conclusive decision on the point because he had not had full argument on it; he did reject a suggestion put on behalf of the Secretary of State that the mother's help amounted to no more than encouragement to give up a bad habit or to take up a good pastime, but the question of whether training the brain could be therapy to avoid a deterioration in health was not argued. Judge Hemingway thought that it possibly could be. He refers to *RH v SSWP (PIP)* [2015] UKUT 281 (AAC) where the UT judge had accepted that a TENS machine that relieved the claimant's pain could be regarded as therapy because it improved his health in the sense of making him more comfortable and hence its absence might be regarded as a deterioration in health. In the present case the judge thought it was arguable that the exercises might amount to therapy (they were advised by a health professional) if they facilitated her ability to hear and that, without them, her hearing would be reduced by more than a minimal degree.

The meaning of "therapy" has been touched on by Judge Perez in *PM v SSWP (PIP)* [2018] UKUT 138 (AAC). There the claimant, who suffered extensively from arthritis had been advised by her consultant to apply a compression bandage to her lower leg daily. She said that doing so caused her pain and that she was slow in doing it. It was not suggested that the bandage was medicated. The UT judge found that there were sufficient findings of fact in the case file to be able to award 2 points under Descriptor c - needs assistance to manage therapy that takes no more than 3.5 hours a week.

In *TK v SSWP (PIP)* [2020] UKUT 22 (AAC) Judge Markus QC has made clear that managing therapy can include things that are done by another for the claimant, as well as assistance that is given to the claimant in doing things themselves. This point was necessary because the wording of s.78 of the Welfare Reform Act 2012 that makes provision for the Daily Living Component of Personal Independence Payment, refers to a person's ability to "carry out activities" being limited by that persons physical or mental condition. The claimant was a young man who suffered from cystic fibrosis and several other conditions. The therapy required to maintain his health was exhaustive and exhausting. The claimant's argument was, in effect, that even if he were able to carry out the regime of therapy required himself, that it was so onerous as to make that impossible for him (or anyone else) to do so without assistance from another person. Judge Markus had regard to the preparatory legislative materials that led to the introduction of PIP in replacing DLA. She concludes that, although the assistance given must relate to the physical or mental condition of the claimant, there is nothing in the wording of section 78 that requires it to be the *direct* result of that condition. In the present case the claimant's need for assistance arose from either, his physical fatigue, or from want of mental persistence in doing the therapy, neither of which could be regarded as "irresponsible behaviour" as referred to in *R(A)* 2/92. As the judge put it:

> "The tasks within activity 3 are all carried out by reason of a person's health condition. If a claimant needs assistance in carrying out those tasks, it can be said that the need arises from their physical or mental condition. This is the position even where a claimant is not physically or mentally impaired in performing the tasks involved in managing their therapy but where, nonetheless, they require assistance to do so because of the nature of the tasks themselves."

An example (not apparently relevant in this case) would be where the cystic fibrosis patient is treated by percussive physiotherapy to his chest and back- clearly an activity that he could not perform himself. In this case the judge considered that it was possible that the same might be true of therapy that he could perform himself but was prevented from doing so by his own fatigue both physical and mental. The case was remitted to be heard by a fresh tribunal.

The importance of understanding the use of each term is brought out by the facts of *MF v SSWP (PIP)* [2015] UKUT 554 (AAC); [2016] AACR 20. The claimant suffered from a condition that necessitated daily use of a dilator to maintain the function of her urethra. She used this device herself for about an hour each day at home in the evening. Clearly the dilator was an "aid" and its use would seem to constitute managing therapy rather than medication. The claimant could not, therefore, manage her therapy "unaided" because she needed to use an appliance, but neither subparagraph of Descriptor 3b seems applicable because subpara.(i) refers only to managing medication, while subpara.(ii) relates only to supervision, prompting or assistance, and in this case the claimant managed the therapy for herself. Nor could she satisfy any of the remaining descriptors because none of them refers to the use of an aid. This meant that the claimant was forced to argue that she needed supervision, prompting or assistance to manage her therapy, which would have scored four points under Descriptor 3c. The judge appears to have accepted (perhaps just for the sake of argument) the claimant's argument that the prescribing and recommendation by her doctor and advice from a nurse, could amount to the necessary supervision, prompting or assistance, but of these, supervision and assistance are defined art.1 of the schedule so as to require the presence of the person supervising or assisting which did not appear to be the case here, and neither did it appear that the claimant required any prompting. It appears, therefore, that the only way this claimant could have scored even one point, would be if her use of the dilator could be regarded as "managing medication" with use of an aid. While it is now clear that therapy cannot include giving medication or monitoring of health, the difference between medication and therapy is still not entirely clear; hence it might be possible to argue that the converse could still apply – therapy (in this case by oneself with an appliance) might also be a form of medication and therefore score under para.3.b.(i), but only so as to gain one point.

The distinction between medication and therapy may also be important in relation to the various forms in which medication is delivered to the claimant. While an inhaler (or rather the medicine that it contains) and insulin needles are a medication they can usually be handled by the claimant themselves and therefore score no points under Descriptor 3.a.(ii). (It will be otherwise where, for example the claimant has a needle phobia, and needs another person to administer the injection – he will score 1 point under 3.b.(ii)). A question also remains as to whether certain forms of treatment are medication. Clearly physiotherapy is not, but is the delivery of oxygen to the lungs of a person who suffers from COPD medication, or is it therapy? If it is the latter then the claimant could qualify under paras c–f – but then only if he requires help with the equipment and then to score points only in respect of the time for which the assistance is necessary. The same question might be asked if the claimant requires help with a nebuliser; the *PIP Assessment Guide* says that the use of nebuliser is therapy. If these claimants need no help they could score points then only if the equipment can be regarded as an "aid or appliance" and so score 1 point under para b.(i). Cases of *KR* and *RB* discussed below leave open the question of whether equipment such as this could be a device and hence an aid for this purpose. Because the meaning of therapy is unclear it is not uncommon for a claim to be made for points to be scored under this Activity at the same time as points are claimed in respect of the same disability under another Activity. While it is common place for a disability to affect a claimant's ability in several different ways and hence score points under more than one Activity (see *MF v SSWP (PIP)* [2015] UKUT 554 (AAC); [2016] AARC 20) and *PE v SSWP (PIP)* [2015] UKUT 309 (AAC); [2016] AACR 10) what is in question is whether points can be scored more than once in respect of the same action by the claimant. See, for example *AS v SSWP (PIP)* [2017] UKUT 104 (AAC); [2017] AACR 31 where Judge Bano (applying a principle first stated by Judge Gamble in *CSPIP/386/2015*) held that the claimant who needed help with using a catheter could not score under both this Activity and under Activity 5 for toilet needs. The principle to be applied was that where words are used in a statute that refer specifically to the matter in question they displace any more general reference that might otherwise be thought to apply. On that basis, to allow the claimant to score in more than one Activity would be double counting by allowing them to score points for exactly the same limitation. This principle has been applied again by Judge Mesher in *SSWP v KS (PIP)* [2018] UKUT 102 (AAC) where he accepted that the claimant could not score for both this Activity (Managing therapy) and Activity 2 (Taking nutrition) when it was the same process of using her therapeutic resource that was the basis of the claim. Judge Mesher points out that the *AS* decision should now be regarded as having the general agreement of judges in the Administrative Appeals Chamber of the Upper Tribunal because it is now reported there, but he does mention that it may be considered again by a three-judge panel and also suggests that it could be confined to the instance of assistance being required, rather than of prompting or supervision. **4.245**

An aid or appliance can be something as simple as a tablet organiser box (referred to in the *PIP Assessment Guide* as a dosette box) – see decision of Judge May QC in *AK v SSWP (CSPIP)* [2016] UKUT 256 (AAC). Certainly if the box is used to help a claimant who otherwise could not be relied upon to get their medication correct it would seem to comply with this definition, though, if the use of the box is to avoid a risk to the claimant's safety, then "supervision" might be equally appropriate. Where, however the box is prepared by a person who will not be present (as in the case of a dispenser prepared by the pharmacy or by a person who visits) the box will have to be an "aid or appliance"—in this case it would make no difference as the descriptors have the same score. It now seems reasonably clear that an inhaler is not an aid when used to deliver medication – see *KR v SSWP (PIP)* [2015] UKUT 547 (AAC). This was a case on mobility component where the claimant had argued that he needed the inhaler as an aid to move more than 50 metres, but the principle should be the same for this Activity. The UT held that the inhaler was a means by which the medicine was delivered (cf. a teaspoon for a linctus) and not an aid to improving his physical function – that was done by the medicine not the inhaler. The same has been held in the case of a nebuliser in *RB v SSWP (PIP)* [2016] UKUT 556 (AAC) though there the judge left open the possibility that a nebuliser might be an aid in delivering medication when an inhaler was insufficient for that patient – see the discussion of this case in the Notes to regulation 2.

"Monitor a health condition" means that the claimant needs someone to detect significant changes in the claimant's health that may lead to a likely deterioration, to be followed by taking action to avoid that deterioration— the action having been advised by a registered doctor, nurse or health professional who is regulated by a Health Professions Council. Presumably this includes action advised in advance of the event as well as advice that is sought immediately and could be as simple as calling an ambulance. See for an example of monitoring health the case of *SSWP v IM (PIP)* [2015] UKUT 680 (AAC) referred to above and also *DC v SSWP (PIP)* [2016] UKUT 11 (AAC) where the claimant was a schizophrenic who lived in sheltered accommodation. He was required to attend at the nurse's room each day to ensure that he took his medication, but otherwise took care of himself. It was held that he could score, at most, two points on the basis that he might need prompting to take his medication though Descriptor 3 b(ii) seems equally appropriate.

"therapy" means treatment (therapy) to be undertaken at home and which is prescribed or recommended by a registered doctor, nurse, pharmacist or other health professional who is regulated by a Health Professions Council. Under the amendment to this definition, referred to above, it is made clear that therapy cannot include the taking of medication in any way, nor any action that can constitute monitoring of a health condition. Therapy will include renal dialysis and physiotherapy, especially for claimants such as those with cystic fibrosis. Note that PIP will be available for renal dialysis only when the claimant dialyses at home whereas AA and DLA could be available in a hospital if no help was given by hospital staff. Whether the claimant will be entitled to benefit on the basis of this activity alone will depend upon the time for which therapy is needed each week. In the case of renal dialysis, the time will be that for which the claimant needs assistance, supervision etc not the time spent dialysing—see *HH v SSWP (PIP)* [2015] UKUT 558 (AAC) discussed above.

Activity 4—Washing and bathing

4.246 A claimant will score points if he is unable either to wash or to bathe unaided.

"Wash" is not defined but will probably involve the use of water—using "wet-wipes" alone should not suffice, but sponging down will.

"bathe" includes the process of getting into and out of an unadapted bath or shower.

There are many devices designed to make it safer to get into and out of a bath or shower; most of which should be classed as an "aid or appliance". A single grab-handle that might be just as likely to be used by an able person would not be an aid for this purpose (See *CW v SSWP (PIP)* [2016] UKUT 197 (AAC); [2016] AACR 44) discussed above in Note to regulation 2 but any extra handles that are necessary for the claimant to use in bathing or showering probably will be. Lever arm taps that were accepted as an aid in *GB v SSWP (PIP)* [2015] UKUT 546 (AAC) and were suggested in the original version of the *PIP Assessment Guide* have been doubted in the *CW* case. The *Guide* now suggests that items that are in common use by non-disabled persons are unlikely to be accepted as aids. (See discussion of these cases in Note to regulation 2 above). The use of a chair in the shower was accepted in *NA v SSWP (PIP)* [2015] UKUT 572 (AAC).

The meaning of Descriptor e has been examined by Judge Rowley in *SP v SSWP (PIP)* [2016] UKUT 190 (AAC); [2016] AACR 43. The claimant had moved into a house where there was a walk-in bath left by a previous occupier. He said on his claim form that he would require assistance to get in or out of an unadapted bath, but it appears to be accepted that he could use the walk-in bath unaided. The judge had to decide two points. First, whether Descriptor e prescribed a test that was disjunctive or whether it was conjunctive. In other words would it suffice for a claimant to show that he could not climb in and out of a bath unaided, even though he might be able to use a shower, or must he show that he was capable of using neither the bath, nor the shower, without assistance? The judge found the word "or" was disjunctive and therefore the former test applied. (For especially clear explanation of this distinction see paras.11–16 of this judgment). Secondly, she had to decide if the "bath or shower" referred to in Descriptor e was an unadapted bath etc or whether it might suffice if the claimant could use the walk-in bath with which he was provided. The judge had little difficulty in accepting that Descriptor e must be taken to refer to an unadapted bath- that was the meaning given to the word "bathe" as defined in Part 1 of the Schedule and as used elsewhere in this activity. The word bathe does not appear in Descriptor e, but that is the consequence of the history of this provision. In this case it appears that the FTT had taken the claimant's ability to use his walk-in bath as determinative and the case was returned for rehearing.

A decision of Judge Mitchell in *MB v SSWP (PIP)* [2018] UKUT 139 (AAC) has considered the meaning of Descriptor f in this Activity. The claimant had said that she could not wash the upper part of her back satisfactorily and therefore needed assistance to do so. The FTT had found that most people are unable to reach the upper spinal region of their body and that therefore the claimant's inability to do so could not score points under this descriptor. The Judge finds that this was an error of law. He says that doubtless the tribunal was correct in their assumption about the ability of most people, but that such people are able to wash their back to a satisfactory extent by the use of a sponge or other appliance. The question that they should have considered was whether the claimant was unable to do that in a similar way so as to achieve a similar result without requiring the assistance of another. The claimant had raised a separate point about her ability to dry her back. Although neither the definitions of wash or bathe nor the words of Activity 4 refer to drying oneself, the judge was able to conclude that in this case (and probably in almost all others) the two activities are so closely related in functional terms that an ability to do the one will inevitably include an ability to do the other.

Note that in *SH v SSWP (PIP)* [2018] UKUT 251 (AAC) Judge Hemingway has made the point that just because the claimant may have to remove cochlear implants when washing and bathing does not mean that they must always qualify to have a need for supervision. That was the same situation in *RJ and others v SSWP (PIP)* [2017] UKUT 105 (AAC); [2017] AACR 32 where the judges had suggested that supervision might be necessary to ensure the safety of the claimant when her implants were removed. In the present case Judge Hemingway suggests that so long as the question of safety is considered correctly in accordance with the meaning of safety in reg.4, and on the evidence before them, an FTT might still conclude that the claimant does not require supervision while bathing. But note that the judge rejects an argument made on behalf of the Secretary of State that the claimant could be expected to minimise risk by reducing the time that she took to shower.

Two cases heard together by Judge Perez, *KT and SH v SSWP (PIP)* [2020] UKUT 252 (AAC), both concern claimants who were required to remove the cochlear implants with which they were fitted while they were using a shower or bath. Without those devices neither claimant could hear an alarm that would warn them of either a fire or a burglary in the house. In both cases the argument was put that this required the presence of another person in the home to warn them of danger and would qualify them for two points under Descriptor 4c (needs supervision to be able to wash or bathe). Alternatively, if the risk could be managed by a visual alarm that would qualify for the same score under Descriptor 4b (needs an aid or appliance to be able to wash or bathe). Counsel for the Secretary of State had agreed that, in both cases, applying the test established in *RJ v SSWP (PIP)* [2017] UKUT 105 (AAC); [2017] AACR 32 the FTT had made an error of law in applying the test of whether a claimant could accomplish a task "safely" when they failed to explain why, given the claimants' inability to hear an alarm, that the risk created could reasonably or sensibly be ignored. Subsequently, they agreed also, that it would not be washing or bathing to an acceptable standard if the claimant were required to do so with the bathroom door open, thereby making it more possible to hear the alarm or possibly to see signs of the danger.

Rather than remit the cases for rehearing, Judge Perez substituted a decision of her own. In deciding not to remit the judge was mindful of the fact that typical FTT hearings are scheduled to be completed in 60 to 90 minutes. In rehearing these cases counsel for the Secretary of State had argued that the FTT should consider statistical evidence as to the likelihood of fire occurring, or of burglary, together with, evidence of the extent of harm to be expected in either case. In the judge's view this would be too onerous a task to be undertaken in the allotted time, but, in any case, she also took the view that neither an FTT, nor herself in reaching the current decision, should have regard to such evidence because it would mean that the risk to be assessed would vary according to the area in which the claimant lived as well as to the type and construction of the premises. In her view the ability for a claimant to succeed should depend only upon factors that relate to the condition of the claimant themselves and not to other external factors. This was not to say that every claimant who was required to remove their hearing devices was entitled to succeed on a claim such as this; it would still be necessary for the claimant to show the extent of their hearing impairment, whether they needed to remove the aid when showering or bathing, whether without the aid they were unable to hear a normal warning device and, consequently, whether it was necessary for them to have an aid or appliance or supervision whilst they were showering or bathing. Judge Perez had been presented with extensive statistical evidence to show that the risk of harm from fire occurring in domestic premises was slight. For the period covered by that evidence the risk of domestic fires at which fire services had attended was 1 in 270,000. Counsel had argued that this risk was de minimis, or at least so small that it could reasonably and sensibly be ignored. The judge disagreed. She refers to the case of *R(A)2/89* in which Commissioner Monroe had decided that, in the case of a claimant who was tetraplegic, the risk to him from a fire in the home was such that it could not reasonably be ignored even if it was remote. Using that test, which she found to be consistent with the views of the panel of three judges in the RJ case, she found that the risk to claimants in the present cases was such that it could not reasonably or sensibly be ignored. Judge Perez goes on to find that on the evidence submitted by both claimants each should be entitled to two points under Activity 4.

In this decision Judge Perez has held that entitlement should not depend upon the different views that might be taken by an FTT of the degree or the acceptability of risk from fire, except in so far as there might be differences in the degree of the claimant's hearing impairment and the need for them to remove their hearing devices and the consequent need for aid or supervision. In all other respects, the risk from fire should be treated as unacceptable so as to make the act of showering and bathing unsafe. Other means of washing were not raised in these cases. Nor was it necessary for the judge to decide on risks arising from burglary because counsel had conceded that if the risk of fire made the activity unsafe the claimant was entitled to succeed.

Note that in this case the judge finds specifically (in para.149) on evidence presented on behalf of the Secretary of State, that a person without hearing impairment would be able to hear a normal alarm whilst showering with the bathroom door shut. This is important because were that not so it could be argued, on the same basis as in *CW v SSWP (PIP)* [2016] UKUT 197 (AAC); [2016] AACR 33 that an inability to hear an alarm while in the shower was not a measure of disability for the purpose of claiming PIP.

Activity 5—Managing toilet needs or incontinence

4.247 "toilet needs" include getting on and off an unadapted toilet, evacuating the bowel or bladder and cleaning oneself afterwards.

Extra handles and support bars in the toilet area will constitute an "aid or appliance" in this context. The use of grab handles and support bars to assist when using the toilet (and elsewhere in the bathroom) has been accepted in *FK v SSWP (PIP)* [2017] UKUT 375 (AAC). There, the point was made that such handles and bars are not mentioned in the list of items suggested to be aids and that a claimant is invited to consider when answering the relevant question on the PIP claim form. The judge suggests that might lead a claimant to answer "no" to that question, but he confirms that the handles are an aid or appliance when used to access the toilet. Note that it must be shown that it is necessary for the claimant to use those handles and that they are not there merely as a matter of convenience (see above in relation to Activity 4—Washing and bathing).

In *RB v SSWP (PIP)* [2019] UKUT 186 (AAC) the claimant suffered from peripheral neuropathy which meant that his hands were frequently so stiff and numb that it made the performance of several of the daily living activities difficult. This was especially so in the early morning after rising and in order to be able to manage his toilet needs the claimant had developed the strategy of warming his hands with a fan heater or a hair dryer or, on some occasions, by first running warm water over his hands in a basin. This action was necessary particularly when cleaning himself after defecating in the morning. The FTT that had heard his appeal had awarded 7 points under various activities that included the use of aids, but they had allowed no points in respect of his toilet needs. Judge Hemingway, though accepting that this was a marginal case, found that it was an error of law not to have considered his need to use the devices he described, as aids and referred the case for a rehearing. The claimant had conceded that the condition of his hands did improve as the day went on. The FTT appear to have thought that it was therefore unlikely that he would need such assistance with his toilet needs for more than 50% of the time, but neither in that decision, nor in the UT, does it appear that consideration was given to the regularity or timing of his toileting.

Different toilet arrangements that arise from cultural differences should be taken into account.

"managing incontinence" involves dealing with involuntary evacuation of the bowel or bladder and includes doing so with the use of devices such as colostomy bags and a catheter. In previous versions of the note to this Activity it was suggested that this definition meant using such devices would mean that the claimant could manage toilet needs unaided and would therefore score no points. Two cases in the UT have shown that to be wrong.

In the first of these, *JM v SSWP (PIP)* [2016] UKUT 296 (AAC), the claimant was given a stoma following surgery for a bowel cancer that meant the use of colostomy bags to manage incontinence. In the FTT the two points that he had been awarded under this Activity by the DM were removed. In the UT however, attention was given to the inconsistency that then arises between Descriptor 5(a) where the claimant might be regarded as managing incontinence unaided, and Descriptor 5(b) where he might be regarded as needing to use an aid or appliance to manage incontinence. A colostomy bag would certainly fall within the definition of an "aid or appliance" in reg.2 as a "device that improves, provides or replaces C's impaired physical function". It would be only if that definition should be read to exclude a colostomy bag because of the reference to a collecting device in the subsequent definition of "managing incontinence" found in Part 1 of the schedule that the claimant could be deprived of the two points awarded under 5(b). In the UT Judge Lane found that the ambiguity appearing in these descriptors, coupled with what she saw as the absurdity that might then to be said to arise if a claimant such as this scored no points when someone using something as simple as a dosette box did, would justify her in having recourse to the legislative preparatory materials under the principles in *Pepper v Hart* [1992] UKHL 3. From these it was clear that a colostomy bag (referred to there as a stoma bag) was intended to be treated as an aid or appliance.

Following this case a similar conclusion has been reached in respect of incontinence pads – see *BS v SSWP (PIP)* [2016] UKUT 456 (AAC). The precautionary use of incontinence pads on a daily basis, even though they were soiled only infrequently, has been held to satisfy the 50 percent rule required by reg.7: see *SSWP v NH (PIP)* [2017] UKUT 258 (AAC). Further it is important to note that what is in issue is whether the claimant has a need for incontinence pads - whether they actually use them or not—see *KO v SSWP (PIP)* [2018] UKUT 78 (AAC). In this case there was evidence that the claimant wet the bed at night (frequency not specified); it was unclear from the FTT decision whether they had found that the claimant did not wear incontinence pads during the day or whether she wore them neither by day nor by night. The case was remitted with a reminder that the test was that of need rather than of actual use. Catheters are not mentioned in the preparatory material, but by a parity of reasoning it would seem right to say that any catheter used (whether by self-insertion or fitted more permanently) is equally an aid or appliance used in accordance with Descriptor 5(b). That much seems to have been accepted by the UT judge in *AS v SSWP (PIP)* [2017] UKUT 104 (AAC); [2017] AACR 31. There the claimant was a woman who had to use a catheter several times a day to empty her bladder; she claimed that she was unable to catheterise herself and needed help from her partner to do so. The FTT hearing her appeal had granted two points on the ground that she was using an aid or appliance to manage toilet needs, but did not accept that she needed help for which she would have scored four points. An appeal was allowed because Judge Bano, in the UT, thought that the FTT had failed to deal adequately with the evidence that was before them. It appears, however that the claimant alleged that she should also score points under Activity 3 by needing assistance to manage therapy. Judge Bano held that it should not be so. Where, as here, an action is dealt with specifically under one Activity it should not be considered again under a more general Activity. Although it will be common for a claimant's disability to affect more than one daily living Activity (as has been accepted in several cases (see *MF v SSWP (PIP)* [2015] UKUT 554 (AAC), [2016] AARC 20 and *PE v SSWP (PIP)* [2015] UKUT 309 (AAC); [2016] AACR 10) it is an accepted principle of statutory construction that the specific should displace the general (see an expression of this principle by Judge Gamble in *CSPIP/386/2015*). And note too that in this case it is not just the claimant's form of disability that affects more than one Activity, but precisely the same action that is being offered as the reason to score in both Activities.

In the case of *GP v SSWP (PIP)* [2015] UKUT 498 (AAC) Judge Hemingway has dealt with the question whether a difficulty in dressing and undressing could count for both Activity 6 and for this activity when it was necessary for the claimant to remove and replace clothing when using the toilet. He held that it does not, but not because, as argued by the representative of the Secretary of State, that to do so would amount to "double counting"—he observes that the same disability will frequently entitle a claimant to score under more than one activity. The reason why dressing and undressing does not count here, is because of the way that "toilet needs" and "managing incontinence" are defined in Part 1 of this schedule. Each is defined in such a way that the process of undressing and dressing does not form part of that activity- hence no points can be scored in respect of difficulty in doing so.

The decision in *GW v SSWP* [2015] UKUT 570 (AAC) also explains the meaning of "toilet needs" as defined in Part1 of the schedule. There, getting on and off the toilet, evacuating bowels and bladder, and cleaning oneself afterwards, are all linked by the conjunction "and". In the FTT it was held that this meant that a claimant must be unable to accomplish all three parts of this definition before they could qualify for two points under Descriptor 5b. In the UT Judge Rowley held that this was wrong. In this context, she said, the word was used disjunctively and hence an inability to accomplish any one of these parts would qualify. In this case the claimant was an obese man. He had been allowed points under both Activity 4 (Washing and bathing) and under Activity 6 (Dressing and undressing) because he needed to use an aid to assist in those functions. In the toilet he needed to use a shower head or brush to clean himself and so was awarded two points under this descriptor also.

The decision in *MF v SSWP (PIP)* [2015] UKUT 554 (AAC); [2016] AACR 20 deals with a possible relationship between this activity and Activity 3 (Managing therapy etc). The claimant in that case needed to use a dilator on a daily basis in order to maintain the use of her urethra—if she did not do so she would need to undergo surgery to reopen the urethra and permit her to evacuate her bladder. It did not appear from the evidence recorded that she used the dilator when actually using the toilet, but her claim seems to have been based on the argument that she needed to use an aid (the dilator) to manage her toilet needs—Descriptor 5b. The FTT had rejected her claim on the basis that they did not see a sufficiently direct connection between the use of the dilator and the use of the toilet, but they seem also to have taken the view that because the claimant's use of the dilator was pertinent in relation to Activity 3, it could not be considered, as well, in relation to Activity 5. Judge Williams allowed an appeal and returned the case for consideration by a fresh tribunal. In doing so he deals first with this point about overlap between the activities. As he puts it, simply because a particular disability is relevant in relation to one activity is no reason why it should not apply also to another- there will be numerous cases where upper body disabilities or mental disabilities affect several activities. What was not clear, and was why the judge returned the case to another tribunal, was whether the claimant did, at the relevant time, have to use a catheter to empty her bladder, or to use incontinence pads, both of which would be aids or appliances that she used to manage toiletry needs. But the real question in this case is, if the dilator is used only as device that will subsequently facilitate the passing of urine, as and when that may be necessary, can it be said to be used to manage toiletry needs? There must be some point at which the management of a condition relates to the medical treatment of the claimant, rather to the management of their toiletry needs otherwise the surgery that the claimant had undergone, on at least two occasions, would be "assistance" in managing her toiletry needs. It was only the daily repetition of the dilation procedure that might seem to make it a part of her toileting management.

Managing incontinence, as defined in Pt 1, also involves "cleaning oneself" afterwards, but cleaning oneself does not include washing soiled clothes or bedding. (cf. *Cockburn R(DLA) 2/98* where the immediate cleaning of the bedding was regarded as sufficiently close to a bodily function to qualify for DLA, though not doing the laundry next day). Someone who needs help only in dealing with the aftermath will not qualify. Note too, that although managing incontinence includes "cleaning oneself" afterwards, if the claimant uses devices in doing that cleaning those devices can only be an aid or appliance if it is the action involved in cleaning oneself that is the function that is impaired–see *DA v SSWP (PIP)* [2019] UKUT 320 (AAC) discussed in the Note following regulation 2 above.

Activity 6—Dressing and undressing

"dress and undress" includes both putting on and taking off socks and shoes. **4.248**
But note that it is not necessary that a claimant has difficulty in both dressing and undressing; difficulty with either function will suffice. Also, if the claimant needs to use a device to put on socks though not his shoes, that will suffice. For both of these points see *JM v SSWP (PIP)* [2016] UKUT 542 (AAC). In that case it was also held that a claimant who could manage slip-on shoes, though not shoes with laces, could not score points for this Activity. This was a decision of Judge Rowley applying the same reasoning as had been done in the case of *CW* and others discussed below.

Dressing and undressing unaided will require that the claimant can manage all buttons, zips and other fasteners and it will require that the claimant is able to dress in garments that are appropriate to themselves in a cultural sense, as well as being able to choose clothes that are appropriate to the weather conditions and to the event, or the circumstances, in which they are to be worn. The reference here to clothes that are appropriate in a cultural sense was based originally on the inclusion of that element in the first version of the *PIP Assessment Guide* for DM. Those words have now been removed from the *Guide*. Nevertheless it remains the role of the tribunal to reach a decision on the basis of the claimant's ability to dress and undress in clothing that is appropriate for them. There seems no reason why this should not take account of what is culturally appropriate clothing. What might be doubted is whether dressing in such clothing, when the claimant is accustomed to doing so, should be any more difficult than any other mode of dress. Presumably if dressing in this way takes longer, the time taken is to be compared with time that would be taken to dress that way by a non-disabled person.

Note that the descriptors for PIP make no distinction between activities by day and by night. This will be of most relevance in relation to dressing, undressing, washing and bathing and undertaking toilet needs. In *DP v SSWP (PIP)* [2017] UKUT 156 (AAC) Judge Hemingway has held that a claimant may be said to require help in dressing if, because of mental or physical disability, he might select items of clothing that are malodorous or are unhygienic. In *ML v SSWP (PIP)* [2017] UKUT 171 (AAC) Judge Hemingway has considered the case of a claimant whose medical condition caused her to hesitate and prolong the process of dressing. The FTT had accepted that her condition might extend the time that she took to dress—they said that "she was able to make a decision eventually", but they made no finding as to how long the delay might be and in particular did not refer to reg.4(4) and the definition there of what might be a reasonable time. For that reason the case was returned to a new tribunal, but in doing so the judge affirms that hesitation in choosing clothes, even on the basis of the appearance presented, could be reason to satisfy Activity 6, provided always that the claimant's difficulty in doing so could be attributed to their physical or mental condition.

In *NA v SSWP (PIP)* [2015] UKUT 572 (AAC) Judge Mark held that the claimant's use of a chair, or a bed, to dress and undress could satisfy Descriptor 6b. It mattered not that able people might similarly use a chair or bed to dress or to help put on their shoes; what mattered was whether the claimant was *unable* to do those things without that aid to assist them.

However, a different conclusion on similar facts has now been reached by Judge Jacobs in *CW v SSWP* [2016] UKUT 197 (AAC); [2016] AACR 44. There the claimant said that she had to sit on her bed in order to dress herself. The judge held that a bed, which might equally be used by a non-disabled person should not, in these circumstances be regarded as an aid to dressing. While he begins by agreeing with the decision of Judge Mark that an ordinary object may become an aid to a disabled person if that person cannot accomplish the task without it, he goes on to say that the need for assistance must relate to the particular function in question-what might be necessary as an aid in washing and toileting will not necessarily be an aid in dressing. The use of the aid must then be related to the function:

> "The question is this: would this 'aid' usually or normally be used by someone without any limitation in carrying out this particular aspect of the activity? If it would, the 'aid' is not assisting to overcome the consequences of an impaired function that is involved in the activity and its descriptors".

On this basis he concludes that while the claimant needed to sit whilst she took her jeans on and off it was just as normal for able persons to do the same— in effect the claimant was not disabled in respect of the function of dressing and undressing because that is commonly the way that dressing etc is done. The decision of Judge Jacobs in *CW v SSWP (PIP)* [2016] UKUT 197 (AAC); [2016] AACR 44 has been followed by Judge Markus QC in *AP v SSWP (PIP)* [2016] UKUT 501 (AAC). She supports the reasoning in that decision and adds to it herself in the following way:

> "The activities in Schedule 1 to the Regulations can be performed in a variety of ways. Dressing and undressing is no exception. A person who has little or no choice as to the manner in which they can carry out an activity but who can do it nonetheless, is not limited in doing so. I respectfully agree with Judge Jacobs'

reasoning at paragraph 31 and 32 of CW. Otherwise a claimant who can eat sitting down but needs an aid or assistance to eat standing up would qualify for points under activity 2, and a claimant who can sit in a bath but needs an aid or assistance to lie down in it would qualify for points under activity 4. Once that is understood, it can be seen that what is usual or normal is both a relevant and a necessary consideration. It provides the limits for what a claimant can be expected to do and not to do (see Judge Jacobs' example at paragraph 30 of his decision) in order to undertake an activity."

And see the discussion of these cases in the note that follows regulation 2 above. The approach in *CW v SSWP (PIP)* [2016] UKUT 197 (AAC); [2016] AACR 44 has been followed by Judge Ward in *MR v SSWP (PIP)* [2019] UKUT 293 (AAC) though, in that case, he allowed an appeal because the FTT had failed to consider the claimant's need to use a further aid when he dressed. Although the claimant commenced the process of dressing by sitting on his bed the evidence showed that at some point he had to stand, balancing himself with the aid of a crutch, to complete the process of putting his trousers on and doing them up. The case was returned to a new tribunal, but the rehearing was limited only to a consideration of this Activity.

The meaning of "dressing" has been explored by Judge Jacobs in *PE v SSWP (PIP)* [2015] UKUT 309 (AAC); [2016] AACR 10. The claimant had failed in her claim because although in her claim pack she had stated that she needed help when dressing, when before the FTT, she said that she managed to dress by wearing "easy to wear" clothing. The judge allowed her appeal on the basis that the test in Activity 6 was based upon an abstract test of normal clothing which the representative of the Secretary of State appears to have accepted means "clothing which is appropriate to the general norms of society at large." In this case she argued the FTT had clearly found that the claimant's "easy to wear" clothing was appropriate. The judge returned the case for rehearing. In his view, just as a claimant could not elevate their degree of disability by insisting on wearing clothes that were particularly difficult to manage, so too, they would not be required to reduce their disability by wearing only loose fitting and elasticated clothes. The judge suggested that the new tribunal should focus first upon the ways in which the claimant's disability affected her ability to dress - bending, reaching, and twisting, together with any degree of pain associated with the process. They should also consider the effect that reg.4(2A) might have in assessing her ability to do so to an acceptable standard and within a reasonable time.

In this case it does not appear that the judge had been referred to the *PIP Assessment Guide* as has been done in other cases. Although the *Guide* is not determinative of meaning in the regulations it has been accepted as helpful in interpreting them. The judge might have found helpful the first paragraph relating to Activity 6 which reads as follows:

"This activity assesses a claimant's ability to put on and take off [. . .] un-adapted clothing that is suitable for the situation. This may include the need for fastenings, such as zips or buttons and considers the ability to put on/take off socks and shoes."

In *LC v SSWP (PIP)* [2016] UKUT 150 (AAC) the point was also made that the claimant who had lost the use of one arm and her hand in a motor accident would not be able to manage buttons, zips and most other fasteners. Judge Gray observed that this would make it difficult for the claimant to put on most outer garments without assistance from another person. For much of the time a coat would be required when out of doors and this would be relevant to the 50% rule under reg.7.

Activity 7—Communicating verbally

This Activity is entitled communicating verbally. Taken literally that could **4.249**
mean both spoken and written communication, but it appears that the use of

the term verbal occurs because this Activity was originally combined with that in Activity 8 – written communication. It is now clear that this Activity is concerned only with making and receiving oral/aural communication. This is established in the decision of Judge Gray in *EG v SSWP (PIP)* [2017] UKUT 101 (AAC). In that case it became clear that the DWP does not now use the claimant's ability to lip-read as a way to receive oral information, although there are several reported decision in which lip-reading has been taken account of in the past. Judge Gray could find no basis upon which she could read that limitation into the PIP legislation, but accepted, at least for the purposes of this case, that it was a concession properly made on the basis of a pragmatic approach to the matter under regulation 4 – in other words lip-reading might be thought to be so ineffective and unreliable that it should not be regarded as a way of receiving information to an acceptable standard.

Judge Gray has referred again to the matter of lip-reading in *CC v SSWP (PIP)* [2017] UKUT 429 (AAC). The same concession was made by counsel representing the Secretary of State and although no general direction has been issued to judges in the Social Entitlement Chamber as the judge had requested, she was advised that guidance to this effect has been issued to decision makers, and that this should ensure a common treatment across all claimants. Judge Gray observes that DM guidance is not binding on tribunals, but suggests that, were a tribunal to reject that advice, they would need to explain their reasons with some particularity.

The matter of whether lip-reading should be taken account of in assessing a claimant's ability to communicate has been considered again in *MM v SSWP (PIP)* [2018] UKUT 193 (AAC) and also in *SB v SSWP (PIP)* [2018] UKUT 122 (AAC). In both cases the UT has held that for an FTT to take lip-reading into account amounts to an error of law so long as the Secretary of State continues to direct DMs that it is not an acceptable means of communication. In *P v SSWP (PIP)* [2018] UKUT 376 (AAC) Judge Mitchell has put this matter beyond any doubt (at least so far as the FTT is concerned) by holding that lip-reading is not a means of communicating verbally. He holds that this is not because of any concession by the Secretary of State but because that is the correct interpretation of the law having regard to reg.4(2A) that would require communication to an acceptable standard.

Confining Article 7 to oral/aural communication also means that use of telephones and other devices to send and receive text messages plays no part in Activity 7. Judge Gray takes the view that this Activity requires that the claimant can both speak and hear; thus someone who can speak, but not hear and uses a hearing aid, or, someone who can hear, but not speak and uses a text-to-speech machine, is in each case communicating only with the use of an aid or appliance and will score 2 points under Descriptor b. This case concerned a young person who suffered from a serious hearing loss from an early age. She had learned to speak and had some benefit from hearing aids, but had difficulty in using a telephone and sought out quiet places to in which she could communicate more easily. A major point made in this case is the need for a tribunal to assess the claimant's ability in the range of environments that might be regard as normal for that claimant. The claimant should not be judged in a quiet environment if she chooses to go there only because her disability. This means that the tribunal must try to distinguish between what the claimant does as a matter of her genuine preference and what she does because of her disability. (cf. *PE v SSWP (PIP)* [2015] 309 (AAC); [2016] AACR 10 where the issue was claimant's choice of clothes).

"Basic verbal information" means information in the claimant's native language. It is "basic if it is in just one simple sentence.

"Complex verbal information" is more than one sentence or, just one complex sentence- again in the claimant's native language.

In *SSWP v GJ (PIP)* [2016] UKUT 8 (AAC) Judge Hemingway has underlined the need for tribunals to make clear in their reasons that they have taken account of the meaning of "complex" communications as defined in Part 1 of the schedule. Although it might have been inferred, at least in relation to written communication where the claimant had been found to have difficulty in dealing with correspondence from the DWP and in completing his PIP claim form, that he did have difficulty with complex information in the requisite sense, the judge held that the FTT should have made specific reference to that matter.

This case is important also in dealing with the relationship between Activity 7 and Activity 9. The claimant was a schizophrenic who needed support in relation to both activities. But the judge accepts that the sort of support that is necessary in relation to Activity 9—help in dealing with other people in a face to face situation will not be sufficient to satisfy Activity 7 as well. There the difficulty experienced by the claimant must be such as to make him unable to communicate as distinct from just relate socially to others. He explains this as follows:

> "I accept that anxiety caused by mental health difficulties can potentially lead to the scoring of points under activity 7 such that the activity and its associated descriptors are not simply concerned with physical or sensory impairments to communication. I also accept though, as highlighted in the government response, that there is a distinction to be drawn between the sorts of tasks the two different activities, and the associated descriptors, are seeking to test. In this context there is a difference between communication and engagement. If a claimant has difficulty in speaking as a result of anxiety, or perhaps some other mental health problem, it must be asked what it is that causes that difficulty. Is it a fear of social engagement? Or is it something simply connected to the activity of communicating verbally? It could, of course, be both but, equally, it could be one or the other. So, it seems to me an anxious claimant who, for example, is not able to communicate with strangers or persons who are not well known to him or is not able to do so when in the company of a large number of people but is able to verbally express himself or herself and understand communication with a person with whom they are familiar and comfortable would, in all probability, score points under activity 9 but not under activity 7. That is because, in such a case, it is likely to be the engagement with others which is triggering the difficulty. So, such a claimant would not be able to score points under both activity 9 and activity 7 as a consequence of an anxiety problem impacting upon the ability to engage with other people. However, if a claimant was so anxious that not only was he impaired with respect to engaging with others but was also impaired with respect to the function of communicating verbally, perhaps a most unlikely eventuality, he might score under both activities."

In this case the claimant would probably show that he could satisfy Activity 9 more easily than he could Activity 7. The converse was probably the case in *HB v SSWP (PIP)* [2016] UKUT 160 (AAC). There the claimant was a girl who was bilaterally deaf though she could lip-read and used hearing aids. Judge Rowley agreed with the view expressed in the case above and returned the case to an FTT for further facts to be found relating to the claimant's need for social support.

"communication support" is help given by a person with training or experience in assisting people with specific communication needs. Superficially this could cover any communication need, but limiting the test to the claimant's native language will have the effect of eliminating the foreign language interpreter. The most obvious cases of a person giving communication support will be a signer for the deaf. Note that communication support (which satisfies Descriptor c.) must be given by a person, so that a claimant who uses a computer generated voice will be using an aid or appliance to communicate and will satisfy only Descriptor b.

In *TC v SSWP (PIP)* [2016] UKUT 550 (AAC) Judge Rowley has held that communication support should be treated in the same way as is social support in relation to Activity 9. That means that it is not only persons who have been trained to provide support to persons in general who qualify, but also persons, such as friends and family, who have experience in supporting that claimant. 4.250

It is interesting to note that, at a time when the use of a hearing aid, at least among the elderly, has become almost commonplace; it will still count as the use of an appliance in order to communicate and therefore, satisfy Descriptor b. (cf. the wearing of spectacles below).

Activity 8—Reading and understanding signs, symbols and words

4.251 The definitions of basic and complex written information approach the difference in a similar manner to that for verbal information in Activity 7.

"basic written information" is signs symbols or dates in standard size text written in the claimant's native language.

"complex written information" is more than one sentence written in standard size text in the claimant's native language. By implication then, basic information is limited to one sentence.

"read" means the ability to understand signs, symbols and words in the claimant's native language and in standard size text. To "read" does not include Braille, so a person who is visually impaired so as not to be able to read standard size text will score under Descriptor d. (four points). In order to score under Descriptor e (eight points) the claimant would need to show that he cannot read signs, symbols or words at all, and the shift from "written information" (i.e. standard size text) in the preceding Descriptors, to any words seems to be deliberate. Note that the shift to the use of "words" and the use of that word in the definition of "read" in contrast to "signs and symbols" may mean that a claimant who can understand numbers and other symbols, might succeed under this Activity if he cannot understand words though he may still understand symbols. The importance of examining the claimant's ability to read all kinds of information has been emphasised by Judge Lane in *SSWP v SH (PIP)* [2017] UKUT 301 (AAC). There the FTT had focused on her ability to read official letters, and her tendency to have difficulty when she got upset, rather than the whole range of any possible literature and signage. The judge said that they had erred too, in relying on the oral evidence given to them at the hearing, when there was other and contradictory evidence in the tribunal file.

A helpful decision has been made by Judge Ward in *SE v SSWP (PIP)* [2021] UKUT 1 (AAC). The judge begins by observing that this Activity caters for two distinct kinds of disability -those whose disability results from a want of visual capability and those whose disability arises from a lack of understanding. The claimant in this case was of the latter kind. The judge had reserved his decision for further evidence but gave guidance on the meaning of these Descriptors and of the relevant definitions for the benefit of others. He finds, and counsel for the Secretary of State agreed, that the definitions of both basic and complex written information are essentially about an ability to read words. Thus, the reference in both to signs means something in the form of words that is displayed as a warning or instruction e.g. "Private Property Keep Out" or "Danger High Voltage Electricity". Similarly, the reference to dates he finds to be as expressed in words e.g. "Monday, January 1st"- otherwise, as he points out, what would be the significance of matters being expressed in the claimant's native language and is also consistent with the definition of read. By implication this confirms also that the list of signs, symbols and words must be conjunctive – a claimant must be able to read all three forms of information. The words written or printed, by contrast, are probably alternatives because by written the judge suggests is meant handwritten and printed standard size text means of a size appropriate to the form that the words are displayed in e,g. a notice as above.

Prompting, he notes, may take the form of reminding or encouraging though explaining must be understood to mean not simply telling the claimant what the words say because that is what the Descriptors require that the claimant can do for themselves.

As to satisfying reg.4(2A), being able to read even basic information safely must require that they also do so to an acceptable standard, which will mean that they can do so reliably because a person who makes a guess at what a warning notice might say, rather than ask for assistance, could not be said to do so either safely or to an acceptable standard. Reading basic information within a reasonable time might be more problematic because for an able person the process will be almost instantaneous and hence a test of no more than twice as long will require some further judgment.

Finally, Judge Ward finds that where Descriptor (e) says that the claimant cannot read signs symbols or words "at all" this does not mean a total inability to read any word, but only that the claimant is unable to do so even to the extent prescribed by Descriptor (d). In the subsequent report of the case after receiving further evidence it was found that the claimant satisfied that Descriptor. The further report is significant in that the respondent had submitted further evidence in the form of decisions relating to the same claimant's assessment of work capability in her claims for Universal Credit. On three occasions she had been found to have limited capability for work-related activity. Judge Ward found that though the benefits were different, in cases of this kind the evidence provided in the UC claim was relevant also to the claim for PIP. He suggested that where this was so, representatives of the claimant and of the Secretary of State might bear in mind the obligation under FTT rules to provide "all documents relevant to the case in the decision maker's possession". (See *SE v SSWP (PIP)* [2021] UKUT 79 (AAC)).

Two cases have been decided that show that illiteracy is not relevant to this Activity unless it can be shown to derive from the claimant's mental or physical condition – see *SSWP v IV (PIP)* [2016] UKUT 420 (AAC) which was a case on the mobility component and *KP v SSWP (PIP)* [2017] UKUT 30 (AAC). In both cases the illiteracy was from a failure to learn to read rather than any demonstrated relevant condition.

The descriptors for written communication make no reference to communication support. This means that someone who is blind so as to require the services of a reader will qualify under Descriptor e.

The benchmark of normality in this case includes the use of spectacles or contact lenses- Descriptor a. A person who chooses to use a magnifying glass rather than spectacles, will also be treated as meeting Descriptor a. so long as it is possible (and reasonable) to expect him to so—see reg.4(2)(b) above. Where it is not, the use of a magnifier will mean that the claimant is using an aid or appliance.

Activity 9—Engaging with other people face to face

"engage socially" means to interact with people in an appropriate manner both contextually and socially and it will require the claimant to understand body language and to be able to establish relationships. It is important to note that the function required here of the claimant is to engage socially. Although those words do not appear directly in the Activity it has been accepted that they are to be imported from the definitions in Part 1 of the schedule. This means that it is the claimant's ability to meet and engage with others in a social context that is to be tested. Evidence that the claimant engaged effectively with the HCP, or that he could attend for hospital appointments, or take part in work related group sessions does not meet the point – see *SF v SSWP (PIP)* [2016] UKUT 543 (AAC). In *HA v SSWP (PIP)* [2018] UKUT 56 (AAC) Judge Rowley has emphasised the need for a tribunal in considering this Activity to examine the claimant's ability to satisfy all three parts of engaging socially—i.e. to interact in a contextually and socially appropriate manner, to understand body language and to establish relationships. In this case the claimant had profound difficulty in relating to adults and the judge directed that being able to engage only with other young people or with others who were already known to him would not suffice. The requirement that the claimant must be able to engage "face to face" also precluded a finding that he could engage with others by sending texts on his telephone. 4.252

But note the points made by Coulson LJ in the CA decision in *Hickey v SSWP* [2018] EWCA Civ 851. The claimant's appeal failed in that case because the court found that facts, as found by the FTT, that the claimant could form appropriate social relationships with only a need for prompting rather than other forms of support were clearly supported by the evidence. In doing so, Coulson LJ holds that first, although the claimant might need to be shown to achieve each of these 3 elements, the FTT need not do so for each separately but could consider them all "in the round". Secondly, he holds that a finding that the claimant ""does not shy away from people" and that she "engaged well" with the HP, the FTT and "whoever she needs to" are more than sufficient to demonstrate that the appellant had a clear ability to establish relationships". He rejects the suggestion that a "relationship" must be of a long-lasting nature; as he puts it, relationships encompass all forms of social engagement whether it "lasts ten minutes, ten days or ten years" and he adopts the phrase used by counsel for the Secretary of State that "it is a low threshold".

A further example of where the claimant might be said to engage successfully but only with a limited range of people is found in *AC v SSWP (PIP)* [2021] UKUT 216 (AAC). The claimant had Asperger's syndrome and Prader Willi Syndrome. Evidence was given to the FTT that he was able to relate to others when he visited a shop selling wargames and that he could take part, in person, at wargaming competitions. Judge Church, in the UT, allowed an appeal on the ground that the tribunal had placed disproportionate emphasis on his ability to participate in wargaming and had drawn impermissible inferences from that about his ability to form social relationships for which they had allowed zero points.

"social support" means help from a person who is trained or experienced in assisting people to engage in social situations. It is not clear whether "social" in this context is intended to be confined to what might be described as non-business relationships or whether it might extend to all inter-personal contacts. As the descriptors refer only to "engaging with other people" and that must be in a contextually appropriate (as well as a socially appropriate) manner it is suggested that the wider meaning should be preferred. In *AM v SSWP (PIP)* [2017] UKUT 7 (AAC) Judge Jacobs has held that engaging face to face means engaging one to one or within a small group and does not necessarily require the ability to cope with a crowd.

The application of this Activity in the case of a claimant whose sight is severely restricted is examined by Judge Sutherland Williams in *DV v SSWP (PIP)* [2017] UKUT 244 (AAC); [2017] AACR 38. The judge reviewed several helpful passages drawn from earlier cases. The case was returned to fresh tribunal who would be required to make findings, in particular of the extent to which the claimant could read the body language of those with whom he was interacting, and of the extent to which prompting or support would assist him in that situation. The judge emphasised also, that the test was of the claimant's ability to interact generally one to one, or in a small group and in social situations. Inferences that the FTT had drawn from the claimant's interaction with them in the hearing room were either of limited relevance, or, if they were to be relied upon as the reason for their decision, they should have been put to the claimant as a part of the hearing.

A decision of Judge Mark *PR v SSWP (PIP)* [2015] UKUT 584 (ACC) has clarified two points in applying this descriptor. First, the definition in para.1 of this Schedule of "social support" as support from a person "trained or experienced in assisting people to engage in social situations" might reasonably have been thought to include only those people who have had training or experience in handling this situation for people in general, but this case establishes that it will suffice if the person assisting does so in light of experience only of that particular claimant. This means that assistance from family members and friends will qualify as social support. This was pointed out by the representative of the Secretary of State as having been explained in the Government's response to consultation on the assessment guide and is now contained in the *Guide* itself. In this case it appears that the family and friends had not in fact supplied any social support—indeed, as the judge put it, they showed a singular lack of empathy with her. It seems that doubt has been expressed as to whether the decision of Judge Mark does then settle that point. For that reason the matter has been decided again in *SL v SSWP (PIP)* [2016] UKUT 147 (AAC) and should now be regarded as settled.

The second point made by Judge Mark is that for social support to be given, does not require that the assistant is there at the time of engaging face to face; the support may be given by counselling beforehand, but without which, the claimant would be unable to engage with other people. Indeed, the *PIP Assessment Guide* goes even further—it points out that the claimant may not have support at all—what is required is that the claimant *needs* social support and that may be the case even when none has been provided.

The meaning of "social support" in Descriptor 9c (for which 4 points are awarded) and the difference between that and "prompting" in 9b (only 2 points) has given rise to a number of cases. In the Scottish case of *SSWP v MMcK* [2017] CSIH 57 the Inner House of the Court of Session upheld a decision of Judge Agnew that had held the difference to depend mainly on the fact that social support could be given only by a person trained or experienced (in the wider sense that had been accepted by Judge Mark in the *PR* case above). The Court of Session affirmed also that support given in advance of the occasion could qualify, though they did suggest that there must be some "temporal or causal" link between help given and the event to which it was related. In England, at the same time, a number of cases had been decided by the UT in which it was said that there must be something more than just the training and experience of the person giving support to justify the difference in the points awarded. There must be, it was said, some qualitative difference between the actions that were social support and those that amounted only to prompting. That was the view taken by Judge Humphrey in *AH v SSWP (PIP)* [2016] UKUT 147 (AAC). That case was appealed to the CA where it is reported as *Hickey v Secretary of State for Work and Pensions* [2018] EWCA Civ 851, but in which the court found it unnecessary to reach a decision on the points raised above. Clarification has now been provided by the decision of the Supreme Court on the appeal from the Court of Session in the *MMcK* case reported as *Secretary of State for Work and Pensions v MM* [2019] UKSC 34. The appeal was allowed, but only because the unanimous decision of the Court (given by Lady Black) was for slightly different reasons than those in the court below; the result remains the same.

The decision of the court begins by accepting that the definition of "engage socially" in para.1 of this schedule is appropriate to be used when considering a claimant's ability to engage with other people face to face–Activity 9.

The court then proceeds to deal with the matters to be decided in two parts. First, what was called the "qualitative issue". In the Supreme Court the Secretary of State accepted that "prompting" could also qualify as "support". This meant that the difference between assistance that would satisfy Descriptor 9c rather than 9b will turn upon the need for the person giving it, to be trained or experienced in that regard. Again, the Secretary of State was happy to affirm that the training and experience required could be that of family or friends. Lady Black first emphasised the matter of the claimant's "need" for support. She puts it thus:

> "30. The obvious starting point, in determining which of the Activity 9 descriptors applies, is to establish what help the particular person needs in order to be able to engage with other people face to face, remembering that this is not about the help the person is actually receiving, but about the help that they need, although the one may of course inform the other. It is worth stressing that the provisions are not concerned with support that the person would like to have, or would appreciate as generally comforting; the particular support has to be needed to enable the activity to take place."

Lady Black then returned to the central question of the difference between support that deserves the award of 4 points and that which results in only 2 points.

The difference, she says, lies in the fact that the support given will help the claimant only when it is provided by a person who is trained or experienced.

> "34. The Secretary of State's anxiety that the provision will be taken to include the sort of confidence-boosting and reassurance that occurs in most close relationships can be allayed by keeping the focus very firmly on the twin requirements of necessity and relevant training or experience. Applied in the family/ friends setting, to qualify for points under 9c, the claimant has to need support from someone who is not just familiar with him or her, but who is also experienced in assisting engagement in social situations. It is the training/experience of the helper upon which the claimant depends in order to enable the face to face engagement with others to take place, not simply the close and comforting relationship that may exist between the claimant and the helper.
> 35. Having dispatched the idea that "prompting" can never constitute "social support", the words of descriptor 9c, taken with the definition of "social support", clearly define the ambit of the category and distinguish it from descriptor 9b. There is no need to complicate them. As the Inner House observed in para 55 of its opinion [...] the nature of the support provided might not differ between 9b and 9c. What brings the claimant into 9c rather than 9b is that, to be able to engage with others, he or she needs that support to come from someone trained or experienced in assisting people to engage in social situations. As the Inner House helpfully put it, the support "will only be effective if delivered by someone who is trained or experienced"."

Lady Black goes on to disagree with the suggestion made in the Inner House that it might suffice if the training or experience *increased* the effectiveness of the support that was given. In her view that would not suffice; the test was whether, without that training and experience, the support would be effective at all. This was because the claimant must "need" that sort of help, if they could relate to others face to face with untrained help, then it could not be said that they needed the more specialised help of a trained or experienced person. But this point must be nuanced by reference to reg.4(2A), because if, with what Lady Black described as "lay" help, the claimant could not relate to others to "an acceptable standard" then it would be right to say that more qualified help was needed by the claimant and thus the effectiveness of support would be increased.

In the second part–the "timing issue", the Supreme Court rejected the Secretary of State's argument that support must be contemporaneous with the event at which it is required. There were, in Lady Black's view, too many instances where support given prior to the event would be helpful in assisting the claimant to relate successfully and therefore, it would be undesirable to adopt an interpretation that excluded that support.

> "46. In short, I do not consider that descriptor 9c is limited to cases where a claimant needs social support actually during the face to face engagement. Given that social support is likely to take many different forms, depending on the individual needs of the claimant, it is undesirable to attempt to prescribe, in the abstract, which other forms of support will be sufficient. It will be a question of fact and degree, and is something that will have to be worked out on a case by case basis, by those with expertise in making assessments and decisions in relation to claims, keeping the wording of the provision firmly in mind. I am hopeful that it will prove possible to do this without the Secretary of State's fears of inconsistent and arbitrary decisions being realised."

Clearly, it will still be necessary to demonstrate that there is a sufficiently close connection between the support given and the event for which it is needed. The court accepts that psychiatric or psychological help given in the past will cease, at some point, to be needed by the claimant so as to satisfy this Activity–relating to other people face to face will have become a part of the claimant's life skills. But

Lady Black does not find the expression "temporal or causal link" used by the Inner House to be helpful, if only because, as she says, it would be hard to imagine help that was timely (temporal) and would not also be causal; perhaps temporal and causal would be a better formulation so long as it is not applied too restrictively.

In *SSWP v AM (PIP)* [2015] UKUT 215 (AAC) Judge Mark has upheld the decision of an FTT that awarded benefit to a claimant who suffered from both Asperger's Syndrome and from OCD (obsessive compulsive disorder). The judge held that while they may have failed to give sufficient reasons for one part of their decision (see Activity 1, above) this would make no difference to the outcome of the case. In upholding the decision in respect of Activity 9, an award of 8 points under Descriptor d, the judge found no mistake. He did, though, point up some difficulties with the wording of this activity. First, although Part 1 of this Schedule contains a definition of "engage socially" that expression does not appear in this activity or, indeed, anywhere else in the Schedule. But that definition does serve to identify the factors that might be involved in measuring a claimant's ability to engage effectively. More problematically, there may be difficulty in reconciling the requirements under reg.4(2A) for the claimant to engage with other people safely and to an acceptable standard, and for the need in Descriptor d for the claimant to do so without overwhelming psychological distress or causing a substantial risk of harm. If the evidence shows that the claimant cannot (on at least 50% of the days in the relevant period) engage safely and to a satisfactory extent is it necessary to find, as well, that the same behaviour shows the necessary overwhelming distress and risk to safety? In the view of Judge Mark it was sufficient for the tribunal to have found, on the evidence that was before them, that the claimant could not engage socially safely and to an acceptable extent; it was not necessary for them then to make a separate finding that this was because of overwhelming psychological distress or the risk of substantial harm. Perhaps the best explanation is that the same evidence fulfilled both requirements. And see below the further decision of Judge Jacobs in *RC v SSWP (PIP)* [2017] UKUT 352 (AAC) 4.253

In *HJ v SSWP (PIP)* [2016] UKUT 487 (AAC) Judge Markus QC has considered the requirements that must be shown for a claimant to be engaging with other people to a satisfactory extent. She accepts, as had Judge Mark in *SSWP v AM (PIP)* [2015] UKUT 215 (AAC), that although the words "engage socially" do not appear in the descriptors for this activity, the definition that is given for them in Part 1 of the Schedule should be used as a guide to what engaging face to face might involve. In this case the claimant, who was an alcoholic and suffered from depression, had said that she visited one or other of three pubs each day. The FTT had dismissed the appeal against refusal of her claim taking the view that this was inconsistent with any claimed inability to engage with others. The claimant had said that at the pub she stood at the bar alone and moved away if anyone tried to talk with her. She also gave evidence of self-harming when under stress. Judge Markus thought that this, and other evidence, had been overlooked by the FTT so as to be an error of law or, at any rate, they had failed to give sufficient reasons to explain why they had done so. The judge thought it may have been possible that the claimant's behaviour at the pub and her other dealings with people, did not evince an interaction that was "in a contextually and socially appropriate manner", and that the evidence showed that she might not be able to "establish relationships with others". The case was returned to a fresh tribunal. A helpful analysis of the requirements to be examined in establishing whether the claimant can engage to a satisfactory extent can be found in the decision of Judge Sutherland Williams in *DV v SSWP (PIP)* [2017] UKUT 244 (AAC), where the claimant suffered from a visual impairment that affected his ability to read the body language when making a face-to-face engagement.

A decision of Judge Jacobs in *RC v SSWP (PIP)* [2017] UKUT 352 (AAC) has considered further the meaning of engaging socially and in particular what might be required to "establish relationships". The claimant suffered from a mental health condition which caused him to have thoughts of a homosexual nature whenever he came into contact with other men. He found this extremely distressing and said that he wished he could kill himself. The FTT had awarded 2 points for Descriptor 9(b) on the basis that, with prompting (though their reasons would suggest that they should have awarded 4 points under 9(c)), he could engage with other men (he had no difficulty in respect of women) to the extent of making a reciprocal exchange. Judge Jacobs held that this was not sufficient to constitute establishing a relationship. As he points out a brief conversation about the weather with a stranger, would be a reciprocal exchange, but we would not, as a matter of ordinary language, call that establishing a relationship. The judge returned the case to a new tribunal without attempting to prescribe what would be necessary to establish a relationship. He considered that it would be impossible to list the essential characteristics of a relationship in all circumstances—he doubted, for example, that he would have been able to anticipate the facts of this case if he had tried to list the situations that such a list might be required to encompass. This means that these words, as ordinary words of the English language, should be interpreted by a new tribunal (as the finders of the facts) relying upon their own experience and common sense.

One further point that arises from this case is the relationship between a claimant's ability to achieve an Activity to an acceptable standard, in accordance with reg.4(2A)(b), and the need to show, in Activity 9(d)(i), overwhelming psychological distress. In *SSWP v AM (PIP)* [2015] UKUT 215 (AAC) Judge Mark held that where the claimant had been unable to engage socially in a manner that was safe and to an acceptable standard, that it was not necessary to find, as well, that he would suffer overwhelming distress. In this case Judge Jacobs does not refer to the earlier case and his disposition of the case suggests that he did expect the new tribunal to make a finding about the level of distress that the claimant might suffer. Yet, he also suggests that neither prompting nor support might be sufficient to enable the claimant to engage socially to a satisfactory standard in accordance with reg.4(2A). It therefore seems open to a new tribunal, following the *AM* case, to find in the claimant's favour without needing to find overwhelming distress. The trouble with this conclusion is that the Descriptor 9(d)(i) is satisfied only when such a finding has been made. This creates the same conundrum that emerges from cases such as *GP v SSWP (PIP)* [2016] UKUT 444 (AAC) where the FTT was forced to conclude that the claimant could not wash himself at all (because he took more than twice as long as a normal person would to do so) when the descriptor to be satisfied read "cannot wash and bathe at all and needs another person to wash their entire body". While that might have been physically possible (though unlikely) in that case, it is difficult to see how Descriptor 9(d)(i) can be said to be satisfied at all unless the overwhelming distress is shown.

But an alternative and perhaps more viable approach to this conundrum is suggested by Judge Ovey in *AB v SSWP (PIP)* [2017] UKUT 217 (AAC). This was another case where the claimant's evidence suggested that he suffered distress when he tried to engage socially with others. Judge Ovey suggests that the requirements of reg.4(2A) should apply only to those descriptors which test what the claimant *can* do, and are not applicable to those descriptors that describe what the claimant *cannot* do. In her view the structure of PIP Activities ranges from a descriptor at one end that specifies a claimant who can accomplish the activity described without any need for assistance at all, to another at the other extreme where the claimant cannot accomplish that activity at all. By way of illustration she refers to Activity 6—dressing and undressing; that ranges from "can dress and undress unaided" to "cannot dress or undress at all". It makes sense applying reg.4(2A) to test whether a claimant can dress (with or without aid) to a satisfactory extent, safely and in a reasonable time, but it does not, she says, make sense to ask whether someone who cannot dress at all does so satisfactorily, safely and timeously.

The inference is that reg.4(2A) was not intended to apply to the "cannot-do" descriptors. Regulation 4(2A) was a late addition to the regulations (as can be seen from the numbering) and in this, as well as other respects, the regulations as a whole, and the descriptors in particular, have evolved somewhat piecemeal. The advantage of this approach in relation to Activity 9 is that the tribunal can sensibly decide if the claimant can engage with others with or without prompting or support, to a satisfactory extent and do so safely, but, if it is shown that he cannot do that, then the sole question is whether, when he tries to engage, he suffers either overwhelming psychological distress or becomes a danger to himself or others.

The relationship between this Activity, in particular Descriptor 9d, and reg.4(2A) **4.254**
has been considered again in *JT v SSWP (PIP)* [2020] UKUT 186 (AAC). The claimant suffered from paranoid schizophrenia and although he had been well controlled for a number of years still had difficulty in meeting with other people because of anxiety and stress. In the FTT the claimant had been awarded 4 points under Descriptor 9c. He appealed on the ground that the FTT had not dealt adequately with his claim under Descriptor 9d. Evidence found by the FTT suggested that he met occasionally with people to whom he was known including some students and a neighbour, and that when accompanied by his mother he was able to attend his doctor's surgery, at the HCP interview, and, on two occasions, at a FTT hearing (though he did not attend at the hearing from which he was appealing). Judge Rowland deals at some length with the relationship between Activity 9 and reg.4(2A). He begins by reminding us that the provisions in reg.4(2A) were written originally to appear in the *Assessment Guide* but were moved by amending regulations that came into force at the same time as the main regulations. That may explain, he suggests, why they might have been written without the same attention to linguistic precision and may explain the ill-fit that there is sometimes between the regulation and the Activities. In the judge's view neither the words of reg.4(2A) nor those of Activity 9 can be read in a literal sense but must be approached in a way that gives reasonable effect to both. He rejects the possibility that the words might be read so that, having concluded that a claimant "cannot" form a relationship safely and satisfactorily but for a reason other than those specified in Descriptor 9d, he could then fail to score under any other part of Activity 9 because those Descriptors require that the claimant "can" form a relationship albeit with help or support. Activity 9d and reg 4(2A) must be read, he suggests, as if the word "cannot" means that the claimant is able to relate to others (either with or without support), but, if in doing so, he suffers overwhelming anxiety or endangerment then reg.4(2A) is not satisfied and at the same time the claimant "cannot" be said to be able to form a relationship.

Counsel for the Secretary of State had also put to Judge Rowland that the decision of the three-judge panel in *MR v SSWP (PIP)* [2016] UKUT 531 (AAC); [2018] AACR 12 had said that the word "overwhelming" in Descriptor 9d. set a very high threshold and that being anxious, worried or emotional would not be enough to meet that standard. Judge Rowland says that a ``very high threshold" is still a relative term and that the panel should not be regarded as having made a gloss on the statutory words. In MR, he suggests, the panel was merely explaining that, on the facts of two of the cases before them, the claimant had not met the required standard.

The decision of Judge Gray in *EG v SSWP (PIP)* [2017] UKUT 101 (AAC) discussed in the Note to Activity 7 above, has also made extensive and helpful observations in relation to this Activity and to the relationship between both Activities. She emphasises that the help (prompting, supervision or assistance) that might be given to the claimant will need to be different in respect of each Activity. Help given in respect of verbal communication cannot also be the basis of a score for social support in engaging with other people. This is a further example of a disability that is dealt with specifically in one Activity not being acceptable as the basis of a score in another, more general Activity – see *AS v SSWP (PIP)* [2017] UKUT 104 (AAC); [2017] AACR 31 discussed in Note to Activity 5 above. In her view also "social support" requires something more than "prompting". There is a qualitative difference between what is required of social support and prompting and in her view social support requires the presence of the person giving that support, though she agrees with Judge Parker in *CSPIP/203/2015* that this will not require constant vigilance.

Again in *PM v SSWP (PIP)* [2017] UKUT 154 (AAC) Judge Gray has dealt with the nature of the face-to-face event that this Activity involves. It is not sufficient that the claimant should be competent in dealing with friends and other persons that she knows, or those with whom there is a specific objective such as a health professional. The definition of "interact socially" informs this Activity and seems to envisage the ability to interact with others so as to *establish* relationships.

"psychological distress" means distress that relates to an "enduring mental health condition or to an intellectual or cognitive impairment".

Psychological distress could have a physical trigger as in the case of the person who has episodes of incontinence, but to satisfy this Descriptor that would need to link with a mental health condition or impairment. A person who suffers acute embarrassment as a result of episodes of incontinence will qualify only under Activity 5, if at all.

The duty of an FTT in acting in an inquisitorial role is demonstrated in *SM v SSWP (PIP)* [2019] UKUT 292 (AAC). There the claimant was an ex-prisoner who had been released on a lifetime licence. There was evidence before the FTT in statements from a consultant psychologist that showed he suffered from extreme anxiety when interacting with others and that his propensity to anger caused him to avoid making contact for fear of being sent back to prison. Judge Poole QC, in the UT, held that they had made an error of law in considering only his entitlement under Descriptor 9c. when this evidence clearly raised the possibility that he might succeed under 9d.

Activity 10—Making budgeting decisions

4.255 This is the only Activity in which no Descriptor will give a qualifying score on its own and any score must, therefore be combined with a score from another Activity.

"simple budgeting decisions" are those relating to calculating the cost of goods and the change required after making a purchase. Presumably, the touchstone for this Activity would be if the claimant could be relied upon to go shopping on their own.

"complex budgeting decisions" will require the claimant to be able to calculate household and personal budgets as well as managing the payment of bills and planning for future purchases. Again, it will usually be fairly obvious when someone needs another to take over the management of their affairs, though that must be in consequence of the claimant's mental or physical condition; irresponsible indebtedness is not unknown among those who are not disabled!

In *SE v SSWP (PIP)* [2021] UKUT 1 (AAC) Judge Ward has given helpful guidance on the operation of this Activity. First, he observes that the elements of both simple budgeting decisions and complex budgeting decisions are cumulative. Further, that in complex decisions the first two elements each contain two sub-elements. The result is that the claimant must be shown to be capable in respect of not just personal budgets but of household budgets and of not just paying bills but of managing them (which may involve a much greater intellectual process) and finally of planning future purchases. For simple budgeting decisions he notes that the claimant must be capable of calculating the cost of goods and that may require more than just knowing the cost. Although the judge accepts that the focus in this Activity is on "decisions" that relate to budgeting he accepts that these are "decisions involving" the required elements and that may mean a more flexible result just being able to pay the bill – it may mean, for example, being able to reflect upon the consequences of making that purchase-see e.g. the example of impulsive spending referred to by Judge Hemingway in *DP v SSWP (PIP)* [2017] UKUT 156 (AAC) referred to below.

Finally, Judge Ward makes the point that the words "at all" as used in Descriptor 10(d) do not mean that the claimant has absolutely no budgeting ability, but only that he cannot budget to the extent required by Descriptor 10(c).

The distinction between the ability to make complex budgeting decisions and simple ones is explored in *CPIP/3015/2015*. The claimant had a number of disabling conditions including alcohol dependency. The judge, by way of illustration, suggests that an alcoholic who had no control over his addiction might be compelled to spend every penny on drink so as to be incapable of planning and undertaking complex budgeting decisions, but be quite capable of the simple decisions involved in purchasing items and accounting for the change. In *RB v SSWP (PIP)* [2016] UKUT 393 (AAC) Judge White accepted that the claimant's physical condition as well as his mental condition could be relevant in relation to this activity. The claimant had argued that the pain he suffered from osteoarthritis interfered with his ability to make complex budgeting decisions – he said that he had to leave all such matters for his wife to deal with. The judge accepted that while this might be so he thought that it could arise only in extreme conditions and that was not shown in this case. It should be noted too that all the descriptors for this activity involve the claimant's ability to make "decisions", so a physical disability that affects only the claimant's ability to undertake the physical part of a transaction such as to go shopping, or to handle money, or write a cheque will not qualify under this activity. (See for example in *CPIP/0184/2016)*.

A decision of Judge Markus in *CPIP/1650/2015*, cited by Judge Mesher in the case of *SSWP v LB* below, carries this a step further. Judge Markus QC accepted the argument of the Secretary of State that the focus of this activity is upon the cognitive process of decision making rather than the claimant's inability to obtain the information necessary to make that decision. Thus a person who is blind and not able to read braille, but has full cognitive ability, would score no points because, given the information, they would be able to make budgeting decisions. This argument was put to Judge Mesher in *SSWP v LB (PIP)* [2016] UKUT 530 (AAC), discussed above in relation to Activity 3. The claimant suffered from diabetes and depression and was dyslexic. She had been allowed two points under this activity by the HCP on the ground that because of her dyslexia she needed prompting or assistance to be able to take complex budgeting decisions. This had not been the subject of her appeal to the FTT, but in the UT counsel for the Secretary of State put the argument as above, that this was not help with the cognitive process of decision making, but with the gathering of information to begin that process. He found support for this in the definition of "assistance" (in Part 1 of the schedule) because that does not include assistance given by speech, and assistance would seem the most apt way to describe the help given to a person who is dyslexic (or blind) when a bill or other information is read to them. (Note though, that "prompting" as defined includes explaining to the claimant, which might be equally apt). Counsel argued, too that an inability to read that was the result of some physical or mental condition was covered by Activity 8 (Reading and understanding signs symbols and words) and to allow points under this activity as well, would be providing a double benefit. This argument is unconvincing; many activities will involve the claimant scoring twice, or even multiple times, as a result of the same physical or mental condition – a person who suffers badly from arthritis in their arms and hands, for example, might score for difficulty in dressing, as well as washing and cooking and other activities. The counter argument put by counsel for the claimant focused chiefly on the words of the descriptors – "needs prompting or assistance *to be able* to make budgeting decisions"; this, he thought, should include help in obtaining the information necessary to make decisions. Judge Mesher did not find it necessary or appropriate for him to reach a decision on these arguments because his decision on other activities gave the claimant sufficient points to be awarded benefit at the enhanced rate and hence a decision on this activity would serve no useful purpose, but he thought that an arguable case could be put that deserved a decision where the facts were fully explored and after argument had been heard.

The need to be able to make budgeting decisions, even complex ones, has been accepted as a proper Activity in respect of a claimant who was 16 or 17 years old by Judge Hemingway in *DP v SSWP (PIP)* [2017] UKUT 156 (AAC). In that case he also suggests that where the claimant, because of his condition (he was considering the suggestion of someone suffering from ADHD), is able to make a complex budgeting decision about the need to prioritise certain expenses, but then goes out and spends his money impulsively on something else, he might yet satisfy this Activity because his behaviour would be about "decisions involving . . . paying bills" within the definition in Part 1 of the Schedule.

The Mobility Component—Activities and Descriptors

4.256 The test of mobility has been reduced to just two activities—planning a journey and moving about.

Activity 1—Planning and following journeys

4.257 The mobility component for PIP is not restricted to a physical disability. Section 79 of WRA 2012 refers specifically to a person's "physical or mental condition". In *NK v SSWP (PIP)* [2016] UKUT 146 (AAC) Judge Rowley affirmed that this could include a claimant whose psychosomatic condition caused her to believe that she was unable to walk even though there was no physical reason that prevented her from doing so. The sole question was whether that belief, or the pain she experienced was real to the claimant; though on the evidence available in this case the judge was able to find that the claimant was able to move satisfactorily and the appeal was dismissed. This means that PIP will be available to an agoraphobic person. Whether they will qualify under Descriptor b or under Descriptor e will depend upon whether they can be persuaded to go out with prompting, or whether they will not go out at all without overwhelming psychological distress.

"psychological distress" must relate to the claimant's mental health condition or an intellectual or cognitive impairment. This means that the claimant who is inhibited from going out just because of a fear of being embarrassed by an episode of incontinence would not succeed unless their distress was linked to such a health condition. (cf. *SSWP v DC* [2011] UKUT 235 (AAC) where the claim failed because the claimant's reluctance to go out arose just from fear and anxiety). A fear of meeting a dog, or at least of meeting a dog running free, so as to cause overwhelming psychological distress has been accepted as relevant if it arises from a person's mental or physical condition. In *EE v SSWP (CPIP)* [2021] UKUT 17 (AAC) the claimant, who was autistic and suffered from depression, said that she could not undertake an unfamiliar journey unless accompanied for fear of meeting with a dog not on its lead. The FTT had refused her appeal but failed to give adequate reasons for doing so. In the UT Judge Hemingway allowed an appeal and directed a rehearing.

Following a journey in this context means being able to follow a route. The route may have been prepared in advance (planned) by the claimant or by someone else, but the benchmark for this activity requires that the claimant must be able to both plan and to follow a route. If the claimant can follow, though not plan, a route he will score under Descriptor c. If the claimant can plan a route, but is then unable to follow that route without some level of assistance or encouragement he will score under which ever of the descriptors is appropriate for that assistance etc.

Further points concerned in the ability to make a journey are explored by Judge Wikeley in *JC v SSWP (PIP)* [2019] UKUT 181 (AAC). There an appeal had been dismissed by the FTT because they found that the claimant was able to make journeys, both familiar and unfamiliar, by driving in her car. When the journey was unfamiliar, they found that she would make a "practice run", but they had not determined whether, in making either that practice run, or when making her journey subsequently, she required the assistance of another person to do so. They failed also to consider whether she could complete her car journey to reach a destination on foot. More fundamentally perhaps, they did not consider whether she could make either journey by public transport should she need to do so. This part of the test is suggested in the *PIP Assessment Guide Part 2: The Assessment Criteria.*

Judge Wikeley concedes that the *Guide* is not determinative of the law, but notes the statement found there "A person should only be considered able to follow an unfamiliar journey if they would be capable of using public transport – the assessment of which should focus on ability rather than choice" and he suggests that, by the same token, the claimant's ability to plan and follow a journey on foot should form part of an overall and holistic approach to the test.

A different view on this matter has been taken by Judge Hemingway in *JB v SSWP (PIP)* [2019] UKUT 203 (AAC). The judge rejected the quotation cited above (which does still appear in the current *Guide*) on the ground that entitlement to PIP was determined by the interpretation of statute and the *Guide* was indicative only of one view. He does, however, adopt the same approach in relation to the commencement and completion of any journey made substantially by car; the FTT had erred in failing to consider the claimant's ability at both ends of a journey.

Judge Hemingway has given further consideration to this matter in *SB v SSWP (PIP)* [2019] [UKUT 274 (AAC). In this case he was referred by the representative of the Secretary of State to the passage in the *Assessment Guide*; the representative had advanced the view that failing to consider the claimant's ability to use public transport was, of itself, an error of law. The judge did not go that far, but he did agree that the ability to make a journey should be tested by adopting a more holistic approach that would include considering his ability by driving, by walking and by using public transport.

The statement in the *PIP Assessment Guide* concerning the ability to use public transport and the meaning to be given to it has been considered again by Judge Wikeley in *HO'H v SSWP* (PIP) [2020] UKUT 135 (AAC). The claimant was disabled because of a stroke. It appears that he was able to make some progress on foot, probably with the aid of a stick, but the history of his PIP awards left the extent of that ability unclear. However, the claimant contended that this disability made it impossible for him to walk to any bus stop or to any train station. He said, as well, that he would be unable to use a bus or train when he got there. There appeared to be no evidence as to why he might not be able to use the bus or train, but the case proceeded on the basis that it was accepted that he could not access either form of public transport. The claimant's argument was that he should, therefore, score at least another 10 points under Descriptor 1(d) to add to whatever score he had for Activity 2.

Judge Wikeley first reiterates the view that the *PIP Assessment Guide* is not a statement of what the law is but an expression of what the Secretary of State might have thought it to be. More importantly, however, he goes on to examine how that statement should be understood when read in the context of the *Guide*. While the decision of the three-judge panel in *MH v SSWP (PIP)* [2016] UKUT 531 (AAC) accepts that there may be interaction between mental and physical disabilities for both mobility Activities, they accept that the primary distinction is that Activity 1 is concerned mainly with mental disabilities and Activity 2 with physical ones.

When read in the context of the *Guide* it then becomes clear that the ability to use public transport to make an unfamiliar journey was to be a way of measuring the claimant's cognitive, psychological or sensory capability. A physical inability to access, or even to use public transport, should therefore be relevant mainly when measuring Activity 2.

Another difference of opinion that had arisen between judges of the UT in the application of this Activity has been resolved by a decision of a three judge panel in *MH v SSWP (PIP)* [2016] UKUT 531 (AAC); [2018] AACR 12. The disagreement revealed in the previous decisions turned upon the meaning to be given to Descriptors d and f of this Activity. In two decisions (*DA v SSWP (PIP)* [2015] UKUT 344 (AAC) and *HL v SSWP (PIP)* [2015] UKUT 694 (AAC)) the judges took the view that the words "follow the route" meant only an ability to navigate a route, while in another (*RC v SSWP (PIP)* [2015] UKUT 386 (AAC)) the judge thought that the words should include the case of a claimant who was prevented from following the route by a fear of, or an inability to interact with, other people along the route if, for example, it became necessary to ask for alternative or better directions. Such a claimant might then be able to follow the route if he were accompanied by another person as required in Descriptors d and f. The second view would mean that both of these Descriptors were available to a claimant who could not undertake a journey because of overwhelming psychological distress and in particular a person who suffered from agoraphobia might qualify for the higher rate (12 points) under Descriptor f and not the lower rate (10 points) under Descriptor e. The three judge panel decided in favour of that second view- though they restricted their conclusion to claimants for whom they thought the psychological distress would be truly exceptional. The Personal Independence Payment (Amendment) Regulations 2017 (SI 2017/194) were made, in part, to reverse the effect of this decision, but para.4(2) of reg.2 of those regulations that effected the change was held (in *RF v SSWP* [2017] EWHC 3375; [2018] AACR 13) to have been made *ultra vires* the regulation-making power in Part 4 of the Welfare Reform Act 2014 and hence to be of no effect. The text of Descriptors in Activity 1 of Part 3 of the schedule has been restored to its original form in this volume. The appeal that had been lodged by the DWP against the decision in *MH* has also been withdrawn and hence decisions on this Activity should now be decided in accordance with the decision of the three-judge panel.

Note that the same effect as the decision in *RF v SSWP* has been given to the regulations in Northern Ireland by a decision of a Tribunal of Commissioners in that jurisdiction – see *HH v Department for Communities (PIP)* [2024] NI Com 8.

Several issues arising from the application of psychological distress and anxiety under the Descriptors to Activity 1 have been considered in *AA v SSWP (PIP)* [2018] UKUT 339 (AAC). The claimant suffered from paranoid schizophrenia. He had periods of low mood, lacked motivation and suffered high levels of anxiety. His evidence, which was accepted by the FTT, was that he would usually need encouragement to venture out of doors at all; that he could sometimes accomplish familiar journeys on his own, but that he would never go somewhere unfamiliar without someone to accompany him. Evidence was given that when he did go out alone he wore earphones and looked at the ground. Even when accompanied he might wear the earphones—his companion was there to provide what he described as "moral support" rather than to tell him where to go. The FTT allowed him 4 points under Descriptor 1b. Judge Hemingway, in the UT, observed that this meant that they accepted that he did need at least encouraging to avoid overwhelming psychological distress in order to leave his home. But they did not think that he qualified under Descriptor 1d or 1f. (It seems that they did not consider 1e because it was clear that he could undertake journeys so long as he had a companion). Judge Hemingway thought that they had probably refused his claim under 1d or 1f because they thought that his companion should need to provide some more positive intervention, that was more than just passive presence, to satisfy those Descriptors.

Judge Hemingway thought that two questions arose—does the companion have to play an active role when he accompanies the claimant; and can a claim succeed under Descriptor 1f if the claimant can undertake some familiar journeys but not others. As to the first Judge Hemingway decided that active intervention was not necessary; with this the representative of the Secretary of State agreed and as the judge demonstrated this was in accordance with the reasoning of the UT in the *MH* case. As to the second, the representative of the Secretary of State had observed that the wording of both 1d and 1f is "a" journey rather than "any" journey; therefore she said it should suffice that the claimant was sometimes unable to accomplish that journey without support. The judge held that thereafter the matter would be governed by reg.7—does the situation apply on more than 50% of the days on which it might arise. This was a helpful conclusion for the claimant in this case but the judge anticipated a further argument that could arise from this distinction between "a" journey and "any" journey. He thought that in applying the same reasoning to Descriptors 1b and 1e that the claimant might fail if they were able to make a journey occasionally because the wording suggests that they would need to be incapable of "any" journey. He suggests that he would reject that argument; the use of the word "any" in that context means, he suggests, simply there is no distinction between familiar and unfamiliar journeys. He then goes on to consider the case of a claimant who can make some familiar journeys on most, but not on all days, and other familiar journeys on some but not most days! This is not a case for the application of reg.7 because it is not a matter of the days so much as the various journeys. Judge Hemingway says that the answer is to approach the question as a broad assessment of the claimant's ability to tackle familiar routes in general.

When the amending regulations were before Parliament they met with considerable criticism on the ground that they refuted the principle stated in the enabling act (s.79 WRA 2012) that PIP would be available equally to claimants whose disability was mental as to those that were physical. The DWP was challenged to produce examples where Descriptors c, d and f might still be satisfied by claimants whose disability was mental in origin. The DWP responded in a House of Commons Briefing Paper Number 7911 (April 13, 2017) entitled *Changes to the Personal Independence Payment eligibility criteria* by giving the following four examples (although these examples are no longer necessary to serve the original purpose for which they were produced they may be useful to tribunals and advisers to illustrate further cases where there should be no difficulty in satisfying the terms of these Descriptors):

A person (person A) with a cognitive impairment who cannot, due to their impairment, work out where to go, follow directions or deal with unexpected changes in their journey, even when the journey is familiar, would score 12 points under descriptor f in mobility activity 1 ("planning and following journeys"), and hence be entitled to the enhanced rate of the mobility component. Examples of such conditions could include dementia, or a learning disability such as Down's Syndrome. (Some people covered by this example may experience psychological distress as well, and may also meet descriptor b, requiring "prompting" – i.e. reminding, encouraging or explaining – from another person in order to be able to undertake a journey. They will still receive 12 points under Descriptor f and be entitled to the enhanced rate.)

A person (person B) with a developmental disorder could qualify on a similar basis to person A if the disorder affects their ability to work out where to go, follow directions or deal with unexpected changes in their journey. If their disorder results in them having difficulty assessing and responding to risks, or in impulsivity, then they could also score 12 points under Descriptor f on the basis that they need to be accompanied for their own safety. Examples of developmental disorders which could have these effects include Autistic Spectrum Disorder and Attention Deficit Hyperactivity Disorder (ADHD).

A person (person C) who suffers psychosomatic pain could qualify for the enhanced rate through satisfying Descriptors e or f in mobility activity 2 ("moving around"). The case of *NK v SSWP (PIP)* [2016] UKUT 146 (AAC) concerned a claimant who suffered significant pain when moving around, but the pain resulted from a mental condition rather than any physical impairment. The Upper Tribunal found that the claimant could score points towards an award of the mobility component under mobility activity 2, even though her pain did not have a physical cause. **4.258**

A person (person D) who has chronic fatigue syndrome (CFS) and experiences symptoms including significant fatigue following physical exertion, muscular and joint pain and balance problems, together with psychological difficulties which manifest as depression and panic attacks, could qualify for the enhanced rate under mobility activity 2, or by scoring points on a combination of mobility activity 1 (4 points under Descriptor b, for requiring prompting to avoid psychological distress when undertaking any journey) and mobility activity 2 (eight points under descriptor c, for being able to stand and then move unaided more than 20m but no more than 50m). As explained above, Chronic Fatigue Symptom (CFS), also known as myalgic encephalomyelitis (ME), has complex causes which are still not well understood, but which may involve both physical and psychological factors. Note that where the claim is based upon an argument that the claimant needs to be accompanied when undertaking a journey, it is necessary to demonstrate, with evidence in support, that without that company the claimant would be at risk of harm in some way. See the decision of Judge May QC in *AR v SSWP (PIP)* [2018] UKUT 313 (AAC). The claimant suffered from epilepsy, but there was no evidence that he was prone to having a seizure when he was out.

An "assistance dog" is a dog that has been trained to guide or assist a person with sensory perception.

The obvious example is a guide-dog for the blind, but it could include a hearing-dog if the claimant is deaf and needs to be warned of a danger of which others would be alerted by sound.

An "orientation aid" is a specialist aid designed to enable a disabled person to follow a route safely so that should include a long cane or white stick that is used to give the claimant information to locate objects, kerbs etc. It will include too, any echolocation device that provides similar information to the claimant, though it is presumably not a "device" if the claimant uses his own tongue to emit clicks. It is doubtful if a white stick that is used only to inform other people that the claimant is visually impaired could be regarded as an orientation aid.

In *RB v SSWP (PIP)* [2016] UKUT 304 (AAC) Judge Rowley has considered the question whether a satellite navigation device (a SatNav) could be considered to be an orientation aid so as to qualify a claimant for points under Descriptors 1d and 1f of this activity. She held that it did not. The same conclusion had been reached by Judge May QC in *CSPIP/229/2015* and the reason, in both cases, was the same; an orientation aid is defined in Part 1 of the schedule to mean "a specialist aid designed to assist disabled people to follow a route safely". The device in each of these cases was a standard SatNav and although the equipment in this later case was a built-in version, that would not mean that it had been designed specifically to aid disabled people. The consequence would seem to be that a person who is blind and uses an ordinary walking stick, rather than a white stick or an extending stick, to guide himself would not satisfy this descriptor either. This reasoning also throws doubt on the use of an eye patch that was in question in *SSWP v SS (PIP)* [2015] UKUT 240 (AAC) The claimant needed to wear a patch over one eye because without it he suffered from dazzling that disorientated him. It would seem that the eye patch, as used there, would still be an aid, though not an orientation aid. While it might be said that an eyepatch was designed to assist disabled people, it would not normally be thought to have been designed to assist them to follow a route safely. The claimant in that case would then not satisfy descriptor 1a for zero points (because he could not follow a route *unaided*), but it is difficult to see which of the Descriptors that follow could be applied to him. The same point might have been made in the current case, but it would still be necessary to show that the claimant was unable to follow a route without the use of her SatNav and that the inability arose from some mental or physical condition; such inability had been accepted in the earlier case.The same conclusion regarding the use of a SatNav has been reached by Judge Humphrey in *SSWP v NF (PIP)* [2017] UKUT 480 (AAC). There the claimant suffered from memory problems as a result of a stroke. Although she was able to drive, she was unable to remember a route for any journey, even a very simple one with which she had been familiar, and consequently she needed to use her SatNav to make any journey at all. The judge allowed the Secretary of State's appeal following the cases above because the SatNav had not been designed for use as a specialist aid for disabled people, but in this case the claimant might have succeeded in scoring 8 points under Descriptor 1c if it could be shown that she was incapable of planning the route of a journey.

In *SSWP v IV (PIP)* [2016] UKUT 420 (AAC) Judge Jacobs has decided two important points about Activity 1. First, that the journey to be undertaken and the route to be followed is not necessarily a local one. The *PIP Assessment Guide* directs the DM to consider only a local journey in respect of both a familiar route and an unfamiliar one. Nowhere in the legislation to be applied does this limitation appear. In this case, the FTT which had allowed the claimant's appeal, had asked the claimant if he could find his way to London – a considerable distance away. Judge Jacobs accepted that the destination was irrelevant; what mattered was the claimant's ability to follow the route wherever that was leading to. The FTT were entitled to test that ability by posing a variety of journeys including one that might be intimidating to many people. In this case the FTT had in fact also discussed with the claimant his ability to follow several other more local routes. Secondly, and more importantly, the judge emphasises that any inability to satisfy a Descriptor must be as a result of the claimant's mental or physical condition. In this case the claimant, who suffered also some physical disabilities, was illiterate. It was for that reason that the FTT were satisfied that he could not undertake an unfamiliar journey on his own. But the claimant's illiteracy was not shown on the evidence to be the result of any mental or physical condition. It appeared that his illiteracy was because he had failed to learn, rather than because he was incapable of learning; the FTT had already rejected his claim in respect of Activity 8 (reading and understanding signs symbols and words) for the daily living component, and their finding in relation to mobility was inconsistent with that.

A similar point is made in *MC v SSWP (PIP)* [2019] UKUT 264 (AAC). Judge Hemingway held that the journey to be considered in this Activity is not limited to a short one. The FTT had found in favour of the claimant in finding that she qualified under Descriptor 1e, but that she could not satisfy Descriptor 1f because she was able to follow the route of a "short familiar journey". The judge held that it was an error of law to confine the length of the journey in this way. Following what had been said by Judge Jacobs in *SSWP* v *IV (PIP)* [2016] UKUT 420 (AAC) that the journey need not necessarily be a local one he holds that, conversely, the journey need not be a long one. The test should focus on an overall assessment of the claimant's ability to make journeys by adopting a more holistic approach.

Activity 2—Moving around

In discussing this activity it should be noted first of all, that the general prerequisite in reg.4 that an assessment of the claimant's capability must be made using or wearing any aid or appliance that he normally uses, or which he can reasonably be expected to use, must be suspended because some of the descriptors in this activity specify the claimant's ability when unaided. In *KL v SSWP (PIP)* [2015] UKUT 612 (AAC) Judge Mitchell accepts that the well-recognised principle of statutory interpretation to the effect that a specific provision in a piece of legislation overrides the more general expression in that same legislation means, in this instance, that the assessment of the claimant must be made when unaided if that is what is specified. **4.259**

Although there is no definition of "move" in the regulations it must be taken to mean that the claimant must progress by the movement of his own limbs or, where appropriate, by the aid of a prosthesis, a crutch or a stick. Any of these things can be regarded as an "aid or appliance" Query whether a wheelchair should be regarded as an appliance? If it is, that might lead to difficulty in applying Descriptor f of this activity. The guidance given by DWP to the HCP explains this by saying that the requirement for most of these Descriptors is that the claimant must be able to "stand" and then "move" which means that the moving must be whilst he is still standing. In broad terms moving will equate with the popular notion of walking even though the walking may be with the use of sticks, walking frames or crutches. Note that for PIP making forward progress even with two crutches will still be "moving". (cf. for DLA where progressing by "swinging through" was not regarded as walking).

The prerequisite to any degree of movement in these Descriptors is for the claimant to be able to stand. "stand" is defined as being able to stand upright with at least one biological foot on the ground; so a double lower-limb amputee, even an Olympic champion, will qualify under Descriptor f.

In *DT v SSWP (PIP)* [2016] UKUT 240 (AAC) Judge Rowley has considered the nature of the terrain over which the ability to move around must be judged. She accepts the concession made by the representative for the Secretary of State that the surface must be of a type that is commonly experienced by pedestrians when walking out of doors. This meant a reasonably flat pavement taking into account the usual rise and fall that one might normally encounter, including the need to negotiate kerbs, but not necessarily involving steps and slopes. In this case the claimant, who had a back problem, reported difficulty in stepping on and off the kerb; the FTT had not addressed that matter and the case was returned to a fresh tribunal.

Provided that the claimant can stand, then the extent of ability to move depends upon both the distance over which the claimant can move and whether there is a need for "aid", which in most cases will include either an appliance or some form of assistance, encouragement or supervision.

A single lower-limb amputee who is able to use a prosthesis and can stand and then move, even if he uses an aid to do so, may find that he does not qualify at all.

Descriptor a. The benchmark of normality, in this instance, is being able to stand and move more than 200 metres, even if that is possible only with the use of an aid or with assistance etc. If the claimant can do this, he scores no points.

Descriptor b. is satisfied if the claimant can move at least 50 metres, but no more than 200 metres, even if he can do that only by using an aid or with assistance, encouragement or supervision etc.

Descriptor c. (which marks the point at which a claimant could qualify, on movement grounds alone, for the standard rate) is satisfied if the claimant can move more than 20 metres but no more than 50 metres without using an appliance or having assistance etc. If, to go further, he needs to use an aid, appliance or have supervision, prompting (which itself means reminding, encouraging or explaining) or assistance, then he will qualify at the standard rate.

There are now two conflicting decisions on the interpretation of Descriptor c. This is important because that descriptor awards eight points—sufficient to qualify the claimant at the standard rate for the mobility component. The application of Activity 2 was always going to be difficult. Reading Descriptor c. literally, a person who could move more than 20 but no more than 50 metres unaided, satisfies that descriptor and that could be said to be the case even if, with an aid or appliance, they could then progress a further 1000 metres! That was the meaning accepted originally in the commentary to this descriptor, but is now questioned because if this descriptor is given its literal meaning it then makes nonsense of Descriptor a. That descriptor says a claimant who can move more than 200 metres *aided or unaided* scores nothing. It is not, of course unusual for a claimant to satisfy more than one of the descriptors in any particular activity and if he does reg.7 prescribes that he should take the higher or highest score. But in this instance it could be argued that the claimant who could move unaided up to 50 metres and thereafter required the use of a stick would be treated more favourably than someone who needed to use his stick from the outset. This was the argument accepted by Judge Hemingway in *JP v SSWP (PIP)* [2015] UKUT 529 (AAC) As the representative of the Secretary of State had put it to him, a claimant who could walk, more than 200 metres, but only with the aid of a stick or other appliance used for the *whole* of that journey, would be treated less favourably that one who could walk up to 50 metres unaided and could then carry on indefinitely with the aid of a stick—arguably the former person was the more disabled and therefore more deserving. He suggests that, reading Descriptor c. in the context of all the other descriptors, it must be read as applying only to a person who can move up to 50 metres without an aid, but then can move no further at all even if aided. (The difference between c.—(eight points) and d.—(10 points) then depends upon whether the claimant can do that unaided or only with an aid).

This interpretation of Descriptor c. has been rejected in *KL v SSWP (PIP)* [2015] UKUT 612 AAC by Judge Mitchell. In this case the claimant had a condition of her ankle which required her to use a crutch or walking stick. With that aid she could walk more than 200 metres. It does not appear from the evidence whether, without an aid she could move at all. The FTT to whom she had appealed rejected that appeal applying the words of Descriptor a: "can stand and move more than 200 metres aided or unaided". They did not consider her ability to move unaided and hence did not refer to Descriptor c. Judge Mitchell finds that it was an error of law not to do so and referred the case back for rehearing. The argument made in the case above, *JP v SSWP,* was not put to the judge in this case, but he refers to it on the basis that it might well be put before the new FTT on rehearing. In his view the logic, or lack of it, in the construction of this activity and the descriptors provided there, was not a sufficient reason to depart from what he found to be the clear literal meaning of Descriptor c.

The conflict between the decision in *JP v SSWP (PIP)* [2015] UKUT 529 (AAC) and that in *KL v SSWP (PIP)* [2015] UKUT 612 (AAC) is addressed again by Judge Markus QC in *AP v SSWP (PIP)* [2016] UKUT 501 (AAC). Her decision is in agreement with that of Judge Hemingway in the former case. This decision is reached after full argument based on the submissions of both parties and should before an FTT, for that reason, be regarded as settling the matter unless and until there has been an appeal to the Court of Appeal or a contrary decision of a three-judge panel.

Descriptor d. will be satisfied if the claimant needs to use an aid or appliance to move a distance between 20 and 50 metres. This level of disability scores 10 points, but unless the claimant also has problems in planning a journey, he will have no further points to aggregate and will therefore qualify only for the standard rate of benefit. **4.260**

Descriptor e. is satisfied if the claimant can stand and move at least 1 metre but no more than 20 metres even with an aid or with assistance etc.

Descriptor f. requires that the claimant can either not stand, or cannot move more than one metre, in either case even with aid or assistance etc.

Although both descriptors e. and f. carry the same score of 12 points (and hence qualify the claimant for the component at the enhanced rate) Descriptor f. has probably been included because it best describes the extreme case of a claimant who needs to use a wheelchair to be able to move, effectively, at all.

A claimant's ability to walk may fluctuate over a period of time and even on a day to day basis. Such cases will need to satisfy the 50% rule in reg.7 and the appropriate Descriptor to be applied will be determined in accordance with that regulation, but there is no reason why, in applying that regulation, account should not be taken of days on which the claimant is so afflicted as to not be able to walk at all. In *BM v SSWP (PIP)* [2017] UKUT 486 (AAC) Judge Bano considered the case of a claimant whose condition was such that on seven to ten days each month he was bedridden. The judge held that to ignore these days in the overall assessment of how limited the claimant's ability to walk was, and on how many days it was so limited, was an error of law.

In these descriptors there is no explicit criterion that relates to time and speed, but reg.4(2A) does require that he must be able to accomplish the task "within a reasonable time". A reasonable time is defined in reg.4(2A) as being, no more than twice the time that would be taken by an able-bodied person.

Regulation 4(2A) also requires that the claimant can perform a task "repeatedly". This is defined in that regulation as being as often as it might reasonably be expected to be completed. This will introduce consideration of the claimant's condition when he completes a journey and the recovery time that would be needed, if it were reasonable to expect the journey to be done again. So a claimant who could walk more than, say, 200 metres to the shops, but would need then to rest for an hour before he could return, would not have satisfied Descriptor a.

In applying any of these Descriptors due account will need to be taken of pain, breathlessness and other forms of discomfort such as dizziness, vertigo, etc. Where the exertion involved in completing the task might endanger the claimant's health the Descriptor will not be satisfied unless such harm would be "unlikely"—see reg.4(4). But this must now be read in the sense decided in *RJ v SSWP (PIP)* UKUT [2017] UKUT 105 (AAC); [2017] AACR 32 so that the Descriptor will be satisfied when there is a real risk of harm such that it would not be sensible to ignore 3– see above in the note that follows reg.4.

The number and extent of any rests that the claimant might need to take will also be relevant to the question of whether the claimant can complete the Descriptor "to an acceptable standard".

Given the precise distances that have been prescribed and the wording of most descriptors as "stand and then move" it might be argued that the test should envisage a single unbroken progress to the requisite distance. But that approach has been rejected in two UT decisions; the preferred view in both decisions is that stops and pauses should be taken account of as a part of the overall assessment of a claimant's ability to move when regard is had to the criteria specified in reg. 4(2A). In particular the need to accomplish the distance repeatedly and within a reasonable time, but regard might be had also to achieving movement "to an acceptable standard". A person who could achieve the distance only by taking long rests would be unlikely to satisfy the definition of a reasonable time period in that regulation (no more than twice as long as an able bodied person), but it may still be possible for a claimant to succeed if they can accomplish the distance only with a great deal of effort or with a great deal of pain; such a person might not be said to carry out the activity to an acceptable standard. This was the view taken by Judge Parker in *TF v SSWP (PIP)* [2015] UKUT 661 (AAC) and that decision was followed by Judge Hemingway in *KN v SSWP* [2016] UKUT 261 (AAC). In the latter case the judge thought it was unclear if the FTT had taken account of the claimant's need to "stop" and to "pause" (though if they had done so, would have made no difference to the decision), but he did allow the appeal because the tribunal had not then gone on to consider, specifically, the time that the claimant needed to cover the distance.

In *PS v SSWP (PIP)* [2016] UKUT 326 (AAC) Judge Markus QC refers again to the matter of pain suffered by a claimant while walking and the effect that might have on the application of regulation 4(2A) – ability to achieve the activity to an acceptable standard. In this case the claimant suffered from spinal stenosis and his evidence was that he could walk a distance of about 50 yards but always in considerable pain and that, at that point, the pain was such that he was forced to stop. In the view of Judge Markus the FTT had failed to give proper consideration to this part of the evidence and the case was returned to a fresh tribunal. In *PM v SSWP (PIP)* [2017] UKUT 154 (AAC) Judge Gray has added further to the consideration of what walking might reasonably be required under regulation 4 by emphasising that the test should reflect the claimant's choice as to how far and how often she might wish to do so at least to the extent that she wishes to lead a normal life. The judge refers to the test adopted in the House of Lords in *Secretary of State v Fairey* (*R(A)2/98*). When a claimant walks slowly but can nevertheless achieve the distance prescribed in less than twice the time required by an able person (so that the test relating to speed in regulation 4(4) is satisfied) the question can then arise whether that slowness might still be taken into account in determining whether the claimant can walk "to an acceptable standard". In *KL v SSWP (PIP)* [2017] UKUT 545 (AAC) Judge Hemingway has held that it should not. In his view, because slowness is specifically provided for by the test in regulation 4(4)(c) it would result in inconsistency if it were to be taken account of elsewhere as well.

But he does say that this conclusion is limited to the context of speed in relation to the walking test.

It seems that it is not uncommon for an FTT to be provided with evidence that a claimant has made a journey by air and are therefore invited to reach a conclusion on the basis of that information about the claimant's ability to walk within the airport. In *LG v SSWP (PIP)* [2020] UKUT 343 (AAC) the claimant was reported to have made three such journeys to Egypt, each involving a change of aircraft in Turkey. There was evidence that she had a wheelchair and assistance each time at Manchester airport, but not at the other airports. Judge Hemingway allowed an appeal and directed a rehearing of the appeal. In doing so he refers to the earlier case of *JT v SSWP (DLA)* [2013] UKUT 221 (AAC) where, on similar evidence, Judge Wright had remitted the case because the FTT had failed to examine in sufficient detail exactly what walking had been involved and then to take account of pain or discomfort that the claimant might have experienced as well as to allow for the time taken and the need for any periods of rest. He noted also that the majority, if not all, of the walking involved would have been indoors whereas the test for DLA required also consideration of the claimant's ability to walk outdoors. While this last element does not arise in relation to PIP mobility, Judge Hemingway thought that all the rest of the judge's reservations were equally applicable to a claim for PIP by reference to reg.4 and in particular reg.4(2A). A submission of behalf of the Secretary of State had accepted that the strictures set out in the earlier case were equally applicable to a claim for PIP. What is worth noting also, is that, in both cases, the judges include as a factor to be taken into account that a claimant may be motivated to make an exceptional effort, or to endure more pain, by the occasion of making such a journey and possibly the reason for which they are doing so.

An FTT is sometimes left to make inferences about the distances described by a claimant as being the limits of their walking ability. The danger of being too inventive is shown in *PR v SSWP (PIP)* [2021] UKUT 35 (AAC). There the FTT had calculated the distance between the claimant's home and a local store. The claimant described the shop as being "less than 5 minutes away". Taking this as the walking time of a non-disabled person (the claimant had said that it took her 10 minutes) the FTT found the distance to be over 300 metres so that the claimant could score no points. On appeal to the UT evidence was produced derived from a computer programme and Google maps that the distance was in fact only 140 metres. Judge Church held that the new evidence (which neither the claimant nor her then advisers could have been expected to provide) showed the decision of the FTT disclosed an error of law.

SCHEDULE 2

MEMBERS OF HER MAJESTY'S FORCES: EXCLUDED PERSONS

1. The following persons are not members of Her Majesty's forces for the purpose of these Regulations— **4.261**

(a) subject to paragraph (2), any person who is serving as a member of any naval force of Her Majesty's forces and who locally entered that force at a naval base outside the UK;

(b) any person who is serving as a member of any military force of Her Majesty's forces and who entered that force, or was recruited for that force, outside the UK, and the depot of whose unit is situated outside the UK;

(c) any person who is serving as a member of any air force of Her Majesty's forces and who entered that force, or was recruited for that force, outside the UK, and is liable under the terms of engagement to serve only in a specified part of the world outside the UK.

2. Paragraph (1)(a) does not include any person who—

(a) has previously been an insured person under Part 1 of the National Insurance Act 1965; or

(b) is paying or has previously paid one or more of the following classes of contributions under the Social Security Act 1975 or the Social Security Contributions and Benefits Act 1992—

(i) primary Class 1;

(ii) Class 2; or

(iii) Class 3.

The Personal Independence Payment (Transitional Provisions) Regulations 2013

(SI 2013/387)

ARRANGEMENT OF REGULATIONS

The Secretary of State, in exercise of the powers conferred by sections 93 and 94 of, and Schedule 10 to, the Welfare Reform Act 2012, makes the following regulations.

These Regulations are made under the provisions of that Act and are made before the end of a period of six months beginning with the coming into force of those provisions of that Act.

Citation, commencement and interpretation

4.263 **1.** These Regulations may be cited as the Personal Independence Payment (Transitional Provisions) Regulations 2013 and come into force on 8th April 2013.

2.—(1) In these Regulations—

"the Act" means the Welfare Reform Act 2012;

"the 1987 Regulations" means the Social Security (Claims and Payments) Regulations 1987;

"the 1991 Regulations" means the Social Security (Disability Living Allowance) Regulations 1991;

"the 1992 Act" means the Social Security Contributions and Benefits Act 1992;

"the 1998 Act" means the Social Security Act 1998;

"the 1999 Regulations" means the Social Security and Child Support (Decisions and Appeals) Regulations 1999;

"the Claims and Payments Regulations" means the Universal Credit, Personal Independence Payment, Jobseeker's Allowance and Employment and Support Allowance (Claims and Payments) Regulations 2013;

"the PIP Regulations" means the Social Security (Personal Independence Payment) Regulations 2013;

"the Decisions and Appeals Regulations" means the Universal Credit, Personal Independence Payment, Jobseeker's Allowance and Employment and Support Allowance (Decisions and Appeals) Regulations 2013;

"appropriate office" has the meaning given by regulation 2 (interpretation) of the Claims and Payments Regulations;

"assessment determination" means the determination, under regulation 4 (assessment of ability to carry out activities) of the PIP Regulations, of a claim for personal independence payment made by a transfer claimant;

"change of circumstances" means a change of circumstances which a person might reasonably have been expected to know might affect the continuance of that person's entitlement to disability living allowance (by ending entitlement to one component or both components or resulting in entitlement to one or both components being at a different rate);

"component", in relation to disability living allowance, means one of the components of disability living allowance referred to in section 71 (disability living allowance) of the 1992 Act;

"disability living allowance" means the benefit known by that name that is provided for in sections 71 to 76 of the 1992 Act;

"DLA entitled person" means a person aged 16 or over who is entitled to either component or both components of disability living allowance;
"electronic communication" has the meaning given by subsection (1) of section 15 (general interpretation) of the Electronic Communications Act 2000;
[2 "exempt person" means a DLA entitled person in respect of whom, by virtue of regulation 8(2B) or 12A(3) of the 1991 Regulations (person under the age of 18 on the day of entry into hospital), a disability living allowance is payable even though they are maintained free of charge while undergoing medical or other treatment as an in-patient in a hospital or other similar institution;]
"notified person" means a DLA entitled person who has been sent a notification by the Secretary of State under regulation 3(1);
"pay day", in relation to disability living allowance, means—
(a) in the case of a payment of disability living allowance in respect of a period to which paragraph (2) of regulation 25 of the 1987 Regulations applies, the day on which the payment is made in accordance with paragraph (1) of that regulation;
(b) in the case of any other payment of disability living allowance, the day on which the allowance is payable in accordance with paragraph 1 of Schedule 6 (days for payment of long term benefits) to the 1987 Regulations.
[1 "relevant date" means the date, specified by the Secretary of State in relation to any category of DLA entitled person, from which the Secretary of State is satisfied that satisfactory arrangements will be in place to assess the entitlement of persons in that category to personal independence payment;]
"transfer claimant" means a person who is either—
(a) a notified person who has claimed personal independence payment in response to a notification sent by the Secretary of State under regulation 3(1), or
(b) a voluntary transfer claimant;
"voluntary transfer claimant" means a DLA entitled person who has claimed personal independence payment under regulation 4.

(2) For the purpose of these Regulations, except regulations 8, 12 and 16—

(a) a claim for personal independence payment is made—
  (i) in the case of a claim made in writing other than by means of an electronic communication, on the day on which a form, authorised by the Secretary of State for the purpose, containing all the information requested in the form is delivered to or received at the appropriate office,
  (ii) in the case of a claim made in writing by means of an electronic communication made in accordance with the provisions set out in Part 1 of Schedule 2 (use of electronic communications) to the Claims and Payments Regulations, on the day on which an electronic communication containing all the information requested by the Secretary of State in the form referred to in paragraph (i), or completing that information, is received at the appropriate office, and
  (iii) in the case of a claim made by telephone, on the day on which a telephone call takes place during which all the information

requested by the Secretary of State in the form referred to in paragraph (i) is supplied or which results in all that information having been supplied; and

(b) references to the making of a claim do not include the making of a defective claim.

(3) The Claims and Payments Regulations, the PIP Regulations and the Decisions and Appeals Regulations apply to the claims for personal independence payment referred to in these Regulations except where—

(a) these Regulations provide otherwise, or

(b) the application of those Regulations would be inconsistent with the application of these Regulations.

[1(4) As soon as practicable after specifying a relevant date in relation to any category of DLA entitled person, the Secretary of State must publish, in such manner as the Secretary of State considers appropriate, information sufficient to enable any DLA entitled person to ascertain the relevant date, if any, which applies in their case.]

AMENDMENTS

1. Personal Independence Payment (Transitional Provisions) (Amendment) (No.2) Regulations 2013 (2013/2698) reg.2(2) (October 25, 2013).

2. Social Security (Disability Living Allowance and Personal Independence Payment) (Amendment) Regulations 2016 (SI 2016/556) reg.4(2) (June 29, 2016).

Invitations to persons entitled to disability living allowance to claim personal independence payment

4.264 **3.**—(1) At any time after [1 27th October 2013], the Secretary of State may by written notification invite a DLA entitled person to make a claim for personal independence payment.

(2) The Secretary of State must not send a notification under paragraph (1) to any person who, on 8th April 2013, was 65 or over.

(3) [2Subject to paragraphs [4 [5*omitted*]] [3 (3A), (4) and (4A)],] The Secretary of State must send a notification under paragraph (1) to a DLA entitled person who reaches 16 after [1 27th October 2013] as soon as reasonably practicable after the person reaches that age.

[4 [5*omitted*]].

[2(3A) Paragraph (3) does not apply unless—

(a) the Secretary of State has specified a relevant date which applies in the case of the DLA entitled person, and

(b) that person reaches 16 on or after that relevant date.]

(4) Paragraph (3) does [4 [5*omitted*]] not apply to a DLA entitled person whose entitlement, on the day that the person reaches 16, is on the basis that the person is terminally ill within the meaning given by subsection (2) of section 66 (attendance allowance for the terminally ill) of the 1992 Act.

[3 (4A) If the DLA entitled person referred to in paragraph (3) [4 [5*omitted*]] is an exempt person, the Secretary of State must not send the notification required by paragraph (3) [4 [5*omitted*]] until the DLA entitled person ceases to be an exempt person.]

(5) [2Subject to [3 paragraph (5A) and (5B)]] where, after [1 27th October 2013], a DLA entitled person who has neither—

(a) been sent a notification under paragraph (1), nor

(b) made a claim for personal independence payment under regulation 4, notifies the Secretary of State of a change of circumstances other than a change to which paragraph (6) applies, the Secretary of State must, as soon as reasonably practicable, send the person a notification under paragraph (1).

([[2](5A) Paragraph (5) does not apply unless—

(a) the Secretary of State has specified a relevant date which applies in the case of the DLA entitled person, and

(b) that person notifies the Secretary of State of the change of circumstances on or after that relevant date.]

[[3] (5B) If the DLA entitled person referred to in paragraph (5) is an exempt person, the Secretary of State must not send the notification required by paragraph (5) until the DLA entitled person ceases to be an exempt person.]

(6) This paragraph applies to a change of circumstances where the change notified is that the DLA entitled person is to become or has become absent, whether temporarily or permanently, from Great Britain.

AMENDMENTS

1. Personal Independence Payment (Transitional Provisions) (Amendment) Regulations 2013 (SI 2013/2231) reg.2(2) (October 6, 2013).

2. Personal Independence Payment (Transitional Provisions) (Amendment) Regulations 2013 (SI 2013/2689) reg.2(3) (October 25, 2013).

3. Social Security (Disability Living Allowance and Personal Independence Payment) (Amendment) Regulations 2016 (SI 2016/556) reg.4(3) (June 29, 2016).

4. Personal Independence Payment (Transitional Provisions) Amendment (Scotland) Regulations 2020 (SSI 2020/218) reg.2(2) (September 1, 2020, effective only in Scotland). This substitutes the words in italics for the pre-existing text, which therefore now applies only in England and Wales).

5. Disability Assistance for Working Age People (Transitional Provisions and Miscellaneous Amendment) (Scotland) Regulations 2022 (SSI 2022/217), reg.17 (August 29, 2022). Note these regulations omit paras (3) to (6) of reg.1 but extend only to Scotland. The text of this regulation for England and Wales has therefore been returned to its original format.

DEFINITIONS

"change of circumstances"—see reg.2(1). **4.265**
"DLA entitled person"—see reg.2(1).

GENERAL NOTE

In *DC v SSWP (PIP)* [2016] UKUT 117 (AAC); [2019] AACR 15 (CA only) **4.266**
the claimant contacted the DWP to enquire about transition from his current award of DLA. The DWP treated this contact as if it were notice of a change of circumstances and sent him a claim form for PIP which he duly completed. That claim for PIP failed entirely and his DLA entitlement terminated. The claimant appealed. He argued first, that his original communication to the DWP was not in fact notice of a change of circumstances (that would have triggered an obligation on the part of the Secretary of State to send a claim form), but was merely an enquiry as to his position in the future when transition to PIP might occur. His communication was not in fact available to the FTT that heard his appeal, but Judge Mitchell in the UT found that that did not matter because, in any case, the Secretary of State had a more general power under reg.3(1) to invite a claim from a DLA entitled person at any time. Once the process was begun the claimant was effectively on a conveyer-belt towards the determination of a PIP claim. (The case was in fact returned for rehearing but that was because the FTT appeared to have misunderstood the evidence that was before them).

An attempt to have these regulations declared invalid was unsuccessful in *TW v SSWP (PIP)* [2017] UKUT 25 (AAC). The claimant had been entitled to DLA and on mandatory transfer to PIP she was awarded a greater amount of benefit – she was a PIP "winner". But under these regulations by reg.17 her award of PIP was delayed for 28 days and her entitlement to DLA continued at the lower rate. She argued that this discriminated against her as a PIP transfer claimant because a payment of PIP to a new claimant would have been made from the date of claim. She argued that this meant the regulations were in breach of her art.14 rights under the ECHR and should be disapplied. A three judge panel of the UT rejected her argument. The delay applied equally to those claimants who were PIP "losers" and was a part of a necessarily complex scheme to provide for a fair and efficient system to transfer claimants. That being so the delay was, they said, objectively justified.

This case and the reasoning used has been upheld by the Court of Appeal reported as *Worley v SSWP (PIP)* [2019] EWCA Civ 15; [2019] AACR 15.

Claims by persons entitled to disability living allowance for personal independence payment other than by invitation

4.267 [[1]**4.** A DLA entitled person who has not been sent a notification under regulation 3(1) may not make a claim for personal independence payment unless—

(a) they were aged under 65 on 8th April 2013,
(b) the Secretary of State has specified a relevant date which applies in their case, and
(c) they make the claim on or after that relevant date.]

AMENDMENTS

1. Personal Independence Payment (Transitional Provisions) (Amendment) Regulations 2013 (SI 2013/2689) reg.2(3) (October 25, 2013).

GENERAL NOTE

4.268 For the period from October 6, 2013 until October 25, 2013 reg.4 in its original form was amended in reg.4(2) to read as the date October 28, 2013.

DEFINITIONS

4.269 "DLA" entitled person"—see reg.2(1).
"disability living allowance"—see reg.2(1).

[[1] (Scotland) ***Claims by persons entitled to disability living allowance for personal independence payment upon becoming resident in Scotland***

4.270 *4A.—(1) Paragraphs (2) to (4) apply where a DLA entitled person who reaches the age of 16 on or after 1 September 2020—*

(a) has been sent a notification under regulation 3(1) whilst resident in England or Wales, and

(b) becomes resident in Scotland before an assessment determination is made.

(2) From the date on which the person becomes resident in Scotland—

(a) the notification sent under regulation 3(1) ceases to have effect,
(b) regulations 8 to 11 are of no effect in respect of that notification,
(c) regulations 3(3ZA) and 18A apply in respect of the person, and
(d) for the purposes of regulation 4, the person is treated as though they have not been sent a notification under regulation 3(1).

(3) If the person described in paragraph (1) has made a claim for personal independence payment—

(a) for the avoidance of doubt, nothing in paragraph (2) affects the validity of a claim for personal independence payment that has been made in pursuance of the notification,

(b) the claim will continue towards an assessment determination, unless it is withdrawn under regulation 31 (withdrawal of claim) of the Claims and Payments Regulations.

(4) If the person described in paragraph (1) has made a claim for personal independence payment in pursuance of the notification, and then withdraws their claim under regulation 31 (withdrawal of claim) of the Claims and Payments Regulations before an assessment determination is made, regulation 15 does not apply in respect of that withdrawal.]

AMENDMENT

1. Personal Independence Payment (Transitional Provisions) Amendment (Scotland) Regulations 2020 (SSI 2020/218) reg.2(3) (September 1, 2020, effective only in Scotland).

Persons under 16 not entitled to claim personal independence payment

5.—(1) No claim for personal independence payment may be made by a person who has not reached 16. 4.271

(2) Paragraph (1) applies whether or not a person is entitled to disability living allowance.

GENERAL NOTE

In the case of a child who has an appointee in in respect of their claim to DLA the DWP has a process that they follow when the claimant approaches the age of 16. A letter sent to the claimant enquires as to whether they will still require an appointee for the purposes of a claim to PIP. If they reply to the effect that they will, then an appointment is made, by the Secretary of State, under the powers that she has in reg. 28 to appoint for persons unable to act. In *P v SSWP (PIP)* [2018] UKUT 359 (AAC) there was no evidence before the FTT of such a process having been followed but the judge held that the tribunal (had they been aware of the deficiency) would be entitled to assume (applying the presumption of regularity) that the correct procedure had been followed in the absence of any evidence to the contrary. 4.272

Persons in the course of claiming disability living allowance not entitled to claim personal independence payment

6.—(1) This regulation applies to a person who is not entitled to disability living allowance if— 4.273

(a) the person claimed disability living allowance before [[1]28th October 2013], and

(b) that claim remains under consideration on that date.

(2) A person to whom this regulation applies may not claim personal independence payment while the person's claim for disability living allowance remains under consideration.

(3) For the purpose of this regulation a person's claim for disability living allowance remains under consideration only if it has not—

(a) been decided by the Secretary of State under section 8 (decisions by the Secretary of State) of the Social Security Act 1998,
(b) been withdrawn in accordance with paragraph (2) of regulation 5 (amendment and withdrawal of claim) of the 1987 Regulations, or
(c) otherwise ceased to be under consideration before being decided by the Secretary of State as mentioned in subparagraph (a).

AMENDMENT

1. Personal Independence Payment (Transitional Provisions) (Amendment) Regulations 2013 (SI 2013/2231) reg.2(4) (October 6, 2013).

DEFINITIONS

"disability living allowance"—see reg.2(1).
"the 1987 Regulations—see reg. 2(1).

Form of notification inviting a person to claim personal independence payment

4.274 **7.** A notification to a DLA entitled person under regulation 3(1) inviting the person to claim personal independence payment must—
(a) explain that the person's entitlement to disability living allowance will end if the person does not claim personal independence payment,
(b) state the date of the last day of the period within which the person should claim personal independence payment, that period being one of 28 days starting with the day that is the stated date of notification,
(c) tell the person how to claim personal independence payment,
and may contain such additional guidance and information as the Secretary of State considers appropriate.

DEFINITIONS

4.275 "disability living allowance"—see reg.2(1).
"DLA entitled person"—see reg.2(1).

Making a claim for personal independence payment following notification

4.276 **8.**—(1) In this regulation and regulation 9 "the claim period" means the period of 28 days referred to in regulation 7(b).

(2) For the purposes of this regulation a claim, whether or not it is defective as mentioned in paragraph (3) or (4) of regulation 11 (making a claim for personal independence payment) of the Claims and Payments Regulations, must be made in accordance with and by a means set out in paragraph (1)(a), (b) or (c) of that regulation.

(3) Such a claim is made—
(a) in the case of a claim made in writing, other than by means of an electronic communication, on a form authorised by the Secretary of State, on the day on which it is delivered to or received at the appropriate office,
(b) in the case of a claim in writing made by means of an electronic communication in accordance with the provisions set out in Part 2 of Schedule 2 to the Claims and Payments Regulations, on the day on which it is received at the appropriate office, and

(c) in the case of a claim made by telephone, on the day on which the telephone call takes place.

(4) Neither paragraph (6) of regulation 11 of the Claims and Payments Regulations nor paragraph (2) of regulation 12 (date of claim for personal independence payment) of those Regulations shall apply in relation to a claim made by a notified person but—

(a) in a case where the claim is defective as mentioned in paragraph (3) or (4) of the said regulation 11, the Secretary of State must extend the claim period by a period of 28 days, or such longer period as the Secretary of State thinks fit, starting with the day following the last day of the claim period, and

(b) in any other case the Secretary of State may extend the claim period by such further period as the Secretary of State thinks fit.

(5) The duty in paragraph (4)(a) and power in paragraph (4)(b) to extend the claim period may be exercised before the claim period would otherwise have expired or after it has expired.

(6) The Secretary of State may further extend a claim period extended under paragraph (4) either before the extended period would have expired or after it has expired.

(7) Where the claim period has been extended under paragraph (4), the Secretary of State must treat the claim as properly made if a claim is made—

(a) before the end of the period by which the claim period was extended or further extended, and

(b) in accordance with any instructions of the Secretary of State as to the way in which the claim is to be completed.

DEFINITIONS

"the Claims and Payments Regulations"—see reg.2(1). 4.277
"appropriate office"—see reg.2(1).
"electronic communication"—see reg.2(1).

Suspension of disability living allowance where no claim for personal independence payment made

9.—(1) Where a notified person makes no claim for personal independence payment before the end of the claim period or, where applicable, that period as extended under regulation 8(4) or (6), the person's entitlement to disability living allowance shall be suspended. 4.278

(2) The suspension shall take effect on the first pay day after the last day of the claim period or, where applicable, of that period as extended or further extended.

DEFINITIONS

"notified person"—see reg.2(1). 4.279
"disability living allowance"—see reg.2(1).

Further opportunity to claim personal independence payment

10.—(1) The Secretary of State must send any notified person in relation to whom regulation 9 takes effect a notice in writing informing the person— 4.280

(a) that the person's entitlement to disability living allowance will be or has been suspended,
(b) of the day on which the suspension takes or took effect, and
(c) that the person's entitlement to disability living allowance will be terminated unless the person makes a claim for personal independence payment before the end of the period of 28 days beginning with the day on which the suspension takes or took effect.

(2) The Secretary of State must send a notice under paragraph (1) before, on or as soon as practicable after, the day on which the suspension takes effect in accordance with regulation 9(2).

(3) Where a notice is sent to a notified person under paragraph (1), and the person makes a claim for personal independence payment before the end of the period specified in paragraph (1)(c), the person's entitlement to disability living allowance shall be reinstated as if the suspension of the entitlement had never taken effect.

DEFINITIONS

4.281 "notified person"—see reg.2(1).
"disability living allowance"—see reg.2(1).

Termination of entitlement to disability living allowance following failure to claim personal independence payment

4.282 **11.**—(1) Where a notice is sent to a notified person under paragraph 10(1) and the person makes no claim for personal independence payment before the end of the period specified in regulation 10(1)(c), the person's entitlement to disability living allowance shall terminate with effect from the day on which the suspension of the person's entitlement took effect in accordance with regulation 9(2).

(2) The Secretary of State must send any person in relation to whom paragraph (1) takes effect a notice in writing—
(a) informing the person that the person's entitlement to disability living allowance has terminated and of the date on which the termination took effect, and
(b) explaining that it is no longer possible for the person's entitlement to disability living allowance to be reinstated but that it remains open to the person to claim personal independence payment.

DEFINITIONS

4.283 "notified person"—see reg.2(1).
"disability living allowance"—see reg.2(1).

Defective claims by voluntary transfer claimants

4.284 **12.**—(1) This regulation applies in relation to a claim for personal independence payment by a voluntary transfer claimant if—
(a) the claim was defective as mentioned in paragraphs (3) or (4) of regulation 11 of the Claims and Payments Regulations, and
(b) no claim completed in accordance with the instructions of the Secretary of State is received within the period of one month or longer which applies under paragraph (6) of that regulation.

(2) Where this regulation applies—

(a) regulation 9(1) shall apply to the voluntary transfer claimant as if the claimant were a notified person who has failed to claim before the end of the claim period, and

(b) for the purpose of that regulation the claim period for the voluntary transfer claimant shall be treated as ending on the last day of the period of one month or longer referred to in paragraph (6) of regulation 11 of the Claims and Payments Regulations, and regulations 9(2), 10 and 11 shall apply as if the voluntary transfer claimant were a notified person.

DEFINITIONS

"voluntary transfer claimant"—see reg.2(1). 4.285

Failure to provide information etc.

13.—(1) Where, in relation to a claim for personal independence payment made by a transfer claimant— 4.286

(a) a negative determination is made in relation to both components under regulation 8 (information or evidence required for determining limited or severely limited ability to carry out activities) of the PIP Regulations or paragraph (2) of regulation 9 (claimant may be called for consultation to determine whether the claimant has limited or severely limited ability to carry out activities) of the PIP Regulations, or

(b) there is a determination by the Secretary of State that the transfer claimant has—

(i) unreasonably failed to comply with a requirement imposed on the claimant by the Secretary of State under regulation 35 (attendance in person) of the Claims and Payments Regulations, or

(ii) failed to comply with a requirement imposed on the claimant by the Secretary of State under regulation 37 (evidence and information in connection with a claim) of the Claims and Payments Regulations,

the transfer claimant's entitlement to disability living allowance shall terminate with effect from the last day of the period of 14 days starting with the first pay day after the day on which the determination is made.

(2) Where—

(a) for any reason an assessment determination is made on a claim by a transfer claimant in respect of which there has been a determination referred to in paragraph (1)(a) or (b) (for example, because the determination is revised by the Secretary of State under section 9 of the 1998 Act or there is a successful appeal in respect of the determination under section 12 of that Act), and

(b) personal independence payment is awarded to the transfer claimant,

the transfer claimant shall be entitled to personal independence payment in accordance with regulation 17(2)(b).

DEFINITIONS

"transfer claimant"—see reg.2(1). 4.287

"the PIP Regulations—see reg.2(1).

"the Claims and Payments Regulations—see reg.2(1).

"disability living allowance"—see reg.2(1).

"assessment determination"—see reg.2(1).

Express intention not to claim personal independence payment

4.288 **14.**—(1) This regulation applies where a DLA entitled person who has not made a claim for personal independence payment informs the Secretary of State, whether in writing or by telephone, that the person does not intend to claim personal independence payment.

(2) Where this regulation applies the person's entitlement to disability living allowance shall terminate with effect from the last day of the period of 14 days starting with the first pay day after the day on which the Secretary of State decides that the person has informed the Secretary of State as mentioned in paragraph (1).

(3) Paragraph (2) does not apply unless the Secretary of State is satisfied that the person was told, before the person informed the Secretary of State of the person's intention not to claim personal independence payment, that the person's entitlement to disability living allowance would terminate if the person expressed that intention.

DEFINITIONS

4.289 "DLA entitled person"—see reg.2(1).
"disability living allowance"—see reg.2(1).

Withdrawal of claim for personal independence payment

4.290 **15.** Where a claim for personal independence payment is withdrawn by a transfer claimant under regulation 31 (withdrawal of claim) of the Claims and Payments Regulations before an assessment determination is made in relation to it, the claimant's entitlement to disability living allowance shall terminate with effect from the last day of the period of 14 days starting with the first pay day after the day on which the Secretary of State decides that the transfer claimant has withdrawn the claim.

DEFINITIONS

4.291 "transfer claimant"—see reg.2(1).
"the Claims and Payments Regulations"—see reg.2(1).
"assessment determination"—see reg. 2(1).
"disability living allowance"—see reg. 2(1).

Death before or after making claim for personal independence payment

4.292 **16.**—(1) Where a notified person dies before making a claim for personal independence payment the law relating to the person's entitlement to disability living allowance shall apply as if the notification had never been sent.

(2) Where a transfer claimant dies—

(a) before any assessment determination is made in relation to the claim, or

(b) where an assessment determination is made in relation to the claim, before the day on which the claimant becomes entitled to personal independence payment in accordance with regulation 17(2), the claim shall be treated as if it had never been made and, if the transfer claimant is a notified person, as if no notification under regulation 3(1) had been sent.

DEFINITIONS

"notified person"—see reg.2(1). 4.293
"disability living allowance"—see reg.2(1).
"transfer claimant"—see reg.2(1).
"assessment determination"—see reg.2(1).

Procedure following and consequences of determination of claim for personal independence payment

17.—(1) Upon an assessment determination being made on a claim by a transfer claimant— 4.294

(a) the Secretary of State must, as soon as practicable, send the claimant written notification of the outcome of the determination, and

[1 (b) except where paragraph (2) of regulation 13 applies to the claimant, the claimant's entitlement to disability living allowance shall terminate—

(i) where paragraph (1B) applies, on the earlier of—

(aa) the last day of the payment period during which the assessment determination is made, or

(bb) the first Tuesday after the making of the assessment determination;

(ii) in any other case, on the last day of the period of 28 days starting with the first pay day after the making of the assessment determination.]

[1 (1A) In paragraph (1), "payment period" means a period in respect of which disability living allowance is paid to the claimant in accordance with regulation 22 of the 1987 Regulations.

(1B) This paragraph applies if—

(a) the transfer claimant is terminally ill for the purposes of section 82 of the Act,

(b) the outcome of an assessment determination in respect of that claimant is an award of personal independence payment, and

(c) the total weekly rate of personal independence payment payable by virtue of that award is greater than the total weekly rate of disability living allowance payable by virtue of that claimant's existing award of disability living allowance.]

(2) Where the outcome of an assessment determination is an award in respect of either or both components of personal independence payment, the claimant's entitlement to personal independence payment starts with effect from the day immediately following—

[1 (a) the day on which the claimant's entitlement to disability living allowance terminates in accordance with paragraph (1)(b) of this regulation,]

(b) where paragraph (2) of regulation 13 applies to the claimant, the day [1 ...] on which the claimant's entitlement to disability living allowance terminated under regulation 13(1).

(3) The notification referred to in paragraph (1) must state—

(a) except where paragraph (2) of regulation 13 applies to the claimant, the day on which the claimant's entitlement to disability living allowance will terminate in accordance with paragraph (1)(b), and

(b) if personal independence payment is awarded, the day on which the claimant's entitlement to personal independence payment starts in accordance with paragraph (2).

(4) This paragraph applies to a person—

(a) whose claim for disability living allowance was refused,

(b) who claimed personal independence payment after that refusal, and

(c) who, as a result of the determination of legal proceedings initiated under the 1998 Act in relation to that refusal, becomes entitled, after the assessment determination, to disability living allowance.

(5) The entitlement of a person to whom paragraph (4) applies to disability living allowance shall terminate—

(a) where personal independence payment is awarded, on the day before that on which the person becomes entitled to personal independence payment, and

(b) where personal independence payment is not awarded, on the last day of the period of 28 days starting with the first pay day after the making of the assessment determination.

DEFINITIONS

4.295 "assessment determination"—see reg.2(1).
"transfer claimant"—see reg.2(1).
"disability living allowance"—see reg.2(1).
"the 1998 Act"—see reg.2(1).

AMENDMENT

1. The Personal Independence Payment (Transitional Provisions) (Amendment) Regulations 2016 (SI 2016/189) reg.2 (April 4, 2016).

Extension of certain fixed term period awards of disability living allowance for persons reaching 16

4.296 **18.**—(1) E & W Where [2 (Scotland) *Subject to regulation 18A, where*] there is an award of disability living allowance to a DLA entitled person and—

(a) the award is of—

(i) both components and the award in respect of either or both is for a fixed term period, or

(ii) one component only and for a fixed term period,

(b) the person reaches 16 after [1 27th October 2013], and

(c) the fixed term period expires in the period starting with the day before the person reaches 16 and ending with the day before the person reaches 16 years and six months, the fixed term period shall be extended.

(2) A fixed term period extended under paragraph (1) shall expire on the day before the person reaches 17 or, where these Regulations have the effect that the person's entitlement to disability living allowance terminates on an earlier day, on that day.

AMENDMENTS

1. Personal Independence Payment (Transitional Provisions) (Amendment) Regulations (SI 2013/2231) reg.2(5) (October 6, 2013).

2. Personal Independence Payment (Transitional Provisions) Amendment (Scotland) Regulations 2020 (SSI 2020/218) reg.2(4) (September 1, 2020, effective

only in Scotland). This substitutes the words in italics for the pre-existing text, which therefore now applies only in England and Wales).

DEFINITIONS

"disability living allowance"—see reg.2(1).
"components"—see reg.2(1).

[1(Scotland) Extension of certain fixed term period awards of disability living allowance for persons resident in Scotland reaching 16

***18A.**—(1) Where there is an award of disability living allowance to a DLA entitled person and—* 4.297

(a) the award is of—

(i) both components and the award in respect of either or both is for a fixed term period, or

(ii) one component only and for a fixed term period,

(b) the person reaches the age of 16 on or after 1 September 2020,

(c) the fixed term period will expire in the period starting with the day before the person reaches the age of 16 and ending with the day before the person reaches the age of 18, and

(d) the person is resident in Scotland,

the fixed term period shall be extended.

(2) A fixed term period extended under paragraph (1) shall expire on the day before the person reaches 18 years and 6 months, or where these Regulations have the effect that the person's entitlement to disability living allowance terminates on an earlier day, on that day.]

AMENDMENT

1. Personal Independence Payment (Transitional Provisions) Amendment (Scotland) Regulations 2020 (SSI 2020/218) reg.2(5) (September 1, 2020, effective only in Scotland).

General power to extend fixed term period awards of disability living allowance

19.—(1) Where there is an award of disability living allowance to a DLA entitled person and— 4.298

(a) the award is of—

(i) both components and the award in respect of either or both is for a fixed term period, or

(ii) one component only and for a fixed term period, and

(b) the Secretary of State considers that the fixed term period may expire [1 while the DLA entitled person is an exempt person to whom a notification cannot be sent by virtue of regulation 3(4A) or (5B), or] before an assessment determination can be made, the Secretary of State may extend the period by such further period as the Secretary of State considers appropriate.

(2) The Secretary of State may extend a fixed term period under paragraph (1)—

(a) regardless of whether the person has yet made a claim for personal independence payment,

(b) where the fixed term period has already been extended under regulation 18, and
(c) on more than one occasion.

(3) A fixed term period extended under paragraph (1) shall expire—
(a) on the last day of the period by which the Secretary of State extended or last extended it, or
(b) where these Regulations have the effect that the person's entitlement to disability living allowance terminates on an earlier day, on that day.

AMENDMENTS

1. Social Security (Disability Living Allowance and Personal Independence Payment) (Amendment) Regulations 2016 (SI 2016/556) reg.4(4) (June 29, 2016).

DEFINITIONS

4.299 "disability living allowance"—see reg.2(1).
"DLA entitled person"—see reg.2(1).
"components"—see reg.2(1).
"assessment determination"—see reg.2(1).

Notifications of change of circumstances

4.300 **20.**—(1) This regulation applies where—
(a) a person notifies the Secretary of State of a change of circumstances, and
(b) paragraph (3), (4) or (5) applies.

(2) If this regulation applies—
(a) the notification shall not be regarded as relating to disability living allowance and accordingly neither section 10 (decisions superseding earlier decisions) nor any other provision of the 1998 Act shall apply, and
(b) the notification to the Secretary of State must be treated in all respects as if it were a notification under paragraph (4) of regulation 38 (evidence and information in connection with an award) of the Claims and Payments regulations of a change of circumstances which the person might reasonably be expected to know might affect the continuance of entitlement to personal independence payment.

(3) This paragraph applies where a notified person notifies the Secretary of State of a change of circumstances before the person makes a claim for personal independence payment.

(4) This paragraph applies where a transfer claimant notifies the Secretary of State of a change of circumstances.

(5) This paragraph applies where a DLA entitled person notifies the Secretary of State of a change of circumstances and, as a result, the Secretary of State is required by regulation 3(5) to send a notification under regulation 3(1) inviting the person to claim personal independence payment.

(6) Paragraphs (3) and (4) do not apply where the change of circumstances notified is that the notified person or the transfer claimant, as the case may be, is to become or has become absent, whether temporarily or permanently, from Great Britain.

DEFINITIONS

4.301 "change of circumstances"—see reg.2(1).

"disability living allowance"—see reg.2(1).
"the 1998 Act"—see reg.2(1).
"the Claims and Payments Regulations"—see reg.2(1).
"notified person"—see reg.2(1).
"transfer claimant"—see reg.2(1).
"DLA entitled person"—see reg.2(1).

Extinguishment of rights of appeal etc. under disability living allowance regime

21. No suspension of a person's entitlement to disability living allowance that takes place by virtue of the application of these Regulations is to be regarded as a decision of the Secretary of State to which section 8 (decisions by the Secretary of State) or 10 (decisions superseding earlier decisions) of the 1998 Act applies, and accordingly— 4.302

(a) no revision by the Secretary of State may take place in relation to the suspension under section 9 (revision of decisions) of that Act, and
(b) no right of appeal in respect of the suspension is to be available to the person under section 12 (appeal to appeal tribunal) of that Act.

DEFINITIONS

"disability living allowance"—see reg.2(1). 4.303
"the 1998 Act"—see reg.2(1).

Extinguishment of right to claim disability living allowance

22.—(1) No person may claim disability living allowance who is— 4.304

(a) entitled to personal independence payment, or
(b) entitled to claim personal independence payment.

(2) Paragraph (1) does not apply to a person whose award of disability living allowance is of—

(a) both components and the award in respect of either or both is for a fixed term period, or
(b) one component only and the award is for a fixed term period,

if, [1 [2 *omitted*], the person has been notified by the Secretary of State that, because the fixed term period is due to come to an end, the person needs to claim disability living allowance again, or to apply for a supersession of the award, if the person wishes to continue to be entitled to disability living allowance in respect of the component or components subject to the fixed term period.

DEFINITIONS

"disability living allowance"—see reg.2(1). 4.305
"component"—see reg.2(1).

AMENDMENTS

1. Personal Independence Payment (Transitional Provisions) (Amendment) Regulations 2013 (SI 2013/2231 reg.2(6) (October 6, 2013).
2. Personal Independence Payments (Transitional Provisions) (Amendment) (No.2) Regulation 2013 (SI 2013/2689) reg.2(5) (October 25, 2013).

General Note

4.306 For the period between October 6, 2013 and October 25, 2013 this regulation was amended to read "before 28th October 2013".

Assessment of claim: transfer claimants to be taken to meet part of required period condition

4.307 **23.**—(1) In applying the required period condition under Part 3 (required period condition) of the PIP Regulations to a claim by a transfer claimant or by a person to whom paragraph (2) or (3) applies, the claimant shall be regarded as meeting such of the conditions contained in the following provisions of Part 3 (which relate to a claimant's abilities in the past) as are relevant to the claim regardless of whether those conditions have been met—

(a) in regulation 12 (required period condition: daily living component), paragraph (1)(a) or (2)(a),
(b) in regulation 13 (required period condition: mobility component), paragraph (1)(a) or (2)(a).

(2) This paragraph applies to a person claiming personal independence payment who—

(a) had not reached 65 on 8th April 2013,
(b) was not entitled to disability living allowance on the day the claim was made but was so entitled on the day falling twenty four months before that day or at any time between those days, and
(c) is not a person to whom paragraph (3) applies.

(3) This paragraph applies to a person claiming personal independence payment who—

(a) was aged 65 or over on the day the claim was made, and
(b) was not entitled to disability living allowance on that day but was so entitled on the day falling 12 months before that day or at any time between those days.

Definitions

4.308 "the PIP Regulations"—see reg.2(1).
"transfer claimant"—see reg.2(1).
"disability living allowance"—see reg.2(1).

General Note

4.309 This regulation provides that in the case of a transfer claimant (defined in reg.2 of these regulations as a person who is transferring from an award of DLA to one of PIP) the 3 month past period condition required by reg.12 of the PIP regulations should be deemed to have been satisfied. The complication that arose in *EB v SSWP (PIP)* [2017] UKUT 311 (AAC) was that one of the possible disabling conditions that the claimant suffered from at the time his PIP claim came to be determined may have not existed then for 3 months (it arose from prostate surgery and the FTT had not determined the exact date of the surgery) and neither did it form any part of the basis on which the claimant had been awarded DLA—(that much was clear because his DLA award had been only for the mobility component). The claimant argued that on the literal interpretation of reg.23 he should be deemed to have satisfied the past period condition, but Judge Farbey QC held that a proper interpretation of this regulation confined its meaning to those conditions that existed at the time of the DLA award and on which that award was based. The judge does this on the basis that transitional legislation is intended to facilitate transfer from one regime to another, but not to authorise innovation. (See the HL in *Britnell v Secretary of State for Social Security* [1991] 1 W.L.R. 198). But an appeal was allowed on the basis that the FTT should have gone on to consider the claim under reg.33 of the Claims and Payments Regulations which allows for an advance award for conditions arising in the 3 months period after the DM decision. As the claimant had been scored 6 points in respect of other daily living Activities this meant that he might have succeeded on a claim for the daily living component under PIP when regard was had to Activity 5—Managing toilet needs or incontinence. The case was returned for rehearing.

Assessment of claim: date by reference to which assessment is to be made

24. In applying the required period condition under Part 3 of the PIP Regulations to a claim by a transfer claimant the "prescribed date" referred to in— 4.310

(a) paragraphs (1) and (2) of regulation 12 of those Regulations, and
(b) paragraphs (1) and (2) of regulation 13 of those Regulations,

is the date on which the claim is made.

DEFINITIONS

"the PIP Regulations"—see reg.2(1). 4.311
"transfer claimant"—see reg.2(1).

Treatment of persons in hospital or care home during transfer to personal independence payment

25.—(1) This regulation applies to a transfer claimant awarded personal independence payment if, on the day on which the claimant's entitlement to disability living allowance terminates in accordance with regulations 13(1) or 17(1)(b), the claimant is a person who— 4.312

(a) fails to meet the condition in paragraph (1) of regulation 8 (hospitalisation) of the 1991 Regulations but is nevertheless entitled to payment of the care component by reason of the application of regulation 10 (exemption from regulations 8 and 9) of the 1991 Regulations,
(b) fails to meet the condition in paragraph (1) of regulation 12A (hospitalisation in mobility component cases) of the 1991 Regulations but is nevertheless entitled to payment of the mobility component by reason of the application of regulation 12B of the 1991 Regulations (exemption from regulation 12A), or
(c) fails to meet both of the conditions referred to in subparagraphs (a) and (b) but is nevertheless entitled to payment of both components by reason of the application of regulations 10 and 12B of the 1991 Regulations, and, on the day on which the claimant's entitlement to personal independence payment starts in accordance with regulation 17(2), the claimant meets the condition in subsection (2) of section 86 (hospital in-patients) of the Act.

(2) This regulation also applies to a transfer claimant awarded personal independence payment if—

(a) on the day on which the claimant's entitlement to disability living allowance terminates in accordance with regulations 13(1) or 17(1)(b), the claimant is a person—
   (i) to whom the care component of disability living allowance is not payable under paragraph (1) of regulation 9 (persons in care homes) of the 1991 Regulations, but

(ii) who is nevertheless entitled to payment of that component by reason of the application of regulation 10 of the 1991 Regulations, and

(b) on the day on which the claimant's entitlement to personal independence payment starts in accordance with regulation 17(2), the claimant meets the condition in subsection (2) of section 85 (care home residents) of the Act.

(3) Where this regulation applies to a transfer claimant—

(a) the day on which the claimant's entitlement to personal independence payment starts in accordance with regulation 17(2) shall be treated as being the first day of the period referred to in paragraph (1) of regulation 30 (payability exceptions: care homes and hospitals) of the PIP Regulations, and

(b) paragraph (2) of regulation 30 of the PIP Regulations shall not apply to the claimant in respect of either that day or any consecutive period of days starting with that day during which the claimant meets the condition in section 85(2) of the Act (care home residents: costs of qualifying services borne out of public or local funds) or section 86(2) of the Act (in-patient treatment: costs of treatment, accommodation and related services borne out of public funds).

DEFINITIONS

4.313 "transfer claimant"—see reg.2(1).
"disability living allowance"—see reg.2(1).
"the 1991 Regulations"—see reg.2(1).
"the Act"—see reg.2(1).
"the PIP Regulations"—see reg.2(1).

Temporary absence from Great Britain when transfer claimant becomes entitled to personal independence payment

4.314 **26.**—(1) This paragraph applies to a transfer claimant awarded personal independence payment if, on the day that the claimant's entitlement to disability living allowance terminates in accordance with regulations 13(1) or 17(1)(b), the claimant would otherwise be temporarily absent from Great Britain but is treated as present in Great Britain by virtue of—

(a) paragraph (2)(d) of regulation 2 (conditions as to residence and presence in Great Britain) of the 1991 Regulations), because the first 13 weeks of absence referred to in that regulation have not expired, or

(b) paragraph (3B) of regulation 2 of the 1991 Regulations, because the first 26 weeks of absence referred to in that regulation have not expired.

(2) In applying regulation 17 (absence from Great Britain) of the PIP Regulations to a transfer claimant to whom paragraph (1)(a) applies, the period—

(a) starting with the first day on which the claimant was treated as present in Great Britain by virtue of regulation 2(2)(d) of the 1991 Regulations, and

(b) ending with the day on which the claimant's entitlement to disability living allowance terminates in accordance with regulations 13(1) or

17(1)(b) shall be counted towards the 13 weeks of absence referred to in regulation 17 of the PIP Regulations.

(3) In applying regulation 18 (absence from Great Britain to receive medical treatment) of the PIP Regulations to a transfer claimant to whom paragraph (1)(b) applies the period—

(a) starting with the first day of absence for the purpose of regulation (3B) of the 1991 Regulations, and

(b) ending with the day on which the claimant's entitlement to disability living allowance terminates in accordance with regulation 13(1) or 17(1)(b) shall be counted towards the 26 weeks of absence referred to in regulation 18 of the PIP Regulations.

DEFINITIONS

"transfer claimant"—see reg.2(1). **4.315**
"disability living allowance"—see reg.2(1).
"the 1991 Regulations"—see reg.2(1).
"the PIP Regulations"—see reg.2(1).

Persons aged 65 and over to be entitled to personal independence payment in certain circumstances

27.—(1) Section 83(1) (persons of pensionable age) of the Act does not apply to a person to whom this regulation applies. **4.316**

(2) This regulation applies to a person who—

(a) had not reached 65 on 8th April 2013,

(b) is a DLA entitled person, and

(c) claims personal independence payment—

(i) in response to a notification sent to the person by the Secretary of State under regulation 3(1), or

(ii) under regulation 4.

(3) This regulation also applies to a person who—

(a) had not reached 65 on 8th April 2013,

(b) claims personal independence payment, and

(c) is not entitled to disability living allowance on the day the claim is made but was so entitled on the day falling 12 months before that day or at any time between those days.

DEFINITIONS

"DLA entitled person"—see reg.2(1). **4.317**
"disability living allowance"—see reg.2(1).

[[1]Revision and supersession of an award of personal independence payment in certain circumstances

27A. (1) Subject to paragraph (2), section 83(1) of the Act (persons of pensionable age) does not apply to a person who— **4.318**

(a) met the conditions at paragraph (2) or (3) of regulation 27, and

(b) is entitled to an award of personal independence payment ("the original award"), and that award is revised or superseded within the meaning of section 9 or 10 of the 1998 Act) respectively.

(2) Where the original award includes the mobility component of personal independence payment and is superseded, paragraphs (2) and (3) of regulation 27 of the PIP Regulations apply in relation to the supersession.

(3) In this regulation, the references to an original award are to be read as including a concessionary payment made in lieu of personal independence payment under arrangements by the Secretary of State with the consent of the Treasury.]

AMENDMENT

1. Personal Independence Payment (Transitional Provisions) (Amendment) Regulations 2019 (SI 2019/1011) reg.2 (July 4, 2019).

GENERAL NOTE

4.319 This amendment fills an unintended gap that occurred when DLA transfer claimants transferred to PIP at 65 years of age or older and whose award of benefit was subsequently revised or superseded. See further *RJ v SSWP (PIP)* [2020] UKUT 107 (AAC).

Persons unable to act: claims for personal independence payment

4.320 **28.**—(1) This regulation applies where, immediately before any claim for personal independence payment is made by or on behalf of a person entitled to disability living allowance, there is a person ("the appointed person")—

(a) appointed by the Secretary of State in accordance with paragraph (1) of regulation 33 (persons unable to act) of the 1987 Regulations, or

(b) treated, by virtue of paragraph (1A) of the said regulation 33, as being a person appointed by the Secretary of State in accordance with paragraph (1) of that regulation, to exercise rights on behalf of the person entitled to disability living allowance and receive and deal with any sums payable to that person.

(2) Where this regulation applies the appointed person shall be regarded as acting on behalf of the person entitled to disability living allowance for the purposes of the making and pursuit of a claim for personal independence payment under these Regulations and, where applicable, the Claims and Payments Regulations.

DEFINITIONS

4.321 "disability living allowance"—see reg.2(1).
"the 1987 Regulations"—see reg.2(1).
"the Claims and Payments Regulations"—see reg.2(1).

Persons unable to act: transfer to personal independence payment

4.322 **29.**—(1) This regulation applies if a transfer claimant is awarded personal independence payment and, on the day that the person's entitlement to disability living allowance terminates in accordance with regulations 13(1) or 17(1)(b), there is a person ("the appointed person") who, under paragraph (2) of regulation 28, is to be regarded as acting on behalf of the claimant for the purposes set out in that paragraph.

(2) Where this regulation applies then, with effect from the first day on which the transfer claimant is entitled to personal independence payment in accordance with regulation 17(2), the appointed person shall be treated as being a person appointed by the Secretary of State in accordance with regulation 57(1) (persons unable to act) of the Claims and Payments Regulations to exercise rights on behalf of the transfer claimant and receive and deal with any sums payable to the transfer claimant.

DEFINITIONS

"transfer claimant"—see reg.2(1). 4.323
"disability living allowance"—see reg.2(1).
"the Claims and Payments Regulations"—see reg.2(1).

Application of these Regulations to certain persons becoming entitled to disability living allowance while claiming personal independence payment

30.—(1) If paragraph (2) applies to a person then, with effect from the date of the determination referred to in subparagraph (c) of paragraph (2), the regulations referred to in paragraphs (3), (4), (5) and (6) shall apply in relation to that person in accordance with the provisions of those paragraphs. 4.324

(2) This paragraph applies to a person—

(a) whose claim for disability living allowance was refused,
(b) who claimed personal independence payment after that refusal, and
(c) who, as a result of the determination of legal proceedings initiated under the 1998 Act in relation to that refusal, becomes entitled, before the assessment determination, to disability living allowance.

(3) Regulations 13, 15, 16(2), 17(1) to (3), 20(1), (2), (4) and (6) (so far as it applies to paragraph (4) of regulation 20), 23(1) (in its application to transfer claimants), 24, 25, and 26 shall apply to the person as if the person were a transfer claimant.

(4) Regulations 18 and 19 shall apply to the person as if the person were a DLA entitled person.

(5) Where a person to whom paragraph (2) applies also satisfies the condition in regulation 27(2)(a), regulation 27 shall be treated as applying to the person as if the person satisfied all the conditions in regulation 27(2).

(6) Regulation 29 shall apply to the person as if the person were a transfer claimant if, on the day that the person's entitlement to disability living allowance terminates in accordance with regulation 13(1) or 17(1)(b), there is a person ("the appointed person")—

(a) appointed by the Secretary of State in accordance with paragraph (1) of regulation 33 of the 1987 Regulations, or
(b) treated by virtue of paragraph (1A) of the said regulation 33 as being a person appointed by the Secretary of State in accordance with paragraph (1) of that regulation, to exercise rights on behalf of the person entitled to disability living allowance and receive and deal with any sums payable to that person.

DEFINITIONS

"disability living allowance"—see reg.2(1). 4.325

"the 1998 Act"—see reg.2(1).
"assessment determination"—see reg.2(1).
"transfer claimant"—see reg.2(1).
"DLA entitled person"—see reg.2(1).
"the 1987 Regulations"—see reg.2(1).

Disabled people: badges for motor vehicles

4.326 **31.**—(1) In this regulation, "the 2000 Regulations" means the Disabled Persons (Badges for Motor Vehicles) (England) Regulations 2000.

(2) Where a person satisfies paragraph (3)—

(a) the person shall be treated as being a disabled person for the purpose of regulation 7 of the 2000 Regulations, and

(b) regulation 9(1)(c) of the 2000 Regulations shall not apply to the person, until the expiration of the period for which the disabled person's badge referred to in paragraph (3)(b)(i) was issued.

(3) A person satisfies this paragraph if—

(a) the entitlement of the person to disability living allowance terminates in accordance with these Regulations,

(b) on the last day on which the person is entitled to disability living allowance the person—

(i) is a holder of a disabled person's badge in accordance with the 2000 Regulations, and

(ii) is a disabled person for the purposes of the 2000 Regulations by virtue of satisfying regulation 4(1)(a) and (2)(a) of the 2000 Regulations,

(c) with effect from the following day the person is no longer a disabled person for the purposes of the 2000 Regulations because the person does not satisfy regulation 4(1)(a) and (2)(g) of the 2000 Regulations, and

(d) the period for which the badge mentioned above in sub-paragraph (b) was issued has not yet expired.

DEFINITIONS

4.327 "disability living allowance"—see reg.2(1).

PART V

MATERNITY BENEFITS

The Social Security (Maternity Allowance) Regulations 1987

(SI 1987/416) (*as amended*)

ARRANGEMENT OF REGULATIONS

The Secretary of State for Social Services, in exercise of the powers conferred by section 22(3) of, and Schedule 20 to, the Social Security Act 1975 and sections 84(1) and 89(1) of the Social Security Act 1986, and of all other powers enabling him in that behalf, by this instrument, which is made before the end of the period of 12 months from the commencement of the enactments under which it is made, makes the following Regulations:

Citation, commencement and interpretation

1.—(1) These regulations may be cited as the Social Security (Maternity Allowance) Regulations 1987 and shall come into operation on 6th April 1987. 5.2

(2) In these regulations—

"the Act" means the Social Security Act 1975;

"the 1986 Act" means the Social Security Act 1986.

[[1]"the 1992 Act" means the Social Security Contributions and Benefits Act 1992.]

(3) Unless the context otherwise requires, any reference in any of these regulations—

(a) to a numbered paragraph is a reference to the paragraph bearing that number in that regulation; and

(b) in these regulations to a Schedule is to the Schedule to these regulations.

AMENDMENT

1. Social Security (Maternity Allowance) (Miscellaneous Amendments) Regulations 2014 (SI 2014/884) reg.2 (May 18, 2014).

[[1] Disapplication of section 1(1A) of the Administration Act

[[2] **1A.** Section 1(1A) of the Social Security Administration Act 1992 (requirement to state a national insurance number) shall not apply to an adult dependant who— 5.3

(a) is a person in respect of whom a claim for an increase of maternity allowance is made;

(b) is subject to immigration control within the meaning of section 115(9)(a) of the Immigration and Asylum Act 1999; and

(c) has not previously been allocated a national insurance number.]

AMENDMENTS

1. Social Security (National Insurance Information: Exemption) Regulations (SI 1997/2676) (December 1, 1997).

2. Social Security (National Insurance Number Information: Exemption) Regulations 2009 (SI 2009/471) reg.4 (April 6, 2009).

Disqualification for the receipt of a maternity allowance

5.4 [[1]**2.** (1) A woman shall be disqualified for receiving a maternity allowance under section 35 of the 1992 Act if during the maternity allowance period she does any work in employment as an employed or self-employed earner, for more than 10 days, whether consecutive or not, falling within that period.

(2) The disqualification referred to in paragraph (1) shall be for such part of the maternity allowance period as may, in the opinion of the Secretary of State, be reasonable in the circumstances, provided that the disqualification shall, in any event, be for at least the number of days on which she so worked in excess of 10 days.

(3) A woman shall be disqualified for receiving a maternity allowance under section 35B of the 1992 Act if during the maternity allowance period—

(a) she works with S (as defined in subsection (1)(b) of that section); or

(b) she does any work in employment as an employed or self-employed earner.

(4) The disqualification referred to in paragraph (3) shall be for such part of the maternity allowance period as may, in the opinion of the Secretary of State, be reasonable in the circumstances and in any event shall be for at least the number of days she so worked.

(5) [[2] *omitted*]

(6) [[2] omitted]

(7) A woman shall be disqualified for receiving maternity allowance under section 35 or 35B of the 1992 Act if at any time before she is confined she fails without good cause to attend for or to submit herself to any medical examination for which she was given at least 3 days notice in writing by or on behalf of the Secretary of State.

(8) The disqualification referred to in paragraph (7) shall be for such part of the maternity allowance period (being a part beginning not earlier than the day on which the failure occurs) as may, in the opinion of the Secretary of State, be reasonable in the circumstances, except that in the event of her being confined after such failure the woman shall not by reason of such failure be so disqualified for the day on which the confinement occurs or any day thereafter.]

AMENDMENT

1. Social Security (Maternity Allowance) (Miscellaneous Amendments) Regulations 2014 (SI2014/884) reg.2 (May 18, 2014).

2. Social Security (Miscellaneous Amendments) Regulations 2015 (SI 2015/67) reg.3 (February 23, 2015).

Modification of the maternity allowance period

5.5 **3.**—(1) [Section 35(2)] of the Social Security Contributions and Benefits Act 1992] (which relates to the maternity allowance period) shall be modified in accordance with [[5]paragraph (2A)].

(2) [[3]omitted].

[[1] (2A) In relation to a woman who—

(a) is not entitled to maternity allowance at the 11th week before the expected week of confinement; and

(b) subsequently becomes entitled to maternity allowance before being confined; and

(c) has stopped work

the maternity allowance period shall be a period of [[4]39 weeks commencing no earlier than the day she becomes entitled to maternity allowance and no later than the day following the day on which she is confined]]

[[5](2B) The provisions of section 35B of the 1992 Act which relate to the maternity allowance period shall, in relation to a woman who–

(a) is not entitled to maternity allowance at the 11th week before the expected week of confinement;

(b) subsequently becomes entitled to maternity allowance before being confined; and

(c) has ceased to work with S,

be modified in accordance with paragraph (2C).

(2C) The maternity allowance period shall be a period of 14 weeks commencing—

(a) on the day after she ceases work, or, if later, the day she becomes entitled to maternity allowance; and

(b) no later than the day following the day on which she is confined.]

(3)–(6) [[3]*omitted*].

AMENDMENTS

1. Social Security Maternity Benefits and Statutory Sick Pay (Amendment) Regulations 1994 (SI 1994/1367) reg.3 (where the expected week of confinement begins after October 16, 1994).

2. Social Security (Miscellaneous Amendments) (No. 2) Regulations 1997 (SI 1997/793) reg.18 (April 7, 1997).

3. Social Security, Statutory Maternity Pay and Statutory Sick Pay (Miscellaneous Amendment) Regulations 2002 (SI 2002/2690) Reg.15 (November 24, 2002).

4. Statutory Maternity Pay, Social Security (Maternity Allowance) and Social Security (Overlapping Benefits) (Amendment) Regulations 2006 (SI 2006/2379) reg.4(3)(October 1, 2006).

5. Social Security (Maternity Allowance) (Miscellaneous Amendments) Regulations 2014 (SI 2014/884) reg.2 (May 18, 2014).

The Social Security (Maternity Allowance) (Work Abroad) Regulations 1987

(SI 1987/417) (*as amended*)

ARRANGEMENT OF REGULATIONS

The Secretary of State for Social Services, in exercise of the powers conferred by section 131 of and Schedule 20 to the Social Security Act 1975 and of all other powers enabling him in that behalf, after agreement by the Social Security Advisory Committee that proposals to make these Regulations should not be referred to it, hereby makes the following Regulations:

Citation and commencement

5.7 **1.**—(1) These regulations may be cited as the Social Security (Maternity Allowance) (Work Abroad) Regulations 1987 and shall come into force on 6th April 1987.

(2) In these regulations—

"the Act" means the Social Security Act 1975;

"the Contributions Regulations" means the Social Security (Contributions) Regulations 1979.

Special provision for certain persons who have been employed abroad

5.8 **2.**—(1) This regulation applies, subject to paragraph (5), for the purpose of determining entitlement to a maternity allowance in respect of a woman who—

(a) has been absent from Great Britain;

(b) has returned to Great Britain; and

(c) throughout the whole period of her absence was ordinarily resident in Great Britain.

(2) [1 Where a woman has paid, or is treated as having actually paid, Class 1 contributions under the Act either]

(a) to the full extent of her liability under regulation 120 of the Contributions Regulations; or

(b) in respect of the first 52 weeks of her employment abroad by virtue of either—

(i) an Order in Council made under section 143 of the Act (reciprocity with countries outside the United Kingdom); or

(ii) Council Regulation No. 1408/71 EEC [3, as amended from time to time,] (application of social security schemes to employed persons and their families moving within the Community), [3 or Regulation (EC) No. 833/2004 of the European Parliament and of Council of 29 April 2004, as amended from time to time, on the coordination of social security systems]

and the employment by reference to which the liability arose continued throughout the first 52 weeks after the commencement of that liability, she shall be treated for any week in which she was in fact engaged in gainful employment as having been engaged in employment as an employed earner [1 and for any such week, and for any weeks following the period of that liability and before the date of her return to Great Britain so far as those weeks are relevant to her claim for a maternity allowance, as having received an amount of specified payments for the purposes of section 35A(4) of the Social Security Contributions and Benefits Act 1992 equal to the lower earnings limit in force on the last day of that week.]

(3) Where—

(a) a woman would have been liable to pay Class 1 contributions under regulation 120 of the Contributions Regulations but for the provisions of an Order in Council made under section 143 of the Act,

(b) in relation to her case the Order does not provide for periods of insurance, employment or residence in the other country to which the Order relates to be taken into account in determining title to benefit, and

(c) the employment by reference to which she would have been liable under that regulation continued throughout the first 52 weeks,

she shall be treated for any week during her absence in which she was in fact engaged in gainful employment as having been engaged in employment as an employed earner [1 and for each week of her absence as having received an amount of specified payments for the purposes of section 35A(4) of the Social Security Contributions and Benefits Act 1992 equal to the lower earnings limit in force on the last day of the week].

(4) Where—

(a) a woman would have been liable to pay Class 1 contributions under regulation 120 of the Contributions Regulations but for the provisions of either an Order in Council made under section 143 or Council Regulation No. 1408/71/EEC [3, as amended from time to time, or Regulation EC No. 883/2004 of the European Parliament and of the Council of 29 April 2004, as amended from time to time];

(b) the employment by reference to which she would have been liable under regulation 120 continued throughout the first 52 weeks from the time that the liability would have commenced; and

(c) the Order of the Council Regulations [3 or Regulation of the European Parliament and of the Council], as the case may be, provides for aggregation of periods of insurance, employment or residence only if an insurance period has been completed since her return to Great Britain, and an insurance period has not been so completed,

any period of insurance, or employment in the other country to which that Order of Council Regulations [3 or Regulation of the European Parliament and of the Council], as the case may be, relates which falls in the [266 weeks immediately preceding] the expected week of confinement shall be treated as a period in respect of which she was engaged in employment as employed earner [1 and in eachweek of which she received an amount of specified payments for the purposes of section 35A(4) of the Social Security Contributions and Benefits Act 1992 equal to the lower earnings limit in force on the last day of that week.]

(5) Paragraphs (2) (except in a case to which paragraph (2)(a) applies), (3) and (4) shall not apply in relation to a claim for maternity allowance for any day in respect of which the woman concerned is entitled to a corresponding benefit under the social security scheme of the country in which she was employed.

(6) Where a woman satisfies the requirements of paragraph (3)(a) or (4)(a) but the employment did not continue for 52 weeks, she shall be treated in respect of those weeks in which her employment did continue as having been engaged in employment as an employed earner [1 and as having received an amount of specified payments for the purposes of section 35A(4) of the Social Security Contributions and Benefits Act 1992 equal to the lower limit in force on the last day of each of those weeks].

AMENDMENTS

1. Social Security (Maternity Allowance) (Work Abroad) (Amendment) Regulations 2000 (2000/691) reg.2 (April 2, 2000).

2. Social Security Maternity Benefits and Statutory Sick Pay (Amendment) Regulations 1994 (SI 1994/1367) reg.8 (where the expected week of confinement begins after October 16, 1994).

3. Social Security (Uprating of EU References) (Amendment) Regulations (SI 2018/1084) reg.4 and Sch. para. 4 (November 15, 2018).

The Social Security (Maternity Allowance) (Earnings) Regulations 2000

(SI 2000/688) *(as amended)*

ARRANGEMENT OF REGULATIONS

The Secretary of State for Social Security, in exercise of powers conferred by sections 35A(4), (5) and (6)(c), 122(1) and 175(1) to (4) of the Social Security Contributions and Benefits Act 1992 and of all other powers enabling him in that behalf by this instrument, which is made before the end of the period of six months beginning with the coming into force of the enactments under which it is made, hereby makes the following Regulations:

Citation, commencement and interpretation

5.10 **1.**—(1) These regulations may be cited as the Social Security (Maternity Allowance) (Earnings) Regulations 2000 and shall come into force on April 2, 2000.

(2) In these Regulations—

[1 *omitted*]

"the Contributions Regulations" means the [2 Social Security (Contributions) Regulations 2001]

"the Contributions and Benefits Act" means the Social Security Contributions and Benefits Act 1992;

"test period" means the period of 66 weeks specified in section 35(1)(b) of the Contributions and Benefits Act.

AMENDMENT

1. Social Security (Maternity Allowance) (Earnings) (Amendment) Regulations 2015 (SI 2015/342) reg.2 (April 6, 2015).

Specified payments for employed earners

5.11 **2.**—(1) Subject to paragraph (2), for the purposes of section 35A(4)(a) of the Contributions and Benefits Act, the payments specified for a woman who is an employed earner in any week falling within the test period shall be all payments made to her or for her benefit as an employed earner including—

[2 (za) any amount retrospectively treated as earnings by regulations made by virtue of section 4B(2) of the Contributions and Benefits Act];

(a) any sum payable in respect of arrears of pay in pursuance of an order for reinstatement under section 114 or re-engagement under section 115 of the Employment Rights Act 1996 (orders for reinstatement and re-engagement);

(b) any sum payable by way of pay in pursuance of an order made under section 129 of the Employment Rights Act 1996 (procedure on hearing of application and making of order) for the continuation of a contract of employment;

(c) any sum payable by way of remuneration in pursuance of a protective award under section 189 of the Trade Union and Labour Relations (Consolidation) Act 1992 (complaint and protective award);

(d) any sum payable by way of statutory sick pay, including sums payable in accordance with regulations made under section 151(6) of the Contributions and Benefits Act (employers' liability);

(e) any sum payable by way of statutory maternity pay, including sums payable in accordance with regulations made under section 164(9)(b) of the Contributions and Benefits Act.

[1(f) any sum payable by way of statutory paternity pay, including any sums payable in accordance with regulations made under section 171ZD(3) of the Contributions and Benefits Act;

(g) any sum payable by way of statutory adoption pay, including any sums payable in accordance with regulations made under section 171ZM(3) of the Contributions and Benefits Act,]

[3 (h) any sum payable by way of statutory shared parental pay, including any sums payable in accordance with regulations made under section 171ZX(3) of the Contributions and Benefits Act

[4 (i) any sum payable by way of statutory parental bereavement pay, including any sums payable in accordance with regulations made under section 171ZZ8(3) of the Contributions and Benefits Act.]]

(2) The payments specified shall not include any sum excluded from the computation of a person's earnings under regulation [225, 27 or 123 of Schedule 3 to] the Contributions Regulations (payments to be disregarded).

AMENDMENTS

1. Social Security, Statutory Maternity Pay and Statutory Sick Pay (Miscellaneous Amendments) Regulations (SI 2002/2690) reg.16 (December 8, 2002).

2. Social Security, Occupational Pensions Schemes and Statutory Payments (Consequential Provisions) Regulations 2007 (SI 2007/1154) reg.3 (April 6, 2007).

3. Shared Parental Leave and Statutory Shared Parental Pay (Consequential Amendments to Subordinate Legislation) Order 2014 (SI 2014/3255) art.8 (December 31, 2014).

4. Parental Leave and Pay (Consequential Amendments to Subordinate Legislation) Regulations 2020 (SI 2020/354) reg.9 (April 6, 2020).

Specified payments for self-employed earners

3.—For the purposes of section 35A(4)(b) of the Contributions and Benefits Act, where a woman is a self-employed earner in any week falling 5.12
within the test period, the payments treated as made to her or for her benefit shall be—

(a) a payment equal to [1 an amount 90 per cent of which is equal to the weekly rate prescribed under section 66(1)(b) of the Contributions and Benefits Act that is in force] on the last day of that week where she has paid a Class 2 contribution [2 . . .]

(b) a payment equal to the maternity allowance threshold in force on the last day of that week, [2 if she could have paid but has not paid such a contribution] in respect of that week

AMENDMENT

1. Social Security, Statutory Maternity Pay and Statutory Sick Pay Regulations 2002 (SI 2002/2690) reg.17 (November 24, 2002).

2. Social Security (Maternity Allowance) (Earnings) (Amendment) Regulations 2015 (SI 2015/342) reg.2 (April 6, 2015).

Aggregation of specified payments

5.13 **4.**—(1) In a case [1. . .] where a woman, either in the same week or in different weeks falling within the test period, is engaged in two or more employments (whether, in each case, as an employed earner or a self-employed earner), any payments which are made, or treated in accordance with these Regulations as made to her or for her benefit shall be aggregated for the purpose of determining the average weekly amount of specified payments applicable in her case.

(2) In a case to which regulation 5(2) applies, any payments which are made or treated in accordance with these Regulations as made, to her or for her benefit shall not be aggregated for the purpose of determining the average weekly amount of specified payments applicable in her case.

AMENDMENT

1. Social Security, Statutory Maternity Pay and Statutory Sick Pay Regulations 2002 (SI 2002/2690) reg.17 (November 24, 2002).

[1 [2 The specified period

5.14 **5.**—(1) Subject to paragraph (2) below, for the purposes of section 35A(4) and (5) of the Contributions and Benefits Act, the specified period shall be the test period.

(2) Where a woman is treated by virtue of regulation 3(a) above as having received payments for at least 13 weeks (whether consecutive or not) falling within the test period, the first 13 weeks shall be the specified period.]]

AMENDMENTS

1. Social Security Statutory Maternity Pay and Statutory Sick Pay (Miscellaneous Amendments) Regulations 2002 (SI 2002/2690) reg.19 (November 24,2002).

2. Social Security Maternity Allowance (Earnings) (Amendment) Regulations 2003 (SI 2003/659) reg.2 (April 6, 2003).

Determination of average weekly amount of specified payments

5.15 **6.**—[1 [2 (1) For the purposes of section 35A(4) of the Contributions and Benefits Act a woman's average weekly amount of specified payments shall, subject to paragraph (2), be determined by dividing by 13 the payments made, or treated in accordance with these Regulations as made, to her or for her benefit—

(a) in the case of a woman to whom paragraph (2) of regulation 5 applies, in the 13 weeks referred to in that paragraph;
(b) in any other case, in the 13 weeks (whether consecutive or not) falling within the specified period in which such payments are greatest.]]

(2) In any case where a woman receives a back-dated pay increase after the end of the period specified in regulation 5 above which includes a sum in respect of any week falling within that period, her average weekly amount of specified payments shall be determined as if such sum had been paid in that week.

[2 (3) Where a woman is normally paid other than weekly, the payments made or treated as made to her or for her benefit for the purposes of paragraph (1) shall be calculated by dividing the payments made to her in any week by the nearest whole number of weeks in the period in respect of which she is paid.]

[3 (4) Paragraph (5) applies in respect of a week where–
(a) a woman is a furloughed employee;
(b) the woman's employer has claimed and is in receipt of financial support in respect of the woman's earnings under the Coronavirus Job Retention Scheme; and
(c) the woman's earnings are lower than they would otherwise have been as a result of that woman being a furloughed employee.

(5) Where any of the weeks in the period of 13 weeks referred to in paragraph (1)(a) or (b) is a week to which this paragraph applies, the average weekly amount of the specified payments are to be determined as if for that week she were paid the amount she would have derived from her employment had she not been a furloughed employee.

(6) For the purposes of paragraphs (4) and (5)—

"Coronavirus Job Retention Scheme" ("the Scheme") means any scheme to provide for payments to be made to employers on a claim made in respect of them incurring costs of employment in respect of furloughed employees arising from the health, social and economic emergency in the United Kingdom resulting from coronavirus and coronavirus disease and contained in such Directions as may be issued from time to time pursuant to section 76 of the Coronavirus Act 2020;

"coronavirus" and "coronavirus disease" have the meanings given in section 1 of that Act.

"furloughed employee" has the meaning given for the purposes of the Scheme.]

AMENDMENTS

1. Social Security Statutory Maternity Pay and Statutory Sick Pay (Miscellaneous Amendments) Regulations 2002 (SI 2002/2690) reg.20 (November 24, 2002)

2. Social Security Maternity Allowance (Earnings) (Amendment) Regulations 2003 (SI 2003/659 reg.3 (April 6, 2003).

3. Maternity Allowance, Statutory Maternity Pay, Statutory Paternity Pay, Statutory Adoption Pay, Statutory Shared Parental Bereavement Pay (Normal Weekly Earnings etc.) (Coronavirus) (Amendment) Regulations 2020 (SI 2020/450) reg.4 (April 25, 2020).

The Maternity Allowance (Curtailment) Regulations 2014

(SI 2014/3053)

ARRANGEMENTS OF REGULATIONS

5.16 This instrument contains only regulations made by virtue of, or consequential upon, section 120(1) and (2) of the Children and Families Act 2014 and is made before the end of the period of 6 months beginning with the coming into force of that enactment.

The Secretary of State for Work and Pensions, in exercise of the powers conferred by sections 35(3A), (3B), (3C) and (3D) and 175(1), (3), (4) and (5) of the Social Security Contributions and Benefits Act 1992, makes the following Regulations:

Citation and commencement

5.17 **1.** These Regulations may be cited as the Maternity Allowance (Curtailment) Regulations 2014 and come into force on 1st December 2014.

Interpretation

5.18 **2.** In these Regulations—

"the 1992 Act" means the Social Security Contributions and Benefits Act 1992;

"the 1996 Act" means the Employment Rights Act 1996;

"C" means the child in respect of whom an entitlement to—

(a) shared parental leave arises under section 75E (entitlement to shared parental leave: birth) of the 1996 Act; or

(b) statutory shared parental pay arises under section 171ZU (entitlement: birth) of the 1992 Act;

"M" means the mother (or expectant mother) of C;

"maternity allowance period curtailment date" means, subject to regulation 5(5), the date specified in a maternity allowance period curtailment notification;

"maternity allowance period curtailment notification" means a notification given in accordance with regulation 5 and regulation 6(4);

"P" means the father of C, or the person who is married to, or the civil partner or the partner of, M;

"partner" in relation to M, means a person (whether of a different sex or the same sex) who lives with M and C in an enduring family relationship but is not M's child, parent, grandchild, grandparent, sibling, aunt, uncle, niece or nephew;

"SPL Regulations" means the Shared Parental Leave Regulations 2014;

"ShPP Regulations" means the Statutory Shared Parental Pay (General) Regulations 2014.

Curtailment of maternity allowance period (statutory shared parental pay: P)

3. M's maternity allowance period shall end on the maternity allowance period curtailment date if— 5.19

(a) M gives a maternity allowance period curtailment notification (unless the notification is revoked under regulation 6);

(b) P satisfies the condition in sub-paragraph (a) of regulation 5(2) (entitlement of father or partner to statutory shared parental pay (birth)) of the ShPP Regulations; and

(c) M satisfies the conditions in sub-paragraphs (b) and (c) of regulation 5(3) of the ShPP Regulations.

Curtailment of maternity allowance period (shared parental leave: P)

4. M's maternity allowance period shall end on the maternity allowance period curtailment date if— 5.20

(a) M gives a maternity allowance period curtailment notification (unless the notification is revoked under regulation 6);

(b) P satisfies the condition in sub-paragraph (a) of regulation 5(2) (father's or partner's entitlement to shared parental leave) of the SPL Regulations; and

(c) M satisfies the conditions in sub-paragraphs (a) and (c) of regulation 5(3) of the SPL Regulations.

Maternity allowance period curtailment notification

5.—(1) A maternity allowance period curtailment notification must— 5.21

(a) be given to the Secretary of State; and

(b) specify the date on which M wants her maternity allowance period to end.

(2) The date specified in accordance with paragraph (1)(b) must be—

(a) the last day of a week;

(b) if M has the right to maternity leave under section 71 (ordinary maternity leave) of the 1996 Act, at least one day after the end of the compulsory maternity leave period or, if M does not have that right, at least two weeks after the end of the pregnancy;

(c) at least eight weeks after the date on which M gives the maternity allowance period curtailment notification; and

(d) at least one week before the last day of M's maternity allowance period.

(3) Where the Secretary of State considers it appropriate the eight week period set out in paragraph (2)(c) may be reduced in any particular case.

(4) In paragraph (2)(b) "the end of the compulsory maternity leave period" means whichever is the later of—

(a) the last day of the compulsory maternity leave period provided for in regulations under section 72(2) (compulsory maternity leave) of the 1996 Act; or

(b) where section 205 of the Public Health Act 1936 (women not to be employed in factories or workshops within four weeks after birth of a child) applies to M's employment, the last day of the period in which an occupier of a factory is prohibited from knowingly allowing M to be employed in that factory.

(5) Where M—

(a) returns to work before giving a notification under paragraph (1); and

(b) subsequently gives such a notification;

the "maternity allowance period curtailment date" shall be the last day of the week in which that notification is submitted (irrespective of the date given in that notification under paragraph (1)).

(6) For the purposes of paragraphs (2)(a) and (5), "week" has the meaning given in section 165(8) of the 1992 Act (the maternity pay period).

(7) For the purposes of paragraph (5)(a), a woman is treated as returning to work where maternity allowance is not payable to her in accordance with regulation 2(1) of the Social Security (Maternity Allowance) Regulations 1987 (disqualification for the receipt of a maternity allowance).

Revocation (maternity allowance period curtailment notification)

5.22 **6.**—(1) Subject to paragraph (2), M may revoke a maternity allowance period curtailment notification before the maternity allowance period curtailment date if—

(a) M provided the maternity allowance period curtailment notification before the birth of C; or

(b) P dies.

(2) Revocation is effective under paragraph (1) where M gives a notification ("a revocation notification") to the Secretary of State that—

(a) if given under paragraph (1)(a), is given within six weeks of the date of C's birth;

(b) if given under paragraph (1)(b), is given within a reasonable period from the date of P's death.

(3) A revocation notification must—

(a) state that M revokes the maternity allowance period curtailment notification; and

(b) if given under paragraph (1)(b), state the date of P's death.

(4) M may not give a maternity allowance period curtailment notification in respect of the same maternity allowance period subsequent to giving a revocation notification unless the revocation was made in accordance with paragraph (1)(a).

PART VI

PENSIONS, SURVIVORS' BENEFITS AND GRADUATED RETIREMENT BENEFIT

The Social Security (Deferral of Retirement Pensions) Regulations 2005

(SI 2005/453) (*as amended*)

ARRANGEMENT OF REGULATIONS

The Secretary of State for Work and Pensions, in exercise of the powers conferred upon him by sections 54(1), 122(1) and 175(3) of, and paragraphs 2(2), 3(1), 3B(2) and (5)(b)(iii) and 7B(2) and (5)(b)(iii) of Schedule 5 to, the Social Security Contributions and Benefits Act 1992, and of all other powers enabling him in that behalf, after agreement by the Social Security Advisory Committee that proposals in respect of regulation 4 should not be referred to it, the remainder of this Instrument containing only regulations made under provisions introduced by section 297 of, and Schedule 11 to, the Pensions Act 2004 and being made before the end of the period of 6 months beginning with the coming into force of those provisions, hereby makes the following Regulations:

Citation, commencement and interpretation

1.—(1) These Regulations may be cited as the Social Security (Deferral of Retirement Pensions) Regulations 2005 and shall come into force on 6th April 2005. 6.2

(2) In these Regulations—

"the Act" means the Social Security Contributions and Benefits Act 1992;

"retirement pension" means a Category A or Category B retirement pension.

[1 "shared additional pension" means a shared pension under section 55A [2 or 55AA] of the Act.]

AMENDMENTS

1. Shared Additional Pensions (Miscellaneous Amendments) Regulations 2005 (SI 2005/1551) (July 6, 2005).

2. The Pensions Act 2014 (Consequential, Supplementary and Incidental Amendments) Order 2015 (SI 2015/1985) art.26 (April 6, 2016).

GENERAL NOTE

Following the reforms introduced from April 6, 2016 by the Pensions Act 2014 these regulations only apply directly to periods before that date. For the provisions that apply from that date see Part 3 of the State Pension Regulations 2015 below. 6.3

Beginning of accrual period

[1**2.**—(1) This regulation applies for the purposes of paragraphs 3B and 7B of Schedule 5 and paragraph 5 of Schedule 5A to the Act (calculation of lump sum). 6.4

(2) In the case of a retirement pension or shared additional pension to which regulation 22 (long term benefits) of the Social Security (Claims and Payments) Regulations 1987 ("the 1987 Regulations") applies, the accrual period shall begin with the day of the week on which benefit would have been payable had entitlement not been deferred.

(3) In the case of a retirement pension to which regulation 22C (retirement pension for persons reaching pensionable age on or after 6th April 2010) of the 1987 Regulations applies, the accrual period shall begin with the first day of the benefit week in relation to which benefit would have been payable had entitlement not been deferred.

(4) In this regulation, "benefit week" has the same meaning as in regulation 22D (payment of retirement pension at a daily rate) of the 1987 Regulations.]

AMENDMENT

1. Social Security (Deferral of Retirement Pensions) (Amendment) Regulations 2011 (SI 2011/786) reg.2 (April 5, 2011).

Amount of retirement pension not included in the calculation of the lump sum

6.5 **3.**—(1) For the purposes of the calculation of the lump sum under paragraphs 3B and 7B of Schedule 5 to the Act, the amount of retirement pension to which the person ("the deferrer") would have been entitled for the accrual period if his entitlement had not been deferred shall not include any such pension where, for the entire accrual period—

(a) the deferrer has received any of the following benefits—

(i) any benefit under Parts II and III of the Act other than child's special allowance, attendance allowance, disability living allowance [1, a shared additional pension] and guardian's allowance;

(ii) any severe disablement allowance under sections 68 and 69 of the Act as in force before 6th April 2001;

(iii) any unemployability supplement within the extended meaning in regulation 2(1) of the Social Security (Overlapping Benefits) Regulations 1979 and including benefit corresponding to an unemployability supplement by virtue of regulations under paragraph 7(2) of Schedule 8 to the Act;

[3(iv) state pension credit under section 1 of the State Pension Credit Act 2002;]

[5(v) carer support payment under the Carer's Assistance (Carer's Support Payment) (Scotland) Regulations 2023;]

[3(aa) in the case of a deferrer who was a member of a couple, the other member of the couple was in receipt of—

(i) income support under section 124 of the Act;

(ii) income-based jobseeker's allowance under section 1 of the State Pension Credit Act 2002; or

(iii) state pension credit under section 1 of the State Pension Credit Act 2002;

(iv) income-related employment and support allowance under section 1 of the Welfare Reform Act 2007;]

[4 or

(v) universal credit under Part 1 of the Welfare Reform Act 2012;]

(b) an increase of any of the benefits specified in sub-paragraph (a) is being paid to a married man in respect of his wife where the wife is a deferrer whose period of deferment began before 6th April 2005 and who would have been entitled to a Category B retirement pension or to an increase under section 51A(2) of the Act;

(c) an increase of any of the benefits specified in sub-paragraph (a) is being paid to any person in respect of a deferrer whose period of deferment began on or after 6th April 2005 except where that deferrer is neither married to [2 or in a civil partnership with,], nor residing with, that person;

(d) the deferrer would have been disqualified for receiving retirement pension by reason of imprisonment or detention in legal custody.

[1 (1A) For the purposes of the calculation of the lump sum under paragraph 5 of Schedule 5A to the Act, the amount of a shared additional pension to which a person ("the deferrer") would have been entitled for the accrual period if his entitlement had not been deferred shall not include any such pension where, for the entire accrual period, the deferrer would have been disqualified for receiving shared additional pension by reason of imprisonment or detention in legal custody.]

(2) Where any of the benefits referred to in paragraph (1)(a) [3 or (aa)] or an increase referred to in paragraph (1)(b) or (c) has been received for part only of an accrual period, the amount of retirement pension not included by paragraph (1) shall be reduced by 1/7th for each day of the accrual period in respect of which the benefit or increase has not been received.

(3) Where the deferrer would have been disqualified for receiving retirement pension as specified in paragraph (1)(d) [1 or a shared additional pension as specified in paragraph (1A)] for part only of an accrual period, the amount of retirement pension not included by paragraph (1) [1 or a shared additional pension not included by paragraph (1A)] shall be reduced by 1/7th for each day of the accrual period for which he would not have been so disqualified.

(4) Subject to paragraph (5), where—

(a) a person has, in respect of any day in an accrual period, received one or more of the benefits referred to in paragraph (1)(a) [3 or (aa)] or increases referred to in paragraph (1)(b) and (c) or both;

(b) the determining authority has determined that in respect of that day, he was not entitled to the benefit or increase; and

(c) the whole of the benefit or increase in respect of that day has been repaid or, as the case may be, recovered on or before the relevant date,

that day shall be treated as a day in respect of which he did not receive that benefit or increase or both.

(5) Where the benefit or increase in respect of a day to which paragraph (4)(a) and (b) applies is repaid or, as the case may be, recovered on or after the relevant date, that day shall only be treated as a day in respect of which that person did not receive that benefit or increase once the benefit or increase has been repaid in respect of all the days to which those sub-paragraphs relate and which fall within the period of deferment.

[3[4(5A) In paragraph (1), couple has the meaning—

(a) in relation to universal credit, given by section 39 of the Welfare Reform Act 2012; and

(b) in relation to the other benefits referred to in paragraph (1)(a) or (aa), given by section 137(1) of the Act.]]

(6) In paragraph (4), "the determining authority" means as the case may require, the Secretary of State, an appeal tribunal constituted under

Chapter I of Part I of the Social Security Act 1998 or a Commissioner, or a tribunal consisting of three or more such Commissioners constituted in accordance with section 16(7) of that Act.

(7) In paragraphs (4) and (5), "relevant date" means—

(a) the last day of the period of deferment; or

(b) where entitlement to a lump sum arises under paragraph 7A of Schedule 5 to the Act, the date of S's death.

(8) Any amount of retirement pension [1 or a shared additional pension] not included in the calculation of the lump sum in accordance with this regulation must be rounded to the nearest penny, taking any 1/2 p as nearest to the next whole penny above.

AMENDMENTS

1. Shared Additional Pension (Miscellaneous Amendments) Regulations 2005 (SI 2005/1551) (July 6, 2005).

2. Civil Partnership (Consequential Amendments) Regulations 2005 (SI 2005/2878) (December 6, 2005).

3. Social Security (Deferral of Retirement Pensions) Regulations 2011 (SI 2011/634) reg.3 (April 6, 2011).

4. Universal Credit (Consequential, Supplementary, Incidental and Miscellaneous Provisions) Regulations 2013 (SI 2013/630) reg.34 (April 29, 2013).

5. Carer's Assistance (Carer Support Payment) (Scotland) Regulations 2023 (Consequential Amendments) Order 2023 (SI 2023/1218) art.15 (November 19, 2023).

GENERAL NOTE

6.6 The amendment effected by the Deferral of Retirement Pensions Regulations, 2011 will apply only in relation to an accrual period, or part of a period, falling on or after April 6, 2011.

Amendment of the Social Security (Widow's Benefit and Retirement Pensions) Regulations 1979

6.7 **4.**—*Taken into account in the text of those regulations.*

The Social Security (Additional Pension) (Contributions Paid in Error) Regulations 1996

(SI 1996/1245)

6.8 ARRANGEMENT OF REGULATIONS

The Secretary of State for Social Security, in exercise of the powers conferred by sections 61A, 122(1) and 175(1) to (4) of, and paragraph 8(1)(m) of Schedule 1 to, the Social Security Contributions and Benefits Act 1992 and of all other powers enabling him in that behalf, after agreement by the Social Security Advisory Committee that proposals in respect of these Regulations should not be referred to it, hereby makes the following regulations:

Citation, commencement and interpretation 6.9

1. – (1) These Regulations may be cited as the Social Security (Additional Pension) (Contributions Paid in Error) Regulations 1996 and shall come into force on 4th June 1996.

(2) In these Regulations "the Contributions and Benefits Act" means the Social Security Contributions and Benefits Act 1992.

Prescribed conditions for the application of section 61A of the Contributions and Benefits Act 6.10

2. – (1) The prescribed conditions for the application, in the case of an individual, of section 61A of the Contributions and Benefits Act (which provides for cases where primary Class 1 contributions have been paid in error) are—

(a) that the [1 Commissioners of Inland Revenue are] satisfied that the error was not made with the individual's consent or connivance or attributable to any negligence on the individual's part;

(b) that none of the contributions in question have been returned to the individual in accordance with regulation 32 of the Social Security (Contributions) Regulations 1979 (which provides for the return of contributions overpaid or paid in error); and

(c) that, by the date on which the individual reaches pensionable age, or such later date as the [1 Commissioners of Inland Revenue consider] reasonable in a particular case, the [1 Commissioners of Inland Revenue have] not received written notification from the individual in accordance with paragraph (2).

(2) The written notification referred to in paragraph (1)(c) is a notice stating that the individual does not wish regulation 3 to apply in his case.

(3) In a case where the individual in question has died, a reference to the individual in this regulation, except in paragraph (1)(a), shall include a reference to his surviving spouse.

AMENDMENT

1. Social Security Contributions (Transfer of Functions, etc) Act 1999 Sch.2 (April 1, 1999).

Purposes for which primary Class 1 contributions paid in error are to be treated as properly paid 6.11

3. – (1) Where section 61A of the Contributions and Benefits Act applies in the case of an individual and the [1Commissioners of Inland Revenue are] of the opinion that it is appropriate for this regulation to apply—

(a) the entitlement of the individual to, and the amount of, additional pension shall be determined as if the individual had been an employed earner and, accordingly, all of the primary Class I contributions in question had been properly paid;

(b) in the case of an individual who is entitled to a transitional award of incapacity benefit, regulations made by virtue of section 4(8) of the Social Security (Incapacity for Work) Act 1994 (provision during transition from invalidity benefit to incapacity benefit for incapacity benefit to include the additional pension element of invalidity pension) shall have effect as if, in relation to the provisions in force before the commencement of that section with respect to that additional pension element, the individual had been an employed earner and, accordingly, all of the primary Class 1 contributions in question had been properly paid; and

(c) where any amount calculated by reference to the contributions in question has been paid in respect of the individual by way of minimum contributions under section 43 of the Pension Schemes Act 1993 (contributions to personal pension schemes) the individual shall be treated for the purposes of that Act as if he had been an employed earner and, accordingly, the amount had been properly paid.

(2) The reference in paragraph (1)(a) to additional pension is to additional pension for the individual or the individual's spouse falling to be calculated under section 45 of the Contributions and Benefits Act for the purposes of—

(a) Category A retirement pension;
(b) Category B retirement pension for widows or widowers;
(c) widowed mother's allowance and widow's pension; and
(d) incapacity benefit (except in transitional cases).

AMENDMENT

1. Social Security Contributions (Transfer of Functions, etc) Act 1999, Sch.2 (April 1, 1999).

The Social Security (Deferral of Retirement Pensions, Shared Additional Pension and Graduated Retirement Benefit) (Miscellaneous Provisions) Regulations 2005

(SI 2005/2677)

ARRANGEMENT OF REGULATIONS

PART 1

GENERAL

PART 2

DEFERRAL OF RETIREMENT PENSIONS AND SHARED ADDITIONAL PENSION

PART 1

GENERAL

Citation, commencement and interpretation

1. —(1) These Regulations may be cited as the Social Security (Deferral of Retirement Pensions, Shared Additional Pension and Graduated Retirement Benefit) (Miscellaneous Provisions) Regulations 2005 and shall come into force on 6th April 2006. **6.13**

(2) In these Regulations—

"the Claims and Payments Regulations" means the Social Security (Claims and Payments) Regulations 1987;

"the Housing Benefit Regulations" means the Housing Benefit (General) Regulations 1987.

PART 2

DEFERRAL OF RETIREMENT PENSIONS AND SHARED ADDITIONAL PENSION

Interpretation

2.—(1) In this Part— **6.14**

"elector" means the person who may make an election under paragraph A1(1) or 3C(2) of Schedule 5 or paragraph 1(1) of Schedule 5A;

"retirement pension" means a Category A or a Category B retirement pension.

(2) In this Part, references to Schedules 5 and 5A are to those Schedules to the Social Security Contributions and Benefits Act 1992.

Timing of election

3.—(1) The period for making an election under— **6.15**

(a) paragraph A1(1) of Schedule 5 (choice between increase of pension and lump sum where pensioner's entitlement is deferred); and

(b) paragraph 1(1) of Schedule 5A (choice between pension increase and lump sum where entitlement to shared additional pension is deferred),

is, subject to paragraph (4), three months starting on the date shown on the notice issued by the Secretary of State following the claim for retirement pension or shared additional pension, confirming that the elector is required to make that election.

(2) The period for making an election under paragraph 3C(2) of Schedule 5 (choice between increase of pension and lump sum where pensioner's deceased spouse or civil partner has deferred entitlement) is, subject to paragraph (4), three months starting on the date shown on the notice issued by the Secretary of State following W's claim for retirement pension or, if later, the date of S's death, confirming that the elector is required to make that election.

(3) Where more than one notice has been issued by the Secretary of State in accordance with paragraph (1) or (2), the periods prescribed in those paragraphs shall only commence from the date shown on the latest such notice.

(4) The periods specified in paragraphs (1) and (2) may be extended by the Secretary of State if he considers it reasonable to do so in any particular case.

(5) Nothing in this regulation shall prevent the making of an election on or after claiming retirement pension or, as the case may be, shared additional pension but before the issue of the notice referred to in paragraph (1) or (2).

Manner of making election

6.16 **4.**—An election under paragraph A1(1) or 3C(2) of Schedule 5 or under paragraph 1(1) of Schedule 5A may be made—

(a) in writing to an office specified by the Secretary of State for accepting such elections; or

(b) except where the Secretary of State directs in any particular case that the election must be made in accordance with paragraph (a), by telephone call to the telephone number specified by the Secretary of State.

Change of election

6.17 **5.**—(1) Subject to paragraphs (2) and (6), this regulation applies in the case of an election which—

(a) has been made under paragraph A1(1) or 3C(2) of Schedule 5 or under paragraph 1(1) of Schedule 5A; or

(b) has been treated as made under paragraph A1(2) or 3C(3) of Schedule 5 or under paragraph 1(2) of Schedule 5A.

(2) This regulation does not apply in the case of an election which is—

(a) made, or treated as made, by an elector who has subsequently died; or

(b) treated as having been made by virtue of [[1] regulation 30(5E) or (5G)] of the Claims and Payments Regulations.

(3) An election specified in paragraph (1) may be changed by way of application made no later than the last day of the period specified in paragraph (4).

(4) The period specified for the purposes of paragraph (3) is, subject to paragraph (5), three months starting on the date shown on the written notification issued by the Secretary of State to the elector, confirming the election which the elector has made or is treated as having made.

(5) The period specified in paragraph (4) may be extended by the Secretary of State if he considers it reasonable to do so in any particular case.

(6) An election specified in paragraph (1) may not be changed where—

(a) there has been a previous change of election under this regulation in respect of the same period of deferment;

(b) the application is to change the election to one under paragraph A1(1)(a) or 3C(2)(a) of Schedule 5 or paragraph 1(1)(a) of Schedule 5A and any amount paid to him by way of, or on account of, a lump sum pursuant to Schedule 5 or 5A, has not been repaid in full to the Secretary of State within the period specified in paragraph (4) or, as the case may be, (5); or

(c) the application is to change the election to one under paragraph A1(1)(b) or 3C(2)(b) of Schedule 5 or paragraph 1(1)(b) of Schedule 5A and the amount actually paid by way of an increase of retirement pension or shared additional pension, or actually paid on account of such an increase, would exceed the amount to which the elector would be entitled by way of a lump sum.

(7) For the purposes of paragraph (6)(b), repayment in full of the amount paid by way of, or on account of, a lump sum shall only be treated as having occurred if repaid to the Secretary of State in the currency in which that amount was originally paid.

(8) Where the application is to change the election to one under paragraph A1(1)(b) or 3C(2)(b) of Schedule 5 or paragraph 1(1)(b) of Schedule 5A and paragraph (6)(c) does not apply, any amount paid by way of an increase of retirement pension or shared additional pension, or on account of such an increase, in respect of the period of deferment for which the election was originally made, shall be treated as having been paid on account of the lump sum to which the elector is entitled under paragraph 3A or 7A of Schedule 5 or, as the case may be, paragraph 4 of Schedule 5A.

(9) An application under paragraph (3) to change an election may be made—

(a) in writing to an office specified by the Secretary of State for accepting such applications; or

(b) except where the Secretary of State directs in any particular case that the application must be made in accordance with sub-paragraph (a), by telephone call to the telephone number specified by the Secretary of State.

Amendment of the Social Security (Retirement Pensions etc.) (Transitional Provisions) Regulations 2005

6.—Regulation 2(6)(a) of the Social Security (Retirement Pensions etc.) (Transitional Provisions) Regulations 2005 (modification of Schedule 5) is omitted. 6.18

AMENDMENT

1. Social Security (Deferral of Retirement Pensions etc) Regulations 2006 (SI 2006/516) reg.4 (April 6, 2006).

The Social Security (Graduated Retirement Benefit) (No. 2) Regulations 1978

(SI 1978/393) (*as amended*)

ARRANGEMENT OF REGULATIONS

The Secretary of State for Social Services, in exercise of the powers conferred on him by section 2(1) of and paragraphs 3, 7 and 9 of Schedule 3 to the Social Security (Consequential Provisions) Act 1975 and section 24(1) of the Social Security Pensions Act 1975, and of all other powers enabling him in that behalf, hereby makes the following regulations, which only make provision consequential on the passing of the last-mentioned Act and accordingly by virtue of section 61(1)(e) of that Act are exempt from the requirements of section 139(1) of the Social Security

Act 1975 (duty to consult National Insurance Advisory Committee about proposed regulations):

GENERAL NOTE

6.20 Responsibility for decisions made in respect of Graduated Retirement Pension, even those relating to contributions and the record of the claimant's contributions, remains that of the Department for Work and Pensions. This is because no transfer of function in this respect was made when other aspects of the administration of contributions was transferred to HRMC. The consequence is that all such decisions made in relation to GRP entitlement that depend upon contribution questions, must either be made by officers of Department for Work and Pensions, or, if made by HMRC, must be made by them as agents of that department. The result is that all such decisions are appealable only to the Social Entitlement Chamber of the First-tier Tribunal rather than the Tax Chamber. See First-tier Tribunal and Upper Tribunal (Chambers) Order (SI 2008/2684), art.4.

Citation, commencement and interpretation

6.21 **1.**—(1) These regulations may be cited as the Social Security (Graduated Retirement Benefit) (No.2) Regulations 1978.

(2) This regulation and regulation 2 below shall come into operation on 6th April 1978.

(3) The remainder of these regulations shall, for the purpose only of determining, before 6th April 1979, claims for, or questions arising as to, benefit for any period after 5th April 1979, come into operation on 6th December 1978.

(4) Except as mentioned in paragraphs (2) and (3) above, these regulations shall come into operation on 6th April 1979.

(5) In these regulations—

"the Act" means the Social Security Act 1975;

"the Pensions Act" means the Social Security Pensions Act 1975;

"the 1965 Act" means the National Insurance Act 1965;

"the 1975 regulations" means the Social Security (Graduated Retirement Benefit) Regulations 1975, as amended;

"the 1978 regulations" means the Social Security (Graduated Retirement Benefit) Regulations 1978;

and other expressions have the same meanings as in the Act.

(6) Any reference in these regulations to any provision made by or contained in any enactment or instrument shall, except in so far as the context otherwise requires, be construed as a reference to that provision as amended or extended by any enactment or instrument and as including a reference to any provision which it re-enacts or replaces, or which may re-enact or replace it, with or without modification.

(7) The rules for the construction of Acts of Parliament contained in the Interpretation Act 1889 shall apply in relation to this instrument and in relation to the revocations effected by it as if this instrument and the regulations revoked by it were Acts of Parliament and as if the revocations were repeals.

[2 Application of sections 150 and 155 of the Social Security Administration Act 1992

6.22 **2.**—The provisions of sections 150 and 155 of the Social Security Administration Act 1992, (annual up-rating of benefits and effect of alteration of rates of benefit) shall apply to—

(a) the amount of graduated retirement benefit payable for each unit of graduated contributions;
(b) increases of such benefit under the provisions of Schedule 2 to these Regulations; and
(c) any addition under section 37(1) of the 1965 Act (addition to weekly rate of retirement pension for [[1] widows, widowers and surviving civil partners]) to the amount of such benefit.

as if that amount, those increases and that addition were included in the sums mentioned in section 150(1) and (3) and graduated retirement benefit were a benefit referred to in section 155(2).]

AMENDMENT

1. Social Security (Retirement Pensions and Graduated Retirement Benefit) (Widowers and Civil Partnership) Regulations 2005 (SI 2005/3078) (April 6, 2006).

Continuation in force of sections 36, 37 and 118(1) of the 1965 Act

3.—(1) The provisions of this regulation shall have effect for the purpose of securing continuity between the Act and the 1965 Act in the case of persons who had, immediately before 6th April 1975, rights or prospective rights to or expectations of graduated retirement benefit under sections 36 and 37 of the 1965 Act, by preserving those rights and temporarily retaining the effect of those sections for transitional purposes. 6.23

(2) Paragraph (3) below shall have effect so that notwithstanding their repeal by the Social Security Act 1973 those sections shall, for the purpose aforesaid, continue in force subject to the making in them of the modifications required—

(a) to bring them into conformity with the provisions of the Act and the Pensions Act and to enable them to have effect as if contained in the scheme of social security benefits established by those Acts;
(b) to replace section 36(4) of the 1965 Act (increase of graduated retirement benefit in cases of deferred retirement) with provisions corresponding to those of paragraphs 1 to 3 of Schedule 1 to the Pensions Act;
(c) to extend section 37 of the 1965 Act (increase of woman's retirement pension by reference to her late husband's graduated retirement benefit) to men and their late wives. [[1]; [[2] …]
(d) to extend section 37 of the 1965 Act (increase of women's retirement pension by reference to her late husband's graduated retirement benefit) to civil partners and surviving civil partners.] [[2]and
(e) to extend section 37 of the 1965 Act to men and their late husbands, and women and their late wives.]

(3) On and after 6th April 1979 those sections shall continue in force in the modified form in which they are set out in Schedule 1 to these regulations, but not so as to save the National Insurance (Graduated Retirement Benefit and Consequential Provisions) Regulations 1961, so far as deemed to have been made under those sections, from being invalidated by the repeal; and section 118(1) of the 1965 Act (short title) shall also continue in force.

AMENDMENTS

1. Social Security (Retirement Pensions and Graduated Retirement Benefit) (Widowers and Civil Partnership) Regulations 2005 (SI 2005/3078) (April 6, 2006).

2. Social Security (Graduated Retirement Benefit) (Marriage Same Sex Couples) Regulations 2014 (SI 2014/76) reg.3 (March 13, 2014). See also the Marriage

and Civil Partnership (Scotland) Act 2014 and Civil Partnership Act 2004 (Consequential Provisions and Modifications) Order 2014 (SI 2014/3229) Sch.6 art.3 (December 12, 2014).

Modification of regulations concerning graduated retirement benefit

6.24 **4.**—The provisions of regulations 2 and 3 of the 1978 regulations (which were made under sections 36 and 37 of the 1965 Act) shall continue in force in the modified form set out in Schedule 3 to these regulations; and paragraphs (1) (so far as it relates to citation), (2) and (3) (interpretation) of regulation 1 of the 1978 regulations shall also continue in force.

Revocations

6.25 **5.**—*Omitted.*

SCHEDULES

SCHEDULE 1 **Regulation 3(3)**

SECTIONS 36 AND 37 OF THE NATIONAL INSURANCE ACT 1965 AS CONTINUED IN FORCE BY THESE REGULATIONS

Graduated retirement benefit

6.26 **36.**—(1) Subject to the provisions of the Act, graduated retirement benefit shall be payable to any person who is over pensionable age and who [[1] is entitled to a retirement pension], and shall be an increase in the weekly rate of his retirement pension equal to [[12] 14.92] pence for each unit, ascertained in accordance with subsections (2) and (3) of this section, of the graduated contributions properly paid by him as an insured person, the result being rounded to the nearest whole penny, taking 1/2p as nearest to the next whole penny above.

(2) For the purpose of graduated retirement benefit [[9]a unit of graduated contributions shall be £7.50.]

(3) Where a person's graduated contributions calculated at the said rate do not make an exact number of units any incomplete fraction of a unit shall, if it is one-half or more, be treated as a complete unit.

[[7](4) Where a person's entitlement to graduated retirement benefit is deferred—

(a) Schedule 2 to the Social Security (Graduated Retirement Benefit) (No.2) Regulations 1978; and

(b) Schedule 1 to the 2005 Regulations,

shall have effect and both those Schedules shall be construed and have effect as if they were part of this subsection.

(4A) For the purposes of subsection (4), a person's entitlement to graduated retirement benefit is deferred—

(a) where he would be entitled to a Category A or Category B retirement pension but for the fact that his entitlement is deferred within the meaning in section 55(3) of the Social Security Contributions and Benefits Act 1992, if and so long as his entitlement to such a pension is deferred;

(b) where he is treated under subsection (7) as receiving a Category A or a Category B retirement pension at a nominal weekly rate, if and so long as he does not become entitled to graduated retirement benefit by reason only of not satisfying the conditions in section 1 of the Social Security Administration Act 1992 (entitlement to benefit dependent on claim),

and in relation to graduated retirement benefit, "period of deferment" shall be construed accordingly.]

(5) For the purposes of subsection (4) of this section, the Secretary of State may by regulations provide for treating all or any of the graduated contributions paid by a person in the tax year in which he attained pensionable age as having been paid before, or as having been paid after, the day on which he attained that age, whether or not the contribution in question was so paid.

(7) A person who has attained pensionable age and [[1]has claimed], but is not entitled to a retirement pension [[2](except a person who is not so entitled because of an election under

section 54(1) of the Social Security Contributions and Benefits Act 1992 or because he has withdrawn his claim)], shall be treated for the purposes of the foregoing provisions of this section as receiving a retirement pension at a nominal weekly rate:

Provided that—

(a) this subsection shall not confer any right to graduated retirement benefit on a person who would be entitled to a retirement pension but for some provision of the Act or of regulations disqualifying him for receipt of it; and

(b) regulations may provide that any right by virtue of this subsection to benefit at less than a specified weekly rate shall be satisfied either altogether or for a specified period by the making of a single payment of the prescribed amount.

(8) In this section and in section 37 below—

"graduated contributions" means graduated contributions under the National Insurance Act 1965 or the National Insurance Act 1959;

"insured person" means insured person under the National Insurance Act 1965 or the National Insurance Act 1946;

"retirement pension" means retirement pension of any category;

"the Act" means the Social Security Act 1975;

[[7] "the 2005 Regulations" means the Social Security (Graduated Retirement Benefit) Regulations 2005;]

and any reference in section 37 below to "section 36 of this Act" or to any of its subsections is a reference to that section or subsection as it is here set out.

(9) This section and section 37 below and the Act shall be construed and have effect as if this section and section 37 below were included in Chapter I of Part II of that Act (contributory benefits); and references to that Chapter, that Part or that Act in any other enactment or in any instrument shall be construed accordingly:

Provided that nothing in this subsection shall affect the construction of any reference to section 36 or 37 of this Act or of that Act or to any of the subsections of those sections; and any increase in the weekly rate of a person's retirement pension, to the extent that it is attributable to subsection (4) of this section, shall be left out of account in determining the weekly rate of that pension for the purposes of [[3]section 30B(3) of the Social Security Contributions and Benefits Act 1992 regulations 11(1) and 18(7) of the Social Security (Incapacity Benefit) (Transitional Regulations 1995] and [[4] regulation 10(6) of the Jobseeker's Allowance (Transitional Provisions) Regulations 1996] (rates of incapacity benefit and jobseeker's allowance in transitional cases for persons over pensionable age)].

(10) [[5] . . .]

37.—(1) Subject to the provisions of this section [[7] and to Schedule 1 to the 2005 Regulations]—

[[10], where a person, having paid graduated contributions as an insured person, dies leaving a widow, widower [[11] surviving same sex spouse] or surviving civil partner and the survivor—

(a) has attained pensionable age at the time of the death; or

(b) remains that person's widow, widower [[11] surviving same sex spouse] or surviving civil partner (as the case may be) when attaining pensionable age,] [[8] ; or

(c) where a person, having paid graduated contributions as an insured person, dies on or after 5th December 2005 leaving a surviving civil partner, and they have both attained pensionable age at the time of his or her death,] [[11] ; or

(d) where a man, having paid graduated contributions as an insured person, dies leaving a widower, and they have both attained pensionable age at the time of his death; or

(e) where a woman, having paid graduated contributions as an insured person, dies leaving a widow, and they have both attained pensionable age at the time of her death,]

then section 36 of this Act shall apply as if the increase in the weekly rate of the retirement pension of the [[8] widow, widower [[11] surviving same sex spouse] or surviving civil partner], as the case may be, provided for by subsection (1) thereof were the amount there specified by reference to his or her graduated contributions with the addition of one-half of the weekly rate of the graduated retirement benefit of his or her former spouse [[8] or civil partner] (any amount including 1/2p being rounded to the next whole penny above) [[10] . . .]

(2) For the purposes of subsection (1) of this section, the weekly rate of the deceased spouse's [[8] or civil partner's] graduated retirement benefit shall (whether or not he or she was receiving or entitled to receive any such benefit) be taken to have been the weekly rate appropriate to the amount of graduated contributions paid by him or her (determined as if any orders which have come into force under section 124 of the Act (increases in rates of benefit) since the date of the deceased spouse's [[8] or civil partner's] death had come into force before that date), excluding any addition under section 37(1) of this Act, but including any addition under section 36(4), thereof (and for the purpose of calculating the addition

under section 36(4) taking into account any addition under section 37(1)); and where at his or her death he or she had attained pensionable age but had [1not] become entitled to graduated retirement benefit, that addition shall be computed as if he or she had [1 . . .] become entitled to graduated retirement benefit immediately before his or her death.

(3) A person's right to graduated retirement benefit by virtue of this section shall be brought into account under section 36(4) of this Act in determining the graduated retirement benefit payable to him or her under the said section 36:

Provided that, if the termination of the marriage [8 or civil partnership] by death occurred after he or she attained pensionable age, he or she shall for the purposes of this subsection be treated as not having attained pensionable age until the date of that termination.

(4) A person's right to graduated retirement benefit by virtue of this section in respect of a spouse he or she marries [8 or as the case may be, a civil partner he or she forms a civil partnership with] after attaining pensionable age shall be subject to such additional conditions as may be prescribed; and except as may be provided by regulations a person more than once married [8 or who has formed a civil partnership more than once or who has been both married and a civil partner] shall not be entitled for the same period to any graduated retirement benefit by virtue of this section in respect of more than one of his or her spouses [8 or civil partners].

(5) Regulations may provide that where a woman is entitled to graduated retirement benefit and to a widowed mother's allowance the graduated retirement benefit shall be an increase in the weekly rate of that allowance; and where the benefit is such an increase, section 36(7) of this Act shall not apply.

GENERAL NOTE

6.27 The amendments made to ss.36(1) and 37(1) above by the Social Security (State Pension and National Insurance Credits) Regulations 2009 (SI 2009/2206), which have effect from April 6, 2010, do not apply in the case of a woman who attained pensionable age before that date or, in the case of a deceased person in accordance with s.37, where that person is a woman who would have reached pensionable age before that date. Nor does the amendment in s.37(1) apply where the survivor attained pensionable age before that date and it is immaterial in that case when the deceased person died. (See reg.3(2) and reg.4(4) of those regulations). For the text of the original sections applicable in those cases please see earlier editions of this book.

SCHEDULE 2 **Regulation 3(3)**

PROVISIONS REPLACING SECTION 36(4) OF THE NATIONAL INSURANCE ACT 1965

6.28 **1.**—Where a person [1defers his entitlement to a Category A or Category B retirement pensions] after attaining pensionable age, or has made an election by virtue of section 30(3) of the Act and has not revoked it, then for the purpose of calculating the graduated retirement benefit payable to him from the date of his retirement—

(a) there shall be added to the amount of the graduated contributions properly paid by him as an insured person one-half of the aggregate graduated retirement benefit which would have been payable to him for any period before 6th April 1979 (disregarding the effect of any order made under section 124 of the Act) if he had retired from regular employment on attaining pensionable age and had received that benefit for the whole of the period without any interruption or abatement:

Provided that, in computing the addition to be made in accordance with this paragraph in the case of a person who has made an election by virtue of section 30(3) of the Act (re-entry into regular employment) or the corresponding provisions of any earlier Act, no account shall be taken of any period between 6th April 1975 and 5th April 1979 (both dates inclusive) which falls between the date of that election and the date of his previous [1entitlement]; and

[7*omitted*]

GENERAL NOTE

6.29 This version of Schedule 2 is applicable to periods of deferment ending before April 6, 2005 and to incremental periods beginning after that date. For earlier periods see the text of this Schedule as it was in SI 1978/393 and in earlier editions of this book.

The sums which, under Sch.2, are the increases of graduated retirement benefit were increased, with effect from April 8, 2024, by 6.7 per cent: see art.11(2) of the Social Security Benefits Up-rating Order 2024 (SI 2024/242). For previous years' increases, see previous editions of this work.

SCHEDULE 3 **Regulation 4**

REGULATIONS 2 AND 3 OF THE 1978 REGULATIONS AS MODIFIED BY THESE REGULATIONS

Graduated retirement benefit when retirement is deferred

2.—For the purposes of paragraph 1(a) of Schedule 2 to the Social Security (Graduated Retirement Benefit) (No. 2) Regulations 1978 (provision, where a person attains pensionable age before 6th April 1979 but does not retire from regular employment until after 5th April 1979, for calculating the graduated retirement benefit payable to him from the date of his retirement) all the graduated contributions paid by a person in the income tax year in which he attained pensionable age shall be treated as having been paid before the day on which he attained that age: **6.30**

Provided that where, in any case, the aggregate amount of the graduated contributions paid by him in that year exceeded the aggregate amount of graduated contributions which would have been payable by him in that part of the year which ended with the income tax week, in which he attained pensionable age if, in each income tax week beginning in that part of the year, a graduated contribution as for an employment which was not a non-participating employment had been payable by him in respect of a weekly payment of remuneration made in that week at a level equal to the upper limit on the amount of weekly pay then taken into account under section 4(1)(c) of the 1965 Act as amended, the excess shall be treated as having been paid after the day on which he attained that age.

Graduated retirement benefit for persons who have been married more than once

3.—For the purposes of section 37 of the 1965 Act (special provisions as to graduated retirement benefit for widows and widowers) a person who has been married more than once [[8] or has formed more than one civil partnership or who has been both married and a civil partner] and who is entitled to graduated retirement benefit for any period by virtue of the provisions of that section in respect of a second or subsequent spouse [[8] or civil partner] shall not be precluded from entitlement to graduated retirement benefit for that period by virtue of that section in respect of a former spouse [[8] or civil partner], but shall be so entitled to the extent only that it is payable to him or her by the application of section 36(4) of the 1965 Act in respect of any period before the death of the first-mentioned spouse [[8] or civil partner].

AMENDMENTS

1. Social Security (Abolition of Earnings Rule) Regulations 1989 (SI 1989/1642) reg.5 (October 1, 1989).
2. Social Security (Graduated Retirement Benefit) Amendment Regulations 1995 (SI 1995/2606) reg.2 (November 1, 2005).
3. Social Security and Child Support (Jobseeker's Allowance) (Consequential Amendments) Regulations 1996 (SI 1996/1345) reg.18 (July 10, 1996).
4. Social Security (Miscellaneous Amendments) Regulations 1997 (SI 1997/454) reg.5 (March 21, 1997).
5. Social Security Act 1998 (Commencement No.9, and Savings and Consequential and Transitional Provisions) Order 1999 (SI 1999/2422) (September 6, 1999).
6. Social Security Benefits Up-rating Order 2015 (SI 015/457) art.8 (April 8, 2015).
7. Social Security (Graduated Retirement Benefit) Regulations 2005 (SI 2005/454) reg.2 and reg.3 (April 6, 2005).
8. Social Security (Retirement Pensions and Graduated Benefit) (Widowers and Civil Partnership) Regulations 2005 (SI 2005/3078) (April 6, 2006).
9. Social Security (State Pension and National Insurance Credits) Regulations 2009 (SI 2009/2206) reg.3 (April 6, 2010).
10. Social Security (State Pension and National Insurance Credits) Regulations 2009 (SI 2009/2206) reg.4 (April 6, 2010).

11. Social Security (Graduated Retirement Benefit) (Married Same Sex Couples) Regulations 2014 (SI 2014/76) reg.2, (March 13, 2014).
12. The Social Security Benefits Up-rating Order 2021 (SI 2021/162) art.12(1) (April 11, 2021).

General Note

6.31 Regulation 3 of the Graduated Retirement Benefit Regulations 2005 makes further changes to Sch.2 of these regulations but only in respect of periods of deferment ending after April 6, 2005. Regulation 5 of the same regulations makes provision for transitional cases, being those cases where the period of deferment begins before April 6, 2005 but ends after that date.

The Additional Pension and Social Security Pensions (Home Responsibilities) (Amendment) Regulations 2001

(SI 2001/1323) (*as amended*)

Arrangement of Regulations

The Secretary of State for Social Security, in exercise of powers conferred by sections 44A(2)(c)(ii), 122(1) and 175(1) and (5) of, and paragraph 5(7A) of Schedule 3 to and paragraph 9 of Schedule 4A to, the Social Security Contributions and Benefits Act 1992 and of all other powers enabling him in that behalf, by this instrument, which contains only regulations made before the end of the period of 6 months beginning with the coming into force of sections 30(3) and 40 of, and Schedule 4 to, the Child Support, Pensions and Social Security Act 2000 makes the following Regulations:

Citation, commencement and interpretation

6.33 **1.**—(1) These Regulations may be cited as the Additional Pension and Social Security Pensions (Home Responsibilities) (Amendment) Regulations 2001 and shall come into force on 6th April 2002.

(2) In these Regulations—

[1"the 2007 Act" means the Welfare Reform Act 2007;]

"the Administration Act" means the Social Security Administration Act 1992;

[4 "appropriate personal pension scheme" means an appropriate scheme within the meaning of section 7B(6) (meaning of "contracted-out scheme" etc) of the Pension Schemes Act 1993;]

"appropriate table" means—

(a) in the case of a person attaining pensionable age after the end of the year 2002–2003 but before 6th April 2009, Table 5 of paragraph 7(3) of Schedule 4A to the Contributions and Benefits Act,

(b) in the case of a person attaining pensionable age on or after 6th April 2009, Table 6 of paragraph 7(4) of that Schedule;

"the Contributions and Benefits Act" means the Social Security Contributions and Benefits Act 1992;

"the 1994 Regulations" means the Social Security Pensions (Home Responsibilities) Regulations 1994;

"contracted-out employment" means [1subject to regulation 3(5),] employed earner's employment qualifying a person for a pension provided by a salary related contracted-out scheme or a money purchase contracted-out scheme or an appropriate personal pension scheme, as the case may be;

[4 "contributions equivalent premium" has the meaning given in section 181(1) (general interpretation) of the Pension Schemes Act 1993;]

[4 "money purchase contracted-out scheme" has the meaning given in section 7B(5) of the Pension Schemes Act 1993;]

[4 "salary related contracted-out scheme" has the meaning given in section 7B(4) of the Pension Schemes Act 1993;]

"contributions equivalent premium" means the premium referred to in section 55(2) of the Pension Schemes Act 1993;

"non-contracted-out employment" means employed earner's employment which is not contracted-out employment;

"year" means a tax year.

Calculation of additional pension where contributions equivalent premium paid or treated as paid

2. Where a contributions equivalent premium— 6.34

(a) is paid in accordance with the provisions of sections 55 to 61 of the Pension Schemes Act 1993 (which deal with the payment of a contributions equivalent premium in respect of specified periods of contracted-out employment) and regulations made thereunder; or

(b) is treated as having been paid in accordance with the provisions of paragraph 5(3) to (3E) of Schedule 2 to that Act (which provide for a contributions equivalent premium to be treated as paid in respect of contracted-out employment in certain circumstances) and regulations made thereunder,

the amount referred to in [1section 45(2)(c) or (d) of the Contributions and Benefits Act] (which provides for the calculation of the amount of additional pension in a Category A retirement pension in relation to the 2002–2003 tax year and subsequent tax years) is to be calculated in accordance with Parts I and II of [1Schedule 4A to the Contributions and Benefits Act or, as the case may be, Parts 1 and 2 of Schedule 4B to that Act] (additional pension) as if the employment in respect of which a premium is paid, or treated as paid, had not been contracted-out employment.

Calculation of additional pension: earnings partly from employment with contracted-out scheme membership

6.35 **3.**—(1) This regulation applies in relation to any year where earnings are paid to or for the benefit of an earner—

(a) partly in respect of non-contracted-out employment; and
(b) partly in respect of employment qualifying him for a pension provided by a salary related contracted-out scheme or a money purchase contracted-out scheme, or both.

(2) For any year in relation to which this regulation applies, the amount referred to in paragraph 1(1)(a) of Schedule 4A [[1]or, as the case may be, in paragraph 1(1) of Schedule 4B] to the Contributions and Benefits Act shall be amount C where—

(a) amount C is equal to amount A minus amount B; and
(b) amounts A and B are calculated in accordance with the following paragraphs.

(3) Amount A is to be calculated in accordance with paragraph 5 of Schedule 4A [[1]or, as the case may be, in paragraphs 8 and 9 of Schedule 4B] to the Contributions and Benefits Act.

(4) Amount B is to be calculated as follows:—

(a) find the earnings factor derived from the aggregate of the amounts of weekly earnings paid in that year in respect of the employment referred to in paragraph (1)(b) above;
(b) deduct from that earnings factor an amount equal to the weekly lower earnings limit for the year multiplied by the number of tax weeks in which earnings were paid in respect of weeks of that employment;
(c) multiply the amount found under sub-paragraph (b) above in accordance with the last order under section 148 of the Administration Act to come into force before the end of the final relevant year;
(d) multiply the amount found under sub-paragraph (c) above by the percentage specified in paragraph 6(3) of Schedule 4A [[1]or, as the case may be, in paragraph 10(1)(c) of Schedule 4B] to the Contributions and Benefits Act which is applicable in the case of the earner.

[[1](5) In so far as paragraphs (1) to (4) apply in respect of the calculation of additional pension under Schedule 4B to the Contributions and Benefits Act, the definition of "contracted-out employment" has effect as if the words from "or a money purchase contracted-out scheme" to the end were omitted.]

Calculation of additional pension: earnings partly from employment with scheme membership

6.36 **4.**—(1) This regulation applies in relation to any year where earnings are paid to or for the benefit of an earner—

(a) partly in respect of non-contracted-out employment; and
(b) partly in respect of employment qualifying him for a pension provided by an appropriate personal pension scheme.

(2) For any year in relation to which this regulation applies, the amount referred to in paragraph 1(1)(a) of Schedule 4A [[1]or, as the case may be, in paragraph 1(1) of Schedule 4B] to the Contributions and Benefits Act shall be amount C where—

(a) amount C is equal to amount A minus amount B; and
(b) amounts A and B are calculated in accordance with the following paragraphs.

(3) Amount A is to be calculated in accordance with paragraph 5 of Schedule 4A to the Contributions and Benefits Act.

(4) Amount B is to be calculated as follows:—

(a) find the earnings factor derived from the aggregate of the amounts of weekly earnings paid in that year in respect of employment qualifying the earner for a pension provided by an appropriate personal pension scheme;

(b) deduct from that earnings factor an amount equal to the qualifying earnings factor for that year;

(c) calculate the part of the amount found under sub-paragraph (b) above falling into each of the bands specified in the appropriate table;

(d) multiply the amount of each such part in accordance with the last order under section 148 of the Administration Act to come into force before the end of the final relevant year;

(e) multiply each amount found under sub-paragraph (d) above by such percentage specified in the appropriate table in relation to the appropriate band as is applicable in the case of the earner;

(f) add together the amounts calculated under sub-paragraph (e) above.

Calculation of additional pension: other cases of mixed forms of contracted-out employment

5.—(1) This regulation applies in relation to any year where earnings are paid to or for the benefit of an earner— 6.37

(a) partly in respect of—

(i) employment qualifying him for a pension provided by a salary related contracted-out scheme or a money purchase contracted-out scheme, or both, and

(ii) employment qualifying him for a pension provided by an appropriate personal pension scheme; or

(b) partly in respect of—

(i) non-contracted-out employment,

(ii) employment qualifying him for a pension provided by a salary related contracted-out scheme or a money purchase contracted-out scheme, or both, and

(iii) employment qualifying him for a pension provided by an appropriate personal pension scheme.

(2) For any year in relation to which this regulation applies, the amount referred to in paragraph 1(1)(a) of Schedule 4A to the Contributions and Benefits Act shall be amount C where—

(a) amount C is equal to amount A minus amount B; and

(b) amounts A and B are calculated in accordance with the following paragraphs.

(3) Amount A is to be determined in accordance with paragraph 5 of Schedule 4A to the Contributions and Benefits Act.

(4) Amount B is the sum of amount D and amount E and—

(a) amount D is to be found as follows:—

(i) find the earnings factor derived from the aggregate of the amounts of weekly earnings paid in that year in respect of the employment referred to in paragraph (1)(a)(i) or, as the case may be, (1)(b)(ii) above,

(ii) deduct from that earnings factor an amount equal to the weekly lower earnings limit for the year multiplied by the number of tax weeks in which earnings were paid in respect of that employment,

(iii) multiply the amount found under head (ii) above in accordance with the last order under section 148 of the Administration Act to come into force before the end of the final relevant year,

(iv) multiply the amount found under head (iii) above by the percentage specified in paragraph 6(3) of Schedule 4A to the Contributions and Benefits Act which is applicable in the case of the earner;

(b) amount E is to be found as follows:—

(i) find the earnings factor derived from the aggregate of the amounts of weekly earnings paid in the year in which this regulation applies in respect of the employment referred to in paragraph (1)(a)(ii) or, as the case may be, (1)(b)(iii) above,

(ii) add to that earnings factor an amount equal to the weekly lower earnings limit for the year multiplied by the number of tax weeks in which earnings were paid in respect of the employment referred to in paragraph (1)(a)(i) or, as the case may be, (1)(b)(ii) above,

(iii) deduct from the amount found under head (ii) above an amount equal to the qualifying earnings factor for that year,

(iv) calculate the part of the amount found under head (iii) above falling into each of the bands specified in the appropriate table,

(v) multiply the amount of each such part in accordance with the last order under section 148 of the Administration Act to come into force before the end of the final relevant year,

(vi) multiply each amount found under head (v) above by such percentage specified in the appropriate table in relation to the appropriate band as is applicable in the case of the earner;

(vii) add together the amounts calculated under head (vi) above.

[[1]Earnings factor credits eligibility for pensioners to whom employment and support allowance was payable

6.38 **5A.**—(1) For the purposes of subsection (3) of section 44C (earnings factor credits) of the Contributions and Benefits Act(**9**), a pensioner is eligible for earnings factor enhancement in respect of a week if that pensioner satisfies one or more of the conditions in paragraph (2) and was—

(a) a person to whom employment and support allowance was payable for any part of that week;

(b) a person to whom that allowance would have been payable but for the fact that that person did not satisfy the contribution condition in paragraph 1 or paragraph 2 of Schedule 1 to the 2007 Act; or

(c) a person to whom that allowance would have been payable but for the fact that under regulations the amount was reduced to nil because of—

(i) receipt of other benefits; or

(ii) receipt of payments from an occupational pension scheme or personal pension scheme.

(2) The conditions are—
(a) immediately prior to that week, employment and support allowance was payable or would have been payable for—
(i) a continuous period of 52 weeks; or
(ii) a period of 52 weeks treated as continuous by virtue of regulations made under paragraph 4 of Schedule 2 to the 2007 Act;
(b) that allowance included or would have included the support component under section 2(2) of the 2007 Act; or
(c) immediately prior to that week, in the case of—
(i) a man born in the period beginning with 6th April 1946 and ending with 5th April 1947; or
(ii) a woman born in the period beginning with 6th October 1950 and ending with 5th April 1951,

that allowance was payable or would have been payable for a continuous period of 13 weeks immediately following a period throughout which statutory sick pay was payable.

(3) In this regulation [3 and regulation 5C], "employment and support allowance" means an employment and support allowance under Part 1 (employment and support allowance) of the 2007 Act.]

[2 Earnings factor credits eligibility for certain persons entitled to universal credit

5B.—(1) For the purposes of subsection (3) of section 44C (earnings factor credits) of the 6.39

Contributions and Benefits Act, a pensioner is eligible for earnings factor enhancement in respect of a week if that pensioner was a person entitled to an award of universal credit under Part 1 of the Welfare Reform Act 2012 in respect of any part of that week which includes—
(a) if the person satisfies the condition in paragraph (2), an amount under regulation 27(1)(a) of the Universal Credit Regulations 2013 in respect of the fact that the person has limited capability for work;
(b) an amount under regulation 27(1)(b) of those Regulations in respect of the fact that the person has limited capability for work and work-related activity; or
(c) an amount under regulation 29(1) of those Regulations where the person has regular and substantial caring responsibilities for a severely disabled person, or would include any of those amounts but for regulation 27(4) or 29(4) of those Regulations.

(2) The condition referred to in paragraph (1)(a) is that for each of the 52 weeks immediately prior to that week—
(a) the person was entitled to universal credit inrespect of the fact that the person had limited capability for work or would have included an amount in respect of the fact that the person had limited capability for work but for regulation 27(4) or 29(4) of the Universal Credit Regulations 2013; or
(b) employment and support allowance under Part 1 (employment and support allowance) of the Welfare Reform Act 2007 ("the 2007 Act")—

(i) was payable to the person;
(ii) would have been payable to the person but for the fact that the person did not satisfy the contribution condition in paragraph 1 or paragraph 2 of Schedule 1 to the 2007 Act;
(iii) would have been payable to the person but for the fact that the person had been entitled to it for the relevant maximum number of days under section 1A of the 2007 Act; or
(iv) would have been payable to the person but for the fact that under regulations the amount was reduced to nil because of—
(aa) receipt of other benefits; or
(bb) receipt of payments from an occupational pension scheme or personal pension scheme.

(3) Paragraph (2)(b) of this regulation is satisfied in respect of a week which falls between periods which are linked by virtue of regulations under paragraph 4 (linking periods) of Schedule 2 to the 2007 Act.].

[3 Earnings factor credit eligibility for pensioners to whom section 1A of the 2007 Act applied

6.40 **5C.**—(1) For the purposes of section 44C(3) (earnings factor credits) of the Contributions and Benefits Act, a pensioner is eligible for earnings factor enhancement in respect of a week to which paragraph (2) applies.

(2) This paragraph applies to a week in which, in relation to the pensioner concerned, each of the days would have been—
(a) a day of limited capability for work; or
(b) a day on which that pensioner would have been treated as having limited capability for work,

for the purposes of Part 1 of the 2007 Act (limited capability for work) where that pensioner would have been entitled to an employment and support allowance but for the application of section 1A of the 2007 Act.]

Preclusion from regular employment

6.41 **6.**—The condition referred to in section 44A(2)(c)(ii) of the Contributions and Benefits Act (which relates to the condition to be satisfied for a person to be taken to be precluded from regular employment by responsibilities at home throughout a year for the purposes of paragraph 5(7)(b) of Schedule 3 to that Act) is that specified in regulation 2(2)(b) or (3) of the 1994 Regulations (which refer respectively to a person to whom income support is payable and a person regularly engaged in caring for at least 35 hours a week for someone in receipt of certain benefits).

AMENDMENTS

1. Social Security (State Pensions and National Insurance Credits) Regulations 2009 (SI 2009/2206) regs 23–27 (April 6, 2010).

2. Universal Credit (Consequential, Supplementary, Incidental and Miscellaneous Amendments) Regulations 2013 (SI 2013/630 (April 29, 2013).

3. Social Security (Miscellaneous Amendments) Regulations 2014 (SI 2014/591) reg.2 (April 28, 2014).

4. Pensions Act 2014 (Abolition of Contracting-out for Salary Related Pension Schemes) (Consequential Amendments and Savings) Order 2016 (SI 2016/200) art.19 (April 6, 2016).

The Social Security (Graduated Retirement Benefit) Regulations 2005

(SI 2005/454)

ARRANGEMENT OF REGULATIONS

The Secretary of State for Work and Pensions, in exercise of the powers conferred upon him by sections 62(1)(a) and (c) and 175(3) and (4) of the Social Security Contributions and Benefits Act 1992, and of all other powers enabling him in that behalf, after agreement by the Social Security Advisory Committee that proposals in respect of regulations 3 and 4, and paragraphs 2, 3, 7, 13, 14 and 18 of Schedule 1 in so far as they apply to regulation 4, should not be referred to it, the remainder of this Instrument containing only regulations made under provisions introduced by section 297 of, and Schedule 11 to, the Pensions Act 2004 and being made before the end of the period of 6 months beginning with the coming into force of those provisions, hereby makes the following Regulations:

Citation, commencement, effect and interpretation

1.—(1) These Regulations may be cited as the Social Security (Graduated Retirement Benefit) Regulations 2005 and shall come into force on 6th April 2005. **6.43**

(2) Regulation 4 and paragraphs [[1]4(2) and (3) and 14(2) and (3)] of Schedule 1 in so far as they apply to that regulation, shall not have effect in relation to incremental periods beginning before 6th April 2005.

(3) In these Regulations—

"the 1965 Act" means the National Insurance Act 1965;

"the Administration Act" means the Social Security Administration Act 1992;

"the Benefits Act" means the Social Security Contributions and Benefits Act 1992 and references to Schedule 5 are to Schedule 5 to that Act;

"incremental period" shall have the meaning ascribed to it in paragraph 4(6) of Schedule 1.

Amendment of the 1965 Act

2.—*Omitted as taken into account in the text of the Act set out in the Social Security (Graduated Retirement Benefit) (No.2) Regulations 1978.* **6.44**

Amendment of Schedule 2 to the Social Security (Graduated Retirement Benefit) (No.2) Regulations 1978 and saving

6.45 **3.**—(1) Subject to paragraph (2), in Schedule 2 to the Social Security (Graduated Retirement Benefit) (No.2) Regulations 1978—

(a) the word "and" at the end of paragraph 1(a) and paragraph 1(b); and

(b) paragraphs 2 to 4,

shall be omitted.

(2) Schedule 2 to those Regulations shall have effect as if the amendments made by paragraph (1) had not been made in the case of—

(a) periods of deferment (as defined by section 36(4A) of the 1965 Act) ending before 6th April 2005; and

(b) incremental periods beginning before that date.

Schedule 1

6.46 **4.**—Schedule 1 to these Regulations (which makes further provision replacing section 36(4) of the 1965 Act) shall have effect.

Modification of Schedule 1 in transitional cases

6.47 **5.**—Schedule 1 shall be modified by Schedule 2 in relation to transitional cases and in this regulation, a "transitional case" means a case where a person's entitlement to graduated retirement benefit is deferred and the period of deferment begins before 6th April 2005 and continues on or after that day.

SCHEDULE 1 **Regulation 4**

FURTHER PROVISIONS REPLACING SECTION 36(4) OF THE NATIONAL INSURANCE ACT 1965: INCREASES OF GRADUATED RETIREMENT BENEFIT AND LUMP SUMS

PART 1

INCREASE AND LUMP SUM WHERE ENTITLEMENT TO RETIREMENT PENSION IS DEFERRED

Scope

6.48 **1.**—This Part applies only in respect of a person who is deferring entitlement to graduated retirement benefit by virtue of section 36(4A)(a) of the 1965 Act.

Increase or lump sum where pensioner's entitlement is deferred

2.—(1) Where a person's entitlement to a Category A or Category B retirement pension is deferred and that person elects, [2 . . .]—

(a) that paragraph 1 of Schedule 5 (increase of pension) is to apply in relation to the period of deferment, paragraph 3 of this Schedule shall also apply in relation to that period;

(b) that paragraph 3A of Schedule 5 (lump sum) is to apply in relation to the period of deferment, paragraph 5 of this Schedule shall also apply in relation to that period.

(2) The reference to an election in sub-paragraph (1) includes an election a person is treated as having made under paragraph A1(2) of Schedule 5.

Increase where pensioner's entitlement is deferred

6.49 **3.**—(1) This paragraph applies where—

(a) entitlement to a Category A or Category B retirement pension is deferred and the period of deferment is less than 12 months; or

(b) paragraph 2(1)(a) applies.

(2) The rate of the person's graduated retirement benefit shall be increased by an amount equal to the aggregate of the increments to which he is entitled under paragraph 4 but only if that amount is enough to increase the rate of the benefit by at least 1 per cent.

Calculation of increment

4.—(1) A person is entitled to an increment under this paragraph for each complete incremental period in his period of deferment.

(2) The amount of the increment for an incremental period shall be 1/5th per cent. of the weekly rate of the graduated retirement benefit to which the person would have been entitled for the period if his entitlement to a Category A or Category B retirement pension had not been deferred.

(3) For the purposes of sub-paragraph (2), the weekly rate of graduated retirement benefit shall be taken to include any increase in the weekly rate of that benefit and the amount of the increment in respect of such an increase shall be 1/5th per cent. of its weekly rate for each incremental period in the period of deferment beginning on the day the increase occurred.

(4) Amounts under sub-paragraphs (2) and (3) shall be rounded to the nearest penny, taking any 1/2p as nearest to the next whole penny.

(5) Where an amount under sub-paragraph (2) or (3) would, apart from this sub-paragraph, be a sum less than 1/2p, the amount shall be taken to be zero, notwithstanding any provision of the Benefits Act, the Administration Act or the Pension Schemes Act 1993.

(6) In this paragraph, "incremental period" means any period of six days which are treated by the Social Security (Widow's Benefit and Retirement Pensions) Regulations 1979 as days of increment for the purposes of paragraph 2 of Schedule 5 in relation to the person and pension in question.

(7) Where one or more orders have come into force under section 150 of the Administration Act during the period of deferment, the rate for any incremental period shall be determined as if the order or orders had come into force before the beginning of the period of deferment.

Lump sum where pensioner's entitlement is deferred

5.—(1) This paragraph applies where paragraph 2(1)(b) applies. **6.50**

(2) The person is entitled to an amount calculated in accordance with paragraph 6 (a "lump sum").

Calculation of lump sum

6.—(1) The lump sum is the accrued amount for the last accrual period beginning during the period of deferment.

(2) In this paragraph—

"accrued amount" means the amount calculated in accordance with sub-paragraph (3);

"accrual period" means any period of seven days beginning with the day of the week on which Category A or Category B retirement pension would have been payable to a person in accordance with regulation 22(3) of, and paragraph 5 of Schedule 6 to, the Social Security (Claims and Payments) Regulations 1987 [5 or in accordance with regulation 22C(3) or (4) of those Regulations], if his entitlement to a retirement pension had not been deferred, where that day falls within the period of deferment.

(3) The accrued amount for an accrual period for a person is—

$$(A + P) \times \sqrt[52]{(1 + R/100)}$$

where—

A is the accrued amount for the previous accrual period (or, in the case of the first accrual period beginning during the period of deferment, zero);

P is, subject to sub-paragraph (5), the amount of graduated retirement benefit to which the person would have been entitled for the accrual period if his entitlement to a Category A or Category B retirement pension had not been deferred;

R is—

(a) a percentage rate two per cent. higher than the Bank of England base rate; or

(b) if a higher rate is prescribed for the purposes of paragraphs 3B and 7B of Schedule 5, that higher rate.

(4) For the purposes of sub-paragraph (3), any change in the Bank of England base rate is to be treated as taking effect—

(a) at the beginning of the accrual period immediately following the accrual period during which the change took effect; or
(b) if regulations under paragraph 3B(4) of Schedule 5 so provide, at such other time as may be prescribed in those Regulations.

(5) Regulation 3 of the Social Security (Deferral of Retirement Pensions) Regulations 2005 shall have effect for the purposes of this paragraph in like manner to graduated retirement benefit as it does to retirement pension in the calculation of the lump sum under paragraph 3B of Schedule 5.

Increase or lump sum where pensioner's deceased spouse [2 or civil partner] has deferred entitlement

6.51 7.—(1) This paragraph applies where—
(a) a [2 widow, widower or surviving civil partner] ("W") is entitled to a Category A or Category B retirement pension;
(b) W was married to [2 or in a civil partnership with] the other party to the marriage [2 or civil partnership] ("S") when S died;
(c) S's entitlement to a Category A or Category B retirement pension was deferred when S died; and
(d) S's entitlement had been deferred throughout the period of 12 months ending with the day before S's death.

(2) Where W elects—
(a) that paragraph 4 of Schedule 5 (increase of pension) is to apply in relation to the period of deferment, paragraph 8 of this Schedule shall also apply in relation to that period;
(b) that paragraph 7A of Schedule 5 (lump sum) is to apply in relation to the period of deferment, paragraph 9 of this Schedule shall also apply in relation to that period.

(3) The reference to an election in sub-paragraph (2) includes an election W is treated as having made under paragraph 3C(3) of Schedule 5.

Increase where pensioner's deceased spouse [2 or civil partner] has deferred entitlement

6.52 8.—(1) This paragraph applies where a [2 widow, widower or surviving civil partner] is entitled to a Category A or Category B retirement pension, was married to [2 or in a civil partnership with] the other party to the marriage [2 or civil partnership] when S died and one of the following conditions is met—
(a) S was entitled to graduated retirement benefit with an increase under this Schedule;
(b) paragraph 7(2)(a) applies; or
(c) paragraph 7 would apply to W but for the fact that the condition in sub-paragraph (1)(d) of that paragraph is not met.

(2) The increase in the weekly rate of W's graduated retirement benefit shall, in a case to which sub-paragraph (1) applies, be determined in accordance with section 37 of the 1965 Act as continued in force by virtue of regulations made under Schedule 3 to the Social Security (Consequential Provisions) Act 1975 or under Schedule 3 to the Social Security (Consequential Provisions) Act 1992.

Entitlement to lump sum where pensioner's deceased spouse [2 or civil partner] has deferred entitlement

6.53 9.—(1) This paragraph applies where paragraph 7(2)(b) applies.

(2) W is entitled to an amount calculated in accordance with paragraph 10 (a "widowed person's [2 or surviving civil partner's] lump sum").

Calculation of widowed person's [2 or surviving civil partner's] lump sum

6.54 10.—(1) The widowed person's [2 or surviving civil partner's] lump sum is the accrued amount for the last accrual period beginning during the period which—
(a) began at the beginning of S's period of deferment; and
(b) ended on the day before S's death.

(2) In this paragraph—

"S" means the other party to the marriage [2 or civil partnership];
"accrued amount" means the amount calculated in accordance with sub-paragraph (3);
"accrual period" means any period of seven days beginning with the day of the week on which Category A or Category B retirement pension would have been payable to S in accordance with regulation 22(3) of, and paragraph 5 of Schedule 6 to, the Social Security (Claims and Payments) Regulations 1987 [5 or in accordance with regulation 22C(3) or (4) of those Regulations], if his entitlement to a retirement pension had not been deferred, where that day falls within S's period of deferment.

(3) The accrued amount for an accrual period for W is—

$$(A + P) \times \sqrt[52]{(1 + R/100)}$$

where—

A is the accrued amount for the previous accrual period (or, in the case of the first accrual period beginning during the period mentioned in sub-paragraph (1), zero);

P is, subject to sub-paragraph (5), one-half of the graduated retirement benefit to which S would have been entitled for the accrual period if his entitlement had not been deferred during the period mentioned in sub-paragraph (1);

R is—

(a) a percentage rate two per cent. higher than the Bank of England base rate; or
(b) if a higher rate is prescribed for the purposes of paragraphs 3B and 7B of Schedule 5, that higher rate.

(4) For the purposes of sub-paragraph (3), any change in the Bank of England base rate is to be treated as taking effect—

(a) at the beginning of the accrual period immediately following the accrual period during which the change took effect; or
(b) if regulations under paragraph 7B(4) of Schedule 5 so provide, at such other time as may be prescribed.

(5) Regulation 3 of the Social Security (Deferral of Retirement Pensions) Regulations 2005 shall have effect for the purposes of this paragraph in like manner to graduated retirement benefit as it does to retirement pension in the calculation of the lump sum under paragraph 7B of Schedule 5.

(6) In any case where—

(a) there is a period between the death of S and the date on which W becomes entitled to a Category A or Category B retirement pension; and
(b) one or more orders have come into force under section 150 of the Administration Act during that period,

the amount of the lump sum shall be increased in accordance with that order or those orders.

PART 2

INCREASE OR LUMP SUM WHERE PERSON IS TREATED AS RECEIVING RETIREMENT PENSION AT A NOMINAL WEEKLY RATE

Scope

11.—This Part applies only in respect of a person who is deferring entitlement to graduated retirement benefit by virtue of section 36(4A)(b) of the 1965 Act. **6.55**

Choice between increase and lump sum

12.—(1) Where the period of deferment is at least 12 months, a person shall, on becoming entitled to graduated retirement benefit, elect that— **6.56**

(a) paragraph 13; or
(b) paragraph 15, is to apply in respect of that period.

[2 (2) The election referred to in sub-paragraph (1) shall be made—

(a) on the date on which he claims graduated retirement benefit; or
(b) within the period after claiming graduated retirement benefit prescribed in paragraph 20B,

and in the manner prescribed in paragraph 20C.]

(3) If no election under sub-paragraph (1) is made within the period referred to in sub-paragraph (2)(b), the person is to be treated as having made an election under sub-paragraph (1)(b).

(4) A person who has made an election under sub-paragraph (1) (including one that the person is treated by sub-paragraph (3) as having made) may change the election in the circumstances [2, manner and within the period prescribed, in paragraph 20D].

Increase

13.—(1) This paragraph applies where— **6.57**

(a) the period of deferment is less than 12 months; or
(b) the person has made an election under paragraph 12(1)(a) in respect of the period of deferment.

(2) The rate of the person's graduated retirement benefit shall be increased by an amount equal to the aggregate of the increments to which he is entitled under paragraph 14 but only if that amount is enough to increase the rate of the benefit by at least one per cent.

Calculation of increment

6.58 **14.**—(1) A person is entitled to an increment under this paragraph for each complete incremental period in the period of deferment.

(2) The amount of the increment for an incremental period shall be 1/5th per cent. of the weekly rate of the graduated retirement benefit to which the person would have been entitled for the period if his entitlement to graduated retirement benefit had not been deferred.

(3) For the purposes of sub-paragraph (2), the weekly rate of graduated retirement benefit shall be taken to include any increase in the weekly rate of that benefit and the amount of the increment in respect of such an increase shall be 1/5th per cent. of its weekly rate for each incremental period in the period of deferment beginning on the day the increase occurred.

(4) Amounts under sub-paragraphs (2) and (3) shall be rounded to the nearest penny, taking any 1/2p as nearest to the next whole penny.

(5) Where an amount under sub-paragraph (2) or (3) would, apart from this sub-paragraph, be a sum less than 1/2p, the amount shall be taken to be zero, notwithstanding any provision of the Benefits Act, the Administration Act or the Pension Schemes Act 1993.

(6) Where one or more orders have come into force under section 150 of the Administration Act during the period of deferment, the rate for any incremental period shall be determined as if the order or orders had come into force before the beginning of the period of deferment.

Lump sum

6.59 **15.**—(1) This paragraph applies where paragraph 12(1)(b) applies.

(2) The person is entitled to an amount calculated in accordance with paragraph 16 (a "lump sum").

Calculation of lump sum

6.60 **16.**—(1) The lump sum is the accrued amount for the last accrual period beginning during the period of deferment.

(2) In this paragraph—

"accrued amount" means the amount calculated in accordance with sub-paragraph (3);

"accrual period" means any period of seven days beginning with the day of the week on which Category A or Category B retirement pension would have been payable to a person in accordance with regulation 22(3) of, and paragraph 5 of Schedule 6 to, the Social Security (Claims and Payments) Regulations 1987 [5 or in accordance with regulation 22C(3) or (4) of those Regulations], if he had been entitled to it, where that day falls within the period of deferment.

(3) The accrued amount for an accrual period for a person is—

$$(A + P) \times \sqrt[52]{(1 + R/100)}$$

where—

A is the accrued amount for the previous accrual period (or, in the case of the first accrual period beginning during the period of deferment, zero);

P is, subject to sub-paragraph (5), the amount of graduated retirement benefit to which the person would have been entitled for the accrual period if he had been entitled to it;

R is—

(a) a percentage rate two per cent. higher than the Bank of England base rate; or
(b) if a higher rate is prescribed for the purposes of paragraphs 3B and 7B of Schedule 5, that higher rate.

(4) For the purposes of sub-paragraph (3), any change in the Bank of England base rate is to be treated as taking effect—

(a) at the beginning of the accrual period immediately following the accrual period during which the change took effect; or
(b) if regulations under paragraph 3B(4) of Schedule 5 so provide, at such other time as may be prescribed in those Regulations.

(5) Regulation 3 of the Social Security (Deferral of Retirement Pensions) Regulations 2005 shall have effect for the purposes of this paragraph in like manner to graduated retirement

benefit as it does to retirement pension in the calculation of the lump sum under paragraph 3B of Schedule 5.

Choice between increase and lump sum where person's deceased spouse [3 or civil partner] has deferred entitlement to graduated retirement benefit

17.—(1) This paragraph applies where— **6.61**

(a) a [3 widow, widower or surviving civil partner] ("W") is entitled to a Category A or Category B retirement pension;
(b) W was married to [3 or in a civil partnership with] the other party to the marriage [3or civil partnership] ("S") when S died;
(c) S's entitlement to graduated retirement benefit was deferred when S died; and
(d) S's entitlement had been deferred throughout the period of 12 months ending with the day before S's death.

(2) W shall elect either that—

(a) paragraph 18; or
(b) paragraph 19,

is to apply in respect of S's period of deferment.

[2 (3) The election referred to in sub-paragraph (2) shall be made within the period prescribed in paragraph 20B and in the manner prescribed in paragraph 20C.]

(4) If no election under sub-paragraph (2) is made within the period referred to in sub-paragraph [2 (3)], the person is to be treated as having made an election under subparagraph (2)(b).

[2 (5) A person who has made an election under sub-paragraph (2) (including one that the person is treated by sub-paragraph (4) as having made) may change the election in the circumstances, manner and within the period prescribed in paragraph 20D.]

Increase where person's deceased spouse [3 or civil partner] has deferred entitlement to graduated retirement benefit

18.—(1) This paragraph applies where a [3 widow, widower or surviving civil partner] is entitled to graduated retirement benefit, was married to [3 or in a civil partnership with] the other party to the marriage [3or civil partnership] when S died and one of the following conditions is met— **6.62**

(a) S was entitled to graduated retirement benefit with an increase under this Schedule;
(b) W is a widow or widower to whom paragraph 17 applies and has made an election under paragraph 17(2)(a); or
(c) paragraph 17 would apply to W but for the fact that the condition in sub-paragraph (1)(d) of that paragraph is not met.

(2) The increase in the weekly rate of W's graduated retirement benefit shall, in a case to which sub-paragraph (1) applies, be determined in accordance with section 37 of the 1965 Act as continued in force by virtue of regulations made under Schedule 3 to the Social Security (Consequential Provisions) Act 1975 or under Schedule 3 to the Social Security (Consequential Provisions) Act 1992.

Entitlement to lump sum where person's deceased spouse [3 or civil partner] has deferred entitlement to graduated retirement benefit

19.—(1) This paragraph applies where paragraph 17(2)(b) applies. **6.63**

(2) W is entitled to an amount calculated in accordance with paragraph 20 (a "widowed person's [3 or surviving civil partner's] lump sum").

Calculation of widowed person's [3 or surviving civil partner's] lump sum

20.—(1) The widowed person's lump sum is the accrued amount for last accrual period beginning during the period which— **6.64**

(a) began at the beginning of S's period of deferment; and
(b) ended on the day before S's death.

(2) In this paragraph—

"S" means the other party to the marriage [3 or civil partnership];
"accrued amount" means the amount calculated in accordance with sub-paragraph (3);
"accrual period" means any period of seven days beginning with the day of the week on which Category A or Category B retirement pension would have been payable to S in accordance with regulation 22(3) of, and paragraph 5 of Schedule 6 to, the Social Security (Claims and Payments) Regulations 1987 [5 or in accordance with regulation 22C(3) or (4) of those Regulations], if he had been entitled to it, where that day falls within S's period of deferment.

(3) The accrued amount for an accrual period for W is—

$$(A + P) \times \sqrt[52]{(1 + R/100)}$$

where—

A is the accrued amount for the previous accrual period (or, in the case of the first accrual period beginning during the period mentioned in sub-paragraph (1), zero);

P is, subject to sub-paragraph (5), one-half of the graduated retirement benefit to which S would have been entitled for the accrual period if he had been entitled to it during the period mentioned in sub-paragraph (1);

R is—

(a) a percentage rate two per cent. higher than the Bank of England base rate; or
(b) if a higher rate is prescribed for the purposes of paragraphs 3B and 7B of Schedule 5, that higher rate.

(4) For the purposes of sub-paragraph (3), any change in the Bank of England base rate is to be treated as taking effect—

(a) at the beginning of the accrual period immediately following the accrual period during which the change took effect; or
(b) if regulations under paragraph 7B(4) of Schedule 5 so provide, at such other time as may be prescribed.

(5) Regulation 3 of the Social Security (Deferral of Retirement Pensions) Regulations 2005 shall have effect for the purposes of this paragraph in like manner to graduated retirement benefit as it does to retirement pension in the calculation of the lump sum under paragraph 7B of Schedule 5.

(6) In any case where—

(a) there is a period between the death of S and the date on which W becomes entitled to graduated retirement benefit; and
(b) one or more orders have come into force under section 150 of the Administration Act during that period,

the amount of the lump sum shall be increased in accordance with that order or those orders.

[3 Transitional provision relating to widower's entitlement to increase of graduated retirement benefit or lump sum

6.65 **20ZA.**—In the case of a widower who attains pensionable age before 6th April 2010, paragraphs 17 to 19 shall not apply unless he was over pensionable age when his wife died.

Transitional provision relating to civil partner's entitlement to increase of graduated retirement benefit or lump sum

6.66 **20ZB.**—In the case of a civil partner who attains pensionable age before 6th April 2010, paragraphs 17 to 19 shall not apply unless he or she was over pensionable age when his or her civil partner died.]

[2 PART 2A

ELECTIONS UNDER PART 2

Scope and interpretation

6.67 **20A.**—(1) This Part applies in respect of elections which a person makes or is treated as having made under Part 2.

(2) In this Part, "elector" means the person who may make an election under paragraph 12(1) or 17(2).

Timing of election

6.68 **20B.**—(1) The period for making an election under paragraph 12(1) is, subject to sub-paragraph (4), three months starting on the date shown on the notice issued by the Secretary of State following the claim for graduated retirement benefit, confirming that the elector is required to make that election.

(2) The period for making an election under paragraph 17(2) is, subject to sub-paragraph (4), three months starting on the date shown on the notice issued by the Secretary of State following W's claim for a Category A or Category B retirement pension or, if later, the date of S's death, confirming that the elector is required to make that election.

(3) Where more than one notice has been issued by the Secretary of State in accordance with sub-paragraph (1) or (2), the periods prescribed in those sub-paragraphs shall only commence from the date shown on the latest such notice.

(4) The periods specified in sub-paragraphs (1) and (2) may be extended by the Secretary of State if he considers it reasonable to do so in any particular case.

(5) Nothing in this paragraph shall prevent the making of an election on or after claiming graduated retirement benefit or, as the case may be, Category A or Category B retirement pension, but before the issue of the notice referred to in sub-paragraph (1) or (2).

Manner of making election

20C.—An election under paragraph 12(1) or 17(2) may be made— **6.69**

(a) in writing to an office specified by the Secretary of State for accepting such elections; or

(b) except where the Secretary of State directs in any particular case that the election must be made in accordance with sub-paragraph (a), by telephone call to the telephone number specified by the Secretary of State.

Change of election

20D.—(1) Subject to sub-paragraphs (2) and (6), this paragraph applies in the case of an election which— **6.70**

(a) has been made under paragraph 12(1) or 17(2); or

(b) has been treated as made under paragraph 12(3) or 17(4).

(2) This paragraph does not apply in the case of an election which is—

(a) made, or treated as made, by an elector who has subsequently died; or

(b) treated as having been made by virtue of regulation [4 30(5E) or (5G)] of the Social Security (Claims and Payments) Regulations 1987.

(3) An election specified in sub-paragraph (1) may be changed by way of application made no later than the last day of the period specified in sub-paragraph (4).

(4) The period specified for the purposes of sub-paragraph (3) is, subject to sub-paragraph (5), three months after the date shown on the written notification issued by the Secretary of State to the elector, confirming the election which the elector has made or is treated as having made.

(5) The period specified in sub-paragraph (4) may be extended by the Secretary of State if he considers it reasonable to do so in any particular case.

(6) An election specified in sub-paragraph (1) may not be changed where—

(a) there has been a previous change of election under this paragraph in respect of the same period of deferment;

(b) the application is to change the election to one under paragraph 12(1)(a) or 17(2)(a) and any amount paid to him by way of, or on account of, a lump sum pursuant to paragraph 15 or 19, has not been repaid in full to the Secretary of State within the period specified in sub-paragraph (4) or, as the case may be, (5); or

(c) the application is to change the election to one under paragraph 12(1)(b) or 17(2)(b) and the amount actually paid by way of an increase of graduated retirement benefit, or actually paid on account of such an increase, would exceed the amount to which the elector would be entitled by way of a lump sum.

(7) For the purposes of sub-paragraph (6)(b), repayment in full of the amount paid by way of, or on account of, a lump sum shall only be treated as having occurred if repaid to the Secretary of State in the currency in which that amount was originally paid.

(8) Where the application is to change the election to one under paragraph 12(1)(b) or 17(2)(b) and sub-paragraph (6)(c) does not apply, any amount paid by way of an increase of graduated retirement benefit, or on account of such an increase, in respect of the period of deferment for which the election was originally made, shall be treated as having been paid on account of the lump sum to which the elector is entitled under paragraph 15 or 19.

(9) An application under sub-paragraph (3) to change an election may be made—

(a) in writing to an office specified by the Secretary of State for accepting such applications; or

(b) except where the Secretary of State directs in any particular case that the application must be made in accordance with paragraph (a), by telephone call to the telephone number specified by the Secretary of State].

PART 3

SUPPLEMENTARY

Supplementary

6.71 **21.**—Any lump sum calculated under paragraph 6, 10, 16 or 20 must be rounded to the nearest penny, taking any 1/2p as nearest to the next whole penny above.

GENERAL NOTE

6.72 The sums which are lump sums to which surviving spouses or civil partners will become entitled under Sch.1 were increased, with effect from April 8, 2024, by 6.7 per cent: see art.11(3) of the Social Security Benefits Up-rating Order 2024 (SI 2024/242). For previous years' increases, see previous editions of this work.

SCHEDULE 2 **Regulation 5**

MODIFICATION OF SCHEDULE 1

6.73 **1.**—In paragraph 2(1), for paragraph (b) there shall be substituted the following paragraph—

"(b) that paragraph 1 of Schedule 5 is to apply in relation to so much of the period of deferment which falls before the first day of the first accrual period (as defined by paragraph 3B(2) of that Schedule) beginning on or after 6th April 2005 ('the first part') and that paragraph 3A of that Schedule is to apply in relation to the remainder of the period of deferment ('the second part'), paragraph 3 of this Schedule shall apply in relation to the first part and paragraph 5 of this Schedule shall apply in relation to the second part.".

2.—In paragraph 3(2), for the words from "that amount" to the end of the sub-paragraph, there shall be substituted—

"—

(a) there are at least 7 incremental periods in the period of deferment;
(b) there are at least 5 incremental periods in the period of deferment and the amount of the increment for at least one of those periods is calculated in accordance with paragraph 4(2); or
(c) paragraph 2(1)(b) applies and there is at least one incremental period before the first day of the first accrual period.".

3.—At the end of paragraph 6(1), there shall be added the words "or, if greater, the amount equal to the total amount of graduated retirement benefit which would have been payable to the person during the period of 12 months ending with the last day of the period of deferment if his entitlement had not been deferred".

4.—In paragraph 7—

(a) at the end of sub-paragraph (1)(d), there shall be added the words "and throughout the period of 12 months falling after 5th April 2005";
(b) for sub-paragraph (2)(b) there shall be substituted the following sub-paragraph—

"(b) that paragraph 4 of Schedule 5 is to apply in relation to so much of S's period of deferment which falls before the first day of the first accrual period (as defined by paragraph 7B(2) of that Schedule) beginning on or after 6th April 2005 ('the first part') and that paragraph 7A of that Schedule is to apply in relation to the remainder of the period of deferment ('the second part'), paragraph 8 of this Schedule shall apply in relation to the first part and paragraph 9 of this Schedule shall apply in relation to the second part.".

5.—[[2] *Omitted*].

6.—In paragraph 12(1)—

(a) after the words "12 months" there shall be inserted the words "and at least 12 months of that period falls after 5th April 2005";
(b) for sub-paragraph (b), there shall be substituted the following sub-paragraph—

"(b) that paragraph 13 is to apply in relation to so much of the period of deferment which falls before the first day of the first accrual period (as defined in paragraph 16(2)) for the purposes of paragraph 15 and that paragraph 14 is to apply in relation to the remainder of the period of deferment.".

7.—In paragraph 13(2), for the words from "that amount" to the end of the sub-paragraph, there shall be substituted—

"—

(a) there are at least 7 incremental periods in the period of deferment;
(b) there are at least 5 incremental periods in the period of deferment and the amount of the increment for at least one of those periods is calculated in accordance with paragraph 14(2); or
(c) the person has made (or is treated as having made) an election under paragraph 12(1)(b) and there is at least one incremental period before the first day of the first accrual period.".

8.—At the end of paragraph 16(1), there shall be added the words "or, if greater, the amount equal to the total amount of graduated retirement benefit to which the person would have been entitled for the period of 12 months ending with the last day of the period of deferment if his entitlement had not been deferred".

9.—In paragraph 17—

(a) at the end of sub-paragraph (1)(d), there shall be added the words "and throughout the period of 12 months falling after 5th April 2005";
(b) for sub-paragraph (2)(b), there shall be substituted the following paragraph—

"(b) that paragraph 18 is to apply in relation to so much of S's period of deferment which falls before the first day of the first accrual period (as defined in paragraph 20(2)) for the purposes of paragraph 19 and that paragraph 19 is to apply in relation to the remainder of that period of deferment.".

10.—[2 *Omitted*].

AMENDMENTS

1. Social Security (Graduated Retirement Benefit)(Amendment) Regulations 2005 (SI 2005/846) reg.2 (April 5, 2005)
2. Social Security (Deferral of Retirement Pensions, Shared Additional Pensions and Graduated Retirement Benefit) (Miscellaneous Provisions) Regulations 2005 (SI 2005/2677) (April 6, 2006).
3. Social Security (Retirement Pensions and Graduated Retirement Benefits) (Widowers and Civil Partnership) Regulations 2005 (SI 2005/3078) (April 6, 2006).
4. Social Security (Deferral of Pensions etc) Regulations 2006 (SI 2006/516) (April 6, 2006).
5. Occupational Pension Schemes and Social Security (Schemes that were Contracted-out and Graduated Retirement Benefit) (Miscellaneous Amendments) Regulations 2017 (SI 2017/354) reg.3 (April 6, 2017).

The Social Security (Maximum Additional Pension) Regulations 2010

(SI 2010/426) *(as amended)*

ARRANGEMENT OF REGULATIONS

The Secretary of State for Work and Pensions makes the following Regulations in exercise of the powers conferred by sections 52(3), 122(1), 175(1) of the Social Security Contributions and Benefits Act 1992.

The Social Security Advisory Committee has agreed that proposals in respect of these Regulations should not be referred to it.

Citation and commencement

6.75 **1.**—These Regulations may be cited as the Social Security (Maximum Additional Pension) Regulations 2010 and shall come into force on 6th April 2010.

GENERAL NOTE

6.76 Following the reforms introduced from April 6, 2016 by the Pensions Act 2014, these regulations only apply directly to periods before that date, save for the new reg.3A. For the provisions that apply from that date see the State Pension Regulations 2015 below.

Interpretation

6.77 **2.**—(1) In these Regulations—

"applicable limit" has the meaning given by section 44(7)(c);

[1 "relevant day" means the day on which the survivor would, but for section 43 (persons entitled to more than one retirement pension), have become entitled to both—

(a) a Category A retirement pension; and

(b) a Category B retirement pension by virtue of the contributions of a spouse or civil partner who has died,

or would have become so entitled if the survivor's entitlement to a Category A or Category B retirement pension had not been deferred;]

"relevant year" has the meaning given by section 44(7)(a);

"survivor" means surviving spouse or surviving civil partner.

(2) In these Regulations a reference to a section by number alone is a reference to the section so numbered in the Social Security Contributions and Benefits Act 1992.

AMENDMENT

1. Pensions Act (Consequential, Supplementary and Incidental Amendments) Order 2015 (SI 2015/1985) art.33 (April 6, 2016).

Prescribed maximum additional pension

6.78 **3.**—[1 (A1) This regulation applies to a survivor whose relevant day is before 6th April 2016.]

(1) For the purposes of section 52(3) (increase of additional pension in the Category A retirement pension for surviving spouses) the maximum additional pension shall be the amount of additional pension to which a person is entitled where that person—

(a) has reached pensionable age on [1 the survivor's relevant day]; and

(b) in respect of each relevant year has an earnings factor specified in paragraph (3).

(2) [1 ...]

(3) For the purposes of paragraph (1)(b), the specified earnings factor is an earnings factor which—

(a) is equal to 53 times that year's applicable limit, before any increase under section 148 of the Social Security Administration Act 1992 (revaluation of earnings factors); and
(b) is derived from earnings on which primary Class 1 contributions were paid.

AMENDMENT

1. Pensions Act (Consequential, Supplementary and Incidental Amendments) Order 2015 (SI 2015/1985) art.33 (April 6, 2016).

[1 Prescribed maximum additional pension for survivors who become entitled on or after 6th April 2016 6.79

3A.—(1) This regulation applies to a survivor whose relevant day is on or after 6th April 2016.

(2) For the purposes of section 52(3), the maximum additional pension shall be [2 £218.39.]

AMENDMENTS

1. Pensions Act (Consequential, Supplementary and Incidental Amendments) Order 2015 (SI 2015/1985) art.33 (April 6, 2016).
2. The Social Security Benefits Up-rating Order 2024 (SI 2014/242) art.13 (April 8, 2024).

The Social Security (Retirement Pensions etc.) (Transitional Provisions) Regulations 2005

(SI 2005/469) (as amended)

ARRANGEMENT OF REGULATIONS

The Secretary of State for Work and Pensions, in exercise of the powers conferred upon him by paragraph 27 of Schedule 11 to the Pensions Act 2004 and of all other powers enabling him in that behalf, hereby makes the following Regulations:

Citation, commencement and interpretation

1.—(1) These Regulations may be cited as the Social Security (Retirement Pensions etc.) (Transitional Provisions) Regulations 2005 and shall come into force on 6th April 2005. 6.81

(2) In these Regulations—

"the Act" means the Social Security Contributions and Benefits Act 1992;

"period of deferment" shall be construed in accordance with section 55(3) or, as the case may be, section 55C(3), of the Act;

"transitional case" means a case where a person's entitlement to retirement pension or shared additional pension is deferred and the period of deferment begins before 6th April 2005 and continues on or after that day.

General Note

6.82 Following the reforms introduced from April 6, 2016 by the Pensions Act 2014 these regulations only apply directly to periods before that date. For the provisions that apply from that date see the State Pension Regulations 2015 below.

Modification of Schedule 5 to the Act

6.83 **2.**—(1) Schedule 5 to the Act (pension increase or lump sum where entitlement to retirement pension is deferred) shall be modified in relation to transitional cases in accordance with the following paragraphs.

(2) In paragraph A1(1) (choice between increase of pension and lump sum where pensioner's entitlement is deferred)—

(a) after the words "12 months" there shall be inserted the words "and at least 12 months of that period fall after 5th April 2005";

(b) for paragraph (b) there shall be substituted the following paragraph—

"(b) that paragraph 1 is to apply in relation to so much of the period of deferment as falls before the first day of the first accrual period (as defined by paragraph 3B(2)) beginning on or after 6th April 2005 and that paragraph 3A (entitlement to lump sum) is to apply in relation to the remainder of the period of deferment.".

(3) In paragraph 1(2) (increase of pension where pensioner's entitlement is deferred), for the words from "that amount" to the end of the sub-paragraph, there shall be substituted—

"(a) there are at least 7 incremental periods in the period of deferment;

(b) there are at least 5 incremental periods in the period of deferment and the amount of the increment for at least one of those periods is calculated in accordance with paragraph 2(3) as in force in relation to incremental periods beginning on or after 6th April 2005; or

(c) the person has made (or is treated as having made) an election under paragraph A1(1)(b) and there is at least one incremental period before the first day of the first accrual period (as defined by paragraph 3B(2)) beginning on or after 6th April 2005.".

(4) In paragraph 3B (calculation of lump sum)—

(a) at the end of sub-paragraph (1), there shall be added the words "or, if greater, the amount equal to the total amount of Category A or Category B retirement pension [2 (excluding any increase under section 83, 84 or 85)] which would have been payable to the person during the period of 12 months ending with the last day of the period of deferment if his entitlement had not been deferred";

(b) in the definition of "accrual period" in sub-paragraph (2), for the words "a prescribed day of the week", there shall be substituted the words "the day of the week on which the person's retirement pension would have been payable had his entitlement not been deferred";

(5) In paragraph 3C (choice between increase of pension and lump sum where pensioner's deceased spouse has deferred entitlement)—

(a) at the end of paragraph (1)(d), there shall be added the words "and throughout the period of 12 months beginning with 6th April 2005";

(b) for paragraph (2)(b) there shall be substituted the following paragraph—

"(b) that paragraph 4 is to apply in relation to so much of S's period of deferment as falls before the first day of the first accrual period (as defined by paragraph 7B(2)) beginning on or after 6th April 2005 and that paragraph 7A (entitlement to lump sum) is to apply in relation to the remainder of that period of deferment.".

(6) In paragraph 7B (calculation of lump sum)—

(a) [[1] *omitted*];

(b) in the definition of "accrual period" in sub-paragraph (2), for the words "a prescribed day of the week", there shall be substituted the words "the day of the week on which S's retirement pension would have been payable had his entitlement not been deferred".

AMENDMENTS

1. Social Security (Deferral of Retirement Pensions, Shared Additional Pensions and Graduated Retirement Benefit) (Miscellaneous Provisions) Regulations 2005 (SI 2005/2677) (April 6, 2006).

2. Social Security (Deferral of Retirement Pensions etc.) Regulations 2006 (SI 2006/516) (April 6, 2006)

Modification of Schedule 5A to the Act

3.—(1) Schedule 5A to the Act (pension increase or lump sum where entitlement to shared additional pension is deferred) shall be modified in relation to transitional cases in accordance with the following paragraphs. 6.84

(2) In paragraph 1(1) (choice between increase of pension and lump sum where pensioner's entitlement is deferred)—

(a) after the words "12 months" there shall be inserted the words "and at least 12 months of that period fall after 5th April 2005";

(b) for paragraph (b) there shall be substituted the following paragraph—

"(b) that paragraph 2 is to apply in relation to so much of the period of deferment as falls before the first day of the first accrual period (as defined by paragraph 5(2)) beginning on or after 6th April 2005 and that paragraph 4 (entitlement to lump sum) is to apply in relation to the remainder of the period of deferment.".

(3) In paragraph 2(2) (increase of pension where pensioner's entitlement is deferred), for the words from "that amount" to the end of the sub-paragraph, there shall be substituted—

"(a) there are at least 7 incremental periods in the period of deferment;

(b) there are at least 5 incremental periods in the period of deferment and the amount of the increment for at least one of those periods is calculated in accordance with paragraph 3(2); or

(c) the person has made (or is treated as having made) an election under paragraph 1(1)(b) and there is at least one incremental period before the first day of the first accrual period (as defined by paragraph 5(2)) beginning on or after 6th April 2005."

(4) In paragraph 5 (calculation of lump sum)—

(a) at the end of sub-paragraph (1), there shall be added the words "or, if greater, the amount equal to the total amount of shared additional pension which would have been payable to the person during the period of 12 months ending with the last day of the period of deferment if his entitlement had not been deferred";

(b) in the definition of "accrual period" in sub-paragraph (2), for the words "a prescribed day of the week", there shall be substituted the words "the day of the week on which the person's shared additional pension would have been payable had his entitlement not been deferred".

Social Security (Widow's Benefit and Retirement Pensions) Regulations 1979

(SI 1979/642) (*as amended*)

ARRANGMENT OF REGULATIONS

The Secretary of State for Social Services, in exercise of the powers conferred upon him by sections 29(5), 30(3), 33, 39(1) and (4), 40(2), 85(1) and 162 of, and Schedule 20 to, the Social Security Act 1975, section 20 of, and paragraphs 2(2)(a) and 3 of Schedule 1 to, the Social Security Pensions Act 1975 and of all other powers enabling him in that behalf, hereby makes the following regulations which only consolidate the regulations herein revoked and which accordingly, by virtue of paragraph 20 of Schedule 15 to the Social Security Act 1975, are not subject to the requirement of section 139(1) of that Act for prior reference to the National Insurance Advisory Committee:

Citation, commencement and interpretation

1.—(1) These regulations may be cited as the Social Security (Widow's Benefit and Retirement Pensions) Regulations 1979 and shall come into operation on 10th July 1979. **6.86**

(2) In these regulations, unless the context otherwise requires—

"the Act" means Social Security Act 1975

[1 "bereavement allowance" means an allowance awarded in accordance with section 39B of the Social Security Contributions and Benefits Act 1992 [11 (as in force immediately before it was repealed by paragraph 13 of Schedule 16 to the Pensions Act 2014)];]

[2 "civil partner" in relation to any person who has been in a civil partnership more than once means the last civil partner;]

[9 . . .]

"husband", "wife" or "spouse" in relation to any person who has been married more than once means the last husband, last wife or last spouse respectively;

"a period of at least 10 years" means a period of, or periods amounting in the aggregate to, at least 3,652 days;

[5 . . .]

[9 . . .]

[3 "the determining authority" means, as the case may require, the Secretary of State, [8 the First tier Tribunal or the Upper Tribunal]]

"section 9(2), 9(3) or 10(2) increase" means an increase under section 9(2), 9(3) or 10(2), respectively, of the Act of a person's Category A retirement pension attributable to his spouse's contributions;

"Service Pensions Instrument" means a provision and only a provision of any Royal Warrant, Order in Council or other instrument (not being a 1914–18 War Injuries Scheme) under which a disablement pension (not including a pension calculated or determined by reference to length of service) may be paid out of public funds in respect of any disablement, wound, injury or disease due to service in the naval, military or air force of the Crown or in any nursing service or other auxiliary service of any of the said forces or in the Home Guard or in any other organisation established under the control of the Defence Council or formerly established under the control of the Admiralty, the Army Council, or the Air Council;

[6 "shared additional pension" means a shared additional pension under Section 55A [10 or 55AA] of the Social Security Contributions and Benefit Act 1992;]

"1914–18 War Injuries Scheme" means any scheme made under the Injuries in War (Compensation) Act 1914 or under the Injuries in War Compensation Act 1914 (Session 2) or any Government scheme for compensation in respect of persons injured in any merchant ship or fishing vessel as the result of hostilities during the 1914–18 war;

"unemployability supplement" has the extended meaning assigned to it in regulation 2 of the Social Security (Overlapping Benefits) Regulations 1979 and further includes benefit corresponding to an unemployability supplement by virtue of regulations under section 159(3) (a) of the Act;

[12 widowed mother's allowance" means an allowance referred to in section 37 of the Social Security Contributions and Benefits Act 1992 (widowed mother's allowance: deaths before 9 April 2001).]

[1 "widowed parent's allowance" means an allowance referred to in section 39A of the Social Security Contributions and Benefits Act 1992;]

"year" means tax year.

(3) For the purposes of these regulations a person who has obtained a decree absolute of presumption of death and dissolution of marriage under the Matrimonial Causes Act 1973 shall, notwithstanding that the spouse whose death has been presumed is dead, be treated as a person whose marriage has been terminated otherwise than by the death of his spouse unless the date of his death is established to the satisfaction of the determining authority, and, in relation to a person who is so treated, the marriage in question shall be treated as having been terminated on the date of the decree absolute.

[4 (3A) For the purposes of regulation 8 of these Regulations, where, before the coming into force of the Nullity of Marriages Act 1971 a decree of nullity was granted in relation to a person on the ground that the marriage was voidable, that person shall be treated as a person whose marriage has been terminated by divorce from the date on which that decree was made absolute.]

(4) For the purposes of regulations 11(1)(d), 12(3) and 13(2) a person shall be deemed to be, or to have been, entitled to a pension or benefit if he would have been entitled had he made a claim for it.

AMENDMENTS

1. Social Security (Benefits for Widows and Widowers) (Consequential Amendments) Regulation 2000 (SI 2000/1483) reg.8 (April 9, 2001).

2. Social Security (Abolition of Earnings Rule) (Consequential) Regulations 1989 (SI 1989/1642), reg.11 (October 1, 1989).

3. Social Security Act 1998 (Commencement No. 9, and Savings and Consequential and Transitional Provisions) Order 1999 (SI 1999/2422) (September 6, 1999).

4. Social Security (Widows' Benefit and Retirement Pensions) Amendment Regulations 1995 (SI 1995/74) reg.1 (February 10, 1995).

5. Social Security (Deferral of Retirement Pensions) Regulations 2005 (SI 2005/453) reg.4 (April 6, 2005).

6. Shared Additional Pensions (Miscellaneous Amendments) regulations 2005 (SI 2005/1551) (July 6, 2005).

7. Civil Partnership (consequential amendments) Regulations 2005 (SI 2005/2878) (December 5, 2005).

8. Tribunals, Courts and Enforcement Act 2007 Sch.1 (November 3, 2008).

9. Social Security (State Pensions and National Insurance Credits) Regulations 2009 (SI 2009/2206) reg.6 (April 6, 2010).

10. The Pensions Act 2014 (Consequential, Supplementary and Incidental Amendments) Order 2015 (SI 2015/1985) art.5 (April 6, 2016).

11. The Pensions Act 2014 (Consequential, Supplementary and Incidental Amendments) Order 2017 (SI 2017/422) art.7 (April 6, 2017).
12. Social Security (Miscellaneous Amendments) Regulations 2017 (SI 2017/1015) reg.3(2) (December 6, 2018).

GENERAL NOTE

Following the reforms introduced from April 6, 2016 by the Pensions Act 2014 these regulations only apply directly to retirement pensions in or for periods before that date. For the provisions that apply from that date see the State Pension Regulations 2015 below. 6.87

Note that the amendment effected by the Social Security (State Pensions and National Insurance Credits) Regulations 2009 (SI 2009/2206) above, does not apply where the person concerned reached pensionable age before April 6, 2010. For the text applicable in such cases please see earlier editions of this book.

[1 Disapplication of section 1(1A) of the Administration Act for the purposes of retirement pension

1A.—Section 1(1A) of the Administration Act (requirement to state national insurance number) shall not apply— 6.88
(a) [2 *omitted*];
(b) to an adult dependant in respect of whom a claim for an increase of retirement pension is made or treated as made before 5th October, 1998.]
[3(c) to an adult dependant who—
(i) is a person in respect of whom a claim for an increase of retirement pension is made;
(ii) is subject to immigration control within the meaning of section 115(9)(a) of the Immigration and Asylum Act 1999; and
(iii) has not previously been allocated a national insurance number.]

AMENDMENTS

1. Social Security (National Insurance Information: Exemption) Regulations (SI 1997/2676) (December 1, 1997).
2. Social Security (Working Tax Credit and Child Tax Credit) (Consequential Amendments) (No. 2) Regulations 2003 (SI 2003/937) reg.2 (April 6, 2003).
3. Social Security (National Insurance Number Information: Exemption) Regulations 2009, (SI 2009/471) reg.3 (April 6, 2009).

Election to be treated as not having retired

2.—(1) Subject to the provisions of these regulations, where any person (other than one mentioned in paragraph (2))— 6.89
(a) has become entitled to either a Category A or a Category B retirement pension [3 or a shared additional pension] [2 . . .]; and
(b) elects that this regulation shall apply in his case,
the Act shall have effect as if that person had not become entitled as aforesaid.

[4(2) Paragraph (1) shall not apply to a person who has previously made such an election.]

[2(3) Notice of election for the purposes of this regulation may be given by telephone call to the telephone number specified by the Secretary of State unless the Secretary of State directs in any particular case that the notice [4 . . .] must be given in writing.

(4) Subject to [4paragraph (6)], an election shall take effect—

(a) on the date on which it is given; or

(b) on such other date specified by the person making the election, being no earlier than the date on which it is given and no later than 28 days after the date on which it is given.]

(5) [4. . .]

(6) Where a woman entitled to a Category B retirement pension under section 29(4) of the Act has, on or after 6th April 1979, made an election and has not revoked it, then, for the purpose only of determining her right to increments under paragraph 2 of Schedule 1 to the Pensions Act, her election shall be treated as if it took effect from 6th April, 1979 or, if later, the date of the death of her husband by virtue of whose contributions she is so entitled.

AMENDMENTS

1. Social Security Miscellaneous Provisions Regulations 1989 (SI 1989/893) reg.4 (May 28, 1989).

2. Social Security (Deferral of Retirement Pensions) Regulations 2005 (SI 2005/453) reg.4 (April 6, 2005).

3. Shared Additional Pensions (Miscellaneous Amendments) Regulations 2005 (SI 2005/1551) (July 6, 2005).

4. Social Security (State Pensions and National Insurance Credits) Regulations 2009 (SI 2009/2206) reg.7 (April 6, 2010).

GENERAL NOTE

Paragraph (5)

6.90 For the circumstances in which it is suggested that a wife's consent might be unreasonably withheld, see note to s.55 of the Act.

Provisions applying after election

6.91 **3.**—Where an election has been made in accordance with regulation 2—

(a) subject to the provisions of regulations made under section 82(2)(a) of the Act (adjustment to prevent payments for periods of less than a week or at different rates for different parts of a week), no Category A or B retirement pension [2 or a shared additional pension] shall be payable to a person [3 . . .] for any period on or after the date of his election and before he subsequently [1 becomes entitled to a Category A or Category B retirement pension] [2 or a shared additional pension] or dies; and

(b) where the person who has made the election is a woman who became entitled to a Category B retirement pension in accordance with section 29(4) of the Act and she revokes her election, she shall cease to be treated as if she had not become entitled to such a retirement pension; [3 . . .]

(c) [3 . . .]

AMENDMENTS

1. Social Security (Abolition of Earnings Rule) (Consequential) Regulations 1989 (SI 1989/1642) reg.3 (October 1, 1989).

2. Shared Additional Pensions (Miscellaneous Amendments) Regulations 2005 (SI 2005/1551) (July 6, 2005).

3. Social Security (State Pensions and National Insurance Credits) Regulations 2009 (SI 2009/2206) reg.8 (April 6, 2010).

Calculating periods of incapacity for work for welfare to work beneficiaries entitled to an increase of long-term incapacity benefit

[1 **3A.**—Section 47(1) of the Social Security Contributions and Benefits Act 1992 (increase of Category A retirement pension for long-term incapacity) shall have effect, in any case where a person is treated in accordance with regulation 13A of the Social Security (Incapacity for Work) (General) Regulations 1995 as a welfare to work beneficiary, as if for the reference to 8 weeks there were substituted a reference to [2 104] weeks.] **6.92**

AMENDMENTS

1. Social Security (Welfare to Work) Regulations 1998 (SI 1998/2231), reg.7 (October 5, 1998).
2. Social Security (Miscellaneous Amendment) (No.4) Regulations 2006 (SI 2006/2378), reg.2 (October 9, 2006).

Days to be treated as days of increment

4.—(1) For the purposes of paragraph 2 of Schedule 1 to the Pensions Act a day shall be treated as a day of increment in relation to any person if it is a day in that person's [1 period of [5 deferment]] other than a Sunday, in respect of which— **6.93**

[1 (a) if that person had not deferred his entitlement to a Category A or Category B retirement pension, [9 . . .] that person would have been entitled to such a pension (and would not have been disqualified for receiving it by reason of imprisonment or detention in legal custody); and]

(b) that person had not received any of the following benefits:—

(i) any benefit under Chapters I and II of Part II of the Act other than child's special allowance, attendance allowance, [2 disability living allowance] and guardian's allowance; or

[8 (ii) graduated retirement benefit where that person's period of deferment ended on or before 5th April 2006; or

(iii) an unemployability supplement;] [10 or]

[10 (iv) state pension credit under section 1 of the State Pension Credit Act 2002; and]

[12 (v) carer support payment under the Carer's Assistance (Carer's Support Payment) (Scotland) Regulations 2023; and]

(c) in the case of a married woman who would have been entitled to a Category B retirement pension or a section 10(2) increase [5 and whose period of deferment began before 6th April 2005], her husband had not received an increase of any of the benefits mentioned in paragraph (1)(b) in respect of her.

[5 and

(d) in the case of a person who would have been entitled to a Category A or Category B retirement pension ("the deferrer") and whose period of deferment begins on or after 6th April 2005—

(i) no other person has received an increase of any of the benefits mentioned in sub-paragraph (b) in respect of the deferrer; or

(ii) another person has received such an increase in respect of the deferrer and the deferrer is neither married to, [7 or in a civil partnership with,] nor residing with, that other person.]

[10 and

(e) in the case of a person who was a member of a couple, the other member of the couple was not in receipt of—

(i) income support under section 124 of the Social Security Contributions and Benefits Act 1992;

(ii) income-based jobseeker's allowance under section 1 of the Jobseeker's Act 1995;

(iii) state pension credit under section 1 of the State Pension Credit Act 2002; or

(iv) income-related employment and support allowance under section 1 of the Welfare Reform Act 2007.]

[11 or

(v) universal credit under Part 1 of the Welfare Reform Act 2012;]

(2) Subject to the following paragraph, for the purposes of this regulation, where in respect of any day—

(a) a person has received one or more of the benefits mentioned in paragraph (1)(b) or (c), and

(b) either—

(i) the determining authority, has determined that in respect of that day he was not entitled to that benefit; or

(ii) by virtue of the provisions of the Employment Protection (Recoupment of Unemployment Benefit and Supplementary Benefit) Regulations 1977 the Secretary of State has recovered from that person's employer sums on account of [4[1. . .] jobseeker's allowance] received by that person in respect of that day; and

(c) the whole of the benefit or sum on account of benefit in respect of that day has been repaid or, as the case may be, recovered before the relevant date,

that day shall be treated as a day in respect of which he did not receive that benefit; and in this paragraph "relevant date" means—

(i) where a person's entitlement to increments under paragraph 2 of Schedule 1 to the Pensions Act is in question, the end of his [1 period of [5deferment;]] or

(ii) where a person's entitlement to increments under paragraph 4 or 4A of that Schedule in relation to the [1deferred entitlement] of a deceased spouse is in question, the date of the death of that spouse.

(3) Where the benefit or sum on account of benefit in respect of a day to which paragraph (2)(a) and (b) applies is repaid or, as the case may be, recovered on or after the said relevant date, that day shall not be treated as a day in respect of which that person did not receive that benefit until the benefit has been repaid or, as the case may be, sums on account of the benefit have been recovered in respect of all the days to which those sub-paragraphs relate and which fall within the period to which this regulation applies.

[6 (4) For the purpose of paragraph 3 of Schedule 5A to the Social Security Contributions and Benefits Act 1992 a day shall be treated as a day of increment in relation to any person if it is a day in that person's period of deferment, other than a Sunday, in respect of which if that person had not deferred his entitlement to a shared additional pension he would have been entitled to it (and would not have been disqualified from receiving it by reason of imprisonment or detention in legal custody).]

[10 [11(5) In this regulation—

(a) in paragraph (1), "couple" has the meaning—

(i) apart from in relation to universal credit, given by section 137(1) of the Social Security Contributions and Benefits Act 1992 (interpretation of Part VII and supplementary provisions);

(ii) in relation to universal credit, given by section 39 of the Welfare Reform Act 2012 (couples);

(b) in paragraph (2), "jobseeker's allowance" means an allowance under the Jobseekers Act 1995 as amended by the provisions of Part 1 of Schedule 14 to the Welfare Reform Act 2012 that remove references to an income-based allowance, and a contribution-based allowance under the Jobseekers Act 1995 as that Act has effect apart from those provisions; and

(c) "universal credit" means universal credit under Part 1 of the Welfare Reform Act 2012.]]

AMENDMENTS

1. Social Security (Abolition of Earnings Rule) (Consequential) Regulations 1989 (SI 1989/1642) reg.11 (October 1, 1989).

2. Social Security Disability Living Allowance and Disability Working Allowance (Consequential Provisions) Regulations 1991 (SI 1991/2742) reg.6 (April 6, 1992).

3. Social Security (Widows' Benefit and Retirement Pensions) (Amendment) Regulations 1992 (SI 1992/1692) reg.2 (August 5, 1992).

4. Social Security and Child Support (Jobseeker's Allowance) (Consequential Amendments) Regulations 1996 (SI 1996/1345) reg.26 (October 7, 1996).

5. Social Security (Deferral of Retirement Pensions) Regulations 2005 (SI 2005/453) reg.4 (April 6, 2005).

6. Shared Additional Pensions (Miscellaneous Amendments) Regulations 2005 (SI 2005/1551) (July 6, 2005).

7. Civil Partnership (Consequential Amendments) Regulations (SI 2005/2878) (December 5, 2005).

8. Social Security (Deferral of Retirement Pensions etc) Regulations 2006 (SI 2006/516) (April 6, 2006).

9. Social Security (State Pensions and National Insurance Credits) Regulations 2009 (SI 2009/2206) reg.9 (April 6, 2010).

10. Social Security (Deferral of Retirement Pensions) Regulations 2011 (SI 2011/634) reg.2 (April 6, 2011).

11. Universal Credit (Consequential, Incidental, Supplementary, Incidental and Miscellaneous Provisions) Regulations 2013 (SI 2013/630) reg.26 (April 29, 2013).

12. Carer's Assistance (Carer Support Payment) (Scotland) Regulations 2023 (Consequential Amendments) Order 2023 (SI 2023/1218) art.4(2) (November 19, 2023).

GENERAL NOTE

Regulation 4(1)(a) is difficult to follow but an unreported Commissioner's decision (*CP/037/1991*) confirms that the increment accrues in respect of a married woman and her Category B pension only if both that pension and her husband's Category A pension have been deferred. In this case the husband had reached retirement age and had deferred his pension for four years. He then retired some eight months before his wife reached the age of 60 and claimed her Category B pension. In such a case the husband has an increment to his Category A pension because entitlement to that has been deferred, but his wife has no increment because her entitlement was not deferred. 6.94

Sub-paragraph (1)

6.95 Regulation 4(1)(b)(ii) has been amended to include graduated retirement pension with effect from August 5, 1992. This amendment is the response to the case of *Chief Adjudication Officer and Sec. of State v Pearse (R(P) 2/93)*. Mr Pearse had deferred his retirement and accrued increments to his Category A retirement pension. Mrs Pearse had, however, been refused increments to her Category B pension because she had during the deferred period been in receipt of Graduated Retirement Pension. The Department argued that GRP was covered by sub-para. (i) of reg.4(1)(b). The Commissioner, and the Court of Appeal, held that it was not. (Regulations deeming GRP to be a benefit under Pt II of the Act applied only for the purpose of continuity.) Mrs Pearse was therefore entitled to receive the increments to her Category B pension. The Department has now closed the door on this argument by amending sub-para.(ii) specifically to include GRP. But the amendment applies only from August 5, 1992. Married women whose husbands deferred their retirement for a period before that date and who were refused increments for the same reasons as Mrs Pearse will be entitled to arrears of their pension. Also married women who opted not to take the GRP so as to be allowed to accrue increments should now receive a payment of arrears for the GRP.

Sub-paragraph (1) has been further amended by the Deferral of Retirement Pensions Regulations 2011, to disqualify a claimant who is in receipt of that benefit or other income-related benefits, during the relevant period, but this amendment affects only a period after April 6, 2011.

Modification of paragraph 2(1) to (3) of Schedule 1 to the Pensions Act

6.96 **5.**—(1) This regulation applies to a person referred to in paragraph 1 of Schedule 1 to the Pensions Act during whose [2period of [3 deferment]] there has been an increase, other than an increase made by an order under [1 section 63 of the Social Security Act 1986] in the rate of the Category A or Category B retirement pension to which he would have been entitled if his [2 entitlement to the pension had commenced on the day on which he attained pensionable age.]

(2) In relation to a person to whom this regulation applies, paragraph 2(1) to (3) of the said Schedule 1 shall have effect with the additions, omissions and amendments prescribed below.

(3) In paragraph 2(1) for the words after "incremental period" there shall be substituted—

"(a) in his [2 period of [3 deferment]] and

(b) in each period beginning with the day on which an increase in the weekly rate of his pension took place and ending with the day before [2 his entitlement arose]".

(4) After paragraph 2(2)(b) there shall be added—

"and

(c) 'weekly rate of his pension' means the weekly rate of the Category A or Category B retirement pension to which that person would have been entitled on attaining pensionable age; and

(d) 'increase' means an increase in the weekly rate of his pension other than an increase made by such an order as is mentioned in sub-paragraph (5) below".

(5) In paragraph 2(3) for the words after "incremental period" there shall be substituted—

"(a) in the case of an incremental period specified in paragraph 2(1)(a) above, shall be [3 1/5th per cent.] of the weekly rate of his pension immediately after he attained pensionable age; and

(b) in the case of an incremental period specified in paragraph 2(1)(b) above, shall be [3 1/5th per cent.] of that increase".

AMENDMENTS

1. Social Security (Widow's Benefits and Retirement Pensions) Amendment Regulations 1987 (SI 1987/1854) reg.2 (April 11, 1988).
2. Social Security (Abolition of Earnings Rule) (Consequential) Regulations 1989 (SI 1989/1642) reg.11 (October 1, 1989).
3. Social Security (Deferral of Retirement Pensions) Regulations 2005 (SI 2005/453) reg.4 (April 6, 2005).

[5Rate of benefit where the second contribution condition in paragraph 5 of Schedule 3 to the Social Security Contributions and Benefits Act 1992 is not satisfied]

[2 **6.**—(1) Subject to paragraph (2) of this regulation, where the second contribution condition specified in paragraph 5(3) of Schedule 3 to the Act is not satisfied a person shall be entitled to— 6.97

(a) widowed mother's allowance;
[1(aa) widowed parent's allowance;
(ab) [6 . . .];]
(b) widow's pension;
(c) Category A retirement pension; or
(d) Category B retirement pension,

provided the percentage of the number of qualifying years in the working life of that person calculated in accordance with paragraph (3B) of this regulation is 25 per cent. or more.

(2) Where a person to whom paragraph (1) alone would otherwise apply is not entitled to benefit under that paragraph because the percentage of the number of qualifying years in his working life, calculated in accordance with paragraph (3B) of this regulation, is less than 25 per cent., but there are one or more surpluses in that person's earnings factors for the relevant years, that person shall be entitled to—

(a) widowed mother's allowance;
[1(aa) widowed parent's allowance;]
(b) widow's pension;
(c) Category A retirement pension; or
(d) Category B retirement pension

consisting only of the additional pension in that benefit.

(3) Where a person is entitled to benefit under paragraph (1) of this regulation, the benefit payable shall be—

(a) the basic pension in that benefit at a reduced rate calculated in accordance with paragraph (3B) of this regulation as a percentage of the higher of the sums specified in section 6(1)(a) of the Pensions Act; and
(b) any additional pension arising from one or more surpluses in the pensioner's earnings factors for the relevant years; and
(c) any increase of benefit to which he may be entitled under sections 41, 45, 45A and 46 of the Act—
  (i) in respect of an adult dependant calculated in accordance with paragraph (3B) of this regulation as a percentage of the appropriate increase specified in Part IV of Schedule 4 to the Act;
  (ii) [2 *omitted*].

(3A) Where a person is entitled to benefit under paragraph (2) of this regulation, the benefit payable shall be only the additional pension in that benefit.

(3B) [5The] percentage referred to in paragraphs (1), (2), (3)(a) and (3)(c)(i) of this regulation shall be ascertained by taking the number of qualifying years in the working life of the contributor concerned, expressing that number as a percentage of the requisite number of years specified for that working life in paragraph 5(4) of Schedule 3 to the Act and rounding up that percentage to the next whole number.]

(4) [5 *omitted*]

(5) Where a person is entitled by virtue of this regulation to a Category A retirement pension and also to a section 9(2), 9(3) or 10(2) increase, an uprating order shall have the effect of increasing—

(a) the [4 basic pension] in that pension

(i) where there is a section 10(2) increase, in proportion to the increase under that order of the [3 higher of the sums] specified in section 6(1)(a) of the Pensions Act 10(2) and

(ii) where there is a section [53(2)] increase, in proportion to the increase under that order of the sum specified in paragraph 9 of Part I of Schedule 4 to the Act;

(b) the [4 additional pension] where there is a section 9(2) increase, by the percentage specified in that order for an increase of the sums [3 which are the additional pensions in the rates of long-term benefits.]

[5(6) For the purposes of this regulation, "qualifying year" means a year for which a person's earnings factor is sufficient to satisfy paragraph 5(3)(b) of Schedule 3 to the Social Security Contributions and Benefits Act 1992 and includes a year which is treated as such a year by virtue of regulation 8(4).]

AMENDMENTS

1. Social Security (Benefits for Widows and Widowers) (Consequential Amendments) Regulations 2000 (SI 2000/1483) reg.7 (April 9, 2001).

2. Social Security (Working Tax Credit and Child Tax Credit) (Consequential Amendments) (No. 2) Regulations 2003 (SI 2003/937) reg.2 (April 6, 2003).

3. Social Security (Widows' Benefits and Retirement Pensions) Amendment Regulations 1990 (SI 1990/2642) reg.2 (January 29, 1991).

4. Social Security Act 1986 s.18 (April 6, 1987).

5. Social Security (State Pensions and National Insurance Credits) Regulations 2009 (SI 2009/2206) regs 10 and 11 (April 6, 2010).

6. The Pensions Act 2014 (Consequential, Supplementary and Incidental Amendments) Order 2017 (SI 2017/422) art.7 (April 6, 2017).

GENERAL NOTE

6.98 Note that the amendments made by the Social Security (State Pensions and National Insurance Credits) Regulations 2009 (SI 2009/2206) above, do not apply where the contributor concerned attained pensionable age, or died, before April 6, 2010. For the text applicable in such cases please see earlier editions of this book.

The operation of regulation 6 was explained by Upper Tribunal Judge Wikeley in *BB v Secretary of State for Work & Pensions* (RP) [2021] UKUT 141 (AAC) as follows:

> "19. Those persons who did not satisfy the second contribution condition [provided for by paragraph 5 of Part I to Schedule 3 to the Social Security Contributions and Benefits Act 1992] were nevertheless entitled to a reduced Category A retirement pension if they had either paid or been credited with

sufficient contributions in at least 25% of the requisite number of years of their working lives (see regulation 6 of the Social Security (Widow's Benefit and Retirement Pensions) Regulations 1979 (SI 1979/642)). The Appellant fell into this category. His national insurance record showed that he had 36 qualifying years of insurance paid into the UK scheme (as against 44 years for the requisite number of years for the full rate pension). The Appellant was therefore entitled to a reduced Category A retirement pension representing 82% of the full rate pension (36/44, when rounded up, equates to 82%)."

[[1]Proportion of retirement pension where the contribution condition in paragraph 5A of Schedule 3 to the Social Security Contributions and Benefits Act 1992 is not satisfied

6A.—(1) This regulation applies where the contribution condition in paragraph 5A of Schedule 3 (contribution conditions for entitlement to benefit) to the Social Security Contributions and Benefits Act 1992 ("the 1992 Act") is not satisfied in relation to a benefit to which that paragraph applies. **6.99**

(2) The amount of such a benefit to which a person is nevertheless entitled shall be—

- (a) 1/30th of the weekly rate of basic pension in that benefit for each year in the contributor's working life in relation to which the requirements of paragraph 5A(2)(a) and (b) of Schedule 3 to the 1992 Act are satisfied; and
- (b) any additional pension in that benefit arising from one or more surpluses in the contributor's earnings factors for the relevant years.

(3) For the purposes of paragraph (2)(a), satisfaction of the requirements of paragraph 5A(2)(a) and (b) of Schedule 3 to the 1992 Act in relation to a year includes satisfaction of those requirements by virtue of regulation 8.

(4) Paragraph (5) of regulation 6 applies to entitlement to a Category A retirement pension by virtue of this regulation as it does to such entitlement by virtue of that regulation.

Regulations 6 and 6A: supplemental

6B.—In regulations 6 and 6A, "basic pension" includes the weekly rate of Category B retirement pension specified in paragraph 5 of Part 1 (contributory periodical benefits) of Schedule 4 (rates of benefit, etc) to the Social Security Contributions and Benefits Act 1992.] **6.100**

AMENDMENT

1. These regulations were inserted by the Social Security (State Pensions and National Insurance Credits) Regulations 2009 (SI 2009/2206) reg.12 (April 6, 2010).

Category B retirement pension for certain widows by virtue of husband's contributions

7.—For the purposes of a woman's entitlement to a Category B retirement pension under section 29(5) of the Act, she shall be treated as being entitled to a widow's pension if she would have been so entitled but for any one or more of the following circumstances: **6.101**

- (a) her failure to make, or delay in making, a claim for that widow's pension;
- (b) her entitlement to a widowed mother's allowance;

(c) the operation of section 82 of the Act (disqualification and suspension) or section 85 of the Act (overlapping benefits and hospital in-patients) or any regulations made under either of those sections, except for the operation of section 82(5)(a) of the Act (absence from Great Britain);

(d) the operation of any provision of the Act or any regulations made under the Act disqualifying her for the receipt of that widow's pension for any period, except for the operation of the said section 82(5)(a);

(e) her having attained [1 pensionable age];

(f) her remarriage after 4th April 1971,

[1 (g) her having ceased to be entitled to a widowed mother's allowance at a time when she had reached the age of 65 but was under pensionable age,]

and for the purposes of section 29(7)(c) of the Act the weekly rate of the widow's pension shall be the weekly rate to which she would have been entitled but for any one or more of the said circumstances.

AMENDMENTS

1. Social Security (Miscellaneous Amendments No.4) Regulations 2017 (SI 2017/1015) reg.3(3) (December 6, 2018).

[1 Category B retirement pension for surviving spouses [2 and surviving civil partners] by virtue of deceased spouse's [2 or deceased civil partner's] contributions

6.102 **7A.**—(1) For the purposes of entitlement of any person ("the pensioner") to a Category B retirement pension under section 48BB of the Social Security Contributions and Benefits Act 1992 (Category B retirement pension: entitlement by reference to benefit under section 39A or 39B) ("the 1992 Act"), the pensioner shall be treated as being entitled to a widowed parent's allowance or a bereavement allowance as the case may be, if he would have been so entitled but for any one or more of the circumstances specified in paragraph (2) below.

(2) The circumstances referred to in paragraph (1) above are—

(a) the pensioner's failure to make, or his delay in making, a claim for that widowed parent's allowance or bereavement allowance;

(b) the operation of section 113 of the 1992 Act (disqualification and suspension) or section 73 of the Social Security Administration Act 1992 (overlapping benefits) or any regulations made under either of those sections, except for the operation of section 113(1)(a) of the 1992 Act (absence from Great Britain);

(c) the operation of any provision of the 1992 Act or any regulations made under the 1992 Act, disqualifying the pensioner from receipt of that widowed parent's allowance or bereavement allowance for any period except for the operation of the said section 113(1)(a);

(d) the pensioner's having attained pensionable age;

(e) the pensioner's having remarried [2 or formed a civil partnership].

(3) Where this regulation applies the weekly rate of a Category B pension shall—

(a) in the case of a pensioner treated as being entitled to widowed parent's allowance immediately before attaining pensionable age in consequence of the death of his or her spouse [2 or civil partner], be that specified in section 48BB(2) of the 1992 Act;

(b) in the case of a pensioner treated as being entitled to—

(i) widowed parent's allowance at any time when over the age of 45 but not immediately before attaining pensionable age, or

(ii) bereavement allowance at any time prior to obtaining pensionable age,

be that specified in section 48BB(5) and (6) of the 1992 Act as the case may be.]

AMENDMENTS

1. Social Security (Benefits for Widows and Widowers) (Consequential Amendments) Regulations 2000 (SI 2000/1483) reg.7 (April 9, 2001).

2. Civil Partnership (Pensions, Social Security and Child Support) (Consequential, etc. Provisions) Regulations 2005 (SI 2005/2877) art.10(2) (December 5, 2005).

[1 Notional entitlement to Category B retirement pension for new State Pension purposes

7B.—(1) This regulation applies for the purposes of determining whether, in accordance with paragraph 3(1)(d) of Schedule 3 to the Pensions Act 2014 (survivor's pension inherited amount: dead spouse or civil partner in old state pension scheme)(5), a person ("the pensioner") would have been entitled to a Category B retirement pension. **6.103**

(2) The pensioner shall be treated as being entitled to bereavement support payment if the pensioner would have been so entitled but for one or both of the circumstances specified in paragraph (3).

(3) The circumstances referred to in paragraph (2) are—

(a) the pensioner's failure to make, or the pensioner's delay in making, a claim for that bereavement support payment;

(b) the operation of section 32 of the Pensions Act 2014 (bereavement support payment: prisoners) or any regulations made under that section.]

AMENDMENTS

1. The Pensions Act 2014 (Consequential, Supplementary and Incidental Amendments) Order 2017 (SI 2017/422) art.7 (April 6, 2017).

Substitution of former spouse's [3 or former civil partner's] contribution record to give entitlement to a Category A retirement pension

8.—(1) This regulation applies to— **6.104**

(a) any person whose last marriage terminated before he attained pensionable age and who did not remarry [3 or, as the case may be, form a civil partnership] before that date;

[3 (aa) any person whose last civil partnership terminated before he attained pensionable age and who did not form a subsequent civil partnership or, as the case may be, marry before that date;]

[1 (b) any man or woman widowed on or after attaining pensionable age [3 or whose civil partner died on or after the man or woman had attained that age], his or her former spouse [3 or former civil partner], as the case may be, being under pensionable age when she or he died; and]

(c) any person [4other than one to whom regulation 8A applies,] whose last marriage [3 or last civil partnership] terminated on or after the date on which he attained pensionable age otherwise than by the death of his spouse [3 or, as the case may be, his civil partner],

and any such person shall be referred to in this regulation as "the beneficiary".

(2) Where the beneficiary does not, in respect of the year in which his marriage [3 or civil partner] terminated or any previous year, with his own contributions satisfy the contribution conditions for a Category A retirement pension specified in paragraph 5 of Schedule 3 [4to the Social Security Contributions and Benefits Act 1992 ("the 1992 Act") or the contribution condition for such a pension specified in paragraph 5A of that Schedule to that Act], then, for the purpose of enabling him to satisfy those conditions, the contributions of his former spouse [3 or former civil partner] may, if it is advantageous to him, be treated to the extent specified in paragraphs (3) to (6) as though they were his own.

[4 (3) The beneficiary shall be treated as satisfying the first contribution condition specified in paragraph 5 of Schedule 3 to the 1992 Act if his former spouse or former civil partner—

(a) had satisfied that condition; or

(b) would have satisfied that condition had paragraph 5A of Schedule 3 not been applicable,

as respects any year of his working life up to (inclusive) the year in which the marriage or civil partnership terminated.]

[5 (3A) The beneficiary shall be treated as satisfying the first contribution condition specified in paragraph 5 of Schedule 3 to the 1992 Act if his former spouse or former civil partner would have satisfied that condition had Part 1 of the Pensions Act 2014 not been applicable, as respects any year of his working life up to the year ending on 5th April 2016 (inclusive).]

(4) The beneficiary shall be treated as satisfying the second contribution condition [4specified in paragraph 5 of Schedule 3 to the 1992 Act or the contribution condition specified in paragraph 5A of that Schedule to that Act] as respects the number of years arrived at under paragraph 2 or 3 of Schedule 1 to these regulations, whichever is the more beneficial to him.

(5) Where a person is entitled for any period to any [2 basic pension] in his Category A retirement pension by virtue of this regulation and regulation 6 [4or 6A], he shall not be entitled for that period to a section 9(2) increase.

(6) [4*omitted*].

AMENDMENTS

1. Social Security (Benefits for Widows and Widowers) (Consequential Amendments) Regulations 2000 (SI 2000/1483) reg.7 (April 9, 2001).

2. Social Security Act 1986 s.18 (April 6, 1987).

3. Civil Partnership (Pensions, Social Security and Child Support) (Consequential etc. Provisions) Regulations 2005 (SI 2005/2877) (December 5, 2005).

4. Social Security (State Pensions and National Insurance Credits) Regulations 2009 (SI 2009/2206) reg.13 (April 6, 2010).

5. Pensions Act (Consequential, Supplementary and Incidental Amendments) Order 2015 (SI 2015/1985) art.5 (April 6, 2016).

General Note

For the meaning of marriage, see the notes following s.39c of the Act. 6.105

A marriage terminated by divorce or by a decree of nullity is terminated from the date of decree absolute. A marriage terminated by a decree of presumption of death and dissolution of marriage is treated as terminated otherwise than by death, and is treated as terminated from the date of the decree absolute unless the Secretary of State or the determining authority is satisfied as to the date of the death, in which case it is presumably also treated as terminated by death (see reg.1(3) above).

The omission of reg.8(6) above does not apply where the person concerned attained pensionable age before April 6, 2010. For the text to be applied in such cases please see earlier editions of this book.

[[1]8A.—(1) This regulation applies to a person— 6.106

(a) whose marriage or civil partnership terminated otherwise than by the death of that person's spouse or civil partner;

(b) whose marriage or civil partnership terminated after—

(i) that person; and

(ii) that person's former spouse or former civil partner, attained pensionable age;

(c) who attained pensionable age on or after 6th April 2010;

(d) whose former spouse or former civil partner attained pensionable age on or after 6th April 2010; and

[[2] (e) whose former spouse or former civil partner—

(i) satisfied the contribution condition specified in paragraph 5A(2) of Schedule 3 (contribution conditions for entitlement to benefit) to the Social Security Contributions and Benefits Act 1992 ("the 1992 Act"); or

(ii) would have satisfied the contribution condition specified in paragraph 5A(2) of Schedule 3 to the 1992 Act in respect of contributions paid before 6th April 2016 had Part 1 of the Pensions Act 2014 not been applicable.]

(2) Where a person to whom this regulation applies does not satisfy the contribution condition specified in paragraph 5A(2) of Schedule 3 to the 1992 Act, that person shall be treated as having satisfied that condition by virtue of the contributions of the former spouse or civil partner.]

Amendments

1. This regulation has been inserted by the Social Security (State Pensions and National Insurance Credits) Regulations 2009 (SI 2009/2206) reg.14 (April 6, 2010).

2. Pensions Act (Consequential, Supplementary and Incidental Amendments) Order 2015 (SI 2015/1985) art.5 (April 6, 2016).

Conditions for entitlement to a Category C retirement pension

9.—The conditions for entitlement to a Category C retirement pension shall be that the person concerned— 6.107

(a) was resident in Great Britain for a period of at least 10 years between 5th July 1948 and 1st November 1970, inclusive of both dates; and

(b) was ordinarily resident in Great Britain on 2nd November 1970 or on the date of his claim for that pension.

GENERAL NOTE

6.108 Category C pensions were abolished by the Pensions Act 2014 with respect to any prior from April 6, 2016. The amendment to reg.11 below converts the entitlements that continue into a specific rate of state pension rather than a category.

For the meaning of "resident" and "ordinarily resident", see the notes to Persons Abroad Regulations.

Conditions for entitlement to a Category D retirement pension

6.109 **10.**— [2(1)] The conditions for entitlement to a Category D retirement pension shall be that the person concerned—

[1(a) was resident in Great Britain for a period of at least 10 years in any continuous period of 20 years which included the day before that on which he attained the age of 80 or any day thereafter; and]

(b) was ordinarily resident in Great Britain either—

(i) on the day he attained the age of 80; or

(ii) if he was not so ordinarily resident on that day and the date of his claim for the pension was later than that day, on the date of his claim, so however that where a person satisfies this condition under this head he shall be deemed to have satisfied it on the date that he became so ordinarily resident.

[2 (2) Paragraph (1)(b) does not apply where, on the day or date determined in accordance with that paragraph, the person is ordinarily resident in an EEA state or Switzerland and one of the following provisions applies to that person—

(a) the Convention on Social Security between the Government of the United Kingdom of Great Britain and Northern Ireland and the Government of Ireland, signed on 1st February 2019;

(b) the Agreement between the United Kingdom of Great Britain and Northern Ireland and the Swiss Confederation on Citizens' Rights following the Withdrawal of the United Kingdom from the European Union and the Free Movement of Persons Agreement, signed on 25th February 2019;

(c) the Agreement on the Withdrawal of the United Kingdom of Great Britain and Northern Ireland from the European Union and the European Atomic Energy Community, signed on 24th January 2020;

(d) the Agreement on arrangements between Iceland, the Principality of Liechtenstein, the Kingdom of Norway and the United Kingdom of Great Britain and Northern Ireland following the withdrawal of the United Kingdom from the European Union, the EEA Agreement and other agreements applicable between the United Kingdom and the EEA EFTA States by virtue of the United Kingdom's membership of the European Union, signed on 28th January 2020;

(e) the Protocol on Social Security Coordination to the Trade and Cooperation Agreement between the United Kingdom of Great Britain and Northern Ireland, of the one part, and the European Union and the European Atomic Energy Community, of the other part, signed on 30th December 2020;

(f) the Convention on Social Security Coordination between the United Kingdom of Great Britain and Northern Ireland and the Swiss Confederation, signed on 9th September 2021;

(g) the Convention on Social Security Coordination between Iceland, the Principality of Liechtenstein, the Kingdom of Norway and the United Kingdom of Great Britain and Northern Ireland, signed on 30th June 2023.]

AMENDMENTS

1. Social Security (Widows' Benefit and Retirement Pensions) Amendment Regulations 1984 (SI 1984/1704) reg.2 (November 26, 1984).
2. Social Security (Widow's Benefit and Retirement Pensions) (Amendment) Regulations 2023 (SI 2023/1237) reg.2 (December 31, 2023).

GENERAL NOTE

For the meaning of "resident" and "ordinarily resident", see the notes to Persons Abroad Regulations. **6.110**

Regulation 10(2) enables a person resident in a European Economic Area (EEA) state or Switzerland to continue to claim a Category D retirement pension provided that the claimant is covered by one of the Conventions or Agreements specified in the regulation. This provision is necessary in anticipation of the Retained EU Law (Revocation and Reform) Act 2023 which will disapply the effect of the European Court of Justice's judgment in *Stewart v Secretary of State for Work & Pensions* (C-503/09) EU:C:2011:500; [2012] P.T.S.R. 1. *Stewart* effectively modifies the Great Britain residency conditions in reg.10(1) so that residents in an EEA state or Switzerland may nevertheless claim a Category D pension. Regulation 10(2) maintains the *Stewart* position, following implementation of the 2023 Act, in respect of persons falling within reg.10(2).

Category C retirement pension for widows of men over pensionable age on 5th July, 1948

11.—(1) Subject to the provisions of these regulations, a widow whose husband was over pensionable age on 5th July 1948 shall be entitled to a Category C retirement pension at a rate ascertained in accordance with paragraph (3) if— **6.111**

(a) she is over pensionable age; and
(b) [1 . . .]
(c) she was over the age of [2 45] either—
  (i) when her husband died; or
  (ii) if she was entitled under regulation 14 to benefit corresponding to a widowed mother's allowance, when she ceased to be so entitled; and either
(d) her husband was at any time entitled to a Category C retirement pension or a retirement pension under section 1(1)(a) of the National Insurance Act 1970; or
(e) her husband died before 2nd November 1970 and—
  (i) she was resident in Great Britain for a period of at least 10 years between 5th July 1948 and 1st November 1970, inclusive of both dates; and
  (ii) she was ordinarily resident in Great Britain on 2nd November 1970 or on the date of her claim for a Category C retirement pension; and
  (iii) he was ordinarily resident in Great Britain on the date of his death.

(2) A pension payable under paragraph (1) shall commence on 6th April 1975 or the date on which the requirements of sub-paragraphs (a) to (c)

and either (d) or (e) of that paragraph are satisfied in relation to the beneficiary, whichever is the later, and shall be payable for life.

(3) The pension under paragraph (1) shall be at the [3 weekly rate of [4£101.55]] so however that—

(a) in the case of a widow who was under the age of [2 55] either when her husband died, or, if she was entitled under regulation 14 to benefit corresponding to a widowed mother's allowance, when she ceased to be so entitled, the rate of such pension shall be reduced as if the provisions of section 26(2) of the Act applied to it;

(b) [1 . . .].

AMENDMENTS

1. Social Security (Abolition of Earnings Rule) (Consequential) Regulations 1989 (SI 1989/1642) reg.11 (October 1, 1989).
2. Social Security (Widows' Benefit and Retirement Pensions) Amendment Regulations 1987 (SI 1987/1854) reg.2 (April 11, 1988).
3. Pensions Act (Consequential, Supplementary and Incidental Amendments) Order 2015 (SI 2015/1985) art.5 (April 6, 2016).
4. The Social Security Benefits Up-rating Order 2024 (SI 2014/242) art.12 (April 8, 2024).

GENERAL NOTE

6.112 For the meaning of "resident" and "ordinarily resident", see the notes to Persons Abroad Regulations.

For the purpose of para.(1)(d) a person is entitled to the benefit if he would have been entitled had he made a claim for it. (See reg.1(4).)

Category C pensions were abolished by the Pensions Act 2014 with respect to any prior from April 6, 2016. The amendment to reg.11(3) converts the entitlements that continue into a specific rate of state pension rather than a category.

Category C retirement pension for certain women whose marriage has been terminated otherwise than by death

6.113 **12.**—(1) Subject to the provisions of these regulations, a woman whose marriage to a husband who was over pensionable age on 5th July 1948 was terminated otherwise than by his death shall be entitled to a Category C retirement pension at the higher rate specified in relation to such a pension in Part III of Schedule 4 to the Act if—

(a) she had attained pensionable age before the date of the termination of the marriage; and

(b) [1 . . .]

(c) the conditions set out in paragraph (2) or (3), as the case may be, are satisfied.

(2) The conditions applicable in the case of a woman whose marriage was terminated before 2nd November 1970 shall be—

(a) that she was resident in Great Britain for a period of at least 10 years between 5th July 1948, and 1st November 1970, inclusive of both dates; and

(b) that she was ordinarily resident in Great Britain on 2nd November 1970, or on the date of her claim for a Category C retirement pension; and

(c) that her husband was ordinarily resident in Great Britain on the date of the termination of the marriage; and

(d) that she did not remarry between the date of that termination and 2nd November 1970.

(3) The conditions applicable in the case of a woman whose marriage was terminated on or after 2nd November 1970 shall be that her husband was entitled to a Category C retirement pension or a retirement pension under section 1(1)(a) of the National Insurance Act 1970.

(4) A pension payable under paragraph (1) shall commence on 6th April 1975 or the date on which the requirements of sub-paragraphs (a) to (c) of that paragraph are satisfied in relation to the beneficiary, whichever is the later, and shall be payable for life.

AMENDMENT

1. Social Security (Abolition of Earnings Rule) (Consequential) Regulations 1989 (SI 1989/1642) reg.11 (October 1, 1989).

GENERAL NOTE

For the meaning of "resident" and "ordinarily resident", see the notes to Persons Abroad Regulations. **6.114**

For the purposes of para.(3) a person is entitled to the benefit if he would have been entitled had he made a claim for it. (See reg.1(4).)

Benefit corresponding to a widow's pension for widows of men over pensionable age on 5th July 1948

13.—(1) Subject to the provisions of these regulations, a widow whose husband was over pensionable age on 5th July 1948 shall be entitled to benefit corresponding to a widow's pension at a rate ascertained in accordance with paragraph (3) if— **6.115**

(a) she was over the age of [1 45] but under the age of 65 either—
  (i) when her husband died; or
  (ii) if she was entitled under regulation 14 to benefit corresponding to a widowed mother's allowance, when she ceased to be so entitled; and
(b) the requirements of sub-paragraph (d) or (e) of regulation 11(1) are satisfied in her case.

(2) The period for which benefit is payable under paragraph (1) shall be any period commencing on the date on which the requirements of sub-paragraph (d) or (e) of regulation 11(1) are first satisfied in the case of the widow, and during which she is under the age of 65 and for which she is not entitled under regulation 14 to benefit corresponding to a widowed mother's allowance; so however that the benefit shall not be payable for any period after the widow's remarriage or for any period during which she and a man to whom she is not married are living together as husband and wife.

(3) The benefit under paragraph (1) shall be at the higher rate specified in relation to a Category C retirement pension in Part III of Schedule 4 to the Act; so however that in the case of a widow who was under the age of [1 55] either when her husband died, or, if she was entitled under regulation 14 to benefit corresponding to a widowed mother's allowance, when she ceased to be so entitled, the rate of such benefit shall be reduced as if the provisions of section 26(2) of the Act applied to it.

AMENDMENT

1. Social Security (Widows' Benefit and Retirement Pensions) Amendment Regulations 1987 (SI 1987/1854) reg.2 (April 11, 1988).

GENERAL NOTE

6.116 For the purposes of para.(2) a person is entitled to the benefit if he would have been entitled had he made a claim for it. (See reg.1(4).)

Benefit corresponding to a widowed mother's allowance for widows of men over pensionable age on 5th July 1948

6.117 **14.**—(1) Subject to the provisions of these regulations, a widow whose husband was over pensionable age on 5th July 1948 shall be entitled to benefit corresponding to a widowed mother's allowance, which shall be at the higher rate specified in relation to a Category C retirement pension in Part III of Schedule 4 to the Act, for any period commencing on the date on which the requirements of sub-paragraph (d) or (e) of regulation 11(1) are first satisfied in her case and during which she would have been entitled to a widowed mother's allowance under section 25 of the Act had her husband satisfied the contribution conditions set out in paragraph 5 of Schedule 3 to the Act; so however that the benefit shall not be payable for any period after the widow's remarriage or for any period during which she and a man to whom she is not married are living together as husband and wife.

(2) The provisions of section 41(4) of the Act (which related to increases of widowed mother's allowance in respect of children) shall apply to benefit payable under this regulation as they apply to an allowance payable under section 25(1)(A) of the Act.

Restriction on benefit under regulations 13 and 14 in certain cases

6.118 **15.**—(1) In the case of a widow of a member of a police force or of a special constable who, as such a widow, is in receipt of a pension under regulations from time to time in force made under—

(a) the Police Pensions Act 1976;
(b) section 34 of the Police Act 1964;
(c) section 26 of the Police (Scotland) Act 1967,

benefit under regulation 13 or 14 corresponding to a widow's pension or a widowed mother's allowance shall not be payable in respect of any week during which she is receiving an increase of the said pension under either—

(i) the provisions of regulation 12 or 15 of the Police Pensions Regulations 1971, or of any corresponding regulations from time to time in force and made as mentioned in sub-paragraph (a); or
(ii) those provisions as applied by regulations from time to time in force and made as mentioned in sub-paragraph (b) or (c).

(2) For the purposes of paragraph (1), any reference in that paragraph to an enactment or regulation shall include a reference to any corresponding Northern Ireland legislation, or, as the case may be, any order or regulation having effect by virtue of such legislation, being in each case passed or made for purposes similar to the purposes of the enactment or regulation specified in that paragraph.

Provision in relation to entitlement to child benefit for the purposes of a widowed mother's allowance

16.—(1) For the sole purpose of determining whether a woman who has been widowed satisfies the requirements of section 25(1)(a) of the Act (entitlement to a widowed mother's allowance)— **6.119**

[[1](a) [[2] any person under the age of 20 residing with the widow shall be deemed to be] within section 25(2) of the Act if—

(i) the requirements of section 25(2)(a) are satisfied in his case and child benefit would have been payable in respect of him had he not been absent from Great Britain and had a claim for it been made in the manner prescribed under section 6 of the Child Benefit Act 1975, or

(ii) the requirements of section 25(2)(b) or (c) would have been satisfied, and child benefit would have been payable in respect of him continuously since the date of death of the late husband, had he not been absent from Great Britain and had a claim for child benefit been made in respect of him in the manner prescribed under section 6 of the Child Benefit Act 1975 and]

(b) a widow shall be treated as entitled to child benefit in respect of any person deemed, in accordance with sub-paragraph (a), to be [[2] . . .] within the said section 25(2).

(2) In determining whether a woman who has been more than once married and who was not residing with her late husband immediately before his death is entitled to a widowed mother's allowance under section 25 of the Act, her late husband shall, for the purposes of section 25(2)(b) of the Act, be treated as having been entitled to child benefit in respect of any child [[2] or qualifying young person] in respect of whom—

(a) a previous husband of that woman by a marriage which ended with that husband's death was, immediately before his death, entitled or treated as entitled to child benefit; and

(b) that woman was entitled or treated as entitled to child benefit immediately before the death of her late husband.

(3) For the purposes of paragraph (2)(a) or (b), if the death there referred to occurred before 4th April 1977 the previous husband or, as the case may be, the woman, shall be treated as entitled to child benefit in respect of the child [[2] or qualifying young person] in question if he or she satisfied the relevant requirement in section 25(2)(c) of the Act as originally enacted.

Amendments

1. Social Security (Widows' Benefit and Retirement Pensions) Amendment Regulations 1987 (SI 1987/1854) reg.2 (April 11 1988).

2. Social Security (Provisions Relating to Qualifying Young Persons) (Amendment) Regulations 2006 (SI 2006/692) reg.3(2) (April 10, 2006).

General Note

Regulation 16(1)(a) has been amended as from April 11, 1988 to make it clear that children under 19 living with the widow will be the basis for an award of widowed mother's allowance only so long as child benefit is payable in respect of them—in other words, so long as they remain in full-time education, or are deemed so to remain. The original drafting of this regulation, under which a widow qual- **6.120** ified by virtue of any child living with her and under the age of 19, appears to have been accidental, but nevertheless a saving provision in favour of such widows who qualify for widowed mother's allowance before April 11, 1988 was contained in the Widow's Benefit and Retirement Pension Amendment Regs 1987. For text of the earlier version of this reg., see earlier editions of this work.

[1 Provision in relation to entitlement to child benefit for the purposes of a widowed parent's allowance

6.121 **16ZA.**—(1) For the purpose only of determining whether a man or a woman who has been widowed ("the surviving spouse") [2 or where civil partner has died ("surviving civil partner")] satisfies the requirements of subsection (2)(a) of section 39A of the Social Security Contributions and Benefits Act 1992 ("the 1992 Act")—

(a) a person shall be treated for the purposes of subsection (3)(b) or (c) of that section as having been entitled to child benefit in respect of a child [3 or qualifying young person] where that person would have been so entitled had—
 (i) that child [3 or qualifying young person] not been absent from Great Britain, and
 (ii) a claim for child benefit been made in respect of the child [3 or qualifying young person] in the manner prescribed under section 13 of the Social Security Administration Act 1992; and

(b) the surviving spouse [2 or surviving civil partner] shall be treated, for the purposes of subsection (2)(a) of section 39A, as entitled to child benefit in respect of the child [3 or qualifying young person] who, by virtue of sub-paragraph (a) above, falls within subsection (3) of that section.

(2) In determining whether a surviving spouse [2 or surviving civil partner] who has been more than once married [2 has formed more than one civil partnership, or who has been both married and formed a civil partnership] and who was not residing with the deceased spouse [" or, as the case may be, the deceased civil partner] immediately before his or her death is entitled to a widowed parent's allowance under section 39A of the 1992 Act, the deceased spouse [" or deceased civil partner] shall, for the purposes of subsection (3)(b) of that section, be treated as having been entitled to child benefit in respect of any child [3 or qualifying young person] in respect of whom—

(a) a previous spouse [2 or civil partner] of that surviving spouse [2 or civil partner] by a marriage [2 or, as the case may be, by the formation at a civil partnership] which ended with that previous spouse's [2 or previous civil partner's] death was, immediately before his or her death, entitled or treated as entitled to child benefit; and

(b) that surviving spouse [2 or civil partner] was entitled or treated as entitled to child benefit immediately before the death of the deceased spouse [2 or civil partner].]

AMENDMENTS

1. Social Security (Widow's Benefits and Retirement Pensions) Amendment Regulations 2001 (SI 2001/1235) (April 9, 2001).

2. Civil Partnership (Pensions Social Security and Child Support) (Consequential etc. Provisions) order 2005 (SI 2005/2877) (December 5, 2005).

3. Social Security (Provisions relating to QualifyingYoung Persons) (Amendment) Regulations (SI 2006/692) reg.3(3) (April 10, 2006).

[1 Disapplication of section 1(1A) of the Administration Act for the purposes of widowed mother's allowance

16A.—Section 1(1A) of the Administration Act (requirement to state national insurance number) shall not apply to a child [3 or qualifying young person] in respect of whom an increase of widowed mother's allowance [2 or widowed parent's allowance] is claimed.] 6.122

AMENDMENTS

1. Social Security (National Insurance Information: Exemption) Regulations (SI 1997/2676) (December 1, 1997).
2. Social Security (Widow's Benefit and Retirement Pensions) Amendment Regulations 2001 (SI 2001/1235) (April 9, 2001).
3. Social Security (Provisions relating to Qualifying Young Persons) Regulations (SI 2006/692) reg.3(4) (April 10, 2006).

Provisions relating to age addition for persons not in receipt of a retirement pension

17.—(1) For the purposes of section 40(2) of the Act (age addition for persons over the age of 80 who are not entitled to a retirement pension but are in receipt of certain other payments) the prescribed enactments and instruments shall be— 6.123

(a) Chapter IV or V of Part II of the Act;
(b) any scheme made under section 5 of the Industrial Injuries and Diseases (Old Cases) Act 1975;
(c) any Service Pensions Instrument;
(d) any scheme made under the Personal Injuries (Emergency Provisions) Act 1939 or under the Pensions (Navy, Army, Air Force and Mercantile Marine) Act 1939;
(e) any 1914–18 War Injuries Scheme;
(f) section 36 of the Act ([3 severe disablement allowance]);
(g) section 37 of the Act ([1 carer's allowance]);
[4 (ga) the Carer's Assistance (Carer's Support Payment) (Scotland) Regulations 2023;]
[2 (h) sections 36 and 37 of the National Insurance Act 1965 as continued in force by the Social Security (Graduated Retirement Benefit) (No. 2) Regulations 1978.]

(2) The following shall [2 subject to paragraph (3)] be additional conditions of entitlement to age addition under section 40(2) of the Act—

(a) that the person concerned is in receipt of a payment under an enactment or instrument specified in paragraph (1), by reference to which the amount of a retirement pension would, if it were otherwise payable to him, be extinguished by virtue of any regulations made under section 85(1)(a) of the Act (overlapping benefits); and
(b) that had he made a claim for it, he would have been entitled to a retirement pension of any category by virtue of any provision of the Act or any regulations made under it.

[2 (3) Paragraph (2) shall not apply to a person who is in receipt of a payment under the enactment specified in paragraph (1)(h)].

AMENDMENTS

1. Social Security Amendment (Carer's Allowance) Regulations 2002 (SI 2002/2497) reg.3 (April 1, 2003).

2. Social Security (Widows' Benefit and Retirement Pensions) Amendment Regulations 1993 (SI 1993/1242) reg.2 (June 7, 1993).

3. Social Security (Severe Disablement Allowance) Regulations 1984 (SI 1984/1303) Sch.2 (November 29, 1984).

4. Carer's Assistance (Carer Support Payment) (Scotland) Regulations 2023 (Consequential Amendments) Order 2023 (SI 2023/1218) art.4(3) (November 19, 2023).

6.124 *Regulation 18 omitted.*

SCHEDULE 1

6.125 **Method of treating former spouse's [1 or former civil partner's] contributions as those of the beneficiary so as to entitle him to a Category A retirement pension**

1. In this Schedule—

(a) A is the number of former spouse's or [1 former civil partner's] qualifying years up to (exclusive) the year in which the marriage [1or, as the case may be the former civil partnership] terminated [3 but where Part 1 of the Pensions Act 2014 applies to the former spouse or former civil partner, A is the number of his qualifying years up to the year ending on 5th April 2016 (inclusive)];

(b) B is the number of years in the former spouse's [1 or former civil partner's] working life up to (exclusive) the year in which the marriage [1 or, as the case may be the former civil partnership] terminated. [2; and

(c) "qualifying year" means a year for which the former spouse's or former civil partner's earnings factor is sufficient to satisfy—

(i) paragraph 5(3)(b); or

(ii) paragraph 5A(2)(b),

of Schedule 3 to the Social Security Contributions and Benefits Act 1992 and does not include a year which is treated as such a year by virtue of regulation 8(4).]

2. The number of years arrived at under this paragraph is that which is obtained by—

(a) taking the number of years in the beneficiary's working life between (inclusive) the first year in that working life and (inclusive) the year in which the marriage [1 or former civil partnership] terminated, multiplying it by A/B and rounding up the result to the next whole number; and

(b) adding to that number of years the number of the beneficiary's qualifying years falling after the year in which the marriage [1 or former civil partnership] terminated.

3. The number of years arrived at under this paragraph is that which is obtained by—

(a) taking the number of years in the beneficiary's working life between (inclusive) the year in which the marriage took place [1 or the civil partnership was formed] and (inclusive) the year [1 in which the marriage or civil partnership terminated], multiplying it by A/B and rounding up the result to the next whole number; and

(b) adding to that number of years the number of the beneficiary's qualifying years falling—

(i) before the year in which the marriage took place [1 or the civil partnership was formed] and

(ii) after that in which the marriage [1 or civil partnership] terminated.

AMENDMENTS

1. Civil Partnership (Pensions Social Security and Child Support) (Consequential etc. Provisions) order 2005 (SI 2005/2877) (December 5, 2005).

2. Social Security (State Pensions and National Insurance Credits) Regulations 2009 (SI 2009/2206) reg.15 (April 6, 2010).

3. Pensions Act (Consequential, Supplementary and Incidental Amendments) Order 2015 (SI 2015/1985) art.5 (April 6, 2016).

General Note

Note that the inclusion of sub-para.(c) does not apply so as to include in the definition of "qualifying year" any years credited by virtue of s.23A(5) of the Social Security Contributions and Benefits Act 1992 where the marriage or civil partnership terminated before April 6, 2010. **6.126**

The Social Security (Widow's Benefit, Retirement Pensions and Other Benefits) (Transitional) Regulations 1979

(SI 1979/643) (*as amended*)

The Secretary of State for Social Services, in exercise of the powers conferred upon him by section 2 of, and paragraphs 3, 4, 5, 7 and 9 of Schedule 3 to, the Social Security (Consequential Provisions) Act 1975 and section 63 of the Social Security Pensions Act 1975 and of all other powers enabling him in that behalf, hereby makes the following regulations which only consolidate other regulations herein revoked and which, accordingly, by virtue of paragraph 20 of Schedule 15 to the Social Security Act 1975, are not subject to the requirement of section 139(1) of that Act for prior reference to the National Insurance Advisory Committee. **6.127**

Arrangement Of Regulations

Citation and commencement

6.129 **1.**—These regulations may be cited as the Social Security (Widow's Benefit, Retirement Pensions and Other Benefits) (Transitional) Regulations 1979 and shall come into operation on 10th July 1979.

GENERAL NOTE

6.130 Those provisions in these regulations that apply to entitlement to a state pension must now be read subject to the Pensions Act 2014 and State Pension Regulations 2015. These abolish Category B pensions with effect from April 6, 2016 and replace all relevant provisions about entitlement to a state pension with new provisions from that date. However, they protect transitional cases where a person's entitlement has arisen under this law and many of these provisions continue in effect subject to the new scheme.

Interpretation

6.131 **2.**—(1) In these regulations, unless the context otherwise requires:—

[1" the 1992 Act" means the Social Security Contributions and Benefits Act 1992;]

"the Act" means the Social Security Act 1975;

"the former principal Act" means the National Insurance Act 1965;

"the Pensions Act" means the Social Security Pensions Act 1975;

"contribution week" means a period of 7 days beginning with midnight between Sunday and Monday;

"the Contributory Pensions Acts" means the Widows', Orphans' and Old Age Contributory Pensions Acts 1936 to 1941;

"pre-1975 beneficiary" means—

(a) a person to or in respect of whom benefit under the former principal Act (including such benefit, pension or allowance as is mentioned in paragraph 17(2)(b) of Schedule 11 to that Act is, or but for a disqualification or forfeiture would be, payable immediately before 6th April 1975; and

(b) a person who immediately before that date had a prospective right to, or expectation of, such benefit;

" pre-1975 contribution" means a contribution of any class paid under the former principal Act in respect of a week before the contributor concerned attained pensionable age and also means—

(a) in relation to widowed mother's allowance, widow's pension, child's special allowance and a Category B retirement pension to which a woman is entitled by virtue of section 29(5) of the Act, a contribution paid under the Contributory Pensions Acts by a pre-1948 contributor in respect of a period between the date of the contributor's last entry into insurance under those Acts and 5th July 1948 and paid for purposes which included widows' and orphans' pensions purposes; and

(b) in relation to a Category A retirement pension or a Category B retirement pension, other than such a pension as is referred to in the preceding sub-paragraph, a contribution paid under the Contributory Pensions Acts by a pre-1948 contributory in respect of a period between the date of his last entry into insurance under those Acts and 5th July 1948 and paid for purposes which included old age pensions purposes;

"pre-1975 contributor" means a person who was insured under the former principal Act;

"pre-1948 contributor" means a person who, within the prescribed time referred to in paragraph 17(1)(a) of Schedule 11 to the former principal Act, was, or was deemed to be, or was treated as insured under the Contributory Pensions Acts;

"reckonable year" for the purposes of the contribution conditions for any benefit means a tax year before 6th April 1978 in which the contributor concerned paid or was credited with contributions of a relevant class and the earnings factor derived from those contributions amounted to not less than that year's lower earnings limit multiplied by 50; " year" means tax year.

(2) Any reference in these regulations to a pre-1975 beneficiary who is entitled to benefit under the former principal Act shall include a person who but for any disqualification or forfeiture would be entitled to such benefit; and where, on or after 6th April 1975, a person is, by virtue of these regulations, entitled to benefit under the Act or the Pensions Act, such entitlement shall be subject to any disqualification or forfeiture and subject to any reduction in the rate of benefit payable to which that person's entitlement to benefit under the former principal Act would have been subject if that Act had continued on or after 6th April 1975.

(3) For the purposes of these regulations a person who has obtained a decree absolute of presumption of death and dissolution of marriage under the Matrimonial Causes Act 1973 shall, notwithstanding that the spouse whose death has been presumed is dead, be treated as a person whose marriage has been terminated otherwise than by the death of his spouse unless the date of his death is established to the satisfaction of the Secretary of State, a Commissioner [2 or an appeal tribunal constituted under Chapter I of Part I of the Social Security Act 1998], whichever is appropriate; and, in relation to a person who is so treated, the marriage in question shall be treated as having been terminated on the date of the decree absolute.

AMENDMENTS

1. Social Security (Widow's Benefit, Retirement Pensions and other Benefits) (Transitional) Amendment Regulations 1981 (SI 1981/1627) regs 2, 3 (December 14, 1981).

2. Social Security Act 1998 (Commencement No. 9, and Savings and Consequential and Transitional Provisions) Order (SI 1999/2422) Sch.4 para.2 (September 6, 1999).

Modifications of [1 pensions legislation in its] application to pre-1975 beneficiaries and pre-1975 contributors

6.132 **3.**—In relation to pre-1975 beneficiaries and pre-1975 contributors the provisions of [1the Act, the Pensions Act and the 1992 Act] and the orders and regulations for the time being in force thereunder shall have effect subject to the modifications made by these regulations.

AMENDMENTS

1. Social Security (State Pension and National Insurance Credits) Regulations 2009 (SI 2009/2206) regs 16–22 (April 6, 2010).

Benefit in respect of events or for periods commencing before 6th April 1975

6.133 **4.**—Where, on or after 6th April 1975, a person claims, in respect of an event falling or for a period commencing before 6th April 1975, benefit under the former principal Act of a description specified in Column (1) of Schedule 1to these regulations, the claim shall, subject to the provisions of regulation 5, be determined as respects such event or for such period as if the provisions of the former principal Act and the enactments specified in the third column of Schedule 1 to the Social Security (Consequential Provisions) Act 1975 covering entitlement to such benefit had continued in force in place of the provisions of the Act and the Pensions Act covering entitlement to benefit of a corresponding description.

Provision of alternative rights to benefit

6.134 **5.**—(1) Subject to regulation 2(2) where, immediately before 6th April 1975, a pre-1975 beneficiary was entitled to benefit under the former principal Act of a description specified in Column (1) of Schedule 1 to these regulations or to any increase of such benefit for a child or adult dependant, he shall as from that date be entitled, without any claim being made therefore, or award being made thereof, to benefit under the Act or the Pensions Act of a description set out in Column (2) of that Schedule opposite the said benefit under the former principal Act specified in Column (1) as if such benefit had been claimed and awarded under the Act or the Pensions Act, and to any increase of such benefit for a child or adult dependant to which he may be entitled under or by virtue of those Acts.

(2) Where, immediately before 6th April 1975, a woman was entitled to a widow's pension under the former principal Act by virtue of regulation 13 of the National Insurance (Widow's Benefit and Retirement Pensions) Regulations 1972 as being incapable of self-support by reason of an infirmity, she shall, subject to regulation 2(2), be entitled as from 6th April 1975 to a widow's pension under the Act for any period for which she would have been entitled to such a pension under the former principal Act if the said regulation 13 and the provisions referred to in that regulation had continued in force.

Modifications relating to the first contribution condition for widowed mother's allowance, widow's pension and Category A and B retirement pension

6.—(1) The first contribution condition for a widowed mother's allowance, a widow's pension or a Category A or Category B retirement pension specified in paragraph 5(2) of Schedule 3 to the Act shall be deemed to be satisfied in any case where the contributor concerned is, or was, a pre-1975 contributor who had paid not less than 50 pre-1975 contributions. **6.135**

(2) The said contribution condition for a Category A retirement pension shall be deemed to be satisfied in the case of a woman who attains pensionable age on or after 6th April 1975 if—

(a) she was a widow who was entitled to a widow's allowance or a widowed mother's allowance under the former principal Act at any time before 6th April 1975 and has not re-married before attaining pensionable age; or

(b) her marriage was terminated before 6th April 1975 otherwise than by the death of her husband and she has not re-married before attaining pensionable age and her husband had paid not less than 50 pre-1975 contributions before the termination of the marriage.

Modifications relating to the second contribution condition for widowed mother's allowance, widow's pension and Category A and B retirement pension [2and to the contribution condition for Category A and B retirement pension for those attaining pensionable age on or after 6th April 2010]

7.—(1) The following provisions of this regulation shall, except where expressly provided otherwise, have effect [2for the purposes of— **6.136**

(a) the second contribution condition for a widowed mother's allowance, a widow's pension or a Category A or Category B retirement pension specified in paragraph 5(3) of Schedule 3 to the 1992 Act; and

(b) the contribution condition for a Category A or Category B retirement pension specified in paragraph 5A(2) of that Schedule.]

(2) Subject to paragraph (3), where the contributor concerned is, or was, a pre-1975 contributor he shall, in respect of that part of his working life falling before 6th April 1975, have the number of reckonable years obtained by taking the total number of contributions of any class paid by or credited to him, in accordance with the provisions of the former principal Act or regulations made thereunder, for each week in the said part of his working life or credited to him by any provision of these regulations and dividing it by 50 and, if the resultant quotient is not a whole number, by rounding it up to the nearest whole number;

provided that the number of reckonable years so obtained shall not exceed the number of years of a person's working life falling before 6th April 1975.

(3) For the purposes of a Category B retirement pension under section 29(2)or (3) of the Act where the contributor concerned was a pre-1975 contributor who attained pensionable age before 6th April 1975, the second contribution condition shall be deemed to be satisfied to the same extent as it was satisfied in relation to that contributor for the purposes of his Category A retirement pension; so however that this paragraph shall not apply where that contributor died on or after that date.

(4) A contribution as payable by a non-employed person under the former principal Act shall be credited to a pre-1975 contributor—

(a) if he was a pre-1948 contributor, for each contribution week during the period from 6th April 1936, or if later, 6th April of the year in which he last entered into insurance under the Contributory Pensions Acts, to 4th July 1948; or

(b) if he was not a pre-1948 contributor but was insured under the former principal Act and—

(i) he was over the age of 16 on 5th July 1948, for each contribution week in the period from 6th April 1948 to 4th July 1948; or

(ii) he attained the age of 16 on or after 5th July 1948, for each contribution week in the period from 6th April of the year in which he attained the age of 16 up to the contribution week immediately before that in which he reached the upper limit of compulsory school age or, if later, the contribution week immediately before that in which he attained the age of 16;

provided that a contribution credited to a pre-1975 contributor under this paragraph for any contribution week specified therein shall be treated as credited in place of any contribution under the Contributory Pensions Acts or a contribution of any class under the former principal Act that may have been paid by, or otherwise credited to, that contributor in respect of such a week.

(5) In any case where the contributor concerned attained the age of 16 before 6th April 1975 and is not a pre-1975 contributor, a contribution as payable by a non-employed person under the former principal Act shall be credited to him—

(a) if he attained the age of 16 before 5th July 1948, for each contribution week in the period from 6th April 1948 to 4th July 1948;

(b) if he attained the age of 16 on or after 5th July 1948, for each contribution week from 6th April of the year in which he attained the age of 16 up to the contribution week immediately before that in which he attained that age;

provided that the maximum number of weeks for which a contribution may be credited to any person by virtue of the provisions of this paragraph shall be 50.

(6) For the purposes of paragraphs (4) and (5), if the period for which contributions are to be credited does not commence with midnight between Sunday and Monday, the days from the beginning of such period up to the first such midnight shall be treated as constituting a contribution week and if the period for which contributions are to be credited does not cease with midnight between Sunday and Monday, the days from the last such midnight to the end of such period shall be disregarded.

(7) Subject to paragraph (8), the working life of a person who attained the age of 16 before 5th July 1948 shall—

(a) if he was a pre-1948 contributor, be the period between 6th April 1936 or, if later, 6th April of the year in which he last entered into insurance under the Contributory Pensions Acts, and the end of the year immediately before that in which he attains pensionable age or dies under that age; or

(b) if he was not a pre-1948 contributor, be the period between 6th April 1948 and the end of the year immediately before that in which he attains pensionable age or dies under that age.

(8) Where the contributor concerned has died on or after 6th April 1975 and he was—

(a) a pre-1948 contributor whose last date of entry into insurance under the Contributory Pensions Acts was before 30th September 1946 and who at that date of entry was within 5 years of pensionable age; or

(b) a pre-1948 contributor whose last date of entry into insurance under the Contributory Pensions Acts was on or after 30th September 1946 and who at that date of entry was within 10 years of pensionable age; or

(c) a person who was not a pre-1948 contributor and who was, immediately before 5th July 1948, within 10 years of pensionable age,

his working life shall be—

(d) where the contributor concerned is a person to whom paragraph (a) or (b) applies, the period from 6th April of the year in which he last entered into insurance under the Contributory Pensions Acts to 5th April immediately before the date on which he completed—

(i) where paragraph (a) applies, the said period of 5 years; (ii) where paragraph (b) applies, the said period of 10 years;

(e) where the contributor concerned is a person to whom paragraph (c) applies, the period from 6th April 1948 to 5th April 1958,

and the provisions of paragraph (2) shall apply as if any employer's contribution paid in respect of any person to whom this paragraph applies for any period after such person reached pensionable age were a contribution paid by that person.

(9) If a pre-1948 contributor's last dates of entry into insurance under the Contributory Pensions Acts were different dates for widows' and orphans' pensions purposes and old age pensions purposes, his date of entry into insurance under those Acts for the purposes of the second contribution condition for a widowed mother's allowance, a widow's pension or a Category B retirement pension for a widow by virtue of her husband's contributions shall be his last date of entry into insurance for widows' and orphans' pensions purposes, and for the purpose of the said contribution condition for a Category A retirement pension shall be his last date of entry into insurance for old age pensions purposes.

(10) In the case of a person (hereinafter called " the beneficiary") whose former spouse [3 or former civil partner]:- was a pre-1975 contributor and who has the contributions of his said spouse [3 or former civil partner] treated, by virtue of regulation 8 of, and Schedule 1 to, the Social Security (Widow's Benefit and Retirement Pensions) Regulations 1979 as if they were contributions of his own so as to entitle him to a Category A retirement pension—

(a) the number of any qualifying years before 6th April 1975 which, by virtue of regulations 7(2) and 13 , were or could have been obtained by his former spouse [3 or former civil partner]:- and which may be taken into account towards the beneficiary's said entitlement, shall be ascertained by reference to the number of contributions of any class paid by or credited to his former spouse [3 or former civil partner]:- [1in respect of] the period of the former spouse's [3 or former civil partner's] working life between (inclusive) the first year of his working life and (exclusive) the year in which the marriage terminated or the year 1975/76, whichever is the earlier, [3 (or, in the case of a civil partnership, the year 1975/76)] and shall not exceed the number of years in that period; and

(b) the number of any qualifying years before 6th April 1975 which, by virtue of regulations 7(2) and 13, are obtained by the beneficiary by virtue of paragraph 2(b)or, as the case may be, paragraph 3(b)of the said Schedule and which may be taken into account towards his said entitlement shall be ascertained by reference to the number of contributions of any class paid by or credited to him during the period or periods specified in the said paragraphs which fell before 6th April 1975 and shall not exceed the number of years in that period or in each of those periods, as the case may be;

(c) where the beneficiary is a woman, if her husband died on or after 5th July 1948 and immediately before that date he was insured under the Contributory Pensions Acts for purposes which included widows' and orphans' pensions purposes, the working life of her said husband may, if it would be more favourable to her, be treated as the period between 6th April 1936 or, if later, 6th April of the year in which he last entered into insurance for widows' and orphans' pensions purposes and the end of the year immediately before that in which he attained pensionable age or died under that age.

AMENDMENTS

1. Social Security (Widow's Benefit, Retirement Pensions and other Benefits) (Transitional) Amendment Regulations 1981 (SI 1981/1627) regs 2, 3 (December 14, 1981).

2. Social Security (State Pension and National Insurance Credits) Regulations 2009 (SI 2009/2206) regs 16–22 (April 6, 2010).

3. Marriage (Same Sex Couples) Act 2013 and Marriage and Civil Partnership (Scotland) Act 2014 (Consequential Provisions) Order 2014 (SI 2014/3061) art.2 and Sch.1 (December 10, 2014 and in respect of Scotland December 16, 2014).

Modifications relating to the contribution condition for child's special allowance

6.137 **8.**—The contribution condition for a child's special allowance specified in paragraph 6(1) of Schedule 3 to the Act shall be deemed to be satisfied in any case where the contributor concerned is, or was, a pre-1975 contributor who attained pensionable age or died under that age on or after 6th April 1975 and had paid not less than 50 pre-1975 contributions.

Modifications in respect of claims and questions relating to persons who attained pensionable age before 6th April 1975 but who retire thereafter

6.138 **9.**—Where a person who, having attained pensionable age before 6th April 1975, retires on or after that date or, having made an election before that date under section 35 of the former principal Act, retires on or after that date—

(a) any question under the former principal Act relating to that person's entitlement to a retirement pension determined in advance of a claim before 6th April 1975 shall be treated, for the purpose of facilitating the determination of a subsequent claim to a Category A or a Category B retirement pension, as a question determined under the Act in relation to that person's entitlement to such a pension; and

(b) subject to regulation 4, any claim for, or question relating to, that person's entitlement to a retirement pension that has not been determined before 6th April 1975 shall be for determination as a claim for, or a question under the Act relating to that person's entitlement to, a Category A or, as the case may be, a Category B retirement pension.

Modifications relating to increases of retirement pension for deferred retirement

10.—(1) In this regulation and in regulations 11 and 12— 6.139

" a pre-1975 increment" means an increase of retirement pension under section 31(1) or 34(1) of the former principal Act;

" a post-1975 increment" means an increase of a Category A or B retirement pension which accrued under section 28(4), 28(5) or 29(10) of the Act between 6th April 1975 and 5th April 1979 (both dates inclusive);

and the pre-1975 beneficiaries to whom the said regulations relate are those who, immediately before 6th April 1975, were, or but for any disqualification or forfeiture would be, entitled to, or who have prospective rights to, or expectation of, a pre-1975 increment.

(2) The weekly rate of a Category A or B retirement pension payable to a pre-1975 beneficiary to whom this regulation relates shall, in addition to any post-1975 increments that fall to be made, be increased by the amount of any pre-1975 increments to which, immediately before 6th April 1975 he was, or but for any disqualification or forfeiture would have been, entitled or to which he had a prospective right or expectation, together with increases (if any) of the said amount calculated in accordance with the provisions of section 124 of the Act and section 23(3) of the Pensions Act.

(3) The weekly rate of a Category B retirement pension payable to the widow of a pre-1975 beneficiary to whom this regulation applies, whom she married on or after 6th April 1975 shall, in addition to any post-1975 increments that fall to be made, be increased by one half of the amount of any pre-1975 increments by which the Category A retirement pension of her husband would, if were still alive, be increased for him by the provisions of paragraph (2).

(4) Where a pre-1975 beneficiary to whom this regulation relates has, immediately before 6th April 1979, entitlement, or a prospective right, to at least one pre-1975 increment, paragraph 1 of Schedule 1 to the Pensions Act shall apply to his case as if—

(a) the words " " but only if that amount is enough to increase the rate of the pension by at least 1 per cent" " were omitted from that paragraph, and

(b) any contribution as an employed or self-employed person, paid by him under the former principal Act in respect of any period after he attained pensionable age and not taken into account for a pre-1975 or a post-1975 increment, were treated as an incremental period for the purposes of Schedule 1 to the Pensions Act.

(5) Where a pre-1975 beneficiary to whom this regulation relates is a woman who has attained pensionable age but has not yet attained the age of 65, any Category B retirement pension payable to her by virtue of regulation 18 for any day before the day on which she attains the age of 65 or retires before attaining that age shall be disregarded for the purposes

of regulation 4 of the Social Security (Widow's Benefit and Retirement Pensions) Regulations 1979.

Modifications in respect of increases of retirement pension relating to persons who attained pensionable age before 6th April 1979 but who retire thereafter

6.140 **11.**—(1) The following provisions of this regulation relate to a person who, having attained pensionable age before 6th April 1979, retires from regular employment on or after that date or, having made an election before that date under section 30(3) of the Act or section 35 of the former principal Act, retires on or after that date.

(2) Where a person, before 6th April 1979, satisfied the condition in section 28(4) of the Act that the number of days of increment was at least 48, paragraph 1 of Schedule 1 to the Pensions Act shall apply to his case as if the words " but only if that amount is enough to increase the rate of the pension by at least 1 per cent" were omitted from that paragraph.

(3) Where a person, before 6th April 1979, did not satisfy the condition in section 28(4) of the Act that the number of days of increment was at least 48, then, subject to the condition specified in paragraph 1 of Schedule 1 to the Pensions Act (that an increase under that paragraph is payable only if its amount would increase the retirement pension by at least 1 per cent)—

(a) that person's retirement pension shall be increased by 1/8th per cent of its rate for each period of six days of increment which fell before 6th April 1979, and

(b) any such day of increment which does not form part of a period as aforesaid shall be treated as a day of increment for the purposes of Schedule 1 to the Pensions Act.

(4) For the sole purpose of determining whether the condition specified in paragraph 1 of Schedule 1 to the Pensions Act (referred to in paragraph (3) above) has been satisfied by a married woman whose husband's days of increment before 6th April 1979 amounted to less than 48, her entitlement to an increase of a Category B retirement pension in respect of the period before 6th April 1979 shall be calculated on the basis of an increase of 1/8th per cent for each incremental period which fell within the period beginning with the day on which her husband attained pensionable age, she attained pensionable age or they were married, whichever is the latest, and ending on 5th April 1979.

Provision relating to increase of retirement pension where pensioner's deceased spouse [2or deceased civil partner] had deferred retirement

6.141 **12.**—For the purpose of calculating entitlement to an increase of retirement pension under paragraph 4 of Schedule 1 to the Pensions Act (increase of Category A or Category B retirement pension by amount to which deceased spouse [2or deceased civil partner] was entitled) in the case of a person whose spouse dies on or after 6th April 1979 [2 or whose civil partner dies on or after 5th December 2005] , or, in the case of a widow, who attains pensionable age on or after [26th April 1979] , any pre-1975 increment or post-1975 increment to which the deceased spouse [2or deceased civil partner] was entitled or [1would at his death have been entitled if his entitlement had not been deferred] shall be treated as an increase to which he was entitled under the said Schedule.

AMENDMENTS

1. Social Security (Abolition of Earnings Rule) (Consequential) Regulations (SI 1989/1642) reg.12(4) (October 1, 1989).
2. Social Security (State Pension and National Insurance Credits) Regulations 2009 (SI 2009/2206) regs 16–22 (April 6, 2010).

[1 Provision relating to increase of a woman's Category A or B retirement pension on termination of marriage

12A.—In the case of a woman— 6.142

(a) who before 6th April 1979 was or, if both she and her husband had retired immediately before that date, would have been entitled under section 29(10)(a) of the Act (increase of a woman's Category B retirement pension where her husband deferred his retirement) to an increase of the weekly rate of her Category B retirement pension, and

(b) whose marriage has terminated on or after 6th April 1979,

the weekly rate of her Category B retirement pension or, where by virtue of section 9 or section 20 of the Pensions Act she has become entitled to a Category A retirement pension, the weekly rate of her Category A retirement pension shall be increased, with effect from the date on which this regulation comes into operation or of the said termination or, in the case of a Category A retirement pension, her retirement, whichever is the latest, by the amount by which her Category B retirement pension was, or would have been, increased under the said section 29(10)(a) together with any increase of that amount by virtue of section 124 of the Act (increase of rates of benefit).]

AMENDMENT

1. Social Security (Widow's Benefit, Retirement Pensions and other Benefits) (Transitional) Amendment Regulations 1981 (SI 1981/1627), reg 3, (December 14, 1981).

Provision relating to treatment of reckonable years

13.—(1) For the purposes of [1paragraph 5(2)(b) and (3)(b) and paragraph 5A(2)(b) of Schedule 3 to the 1992 Act] and Schedule 1 to the Social Security (Widow's Benefit and Retirement Pensions) Regulations 1979 any reckonable year or years shall be treated as a qualifying year or years. 6.143

(2) In this regulation " qualifying year" means a year in which a person's earnings factor is sufficient for satisfaction of paragraph (b) of the second contribution condition specified in paragraph 5(3) of Schedule 3 [1to the 1992 Act or paragraph (b) of the contribution condition specified in paragraph 5A(2) of that Schedule.]

AMENDMENT

1. Social Security (State Pension and National Insurance Credits) Regulations 2009 (SI 2009/2206) regs 16–22 (April 6, 2010).

Provision relating to Category B retirement pension for widowers

14.—The condition in section 8(1)(c) of the Pensions Act (that the deceased wife satisfied the contribution conditions in paragraph 5 of Schedule 3 to the Act) shall not be satisfied by virtue of any contributions 6.144

of a woman's former husband which were treated as her own by virtue of section 28(3) of, and Schedule 7 to, the Act or regulation 4(1) of, and the Schedule to, the Social Security (Benefit) (Married Women and Widows Special Provisions) Regulations 1974 as in force immediately before 6th April 1979.

Provision relating to widow's election to be treated as not having retired

6.145 **15.**—Where a woman who became entitled to a Category B retirement pension under section 29(4) of the Act before 6th April 1979, has, on or after that date, made an election under section 30(3) of the Act and has not revoked it then, for the purpose only of determining her right to increments under Schedule 1to the Pensions Act, her election shall be treated as if it took effect from 6th April 1975 or, if later, the date of the death of her husband by virtue of whose contributions she is so entitled.

Provision relating to increase under Schedule 1 to the Pensions Act of married woman's Category B retirement pension

6.146 **16.**—In relation to a woman who—

(a) attained pensionable age before 6th April 1979, and
(b) is married to a man who attained pensionable age before 6th April 1979, and
(c) on or after 6th April 1979 is entitled to a Category B retirement pension under section 29(2) or 29(3) of the Act,

regulation 4(1)(b)(i) of the Social Security (Widow's Benefit and Retirement Pensions) Regulations 1979 (days of deferred retirement not to be treated as days of increment when certain benefits have been received) shall not apply by reason only of the fact that the woman has received graduated retirement benefit by virtue of her having paid graduated contributions as an insured person.

[1Disapplication of section 1(1A) of the Administration Act for the purposes of widowed mother's allowance

6.147 **16A.**—Section 1(1A) of the Administration Act (requirement to state national insurance number) shall not apply to a child in respect of whom an increase of widowed mother's allowance is claimed.]

AMENDMENT

1. Social Security (National Insurance Number Information: Exemption) Regulations 1997 (SI 1997/2676) reg.15(3) (December 1, 1997).

Alternative benefit rights in place of widow's basic pension

6.148 **17.**—(1) Subject to regulation 2(2) where, immediately before 6th April 1975, a pre-1975 beneficiary was entitled to a widow's basic pension under the former principal Act, she shall be entitled, as from that date and until she either attains pensionable age and [1 is entitled to a Category A or Category B retirement pension], to a widow's pension under the Act as through she had been 40 years of age at her husband's death.

(2) A person entitled to a widow's pension by virtue of this regulation shall be treated as having not been so entitled immediately before attaining

pensionable age for the purposes of any regulations under the Act disqualifying a widow, not ordinarily resident in Great Britain, for receiving a retirement pension at a rate higher than the rate of widow's pension to which she was entitled immediately before attaining pensionable age.

AMENDMENT

1. Social Security (Abolition of Earnings Rule) (Consequential) Regulations (SI 1989/1642) reg.12(4) (October 1, 1989).

Alternative benefit rights in place of contributory old age pension

18.—(1) Subject to regulation 2(2)where, immediately before 6th April 1975, a pre-1975 beneficiary was entitled to a contributory old age pension under the former principal Act, such beneficiary shall, as from that date, be entitled— **6.149**

(a) if entitled to a contributory old age pension by virtue of his or her own insurance, to a Category A retirement pension;
(b) if she is a woman who was entitled to a contributory old age pension by virtue of her husband's insurance, to a Category B retirement pension;

and, in either case, the rate of retirement pension to which any such person becomes entitled on 6th April 1975 shall, subject to the provisions of *regulation 5*, be at the same rate as the contributory old age pension to which that person was entitled immediately before that date.

(2) [1. . .]

AMENDMENT

1. Social Security (Abolition of Earnings Rule) (Consequential) Regulations (SI 1989/1642) reg.12(4) (October 1, 1989).

Provision relating to widow's pension for certain widows incapable of self-support by reason of an infirmity

19.—(1) Where before 7th January 1957 a widow ceased to be entitled to a widow's benefit under the former principal Act and when she so ceased she was incapable of self-support by reason of an infirmity, she shall for any subsequent period during which she is under the age of 65 and is incapable of self-support by reason of that infirmity have the same right (if any) to a widow's pension in respect of the marriage in respect of which she was entitled to the widow's benefit as if she was over the age of 50 when her husband died. **6.150**

(2) [1 [2. . .]

AMENDMENTS

1. Social Security (Widow's Benefit, Retirement Pensions and other Benefits) (Transitional) Amendment Regulations 1981 (SI 1981/1627) regs 2, 3 (December 14, 1981).
2. Social Security Act 1998 (Commencement No. 9, and Savings and Consequential and Transitional Provisions) Order (SI 1999/2422) Sch.4 para.2 (September 6, 1999).

Revocations

20.—*Omitted.* **6.151**

SCHEDULE 1

ALTERNATIVE RIGHTS TO BENEFIT

6.152

Column (1)	**Column (2)**
Benefits under the former principal Act	**Benefits under the Act or the Pensions Act**
widowed mother's allowance	widowed mother's allowance
widow's pension	widow's pension
retirement pension by virtue of own insurance	Category A retirement pension
retirement pension by virtue of husband's insurance whilst husband alive	Category B retirement pension at the rate specified in paragraph 9 of Part I of Schedule 4 to the Act
retirement pension by virtue of husband's insurance and husband no longer alive	Category B retirement pension at the rate specified in section 6(1)(a) of the Pensions Act for the [1basic pension of a Category A retirement] pension
retirement pension for, or in respect of, person over pensionable age on 5th July 1948	Category C retirement pension at rate determined in accordance with section 39(2) of the Act
retirement pension for person over 80 years of age	Category D retirement pension
age addition	age addition
invalidity increase of retirement pension	invalidity increase of Category A retirement pension
widow's basic pension	widow's pension as provided for by regulation 17
contributory old age pension	Category A or B retirement pension as provided for by *regulation 18*
child's special allowance	child's special allowance
death grant	death grant
widow's pension by virtue of section 1(1) of the National Insurance Act 1970	benefit by virtue of section 39(4) of the Act corresponding to a widow's pension
widowed mother's allowance by virtue of the said section 1(1)	benefit by virtue of the said section 39(4) corresponding to a widowed mother's allowance

AMENDMENT

1. Social Security Act 1986 s.18(1) (April 6, 1987).

The Rate of Bereavement Benefits Regulations 2010

(SI 2010/2818)

ARRANGEMENT OF REGULATIONS

The Secretary of State makes the following Regulations in exercise of the powers conferred by sections 39(2A), 39C(1A), 122(1) and 175(1) of the Social Security Contributions and Benefits Act 1992.

The Social Security Advisory Committee has agreed that proposals in respect of these Regulations should not be referred to it.

Citation and commencement

1. These Regulations may be cited as the Rate of Bereavement Benefits Regulations 2010 and shall come into force on 1st January 2011. 6.154

Rate of widowed mother's allowance and widow's pension

2. The amount prescribed for the purposes of subsection (2A) of section 39 (rate of widowed mother's allowance and widow's pension) of the Social Security Contributions and Benefits Act 1992 is [[2] £148.40]. 6.155

Rate of widowed parent's allowance and bereavement allowance

3. The amount prescribed for the purposes of subsection (1A) of section 39C (rate of widowed parent's allowance [[1] . . .]) of the Social Security Contributions and Benefits Act 1992 is [[2] £148.40]. 6.156

AMENDMENTS

1. Pensions Act 2014 (Consequential, Supplementary and Incidental Amendments) Order (SI 2017/422) art.38 (April 6, 2017). There are saving provisions in arts 2 and 3 of this Order in respect of persons who would have been entitled to the benefits had a claim been made before that date.

2. Social Security Benefits Up-rating Order 2024 (SI 2024/242) art.18 (April 8, 2024).

The Marriage and Civil Partnership (Scotland) Act 2014 and Civil Partnership Act 2004 (Consequential Provisions and Modifications) Order 2014

(SI 2014/3229)

The Secretary of State makes the following Order in exercise of the powers conferred by sections 104, 112(1) and 113(2) to (5) and (7) of the Scotland Act 1998 and section 259(1) of the Civil Partnership Act 2004. In accordance with paragraphs 1, 2 and 3 of Schedule 7 to the Scotland Act 1998 and section 259(8) of the

Civil Partnership Act 2004, a draft of this Order has been laid before and approved by a resolution of each House of Parliament.

Part 1

Introduction

Citation and commencement

6.157 **1.—**(1) This Order may be cited as the Marriage and Civil Partnership (Scotland) Act 2014 and Civil Partnership Act 2004 (Consequential Provisions and Modifications) Order 2014.

(2) This Order comes into force on 16th December 2014.

Interpretation

6.158 **2.-** In this Order—

"the 1977 Act" means the Marriage (Scotland) Act 1977;

"the 1992 Act" means the Social Security Contributions and Benefits Act 1992;

"the 2004 Act" means the Gender Recognition Act 2004;

"the 2006 Act" means the Armed Forces Act 2006;

"the 2013 Act" means the Marriage (Same Sex Couples) Act 2013;

"the 2014 Act" means the Marriage and Civil Partnership (Scotland) Act 2014.

Extent

6.159 **3.**—(1) Articles 1 to 3, 7, 29, paragraph 15(7) and paragraph 16 of Schedule 5 extend to England and Wales, Scotland and Northern Ireland.

(2) Articles 12 to 28, paragraph 2(7) of Schedule 4 and paragraphs 15(1), (2), (3), (4) and 19 of Schedule 5 extend to England and Wales and Scotland only [[1] but see regulation 43(1) of the Marriage (Same-sex Couples) and Civil Partnership (Opposite-sex Couples) (Northern Ireland) Regulations 2019)].

(3) Paragraph 15(6) of Schedule 5 extends to England and Wales only.

(4) Articles 4, 5, 8 to 11, and Schedule 1, Schedule 2, Schedule 3, Schedule 4 (except as specified in paragraph (2) of this article), Schedule 5 (except as specified in paragraphs (1), (2) and (3) of this article) and Schedule 6 extend to Scotland only.

(5) Article 6 extends to Northern Ireland only.

Amendment

1. Marriage (Same-sex Couples) and Civil Partnership (Opposite-sex Couples) (Northern Ireland) Regulations 2019 (SI 2019/1514), reg.52 (January 13, 2020).

PART 2

CONSEQUENTIAL PROVISIONS

Omitted 6.160

PART 3

SCOTTISH SAME SEX MARRIAGE IN NORTHERN IRELAND

Omitted 6.161

PART 4

STATE PENSIONS

Articles 8, 9, 10 and 12 of this Order were revoked with effect from April 6, 2016 by Pensions Act (Consequential, Supplementary and Incidental Amendments) Order 2015 (SI 2015/1985) art.44. 6.162

Adult dependency increases

11.—(1) In a case where a full gender recognition certificate is issued to a person under the 2004 Act— 6.163

(a) section 83 of the 1992 Act (pension increase (wife)) does not cease to apply by virtue of the change of gender; and

(b) in the continued application of section 83 in such a case, references to a pension payable to a man, or references to his wife, are to be construed accordingly.

(2) In a case where a full gender recognition certificate is issued to a person under the 2004 Act—

(a) section 84 of the 1992 Act (pension increase (husband)) does not cease to apply by virtue of the change of gender; and

(b) in the continued application of section 84 in such a case, references to a pension payable to a woman, or references to her husband, are to be construed accordingly.

SCHEDULE 5

CONSEQUENTIAL MODIFICATIONS TO PRIMARY LEGISLATION

The relevant legislation is amended elsewhere in the volume 6.164

The Pensions Act 2014 (Commencement No.4) Order 2015

(SI 2015/134)

The Secretary of State for Work and Pensions makes the following Order in exercise of the powers conferred by section 56(1), (4) and (7) of the Pensions Act 2014.

Citation

6.165 **1.-** This Order may be cited as the Pensions Act 2014 (Commencement No.4) Order 2015.

Commencement of provisions

6.166 **2.—**(1) 5th February 2015 is the day appointed for the coming into force of the provisions of the Pensions Act 2014 listed in paragraph (4) for the purposes of making regulations.

(2) 23rd February 2015 is the day appointed for the coming into force of section 24(2) to (9) of, and Schedule 14 to, the Pensions Act 2014.

(3) 1st October 2015 is the day appointed for the coming into force of section 36 of the Pensions Act 2014.

(4) The provisions of the Pensions Act 2014 mentioned in paragraph (1) are—

(a) section 2(3);
(b) section 4(2);
(c) section 8(3), (7) and (8);
(d) section 16(1) and (6);
(e) section 17(4) and (5);
(f) section 18(1);
(g) section 19(1) and (3);
(h) section 22(1);
(i) paragraph 4 of Schedule 8 and section 13(2) in so far as it relates to that paragraph;
(j) paragraph 4 of Schedule 10 and section 14(2) in so far as it relates to that paragraph; and
(k) paragraph 11 of Schedule 11 and section 15 in so far as it relates to that paragraph.

General Note

6.167 This is the fourth Commencement Order made under the Pensions Act 2014. This Order brings into force provisions relating to the new state pension for people reaching pensionable age on or after 6th April 2016 (see Part 1 of that Act)and provisions relating to occupational pension schemes on short service benefits and on the abolition of contracting-out for salary related schemes. Article 2(1) and (4) brings provisions into force to enable the State Pensions Regulations 2015 (SI 2015/119) to be made. Those Regulations set out some of the detailed rules relating to the new state pension, in particular relating to prisoners, deferral of state pension, the minimum number of qualifying years and pension sharing on divorce or dissolution of a civil partnership. The provisions are brought into force on 5th February 2015 for the purposes of enabling the Regulations to be made. (Section 56(4) of the Pensions Act 2014 brings the provisions into force on 6th April 2016 for all other purposes – that is the date the new state pension is introduced.)

(SI 2015/134 reg.2)

Earlier commencement orders

The earlier commencement orders (bringing in provisions not relevant to the current year save for regulation powers) are SI 2014/1965 with effect from September 11, 2014 and SI 2014/2377 with effect from October 1, 2014. **6.168**

The State Pension Regulations 2015

(SI 2015/173)

ARRANGEMENT OF REGULATIONS

PART 1

GENERAL

PART 1A

PART 2

PRISONERS

PART 3

DEFERRAL OF STATE PENSION

PART 8

NATIONAL INSURANCE CREDITS

CHAPTER 1

GENERAL

CHAPTER 2

Crediting earnings or contributions in respect of a pre-commencement qualifying year

CHAPTER 3

Crediting earnings or contributions in respect of a qualifying year or a post-commencement qualifying year

SCHEDULE

The Secretary of State for Work and Pensions makes the following Regulations in exercise of the powers conferred by sections 55A(6) and 175(4) of the Social Security Contributions and Benefits Act 1992), sections 23(1)(a), (b)(ii) and (c)(i) and (2), 48(1)(f)(ii) and 49(4) and (4A) of the Welfare Reform and Pensions Act 1999) and sections 2(3), 4(2), 8(3), (7) and (8), 16(1) and (6), 17(4) and (5), 18(1), 19(1) and (3), 22(1) and 54(5) and (6) of, and paragraph 4 of Schedule 8 and paragraph 4 of Schedule 10 to, the Pensions Act 2014).

The Social Security Advisory Committee has agreed that the proposals in respect of Part 5 of these Regulations should not be referred to it).

The remainder of these Regulations have not been referred to the Social Security Advisory Committee because they are made before the end of the period of six months beginning with the coming into force of the provisions of the Pensions Act 2014 under which they are made).

In accordance with section 83(11) of the Welfare Reform and Pensions Act 1999, due to the exercise of powers to make regulations under Part 4 of that Act, the Secretary of State has consulted such persons as he considers appropriate about Part 5 of these Regulations).

A draft of these Regulations has been laid before Parliament in accordance with section 54(2)(a) of the Pensions Act 2014 and approved by a resolution of each House of Parliament.

GENERAL NOTE

6.170 The 2015 Regulations are modified to the extent necessary to give effect to a Convention on Social Security entered into on February 1, 2019, by the Government of the United Kingdom and the Government of Ireland (Article 2(1) of the Social Security (Ireland) Order 2019 (SI 2019/622). The Convention seeks to maintain, following the UK's departure from the European Union, certain UK social security entitlements of citizens of the Republic of Ireland. This includes rules for mutual recognition of social security contributions for the purposes of the state pension provided for by the Pensions Act 2014 and the 2015 Regulations.

PART 1

GENERAL

Citation, commencement, application and interpretation

6.171 **1.**—(1) These Regulations may be cited as the State Pension Regulations 2015.

(2) These Regulations come into force on 6th April 2016.

(3) These Regulations (except Part 5) do not apply to a person who reaches pensionable age before 6th April 2016.

[1 (4) In these Regulations—

"the 1965 Act" means the National Insurance Act 1965;

"the 2014 Act" means the Pensions Act 2014;

"deferral period" means the period during which a person's entitlement to a state pension under Part 1 of the 2014 Act is deferred;

"graduated retirement benefit" means any benefit under section 36 (graduated retirement benefit) or 37 (special provisions as to graduated retirement benefit for widows) of the 1965 Act.]

(5) For the purposes of these Regulations (except this paragraph), two people are to be treated as if they are not married to each other in relation to times when either of them is married to a third person.

AMENDMENT

1. State Pension Regulations 2015 (SI 2015/173) reg.2 (April 6, 2016).

[1 PART 1A

FULL RATE OF STATE PENSION

Full rate of state pension

6.172 **1A.** The full rate of the state pension for the purposes of section 3(1) of the 2014 Act (full rate of state pension) is [2 £221.20 per week.]

AMENDMENTS

1. State Pension (Amendment) Regulations 2016 (SI 2016/227) reg.2 (April 6, 2016).
2. The Social Security Benefits Up-rating Order 2024 (SI 2014/242) art.6(1) (April 8, 2024).

PART 2

PRISONERS

Prisoners who are not to be paid state pension

2.—(1) Subject to regulation 3, a person is not to be paid a state pension under Part 1 of the 2014 Act (state pension) for any period during which the person is a prisoner who is mentioned in paragraph (2). 6.173

(2) Except where paragraph (3) applies, a person is a prisoner for the purposes of paragraph (1) where the person is—

(a) a prisoner in Great Britain or elsewhere who is imprisoned or detained in legal custody in connection with, or as a result of, criminal proceedings;
(b) a prisoner in Great Britain or elsewhere who is unlawfully at large;
(c) a prisoner in Great Britain who is being detained—
 (i) under section 47 of the Mental Health Act 1983 (removal to hospital of persons serving sentences of imprisonment etc); and
 (ii) on or before the day which the Secretary of State certifies to be the person's release date (if any) within the meaning in section 50(3) of that Act;
(d) a prisoner in Great Britain who is being detained under section 136 of the Mental Health (Care and Treatment) (Scotland) Act 2003 (transfer of prisoners for treatment of mental disorder).

(3) Where a person outside Great Britain is a prisoner within paragraph (2)(a) or (b) and, in similar circumstances in Great Britain, the person would not have been a prisoner, the person is not a prisoner within paragraph (2)(a) or (b).

Paying state pension to persons who are remanded in custody

3.—(1) Where a person is remanded in custody for an offence, regulation 2(1) does not apply unless a sentence described in paragraph (2) is later imposed on the person for the offence. 6.174

(2) Subject to paragraph (3), the described sentences for the purposes of paragraph (1) are—

(a) a sentence of imprisonment or detention in legal custody as a result of criminal proceedings;
(b) a sentence of detention where the provisions mentioned in regulation 2(2)(c)(i) or (d) apply;
(c) a suspended sentence within the meaning in [1 section 286 of the Sentencing Code] (suspended sentences of imprisonment).

(3) A sentence described in paragraph (2)(a) which is imposed outside Great Britain is not a described sentence for the purposes of paragraph (1) if, in similar circumstances in Great Britain, a sentence described in paragraph (2)(a) would not have been imposed.

AMENDMENT

1. Sentencing Act 2020, Sch. 24, para. 427 (December 1, 2020).

PART 3

DEFERRAL OF STATE PENSION

When a choice of lump sum or survivor's pension may be made

6.175 **4.**—(1) Where a person falls within section 8(1) of the 2014 Act (choice of lump sum or survivor's pension under section 9 in certain cases), paragraphs (2) and (3) set out the period within which that person is to make any choice under section 8(2) of that Act to be paid—

(a) a lump sum under section 8 of that Act; or

(b) a state pension under section 9 of that Act (survivor's pension based on inheritance of deferred old state pension).

(2) Where the Secretary of State has issued a notice which confirms that the person may make the choice, the period is three months starting on the date in that notice (or, where there is more than one notice which confirms that the person may make that choice, the date in the most recent such notice).

(3) Where the person makes the choice before the Secretary of State has issued any such notice, the period—

(a) starts on the later of the date—

(i) the person claims a state pension; or

(ii) the person's spouse or civil partner died; and

(b) ends on the date the person makes the choice.

(4) A person may make a late choice after the period set out in this regulation in circumstances where—

(a) the Secretary of State considers it is reasonable in any particular case; and

(b) any amount paid by way of (or on account of) a lump sum under section 8(4) of the 2014 Act has been repaid to the Secretary of State—

(i) in full; and

(ii) in the currency in which that amount was originally paid.

(5) The amount of any lump sum to be paid to the person under section 8(4) is reduced to nil where the person makes a late choice under paragraph (4) to be paid a state pension under section 9 of the 2014 Act.

How a choice of lump sum or survivor's pension may be made

6.176 **5.**—(1) Where a person falls within section 8(1) of the 2014 Act, this regulation sets out the manner in which that person is to make any choice under section 8(2) of that Act to be paid—

(a) a lump sum under section 8 of that Act; or

(b) a state pension under section 9 of that Act.

(2) The manner is—

(a) in writing to an office which is specified to the person in writing by the Secretary of State as accepting any such choice; or

(b) by telephone to a telephone number which is specified to the person in writing by the Secretary of State as accepting any such choice.

(3) The person must use the manner set out in paragraph (2)(a) where the Secretary of State directs in any particular case that that manner must be used.

Changing a choice of lump sum or survivor's pension

6.—(1) Any choice under section 8(2) of the 2014 Act to be paid— 6.177

(a) a lump sum under section 8 of that Act; or

(b) a state pension under section 9 of that Act,

may be altered in the circumstances specified in paragraph (2).

(2) The circumstances referred to in paragraph (1) are—

(a) the person who made the choice has not subsequently died;

(b) an application is made to alter the choice;

(c) the application is made within—

(i) the period of three months starting on the date in the notification issued by the Secretary of State which confirms the choice that has been made; or

(ii) such longer period as the Secretary of State considers reasonable in any particular case;

(d) the application is made in the manner set out in—

(i) regulation 5(2)(a), where the Secretary of State directs in any particular case that the manner in regulation 5(2)(a) must be used; or

(ii) regulation 5(2)(a) or (b), in all other cases;

(e) where the application is to alter the choice so that it becomes a choice to be paid a state pension under section 9 of the 2014 Act, any amount paid by way of (or on account of) a lump sum under section 8 of the 2014 Act has been repaid to the Secretary of State—

(i) in full;

(ii) within the period mentioned in sub-paragraph (c); and

(iii) in the currency in which that amount was originally paid;

(f) where the application is to alter the choice so that it becomes a choice to be paid a lump sum under section 8 of the 2014 Act, any amount paid by way of (or on account of) a state pension under section 9 of the 2014 Act would be less than the amount which would be paid as a lump sum under section 8 of the 2014 Act;

(g) no previous alteration has been made under this regulation in respect of the same deferral mentioned in section 8(1)(c) of the 2014 Act; and

(h) the choice has not been treated as made under regulation 30(5G) [[1] or (5H)] of the Social Security (Claims and Payments) Regulations 1987 (payments on death).

(3) Where the circumstance in paragraph (2)(f) applies, any amount paid by way of (or on account of) a state pension under section 9 of the 2014 Act in respect of the deferral mentioned in section 8(1)(c) of the 2014 Act for which the choice was originally made is to be treated as having been paid on account of the lump sum to be paid under section 8 of the 2014 Act.

AMENDMENT

1. Pensions Act (Consequential, Supplementary and Incidental Amendments) Order 2015 (SI 2015/1985) art.45 (April 6, 2016).

How entitlement to a state pension may be suspended

6.178 **7.**—(1) A person who has become entitled to a state pension under Part 1 of the 2014 Act may opt to suspend their entitlement if they give notice to the Secretary of State.

(2) The manner in which the notice must be given is—

(a) in writing to an office which is specified to the person in writing by the Secretary of State as accepting any such notice; or

(b) by telephone to a telephone number which is specified to the person in writing by the Secretary of State as accepting any such notice.

(3) But the person must use the manner set out in paragraph (2)(a) where the Secretary of State directs in any particular case that that manner must be used.

Date from which a suspension of a state pension begins

6.179 **8.**—(1) Where a person exercises their option to suspend their entitlement to a state pension under Part 1 of the 2014 Act, the suspension takes effect from the date set out in this regulation.

(2) The date is any date which the person specifies that is—

(a) not before the date on which the option was exercised; and

(b) not after 28 days starting with the date on which the option was exercised.

(3) Where the person does not specify a date in accordance with paragraph (2), the date is the date on which the option was exercised.

Cancelling a suspension of a state pension

6.180 **9.**—(1) Where a person has opted to suspend their entitlement to a state pension under Part 1 of the 2014 Act, the person may cancel the exercise of that option in relation to the whole of, or part of, a past period referred to in paragraph (3).

(2) The person cancels the suspension by making a claim for their state pension whilst their state pension is suspended.

(3) The past period mentioned in paragraph (1) is any period of up to 12 months before the date on which the person cancels the suspension.

Percentage for the weekly rate of increases resulting from deferral of state pension

6.181 **10.** For the purposes of section 17(4) of the 2014 Act (effect of pensioner postponing or suspending state pension), the specified percentage is one-ninth of 1%.

Days which are not included in determining the period of deferral

6.182 **11.**—(1) In the circumstances set out in paragraph (2), a day does not count in determining a number of whole weeks for the purposes of section 17(3) of the 2014 Act.

(2) The circumstances mentioned in paragraph (1) are where the day is—

(a) a day on which the person whose entitlement to a state pension under Part 1 of the 2014 Act is deferred has received any of the following benefits—

(i) state pension credit under section 1 of the State Pension Credit Act 2002 (entitlement to state pension credit);

(ii) income support under section 124 of the Contributions and Benefits Act (income support);
(iii) an income-related employment and support allowance (which means an income-related allowance under Part 1 of the Welfare Reform Act 2007 (employment and support allowance);
(iv) an income-based jobseeker's allowance within the meaning in section 1(4) of the Jobseekers Act 1995 (the jobseeker's allowance);
(v) universal credit under Part 1 of the Welfare Reform Act 2012 (universal credit);
(vi) a carer's allowance under section 70 of the Contributions and Benefits Act (carer's allowance);
[[1](via) carer support payment under the Carer's Assistance (Carer's Support Payment) (Scotland) Regulations 2023 ("carer support payment");]
(vii) an unemployability supplement within the meaning in regulation 2(1) of the Social Security (Overlapping Benefits) Regulations 1979 (interpretation);
(viii) severe disablement allowance under section 68 of the Contributions and Benefits Act (entitlement and rate of severe disablement allowance);
(ix) a widow's pension under section 39 of the Contributions and Benefits Act (rate of widowed mother's allowance and widow's pension);
(x) a widowed mother's allowance under section 37 of the Contributions and Benefits Act (widowed mother's allowance);
(xi) incapacity benefit under section 30A of the Contributions and Benefits Act (incapacity benefit: entitlement);

(b) a day on which a person—
(i) has received an increase of any of the benefits mentioned in sub-paragraph (a) in respect of the person whose entitlement to a state pension under Part 1 of the 2014 Act is deferred; and
(ii) is married to, in a civil partnership with or residing with the person whose entitlement to a state pension under Part 1 of the 2014 Act is deferred; or

(c) a day on which the person whose entitlement to a state pension under Part 1 of the 2014 Act is deferred would not, if their entitlement was not deferred, be paid that state pension because they were a prisoner (see section 19 of the 2014 Act (prisoners) and regulations 2 and 3).

AMENDMENT

1. Carer's Assistance (Carer Support Payment) (Scotland) Regulations 2023 (Consequential Amendments) Order 2023 (SI 2023/1218) art.27(2) (November 19, 2023).

Part weeks treated as whole weeks in determining the amount of entitlement during deferral

12.—(1) In the circumstances set out in paragraph (2), a part of a week is to be treated as a whole week for the purposes of section 17(3) of the 2014 Act. **6.183**

(2) The circumstances mentioned in paragraph (1) are where there is a part of a week in the total period during which the person's entitlement to a state pension was deferred, after any days have been discounted under regulation 11.

[1 Modification of the amount of an increment for other cases during deferral

6.184 **12A.**—(1) Subject to regulation 23, this regulation applies in cases where, at any time in the deferral period, the weekly rate of the person's state pension, had the person's entitlement not been deferred, would have changed otherwise than because of an up-rating increase ("a non-uprating change").

(2) Section 17(4) of the 2014 Act (amount of an increment for pensioner postponing or suspending state pension) is modified to provide that the amount of an increment for each modification period is equal to a percentage specified in regulations of the weekly rate of the state pension to which the person, if their entitlement had not been deferred, would have been entitled immediately before the end of the modification period.

(3) The first modification period begins at the start of the deferral period and ends immediately before the date of the first or only non-uprating change.

(4) Further modification periods begin on the date of the most recent or only non-uprating change and end—

(a) immediately before the end of the deferral period, where there is no subsequent non-uprating change; or

(b) immediately before the date of the subsequent non-uprating change, where there is a subsequent non-uprating change.]

AMENDMENT

1. State Pension and Occupational Pension Schemes (Miscellaneous Amendments) Regulations 2016 (SI 2016/199) reg.3 (April 6, 2016).

PART 4

MINIMUM QUALIFYING PERIOD

Minimum number of qualifying years

6.185 **13.**—(1) For the purposes of section 2(3) of the 2014 Act (entitlement to state pension at full or reduced rate), the minimum number of qualifying years(**a**) for a state pension payable at the reduced rate is ten.

(2) For the purposes of section 4(2) of the 2014 Act (entitlement to a state pension at transitional rate), the minimum number of qualifying years for a state pension payable at the transitional rate is ten.

PART 5

AMENDMENTS TO OTHER LEGISLATION

Sharing of state pension scheme rights

6.186 **14.** The Schedule to these Regulations (which makes amendments relating to the sharing of state pension rights) has effect.

[1 PART 6

GRADUATED RETIREMENT BENEFIT

Survivor's state pension based on inheritance of graduated retirement benefit

15.—(1) A person whose dead spouse or civil partner paid graduated contributions as an insured person is entitled to a state pension in accordance with this regulation. 6.187

(2) Such a person is entitled to a state pension if—

(a) that person has reached pensionable age;

(b) that person's spouse died while they were married or that person's civil partner died while they were civil partners of each other;

(c) the marriage took place, or the civil partnership was formed, before 6th April 2016; and

(d) that person is entitled to an inherited amount under regulation 16(1), (2) or (3).

(3) A state pension under this regulation is payable at a weekly rate equal to the inherited amount determined in accordance with regulation 16(4) to (6).

(4) The rate of the state pension for a person under this regulation is to be increased from time to time in accordance with regulation 17.]

AMENDMENT

1. State Pension and Occupational Pension Schemes (Miscellaneous Amendments) Regulations 2016 (SI 2016/199) reg.4 (April 6, 2016).

[1 Survivor's state pension under regulation 15: inherited amount

16.—(1) For the purposes of regulation 15(2)(d), a person is entitled to an inherited amount if— 6.188

(a) their spouse or civil partner died before 6th April 2016;

(b) they were under pensionable age when their spouse or civil partner died; and

(c) they have not married or formed a civil partnership after the death and before the time they reach pensionable age.

(2) For the purposes of regulation 15(2)(d), a person is entitled to an inherited amount if—

(a) their spouse or civil partner reached pensionable age before 6th April 2016 but died on or after 6th April 2016;

(b) they were under pensionable age when their spouse or civil partner died; and

(c) they have not married or formed a civil partnership after the death and before the time they reach pensionable age.

(3) For the purposes of regulation 15(2)(d), a person is entitled to an inherited amount if—

(a) their spouse or civil partner reached pensionable age before 6th April 2016 but died on or after 6th April 2016; and

(b) they were over pensionable age when their spouse or civil partner died.

(4) The inherited amount is half of the weekly rate of the deceased spouse's or civil partner's graduated retirement benefit, determined in

accordance with paragraph (5), on the date referred to in paragraph (6) (whether or not the deceased was receiving, or entitled to receive, any such benefit).

(5) The determination for the purposes of paragraph (4) is carried out by—

(a) taking the weekly rate of graduated retirement benefit appropriate to the amount of graduated contributions paid by the deceased;

(b) determining that weekly rate as if any provisions in orders under section 150 of the Administration Act (annual up-rating of benefits) (**a**) which—

(i) increase that weekly rate; and

(ii) have come into force since the date of the deceased's death, had come into force before that date; and

(c) excluding any addition under—

(i) section 36(4) of the 1965 Act; or

(ii) section 37(1) of that Act.

(6) The date mentioned in paragraph (4) is—

(a) where the person falls within paragraph (1) or (2), the date on which the person reaches pensionable age; or

(b) where the person falls within paragraph (3), the date on which the person's spouse or civil partner died.]

AMENDMENT

1. State Pension and Occupational Pension Schemes (Miscellaneous Amendments) Regulations 2016 (SI 2016/199) reg.4 (April 6, 2016).

[[1] Survivor's state pension under regulation 15: up-rating

6.189 **17.**—(1) The rate of a person's state pension under regulation 15 is to be increased as follows.

(2) In this regulation, a reference to the rate of a person's state pension is to the rate—

(a) without any reduction under Regulations made under section 7(4) (survivor's pension based on inheritance of additional old state pension) of the 2014 Act (in the case of a state pension under section 7 of the 2014 Act);

(b) taking into account any reduction under section 14 (pension sharing: reduction in the sharer's section 4 pension) of the 2014 Act (in the case of a state pension under section 4 of the 2014 Act); and

(c) without any increase under section 17 of the 2014 Act.

(3) The rate of the person's state pension is increased in accordance with paragraph (4) where—

(a) that rate, when added to the sum of the rate of any state pension to which the person is entitled under section 7 and section 2, 4 or 12 of the 2014 Act (entitlement to state pension at various rates), is equal to or less than the full rate of the state pension; and

(b) the full rate of the state pension is increased at any time.

(4) Where paragraph (3) applies—

(a) the rate of the person's state pension is increased by the same percentage as the increase in the full rate; and

(b) that increase of the person's state pension is to be made at the same time as the increase in the full rate.

(5) The rate of the person's state pension is increased in accordance with either or both of paragraphs (6) and (7) where—

(a) both—

(i) that rate, when added to the sum of the rate of any state pension to which the person is entitled under section 7 and section 2, 4 or 12 of the 2014 Act, exceeds the full rate of the state pension; and

(ii) the sum of the rate of any state pension to which the person is entitled under section 7 and section 2, 4 or 12 of the 2014 Act is less than the full rate of the state pension; and

(b) either or both of the following occurs at any time—

(i) the full rate of the state pension is increased;

(ii) an uprating order comes into force.

(6) Where paragraph (5)(a) and (b)(i) applies, the rate of the person's state pension is increased—

(a) by an amount equal to the appropriate percentage of the shortfall immediately before the full rate of the state pension is increased ("the appropriate percentage" means the percentage by which the full rate is increased); and

(b) at the same time as paragraph (5)(b)(i) applies.

(7) Where paragraph (5)(a) and (b)(ii) applies, the rate of the person's state pension is increased—

(a) by an amount equal to the appropriate percentage of the excess immediately before the uprating order mentioned in paragraph (5)(b)(ii) comes into force ("the appropriate percentage" means the percentage specified in that uprating order); and

(b) at the same time as that uprating order comes into force.

(8) The rate of the person's state pension is increased in accordance with paragraph (9) where—

(a) the sum of the rate of any state pension to which the person is entitled under section 7 and section 2, 4 or 12 of the 2014 Act is equal to or higher than the full rate of the state pension; and

(b) an uprating order comes into force at any time.

(9) Where paragraph (8) applies—

(a) the rate of the person's state pension is increased by the percentage specified in the uprating order mentioned in paragraph (8)(b); and

(b) that increase of the person's state pension is to be made at the same time as that uprating order comes into force.

(10) In this regulation—

"the excess" means the amount by which the rate of the state pension, when added to the sum of the rate of any state pension to which the person is entitled under section 7 and section 2, 4 or 12 of the 2014 Act, exceeds the full rate;

"the shortfall" means the amount by which the sum of the rate of any state pension to which the person is entitled under section 7 and section 2, 4 or 12 of the 2014 Act, is less than the full rate;

"uprating order" means an order under section 151A of the Administration Act (uprating of transitional state pensions under the 2014 Act).]

AMENDMENT

1. State Pension and Occupational Pension Schemes (Miscellaneous Amendments) Regulations 2016 (SI 2016/199) reg.4 (April 6, 2016).

[1 Choice of lump sum or state pension based on inheritance of deferred graduated retirement benefit

6.190 **18.**—(1) Subject to paragraph (8), a person is entitled to a choice under this regulation if—

(a) that person has reached pensionable age;

(b) that person's spouse died while they were married or that person's civil partner died while they were civil partners of each other;

(c) the spouse's or civil partner's entitlement to graduated retirement benefit was deferred at the time of death and throughout the period of 12 months ending with the day before the death; and

(d) either—

(i) that person was under pensionable age when the spouse or civil partner died and did not marry or form a civil partnership between the date of death and the date that person reached pensionable age; or

(ii) that person was over pensionable age when the spouse or civil partner died.

(2) The person may choose to be paid—

(a) a lump sum under regulation 19; or

(b) a state pension under regulation 20.

(3) The manner in which that choice is to be made is the manner set out in regulation 5(2) and (3).

(4) The period within which that choice is to be made is the period set out in regulation 4(2) and (3) and a person may make a late choice after that period where—

(a) the Secretary of State considers it is reasonable in any particular case; and

(b) any amount paid by way of (or on account of) a lump sum under regulation 19 has been repaid to the Secretary of State—

(i) in full; and

(ii) in the currency in which that amount was originally paid.

(5) Where the person fails to make a choice within the period set out in regulation 4(2) and (3), they are to be paid a lump sum under regulation 19.

(6) The amount of any lump sum to be paid to the person under regulation 19 is reduced to nil where the person makes a late choice under paragraph (4) to be paid a state pension under regulation 20.

(7) A choice under this regulation may be altered in the circumstances specified in regulation 6(2), and for that purpose—

(a) regulation 6(3) applies where the circumstance in regulation 6(2)(f) applies;

(b) any references in regulation 6(2) and (3) to section 8 of the 2014 Act are to be read as references to regulation 19; and

(c) any references in regulation 6(2) and (3) to section 9 of the 2014 Act are to be read as references to regulation 20.

(8) A person is not entitled to a choice under this regulation if they are entitled to a choice under section 8(2) of the 2014 Act.

(9) Where paragraph (1) applies to a person and that person makes a choice under—

(a) section 8(2)(a) of the 2014 Act, they are to be paid a lump sum under regulation 19 (subject to paragraph (10));

(b) section 8(2)(b) of the 2014 Act, they are to be paid a state pension under regulation 20 (subject to paragraph (10)).

(10) Where paragraph (1) applies to a person and that person alters a choice under regulation 6—

(a) they are to be paid a lump sum under regulation 19 where their new choice is to be paid a lump sum under section 8 of the 2014 Act;

(b) they are to be paid a state pension under regulation 20 where their new choice is to be paid a state pension under section 9 of the 2014 Act.

(11) Where paragraph (1) applies to a person and that person fails to make a choice under section 8(2) of the 2014 Act, they are to be paid a lump sum under regulation 19.]

AMENDMENT

1. State Pension and Occupational Pension Schemes (Miscellaneous Amendments) Regulations 2016 (SI 2016/199) reg.4 (April 6, 2016).

[1 Survivor's lump sum based on inheritance of deferred graduated retirement benefit

19.—(1) Where a person is to be paid a lump sum by virtue of regulation 18, they are entitled to a lump sum calculated in accordance with paragraph 10 or, where appropriate, paragraph 20 of Schedule 1 to the Social Security (Graduated Retirement Benefit) Regulations 2005. 6.191

(2) In paragraphs 10(6) and 20(6) of Schedule 1 to those Regulations as they apply for the purposes of this regulation, the references to the date on which the person becomes entitled to a Category A or Category B retirement pension or to graduated retirement benefit are to be read as a reference to the date on which the person becomes entitled to make a choice under regulation 18.]

AMENDMENT

1. State Pension and Occupational Pension Schemes (Miscellaneous Amendments) Regulations 2016 (SI 2016/199) reg.4 (April 6, 2016).

[1 Survivor's state pension based on inheritance of deferred graduated retirement benefit

20.—(1) A person is entitled to a state pension under this regulation if— 6.192

(a) that person has reached pensionable age;

(b) that person's spouse died while they were married or that person's civil partner died while they were civil partners of each other;

(c) either—

(i) that person was under pensionable age when the spouse or civil partner died and did not marry or form a civil partnership between the date of death and the date that person reached pensionable age; or

(ii) that person was over pensionable age when the spouse or civil partner died;

(d) either—

(i) that person's spouse or civil partner was entitled to an increase in graduated retirement benefit; or

(ii) that person's spouse's or civil partner's entitlement to graduated retirement benefit was deferred when the spouse or civil partner died;

(e) in the case of a person entitled to a choice under regulation 18, that person has chosen to be paid a state pension under this regulation; and

(f) in the case of a person who is not entitled to a choice under regulation 18 because regulation 18(8) applies to them, that person is to be paid a state pension under this regulation by virtue of regulation 18(9)(b) or (10)(b).

(2) Subject to paragraph (3), a state pension under this regulation is payable at a weekly rate equal to half of the weekly rate of—v

(a) the deceased spouse's or civil partner's increase in graduated retirement benefit; or

(b) where the deceased spouse's or civil partner's entitlement to graduated retirement benefit was deferred when they died, the increase in graduated retirement benefit, determined in accordance with paragraph (4), that would have been payable if the deferral had ended immediately before their death.

(3) For the purposes of paragraph (2), if at any time an order under section 151A of the Administration Act comes into force, the rate of the person's state pension under this regulation is increased (at that time) by the percentage specified in the order.

(4) For the purposes of paragraph (2), the increase is to be determined as if—

(a) any provisions in orders under section 150 of the Administration Act which—

(i) increase the weekly rate of the graduated retirement benefit; and

(ii) have come into force between the date of the deceased's death and the date on which the person reaches pensionable age, had come into force before the date of death; and

(b) the weekly rate of the deceased spouse's or civil partner's increase did not include any addition under section 37(1) of the 1965 Act.

(5) In this regulation, "increase in graduated retirement benefit" means an increase determined in accordance with section 36(4) of the 1965 Act.]

AMENDMENT

1. State Pension and Occupational Pension Schemes (Miscellaneous Amendments) Regulations 2016 (SI 2016/199) reg.4 (April 6, 2016).

PART 7

OVERSEAS RESIDENTS

Entitlement to state pension for overseas residents

6.193 **21.**—(1) An overseas resident who is entitled to a state pension under Part 1 of the 2014 Act is not entitled to up-rating increases in accordance with this regulation.

(2) This regulation—

(a) applies in relation to an up-rating increase if Regulations are made—

(i) in consequence of an order under section 150A (annual up-rating) or 151A of the Administration Act or in consequence of any other legislation; and

(ii) which provide that this regulation applies to that up-rating increase; and

(b) is subject to the Regulations made as mentioned in sub-paragraph (a).

(3) Paragraph (4) applies in a case where—

(a) a person's entitlement to a state pension under Part 1 of the 2014 Act has been deferred for a period; and

(b) when the deferral period ends, that person is—

(i) entitled to a state pension under Part 1 of the 2014 Act; and

(ii) an overseas resident.

(4) Where this paragraph applies, the person mentioned in paragraph (3) is not entitled to any up-rating increases—

(a) in respect of the deferral period if—

(i) the person was an overseas resident at the time of that increase; and

(ii) the person continued to be an overseas resident until the deferral period ended; and

(b) after the deferral period ended if the person is an overseas resident at the time of that increase.

(5) In all other cases, a person is not entitled to up-rating increases where, immediately before the up-rating increase comes into force, they were—

(a) entitled to a state pension under Part 1 of the 2014 Act; and

(b) an overseas resident.

(6) For the purposes of sections 18(4) and 20(2) and (3) of the 2014 Act, the territory specified is any part of the Channel Islands which is not subject to an Order made under section 179 of the Administration Act.]

AMENDMENT

1. State Pension and Occupational Pension Schemes (Miscellaneous Amendments) Regulations 2016 (SI 2016/199) reg.4 (April 6, 2016).

GENERAL NOTE

Regulation 3 of the Social Security Benefits Up-rating Regulations 2024 (SI 2014/386) applies reg.21 to any up-rating increase as defined in s.22(1) of the Pensions Act 2014. Each year's up-rating regulations invariably include this provision. 6.194

Modification of the amount of an increment for an overseas resident

22.—(1) Subject to regulation 23, this regulation applies in cases where, during any part of the deferral period, a person has been an overseas resident. 6.195

(2) For any part of the deferral period during which the person was an overseas resident and was not in Great Britain or a territory specified in regulation 21(6), section 17(4) of the 2014 Act is modified to provide that the amount of an increment is equal to a percentage specified in regulations of the weekly rate of the state pension to which the person would have been entitled immediately before the start of that part of the deferral period if the person's entitlement had not been deferred.

(3) For any part of the deferral period during which the person was not an overseas resident, section 17(4) of the 2014 Act is modified to provide that the amount of an increment is equal to a specified percentage of the weekly rate of the state pension to which the person would have been

entitled immediately before the end of that part of the deferral period if the person's entitlement had not been deferred.]

AMENDMENT

1. State Pension and Occupational Pension Schemes (Miscellaneous Amendments) Regulations 2016 (SI 2016/199) reg.4 (April 6, 2016).

Modification of the amount of an increment where regulations 12A and 22 both apply

6.196 **23.**—(1) This regulation applies in a case where section 17(4) of the 2014 Act falls to be modified under both regulations 12A and 22 at the same time.

(2) Section 17(4) of the 2014 Act is modified to provide that the amount of an increment is determined as set out in the following paragraphs.

(3) The amount of the increment is first determined in accordance with the modifications set out in regulation 22.

(4) The amount of the increment is then determined in accordance with the modifications set out in regulation 12A as if the reference in regulation 12A(2) to the weekly rate of the state pension were a reference to the weekly rate referred to in—

(a) regulation 22(2), for any part of the deferral period during which the person was an overseas resident and was not in Great Britain or a territory specified in regulation 21(6); and

(b) regulation 22(3), for any part of the deferral period during which the person was not an overseas resident.

(5) Any increase or decrease of the increment as determined in accordance with paragraph (4) is then added to, or subtracted from, the amount of the increment as determined in accordance with paragraph (3).]

AMENDMENT

1. State Pension and Occupational Pension Schemes (Miscellaneous Amendments) Regulations 2016 (SI 2016/199) reg.4 (April 6, 2016).

[1 PART 8

NATIONAL INSURANCE CREDITS

CHAPTER 1

GENERAL

Interpretation

6.197 **24.**—(1) In this Part—

"the 1975 Regulations" means the Social Security (Credits) Regulations 1975;

"the 1992 Act" means the Social Security Contributions and Benefits Act 1992;

"the 2012 Act" means the Welfare Reform Act 2012;

"post-commencement qualifying year" and "pre-commencement qualifying year" have the same meaning as in section 4(4) of the 2014 Act;

"qualifying year" has the same meaning as in section 2(4) of the 2014 Act;

"working tax credit" means a working tax credit under section 10 of the Tax Credits Act 2002;

"year" means a tax year.

(2) Nothing in Chapter 3 is to be construed as entitling any person to be credited with earnings or contributions for any day or in respect of any event occurring before 6th April 2016.

General provisions relating to the crediting of earnings or contributions

25.—(1) For the purposes of Part 1 of the 2014 Act— **6.198**

(a) Chapter 2 makes provision for crediting earnings or contributions in respect of a pre-commencement qualifying year;

(b) Chapter 3 makes provision for crediting earnings or contributions in respect of a qualifying year or a post-commencement qualifying year.

(2) Where under this Part a person would, but for this paragraph, be entitled to be credited with any earnings or contributions for a year, or in respect of any week in a year, that person is only to be credited to the extent necessary to make that year a qualifying year.

(3) Where under this Part a person is entitled to be credited with earnings or a contribution in respect of a week that falls partly in one tax year and partly in another, that week is to be treated as falling in the year in which it begins and not in the following year.

GENERAL NOTE

Part 6 of the Regulations is in effect a partial code for dealing with all contributions credits entitlement issues in connection with pension claims arising on or after April 6, 2016. Note that Chapter 2 deals with years before that date, while Chapter 3 deals with years after that date. Both Chapter 2 (reg.26) and Chapter 3 (reg.29) keep in being provisions of the Social Security (Credits) Regulations 1975 (above in this volume). But they do not do so in entirety, with some of the regulations being rewritten by these provisions while others are accepted without change. **6.199**

CHAPTER 2

Crediting earnings or contributions in respect of a pre-commencement qualifying year

Credits under the 1975 Regulations

26. A person is to be credited with the earnings or contributions to which the person would have been entitled under the 1975 Regulations for the purposes of entitlement to a Category A retirement pension had— **6.200**

(a) the amendment made by paragraph 55 of Schedule 12 to the 2014 Act (which limits Category A retirement pensions to people who reach pensionable age before 6th April 2016) not come into force, and

(b) the person attained pensionable age on 6th April 2016.

Credits for parents and carers

6.201 **27.** A person is to be credited with a Class 3 contribution to which the person would have been entitled under section 23A of the 1992 Act (contributions credits for relevant parents and carers), or regulations made under that section, for the purposes of entitlement to a Category A retirement pension had—

(a) the amendment made by paragraph 55 of Schedule 12 to the 2014 Act (which limits Category A retirement pensions to people who reach pensionable age before 6th April 2016) not come into force, and

(b) the person attained pensionable age on 6th April 2016.

Credits for spouses and civil partners of members of Her Majesty's forces

6.202 **28.**—(1) Subject to paragraph (5), a person who satisfies the conditions in paragraph (2) for any part of a week to which this regulation applies is to be credited with a Class 3 contribution in respect of that week.

(2) The conditions are that the person—

(a) is a spouse or civil partner of a member of Her Majesty's forces, or is treated as such by the Secretary of State for the purposes of occupying accommodation, and

(b) is accompanying the member of Her Majesty's forces on an assignment outside the United Kingdom, or is treated as such by the Secretary of State.

(3) This regulation applies to a week which falls within a year beginning on or after 6th April 1975 and ending before 6th April 2016 for which the earnings factors of the member of Her Majesty's forces exceed the qualifying earnings factor.

(4) Paragraph (1) does not apply to—

(a) a person in respect of a week in which the person is entitled to be credited with earnings under—

(i) regulation 7A (credits for carer's allowance [1 or carer support payment]),

(ii) regulation 8A (credits for unemployment),

(iii) regulation 8B (credits for incapacity for work or limited capability for work), or

(iv) regulation 9E (credits for certain spouses and civil partners of members of Her Majesty's forces), of the 1975 Regulations; or

(b) a woman in respect of a week in any part of which an election made by her under regulations under section 19(4) of the 1992 Act (reduced rate election for married women) is in force.

(5) A person is not entitled to be credited with a Class 3 contribution under paragraph (1) unless an application to be so credited is received by the Secretary of State in accordance with paragraph (6).

(6) An application under paragraph (5) may only be made in respect of a past period and must—

(a) be on a form approved by the Secretary of State, or made in such manner as the Secretary of State accepts as sufficient in the circumstances, and

(b) include such information as may be specified by the Secretary of State or the Commissioners for Her Majesty's Revenue and Customs.

AMENDMENT

1. Carer's Assistance (Carer Support Payment) (Scotland) Regulations 2023 (Consequential Amendments) Order 2023 (SI 2023/1218) art.27(3) (November 19, 2023).

CHAPTER 3

Crediting earnings or contributions in respect of a qualifying year or a post-commencement qualifying year

Credits under the 1975 Regulations

29.—(1) Where a person is credited with earnings or contributions under the provisions of the 1975 Regulations specified in paragraph (2), the person is also to be credited with those earnings or contributions for the purposes of Part 1 of the 2014 Act. 6.203

(2) The provisions specified are—

(a) regulation 7 (credits for approved training);

(b) regulation 7A (credits for carer's allowance [1 or carer support payment]);

(c) regulation 7B (credits for disability element of working tax credit);

(d) regulation 8A (credits for unemployment);

(e) regulation 8B (credits for incapacity for work or limited capability for work);

(f) regulation 9B (credits for jury service);

(g) regulation 9C (credits for maternity pay etc.);

(h) regulation 9D (credits for certain periods of imprisonment or detention in legal custody);

(i) regulation 9E (credits for certain spouses and civil partners of members of Her Majesty's forces).

AMENDMENT

1. Carer's Assistance (Carer Support Payment) (Scotland) Regulations 2023 (Consequential Amendments) Order 2023 (SI 2023/1218) art.27(4) (November 19, 2023).

Credits for persons in receipt of working tax credit

30.—(1) Where working tax credit is paid to a person in respect of a week in which the person is— 6.204

(a) an employed earner,

(b) a self-employed earner whose profits for the year are below the small profits threshold specified by [1 section 11(4)(b)] of the 1992 Act, who would otherwise [2...[1 be treated as having actually paid,] a Class 2 contribution, or

(c) excepted from [2 being treated as having actually paid] a Class 2 contribution by virtue of regulation 43 of the Social Security (Contributions) Regulations 2001, the person is to be credited with earnings equal to the lower earnings limit then in force in respect of that week.

(2) Where working tax credit is paid in respect of a couple, the reference in paragraph (1) to the person in respect of whom working tax credit is paid is a reference to —

(a) where only one member of the couple is assessed for the purposes of the award of working tax credit as having income consisting of earnings, that member, or

(b) where the earnings of each member are assessed, the member of the couple to whom working tax credit is paid.

(3) Paragraph (1) does not apply to—

(a) a person in respect of a week in which the person is entitled to be credited with earnings under—

(i) regulation 7B (credits for disability element of working tax credit),

(ii) regulation 8A (credits for unemployment), or

(iii) regulation 8B (credits for incapacity for work or limited capability for work), of the 1975 Regulations; or

(b) a woman in respect of a week in any part of which an election made by her under regulations under section 19(4) of the 1992 Act (reduced rate election for married women) is in force.

(4) In this regulation, "couple" has the same meaning as in section 3(5A) of the Tax Credits Act 2002.

AMENDMENTS

1. The Social Security (Class 2 National Insurance Contributions Increase of Threshold) Regulations 2022 (SI 2022/1329) reg.6(3)(b) (April 6, 2022; the Regulations came into force on December 14, 2022 but have effect from April 6, 2022: see reg.1).

2. The Social Security (Class 2 National Insurance Contributions) (Consequential Amendments and Savings) Regulations 2024 (SI 2024/377) reg.8(22)(a) (amendment has effect for tax year 2024–25 and subsequent tax years).

Credits for persons entitled to universal credit

6.205 **31.** A person is to be credited with a Class 3 contribution in respect of a week for any part of which the person is entitled to universal credit under Part 1 of the 2012 Act.

Credits for persons approaching pensionable age

6.206 **32.**—(1) Subject to paragraph (4), a man born before 6th October 1953 is to be credited with earnings equal to the lower earnings limit then in force in respect of a week to which paragraph (2) applies.

(2) This paragraph applies to a week which falls within—

(a) the year in which the man attains the age which is pensionable age in the case of a woman born on the same day, and

(b) a subsequent year prior to that in which he attains the age of 65.

(3) Paragraph (2) does not apply to a week which falls within a year during which the man is absent from Great Britain for more than 182 days.

(4) Paragraph (1) applies to a man who is a self-employed earner only if he—

(a) [2...] would be treated as having actually paid,] a Class 2 contribution but for the fact that his profits for the year are below the small profits threshold specified by [1 section 11(4)(b)] of the 1992 Act, or

(b) is excepted from [2 being treated as having actually paid] a Class 2 contribution by virtue of regulation 43 of the Social Security (Contributions) Regulations 2001 in respect of any week in a year to which this regulation applies.

AMENDMENTS

1. The Social Security (Class 2 National Insurance Contributions Increase of Threshold) Regulations 2022 (SI 2022/1329) reg.6(3)(b) (April 6, 2022; the Regulations came into force on December 14, 2022 but have effect from April 6, 2022: see reg.1).

2. The Social Security (Class 2 National Insurance Contributions) (Consequential Amendments and Savings) Regulations 2024 (SI 2024/377) reg.8(22)(b) (amendment has effect for tax year 2024–25 and subsequent tax years).

Credits for spouses and civil partners of members of Her Majesty's forces

33.—(1) Subject to paragraph (5), a person who satisfies the conditions in paragraph (2) for any part of a week to which this regulation applies is to be credited with a Class 3 contribution in respect of that week. 6.207

(2) The conditions are that the person—

(a) is a spouse or civil partner of a member of Her Majesty's forces, or is treated as such by the Secretary of State for the purposes of occupying accommodation, and

(b) is accompanying the member of Her Majesty's forces on an assignment outside the United Kingdom, or is treated as such by the Secretary of State.

(3) This regulation applies to a week which falls within a year beginning on or after 6th April 2016 for which the earnings factors of the member of Her Majesty's forces exceed the qualifying earnings factor.

(4) Paragraph (1) does not apply to—

(a) a person in respect of a week in which the person is entitled to be credited with earnings under—

(i) regulation 7A (credits for carer's allowance [1 or carer support payment]),

(ii) regulation 8A (credits for unemployment),

(iii) regulation 8B (credits for incapacity for work or limited capability for work), or

(iv) regulation 9E (credits for certain spouses and civil partners of members of Her Majesty's forces), of the 1975 Regulations; or

(b) a woman in respect of a week in any part of which an election made by her under regulations under section 19(4) of the 1992 Act (reduced rate election for married women) is in force.

(5) A person is not entitled to be credited with a Class 3 contribution under paragraph (1) unless an application to be so credited is received by the Secretary of State in accordance with paragraph (6).

(6) An application under paragraph (5) may only be made in respect of a past period and must—

(a) be on a form approved by the Secretary of State, or made in such manner as the Secretary of State accepts as sufficient in the circumstances, and

(b) include such information as may be specified by the Secretary of State or the Commissioners for Her Majesty's Revenue and Customs.

AMENDMENT

1. Carer's Assistance (Carer Support Payment) (Scotland) Regulations 2023 (Consequential Amendments) Order 2023 (SI 2023/1218) art.27(5) (November 19, 2023).

Credits in respect of an award of child benefit

6.208 **34.**—(1) A person is entitled to be credited with a Class 3 contribution in respect of a week in which the person is—

(a) awarded child benefit for any part of that week in respect of a child under the age of 12, or

(b) in the circumstances specified by paragraph (2) and subject to paragraph (3), the partner of a person to whom child benefit is awarded.

(2) The circumstances are that the partner—

(a) resides with the person to whom child benefit is awarded,

(b) shares responsibility for the child in respect of whom child benefit is awarded with that person,

(c) is ordinarily resident in Great Britain,

(d) is not undergoing imprisonment or detention in legal custody, and7

(e) makes an application to the Commissioners for Her Majesty's Revenue and Customs to be so credited in accordance with regulation 39.

(3) Paragraph (1)(b) only applies in respect of a week that falls within a year for which the earnings factors of the person to whom child benefit is awarded exceed the qualifying earnings factor.

(4) In calculating the earnings factors for the purpose of paragraph (3), no account is to be taken of any earnings factors derived from contributions credited by virtue of that person being awarded child benefit.

Credits for persons providing care for a child under the age of 12

6.209 **35.**—(1) Subject to paragraphs (3) and (4), a person is to be credited with a Class 3 contribution in respect of a week ("the relevant week") in which the conditions in paragraph (2) are satisfied.

(2) The conditions are that in the relevant week the person—

(a) provided care in respect of a child under the age of 12,

(b) is, in relation to that child, a person specified in paragraph (6), and

(c) was ordinarily resident in Great Britain.

[[1] (3) The person ('A') referred to in paragraph (1) is not entitled to be credited with a Class 3 contribution unless—

(a) child benefit was awarded to another person ('B') in respect of—

  (i) the child, or each child, for whom A provided care, and

  (ii) the week in which A provided that care,

(b) B's earnings factors, other than those derived from a Class 3 contribution credit awarded under regulation 34, exceed the qualifying earnings factor for the year in which the relevant week falls, and

(c) A makes an application to the Secretary of State to be so credited in accordance with paragraph (5) and regulation 39.

(4) Where the requirements relating to the provision of care by A in paragraph (3)(a)(i) can be satisfied by more than one person in respect of a week in which B was awarded child benefit—

(a) those persons shall elect, with the agreement of B, which of them is to be credited with a Class 3 contribution credit (and then only the elected person is to be so credited), or

(b) the Secretary of State is to exercise his discretion to determine which of those persons is to be credited with that contribution, in default of the agreement referred to in sub-paragraph (a).]

(5) An application under paragraph [1 (3)(c)] must—
(a) include the name and date of birth of the child [1, or each child,] cared for,
(b) where requested by the Secretary of State or the Commissioners for Her Majesty's Revenue and Customs, include a declaration by B that the conditions in paragraph (2) are satisfied, and
(c) specify the relevant week or weeks in which the child [1, or each child,] was cared for.
(6) The person specified in paragraph (2)(b) is—
(a) a non-resident parent;
(b) a grandparent;
(c) a great-grandparent;
(d) a great-great-grandparent;
(e) a sibling;
(f) a parent's sibling;
(g) a spouse or former spouse of any persons listed in sub-paragraphs (a) to (f);
(h) a civil partner or former civil partner of any persons listed in sub-paragraphs (a) to (f);
(i) a partner or former partner of any persons listed in sub-paragraphs (a) to (h);
(j) a son or daughter of any persons listed in sub-paragraphs (e) to (i);
(k) in respect of a son or daughter of a person listed in sub-paragraph (f), that person's—
(i) spouse or former spouse,
(ii) civil partner or former civil partner, or
(iii) partner or former partner.
(7) For the purposes of paragraph (6)(e) and (f), a sibling includes a sibling of the half blood, a step sibling and an adopted sibling.
(8) For the purposes of paragraph (6)(i) and (k)(iii), a partner is a person who is the other member of a couple who are not married to, or civil partners of, each other but are living together [2 as if they were a married couple or civil partners].

AMENDMENTS

1. Social Security (Miscellaneous Amendments) Regulations 2017 (SI 2017/1015), reg.17 (November 16 2017).
2. The Civil Partnership (Opposite-sex Couples) Regulations 2019 (SI 2019/1458) Sch.3 para. 100 (December 2, 2019).

Credits for being a foster parent

36.—(1) Subject to paragraph (3), a person is to be credited with a Class 3 contribution in respect of a week in which the person is a foster parent and is— **6.210**
(a) ordinarily resident in Great Britain, and
(b) not undergoing imprisonment or detention in legal custody.
(2) For the purposes of this regulation, a foster parent is a person approved as—
(a) a foster parent in accordance with Part 5 (approval of foster parents) of the Fostering Services (England) Regulations 2011,
(b) a kinship carer in accordance with Part 5 (kinship care) of the Looked After Children (Scotland) Regulations 2009,

(c) a foster carer in accordance with Part 7 (fostering) of those Regulations, or

(d) a foster parent in accordance with Part 2 (approvals and placements) of the Foster Placement (Children) Regulations (Northern Ireland) 1996.

(3) A person is not entitled to be credited with a Class 3 contribution under paragraph (1) unless an application to be so credited is received by the Commissioners for Her Majesty's Revenue and Customs in accordance with regulation 39.

Credits for persons engaged in caring

6.211 **37.**—(1) Subject to paragraph (5), a person is to be credited with a Class 3 contribution in respect of a week in which the person is engaged in caring.

(2) A person is engaged in caring in a week if the person is—

(a) caring for another person or persons for a total of 20 or more hours in that week and—

(i) that other person is, or each of the persons cared for are, entitled to a relevant benefit for that week, or

(ii) the Secretary of State considers that level of care to be appropriate; or

(b) a person to whom one or more of paragraphs 4 to 6 (persons caring for another person) of Schedule 1B (prescribed categories of person) to the Income Support (General) Regulations 1987 applies.

(3) A person is not engaged in caring for the purposes of this regulation during any period in respect of which the person is—

(a) not ordinarily resident in Great Britain, or

(b) undergoing imprisonment or detention in legal custody.

(4) For the purposes of paragraph (2)(a)(i), "relevant benefit" means—

(a) attendance allowance in accordance with section 64 of the 1992 Act;

(b) the care component of disability living allowance in accordance with `section 72 of the 1992 Act, at the middle or highest rate prescribed in accordance with subsection (3) of that section;

(c) an increase in the rate of disablement pension in accordance with section 104 of the 1992 Act;

(d) any benefit which is payable as if an injury or disease were one in respect of which a disablement pension would for the time being be payable in respect of an assessment of 100 per cent., by virtue of—

(i) the Pneumoconiosis, Byssinosis and Miscellaneous Diseases Benefit Scheme 1983; or

(ii) regulations made under section 64(3) of the 2012 Act (injuries arising before 5 July 1948);

(e) a constant attendance allowance payable by virtue of—

(i) article 8 (constant attendance allowance) of the Naval, Military and Air Forces etc. (Disablement and Death) Service Pensions Order 2006; or

(ii) article 14 (constant attendance allowance) of the Personal Injuries (Civilians) Scheme 1983;

(f) the daily living component of personal independence payment in accordance with section 78 of the 2012 Act;

(g) armed forces independence payment in accordance with the Armed Forces and Reserve Forces (Compensation Scheme) Order 2011;

[1(h) the care component of child disability payment at the middle or highest rate in accordance with regulation 11 of the Disability Assistance for Children and Young People (Scotland) Regulations 2021;]

[2(i) the daily living component of adult disability payment at the standard or enhanced rate payable in accordance with regulation 5 of the Disability Assistance for Working Age People (Scotland) Regulations 2022].

(5) Except in a case to which paragraph (8) applies, a person is not entitled to be credited with a Class 3 contribution under paragraph (2)(a) unless an application to be so credited is received by the Secretary of State in accordance with paragraph (6) and regulation 39.

(6) An application under paragraph (5) must include—

(a) a declaration by the applicant that the applicant cares for a person or persons for 20 or more hours in a week,

(b) the name and, where known, the national insurance number of each person cared for,

(c) where applicable, which relevant benefit each person cared for is entitled to, and

(d) where requested by the Secretary of State, a declaration signed by an appropriate person as to the level of care which is required for each person cared for.

(7) For the purposes of paragraph (6)(d), an appropriate person is a person who is—

(a) involved in the health care or social care of the person cared for, and

(b) considered by the Secretary of State as appropriate to make a declaration as to the level of care required.

(8) This paragraph applies in the case of a woman in respect of a week in any part of which an election made by her under regulations under section 19(4) of the 1992 Act (reduced rate election for married women) is in force.

AMENDMENTS

1. The Social Security (Scotland) Act 2018 (Disability Assistance for Children and Young People) (Consequential Modifications) (No. 2) Order 2021 (SI 2021/1301) reg.4 (November 17, 2021).

2. The Social Security (Scotland) Act 2018 (Disability Assistance and Information-Sharing) (Consequential Provision and Modifications) Order 2022 (SI 2022/332) art.15 (March 21, 2022).

Credits for an additional period in respect of entitlement to carer's allowance [1 or carer support payment] and relevant benefits

38.—(1) A person is to be credited with a Class 3 contribution for a period of 12 weeks— 6.212

(a) prior to the date on which that person becomes entitled to carer's allowance by virtue of subsection (1) of section 70 of the 1992 Act [1 or carer support payment under the Carer's Assistance (Carer Support Payment) (Scotland) Regulations 2023];

(b) subject to paragraph (2), following the end of the week in which that person ceases to be entitled to carer's allowance by virtue of that subsection [1 or carer support payment by virtue of those Regulations];

(c) following the end of a week in which regulation 37(2)(a) ceases to be satisfied.

(2) A person is not entitled to be credited with a Class 3 contribution under paragraph (1)(b) in a week in respect of which that person is entitled under regulation 7A of the 1975 Regulations to be credited with contributions by virtue of being entitled to an allowance under section 70 of the 1992 Act [[1] or carer support payment under the Carer's Assistance (Carer Support Payment) (Scotland) Regulations 2023].

AMENDMENT

1. Carer's Assistance (Carer Support Payment) (Scotland) Regulations 2023 (Consequential Amendments) Order 2023 (SI 2023/1218) art.27(6) (November 19, 2023).

Time limit for making an application under regulation 34(1)(b), 35, 36 or 37

6.213 **39.** An application must be received—

(a) where the application is under regulation 34(1)(b), 36 or 37—
  (i) before the end of the year following that in which a week, which is the subject of the application, falls, or
  (ii) within such further time as the Secretary of State or the Commissioners for Her Majesty's Revenue and Customs, as the case may be, consider reasonable in the circumstances, or

(b) where the application is under regulation 35, after the end of the year in which a week, which is the subject of the application, falls.]

AMENDMENT

1. State Pension (Amendment) (No 2) Regulations 2016 (SI 2016/240) reg.2 (April 6, 2016).

SCHEDULE **Regulation 14**

6.214 *Omitted as not within the scope of the volume.*

The Pensions Act 2014 (Pension Sharing on Divorce etc.) (Transitional Provision) Order 2016

(SI 2016/39)

The Secretary of State for Work and Pensions makes the following Order in exercise of the power conferred by section 56(8) of the Pensions Act 2014.

Citation, commencement and interpretation

6.215 **1.**—(1) This Order may be cited as the Pensions Act 2014 (Pension Sharing on Divorce etc.) (Transitional Provision) Order 2016 and shall come into force on 6th April 2016.

(2) For the purposes of this Order—

(a) a petition or application is issued on the date entered on the petition or application form by a member of the court staff;

(b) an initial writ or summons is presented on the date entered on the initial writ or summons by a member of the court staff.

Transitional provision in connection with the coming into force of amendments to pension sharing on divorce etc.

2.—(1) This Order applies in a case where section 49A of the Welfare Reform and Pensions Act 1999 (creation of debits and credits: transferor in new state pension system and sharing activated on or after 6 April 2016) would otherwise apply and either— **6.216**

(a) in England and Wales—
  (i) the petition for divorce or nullity of a marriage was issued before 6th April 2016;
  (ii) the application for dissolution or annulment of a civil partnership was issued before 6th April 2016; or
  (iii) in the case of the application for financial relief after overseas divorce or nullity of a marriage or overseas dissolution or annulment of a civil partnership, the application for permission of the court for financial relief was issued before 6th April 2016; or

(b) in Scotland—
  (i) the initial writ or summons in the proceedings for divorce or nullity of a marriage or for dissolution or annulment of a civil partnership was presented before 6th April 2016;
  (ii) the initial writ or summons in the application for an order for financial provision after overseas divorce or nullity of a marriage or overseas dissolution or annulment of a civil partnership was presented before 6th April 2016; or
  (iii) the qualifying agreement, referred to in section 48(1)(f)(i) of the Welfare Reform and Pensions Act 1999 (activation of benefit sharing), was executed by the parties before 6th April 2016.

(2) In a case where this Order applies—

(a) section 49 of the Welfare Reform and Pensions Act 1999 (creation of state scheme pension debits and credits: transferor in old state pension system or pension sharing activated before 6 April 2016) applies;

(b) section 49A of that Act does not apply; and

(c) the relevant order or provision is to be treated as taking effect on 5th April 2016.

The Pensions Act 2014 (Transitional and Transitory Provisions) Order 2016

(SI 2016/408)

The Secretary of State for Work and Pensions makes the following Order in exercise of the power conferred by section 56(8) of the Pensions Act 2014.

Citation, commencement and cessation

1.—(1) This Order may be cited as the Pensions Act 2014 (Transitional and Transitory Provisions) Order 2016. **6.217**

(2) This Order comes into force on 6th April 2016.

(3) Article 2 of this Order ceases to have effect on the day on which section 30 of the Pensions Act 2014 (bereavement support payment) comes fully into force.

GENERAL NOTE

6.218 This Order deal with problems arising because the reforms to the bereavement payments under the Pensions Act 2014 do not come into force at the same time as the reforms to the state pension, the intention being to start them in 2017.

Transitory provision

6.219 **2.** Section 36(1)(a) of the Social Security Contributions and Benefits Act 1992 (bereavement payment) is to be read as if after "under section 44 below" the words "or a state pension under Part 1 of the Pensions Act 2014" appear.

GENERAL NOTE

6.220 This regulation ceased to have effect on April 6, 2017. This was the day on which s.30 of the Pensions Act 2014 came into force: see art.1(3) of this Order.

Transitional provisions

6.221 **3.**—(1) This article applies to a case in which the spouse or civil partner mentioned in paragraph 3(1) of Schedule 3 to the Pensions Act 2014 (survivor's pension: inherited amount where dead spouse or civil partner was in the old state pension system) died—

(a) on or after 6th April 2016; but

(b) before the day on which section 30 of the Pensions Act 2014 comes fully into force.

(2) In a case to which this article applies—

(a) paragraph 3(1)(d) of Schedule 3 to the Pensions Act 2014 is to be read as if it provides—

"(d) the pensioner would, on reaching pensionable age, have been entitled to a Category B retirement pension under section 48BB of the Contributions and Benefits Act if in subsections (1) and (3) of that section the words "before 6 April 2016" were omitted."; and

(b) paragraph 3(2) of that Schedule is to be read as if it provides—

"(2) The inherited amount is equal to the weekly rate at which that Category B retirement pension would have been payable on the day on which the pensioner reached pensionable age if any element of the rate attributable to the basic pension were ignored.".

The Bereavement Support Payment Regulations 2017

(2017/410)

The Secretary of State for Work and Pensions makes the following Regulations in exercise of the powers conferred by sections 30(1)(c), (2), (3), (4)(a) and (7), 32(1) and (3) and 54(5) and (6) of the Pensions Act 2014.

These Regulations have not been referred to the Social Security Advisory Committee because they are made before the end of the period of six months beginning with the coming into force of the provisions of the Pensions Act 2014 under which they are made.

A draft of these Regulations has been laid before Parliament in accordance with section 54(2)(a) of the Pensions Act 2014 and approved by a resolution of each House of Parliament.

Citation and commencement

1.—(1) These Regulations may be cited as the Bereavement Support Payment Regulations 2017. 6.222

(2) These Regulations come into force on the day on which section 30 of the Pensions Act 2014 (bereavement support payment) comes into force for all purposes.

Period for which bereavement support payment is payable

2.—(1) The period for which bereavement support payment is payable [1 is determined— 6.223

(a) in the case mentioned in paragraph (4), in accordance with paragraphs (5) and (6);

(b) in the case mentioned in paragraph (7), in accordance with paragraphs (8) and (9); and

(c) in any other case, in accordance with paragraphs (2) and (3)].

(2) The period starts—

(a) on the date the person's [1 spouse, civil partner or cohabiting partner] died, where the person claims the payment three months or less after that date; or

(b) at the beginning of the period of three months preceding the date the person claims the payment, where the person claims the payment—

(i) more than three months after the date the person's [1 spouse, civil partner or cohabiting partner] died; and

(ii) no more than three months after the date the period finishes under paragraph (3).

(3) The period finishes at the end of the period of 18 months beginning with the day after the date the person's [1 spouse, civil partner or cohabiting partner] died.

[1 (4) Paragraphs (5) and (6) apply where the person is entitled to bereavement support payment—

(a) as a result of the amendments made by the 2023 Remedial Order, and

(b) as a result of the death of their cohabiting partner occurring on or after 30th August 2018 and before the RO commencement day.

(5) The period starts—

(a) with the RO commencement day, where the person claims the payment 12 months or less after that date; or

(b) at the beginning of the period of three months preceding the date the person claims the payment, where the person claims the payment—

(i) more than 12 months after the RO commencement day; and

(ii) no more than three months after the date the period finishes under paragraph (6).

(6) The period finishes at the end of the period of 18 months beginning with the RO commencement day.

(7) Paragraphs (8) and (9) apply where the person is entitled to bereavement support payment—

(a) as a result of the amendments made by the 2023 Remedial Order, and

(b) as a result of the death of their cohabiting partner occurring on or after 6th April 2017 and before 30th August 2018.

(8) The period starts with the RO commencement day.

(9) The period finishes—

(a) at the end of the period of W months beginning with the RO commencement day, where the person claims the payment 12 months or less after the RO commencement day; and

(b) at the end of—

(i) the period described in sub-paragraph (a); or

(ii) if shorter, the period of X months beginning with the RO commencement day,

where the person claims the payment more than 12 months after but no more than 21 months after the RO commencement day

(10) For the purposes of paragraph (9)—

"W months" means the number of months which is 18 less Y;

"X months" means the number of months which is 21 less Z.

(11) For the purposes of paragraph (10)—

"Y" is the number of monthly recurrences of the day of the month on which the person's cohabiting partner died which occur during the period beginning with the day after the date of the cohabiting partner's death and ending with 29th August 2018;

"Z" is the number of monthly recurrences of the day of the month on which the RO commencement day occurs during the period beginning with the day after the RO commencement day and ending with the date on which the person claims the payment.

(12) In paragraph (11)—

(a) for the purposes of the definition of "Y"—

(i) paragraph (7) of regulation 3 applies as if the words "for the purposes of paragraphs (1) and (4)" were omitted, and

(ii) paragraph (8) of regulation 3 applies as if the words "for those purposes" were omitted;

(b) for the purposes of the definition of "Z"—

(i) where the 2023 Remedial Order comes into force on the 31st day of a month, the monthly recurrence of the RO commencement day is to be treated as falling on the last day of the month;

(ii) where the 2023 Remedial Order comes into force on the 29th or 30th day of a month, the monthly recurrence of the RO commencement day in February is to be treated as falling on the last day of February.

(13) In paragraphs (4) to (12)—

"the 2023 Remedial Order" means the Bereavement Benefits (Remedial) Order 2023; and

"the RO commencement day" means the day on which the 2023 Remedial Order comes into force.]

AMENDMENT

1. Bereavement Benefits (Remedial) Order 2023 (SI 2023/134) art.6, (February 9, 2023).

GENERAL NOTE

6.224 Bereavement Support payments will be made for a maximum of 18 monthly payments. This was extended from the original period proposed of 12 months to avoid the last of the payments coinciding with the anniversary of the death on which the payment is based. The payment period begins on the date of the death where the claim is made within three months of the death; where the claim is made more than three months after the death, the payment period begins three months before the date of claim, but it ends 18 months after the day following the date of death. This means that a claim made later than the three months period of grace allowed will be foreshortened; a claim made 20 months after the date of the death will run for only one month.

Special provision is made in paras(4) – (13) in respect of claims made in consequence of the Remedial Order that amends these regulations to extend entitlement to a surviving cohabiting partner. The date that the remedial Order came into force, referred to in these paragraphs as the RO commencement date, was February 9, 2023. A helpful discussion of the amendments made by the Remedial Order including worked out examples of these provisions can be found in Welfare Rights Bulletin No. 293 published by CPAG.

Rate of bereavement support payment

3.—(1) The higher rate of bereavement support payment is £350 for each monthly recurrence of the day of the month on which the person's [1 spouse, civil partner or cohabiting partner] died during the period for which bereavement support payment is payable (see regulation 2). 6.225

[1(2) Where the person claims bereavement support payment 12 months or less after—

(a) the date their spouse or civil partner died;

(b) in the case of a claim in respect of their cohabiting partner who died on or after 30th August 2018 and before the RO commencement day, the RO commencement day;

(c) in the case of a claim in respect of their cohabiting partner who died on or after the RO commencement day, the date their cohabiting partner died,

the higher rate of bereavement support payment is £3,500 for the first month of the period for which bereavement support payment is payable.]

(3) Any higher rate mentioned in paragraph (2) is in addition to any higher rate mentioned in paragraph (1).

(4) The standard rate of bereavement support payment is £100 for each monthly recurrence of the day of the month on which the person's spouse or civil partner died during the period for which bereavement support payment is payable.

(5) Where the person claims bereavement support payment 12 months or less after the date their spouse or civil partner died, the standard rate of bereavement support payment is £2,500 for the first month of the period for which bereavement support payment is payable.

(6) Any standard rate mentioned in paragraph (5) is in addition to any standard rate mentioned in paragraph (4).

(7) Where a person's spouse or civil partner died on the 31st day of a month, the monthly recurrence of the day of death is to be treated for the purposes of paragraphs (1) and (4) as falling on the last day of the month [1 (the same applies where a cohabiting partner dies for the purposes of paragraph (1))]

(8) Where a person's [1 spouse, civil partner or cohabiting partner] died on the 29th or 30th day of a month, the monthly recurrence of the day of death in February is to be treated for those purposes as falling on the last day of February.

[1 (9) In this regulation, "the RO commencement day" has the meaning given in regulation 2(13).]

AMENDMENT

1. Bereavement Benefits (Remedial) Order 2023 (SI 2023/134) art.6 (February 9, 2023).

GENERAL NOTE

6.226 Bereavement Support payments will be made at two rates and in each case will consist of two components. Payments will be made at a higher rate for a claimant who has responsibility for children (as defined in regulation 4 below) and at the standard rate for those without children. In each case the first monthly payment will be enhanced by a lump sum payment again at different rates. Note that, because the lump sum is an enhancement of the monthly payment rather than a separate payment, this means that where the claimant has lost entitlement to a payment altogether, by delaying more than 20 months after the day following the date of death, entitlement to the lump sum will be lost as well. The rates of payment provided in this regulation have remained unchanged. See the annual Social Security Benefits Up-rating Order each year.

Persons entitled to the higher rate of bereavement support payment

6.227 **4.**—(1) A person falling within any of paragraphs (2) to (4) is entitled to the higher rate of bereavement support payment under regulation 3(1) to (3).

(2) A person who was pregnant when their [[1] spouse, civil partner or cohabiting partner] died.

(3) A person who was entitled to child benefit under section 141 of the Social Security Contributions and Benefits Act 1992 (child benefit) when their [[1] spouse, civil partner or cohabiting partner] died.

(4) A person who, after their [[1] spouse, civil partner or cohabiting partner] died, becomes entitled to child benefit under section 141 of that Act for a child or qualifying young person who was residing with the person or their deceased [[1] spouse, civil partner or cohabiting partner] immediately before the [[1] spouse, civil partner or cohabiting partner] died.

(5) Paragraph (4) applies to a person whether or not they later cease to be entitled to child benefit for that child or qualifying young person.

(6) In this regulation, "child" and "qualifying young person" have the same meaning as in section 142 of the Social Security Contributions and Benefits Act 1992 (definitions of "child" and "qualifying young person").

AMENDMENT

1. Bereavement Benefits (Remedial) Order 2023 (SI 2023/134) art.6 (February 9, 2023).

Persons entitled to the standard rate of bereavement support payment

6.228 **5.** A person is entitled to the standard rate of bereavement support payment under regulation 3(4) to (6) if they are not entitled to the higher rate of bereavement support payment.

Prisoners who are not to be paid bereavement support payment

6.229 **6.**—(1) Subject to regulation 7, a person is not to be paid bereavement support payment for any period during which the person is a prisoner.

(2) Except where paragraph (3) applies, a person is a prisoner for the purposes of paragraph (1) where the person is—

(a) a prisoner in Great Britain or elsewhere who is imprisoned or detained in legal custody in connection with, or as a result of, criminal proceedings;

(b) a prisoner in Great Britain or elsewhere who is unlawfully at large;

(c) a prisoner in Great Britain who is being detained—

(i) under section 47 of the Mental Health Act 1983 (removal to hospital of persons serving sentences of imprisonment, etc); and

(ii) on or before the day which the Secretary of State certifies to be the person's release date (if any) within the meaning in section 50(3) of that Act (further provisions as to prisoners under sentence);

(d) a prisoner in Great Britain who is being detained under section 136 of the Mental Health (Care and Treatment) (Scotland) Act 2003 (transfer of prisoners for treatment of mental disorder).

(3) Where a person outside Great Britain is a prisoner within paragraph (2)(a) or (b) and, in similar circumstances in Great Britain, the person would not have been a prisoner, the person is not a prisoner within paragraph (2)(a) or (b).

Paying bereavement support payment to persons who are remanded in custody

7.—(1) Where a person is remanded in custody for an offence, regulation 6(1) does not apply unless a sentence described in paragraph (2) is later imposed on the person for the offence. 6.230

(2) Subject to paragraph (3), the sentences described for the purposes of paragraph (1) are—

(a) a sentence of imprisonment or detention in legal custody as a result of criminal proceedings;

(b) a sentence of detention where the provisions mentioned in regulation 6(2)(c)(i) or (d) apply;

(c) a suspended sentence within the meaning in section 189 of the Criminal Justice Act 2003 [1 or section 286 of the Sentencing Code] (suspended sentences of imprisonment).

(3) A sentence described in paragraph (2)(a) which is imposed outside Great Britain is not a sentence described for the purposes of paragraph (1) if, in similar circumstances in Great Britain, a sentence described in paragraph (2)(a) would not have been imposed.

Territory in which a person may be entitled to bereavement support payment

8. For the purposes of section 30(1)(c) of the Pensions Act 2014 (bereavement support payment), the territory specified is any part of the Channel Islands which is not subject to an Order made under section 179 of the Social Security Administration Act 1992 (reciprocal agreements with countries outside the United Kingdom). 6.231

AMENDMENT

1. Sentencing Act 2020 Sch.24 para.447 (December 1, 2020).

PART VII

NEW STYLE JOBSEEKER'S ALLOWANCE

The Jobseeker's Allowance Regulations 2013

(SI 2013/378) (AS AMENDED)

Made by the Secretary of State for Work and Pensions under ss.2(1)(c), (2A) and (3B)(a), 4(1)(b), (2) and (4), 5(3), 6A(5), 6B(2), 6D(4), 6E(3) and (5), 6F(1), 6H(1)(a), (5) and (6), 6I, 6J(2)(a), (5) and (7), 6K(4), (5) and (9), 12(1) to (4)(a) and (b), 35(1) and (3) and 36(2) to (4) of, and Sch.1 to, the Jobseekers Act 1995, ss.5(1)(i) and (j) and (1A), 189(4), (5) and (6) and 191 of the Social Security Administration Act 1992, ss.171D, 171G(2) and 175(3) to (5) of the Social Security Contributions and Benefits Act 1992 and paras 2(3) and 3 of Sch.5 to the Welfare Reform Act 2012, the Social Security Advisory Committee having agreed that the proposal to make the regulations did not need to be referred to it.

ARRANGEMENT OF REGULATIONS

PART 1

GENERAL

PART 2

CLAIMANT RESPONSIBILITIES

PART 3

SANCTIONS

PART 4

INFORMATION AND EVIDENCE

PART 5

CONDITIONS OF ENTITLEMENT

PART 6

AMOUNTS OF A JOBSEEKER'S ALLOWANCE

PART 7

EARNINGS

PART 8

PART WEEKS

PART 9

SHARE FISHERMEN

PART 10

MODIFICATION OF THE ACT

PART 1

General

Citation, commencement and application

7.2 **1.**—(1) These Regulations may be cited as the Jobseeker's Allowance Regulations 2013.

(2) They come into force on 29th April 2013.

(3) They apply in relation to a particular case on any day on which section 33(1)(a) of the Welfare Reform Act 2012 (abolition of income-based jobseeker's allowance) is in force and applies in relation to that case.

General Note

7.3 Although these Regulations entered into force on April 29, 2013, they only apply in any particular case and to any particular claimant from the day on which the abolition of income-based JSA by s.33(1)(a) of the Welfare Reform Act 2012 came into force in that case and for that claimant (para.(3)). The circumstance that brings about the abolition of IBJSA under s.33(1)(a) of the WRA 2012 and the coming into force of the amendments to the 1995 Act under later provisions is the making of a new claim for JSA (or for other benefits including universal credit and ESA) in an area where "full service" universal credit has been rolled out and where the particular claimant is legally able to make a claim for universal credit (see arts 4(1) and (2) of the Welfare Reform Act 2012 (Commencement No.9 and Transitional and Transitory Provisions and Commencement No.8 and Savings and Transitional Provisions (Amendment) Order 2013 (SI 2013/983) as further applied in later Commencement Orders). The Orders are now set out so far as still relevant in Vol.V of this series, 2021/22 edition as updated in Cumulative Supplements included in Vol.II of this series and in mid-year Supplements. The position was reached in December 2018 where the universal credit rollout for new claims had extended to the whole of Great Britain. Some prohibitions on claiming universal credit remained, in particular the so-called SDP gateway, where a claimant who was entitled to an income-related benefit including the severe disability premium was prohibited from claiming universal credit (reg.4A of the Universal Credit (Transitional Provisions) Regulations 2014 (SI 2014/1230)). That prohibition was removed by the revocation of reg.4A with effect from January 27, 2021. The two further remaining prohibitions have now also been removed. The former exception for "frontier workers" was removed with effect from March 30, 2022 by SI 2022/302 and the discretion given to the Secretary of State under reg.4 of the Transitional Provisions Regulations 2014 to determine (for the safeguarding of efficient administration or ensuring the efficient testing of administrative systems) that no claims for universal credit were to be accepted in an area or category of case was removed with effect from July 25, 2022 by reg.2 of the Universal Credit (Transitional Provisions) Amendment Regulations 2022 (SI 2022/752). There is thus now no exception, however remote, to the proposition that any new claim for JSA can only be for new style JSA.

Note in particular that it is not necessary for a claim for universal credit to be made to bring the new style form of the Jobseekers Act 1995 and the present Regulations into operation. Any claim for JSA or ESA, even if it purports to be for old style JSA or ESA, has the effect set out in art.(1) and (2) of the No.9 Commencement Order, so that the claim can only be for new style JSA or ESA.

Entitlement to old style JSA can only now exist as part of a continuing award made earlier (see now in Vol.V of this series). Since entitlement to contribution-based benefit in old style JSA is limited to 182 days in any jobseeking period (s.5 of the old style Jobseekers Act 1995), no award made at a time when a new claim for old style JSA was still generally possible could survive long after April 2021. In practice continuing awards will overwhelmingly be awards of income-based old style JSA (see Vol.V of this series, 2021/22 edition as updated in Cumulative Supplements included in Vol.II of this series and in mid-year Supplements).

General interpretation

2.—(1) For the purposes of the Act and of these Regulations— 7.4

"employed earner" has the meaning it has in Part 1 of the Benefits Act by virtue of section 2(1)(a) of that Act;

"employment" includes any trade, business, profession, office or vocation, except in section 14 of the Act, where it means employed earner's employment within the meaning in the Benefits Act;

"jobseeking period" means the period described in regulation 37;

"pensionable age" has the meaning it has in Parts 1 to 6 of the Benefits Act by virtue of section 122(1) of that Act.

(2) In these Regulations—

"the Act" means the Jobseekers Act 1995;

"adoption leave" means a period of absence from work on ordinary or additional adoption leave by virtue of section 75A or 75B of the Employment Rights Act 1996;

"attendance allowance" means—

(a) an attendance allowance under section 64 of the Benefits Act;

(b) an increase of disablement pension under section 104 or 105 of the Benefits Act;

(c) a payment by virtue of article 14, 15, 16, 43 or 44 of the Personal Injuries (Civilians) Scheme 1983 or any analogous payment;

(d) any payment based on the need for attendance which is paid as an addition to a war disablement pension (which means any retired pay or pension or allowance payable in respect of disablement under an instrument specified in section 639(2) of the Income Tax (Earnings and Pensions) Act 2003);

"basic rate" has the same meaning as in the Income Tax Act 2007;

"benefit week" means a period of seven days ending with the end day unless, in any particular case or class of case, the Secretary of State arranges otherwise, and for these purposes "end day" means the day in column (2) which corresponds to the series of numbers in column (1) which includes the last two digits of the person's national insurance number—

(1)		(2)
00 to 19		Monday
20 to 39		Tuesday
40 to 59		Wednesday
60 to 79		Thursday
80 to 99		Friday;

[6"carer support payment" means carer's assistance given in accordance with the Carer's Assistance (Carer Support Payment) (Scotland) Regulations 2023;]

"Claims and Payments Regulations 2013" means the Universal Credit, Personal Independence Payment, Jobseeker's Allowance and Employment and Support Allowance (Claims and Payments) Regulations 2013;

"close relative" means a parent, parent-in-law, son, son-in-law, daughter, daughter-in-law, step-parent, step-son, step-daughter, brother, sister or, if any of the preceding persons is one member of a couple, the other member of that couple;

"date of claim" means the date on which the claimant makes, or is treated as making, a claim for a jobseeker's allowance for the purposes of—
(a) regulation 6 of the Social Security (Claims and Payments) Regulations 1987; or
(b) regulation 20, 22 or 24 of the Claims and Payments Regulations 2013;

"earnings", for the purposes of section 35(3) of the Act, has the meaning specified—
(a) in the case of an employed earner, in regulation 58; or
(b) in the case of a self-employed earner, in regulation 60;

[[2]"first year of training" means a period of one year beginning with a person's first day of training.

"Health Service Act" means the National Health Service Act 2006;

"Health Service (Wales) Act" means the National Health Service (Wales) Act 2006;

"maternity leave" means a period during which a woman is absent from work because she is pregnant or has given birth to a child, and at the end of which she has a right to return to work either under the terms of her contract of employment or under Part 8 of the Employment Rights Act 1996;

"net earnings" means such earnings as are calculated in accordance with regulation 59;

"net profit" means such profit as is calculated in accordance with regulation 61;

"occupational pension" means any pension or other periodical payment under an occupational pension scheme but does not include any discretionary payment out of a fund established for relieving hardship in particular cases;

[[5]"parental bereavement leave" means a period of absence from work on leave by virtue of section 80EA of the Employment Rights Act 1996;]

"partner" means, where a claimant—
(a) is a member of a couple, the other member of that couple;
(b) is married polygamously to two or more members of the claimant's household, any such member;

"paternity leave" means a period of absence from work on leave by virtue of section 80A or 80B of the Employment Rights Act 1996;

"payment" includes a part of a payment;

"remunerative work" has the meaning prescribed in regulation 42(1);

[[4] "Scottish basic rate" means the rate of income tax of that name calculated in accordance with section 6A of the Income Tax Act 2007;

"Scottish taxpayer" has the same meaning as in Chapter 2 of Part 4A of the Scotland Act 1998;]

"self-employed earner" is to be construed in accordance with section 2(1)(b) of the Benefits Act;

[[1]"shared parental leave" means a period of absence from work on leave by virtue of section 75E or 75G of the Employment Rights Act 1996;]

"sports award" means an award made by one of the Sports Councils named in section 23(2) of the National Lottery etc. Act 1993 out of sums allocated to it for distribution under that section;

"training allowance" means an allowance (whether by way of periodical grants or otherwise) payable—

(a) out of public funds by a Government department or by or on behalf of the Secretary of State, Skills Development Scotland, Scottish Enterprise, Highlands and Islands Enterprise [3 . . .] or the Welsh Ministers;

(b) to a person for their maintenance or in respect of the maintenance of a member of their family; and

(c) for the period, or part of the period, during which the person is following a course of training or instruction provided by, or in pursuance of arrangements made with, that department or approved by that department in relation to them or provided or approved by or on behalf of the Secretary of State, Skills Development Scotland, Scottish Enterprise, Highlands and Islands Enterprise or the Welsh Ministers,

but it does not include an allowance paid by any Government department to or in respect of a person by reason of the fact that the person is following a course of full-time education, other than under arrangements made under section 2 of the Employment and Training Act 1973 or section 2 of the Enterprise and New Towns (Scotland) Act 1990, or the person is training as a teacher;

"voluntary organisation" means a body, other than a public or local authority, the activities of which are carried on otherwise than for profit;

"voluntary work" means work other than for a member of the claimant's family, where no payment is received by the claimant or the only payment due to be made to the claimant by virtue of being so engaged is a payment in respect of any expenses reasonably incurred by the claimant in the course of being so engaged;

"week" means, in the definition of "Work Experience" and in Parts 5, 6, 7, 9 and 10, a period of seven days;

"Work Experience" means a programme which consists of work experience, job search skills and job skills (and which is not employment), provided in pursuance of arrangements made by or on behalf of the Secretary of State under section 2 of the Employment and Training Act 1973, and which—

(a) subject to paragraph (b), is of between two and eight weeks duration; or

(b) is of between two and 12 weeks duration where, during the first eight weeks of the claimant's participation in Work Experience, and as a result of that participation, the claimant is offered and accepts an apprenticeship made under government arrangements made respectively for England, Wales or Scotland;

"young person" means a person who falls within the definition of "qualifying young person" in section 142 of the Benefits Act (child and qualifying young person).

AMENDMENTS

1. Shared Parental Leave and Statutory Shared Parental Pay (Consequential Amendments and Subordinate Legislation) Order 2014 (SI 2014/3255) art.29(2) (December 31, 2014).

2. Social Security (Members of the Reserve Forces) (Amendment) Regulations 2015 (SI 2015/389) reg.5(2) (April 6, 2015).

3. Deregulation Act 2015 (Consequential Amendments) Order 2015 (SI 2015/971) Sch.3 art.25 (May 26, 2015).

4. Social Security (Scottish Rate of Income Tax etc.) (Amendment) Regulations 2016 (SI 2016/233) reg.7(2) (April 6, 2016).

5. Parental Bereavement Leave and Pay (Consequential Amendments to Subordinate Legislation) Regulations 2020 (SI 2020/354) reg.29(2) (April 6, 2020).
6. Carer's Assistance (Carer Support Payment) (Scotland) Regulations 2023 (Consequential Amendments) Order 2023 (SI 2023/1218) art.24(2) (November 19, 2023).

DEFINITIONS

"the Benefits Act"—see Jobseekers Act 1995 s.35(1).
"claimant"—*ibid.*
"couple"—*ibid.*
"family"—*ibid.* and reg.3(1), (3) and (5).
"occupational pension scheme"—see Jobseekers Act 1995 s.35(1).

GENERAL NOTE

7.5 This sets out key definitions for the application of these Regulations. It is, not, however, the sole provider of relevant definitions. Aside from s.35 of the new style Jobseekers Act 1995, important definitions are also to be found in regs 3, 4, 17 and 67 and occasionally within other provisions, in that last case generally defining a term used solely in that provision.

7.6 *Paragraph (1)*

"Employed earner". The definition refers on to s.2(1)(a) of the SSCBA 1992, where the meaning is "a person who is gainfully employed in Great Britain either under a contract of service, or in an office (including elective office) with earnings".

"Employment". The definition expressly includes any trade, business, profession, office or vocation, except in relation to s.14 (trade disputes) of the new style Jobseekers Act 1995, where it means employed earner's employment for the purposes of the SSCBA 1992.

"Pensionable age". The prescribed meaning of the same as under s.122(1) of the SSCBA 1992, leads on to the rules in para.1 of Sch.4 to the Pensions Act 1995. The rules are now the same for men and women. For anyone born after October 5, 1954 but before April 6, 1960 pensionable age is 66. For anyone born after April 5, 1960 but before March 6, 1961, the pensionable age increases by one month for each month after the first date. For anyone born after March 5, 1961 but before April 6, 1977, pensionable age is 67.

Paragraph (2)

"Close relative". The words "brother" and "sister" include half-brothers and half- sisters *(R(SB) 22/87)*. The same decision confirms that if a child is adopted it becomes the child of its adoptive parents and ceases to have any legal relationship with its natural parents or brothers or sisters. It is legal relationships that are referred to in the definition of "close relative." In *Bristol City Council v JKT (HB)* [2016] UKUT 517 (AAC), a case on the equivalent housing benefit definition, Judge Ward pointed out that what was said in *R(SB) 22/87* about "brother" and "sister" including half-brothers and sisters was obiter, but then went on to reach the same conclusion that half-siblings fall within the definition of "close relative".

From December 5, 2005, references to "step" relationships and "in-laws" in new legislative provisions are to be read as including relationships arising through civil partnerships (s.246 of the Civil Partnership Act 2004).

"Earnings". See the notes to s.35(3) of the new style Jobseekers Act 1995. The prescription here, to take cases out of the general effect of s.35(3), covers only what categories of payments or receipts do or do not count as earnings for employed (reg.58) or self-employed (reg.60) earners. Matters of calculation or estimation and of the attribution of earnings to particular weeks are left by the s.35(3) definition to the operation of the Computation of Earnings Regulations (see Pt III of this volume), made under s.3 of the SSCBA 1992 as referred to in s.35(3). But reg.50

provides that any deduction from benefit for earnings under s.4(1)(b) of the new style Jobseekers Act 1995 is to be the amount of earnings calculated in accordance with Pt. 7 (i.e. regs 53-63). That specific provision would seem to indicate a sufficient contrary intention to oust the s.35(3) and reg.2(2) meaning, which is thus relevant only to the condition of entitlement in s.2(1)(c) of the new style Jobseekers Act 1995 of not having earnings in excess of a prescribed amount. Regulation 48 deals with the consequences for the purposes of s.2(1)(c) of calculating earnings under the Computation of Earnings Regulations.

"Occupational pension". See the notes to the definition of "occupational pension scheme" in s.35(1) of the new style Jobseekers Act 1995. There is no further definition of "pension" or "periodical payment". The reg.2(2) definition is relevant only to the exclusion from the meaning of earnings of employed earners (reg.58(2)(e)).

"Self-employed earner". The definition refers on to s.2(1)(b) of the SSCBA 1992, where the meaning is "a person who is gainfully employed in Great Britain otherwise than in employed earner's employment".

"Young person". The reference to a "qualifying young person" within the meaning of s.142 of the SSCBA 1992 in general covers someone aged 16 or more but less than 20 who is undertaking full-time non-advanced education (see regs 3–7 of the Child Benefit (General) Regulations 2006 in Vol.IV of this series). Anyone aged under 16 is a child (s.35(1)).

Further interpretation

3.—(1) Any reference to the claimant's family or, as the case may be, to a member of the claimant's family, is to be construed for the purposes of these Regulations as if it included, in relation to a polygamous marriage, a reference to any partner and to any child or young person who is treated by the Secretary of State as the responsibility of the claimant or their partner, where that child or young person is a member of the claimant's household. 7.7

(2) In such cases and subject to such conditions or requirements as the Secretary of State may specify by means of a direction, any requirement imposed under these Regulations for a signature may be satisfied by means of an electronic signature (within the meaning given in section 7(2) of the Electronic Communications Act 2000).

(3) A person of a prescribed description for the purposes of the definition of "family" in section 35(1) of the Act is a young person.

(4) [2...]

(5) In this regulation, "polygamous marriage" means any marriage during the subsistence of which a party to it is married to more than one person and the ceremony of marriage took place under the law of a country which permits polygamy.

(6) References in these Regulations to a person participating as a service user are to [1 . . .]—

(a) a person who is being consulted by or on behalf of—
   (i) a body which has a statutory duty to provide services in the field of health, social care or social housing; or
   (ii) a body which conducts research or undertakes monitoring for the purpose of planning or improving such services, in the person's capacity as a user, potential user, carer of a user or person otherwise affected by the provision of those services; or

[1(ab) a person who is being consulted by or on behalf of—
   (i) the Secretary of State in relation to any of the Secretary of State's functions in the field of social security or child support or under section 2 of the Employment and Training Act 1973; or

(ii) a body which conducts research or undertakes monitoring for the purpose of planning or improving such functions,

in their capacity as a person affected or potentially affected by the exercise of those functions or the carer of such a person;]

(b) the carer of a person consulted under [1 sub-paragraphs (a) or (ab)].

(7) In these Regulations, references to obtaining paid work includes obtaining more paid work or obtaining better-paid work.

AMENDMENTS

1. Social Security (Miscellaneous Amendments) Regulations 2015 (SI 2015/67) reg.2 (February 23, 2015).

2. Civil Partnership (Opposite-sex Couples) Regulations 2019 (SI 2019/1458) reg.41(b) and Sch.3 para.97 (December 2, 2019).

DEFINITIONS

"the Act"—see reg.2(2).
"child"—see Jobseekers Act 1995 s.35(1).
"claimant"—*ibid.*
"couple"—*ibid.*
"family"—*ibid.*
"partner"—see reg.2(2).
"young person"—*ibid.*

GENERAL NOTE

7.8 This provides further definitions and interpretative provisions in addition to those in reg.2. Paragraphs (1) and (5) bring polygamous marriages within the ambit of the definitions of "couple" and "family" in s.35(1) of the new style Jobseekers Act 1995. Paragraph (4) was no longer necessary after the December 2019 amendment to the definition of "couple" in s.35(1).

PART 2

CLAIMANT RESPONSIBILITIES

GENERAL NOTE

7.9 Claimant responsibilities in new style JSA cover similar issues to the "labour market" conditions (entering into a jobseeker's agreement, availability for and actively seeking employment) in old style JSA, but with different consequences according to the different structure of the benefit and with some extensions, for instance in requirements to participate in interviews in connection with work-related requirements.

For new style JSA those responsibilities are laid down in ss.6–6L of the new style Jobseekers Act 1995 as set out in Pt I of this volume. Those responsibilities – not all of which are imposed on all claimants – cover work-related requirements and connected requirements under s.6G. They should be set out in the claimant commitment (s.6A) acceptance of which is required of all claimants, other than those exempted by reg.8 (if that regulation was validly made), as a condition of entitlement. Work-related requirements are: a work-focused interview requirement (s.6B); a work preparation requirement (s.6C); a work search requirement (s.6D); and a work availability requirement (s.6E). Connected requirements, such as participation in an interview to verify and assist claimants' compliance with their claimant commitment, fall under s.6G. While acceptance of the claimant commitment is a condition of entitlement to new style JSA under s.1(2)(b) of the new style Jobseekers Act 1995, failure to meet an obligation set out in claimant commitment does not attract any sanction for that reason in itself. It is only non-compliance for no good reason with a requirement imposed under s.6B–6G that leads to a sanction involving a reduction in the amount of benefit payable (s.6J and 6K).

Regulations 5 and 6 below deal with the relationship of the work-related requirements and sanctions regime with universal credit entitlement. Regulations 7 and 8 deal with the acceptance of a claimant commitment, although there is doubt about their validity . Regulations 9–14 deal with the content of work-related requirements. Regulations 15, 16 and 16A set out the circumstances when various work-related requirements are not to be imposed, reg.15 dealing with recent victims of domestic violence. Part 3 of the Regulations deals with sanctions, including circumstances in which a reduction in benefit is not to follow from the existence of a sanctionable failure.

Interpretation

4.—(1) In this Part— 7.10

"relevant carer" means—

(a) a parent of a child who is not the responsible carer, but has caring responsibilities for the child; or

(b) a person who has caring responsibilities for a person who has a physical or mental impairment which makes those caring responsibilities necessary;

"responsible carer", in relation to a child, means—

(a) a person who is the only person responsible for the child; or

(b) a person who is a member of a couple where—

(i) both members of the couple are responsible for the child; and

(ii) the person has been nominated by the couple jointly as responsible for the child;

"responsible foster parent", in relation to a child, means—

(a) a person who is the only foster parent in relation to the child; or

(b) a person who is a member of a couple where—

(i) both members of the couple are foster parents in relation to the child; and

(ii) the person has been nominated by the couple jointly as the responsible foster parent;

"voluntary work preparation" means particular action taken by a claimant and agreed by the Secretary of State for the purpose of making it more likely that the claimant will obtain paid work, but which is not specified by the Secretary of State as a work preparation requirement under section 6C of the Act.

(2) The nomination of a responsible carer or responsible foster parent for the purposes of paragraph (1) may be changed—

(a) once in a 12 month period, beginning with the date of the previous nomination; or

(b) on any occasion where the Secretary of State considers that there has been a change of circumstances which is relevant to the nomination.

(3) Only one person may be nominated as a responsible carer or a responsible foster parent.

(4) The nomination applies to all of the children for whom the claimant is responsible.

DEFINITIONS

"child"—see Jobseekers Act 1995 s.35(1).
"claimant"—*ibid.*
"couple"—see Jobseekers Act 1995 s.35(1) and reg.3(4).

GENERAL NOTE

7.11 In addition to terms already defined in regs 2 and 3, this provides for the purposes of this Part (Pt 2 Claimant responsibilities) a number of important definitions: "relevant carer"; "responsible foster parent"; "responsible carer"; "voluntary work preparation". The definitions of "relevant carer", "responsible carer" and "responsible foster parent" are relevant for the purposes of regs 9, 13 and 14. A child is a person under the age of 16. In contrast to the position in universal credit (see regs 4 and 4A of the UC Regulations 2013, under which the basic test is whether the child normally lives with the person in question) there appear to be no provisions for determining responsibility for a child. The definition of "relevant carer" allows the inclusion in that category of people who do not count as a "responsible carer" but nevertheless have caring responsibilities (not further defined) for the child in question or have caring responsibilities for a person of any age who has a physical or mental impairment (not further defined). If a child has only one foster parent, that person is the "responsible foster parent". If both members of a couple are foster parents of the child, there must be a joint nomination of one of them.

The definition of "voluntary work preparation" is relevant for the purposes of regs 12 and 16.

Application of regulations where there is dual entitlement

7.12 **5.**—(1) This regulation applies where a person is entitled to universal credit and a jobseeker's allowance.

(2) The work-related requirements under sections 6B to 6I of the Act and regulations 9 to16 of these Regulations do not apply to such a person.

(3) Reductions relating to the award of a jobseeker's allowance under section 6J or 6K of the Act and regulations 17 to 29 of these Regulations do not apply to such a person.

DEFINITION

"the Act"—see reg.2(2).

GENERAL NOTE

7.13 This provision, made it appears under ss.6F(1), 6H(1)(a), 6J(7)(a) and 6K(9)(a) of the new style Jobseekers Act 1995, as well as para.2(3) and (4)(b) of Sch.5 to the Welfare Reform Act 2012, constitutes an important element in the structure of new style JSA and its relationship with universal credit. Paragraph (2) provides that where a claimant is entitled to both universal credit and JSA, the work-related and connected requirements regime applicable to new style JSA does not operate at all. Although para.(2) refers to work-related requirements only, the specific reference to the whole of s.6B–6I must bring s.6G (connected requirements) within its scope. The claimant will instead be subject to the comparable universal credit regime. See the UC Regulations 2013 regs 84–114 in Vol.II, *Universal Credit etc.* It appears that the claimant is still subject to the condition of entitlement of accepting a claimant commitment under ss.1(2)(b) and 6A of the new style Jobseekers Act 1995, but it is not clear what could go into that document in terms of a statement of responsibilities under the Act. The document could of course contain other relevant information, but it might be that in the circumstances envisaged in reg.5, where the claimant will by definition have accepted a universal credit claimant commitment or been exempted from needing to accept one (in order to be entitled) the Secretary of State will consider the application of reg.8(b) (unreasonable to expect a claimant to accept a claimant commitment).

Paragraph (3) provides that reductions in the amount of new style JSA payable under the sanctions regime do not apply to a person who is also entitled to universal credit. At first sight that appears somewhat redundant in the light of para.(2). If a claimant cannot be subject to any work-related or connected requirements, there can be no failure to comply that can lead to a sanction. However, sanctionable failures under s.6J are not limited to such failures to comply, but also extend, for example, to the traditional categories of losing employment through misconduct or leaving voluntarily for no good reason. Paragraph (3) will also presumably apply where a sanctionable failure occurred while the new style JSA recipient was not entitled to universal credit, but the person becomes entitled to universal credit before a sanction and reduction decision is made. See reg.6 for the situation where a JSA reduction has already been applied.

The rather odd result appears to follow that if a claimant who is entitled to new style JSA, having satisfied the contribution conditions, and is also entitled to universal credit to top up the income from JSA, commits a sanctionable failure, the reduction in the amount of benefit payable can only eat into whatever is the amount of universal credit payable and not into the amount of JSA payable. Although the amount of the reduction to be applied under the universal credit sanctions regime is expressed in terms of a percentage (100 per cent or 40 per cent) of the claimant's standard allowance, the concept of a reduction cannot allow the amount of universal credit payable to be reduced below nil. By contrast, if a new style JSA recipient does not qualify for a top-up through universal credit, or has not claimed universal credit, reg.5 will not apply and the 100 per cent reduction of benefit following a sanction will be applied to the amount of JSA payable. Similarly, a universal credit recipient who does not qualify for new style JSA will receive correspondingly more in universal credit without that income to be counted, but will then have more benefit to be reduced following a sanction. Note that while a reduction in the amount of universal credit payable following a sanction is in operation, the claimant remains entitled to universal credit, even if nothing is being paid, so that reg.5 continues to apply.

The Welfare Reform Act 2012 contains a regulation-making power that could have been used to avoid these anomalous results. This is in para.2 of Sch.5 (see Vol.II of this series, *Universal Credit etc.*), which applies when a claimant is entitled to both universal credit and a "relevant benefit", i.e. new style JSA or new style ESA. Paragraph 2(2) in particular allows regulations to provide in such circumstances for no amount to be payable by way of the relevant benefit. A Departmental memorandum to the House of Lords Select Committee on Delegated Powers and Regulatory Reform (see para1.271 of Vol.II) indicated that among the intended uses of the powers in para.2 was to specify in cases of dual entitlement whether the claimant would be paid only universal credit or only the relevant benefit or both. It was also intended to set out, if sanctions were applicable, which benefit was to be reduced first and to provide, if appropriate, that the application of a sanction to one benefit did not increase the amount of another. However, no regulations have been made to carry out those intentions. The only use of para.2 appears to have been in making reg.5 in its current form (and reg.42 of the ESA Regulations 2013), under the power in para.2(3), para.2(2) not being mentioned in the list of statutory powers invoked in the preamble to the Regulations. If regulations had provided that when there was dual entitlement no amount of new style JSA or ESA was to be payable, then there would have been no income from the benefit concerned to be taken into account in the calculation of the amount of universal credit payable and any reduction of benefit under a sanction would bite on the whole amount of the universal credit in the ordinary way. The non-application of the work-related and connected requirements and the sanctions regime under new style JSA would then have been part of a coherent structure. But that is not the actual state of the legislation.

It might be asked whether the provisions for reduction periods under the universal credit provisions to be applied to a new style JSA award and vice versa supply a way out of the anomalies. The answer is no. Regulation 30 of the present Regulations only applies where a claimant ceases to be entitled to universal credit and is or becomes entitled to new style JSA, when any universal credit sanction reduction period is applied to the JSA award. Regulation 30 does not apply during any period of dual entitlement. By contrast, when the opposite direction is considered, reg.6 applies only where the claimant is entitled to new style JSA subject to a sanction reduction period, becomes entitled to universal credit and *remains* entitled to new style JSA. But the result is that the reduction ceases to be applicable to the JSA award. That appears merely to reinforce the position under reg.5. Paragraph 2 of Sch.11 to the UC Regulations 2013 (in Vol.II, and see para.1 of Sch.11 for new style ESA) provides that in those circumstances, and also where the claimant ceases to be entitled to new style JSA, the JSA reduction is to be applied to the universal credit award. That works if entitlement to JSA has ceased, but if that entitlement continues, it is still the case that the unreduced amount of JSA counts as income in the calculation of the amount of any universal credit award and so cuts into the amount available for reduction under the universal credit sanction. That sanction cannot as such reduce the amount of new style JSA payable.

In the examination by the Social Security Advisory Committee (SSAC) of the proposal to amend reg.18 (see the notes to reg.18) at its meeting of September 8, 2021, the anomalous results flowing from the prohibition on applying a sanction to new style JSA when the claimant is also entitled to universal credit were raised. The DWP appeared initially not to consider the results problematic, but following the SSAC's expressions of concern, it said that it was starting to look at the issue of dual entitlement (para.1.2 of the minutes of the SSAC meeting of October 7, 2021, published with the minutes of the September meeting). The chair's letter of October 7 recorded the SSAC's strong view that the inconsistency be reviewed and addressed at the earliest opportunity. The Minister's reply of the same date committed to an investigation of whether the effect of reg.5 (and reg.42 of the ESA Regulations 2013) represented the policy intent and, if not, the extent of the issues, and to producing proposals addressing the SSAC's concerns.

There was some further discussion at the April 27, 2022 meeting of the SSAC. A letter to the Committee of April 14, 2022 from the Minister for Employment, Mims Davies, (Annex B to the minutes) had put forward the suggested solution, after consideration of the complexities, of reducing the amount of any new style JSA or ESA payment to nil while a universal credit sanction was being applied. However, at the meeting a somewhat obscure alternative suggestion (para.3.3(c) of the minutes) apparently involving only reducing the amount of the new style payment by the amount of the universal credit sanction, was said by officials to make good logical sense and to require looking into. A process of consideration of delivery implications, to lead to proposals for changes to legislation had been said in the Minister's letter already to be under way.

A letter dated March 6, 2023 (but not published on the internet until April 27, 2023) from the current Minister for Employment, Guy Opperman, revealed that there had been further correspondence and a meeting of officials in June 2022, but that the DWP had concluded that the SSAC alternative would lead to the same result in nearly every case at the cost of additional complexity. In January 2023 Mr Opperman had informed the SSAC that the then Secretary of State had decided to proceed with the original proposal. The letter of March 6, 2023 added that the DWP had been "unable to finalise a realistic delivery date for the digital and process changes required to implement the proposal due to resource constraints". It was unlikely, given the small number of people impacted, that the change would be delivered in the near future, as the DWP was focused on priority items with a greater impact on services and claimants.

Sanction ceases to apply to jobseeker's allowance

6.—(1) This regulation applies where— 7.14

(a) a person is entitled to a jobseeker's allowance;

(b) there is a reduction relating to the person's award of a jobseeker's allowance under section 6J or 6K of the Act;

(c) the person becomes entitled to universal credit; and

(d) the person remains entitled to a jobseeker's allowance.

(2) Any reduction relating to the person's award of the jobseeker's allowance is to cease being applied to the award of the jobseeker's allowance.

DEFINITION

"the Act"—see reg.2(2).

GENERAL NOTE

This regulation appears to have been made under ss.6J(7)(a) and 6K(9)(a) of the new style Jobseekers Act 1995, as well as para.2(3)(b) of Sch.5 to the Welfare Reform Act 2012 (in Vol.II of this series, *Universal Credit etc.*). 7.15

Where a new style JSA reduction is in place following a sanction and the claimant then becomes entitled to universal credit as well as JSA, the JSA reduction ceases to apply. The person will instead be dealt with under the universal credit regime, as explained in the notes to reg.5. In the circumstances covered by reg.6, of continuing dual entitlement, reg.112 of and para.2 of Sch.11 to the UC Regulations 2013 apply to move the unexpired portion of the JSA sanction reduction period to the universal credit award, but with the anomalous consequences explored in the notes to reg.5. If the claimant ceases to be entitled to new style JSA, para.2 of Sch.11 still applies, but nothing needs to be said about that in the JSA legislation because entitlement and thus payment has by definition stopped.

It is not clear whether, if the claimant subsequently ceases to be entitled to universal credit while some part of the original JSA sanction period remains unexpired, the case falls within reg.30 below. Has there been a reduction under s.26 or 27 of the WRA 2012?

Claimant commitment – date and method of acceptance

7.—(1) For the purposes of section 1(2)(b) of the Act, a claimant who has accepted a claimant commitment within such period after making a claim for a jobseeker's allowance as the Secretary of State specifies is to be treated as having accepted that claimant commitment on the first day of the period in respect of which the claim is made. 7.16

(2) The Secretary of State may extend the period within which a claimant is required to accept a claimant commitment or an updated claimant commitment where the claimant requests that the Secretary of State review—

(a) any action proposed as a work search requirement or a work availability requirement; or

(b) whether any limitation should apply to those requirements,

and the Secretary of State considers that the request is reasonable.

(3) A claimant must accept a claimant commitment by one of the following methods, as specified by the Secretary of State—

(a) electronically;

(b) by telephone; or

(c) in writing.

DEFINITIONS

"the Act"—see reg.2(2).
"claimant"—see Jobseekers Act 1995 s.35(1).
"claimant commitment"—see Jobseekers Act 1995 s.6A.
"work availability requirement"—see Jobseekers Act 1995 ss.35(1) and 6E.
"work search requirement"—see Jobseekers Act 1995 ss.35(1) and 6D.
"writing"—see Interpretation Act 1978 Sch.1.

GENERAL NOTE

7.17 By virtue of s.1(2)(b) of the new style Jobseekers Act 1995 it is a condition of entitlement to new style JSA that a claimant has accepted a claimant commitment as described in s.6A. See the notes to s.6A for the nature of a claimant commitment (i.e. a record of the claimant's responsibilities in relation to an award of JSA) and what is entailed in accepting such a record. There are exceptions from that condition in reg.8 below. Regulation 7 deals with the time within which and the method by which a claimant commitment must be accepted. The relevant regulation-making power is in s.6A(5), which requires the most up-to-date version of a claimant commitment to be accepted "in such manner as may be prescribed". However, there appears to be no equivalent to s.4(7) of the Welfare Reform Act 2012 in relation to universal credit (see Vol.II of this series), to allow regulations to specify circumstances in which a claimant is to be treated as having or as not having accepted a claimant commitment (s.6I does not give power as there is no requirement, as opposed to a condition of entitlement, to accept a claimant commitment). Treating a claimant commitment as having been accepted before the date of actual acceptance seems to go beyond a prescription of the "manner" of acceptance under s.6A(5), which plainly authorises the making of reg.7(3). There is therefore considerable doubt about the validity of paras (1) and (2), but as they operate in general beneficially towards claimants a challenge to their validity is unlikely.

Note that, before there can be a question of acceptance, a claimant commitment must have been prepared on behalf of the Secretary of State and offered for acceptance. A claimant should not be found to have failed to satisfy the basic condition in s.1(2)(b) merely by failing to attend and participate in what is called a commitments interview with a work coach.

However, the effect of such a failure is difficult to work out, especially if the interview is on a new claim. In general, such a failure to participate, for no good reason, whether in relation to an interview under s.6B of the new style Jobseekers Act 1995 (work-focused interview requirement) or under s.6G (connected requirements) is a matter for a sanction under s.6K(2), not for a decision that there is no entitlement to new style JSA. But a claimant cannot be allowed to stymie the process of drawing up a claimant commitment into a form in which it can be accepted or not accepted by refusing to take part in that process. It would not appear proper in such circumstances for the work coach to prepare a generic commitment recording work requirements that had not been identified through consideration of the claimant's individual circumstances and present that formally to the claimant for acceptance or not. However, it is suggested that, once the question of any good reason for failing to participate in the interview has been explored, possibly after a second appointment has been offered, a decision could properly be made that the claimant is not entitled to new style JSA from the outset by reason of failing to satisfy the basic condition in s.1(2)(b). The claimant will not have accepted a claimant commitment. Chapter J1 of *Advice for decision making*, on the equivalent universal credit provision, does not seem to deal with this scenario.

By contrast, that chapter does deal in some detail with the situation where a claimant has accepted a claimant commitment and there is a question of review of some work-related requirement recorded in that current version. There seems no reason why that guidance should not also be relevant to new style JSA, although not included in the specific guidance for that benefit. The note to J1031 now says that while a requirement to accept the most up-to-date version of the claimant commitment (see s.6A(5) of the new style Jobseekers Act 1995) does not make it compulsory for there to be an interview before a revised commitment is put to a claimant for acceptance, the public law principles of fairness (ADM Chapter K1) must be met, taking account of the individual circumstances of the case, when notifying a claimant of the requirement to accept any new commitments and of the consequences of failing to do so. If the claimant attends the interview and the work coach draws up a revised commitment, the claimant can accept then or be given a "cooling-off period" usually of seven days in which to do so (during which entitlement continues by virtue of the acceptance of the existing version: J1035). If the claimant does not attend the interview or participate in substance, this guidance is given in J1034 and J1036 (see the previous edition of this volume for the form of the guidance in force at the time of the decision in *FO v SSWP (UC)*, discussed below):

> "J1034 Taking part in an interview can be set as a requirement for the claimant even if taking part in an interview is not included on the current claimant commitment. The claimant must be separately and correctly informed of the date, time and place of the appointment, the reasons for the interview and the consequences of failing to take part in that appointment.
> ...
>
> J1036 If the claimant
>
> 1. fails to attend the interview the DM will consider a sanction (see Note 1) or
> 2. takes part in the interview but fails or refuses to accept the new commitments at the end of the cooling off period the DM will end the award of UC (see Note 2).
>
> Note 1: There is no legal basis to consider ending the award of UC for not having a new claimant commitment since the previous claimant commitment still applies, but requirements can be set outside of the claimant commitment to take part in an interview, if it is reasonable to do so. Any failure to comply with a requirement to participate in a commitments review for no good reason, i.e. they fail to attend the interview, is a sanctionable failure and not reason to suspend or terminate the award of UC. The guidance on low-level sanctions in ADM Chapter K5 will apply.
>
> Note 2: Only if the claimant attends the interview as required but refuses or fails to accept the new commitments can the DM consider terminating the award of UC after a cooling off period."

That guidance appears to have been sharpened up, as compared with that set out in the 2022/23 edition of this volume, but in what is submitted is the wrong direction. It is submitted that note 1 is correct for both universal credit and new style JSA so far as it goes and if properly understood, but that note 2 is incorrect. Note 1 in its terms is restricted to the position as at the point that the claimant fails to participate in the commitment review interview. That in itself does not justify terminating the award of new style JSA for failing to satisfy the basic condition in s.1(2)(b) of the new style Jobseekers Act 1995. There could be a sanction under s.6K(2), as explained above, although note that neither s.6B, with reg.10, nor s.6G(1) allow participation in an interview for the sole purpose of reviewing or discussing the claimant commitment to be required. Under s.6B and reg.10 the purpose must be related to wider matters relating to work prospects, opportunities or activities and under s.6G(1) must be related to the imposition of or compliance with a work-related requirement. However, for similar reasons as discussed above, it would be wrong to allow a claimant to stymie the process of review by refusing to participate in interviews, even though the first sanction might continue until the claimant met the compliance condition of participating in an interview. It is submitted that, just as on a new claim, a point would come where a revised claimant commitment could be put formally to a claimant for acceptance within a reasonable time, despite there having been no interview, so that a failure to accept that most up-to-date version would constitute a failure to satisfy s.1(2)(b). On that ground, it is submitted that Note 2 is wrong in its categorical statement that termination of an award can only be considered after a claimant has attended an interview and refused or failed to accept a new claimant commitment.

The confusion that can result from a misunderstanding of the ADM guidance is well illustrated in *FO v SSWP (UC)* [2022] UKUT 56 (AAC). There, according to the DWP, the appellant claimant's partner (therefore also a claimant) had been set an on-line "To-do" on her universal credit account on March 23, 2020 to accept her claimant commitments (sic) by March 29, 2020 (later extended to April 14, 2020). In the absence of such acceptance, the couple's "claim" was "closed" on April 14, 2020. The appeal against that decision was disallowed by the First-tier Tribunal. Judge Wikeley had no difficulty in allowing the further appeal and substituting a decision that the universal credit award should not have been terminated on April 14, 2020, because the documentary evidence submitted to the First-tier Tribunal was hopelessly inadequate. There was no copy of the claimant commitment document said not have been accepted or of the "To-do", let alone of any existing document or evidence of prior discussions, so that the DWP's submission relied almost entirely on mere assertion about what had happened. Even before the Upper Tribunal the Secretary of State's representative was unable to provide any of that material or explain why, given the suspension of work search and availability requirements from March 30, 2020 due to the coronavirus pandemic, the matter was pursued after that date.

However, in the course of the Upper Tribunal proceedings the Secretary of State's representative made a submission that the First-tier Tribunal erred in law in finding that entitlement would automatically end where a claimant failed to accept a claimant commitment in circumstances where there was an award already in place, repeating the substance of the guidance then in ADM J1034 and now in Notes 1 and 2 to J1036. The difficulty with that submission is that it would seem that if such a "To-do" has been placed on a claimant's account a revised claimant commitment must have been prepared that has become the most up-to-date version. Although the condition, in that case through the combination of ss.4(1)(e) and 14(5) of the WRA 2012, of having accepted the most up-to-date version of the claimant commitment could not be said to have ceased to be satisfied until after the expiry of the time given for acceptance, after that point the existence of the previous claimant commitment would not seem to be an obstacle to the termination of the couple's award. The submission also noted that the representative had been unable to find any documentary evidence of any discussion about the contents of the revised claimant commitment before the "To-do" of March 23, 2020. Such a breach of the duty of fairness or the "prior information duty" (see the notes to ss.6A and 6K of the new style Jobseekers Act 1995) might undermine the validity of the revised claimant commitment on appeal, if the claimant or the subsisting evidence raised an issue as lack of opportunity to make meaningful representations about the contents of the revised claimant commitment (as now acknowledged in ADM J1035). The judge's substituted decision in *FO* that the award of universal credit should not have been terminated on April 14, 2020 might be better supported on that basis (or on the judge's alternative reasoning that by April 14, 2020 there were exceptional circumstances absolving the partner under the equivalent of reg.8(b) from the condition of having accepted a claimant commitment), rather than on the apparent basis of the Secretary of State's submission. But if in other cases the lack of opportunity was created by a claimant's own unreasonable failure to participate in an interview there can hardly be said to have been any unfairness.

Paragraph (1)

7.18 On a new claim, if the claimant commitment is accepted within the time specified by the Secretary of State (as extended under para.(2) if applicable), and by a method prescribed in para.(3), the condition of entitlement in s.1(2)(b) of the new style Jobseekers Act 1995 is deemed to be satisfied from the first day of the period claimed for. Otherwise, the condition would only be met from the date on which the acceptance by a prescribed method actually took place, as would be the case if para.(1) is not validly made. No-one is likely to object to para.(1) being given effect even if invalid. Under s.6A(2) of the Act, the Secretary of State may review and up-date a claimant commitment as he thinks fit and under s.6A(5) a claimant has to accept the most up-to-date version. Such circumstances do not seem to fall within either paras (1) or (2), although para.(2) refers to a period within which a claimant is required to accept an up-dated claimant commitment and its possible extension. There is doubt whether an acceptance of an up-dated claimant commitment after a review strictly takes effect only from its actual date or from the date of the preparation of the up-dated version, but again no-one is likely to complain if the Secretary of State gives retrospective effect to an acceptance of an up-dated version within a specified time, as consistency would suggest is fair.

Paragraph (2)

This paragraph allows the Secretary of State, in defined circumstances, to extend the period within which a person is required (which is only in the sense of required in order to take advantage of giving a retrospective effect to the acceptance) to accept a claimant commitment or an up-dated version. It is arguable that no such authorisation is needed to allow the Secretary of State to extend any period as first specified under para.(1), so that the form of the restrictions in sub-paras (a) and (b) may not matter too much. Those provisions purport to apply when a claimant has requested that the Secretary of State review any action proposed as a work search or work availability requirement (see s.6D and 6E of the new style Jobseekers Act 1995) or whether any limitation should apply to those requirements (see reg.14 below). The main difficulty with them, apart from the fact that s.6E contains no power for the Secretary of State to specify particular action in relation to a work availability requirement, is that the legislation contains no formal process of review of the "proposals" mentioned. The reference must presumably be to the power under s.6H(3) for the Secretary of State to revoke or change any requirement imposed under the Act or any specification of action to be taken and to a request to exercise that power in relation to action specified under s.6D or 6E. Those difficulties perhaps reinforce the argument for the Secretary of State being able to extend the period for acceptance of the claimant whenever it appears reasonable to do so, although that would involve giving no effective force to para.(2). **7.19**

Paragraph (3)

This paragraph, as allowed by s.6A(5) of the new style Jobseekers Act 1995, requires that any acceptance of a claimant commitment can count for the purposes of s.1(2)(b) only if done electronically, by telephone or in writing, with the Secretary of State able to specify which in any particular case. "Electronically" will no doubt cover a range of methods. It seems bizarre that acceptance orally or otherwise face-to-face is not allowed, although the telephone is covered. Both methods are capable of being recorded in some permanent form. In so far as no account is taken of the circumstances of claimants with disabilities and the problem cannot be taken care of under reg.8 this provision must be vulnerable to a challenge under the Human Rights Act 1998 for discrimination contrary to art.14 of the European Convention on Human Rights. **7.20**

Claimant commitment – exceptions

8.—A claimant may be entitled to a jobseeker's allowance without having accepted a claimant commitment if the Secretary of State considers— **7.21**

(a) the claimant cannot accept a claimant commitment because they lack capacity to do so; or
(b) there are exceptional circumstances in which it would be unreasonable to expect the person to accept a claimant commitment.

DEFINITIONS

"claimant"—see Jobseekers Act 1995 s.35(1).
"claimant commitment"—see Jobseekers Act 1995 s.6A.

GENERAL NOTE

7.22 See the notes to s.1(2)(b) of the new style Jobseekers Act 1995 (Pt I of this volume) for the argument that that Act contains no power to make a regulation allowing there to be entitlement to new style JSA without the claimant having accepted a claimant commitment. There must therefore be doubt about the validity of the whole of reg.8, although, as with reg.7(1) and (2), presumably no-one will object to its application in practice. That is especially important since, as argued in the section of the notes to ss.1, 6D and 6E on *Temporary coronavirus provisions* in previous editions of this volume, the use of reg.8(b) appears to have been central to the lifting of conditionality for the three months from March 30, 2020.

The effect of reg.8, if valid, is that the condition of entitlement in s.1(2)(b) of the new style Jobseekers Act 1995 does not have to be met where the claimant either lacks the capacity to accept a claimant commitment (para.(a)) or there are exceptional circumstances in which it would be unreasonable to expect the claimant to accept a claimant commitment (para.(b)). Both provisions, but especially para.(b), contain elements of judgment. If "accepting" a claimant commitment has the restricted meaning suggested in the notes to s.6A of the Act, that will affect when it might be unreasonable to expect a claimant to do so. If a claimant would be unable or experience undue difficulty in accepting a claimant commitment by any of the methods required by reg.7(3), that would suggest that it would be unreasonable to expect the claimant to take those steps to accept the claimant commitment. In a case where a claimant is entitled to both new style JSA and universal credit, so that under reg.5 above no work-related or connected requirements can be imposed in relation to JSA, it is arguable that it would be unreasonable to expect the claimant to accept a JSA claimant commitment.

Expected hours

7.23 **9.**—(1) The expected number of hours per week in relation to a claimant for the purposes of determining any limitations on work search or work availability requirements is 35 unless some lesser number of hours applies in the claimant's case under paragraph (2).

(2) The lesser number of hours referred to in paragraph (1) is—

(a) where—

(i) the claimant is a relevant carer, a responsible carer or a responsible foster parent; and

(ii) the Secretary of State is satisfied that the claimant has reasonable prospects of obtaining paid work, the number of hours, being less than 35, that the Secretary of State considers is compatible with those caring responsibilities;

(b) where the claimant is a responsible carer or a responsible foster carer for a child under the age of 13, the number of hours that the Secretary of State considers is compatible with their caring responsibilities for the child during the child's normal school hours (including the normal time it takes the child to travel to and from school); or

(c) where the claimant has a physical or mental impairment, the number of hours that the Secretary of State considers is reasonable in light of the impairment.

DEFINITIONS

"child"—see Jobseekers Act 1995 s.35(1).
"claimant"—*ibid.*

"relevant carer"—see reg.4(1).
"responsible carer"—*ibid.*
"responsible foster parent"—*ibid.*
"work availability requirement"—see Jobseekers Act 1995 ss.35(1) and 6E.
"work search requirement"—see Jobseekers Act 1995 ss.35(1) and 6D.

General Note

The identification of the expected number of hours under this provision is relevant to reg.12(1)(a) and (2) below (hours of work search needed to avoid being deemed not to have complied with the work search requirement under s.6D of the new style Jobseekers Act 1995) and reg.14(5) (limitations for certain claimants on the work for which they must be available and for which they must search). 7.24

The number of hours under para.(1) is 35, unless some lesser number is applicable under para.(2). Can the number be reduced to zero? Why not? Zero is a number and it is less than 35. There are three alternative categories in para.(2). Sub-paragraph (a) applies where the claimant is a relevant carer, a responsible carer or a responsible foster parent (all as identified in reg.4), and so has some substantial caring responsibility. Then, if the claimant nonetheless has reasonable prospects of obtaining paid work (including obtaining more or better paid work: reg.3(7)), the expected hours are what is compatible with those caring responsibilities. Sub-paragraph (b) applies where the claimant is a responsible carer for a child under the age of 13, when the expected hours are those compatible with the child's normal school and travel hours. That rule apparently applies as much during school holidays as during term-time. Sub-paragraph (c) applies where the claimant has a physical or mental impairment (not further defined), when the expected hours are those reasonable in the light of the impairment.

See the notes to reg.88 of the Universal Credit Regulations in Vol.II of this series for the administrative changes made with effect from October 25, 2023 to the identification of expected hours for universal credit purposes. But note that the press release announcing those changes was expressly in terms of that benefit, so that it appears that no change of approach was intended in relation to new style JSA.

Note that the application of the deeming of non-compliance with the work search requirement under reg.12(1) if action is not taken for the expected number of hours is subject to deductions of hours under reg.12(2), including for temporary circumstances. Also note regs 15–16A on circumstances in which the work availability and work search requirements cannot be imposed or are moderated, particularly reg.16(4) (temporary circumstances etc) and regs 16(5) and 16A (unfitness for work for short periods).

Purposes of a work-focused interview

10.—The purposes of a work-focused interview are any or all of the following— 7.25

(a) assessing the claimant's prospects for remaining in or obtaining work;
(b) assisting or encouraging the claimant to remain in or obtain work;
(c) identifying activities that the claimant may undertake that will make remaining in or obtaining work more likely;
(d) identifying training, educational or rehabilitation opportunities for the claimant which may make it more likely that the claimant will remain in or obtain work or be able to do so;
(e) identifying current or future work opportunities for the claimant that are relevant to the claimant's needs and abilities.

Definition

"claimant"—see Jobseekers Act 1995 s.35(1).

GENERAL NOTE

7.26 This provision sets out the purposes of a work-focused interview for the purposes of the definition in s.6B(2) of the new style Jobseekers Act 1995. The purposes could probably not be set out more widely, especially given that obtaining paid work includes obtaining more or better paid work (reg.3(7)) and that s.6B covers work preparation as well as work. It appears odd that reg.10 uses the word "work" and not "paid work", by contrast with the terms of ss.6C–6E and the regulations related to those sections. The difference may though be deliberate, taking account that s.6B only requires the purposes of the interview to be related to work or work preparation, so that an interview may legitimately include discussion of opportunities that would improve the claimant's prospects of obtaining unpaid work, e.g. as an intern or in voluntary work. Compare ESA Regulations 2008 reg.55 and UC Regulations 2013 reg.93, the latter of which is in terms of paid work. Arguably, even if there is no realistic prospect of a claimant obtaining any kind of work, the purpose of assessing those prospects or lack of prospects in an interview could still be fulfilled.

Note that the permitted purposes of a work-focused interview do not include discussion of the drawing up or review of a claimant commitment as such. However, discussion of the wider opportunities, activities and prospects listed and the encouragement to obtain work would be relevant to what work-related requirements, if any, should be imposed, which would then be recorded in a claimant commitment.

Work search requirement: interviews

7.27 **11.**—A claimant is to be treated as not having complied with a work search requirement to apply for a particular vacancy for paid work where the claimant fails to participate in an interview offered to the claimant in connection with the vacancy.

DEFINITIONS

"claimant"—see Jobseekers Act 1995 s.35(1).

"work search requirement"—see Jobseekers Act 1995 ss.35(1) and 6D(1).

GENERAL NOTE

7.28 This provision, made under s.6I(a) of the new style Jobseekers Act 1995, applies when the Secretary of State has required under s.6D(1)(b) that the claimant take the particular action of applying for a specified vacancy for paid work. A claimant who fails to participate in an interview offered in connection with the vacancy is deemed not to have complied with the work search requirement. See the notes to s.6D, and the notes to ss.6B and 6K for "participation" in an interview.

Work search requirement: all reasonable action

7.29 **12.**—(1) A claimant is to be treated as not having complied with a work search requirement to take all reasonable action for the purpose of obtaining paid work in any week unless—

(a) either—

(i) for the purpose of obtaining paid work, the claimant takes action for the claimant's expected hours per week minus any relevant deductions; or

(ii) the Secretary of State is satisfied that the claimant has taken all reasonable action for the purpose of obtaining paid work despite the number of hours that the claimant spends taking such action being lower than the expected number of hours per week; and

(b) that action gives the claimant the best prospects of obtaining work.

(2) In this regulation "relevant deductions" means the total of any time agreed by the Secretary of State—

(a) for the claimant to carry out paid work in that week;

(b) for the claimant to carry out voluntary work in that week;

(c) for the claimant to carry out a work preparation requirement, or voluntary work preparation, in that week; or

(d) for the claimant to deal with temporary child care responsibilities, a domestic emergency, funeral arrangements or other temporary circumstances.

(3) For the purpose of paragraph (2)(b) the time agreed by the Secretary of State for the claimant to carry out voluntary work must not exceed 50% of the claimant's expected number of hours per week.

DEFINITIONS

"claimant"—see Jobseekers Act 1995 s.35(1).
"expected number of hours"—see reg.9.
"obtaining paid work'—see reg.3(7).
"voluntary work"—see reg.2(2).
"voluntary work preparation"—see reg.4(1).
"week"—see Jobseekers Act 1995 s.35(1).
"work preparation requirement"—see Jobseekers Act 1995 ss.35(1) and 6C(1).
"work search requirement"—see Jobseekers Act 1995 ss.35(1) and 6D(1).

GENERAL NOTE

In old style JSA, the claimant had to be "actively seeking employment", which was a condition of entitlement. For new style JSA, this became the obligation to comply with a work search requirement, which is no longer a condition of entitlement, but a requirement failure to comply with which for no good reason leads to the sanction of reduction in benefit. Section 6D of the new style Jobseekers Act 1995 deals with what is entailed in that requirement, covering both taking all reasonable action for the purpose of obtaining paid work or more or better-paid work (subs.(1)(a)) and taking any particular action specified by the Secretary of State for that purpose (subs.(1)(b)). Further provision is made in ss.6F and 6H and in regs 14–16A below (limitations on the kind of work that a claimant must search for and circumstances in which the requirement cannot be imposed). 7.30

The present regulation, made under s.6I(a) of the Act, deems certain claimants not to have complied with a work search requirement under s.6D(1)(a) to take all reasonable action. Although in form meeting the conditions in para.(1) merely lifts the deeming of non-compliance, there would be no point in making such detailed provision if claimants were not to be positively treated as having complied if the conditions are met. See the notes to s.6D and see reg.14 below for limitations on the kind of work that needs to be searched for. A failure for no good reason to comply with the requirement under s.6D(1)(a) can lead to a medium-level sanction under s.6K(2)(a) of the Act and reg.17 (para.(a) of the definition of "medium-level sanction") below.

To avoid the deeming a claimant must get within *both* sub-paras (a) *and* (b) of para.(1).

There are two alternative routes to getting within sub-para.(a). Although the route in head (i), relating to spending the "expected hours" (starting point under reg.9, 35), has been described as the "primary" rule in some previous editions, it is now submitted that that is misleading. Although head (ii), with the route of having taken all reasonable action in the week in question, is in a sense only needed if the claimant spent less than the expected hours, logically the two routes are of equal status. One of the routes had to appear before the other in sub-para.(a) and the two routes could with the same effect have been put in the opposite order. The effect of reading the two provisions together is that there is no rigid rule that claimants be held to spending the expected hours in work search week after week, even though that may be the easiest point to start the enquiry. The ultimate test is what is reasonable. The sentence in the middle of para.32 of *S v SSWP (UC)* [2017] UKUT 477 (AAC) (see the notes to s.6J of the new style Jobseekers Act 1995 for the details) saying that if "a claimant spends less than 35 hours, or the quality of the work search is disputed, he will need to rely on section 27(2) [i.e. the 'for no good reason' rule] if he seeks to avoid a sanction" is not to be taken to indicate the contrary. That sentence is immediately followed by an acknowledgement of the effect of head (ii).

The para.(1)(a)(i) route applies where the claimant spends at least the "expected number of hours per week" (reg.9), less deductions for work or work-related activities or various emergency, urgent or other temporary difficulties (para.(2), subject to the further condition about voluntary work in para.(3)), in taking action for the purpose of obtaining paid work. Note that the starting point of expected hours under reg.9 may be reduced from 35 (arguably to nil, if appropriate) to take account of regular caring responsibilities and physical or mental impairments. The time to count as a deduction under para.(2) must be agreed by the Secretary of State. The words might suggest that the agreement must come in advance of the activity that might qualify. However, it would seem unrealistic for claimants to predict, say, the future occurrence of domestic emergencies so as to seek the Secretary of State's agreement in advance. Thus, it would seem, and would be in line with the normal pattern of claimants signing a declaration that they have been seeking work in the previous fortnight, that a subsequent agreement will do (although no doubt it would be sensible for claimants to raise potential issues in advance where possible). It must be the case that, while the Secretary of State appears to have an open-ended discretion whether or not to agree to any particular hours being deducted under para.(2), on appeal against any sanction for failure to comply with the work search requirement under s.6D(1)(a) a tribunal is allowed to substitute its own judgment about what should have been agreed. Even if it were to be held that whatever had or had not been agreed by the Secretary of State has to control whether there had been a sanctionable failure, the reasonableness or otherwise of the Secretary of State's view would be relevant to whether a failure to comply was "for no good reason". The deductions for hours spent in paid or voluntary work and work preparation are important. Would para.(2)(d) allow the Secretary of State to allow short "holidays" from work search, under the heading of temporary circumstances or temporary child care responsibilities (cf. reg.19(1)(p) and (2) of the JSA Regulations 1996)? Or would such an allowance fall more naturally under reg.16(4)(a) or (b) (work search requirement not to be imposed where it would be unreasonable to do so because of temporary child care responsibilities or temporary circumstances)?

However, if the claimant does not meet the expected hours condition, which for most claimants will be for 35 hours per week, sub-para.(a) can nevertheless be satisfied under head (ii) if the claimant has taken all reasonable action for the purpose of obtaining paid work. This important provision must never be overlooked. It can render some of the rigours of head (i) irrelevant and can go some way to meet the criticism that, especially for those who have been unemployed for some time, it is impossible to fill 35 hours with meaningful work-search action week after week.

7.31 In *RR v SSWP (UC)* [2017] UKUT 459 (AAC), the First-tier Tribunal, in upholding two medium-level sanctions on the basis that the claimant had not taken work-search action for the 35 expected hours in two weeks, failed to consider whether there should be deductions from 35 hours under the equivalent (though different in form) to reg.12(2) when there was evidence of circumstances (having to deal with the fall-out from divorce or other family proceedings) that could have amounted to a domestic emergency or other temporary circumstances. The tribunal appeared to think that the 35 hours were immutable, which was plainly an error of law. Alternatively, the claimant could have been taken to satisfy the condition in the equivalent of s.6D(1)(a) through the equivalent of reg.12(1)(a)(ii), which applies even though the expected hours, less deductions, are not met. The decision-maker and the tribunal put some emphasis on the claimant having agreed in her claimant commitment to prepare and look for work for 35 hours a week. Judge Wikeley pointed out that the claimant commitment was only in terms of "normally" spending 35 hours a week, but in fact the number of hours specified in a claimant commitment cannot be directly relevant unless they establish a lesser number of hours under reg.9(2) or an agreement to a deduction of hours under reg.12(2). The test is in terms of the expected hours less deductions, which the claimant commitment merely records, or "all reasonable action" under reg.12(1)(a)(ii). It is worth noting that the claimant commitment in *RR* (following what appears to be a standard form) specified 35 hours normally for a combination of work preparation (s.6C of the new style Jobseekers Act 1995) *and* work search, so did incorporate an unquantified deduction under the equivalent of reg.12(2)(c).

The judge, in re-making the decision in the claimant's favour, did not expressly consider the condition that a deduction under para.(2) be agreed by the Secretary of State. He must either have regarded that condition as one on which a First-tier Tribunal was entitled to substitute its own agreement or have regarded the Secretary of State's support of the appeal in the Upper Tribunal and of the substitution of a decision as necessarily involving agreement to a deduction. He also suggested that an alternative way of looking at the case could have been to consider whether a provision similar to reg.16(4)(b) of these Regulations applied (subject to temporary circumstances), so that no work search requirement could be imposed for the weeks in question. See the notes to reg.16.

Under (b), the action under (a) must give the claimant the best prospects of obtaining work, which arguably in the context must mean paid work. Taken at face value, that condition imposes an almost impossibly high standard, because there will nearly always be something extra that the claimant could do to improve prospects of obtaining work. The condition must therefore be interpreted in a way that leaves some work for condition (a) to do and with some degree of common sense, taking account of all the circumstances, especially any factors that have led to a reduction in the expected hours below 35 or a deduction under sub-para.(a)(i) and (2), as well as matters such as the state of the local labour market, what the claimant has done in previous weeks and how successful or otherwise those actions were (compare reg.18(3) of the JSA Regulations 1996). The work search requirement in s.6D(1)(a) is only to take all reasonable action. The reference here to the best prospects of obtaining work cannot be allowed to make the test as set out in the primary legislation stricter than that. There will of course be considerable difficulty in checking on the precise number of hours spent in taking relevant action, depending on what might count as action (see the notes to s.6D) and on what might be required from claimants in the way of record keeping. It may be that it will be much easier to define non-compliance with the requirement in s.6D(1)(b) of the Act to take particular action specified by the Secretary of State, although such a failure will only attract a low-level sanction under s.6K(2)(a) and reg.17 (para.(c) of definition of "low-level sanction") below.

In the Upper Tribunal's substituted decision in *RR* (above), there was no express consideration of the equivalent of the overriding condition in sub-para.(b). That must be regarded as having been satisfied in the absence of it having been raised on behalf of the Secretary of State in the support of the appeal to the Upper Tribunal.

In *S v SSWP (UC)* [2017] UKUT 477 (AAC) (see the notes to s.6J of the new style Jobseekers Act 1995 for the details) the basis on which the First-tier Tribunal seemed to have accepted that the claimant had failed to take all reasonable action for the purpose of obtaining paid work in the various weeks in question was that he had failed to apply for vacancies outside the healthcare sector that the DWP said were suitable. The claimant's evidence was somewhat inconsistent and unconvincing, but he appears to have said that, although he did not apply for any vacancies, he had spent 35 hours in each week checking jobs websites and local newspapers. If that had been accepted, it could have been argued (see the beginning of this note) that, subject to the operation of para.(2)(b), the claimant not only escaped the deeming of non-compliance in para.(1) but fell to be treated as having complied with the eqivalent of the s.6D(1)(a) requirement. That point was not addressed in the Upper Tribunal's substituted decision dismissing the claimant's appeal (on the issue of "no good reason"). There was certainly evidence on which it could have been concluded that the action taken by the claimant, even if taking 35 hours each week, had not given him the best prospects of obtaining work. It would have been better if it had been spelled out just where the inadequacy of the claimant's job search fitted into the legislative structure. Did the claimant fail the expected hours test in para.(2)(a)(i) without being rescued by para.(2)(a)(ii) or did he get within para.(2)(a)(i), but fail the para.(2)(b) test?

Work availability requirement: able and willing immediately to take up paid work

7.32 **13.**—(1) Subject to paragraph (2), a claimant is to be treated as not having complied with a work availability requirement if the claimant is—

(a) not able and willing immediately to attend an interview offered to the claimant in connection with obtaining paid work;

(b) a prisoner on temporary release in accordance with the provisions of the Prison Act 1952 or rules made under section 39(6) of the Prisons (Scotland) Act 1989.

(2) A claimant is to be treated as having complied with a work availability requirement despite not being able immediately to take up paid work, if paragraph (3), (4) or (5) applies.

(3) This paragraph applies where—

(a) a claimant is a responsible carer or a relevant carer;

(b) the Secretary of State is satisfied that as a consequence the claimant needs a period of up to one month to take up paid work, or up to 48 hours to attend an interview in connection with obtaining paid work, taking into account alternative care arrangements; and

(c) the claimant is able and willing to take up paid work, or attend such an interview, on being given notice for that period.

(4) This paragraph applies where—

(a) a claimant is carrying out voluntary work;

(b) the Secretary of State is satisfied that as a consequence the claimant needs a period of up to one week to take up paid work, or up to 48 hours to attend an interview in connection with obtaining paid work; and

(c) the claimant is able and willing to take up paid work, or attend such an interview, on being given notice for that period.

(5) This paragraph applies where a claimant is—

(a) employed under a contract of service;

(b) required by section 86 of the Employment Rights Act 1996, or by the contract of service, to give notice to terminate the contract;

(c) able and willing to take up paid work once the notice period has expired; and

(d) able and willing to attend an interview in connection with obtaining paid work on being given 48 hours notice.

DEFINITIONS

"claimant"—see Jobseekers Act 1995 s.35(1).
"obtaining paid work"—see reg.3(7).
"relevant carer"—see reg.4(1).
"responsible carer"—*ibid.*

"voluntary work"—see reg.2(2).
"work availability requirement"—see Jobseekers Act 1995 ss.35(1) and 6E.

General Note

Temporary Coronavirus Provisions

The effect of the temporary coronavirus provisions relevant to the work availability requirement in new style JSA expired at the end of November 12, 2020. See previous editions of this volume for the details. 7.33

In old style JSA, s.6 of the old style Jobseekers Act 1995 stipulated that a claimant satisfied the condition of entitlement of being available for work if willing and able to take up immediately any employed earner's employment. For new style JSA, this became the obligation to comply with a work availability requirement, which is no longer a condition of entitlement, but a requirement failure to comply with which for no good reason leads to the sanction of reduction in benefit, although it is a condition of entitlement under s.1(2)(b) to accept a claimant commitment that should record the requirement. Section 6E of the new style Jobseekers Act 1995 deals with what is entailed in that requirement, in particular being able and willing immediately to take up paid work or more or better paid work. See reg.14 below for limitations on the kind of work for which a claimant must be available and regs 16 and 16A for other situations in which the "immediately" test is modified.

Paragraph (1) of this regulation specifies that a prisoner on temporary release is to be treated as not available (sub-para.(b)). More generally it provides in sub-para. (a) that a claimant is not available for work if not able and willing immediately to attend an interview offered to the claimant in connection with paid work, unless (as provided in para.(2)) one of the exemptions from the "immediately" requirement set out in paras (3), (4) or (5) applies. See the notes to s.6E for further discussion of the "immediately" test.

Under para.(2) a claimant who falls within paras (3), (4) or (5) is to be treated as complying with the work availability requirement, including as extended by para. (1). Paragraph (3) applies to those with child-care or other caring responsibilities who would need to take up to one month to take up paid work or up to 48 hours to attend an interview and are able and willing to do so if given that length of notice. Can para.(3)(b) allow claimants with caring responsibilities (noting that such claimants do not need to have sole or main responsibility) to have a holiday without needing to arrange some means of taking up work offers or interviews immediately? Or would such an allowance fall more naturally under reg.16(4)(a) or (b) (no need to be available immediately where work search requirement not to be imposed because it would be unreasonable to do so because of temporary child care responsibilities or temporary circumstances)? Paragraph (4) applies to claimants doing voluntary work (as defined in reg.2(2)), subject to the same conditions. Paragraph (5) applies to claimants in employment who are required to give notice to terminate their contract of employment and who are able and willing to take up paid work once that notice has expired and to attend an interview on 48 hours' notice.

Neither reg.13 nor s.6E of the new style Jobseekers Act 1995 says anything about what sort of paid work a claimant subject to the availability requirement must be able and willing to take up immediately. It cannot be the case that a claimant must be prepared to take up any kind of work at any level of remuneration, subject only to the limitations in reg.14 and the exceptions and modifications in regs 15–16A. That would be irrationally inconsistent with the content of the work search requirement under s.6D and reg.12, under which the fundamental obligation is to take all reasonable action for the purpose of obtaining paid work or more paid work, as well as any particular action specified by the Secretary of State (s.6D(1)). The criterion of reasonableness entails consideration of whether the nature of the work and level of remuneration is suitable for the claimant (in addition to the factors specifically mentioned in reg.14). The availability requirement must be applied consistently with whatever kind of work the claimant is being required to search for, as would seem to be further supported by the approach of reg.14 in applying limitations to both requirements.

Work search requirement and work availability requirement: limitations

7.34 **14.**—(1) Paragraphs (2) to (5) set out the limitations on a work search requirement and a work availability requirement.

(2) A work search requirement and a work availability requirement must be limited to work that is in a location which would normally take the claimant—

(a) a maximum of one hour and 30 minutes to travel from home to the location; and

(b) a maximum of one hour and 30 minutes to travel from the location to home.

(3) Where a claimant has previously carried out work of a particular nature, or at a particular level of remuneration, a work search requirement and a work availability requirement must be limited to work of a similar nature, or level of remuneration, for such period as the Secretary of State considers appropriate; but

(a) only if the Secretary of State is satisfied that the claimant will have reasonable prospects of obtaining paid work in spite of such limitation; and

(b) the limitation is to apply for no more than [[1]4 weeks] beginning on the date of claim.

(4) Where a claimant has a physical or mental impairment that has a substantial adverse effect on the claimant's ability to carry out work of a particular nature, or in particular locations, a work search requirement or work availability requirement must not relate to work of such a nature or in such locations.

(5) In the case of a claimant who is a relevant carer or a responsible carer or has a physical or mental impairment, a work search and work availability requirement must be limited to the number of hours that is determined to be the claimant's expected number of hours per week in accordance with regulation 9(2).

AMENDMENT

1. Universal Credit and Jobseeker's Allowance (Work Search and Work Availability Requirements – limitations) (Amendment) Regulations 2022 (SI 2022/108) reg.3 (February 8, 2022).

DEFINITIONS

"claimant"—see Jobseekers Act 1995 s.35(1).
"date of claim"—see reg.2(2).
"obtaining paid work"—see reg.3(7).
"relevant carer"—see reg.4(1).
"responsible carer"—see reg.4(1).
"week"—see Jobseekers Act 1995 s.35(1).
"work availability requirement"—see Jobseekers Act 1995 ss.35(1) and 6E.
"work search requirement"—see Jobseekers Act 1995 ss.35(1) and 6D.

General Note

This regulation is made under ss.6D(4) and (5) (work search requirement) and 6E(3) and (4) (work availability requirement) of the new style Jobseekers Act 1995. It sets out limitations on the kind of work that a claimant can be required to search for or be able and willing immediately to take up. See regs 15, 16 and 16A for other situations in which those requirements cannot be imposed or the ordinary tests are modified. See the notes to reg.13 for the proposition that, in addition to the limitations specified in reg.14, the availability requirement must be applied consistently with whatever kind of work the claimant is being required to search for under s.6D. 7.35

Paragraph (2)

A work search or availability requirement cannot relate to work in a location where the claimant's normal travel time either from home to work or from work to home would exceed 90 minutes, subject to the further limitation in para.(4) for some disabled claimants. Travel times below that limit could be relevant in relation to a sanction for non-compliance with a requirement, on the question whether the claimant had no good reason for the failure to comply. On that question all circumstances could be considered, including the effect of any physical or mental impairment not serious enough to count under para.(4), whereas under this provision time is the conclusive factor unless the location is completely excluded under para.(4). 7.36

Paragraph (3)

A claimant who has previously carried out work of a particular nature or at a particular level of remuneration is to have the kind of work to be considered limited to similar conditions for so long as considered appropriate up to three months (purportedly reduced to four weeks with effect from February 8, 2022, subject to the transitional provision in reg.4 of the amending regulations) from the date of claim. Presumably in the case of level of remuneration the similarity should be in real terms. But the rule only applies if and so long as the claimant will have reasonable prospects of obtaining paid work (or more or better paid work) subject to that limitation. 7.37

This hitherto inoffensive provision, promoting a limited protection of job skills and avoiding a need to make difficult decisions about the proper scope of work search when the period out of work might be short, has been rendered controversial by the nature and manner of the 2022 amendment, though most attention has been given to the corresponding amendment to reg.97(5) of the UC Regulations 2013 (see Vol.II).

Note first that the central part of the provision in para.(3), building on similar rules that had applied to old style JSA and to unemployment benefit, contains considerable flexibility. Although, once its conditions are met, the limitations as to work search and availability must be applied, there are quite complicated hurdles to be jumped before that stage is reached. The claimant must first have previously carried out work of a particular nature or at a particular level of remuneration. That work could have been self-employment. There is no limit as to how far in the past the work could have been carried out, but the further in the past the more likely it is that one of the following two conditions might not be met. The second condition (para.(3)(a)) is that the claimant has reasonable prospects of obtaining paid work subject to the limitations about nature of work and/or level of remuneration. There could be many circumstances, such as the claimant having moved to a different area or suffered some significant deterioration in physical or mental capacity or the lapse of time having rendered the claimant's previous experience redundant, where such reasonable prospects do not exist. The third condition is that the compulsory application of the limitations is to last only for such period as is considered appropriate (subject to the time-limit in para.(3)(b)). Similar factors to those relevant to para.(3)(a) might also be relevant here, avoiding difficult judgments about when prospects of obtaining work are reasonable or not. But the nature of the job skills up for protection, as well as other wider considerations, such as the state of the national and local job market and economy, might also be relevant. The length of the appropriate period could be less than the maximum or possibly no period could be appropriate. Thus, although in practice many claimants with recent work experience might, prior to February 2022, have been allowed three months with limited work search and availability without too much investigation, that was by no means inevitable.

It should also be noted that after the expiry of the maximum period under para.(3)(b) the protection of job skills does not become completely irrelevant. Outside the special circumstances catered for in paras (2), (4) and (5) and regs 15 – 16A, the general work search requirement is only to take all reasonable action for the purpose of obtaining paid work (new style Jobseekers Act 1995, s.6D(1)(a)) and particular actions specified by the Secretary of State under s.6D(1)(b) must as a matter of principle also be reasonable. Although s.6E on the work availability requirement makes no explicit reference to the nature of the work for which the claimant has to be available, it is suggested that by necessary implication, especially considering the power in s.6E(3) for the Secretary of State to specify limitations on the work availability requirement beyond those in regulations, that requirement must be in line with the proper work search requirement. It is plainly arguable that it is reasonable for claimants with specific and recent job skills and who have reasonable prospects of obtaining paid work of that kind and/or level of remuneration to limit their work search for a period beyond the para.(3)(b) maximum, at least until a point where the reasonableness of the prospects is undermined. Such an approach might also produce more enduring beneficial results for the economy as a whole. As it was well put by the Institute for Government and the SSAC at p.33 of their 2021 joint report *Jobs and benefits: The Covid-19 challenge*, a "constructive relationship between work coaches and claimants in finding not just any job but suitable jobs is likely to yield better enduring results for both individuals and the economy than merely enforcing work search conditions".

The impetus for the 2022 amendments, as set out in the Explanatory Memorandum to SI 2022/108, was the adoption of the "Way to Work" campaign, to enable 500,000 people currently out of work into jobs by the end of June 2022. However, that Memorandum gave no other information about the nature of that campaign except that it was launched on January 26, 2022. The thinking behind the campaign was perhaps revealed in paras 7.3 and 7.4:

> "7.3 Claimants with skills and experience for a specific type of role will be permitted up to four weeks to secure employment in that sector from their date of claim. After this period, they will be expected to widen their job search into other suitable sectors where they may find employment that can support them whilst they consider their longer-term career options. This will be part of their work-related requirements for receiving their benefit payment.
>
> 7.4 This change will enable jobcentres to promote wider employment opportunities for claimants, working with employers to fill local vacancies, supporting people back into work more quickly. This could reduce the time claimants spend out of work, thus preventing them from moving further away from the labour market – a factor that makes it increasingly difficult to get a job."

The Secretary of State had written to the Social Security Advisory Committee (SSAC) on February 3, 2022 informing it that she was not going to refer the proposal to make the regulations to it in advance, by reason of urgency, and was also dispensing with the "21-day rule" (i.e. that in general there should be at least a 21-day gap between the making of regulations and their coming into force, to allow Parliamentary scrutiny and give those affected a chance to react to the provisions). Paragraph 3.2 of the Explanatory Memorandum says that "the regulations could not have been made and laid sooner as the policy was only formulated very recently, and they had to come into effect as quickly as possible in order to achieve the target of getting 500,000 people into work by the end of June". Some more information was given at a scrutiny session of the House of Lords Secondary Legislation Scrutiny Committee on March 8, 2022 and in later correspondence, including that there were currently 1.2 million job vacancies nationally (although higher figures were given at some points). According to para.19 of the Committee's highly critical report (33rd Report):

"At the oral evidence session, we were told that the *Way to Work* campaign also included a national team and local employer teams that were focused on producing more vacancies. We also discovered that during the pandemic period DWP had doubled its number of work coaches and opened 200 new jobcentres around the country, and, in consequence, is now in a position to devote 50 minutes a week to each claimant's needs so as to encourage them back into work. Given the current high number of vacancies, DWP takes the view that claimants should broaden their job search at a much earlier stage than previously: the change made by these Regulations provides the ability to enforce that where necessary."

The Committee considered that the 500,000 June 2022 target, and the resulting urgency, was self-imposed and arbitrary and did not justify the avoidance of normal procedures. The Explanatory Memorandum was misleading in several ways, especially in not explaining how the specific amendment would contribute to achieving that target, as opposed to all the other elements of the campaign.

The Joint Committee on Statutory Instruments, in its 30th Report for the session 2021–22 (HL 189, HC 56-xxx), also drew the special attention of both Houses of Parliament to the regulations on the ground of failure to comply with proper legislative practice in respect of the 21-day rule. The SSAC has returned to these issues and the substance of the regulations in the further scrutiny noted below.

A close examination of the way in which reg.14(3) and reg.97(5) of the UC Regulations 2013 work, as set out above, would also have undermined any case for urgency. Given the existing power to set an appropriate period for the operation of the provisions at less than three months, even where a claimant might have reasonable prospects of obtaining paid work subject to the limitations, there was no reason why work coaches should not, immediately on the implementation of the campaign, have taken into account the number of job vacancies nationally and locally, the state of the national and local economy and other measures being undertaken as part of the campaign in determining that the permitted period should be something less than three months, say four weeks. What they could not properly have done, in the absence of the February 2022 amendment, would have been to adopt a rigid or blanket view that the permitted period should be four weeks in all cases. The particular circumstances of individual claimants would have had to be considered. But that is what work coaches are supposed to do in producing a personally tailored set of work requirements to be recorded in the claimant commitment, especially with the additional time made available, and would anyway be necessary outside the permitted period (see further below). The substance of the campaign could have been started immediately without the need for any urgent amendment.

That is important, not merely as a criticism of the processes adopted, but because it raises serious doubts about the validity of the amendments. *Howker v Secretary of State for Work and Pensions* [2002] EWCA Civ 1623, [2003] I.C.R. 405, also reported as *R(IB) 3/03* (see Vol.III of this series at 1.250), established that a failure to follow the mandatory provisions in s.172 of SSAA 1992 for reference to the SSAC of proposals to make regulations led to the invalidity of the regulations and that the then Social Security Commissioners had jurisdiction to decide that that was so. That no doubt now applies to the Upper Tribunal and presumably to the First-tier Tribunal. *Howker* was a case where the SSAC was misled by incorrect information from DWP officials into agreeing under s.173(1)(b) to there being no reference to it. *IC v Glasgow City Council and SSWP (HB)* [2016] UKUT 321 (AAC), reported as [2017] AACR 1, was specifically concerned with the exemption for urgency in s.173(1)(a). Although the three-judge panel of the Upper Tribunal rejected the argument that the Secretary of State had failed to show a need for urgency on the facts of the case, its decision operated on the basis that if that argument had been accepted it would have meant that the regulations in question were invalid. In the case of SI 2022/108 it appears that on any objective analysis urgency could not be shown.

Note also that the Explanatory Memorandum to SI 2022/108, in para. 2.2 as well as in para. 7.2 quoted above, contains misleading statements about the effect of the amendments. The former says that the amendment will require claimants to search more widely for available jobs beyond those of a similar nature or level of remuneration to that of previous work following the fourth week of their claim. The suggestion that that will be an automatic expectation is repeated in para. 7.2. That is misleading because, as explained above, where reg.14(3) has ceased to apply the reasonableness of restricting job search and availability to a similarly limited scope must be considered in the individual circumstances of each particular claimant in asking what is all reasonable action to obtain paid work under s.6D(1).

On June 23, 2022 (published on the internet on July 6, 2022), the Chair of the SSAC wrote to the Secretary of State to say that after careful consideration the Committee had decided not to take the regulations shortening the "permitted period" on formal reference, but wished to record a number of concerns and make some advisory recommendations. It is worth setting out in full the statement of concerns relating to the role of the regulatory changes in enhancing the overall policy intent (footnotes have been omitted):

> "**Scale of the challenge**
>
> In order to assess whether the regulation change could deliver and was proportionate to the policy intent, we were keen to understand the relative size of the role of the regulatory change in combination with the other measures as part of the Way to Work scheme, and the scale of the increase in off-flow into work that would be expected to be required to achieve the 500k target. Officials were unable to provide an estimate of the overall scale of the change from the combined programme or of the expected contribution of the regulatory change. We appreciate that this is difficult to do, but whether this goal involves an increase in off-flow rates of 10%, 50% or 100% compared to an expected counterfactual has a material impact on the proportionality of the policy response.
>
> Given that the off-flow from benefits into employment for the month of February (which would be unlikely to have yet been significantly affected by the programme's components) had been estimated at around 114K -- so that on average only 96.5K per month needed to be achieved over the remaining four months to meet the target – it seems as if the required impact could be at the lower end of the scale, and more aligned to avoiding a drop in off-flow rates rather than appreciably boosting them.
>
> We also sought to understand the number of jobseekers whose search expectations would be changed by these regulations for the duration of the scheme. Unfortunately, officials were not in a position to provide an estimate of the scale of the change.
>
> **Evidence base**
>
> We were informed that the rationale for the reduction in the duration of the permitted period was that there was a unique moment in the labour market as, post-COVID, there were significantly higher than normal levels of sectoral shift and high levels of vacancies – which meant there would be greater benefit from jobseekers expanding their search into new sectors at an earlier point.
>
> We have sought access to evidence that could underpin the basis of the decision to shorten the permitted period. We understand that the choice of four weeks as the new duration was a judgment informed by feedback from work coaches. However, no data or explanation has been made available to indicate what the impact would be of making the change. In fact, the evidence offered indicated that there was no noticeable increase in the historic off-flow rate after the 13-week point, suggesting that the extant pattern of broadening of the work-search expectations, at least at this point, did not have a discernible impact.
>
> Our concerns are compounded by the lack of a clear positive outcome expected as a result of the reduction in the permitted period. We are told that no estimate is available of what a positive outcome would be either in terms of

the number claiming the benefits, or the fiscal impact though presumably these have been incorporated in the latest forecasts produced by the Office for Budget Responsibility and adopted by the Government in the Spring Statement.

We asked your officials for an assessment of the baseline (historic) patterns of off-flow, and how these might have been expected to evolve in coming months absent these change in these regulations, alongside any early indication of patterns in the early months of the programme (see Appendix for details). Unfortunately, this information has not been shared with the Committee.

Potential negative impact

At the time of our scrutiny, no assessment had been made of the risk of individuals entering roles that were inconsistent with their qualifications/ experience, or simply wrong for them in terms of their career path and ambitions, nor of the risk that increased competition from more highly qualified people would make it more difficult for longer-term unemployed people to find work. Similarly, no consideration had been made of the impact on those with part-time, or other flexible, job-search expectations for whom the four-week cut-off could be disproportionate and one that will certainly vary by protected characteristics, most obviously sex and disability.

There was some acknowledgement that there may be negative consequences from these changes, for example increased cycling on and off benefits, and job mismatches leading to more churn for employers and to claimants potentially having career paths hindered. However, there was no analysis of how to mitigate against negative effects, particularly where those with protected characteristics might be disproportionately impacted.

Evaluating the effectiveness of the permitted period change

These regulations were brought in to deal with a unique moment in the economy as it reopened from COVID restrictions, resulting in a very high number of labour market vacancies. However, the regulations do not have a sunset clause and the Committee would be concerned that, without a proper review of the impact of these regulations, they may be left on the statute book, despite the labour market situation having substantially changed. Therefore, the Committee very much welcomes that in your letter to me of 3 February, you committed to undertake such an evaluation of the regulations at the end of June to assess their effectiveness and whether they should be retained.

The way in which the regulations would be reviewed in terms of (a) by what criteria they would be deemed a success, and (b) how such criteria would be evaluated is in need of detailed thought. It will also be important to differentiate the criteria on which the regulations are evaluated with respect to the current unique point in time and the assessment whether they should be retained for what should then be much more normal times ahead. However, when we asked officials how they plan to undertake this, it was clear that such thinking had not yet matured.

Urgency

The regulations had been laid under the urgency provision before being presented to this Committee for scrutiny. I have previously written to you seeking a better understanding of the nature of the urgency in this instance. As you know, this Committee is supportive of the use of "urgency" where legislation is being brought forward as a direct consequence of either an external factor or a fiscal event. Indeed we welcomed the use of urgency, and expedited our own statutory scrutiny process, to ensure that essential support could be introduced quickly in response to recent crises in Afghanistan and Ukraine. However, a compelling argument for urgency in this specific case remains unclear to us.

We were informed that the regulations had to bypass the scrutiny of the Committee before coming into force, as "every day" was essential in ensuring that the Government can meet its own target. However, there was no explanation of what impact there might be in waiting a few weeks for the Committee to complete its statutory scrutiny – either on the specific issue of the target or in terms of the broader proposals.

Similarly, it is not clear why the target could not simply have been put back a short period, or why the rest of the Way to Work programme could not proceed whilst the permitted period proposals were considered by the Committee."

Despite that politely devastating analysis, success of the Way to Work campaign was declared on June 30, 2022 by way of a tweet and a press release asserting that over half a million people had been helped into work thanks to the campaign in five months (later quoted in the House of Commons by the then Prime Minister on July 6, 2022). That declaration was apparently based on an answer to a Parliamentary Question on June 30, 2022 revealing an estimate using management information that as of June 29, 2022 at least 505,400 unemployed universal credit and JSA claimants had moved into work during the campaign. That use of the figures was castigated by the Director General for Regulation in the Office for Statistics Regulation in his letter of July 29, 2022 to the Permanent Secretary of the DWP. He concluded that it was difficult to attribute and quantify the impact of the campaign in the absence of a clearly defined and published target and details of how it would be measured and reported, so that the way that the DWP had communicated information did not uphold the principles of being trustworthy, of high quality and offering public value. A more targeted point might have been to note the speciousness of using evidence of the numbers who moved into work during the campaign to support the assertion that all those claimants had been helped into work by the campaign. A further written answer to a Parliamentary Question on September 5, 2022 revealed that no estimate had been made of the number of unemployed universal credit and JSA claimants who would have moved into work between January and June 2022 in the absence of the Way to Work campaign.

Overall, it is hard to avoid the conclusion that this whole shabby episode was little more than a small-scale exercise in grandiose posturing with every appearance of having been foisted on the DWP with no time for thought or preparation. However, the episode is not over. There has been no public sign of the promised evaluation of the effectiveness of the amending regulations and of whether they should be retained (the September 2022 written answer suggests that there has been no attempt at any real evaluation or at meeting the concerns of the SSAC or of the Office for Statistics Regulation). But the amendments are unlikely to be reversed while a high level of job vacancies continues, even though that state of affairs is likely to produce a high level of off-flow from benefit independently of the amendments' effect. A letter of May 23, 2023 from the Minister for Employment, Guy Opperman, to the Chair of the House of Commons Work and Pensions Select Committee gives the appearance of attempting to rewrite history by saying that the DWP had achieved its ambition to see at least 500,000 people move into work from universal credit and JSA *during* the campaign (emphasis added by commentator). The letter did say that assurances had been given to the Office for Statistics Regulation about future adherence to its principles.

There is a transitional provision in reg.4 of the amending regulations (see 7.204 below). If on February 8, 2022 a claimant had a work search or availability requirement limited under reg.14(3), the limitation is to extend for the length of the existing permitted period or until March 7, 2022 if earlier.

Paragraph (4)

7.38 A claimant who has a physical or mental impairment (not further defined) which has a substantial adverse effect on their ability to carry out work of a particular nature or in particular locations (a significant additional condition over and above that of impairment or disability on its own) is to have the kind of work to be considered under the work search and work availability requirements limited to avoid such work.

Paragraph (5)

7.39 This paragraph establishes an important limitation on the kind of work that can be considered, but only for the particular categories of claimant identified: those with child care responsibilities and those with physical or mental impairments.

Those categories of claimant can only be required to search for or to be able and willing to take up work for no more than the number of hours per week compatible with those circumstances, as worked out under reg.9(2). So far as the work search requirement is concerned, this limitation appears to apply as much to the sort of work in relation to which the Secretary of State may specify particular action under s.6D(1)(b) of the new style Jobseekers Act 1995 as to the requirement under s.6D(1)(a) to take all reasonable action for the purpose of obtaining paid work or more or better paid work.

See the notes to s.6E for the argument that these limitations, and any further limitations imposed under s.6E(3), in terms of hours apply both to the hours of work that the claimant must search for and be available for and to the hours for which the claimant must carry out the work search and during which be prepared immediately to take up paid work or attend an interview.

Victims of domestic violence

15.—(1) Where a claimant has recently been a victim of domestic violence and the circumstances set out in paragraph (3) apply— **7.40**

(a) a requirement imposed on that claimant under sections 6 to 6G of the Act ceases to have effect for a period of 13 consecutive weeks starting on the date of the notification referred to in paragraph (3)(a); and

(b) the Secretary of State must not impose any other such requirement on that claimant during that period.

(2) A person has recently been a victim of domestic violence if a period of six months has not expired since the violence was inflicted or threatened.

(3) The circumstances are that—

(a) the claimant notifies the Secretary of State, in such manner as the Secretary of State specifies, that domestic violence has been inflicted on or threatened against the claimant by a person specified in paragraph (4) during the period of six months ending on the date of the notification;

(b) this regulation has not applied to the claimant for a period of 12 months before the date of the notification;

(c) on the date of the notification the claimant is not living at the same address as the person who inflicted or threatened the domestic violence; and

(d) as soon as possible, and no later than one month, after the date of the notification the claimant provides evidence from a person acting in an official capacity which demonstrates that—

(i) the claimant's circumstances are consistent with those of a person who has had domestic violence inflicted on or threatened against them during the period of six months ending on the date of the notification; and

(ii) the claimant has made contact with the person acting in an official capacity in relation to such an incident, which occurred during that period.

(4) A person is specified in this paragraph if the person is—

(a) where the claimant is, or was, a member of a couple, the other member of the couple;

(b) the claimant's grandparent, grandchild, parent, parent-in-law, son, son-in-law, daughter, daughter-in-law, step-parent, step-son, step-daughter, brother, step-brother, brother-in-law, sister, step-sister or sister-in-law; or

(c) where any of the persons listed in sub-paragraph (b) is a member of a couple, the other member of that couple.

(5) In this regulation—

[1"coercive behaviour" means an act of assault, humiliation or intimidation or other abuse that is used to harm, punish or frighten the victim;

"controlling behaviour" means an act designed to make a person subordinate or dependent by isolating them from sources of support, exploiting their resources and capacities for personal gain, depriving them of the means needed for independence, resistance or escape or regulating their everyday behaviour;

"domestic violence" means any incident, or pattern of incidents, of controlling behaviour, coercive behaviour, violence or abuse, including but not limited to—

(a) psychological abuse;
(b) physical abuse;
(c) sexual abuse;
(d) emotional abuse;
(e) financial abuse,

regardless of the gender or sexuality of the victim;

"health care professional" means a person who is a member of a profession regulated by a body mentioned in section 25(3) of the National Health Service Reform and Health Care Professions Act 2002;

"person acting in an official capacity" means a health care professional, a police officer, a registered social worker, the claimant's employer, a representative of the claimant's trade union or any public, voluntary or charitable body which has had direct contact with the claimant in connection with domestic violence;

"registered social worker" means a person registered as a social worker in a register maintained by—

[3 (a) Social Work England,]
[2 (b) Social Care Wales;]
(c) the Scottish Social Services Council; or
(d) the Northern Ireland Social Care Council.

Amendments

1. Social Security (Miscellaneous Amendments) (No.2) Regulations 2013 (SI 2013/1508) reg.4(1) and (2) (October 29, 2013).

2. Social Security (Social Care Wales) (Amendment) Regulations 2017 (SI 2017/291) reg.3 (April 1, 2017).

3. Children and Social Work Act 2017 (Consequential Amendments) (Social Workers) Regulations 2019 (SI 2019/1094) reg.2(c) and Sch.3 para.31 (July 9, 2019).

Definitions

"the Act"—see reg.2(2).
"claimant"—see Jobseekers Act 1995 s.35(1).
"couple"—*ibid.*
"victim of domestic violence"—see Jobseekers Act 1995 s.6H(6)(b).

General Note

7.41 This regulation, made as required by s.6H(5) and (6) of the new style Jobseekers Act 1995, exempts recent victims of domestic violence from the imposition of any work-related or connected requirements for a period of 13 weeks from the date of notification to the Secretary of State under para.(3)(a) and lifts the effect of any existing imposition for the same period. Equivalent provision has been made in the UC Regulations 2013 reg.98, with a small gap (Vol.II of this series, *Universal Credit etc.*).

Section 6H(6) of the Act, while defining "victim of domestic violence" as a person on or against whom domestic violence had been inflicted or threatened, left the meaning of "domestic violence" and of what is to be treated as recent to regulations. Paragraph (2) of this regulation provides that a person has recently been a victim of domestic violence if no more than six months has elapsed since its infliction or threat. Initially, para.(5) required the meaning of "domestic violence" to be in terms of abuse which is specified on a particular page of the December 2005 Department of Health document *Responding to domestic abuse: a handbook for health professionals*. It was not very satisfactory for an important definition not only not to be set out in the Regulations, but to be in a publication that was difficult to find. Also, its terms were perhaps not well-suited to the particular benefits context. The new definition in para.(5), expanded into various forms of abuse and into further definitions of coercive and controlling behaviour, is still very wide.

The definition uses the terms of the government's official approach to the meaning of domestic violence across departments, which had not previously been used as a statutory definition. Note that the new criminal offence of controlling or coercive behaviour in intimate or familial relationships under s.76 of the Serious Crime Act 2015, while using the terms of controlling and coercive behaviour (the meaning of which is discussed in Home Office Statutory Guidance of December 2015), contains conditions that are different from those in reg.15. While the definition here expressly includes coercive behaviour and controlling behaviour (both given their own definitions in para.(5)), any other incident of abuse of any kind can come within the ambit of domestic violence. Thus, although the specific definition of "coercive behaviour" requires the act or abuse to be used to harm, punish or frighten the victim and the specific definition of "controlling behaviour" is restricted to acts designed to make the victim subordinate or dependant by particular means (as taken to extremes by the vile Rob Titchener in *The Archers*), abuse of similar kinds where that specific form of intention or purpose is not present or is difficult to prove can nonetheless be domestic violence. The width of that approach makes the specification in para.(3) of the circumstances in which reg.15 applies more important. Victims can be of any gender and their sexuality is immaterial. The person perpetrating or threatening the domestic violence must be the claimant's partner, former partner or a family member as set out in para.(4)(b) and (c) to cover a wide range of members of the family.

Paragraph (3)

This paragraph lays down four quite restrictive conditions that must all be satisfied for reg.15 to apply. Under sub-para.(a) the claimant must have notified the Secretary of State of the infliction or threatening of domestic violence by a partner, former partner or family member or relative (as defined in para.(4)) within the previous six months. Under sub-para.(b), reg.15 must not have applied within the 12 months before the notification. Under sub-para.(c), the claimant must not on the date of the notification have been living at the same address as the person named as the assailant. Under sub-para.(d), the claimant must also provide, as soon as possible and no more than one month after the notification, evidence from a person acting in an official capacity (defined quite widely in para.(5)) both that the claimant's circumstances are consistent with having had domestic violence inflicted or threatened in the six months before notification and that the claimant had made contact (apparently not necessarily within the six months) with the person in relation to an incident of infliction or threat of domestic violence that occurred during the six months before notification. **7.42**

The transition from old style JSA

In para.(3)(b) the reference to reg.15 applying to the claimant is, where art.12(1) and (2) of the Welfare Reform Act 2012 (Commencement No.9 and Transitional and Transitory Provisions and Commencement No.8 and Savings and Transitional Provisions (Amendment)) Order 2013 (as amended and set out in Vol.V of this **7.43** series) applies, to be read as if it included a reference to the claimant having been treated as available for employment under reg.14A(2) or (6) of the JSA Regulations 1996 (art.12(3)(a) of that Order).

Circumstances in which requirements must not be imposed

7.44 **16.**—(1) Where paragraph (3), [1(4), (5) or (5B)] applies—

(a) the Secretary of State must not impose a work search requirement on a claimant; and

(b) "able and willing immediately to take up work" under a work availability requirement means able and willing to take up paid work, or attend an interview, immediately once the circumstances set out in paragraph (3), [1(4), (5) or (5B)] no longer apply.

(2) A work search requirement previously applying to the claimant ceases to have effect from the date on which the circumstances set out in paragraph (3), [1(4), (5) or (5B)] apply.

(3) This paragraph applies where—

(a) the claimant is attending a court or tribunal as a party to any proceedings or as a witness;

(b) the claimant is temporarily absent from Great Britain because they are—

(i) taking their child outside Great Britain for medical treatment;

(ii) attending a job interview outside Great Britain; or

(iii) receiving medical treatment outside Great Britain;

(c) it is within six months of the death of—

(i) where the claimant is a member of a couple, the other member;

(ii) a child for whom the claimant or, where the claimant is a member of a couple, the other member, is responsible; or

(iii) a child, where the claimant is the child's parent;

(d) the claimant is receiving and participating in a structured, recovery-orientated, course of alcohol or drug dependency treatment, for a period of up to six months (where the course is for more than six months, this sub-paragraph only applies for the first six months);

(e) the claimant is a person for whom arrangements have been made by a protection provider under section 82 of the Serious Organised Crime and Police Act 2005, for a period of up to three months (where the arrangements are for more than three months, this sub-paragraph only applies for the first three months).

(4) This paragraph applies where the Secretary of State is satisfied that it would be unreasonable to require the claimant to comply with a work search requirement, including if such a requirement were limited in accordance with section 6D(4) of the Act, because the claimant—

(a) has temporary child care responsibilities;

(b) is subject to temporary circumstances;

(c) is carrying out a public duty; or

(d) is carrying out a work preparation requirement or voluntary work preparation.

(5) This paragraph applies where the claimant—

(a) is unfit for work—

(i) for a maximum of 14 consecutive days after the date on which the evidence referred to in sub-paragraph (b) is provided; and

(ii) on no more than two such periods in any period of 12 months; and

(b) provides to the Secretary of State the following evidence—

(i) for the first seven days when they are unfit for work, a declaration made by the claimant in such manner and form as the Secretary of State approves that the claimant is unfit for work; and

(ii) for any further days when they are unfit for work, a statement given [2 ...] in accordance with the rules set out in Part 1 of Schedule 1 to the Social Security (Medical Evidence) Regulations 1976 which advises that the person is not fit for work.

[1(5A) Paragraph (5) does not apply to a claimant—

(a) if it has previously been determined on the basis of an assessment under Part 5 of the Universal Credit Regulations 2013 or Part 4 or 5 of the Employment and Support Allowance Regulations 2013 that the claimant does not have limited capability for work; and

(b) the condition specified in the evidence provided by the claimant in accordance with paragraph (5)(b) is in the opinion of the Secretary of State the same, or substantially the same, as the condition specified in the evidence provided by the claimant before the date of the determination that the claimant does not have limited capability for work.

(5B) This paragraph applies where the Secretary of State is satisfied that it would be unreasonable to require the claimant to comply with a work search requirement or a work availability requirement, including if such a requirement were limited in accordance with section 6D(4) of the Act, because paragraph (5) would apply to the claimant but for paragraph (5A).]

(6) In this regulation, "tribunal" means any tribunal listed in Schedule 1 to the Tribunal and Inquiries Act 1992.

AMENDMENTS

1. Universal Credit (Miscellaneous Amendments, Saving and Transitional Provision) Regulations 2018 (SI 2018/65) reg.4 (April 11, 2018).

2. Social Security (Medical Evidence) and Statutory Sick Pay (Medical Evidence) (Amendment) (No. 2) Regulations 2022 (SI 2022/630) reg.4(4)(a) (July 1, 2022).

DEFINITIONS

"the Act"—see reg.2(2).
"child"—see Jobseekers Act 1995 s.35(1).
"claimant"—*ibid.*
"Great Britain"—*ibid.*
"voluntary work preparation"—see reg.4(1).
"work availability requirement"—see Jobseekers Act 1995 ss.35(1) and 6E.
"work preparation requirement"—see Jobseekers Act 1995 ss.35(1) and 6C.
"work search requirement"—see Jobseekers Act 1995 ss.35(1) and 6D.

GENERAL NOTE

Temporary Coronavirus Provisions

The effect of the temporary coronavirus provisions relevant to the work search and work availability requirements in new style JSA expired at the end of November 12, 2020. See previous editions of this volume for the details. 7.45

This regulation is made under s.6H(1)(a) of the new style Jobseekers Act 1995 in respect of the work search requirement and under s.6E(5) in respect of the work availability requirement. Any claimant falling under paras (3)–(5B) cannot have a work search requirement imposed (para.(1)(a)) and any existing such requirement ceases to have effect (para.(2)). And the requirement in s.6E(2) to be able and willing immediately to take up work means able to take up work, or attend an interview immediately the relevant circumstance under paras (3)–(5B) ceases to exist. Regulation 16 does not affect the imposition of the work-focused interview requirement and the work preparation requirement, although under s.6F(2) of the new style Jobseekers Act 1995 there is a discretion regarding whether or not to impose those requirements, under which all relevant circumstances must be considered.

Paragraph (3)

7.46 Paragraph (3) lists a number of categories of claimant where the circumstances mean that the claimant could not be expected to look for or take up work or attend an interview, generally of a temporary and fairly clear-cut nature. Cases which fall outside para.(3) can come within the much more open-ended provisions in para.(4) subject to the additional express condition that it would be unreasonable to require the claimant to comply with a work search requirement in the circumstances.

(a) Attending a court or tribunal (defined in para.(6)) as a party to proceedings or as a witness, apparently so long as the hearing continues for a party and so long as attendance is required for a witness.

(b) Temporary absence from Great Britain in connection with medical treatment or accompanying a child undergoing such treatment, or to attend a job interview abroad. This provision seems very narrowly drawn by comparison with reg.99(3)(c) of the UC Regulations 2013 on medical treatment, etc. It appears to be restricted to the claimant and a child of the claimant (whatever that precisely means) and does not extend to accompanying a partner or a young person who is a member of the family abroad for medical treatment. Nor is it clear that convalescence would come within "medical treatment". But reg.16 may still apply where reasonable through the operation of para.(4).

(c) The claimant's then partner, a child (but not a young person) for whom the claimant or partner was responsible or a child of the claimant has died within the previous six months.

(d) Attending a structured recovery-oriented course of alcohol or drug dependency treatment, for no more than six months.

(e) Having protection arrangements made under s.82 of the Serious Organised Crime and Police Act 2005 (protection of persons involved in investigations or proceedings whose safety is considered to be at risk), for no more than three months. Arrangements for protection are made by protection providers (e.g. Chief Constables, or any of the Commissioners for His Majesty's Revenue and Customs).

Paragraph (4)

7.47 In four sorts of circumstances the imposition of a work search requirement or the satisfaction of a work availability requirement, even as limited under s.6D(4) of the Act and reg.14, can be further restricted where those circumstances make it unreasonable for the claimant to be required to comply with the requirement. Although, in contrast to reg.99(5) of the UC Regulations 2013, there is no express reference to whether or not it would be reasonable to apply the usual "immediately" test under the work availability requirement, for para.(1)(b) to apply while circumstances identified in para.(4) exist some such reference must be implied. Sub-paragraph (a) applies if the claimant has temporary child care responsibilities (apparently for any child). Sub-paragraph (b) applies where the claimant is subject to any kind of temporary circumstances. Sub-paragraph (c) applies where the claimant is carrying out any kind of public duty (not further defined). Sub-paragraph (d) applies if the claimant is carrying out a work preparation requirement (s.6C(1) of the Act) or voluntary work preparation requirement (reg.4(1)). It appears that voluntary work preparation could include the doing of voluntary work if agreed by the Secretary of State (see the definition in reg.4(1)).

In *RR v SSWP (UC)* [2017] UKUT 459 (AAC) (see the notes to reg.12), Judge Wikeley suggested that another way of looking at the case, rather than exploring deductions from 35 as the expected number of hours under the equivalent of reg.12(2), was to consider whether a work search requirement could not be imposed for the weeks in question on the basis that the claimant was dealing with a domestic emergency or other temporary circumstances (sub-para.(b)) in the form of dealing with the fall-out of divorce or other family proceedings.

It is arguable that under sub-para.(b), or (a) where the claimant has some responsibility for care of a child, the application of the work search requirement and the "immediate" obligations of the work availability requirement can be lifted during a holiday. The crucial test is whether it is unreasonable to expect the claimant to comply with the normal requirements. Claimants in part-time work, not amounting to remunerative work under s.1(2)(e) of the new style Jobseekers Act 1995, will have statutory holiday entitlements and it is arguable, depending of course on all the circumstances (including the likelihood of some actual opportunity arising for the claimant in question during the holiday period), that that should be acknowledged in the new style JSA system. Regulation 19(1)(p) and (2) of the JSA Regulations 1996 allows claimants of old style JSA two weeks off from actively seeking employment within any 12 months if residing away from home, and see the notes to s.6 of the old style Jobseekers Act 1995 in Vol.V of this series, 2021/22 edition as updated in Cumulative Supplements included in Vol.II of this series and in mid-year Supplements, for extensive discussion of the operation of the condition of entitlement of availability for employment during a holiday. If some other member of the claimant's family is in work and contractually entitled to holiday, an argument about reasonableness could still perhaps be made.

Paragraphs (5)–(5B)

A claimant who is unfit for work (not further defined) and provides a self-certificate for the first seven days and, if requested, a statement from a specified healthcare professional under the Medical Evidence Regulations (Vol.III of this series) for any further days falls within the basic rules in this regulation. But the benefit of para.(5) is limited to a period of no more than 14 days after the evidence is provided and to no more than two such periods in any 12 months. There is a possible extension of those restrictions under para.(4)(b). **7.48**

There appears on the original form of para.(5) no reason why a claimant should not take the benefit of its provisions from the first day of entitlement to new style JSA. But to have such entitlement while unfit for work and not to fall foul of the condition of entitlement in s.1(2)(f) (does not have limited capability for work) a claimant would have to get within the terms of reg.46. See the notes to that provision for a full discussion and the difficulty in applying it from the beginning of a period of a new style JSA claim.

From April 2018 an additional limitation on the operation of para.(5) was created by the new para.(5A), designed to deal with the common circumstances where a claimant's entitlement to new style ESA or universal credit was terminated by reason of a determination following an assessment that they do not have limited capability for work and are thereby forced to claim new style JSA. Even if the claimant has appealed against the ESA or universal credit decision after the mandatory reconsideration process, the circumstances in which limited capability for work will be deemed for ESA purposes (so that a claimant can avoid having to claim universal credit if in need of the income) has been severely restricted and there appears to be no such deeming under universal credit. In the circumstances prescribed in para.(5A)(a) a claimant can only take advantage of para.(5) if the condition specified in the medical evidence provided under para.(5)(b) is not the same or substantially the same as the condition specified in the evidence provided by the claimant before the determination of not having limited capability for work. Thus, the claimant is not permitted for these purposes to undermine the judgment on capability for work embodied in the adverse new style ESA or universal credit determination. However, para.(5B) allows the application of para.(5) where it would be unreasonable to require a claimant who would otherwise be caught by para.(5A) to comply with a work search or availability requirement.

The Explanatory Memorandum for SI 2018/65 describes the effect of these amendments as follows in paras 7.14 and 7.15:

> "7.14 This instrument amends regulation 99 of the Universal Credit Regulations (and makes equivalent amendments to regulation 16 of the Jobseeker's Allowance Regulations 2013) to prevent work search and work availability requirements being automatically switched off for illness in certain circumstances. The amendments apply to claimants who have undergone a work capability assessment and been found not to have limited capability for work, and to claimants who have failed to attend a medical examination or comply with a request for information and are treated as not having limited capability for work. In other words, claimants who are, or are treated as being, fit for work. Where such claimants produce evidence that they are unfit for work and the condition mentioned in the evidence is the same, or substantially the same, as the condition for which they were assessed in the work capability assessment, work search and work availability requirements will only be switched off if they have been referred for another assessment as to their capability for work.
>
> 7.15 If such a claimant has not been referred for another assessment, regulations will continue to allow for work search and work availability requirements to be switched off if it would be unreasonable for a claimant to comply with such requirements."

It is, however, hard to see how some elements of that explanation follow from the actual words of the amendments. First, para.(5A)(a) expressly applies only where the new style ESA or universal credit determination of not having limited capability for work was based on an assessment. That means the assessment by a decision-maker or tribunal of the points scored under the appropriate Schedule (ESA Regulations 2013 reg.15(2); UC Regulations 2013 reg.39(2)). Therefore, it appears not to apply in circumstances where the claimant was treated as not having limited capability for work for failing to attend for or submit to a medical examination or for failing to comply with an information request. Second, it is hard to see where the issue of whether or not the claimant has been referred for a further assessment fits in. Paragraphs (5A) and (5B) both appear to operate independently of that issue, although it could be relevant to reasonableness under para.(5B).

A number of other points need brief mention. Note first that para.(5A) only applies where the assessment and determination was for the purposes of new style ESA or universal credit. It does not apply if it was for the purposes of old style ESA. Then on its face it applies whenever in the past the adverse determination was made. It may need to be decided whether in order to operate in a rational and fair way para.(5A) should be limited to the most recent determination of no limited capability for work under new style ESA or universal credit. Third, the comparison to be made in para.(5A)(b) is between the condition(s) specified in the evidence provided by the claimant before the previous adverse determination and the condition(s) specified in the evidence put forward by the claimant in support of the application of para.(5). The evidence provided by the claimant before the adverse determination will presumably cover primarily a GP's fit note, but also any questionnaire completed by the claimant and any other evidence, from medical professionals or otherwise, put forward (and, it would seem, the claimant's oral evidence to any tribunal and any further evidence put forward there). It will not cover the opinions of any approved health care professional who has carried out a medical examination, even though it is usually on the basis of those opinions that adverse determinations are made. The evidence to be provided under para.(5)(b) is a self-certificate for the first week and then a GP's fit note. Difficulties can be anticipated in making a comparison between what may be a fairly informal and short specification in a self-certificate and the previous evidence. And is it enough to trigger para.

(5A)(b) that, say, the sole condition specified in the new self-certificate or fit note is substantially the same as one, but only one, out of several that were specified before the adverse determination?

See reg.16A for the terms on which there can be a similar lifting of restrictions for an extended period of sickness, up to 13 weeks. The application of reg.16A can follow on from a period under reg.16(5) but not vice versa (see the notes to reg.46A).

[[1]Further circumstances in which requirements must not be imposed

16A.—(1) This regulation applies in the case of a claimant who is treated as capable of work or as not having limited capability for work under regulation 46A (extended period of sickness). 7.49

(2) Where the Secretary of State is satisfied that it would be unreasonable to require the claimant to comply with a work search requirement—

(a) the Secretary of State must not impose a work search requirement on the claimant; and

(b) a work search requirement previously applying to the claimant ceases to have effect from the date on which the claimant is first treated as capable of work or as having limited capability for work under regulation 46A.

(3) Paragraph (4) applies where the Secretary of State is satisfied that it would be unreasonable to require the claimant to comply with a work availability requirement to be able and willing to—

(a) take up work; and

(b) attend an interview.

(4) Where this paragraph applies, "able and willing to take up work" under a work availability requirement means able and willing to take up paid work and to attend an interview, immediately once the claimant ceases to be treated as capable of work or as not having limited capability for work under regulation 46A.

(5) Paragraph (6) applies where the Secretary of State is satisfied that it would be—

(a) unreasonable to require the claimant to comply with a work availability requirement to able and willing to take up work; and

(b) reasonable to require the claimant to comply with a work availability requirement to be able and willing to attend an interview.

(6) Where this paragraph applies, "able and willing to take up work" under a work availability requirement means—

(a) able and willing to take up paid work immediately once the claimant ceases to be treated as capable of work or as not having limited capability for work under regulation 46A; and

(b) able and willing to attend an interview before the claimant ceases to be so treated.]

AMENDMENT

1. Jobseeker's Allowance (Extended Period of Sickness) Amendment Regulations 2015 (SI 2015/339) reg.3(2) (March 30, 2015).

DEFINITIONS

"claimant"—see Jobseekers Act 1995 s.35(1).
"paid work"—see reg.3(7).
"work availability requirement"—see Jobseekers Act 1995 ss.35(1) and 6E.
"work search requirement"—see Jobseekers Act 1995 ss.35(1) and 6D.

General Note

7.50 This regulation, together with reg.46A, provides an extension to the rules in regs 16(5) and 46. The latter provisions allow, no more than twice in any 12 months (subject to a temporary coronavirus extension: see the notes to reg.46), qualification for new style JSA while the claimant is unfit for work for a period of up to 14 days, with some new restrictions from April 2018. Regulation 16(5) (with sub-paras (1) and (2)) prevents the application of the work search requirement and modifies the work availability requirement. Regulation 46, under similar but slightly more restrictive conditions, deems the claimant to satisfy the condition of entitlement in s.1(2)(f) of the new style Jobseekers Act 1995 (does not have limited capability for work). The new provisions can produce the same effect for an extended period of up to 13 weeks but only once in any 12 months.

Regulation 16A is directly linked to the application of reg.46A. By virtue of para.(1) it only applies to claimants who are treated under reg.46A as capable of work or as not having limited capability for work (and so satisfy the condition of entitlement in s.1(2)(f)). The assessment of the evidence about fitness to work therefore takes place under reg.46A. By contrast to the position under reg.16, the effect on the work search requirement and the work availability requirement is not automatic but depends on a determination that it would be unreasonable to require the claimant to comply with a work search requirement or to be able and willing to take up work and/or attend an interview.

Regulation 16A does not affect the imposition of the work-focused interview requirement and the work preparation requirement. However, under s.6F(2) of the new style Jobseekers Act 1995 there is a discretion regarding whether or not to impose those requirements, under which all relevant circumstances must be considered.

PART 3

Sanctions

Interpretation

7.51 **17.**—For the purposes of this Part—

[1"current sanctionable failure" means a failure of the following kinds in relation to which the Secretary of State has not yet determined whether the amount of an award of benefit is to be reduced—

(a) a sanctionable failure,

(b) an ESA sanctionable failure, or

(c) a UC sanctionable failure;]

"ESA sanctionable failure" means a failure by a claimant which is sanctionable under section 11J of the Welfare Reform Act 2007;

"higher-level sanction" means a reduction of a jobseeker's allowance in accordance with section 6J of the Act;

"low-level sanction" means a reduction of a jobseeker's allowance in accordance with section 6K of the Act for a sanctionable failure by the claimant to comply with—

(a) a work-focused interview requirement under section 6B(1) of the Act;

(b) a work preparation requirement under section 6C(1) of the Act;

(c) a work search requirement under section 6D(1)(b) of the Act (requirement to take action specified by the Secretary of State to obtain work); or

(d) a requirement under section 6G of the Act (connected requirements);

"medium-level sanction" means a reduction of a jobseeker's allowance in accordance with section 6K of the Act for a sanctionable failure by the claimant to comply with—
(a) a work search requirement under section 6D(1)(a) of the Act (requirement to take all reasonable action to obtain paid work); or
(b) a work availability requirement under section 6E(1) of the Act (requirement to be available for work);
"pre-claim failure" means a sanctionable failure listed in section 6J(3) of the Act;
"reduction period" means the number of days for which a reduction in the amount of an award of a jobseeker's allowance is to have effect;
"sanctionable failure" means a failure by a claimant which is sanctionable under section 6J or 6K of the Act;
"total outstanding reduction period" means the total number of days for which no reduction has yet been applied for all of the claimant's higher-level sanctions, medium-level sanctions, low-level sanctions and reductions to which regulation 30 applies;
"UC sanctionable failure" means a failure by a claimant which is sanctionable under section 26 or 27 of the Welfare Reform Act 2012.

AMENDMENT

1. Social Security (Jobseeker's Allowance, Employment and Support Allowance and Universal Credit) (Amendment) Regulations 2016 (SI 2016/678) reg.6(2) (July 25, 2016).

DEFINITION

"the Act"—see reg.2(2).
"claimant"—see Jobseekers Act 1995 s.35(1).

GENERAL NOTE

The general structure of the sanctions regime for new style JSA is set out in ss.6J and 6K of the new style Jobseekers Act 1995. This regulation provides definitions of various terms for the purposes of the more detailed provisions in the rest of Pt 3. However, the definitions of "higher-level sanction", "medium-level sanction" and "low-level sanction" in fact provide substantive rules about what sorts of failures to comply with work-related and connected requirements give rise to each level of sanction, the consequences of which are identified in regs 19–21 below. 7.52

A "higher-level sanction" is one imposed under s.6J of the Act, which, although headed "higher-level sanctions", does not use those words in its text. A "medium-level sanction" is one imposed under s.6K(2)(a) for a failure to comply with either of two specific requirements: a requirement to take all reasonable action to obtain paid work under s.6D(1)(a) (work search requirement) or a requirement to be available for work under s.6E(1). A "low-level sanction" is imposed for failures to comply with any other work-related or connected requirement.

The only effective purpose of the new definition of "current sanctionable failure" is in its reference to a sanctionable failure (i.e. a failure under s.6J or 6K) in relation to which the Secretary of State has not yet determined whether a reduction of benefit is to be applied. In any subsequent decision to apply a reduction for that failure, and any appeal, the test of whether there have been previous sanctionable failures must therefore be applied as at the date of the current sanctionable failure and not at the date of the decision applying the sanction. The extension of the definition to ESA and universal credit sanctionable failures appears pointless. This Part of the Regulations applies only where sanctionable failures under ss.6J or 6K of the new style Jobseekers Act 1995 are under consideration. It can have no application where the possible existence of sanctionable failures under other benefit regimes is under consideration.

General principles for calculating reduction periods

7.53 **18.**—(1) Subject to [1paragraph (3)], the reduction period is to be determined in relation to each sanctionable failure in accordance with regulations 19, 20 and 21.

(2) Reduction periods are to run consecutively.

(3) Where the reduction period calculated in relation to a sanctionable failure in accordance with regulation 19, 20 or 21 would result in the total outstanding reduction period exceeding 1095 days, the number of days in the reduction period in relation to that failure is to be adjusted so that 1095 days is not exceeded.

(4) [1...]

AMENDMENT

1. Jobseeker's Allowance and Employment and Support Allowance (Amendment) Regulations 2021 (SI 2021/1132) reg.2 (November 1, 2021).

DEFINITIONS

"reduction period"— see reg.17.
"sanctionable failure"—*ibid.*
"total outstanding reduction period"—*ibid.*
"UC sanctionable failure"—*ibid.*

GENERAL NOTE

7.54 Under ss.6J(1) and 6K(1) of the new style Jobseekers Act 1995, the definition of "reduction period" in reg.17 and this provision, the way in which a sanction bites is through a reduction in the amount of an award of JSA for a period determined under regs 19–21 for each sanctionable failure. A sanctionable failure is a failure which is sanctionable under s.6J or 6K of the Act, but that is subject to the rule in reg.5 above that the new style JSA requirements and sanctions regime does not apply at all if the claimant is entitled to universal credit. This regulation contains some general rules on calculating the length of sanction periods, which is where the main differences between higher, medium and low-level sanctions lie.

Under para.(2) reduction periods for separate new style JSA sanctionable failures run consecutively. The effect of reg.30 below is that if a claimant ceases to be entitled to universal credit while a reduction period for a universal credit sanction is running and either continues to be or becomes entitled to new style JSA, the balance of the period is to be to applied to the JSA award. Thus any reduction period for a new JSA sanctionable failure would appear to have to run consecutively after the expiry of the former universal credit reduction period and not concurrently. There appears to be no equivalent provision for the effect of an outstanding ESA sanctionable failure.

The general rule in para.(2) is subject to the general overall three-year limit in para.(3). The drafting is fairly impenetrable but the upshot seems to be that if adding a new reduction period to the end of an existing period or, more likely, chain of reduction periods would take the total days in the periods over 1095 days the new reduction period is to be adjusted to make the total 1095 days exactly. The definition of "total outstanding reduction period" in reg.17 expressly brings in the effect of reg.30, where it applies, to count the outstanding balance of a universal credit reduction period towards the 1095-day limit. The Jobseeker's Allowance and

Universal Credit (Higher-Level Sanctions) (Amendment) Regulations 2019 (SI 2019/1357) have made no change to para.(3) (see the notes to reg.19).

Paragraph (4) was removed entirely with effect from November 1, 2021. That leaves intact the operation of regs 19–21 in allowing an escalation in the length of reduction periods if there is more than one sanctionable failure within a year. A previous amendment with effect from July 25, 2016 should have done that to achieve its obvious purpose. However, it only removed sub-para.(a) of the then existing para. (4), thereby creating a provision whose plain words prevented any escalation, even though that was required under the amendments made to regs 19–21 by the same statutory instrument (the Social Security (Jobseeker's Allowance, Employment and Support Allowance and Universal Credit) (Amendment) Regulations 2016 (SI 2016/678)). It is still necessary to explore the consequences of that position of absurdity, to show the background to the 2021 amendment and to suggest the proper outcome for any sanction decisions in the period from July 25, 2016 to October 31, 2021.

Prior to the 2016 amendment the point of para.(4) was to disregard previous sanctionable failures (including under universal credit and ESA where applicable under regs 19–21 below) giving rise to a reduction in benefit that occurred in the 13 days immediately before the date of the current sanctionable failure. However, the plain words of reg.6(3) of the 2016 amending regulations omitted only sub-para.(a) of para.(4), leaving the opening words and sub-para.(b) in place. Because the form of para.(4) was to require the disregarding of the identified sanctionable failures, the result was that the plain remaining words required the disregarding of all previous sanctionable failures that gave rise to a reduction in benefit at any point in the process of determining the length of the reduction period for the current sanctionable failure. On the face of it, that would have meant that in the new tables in regs 19(1), 20(1) and 21 only the first entry, where there has been no previous relevant sanctionable failure, could ever be applied.

It may be that it can be said that, since that would have rendered inoperative much of the new tables inserted by the amending regulations, those regulations taken as a whole cannot be interpreted in that way. However, even if not, it must be very strongly arguable that the conditions for departing from the plain words of legislation where there has been a drafting mistake, as laid down in *Inco Europe Ltd v First Choice Distribution (a firm)* [2000] UKHL 15; [2000] 1 W.L.R. 586 and applied many times since, are met. There, Lord Nicholls said:

> "Before interpreting a statute in this way the court must be abundantly sure of three matters: (1) the intended purpose of the statute or provision in question; (2) that by inadvertence the draftsmen and Parliament failed to give effect to that purpose in the provision in question; and (3) the substance of the provision Parliament would have made, although not necessarily the precise words Parliament would have used, had the error in the Bill been noticed."

Lord Nicholls also indicated that even if those conditions are met the departure from the plain words of the provision must not be so great as to cross the line between interpretation and legislation.

In the case of the 2016 amendment to para.(4) the intended purpose is clear both from the explanatory note to the amending regulations (to ensure that the 14-day disregard rule applied not just in relation to the current sanctionable failure, but also to previous sanctionable failures) and from what was done by those regulations both in relation to regs 19(1), 20(1) and 21 and in relation to old style JSA and universal credit when a uniform position was intended to be produced over the three varieties of benefit. Then it appears that by mistake the draftsman failed to notice the difference in the form of para.(4) from that of reg.69(2) of the JSA Regulations 1996, which provided conditions for a previous sanctionable failure to count in the calculation of a reduction period, rather than be disregarded (reg.101(4) of the Universal Credit Regulations 2013 was not divided into sub-paragraphs and was removed in its entirety). If that mistake had been noticed, there can be little doubt that the draftsman would have provided for the amendment to omit the whole of para.(4), rather than merely sub-para.(a). That does not go beyond the process of interpretation, as it enables the substance of the amendments made to regs 19–21 to have effect, instead of the great part of them being rendered inoperative.

It might be thought that that conclusion (first expressed in the 2017/18 edition of what was then Vol.II of this series) would have been challenged by or on behalf of some new style JSA claimant relying on the plain words of reg.18 within the period of a little over five years in which reg.18 was in its defective form. That has not happened, so far as the editors are aware. The question of what the law actually was in that period is approached only tangentially in the documents relating to the November 2021 amendment. The Explanatory Note and Explanatory Memorandum to SI 2021/1132 describe the process as the correction of an error, which may possibly be taken as an endorsement of the argument above that the error should be regarded as not having existed from July 25, 2016. However, the Explanatory Memorandum does not spell that out and refers to the 2016 amendment as having raised ambiguity and says that, as the words of the amendment had not been applied in practice, no claimant would be adversely affected by the removal of reg.18(4). That explanation appears on its face to be disingenuous at best, if claimants had in practice been made subject to escalating sanctions from July 25, 2016 when there was no ambiguity in the plain words of the amended reg.18. Some further explanation would be necessary of how those plain words could be ignored as a matter of interpretation. However, the minutes of the meeting of the Social Security Advisory Committee (SSAC) on September 8, 2021 reveal the extraordinary (and only possible to accept following the revelation that the JSAPS computer payment system would not allow the application of reductions of new style JSA for sanctions: see the notes to s.6J of the new style Jobseekers Act 1995) claim made by DWP officials that no sanctions had been imposed on any new style JSA or ESA claimant since 2013, the focus instead having been on engagement and encouragement by work coaches (para.2.2(b)). There was, though, to be a process of applying sanctions for the future, so that the error (that was said to have been identified in 2018, but not corrected through lack of Parliamentary time) now needed to be corrected. In a letter to the Minister for Employment dated October 7, 2021, the chairman of the SSAC said that it had decided, following its September meeting, not to take the 2021 amending regulations on formal reference.

Note also the circumstances prescribed in reg.28 where there is to be no reduction despite the existence of a sanctionable failure under s.6J (and not s.6K).

The transition from old style JSA

7.55 Articles 17 and 18 of the Welfare Reform Act 2012 (Commencement No.9 and Transitional and Transitory Provisions and Commencement No.8 and Savings and Transitional Provisions (Amendment)) Order 2013 (as amended and set out in Vol.V of this series, 2021/22 edition as updated in Cumulative Supplements included in Vol.II of this series and in mid-year Supplements) set out some rules operating where a claimant was, before becoming entitled to new style JSA, subject to a reduction in benefit from old style JSA by reason of a sanction under ss.19 or 19A of the old style Jobseekers Act 1995 or reg.69B of the JSA Regulations 1996. Article 17 deals with the situation where the old style JSA award was not in existence immediately before the first day of entitlement under the new style JSA award. Article 18 deals with the situation where the old style JSA award continues as a new style award without any gap. Essentially the same rules are applied. Where the old style JSA reduction was made under s.19, the circumstances are to be treated as a failure sanctionable under s.6J of the new style Jobseekers Act 1995. Where the old style JSA reduction was made under s.19A or reg.69B, the circumstances are to be treated as a failure sanctionable under s.6K. Then a reduction is to be made to the new style JSA award in accordance with the present Regulations as modified by arts.17(4) and 18(4) and is to be treated as made under s.6J or 6K as appropriate. The reduction period is to be the same as that imposed by the old style JSA reduction decision, reduced by the number of days for which the old style JSA was reduced and (in the case of art.17) the number of days between the end of the old style JSA award and the first day of entitlement under the new style JSA award. Where art.17 applies, the references in reg.18(1) and (3) to regs 19, 20 and 21 are replaced by references to art.17 (art.17(4)). Where art.18 applies, they are replaced by references to art.18 (art.18(4)).

Higher-level sanction

19.—[1(1) Where the sanctionable failure is not a pre-claim failure, the reduction for a higher-level sanction in the circumstances described in the first column of the following table is the period set out in the second column. 7.56

Circumstances in which reduction period applies	*Reduction Period*
Where there has been no previous relevant failure by the claimant	91 days
Where there have been one or more previous relevant failures by the claimant and the date of the most recent relevant failure is not within 365 days beginning with the date of the current sanctionable failure	91 days
Where there have been one or more previous relevant failures by the claimant and the date of the most recent previous relevant failure is within 365 days, but not within 14 days, beginning with the date of the current sanctionable failure and the reduction period applicable to the most recent previous relevant failure is—	
(a) 91 days	182 days
(b) 182 days	[2182 days]
[2...]	
Where there have been one or more previous relevant failures by the claimant and the date of the most recent previous relevant failure is within 14 days beginning with the date of the current sanctionable failure and the reduction period applicable to the most recent previous relevant failure is—	
(a) 91 days	91 days
(b) 182 days	182 days
[2...]]	

(2) But where—

(a) the other sanctionable failure referred to in paragraph (1) was a pre-claim failure; or

(b) the UC sanctionable failure referred to in paragraph (1) was a pre-claim failure under regulation 102(4) of the Universal Credit Regulations 2013,

it is to be disregarded in determining the reduction period in accordance with paragraph (1).

(3) Where the sanctionable failure for which a reduction period is to be determined is a pre-claim failure, the reduction period is the lesser of—

(a) the period which would be applicable to the claimant under paragraph (1) if it were not a pre-claim failure; or

(b) where the sanctionable failure relates to paid work that was due to last for a limited period, the period beginning with the day after the date of the sanctionable failure and ending with the last day of the limited period,

minus the number of days beginning with the day after the date of the sanctionable failure and ending with the day before the date of claim.

[[1](4) In this regulation "relevant failure" means—

(a) a sanctionable failure giving rise to a higher-level sanction, or

(b) a UC sanctionable failure giving rise to a sanction under section 26 of the Welfare Reform Act 2012.]

AMENDMENTS

1. Social Security (Jobseeker's Allowance, Employment and Support Allowance and Universal Credit) (Amendment) Regulations 2016 (SI 2016/678) reg.6(4) (July 25, 2016).

2. Jobseeker's Allowance and Universal Credit (Higher-Level Sanctions) (Amendment) Regulations 2019 (SI 2019/1357) reg.4 (November 27, 2019).

DEFINITIONS

"claimant"—see Jobseekers Act 1995 s.35(1).
"current sanctionable failure"—see reg.17.
"date of claim"—see reg.2(2).
"higher-level sanction"—see reg.17.
"pre-claim failure"—*ibid.*
"reduction period"—*ibid.*
"sanctionable failure"—*ibid.*
"UC sanctionable failure"—*ibid.*

GENERAL NOTE

7.57 Higher-level sanctions are applicable to failures under s.6J of the new style Jobseekers Act 1995 (see the definition in reg.17). Such failures fall outside the scope of regs 20 and 21 and no failures under s.6K can come within the present regulation. Note the effect of reg.28 in preventing there being any reduction in benefit in specified circumstances though there has been a sanctionable failure under s.6J. There is a distinction between "pre-claim failures", i.e. failures under s.6J(3) (before the relevant claim failing for no good reason to take up an offer of paid work or ceasing paid work or losing pay by reason of misconduct or voluntarily and for no good reason), and other failures.

The rules for the latter are set out in paras (1) and (2). The new form of para.(1) in force from July 2016 was intended to spell out more precisely the rules that had applied previously in combination with the now-revoked reg.18(4)(a) and to extend the protection formerly given by that provision in the non-counting of previous sanctionable failures within the previous 14 days from the current sanctionable failure to include all previous sanctionable failures. The whole of reg.18(4) has now, from November 1, 2021, been revoked, ensuring that outcome for the future, with no impediment to the "escalation" process under reg.19. See the notes to reg.18 for the details and the argument that in the intervening period the plain words of reg.18(4) were to be ignored as producing an absurd and obviously unintended result.

The general rule in para.(1) (unhelpfully with no numbering for the four separate heads within the table) is that the reduction period is 91 days where there have been no previous new style JSA sanctionable failures giving rise to a higher-level sanction or universal credit sanctionable failures giving rise to a higher-level sanction under s.26 of the Welfare Reform Act 2012 (see the definition of "relevant failure" in para. (4)) within the past period of 365 days including the date of the sanctionable failure currently under consideration. See the note below on the transition from old style JSA for when an old style JSA sanctionable failure counts for the purposes of para.(1). However, para.(2) secures that pre-claim JSA or universal credit sanctionable failures do not count as previous failures (a "UC sanctionable failure referred to in paragraph (1)" must be taken to cover a "relevant failure" coupled with the definition in para.(4)).

Matters become more complicated when there has been a previous relevant failure within the 365 days. But the amendment with effect from November 27, 2019 has led to a considerable simplification through the removal of the category requiring a reduction period of 1095 days. To start at the end of the table, if the sole or most recent previous sanctionable failure was within the 13 days immediately preceding the date of the current failure, the period of reduction for the current failure is of equal length (either 91 or 182 days) to that for the previous failure. But note that the result of reg.18(2) and (3) is that the new period is to be added on to the end of the previous period, subject to the overall 1095-day limit. If the most recent previous sanctionable failure falls outside that 13-day period but within the 364 days immediately preceding the date of the current failure, the period of reduction for the current failure is 182 days. But note again the effect of reg.18(2) and (3).

The November 2019 amendment was in strict fulfilment of the decision announced by the then Secretary of State, Amber Rudd (written statement to Parliament, HCWS1545, May 9, 2019) to remove three-year sanctions for third or subsequent failures and reduce the maximum sanction length to six months by the end of the year. She considered a three-year sanction to be unnecessarily long and that the additional incentive provided by the three-year period over the already significant incentive provided by a six-month period was outweighed by the unintended impacts on the claimant due to the additional duration. However, as explained above and in the notes to reg.18, in new style JSA and universal credit, by contrast with the position for old style JSA (see reg.70(2) of the JSA Regulations 1996 in Vol.V of this series), the effect of the rules that reduction periods run consecutively, which has not been amended, is that if there have been multiple sanctionable failures within a year, a claimant may have a total outstanding reduction period of up to 1095 days imposed. Thus, the precise terms of the decision have been carried out, but it may be said that the spirit of the reasoning behind it has not been adopted for new style JSA and universal credit.

Regulation 5(1) of the amending regulation made the transitional provision that, where an award of new style JSA was subject to a 1095-day reduction under s.6J as at November 27, 2019, that reduction was to be terminated where the award had been reduced for at least 182 days. That appears to apply whether the 182 days expired before, on or after November 27, 2019, provided that the award was subject to the 1095-day reduction on that date. It then appears that once the 1095-day reduction had been terminated, the reduction period "applicable" to the previous sanctionable failure became 182 days, so that the case would fall within the new form of para.(b) of the third part of the table.

For pre-claim sanctionable failures, under para.(3) the number of days between the date of the failure and the date of the relevant claim is deducted from the number of days in the reduction period calculated as under para.(1). That is subject to the further rule that if the sanctionable failure relates to paid work that was due to last only for a limited period, the period down to the date when the work was due to end is substituted for the para.(2) period in the calculation. Presumably that is to give an incentive to people to take such work. See also reg.28(1)(c) removing the possibility of a reduction of benefit if the new style JSA claim is made outside the period of reduction that would otherwise have applied to the pre-claim failure.

Note that reg.22 below on the start date of the reduction period does not make obvious sense in relation to pre-claim sanctionable failures. By definition, the claimant will not have been paid new style JSA for the benefit week in which the pre-claim sanctionable failure occurred (although just possibly could have been paid old style JSA). In that case the terms of reg.22(a) appear to apply, making the start date the first day of the benefit week in which the sanctionable failure occurred. But that would not fit with the operation of reg.19(3) in excluding the days between the pre-claim sanctionable failure and the date of claim from the reduction period (because those days would in effect be counted twice in diminishing the effect of the sanction). To make sense, it appears that "has not been paid" in reg.22(a) has to be interpreted as meaning "has not been paid in a period covered by the current claim for new style JSA" or as "has not been paid when there is an entitlement to new style JSA". Then the reduction period for a pre-claim failure can start from the beginning of the period claimed for, if JSA has not been paid for the first benefit week, or, if it has been paid, under the reg.22(b) rule.

The transition from old style JSA

7.58 Where there is a sanctionable failure directly under the new style JSA legislation, a reduction of a new style award under art.17 or 18 of the Welfare Reform Act 2012 (Commencement No.9 and Transitional and Transitory Provisions and Commencement No.8 and Savings and Transitional Provisions (Amendment)) Order 2013 (as amended and set out in Vol.V of this series, 2021/22 edition as updated in Cumulative Supplements included in Vol.II of this series and in mid-year Supplements) (see the notes to reg.18) or a reduction of an old style JSA award counts as a previous sanctionable failure for which the reduction period is the number of days equivalent to the length of the period which applied under the old style JSA legislation (art.19 of that Order). However, if a period of entitlement to old style JSA, old style ESA or income support has intervened since the end of the new style JSA reduction under arts 17 or 18, no account is to be taken of that reduction for the present purpose (art.19(3)(a)). The same applies to a reduction of an old style JSA award but only where there has subsequently been entitlement to universal credit, new style JSA or new style ESA followed by entitlement to old style JSA, old style ESA or income support (art.19(3)(b)).

Medium-level sanctions

7.59 [[1]**20.**—(1) The reduction for a medium-level sanction in the circumstances described in the first column of the following table is the period set out in the second column.

Circumstances in which reduction period applies	*Reduction Period*
Where there has been no previous relevant failure by the claimant	28 days
Where there have been one or more previous relevant failures by the claimant and the date of the most recent relevant failure is not within 365 days beginning with the date of the current sanctionable failure	28 days
Where there have been one or more previous relevant failures by the claimant and the date of the most recent previous relevant failure is within 365 days, but not within 14 days, beginning with the date of the current sanctionable failure and the reduction period applicable to the most recent previous relevant failure is—	
(a) 28 days	91 days
(b) 91 days	91 days

Circumstances in which reduction period applies	*Reduction Period*
Where there have been one or more previous relevant failures by the claimant and the date of the most recent previous relevant failure is within 14 days beginning with the date of the current sanctionable failure and the reduction period applicable to the most recent previous relevant failure is—	
(a) 28 days	28 days
(b) 91 days	91 days

(2) In this regulation "relevant failure" means—

(a) a sanctionable failure giving rise to a medium-level sanction, or

(b) a UC sanctionable failure giving rise to a sanction under section 27 of the Welfare Reform Act 2012 to which regulation 103 of the Universal Credit Regulations 2013 applies.]

AMENDMENT

1. Social Security (Jobseeker's Allowance, Employment and Support Allowance and Universal Credit) (Amendment) Regulations 2016 (SI 2016/678) reg.6(5) (July 25, 2016).

DEFINITIONS

"claimant"—see Jobseekers Act 1995 s.35(1).
"current sanctionable failure"—see reg.17.
"medium-level sanction"—*ibid.*
"sanctionable failure"—*ibid.*
"reduction period"—*ibid.*
"UC sanctionable failure"—*ibid.*

GENERAL NOTE

By virtue of the definition of "medium-level sanction" in reg.17, this regulation applies to failures for no good reason to comply with two particular work-related requirements to which the claimant in question is subject: the requirement under s.6D(1)(a) of the new style Jobseekers Act 1995 to take all reasonable action to obtain paid work (but note, not the requirement under s.6D(1)(b) to take particular action specified by the Secretary of State, where failure to comply with a requirement to apply for a particular vacancy for paid work falls within s.6J(2)(b) and the higher-level sanctions regime) and the work availability requirement in s.6E(1). Note in relation to the second category that a failure for no good reason to comply with a work availability requirement by not taking up an offer of paid work falls under s.6J(2)(c) and so is subject to a higher-level sanction and not to any sanction under s.6K (s.6K(3)). Note that reg.28 (failures for which no reduction is applied) does not apply to any sanctionable failure under s.6K. 7.60

The reduction period under para.(1) as from July 25, 2016 is 28 days if there have been no other medium-level sanctionable failures (or equivalent universal credit sanctionable failures) at all or only outside the past period of 365 days including the date of the current sanctionable failure. If the most recent relevant sanctionable failure (see the definition in para.(2)) was in the past period of 14 days including the date of the current sanctionable failure, the length of the reduction period is equal to that for the most recent failure. Where the most recent relevant failure was further in the past but still within the 365 days, the length of the reduction period is 91 days. That is in substance the same result as under the previous form of reg.20 and reg.18(4). The whole of reg.18(4) has now, from November 1, 2021, been revoked, ensuring that outcome for the future, with no impediment to the "escalation" process under reg.20. See the notes to reg.18 for the details and the argument that in the intervening period the plain words of reg.18(4) were to be ignored as producing an absurd and obviously unintended result.

See the notes to regs 19, 25 and 28 for discussion of what sanctionable failures might or might not count for these purposes.

The transition from old style JSA

7.61 Where there is a sanctionable failure directly under the new style JSA legislation, a reduction of a new style award under arts 17 or 18 of the Welfare Reform Act 2012 (Commencement No.9 and Transitional and Transitory Provisions and Commencement No.8 and Savings and Transitional Provisions (Amendment)) Order 2013 (as amended and set out in Vol.V of this series, 2021/22 edition as updated in Cumulative Supplements included in Vol.II of this series and in mid-year Supplements) (see the notes to reg.18) or a reduction of an old style JSA award counts as a previous sanctionable failure for which the reduction period is the number of days equivalent to the length of the period which applied under the old style JSA legislation (art.19 of that Order). However, if a period of entitlement to old style JSA, old style ESA or income support has intervened since the end of the new style JSA reduction under arts 17 or 18, no account is to be taken of that reduction for the present purpose (art.19(3)(a)). The same applies to a reduction of an old style JSA award but only where there has subsequently been entitlement to universal credit, new style JSA or new style ESA followed by entitlement to old style JSA, old style ESA or income support (art.19(3)(b)).

Low-level sanctions

7.62 **21.**—(1) The reduction period for a low-level sanction is the total of the number of days referred to in paragraphs (2) and (3).

(2) The number of days beginning with the date of the sanctionable failure and ending with—

(a) the day before the day on which the claimant meets a compliance condition specified by the Secretary of State;

(b) the day before the day on which the claimant is no longer required to take a particular action specified as a work preparation requirement by the Secretary of State under section 6C(1) of the Act; or

(c) the day on which the award of a jobseeker's allowance is terminated,

whichever is soonest.

[[1](3) In the circumstances described in the first column of the following table, the number of days set out in the second column.

Circumstances applicable to claimant's case	*Number of days*
Where there has been no previous relevant failure by the claimant	7 days
Where there have been one or more previous relevant failures by the claimant and the date of the most recent relevant failure is not within 365 days beginning with the date of the current sanctionable failure	7 days
Where there have been one or more previous relevant failures by the claimant and the date of the most recent previous relevant failure is within 365 days, but not within 14 days, beginning with the date of the current sanctionable failure and the reduction period applicable to the most recent previous relevant failure is—	

Circumstances applicable to claimant's case	*Number of days*
(a) 7 days	14 days
(b) 14 days	28 days
(c) 28 days	28 days
Where there have been one or more previous relevant failures by the claimant and the date of the most recent previous relevant failure is within 14 days beginning with the date of the current sanctionable failure and the reduction period applicable to the most recent previous relevant failure is—	
(a) 7 days	7 days
(b) 14 days	14 days
(c) 28 days	28 days

(4) In this regulation "relevant failure" means—

(a) a sanctionable failure giving rise to a low-level sanction, or

(b) a UC sanctionable failure giving rise to a sanction under section 27 of the Welfare Reform Act 2012 to which regulation 104 of the Universal Credit Regulations 2013 applies, or

(c) an ESA sanctionable failure giving rise to a sanction under section 11J of the Welfare Reform Act 2007 to which regulation 52 of the Employment and Support Allowance Regulations 2013 applies.]

AMENDMENT

1. Social Security (Jobseeker's Allowance, Employment and Support Allowance and Universal Credit) (Amendment) Regulations 2016 (SI 2016/678) reg.6(6) (July 25, 2016).

DEFINITIONS

"claimant"—see Jobseekers Act 1995 s.35(1).
"compliance condition"—see Jobseekers Act 1995 s.6K(6).
"current sanctionable failure"—see reg.17.
"ESA sanctionable failure"—*ibid.*
"low-level sanction"—*ibid.*
"sanctionable failure"—*ibid.*
"UC sanctionable failure"—*ibid.*

GENERAL NOTE

The definition of "low-level sanction" in reg.17 above is in terms of the requirements failure to comply with which lead to a sanction at that level under s.6K of the new style Jobseekers Act 1995: (a) a work-focused interview requirement under s.6B(1) of the Act; (b) a work preparation requirement under s.6C(1); (c) a work search requirement under section 6D(1)(b) of the Act (requirement to take particular action specified by the Secretary of State to obtain paid work); or (d) a requirement under s.6G of the Act (connected requirements). In effect, the low-level sanction covers any sanctionable failure under s.6K not covered by a medium-level sanction, the higher-level sanction being restricted to sanctions under s.6J. Note that reg.28 (failures for which no reduction is applied) does not apply to any sanctionable failure under s.6K. **7.63**

Note in relation to category (b) that a failure for no good reason to comply with a work preparation requirement in the form of undertaking a work placement of a prescribed description falls within s.6J(2)(a) and so is subject to a higher-level sanction and not to any sanction under s.6K (s.6K(3)). But the only such placement prescribed by reg.29 below (the Mandatory Work Activity Scheme) ceased to operate after April 2016. Note in relation to category (c) that a failure for no good reason to comply with a work search requirement to take particular action in the form of applying for a particular vacancy for paid work falls under s.6J(2)(b) and so is subject to a higher-level sanction and not to any sanction under s.6K (s.6K(3)).

The calculation of the reduction period under para.(1) is more complicated than that for higher and medium-level sanctions. It is made up of a period of flexible length depending on the ongoing circumstances under para.(2) plus a fixed period of days under para.(3) to be added to the para.(2) period.

The basic rule in para.(2) is that the period runs until any compliance condition specified by the Secretary of State is met. See the notes to s.6K(5) of the Act for the authorisation for this provision. A compliance condition is that the failure to comply ceases to exist (e.g. attending a work-focused interview) or as to future compliance. The condition must in accordance with s.6K(5)(a) and sub-para.(a)(i) be specified by the Secretary of State. Although s.6K(7)(b) allows the Secretary of State to notify a claimant of a compliance condition in such manner as he determines, the approach of the Supreme Court in *R (on the application of Reilly and Wilson) v Secretary of State for Work and Pensions* [2013] UKSC 68; [2014] 1 A.C. 453 might possibly be relevant to the substance of what must be specified, as discussed further in the notes to s.6K(5). The para.(2) period will also end if the award of JSA terminates. It appears that during the 2020 COVID-19 outbreak, if the same approach was taken as for universal credit, any contact by the claimant with the DWP was treated as compliance with any condition, thus bringing that part of the reduction period to an end.

Under para.(3) as in force from July 25, 2016 the additional number of days is seven if there have been no other low-level sanctionable failures (or equivalent universal credit or ESA sanctionable failures) at all or only outside the past period of 365 days including the date of the current sanctionable failure. If the most recent relevant sanctionable failure (see the definition in para.(4)) was in the past period of 14 days including the date of the current sanctionable failure, the number of days is equal to that for the most recent failure. Where the most recent relevant failure was further in the past but still within the 365 days, the number of days is one step up from that attracted by the most recent failure, up to 28 (14 for 7, 28 for 14, 28 for 28). That is in substance the same result as under the previous form of reg.21 and reg.18(4). The whole of reg.18(4) has now, from November 1, 2021, been revoked, ensuring that outcome for the future, with no impediment to the "escalation" process under para.(3). See the notes to reg.18 for the details and the argument that in the intervening period the plain words of reg.18(4) were to be ignored as producing an absurd and obviously unintended result.

See the notes to regs 19, 25 and 28 for discussion of what sanctionable failures might or might not count for these purposes.

The transition from old style JSA

7.64 Where there is a sanctionable failure directly under the new style JSA legislation, a reduction of a new style award under art.17 or 18 of the Welfare Reform Act 2012 (Commencement No.9 and Transitional and Transitory Provisions and Commencement No.8 and Savings and Transitional Provisions (Amendment)) Order 2013 (as amended and set out in Vol.V of this series, 2021/22 edition as updated in Cumulative Supplements included in Vol.II of this series and in mid-year Supplements) (see the notes to reg.18) or a reduction of an old style JSA award counts as a previous sanctionable failure for which the reduction period is the number of days equivalent to the length of the period which applied under the old style JSA legislation (art.19 of that Order). However, if a period of entitlement to old style JSA, old style ESA or income support has intervened since the end of the new style JSA reduction under arts 17 or 18, no account is to be taken of that reduction for the present purpose (art.19(3)(a)). The same applies to a reduction of an old style JSA award but only where there has subsequently been entitlement to universal credit, new style JSA or new style ESA followed by entitlement to old style JSA, old style ESA or income support (art.19(3)(b)).

Start of the reduction

22.—A reduction period determined in relation to a sanctionable failure takes effect from— 7.65

(a) where the claimant has not been paid a jobseeker's allowance for the benefit week in which the sanctionable failure occurred, the first day of that benefit week;

(b) where the claimant has been paid a jobseeker's allowance for the benefit week referred to in paragraph (a), the first day of the first benefit week for which the claimant has not been paid a jobseeker's allowance; or

(c) where the amount of the award of the jobseeker's allowance for the benefit week referred to in paragraph (a) or (b) is already subject to a reduction because of a previous sanctionable failure, the first day of the first benefit week in respect of which the amount of the award is no longer subject to that reduction.

DEFINITIONS

"benefit week"—see reg.2(2).
"claimant"—see Jobseekers Act 1995 s.35(1).
"reduction period"—see reg.17.
"sanctionable failure"—*ibid.*

GENERAL NOTE

This stipulates in which benefit week the relevant period of reduction appropriate to the sanctionable failure actually takes effect in relation to an award of new style JSA. Under para.(a), if new style JSA has not been paid for the benefit week in which the sanctionable failure occurred, the reduction period starts from that benefit week. Presumably it does not matter that payment of benefit has been made for some subsequent week(s). That award of benefit can be superseded under regs 27(1)(b) and 35(10) of the Universal Credit, Personal Independence Payment, Jobseeker's Allowance and Employment and Support Allowance (Decisions and Appeals) Regulations 2013 (SI 2013/381) (see Vol.III of this series). Under para. (b), if payment has been made for that benefit week, the reduction period starts with the first benefit week for which payment has not been made. Paragraph (c), making the start of the reduction period run on from the end of an existing reduction period, follows from the principle that reduction periods for separate sanctionable failures run consecutively (reg.18(2)). 7.66

The rules above fit together for the great majority of sanctions under ss.6J and 6K, where by definition the claimant must have become subject to work-related or connected requirements under a claim, or in most cases have an award of new style JSA. However, they do not make obvious sense for pre-claim sanctionable failures under s.6J(3) of the new style Jobseekers Act 1995, where the length of the reduction period is set by reg.19(3) above. That is because, as explained in the notes to reg.19(3), by definition the claimant will not have been paid new style JSA for the benefit week in which the pre-claim failure occurred, so that reg.22(a) would apparently apply, but it would not fit with reg.19(3), on excluding the days between the date of the pre-claim sanctionable failure and the date of claim from the reduction period to be applied, for the reduction period to start with that benefit week. That would involve taking those days out of effective application of the reduction period twice. It is submitted that, to make sense, "has not been paid" in reg.22(a) has to be interpreted as meaning "has not been paid in a period covered by the current claim for new style JSA" or as "has not been paid when there is an entitlement to new style JSA". Then the reduction period for pre-claim failure can start from the beginning of the period claimed for or the period of entitlement, if JSA has not been paid for the first benefit week, or, if it has been paid, under the reg.22(b) rule.

Reduction period to continue where award of jobseeker's allowance terminates

7.67 **23.**—(1) Where an award of a jobseeker's allowance terminates while there is an outstanding reduction period—

(a) the period continues to run as if a daily reduction were being applied; and

(b) if the claimant becomes entitled to a new award of a jobseeker's allowance before the period expires, that new award is subject to a reduction for the remainder of the total outstanding reduction period.

(2) Paragraph (3) applies where—

(a) an award of a jobseeker's allowance terminates before the Secretary of State determines that the amount of the award is to be reduced in accordance with section 6J or 6K of the Act in relation to a sanctionable failure; and

(b) that determination is made after the claimant becomes entitled to a new award of a jobseeker's allowance.

(3) Where this paragraph applies—

(a) the reduction period in relation to the sanctionable failure referred to in paragraph (2) is to be treated as having taken effect on the day before the previous award terminated;

(b) that reduction period is treated as having continued to run as if a daily reduction were being applied; and

(c) if the new award referred to in paragraph (2)(b) begins before that reduction period expires, that new award is subject to a reduction for the remainder of the total outstanding reduction period.

DEFINITIONS

"the Act"—see reg.2(2).
"claimant"—see Jobseekers Act 1995 s.35(1).
"reduction period"—see reg.17.
"sanctionable failure"—*ibid.*
"total outstanding reduction period"—*ibid.*

GENERAL NOTE

7.68 If an award of new style JSA terminates while there is an outstanding reduction period, subsequent days count as if an actual reduction of benefit were being applied (thus reducing the days outstanding in the period), so that on any further claim for JSA the claimant is subject to the reduction only for the remainder of the period, if any (para.(1)). If an award of new style JSA terminates before the Secretary of State has made a decision about a reduction for a sanctionable failure, but a new award is in place by the time the decision is made, the reduction period starts as if the decision had been made on the day before the previous award terminated, so that the new award of JSA will be reduced for the remainder of the total outstanding reduction period (paras (2) and (3)). This regulation can only apply to cases that fall outside reg.6 (JSA sanction transfers to universal credit when become entitled to universal credit while JSA entitlement continues) because it operates only when JSA entitlement has ceased.

Suspension of a reduction where a fraud sanction applies

24.—(1) A reduction in the amount of an award of a jobseeker's allowance in accordance with section 6J or 6K of the Act is to be suspended for any period during which section 6B or 7 of the Social Security Fraud Act 2001 applies to the award. 7.69

(2) The reduction ceases to have effect on the day on which that period begins and has effect again on the day after that period ends.

DEFINITION

"the Act"—see reg.2(2).

Termination of a reduction

25.—(1) A reduction in the amount of an award of a jobseeker's allowance in accordance with section 6J or 6K of the Act is to be terminated where, since the date of the most recent sanctionable failure which gave rise to such a reduction, the claimant has been in paid work— 7.70

(a) for a period of at least 26 weeks; or

(b) for more than one period where the total of those periods amounts to at least 26 weeks.

(2) The termination of the reduction has effect—

(a) where the date on which paragraph (1) is satisfied falls within a period of entitlement to a jobseeker's allowance, from the beginning of the benefit week in which that date falls; or

(b) where that date falls outside a period of entitlement to a jobseeker's allowance, from the beginning of the first benefit week in relation to any subsequent award of a jobseeker's allowance.

(3) The claimant is in paid work for the purposes of paragraph (1) where their weekly earnings are at least equal to their expected number of hours per week calculated under regulation 9 multiplied by the national minimum wage which would apply for a person of the claimant's age under the National Minimum Wage Regulations 1999.

DEFINITIONS

"the Act" —see reg.2(2).
"claimant"—see Jobseekers Act 1995 s.35(1).
"benefit week" —see reg.2(2).
"sanctionable failure"—see reg.17.

GENERAL NOTE

Any reduction for any level of sanction or sanctions terminates where, since the date of the most recent sanctionable failure, the claimant has been in paid work for at least 26 weeks, not necessarily consecutive, with weekly earnings at least equal to the expected number of hours per week (see reg.9: normally 35) multiplied by the national minimum wage applicable to a person of the claimant's age under the National Minimum Wage Regulations 1999 (paras (1) and (3)). The 1999 Regulations were revoked and consolidated with subsequent amendments into the National Minimum Wage Regulations 2015 (SI 2015/621), which can therefore be taken as covered by the reference to the 1999 Regulations. The amendments with effect from April 6, 7.71

2016 (SI 2016/68) to implement the "national living wage" made the main rate, with the additional national living wage label, under reg.4 generally applicable, with lower rates for those under 25. The lower age range of the main rate has since been extended, first to 23, and from April 1, 2024 stands at 21. The UC Regulations 2013 were amended from July 25, 2016 by SI 2016/678 to up-date the references, but the amending regulations contain no equivalent for the JSA Regulations 2013. Paragraph (2) sets out the time the termination takes effect dependent on whether or not the day the 26-week period is up falls within or outside a period of entitlement to JSA. If within, termination takes effect from the beginning of the benefit week in which there fell the completion of the 26-week period. If outside, it takes effect from the beginning of the first benefit week of any subsequent JSA award.

Note that it does not matter how long the outstanding reduction period is. A claimant could have had a reduction period of 1095 days imposed, yet after 26 weeks' work at minimum wage level the entire reduction disappears, just as much as if the reduction period affected were much shorter. But note also that this regulation does not take away the status of the sanctionable failure or failures that the reduction was based on. It merely terminates the reduction in benefit. Thus for the purpose of asking in the future whether there have been any other sanctionable failures within the previous 364 days of a new sanctionable failure (see regs 19–21) it might appear that all such sanctionable failures still count for those purposes. However, since the references in regs 19–21 are to other sanctionable failures "giving rise to" a sanction at the appropriate level, it is arguable that if there is no longer any reduction being imposed the sanctionable failure no longer gives rise to a sanction. But if a reduction period was initially actually imposed following the sanctionable failure in question, which is later terminated under reg.25, there is also an argument that the sanctionable failure did give rise to a sanction for the purposes of regs 19–21.

Amount of reduction for each benefit week

7.72 **26.**—Where it has been determined that an award of a jobseeker's allowance is to be reduced in accordance with section 6J or 6K of the Act, the amount of the reduction for each benefit week in respect of which a reduction has effect is to be calculated as follows.

Step 1

Take the number of days—

(a) in the benefit week; or

(b) if lower, in the total outstanding reduction period,

and deduct any days in that benefit week or total outstanding reduction period for which the reduction is suspended in accordance with regulation 24.

Step 2

Multiply the number of days produced by step 1 by the daily reduction rate.

Step 3

Deduct the amount produced by step 2 from the amount of the award of jobseeker's allowance for the benefit week.

DEFINITIONS

"the Act"—see reg.2(2).

"benefit week"—*ibid.*

"daily reduction rate"—see reg.27.

"total outstanding reduction period"—see reg.17.

GENERAL NOTE

This provides the means of calculating for each benefit week the amount of reduction. It translates the daily reduction rate under reg.27 into the appropriate amount for each benefit week, depending on the number of days on the week covered by the reduction period. 7.73

Daily reduction rate

27.—(1) The daily reduction rate for the purposes of regulation 26 is the amount applicable to the claimant under regulation 49 multiplied by 52 and divided by 365. 7.74

(2) The amount of the rate in paragraph (1) is to be rounded down to the nearest 10 pence.

GENERAL NOTE

The effect of this regulation is that the reduction in benefit under a sanction of any level, for the period affected, in substance takes away the whole of the benefit otherwise payable. That is because new style JSA provides no benefit over and above the age-related amounts prescribed for claimants under 25 and aged 25 or over in reg.49. It is possible that the operation of the calculation in para.(1) to translate the figure per week in reg.49 to a daily rate, involving a division by 365, whether in a Leap Year or not, coupled with the rounding down process in para.(2), could result in an amount to be deducted under reg.26 for a full benefit week which is lower than the age-related amount. However, whatever remains is unlikely to be paid to a claimant in the light of the rule in reg.52 that where the weekly amount of new style JSA is less than 10p it is not payable. 7.75

Failures for which no reduction is applied

28.—(1) No reduction is to be made in accordance with section 6J of the Act for a sanctionable failure where— 7.76

(a) the sanctionable failure is listed in section 6J(2)(b) or (c) of the Act (failure to apply for a vacancy for paid work or failure to take up an offer of paid work) and the vacancy has arisen because of a strike arising from a trade dispute;

(b) the sanctionable failure is listed in section 6J(2)(d) of the Act (ceases paid work or loses pay) and the following circumstances apply—

  (i) the claimant's work search and work availability requirements are subject to limitations under sections 6D(4) and 6E(3) of the Act in respect of work available for a certain number of hours;

  (ii) the claimant takes up paid work that is for a greater number of hours; and

  (iii) the claimant voluntarily ceases that paid work, or loses pay, within a trial period;

(c) the sanctionable failure is listed in section 6J(3) of the Act (failures that occur before a claim is made) and the period of the reduction that would otherwise apply under regulation 19 is the same as or shorter than the number of days beginning with the day after the date of the sanctionable failure and ending with the day before the date of that claim;

(d) the sanctionable failure is that the claimant voluntarily ceases paid work, or loses pay, because of a strike arising from a trade dispute;

(e) the sanctionable failure is that the claimant voluntarily ceases paid work as a member of the regular forces or the reserve forces (within the meanings in section 374 of the Armed Forces Act 2006), or loses pay in that capacity; or

(f) the sanctionable failure is that the claimant voluntarily ceases paid work in one of the following circumstances—

(i) the claimant has been dismissed because of redundancy after volunteering or agreeing to be dismissed;

(ii) the claimant has ceased work on an agreed date without being dismissed in pursuance of an agreement relating to voluntary redundancy; or

(iii) the claimant has been laid-off or kept on short-time to the extent specified in section 148 of the Employment Rights Act 1996, and has complied with the requirements of that section.

(2) In this regulation—

"redundancy" has the same meaning as in section 139(1) of the Employment Rights Act 1996;

"strike" has the same meaning as in section 246 of the Trade Union and Labour Relations (Consolidation) Act 1992;

"trade dispute" has the same meaning as in section 244 of that Act.

DEFINITIONS

"the Act"—see reg.2(2).
"claimant"—see Jobseekers Act 1995 s.35(1).
"the regular forces"—see Armed Forces Act 2006 s.374.
"the reserve forces"—*ibid.*
"sanctionable failure"—see reg.17.
"work availability requirement"—see Jobseekers Act 1995 ss.35(1) and 6E.
"work search requirement"—see Jobseekers Act 1995 ss.35(1) and 6D.

GENERAL NOTE

7.77 This is a significant provision in prescribing, under s.6J(7)(a) of the new style Jobseekers Act 1995, cases of sanctionable failure for which no reduction of benefit can be imposed. It is thus limited to the higher-level sanctions regime and does not apply to medium or low-level sanctions under s.6K, although the categories prescribed would not seem to be relevant to the s.6K conditions. Note that if a case comes within this regulation that does not affect the status of the sanctionable failure in question. But, in contrast to the circumstances discussed in the note to reg.25, if no reduction period was ever imposed, it must be strongly arguable that the sanctionable failure in question did not "give rise to" a higher-level sanction for the purposes of reg.19. There remains scope for argument that in some of the circumstances listed there is a good reason for the particular claimant's failure to comply with the requirement in question, so that there is not in fact a sanctionable failure.

The cases are as follows.

Sub-paragraph (a)

7.78 Where the sanctionable failure is failing for no good reason to apply for a particular vacancy for paid work or to take up an offer of paid work (new style Jobseekers Act 1995 s.6J(2)(b) or (c)), no reduction is to be imposed if the vacancy arose because of a strike arising from a trade dispute. "Strike" is defined in para.(2) by reference on to s.246 of the Trade Union and Labour Relations (Consolidation) Act 1992, where it means "any concerted stoppage of work". Paragraph (2) also adopts the meaning of "trade dispute" given there (thus displacing the definition in s.35(1) of the new style Jobseekers Act 1995):

"(1) In this Part a "trade dispute" means a dispute between workers and their employer which relates wholly or mainly to one or more of the following—

(a) terms and conditions of employment, or the physical conditions in which any workers are required to work;
(b) engagement or non-engagement, or termination or suspension of employment or the duties of employment, of one or more workers;
(c) allocation of work or the duties of employment between workers or groups of workers;
(d) matters of discipline;
(e) a worker's membership or non-membership of a trade union;
(f) facilities for officials of trade unions; and
(g) machinery for negotiation or consultation, and other procedures, relating to any of the above matters, including the recognition by employers or employers' associations of the right of a trade union to represent workers in such negotiation or consultation or in the carrying out of such procedures.

(2) A dispute between a Minister of the Crown and any workers shall, notwithstanding that he is not the employer of those workers, be treated as a dispute between those workers and their employer if the dispute relates to matters which—

(a) have been referred for consideration by a joint body on which, by virtue of provision made by or under any enactment, he is represented, or
(b) cannot be settled without him exercising a power conferred on him by or under an enactment.

(3) There is a trade dispute even though it relates to matters occurring outside the United Kingdom, so long as the person or persons whose actions in the United Kingdom are said to be in contemplation or furtherance of a trade dispute relating to matters occurring outside the United Kingdom are likely to be affected in respect of one or more of the matters specified in subsection (1) by the outcome of the dispute.

(4) An act, threat or demand done or made by one person or organisation against another which, if resisted, would have led to a trade dispute with that other, shall be treated as being done or made in contemplation of a trade dispute with that other, notwithstanding that because that other submits to the act or threat or accedes to the demand no dispute arises.

(5) In this section—

"employment" includes any relationship whereby one person personally does work or performs services for another; and

"worker", in relation to a dispute with an employer, means—

(a) a worker employed by that employer; or
(b) a person who has ceased to be so employed if his employment was terminated in connection with the dispute or if the termination of his employment was one of the circumstances giving rise to the dispute."

That is a fairly comprehensive definition, although as compared with s.35(1) of the old style Jobseeker's Act 1995 it does not cover disputes between employees and employees. It is possible that vacancies could arise because of industrial action short of a strike. There seems no good reason why claimants who on principle are not prepared to apply for such vacancies or accept offers should not also be protected. Perhaps it is arguable that in any event they have a good reason for failing to comply with the requirement in question, so that there is no sanctionable failure.

Sub-paragraph (b)

This provision protects current new style JSA claimants who take up work for a trial period (not further defined, so to have its ordinary meaning not subject to the restrictions of reg.74(4) of the JSA Regulations 1996), but is restricted to those who are required only to search for and be available for work subject to limitations as to hours of work under reg.14. It is made under s.6D(4) and 6E(3) of the Act. Then if such a claimant takes up work, or more work, for more than the hours of limitation 7.79

for a trial period, but later voluntarily gives up that work or extra work or loses pay within the trial period, there is to be no reduction. As above, it would be arguable there was good reason for such action, so no sanctionable failure.

Sub-paragraph (c)

7.80 Where there is a pre-claim sanctionable failure and the reduction period normally applicable would expire on or before the date of the relevant JSA claim, there is to be no reduction. It may be that the same result is achieved by reg.19(3).

Sub-paragraph (d)

7.81 This provision provides the same protection as under sub-para.(a) for voluntarily ceasing paid work or losing pay because of a strike arising from a trade dispute.

Sub-paragraph (e)

7.82 Members of the UK armed forces, both regular and reserve forces, who voluntarily cease paid work as such or lose pay, cannot suffer a reduction on that ground, whatever the circumstances.

Sub-paragraph (f)

7.83 This provides protection in the same circumstances as prescribed in reg.71 of the JSA Regulations 1996 for old style JSA purposes, except that there the claimant is deemed not to have left employment voluntarily and so is not subject to any sanction. Here the claimant is merely protected from having a reduction of benefit imposed, subject to any argument that there was a good reason under general principles for voluntarily ceasing work, so no sanctionable failure.

Sanctionable failures under section 6J of the Act: work placements

7.84 [[1]**29.**—(1) A placement on the Mandatory Work Activity Scheme is a prescribed placement for the purpose of section 6J(2)(a) of the Act (sanctionable failure not to comply with a work placement).

(2) In paragraph (1) "the Mandatory Work Activity Scheme" means a scheme provided pursuant to arrangements made by the Secretary of State and known by that name that is designed to provide work or work-related activity for up to 30 hours per week over a period of 4 consecutive weeks with a view to assisting claimants to improve their prospects of obtaining employment.]

AMENDMENT

1. Universal Credit (Consequential, Supplementary, Incidental and Miscellaneous Provisions) Regulations 2013 (SI 2013/630) reg.39 (April 29, 2013).

DEFINITION

"the Act"—see reg.2(2).

GENERAL NOTE

7.85 In order for a higher-level sanction to be imposed under s.6J(2)(a) of the new style Jobseekers Act, the claimant must have failed for no good reason to comply with a work preparation requirement to undertake a work placement of a prescribed description. Paragraph (1) prescribes the Mandatory Work Activity Scheme and para.(2) gives a description of the scheme considered sufficient to meet the test in s.6J(2)(a). See the notes to that section for discussion of the validity of this regulation. The scheme ceased to operate after April 2016.

Sanctions where universal credit ends and the person is entitled to a jobseeker's allowance

30.—(1) This regulation applies where— 7.86

(a) a person ceases to be entitled to universal credit;

(b) there is a reduction relating to the person's award of universal credit under section 26 or 27 of the Welfare Reform Act 2012; and

(c) the person is entitled to a jobseeker's allowance.

(2) Any reduction relating to the award of the universal credit is to be applied to the award of the jobseeker's allowance.

(3) The period for which the reduction relating to the award of the jobseeker's allowance is to have effect is the number of days which apply to the person under regulation 102, 103, 104 or 105 of the Universal Credit Regulations 2013 minus any such days which—

(a) have already resulted in a reduction in the amount of universal credit; or

(b) fall after the date the award of universal credit was terminated and before the date on which the award of a jobseeker's allowance starts.

(4) The daily reduction rate for the reduction relating to the award of the jobseeker's allowance is the amount of the claimant's jobseeker's allowance multiplied by 52 and divided by 365.

(5) The claimant's award of a jobseeker's allowance is to be reduced by the daily reduction amount referred to in paragraph (4) for each day of the period referred to in paragraph (3).

DEFINITION

"claimant"—see Jobseekers Act 1995 s.35(1).

GENERAL NOTE

Where someone subject to one or more universal credit sanctions ceases to be entitled to universal credit and becomes entitled to new style JSA, the remaining reduction period applicable to the universal credit award carries over to reduce the JSA award. The remaining reduction period is calculated by deducting from the period imposed as regards universal credit: (i) the days for which universal credit has been in consequence reduced, and (ii) the days between the cessation of entitlement to universal credit and the beginning of entitlement to new style JSA. The JSA award must be reduced for each day of the remaining reduction period by the daily reduction amount set out in para.(4) (para.(5)), which appears to be the same as the standard reduction under reg.27. 7.87

See the notes to reg.6 above for a question whether, if a new style JSA sanction has transferred to universal credit under that provision and the claimant then ceases to be entitled to universal credit while there are still some unexpired days in the sanction period, reg.30 applies. It is arguable that there was not a reduction under s.26 or 27 of the WRA 2012 (para.(1)(b)), since the sanction was originally imposed under the JSA legislation.

PART 4

Information and evidence

Provision of information and evidence

7.88 **31.**—(1) A claimant must supply such information in connection with the claim for a jobseeker's allowance, or any question arising out of it, as may be required by the Secretary of State.

(2) A claimant must furnish such certificates, documents and other evidence as may be required by the Secretary of State for the determination of the claim.

(3) A claimant must furnish such certificates, documents and other evidence affecting their continuing entitlement to a jobseeker's allowance, whether that allowance is payable to them and, if so, in what amount, as the Secretary of State may require.

(4) A claimant must notify the Secretary of State—

(a) of any change of circumstances which has occurred which the claimant might reasonably be expected to know might affect their entitlement to a jobseeker's allowance or the payability or amount of such an allowance; and

(b) of any such change of circumstances which the claimant is aware is likely to occur.

(5) The notification referred to in paragraph (4) must be given as soon as reasonably practicable after the occurrence or, as the case may be, after the claimant becomes so aware, by giving notice of the change to an office of the Department for Work and Pensions specified by the Secretary of State—

(a) in writing or by telephone (unless the Secretary of State determines in any particular case that notice must be given in writing or may be given otherwise than in writing or by telephone); or

(b) in writing if in any particular case the Secretary of State requires written notice (unless the Secretary of State determines in any particular case to accept notice given otherwise than in writing).

(6) Where, pursuant to paragraph (1), a claimant is required to supply information, they must do so when they participate in a work-focused interview under section 6B of the Act, if so required by the Secretary of State, or within such period as the Secretary of State may require.

(7) Where, pursuant to paragraph (2) or (3), a claimant is required to provide certificates, documents or other evidence they must do so within seven days of being so required or such longer period as the Secretary of State may consider reasonable.

Definitions

"the Act"—see reg.2(2).
"claimant"—see Jobseekers Act 1995 s.35(1).
"writing"—see Interpretation Act 1978 Sch.1.

General Note

Paragraphs (1) and (2)

7.89 See reg.7(1) of the Social Security (Claims and Payments) Regulations 1987 and the annotations to that provision in Vol.III of this series. The general rule in reg.19 of the Universal Credit, Personal Independence Payment, Jobseeker's Allowance and Employment and Support Allowance (Claims and Payments) Regulations 2013 (see Vol.III) is that a person wishing to make claim for new style JSA is to attend an appropriate office at a time specified by the Secretary of State, although there is also provision for claims in writing without attendance and by telephone. If the person attends as specified and provides a properly completed claim form at the time or within any extra time allowed under reg.20(3) of the Claims and Payments Regulations 2013, the claim is treated as made on the later of the first day of the period claimed for or the date of first notification of an intention to claim (reg.20(1)). If the person does not attend or does not provide a properly completed claim form within time, the claim cannot be treated as made before the person does attend or provide a properly completed claim form. It therefore appears that, before an effective claim is made and the person becomes a "claimant" as defined in s.35(1) of the new style Jobseekers Act 1995, the Secretary of State's powers to require the person to provide information and evidence when attending to claim must rest on the appropriate parts of reg.21 of the Claims and Payments Regulations 2013. By contrast with the 1987 Regulations, this does not give an express power for a written claim form to instruct that information or evidence be provided. However, there seems no reason why such an instruction should not be included in a claim form. Then, a written claim on the approved form is properly completed if completed in accordance with the instructions and defective if not so completed (see reg.21(3) and reg.21(4) and (5) for correcting defects). Paragraphs (1) and (2) of the present regulation can only apply once an effective claim has been made, as is confirmed by the mention in para.(6) of the information required under para.(1) being provided at a work-focused interview under s.6B of the Act. A person cannot be required to participate in such an interview until they have become a "claimant". The consequence of a breach of the requirements of paras (1) and (2) would seem to be as discussed in *R(IS) 4/93*, that an initial effective claim has to be decided in the absence of the information or evidence in question, which may mean that the claimant has failed to show qualification for benefit.

Where a requirement under para.(1), (2) or (3) arises in the course of an award of new style JSA, the consequences of a failure to comply are not clear. It can be a connected requirement under s.6G(3)(a) of the new style Jobseekers Act 1995 to provide specified information or evidence for the purpose of verifying compliance with a work-related requirement, where a failure for no good reason to comply gives rise to a low-level sanction under s.6K(2)(b). Similarly, under s.6G(4) the Secretary of State may require a claimant to report any specified changes in circumstances that are relevant to the imposition of a work-related requirement or the claimant's compliance with such a requirement. However, outside those categories, a failure to comply with a para.(1), (2) or (3) requirement would not seem in itself to provide a ground for revision or supersession. It might though be possible to argue, depending on the specifics of the individual case, that adverse inferences could be drawn from a failure to supply the required information or evidence such as to support a finding of a relevant change of circumstances.

Paragraph (3)

See reg.32(1A) of the Claims and Payments Regulations 1987 (Vol.III). 7.90

Paragraphs (4) and (5)

See reg.32(1B) of the Claims and Payments Regulations 1987 (Vol.III). 7.91

Alternative means of notifying changes of circumstances

32.—(1) In such cases and subject to such conditions as the Secretary of State may specify, the duty in regulation 31(4) to notify a change of 7.92

circumstances may be discharged by notifying the Secretary of State as soon as reasonably practicable—

(a) where the change of circumstances is a birth or death, through a local authority, or a county council in England, by personal attendance at an office specified by that authority or county council, provided the Secretary of State has agreed with that authority or county council for it to facilitate such notification; or

(b) where the change of circumstances is a death, by telephone to a telephone number specified for that purpose by the Secretary of State.

(2) In this regulation "local authority" has the same meaning as in section 191 of the Administration Act.

DEFINITION

"the Administration Act"—see Jobseekers Act 1995 s.35(1).

GENERAL NOTE

7.93 See reg.32ZZA of the Claims and Payments Regulations 1987 (Vol.III). "Local authority" seems to be the same as a "relevant authority" there.

Information given electronically

7.94 **33.**—(1) A person may give any certificate, notice, information or evidence required to be given and in particular may give notice of a change of circumstances required to be notified under regulation 31 by means of an electronic communication, in accordance with the provisions set out in Schedule 2 to the Claims and Payments Regulations 2013.

(2) In this regulation, "electronic communication" has the meaning given in section 15(1) of the Electronic Communications Act 2000.

DEFINITION

"Claims and Payments Regulations 2013"—see reg.2(2).

GENERAL NOTE

7.95 See reg.32ZA of the Claims and Payments Regulations 1987 (Vol.III).

PART 5

CONDITIONS OF ENTITLEMENT

The conditions and relevant earnings

7.96 **34.**—(1) A claimant's relevant earnings for the purposes of section 2(2)(b) of the Act are the total amount of the claimant's earnings equal to the lower earnings limit for the base year.

(2) For the purposes of paragraph (1), earnings which exceed the lower earnings limit are to be disregarded.

GENERAL NOTE

7.97 See the notes to s.2(2) of the new style Jobseekers Act 1995 for the place of this provision in the contribution conditions for new style JSA. It has the practical effect that a claimant has to have actually paid Class 1 social security contributions for at least 26 weeks in one of the two last complete tax years ending before the beginning of the benefit year (January – January) containing the beginning of the jobseeking period (see regs 37–39) containing the week for which JSA is claimed. *NH v SSWP (JSA)* [2021] UKUT 227 (AAC), detailed in the notes to s.2 at 1.666, provides a helpful illustration of the effect of reg.34.

Relaxation of the first set of conditions

35.—(1) A claimant who satisfies the condition in paragraph (2) is to be taken to satisfy the first set of conditions if the claimant has— 7.98

(a) paid Class 1 contributions before the relevant benefit week in respect of any one tax year; and

(b) earnings equal to the lower earnings limit in that tax year on which primary Class 1 contributions have been paid or treated as paid which in total, and disregarding any earnings which exceed the lower earnings limit for that year, are not less than that limit multiplied by 26.

(2) The condition referred to in paragraph (1) is that the claimant, in respect of any week during the last complete tax year preceding the relevant benefit year, is entitled to be credited with earnings in accordance with regulation 9E of the Social Security (Credits) Regulations 1975 (credits for certain spouses and civil partners of members of Her Majesty's forces).

(3) In this regulation, "relevant benefit week" means the week in relation to which the question of entitlement to a jobseeker's allowance is being considered.

DEFINITIONS

"benefit week"—see reg.2(2).
"claimant"—see Jobseekers Act 1995 s.35(1).
"tax year"—*ibid.*
"the first set of conditions"—see Jobseekers Act 1995 s.2(3C).

GENERAL NOTE

"The first set of conditions" in para.(1) refers to the contribution conditions in s.2(1)(a) and (2) of the new style Jobseekers Act 1995. From January 1, 2012, some spouses and civil partners, accompanying a member of His Majesty's forces on a posting abroad after April 2010, have on return from that posting been able to benefit from the relaxation of the first contribution condition effected by this regulation when they make a claim for new style JSA where they would not have otherwise met that condition. The regulation covers such spouses and civil partners in respect of any week during the last complete tax year preceding the start of the benefit year in which the claim for benefit was made, provided they have been credited with earnings under reg.9E of the Social Security (Credits) Regulations 1975 in respect of at least one week during the last complete tax year prior to their claim. The relaxation allows them to be taken to have satisfied the first contribution condition when they had paid sufficient Class 1 contributions in any previous complete tax year before the beginning of the relevant benefit year, not one of last two such years. 7.99

Waiting Days

36.—(1) Paragraph 4 of Schedule 1 to the Act does not apply in a case where a person's entitlement to a jobseeker's allowance commences within 12 weeks of an entitlement of theirs to income support, incapacity benefit, employment and support allowance[[2], carer's allowance or carer support payment] coming to an end. 7.100

(2) In the case of a person to whom paragraph 4 of Schedule 1 to the Act applies, the number of days is [1 seven].

Amendments

1. Social Security (Jobseeker's Allowance and Employment and Support Allowance) (Waiting Days) Amendment Regulations 2014 (SI 2014/2309) reg.2(3) (October 27, 2014).

2. Carer's Assistance (Carer Support Payment) (Scotland) Regulations 2023 (Consequential Amendments) Order 2023 (SI 2023/1218) art.24(3) (November 19, 2023).

Definitions

"the Act"—see reg.2(2).
"carer support payment"—*ibid.*
"week"—*ibid.*

General Note

7.101 Unemployment benefit was a daily benefit payable in respect of a six-day week. JSA is a weekly benefit. Nonetheless, through para.4 of Sch.1 to the new style Jobseekers Act 1995, as amplified by this regulation, it deploys the traditional concept of "waiting days".

There is no entitlement to new style JSA for a number of days (now seven, but previously three (see para.(2)) but alterable by regulations) at the start of a jobseeking period. On "jobseeking period" and the effect of "linking", see the notes to regs 37 and 38 below. Note further that the "waiting days" rule does not apply where the claimant's entitlement to new style JSA begins within 12 weeks of the ending of entitlement to income support, incapacity benefit, employment and support allowance, carer's allowance or Scottish carer support payment.

The amendment to increase the number of waiting days to seven does not apply where the relevant jobseeking period began before October 27, 2014 (reg.4(1) of the amending regulations). Seven days' worth of benefit is a substantial amount, so that the provision in the Social Security (Payments on Account of Benefit) Regulations 2013 (Vol.III of this series) for the making of payments on account of benefit, in certain cases of financial need (restrictively defined), has become more important. However, the claimant has to repay the "advance" out of future payments of JSA. There are no waiting days in universal credit, but the first payment will not be made until after the end of the first monthly assessment period unless the claimant takes an advance of that benefit.

The transition from old style JSA

7.102 In para.(1) the reference to jobseeker's allowance is, where art.12(1)(b) of the Welfare Reform Act 2012 (Commencement No.9 and Transitional and Transitory Provisions and Commencement No.8 and Savings and Transitional Provisions (Amendment)) Order 2013 (as amended and set out in Vol.V of this series, 2021/22 edition as updated in Cumulative Supplements included in Vol.II of this series and in mid-year Supplements) applies and the claimant was entitled to old style JSA under reg.46(1)(a) of the JSA Regulations 1996 during what would otherwise have been waiting days when that award continued as an award of new style JSA, to be read as if it included a reference to the old style JSA award (art.12(3)(b) of that Order).

Jobseeking Period

7.103 **37.**—(1) For the purposes of the Act, but subject to paragraph (2), the "jobseeking period" means any period throughout which the claimant satisfies or is treated as satisfying the conditions specified in section 1(2)

(b) and (e) to (i) of the Act (conditions of entitlement to a jobseeker's allowance).

(2) The following periods are not to be, or to be part of, a jobseeking period—

(a) any period in respect of which no claim for a jobseeker's allowance has been made or treated as made;

(b) such period as falls before the day on which a claim for a jobseeker's allowance is made or treated as made;

(c) where a claim for a jobseeker's allowance has been made or treated as made but no entitlement to benefit arises in respect of a period before the date of claim by virtue of section 1(2) of the Administration Act (limits for backdating entitlement), that period;

(d) any week in which a claimant is not entitled to a jobseeker's allowance in accordance with section 14 of the Act (trade disputes); or

(e) any period in respect of which a claimant is not entitled to a jobseeker's allowance because section 1(1A) of the Administration Act (requirement to state national insurance number) applies.

(3) For the purposes of section 5 of the Act (duration of a jobseeker's allowance), a day must be treated as if it was a day in respect of which the claimant was entitled to a jobseeker's allowance where that day—

(a) falls within a jobseeking period; and

(b) is a day—

(i) on which the claimant satisfies the conditions specified in section 2 of the Act (the contribution-based conditions) other than the conditions specified in section 2(1)(c) and (d) of the Act; and

(ii) on which a jobseeker's allowance is not payable to the claimant by virtue of sections 6J or 6K of the Act or by virtue of a restriction imposed pursuant to section 6B, 7, 8 or 9 of the Social Security Fraud Act 2001 (loss of benefit provisions).

DEFINITIONS

"the Act"—see reg.2(2).

"the Administration Act"—see Jobseekers Act 1995 s.35(1).

"claimant"—*ibid.*

GENERAL NOTE

This regulation, read with regs 38 and 39 below and para.3 of Sch.1 to the new style Jobseekers Act 1995, provides some relief to those whose unemployment is intermittent, interspersed with, say, periods of employment, of incapacity for work, of training for work or periods when pregnant. It uses the concept of "linking" and "linked periods" where what would otherwise be separate jobseeking periods are fused into one and certain periods ("linked periods") do not "break" a jobseeking period, although they do not themselves form part of the jobseeking period. There are three particular purposes for which the concept of the jobseeking period is relevant: (a) in the identification of the tax years in which the two contribution conditions in s.2(1)(a) and (b) of the Act must be satisfied; (b) in the application of the waiting days rule in para.4 of Sch.1 to the Act only once in each jobseeking period; and (c) in the possibly redundant provisions in para.(3) about days which count towards the 182-day limit on a period of entitlement under s.5 of the Act. 7.104

Regulation 37 provides the general definition of "jobseeking period" and some important exceptions. Regulations 38 and 39 deal with linking.

A "jobseeking period" is under para.(1) any period throughout which the claimant satisfies (or is treated as satisfying) the conditions of entitlement to JSA set out in the new style Jobseekers Act 1995, s.1(2)(b) and (e)–(i): accepted a claimant commitment; not in remunerative work; does not have limited capability for work; not receiving relevant education; under pensionable age; and in Great Britain. Note that reg.39 below treats certain days as ones meeting those conditions in respect of persons approaching retirement.

None of the periods listed in para.(2) can constitute or form any part of, a jobseeking period. A period for which no claim for JSA has been made cannot count, although the conditions of entitlement mentioned in para.(1) were objectively satisfied in that period (sub-para.(a)). Nor can any period prior to the day on which the claim for JSA is made or treated as made (sub-para.(b)). See reg.29 of the Claims and Payments Regulations 2013 for the circumstances in which a claim can be "backdated" up to three months and treated as made on the first day of the period claimed for, within that three-month limit. If the rule in reg.29 were a great deal more generous, no period prior to the 12-month limit on entitlement before the date of claim (Social Security Administration Act 1992 s.1(2)) could form part of a jobseeking period (sub-para. (c)). Any week in which the claimant is not entitled to benefit under the trade dispute disqualification under s.14 of the new style Jobseekers Act 1995 does not count (sub-para.(d)). Nor does a day on which there is no entitlement by virtue of the provisions of s.1(1A) of the Administration Act connected with national insurance numbers.

Under para.(3), for the purpose only of the rules in s.5 of the Act limiting the duration of entitlement to 182 days, a day which would otherwise fall within a jobseeking period, but on which someone satisfying the two contribution conditions in s.2(2) is subject to a JSA sanction or a fraud sanction so that JSA is not payable, is nonetheless to be treated as a day of entitlement to new style JSA, so that it will count as one of the 182 days. This provision is arguably unnecessary because sanctions under s.6J and 6K of the Act and restrictions under the Social Security Fraud Act 2001 only affect the payability of benefit or the amount payable, not entitlement.

The transition from old style JSA

7.105 Regulation 37 as a whole is, where art.12(1) and (2) of the Welfare Reform Act 2012 (Commencement No.9 and Transitional and Transitory Provisions and Commencement No.8 and Savings and Transitional Provisions (Amendment)) Order 2013 (as amended and set out in Vol.V of this series, 2021/22 edition as updated in Cumulative Supplements included in Vol.II of this series and in mid-year Supplements) applies, to be read as if a jobseeking period includes any period that formed part of a jobseeking period under reg.47 of the JSA Regulations 1996 and in para.(3) as if the reference to a day treated as a day on which the claimant was entitled to new style JSA included a reference to a day treated under reg.47(4) of the JSA Regulations 1996 as a day of entitlement to old style JSA (art.12(3)(c) of that Order).

Jobseeking periods: periods of interruption of employment

7.106 **38.**—(1) For the purposes of section 2(4)(b)(i) of the Act and for determining any waiting days—

(a) where a linked period commenced before 7th October 1996, any days of unemployment which form part of a period of interruption of employment where the last day of unemployment in that period of interruption of employment was no more than eight weeks before the date upon which that linked period commenced;

(b) where a jobseeking period or a linked period commences on 7th October 1996, any period of interruption of employment ending within the eight weeks preceding that date; or

(c) where a jobseeking period or a linked period commences after 7th October 1996, any period of interruption of employment ending within the 12 weeks preceding the day the jobseeking period or linked period commenced, must be treated as a jobseeking period and, for the purposes of sub-paragraph (a), a day must be treated as being, or not being, a day of unemployment in accordance with section 25A of the Benefits Act (determination of days for which unemployment benefit is payable) and with any regulations made under that section, as in force on 6th October 1996.

(2) In this regulation—

"period of interruption of employment" in relation to a period prior to 7th October 1996 has the same meaning as it had in the Benefits Act by virtue of section 25A of that Act as in force on 6th October 1996;

"waiting day" means a day—

(a) at the beginning of a jobseeking period; and

(b) in respect of which a person is not entitled to a jobseeker's allowance.

DEFINITIONS

"the Act"—see reg.2(2).
"the Benefits Act"—see Jobseekers Act 1995 s.35(1).
"jobseeking period"—see reg.37(1).
"linked period"—see reg.39(2).

GENERAL NOTE

Some spells of unemployment are continuous, others intermittent. A jobseeking period can consist of a long chain of such spells, interspersed with spells of work or entitlement to certain other benefits. This regulation enables such a chain to go back to the unemployment benefit regime before October 7, 1996, when JSA was introduced, for the purposes of the contribution conditions and the waiting days rule. Then the relevant concept was a "period of interruption of employment" ("PIE") and the regime worked on an eight-week linking rule where two or more ostensibly separate PIEs were fused into a single one where they were not more than eight weeks apart. New style JSA works on a 12-week linking period (see reg.39(1) and (3)). 7.107

Linking Periods

39.—(1) For the purposes of the Act, two or more jobseeking periods must be treated as one jobseeking period where they are separated by a period comprising only— 7.108

(a) any period of not more than 12 weeks;

(b) a linked period;

(c) any period of not more than 12 weeks falling between—

(i) any two linked periods; or

(ii) a jobseeking period and a linked period; or

(d) a period in respect of which the claimant is summoned for jury service and is required to attend court.

(2) Linked periods for the purposes of the Act are any of the following periods—

(a) to the extent specified in paragraph (4), any period throughout which the claimant is entitled to a carer's allowance under section 70 of the Benefits Act [2 or carer support payment];

(b) any period throughout which the claimant is incapable of work, or is treated as incapable of work, in accordance with Part 12A of the Benefits Act;

(c) any period throughout which the claimant has, or is treated as having, limited capability for work for the purposes of Part 1 of the Welfare Reform Act 2007;

(d) any period throughout which the claimant was entitled to a maternity allowance under section 35 [[1]or 35B] of the Benefits Act;
(e) any period throughout which the claimant was engaged in training for which a training allowance is payable;
(f) a period which includes 6th October 1996 during which the claimant attends court in response to a summons for jury service and which was immediately preceded by a period of entitlement to unemployment benefit.

(3) A period is a linked period for the purposes of section 2(4)(b)(ii) of the Act only where it ends within 12 weeks or less of the commencement of a jobseeking period or of some other linked period.

(4) A period of entitlement to carer's allowance [[2]or carer support payment] is a linked period only where it enables the claimant to satisfy contribution conditions for entitlement to a jobseeker's allowance which the claimant would otherwise be unable to satisfy.

AMENDMENTS

1. Social Security (Maternity Allowance) (Miscellaneous Amendments) Regulations 2014 (SI 2914/884) reg.6(2) (May 18, 2014).

2. Carer's Assistance (Carer Support Payment) (Scotland) Regulations 2023 (Consequential Amendments) Order 2023 (SI 2023/1218) art.24(4) (November 19, 2023).

DEFINITIONS

"the Act"—see reg.2(2).
"the Benefits Act"—see Jobseekers Act 1995 s.35(1).
"carer support payment"—*ibid.*
"claimant"—*ibid.*
"jobseeking period"—see reg.37(1).
"training allowance"—see reg.2(2).
"week"—*ibid.*

GENERAL NOTE

7.109 Under para.(1), two or more jobseeking periods as defined in reg.37 must be fused into a single jobseeking period where separated by no more than 12 weeks, by a linked period (defined in para.(2)), by any period of not more than 12 weeks falling between any two linked periods or a jobseeking period and a linked period, or by a period in respect of which the claimant is summoned for jury service and is required to attend court. Thus, through the list of categories in para.(2) are the intermittently unemployed protected, while oscillating between unemployment and work or training, or unemployment and sickness/disability related inability to work, or unemployment and maternity or performing jury service, or caring, or any combination of these. Not all linked periods count as such for all purposes. Thus, a period of entitlement to a carer's allowance or Scottish carer support payment (para.(2)(a)) counts only to enable the JSA claimant to satisfy the new style JSA contribution conditions (new style Jobseekers Act 1995 s.2(2)(a) and (b)) that otherwise would not be satisfied (para.(4)). Similarly, to rank for the purposes of s.2(4)(b)(ii) (identifying the "relevant benefit year" for contributions conditions purposes as earlier than the start of the benefit year in which the JSA claim is made) a linked period counts only if it ended within 12 weeks of the start of a jobseeking period or another linked period (para.(3)). It is hard to see why this result is not already achieved by para.(1)(a) and (c).

Note that linked periods or intervening periods of 12 weeks or less cannot themselves form part of a jobseeking period.

Persons approaching retirement and the jobseeking period

40.—(1) The provisions of this regulation apply only to days— 7.110

(a) which fall after 6th October 1996 and within a tax year in which the claimant has attained the qualifying age for state pension credit (which is, in the case of a woman, pensionable age and in the case of a man, the age which is pensionable age in the case of a woman born on the same day as the man) but is under pensionable age; and

(b) in respect of which a jobseeker's allowance is not payable because the decision of the determining authority is that the claimant—
   (i) has exhausted their entitlement to a jobseeker's allowance;
   (ii) fails to satisfy one or both of the contribution conditions specified in section 2(1)(a) and (b) of the Act; or
   (iii) is entitled to a jobseeker's allowance but the amount payable is reduced to nil by virtue of deductions made in accordance with regulation 51 for pension payments.

(2) For the purposes of regulation 37(1) (jobseeking period) but subject to paragraphs (3), (4) and (5), any days to which paragraph (1) applies and in respect of which the person does not satisfy the condition specified in section 1(2)(b) of the Act (conditions of entitlement to a jobseeker's allowance), are to be days on which the person is treated as satisfying the condition in section 1(2)(b) and (e) to (i) of the Act.

(3) Where a person is employed as an employed earner or a self-employed earner for a period of more than 12 weeks, then no day which falls within or follows that period is to be a day on which the person is treated as satisfying those conditions, but this paragraph is not to prevent paragraph (2) from again applying to a person who makes a claim for a jobseeker's allowance after that period.

(4) Any day which is, for the purposes of section 30C of the Benefits Act, a day of incapacity for work falling within a period of incapacity for work is not to be a day on which the person is treated as satisfying the conditions referred to in paragraph (2).

(5) Any day which, for the purposes of Part 1 of the Welfare Reform Act 2007, is a day where the person has limited capability for work falling within a period of limited capability for work is not to be a day on which the person is treated as satisfying the conditions referred to in paragraph (2).

DEFINITIONS

"the Act"—see reg.2(2).
"the Benefits Act"—see Jobseekers Act 1995 s.35(1).
"claimant"—*ibid.*
"employed earner"—see reg.2(1).
"pensionable age"—*ibid.*
"self-employed earner"—see reg.2(2).
"tax year"—see Jobseekers Act 1995 s.35(1).
"week"—see reg.2(2).

GENERAL NOTE

This provision benefits persons (in practice only men: para.(1)(a)) for some days falling after October 6, 1996 during the tax year in which they reach the qualifying age for SPC. The days are ones in that tax year prior to actual attainment of pensionable age on which new style JSA is not payable because of exhaustion of entitlement, failure to satisfy one or both contribution conditions (new style Jobseekers Act 1995 7.111

s.2(1)(a) and (b)), or because the JSA amount has been reduced to nil under reg.51 because of pension payments. Any such days (other than those excluded by any of paras (3)–(5)) are to be days in a jobseeking period notwithstanding that no claimant commitment has been accepted.

Days which were ones of incapacity for work within a period of incapacity for work cannot form part of a jobseeking period in this way (para.(4)). Nor can days of limited capability for work forming part of a period of limited capability for work (para.(5)). But both such situations rank as linked periods under reg.39(2)(b). Further, where someone works in employment or self-employment for more than 12 weeks, no day within or after that period can be treated as part of a jobseeking period in this way, but the protection afforded by paras (1) and (2) of the regulation can apply again after such a period when the person makes a claim for JSA (para.(3)).

Persons temporarily absent from Great Britain

7.112 **41.**—(1) For the purposes of the Act, a claimant must be treated as being in Great Britain during any period of temporary absence from Great Britain—

(a) not exceeding four weeks in the circumstances specified in paragraph (2);

(b) not exceeding eight weeks in the circumstances specified in paragraph (3).

(2) The circumstances specified in this paragraph are that—

(a) the claimant is in Northern Ireland and satisfies the conditions of entitlement to a jobseeker's allowance;

(b) immediately preceding the period of absence from Great Britain, the claimant was entitled to a jobseeker's allowance; and

(c) the period of absence is unlikely to exceed 52 weeks.

(3) The circumstances specified in this paragraph are that—

(a) immediately preceding the period of absence from Great Britain, the claimant was entitled to a jobseeker's allowance;

(b) the period of absence is unlikely to exceed 52 weeks;

(c) the claimant continues to satisfy or be treated as satisfying the other conditions of entitlement to a jobseeker's allowance;

(d) the claimant is, or the claimant and any other member of their family are, accompanying a member of the claimant's family who is a child or young person solely in connection with arrangements made for the treatment of that child or young person for a disease or bodily or mental disablement; and

(e) those arrangements relate to treatment—

(i) outside Great Britain;

(ii) during the period whilst the claimant is, or the claimant and any member of their family are, temporarily absent from Great Britain; and

(iii) by, or under the supervision of, a person appropriately qualified to carry out that treatment.

(4) A person must also be treated, for the purposes of the Act, as being in Great Britain during any period of temporary absence from Great Britain where—

(a) the absence is for the purpose of attending an interview for employment;

(b) the absence is for seven consecutive days or less;

(c) notice of the proposed absence is given to the Secretary of State before departure, and is given in writing if so required by the Secretary of State; and

(d) on their return to Great Britain the person satisfies the Secretary of State that they attended for the interview in accordance with their notice.

(5) For the purposes of the Act a claimant must be treated as being in Great Britain during any period of temporary absence from Great Britain if—

(a) the claimant was entitled to a jobseeker's allowance immediately before the beginning of that period of temporary absence; and

(b) that period of temporary absence is for the purpose of the claimant receiving treatment at a hospital or other institution outside Great Britain where the treatment is being provided—

(i) under section 6(2) of the Health Service Act (performance of functions outside England) or section 6(2) of the Health Service (Wales) Act (performance of functions outside Wales);

(ii) pursuant to arrangements made under section 12(1) of the Health Service Act (Secretary of State's arrangements with other bodies), section 10(1) of the Health Service (Wales) Act (Welsh Minister's arrangements with other bodies), paragraph 18 of Schedule 4 to the Health Service Act (joint exercise of functions) or paragraph 18 of Schedule 3 to the Health Service (Wales) Act (joint exercise of functions); or

(iii) under any equivalent provision in Scotland or pursuant to arrangements made under such provision.

(6) For the purposes of the Act, a person must be treated as being in Great Britain during any period of temporary absence from Great Britain not exceeding 15 days where—

(a) the absence is for the purpose of taking part in annual continuous training as a member of any [1 . . .] reserve force prescribed in Part 1 of Schedule 6 to the Social Security (Contributions) Regulations 2001; and

(b) the person was entitled to a jobseeker's allowance immediately before the period of absence.

(7) In this regulation, "appropriately qualified" means qualified to provide medical treatment, physiotherapy or a form of treatment which is similar to, or related to, either of those forms of treatment.

AMENDMENT

1. Social Security (Members of the Reserve Forces) (Amendment) Regulations 2015 (SI 2015/389) reg.5(5) (April 6, 2015).

DEFINITIONS

"the Act"—see reg.2(2).
"child"—see Jobseekers Act 1995 s.35(1).
"claimant"—*ibid.*
"employment"—see reg.2(1).
"family"—see Jobseekers Act 1995 s.35(1).
"Health Service Act" —see reg.2(2)
"week"—*ibid.*
"young person"—*ibid.*

GENERAL NOTE

This provision is made under para.11 of Sch.1 to the new style Jobseekers Act 1995 for the purposes of the condition of entitlement in s.1(2)(i) ("is in Great **7.113**

Britain"). It treats claimants as being in Great Britain during a range of periods of temporary absence. Regulation 47 below deals with the effect of absence in relation to the condition of entitlement in s.1(2)(f) ("does not have limited capability for work"). There is authority on the meaning of temporary absence (see the notes to reg.2 of the Persons Abroad Regulations in Pt III of this volume), but often the specific time-limits in reg.41 will avoid the need to make difficult judgments. Absences clearly intended from the outset to be permanent will not come within reg.41 even if the period of absence has not yet exceeded the relevant time-limit.

Paragraph (1)

Paragraph (1) establishes the deeming of presence in Great Britain rule for circumstances falling within paras (2) and (3), for periods not exceeding four weeks (para.(2)) or eight weeks (para.(3)).

7.114 *Paragraph (2) read with para.(1)(a)*

A claimant entitled to new style JSA immediately prior to the absence is to be treated as being in Great Britain for up to four weeks of temporary absence from Great Britain where the claimant is in Northern Ireland and satisfies the conditions of entitlement to new style JSA (by necessary implication excluding that in s.1(2)(i) despite the absence of the word "other") and the period of absence is unlikely to exceed 52 weeks. It may be that the claimant would be able to satisfy any applicable work-related requirements from Northern Ireland and thus not be exposed to the threat of a sanction for non-compliance.

7.115 *Paragraph (3) read with para.(1)(a)*

A claimant entitled to new style JSA immediately prior to the absence is to be treated as being in Great Britain for up to eight weeks of temporary absence from Great Britain to accompany a child or young person who is a member of the family solely in connection with arrangements for their treatment for a disease or bodily or mental disablement, where the period of absence is unlikely to exceed 52 weeks and during the absence the claimant continues to satisfy or be treated as satisfying the other conditions of entitlement to new style JSA. The treatment must be outside Great Britain, during the period of temporary absence and by or under the supervision of someone appropriately qualified to carry out that treatment. "Appropriately qualified" means qualified to provide medical treatment, physiotherapy or a similar or related form of treatment (para.(7)).

Regulation 16(3)(b)(i), read with paras (1) and (2), provides that a claimant temporarily absent from Great Britain because of taking their child (i.e. under 16) outside Great Britain for medical treatment (not further defined) cannot be subject to a work search requirement or be required to be able and willing to take up work until their return.

See para.(5) for absence for the claimant to be treated.

7.116 *Paragraph (4)*

A person must also be treated as being in Great Britain during any period of temporary absence of up to seven days where the absence is for the purpose of attending an interview for employment, notice (in writing if required) of the absence was given to the Secretary of State before departure, and on return they satisfy the Secretary of State that they attended for the interview in accordance with the notice. "Employment" is defined to include self-employment and it does not appear to matter whether the employment is in Great Britain or not.

Regulation 16(3)(b)(ii), read with paras (1) and (2), provides that a claimant temporarily absent from Great Britain because of attending a job interview outside Great Britain cannot be subject to a work search requirement or be required to be able and willing to take up work until their return.

Paragraph (5) 7.117

A claimant entitled to new style JSA immediately prior to the absence is to be treated as being in Great Britain as long as the absence remains temporary when the absence is to receive treatment at a hospital or other institution provided under specified legislation allowing the NHS to provide services abroad.

Regulation 16(3)(b)(iii), read with paras (1) and (2), provides that a claimant temporarily absent from Great Britain because of receiving medical treatment (not further defined) outside Great Britain cannot be subject to a work search requirement or be required to be able and willing to take up work until their return. Regulations 16(5) (periods of sickness) and 16A (extended periods of sickness) might also be relevant.

Claimants falling within para.(5) cannot claim the benefit of reg.46(1) to be treated as not having limited capability for work for the purposes of s.1(2)(f) (reg.46(5)), but reg.47 applies to so treat them for the period of absence, without any fixed time-limit, provided that they have proved that they are unable to work on account of some specific disease or disablement and, but for that, would satisfy the conditions of entitlement in s.1(2) apart from para.(f).

Paragraph (6) 7.118

This establishes a special rule for members of the reserve forces temporarily absent from Great Britain for no more than 15 days for training of the specified kind who were entitled to new style JSA immediately before the absence.

If the training is properly to be regarded as a "public duty" making it unreasonable to comply with a work search requirement, reg.16(4)(c) could apply so that the claimant could not be subject to a work search requirement or be required to be able and willing to take up work until their return. The claimant will be treated as not engaged in remunerative work for the period (reg.44(1)(c)(v)).

The transition from old style JSA

In paras (2)(b), (3)(a) and (c), (5)(a) and (6)(b) the references to entitlement to jobseeker's allowance are, where art.12(1)(b) of the Welfare Reform Act 2012 (Commencement No.9 and Transitional and Transitory Provisions and Commencement No.8 and Savings and Transitional Provisions (Amendment)) Order 2013 (as amended and set out in Vol.V of this series, 2021/22 edition as updated in Cumulative Supplements included in Vol.II of this series and in mid-year Supplements) applies, to be read as if they included a reference to entitlement under an old style JSA award (art.12(3)(d) of that Order). 7.119

Remunerative work

42.—(1) For the purposes of the Act, "remunerative work" means work— 7.120

(a) for which payment is made or which is done in expectation of payment; and

(b) in which a claimant is—

  (i) engaged for 16 or more hours per week; or

  (ii) where their hours of work fluctuate, engaged on average for 16 or more hours per week.

(2) For the purposes of paragraph (1), the number of hours in which a claimant is engaged in work is to be determined—

(a) where no recognisable cycle has been established in respect of a person's work, by reference to the number of hours or, where those hours are likely to fluctuate, the average of the hours, which they are expected to work in a week;

(b) where the number of hours for which they are engaged fluctuate, by reference to the average of hours worked over—

(i) if there is a recognisable cycle of work, the period of one complete cycle (including, where the cycle involves periods in which the person does not work, those periods but disregarding any other absences);

(ii) in any other case, the period of five weeks immediately before the date of claim or the date of supersession, or such other length of time as may, in the particular case, enable the person's average hours of work to be determined more accurately.

(3) In determining in accordance with this regulation the number of hours for which a person is engaged in remunerative work—

(a) that number must include any time allowed to that person by their employer for a meal or for refreshments, but only where the person is, or expects to be, paid earnings in respect of that time;

(b) no account must be taken of any hours in which the person is engaged in an employment or scheme to which any one of sub-paragraphs (a) to (e) of regulation 44(1) (person treated as not engaged in remunerative work) applies;

(c) no account must be taken of any hours in which the person is engaged otherwise than in an employment as an earner in caring for—

(i) a person who is in receipt of attendance allowance, the care component [1 . . .] the daily living component [1 or armed forces independence payment];

(ii) a person who has claimed an attendance allowance, [1armed forces independence payment,] a disability living allowance [2, child disability payment[4,]] personal independence payment [4or adult disability payment], but only for the period beginning with the date of claim and ending on the date on which the claim is determined or, if earlier, on the expiration of the period of 26 weeks from the date of claim;

(iii) another person and is in receipt of a carer's allowance under section 70 of the Benefits Act [5 or carer support payment]; or

(iv) a person who has claimed either an attendance allowance, [1armed forces independence payment,] a disability living allowance[2, child disability payment[4,]] personal independence payment [4or adult disability payment] and has an award of attendance allowance, [1armed forces independence payment,] the care component or the daily living component for a period commencing after the date on which that claim was made;

(4) In this regulation—

[4"adult disability payment" has the meaning given in regulation 2 of the Disability Assistance for Working Age People (Scotland) Regulations 2022;]

[1"armed forces independence payment" means armed forces independence payment under the Armed Forces and Reserve Forces (Compensation Scheme) Order 2013;]

[3"child disability payment" has the meaning given in regulation 2 of the Disability Assistance for Children and Young People (Scotland) Regulations 2021;]

"disability living allowance" means a disability living allowance under section 71 of the Benefits Act;

[3"care component" means—

(a) the care component of disability living allowance at the highest or middle rate prescribed under section 72(3) of the Benefits Act; or
(b) the care component of child disability payment at the highest or middle rate provided for in regulation 11(5) of the Disability Assistance for Children and Young People (Scotland) Regulations 2021;]

[[4]"daily living component" means —
(a) in respect of personal independence payment, the daily living component of that payment at the standard or enhanced rate referred to in section 78 of the Welfare Reform Act 2012;
(b) in respect of adult disability payment, the daily living component of that payment at the standard or enhanced rate referred to in regulation 5 of the Disability Assistance for Working Age People (Scotland) Regulations 2022;]

"personal independence payment" means an allowance under Part 4 of the Welfare Reform Act 2012.

AMENDMENTS

1. Armed Forces and Reserve Forces Compensation Scheme (Consequential Provisions: Subordinate Legislation) Order 2013 (SI 2013/591) art.7 and Sch. para.52 (April 8, 2013).
2. Social Security (Scotland) Act 2018 (Disability Assistance for Children and Young People) (Consequential Modifications) Order 2021 (SI 2021/786) art.22(2) (July 26, 2021).
3. Social Security (Scotland) Act 2018 (Disability Assistance for Children and Young People) (Consequential Modifications) Order 2021 (SI 2021/786) art.22(3) (July 26, 2021).
4. Social Security (Disability Assistance for Working Age People) (Consequential Amendments) Order 2022 (SI 2022/177 art.15(2)(a) (March 21, 2022).
5. Carer's Assistance (Carer Support Payment) (Scotland) Regulations 2023 (Consequential Amendments) Order 2023 (SI 2023/1218) art.24(5) (November 19, 2023).

DEFINITIONS

"the Act"—see reg.2(2).
"the Benefits Act"—see Jobseekers Act 1995 s.35(1).
"carer support payment"—see reg.2(2).
"claimant"—*ibid.*
"employment"—see reg.2(1).

GENERAL NOTE

A person who is engaged in remunerative work is not entitled to new style JSA (s.1(2)(e) of the new style Jobseekers Act). It does not matter whether the claimant's partner or any other member of the family is or is not in remunerative work or how much they earn. Regulation 42 defines what is remunerative work. Regulation 43 deals with deeming of engagement during some periods of absence or when in receipt of holiday pay. Regulation 44 deems those carrying out certain forms of activity not to be engaged in remunerative work. 7.121

Paragraph (1) 7.122

Paragraph (1) contains the basic rule. Remunerative work is work for which payment is made or which is done in the expectation of payment (sub-para.(a)) in which the claimant is engaged for 16 hours or more on average a week (sub-para.(b)). Paragraph (2) deals with averaging and para.(3) specifies some hours that either do or do not count towards the 16.

Work can thus encompass both employment (which would include office-holders, such as company directors or Church of England clergy) and self-employment or any further form of work that cannot be so classified. That is illustrated in two family credit decisions (where remunerative work was a qualification). In *CFC/7/1989* the claimant's husband was working in connection with Moral Re-Armament, a Christian charity, for about 38 hours a week. He received payment by persuading individuals to covenant income to him. He was not employed by Moral Re-Armament or the covenantors, nor did he contract with them on a self-employed basis. But this did not matter, because what he did was undoubtedly work and he was paid for it. In *R(FC) 2/90* both the claimant and her husband were officers of the Salvation Army. It was accepted, following the decision of the Court of Appeal in *Rogers v Booth* [1937] 2 All E.R. 751, that the relationship of officers to the Salvation Army is spiritual, not contractual. Nevertheless, the onerous duties of officers were "work."

On the other hand, there will be a question whether some activities, such as caring for a relative or neighbour or indeed anyone, constitutes "work", even if some money changes hands. Not all such situations will fall within the deeming not to be engaged in remunerative work in reg.44(1)(a).

7.123 *Remunerative*

Work is remunerative if payment is made for it, or it is done in the expectation of payment. There is a significant difference from the common law test (on which see *R(FIS) 1/83)*, because the mere hope of or desire for payment is not the same as expectation (although note that in *R(IS) 13/99* the Commissioner comments that he did not see any fundamental distinction between "hope of" and "expectation of" payment). In *R(IS) 1/93* the Commissioner holds that the guiding principle on when there is an expectation of payment should be common sense and an appreciation of the realities of the situation. The claimant, a writer, had sent several works to publishers, but had had negligible success in selling anything. She was working "on spec", with only the hope of payment, not an expectation. In *Smith v Chief Adjudication Officer (R(IS) 21/95)* the claimant's partner, who was in receipt of an enterprise allowance, wished to establish herself as an agent for pop groups and spent a lot of time building up contacts in the pop music world. The Court of Appeal, having said that the question was really one of fact, distinguished between work done to set up a business, which is not done in expectation of payment, and work carried out once the business is established, which it would be reasonable to infer was done in expectation of payment. On the facts of that case the claimant's partner was not engaged in remunerative work. On the other side of the line, see *CIS/434/1994* in which a person who had started an estate agent's business and was working without pay until the business became profitable was held to be in remunerative work.

In *R(IS) 22/95* the claimant's wife worked in a general shop owned by the two of them. For several months she had worked without pay and had no expectation of receiving any in the future because the business was making a loss. The Commissioner held that the SSAT had been correct in concluding that on the facts she was not in remunerative work. This decision was upheld by the Court of Appeal in *Chief Adjudication Officer v Ellis* (reported as part of *R(IS) 22/95*). The Court gave some general guidance on the questions to be considered when deciding whether a person is in remunerative work. In particular, it drew a distinction between a person providing a service (such as the claimant carrying on a translation agency in *Perrot v Supplementary Benefits Commission* [1980] 1 W.L.R. 1153 where the unprofitability of her business was irrelevant) and the position of a retail shop. The Court pointed out that the price paid for goods sold in a shop is not payment for the work of the salesman, but the price of the goods sold. Thus simply carrying on a retail business did not necessarily mean that a person was in remunerative work (so *CSIS/39/1994* should not be followed on this point). But if the person was not expecting to make any money the question had to be asked why the shop was being kept open. In this case the answer was clear. The claimant's wife was carrying on the business in the hope of disposing of the goodwill. She was not in remunerative work.

In *R(IS) 5/95* the claimant, who was both a director and an employee of a small limited company, had also worked for some months without pay, due to financial difficulties. The Commissioner states that it was necessary to consider in relation to each week whether he was working in his capacity as an employee or a director (although the functions of a director of a small private company were quite slight (*R(U) 1/93*, para.5)). If this work had been done as an employee it was only remunerative if any payment expected was in that capacity. Moreover expectation of payment meant payment for current work. It may be that that is not the case for the self-employed, although the Court of Appeal in *Ellis* stated that the question of whether work is done in expectation of payment is to be decided at the time the work is done, not at the end of the year or other accounting period.

If a claimant deliberately arranges to work for no remuneration (and therefore has no expectation of payment) then, unsurprisingly, that work does not qualify as remunerative work. In *CTC/626/2001* a husband went into partnership with his wife. He worked 30 hours a week in the partnership business and she worked six. However, in order to save income tax the partners agreed that 100 per cent of the profits was allocated to the wife leaving the husband with no income from the business. The Commissioner upheld the decision of the tribunal that there was no entitlement to WFTC: the wife was in remunerative work but for less than 16 hours a week and the husband, though he worked far more than 16 hours a week, was not in remunerative work at all. As *CTC/626/2001* related to a tax credit, the conclusion that the husband was not in remunerative work was to his disadvantage. However, one logical consequence of the decision is the possibility that a similar partnership arrangement could be used by a self-employed claimant who was in fact working for more than 16 hours a week to retain entitlement to new style JSA. It is suggested that such an arrangement might not in fact be effective because, following the remarks of Millet LJ in *Ellis* that it would often in the case of small husband and wife businesses be appropriate in such circumstances "to treat the partnership as a single economic unit just as if it were carried on by a sole trader". But that approach may not be able to stand in the face of an express partnership agreement on the share of profits. If it did, it would suggest that *CTC/626/2001* was wrongly decided.

In means-tested benefits one would in many cases of non-payment have to consider the possibility of notional income being attributed, but there in no such rule for new style JSA. What matters is the actuality at the relevant time.

If the claimant receives payment, that is the end of the matter without having to consider expectations (*Ellis*), but the payment must be in return for the work (*R(FIS) 1/86*). It need not, though, derive from an employer. Thus the payments by the covenantors in *CFC/7/1989* (see above) counted. So too did the payments from the Salvation Army in *R(FC) 2/90*, although they were not paid under contract and were aimed at providing for the officers' actual needs. There was a distinction from the maintenance grant paid to a student. Provision for actual needs went beyond mere maintenance. A grant is not in return for work (*R(FIS) 1/86*), so that students and trainees (*R(FIS) 1/83*) will still not be said to be in remunerative work. The argument that enterprise allowance was paid in return for work was rejected by the Court of Appeal in *Smith v Chief Adjudication Officer* (above). The Court held that it is a payment to enable people to establish themselves in business, not for work. Presumably the same would apply to the current New Enterprise Allowance.

A payment in kind will count in the same way as a payment in cash. In *CFC/33/1993* the provision of rent-free accommodation and the payment of gas and electricity bills meant that the claimant's work was done for payment.

Engaged in work 7.124

It is hours during which the person is engaged in work and is paid (or at least expects payment) which are crucial. The calculation is usually relatively easy for employees. Thus in *CIS/3/1989* the claimant's paid one-hour lunch break did not count towards the limit. He was not "engaged in" work for that hour. The precise result is reversed from April 1990, by para.(3)(a), but the principle might apply in other situations. *R(FC) 1/92* suggests that where the nature of the job requires a person to work beyond the contractually specified hours, the longer hours count. However, it is not clear just how this translates from the old family credit provisions to new style JSA. For the self-employed the test is not of hours costed and charged to a client, but of hours of activities which are essential to the undertaking *(R(FIS) 6/85)*. Thus time spent in preparation, research, doing estimates and accounts, travel for the purposes of the undertaking, keeping a shop open, etc. may all count. But activities carried on merely in the hope, rather than expectation, of payment are not remunerative. The actual hours of work must be considered. In *R(IS) 22/95*, although the shop in which the claimant's wife worked was open from 08:30–18:30 Monday to Friday, she only spent three hours a day in it. The rest of the time she was in her home (which was in the same premises), ready to go into the shop if the shop bell rang. The Commissioner expressed the view (without finally deciding the point) that on the particular facts of that case (a small shop with little stock and fewer customers) the hours "on call" may not be hours of work. The decision in *R(IS) 22/95* was upheld by the Court of Appeal in *Chief Adjudication Officer v Ellis* (see above), but the Court did not deal with this particular point. But in *R(IS) 13/99* the same Commissioner decided that the time spent by a self-employed minicab driver waiting at the cab office for potential customers (which he was not obliged to do) was work done in expectation of payment. That seems somewhat dubious, in that it was not essential to his work for him to spend that time there. However, the decision was upheld by the Court of Appeal (*Kazantzis v Chief Adjudication Officer*, reported as part of *R(IS) 13/99*). In *R(IS) 12/95* all the hours that a share fisherman was at sea (including those that he was not on watch or was sleeping) counted. The Commissioner referred to *Suffolk CC v Secretary of State for the Environment* [1984] I.C.R. 882 in which the House of Lords had distinguished between a regular fireman required to remain in the station while on duty and a retained fireman free to do as he pleased until called upon. The claimant could not do as he pleased during his rest period. He had to stay on the trawler and could be summoned to assist if, for example, there was a storm. In the *Suffolk* case the House of Lords held that a retained fireman's waiting time could not be taken into account in calculating his contractual hours of employment. The Commissioner in *R(IS) 13/99* found the circumstances not to be analogous. The issue there was not whether the claimant was employed during his waiting time but whether he was "at work" during that time.

CIS/514/1990 held that although recipients of enterprise allowance had to undertake to work for at least 36 hours a week in their business, that did not mean that they had automatically to be treated as doing so for benefit purposes (see *Smith v Chief Adjudication Officer (R(IS) 21/95)* above on whether enterprise allowance was paid in return for work).

7.125 *Paragraph (2)*

Where a person works a fixed number of hours, week in, week out, there is no difficulty in applying the weekly limits in para.(1). But what if a person does not work the same hours each week? What, indeed, if there are some weeks in which they do no work at all? Those are the problems addressed by para.(2) and reg.43(1), problems that have been very troublesome in the context of income support and old style JSA.

Consideration must now begin with the decision of the Tribunal of Commissioners in *R(JSA) 5/03*, dealing with the equivalent old style JSA provisions in the JSA Regulations 1996. The appeals before the Tribunal concerned people who were employees and the principles laid down in its decision must be seen in that context. Other considerations may be relevant in cases where the claimant is self-employed (see below).

The Tribunal's starting point was that:

"11. Defining 'remunerative work' as being work in which someone is engaged for not less than 16 hours a week (24 hours in the case of a claimant's partner) is simple enough. But how do you arrive at the appropriate number of hours when the working hours fluctuate? And how do you deal with those periods during most people's working year, when for some reason or other they are absent from work (and, therefore, not engaged in work at all)?

12. The first step in any analysis is to recognise that periods when a person does no work fall into various categories. Consideration of regulations 51(2) and 52(1) [the equivalent of regs 42(2) and 43(1)] suggests that the relevant categories are:

(a) periods during which someone is without work because he or she is between jobs,
(b) periods of no work (other than holidays) during which someone is without work because work is not provided by his or her employer,
(c) periods during which someone can properly be regarded as being on holiday,
(d) periods of absence due to sickness and maternity leave.
(e) periods of unauthorised absence 'without good cause'.

In these appeals, we are not concerned with periods of absence due to sickness or maternity leave, but it is apparent from the terms of regulation 52(1) that a person who is otherwise in remunerative work ceases temporarily to be so engaged during such absences. We are also not concerned with periods of absence without good cause, but it is equally apparent that such absences are to be treated in the same way as holidays."

The Tribunal's approach to those issues was to look first at whether the person's employment had ended. In doing so, "regard should be had to reality" (at para.25) and not just to the formal legal position:

"22. In our view, the approach taken by decision-makers should be as follows. Where a contract of employment comes to an end at the beginning of what would be a period of absence from work even if the contract continued, the person should be taken still to be in employment if is expected that he or she will resume employment after that period, either because there is some express arrangement, though not necessarily an enforceable contract, or because it is reasonable to assume that a long standing practice of re-employment will continue."

If it is determined that the person is no longer in employment then no question of remunerative work arises. If, on the other hand, the employment relationship is—as a matter of reality—still subsisting, it becomes necessary to decide whether the person is absent from work due to a holiday or for some other reason. This issue is to be decided on the basis that a person is on holiday during those periods of absence for which they are entitled to be paid—either by contract or, from October 1, 1998, under the Working Time Regulations 1998.

The Tribunal continued:

"28. Applying regulation 51(2) is relatively straightforward once it has been established that a person is still engaged in employment and his or her entitlement to holidays has been ascertained. If he works the same number of hours each week when not on holiday, that is the number of hours to be taken into account for the purpose of regulation 51(1). If the number of hours fluctuates, an average is taken. How the average is calculated when there is no cycle of work is determined under regulation 51(2)(b)(ii) which allows some discretion as to the period over which the average is to be calculated. Regulation 51(2)(b)(i) makes more specific provision in a case where there is a recognisable cycle of work."

Specifically, when there was a recognisable cycle of work of one year, the requirement in reg.51(2)(b)(i) [reg.42(2)(b)(i)] to calculate the average taking into account "periods in which the person does no work . . . but disregarding other absences" meant (para.29):

> "dividing the total number of hours worked . . . by 52 less the number of weeks of holiday to which the particular claimant is entitled. The result determines whether the person concerned is in remunerative work or not for the whole period of the cycle (*R(IS) 8/95*) so that it is not necessary where there is a cycle to attribute the holiday entitlement to any particular weeks."

The same approach should presumably be adopted to established cycles of work of less than 52 weeks but which include periods in which the person does no work. On that basis, unpaid "holidays" are "periods in which the person does no work" for the purposes of reg.42(2)(b)(i) and paid holidays and periods of absence through sickness, etc. are "other absences". In cases which pre-date the Working Time Regulations 1998—or to which those Regulations do not apply, see for example *CJSA/4764/2002*—in which the employee has no holiday entitlement, neither the fact that payment of their salary may be spread over the year in equal monthly instalments nor the fact that the rate at which they are paid has been enhanced to reflect the absence of any formal holiday entitlement alters the position that there is no holiday entitlement (although the latter circumstance is relevant to the issue of the claimant's earnings (see para.42)).

In consequence, the Tribunal of Commissioners held that the reasoning in (though not the result of) *R(IS) 15/94* was incorrect and that *R(IS) 7/96*, which had followed that reasoning, was wrongly decided and should no longer be followed.

There is further guidance on when a recognisable cycle has been established in para.4 of *R(JSA) 5/02*, another term-time employee case, referred to in *R(JSA) 5/03*:

> "4. However, the Secretary of State submits that regulation 51(2)(c)[reg.42(2)(b)(i)] does not apply until a claimant has been employed for at least a year, which was not the case when this claimant made her claim during the 1997 summer vacation. I do not accept that submission. It must be established that there is a cycle of work but it seems to me that, if there is a permanent contract—or more accurately, an indefinite contract—which expressly provides for a cycle, the cycle is established from the commencement of the contract. It may be different where there is a fixed-term contract or where a person is employed on a casual or relief basis. In the case of a fixed term contract for a period of less than the length of two cycles, there may not be the degree of recurrence necessarily implied by the concept of a cycle (see *CIS/493/1993* and *CIS/11228/1995*). In the case of a casual or relief arrangement, it may be clear that a person will not work during holidays or vacations but it may not be clear that he or she will work during the whole of the terms and for that reason a cycle may not be established. However, where there has been a series of fixed-term contracts or where the person has in fact been regularly employed albeit on what is formally a casual basis, there may come a time when a cycle is established in practice, although that is likely to require the completion of two cycles. In *R(IS) 8/95* a two-week cycle became established after four weeks. In *R(IS) 15/94*, a yearly cycle was found to be established in the case of a school receptionist after 18 months but, as was pointed out in *CIS/11228/1995*, the receptionist had by then received a written contract specifying the periods of work and no-work, which, I would add, appears to have been of indefinite duration. In *CIS/11228/1995* itself, no cycle had been established in the case of a school bus driver who had worked 20 hours a week during term times for 15 months."

Where no recognisable cycle has been established and hours fluctuate, an average must be taken under para.(2)(b)(ii), with the default period for averaging being the five weeks immediately before the date of claim or the date of supersession (or, to make sense, a potential supersession). There is a broad discretion to adopt another period, e.g. where there has been some significant change of circumstances. In the case of a continuing award, there can be a rolling five-week calculation as evidence of hours worked comes in (see *MS v SSWP (IS)* [2015] UKUT 423 (AAC), followed in *LB v SSWP (ESA)* [2019] UKUT 153). *MS* is an instructive example of the workings of a complex remunerative work calculation.

For an example of the application of the principles in *R(JSA) 5/03* (and, in particular, the treatment of paid public or extra-statutory holidays falling outside term-time) see *R(JSA) 3/04*.

In *KN v DfC (JSA)* [2022] NICom 21, a claim was made after the claimant lost his full-time work but continued to work for the employer on a casual basis, the weekly hours apparently being completely ad hoc. He was paid fortnightly. Since the claimant had said on his claim form that he had been sacked, the effect of that work on entitlement was not examined until some months had passed. The DfC initially considered that the pattern of fortnightly payment meant that there was a recognisable cycle of work under the equivalent of reg.42(2)(b)(i), so that the claimant was not entitled to JSA for fortnights in which the hours worked averaged at least 16 per week and was not excluded by the remunerative work rule for fortnights in which the average fell below that level. An appeal tribunal endorsed that approach. On further appeal, Northern Ireland Commissioner Stockman accepted the DfC's submission that the conflation of the issue of a recognisable cycle of *work* with the period of payment of remuneration was an error of law and that the equivalent of reg.42(2)(b)(ii) should have been applied. The case was remitted to a new tribunal for reconsideration after the DfC had made a fresh submission on the application of that provision to the evidence. The Commissioner expressed no opinion on the claimant's contention that the hours worked should be averaged over the whole period concerned (20 weeks). Thus, the question of whether that approach or a rolling five-week average should be adopted was left open.

Seasonal workers **7.126**

The position of seasonal workers (including term-time only workers) was considered by the Commissioner in *R(JSA) 1/07* and in *CJSA/3832/2006*.

In the former case, the claimants had, for several years, been able to obtain casual work during the summer season in holiday resorts on the Lincolnshire coast but had been unable to find work during the winter months. Their claims for old style JSA were refused on the basis that they had to be treated as having a cycle of work extending over the whole calendar year. The tribunal rejected that argument and found that they were not in a cycle of work at all during periods when they were not in employment. Confirming that decision, the Commissioner held that whether there was an "expectation" that the claimant would resume their employment under the test in para.22 of *R(JSA) 5/03* was a matter of fact for the tribunal and that "there would need to be some element of mutuality in the arrangement or understanding between employer and employee" before such an "expectation" could be found to exist. The Secretary of State's construction was

> "an attempt to start with the calculation provisions by assuming that the whole year is to be included, and then work backwards to distort the meaning of regulation 51(1) [reg.42(1)] as if it contained a deeming provision making people count as in work when in fact they are not".

The recurrence of an inability to get work at all during the winter months did not turn the whole calendar year into one continuous period of the claimant being "engaged in work" for the purposes of reg.51 so as to be able to call the whole year a recognisable cycle of work. Regulation 51(2) was concerned with the calculation of a numerical average of hours at work over a period while a person continues to be in work.

In *CJSA/3832/2006*, the claimant worked as a cleaner during university terms only. At the end of each term his contract of employment was terminated and he and his colleagues were told that if they were interested in re-employment from the beginning of the following term they should contact the facilities manager during the preceding week. The Commissioner stated:

"As was recently stressed in *CJSA/1390/2006* [now *R(JSA) 1/07*], the real question is whether the person claiming benefit can properly be regarded as being 'in' work at the material time. There must be some sort of continuing relationship between the employer and employee, even if it is not technically a subsisting employment relationship. Unless the circumstances show some commitment to a resumption of the employment relationship by a former worker upon which an employer might reasonably place some reliance, it is difficult to see how a person can be regarded as being in employment between periods of work when his contract of employment has expressly been terminated. It seems to me that there needs to be a 'tacit understanding' or a mutual expectation such as was found in *R(U) 1/66* and *R(U) 8/68*, discussed in *R(JSA) 5/03*. In my judgment, the tribunal erred in apparently not distinguishing between a cycle involving periods of employment and periods of unemployment and a cycle of employment involving periods of work and periods of no work."

As there was no evidence of any expectation by the employer that the claimant would resume employment, and as it would not be difficult to find other cleaners if he did not apply in the week before the next term, the claimant was not in remunerative work during the vacation.

In the light of the requirement in *R(JSA) 1/07* for the "expectation" to be mutual to both employer and employee, it is suggested that the result should have been the same if the evidence had shown that the claimant did not have an expectation of being re-employed if he were to apply.

7.127 *Self-employment*

In the case of a self-employed worker who has periods of work interspersed with periods of no work the position is less clear. Paragraph (1) does not state what is the appropriate period to look at when determining whether a person is engaged in remunerative work. Each case will therefore depend to some extent on its own facts. If, for example, a person carries on a business for six months of the year and does no work in connection with that business for the rest of the year, it must be arguable that the period to be looked at is the six months when their business is dormant and that during that time they are not engaged in work. That was the approach originally taken in the Decision Makers Guide (but now see para.20340). However, that was not the conclusion reached by the Commissioner in *CIS 493/1993*.

The claimant ran a guest house with a six-month season and did a minimal amount of work during the closed season. He had argued that there were two cycles, or periods, one in which he worked more than 16 hours every week and the second during which he was not engaged in work at all. The Commissioner stated that the first question was whether there was a recognisable cycle, and the second was whether the claimant's hours fluctuated within that cycle. The basis of this approach seems to have been that para.(2) is to be used to determine the number of hours for which a person is engaged in work. But para.(2) does not provide a rule for deciding the number of hours worked per week in all cases. It applies in the circumstances described in the opening words of sub-paras (a) and (b) *(R(IS) 8/95)*. It is suggested that the first question is what is the appropriate period for deciding whether a claimant is engaged in remunerative work, which will depend on the facts of each case, before going on to consider whether the particular circumstances referred to in para.(2) apply.

That approach was confirmed in *Saunderson v Secretary of State for Work and Pensions* [2012] CSIH 102; [2013] AACR 16, which concerned reg.51 of the JSA Regulations 1996. The claimant had worked as a self-employed golf caddie in St Andrews in the spring and summer months for a number of years. His authorisation to work as a caddie was withdrawn in October 2007 because the demand for caddies reduced in the winter. There was no commitment that he would be able to work as a caddie in St Andrews the following or any future year. The Inner House of the Court of Session stated that the notion that a seasonal worker was, by dint of being a seasonal worker, engaged in an annual cycle of work, with the consequence that his hours or earnings fell to be averaged over 12 months, had its origin in the obiter observations in *R(JSA) 1/03* (see para.12). However, the concept of a "recognisable cycle of work" in reg.51(2) only came into play for the purpose of averaging the weekly hours of work after the primary question under reg.51(1) as to whether the claimant was "in work" at the time of his claim for JSA had been answered. That primary question was not determined by whether there was a recognisable cycle of work but was a matter of fact, giving "in work" its ordinary meaning. The Secretary of State had accepted that in relation to those who were employees in seasonal work (as held in *R(JSA) 1/07*) but contended that seasonal self-employment was an annual activity. The Court of Session, however, rejected this sharp distinction. While there may be many self-employed trading or professional activities in which the activity continues during an idle period, there are also many seasonally pursued activities, which, while treated as self-employment, are in substance little different from employment. What needed to be considered was the primary question of whether the person was "in work" when his seasonal activity came to an end.

See also *TC v DSD (JSA)* [2013] NI Com 65 (a decision of a Northern Ireland Commissioner). The claimant was a self-employed eel fisherman on Lough Neagh who claimed JSA following the breakdown of his boat towards the end of the eel fishing season. The Commissioner followed *Saunderson*. He considered that in the past the Great Britain Commissioners (as they then were) had taken different approaches to the question of seasonal employment and seasonally-based self-employment but, as stated by the Court of Session (see para.20), there was no textual warrant in the legislative definition of remunerative work for any distinction to be drawn between previously employed or self-employed claimants. For the months when fishing was either prohibited or not economically worthwhile, the claimant had ceased self-employment, although he hoped to resume (if he could get his boat repaired, for the next season. The test did not require a permanent cessation of employment.

Paragraph (3)

Note these categories of hours that do not count under para.(2), in particular hours in which a person is engaged in caring for a person who has been awarded one of the main disability benefits, excluding those related to mobility needs (or has a claim not yet determined). The new Scottish child disability payment and adult disability payment, as well as carer support payment, are now covered on the same basis as GB-wide benefits.

Persons treated as engaged in remunerative work

43.—(1) Except in the case of a person on maternity leave, paternity leave, [1 shared parental leave,] [2parental bereavement or adoption leave,] leave or absent from work through illness, a person is to be treated as engaged in remunerative work during any period for which they are absent from work referred to in regulation 42(1) (remunerative work) where the absence is either without good cause or by reason of a recognised, customary or other holiday. 7.128

(2) Subject to paragraph (3), a person who was, or was treated as being, engaged in remunerative work and in respect of that work earnings to which regulation 58(1)(c) (earnings of employed earners) applies are paid, is to be treated as engaged in remunerative work for the period for which those earnings are taken into account in accordance with Part 7.

(3) Paragraph (2) does not apply to earnings disregarded under paragraph 1 of the Schedule to these Regulations.

AMENDMENTS

1. Shared Parental Leave and Statutory Shared Parental Pay (Consequential Amendments and Subordinate Legislation) Order 2014 (SI 2014/3255) art.29(3) (December 23, 2014).

2. Parental Bereavement Leave and Pay (Consequential Amendments to Subordinate Legislation) Regulations 2020 (SI 2020/354) reg.29(3) (April 6, 2020).

DEFINITIONS

"adoption leave"—see reg.2(2).
"maternity leave"—*ibid.*
"parental bereavement leave"—*ibid.*
"paternity leave"—*ibid.*
"remunerative work"—see reg.42(1).
"shared parental leave"—see reg.2(2).

GENERAL NOTE

7.129 *Paragraph (1)*

See the notes to reg.42, and in particular the passages cited from *R(JSA) 5/03*, for the interaction of this provision deeming claimants to be engaged in remunerative work during absence from work without good cause or by reason of a recognised, customary or other holiday. Those passages need to be updated to include the additional kinds of statutory leave that do not attract the deeming, along with absence through illness (not further defined).

There should not usually be difficulty in determining whether a claimant is absent from work due to a holiday. But sometimes there will be problems in drawing the line between such absence and periods when there is no work for the claimant. To activate the deeming a period of no work must be a holiday for the claimant, not just for the employer. The problems have in the past been most apparent in cases of employment in some educational institution.

The Tribunal of Commissioners said this in para.27 of *R(JSA) 5/03*, where the claimants were employed in teaching posts with fluctuating hours during term-time and no work during school holidays or college vacations:

> "27. We consider that the extent to which a person is regarded as being on holiday should, as the claimants in these cases have argued, be determined by reference to their contractual entitlement to holiday and that in the context of an income-related benefit, it makes perfect sense to have regard only to those weeks of holiday for which a person is actually paid. From 1 October 1998, when the Working Time Regulations came into force, it may generally be assumed that a worker is entitled to four weeks' annual leave in the absence of any evidence of greater entitlement."

There seems no reason why that approach should not also be taken in the non-income-related benefit of new style JSA, with no distinction so far as educational institutions are concerned between teaching staff and others.

Absence from work without good cause may obviously cover a wide range of circumstances. Presumably the merits or otherwise of the cause must be assessed in the context of the employment relationship.

7.130 *Paragraphs (2) and (3)*

Where (within four weeks of the termination or interruption of employment) holiday pay (the category covered by reg.58(1)(c)) is paid, the person is treated as in remunerative work for the period covered (on which see regs 54 and 56). The effect of the exclusion in para.(3) of earnings disregarded under para.1 of the Schedule is that this provision will only apply where a person's employment has been suspended.

Persons treated as not engaged in remunerative work

44.—(1) A person is to be treated as not engaged in remunerative work in so far as they are— 7.131

(a) engaged by a charity or a voluntary organisation or are a volunteer where the only payment received by them or due to be paid to them is a payment in respect of any expenses incurred, or to be incurred, if they otherwise derive no remuneration or profit from the employment;

(b) engaged on a scheme for which a training allowance is being paid;

(c) engaged in employment as—

[[1](i) a part-time fire-fighter employed by a fire and rescue authority under the Fire and Rescue Services Act 2004 or by the Scottish Fire and Rescue Service established under section 1A of the Fire (Scotland) Act 2005];

(ii) [[1]. . .];

(iii) an auxiliary coastguard in respect of coastal rescue activities;

(iv) a person engaged part-time in the manning or launching of a lifeboat;

(v) a member of any [[2] . . .] reserve force prescribed in Part 1 of Schedule 6 to the Social Security (Contributions) Regulations 2001;

(d) performing their duties as a councillor, and for this purpose "councillor" has the same meaning as in section 171F(2) of the Benefits Act;

(e) engaged in caring for a person who is accommodated with them by virtue of arrangements made under any of the provisions referred to in regulation 60(2)(b) or (c), and are in receipt of any payment specified in regulation 60(2)(b) or (c);

(f) engaged in an activity in respect of which—

(i) a sports award had been made, or is to be made, to them; and

(ii) no other payment is made or is expected to be made to them;

(g) engaged in the programme known as Work Experience.

(2) In this regulation, "volunteer" means a person who is engaged in voluntary work, otherwise than for a close relative, grand-parent, grand-child, uncle, aunt, nephew or niece, where the only payment received, or due to be paid to the person by virtue of being so engaged, is in respect of any expenses reasonably incurred by the person in connection with that work.

AMENDMENTS

1. Social Security (Miscellaneous Amendments) (No.2) Regulations 2013 (SI 2013/1508) reg.4(1) and (3) (July 29, 2013).

2. Social Security (Members of the Reserve Forces) (Amendment) Regulations 2015 (SI 2015/389) reg.5(5) (April 6, 2015).

DEFINITIONS

"the Benefits Act"—see Jobseekers Act 1995 s.35(1).
"close relative"—see reg.2(2).
"remunerative work"—see reg.42(1).
"sports award"—see reg.2(2).
"training allowance"—*ibid.*
"voluntary organisation"—*ibid.*

"voluntary work"—*ibid.*
"Work Experience"—*ibid.*

GENERAL NOTE

7.132 Claimants must be deemed not to be engaged in remunerative work for the time engaged in these activities. The effect, if excluding the hours involved leaves no more than 16 hours that do count, is that there is no automatic exclusion from entitlement under s.1(2)(e) of the new style Jobseekers Act 1995. Any earnings from employment must still be taken into account under ss.2(1)(c) and 4(1)(b). Most of the categories are self-explanatory, at least once the necessary definitions have been pursued.

Under para.(1)(a), "volunteer" is defined in para.(2), which in turn refers to the definition of "voluntary work" in reg.2(2), which is in almost the same terms. Note that assistance to the relatives specified in para.(2) is excluded, but there is of course a question whether unpaid assistance to relatives constitutes work in the first place.

Under para.(1)(b), ADM R2008 gives examples of schemes that pay training allowances as Training for Work in Scotland, Work Based Learning–Skills Based in Wales and Employment Rehabilitation. The definition in reg.2(2) excludes allowances paid by any Government department for a person following a course of full-time education (apart from courses arranged under prescribed legislation or for a person training to be a teacher).

Under para.(1)(d), the definition of "councillor" in s.171F(2) of the SSCBA 1992 (now repealed) was—

"(a) in relation to England and Wales, a member of a London borough council, a county or county borough council, a district council, a parish or community council, the Common Council of the City of London or the Council of the Isles of Scilly; and
(b) in relation to Scotland, a member of a regional, islands or district council."

Under para.(1)(e) foster parents who receive statutory payments for fostering, or people receiving payments for providing temporary care in their home, are deemed not to be in remunerative work by reason of those payments. Such payments are excluded from the meaning of earnings from self-employment (reg.60(2)).

Under para.(1)(f) a person will be deemed not to be in remunerative work while engaged in activity for which the only payment received, or to be received, is a "sports award" (defined in reg.2(2)). Such an award is not treated as self-employed earnings (reg.60(2)(d)).

Relevant education

7.133 **45.**—(1) For the purposes of the Act—

(a) a person is to be treated as receiving relevant education if they are a qualifying young person[[1], unless the person is participating in a traineeship]; and
(b) [[1]except in circumstances where sub-paragraph (a) applies,] the following are to be treated as relevant education—
  (i) undertaking a full-time course of advanced education; and
  (ii) undertaking any other full-time course of study or training at an educational establishment for which a student loan, grant or bursary is provided for the person's maintenance or would be available if the person applied for it.

[[1](1A) In paragraph (1) "traineeship" means a course which—

(a) is funded (in whole or in part) by, or under arrangements made by, the—
  (i) Secretary of State under section 14 of the Education Act 2002, or
  (ii) Chief Executive of [[2]Education and Skills Funding];

(b) lasts no more than 6 months;
(c) includes training to help prepare the participant for work and a work experience placement; and
(d) is open to persons who on the first day of the course have reached the age of 16 but not 25.]

(2) In paragraph (1)(b)(i), "course of advanced education" means—
(a) a course of study leading to—
  (i) a postgraduate degree or comparable qualification;
  (ii) a first degree or comparable qualification;
  (iii) a diploma of higher education;
  (iv) a higher national diploma; or
(b) any other course of study which is of a standard above advanced GNVQ or equivalent, including a course which is of a standard above a general certificate of education (advanced level), or above a Scottish national qualification (higher or advanced higher).

(3) A claimant who is not a qualifying young person and is not undertaking a course described in paragraph (1)(b) is nevertheless to be treated as receiving relevant education if the claimant is undertaking a course of study or training that is not compatible with any work-related requirement imposed on the claimant by the Secretary of State.

(4) For the purposes of paragraph (1)(b), a person is to be regarded as undertaking a course—
(a) throughout the period beginning on the date on which the person starts undertaking the course and ending on the last day of the course or on such earlier date (if any) as the person finally abandons it or is dismissed from it; or
(b) where a person is undertaking a part of a modular course, for the period beginning on the day on which that part of the course starts and ending—
  (i) on the last day on which the person is registered with the provider of the course, or part of the course, as undertaking that part; or
  (ii) on such earlier date (if any) as the person finally abandons the course or is dismissed from it.

(5) The period referred to in paragraph (4)(b) includes—
(a) where a person has failed examinations or has failed to complete successfully a module relating to a period when the person was undertaking a part of the course, any period in respect of which the person undertakes the course for the purpose of retaking those examinations or that module; and
(b) any period of vacation within the period specified in paragraph (4)(b) or immediately following that period except where the person has registered with the provider of the course, or part of the course, to attend or undertake the final module in the course and the vacation immediately follows the last day on which the person is to attend or undertake the course.

(6) A person is not to be regarded as undertaking a course by virtue of this regulation for any part of the period mentioned in paragraph (4) during which the following conditions are met—
(a) the person has, with the consent of the relevant educational establishment, ceased to attend or undertake the course because they are ill or caring for another person;

(b) the person has recovered from that illness or ceased caring for that person within the past year, but not yet resumed the course; and
(c) the person is not eligible for a grant or student loan.

(7) In this regulation, except where paragraph (8) applies, "qualifying young person" means a person who has reached the age of 16 but not the age of 20—

(a) up to, but not including, the 1st September following their 16th birthday; and
(b) up to, but not including, the 1st September following their 19th birthday, if they are enrolled in, or accepted for, approved training or a course of education—
  (i) which is not a course of advanced education;
  (ii) which is provided at a school or college or provided elsewhere but approved by the Secretary of State; and
  (iii) where the average time spent during term time (excluding meal breaks) in receiving tuition, engaging in practical work, or supervised study, or taking examinations exceeds 12 hours per week.

(8) A person is not a "qualifying young person" within the meaning in paragraph (7) where they—

(a) are aged 19 and have not started the education or training or been enrolled or accepted for it before reaching the age of 19;
(b) fall within paragraph (7)(b) and their education or training is provided by means of a contract of employment; or
(c) are receiving universal credit, an employment or support allowance or a jobseeker's allowance.

(9) In this regulation—

"approved training" means training in pursuance of arrangements made under section 2(1) of the Employment and Training Act 1973 or section 2(3) of the Enterprise and New Towns (Scotland) Act 1990 which is approved by the Secretary of State for the purposes of this regulation;

"modular course" means a course which consists of two or more modules, the successful completion of a specified number of which is required before a person is considered by the educational establishment to have completed the course;

"student loan" means a loan towards a student's maintenance pursuant to any regulations made under section 22 of the Teaching and Higher Education Act 1998, section 73 of the Education (Scotland) Act 1980 or Article 3 of the Education (Student Support) (Northern Ireland) Order 1998, including in Scotland a young student's bursary paid under regulation 4(1)(c) of the Student's Allowances (Scotland) Regulations 2007.

AMENDMENTS

1. Social Security (Traineeships and Qualifying Young Persons) Amendment Regulations 2015 (SI 2015/336) reg.5 (March 27, 2015).

2. Social Security (Qualifying Young Persons Participating in Relevant Training Schemes) (Amendment) Regulations (SI 2017/987) reg.5 (November 6, 2017).

DEFINITIONS

"the Act"—see reg.2(2).

"claimant"—see Jobseekers Act 1995 s.35(1).

General Note

It is a condition of entitlement to new style JSA that a person is not receiving relevant education (new style Jobseekers Act 1995 s.1(1)(g)). This regulation stipulates who is to be treated as receiving it. Note that reg.45 applies only to young persons (i.e. those aged from 16–19) and older students and not to children (i.e. those under 16). That is presumably because it is impossible for a child to have satisfied the contribution conditions for new style JSA in s.2(1)(a) and (b). **7.134**

Under para.(1)(a) a qualifying young person (QYP) is generally to be treated as receiving relevant education, and thus excluded from new style JSA unless participating in a traineeship (defined in para.(1A)). A QYP is someone aged 16–19 meeting all of the criteria set out in para.(7), mainly to do with participation in a course of non-advanced education, but excluding those within one of the exempt heads in para.(8). Traineeships as defined and described in the new para.(1A) are short courses aimed at addressing the skills gaps that employers consider prevalent among young people, combining English and maths tuition when needed with work preparation training and a work experience placement. Such a course would be regarded as not one of advanced education so that a participant would fall within the meaning of QYP and be excluded from entitlement to new style JSA were it not for the new exception to sub-para.(a). The exception is to encourage voluntary take-up of the courses.

In addition, under para.(1)(b)(i) anyone not covered by sub-para.(a) undertaking a full-time course of "advanced education" (as fairly comprehensively defined in para.(2) to cover courses over secondary level) is receiving relevant education and excluded from new style JSA. When a person is regarded as undertaking a course varies according to whether it is modular or not. For a non-modular course, a person is regarded as undertaking a course from when the person starts undertaking the course until the last day of the course, or where the person has been dismissed from it or finally abandoned it, from the date of dismissal or abandonment (para.(4)(a)). For a modular course, a person is regarded as undertaking part of a modular course from when that part of the course starts until the last date on which they are registered with the course provider or the provider of that part for that part of the modular course, or where the person has been dismissed from it or finally abandoned it, from the date of dismissal or abandonment. With modular courses, the person is regarded as undertaking it during vacations other than the vacation following completion of the final module and also when undertaking the course for purposes of retaking failed examinations (paras (4)(b) and (5)). See *RVS v SSWP (ESA)* [2019] UKUT 102 (AAC) holding that a student on a modular course intermitting for a year was not undertaking a part of the course.

There is a discussion of some of the older authority on when a course is full-time in the notes to reg.61 of the Income Support (General) Regulations 1987 in the 2021/22 edition of Vol.V of this series. The principles derived from the case law, which would be equally applicable to new style JSA, have recently been summarised by Judge Rowley in para.19 of *BK v SSWP (UC)* [2022] UKUT 73 (AAC) (some references added by annotator):

"a. Whether or not a person is undertaking a full-time course is a question of fact for the tribunal having regard to the circumstances in each particular case ((*R/SB 40/83* at [13]; *R(SB) 41/83* at [12]). Parameters have been set, as appear below:

b. The words "full-time" relate to the course and not to the student. Specifically, they do not permit the matter to be determined by reference to the amount of time which the student happens to dedicate to their studies (*R/SB 40/83* at [14, 15]; *R(SB) 2/91* at [7]; *R(SB) 41/83* at [11]).

c. Evidence from the educational establishment as to whether or not the course is full-time is not necessarily conclusive, but it ought to be accepted as such unless it is inconclusive on its face, or is challenged by relevant evidence which at least raises the possibility that it ought to be rejected (*R/SB 40/83* at [18]), and any evidence adduced in rebuttal should be weighty in content

(*R/SB 41/83* at [12]). See also *Flemming v Secretary of State for Work and Pensions* [2002] EWCA Civ 641, [2002] 1 W.L.R. 2322 [also reported as *R(G) 2/02*] at [21]-[22] and [38]; and *Deane v Secretary of State for Work and Pensions* [2010] EWCA Civ 699, [2011] 1 W.L.R. 743 [also reported at [2010] AACR 42] where the Court of Appeal repeated an earlier statement in *Flemming* that:

> '38 ... A tribunal of fact should, I think be very slow to accept that a person expects or intends to devote – or does, in fact, devote – significantly less time to the course than those who have conduct of the course expect of him, and very slow to hold that a person who is attending a course considered by the educational establishment to be a part-time course is to be treated as receiving full-time education because he devotes significantly more time than that which is expected of him..."

d. If the course is offered as a full-time course, the presumption is that the recipient is in full-time education. There may be exceptions to the rule, such where a student is granted exemptions from part of the course: *Deane* [51]."

In *BK* itself the claimant was on a one-year MA course at Goldsmiths, University of London, described by that institution as full-time and involving more than 24 hours of study per week. Letters from the Department concerned confirmed six contact hours of teaching in two terms, with an expectation of at least six hours per week in independent study. A dissertation was to be written in the third term. The First-tier Tribunal rejected the claimant's argument that those letters, and the fact that he could arrange his time to be available for work, showed that the course was not full-time. Judge Rowley held that it did not err in law in doing so and that in saying that Goldsmiths' description was "determinative" of the nature of the course it had not strayed into regarding it as conclusive, but had applied the test in para.19(c) above.

Whether the course of advanced education is modular or non-modular, someone who has taken time out of the course with the consent of the educational establishment concerned because of illness or caring responsibilities (not defined), and who has now recovered or whose caring responsibilities have ended, can claim new style JSA until the day before the person resumes the course (subject to a maximum of one year). This does not apply if the person is eligible for a grant or student loan during this period (para.(6)).

Finally anyone aged 20 or over (or possibly 16–19 and not meeting the definition of QYP in para.(7)) undertaking a course of study or training which is not one of full-time advanced education must be treated as receiving relevant education if undertaking it is not compatible with the work-related requirements imposed on them by the Secretary of State (para.(3)).

Short periods of sickness

7.135 **46.**—(1) Subject to the following provisions of this regulation, a person who—

(a) [1 . . .] has been awarded a jobseeker's allowance, or is a person to whom any of the circumstances mentioned in section 6J(2) or (3) or 6K(2) of the Act apply;

(b) proves to the satisfaction of the Secretary of State that they are unable to work on account of some specific disease or disablement; and

(c) [1 during the period of their disease or disablement, satisfies] the requirements for entitlement to a jobseeker's allowance other than those specified in section 1(2)(f) of the Act (capable of work or not having limited capability for work),

is to be treated for a period of not more than two weeks, beginning on the day on which sub-paragraphs (a) to (c) are met, as capable of work or as not having limited capability for work, except where the claimant states in writing that for the period of their disease or disablement they propose to claim or have claimed employment and support allowance [1 or universal credit].

(2) The evidence which is required for the purposes of paragraph (1)(b) is a declaration made by the claimant in writing, in a form approved for the purposes by the Secretary of State, that they have been unfit for work from a date or for a period specified in the declaration.

(3) [1 Paragraph (1) does not apply to a claimant on more than two occasions in any one jobseeking period or, where a jobseeking period exceeds 12 months, in each successive 12 months within that period; and for the purposes of calculating any period of 12 months, the first 12 months in the jobseeking period commences on the first day of the jobseeking period.

(4) [1 Paragraph (1) does not apply to any person where the first day in respect of which they are unable to work falls within eight weeks after the day the person ceased to be entitled to statutory sick pay.

(5) [1 Paragraph (1) does not apply to a claimant who is temporarily absent from Great Britain in the circumstances prescribed by regulation 41(5).

[1(6) Paragraph (1) does not apply to any person—

(a) during any period where the person is treated as capable of work or as not having limited capability for work under regulation 46A (extended period of sickness); or

(b) where the first day in respect of which that person would, apart from this sub-paragraph, have been treated as capable of work or as not having limited capability for work under this regulation falls immediately after the last day on which the person is so treated under regulation 46A.]

[2(7) For the purposes of calculating the number of occasions under paragraph (3), any occasion to which regulation 46A applies to the claimant is to be disregarded.]

AMENDMENTS

1. Jobseeker's Allowance (Extended Period of Sickness) Amendment Regulations 2015 (SI 2015/339) reg.3(3) (March 30, 2015).

2. Jobseeker's Allowance (Extended Period of Sickness) Amendment Regulations 2016 (SI 2016/502) reg.3(2) (May 23, 2016).

DEFINITIONS

"the Act"—see reg.2(2).
"claimant"—see Jobseekers Act 1995 s.35(1).
"Great Britain"—*ibid.*
"jobseeking period"—see reg.37(1).
"writing"—see Interpretation Act 1978 Sch.1.

GENERAL NOTE

Temporary Coronavirus Provisions

The effect of the temporary coronavirus provisions relevant to reg.46 expired at the end of August 31, 2021. See previous editions of this volume for the details. **7.136**

It is a condition of entitlement to new style JSA that the claimant does not have limited capability for work (new style Jobseekers Act 1995 s.1(2)(f)). This regulation permits persons unable to work on account of some specific disease or disablement to be entitled to JSA for up to two weeks on two occasions in any 12-month period by treating them as capable of work or not having limited capability for work, unless they inform the Secretary of State in writing that they have claimed or propose to claim ESA or universal credit. Under para.(5) a person who is treated as being in Great Britain by virtue of reg.41(5) cannot use this provision, but can benefit from reg.47 below. The other conditions of entitlement under s.1(2) of course have to be satisfied, in particular that of having accepted the most up-to-date version of the claimant commitment. The operation of the work-related requirements is heavily modified under reg.16 (see below).

Note that to take advantage of this provision, claimants need only to show that they are unable to work on account of some specific disease or disablement, which test is not further defined. Thus the convolutions of the ESA test for having limited capability for work are not incorporated. The ordinary everyday meaning of the words must be applied. Also, the claimant need not produce any evidence beyond a written declaration on the approved form of unfitness for work (para.(2) but see the conditions in reg.16(5)(b) discussed below), although it may be that in particular cases something more would be needed to satisfy the Secretary of State under para.(1)(b). The operation of reg.46 is voluntary in the sense that if a claimant declares in writing that they intend to or have claimed ESA or universal credit, it does not apply (end of para.(1)).

Under reg.16(5), while a claimant is unfit for work (for up to 14 days no more than twice within 12 months) and provides a signed declaration for the first seven days and a doctor's statement for any subsequent days, no work search requirement can be imposed and the requirement to be able and willing immediately to take up work is lifted for the duration of the operation of reg.16(5). With effect from April 2018, a restriction on the operation of reg.16(5) has been imposed where a claimant has previously been determined not to have limited capability for work for the purposes of new style ESA or universal credit (reg.16(5A) and (5B): see the notes to reg.16 for the details). Regulation 16 does not affect the application of the work-focused interview requirement and the work preparation requirement, but under s.6F(2) of the new style Jobseekers Act 1995 there is a discretion whether to impose those requirement, under which all relevant circumstances (including a claimant's state of health) would have to be considered).

7.137 There has been some discussion of whether reg.46 can apply immediately at the beginning of the period covered by a claim for new style JSA, e.g. where a claimant previously entitled to old style or new style ESA has lost entitlement on being found not to have limited capability for work and is challenging that decision. Can such a claimant (in circumstances where universal credit has already come into operation for them or will do so, with new style JSA, if there is an attempt to claim old style JSA), who claims new style JSA, take advantage of regs 46 and 46A immediately, so as to be able to maintain the contention of incapacity for work while claiming JSA and to maintain a continuity of benefit entitlement without falling between the two stools of ESA and JSA? In some circumstances a claimant who appeals against the decision terminating ESA entitlement can, without making a further claim, be awarded old style or new style ESA pending the determination of the appeal (see reg.147A of the ESA Regulations 2008 in Vol.V of this series and reg.87 of the ESA Regulations 2013 in Pt VIII of this volume). However, even where that is so, there may well be some delay while the mandatory reconsideration process is completed, so that potential entitlement to new style JSA is of practical importance. The difficulty lies mainly in the terms of regs 46(1)(a) and 46A(1)(a). The reference to an award in the past tense (in contrast to the normal use of the present tense in legislation) appears to require that there has already been a decision that the claimant is entitled to new style JSA (even if no benefit is payable, e.g. because of a sanction) under the normal conditions of entitlement (without modification under reg.46 or 46A) before those provisions can operate. The terms of regs 46(1)(c) and 46A(1)(d) are perhaps neutral.

It might be thought that, even if that is correct, a claimant disputing an ESA decision can avoid more than a short-term disadvantage by claiming and being awarded new style JSA on the ordinary conditions and then immediately applying for a supersession in reliance on the rules in reg.46 or 46A as appropriate. The immediate difficulty, though, is that claimants then have to satisfy the condition of entitlement of not having limited capability for work (new style Jobseekers Act 1995 s.1(2)(f)) when they are maintaining that they *do* have limited capability for work.

If it is an old style ESA decision under challenge, the claimant may first have a difficult choice. By definition, we are considering circumstances in which a claim for any form of "legacy benefit" triggers the introduction of universal credit and new style JSA. Since old style ESA may be awarded while an appeal is pending without the need for a claim, claimants who can take advantage of such an award may prefer not to claim JSA. If a claim for new style JSA is made, it is arguable that reg.10 of the Decisions and Appeals Regulations (Vol.III of this series) applies to make the old style ESA determination that the claimant does not have limited capability for work conclusive for the purposes of a subsequent new style JSA decision. Thus the claimant, being forced at that point to accept that conclusive effect may legitimately claim to satisfy all the ordinary conditions of entitlement, if the conditions other than s.1(2)(f) are met. Then there would be no inconsistency in substance in the claimant's immediately maintaining an application for supersession on the basis of a relevant change of circumstances (having been awarded JSA) and in fact being unable to work on account of some specific disease or disablement (in any event a different test from that for limited capability for work in ESA), relying on the terms of reg.46 or 46A (and regs 16(1), (2) and (5), where the test is in terms of unfitness for work, or 16A, which refers directly to reg.46A). If reg.16 or 16A applies, the claimant would be free of the work search and availability requirements while the unfitness lasted, subject to the limits as to time. The claimant would still have to have accepted a claimant commitment under s.1(2)(b). There is no provision under new style JSA, in contrast to old style JSA, for deeming a claimant commitment to have been accepted, although a claimant can be exempted from the condition under reg.8. However, the terms of any claimant commitment would have to reflect the effects of reg.16(5) or 16A and take into account the claimant's state of health in the contents of any work-focused interview or work preparation requirement.

If it is a new style ESA decision under challenge, reg.40 of the Universal Credit etc. (Decisions and Appeals) Regulations 2013 (Vol.III of this series) specifically restricts the conclusive effect of such determinations as to limited capability for work to further ESA decisions. However, the Secretary of State could perfectly properly adopt the same view in determining that the claimant did satisfy the condition of entitlement in s.1(2)(f) even though the claimant did not accept that view. The claimant could not then be regarded as maintaining inconsistent positions in claiming new style JSA while challenging the ESA decision and could pursue an application for supersession on the same basis as suggested in the previous paragraph

It must be stressed that the above arguments do not reflect any accepted Departmental views and have not been tested before the Upper Tribunal. However, elementary considerations of fairness require that some way must be found of preventing claimants being denied entitlement to ESA on the basis that they do not have limited capability for work and also being denied entitlement to JSA on the basis that they maintain that they do have limited capability for work. It may therefore be necessary to consider a more direct route beyond the 13 weeks allowed by reg.46A and perhaps as an alternative to the above argument. This would involve first submitting that the claimant satisfies s.1(2)(b) by virtue of the conclusive effect of the old style ESA determination or the rational effect of the new style ESA determination, regardless of what he says himself about his capability for work. Then the claimant would have to assert that under regs 9(2)(c) and 14(5) his availability could be restricted to nil or something minimal in the light of his actual physical and mental condition and that it was not reasonable to expect him to take more than one or a few simple steps each week under the work search requirement, plus persuade the Secretary of State that those restrictions, and minimal or nil work-focused interview or work preparation requirement, should be incorporated into his claimant commitment.

The new para.(7) confirms that, in identifying under para.(3) the two occasions during any 12 months on which the benefit of reg.46 can be taken, occasions on which the benefit of reg.46A was taken do not count.

Now see reg.46A, allowing the same effect as under reg.46 to operate for a more extended period. Under reg.46(6), the present provision cannot be used while reg.46A applies. Nor can a reg.46 period of deeming follow on immediately from a reg.46A period. However, the converse does not apply. An extended period of sickness under reg.46A may follow on from a reg.46 period, as seems sensible when prediction of the duration of unfitness to work may be very uncertain. It appears, though, from the definition of "the first day" in reg.46A(4), that any days covered by reg.46 will count against the 13-week limit under reg.46A.

The transition from old style JSA

7.138 Where art.13(1) and (2) of the Welfare Reform Act 2012 (Commencement No.9 and Transitional and Transitory Provisions and Commencement No.8 and Savings and Transitional Provisions (Amendment)) Order 2013 (as amended and set out in Vol.V of this series, 2021/22 edition as updated in Cumulative Supplements included in Vol.II of this series and in mid-year Supplements) applies, reg.46 is to be read as if it included the additional provisions set out below (art.12(3)(e) of that Order). The introduction of a new para.(6) for all purposes by the 2015 amending regulations cannot be taken as having revoked this additional para.(6). The two must co-exist.

"(6) Where—

(a) a person has been treated under regulation 55(1) of the Jobseeker's Allowance Regulations 1996 as capable of work or as not having limited capability for work for a certain period; and

(b) these Regulations apply to that person with effect from a day ("the relevant day") within that period,

the person is to be treated for the part of that period that begins with the relevant day as capable of work or as not having limited capability for work.

(7) Where paragraph (6) applies to a person and the conditions in paragraph (1)(a) to (c) are fulfilled in relation to that person on any day within the part of a period referred to in paragraph (6), the requirement of paragraph (1) to treat the person as capable of work or as not having limited capability for work is to be regarded as satisfied with respect to the fulfilment of those conditions on that day.

(8) For the purposes of paragraph (3), where paragraph (6) applies to a person, paragraph (3) is to apply to the person as though the preceding provisions of this regulation had applied to the person with respect to the person having been treated for a period, under regulation 55(1) of the Jobseeker's Allowance Regulations 1996 and paragraph (6), as capable of work or as not having limited capability for work."

[1Extended period of sickness

7.139 **46A.**—(1) This regulation applies to a person who—

(a) has been awarded a jobseeker's allowance or is a person to whom any of the circumstances mentioned in section 6J(2) or 6K(2) of the Act apply;

(b) proves to the satisfaction of the Secretary of State that they are unable to work on account of some specific disease or disablement [2("the initial condition")];

(c) either—

(i) declares that they have been unable to work, or expect to be unable to work, on account of [2the initial condition or any other disease or disablement] for more than 2 weeks but [2not] more than 13 weeks; or

(ii) is not a person to whom regulation 46(1) (short periods of sickness) applies by virtue of paragraph (3) of that regulation [2, and declares that he has been unable to work or expects to be unable to work, on account of the initial condition or any other disease or disablement, for two weeks or less];

(d) during the period of their disease or disablement, satisfies the requirements for entitlement to a jobseeker's allowance except those specified in section 1(2)(f) (capable of work or not having limited capability for work); and

(e) has not stated in writing that for the period of the disease or disablement they propose to claim or have claimed an employment and support allowance or universal credit.

(2) The evidence which is required for the purposes of paragraph (1)(b) in a case where paragraph (1)(c)(i) applies is—

(a) evidence of incapacity for work or limited capability for work in accordance with the Social Security (Medical Evidence) Regulations 1976 (which prescribe the form of a [3 ...] statement or other evidence required in each case; and

(b) any such additional information as the Secretary of State may request.

(3) [2Subject to paragraph (3A),] the evidence which is required for the purposes of paragraph (1)(b) in a case where paragraph (1)(c)(ii) applies is a declaration made by the person in writing, in a form approved for the purposes by the Secretary of State, that the person has been unfit for work from a date or for a period in the declaration.

[2(3A) In a case where paragraph (1)(c)(ii) applies, but the period in which the person has been unable to work or expects to be able to work in fact exceeds 2 weeks, the evidence that is required for the purposes of paragraph (1)(b) is the evidence that is required in a case where paragraph (1)(c)(i) applies.]

(4) Subject to the following paragraphs, a person to whom this regulation applies is to be treated as capable of work or as not having limited capability for work for the continuous period beginning on the first day on which the person is unable to work on account of [2 . . .] disease or disablement ("the first day") and ending on—

(a) the last such day; or

(b) if that period would otherwise exceed thirteen weeks, the day which is thirteen weeks after the first day.

(5) This regulation does not apply to a person on more than one occasion in any period of twelve months starting on the first day applying for the purpose of paragraph (4).

(6) Paragraphs (4) and (5) of regulation 46 apply for the purposes of this regulation as they apply for the purposes of paragraph (1) of regulation 46.]

AMENDMENTS

1. Jobseeker's Allowance (Extended Period of Sickness) Amendment Regulations 2015 (SI 2015/339) reg.3(4) (March 30, 2015).

2. Jobseeker's Allowance (Extended Period of Sickness) Amendment Regulations 2016 (SI 2016/502) reg.3(3) (May 23, 2016).

3. Social Security (Medical Evidence) and Statutory Sick Pay (Medical Evidence) (Amendment) (No. 2) Regulations 2022 (SI 2022/630) reg.4(4)(b) (July 1, 2022).

DEFINITIONS

"the Act"—see reg.2(2).

"writing"—see Interpretation Act 1978 Sch.1.

General Note

Temporary Coronavirus Provisions

7.140 The effect of the temporary coronavirus provisions relevant to reg.46A expired at the end of August 31, 2021. See previous editions of this volume for the details.

This provision, in conjunction with the new reg.16A, produces a similar (but not identical) effect to that under regs 46 and 16, which can extend to 13 weeks rather than two weeks but can only be relied on once within any 12 months, rather than twice (para.(5)). However, it can be relied on by a claimant who has exhausted the two periods allowed under reg.46 (see para.(1)(c)(ii)).

See the note to reg.46 for the general background, and reg.55ZA of the JSA Regulations 1996. For the reasons discussed in that note it seems that reg.46A also cannot be relied on at the very outset of a claim but only where the claimant has been awarded new style JSA at least for some period and then argues for supersession on the basis of existing or intervening unfitness for work. However, if a claimant were able to establish an initial entitlement on the basis discussed there, it is arguable that after the effect of reg.16(5) ran out after 14 days, the claimant could then rely on regs 46A and 16A for a further 11 weeks. The 13-week limit in reg.46A(4) runs from the first day on which the claimant is unable to work on account of the disease or disablement. That plainly goes back to any day on which reg.46 had effect. Although para.(4) on its face refers to the objective state of being unable to work, fairness would dictate that the 13-week period should not be regarded as having started to run before the claimant's inability to work was accepted by the Secretary of State under regs 46(1)(b) or 46A(1)(b).

As in reg.46 the test is whether the claimant is unable to work on account of some specific disease or disablement rather than the ESA test for having limited capability for work, although the claimant must, unless excluded from reg.46 by the "twice in 12 months" rule, declare that they have been, or expect to be, unable to work for more than two weeks, but not more than 13 weeks (para.(1)(c)). The provision is thus aimed at those with a relatively short-term condition, who can be expected to return to the JSA regime. Those with more long-term conditions are still required to claim ESA, unless they are still to be regarded as not having limited capability for work despite protestations to the contrary in an ESA appeal. In contrast to reg.46, no doubt because of the longer period involved, in ordinary cases the claimant is required to produce evidence of incapacity for work or limited capability for work under the Medical Evidence Regulations (usually a specified healthcare professional's statement) or such additional information as requested by the Secretary of State (para.(2)(a)). Claimants falling under para.(1)(c)(ii) and in effect having a third go under reg.46 are only required to produce a written declaration of unfitness (para.(3)). It appears at first sight odd to require evidence in the terms just mentioned but the form of statement prescribed in Pt.2 of Sch.1 to the Medical Evidence Regulations requires the healthcare professional to record advice in terms of being or not being fit for work.

Regulation 46A directly allows the condition of entitlement in s.1(2)(f) of the new style Jobseekers Act 1995 to be satisfied. See reg.16A for the prohibition on imposing a work search requirement and on satisfaction of the work availability requirement while reg.46A applies. In contrast to reg.16, there is an additional condition for the production of this effect. It must be unreasonable to require the particular claimant to comply with any work search requirement or to comply with a work availability requirement to be able and willing to take up work and attend an interview.

Periods of sickness and persons receiving treatment outside Great Britain

7.141 **47.**—(1) A person—

(a) who has been awarded a jobseeker's allowance, or is a person to whom any of the circumstances mentioned in section 6J(2) or (3) or 6K(2) of the Act apply;

(b) who is temporarily absent from Great Britain in the circumstances prescribed by regulation 41(5);

(c) who proves to the satisfaction of the Secretary of State that they are unable to work on account of some specific disease or disablement; and

(d) but for their disease or disablement, would satisfy the requirements for entitlement to a jobseeker's allowance other than those specified in section 1(2)(f) of the Act (capable of work or not having limited capability for work),

is to be treated during that period of temporary absence abroad as capable of work or as not having limited capability for work, except where that person has stated in writing before that period of temporary absence abroad begins that immediately before the beginning of the period of that temporary absence abroad they have claimed employment and support allowance.

(2) The evidence which is required for the purposes of paragraph (1)(c) is a declaration made by that person in writing, in a form approved for the purposes by the Secretary of State, that they are unfit for work from a date or for a period specified in the declaration.

DEFINITIONS

"the Act"—see reg.2(2).
"Great Britain"—see Jobseekers Act 1995 s.35(1).
"writing"—see Interpretation Act 1978 Sch.1.

GENERAL NOTE

The purpose of this provision, together with reg.41(5), is to enable entitlement to new style JSA to continue during any period (not time-limited) that claimants with an award go abroad temporarily for the purpose of receiving treatment provided by the NHS. Regulation 47 treats such persons as capable of work, or as not having limited capability for work, provided that they supply a written declaration on an approved form that they are unfit for work from a stated date or for a specified period, such as to prove that they are unable to work on account of some specific disease or disablement (para.(1)(c)) and would, but for that, satisfy the conditions of entitlement in s.1(2) of the new style Jobseekers Act 1995 apart from para.(f) (does not have limited capability for work). However, they will not be treated as capable of work, or as not having limited capability for work, if they have stated in writing before the absence abroad begins that they have claimed ESA. Thus claimants in these circumstances can choose to remain in receipt of new style JSA or to claim benefit on the ground of limited capability for work if they wish to do so. 7.142

Prescribed amount of earnings

48.—The prescribed amount of earnings for the purposes of section 2(1)(c) of the Act (the contribution-based conditions) is to be calculated by applying the formula— 7.143

$$(A+D) - £0.01$$

where—

A is the age-related amount applicable to the claimant for the purposes of section 4(1)(a) of the Act; and

D is any amount disregarded from the claimant's earnings in accordance with the Schedule to these Regulations and either regulation 59(2) (calculation of net earnings of employed earners) or regulation 61(2) (calculation of net profit of self-employed earners).

DEFINITIONS

"the Act"—see reg.2(2).
"claimant"—see Jobseekers Act 1995 s.35(1).
"earnings"—see Jobseekers Act 1995 s.35(3).

GENERAL NOTE

7.144 It is a condition of entitlement to new style JSA that the claimant does not have earnings in excess of the prescribed amount (new style Jobseekers Act 1995 s.2(1)(c)). This regulation gives the set formula for determining that prescribed amount, which amount is not the same for everyone. The prescribed amount is a level equal to the total of the claimant's personal age-related rate of JSA (determined in accordance with new style Jobseekers Act 1995 s.4 and with reg.49) (A in the formula) and the appropriate disregards from his earnings (D in the formula), minus one penny.

See the notes to the definition of "earnings" in s.35(3) of the new style Jobseekers Act 1995 and in reg.2(2) for why the provision for the adding in of any applicable earnings disregards is necessary and how reg.48 interacts with reg.50.

PART 6

AMOUNTS OF A JOBSEEKER'S ALLOWANCE

Weekly amounts of jobseeker's allowance

7.145 **49.**—(1) In the case of a jobseeker's allowance, the age-related amount applicable to a claimant for the purposes of section 4(1)(a) of the Act is—

(a) in the case of a person who has not attained the age of 25, [1£71.70] per week;

(b) in the case of a person who has attained the age of 25, [1£90.50] per week.

(2) Where the amount of any jobseeker's allowance would, but for this paragraph, include a fraction of one penny, that fraction is to be treated as one penny.

AMENDMENT

1. Social Security Benefits Up-rating Order 2024 (SI 2024/242) art.28 (first day of first benefit week beginning on or after April 8, 2024).

DEFINITIONS

"the Act"—see reg.2(2).
"claimant"—see Jobseekers Act 1995 s.35(1).
"week"—see reg.2(2).

GENERAL NOTE

7.146 If a claimant is entitled to new style JSA, the amount payable ("his personal rate": s.4(1) of the new style Jobseekers Act 1995) is calculated by deducting from the appropriate age-related amount in reg.49 any earnings that they have, subject to deductions and disregards (see reg.50) and pension, PPF (pension protection fund) and FAS (financial assistance scheme) payments (reg.51), in so far as the aggregate of reg.51 payments exceeds £50 a week. The rate of benefit is therefore not related to the level of previous earnings or to household responsibilities and is not generous. The April 2020 up-rating was the first since 2015.

In the Institute for Government and the SSAC's 2021 joint report *Jobs and benefits: The Covid-19 challenge* it was recommended that contributory JSA should be strengthened to provide a more generous short-term buffer against the immediate drop in income on losing employment and that its rates should not be below those provided by the standard allowance in universal credit (pp.20-1 and 34). That recommendation was merely noted in the Government's response of March 22, 2022, with the comment that the benefit system is not intended to replicate the income that a claimant was receiving prior to making a claim.

In R. *(on the application of Carson and Reynolds* [2005] UKHL 37, [2006] 1 A.C. 173, the House of Lords dismissed an appeal against the Court of Appeal's decision in *Reynolds* that the differential treatment of the under-25s was not discriminatory contrary to the Human Rights Act 1998 and art.14 of the ECHR. Lord Hoffmann considered that the circumstances of JSA (then old style JSA) and income support claimants aged up to and over 25 were relevantly different. Those under 25 were likely to have lower living expenses, e.g. from living with parents or otherwise not in an independent household, and to have lower earnings expectations. Also a line had to be drawn somewhere, so that there would have been justification if it had been concluded that similar circumstances had been treated differently. It is not clear how far that reasoning applies to new style JSA if a claimant under 25 has satisfied the contribution conditions.

Deductions in respect of earnings

50.—The deduction in respect of earnings which falls to be made in accordance with section 4(1)(b) of the Act is an amount equal to the weekly amount of the claimant's earnings calculated in accordance with Part 7. **7.147**

DEFINITIONS

"the Act"—see reg.2(2).
"claimant"—see Jobseekers Act 1995 s.35(1).

GENERAL NOTE

If a claimant is entitled to new style JSA, the amount payable ("his personal rate": s.4(1) of the new style Jobseekers Act 1995) is calculated by deducting from the appropriate age-related amount in reg.49 any earnings that they have (reg.50) and pension, PPF (pension protection fund) and FAS (financial assistance scheme) payments (reg.51), in so far as the aggregate of reg.51 payments exceeds £50 a week. **7.148**

Only the claimant's own earnings are relevant under reg.50. On what constitutes "earnings" and their calculation, there is a general provision in s.35(3) (see the notes to that provision and to s.4(1)), which requires the term to be construed in accordance with SSCBA 1992 s.3 (earnings includes any remuneration or profit derived from an employment) and accordingly calculated or estimated in accordance with the Computation of Earnings Regulations made under s.3, but subject to any regulations made for the purposes of s.35(3). However, reg.50 expressly provides that the amount to be deducted under s.4(1)(b) is to be the amount of earnings calculated in accordance with Pt. 7 of these Regulations (i.e. regs 53-63). That specific provision, authorised by s.4(1)(b), would seem to indicate an intention contrary to the general effect of s.35(3) sufficient to displace that meaning, even though it does not expressly mention s.35(3). The earnings to be deducted, encompassing both earnings from employed earner's employment (reg.58) and earnings from self-employment (reg.60), are net of the amounts specified in regs.59 and 62 and of the disregards specified in the Schedule, in particular the general £5 disregard in para.5. Notional earnings under reg.63 are taken into account, in contrast to the position under s.2(1)(c) of the new style Jobseekers Act 1995 and reg.48 where the application of the Computation of Earnings Regulations seems to include only a very restricted category of notional earnings (where earnings are not ascertainable: reg.4) in addition to actual earnings.

Payments by way of pensions

7.149 **51.**—(1) The deduction in respect of pension payments, PPF payments or FAS payments which fall to be made in accordance with section 4(1)(b) of the Act is a sum equal to the amount by which that payment exceeds or, as the case may be, the aggregate of those payments exceed £50 per week.

(2) Where pension payments, PPF payments or FAS payments first begin to be made to a person for a period starting other than on the first day of a benefit week, the deduction referred to in paragraph (1) has effect from the beginning of that benefit week.

(3) Where pension payments, PPF payments or FAS payments are already in payment to a person and a change in the rate of payment takes effect in a week other than at the beginning of the benefit week, the deduction referred to in paragraph (1) has effect from the first day of that benefit week.

(4) In determining the amount of any pension payments, PPF payments or FAS payments for the purposes of paragraphs (1) and (5), there are to be disregarded—

(a) any payments from a personal pension scheme, an occupational pension scheme or a public service pension scheme which are payable to the claimant and which arose in accordance with the terms of such a scheme on the death of a person who was a member of the scheme in question; and

(b) any PPF payments or FAS payments which—

(i) are payable to the claimant; and

(ii) arose on the death of a person who had an entitlement to such payments.

(5) Where a pension payment, PPF payment or FAS payment, or an aggregate of such payments, as the case may be, is paid to a person for a period other than a week, such payments are to be treated as being made to that person by way of weekly pension payments, weekly PPF payments or weekly FAS payments and the weekly amount is to be determined—

(a) where payment is made for a year, by dividing the total by 52;

(b) where payment is made for three months, by dividing the total by 13;

(c) where payment is made for a month, by multiplying the total by 12 and dividing the product by 52;

(d) where payment is made for two or more months, otherwise than for a year or for three months, by dividing the total by the number of months, multiplying the result by 12 and dividing the product by 52; or

(e) in any other case, by dividing the amount of the payment by the number of days in the period for which it is made and multiplying the result by seven.

DEFINITIONS

"the Act"—see reg.2(2).
"claimant"—see Jobseekers Act 1995 s.35(1).
"FAS payments"—*ibid.*
"occupational pension scheme"—*ibid.*
"payment"—see reg.2(2).
"pension payments"—see Jobseekers Act 1995 s.35(1).
"personal pension scheme"—*ibid.*
"PPF payments"—*ibid.*
"public service pension scheme"—*ibid.*
"week"—see reg.2(2).

GENERAL NOTE

Section 4(1)(b) of the new style Jobseekers Act 1995 provides that the amount of JSA is to be the claimant's age-related amount (reg.49) subject to deductions for earnings (reg.50) and for pension payments and cognate payments under this regulation. See the notes to s.4 for the Social Security Advisory Committee's doubts about the rationale for the continuing application of the deduction of pension payments. **7.150**

The deduction under reg.51 operates only to the extent that the aggregate of any of the categories covered (pension payments, FAS payments and PPF payments) exceeds £50 per week (para.(1)). That sum has not altered since the introduction of what is now called old style JSA in 1996. Paragraph (4) provides for the disregard of payments arising on the death of a scheme member. Paragraphs (2) and (3) contain rules for the start of payments or changes to rates to take effect at the start of the benefit week in which they occur. Paragraph (5) contains rules for converting payments for periods other than a week into weekly amounts.

Note that the definition of "pension payments" (see below) is in terms of periodical payments. Thus, the receipt of a lump sum under the scheme in question does not give rise to any amount to be deducted under s.4(1)(b). Since there is no "deprivation" rule in new style JSA, claimants who could have received higher periodical payments if they had opted to receive a smaller lump sum cannot be treated as receiving anything more than the actual amount of the periodical payments. And of course the amount of a claimant's capital is irrelevant. The definitions of "PPF payments" and "FAS payments" are not specifically restricted to periodical payments, but it is submitted that the overall context of reg.51 is clearly to restrict its application to payments in respect of a period and not to extend it to capital payments.

"Pension payments" and the other payments are defined in Jobseekers Act 1995 s.35(1).

"Pension payments" are "periodical payments made in relation to a person, under a personal pension scheme or, in connection with the coming to an end of an employment of his, under an occupational pension scheme or a public service pension scheme". No regulations have been made to prescribe any other payments, as would have been allowed under the s.35(1) definition. See the notes to s.35(1) for the definitions of "personal pension scheme", "occupational pension scheme" and "public service pension scheme".

The PPF (Pensions Protection Fund), payments from which are deducted under reg.51 in the same way as pension payments, is a statutory fund that became operational on April 6, 2005. There is a technical definition in s.35(1). The PPF aims to provide compensation for members of defined benefit occupational pension schemes and the defined benefit element of hybrid pension schemes should the employer become insolvent and the pension scheme is underfunded at a certain level.

The FAS (Financial Assistance Scheme), also with a technical definition in s.35(1), offers help to some people who have lost out on their defined benefit occupational pension because their scheme was underfunded when it wound up and the employer is insolvent or no longer exists. In addition, it also provides assistance for certain surviving spouses and civil partners. The FAS is aimed at pension schemes that began to wind up between January 1, 1997 and April 5, 2005. Schemes that began winding up after this period may be eligible for help from the PPF.

In determining the amount of any pension or other payments for abatement purposes, there must under para.(2) be disregarded any payable to the claimant which arose in accordance with the terms of a personal pension scheme, occupational pension scheme or a public service pension scheme on the death of someone who was a member of that scheme. In effect that covers pensions paid to the spouses or dependants of scheme members on the death of the latter. Thus only a claimant's direct pension entitlements, that could be regarded as a form of deferred pay for the person whose work or contributions earned them, affect the amount of new style JSA.

In *R(JSA) 1/01* Commissioner Howell considered the case of a claimant who was a former civil servant with the Property Services Agency who received annual compensation payments for his redundancy which came about when the agency was sold off to the private sector. Those annual payments were not part of his retirement benefits but were "contractual payments made by his private employer, not under any separate funded scheme but out of its own operational assets, in satisfaction of the redundancy terms negotiated with him as part of his contract of employment on transfer of employment to them" (para.6). Clearly those payments were not earnings under the equivalent of reg.58 since the equivalent of reg.58(2)(b) excluded from the definition of earnings "any periodic sum paid to a claimant on account of the termination of his employment by reasons of redundancy". Following the Court of Appeal in *Westminster CC v Haywood* [1998] Ch. 377 and Hart J in *City and Council of Swansea v Johnson* [1999] Ch. 189, the Commissioner held that the annual payments were ones of occupational pension and subject to the abatement of JSA rules in the equivalent of reg.51. He commented in para.28:

> "I do not for my part consider there to be any absurdity or inconsistency in this result. Periodical payments under an employer's scheme or arrangement of this type after employment terminates appear to me to have the same essential characteristic of deferred or contingent 'pay' for this purpose, whether the reason is permitted early retirement or premature termination on redundancy. It seems to me consistent to treat both in the same way as 'pension payments' under regulation [51] whether or not they come from the same source. Nor do I find any absurdity or inconsistency in their both being taken into account as pension payments though excluded from counting as 'earnings'. The point of excluding both from the definition of 'earnings' in regulation [58] is not to remove them from the reckoning altogether, but to allow the first £50 a week of these types of payment to be left out of account while continued current earnings left within regulation [58] would be fully deductible".

To apply this regulation it is vital to identify the source of the payment. Failure so to do is an error of law *(R(JSA) 2/01; CJSA/4316/1998)*. It would be helpful if the correspondence from employer to claimant indicated the source of the payment (*R(JSA) 2/01*). In the above cases the source of the annual compensation payment was the Civil Service Pension Scheme. Following *R(JSA) 1/01* and the statements of Millett LJ in *Westminster CC v Haywood* [1998] Ch. 377, at 404–405, that was held in both cases to fall within the JSA definitions of pension payment, notwithstanding that in *R(JSA) 2/01* the claimant got the compensation payment because he did not get what the civil service scheme called a pension (para.7 of *R(JSA) 2/01*).

In *R(JSA) 6/02* Commissioner Howell followed *R(JSA) 1/01* to hold that "three months' redundancy payment" under a contractual arrangement on termination of employment with London and Manchester (Management Services) Group constituted periodical pension payments abating the amount of benefit.

By contrast, the police disablement gratuity discussed in *Chief Constable of Derbyshire v Clark* [2023] EAT 135; [2024] I.C.R. 239; and, on appeal, [2024] EWCA Civ 676 (see the notes to the definition of "occupational pension scheme in s.35(1) of the Jobseekers Act 1995 for the details) was not from such a scheme because it was not payable <u>on</u> termination of service. Although it was only payable if the officer had ceased to be a member of a police force, entitlement was only established once the officer was found to be totally and permanently disabled.

Minimum amount of a jobseeker's allowance

7.151 **52.**—Where the amount of a jobseeker's allowance is less than 10 pence a week that allowance is not payable.

PART 7

EARNINGS

Rounding of fractions

53.—Where any calculation under this Part results in a fraction of a penny that fraction must, if it would be to the claimant's advantage, be treated as a penny, but otherwise it must be disregarded. 7.152

Calculation of earnings derived from employed earner's employment

54.—(1) Earnings derived from employment as an employed earner are to be taken into account over a period determined in accordance with the following paragraphs and at a weekly amount determined in accordance with regulation 57 (calculation of weekly amount of earnings). 7.153

(2) Subject to the following provisions of this regulation, the period over which a payment is to be taken into account is to be—

(a) where the payment is monthly, a period equal to the number of weeks beginning with the date on which the payment is treated as paid under regulation 56 and ending with the date immediately before the date on which the next monthly payment would have been so treated as paid whether or not the next monthly payment is actually paid;

(b) where the payment is in respect of a period which is not monthly, a period equal to the length of the period for which payment is made; or

(c) in any other case, a period equal to such number of weeks as is equal to the number obtained (see paragraph (13)) by applying the formula—

$$\frac{E}{J+D}$$

where—

E is the net earnings;

J is the amount of jobseeker's allowance which would be payable had the payment not been made;

D is an amount equal to the total of the sums which would fall to be disregarded from that payment under the Schedule to these Regulations (sums to be disregarded in the calculation of earnings), as is appropriate in the claimant's case,

and that period is to begin on the date on which the payment is treated as paid under regulation 56.

[[1](3)(a) This paragraph applies where earnings are derived by a claimant as a member of a reserve force prescribed in Part 1 of Schedule 6 to the Social Security (Contributions) Regulations 2001—

(i) in respect of a period of annual continuous training for a maximum of 15 days in any calendar year; or

(ii) in respect of training in the claimant's first year of training as a member of a reserve force for a maximum of 43 days in that year.

(b) Earnings, whether paid to the claimant alone or together with other earnings derived from the same source, are to be taken into account—

(i) in the case of a period of training which lasts for the number of days listed in column 1 of the table in sub-paragraph (c), over a period of time which is equal to the number of days set out in the corresponding row in column 2 of that table; or
(ii) in any other case, over a period which is equal to the duration of the training period.
(c) This is the table referred to in sub-paragraph (b)(i)—

Column 1 *Period of training in days*	*Column 2* *Period of time over which earnings are to be taken into account in days*
8 to 10	7
15 to 17	14
22 to 24	21
29 to 31	28
36 to 38	35
43	42]

(4) The period referred to in paragraph (3) over which earnings are to be taken into account is to begin on the date on which they are treated as paid under regulation 56.

(5) Where earnings are derived from the same source but are not of the same kind and the periods in respect of which those earnings would, but for this paragraph, fall to be taken into account, overlap wholly or partly—
(a) those earnings are to be taken into account over a period equal to the aggregate length of those periods; and
(b) that period is to begin with the earliest date on which any part of those earnings would otherwise be treated as paid under regulation 56 (date on which earnings are treated as paid).

(6) In a case to which paragraph (5) applies, earnings falling within regulation 58 (earnings of employed earners) are to be taken into account in the following order of priority—
(a) earnings normally derived from the employment;
(b) any compensation payment;
(c) any holiday pay.

(7) Where earnings to which regulation 58(1)(b) or (c) (earnings of employed earners) applies are paid in respect of part of a day, those earnings are to be taken into account over a period equal to a day.

(8) Subject to paragraph (9), the period over which a compensation payment is to be taken into account is to be the period beginning on the date on which the payment is treated as paid under regulation 56 (date on which earnings are treated as paid) and ending—
(a) subject to sub-paragraph (b), where the person who made the payment represents that it, or part of it, was paid in lieu of notice of termination of employment or on account of the early termination of a contract of employment for a term certain, on the expiry date;
(b) in a case where the person who made the payment represents that it, or part of it, was paid in lieu of consultation under section 188 of the Trade Union and Labour Relations (Consolidation) Act 1992(73), on the latest of—
(i) the date on which the consultation period under that section would have ended;

(ii) in a case where sub-paragraph (a) also applies, the expiry date; or

(iii) the standard date; or

(c) in any other case, on the standard date.

(9) The maximum period over which a compensation payment may be taken into account under paragraph (8) is 52 weeks from the date on which the payment is treated as paid under regulation 56.

(10) In this regulation—

"compensation payment" means any payment" to which regulation 58(4) (earnings of employed earners) applies;

"the expiry date" means in relation to the termination of a person's employment—

(a) the date on which any period of notice (which means the period of notice of termination of employment to which a person is entitled by statute or by contract, whichever is the longer, or, if they are not entitled to such notice, the period of notice which is customary in the employment in question) applicable to the person was due to expire, or would have expired had it not been waived;

(b) subject to paragraph (11), where the person who made the payment represents that the period in respect of which that payment is made is longer than the period of notice referred to in paragraph (a), the date on which that longer period is due to expire; or

(c) where the person had a contract of employment for a term certain, the date on which it was due to expire;

"the standard date" means the earlier of—

(a) the expiry date; and

(b) the last day of the period determined by dividing the amount of the compensation payment by the maximum weekly amount which, on the date on which the payment is treated as paid under regulation 56, is specified in section 227(1) of the Employment Rights Act 1996, and treating the result (less any fraction of a whole number) as a number of weeks.

(11) For the purposes of paragraph (10), if it appears to the Secretary of State in a case to which paragraph (b) of the definition of "expiry date" applies that, having regard to the amount of the compensation payment and the level of remuneration normally received by the claimant when they were engaged in the employment in respect of which the compensation payment was made, it is unreasonable to take the payment into account until the date specified in that paragraph (b), the expiry date is to be the date specified in paragraph (a) of that definition.

(12) For the purposes of this regulation the claimant's earnings are to be calculated in accordance with regulations 58, 59 and 63.

(13) For the purposes of the number obtained as mentioned in paragraph (2)(c), any fraction is to be treated as a corresponding fraction of a week.

AMENDMENT

1. Social Security (Members of the Reserve Forces) (Amendment) Regulations 2015 (SI 2015/389) reg.5(3) (April 6, 2015).

DEFINITIONS

"claimant"—see Jobseekers Act 1995 s.35(1).
"earnings"—see Jobseekers Act 1995 s.35(3).
"employed earner"—see reg.2(1).
"first year of training"—see reg.2(2).
"week"—*ibid.*

GENERAL NOTE

Paragraphs (1)–(7)

7.154 These provisions specify the period over which payments of earnings from employed earner's employment are to be taken into account for the purposes of the deductions from the applicable age-related amount under s.4(1)(b) of the new style Jobseekers Act 1995 and reg.50. The application of regs.53-63 for those purposes is specifically prescribed by reg.50. For the reasons explained in the notes to s.35(3) of the Act and to the definition of "earnings" in reg.2(2), it is submitted that only regs 58 and 60 out of those regulations apply for the purposes of s.2(1)(c) of the Act and the condition of entitlement that earnings do not exceed a prescribed amount. Instead, the amount of earnings from employed earner's employment, as defined in reg.58, to be taken into account in any week is to be calculated or estimated in accordance with the Computation of Earnings Regulations (see Pt III of this volume).

Paragraphs (1)-(7) deal in particular with the period over which a payment is to be taken into account. The start of the period is identified under reg.56. The weekly amount to be taken into account is determined under reg.57. Regulation 58 defines what counts as earnings from employment: in general covering any remuneration or profit derived from the employment, with a number of specific inclusions and exclusions. Regulation 59 specifies the deductions that are to be made in calculating the net earnings to be taken into account.

The general rules on "what period" are found in para.(2). Different rules, however, apply for earnings from certain types of training as a member of a reserve force (paras (3) and (4)). Furthermore, where earnings from the same source but of a different kind overlap, the para.(2) rules are first applied to each kind and then that set by para.(5), so that they are to be taken into account over a period equal to the aggregate length of the periods determined for each under the general rules, beginning on the earliest date on which any of these earnings would be treated as paid in accordance with reg.56, with para.(6) setting an order of priority. Where compensation payments or holiday pay ("earnings to which regulation 58(1)(b) or (c)" apply) are paid in respect of part of a day they are to be treated as applicable to a day (para.(7)).

Paragraphs (8)–(11)

7.155 These provisions define the length of the period for which a "compensation payment" (defined in para.(10) by reference to reg.58(4)) is to be taken into account. There is no equivalent to reg.29(4C) of the Income Support Regulations, so it seems that a compensation payment made on the termination of part-time employment will be taken into account as earnings for the period covered by the payment. The rules for identifying the end date of that period are complicated. Where the "expiry date" cannot be identified by the nature of the payment concerned, a default rule is to use the "standard date". That usually involves dividing the amount of the payment by the "maximum weekly rate" specified in s.227(1) of the Employment Rights Act 1996 and taking the result as the number of weeks covered. The "maximum weekly amount" referred to in para.(b) of the definition of "the standard date" in para.(10) is the amount specified at the relevant time as the amount to be used in calculating the basic award for unfair dismissal and redundancy payments. The figure in effect from April 6, 2024 is £700 (2023, £643; 2022,

£571; 2021, £544; (2020, £538; 2019, £525; 2018, £508; 2017, £489; 2016, £479; 2015, £475).

Note *CJSA 5529/1997* in which the effect of reg.94(6) of the JSA Regulations 1996 (the equivalent of para.(8) here) was that the period to which the claimant's compensation payment was to be attributed ended before it started. On October 1, 1996 the claimant agreed with her employer that her employment would end on December 31, 1996 by way of voluntary redundancy. She was to receive a payment of £41,500 on January 4, 1997, which would not include any sum in lieu of notice. She claimed JSA with effect from January 1, 1997. The Commissioner states that the period for which the compensation period was to be taken into account ended on the "standard date". Under the equivalent of para.(10) here, the standard date was the earlier of the "expiry date" and what might be termed the "apportionment date". The expiry date in this case was no later than December 31, 1996 because the claimant was entitled to 12 weeks' (or three months') notice and the agreement for redundancy had been made on October 1, 1996 (see para.(a) of the definition of "expiry date" in para.(10))). The result was that there was no period in respect of which the compensation payment was to be taken into account and thus no period during which she was to be treated as in remunerative work after December 31, 1996.

Calculation of earnings of self-employed earners

55.—(1) Except where paragraph (2) applies, where a claimant's income consists of earnings from employment as a self-employed earner the weekly amount of their earnings is to be determined by reference to their average weekly earnings from that employment— 7.156

(a) over a period of one year; or

(b) where the claimant has recently become engaged in that employment or there has been a change which is likely to affect the normal pattern of business, over such other period as may, in any particular case, enable the weekly amount of their earnings to be determined more accurately.

(2) Where the claimant's earnings consist of any items to which paragraph (3) applies, those earnings are to be taken into account over a period equal to such number of weeks as is equal to the number obtained (see paragraph (5)) by applying the formula—

$$\frac{E}{J+D}$$

where—

E is the earnings;

J is the amount of jobseeker's allowance which would be payable had the payment not been made;

D is an amount equal to the total of the sums which would fall to be disregarded from the payment under the Schedule to these Regulations (earnings to be disregarded) as is appropriate in the claimant's case.

(3) This paragraph applies to—

(a) royalties or other sums paid as a consideration for the use of, or the right to use, any copyright, design, patent or trade mark; or

(b) any payment in respect of any—

(i) book registered under the Public Lending Right Scheme 1982; or

(ii) work made under any international public lending right scheme that is analogous to the Public Lending Right Scheme 1982,

where the claimant is the first owner of the copyright, design, patent or trade mark, or an original contributor to the book or work concerned.

(4) For the purposes of this regulation the claimant's earnings are to be calculated in accordance with regulations 60 to 62.

(5) For the purposes of the number obtained as mentioned in paragraph (2), any fraction is to be treated as a corresponding fraction of a week.

DEFINITIONS

"claimant"—see Jobseekers Act 1995 s.35(1).
"self-employed earner"—see reg.2(2).

GENERAL NOTE

7.157 This regulation specifies how income in the form of earnings from self-employment are to be taken into account in any particular week for the purposes of the deductions from the applicable age-related amount under s.4(1)(b) of the new style Jobseekers Act 1995 and reg.50. The application of regs.53-63 for those purposes is specifically prescribed by reg.50. For the reasons explained in the notes to s.35(3) of the Act and to the definition of "earnings" in reg.2(2), it is submitted that only regs 58 and 60 out of those regulations apply for the purposes of s.2(1)(c) of the Act and the condition of entitlement that earnings do not exceed a prescribed amount. Instead, the amount of earnings from self-employment, as defined in reg.60, to be taken into account in any week is to be calculated or estimated in accordance with the Computation of Earnings Regulations (see Pt III of this volume). See the notes to reg.30 of the Income Support Regulations in Vol.V of this series (2021/22 edition as updated in Cumulative Supplements included in Vol.II of this series and in mid-year Supplements), including discussion of the effect of the receipt of grants under the Coronavirus Self-Employed Income Support Scheme.

Note the more general exception to the rule in para.(1)(a) that is hidden in reg.61(10) which allows the amount of any item of income or expenditure to be calculated over a different period if that will produce a more accurate figure.

Date on which earnings are treated as paid

7.158 **56.**—A payment of earnings to which regulation 54 (calculation of earnings derived from employed earner's employment) applies is to be treated as paid—

(a) in the case of a payment which is due to be paid before the first benefit week pursuant to the claim, on the date on which it is due to be paid; or
(b) in any other case, on the first day of the benefit week in which it is due to be paid or the first succeeding benefit week in which it is practicable to take it into account.

DEFINITIONS

"benefit week"—see reg.2(2).
"payment"—*ibid.*

GENERAL NOTE

7.159 See the annotations to reg.31(1) of the Income Support Regulations in Vol.V of this series (2021/22 edition as updated in Cumulative Supplements included in Vol.

II of this series and in mid-year Supplements) in so far as they deal with earnings rather than with other income. The identification of the date on which a payment is due to be paid in effect identifies the start of the period as fixed under reg.54 for which it is to be taken into account at the rate fixed under reg.57.

Calculation of weekly amount of earnings

57.—(1) For the purposes of regulation 54 (calculation of earnings derived from employed earner's employment), subject to paragraphs (2) to (5), where the period in respect of which a payment of earnings is made— **7.160**

(a) does not exceed a week, the weekly amount is to be the amount of that payment;

(b) exceeds a week, the weekly amount is to be determined—

(i) in a case where that period is a month, by multiplying the amount of the payment by 12 and dividing the product by 52;

(ii) in a case where that period is three months, by multiplying the amount of the payment by four and dividing the product by 52;

(iii) in a case where that period is a year, by dividing the amount of the payment by 52;

(iv) in any other case, by multiplying the amount of the payment by seven and dividing the product by the number equal to the number of days in the period in respect of which it is made.

(2) Where a payment for a period not exceeding a week is treated under regulation 56(a) (date on which earnings are treated as paid) as paid before the first benefit week and a part is to be taken into account for some days only in that week ("the relevant days"), the amount to be taken into account for the relevant days is to be calculated by multiplying the amount of the payment by the number of relevant days and dividing the product by the number of days in the period in respect of which it is made.

(3) Where a payment is in respect of a period equal to or in excess of a week and a part is to be taken into account for some days only in a benefit week ("the relevant days"), the amount to be taken into account for the relevant days is, except where paragraph (4) applies, to be calculated by multiplying the amount of the payment by the number of relevant days and dividing the product by the number of days in the period in respect of which it is made.

(4) Except in the case of a payment which it has not been practicable to treat under regulation 56(b) as paid on the first day of the benefit week in which it is due to be paid, where a payment of income from a particular source is or has been paid regularly and that payment falls to be taken into account in the same benefit week as a payment of the same kind and from the same source, the amount of that income to be taken into account in any one benefit week is not to exceed the weekly amount determined under paragraph (1)(a) or (b), as the case may be, of the payment which under regulation 56(b) (date on which earnings are treated as paid) is treated as paid first.

(5) Where the amount of the claimant's earnings fluctuates and has changed more than once, or a claimant's regular pattern of work is such that they do not work every week, paragraphs (1) to (4) may be modified so that the weekly amount of their earnings is determined by reference to their average weekly earnings—

(a) if there is a recognisable cycle of work, over the period of one complete cycle (including, where the cycle involves periods in which the claimant does no work, those periods but disregarding any other absences);

(b) in any other case, over a period of five weeks or such other period as may, in the particular case, enable the claimant's average weekly earnings to be determined more accurately.

DEFINITIONS

"benefit week"—see reg.2(2).
"claimant"—see Jobseekers Act 1995 s.35(1).
"payment"—see reg.2(2).
"week"—*ibid.*

GENERAL NOTE

7.161 See the notes to reg.32(1)-(3), (5) and (6) of the Income Support Regulations in Vol.V of this series (2021/22 edition as updated in Cumulative Supplements included in Vol.II of this series and in mid-year Supplements).

Earnings of employed earners

7.162 **58.**—(1) Subject to paragraphs (2) and (4), "earnings" means in the case of employment as an employed earner, any remuneration or profit derived from that employment and includes—

(a) any bonus or commission;
(b) any compensation payment;
(c) any holiday pay except any payable more than four weeks after the termination or interruption of employment but this exception does not apply to a person who is, or would be, prevented from being entitled to a jobseeker's allowance by section 14 of the Act (trade disputes);
(d) any payment by way of a retainer;
(e) any payment made by the claimant's employer in respect of expenses not wholly, exclusively and necessarily incurred in the performance of the duties of the employment, including any payment made by the claimant's employer in respect of—
 (i) travelling expenses incurred by the claimant between their home and place of employment;
 (ii) expenses incurred by the claimant under arrangements made for the care of a member of their family owing to the claimant's absence from home;
(f) any payment or award of compensation made under section 112(4), 113, 117(3)(a), 128, 131 or 132 of the Employment Rights Act 1996 (the remedies: orders and compensation, the orders, enforcement of order and compensation, interim relief);
(g) any payment made or remuneration paid under section 28, 34, 64, 68 or 70 of the Employment Rights Act 1996 (right to guarantee payments, remuneration on suspension on medical or maternity grounds, complaints to employment tribunals);
(h) any award of compensation made under section 156, 161 to 166, 189 or 192 of the Trade Union and Labour Relations (Consolidation) Act 1992 (compensation for unfair dismissal or redundancy on grounds of involvement in trade union activities, and protective awards);
(i) the amount of any payment by way of a non-cash voucher which has been taken into account in the computation of a person's earn-

ings in accordance with Part 5 of Schedule 3 to the Social Security (Contributions) Regulations 2001.

(2) "Earnings" does not include—

(a) subject to paragraph (3), any payment in kind;

(b) any periodic sum paid to a claimant on account of the termination of their employment by reason of redundancy;

(c) any remuneration paid by or on behalf of an employer to the claimant in respect of a period throughout which the claimant is on maternity leave, paternity leave[2, shared paternity leave] [3, parental bereavement leave] or adoption leave or is absent from work because they are ill;

(d) any payment in respect of expenses wholly, exclusively and necessarily incurred in the performance of the duties of the employment;

(e) any occupational pension;

(f) any redundancy payment within the meaning of section 135(1) of the Employment Rights Act 1996;

(g) any lump sum payment made under the Iron and Steel Re-adaptation Benefits Scheme;

(h) any payment in respect of expenses arising out of the claimant's participation as a service user;

[1(i) any bounty paid at intervals of at least one year and derived from employment to which paragraph 6 of the Schedule to these Regulations applies.]

(3) Paragraph (2)(a) does not apply in respect of any non-cash voucher referred to in paragraph (1)(i).

(4) In this regulation, "compensation payment" means any payment made in respect of the termination of employment other than—

(a) any remuneration or emolument (whether in money or in kind) which accrued in the period before the termination;

(b) any holiday pay;

(c) any payment specified in paragraphs (1)(f), (g), or (h) or (2);

(d) any refund of contributions to which the person was entitled under an occupational pension scheme.

AMENDMENTS

1. Universal Credit and Miscellaneous Amendments Regulations 2014 reg.3(7) (April 28, 2014).

2. Shared Parental Leave and Statutory Shared Parental Pay (Consequential Amendments and Subordinate Legislation) Order 2014 (SI 2014/3255) art.29(4) (December 23, 2014).

3. Parental Bereavement Leave and Pay (Consequential Amendments to Subordinate Legislation) Regulations 2020 (SI 2020/354) reg.29(4) (April 6, 2020).

DEFINITIONS

"the Act"—see reg.2(2).
"adoption leave"—*ibid.*
"claimant"—see Jobseekers Act 1995 s.35(1).
"employed earner"—see reg.2(1).
"employment"—*ibid.*
"family"—see Jobseekers Act 1995 s.35(1).
"maternity leave"—see reg.2(2).
"occupational pension"—*ibid.*
"occupational pension scheme"—see Jobseekers Act 1995 s.35(1).

"parental bereavement leave"—see reg.2(2).
"person participating as a service user"—see reg.3(6).
"shared parental leave"—see reg.2(2).
"week"—*ibid.*

General Note

7.163 See the notes to reg.35 of the Income Support Regulations in Vol.V of this series (2021/22 edition as updated in Cumulative Supplements included in Vol.II of this series and in mid-year Supplements).

Note that the definition of "earnings" in reg.2(2) provides specifically for the purposes of s.35(3) of the new style Jobseekers Act 1995 that earnings in the case of an employed earner is to have the meaning specified in reg.58. Thus, although it is argued in the notes to s.35(3) and reg.2(2) that for the purposes of the condition of entitlement in s.2(1)(c) of the Act (does not have earnings in excess of prescribed amount) earnings are to be calculated or estimated under the Computation of Earnings Regulations, what counts as earnings from employment as an employed earner is defined by reg.58. The whole of Pt 7 of the Regulations applies for the purposes of s.4(1)(b) of the Act.

Calculation of net earnings of employed earners

7.164 **59.**—(1) For the purposes of regulation 54 (calculation of earnings of employed earners), the earnings of a claimant derived from employment as an employed earner to be taken into account are to be, subject to paragraph (2), their net earnings.

(2) There is to be disregarded from a claimant's net earnings, any sum, where applicable, specified in the Schedule to these Regulations.

(3) For the purposes of paragraph (1) net earnings are to be calculated by taking into account the gross earnings of the claimant from that employment less—

(a) any amount deducted from those earnings by way of—
   (i) income tax;
   (ii) primary Class 1 contributions payable under the Benefits Act; and
(b) half of any sum paid by the claimant in respect of a pay period (the period in respect of which a claimant is, or expects to be, normally paid by their employer, being a week, a fortnight, four weeks, a month or other longer or shorter period as the case may be) by way of a contribution towards an occupational or personal pension scheme.

Definitions

"the Benefits Act"—see Jobseekers Act 1995 s.35(1).
"claimant"—*ibid.*
"employed earner"—see reg.2(1).
"employment"—*ibid.*
"occupational pension scheme"—see Jobseekers Act 1995 s.35(1).
"personal pension scheme"—*ibid.*
"week"—see reg.2(2).

General Note

7.165 See the annotations to reg.36 of the Income Support Regulations in Vol.V of this series (2021/22 edition as updated in Cumulative Supplements included in Vol.II of this series and in mid-year Supplements).

Earnings of self-employed earners

60.—(1) Subject to paragraph (2), "earnings", in the case of employment as a self-employed earner, means the gross receipts of the employment. 7.166

(2) "Earnings" does not include—

(a) where a claimant is involved in providing board and lodging accommodation for which a charge is payable, any payment by way of such a charge;

(b) any payment made to the claimant with whom a person is accommodated by virtue of arrangements made—

(i) under section 22C(2), (3), (5) or (6)(a) or (b) of the Children Act 1989 (provision of accommodation and maintenance for a child whom the local authority is looking after);

[2(ia) under section 81(2), (3), (5) or (6)(a) or (b) of the Social Services and Well-being (Wales) Act 2014 (ways in which looked after children are to be accommodated and maintained);]

(ii) by a local authority under section 26 [4or 26A] of the Children (Scotland) Act 1995 (manner of provision of accommodation to child looked after by local authority [4and duty to provide continuing care]); or

(iii) by a local authority under regulation 33 or 51 of the Looked After Children (Scotland) Regulations 2009 (fostering and kinship care allowances and fostering allowances); or

(iv) by a voluntary organisation under section 59(1)(a) of the Children Act 1989 (provision of accommodation by voluntary organisations);

[3(ba) any payment made to the claimant under section 73(1)(b) of the Children and Young People (Scotland) Act 2014 (kinship care assistance);]

(c) any payment made to the claimant for a person ("the person concerned"), who is not normally a member of the claimant's household but is temporarily in the claimant's care, by—

(i) [6 NHS England;]

(ii) a local authority but excluding payments of housing benefit made in respect of the person concerned;

(iii) a voluntary organisation;

(iv) the person concerned pursuant to section 26(3A) of the National Assistance Act 1948;

[5(v) an integrated care board established under Chapter A3 of Part 2 of the National Health Service Act 2006]; [1 . . .]

(vi) a Local Health Board established by an order made under section 11 of the Health Service (Wales) Act; [1[2 . . .]

(vii) the person concerned where the payment is for the provision of accommodation in respect of the meeting of that person's needs under section 18 or 19 of the Care Act 2014 (duty and power to meet needs for care and support);] [2or

(vii) the person concerned where the payment is for the provision of accommodation to meet that person's needs for care and support under section 35 or 36 of the Social Services and Well-being (Wales) Act 2014 (duty and power to meet needs for care and support of an adult;]

(d) any sports award.

(3) In this regulation, "board and lodging accommodation" means—

(a) accommodation provided to a person or, if they are a member of a family, to them or any other member of their family, for a charge which is inclusive of—

(i) the provision of that accommodation; and

(ii) at least some cooked or prepared meals which are cooked or prepared (by a person other than the person to whom the accommodation is provided or a member of their family) and consumed in that accommodation or associated premises; or

(b) accommodation provided to a person in a hotel, guest house, lodging house or some similar establishment,

except accommodation provided by a close relative of theirs or of any other member of their family, or other than on a commercial basis.

AMENDMENTS

1. Care Act 2014 (Consequential Amendments) (Secondary Legislation) Order 2015 (SI 2015/643) Sch. art.41 (April 1, 2015).

2. Social Services and Well-being (Wales) Act 2014 and the Regulation and Inspection of Social Care (Wales) Act 2016 (Consequential Amendments) Order 2017 (SI 2017/901) art.17 (November 3, 2017).

3. Social Security and Child Support (Care Payments and Tenant Incentive Scheme) (Amendment) Regulations 2017 (SI 2017/995) reg.8(2) (November 7, 2017).

4. Social Security and Child Support (Care Payments and Tenant Incentive Scheme) (Amendment) Regulations 2017 (SI 2017/995) reg.14(2) (November 7, 2017).

5. Health and Care Act 2022 (Consequential and Related Amendments and Transitional Provisions) Regulations 2022 (SI 2022/634) reg.65 (July 1, 2022).

6. Health and Care Act 2022 (Further Consequential Amendments) (No.2) Regulations 2023 (SI 2023/1071) reg.107 and Sch. para.1 (November 6, 2023).

DEFINITIONS

"claimant"—see Jobseekers Act 1995 s.35(1).
"close relative"—see reg.2(2).
"employment"—see reg.2(1).
"family"—see Jobseekers Act 1995 s.35(1) and reg.3(1).
"Health Service (Wales) Act"—see reg.2(2).
"self-employed earner"—*ibid.*
"sports award"—*ibid.*
"voluntary organisation"—*ibid.*

GENERAL NOTE

7.167 See the notes to reg.37 of the Income Support Regulations in Vol.V of this series (2021/22 edition as updated in Cumulative Supplements included in Vol.II of this series and in mid-year Supplements), including discussion of the effect of the receipt of grants under the Coronavirus Self-Employed Income Support Scheme.

Note that the definition of "earnings" in reg.2(2) provides specifically for the purposes of s.35(3) of the Jobseekers Act 1995 that earnings in the case of a self-employed earner is to have the meaning specified in reg.60. Thus, although it is argued in the notes to s.35(3) and reg.2(2) that for the purposes of the condition of entitlement in s.2(1)(c) of the Act (does not have earnings in excess of prescribed amount) earnings are to be calculated or estimated under the Computation of Earnings Regulations, what counts as earnings from self-employment is defined by reg.60. The whole of Pt 7 of the Regulations applies for the purposes of s.4(1)(b) of the Act.

Note that the new head (vii) inserted into reg.60(2)(c) in November 2017 is clearly numbered as such by the amending regulation, despite there already being a head (vii). The obvious mistake can be corrected and the new head regarded as (viii).

Calculation of net profit of self-employed earners

61.—(1) For the purposes of regulation 55 (calculation of earnings of self-employed earners), the earnings of a claimant to be taken into account are— **7.168**

(a) in the case of a self-employed earner who is engaged in employment on their own account, the net profit derived from that employment;

(b) in the case of a self-employed earner whose employment is carried on in partnership, or is that of a share fisherman within the meaning of regulation 67, the claimant's share of the net profit derived from that employment less—

(i) an amount in respect of income tax and of national insurance contributions payable under the Benefits Act calculated in accordance with regulation 62 (deduction of tax and contributions for self-employed earners); and

(ii) half of any premium paid in the period that is relevant under regulation 55 in respect of a personal pension scheme.

(2) There is to be disregarded from a claimant's net profit any sum, where applicable, specified in paragraphs 1 to 11 of the Schedule to these Regulations.

(3) For the purposes of paragraph (1)(a) the net profit of the employment is, except where paragraph (9) applies, to be calculated by taking into account the earnings of the employment over the period determined under regulation 55 (calculation of earnings of self-employed earners) less—

(a) subject to paragraphs (5) to (7), any expenses wholly and exclusively incurred in that period for the purposes of that employment;

(b) an amount in respect of—

(i) income tax; and

(ii) national insurance contributions payable under the Benefits Act, calculated in accordance with regulation 62 (deductions of tax and contributions for self-employed earners); and

(c) half of any premium paid in the period determined under regulation 55 in respect of a personal pension scheme.

(4) For the purposes of paragraph (1)(b), the net profit of the employment is to be calculated by taking into account the earnings of the employment over the period determined under regulation 55 less, subject to paragraphs (5) to (7), any expenses wholly and exclusively incurred in that period for the purposes of that employment.

(5) Subject to paragraph (6), no deduction is to be made under paragraph (3)(a) or (4) in respect of—

(a) any capital expenditure;

(b) the depreciation of any capital asset;

(c) any sum employed or intended to be employed in the setting up or expansion of the employment;

(d) any loss incurred before the beginning of the period determined under regulation 55;

(e) the repayment of capital on any loan taken out for the purposes of the employment;

(f) any expenses incurred in providing business entertainment.

(6) A deduction is to be made under paragraph (3)(a) or (4) in respect of the repayment of capital on any loan used for—

(a) the replacement in the course of business of equipment or machinery; and

(b) the repair of an existing business asset except to the extent that any sum is payable under an insurance policy for its repair.

(7) The Secretary of State must not make a deduction under paragraph (3)(a) or (4) in respect of any expenses where the Secretary of State is not satisfied that the expense has been incurred or, having regard to the nature of the expense and its amount, that it has been reasonably incurred.

(8) A deduction under paragraph (3)(a) or (4)—

(a) must not be made in respect of any sum unless it has been incurred for the purposes of the business;

(b) must be made in respect of—

(i) the excess of any Value Added Tax paid over Value Added Tax received in the period determined under regulation 55;

(ii) any income expended in the repair of an existing asset except to the extent that any sum is payable under an insurance policy for its repair;

(iii) any payment of interest on a loan taken out for the purposes of the employment.

(9) Where a claimant is engaged in employment as a child-minder the net profit of the employment is to be one-third of the earnings of that employment, less—

(a) an amount in respect of—

(i) income tax; and

(ii) national insurance contributions payable under the Benefits Act, calculated in accordance with regulation 62 (deductions of tax and contributions for self-employed earners); and

(b) half of any premium paid in the period determined under regulation 55 in respect of a personal pension scheme.

(10) Notwithstanding regulation 55 and paragraphs (1) to (9), the Secretary of State may assess any item of a claimant's income or expenditure over a period other than that determined under regulation 55 provided that the other period may, in the particular case, enable the weekly amount of that item of income or expenditure to be determined more accurately.

(11) Where a claimant is engaged in employment as a self-employed earner and they are engaged in one or more other employments as a self-employed or employed earner, any loss incurred in any one of their employments is not to be offset against their earnings in any other of their employments.

DEFINITIONS

"the Benefits Act"—see Jobseekers Act 1995 s.35(1).
"claimant"—*ibid.*
"employed earner"—see reg.2(1).
"employment"—*ibid.*
"personal pension scheme"—see Jobseekers Act 1995 s.35(1).
"self-employed earner"—see reg.2(2).
"share fisherman"—see reg.67.

GENERAL NOTE

See the annotations to reg.38 of the Income Support Regulations in Vol.V of this series (2021/22 edition as updated in Cumulative Supplements included in Vol.II of this series and in mid-year Supplements). Note the width of para.(10). See the annotation to reg.55 above. **7.169**

Deduction of tax and contributions for self-employed earners

62.—(1) Subject to paragraph (2), the amount to be deducted in respect of income tax under regulation 61(1)(b)(i), (3)(b)(i) or (9)(a)(i) (calculation of net profit of self-employed earners) is to be calculated— **7.170**

(a) on the basis of the amount of chargeable income; and

[[2](b) as if that income were assessable to income tax at the basic rate, or in the case of a Scottish taxpayer, the Scottish basic rate, of tax less only the personal reliefs to which the claimant is entitled under Chapters 2, 3 and 3A of Part 3 of the Income Tax Act 2007 as are appropriate to their circumstances;]

(2) If the period determined under regulation 55 is less than a year, the earnings to which the basic rate of tax is to be applied and the amount of the personal allowance deductible under paragraph (1) is to be calculated on a pro rata basis.

(3) Subject to paragraph (4), the amount to be deducted in respect of national insurance contributions under regulation 61(1)(b)(i), (3)(b)(ii) or (9)(a)(ii) is to be the total of—

(a) the amount of Class 2 contributions payable under section [[1] 11(2)] or, as the case may be, [[1] 11(8)] of the Benefits Act at the rate applicable at the date of claim except where the claimant's chargeable income is less than the amount specified in section 11(4) of that Act ([[1] small profits threshold]) for the tax year in which the date of claim falls; and

(b) the amount of Class 4 contributions (if any) which would be payable under section 15 of that Act (Class 4 contributions recoverable under the Income Tax Acts) at the percentage rate applicable at the date of claim on so much of the chargeable income as exceeds the lower limit but does not exceed the upper limit of profits and gains applicable for the tax year in which the date of claim falls.

(4) If the period determined under regulation 55 is less than a year—

(a) the amount specified for the tax year referred to in paragraph (3)(a) is to be reduced pro rata; and

(b) the limits referred to in paragraph (3)(b) are to be reduced pro rata.

(5) In this regulation "chargeable income" means—

(a) except where sub-paragraph (b) applies, the earnings derived from the employment less any expenses deducted under regulation 61(3)(a) or, as the case may be, (4);

(b) in the case of employment as a child minder, one-third of the earnings of that employment.

AMENDMENTS

1. Social Security (Miscellaneous Amendments No.2) Regulations 2015 (SI 2015/478) reg.37 (April 6, 2015).

2. Social Security (Scottish Rate of Income Tax etc.) (Amendment) Regulations 2016 (SI 2016/233) reg.7(3) (April 6, 2016).

DEFINITIONS

"the Benefits Act"—see Jobseekers Act 1995 s.35(1).
"date of claim"—see reg.2(2).
"employment"—see reg.2(1).
"Scottish basic rate"—see reg.2(2)
"Scottish taxpayer"—*ibid.*
"tax year"—see Jobseekers Act 1995 s.35(1).

GENERAL NOTE

7.171 See the annotations to reg.39 of the Income Support Regulations in Vol.V of this series (2021/22 edition as updated in Cumulative Supplements included in Vol.II of this series and in mid-year Supplements).

Notional earnings

7.172 **63.**—(1) Subject to paragraph (2), any earnings which are due to be paid to the claimant but have not been paid to the claimant, are to be treated as possessed by the claimant.

(2) Paragraph (1) does not apply to any earnings which are due to an employed earner on the termination of their employment by reason of redundancy but which have not been paid to them.

(3) Where a claimant's earnings are not ascertainable at the time of the determination of the claim or of any revision or supersession, the Secretary of State must treat the claimant as possessing such earnings as is reasonable in the circumstances of the case having regard to the number of hours worked and the earnings paid for comparable employment in the area.

(4) Subject to paragraph (5), where—

(a) a claimant performs a service for another person; and
(b) that person makes no payment of earnings or pays less than that paid for a comparable employment in the area,

the Secretary of State must treat the claimant as possessing such earnings (if any) as is reasonable for that employment unless the claimant satisfies the Secretary of State that the means of that person are insufficient for that person to pay or to pay more for the service.

(5) Paragraph (4) does not apply—

(a) to a claimant who is engaged by a charity or voluntary organisation or who is a volunteer if the Secretary of State is satisfied in any of those cases that it is reasonable for the claimant to provide those services free of charge;
(b) to a claimant who is participating in a work placement approved by the Secretary of State (or a person providing services to the Secretary of State) before the placement starts.

(6) Where a claimant is treated as possessing any earnings under paragraphs (1) or (2), regulations 54 to 62 apply for the purposes of calculating the amount of those earnings as if a payment had actually been made and as if it were actual earnings which the claimant does possess.

(7) Where a claimant is treated as possessing any earnings under paragraphs (3) or (4), regulations 54 to 62 apply for the purposes of calculating the amount of those earnings as if a payment had actually been made and as if they were actual earnings which the claimant does possess, except that—

(a) regulation 59(3) does not apply; and

(b) the claimant's net earnings are to be calculated by taking into account the earnings which the claimant is treated as possessing less the amounts referred to in paragraph (8).

(8) The amounts mentioned in paragraph (7)(b) are—

(a) where the period over which the earnings which the claimant is treated as possessing are to be taken into account is—

(i) a year or more, an amount in respect of income tax equivalent to an amount calculated in accordance with paragraph (11);

(ii) less than a year, the earnings to which the starting rate of tax is to be applied and the amount of the personal allowance deductible under this paragraph are to be calculated on a pro rata basis;

(b) where the weekly amount of the earnings which the claimant is treated as possessing is not less than the lower earnings limit, an amount representing primary Class 1 contributions under the Benefits Act, calculated by applying to those earnings the initial and main primary percentages in accordance with section 8(1)(a) and (b) of that Act; and

(c) half of any sum payable by the claimant in respect of a pay period by way of a contribution towards an occupational or personal pension scheme.

(9) Paragraphs (1), (3) and (4) do not apply in respect of any amount of earnings derived from employment as an employed earner, arising out of the claimant's participation as a service user.

(10) In this regulation, "work placement" means practical work experience which is not undertaken in expectation of payment.

[[1](11) For the purposes of paragraph (8)(a)(i), the amount is calculated by applying to those earnings the basic rate, or in the case of a Scottish taxpayer, the Scottish basic rate, of tax in the year of assessment less only the personal reliefs to which the claimant is entitled under Chapters 2, 3 and 3A of Part 3 of the Income Tax Act 2007 as are appropriate to the claimant's circumstances.]

AMENDMENT

1. Social Security (Scottish Rate of Income Tax etc.) (Amendment) Regulations 2016 (SI 2016/233) reg.7(4) (April 6, 2016).

DEFINITIONS

"the Benefits Act"—see Jobseekers Act 1995 s.35(1).
"claimant"—*ibid.*
"earnings"—see reg.2(2).
"employment"—see reg.2(1).
"employed earner"—*ibid.*
"occupational pension scheme"—see Jobseekers Act 1995 s.35(1).
"participation as a service user"—see reg.3(6).
"personal pension scheme"—see Jobseekers Act 1995 s.35(1).
"Scottish basic rate"—see reg.2(2)
"Scottish taxpayer"—*ibid.*
"voluntary organisation"—*ibid.*

GENERAL NOTE

7.173 The concept of notional income and capital is familiar from old style JSA and income support. It is also carried forward into universal credit (see reg.60 of the UC Regulations 2013). The concept is that in certain circumstances the benefits regime treats someone as possessing income or capital they do not actually have. This regulation applies that concept to earnings, capital being irrelevant in new style JSA. Note that under para.(9) none of this regulation's "notional earnings" rules applies to any amount of earnings derived from employment as an employed earner that arise out of the claimant's participation as a service user, on which see reg.3(6). See in general the annotations to reg.42 of the Income Support Regulations in Vol.V of this series (2021/22 edition as updated in Cumulative Supplements included in Vol.II of this series and in mid-year Supplements), taking account of the differences noted above and below.

Note the argument in the notes to s.35(3) of the new style Jobseekers Act 1995 and reg.2(2) that for the purposes of the condition of entitlement in s.2(1)(c) of the Act (does not have earnings in excess of prescribed amount) earnings are to be calculated or estimated under the Computation of Earnings Regulations, not Pt 7 of these Regulations apart from regs 58 and 60. The Computation of Earnings Regulations contain only a very restricted notional earnings rule, where earnings are not ascertainable at a relevant date (reg.4)

Paragraphs (1), (2) and (6)

7.174 Earnings as an employee due, but not yet paid, to the claimant are treated as being possessed by the claimant, unless they are earnings not yet paid but due to the claimant on the termination of their employment by reason of redundancy. They are to be calculated under regs 54–62 as if actually paid to and possessed by the claimant.

Paragraph (3)

7.175 Where the claimant's earnings are not ascertainable at the time of the relevant decision, revision or supersession, the claimant must be treated as possessing such earnings as is reasonable in the circumstances of the case having regard to the number of hours worked and the earnings paid for comparable employment in the area. This is a very general discretion. The decision-maker (or tribunal) must have regard to the number of hours worked and the going rate locally for comparable employment in deciding what is reasonable, but is not prevented from considering all relevant circumstances (*R(SB) 25/83, R(SB) 15/86, R(SB) 6/88*). Paragraphs (7), (8) and (11) govern the calculation of the amount to be taken into account, including the making of deductions to take account of income tax, national insurance contributions and pension contributions. Note that reg.59(3), on the making of such deductions from actual earnings from employment does not apply.

Paragraphs (4) and (5)

7.176 See the annotations to reg.42(6) and (6A) of the Income Support Regulations (Vol.V of this series, 2021/22 edition as updated in Cumulative Supplements included in Vol.II of this series and in mid-year Supplements). These provisions apply where a claimant provides services for nothing or for less than the going rate and allow notional earnings of what is reasonable for the employment to be deemed, subject to the means of the person for whom the services are provided not being insufficient to pay any more than the actual rate. There are exceptions in para.(5), including where the claimant is participating in an approved work placement, as defined in para.(10). Paragraphs (7), (8) and (11) on calculation also apply here as for para.(3).

PART 8

PART WEEKS

Amount of a jobseeker's allowance payable

64.—(1) Subject to the following provisions of this Part, the amount payable by way of a jobseeker's allowance in respect of a part-week is to be calculated by applying the formula— 7.177

$$(N \times X) / 7$$

where—

X is the personal rate determined in accordance with section 4(1) of the Act;
N is the number of days in the part-week.

(2) In this Part—
"part-week" means any period of less than a week in respect of which there is an entitlement to a jobseeker's allowance;
"relevant week" means the period of seven days determined in accordance with regulation 65.

DEFINITIONS

"the Act"—see reg.2(2).
"week"—*ibid.*

Relevant week

65.—(1) Where the part-week— 7.178
(a) is the whole period for which a jobseeker's allowance is payable or occurs at the beginning of an award, the relevant week is the period of seven days ending on the last day of that part-week;
(b) occurs at the end of an award, the relevant week is the period of seven days beginning on the first day of the part-week; or
(c) occurs because a jobseeker's allowance is not payable for any period in accordance with sections 6J or 7K of the Act (circumstances in which a jobseeker's allowance is not payable), the relevant week is the seven days ending immediately before the start of the next benefit week to commence for that claimant.

(2) Where a person has an award of a jobseeker's allowance and their benefit week changes, for the purpose of calculating the amounts of a jobseeker's allowance payable for the part-week beginning on the day after their last complete benefit week before the change and ending immediately before the change, the relevant week is the period of seven days beginning on the day after the last complete benefit week.

DEFINITIONS

"the Act"—see reg.2(2).
"benefit week"—*ibid.*
"part-week"—see reg.64(2).

Modification in the calculation of income

7.179 **66.**—For the purposes of regulation 64 (amount of jobseeker's allowance payable for part-weeks), a claimant's income is to be calculated in accordance with Part 7 subject to the following changes—

(a) any income which is due to be paid in the relevant week is to be treated as paid on the first day of that week;
(b) where the part-week occurs at the end of the claim, any income or any change in the amount of income of the same kind which is first payable within the relevant week but not on any day in the part-week is to be disregarded;
(c) where the part-week occurs immediately after a period in which a person was treated as engaged in remunerative work under regulation 43 (persons treated as engaged in remunerative work) any earnings which are taken into account for the purposes of determining that period are to be disregarded;
(d) where only part of the weekly amount of income is taken into account in the relevant week, the balance is to be disregarded.

DEFINITIONS

"part-week"—see reg.64(2).
"relevant week"—see regs 64(2) and 65.

PART 9

SHARE FISHERMEN

GENERAL NOTE

7.180 This Part of the Regulations modifies the usual rules so as to deal with "share fishermen" (defined in reg.67). Individual annotations are not provided below.

Share fishermen are paid by way of a share of the catch or the gross profits of the fishing boat. For contributions purposes they are treated as a special form of self-employed earner and pay a special Class 2 contribution. Normally, of course, those liable to pay Class 2 (self-employed earner's contributions) rather than Class 1 contributions (employed earner's contributions) would not be entitled to JSA where fulfilment of the key contribution conditions depends on paid and/or credited Class 1 contributions (new style Jobseekers Act 1995 s.2). Regulation 69 modifies s.2 to take in for purposes of qualifying for new style JSA the special Class 2 contributions paid by share fishermen at the rate applicable in accordance with reg.125(c) of the Social Security (Contributions) Regulations 2001 (SI 2001/1004).

Regulation 70 modifies the definition of "trade dispute" in s.35(1) of the new style Jobseekers Act 1995. Regulation 71(1) sets an additional condition for the payment of JSA to a share fisherman in respect of any benefit week: where in any benefit week claimants have not worked as a share fisherman (partly defined in reg.71(2)) they must prove that they have not neglected to avail themselves of a reasonable opportunity of employment as a share fisherman. Regulation 71(3) sets an additional condition that where claimants are master or a member of the crew of a fishing boat of which either the master or any member of the crew is the owner or part owner, they must also prove that in respect of any period in that benefit week when they were not working as a share fisherman the fishing boat did not put to sea with a view to fishing for one of the reasons specified in reg,71(3)(a)–(c) or that "any other good cause necessitated abstention from fishing" (reg.71(3)(d)). Hours of engagement in work as a share fisherman are not to be counted "in determining the number of hours in which a person is engaged in remunerative work for the purposes of establishing entitlement to a jobseeker's allowance" (reg.72). Regulation 73 deals with calculation of the earnings of share fishermen, effecting modifications to the wording of standard rules in these Regulations, enabling them to be applied differently in the case of share fishermen. Regulation 74 provides that the amount of JSA payable is to be determined under its provisions and not those in Pt 8 above. For this purpose it also affords a different definition of "benefit week" (reg.74(3)).

Interpretation

67.—In this Part— **7.181**

"fishing boat" means a fishing vessel as defined by section 313 of the Merchant Shipping Act 1995;

"owner" has the same meaning as in the Social Security (Mariners' Benefits) Regulations 1975;

"share fisherman" means any person who—

(a) is ordinarily employed in the fishing industry otherwise than under a contract of service, as a master or member of the crew of any fishing boat manned by more than one person, and is remunerated in respect of that employment in whole or in part by a share of the profits or gross earnings of the fishing boat; or

(b) has ordinarily been so employed, but who by reason of age or infirmity permanently ceases to be so employed and becomes ordinarily engaged in employment ashore in Great Britain, otherwise than under a contract of service, making or mending any gear relevant to a fishing boat or performing other services ancillary to or in connection with that boat and is remunerated in respect of that employment in whole or in part by a share of the profits or gross earnings of that boat and has not ceased to be ordinarily engaged in such employment.

Special provisions in respect of share fishermen

68.—The Act and above provisions of these Regulations have effect in relation to share fishermen subject to the provisions of this Part. **7.182**

Modifications of section 2

69.—(1) Section 2 of the Act (the contribution-based conditions) applies to share fishermen with the modifications set out in the following provisions of this regulation. **7.183**

(2) After the words "Class 1 contributions" in each place where they appear there is to be inserted the words "or special Class 2 contributions".

(3) In subsection (4) after the definition of "the relevant benefit year" there is to be inserted the following definition—

> "special Class 2 contributions" means any Class 2 contributions paid by a share fisherman at the rate applicable to share fishermen in accordance with regulation 125(c) of the Social Security (Contributions) Regulations 2001.".

Modification of section 35

70.—(1) The definition of "trade dispute" in section 35(1) of the Act (interpretation) applies to share fishermen with the effect that the owner **7.184**

(or managing owner if there is more than one owner) of a fishing boat is to be treated as the employer of any share fisherman (other than themselves) ordinarily employed as master or member of the crew of, or making or mending any gear relevant to, or performing other services ancillary to or in connection with, that fishing boat, and any such share fisherman is to be treated as their employee.

(2) In this regulation, "managing owner" means that the owner of any ship or vessel who, where there is more than one such owner, is responsible for the control and management of that ship or vessel.

Additional conditions for payment of a jobseeker's allowance

7.185 **71.**—(1) It is to be an additional condition with respect to the payment of a jobseeker's allowance to a share fisherman in respect of any benefit week, that in respect of any period in that benefit week when they have not worked as a share fisherman, they prove that they have not neglected to avail themselves of a reasonable opportunity of employment as a share fisherman.

(2) The following provisions apply for the purposes of the application of paragraph (1)—

(a) work as a share fisherman within the meaning of paragraph (1) includes any of the work specified in sub-paragraph (b) which—

(i) at the time of its performance is necessary for the safety or reasonable efficiency of the fishing boat, or is likely to become so necessary in the near future; and

(ii) it is the duty of the share fisherman (whether by agreement, custom, practice or otherwise) to undertake without remuneration other than by way of a share in the profits or gross earnings of the fishing boat, but any other work done to the fishing boat or its nets or gear is to be disregarded; and

(b) the work so included by sub-paragraph (a) is any work done to the fishing boat or its nets or gear by way of repairs (including running repairs) or maintenance, or in connection with the laying up of the boat and its nets and gear at the end of a fishing season or their preparation for a season's fishing.

(3) It is to be a further additional condition with respect to the payment of a jobseeker's allowance to a share fisherman in respect of any benefit week that, where they are master or a member of the crew of a fishing boat of which either the master or any member of the crew is the owner or part owner, they must also prove that in respect of any period in that benefit week when they were not working as a share fisherman, the fishing boat did not put to sea with a view to fishing, for the reason that—

(a) on account of the state of the weather the fishing boat could not reasonably have put to sea with a view to fishing;

(b) the fishing boat was undergoing repairs or maintenance, not being repairs or maintenance to which paragraph (2) relates;

(c) there was an absence of fish from any waters in which the fishing boat could reasonably be expected to operate; or

(d) any other good cause necessitated abstention from fishing.

(4) In this regulation, "benefit week" in relation to a jobseeker's allowance has the meaning it has in regulation 74 (share fisherman: amount payable).

Remuneration work

72.—In determining the number of hours in which a person is engaged in remunerative work for the purposes of establishing entitlement to a jobseeker's allowance, no account is to be taken of any hours in which a person is engaged in work as a share fisherman. 7.186

Calculation of earnings

73.—(1) In the calculation of earnings derived from work as a share fisherman for the purposes of establishing entitlement to a jobseeker's allowance, the provisions of Part 7 apply subject to the following provisions of this regulation. 7.187

(2) Regulation 55 (calculation of earnings of self-employed earners) is to be omitted.

(3) For regulation 61 (calculation of net profit of self-employed earners) there is to be substituted the following regulation—

"**Calculation of earnings derived from work as a share fisherman**

61.—(1) Earnings derived from work as a share fisherman within the meaning of regulation 67 (interpretation) are to be calculated in accordance with the following provisions of this regulation.

(2) Any such earnings are to be treated as paid in the benefit week in respect of which they are earned.

(3) The amount of earnings to be taken into account in respect of any benefit week are to be the claimant's share of the net profit derived from the work as a share fisherman less—

(a) an amount in respect of income tax and national insurance contributions under the Benefits Act calculated in accordance with regulation 62 (deduction of tax and contributions for self-employed earners); and

(b) half of any premium paid in respect of a personal pension scheme.

(4) Subject to paragraph (5), there is to be disregarded from a claimant's share of the weekly net profit—

(a) £20; and

(b) the amount of any earnings specified in paragraphs 4 and 10 of the Schedule to these Regulations, if applicable.

(5) Where a share fisherman has earnings from work other than work as a share fisherman, and an amount is disregarded from those earnings in accordance with paragraph 5, 6 or 7 of the Schedule—

(a) if the amount so disregarded is £20, paragraph (4)(a) does not apply;

(b) if the amount so disregarded is less than £20, the amount disregarded under paragraph (4)(a) must not exceed the difference between the amount disregarded from those other earnings and [[1]£20].

(6) For the purposes of paragraph (3), the net profit is to be calculated by taking into account the earnings less, subject to paragraphs (7) to (9), any expenses relevant to that benefit week which were wholly, exclusively and necessarily incurred for the purposes of the employment.

(7) Subject to paragraph (8), no deduction is to be made under paragraph (6) in respect of—

(a) any capital expenditure;

(b) the depreciation of any capital asset;

(c) any sum employed or intended to be employed in the setting up or expansion of the employment;

(d) the repayment of capital on any loan taken out for the purposes of the employment;

(e) any expenses incurred in providing business entertainment.

(8) A deduction is to be made under paragraph (6) in respect of the repayment of capital on any loan used for—

(a) the replacement in the course of business of equipment or machinery; and

(b) the repair of an existing business asset except to the extent that any sum is payable under an insurance policy for its repair.

(9) No reduction is to be made under paragraph (6) in respect of any expenses where the Secretary of State is not satisfied that the expense has been incurred or, having regard to the nature of the expense and its amount, that it has been reasonably incurred.

(10) A deduction under paragraph (6)—

(a) must not be made in respect of any sum unless it has been incurred for the purposes of the business;

(b) must be made in respect of—

(i) the excess of any Value Added Tax paid over Value Added Tax received in the benefit week;

(ii) any expense incurred in the repair of an existing asset except to the extent that any sum is payable under an insurance policy for its repair;

(iii) any payment of interest on a loan taken out for the purposes of the employment.

(11) Notwithstanding paragraphs (1) to (10), the Secretary of State may calculate earnings or expenditure over a period other than the benefit week if the Secretary of State considers it is reasonable to do so having regard to all the facts of the case and in particular whether the earnings earned or expenditure incurred in respect of a benefit week are unusually high or low.

(12) In this regulation "benefit week" has the same meaning as in regulation 74 (share fishermen: amount payable)."

(4) In regulation 62 (deduction of tax and contributions for self-employed earners)—

(a) in paragraphs (1) and (3), for the words "regulation 61(1)(b)(i)" there is to be substituted the words "regulation 61(3)(a)";

(b) paragraphs (2) and (4) are to be omitted;

[[2](ba) in paragraph (3) for "Subject to paragraph (4), the" substitute "The";]

(c) in paragraph (5)(a) for the words "regulation 61(3)(a) or, as the case may be, (4)" there is to be substituted the words "regulation 61(6)";

(d) at the end of the regulation there is to be added the following paragraph—

"(6) For the purposes of paragraphs (1) and (3) the earnings to which the basic rate of tax is to be applied and the amount of personal relief deductible, the amount specified in section 11(4) of the Benefits Act, and the upper limit of profits and gains referred to in paragraph (3)(b), are to be apportioned pro rata according to the period over which the earnings are assessed in accordance with regulation 61.".

AMENDMENTS

1. Social Security (Miscellaneous Amendments) (No.2) Regulations 2013 (SI 2013/1508) reg.4(4) (July 29, 2013).

2. Social Security (Scottish Rate of Income Tax etc.) (Amendment) Regulations 2016 (SI 2016/233) reg.7(5) (April 6, 2016).

Amount payable

74.—(1) The amount payable to a share fisherman by way of a jobseeker's allowance is to be calculated in accordance with regulations 49 to 51 (weekly amounts of jobseeker's allowance, deductions in respect of earnings and payments by way of pensions) and this regulation, and Part 8 does not apply. **7.188**

(2) Regulations 49 to 51 apply in respect of share fishermen so that the amount payable is calculated by reference to earnings earned and pension payments received in the benefit week.

(3) In this regulation "benefit week" means—

(a) in respect of the week in which the claim is made, the period of seven days beginning with the date of claim; and

(b) in respect of any subsequent week, the period of seven days beginning with the day after the last day of the previous benefit week.

PART 10

MODIFICATION OF THE ACT

Modification of section 2 of the Act

75.—Section 2 of the Act (the contribution-based conditions) applies with the modifications that after the words "Class 1 contributions" in each place where they appear there is to be inserted the words "or Class 2 contributions under Case G of Part 9 of the Social Security (Contributions) Regulations 2001". **7.189**

DEFINITION

"the Act"—see reg.2(2).

GENERAL NOTE

This modifies s.2 of the new style Jobseekers Act 1995 (already modified by reg.69, above in making the special class 2 contributions paid by share fishermen count for the contribution conditions) so as to make count for JSA entitlement "Class 2 contributions under Case G of Part 9 of the Social Security (Contributions) Regulations 2001". These cover a "volunteer development worker": someone who is ordinarily resident in Great Britain or Northern Ireland (as the case may be), but is employed outside Great Britain, who has been allowed to pay Class 2 contributions because HMRC has certified that it is consistent with the proper administration of the Benefits Act that, subject to the satisfaction of further conditions, that person should be entitled to pay Class 2 contributions under reg.151 of the Contributions Regulations. The modification is set out in the text of s.2. **7.190**

SCHEDULE

Regulations 59(2) and 61(2)

SUMS TO BE DISREGARDED IN THE CALCULATION OF EARNINGS

7.191 **1.**—(1) In the case of a claimant who has been engaged in remunerative work as an employed earner or, had the employment been in Great Britain, would have been so engaged—

(a) any earnings, other than items to which sub-paragraph (2) applies, paid or due to be paid from the employment which was terminated before the first day of entitlement to a jobseeker's allowance;

(b) any earnings, other than a payment of the nature described in sub-paragraph (2)(a) or (b)(ii), paid or due to be paid from the employment which has not been terminated where the claimant is not—

(i) engaged in remunerative work; or

(ii) suspended from their employment.

(2) This sub-paragraph applies to—

(a) any payment of the nature described in—

(i) regulation 58(1)(d); or

(ii) section 28, 64 or 68 of the Employment Rights Act 1996 (guarantee payments, suspension from work on medical or maternity grounds); and

(b) any award, sum or payment of the nature described in—

(i) regulation 58(1)(f) or (h); or

(ii) section 34 or 70 of the Employment Rights Act 1996 (guarantee payments and suspension from work: complaints to employment tribunals),including any payment made following the settlement of a complaint to an employment tribunal or of court proceedings.

2.—(1) In the case of a claimant to whom this paragraph applies, any earnings (other than items to which paragraph 1(2) applies) which relate to employment which ceased before the first day of entitlement to a jobseeker's allowance whether or not that employment has been terminated.

(2) This paragraph—

(a) applies to a claimant who has been engaged in part-time employment as an employed earner or, had the employment been in Great Britain, would have been so engaged;

(b) does not apply to a claimant who has been suspended from their employment.

3.—Any payment to which regulation 58(1)(f) applies—

(a) which is due to be paid more than 52 weeks after the date of termination of the employment in respect of which the payment is made; or

(b) which is a compensatory award within the meaning of section 118(1)(b) of the Employment Rights Act 1996 for so long as such an award remains unpaid and the employer is insolvent within the meaning of section 127 of that Act.

4.—In the case of a claimant who has been engaged in remunerative work or part-time employment as a self-employed earner or, had the employment been in Great Britain, would have been so engaged and who has ceased to be so engaged, from the date of the cessation of their employment any earnings derived from that employment except earnings to which regulation 55(2) (royalties etc) applies.

5.—In a case to which neither of paragraphs 6 and 7 applies to the claimant, £5.

6.—£20 of the total earnings derived from one or more employments as—

[[1](a) a part-time fire-fighter employed by a fire and rescue authority under the Fire and Rescue Services Act 2004 or by the Scottish Fire and Rescue Service established under section 1A of the Fire (Scotland) Act 2005];

(b) [[1] . . ..];

(c) an auxiliary coastguard in respect of coast rescue activities;

(d) a person engaged part-time in the manning or launching of a lifeboat;

(e) a member of any territorial or reserve force prescribed in Part I of Schedule 6 to the Social Security (Contributions) Regulations 2001.

7.—Where the claimant is engaged in one or more employments specified in paragraph 6 but their earnings derived from such employments are less than £20 in any week and they are also engaged in any other part-time employment, so much of their earnings from that other employment up to £5 as would not in aggregate with the amount of their earnings disregarded under paragraph 6 exceed £20.

8.—Notwithstanding paragraphs 1 to 7 of this Schedule, where two or more payments of the same kind and from the same source are to be taken into account in the same benefit week, because it has not been practicable to treat the payments under regulation 56(b) (date on which earnings are treated as paid) as paid on the first day of the benefit week in which they were due to be paid, there is to be disregarded from each payment the sum that would have been disregarded if the payment had been taken into account on the date on which it was due to be paid.

9.—Any earnings derived from employment which are payable in a country outside the United Kingdom for such period during which there is a prohibition against the transfer to the United Kingdom of those earnings.

10.—Where a payment of earnings is made in a currency other than sterling, any banking charge or commission payable in converting that payment into sterling.

11.—Any earnings which are due to be paid before the date of claim and which would otherwise fall to be taken into account in the same benefit week as a payment of the same kind and from the same source.

12.—(1) Where by reason of earnings to which sub-paragraph (2) applies (in aggregate with the claimant's other earnings (if any) calculated in accordance with this Part) the claimant would (apart from this paragraph) have a personal rate of less than 10 pence, the amount of such earnings but only to the extent that that amount exceeds the claimant's personal rate less 10 pence.

(2) This sub-paragraph applies to earnings, in so far as they exceed the amount disregarded under paragraph 6, derived by the claimant from employment as a member of any [2 . . .] reserve force prescribed in Part 1 of Schedule 6 to the Social Security (Contributions) Regulations 2001 in respect of a period of annual continuous training for a maximum of 15 days in any calendar year [2 or in respect of training in the claimant's first year of training as a member of a reserve force for a maximum of 43 days in that year.]

(3) In sub-paragraph (1), "personal rate" means the rate for the claimant calculated as specified in section 4(1) of the Act.

13.—In this Schedule "part-time employment" means employment in which the person is not to be treated as engaged in remunerative work under regulation 43 or 44 (persons treated as engaged, or not engaged, in remunerative work).

AMENDMENTS

1. Social Security (Miscellaneous Amendments) (No.2) Regulations 2013 (SI 2013/1508) reg.4(5) (July 29, 2013).

2. Social Security (Members of the Reserve Forces) (Amendment) Regulations 2015 (SI 2015/389) reg.5(4) (April 6, 2015).

DEFINITIONS

"the Act"—see reg.2(2).
"benefit week"—*ibid.*
"claimant"—see Jobseekers Act 1995 s.35(1).
"date of claim"—see reg.2(2).
"earnings"—see Jobseekers Act 1995 s.35(3).
"employed earner"—see reg.2(1).
"employment"—*ibid.*
"Great Britain"—see Jobseekers Act 1995 s.35(1).
"payment"—see reg.2(2).
"remunerative work"—see regs 2(2) and 42(1).
"self-employed earner"—see reg.2(2).

GENERAL NOTE

The Schedule sets out—for the purposes of regs 59 and 61, dealing respectively with the calculation of the earnings of employed earners and self-employed earners—a range of payments which are wholly or to a degree to be disregarded in 7.192

calculating those earnings, for the purposes of s.4(1)(b) of the new style Jobseekers Act 1995, but not for that of the condition of entitlement in s.2(1)(c), where the Computation of Earnings Regulations apply (see the notes to the definition of "earnings" in reg.2(2) and to s.35(3) of the Act).

The provisions of the Schedule are substantially equivalent to many of those in Sch.8 to the Income Support Regulations (see Vol.V of this series, 2021/22 edition as updated in Cumulative Supplements included in Vol.II of this series and in mid-year Supplements). Paragraphs 1-4 equate to paras 1-3 (including (1A)) of Sch.8. Paragraphs 5-7 on £20 or £5 disregards for various categories of employment are much simpler than paras 4-9 of Sch.8, mainly because the complication of having to take a partner's earnings into account is avoided. Paragraphs 8-11 equate to paras 10-13 of Sch.8. Paragraphs 12 and 13 equate to paras 15A and 16 of Sch.8.

The Social Security (Coronavirus) (Further Measures) Regulations 2020

(SI 2020/371)

7.193 *[The effect of these Regulations expired on various dates, the latest being August 31, 2021. See previous editions of this volume for the details]*

The Universal Credit and Jobseeker's Allowance (Work Search and Work Availability Requirements – limitations) (Amendment) Regulations 2022

(SI 2022/108)

Made by the Secretary of State at 10.35 a.m. on February 7, 2022 under sections 6D(4), 6E(3), 35 and 36(2) and (4) of the Jobseekers Act 1995 and sections 17(4), 18(3) and 42(1) to (3) of the Welfare Reform Act 2012), it appearing to the Secretary of State inexpedient, by reason of urgency, to refer the proposals in respect of these Regulations to the Social Security Advisory Committee.

Citation, commencement and extent

7.194 **1.**—(1) These Regulations may be cited as the Universal Credit and Jobseeker's Allowance (Work Search and Work Availability Requirements – limitations) (Amendment) Regulations 2022 and come into force on 8th February 2022.

(2) Any amendment made by these Regulations has the same extent as the provision amended.

Amendment of the Universal Credit Regulations 2013

7.195 **2.** [*Amendment incorporated into the text of reg.97(5) of the Universal Credit Regulations 2013 in Vol.II of this series*]

Amendment of the Jobseeker's Allowance Regulations 2013

3. [*Amendment incorporated into the text of reg.14(3)(b) of the JSA Regulations 2013*] 7.196

Transitional provision

4. Where, on the date that these Regulations come into force, a work search requirement or work availability requirement is limited under regulation 97(4) of the Universal Credit Regulations 2013 or regulation 14(3) of the Jobseeker's Allowance Regulations 2013, the limitation is to end on— 7.197

(a) the day before the day on which the limitation no longer applies; or

(b) if earlier, 7th March 2022.

GENERAL NOTE

These Regulations, in particular the amendments made by regs 2 and 3, that have a continuing purported application, are of very doubtful validity because on any objective analysis there was no urgency in bringing them into operation before carrying out the Social Security Advisory Committee (SSAC) referral process. See the notes to reg.14 of the JSA Regulations 2013 for the detailed argument on invalidity and the very limited nature of the amendment actually achieved by reg.3. *Howker v Secretary of State for Work and Pensions* [2002] EWCA Civ 1623, [2003] I.C.R. 405, also reported as *R(IB) 3/03*, establishes that a failure to follow the required reference procedure under s.172 of the SSCBA 1992 (there through misleading the SSAC about the nature of the proposal, so that it agreed to no reference) leads to invalidity. In *IC v Glasgow City Council and SSWP (HB)* [2016] UKUT 321 (AAC), reported as [2017] AACR 1, although the three-judge panel rejected the argument that the Secretary of State had failed to show a need for urgency on the facts of the case, the decision operated on the basis that if that argument had been accepted it would have meant that the regulations in question were invalid. 7.198

PART VIII

NEW STYLE EMPLOYMENT AND SUPPORT ALLOWANCE

The Employment and Support Allowance Regulations 2013

(SI 2013/379) (*as amended*)

ARRANGEMENT OF REGULATIONS

PART 1

General

PART 2

The assessment phase

PART 3

Conditions of entitlement

PART 4

Limited Capability for Work

PART 5

Limited Capability for Work-related Activity

PART 6

Effect of work on entitlement to an Employment and Support Allowance

PART 7

Claimant responsibilities

PART 8

Sanctions

PART 9

Amounts of Allowance

PART 10

Income and earnings

PART 11

Supplementary provisions

PART 12

Disqualification

PART 13

Periods of less than a week

The Secretary of State for Work and Pensions makes the following Regulations in exercise of the powers conferred by sections 2(1)(a) and (c) and (4)(a)and (c), 3(1)(c), (2)(b)and (d)and (3), 8(1) to (3), (4)(a) and (b), (5) and (6), 9(1) to (3) and (4)(a)and (b), 11A(5), 11B(2) and (3), 11D(2)(d), 11E(1), 11H(5) and (6), 11J(3), (4) and (8), 17(1), (2) and (3)(a) and (b), 18(1), (2) and (4), 20(2) to (7), 24(1), (2)(b) and (3) and 25(2) to (5) of, and paragraphs 1(3) and (4), 3(2) and 4(1)(a) and (c), (3) and (4) of Schedule 1 and paragraphs 1 to 4A, 5, 6, 9 and 10 of Schedule 2 to, the Welfare Reform Act 2007, sections 5(1A), 189(4) to (6) and 191 of the Social Security Administration Act 1992, section 21(1)(a) of the Social Security Act 1998 and paragraphs 2(3) and 3 of Schedule 5 to the Welfare Reform Act 2012. 8.2

The Social Security Advisory Committee has agreed that the proposals in respect of these Regulations should not be referred to it.

A draft of these Regulations has been laid before Parliament in accordance with section 26(1) of the Welfare Reform Act 2007 and approved by a resolution of each House of Parliament.

GENERAL NOTE

These regulations govern eligibility for "new style ESA". This is a wholly contribution-based benefit for those who have a health condition or disability which limits their capability for work. Those entitled to it whose "resources" are insufficient to meet "needs" will have to seek a top-up through Universal Credit (UC). In the longer term, when the UC scheme is fully rolled out and the legacy benefits withdrawn, the result will be a simpler system, since there will then be only one income-related benefit—UC—for persons of working age, rather than the current system of several income-related benefits each for different categories of claimant and administered by different authorities: IS, IBJSA and IRESA (by DWP/JobCentres), tax credits (by HMRC) and housing benefit (by local authorities). But until that time UC is an additional benefit rather than a benefit replacing all those other income related benefits. The roll-out of UC has been slow and complicated. However, by December 12, 2018 the position had been reached that most new claimants had to claim UC rather than one of the former legacy benefits. 8.3

New claimants – to start with at least – could only claim IRESA in three narrowly-defined sets of circumstances.

The first exception covered claimants in the so-called SDP gateway, i.e. claimants who were (or had been in the last month) entitled to a legacy benefit whose award included the severe disability premium and who had not been given a 'migration notice' that they would be transferred to UC. This class is now an empty class because the SDP gateway was closed with effect from January 27, 2021 by reg.7 of the Universal Credit (Managed Migration Pilot and Miscellaneous Amendments) Regulations 2019 (SI 2019/1152), which revoked reg.4A of the Universal Credit (Transitional Provisions) Regulations 2014 (SI 2014/1230).

The second exception covered frontier workers, e.g. claimants who lived in the Republic of Ireland but worked in Northern Ireland. This category was abolished with effect from March 30, 2022 by art.4 of the Welfare Reform Act 2012 (Commencement No. 34 and Commencement No. 9, 21, 23, 31 and 32 and Transitional and Transitory Provisions (Amendment)) Order 2022 (SI 2022/302), which removed the restriction on frontier workers claiming UC.

The third exception concerned claimants who fell within a category of case in respect of which it had been decided not to accept claims for UC in order to safeguard or effectively test the efficient administration of UC (see reg.4 of the Universal Credit (Transitional Provisions) Regulations 2014 (SI 2014/1230). No such category of cases was ever prescribed and the exception was revoked with effect from July 25, 2022 by reg.2 of the Universal Credit (Transitional Provisions) Amendment Regulations 2022 (SI 2022/752).

The entitlement of all claimants who remain on old-style ESA (either or both CESA and IRESA) continues to be governed by the WRA 2007 and the ESA Regs 2008, as set out in Vol.V of this series. However, UC claimants can only claim new-style ESA in its exclusively contributory form, as governed by the WRA 2007 (as amended) and the ESA Regs 2013 in this volume.

Existing IRESA claimants will find their awards will continue for the time being unless and until a change of circumstances results in 'natural migration' to UC or unless and until they are subject to 'managed migration' to the new benefit. Managed migration is now underway in selected areas. The Government's current plan is that all tax credits legacy cases (including those on both IRESA and tax credits) will be subject to managed migration to UC by the end of 2024/25 (along with all cases on income support and jobseeker's allowance, and all housing benefit only cases). However, the Autumn Statement 2022 announced that the moving of some 800,000 IRESA and IRESA/HB cases will be delayed until 2028/29.

Most of the key rules on "new style ESA" remain the same in terms of effect as those applicable to CESA in the ESA Regulations 2008, but the DWP considers that in drawing up the ESA Regulations 2013 "opportunities have been taken to make simplifications and improvements". In addition, the regulations specific to IRESA are not carried into the 2013 Regulations. This means that material may be differently distributed within the same-numbered regulation in these ESA Regulations 2013 as compared to the ESA Regulations 2008, or be found in a differently numbered one. In addition, in the ESA Regulations 2013, there is a regime of claimant commitments and sanctions analogous in some respects to those applicable to UC and "new style JSA".

For detailed commentary on regs 15–36 of, and Sch.2–3 to, the ESA Regulations 2013 see the annotations to the equivalent provisions in regs 19–39 of, and Sch.2–3 to, the ESA Regulations 2008 in the next Part of this Volume.

Conversion to ESA from IB, IS on the basis of incapacity or disability and SDA is ongoing. It is governed by the ESA (Existing Awards) (No.2) Regs 2010 (SI 2010/1907). These apply to "new style" ESA with modifications made by art.9 and Sch.4 of the Welfare Reform Act 2012 (Commencement No.9 and Transitional and Transitory Provisions and Commencement No.8 and Savings and Transitional Provisions (Amendment)) Order 2013 (SI 2013/983). See further the General Note to the ESA (Existing Awards) (No. 2) Regs 2010 in Pt IX of this book in Vol.V of this series.

PART 1

General

Citation, commencement and application

1.—(1) These Regulations may be cited as the Employment and Support Allowance Regulations 2013. 8.4

(2) They come into force on 29th April 2013.

(3) They apply in relation to a particular case on any day on which section 33(1)(b) of the Welfare Reform Act 2012 (abolition of income-related employment and support allowance) is in force and applies in relation to that case.

GENERAL NOTE

Paras 2, 3.

Although these regulations entered into force on April 29, 2013, they do not as yet apply to all claimants. They will only do so once there has been a full rolling out of Universal Credit and consequent total abolition of IRESA. An important step on the way to this goal was the conversion of all UC 'gateway' or 'live service' areas to 'full service' areas by December 12, 2018, meaning that most new claimants must now claim UC rather than one of the former legacy benefits. New claimants may now only claim IRESA in very narrowly-defined circumstances (see General Note above). Existing awards of IRESA continue for the time being unless and until the claimant has a change in circumstances that results in 'natural migration' to UC. The timetable for the DWP-instigated process of 'managed migration' of existing claimants of legacy benefits (such as IRESA) has continued to slip. 8.5

Interpretation

2.—In these Regulations— 8.6

"the Act" means the Welfare Reform Act 2007;

"advanced education" means education for the purposes of—

(a) a course in preparation for a degree, a diploma of higher education, a higher national diploma, a higher national diploma of the Business and Technology Education Council or the Scottish Qualifications Authority, or a teaching qualification; or

(b) any other course which is of a standard above ordinary national diploma, a diploma of the Business and Technology Education Council or a higher or advanced higher national certificate of the Scottish Qualifications Authority or a general certificate of education (advanced level);

"benefit week" means a period of seven days ending on such day as the Secretary of State may direct, but for the purposes of calculating any payment of income "benefit week" means the period of seven days ending on—

(a) the day before the first day of the first period of seven days which—

(i) ends on such day as the Secretary of State may direct; and

(ii) follows the date of claim for an employment and support allowance; or

(b) the last day on which an employment and support allowance is paid if it is in payment for less than a week;

"carer's allowance" means an allowance under section 70 of the Contributions and Benefits Act;

[7 "carer support payment" means carer's assistance given in accordance with the Carer's Assistance (Carer Support Payment) (Scotland) Regulations 2023;]

"child" means a person under the age of 16;

"Claims and Payments Regulations 2013" means the Universal Credit, Personal Independence Payment, Jobseeker's Allowance and Employment and Support Allowance (Claims and Payments) Regulations 2013;

"close relative" means a parent, parent-in-law, son, son-in-law, daughter, daughter-in-law, step-parent, step-son, step-daughter, brother, sister or, if any of the preceding persons is one member of a couple, the other member of that couple;

"confinement" has the meaning given to it by section 171(1) of the Contributions and Benefits Act;

"councillor" means—

(a) in relation to England and Wales, a member of a London borough council, a county council, a county borough council, a district council, a parish or community council, the Common Council of the City of London or the Council of the Isles of Scilly; and

(b) in relation to Scotland, a member of a council constituted under section 2 of the Local Government etc. (Scotland) Act 1994;

"councillor's allowance" means—

(a) in England, an allowance under or by virtue of—

(i) section 173 or 177 of the Local Government Act 1972; or

(ii) a scheme made by virtue of section 18 of the Local Government and Housing Act 1989,

other than such an allowance as is mentioned in section 173(4) of the Local Government Act 1972;

(b) in Wales, an allowance under or by virtue of a scheme made by virtue of section 18 of the Local Government and Housing Act 1989 other than such an allowance as is mentioned in section 173(4) of the Local Government Act 1972; or

(c) in Scotland, an allowance or remuneration under or by virtue of—

(i) a scheme made by virtue of section 18 of the Local Government and Housing Act 1989; or

(ii) section 11 of the Local Governance (Scotland) Act 2004;

[1,2"couple" means—

(a) two people who are married to, or civil partners of, each other and are members of the same household; or

(b) two people who are not married to, or civil partners of, each other but are living together [5 as if they were a married couple or civil partners];]

"Decisions and Appeals Regulations 1999" means the Social Security and Child Support (Decisions and Appeals) Regulations 1999;

"Decisions and Appeals Regulations 2013" means the Universal Credit, Personal Independence Payment, Jobseeker's Allowance and Employment and Support Allowance (Decisions and Appeals) Regulations 2013;

"descriptor" means, in relation to an activity specified in column (1) of Schedule 2, a descriptor in column (2) of that Schedule which describes a person's ability to perform that activity;

"employed earner" is to be construed in accordance with section 2(1)(a) of the Contributions and Benefits Act;
"employment" includes any trade, business, profession, office or vocation; and "employed" has a corresponding meaning;
"enactment" includes an enactment comprised in, or in an instrument made under, an Act of the Scottish Parliament or the National Assembly of Wales;
"family" means—
(a) a couple;
(b) a couple and a member of the same household for whom one of them is or both are responsible and who is a child or a young person;
(c) a person who is not a member of a couple and a member of the same household for whom that person is responsible and who is a child or a young person;
"first contribution condition" means the condition set out in paragraph 1(1) of Schedule 1 to the Act;
"First-tier Tribunal" has the meaning given by section 3(1) of the Tribunals, Courts and Enforcement Act 2007;
"health care professional" means—
(a) a registered medical practitioner;
(b) a registered nurse; or
(c) an occupational therapist or physiotherapist registered with a regulatory body established by an Order in Council under section 60 of the Health Act 1999;
"Health Service Act" means the National Health Service Act 2006;
"Health Service (Wales) Act" means the National Health Service (Wales) Act 2006;
"Income Support Regulations" means the Income Support (General) Regulations 1987;
"limited capability for work assessment" means the assessment described in regulation 15(2) and in Schedule 2;
"Medical Evidence Regulations" means the Social Security (Medical Evidence) Regulations 1976;
"medical treatment" means medical, surgical or rehabilitative treatment (including any course or diet or other regimen), and references to a person receiving or submitting to medical treatment are to be construed accordingly;
"member of Her Majesty's forces" means a person, other than one mentioned in Part 2 of Schedule 1, who is—
(a) over 16 years of age; and
(b) a member of an establishment or organisation specified in Part 1 of that Schedule, but does not include any such person while absent on desertion;
[4 "member of the work-related activity group" means a claimant who has or is treated as having limited capability for work under either—
(a) Part 5 of the Employment and Support Allowance Regulations 2008 other than by virtue of regulation 30 of those Regulations; or
(b) Part 4 of these Regulations other than by virtue of regulation 26;]
"National Minimum Wage" means the rate of the national minimum wage specified in regulation 11 of the National Minimum Wage Regulations 1999 (rate of the national minimum wage);

"net earnings" means such earnings as are calculated in accordance with regulation 81;

"occupational pension scheme" has the meaning given by section 1 of the Pension Schemes Act 1993;

"part-time employment" means, if the claimant were entitled to income support, employment in which the claimant is not to be treated as engaged in remunerative work under regulation 5 or 6(1) and (4) of the Income Support Regulations (persons treated, or not treated, as engaged in remunerative work);

"partner" means—

(a) where a claimant is a member of a couple, the other member of that couple; or

(b) where a claimant is a husband or wife by virtue of a polygamous marriage, the other party to the marriage or any spouse additional to either party to the marriage;

"payment" includes a part of a payment;

"pay period" means the period in respect of which a claimant is, or expects to be, normally paid by the claimant's employer, being a week, a fortnight, four weeks, a month or other shorter or longer period as the case may be;

"period of limited capability for work" means, except in regulation 3(2), a period throughout which a person has, or is treated as having, limited capability for work under these Regulations, and does not include a period which is outside the prescribed time for claiming as specified in regulation 28 of the Claims and Payments Regulations 2013;

"permanent health insurance payment" means any periodical payment arranged by an employer under an insurance policy providing benefits in connection with physical or mental illness or disability, in relation to a former employee on the termination of that person's employment;

"personal pension scheme" means—

(a) a personal pension scheme as defined by section 1 of the Pension Schemes Act 1993;

(b) an annuity contract, trust scheme or substituted contract which is treated as having become a registered pension scheme by virtue of paragraph 1(1)(f) of Schedule 36 to the Finance Act 2004;

(c) a personal pension scheme which is treated as having become a registered pension scheme by virtue of paragraph 1(1) (g) of Schedule 36 to the Finance Act 2004;

"polygamous marriage" means any marriage entered into under a law which permits polygamy where—

(a) either party has for the time being any spouse additional to the other party; and

(b) the claimant, the other party to the marriage and the additional spouse are members of the same household;

"qualifying young person" has the meaning given by section 142 of the Contributions and Benefits Act (child and qualifying young person);

"relative" means close relative, grand-parent, grand-child, uncle, aunt, nephew or niece;

"second contribution condition" means the condition set out in paragraph 2(1) of Schedule 1 to the Act;

"self-employed earner" is to be construed in accordance with section 2(1)(b) of the Contributions and Benefits Act;

"state pension credit" means a state pension credit under the State Pension Credit Act 2002;

"Tax Credits Act" means the Tax Credits Act 2002;

"terminally ill", in relation to a claimant, means the claimant is suffering from a progressive disease and death in consequence of that disease can reasonably be expected within [6 12 months];

"training" means—

(a) training in pursuance of arrangements made under section 2(1) of the Employment and Training Act 1973 or section 2(3) of the Enterprise and New Towns (Scotland) Act 1990; or

(b) any training received on a course which a person attends for 16 hours or more a week, the primary purpose of which is the teaching of occupational or vocational skills;

"training allowance" means an allowance (whether by way of periodical grants or otherwise) payable—

(a) out of public funds by a Government department or by or on behalf of the Secretary of State, Skills Development Scotland, Scottish Enterprise, Highlands and Islands Enterprise [3 . . .] or the Welsh Ministers;

(b) to a person for that person's maintenance or in respect of a member of that person's family; and

(c) for the period, or part of the period, during which the person is following a course of training or instruction provided by, or in pursuance of arrangements made with, that department or approved by that department in relation to that person or provided or approved by or on behalf of the Secretary of State, Skills Development Scotland, Scottish Enterprise, Highlands and Islands Enterprise, or the Welsh Ministers,

but does not include an allowance paid by any Government department to or in respect of a person by reason of the fact that that person is following a course of full-time education, other than under arrangements made under section 2 of the Employment and Training Act 1973 or section 2 of the Enterprise and New Towns (Scotland) Act 1990, or is training as a teacher;

"voluntary organisation" means a body, other than a public or local authority, the activities of which are carried on otherwise than for profit;

"week" means a period of seven days except in relation to regulation 22;

"working tax credit" means a working tax credit under section 10 of the Tax Credits Act;

"young person" is a person who, except where section 6 of the Children (Leaving Care) Act 2000 (exclusion from benefits) applies, falls within the definition of qualifying young person in section 142 of the Contributions and Benefits Act (child and qualifying young person).

AMENDMENTS

1. Marriage (Same Sex Couples) Act 2013 (Consequential Provisions) Order 2014 (SI 2014/107), reg.2, Sch.1 para.55 (March 13, 2014). (England and Wales only: see art.1(4)).

2. Marriage and Civil Partnership (Scotland) Act 2014 and Civil Partnership Act 2004 (Consequential Provisions and Modifications) Order 2014 (SI 2014/3229) art.29 and Sch.6 para.23 (December 16, 2014: throughout the United Kingdom: see art.3(1)).

3. Deregulation Act 2015 (Consequential Amendments) Order 2015 (SI 2015/971) Art.2 and Sch.3 para.26 (May 26, 2015).

4. Employment and Support Allowance and Universal Credit (Miscellaneous Amendments and Transitional and Savings Provisions) Regulations 2017 (SI 2017/204) reg.3(2) (April 3, 2017).

5. Civil Partnership (Opposite-sex Couples) Regulations 2019 (SI 2019/1458) reg.41(b) and Sch.3 Part 2 para.98 (December 2, 2019).

6. Universal Credit and Employment and Support Allowance (Terminal Illness) (Amendment) Regulations 2022 (SI 2022/260) reg.2(3) (April 4, 2022).

7. Carer's Assistance (Carer Support Payment) (Scotland) Regulations 2023 (Consequential Amendments) Order 2023 (SI 2023/1218) art.25(2) (November 19, 2023).

GENERAL NOTE

8.7 *"couple"*

This definition, initially applicable only in England and Wales, is now applicable throughout the United Kingdom, reflecting the different pace of legal acceptance of civil partnerships and same sex marriage in the various parts of the United Kingdom.

Under the Marriage (Same Sex Couples) Act 2013 (Consequential and Contrary Provisions and Scotland) Order 2014 (SI 2014/560) art.5, effective from March 13, 2014, a same sex marriage in England and Wales was treated as a civil partnership in Scotland. That provision was revoked by the Marriage (Same Sex Couples) Act 2013 (Consequential and Contrary Provisions and Scotland) and Marriage and Civil Partnership (Scotland) Act 2014 (Consequential Provisions) Order 2014 (SI 2014/3168) art.4, with effect from December 16, 2014, no longer being necessary since Scotland's acceptance of same sex marriage. Northern Ireland, however, has no same sex marriage legislation. Hence, the Marriage (Same Sex Couples) Act 2013, s.10(3) and Sch.2 para.2 provided that from March 13, 2014 a same sex marriage in England and Wales was to be treated as a civil partnership in Northern Ireland. Similarly, art.6 of the Marriage and Civil Partnership (Scotland) Act 2014 and Civil Partnership Act 2004 (Consequential Provisions and Modifications) Order 2014 (SI 2014/3229) stipulates that a same sex marriage in Scotland is from December 16, 2014 to be treated in Northern Ireland as a civil partnership.

Further interpretation

8.8 **3.**—(1) In these Regulations, any reference to the claimant's family is to be construed as if it included in relation to a polygamous marriage a reference to any partner and any child or young person who is a member of the claimant's household.

(2) For the purposes of paragraph 4 of Schedule 1 to the Act (condition relating to youth), "period of limited capability for work" means a period throughout which a person has, or is treated as having, limited capability for work.

(3) For the purposes of paragraph 5 of Schedule 1 to the Act, "week" means a period of seven days.

DEFINITIONS

"child"—see reg.2.
"partner"—see reg.2.
"period of limited capability for work"—see para.(2).
"week"—see para.(3).
"young person"—see reg.2.

Rounding of fractions

4.— For the purposes of these Regulations— 8.9

(a) where any calculation under these Regulations results in a fraction of a penny, that fraction is, if it would be to the claimant's advantage, to be treated as a penny, but otherwise it must be disregarded;

(b) where an employment and support allowance is awarded for a period which is not a complete benefit week and the applicable amount in respect of the period results in an amount which includes a fraction of a penny, that fraction is to be treated as a penny.

DEFINITIONS

"benefit week"— see reg.2.

GENERAL NOTE

As with ESA Regs 2008 reg.3, fractions are always rounded in favour of the claimant. 8.10

PART 2

The assessment phase

The end of the assessment phase

5.—(1) Subject to paragraphs (2) and (3) and regulation 6, the assessment phase in relation to a claimant ends on the last day of [1 the relevant period]. 8.11

(2) Where paragraph (3) applies, the assessment phase is to end when it is determined whether the claimant has limited capability for work.

(3) This paragraph applies where, at the end of [1 the relevant period]—

(a) the claimant has not been assessed in accordance with a limited capability for work assessment; and

(b) the claimant has not been treated as having limited capability for work in accordance with regulation 16, 21, 22 or 25.

[1(4) In this regulation, "the relevant period" means the period of 13 weeks beginning with—

(a) the first day of the assessment phase as determined under section 24(2)(a) of the Act; or

(b) where that day immediately follows an extended period of sickness, the first day of the extended period of sickness.

(5) In paragraph (4), "extended period of sickness" means a period in which the claimant was—

(a) entitled to a jobseeker's allowance; and

(b) treated as capable of work or as not having limited capability for work under regulation 55ZA of the Jobseeker's Allowance Regulations 1996 or regulation 46A of the Jobseeker's Allowance Regulations 2013 (extended period of sickness).]

AMENDMENT

1. Jobseeker's Allowance (Extended Period of Sickness) Amendment Regulations 2015 (SI 2015/339) reg.5 (March 30, 2015).

DEFINITIONS

"the assessment phase"—see WRA 2007 s.24(2).
"claimant"—see WRA 2007 s.24(1).
"extended period of sickness"—see para.(5).
"limited capability for work"—see WRA 2007 s.1(4).
"limited capability for work assessment"—see reg.2(1).
"the relevant period"—see para.(4).
"week"—see reg.2(1).

GENERAL NOTE

8.12 This regulation has the same effect as ESA Regs 2008, reg.4. During an initial "assessment phase", generally (reg.7, below, affords exceptions) a claimant can only be entitled to "basic allowance" ESA; entitlement to the additional support component (where applicable) only arises after the end of that initial phase (WRA 2007 s.2(2)). The assessment phase ends on the last day of the "relevant period" (para.(1)). That period is one of 13 weeks beginning either with the first day of the assessment phase determined by WRA 2007 s.24(2)(a) or, if that day followed an extended period of sickness in which the claimant remained entitled to JSA under the specified regulations, with the first day of that extended period of sickness (paras (4), (5)). Section 24(2)(a) of the WRA 2007 stipulates that the "assessment phase" begins on the first day of entitlement to ESA, i.e. the first day of limited capability for work after serving the "waiting days" (these are days of non-entitlement: see WRA 2007 Sch.2, para.2 and reg.85). This regulation, in contrast, sets out when the "assessment phase" ends. It ends after 13 weeks, unless at that time it still has not been determined whether the claimant has, or is to be treated under the regulations enumerated in para.(3) as having, limited capability for work. In that case the "assessment phase" lasts longer than the 13-week period and ends when the limited capability for work determination is made, that is, when it is decided whether or not the person has, or is to be treated as having, limited capability for work.

In short, the assessment phase ends after the later of 13 weeks or the decision on whether the claimant has (or is to be treated as having) limited capability for work. Where, however, the claimant appeals a decision embodying an adverse determination on limited capability for work, the assessment phase ends only when the appeal is determined by an appeal tribunal (see regs 6(5) and 87).

In *SSWP v NC (ESA)* [2013] UKUT 477 (AAC), Judge Bano held that, despite poor wording, the effect of the then reg.4(2) of the ESA Regs 2008 was that "subject to exceptions in cases involving appeals, the assessment phase lasts until the end of the three month period, or until a determination that a claimant has (or is to be treated as having) limited capability for work, whichever is the later" (para.9). In *SSWP v RM (ESA)* [2014] UKUT 42 (AAC), Judge Jacobs agreed with Judge Bano both as to the result of a proper reading of reg.4 and that reg.4(2) as worded before the October 2013 amendments was poorly worded, but considered that it could be rendered coherent by inserting "by" at the beginning of the then para.(2)(a). Fortunately, the October 2013 amendment to the ESA Regs 2008 made things much clearer and with the same effect as in these two decisions.

In para.(3) (b), the renumbered regs compare with the equivalent ones in the ESA Regs 2008 as follows:

2013 Regs	2008 Regs	Coverage
16	20	Certain claimants to be treated as having limited capability for work
21	25	Hospital patients
22	26	Claimants receiving certain treatment
25	29	Exceptional circumstances

There is no equivalent in the ESA Regs 2013 to reg.33(2) of the ESA Regs 2008, which dealt with ability to treat as having limited capability with respect only to IRESA, a benefit abolished in all cases in which these 2013 Regulations apply.

The assessment phase – previous claimants

6.—(1) Where the circumstances in paragraph (2) apply in relation to a claimant, the assessment phase— 8.13

(a) begins on the first day of the period for which the claimant was previously entitled to an employment and support allowance; and

(b) subject to paragraphs (3), (4) and (5), ends on the day when the sum of the period for which the claimant was previously entitled to an employment and support allowance and the period for which the claimant is currently entitled to such an allowance is 13 weeks.

[1(1A) For the purposes of paragraph (1), any period when the claimant was—

(a) entitled to a jobseeker's allowance; and

(b) treated as capable of work or as not having limited capability for work under regulation 55ZA of the Jobseeker's Allowance Regulations 1996 or regulation 46A of the Jobseeker's Allowance Regulations 2013,

is to be treated as a period when the claimant was previously entitled to an employment and support allowance.]

(2) The circumstances are that—

(a) all of the following apply—

(i) the claimant's current period of limited capability for work is to be treated as a continuation of an earlier period of limited capability for work under regulation 86;

(ii) the claimant was entitled to an employment and support allowance in the earlier period of limited capability for work;

(iii) the assessment phase had not ended in the previous period for which the claimant was entitled to an employment and support allowance; and

(iv) the period for which the claimant was previously entitled was no more than 13 weeks;

(b) all of the following apply—

(i) the claimant's current period of limited capability for work is to be treated as a continuation of an earlier period of limited capability for work under regulation 86;

(ii) the claimant was entitled to an employment and support allowance in the earlier period of limited capability for work;

(iii) the previous period of limited capability for work was terminated by virtue of a determination that the claimant did not have limited capability for work;

(iv) the period for which the claimant was previously entitled was no more than 13 weeks; and

(v) a determination is made in relation to the current period of limited capability for work that the claimant has or is treated, other than under regulation 26, as having limited capability for work; or

(c) all of the following apply—

(i) the claimant's current period of limited capability for work is to be treated as a continuation of an earlier period of limited capability for work under regulation 86;

(ii) the claimant was entitled to an employment and support allowance in the earlier period of limited capability for work;

(iii) in relation to the previous award of an employment and support allowance, a determination was made that the claimant had limited capability for work or was treated, other than under regulation 26, as having limited capability for work; and

(iv) the period for which the claimant was previously entitled was no more than 13 weeks.

(3) Where paragraph (4) applies, the assessment phase is to end when it is determined whether the claimant has limited capability for work.

(4) This paragraph applies where, on the day referred to in paragraph (1)(b)—

(a) the claimant has not been assessed in accordance with a limited capability for work assessment; and

(b) the claimant has not been treated as having limited capability for work in accordance with regulation 16, 21, 22 or 25.

(5) Where a person has made and is pursuing an appeal against a decision of the Secretary of State that embodies a determination that the claimant does not have limited capability for work—

(a) paragraphs (3) and (4) do not apply; and

(b) paragraph (1) does not apply to any period of limited capability for work to which regulation 87(2) applies until a determination of limited capability for work has been made following the determination of the appeal by the First-tier Tribunal.

AMENDMENT

1. Jobseeker's Allowance (Extended Period of Sickness) Amendment Regulations 2015 (SI 2015/339) reg.5 (March 30, 2015).

DEFINITIONS

"the assessment phase"—see WRA 2007 s.24(2).
"claimant"—see WRA 2007 s.24(1).
"limited capability for work"—see WRA 2007 s.1(4).
"limited capability for work assessment"—see reg.2(1).
"week"—see reg.2(1).

GENERAL NOTE

8.14 This is the equivalent of ESA Regs 2008 reg.5. On the 2008 equivalents of the renumbered regs in para.(4) (b), see the Table in the annotations to reg.6, above. Reg.86 referred to in para.(2) (a) (i), (b) (i) and (c)(i) is the equivalent of reg.145(1) of the ESA Regs 2008. Reg.26 referred to in para.(2) (b) (v) is the equivalent of reg.30 of the ESA Regs 2008. Reg.87(2) in para.(5) (b) corresponds to reg.147A(2) of the ESA Regs 2008.

This regulation deals with determining the end of the "assessment phase" in cases of intermittent limited capability for work (where spells of limited capability for work are interspersed with spells in which capability for work is not limited), where the ostensibly separate spells of limited capability are fused into one by the operation of the "linking rule" in reg.86. This will happen where the two spells are not separated by more than 12 weeks (until May 1, 2012, the permissible separation period in some cases could have been as long as 104 weeks).

A period in which a claimant remained entitled to JSA during an extended period of sickness under the specified JSA Regs counts as a period of previous entitlement to ESA (paras (1), (1A)). The effect of reg.6 is that the weeks of entitlement to ESA in each period thus linked are added together and the assessment phase ends when their sum reaches 13, unless no limited capability for work determination (see commentary to reg.5) has by then been made, in which case, as with continuous periods of limited capability for work under reg.5, it ends when that determination has been made. In short, the assessment phase ends after the later of 13 weeks (in two or more linked spells of limited capability) or the decision on whether the claimant has (or is to be treated as having) limited capability for work. Where, however, the claimant appeals a decision embodying an adverse determination on limited capability for work, the assessment phase ends only when the appeal is determined by an appeal tribunal (see reg.87).

Circumstances where the condition that the assessment phase has ended before entitlement to the support component [‘. . .] arises does not apply

7.—(1) Subject to paragraph (4), section 2(2)(a) [‘. . .] of the Act does not apply where— **8.15**

(a) a claimant is terminally ill and has either—
 (i) made a claim expressly on the ground of being terminally ill; or
 (ii) made an application for supersession or revision in accordance with the Decisions and Appeals Regulations 1999 or the Decisions and Appeals Regulations 2013 which contains an express statement that the claimant is terminally ill;

(b) the case is a relevant linked case;

(c) the case is one where—
 (i) the claimant's entitlement to an employment and support allowance commences within 12 weeks of the claimant's entitlement to income support coming to an end;
 (ii) in relation to that entitlement to income support, immediately before it ended, the claimant's applicable amount included the disability premium by virtue of their satisfying the conditions in paragraphs 11 and 12 of Schedule 2 to the Income Support Regulations; and
 (iii) that entitlement to income support ended only by virtue of the coming into force, in relation to the claimant, of the Social Security (Lone Parents and Miscellaneous Amendments) Regulations 2008; or

(d) a claimant is entitled to an employment and support allowance by virtue of section 1B of the Act (further entitlement after time-limiting).

(2) For the purposes of paragraph (1) (b) a relevant linked case is a case mentioned in paragraph (3) where a period of limited capability for work is to be treated as a continuation of an earlier period of limited capability for work under regulation 86.

(3) For the purposes of paragraph (2), the cases are as follows—

(a) case 1 is where—
 (i) the claimant was entitled to an employment and support allowance (including entitlement to a component under section 2(2) [1. . .] of the Act [1 or they were a member of the work-related activity group]) in the earlier period of limited capability for work; and

(ii) the previous period for which the claimant was entitled to an employment and support allowance was terminated other than by virtue of a determination that the claimant did not have limited capability for work;

(b) case 2 is where—

(i) the claimant was entitled to an employment and support allowance in the earlier period of limited capability for work;

(ii) the previous period for which the claimant was entitled to an employment and support allowance was 13 weeks or longer;

(iii) the previous period for which the claimant was entitled to an employment and support allowance was terminated by virtue of a determination that the claimant did not have, or was treated as not having, limited capability for work; and

(iv) it is determined in relation to the current period of limited capability for work that the claimant has limited capability for work or is treated, other than under regulation 26, as having limited capability for work;

(c) case 3 is where—

(i) the claimant was entitled to an employment and support allowance in the earlier period of limited capability for work;

(ii) the previous period for which the claimant was entitled to an employment and support allowance was 13 weeks or longer;

(iii) the previous period for which the claimant was entitled to an employment and support allowance was terminated before it could be determined whether the claimant had limited capability for work or was treated, other than under regulation 26, as having limited capability for work; and

(iv) it is determined in relation to the current period of limited capability for work that the claimant has limited capability for work or is treated, other than under regulation 26, as having limited capability for work; and

(d) case 4 is where—

(i) the claimant was entitled to an employment and support allowance (including entitlement to a component under section 2(2) [‘. . .] of the Act [[1] or they were a member of the work-related activity group]) in the earlier period of limited capability for work;

(ii) the previous period for which the claimant was entitled to an employment and support allowance was terminated because it was determined that the claimant did not have limited capability for work or was treated as not having limited capability for work; and

(iii) it is determined in relation to the current period of limited capability for work that the claimant has limited capability for work or is treated, other than under regulation 26, as having limited capability for work.

(4) Paragraph (1) (b) does not apply to any period of limited capability for work to which regulation 87(2) applies until the determination of limited capability for work has been made following the determination of the appeal by the First-tier Tribunal.

AMENDMENT

1. Employment and Support Allowance and Universal Credit (Miscellaneous Amendments and Transitional and Savings Provisions) Regulations 2017 (SI 2017/204) reg.3(3) (April 3, 2017).

DEFINITIONS

"claimant"—see WRA 2007 s.24(1).
"entitled"—see WRA 2007 s.24(1).
"limited capability for work"—see WRA 2007 s.1(4).
"period of limited capability for work"—see reg.2(1).
"relevant linked case"—see paras (2)(b), (3).
"terminally ill"—see reg.2(1).
"the assessment phase"—see WRA 2007 s.24(2).

GENERAL NOTE

This is the equivalent of reg.7 of the ESA Regs 2008. **8.16**

Reg.86 referred to in para.(2) is the equivalent of reg.145(1) of the ESA Regs 2008. Reg.26 referred to in para.(3) (b), (c) and (d) is the equivalent of reg.30 of the ESA Regs 2008. Reg.87(2) in para.(4) corresponds to reg.147A(2) of the ESA Regs 2008.

WRA 2007 ss.2 and 4 provide that, until the "assessment phase" ends, there can be no entitlement other than to basic allowance ESA; entitlement to the support component normally cannot arise until the assessment phase has ended (on which see WRA 2007 s.24(2) and ESA Regs 2013 regs 5–6). This regulation provides that the general rule precluding entitlement does not apply in four situations.

First of all it does not apply to someone terminally ill who has claimed ESA expressly on that basis or has sought supersession or revision expressly stating that he is terminally ill (para.(1)(a)). Note that someone is terminally ill where he is suffering from a progressive disease and death as a consequence of it can reasonably be expected within 12 months (reg.2(1)).

The second situation where the general preclusive rule is disapplied is where the claimant's entitlement to ESA arises within 12 weeks of entitlement to IS which had included the disability premium, ending solely because of the entry into force in relation to him of the Social Security (Lone Parents and Miscellaneous Amendments) Regulations 2012 (para.(1)(c)).

The third situation of disapplication of the general preclusive rule is where the claimant is entitled to ESA because of the further entitlement after time-limiting provisions in WRA 2007 s.1B (para.(1)(d)).

The fourth situation in which the general preclusive rule is disapplied is where the claimant's position falls within one of the four cases each constituting "a relevant linked case" (paras (1)(b), (2), (3)). A "relevant linked case" is one of those in para.(3) in which a period of limited capability for work is to be treated as a continuation of an earlier one under reg.86 (the 12 week linking rule) (paras (1)(b), (2)). Case 1 covers the situation in which the previous entitlement to ESA was one in which there was entitlement to the support component and that entitlement to ESA ended other than by virtue of it being determined that the claimant did not have limited capability for work (para.(3)(a))). Case 2 embraces the situation in which the previous period of entitlement to ESA lasted 13 weeks or more, was ended because of a determination that the claimant did not have, or was treated as not having, limited capability for work and in the current period of ESA entitlement it has been decided that the claimant has limited capability for work or is to be treated as having it other than through reg.30 (treating someone as having limited capability for work pending an actual determination) (para.(3)(b)). Case 3 covers the situation in which the previous period of ESA entitlement lasted 13 weeks or more but was ended before a determination of actual or deemed limited capability for work had been made (other than under reg.30), and in the current period of ESA entitlement it has been decided that the claimant has limited capability for work or is to be treated as having it other than through reg.30 (treating someone as having limited capability for work pending an actual determination) (para.(3)(c)). Case 4 embraces the situation where the claimant's previous period of entitlement to ESA included a component, was ended because it was decided the claimant did not have limited capability for work or was to be treated as not having it, and in the current period of ESA entitlement it has been decided that the claimant has limited capability for work or is to be treated as having it other than through reg.30 (para.(3)(d)).

PART 3

Conditions of entitlement

Conditions relating to national insurance and relevant earnings

8.17 **8.**—(1) A claimant's relevant earnings for the purposes of paragraph 1(2)(a) of Schedule 1 to the Act (employment and support allowance: conditions relating to national insurance) are the total amount of the claimant's earnings equal to the lower earnings limit for the base tax year.

(2) For the purposes of paragraph (1), earnings which exceed the lower earnings limit are to be disregarded.

GENERAL NOTE

8.18 The changes effected by s.13 of the Welfare Reform Act 2009 to Sch.1, para.1 to the Welfare Reform Act 2007, and this regulation made in consequence, significantly tighten the contribution conditions for new style ESA. Together they mean that the requisite level of "relevant earnings" in the tax year relied on for the first contribution condition is now 26 times that year's lower earnings limit, rather than 25. However, this regulation defines "relevant earnings" to cover only earnings at that lower earnings limit (see para.(2)), so that new claimants will have to have worked for at least 26 weeks in one of the last two complete tax years (April 6–April 5) before the start of the benefit year (beginning in early January) which includes the first day of claim in the relevant period of limited capability for work.

Relaxation of the first contribution condition

8.19 **9.**—(1) A claimant who satisfies any of the conditions in paragraph (2) is to be taken to satisfy the first contribution condition if—

(a) the claimant paid Class 1 or Class 2 contributions before the relevant benefit week in respect of any one tax year; and

(b) the claimant has—

   (i) earnings equal to the lower earnings limit in that tax year on which primary Class 1 contributions have been paid or treated as paid which in total, and disregarding any earnings which exceed the lower earnings limit for that year, are not less than that limit multiplied by 26; or

   (ii) earnings factors in that tax year derived from Class 2 contributions multiplied by 26.

(2) The conditions referred to in paragraph (1) are that the claimant—

(a) was entitled to a carer's allowance [1 or carer support payment] in the last complete tax year immediately preceding the relevant benefit year;

(b) had been—
  (i) engaged in qualifying remunerative work (which has the meaning given by Part 1 of the Tax Credits Act) for a period of more than two years immediately before the first day of the period of limited capability for work; and
  (ii) entitled to working tax credit where the disability element or the severe disability element of working tax credit specified in regulation 20(1)(b) or (f) of the Working Tax Credit (Entitlement and Maximum Rate) Regulations 2002 was included in the award;
(c) in respect of any week in any tax year preceding the relevant benefit year—
  (i) is entitled to be credited with earnings or contributions in accordance with regulation 9D of the Social Security (Credits) Regulations 1975 (credits for certain periods of imprisonment or detention in legal custody); or
  (ii) would have been so entitled had an application to the Secretary of State been made for the purpose of that regulation; or
(d) in respect of any week in the last complete tax year preceding the relevant benefit year, is entitled to be credited with earnings in accordance with regulation 9E of the Social Security (Credits) Regulations 1975 (credits for certain spouses and civil partners of members of Her Majesty's forces).

AMENDMENT

1. Carer's Assistance (Carer Support Payment) (Scotland) Regulations 2023 (Consequential Amendments) Order 2023 (SI 2023/1218) art.25(3) (November 19, 2023).

DEFINITIONS

"benefit week"—see reg.2(1).
"carer's allowance"—see reg.2(1).
"claimant"—see WRA 2007 s.24(1).
"Class 1 contributions"—see WRA 2007 s.1, Sch.1 Pt 1 para.3(1)(b).
"Class 2 contributions—see WRA 2007 s.1, Sch.1 Pt 1 para.3(1)(b).
"earnings"—see WRA 2007 s.1, Sch.1 Pt 1 para.3(1)(c).
"earnings factor"—see WRA 2007 s.1, Sch.1 Pt 1 para.3(1)(d).
"first contribution condition"—see reg.2(1); WRA 2007 Sch.1 para.1(1).
"lower earnings limit"—see WRA 2007 s.1, Sch.1 Pt 1 para.3(1)(e).
"period of limited capability for work,"—see reg.2(1).
"primary Class 1 contributions"—see WRA 2007 s.1, Sch.1 Pt 1 para.3(1)(b).
"relevant benefit year"—see WRA 2007 s.1, Sch.1 Pt 1 para.3(1) (f).
"tax year"—see WRA 2007 s.1, Sch.1 Pt 1 para.3(1)(g).
"week"—see reg.2(1).

GENERAL NOTE

See reg.8 of the ESA Regs 2008. 8.20

Condition relating to youth – claimants aged 20 or over but under 25

10.—(1) For the purposes of paragraph 4(1)(a) of Schedule 1 to the Act, a claimant who satisfies the conditions specified in paragraph (2) falls within a prescribed case. 8.21

(2) The conditions are that the claimant—

(a) registered on a course of—

(i) full-time advanced or secondary education; or

(ii) training,

at least three months before attaining the age of 20; and

(b) not more than one academic term immediately after registration attended one or more such courses in respect of a period referred to in paragraph (3).

(3) The period mentioned in paragraph (2) (b) is a period which—

(a) began on or before a day at least three months before the day the claimant attained the age of 20; and

(b) ended no earlier than the beginning of the last two complete tax years before the relevant benefit year which would have applied if the claimant was entitled to an employment and support allowance having satisfied the first contribution condition and the second contribution condition.

(4) For the purposes of this regulation a claimant is to be treated as attending a course on any day on which the course is interrupted by an illness or domestic emergency.

(5) In this regulation—

"full-time" includes part-time where the person's disability prevents attendance at a full-time course;

"secondary education" means a course of education below a course of advanced education by attendance—

(a) at an establishment recognised by the Secretary of State—

(i) as being a university, college or school; or

(ii) as comparable to a university, college or school;

(b) at an establishment that is not mentioned in paragraph (a) where the Secretary of State is satisfied that the education is equivalent to that given in an establishment recognised—

(i) as being a university, college or school; or

(ii) as comparable to a university, college or school.

(6) A claimant is to be treated as not having limited capability for work on a day which is not, for the purposes of paragraph 4(1)(d)(ii) of Schedule 1 to the Act (period of 196 consecutive days preceding the relevant period of limited capability for work), part of a period of consecutive days of limited capability for work.

DEFINTIONS

"advanced education"—see reg.2(1).
"claimant"—see WRA 2007 s.24(1).
"first contribution condition"—see reg.2(1); WRA 2007 Sch.1 para.1(1).
"full-time"—see para.(5).
"relevant benefit year"—see WRA 2007 s.1, Sch.1 Pt 1 para.3(1) (f).
"secondary education"—see para.(5).
"second contribution condition"—see reg.2(1); WRA 2007 Sch.1 para.2(1).
"tax year"—see WRA 2007 s.1, Sch.1 Pt 1 para.3(1) (g).
"training"—see reg.2(1).

GENERAL NOTE

8.22 This is the same as ESA Regs 2008 reg.9.

Condition relating to youth – previous claimants

11.—(1) Paragraph 4(1)(a) of Schedule 1 to the Act does not apply to a claimant— **8.23**

(a) who has previously ceased to be entitled to an employment and support allowance to which the claimant was entitled by virtue of satisfying the condition set out in paragraph 4(1) of Schedule 1 to the Act;

(b) whose previous entitlement had not been ended by a decision which embodied a determination (other than a determination in the circumstances applicable to a claimant under paragraph (2)(a)) that the claimant did not have limited capability for work;

(c) in relation to whom regulation 86 (linking rules) does not apply;

(d) who is aged 20 or over or, where regulation 10 would otherwise apply to the person, aged 25 or over; and

(e) to whom paragraph (2) applies.

(2) This paragraph applies to a claimant—

(a) whose previous entitlement to an employment and support allowance ended only with a view to that person taking up employment or training;

(b) whose earnings factor from an employment or series of employments pursued in the period from the end of the previous entitlement to the beginning of the period of limited capability for work, was below the lower earnings limit multiplied by 25 in any of the last three complete tax years before the beginning of the relevant benefit year; and

(c) who—

(i) in respect of the last two complete tax years before the beginning of the relevant benefit year has either paid or been credited with earnings equivalent in each of those years to the year's lower earnings limit multiplied by 50, of which at least one such payment or credit, in the last complete tax year, was in respect of the disability element or severe disability element of working tax credit; or

(ii) makes a claim for an employment and support allowance within the period of 12 weeks after the day on which the last employment referred to in sub-paragraph (b) ceased.

DEFINITIONS

"claimant"—see WRA 2007 s.24(1).
"earnings factor"—see WRA 2007 s.1, Sch.1 Pt 1 para.3(1) (d).
"employment"—see reg.2(1).
"limited capability for work"—see WRA 2007 s.1(4).
"lower earnings limit"—see WRA 2007 s.1, Sch.1 Pt 1 para.3(1)(e).
"period of limited capability for work"—see reg.2(1).
"relevant benefit year"—see WRA 2007 s.1, Sch.1 Pt 1 para.3(1)(f).
"tax year"—see WRA 2007 s.1, Sch.1 Pt 1 para.3(1)(g).
"training"—see reg.2(1).
"week"—see reg.2(1).
"working tax credit"—see reg.2(1).

GENERAL NOTE

This is the same as ESA Regs 2008 reg.10. The equivalent in the 2008 Regs of reg.86 (linking rules) referred to in para.(1) is reg.145. **8.24**

Condition relating to youth – residence or presence

8.25 **12.**—(1) The conditions prescribed for the purposes of paragraph 4(1)(c) of Schedule 1 to the Act as to residence and presence in Great Britain are that the claimant—

(a) is ordinarily resident in Great Britain;
(b) is not a person subject to immigration control within the meaning of section 115(9) of the Immigration and Asylum Act 1999 or is a person to whom paragraph (3) applies;
(c) is present in Great Britain; and
(d) has been present in Great Britain for a period of, or for periods amounting in aggregate to, not less than 26 weeks in the 52 weeks immediately preceding the relevant benefit week.

(2) For the purposes of paragraph (1), a claimant is to be treated as being resident and present in Great Britain where the claimant is absent from Great Britain by reason only of being—

(a) the spouse, civil partner, son, daughter, father, father-in-law, mother or mother-in-law of, and living with, a member of Her Majesty's forces who is abroad in that capacity;
(b) in employment prescribed for the purposes of paragraph 7(1)(c) of Schedule 2 to the Act in connection with continental shelf operations; or
(c) abroad in the capacity of being an aircraft worker or mariner.

(3) This paragraph applies where a person is—

(a) a member of a family of a national of an European Economic Area state;
(b) a person who is lawfully working in Great Britain and is a national of a State with which the European Union has concluded an agreement under Article 217 of the Treaty on the Functioning of the European Union providing, in the field of social security, for the equal treatment of workers who are nationals of the signatory State and their families;
(c) a person who is a member of a family of, and living with, a person specified in subparagraph (b) ; or
(d) a person who has been given leave to enter, or remain in, the United Kingdom by the Secretary of State upon an undertaking by another person or persons pursuant to the immigration rules within the meaning of the Immigration Act 1971 to be responsible for that person's maintenance and accommodation.

(4) A person is to be treated as having satisfied the residence or presence conditions in paragraph (1) throughout a period of limited capability for work where those conditions are satisfied on the first day of that period of limited capability for work.

(5) In this regulation—

"aircraft worker" means a person who is, or has been, employed under a contract of service either as a pilot, commander, navigator or other member of the crew of any aircraft, or in any other capacity on board any aircraft where—

(a) the employment in that other capacity is for the purposes of the aircraft or its crew or of any passengers or cargo or mail carried on that aircraft; and
(b) the contract is entered into in the United Kingdom with a view to its performance (in whole or in part) while the aircraft is in flight, but does not include a person who is in employment as a member of Her Majesty's forces;

"mariner" means a person who is, or has been, in employment under a contract of service either as a master or other member of the crew of any ship or vessel, or in any other capacity on board any ship or vessel where—

(a) the employment in that other capacity is for the purposes of that ship or vessel or its crew or any passengers or cargo or mail carried by the ship or vessel; and

(b) the contract is entered into in the United Kingdom with a view to its performance (in whole or in part) while the ship or vessel is on its voyage, but does not include a person who is in employment as a member of Her Majesty's forces.

(6) In the definition of "mariner" in paragraph (5), "passenger" means any person carried on a ship or vessel except—

(a) a person employed or engaged in any capacity on board the ship or vessel on the business of the ship or vessel; or

(b) a person on board the ship or vessel either in pursuance of an obligation to carry shipwrecked, distressed or other persons, or by reason of any circumstance that neither the master nor the owner nor the charterer (if any) could have prevented or forestalled.

DEFINITIONS

"aircraft worker"—see para.(5)).
"benefit week"—see reg.2(1).
"claimant"—see WRA 2007 s.24(1).
"continental shelf operations"—see WRA 2007 s.22, Sch.2, para.7(3).
"employment"—see reg.2(1).
"family"—see reg.2(1).
"member of Her Majesty's forces"—see reg.2(1).
"mariner"—see para.(5).
"passenger"—see para.(5).
"period of limited capability for work"—see reg.2(1).
"prescribed"—see WRA 2007 s.24(1).
"week"—see reg.2(1).

GENERAL NOTE

This is the same as ESA Regs 2008 reg.11. **8.26**

Condition relating to youth – full-time education

13.—(1) For the purposes of paragraph 4(1)(b)of Schedule 1 to the Act, a claimant is to be treated as receiving full-time education for any period during which the claimant— **8.27**

(a) is at least 16 years old but under the age of 19; and

(b) attends a course of education for 21 hours or more a week.

(2) For the purposes of paragraph (1)(b), in calculating the number of hours a week during which a claimant attends a course, no account is to be taken of any instruction or tuition which is, in the opinion of the Secretary of State, not suitable for persons of the same age who do not have a disability.

(3) In determining the duration of a period of full-time education under paragraph (1) any temporary interruption of that education may be disregarded.

(4) A claimant who is 19 years of age or over is not to be treated for the purposes of paragraph 4(1)–(b) of Schedule 1 to the Act as receiving full-time education.

DEFINITIONS

"claimant"—see WRA 2007 s.24(1).
"week"—see reg.2(1).

GENERAL NOTE

8.28 This is exactly the same as ESA Regs 2008 reg.12.

Modification of the relevant benefit year

8.29 **14.**—(1) Where paragraph (2) applies, paragraph 3(1)(f) of Schedule 1 to the Act has effect as if the "relevant benefit year" were any benefit year which includes all or part of the period of limited capability for work which includes the relevant benefit week.

(2) This paragraph applies where a claimant has made a claim for employment and support allowance but does not satisfy—

(a) the first contribution condition;
(b) the second contribution condition; or
(c) either contribution condition,

but would satisfy both of those conditions if the modified definition of "relevant benefit year" provided in paragraph (1) applied.

DEFINTIONS

"claimant"—see WRA 2007 s.24(1).
"first contribution condition"—see reg.2(1); WRA 2007 s.1, Sch.1 para.1(1).
"period of limited capability for work"—see reg.2(1).
"relevant benefit year"—see para.(1).
"second contribution condition"—see reg.2(1); WRA 2007 s.1, Sch.1 para.2(1).

GENERAL NOTE

8.30 This is exactly the same as ESA Regs 2008 reg.13.

PART 4

Limited Capability for Work

Determination of limited capability for work

8.31 **15.**—(1) For the purposes of Part 1 of the Act, whether a claimant's capability for work is limited by the claimant's physical or mental condition and, if it is, whether the limitation is such that it is not reasonable to require the claimant to work is to be determined on the basis of a limited capability for work assessment of the claimant in accordance with this Part.

(2) The limited capability for work assessment is an assessment of the extent to which a claimant who has some specific disease or bodily or mental disablement is capable of performing the activities prescribed in Schedule 2 or is incapable by reason of such disease or bodily or mental disablement of performing those activities.

(3) Subject to paragraph (6), for the purposes of Part 1 of the Act a claimant has limited capability for work if, by adding the points listed in column (3) of Schedule 2 against each descriptor listed in that Schedule which applies in the claimant's case, the claimant obtains a total score of at least—

(a) 15 points whether singly or by a combination of descriptors specified in Part 1 of that Schedule;
(b) 15 points whether singly or by a combination of descriptors specified in Part 2 of that Schedule; or
(c) 15 points by a combination of descriptors specified in Parts 1 and 2 of that Schedule.

(4) In assessing the extent of a claimant's capability to perform any activity listed in Part 1 of Schedule 2, the claimant is to be assessed as if—
(a) fitted with or wearing any prosthesis with which the claimant is normally fitted or normally wears; or, as the case may be,
(b) wearing or using any aid or appliance which is normally, or could reasonably be expected to be, worn or used.

(5) In assessing the extent of a claimant's capability to perform any activity listed in Schedule 2, it is a condition that the claimant's incapability to perform the activity arises—
(a) in respect of any descriptor listed in Part 1 of Schedule 2, from a specific bodily disease or disablement;
(b) in respect of any descriptor listed in Part 2 of Schedule 2, from a specific mental illness or disablement; or
(c) in respect of any descriptor or descriptors listed in—
  (i) Part 1 of Schedule 2, as a direct result of treatment provided by a registered medical practitioner for a specific physical disease or disablement; or
  (ii) Part 2 of Schedule 2, as a direct result of treatment provided by a registered medical practitioner for a specific mental illness or disablement.

(6) Where more than one descriptor specified for an activity applies to a claimant, only the descriptor with the highest score in respect of each activity which applies is to be counted.

(7) Where a claimant—
(a) has been determined to have limited capability for work; or
(b) is to be treated as having limited capability for work under regulation 16, 21, 22 or 25, the Secretary of State may, if paragraph (8) applies, determine afresh whether the claimant has or is to be treated as having limited capability for work.

(8) This paragraph applies where—
(a) the Secretary of State wishes to determine whether there has been a relevant change of circumstances in relation to the claimant's physical or mental condition;
(b) the Secretary of State wishes to determine whether the previous determination of limited capability for work or that the claimant is to be treated as having limited capability for work, was made in ignorance of, or was based on a mistake as to, some material fact; or
(c) at least three months have passed since the date on which the claimant was determined to have limited capability for work or to be treated as having limited capability for work.

DEFINITIONS

"claimant"—see WRA 2007 s.24(1).
"descriptor"—see reg.2(1).
"limited capability for work"—see WRA 2007 s.1(4).
"limited capability for work assessment"—see para.(2).

General Note

8.32 This replicates ESA Regs 2008 reg.19.

For detailed commentary on regs 15-36 of, and Sch.2-3 to, the ESA Regulations 2013 see the annotations to the equivalent provisions in regs 19-39 of, and Sch.2-3 to, the ESA Regulations 2008 in the next Part of this Volume.

In para.(7)(b), the renumbered regs compare with equivalent ones in the ESA Regs 2008 as follows:

2013 Regs	2008 Regs	Subject Matter
16	20	Certain claimants to be treated as having limited capability for work
21	25	Hospital patients
22	26	Claimants receiving certain treatment
25	29	Exceptional circumstances

There is no equivalent in the ESA Regs 2013 of ESA Regs 2008 reg.33(2) which dealt with ability to treat as having limited capability with respect only to IRESA, a benefit abolished in the cases and areas in which these 2013 Regulations apply.

Certain claimants to be treated as having limited capability for work

8.33 **16.**—(1) A claimant is to be treated as having limited capability for work if—

(a) the claimant is terminally ill;

(b) the claimant is—

(i) receiving treatment for cancer by way of chemotherapy or radiotherapy;

(ii) likely to receive such treatment within six months after the date of the determination of capability for work; or

(iii) recovering from such treatment, and the Secretary of State is satisfied that the claimant should be treated as having limited capability for work;

(c) the claimant is—

(i) excluded or abstains from work pursuant to a request or notice in writing lawfully made or given under an enactment; or

(ii) otherwise prevented from working pursuant to an enactment,

by reason of it being known or reasonably suspected that the claimant is infected or contaminated by, or has been in contact with a case of, a relevant infection or contamination;

(d) in the case of a pregnant woman, there is a serious risk of damage to her health or to the health of her unborn child if she does not refrain from work;

(e) in the case of a pregnant woman, she—

(i) is within the maternity allowance period (which has the meaning it has in section 35(2) of the Contributions and Benefits Act); and

(ii) is entitled to a maternity allowance under section 35(1) of the Contributions and Benefits Act;

(f) in the case of a pregnant woman whose expected or actual date of confinement has been certified in accordance with the Medical Evidence Regulations, on any day in the period—

(i) beginning with the first date of the 6th week before the expected week of her confinement or the actual date of her confinement, whichever is earlier; and

(ii) ending on the 14th day after the actual date of her confinement,

if she would have no entitlement to a maternity allowance or statutory maternity pay were she to make a claim in respect of that period;

(g) the claimant meets any of the descriptors at paragraph 15 or 16 of Schedule 3 in accordance with regulation 30(2), (3) and (6) where applicable; or

(h) the claimant is entitled to universal credit and it has previously been determined that the claimant has limited capability for work on the basis of an assessment under Part 5 of the Universal Credit Regulations 2013.

(2) In this regulation, "relevant infection or contamination" means—

(a) in England and Wales—

(i) any incidence or spread of infection or contamination, within the meaning of section 45A(3) of the Public Health (Control of Disease) Act 1984 in respect of which regulations are made under Part 2A of that Act (public health protection) for the purpose of preventing, protecting against, controlling or providing a public health response to, such incidence or spread; or

(ii) tuberculosis or any infectious disease to which regulation 9 of the Public Health (Aircraft) Regulations 1979 (powers in respect of persons leaving aircraft) applies or to which regulation 10 of the Public Health (Ships) Regulations 1979 (powers in respect of certain persons on ships) applies; and

(b) in Scotland, any—

(i) infectious disease within the meaning of section 1(5) of the Public Health etc (Scotland) Act 2008, or exposure to an organism causing that disease; or

(ii) contamination within the meaning of section 1(5) of that Act, or exposure to a contaminant, to which sections 56 to 58 of that Act (compensation) apply.

DEFINITIONS

"claimant"—see WRA 2007 s.24(1).
"confinement"—see reg.2(1).
"Contributions and Benefits Act"—see WRA 2007 s.65.
"limited capability for work"—see WRA 2007 s.1(4).
"maternity allowance period" —see para.(1)(e)(i).
"Medical Evidence Regulations"—see reg.2(1).
"relevant infection or contamination"—see para.(2).
"terminally ill"—see reg.2(1).
"week"—see reg.2(1).

GENERAL NOTE

This is much the same as ESA Regs 2008 reg.20. See the next Part of this Volume.

Information required for determining capability for work

17.—(1) Subject to paragraphs (2) and (3), the information or evidence required to determine whether a claimant has limited capability for work is— **8.34**

(a) evidence of limited capability for work in accordance with the Medical Evidence Regulations (which prescribe the form of [1...] statement or other evidence required in each case);
(b) any information relating to a claimant's capability to perform the activities referred to in Schedule 2 as may be requested in the form of a questionnaire; and
(c) any such additional information as may be requested.

(2) Where the Secretary of State is satisfied that there is sufficient information to determine whether a claimant has limited capability for work without the information specified in paragraph (1)(b), that information must not be required for the purposes of making the determination.

(3) Paragraph (1) does not apply in relation to a determination whether a claimant is to be treated as having limited capability for work under any of regulations 16 (certain claimants to be treated as having limited capability for work), 21 (hospital in-patients) and 22 (claimants receiving certain treatment).

Amendment

1. Social Security (Medical Evidence) and Statutory Sick Pay (Medical Evidence) (Amendment) (No. 2) Regulations 2022 (SI 2022/630) reg.4(5) (July 1, 2022).

Definitions

"claimant"—see WRA 2007 s.24(1).
"limited capability for work"—see WRA 2007 s.1(4).
"Medical Evidence Regulations"—see reg.2(1).

General Note

8.35 This corresponds to ESA Regs 2008 reg.21. See the next Part of this Volume.

Failure to provide information in relation to limited capability for work

8.36 **18.**—(1) Where a claimant fails without good cause to comply with the request referred to in regulation 17(1)(b), that claimant is, subject to paragraph (2), to be treated as not having limited capability for work.

(2) Paragraph (1) does not apply unless—
(a) the claimant was sent a further request at least three weeks after the date of the first request; and
(b) at least one week has passed since the further request was sent.

Definitions

"claimant"—see WRA 2007 s.24(1).
"limited capability for work"—see WRA 2007 s.1(4).
"week"—see reg.2(1).

General Note

8.37 This is the same as ESA Regs 2008 reg.22. See the next Part of this Volume.

Claimant may be called for a medical examination to determine whether the claimant has limited capability for work

19.—(1) Where it falls to be determined whether a claimant has limited capability for work, that claimant may be called by or on behalf of a health care professional approved by the Secretary of State to attend for a medical examination [[1]in person, by telephone or by video]. **8.38**

(2) Subject to paragraph (3), where a claimant fails without good cause to attend for or to submit to an examination mentioned in paragraph (1), the claimant is to be treated as not having limited capability for work.

(3) Paragraph (2) does not apply unless—

(a) written notice of the date, time and place for the examination was sent to the claimant at least seven days in advance; or

(b) that claimant agreed to accept a shorter period of notice whether given in writing or otherwise.

AMENDMENT

1. Social Security (Claims and Payments, Employment and Support Allowance, Personal Independence Payment and Universal Credit) (Telephone and Video Assessment) (Amendment) Regulations 2021 reg.6(2) (March 25, 2021).

DEFINITIONS

"claimant"—see WRA 2007 s.24(1).
"health care professional"—see reg.2(1).
"limited capability for work"—see WRA 2007 s.1(4).

GENERAL NOTE

This is the same as ESA Regs 2008 reg.23. See the next Part of this Volume. **8.39**

Matters to be taken into account in determining good cause in relation to regulations 18 or 19

20. The matters to be taken into account in determining whether a claimant has good cause under regulation 18 (failure to provide information in relation to limited capability for work) or 19 (failure to attend a medical examination to determine limited capability for work) include— **8.40**

(a) whether the claimant was outside Great Britain at the relevant time;

(b) the claimant's state of health at the relevant time; and

(c) the nature of any disability the claimant has.

DEFINITION

"claimant"—see WRA 2007 s.24(1).

GENERAL NOTE

This corresponds to ESA Regs 2008 reg.24. See the next Part of this Volume. **8.41**

Hospital patients

21.—(1) A claimant is to be treated as having limited capability for work on any day on which that claimant is undergoing medical or other treatment as a patient in a hospital or similar institution [[1]on any day], or which is a day of recovery from that treatment. **8.42**

(2) The circumstances in which a claimant is to be regarded as undergoing treatment falling within paragraph (1) include where the claimant is attending a residential programme of rehabilitation for the treatment of drug or alcohol addiction.

(3) For the purposes of this regulation, a claimant is to be regarded as undergoing treatment as a patient in a hospital or similar institution only if that claimant has been advised by a health care professional to stay [[1]for a period of 24 hours or longer] following medical or other treatment.

(4) For the purposes of this regulation, "day of recovery" means a day on which a claimant is recovering from treatment as a patient in a hospital or similar institution as referred to in paragraph (1) and the Secretary of State is satisfied that the claimant should be treated as having limited capability for work on that day.

AMENDMENT

1. Social Security (Miscellaneous Amendments) (No.2) Regulations 2013 (SI 2013/1508) reg.5(1), (2) (July 29, 2013).

DEFINITIONS

"claimant"—see WRA 2007 s.24(1).
"day of recovery"—see para.(4).
"limited capability for work"—see WRA 2007 s.1(4).
"medical treatment"—see reg.2(1).

GENERAL NOTE

8.43 This is the same as ESA Regs 2008 reg.25. See the next Part of this Volume.

Claimants receiving certain treatment

8.44 **22.**—(1) Subject to paragraph (2), a claimant receiving—

(a) regular weekly treatment by way of haemodialysis for chronic renal failure;
(b) treatment by way of plasmapheresis; or
(c) regular weekly treatment by way of total parenteral nutrition for gross impairment of enteric function,

is to be treated as having limited capability for work during any week in which that claimant is engaged in receiving that treatment or has a day of recovery from that treatment.

(2) A claimant who receives the treatment referred to in paragraph (1) is only to be treated as having limited capability for work from the first week of treatment in which the claimant undergoes no fewer than—

(a) two days of treatment;
(b) two days of recovery from any of the forms of treatment listed in paragraph (1) (a) to (c); or
(c) one day of treatment and one day of recovery from that treatment,

but the days of treatment or recovery from that treatment or both need not be consecutive.

(3) For the purpose of this regulation "day of recovery" means a day on which a claimant is recovering from any of the forms of treatment listed in paragraph (1) (a) to (c) and the Secretary of State is satisfied that the claimant should be treated as having limited capability for work on that day.

Definitions

"claimant"—see WRA 2007 s.24(1).
"day of recovery"—see para.(3).
"limited capability for work"—see WRA 2007 s.1(4).
"week"—see reg.2(1).

General Note

This replicates ESA Regs 2008 reg.26. See the next Part of this Volume. **8.45**

Claimant to be treated as having limited capability for work throughout a day

23. A claimant who, at the commencement of any day has, or after that develops, limited capability for work as determined in accordance with the limited capability for work assessment is to be treated as having limited capability for work on that day. **8.46**

Definitions

"claimant"—see WRA 2007 s.24(1).
"limited capability for work"—see WRA 2007 s.1(4).
"limited capability for work assessment"—see reg.2(1).

General Note

This is identical to ESA Regs 2008 reg.27. See the next Part of this Volume. **8.47**

Night workers

24.—(1) Where a claimant works for a continuous period which extends over midnight into the following day, that claimant is to be treated as having limited capability for work on the day on which the lesser part of that period falls if that claimant had limited capability for work for the remainder of that day. **8.48**

(2) Where, in relation to a period referred to in paragraph (1), the number of hours worked before and after midnight is equal—

(a) if the days in question fall at the beginning of a period of limited capability for work, the claimant is to be treated as having limited capability on the second day; and
(b) if the days in question fall at the end of a period of limited capability for work, the claimant is to be treated as having limited capability for work on the first day.

Definitions

"claimant"—see WRA 2007 s.24(1).
"limited capability for work"—see WRA 2007 s.1(4).
"period of limited capability for work"—see reg.2(1).

General Note

This replicates ESA Regs 2008 reg.28. See the next Part of this Volume. **8.49**

Exceptional circumstances

25.—(1) Aclaimant who does not have limited capability for work as determined in accordance with the limited capability for work assessment is **8.50**

to be treated as having limited capability for work if paragraph (2) applies to the claimant.

(2) Subject to paragraph (3), this paragraph applies if—

(a) the claimant is suffering from a life-threatening disease in relation to which—

(i) there is medical evidence that the disease is uncontrollable, or uncontrolled, by a recognised therapeutic procedure; and

(ii) in the case of a disease that is uncontrolled, there is a reasonable cause for it not to be controlled by a recognised therapeutic procedure; or

(b) the claimant suffers from some specific disease or bodily or mental disablement and, by reason of such disease or disablement, there would be a substantial risk to the mental or physical health of any person if the claimant were found not to have limited capability for work.

(3) Paragraph (2)(b) does not apply where the risk could be reduced by a significant amount by—

(a) reasonable adjustments being made in the claimant's workplace; or

(b) the claimant taking medication to manage the claimant's condition where such medication has been prescribed for the claimant by a registered medical practitioner treating the claimant.

(4) In this regulation "medical evidence" means—

(a) evidence from a health care professional approved by the Secretary of State; and

(b) evidence (if any) from any health care professional or a hospital or similar institution, or such part of such evidence as constitutes the most reliable evidence available in the circumstances.

DEFINITIONS

"claimant"—see WRA 2007 s.24(1).

"limited capability for work"—see WRA 2007 s.1(4).

"limited capability for work assessment"—see reg.2(1).

"medical evidence"—see para.(4).

GENERAL NOTE

8.51 This replicates ESA Regs 2008 reg.29. See the next Part of this Volume.

Conditions for treating a claimant as having limited capability for work until a determination about limited capability for work has been made

8.52 **26.**—(1) A claimant is, if the conditions set out in paragraph (2) are met, to be treated as having limited capability for work until such time as it is determined—

(a) whether or not the claimant has limited capability for work;

(b) whether or not the claimant is to be treated as having limited capability for work otherwise than in accordance with this regulation; or

(c) whether the claimant falls to be treated as not having limited capability for work in accordance with regulation 18 (failure to provide information in relation to limited capability for work) or 19 (failure to attend a medical examination to determine limited capability for work).

(2) The conditions are—

(a) that the claimant provides evidence of limited capability for work in accordance with the Medical Evidence Regulations; and

[1(b) in relation to the claimant's entitlement to any benefit, allowance or advantage which is dependent on the claimant having limited capability for work, it has not been determined—

(i) in the last determination preceding the date of claim for an employment and support allowance, that the claimant does not have limited capability for work; or

(ii) within the 6 months preceding the date of claim for an employment and support allowance, that the claimant is to be treated as not having limited capability for work under regulation 22 or 23,

unless paragraph (4) applies;]

[1(3) Paragraph 2(b) does not apply where a claimant has made and is pursuing an appeal against a relevant decision of the Secretary of State, and that appeal has not yet been determined by the First-tier Tribunal.]

(4) This paragraph applies where—

(a) the claimant is suffering from some specific disease or bodily or mental disablement from which the claimant was not suffering at the time of that determination;

(b) a disease or bodily or mental disablement from which the claimant was suffering at the time of that determination has significantly worsened; or

(c) in the case of a claimant who was treated as not having limited capability for work under regulation 18 (failure to provide information), the claimant has since provided the information requested under that regulation.

[1(5) In this regulation a "relevant decision" means—

(a) a decision that embodies the first determination by the Secretary of State that the claimant does not have limited capability for work; or

(b) a decision that embodies the first determination by the Secretary of State that the claimant does not have limited capability for work since a previous determination by the Secretary of State or appellate authority that the claimant does have limited capability for work.

(6) In this regulation, "appellate authority" means the First-tier Tribunal, the Upper Tribunal, the Court of Appeal, the Court of Session, or the Supreme Court.]

AMENDMENT

1. Employment and Support Allowance (Repeat Assessments and Pending Appeal Awards) (Amendment) Regulations 2015 (SI 2015/437) reg.4 (March 30, 2015).

DEFINITIONS

"appellate authority"—see para.(6).
"claimant"—see WRA 2007 s.24(1).
"limited capability for work"—see WRA 2007 s.1(4).
"Medical Evidence Regulations"—see reg.2(1).
"relevant decision"—see para.(5)

GENERAL NOTE

This corresponds to ESA Regs 2008 reg.30. See the next Part of this Volume. **8.53**

Certain claimants to be treated as not having limited capability for work

8.54 **27.**—(1) A claimant who is or has been a member of Her Majesty's forces is to be treated as not having limited capability for work on any day which is recorded by the Secretary of State as a day of sickness absence from duty.

(2) A claimant is to be treated as not having limited capability for work on any day on which the claimant attends a training course in respect of which the claimant is paid a training allowance or premium pursuant to arrangements made under section 2 of the Employment and Training Act 1973 or section 2(3) of the Enterprise and New Towns (Scotland) Act 1990.

(3) Paragraph (2) is not to apply—

(a) for the purposes of any claim to an employment and support allowance for a period commencing after the claimant ceased attending the training course in question; or

(b) where any training allowance or premium paid to the claimant is paid for the sole purpose of travelling or meal expenses incurred or to be incurred under the arrangements made under section 2 of the Employment and Training Act 1973 or section 2(3) of the Enterprise and New Towns (Scotland) Act 1990.

(4) A claimant is to be treated as not having limited capability for work where—

(a) it has previously been determined, within the six months preceding the date of claim for employment and support allowance, on the basis of an assessment under Part 5 of the Universal Credit Regulations 2013 that the claimant does not have limited capability for work; and

(b) it appears to the Secretary of State that—

(i) the determination was not based on ignorance of, or mistake as to, a material fact; and

(ii) there has been no relevant change of circumstances in relation to the claimant's physical or mental condition since the determination.

DEFINITIONS

"claimant"—see WRA 2007 s.24(1).
"limited capability for work"—see WRA 2007 s.1(4).

GENERAL NOTE

8.55 This is much the same as ESA Regs 2008 reg.32. See the next Part of this Volume.

Claimants to be treated as not having limited capability for work at the end of the period covered by medical evidence

8.56 **28.**—(1) Where the Secretary of State is satisfied that it is appropriate in the circumstances of the case, a claimant may be treated as not having limited capability for work if—

(a) the claimant has supplied medical evidence;

(b) the period for which medical evidence was supplied has ended;

(c) the Secretary of State has requested further medical evidence; and

(d) the claimant has not, before whichever is the later of either the end of the period of six weeks beginning with the date of the Secretary of

State's request or the end of six weeks beginning with the day after the end of the period for which medical evidence was supplied—

(i) supplied further medical evidence; or

(ii) otherwise made contact with the Secretary of State to indicate that they wish to have the question of limited capability for work determined.

(2) In this regulation "medical evidence" means evidence provided under regulation 2 or 5 of the Medical Evidence Regulations.

General Note

This is the same as ESA Regs 2008 reg.32A. See the next Part of this Volume. 8.57

Additional circumstances where claimants are to be treated as having limited capability for work

29. For the purposes of paragraph 4(1)(d)(ii) of Schedule 1 to the Act, a claimant is to be treated as having limited capability for work on any day in respect of which that claimant is entitled to statutory sick pay. 8.58

General Note

This is exactly the same as ESA Regs 2008 reg.33(1). See the next Part of this Volume. 8.59

PART 5

Limited Capability for Work-related Activity

Determination of limited capability for work-related activity

30.—(1) For the purposes of Part 1 of the Act, where, by reason of a claimant's physical or mental condition, at least one of the descriptors set out in Schedule 3 applies to the claimant, the claimant has limited capability for work-related activity and the limitation must be such that it is not reasonable to require that claimant to undertake such activity. 8.60

(2) A descriptor applies to a claimant if that descriptor applies to the claimant for the majority of the time or, as the case may be, on the majority of the occasions on which the claimant undertakes or attempts to undertake the activity described by that descriptor.

(3) In determining whether a descriptor applies to a claimant, the claimant is to be assessed as if—

(a) the claimant were fitted with or wearing any prosthesis with which the claimant is normally fitted or normally wears; or, as the case may be

(b) wearing or using any aid or appliance which is normally, or could reasonably be expected to be, worn or used.

(4) Where a determination has been made about whether a claimant—

(a) has limited capability for work-related activity;

(b) is to be treated as having limited capability for work-related activity; or

(c) is to be treated as not having limited capability for work-related activity,

the Secretary of State may, if paragraph (5) applies, determine afresh whether the claimant has or is to be treated as having limited capability for work-related activity.

(5) This paragraph applies where—

(a) the Secretary of State wishes to determine whether there has been a relevant change of circumstances in relation to the claimant's physical or mental condition;

(b) the Secretary of State wishes to determine whether the previous determination about limited capability for work-related activity or about treating the claimant as having or as not having limited capability for work-related activity, was made in ignorance of, or was based on a mistake as to, some material fact; or

(c) at least three months have passed since the date of the previous determination about limited capability for work-related activity or about treating the claimant as having or as not having limited capability for work-related activity.

(6) In assessing the extent of a claimant's capability to perform any activity listed in Schedule 3, it is a condition that the claimant's incapability to perform the activity arises—

(a) in respect of descriptors 1 to 8, 15(a), 15(b), 16(a)and 16(b)—

(i) from a specific bodily disease or disablement; or

(ii) as a direct result of treatment provided by a registered medical practitioner for a specific physical disease or disablement; or

(b) in respect of descriptors 9 to 14, 15(c), 15(d), 16(c)and 16(d)—

(i) from a specific mental illness or disablement; or

(ii) as a direct result of treatment provided by a registered medical practitioner for a specific mental illness or disablement.

DEFINITIONS

"the Act"—see reg.2(1).
"claimant"—see WRA 2007 s.24(1).
"descriptor"—see reg.2(1).
"limited capability for work-related activity"—see WRA 2007 s.2(5).
"work-related activity"—see WRA 2007 ss.24(1), 13(7).

GENERAL NOTE

8.61 This corresponds to ESA Regs 2008 reg.34. For detailed commentary on regs 15–36 of, and Sch.2–3 to, the ESA Regulations 2013 see the annotations to the equivalent provisions in regs 19–39 of, and Sch.2–3 to, the ESA Regulations 2008 in the next Part of this Volume.

Certain claimants to be treated as having, or not having, limited capability for work-related activity

8.62 **31.**—(1) A claimant is to be treated as having limited capability for work-related activity if—

(a) the claimant is terminally ill;

(b) the claimant is—

(i) receiving treatment for cancer by way of chemotherapy or radiotherapy;

(ii) likely to receive such treatment within six months after the date of the determination of capability for work-related activity; or
(iii) recovering from such treatment,

and the Secretary of State is satisfied that the claimant should be treated as having limited capability for work-related activity;

(c) in the case of a woman, she is pregnant and there is a serious risk of damage to her health or to the health of her unborn child if she does not refrain from work-related activity; or
(d) the claimant is entitled to universal credit and it has previously been determined that the claimant has limited capability for work and work-related activity on the basis of an assessment under Part 5 of the Universal Credit Regulations 2013.

(2) A claimant who does not have limited capability for work-related activity as determined in accordance with regulation 30(1) is to be treated as having limited capability for work-related activity if—

(a) the claimant suffers from some specific disease or bodily or mental disablement; and
(b) by reason of such disease or disablement, there would be a substantial risk to the mental or physical health of any person if the claimant were found not to have limited capability for work-related activity.

(3) A claimant is to be treated as not having limited capability for work-related activity where—

(a) it has previously been determined, within the six months preceding the date of claim for employment and support allowance, on the basis of an assessment under Part 5 of the Universal Credit Regulations 2013 that the claimant does not have limited capability for work and work-related activity; and
(b) it appears to the Secretary of State that—
  (i) the determination was not based on ignorance of, or mistake as to, a material fact; and
  (ii) there has been no relevant change of circumstances in relation to the claimant's physical or mental condition.

Definitions

"claimant"—see WRA 2007 s.24(1).
"limited capability for work-related activity"—see WRA 2007 s.2(5).
"terminally ill"—see reg.2(1).
"work-related activity"—see WRA 2007 ss.24(1), 13(7).

General Note

This is the same as ESA Regs 2008 reg.35. See the next Part of this Volume. 8.63

Relevant linked cases – limited capability for work-related activity

32. A claimant is to be treated as having limited capability for work-related activity where— 8.64

(a) they fall within case 1, as defined in regulation 7(3)(a); and
(b) in respect of the earlier period of limited capability for work referred to in regulation 7(3)(a)(i), they had been entitled to a support component under section 2(2) of the Act.

General Note

8.65 This corresponds to ESA Regs 2008 reg.35A. See the next Part of this Volume.

Information required for determining capability for work-related activity

8.66 **33.**—(1) Subject to paragraph (2), the information or evidence required to determine whether a claimant has limited capability for work-related activity is—

(a) any information relating to the descriptors set out in Schedule 3 as may be requested in the form of a questionnaire; and

(b) any such additional information as may be requested.

(2) Where the Secretary of State is satisfied that there is sufficient information to determine whether a claimant has limited capability for work-related activity without the information specified in paragraph (1)(a), that information must not be required for the purposes of making the determination.

Defintions

"claimant"—see WRA 2007 s.24(1).
"limited capability for work-related activity"—see WRA 2007 s.2(5).
"work-related activity"—see WRA 2007 ss.24(1), 13(7).

General Note

8.67 This is the same as ESA Regs 2008 reg.36. See the next Part of this Volume.

Failure to provide information in relation to work-related activity

8.68 **34.**—(1) Where a claimant fails without good cause to comply with the request referred to in regulation 33(1)(a), the claimant is, subject to paragraph (2), to be treated as not having limited capability for work-related activity.

(2) Paragraph (1) does not apply unless—

(a) the claimant was sent a further request at least three weeks after the date of the first request; and

(b) at least one week has passed since the further request was sent.

Definitions

"claimant"—see WRA 2007 s.24(1).
"limited capability for work-related activity"—see WRA 2007 s.2(5).
"week"—see reg.2(1).
"work-related activity"—see WRA 2007 ss.24(1), 13(7).

General Note

8.69 This corresponds to ESA Regs 2008 reg.37. See the next Part of this Volume.

Claimant may be called for a medical examination to determine whether the claimant has limited capability for work-related activity

8.70 **35.**—(1) Where it falls to be determined whether a claimant has limited capability for work-related activity, that claimant may be called by or on behalf of a health care professional approved by the Secretary of State to attend for a medical examination [[1]in person, by telephone or by video].

(2) Subject to paragraph (3), where a claimant fails without good cause to attend for or to submit to an examination mentioned in paragraph (1), the claimant is to be treated as not having limited capability for work-related activity.

(3) Paragraph (2) does not apply unless—

(a) written notice of the date, time and place for the examination was sent to the claimant at least seven days in advance; or

(b) the claimant agreed to accept a shorter period of notice whether given in writing or otherwise.

AMENDMENT

1. Social Security (Claims and Payments, Employment and Support Allowance, Personal Independence Payment and Universal Credit) (Telephone and Video Assessment) (Amendment) Regulations 2021 reg.6(3) (March 25, 2021).

DEFINITIONS

"claimant"—see WRA 2007 s.24(1).
"health care professional"—see reg.2(1).
"limited capability for work-related activity"—see WRA 2007 s.2(5).
"work-related activity"—see WRA 2007 ss.24(1), 13(7).

GENERAL NOTE

This is the same as ESA Regs 2008 reg.38. See the next Part of this Volume. 8.71

Matters to be taken into account in determining good cause in relation to regulations 34 or 35

36. The matters to be taken into account in determining whether a claimant has good cause under regulation 34 (failure to provide information in relation to work-related activity) or 35 (failure to attend a medical examination to determine limited capability for work-related activity) include— 8.72

(a) whether the claimant was outside Great Britain at the relevant time;

(b) the claimant's state of health at the relevant time; and

(c) the nature of any disability the claimant has.

DEFINITION

"claimant"—see WRA 2007 s.24(1).

GENERAL NOTE

This corresponds to ESA Regs 2008 reg.39. See the next Part of this Volume. 8.73

PART 6

Effect of work on entitlement to an Employment and Support Allowance

A claimant who works to be treated as not entitled to an employment and support allowance

8.74 **37.**—(1) Subject to the following paragraphs, a claimant is to be treated as not entitled to an employment and support allowance in any week in which that claimant does work.

(2) Paragraph (1) does not apply to—

(a) work as a councillor;

(b) duties undertaken on either one full day or two half-days a week as a member of the First-tier Tribunal where the member is eligible for appointment to be such a member in accordance with article 2(3) of the Qualifications for Appointment of Members to the First-tier Tribunal and Upper Tribunal Order 2008;

(c) domestic tasks carried out in the claimant's own home or the care of a relative;

(d) duties undertaken in caring for another person who is accommodated with the claimant by virtue of arrangements made under any of the provisions referred to in paragraph (7) or where the claimant is in receipt of any payment specified in that paragraph;

(e) any activity the claimant undertakes during an emergency to protect another person or to prevent serious damage to property or livestock; or

(f) any of the categories of work set out in regulation 39(1) (exempt work).

(3) This regulation is subject to regulation 40 (effect of work on entitlement to an employment and support allowance where claimant is receiving certain treatment).

(4) A claimant who does work to which this regulation applies in a week which is—

(a) the week in which the claimant first becomes entitled to a benefit, allowance or advantage on account of the claimant's limited capability for work in any period; or

(b) the last week in any period in which the claimant has limited capability for work or is treated as having limited capability for work, is to be treated as not entitled to an employment and support allowance by virtue of paragraph (1) only on the actual day or days in that week on which the claimant does that work.

(5) Regulation 86 (linking rules) does not apply for the purposes of calculating the beginning or end of any period of limited capability for work under paragraph (4).

(6) The day or days in a week on which a night worker works, for the purposes of paragraph (4), are to be calculated by reference to regulation 24 (night workers).

(7) The payments and provisions mentioned in paragraph (2)(d) are—

(a) any payment made to the claimant with whom a person is accommodated by virtue of arrangements made—

(i) by a local authority under section 22C(2), (3), (5) or (6)(a) or (b) of the Children Act 1989 (provision of accommodation and maintenance for a child whom the local authority is looking after);

(ii) by a local authority under section 26 [2 or 26A] of the Children (Scotland) Act 1995 (manner of provision of accommodation to child looked after by local authority [2 and duty to provide continuing care]);

(iii) by a local authority under regulations 33 or 51 of the Looked After Children (Scotland) Regulations 2009 (fostering and kinship care allowances and fostering allowances); or

(iv) by a voluntary organisation under section 59(1)(a) of the 1989 Act (provision of accommodation by voluntary organisations);

[2 (aa) any payment made to the claimant under section 73(1)(b) of the Children and Young People (Scotland) Act 2014 (kinship care assistance);]

(b) any payment made to the claimant or the claimant's partner for a person ("the person concerned"), who is not normally a member of the claimant's household but is temporarily in the claimant's care, by—

(i) [4 NHS England;]

(ii) a local authority but excluding payments of housing benefit made in respect of the person concerned;

(iii) a voluntary organisation;

(iv) the person concerned pursuant to section 26(3A) of the National Assistance Act 1948;

[3(v) an integrated care board established under Chapter A3 of Part 2 of the National Health Service Act 2006;]

(vi) a Local Health Board established by an order made under section 11 of the Health Service (Wales) Act. [1; or

(vii) the person concerned where the payment is for the provision of accommodation in respect of the meeting of that person's needs under section 18 or 19 of the Care Act 2014 (duty and power to meet needs for care and support).]

(8) In this regulation—

"week" means a week in respect of which a claimant is entitled to an employment and support allowance;

"work" means any work which a claimant does, whether or not that claimant undertakes it in expectation of payment;

"work as a councillor" includes any work which a claimant undertakes as a member of any of the bodies referred to in section 177(1) of the Local Government Act 1972 or section 49(1) or (1A) of the Local Government (Scotland) Act 1973(a), of which the claimant is a member by reason of being a councillor.

AMENDMENTS

1. Care Act 2014 (Consequential Amendments) (Secondary Legislation) Order 2015 (SI 2015/643) art.2, Sch para.42 (April 1, 2015).

2. Social Security and Child Support (Care Payments and Tenant Incentive Scheme) (Amendment) Regulations 2017 (SI 2017/995), regs 9(2) and 15(2) (November 7, 2017).

3. Health and Care Act 2022 (Consequential and Related Amendments and Transitional Provisions) Regulations 2022 (SI 2922/634) reg.66 (July 1,2022).

4. Health and Care Act 2022 (Further Consequential Amendments) (No.2) Regulations 2023 (SI 2023/1071) Sch. para.1 (November 6, 2023).

DEFINITIONS

"claimant"—see WRA 2007 s.24(1).
"entitled"—see WRA 2007 s.24(1).
"relative"—see reg.2(1).
"week"—see para.(8) and reg.2(1).
"work"—see para.(8).
"work as a councillor"—see para.(8).

GENERAL NOTE

8.75 This regulation, which corresponds to ESA Regs 2008 reg.45, needs to be read in conjunction with regs 38–40.

To find in any incapacity regime a general rule that working (whether or not for payment) negatives incapacity for work is unsurprising since, in principle, it is fairly obviously a strong indication of an ability to work. This regulation contains just such a rule, precluding entitlement to ESA in any week in which a claimant does work. Moreover, in that period of non-entitlement, he or she will be treated as not having limited capability for work (reg.38). That can happen in that work done in a week when someone, entitled to new style ESA, is receiving or recovering from certain regular treatments, does not negative title to ESA (regs 40 (to which para.(3) makes this regulation subject) and 38(2)). But like the former incapacity benefit regime, the general preclusive rule is modified to permit engagement in a range of work without loss of benefit (see para.(1) and "subject to the following paragraphs", one of which (para.(2)(f)) links this regulation to reg.39 and the concept of "exempt work"). These modifications recognize that work can assist recovery or help the claimant into thinking about work and a possibility to return to work, or merely not wanting to exclude the sick and disabled from participation in civic office or a range of voluntary or charitable work.

Although, unlike its IB comparator (Incapacity for Work Regs, reg.16) the point is no longer explicit, it is submitted that the regulation can operate despite the fact that, applying the limited capability for work assessment, the person in fact has limited capability for work, or is someone treated as having such limited capability by virtue of other regs.

Paragraph (1) sets out the general preclusive rule: a person must be treated as capable of work on each day of any week during which he does work. "Work" for the purposes of the regulation is defined in para.(8) as any work done whether or not undertaken in expectation of payment. "Week" is a period of seven days beginning with Sunday (para.(8)).

Note, however, that this ostensibly very wide general preclusive rule is subject to the partial relief afforded by para.(4) and by reg.40 (see para.(3)) and the complete relief afforded by para.(2). Execution of some de minimis tasks can also be ignored as not constituting "work". Discussion is divided accordingly.

Partial relief

8.76 *Paras (4), (5)*: Together these paragraphs afford some relief from the general preclusive rule set out in para.(1). Paragraph (4) contains an obviously necessary one, it covers the worker who initially falls sick part way through his working week and/or the period in which he is incapable of work finishes part way through a week in the course of which he returns to work. Here, the preclusive effect of the regulation is confined to ruling out only the days actually worked in that week or those weeks.

Note that the linking rules in reg.86 do not apply for determining when, for the purposes of this relieving rule, a period of limited capability for work begins and ends (para.(5)). In effect, each "spell" of limited capability for work" is treated separately, thus helping those whose limited capability for work is intermittent and removing a disincentive to trying work for a while.

Para.(3): This regulation is "subject to regulation 40". That provides that those treated under reg.22 as having limited capability for work on days when receiving or recovering from certain regular treatments (e.g. chemotherapy), who work on other days of the week in which they receive or are recovering from such treatment such treatment, will not have their entitlement to new style ESA affected by doing that work.

Complete relief

Para.(2) prevents the general preclusive rule in para.(1) applying to: **8.77**

(i) any of the categories of work in reg.39(1) (para.(2)(f));

(ii) work as a councillor (see para.(8) for its breadth) (para.(2)(a);

The scheme, as before, seeks to encourage sick and disabled people to participate in civic office by enabling them to receive CESA reduced or abated by the amount by which their councillor's allowance applicable to that week exceeds a specified amount (reg.69).

(iii) care of a relative or domestic tasks carried out in his own home (para.(2)(c);

(iv) work as a foster parent or other specified carer in respect of someone accommodated in one's home or where the claimant is in receipt of any payment specified in para.(7) (para.(2)(d));

(v) limited duties (one full day or two half days per week) as a First-tier Tribunal member with a disability qualification (para.(2)(b)) (i.e. someone other than a registered medical practitioner, who is experienced in dealing with the physical or mental needs of disabled persons because they work with disabled persons in a professional or voluntary capacity, or are themselves disabled (see art.2(3) of the Qualifications for Appointment of Members to the First-tier Tribunal and Upper Tribunal Order 2008 (SI 2008/2692));

(vi) any activity undertaken during an emergency solely to protect another person or to prevent serious damage to property or livestock (para.(2)(e)).

This exemption is essential to protect the benefit position of the rescuer; of the good neighbour who looks after his/her neighbour's children when she is rushed to hospital; or of the person who helps round up livestock which have strayed into a busy road; or of the good neighbour who helps fight a fire until the emergency services arrive; or the husband on ESA who is compelled to drive to rush his pregnant wife in labour to hospital because the ambulance has not arrived. These can be but speculative examples.

"Emergency" is not defined. However, note it is not qualified by terms such as "severe" or "serious" or "great", so it ought not to be construed too narrowly. By way of comparison, in the industrial injuries context, case law dealing with "in the course of employment" has brought within that phrase persons responding to emergency. There "emergency" was construed broadly to encompass a wide range of unexpected occurrences (see commentary to SSCBA 1992, s.100). Arguably a broad approach ought to be taken, similarly, to the notion of "any activity to protect another person".

Applying the de minimis principle to ignore trivial or negligible amounts of work

It is submitted that this long-standing principle, which has applied to previous incapacity for work regimes, is equally applicable to ESA and that previous case law applies here. *CIB/5298/1997* supports the view (then found in AOG, paras 18782 and 18783) that the *de minimis* principle applies to enable trivial or negligible amounts of work to be ignored (paras 5–12), recognising as a practical proposition something seen as a theoretical one in *CIB/14656/96*. Deputy Commissioner Wikeley's decision in *CIB/6777/1999* contains a thorough review of the authorities on this matter. He notes that the rule here can apply irrespective of whether the work might in any event be treated as exempt under Incapacity for Work Regs reg.17 (and thus ESA Regs 2013 regs 37, 39). Whether work done is trivial or negligible is a matter of fact and degree. Like Commissioner Williams in *CIB/5298/1997*, who had approved guidance in the AOG, the Deputy Commissioner supported as illustrative but not exhaustive, relevant factors, those set out in DMG para.13867: **8.78** "whether work on a day is negligible depends on its proportion to the normal working hours, the type of work and the effort required in relation to normal working duties."

Stressing the role of incapacity benefit as "an earnings replacement . . . benefit for those with the appropriate contributions record who cannot work in the labour market" he (rightly in the opinion of this commentator) disagreed with Commissioner Williams in *CIB/5298/1997* who took the view that the amount of remuneration earned was always wholly irrelevant since para.(8) states that work is "work" whether or not undertaken in expectation of payment. That means, of course, that the lack of remuneration or of the expectation of it is irrelevant. The key question is really what the tasks performed tell one about the person's capacity for work. But, in contrast to the irrelevance of lack of remuneration, this author, like the Deputy Commissioner, believes that the amount of remuneration received for a relatively small degree of work-like activity, when contrasted with the weekly rate of incapacity benefit (and now ESA), surely is a relevant factor in deciding whether work done should be disregarded as trivial or negligible—it brings into play the "anti-abuse" element of the rules here, which arguably takes one into the realm of when the public (including other recipients of benefit) might view as inappropriate receipt of incapacity benefit or ESA by someone with what looks like a source of income from "employment", albeit only in that one week. Is that not one purpose behind the earnings limits on exempt work in Incapacity for Work Regs, reg.17 (ESA Regs 2013 reg.39)? However, that Incapacity for Work Regs reg.16 (ESA Regs reg.37) stipulates particular worthy tasks as ones to be disregarded seems to cast doubt on the Deputy Commissioner's view that the identity of the person for whom the task is performed may be a material factor in applying the de minimis rule.

CIB/3507/2002 affords another illustration of work being disregarded as *de minimis*. The work in question was described by the Commissioner as follows:

"On 28th November 2001, DW Windows wrote a letter in which they said: 'In July of this year we approached [the claimant] to see if he would like to do a couple of hours each week at [DW Windows] doing various light duties. i.e. Making coffees, emptying bins etc and occasionally driving a vehicle to transport [Mr S. E.] the Manager who holds no driving license. There is no dispute about what DW Windows say. Nor is there any dispute about the fact that the claimant was paid £3.85 per hour and that he worked between one and three hours per week. A schedule of his weekly hours and earnings between the beginning of July and the first week of October 2001 has been produced by DW Windows. He never worked for more than three hours and consequently never earned more than £11.55, in any one week. The period covered is one of 14 weeks. During three of those weeks he worked for 1 hour only. He worked for two hours for five of those weeks and for three hours for the remaining six weeks. The average is a little above two hours per week"' (paras 6, 7).

In marked contrast, in *CIB/4684/2003*, Commissioner Jacobs found the work done by the claimant was not so minimal that it could be disregarded. He did so, however, for a different reason to the tribunal which had so found on the basis that the claimant's contribution to the earnings from the post office was significant when compared to his wife's. Instead Commissioner Jacobs approached the matter thus:

"For 8 hours a week, spread over 2 mornings, the claimant manned the post office. He was not there merely to summon his wife if a customer arrived. He was there to serve any customer who wanted any of the services offered by the office. Covering the office in those circumstances amounted to work, even if there were no customers at all. He was in exactly the same position as a stallholder on a market who had no customers. Surely that stallholder would be working, even if no one bought from, or even visited, the stall? How the claimant spent his time when he was not actually serving customers is irrelevant. It would be just as irrelevant whether a market stallholder at a market spent the time trying to entice customers to the stall or merely sat reading a book" (paras 10, 11).

Claimants who are treated as not entitled to any allowance at all by reason of regulation 37(1) are to be treated as not having limited capability for work

38.—(1) Where a claimant is treated as not entitled to an employment and support allowance by reason of regulation 37(1), the claimant is to be treated as not having limited capability for work. 8.79

(2) Paragraph (1) applies even if—

(a) it has been determined that the claimant has or is to be treated as having, under any of regulations 16 (certain claimants to be treated as having limited capability for work), 21 (hospital in-patients), 22 (claimants undergoing certain treatment) and 25 (exceptional circumstances), limited capability for work; or

(b) the claimant meets the conditions set out in regulation 26(2) for being treated as having limited capability for work until a determination is made in accordance with the limited capability for work assessment.

General Note

Regulation 37(1) precludes entitlement to ESA in any week in which a claimant does work. In the light of that, this regulation provides, moreover, that in that period of non-entitlement, he or she will be treated as not having limited capability for work (para.(1)). Such a situation can arise where reg.40 applies in that work done in a week when someone, entitled to ESA, is receiving or recovering from certain regular treatments, does not negative title to ESA. Paragraph (2) makes clear that the regulation can operate despite the fact that, applying the limited capability for work assessment, the person in fact has limited capability for work incapable of work, or is someone treated as having such limited capability by virtue of certain other regs: 16 (certain claimants to be treated as having limited capability for work); 21 (hospital in-patients); 22 (claimants undergoing certain regular treatment); or 25 (exceptional circumstances). This suggests that this rule on treating the person as not having limited capability for work will not operate in other cases where regs treat someone (whatever the reality) as having limited capability for work, e.g. reg 26 (treated as having limited capability pending assessment). In those cases there will be no entitlement to ESA where the person is caught by reg.37, but the days might still rank as ones of limited capability for work. 8.80

Exempt work

39.—(1) The categories of work referred to in regulation 37(2)(f) are— 8.81

(a) work for which the total earnings in any week does not exceed £20;

(b) work for which the total earnings in any week does not exceed 16 multiplied by the National Minimum Wage, subject to paragraph (4), and which—

(i) is part of the claimant's treatment programme and is done under medical supervision while the claimant is an in-patient, or is regularly attending as an out-patient, of a hospital or similar institution; or

(ii) is supervised by a person employed by a public or local authority or by a voluntary organisation or community interest company engaged in the provision or procurement of work for persons who have disabilities;

(c) work which is done for less than 16 hours a week, for which total earnings in any week does not exceed 16 multiplied by the National Minimum Wage, subject to paragraph (4); [1. . .]

(d) work done in the course of receiving assistance in pursuing self-employed earner's employment whilst participating in a programme provided, or in other arrangements made, under section 2 of the Employment and Training Act 1973 (functions of the Secretary of State) or section 2 of the Enterprise and New Towns (Scotland) Act 1990 (functions in relation to training for employment etc);

(e) work done where the claimant receives no payment of earnings and where the claimant is—

(i) engaged by a charity or voluntary organisation; or

(ii) a volunteer,

and where the Secretary of State is satisfied in either of those cases that it is reasonable for the claimant to do the work free of charge;

(f) work done in the course of participating in a work placement approved in writing by the Secretary of State before the placement starts.

(2) The number of hours for which a claimant is engaged in work is to be determined—

(a) where no recognisable cycle has been established in respect of a claimant's work, by reference to the number of hours or, where those hours are likely to fluctuate, the average of the hours, which the claimant is expected to work in a week;

(b) where the number of hours for which the claimant is engaged fluctuate, by reference to the average of hours worked over—

(i) if there is a recognisable cycle of work, the period of one complete cycle (including, where the cycle involves periods in which the claimant does no work, those periods but disregarding any other absences);

(ii) in any other case, the period of five weeks immediately before the date of claim or the date on which a superseding decision is made under section 10 of the Social Security Act 1998 (decisions superseding earlier decisions), or such other length of time as may, in the particular case, enable the claimant's average hours of work to be determined more accurately.

(3) For the purposes of determining the number of hours for which a claimant is engaged in work, that number is to include any time allowed to that claimant by the claimant's employer for a meal or for refreshment, but only where that claimant is, or expects to be, paid earnings in respect of that time.

(4) Where the amount determined by the calculation in paragraph (1)(b)or (c) would, but for this paragraph, include an amount of—

(a) less than 50p, that amount is to be rounded up to the nearest 50p; or

(b) less than £1 but more than 50p, that amount is to be rounded up to the nearest £1.

(5) Part 10 applies for the purposes of calculating any income which consists of earnings under this regulation.

(6) In this regulation—

[1...]

"volunteer" means a person who is engaged in voluntary work otherwise than for a relative, where the only payment received or due to be paid to the person by virtue of being so engaged is in respect of any expenses reasonably incurred by the person in connection with that work;

[1...]

"work placement" means practical work experience with an employer, which is neither paid nor undertaken in expectation of payment.

(7) [1...]

AMENDMENTS

1. Employment and Support Allowance (Exempt Work & Hardship Amounts) (Amendment) Regulations 2017 (SI 2017/205) reg.4 (April 3, 2017).

DEFINITIONS

"the Act"—see reg.2(1).
"claimant"—see WRA 2007 s.24(1).
"Contributions and Benefits Act"—see WRA 2007 s.65.
"employment"—see reg.2(1).
"relevant benefit"—see para.(6).
"self-employed earner"—see reg.2(1).
"voluntary organisation"—see reg.2(1).
"volunteer"—see para.(6).
"week"—see reg.2(1).
"work period"—see para.(6).
"work placement"—see para.(6).

GENERAL NOTE

This regulation needs to be read in conjunction with reg.37(1) which precludes entitlement to ESA in any week in which a claimant does work. "Work" for the purposes of that regulation is defined in reg.37(8) as any work done whether or not undertaken in expectation of payment. "Week" is a period of seven days beginning with Sunday (reg.37(8)). This regulation in contrast defines a variety of work which ranking as "exempt work" does not pursuant to reg.37(2)(f) preclude entitlement to ESA under the general preclusive rule in reg.37(1). The regulation is part of the welfare to work strategy, of encouraging people to try out work, the better to enable a return to work. 8.82

The current categories of exempt work

Some embody an earnings limit, others both an earnings and hours limit. The matters of determining the hours of engagement and assessing earnings are examined further below, after considering the seven categories of exempt work: 8.83

(1) *Work for which the earnings in any week do not exceed £20 (para.(2))*: there is no hours limit as such here, but it is anticipated that in practice the effect of the minimum wage laws will mean that DWP staff will expect a claimant in this category to be working less than 5 hours a week. Its prime role is the encouragement of social contact.

(2) *Unpaid work for a charity or voluntary organization (para.(1)(e))*: Work done where the claimant is engaged by a charity or voluntary organization is exempt where he receives no payment of earnings and the Secretary of State is satisfied that it is reasonable for him to provide the service free of charge. "Charity" is not defined in the ESA Regs, so must bear the meaning it does in charity law. "Voluntary organization" means a body, other than a public or local authority, the activities of which are carried on otherwise than for profit (reg.2(1)).

(3) *Work done as a volunteer (paras (1)(e), (6))*: Voluntary work other than that covered by para.(1)(e) is thus also protected where the claimant receives no payment of earnings and the Secretary of State is satisfied that it is reasonable for him to provide the service free of charge. "Volunteer" is defined in para.(6) to embrace a person who is engaged in voluntary work otherwise than for a relative, where the only payment received by him or due to be paid to him by virtue of being so engaged is in respect of any expenses reasonably incurred by him in connection with that work. "Relative" is widely defined: it means a close relative, grand-parent, grand-child, uncle, aunt, nephew or niece (reg.2(1)). "Close relative" covers a parent, parent-in-law, son, son-in-law, daughter, daughter-in-law, step-parent, step-son, step-daughter, brother, sister, or the spouse of any of these persons, or if that person is one of an unmarried couple, the other member of that couple (reg.2(1)). There are no hours or earnings limits.

(4) *Supervised work (para (1)(b))*: there are two categories here. First, work done with the supervision of bodies providing or finding work for disabled people (para. (1)(b)(ii)). The bodies in question are a public or local authority or a voluntary organisation (that is, a body, other than a public or local authority, whose activities are carried on otherwise than for profit (reg.2(1)). The second category covers work while a patient of a hospital or similar institution under medical supervision as part of a treatment programme. The patient must be an in-patient or a regularly attending out-patient (para.(1)(b)(i)). Whichever of the two categories, the earnings from the work must not exceed 16 x National Minimum Wage a week (see further para.(4)). On "hospital or similar institution", some guidance is given in DMG, paras 18031–18033, 24018–24023. But this is not binding on tribunals or courts.

(5) *Work done in the course of receiving assistance in pursuing self-employed earner's employment whilst participating in certain programmes or arrangements (para.(1)(d))*: this makes it easier for people receiving ESA to attempt self-employment. Test Trading allows people to try out 'self-employment' for a period of up to 26 weeks. Its introduction prevents participants being regarded as in work with the possibility of a loss of benefit should earnings exceed the permitted work limits.

(6) *Permitted work for up to 16 hours a week where earnings do not exceed national minimum wage para. (1)(c)*: The work must be done for less than 16 hours a week (see further below) and the earnings in any week must not exceed 16 x National Minimum Wage (and note the rounding rule in para. (4)). The previous 52-week restriction on undertaking permitted work for ESA claimants in the work-related activity group and the assessment phase of the benefit was abolished with effect from April 3, 2017, with a view to improving work incentives. As a result, ESA claimants are now able to continue to undertake permitted work while retaining all their benefit for an indefinite period.

(7) *Approved, unpaid work placements (paras (1)(f), (6))*: "Work placement" is practical work experience with an employer, which is neither paid nor taken on in expectation of payment (para.(6)). The work placement must have been approved by the Secretary of State in writing prior to its commencement.

In determining the number of hours of engagement in work (paras (2), (3)) an averaging approach applies, varying according to whether there is or is not a recognizable cycle and whether the claimant's hours fluctuate (para.(2)). With regard to para.(2) (averaging of hours) and the non-applicability of the Computation of Earnings Regulations for the purpose of averaging earnings, see also *LB v Secretary of State for Work and Pensions (ESA)* [2019] UKUT 153 (AAC). The hours of engagement include time the employer allows for meals or refreshment where the claimant is, or expects to be, paid earnings in respect of that time (para.(3)).

The earnings limit—Computation of Earnings Regs not applicable here

8.84 Unlike the position as it used to be with IB, ESA is not within the sphere of the SSCBA 1992 and so the Computation of Earnings Regs cannot apply. Calculation of earnings is to be done under the rules in the ESA Regs.

Effect of work on entitlement to an employment and support allowance where claimant is receiving certain treatment

40. Where a claimant who is entitled to an employment and support allowance and is treated as having limited capability for work by virtue of regulation 22 works on any day during a week when the claimant is receiving certain treatment mentioned in regulation 22 or recovering from that treatment, that work is to have no effect on the claimant's entitlement to the employment and support allowance. 8.85

DEFINITIONS

"claimant"—see WRA 2007 s.24(1).
"entitled"—see WRA 2007 s.24(1).
"limited capability for work"—see WRA 2007 s.24(1).
"week"—see reg.2(1), WRA 2007 s.24(1).

GENERAL NOTE

This regulation (affording an exception to the preclusive rule on work in reg.37(1)) provides that those treated under reg.22 as having limited capability for work on days when receiving or recovering from certain regular treatments (e.g. chemotherapy), who work on other days of the week in which they receive or are recovering from such treatment such treatment, will not have their entitlement to ESA affected by doing that work. 8.86

PART 7

Claimant responsibilities

Interpretation

41.—(1) In this Part— 8.87
"responsible carer", in relation to a child, means—
(a) a person who is the only person responsible for the child; or
(b) a person who is a member of a couple where—
(i) both members of the couple are responsible for the child; and
(ii) the person has been nominated by the couple jointly as responsible for the child;
"responsible foster parent", in relation to a child, means—
(a) a person who is the only foster parent in relation to the child; or
(b) a person who is a member of a couple where—
(i) both members of the couple are foster parents in relation to the child; and
(ii) the person has been nominated by the couple jointly as the responsible foster parent.

(2) The nomination of a responsible carer or responsible foster parent for the purposes of paragraph (1) may be changed—
(a) once in a 12 month period, beginning with the date of the previous nomination; or
(b) on any occasion where the Secretary of State considers that there has been a change of circumstances which is relevant to the nomination.

(3) Only one person may be nominated as a responsible carer or a responsible foster parent.

(4) The nomination applies to all of the children for whom the claimant is responsible.

DEFINITIONS

"child"—see reg.2(1).
"claimant" see WRA 2007 s.24(1).
"couple"—see reg.2(1).
"responsible carer"—see para.(1).
"responsible foster parent"—see para.(1).

GENERAL NOTE

8.88 Compare Universal Credit Regs 2013 regs 85, 86.

Application of regulations where there is dual entitlement

8.89 **42.**—(1) This regulation applies where a person is entitled to universal credit and an employment and support allowance.

(2) The work-related requirements under sections 11B to 11I of the Act and regulations 46 to 49 of these Regulations do not apply to such a person.

(3) Reductions relating to the award of an employment and support allowance under section 11J of the Act and regulations 50 to 60 of these Regulations do not apply to such a person.

GENERAL NOTE

8.90 This provides that where a person is entitled to UC and ESA, the work-related requirements and sanctions regime applicable to ESA does not apply. The person will instead be subject to the comparable UC regime. See Universal Credit Regs 2013, regs.83–104.

Sanction ceases to apply to employment and support allowance

8.91 **43.**—(1) This regulation applies where—

(a) a person is entitled to an employment and support allowance;
(b) there is a reduction relating to the award of the employment and support allowance under section 11J of the Act;
(c) the person becomes entitled to universal credit; and
(d) the person remains entitled to an employment and support allowance.

(2) Any reduction relating to the award of the employment and support allowance is to cease being applied to the award of the employment and support allowance.

GENERAL NOTE

Where an ESA reduction in place and the person then becomes entitled to UC as well as ESA, the ESA reduction ceases to apply. The person will instead be dealt with under the UC regime. See Universal Credit Regs 2013, regs.84–114.

Claimant commitment—date and method of acceptance

8.92 **44.**—(1) For the purposes of section 1(3)(aa) of the Act, a claimant who has accepted a claimant commitment within such period after making a claim for an employment and support allowance as the Secretary of State specifies is to be treated as having accepted that claimant commitment on the first day of the period in respect of which the claim is made.

(2) In a case where an award of an employment and support allowance may be made without a claim, a claimant who accepts a claimant commitment within such period as the Secretary of State specifies is to be treated as having accepted a claimant commitment on the day that would be the first day of the first benefit week in relation to the award.

(3) The Secretary of State may extend the period within which a claimant is required to accept a claimant commitment or an updated claimant commitment where the claimant requests an extension and the Secretary of State considers that the request is reasonable.

(4) A claimant must accept a claimant commitment by one of the following methods, as specified by the Secretary of State—

(a) electronically;
(b) by telephone; or
(c) in writing.

DEFINITIONS

"benefit week"—see reg.2(1).

GENERAL NOTE

This provides for a claimant commitment accepted within a period after the claim to be backdated to the first day of the claim period (para.(1). As regards an award of ESA without a claim, acceptance of a claimant commitment within a period can be attributed to the first day of the first benefit week of the award (para.(2). A period can be extended by the Secretary of State where the claimant reasonably requests an extension (para.(3)). The commitment must be accepted electronically, in writing or by telephone, whichever is specified by the Secretary of State (para.(4)). 8.93

Claimant commitment—exceptions

45. [1(1)] A claimant may be entitled to an employment and support allowance without having accepted a claimant commitment if the Secretary of State considers that— 8.94

(a) the claimant cannot accept a claimant commitment because they lack capacity to do so; or
(b) there are exceptional circumstances in which it would be unreasonable to expect the person to accept a claimant commitment.

[1(2) A claimant may be entitled to an employment and support allowance without having accepted a claimant commitment if the claimant is terminally ill.]

AMENDMENTS

1. Universal Credit and Employment and Support Allowance (Claimant Commitment Exceptions) (Amendment) Regulations 2022 (SI 2022/60) reg.3 (February 15, 2022).

GENERAL NOTE

This allows the Secretary of State to release the claimant from the requirement to accept a claimant commitment as a condition of receiving ESA where the Secretary of State considers that exceptional circumstances pertain in which it would be unreasonable to expect acceptance or where the claimant lacks capacity to accept a claimant commitment, 8.95

Purposes of a work-focused interview

8.96 **46.** The purposes of a work-focused interview are any or all of the following—

(a) assessing the claimant's prospects for remaining in or obtaining work;
(b) assisting or encouraging the claimant to remain in or obtain work;
(c) identifying activities that the claimant may undertake that will make remaining in or obtaining work more likely;
(d) identifying training, educational or rehabilitation opportunities for the claimant which may make it more likely that the claimant will remain in or obtain work or be able to do so;
(e) identifying current or future work opportunities for the claimant that are relevant to the claimant's needs and abilities.

General Note

8.97 This sets out the purposes of a work-focused interview. Compare ESA Regs 2008 reg.55 and Universal Credit Regulations 2013 reg.93.

Claimants subject to no work-related requirements

8.98 **47.**—(1) A claimant falls within section 11D of the Act (persons subject to no work-related requirements) if they are a claimant who—

(a) has caring responsibilities for one or more severely disabled persons for at least 35 hours a week but does not meet the conditions of entitlement to a carer's allowance [1 or have entitlement to carer support payment];
(b) is the responsible foster parent of a child under the age of one;
(c) is an adopter and it is 52 weeks or less since—
 (i) the date on which the child was placed with the claimant; or
 (ii) if the claimant requested that the 52 weeks should run from a date within 14 days before the child was expected to be placed, that date;
(d) has been enrolled on, been accepted for or is undertaking, a full-time course of study or training which is not a course of advanced education and—
 (i) is under the age of 21, or is 21 and reached that age whilst undertaking the course; and
 (ii) is without parental support;
(e) is entitled to an employment and support allowance which is payable at a nil rate;
(f) is pregnant and it is 11 weeks or less before her expected week of confinement; or
(g) was pregnant and it is 15 weeks or less since the date of her confinement.

(2) Subject to paragraph (3), for the purposes of section 11D of the Act, a person has regular and substantial caring responsibilities for a severely disabled person if the person—

[1 (a) satisfies the conditions for entitlement to a carer's allowance, or would do so but for the fact that—
 (i) their earnings have exceeded the limit prescribed for the purposes of that allowance; or
 (ii) they are—

(aa) resident, or treated as resident, in Scotland; or
(bb) resident outside of Great Britain and have a genuine and sufficient link to Scotland; or

(b) is entitled to carer support payment.]

(3) A person does not have regular and substantial caring responsibilities for a severely disabled person if the person derives earnings from those caring responsibilities.

(4) Paragraph (2) applies whether or not the person has made a claim for a carer's allowance.

(5) In this regulation—

"adopter" means a person who has been matched with a child for adoption and who is, or is intended to be, the responsible carer for the child, but excluding a person who is a foster parent or close relative of the child;

"matched with a child for adoption" means an adoption agency has decided that the person would be a suitable adoptive parent for the child;

"severely disabled" has the meaning in section 70 of the Contributions and Benefits Act;

[1 "sufficient" has the meaning given in paragraph 3 of Schedule 1 to the Carer's Assistance (Carer Support Payment) (Scotland) Regulations 2023;]

"without parental support" means the person is not being looked after by a local authority and—

(a) has no parent (in this definition, "parent" includes any person acting in the place of a parent);
(b) cannot live with their parents because the person is estranged from them or there is a serious risk—
  (i) to the person's physical or mental health; or
  (ii) that the person would suffer significant harm if the person lived with them; or
(c) is living away from their parents, and neither parent is able to support the person financially because that parent—
  (i) has a physical or mental impairment;
  (ii) is detained in custody pending trial or sentence upon conviction or under a sentence imposed by a court; or
  (iii) is prohibited from entering or re-entering Great Britain.

AMENDMENT

1. Carer's Assistance (Carer Support Payment) (Scotland) Regulations 2023 (Consequential Amendments) Order 2023 (SI 2023/1218) reg.25(4) (November 19, 2023).

DEFINITIONS

"adopter"—see para.(5).
"carer's allowance—see reg.2(1).
"close relative" —see reg.2(1).
"matched with a child for adoption"—see para.(5).
"parent" —see para.(5).
"severely disabled"—see para.(5).
"without parental support"—see para.(5).

General Note

8.99 This specifies the persons who under s.11D of the WRA 2012 are not subject to any work-related requirements. Compare Universal Credit Regulations 2013 reg.89.

Claimants subject to work-focused interview requirement only

8.100 **48.**—(1) For the purposes of section 11E(1)(a) of the Act (claimant is the responsible carer for a child aged at least one and under a prescribed age) the prescribed age is [[1]three].

(2) A claimant falls within section 11E of the Act (claimants subject to work-focused interview requirement only) if—

(a) the claimant is the responsible foster parent in relation to a child aged at least one;

(b) the claimant is the responsible foster parent in relation to a qualifying young person and the Secretary of State is satisfied that the qualifying young person has care needs which would make it unreasonable to require the claimant to comply with a work preparation requirement;

(c) the claimant is a foster parent, but not the responsible foster parent, in relation to a child or qualifying young person and the Secretary of State is satisfied that the child or qualifying young person has care needs which would make it unreasonable to require the claimant to comply with a work preparation requirement;

(d) the claimant is a foster parent who—

(i) does not have a child or qualifying young person placed with them, but intends to; and

(ii) fell within sub-paragraph (a) within the past eight weeks; or

(e) the claimant has become a friend or family carer in relation to a child within the past 12 months and is also the responsible carer in relation to that child.

(3) In paragraph (2) (e), "friend or family carer" means a person who is responsible for a child, but is not the child's parent or step-parent, and has undertaken the care of the child in the following circumstances—

(a) the child has no parent or has parents who are unable to care for the child; or

(b) it is likely that the child would otherwise be looked after by a local authority because of concerns in relation to the child's welfare.

Amendment

1. Income Support (Work-Related Activity) and Miscellaneous Amendments Regulations 2014 (SI 2014/1097), reg.17 (April 27, 2014).

Definitions

"child"—see reg.2(1).
"friend of family carer"—see para.(3).
"qualifying young person"—see reg.2(1).

General Note

8.101 This lists for the purposes of s.11E of the WRA 2007 the persons who are to be subject only to a work-focused interview requirement. Compare Universal Credit Regulations 2013 reg.91, as amended.

Victims of domestic violence

49.—(1) Where a claimant has recently been a victim of domestic violence and the circumstances set out in paragraph (3) apply— 8.102

(a) a requirement imposed on that claimant under sections 11 to 11G of the Act ceases to have effect for a period of 13 consecutive weeks starting on the date of the notification referred to in paragraph (3)(a); and

(b) the Secretary of State must not impose any other such requirement on that claimant during that period.

(2) A person has recently been a victim of domestic violence if a period of six months has not expired since the violence was inflicted or threatened.

(3) The circumstances are that—

(a) the claimant notifies the Secretary of State, in such manner as the Secretary of State specifies, that domestic violence has been inflicted on or threatened against the claimant by a person specified in paragraph (4) during the period of six months ending on the date of the notification;

(b) this regulation has not applied to the claimant for a period of 12 months before the date of the notification;

(c) on the date of the notification the claimant is not living at the same address as the person who inflicted or threatened the domestic violence; and

(d) as soon as possible, and no later than one month, after the date of the notification the claimant provides evidence from a person acting in an official capacity which demonstrates that—

(i) the claimant's circumstances are consistent with those of a person who has had domestic violence inflicted on or threatened against them during the period of six months ending on the date of the notification; and

(ii) the claimant has made contact with the person acting in an official capacity in relation to such an incident, which occurred during that period.

(4) A person is specified in this paragraph if the person is—

(a) where the claimant is, or was, a member of a couple, the other member of the couple;

(b) the claimant's grandparent, grandchild, parent, parent-in-law, son, son-in-law, daughter, daughter-in-law, step-parent, step-son, step-daughter, brother, step-brother, brother-in-law, sister, step-sister or sister-in-law; or

(c) where any of the persons listed in sub-paragraph (b) is a member of a couple, the other member of that couple.

(5) In this regulation—

[[1]"coercive behaviour" means an act of assault, humiliation or intimidation or other abuse that is used to harm, punish or frighten the victim;

"controlling behaviour" means an act designed to make a person subordinate or dependent by isolating them from sources of support, exploiting their resources and capacities for personal gain, depriving them of the means needed for independence, resistance or escape or regulating their everyday behaviour;

"domestic violence" means any incident, or pattern of incidents, of controlling behaviour, coercive behaviour, violence or abuse, including but not limited to—

(a) psychological abuse;
(b) physical abuse;
(c) sexual abuse;
(d) emotional abuse;
(e) financial abuse,

regardless of the gender or sexuality of the victim;]

"person acting in an official capacity" means a person who is a member of a profession regulated by a body mentioned in section 25(3) of the National Health Service Reform and Health Care Professions Act 2002, a police officer, a registered social worker, the claimant's employer, a representative of the claimant's trade union or any public, voluntary or charitable body which has had direct contact with the claimant in connection with domestic violence;

"registered social worker" means a person registered as a social worker in a register maintained by—

[2[4(a) Social Work England;]]
[3 (b) Social Care Wales;]
(c) the Scottish Social Services Council; or
(d) the Northern Ireland Social Care Council.

AMENDMENTS

1. Social Security (Miscellaneous Amendments) (No.2) Regulations 2013 (SI 2013/1508 reg.5(1), (3) (October 29, 2013).
2. Universal Credit and Miscellaneous Amendments Regulations 2014 (SI 2014/597) reg.4(1), (2) (April 28, 2014).
3. Social Security (Social Care Wales) (Amendment) Regulations 2017 (SI 2017/291), reg.4 (April 1, 2017).
4. Children and Social Work Act 2017 (Consequential Amendments) (Social Workers) Regulations 2019 (SI 2019/1094) reg.2(c) and Sch.3 para.32 (December 2, 2019).

DEFINITIONS

"coercive behaviour"—see para.5.
"controlling behaviour"—see para.5.
"couple"—see reg.2(1).
"domestic violence"—see para.5.
"person acting in an official capacity"—see para.5.
"registered social worker"—see para.5.

GENERAL NOTE

8.103 This enables recent victims (v) of domestic violence to obtain a "breathing space" during which work-related requirement already imposed are lifted and others can not be imposed. Compare Universal Credit Regulations 2013 reg.98 and JSA Regs 1996, reg.14A.

Domestic violence is defined in para.(5). The reg covers both its infliction and it being threatened. V is a recent victim if no more than 6 months have elapsed since domestic violence was inflicted or threatened (para.2).

V can obtain this 13 week period of respite commencing with V's notification to the Secretary of State so long as V provides within one month of the notification evidence from a person acting in an official capacity confirming that the claimant is indeed such a victim in the last six months and has been in contact with that person about an incident of domestic violence. The claimant must not be living on the date of notification at the same address as the person who inflicted or threatened the domestic violence. The person inflicting or threatening the domestic violence must be someone specified in para.(4) (covering a very wide range of "family" members or relatives). There can only be one respite period in any 12 months (para.(3)(b)).

PART 8

Sanctions

Interpretation

50. For the purposes of this Part— 8.104

[1 "current sanctionable failure" means a failure of the following kinds in relation to which the Secretary of State has not yet determined whether the amount of an award of benefit is to be reduced—

(a) a sanctionable failure,

(b) a JSA sanctionable failure, or

(c) a UC sanctionable failure;]

"JSA sanctionable failure" means a failure by a claimant which is sanctionable under section 6K of the Jobseekers Act 1995;

"low-level sanction" means a reduction of an employment and support allowance in accordance with section 11J of the Act for a sanctionable failure by the claimant to comply with—

(a) a work-focused interview requirement imposed under section 11F(2) of the Act (persons subject to work preparation requirement and work-focused interview requirement);

(b) a work preparation requirement imposed under section 11F(2) of the Act; or

(c) a requirement under section 11G of the Act (connected requirements);

"lowest-level sanction" means a reduction of an employment and support allowance in accordance with section 11J of the Act for a sanctionable failure by the claimant to comply with a requirement imposed under section 11E(2) of the Act (persons subject to work-focused interview requirement only);

"reduction period" means the number of days for which a reduction in the amount of an award of an employment and support allowance is to have effect;

[1 "relevant failure" means—

(a) a sanctionable failure giving rise to a low-level sanction,

(b) a UC sanctionable failure giving rise to a sanction under section 27 of the Welfare Reform Act 2012 to which regulation 104 of the Universal Credit Regulations 2013 applies, or

(c) a JSA sanctionable failure giving rise to a sanction under section 6K of the Jobseekers Act 1995 to which regulation 21 of the Jobseeker's Allowance Regulations 2013 applies;]

"sanctionable failure" means a failure which is sanctionable under section 11J of the Act;

"total outstanding reduction period" means the total number of days for which no reduction has yet been applied for all of the claimant's low-level sanctions, lowest-level sanctions and reductions to which regulation 61 applies;

"UC sanctionable failure" means a failure by a claimant which is sanctionable under section 26 or 27 of the Welfare Reform Act 2012.

AMENDMENT

1. Social Security (Jobseeker's Allowance, Employment and Support Allowance and Universal Credit) (Amendment) Regulations 2016 (SI 2016/678) reg.7(2) (July 25, 2016).

General principles for calculating reduction periods

8.105 **51.**—(1) Subject to [[1]paragraph (3)], the reduction period is to be determined in relation to each sanctionable failure in accordance with regulations 52 and 53.

(2) Reduction periods are to run consecutively.

(3) Where the reduction period calculated in relation to a sanctionable failure in accordance with regulation 52 or 53 would result in the total outstanding reduction period exceeding 1095 days, the number of days in the reduction period in relation to that failure is to be adjusted so that 1095 days is not exceeded.

(4) [[1] ...]

AMENDMENT

1. Jobseeker's Allowance and Employment and Support Allowance (Amendment) Regulations 2021 (SI 2021/1132) reg.3 (November 1, 2021).

DEFINITIONS

"JSA sanctionable failure"—see reg.50.
"reduction period"—see reg.50.
"sanctionable failure"—see reg.50.
"total outstanding reduction period"—see reg.50.
UC sanctionable failure—see reg.50.

GENERAL NOTE

8.106 This deals with the general principles applicable to sanctionable failures with respect to work-related requirements as regards ESA under s.11J of the WRA 2007. Sanctions consist of periods for which ESA is reduced. The reduction period is to be set in accordance with regs 52, 53 below (para.1). Reduction periods run consecutively (para.(2) That is subject to the general overall three-year limit in para.(3): a reduction in accordance with regs 52 and 53 cannot take over three years (1095 days) in length the total outstanding reduction period for all the claimants low-level or lowest level sanctions (whether under ESA, JSA or UC) and those under reg.61. This drafting is somewhat opaque. The idea appears to be that if adding a new reduction period to the end of what is likely to be a chain of reduction periods would take the total days in the chain over 1095 days the new reduction period must be adjusted to make the total 1095 days in all.

Para.(4) purports to stipulate when previous sanctionable failures or ones sanctionable under UC and JSA are to be ignored. However, the July 2016 amendment to para.(4) appears to create an absurdity. Before that amendment, the purpose of para.(4) was to disregard previous sanctionable failures giving rise to a reduction in benefit that occurred in the 13 days immediately before the date of the current sanctionable failure. Yet the clear words of reg.7(3) of the amending regulations omit only sub-para.(a) of para.(4), leaving the opening words and sub-para.(b) in place. Because the form of para.(4) is to require the disregarding of the identified sanctionable failures, the result is that the remaining words require the disregarding of *all* previous sanctionable failures that gave rise to a reduction in benefit *at any point* in the process of determining the length of the reduction period for the current sanctionable failure. If that is right, then in the new tables (see e.g. reg.54) only the first entry (and so the shortest sanction), i.e. where there has been no previous relevant sanctionable failure, could ever be applied. See further by analogy the more detailed analysis above commenting on reg.18(4) of the JSA Regulations 2013.

Low-level sanction

52. The reduction period for a low-level sanction is the total of— 8.107

(a) the number of days beginning with the date of the sanctionable failure and ending with—

(i) the day before the date on which the claimant meets a compliance condition specified by the Secretary of State;

(ii) the day before the date on which the claimant falls within section 11D of the Act;

(iii) the day before the date on which the claimant is no longer required to take a particular action specified as a work preparation requirement by the Secretary of State under section 11C(1) or 11F(2) of the Act; or

(iv) the day on which the award of an employment and support allowance is terminated,

whichever is soonest; and

[1 (b) in the circumstances described in the first column of the following table, the number of days set out in the second column.

Circumstances applicable to claimant's case	Number of days
Where there has been no previous relevant failure by the claimant	7 days
Where there have been one or more previous relevant failures by the claimant and the date of the most recent previous relevant failure is not within 365 days beginning with the date of the current sanctionable failure	7 days
Where there have been one or more previous relevant failures by the claimant and the date of the most recent previous relevant failure is within 365 days, but not within 14 days, beginning with the date of the current sanctionable failure and the reduction period applicable to the most recent previous relevant failure is—	
(a) 7 days	14 days
(b) 14 days	28 days
(c) 28 days	28 days
Where there have been one or more previous relevant failures by the claimant and the date of the most recent previous relevant failure is within 14 days beginning with the date of the current sanctionable failure and the reduction period applicable to the most recent previous relevant failure is—	
(a) 7 days	7 days
(b) 14 days	14 days
(c) 28 days	28 days.]

AMENDMENT

1. Social Security (Jobseeker's Allowance, Employment and Support Allowance and Universal Credit) (Amendment) Regulations 2016 (SI 2016/678) reg.7(4) (July 25, 2016).

DEFINITIONS

"compliance condition"—see WRA 2007 s.11J(5).

"JSA sanctionable failure" —see reg.50.
"low-level sanction" —see reg.50.
"reduction period" —see reg.50.
"sanctionable failure" —see reg.50.
"UC sanctionable failure" —see reg.50.

General Note

8.108 This regulation deals with the period of reduction of ESA in respect of a low-level sanction. See also, reg.54 on when the period takes effect.

This regulation specifies the reduction period as the sum of two periods. Under para (a) the first period begins on the day of the sanctionable failure and ends on whichever is the earliest of the days identified in para. (a)(i)(iv) which apply in the particular case. Sub-para.(i)in effect means the day before the one on which the claimant does what the Secretary of State wants in terms of work-related requirements (remedies the failure). Sub-para. (ii) sets the end of this first period as the day before that on which the claimant becomes exempt from work-related requirements under s.11D of the WRA 2007 read with reg.47, above. Sub-para. (iii) envisages this first period ending where the claimant is no longer required to take a particular action as a work preparation requirement under s.11C(1) of 11F(2) of the WRA 2007 Finally, sub-para. (iv) sees the end of the first period as the day on which an ESA award is terminated.

Para. (b) sets the second period at varying lengths (7, 14 or 28 days) depending on whether the failure was a first, second or subsequent offence (whether with respect to ESA, JSA or UC) in the 364 days preceding the failure in question. Note, however, that sanctionable failures attracting a JSA, ESA or UC reduction occurring in the 13 days before the sanctionable failure in question are to be disregarded (reg.51(4)).

Lowest-level sanction

8.109 **53.** The reduction period for a lowest-level sanction is the number of days beginning with the date of the sanctionable failure and ending with—

(a) the day before the date on which the claimant meets a compliance condition specified by the Secretary of State;

(b) the day before the date on which the claimant falls within section 11D of the Act; or

(c) the day on which the claimant's award of an employment and support allowance is terminated, whichever is soonest.

Definitions

"compliance condition"—see WRA 2007 s.11J(5).
"lowest-level sanction"—see reg.50.
"sanctionable failure"—see reg.50.

General Note

8.110 This deals with the reduction period in respect of a lowest-level sanction. Such a sanction is in respect of a failure by the claimant to comply with a requirement imposed under section 11E(2) of the Act (persons subject to work-focused interview requirement only). The period ends on whichever is the earliest of the days specified in paras (a), (b) or (c) as is applicable to the particular case. Para. (a) specifies this as the day before that on which the claimant complies with the condition. Para. (b) sets it as the day before that on which the claimant becomes exempt from work-related requirements under s.11D of the WRA 2007 read with reg.47 above. Para. (c) deals with the case where an award of ESA is terminated.

Start of the reduction

54. A reduction period determined in relation to a sanctionable failure takes effect from— 8.111

(a) where the claimant has not been paid an employment and support allowance for the benefit week in which the Secretary of State determines that the amount of the award of employment and support allowance is to be reduced under section 11J of the Act, the first day of that benefit week;

(b) where the claimant has been paid an employment and support allowance for the benefit week referred to in paragraph (a), the first day of the first benefit week for which the claimant has not been paid an employment and support allowance; or

(c) where the amount of the award of the employment and support allowance for the benefit week referred to in paragraph (a) or (b) is already subject to a reduction because of a previous sanctionable failure, the first day in respect of which the amount of the award is no longer subject to that reduction.

Definitions

"benefit week"—see reg.2.
"reduction period"—see reg.50.
"sanctionable failure"—see reg.50

General Note

This regulation deals with the matter of when a reduction period is to be given effect. 8.112

Reduction period to continue where award of employment and support allowance terminates

55.—(1) Where an award of an employment and support allowance terminates while there is an outstanding reduction period— 8.113

(a) the period continues to run as if a daily reduction were being applied; and

(b) if the claimant becomes entitled to a new award of an employment and support allowance before the period expires, that new award is subject to a reduction for the remainder of the total outstanding reduction period.

(2) Paragraph (3) applies where—

(a) an award of an employment and support allowance terminates before the Secretary of State determines that the amount of the award is to be reduced under section 11J of the Act in relation to a sanctionable failure; and

(b) that determination is made after the claimant becomes entitled to a new award of an employment and support allowance.

(3) Where this paragraph applies—

(a) the reduction period in relation to the sanctionable failure referred to in paragraph (2) is to be treated as having taken effect on the day before the previous award terminated;

(b) that reduction period is treated as having continued to run as if a daily reduction were being applied; and

(c) if the new award referred to in paragraph (2)(b) begins before that reduction period expires, that new award is subject to a reduction for the remainder of the total outstanding reduction period.

DEFINITIONS

"reduction period"—see reg.50.
"sanctionable failure"—see reg.50.
"total outstanding reduction period"—see reg.50.

GENERAL NOTE

8.114 If an award of ESA terminates while there is an outstanding reduction period, subsequent days count as if an actual reduction of benefit were being applied (thus reducing the days outstanding in the period), so that on any further claim for ESA the claimant is subject to the reduction only for the remainder of the period, if any (para.(1)). If an award of ESA terminates before the Secretary of State has made a decision about a reduction for a sanctionable failure, but a new award is in place by the time the decision is made, the reduction period starts as if the decision had been made on the day before the previous award terminated, so that the new award of ESA will be reduced for the remainder of the total outstanding reduction period (paras (2), (3)).

Suspension of a reduction where a fraud sanction applies

8.115 **56.**—(1) A reduction in the amount of an award of an employment and support allowance in accordance with section 11J of the Act is to be suspended for any period during which section 6B or 7 of the Social Security Fraud Act 2001 applies to the award.

(2) The reduction ceases to have effect on the day on which that period begins and has effect again on the day after that period ends.

Termination of a reduction

8.116 **57.**—(1) A reduction in the amount of an award of an employment and support allowance under section 11J of the Act is to be terminated where, since the date of the most recent sanctionable failure which gave rise to such a reduction, the claimant has been in paid work—

(a) for a period of at least 26 weeks; or
(b) for more than one period where the total of those periods amounts to at least 26 weeks.

(2) The termination of the reduction has effect—

(a) where the date on which paragraph (1) is satisfied falls within a period of entitlement to an employment and support allowance, from the beginning of the benefit week in which that date falls; or
(b) where that date falls outside a period of entitlement to an employment and support allowance, from the beginning of the first benefit week in relation to any subsequent award of an employment and support allowance.

(3) The claimant is in paid work for the purposes of paragraph (1) where their weekly earnings are at least equal to 16 multiplied by the national minimum wage which would apply for a person of the claimant's age under the National Minimum Wage Regulations 1999.

DEFINITIONS

"benefit week"—see reg.2.
"in paid work"—see para.(3).
"sanctionable failure"—see reg.50

General Note

Any reduction for any level of sanction or sanctions terminates where since the date of the most recent sanctionable failure the claimant has been in paid work for at least 26 weeks, not necessarily consecutive, with weekly earnings at least equal to 16 multiplied by the national minimum wage applicable to a person of the claimant's age under the National Minimum Wage Regulations 1999 (paras (1), (3)). Para.(2) sets out the time the termination takes effect dependent on whether or not the day the 26 week period is up falls within or outside a period of entitlement to ESA. If within, termination takes effect from the beginning of the benefit week in which there fell the completion of the 26 week period. If outside, it takes effect from the beginning of the first benefit week of any subsequent ESA award. 8.117

Amount of reduction for each benefit week

58. Where it has been determined that an award of an employment and support allowance is to be reduced in accordance with section 11J of the Act, the amount of the reduction for each benefit week in respect of which a reduction has effect is to be calculated as follows. 8.118

Step 1

Take the number of days—

(a) in the benefit week; or

(b) if lower, in the total outstanding reduction period,

and deduct any days in that benefit week or total outstanding reduction period for which the reduction is suspended in accordance with regulation 56.

Step 2

Multiply the number of days produced by step 1 by the daily reduction rate.

Step 3

Deduct the amount produced by step 2 from the amount of the award of employment and support allowance for the benefit week.

Definitions

"benefit week"—see reg.2.
"daily reduction rate"—see regs 59(1), 60.
"total outstanding reduction period"—see reg.50

General Note

This provides the means of calculating for each benefit week the amount of reduction depending on whether the claimant's case fits within reg.58(1) (daily reduction rate) or reg.60 (lower daily reduction rate) 8.119

Daily reduction rate

59.—(1) The daily reduction rate for the purposes of regulation 58 is, unless regulation 60 applies, the amount prescribed for the claimant under regulation 62(1) or, where applicable, regulation 63(2), multiplied by 52 and divided by 365. 8.120

(2) The amount of the daily reduction rate is to be rounded down to the nearest 10 pence.

General Note

Unless the lower daily reduction rate in reg.60 applies, the daily reduction rate is the weekly prescribed amount appropriate for the particular claimant under 8.121

reg.62, or if the claimant is a special case within reg.62, the weekly amount there prescribed. The pertinent prescribed amount is then multiplied by 52 and divided by 365 to produce the daily reduction rate. The daily rate must be rounded down to the nearest 10 pence.

Lower daily reduction rate

8.122 **60.**—(1) The daily reduction rate is 40% of the rate applicable under regulation 59(1) if, at the end of the benefit week, the claimant falls within—

(a) section 11E of the Act;
(b) section 11D(2)(c) of the Act; or
(c) regulation 47(1)(b), (c), (f) or (g).

(2) The daily reduction rate is nil if, at the end of the benefit week, the claimant falls within section 11D(2)(a) of the Act.

DEFINITIONS

"benefit week"—see reg.2.

GENERAL NOTE

8.123 If at the end of the benefit week the claimant falls within s.11E (person subject only to work-focused interview requirement) or s.11D(2) (c) (someone subject to no work-related requirements as a single person responsible for a child aged less than one) of the Welfare Reform Act 2007, the daily reduction rate is instead 40 per cent of the daily reduction rate determined under reg.58(1). Similarly if at the end of the benefit week the claimant falls with reg.47(1)(b) (responsible foster parent of a child aged under one), (1)(c) (an adopter in the first year of the adoption), (1)(f) (pregnant with 11 weeks or less to confinement), or (1)(g) (was pregnant and it is 15 weeks or less since confinement). If, however, the claimant falls within s.11D(2)(a) of the 2007 Act (as someone with limited capability for work and work related activity—a member of the support group) the reduction rate is nil.

Sanctions where universal credit ends and the person is entitled to an employment and support allowance

8.124 **61.**—(1) This regulation applies where—

(a) a person ceases to be entitled to universal credit;
(b) there is a reduction relating to the person's award of universal credit under section 26 or 27 of the Welfare Reform Act 2012; and
(c) the person is entitled to an employment and support allowance.

(2) Any reduction relating to the award of the universal credit is to be applied to the award of the employment and support allowance.

(3) The period for which the reduction relating to the award of employment and support allowance is to have effect is the number of days which apply to the person under regulation 102, 103, 104 or 105 of the Universal Credit Regulations 2013 minus any such days which—

(a) have already resulted in a reduction in the amount of universal credit; or
(b) fall after the date on which the person ceases to be entitled to universal credit and before the date on which the person becomes entitled to an employment and support allowance.

(4) The daily reduction rate for the reduction relating to the award of employment and support allowance is—

(a) the amount referred to in regulation 60(1) where, on the date the claimant becomes entitled to an employment and support allowance, the claimant falls within—

(i) section 11E of the Act;
(ii) section 11D(2)(c) of the Act; or
(iii) regulation 47(1)(b), (c), (f) or (g);

(b) zero where the claimant falls within section 11D(2)(a) of the Act; or

(c) the amount referred to in regulation 59(1) in all other cases.

(5) The amount of the reduction of the claimant's award of an employment and support allowance is the number of days arrived at under paragraph (3) multiplied by the daily reduction rate referred to in paragraph (4).

GENERAL NOTE

Where someone subject to a UC sanction ceases to be entitled to UC and becomes entitled to ESA, the remaining reduction period applicable to the UC award carries over to reduce the ESA award. The remaining reduction period is calculated by deducting from the period imposed as regards UC (i) the days for which UC has been in consequence reduced and (ii) the days between the cessation of entitlement to UC and the beginning of entitlement to ESA. Para.(4) identifies the appropriate daily reduction rate according to whether the claimant falls within reg.61 (paras (4)(a)and (b)) or reg.59(1) (para.(4)(c)). 8.125

PART 9

Amounts of Allowance

Prescribed amounts

62.—(1) Subject to regulation 63 (special cases) the amount prescribed for the purposes of the calculation of the amount of a claimant's employment and support allowance under section 2(1)(a) of the Act is— 8.126

(a) where the claimant satisfies the conditions set out in section 2(2) of the Act [2 or the claimant is a member of the work-related activity group and satisfies the conditions set out in Part 1 to Schedule 1 to the Act], [3 £90.50]; or

(b) where the claimant does not satisfy the conditions set out in section 2(2) of the Act [3 or the claimant is a member of the work-related activity group and satisfies the conditions set out in Part 1 to Schedule 1 to the Act] —
(i) where the claimant is aged not less than 25, [3 £90.50]; or
(ii) where the claimant is aged less than 25, [3 £71.70].

[2 (2) Subject to regulation 63 the amount of the support component is [3 £47.70].]

AMENDMENTS

1. Employment and Support Allowance and Universal Credit (Miscellaneous Amendments and Transitional and Savings Provisions) Regulations 2017 (SI 2017/204) reg.3(4) (April 3, 2017).

2. Employment and Support Allowance (Miscellaneous Amendments and Transitional and Savings Provision) Regulations 2017 (SI 2017/581) reg.8 (June 23, 2017).

3. Social Security Benefits Up-rating Order 2024 (SI 2024/242) art.31(1) (April 8, 2024).

General Note

8.127 This sets the prescribed amounts of ESA, for claimants who are not special cases under reg.63. Where the assessment phase has ended, the weekly rate is £90.50, to which will be added a further £47.70 support component if the claimant has limited capability for work and work-related activity (members of the support group).

Where the assessment phase has not yet ended for the claimant, the rate of basic ESA depends on age: £90.50 for those aged 25 or over; £71.70 for those under 25.

Special cases

8.128 **63.**—(1) The amount prescribed for the purposes of the calculation of the amount of a claimant's employment and support allowance under section 2(1)(a) of the Act in respect of a claimant who—

(a) satisfies either of the conditions in paragraphs (3) or (4); or

(b) has been a patient for a continuous period of more than 52 weeks,

is the amount applicable under regulation 62(1) and the amount of nil under regulation 62(2).

(2) The amount prescribed for those purposes in respect of a claimant who is a person in hardship, is the amount to which the claimant is entitled—

(a) under regulation 62(1) reduced by 20%; and

(b) under regulation 62(2).

(3) The first condition mentioned in paragraph (1) (a) is that—

(a) the claimant is being detained under section 45A or 47 of the Mental Health Act 1983 (power of higher courts to direct hospital admission; removal to hospital of persons serving sentences of imprisonment etc); and

(b) in any case where there is in relation to the claimant a release date within the meaning of section 50(3) of that Act, the claimant is being detained on or before the day which the Secretary of State certifies to be that release date.

(4) The second condition mentioned in paragraph (1) (a) is that the claimant is being detained under—

(a) section 59A of the Criminal Procedure (Scotland) Act 1995 (hospital direction); or

(b) section 136 of the Mental Health (Care and Treatment) (Scotland) Act 2003 (transfer of prisoners for treatment of mental disorder).

(5) In this regulation—

"patient" means a person (other than a prisoner) who is regarded as receiving free in-patient treatment within the meaning of regulation 2(4) and (5) of the Social Security (Hospital In- Patients) Regulations 2005;

"prisoner" means a person who—

(a) is detained in custody pending trial or sentence on conviction or under a sentence imposed by a court; or

(b) is on temporary release in accordance with the provisions of the Prison Act 1952 or the Prisons (Scotland) Act 1989,

other than a person who is detained in hospital under the provisions of the Mental Health Act 1983 or, in Scotland, under the provisions of the Mental Health (Care and Treatment) (Scotland) Act 2003 or the Criminal Procedure (Scotland) Act 1995.

(6) For the purposes of this regulation—

(a) except where sub-paragraph (b) applies, a person is a "person in hardship" if they satisfy regulation 94; and

(b) where a person satisfies regulation 94 for more than six weeks, they are a "person in hardship" only for the first six weeks.

DEFINITIONS

"patient"—see para.(5).
"person in hardship"—see para.(5).
"prisoner"—see para.(5).

GENERAL NOTE

This sets the prescribed amounts of ESA awards for claimants who are special cases either as patients, certain persons detained under specified provisions of the applicable mental health legislation, persons in hardship and some remand prisoners or ones on temporary release. **8.129**

Permanent health insurance

64. For the purposes of sections 2(1)(c) and 3(3) of the Act (deductions from an employment and support allowance) "pension payment" is to include a permanent health insurance payment. **8.130**

DEFINITIONS

"pension payment"—see WRA 2007 s.3(3).
"permanent health insurance payment"—see reg.2.

GENERAL NOTE

WRA 2007 ss.2(1)(c) and 3(1)(a) stipulate that deductions are to be made from new style ESA in respect of pension payments. "Pension payments" are defined in s.3(3) in terms enabling expansion by regulations (category (c) in the definition). This regulation does just that, specifying "permanent health insurance payment", defined in reg.(2), as included in the term "pension payment". Note, however, that reg.68(f) means that any such payment in respect of which the employee had contributed more than 50% to the premium will be treated as not counting for reduction purposes. **8.131**

Financial Assistance Scheme

65.—(1) For the purposes of sections 2(1)(c) and 3(3) of the Act (deductions from an employment and support allowance) "pension payment" is to include a Financial Assistance Scheme payment. **8.132**

(2) In this regulation "Financial Assistance Scheme payment" means a payment made under the Financial Assistance Scheme Regulations 2005.

DEFINITIONS

"Financial Assistance Scheme payment"—see para.(2).
"pension payment"—see WRA 2007 s.3(3).

GENERAL NOTE

WRA 2007, ss.2(1)(c) and 3(1)(a) stipulate that deductions are to be made from new style ESA in respect of pension payments. "Pension payments" are defined in s.3(3) in terms enabling expansion by regulations (category (c) in the definition). This regulation does that by specifying a "Financial Assistance Scheme payment" (defined in para.(2)) as a pension payment. **8.133**

Councillor's allowance

8.134 **66.** For the purposes of section 3(1)(c) of the Act—

(a) a councillor's allowance is a payment of a prescribed description; and

(b) the prescribed bodies carrying out public or local functions are—

(i) in relation to England and Wales, a London borough council, a county council, a county borough council, a district council, a parish or community council, the Common Council of the City of London or the Council of the Isles of Scilly; and

(ii) in relation to Scotland, a council constituted under section 2 of the Local Government etc. (Scotland) Act 1994.

DEFINITIONS

"councillor"—see reg.2.
"councillor's allowance"—see reg.2.

GENERAL NOTE

8.135 Whatever the amount of new-style ESA set by regs 62 (usual cases) or 63 (special cases), it is, under WRA 2007, ss.2(1)(c) and 3, subject to reduction in respect of a variety of payments: including prescribed payments to members of prescribed bodies carrying out public or local functions. This regulation defines councillor's allowance as a prescribed payment and stipulates that "prescribed bodies carrying out public or local functions" are those bodies in the definition of councillor in reg.2. On the reductive effect of councillor's allowance see reg.69.

Deductions for pension payment and PPF payment

8.136 **67.**—(1) Where—

(a) a claimant is entitled to an employment and support allowance in respect of any period of a week or part of a week;

(b) there is—

(i) a pension payment;

(ii) a PPF periodic payment; or

(iii) both of the payments specified in paragraphs (i) and (ii),

payable to that person in respect of that period (or a period which forms part of that period or includes that period or part of it); and

(c) the amount of the payment, or payments when taken together, exceeds—

(i) if the period in question is a week, £85; or

(ii) if that period is not a week, such proportion of £85 as falls to be calculated in accordance with regulation 79(1) or (5) (calculation of weekly amount of income),

the amount of that allowance is to be reduced by an amount equal to 50% of the excess.

(2) For the purposes of regulations 67 to 72 "payment" means a payment or payments, as the case may be, referred to in paragraph (1)(b).

DEFINITIONS

"claimant"—see WRA 2007 s.24(1).
"payment"—see para.(2).
"pension payment"—see WRA 2007 s.3(3); regs 64, 65.
"PPF periodic payment"—see WRA 2007 s.3(3).

GENERAL NOTE

WRA 2007 ss.2(1)(c) and 3(1)(a) stipulate that deductions are to be made from new style ESA in respect of "pension payments" and "PPF periodic payments". This regulation provides that where one or more of these is payable to a claimant in respect of a week in respect of which he is entitled to ESA, then where the amount (or combined amount) of that payment (those payments) exceeds £85, the amount of ESA otherwise due is to be reduced by half of the excess over £85. Where the period of ESA entitlement is less than a week, 50% of the excess over an appropriate proportion of the amount of £85 as determined under reg.79(1) and (5) (calculation of amount of income) is instead to be deducted. 8.137

Payments treated as not being payments to which section 3 applies

68. The following payments are to be treated as not being payments to which section 3 of the Act applies— 8.138

(a) any pension payment made to a claimant as a beneficiary on the death of a member of any pension scheme;
(b) any PPF periodic payment made to a claimant as a beneficiary on the death of a person entitled to such a payment;
(c) where a pension scheme is in deficit or has insufficient resources to meet the full pension payment, the extent of the shortfall;
(d) any pension payment made under an instrument specified in section 639(2) of the Income Tax (Earnings and Pensions) Act 2003;
(e) any guaranteed income payment (which means a payment made under article 15(1)(a) or 29(1)(a) of the Armed Forces and Reserved Forces (Compensation Schemes) Order 2011);
(f) any permanent health insurance payment in respect of which the employee had contributed to the premium to the extent of more than 50%.

DEFINITIONS

"claimant"—see WRA 2007 s.24(1).
"guaranteed income payment"—see para.(e).
"pension payment"—see WRA 2007 s.3(3); regs 64, 65.
"permanent health insurance payment"—see reg.2.
"PPF periodic payment"—see WRA 2007 s.3(3).

GENERAL NOTE

WRA 2007 ss.2(1)(c) and 3(1)(a) stipulate that deductions are to be made from new style ESA in respect of "pension payments" and "PPF periodic payments". This regulation provides that the payments listed in it, which would otherwise so rank, are not to be treated as payments to which s.3 applies, and so are not to be deducted from ESA. 8.139

Deductions for councillor's allowance

69.—(1) Where the net amount of councillor's allowance to which a claimant is entitled in respect of any week exceeds 16 multiplied by the National Minimum Wage, subject to paragraph (3), an amount equal to the excess is to be deducted from the amount of an employment and support allowance to which that claimant is entitled in respect of that week, and only the balance remaining (if any) is to be payable. 8.140

(2) In paragraph (1) "net amount", in relation to any councillor's allowance to which a claimant is entitled, means the aggregate amount of the councillor's allowance or allowances, or remuneration to which that claimant is entitled for the week in question, reduced by the amount of any payment in respect of expenses wholly, exclusively and necessarily incurred by that claimant, in that week, in the performance of the duties of a councillor.

(3) Where the amount determined by the calculation in paragraph (1) would, but for this paragraph, include an amount of—

(a) less than 50p, that amount is to be rounded up to the nearest 50p; or

(b) less than £1 but more than 50p, that amount is to be rounded up to the nearest £1.

DEFINITIONS

"councillor's allowance"—see reg.2.
"net amount"—see para.(2).

GENERAL NOTE

8.141 This regulation provides that where the net amount of councillor's allowance or remuneration to which the claimant is entitled in any week exceed 16 × National Minimum Wage (rounded as per para.(3)), the amount of the excess must be deducted from the amount of new style ESA to which he would otherwise be entitled in respect of that week. The reduction can be to nil. Only the balance of ESA remaining (if any) is to be payable. On para.(2) (determination of net amount), compare SSCBA 1992 s.30E(3). That is in similar terms, apart from not specifying as para.(2) of this regulation does that the expenses must be "wholly, exclusively and necessarily incurred by that claimant, in that week, in the performance of the duties of a councillor". The IB provision specified that the expenses must have been incurred in that week in connection with his membership of the [relevant council(s)]. Subject to that, however, existing IVB and IB case law on "net amount" is relevant.

Unlike the position with computation of earnings under the Computation of Earnings Regs, no concept of averaging across the year is to be applied. In *CS/7934/95*, Commissioner Rice decided:

> "that the expenses incurred in any week by the claimant for the performance of her duties as a local authority councillor (whether for clothes, telephone rental, telephone calls, subscriptions, travel, or whatever it might be) shall for the purposes of calculating her entitlement to invalidity benefit [pursuant to SSCBA 1992, s.58(4), the similarly worded precursor of para.(3) of this section, defining 'net amount'], be deducted from the allowance or allowances to which she is entitled in respect of that week" (para.1).

It is immaterial that the benefits of expenses incurred in that week (e.g. the purchase of a dress to be worn more than once for official functions) are enjoyed in future weeks (para.9). In *CIB/2858, /2859* and *2864/2001*, Commissioner Jacobs supported as correct the approach taken by Commissioner Rice in *CS/7934/95*. He disagreed with Commissioner Williams in *R(IB) 3/01*. He accepted that s.30E should be interpreted as a whole. The phrase "in connection with" membership of the council set a limit of reasonableness on the expenditure. An expense is incurred when the liability to discharge it arises (a matter on which he agreed with Commissioner Williams), but it is not incurred in the week in which the item is used (a matter of disagreement with Commissioner Williams). In Commissioner Jacobs's view the result is that s.30E has to be applied week by week, either in each week or retrospectively over a past period. The change of wording to the stricter "in the performance of the duties of a councillor" (the stricter tax approach noted by Commissioner Williams in *R(IB) 3/01*, para.22) may well affirm that approach. An expense is incurred in the week in which the liability arises and can only be used to reduce the reduction in incapacity benefit for that week. Income tax and national insurance deductions do not rank as "expenses in connection with a claimant's membership of a council" and cannot be deducted from the gross councillor's allowances for purposes of incapacity benefit (*R(IB) 3/01*). It is difficult to see that the alteration to "in the performance of his duties as a councillor" alters the status of income tax and NI deductions in this respect.

Date from which payments are to be taken into account

70. Where regulation 67(1) or 69(1) applies, a deduction must have effect, calculated where appropriate in accordance with regulation 79(1) or (5), from the first day of the benefit week in which the payment or councillor's allowance is paid to a claimant who is entitled to an employment and support allowance in that week. **8.142**

DEFINITIONS

"benefit week"—see reg.2.
"claimant"—see WRA 2007 s.24(1).
"councillor's allowance"—see reg.2.
"payment—see reg.67(2).

GENERAL NOTE

Deductions for pension payments, PPF periodic payments and councillor's allowance, calculated where appropriate under reg.79(1) and (5) (calculation of weekly amount of income) are to have effect from the first day of the benefit week in which they are paid to a claimant entitled to new style ESA in that week. **8.143**

Date from which a change in the rate of the payment takes effect

71. Where a payment or councillor's allowance is already being made to a claimant and the rate of that payment or that allowance changes, the deduction at the new rate must take effect, calculated where appropriate in accordance with regulation 79(1) or (5), from the first day of the benefit week in which the new rate of the payment or councillor's allowance is paid. **8.144**

DEFINITIONS

"benefit week"—see reg.2.
"claimant"—see WRA 2007 s.24(1).
"councillor's allowance"—see reg.2.
"payment—see reg.67(2).

GENERAL NOTE

Changes in the rate of pension payments, PPF periodic payments and councillor's allowance affect the amount to be deducted from new style ESA. The deduction at the new rate, calculated where appropriate under reg.79(1) or (5) (calculation of weekly amount of income), is to have effect from the first day of the benefit week in which the new rate of payment or councillor's allowance is paid to a claimant entitled to ESA in that week. **8.145**

Calculation of payment made other than weekly

72.—(1) Where the period in respect of which a payment or councillor's allowance is paid is otherwise than weekly, an amount calculated or estimated in accordance with regulation 79(1) or (5) is to be regarded as the weekly amount of that payment or allowance. **8.146**

(2) In determining the weekly payment, where two or more payments are payable to a claimant, each payment is to be calculated separately in accordance with regulation 79(1) or (5) before aggregating the sum of those payments for the purposes of the reduction of an employment and support allowance in accordance with regulation 67.

DEFINITIONS

"benefit week"—see reg.2.
"claimant"—see WRA 2007 s.24(1).
"councillor's allowance"—see reg.2.
"payment—see reg.67(2).

GENERAL NOTE

8.147 This provides for the case where pension payments, PPF periodic payments and councillor's allowance are paid otherwise than weekly. The amount to be deducted is to be calculated or estimated, taking each payment or allowance separately, in accordance with reg.79(1) or (5) to ascertain an appropriate weekly equivalent for the pension payment, the PPF periodic payment and the councillor's allowance (para.(1)) For the purposes of the deduction rule in reg.67, the weekly equivalents for each pension payment or PPF payment are then to be aggregated (para.(2)).

Effect of statutory maternity pay on an employment and support allowance

8.148 **73.**—(1) This regulation applies where—
(a) a woman is entitled to statutory maternity pay and, on the day immediately preceding the first day in the maternity pay period, she—
(i) is in a period of limited capability for work; and
(ii) satisfies the conditions of entitlement to an employment and support allowance in accordance with section 1(2)(a) of the Act; and
(b) on any day during the maternity pay period—
(i) she is in a period of limited capability for work; and
(ii) that day is not a day where she is treated as not having limited capability for work.

(2) Where this regulation applies, notwithstanding section 20(2) of the Act, a woman who is entitled to statutory maternity pay is to be entitled to an employment and support allowance in respect of any day that falls within the maternity pay period.

(3) Where by virtue of paragraph (2) a woman is entitled to an employment and support allowance for any week (including part of a week), the total amount of employment and support allowance payable to her for that week is to be reduced by an amount equivalent to any statutory maternity pay to which she is entitled in accordance with Part 12 of the Contributions and Benefits Act for the same week (or equivalent part of a week where entitlement to an employment and support allowance is for part of a week), and only the balance, if any, of the employment and support allowance is to be payable to her.

DEFINITIONS

"the Act"—see reg.2.
"Contributions and Benefits Act"—see WRA 2007 s.65.
"maternity pay period"—see WRA 2007 s.20(8); SSCBA 1992 s.165(1).
"week"—see reg.2.

General Note

In essence this provides that, where a woman's ongoing entitlement to new style ESA and statutory maternity pay (SMP) overlap, then during the period they coincide, despite WRA 2007, s.20(2), entitlement to ESA is preserved, but the amount payable in respect of the week or part week, as appropriate, is to be reduced (even to nil) by the amount of SMP for that week or part week—only the balance (if any) of ESA is payable. 8.149

Effect of statutory adoption pay on an employment and support allowance

74.—(1) This regulation applies where— 8.150

(a) a claimant is entitled to statutory adoption pay and, on the day immediately preceding the first day in the adoption pay period, she—
  (i) is in a period of limited capability for work; and
  (ii) satisfies the conditions of entitlement to an employment and support allowance in accordance with section 1(2)(a) of the Act; and

(b) on any day during the adoption pay period—
  (i) that claimant is in a period of limited capability for work; and
  (ii) that day is not a day where that claimant is treated as not having limited capability for work.

(2) Where this regulation applies, notwithstanding section 20(4) of the Act, a claimant who is entitled to statutory adoption pay is to be entitled to an employment and support allowance in respect of any day that falls within the adoption pay period.

(3) Where by virtue of paragraph (2) a claimant is entitled to an employment and support allowance for any week (including part of a week), the total amount of employment and support allowance payable to that claimant for that week is to be reduced by an amount equivalent to any statutory adoption pay to which that claimant is entitled in accordance with Part 12ZB of the Contributions and Benefits Act for the same week (or equivalent part of a week where entitlement to an employment and support allowance is for part of a week), and only the balance, if any, of the employment and support allowance is to be payable to that claimant.

Definitions

"the Act"—see reg.2.
"adoption pay period"—see WRA 2007 s.20(8).
"claimant"—see WRA 2007 s.24(1).
"Contributions and Benefits Act"—see WRA 2007 s.65.
"week"—see reg.2.

General Note

In essence this provides that, where a claimant's ongoing entitlement to new style ESA and statutory adoption pay (SAP) overlap, then during the period they coincide, despite WRA 2007 s.20(2), entitlement to ESA is preserved, but the amount payable in respect of the week or part week, as appropriate, is to be reduced (even to nil) by the amount of SAP for that week or part week—only the balance (if any) of ESA is payable. 8.151

Effect of additional statutory paternity pay on an employment and support allowance

8.152 **75.** — [[1]. . .].

REVOCATION

1. Shared Parental Leave and Statutory Shared Parental Pay (Consequential Amendments to Subordinate Legislation) Order 2014 (SI 2014/3255) art.30 (1), (2) (April 5, 2015).

[[1]Effect of statutory shared parental pay on an employment and support allowance

8.153 **75A.**—(1) This regulation applies where—

(a) a claimant is entitled to statutory shared parental pay and, on the day immediately preceding the first day in the shared parental pay period the claimant—

(i) is in a period of limited capability for work; and

(ii) satisfies the conditions of entitlement to an employment and support allowance in accordance with section 1(2)(a) of the Act; and

(b) on any day during the statutory shared parental pay period—

(i) that claimant is in a period of limited capability for work; and

(ii) that day is not a day where that claimant is treated as not having limited capability for work.

(2) Where this regulation applies, notwithstanding section 20(6) of the Act, a claimant who is entitled to statutory shared parental pay is to be entitled to an employment and support allowance in respect of any day that falls within the shared parental pay period.

(3) Where by virtue of paragraph (2) a person is entitled to an employment and support allowance for any week (including part of a week), the total amount of such benefit payable to that claimant for that week is to be reduced by an amount equivalent to any statutory shared parental pay to which that claimant is entitled in accordance with Part 12ZC of the Contributions and Benefits Act for the same week (or equivalent part of a week where entitlement to an employment and support allowance is for part of a week), and only the balance, if any, of the employment and support allowance is to be payable to that claimant.

(4) In this regulation "statutory shared parental pay period" means the weeks in respect of which statutory shared parental pay is payable to a person under section 171ZY(2) of the Social Security Contributions and Benefits Act 1992.]

AMENDMENT

1. Shared Parental Leave and Statutory Shared Parental Pay (Consequential Amendments to Subordinate Legislation) Order 2014 (SI 2014/3255) art.30 (1), (3) (December 31, 2014).

DEFINITIONS

"the Act"—see reg.2(1).
"claimant"—see WRA 2007, s.24(1).
"contributory allowance"—see WRA 2007 s.1(7).
"Contributions and Benefits Act"—see WRA 2007 s.65.

"statutory shared parental pay period"—see para.(4).
"week"—see reg.2(1).

GENERAL NOTE

In essence this provides that, where a claimant's ongoing entitlement to new style ESA and statutory shared parental pay (SSPP) overlap, then during the period they coincide, despite WRA 2007, s.20(6), entitlement to ESA is preserved, but the amount payable in respect of the week or part week, as appropriate, is to be reduced (even to nil) by the amount of SSPP for that week or part week—only the balance (if any) of ESA is payable. **8.154**

PART 10

Income and earnings

Calculation of earnings derived from employed earner's employment and income other than earnings

76.—(1) Earnings derived from employment as an employed earner and income which does not consist of earnings are to be taken into account over a period determined in accordance with the following provisions of this regulation and at a weekly amount determined in accordance with regulation 79 (calculation of weekly amount of income). **8.155**

(2) Subject to the following provisions of this regulation, the period over which a payment is to be taken into account is to be—

(a) where the payment is monthly, a period equal to the number of weeks beginning with the date on which the payment is treated as paid and ending with the date immediately before the date on which the next monthly payment would have been treated as paid whether or not the next monthly payment is actually paid;
(b) where the payment is in respect of a period which is not monthly, a period equal to the length of the period for which payment is made;
(c) in any other case, a period equal to such number of weeks as is equal to the number obtained (see paragraph (9)) by applying the formula—

$$\frac{E}{J}$$

where—
E is the net earnings;
J is the amount of an employment and support allowance which would be payable had the payment not been made;

and that period is to begin on the date on which the payment is treated as paid under regulation 78 (date on which income is treated as paid).

(3) Where—

(a) earnings are derived from the same source but are not of the same kind; and
(b) but for this paragraph, the periods in respect of which those earnings would fall to be taken into account overlap, wholly or partly,

those earnings are to be taken into account over a period equal to the aggregate length of those periods, and that period is to begin with the earliest date on which any part of those earnings would be treated as paid under regulation 78.

(4) In a case to which paragraph (5) applies, earnings under regulation 80 (earnings of employed earners) are to be taken into account in the following order of priority—

(a) earnings normally derived from the employment;
(b) any payment to which paragraph (1)(b) or (c) of that regulation applies;
(c) any payment to which paragraph (1)(j) of that regulation applies;
(d) any payment to which paragraph (1)(d) of that regulation applies.

(5) Where earnings to which regulation 80(1)(b) to (d) applies are paid in respect of part of a day, those earnings are to be taken into account over a period equal to a day.

(6) Any earnings to which regulation 80(1)(j) applies which are paid in respect of, or on the termination of, part-time employment, are to be taken into account over a period of one week.

(7) For the purposes of this regulation the claimant's earnings are to be calculated in accordance with regulations 80 and 81.

(8) For the purposes of paragraph 10 of Schedule 2 to the Act (effect of work), the income which consists of earnings of a claimant is to be calculated on a weekly basis by determining the weekly amount of those earnings in accordance with regulations 77 to 84.

(9) For the purposes of the number obtained as mentioned in paragraph (2)(c), any fraction is to be treated as a corresponding fraction of a week.

DEFINITIONS

"the Act"—see reg.2.
"claimant"— see WRA 2007 s.24(1).
"employed earner"—see reg.2.
"employment"—see reg.2.
"net earnings"—see reg.2.
"week"—see reg.2.

GENERAL NOTE

8.156 This has affinities with ESA Regs 2008 reg.91, save with respect to the formula in para.(2)(c) of this regulation.

Calculation of earnings of self-employed earners

8.157 **77.**—(1) Where a claimant's income consists of earnings from employment as a self-employed earner, the weekly amount of the claimant's earnings is to be determined by reference to the claimant's average weekly earnings from that employment—

(a) over a period of one year; or
(b) where the claimant has recently become engaged in that employment or there has been a change which is likely to affect the normal pattern of business, over such other period as may, in any particular case, enable the weekly amount of the claimant's earnings to be determined more accurately.

(2) For the purposes of this regulation the claimant's earnings are to be calculated in accordance with regulations 82 to 84.

DEFINITIONS

"claimant"—see WRA 2007 s.24(1).
"self-employed earner"—see reg.2.

GENERAL NOTE

This is much the same as ESA Regs 2008 reg.92(1), (3). 8.158

Date on which income is treated as paid

78. A payment of income to which regulation 76 (calculation of earnings derived from employed earner's employment and income other than earnings) applies is to be treated as paid— 8.159

(a) in the case of a payment which is due to be paid before the first benefit week pursuant to the claim, on the date on which it is due to be paid;
(b) in any other case, on the first day of the benefit week in which it is due to be paid or the first succeeding benefit week in which it is practicable to take it into account.

DEFINITIONS

"benefit week"—see reg.2.
"claimant"—see WRA 2007 s.24(1).
"employed earner"—see reg.2.
"employment"—see reg.2.

GENERAL NOTE

This is the equivalent of ESA Regs 2008 reg.93(1). 8.160

Calculation of weekly amount of income

79.—(1) For the purposes of regulation 76 (calculation of earnings derived from employed earner's employment and income other than earnings) and regulations 64 to 72 (deductions from employment and support allowance), subject to paragraphs (2) to (5), where the period in respect of which a payment is made— 8.161

(a) does not exceed a week, the weekly amount is to be the amount of that payment;
(b) exceeds a week, the weekly amount is to be determined—
  (i) in a case where that period is a month, by multiplying the amount of the payment by 12 and dividing the product by 52;
  (ii) in a case where that period is three months, by multiplying the amount of the payment by four and dividing the product by 52;
  (iii) in a case where that period is a year and the payment is income, by dividing the amount of the payment by 52;
  (iv) in any other case, by multiplying the amount of the payment by seven and dividing the product by the number equal to the number of days in the period in respect of which it is made.

(2) Where a payment for a period not exceeding a week is treated under regulation 78(a) (date on which income is treated as paid) as paid before the first benefit week and a part is to be taken into account for some days only in that week (the relevant days), the amount to be taken into account for the relevant days is to be calculated by multiplying the amount of the payment by the number of relevant days and dividing the product by the number of days in the period in respect of which it is made.

(3) Where a payment is in respect of a period equal to or in excess of a week and a part thereof is to be taken into account for some days only in a benefit week (the relevant days), the amount to be taken into account for the relevant days is to be calculated by multiplying the amount of the payment by the number of relevant days and dividing the product by the number of days in the period in respect of which it is made.

(4) Except in the case of a payment which it has not been practicable to treat under regulation 78(b) (date on which income is treated as paid) as paid on the first day of the benefit week in which it is due to be paid, where a payment of income from a particular source is or has been paid regularly and that payment falls to be taken into account in the same benefit week as a payment of the same kind and from the same source, the amount of that income to be taken into account in any one benefit week is not to exceed the weekly amount determined under paragraph (1)(a) or (b) of the payment which under regulation 78(b) is treated as paid first.

(5) Where the amount of the claimant's income fluctuates and has changed more than once, or a claimant's regular pattern of work is such that the claimant does not work every week, the foregoing paragraphs may be modified so that the weekly amount of the claimant's income is determined by reference to the claimant's average weekly income—

(a) if there is a recognisable cycle of work, over the period of one complete cycle (including, where the cycle involves periods in which the claimant does no work, those periods but disregarding any other absences);

(b) in any other case, over a period of five weeks or such other period as may, in the particular case, enable the claimant's average weekly income to be determined more accurately.

DEFINITIONS

"benefit week"—see reg.2.
"claimant"—see WRA 2007 s.24(1).

GENERAL NOTE

8.162 This equates to ESA Regs 2008 reg.94 (1)–(3), (5), (6).

Earnings of employed earners

8.163 **80.**—(1) Subject to paragraphs (2) and (3), "earnings" means, in the case of employment as an employed earner, any remuneration or profit derived from that employment and includes—

(a) any bonus or commission;

(b) any payment in lieu of remuneration except any periodic sum paid to a claimant on account of the termination of the claimant's employment by reason of redundancy;

(c) any payment in lieu of notice;
(d) any holiday pay except any payable more than four weeks after the termination or interruption of employment;
(e) any payment by way of a retainer;
(f) any payment made by the claimant's employer in respect of expenses not wholly, exclusively and necessarily incurred in the performance of the duties of the employment, including any payment made by the claimant's employer in respect of—
(i) travelling expenses incurred by the claimant between the claimant's home and place of employment;
(ii) expenses incurred by the claimant under arrangements made for the care of a member of the claimant's family owing to the claimant's absence from home;
(g) any award of compensation made under section 112(4) or 117(3)(a) of the Employment Rights Act 1996 (the remedies: orders and compensation, enforcement of order and compensation);
(h) any payment made or remuneration paid under [1section] 28, 34, 64, 68 [1or] 70 of the Employment Rights Act 1996 (right to guarantee payments, remuneration on suspension on medical or maternity grounds, complaints to employment tribunals);
(i) any such sum as is referred to in section 112(3) of the Contributions and Benefits Act (certain sums to be earnings for social security purposes);
(j) where a payment of compensation is made in respect of employment which is part-time employment, the amount of the compensation;
(k) the amount of any payment by way of a non-cash voucher which has been taken into account in the computation of a person's earnings in accordance with Part 5 of Schedule 3 to the Social Security (Contributions) Regulations 2001.

(2) "Earnings" are not to include—
(a) subject to paragraph (3), any payment in kind;
(b) any remuneration paid by or on behalf of an employer to the claimant in respect of a period throughout which the claimant is on maternity leave, paternity leave[2,] adoption leave (which means a period of absence from work on ordinary or additional adoption leave under section 75A or 75B of the Employment Rights Act 1996)[2, shared parental leave under section 75E or 75G of that Act] [3, parental bereavement leave under section 80EA of that Act] or is absent from work because the claimant is ill;
(c) any payment in respect of expenses wholly, exclusively and necessarily incurred in the performance of the duties of the employment;
(d) any occupational pension (which means any pension or other periodical payment under an occupational pension scheme but does not include any discretionary payment out of a fund established for relieving hardship in particular cases);
(e) any lump sum payment made under the Iron and Steel Re-adaptation Benefits Scheme;
(f) any payment in respect of expenses arising out of the claimant participating as a service user;
[1 (g) any bounty paid at intervals of at least one year and derived from employment as—

(i) a part-time fire-fighter in a fire brigade maintained in pursuance of the Fire and Rescue Services Act 2004;
(ii) a part-time fire-fighter employed by a fire and rescue authority under that Act;
(iii) a part-time fire-fighter employed by the Scottish Fire and Rescue Service established under section 1A of the Fire (Scotland) Act 2005;
(iv) an auxiliary coastguard in respect of coast rescue activities;
(v) a person engaged part-time in the manning or launching of a lifeboat;
(vi) a member of any territorial or reserve force prescribed in Part 1 of Schedule 6 to the Social Security (Contributions) Regulations 2001.]

(3) Paragraph (2)(a) is not to apply in respect of any non-cash voucher referred to in paragraph (1)(k).

(4) In this regulation—

"compensation" means any payment made in respect of, or on the termination of, employment in a case where a claimant has not received or received only part of a payment in lieu of notice due or which would have been due to the claimant had that claimant not waived the right to receive it, other than—

(a) any payment specified in paragraph (1)(a) to (i);
(b) any payment specified in paragraph (2)(a) to (f);
(c) any redundancy payment within the meaning of section 135(1) of the Employment Rights Act 1996;
(d) any refund of contributions to which that person was entitled under an occupational pension scheme; and
(e) any compensation payable by virtue of section 173 of the Education Reform Act 1988;

"paternity leave" means a period of absence from work on ordinary paternity leave by virtue of section 80A or 80B of the Employment Rights Act 1996 or on additional paternity leave by virtue of section 80AA or 80BB of that Act.

(5) The reference in paragraph (2)(f) to a person participating as a service user is to—

(a) a person who is being consulted by or on behalf of—
(i) a body which has a statutory duty to provide services in the field of health, social care or social housing; or
(ii) a body which conducts research or undertakes monitoring for the purpose of planning or improving such services, in the person's capacity as a user, potential user, carer of a user or person otherwise affected by the provision of those services; or
(b) the carer of a person consulted under sub-paragraph (a).

AMENDMENTS

1. Universal Credit and Miscellaneous Amendments Regulations 2014 (SI 2014/597) reg.4(1), (5) (April 28, 2014).

2. Shared Parental Leave and Statutory Shared Parental Pay (Consequential Amendments to Subordinate Legislation) Order 2014 (SI 2014/3255) art.30 (1), (4)(a) (December 31, 2014).

3. Parental Bereavement Leave and Pay (Consequential Amendments to Subordinate Legislation) Regulations 2020 (SI 2020/354) reg.30 (April 6, 2020).

DEFINITIONS

"claimant"—see WRA 2007 s.24(1).
"compensation"—see para.(4).
"employed earner"—see reg.2.
"employment"—see reg.2.
"part-time employment"—see reg.2.
"paternity leave"—see para.(4).
"person participating as a service user"—see para.(5).

GENERAL NOTE

This is much the same as ESA Regs 2008 reg.95. **8.164**

Calculation of net earnings of employed earners

81.—(1) For the purposes of regulation 76 (calculation of earnings derived from employed earner's employment and income other than earnings) the earnings of a claimant derived from employment as an employed earner to be taken into account are the claimant's net earnings. **8.165**

(2) For the purposes of paragraph (1) net earnings are to be calculated by taking into account the gross earnings of the claimant from that employment less—

(a) any amount deducted from those earnings by way of—
 (i) income tax;
 (ii) primary Class 1 contributions under section 6(1)(a) of the Contributions and Benefits Act;
(b) one-half of any sum paid by the claimant in respect of a pay period by way of a contribution towards an occupational or personal pension scheme.

DEFINITIONS

"claimant"—see WRA 2007 s.24(1).
"employed earner"—see reg.2.
"occupational pension scheme"—see reg.2.
"pay period"—see reg.2.
"personal pension scheme"—see reg.2.

GENERAL NOTE

Compare ESA Regs 2008 reg.96(1), (3). **8.166**

Earnings of self-employed earners

82.—(1) Subject to paragraph (2), "earnings", in the case of employment as a self-employed earner, means the gross receipts of the employment and include any allowance paid under section 2 of the Employment and Training Act 1973 or section 2 of the Enterprise and New Towns (Scotland) Act 1990 to the claimant for the purpose of assisting the claimant in carrying on the claimant's business. **8.167**

(2) "Earnings" do not include—

(a) where a claimant is involved in providing board and lodging accommodation for which a charge is payable, any payment by way of such a charge;
(b) any award made by one of the Sports Councils named in section 23(2) of the National Lottery etc Act 1993 out of sums allocated to it for distribution under that section.

(3) In this regulation, "board and lodging" means—

(a) accommodation provided to a person or, if the person is a member of a family, to that person or any other member of that person's family, for a charge which is inclusive of the provision of that accommodation and at least some cooked or prepared meals which both are cooked or prepared (by a person other than the person to whom the accommodation is provided or a member of that person's family) and are consumed in that accommodation or associated premises; or

(b) accommodation provided to a person in a hotel, guest house, lodging house or some similar establishment, except accommodation provided by a close relative of the person or any other member of the person's family, or other than on a commercial basis.

DEFINITIONS

"board and lodging"—see para.(3).
"claimant"—see WRA 2007 s.24(1).
"self-employed earner"—see reg.2.

GENERAL NOTE

8.168 This is the same as ESA Regs 2008 reg.97.

Calculation of net profit of self-employed earners

8.169 **83.**—(1) For the purposes of regulation 77 (calculation of earnings of self-employed earners), the earnings of a claimant to be taken into account are to be—

(a) in the case of a self-employed earner who is engaged in employment on that self-employed earner's own account, the net profit derived from that employment;

(b) in the case of a self-employed earner whose employment is carried on in partnership or is that of a share fisherman within the meaning of the Social Security (Mariners' Benefits) Regulations 1975, that self-employed earner's share of the net profit derived from that employment less—

(i) an amount in respect of income tax and of National Insurance contributions payable under the Contributions and Benefits Act calculated in accordance with regulation 84 (deduction of tax and contributions for self-employed earners); and

(ii) one half of any contribution paid in the period that is relevant under regulation 77 (calculation of earnings of self-employed earners) in respect of a personal pension scheme.

(2) For the purposes of paragraph (1)(a) the net profit of the employment, except where paragraph (8) applies, is to be calculated by taking into account the earnings of the employment over the period determined under regulation 77 less—

(a) subject to paragraphs (4) to (6), any expenses wholly and exclusively defrayed in that period for the purposes of that employment;

(b) an amount in respect of—

(i) income tax; and

(ii) National Insurance contributions payable under the Contributions and Benefits Act, calculated in accordance with regulation 84 (deduction of tax and contributions for self-employed earners); and

(c) one half of any contribution paid in the period that is relevant under regulation 77 in respect of a personal pension scheme.

(3) For the purposes of paragraph (1)(b), the net profit of the employment is to be calculated by taking into account the earnings of the employment over the period determined under regulation 77 less, subject to paragraphs (4) to (6), any expenses wholly and exclusively defrayed in that period for the purpose of that employment.

(4) Subject to paragraph (5), a deduction is not to be made under paragraph (2)(a) or (3) in respect of—

(a) any capital expenditure;

(b) the depreciation of any capital asset;

(c) any sum employed or intended to be employed in the setting up or expansion of the employment;

(d) any loss incurred before the beginning of the period determined under regulation 77 (calculation of earnings of self-employed earners);

(e) the repayment of capital on any loan taken out for the purposes of the employment;

(f) any expenses incurred in providing business entertainment.

(5) A deduction is to be made under paragraph (2)(a) or (3) in respect of the repayment of capital on any loan used for—

(a) the replacement in the course of business of equipment or machinery; and

(b) the repair of an existing business asset except to the extent that any sum is payable under an insurance policy for its repair.

(6) The Secretary of State must refuse to make a deduction in respect of any expenses under paragraph (2)(a) or (3) where the Secretary of State is not satisfied that the expense has been defrayed or, having regard to the nature of the expense and its amount, that it has been reasonably incurred.

(7) A deduction—

(a) is not to be made under paragraph (2)(a) or (3) in respect of any sum unless it has been expended for the purposes of the business;

(b) is to be made under paragraph (2)(a) or (3) in respect of—

(i) the excess of any Value Added Tax paid over Value Added Tax received in the period determined under regulation 77;

(ii) any income expended in the repair of an existing asset except to the extent that any sum is payable under an insurance policy for its repair;

(iii) any payment of interest on a loan taken out for the purposes of the employment.

(8) Where a claimant is engaged in employment as a child minder the net profit of the employment is to be one-third of the earnings of that employment, less—

(a) an amount in respect of—

(i) income tax; and

(ii) National Insurance contributions payable under the Contributions and Benefits Act, calculated in accordance with regulation 84 (deduction of tax and contributions for self-employed earners); and

(b) one half of any contribution paid in respect of a personal pension scheme.

(9) Notwithstanding regulation 77 (calculation of earnings of self-employed earners) and the foregoing paragraphs, the Secretary of State may assess any item of a claimant's income or expenditure over a period other than that determined under regulation 77 as may, in the particular case, enable the weekly amount of that item of income or expenditure to be determined more accurately.

(10) Where a claimant is engaged in employment as a self-employed earner and that claimant is also engaged in one or more other employments as a self-employed or employed earner, any loss incurred in any one of the claimant's employments is not to be offset against the claimant's earnings in any other of the claimant's employments.

DEFINITIONS

"claimant"—see WRA 2007 s.24(1).
"employment"—see reg.2.
"personal pension scheme"—see reg.2.
"self-employed earner"—see reg.2.

GENERAL NOTE

8.170 This is much the same as ESA Regs 2008 reg.98.

Deduction of tax and contributions for self-employed earners

8.171 **84.**—(1) Subject to paragraph (2), the amount to be deducted in respect of income tax under regulation 83(1)(b)(i), (2)(b)(i) or (8)(a)(i) (calculation of net profit of self-employed earners) is to be calculated on the basis of the amount of chargeable income and as if that income were assessable to income tax at the basic rate [1, or in the case of a Scottish taxpayer, the Scottish basic rate,] of tax less only the [1 personal reliefs to which the claimant is entitled under Chapters 2, 3 and 3A of Part 3 of the Income Tax Act 2007 as are] appropriate to the claimant's circumstances.

(2) If the period determined under regulation 77 is less than a year, the earnings to which the basic rate [1, or the Scottish basic rate,] of tax is to be applied and the amount of the personal reliefs deductible under paragraph (1) are to be calculated on a pro rata basis.

(3) The amount to be deducted in respect of National Insurance contributions under regulation 83(1)(b)(i), (2)(b)(ii)or (8)(a)(ii) is to be the total of—

(a) [2...]
(b) the amount of Class 4 contributions (if any) which would be payable under section 15 of that Act (Class 4 contributions recoverable under the Income Tax Acts) at the percentage rate applicable at the date of claim on so much of the chargeable income as exceeds the lower limit but does not exceed the upper limit of profits applicable for the tax year in which the date of claim falls; but if the assessment period is less than a year, those limits are to be reduced pro rata.

(4) In this regulation—

"assessment period" means the period mentioned in regulation 77 over which the weekly amount of the claimant's earnings is to be determined;

"basic rate" has the same meaning as in the Income Tax Act 2007 (see section 989 of that Act);

"chargeable income" means—

(a) except where paragraph (b) applies, the earnings derived from the employment less any expenses deducted under paragraph (2)(a) or, as the case may be, (3) of regulation 83;

(b) in the case of employment as a child minder, one-third of the earnings of that employment.

[1 "Scottish basic rate" means the rate of income tax of that name calculated in accordance with section 6A of the Income Tax Act 2007;

"Scottish taxpayer" has the same meaning as in Chapter 2 of Part 4A of the Scotland Act 1998]

AMENDMENTS

1. Social Security (Scottish Rate of Income Tax etc.) (Amendment) Regulations 2016 (SI 2016/233) reg.8 (April 6, 2016).

2. Social Security (Class 2 National Insurance Contributions) (Consequential Amendments and Savings) Regulations 2024 (SI 2024/377) reg.8(21) (April 6, 2024).

DEFINITIONS

"claimant"—see WRA 2007 s.24(1).

"Contributions and Benefits Act"—see WRA 2007 s.65.

GENERAL NOTE

This is much the same as ESA Regs 2008 reg.99. 8.172

PART 11

Supplementary provisions

Waiting days

85.—(1) The number of days prescribed for the purposes of paragraph 2 of Schedule 2 to the Act (days during which a person is not entitled to an employment and support allowance at the beginning of a period of limited capability for work) is [1 seven]. 8.173

(2) Paragraph 2 of Schedule 2 to the Act does not apply where—

(a) the claimant's entitlement to an employment and support allowance commences within 12 weeks of the claimant's entitlement to income support, incapacity benefit, severe disablement allowance, state pension credit, a jobseeker's allowance, a carer's allowance, [2 carer support payment,] statutory sick pay or a maternity allowance coming to an end;

(b) the claimant is terminally ill and has—

(i) made a claim expressly on the ground of being terminally ill; or

(ii) made an application for supersession or revision in accordance with the Decisions and Appeals Regulations 1999 or the Decisions and Appeals Regulations 2013 which contains an express statement that the claimant is terminally ill;

(c) the claimant has been discharged from being a member of Her Majesty's forces and three or more days immediately before that discharge were days of sickness absence from duty, which are recorded by the Secretary of State; or

(d) the claimant is entitled to an employment and support allowance by virtue of section 1B of the Act (further entitlement after time-limiting).

AMENDMENTS

1. Social Security (Jobseeker's Allowance and Employment and Support Allowance) (Waiting Days) Amendment Regulations 2014 (SI 2014/2309) reg.2(4) (October 27, 2014).

2. Carer's Assistance (Carer Support Payment) (Scotland) Regulations 2023 (Consequential Amendments) Order 2023 (SI 2023/1218) art.25(5) (November 19, 2023).

DEFINITIONS

"claimant"—see WRA 2007 s.24(1).
"a member of Her Majesty's forces"—see reg.2(1).
"terminally ill"—see reg.2(1).

GENERAL NOTE

8.174 WRA 2007, s.22 and Sch.2 para.2 provide that "except in prescribed circumstances" a claimant cannot be entitled to ESA for a prescribed number of days at the beginning of a period of limited capability for work. This regulation originally set the number of these days of non-entitlement ("waiting days") at three, but that was increased to seven days with effect from October 27, 2014. It further provides in para.(2) for the exceptions to that general rule:

- where entitlement to ESA begins within 12 weeks of entitlement to IS, SPC, JSA, carer's allowance or SSP coming to an end (sub-para.(a));
- terminally ill claimants (including those seeking revision or supersession on the basis of being terminally ill) (sub-para.(b));
- discharge from His Majesty's forces where three or more days of recorded sickness absence from duty preceded it (sub-para.(c));
- where for someone not in the support group entitlement to ESA ended because of the time limit set by WRA 2007 s.1A (currently 365 days), but further entitlement arises under s.IB of that Act because subsequent deterioration in health now places that person in the support group (sub- para.(d)).

In addition, the general rule is, of course, affected by the "linking rule" (on which see reg.86) in a case of intermittent incapacity where that rule fuses into one ostensibly separate spells of limited capability for work: the "waiting days" only have to be served once in a period of limited capability for work.

Linking period

86. Any period of limited capability for work which is separated from another such period by not more than 12 weeks is to be treated as a continuation of the earlier period.

DEFINITIONS

"claimant"—see WRA 2007 s.24(1).
"week"—see reg.2.

GENERAL NOTE

8.175 Linking rules are crucial for those suffering from intermittent incapacity. They impact, to the claimant's benefit, as regards "waiting days"; those days of non-entitlement (see ESA Regs 2013, reg.85) only have to be served once in any period of limited capability for work. They are also relevant to determining the relevant benefit year and hence the appropriate tax years to which to have regard with respect to the application of the national insurance contribution conditions (see further the commentary to WRA 2007 Sch.1 Pt 1 paras 1–3). There is now only one linking rule: two ostensibly separate spells of limited capability for work will be fused into one where the separation period between the spells is not more than 12 weeks. This fusing does not, however, mean that days in the separation period thereby become ones of limited capability for work (*Chief Adjudication Officer v Astle* (Court of Appeal, judgment of March 17, 1999, noted in [1999] 6 J.S.S.L. 203). See further for more detail the commentary to SSCBA 1992, s.30C(1)(c) (the "linking" rule) in the 2011/12 edition of this Volume at 1.67–1.77). A period of limited capability for work can only be formed of days of actual limited capability for work and/or ones which the legislative scheme treats as ones of limited capability for work.

Claimants appealing a decision

87.—[1(1) This regulation applies where a claimant has made and is pursuing an appeal against a relevant decision of the Secretary of State as defined in regulation 26.] **8.176**

(2) Subject to paragraph (3), where this regulation applies, a determination of limited capability for work by the Secretary of State under regulation 15 must not be made until the appeal is determined by the First-tier Tribunal.

(3) Paragraph (2) does not apply where either—

(a) the claimant suffers from some specific disease or bodily or mental disablement from which the claimant was not suffering when entitlement began; or

(b) a disease or bodily or mental disablement from which the claimant was suffering when entitlement began has significantly worsened.

(4) Where this regulation applies and the Secretary of State makes a determination—

(a) in a case to which paragraph (3) applies (including where the determination is not the first such determination) that the claimant does not have or, by virtue of regulation 18 or 19, is to be treated as not having limited capability for work; or

(b) subsequent to a determination that the claimant is to be treated as having limited capability for work by virtue of a provision of these Regulations other than regulation 26, that the claimant is no longer to be so treated, this regulation and regulation 26 have effect as if that determination had not been made.

(5) Where this regulation applies and—

(a) the claimant is entitled to an employment and support allowance by virtue of being treated as having limited capability for work in accordance with regulation 26;

(b) neither of the circumstances in paragraph (3) applies, or, subsequent to the application of either of those circumstances, the claimant has been determined not to have limited capability for work; and

(c) the claimant's appeal is dismissed, withdrawn or struck out,

the claimant is to be treated as not having limited capability for work with effect from the day specified in paragraph (6).

(6) The day specified for the purposes of paragraph (5) is the first day of the benefit week following the date on which the Secretary of State receives

the First-tier Tribunal's notification that the appeal is dismissed, withdrawn or struck out.

(7) Where a claimant's appeal is successful, subject to paragraph (8), any finding of fact or other determination embodied in or necessary to the decision of the First-tier Tribunal or on which the First-tier Tribunal's decision is based is to be conclusive for the purposes of the decision of the Secretary of State, in relation to an award made in a case to which this regulation applies, as to whether the claimant has limited capability for work or limited capability for work-related activity.

(8) Paragraph (7) does not apply where, due to a change of circumstances after entitlement began, the Secretary of State is satisfied that it is no longer appropriate to rely on such finding or determination.

AMENDMENT

1. Employment and Support Allowance (Repeat Assessments and Pending Appeal Awards) (Amendment) Regulations 2015 (SI 2015/437) reg.4 (March 30, 2015).

DEFINITIONS

"claimant"—see WRA 2007 s.24(1).
"First-tier Tribunal"—see reg.2.

GENERAL NOTE

8.177 See the detailed commentary on that provision in the 2021/22 edition of Volume V at paras 4.330-4.335.

Absence from Great Britain

8.178 **88.**—(1) A claimant who is entitled to an employment and support allowance is to continue to be so entitled during a period of temporary absence from Great Britain only in accordance with regulations 89 to 92.

(2) A claimant who continues to be entitled to an employment and support allowance during a period of temporary absence is not disqualified for receiving that allowance during that period under section 18(4) of the Act.

DEFINITIONS

"claimant"—see WRA 2007 s.24(1).

GENERAL NOTE

8.179 Under s.1(3) of the WRA 2007, it is a condition of entitlement to ESA that the claimant should be "in Great Britain". However, para.5 of Sch.2 to that Act empowers the Secretary of State to "make provision . . . as to the circumstances in which a person is to be treated as being, or not being, in Great Britain". In addition, those entitled to new style ESA are disqualified under s.18(4)(a) while they are absent from Great Britain "except where regulations otherwise provide". Paragraph 6 of Sch.2 to the Act provides that "regulations may provide that in prescribed circumstances a claimant who is not in Great Britain may nevertheless be entitled to" ESA. The regulations in this Chapter are made under those powers.

Short absence

8.180 **89.** A claimant is to continue to be entitled to an employment and support allowance during the first four weeks of a temporary absence from Great Britain if—

(a) the period of absence is unlikely to exceed 52 weeks; and
(b) while absent from Great Britain, the claimant continues to satisfy the other conditions of entitlement to that employment and support allowance.

Definitions

"claimant"—see WRA 2007 s.24(1).
"week"—see reg.2.

General Note

This is identical to ESA Regs 2008 reg.152. 8.181

Absence to receive medical treatment

90.—(1) A claimant is to continue to be entitled to an employment and support allowance during the first 26 weeks of a temporary absence from Great Britain if— 8.182

(a) the period of absence is unlikely to exceed 52 weeks;
(b) while absent from Great Britain, the claimant continues to satisfy the other conditions of entitlement to that employment and support allowance;
(c) the claimant is absent from Great Britain only—
 (i) in connection with arrangements made for the treatment of the claimant for a disease or bodily or mental disablement directly related to the claimant's limited capability for work which commenced before leaving Great Britain; or
 (ii) because the claimant is accompanying a dependent child (which means any child or qualifying young person who is treated as the responsibility of the claimant or the claimant's partner, where that child or young person is a member of the claimant's household) in connection with arrangements made for the treatment of that child for a disease or bodily or mental disablement; and
(d) those arrangements relate to treatment—
 (i) outside Great Britain;
 (ii) during the period whilst the claimant is temporarily absent from Great Britain; and
 (iii) by, or under the supervision of, a person appropriately qualified to carry out that treatment.

(2) In this regulation, "appropriately qualified" means qualified to provide medical treatment, physiotherapy or a form of treatment which is similar to, or related to, either of those forms of treatment.

Definitions

"appropriately qualified"—see para.(2).
"child"—see reg.2.
"claimant"—see WRA 2007 s.24(1)
"dependent child"—see para.(1) (c) (ii)
"partner"—see reg.2.
"qualifying young person"—see reg.2.

General Note

Where the temporary absence is in connection with receiving medical treatment for a condition related to the claimant's limited capacity for work, or because the 8.183

claimant is accompanying a dependent child who is receiving medical treatment, ESA remains payable for the first 26 weeks of absence, as long as the total length of the absence is unlikely to exceed 52 weeks. The former requirement in ESA Regs 2008 to obtain the Secretary of State's permission before departure was removed as from October 26, 2009. Where the medical treatment abroad is paid for by the NHS, see reg.91 below.

Absence in order to receive NHS treatment

8.184 **91.** A claimant is to continue to be entitled to an employment and support allowance during any period of temporary absence from Great Britain if—

(a) while absent from Great Britain, the claimant continues to satisfy the other conditions of entitlement to that employment and support allowance; and

(b) that period of temporary absence is for the purpose of the claimant receiving treatment at a hospital or other institution outside Great Britain where the treatment is being provided—

(i) under section 6(2) of the Health Service Act (Performance of functions outside England) or section 6(2) of the Health Service (Wales) Act (Performance of functions outside Wales);

(ii) pursuant to arrangements made under section 12(1) of the Health Service Act (Secretary of State's arrangements with other bodies), section 10(1) of the Health Service (Wales) Act (Welsh Ministers' arrangements with other bodies), paragraph 18 of Schedule 4 to the Health Service Act (joint exercise of functions) or paragraph 18 of Schedule 3 to the Health Service (Wales) Act (joint exercise of functions); or

(iii) under any equivalent provision in Scotland or pursuant to arrangements made under such provision.

DEFINITIONS

"claimant"—see WRA 2007 s.24(1).

GENERAL NOTE

8.185 This is the same as ESA Regs 2008 reg.154.

Absence of member of family of member of Her Majesty's forces

92.—(1) A claimant is to continue to be entitled to an employment and support allowance during any period of temporary absence from Great Britain if the claimant is a member of the family of a member of Her Majesty's forces and temporarily absent from Great Britain by reason only of the fact that the claimant is living with that member.

(2) In this regulation "member of the family of a member of Her Majesty's forces" means the spouse, civil partner, son, daughter, step-son, step-daughter, father, father-in-law, step-father, mother, mother-in-law or step-mother of such a member.

DEFINITIONS

"claimant"—see WRA 2007 s.24(1).
"member of Her Majesty's forces"—see reg.(2) and Sch.1.
"member of the family of a member of Her Majesty's forces"—see para.(2).

General Note

This corresponds to ESA Regs 2008 reg.155. 8.186

PART 12

Disqualification

Disqualification for misconduct etc

93.—(1) Subject to paragraph (3), paragraph (2) applies where a claimant— 8.187

(a) has limited capability for work by reason of the claimant's own misconduct, except in a case where the limited capability is due to a sexually transmitted disease;

(b) fails without good cause to attend for or submit to medical or other treatment (excluding vaccination, inoculation or surgery which the Secretary of State considers is major) recommended by a doctor with whom, or a hospital or similar institution with which, the claimant is undergoing medical treatment, which would be likely to remove the limitation on the claimant's capability for work;

(c) fails without good cause to refrain from behaviour calculated to retard the claimant's recovery to health; or

(d) is, without good cause, absent from the claimant's place of residence without informing the Secretary of State where the claimant may be found.

(2) A claimant referred to in paragraph (1) is to be disqualified for receiving an employment and support allowance for such period not exceeding six weeks as the Secretary of State may determine in accordance with Chapter 2 of Part 1 of the Social Security Act 1998.

(3) Paragraph (2) does not apply where the claimant—

(a) is disqualified for receiving an employment and support allowance by virtue of regulations made under section 6B or 7 of the Social Security Fraud Act 2001; or

(b) is a person in hardship.

(4) In this regulation, "doctor" means a registered medical practitioner, or in the case of a medical practitioner practising outside the United Kingdom, a person registered or recognised as such in the country in which the person undertakes medical practice.

Definitions

"claimant"—see WRA 2007 s.24(1).
"doctor"—see para.(4).
"medical treatment"—see reg.2.
"person in hardship"—see reg.94.
"week"—see reg.2.

General Note

Disqualification here reflects the policy intention to deny ESA to those whose behaviour has in some way brought about their limited capability for work, or has worsened it, or where the claimant has behaved inappropriately in some other way. 8.188

This regulation provides that (subject to the two exceptions in para.(3)), someone who falls within one of the several "heads" of disqualification examined below must be disqualified for receiving ESA. As under the previous sickness and invalidity benefits regime and the incapacity benefit system, the maximum period imposable is six weeks. No minimum is specified (unlike disqualification in JSA where one week is specified—Jobseekers Act 1995 s.19(3)). Although, like JSA, ESA is in principle a weekly benefit, payment for less than a week is possible, so arguably the minimum should still be one day (the minimum unit for benefit purposes). While there have been some changes of wording from that in USI Regs reg.17, governing sickness and invalidity benefits disqualifications, and from Incapacity for Work (General) Regulations 1995 reg.18, in so far as the wording remains the same as that incapacity benefit provision, case authorities on that regime and its predecessors remain authoritative. Some of the "heads" are subject to a "good cause" saving. However, the rule-making power to further define or restrict "good cause" has not been exercised in this context (WRA 2007 s.18(3)).

If one or more of the "heads" apply, there must be some disqualification: the discretion afforded by the regulation goes only to the length of the period (maximum six weeks). As with exercising the equivalent discretion for JSA purposes, the determining authorities must act judicially and consider each case in the light of its circumstances and give reasons for their choice of period (see *R(U) 8/74(T)*; *R(S) 1/87*; *CS/002/1990*, para.6). The same rules on considering and recording decisions on the matter would apply (*R(U) 4/87*). Some of the factors relevant in exercising the discretion in that context may equally be relevant here. The burden lies on the decision maker to show that the claimant falls clearly and squarely within the head of disqualification (*R(S) 7/83*). Where "good cause" is the issue, it falls to the claimant to establish that he had it (*R(S) 9/51*). *R(S) 1/87* made it abundantly clear that in the same case the same facts could put in issue more than one of the heads of disqualification in USI Regs reg.17(1). There the heads at issue were paras 17(1)(b) and (1)(d)(ii). The poorly completed record of the SSAT's decision did not make clear on which head they rested disqualification. This was an error of law, a breach of the duty to record reasons for the decision and the material facts on which it is based. Presumably as well as complying with this duty, a tribunal should also comply with *R(U) 2/71* where the case involves the Secretary of State relying on a head of disqualification not set out in the appeal papers or the tribunal relying on a different ground to that relied on by the Secretary of State.

Paragraph (1)(a)

8.189 This penalises certain behaviour by the claimant. Disqualification must be imposed if his incapacity is due to his own misconduct, but two instances where incapacity may have arisen in consequence of what might otherwise be treated as sexual misconduct are expressly stated not to ground disqualification: (a) where the incapacity is due to a sexually transmitted disease; and (b) the case of pregnancy.

Misconduct has not been exhaustively defined. Presumably, by analogy with its use in the unemployment benefit and jobseeker's allowance contexts, it denotes conduct which is blameworthy, reprehensible and wrong. It is unclear in this context, whether merely reckless or negligent conduct will suffice. *R(S)2/53* has been thought to import a requirement of wilfulness, but this may be to read too much into a particular example of misconduct. In that case the Commissioner considered alcoholism, and upheld disqualification. Drinking to such an extent to endanger health raises a prima facie inference of misconduct which can only be rebutted if the claimant proves that the alcoholism was involuntary, the result of disease or disablement which destroyed his willpower, so that he was *unable* to refrain from excessive drinking. The particular evidence in that case of an anxiety state was insufficient to rebut the presumption. Whether in the current medical and social climate the provision could apply to incapacity through heavy smoking remains to be seen.

Paragraph (1)(b)

This seems designed to deal with a specific aspect of behaviour which may contribute to further limited capability for work or hinder recovery. Disqualification must be imposed where the claimant fails to attend for or submit to medical or other treatment. The medical or other treatment must be recommended by a doctor with whom, or a hospital or similar institution with which, he is undergoing medical treatment and be such as would be likely to render him capable of work. This formulation may reverse *R(S) 3/57*, depending on the scope of "other treatment". There the blind claimant gave up a vocational training course when she became pregnant and refused to resume it thereafter; under USI Regs reg.17(1)(c) she had not refused treatment for her disablement since the course could have no effect on her blindness (para.6; *cf. R2/60SB*). Failure to attend for or submit to certain medical or other treatment is explicitly exempt from the sanction, namely failure to attend for or submit to vaccination or inoculation of any kind or to major surgery. Establishing "good cause" for non-compliance precludes disqualification. In *R(S) 9/51* the claimant did so. Her non-attendance was founded on her own firm conviction that her religious beliefs (Christian Scientist) required her not to. It would not have been enough merely to establish membership of a sect whose religious rules forbade submission to treatment or examination. **8.190**

Paragraph (1)(c)

Disqualification here penalises a claimant who fails to refrain from behaviour calculated to retard his recovery. "Calculated to retard his recovery" does not import an intention on his part to do so; the test is an objective one: was his behaviour likely to do so. Thus in *R(S) 21/52* the Commissioner upheld disqualification of the claimant, suffering from influenza bronchitis who was taken ill after undertaking a 60-mile drive when so suffering. However in *R(S) 3/57* (above para.(1)(b)) the course was irrelevant to recovery from blindness, so leaving and refusing to resume the course could not ground disqualification. Establishing good cause for the failure precludes disqualification. Mere ignorance of the rules is not good cause (*R(S) 21/52*). **8.191**

Paragraph (1)(d)

This requires the claimant not to be absent from his place of residence without leaving word as to where he can be found. It is designed to penalise those who deliberately seek to avoid the Department's visiting officers who may (albeit nowadays very rarely) call as part of the Department's claims control mechanisms. It will only be invoked where visits have already proved ineffective, and as a matter of law the absence must have occurred during the currency of a claim. The rule cannot apply unless the claimant has a residence; it is not to be interpreted as imposing a requirement to have one (*R(S) 7/83*), so claimants of no fixed abode cannot be caught by it. *R(S) 1/87* requires findings be made as to place of residence, any absence in the relevant period, and on whether the claimant had failed to leave word where he could be found. If those findings showed the claimant's absence from his residence without leaving word as to his whereabouts, it would then fall to the claimant to establish good cause for so acting (see para.12). A claimant's genuine difficulty in leaving word where he might be found was held to constitute good cause in *R(S) 6/55*. There the claimant lived with relatives who were out at work on the three occasions that the visiting officer called. The claimant was out in the park or at the cinema on those occasions, and there was no one with whom he could leave a message. His doctor had advised him to get out as much as possible. Mere ignorance of the rules is not good cause (*R(S) 21/52*). **8.192**

Exceptions (paragraph (3))

Someone disqualified under the specified fraud provision cannot be disqualified under this regulation (sub-para.(a)). Nor can someone who qualifies as a "person in hardship" as defined in reg.94 (sub-para.(b)). **8.193**

Meaning of "person in hardship"

8.194 **94.**—(1) A claimant is a "person in hardship" if the claimant—

(a) has informed the Secretary of State of the circumstances on which the claimant relies to establish that fact; and

(b) falls within paragraph (2), (3) or (5).

(2) A claimant falls within this paragraph if—

(a) she is pregnant;

(b) a member of the claimant's family is pregnant;

(c) the claimant is single and aged less than 18; or

(d) the claimant is a member of a couple and both members are aged less than 18.

(3) Subject to paragraph (4), the claimant falls within this paragraph if the claimant or the claimant's partner—

(a) has been awarded an attendance allowance, [1armed forces independence payment] the care component or the daily living component;

(b) has claimed attendance allowance, [1armed forces independence payment] [3, child disability payment] [4,] personal independence payment [4 or adult disability payment] and the claim has not been determined;

(c) devotes what the Secretary of State considers is a considerable portion of each week to caring for another person who—

(i) has been awarded an attendance allowance, [1armed forces independence payment] the care component or the daily living component; or

(ii) has claimed attendance allowance, [1armed forces independence payment] [3, child disability payment] [4,] personal independence payment [4 or adult disability payment] and the claim has not been determined; or

(d) has attained the qualifying age for state pension credit, which has the meaning given in section 1(6) of the State Pension Credit Act 2002.

(4) A claimant to whom paragraph (3)(b) or (3)(c)(ii) applies is a person in hardship only for 26 weeks from the date of the claim unless the claimant is a person in hardship under another provision of this regulation.

(5) The claimant falls within this paragraph where the Secretary of State is satisfied, having regard to all the circumstances and, in particular, the matters set out in paragraph (6), that unless an employment and support allowance is paid, the claimant, or a member of the claimant's family, will suffer hardship.

(6) The matters referred to in paragraph (5) are—

(a) the resources which are likely to be available to the claimant and the claimant's family and the length of time for which they might be available; and

(b) whether there is a substantial risk that essential items, including food, clothing and heating, will cease to be available to the claimant or a member of the claimant's family, or will be available at considerably reduced levels and the length of time for which this might be so.

(7) In this regulation—

[4"adult disability payment" has the meaning given in regulation 2 of the Disability Assistance for Working Age People (Scotland) Regulations 2022;]

[1"armed forces independence payment" means armed forces independence payment under the Armed Forces and Reserve Forces (Compensation Scheme) Order 2011;]

"attendance allowance" means—

(a) an attendance allowance under section 64 of the Contributions and Benefits Act;

(b) an increase of disablement pension under section 104 or 105 of that Act;

(c) [1*omitted*]

(d) [1*omitted*];

(e) a payment by virtue of article 14, 15, 16, 43 or 44 of the Personal Injuries (Civilians) Scheme 1983 or any analogous payment;

(f) any payment based on the need for attendance which is paid as an addition to a war disablement pension (which means any retired pay or pension or allowance payable in respect of disablement under an instrument specified in section 639(2) of the Income Tax (Earnings and Pensions) Act 2003);

[3"care component" means—

(a) the care component of disability living allowance at the highest or middle rate prescribed under section 72(3) of the Contributions and Benefits Act; or

(b) the care component of child disability payment at the highest or middle rate provided for in regulation 11(5) of the Disability Assistance for Children and Young People (Scotland) Regulations 2021;]

[3"child disability payment" has the meaning given in regulation 2 of the Disability Assistance for Children and Young People (Scotland) Regulations 2021;]

[4"daily living component" means—

(a) in respect of personal independence payment, the daily living component of that payment at the standard or enhanced rate referred to in section 78 of the Welfare Reform Act 2012;

(b) in respect of adult disability payment, the daily living component of that payment at the standard or enhanced rate referred to in regulation 5 of the Disability Assistance for Working Age People (Scotland) Regulations 2022.]

"disability living allowance" means a disability living allowance under section 71 of the Contributions and Benefits Act;

"personal independence payment" means an allowance under Part 4 of the Welfare Reform Act 2012.

AMENDMENTS

1. Armed Forces and Reserve Forces Compensation Scheme (Consequential Provisions: Subordinate Legislation) Order 2013 (SI 2013/591) Sch.1 para.51(2)(a) (April 29, 2013).

2. Social Security (Miscellaneous Amendments) (No.2) Regulations 2013 (SI 2013/1508) reg.5(1), (4) (October 29, 2013).

3. Social Security (Scotland) Act 2018 (Disability Assistance for Children and Young People) (Consequential Modifications) Order 2021 (SI 2021/786) art.23 (July 26, 2021).

4. Social Security (Disability Assistance for Working Age People) (Consequential Amendments) Order 2022 (SI 2022/177) art.16 (March 21, 2022).

DEFINITIONS

"attendance allowance"—see para.(7).
"care component"—see para.(7).
"claimant"—see WRA 2007 s.24(1).
"Contributions and Benefits Act"—see WRA 2007 s.65.
"daily living component"—see para.(7).
"disability living allowance"—see para.(7).
"family"—see reg.2.
"person in hardship"—see para.(1).
"personal independence payment"—see para.(7).

8.195 GENERAL NOTE

Paragraph (1)

8.196 A person in hardship cannot be disqualified from receiving new style ESA under reg.93 (see para.(3)(b) of that regulation). This paragraph defines someone as a "person in hardship" who notifies the Secretary of State of the circumstances relied on to establish this, so long as he satisfies the conditions set in paras (2), (3) or (5).

Paragraph (2)

8.197 This covers a claimant who is pregnant; a claimant where a family member is pregnant; the claimant is single and under 18; and the claimant who is a member of a couple and both the claimant and partner are under 18.

Paragraphs (3), (4)

8.198 This covers someone aged 60 or over; someone responsible for a child or young perso who is a member of his household someone who has been awarded attendance allowance, the care component (middle or higher rate) of disability living allowance or an equivalent benefit (see also para.(7)); and a carer who devotes a considerable portion of a week to caring for another who has been awarded a relevant benefit (see also para.(7)). The paragraph also brings in, but only for 26 weeks unless the claimant also qualifies under another head, someone who has claimed one of the relevant benefits, but the claim remains undetermined, or the carer devoting a substantial portion of the week to caring for someone in that position (paras (3)(c), (d)(ii), (4)).

Paragraphs (5), (6)

8.199 These cover the claimant where the Secretary of State is satisfied that unless ESA is paid, the claimant or a member of his family will suffer hardship. In considering whether that is the case, he must have regard to all the circumstances, particularly those set out in para.(6).

Treating a claimant as not having limited capability for work

8.200 **95.** The claimant is to be treated as not having limited capability for work if the claimant is disqualified for receiving an employment and support allowance during a period of imprisonment or detention in legal custody if that disqualification is for more than six weeks.

DEFINITIONS

"claimant"—see WRA 2007 s.24(1).
"week"—see reg.2.

GENERAL NOTE

Those disqualified for new style ESA under WRA 2007 s.18(4) for more than six weeks because they are imprisoned or detained in custody are treated as not having limited capability for work. 8.201

Exceptions from disqualification for imprisonment

96.—(1) Notwithstanding section 18(4)(b) of the Act, a claimant is not disqualified for receiving an employment and support allowance for any period during which that claimant is undergoing imprisonment or detention in legal custody— 8.202

(a) in connection with a charge brought or intended to be brought against the claimant in criminal proceedings;
(b) pursuant to any sentence of a court in criminal proceedings; or
(c) pursuant to any order for detention made by a court in criminal proceedings,

unless paragraph (2) applies.

(2) This paragraph applies where—

(a) a penalty is imposed on the claimant at the conclusion of the proceedings referred to in paragraph (1); or
(b) in the case of default of payment of a sum adjudged to be paid on conviction, a penalty is imposed in respect of such default.

(3) Notwithstanding section 18(4)(b) of the Act, a claimant ("C") is not to be disqualified for receiving an employment and support allowance, for any period during which C is undergoing detention in legal custody after the conclusion of criminal proceedings if it is a period during which C is detained in a hospital or similar institution in Great Britain as a person suffering from mental disorder unless C satisfies either of the following conditions.

(4) The first condition is that—

(a) C is being detained under section 45A or 47 of the Mental Health Act 1983 (power of higher courts to direct hospital admission; removal to hospital of persons serving sentences of imprisonment etc); and
(b) in any case where there is in relation to C a release date within the meaning of section 50(3) of that Act, C is being detained on or before the day which the Secretary of State certifies to be that release date.

(5) The second condition is that C is being detained under—

(a) section 59A of the Criminal Procedure (Scotland) Act 1995 (hospital direction); or
(b) section 136 of the Mental Health (Care and Treatment) (Scotland) Act 2003 (transfer of prisoners for treatment of mental disorder).

(6) For the purposes of this regulation—

(a) "court" means any court in the United Kingdom, the Channel Islands or the Isle of Man or in any place to which the Colonial Prisoners Removal Act 1884 applies or any naval court-martial, army court-martial or air force court-martial within the meaning of the Courts-Martial (Appeals) Act 1968 or the Courts-Martial Appeal Court;
(b) "hospital or similar institution" means any place (not being a prison, a young offender institution, a secure training centre,

secure accommodation in a children's home [1, a place at which a secure accommodation service within the meaning of Part 1 of the Regulation and Inspection of Social Care (Wales) Act 2016 is being provided] or a remand centre, and not being at or in any such place) in which persons suffering from mental disorder are or may be received for care or treatment;

(c) "penalty" means a sentence of imprisonment or detention under section 90 or 91 of the Powers of Criminal Courts (Sentencing) Act 2000, [2or section 250 or 259 of the Sentencing Code] a detention and training order under section 100 of that Act, [2section 100 of the Powers of Criminal Courts (Sentencing) Act 2000 or Chapter 2 of Part 10 of the Sentencing Code] a sentence of detention for public protection under section 226 of the Criminal Justice Act 2003 or an extended sentence under section 228 of that Act or, in Scotland, under section 205, 207 or 208 of the Criminal Procedure (Scotland) Act 1995;

(d) in relation to a person who is liable to be detained in Great Britain as a result of any order made under the Colonial Prisoners Removal Act 1884, references to a prison must be construed as including references to a prison within the meaning of that Act;

(e) criminal proceedings against any person must be deemed to be concluded upon that person being found insane in those proceedings so that the person cannot be tried or that person's trial cannot proceed.

(7) Where a claimant outside Great Britain is undergoing imprisonment or detention in legal custody and, in similar circumstances in Great Britain, the claimant would, by virtue of this regulation, not have been disqualified for receiving an employment and support allowance, the claimant is not disqualified for receiving that allowance by reason only of the imprisonment or detention.

AMENDMENTS

1. Social Security and Child Support (Regulation and Inspection of Social Care (Wales) Act 2016) (Consequential Provision) Regulations 2018 (SI 2018/228) reg.15(2) (April 2, 2018).

2. Sentencing Act 2020 Sch.24 para.413 (December 1, 2020).

DEFINITIONS

"claimant"—see WRA 2007 s.24(1).
"court"—see para.(6) (a).
"hospital or similar institution"—see para.(6)(b).
"penalty"—see para.(6)(c).
"prison"—see para.(6)(d)

GENERAL NOTE

8.203 Under s.18(4) of the WRA 2007, a claimant is disqualified for new style ESA while "undergoing imprisonment or detention in legal custody". This regulation establishes exceptions to that rule. Under paras (1) and (2), there is no disqualification while the claimant is in custody pending trial or sentence unless a penalty is imposed. For these purposes "the definition of 'penalty' is intended to include all sentences of imprisonment and those forms of detention for persons under 21 that may be regarded as equivalent" *(SSWP v NC (ESA)* [2023] UKUT 124 (AAC), a decision on the equivalent reg.160 of the ESA Regs 2008). Payment of ESA is suspended under reg.97 below during the period when it is not known whether a penalty will eventually be imposed. By para.(7), the same rule is applied to claimants imprisoned outside Great Britain Under para.(3), there is no disqualification where the claimant is compulsorily detained in hospital following the conclusion of criminal proceedings unless a prison sentence is imposed and the claimant is subsequently transferred to hospital under the specified legislation.

Suspension of payment of an employment and support allowance during imprisonment

97.—(1) Subject to the following provisions of this regulation, the payment of an employment and support allowance to any claimant— 8.204

(a) which is excepted from the operation of section 18(4)(b) of the Act by virtue of the provisions of regulation 96(1), (3) or (7); or

(b) which is payable otherwise than in respect of a period during which the claimant is undergoing imprisonment or detention in legal custody, is suspended while that claimant is undergoing imprisonment or detention in legal custody.

(2) An employment and support allowance is not to be suspended while the claimant is liable to be detained in a hospital or similar institution, as defined in regulation 96(6), during a period for which in the claimant's case, the allowance is or would be excepted from the operation of section 18(4)(b) by virtue of the provisions of regulation 96(3).

(3) Where, by virtue of this regulation, payment of an employment and support allowance is suspended for any period, the period of suspension is not to be taken into account in calculating any period under the provisions of regulation 55 of the Claims and Payments Regulations 2013 (extinguishment of right to payment if payment is not obtained within the prescribed time).

DEFINITIONS

"claimant"—see WRA 2007 s.24(1).
"hospital or similar institution"—see reg.96(6).

GENERAL NOTE

See the annotation to reg.96 above. 8.205

PART 13

Periods of less than a week

Entitlement for less than a week – amount of an employment and support allowance payable

98.—(1) This regulation applies where the claimant is entitled to an employment and support allowance for a part-week and this regulation is subject to the following provisions of this Part. 8.206

(2) The amount payable by way of an employment and support allowance in respect of a part-week is to be calculated by applying the formula—

$$(N\chi X)/7$$

where—

X is the amount calculated in accordance with section 2(1) of the Act;

N is the number of days in the part-week.

(3) In this Part—

"part-week" means an entitlement to an employment and support allowance in respect of any period of less than a week; and

"relevant week" means the period of seven days determined in accordance with regulation 99.

DEFINITIONS

"claimant"—see WRA 2007 s.24(1).
"part-week"—see para.(3).
"relevant week"—see para.(3).

GENERAL NOTE

8.207 This has much the same effect as ESA Regs 2008 reg.165.

Relevant week

8.208 **99.**—(1) Where a part-week—

(a) is the whole period for which an employment and support allowance is payable, or occurs at the beginning of an award, the relevant week is the period of seven days ending on the last day of that part-week; or
(b) occurs at the end of an award, the relevant week is the period of seven days beginning on the first day of the part-week.

(2) Where a claimant has an award of an employment and support allowance and that claimant's benefit week changes, for the purpose of calculating the amounts of an employment and support allowance payable for the part-week beginning on the day after the last complete benefit week before the change and ending immediately before the change, the relevant week is the period of seven days beginning on the day after the last complete benefit week.

DEFINITIONS

"benefit week"—see reg.2.
"claimant"—see WRA 2007 s.24(1).
"part-week"—see reg.98(3).
"relevant week"— see reg.98(3).

GENERAL NOTE

8.209 This has the same effect as ESA Regs 2008 reg.166.

Modification in the calculation of income

8.210 **100.** For the purposes of regulation 98 (entitlement for less than a week – amount of an employment and support allowance payable), a claimant's income is to be calculated in accordance with regulations 76 to 84 subject to the following changes—

(a) any income which is due to be paid in the relevant week is to be treated as paid on the first day of that week;

(b) any widow's benefit, training allowance, widowed parent's allowance, [1 bereavement support payment under section 30 of the Pensions Act 2014], carer's allowance [2, carer support payment] and any increase in disablement pension payable in accordance with Part 1 of Schedule 7 to the Contributions and Benefits Act (unemployability supplement) which is payable in the relevant week but not in respect of any day in the part-week is to be disregarded;
(c) where the part-week occurs at the end of the claim—
   (i) any income; or
   (ii) any change in the amount of income of the same kind,
   which is first payable within the relevant week but not on any day in the part-week is to be disregarded;
(d) where only part of the weekly balance of income is taken into account in the relevant week, the balance is to be disregarded.

AMENDMENTS

1. Pensions Act 2014 (Consequential, Supplementary and Incidental Amendments) Order 2017 (SI 2017/422) art.44 (April 6, 2017).
2. Carer's Assistance (Carer Support Payment) (Scotland) Regulations 2023 (Consequential Amendments) Order 2023 (SI 2023/1218) art.25(6) (November 19, 2023).

DEFINITIONS

"carer's allowance"—see reg.2.
"claimant"—see WRA 2007 s.24(1).
"training allowance"—see reg.2.
"week"—see reg.2.
"part-week"—see reg.98(3).
"relevant week"— see reg.98(3).

GENERAL NOTE

This has the same effect as ESA Regs 2008 reg.167. 8.211

Reduction in certain cases

101.—(1) Where a disqualification is to be made in accordance with regulation 93 in respect of a part-week, the amount referred to in paragraph (2) is to be payable by way of an employment and support allowance in respect of that part-week. 8.212
(2) The amount mentioned in paragraph (1) is—
(a) one seventh of the employment and support allowance which would have been paid for the part-week if—
   (i) there was no disqualification under regulation 93; and
   (ii) it was not a part-week; multiplied by
(b) the number of days in the part-week in respect of which no disqualification is to be made in accordance with regulation 93.

DEFINITIONS

"claimant"—see WRA 2007 s.24(1).
"part-week"—see reg.98(3).
"relevant week"— see reg.98(3).

GENERAL NOTE

This has the same effect as ESA Regs 2008 reg.168. 8.213

Payment of an employment and support allowance for days of certain treatment

8.214 **102.**—(1) Where a claimant is entitled to an employment and support allowance as a result of being treated as having limited capability for work in accordance with regulation 22, the amount payable is to be equal to one seventh of the amount of the employment and support allowance which would be payable in respect of a week in accordance with section 2(1) of the Act multiplied by N.

(2) In paragraph (1), N is the number of days in that week on which the claimant was receiving treatment referred to in regulation 22 or recovering from that treatment, but does not include any day during which the claimant does work.

SCHEDULE 1

Regulation 2

HER MAJESTY'S FORCES

PART 1

PRESCRIBED ESTABLISHMENTS AND ORGANISATIONS

8.215

1. Any of the regular naval, military or air forces of the Crown.

2. Royal Fleet Reserve.

3. Royal Navy Reserve.

4. Royal Marines Reserve.

5. Army Reserve.

6. Territorial Army.

7. Royal Air Force Reserve.

8. Royal Auxiliary Air Force.

9. The Royal Irish Regiment, to the extent that its members are not members of any force falling within paragraph 1.

PART 2

ESTABLISHMENTS AND ORGANISATIONS OF WHICH HER MAJESTY'S FORCES DO NOT CONSIST

8.216 **10.** Her Majesty's forces are not to be taken to consist of any of the establishments or organisations specified in Part 1 of this Schedule by virtue only of the employment in such establishment or organisation of the following persons—

(a) any person who is serving as a member of any naval force of Her Majesty's forces and who (not having been an insured person under the National Insurance Act 1965 and not having been a contributor under the Social Security Act 1975 or not being a contributor under the Contributions and Benefits Act) locally entered that force at an overseas base;

(b) any person who is serving as a member of any military force of Her Majesty's forces and who entered that force, or was recruited for that force outside the United Kingdom, and the depot of whose unit is situated outside the United Kingdom;

(c) any person who is serving as a member of any air force of Her Majesty's forces and who entered that force, or was recruited for that force, outside the United Kingdom, and is liable under the terms of engagement to serve only in a specified part of the world outside the United Kingdom.

General Note

This is the same as ESA Regs 2008 Sch.1. 8.217

SCHEDULE 2 **Regulation 15(2) and (3)**

Assessment of Whether a Claimant has Limited Capability for Work

PART 1

Physical Disabilities 8.218

(1) Activity	(2) Descriptors	(3) Points
1. Mobilising unaided by another person with or without a walking stick, manual wheelchair or other aid if such aid is normally or could reasonably be worn or used.	1 (a) Cannot, unaided by another person, either: (i) mobilise more than 50 metres on level ground without stopping in order to avoid significant discomfort or exhaustion; or (ii) repeatedly mobilise 50 metres within a reasonable timescale because of significant discomfort or exhaustion.	15
	(b) Cannot, unaided by another person, mount or descend two steps even with the support of a handrail.	9
	(c) Cannot, unaided by another person, either: (i) mobilise more than 100 metres on level ground without stopping in order to avoid significant discomfort or exhaustion; or (ii) repeatedly mobilise 100 metres within a reasonable timescale because of significant discomfort or exhaustion.	9
	(d) Cannot, unaided by another person, either: (i) mobilise more than 200 metres on level ground without stopping in order to avoid significant discomfort or exhaustion; or (ii) repeatedly mobilise 200 metres within a reasonable timescale because of significant discomfort or exhaustion.	6
	(e) None of the above applies.	0

(1) Activity	(2) Descriptors	(3) Points
2. Standing and sitting.	2 (a) Cannot move between one seated position and another seated position which are located next to one another without receiving physical assistance from another person.	15
	(b) Cannot, for the majority of the time, remain at a work station: (i) standing unassisted by another person (even if free to move around); (ii) sitting (even in an adjustable chair); or (iii) a combination of paragraphs (i) and (ii), (for more than 30 minutes, before needing to move away in order to avoid significant discomfort or exhaustion.	9
	(c) Cannot, for the majority of the time, remain at a work station: (i) standing unassisted by another person (even if free to move around); (ii) sitting (even in an adjustable chair); or (iii) a combination of paragraphs (i) and (ii), for more than an hour before needing to move away in order to avoid significant discomfort or exhaustion.	6
	(d) None of the above applies.	0
3. Reaching.	3 (a) Cannot raise either arm as if to put something in the top pocket of a coat or jacket.	15
	(b) Cannot raise either arm to top of head as if to put on a hat.	9
	(c) Cannot raise either arm above head height as if to reach for something.	6
	(d) None of the above applies.	0
4. Picking up and moving or transferring by the use of the upper body and arms.	4 (a) Cannot pick up and move a 0.5 litre carton full of liquid.	15
	(b) Cannot pick up and move a one litre carton full of liquid.	9
	(c) Cannot transfer a light but bulky object such as an empty cardboard box.	6
	(d) None of the above applies.	0
5. Manual dexterity.	5 (a) Cannot press a button (such as a telephone keypad) with either hand or cannot turn the pages of a book with either hand.	15
	(b) Cannot pick up a £1 coin or equivalent with either hand.	15
	(c) Cannot use a pen or pencil to make a meaningful mark with either hand.	9
	(d) Cannot single-handedly use a suitable keyboard or mouse.	9
	(e) None of the above applies.	0

(1) Activity	(2) Descriptors		(3) Points
6. Making self understood through speaking, writing, typing, or other means which are normally or could reasonably be used, unaided by another person, to strangers.	6	(a) Cannot convey a simple message, such as the presence of a hazard.	15
		(b) Has significant difficulty conveying a simple message	15
		(c) Has some difficulty conveying a simple message to strangers.	6
		(d) None of the above applies.	0
7. Understanding communication by: (i) verbal means (such as hearing or lip reading) alone; (ii) non-verbal means (such as reading 16 point print or Braille) alone; or (iii) a combination of sub-paragraphs (i) and (ii), using any aid that is normally or could reasonably be used, unaided by another person.	7	(a) Cannot understand a simple message, such as the location of a fire escape, due to sensory impairment.	15
		(b) Has significant difficulty understanding a simple message from a stranger due to sensory impairment.	15
		(c) Has some difficulty understanding a simple message from a stranger due to sensory impairment.	6
		(d) None of the above applies.	0
8. Navigation and maintaining safety using a guide dog or other aid if either or both are normally used or could reasonably be used.	8	(a) Unable to navigate around familiar surroundings, without being accompanied by another person, due to sensory impairment.	15
		(b) Cannot safely complete a potentially hazardous task such as crossing the road, without being accompanied by another person, due to sensory impairment.	15
		(c) Unable to navigate around unfamiliar surroundings, without being accompanied by another person, due to sensory impairment.	9
		(d) None of the above applies.	0
9. Absence or loss of control whilst conscious leading to extensive evacuation of the bowel and/or bladder, other than enuresis (bedwetting), despite the wearing or use of any aids or adaptations which are normally or could reasonably be worn or used.	9	(a) At least once a month experiences: (i) loss of control leading to extensive evacuation of the bowel and/or voiding of the bladder; or (ii) substantial leakage of the contents of a collecting device sufficient to require cleaning and a change in clothing.	15
		(b) The majority of the time is at risk of loss of control leading to extensive evacuation of the bowel and/or voiding of the bladder, sufficient to require cleaning and a change in clothing, if not able to reach a toilet quickly.	6
		(c) Neither of the above applies.	0
10. Consciousness during waking moments.	10	(a) At least once a week, has an involuntary episode of lost or altered consciousness resulting in significantly disrupted awareness or concentration.	15

(1) Activity	(2) Descriptors	(3) Points
	(b) At least once a month, has an involuntary episode of lost or altered consciousness resulting in significantly disrupted awareness or concentration.	6
	(c) Neither of the above applies.	0

PART 2

Mental, cognitive and intellectual function assessment

(1) Activity	(2) Descriptors	(3) Points
11. Learning tasks.	11 (a) Cannot learn how to complete a simple task, such as setting an alarm clock.	15
	(b) Cannot learn anything beyond a simple task, such as setting an alarm clock.	9
	(c) Cannot learn anything beyond a moderately complex task, such as the steps involved in operating a washing machine to clean clothes.	6
	(d) None of the above applies.	0
12. Awareness of everyday hazards (such as boiling water or sharp objects).	12 (a) Reduced awareness of everyday hazards leads to a significant risk of: (i) injury to self or others; or (ii) damage to property or possessions, such that the claimant requires supervision for the majority of the time to maintain safety.	15
	(b) Reduced awareness of everyday hazards leads to a significant risk of: (i) injury to self or others; or (ii) damage to property or possessions, such that the claimant frequently requires supervision to maintain safety.	9
	(c) Reduced awareness of everyday hazards leads to a significant risk of: (i) injury to self or others; or (ii) damage to property or possessions, such that the claimant occasionally requires supervision to maintain safety.	6
	(d) None of the above applies.	0

(1) Activity	(2) Descriptors			(3) Points
13. Initiating and completing personal action (which means planning, organisation, problem solving, prioritising or switching tasks).	13	(a)	Cannot, due to impaired mental function, reliably initiate or complete at least two sequential personal actions.	15
		(b)	Cannot, due to impaired mental function, reliably initiate or complete at least two sequential personal actions for the majority of the time.	9
		(c)	Frequently cannot, due to impaired mental function, reliably initiate or complete at least two sequential personal actions.	6
		(d)	None of the above applies.	0
14. Coping with change.	14	(a)	Cannot cope with any change to the extent that day to day life cannot be managed.	15
		(b)	Cannot cope with minor planned change (such as a prearranged change to the routine time scheduled for a lunch break), to the extent that, overall, day to day life is made significantly more difficult.	9
		(c)	Cannot cope with minor unplanned change (such as the timing of an appointment on the day it is due to occur), to the extent that, overall, day to day life is made significantly more difficult.	6
		(d)	None of the above applies	0
15. Getting about.	15	(a)	Cannot get to any place outside the claimant's home with which the claimant is familiar.	15
		(b)	Is unable to get to a specified place with which the claimant is familiar, without being accompanied by another person.	9
		(c)	Is unable to get to a specified place with which the claimant is unfamiliar without being accompanied by another person.	6
		(d)	None of the above applies.	0
16. Coping with social engagement due to cognitive impairment or mental disorder.	16	(a)	Engagement in social contact is always precluded due to difficulty relating to others or significant distress experienced by the claimant.	15
		(b)	Engagement in social contact with someone unfamiliar to the claimant is always precluded due to difficulty relating to others or significant distress experienced by the claimant.	9

(1) Activity	(2) Descriptors		(3) Points
	(c)	Engagement in social contact with someone unfamiliar to the claimant is not possible for the majority of the time due to difficulty relating to others or significant distress experienced by the claimant.	6
	(d)	None of the above applies.	0
17. Appropriateness of behaviour with other people, due to cognitive impairment or mental disorder.	17 (a)	Has, on a daily basis, uncontrollable episodes of aggressive or disinhibited behaviour that would be unreasonable in any workplace.	15
	(b)	Frequently has uncontrollable episodes of aggressive or disinhibited behaviour that would be unreasonable in any workplace.	15
	(c)	Occasionally has uncontrollable episodes of aggressive or disinhibited behaviour that would be unreasonable in any workplace.	9
	(d)	None of the above applies.	0

General Note

8.219 This Sch. is the same as ESA Regs 2008 Sch.2, as amended.

SCHEDULE 3

Regulation 30(1)

8.220 Assessment of whether a claimant has limited capability for work-related activity

Activity	Descriptors
1. Mobilising unaided by another person with or without a walking stick, manual wheelchair or other aid if such aid is normally or could reasonably be worn or used.	1. Cannot either: (a) mobilise more than 50 metres on level ground without stopping in order to avoid significant discomfort or exhaustion; or (b) repeatedly mobilise 50 metres within a reasonable timescale because of significant discomfort or exhaustion.
2. Transferring from one seated position to another.	2. Cannot move between one seated position and another seated position located next to one another without receiving physical assistance from another person.
3. Reaching.	3. Cannot raise either arm as if to put something in the top pocket of a coat or jacket.
4. Picking up and moving or transferring by the use of the upper body and arms (excluding standing, sitting, bending or kneeling and all other activities specified in this Schedule).	4. Cannot pick up and move a 0.5 litre carton full of liquid.
5. Manual dexterity.	5. Cannot press a button (such as a telephone keypad) with either hand or cannot turn the pages of a book with either hand.

Activity	Descriptors
6. Making self understood through speaking, writing, typing, or other means which are normally, or could reasonably be, used unaided by another person.	6. Cannot convey a simple message, such as the presence of a hazard.
7. Understanding communication by: (i) verbal means (such as hearing or lip reading) alone; (ii) non-verbal means (such as reading 16 point print or Braille) alone; or (iii) a combination of subparagraphs (i) and (ii), using any aid that is normally, or could reasonably, be used unaided by another person.	7. Cannot understand a simple message, such as the location of a fire escape, due to sensory impairment.
8. Absence or loss of control whilst conscious leading to extensive evacuation of the bowel and/or voiding of the bladder, other than enuresis (bed-wetting), despite the wearing or use of any aids or adaptations which are normally or could reasonably be worn or used.	8. At least once a week experiences (a) loss of control leading to extensive evacuation of the bowel and/or voiding of the bladder; or (b) substantial leakage of the contents of a collecting device sufficient to require the individual to clean themselves. and change clothing.
9. Learning tasks.	9. Cannot learn how to complete a simple task, such as setting an alarm clock, due to cognitive impairment or mental disorder.
10. Awareness of hazard.	10. Reduced awareness of everyday hazards, due to cognitive impairment or mental disorder, leads to a significant risk of: (a) injury to self or others; or (b) damage to property or possessions such that the claimant requires supervision for the majority of the time to maintain safety.
11. Initiating and completing personal action (which means planning, organisation, problem solving, prioritising or switching tasks).	11. Cannot, due to impaired mental function, reliably initiate or complete at least two sequential personal actions.
12. Coping with change.	12. Cannot cope with any change, due to cognitive impairment or mental disorder, to the extent that day to day life cannot be managed.
13. Coping with social engagement, due to cognitive impairment or mental disorder.	13. Engagement in social contact is always precluded due to difficulty relating to others or significant distress experienced by the claimant.
14. Appropriateness of behaviour with other people, due to cognitive impairment or mental disorder.	14. Has, on a daily basis, uncontrollable episodes of aggressive or disinhibited behaviour that would be unreasonable in any workplace.

Activity	Descriptors
15. Conveying food or drink to the mouth.	15 (a) Cannot convey food or drink to the claimant's own mouth without receiving physical assistance from someone else; (b) Cannot convey food or drink to the claimant's own mouth without repeatedly stopping or experiencing breathlessness or severe discomfort; (c) Cannot convey food or drink to the claimant's own mouth without receiving regular prompting given by someone else in the claimant's presence; or (d) Owing to a severe disorder of mood or behaviour, fails to convey food or drink to the claimant's own mouth without receiving: (i) physical assistance from someone else; or (ii) regular prompting given by someone else in the claimant's presence.
16. Chewing or swallowing food or drink.	16 (a) Cannot chew or swallow food or drink; (b) Cannot chew or swallow food or drink without repeatedly stopping or experiencing breathlessness or severe discomfort; (c) Cannot chew or swallow food or drink without repeatedly receiving regular prompting given by someone else in the claimant's presence; or (d) Owing to a severe disorder of mood or behaviour, fails to: (i) chew or swallow food or drink; or (ii) chew or swallow food or drink without regular prompting given by someone else in the claimant's presence.

GENERAL NOTE

8.221 This Sch. is the same as ESA Regs 2008 Sch.3, as amended.

PART IX

LIMITED CAPABILITY FOR WORK AND LIMITED CAPABILITY FOR WORK-RELATED ACTIVITY FOR "OLD-STYLE" EMPLOYMENT AND SUPPORT ALLOWANCE

The Employment and Support Allowance Regulations 2008

(SI 2008/794) (as amended)

ARRANGEMENT OF (SELECTED) REGULATIONS

PART 1

GENERAL

PART 5

LIMITED CAPABILITY FOR WORK

PART 6

LIMITED CAPABILITY FOR WORK-RELATED ACTIVITY

SCHEDULE 2

ASSESSMENT OF WHETHER A CLAIMANT HAS LIMITED CAPABILITY FOR WORK

PART 1 PHYSICAL DISABILITIES

PART 2 MENTAL, COGNITIVE AND INTELLECTUAL FUNCTION ASSESSMENT

SCHEDULE 3

ASSESSMENT OF WHETHER A CLAIMANT HAS LIMITED CAPABILITY FOR WORKRELATED ACTIVITY

9.1 The Secretary of State for Work and Pensions, in exercise of the powers conferred by sections 2(1)(a) and (c), (4)(a) and (c), 3(1)(c), (2)(b) and (d) and (3)(1), 4(2)(a), (3), (6)(a) and (c), 5(2) and (3), 8(1) to (3), (4)(a) and (b), (5) and (6), 9(1) to (3) and (4)(a) and (b), 11(1), (2) (a) to (g), (3) to (5), (6)(a) and (7)(c), 12(1), (2)(a) to (h), (3) to (7), 14(1) and (2) (a) and (b), 16(2)(a) and (4), 17, 18(1), (2) and (4), 20(2) to (7), 22(2), 23(1) and (3), 24(1)(3), (2) (b) and (3), 25(1) to (5) and 26(2) of, and paragraphs 1(4), 3(2), 4(1)(a) and (c), (3) and (4) and 6(1)(b), (2) to (5) (4), (7) and (8) of Schedule 1 to, and paragraphs 1 to 7, 8(1), 9, 10, 12 and 14 of Schedule 2 to, the Welfare Reform Act 2007, section 5(1) of the Social Security Administration Act 1992 and section 21(1)(a) of the Social Security Act 1998(7) makes the following Regulations, which are made by virtue of, or consequential on, the provisions of the Welfare Reform Act 2007 and which are made before the end of a period of 6 months beginning with the coming into force of those provisions:

PART 1

GENERAL

9.2 **[1 Citation, commencement and application]**

1. These Regulations may be cited as the Employment and Support Allowance Regulations 2008 and shall come into force—

(a) subject to paragraphs (b) and (c), on 27th October 2008;

(b) in relation to regulation 128(6)(a) and paragraph 15(2) of Schedule 6, so far as it applies to a maintenance calculation, in relation to a particular case, on the day on which paragraph 11(20)(d) of Schedule 3 to the 2000 Act comes into force for the purposes of that type of case;

(c) [2 . . .]

[1 (2) These Regulations do not apply to a particular case on any day on which section 33(1)(b) of the 2012 Act (abolition of income-related employment and support allowance) is in force and applies in relation to that case.]

AMENDMENTS

1. Universal Credit (Consequential, Supplementary, Incidental and Miscellaneous Provisions) Regulations 2013 (SI 2013/630) reg.37(1) and (2) (April 29, 2013).

2. Shared Parental Leave and Statutory Shared Parental Pay (Consequential Amendments to Subordinate Legislation) Order 2014 art.20(2) (April 5, 2014).

GENERAL NOTE

The ESA Regulations 2008, which govern "old style" ESA, have been reproduced here only insofar as they include statutory material related to the tests for limited capability for work and limited capability for work-related activity (see further Parts 5 and 6 of these Regulations (regs.19-39) and Schedules 2 and 3). This material is replicated here in Vol I for the convenience of readers. For the full text of the ESA Regulations 2008, with commentary and notes on amendments, readers should consult the full version of those Regulations in Vol.V of this series. **9.3**

Interpretation

2.—(1) In these Regulations— **9.4**

...

"the Act" means the Welfare Reform Act 2007;

...

"confinement" has the meaning given to it by section 171(1) of the Contributions and Benefits Act;

...

"descriptor" means, in relation to an activity specified in column (1) of Schedule 2, a descriptor in column (2) of that Schedule which describes a person's ability to perform that activity;

...

"doctor" means a registered medical practitioner, or in the case of a medical practitioner practising outside the United Kingdom of whom the Secretary of State may request a medical opinion, a person registered or recognised as such in the country in which the person undertakes medical practice;

...

"health care professional" means—

(a) a registered medical practitioner;

(b) a registered nurse; or

(c) an occupational therapist or physiotherapist registered with a regulatory body established by an Order in Council under section 60 of the Health Act 1999;

...

"limited capability for work assessment" means the assessment of whether a person has limited capability for work as set out in regulation 19(2) and in Schedule 2;

...

"Medical Evidence Regulations" means the Social Security (Medical Evidence) Regulations 1976;

...

"medical treatment" means medical, surgical or rehabilitative treatment (including any course or diet or other regimen), and references to a person receiving or submitting to medical treatment are to be construed accordingly;

...

"period of limited capability for work" means except in paragraph (5), a period throughout which a person has, or is treated as having, limited capability for work, and does not include a period which is outside the prescribed time for claiming as specified in regulation 19 of the Social Security (Claims and Payments) Regulations 1987;

...

"qualifying young person" has the meaning given by section 142 of the Contributions and Benefits Act (child and qualifying young person);

...

"terminally ill", in relation to a claimant, means the claimant is suffering from a progressive disease and death in consequence of that disease can reasonably be expected within [[1]12 months];

...

"week" means a period of 7 days except in relation to regulation 26;

...

AMENDMENT

1. Universal Credit and Employment and Support Allowance (Terminal Illness) (Amendment) Regulations 2022 (SI 2022/260) reg.2(1) (April 4, 2022).

GENERAL NOTE

9.5 Regulation 2 has been reproduced here only insofar as it includes definitions which are relevant to Parts 5 and 6 of these Regulations (regs.19-39). For the full text of reg.2, and notes on amendments, readers should consult the version of the ESA Regulations 2008 in Vol.V of this series.

PART 5

LIMITED CAPABILITY FOR WORK

Determination of limited capability for work

9.6 **19.**—(1) For the purposes of Part 1 of the Act, whether a claimant's capability for work is limited by the claimant's physical or mental condition and, if it is, whether the limitation is such that it is not reasonable to require the claimant to work is to be determined on the basis of a limited capability for work assessment of the claimant in accordance with this Part.

(2) The limited capability for work assessment is an assessment of the extent to which a claimant who has some specific disease or bodily or mental disablement is capable of performing the activities prescribed in Schedule 2 or is incapable by reason of such disease or bodily or mental disablement of performing those activities.

(3) Subject to paragraph (6), for the purposes of Part 1 of the Act a claimant has limited capability for work if, by adding the points listed in column (3) of Schedule 2 against [[2] each descriptor] listed in that Schedule [[2] which applies in the claimant's case], the claimant obtains a total score of at least—

(a) 15 points whether singly or by a combination of descriptors specified in Part 1 of that Schedule;

(b) 15 points whether singly or by a combination of descriptors specified in Part 2 of that Schedule; or

(c) 15 points by a combination of descriptors specified in Parts 1 and 2 of that Schedule.

[[1](4) In assessing the extent of a claimant's capability to perform any activity listed in Part 1 of Schedule 2, the claimant is to be assessed as if—

(a) fitted with or wearing any prosthesis with which the claimant is normally fitted or normally wears; or, as the case may be,
(b) wearing or using any aid or appliance which is normally, or could reasonably be expected to be, worn or used.

(5) In assessing the extent of a claimant's capability to perform any activity listed in Schedule 2, it is a condition that the claimant's incapability to perform the activity arises—
(a) in respect of any descriptor listed in Part 1 of Schedule 2, from a specific bodily disease or disablement;
(b) in respect of any descriptor listed in Part 2 of Schedule 2, from a specific mental illness or disablement; or
(c) in respect of any descriptor or descriptors listed in—
(i) Part 1 of Schedule 2, as a direct result of treatment provided by a registered medical practitioner for a specific physical disease or disablement; [2 or]
(ii) Part 2 of Schedule 2, as a direct result of treatment provided by a registered medical practitioner for a specific mental illness or disablement.]

(6) Where more than one descriptor specified for an activity [2 applies] to a claimant, only the descriptor with the highest score in respect of each activity which applies is to be counted.

(7) Where a claimant—
(a) has been determined to have limited capability for work; or
(b) is to be treated as having limited capability for work under regulations 20, 25, 26, 29 or 33(2),

the Secretary of State may, if paragraph (8) applies, determine afresh whether the claimant has or is to be treated as having limited capability for work.

(8) This paragraph applies where—
(a) the Secretary of State wishes to determine whether there has been a relevant change of circumstances in relation to the claimant's physical or mental condition;
(b) the Secretary of State wishes to determine whether the previous determination of limited capability for work or that the claimant is to be treated as having limited capability for work, was made in ignorance of, or was based on a mistake as to, some material fact; or
(c) at least 3 months have passed since the date on which the claimant was determined to have limited capability for work or to be treated as having limited capability for work.

AMENDMENTS

1. Employment and Support Allowance (Amendment) Regulations 2012 (SI 2012/3096) reg.3(2) (January 28, 2013, subject to application, transitional and savings provisions in reg.2 of this amending instrument, below, para.9.614).
2. Social Security (Miscellaneous Amendments) (No. 3) Regulations 2013 (SI 2013/2536) reg.13(7) (October 29, 2013).

DEFINITIONS

"claimant"—see WRA 2007 s.24(1).
"descriptor"—see reg.2(1).
"limited capability for work"—see WRA 2007 s.1(4).
"limited capability for work assessment"—see para.(2).

General Note

9.7 Entitlement to ESA requires that the claimant has limited capability for work (WRA 2007, s.1(3)(a)). Whether his capability for work is limited by his physical or mental condition such that it is not reasonable to require him to work is to be determined in accordance with regulations (WRA 2007 s.8(1)). This regulation, setting out how "actual" limited capability to work is to be determined through the limited capability for work assessment is the product. The remainder of this Part (regs 20–33), deal with situations in which someone, whatever the reality, is to be treated as having limited capability for work, and also with aspects of the decision-making process.

Note, however, that the days of the WCA now appear to be numbered. In March 2023 a Government White Paper announced that the WCA would be abolished, as would the concepts of LCW and LCWRA. Instead, a new income-related 'health element' will be available under the universal credit scheme for claimants who receive PIP. The proposed reforms will be rolled out to new claims only "from no earlier than 2026/27" (see *DWP, Transforming Support: The Health and Disability White Paper* (March 2023) ch.4 para.156).

Paragraph (1)

9.8 ESA is a benefit designed to help people with a limiting health condition overcome barriers, and where appropriate move into work and improve their lives. The Work Capability Assessment (WCA) seeks more accurately to relate to modern context than the IB/IS system, and to focus more on what people can do, rather on what they are unable to do. The matter of whether the claimant's capability for work is limited by his physical or mental condition, and, if so, whether the limitation is to such an extent that it is not reasonable to require him to work, is to be decided on the basis of the "limited capability for work assessment" (WCAt or LCWA). This is the first element in a new three-part "work capability assessment" (WCA), developed out of the review of the IB "personal capability assessment" (PCA), which governs entitlement to the basic allowance and the additional components of ESA. The new WCA underpinning ESA was devised by the DWP's Health Work and Wellbeing Directorate with input from two technical working groups, one focusing on mental health and learning difficulties, the other on physical function and conditions (hereinafter "review group"). The review group consisted of medical and other relevant experts. It examined how the IB Personal Capability Assessment (PCA) (characterized by them as "the best assessment of its type in the world" could nonetheless be improved and updated so as to reflect the many changes since its inception:

> "in the prevalence of disabling conditions; in advances in medical science resulting in the availability of new and more effective medical interventions; and in the workplace environment. The Disability Discrimination Act, introduced after the PCA had been developed, has influenced the ability of employers to make reasonable adjustments to accommodate people with long term disabilities. It has also raised the expectations of disabled people that adjustments should be made to enable them to work."

The three-element WCA is not merely an incapacity-based tool for determining entitlement to ESA. That remains true of its first element the subject of this regulation. However, its second element is rather a more positive assessment considering ability to benefit from work-related activity with a view to promoting capacity for work. The assessment has two aspects: an assessment of limited capability to work (WCAt) and an assessment of limited capacity to engage in work-related activity (WRAAt). Both assessments will generally be conducted at the same time. The WCAt is a more rigorous test than the PCA and far fewer groups are exempted from it.

Paragraphs (2) and (5)

9.9 This defines the "limited capability for work assessment" (WCAt). Like the IB "personal capability assessment" (PCA) and its predecessor, the "all work" test, the

ESA WCAt is an assessment of the extent to which someone with a specific disease or bodily or mental disablement is (despite that) capable of performing the activities set out in Sch.2 or is because of it incapable of performing them. Since the test is thus so similar to that in IB (see Incapacity for Work Regs, reg.24 and Sch.), the position taken here is that case authorities (whether Commissioner or court) on the PCA will also apply to the WCAt. As with the IB PCA, the tasks involved in applying the WCAt are twofold:

1. ascertaining from all the evidence in the case which descriptors apply (paras (2), (5) and Sch.2);
2. computing the scores (paras (3), (6)).

The terms of para.(2) require the incapacity to perform the Sch.2 activities to arise by reason of "some specific disease or bodily or mental disablement". This is further stressed in paras (5)(a) and (b), the latter of which specifically also brings in "mental illness", while para.(5)(c) in effect adds that the rubric will also cover incapability as a direct result of treatment provided by a registered medical practitioner for such a disease, illness or disablement. Para.(5) was introduced with effect from January 28, 2013 and was not explicitly subject to the transitional protection afforded by reg.2 of the amending instrument to claimants who had completed an ESA questionnaire issued to them based on the pre-January 28, 2013 versions of Schs 2 and 3; that reg on its face appeared only to give protection in respect of the changes to the Schs themselves, effected by reg.5 of the amending instrument, whereas the para.(5) amendment was effected by reg.3 (see, below, para.9.614). In *FR v SSWP (ESA)* [2015] UKUT 175 (AAC), however, Judge Ward accepted the Secretary of State's submission that the tribunal had erred in law in applying the para.(5) "split" to this claimant who had completed such a questionnaire. Judge Ward interpreted the Secretary of State's concession "as being that the requirement for the provisions of Schedule 2 "to continue to apply. . .*as they had effect* immediately before the commencement date" [Judge Ward's emphasis] is sufficient [in a case such as this] to maintain the pre-2013 position of no physical/mental split as part of how Schedule 2 "had effect"" (para.2). This "specific disease or bodily or mental disablement" phraseology was found in the sickness/invalidity benefits statutory test and in both the "own occupation" test and the IB PCA, so decisions on this phraseology from those regimes will still be authoritative here. In *VT v SSWP (ESA)* [2016] UKUT 241 (AAC) Judge Ward subsequently rejected an attempt by the Secretary of State to resile from the concession made in *FR v SSWP (ESA)*.

"Specific" means "of a kind identified by medical science" (*CS/57/82*, noted in [1983] J.S.W.L. 306). "Specific" is designed to keep out conditions that may in some ordinary sense be said to be mental illness or disablement but which are not (as yet) recognised, or accounted for, as physical or mental conditions by medical science" (*JG v SSWP (ESA)* [2013] UKUT 37 (AAC); [2013] AACR 23 (a decision of a three judge panel of Upper Tribunal Judges, para.38, citing to similar effect (*R(IB)2/98*, para.7). A "specific mental illness" is a mental disease and also falls within the term "mental disablement" (*JG*, paras 36, 37). "Disease" has been described as "a departure from health capable of identification by its signs and symptoms, an abnormality of some sort", and sickness falls within the definition (*CS/221/49*, para.3; *CS/7/82*, noted in [1983] J.S.W.L. 306). "Disablement"—which may be bodily or mental—constitutes a state of deprivation or incapacitation of ability measured against the abilities of a normal person (*CS/7/82*, *ibid.*).

In most cases there will be little problem, given the medical evidence, as to whether the claimant's condition amounts to disease or disablement; disagreement will generally centre on whether it prevents him carrying out the activities in Sch.2. However, a number of areas can be identified where difficult lines may have to be drawn on whether or not the condition comes within the rubric "disease or . . . disablement" at all. Pregnancy alone does not, but a disease or disablement associated with, but going beyond the normal incidents of, pregnancy does, as in *CS/221/49* where the certified incapacity, "sickness of pregnancy", was suffered throughout the day. See also *R(S) 4/93*. But note now that certain pregnant women are to be treated as incapable of work (see reg.20(e)). Alcoholism can come within the rubric, but in some circumstances might bring about a period of disqualification from benefit (see reg.157). Whether certain conditions constitute a disease of the mind or a mental disablement can be problematical in that the line between a recognisable mental illness or disablement, on the one hand, and states of malingering or being workshy on the other, can be fine and uncertain. The difficulty is to decide from the available evidence whether the claimant is genuinely ill or disabled and thereby incapacitated for work in the sense understood above, or whether his is a voluntary attitude of work shyness where he could but will not work. The problem will be compounded where the outward symptoms of these alternative states are the same. What will be crucial will be the terms in which the medical (psychiatric) evidence is cast, and the inevitable value judgments about whether a particular claimant's attitudes to doing work are voluntary or involuntary. Perhaps here the appellate authorities' jurisdiction to seek further medical (in this case psychiatric) reports at public expense could prove valuable. In *R(S) 6/59*, the Commissioner considered a particular case of Munchausen's syndrome, under which condition a person repeatedly presents himself for treatment to a hospital or series of hospitals recounting symptoms of a particular disease or disability from which he is not in fact suffering, which the Commissioner there described as a strange condition in the nature of malingering. The Commissioner in that case was not satisfied on the evidence that the claimant believed the symptoms actually to exist, and felt unable to regard the condition as a psychosis, which would have come within the statutory rubric. The claim for benefit failed, the Commissioner stating as an additional ground for the decision his view that the syndrome in any event did not affect that particular claimant's capacity to work since he had driven from hospital to hospital in his lorry. In effect, the condition was treated as a defect of character. In *CS/1/81* (noted in [1982] J.S.W.L. 48), the dispute initially centred on whether the claimant, suffering from what the RMO (now a DWP MS doctor) and his own doctor described as an anxiety state, was as a result incapable of work. The consultant psychiatrist to whom the claimant was referred considered him an inadequate personality by reason of his total self-indulgence and extreme degree of sheltering behind psychiatric symptoms to avoid responsibility. His condition resulted from a dismal personality structure rather than illness. Accordingly the Commissioner held that he was incapable of work but not by reason of disease or disablement, so the claim failed. Mesher (later Commissioner Mesher) suggests in [1982] J.S.W.L. 48 that the Commissioner there gave inadequate consideration to whether the defect (clearly on the evidence not an illness) could nevertheless be a mental disablement. In contrast, *CS 7/82* (noted in [1983] J.S.W.L. 306) dealt with a situation in which the claimant was said to have a severe personality disorder but not to be mentally ill. "Personality disorder" is a term sometimes used as a euphemism for workshy. The Commissioner held that its use in the particular case conveyed a notion of disability of mind sufficient to bring the claimant within the statutory rubric. It is submitted that one should avoid using euphemisms which may confuse; the loser in the case is entitled to know why he has lost. If he is thought workshy, that should be stated and reasons given for that conclusion. Sheltering behind euphemisms may also cloud the steps in reasoning which go towards good adjudication and decision-making.

In *DMcK v SSWP (ESA)* [2014] UKUT 45 (AAC), having allowed the appeal on other grounds, Judge Wikeley went on to consider the fact that the tribunal had found that the appellant had exhibited "illness behaviour" so that it did not find credible the level of her claimed physical disabilities. Judge Wikeley gave some guidance for the new tribunal to which the case was remitted. He thought it unclear whether the tribunal's rejection of the claimant's appeal "was indeed a recognition that she was displaying genuine but abnormal responses or whether it was a polite way of suggesting that she was malingering" (para.18). Citing para.43(ii) of the panel of three Upper Tribunal Judges in *JG*, below, an adjournment would have enabled the claimant to deal with a new point not taken by the Secretary of State, namely whether she had a recognized disease or disablement. On "illness behaviour" itself, Judge Wikeley referred the new tribunal to two unreported cases, one from the industrial injuries area, the other on incapacity benefit. In *CSI/1180/2001*, Commissioner (now Judge) Parker observed

"The new tribunal, if it considers that there is an insufficient organic basis for all of the claimant's problems, must decide if he is consciously exaggerating or if he is genuine and his complaints form part of an abnormal illness behaviour linked to his accident. In the latter situation, it can form part of the relevant loss of faculty. The courts have long recognised there can be compensation for an unconscious reaction to physical injury sustained, provided the latter remains a material cause of the former" (para.8).

In *CIB/4841/2002*, Commissioner (now Judge) Jacobs gave this guidance:

"10. The Secretary of State's medical advice, which I accept, is in summary this. Abnormal illness behaviour is one of a number of terms used to describe symptoms which are caused by the influence of psychological makeup and social environment on the perception of the disabling effects of a medical condition. This phenomenon is reflected by more modern approaches to treatment, which address the psychosocial as well as the medical factors. The symptoms are subjective in the sense that they depend on an experience of pain or fatigue. In order to distinguish between claimants who genuinely experience a particular disability from those who merely claim to do so, it is helpful to consider the history of their daily activity and unobtrusive observations. This can identify consistency or inconsistency.
11. In this case, the examining doctor detected resistance on examination and exaggeration of response to the testing of the reflexes. The claimant was also observed to walk normally and to be able to stand erect, albeit briefly. The claimant's performance on examination and the observations recorded by the doctor are not consistent with a genuine experience of illness behaviour. This was confirmed by the tribunal, who observed the claimant to walk differently at the beginning and end of the hearing. All of this was in conflict with the Surgeon's evidence, which accepted that the claimant was genuinely experiencing the symptoms he exhibited. In view of the actual observations of the examining doctor and the tribunal, the Surgeon's opinion could obviously not be accepted."

What has to be established, to what standard of proof, and by what evidence, is **9.10** analysed well by Commissioner Jacobs in *CIB/26/2004*. There must be established, on the civil standard of balance of probabilities, that the claimant has a recognised medical condition (paras 18, 25, citing *R2/99 (IB)*, para.8; *CSDLA/552/2001*, para.27; and *CDLA/944/2001*, paras 9 and 10). A medical diagnosis is useful evidence, but is not decisive in that an appeal tribunal, giving appropriate reasons, can refuse to accept it. The cogency of a diagnosis varies according to a number of factors: the nature of the condition (some being easier to diagnose than others); how well qualified in the relevant area of medicine the doctor is who makes the diagnosis; the range of information and material on which the diagnosis is based; and the degree of certainty with which it is made (e.g. is the diagnosis "firm", or qualified as "working", "presumptive" or "provisional") (para.22). If there is general consensus among medical authorities as to the existence of a particular condition, a tribunal (even one containing a medical member) will normally err in law if, being sceptical, it denies its existence (para.21, citing a Northern Ireland Tribunal of Commissioners in *C38/03–04 (DLA)*, para.20(3)). If a medical diagnosis is not necessarily decisive, nor is the lack of one necessarily fatal; in appropriate circumstances a tribunal can make a diagnosis without medical evidence (para.19). While agreeing to some extent with Commissioner Brown's view (*R 2/99 (IB)*, para.11) that a tribunal should be cautious of making a diagnosis of mental disease or disablement in the absence of supportive medical evidence, Commissioner Jacobs qualified that by noting that at the time of that decision there was no medical member on the tribunal—it merely then had advice from an assessor—that change in composition rendering it easier now for a tribunal to make a diagnosis on the evidence available (para.20).

In *AD v SSWP (ESA)* [2011] UKUT 307 (AAC), Judge Levenson considered a case where the First-tier tribunal had upheld a decision that the claimant did not have limited capability for work on the basis that the claimant's abuse of alcohol and drugs were "a lifestyle choice" rather than coming about because of a specific physical or mental illness or disability. He held that it had erred in law. Alcohol or drug dependence, whether for DLA, incapacity benefit or ESA, constitutes a "mental condition". That was decided as regards DLA by a tribunal of Commissioners in *R (DLA) 6/06 (T)* and correctly applied to incapacity benefit by Commissioner Jacobs in *CIB/1296/2007*. Judge Levenson thought mistaken Judge May's decision in *RA v SSWP (ESA)* [2010] UKUT 301 (AAC) to disapprove Commissioner Jacob's decision on incapacity benefit and to seek there to confine *R (DLA) 6/06(T)* to the effects of the wording in ss.72 and 73 of the SSCBA 1992. In *RA*, Judge May stated that a "mental condition" is not necessarily the same as "specific disease or bodily or mental disablement" (para.13), but had already held that the claimant could not succeed under Activity 11 of the original ESA Regs, Sch.2 because that required a link to a *physical* disease or disablement.

In *JG v SSWP (ESA)* [2013] UKUT 37 (AAC); [2013] AACR 23 a three judge panel of Upper Tribunal Judges held that Parliament clearly intended that alcohol dependency falls within the phrase "specific disease or bodily or mental disablement". Were that not so, WRA 2007 s.15A and Sch.1A would have nothing to bite on. WRA 2007 s.18 and ESA Regs reg.157 on disqualification indicate that self-induced or self-inflicted physical or mental conditions can still amount to a "specific disease or bodily or mental disablement" (paras 18–20). Moreover, the three judge panel held that the summary of the expert evidence on alcohol dependence in *R(DLA)6/06*, itself a decision of a tribunal of Commissioners, "can and should be adopted by decision makers and tribunals in ESA cases as representing the currently accepted and mainstream medical view in respect of alcohol dependence" (para.47). That expert evidence is summarised in paras 16–19 of *R(DLA)6/)06* and set out in para.44 of *JG v* SSWP *(ESA)*. The three judge panel thus disapproved Judge May's rejection of this approach in *RA v SSWP (ESA)*, above, and saw nothing wrong with Judge Jacobs's direction in *CIB/1296/2007* that alcohol dependence was a mental condition rather than a physical one. See further, on drug dependency, *SD v SSWP (ESA)* [2016] UKUT 100 (AAC); [2016] AACR 35, discussed in the ESA commentary.

The current version of para.(5) entered into force on January 28, 2013, subject to application, transitional and savings provisions in reg.2 of the amending instrument (see, below, para.9.614). It brings in the requirement—familiar from the IB regime—that Pt 1 of Sch.2 must be linked to incapability arising from a specific bodily disease or disablement or as a direct result of treatment provided by a registered medical practitioner for such a disease or disablement. Similarly it introduces the requirement that Pt 2 of Sch.2 must be linked to incapability arising from a specific mental illness or disablement or as a direct result of treatment provided by a registered medical practitioner for such an illness or disablement. Commenting on the new wording, Judge Rowland in *MC v SSWP (ESA)* [2015] UKUT 646 (AAC) has observed as follows:

> "the correct approach, best giving effect to the purpose behind the legislation – is that the claimant's "specific mental illness or disablement" had to be an *effective* cause of her inability to go out unaccompanied. That is not the same as being the root cause or the primary cause. In my judgement, where a specific mental illness or disablement would not by itself have been sufficiently serious to enable a claimant to satisfy a descriptor, it is enough for the purposes of regulation 19(5)(b) that it has made the difference between the claimant being able to satisfy a descriptor and not being able to do so even though there may have been another, perhaps more important, cause" (at para.9).

Under the previous wording of the paragraph (still applicable to some cases after January 28, 2013—see reg.2 of the amending instrument, below, para.9.614), there was no such link (*JG v SSWP (ESA)* [2013] UKUT 37 (AAC); [2013] AACR 23 (a decision of a three judge panel of Upper Tribunal Judges, disapproving Judge May's decision in *RA v SSWP*, above, which should not be followed on this issue); *KP v SSWP (ESA)* [2011] UKUT 216 (AAC); *KN v SSWP (ESA)* [2011] UKUT 229 (AAC); *RM v SSWP (ESA)* [2011] UKUT 454 (AAC); *AH v SSWP (ESA)* [2011] UKUT 333 (AAC)).

See also *NC v SSWP (ESA)* [2016] UKUT 401 (AAC) (Judge Gray) for confirmation that the term 'mental illness or disablement' in reg.19(5)(b) as amended "encompasses not merely mental ill-health in the form of conditions such as depression or schizophrenia but mental disablement of all kinds, for example learning difficulties and cognitive deficiency whether that be by reason of age or acquired brain injury" (at para.13).

Paragraph (4)

The current version of para.(4) entered into force on January 28, 2013, subject to application, transitional and savings provisions in reg.2 of the amending instrument (see, below, para.9.614). In *RP v SSWP* (ESA) [2011] UKUT 449 (AAC), Judge Levenson had thought the approach now embodied in sub-para.(b) was implicit in the previous wording. In addition, however, he thought that there had to be some "explanation of how the aid or appliance could help the particular claimant .... The degree of detail is a matter for the tribunal on the facts of each particular case, but in my view, in the absence of actual use or prescription, there does need to be some explanation" (para.16). See also *TM v SSWP (ESA)* [2018] UKUT 9 (AAC), where Judge Wikeley accepted a concession by the Secretary of State that reg.19(4) limits consideration of aids and appliances to the *physical health* descriptors in Part 1 of Sch.2. and so in the context of activity 15 (getting about) the FTT should not have considered the claimant's ability to navigate by a mobile phone app. 9.11

Paragraphs (3) and (6)

Computing the scores: Achievement of a particular score is required before the claimant can be found to have limited capability for work. Under ESA, the scoring system is simpler. The score attained must be at least 15 points whether from Sch.2, Pt 1 alone (physical disabilities), Pt 2 alone (mental, cognitive and intellectual function assessment), or from a combination of the descriptors in both parts. In each case, where more than one descriptor for an activity applies, only the highest scoring one counts (para.(6)). Following the approach to the IB PCA), it is submitted that there are no implied limits on simply adding together the highest scores from each activity (*R(IB) 3/98*). 9.12

Paragraphs (7), (8)

These make clear that the matters of whether someone actually has limited capability for work, or whether he is to be treated as having it under regs 20, 25, 26, 29 or 33(2), are ones that can be revisited where one or more of the situations in para.(8) arise: 9.13

- a desire to determine whether there has been a relevant change of circumstances in relation to the claimant's health condition (is he getting better or worse?) (sub-para.(a);
- a wish to determine whether the prior determination of actual or deemed limited capability was made in ignorance of, or was based on a mistake as to, a material fact (sub-para.(b);
- at least three months have elapsed since the previous decision on actual or deemed limited capability (sub-para.(c)).

Certain claimants to be treated as having limited capability for work

20.—[[2](1)] A claimant is to be treated as having limited capability for work if— 9.14

(a) the claimant is terminally ill;
(b) the claimant is—
(i) receiving treatment for cancer by way of chemotherapy or radiotherapy;
(ii) likely to receive such treatment within six months after the date of the determination of capability for work; or
(iii) recovering from such treatment,

and the Secretary of State is satisfied that the claimant should be treated as having limited capability for work];
(c) the claimant is—
(i) excluded or abstains from work [2...] pursuant to a request or notice in writing lawfully made [2or given] under an enactment; or
(ii) otherwise prevented from working pursuant to an enactment, by reason of it being known or reasonably suspected that the claimant is infected or contaminated by, or has been in contact with a case of, a relevant infection or contamination;
(d) in the case of a pregnant woman, there is a serious risk of damage to her health or to the health of her unborn child if she does not refrain from work;
(e) in the case of a pregnant woman, she—
(i) is within the maternity allowance period [2(which has the meaning it has in section 35(2) of the Contributions and Benefits Act)]; and
(ii) is entitled to a maternity allowance under section 35(1) of the Contributions and Benefits Act;
(f) in the case of a pregnant woman whose expected or actual date of confinement has been certified in accordance with the Medical Evidence Regulations, on any day in the period—
(i) beginning with the first date of the 6th week before the expected week of her confinement or the actual date of her confinement, whichever is earlier; and
(ii) ending on the 14th day after the actual date of her confinement,

if she would have no entitlement to a maternity allowance or statutory maternity pay were she to make a claim in respect of that period.
(g) [2the claimant meets] [1any of the descriptors at paragraph 15 or 16 of Schedule 3] [2in accordance with regulation 34(2), (3) and (6) where applicable].

[2(2) In this regulation, "relevant infection or contamination" means—
(a) in England and Wales—
(i) any incidence or spread of infection or contamination, within the meaning of section 45A(3) of the Public Health (Control of Disease) Act 1984 in respect of which regulations are made under Part 2A of that Act (public health protection) for the purpose of preventing, protecting against, controlling or providing a public health response to, such incidence or spread; or
(ii) tuberculosis or any infectious disease to which regulation 9 of the Public Health (Aircraft) Regulations 1979 (powers in respect of persons leaving aircraft) applies or to which regulation 10 of the Public Health (Ships) Regulations 1979 (powers in respect of certain persons on ships) applies; and

(b) in Scotland, any—
  (i) infectious disease within the meaning of section 1(5) of the Public Health etc (Scotland) Act 2008, or exposure to an organism causing that disease; or
  (ii) contamination within the meaning of section 1(5) of that Act, or exposure to a contaminant,

to which sections 56 to 58 of that Act (compensation) apply.]

AMENDMENTS

1. Employment and Support Allowance (Limited Capability for Work and Limited Capability for Work-Related Activity) (Amendment) Regulations 2011 (SI 2011/228) reg.3(2) (March 28, 2011).

2. Social Security (Miscellaneous Amendments) (No. 3) Regulations 2013 (SI 2013/2536) reg.13(8) (October 29, 2013).

DEFINITIONS

"claimant"—see WRA 2007 s.24(1).
"confinement"—see para.(1)(e)(i).
"Contributions and Benefits Act"—see WRA 2007 s.65.
"limited capability for work"—see WRA 2007 s.1(4).
"maternity allowance period"—see para.(1)(e)(i).
"Medical Evidence Regulations"—see reg.2(1).
"relevant infection or contamination"—see para.(2).
"terminally ill"—see reg.2(1).
"week"—see reg.2(1).

GENERAL NOTE

This regulation—the parent power for which is WRA 2007 s.22 and Sch.2, para.9—sets out the situations in which a claimant is to be treated as having limited capability for work. This is important because such claimants will be exempt from the WCA and its information gathering processes (see reg.21). Those exempt are: **9.15**

- the terminally ill (para.(1)(a))—"suffering from a progressive disease and death in consequence of that disease can reasonably be expected within 6 months" (reg.2(1));
- provided that the Secretary of State is satisfied that the claimant should be treated as having limited capability for work (note the discretion), the claimant is receiving treatment for cancer by way of chemotherapy or radiotherapy; likely to receive such treatment within six months from the date of the determination of capability for work; or recovering from such treatment (para.(1)(b));
- those excluded or prevented from working by reason of it being known or reasonably suspected that the claimant is infected or contaminated by, or has been in contact with a case of, a relevant infection or contamination covered by a variety of public health enactments) (paras (1)(c), (2));
- pregnant women where there is a serious risk of damage to their or their unborn child's health if they do not refrain from work (para.(1)(d));
- pregnant women at a certain stage in pregnancy (paras (1)(e), (f)). Paragraph (1)(e) covers the pregnant woman during the maternity allowance period (see reg.2(1) and SSCBA 1992, s.35(2)) entitled to a maternity allowance under SSCBA 1992, s.35. Para.(1)(f) in contrast deals with the pregnant woman whose expected or actual date of confinement has been duly certified in accordance with the Medical Evidence Regulations. It covers her during a period beginning with the earlier of the actual date of confinement or the first day of the sixth week before the expected week of confinement and ending on

the 14th day after the actual date of confinement. But it does so only where she would not be entitled to maternity allowance or SMP if she were to claim in respect of that period.

- in accordance with reg.34(2), (3) and (6), where applicable, those to whom there applies any of the descriptors in para.15 or 16 of Sch.2 operable from that date (para.(1)(g)).

Paragraph (1)(b): "recovering" from treatment for cancer by way of chemotherapy or radiotherapy

9.16 In *W Da-C v SSWP (ESA)* [2015] UKUT 158 (AAC), Judge Markus considered that, since "recovering" was not defined in the legislation, it had to bear its ordinary meaning. She had no doubt

> "that, when used in a health context, "recovering" refers to a process of getting better. It may not result in a person's condition reverting to the way it was before the treatment in question, but it denotes a process of some improvement or, at the very least, hoped-for improvement. Thus the Shorter Oxford English Dictionary defines the word, in so far as it relates to health, as "restoration or return to health from sickness". At some stage a person will cease to recover. This may occur when they are completely better. Or it may occur when they have reached a point when no further recovery will take place" (para.12).

Looking at the wider legislative context confirmed her view that this was "the only sensible way" in which the term could be understood; other ESA Regulations (e.g. regs 25, 26) suggested a period of recovery was time-limited. Moreover, interpreting para.(1)(b) to be without limit of time would jar with the underlying policy with respect to ESA that it should not simply be assumed that someone with a significant health condition or disability must be incapable of work.

The case concerned recovery from radiotherapy. Judge Markus accepted the Secretary of State's argument that

> "the normal recovery period following the immediate side effects of radiotherapy is up to six months and that the evidence in this case indicates that after six months the appellant had [completely] recovered from the short term effects of radiotherapy . . . [so] that where the long-term effects of radiotherapy are chronic it cannot be said that the appellant is recovering. The treatment has caused a separate health condition from which she has not recovered" (para.10).

In essence in this case, since there was no prospect of recovery, the claimant could not be said to be "recovering" (para.16).

Information required for determining capability for work

9.17 **21.**—(1) Subject to paragraphs (2) and (3), the information or evidence required to determine whether a claimant has limited capability for work is—

(a) evidence of limited capability for work in accordance with the Medical Evidence Regulations (which prescribe the form of [2...] statement or other evidence required in each case);

(b) any information relating to a claimant's capability to perform the activities referred to in Schedule 2 as may be requested in the form of a questionnaire; and

(c) any such additional information as may be requested.

(2) Where the Secretary of State is satisfied that there is sufficient information to determine whether a claimant has limited capability for work without the information specified in paragraph (1)(b), that information [1 must] not be required for the purposes of making the determination.

(3) Paragraph (1) does not apply in relation to a determination whether a claimant is to be treated as having limited capability for work under any of regulations 20 (certain claimants to be treated as having limited capability for work), 25 (hospital in-patients), 26 (claimants receiving certain regular treatment) and 33(2) (additional circumstances in which a claimant is to be treated as having limited capability for work).

AMENDMENTS

1. Social Security (Miscellaneous Amendments) (No.3) Regulations 2013 (SI 2013/2536) reg.13(9) (October 29, 2013).
2. Social Security (Medical Evidence) and Statutory Sick Pay (Medical Evidence) (Amendment) (No. 2) Regulations 2022 (SI 2022/630) reg.4(2) (July 1, 2022).

DEFINITIONS

"claimant"—see WRA 2007 s.24(1).
"doctor"—see reg.2(1).
"limited capability for work"—see WRA 2007 s.1(4).
"Medical Evidence Regulations"—see reg.2(1).

GENERAL NOTE

This regulation deals with the information required for determining whether someone has limited capability for work. It is designed to give the decision-maker sufficient information to decide that matter for himself (the minority of cases), or whether to seek advice from a health care professional on the basis of the papers in respect of that decision, or to refer the claimant for a face to face WCAt, including a medical examination (see reg.23). **9.18**

Unless para.(3) operates, the claimant will have to supply: (i) evidence of his incapacity for work in accordance with the Medical Evidence Regs (para.(1)(a)); and (ii) such additional information relating to the relevant test as the Secretary of State asks for (para.(1)(c)). Furthermore, he must generally complete and return the appropriate questionnaire (para.(1)(b)), unless para.(3) operates or the Secretary of State decides that completion of the questionnaire is not necessary because without it he has sufficient information to determine whether the claimant does or does not have limited capability for work (para.(2)). Note that where the claimant is requested by the Secretary of State to complete and return the questionnaire, failure to do so can result in his being treated as capable of work (and thus not entitled to ESA) (reg.22).

The impact on claimants with mental health problems (MHP) of the information collecting and assessment process originally administered by Atos Healthcare, the medical services provider for the DWP (although Atos was subsequently replaced by MAXIMUS Health and Human Services Ltd from March 2015) was the subject of challenge by way of the Upper Tribunal's judicial review jurisdiction, as constituting disability discrimination under the Equality Act 2010. The decision of a three judge tribunal in favour of the applicants in *MM & DM* v *SSWP* [2013] UKUT 259 (AAC) was appealed to the Court of Appeal by the Secretary of State.

On December 4, 2013, that Court rejected the appeal as to several matters and upheld it as to another in *Secretary of State for Work and Pensions* v *The Queen on the application of MM and DM (as respondents) and MIND, the National Autistic Society, Rethink Mental Illness and the Equality and Human Rights Commission (as interveners)* [2013] EWCA Civ 1565; [2016] AACR 11. The Court held that the Upper Tribunal was correct in holding that it had jurisdiction to deal with the matter of discrimination contrary to the Equality Act 2010 by way of judicial review, and that the applicants and the interveners had the requisite standing to maintain the application for judicial review. The Court also found that the Upper Tribunal's declaration that the information and examination process caused substantial disadvantage to claimants with mental health problems (and was thus discriminatory) was not erroneous in law nor, in the light of the evidence, was it perverse or irrational. However, the Court held that the Upper Tribunal had misunderstood the scope of its powers and should not have directed the Secretary of State to carry out an investigation or assessment within a specified time to see how the "Evidence Seeking Recommendation" (see below) could be implemented. Rather it was for the applicants to advance a reasonable adjustment proposal, leaving "the Secretary of State to adduce such evidence and advance such arguments as he thinks appropriate in order to discharge the burden now falling on him" of showing that such adjustment cannot reasonably be made (para.83).

The "Evidence Seeking Recommendation" was a less rigorous one than the proposal that in every case involving a mental health patient the decision-maker should always be required to seek further medical evidence (FME) before a decision was reached thus in many cases obviating the need for the ESA50 questionnaire and/or the face to face interview, both of which substantially disadvantaged mental health patients. The Upper Tribunal had rejected that as unduly onerous. Instead, the "Evidence Seeking Recommendation", seen by the Upper Tribunal as a prima facie "reasonable adjustment", proposes that "the decision-maker should at least be required to consider obtaining FME in the case of MHP claimants and if FME was not sought, should explain why it was thought to be unnecessary" (para.2).

It should be noted that the need for this change was also supported as part of the independent review undertaken by Professor Harrington (see para.40 of his third report, cited in para.21 of the Court of Appeal judgment).

The judicial review challenge then returned to the Upper Tribunal for a renewed hearing on remedies (*R (MM and DM) v SSWP* [2015] UKUT 107 (AAC); [2016] AACR 11). The three judge panel disallowed the applications, holding that it was clear from the Court of Appeal's decision that ss.20 and 21 of the Equality Act created a two stage approach to determining whether an individual applicant could establish discrimination, namely: (i) has there been a failure to comply with a duty to make reasonable adjustments; and (ii) has the individual applicant shown a failure to comply with that duty in relation him or her. At the second stage, the individual applicant has to show that he or she was put at such a disadvantage by the failure to comply with the duty to make reasonable adjustments (paragraphs 49 and 51). The Upper Tribunal ruled that the individual applicants could not show that the alleged failure of the Secretary of State to comply with his anticipatory duty by making the adjustments said to be reasonable had caused (or indeed was causing or would cause) them any substantial disadvantage or had, was or would subject them to any detriment that caused them an unreasonably adverse experience. This was fatal to the applicants' claims for judicial review (para.58). Thus, despite proceeding on the assumption that the Secretary of State had failed to establish that the adjustments suggested by the applicants were not reasonable, the applicants had failed to establish that there had been an individual breach, and so discrimination, as required by s.21(2) of the Equality Act 2010 (paragraphs 60 to 62, 78 and 90).

Following the Upper Tribunal decision, the Secretary of State subsequently issued new guidance in the form of Memo DMG 13/17 about the circumstances in which further medical evidence (FME) for assessing limited capability for work should be obtained. This circular states that additional medical evidence should be gathered at the scrutiny (or "filework") stage "where the HCP considers that further information would be helpful to the assessing HCP and Decision Maker. This is FME to inform the assessment." It adds that "there MUST be a reasonable expectation that the FME would assist the assessing HCP and subsequently the Decision Maker."

Failure to provide information in relation to limited capability for work

9.19 **22.**—(1) Where a claimant fails without good cause to comply with the request referred to in regulation 21(1)(b), that claimant is, subject to paragraph (2), to be treated as not having limited capability for work.

(2) Paragraph (1) does not apply unless—
(a) [2(a) the claimant was sent a further request at least three weeks after the date of the first request;]
(b) [2. . .] at least [11 week has] passed since the further request was sent.

AMENDMENT

1. Social Security (Miscellaneous Amendments) (No.3) Regulations 2011 (SI 2011/2425) reg.23(5), (6) (October 31, 2011).
2. Social Security (Miscellaneous Amendments) (No.3) Regulations 2013 (SI 2013/2536) reg.13(10) (October 29, 2013).

DEFINITIONS

"claimant"—see WRA 2007 s.24(1).
"limited capability for work"—see WRA 2007 s.1(4).
"week"—see reg.2(1)

GENERAL NOTE

If a claimant fails without good cause (on which more, below) to comply with the requirement to complete and return a limited capability for work questionnaire, he must be treated as not having limited capability for work, that is, as having no entitlement to ESA. This can only happen, however, if a further request for information was sent at least three weeks after the first and at least one week has gone by since the second request was sent. Commissioners' decisions on IB establish that as regards calculating a period before the end of which something cannot be done (e.g. "at least six weeks have passed"—para.(2)(a)), one must ignore the day from which the period runs as well as the day on which it expires (per Commissioner Jacobs in *R(IB) 1/00*). "Week" here means any period of seven days (reg.2(1)). But note that the para refers, like the IB provision, to a request being "sent" rather than "received" (as stressed by Commissioner Rowland in *CIB/3512/1998*). Non-receipt has, however, an important bearing on "good cause". "Good cause" is not exhaustively defined in legislation, although reg.24 non-exhaustively prescribes certain matters which must be taken into account in determining the issue. Some guidance may be found in authorities on the corresponding area in unemployment benefit (see USI Regs regs 7(1)(i), (j)—see pp.720–21 of Bonner, Hooker and White, *Non Means Tested Benefits: The Legislation* (1996)), the matter of relief from disqualification from sickness and invalidity benefit under the now revoked USI Regs reg.17 (see pp.737–740 of the 1994 edition of *Non Means Tested Benefits, The Legislation*), and that from disqualification/being treated as incapable under Incapacity for Work Regs reg.18 or, in time, reg.157 of these ESA Regs. 9.20

Determining when a request/reminder was "sent"

In *CT* v *SSWP (ESA)* [2013] UKUT 414 (AAC), Judge Mark (following his decision in *CIB/4012/2004*) stressed the need for very careful appraisal of the evidence to determine exactly when requests and reminders were sent and their exact nature. However, it appears that elsewhere in this decision Judge Mark arguably set the bar too high for the Secretary of State and those acting on his behalf. Three other Upper Tribunal decisions have adopted a rather more pragmatic approach to the evidential requirements imposed on the Secretary of State. In *AL v SSWP (ESA)* [2011] UKUT 512 (AAC), Judge May QC held that a tribunal was entitled to make a finding that an appointment letter had been sent on the basis of a computer generated letter history log. In particular, he accepted (at para.27) the Secretary of State's submission that the fact that the word "triggered" was used in the log did not mean it was uncertain whether that letter was actually posted. Similarly, in *SH v SSWP (ESA)* [2014] UKUT 574 (AAC), Judge Ward expressed the view that "printouts of the type in issue are capable of providing evidence from 9.21

which a tribunal may draw inferences that a document was 'sent'. It is then for the tribunal of fact to decide what weight to put on it" (at para.36). Both those decisions were approved and followed by Judge Wright in *DW v SSWP (ESA)* [2016] UKUT 179 (AAC), a decision which contains a useful review of the authorities.

Claimant may be called for a medical examination to determine whether the claimant has limited capability for work

9.22 **23.**—(1) Where it falls to be determined whether a claimant has limited capability for work, that claimant may be called by or on behalf of a health care professional approved by the Secretary of State to attend for a medical examination [2in person, by telephone or by video].

(2) Subject to paragraph (3), where a claimant fails without good cause to attend for or to submit to an examination [1mentioned] in paragraph (1), the claimant is to be treated as not having limited capability for work.

[1(3) Paragraph (2) does not apply unless—

(a) written notice of the date, time and place for the examination was sent to the claimant at least seven days in advance; or

(b) that claimant agreed to accept a shorter period of notice whether given in writing or otherwise.]

AMENDMENTS

1. Social Security (Miscellaneous Amendments) (No.3) Regulations 2013 (SI 2013/2536) reg.13(11) (October 29, 2013).

2. Social Security (Claims and Payments, Employment and Support Allowance, Personal Independence Payment and Universal Credit) (Telephone and Video Assessment) (Amendment) Regulations 2021 (SI 2021/230) reg.3(2) (March 25, 2021).

DEFINITIONS

"claimant"—see WRA 2007 s.24(1).

"health care professional"—see reg.2(1).

"limited capability for work"—see WRA 2007 s.1(4).

GENERAL NOTE

Introduction

9.23 This regulation enables the DWP to have a claimant medically examined by a health care professional (technically any health service professional approved by the Secretary of State) when a question arises as to the claimant's capability for work (see para.(1)). Failure without good cause to attend for or submit to such an examination (see para.(2)), of which he was given proper written notice (see para.(3)), will result in the claimant being treated as not having limited capability for work and not entitled to ESA.

An appeal against a decision under reg.23 is heard by a judge sitting alone: *CH v SSWP (ESA)* [2017] UKUT 6 (AAC). See also the annotation to regulation 21, above, on the judicial review challenge under the Equality Act 2010 with regard to the system of medical examinations and its impact on those with mental health problems.

Para.(1)

9.24 Paragraph (1) vests the Secretary of State with a discretion – where a question as to limited capability for work arises, a claimant "*may* be called ... to attend for a medical examination" (emphasis added). In principle, and probably only in exceptional cases, if it was unreasonable of the Secretary of State to arrange a medical examination, the claimant can argue that he had good cause for refusing to submit to it (*CIB/2645/99*; *CIB/2011/2001*, para.16). But since, as Commissioner Rowland stressed, "the integrity of the system depends upon their being appropriate tests in place" (*CIB/2011/2001*, para.16), establishing unreasonableness in that context is unlikely to be easy.

Para.(2)
"where a claimant fails..."

The question of what is meant by the phrase "where a claimant *fails*..." (emphasis added) was examined by Judge Poynter in *PPE v SSWP (ESA)* [2020] UKUT 59 (AAC), where he held (at para.56) that "regulation 23(2) does not permit the Secretary of State to treat a claimant as not having limited capability for work unless: (a) she was under a legal obligation to attend for and submit to a medical examination; (b) in breach of that obligation she did not do so; and (c) she did not have good cause for her breach of that obligation." Moreover, there was "a clear line of authority in the case law of the Social Security Commissioners, the Upper Tribunal and the higher courts that, before the Secretary of State can subject a claimant to adverse consequences for failing to do something—whether that something is to provide information, notify a change of circumstances, or to attend a specified place and undertake a specified activity—she must tell the claimant in the most unambiguous terms: (a) that it must be done; and (b) what it is that must be done. In short, there needs to be "the language of clear and unambiguous mandatory requirement" and there needs to be "crystal clarity" (para.57). Judge Poynter accordingly concluded as follows: 9.25

> "76. If the Secretary of State has the power to impose a legal obligation on claimants to do something, she can impose that obligation on a particular claimant simply by telling that claimant unambiguously that she must do it.
> 77. However, the Secretary of State must use "the language of clear and unambiguous mandatory requirement". No legal obligation is imposed if either:
> (a) the Secretary of State merely invites, advises, or encourages the claimant to do the thing, as opposed to telling her she must do it; or
> (b) it is unclear whether the Secretary of State has told the claimant that she must do the thing, as opposed to merely inviting, advising, or encouraging her to do it.
> 78. Moreover, the requirement to use "clear and unambiguous language" is to be applied strictly. The Secretary of State must be "crystal clear"."

On the evidence in that case, there were only two sentences that "could even arguably be read as imposing a legal obligation on the claimant to attend the examination rather than merely inviting her to do so". One was the statement that "It is very important you go to your assessment on [date]." The other was that "**You could lose your ESA payments and/or National Insurance credits if you don't go to your Work Capability Assessment**" (original emphasis) (at paras 92-95). Judge Poynter concluded that "the wording of the standard letter that was sent to the claimant did not include anything that unambiguously expressed the element of compulsion to that was necessary to impose a legal requirement on the claimant to attend the medical examination" (at para.100). It followed that the claimant "did not fail to attend for examination because she was never under any legal obligation to do so" (para.124). In terms of the proper approach in such appeals, Judge Poynter held that tribunals should "allow the appeal and reinstate the claimant's benefit unless both: (a) the papers before it include either: (i) a copy of the letter that was sent to the claimant calling him or her for examination; or (ii) a specimen of the standard letter that would have been sent and evidence from the relevant computer system that a letter in that form was generated and despatched; and (b) that letter imposes a legal obligation on the claimant to attend for the examination, as opposed to merely inviting, advising, or encouraging her to do so" (at para.6).

"without good cause"

9.26 The notion of "good cause" (see also reg.24) will necessarily be fact and context-specific, as reinforced by Judge Church in *SA v SSWP (ESA)* [2019] UKUT 118 (AAC). There the claimant, who had epilepsy, had a seizure on the day of his appointment and did not attend. The DWP argued that, having also missed previous appointments due to seizures, the claimant should have anticipated the possibility that he might have a seizure on the day and should therefore have requested a home visit. Judge Church held that the FTT's findings that the claimant did not act reasonably when he failed to ask in advance for a home visit, and that his state of health at the relevant time did not amount to good cause for his failure to attend, fell outside the range of reasonable decisions open to it on the facts. See also *JS v SSWP (ESA)* [2019] UKUT 303 (AAC) on the significance to be attached to previously missed appointments (see note to reg.24).

Several decisions have involved cases which have involved some form of 'stand-off' between the claimant and the HCP. If a claimant makes it clear that he or she will not be medically examined, then that arguably constitutes failure to "submit to" an examination. Going to the medical examination but refusing to be examined, constitutes attendance but also a failure to submit. In *CIB/849/2001*, Commissioner Turnbull stated:

> "The purpose of the medical examination was of course to enable the adjudication officer, with the benefit of the doctor's report, to determine whether the Claimant passed the all work test. The condition which the Claimant wished to impose on his submitting to an examination—i.e. that the doctor's report should not be passed to any layman, including an adjudication officer—rendered an examination useless for the purpose for which it was required. I have no doubt that, by imposing such a condition, the Claimant was failing to submit himself to a medical examination within the meaning of reg.8(2) [by analogy ESA Regs, reg.23(2)]. A person 'fails' to submit himself to an examination not only if he absolutely refuses to be examined, but also if he seeks to impose as a condition of being examined a term which would render the examination useless for the purpose for which it is required" (para.11).

The importance of careful fact-finding in such cases is demonstrated by *PH v SSWP (ESA)* [2016] UKUT 119 (AAC). In that case the claimant (Mr H) attended the examination centre and entered the examination room with the HCP, who asked him to sign an audio-recording agreement. Mr H could not take in its contents so signed the form but added "unread". The HCP informed him this was not acceptable, but added he could take the agreement away to read and another examination would be arranged for another date. On the day Mr H could not agree a new date as he did not have his diary with him. After having remonstrated with staff at the reception desk, security guards were called and he then left the centre. A tribunal dismissed his appeal against the Secretary of State's decision that he had "failed to participate" without good cause in a medical examination. As Judge Mitchell notes, reg.23 does not use the concept of "participating". Rather, it deals with failing to (a) "attend for" or (b) "submit to" a medical examination: "To put it in more everyday terms, (a) refers to a person who fails to turn up for an examination of which s/he has been duly notified and (b) refers to a person who fails to co-operate with the examination process so as to thwart its purpose" (at para.22). On the undisputed facts of the case, Mr H had plainly attended for a medical examination but the examination itself had never started, so he could not have failed to "submit to" such an examination:

> "32. On this case's undisputed facts, Mr H's medical examination did not begin. The evidence cannot support a contrary finding. The planned medical examination was abandoned or cancelled once it became clear to the healthcare professional that Mr H would not, on the day, complete the audio-recording form in

the way the centre's management thought he should. If Mr H's refusal was in the circumstances unreasonable, in the light of the examination's purpose, he could properly be said to have failed to submit to the examination. However, it was not viewed as unreasonable by the assessment staff as is shown, in my view, by the staff informing Mr H that another examination could be arranged. For that reason, I conclude that Mr H's conduct before the planned examination was cancelled was not unreasonable. And what happened afterwards is not relevant to the question whether he failed to submit to the medical examination."

The decision in *PH v SSWP (ESA)* may be usefully contrasted with that in *JW v SSWP (ESA)* [2016] UKUT 207 (AAC), where the assessment interview did actually commence, only to be abandoned when the claimant began cross- examining the HCP about her qualifications and insisted on recording the interview on his mobile phone. Judge Hemingway held "that if a claimant seeks to impose an unreasonable condition and, absent that unreasonable condition's fulfilment, withholds consent to the examination taking place, then he does not submit to the examination" (at para.13). However, in that case the tribunal's failure to find sufficient facts resulted in the decision being set aside and the appeal remitted for rehearing. See also *JW v SSWP (ESA)* [2016] UKUT 208 (AAC), where the claimant had sought to insist on e.g. knowing the details of the HCP's experience as a nurse, the history of her nursing career and the qualifications she had over and above the fact that she was a qualified general nurse. Judge Hemingway upheld the tribunal's decision that the appellant had failed without good cause to submit to a medical examination:

"38. It seems to me that, given my acceptance that, as a matter of law, a person can fail to submit by imposing unreasonable conditions and given the tribunal's findings it was clearly open to it to conclude that the additional information he was seeking, as a condition of allowing the examination to proceed, was being unreasonably required and did amount to a failure to submit. He already knew he was to be examined by a person whose name he was aware of and he knew that she was qualified as a registered general nurse. He also knew that she was authorised to carry out the examination for the purpose for which it was required. That ought to have been sufficient to reassure him as to any genuine concerns he might have had. It was open to the tribunal to conclude his insistence on more than that, even absent the intimidating behaviour it found him guilty of, amounted to a failure to submit."

Judge Hemingway's decision in *JW v SSWP (ESA)* [2016] UKUT 208 (AAC) was followed by Judge Mitchell in *RO v SSWP (ESA)* [2016] UKUT 402 (AAC), in which the claimant insisted on proof that the HCP (who was not wearing a name badge) was a registered nurse. The claimant (Mr O) was offered access to the relevant website but declined that offer in the absence of photographic evidence and left the examination centre. The First-tier Tribunal decided he did not have good cause for failing to participate in the medical examination. Judge Mitchell, having referred to the terms of the statutory provisions defining who is qualified to be a HCP, ruled that "a claimant is entitled to make a reasonable request for proof that a purported healthcare professional is in fact a health care professional" (at para.17), not least because a medical examination is an invasion of privacy (at para.22). However, the claimant's appeal failed on the facts.

RO v SSWP (ESA) was followed by Judge Gray in *CH v SSWP (ESA)* [2017] UKUT 6 (AAC), where she expressed the view (obiter on the facts) that "it is for the Secretary of State to decide on the type of health care professional who will conduct the examination, and for a claimant to refuse to submit to the examination on the basis that the healthcare professional chosen was not a doctor, or to insist as a precondition of attendance that it must be a doctor conducting the examination, would amount to a failure to attend" (para.22). The nature and extent of the medical examination to which the claimant must submit is a matter for the examining health care professional rather than the claimant, tribunal or Commissioner, "fundamentally a medical matter and for the judgment of the clinician in each individual case" (*C1/07–08(IB)*, para.12). The health care professional's demands of the claimant must, however, fall within the bounds of a "medical examination" and there remains the issue of whether a claimant has good cause for refusing to submit to the examination (*C1/07–08(IB)*, para.15).

A health care professional can insist on the presence of a suitable chaperone (e.g. a DWP employee bound by confidentiality not to broadcast details to the world at large), and unreasonable refusal to allow such a chaperone to be present constitutes refusing to submit to the examination (*CIB/2645/99*; *CIB/2011/2001*, para.15). Claimants cannot expect their medical details to be kept from those who must determine their claims; those who insist on strict medical confidentiality can do so, but only at the cost of foregoing their rights to benefit or credits (*CIB/2011/2001*, para.15).

The effect of a finding of lack of good cause precludes benefit until a new claim is submitted and a new period of incapacity for work begins. It may also prevent the claimant being treated under reg.30 as incapable of work pending a limited capability for work assessment. However, if the claimant is found to have limited capability for work in that assessment, benefit can be backdated to the beginning of the period covered by the new claim or application. See also on this aspect *R(IB)2/01* and para.8 of *CIB/3512/1998*. On "good cause", see also the commentary to reg.22 and note the non-exhaustive prescription in reg.24 of matters which must be taken into account in determining good cause.

Para.(3)

9.27 Paragraph (3) imposes a due notice requirement. If this condition is not met, then whether the claimant has good cause or not becomes irrelevant. Note that proper written notice means written notice of the date, time and place of the examination, sent to the claimant at least seven days beforehand, unless the person agreed to accept a shorter period of notice, whether given in writing or otherwise. On determining whether and when a written notice was sent, see also the commentary to reg.22, above. Interpreted by analogy with the approach to another time period issue in *R(IB)2/00*, para.(3) requires at least seven days' clear notice so that neither the day of sending nor that of receipt count in determining that period (*CIB/2576/2007*, para.6). The notice may be given by or on behalf of the approved (generally DWPMS) health care professional concerned (para.(1)). The notice must, however, be written. So, where an appointment had been made over the telephone by leaving a message with the claimant's sister, which the claimant asserted was not passed on, he could not properly be treated as capable of work for not having attended without good cause, since the regulation's clear requisite of written notice had not been satisfied (see *CIB/969/97*). In *R(IB) 1/01*, Commissioner Rowland considered that where, when a claimant stated that he would not be able to attend a medical examination, the Department in consequence said they would cancel it, the claimant cannot be held not to have attended it.

As to the meaning of "sent", in *CIB/1381/2003* Deputy Commissioner Wikeley declined, after reviewing a range of authority on analogous provisions in child support and jobseeker's allowance, to determine whether "sent" meant "despatched" or "delivered", since a failure to attend because of not receiving the notice could in any event constitute "good cause" as the tribunal had held. In *CSIB/721/2004*, however, Commissioner Parker was of the view that where the claimant proved that the notification duly despatched (a matter for the Secretary of State to establish) had not in fact been received by him, in the ordinary course of post or at all, then it had not been "sent" within the meaning of para.(3), thus precluding treating the claimant as capable of work for "failure to attend or submit to examination" so that the issue of "good cause" never arose. She there took account of a Secretary of State concession on the point noted in *CIB/4512/2002* (not on the Commissioners' website), to which the Secretary of State's representative referred her. But in contrast note that Commissioner Rowland in *CIB/3512/1998*, dealing with an analogous Incapacity for Work Reg., stressed that it said "sent" rather than "received", albeit that non-receipt would be a matter as regards "good cause".

The Northern Ireland decision *C11/03–04(IB)* is a useful reminder of the need to ascertain the precise facts and be careful in applying to them the concept of "good cause". The case concerned a common "defence", where the claimant alleged he had never received a particular letter sent by the Department, a typical case of conflict of evidence. Deputy Commissioner Powell thought that sometimes it is right to reject such allegations in a robust manner, for example, where the excuse extends to a number of letters, or is coupled with suspicious circumstances, or if the non-receipt of mail is selective so that only certain letters are not received. The case before him, however, concerned a rather different situation—the uncontradicted evidence of the claimant, who did not attend the appeal hearing, of the non-receipt of a single letter in plausible circumstances, namely, a communal delivery of mail to particular premises and the possibility that another went through it before the claimant had a chance to do so. The Commissioner could not see how an effective challenge could be mounted to the claim and that, in these circumstances, the claimant had established good cause. The Secretary of State bears the burden of proof in establishing that the requirements of para.(3) have been met, a precondition for being able to find the claimant capable of work for non-attendance etc.

In *CIB/4012/2004*, Deputy Commissioner Mark, considering the cases noted above, found that the burden had not been discharged. Computer records showing that a letter had been issued were not sufficient evidence of it being "sent" on the facts of that case. However, in other respects it appears that Judge Mark arguably set the bar too high for the Secretary of State and those acting on his behalf. Three other Upper Tribunal decisions have adopted a rather more pragmatic approach to the evidential requirements imposed on the Secretary of State. See further *AL v SSWP (ESA)* [2011] UKUT 512 (AAC), *SH v SSWP (ESA)* [2014] UKUT 574 (AAC) and *DW v SSWP (ESA)* [2016] UKUT 179 (AAC)—the last a decision which contains a useful review of the authorities—all discussed in the commentary to reg.22 above.

Matters to be taken into account in determining good cause in relation to regulations 22 or 23

24. The matters to be taken into account in determining whether a claimant has good cause under regulations 22 (failure to provide information in relation to limited capability for work) or 23 (failure to attend a medical examination to determine limited capability for work) include— 9.28

(a) whether the claimant was outside Great Britain at the relevant time;
(b) the claimant's state of health at the relevant time; and
(c) the nature of any disability the claimant has.

DEFINITION

"claimant"—see WRA 2007 s.24(1).

GENERAL NOTE

This regulation, made pursuant to WRA 2007 s.8(4), stipulates that in determining whether someone had good cause for failing to provide information (under reg.22) or for failing to attend for or submit to a medical examination (under reg.23) decision-makers and appellate bodies must take into account (i) whether the person was outside Great Britain at the relevant time, (ii) his state of health at the relevant time, and (iii) the nature of his disability. This list is not, however, exhaustive (the regulation says "shall include"). On "good cause", see further the commentary to regs 22 and 23. 9.29

On the relevance of previously missed appointments when assessing whether a claimant has shown good cause for not attending an HCP appointment, see *JS v SSWP (ESA)* [2019] UKUT 303 (AAC), where Judge Jacobs held as follows:

"16. Take first a claimant whose explanations refer to the same condition. Much will depend on the nature of that condition. It should come as no surprise if there are repeated failures to attend on account of agoraphobia. There would be no cause for suspicion. Quite the contrary, an ability to attend sometimes but not others could call into question the claimant's asserted disability. In contrast, if the claimant's condition is variable, chronic fatigue syndrome say, variation is to be expected and not of itself a cause for suspicion.
17. The position may be more complicated if the claimant gives different reasons for not attending on successive occasions. By definition, the decisionmaker will have accepted good cause on the earlier occasions. There is no question of changing those decisions, but a later decision-maker may conclude, looking back at the history of the case and taking account of evidence now available, that there has been a pattern of avoidance by the claimant. Even then, it is important to focus on the current failure. The previous conduct may justify careful scrutiny of the current failure, with perhaps a request for supporting evidence. But even a claimant with a lengthy history of failing to attend for what appear, in hindsight, to be highly dubious reasons may still be delayed by inclement weather or have a domestic emergency. And a claimant who has more than one disabling condition may be prevented from attending for different reasons on different occasions.
18. In short, it all depends, which means that tribunals need to take care in their reasoning to show whether they took any account of a claimant's previous failures and, if so, how in order to demonstrate that their relevance was assessed rationally, taking account of points both for and against the claimant."

A judicial review claim challenging the legality of the DWP's safeguarding policies for vulnerable claimants was brought in *R (on the application of Turner) v Secretary of State for Work and Pensions* [2021] EWHC 465 (Admin). Ms Turner brought the proceedings following the inquest into the death of her relative Errol Graham, who had starved to death after his benefits (including ESA) had been stopped when he had failed to attend a fitness for work assessment and not responded to other communications. The grounds of challenge related to the lawfulness of both the DWP's safeguarding policy and the decision to stop Mr Graham's benefits respectively. Bourne J dismissed both grounds of judicial review.

As to the former, Bourne J rejected the argument that putting the burden of proof on the claimant to show good cause under reg.24 was unlawful. However, the judge ruled that "Where the issue is `good cause' for a claimant's failure to attend an assessment, it is logical and reasonable to look to the claimant for the explanation. However, cases such as Kerr are a reminder that the claimant is not the only possible source of an explanation and, moreover, that the Defendant's officials must consider any relevant information which is reasonably available to them" (para.71). Moreover, "The point being made under regulation 24 is straightforward. That regulation, quoted above, requires decision makers to have regard to matters including the claimant's state of health and any disability he may have. A public law decision maker must in general ask himself the right question and `take reasonable steps to acquaint himself with the relevant information to enable him to answer it correctly': *Secretary of State for Education and Science v Tameside MBC* [1977] AC 1014 at 1065B per Lord Diplock" (at para.76). Furthermore, s.149 of the Equality Act 2010 did not materially affect the interpretation of that duty (para.88).

As to the latter, Bourne J. held that while the DWP was aware of some of Mr Graham's circumstances it did not know of the acute illness he had suffered more recently or of any individual other than his GP (who was contacted by the DWP but had little to report) who might have been expected to provide relevant information. In all the circumstances the DWP was not bound to make further inquiries into Mr Graham's health.

[1Hospital patients

25.—(1) A claimant is to be treated as having limited capability for work on any day on which that claimant is undergoing medical or other treatment as a patient in a hospital or similar institution, or on any day which is a day of recovery from that treatment. 9.30

(2) The circumstances in which a claimant is to be regarded as undergoing treatment falling within paragraph (1) include where the claimant is attending a residential programme of rehabilitation for the treatment of drug or alcohol addiction.

(3) For the purposes of this regulation, a claimant is to be regarded as undergoing treatment as a patient in a hospital or similar institution only if that claimant has been advised by a health care professional to stay in a hospital or similar institution for a period of 24 hours or longer.

(4) For the purposes of this regulation, "day of recovery" means a day on which a claimant is recovering from treatment as a patient in a hospital or similar institution and the Secretary of State is satisfied that the claimant should be treated as having limited capability for work on that day.]

AMENDMENT

1. Employment and Support Allowance (Amendment) Regulations 2012 (SI 2012/3096), reg.3(4) (January 28, 2013, subject to application, transitional and savings provisions in reg.2 of this amending instrument, below, para.9.614).

DEFINITIONS

"claimant"—see WRA 2007 s.24(1).
"day of recovery"—see para.(4).
"limited capability for work"—see WRA 2007 s.1(4).
"medical treatment"—see reg.2(1).

GENERAL NOTE

Paragraphs (1), (3)

This regulation stipulates that those undergoing medical or other treatment as a patient in a hospital or other institution, must be treated as having limited capability for work on any day on which they are undergoing that treatment, or on any day of recovery from that treatment. 9.31

The notion of "undergoing treatment as a patient in a hospital or similar institution" was initially not defined at all and was the subject of criticism and guidance by Judge Williams in *CJ v SSWP (ESA)* [2012] UKUT 201 (AAC) which still has application to those cases still subject, after the amended version of reg.25 inserted from January 28, 2013, to the previously worded reg.25.

The current wording was subject to analysis by Judge Mitchell in *SJ v SSWP (ESA)* [2015] UKUT 180 (AAC). He regarded himself as bound in several respects by the Court of Appeal decision in *Secretary of State for Work and Pensions* v *Slavin* [2012] AACR 30, interpreting similar terms in the DLA Regs 1991 reg.9, the appeal from Judge Turnbull's decision in *AS v SSWP (DLA)* [2010] UKUT 482 (AAC) (see, above, para.4.53) (hereinafter "*Slavin*").

Judge Mitchell considered that the regulation has to be "read as a whole". Para.(1) read with para.(3) sets out four elements all of which must be fulfilled for a day to be treated as one of limited capability for work:

"(a) the claimant must be undergoing medical or other treatment; and

(b) the treatment must be as a patient; and

(c) the treatment must be in a hospital or similar institution; and

(d) the claimant must have been advised by a health care professional to stay in the hospital or other institution for a period of 24 hours or longer" (para.15).

If any element is absent, the claim based on para.(1) must fail. Therefore, a tribunal can reject an argument founded on para.(1) "simply by reference to the non-satisfaction of any one element" (para.16).

"Hospital or similar institution": this is not defined in the ESA Regs, but features in a number of social security legislative contexts and its meaning has been elucidated by case law on them and is to be applied to the term in this regulation (para.52). Essentially, a hospital is any institution for the reception and treatment of persons suffering from illness, with "illness" being defined as including mental illness and any injury or disability requiring medical or dental treatment or nursing (para.38).

"Medical or other treatment": "medical treatment" is defined in reg.2(1), above, as

> "medical, surgical or rehabilitative treatment (including any course or diet or other regimen), and references to a person receiving or submitting to medical treatment are to be construed accordingly".

Judge Mitchell considered that *Slavin* (binding on him) held that "medical or other treatment is confined to medical treatment, dental treatment or nursing care" (para.42). He also approved Judge Turnbull's view in para.88 of *AS*, noting that nothing in the Court of Appeal's decision in *Slavin* upholding that of Judge Turnbull in *AS* indicated disapproval of it. Judge Turnbull accepted counsel's view that "nursing" and "treatment" could not be confined to "care and skill exercised by doctors and nurses", but had to extend to that administered by other health care professionals (e.g. physiotherapy or occupational therapy) (paras 46-48, 60). Para.(2) of reg.25 (see further, below) stipulates that treatment falling within para.(1) includes attendance at "a residential programme of rehabilitation for the treatment of drug or alcohol addiction".

Accordingly, Judge Mitchell upheld the tribunal's decision that the refuge in which the claimant was staying as a victim of domestic violence did not fall within para.(1) because she was not undergoing medical or other treatment there. Nor had she been advised by a health care professional to stay in the refuge for a period of at least 24 hours so that the condition in para.(3) was not met. Judge Mitchell considered that his decision did not mean that all refuges would fall outside reg.25; labels "are of no intrinsic significance... What matters is whether the facts of a particular case come within regulation 25" (para.67), but stated, by way of general guidance, that he "would not be surprised if most refuge placements have characteristics matching, in material respects, [this claimant's] so that their residents fall outside regulation 25(1)" (para.68).

Paragraphs (1), (4)

9.32 The regulation protects not only those "undergoing medical or other treatment as a patient in a hospital or other institution" but also their days of "recovery from that treatment". "Day of recovery" is defined in para.(4). Note the discretion given to the Secretary of State—the day on which the former in-patient is recovering from that treatment will only count if the Secretary of State is satisfied that the claimant should on that day be treated as having limited capability for work. In *SI v SSWP (ESA)* [2013] UKUT 453 (AAC), Judge Mark was not satisfied

> "that the tribunal did properly consider the question whether the claimant was still recovering from the treatment. It does not follow just because the wound had scarred over and he had restricted movement back in his joint that he was fully

recovered. The remaining limitations could in part still be due to the fact that he had not fully recovered. There does not appear to have been any investigation of the extent of his limitation previously or the nature of the operation or of his prognosis or the reasons for his continuing therapies and consultations or of the expected period within which recovery from the operation was to be expected" (para.10).

This lapse did not assist the claimant because the tribunal on the facts was entitled to conclude that there was no good ground for treating him as incapable of work.

Paragraphs (1), (2)

Attendance at a residential programme of rehabilitation for the treatment of drug or alcohol addiction counts as undergoing "treatment falling within paragraph (1)". This statutory stipulation is exhaustive and does not permit extension by analogy so as to cover other rehabilitation programmes (*SJ v SSWP (ESA)* [2015] UKUT 180 (AAC), paras 65, 66). 9.33

Regulation 21(1) (information gathering requirements) does not apply to a determination under this regulation (see reg.21(3)).

Claimants receiving certain regular treatment

26.—(1) Subject to paragraph (2), a claimant receiving— 9.34

(a) regular weekly treatment by way of haemodialysis for chronic renal failure;

(b) treatment by way of plasmapheresis [2. . .]; or

(c) regular weekly treatment by way of total parenteral nutrition for gross impairment of enteric function,

is to be treated as having limited capability for work during any week in which that claimant is engaged in [3receiving] that treatment or has a day of recovery from that treatment.

[1(2) A claimant who receives the treatment referred to in paragraph (1) is only to be treated as having limited capability for work from the first week of treatment in which the claimant undergoes no fewer than—

(a) two days of treatment;

(b) two days of recovery from any of the forms of treatment listed in paragraph 1(a) to (c); or

(c) one day of treatment and one day of recovery from that treatment,

but the days of treatment or recovery from that treatment or both need not be consecutive.]

(3) For the purpose of this regulation "day of recovery" means a day on which a claimant is recovering from any of the forms of treatment listed in paragraph (1)(a) to (c) and the Secretary of State is satisfied that the claimant should be treated as having limited capability for work on that day.

AMENDMENTS

1. Employment and Support Allowance (Miscellaneous Amendments) Regulations 2008 (SI 2008/2428) reg.5(1) (October 27, 2008).

2. Employment and Support Allowance (Amendment) Regulations 2012 (SI 2012/3096) reg.3(5) (January 28, 2013, subject to application, transitional and savings provisions in reg.2 of this amending instrument, below, para.9.614).

3. Social Security (Miscellaneous Amendments) (No.3) Regulations 2013 (SI 2013/2536) reg.13(12) (October 29, 2013).

DEFINITIONS

"claimant"—see WRA 2007 s.24(1).

"day of recovery"—see para.(3).

"limited capability for work"—see WRA 2007 s.1(4).
"week"—see WRA 2007 s.24(1); reg.2(1).

GENERAL NOTE

9.35 Someone undergoing certain treatments is treated as having limited capability for work on during any week in which he is engaged in that treatment or has a day of recovery from that treatment (para.(1)). The treatments concerned are: regular weekly treatment by way of haemodialysis for chronic renal failure (para.(1)(a)); treatment by way of plasmapheresis (para.(1)(b); or regular weekly treatment by way of total parenteral nutrition for gross impairment of enteric function (para. (1)(c)). "Day of recovery" is defined in para.(3) as one on which the claimant is recovering from any of the forms of treatment so long as the Secretary of State (note the discretion) is satisfied that the claimant should be treated as having limited capability for work on that day. Paragraph (2) deals with the first week of any such treatment. During that week, the claimant can only be treated as having limited capability for work if in that week he undergoes no fewer than two days of treatment, or two days of recovery from such treatment or one day of treatment and one day of recovery. The days of treatment or recovery from it need not be consecutive.

Regulation 21(1) (information gathering requirements) does not apply to a determination under this regulation (see reg.21(3)).

Claimant to be treated as having limited capability for work throughout a day

9.36 **27.** A claimant who at the commencement of any day has, or thereafter develops, limited capability for work as determined in accordance with the limited capability for work assessment is to be treated as having limited capability for work throughout that day.

DEFINITIONS

"claimant"—see WRA 2007 s.24(1).
"limited capability for work"—see WRA 2007 s.1(4).
"limited capability for work assessment"—see reg.2(1).

GENERAL NOTE

9.37 The situation encompassed here in which someone is to be treated as having limited capability for work, confers no exemption from the information gathering processes for the limited capability for work assessment (reg.21(3)).

The effect of this regulation is that those with limited capability for work at the start of a day or who thereafter develop it on that day are to be treated as having limited capability for work throughout that day. In *CIB/6244/1997*, Commissioner Jacobs considered the application of the IB regulation to intermittent and variable conditions. He considered that the provision must be read in the light that, under the all work test/PCA and its descriptors, one cannot confine consideration merely to a particular time on a particular day—otherwise a claimant could always satisfy the "cannot" descriptors and the "sometimes" ones (not in any event in the ESA limited capability for work assessment activities and descriptors) would never apply. The "cannot" and "sometimes" descriptors inevitably require a focus over a period and not at a specific moment in time. Thus he thought that Incapacity for Work Regs, reg.15 "does not operate to ensure that a claimant with a variable condition that incapacitates him for a part of each day must be considered as incapable throughout the whole of every day" (para.23).However, it will "apply where there is a sudden onset of or recovery from an incapacitating condition, including an intermittent incapacitating condition or the incapacitating intermittent features of a condition" (*ibid.* and see also *CIB/15482/1996*, paras 7–9). In *CIB/243/1998*. Deputy Commissioner Mark considered that a claimant who suffered an asthma attack for part of a day had to be treated as incapable of work throughout that day under this regulation, provided that the effect of the attack when ongoing was such that he would score at least 15 points for more than a minimal period on that day. In *CIB/399/2003*, Commissioner Mesher very firmly rejected that approach of Deputy Commissioner Mark in *CIB/243/1998* and preferred the approach taken by Commissioner Jacobs in *CIB/6244/1997* and by Deputy Commissioner Ramsay in *CIB/15482/1996*, thus establishing a strong line of authority against Deputy Commissioner Mark's view of the application of Incapacity for Work Regs, reg.15. Commissioner Mesher thought the rejected approach to be inconsistent with the concept of "reasonable regularity" applicable to the "cannot" descriptors and out of tune with the tenor of *R(IB)2/99(T)* (on which see further the commentary to Sch.2).

Night workers

28.—(1) Where a claimant works for a continuous period which extends over midnight into the following day, that claimant is to be treated as having limited capability for work on the day on which the lesser part of that period falls if that claimant had limited capability for work for the remainder of that day. 9.38

(2) Where, in relation to a period referred to in paragraph (1), the number of hours worked before and after midnight is equal—

(a) if the days in question fall at the beginning of a period of limited capability for work, the claimant is to be treated as having limited capability on the second day; and

(b) if the days in question fall at the end of a period of limited capability for work, the claimant is to be treated as having limited capability for work on the first day.

DEFINITIONS

"claimant"—see WRA 2007 s.24(1).
"limited capability for work"—see WRA 2007 s.1(4).
"period of limited capability for work"—see reg.2(1).

GENERAL NOTE

Although unlike IB, ESA is a weekly rather than a daily benefit, there is still need to be able to attribute limited capability for work to a particular day, where the person doing nightwork has a shift spanning midnight and thus covering two days. The ESA scheme in some circumstances permits awards for periods of less than a week (the amount payable being determined under regs 165–169) (e.g. the period at the start or end of a claim; persons receiving certain regular treatments). Although the ESA scheme neither in Act or Regs defines "day", the general rule for benefit purposes has been that a day is the period midnight to midnight, and performance of work on a day will generally preclude the week in which it is done ranking as one of entitlement to ESA (see reg.40(1)). But there are exceptions to that preclusive rule (regs 40(4), 46) where the preclusion is only to affect the day(s) actually worked. There is thus a need to attribute a nightshift spanning two days to one day or the other. Otherwise, the application of the rules to nightworkers whose shifts span midnight could cause hardship since they would, without this regulation, be regarded as working on two days and thus be treated less favourably than their day worker counterparts whose shift of exactly the same length (period of work) would be attributed to one day. Equally, even though the nightworker suffered the same degree of limited capability for work on one of those days, the day could not count as one of limited capability for work This regulation attempts some easing of the position of nightworkers in this regard. 9.39

Paragraph (1) provides that where someone works for a continuous period beginning one day and spanning midnight into the following day, the day on which there falls the lesser part of the period worked will be treated as one of limited capability for work if the claimant has limited capability for work for the rest of that day. To put it another way, the day with the longer period worked is to be treated for the purpose of the exceptions to the preclusive rules noted above as the day of work. Paragraph (2) deals with the situation in which the hours worked each side of midnight are equal. If the two days in question fall at the beginning of a period of limited capability for work, the second day is to be treated as one of incapacity and the first as the one of work. If the two days fall at the end of a period of incapacity for work, the first day is the one to be regarded as a day of limited capability for work and the second as the one of work.

Exceptional circumstances

9.40 **29.**—(1) A claimant who does not have limited capability for work as determined in accordance with the limited capability for work assessment is to be treated as having limited capability for work if paragraph (2) applies to the claimant.

(2) [1 Subject to paragraph (3)] this paragraph applies if—

(a) the claimant is suffering from a life threatening disease in relation to which—

(i) there is medical evidence that the disease is uncontrollable, or uncontrolled, by a recognised therapeutic procedure; and

(ii) in the case of a disease that is uncontrolled, there is a reasonable cause for it not to be controlled by a recognised therapeutic procedure; or

(b) the claimant suffers from some specific disease or bodily or mental disablement and, by reasons of such disease or disablement, there would be a substantial risk to the mental or physical health of any person if the claimant were found not to have limited capability for work.

[1(3) Paragraph (2)(b) does not apply where the risk could be reduced by a significant amount by—

(a) reasonable adjustments being made in the claimant's workplace; or

(b) the claimant taking medication to manage the claimant's condition where such medication has been prescribed for the claimant by a registered medical practitioner treating the claimant.]

[2(4) In this regulation "medical evidence" means—

(a) evidence from a health care professional approved by the Secretary of State; and

(b) evidence (if any) from any health care professional or a hospital or similar Institution,

or such part of such evidence as constitutes the most reliable evidence available in the circumstances.]

AMENDMENTS

1. Employment and Support Allowance (Amendment) Regulations 2012 (SI 2012/3096) reg.3(6) (January 28, 2013, subject to application, transitional and savings provisions in reg.2 of this amending instrument, below, para.9.614).

2. Social Security (Miscellaneous Amendments) (No.3) Regulations 2013 (SI 2013/2536) reg.13(13) (October 29, 2013).

DEFINITIONS

"claimant"—see WRA 2007 s.24(1).

"limited capability for work"—see WRA 2007 s.1(4).

"limited capability for work assessment"—see reg.2(1).
"medical evidence"—see para.(4).

GENERAL NOTE

Paragraph (1): background and role

Like reg.27 in the IB scheme, this regulation reflects the fact that functional assessment systems like the IB PCA or the ESA LCWA would not properly measure the incapacitating effect of certain conditions, and so would "fail" some people who properly ought to be regarded as being incapable of work (IB) or having limited capability for work (ESA). Headed "exceptional circumstances", the regulation can only come into play where the claimant has been found *not* to have limited capability for work under reg.19 and Sch.2; where s/he has attained an insufficient score (less than 15 points) applying those descriptors. 9.41

The regulation envisages two classes of case in which someone assessed as not having limited capability for work can nonetheless be treated as having it.

Paragraph (2)(a): claimant suffering from a life threatening disease uncontrolled or uncontrollable by a recognised therapeutic procedure

The first class of case is where the claimant suffers from a life threatening disease (the IB requirement that it be "severe" is not continued into ESA) which *medical evidence establishes* is uncontrollable by a recognized therapeutic procedure or (but only with reasonable cause) is uncontrolled by such a procedure. 9.42

Dealing with the substantially similarly worded IB provision in *CIB/4506/01*, Commissioner Howell stated that here:

> "the question is only whether the nature of [the claimant's] condition is such that it is capable of being controlled by medical science, or not. Consequently the tribunal were right in taking account not only of the inhalers and adrenaline injector she is able to use for herself, but also the hospital treatment which unhappily she finds also has to be used on occasions as a means of bringing the condition under control. On the tribunal's findings the claimant's condition is thus controllable in the relevant sense, and their reasons are clearly and adequately given" (para.10).

The tribunal had not erred in law.

What level of "control" does the provision envisage? In *CIB/155/2004*, Commissioner Jacobs thought it inappropriate to deploy as a test whether the level of control would suffice to allow the claimant to work; since that test would always be satisfied. Rather, he thought that IB reg.27 [ESA reg.29] comes into play where a claimant is capable of work but has a condition that makes it inappropriate that he be expected to work. Since, as regards para.(2)(a) what makes that inappropriate is the fact that the condition is a threat to the claimant's life, the threshold for control should be whether the control is sufficient to remove the threat to the claimant's life. In the case at hand, while the evidence disclosed that the claimant's diabetes was poorly controlled, it was nonetheless sufficiently controlled that para.(2)(a) was inapplicable. While there were longer-term complications to which the Consultant referred, they were not yet present, and not currently threatening the claimant's life.

"Reasonable cause for it not to be controlled by a recognised therapeutic procedure": even where a tribunal with the assistance of its medical member considers that a procedure would be of benefit, a claimant had reasonable cause for not taking advantage of it where two cardiologists had advised him not to do so and it had not been offered to him (*KR v SSWP (ESA)* [2013] UKUT 637 (AAC), para.6). 9.43

There must be "medical evidence" that the disease is uncontrollable or uncontrolled. The term "medical evidence" embraces (i) evidence from a health care professional approved by the Secretary of State, (ii) evidence (if any) from any other health care professional, hospital or similar institution, or such part of evidence in (i) or (ii) as constitutes the most reliable evidence available in the circumstances (para.(4)). "Health care professional" covers a registered medical practitioner, a registered nurse or an occupational therapist or physiotherapist registered with a regulatory body established by an Order in Council under section 60 of the Health Act 1999 (reg.2(1)). In a Northern Ireland decision *C5/00–01(IB)* Commissioner Brown stressed that the evidence "must relate to the claimant himself, it is not constituted by extracts from medical textbooks unless the doctor relates them to the claimant" (para.16). The medical evidence must have been issued before the Secretary of State's decision in the case. In *GC* v *SSWP (ESA)* [2013] UKUT 271 (AAC), the claimant sought to rely on medical evidence issued after the Secretary of State had made his decision, on the evidence then before him, that the claimant's disease (bladder cancer) was controlled. Judge Jacobs considered reg.29 in the context of SSA 1998 s.12(8)(b) (an appeal tribunal shall not take into account any circumstances not obtaining at the time when the decision appealed against was made). He held that this was not the same situation as that in *R(DLA) 2 & 3/01* where later evidence could properly be adduced to show the circumstances prevailing at the date of decision:

> "Regulation 29([2])(a)(i) is different. It does not refer to the claimant having a disease that is uncontrolled or uncontrollable. It refers to the need for *medical evidence* that that is so. In applying section 12(8)(b), the relevant circumstance is the existence of the evidence of the state of the claimant's condition. In Mr C's case, the evidence that his cancer had returned and required surgery did not exist until after the Secretary of State made the decision under appeal. In such a case, it makes no sense to say that later evidence shows that there was evidence at the time of the decision. Such talk is entirely inconsistent with the requirements of [regulation 29(2)(a)] as it renders the requirement for contemporaneous evidence redundant" (para.12).

Paragraph (2)(b), (3): "by reasons of [the claimant's health condition or disability] there would be a substantial risk to the mental or physical health of any person if the claimant were found not to have limited capability for work"

9.44 The second class of case in which someone not assessed as having limited capability for work can nonetheless be treated as having it, concerns a claimant, suffering from some specific disease or bodily or mental disablement, and by reasons of such there would be substantial risk to the mental or physical health of any person if the claimant were found not to have limited capability for work. The scheme thus carries into ESA something the Department had tried unsuccessfully to remove as regards IB in 1997.

With effect from January 28, 2013, para.(2) was made "subject to paragraph (3)", so that the "substantial risk" provision in para.(2)(b) does not apply if the risk could be reduced by a "significant amount" by reasonable adjustments being made in the claimant's workplace or by the claimant taking medication prescribed by a registered medical practitioner treating the patient (para.(3)). "Significant amount" unfortunately is not defined but, given the protective purpose of para.(2)(b) should preferably be interpreted as one reducing the risk to a level describable as less than "substantial". The *Explanatory Memorandum* to the amending instrument refers to the risk being "greatly reduced" (See para.7.14) (*http:// www.legislation.gov.uk/uksi/2012/3096/pdfs/uksiem_20123096_en.pdf*). In contrast the two examples given in para.7.15 of Memo *DMG 1/13* to the *Decision Makers Guide* (*http://www.dwp.gov.uk/docs/m-1-13.pdf*) rather confusingly refer respectively to "the risk to his health could be alleviated" and "the risk could be substantially reduced". It is to be expected that the proper interpretation will be a matter appealed to the Upper Tribunal in due course.

Note that the old wording of para.(2) will still apply to some cases after January 28, 2013 (see reg.2 of the amending instrument, below, para.9.614).

On "specific disease or bodily or mental disablement", see the commentary to reg.19.

The "substantial risk" must arise "by reasons of" a specific disease or bodily or mental disablement: In *DR v SSWP (ESA)* [2014] UKUT 188 (AAC); [2014] AACR 38, Judge May held erroneous in law a tribunal decision that the claimant satisfied reg.29 because it had not made the necessary connection between the risk and the disease or disablement (see para.3). Alcohol misuse in itself is not such a disablement. To rank as disablement the misuse of alcohol must rank as "alcohol dependency" in terms of the "constellation of markers" found in quotations from *R(DLA) 6/06* in the Three-Judge Panel's decision in *JG v SSWP (ESA)* [2013] UKUT 37 (AAC); [2013] AACR 23 (see paras 5-7, 10 of *DR*). Para.45 of the panel decision sets out the constellation of markers as follows: 9.45

> "A maladaptive pattern of substance use, leading to clinically significant impairment or distress, as manifested by three (or more) of the following, occurring at any time in the same 12-month period
>
> (1) tolerance, as defined by either of the following:
> (a) a need for markedly increased amounts of the substance to achieve intoxication or desire effect
> (b) markedly diminished effect with continued use of the same amount of the substance
>
> (2) withdrawal, as manifested by either of the following:
> (a) the characteristic withdrawal syndrome for the substance . . .
> (b) the same (or a closely related) substance is taken to relieve or avoid withdrawal symptoms
>
> (3) the substance is often taken in larger amounts or over a longer period than was intended
> (4) there is a persistent desire or unsuccessful efforts to cut down or control substance use
> (5) a great deal of time is spent in activities necessary to obtain the substance (e.g. visiting multiple doctors or driving long distances), use the substance (eg chain-smoking), or recover from its effects
> (6) important social, occupational, or recreational activities are given up or reduced because of substance use
> (7) the substance use is continued despite knowledge of having a persistent or recurrent physical or psychological problem that is likely to have been caused or exacerbated by the substance (e.g. current cocaine use despite recognition of cocaine-induced depression, or continued drinking despite recognition that an ulcer was made worse by alcohol consumption)."

These various factors were adopted from those listed in the category of Substance Dependence contained in the Diagnostic and Statistical Manual of Mental Disorders of the American Psychiatric Association (DSM IV). In *SD v SSWP (ESA)* [2016] UKUT 100 (AAC); [2016] AACR 35, in which the claimant used street heroin (an opoid), Judge Knowles QC held that the factors pointing towards alcohol dependence as set out in *JG v SSWP (ESA)* (above) also have application in the case of drug dependency:

> "31. I note that the factors listed in the category of Substance Dependence in DSM-IV are not alcohol specific [see (vii) above for example] and thus, as a matter of logic, they must apply to other substances such as heroin and cocaine. I find that the constellation of markers set out in paragraph 45 is therefore equally applicable to drug dependence (such as that probably seen in this particular case)."

Judge Knowles QC observed that DSM-IV has now been superseded by DSM-5, in which substance-related/addictive disorders are divided into two categories, namely substance use disorders (including opioid use disorder) and substance induced disorders. Judge Knowles QC concluded as follows:

"37. The diagnostic criteria for opioid use disorder (heroin being an opioid) are as follows:

"*a problematic pattern of opioid use leading to clinically significant impairment or distress as manifested by at least two of the following occurring within a 12 month period:*

i) opioids are often taken in larger amounts or over a longer period than was intended;
ii) a persistent desire or unsuccessful attempts to cut down or control opiate use;
iii) a great deal of time is spent in activities necessary to obtain the opioid, use the opioid or recover from its effects;
iv) craving or a strong desire to use opioids;
v) recurrent opioid use resulting in a failure to fulfil major role obligations at work, school or home;
vi) continued opioid use despite having persistent or recurrent social or interpersonal problems caused or exacerbated by the use of opioids;
vii) important social, occupational or recreational activities are given up or their engagement is reduced because of opioid use;
viii) recurrent opioid use in situations in which it is physically hazardous;
ix) continued opioid use despite knowledge of having a persistent or recurrent physical of psychological problem that is likely to have been caused or exacerbated by the substance;
x) tolerance as defined by either a need for markedly increased amounts of opioids to achieve intoxication/desired effect or a markedly diminished effect with continued use of the same amount of opioid;
xi) and withdrawal as manifested by either the characteristic opioid withdrawal syndrome or opioids (or a closely related substance) being taken to relieve or avoid withdrawal symptoms."

38. Severity is specified as follows: mild substance use disorder is the presence of 2-3 of the above symptoms; moderate is the presence of 4-5 symptoms; and severe is the presence of six or more symptoms.
39. The category of opioid induced disorders includes opioid intoxication, opioid withdrawal; opioid induced anxiety disorder and opioid induced depressive disorder.
40. *JG* concluded that a diagnosis of alcohol dependence or alcohol dependency syndrome plainly brought that condition within regulation 19(5) of the Regulations [paragraph 48]. The position now is rather more complex given the adjustments made by DSM-5 to the category of substance related disorders.
41. I have come to the conclusion that a diagnosis of mild substance abuse disorder in accordance with DSM-5 would not bring that condition within regulation 19(5) or 29(2)(b) of the Regulations. I consider that, in order to fall within the ambit of the relevant regulations, the substance abuse disorder must fall within either the moderate or severe categories. My reasons for so concluding are as follows.
42. A DSM-IV diagnosis of alcohol dependency required three or more symptoms from the list occurring at any time in the same 12 month period. It is clear that all of the factors listed in DSM-IV are incorporated into the factors for substance abuse disorder listed in paragraph 37. The presence of three or more factors in a twelve month period from the DSM-5 list would establish a diagnosis of mild substance use disorder. However a DSM-5 diagnosis of substance use disorder equivalent to DSM-IV substance dependency requires, in my view, the presence of, at least 4-5 symptoms from the eleven listed, thus bringing it within the moderately severe category of substance use disorder. This is because the distinction between abuse and dependence In DSM-IV was based on the concept of substance abuse as a mild or early phase and substance dependence as the more

severe manifestation." Judge Knowles QC's decision was followed in CT v SSWP (ESA) [2021] UKUT 131 (AAC).

"Substantial risk to the mental or physical health of any person": "Substantial" does not only refer to the likelihood of the risk occurring: "a risk may be 'substantial' if the harm would be serious, even though it was unlikely to occur and, conversely, may not be 'substantial' if the harm would be insignificant, even though the likelihood of some such harm is great. Paragraph (b) must be viewed in the light of the other paragraphs of regulation 27 [now ESA Regs reg.29] and the general scheme of the Regulations" (*CIB/3519/2002*, para.7). Commissioner Fellner accepted this as "probably right" in *CIB/2767/2004*, but added that: **9.46**

> "invocation of the other paragraphs of regulation 27 as guides to interpretation suggests that the interpretation should be rather narrow. . . . the other paragraphs refer to more or less factual medical questions—presence of life-threatening or severe uncontrolled or uncontrollable disease, need for an identified major medical procedure within a short time" (para.6).

In *MW v SSWP (ESA)* [2012] UKUT 31 (AAC) Judge Parker was of the opinion that the question of "substantial risk" is an objective one and, as regards physical health, one to which the claimant's personal belief system and subjective views are not likely to be pertinent. In contrast, the position may well be different as regards mental health:

> "while the determination of the point is still an objective one, what are the subjective beliefs of a claimant must form part of the background to the question whether, looked at objectively, she might suffer a significant deterioration in mental health, faced with the thought that, in work, she could not follow out her preferred therapeutic regime. The tribunal erred in concentrating only on a reaction mentally to the distressing news of a cancer diagnosis or on whether the state of her cancer was at the relevant date physically harmful. It ought also to have applied an objective test in consideration of the question whether, in all her circumstances, the prospect of having to give up her daily time-consuming regime which she believed was the right and only way to combat her cancer, could constitute the necessary substantial risk" (para.3).

In relation to which employment contexts must the "substantial risk to health" be evaluated? Charlton *and its application:* Whether "substantial risk to health" had to be evaluated against specific employments or in the abstract generated a number of conflicting Commissioners' decisions on IFW Regs, reg.27(b), but its meaning and the approach to take to its application was resolved by the Court of Appeal in *Charlton v Secretary of State for Work and Pensions* [2009] EWCA Civ 42 (the appeal from the decision of Commissioner Williams in *CIB/143/2007*) in judgments that make it clear that they apply also to the same terms in the relevant ESA Regulations. **9.47**

Regulation 29(2)((b) requires (as noted above) a decision firstly that a person suffers as a consequence of some specific disease or bodily or mental disablement which does not of itself cause such functional limitation as to justify a total score warranting a finding of limited capability for work; it can only come into play where it has been found that the claimant does not have limited capability for work under the LCWA. It requires, secondly, a decision on whether because of the disease or disablement there would be a substantial risk to the mental or physical health of *any person* if the claimant were found capable of work (*Charlton*, para.30). The risk to be assessed must arise as a consequence of work the claimant would be found capable of undertaking, but for reg.29 (*Charlton*, para.33). Paragraph 2(b) might be satisfied

> "where the very finding of capability might create a substantial risk to a claimant's health or that of others, for example when a claimant suffering from anxiety or depression might suffer a significant deterioration on being told that the benefit

claimed was being refused. Apart from that, probably rare, situation, the determination must be made in the context of the journey to or from work or in the workplace itself" (*Charlton*, para.34).

Although the regulation is headed "exceptional circumstances" and the wording of para.(2)(b) refers to the the health of "any person", in *HR v SSWP (ESA)* [2013] UKUT 55 (AAC), Judge Wikeley rightly pointed out that its coverage is in law determined by the words used in the body of the regulation. It cannot cover any circumstance describable as "exceptional". There was no evidence before the tribunal to enable it to conclude that the claimant being found capable of work posed any substantial risk to her. She did have an adult daughter recently diagnosed with terminal cancer, but again there was no evidence to show that the claimant being found capable of work would put the daughter's health at substantial risk. Indeed the claimant's regular visits to her daughter of about two hours a day were maintainable if having to claim JSA or being in full or part-time work. He thought the tribunal entitled to proceed and not adjourn to seek more evidence on that. ESA was not designed to cover a difficult case such as this. The more appropriate benefits might be DLA for the daughter and carer's allowance for the mother.

On one view the "proper approach" to para.(2)(b)—accepted as such in *CF v SSWP (ESA)* [2012] UKUT 29 (AAC) (Judge Parker); *SP v SSWP (ESA)* [2014] UKUT 522 (AAC) (Judge Parker); *SD v SSWP (ESA)* [2014] UKUT 240 (AAC) (Judge Mark); *GS v SSWP (ESA)* [2014] UKUT 16 (AAC) (Judge Mark)—is to start with the statement of Judge Mark in *IJ v SSWP (IB)* [2010] UKUT 408 (AAC):

> "the test is not limited to whether there would be a substantial risk to the claimant from any work he may undertake. *The test is as to the risk as a result of being found capable of work.* If he was found capable of work, he would lose his incapacity benefit, and would very possibly need to seek work and apply for jobseeker's allowance. That would involve his attending interviews, and going through all the other steps that would be needed to obtain and keep jobseeker's allowance. In the present economic climate, a claimant who is 62 years old with mental health problems, and who has not worked since the early 1990's is unlikely to find work quickly and would very possibly never find it. His GP's assessment that it is inconceivable that he would ever be able to earn his living may be right. The tribunal would then have to determine how this change from his being in receipt of incapacity benefit would affect the claimant's mental health, looking not at some work he may do, but at the effect on his mental health of fruitless and repeated interviews and the possibly hopeless pursuit of jobs until he reached retirement age. These factors were not considered by the tribunal, and indeed they did not elicit the information necessary to enable them to be considered, such as whether he had in fact applied for jobseeker's allowance and if not, how he was coping or would cope" (para.10, emphasis supplied by commentator).

Such cases will be rare (*Charlton*, para.34; *MB v SSWP (ESA)* [2012] UKUT 228 (AAC), para.14 (Judge Jacobs)), so that in most cases the key task is to identify the nature of the relevant work and workplace and to consider the nature of the risk to the health of the claimant or another person in the context of that work, that workplace, and the journey to and from it.

The passage from Judge Mark's decision in *IJ v SSWP (IB)* [2010] UKUT 408 (AAC) (at para.10) cited immediately above was approved by Judge White in *NS v SSWP (ESA)* [2014] UKUT 115 (AAC); [2014] AACR 33, with the observation that reg.29(2)(b) "is not just about whether there is any work or type of work which a claimant can do without substantial risk to the mental or physical health of any person. It is about whether a substantial risk would arise from a claimant's being found not to have limited capability for work" (para.45). The same passage in *IJ v SSWP (IB)* was criticised by Judge Lane in *MW v SSWP (ESA)* [2015] UKUT 665 (AAC); however, Judge Lane's decision makes no reference to the previous reported decision of *NS v SSWP (ESA)*, which would appear to settle the point that e.g. conditionality issues *may* be relevant to the regulation 29 assessment. See further *JT v SSWP (ESA)* [2018] UKUT 124 (AAC). See also *ET v SSWP (UC)* [2021] UKUT 47 (AAC), not following *MW v SSWP (ESA)* and confirming that journeys to the Jobcentre or for job interviews are relevant to the reg.29 risk assessment.

Be that as it may, the Court in *Charlton* held that the correct approach to identifying the nature of the relevant work and workplace for the claimant was that identified with respect to IFW Regs, reg.27(b) in paras 17-18 of Deputy Commissioner Paines' decision in *CIB/360/2007*. It rejected the view that decision-makers and tribunals had to speculate as to the type of job which would have been set out for purposes of a JSA claim in a hypothetical Jobseeker's Agreement. Rather (reading Personal Capability Assessment as LCWA):

> "The decision-maker must assess the range or type of work which a claimant is capable of performing sufficiently to assess the risk to health either to himself or to others.
>
> Sufficient information may be elicited by reference to the claimant's completion of the initial questionnaire, questioning during his medical examination, or by any evidence he may choose to give on an appeal to the Tribunal. The process to be adopted by the decision-maker or Tribunal is to be regarded as inquisitorial and not adversarial. It is a process described by Diplock J. in *R. v Medical Appeal Tribunal (North Midland Region ex-parte Hubble)* 1958 2 QB 228 at 240 as a fact gathering exercise in which there is no formal burden of proof on either side. There should be no difficulty provided the decision-maker or Tribunal recall that the essential question is whether there is an adequate range of work which the claimant could undertake without creating a substantial risk to himself or to others. This conclusion is consistent with the practical application of these regulations. Any interpretation must bear in mind that the regulations are designed to provide a fair and effective system for assessing entitlement to incapacity benefit and to allied benefits when a claimant has passed the Personal Capability Assessment. It would not be possible to achieve the aim of those regulations were the decision-maker to be required to make findings of the particularity for which the claimant contends. The decision-maker, it must be recalled, will be provided only with the report of the doctor based upon the doctor's interview with the claimant and the claimant's completion of the questionnaire. It is quite impossible for the decision-maker to identify actual positions of employment or the nature of the duties and location of any job which the claimant might undertake, not least because the decision-maker may often be based in Belfast, or elsewhere, and can have no possible means of discovering employment circumstances throughout the country. The conclusion which requires no more than that the decision-maker or Tribunal assess the range of work of which the claimant is capable for the purposes of assessing risk to health has the merit of achieving the objective of the regulations" (*Charlton*, paras 45-47).

The Court upheld Commissioner Williams' finding that Mr Charlton was capable of performing the kind of work:—

> ". . . to which a person with no physical limitations, no qualifications, no skills and no experience might be directed ([section] 48) and that he could undertake straightforward and unstructured, unskilled work."

There is undoubtedly a tension between the approach of Judge Mark in *IJ v SSWP (IB)* and that of Judge Lane in *MW v SSWP (ESA)*, as recognised by Judge Bano in *JT v SSWP (ESA)* [2018] UKUT 124 (AAC). In the circumstances of that case, Judge Bano did not find it necessary to resolve that tension, although the tenor of his decision is more in keeping with the approach in *IJ v SSWP (IB)*. Thus Judge Bano held that "in the case of claimants with fragile mental health the possible effects on a claimant of any compulsion to perform a particular type of work may have to be taken into account when considering regulation 29(2)(b)." Furthermore, the inquiry necessary under reg.29(2)(b):

> "can only be sensibly undertaken if full account is taken of risks to a particular claimant resulting from any compulsion to undertake the work because of an element of 'conditionality' in the relevant benefits regime. Regulation 29(2)(b) is intended to protect third parties as well as claimants, and there is no indication in the legislation that any matter which is relevant to an assessment of the risks resulting from a claimant carrying out a particular type of work should not be taken into account."

The tension between *IJ v SSWP (IB)* and *MW v SSWP (ESA)* was tackled head on by Judge Wright in *ET v SSWP (UC)* [2021] UKUT 47 (AAC), who held that consideration of the question of substantial risk (in that context under para.4 of Sch. 8 to the United Credit Regulations) can include travel to and from the Jobcentre and job interviews as well as to and from work. Furthermore, Judge Wright held (at paras 25-30) that *MW v SSWP (ESA)* was itself wrongly decided, given both the statutory language and the reasoning in *Charlton* and *NS v SSWP (ESA)*:

> "29. Therefore, the statutory language does not provide any statutory restriction or fetter against taking into account, where relevant, travelling to and from the Jobcentre and job interviews (and engaging with others in so doing and at the Jobcentre or job interview). In the context of income-replacement benefits, it will very often be the inevitable consequence of claimants being found not to have limited capability for work that they will have to take such steps in order to satisfy the conditions of entitlement to jobseeker's allowance or universal credit. Indeed, I struggle to understand the basis on which the statutory language could be taken as importing such a restriction in a context where, per *Charlton*, the reaction to the `fit for work' decision itself and being in, and travelling to and from, work **are** to be taken as relevant consequences of the decision. To exclude what will in all likelihood be the more immediate or proximate consequences of the decision - for example, attending at the Jobcentre - but include what may perhaps be a remoter consequence of being found work, seems in my judgment to lack rationality, and is not justified on the statutory language alone."

Should a tribunal consider whether a claimant could work from home? It is submitted that the better view is that it should *not* do so, save perhaps in one rare case.

In *SM v SSMP (ESA)* [2014] UKUT 241 (AAC), Judge Wikeley held that a tribunal erred in law by looking at work from home That approach is supported by references in *Charlton* to travelling to and from a workplace and by the amendment to the regulation about taking account of an employer's reasonable adjustments to the workplace. Although working from home is more common that in the past it is entirely dependent on an employer's discretion and to take it into account would deprive the regulation of any real purpose for large number of cases and defeat the legislative purpose of protecting exceptionally vulnerable people, especially those with mental health problems (paras 7–11). He cited in support of his interpretation the tenor of Judge Ward's decision in *PD v SSWP (ESA)* [2014] UKUT 148. Judge Wikeley noted that Judge Ward there

> "identified the central issue in that appeal as being the impact of regulation 29 "on persons who by reason of mental ill-health have an impaired ability to get to places, such as a hypothetical workplace" (at paragraph 1). If claimants could not avail themselves of regulation 29 simply because they could get a home-working job, then the whole premise of Judge Ward's analysis was flawed. I do not accept that it was" (para.11).

It should be noted, however, that later in *PD*, Judge Ward seemed to indicate that a tribunal *could* look at the viability and suitability of work from home before looking at ability to travel to a workplace. Judge Ward stated

"The tribunal may wish to explore types of work which the person could do from home. Even if the traditional fields for such activity have declined, information technology must bring with it a number of such opportunities for some people. But if such work is not appropriate to the particular claimant, the tribunal will have to conduct the assessment of risk, which is the primary purpose of regulation 29, as best it can in relation to the sort of range of work mandated by *Charlton*, outside the home. If someone has been found to be unable to do something, I find it hard to see how it might be possible to hold that there would be no substantial risk to their health on an assumption that they were effectively made to do that which had been found to be impossible for them (i.e. go to work unaccompanied), though I do not intend to lay that down as a proposition of law. Far more likely is it that what is required is an evaluation of their circumstances when making the hypothetical journey, in particular in relation to being accompanied, in order to see whether the conditions could be satisfied which would alleviate or avoid the risk to health" (para.16).

Agreeing that Judge Wikeley was correct on the facts of *SM*, in *CL v SSWP (ESA)* [2015] UKUT 375 (AAC), Judge Jacobs declined to find in *SM* an absolute prohibition on considering home working under this regulation, stating that it was possible, albeit rare, "that the only type of work for which the claimant is suitable might be in an industry where home working is possible, even encouraged" (para.12).

Where the claimant has an existing job to go back to but is as yet unable to do so, the relevance of that job to the reg.29(2) question lies solely in the reasons why the claimant cannot return to that job. In *AJ v SSWP (ESA)* [2013] UKUT 279 (AAC), Judge Wright stated: 9.48

"For example, and these are no more than examples, if the appellant was not then doing the job because the police had in place a temporary cleaner whose contract still had a month to run and they did not want to have the appellant back at the same time, that may have little or nothing relevant to say about risk in terms of the appellant carrying out such a job. On the other hand, if the police had made its own assessment and found that the appellant needed until, say, the end of August 2010 before she could safely work as a cleaner then that would have been very relevant to regulation 29(2)(b) risk assessment. That may then have ruled out dexterous manual work as relevant work and would have needed the tribunal to look elsewhere for work the appellant was suited both as a matter of training and aptitude" (para.13).

Regulation 29(2)(b) looks to risk and not to more remote matters such as the ultimate or longer-term benefit to the claimant. What is at issue is not the claimant's positive attitude to work but rather whether there is a substantial risk to health if he were found not to have limited capability for work; if that risk exists it is not altered by the claimant's attitude to it (*JW v SSWP* (ESA) [2011] UKUT 416 (AAC), para.12). Similarly, whether work would be good for the claimant is not the correct test (*CH v SSMP) (ESA*) [2014] UKUT 11 (AAC)).

In terms of timescale, the claimant being found not to have limited capability for work occurs when the Secretary of State makes his decision and tribunals must look at the risk as at that date. But that decision has to look to the future, at what will be the effect of the finding given that *Charlton* widened the scope of the enquiry to take account of how the claimant would function in work (*CH v SSWP (ESA)* [2014] UKUT 11 (AAC), paras11-13). As Judge Mark put it in *GS v SSWP (ESA)* [2014] UKUT 16 (AAC):

"the job of the tribunal was to assess . . ., as at the date of the decision, the risk to the claimant's health of her being found not to have limited capability for work. As pointed out repeatedly, this does not prevent tribunals from having regard to evidence coming into existence after the date of the decision, or of events after the decision under appeal, so long as it is relevant to the prognosis at that date. Thus in *R(DLA) 3/01* the actual rate of recovery of a claimant from a health problem was held to be relevant to the question whether as at the date of the decision the claimant was likely to satisfy the relevant conditions for benefit for 6 months after the date of the decision. So too, in the present case, the tribunal needed to assess whether there was a deterioration in the claimant's health following the decision, the extent of the deterioration, and the extent to which it was as a result of her being found not to have limited capability for work. This includes the stress from an appeal, successful or otherwise, the stress of dealing with the Jobcentre and possible interviews, the prospects of employment, and the ways in which it is said that the claimant's mental health can be kept stabilised bearing in mind, if the evidence is accepted, that it appears to have deteriorated even without seeking or obtaining work and without both the pressures of work and the additional pressures on daily life if she did spend part of it working" (paras 16, 17).

In *MB v SSWP (ESA)* [2012] UKUT 228 (AAC), Judge Jacobs was concerned with the case of a claimant (Mr B) addicted to drugs and taking part in a drug recovery programme. The argument was made that since wages from work which were higher than benefit income would enable him to buy more drugs than when on benefit, this would increase the risk to his health and so reg.29(2)(b) should apply. Judge Jacobs identified the issue as: what connection does there have to be between the risk and being found capable of work? Must the risk arise from the work itself or is it enough that it arises from some consequence (in this case increased income) that follows from the work but is unrelated to the nature of the work? Applying *Charlton*, he accepted the Secretary of State's argument (see para.10) that the provision did not embrace the claimant's argument. As Judge Jacobs saw it, *Charlton*

"decided that the trigger for the risk had to be found in the work the claimant would be undertaking. It had to arise from: (i) the decision that the claimant had capability for work; (ii) the work that the claimant might do; or (iii) travelling to and from work. (i) will be rare.

The argument for Mr B is that the wages he would receive for the work would put more money in his pocket than he would spend on drugs. That is not a risk that arises from the work. The work is merely the circumstance that gives rise to it. It would not arise if his wages were so low that he would have been better off on benefit. Nor would it arise if the street price for the drugs increased in line with his income so that he could not afford any more drugs than previously. In other words, the risk arises from the comparative value of Mr B's benefit and the wages he might receive relative to the price of drugs" (paras 14, 15).

9.49 *Where travelling to work unaccompanied is the potential risk, a question arises as to whether third party assistance can be considered as alleviating it.* In *PD* v *SSWP (ESA)* [2014] UKUT 148 (AAC), Judge Ward considered that the risk with respect to travelling to work arising from physical elements was likely to be rare; the traveller contemplated by the Court of Appeal in *Charlton* was "the person whose mental health problems cause difficulties with the journey to work" (para.15). Judge Ward's starting point was that where there was appropriate evidence third party help could be taken into account, that line of argument was open to the Secretary of State (paras 23, 26):

"There will be cases, for instance where a partner is not working, there is no one else at home who uses the car and where the evidence shows a pattern of the partner driving the claimant to wherever s/he wants or needs to go, that it may be open to a tribunal to infer that such help would similarly be available to get a claimant to the *Charlton*-mandated hypothetical workplace. If a scheme such as Access to Work were available on a sufficiently reliable basis, it is hard to see why it should not be taken into account. Such are ultimately conclusions of fact and not matters on which I need say more, except to observe that this may be, par excellence, a field in which tribunals can look to the principles of *Kerr v Department for Social Development* [2004] UKHL 23; [2004] 1 WLR 1372" (para.26).

Judge Ward also stated that

> "What is difficult in relation to transport is yet harder in relating to accompaniment within the workplace. Such a setup would be highly unusual, even if only to help with the first few days. I did not hear argument on whether that, unlike the provision of transport, could constitute a reasonable adjustment for Equality Act purposes" (para.27).

Judge Hemingway in *HT v SSWP (ESA)* [2018] UKUT 174 (AAC) has agreed with Judge Ward in *PD v SSWP (ESA)* [2014] UKUT 148 (AAC) that the risk within reg.29 with respect to travelling to work is likely to be "rare (though not impossible)" in the context of "physical health difficulties in circumstances where those same difficulties do not lead to the risk arising in the workplace itself" (at para.19). Likewise, "the prospect of third party assistance on the journey will be a potentially relevant consideration though the availability of such cannot simply, without evidence, be assumed. Where the arguments as to risk relate to falling the use of such as walking sticks and walking frames will need to be considered."

Where someone satisfies descriptor 15(c) in Sch.2 (needs assistance to get to an unfamiliar place), third party assistance might be a possibility of avoiding the risk to health for an initial period until the journey to and from the workplace became familiar (*EJ v SSWP (ESA)* [2014] UKUT 551 (AAC) paras 19, 21 (Judge Wikeley)). But practicalities need to be looked at (*SS v SSWP (ESA)* [2015] UKUT 101 (AAC), para.5 (Judge Rowland)) and a sound evidential basis shown for relevant findings of fact (*ET v SSWP (UC)* [2021] UKUT 47 (AAC)). In another context, the three-judge panel in *JC v SSWP (ESA)* [2014] UKUT 352 (AAC); [2015] AACR 12, did not consider that a person could properly be regarded "as able to engage in social contact if she or he can do so only if accompanied by someone, *at least without further explanation as to how it is envisaged that that might be realistic in the workplace*" (para.45, emphasis supplied by commentator).

It should also be noted that in stark contrast in *MT v SSWP (ESA)* [2013] UKUT 545 (AAC), in the context of reg.35(2), Judge Gray firmly rejected looking at capacity to perform activities with third party assistance, observing:

> "I do need to deal however with the observation of the FTT in its statement of reasons that the appellant could take another person with her to any work-related activities. It may be that the Secretary of State would be facilitative in any matter which helped a claimant engage so as to improve their ultimate prospects of retaining work. I do not know. Whether or not that is so, is not relevant. As a matter of law any work-related activity which could only be accomplished because of the presence of another person must be looked upon as not being an activity that the claimant can carry out. *The issue under regulation 35 (2) (b) as to whether there would be a substantial risk to the mental or physical health of any person if the claimant were found not to have limited capability for work-related activity cannot be assessed as if the claimant under consideration had somebody else by their side.* There will be claimants who have a need for the personal reassurance of another person, but who do not have anybody available to perform that role. Even if they did, it would not be reasonable for such an assessment to be made on the basis of reliance on another's goodwill. Legal tests cannot depend upon that. Where an appellant who is found to have limited capability for work-related activities wishes to engage voluntarily, it may be that they choose to do so with the help of another person, and it may (or may not, I do not know) be possible for them to do so, but the capacity to engage only with that assistance cannot be part of the test of capability" (para.34, emphasis added by commentator).

In *PD*, Judge Ward agreed with the italicised passage insofar as it meant "without consideration as to whether the third party's presence would be made out in fact" (para.21), but otherwise distinguished the passage as focussing on the claimant's capability to perform activities (agreeing that there third party assistance should be ignored) rather than the different question of what risks would ensue (where, with respect to travelling, at least, third party assistance available in fact might obviate the risk). See also *SP v SSWP (ESA)* [2014] UKUT 522 (AAC), where Judge Parker did not categorically reject as inadmissible the Secretary of State's submission that the claimant could be accompanied (at least initially) to some interviews, but instead concluded that "this would not address some of the potential stress to which Judge Mark referred [in *IJ v SSWP (IB)* [2010] UKUT 408 (AAC)" (para.7).

9.50 *As the foregoing discussion makes clear* Charlton *must be applied in the light of all the available evidence.* In *LD v SSWP (ESA)* [2014] UKUT 131 (AAC), Judge Ward held that retirement on health grounds 17 years earlier could be of probative value and ongoing relevance since it had involved an assessment by experts that at that time the claimant was permanently incapable of doing a particular type of job and other evidence before the tribunal had indicated a deterioration rather than an improvement in the claimant's condition since that time. In *GS v SSWP (ESA)* [2014] UKUT 16 (AAC), Judge Mark held:

> "It was the duty of the decision maker in relation to the present appeal, under rule 24(4)(b) of the Tribunal Procedure (First-tier Tribunal) (SEC) Rules 2008, to provide with the response to the appeal copies of all documents relevant to the case in the decision maker's possession. It was also the duty of the Secretary of State, under rule 2(4) of the same Rules, to help the tribunal to deal with the case fairly and justly. Under one head or the other, if not both, the tribunal ought to have been provided with copies of the evidence before the previous tribunal which had heard the appeal only 7 months before the new decision now under appeal. It is a duty which the new tribunal [to which he remitted the case] ought to have enforced" (para.5).

The effect of failure to follow the steps required by Charlton: Generally failing to follow the steps approved in *Charlton* will mean that the tribunal errs in law as in *JW v SSWP* (ESA) [2011] UKUT 416 (AAC). In *SSWP v Cattrell* [2011] EWCA Civ 572; [2011] AACR 35, however, the Court of Appeal held that while tribunals should normally identify the range of work that a claimant might be capable of, in this particular case because the first-tier tribunal had accepted evidence that there was no prospect of this claimant finding any suitably safe work, adopting the approach in *Charlton* and speculating about a range of possible work was not appropriate. But so doing was not here an error of law and the decision that this claimant was entitled to IB on the basis of "substantial risk" (there IFW Regs, reg.27(b), the equivalent of ESA Regs, reg.29(2)(b)) should stand. In contrast, in *RB v SSWP (ESA)* [2012] UKUT 431 (AAC), the tribunal merely stated that there was no evidence to suggest that reg.29 applied. Judge Ward held that it had erred in law in not identifying in its reasons that it had considered the range of work the claimant might be expected to do; given his knee problem and work background the answer was not self-evident (paras 4–7).

9.51 *A question which has troubled tribunals at both levels is whether reg.29(2)(b) must always be considered where the claimant has failed to achieve a sufficient score on the LCWA?* It need not be considered as a matter of routine, but whether it should be considered in any particular case depends on all the circumstances of that case (*PC v SSWP (ESA)* [2014] UKUT 1 (AAC); *SP v SSWP (ESA)* [2014] UKUT 10 (AAC); *DB v SSWP (ESA)* [2014] UKUT 41 (AAC); *NS v SSWP (ESA)* [2014] UKUT 115 (AAC); [2014] AACR 33). If a competent representative chooses not to raise it, then, absent unusual circumstances, a tribunal need not consider it. However, the more narrowly focused the descriptors in the LCWA become, the more likely it is that reg.29(2)(b) will be put in issue (*RB v SSWP (ESA)* [2012] UKUT 431 (AAC), para.7; *NS v SSWP (ESA)* [2014] UKUT 115 (AAC); [2014] AACR 33, para.50). It is likely particularly to be relevant where mental health issues are involved. In *NS v SSWP (ESA)* [2014] UKUT 115 (AAC); [2014] AACR 33, Judge White proffered the following useful guidance to tribunals:

> "There will be some cases in which a tribunal need say nothing about regulation 29(2)(b). I give one clear example. Where a claimant is represented, claims only problems with physical functions, is found to score no points under Part 1 of Schedule 2 to the Employment and Support Allowance Regulations 2008, and where the representative does not put regulation 29(2)(b) in issue, a tribunal can safely leave out any mention of regulation 29(2)(b). However, in such a case a wise tribunal would seek confirmation from the representative that no issue is raised under regulation 29(2)(b) if they were to find that no points are scored under the Part 1 descriptors.
>
> There will be some cases in which a tribunal must address regulation 29(2)(b). Clearly, if it is put in issue by a claimant, it must be fully and properly addressed. This will not require repetition of the findings of fact made in respect of the descriptors in Schedule 2, but that will be the obvious starting point for the explanation of why regulation 29(2)(b) does or does not apply.
>
> In cases in which the descriptors relating to mental, cognitive and intellectual functions are in issue, it is more likely that regulation 29(2)(b) will be relevant. After all, in cases which come before the tribunal, more often than not the claimant's GP has issued a certificate that the claimant is incapable of work (though I accept that the GP may not be making that judgment against the Schedule 2 assessment). If the GP has submitted a letter in support of the claimant's appeal, that will often indicate why the GP considers that the claimant is incapable of work" (paras 47–49).

That guidance was followed by Judge Gray in *KB v SSWP (ESA)* [2014] UKUT 303 (AAC).

Although reg.29(2)(b) can only come into play where the person has failed to achieve a sufficient score in the LCWA, the question of which descriptors a claimant satisfies is relevant to the application of the paragraph because one is determining the matter taking due account of the claimant's disabilities (*CF v SSWP (ESA)* [2012] UKUT 29 (AAC), paras 14, 15). Indeed, a claimant's satisfaction of descriptor 15(b) (9 points) must inevitably raise the question of the applicability of reg.29 since that means that the claimant has been found to be "unable to get to a particular place with which the claimant is familiar, without being accompanied by another person", thus raising issues about substantial risk to the claimant's health in terms of the journey to work (*SS v SSWP (ESA)* [2015] UKUT 101 (AAC), para.4 (Judge Rowland)).

While a Med 3 issued by the claimant's GP is not conclusive on the issue under reg.29(2), the implications of the certificate must be addressed and facts found to the extent possible (*SP v SSWP (ESA)* [2014] UKUT 278 (AAC), para.16). In *RU v SSWP (ESA)* [2014] UKUT 77 (AAC), Judge Ward held that:

> "if the claimant's GP was advising his or her patient to refrain from work for 6 months by a Med 3 issued more or less contemporaneously with the decision under appeal, it was incumbent on the tribunal to consider the implications of that. The work capability assessment is an artificial construct, which looks at certain activities only, and there is no necessary correlation between a doctor's views as to what the patient can manage and the outcome of the WCA applied to that person, or vice versa. Regulation 29 has the function of a safety valve addressing that lack of correlation, protecting claimants (and others) from the effect of determinations which in the circumstances set out in that regulation would otherwise result in substantial risk to health" (para.6).

In addition, the existence of a recent DLA award on the ground of day supervision is likely to be material evidence and required to be addressed (*NA (by ST) v SSWP (ESA)* [2012] UKUT 428 (AAC), para.3).

9.52 *The standard of tribunal decision-making and giving of reasons as the applicability or otherwise of reg.29(2)(b) has caused concern among Upper Tribunal Judges.* If a tribunal chooses to address the provision, whether at the request of the claimant, representative or of its own volition, "it must do so properly . . . and an inadequate analysis" will not suffice (*EJ v SSWP (ESA)* [2014] UKUT 551 (AAC), para.18). Its findings on reg.29(2)(b) must be consistent with those it has made on the application of the Sch.2 descriptors (*CC v SSWP (ESA)* [2015] UKUT 62 (AAC), para.22; *SS v SSWP (ESA)* [2015] UKUT 101 (AAC), para.4). In *NS v SSWP (ESA)* [2014] UKUT 115 (AAC); [2014] AACR 33, Judge White proffered the following useful guidance to tribunals:

> "I do not consider that the level of detail required for proper reasons on the application of regulation 29(2)(b) is high. The more obvious it is that regulation 29(2)(b) does not apply, the easier it should be to give reasons why that is so.
>
> What is frequently missing from brief statements that regulation 29(2)(b) does not apply is the addition of a statement as to why it does not apply. This is exemplified by the statement in the appeal before me, where the tribunal said:
>
> > Regulation 29 does not apply as the Tribunal was not satisfied that there was a substantial risk to the appellant or to any person if he were not found to have limited capability for work.
>
> What is needed is for that sentence to end in a comma and to be followed by the word "because" and then a phrase or two explaining why regulation 29(2) (b) does not apply. After all, if the tribunal has done a proper job in considering regulation 29(2)(b) they must have considered why the regulation did not apply. Otherwise, this is a mere formulaic response to the issue. A tribunal which embarks upon a consideration of regulation 29(2)(b) must do a proper job of considering it" (paras 50–53).

For a further example of a case in which the Upper Tribunal followed the same approach, namely that the more obvious it is that reg.29 does not apply, the easier it is to say why that is so, see *JH(S) v Secretary of State for Work and Pensions (ESA)* [2015] UKUT 567 (AAC). The following observation was made by Judge Hemingway in *RK v Secretary of State for Work and Pensions (ESA)* [2015] UKUT 549 (AAC), allowing an appeal on the reg.29 point:

> "16. I would just wish to add one brief final comment. It seems to me that a consideration of the type or range of work a claimant might reasonably be expected to undertake is something which is often (though by no means always) missed by a tribunal. Often that will not be fatal. Indeed, as was made clear in *NS*, cited above, it will sometimes not be fatal even if regulation 29 is not referred to at all. However, there will be cases, as here, and it seems to me they are not infrequent, where there are indications that the range might be limited for various reasons, perhaps a lack of experience of or aptitude for certain categories of work, perhaps a difficulty with written or spoken English, perhaps an established physical or mental disablement, perhaps something else, such that a proper consideration of this aspect is needed. Of course, the test does not require anything like the sort of detailed analysis which might be involved in, say, testing the degree of risk to health by reference to specific jobs or job descriptions. A short assessment, perhaps only a couple of sentences or so, will often be enough. A tribunal will often already have some background information in the documents before it and will be able to ask questions about the sorts of matters referred to above if an oral hearing is held. Where competent representatives are involved it may well assist a tribunal if any written submission

lodged in advance of a hearing can specify whether and on what basis regulation 29 is relied upon and can deal with, if thought to be relevant, the question of the range or type of work."

Merely reiterating the statutory test in negative form will not suffice. As Judge Bano rightly stressed in *PH v SSWP (ESA)* [2014] UKUT 502 (AAC)

> "[t]he difficult issues which may arise under regulation 29 will often require detailed findings of fact to be made by the tribunal, rather than mantra-like recitations of the terms of the legislation and unparticularised references to adjustments in the workplace" (para.5).

In *MF v SSWP (ESA)* [2014] UKUT 523 (AAC), Judge Mark allowed the appeal stating that

> "...The tribunal does not indicate what occupation or range of occupations it had in mind. More seriously it totally failed to deal with the points actually made in the written submissions. It was dealing with a claimant who had not worked for 20 years, whose appearance was described by the disability analyst as unkempt, and whose behaviour was described as restless with reduced facial expression, and whom it had found was prone to episodes of depression when he may lack the motivation to do things.
>
> The tribunal needed to address how he would have coped not just with an interview and with some unspecified job when not having a depressive episode, but with all the matters identified by the claimant's representative in his written submissions and then determine whether there was a substantial risk to his mental or physical health (or that of anybody else) if he were found not to have limited capability for work. There have also been raised, at least before me, issues as to the extent to which the claimant can use public transport or travel at busy times and the tribunal may need to consider this both in connection with any requirements imposed in connection with jobseeker's allowance and in connection with any employment he may obtain. In failing to identify the correct issues and to make appropriate reasoned findings, the tribunal was in error of law. Its decision must be set aside and the matter remitted for rehearing by a new tribunal" (paras 7–8).

Similarly, Judge Wikeley in *CC v SSWP (ESA)* [2015] UKUT 62 (AAC) held erroneous in law a tribunal decision which inadequately explained why reg.29(2)(b) failed to apply. It had awarded the claimant 9 points under descriptor 8(c): "unable to navigate around unfamiliar surroundings, without being accompanied by another person, due to sensory impairment". The tribunal's finding that the claimant could "get about safely and see right in front of him at a short distance" was not, without further explanation, consistent with its decision on that descriptor (para.22).

Ultimately the adequacy of reasons required is going to be context-specific. For example, in *DB v SSWP (ESA)* [2016] UKUT 493 (AAC) Judge Gray, in dismissing the claimant's appeal, observed as follows:

> "21. Regulation 29 whilst relevant at the outset of the appeal, really ceased to be so in view of the findings of the tribunal that the somewhat extreme difficulties the appellant put forward as being caused by her continuing chronic pain were not made out. The tribunal ... simply did not accept that she would have either the problems that she said she had, or, indeed, any problems at all under the descriptors. In those factual circumstances there could be no question of substantial risk. It would not have been inappropriate for the tribunal, having made its findings, to have decided not to formally consider regulation 29, or, to put it perhaps more accurately, to consider it only in order to confirm that it was not, or

was not any longer, an applicable consideration in the light of those findings. In any event read as a whole the explanation satisfied the test set out by the Court of Appeal in *Charlton*."

In *DB v Secretary of State for Work and Pensions (ESA)* [2017] UKUT 251 (AAC) Judge Bano gave the following guidance on the application of reg.29:

"9. It is clear from the judgment of the Court of Appeal in *Charlton* that the question of whether regulation 29 applies to a claimant is fact-specific and that a tribunal's findings in relation to the Regulation must therefore be based specifically on a claimant's individual circumstances. That is not to say that the reasons for a tribunal's decision on whether regulation 29 applies to a claimant need necessarily be long or elaborate, and in many cases the tribunal's findings in relation to matters such as the nature and extent of a claimant's disablement will also provide a basis for their conclusions in relation to regulation 29. However, in carrying out the risk assessment required by the Regulation, it is in my view necessary that it should be reasonably apparent from the reasons, read as a whole, that the individual circumstances of the particular claimant have been fully and properly taken into account when deciding whether the Regulation applies."

The (in)applicability of the Equality Act 2010: the Equality Act 2010 has been mentioned and subject to varying degrees of consideration in a number of Upper Tribunal decisions in a number of contexts. But its specific applicability in the context of reg.29(2)(b) was most fully argued before Judge Wright in *JS v SSWP (ESA)* [2014] UKUT 428; [2015] AACR 12, a case in which an oral hearing was held, and the matter analysed in a judgment running to 78 paragraphs. His conclusion was that

"the assessment of risk under regulation 29(2)(b) of the ESA Regs does not require or involve the decision maker (be that the Secretary of State's delegate or the First-tier Tribunal) in making an assessment as to whether employers would owe a duty under the Equality Act 2010 to make reasonable adjustments in respect of the individual claimant whose case falls for decision, and in my judgment the tribunal therefore erred in law in relying on the Equality Act 2010 to that effect" (para.5).

It is submitted that his conclusion that the Equality Act 2010 is not applicable is the correct approach to the matter, for the reasons he gave (summarised below). His decision has been reported, and is accepted as the correct approach by the Secretary of State; in *SB v SSWP (ESA)* [2015] UKUT 88 (AAC), Judge Ward accepted as "properly made" the concession by the Secretary of State in the appeal. The Secretary of State considered that in *JS*

"Judge Wright held that:

- it is not sufficient for the First-tier Tribunal (FtT) to assume that because the Equality Act 2010 will require an employer not to discriminate against and make reasonable adjustments in the work place to accommodate a disabled person, there will be no risk arising from the person being found fit for work;
- the assessment of risk under regulation 29(2)(b) of the ESA Regs 2008 however does not require or involve the SSWP or FtT in making an assessment as to whether employers would owe a duty under the Equality Act to make reasonable adjustments in respect of the individual claimant (specifically disagreeing with Judge Mark in *JB v SSWP (ESA)* [2013] UKUT 518 AAC.)"

The Secretary of State conceded that in practical terms, this meant "that in assessing [any] reg.29 risk, SSWP [and the First-tier Tribunal] must make a claimant specific risk assessment". While this includes the matter of what steps could reasonably and realistically be taken on the facts of the specific case to avoid substantial risk (a requirement now statutorily set by reg.29(3)(a)), it does not require evidence of what a potential employer would or might do by way of reasonable adjustments in compliance with any Equality Act duties the employer might be subject to.

Judge Wright supported his conclusion with a number of lines of reasoning which he saw as "incremental" (para.46).

He argued, firstly, that the Equality Act 2010 and employment and support allowance schemes have different statutory aims and materially different statutory contents. That the ESA Regs are not to be divorced from the real world (see *AS* and *SI*, above) points to the 2010 Act having potential relevance to the ESA Regs. But, as regards "statutory intendment", against that must be set the plain fact that the ESA Regs (and their predecessors for IB) have never on their face made any express link to the Equality Act 2010 or its predecessor, the Disability Discrimination Act 1995. Indeed, even where as now, para.(3)(a) requires consideration in applying para.(2)(b) to be given to "reasonable adjustments being made in the claimant's workplace" no link was made, pointing to para.(2)(b) "being intended to embody a test separate to the tests under the Equality Act 2010" (para.48). In addition, the ESA scheme applies to persons not in employment and unable to work, whereas the duties under the Equality Act 2010 apply only to employees or applicants for employment who have made known to the employer their disability. Moreover key elements for assessing disability are different, and noticeably different, under the two schemes (paras 53, 54).

Secondly, the Equality Act 2010 test sits uneasily with *Charlton*. That case eschewed an "actual employment" test which is essentially the test embodied in that Act (para.51). *Charlton* embraces the impact in respect of travelling to work; the 2010 Act does not (para.55). In addition, *Charlton* took account of the test under para (2)(b) "having to be applied practicably". Requiring a decision-maker to consider whether "the claimant would be likely to be owed a duty by an employer or employers to make reasonable adjustments under the statutory machinery contained within the Equality Act 2010" would be likely to render impracticable "a timeous decision" (para. 58).

Thirdly, the First-tier Tribunal is ill-equipped to make proper assessments under the Equality Act 2010, which matters are vested in the specialist employment tribunal. While the First-tier tribunal is also specialist in its sphere of operation, "on its face it is not concerned with assessing whether an employer will in fact owe a duty to make reasonable adjustments in respect of an individual disabled person" (para.57).

Finally, *recourse to the Equality Act 2010 is simply unnecessary*. The matter of applying the para.(2)(b) test in the light of reasonable adjustments which might be made in the envisaged range of workplaces is now explicit in para.(3)(a), but has also always been inherent in the risk assessment required by para.(2)(b),as interpreted in *Charlton*; as Judge Wright put it the wording is:

> "wide enough and flexible enough to encompass reasonable steps that realistically on the evidence may be taken by, or in respect of, the [specific individual] claimant, including by prospective employers. But that does not require an assessment to be made of employers' duties under the Equality Act 2010" (para.61).

There must first be analysis of the range and types of work which as a matter of training or aptitude the claimant is suited to do "and which his or her disabilities do not render him [or her] incapable of performing". There must then be assessed the risk the individual's disease(s) or disablement(s) would, on the balance of probabilities, give rise to

> "if the claimant was travelling to and from, and working in, employments he or she was otherwise suited to do. Part of that risk assessment will involve consideration of the steps that, on the evidence and having regard to the individual claimant's health conditions and other circumstances, could reasonably and realistically be taken to avoid any substantial risk to health" (para.62).

SB v SSWP (ESA) [2015] UKUT 88 (AAC) has been considered and followed in *SP v SSWP (ESA)* [2018] UKUT 205 (AAC), where the claimant had a latex allergy and appealed a refusal to award ESA on the basis of reg.29(2)(b). The tribunal dismissed her appeal, noting the duty of an employer to make adjustments under the Equality Act 2010, the claimant's responsibility to also consider making adjustments at work to minimise risk, and the claimant's failure to check for latex the chair she sat on at the tribunal hearing. Judge Poole QC held that the tribunal had made adequate findings of fact to support its conclusion under reg.29(2)(b). These included identifying the gravity of risk to health from the potential effects of allergic reactions to latex, the likelihood of the risk occurring, and risk mitigation measures (such as the claimant's use of medication and her experience in monitoring the environment around her to check for latex).

Paragraph (3)(a): reasonable adjustments in the claimant's workplace

9.53 See *SP v SSWP (ESA)* [2018] UKUT 205 (AAC), where the claimant had a latex allergy and had appealed a refusal to award ESA on the basis of reg.29(2)(b) (discussed above). Judge Poole QC held as follows (at para.11):

> "The wording of regulation 29(3)(a) refers to reasonable adjustments in the claimant's workplace, without confining its application to adjustments made only by an employer. It is normal in the workplace to expect both employer and employee to play their parts in keeping the working environment as risk free as practicable. In my view both employer and employee can be expected to take reasonable measures. Accordingly, measures that a claimant may reasonably take to reduce risk are relevant either under the reasonable adjustment wording in regulation 29(3)(a), or even if that was wrong to the general consideration of whether a risk is substantial under regulation 29(2)(b)."

Conditions for treating a claimant as having limited capability for work until a determination about limited capability for work has been made

9.54 **30.**—(1) A claimant is, if the conditions set out in paragraph (2) are met, to be treated as having limited capability for work until such time as it is determined—

(a) whether or not the claimant has limited capability for work;
(b) whether or not the claimant is to be treated as having limited capability for work otherwise than in accordance with this regulation; or
(c) whether the claimant falls to be treated as not having limited capability for work in accordance with regulation 22 (failure to provide information in relation to limited capability for work) or 23 (failure to attend a medical examination to determine limited capability for work).

(2) The conditions are—

(a) that the claimant provides evidence of limited capability for work in accordance with the Medical Evidence Regulations; and
[[3](b) in relation to the claimant's entitlement to any benefit, allowance or advantage which is dependent on the claimant having limited capability for work, it has not been determined—
  (i) in the last determination preceding the date of claim for an employment and support allowance, that the claimant does not have limited capability for work; or
  (ii) within the 6 months preceding the date of claim for an employment and support allowance, that the claimant is to be treated as not having limited capability for work under regulation 22 or 23,

unless paragraph (4) applies;]

(c) [[2]*omitted*].

[[3](3) Paragraph 2(b) does not apply where a claimant has made and is pursuing an appeal against a relevant decision of the Secretary of State, and that appeal has not yet been determined by the First-tier Tribunal.]

[[2](4) This paragraph applies where—

(a) the claimant is suffering from some specific disease or bodily or mental disablement from which the claimant was not suffering at the time of that determination;

(b) a disease or bodily or mental disablement from which the claimant was suffering at the time of that determination has significantly worsened; or

(c) in the case of a claimant who was treated as not having limited capability for work under regulation 22 (failure to provide information), the claimant has since provided the information requested under that regulation.]

[[3](5) In this regulation a "relevant decision" means—

(a) a decision that embodies the first determination by the Secretary of State that the claimant does not have limited capability for work; or

(b) a decision that embodies the first determination by the Secretary of State that the claimant does not have limited capability for work since a previous determination by the Secretary of State or appellate authority that the claimant does have limited capability for work.

(6) In this regulation, "appellate authority" means the First-tier Tribunal, the Upper Tribunal, the Court of Appeal, the Court of Session, or the Supreme Court.]

AMENDMENTS

1. Social Security (Miscellaneous Amendments) Regulations 2011 (SI 2011/674) reg.16(3) (April 11, 2011).

2. Social Security (Miscellaneous Amendments) (No.3) Regulations 2013 (SI 2013/2536) reg.13(14) (October 29, 2013).

3. Employment and Support Allowance (Repeat Assessments and Pending Appeal Awards) (Amendment) Regulations 2015 (SI 2015/437) reg.3 (March 30, 2015).

MODIFICATION

Regulation 30 is modified by Sch.1 para.10 of the Employment and Support Allowance (Transitional Provisions, Housing Benefit and Council Tax Benefit) (Existing Awards) (No.2) Regulations 2010 (SI 2010/1907) (as amended) for the purposes specified in reg.6(1). For details of the modification, see the text of those Regulations, below.

DEFINITIONS

"appellate authority"—see para.(6).
"claimant"—see WRA 2007 s.24(1).
"limited capability for work"—see WRA 2007 s.1(4).
"Medical Evidence Regulations"—see reg.2(1).
"relevant decision"—see para.(5).

GENERAL NOTE

This regulation deals with the position of claimants for ESA pending a decision 9.55
on eligibility. As amended with effect from March 30, 2015, it applies (a) where the

claimant makes, or is treated as making a claim for ESA on or after that date, and (b) where, in respect of such a claim, the claimant makes and pursues an appeal against a Secretary of State's decision that s/he does not have limited capability for work (see reg.2 of the amending Regs). Claims made before March 30, 2015 and appeals in respect of them are instead regulated by the previous version of this regulation (for which see the 2014/15 edition of this book and the detailed analysis by Judge Wright in *EI v SSWP (ESA)* [2016] UKUT 397 (AAC))).

The March 2015 amendments were made to rectify an unintended consequence of the previous version of this regulation whereby someone whose entitlement had ended because of a finding that s/he did not have limited work could make a repeat claim after six months and gain a further period of entitlement to ESA pending a decision on eligibility even where the claimant could provide no evidence to suggest that their condition had significantly worsened or that they had a new health condition to be considered. One unwanted effect was that even where a First-tier Tribunal had upheld a fit for work decision, if the appeal process had taken longer than six months, a claimant could immediately make a repeat claim for ESA on the basis of exactly the same condition, and would be entitled to receive ESA at the assessment phase rate (the same rate as JSA) pending a new LCWA. The cycle between ESA claim, LCWA and disallowance would begin again.

As amended, the regulation provides that on a "repeat claim" for ESA (see below) the claimant will *not* be treated as having limited capability for work (and thus ESA entitlement at assessment rate pending determination of the claim) unless they can demonstrate either a significant deterioration in their health condition or that a new health condition has developed.

Note that *R. (Connor) v SSWP* [2020] EWHC 1999 holds that the requirement to undertake the mandatory reconsideration process before appealing is unlawful in its application to ESA claimants who meet the conditions for payment while an appeal is pending. Swift J concluded "that regulation 3ZA of the Decisions and Appeals Regulations is a disproportionate interference with the right of access to court, so far as it applies to claimants to ESA who, once an appeal is initiated, meet the conditions for payment pending appeal under reg.30(3) of the ESA Regulations" (at [28]). Swift J explained his reasoning as follows (at [31]):

> "when it comes to ESA claimants such as Mr Connor who, were an appeal to be in progress would meet the conditions for payment pending appeal under regulation 30(2) of the ESA Regulations, the requirement under regulation 3ZA is disproportionate having regard to the combined effect of (a) the period of time the benefits claimant will now need to wait before the right of appeal arises; and (b) the unexplained absence of any provision for payment of ESA during that period equivalent to the payment pending appeal arrangements that arise once an appeal has been started."

Swift J accordingly made "a declaration to the effect that regulation 3ZA of the Decisions and Appeals Regulations is unlawful insofar as it is applied to ESA claimants who would, if pursuing an appeal to the First-tier Tribunal, subject to compliance with the condition at regulation 30(2) of the ESA Regulations, be entitled to receive payment pending appeal pursuant to regulation 30(3)" (at [35]).

Paragraphs (1), (2)

9.56 If the conditions in para.(2) are met, this treats the claimant as having limited capability for work (thus grounding eligibility for ESA) until:

(a) the matter of actual capability is determined in accordance with the work capability assessment (LCWA) under reg.19 and Sch.2;

(b) it is decided whether some other "treated as having limited capability for work" regulation applies (e.g. person receiving certain regular treatment); or

(c) a decision is made that, as a sanction for non-compliance with information gathering or medical examination aspects of the assessment process under

regs 22 and 23, he is to be treated as not having limited capability for work and thus disentitled to ESA (para.(1)).

Since the regulation only applies until the claimant has been "assessed", it cannot apply where the claimant is immediately assessed (*CIB/1959/1997 and CIB/2198/1997*, paras 28, 29).

Clearer analysis is afforded if one distinguishes between "a new claim" and a "repeat claim".

The position in respect of a "new claim": by "new claim" is envisaged the situation where there has never been a "determination" that the claimant does not have, or cannot be treated as having, limited capability for work. For example, this is the first ever claim for ESA. In such a case this regulation applies to treat the claimant as having that limited capability, provided that the claimant continues to provide a doctor's statement in accordance with the Medical Evidence Regs (paras (1), (2)(a)). "Determination" here is not confined to one on ESA eligibility but encompasses one on entitlement to any benefit, allowance or advantage dependent on the claimant having limited capability for work (para.(2)(b)).

The position in respect of a "repeat claim": by "repeat claim is here envisaged a situation in which there has been a previous "determination" that the claimant does not have limited capability for work, or was treated as not having such limited capability because of non-compliance with the medical examination aspect of assessment. On such a claim, the claimant can only be treated as having limited capability for work under this regulation in two situations (paras (2)(b), (4)(a), (b)):- 9.57

(i) if suffering from some specific disease or bodily or mental disablement from which he was not suffering at the time of that "determination" (a "new health condition"); or

(ii) there has been significant worsening of the disease or bodily or mental disablement suffered at the time of that "determination".

Similarly, if within the six months prior to the ESA claim, there has been a determination that the claimant is to be treated as not having limited capability for work under reg.22 (in effect one thereby applying a sanction for non-compliance with information gathering aspect of the assessment process), the claimant can nonetheless be treated as having limited capability for work (i) if s/he has since provided the information requested (paras (2)(b), (4)); or (ii) if they have a "new health condition" or their existing condition has significantly worsened. In addition, the claimant treated as not having limited capability for work under reg. 22 who reclaims more than six months after that determination can again be treated as having limited capability for work pending assessment (para.(2)(b)(ii)).

The words "significantly worsened", as regards the claimant's condition, must be related to the limited capability for work assessment (LCWA), so that it will only have significantly worsened if it has done so to an extent that it is fair to assume the claimant would satisfy that test of limited capability for work if he were subjected to it (see *EI v SSWP (ESA)* [2016] UKUT 397 (AAC) at paragraphs 34-42). If there is actual evidence that he would fail to satisfy that test, the Secretary of State can proceed on the basis that the condition has not significantly worsened (*CIB/1959/1977* and *CIB/2198/1997*, para.30). See further *EI v SSWP (ESA)* [2016] UKUT 397 (AAC) at paras 34–42 (but query whether this applies in relation to the period from the date of the repeat claim to the date of the assessment). That decision is also noteworthy because of the detailed but obiter consideration of whether there should be a right of appeal regarding whether a person's consideration has "significantly worsened" (see at paras 43–59). For the approach of decision-makers, see *Memo DMG 10/15*, paras 24–28.

In *CM v SSWP (ESA)* [2019] UKUT 284 (AAC) Judge Wright has revisited his decision in *EI v SSWP* (ESA) [2016] UKUT 397 (AAC). In particular, Judge

Wright was asked to find that the decision in *EI v SSWP* (ESA) was wrong in two respects. First, if the DWP has decided a repeat claim on the basis that the claimant does not have limited capability for work (and cannot be treated as having limited capability for work under regulations other than regulation 30) then, on any appeal against such a decision, the sole issue for the FTT to decide was whether the claimant has limited capability for work under reg.19 and Sch.2 to the ESA Regs (or can be treated as having limited capability for work under the ESA Regs other than under reg.30). Second, once the determination as to limited capability for work in fact was made on a repeat claim, it always took effect from the date of the repeat claim (whether the determination finds the claimant has limited capability for work or not).

In *CM v SSWP (ESA)* Judge Wright and the Secretary of State agreed with submissions on behalf of the claimant by CPAG that (1) the decision on entitlement to ESA on a repeat claim will typically include determinations (a) on whether the claimant can be treated as having limited capability for work under reg.30 and (b) whether the claimant in fact had limited capability for work under reg.19 (or could be treated as having limited capability for work under reg.29); and (2) following *R(IB) 2/04*, on an appeal against such an entitlement decision, the FTT can give any decision that the decision maker could have made on the repeat claim.

As a result, the FTT is not in any sense bound by the Secretary of State's decision on that claim, even where the DWP's decision was to the effect that the claimant did not have limited capability for work in fact at the date of the repeat claim. Accordingly, in the instant appeal Judge Wright found the FTT was in error of law in not considering whether the claimant could have had an award of ESA on her repeat claim as a result of satisfying reg.30. Moreover, that error of law was material because it ought to have led to her at least being awarded ESA from the date of her repeat claim down to the date of the decision on that claim (subject to any waiting days).

For further discussion of *CM v SSWP (ESA)*, see Vol.III.

On "specific disease or bodily or mental disablement", see commentary to reg.19.

Those making a "repeat claim" who do not satisfy these conditions will not be treated as having limited capability for work pending assessment, and will thus not be entitled to ESA. Instead, if they wish to obtain a benefit they would have to resort to JSA (paid at the same rate as the assessment rate in ESA) and be subject to the JSA conditionality regime. The Government was not prepared to accept the SSAC's recommendation that, in such cases, claimants "should be offered back to work support on a voluntary basis but exempted from conditionality beyond attendance at a work-focused interview". The Government took the view that the recently introduced "extended period of sickness" changes and the flexibility of availability and actively seeking work rules afforded sufficient protection.

Paragraph (3): Continued entitlement to ESA pending appeal

9.58 This paragraph, when read with paras (2) and (4), has the effect that the supply of medical certificates will ground continued ESA entitlement pending an appeal against a "relevant decision", as defined in paragraph.(5). This covers only appeals against the first ever decision that the claimant does not have limited capability for work, either in the context of a decision on a wholly new claim or on an ongoing claim where previous determinations (whether by the Secretary of State or an appellate authority) had found limited capability for work. In such cases, no claim is required (see Claims and Payments Regs 1987, reg.3(1)(l)) and ESA Regs. 2008, reg.147A applies.

Where, however, one is dealing with a "repeat claim", the position is different. By "repeat claim is here envisaged a situation in which there *has been* a previous "determination" that the claimant does not have limited capability for work, or was treated as not having such limited capability. Where the claimant appeals in such a case, para. (3) does not operate to disapply para. (2)(b) since this appeal is not one against a "relevant decision", and the condition for continued entitlement in para.(2)

cannot be met. For the approach of decision-makers, see *Memo DMG 10/15*, paras 31–35. The intention of this as the DWP explained in the *Explanatory Memorandum* to the amending Regs, is

> "to align ESA with what happens for all other social security benefits where if a claimant is found not to be entitled, no benefit is paid whilst awaiting the outcome of the appeal. We believe this is reasonable because in their previous claim, the claimant will have had the opportunity to appeal to a tribunal if they disagreed with the decision. Claimants will instead be signposted to JSA as it is the appropriate benefit for someone who has been found fit for work. JSA provides claimants with personalised support to return to work taking into account their health condition or disability. It is acknowledged that not all ESA claimants will be eligible for JSA because they may not meet the conditions of entitlement" (para.7.5).

See also *R. (Connor) v SSWP* [2020] EWHC 1999 (discussed above), holding that the requirement to undertake the mandatory reconsideration process before appealing is unlawful in its application to ESA claimants who meet the conditions for payment while an appeal is pending.

Claimant who claims jobseeker's allowance to be treated as not having limited capability for work

31. [1 *Revoked.*] **9.59**

AMENDMENT

1. Employment and Support Allowance (Transitional Provisions, Housing Benefit and Council Tax Benefit) (Existing Awards) (No. 2) Regulations 2010 (SI 2010/1907) reg.25(1) (October 1, 2010).

Certain claimants to be treated as not having limited capability for work

32. [1(1)] A claimant [2who is or has been a member of Her Majesty's Forces] is to be treated as not having limited capability for work on any day which is recorded by the Secretary of State [4. . .] as a day of sickness absence from duty. **9.60**

[3(2) A claimant is to be treated as not having limited capability for work on any day on which the claimant attends a training course in respect of which the claimant is paid a training allowance or premium pursuant to arrangements made under section 2 of the Employment and Training Act 1973 or section 2(3) of the Enterprise and New Towns (Scotland) Act 1990.

(3) Paragraph (2) is not to apply—

(a) for the purposes of any claim to employment and support allowance for a period commencing after the claimant ceased attending the training course in question; or

(b) where any training allowance or premium paid to the claimant is paid for the sole purpose of travelling or meal expenses incurred or to be incurred under the arrangement made under section 2 of the Employment and Training Act 1973 or section 2(3) of the Enterprise and New Towns (Scotland) Act 1990.]

AMENDMENTS

1. Employment and Support Allowance (Miscellaneous Amendments) Regulations 2008 (SI 2008/2428) reg.5(2)(a) (October 27, 2008).

2. Employment and Support Allowance (Miscellaneous Amendments) Regulations 2008 (SI 2008/2428) reg.5(2)(b) (October 27, 2008).
3. Employment and Support Allowance (Miscellaneous Amendments) Regulations 2008 (SI 2008/2428) reg.5(2)(c) (October 27, 2008).
4. Social Security (Miscellaneous Amendments) (No.3) Regulations 2013 (SI 2013/2536) reg.13(15) (October 29, 2013).

DEFINITIONS

"claimant"—see WRA 2007 s.24(1).
"limited capability for work"—see WRA 2007 s.1(4).

GENERAL NOTE

Paragraph (1)

9.61 This draws a boundary between ESA and the sickness payment scheme operated by the Ministry of Defence. Days recorded by the Secretary of State as ones of sickness absence from duty are to be treated for ESA purposes as ones on which the person concerned does not have limited capability for work.

[1Claimants to be treated as not having limited capability for work at the end of the period covered by medical evidence

9.62 **32A.** [2(1)] Where the Secretary of State is satisfied that it is appropriate in the circumstances of the case [3 . . .] a claimant may be treated as not having limited capability for work if—

(a) the claimant has supplied medical evidence [2 . . .];
(b) the period for which medical evidence was supplied has ended;
(c) the Secretary of State has requested further medical evidence; and
(d) the claimant has not, before whichever is the later of either the end of the period of 6 weeks beginning with the date of the Secretary of State's request or the end of 6 weeks beginning with the day after the end of the period for which medical evidence was supplied—
 (i) supplied further medical evidence, or
 (ii) otherwise made contact with the Secretary of State to indicate that they wish to have the question of limited capability for work determined.]

[2(2) In this regulation "medical evidence" means evidence provided under regulation 2 or 5 of the Medical Evidence Regulations.]

AMENDMENTS

1. Social Security (Miscellaneous Amendments) (No. 3) Regulations 2010 (SI 2010/840) reg.9(9) (June 28, 2010).
2. Social Security (Miscellaneous Amendments) Regulations 2011 (SI 2011/674) reg.16(4) (April 11, 2011).
3. Social Security (Miscellaneous Amendments) (No.3) Regulations 2013 (SI 2013/2536) reg.13(16) (October 29, 2013).

Additional circumstances where claimants are to be treated as having limited capability for work

9.63 **33.**—(1) For the purposes of paragraph 4(1)(d)(ii) of Schedule 1 to the Act, a claimant is to be treated as having limited capability for work on any day in respect of which that claimant is entitled to statutory sick pay.

(2) For the purposes of an income-related allowance, a claimant is to be treated as having limited capability for work where—

(a) that claimant is not a qualifying young person;

(b) that claimant is receiving education; and

(c) paragraph 6(1)(g) of Schedule 1 to the Act does not apply in accordance with regulation 18.

DEFINITIONS

"claimant"—see WRA 2007 s.24(1).
"income-related allowance"—see WRA 2007 s.1(7).
"limited capability for work"—see WRA 2007 s.1(4).
"qualifying young person"—see reg.2(1).

GENERAL NOTE

Paragraph (1)

Like WRA 2007, s.20(1), this regulation deals with the relationship between ESA and employer paid statutory sick pay (SSP). Days of entitlement to SSP cannot rank as ones of entitlement to ESA. However, para.(1) of this regulation stipulates that such days are to be treated as ones of limited capability for work for the purposes of computing the 196 consecutive days of limited capability for work essential if someone is to qualify through the "condition relating to youth route" to CESA (WRA 2007, Sch.1, para.4(1)(d)(ii)). Being so treated confers no exemption from the information gathering requirements in reg.21 (see para.(3) of that regulation). 9.64

Paragraph (2)

This deals only with IRESA. It treats certain disabled students as having limited capability for work. It covers someone receiving education (sub-para.(b)) but not debarred from IRESA on account of that because he is receiving PIP, DLA or armed forces independence payment (sub-para.(c) [WRA 2007, Sch.1, para.6(1)(g) disapplied by reg.18]). If this person is not a qualifying young person, he is to be treated as having limited capability for work. A qualifying young person bears the same meaning as in SSCBA 1992, s.142 (see reg.2(1)): someone aged 16–19 inclusive undergoing a full-time course of non-advanced education or approved training which commenced before he attained 19 (see Child Benefit Regs, reg.3). See also *MW v SSWP (ESA)* [2018] UKUT 304 (AAC), confirming that although there is a general entitlement condition that a claimant "is not receiving education" (see Welfare Reform Act 2007, Sch.1, para. 6(1)(g) this is disapplied to a claimant entitled to PIP, DLA or armed forces independence payment by virtue of reg.18. 9.65

Being treated as having limited capability for work in this way confers exemption from the information gathering requirements in reg.21 (see para.(3) of that regulation).

PART 6

LIMITED CAPABILITY FOR WORK-RELATED ACTIVITY

Determination of limited capability for work-related activity

34.—(1) For the purposes of Part 1 of the Act, where, by reason of a claimant's physical or mental condition, at least one of the descriptors set out in Schedule 3 applies to the claimant, the [2 claimant has limited] capability for work-related activity [2 . . .] and the limitation [2 must] be such that it is not reasonable to require that claimant to undertake such activity. 9.66

(2) A descriptor applies to a claimant if that descriptor applies to the claimant for the majority of the time or, as the case may be, on the majority of the occasions on which the claimant undertakes or attempts to undertake the activity described by that descriptor.

[[1](3) In determining whether a descriptor applies to the claimant, the claimant is to be assessed as if—

(a) the claimant were fitted with or wearing any prosthesis with which the claimant is normally fitted or normally wears; or, as the case may be,

(b) wearing or using any aid or appliance which is normally, or could reasonably be expected to be, worn or used.]

(3A) [[2] *Omitted.*]

(4) Where a determination has been made about whether a claimant—

(a) has limited capability for work-related activity;

(b) is to be treated as having limited capability for work-related activity; or

(c) is to be treated as not having limited capability for work-related activity,

the Secretary of State may, if paragraph (5) applies, determine afresh whether the claimant has or is to be treated as having limited capability for work-related activity.

(5) This paragraph applies where—

(a) the Secretary of State wishes to determine whether there has been a relevant change of circumstances in relation to the claimant's physical or mental condition;

(b) the Secretary of State wishes to determine whether the previous determination about limited capability for work-related activity or about treating the claimant as having or as not having limited capability for work-related activity, was made in ignorance of, or was based on a mistake as to, some material fact; or

(c) at least 3 months have passed since the date of the previous determination about limited capability for work-related activity or about treating the claimant as having or as not having limited capability for work-related activity.

[[2](6) In assessing the extent of a claimant's capability to perform any activity listed in Schedule 3, it is a condition that the claimant's incapability to perform the action arises—

(a) in respect of descriptors 1 to 8, 15(a), 15(b), 16(a) and 16(b)—

(i) from a specific bodily disease or disablement; or

(ii) as a direct result of treatment provided by a registered medical practitioner for a specific physical disease or disablement; or

(b) in respect of descriptors 9 to 14, 15(c), 15(d), 16(c) and 16(d)—

(i) from a specific mental illness or disablement; or

(ii) as a direct result of treatment provided by a registered medical practitioner for a specific mental illness or disablement.]

AMENDMENTS

1. Employment and Support Allowance (Amendment) Regulations 2012 (SI 2012/3096) reg.4(2) (January 28, 2013, subject to application, transitional and savings provisions in reg.2 of this amending instrument, below, para.9.614).

2. Social Security (Miscellaneous Amendments) (No.3) Regulations 2013 (SI 2013/2536) reg.13(17) (October 29, 2013).

DEFINITIONS

"the Act"—see reg.2(1).

"claimant"—see WRA 2007 s.24(1).

"descriptor"—see reg.2(1).
"limited capability for work-related activity"—see WRA 2007 s.2(5).
"work-related activity"—see WRA 2007 ss.24(1), 13(7).

General Note

Establishing limited capability for work is the central condition governing entitlement to ESA. Establishing limited capacity for work related activity is, in contrast, the core condition of entitlement to support component, the more generous of the two components (support or work-related activity) only one of which can be added to ESA basic allowance. This regulation, read with WRA 2007, s.9 and Sch.3 to these Regs, sets out how limited capacity for work related activity is assessed and determined. 9.67

The assumption behind ESA is that the vast majority of claimants, if given the right support, are in fact capable of some work. Government anticipated that only some 10 per cent of claimants (those with more severe health conditions) will be entitled to the support allowance and so not be subject to work-related activity conditionality requirements (DWP, *Employment and Support Allowance Regulations 2008: Equality Impact Assessment* in *Explanatory Memorandum to Employment and Support Allowance Regulations 2008 (SI 2008/794)* and the *Employment and Support Allowance (Transitional Provisions) Regulations 2008 (SI 2008/795)*, p.19). Recent statistics indicate, however, that some 27 per cent of new claimants are put into the support group (DWP Press Release, April 24, 2012: see *http://www.dwp.gov.uk/newsroom/press-releases/2012/apr-2012/dwp042-12.shtml*). Entry to this protected support group depends on it being established—generally through a work-related activity assessment (WRAAt) of a more stringent nature than the WCAt—that the claimant has limited capacity for work related activity. The WRAAt is the second element in the new Work Capability Assessment (WCA) which will eventually replace the IB PCA. Establishing limited capability for work related activity is based on someone demonstrating that they have a severe level of functional limitation. This is established when by reason of the claimant's physical or mental condition, at least one of the ranges of descriptors in Sch.3 applies to the claimant (WRA 2007, s.9; para.(1)).

There is no scoring system (it is a matter of the descriptor being applicable that counts) and the criteria are deliberately more stringent than in the WCAt:

> "The levels of functional limitation used in the descriptors for determining limited capability for work-related activity are greater because we intend to place in the support group only the minority of customers who are so severely impaired that it would not be reasonable to require them to undertake work-related activity . . . People with less severe functional limitations across a range of descriptors might score highly and be inappropriately included in the support group when they might benefit from work-related activity. . . . A number of case studies were provided in the background information, which hon. Members will find helpful [see DWP, *Welfare Reform Bill: Draft Regulations and Supporting Material* (January 2007), pp.13–17]. Under the revised PCA, someone with a moderate learning disability would score 50 points. They would be significantly above the 15-point threshold, but we clearly would not wish to put even someone with 50 points into the support group automatically, because we are determined to ensure that the new system does not write off people with learning disabilities. The technical groups considered all the options. A crude points-based system would have unintended consequences." (*Hansard*, Standing Committee A, October 19, 2006 (afternoon), col.120 (Mr Jim Murphy MP, Minister for Employment and Welfare Reform)).

Paragraph (2)

Paragraph (2) makes clear (as indeed does the expected transposition to the WRAAt of central elements in existing case law on approaching the PCA) that a descriptor applies to a claimant if it applies to him for the majority of the time or, as the case may be, on the majority of the occasions on which he undertakes 9.68

or attempts to undertake the relevant activity. Moreover, as is the case with the IB PCA and the ESA WCAt, in matching claimant to descriptor, the claimant is to be assessed as if fitted with or wearing any prosthesis with which the claimant is normally fitted or normally wears; or wearing or using any aid or appliance which is normally, or could reasonably be expected to be, worn or used (para.(3), and see commentary to reg.19(4)). The interrelationship of para.(2) with descriptors in Sch.3 deploying differing wording on periodicity ("at least once a week" [activity/descriptor 8], "always" [activity/descriptor 13], "on a daily basis" [activity/descriptor 14],) has been explored in a number of cases.

In *KB* v *SSWP (ESA)* [2013] UKUT 152 (AAC), Judge Parker considered the relationship between this wording (the requisite of "always") and the stipulation in reg.34(2) that "a descriptor applies to a claimant if that descriptor applies to the claimant for the majority of the time or, as the case may be, on the majority of the occasions on which the claimant undertakes or attempts to undertake the activity described by that descriptor". Having looked at definitions of "always" in the Concise Oxford Dictionary, Judge Parker concluded that neither this activity and descriptor, nor its counterpart in Activity 16 of Sch.2 set out an "all or nothing test". Rather "always" here "means 'repeatedly' or 'persistent' or 'often':

> "A 'majority' may be constituted by events which happen only on 50.1 per cent of the possible occasions, but a greater frequency is required by the use of the word 'always'. It is a question of degree, but a fact finding tribunal is eminently suited to applying these subtle nuances of difference in a common sense way. It suffices to say in the present case, that because a claimant attends one tribunal hearing, and his GP accepts that he comes to the surgery very occasionally, does not necessarily entail the conclusion, as the tribunal clearly considered that it did, that it 'cannot be said that engagement in social contact is always precluded'" (para.14).

Judge Fordham took much the same approach in *CH* v *SSWP (ESA)* [2013] UKUT 207 (AAC) (para.8).

In *LM* v *SSWP (ESA)* [2013] UKUT 552 (AAC) (see update to p. 1076), however, Judge Mark agreed that "always" meant repeatedly or "persistent" but considered it did not mean "often" or "for the majority of the time".

In *WT* v *SSWP (ESA)* [2013] UKUT 556 (AAC), Judge Gray was more definitive than Judge Parker on the relationship between reg.34(2) and activity/descriptor 14, stating that "the terminology of the descriptor in question excludes the application of regulation 34 (2), in that it cannot apply to qualify the meaning of the words "on a daily basis" to mean "the majority of the time" or, "on the majority of occasions that the claimant undertakes or tries to undertake the activity", which would in logic lead to satisfaction of the test if it was satisfied on more than half of the days or attempts. That would drive a coach and horses through the descriptor, rendering the inclusion of any reference to the word "daily" pointless. That cannot be what was intended. Regulation 34(2) does not apply to a schedule 3 descriptor where the "majority of the time" approach would be inconsistent with the actual wording of the descriptor" (para.36).

Judge Parker's decision was appealed to the Court of Session. In *SSWP v Brade* [2014] CSIH 39 XA81/13 (May 1, 2014); [2014] AACR 29, the Court held that the wording cannot have been intended to mean "always" in the sense of the claimant never, at any time, whatever the circumstances, being able to engage in "social contact " (para. 35). Instead, the provision required a purposive construction:

> "descriptor 13 must apply if a claimant suffers from a mental disorder which has the consequence that, for the majority of the time, he cannot engage in social contact. That construction properly embraces regulation 34(1), 34(2) and the terms of descriptor 13 and accords with their evident intention. Such a person is not likely to have labour market potential and, moreover, if, for the majority of the time, that person cannot engage in social contact,

requiring participation in the work focused interview would be not only unreasonable but pointless. Further, that construction avoids the fact finder being necessarily driven to the absurd conclusion that descriptor 13 is not satisfied if, for instance, on a single occasion, a claimant has given instructions to a representative for the purposes of a tribunal hearing. The question of whether or not a person is wholly precluded from engagement in social contact for the majority of the time is one of fact having regard to the statutory provisions as understood by the guidance we have sought to provide. That question is not answered by the application of any precise mathematical approach but by the fact finding tribunal having regard to the evidence in the particular case of the effects of the claimant's condition in a realistic way whilst bearing in mind the purpose of the legisation" (para.37).

Activities in Sch.3

There are now 16 activities in Sch.3: mobilising unaided; transferring from one seated position to another; reaching; picking up and moving or transferring; manual dexterity; making self understood; understanding communication; absence or loss of control leading to extensive evacuation of the bowel and/or voiding of the bladder; learning tasks; awareness of hazard; initiating and completing personal action; coping with change; coping with social engagement; appropriateness of behaviour; conveying food or drink to the mouth; chewing or swallowing food or drink. The terms of the descriptors are also more stringent than in the WCAt, to avoid removing too many people from the group which affords incentive to engage in work-related activity and thus denying them the opportunity to take steps to make real their fundamental right to work. Thus, as regards walking, the single descriptor can only be met where a claimant cannot "mobilise" more than 50 metres on level ground without stopping to avoid significant discomfort or exhaustion (or cannot "repeatedly mobilise 50 metres...(etc)"). Most, with counterparts in the WCAt, are couched in terms equivalent to the more difficult of their 15 point descriptors. With effect from January 28, 2013, in deciding which descriptor applies, incapability must arise in respect of descriptors 1 to 8, 15(a), 15(b), 16(a) and 16 (b), from a specific bodily disease or disablement or as a direct result of treatment provided by a registered medical practitioner for such a disease or disablement (para.(3A)(a), (c)(i)). Similarly, as regards descriptors 9 to 14, 15(c), 15(d), 16(c) and 16 (d), incapability must arise from a specific mental illness or disablement; or as a direct result of treatment provided by a registered medical practitioner for such an illness or disablement (para.(3A)(b), (c)(i)). Note that for some cases after January 28, 2013, for a six month period, the previous version of reg.34 can be applicable (see reg.2 of the amending instrument, below, para.9.614). 9.69

Those meeting the WRAAt test will be placed in the support group and receive support component without having to satisfy work-related activity conditions, although they can voluntarily participate in those programmes. Their position can be reviewed periodically or where there has been a change of circumstances in the claimant's physical or mental condition or it is thought that a previous determination was made in ignorance of or a mistake as to some material fact (paras (4), (5)) The threshold for membership of the support group is high; CPAG consider that "many claimants in receipt of the middle and higher rates of Disability Living Allowance (DLA) may not meet the eligibility criteria". Those who fail to establish limited capability for work-related activity will instead be in the work-related activity group, which has stringent conditions attached in terms of appropriate behaviour (participation in work focussed health related assessments, work focused interviews and, eventually, specified work-related activity (see regs 47–60), involving the private and voluntary sector as well as JobCentre Plus).

Certain claimants to be treated as having limited capability for work-related activity

9.70 **35.**—(1) A claimant is to be treated as having limited capability for work-related activity if—

(a) the claimant is terminally ill;

[1(b) the claimant is—

(i) receiving treatment for cancer by way of chemotherapy or radiotherapy;

(ii) likely to receive such treatment within six months after the date of the determination of capability for work-related activity; or

(iii) recovering from such treatment,

and the Secretary of State is satisfied that the claimant should be treated as having limited capability for work-related activity; or]

(c) in the case of a woman, she is pregnant and there is a serious risk of damage to her health or to the health of her unborn child if she does not refrain from work-related activity.

(2) A claimant who does not have limited capability for work-related activity as determined in accordance with regulation 34(1) is to be treated as having limited capability for work-related activity if—

(a) the claimant suffers from some specific disease or bodily or mental disablement; and

(b) by reasons of such disease or disablement, there would be a substantial risk to the mental or physical health of any person if the claimant were found not to have limited capability for work-related activity.

AMENDMENT

1. Employment and Support Allowance (Amendment) Regulations 2012 (SI 2012/3096) reg.4(3) (January 28, 2013, subject to application, transitional and savings provisions in reg.2 of this amending instrument, below, para.9.614).

DEFINITIONS

"claimant"—see WRA 2007 s.24(1).
"limited capability for work-related activity"—see WRA 2007 s.2(5).
"terminally ill"—see reg.2(1).
"work-related activity"—see WRA 2007 ss.24(1), 13(7).

GENERAL NOTE

Paragraph (1)

9.71 This has affinities with reg.20 (treating someone as having limited capability for work). Regulation 35 (1) treats someone as having limited capability for work-related activity but the range of groups so treated is much narrower. The terminally ill (para.(1)(a)) and those undergoing or (as amended from March 28, 2011) likely to undergo within six months, or recovering from chemotherapy (para.(1)(b)) are so treated, as is a pregnant woman where there is a serious risk of damage to her health or that of her unborn child if she does not refrain from work-related activity (para. (1)(c). Unlike reg.20 there is no protection for other pregnant women or for those receiving hospital treatment or certain regular treatments such as dialysis.

Paragraph (2)

9.72 This is a partial equivalent of the "exceptional circumstances" provision (reg.29) applicable to the limited capability for work question, considered above. *A claimant who does not pass the LCWRA* can nonetheless be treated as having the requisite limited capability for work-related activity grounding membership of the support group where, by reasons of the specific disease or bodily or mental disablement from which s/he suffers, "there would be a substantial risk to the mental or physical health of any person if the claimant were found not to have limited capability for work-related activity". Given the structure of the ESA legislative scheme, it is axiomatic that reg.35(2) can only come into play where the claimant has been found to have limited capability for work (either under the LCWA scoring 15 or more in terms of Sch.2 descriptors or through the operation of reg.29) and has also failed to satisfy any of the Sch.3 descriptors, thus being found not to have limited capability for work-related activity (*LH v SSWP (ESA)* [2015] UKUT 154 (AAC)). In such a case, reg.35(2) becomes that claimant's last hope of being placed in the support group by being treated as having limited capability for work-related activity. On "specific disease or bodily or mental disablement", see commentary to reg.19(2).

For an extreme example of reg.35(2) being found to apply, see *JL v SSWP (ESA)* [2018] UKUT 346 (AAC). The claimant had previously been placed in the support group. The evidence of two ESA medical assessments and the claimant's own GP showed that the claimant's blood pressure was indisputably high and uncontrolled. Moreover, the DWP's own guidance to decision-makers (Memo DMG 17/15, paragraph 25(3)) gives the example of a claimant with hypertension which is uncontrolled despite medication as an instance of "immediate substantial risk" in the context of reg.35(2). The FTT's decision (upholding the conclusion that reg.35(2) did not apply, despite the HCP terminating the assessment and advising the claimant to attend A&E forthwith) was set aside for inadequate reasoning and the decision re-made.

On "substantial risk to the mental or physical health of any person if the claimant were found not to have limited capability for work-related activity", see the commentary to reg.29, but note that there is in reg.35(2) no statutory counterpart to the modification effected by reg.29(3) (medication and reasonable adjustments to the claimant's workplace). As with reg. 29(2)(b), the key case is *Charlton v Secretary of State for Work and Pensions* [2009] EWCA Civ. 42.

The application of Charlton *to reg.35(2)*: in *AH v SSWP (ESA)* [2013] UKUT 118 (AAC); [2013] AACR 32 Judge Jacobs considered how (if at all) the approach in *Charlton* on the predecessor of reg.29 should be applied to the differently worded context of reg.35 dealing as it does not with "work" but "work-related activity". He thought the Court of Appeal's conclusion on reg.29(2)(b) equally applicable to reg.35(2) so that the paragraph applies both to the effect of work-related activity and not just to the effect of being found capable of it; so that it applies (i) not only to the immediate effects of the decision on capability, but (ii) to the consequences of having to undertake work-related activity and (iii) to having to travel to and from it. Translating the Court's language on the range of work to be contemplated to fit this analogous context of "work-related activity" means that the 9.73

> "decision-maker must assess the range or type of work-related activity which a claimant is capable of performing and might be expected to undertake sufficiently to assess the risk to health either to himself or to others" (para.26).

The Secretary of State ought in such cases to provide some evidence of the range of "work- related activity" in contemplation. The tribunal should then assess that in light of evidence on the claimant's conditions and limitations for it. It would need to be able to consider, for example, what type of adjustments might be reasonable in the claimant's case, and what type of support the Advisor might provide (para.32). *KB v SSWP (ESA)* [2013] UKUT 152 (AAC) also took this approach to the applicability of *Charlton* reasoning to para.(2):

> "it is necessary, under regulation 35, to make the evaluation of substantial risk, not just an exercise limited to the ability to cope with the work related interview at the Job Centre, but also "in the context of the journey to or from" such an interview. This point has particular relevance to a claimant arguing under activity 13 of Schedule 3. The tribunal therefore went wrong in applying too narrow a statutory test, saying only "he should be able to cope with a work related interview at the Jobcentre" (para.18).

In *MN v SSWP (ESA)* [2013] UKUT 262 (AAC); [2014] AACR 6, Judge Wright endorsed Judge Jacobs's point in *AH* on the Secretary of State and evidence, but added two slight caveats. First, it might be enough in most cases to give a general indication of what is involved in work-related activity. Secondly, where the claimant's grounds of appeal specifically raise reg.35(2), r.24(2)(e) of the Tribunal Procedure Rules mandates the Secretary of State to say whether he opposed the appellant's case on reg.35(2) and state "any grounds for such opposition which are not set out in documents which are before the Tribunal" (paras 16, 17).

In *ML v SSWP (ESA)* [2013] UKUT 174 (AAC); [2013] AACR 33, a follow-up decision to *AH*, Judge Jacobs stressed the need for the Secretary of State to go beyond general formulaic statements to make effective the statutory right of appeal by providing the necessary information to enable claimants to participate in the appeal and the tribunal to make a decision" (para.15). He also considered the relationship between regs 29 and 35. He accepted that a paragraph in the DWP, Medical Services Handbook for ESA was merely guidance but also incorrect in stating that someone found to be "at substantial risk for work" would be extremely unlikely to be found not to be at "substantial risk for work-related activity". Instead Judge Jacobs stated that it all depends on the precise circumstances of each case:

> "Regulations 29 and 35 use similar wording, but they do so for different purposes. The claimant's condition is a constant for both provisions. But the activities to which the provisions apply differ. The former is concerned with the risk of work; the latter is concerned with the risk of work-related activity. There is no reason why the former should automatically be determinative of the latter. This will depend on: (i) the nature of the claimant's condition; (ii) its effects; and (iii) the nature of the work-related activity. It may be that the condition will give rise to the same risk whether the claimant undertakes work or work-related activity. Or it may give rise to different risks. Or it may give rise to risk in respect of one but not the other" (para.14).

9.74 *What evidence of work-related activity must be provided by the Secretary of State and what can a tribunal do where no such evidence is supplied?* How to deal with the practical difficulties posed for tribunals by the decisions in *AH*, *MN* and *ML* produced divergent views from Upper Tribunal judges (see *AK v SSWP (ESA)* [2013] UKUT 435 (AAC); *MT v SSWP (ESA)* [2013] UKUT 545 (AAC); *DH v SSWP (ESA)* [2013] UKUT (ESA) 573 (AAC); *HS v SSWP (ESA)* [2013] UKUT 591 (AAC); *AP v SSWP (ESA)* [2014] UKUT 35 (AAC); *AP v SSWP (ESA)* [2013] UKUT 553 (AAC); *PF v SSWP (ESA)* [2013] UKUT 634 (AAC); and *NA v SSWP (ESA)* [2014] UKUT 305 (AAC)). Those difficulties relate to avoiding the need for adjournments clogging up the adjudication system in a context in which the decision appealed against will have been made *before* the claimant has had an initial consultation with an adviser on appropriate work-related activity and in which there is generally no representative of the Secretary of State present at First-tier tribunals to be questioned as to what activity might be appropriate. In *NA*, Judge Gray deprecated the Secretary of State's failure to provide sufficient information to the tribunal; had the "action plan" seen by Judge Gray on appeal, and which predated the hearing before the First-tier Tribunal, been made available to that tribunal the further appeal to the Upper Tribunal might well have been avoided (presumably because that tribunal would then have applied the regulation in the claimant's favour).

Fortunately, this divisive issue has now been dealt with authoritatively by a panel of three Upper Tribunal judges. In *IM v SSWP (ESA)* [2014] UKUT 412 (AAC); [2015] AACR 10, the panel dealt with the question of "the amount of detail the regulation 35(2) decision-makers should have of the possible results of the work-focused interview" to which those found not to be incapable of work-related activity will be subject. Lest there were any doubt about the matter, the decision in IM v SSWP (ESA), is binding on First-tier Tribunals: see CT v SSWP (ESA) [2021] UKUT 131 (AAC).

The panel considered that the problem with decision-making on reg.35(2) arises because at the stage the decision maker (Secretary of State or First-tier tribunal) has to decide the matter of "substantial risk" exactly what will be required of this particular claimant at any such work-focused interview is unknown, a matter of conjecture, and the decision-maker must perforce engage in a degree of "crystal ball gazing" (para.75), with "substantial risk" bearing the commonly agreed meaning of a risk "that cannot sensibly be ignored having regard to the nature and gravity of the feared harm in the particular case" (para.65).

Having considered the range of case law on the provision noted above, the panel rightly held that a purposive approach, reflecting practicalities apparent in *Charlton*, must be taken to the regulation (para.83). In the view of the panel,

> "the absence of any system for ensuring that relevant information obtained, and findings made, in the course of carrying out a work capability assessment and applying regulation 35(2) and the reasoning behind the decision made on regulation 35(2) are made available to a person considering whether a requirement to engage in work-related activity should be imposed on the claimant effectively destroys the Secretary of State's argument that only generalised information about some types of work-related activity need be taken into account by the regulation 35(2) decision-maker when considering the possible consequences of a particular claimant being found not to have limited capability for work-related activity. The purpose underlying regulation 35(2) requires that those applying it make predictions about the consequences to the particular claimant of him being found not to have limited capability for work-related activity. In a few cases, the risks of an inappropriate requirement to engage in work-related activity being imposed will be too great to be ignored" (para.101).

Given the present system of administering the legislation, the First-tier Tribunal needs to know

> "not only what the least demanding types of work-related activity are but also what the most demanding types are in the area where the claimant lives.
>
> . . . .
>
> [O]n an appeal in which regulation 35(2) is in issue, [the Secretary of State] cannot be expected to anticipate exactly what work-related activity a particular claimant would in fact be required to do. This is axiomatic.
>
> But what the Secretary of State can and should provide is evidence of the types of work-related activity available in each area [Wolverhampton in this claimant's case] and by reference thereto what the particular claimant may be required to undertake and those which he considers it would be reasonable for the provider to require the claimant to undertake. The First-tier Tribunal would then be in a position to assess the relevant risks.
>
> [T]he types of work-related activity available may vary from provider to provider, but it should not be beyond the wit of the Department and providers to produce and maintain a list, perhaps for each of the regions into which the First-tier Tribunal is organised, of what is available in each area within the region. The relevant information could then be included in submissions in individual cases. The First-tier Tribunal would be able to assess the evidential force of such a submission.
>
> . . .

> Being unable to carry out an activity does not necessarily imply that there will be a substantial risk to anyone's health if the claimant is required to engage in the activity. Nor does the risk of being sanctioned. Therefore, it may be fairly obvious in most cases that the claimant does not have any realistic argument under regulation 35 and indeed, if made aware of the issues, the claimant may often accept that that is so. But where there turns out to be a serious argument in relation to regulation 35, the provision of the basic information about the more demanding types of work-related activity would enable the First-tier Tribunal to make the necessary predictions by reference to possible outcomes for the particular claimant" (paras.104-107, 110).

The panel considered that where the Secretary of State has accepted that the claimant has limited capability for work, the Secretary of State will be able to aid the tribunal with a more focused submission on why, given the claimant's disablement, reg. 35(2) does not apply. It noted that in some cases (see e.g. *CMcC v SSWP (ESA)* [2014] UKUT 176 (AAC); [2015] AACR 9) the work-focused interview will have taken place before the tribunal hears the appeal and its outcome and basis should be provided to it where possible, thereby reducing the element of prediction required, but always remembering that, because of SSA 1998 s.12(8)(b) any such evidence "should only be taken into account so far as it is relevant to the position at the time of the decision of the Secretary of State" (para.113).

The panel held that merely identifying that there is some work-related activity that a claimant could do is insufficient to ground a finding

> "that there would not be risk to someone's health if the claimant were found not to have limited capability for work-related activity. That is because it does not wholly answer the statutory question" (para.116).

In *CL v SSWP (ESA)* [2015] UKUT 375 (AAC), Judge Jacobs considered it permissible to take into account work-related activity that the claimant could carry out at home (para.17).

9.75 *But what if the Secretary of State fails to provide the required evidence?* In such a case, the panel considered that the First-tier Tribunal has a number of options as to how to proceed. It can use its own knowledge, if it is confident that it is up-to-date and complete as to the more demanding types of work-related activity. It may instead adjourn to obtain that evidence or decide that it can properly determine the case one way or the other without it. The right approach depends on the circumstances and, in particular, on how vulnerable the claimant is (para. 118).

Interestingly, the panel also made clear that there were ways in which the reg.35(2) risk could be greatly reduced or even eliminated by a change of practice in the way in which the scheme is administered (paras 98-100). But, unless and until the scheme of decision-making and the legislation is changed the approach in *IM* must be followed (see *EH v SSWP (ESA)* [2014] UKUT 473 (AAC); *KW v SSWP (ESA)* [2015] UKUT 131 (AAC); *GB v SSWP (ESA)* [2015] UKUT 200 (AAC)). Problems of decision-making are likely to be exacerbated where the claimant is unlikely to be able to engage in social contact with the provider so as explain their difficulties (*IM, GB*).

9.76 Thus the decision of the three-judge panel in *IM* highlighted:

> "that, because the results of work capability assessments are not routinely passed to providers who determine what work-related activity a claimant should be required to do, there may a risk of a provider requiring a person with, say, mental health problems to perform unsuitable work-related activity, due to the provider's ignorance of the those problems or their extent. This difficulty is liable to be exacerbated if, as in both *IM* and the present case, the claimant is, or is likely to be, unable to engage in social contact with the provider and so explain her difficulties herself" (see also *GB v SSWP (ESA)* [2015] UKUT 200 (AAC), *per* Judge Rowland).

This point was further emphasised by Judge Gray in *XT v SSWP (ESA)* [2015] UKUT 581 (AAC). There the First-tier Tribunal had decided that the appellant could undertake all likely work-related activities with the exception of work placements and work experience (because of her fragile mental health). The tribunal found she did not qualify for the support group, working on the assumption that its reservations would be communicated to the relevant provider of work-related activity. That assumption was misplaced in the light of *IM v SSWP (ESA)*. Judge Gray accordingly held the tribunal's decision to be in error of law; she went ahead to re-make the decision in the appellant's favour, explaining why there was a substantial risk within the terms of reg.35(2).

For another helpful example of a case in which the Upper Tribunal allowed the claimant's appeal and re-made the decision under reg.35, finding and explaining its reasoning as to why the claimant qualified on mental health grounds for the support group, see *SL v SSWP (ESA)* [2016] UKUT 170 (AAC). In that case Judge Sutherland Williams also approved of the DWP's guidance since *IM* (Memo ADM 7/16), which encourages decision makers to make better and more informed decisions in relation to reg.35 and LCRWA:

> "80. I might go further. If the Secretary of State can provide a tribunal with the types of work-related activity available in each area after the DM's decision is made, then it does not appear to me to be overly onerous on the DWP to provide HCP's with similar information before the decision is made, assuming that is not happening already. The HCP should then be able to provide a more reasoned statement in relation to regulation 35(2) in appropriate cases; and in turn the decision-maker could make a more informed decision in terms of predicative risk or otherwise, without that function being essentially passed onto the FTT."

The DWP's guidance since *IM* (both in its original format in Memo DMG 17/15 and its subsequent form in Memo ADM 7/16) was critiqued in more detail in *KC and MC v SSWP (ESA)* [2017] UKUT 94 (AAC). Judge Wright expressed the opinion that the DWP guidance for the most part accurately reflected the ruling in *IM*, subject to two notable exceptions.

The first was the erroneous suggestion in Memo DMG 17/15 that *IM* does not require a list of the most and least demanding types of work-related activity to be produced in appeals against whether a claimant even has limited capability for work (see paragraphs 87-90).

The second was in relation to para.36 of Memo DMG 17/15, which stated that tribunals should be provided with "examples of the most and last demanding WRA which it is considered the claimant *could* undertake" (emphasis added) rather than the whole list. Judge Wright took the view that "might be required to" was a better form of words than "could", which elided the two-stage approach required by *IM*. The first stage was to compile a list of work related activities in a given area, identifying the most and least demanding activities. The second stage was to explain the range of such activities that the particular appellant was capable of doing and might have been expected to undertake (see paragraphs 111-114).

The decision in *KC and MC v SSWP (ESA)* is also significant for the light it sheds on the DWP's provision of work-related activity through the so-called 'Jobcentre Plus Offer', a process which remarkably had not been properly disclosed to, and clarified before, the three-judge panel in *IM*. It transpired that the key distinction was between work-related activity delivered via an external work programme provider and such activity organised internally through the Jobcentre Plus Offer. Between June 2011 and April 2013, if the claimant's reassessment was scheduled for more than 6 months, then the Jobcentre Plus Offer applied. In April 2013 the prognosis criterion for the Jobcentre Plus Offer to apply increased to 12 months. The detailed arrangements under this internal form of provision are explained in Judge Wright's decision (at para.48), which also noted that the Jobcentre Plus Offer applied to all contributory ESA claimants living elsewhere in the EU (see para.95). The 'information gap' identified by the three-judge panel in *IM* still existed, at least until September 2016 (para.102). Judge Wright criticised the fact that the Jobcentre Plus Offer appeared to be unknown to large parts of the DWP responsible for applying regulation 35(2) (para.103). The judge also criticised the deficiencies in external work provider lists (paragraphs 104-110) relating to regulation 35(2).

In *RP v SSWP (ESA)* [2020] UKUT 148 Upper Tribunal Judge Wright further considered three main issues. The first was the progress the Secretary of State had made in providing a claimant's ESA 'adjudication history' with the appeal response to the FTT (paras 34-39). The second was the role of the 'Work Coach' in Jobcentre Plus in setting work-related activity for an individual claimant (paras 16-28). The third was the provision by the Secretary of State of the appellant's ESA 'action plan' to the First-tier Tribunal in an appeal where reg.35(2) was in issue (paras 29-33). It was held that the Secretary of State's appeals responses in ESA work capability appeals ought, where relevant, to include the claimant's ESA adjudication history and action plan since July 2018. Allowing the claimant's appeal, the Judge highlighted two main errors on the part of the FTT:

> "14. First, the tribunal's lack of curiosity or concern about the mangled and adjudication history it was provided with in the Secretary of State's appeal response meant that it failed properly to appraise itself of the decision the appellant was seeking to have superseded and changed. …
> 15. Second, as is now rightly accepted by the Secretary of State, if the 'Work Coach' (or 'Job Coach', the titles appear to be used interchangeably) had advised the appellant to seek placement in the support group then that was plainly relevant evidence, and so the First-tier Tribunal's apparent lack of interest in this evidential area was a further material error of law. …"

The Secretary of State's failure to provide accurate lists of work-related activity in appeals which concerned the assessment of 'substantial risk' under reg.35(2) was revisited again in *MR v SSWP (ESA)* [2020] UKUT 210 (AAC). The FTT in that case, which had been provided with a list of 'soft skills' (e.g. setting an alarm clock, getting out of bed and leaving the house), had concluded that the claimant did not meet the terms of reg.35(2) as he could manage those 'soft skills'. However, on appeal to the Upper Tribunal, Judge Wright held that the FTT "was misled in so concluding because the 'soft skills' of work-related activities was a not a true reflection of the extent of the work-related activities claimants may have been expected to undertake in March 2017. Perhaps most critically (and worryingly), the list being of soft skills, it did not contain the more, or most, onerous forms of work-related activities." Judge Wright further explored in detail why it was that the Secretary of State's responses to such FTT appeals failed to comply with the relevant legal requirements. Having reviewed that sorry saga, Judge Wright concluded as follows:

> "42. The 'soft skills' list, therefore, ought not in fact have appeared in any ESA work capability appeal after January 2018, and in any event was irrelevant as accurate lists of the most and least onerous types of available work-related activity even before that date. In consequence, First-tier Tribunals will need to investigate with conspicuous care any work capability assessment appeals in which the 'soft skills' list is put forward as evidence of the available work-related activity."

See, to similar effect, *MD v SSWP (UC)* [2020] UKUT 215 (AAC).

Proper application of reg.35(2) requires "a determination to be made as to *the extent to which* a person has met Schedule 2 [the LCWA] at the date of the decision under appeal as that informs the factors to be take into account in assessing the regulation 35(2) risk" (*KW v SSWP (ESA)* [2015] UKUT 131 (AAC), para.8 (Judge Wright), emphasis in the original). For further examples of the need for sufficient fact-finding and adequate reasons in appeals where reg.35 is in issue, see *MH v SSWP (ESA)* [2021] UKUT 90 (AAC) and *CT v SSWP (ESA)* [2021] UKUT 131 (AAC). On the importance of tribunals in universal credit appeals (that turn on the equivalent provision to reg.35 in Schedule 9, paragraph 4) ensuring they have been provided with an accurate list of work-related activities, see *KS v SSWP (UC)* [2021] UKUT 132 (AAC). Secretary of State appeal responses on such appeals may not have included accurate lists of work-related activities until after July 2020.

The burgeoning case law on this regulation covers five more issues, dealt with in turn, below.

Issue 1: how does reg.35(2) apply if the claimant could never work again or if there is no work-related activity that could reasonably be required of him? Here Judge Mark and Judge Jacobs take diametrically opposed positions, the former arguing that in such circumstances the provision can have no application, the latter arguing that it can and must in order to protect the most vulnerable by affording them an opportunity to be placed in the support group in circumstances in which their condition has not met the tailored specifics of ESA Regs 2008, Sch. 3. It is submitted that Judge Jacobs' approach is the better one in that promotes the purpose behind reg.35(2) and thus sits better with the purposive approach taken to the provision by the panel in *IM*, above. 9.77

Both judges rightly see the position as involving consideration of the WRA 2007, the ESA Regs 2008 and the Employment and Support Allowance (Work-Related Activity) Regulations 2011 (SI 2011/1349) ("the W-RA Regs"). Both note the definition of "work-related activity" in WRA 2007, s.13(7): "activity which makes it more likely that the person will obtain or remain in work or be able to do so". Although s.13(8) was not in force at the date of the decisions concerned, both judges noted its stipulation that such activity "includes work experience or a work placement". Similarly both took on board, reg. 3 of the W-RA Regs (see para.9.590) giving the Secretary of State discretion on whether or not to require a person in the work-related activity group actually to undertake any such activity, and providing that any such requirement imposed "must be reasonable in the view of the Secretary of State, having regard to the person's circumstances", and may not require him/her to undergo medical treatment or to apply for a job or undertake work, whether as an employee or otherwise.

In *JS v SSWP (ESA)* [2013] UKUT 635 (AAC), followed by him in *RV v SSWP (ESA)* [2014] UKUT 56 (AAC), Judge Mark held that the initial work-focused interview cannot constitute work-related activity since work-related activities can only be required once it has taken place (para.16). Moreover, the work-focused health assessment was also separate from such activity being an assessment, dealt with separately, and not meeting the s.13(7) definition, above (para.16). Given that definition, he considered "that if a person is patently not going to be able to obtain work at any stage, it is difficult to see how they could be required to carry out work-related activities" (para.15). Accordingly in his judgment, in this case reg.35(2) could not assist this claimant:

> "On the basis of the tribunal's finding as to his health problems, there would seem to be no real possibility of his resuming work and it is difficult to see how any interview could come within the definition of work-focused interview in section 12(7) of the 2007 Act since, due to his ill health, there would seem to be no prospect of his getting into work. For the same reason, there would not seem to be any work-related activity that the claimant could be required to do, in that, because of his health problems, there would be no activity which would make it even arguably more likely that he would be able to obtain work.
>
> It follows that, on the basis of the tribunal's findings of fact, there are no work-focused interviews or work-related activities that the Secretary of State could lawfully require the claimant to attend or undertake and that, in the absence of any other issue, there is no risk to his health as a result of not being found to have limited capability for work-related activity. Accordingly he does not fall within regulation 35(2)." (paras 27–28).

Judge Mark reiterated this in *GS v SSWP (ESA)* [2014] UKUT 16 (AAC), para.26.

In marked contrast, in *NS* v *SSWP (ESA)* [2014] UKUT 149 (AAC), Judge Jacobs rejected this way of looking at reg.35(2). Nor, in that case, did the Secretary of State support Judge Mark's analysis. There, Ms Wilkinson, appearing for the Secretary of State, argued that his analysis could not be right because it would remove from the most vulnerable claimants "who will not work again and for whom any WRA [work-related activity] will pose a substantial risk to their health" their final chance of being placed in the support group, final, of course, because reg.35(2) can only be applied where the claimant was not regarded as having limited capability for work-related activity, applying reg.34(1) and Sch.3 (para.23). Her suggested approach, based on s.13(7) requiring only that the activity make it "more likely" that the claimant will be able to obtain work and the chance that circumstances might change (e.g. "through a new form of treatment or medication"), was not accepted by Judge Jacobs as enough to cover the claimant who would clearly never work again. The approach, he thought, required a tribunal to make contradictory findings and, viewed as a statement that there was *at present* no work the claimant could do, left unresolved the question of whether reg.35(2) applied for the time being (para.24). The provision had to be applied effectively, whether before or after consideration had been given to the sort of work-related activity appropriate for a claimant (para.25). For him, it was critical to see reg.35(2) as being a *hypothesis* requiring the identification of "the possible consequences of a particular postulate (the *if* bit)" (para.26). The flaw in Judge Mark's analysis was to ignore the postulate. Judge Jacobs explained further:

> "If a possible consequence would be a substantial risk to health, the provision is satisfied and the claimant qualifies for the support group. As I have already said, the postulate cannot be read literally. The tribunal does not simply have to postulate the claimant being found not to have limited capability for work-related activity. It also has to postulate the claimant actually undertaking such activity.
>
> It does not have to identify that activity with precision. That is a separate stage that will only be reached if the tribunal decides that the claimant does not qualify for the support group. If and when that stage is reached, it is a matter for the Secretary of State, not the tribunal. The tribunal's task is preliminary to and necessarily more speculative and more general than the actual application of regulation 3 of the 2011 Regulations. The tribunal has to apply the hypothesis embodied in regulation 35(2). In doing so, it cannot deny the postulate. That, with respect to Judge Mark, is what he did. He denied that the postulate (the *if* bit) could ever apply in certain circumstances. But that is the very foundation of the provision. It is what the tribunal is required to accept. It cannot reject the basis of the hypothesis that forms the structure of regulation 35(2).
>
> In doing so, the tribunal has to limit itself to applying regulation 35(2) and avoid trespassing into the Secretary of State's decision-making under regulation 3 of the 2011 Regulations. . . . The way to remain properly within the tribunal's jurisdiction lies in the level of generality at which the tribunal has to consider work-related activity. Ms Wilkinson accepted that my decision in *AH* was correct. What the tribunal has to do is to identify in a general way 'the range and type of work-related activity which a claimant is capable of performing and might be expected to undertake' (to quote *AH*); and it must do so regardless of whether the Secretary of State would actually require the claimant to undertake any activity and regardless of whether any such activity would have any effect on the claimant's ability to 'obtain or remain in work' (to quote section 13(7))" (paras 26-28).

Judge Jacobs, in effect, requires the tribunal to ignore what might be done under reg.3 of the W-RA Regs. Judge Ward calls this a "thought experiment" and in *KB v SSWP (ESA)* [2015] UKUT 179 (AAC) applied it to require to be ignored in the application of reg. 35(2) the fact that this claimant, a carer entitled to carer's allowance, could not lawfully under the W-RA Regs be required to undertake work-related activity. This approach chimes well with the answer given by the three-judge panel in *IM* to the question in Issue 2, which must now be examined

Issue 2: given that reg. 3 of the Employment and Support Allowance (Work-Related Activity) Regulations 2011 (SI 2011/1349) ("the W-RA Regs") stipulates that the work-related activity required must be "reasonable ..., having regard to the person's circumstances", does this mean that the condition in reg.35(2) cannot be met? In *IM v SSWP (ESA)* [2014] UKUT 412 (AAC); [2015] AACR 10), the panel of three Upper Tribunal judges answered this in the negative since an affirmative answer would undermine the purpose of the provision. In so deciding they endorsed the decisions on this point given by Judge Jacobs in *NS v SSWP (ESA)* [2014] UKUT 149 (AAC) (paras 30, 34) and Judge Bano in *CMcC v SSWP (ESA)* [2014] UKUT 176 (AAC); [2015] AACR 9. As Judge Bano put it (in a passage endorsed by Judge Jacobs as consonant with his own view in *NS*): 9.78

> "If regulation 35(2) is to have any real meaning, it is not open to a tribunal to find that work-related activity does not present a risk of harm to a claimant on the basis that the claimant will not actually be required to undertake *any* meaningful activity if it turns out to be harmful. I therefore consider that the action of the employment adviser of effectively bringing the claimant's action plan to an end out of concern for her health was evidence which the tribunal should have taken into account when evaluating the risk of harm to the claimant if she were not found to have limited capability for work-related activity" (para.12).

Judge Gray's decision in *YA and SA v SSWP (ESA)* [2017] UKUT 80 (AAC) is authority for two propositions in this context. First, the duty under s.26(6) of the Equality Act 2010 to make reasonable adjustments added nothing to the duty under regulation 3 of the W-RA Regs that the WRA activity is reasonable (paragraphs 49-53). Second, subject to safeguards, the WRA requirements made between the date of the decision under appeal and the FTT hearing may be considered. In particular, tribunals cannot simply assume that a claimant will not be required to undertake any more onerous types of WRA than those already stipulated (paragraphs 39-48).

Issue 3: the "substantial risk" must arise "by reasons of" a specific disease or bodily or mental disablement: in *DR v SSWP (ESA)* [2014] UKUT 188 (AAC); [2014] AACR 38, Judge May held erroneous in law a tribunal decision that the claimant satisfied reg.29 because it had not made the necessary connection between the risk and the disease or disablement (see para.3). He considered the same principle applied to reg.35 (para.10). Alcohol misuse in itself is not such a disablement. To rank as disablement the misuse of alcohol must rank as "alcohol dependency" in terms of the "constellation of markers" found in quotations from *R(DLA) 6/06* in the Three-Judge Panel's decision in *JG v SSWP (ESA)* [2013] UKUT 37 (AAC); [2013] AACR 23 (see paras 5-7, 10 of *DR*). See further, commentary to reg.29(2)(b), above.

Issue 4: can the availability of third party assistance be taken into account? In *MT v SSWP (ESA)* [2013] UKUT 545 (AAC), in the context of reg.35(2) Judge Gray firmly rejected looking at capacity to perform activities with third party assistance, observing: 9.79

> "I do need to deal however with the observation of the FTT in its statement of reasons that the appellant could take another person with her to any work-related activities. It may be that the Secretary of State would be facilitative in any matter which helped a claimant engage so as to improve their ultimate prospects of retaining work. I do not know. Whether or not that is so, is not relevant. As a matter of law any work-related activity which could only be accomplished because of the presence of another person must be looked upon as not being an activity that the claimant can carry out. *The issue under regulation 35 (2) (b)*

> *as to whether there would be a substantial risk to the mental or physical health of any person if the claimant were found not to have limited capability for work-related activity cannot be assessed as if the claimant under consideration had somebody else by their side.* There will be claimants who have a need for the personal reassurance of another person, but who do not have anybody available to perform that role. Even if they did, it would not be reasonable for such an assessment to be made on the basis of reliance on another's goodwill. Legal tests cannot depend upon that. Where an appellant who is found to have limited capability for work-related activities wishes to engage voluntarily, it may be that they choose to do so with the help of another person, and it may (or may not, I do not know) be possible for them to do so, but the capacity to engage only with that assistance cannot be part of the test of capability" (para.34, emphasis added by commentator).

In *PD v SSWP (ESA)* [2014] UKUT 148 (AAC), in the context of the similarly worded reg. 29(2)(b), Judge Ward agreed with the italicised passage insofar as it meant "without consideration as to whether the third party's presence would be made out in fact" (para.21), but otherwise distinguished the passage as focussing on the claimant's capability to perform activities (agreeing that there third party assistance should be ignored) rather than the different question of what risks would ensue (where, with respect to travelling, at least, third party assistance available in fact might obviate the risk). See further commentary to reg.29(2)(b), above, substituting for "in the workplace" the different context of "the places where work-related activities might be performed".

Insofar as there is a difference of view between the two decisions in *MT v SSWP (ESA)* [2013] UKUT 545 (AAC) and *PD v SSWP (ESA)* [2016] UKUT 148 (AAC), Judge Hemingway in *MP v SSWP (ESA)* [2016] UKUT 502 (AAC) expressed a preference for the latter approach, noting that he could not:

> "see any reason why a third party's assistance ought not to be taken into account, in principle, when assessing whether or not the risk envisaged by the regulation would arise. There is nothing within the legislation which suggests that third party assistance cannot be relevant. The language of the test focuses upon risk. It would be artificial to approach the question of risk in a vacuum and without having regard to the prevailing circumstances. Such circumstances might include the availability of assistance" (at para.22).

See also *KN v SSWP (ESA)* [2016] UKUT 521 (AAC). In addition, Judge Gray in *YA and SA v SSWP (ESA)* [2017] UKUT 80 (AAC) accepted that third-party assistance may be considered, but "the circumstances need to be closely investigated and assessed prior to a finding that such assistance is reasonably available" (para.54). Thus "what should not be assumed is regular and open ended input from another person" (para.58). See also, on the importance of appropriate fact-finding in such cases, *ET v SSWP (UC)* [2021] UKUT 47 (AAC) (paras 6-12).

9.80 In *NN-K v Secretary of State for Work and Pensions (ESA)* [2015] UKUT 385 (AAC) Judge Jacobs reminded tribunals that, as a result of the decision in *IM v Secretary of State for Work and Pensions* [2014] UKUT 412 (AAC), a tribunal applying reg.35 must have regard to the type of work-related activity that the claimant might be expected to undertake in her area; in doing so, the tribunal must consider whether the activity would "be reasonable ... having regard to the person's circumstances" (reg.3(4)(a)). In that context the compatibility of any such activity with a claimant's existing education course would be one of those circumstances (para.9). However:

> "10. But such factors are only relevant in so far as they relate to the existence of a substantial risk to health. The tribunal should ignore any factor that is not relevant to that. If the tribunal does not have, and is not to be treated as having, limited capability for work-related activity, any issues such as the reasonableness of the activity would arise subsequently. In particular, the issue might arise whether to give a direction on work-related activity or whether she had good

cause for not undertaking it or whether to reduce her benefit for failing to comply with the direction."

Issue 5: how does reg.35(2) operate if the claimant lives outside the UK? In *BB v Secretary of State for Work and Pensions (ESA)* [2015] UKUT 545 (AAC) the claimant lived in Spain and later in the Republic of Ireland. Following a conversion decision, he was found to qualify for ESA without the support component. A tribunal dismissed his appeal, finding that reg.35(2) was not satisfied. On appeal to the Upper Tribunal, the Secretary of State's representative confirmed that there were no arrangements in place to provide work-related activities in countries outside the UK and argued that the reg. 35(2) test has to be applied on a hypothetical basis, namely "what could happen if a claimant were required to undertake work-related activity, not what would happen" (para.14(b)). Judge Mitchell allowed the claimant's appeal, as he had not had "a fair opportunity to put forward a case in relation to regulation 35(2) because he was unaware of the type of work-related activity by reference to which regulation 35(2) would be applied" (para.20). The Secretary of State's representative further argued that "Where the claimant lives outside the UK and elects to have a paper hearing (as in this case) the hearing is almost always going to take place in Newcastle. However if the claimant chooses to attend in person they can choose a venue suitable to them. Thus, in such cases the relevant WRA evidence will be from the Newcastle area, or the area in which the tribunal was that the claimant attended" (para.17). Remitting the appeal to a new tribunal, Judge Mitchell observed as follows:

> "22. I acknowledge the conceptual difficulties raised by the application of regulation 35(2), given the existing authorities, in foreign cases such as this. The Secretary of State's proposed solution has the benefit of levelling, to an extent, the playing field. It reduces the chances of different reg. 35(2) outcomes solely by reason of a person's country of residence. If an appellant does not object, the First-tier Tribunal ought to adopt the course suggested by the Secretary of State. If the appellant does object, the Tribunal will need to decide for itself how to proceed taking into account the reasons for the objection and any submissions of the Secretary of State" (para.22).

[1Relevant linked cases—limited capability for work-related activity

35A.—A claimant is to be treated as having limited capability for work-related activity where– 9.81

(a) they fall within case 1, as defined in regulation 7(1B)(a); and
(b) in respect of the earlier period of limited capability for work referred to in regulation 7(1B)(a)(i), they had been entitled to a support component under sections 2(2) or 4(4) of the Act.]

AMENDMENT

1. Employment and Support Allowance (Amendment of Linking Rules) Regulations 2012 (SI 2012/919) reg.5(5) (May 1, 2012).

Information required for determining capability for work-related activity

36.—(1) Subject to paragraph (2), the information or evidence required to determine whether a claimant has limited capability for work-related activity is— 9.82

(a) any information relating to the descriptors set out in Schedule 3 as may be requested in the form of a questionnaire; and
(b) any such additional information as may be requested.

(2) Where the Secretary of State is satisfied that there is sufficient information to determine whether a claimant has limited capability for work-related activity without the information specified in paragraph (1)(a), that information [1must] not be required for the purposes of making the determination.

AMENDMENT

1. Social Security (Miscellaneous Amendments) (No.3) Regulations 2013 (SI 2013/2536) reg.13(18) (October 29, 2013).

DEFINITIONS

"claimant"—see WRA 2007 s.24(1).
"limited capability for work-related activity"—see WRA 2007 s.2(5).
"work-related activity"—see WRA 2007 ss.24(1), 13(7).

GENERAL NOTE

9.83 This regulation deals with the information required for determining whether someone has limited capability for work-related activity. It is designed to give the decision-maker sufficient information to decide that matter for himself (the minority of cases), or whether to seek advice from a health care professional on the basis of the papers in respect of that decision, or to refer the claimant for a face to face WRAAt, including a medical examination (see reg.38).

Unless para.(2) operates, the claimant will have to supply (i) any information relating to the descriptors set out in Sch.3 as may be requested in the form of a questionnaire (para.(1)(a)), and (ii) such additional information relating to the relevant test as the Secretary of State asks for (para.(1)(b)). He must generally complete and return the appropriate questionnaire (para.(1)(a)), unless the Secretary of State decides that completion of the questionnaire is not necessary because without it he has sufficient information to determine whether the claimant does or does not have limited capability for work-related activity (para.(2)). Note that where the claimant is requested by the Secretary of State to complete and return the questionnaire, failure to do so can result in his being treated as not having limited capability for work-related activity (and thus not entitled to support component) (reg.37).

Failure to provide information in relation to work-related activity

9.84 **37.**—(1) Where a claimant fails without good cause to comply with the request referred to in regulation 36(1)(a), the claimant is, subject to paragraph (2), to be treated as not having limited capability for work-related activity.

(2) Paragraph (1) does not apply unless—

(a) at least [14] weeks have passed since the claimant was sent the first request for the information; and

(b) [2. . .] at least [11 week has] passed since the further request was sent.

AMENDMENTS

1. Social Security (Miscellaneous Amendments) (No. 3) Regulations 2011 (SI 2011/2425) reg.23(5), (6) (October 31, 2011).

2. Social Security (Miscellaneous Amendments) (No.3) Regulations 2013 (SI 2013/2536) reg.13(19) (October 29, 2013).

DEFINITIONS

"claimant"—see WRA 2007 s.24(1).
"limited capability for work-related activity"—see WRA 2007 s.2(5).
"week"—see reg.2(1).
"work-related activity"—see WRA 2007 ss.24(1), 13(7).

General Note

If a claimant fails without good cause (on which more, below) to comply with the requirement in reg.36(1)(a) to complete and return a limited capability for work-related activity questionnaire, he must be treated as not having limited capability for work-related activity, that is, as having no entitlement to support component. This can only happen, however, if a further request for information was sent at least three weeks after the first and at least one week has gone by since the second request was sent. 9.85

On applicable IB case law on calculating periods and on the matter of good cause, see further the commentary to the analogous reg.22, applicable in respect of similar processes with respect to determination of limited capability for work questions.

Claimant may be called for a medical examination to determine whether the claimant has limited capability for work-related activity

38.—(1) Where it falls to be determined whether a claimant has limited capability for work-related activity, that claimant may be called by or on behalf of a health care professional approved by the Secretary of State to attend for a medical examination [2in person, by telephone or by video]. 9.86

(2) Subject to paragraph (3), where a claimant fails without good cause to attend for or to submit to an examination [1mentioned] in paragraph (1), the claimant is to be treated as not having limited capability for work-related activity.

[1(3) Paragraph (2) does not apply unless—

(a) written notice of the date, time and place for the examination was sent to the claimant at least seven days in advance; or

(b) the claimant agreed to accept a shorter period of notice whether given in writing or otherwise.]

Amendment

1. Social Security (Miscellaneous Amendments) (No.3) Regulations 2013 (SI 2013/2536) reg.13(20) (October 29, 2013).

2. Social Security (Claims and Payments, Employment and Support Allowance, Personal Independence Payment and Universal Credit) (Telephone and Video Assessment) (Amendment) Regulations 2021 (SI 2021/230) reg.3(3) (March 25, 2021).

Definitions

"claimant"—see WRA 2007 s.24(1).

"health care professional"—see reg.2(1).

"limited capability for work-related activity"—see WRA 2007 s.2(5).

"work-related activity"—see WRA 2007 ss.24(1), 13(7).

General Note

This regulation enables the DWP to have a claimant medically examined by a DWP Medical Service (DWPMS) health service professional (technically any health service professional approved by the Secretary of State) when a question arises as to the claimant's capability for work-related activity. Failure without good cause to attend for or submit to such an examination, of which he was given proper written notice (see para.(3)), will result in the claimant being treated as not having limited capability for work-related activity and thus be excluded from the support group. 9.87

This regulation is a direct analogue of reg.23 with respect to medical examination as regards the matter of limited capability for work. The points, including the application of relevant IB case law, made in the commentary to reg.23 are equally applicable here.

Matters to be taken into account in determining good cause in relation to regulations 37 or 38

9.88 **39.** The matters to be taken into account in determining whether a claimant has good cause under regulations 37 (failure to provide information in relation to work-related activity) or 38 (failure to attend a medical examination to determine limited capability for work-related activity) include—
(a) whether the claimant was outside Great Britain at the relevant time;
(b) the claimant's state of health at the relevant time; and
(c) the nature of any disability the claimant has.

DEFINITION

"claimant"—see WRA 2007 s.24(1).

GENERAL NOTE

9.89 This regulation, made pursuant to WRA 2007 s.9(4), stipulates that in determining whether someone had good cause for failing to provide information (under reg.37) or for failing to attend for or submit to a medical examination (under reg.38) decision-makers and appellate bodies must take into account: (i) whether the person was outside Great Britain at the relevant time; (ii) his state of health at the relevant time; and (iii) the nature of his disability. This list is not, however, exhaustive (the regulation says "shall include"). On "good cause", see further the commentary to regs 22 and 23.

9.90 [[1]SCHEDULE 2 **Regulation 19(2) and (3)**

ASSESSMENT OF WHETHER A CLAIMANT HAS LIMITED CAPABILITY FOR WORK

PART 1

PHYSICAL DISABILITIES

(1) *Activity*	*(2)* *Descriptors*	*(3)* *Points*
1. [[2]Mobilising unaided by another person with or without a walking stick, manual wheelchair or other aid if such aid is normally, or could reasonably be, worn or used.]	1 (a) Cannot [[3]unaided by another person] either: (i) mobilise more than 50 metres on level ground without stopping in order to avoid significant discomfort or exhaustion; or (ii) repeatedly mobilise 50 metres within a reasonable timescale because of significant discomfort or exhaustion.	15
	(b) Cannot [[3]unaided by another person] mount or descend two steps [[3]...] even with the support of a handrail.	9
	(c) Cannot [[3]unaided by another person] either (i) mobilise more than 100 metres on level ground without stopping in order to avoid significant discomfort or exhaustion; or (ii) repeatedly mobilise 100 metres within a reasonable timescale because of significant discomfort or exhaustion.	9

(1) *Activity*	*(2)* *Descriptors*	*(3)* *Points*
	(d) Cannot [3unaided by another person] either: (i) mobilise more than 200 metres on level ground without stopping in order to avoid significant discomfort or exhaustion; or (ii) repeatedly mobilise 200 metres within a reasonable timescale because of significant discomfort or exhaustion.	6
	(e) None of the above [3applies].	0
2. Standing and sitting.	2 (a) Cannot move between one seated position and another seated position located next to one another without receiving physical assistance from another person.	15
	(b) Cannot, for the majority of the time, remain at a work station, either: (i) standing unassisted by another person (even if free to move around); or (ii) sitting (even in an adjustable chair) [2; or (iii) a combination of (i) and (ii),] for more than 30 minutes, before needing to move away in order to avoid significant discomfort or exhaustion.	9
	(c) Cannot, for the majority of the time, remain at a work station, either: (i) standing unassisted by another person (even if free to move around); or (ii) sitting (even in an adjustable chair) [2; or (iii) a combination of (i) and (ii),] for more than an hour before needing to move away in order to avoid significant discomfort or exhaustion.	6
	(d) None of the above apply	0
3. Reaching.	3 (a) Cannot raise either arm as if to put something in the top pocket of a coat or jacket.	15
	(b) Cannot raise either arm to top of head as if to put on a hat.	9
	(c) Cannot raise either arm above head height as if to reach for something.	6
	(d) None of the above apply.	0
4. Picking up and moving or transferring by the use of the upper body and arms.	(a) Cannot pick up and move a 0.5 litre carton full of liquid.	15
	(b) Cannot pick up and move a one litre carton full of liquid.	9
	(c) Cannot transfer a light but bulky object such as an empty cardboard box.	6
	(d) None of the above apply.	0

(1) *Activity*	*(2)* *Descriptors*	*(3)* *Points*
5. Manual dexterity.	5. [[3](a) Cannot press a button (such as a telephone keypad) with either hand or cannot turn the pages of a book with either hand.]	15
	(b) Cannot pick up a £1 coin or equivalent with either hand.	15
	(c) Cannot use a pen or pencil to make a meaningful mark [[3] with either hand].	9
	(d) Cannot [[2] single-handedly] use a suitable keyboard or mouse.	9
	(e) None of the above [[3] applies].	0
[[2] 6. Making self understood through speaking, writing, typing, or other means which are normally, or could reasonably be, used, unaided by another person.]	6 (a) Cannot convey a simple message, such as the presence of a hazard.	15
	(b) Has significant difficulty conveying a simple message to strangers.	15
	(c) Has some difficulty conveying a simple message to strangers.	6
	(d) None of the above apply.	0
[[2] 7. Understanding communication by— (i) verbal means (such as hearing or lip reading) alone, [(ii) non-verbal means (such as reading 16 point print or Braille) alone, or (iii) a combination of (i) and (ii), using any aid that is normally, or could reasonably be, used, unaided by another person.]	7. (a) Cannot understand a simple message [[3],such as the location of a fire escape,] due to sensory impairment [[3]...].	15
	(b) Has significant difficulty understanding a simple message from a stranger due to sensory impairment.	15
	(c) Has some difficulty understanding a simple message from a stranger due to sensory impairment.	6
	(d) None of the above [[3] applies].	0
[[2] 8. Navigation and maintaining safety, using a guide dog or other aid if either or both are normally, or could reasonably be, used.]	8 (a) Unable to navigate around familiar surroundings, without being accompanied by another person, due to sensory impairment.	15
	(b) Cannot safely complete a potentially hazardous task such as crossing the road, without being accompanied by another person, due to sensory impairment.	15
	(c) Unable to navigate around unfamiliar surroundings, without being accompanied by another person, due to sensory impairment.	9
	(d) None of the above apply.	0
[[2] 9. Absence or loss of control whilst conscious leading to extensive evacuation of the bowel and/or bladder, other than enuresis (bed-wetting), despite the wearing or use of any aids or adaptations which are normally, or could reasonably be, worn or used.]	9 (a) At least once a month experiences: (i) loss of control leading to extensive evacuation of the bowel and/or voiding of the bladder; or (ii) substantial leakage of the contents of a collecting device sufficient to require cleaning and a change in clothing.	15

(1) Activity	*(2) Descriptors*	*(3) Points*
	(b) [[2] The majority of the time is at risk] of loss of control leading to extensive evacuation of the bowel and/or voiding of the bladder, sufficient to require cleaning and a change in clothing, if not able to reach a toilet quickly.	6
	(c) [[3] Neither of the above applies.]	0
10. Consciousness during waking moments.	10 (a) At least once a week, has an involuntary episode of lost or altered consciousness resulting in significantly disrupted awareness or concentration.	15
	(b) At least once a month, has an involuntary episode of lost or altered consciousness resulting in significantly disrupted awareness or concentration.	6
	(c) None of the above apply.	0

PART 2

MENTAL, COGNITIVE AND INTELLECTUAL FUNCTION ASSESSMENT

(1) Activity	*(2) Descriptors*	*(3) Points*
11. Learning tasks.	11 (a) Cannot learn how to complete a simple task, such as setting an alarm clock.	15
	(b) Cannot learn anything beyond a simple task, such as setting an alarm clock.	9
	(c) Cannot learn anything beyond a moderately complex task, such as the steps involved in operating a washing machine to clean clothes.	6
	(d) None of the above apply.	0
12. Awareness of everyday hazards (such as boiling water or sharp objects).	12.(a) Reduced awareness of everyday hazards leads to a significant risk of: (i) injury to self or others; or (ii) damage to property or possessions such that [[4]the claimant requires] supervision for the majority of the time to maintain safety.	15
	(b) Reduced awareness of everyday hazards leads to a significant risk of (i) injury to self or others; or (ii) damage to property or possessions such that [[4]the claimant frequently requires] supervision to maintain safety	9
	(c) Reduced awareness of everyday hazards leads to a significant risk of: (i) injury to self or others; or (ii) damage to property or possessions such that [[4]the claimant occasionally requires] supervision to maintain safety.	6
	(d) None of the above apply.	0

(1) *Activity*	*(2)* *Descriptors*	*(3)* *Points*
13. Initiating and completing personal action (which means planning, organisation, problem solving, prioritising or switching tasks).	13 (a) Cannot, due to impaired mental function, reliably initiate or complete at least 2 sequential personal actions.	15
	(b) Cannot, due to impaired mental function, reliably initiate or complete at least 2 [4 sequential] personal actions for the majority of the time.	9
	(c) Frequently cannot, due to impaired mental function, reliably initiate or complete at least 2 [4 sequential] personal actions.	6
	(d) None of the above [4 applies].	0
14. Coping with change.	14 (a) Cannot cope with any change to the extent that day to day life cannot be managed.	15
	(b) Cannot cope with minor planned change (such as a pre-arranged change to the routine time scheduled for a lunch break), to the extent that overall day to day life is made significantly more difficult.	9
	(c) Cannot cope with minor unplanned change (such as the timing of an appointment on the day it is due to occur), to the extent that overall, day to day life is made significantly more difficult.	6
	(d) None of the above apply.	0
15. Getting about.	15 [2(a) Cannot get to any place outside the claimant's home with which the claimant is familiar.]	15
	(b) Is unable to get to a specified place with which the claimant is familiar, without being accompanied by another person.	9
	(c) Is unable to get to a specified place with which the claimant is unfamiliar without being accompanied by another person.	6
	(d) None of the above apply.	0
16. Coping with social engagement due to cognitive impairment or mental disorder.	16 (a) Engagement in social contact is always precluded due to difficulty relating to others or significant distress experienced by the [4 claimant].	15
	(b) Engagement in social contact with someone unfamiliar to the claimant is always precluded due to difficulty relating to others or significant distress experienced by the [4 claimant].	9
	(c) Engagement in social contact with someone unfamiliar to the claimant is not possible for the majority of the time due to difficulty relating to others or significant distress experienced by the [4 claimant].	6
	(d) None of the above [4 applies].	0

(1) *Activity*	*(2)* *Descriptors*	*(3)* *Points*
17. Appropriateness of behaviour with other people, due to cognitive impairment or mental disorder.	17 (a) Has, on a daily basis, uncontrollable episodes of aggressive or disinhibited behaviour that would be unreasonable in any workplace.	15
	(b) Frequently has uncontrollable episodes of aggressive or disinhibited behaviour that would be unreasonable in any workplace.	15
	(c) Occasionally has uncontrollable episodes of aggressive or disinhibited behaviour that would be unreasonable in any workplace.	9
	(d) None of the above apply.	0.]

AMENDMENTS

1. Employment and Support Allowance (Limited Capability for Work and Limited Capability for Work-Related Activity) (Amendment) Regulations 2011 (SI 2011/228) reg.4(1) (March 28, 2011).
2. Employment and Support Allowance (Amendment) Regulations 2012 (SI 2012/3096) reg.5(2) (January 28, 2013, subject to application, transitional and savings provisions in reg. 2 of this amending instrument, below, para.9.601).
3. Social Security (Miscellaneous Amendments) (No.3) Regulations 2013 (SI 2013/2536) reg.13(32) (October 29, 2013).
4. Social Security (Miscellaneous Amendments) (No.3) Regulations 2013 (SI 2013/2536) reg.13(33) (October 29, 2013).

DEFINITION

"claimant"—see WRA 2007 s.24(1).

GENERAL NOTE

I. A Note on the Background to the WCA and the new Schs 2 and 3 inserted on March 28, 2011

In 1995, a new test for incapacity for work was introduced: the "all work test". In 2000 this was renamed the personal capability assessment (PCA). This, like the "all work" test, lay at the heart of the reform effected by the Social Security (Incapacity for Work) Act 1994. According to Government, the results of two large scale evaluation studies to assess the validity and reliability of this essentially medical and functional test indicated: 9.91

> "that [it provided] a more effective means of assessing incapacity, which [would] help ensure that benefit is targeted on those people who are incapable of work, because of their medical condition" (DSS/Benefits Agency, *The medical assessment for incapacity benefit* (HMSO, 1994), p.35).

The "personal capability assessment" was one which—like the WCA—ignored the other personal/environmental factors governing access to employment by people with disabilities (R. Berthoud, "The 'medical' assessment of incapacity: a case study of the (lack of) influence of research on policy" [1995] 2 J.S.S.L. 61, at pp.70, 75). It did not measure people against the requirements of specific jobs (the "personal capability assessment" contained no definition of work for none was required given its nature). Its exclusionary effect would, it was thought by Berthoud, largely deny benefit to persons who probably were capable of work (*ibid.* at p.82). However, it was thought possible that some, who would have failed the previously applicable informal and more holistic test, might qualify as incapable on the AWT/PCA, while some, who failed the AWT/PCA, might well in fact be incapable of work.

The "personal capability assessment" was an assessment of the extent of the claimant's incapacity, by reason of some specific disease or bodily or mental disablement which he has, to perform the activities prescribed in the Schedule [to the IFW Regulations], entitled "disabilities which may make a person incapable of work" (IFW Regulations reg.24).

The new Work Capability Assessment (WCA) underpinning ESA followed similar lines, but embodied important changes to reflect the demands of the modern workplace, the development and availability of adaptive technology, and the legal obligations on employers to make reasonable adjustments better to accommodate those people with long term disabilities. In consequence, the 15 physical activities in the AWT/PCA were reduced to 11, in order to better reflect the activities that an employer might reasonably expect of his workforce. More radically, the mental health provisions in the IFW Regulations were thought not to be the most relevant to activities requisite for remaining in or returning to work. Consequently, the four activities dealing with mental functions in the AWT/PCA were increased to the ten activities in the original WCA with respect to mental, cognitive and intellectual function, reflecting a desire to deal better with the problems of a client group which made up some 41 per cent of the IB caseload.

The difficulties of applying the AWT/PCA are evident in a burgeoning case law. The difficulties of devising a test which accurately ascertains capability for work or for work-related activity are emphasized by ongoing review and the frequent amendments that are the subject of this commentary. Less than three years after its introduction, the WCA was thoroughly revised with new Schs 2 and 3 operating from March 28, 2011 for all new claims after that date, and for most determinations and assessments made after that date. The development of the WCA from the AWT/PCA and its recent revision are examined in some depth here on the basis that this will aid the task of decision-makers and tribunals, who must interpret and apply the wording of the activities and descriptors to the varied circumstances of individual cases, by casting light on the changes and their purpose. It is, of course, for decision-makers and tribunals to decide what the wording chosen to achieve those purposes actually means. Setting out the antecedents of the current provisions also highlights the continued application to similar or identical wording of pertinent case law authorities both on the AWT/PCA and the previous version of the WCA itself, which can be found in para.9.365 of the 2012/13 edition of this volume as updated by the 2012/13 Supplement.

The original WCA was devised by the DWP's Health Work and Wellbeing Directorate with input from two technical working groups, one focusing on mental health and learning difficulties, the other on physical function and conditions (hereinafter "review group"). The review group consisted of medical and other relevant experts. It examined how the incapacity benefits regime's Personal Capability Assessment (PCA) could be improved and updated so as to reflect the many changes since its inception:

> "in the prevalence of disabling conditions; in advances in medical science resulting in the availability of new and more effective medical interventions; and in the workplace environment. The Disability Discrimination Act, introduced after the PCA had been developed, has influenced the ability of employers to make reasonable adjustments to accommodate people with long term disabilities. It has also raised the expectations of disabled people that adjustments should be made to enable them to work."

The work of the review group fed into the drafting of the regulations on the WCA. After that first element had been developed work continued on the second and third elements of the WCA, although nothing has been published on this. Government anticipated that the WCA would "fail" some 60,000 claimants a year who would have "passed" the PCA (DWP, *Impact Assessment of the Employment and Support Allowance*

Regulations 2008—Public sector Impact Only in *Explanatory Memorandum to Employment and Support Allowance Regulations 2008 (SI 2008/794) and the Employment and Support Allowance (Transitional Provisions) Regulations 2008 (SI 2008/795)*, p.9). Statistics from 2012 suggested that some 54 per cent of new claimants were found capable of work (DWP Press Release, April 24, 2012: see *http://www.dwp.gov.uk/newsroom/press-releases/2012/apr-2012/dwp042-12.shtml*), exceeding the DWP's expectations of 38 per cent (DWP, Explanatory Memorandum to the SSAC on the Amending Regulations: App 1a: Revising the WCA – assessment of impact, para.9). Figures published by the DWP in January 2014, however, indicated that 61% of new claimants with a completed claim were found to have limited capability of work. But the WCA is not merely an incapacity-based tool for determining entitlement to ESA. That remains true of its first element, but its second element is rather a more positive assessment considering ability to benefit from work-related activity with a view to promoting capacity for work. The first element is an assessment of limited capability to work (hereinafter the LCWA) (the subject of this Schedule). The second element is an assessment of limited capacity to engage in work-related activity (hereinafter LCWRA) (the subject of Sch.3). Both assessments will generally be conducted at the same time by the same health care professional. Those found not to have limited capacity for work-related activity (expected to be some 90 per cent of new claimants) were originally required to undergo the third element of the WCA: a work-focused health related assessment (WFHRAt).

In many cases, it was envisaged all three elements of the new WCA would be covered in a single appointment with a health care professional working for Atos Origin Medical Services (MS), the company which originally contracted with the DWP to deliver these assessments. However, the WFHRAt was suspended for a two-year period beginning July 19, 2010; ongoing external evaluation of it had shown mixed results, and the suspension affords an opportunity for the DWP to reconsider the assessment's purpose and delivery and frees up capacity to deal with the "migration" of existing incapacity benefits customers to ESA or a more appropriate benefit (typically JSA). The regs dealing with it were revoked from June 1, 2011.

Schedule 2 deals with the LCWA and establishing limited capability for work: the core element of entitlement to ESA. The vast majority of claimants for ESA will be subject to this first element of the new WCA through a face to face assessment with a trained healthcare professional testing the claimant against the activities and descriptors in the Schedule, in the light of the material in the claimant's questionnaire, any evidence from the GP and the professional's examination. Assessment will take place much earlier than in an equivalent claim for IB.

The Government's view remains that the overwhelming majority of customers are capable of some work, given the right support. The approach is designed to treat people in line with their capabilities, instead of making assumptions based on their condition. Hence, because the ESA tests are designed to assess which claimants can benefit from the help towards work afforded by work-related activity, to "write off" from the chance of work as few people as possible, very few groups are exempt from the LCWA: the terminally ill; those receiving treatment by way of intravenous, intraperitoneal or intrathecal chemotherapy; such of those recovering from such treatment as the Secretary of State is satisfied should be treated as having limited capability for work; (from March 28, 2011) those likely to receive such treatment in the next six months; those excluded or prevented from working as a carrier, or having been in contact with a case of relevant disease (food poisoning, infectious or notifiable diseases covered by a variety of public health enactments); pregnant women at a certain stage in pregnancy or where there is a serious risk of damage to their or their unborn child's health if they do not refrain from work (reg.20); and (from March 28, 2011) those who would be found to have limited capability for work-related activity under any of the descriptors in paras 15 and 16 of the revised Sch.3. Hospital inpatients (reg.25) and persons undergoing or recovering from certain regular treatments (e.g. plasmapheresis, radio therapy, dialysis, parenteral nutrition) for at least two days a week (reg.26) are also treated as having limited capability for work. All such persons are exempt from the information gathering requirements with respect to the LCWA (reg.21(3)).

Decision-makers have discretion in respect of all claimants on whether it is necessary in their case to complete the questionnaire or require more information than is provided by the claimant's doctor under the Medical Evidence Regs (reg.21(2)). Whether someone is required to undergo a medical examination is also a matter of decision-maker discretion (reg.23). Typically, most claimants will have to both complete the questionnaire (form ESA50) and undergo medical examination, usually at a medical examination centre, but sometimes in the claimant's home. Failure to do so, without good cause, is as usual sanctioned by treating the person as not having limited capability for work, thus denying benefit (regs 22–24). The Work Capability Assessment is a face-to-face meeting, lasting between 75 and 90 minutes, depending on whether just two or (originally) all three elements of the WCA are carried out. It explores how the claimant's illness or disability affects their ability to work and carry out day-to-day activity Each part of the assessment will be carried out by specially trained healthcare professionals (whether doctor or nurse) approved by the Secretary of State to assess these matters and report to the decision-maker, generally in the form of a computer-generated report.

The WRA 2007 stipulates merely that whether a person's capability for work is limited by his physical or mental condition and, if so, whether the limitation is such that it is not reasonable to require him to work is to be determined in accordance with regulations. ESA Regs, reg.19(1) elaborates that this is to be determined on the basis of a limited capability for work assessment (LCWA), that is by:

> "an assessment of the extent to which a claimant who has some specific disease or bodily or mental disablement is capable of performing the activities prescribed in Schedule 2 or is incapable by reason of such disease or bodily or mental disablement of performing those activities" (reg.19(2)).

This is familiar stuff for those who have worked with the AWT/PCA. The claimant is to be matched, in the light of all the evidence, by the decision-maker or tribunal against a reformulated range of activities and descriptors, and an appropriate "score" awarded. The threshold "score" for entitlement under the WCA remains 15 points, but as regards its computation, there are both "old" and "new" elements.

It is stressed that incapability to perform an activity must arise from a specific bodily disease or disablement, a specific mental illness or disablement, or as a direct result of treatment provided by a registered medical practitioner, for such a disease, illness or disablement (reg.19(5)). The extent of capability to perform a physical activity has, as with IB, to be assessed as if the claimant is wearing any prosthesis with which he is fitted or wearing or using any aid or appliance which is normally worn or used. In computing the score, where more than one descriptor in respect of a particular activity applies, only the highest is counted towards the total "score" (reg.19(4)). Otherwise one simply adds up the total of the particular scores in respect of each activity, whether physical or mental, to see if the threshold of 15 points is reached. If it is, or is exceeded, the claimant has established limited capability for work, grounding entitlement to the basic allowance in ESA. The matter may be determined afresh where the Secretary of State wishes to ascertain: (i) whether there has been a relevant change of circumstances in relation to the claimant's physical or mental condition; (ii) whether the previous decision was made in ignorance of, or was based on a mistake as to, some material fact; or at least three months have passed since the last decision (reg.19(7), (8)).

If the threshold score is not attained, limited capability for work has not been established, there can be no entitlement to ESA and the unsuccessful claimant (subject to retention of ESA pending appeal) will have to look for income maintenance, typically to JSA or, more rarely, IS.

9.92 *The radical revision of Schs 2 and 3, effective March 28, 2011:* Given the careful preparatory work in devising the WCA, which came into being on October 27, 2008, it might be thought surprising that it was thought necessary to wholly replace Schs 2 and 3 with effect from March 28, 2011, especially as the precise wording of the original ESA Regs had further been honed even before they had entered into force. In fact, the process of review began very early in the operative life of the WCA, with a DWP-led review being announced in the December 2008 White Paper, *Raising*

Expectations (Cm.7506). It was thought important that the WCA continued to "provide an up-to-date accurate assessment of a person's functional capability for work and work related activity" (Secretary of State's Statement in accordance with s.174(2) of the SSAA 1992). Led by officials in the DWP, the review began in March 2009, a mere six months after the introduction of ESA. The review, however, also involved representatives of stakeholder groups and employers, experts from the fields of physical, mental and occupational health, and a member of the Social Security Advisory Committee attending in her personal capacity. This Departmental-led review (hereinafter "*Review*") reported in October 2009 and its report can be found online at *http://www.dwp.gov.uk/docs/work-capability-assessment-review.pdf.*

Representations were made by disability groups that some of the recommendations from that the *Review* did not adequately address their concerns. Consequently, the Secretary of State asked the Chief Medical Adviser (CMA) to undertake a further technical review, part of which involved work with representatives of those specialist disability groups which had been part of the group conducting the internal *Review*. This CMA honing with stakeholders (hereinafter "*CMA*") was published in March 2010 and can be found online as an addendum to the *Review* at *http://www.dwp.gov.uk/docs/work-capability-assessment-review.pdf.* This technical review, led by the CMA and taking into account the work done by the *Review* group, saw work undertaken by medical experts within the DWP "with the aim of ensuring that the recommendations of the internal review would lead to a revised WCA which would more accurately and fairly assess an individual's capability for work and thus their entitlement to benefits" (*CMA*, p.3). That technical review proposed a number of changes to the proposals of the internal review and those changes were accepted by the Secretary of State and embodied in the amending Regulations which inserted the new Schedules now under consideration. The draft amending Regulations were also the subject of consideration and report by the SSAC. Its unsupportive Report and recommendations as regards the new Schedules was considered by the Secretary of State. The SSAC Report, material submitted to it by the DWP explaining the draft Regulations, and the Secretary of State's reasons for rejecting the SSAC recommendations (hereinafter "*SSAC Report*") can be found online at *http://www.official-documents.gov.uk/document/other/9780108509698/9780108509698.pdf*).

This DWP-led review and subsequent CMA honing was distinct from the independent annual review envisaged by the WRA 2007 s.10. The first of those five statutory reviews was undertaken by Professor Michael Harrington and published in November 2010.

The DWP-led *Review* saw ESA as an "active benefit", a temporary benefit for the **9.93**
majority of claimants, providing support and encouragement to assist the journey of an individual from an ESA claimant into the workplace. The policy behind ESA is premised on a large body of research evidence (described by Harrington as "incontrovertible") which shows both that work is generally good for physical and mental health and well-being and also the converse—that there is a strong association between worklessness and ill-health, with prolonged time away from work rendering recovery and return to work progressively less likely. The *Review* considered that the WCA was generally working well:

> "There was broad consensus amongst the experts that the WCA was performing according to design. The descriptors used in the WCA were indeed reliably identifying individuals according to capability" (*Review*, para.4.1, p.16).

Despite involvement of stakeholders in that process it is clear that this view not altogether shared by them. The SSAC commented:

> "We recognise that any assessment of benefit entitlement that necessarily involves testing and scoring an individual's functional capabilities is going to be both potentially challenging and controversial. As many of our respondents have pointed out, the assessment process, and the experience of the benefit claimant, can be stressful and frustrating. We have also noted the concern expressed

by respondents about the Department's conclusions with regard to the internal review of the WCA, and the manner in which they have been presented with regard to the current proposals. It appears to us that there is a disagreement of substance between the Department and the external stakeholders who participated in the review as to whether the WCA in its present form could be said to be working satisfactorily" (*SSAC Report*, para.6.2).

In particular, the SSAC thought that the view that the WCA was not working well was supported by the high rate of success on appeal (some 40 per cent of appeals are upheld) (*SSAC Report*, para.4.10). Harrington also found that the WCA:

> "is not working as well as it should. There are clear and consistent criticisms of the whole system and much negativity surrounding the process. There is strong evidence that the system can be impersonal and mechanistic, that the process lacks transparency and that a lack of communication between the various parties involved contributes to poor decision making and a high rate of appeals".

He did not, however, consider the system as "broken or beyond repair", and proposed a substantial series of recommendations to improve its effectiveness—all of which have been accepted by the Government—which would have a positive impact on the WCA process "making it fairer and more effective, changing perceptions so the WCA is seen as a positive first step towards work, and reducing the rate on appeals". He noted that more subjective conditions such as mental health and fluctuating conditions were difficult to assess so that "some of the descriptors used in the assessment may not adequately measure or reflect the full impact of such conditions on the individual's capability for work". He recommended for the second WRA 2007 s.10 review further work on the descriptors, particularly in assessing fluctuating conditions and, possibly, generalised pain. Harrington established a review group (composed of Mind, Mencap and the National Autistic Society to look in detail at the mental, intellectual and cognitive descriptors, to make recommendations to him about any refinements to the descriptors as a basis for his consideration of recommendations to be made to Ministers early in 2011. Like Harrington, the judicial review decision of the Upper Tribunal (AAC) in *MM & DM v SSWP* [2013] UKUT 259; [2016] AACR 11 also called for amendment of the testing procedures in mental health cases so as to increase the gathering of further medical evidence. See further the annotation to reg. 21, above, on the judicial review challenge under the Equality Act 2010 with respect to aspects of the decision-making process. The January 2013 changes do not respond to these pressures, however, but are rather the governmental response to a number of Upper Tribunal decisions seen as thwarting the policy intention behind the statutory provisions.

9.94 The substantial redrawing of Schs 2 and 3 effective from March 28, 2011 was designed to fulfil a number of aims or objectives:

- Removing unnecessary complexities and overlaps in order to simplify the descriptors, to remove inappropriate double counting and to ensure ease of administration and greater transparency for the claimant.
- Expanding the support group in relation to certain mental function and communication problems.
- Improving the assessment of fluctuating conditions by ensuring that the effects of exhaustion and discomfort are recognised.
- Taking greater account of the effects of adaptations and aids in improving an individual's function so as more accurately to identify those lacking the capability to work rather than simply assuming lack of capability merely because of a particular functional impairment.

It was expected that the changes to the LCWA would increase by some five per cent the number of new claims not eligible for ESA, but that the revisions to the LCWRA would slightly increase the percentage of successful claims allocated to the support group *(Review*, para.5.2). The DWP-led review group tested the proposed new activities and descriptors through a detailed analysis of ESA cases. That analysis:

> "revealed that in the vast majority of cases experts thought that the new descriptors would result in appropriate changes in the entitlement decision. The descriptors were thought to be functioning as anticipated and providing a more concise and clearer assessment. The re-focusing of the physical function areas better reflect the activities most applicable to the workplace. The mental function descriptors were found to be clearer and consequently minimised double scoring in addition to providing improved clarity.
>
> The small number of cases that members felt would be inappropriately assessed resulted in further minor refinements of the descriptors" (*Review*, para.5.4).

The *Review* considered that while the existing WCA was working well, the wholesale revision effected would represent "a more robust and accurate evaluation of limited capability for work", because it was founded on recent experience with ESA, simplifying the LCWA, reflecting reasonable adaptation of the disabled to their disability and, because of the Disability Discrimination Act (now the Equality Act 2010), of the reasonable adjustment of workplaces and further consideration of the necessary functions of the modern workplace (*Review*, para.5.5).

The SSAC, in contrast was less sanguine, both about the original WCA and the proposed revisions to it. It saw the WCA as rigid and unnecessarily prescriptive, encouraging a focus on the claimant's specific condition or disability covered by the descriptors, rather than looking at their capability for work, and adaptation to their disability, holistically. A functional assessment cannot easily measure the significance of the many factors which in reality determine capability for work. It regarded the result of the WCA as essentially an expression of the judgment and opinion of the assessor, albeit something based on professional knowledge, training, experience and observation. It considered that some of the streamlining in the proposed new Schedules had removed some of the assessment's necessary subtleties without enhancing its relevance to the real world. It thought that theoretical work capability had not enabled significant numbers to move into work and called for a cost-benefit analysis of the end-to-end process of assessing an ESA claimant where in reality what was determined was not "benefit or work" but rather which out-of-work benefit (ESA or JSA) was the more appropriate. It reported:

> "a widespread perception that, overall, rather than simplifying, streamlining and refining the test, these amendments will make it harder in practice for claimants to demonstrate that they have limited capacity for work or work related activity" (*SSAC Report*, para.4.3).

While it welcomed some of the changes (e.g. the extension of the "deemed" limited capability for work categories), the SSAC recommended that the DWP not proceed with the revisions to the Schs until these had been considered in the light of Harrington and the experience of the trial of the migration of IB claimants to ESA (*SSAC Report*, para.7.3).

In February 2011, having considered Harrington, the Secretary of State declined to do so. The amending Regulations were a carefully-crafted package following a thorough, holistic DWP-led review and CMA honing. The WCA would remain subject to ongoing review, but the Government must retain freedom to implement changes when it considers them necessary to improve the assessment without always awaiting the outcome of the next stage of the review process. (*SSAC Report*, Secretary of State's Response, para.24). The DWP Explanatory Memorandum to the SSAC on the amending Regulations indicated that it was expected that the changes to the mental, cognitive and intellectual function descriptors would have a minimal impact on the disallowance rate (para.4.6), but that overall the changes both to physical and mental descriptors would increase by five per cent the number of claimants being found capable of work (para.4.9). Changes to the LCWRA assessment would increase the numbers in the support group from 6.4 to 6.9 per cent (para.4.9).

The revised Schedules thus appear centrally as the product of the internal *Review* and *CMA* honing, rather than Harrington. The process whereby they came into being has been set out at some length, not only as background. The view taken in this commentary is that, while decision-makers and tribunals must focus on the wording of the Schedules, light can be thrown on particular activities and descriptors both by consideration of the reports that led to them and by consideration, where appropriate, of Upper Tribunal and other court decisions on the predecessors of the current WCA; the AWT/PCA from the incapacity benefits regime and from the pre-March 28, 2011 version of the WCA (see pp.1080–1114, paras 9.457–9.489).

The second Harrington report was published in November 2011: *An Independent Review of the Work Capability Assessment – year two*. This reported that "The WCA has, in my view, noticeably changed for the better. However there is still further to go" (p.7 para.5). The recommendations in the second report were aimed at improving the fairness and effectiveness of the assessment by better communications and sharing of information between all parts of the system, increasing and improving the transparency of the assessment, ensuring quality decisions were made and monitoring the impact of recommendations from the Independent Reviews. For the Government's Response, see Cm 8229 (also November 2011).

A year later the picture was very much the same. The third Harrington report was published in November 2012: *An Independent Review of the Work Capability Assessment – year three*. It reported that "real progress has been made but the pace and scope of the improvements has been slower than the Review would have hoped" (p.8 para. 6). The main areas where further changes were needed were continuing to improve communications with claimants and within DWP Operations, improve the face-to-face assessment and establishing quality dialogue between DWP and First-tier Tribunals. In addition, Harrington advocated keeping the Decision Maker central to the assessment process (and providing them with all the further documentary evidence they need to get the decision "right first time") and stressed the need to continually monitor changes to the WCA and to complete work that was under way on the descriptors. For the Government's Response, see Cm 8474 (also November 2012).

A number of relatively minor changes were made on October 29, 2013 to clarify the drafting of the descriptors and to align the Schedules in these Regulations with those in the ESA Regulations 2013 applicable to "new style" ESA (on which see Part XIII of this volume).

Dr Paul Litchfield conducted the final two reviews. His first was *An Independent Review of the Work Capability Assessment – year four* (December 2013). Dr Litchfield acknowledged at the outset that "the length and complexity of the process contributes to dissatisfaction and negative perceptions surrounding the assessment. People need to feel that they are being treated fairly when dealing with an organisation and it is their perception that drives attitudes and behaviours more than any objective assessment of what has happened" (p.7 para.3). On the WCA itself, he recommended that the DWP review its use of WCA scores, place less emphasis on the number attained and simply use the calculation to determine whether the threshold for benefit has been reached. Further recommendations were designed to improve objectivity, improve decision making and simplify the process. Other changes were suggested with a view to addressing the needs of claimants with mental health conditions. The Government did not publish its response until March 2014 (Cm 8843).

The last report was published in November 2014: *An Independent Review of the Work Capability Assessment – year five* (for the Government's Response see Cm 9014, February 2015). This fifth report contained a total of 33 further recommendations. The report recognised the difficulties created by the frequent changes to the WCA, noted the marked increase in the proportion of claimants being allocated to the support group and yet again emphasised the need to address negative perceptions of the WCA and to improve decision-making standards. The importance of meeting the needs of claimants with mental health problems and/or learning disabilities was also reiterated. The report also set out a number of principles which it recommended should be taken into account it was decided to undertake a fundamental redesign of the WCA, as had been recommended by the House of Commons Work and Pensions Committee in its report *Employment and Support Allowance and Work Capability Assessments* (HC 302, 2014).

Meanwhile the HC Public Accounts Committee has noted how the DWP has increasingly used third-party contractors to provide health and disability assessments *Contracted out health and disability assessments*, 33rd Report of 2015–16, HC 727). In 2005, the Department awarded a contract to Atos Healthcare (Atos) for Incapacity Benefit and, from 2008, ESA assessments. After Atos requested to exit the ESA contract early, the Centre for Health and Disability Assessments (CHDA), a wholly-owned subsidiary within MAXIMUS, took over ESA assessments from March 2015. The Committee noted that the DWP and its contractors have reduced the backlogs that previously existed; outstanding ESA assessments fell from 724,000 in early 2014 to 410,000 in August 2015. However, the Committee also considered that contractors' performance still does not meet claimants', the Department's and taxpayers' expectations, in particular with continuing concerns about the quality of assessments. Thus ESA assessments still take on average 23 weeks. In addition, a significant proportion of the assessment reports sampled by contractors (ranging from 7 per cent to 20 per cent) do not meet the contractual standard required and yet the DWP only returns less than 1 per cent of all assessment reports to contractors because they cannot be used to make a decision. As the DWP increases the number of assessments to be completed by contractors, the Committee states it must learn from past experience to ensure contractors are set challenging but realistic targets against which they are held to account. In addition, the Committee considered the DWP also needs to develop a competitive market for health and disability assessments to ensure that there are sufficient credible bidders for contracts as they come up for renewal.

For the latest and comprehensive Parliamentary report, see HC Work and Pensions Committee, *PIP and ESA Assessments*, Seventh Report of Session 2017-19 (HC 829, February 2018) and *PIP and ESA Assessments: claimant experiences*, Fourth Report of Session 2017-19 (HC 355, January 2018); the Government's response has been published by the Committee as its Eighth Special Report, *PIP and ESA assessments: Government Response to the Committee's Seventh Report of 2017–19*.

The structure of the current Sch.2: As with its predecessor, Sch.2 has two Parts. Part **9.95**
I deals with physical disabilities. Part II covers the mental, cognitive and intellectual function assessment.

Part I (physical disabilities) now contains only ten activities, rather than the eleven in the original Sch.2. They cover: mobilising; standing and sitting; reaching; picking up and moving or transferring by the use of the upper body and arms; manual dexterity; making oneself understood; understanding communication; navigation and maintaining safety; continence (absence or loss of control) other than enuresis; and consciousness during waking moments. The coverage and formulation of the activities and descriptors in the Schedule very much reflects the favoured principle of taking into account adaptations to condition and the use of suitable aids (e.g. walking stick, manual wheelchair, guide dog). This is on the basis that by accounting for any aids or adaptations which an individual may successfully and reasonably use to mitigate the disabling impact of their condition, their actual capability can the better be determined, and was thought to be consistent with the principle that as few people should be written off from re-engagement with work as possible merely because of their condition (*Review*, para.3.2). "Bending or kneeling" (Activity 3 in the original Sch.2) has been dropped. It was considered that activities 1–3 in the original Sch.2 (walking; standing and sitting; bending or kneeling) provided a significant level of overlap, whereby an individual (e.g. a wheelchair user) could score in each activity for what was in the modern workplace essentially the same disability, thus affording an inaccurate assessment of the individual's true level of functional limitation. "Bending or kneeling" was seen as:

> "an unnecessary requirement for the workplace. This is highlighted by the fact that wheelchair users who may be capable of work, may also be unable to bend or kneel. Changes to the [other] two activities [walking/mobilising; standing and sitting] mean that Bending or Kneeling is redundant as an activity. The removal of this activity is also in line with active encouragement in the workplace not to bend forward when lifting for health and safety reasons" (*Review*, para.4.3.1, p.19).

Activity 10 of the original Sch.2 (continence other than enuresis) has been shortened and simplified and is now Activity 9 in the new Sch.2.

Part II of Sch.2 (mental, cognitive and intellectual function assessment) contains seven activities rather than the ten in the original WCA. They cover: learning tasks; awareness of everyday hazards; initiating and completing personal action; coping with change; getting about; coping with social engagement due to cognitive impairment or mental disorder; appropriateness of behaviour with other people, due to cognitive impairment or mental disorder. It was thought that this revision and reduction removed unnecessary complexities and overlaps.

However, the days of the WCA now appear to be numbered. In March 2023 a Government White Paper announced that the WCA would be abolished, as would the concepts of LCW and LCWRA. Instead, a new income-related 'health element' will be available under the universal credit scheme for claimants who receive PIP. The proposed reforms will be rolled out to new claims only "from no earlier than 2026/27" (see *DWP, Transforming Support: The Health and Disability White Paper* (March 2023) ch.4 para.156).

II. The importance of the amendments effected on January 28, 2013

9.96 As reg.2 of the amending instrument makes clear (see para.9.614, below), these apply to all claims made on or after January 28, 2013 and to most decisions made on or after that date, whether the claim was made before that date or not. For a six month period, however, some cases where questionnaires were sent out before that date remained subject to the unamended regime, on which see the 2012/13 edition of this volume.

The amendments relevant to the application of this Schedule concern the assessment process (reg.19(4), (5)); the wording of activities 1, 6, 7, 8, 9; and descriptors 2(b), (c), 5(d), 9(b) and 15(a).

As regards the assessment process, reg.19(4) now provides that in assessing someone's capability to perform the activities in Pt 1 of this Schedule (physical disabilities) the person is to be assessed as if fitted with or wearing any prosthesis with which that person is normally fitted or normally wears, or, as the case may be, wearing or using any aid or appliance which is normally, or could reasonably be expected to be, worn or used. In addition, reg.19(5) brings in the requirement—familiar from the IB regime—that Pt 1 of this Schedule (physical disabilities) must be linked to incapability arising from a specific bodily disease or disablement or as a direct result of treatment provided by a registered medical practitioner for such a disease or disablement. Similarly it introduces the requirement that Pt 2 of this Schedule (mental, cognitive and intellectual function assessment) must be linked to incapability arising from a specific mental illness or disablement or as a direct result of treatment provided by a registered medical practitioner for such an illness or disablement. Under the previous wording of the paragraph (still applicable to some cases after January 28, 2013—see reg.2 of the amending instrument, below, para.9.614), there was no such link (*KP* v *SSWP (ESA)* [2011] UKUT 216 (AAC); *KN* v *SSWP (ESA)* [2011] UKUT 229 (AAC); *RM* v *SSWP (ESA)* [2011] UKUT 454 (AAC); *AH* v *SSWP (ESA)* [2011] UKUT 333 (AAC)).

The changes to particular activities and descriptors are reflected in the commentary to each of them.

III Order of treatment in this commentary

9.97 In the nature of things, this is a lengthy annotation to a Schedule which lies at the heart of determining the key question whether a claimant for ESA has limited capability for work. It aims to identify and highlight key issues and concerns and to indicate which features of a burgeoning case law on the AWT/PCA and the original WCA remain of significance and assistance: (a) in approaching what is in essence a similar task to those earlier regimes (matching a claimant's health condition to a range of activities and descriptors and assigning a score); and (b) more specifically in interpreting and applying any similarly worded terms of the activities and descriptors in the revised LCWA. The commentary is sub-divided as follows:

[A] Approaching the interpretation of the Schedule as a whole.
[B] Interpreting specific activities and descriptors: Pt I: physical disabilities.
[C] Approaching Pt II: mental, cognitive and intellectual function assessment.

[A] Approaching the interpretation of the Schedule as a whole

9.98 *Evidence and attention to detail:* Decision-makers must pay very close attention to the precise wording of the activities and descriptors and to the matter of appropriate evidence to ground their findings (*CSIB/12/96*). Cases must be decided in the light of the totality of the evidence, medical or otherwise, including that from the claimant (*CIB/15663/1996*). His evidence does not require corroboration unless self-contradictory or improbable (*R(I) 2/51*). Differing medical opinions and reports must carefully be appraised, without rigid preconceptions on whether the report of the examining health professional is always to be preferred as more disinterested and informed than that of the claimant's GP or consultant, or vice versa (contrast *CIB/13039/1996* and *CIB/3968/1996* with *CIB/17257/1996*; *CW v SSWP (ESA)* [2011] UKUT 386 (AAC), para.24). Both types of evidence can, from different perspectives, prove valuable (*CIB/17257/1996*; *CIB/21/2002*). A tribunal is not *bound to* decide in the same way as any particular doctor certifies; when faced with a conflict of medical opinion, they are at liberty to prefer, giving reasons, one view rather than another (*R(S) 1/53*; *CSIB/684/1997*; *CSIB/848/1997*; *CIB/309/1997*; *R. v Social Security Commissioner Ex p. Dobie* (QBD, October 26, 1999)—but cf. *CIB/17257/1996*). But that does not warrant underestimating a DWPMS personal capability assessment report, which is based on a more intensive and detailed clinical examination and history-taking than the invalidity benefit system (*CIB/15663/1996*). To prefer a DWPMS doctor's report on the grounds that it is more detailed is not, as such, irrational (*R. v Social Security Commissioner Ex p. Dobie*, QBD (October 26, 1999)). A tribunal should not reject a claimant's appeal on the basis that he was "not a reliable or credible witness" without giving reasons for that finding (*CSIB/459/1997*). It should be made clear that the claimant's evidence has been considered, what account has been taken of it, and, if rejected, why it has been rejected (*CIB/309/1997*; *CW v SSWP (ESA)* [2011] UKUT 386 (AAC), para.24). Nor should a tribunal simply record acceptance of the DWPMS doctor's findings; rather it should make and record its own findings on the descriptors (*CSIB/459/1997*; *CIB/4232/2007*). The correct approach is to weigh all the evidence in the context of the case (*CIB/3620/1998*); *CIB/2308/2001*, para.20; *FR v SSWP (ESA)* [2015] UKUT 151 (AAC), paras 9–12). In *CIB/3074/2003* Commissioner Bano allowed the claimant's appeal because the tribunal had dismissed the appeal "on the basis of a formulaic endorsement of the examining medical practitioner's report", rather than looking at it in the light of its nature and the evidence as a whole. Although a tribunal cannot conduct a physical examination of the claimant, it can use all its senses, including ocular observation of the claimant during the hearing, when considering whether the LCWA is satisfied (*R1/01(IB) (T)*; *R4/99 (IB)*) and a tribunal medical member can properly look at x-rays put in evidence (*R(IB) 2/06*). Getting a claimant to roll up his trouser leg so that the tribunal could ascertain whether he had muscle wastage was impermissible (*MA v SSWP (ESA)* [2015] UKUT 290 (AAC), paras 14-19). Tribunals should also consider carefully evidence that the medical examination was perfunctory. Where a claimant criticises as inadequate a WCA examination, it would, however, be extremely unusual to use in such a case the tribunal's power to exclude otherwise admissible evidence on the basis that its admission would be unfair; but where, as usual, the report of that examination is admitted, questions about the adequacy of the report and the examination are relevant to the weight that the tribunal should accord to the report (*JM v SSWP (IB)* [2010] UKUT 386 (AAC), paras 18, 19). Equally, where the health practitioner's report disputes the claimant's account of his disabilities in his questionnaire, natural justice requires that tribunals hear the claimant's oral evidence about his condition, before deciding which account to prefer (*CIB/5586/1999*). Tribunals should be wary of adviser/representative revision of the picture painted by the claimant's questionnaire answers and the health professional's report, and should look for supporting evidence where such statements differ significantly from the claimant's original own assessment of his or her condition (*CIB/2913/2001*).

The issue of the claimant's credibility arose in *KN v SSWP (ESA)* [2016] UKUT 521 (AAC). Judge Gray held that the fact that a claimant did not make a complaint to the organisation responsible for the HCP did not undermine his or her credibility if the report and/or examination is subsequently criticised on any appeal: "There is no legal requirement for a complaint to be made in tandem with an appeal, and it seems to me wholly wrong to use the absence of such a complaint as a significant credibility pointer" (at para.24).

Now that assessments are carried out by a wider range of HCPs, consideration has been given to the weight that should be placed on their evidence, particularly in mental health cases, where the particular experience of the HCP lies in a non-mental health field.

In *(1) ST, (2) GF v SSWP (ESA)* [2014] UKUT 547 (AAC); [2015] AACR 23, a panel of three Upper Tribunal judges categorically rejected Judge Mark's comments in *JH v SSWP (ESA)* [2013] UKUT 269 (AAC), para.22—which it saw as *obiter*—as

> "wrong if and to the extent that they purport to create a rule of law or starting point that observations on mental health descriptors by HCP physiotherapists are of no probative value whatsoever or are highly likely or likely to have little probative value and thus should be accorded no or little weight by the decision maker and the First-tier tribunal" (para.33).

Instead the proper approach is that the probative value of an HCP physiotherapist's report is a matter for the decision maker or tribunal dealing with the case, just as it is with other reports and evidence.

The panel so held, firstly, because the legislation makes no distinction between an HCP's ability to deal with mental health descriptors as opposed to physical ones. It merely requires approval by the Secretary of State and registration with the appropriate regulatory body. So any such rule as Judge Mark's would frustrate the statutory framework (para.34). The panel's second rationale noted the difference between the LCW assessment (how a condition affects the claimant's functional capacity) and "a medical examination carried out as part of a process of diagnosis and treatment" (para.35), a distinction acknowledged in Professor Harrington's *First Review* of the ESA process. The panel thus considered that the medical examination carried out by a HCP for the LCW did not require that HCP to be a medical specialist in all the physical and mental problems that might be exhibited by a particular claimant. To require the HCP to be such a specialist "would create insurmountable problems for the assessment process" since many claimants have a variety of problems which might then require assessment in a particular case by several HCPs rather than one (para.35).

What is required, however, is that the HCP have an informed understanding of the claimant's medical conditions and the difficulties flowing from them. This requires adequate training and supervision. The panel had received detailed information on the current training process (see paras 11-19)—something not available to Judge Mark in *JH*—and, while not commenting on that programme, did observe that none of the independent reviews of the ESA assessment process had criticised the performance of physiotherapists relative to HCPs from other disciplines and that training for HCPs on mental health problems was being reviewed with the aim of increasing the knowledge of all HCPs (para.36).

There is, therefore, no need for a tribunal to adjourn for further particulars on the qualifications of the HCP in a particular case. The specialist tribunal with its medical member must "make its own findings having regard to all the evidence before it" (para.37). The correct starting point was that identified by Judge Ovey in an incapacity benefit appeal (*JF v SSWP (IB)* [2011] UKUT 385 (AAC) at para.25:

> "...the report is prepared by an HCP who has been trained (whether as part of the training as an HCP or through other training) at least to the level thought appropriate by the Department of Work and Pensions for carrying out examinations where mental health issues are raised. In other words the selection and training procedures ought to have produced an HCP who can conduct a mental health examination competently. It follows that evidence that the HCP has not undergone separate specialist training should not of itself have any effect on the weight which the tribunal attaches to the report..."

The panel held that the weight to be accorded to any report "addressing the functional impact of any medical condition on a claimant" is a matter for the specialist tribunal which should consider

> "(a) the level of the author's expertise (for example, an HCP or a consultant psychiatrist) and (b) the knowledge of the claimant possessed by the author (for example, knowledge gained from a one-off assessment or that gained as a treating clinician). Additionally the date of the evidence, its comprehensiveness, and its relevance to the issues the tribunal has to determine are also key matters for the tribunal to consider. Importantly the tribunal should explain its reasoning for attaching weight to one type or piece of evidence rather than to another" (para.38 of *ST/GF*).

In *ST* v *SSWP (ESA)* [2012] UKUT 469 (AAC), Judge Wright held that with respect to a decision to supersede an award of benefit on the basis of a new work capability assessment, natural justice and the right to a fair trial under art.6(1) ECHR required that the Secretary of State make available to the tribunal the previous work capability assessment (ESA85). In *CA* v *SSWP (ESA)* [2013] UKUT 442 (AAC), Judge Ward stated that it was likely to be an exceptional case in which a change in descriptors would exempt the Secretary of State from that duty, since a previous WCA assessment, particularly one close in time and where the condition in question is not said to be changing can prove of evidential value and assist the tribunal to assess the robustness of the latest assessment at issue, by giving a picture of the claimant's history and considering the descriptors thought by the previous HCP then to be relevant. It is ultimately for the tribunal what to make of that previous assessment. The scope and extent of the obligation of Secretary of State for Work and Pensions to produce previous medical reports, or records of them, in every case has now been considered by a three-judge panel of the Upper Tribunal in *FN v SSWP (SA)* [2015] UKUT 670 (AAC); [2016] AACR 24 (formerly *CSE/422/2013*, *CSE/435/2013* and *CSE/19/2014*). The panel broadly agreed with decisions such as *JC v DSD (IB)* [2011] NICom 177; [2014] AACR 30 and also both *ST v SSWP (ESA)* [2012] UKUT 469 (AAC) and *AM v SSWP (ESA)* [2013] UKUT 458 (AAC). The three-judge panel stressed that the previous adjudication history and associated evidence is not *always* relevant to an employment and support allowance appeal and that, even if the Secretary of State has not produced all the information and evidence that he should have produced with his response to an appeal, it does not necessarily follow that the First-tier Tribunal's decision will be wrong in law and liable to be set aside:

> "79. ... We can envisage a situation where a First-tier Tribunal considers that it has sufficient relevant evidence before it to determine the issues arising in the appeal without the requirement to call for evidence which is missing because the Secretary of State has failed in his duty to provide it.

> 80. … Our view is that the first choice for the tribunal should not be to adjourn but to get on with the task of determining the issues arising in the appeal when satisfied that it has the necessary relevant evidence before it. It might be the case that having weighed and assessed the appellant's oral evidence, the tribunal might be satisfied that the evidence is credible, should be accepted and the appeal be allowed …"

In *CA v SSWP (ESA)* [2016] UKUT 523 (AAC) the claimant had failed a previous WCA, not appealed that decision and claimed and received JSA for nine months before making a further (and again unsuccessful) ESA claim. This time she appealed the adverse WCA decision, but did not mention the previous ESA assessment. Judge Lane, dismissing the further appeal, held that the FTT had not failed in its inquisitorial duty:

> "15. Tribunals in the Social Entitlement Chamber are alert to legal and evidential matters that are relevant but which would be obscure to a layman. They are accustomed to being proactive in a way that would be foreign in other Chambers. But, as *FN* establishes, their proactivity is not boundless. A tribunal cannot pull a rabbit out of a hat unless it is given a hat to work with. The hat, in this case, is evidence from the appellant that there has been no change in their medical condition or disablement since a previous award or assessment."

See further the commentary in Vol III of this series to the Social Security and Child Support (Decisions and Appeals) Regulations 1999 (SI 1999/991) reg.6(2)(g) and (r) (Supersession of decisions) and to Tribunal Procedure (First-tier Tribunal) (Social Entitlement Chamber) Rules 2008 (SI 2008/2685) r.24(1)–(5) (Responses).

Where the claimant has complained about a medical examination and no response to that has been received by the tribunal, or any relevant medical report is not before the tribunal, it is appropriate to consider whether to adjourn., but it does not follow that it must adjourn (*SA* v *SSWP (ESA)* [2013] UKUT 616 (AAC), per Judge Mark):

> "It needs to consider all the matters in issue in the complaint, the likelihood of their being resolved or at least further illuminated by the report, the relevance of the complaints to the matters before it and the likely relevance of any possible response by ATOS in addition to any other relevant matters. Having considered all relevant matters it needs to decide whether it was better to proceed or to adjourn in order to deal with the case fairly and justly in accordance with the overriding objective in rule 2 of the Tribunal Procedure (First-tier Tribunal) (SEC) Rules 2008 (see further *MA v SoS* [2009] UKUT 221 (AAC)). It also needs to give reasons for its decision."

The computerised medical examination report is the end product of the system. In that report statements or phrases can be produced mechanically by the software, which produces relevant phrases from its memory bank, and, unless the examining health professional using it is very careful, the statements in the report may not necessarily represent actual wording chosen and typed in by him. This generates an increased risk of accidental mistakes or discrepancies being left undetected in the final product of the process. The need for careful appraisal of the computerized report has been stressed by Commissioners Howell and Williams (*CIB/511/2005*; *CIB/476/2005*; *CIB/1522/2005*; *CIB/0664/2005*; *CIB/3950/2007*; *CIB/1006/2008*). It is submitted that reports under the revised WCA ought to be scrutinized even more carefully because further glitches might have crept in during the necessary software revision undertaken in a relatively short period of time.

Section 7 of the Electronic Communications Act 2000 has no application to the computerised report form (*R(IB) 7/05*).

In *NH v SSWP (ESA)* [2014] UKUT 114 (AAC), concerns about the qualifications of the examining health care professional, a nurse, and the computerized report combined so that Judge Williams had to set aside the decision superceding entitlement which had been upheld by the tribunal:

"this report not only calls into question whether the nurse actually conducted a mental health examination as reported or even read the report she submitted before doing so but also more generally the evidential value of a report conducted or purportedly conducted by a nurse when there is no indication that the nurse had any specific qualifications to conduct that aspect of the examination. Was she aware of the importance in this case of examining the mental health issues? Was she qualified to give the advice she gave about them? If so, why is this report so deficient in that area? It also calls into question the validity of a report produced by a computer programme that allows the operator to delete the whole of the relevant parts of the report which should record results of a clinical physical examination so that there is no "supporting medical evidence" while still generating unqualified opinions about unexamined physical functions for which there is no such evidence" (para.10).

Judge Williams thought the case to be "one of the most disturbing examples of repeated failure fairly to assess the actual medical problems of an appellant that I have seen for some time. Indeed, it is disturbing enough to call aspects of the system itself into question" (para.18).

To reiterate: the first task is to decide from all the evidence in the case which descriptors apply, the second to calculate the scores. Decision-makers and tribunals must in the light of all relevant evidence identify the relevant health condition and consider carefully the full range of activities which may be impaired by it (*CIB/5797/1997*; *CIB/3589/2004*). Scoring should proceed from top to bottom, so as to properly identify the highest ranking descriptor in the range attached to the particular activity which can properly be said to apply to the claimant (*CIB/5361/1997*; reg.19(6)).

The LCWA is not a snapshot—the need for an approach characterized by "reasonableness": 9.99
The "sometimes" descriptors in the AWT/PCA were not carried over into ESA, but this merely means that there is no descriptor under which the claimant can score points simply because he is sometimes unable to perform the relevant activity. Their removal did not mean that there was no longer a need for the decision-makers to take into account whether the claimant can perform the relevant activity with some degree of repetition. That need subsists in relation to the WCA descriptors as in relation to its predecessors in the AWT/PCA (*AF v SSWP (ESA)* [2011] UKUT 61 (AAC), para.11; *AG* v *SSWP (ESA)* [2013] UKUT 77 (AAC), paras.14–18; *SAG v Department for Social Development (ESA)* [2012] AACR 6). Indeed such a requirement seems inherent in any test of capability for work designed to be attuned to the needs of the modern workplace and a level of activity an employer would expect. The Government emphasised that, like the PCA, the LCWA was not intended to be a simple snapshot. The review group whose work led to the original WCA rightly stressed that guidance to decision-makers and to the healthcare professionals involved in the assessments of capacity would indicate the factors to be taken into account in ascertaining whether a claimant can perform a particular function: ability to do it just once is not enough (the person must reliably be able to sustain or repeat the activity); distress, pain, and fatigue involved in carrying out the activity; and the detrimental effects of medication. The *Review* leading to the revised WCA commented:

"Individuals whose conditions fluctuate in an unpredictable manner may provide a more significant challenge in relation to employment as employers are less able to predict and manage their absence.

. . . [T]he WCA has afforded individuals greater opportunity to detail the variations in their condition, specifically in the questionnaire which they are asked to complete. Rather than a yes/no format, the potential responses also include 'it varies', and space is provided for the detailing of the variation.

In the course of the assessment itself, healthcare professionals take into account fluctuations which an individual may experience in their capability. The assessment seeks to identify whether an individual is capable of carrying out an activity reliably and repeatedly for the majority of the time. If an individual is unable to do so, then they are considered unable to carry out the activity at all, and will be awarded points accordingly" (para.4.10.1).

The *CMA* honing report also commented on fluctuating conditions, echoed this last point, and emphasised that:

"Guidance states that if an individual cannot complete an action safely, reliably and repeatedly they should be considered unable to complete it at all. Recognising the challenges associated with assessing fluctuating conditions, there is ongoing work which aims to enhance the training that healthcare professionals (HCPs) receive and ensure that advice in this area is comprehensive.

In recognition, however, of the importance of accurately assessing fluctuating conditions, changes have been suggested to certain descriptors where exertion is a significant component. This ensures that where an individual is unable to do something as a result of exhaustion experienced, rather than discomfort, that is captured in the assessment" (*CMA*, para.2.1).

Those changes to specific descriptors have been embodied in the revised Schedules.

But (save where embodied in specific descriptors and thus as specific legal elements) this approach is not just a matter of guidance. It is submitted that it is embodied in legal rules established by the extensive jurisprudence on approaching the very similar exercise in the PCA. The requirement is for ability to perform the specified activities with "reasonable regularity"; there must be an element of reasonableness in the approach to the question of what someone is or is not capable of doing, including consideration of his ability to perform the activities most of the time (*C1/95(IB)*; *CSIB/17/96*), so that the question becomes whether the claimant would normally be able to perform the stated activity if and when called upon to do so (*CIB/13161/96*; *CIB/13508/96*). The nature of a *specific* working environment and the matter of employability are both irrelevant (*C1/95*; *CIB/13161/96*; *CIB/13508/96*), but there is some relationship between Sch.2 and the work context. In *AS* v *SSWP (ESA)* [2013] UKUT 587 (AAC), approved by the Northern Ireland Court of Appeal in *O'Neill v Department for Communities* [2018] NICA 29 (a ruling refusing permission to appeal), Judge Wikeley considered in some depth the nature of that relationship, stating that he accepted as correctly made a concession by the Secretary of State's representative.

"that the various activities in Schedule 2 have "a connection with the workplace", albeit that the descriptors are not concerned with any one specific working environment and do not bring in wider questions of employability. This concession properly reflects the direction of policy travel as embodied in legislative change in this area. The first clue is in the change of name; Parliament has approved the shift from the "personal capability assessment" in the incapacity benefit scheme to the "work capability assessment" under the ESA regime. The second clue lies in the drafting of the various activities and individual descriptors, and in particular the amendments which took effect on March 28, 2011 (see further the Explanatory Memorandum to the draft 2011 Regulations, sent to the Social Security Advisory Committee on 13 August 2010). Thus the first three activities in the original Schedule 2 to the ESA Regulations—walking, standing and sitting, bending or kneeling—were seen as providing a high degree of overlap for e.g. wheelchair users, so providing an inaccurate assessment of an individual's true level of functional limitation in the workplace. This resulted in a radical rewriting of the first activity, transforming it from "walking" to "mobilising", the specific inclusion of the "work station" test in the second activity (standing and sitting) and the abolition of the third activity (bending or kneeling) as being both an unnecessary and undesirable requirement in the modern workplace.

It follows that the activities and descriptors in Schedule 2 do not exist in some sort of artificial or parallel universe, entirely divorced from the real world of work. They have to be applied on their own terms, but understood against the backdrop of the modern workplace. In deciding whether a particular descriptor is met, decision makers and tribunals may therefore find it helpful to consider the claimant's ability to undertake the activity in question in a range of different working contexts. However, claimants will not be awarded a defined descriptor simply because they can show that it would apply to them if they were employed to do a particular job in a specific type of working environment.

This is entirely consistent with the well-established principle that decision makers and tribunals must consider whether a claimant can perform a particular activity with a reasonable degree of repetition, sometimes referred to as [the] "reasonable regularity" principle. This principle applies to the ESA scheme just as it did to the previous incapacity benefit regime. As Upper Tribunal Judge Turnbull has explained, "if the effect of performing the activity is likely to be to disable the claimant from performing it for a substantial period, that will need to be taken into account" (see *AF v Secretary of State for Work and Pensions* (ESA) [2011] UKUT 61 at para.11, approved and followed in *SAG v Department for Social Development* (ESA) [2012] AACR 6). Judge Nicholas Paines QC has described the principle in similar terms: "it is implicit in this that a description set out in a descriptor will not fit a claimant who can only perform the relevant task exceptionally or infrequently" *(AG v Secretary of State for Work and Pensions (ESA)* [2013] UKUT 77 (at para.18).

Within the legislative scheme as a whole, this principle only makes sense in the context of the needs of a modern workplace and the level of activity that an employer attuned to the requirements of disability discrimination law can reasonably expect. Plainly, the test is not about a high-pressure working environment, e.g. a call-centre with demanding targets or a factory production line with a fast-moving conveyor belt. Equally, however, the test is not about what the person can do in their own home and entirely in their own time and at their own pace, subject to no external constraints or pressures whatsoever. If reasonable regularity is judged by the latter criterion, then the test has ceased to be a test of "whether a claimant's capability for work is limited by the claimant's physical or mental condition within regulation 19(1) of the ESA Regulations" (paras 18-21).

Judge Wikeley further held that the Court of Appeal decision in *Charlton* v *SSWP* [2009] EWCA Civ 42 (reported as *R(IB) 2/09*), which in the context of ESA Regs 2008, reg.29 required an examination of the work required, does not assist in interpreting the Sch. descriptors (para.17).

Just as the failure to carry over to the WCA the "sometimes" descriptors which featured in the AWT/PCA did not remove this requirement of a reasonable degree of repetition of performance (see *AF* v *SSWP (ESA)* [2011] UKUT 61 (AAC), para.11; *SAG v Department for Social Development (ESA)* [2012] AACR 6), so it is submitted that the incorporation into specific descriptors of an "exertion" element does not remove the overall requirement of "reasonable regularity". It must govern the overall approach to assessment.

Where variable, intermittent and sporadic conditions and their impact on earning **9.100**
capacity are involved, difficult questions of judgment in assessing incapacity for work arise where the claimant can sometimes do things but at other times not. Neither the PCA nor the LCWA were designed to be a simple "snapshot". The system aims to assess the claimant's condition over a particular period, taking account of pain and fatigue (*CIB/14587/1996*; *CIB/13161/96*; *CIB/13508/96*), fears for health and the medical advice received by the claimant (*CSIB/12/96*). The questionnaire asks about variability—the claimant's own doctor can include material on this in the MED 4, and examining health care professionals with Medical Services have been trained to conduct examinations with these issues in mind. The structure of the legislative scheme, however, produces a problem. It embodies a test based on an examination on a particular day designed to provide information on, and assessment of, a claimant over a period of time. The "normality" approach as part of "reasonable regularity" deals with one aspect of the problem: the reference in *C1/95(IB)* to a claimant being

able to accomplish a task most of the time is to be read as meaning "as and when called upon to do so". On this basis, one looks at the position which normally prevails in the period (see *CSIB/459/1997*, para.13; *CIB/911/1997*, paras 12, 13). The more difficult situation is where it is accepted that the claimant's condition is such that for certain periods he is able to cope satisfactorily with normal activities; the problem of the sporadic or intermittent condition. The problem generated significant disagreement among Commissioners on approach. The authoritative Tribunal of Commissioners' decision is *R(IB) 2/99(T)*, endorsed by a tribunal of Commissioners in Northern Ireland in *R1/02(IB) (T)*. *R(IB) 2/99* concerned the situation where a claimant suffered from a condition causing greater disability on some days than on others. The key question was whether the claimant was incapable of work under the PCA on days on which, if the days were viewed in isolation, he or she might not satisfy that test (para.2). While the Tribunal decision does not prescribe any one approach as *universally* applicable, the central thrust of the decision is to see as justified for the majority of cases, the "broad approach" typified by *CIB/6244/97* rather than the stricter "daily approach" exemplified by *CIB/13161/96* and *CIB/13508/96*. The Tribunal did not, however, find helpful the distinction drawn between "variable" and "intermittent" conditions in *CIB/6244/97*. Moreover, the Tribunal recognised that in some cases at least—generally when looking backwards over a prolonged period in the course of which the claimant has only had "short episodes of disablement" (for example, in the dwindling number of cases where the First-tier Tribunal had to consider matters "down to the date of the hearing", or in "review or overpayment cases")—something akin to the meticulous approach in *CIB/13161/96* and *CIB/13508/96* along the lines of Commissioner Jacobs' approach to intermittent conditions in *CIB/6244/1997* would be appropriate (para.17).

The practical reality is that most cases which fall to be decided by the decision-maker in the Department do not concern entitlement to benefit for a past period. Generally, a decision on the award of benefit is "forward looking" and usually made for an indefinite period. Although the decision-maker must of course consider the period from the medical examination up to the date of his decision, that decision will rarely be concerned with entitlement to benefit for a substantial period in the past. While both the "broad" and the "daily basis" approaches are each consistent with the wording of the legislation, the "broad approach" is "the only approach that can sensibly be applied by a decision-maker, making what is in effect a prospective determination for an extended period" (para.11). The Tribunal considered the broader-based approach adopted in *R(A) 2/74* to the attendance allowance issue—was there a period *throughout* which the claimant could be said to be so severely disabled as to require at night prolonged or repeated attention in connection with bodily functions? The Tribunal decided that such an approach applied equally to incapacity benefit despite its daily basis. It noted (without using those statements to support its construction of the legislation) that such an approach accorded with ministerial statements in Parliament on the introduction of the all work test (for example, that the "all work test" (now the "personal capability assessment") is not a "snapshot"). Nonetheless, the Tribunal stressed that:

> "the words of the legislation cannot be ignored . . . [I]n those cases where relevant descriptors are expressed in terms that the claimant 'cannot', rather than 'sometimes cannot', perform the activity, one should not stray too far from an arithmetical approach that considers what the claimant's abilities are 'most of the time'—the phrase used in *C1/95(IB)*. Nevertheless, we agree that all the factors mentioned by counsel [neither of whom argued for a 'daily basis' approach]—the frequency of 'bad' days, the lengths of periods of 'bad' days and of intervening periods, the severity of the claimant's disablement on both 'good' and 'bad' days and the unpredictability of 'bad' days—are relevant when applying the broad approach. Thus a person whose condition varies from day to day and who would easily satisfy the 'all work test' on three days a week and would nearly satisfy it on the other four days might well be considered to be incapable of work for the whole week. But a person who has long periods of illness separated

> by periods of remission lasting some weeks during which he or she suffers no significant disablement, might well be considered to be incapable of work during the periods of illness but not to be incapable of work during the periods of remission, even if the periods of illness are longer than the periods of remission. Each case must be judged on its merits and . . . there are some cases where a claimant can properly be regarded as incapable of work both on days when the 'all work test' is clearly satisfied and on other days in between those days and that there are other cases where the claimant can be regarded as incapable of work only on 'bad days' . . ." (para.15).

That ESA is a weekly benefit, coupled with the demise of the "sometimes" descriptors, emphasises the continued authority and propriety of this approach to the LCWA tasks. Hence, as regards forward-looking decisions, claimants whose condition is such as only to satisfy the test on four or five days a month (albeit days of severe disablement) cannot, however unpredictable those days may be, properly be regarded as satisfying the test for the whole month. It thus may be that some claimants who are unemployable nonetheless are seen as "capable of work" under the PCA or the LCWA.

In *R1/02(IB)(T)*, a Northern Ireland tribunal of Commissioners endorsed the "broad brush" approach to variable conditions in *R(IB)2/99(T)*, but also laid emphasis on para.15 of it, set out above, with one reservation. They were unhappy with the phrase "the unpredictability of 'bad' days", commenting that those who decide cases:

> "will simply have to try to determine the likely patterns of functional limitation. Uncertainty as to the possibility of a future recurrence would not of itself usually be enough to satisfy the test which must be satisfied on the balance of probability at the time of the decision maker's decision" (para.26).

Applying para.15 of *R(IB)2/99* in *CIB/2620/2000*, Commissioner Bano held that the case before him (a sufferer from dysmenorrhoea) was one of the minority of cases in which the broad approach could not be applied, one where the claimant could only be considered incapable of work on "bad days".

Making and recording decisions: Setting rigorous standards for tribunals (cf. his approach to activity 3 in *CSIB/12/96*), Commissioner Walker in *CSIB 324/97* stipulated the following approach to making and recording decisions under the "all work" test [the predecessor of the IB PCA]: 9.101

> "the best and safest practice is for a tribunal to consider and make findings of fact about, first, the disability or disabilities, be they disease or bodily or mental problems, from which an individual has been proved on the evidence to suffer. Second, they should consider and make findings of fact about which, if any of the activities set out in the Schedule, are established to be adversely affected by any of those disabilities. Thirdly, and based upon appropriate findings of fact, in the case of each and every activity the tribunal should determine which descriptor best fits the case having regard to the evidence, in their view. Finally, in the reasons, they should explain why a particular activity has been held not to be adversely affected where there was a contention that it was so affected, and why a particular descriptor has been preferred to any other contended for" (para.11).

But that best and safest practice need not necessarily always be followed. For example, where the issue is whether or not the tribunal believes the claimant on a matter fundamental and relevant, if on reasonable grounds the tribunal did not believe the claimant when he alleged that his responses in the questionnaire were not accurate, then the finding that the tribunal did not believe that he had been mistaken when providing those responses covered in reality all the disputed areas raised at the hearing, and it was not necessary to record specific findings of fact on each of the activity questions brought up by the claimant (per Northern Ireland

Chief Commissioner Martin in *C46/97(IB)*, drawing with approval on Deputy Commissioner Ramsay's decision in *CIB/16572/96*). In para.5 of *CIB/4497/1998*, Commissioner Rowland sets out useful guidance on the minimum requirements of giving reasons. He noted that:

> "a statement of reasons may be adequate even though it could be improved on and, in particular, a failure to observe the 'best and safest practice' recommended in *CSIB 324/97* . . . is not necessarily an error of law . . . What is required by way of reasoning depends very much on the circumstances of the case before the tribunal. Those challenging reasoning must explain its inadequacy and show the significance of the inadequacy."

Where a tribunal has heard oral evidence from a claimant on the effect of his/her condition, it must ensure that, when considering the report of the HCP, it makes clear what it makes of the claimant's evidence, whether that agrees or disagrees with findings in the HCP report (*YD v SSWP (IB)* [2010] UKUT 290 (AAC), para.12). In that case, Judge Turnbull also said that where the claimant has given oral evidence, a tribunal will not necessarily then have to deal with each of the mental health descriptors at issue, "although it may often be desirable to do so" (para.13).

When applying the principles to a particular case, it should be remembered that a First-tier Tribunal has an inquisitorial role (*CIB/14442/96*). It should be cautious about exercising that role when considering mental disablement (*CIB/14202/1996*, see head [C] below). Where the claimant is represented by a competent adviser (e.g. a Welfare Rights officer employed by a "responsible" local authority), a tribunal is entitled to proceed on the basis that the representative will put forward all relevant points on his client's behalf and to know the case that is being made for the client. The tribunal in such a case should not be expected to inquire further into the claimant's case; to require that would be to place an impossible administrative burden on tribunals (*CSIB/389/1998*). Overall, the tribunal's task is rendered easier now in that, because of the SSA 1998, the focus is on matters as at the date of the Secretary of State's decision rather than covering matters in the often lengthy period down to the date of the hearing (see further Vol.III: *Administration, Adjudication and the European Dimension*).

[B] Interpreting specific activities and descriptors: Pt I: physical disabilities

9.102 Note that from January 28, 2013, reg.19(4) provides that in assessing someone's capability to perform the activities in this Part of this Schedule (physical disabilities) the person is to be assessed as if fitted with or wearing any prosthesis with which that person is normally fitted or normally wears, or, as the case may be, wearing or using any aid or appliance which is normally, or could reasonably be expected to be, worn or used. In addition, reg.19(5) brings in the requirement—familiar from the IB regime—that this Part of this Schedule (physical disabilities) must be linked to incapability arising from a specific bodily disease or disablement or as a direct result of treatment provided by a registered medical practitioner for such a disease or disablement.

Activity 1: Mobilising unaided by another person with or without a walking stick, manual wheelchair or other aid if such aid is normally, or could reasonably be, worn or used: On a preliminary note, there are of course important differences in the drafting of the mobility descriptors for ESA and PIP respectively. It follows that what may appear to be inconsistent decisions relating to a particular individual's ability to mobilise under ESA and PIP regimes may be more apparent than real. However, there may be circumstances in which on the facts the FTT needs to consider whether to adjourn to have sight of the relevant PIP reports etc when deciding an ESA appeal: see e.g. *JB v SSWP (ESA)* [2017] UKUT 20 (AAC). On the potential significance of an award of PIP to an ESA appeal concerned with mobilising unaided, see *AG v SSWP (ESA)* [2017] UKUT 413 (AAC), where Judge Hemingway ruled as follows on the comparability (if any) of a PIP award and an ESA award (at para.9):

"The statutory tests are not the same. One is concerned with standing and moving and the other with mobilising which includes the possible use, where appropriate, of a manual wheelchair. Anyway a tribunal, whatever award has been made in respect of a different benefit, will be entitled to make its own decision with respect to entitlement to the benefit with which it is concerned on the appeal before it. It should not simply ignore the possible relevance of an award of a different benefit but that relevance is likely to be in relation to the possibility of there being further relevant evidence which might not be before the tribunal on the appeal and the appropriateness or otherwise of adjourning to get it."

See also *MH v SSWP (ESA)* [2018] UKUT 194 (AAC) where Judge Poole QC held that the tribunal did not act in error of law by failing to adjourn (or to record its reasons for not adjourning) for evidence about a PIP award, nor in either determining the ESA appeal without having before it that evidence or in failing directly to address the claimant's PIP award in its statement of reasons.

As Judge Rowland noted in *KB v SSWP (ESA)* [2014] UKUT 126 (AAC)

"The scheme of this legislation is clear. For each of descriptors 1(a), (c) and (d), two questions must be asked. First, can the claimant mobilise more than the relevant distance without stopping. If the answer is "no", the descriptor is satisfied. If the answer is "yes", the second limb must be considered and it must be asked whether the claimant can repeatedly mobilise the relevant distance. Again, if the answer is "no", the descriptor is satisfied. Only if the answer is "yes" to both questions is the descriptor not satisfied so that one must consider the next descriptor" (para.6).

To the same effect see *GC* v *SSWP (ESA)* [2014] UKUT 117 (AAC), applying *HD v SSWP (ESA)* [2014] UKUT 72 (AAC), a decision on Activity 1 in Sch.3.

The profound change here from the PCA/WCA is from "walking" to "mobilizing" and the removal of the "cannot walk at all" descriptor, thus encompassing adaptation to disability, namely manual wheelchair use. On wheelchair or other aids, the question is whether the wheelchair or other aid "could reasonably be worn or used" or "is normally worn or used". Until the decision of a panel of three Upper Tribunal judges in *SI v SSWP (ESA)* [2014] UKUT 308 (AAC); [2015] AACR 5, there was marked judicial disagreement on the range of factors to be taken into account in determining "reasonableness". Some judges favoured taking account of a broad range (see e.g. *M v SSWP (ESA)* [2012] UKUT 376; *NT v SSWP (ESA)* [2013] UKUT 360 (AAC); *BG v SSWP (ESA)* [2013] UKUT 504 (AAC)). Others saw as pertinent a narrower range of factors, focusing on a predominantly (and sometimes an exclusively) functional approach (see e.g. *TB v SSWP (ESA)* [2013] UKUT 408 (AAC); *AR* v *SSWP (ESA)* [2013] UKUT 417 (AAC); *MG v Department for Social Development (ESA)* [2013] NI Com 359). In *SI*, the panel of three Upper Tribunal judges held that the approach to be followed was the broader "in all the circumstances" one. The panel considered that

"if a person is in practice precluded from using an aid *for any reason and would on that ground be excluded from part of the job market*, it is unfair to assess his or her entitlement to ESA on the basis that he or she could use the aid" (para.58, emphasis supplied by commentator).

Like Judge Wikeley in *AS v SSWP (ESA)* [2013] UKUT 587 (AAC), the panel saw the LCWA as a functional one related to the circumstances of the modern workplace. Like the "cooking test" for disability benefits the WCA is a "thought experiment" so that the LCWA is applied "on the basis that the notional employer from whom the claimant might obtain employment has a modern workplace and is prepared to make reasonable adjustments in order to enable the claimant to be employed" (para.76).

Given that panel decision, it is submitted that the following factors or circumstances—identified from pre- and post-*SI* case law and *SI* itself—are ones of relevance, but this list is not advanced as an exhaustive one:—

- whether use of a wheelchair rather than crutches was medically suitable and had been suggested by medical personnel (*M v SSWP (ESA)* [2012] UKUT 376)—note, however,in contrast,, in a rare case where the claimant inappropriately used a wheelchair (on the medical evidence he did not need one), the tribunal was entitled to assess his ability to mobilize on the basis of his using the wheelchair (*MA v SSWP (ESA)* [2015] UKUT 290 (AAC), paras 23-31);
- whether or not the claimant had been referred for assessment for an NHS wheelchair as an aid to determining whether a wheelchair would normally be used by someone with the claimant's disabilities (*MG v Department for Social Development (ESA)* [2013] NI Com 359, paras 35–44; *TB v SSWP (ESA)* [2013] UKUT 408 (AAC)—although such a referral is not, however, conclusive of whether a wheelchair could in fact reasonably be used by the particular claimant (*TB*);
- whether in light of the claimant's condition and the availability of wheel chairs by local providers, the claimant would in reality have access to one (*M v SSWP (ESA)* [2012] UKUT 376).

  If a claimant does not have a wheelchair, the panel in *SI* stated that Secretary of State should produce evidence on their availability, but it also considered that this would not in practice be problematic given the Access to Work scheme or similar schemes operated by Jobcentres. The panel were mistaken in that the Access to Work scheme does not cover wheelchairs (*CS v SSWP (ESA)* [2014] UKUT 519 (AAC), para.42). But, as noted in *BG* v *SSWP (ESA)* [2013] UKUT 504 (AAC), while "it is even possible that inability to afford a wheelchair may be relevant . . . it would not normally be so given their relative cheapness and their availability from the NHS and charities where reasonably required" (para.15);
- the claimant's home environment (*M v SSWP (ESA)* [2012] UKUT 376; *BG v SSWP (ESA)* [2013] UKUT 504 (AAC)), but in *SI* the panel thought its importance in this context is lessened by the fact that a manual wheelchair could be kept available at the workplace if the home environment does not enable its storage there. It is submitted that this approach focuses too much on the workplace itself, ignoring the issue of how such a claimant would be able to get to and from the workplace, something inherent as a focus in a number of the Sch.2 descriptors and the approach in *Charlton* to regs. 29 and 35.

The mobilization test is an actual rather than hypothetical test; "if the claimant had a manual wheelchair could he or she reasonably use it". As *SI* and the above factors show, the answer to this is not purely a matter of whether, when in the wheelchair, the claimant can mobilize. But even looking at the issue from a purely functional point of view, as Judge Williams made clear in *AR v SSWP (ESA)* [2013] UKUT 417 (AAC), reasonable use of a wheelchair involves several aspects of functional ability aside from the lower limbs. While there is no longer a "rising from sitting" activity in Sch.2, one must nonetheless consider it in the context of whether a wheelchair can reasonably be used. On a functional analysis, "can a claimant reasonably be expected to use a wheelchair (including getting into and out of it) without the aid of another person if he or she cannot reasonably be expected to handle the wheelchair whilst preparing to get into it, or after getting out of it?" (para.35). Unfortunately, the standard forms (ESA50 and ESA85) do not deal with such issues because they are no longer dealt with elsewhere in the Schedules. Tribunals must be wary of falling into the trap of assuming that every claimant who can reasonably use a wheelchair must thereby be able to propel it for more than 50 metres; this is especially so in a case where there is no evidence that the claimant in question has actually used a wheelchair under his own propulsion. Likewise the mere fact of a forthcoming assessment for wheelchair use is not evidence that a wheelchair could be reasonably used (*SG v SSWP (ESA)* [2018] UKUT 34 (AAC)). Note further that a powered wheelchair cannot be an "other aid" for the purposes of Activity 1; see *WT v SSWP (ESA)* [2016] UKUT 472 (AAC);[2017] AACR 16 at para.20.

Descriptor 1(a) is now coterminous with Activity 1 in Sch.3 on LCWRA. That the activity is now mobilising renders this aspect of the LCWA more difficult to satisfy than under the original WCA. Note that "severe discomfort" in the original Sch.2, thought to be ambiguous, has been replaced by "significant discomfort" as part of the CMA honing. Specific provision is made to deal with fluctuating conditions by including "exhaustion" as factor necessitating "stopping" mobilising and by including as an alternative in each of descriptors (a), (c) and (d), the idea of "cannot repeatedly mobilise . . . within a reasonable timescale".

Insofar as the descriptors deal with "walking" as a form of mobilising, no regard should be paid to the case law on "virtually unable to walk" in DLA (*CSIB/60/1996*; *LD v SSWP* [2009] UKUT 208 (AAC)). However, that there is an award of the mobility component of DLA or PIP is pertinent as regards an ESA claim in respect of this activity in that the *evidence* underpinning the award of that component can throw light on whether the descriptors for Activity 1 are satisfied, but whether it does so or nor depends on all the circumstances (e.g. the nature and date of the award as compared to the date of the ESA decision), so that a decision to adjourn or not for the DLA papers is similarly dependent on circumstances (*DF v SSWP (ESA)* [2014] UKUT 129 (AAC); *ML v SSWP (ESA)* [2013] UKUT 174 (AAC); [2013] AACR 33; *MI v SSWP (ESA)* [2013] UKUT 447 (AAC); *GC v SSWP (ESA)* [2014] UKUT 117 (AAC) *MA v SSWP (ESA)* [2014] UKUT 185 (AAC); *JC v SSWP (ESA)* [2014] UKUT 257 (AAC)). A tribunal need not do so, however, where that evidence would add nothing of significance to the other evidence before the tribunal, for example, because the claimant's condition has fundamentally altered since that award or because that award was made in respect of a temporary condition (e.g. restrictions on walking due to an operation) no longer pertaining (*JC*, paras 4–7). A tribunal faced with evidence of a claimant's ability or lack thereof to walk to identified local shops known to the tribunal can draw appropriate inferences from the representative walking ability of the claimant having regard to what she regularly accomplished (*LD v SSWP* [2009] UKUT 208 (AAC)).

Unlike its immediate predecessor ("without stopping or severe discomfort"), descriptors (a), (c) and (d) stipulate "without stopping in order to avoid significant discomfort or exhaustion". While there is still no explicit requirement that the "significant discomfort" be caused by walking or otherwise mobilising, it would seem that since the stopping must be to avoid "severe discomfort", the reformulation may cast some doubt on the applicability to these reformulated descriptors of *AW v SSWP (ESA)* [2011] UKUT 75 (AAC), where Judge Ward held that the previous formulation covered a claimant whose discomfort was always there.

"Pausing" is to be equated with "stopping" for the purposes of descriptors (a), (c) and (d) (*GC v SSWP (ESA)* [2014] UKUT 117 (AAC), para.21; *DB v SSWP (ESA)* [2014] UKUT 471 (AAC), para.4). So that if a tribunal found that a claimant paused for a few seconds after 30 metres, it should go on to ask "why?" (*DB*, para.5). In addition a tribunal should not confine consideration merely to mobilising on foot but should also consider possible wheelchair use (*DB*, para.7).

In *DJ v SSWP (ESA)* [2016] UKUT 93 (AAC) Judge Wright was concerned with the terms of descriptor 1(b) before its amendment with effect from January 28, 2013. The issue was whether the words "unaided by another person" in that context were limited to physical aid by another person. Judge Wright concluded that no such limitation was in place as regards the pre-January 2013 version of the regulations (at para.45):

> "47. I do accept, however, the Secretary of State's argument that the aid from another person which is (and was) contemplated by activity 1 and descriptor 1(b) in Schedule 2 to the ESA Regs means active aid and does not cover passively

standing by waiting to intervene if help were to become needed. It seems to me that this flows both (a) from the word "aid" as a verb, which has clear connotations of actively providing help to the other person rather than just standing by, as well as (b) the aid given by another person which would usually be necessary to help a claimant to carry out an activity when their incapability to do so is a mental restriction. Reassuring and cajoling the claimant so as to aid them to surmount their acute anxiety about using stairs will involve talking to them and perhaps hand movements rather than just standing behind or in front of them doing and saying nothing. The latter is not, in my judgment, another person providing aid to the claimant."

However, in holding that the words "unaided by another person" in descriptor 1(a) were not limited to *physical* aid by another person, Judge Wright specifically left open the question of whether the position was different on the terms of the descriptor *after* January 28, 2013, given the amendments at the same time to reg.19(5) (see para.45).

Activity 1: descriptors (a)(ii), (c)(ii) and (d)(ii): "repeatedly mobilise [X metres] within a reasonable timescale: In *AS* v *SSWP (ESA)* [2013] UKUT 587 (AAC), Judge Wikeley considered the meaning of this phrase, which he saw as a legislative variant on the case law principle of "reasonable regularity" (para. 28). He regarded as an "excellent starting point" Judge Jacobs's decision in *AH* v *SSWP (ESA)* [2013] UKUT 118 (AAC) (noted fully in the annotation to Sch.3 activity/descriptor 1 (para.9.398)). From that case, he took two points. First of all, the need, when considering the "reasonable regularity" principle to focus on the particular wording of the descriptors so that in this context the use of "repeatedly in descriptors (a)(ii), (c)(ii) and (d)(ii) meant that the principle did not apply to limb (i) of each of those descriptors (para.27). Secondly, he took the point that it was important "where the legislative text contains irreducible terms, [to apply] the statutory language without any gloss" (para.29). Like Judge Jacobs, he took the view that it was not for the Upper Tribunal to proffer a precise definition of these terms, but considered that in this case the tribunal's findings went beyond the bounds envisaged by case law. The provisions of the Sch. had to be construed "against the background of a working environment" (see para.9.374, above). He continued:

"What might well be a reasonable timescale for the Appellant at home would not necessarily be a reasonable timescale in the workplace. The consequence of the tribunal's approach was to rob the word "repeatedly" of any real meaning, as the tribunal's findings would equally well meet a statutory test predicated on the activity in question being performed only "occasionally ... in the course of a day". Whilst I am not prepared to draw a precise line, I am satisfied that on any reasonable analysis this tribunal's conclusion was the wrong side of the line. The ability to perform a function in a working environment "repeatedly ... within a reasonable timescale" must be something more than "occasionally ... in the course of a day" (para.32).

In *CS v SSWP (ESA)* [2014] UKUT 519 (AAC), Judge White considered descriptor 1(a).He held that although the phrase "on level ground" appears only in para.(a)(i) and is absent from para.(a)(ii), "the only possible interpretation of the repeatability test is that it is on the same terms as the primary test. That is on level ground" (para.30). It is submitted that this interpretation must also govern paras (c) and (d).

A claimant's ability to mobilise *with* significant discomfort or exhaustion should be disregarded for the purposes of Activity 1: see *GL v Secretary of State for Work and Pensions (ESA)* [2015] UKUT 503 (AAC).

A tribunal's fact-finding (and the relevance to that process of a claimant's own estimate as to how far s/he can walk) was in issue in *MM v SSWP (ESA)* [2017] UKUT 236 (AAC). Judge Hemingway held that it is perfectly permissible for a tribunal to attach weight to the claimant's own estimate as to how long in terms of time (usually expressed in minutes) he/she is able to walk for. It is also permissible for a tribunal to extrapolate as to what such an estimate, if reliable, might translate into in terms of distance. However, there is no rule to say that where a time estimate is offered it has to be accepted unless there is something specific to contradict it or to suggest it is unreliable. Further, it may be appropriate for a tribunal to consider whether such an estimate is, or is not, likely to be reliable and to probe this in questioning with a claimant. There may be reason to think that time estimates as to journeys which are undertaken regularly might be more reliable than other estimates. Finally, "the tribunal was not required to make a precise finding as to exactly how many metres the claimant could mobilise for. Absolutely precise findings as to something like that will often, realistically, be simply impossible. All it was required to do was make a finding as to which category the claimant fell into as to the range of distances contained within the relevant set of descriptors" (at para.13).

Fact-finding was also an issue in *GZ v SSWP (ESA)* [2017] UKUT 447 (AAC). There the tribunal, dismissing the claimant's appeal found that she qualified for 6 points for mobilising, making the following finding: "We find that she cannot unaided by another person mobilise more than 200 metres on level ground without stopping in order to avoid significant discomfort or exhaustion, or repeatedly mobilise 200 metres within a reasonable timescale because of significant discomfort or exhaustion." Judge Mesher explained why such a finding, without defining which limb of descriptor 1(d) applied, was inadequate:

> "6. That [error of law] is in the form of the tribunal's finding of fact in the middle of paragraph 17 of the statement of reasons which adopted the terms of descriptor 1(d) without saying which of the two alternatives within the descriptor was satisfied. That in my judgment is not good enough as a finding of fact, because of the relationship of descriptor 1(d) with descriptors 1(a) and (c). If the tribunal considered that the claimant fell only within descriptor 1(d)(ii), because she could mobilise for more than 200 metres without stopping but could not achieve 200 metres repeatedly within a reasonable timescale, that would necessarily entail that she did not satisfy 1(c)(i) (because she could mobilise more than 100 metres) and would perhaps make it unlikely that she could satisfy descriptor 1(c)(ii) on the basis of not being able to mobilise 100 metres repeatedly. However, if the tribunal considered that the claimant fell within descriptor 1(d)(i), because she could not mobilise more than 200 metres without stopping, that would not as a matter of logical necessity exclude satisfaction of descriptor 1(c). Thus it might be necessary for a tribunal to explain why it chose descriptor 1(d)(i) rather than 1(c)(i). But more pertinently for the present case, if a claimant can only mobilise without stopping for some distance between 100 metres and 200 metres, that does not exclude the possibility that the claimant, while able to mobilise more than 100 metres without stopping, cannot achieve 100 metres repeatedly within a reasonable timescale and so satisfies descriptor 1(c)(ii). The same could potentially be said in relation to descriptor 1(a)(ii) and 50 metres. As a result, while it may not be necessary to the award of 6 points under descriptor 1(d) to specify which alternative is satisfied, in terms of the required underlying findings of fact on the whole activity of mobilising it is necessary in any statement of reasons to be more specific. It seems to me that there are two ways out where descriptor 1(d) is satisfied. The tribunal can identify the distance that it finds that the claimant can mobilise without stopping in order to avoid significant discomfort or exhaustion without considering the issue of repetition. There can then be a firm factual basis, allied to whatever explanation is appropriate, for not applying descriptor 1(c) or 1(a) and in particular for not applying descriptor 1(c)(ii). Alternatively, if the tribunal is unable to be so specific, it may be sufficient for it to explain that, while not sure precisely how far the claimant can mobilise beyond 100 metres without stopping, it has expressly considered descriptor 1(c)(ii) and is satisfied (and why) that the claimant can repeatedly mobilise 100 metres within a reasonable timescale. The question of what sort of range of estimates would be acceptable

would very much depend on the circumstances of particular cases. What in my judgment is plainly not sufficient is to make a finding of fact simply in the terms used in the present case and then to say nothing at all in the statement of reasons about descriptor 1(c)."

9.103 *Activity 2: standing and sitting:* The six scoring descriptors—which differentiated standing and sitting more clearly—in the original WCA have been reduced to three. This represents an amalgamation predicated on the modern workplace requiring an individual to remain at their work station long enough to do their job.

As regards descriptor (a), this looks to "without physical assistance from another person", rather than (as in the PCA) "without the help of another person", so ability to do so with encouragement from another person would preclude a score under this head. Ability only to move between one seated position and another located next to one another by using the seat or back of the chair to deliver the force necessary to move cannot score; the precluded assistance is merely "physical assistance from another person" (compare *(R(IB) 2/03*).

As regards descriptors (b) and (c), there is now no requirement that the individual can both stand and sit; being able to do one or the other for the requisite length of time will preclude scoring under descriptors (b) and (c) (*MC v SSWP (ESA)* [2012] UKUT 324 (AAC); [2013] AACR 13, paras 4, 5; *EW v SSWP (ESA)* [2013] UKUT 228 (AAC), paras 9, 10), something put beyond any doubt by the addition from January 28, 2013 of sub-para.(iii) to descriptors 2(b) and (c). There is no longer any stipulation about the type of chair (it used to be "a chair with a high back and no arms" or "an upright chair")—this was thought unnecessary given the range of adaptable chairs available and the employers' legal duty to provide one as part of the obligation to make reasonable adjustments to the workplace to accommodate persons with disabilities.

While it should be noted that in *MM v Department for Social Development (ESA)* [2014] NI Com 48 a tribunal of three Northern Ireland Commissioners disagreed with Judge Wikeley's approach in *MC* to the interpretation of Activity 2 descriptors *prior to the January 2013 amendment*, that decision is of persuasive authority only and thus, in terms of judicial precedent, ranks lower than that of Judge Wikeley in *MC* which is directly binding in Great Britain (*CC v SSWP (ESA)* [2015] UKUT 62 (AAC)).

The decision of Judge Ward in *EC v SSWP (ESA)* [2015] UKUT 618 (AAC) considers the conflict in the case law on the pre-March 2011 version of the activity 2 descriptors. Judge Ward held that there were "compelling reasons" to depart from the decision of the Northern Ireland Tribunal of Commissioners in *MM v Department for Social Development (ESA)*. In doing so, he analysed a range of materials which shed light on the issues relevant to the interpretation of the Activity 2 descriptors:

> "57. In conclusion, it seems to me that an argument based on informed interpretation, if relying on a committee report, needs to be based on its final form and to take into account other material which Parliament must be taken as having had in mind when approving the legislation. In the light of the totality of the material before me, I accept that the mischief at which the legislation was aimed, on this aspect, included ensuring that people who could remain at a workstation for the requisite period by combining sitting and standing would not get points. Seen against that background, the ambiguity in the use of the 'either … or' construction in the descriptors in activity 2 between 2011 and 2013 would fall to be resolved in accordance with Judge Wikeley's obiter views in *MT*. The Tribunal of Commissioners in *MM* did not have the advantage that I have now had, through oral submissions and subsequent written submissions, of comprehensive examination of the background materials leading up to the making of the Regulations. In those circumstances, while I have applied a test of whether there is a 'compelling reason' to depart from the decision in *MM*, I have concluded that there is. With the benefit of those fuller submissions (which it appears were not made in *MC* or *MT*

either) I conclude that a person who can remain at a workstation by a combination of sitting and standing for the requisite period is not entitled to points."

In addition, as regards descriptors (b) and (c), the meaning of "at a workstation" was considered by Judge Mitchell in *LC v SSWP (ESA)* [2015] UKUT 664 (AAC). The judge held that the First-tier Tribunal had erred in law by failing to address whether the claimant could fairly be said to have been capable of performing a job of work while remaining sat "at a workstation" in the light of her evidence that she needed to sit with one leg stretched rigidly out in front of her. Judge Mitchell concluded as follows:

> "23. I conclude, therefore, that when descriptors 2(b) and 2(c) refer to a person remaining 'at a workstation' they refer to the person being orientated towards a workstation, whether sitting or standing, in such a manner that they may fairly be described as capable of performing a job of work. I do not think I need to go any further than this in interpreting the descriptor by, for example, attempting to define a workstation. I can leave it to the good sense of tribunals, using their knowledge of everyday life and their specialist expertise, to apply that test.
> 24. If, therefore, a person needs to sit with a rigidly outstretched leg so that s/he could not fairly be said to be capable of doing a job of work at a workstation, even with the benefits supplied by an adjustable chair, this would not amount to the person remaining sat 'at a work station'.
> 25. So far as section 20 of the Equality Act 2010 (reasonable adjustments) is concerned, I see no need for tribunals to try and predict how it might operate in a particular case. Attempting to identify the content of any particular reasonable adjustment divorced from a real world case is very difficult and liable to introduce unnecessary confusion and complexity. The question of what is reasonable is informed by two sets of variables: the characteristics of the disabled person and the entity obliged to make the adjustment. What might be reasonable for a small independent trader could well differ from what is required of a well-resourced multinational corporation. Instead, tribunals should simply rely on their own knowledge and expertise in applying the descriptors by envisaging the typical workstations and adjustable chairs with which I suspect we are all familiar."

Note again the replacement of "severe discomfort", thought to be ambiguous, with "significant discomfort" as part of CMA honing, and also the inclusion in descriptors (b) and (c) of "exhaustion" and "for the majority of the time" as one aspect of dealing with fluctuating conditions and the requirement of "reasonable regularity". The degree of discomfort must be such as to require the claimant to move away from the workstation; it is not enough if it merely disrupts, even very significantly, the claimant's concentration at the workstation (*DT v SSWP (ESA)* [2013] UKUT 244 (AAC) in the context of the pre-March 28, 2011 descriptors).

"Standing" does not mean standing stock-still. The normal person (the yardstick for applying the descriptors) does not do so for any length of time. As Commissioner Lloyd-Davies stated in *R(IB) 6/04*:

> "The quasi-involuntary movements that most people make in standing for prolonged periods do not . . . count. Instead the tribunal should concentrate on how long a claimant can stand before needing or having to move around or sit down (usually because of pain in the back or legs)" (para.5).

Activity (3): reaching: this assesses a person's ability to raise their upper limbs above waist height. It also identifies those with very restricted shoulder movement. This is almost identical to the reaching Activity 4 in the original WCA, the only omission being that Activity 4 descriptor (b) ("cannot put either arm behind back as if to put on a coat or jacket"). That was thought inappropriate since, by not requiring ability to put both hands behind the back inadequately identified these limitations. Moreover, it was superfluous as this was not a required function in many workplaces. **9.104**

Descriptor (b) scores only 9, as opposed to 15 under the AWT/PCA in the IB regime. It does not involve raising the upper arm above head level (*CIB 2811/1995*). In contrast, descriptor (c) ("cannot raise either arm above head height as if to reach for something") requires that more than a minimal amount of the arm must be above head level. Reaching involves a degree of stretching, and involves being able to raise the upper arm above shoulder level and to go at least some way towards straightening the arm in moving it towards a notional object" (*CIB 2811/1995*, para.7) so that a claimant with full elbow flexion could probably achieve the task in (b) but not (c).

9.105 *Activity 4: picking up and moving or transferring by use of the upper body or arms:* this is similar to the corresponding activity in the original WCA (Activity 5). Like their immediate predecessor, the formulations avoid previous ambiguity over the meaning of "carry", and make it clear that what is covered is picking up and moving, using the upper body and arms (compare *R(IB) 5/03*). The key difference is that under the original WCA the descriptors variously referred to the use of either hand (descriptors (a) and (b)) or of both hands together (descriptor (c)). They thus assumed only persons with two hands. The Review thought this inappropriate; two hands were not necessarily required to perform the activity:

> "For example, an item may be transferred by wedging it against the body, or another limb, to achieve the same outcome. Many amputees chose not to have a prosthetic limb in order to retain the sensation of touch; however they remain able to complete the task" (para.4.3.2, p.23).

The new descriptors thus deliberately make no mention of hands thus rendering *MH v SSWP (ESA)* [2011] UKUT 492 (AAC) inapplicable here (see para.8). But as with its predecessor the wording of the activity (use of the upper body or arms) means that it is thus not sufficient only to focus on problems with arms. Problems with shoulder(s) or neck should also be taken into account (*TO'B v SSWP (ESA)* [2011] UKUT 461 (AAC)), as should the effect on a back condition (*AG v SSWP (ESA)* [2018] UKUT 137 (AAC).

This descriptor has been considered in two other cases, each dealing with whether the task can be achieved by someone with only one good arm, given that the descriptor, unlike its predecessors no longer stipulates using both hands together.

In *KH v SSWP (ESA)* [2014] UKUT 455 (AAC), Judge Mark accepted that the change in wording means that the use of both hands together is no longer essential, so that if a person could pick the box up and move it by the use of one arm and the upper body, that is by wedging it under the arm, that would suffice as capability to complete the task. But he rightly cautioned that not everyone can be expected to do that. It would depend on all the circumstances of the claimant's condition so that, in this particular case, he considered that the tribunal was entitled to conclude that this claimant "would reasonably require both arms to perform the task", especially so since the object in question is "bulky" (para.4).

In *MT v SSWP (ESA)* [2014] UKUT 548 (AAC), Judge Hemingway agreed with Judge Mark's approach in *KH*, accepting that in principle the task could sometimes be performed by someone with one arm in the way suggested. But he rightly commented that completion of the task is undoubtedly easier for those with two good arms and that it cannot simply be assumed, given the bulky size of the object in question, that someone with one good arm will be capable of accomplishing it (paras 18, 19). It is dependent on all the circumstances of the case. A tribunal should

> "offer some explanation as to how it concludes (if it does so conclude) that the task can be achieved by a claimant who is incapacitated in the way this appellant says he is. In the passage quoted above, the F-tT has not made it clear whether it thinks the appellant could use his left upper limb at all in attempting the task. On the assumption that it does not think he could, it has not explained how it thinks the task might practically be achieved with the use of the rest of his upper

body and his right upper limb. Its finding that he is "resolute" does indicate its view that he has determination but that, of itself, will not always be sufficient for a claimant to overcome physical difficulties and does not, of itself, therefore, represent an adequate explanation for its ultimate conclusion. The task of an F-tT in such a case need not be regarded as an exacting one but the standard required has not, for the above reasons, been reached here" (para.20).

A different issue arose in *MK v SSWP (ESA)* [2016] UKUT 74 (AAC), namely whether the ½ or 1 litre carton full of liquid to be picked up and moved under descriptors 4(a) and (b) respectively is a closed or open carton. Judge Wright concluded that the context necessarily implied that it had to be read as a closed carton, and so spillage in the act of picking up and moving is not relevant. The descriptors are therefore limited to the tasks of "picking up" and "moving" and not the manner in which they are achieved (at para.24). However, this is subject to the following qualification:

> "20. Different considerations might apply where the activity of picking up and moving cannot be completed because the item is dropped or thrown away involuntarily before it is moved or transferred. Then issues of whether the activity can be carried out reliably and repeatedly might come in to play. I would accept that the movement or transfer needs to be to a specific place and cannot involve random and involuntary throwing of the item (even though in one sense it would nonetheless have moved if thrown). This is not, however, to do with manner in which the activity is carried out but whether the activity can in any reasonable sense be done at all."

It follows that "if balance and a steady hand are relevant considerations at all then they fall to be considered under manual dexterity and not picking up and moving" (at para.24).

Activity 5: manual dexterity: As compared with its immediate predecessor, gone are the descriptors dealing with a "star-headed" sink tap and doing up or undoing small buttons. The former was thought to have awarded individuals a disproportionately high number of points for an identified disability which was not necessarily an activity for functioning in the workplace, thus misidentifying affected individuals for ESA purposes. Also removed are the six-point descriptors to make scoring more equitable across the activities. Ability to use a pen and pencil now specifically requires ability to use either "to make a meaningful mark" whereas its predecessor had been interpreted to require ability to use either, with either hand, so as to write in a normal manner. The new formulation arguably requires less ability. Ability to do things with one hand was thought by the *Review* to show capability to perform the specified activity. As regards descriptor (d), use of a keyboard, this jarred with the approach taken by Judge May in *DW* v *SSWP (ESA)* [2010] UKUT 245 (AAC) where he considered a case where a claimant sometimes could physically use a keyboard using one hand, but was unable to do so using two, thus preventing him using "a shift key to form capital letters or for example the sign '@'" (para.3). The approach in the *Review* would suggest that inability to use the shift key does not score so long as the keyboard can be used with one hand. The insertion from January 28, 2013 of "single-handedly" gives effect to that policy intention. 9.106

Taking the interpretation implicit in Judge May's decision in *DW*, Judge Mark in *CL v SSWP (ESA)* [2013] UKUT 434 (AAC) thought that inability to use either a keyboard or a mouse is enough to score points; it was not necessary to show inability to use both. He approved Judge May's approach in *DW*, following *Moyna*, on the need to take a broad view on whether a claimant could or could not satisfy the descriptor, stating that there are no absolutes by reference to which "can" and "cannot" are to be defined. The fact that a claimant could use a mouse or keyboard to a limited extent does not mean that s/he can use it in the way it was intended to be used. He disagreed with this commentator's view in the annotation, above, that the reformulation of the descriptor jarred with Judge May's approach, with the Judge himself being able to use a conventional key board with one hand, but did, however, accept that only being able to use one hand was more difficult, would be slower and that, on a conventional keyboard, combinations of three keys (typically control, alt and delete) – often used for logging on and security or recovery purposes – would not be possible on a conventional keyboard. The principle of "reasonable regularity" may also have relevance (see *KE* v *Department for Social Development (ESA)* [2013] NI Com 59, a decision of Chief Commissioner Mullan, on the previous wording of the descriptor). Since the descriptor now refers to a suitable keyboard or mouse, it is a submitted that for a tribunal properly to decide on this descriptor it needs evidence on the nature of the keyboard or mouse envisaged.

The above interpretation arguably chimes with an approach of reading the words of the Schedule in the context of the "work environment" in the sense that it is looking to ability physically to use a normal or adapted computer although not to test "computer literacy" in the same way as descriptor 5(c) no longer tests ability to write in a meaningful manner. But , as Judge Wright held in *DG v SSWP (ESA)* [2014] UKUT 100 (AAC), that analogy with descriptor 5(c) surely means that descriptor 5(d) can be satisfied with a very low level of ability (e.g. using a mouse alone to insert a check in a tick box); that what is being tested is not overall use of a computer with a mouse; but rather—as with Judge Jacobs' "functional approach" in *GS v SSWP (ESA)* [2010] UKUT 244 (AAC) to the descriptor on doing up or undoing small buttons in the predecessor of the manual dexterity activity and the appropriate inference from the analogy with descriptor 5(c) as regards the use of a pen or pencil to make a meaningful *mark*—a very basic degree of dexterity "in terms of use of a suitable keyboard or mouse [reading the "or" conjunctively rather than disjunctively] (e.g. gripping the mouse and moving it over an icon or box and then using a finger to click on it and using the keyboard to type out letters, numbers or symbols" (para.48). In other words, descriptor 5(d), like 5(c), cannot be satisfied if the claimant can do one of the activities: "the nine points only fall to be awarded … if the claimant cannot do both of the tasks [set out in descriptor 5(d)]; in other words, he can do neither of them" (para.3). Judge Wright preferred the "functional approach" and considered *DW* and *CL* to be wrongly decided and, guided by *R(I)12/75,* declined to follow them (paras 3, 55). He saw this interpretation as consonant with that taken by then Commissioner Howell in *R(IB)3/02* ("bending or kneeling") and (building on that analysis) that by Judge Wikeley in *MC v SSWP (ESA)* [2012] UKUT 324; [2013] AACR 13 ("standing or sitting"). He respectfully disagreed with the view of the Chief Commissioner in Northern Ireland, Judge Martin, in *R1/03 (IB)* that "or" was generally to be read disjunctively and only rarely conjunctively, as not fully reflecting the nuances of the English language and failing to focus adequately on the import of the word "cannot" when used with "or". Underscoring all this, Judge Wright considered that the "conjunctive" interpretation meant that the descriptor properly assessed separately different types of "manual dexterity activities", albeit that there was some "crossover":

> "The test of "use of a suitable [keyboard]" or "use of a mouse" focuses on the parts of the hands and fingers that are needed to use such an item. Thus with the suitable [keyboard] it is primarily looking at the power, sense and spacing in the finger or fingers of the hand so as to be able to press the buttons on the keyboard. Grip plays little or no role. On the other hand, the use of a mouse is likely to involve in part, different manual dexterity functions. The primary function may be to grip and then move the mouse, though the ability to click and click and drag, the cursor may also be important, so the flexing of fingers in the hand gripping the mouse is also likely to be important" (para.50).

In addition, if the legislative purpose had been to test the use of a keyboard with a mouse the descriptor could easily have been worded in that way.

Legally speaking, it is open to tribunal judges at either First-tier or Upper level, to choose which of these conflicting decisions to follow. Which is ultimately to be preferred will eventually be decided by the weight of authority or by one but not the other being reported in the AACR. It may be relevant that the issue was the subject of full argument by one of the parties in *DG* but not in *CL*. Perhaps this is an area requiring decision by a panel of three Upper Tribunal judges.

As Judge Mark notes in *KH v SSWP (ESA)* [2014] UKUT 455 (AAC), the disagreement between himself and Judge Wright remains to be resolved on another occasion. As described above, they disagree on whether scoring under this descriptor requires inability to use both these items of computer equipment (Judge Wright) or inability to use one (Judge Mark). But in *KH*, Judge Mark agrees with Judge Wright that it is not computer literacy that is being tested, but that rather

> "what is being tested is the physical ability, so far as manual dexterity is concerned, to use a suitable keyboard or mouse. His description in paragraph 48 of his decision of the test is whether the mouse can be gripped and moved over an icon or box and then clicked and using the keyboard to type out letters, numbers and symbols. Again, I would not dissent from that, subject to questions relating to such matters as reasonable repetition and the effects of, for example, repetitive strain injury, and that the purpose of the so using the mouse or typing out letters etc. is to achieve certain results on the computer they are being used with. It is possible that a person may have sufficient control of the hands to be able to move and click the mouse or type letters but insufficient control to do so with any degree of accuracy or with any regularity or for any reasonable time.
>
> When the descriptor speaks of using a keyboard or mouse, as Judge Wright's examples make clear, the use can only be to achieve results on a computer. It follows that in assessing whether hands are so lacking in dexterity as to score points on this descriptor it must be in relation to the operation of a computer. Why that scores the same number of points as not being able to make a meaningful mark with a pen or pencil is unclear, but what is clear is that even Judge Wright's description of what is required is far more demanding than a physical ability to make a cross on a piece of paper" (paras 10, 11).

In *SM v SSWP (ESA)* [2015] UKUT 617 (AAC) the appellant had been with congenital deformities to both hands, involving the fusion of certain fingers. One of the issues on the appeal was descriptor 5c: "cannot use a pen or pencil to make a meaningful mark with either hand". The claimant's appeal was allowed on a reg.29 point. However, Judge Ward expressed the following view:

> "7. It follows that I have received only brief submissions from the parties about descriptor 5 (c). The tribunal found as fact that the claimant could write his signature. It certainly is an issue before me (I am not clear whether it was before the First-tier Tribunal) whether he can do so with reasonable regularity but that is something for the tribunal to which this case is remitted to explore. The claimant's representative draws attention to varies definitions of 'meaningful'. In my view descriptor 5(c) is not concerned with marks that are 'meaningful' in the sense of 'having great meaning, eloquent, expressive' (per Collins dictionary). That is a sense which might be appropriate when 'meaningful' is applied to, for instance, glances, but is not a natural sense when applied to something such as rudimentary as a mark with a pen or pencil. Rather, I consider that it in this context means 'having meaning' as opposed to 'not having meaning'. Further than that I prefer not to go in this case."

And see, to the same effect, Judge Jacobs in *SSWP v LH (ESA)* [2017] UKUT 475 (AAC):

> "14. The mark has to be meaningful, so it must be capable of conveying some meaning and, inevitably, be a mark that is directed in the sense of the claimant having a meaning in mind. But that does not make the descriptor a test of intellectual capacity, which is the exclusive province of Part 2 of the Schedule (regulation

19(5)(b)). The level of the claimant's literacy is not in issue. This is a test of physical function, whereas literacy is a mental matter. And the test is limited to the claimant's fingers, hands and wrists, which are not related to literacy.
15. I agree with Judge Ward in *SM* that descriptor 5(c) is not concerned with the content of what is written. The only issue is whether it is meaningful. It has to be capable of conveying meaning. Random doodling or scribbling is not sufficient. It is not, though, necessary to convey any particular meaning. None is specified, so any meaning will do. It might be in the form of words, like a person's name or signature. Or it might be in the form of some symbol, such as a tick that could indicate agreement on a form or a cross that could indicate a vote at an election."

SM v SSWP (ESA) and *SSWP v LH (ESA)* were both followed and endorsed by Judge Wright in *NA v SSWP (ESA)* [2018] UKUT 399 (AAC). As regard descriptor 5(c), the judge stressed that the language of the test requires consideration to be given to the claimant's ability to use both the right and the left hand – so no points are scored if the person can carry out the function with at least one hand. In addition, the statutory test is not whether the person can write a word or a sentence with either hand (as under the old law) but rather the more limited test of not being able to make a meaningful mark with either hand. In that context, the use of the word 'cannot' in the descriptor requires attention to be given to a claimant's functional ability to make a meaningful mark with either hand across a range of potential situations. On the facts of the case, the tribunal's error lay in:

"its failure to consider in the round and across a number of potential or actual situations whether the claimant was unable with his right hand or his left hand to make a meaningful mark with a pen or pencil. For example, could he make the mark of a tick or a cross with either his right or his left hand on a census form or an election card? If he could, even if it was only with one hand, it is not apparent on what basis it could be concluded that he could not make a meaningful mark with either hand" (para.26).

Finally, Judge Mitchell has expressed the view (obiter) that the reference to a £1 coin in descriptor 5(b) includes "the £1 coin in the form in which it exists whenever the assessment is applied in an individual case" (para.26) and so can include the new-style £1 coin: *R v SSWP* [2018] UKUT 326 (AAC).

Activity 6: making self understood through speaking, writing, typing, or other means which are normally, or could reasonably be, used, unaided by another person: The immediate predecessor of this Activity dealt solely with communicating and making oneself understood through speech. The *Review* considered that the activities in the original WCA dealing with speech, hearing and vision, focused too much on the impairment rather than the disability it engendered. To do so was to ignore the adaptations that those with disabilities have made, thereby reducing their level of disability. Hence the removal of the "cannot speak at all" descriptor because that removed the message that those who cannot speak at all or only with very significant pain (see *CIB/4306/1999*) inherently cannot work. The *Review* considered that speech was not the sole mode by which individuals conventionally make themselves understood, so the modes of communicating were broadened to reflect this. The yardstick now is ability to convey a simple message, such as the presence of a hazard, whether at all (descriptor (a)), or to strangers (descriptors (b) and (c)).

"Normally used" means normally used by people in the claimant's situation acting reasonably in all the circumstances (*CIB/14499/1996*).

9.107 *Activity 7: Understanding communication by (i) verbal means (such as hearing or lip reading) alone, (ii) non-verbal means (such as reading 16 point print or Braille) alone, or (iii) a combination of (i) and (ii), in each case using any aid that is normally, or could reasonably be, used, unaided by another person:* The version of Activity 7 in force before January 28, 2013 was analysed by Judge Markus QC in *AT and VC v Secretary of State for Work and Pensions (ESA)* [2015] UKUT 445 (AAC); [2016]

AACR 8. However, her decision is also relevant to the current formulation of the descriptors (see para.54). At the outset Judge Markus noted that the terms 'verbal' and 'non-verbal' are confusing 'because both forms of understanding in Activity 7 relate to verbal communications, in that the activity is about understanding words whether written or spoken'. Thus "'verbal' is used to mean 'spoken' and 'non-verbal' is used to mean 'written'" (para.37). Further, the drafting left it ambiguous as to "whether a claimant must be unable to understand or have difficulty in understanding communication by both verbal and non-verbal means in order to satisfy the relevant descriptors, or whether inability/difficulty by only one of those means is sufficient" (para.1).

Judge Markus therefore considered the legislative history of Activity 7 and its antecedents. This led her to conclude "that in order to qualify under a relevant descriptor a claimant need be impaired in either hearing or vision (but not both) or, as amended, in understanding either spoken or written communication (but not both)" (para.48). The current formulation "is not much of an improvement on the previous wording" (para.50), but the judge was satisfied "that the word "alone" was inserted after each of (i) and (ii) with the intention of making clear that it is sufficient if a person is unable to understand a message by either verbal or non-verbal means" (para.51). Judge Markus's decision was followed in the context of the post-January 2013 version of the regulations by Judge Ward in *CM v SSWP (ESA)* [2016] UKUT 242 (AAC) (dealing with the parallel descriptor in a Sch.3 case).

The decisions in *AT and VC v SSWP (ESA)* [2015] UKUT 445 (AAC); [2016] AACR 6 and *CM v SSWP (ESA)* [2016] UKUT 242 (AAC) were followed by Judge Church in *RK v SSWP (ESA)* [2019] UKUT 345 (AAC), where it was held that a tribunal could find a claimant suffering from hearing loss was able to understand written communication even if she could only understand writing in Urdu: "The activities set out in Schedule 2 are broad proxies for the kinds of activities a claimant may be expected to do in a workplace or in getting to and from work, but any limitation in a claimant's ability to perform an activity which doesn't result from a health condition is not relevant to the assessment of their entitlement... A claimant cannot, therefore, score points for difficulties with communicating with others or understanding communication if the difficulty stems simply from the claimant and the (hypothetical) other people in question not speaking the same language" (at paras 14 and 15).

The predecessor of this dealt only with hearing. The reformulation here again, as with Activity 6, reflects the view that the activities in the original WCA dealing with speech, hearing and vision, focused too much on the impairment rather than the disability it engendered, sending an erroneous message that those who cannot hear at all are inherently unable to work. The yardstick now is that the claimant, due to sensory impairment, cannot understand a simple message, such as the location of a fire escape, either at all (descriptor (a)) or from a stranger (descriptors (b) and (c)). As regards reading 16 point print, what is being tested is the ability to understand a message contained in something with that size print.

Activity 8: Navigation and maintaining safety, using a guide dog or other aid if either or both are normally, or could reasonably be, used: The predecessor of this tested vision (visual acuity). The reformulation here again, as with Activity 6, reflects the view that the activities in the original WCA dealing with speech, hearing and vision, focused too much on the impairment rather than the disability it engendered, sending an erroneous message that those who cannot see at all are inherently unable to work. The key disabling features of visual impairment were thought by the *Review* to be inability or reduced ability, due to sensory impairment, to navigate and maintain safety. It was considered that these would be greater in unfamiliar surroundings, hence the gradations in scoring. Note that "crossing the road" is merely an example of "a potentially hazardous task" and not the sole context for descriptor (b) (*CC v SSWP(ESA)* [2015] UKUT 62 (AAC)). **9.108**

"Normally used" means normally used by people in the claimant's situation acting reasonably in all the circumstances (*CIB/14499/1996*).

The policy intent behind the change in wording from January 28, 2013 was

> "that this activity should examine the ability to understand communication sufficiently clearly to be able to comprehend a simple message by either verbal or non-verbal means or both. The descriptors may therefore apply if a claimant has hearing impairment alone, visual impairment alone or a combination of hearing and visual impairment" (Explanatory Memorandum, *http://www.legislation.gov.uk/uksi/2012/3096/pdfs/uksiem_20123096_en.pdf*)

The meaning of "due to sensory impairment" was touched on in *Secretary of State for Work and Pensions v AI (rule 17) (ESA)* [2017] UKUT 346 (AAC). Strictly the decision is not a binding authority as it is a decision consenting to the Secretary of State (SSWP) withdrawing his appeal to the Upper Tribunal on the meaning of "sensory impairment" under descriptor 8(b) in Sch. 2. The claimant had serious balance problems caused by Meniere's disease. The SSWP appealed to the Upper Tribunal on the ground that "sensory impairment" meant a direct impairment of one the five physical senses of sight, hearing, smell, taste and touch. The SSWP subsequently sought the Upper Tribunal's consent to withdraw the appeal, having obtained further expert evidence on the nature of Meniere's disease. However, this specialist evidence may be useful in other cases.

9.109 *Activity 9: Absence or loss of control whilst conscious leading to extensive evacuation of the bowel and/or bladder, other than enuresis (bed-wetting), despite the wearing or use of any aids or adaptations which are normally, or could reasonably be, worn or used*: This is a significant simplification compared to the original WCA and its coverage of "continence", although the new WCA does not use that term. Like its predecessors, this Activity does not directly deal with capability to work, but rather with matters of personal dignity and social acceptability; "the loss of dignity resulting from the associated soiling is considered severe enough to make it unreasonable to expect an individual with severe incontinence to work" (*Review*, p.33). As Judge Mitchell pointed out in *PC v SSWP (ESA)* [2015] UKUT 285 (AAC), descriptor (a) has a different logic to the other LCWA activities and descriptors. They relate directly to ability to perform tasks in the workplace. In contrast descriptor 9(a) is

> "not about bodily and mental processes used to do work. A monthly incontinence event of the type prescribed is of itself unlikely to have any significant bearing on the performance of work tasks. There must be a different reason for the legislator deciding that anyone within descriptor 9(a) meets the condition of having limited capability for work. I think it is obvious that this is connected to the deeply personal and potentially embarrassing and distressing nature of significant continence problems" (para.30).

That is why the focus is on absence or loss of control, rather than mere urgency. The frequency of urination experienced by a diabetic because of the condition or medication is to be distinguished from urgency leading to a loss of control (*NH v SSWP (ESA)* [2011] UKUT 82 (AAC)). As regards descriptor (b) the requirement from January 28, 2013 is that the claimant is *for the majority of the time* at risk of loss of control. Note that it deals with "risk" and not the materialisation of that risk; there can be a risk without it ever materialising or doing so on only a few occasions (*NH v SSWP (ESA)* [2011] UKUT 82 (AAC)); *KB v SSWP (ESA)* [2014] UKUT 126 (AAC); *DG v SSWP (ESA)* [2015] UKUT 370 (AAC), paras 15–17)). The aspect of being unable to control the full voiding of the bladder essentially involves asking:

> "no more than, if the appellant starts to urinate, will he be able to stop before his bladder is completely empty? The tribunal is most likely to be able to arrive at a reasoned conclusion on this by applying its expert knowledge to the surrounding evidence including the ESA50, GP and medical reports provided by the appellant or obtained by the tribunal, ESA85 (particularly the typical day) and lifestyle" (*NH v SSWP (ESA)* [2011] UKUT 82 (AAC), para.14).

In *NL v SSWP (ESA)* [2017] UKUT 397 (AAC), allowing the claimant's appeal, Judge Rowland considered it possible that the tribunal had:

> "placed too much weight on the distinction between urgency and incontinence. The word 'continence', which at one time featured in the Schedules, no longer does so: the question is simply whether the claimant loses control, or is at risk of doing so, to the extent that he requires, or would require, cleaning and a change of clothing. Moreover, the words 'evacuation' of the bowel and 'voiding' of the bladder in descriptor 9(a)(i) need to be read in the light of descriptor 9(a)(ii) and I agree with the Secretary of State that the revised WCA Handbook (5 July 2016) accurately describes their effect –
>
> > 'The descriptors relate to a substantial leakage of urine or faeces – such that there would be a requirement for the person to have a wash and change their clothing' (para.6)."

Judge Rowland added that "Descriptor 9(b) is satisfied when the claimant has only rare occasions of such a substantial leakage but is, for the majority of the time, at risk of having one unless able to reach a toilet quickly" (para.7).

An important starting point for these descriptors is that the "absence or loss of control" experienced must be "whilst conscious", on which see *CL v SSWP (ESA)* [2019] UKUT 39 (AAC). There Judge West held (at para.28) that:

> "a claimant who loses control of his bowel or bladder whilst in a state of altered, as opposed to lost, consciousness, cannot score points under the descriptors linked to activity 9. If a person has lost consciousness, it clearly cannot be said that that person is "conscious" for the purposes of activity 9. A person who is in a state of altered consciousness, as a claimant may be when experiencing a seizure and possibly for a time in its aftermath, equally cannot be said to be "conscious" within the meaning of activity 9."

In *NH*, approved in *CP v SSWP (ESA)* [2011] UKUT 507 (AAC), Judge Lane sets out a number of helpful questions in para.14. That the yardstick is now "extensive evacuation of the bowel and/or voiding of the bladder" precludes, as did its predecessor, application of IB decisions bringing dribbling and leaking within the "loss of control" rubric (see e.g. *CSIB/880/2003*). Sufferers of stress incontinence may thus find it difficult to score. The necessary extent of the disability is measured by the need for "cleaning and a change of clothing". "Change of clothing" does not require a complete change since that would rarely be a consequence even of considerable levels of incontinence (*EM v SSWP (ESA)* [2014] UKUT 34 (AAC), paras 22, 23). Sanitary pads do not constitute "clothing" for this purpose. Nor, in this context, do disposable pants. In *EM*, Judge Mark said:

> "In practical terms, bearing in mind that the activity is dealing with matters of personal dignity and social acceptability, it appears to me that almost any change of clothing would count for this purpose since the soiled clothing would then have to be retained in the workplace for the rest of the day by the person who has soiled him or herself with the real risk of the clothing in question being seen or smelled by others in the workplace. If, however, pants are disposable, then in my view it would be likely to be the responsibility of the employer to ensure that there were facilities for them to be disposed of. Further it does not appear to me to have been intended that a change of disposable protective sanitary wear was to be relevant, since that would normally be needed in the event of the sort of accident contemplated by the descriptor. For those reasons, I would not consider that in most, if not all, circumstances a change of such wear was properly to be included in a change of clothing" (para.23).

Descriptor (a), through sub-para.(ii), recognises that the impact on the individual of such a need for cleaning and a change of clothing "is just as great where it results from leaking of a collecting device rather than loss of control of bladder or bowels". The precise scope of "collecting device" remains untested—does it include incontinence pads, or just catheter bags or stoma bags? The scope of "aids or adaptations" is not wholly clear; as Judge Mark noted in *EM*, the aids and adaptations envisaged might be thought mainly to cover internal devices, such as an artificial valve manually operated to open and close the bladder, which control such opening and closing or the evacuation of the bowel thus not embracing "sanitary pads and similar devices" since they "do not affect control over the evacuation of the bowel or the voiding of the bladder but only the consequences of such an event occurring" (para. 20). However, the wider wording ("aids or adaptations which are normally, or could reasonably be worn or used") suggests the terms are not so limited, so that "sanitary pads are aids which affect a claimant's ability to perform an activity in that their use may result in there being no need for a change of clothing" (para.20). In *PC v SSWP (ESA)* [2015] UKUT 285 (AAC), Judge Mitchell agreed with Judge Mark that "the aids and adaptations encompassed ...are limited" (para.20) to "those which prevent or minimise a loss of control" (para.38). A bucket thus cannot amount to an aid or adaptation. Nor can it amount to an "aid or appliance" for purposes of descriptors (a) and (b):

> "A bucket cannot reasonably be used in any workplace, apart from perhaps an incredibly unusual one like a one-person lighthouse, to deal with incontinence. That would run counter to, and undermine, the purpose of the continence activity and descriptors. It would be impossible to maintain dignity in those circumstances. The range of permissible aids and appliances must be restricted to achieve that aim and discounted if use in the workplace would be likely to expose an individual to the indignity against which these descriptors are designed to protect. But this does not mean that a less intrusive receptacle than a bucket must be discounted, if it can be used by a person without that associated indignity. I have no idea whether such things exist" (para.39).

Nor is a bucket a "toilet" (ibid).

As with all its predecessors, applying these descriptors involves intrusive scrutiny of the lives of claimants, embracing intimate and embarrassing areas affecting a claimant's dignity. It is necessary to appreciate the nature of the problems of sufferers, the varied nature and disabling effects of irritable bowel syndrome (IBS) (see *CIB/14332/96*) the role of diet (*CSIB/889/1999*), and the nature and role of various urinary or fecal collecting devices. It is also necessary to define and apply carefully the terms used in the descriptors.

Aids or adaptations "normally used" means if the aid or adaptation in question is normally used by people in the claimant's situation acting reasonably in all the circumstances (*CIB/14499/1996*). In *LB* v *SSWP (ESA)* [2013] UKUT 352 (AAC), Judge Mark considered the use of aids or adaptations. He thought that the DWP guidance to decision-makers in Memo DMG 24/12, issued after Judge Levenson's decision in *RP* v *SSWP* [2011] UKUT (ESA) 449 (AAC) (noted in the annotation to reg.19(4) (see para.9.49), embodied a non-exhaustive set of useful matters to be considered in cases, but stressed, as does the guidance itself, that those set out are not the only factors which may be relevant. Judge Mark summarized the relevant parts of the guidance thus:

> "In relation to those physical descriptors which specifically refer to the use of aids, including continence, it observes that decision makers should apply the test in a way that displays consistency between the work capability assessment as a whole and the assessment of each descriptor in particular (para.6). It goes on to state that the decision maker should establish whether the claimant normally uses an aid or appliance, and if not, whether the use of it has been prescribed or advised. If a claimant does not have an aid or appliance which they have been prescribed or advised to use, the decision maker should establish whether it would help the claimant, why they are not using one and whether the explanation is reasonable.

The guidance goes on to state that the decision maker must consider all the circumstances in deciding whether it would be reasonable to assess the claimant as using an aid that they have not been prescribed or that they have not been advised to use. Factors identified include whether (1) the claimant possesses the aid or appliance; (2) the claimant was given specific medical advice about managing their condition, and it is reasonable for them to continue to follow that advice; (3) the claimant would be advised to use an aid or appliance if they raised it with the appropriate authority such as a GP or occupational therapist; (4) if it is medically reasonable for them to use an aid or appliance; (5) the health condition or disability is likely to be of short duration; (6) an aid or appliance is widely available; (7) an aid or appliance is affordable in the claimant's circumstances; (8) the claimant is able to use and store the aid or appliance; and (9) the claimant is unable to use an aid or appliance due to their physical or mental health condition" (paras 11, 12).

He noted that the HCP had not carried out the recommended enquiries. Nor had the tribunal done so. It had referred to the claimant's urine well which he kept in his car as "an aid which he used". But this failed to address the fact it was only of use in the car and even there did not always prove adequate because he could not get to it in time or was not in a suitably quiet place to use it. It could not reasonably be expected to be used in non-private places (para.20). As regards the possible use of pads—which the claimant did not use because he felt shame at the continence problem at his age—Judge Ward stressed that while they could deal with post-urinary dribbling (which does not count for scoring purposes anyway), he was less clear how they could deal adequately with extensive evacuation of the bladder. Moreover—as an additional factor not mentioned in the DWP guidance—the tribunal should consider whether their use might actually exacerbate the problem of "accidents" where the claimant could reach a toilet in time "because they might increase the time required for the claimant to prepare himself to urinate" (para.22).

The descriptors should be applied bearing in the context of the claimant's personal circumstances and any mobility problems experienced by the claimant (*EM v SSWP (ESA)* [2014] UKUT 34 (AAC); *FR v SSWP (ESA)* [2015] UKUT 151 (AAC)). In *EM*, Judge Mark highlighted the error in the then guidance in the DWP Medical Services Handbook which stated that mobility problems should be ignored as regards this descriptor since those problems were dealt with elsewhere in Sch.2. He considered that

> "This statement is wholly misguided both in relation to the descriptor as it was at the time of the decision and as it now is. In descriptor 9(a)(i) the only question is whether at least once a month the claimant experiences loss of control leading to extensive evacuation of the bowel and/or voiding of the bladder sufficient to require cleaning and a change of clothes. The fact that this is because the claimant is unable to reach a toilet in time because of other physical problems is irrelevant, as one would expect bearing in mind that the purpose of the descriptor is to deal with questions of personal dignity and social acceptability. This is made even clearer, if that were possible, by the wording of descriptor 9(b) where the question is whether there is a risk of loss of control if not able to reach a toilet quickly. Loss of control at least once a month because the claimant cannot reach a toilet quickly plainly qualifies for 15 points if the other requirements are met" (para.25).

The guidance in that handbook has been revised to take account of *EM* (see *FR v SSWP (ESA)* [2015] UKUT 151 (AAC), para.21). Rightly so, since, as Judge Grey QC put it in *FR*:

> "The effect of the "loss of control" set out in descriptor 9 must be assessed in the light of an individual's personal circumstances. If, as a result of limited mobility, he or she is more adversely affected than someone who has greater mobility and

an associated ability to better manage the effects of any threatened loss of control, this should be taken into account by the decision-maker. The alternative would be to divorce the assessment of this activity and the descriptors from the reality of an individual's ability to cope with their condition and to replace an assessment which is claimant-centred with one based on (here) the ability of a 'hypothetical', reasonably mobile individual to reach toilets. The activity seeks to assess the likelihood of loss of personal dignity and shame in the workplace associated with significant 'accidents'. It should make no difference whether soiling may occur because an individual's restricted mobility slows down the process of reaching a toilet, or because the loss of control is comparatively rapid. The effect on the individual and their ability to work is the same" (para.19).

For mobilising difficulties to be relevant to Activity 9 and its descriptors, however, there must exist an underlying problem of bowel or bladder functioning; mobilising difficulties alone are not enough. there must be a disease or disablement affecting the control mechanisms of bowel or bladder (*PC v SSWP (ESA)* [2015] UKUT 285 (AAC). paras 33-36, 45; *DG v SSWP (ESA)* [2015] UKUT 370 (AAC), para.18).

For a successful reasons challenge, see *VH v SSWP (ESA)* [2018] UKUT 290 (AAC) (at paras.15 and 16).

9.110 *Activity 10: Consciousness during waking moments:* The focus here is on "involuntary episodes of lost or altered consciousness" which result in "significantly disrupted awareness or concentration". If experienced at least once a week, 15 points are scored and thus limited capability for work established. If experienced at least once a month, six points are scored. With no reference now being made to "epileptic or similar seizures" and the descriptors referring to "significantly disrupted awareness or concentration", the strict and narrow approach in *R(IB) 2/07(T)* is no longer warranted. It cast doubt on earlier authorities on "altered consciousness", finding *CSIB/14/1996*, which had given hope to those who suffered severe headaches, to have been wrongly decided. *R(IB) 2/07(T)* required alteration of consciousness such that the sufferer was "incapable of any deliberate act". In *BB v SSWP (ESA)* [2011] UKUT 158 (AAC); [2012] AACR 2, Judge Ward considered that the Tribunal of Commissioners decision in *R(IB) 2/07(T)*, insofar as it created a test of severity of an episode of altered consciousness should be seen purely as a decision of the previous IB regime. The ESA regime, by providing a statutory yardstick of "results in significantly disrupted awareness or concentration", rendered inapplicable to ESA the test of being "incapable of any deliberate act" (para.14), and the matter of the meaning of the statutory phrase in the ESA regime should be considered "untrammeled as regards the extent of the effects of the episode" by *R(IB) 2/07(T)* (para.15).

In *CB v SSWP (ESA)* [2015] UKUT 287 (AAC), Judge Rowley considered "lost consciousness" self-explanatory in most cases. As regards "altered consciousness", she adopted the proposition set out in the Training and Development Handbook for HCPs, while recognizing that that work is in no way binding on decision-makers or tribunals:

> "'Altered consciousness' implies that, although the person is not fully unconscious, there is a definite clouding of mental faculties resulting in loss of control of thoughts or actions" (PC, para. 10).

The matter of giving substance to the concepts "lost or altered consciousness resulting in significantly disrupted awareness or concentration" and applying them to the facts of disputed cases is very directly the task of the tribunal in the light of all the evidence. In the context of the similarly-worded activity 11 in the Sch. in force at March 27, 2011, *RA v SSWP (ESA)* [2010] UKUT 301 (AAC) considered that the transient and immediate effects of consuming alcohol should not count towards meeting the descriptors of this activity (para.10). Moreover alcohol dependence did not raise issues here since it ranked as a "mental condition" and not, as required, a physical disease or disablement (para.18). In that same context, in *AB v SSWP (ESA)* [2012] UKUT 151 (AAC) Judge Jacobs held that the effects of sleep apnoea were not covered. It takes effect only when asleep and not during waking moments, thus not directly affecting capability for work. Although sleep so interrupted because of the condition does, however, mean that a sufferer may be unrefreshed, tired and liable to fall asleep during the day because of natural tiredness, Judge Jacobs considered that this, even where due to a medical condition could not properly be described as involuntary but rather something subject to control, something we all experience. Nor did he consider it properly describable as disrupting awareness or concentration in this context.

In *JG* v *SSWP (ESA)* [2013] UKUT 496 (AAC), Judge Mark considered the case of a claimant whose drowsiness was a direct side effect of his Parkinson's medication. Applying ESA Regs 2008, reg.19(5)(c), it arose as a direct result of treatment by a medical practitioner for that disease. As tiredness induced by medication, it was thus distinguishable from the "natural tiredness" considered by Judge Jacobs in *AB* v *SSWP (ESA)* [2012 UKUT 151 (AAC). As regards Judge Jacobs's comments on "natural tiredness" in that case, Judge Ward agreed that in general it was something one can control and cannot in the context of descriptor (a) be described as "involuntary", but stated further that

> "[i]t would not, however, be true of somebody suffering from narcolepsy, nor would it be true of somebody who has been administered a sedative designed to cause them to fall asleep, or which has that consequence. There will be occasions when the tiredness or drowsiness is so extreme that voluntary control is lost. Whether there are occasions when the claimant's medication results in such occasions, and if so, how frequently this occurs, is a matter for the tribunal to determine. ... [T]he descriptor clearly refers both to lost and altered consciousness. Sleep is a form of lost consciousness just as much as a state induced by an epileptic fit. A person is not awake if they have lost consciousness and the reference to 'remaining conscious during waking moments' or, as here, 'consciousness during waking moments' is plainly concerned with involuntary loss of consciousness of any type. I can see no difference between losing consciousness due to narcolepsy and losing consciousness due to any other cause. ... [D]rug induced drowsiness can, if severe enough, amount to or result in an involuntary episode of lost or altered consciousness resulting in significantly disrupted awareness or concentration. It is for the tribunal to investigate the cause, nature and extent of the problem and to determine whether there are occasions when the side effects of the claimant's medication have that effect on him, and if so, how frequently they occur" (paras 9–11).

In a Northern Ireland decision, *DM* v *Department for Social Development (ESA)* [2013] NI Com 17, following Judge Jacobs in *AB*, Commissioner Stockman considered that the "correct approach to the activity excludes considerations of periods of normal sleep. Falling asleep during the day does not equate to loss of consciousness" (para.24). *SY v SSWP (ESA)* [2016] UKUT 378 (AAC) confirms that falling asleep during the day due to the effects of a medical condition does not amount to "an involuntary episode of lost or altered consciousness" for the purpose of descriptors (a) or (b) of Activity 10.

[C] Approaching and interpreting specific descriptors: Pt II: mental, cognitive and intellectual function assessment

The terms of the activities and descriptors in Pt II are so different from those in the PCA that no specific IB case law on the PCA descriptors and activities can readily be made relevant. Not so, however, IB case law on the general approach to be taken, namely that, while a tribunal has an inquisitorial function, it should be cautious about exercising it when considering mental disablement (*CIB/14202/1996*), unless the matter has been raised beforehand and there is in addition some medical or other evidence on the point (*R(IB) 2/98*). Now that assessments are carried out **9.111** by a wider range of HCPs, consideration has been given to the weight that should be placed on their evidence, particularly in mental health cases, where the particular experience of the HCP lies in a non-mental health field. In *JH v SSWP (ESA)* [2013] UKUT 269 (AAC), the claimant was assessed in a 15-minute interview by a HCP who was a physiotherapist. Judge Mark thought that when dealing with mental health problems:

> "the opinion of the physiotherapist as to the conclusions to be drawn have no probative value whatsoever. This is because the physiotherapist has no professional expertise in mental health matters. Although the strict rules of evidence do not apply, a tribunal can only take into account evidence that has probative value" (para.22).

He thought that in such cases the disability analyst should have mental health qualifications. But he further noted that even where that is the case, "tribunals should beware of placing too much weight on such reports, based as they are on a very short interview with a claimant and without access to medical records" (para.23). In *ST & GF v SSWP (ESA)* [2014] UKUT 547 (AAC); [2015] AACR 23, a panel of three Upper Tribunal judges categorically rejected Judge Mark's comments—which it saw as *obiter*—as

> "wrong if and to the extent that they purport to create a rule of law or starting point that observations on mental health descriptors by HCP physiotherapists are of no probative value whatsoever or are highly likely or likely to have little probative value and thus should be accorded no or little weight by the decision maker and the First-tier tribunal" (para.33).

Instead the proper approach is that the probative value of an HCP physiotherapist's report is a matter for the decision maker or tribunal dealing with the case, just as it is with other reports and evidence.

The panel so held, firstly, because the legislation makes no distinction between an HCP's ability to deal with mental health descriptors as opposed to physical ones. It merely requires approval by the Secretary of State and registration with the appropriate regulatory body. So any such rule as Judge Mark's would frustrate the statutory framework (para.34). The panel's second rationale noted the difference between the LCW assessment (how a condition affects the claimant's functional capacity) and "a medical examination carried out as part of a process of diagnosis and treatment" (para.35), a distinction acknowledged in Professor Harrington's *First Review* of the ESA process. The panel thus considered that the medical examination carried out by a HCP for the LCW did not require that HCP to be a medical specialist in all the physical and mental problems that might be exhibited by a particular claimant. To require the HCP to be such a specialist "would create insurmountable problems for the assessment process" since many claimants have a variety of problems which might then require assessment in a particular case by several HCPs rather than one (para.35).

What is required, however, is that the HCP have an informed understanding of the claimant's medical conditions and the difficulties flowing from them. This requires adequate training and supervision. The panel had received detailed information on the current training process (see paras 11-19)—something not available to Judge Mark in *JH*—and, while not commenting on that programme, did observe that none of the independent reviews of the ESA assessment process had criticised the performance of physiotherapists relative to HCPs from other disciplines and that training for HCPs on mental health problems was being reviewed with the aim of increasing the knowledge of all HCPs (para.36).

There is, therefore, no need for a tribunal to adjourn for further particulars on the qualifications of the HCP in a particular case. The specialist tribunal with its medical member must "make its own findings having regard to all the evidence before it" (para.37). The correct starting point was that identified by Judge Ovey in an incapacity benefit appeal (*JF v SSWP (IB)* [2011] UKUT 385 (AAC) at para.25:

> "...the report is prepared by an HCP who has been trained (whether as part of the training as an HCP or through other training) at least to the level thought appropriate by the Department of Work and Pensions for carrying out examinations where mental health issues are raised. In other words the selection and training procedures ought to have produced an HCP who can conduct a mental health examination competently. It follows that evidence that the HCP has not undergone separate specialist training should not of itself have any effect on the weight which the tribunal attaches to the report..."

The panel held that the weight to be accorded to any report "addressing the functional impact of any medical condition on a claimant" is a matter for the specialist tribunal which should consider:

> "(a) the level of the author's expertise (for example, an HCP or a consultant psychiatrist) and (b) the knowledge of the claimant possessed by the author (for example, knowledge gained from a one-off assessment or that gained as a treating clinician). Additionally the date of the evidence, its comprehensiveness, and its relevance to the issues the tribunal has to determine are also key matters for the tribunal to consider. Importantly the tribunal should explain its reasoning for attaching weight to one type or piece of evidence rather than to another" (para.38 of *ST & GF*).

In *JS v SSWP (ESA)* [2011] UKUT 243 (AAC), Judge Ward, following *R(DLA) 2/01* and *R(DLA) 3/01*, held that evidence coming into existence after the date of the decision could be relied on so far as relevant to showing the circumstances pertaining at the date of the decision. Accordingly, here, where there was evidence of a recent diagnosis of depression, of recent weight loss, low weight and a very low body mass index (BMI), the tribunal in the exercise of its inquisitorial jurisdiction ought to have followed this up to see if this was a symptom of untreated depression or, at the very least, to have made clear in its reasons what it made of this evidence. There is only a very limited carry-over of case authorities on the original LCWA, given the degree of revision of activities and descriptors undertaken in the amending Regulations.

From January 28, 2013 reg.19(5) requires that incapability to perform the activities in this Part of this Schedule (mental, cognitive and intellectual function assessment) must be linked to incapability arising from a specific mental illness or disablement or as a direct result of treatment provided by a registered medical practitioner for such an illness or disablement. Under the previous wording of the paragraph (still applicable to some cases after January 28, 2013—see reg.2 of the amending instrument, below, para.9.614), there was no such link (*KP v SSWP (ESA)* [2011] UKUT 216 (AAC); [2012] AACR 5; *KN v SSWP (ESA)* [2011] UKUT 229 (AAC); *RM v SSWP (ESA)* [2011] UKUT 454 (AAC); *AH v SSWP (ESA)* [2011] UKUT 333 (AAC)), but the specific language of activities 16 and 17 then as now specifically required causation by cognitive impairment or mental disorder.

The revised LCWA contains only seven activities rather than the ten in the original LCWA. This revision and reduction were designed to remove unnecessary complexities and overlaps and prevent double scoring.

Activity 11: Learning tasks: This aims to identify individuals who have difficulty learning **9.112**
new tasks. The equivalent in the original LCWA covered learning and comprehension but the latter was considered superfluous by the *Review* on the basis that understanding how to do something was built in to the process of retaining that knowledge. The complexity of the task affords the necessary gradation between descriptors. Note that the instances given in each descriptor (setting an alarm clock (descriptors (a) and (b)); operating a washing machine to clean clothes (descriptor (c)) are merely examples.

See by analogy the guidance from Judge Rowley on this activity in the context of Sch.3 in *Secretary of State for Work and Pensions v AT (ESA)* [2017] UKUT 338 (AAC). Note also her observation that "the words 'due to cognitive impairment or mental disorder' do not appear in the descriptors for that activity, presumably because the activity falls under Part 2 of Schedule 2 which is headed 'mental, cognitive and intellectual function assessment.' In my judgment, nothing turns on the difference" (at para.9).

See also *TM v SSWP (ESA)* [2018] UKUT 9 (AAC), dealing with descriptor 11c, where Judge Wikeley observed (at para. 22) that "The method by which the person learns the task in question is irrelevant. They may be able to do so by reading the information booklet. They may be able to do so by having the necessary steps being demonstrated to them. The route is irrelevant. As [the Secretary of State's representative] neatly puts it, 'Reading a manual is just one way of learning to use something, show and tell is another'."

9.113 *Activity 12: Awareness of everyday hazards (such as boiling water or sharp objects):* The focus here is on significant risk of injury to people or damage to property or possessions (rather than, as originally proposed, on risk of significant injury or significant damage). "Everyday hazards" means commonplace or ordinary hazards that are similar in kind to boiling water and sharp objects; it does not extend to social hazards, e.g. the risk of financial exploitation or sexual abuse that a vulnerable claimant with low social intelligence may face because of her suggestibility (*RR v SSWP (ESA)* [2018] UKUT 143 (AAC)). The gradation between descriptors flows from the level of supervision required to manage the risk (supervision needed for: majority of time (15); frequently (9); occasionally (6)). The requisite "reduced awareness of the risks of everyday hazards" could stem from learning difficulties, affected concentration and self-awareness, or the effects of medication (*Review*, para.4.4.2).

9.114 *Activity 13: Initiating and completing personal action (which means planning, organization, problem solving, prioritizing or switching tasks):* The overall intention of the Activity is to assess someone's capability to carry out routine activity. Note the meaning of "personal action" set out in the Activity itself. This part of the revised LCWA seeks to combine in one activity disabilities covered by three activities in the original LCWA: memory and concentration; execution of tasks; initiating and sustaining personal action. This was done because the original three were perceived by the *Review* as each identifying the same disability, namely, the inability to complete a task. The amalgamation thus precludes the double or triple scoring available under the former LCWA. The descriptors focus on completion of at least two sequential tasks, since it was unlikely that in a work context an individual would only be required to undertake a single task. The gradation between descriptors (b) and (c) turns on how often verbal prompting from another is needed to complete the personal action ((b) "most of the time"; (c) "frequent"). The *Review* specifically stated that:

> "if the time it takes an individual to complete a task means it cannot be executed reliably and repeatedly, then they will be considered unable to do so" (p.45).

Conditions potentially involving this Activity were thought to be lapses in memory and concentration, due to fatigue, depression or neurological impairment, apathy, obsessive compulsive behaviours, overwhelming fear or delusions.

In *MW v SSWP (ESA)* [2014] UKUT 112 (AAC), a case of a claimant with obsessive compulsive disorder, Judge Rowland held that the tribunal had erred in law:

> "It neither addressed the consequences of the claimant's need constantly to check that what he had done was right nor paid sufficient attention to the precise language of the legislation. The main consequence of the claimant's disorder was that everything took much longer, but there is also evidence that, for instance, turning gas hobs on and off when cooking had resulted a build-up of gas and in him being a danger to himself to the extent that his mother had taken over his cooking from him. The material features of the legislation are, first, that it is not enough that the claimant can initiate and complete personal actions – he or she must be able to do so "reliably"—and, secondly, a finding that a person can sometimes reliably initiate or complete actions may rule out descriptor 13(a)—at least on a literal construction of that descriptor—but it leaves open the possibility of either of descriptors 13(b) or 13(c) being satisfied since those descriptors are

satisfied if the claimant cannot reliably initiate or complete at least two [personal] actions "for the majority of the time" or "frequently".

The word "reliably" makes it unnecessary to go as far as is argued on behalf of the claimant and hold that a person is to be treated as not being able to initiate and complete actions at all if he or she can do so only with excessive delay. The Secretary of State is right to argue that one should consider separately whether there is a difficulty in initiating an action and whether there is a difficulty in completing it and that in this case the difficulty lay in completing actions, although arguably the difficulty in completing the first action creates a difficulty in initiating the second. In any event, the practical point is that, if compulsive behaviour means that it takes an excessive amount of time to complete at least two actions, it can be said that the claimant cannot "reliably" complete them. The First-tier Tribunal did not consider whether that was, at least frequently, so in this case or, if it did, it gave inadequate reasons for its conclusion" (paras 6, 7).

Activity 13 was further considered by Judge Jacobs in *MP v Secretary of State for Work and Pensions (ESA)* [2015] UKUT 458 (AAC), where he noted it was "neither necessary nor appropriate to define 'personal action'. They are ordinary words that have to be given their normal meaning" (see *Moyna v Secretary of State for Work and Pensions* [2003] 1 W.L.R. 1929 at [24]). Accordingly, "At the risk of stating the obvious, it means something undertaken by someone on their own" (para.23). Judge Jacobs held that the tribunal "must apply common sense in deciding what constitutes an action. It is possible to render the legislation redundant by splitting an action into its component parts. The definition of Activity 13 recognises this by referring to 'tasks' as components of a single action" (para.28). See further the analysis at paras.30–41, including this passage at paras 34–35:

"34. The tribunal's decision on Activity 13 must relate only to actions that involve all these tasks. This does not mean that the tribunal must find evidence of an action involving all those tasks that the claimant cannot complete. It may be that there will be evidence from, say, dressing that shows the claimant being unable to plan by selecting appropriate clothing to wear outdoors, which can be put together with evidence from, say, cooking, that shows the claimant being unable to prioritise tasks. This specific evidence may have to be supplemented by inferences drawn from the nature of the claimant's condition or other factors.

35. This does not mean that the action considered need necessarily be complicated, so long as the tribunal takes all potential tasks into account. Take dressing as an example. Most of the time dressing may simply be routine. It may even involve nothing more than putting on the clothing selected and laid out by the claimant's partner. But it can require planning (deciding what to wear), organising (assembling the different items required), problem solving (finding an alternative item of clothing for something that is in the wash), prioritising (deciding whether it is more important to get dressed or to wash a particular item of clothing) or switching tasks (going to iron a shirt to wear). To put it differently. The tribunal must always be sure that the evidence on which it relies actually demonstrates an ability to undertake all the tasks required by the activity."

See, for a successful reasons challenge, *VH v SSWP (ESA)* [2018] UKUT 290 (AAC) (at paras.17-20).

Activity 14: Coping with change: This assesses ability to cope with change. The focus in descriptors (b) and (c) is now on whether the change is "planned" or "unplanned", rather than "expected", "unexpected" or "unforeseen". Decision-makers and tribunals should look at all the evidence about the person's daily life. **9.115**

In mental health descriptor cases the context of a particular piece of evidence can be very important (see *PD* v *SSWP (ESA)* [2012] UKUT 255 (AAC)). In *GC v SSWP (ESA)* [2013] UKUT 405 (AAC) work-related stress had been the reason the claimant left his previous job as a driver. Being required to change his planned-out driving route part way through a shift, caused him stress, made him bad-tempered, such that he had to leave that job. The decision reflects Judge Ward's important reminder that different people have different abilities to cope with change.

On the evidence Judge Ward found the claimant's ability to cope with change very low and that he satisfied descriptor (c) and had limited capability for work.

What does "cope" mean? In *GC* v *SSWP (ESA)* [2013] UKUT 405 (AAC), Judge Ward considered it to be

> "a word of general application. It significance in the present context is well expressed by a definition given in the Oxford English Dictionary (Online Edition) of 'To manage, deal (competently) with, a situation or problem'. It seems to me that a variety of human behaviours and responses may be indicative of a failure to "cope" in such a sense. Among them may be stress reactions and discomfort sufficient to require the intervention of another in circumstances where such intervention would not normally be expected" (para.6).

9.116 *Activity 15: Getting about:* The differential here between descriptors is one of familiarity. That was thought in the *Review* to ensure the work-related nature of the activity, since the workplace would be a familiar environment. From January 28, 2013, descriptor (a) reads: "cannot get to any place outside the claimant's home with which the claimant is familiar", rather than to "any specified place" thus attempting to make clear that the need is based on most places a claimant cannot get to rather than a single specified place, and aiming to give effect to a policy intention that this activity is to reflect inability to travel unaccompanied by someone for those individuals that are severely affected by a mental health condition (e.g. agoraphobia). "Any place outside the claimant's home" means more than simply beyond their front door. According to Judge Bano in *PC v Secretary of State for Work and Pensions (ESA)* [2015] UKUT 531 (AAC):

> "For my part, I do not consider that putting out the bins or going outside to have a cigarette amounts to 'getting about', even if there is a chance of meeting a neighbour or visitor to the building when doing so. In my judgment, descriptor 1 of Activity 15 requires an investigation of whether a claimant can go to a place outside the immediate vicinity of their home, and that in order to satisfy the descriptor it is not necessary for a claimant to establish that he or she cannot go beyond their front door" (para.8).

The other descriptors refer to "any specified place" or a "specified place", just as did those in Activity 18 in the original LCWA. This phraseology was considered in *DW v SSWP (ESA)* [2011] UKUT 79 (AAC). There, Judge Turnbull dealt with the case of a claimant, suffering from a stress-related illness brought about because of the circumstances of her dismissal from her previous employment, who was found by the tribunal to be fearful of seeing anyone involved with her former employment or reminders of it, such as vans or lorries and who would be unable to visit her employer's premises at all or, at best, accompanied. He took the view that this could not bring her within descriptors 18(a) (as originally worded) or 18(b):

> "the words 'cannot get to any specified place . . .' in 18(a) . . . clearly mean that there is no place with which the claimant is familiar (or would be familiar with if she went out) which she could get to on her own. The words 'is unable to get to a specified place . . . without being accompanied by another person on each occasion' in 18(b) . . . mean that the claimant always needs to be accompanied when getting to a familiar place" (para.15).

Evidence that a claimant had gone unaccompanied to familiar places and accompanied to an unfamiliar one where she was trembling and sweating cannot support a finding that she could go unaccompanied to an unfamiliar place (*LM* v *SSWP*

(ESA) [2013] UKUT 552 (AAC)). See also *MC v SSWP (ESA)* [2015] UKUT 646 (AAC), discussed in the commentary to reg.19 above.

In *AB v SSWP (ESA)* [2016] UKUT 96 (AAC) the issue was whether, if a claimant undertakes a journey by taxi, is that claimant "accompanied" by the taxi driver. Judge Hemingway held that "if a claimant can only undertake a journey to an unfamiliar place by taxi because of a requirement of undertaking the journey in the presence of another person or because the assistance of that other person is required, then that journey is, for the purposes of the relevant descriptor, an accompanied one" (at para.12). The tribunal had therefore erred in law by assuming that a journey in a taxi would be an unaccompanied journey without enquiring into whether the presence of the taxi driver was essential or important to the appellant's ability to make a journey to a specified place with which he was unfamiliar.

See also *TM v SSWP (ESA)* [2018] UKUT 9 (AAC), where Judge Wikeley accepted a concession by the Secretary of State that reg.19(4) limits consideration of aids and appliances to the *physical health* descriptors in Part 1 of Sch.2. and so in the context of activity 15 the FTT should not have considered the claimant's ability to navigate by a mobile phone app.

Activity 16: Coping with social engagement due to cognitive impairment or mental disorder: The primary aim here is to assess functional capability in terms of social contact with the ability to get around being dealt with by other activities. The gradation between descriptors (a), on the one hand, and (b) and (c), on the other, is that the latter two look to inability to engage with strangers, the former with anyone ("social contact is always precluded"). The *Review* thought familiarity an appropriate measure in relation to the workplace. That between (b) and (c) turns on whether that engagement is "never possible" (descriptor (b)) or "not possible for the majority of the time" (descriptor (c)). The preclusion of engagement (descriptor (a)) or the difficulty of engagement (descriptors (b) and (c)) must in each case be "due to difficulty relating to others or significant distress experienced by the individual being assessed for LCW". Contact which involves or would involve "significant distress" must be excluded from consideration" *(DW v SSWP (ESA)* [2014] UKUT 20 (AAC), para.4). 9.117

What does "cope" mean? In *GC* v *SSWP (ESA)* [2013] UKUT 405 (AAC), Judge Ward considered it to be:

> "a word of general application. It significance in the present context is well expressed by a definition given in the Oxford English Dictionary (Online Edition) of 'To manage, deal (competently) with, a situation or problem'. It seems to me that a variety of human behaviours and responses may be indicative of a failure to "cope" in such a sense. Among them may be stress reactions and discomfort sufficient to require the intervention of another in circumstances where such intervention would not normally be expected" (para.6).

In *LM* v *SSWP (ESA)* [2013] UKUT 552 (AAC), Judge Mark considered that descriptor (b) is satisfied if for the majority of the time, social engagement is always precluded (paras 12, 13). As regards descriptors (a) and (b) he could not read "always" as "often" or "for the majority of the time" (the term in descriptor (c)), but rather as "persistently or repeatedly". To say otherwise would have the odd result that a claimant could not satisfy descriptors (a) and (b) but, because of ESA Regs 2008, reg.34(2) would satisfy descriptor 13 in Sch.3 (see para.15). Judge Mark continued:

> "the tribunal is required to form an overall picture of the claimant's ability to engage in social conduct over a period and it does not appear to me that occasional very limited engagement in such conduct need prevent a tribunal concluding that overall the claimant is always unable to do so. To take an extreme example, a person in a coma who surfaces occasionally and is able to engage briefly during that period with familiar and unfamiliar persons before lapsing into unconsciousness should nevertheless be found in this context always to be unable to engage in social contact" (para.16).

He awarded the claimant points under descriptor (b).

See also, however, the annotation to reg.34(2) and the decision of the Court of Session in *SSWP v Brade* [2014] CSIH 39 XA81/13 (May 1,2014); [2014] AACR 29.

The precise scope of "social", of "engagement" and of "contact" has troubled Upper Tribunal Judges and generated different opinions. It has therefore recently been considered by a panel of three Upper Tribunal Judges, but to understand the panel's judgment it is necessary to first take on board the conflicting decisions.

In *KB* v *SSWP (ESA)* [2013] UKUT 152 (AAC), noted in the annotation to Sch.3, activity and descriptor 13 (see para.9.425), as regards "social engagement" and "social contact", Judge Parker, accepting the approach advanced by the Secretary of State's representative, thought "social" to be "a simple reference to relations with other human beings" carrying no connotations of "leisure, pleasure or mutuality", so that a tribunal could properly look at evidence about business visits or contacts with professionals, as well as with friends, relatives and strangers. It was not tied to contact in an informal setting (see paras 15–17). Judge Ward disagreed with this in *AR* v *SSWP (ESA)* [2013] UKUT 446 (AAC). It rendered "social" virtually otiose, placing the focus purely on "engagement with others". It also jarred with the ordinary meaning of the word in the Concise Oxford Dictionary, a meaning Judge Ward thought closer to the legislator's intention. Looking at the legislative history, he considered that the difficulties faced by those with autistic spectrum disorder were very much in mind. Material from the National Autism Society showed the difficulties faced in understanding the rules on social contact and distinguishing a "true friend" from a "pretend friend". Accordingly, in Judge Ward's view,

> "social contact in this sense is not the same as contact for business or professional purposes. If one goes to a medical examination, or a tribunal hearing, the rules are firmly established by the process and/or the person conducting it, and are typically clearly defined, often in writing. If the person being examined or whose case it is does not respond in a way that a person without disability might, the person conducting it may because of their professional responsibilities be expected within generous limits to accommodate the non-conforming response and certainly not, as it were, to take a poorer view of, or attempt to avoid further contact with, the person because of it. That is precisely what is lacking in the social sphere, where people are free to interact on their own terms and to accept the behaviour of another or to reject it, and largely do so on the basis of the sort of unwritten rules to which the National Autism Society guidance makes reference, an inability to respect which could, in the words of the descriptor, be an indication of "difficulty relating to others" (para.18).

In *LM* v *SSWP (ESA)* [2013] UKUT 552 (AAC), Judge Mark cited this paragraph and gave it qualified support, stating that while he agreed that

> "merely attending a medical examination or tribunal hearing does not establish an ability to engage in social contact, but it does not follow that in the course of that examination or hearing the party will not demonstrate an ability to respond appropriately and engage in limited social contact despite the distress that the meeting is causing and that such contact causes. The fact that a person is not so far along the autistic spectrum as to be wholly unable to engage in social contact does not mean that a person might not experience significant distress if required to engage in such contact. A tribunal needs to assess the ability to engage in social contact, which can be in any context, the extent to which a person has the capacity so to engage, the distress it causes when engagement occurs and the impact of that distress on the ability so to engage" (para.18).

9.118 In *JM v SSWP (ESA)* [2014] UKUT 22 (AAC), Judge Gray endorsed Judge Ward's view and added "the observation that because for the important purpose of benefit entitlement, or indeed in order to effect treatment for a mental health condition, one may be able to summon up reserves to attend such an appointment that may not be sufficient in relation to a test which is of the ability to perform an activity reliably and repeatedly" (para.16).

In *AP* v *SSWP (ESA)* [2013] UKUT 293 (AAC), Judge Turnbull considered descriptor (c). He accepted that

> "difficulty, from a mental point of view, in simply getting alone to the destination does not fall to be taken into account under activity 16 (unless the difficulty getting there is itself due to problems with engaging in social contact (e.g. on public transport)). In other words, a claimant does not qualify for points under activity 16(c) merely because he could not put himself in most of the situations where he might engage in social contact with someone unfamiliar, because he could not leave the house unaccompanied in order to do so" (para.11).

"The difficulty with others" aspect of the descriptor envisaged the situation in which it is the need to engage with others which caused the problem. In contrast, however, the alternative—"significant distress experienced by the individual"—did not, in his view,

> "require that it is the need to interact with others which per se causes the distress. ... the wording is satisfied whatever the immediate cause of the distress may be, provided that it is due to cognitive impairment or mental disorder, and that it is sufficiently severe and occurs on sufficient occasions to prevent the claimant engaging with others "for the majority of the time."
>
> Thus, if the effect of having to leave his home unaccompanied, or to enter unfamiliar buildings, is to cause distress which prevents the claimant then being able to engage with someone unfamiliar, ... 16(c) could apply, even if the claimant would have been perfectly capable of engaging with that unfamiliar person if he had been accompanied by friend or family, or if he had been in familiar surroundings.
>
> Thus, the Claimant in the present case was not in my judgment prevented from satisfying 16(c) merely because it was not the process of interacting with unfamiliar persons per se which caused her difficulty" (paras 12–14).

In *SSWP v LC (ESA)* [2014] UKUT 268 (AAC), Judge Williams agreed with Judge Ward's comments on "social contact" in *AR v SSWP (ESA)* [2013] UKUT 446 (AAC) and with Judge Mark's "persuasive analysis" of the meaning of "always" in *LM v SSWP (ESA)* [2013] UKUT 552 (AAC). Judge Williams considered that it "can be read as meaning "every day" but not "every moment", something important where the problems of a claimant are variable. His construction of "always" was, however, made without knowing of the decision of the Court of Session in *SSWP v Brade* [2014] AACR 29 (see annotation to ESA Regs 2008 reg.34(2)), and reads "always" somewhat more narrowly than the Court of Session which saw it as connoting "cannot 'for the majority of the time' engage". In addition, his decision was made before that in *JC v SSWP (ESA)* [2014] UKUT 352 (AAC); [2015] AACR 6 in which a panel of three Upper Tribunal Judges considered this activity and the case law on it, in particular the conflicting approaches of Judge Parker in *KB v SSWP (ESA)* [2013] UKUT 152 (AAC) and Judge Ward in *AR*, above. Insofar as other decisions are at variance with that of the Three-Judge Panel, *JC* is the authoritative decision to be followed.

In *JC*, the panel considered it "common ground" that the phrases "coping with social engagement" in the definition of the activity and "engagement in social contact" in the definition of the descriptor have the same meaning (para.6). It accepted the submission that "the Activities and their descriptors are intended to assess whether a person is able to engage with others for the purpose of work" (para.16). It also agreed with Judge Wikeley's comments in para.19 of his decision in *AS v SSWP (ESA)* [2013] UKUT 587 (AAC) that the activities and descriptors must be "applied on their own terms, but understood against the backdrop of the modern workplace" (para.16). The panel took the view that the differences between Judges Parker and Ward were less than appeared at first sight (para.22). Like Judge Ward it disagreed with Judge Parker that "social" simply meant "relations with other human beings" and did not "carry connotations of leisure and pleasure", but, unlike Judge Ward, did not accept that Parliament's intention was directed only at the difficulties in communication experienced by these with Autistic Spectrum Disorder (ASD) or similar difficulties, although it agreed that Parliament would have had the difficulties of those with ASD in mind (para.25). Instead, the causes "referred to in the Activities and their Descriptors" when read in the context of other relevant provisions in the legislation "show that the intention was not so confined but was directed to the possible impact of a wider range of impairments or disorders" (para.26). The panel saw the words of the definitions in the Activities and Descriptors at issue as a whole and the underlying statutory purposes as being "the most important factors that determine the nature and quality of the behaviour and communications covered by the Activities and their descriptors" (para. 27). Applying these factors requires decision-makers and tribunals to consider the following:

"(i) the range of meanings in common usage of the individual words that are used and so of "coping", "engagement", "social" and "contact" in the context of their combined effect,

(ii) the causes referred to in the Activities for the problems with coping with and engaging in social contact,

(iii) the causes referred to in the Descriptors and their link with the relevant cognitive impairment or mental disorder, and

(iv) the underlying purposes of the legislation and so of the assessments" (para.27).

Given the underlying purposes (whether a person is able to engage with others for the purpose of work and the context of the modern workplace), the panel could not endorse limitation to

> "the nature and quality of the contact or engagement . . . to contact for pleasure or leisure or characterised by friendliness, geniality or companionship and so the choices that that involves [since such a limitation] would be surprising because that limitation (a) would exclude aspects of communication in the workplace, and (b) would not take proper account of the distinction in the descriptors between communication with people with whom the claimant is familiar and all communication. Indeed, it seems to us that points (a) and (b) dictate that the tests in the Activities and their Descriptors extend to contact for the purposes of work and so to contact with other characteristics and purposes that involve different degrees of choice or no choice because they relate to a structured situation or professional relationship (e.g. doctor and patient, lawyer and client)" (para.28).

On that basis the panel agreed with Judge Parker and the Secretary of State that, taken in isolation, "social" is a reference to "with other human beings" (para.29). However, since "social" is not isolated but qualifies "engagement" or "contact", this left open

> "the nature and quality of the "engagement" or "contact" that is precluded or not possible for the given reasons and thus the assessment of what "engagement or contact with other people" the claimant can cope with due to his cognitive impairment or mental disorder" (para.30).

9.119 Key elements here, viewing "coping" and "engagement" in the context of the statutory purposes underlying assessment, were ones of "reciprocity, give and take, initiation and response" (para.32). These can be demonstrated not only by contact characterised by friendliness, geniality or companionship but also "without those elements (and the choices they involve) being present" such as "is often the case in the workplace and elsewhere", although those other contexts might also sometimes display them (para.32). The panel usefully pointed to examples which could equally demonstrate "the necessary degree of reciprocity, give and take, initiation and response": buying a ticket or groceries; contact with a medical examiner or other professional; conversation with a stranger on a park bench or elsewhere; or contact with the First-tier Tribunal itself (para.33). The panel saw the issues, fact finding and value judgements involved as eminently suitable for the First-tier Tribunal, and in the view of the panel:

> "it is open to a decision maker to base his decision on an example or examples chosen from a wide range of situations. Whether the evidence and findings relating to the claimant's communications with others and behaviour in the chosen example or examples have the necessary degree of reciprocity, give and take, initiation and response raises issues of fact and degree and of judgment having regard to all the circumstances relating to them. As with other such issues, the authorities show that it is not practical or appropriate to identify the statutory criterion by reference to abstract examples or by reference to a general classification or description other than the statutory test" (para.34).

The proper approach for a tribunal in each case is to consider and determine how

> "The nature and quality of the examples of communications and behaviour they take into account (and thus the reciprocity, give and take, initiation and response shown thereby) would, for the reasons given in the Activities and their Descriptors, be likely to be an effective barrier to the claimant working" (para.35).

The panel accepted that, because the conceptual test thus set out involves value judgments, this leaves "room for different decision-makers applying the right approach in the right way to reach different answers" (para.36 read with paras 9–12).

Good decision-making here involves carrying out the necessary fact-finding "separately from, although with an eye to, the value judgements that have to be applied to those findings" so as to identify and particularise "by reference to primary facts, the situations and events that will be taken into account and so the bedrock of the decision" (para.38). To reach their decision the tribunal must

> "address and decide whether those findings show that:
>
> (i) the claimant has cognitive impairment or mental disorder,
> (ii) a causative link between that impairment or disorder and his difficulty relating to others or significant distress, and
> (iii) a causative link between that difficulty and distress and a preclusion for all of the time or an impossibility for a majority of the time of contact with all other people, or those who are unfamiliar to the claimant, that has the necessary degree of reciprocity, give and take, initiation and response.
>
> In addressing whether the contact with other people has the necessary nature and quality the tribunal should consider in each individual case how the nature and quality of the communications and behaviour would impact on the ability of the individual to work and so whether or not it would be an effective barrier to him working" (paras 38–39).

As regards the first case under appeal, the panel considered that the tribunal had erred in law in that it may not have understood or applied the statutory test correctly. It had seemed to be concerned about the claimant being able to be helped by someone. The panel did not consider that a person could properly be regarded "as able to engage in social contact if she or he can do so only if accompanied by someone, at least without further explanation as to how it is envisaged that that might be realistic in the workplace" (para.45). The matter was remitted for decision by another tribunal to be decided in light of the guidance proffered by the panel's decision. The panel found no error of law in the second case under appeal (paras 49–60).

9.120 *Activity 17: Appropriateness of behaviour with other people, due to cognitive impairment or mental disorder*: This was revised to remove some of the more negative phraseology of its predecessor, to find more "neutral" terms than "bizarre" or "outbursts". Gradation between descriptors is set in terms of the frequency of the episodes of the relevant behaviour: (a) "on a daily basis"; (b) "frequently"; (c) "occasionally". The episodes must in each case be "uncontrollable". In each case, the behaviour must be "aggressive or disinhibited". A key standard in each descriptor is whether this behaviour "would be unreasonable in any workplace".

As regards descriptor (a), in *WT* v *SSWP (ESA)* [2013] UKUT 556 (AAC), Judge Gray considered the meaning of "on a daily basis". While this was a decision dealing with identical wording in Sch.3, activity/descriptor 14, Judge Gray also applied it to descriptor (a), its "mirror descriptor". Rather than merely deploy a dictionary definition, he took the "mischief" approach to interpretation and reasoned thus:

> "The mischief that the descriptor must be intended to remedy is the creation of an unsafe or otherwise unacceptable work environment for co-workers. The way in which the avoidance of that is accomplished is to exclude from the workplace those who, due to their mental health condition exhibit certain behaviour. If on virtually every day that they were at work they displayed such behaviour, would the fact that there were very rare days on which they did not prevent them from falling within the meaning of the descriptor? To answer "yes" to that question would not be to address the mischief. The descriptor must, then, be interpreted more widely than literally every day.
>
> I fortify myself in this view because the ordinary meaning of the words "on a daily basis" seem to me to connote a lesser test than "every day". The phrase is not confined to events which happen literally every day. Someone might be said to read a particular newspaper on a daily basis even though there were periods when they did not, such as where they were abroad on holiday when it was not available. Walking the dog on a daily basis is an activity which may be interrupted by the ill-health of either dog or walker, but a short break would not change the very regular nature of the activity or make that description inapt.
>
> The words "on a daily basis", then, in the context of schedule 3 descriptor 14, and its mirror descriptor under schedule 2, regulation 17 (a), means certainly more than for the majority of the time, that being the regulation 34 (2) test, and must mean more than frequently, that being the test of periodicity in regulation 17(b), but it does not mean literally every day or even on every working day. The essence is of this being an enduring position; one which is happening regularly, constantly or continually. It is for the tribunal to find the facts as to the frequency of the behaviour set out in the descriptor, and then apply this approach to those facts with their usual common sense" (paras 40-42).

As regards descriptor (c), in *KE* v *SSWP (ESA)* [2013] UKUT 370 (AAC), Judge Williams noted that "the incidence [of disinhibited behaviour] is at a lower level of occurrence but at a higher level of intensity than the previous test, although the underlying issue manifested by these forms of conduct is the same" (para.17). It now attracts three more points than its predecessor (9 rather than 6). The claimant had several times been required to leave the Jobcentre because of abusive and insulting things he said rather than did, "a classic form of disinhibited behaviour". As regards the criterion "unreasonable in any workplace, Judge Williams thought a Jobcentre unlikely to "apply a lower test than an employer would be expected to apply" (para.18).

In *WC v SSWP (ESA)* [2014] UKUT 363, Judge Rowley commended to tribunals considering descriptors under this Activity the following list of questions constituting a "methodical approach":

"(a) Does the claimant have cognitive impairment or mental disorder?

(b) If so, does that cause the claimant to behave in the way described by the descriptor, namely:

(i) Does the claimant have episodes of aggressive or disinhibited behaviour?
(ii) Are any such episodes uncontrollable?
(iii) How often do they occur (noting the words of the descriptor: "on a daily basis," "frequently," "occasionally,").
(iv) Would such behaviour be unreasonable in any workplace?" (para.10).

Judge Rowley, adopting Judge Gray's observations in the quotation from *WT*, considered that the relevant behaviour could include "sufficiently serious verbal aggression" since its use

> "may well create an unacceptable work environment for co-workers, or indeed others with whom the person exhibiting the behaviour may come into contact in the workplace. It would be wrong to say that such conduct can never be enough to satisfy activity 17. Further, in my view it is not necessary for the claimant to have been involved in a fight or argument for activity 17 to apply. There may be examples where his or her behaviour has been aggressive or disinhibited but has not led to another person responding by fighting or arguing. Indeed, in many cases when faced with such behaviour, some people's natural reaction is to walk away. That does not necessarily make the aggressive or disinhibited behaviour any less serious, nor does it necessarily render it any more acceptable to co-workers or others in the workplace. In each case it will be for the tribunal to consider the evidence, find the facts and decide, in the light of those findings, whether a particular claimant's behaviour, whether physical or verbal, is sufficient to satisfy the relevant criteria" (para.16).

Moreover, since the wording of Activity 17 applies to "any workplace", he rejected as an "unnecessary gloss" on that wording the submission of the Secretary of State that "the claimant's behaviour would have to be considered unacceptable in an average workplace such as a call centre" (para.18).

It is vital to note that under ESA Regs 2008, reg.19(2), (5) incapability of performing the activity in respect of any descriptor in Pt 2 of Sch.2 must arise from a specific mental illness or disablement. Alcohol misuse in itself is not such a disablement. To rank as disablement the misuse of alcohol must rank as "alcohol dependency" in terms of the "constellation of markers" found in quotations from *R(DLA) 6/06* in the Three-Judge Panel's decision in *JG v SSWP (ESA)* [2013] UKUT 37 (AAC); [2013] AACR 23. Accordingly, in *DR v SSWP (ESA)* [2014] UKUT 188 (AAC); [2014] AACR 38, Judge May held the tribunal were right to hold that the descriptors did not apply. Moreover, he was persuaded that

> "the volume of alcohol the claimant is said to drink on a daily basis would not in itself amount to the disinhibited behaviour referred to in descriptors 17(a) in Schedule 2 and 14 in Schedule 3. I see the force in Mr Webster's submission that disinhibited behaviour requires the context of an inhibition. I cannot see, and it has not been established, what the inhibition in this case is and how the drinking of a certain volume of alcohol amounts in itself to disinhibited behaviour. Disinhibited behaviour may result as a consequence of drinking specific quantities of alcohol but that is not the basis upon which the claimant's argument is put. Mr Orr seeks to widen "disinhibition" beyond the scope of what the statutory provisions can bear. The activity for both descriptors relates to the appropriateness of behaviour "with" other people, which suggests that the descriptor is intended to be applied in respect of behaviour which is more than the passive drinking of alcohol" (para.8).

Consideration of Activity 17 may require the disclosure of Unacceptable Customer Behaviour (UCB) forms as provided in confidence by the DWP to HMCTS: *MH v SSWP (ESA)* [2021] UKUT 90 (AAC).

[1SCHEDULE 3 **Regulation 34(1)**

9.121 ASSESSMENT OF WHETHER A CLAIMANT HAS LIMITED CAPABILITY FOR WORK-RELATED ACTIVITY

Activity	*Descriptors*
[2 1. Mobilising unaided by another person with or without a walking stick, manual wheelchair or other aid if such aid is normally, or could reasonably be, worn or used.]	Cannot either: (a) mobilise more than 50 metres on level ground without stopping in order to avoid significant discomfort or exhaustion; or (b) repeatedly mobilise 50 metres within a reasonable timescale because of significant discomfort or exhaustion.
2. Transferring from one seated position to another.	Cannot move between one seated position and another seated position located next to one another without receiving physical assistance from another person.
3. Reaching.	Cannot raise either arm as if to put something in the top pocket of a coat or jacket.
4. Picking up and moving or transferring by the use of the upper body and arms (excluding standing, sitting, bending or kneeling and all other activities specified in this Schedule).	Cannot pick up and move a 0.5 litre carton full of liquid.
5. Manual dexterity.	[3Cannot press a button (such as a telephone keypad) with either hand or cannot turn the pages of a book with either hand.]
[2 6. Making self understood through speaking, writing, typing, or other means which are normally, or could reasonably be, used, unaided by another person.]	Cannot convey a simple message, such as the presence of a hazard.
[2 7. Understanding communication by: (i) verbal means (such as hearing or lip reading) alone, (ii) non-verbal means (such as reading 16 point print or Braille) alone, or (iii) a combination of (i) and (ii), using any aid that is normally, or could reasonably be, used, unaided by another person.]	Cannot understand a simple message [3,such as the location of a fire escape due to sensory impairment [3...] .
[2 8. Absence or loss of control whilst conscious leading to extensive evacuation of the bowel and/or voiding of the bladder, other than enuresis (bed-wetting), despite the wearing or use of any aids or adaptations which are normally, or could reasonably be, worn or used.]	At least once a week experiences: (a) loss of control leading to extensive evacuation of the bowel and/or voiding of the bladder; or (b) substantial leakage of the contents of a collecting device sufficient to require the individual to clean themselves and change clothing.

Activity	*Descriptors*
9. Learning tasks.	Cannot learn how to complete a simple task, such as setting an alarm clock, due to cognitive impairment or mental disorder.
10. Awareness of hazard.	Reduced awareness of everyday hazards, due to cognitive impairment or mental disorder, leads to a significant risk of: (a) injury to self or others; or (b) damage to property or possessions such that [3 the claimant requires] supervision for the majority of the time to maintain safety.
11. Initiating and completing personal action (which means planning, organisation, problem solving, prioritising or switching tasks).	Cannot, due to impaired mental function, reliably initiate or complete at least 2 sequential personal actions.
12. Coping with change.	Cannot cope with any change, due to cognitive impairment or mental disorder, to the extent that day to day life cannot be managed.
13. Coping with social engagement, due to cognitive impairment or mental disorder.	Engagement in social contact is always precluded due to difficulty relating to others or significant distress experienced by the [3 claimant].
14. Appropriateness of behaviour with other people, due to cognitive impairment or mental disorder.	Has, on a daily basis, uncontrollable episodes of aggressive or disinhibited behaviour that would be unreasonable in any workplace.
15. Conveying food or drink to the mouth.	(a) Cannot convey food or drink to the claimant's own mouth without receiving physical assistance from someone else; (b) Cannot convey food or drink to the claimant's own mouth without repeatedly [3 stopping or] experiencing breathlessness or severe discomfort; (c) Cannot convey food or drink to the claimant's own mouth without receiving regular prompting given by someone else in the claimant's physical presence; or (d) Owing to a severe disorder of mood or behaviour, fails to convey food or drink to the claimant's own mouth without receiving: (i) physical assistance from someone else; or (ii) regular prompting given by someone else in the claimant's presence.

Activity	*Descriptors*
16. Chewing or swallowing food or drink.	(a) Cannot chew or swallow food or drink; (b) Cannot chew or swallow food or drink without repeatedly stopping, experiencing breathlessness or severe discomfort; (c) Cannot chew or swallow food or drink without repeatedly receiving regular prompting given by someone else in the claimant's presence; or (d) Owing to a severe disorder of mood or behaviour, fails to: (i) chew or swallow food or drink; or (ii) chew or swallow food or drink without regular prompting given by someone else in the claimant's presence.]

AMENDMENTS

1. Employment and Support Allowance (Limited Capability for Work and Limited Capability for Work-Related Activity) (Amendment) Regulations 2011 (SI 2011/228) reg.4(2) (March 28, 2011).
2. Employment and Support Allowance (Amendment) Regulations 2012 (SI 2012/3096) reg.5(2) (January 28, 2013, subject to application, transitional and savings provisions in reg.2 of this amending instrument, para.9.614).
3. Social Security (Miscellaneous Amendments) (No.3) Regulations 2013 (SI 2013/2536) reg.13(34) (October 29, 2013).

DEFINITIONS

"claimant"—see WRA 2007 s.24(1).

GENERAL NOTE

9.122 Establishing limited capability for work-related activity might be said to be the central condition of entitlement to support component. The assumption behind ESA is that the vast majority of claimants, if given the right support, are in fact capable of some work. Government anticipates that only some 10 per cent of claimants (those with more severe health conditions) will be entitled to the support component and so not be subject to work-related activity conditionality requirements. Entry to this protected support group depends on it being established—generally through a work-related activity assessment (LCWRA) of a more stringent nature than the LCWA covered by reg.19 and Sch.2—that the claimant has limited capability for work-related activity: the LCWRA is thus the second element in the revised Work Capability Assessment.

Entry to the support group is based on someone demonstrating that they have a severe level of functional limitation. Until January 28, 2013, this was established when by reason of the claimant's physical or mental condition, at least one of the range of descriptors in this revised Sch.3 to the ESA Regs applies to the claimant. From that date, reg.34(3A) provides that in deciding which descriptor applies, incapability must arise in respect of descriptors 1 to 8, 15(a), 15(b), 16(a) and 16 (b), from a specific bodily disease or disablement or as a direct result of treatment provided by a registered medical practitioner for such a disease or disablement (para.

(3A)(a), (c)(i)). Similarly, as regards descriptors 9 to 14, 15(c), 15(d), 16(c) and 16 (d), incapability must arise from a specific mental illness or disablement; or as a direct result of treatment provided by a registered medical practitioner for such an illness or disablement (para.(3A)(b), (c)(i)). Note that for some cases after January 28, 2013, for a six month period, the previous version of reg.34 can be applicable (see reg.2 of the amending instrument, below, para.9.614). Under both original and amended forms of reg.34, assessment has to take account of prostheses, aids and appliances (para.(3)). It is submitted here that the key elements of IB case law and ESA case law which carry across into interpreting and applying the provisions in Sch.2 on the revised LCWA will also apply here: decide in the light of the totality of the evidence, making a careful appraisal of differing medical reports; the need for careful attention to detail; the concept of reasonable regularity (the test is not a snapshot); relevant factors of pain, discomfort and of fears for the claimant's health; and the need carefully to approach conditions which vary and fluctuate. But here reg.34(2) makes clear that a:

> "descriptor applies to a claimant if that descriptor applies to the claimant for the majority of the time or, as the case may be, on the majority of the occasions on which the claimant undertakes or attempts to undertake the activity described by that descriptor."

This, in broad terms appears to put on a statutory footing for the LCWRA assessment, the "reasonable regularity" test approved for incapacity benefit in *R(IB) 2/99* and by analogy applicable to ESA assessments (*EH v SSWP (ESA)* [2011] UKUT 21 (AAC), para.31). In considering issues under Sch.3, a tribunal should also consider the full ESA85 report and not simply the section stating the EMP's opinion on the Sch.3 issues, as well as other applicable medical evidence with respect to the claimant (*EH v SSWP (ESA)* [2011] UKUT 21 (AAC), paras 27–30, 41–44). The focus, as in Sch.2, should be on "the claimant's functional ability to perform the particular aspect of the activity covered by a descriptor" (*EH v SSWP (ESA)* [2011] UKUT 21 (AAC), para.38, approving Judge Jacobs's in *GS v SSWP (ESA)* [2010] UKUT 244 (AAC), para.14). On the importance of a consistent approach to the descriptors under Sch.2 and Sch.3 respectively, see *SSWP v JL (ESA)* [2018] UKUT 291 (AAC).

There is no scoring system and the criteria are deliberately more stringent than in the LCWA. In Committee, the Minister for Employment and Welfare Reform explained both characteristics: **9.123**

> "The levels of functional limitation used in the descriptors for determining limited capability for work-related activity are greater because we intend to place in the support group only the minority of customers who are so severely impaired that it would not be reasonable to require them to undertake work-related activity . . . People with less severe functional limitations across a range of descriptors might score highly and be inappropriately included in the support group when they might benefit from work-related activity . . . A number of case studies were provided in the background information, which hon. Members will find helpful. [See DWP, *Welfare Reform Bill: Draft Regulations and Supporting Material* (January 2007), pp.13–17.] Under the revised PCA, someone with a moderate learning disability would score 50 points. They would be significantly above the 15-point threshold, but we clearly would not wish to put even someone with 50 points into the support group automatically, because we are determined to ensure that the new system does not write off people with learning disabilities. The technical groups considered all the options. A crude points-based system would have unintended consequences." (*Hansard*, Standing Committee A, October 19, 2006 (afternoon), col.120 (Mr Jim Murphy MP)).

In *CD v SSWP (ESA)* [2012] UKUT (AAC) 289; [2013] AACR 12, Judge Levenson considered the relationship between the terms of descriptors in Sch.2 and the correlative provision in Sch.3, albeit in the context of the Schedules as at March 27, 2011:

> "Irrespective of what the Minister told the relevant committee, looking at the wording of the legislation and regulations I cannot find any support for the Secretary of State's argument that a person qualifying under Sch.3 must inevitably be more severely impaired than one who qualifies under Sch.2. The claimant's reference to the reaching descriptors [now Sch.2 para.3(a); Sch.3, para.3] is persuasive on this point" (para.21).

In *CN v SSWP (ESA)* [2014] UKUT 286 (AAC), Judge Markus applied *CD v SSWP (ESA)* [2012] UKUT 289 (AAC); [2013] AACR 12 to find erroneous in law a tribunal decision finding the claimant not to have limited capability for work-related activity when it had accepted that he had limited capability for work without reviewing the basis on which the decision-maker had proceeded (he had used the "old" pre January 2011Sch.2), since that limited capability was not disputed. Judge Markus accepted that there are more substantial differences in wording between the two relevant descriptors in this case than between those in issue in *CD*, but was of the opinion that a claimant who fell within old activity 16(a) would fall within new activity 13(a) in the current version of Sch.2 and so would also fall within activity 11 in Sch.3. Moreover a person who satisfies activity 17(a) under the old Sch.2 must satisfy activity 12 of the current Sch.3, as long as the inability is due to cognitive impairment or mental disorder.

There is an equivalent of the "exceptional circumstances" provision applicable to the limited capability for work question, considered above. A claimant who does not pass the LCWRA can nonetheless be treated as having the requisite limited capability for work-related activity grounding membership of the support group where, by reason of the specific disease or bodily or mental disablement from which s/he suffers, "there would be a substantial risk to the mental or physical health of any person if the claimant were found not to have limited capability for work-related activity" (reg.35(2)).

There were only 11 activities in the original Sch.3. They covered walking or moving on level ground; rising from sitting and transferring from one seated position to another; picking up and moving or transferring by means of the upper body and arms; reaching; manual dexterity; continence; maintaining personal hygiene; eating and drinking (conveying food or drink to the mouth and chewing or swallowing it); learning or comprehension in the completion of tasks; personal action (planning, organisation, problem solving, prioritising or switching tasks); and communication. The terms of the descriptors were also more stringent than in the LCWA, to avoid removing too many people from the group which affords incentive to engage in work-related activity and thus denying them the opportunity to take steps to make real their fundamental right to work. Thus, as regards walking, the single descriptor (since amended) could only be met where a claimant could not "walk" more than 30 metres without repeatedly stopping, experiencing breathlessness or severe discomfort. "Walk" covered walking with a walking stick, other aid or crutches, each if normally used; and embraced the claimant moving by manually propelling a wheelchair. That on rising from sitting etc, required in effect that the claimant fulfilled two of the 15 point descriptors in the LCWA. Most, with counterparts in the LCWA, were couched in terms equivalent to the more difficult of their 15 point descriptors. That original Sch.2 will apply to all decisions made before March 28, 2011 and also beyond that date where ESA questionnaires had before that date been sent out to claimants or notified persons under the Migration Regulations (transferees from IB, IS (incapacity based) or SDA. But that concession on questionnaires sent out before March 28 will cease after six months (September 28, 2011) (see reg.2 of the amending Regulations).

Those meeting the LCWRA test (or satisfying the "exceptional circumstances" provision) were placed in the support group and received the support component without having to satisfy work-related activity conditions, although they could voluntarily participate in those programmes. Their position could be reviewed periodically or where there had been a change of circumstances in the claimant's physical or mental condition or it was thought that a previous determination was made in ignorance of or a mistake as to some material fact (reg.34(4), (5)). The threshold for membership of the support group was high; many claimants in receipt of the middle and higher rates of Disability Living Allowance (DLA) may not meet it. Those who fail to establish limited capability for work-related activity instead receive the work-related activity component.

Under the revised LCWRA assessment the subject of this commentary, now comprising 16 activities, the threshold remains high, and the same basic rules on the support group continue to apply. But Government anticipated that the revisions and reformulations effected by the *Review* and *CMA* honing (see further the commentary to Sch.2, above) would mean a slight expansion of the numbers allocated to the support group because of a relaxed mobility descriptor (Activity 1 now aligns its requisite distance at 50 metres, as opposed to 30 metres, the same as its highest scoring LCWA counterpart), changes to the mental function assessment and the addition of another sensory impairment-related support group (*Review*, para.5.2). As regards Activities 1–15, each activity and single descriptor corresponds to descriptor (a) (usually the highest scoring but always the one hardest to satisfy) in the corresponding Activity in the LCWA in the revised Sch.2, above. Consequently, it is submitted that any case law on corresponding terms in those revised Sch.2 descriptors is applicable to those in Sch.3, as effective from March 28, 2011. Note, however, that the numbering does not correspond as between Schs 2 and 3. Thus in Sch.3 (LCWRA), there is no equivalent of Sch.2 (LCWA) activity 8 (Navigation and maintaining safety, using a guide dog or other aid if normally used), activity 10 (Consciousness during waking moments) or activity 15 (getting about). Similarly, there is in Sch.2 (LCWA) itself, no equivalent of Sch.3 (LCWRA) multi-descriptor activities 15 (conveying food or drink to the mouth) or 16 (Chewing or swallowing food or drink). Instead, persons covered by those activities in the terms set out in Sch.3 (LCWRA) are from March 28, 2011 treated as having limited capability for work under ESA Regs, reg.20(g).

On the need to interpret the terms of both this Sch and Sch.2 against the background of a working environment, see the annotation to Sch.2 *(Approaching the Interpretation of the Schedule as a whole) (the LCWA is not a snapshot—the need for an approach characterized by "reasonableness").*

Interpreting specific activities and descriptors

Activity 1: "Mobilising unaided by another person with or without a walking stick, manual wheelchair or other aid if such aid can reasonably be used": This descriptor contains two tests. As Judge Williams put it in *HD v SSWP (ESA)* [2014] UKUT 72 (AAC): **9.124**

> "the "cannot either" ... "or" wording is properly interpreted as meaning "one or the other of (a) and (b)". In other words, a claimant who can satisfy the Secretary of State or a tribunal that he or she cannot mobilise to the level of one or other of (a) and (b) is entitled to be regarded as meeting the descriptor as a whole even if he or she can mobilise to the extent that the other is met" (para.4, citing para.15 of his decision granting leave to appeal).

The Secretary of State accepted that interpretation (*ibid.*, para.5) to the same effect see *GC* v *SSWP (ESA)* [2014] UKUT 117 (AAC), applying *HD*, and *KB v SSWP (ESA)* [2014] UKUT 126 (AAC), both decisions on Activity 1 in Sch.2. In *AH* v *SSWP (ESA)* [2013] UKUT 118 (AAC); [2013] AACR 32, Judge Jacobs pointed up the difference in wording between descriptors 1(a) and 1(b). With 1(a), he saw it as impossible to read into it "the need for regularity" (para.14). In contrast the wording of 1(b), taking due account also of reg.34(2), demands mobilising "repeatedly", without "significant discomfort or exhaustion" and within a "reasonable timescale". Judge Jacobs saw these as "normal words in everyday use" and as being coloured by their context. But he saw

"no reason why they should have a different meaning just because they appear in Schedule 3. The purpose of that Schedule is to identify claimants who are not required to take part in work-related activity. But it does so by reference to the nature and extent of their disabilities, not by reference to work-related activity itself. The effect of coming within Schedule 3 may differ from the effect of coming within Schedule 2, but the criteria for classifying claimants are the same. I am not going to attempt to define what these words mean. That would be wrong. It would be the wrong approach to statutory interpretation and would trespass impermissibly into the role of the First-tier Tribunal. It is not for the Upper Tribunal to give more specific content to the law than the language used in the legislation. The Upper Tribunal will not decide that 'repeatedly' means five times, ten times or any other number. Nor will the Upper Tribunal decide that 'reasonable timescale' means five seconds, five minutes or any other time.
The correct approach was explained by Lord Upjohn in *Customs and Excise Commissioners* v *Top Ten Promotions Ltd* [1969] 1 W.L.R. 1163, at 1171:

> 'It is highly dangerous, if not impossible, to attempt to place an accurate definition upon a word in common use; you can look up examples of its many uses if you want to in the Oxford Dictionary but that does not help on definition; in fact it probably only shows that the word normally defies definition. The task of the court in construing statutory language such as that which is before your Lordships is to look at the mischief at which the Act is directed and then, in that light, to consider whether as a matter of common sense and every day usage the known, proved or admitted or properly inferred facts of the particular case bring the case within the ordinary meaning of the words used by Parliament.'

The key to applying the words of Activity 1 lies in making findings of fact relevant to those words that are as specific as the evidence allows. And, if the claimant is present at the hearing, the tribunal should ensure that it obtains evidence that is sufficient to that purpose. Just to take one example: the tribunal should have probed Mr H's evidence that he 'could not repeatedly do 50 metres'. How far could he walk before stopping? What made him stop? How did he feel? How soon could he proceed? How often could he repeat that process? This was particularly important in this case, because of the content of Mr H's evidence to the tribunal. At least as it was recorded by the judge—the record of proceedings does not have to be verbatim—his evidence was expressed in the language of the Schedule. The tribunal had to obtain evidence that would allow it to assess Mr H's answers by reference to that language. It could not do that if the evidence repeated that language. The tribunal would at least need to know what Mr H meant by 'repeatedly', as he might not be using it in the same way as in Activity 1" (paras 18–21).

As regards "could reasonably be … used", Upper Tribunal Judges are divided on the permissible range of matters to examine, and the issue of the proper approach to take is to be decided by a tribunal of three Upper Tribunal Judges. See further the annotation to Sch.2, Activity 1, above.

9.125 *Activity 7: "understanding communication"; Descriptor "cannot understand a simpler message such as the location of a fire escape due to sensory impairment"*: In *AT and VC v SSWP (ESA)* [2015] UKUT 445 (AAC); [2016] AACR 8, Judge Markus QC was "satisfied that Activity 7 in Schedule 3 was intended to correspond with the highest descriptor in Activity 7 of Schedule 2" (para.53). Furthermore, as with Sch.2, Activity 7 (both in its current and previous formulations: see para 54) "applied to a claimant who was unable to communicate by either verbal means or non-verbal means and it was not necessary for the claimant to be unable to communicate by both means" (para.53). Judge Markus's decision was followed in the context of the post-January 2013 version of the regulations by Judge Ward in *CM v SSWP (ESA)* [2016] UKUT 242 (AAC). Both decisions were followed by Judge Church in *RK v SSWP (ESA)* [2019] UKUT 345 (AAC).

Activity 9: "learning tasks"; Descriptor: "Cannot learn how to complete a simple task, such as setting an alarm clock, due to cognitive impairment or mental disorder: See the following guidance from Judge Rowley on this activity in *Secretary of State for Work and Pensions v AT (ESA)* [2017] UKUT 338 (AAC): 9.126

> *"cannot learn"*
> 3. The activity is concerned with a claimant's ability to "learn" a new task, i.e. their ability to absorb, understand and retain information. As the WCA Handbook recognises, different people learn in different ways. They may prefer to watch a visual demonstration, have verbal instruction or read instructions. An inability to learn using one method would not generally lead to an overall inability to learn a new task if another way could be employed.
>
> *"how to complete a simple task"*
> 4. "Simple task" is not defined. It would be inappropriate for me to offer any further definition, save perhaps to note the obvious – a simple task is one which is easy and straightforward. It is unlikely to involve more than one or two steps.
>
> *"such as setting an alarm clock"*
> 5. The words "such as" are important. They confirm that the illustration given – of setting an alarm clock – is merely an example. Other instances may need to be considered by decision makers and tribunals. Further examples are listed in the WCA Handbook:
>
> > "Brushing teeth. This would involve remembering to put toothpaste onto a brush and brushing all areas of teeth.
> > Washing. This would involve the ability to use soap/shower gel and wash their body.
> > Brushing hair.
> > Turning on the television/using basic functions on the TV remote control.
> > Getting a glass of water."

Judge Rowley also stressed the further fundamental requirement that the inability to learn a simple task be "due to cognitive impairment or mental disorder", as reinforced by the requirements of reg.34(6)(b).

Activity 12: "coping with change": Descriptor: "Cannot cope with any change, due to cognitive or mental disorder, to the extent that day to day life cannot be managed": In *CH v SSWP (ESA)* [2013] UKUT 207 (AAC), Judge Fordham held that 9.127

> "the word 'any' brings in changes of differing degree of significance. An individual will fail if, the majority of the time: (a) they cannot cope with significant change but (b) they can cope with less significant change. That is the consequence of the word 'any' in descriptor 12. An individual will succeed if, the majority of the time they cannot cope with 'any' change, even a less significant change. It is not of itself fatal that the claimant can sometimes cope with a change" (para.7).

Activity 13: "coping with social engagement due to cognitive impairment or mental disorder"; Descriptor: "engagement in social contact is always precluded due to difficulty relating to others or significant distress experienced by the individual": In *KB v SSWP* (ESA) [2013] UKUT 152 (AAC), Judge Parker considered the relationship between this wording (the requisite of "always") and the stipulation in reg.34(2) that "a descriptor applies to a claimant if that descriptor applies to the claimant for the majority of the time or, as the case may be, on the majority of the occasions on which the claimant undertakes or attempts to undertake the activity described by that descriptor". Having looked at definitions of "always" in the *Concise Oxford Dictionary*, Judge Parker concluded that neither this activity and descriptor, nor its counterpart in Activity 16 of Sch.2 set out an "all or nothing test". Rather "always" here 9.128

> "means 'repeatedly' or 'persistent' or 'often'. A 'majority' may be constituted by events which happen only on 50.1% of the possible occasions, but a greater

frequency is required by the use of the word 'always'. It is a question of degree, but a fact finding tribunal is eminently suited to applying these subtle nuances of difference in a common sense way. It suffices to say in the present case, that because a claimant attends one tribunal hearing, and his GP accepts that he comes to the surgery very occasionally, does not *necessarily* entail the conclusion, as the tribunal clearly considered that it did, that it 'cannot be said that engagement in social contact is always precluded'" (para.14).

Judge Fordham took much the same approach in *CH v SSWP (ESA)* [2013] UKUT 207 (AAC) (para.8).

As regards "social engagement" and "social contact", Judge Parker, accepting the approach advanced by the Secretary of State's representative, thought that "social" to be "a simple reference to relations with other human beings" carrying no connotations of "leisure, pleasure or mutuality", so that a tribunal could properly look at evidence about business visits or contacts with professionals, as well as with friends, relatives and strangers. It was not tied to contact in an informal setting (see paras 15–17). What conduct constitutes the necessary "contact" or engagement" is

> "a matter of fact and degree, likewise eminently suitable for consideration by a tribunal as a matter of common sense having regard to all the circumstances. At one end of the scale, if a claimant sat silently throughout his tribunal hearing then, outwith exceptional circumstances, a reasonable tribunal could hold that this did not amount to the necessary 'contact' or 'engagement'; similarly, monosyllabic responses in such a context is a borderline scenario. However, where, as here, the claimant communicated with the tribunal on an extensive basis, according to the record, then a conclusion that such did not amount to any 'social engagement' or 'social contact' would have been irrational" (para.18).

See also the annotation to Sch.2, Activity 16 for Judge Mark's narrower view that "always" did not mean "often" (*LM v SSWP (ESA)* [2013] UKUT 553 (AAC)), and for Judge Ward's disagreement with Judge Parker's interpretation of "social" (*AR v SSWP (ESA)* [2013] UKUT 446 (AAC)) and Judge Mark's qualified support for Judge Ward's approach (*LM v SSWP (ESA)* [2013] UKUT 553 (AAC)). See also, however, the annotation to reg.34(2) and the decision of the Court of Session in *SSWP v Brade* [2014] CSIH 39 XA81/13 (May 1, 2014); [2014] AACR 29.

See further the annotation to Sch.2, Activity 16 and in particular the decision of the three-judge panel in *JC v SSWP (ESA)* [2014] UKUT 352 (AAC); [2015] AACR 6, which follows Judge Parker on the meaning of "social", identifies the key elements of "engagement" and "coping" as "reciprocity, give and take, initiation and response", and identifies the conceptual test to be applied and the decision-making process to be followed for its application by tribunals.

Activity 14: Appropriateness of behaviour with other people, due to cognitive impairment or mental disorder: descriptor: Has, on a daily basis, uncontrollable episodes of aggressive or disinhibited behaviour that would be unreasonable in any workplace.

In *WT v SSWP (ESA)* [2013] UKUT 556 (AAC), Judge Gray considered the meaning of "on a daily basis". Rather than merely deploy a dictionary definition, he took the "mischief" approach to interpretation and reasoned thus:

> "The mischief that the descriptor must be intended to remedy is the creation of an unsafe or otherwise unacceptable work environment for co-workers. The way in which the avoidance of that is accomplished is to exclude from the workplace those who, due to their mental health condition exhibit certain behaviour. If on virtually every day that they were at work they displayed such behaviour, would the fact that there were very rare days on which they did not prevent them from falling within the meaning of the descriptor? To answer "yes" to that question would not be to address the mischief. The descriptor must, then, be interpreted more widely than literally every day.

I fortify myself in this view because the ordinary meaning of the words "on a daily basis" seem to me to connote a lesser test than "every day" . The phrase is not confined to events which happen literally every day. Someone might be said to read a particular newspaper on a daily basis even though there were periods when they did not, such as where they were abroad on holiday when it was not available. Walking the dog on a daily basis is an activity which may be interrupted by the ill-health of either dog or walker, but a short break would not change the very regular nature of the activity or make that description inapt.

The words "on a daily basis", then, in the context of schedule 3 descriptor 14, and its mirror descriptor under schedule 2, regulation 17 (a), means certainly more than for the majority of the time, that being the regulation 34 (2) test, and must mean more than frequently, that being the test of periodicity in regulation 17(b), but it does not mean literally every day or even on every working day. The essence is of this being an enduring position; one which is happening regularly, constantly or continually. It is for the tribunal to find the facts as to the frequency of the behaviour set out in the descriptor, and then apply this approach to those facts with their usual common sense" (paras 40–42).

It is vital to remember that under ESA Regs 2008 reg.34(6)(b), incapability of performing the activity in respect of this descriptor must arise from a specific mental illness or disablement. Alcohol misuse in itself is not such a disablement. To rank as disablement the misuse of alcohol must rank as "alcohol dependency" in terms of the "constellation of markers" found in quotations from *R(DLA) 6/06* in para.44 of the Three-Judge Panel's decision in *JG v SSWP (ESA)* [2013] UKUT 37 (AAC); [2013] AACR 23 (see annotation to ESA Regs 2008 reg.19) Accordingly, in *DR v SSWP (ESA)* [2014] UKUT 188 (AAC); [2014] AACR 38, Judge May held the tribunal were right to hold that the descriptor did not apply. Moreover, he was persuaded that:

"the volume of alcohol the claimant is said to drink on a daily basis would not in itself amount to the disinhibited behaviour referred to in descriptors 17(a) in Schedule 2 and 14 in Schedule 3. I see the force in Mr Webster's submission that disinhibited behaviour requires the context of an inhibition. I cannot see, and it has not been established, what the inhibition in this case is and how the drinking of a certain volume of alcohol amounts in itself to disinhibited behaviour. Disinhibited behaviour may result as a consequence of drinking specific quantities of alcohol but that is not the basis upon which the claimant's argument is put. Mr Orr seeks to widen "disinhibition" beyond the scope of what the statutory provisions can bear. The activity for both descriptors relates to the appropriateness of behaviour "with" other people, which suggests that the descriptor is intended to be applied in respect of behaviour which is more than the passive drinking of alcohol" (para.8).

Activity 16: Chewing or swallowing food or drink: In *WC v SSWP (ESA)* [2015] UKUT 304 (AAC); [2016] AACR 1, Judge Wikeley held that (given that one cannot "chew" drink) "this phrase means, in effect, and adding words to ensure clarity of meaning", "cannot *either* chew *and* swallow food or *swallow* drink" (para. 1). That decision was considered by Judge Jacobs in *IC v SSWP (ESA)* [2015] UKUT 615 (AAC), where the specific question that arose was whether a claimant can satisfy either descriptor 16a or 16b on account of the difficulties he experiences as a result of his false teeth. Judge Jacobs held that there was simply no evidence that activity 16 could apply on the facts of the instant case, given the requirements of reg.34(6)(b); thus there was no evidence that the claimant's difficulties with his false teeth arose from a specific bodily disease or disablement or from treatment (para.13). Judge Jacobs continued, without deciding, to consider whether false teeth are and aid or appliance (within reg.34(3)(b)) or a prosthesis (within reg.35(3)(a)) (para.14). Judge Jacobs stressed further the importance of applying the statutory test, rather than a substitute test, and gave the following guidance:

"16. This brings me to another way to frame the issue, which is to concentrate on the food rather than the chewing. As I put it in my preliminary observations: what sort of food is envisaged by the descriptor? Again, there is a range of possibilities. It is not necessary to be able to eat any food, from the most tender to the toughest. That would set too demanding a standard. But liquidised food is a liquid, more akin to a drink than food, and does not require chewing.

17. A third, and better, way to frame the issue is to take the whole expression and ask: what is involved in chewing food? That at least preserves the immediate context. It makes the expression as a whole the object of the enquiry, rather than its individual components. It does not, though, produce any clear answer.

18. On any formulation, it is important to remember the context, which is a test of whether a claimant's capability for work and for work-related activity is restricted sufficiently to qualify for an employment and support allowance. The disability need not have a direct effect on the performance of work or work-related activity, as feeding oneself is not going to be involved in either case. So the scope of the Activity cannot be calibrated by its effect in those contexts. Nevertheless the effect of satisfying a descriptor in terms of benefit entitlement indicates that the disability should be significant. It must be such that 'it is not reasonable to require' the claimant to undertake work or the activity, to use the language of section 8(1) and 9(1) of the Welfare Reform Act 2007. The passage in the WCA Handbook reflects that, although it is not presented (and must not be taken) as a comprehensive statement of the physical conditions that can lead to the disabilities in Activity 16(a) and (b)."

PART X

INDUSTRIAL INJURIES AND PRESCRIBED DISEASES

The Social Security (Claims and Payments) Regulations 1979

(SI 1979/628) (*as amended*)

ARRANGEMENT OF REGULATIONS

PART I

GENERAL

PART IV

SPECIAL PROVISIONS RELATING TO INDUSTRIAL INJURIES BENEFIT ONLY

SCHEDULES

The Secretary of State for Social Services, in exercise of powers conferred upon him by sections 45(3), 79 to 81, 88 to 90, 146(5) and 115(1) of, and Schedule 13 to, the Social Security Act 1975 and paragraphs 9(1)(a) and (c) of Schedule 13 to, the Social Security (Consequential Provisions) Act 1975 and of all other powers enabling him in that behalf, hereby makes the following regulations, which consolidate the regulations hereby revoked and which accordingly by virtue of sections 139(1) and 141(2) of the Social Security Act 1975—and paragraphs 20 of Schedule 15 and 12 of Schedule 16—are not subject to the requirements of section 139(1) and 141(2) of that Act for prior reference to the National Insurance Advisory Committee and the Industrial Injuries Advisory Council respectively:—

PART I

GENERAL

Citation and commencement

10.2 **1**. These regulations may be cited as the Social Security (Claims and Payments) Regulations 1979 and shall come into operation on 9th July 1979.

Interpretation

10.3 **2**.—(1) In these regulations, unless the context otherwise requires—

"the Act" means the Social Security Act 1975;

"approved place" means a place approved by the Secretary of State for the purpose of obtaining payment of benefit;

"benefit order" means an order for the payment of a weekly sum on account of benefit to which regulation 16 applies or of a weekly instalment of a gratuity;

"claim for benefit" includes an application for a declaration that an accident was an industrial accident and an application for the review of an award or a decision for the purpose of obtaining any increase of benefit mentioned in Schedule 1 to these regulations but does not include any other application for the review of an award or a decision and the expression "claim benefit" and every reference to a claim shall be construed accordingly;

[3 "health care professional" means—

(a) a registered medical practitioner,

(b) a registered nurse,

(c) an occupational therapist or physiotherapist registered with a regulatory body established by an Order in Council under section 60 of the Health Care Act 1999, or

(d) a member of such other profession, regulated by a body mentioned in section 25(3) of the National Health Service Reform and Health Care Professions Act 2002, prescribed by the Secretary of State in accordance with powers under section 39(1) of the Social Security Act 1998.]

[1 . . .]

"instrument of payment" means a serial order, benefit order, or any other instrument whatsoever which is intended to enable a person to obtain payment of benefit;

"serial order" means one of a series of orders, including benefit orders, for the payment of a sum on account of benefit which is or has been contained in a book of such orders;

"unemployment benefit office" means any office or place appointed by the Secretary of State for the purpose of claiming unemployment benefit;

and other expressions have the same meaning as in the Act.

[2(1A) The provision in paragraph (1) for the interpretation of the words "claim for benefit" shall not be taken to preclude the application of the regulations to a claim for attendance allowance expressed as an application for review of an earlier determination but which discloses no grounds on which such a determination could be reviewed.]

(2) Unless the context otherwise requires, any reference in these regulations to—

(a) a numbered section is a reference to the section of the Social Security Act 1975 bearing that number;

(b) a numbered regulation is a reference to the regulation bearing that number in these regulations and any reference in a regulation to a numbered paragraph is a reference to the paragraph of that regulation bearing that number;

(c) any provision made by or contained in an enactment or instrument shall be construed as a reference to that provision as amended or extended by any enactment or instrument and as including a reference to any provision which it re-enacts or replaces, or which may re-enact or replace it, with or without modification.

(3) For the purposes of the provisions of these regulations relating to the making of claims every increase of benefit mentioned in Schedule 1 to these regulations shall be treated as a separate benefit.

(4) The provisions of Schedule 1 and 2 to these regulations shall have effect; and the following provisions of these regulations shall, in relation to any particular benefit, have effect subject to any provisions in those Schedules affecting that benefit.

AMENDMENTS

1. Social Security Act 1998 (Commencement No.8, and Savings and Consequential and Transitional Provisions) Order 1999 (SI 1999/1958) Sch.4 para.1 (July 4, 1999)

2. Social Security (Attendance Allowance) Amendment Regulations 1980 (SI 1980/1136) reg.6(1) (August 25, 1980).

3. The Social Security (Miscellaneous Amendments) (No. 2) Regulations 2007, (SI 2007/1626) (July 3, 2007).

GENERAL NOTE

Most of the rules relating to claims and payments can now be found in the Claims and Payments Regulations 1987. The only surviving part of these regulations relates to specific aspects of claims and payments in industrial injuries cases. **10.4**

Regulations 3–23 revoked. **10.5**

PART IV

SPECIAL PROVISIONS RELATING TO INDUSTRIAL INJURIES BENEFIT ONLY

Notice of accidents

24.—(1) Every employed earner who suffers personal injury by accident in respect of which benefit may be payable shall give notice of such accident either in writing or orally as soon as is practicable after the happening thereof. **10.6**

Provided that any such notice required to be given by an employed earner may be given by some other person acting on his behalf.

(2) Every such notice shall be given to the employer, or (if there is more than one employer) to one of such employers, or to any foreman or other official under whose supervision the employed earner is employed at the time of the accident, or to any person designated for the purpose by the employer, and shall give the appropriate particulars.

(3) Any entry of the appropriate particulars of an accident made in a book kept for that purpose in accordance with the provisions of regulation 25 shall, if made as soon as practicable after the happening of an accident by the employed earner or by some other person acting on his behalf, be sufficient notice of the accident for the purposes of this regulation.

(4) In this regulation—

"employer" means, in relation to any person, the employer of that person at the time of the accident and "employers" shall be construed accordingly; and

"employed earner" means a person who is or is treated as an employed earner for the purposes of industrial injuries benefit.

(5) In this regulation and regulation 25, "appropriate particulars" mean the particulars indicated in Schedule 4 to these regulations.

Obligations of employers

10.7 **25.**—(1) Every employer shall take reasonable steps to investigate the circumstances of every accident of which notice is given to him or to his servant or agent in accordance with the provisions of regulation 24 and, if there appear to him to be any discrepancies between the circumstances found by him as a result of his investigation and the circumstances appearing from the notice so given, he shall record the circumstances so found.

(2) Every employer who is required to do so by the Secretary of State shall furnish to an officer of the Department within such reasonable period as may be required, such information and particulars as shall be required—

(a) of any accident or alleged accident in respect of which benefit may be payable to, or in respect of the death of, a person employed by him at the time of the accident or alleged accident; or

(b) of the nature of and other relevant circumstances relating to any occupation prescribed for the purposes of Chapter V of Part II of the Act in which any person to whom or in respect of whose death benefit may be payable under that Chapter was or is alleged to have been employed by him.

(3) Every owner or occupier (being an employer) of any mine or quarry or of any premises to which any of the provisions of the Factories Act 1961 applies and every employer by whom 10 or more persons are normally employed at the same time on or about the same premises in connection with a trade or business carried on by the employer shall, subject to the following provisions of this paragraph—

(a) [[1] keep readily accessible a means (whether in a book or books or by electronic means), in a form approved by the Secretary of State, by which a person employed by the employer or some other person acting on his behalf may record the appropriate particulars (as defined in regulation 24) of any accident causing personal injury to that person; and

(b) preserve every such record for the period of at least 3 years from the date of its entry.]

AMENDMENT

1. Social Security (Claims and Payments) Amendment (No. 3) Regulations 1993 (SI 1993/2113) reg.2 (September 27, 1993)

Obligations of claimants for, and beneficiaries in receipt of [1. . .] disablement benefit

26.—(1) Subject to the following provisions of this regulation, every claimant for, and every beneficiary in receipt of [1. . .] disablement benefit shall comply with every notice given to him by the Secretary of State which requires him either— 10.8

(a) to submit himself to a medical examination [5in person, by telephone or by video] by a [2[4 health care professional approved by the Secretary of State] who has experience in the issues specified in regulation 12(1) of the Social Security and Child Support (Decisions and Appeals) Regulations 1999] for the purpose of determining the effects of the relevant accident or the treatment appropriate to the relevant injury or loss of faculty; or

(b) to submit himself to such medical treatment for the said injury or loss of faculty as is considered appropriate in his case by the medical practitioner in charge of the case [2. . .]

(2) Every notice given to a claimant or beneficiary requiring him to submit himself to medical examination shall be given in writing and shall specify the time and place for examination and shall not require the claimant or beneficiary to submit himself [2 to examination before the expiration of the period of 6 days beginning with the date of the notice or such shorter period as may be reasonable in the circumstances]

(3) Every claimant and every beneficiary who, in accordance with the foregoing provisions of this regulation, is required to submit himself to a medical examination or to medical treatment—

(a) shall attend at every such place and at every such time as may be required; and

(b) may, in the discretion of the Secretary of State, be paid such travelling and other allowances (including compensation for loss of remunerative time) as the Secretary of State may with the consent of the Minister for the Civil Service determine.

(4) [3. . .]

AMENDMENTS

1. Social Security (Abolition of Injury Benefit) (Consequential) Regulations 1983 (SI 1983/186) reg.11 (April 6, 1983).

2. Social Security Act 1998 (Commencement No.8, and Savings and Consequential and Transitional Provisions) Order 1999 (SI 1999/1958) Sch.4 para.2 (July 4, 1999).

3. Social Security Act 1998 (Commencement No.8, and Savings and Consequential and Transitional Provisions) Order 1999 (SI 1999/1958) Sch.4 para.2(c) (July 4, 1999).

4. The Social Security (Miscellaneous Amendments) (No. 2) Regulations 2007, (SI 2007/1626) (July 3, 2007)

5. Social Security (Claims and Payments, Employment and Support Allowance, Personal Independence Payment and Universal Credit) (Telephone and Video Assessment) (Amendment) Regulations 2021 (SI 2022/230) reg.2 (March 25, 2021).

10.9 *Regulations 27–30 revoked.*

10.10 *Regulation 31 omitted*

10.11 *Regulation 32 revoked*

10.12 *Schedules 1–3 revoked.*

SCHEDULE 4 **Regulations 24 and 25**

PARTICULARS TO BE GIVEN OF ACCIDENTS

10.13 (1) Full name, address and occupation of injured person;
(2) Date and time of accident;
(3) Place where accident happened;
(4) Cause and nature of injury;
(5) Name, address and occupation of person giving the notice, if other than the injured person.

10.14 *Schedule 5 revoked.*

The Social Security (General Benefit) Regulations 1982

(SI 1982/1408) (*as amended*)

ARRANGEMENT OF REGULATIONS

PART II

PROVISIONS RELATING TO BENEFIT OTHER THAN INDUSTRIAL INJURIES BENEFIT

PART III

PROVISIONS RELATING TO INDUSTRIAL INJURIES BENEFIT ONLY

Principles of assessment

Disablement benefit

16. Earnings level for the purposes of unemployability supplement under section 58 of the Act.

Increase of disablement benefit

17. Circumstances in which, for the purposes of section 60, a beneficiary may be treated as being incapable of following an occupation or employment notwithstanding that he has worked thereat.
18. Payments in respect of special hardship where beneficiary is entitled to a gratuity.
19. Increase of disablement pension for constant attendance.
20. Determination of degree of disablement for constant attendance allowance.
21. Condition for receipt of increase of disablement pension for constant attendance under section 61 while receiving medical treatment as an inpatient.
22. Treatment of distinct periods of hospital in-patient treatment as continuous for the purposes of section 62 of the Act.

Industrial death benefit

Regulations 23–37 omitted.

Adjustment of benefit for successive accidents

38. Adjustment of benefit for successive accidents where a disablement gratuity is payable.
39. Adjustment of increase of benefit in respect of successive accidents.

Disqualification for receipt of benefit, suspension of proceedings on claims and suspension of benefit

40. Disqualification for receipt of benefit, suspension of proceedings on claims and suspension of payment of benefit.

Payments under the act to certain persons who contracted diseases or who were injured before 5 July 1948

Regulations 42–45 omitted.

Regulation 46 revoked.

PART IV

47. Revocation and transitional provisions.

SCHEDULES

Schedule 1—Provisions for the purpose of which disqualifications under the Act are to be disregarded.
Schedule 2—Prescribed degrees of disablement.
Schedule 3—Scale of disablement gratuities.

Schedule 4—Rate of disablement pension payable in lieu of disablement gratuity in accordance with regulation 18.

Schedules 5–9 Omitted.

SCHEDULES

Schedule 2—Prescribed degrees of disablement.

The Secretary of State for Social Services, in exercise of the powers conferred upon him by sections 50(4), 56(7), 57(5), 58(3), 60(4) and (7), 61(1), 62(2), 67(1), 68(2), 70(2), 72(1) and (8), 74(1), 81(6), 82(5) and (6), 83(1), 85(1), 86(2) and (5), 90(2), 91(1), 119(3) and (4) and 159(3) of and paragraphs 2, 3 and 6 of Schedule 8, paragraphs 1 and 8 of Schedule 9 and Schedule 14 of the Social Security Act 1975 and all other powers enabling him in the behalf, hereby makes the following regulations, which only consolidate the regulations hereby revoked, and which accordingly, by virtue of paragraph 20 of Schedule 3 to the Social Security Act 1980, are not subject to the requirements of section 10 of that Act for prior references to the Social Security Advisory Committee and by virtue of section 141(2) and paragraph 12 of the Schedule 16 of the Social Security Act 1975, do not require prior reference to the Industrial Injuries Advisory Council.

PART I

GENERAL

10.16 *For regs 1-4 see Vol.III: Administration, Appeals and the European Dimension.*

PART II

PROVISIONS RELATING TO BENEFIT OTHER THAN INDUSTRIAL INJURIES BENEFIT

Payment of benefit and suspension of payments pending a decision on appeals or references, arrears and repayments

10.17 **9.** *Omitted.*

Disqualifications to be disregarded for certain purposes

10.18 **10.**—(1) Subject to paragraph (2), where a person of any class mentioned in column (1) of Schedule 1 to these regulations would be entitled to the benefit set opposite that class in column (2) of that Schedule but for the operation of any provision of the Act disqualifying him for the receipt of that benefit, that person shall be treated as if entitled to that benefit for the purpose of the provisions of the Act set opposite thereto in column (3) of the said Schedule and of any regulations made thereunder. (2) For the purposes of determining whether the condition contained in section 79(1) of the Act (which makes a claim a condition of any person's right to any benefit) is satisfied, a person who would be entitled to any benefit but for the operation of any provision of the Act disqualifying him for the receipt of it, and who ceases to be so disqualified within a period of 3 months from the commencement of the disqualification, shall be treated as if entitled to it.

Part III

Provisions Relating to Industrial Injuries Benefit Only

Principles of assessment

Further definition of the principles of assessment of disablement and prescribed degrees of disablement

11.—(1) Schedule [6] to the [SSCBA 1992] (general principles relating to the assessment of the extent of disablement) shall have effect subject to the provisions of this regulation. 10.19

(2) When the extent of disablement is being assessed for the purposes of section [103], any disabilities which, though resulting from the relevant loss of faculty, also result, or without the relevant accident might have been expected to result, from a cause other than the relevant accident (hereafter in this regulation referred to as "the other effective cause") shall only be taken into account subject to and in accordance with the following provisions of this regulation.

(3) [1 Subject to paragraphs (5A) and (5B)] an assessment of the extent of disablement made by reference to any disability to which paragraph (2) applies, in a case where the other effective cause is a congenital defect or is an injury or disease received or contracted before the relevant accident, shall take account of all such disablement except to the extent to which the claimant would have been subject thereto during the period taken into account by the assessment if the relevant accident had not occurred.

(4) [1 Subject to paragraphs (5A) and (5B)] any assessment of the extent of disablement made by reference to any disability to which paragraph (2) applies, in a case where the other effective cause is an injury or disease received or contracted after and not directly attributable to the relevant accident, shall take account of all such disablement to the extent to which the claimant would have been subject thereto during the period taken into account by the assessment if that other effective cause had not arisen and where, in any such case, the extent of a disablement would be assessed at not less than 11 per cent. if that other effective cause had not arisen, the assessment shall also take account of any disablement to which the claimant may be subject as a result of that other effective cause except to the extent to which he would have been subject thereto if the relevant accident had not occurred.

(5) [1 Subject to paragraphs (5A) and (5B)] any disablement to the extent to which the claimant is subject thereto as a result both of an accident and a disease or two or more accidents or diseases (as the case may be), being accidents arising out and in the course of, or diseases due to the nature of, employed earners' employment, shall only be taken into account in assessing the extent of disablement resulting from one such accident or disease being the one which occurred or developed last in point of time.

[1 (5A) Where—

(a) a person has an award of industrial injuries disablement benefit in respect of the disease specified in paragraph D1 of Part I of Schedule 1 to the Social Security (Industrial Injuries) (Prescribed

Diseases) Regulations 1985 (in this paragraph and in paragraph (5B) referred to as "disease D1"); and

(b) by virtue of either paragraph (3) or (4) that award takes account of disablement resulting from the effects of chronic bronchitis or emphysema, not being chronic bronchitis or emphysema prescribed in paragraph D12 of Part I of Schedule 1 to the Social Security (Industrial Injuries) (Prescribed Diseases) Regulations 1985 (in this paragraph and paragraph (5B) referred to as "disease D12"); and

(c) after the date on which the award referred to in sub-paragraph (a) of this paragraph was made the person becomes entitled to industrial injuries disablement benefit in respect of disease D12,

then, during any period when such disablement benefit is payable in respect of disease D12, paragraphs (3), (4) and (5) shall not apply to the assessment in respect of disease D1 for the purpose of assessing the extent of disablement resulting from disease D12.

(5B) Where—

(a) a person has an award of industrial injuries disablement benefit in respect of the disease D12; and

(b) by virtue of either paragraph (3) or (4) that award takes account of disablement resulting from the effects of pneumoconiosis, not being disease D1; and

(c) after the date on which the award referred to in sub-paragraph (a) of this paragraph was made the person becomes entitled to industrial injuries disablement benefit in respect of disease D1,

then, during any period when such disablement benefit is payable in respect of disease D1, paragraphs (3), (4) and (5) shall not apply to the assessment in respect of disease D12 for the purpose of assessing the extent of disablement resulting from disease D1.]

(6) Where the sole injury which a claimant suffers as a result of the relevant accident is one specified in column 1 of Schedule 2 to these regulations, whether or not such injury incorporates one or more other injuries so specified, the loss of faculty suffered by the claimant as a result of that injury shall be treated for the purposes of section [103] of, and Schedule [6] to, the Act as resulting in the degree of disablement set against injury in column 2 of the said Schedule 2 subject to such increase or reduction of that degree of disablement as may be reasonable in the circumstances of the case where, having regard to the provisions of the said Schedule [6] to the Act and to the foregoing paragraphs of this regulation, that degree of disablement does not provide a reasonable assessment of the extent of disablement resulting from the relevant loss of faculty.

(7) For the purposes of paragraph (6) where the relevant injury is one so specified in the said column 1 against which there is set in the said column 2 the degree of disablement of 100 per cent. and the claimant suffers some disablement to which he would have been subject whether or not the relevant accident had occurred, no reduction of that degree of disablement shall be required if [[2] the Secretary of State or, as the case may be,] [[3] the First-tier Tribunal] is satisfied that, in the circumstances of the case, 100 per cent is a reasonable assessment of the extent of disablement from the relevant loss of faculty.

(8) For the purposes of assessing, in accordance with the provisions of Schedule [6] to the [SSCBA 1992], the extent of disablement resulting from

the relevant injury in any case which does not fall to be determined under paragraph (6) or (7), [2 the Secretary of State or, as the case may be,] [3 the First-tier Tribunal] may have such regard as may be appropriate to the prescribed degrees of disablement set against the injuries specified in the said Schedule 2.

AMENDMENTS

1. Social Security (Industrial Injuries) (Prescribed Diseases) Amendment (No. 2) Regulations 1993 (SI 1993/1985) reg.7 (September 13, 1993).
2. Social Security Act 1998 (Commencment No.8, and Savings and Consequential and Transitional Provisions) Order 1999 (SI 1999/1958) (July 5, 1999).
3. Tribunals, Courts and Enforcement Act 2007 (Transitional and Consequential Provisions) Order 2008 (SI 2008/2683) art.6(1) and Sch.1 para.25 (November 3, 2008).

GENERAL NOTE

This regulation provides for the assessment of the extent of disablement in cases **10.20**
where a disability is due both to the relevant accident and another cause; and it also introduces Sch.2 to the Regs which sets out the prescribed degrees of disablement. S.57 of, and Sch.8 to, the SSA 1975 have been replaced by s.103 of, and Sch.6 to the SSCBA 1992. The purpose of reg.11 was explained in these terms by Judge Parker in *AR v SSWP (II)* [2016] UKUT 111 (AAC):

> "10. The provisions of regulation 11 of the general benefit regulations (regulation 11) set out the formula for assessing disablement where there is more than one cause of it; except for regulation 11(5), it is concerned with other causes which are not industrial ones. (Schedule 2 to the prescribed diseases regulations modifies regulation 11 so that it always covers prescribed diseases as well as accidents as appropriate.). The objective is an assessment based solely on that disablement to which any relevant accident or prescribed disease has subjected a claimant, to prevent double-counting; but also to ensure that a claimant is compensated for any greater disablement due to the interaction of the effects of two accidents or diseases i.e. where a claimant's total disablement is more than a simple sum of the two separate disablements considered individually: for example, the loss of vision of one eye is 30% but total loss of sight is 100%."

For an illustration of the operation of these rules and a framework of questions for approaching these matters, see the decision of Commissioner Williams in *CI/2930/2005*, noted in the commentary to SSCBA 1992 s.103 (disablement pension).

For an illustration of the complexities of applying the "multiple effective cause" provisions of this reg., see *CI/3745/2006*. The Schedule to the decision also contains useful evidence from the medical adviser to the DWP (Dr Reed) on PD A8 (tenosynovitis) and PD A12 (carpal tunnel syndrome), on which see also *SM v SSWP (IIDB)* [2020] UKUT 287 (AAC).

For consideration of the current form BI 118A and the need to consider the connection factor arising out of two injuries both due to the same relevant accident, something not considered in *R(I) 1/95*, see *CI/3384/2006*.

In *KW v SSWP (II)* [2012] UKUT 181 (AAC), Judge Parker considered the case of a claimant appealing an assessment in relation to PD A14 where assessment decisions had earlier been made with respect to other industrial accidents. Judge Parker rightly regarded proper identification of the date of onset of the disease under appeal, as being as critical to establish the correct chronology for purposes of applying reg.11. She noted, applying Prescribed Diseases Regs, reg.6(2)(b) and *CI/6027/1999*, that the date of onset is that date the claimant first suffered from the loss of faculty after July 4, 1948, that is, when the disease reached the extent necessary to fit the statutory prescription and that, applying *R(I) 4/96*, that could be before the claimant had worked the 10 years necessary to satisfy the prescribed occupation. That would in the claimant's case be when osteoarthritis of the knee first existed as a matter of fact in his case, something that was not an easy issue to resolve. But how reg.11 applied would depend on whether that date of onset preceded or came after the other industrial accidents. Judge Parker noted that use

> "of regulation 11(4) almost certainly falls out of the analysis, except in the very rare instance when a later effective non-industrial cause of disability, which also results from an earlier relevant accident or disease, actually arises after the 'accident or disease being the one which occurred or developed last in point of time.' Where, as here, there is a string of industrial accidents and diseases under consideration for a new exercise of assessment and aggregation, only regulation 11(3) and (5) will usually be applicable" (para.25).

See further on para.(1) *AR v SSWP (II)* [2016] UKUT 111 (AAC).

Paragraph (2)

10.21 Adjudicating medical authorities used to distinguish between conditions that were regarded as "partly relevant" ("O pre" or "O post") and those that were regarded as merely "connected" ("C"). The former were those conditions considered to have more than one cause and the latter were those conditions considered to be quite separate from the one arising from the relevant accident but which were nonetheless thought to have some effect on the disability arising from the condition caused by the relevant accident. That approach (and Form BI 113 Accident) which reflected it has been criticised in *R(I) 4/94* and *R(I) 1/95*. Any contributory factor is either to be included in the relevant loss of faculty or else is an "other effective cause" within para.(2), in which case it is taken into account under paras (3), (4) or (5).

Paragraph (3)

10.22 This makes provision for a case where the "other effective cause" is either a congenital defect or is an injury or disease received or contracted *before* the relevant accident. In *R(I) 13/75*, the Commissioner said:

> "In the context of regulation [11(3)] I do not think that 'congenital' should receive its primary meaning, which is 'begotten' or 'born with'; see Shorter Oxford English Dictionary. In my view, the word is used in this regulation in a rather wider sense. I think that it must be taken to mean 'inherent' or 'constitutional,' this is to say that it refers to a defect which is a natural constituent of the person's make-up whether physical or mental. Since Dr. Wright [a principal medical officer of the Department of Health and Social Security] stated that a functional overlay is 'a manifestation of constitutional mental make-up,' I cannot hold that it is not covered by the phrase 'congenital defect' in regulation [11(3)]."

Disablement due to the "other effective cause" must be taken into account except to the extent to which the claimant would have been disabled if the relevant accident had not occurred. Usually this is done by making an assessment of the full extent of disablement resulting from the condition and then applying an "offset" in respect of disablement which would have been present even if the relevant accident had not occurred (*CI/2746/2002*, para.5). There should be no offset in respect of a mere *predisposition* to hysteria (*R(I) 2/74*), functional overlay (*R(I) 13/75*), detachment of retina (*R(I) 3/76*) or development of multiple sclerosis (*R(I) 1/81*). In *R(I) 1/81*, it was held that

> "constitutional liability to develop the disease cannot have been a 'disability' because it was wholly symptomless. Such liability corresponds with the statutory concept of 'loss of faculty,' that is to say it is a potential cause of disability but not itself a disability."

The Commissioner emphasised that the assessment was an assessment of disablement and not an assessment of loss of faculty. However, it does not follow that there can never be an offset in respect of a condition which was symptomless before the relevant accident. An adjudicating authority might legitimately apply an offset if a pre-existing, and previously symptomless, condition could have been expected to produced disability at some time even if the accident had not occurred. Nevertheless, such reasoning must be clear, and a tribunal which fails to record good reasons for applying an offset in a case where a claimant has asserted that he or she had no symptoms before the relevant accident is liable to find its decision set aside on appeal (*CI/34/93*). On the other hand, there are some conditions, such as arthritis, from which many older people suffer. That is not a ground for an offset. Rather, it is a ground for not including the effects of the arthritis, to the extent to which other people of the same age would suffer from them, in the assessment of total disability at all. That is because that assessment should be made by comparing the claimant "with a person of the same age and sex whose physical and mental condition is normal" (SSCBA 1992 Sch.6, para.1(a)). There is no reason why an adjudicating authority should not make an assessment which is tapered to take account of the fact that the claimant would have become increasingly disabled even if the accident had not occurred. Whether that is done by increasing an offset over the period of assessment or by simply reducing the total assessment of disablement depends on whether or not the increasing disability is something from which the "normal" person would suffer. In a case where the assessment of total disablement is 100 per cent, see para.(7).

Where the "other effective cause" is a different type of condition or an injury to a different part of the body, it is conventional to talk of a "connection factor" which is expressed as an increase of the disablement resulting from the relevant accident. Like an "offset", a "connection factor" is not a statutory concept, but both concepts are useful ways of explaining decisions. Use of the concepts enables a claimant to be told the proportion of his or her total disablement that is attributable to the relevant accident (*R(I) 2/74*, *R(I) 1/95*). A claimant ought to know the assessment of the total disablement to which he or she is thought to be subject, as well as the assessment of the disablement attributed to the relevant accident. In *R(I) 1/95*, it was observed that **10.23**

> "[a]n inability to lift moderate weights with one hand may not be particularly significant when the claimant can use the other hand instead, but it is obviously a substantial handicap if the claimant has only the one hand and cannot be provided with a functional artificial limb".

The "connection factor" represented that additional degree of disablement from which the claimant would not have suffered but for the relevant accident, over and above the degree of disablement suffered by a person who had a fully functional second hand. The same result is reached if the claimant's total disablement is assessed and there is an "offset" in respect of the disablement from which he would have suffered had the relevant accident not occurred. Ideally, both the "connection factor" and the "offset" should be assessed so that it is quite clear that reg.11(3) has been applied correctly (*R(I) 1/95*). In *R(I) 23/61*, the claimant had a pre-existing disability arising from a defective forefinger and then lost a thumb in the relevant accident. The Commissioner said that:

> "where the medical authorities are dealing with an injury to a hand, the possibility of a connection factor is so obvious, or at any rate will seem so obvious to the claimant, that it is essential that they should satisfy themselves specifically whether or not there is any other defect in the hand which might bring the case within regulation [11(3)] and should give a clear decision on it one way or the other."

In *Murrell v Secretary of State for Social Services* (reported as an appendix to *R(I) 3/84*), a blind man who suffered an injury to his elbow, which resulted in a loss of sensation in his hand rendering him unable to read braille, had the 15 per cent assessment in respect of the elbow injury increased by a further 15 per cent to take account of the extra disability arising from that injury because of his pre-existing blindness. The Court of Appeal thought that the increase was rather on the low side.

The fact that the claimant is entitled to a disablement pension under the war pensions scheme in respect of the previous injury is not a ground for reducing the assessment in respect of the later one (*R(I) 1/79*).

Paragraph (4)

10.24 This applies where the "other effective cause" arises *after* the relevant accident. The paragraph is in two parts. First, account must be taken of all disablement "to the extent to which the claimant would have been subject thereto . . . if *that other effective cause* had not arisen". Thus, a claimant who has lost his right forefinger in an industrial accident and then loses his right hand in a non-industrial accident continues to be entitled to an assessment based on the loss of the forefinger, notwithstanding that he or she would have lost it in the second accident even if the first had not occurred. Secondly, effect is given to the "connection factor", but only in a case where the disablement from which the claimant would have suffered would have been at least 11 per cent without the "other effective cause" arising. In such a case, account must be taken of all disablement to which the claimant is subject "*except* to the extent to which he would have been subject thereto if *the relevant accident* had not occurred". In the example given above concerning the loss of a forefinger followed by the loss of the rest of the hand, no increase would be awarded under the second part of the paragraph because the claimant would have been just as disabled after the second accident even if the first had never occurred. However, an assessment may be increased where a subsequent injury results in greater disablement than it normally would because of the effects of the relevant accident. In *R. v Medical Appeal Tribunal Ex p. Cable* (reported as an appendix to *R(I) 11/66* and decided under earlier legislation), a man who had lost the sight of one eye in an industrial accident was held by the Court of Appeal to be entitled to the benefit of the "connection factor" when he lost the sight of the other as the result of a non-industrial disease. If the assessment of total disablement is 100 per cent, adjudicating medical authorities must bear in mind paras (7) and (8) when considering the "connection factor" under this para.

See further *PA v SSWP (II)* [2021] UKUT 257 (AAC), where the claimant injured his back in an industrial accident in 1981 and later had surgery to correct the effects of the accident. In 1986 he was awarded industrial injuries disablement benefit, based on an assessment of disablement at 7 per cent 'final' for life. In 2019 the claimant then appealed a refusal of his second attempt to supersede the award on the ground that his condition had deteriorated. The FTT dismissed the appeal, finding that some of the deterioration was due to general wear and tear. As the FTT acknowledged that at least some of the deterioration caused by the surgery resulted from the accident, Judge Poynter held that "... regulation 11(4) required it to perform a notional assessment as a building block towards the actual assessment. The tribunal should have assessed how disabled the claimant would have been 'during the period taken into account by the assessment' if the constitutional degenerative changes had not occurred'" (para. 14). Furthermore, "...Even if the notional assessment was less than 11 per cent, the claimant would nevertheless have been entitled to have the existing assessment of 7 per cent increased to reflect any additional disability caused by the deterioration attributable to the accident. The only exception to that would be if the additional disability was so trivial that it was insufficient to affect the 7 per cent assessment. If that was the case, the written statement of reasons should have explained why that it was the case" (paras 29 and 30).

Paragraph (5)

10.25 Where a person suffers disablement as a result of two or more industrial accidents or prescribed diseases, it may be appropriate simply for the adjudication officer to aggregate the resulting disablements under s.103(2) of the SSCBA 1992 (if all the causes were accidents) or reg.15A of the Prescribed Diseases Regs 1985. However, the total disablement resulting from the two accidents may be greater than the aggregate of the individual disablements; the loss of two eyes is more than twice as disabling as the loss of one eye. Effect must be given to that "connection factor" in assessing the extent of disablement resulting from the latest accident or disease for which it is relevant (*R(I) 3/91*). See further on para.(5) *AR v SSWP (II)* [2016] UKUT 111 (AAC).

Paragraph (6)

This introduces Sch.2 which sets out the prescribed degrees of disablement. The degree of disablement may be increased or reduced "as may be reasonable in the circumstances of the case" if the prescribed degree of disablement "does not provide a reasonable assessment of the extent of disablement". Thus a righthanded person who loses his or her right hand might be assessed as more disabled than a left-handed person would be, at least at the beginning of the period of assessment. It would also seem appropriate to make a higher assessment in a case where a person has had a limb amputated and has not yet been fitted with an artificial limb. The disabling effect of any unusual amount of pain must also be taken into account, a statement approved by Commissioner Williams in *CI/2553/2001*, para.17. 10.26

In *R(I) 4/04*, Commissioner Jacobs considered entries 26–28 dealing with amputations in lower limbs and, in particular, the need for a tribunal to specify where the measurement of the stump began and ended. What is assessed is the loss of function consequent upon anatomical loss, rather than the latter itself. The legislation does not specify the start and end points for measurement, but the length of the stump must be related to the likely disablement that will result. Given the possibility of fitting a prosthesis, the length of the stump is likely to relate to the effectiveness of that prosthesis. He concluded that

> "In a perfect world, the precise measurement would not matter. The tribunal would take account of the Scheduled assessments as a whole. It would realise that the length of the stump would affect the effectiveness of the prosthesis, which would affect the claimant's disablement. It would take account of the Scheduled assessment only as a starting point. It would adjust this as authorised by regulation 11(6). This process of adjustment, with a focus on disablement, would counteract any variation between adjudicating authorities on the precise way in which the measurement was taken.
>
> But life, in my experience, is not always perfect. This analysis presupposes an impossible degree of precision on a matter that is imprecise and impressionistic. In practice, tribunals begin their assessment of disablement with the Scheduled assessment, if there is one. That is the proper approach under regulation 11(6). Despite the infinite flexibility that regulation 11(6) allows in theory, the reality is that the starting point of the Scheduled assessment will affect the outcome.
>
> Disablement depends on the effectiveness of the prosthesis. That depends on the length of bone rather than soft tissue. So, it is obvious that it is only the supporting bone that should be measured. The key bone is the tibia, not the fibula. As the tibia is the inner of the two bones in the lower limb, the measurement should be made on the inner surface of the remaining stump, not the outer. So far, the Secretary of State's guidance does no more than put those conclusions into medical language. All that remains is the position of the leg when the measurement is taken. The Secretary of State recommends that the knee be flexed, which obviously is the best way to obtain the precise measurement required. In conclusion, therefore, the Secretary of State's guidance agrees with the measurement that can be deduced by normal interpretive principles from the legislation" (paras 23–25).

Paragraph (7)

In a case where the assessment of total disablement is 100 per cent, "not because that in fact is the proper figure, but because the law permits no greater figure" a smaller offset or even no offset at all in respect of a pre-existing injury might be reasonable (*R(I) 34/61*). That reflects the fact that an assessment of 100 per cent does not imply total disability. 10.27

Paragraph (8)

10.28 In a case where there is no prescribed degree of disablement, the adjudicating authority "may have such regard as may be appropriate" to the Schedule (see *R(I) 1/04* and *R(I) 5/95*). This is necessary in the interests of consistency and fairness as between claimants. Both the unified tribunal and the Commissioners now have jurisdiction over medical and non-medical matters. A Commissioner, allowing an appeal on a point of law, can now take his or her own decision on the facts rather than remitting it to another tribunal. Commissioner Williams did so in *CI/1307/1999* giving a staged assessment of disablement in respect of post-traumatic stress disorder. The decision considers the medical aspects of the claimant's case found to be an industrial accident in *CI/15589/1996*, noted in the annotation to "accident" to SSCBA 1992, s.94. In paras 15–17, Commissioner Williams distinguished "diagnosis" and "disablement" decisions. The former is essentially "a question of medical expertise". A "disablement" decision in contrast is not dissimilar to the tasks performed by judges in assessing common law damages or in applying the tariff of the Criminal Injuries Compensation Authority. In assessing disablement for industrial injuries benefits, however, that Criminal Injuries tariff is not an appropriate yardstick. Instead, supplementing SSCBA 1992 s.103 and Sch.6, regard should be had also to this regulation and Sch.2 to these Regulations. Nonetheless, the import of para. 37 of the decision is that exercise of the Commissioner's power to decide on the facts, rather than remitting to another tribunal, may well be rare. Even so, the decision contrasts markedly with the traditional view of such matters as ones for medical rather than legal judgment (see, for example, Commissioner Howell in *CI/636/93*). That assessment of disablement is ultimately a matter of judgment for the tribunal which hears and sees the evidence was stressed by a Tribunal of Commissioners in *R(I)2/06*. That decision also elaborates on the nature of an error of law, and on the difference between that and a disputed judgment of degree on a question of fact. It also proffers guidance on reference to Sch.2 in non-prescribed cases, on consideration of the judicial guidelines on the assessment of damages in civil personal injury cases, on cross-reference to other schemes such as that for criminal injuries, and on the status of official departmental guidance such as the Medical Assessment Framework (MAF). See further the annotation to SSCBA 1992 Sch.6.

[1. . .] Disablement benefit

10.29 *Regulations 12 and 13 revoked by SI 1983/186 reg.13 (April 6, 1983)*

Amount of disablement gratuities

10.30 **14.**—(1) Where the extent of a claimant's disablement is assessed at any of the degrees of disablement severally specified in column 1 of Schedule 3 to these regulations, the amount of any disablement gratuity payable shall—

(a) if the period taken into account by that assessment is limited by reference to the claimant's life or is not less than 7 years, be the amount calculated as the percentage of the maximum disablement gratuity (specified in paragraph 2 of Part V of Schedule 4 to the Act) which is shown in column 2 of Schedule 3 to these regulations as being appropriate to that degree of disablement;

(b) in any other case, be the amount calculated as such a percentage of the maximum disablement gratuity as bears the same proportion to the percentage shown in column 2 of Schedule 3 to these regulations as being appropriate to that degree of disablement as the period taken into account by the assessment bears to a period of 7 years, a fraction of 5 pence being, for this purpose, treated as 5 pence.

[1 (1A) Paragraph (1) applies in relation to cases where the claim for benefit was made before 1st October 1986.]

(2) For the purposes of this regulation, whenever such maximum disablement gratuity is altered by virtue of the passing of an Act or the making of an up-rating order, corresponding variations in the scale of gratuities payable under this regulation shall be payable only where the period taken into account by the assessment of the extent of disablement in respect of which the gratuity is awarded begins on or after the date of coming into operation of the provision altering the amount of the maximum disablement gratuity.

AMENDMENT

1. Social Security (Industrial Injuries and Diseases) Miscellaneous Provisions Regulations 1986 (SI 1986/1561) reg.7 (October 1, 1986).

Weekly value of gratuity for purposes of reduction of increase of disablement benefit during hospital treatment

15. For the purpose of reducing the weekly rate of disablement pension payable by virtue of section 62 to a person awarded a disablement gratuity wholly or partly in respect of the same period, the weekly value of the gratuity shall be the weekly rate of disablement pension which would be payable to that person in lieu thereof in accordance with regulation 18(2) if that regulation applied to his case. 10.31

Earnings level for the purpose of unemployability supplement under section 58 of the Act

[1**16.**—(1) For the purposes of section 58(3) (earnings level that does not disqualify for unemployability supplement) the prescribed amount of earnings in a year is determined as follows– 10.32

(a) multiply the National Minimum Wage by 16;

(b) where the amount determined by the calculation in sub-paragraph (a) would, but for this sub-paragraph, include an amount of—

(i) less than 50p, the amount determined under sub-paragraph (a) shall be rounded up to the nearest 50p, or

(ii) less than £1 but more than 50p, the amount determined under sub-paragraph (a) shall be rounded up to the nearest £1; and

(c) multiply the amount resulting from sub-paragraph (a) or (b) by 52.

(2) In this regulation "National Minimum Wage" means the rate of the national minimum wage specified in regulation 11 of the National Minimum Wage Regulations 1999 (rate of the national minimum wage).]

AMENDMENT

1. Social Security (Miscellaneous Amendments) Regulations 2011 (SI 2011/674) reg.2 (April 11, 2011).

Increase of [1. . .] Disablement Benefit

Circumstances in which, for the purposes of section 59A, a beneficiary may be treated as being incapable of following an occupation or employment notwithstanding that he has worked thereat

10.33 17.—(1) For the purposes of [2 section 59A (reduced earnings allowance)], when it is being determined whether a beneficiary has at all times since the end of [2 the period of 90 days referred to in section 57(4) been incapable of following his regular occupation or employment of an equivalent standard which is suitable in his case, and in determining that question only, the fact that since the end of that period of 90 days] such beneficiary had worked at that occupation or any such employment (as the case may be)—

(a) for the purpose of rehabilitation or training or of ascertaining whether he had recovered from the effects of the relevant injury; or

(b) before obtaining surgical treatment for the effects of the said injury;

shall be disregarded in respect of the periods specified in the next following paragraph.

(2) The periods during which the beneficiary worked at his regular occupation or at employment of equivalent standard, which shall be disregarded in accordance with the provision of the preceding paragraph, shall be—

(a) in any case to which sub-paragraph (a) of that paragraph applies—

(i) any period during which he worked thereat for any of the said purposes with the approval of the Secretary of State or on the advice of a medical practitioner, and

(ii) any other period or periods during which he worked thereat for any of the said purposes and which did not exceed six months in the aggregate, and

(b) in any case to which sub-paragraph (b) of that paragraph applies—

(i) any period during which he worked thereat and throughout which it is shown that having obtained the advice of a medical practitioner to submit himself to such surgical treatment he was waiting to undergo the said treatment in accordance therewith, and

(ii) any other period during which he worked thereat and throughout which is shown that he was in process of obtaining such advice.

AMENDMENTS

1. Social Security (Abolition of Injury Benefits) (Consequential) Regulations 1983 (SI 1983/186) reg.13 (April 6, 1983).

2. Social Security (Industrial Injuries and Diseases) Miscellaneous Provisions Regulations 1986 (SI 1986/1561) reg.7 (October 1, 1986).

GENERAL NOTE

10.34 The regulation permits both the fact of work and the period for which it has been undertaken to be disregarded where the claimant seeks to establish entitlement to reduced earnings allowance under the "continuous condition", so long as the work is undertaken for either of the purposes specified in the regulation. (See generally, *R(I)1/51, R(I)35/55, R(I)35/58.)*

If the claimant relies upon the purpose in para.(1)(a), the extent of the qualifying period depends upon whether the return to work is upon the advice of a medical practitioner or with the approval of the Secretary of State—without such authorisation the period (or aggregate periods) may not exceed six months. "Rehabilitation", means getting better (*R(I)69/53*), but "ascertaining the results of the relevant injury" has been more widely interpreted to mean discovering whether the claimant can still do the job (*R(I)1/69*). The "advice" of the doctor referred to in the paragraph does not have to be specifically directed to value of a resumption of work, but there must be something which the claimant can point to in the general advice he receives which is relevant to one of the specified purposes—the "general approval and consent of his doctor" (*R(I)93/53*), or "in allowing the claimant to continue at work while in receipt of treatment the doctor must be taken to have advised him to remain at work" (*R(I)69/53*).

If the claimant relies upon the purpose in para.(1)(b), the periods he may use depend upon whether he has actually received advice on surgical treatment, or is in the process of obtaining it. Note that, in this paragraph, the advice must be much more clear and the doctor must have given a specific opinion that surgical treatment should be carried out—further, the claimant must intend to give up work and undergo the treatment as soon as it can be arranged (*R(I)81/53*). The claimant can only avail himself of this paragraph if he has been seeking advice "throughout" the period he has been working, or he has been waiting for the treatment "throughout" the period, and he is not entitled to delay unduly in seeking treatment. He must use "reasonable zeal and expedition" to secure the treatment (*R(I)35/57*).

Payments in respect of special hardship where beneficiary is entitled to a gratuity

18.—(1) Where in any case a beneficiary is entitled to or has received a disablement gratuity, such beneficiary shall as respects that gratuity have the like rights to payments in respect of special hardship as he would have had by way of increase of disablement pension under section 60 if the disablement gratuity had been a disablement pension payable during the period taken into account by the assessment. **10.35**

(2) A beneficiary who is entitled as respects a disablement gratuity to payments in respect of special hardship by virtue of the preceding paragraph shall, if he makes an application in that behalf at any time before that gratuity or any part thereof has been paid to him, be entitled, subject to the proviso to section 57(6), to a disablement pension in lieu of such gratuity for any part of the period taken into account by the assessment during which he may be entitled to an increase of such pension in respect of special hardship under section 60, and the weekly rate of such pension shall be determined in accordance with Schedule 4 of these regulations.

(3) For the purposes of paragraph (2) and notwithstanding the provisions of regulation 14(2) whenever the weekly rate of such pension is altered consequent upon the passing of an Act or the making of an uprating order, such variation shall have effect as from the date on which the provision varying the amount of the disablement pension specified in paragraph 3 of Part V of Schedule 4 to the Act comes into force, whether the period taken into account by the assessment began before or after that date.

(4) Where a pension has been payable under paragraph (2) in lieu of a gratuity for any period and the beneficiary ceases to be entitled to an increase of such pension under the provisions of section 60, the amount of that gratuity shall be treated as reduced by the amounts which have been paid to the beneficiary by way of such pension, other than an increase

thereof under the said section 60 and, subject to the provisions of these regulations, the balance (if any) shall then be payable accordingly.

GENERAL NOTE

10.36 This regulation will only continue in force to cover those claimants who were in receipt of special hardship allowance under this regulation as at October 1, 1986. A claimant in that group became entitled to reduced earnings allowance on that day and will remain so entitled under this regulation until either the period of assessment has expired or the assessment is reviewed, or until reduced earnings allowance has ceased to be payable (whichever is the earlier). See the Social Security (Industrial Injuries and Diseases) Miscellaneous Provisions Regulations 1986 (SI 1986/1561) reg.7(5), (6).

Increase of disablement pension for constant attendance

10.37 **19.** The amount by which the weekly rate of disablement pension may be increased under [section 104 of the Social Security Contributions and Benefits Act 1992] where constant attendance is required by a beneficiary as a result of the relevant loss of faculty shall—

(a) where the beneficiary (not being a case to which paragraph (b) of this regulation relates) is to a substantial extent dependent on such attendance for the necessities of life and is likely to remain so dependent for a prolonged period, be the amount specified in paragraph [2](a) of Part V of Schedule 4 to the Act (unless the attendance so required is part-time only, in which case the amount shall be such sum as may be reasonable in the circumstances) or, where the extent of such attendance is greater by reason of the beneficiary's exceptionally severe disablement, a sum not exceeding one and a half times the amount specified in paragraph [2](a) of Part V of the said Schedule, a fraction of five pence being for this purpose treated as five pence;

(b) where the beneficiary is so exceptionally severely disabled as to be entirely, or almost entirely, dependent on such attendance for the necessities of life, and is likely to remain so dependent for a prolonged period and the attendance so required is whole-time, be the amount specified in paragraph [2](b) of Part V of Schedule 4 to the Act.

Determination of degree of disablement for constant attendance allowance

10.38 **20.**—(1) For the purpose of determining whether a person is entitled to an increase by way of constant attendance allowance under section 61 or to a corresponding increase by virtue of section 159(3)(b) of the Act or section 7(3)(b) of the Industrial Injuries and Diseases (Old Cases) Act 1975 of any other benefit, the Secretary of State shall, in a case where that person is subject to disabilities in respect of which payments of two or more of the descriptions set out in the next following paragraph of this regulation fall to be made, determine the extent of that person's disablement by taking into account all such disabilities to which that person is subject.

(2) The payments which may be taken into account are those of the following descriptions:—

(a) payments by way of disablement pensions under the Act;

(b) weekly payments to which that person is or has been at any time after 4 July 1948 entitled in respect of injury or disease being payments by way of compensation under the Workmen's Compensation Acts or under any contracting-out scheme duly certified thereunder;

(c) payments to which that person is or has been at any time after 4 July 1948 entitled as a former constable or fireman on account of an injury pension under or by virtue of any enactment in respect of an injury received or disease contracted by that person before 5 July 1948 or in respect of his retirement in consequence of such an injury or disease;

(d) payments by way of benefit under the Industrial Injuries and Diseases (Old Cases) Act 1975; and

(e) payments of personal benefit by way of disablement pension or gratuity under any Personal Injuries Scheme or Service Pensions Instrument or 1914–18 War Injuries Scheme.

(3) In sub-paragraph (2)(e) the expressions "personal benefit", "disablement pension", "Personal Injuries Scheme" and "Service Pensions Instrument" have the meanings which are assigned to them by the Social Security (Overlapping Benefits) Regulations 1979 for the purposes of those regulations.

Condition for receipt of increase of disablement pension for constant attendance under section 61 while receiving medical treatment as an in-patient

21.—(1) For the purposes of section 61 (increase of disablement pension in respect of the need of constant attendance), subject to paragraph (2) it shall be a condition for the receipt of an increase of disablement pension under the said section 61 for any period in respect of any person that during that period he is not receiving, or has not received, free in-patient treatment, and for this purpose a person shall be regarded as receiving or having received free in-patient treatment if he would be so regarded for the purposes of the Social Security (Hospital In-Patients) Regulations 1975. **10.39**

(2) Where a person was entitled to an increase of disablement pension under the said section 61 in respect of the period immediately before he commenced to undergo any treatment mentioned in paragraph (1), that paragraph shall not apply in respect of the first 4 weeks of any continuous period during which he is undergoing such treatment.

(3) For the purposes of paragraph (2), 2 or more distinct periods separated by an interval not exceeding 28 days, or by 2 or more such intervals, shall be treated as a continuous period equal in duration to the total of such distinct periods and ending on the last day of the later or last such period.

Treatment of distinct periods of hospital in-patient treatment as continuous for the purposes of section 62 of the Act

22. For the purposes of section 62 (increase of disablement benefit during hospital treatment) a person who receives medical treatment as an in-patient for 2 or more distinct periods separated by an interval of less than a week in each case shall be treated as receiving such treatment continuously from the beginning of the first period until the end of the last. **10.40**

GENERAL NOTE

Section 62 of the Social Security Act 1975 has been replaced by para.10 of Sch.7 to the Social Security Contributions and Benefits Act 1992. **10.41**

10.42 *Regulations 23–37 omitted.*

Adjustment of Benefit for Successive Accidents

Adjustment of benefit for successive accidents where a disablement gratuity is payable

10.43 **38.**—(1) In a case where—

(a) a person who is entitled, as a result of an accident, to a disablement pension (hereafter in this paragraph referred to as an "existing pension") which is payable in respect of an assessment for a period which is limited by reference to that person's life, becomes as a result of any other accident, entitled to an award as a result of an assessment of disablement in respect of which a disablement gratuity would, but for this regulation, be payable; and

(b) the aggregate amount of the assessment in respect of the existing pension and of the assessment in respect of which such disablement gratuity would be payable would, if it were the amount of the assessment of the extent of the disablement resulting from any one accident suffered by that person, have entitled him to receive a disablement pension at a higher rate than the rate of such existing pension;

then, if at any time before his claim for disablement benefit is determined, he so elects, that person shall be entitled to a disablement pension in lieu of the said disablement gratuity at a rate equal to the difference between the said higher rate and the rate of the existing pension.

(2) In a case in which a person who is entitled as a result of any accident to a disablement pension would but for the provisions of this paragraph become entitled in respect of any other accident to a disablement gratuity (not being a case in which he is entitled to a disablement pension in lieu of such gratuity)—

(a) if the assessment in respect of which such pension is payable to him amounts to not less than 100 per cent, such person shall not be entitled to receive any disablement gratuity in respect of such other accident;

(b) in any other case, such person shall not be entitled to receive, by way of disablement gratuity in respect of such other accident, an amount exceeding that which would be payable in respect of an assessment equal to the difference between 100 per cent. and the percentage of the assessment in respect of which such pension is payable to him.

(3) For the respective purposes of the two preceding paragraphs of this regulation—

(a) references to an existing pension within the meaning of paragraph (1) and to any disablement pension in paragraph (2) respectively shall include references to all such pensions which may be payable to the person concerned, and references to the amount of the assessment in respect of which, and the rate at which, any such pension is payable shall include references to the aggregate amount of the assessments in respect of which or the aggregate of the rates at which all such pensions are payable as aforesaid;

(b) the extent by which an assessment is increased by virtue of the provisions of section 62 of the Act (increase of disablement benefit during hospital treatment) shall be disregarded;

(c) for the purposes of paragraph (1)(a) a person shall be deemed to be entitled to a disablement pension and to an award as described in the said sub-paragraph from the respective dates of commencement of the periods taken into account by the assessments relating to such pension and to such award.

Adjustment of increase of benefit of successive accidents

39.—(1) Where a person who is entitled to a disablement pension in respect of any accident suffered by him— **10.44**

(a) has received, or is entitled to, a disablement gratuity in respect of any other accident; and

(b) as a result of the loss of faculty in respect of which he has received, or is entitled to that gratuity, is incapable of work and is likely to remain permanently so incapable;

the provisions of section 58 (increase of disablement pension by way of unemployability supplement) shall apply as if that loss of faculty resulted from the accident in respect of which such disablement pension is payable.

(2) Where a person—

(a) would be entitled to a disablement pension in respect of any accident but for the provisions of section 91(1)(a) (limitations on the aggregate weekly rates of benefit payable for the same period in respect of successive accidents); and

(b) by reason only of those provisions, is unable to satisfy the conditions for the receipt of an increase of that pension by way of unemployability supplement under section 58;

the provisions of the said section 58 shall apply as if such disablement pension were payable to that beneficiary.

(3) At any time at which the sum total of the several assessments in respect of two or more accidents suffered by any person amounts to not less than 100 per cent during the continuance of the periods respectively taken into account thereby, the weekly rate of any disablement pension which is payable to him may be increased in accordance with the provisions of section 61 if he requires constant attendance as a result of the loss of faculty resulting from any one or more of such accidents, whether or not that pension is payable in respect of an assessment of 100 per cent or in respect of that loss of faculty.

(4) A beneficiary who has suffered two or more accidents shall not be entitled at any time to more than one of each of the following increases of benefit, that is to say—

(a) by way of unemployability supplement under section 58;

(b) in respect of the need of constant attendance under section 61;

(c) in respect of a child, under section 64;

(d) in respect of an adult dependant, under section 66.

Disqualification for Receipt of Benefit and Suspension of Benefit Pending Appeals etc.

Disqualification for receipt of benefit, suspension of proceedings on claims and suspension of payment of benefit

10.45

40.—(1)[1. . .]

(2) If, without good cause—

(a) a claimant fails to furnish to the prescribed person any information required for the determination of the claim or of any question arising in connection therewith; or

(b) a beneficiary fails to give notice to the prescribed person of any change of circumstances affecting the continuance of the right to benefit or to the receipt thereof, or to furnish as aforesaid any information required for the determination of any question arising in connection with the award; or

(c) a claimant for, or a beneficiary in receipt of, disablement benefit fails to comply with any requirement of regulation 26 of the Social Security (Claims and Payments) Regulations 1979 (obligations of claimants for, and beneficiaries in receipt of [1. . .] disablement benefit);

he shall, subject to the following provisions of this regulation, if the [2 determining authority] so decide, be disqualified for receiving any benefit claimed in respect of the period of such failure.

(3) If a claimant or beneficiary wilfully obstructs, or is guilty of other misconduct in connection with any examination or treatment to which he is required under regulation 26 of the Social Security(Claims and Payments) Regulation 1979 to submit himself, or any proceedings under the Act for the determination of his right to benefit or to the receipt thereof, he shall, subject to the provisions of this regulation, be disqualified for receiving any benefit claimed for such period as the [2 determining authority] shall determine.

(4) In any case to which any of the foregoing paragraphs of this regulation relates, proceedings on the claim or payment of benefit, as the case may be, may be suspended for such period as the [2 determining authority] may determine.

(5) Nothing in this Regulation providing for the disqualification for the receipt of benefit for any of the following matters, that is to say—

(a) [1. . .]

(b) for failure to comply with the requirements of regulation 26 of the Social Security (Claims and Payments) Regulation 1979;

(c) for obstruction of, or misconduct in connection with, medical examination or treatment;

shall authorise the disentitlement of a claimant or beneficiary to benefit for a period exceeding six weeks on any disqualification.

(6) No person shall be disqualified for receiving any benefit for refusal to undergo a surgical operation not being one of minor character.

(7) A person who would be entitled to any benefit but for the operation of any of the foregoing provisions of this regulation shall be treated as if he were entitled thereto for the purpose of any rights or obligations under the Act (whether of himself or any other person) which depend on his being so entitled other than the right to payment of that benefit.

AMENDMENTS

1. Social Security (Abolition of Injury Benefit) (Consequential) Regulations 1983 (SI 1983/186) reg.13 (April 6, 1983).

2. Social Security Act 1998 (Commencement No. 12 and Consequential and Transitional Provisions) Order 1999 Sch.3 para.3 (November 29, 1999).

(SI 1982/1408 reg.40) (as amended)

Regulation 41 revoked by the Social Security (Claims and Payments) 10.46

Regulations 1987 (SI/1987/1968), reg.48 (April 11, 1988). 10.47

Regulations 42–45 omitted. 10.48

Regulation 46 was revoked by the Social Security Benefits Up-rating Regulations 1992 (SI 1992/469) reg.7 (April 6, 1992). 10.49

Regulation 47 omitted. 10.50

SCHEDULE 1 **Regulation 10**

PROVISIONS FOR THE PURPOSE OF WHICH DISQUALIFICATION UNDER THE ACT ARE TO BE DISREGARDED

10.51

Class of person (1)	*Class of Benefit for which person is disqualified (2)*	*Section of the Act for the purposes of which disqualification is to be disregarded (3)*	*Subject matter (4)*
A widow	Widow's allowance	25(3)	Period for which a widowed mothers allowance is payable (being a period for which she is not entitled to widow's allowance
	Widow's allowance or widowed mother's allowance	26(3)	Period for which a widow's pension is payable (Being a period for which she is not entitled to a widow's allowance or a widowed mother's allowance
	Widowed mother's allowance	26(1)(b)	Widow's pension for certain widows ceasing to be entitled to widowed mother's allowance
The husband of a widow	Category A retirement pension	24(1)(a)	Widow's allowance for the widow of a husband who at the date of his death was not entitled to a Category A retirement pension

In this Schedule "widowed mother's allowance" and "widow's pension" include benefit under section 39(4) corresponding to a widowed mother's allowance and a widow's pension respectively

SCHEDULE 2 **Regulation 11**

PRESCRIBED DEGREES OF DISABLEMENT

10.52

Description of injury	*Degree of disablement per cent*
1. Loss of both hands or amputation at higher sites	100
2. Loss of a hand and a foot	100
3. Double amputation through leg or thigh, or amputation through leg or thigh on one side and loss of other foot	100
4. Loss of sight to such an extent as to render the claimant unable to perform any work for which eyesight is essential	100
5. Very severe facial disfiguration	100
6. Absolute deafness	100
7. Forequarter or hindquarter amputation	100
Amputation cases—upper limbs (either arm)	
8. Amputation through shoulder joint	90
9. Amputation below shoulder with stump less than 20.5 centimetres from tip of acromion	80
10. Amputation from 20.5 centimetres from tip of acromion to less than 11.5 centimetres below tip of olecranon	70
11. Loss of a hand or of the thumb and four fingers of one hand or amputation from 11.5 centimetres below tip of olecranon	60
12. Loss of thumb	30
13. Loss of thumb and its metacarpal bone	40
14. Loss of four fingers of one hand	50
15. Loss of three fingers of one hand	30
16. Loss of two fingers of one hand	20
17. Loss of terminal phalanx of thumb	20
Amputation cases—lower limbs	
18. Amputation of both feet resulting in end-bearing stumps	90
19. Amputation through both feet proximal to the metatarso-phalangeal joint	80
20. Loss of all toes of both feet through the metatarso-phalangeal joint	40
21. Loss of all toes of both feet proximal to the proximal inter-phalangeal joint	30
22. Loss of all toes of both feet distal to the proximal inter-phalangeal joint	20
23. Amputation at hip	90
24. Amputation below hip with stump not exceeding 13 centimetres in length measured from tip of great trochanter	80
25. Amputation below hip and above knee with stump exceeding 13 centimetres in length measured from tip of great trochanter, or at knee not resulting in end-bearing stump	70
26. Amputation at knee resulting in end-bearing stump or below knee with stump not exceeding 9 centimetres	60
27. Amputation below knee with stump exceeding 9 centimetres but not exceeding 13 centimetres	50
28. Amputation below knee with stump exceeding 13 centimetres	40
29. Amputation of one foot resulting in end-bearing stump	30
30. Amputation through one foot proximal to the metatarso-phalangeal joint	30
31. Loss of all toes of one foot through the metatarso-phalangeal joint	20

Other injuries	*Degree of disablement per cent*
32. Loss of one eye, without complications, the other being normal	40
33. Loss of vision of one eye, without complications or disfigurement of the eyeball, the other being normal	30

Loss of:
A Fingers of right or left hand

Index finger—	
34. Whole	14
35. Two phalanges	11
36. One phalanx	9
37. Guillotine amputation of tip without loss of bone	5
Middle finger—	
38. Whole	12
39. Two phalanges	9
40. One phalanx	7
41. Guillotine amputation of tip without loss of bone	4
Ring or little finger—	
42. Whole	7
43. Two phalanges	6
44. One phalanx	5
45. Guillotine amputation of tip without loss of bone	2

B Toes of right or left foot

Great toe—	
46. Through metatarso-phalangeal joint	14
47. Part, with some loss of bone	3
Any other toe—	
48. Through metatarso-phalangeal joint	3
49. Part, with some loss of bone	1
Two toes of one foot, excluding great toe—	
50. Through metatarso-phalangeal joint	5
51. Part, with some loss of bone	2
Three toes of one foot, excluding great toe—	
52. Through metatarso-phalangeal joint	6
53. Part, with some loss of bone	3
Four toes of one foot, excluding great toe—	
54. Through metatarso-phalangeal joint	9
55. Part, with some loss of bone	3

GENERAL NOTE

See the notes to reg.11. 10.53

SCHEDULE 3 **Regulation 14**

SCALE OF DISABLEMENT GRATUITIES

10.54

Degree of disablement (1)	*(1) Appropriate proportion of maximum disablement gratuity (as specified in paragraph 2 of Part V of Schedule 4 to the Act (2)*
	per cent
1 per cent	10
2 per cent	15
3 per cent	20
4 per cent	25
5 per cent	30
6 per cent	35
7 per cent	40
8 per cent	45

Degree of disablement (1)	*(1) Appropriate proportion of maximum disablement gratuity (as specified in paragraph 2 of PartV of Schedule 4 to the Act (2)*
9 per cent	50
10 per cent	55
11 per cent	60
12 per cent	65
13 per cent	70
14 per cent	75
15 per cent	80
16 per cent	85
17 per cent	90
18 per cent	95
19 per cent	100

SCHEDULE 4 **Regulation 18**

[*Schedule 4 saved for certain purposes by regulation 7(5) and (6) of The Social Security (Industrial Injuries and Diseases) Miscellaneous Provisions Regulations 1986, SI 1986/1561.*]

RATE OF DISABLEMENT PAYABLE IN LIEU OF DISABLEMENT GRATUITY IN ACCORDANCE WITH REGULATION 18

10.55 Where the degree of disablement is as specified in column (1) of the following table, the weekly rate of the pension shall be determined in accordance with column (2) of that table:

Degree of disablement (1)	*Rate of pension (2)*
less than 20 per cent but not less than 16 per cent	the appropriate weekly amount of disablement pension payable in respect of a degree of disablement of 20 per cent as specified in paragraph 3 of Part V of Schedule 4 to the Act;
less than 16 per cent but not less than 11 per cent	75 per cent of the appropriate weekly amount of disablement pension payable in respect of a degree of disablement of 20 per cent as specified in the said paragraph 3:
less than 11 per cent but not less than 6 per cent	50 per cent of the appropriate weekly amount of disablement pension payable in respect of a degree of disablement of 20 per cent as specified in the said paragraph 3:
less than 6 per cent	25 per cent of the appropriate weekly amount of disablement pension payable in respect of a degree of disablement of 20 per cent as specified in the said paragraph 3: a fraction of a penny, being for this purpose treated as a penny.

Schedules 5–9 omitted **10.56**

The Social Security (Industrial Injuries) (Prescribed Diseases) Regulations 1985

(SI 1985/967) (*as amended*)

ARRANGEMENT OF REGULATIONS

PART I

GENERAL

PART II

PRESCRIPTION OF DISEASES AND PRESUMPTION AS TO THEIR ORIGIN

PART III

DATE OF ONSET AND RECRUDESCENCE

PART IV

APPLICATION OF SECTIONS 94 TO 107 OF THE SOCIAL SECURITY CONTRIBUTIONS AND BENEFITS ACT 1992 AND SECTIONS 8 TO 10 OF THE SOCIAL SECURITY ADMINISTRATION ACT 1992 AND OF REGULATIONS MADE THEREUNDER

PART V

SPECIAL PROVISIONS AS TO PNEUMOCONIOSIS, BYSSINOSIS, OCCUPATIONAL DEAFNESS AND CERTAIN OTHER DISEASES

Section A—Benefit

PART VI

TRANSITIONAL PROVISIONS AND REVOCATION

SCHEDULES

The Secretary of State for Social Services, in exercise of powers conferred by sections 76, 77, 78, 113 and 155 of and Schedule 20 to the Social Security Act 1975, and of all other powers enabling him in that behalf, and for the purpose only of consolidating regulations hereinafter revoked, after consultation with the Council of Tribunals in so far as is required by section 10 of the Tribunals and Inquiries Act 1971, hereby makes the following regulations:

PART I

GENERAL

Citation, commencement and interpretation

1.—(1) These regulations may be cited as the Social Security (Industrial Injuries) (Prescribed Diseases) Regulations 1985 and shall come into operation on 31st July 1985. **10.58**

(2) In these regulations, unless the context otherwise requires—

"the Act" means the [Social Security Contributions and Benefits Act 1992];

[[1] "the 1998 Act" means the Social Security Act 1998;]

"the Workmen's Compensation Acts" means the Workmen's Compensation Acts 1925 to 1945, or the enactments repealed by the Workmen's Compensation Act 1925, or the enactments repealed by the Workmen's Compensation Act 1906;

"the Adjudication Regulations" means the Social Security (Adjudication) Regulations 1984;

"the Benefit Regulations" means the Social Security (General Benefit) Regulations 1982;

"the Claims and Payments Regulations" means the Social Security (Claims and Payments) Regulations 1979;

[[1] . . .]

"asbestosis" means fibrosis of the parenchyma of the lungs due to the inhalation of asbestos dust;

"asbestos textiles" means yarn or cloth composed of asbestos or of asbestos mixed with any other material;

"coal mine" means any mine where one of the objects of the mining operations is the getting of coal (including bituminous coal, cannel coal, anthracite, lignite, and brown coal);

"diffuse mesothelioma" means the disease numbered D3 in Part I of Schedule 1 to these regulations;

"employed earner" means employed earner for the purposes of industrial injuries benefit and the term "employed earner's employment" shall be construed accordingly;

"foundry" means those parts of industrial premises where the production of metal articles (other than pig iron or steel ingots) is carried on by casting (not being diecasting or other casting in metal moulds), together with any part of the same premises where any of the following processes are carried on incidentally to such production, namely, the drying and subsequent preparation of sand for moulding (including the reclamation of used moulding sand), the preparation of moulds and cores, knock-out operations and dressing or fettling operations;

"grindstone" means a grindstone composed of natural or manufactured sandstone and includes a metal wheel or cylinder into which blocks of natural or manufactured sandstone are fitted;

[[2] "knock out and shake out grid" means a grid used for mechanically separating moulding sand from mouldings and castings;]

"a local office" means any office appointed by the Secretary of State as a local office for the purposes of the Act or of these regulations;

[[3] . . .]

"medical board" has the same meaning as in regulation 30 of the Adjudication Regulations;

[[1] "medical practitioner" means a medical practitioner who has experience in the issues specified in regulation 12(1) of the Social Security and Child Support (Decisions and Appeals) Regulations 1999;]

[[4] "metal" for the purposes of the disease number A10 in Part I of Schedule 1 to these Regulations, does not include stone, concrete, aggregate or similar substances for use in road or railway construction;]

"mine" includes every shaft in the course of being sunk, and every level and inclined plane in the course of being driven, and all the shafts, levels, planes, works, tramways and sidings, both below ground and above ground, in and adjacent to and belonging to the mine, but does not include any part of such premises on which any manufacturing process is carried on other than a process ancillary to the getting or dressing of minerals or the preparation of minerals for sale;

"occupational asthma" means the disease numbered D7 in Part I of Schedule 1 to these regulations;

"occupational deafness" means the disease numbered A10 in Part I of Schedule 1 to these regulations;

"the old regulations" means the Social Security (Industrial Injuries) (Prescribed Diseases) Regulations 1980, as amended by the Social Security (Industrial Injuries) (Prescribed Diseases) Amendment Regulations 1980, the Social Security (Industrial Injuries) (Prescribed Diseases) Amendment Regulations 1982 and the Social Security (Industrial Injuries) (Prescribed Diseases) Amendment (No. 2) Regulations 1982;

"prescribed disease" means a disease or injury prescribed under Part II of these regulations, and references to a prescribed disease being contracted shall be deemed to include references to a prescribed injury being received;

[3 "primary carcinoma of the lung" means the diseases numbered D8, [7 D8A,] D10 and D11 in Schedule 1 to these Regulations;]

"the Secretary of State" means the Secretary of State for Social Services;

"silica rock" means quartz, quartzite, ganister, sandstone, gritstone and chert, but not natural sand or rotten rock;

[2 "skid transfer bank" means the area of a steel mill where the steel product is moved from the area of its formation to the finishing area;]

"special medical board" has the same meaning as in regulation 30 of the Adjudication Regulations;

[5 "specially qualified adjudicating medical practitioner" means a specially qualified adjudicating medical practitioner appointed by virtue of section 62 of the Social Security Administration Act 1992;]

"tuberculosis" in the description of the disease numbered B5 in Part I of Schedule 1 to these regulations means disease due to tuberculosis infection, but when used elsewhere in these regulations in connection with pneumoconiosis means tuberculosis of the respiratory system only;

and other expressions have the same meanings as in the Act.

(3) Unless the context otherwise requires, any reference in these regulations—

(a) to a numbered section or Schedule is to the section of or, as the case may be, the Schedule to the Act bearing that number; and
(b) to a numbered regulation is a reference to the regulations bearing that number in these regulations, and any reference in a regulation to a numbered paragraph is a reference to the paragraph of that regulation bearing that number; and
(c) to any provision made by or contained in any enactment or instrument shall be construed as including a reference to any provision which it re-enacts or replaces, with or without modification.

[6 (4) In these Regulations, any reference to death benefit shall be taken as including also a reference to any benefit in respect of which contribution conditions are taken as having been satisfied in accordance with paragraph 10 of Schedule 3 to the Social Security Act 1986.]

AMENDMENTS

1. Social Security Act 1998 (Commencement No. 8, and Savings and Consequential and Transitional Provisions) Order 1999 (SI 1999/1958) Sch.8 para.1 (July 5, 1999).

2. Social Security (Industrial Injuries) (Prescribed Diseases) Amendment Regulations 1994 (SI 1994/2343) reg.2 (October 10, 1994).

3. Social Security (Industrial Injuries) (Prescribed Diseases) Amendment Regulations 1993 (SI 1993/862) reg.2 (April 19, 1993).

4. Social Security (Industrial Injuries) (Prescribed Diseases) Amendment Regulations 1990 (SI 1990/2269) reg.2 (December 13, 1990).

5. Social Security (Industrial Injuries and Adjudication) Regulations 1993 (SI 1993/861) reg.17 (April 19, 1993).

6. Social Security (Industrial Injuries) (Miscellaneous Amendment) Regulations 1988 (SI 1988/553) reg.5 (April 11, 1988).

7. Social Security (Industrial Injuries) (Prescribed Diseases) Amendment Regulations 2006 (SI 2006/586) reg.2(1) (April 6, 2006).

PART II

PRESCRIPTION OF DISEASES AND PRESUMPTION AS TO THEIR ORIGIN

Prescription of diseases and injuries and occupations for which they are prescribed

10.59 **2.**—For the purposes of [sections 108–110] of the Act—

(a) subject to [1 the following paragraphs] of this regulation and to regulation 43(3), (5) and (6), each disease or injury set out in the first column of Part I of Schedule 1 hereto is prescribed in relation to all persons who have been employed on or after 5th July 1948 in employed earner's employment in any occupation set against such disease or injury in the second column of the said Part;

(b) pneumoconiosis is prescribed—

(i) in relation to all persons who have been employed on or after 5th July 1948 in employed earner's employment in any occupation set out in Part II of the said Schedule; and

(ii) in relation to all other persons who have been so employed in any occupation involving exposure to dust and who have not worked at any time (whether in employed earner's employment or not) in any occupation in relation to which pneumoconiosis is prescribed by virtue of regulations (apart from this sub-paragraph) in force—

(i) in the case of any claim for disablement benefit or a claim for death benefit in respect of the death of a person to whom disablement benefit has been awarded in respect of pneumoconiosis, on the date of the claim for disablement benefit;

(ii) in the case of a claim for death benefit in respect of the death of any other person, on the date of the death of that person;

(c) occupational deafness is prescribed in relation to all persons who have been employed in employed earner's employment—

(i) at any time on or after 5th July 1948; and

(ii) for a period or periods (whether before or after 5th July 1948) amounting in the aggregate to not less than 10 years in one or more of the occupations set out in the second column of paragraph A10 of Part I of Schedule 1 to these regulations [4 . . .]

[2 (d) the disease specified in paragraph D12 of Part I of Schedule 1 is not prescribed in relation to persons to whom regulation 22 applies.]

[3 (e) cataract is not prescribed unless the person was employed in employed earner's employment in an occupation set out in the second column of paragraph A2 of Part I of Schedule 1 to these regulations for a period or periods amounting in aggregate to not less than 5 years.]

AMENDMENTS

1. Social Security (Industrial Injuries) (Prescribed Diseases) Amendment Regulations 2000 (SI 2000/1588) reg.2(2) (July 10, 2000).

2. Social Security (Industrial Injuries) (Prescribed Diseases) Amendment (No. 2) Regulations 1993 (SI 1993/1985) reg.2 (September 13, 1993).

3. Social Security (Industrial Injuries) (Prescribed Diseases) Amendment Regulations 2000 (SI 2000/1588) reg.2(3) (July 10, 2000).

4. Social Security (Industrial Injuries) (Prescribed Diseases) Amendment Regulations 2005 (SI 2005/324) reg.2(1) (March 14, 2005).

Definitions

"employed earner's employment"—see SSCBA 1992 s.95, and note.
"pneumoconiosis"—see SSCBA 1992 s.122(1), above.

General Note

This regulation links with Sch.1 to the Regulations (below) to establish a list of diseases, and a list of the occupations in respect of which they are prescribed. It is not enough to suffer from a disease which happens to be in the list, it must have been linked to the occupation. Each disease is prescribed only in relation to claimants who have been employed in the occupations described in the Schedule. That is a significant limitation. It is also necessary for the occupation to have caused the disease but that is usually presumed under reg.4. **10.60**

On July 5, 1999, AOs' functions with respect to industrial injuries benefits and the making of an industrial accident declaration were transferred to the Secretary of State (SSA 1998 ss.1, 8 and Commencement Order No. 8). He may, however, refer certain issues for report to a medical practitioner who has experience of the issues. The issues so referable are.

(a) the extent of a personal injury for the purposes of s.94

(b) whether the claimant has a prescribed industrial disease and the extent of resulting disablement; and

(c) whether, for disablement benefit purposes, the claimant has a disablement and its extent (Decisions and Appeals Regulations 1999 reg.12).

Decisions on industrial injuries benefits and on the matter of an industrial accident declaration, are appealable to a "unified" appeal tribunal composed of a legally qualified member and up to two medically qualified members (SSA 1998 ss.4, 12, Schs 2 and 3; Decisions and Appeals Regulations 1999 reg.36(2)). Like the Secretary of State, that tribunal is competent to deal with both the medical and non-medical aspect of industrial injuries matters. Note, however, that whether a claimant is an employed or self-employed earner, and whether a specific employment is, or is not, employed earner's employment is to be decided not by the Secretary of State, but by officers of the Board of Revenue and Customs (Social Security Contributions (Transfer of Functions, etc.) Act 1999, s.8(1)). Accordingly, such decisions are not matters of appeal for the "unified" appeal tribunal but rather for appeal to the tax appeal Commissioners (*ibid.*, s.11). Such decisions and appeals are regulated by the Social Security Contributions (Decisions and Appeals) Regulations 1999 (SI 1999/1027).

The key point from all this for industrial injuries matters, is that the distinction between medical issues (the disablement questions) and non-medical issues—previously crucial as demarcating the respective jurisdictions of MATs and SSATs—is no longer relevant.

Regulation 2 requires persons to have been "employed in" an occupation prescribed as relevant for the disease in question in Sch.1 to the regulations. Para.(c) (occupational deafness) further requires the employment in the relevant occupation to have been for a period or periods amounting in the aggregate to not less than 10 years. *R(I) 2/79(T)*, an occupational deafness case, makes it clear that

> "the focus of the regulations is directed to the work done rather than to the contractual obligation to do it. The benefit is for disablement incurred whilst working in any of the prescribed occupations and undergoing exposure to noise whilst so working." (para.15).

At the time that case was considered, an otherwise very similar regulation required 20 years' employment. The Tribunal of Commissioners said that to compute the relevant period, one should use this actual work test. However, one cannot look to whether the person worked on every available day. Normal breaks (weekends, holidays, short-term absences for sickness or absenteeism, short-term interruptions for industrial trouble) should be ignored in the sense of not breaking the period of employment. In contrast, abnormal interruptions would break the period of employment and not count towards the 20-year requirement. What, then, was an abnormal interruption? The Commissioners thought it undesirable to lay down an inflexible rule as to what constituted an abnormal interruption, considering the matter to be one of fact and degree in each case. But they considered that an abnormal interruption "should be a substantial or prolonged period of absence from work" and thought "that it would be a most exceptional case where it could be said that a man had been working during a continuous break in actual work of three calendar months or more for whatever reason" and opined that "such periods of absence should normally be excluded from the computation of the period of 20 years." (see especially paras 19, 20). The same approach had to be taken to determining when a person was last employed in a relevant occupation for the purposes of time limits on claims (see further annotation to reg.25, below).

10.61 Where an employed earner works for less than half the time in a prescribed occupation, he or she cannot be said to be working "wholly or mainly" in that occupation during the whole period of employment. However, there may have been parts of the period of employment during which the claimant was working for most of the time in a prescribed occupation and other parts when he or she was not. It is therefore wrong, on a claim in respect of occupational deafness, to look at the whole period of employment and consider whether the claimant was working "wholly or mainly" in a prescribed occupation throughout that period. The question is whether the parts of the period (or periods) of employment during which the claimant was working in a prescribed occupation total in the aggregate to not less than 10 years (*CI/1446/98*).

Special provision is made for pneumoconiosis and occupational deafness. In respect of pneumoconiosis, para.(b)(ii) gives potential entitlement to a group of people who do not work in the specific occupations for which the disease is prescribed in Pt II of the Schedule. Note that this group do not have the benefit of the presumption that the prescribed disease resulted from employment in the specified occupation (see reg.4, below), and the claimant bears the burden of proving that the disease results from being employed, "in any occupation involving exposure to dust". This means that the exposure to dust must be in excess of that met with in ordinary life (*R(I) 40/57*). The requirement was most recently considered in *R(I) 1/85*, which dealt with the same phrase in relation to the prescribed disease D4 (Inflammation of the mucous membrane etc.).

The amendment inserting para.(e) (cataract) is subject to a transitional provision in reg.7(2) and (3) of the amending instrument such that it

> "shall not apply in the case of a person—
>
> (a) who had an assessment of disablement in respect of the relevant disease for a period up to the date 3 months after the commencement date; or
> (b) in respect of whom a decision in relation to a relevant disease on a claim for disablement benefit made before or within 3 months after the commencement date is revised or superseded after that date under section 9 or 10 of the Social Security Act 1998 resulting in an assessment;
>
> during any period when there is in respect of him a continuous assessment of disablement in respect of that disease, and for this purpose two or more assessments, one of which begins on the day following the end of a preceding assessment, shall be treated as continuous." (reg.7(2)).

Nor will it apply

"in the case of a person—

(a) who had an assessment of disablement in respect of the relevant disease for a period which ended before or within 3 months after the commencement date;
(b) who suffers a further attack of that relevant disease before or within 3 months after the commencement date;
(c) who makes a claim for disablement benefit in respect of that disease after the commencement date; and
(d) in respect of whom it is decided under regulation 7 of the principal Regulations (recrudescence) that the further attack is a recrudescence of that disease." (reg.7(3))

The commencement date is July 10, 2000 and "relevant disease" means the disease referred to in the amendment, or the regulation amended by the amendment (reg.7(4)).

Sequelae or resulting conditions

3.—Where a person— 10.62

(a) is or was in employed earner's employment and a disease is or was prescribed under the Act and these regulations in relation to him in such employment; and
(b) is suffering from a condition which, in his case, has resulted from that disease;

the provisions of [sections 108–110] of the Act and of these regulations shall apply to him as if he was suffering from that disease, whether or not the condition from which he is suffering is itself a prescribed disease.

GENERAL NOTE

Disablement resulting from a condition which is not prescribed but which has resulted from a prescribed disease is to be included in any assessment. 10.63

In *CI/5972/99*, Commissioner Howell held that a tribunal erred in law when, in respect of someone who was a carrier of viral hepatitis (having had an attack of it in the past) they merely recorded that he was not suffering from the disease. They ought to have considered (as the AMA had) whether he suffered from a sequela of the disease.

[1Presumption that a disease is due to the nature of employment

4.—(1) Where a person has developed a disease which is prescribed in Part I of Schedule 1 in paragraphs A3(a), A4, A5, A6, A7, A8, A11, B1(a), B3, B4(a), B9, B10, B11, B12, B14, B15, C3, C24A, D4 or D7, that disease shall, unless the contrary is proved, be presumed to be due to the nature of that person's employed earner's employment if— 10.64

(a) that employment was in any occupation set against that disease in the second column of that Part; and
(b) the person was so employed on, or at any time within one month immediately preceding, the date on which, under these Regulations, that person is treated as having developed the disease.

(2) Where a person has developed a disease which is prescribed in Part I of Schedule 1 in paragraphs A1, A2, A3(b), A10, A13, A14, [3 A15,] B2, B6, B8B, B13, C17, C18, C22(a), C24, C31, C32, [2 C34,]D2, D3, D6, D8, D8A, D9, D10, D11, D12 or D13, that disease shall, unless the

contrary is proved, be presumed to be due to the nature of that person's employed earner's employment if that employment was in any occupation set against that disease in the second column of that Part.

(3) Where a person in relation to whom tuberculosis is prescribed in paragraph B5 of Part I of Schedule 1 in respect of the occupation set out in sub-paragraph (a) in the second column of the entry relating to that disease, develops that disease, that disease shall, unless the contrary is proved, be presumed to be due to the nature of that person's employed earner's employment if the date on which, under these Regulations, that person is treated as having developed the disease is—

(a) not less than six weeks after the date on which that person was first employed in that occupation; and

(b) not more than two years after the date on which that person was last so employed in that occupation.

(4) Where a person has developed a disease which is prescribed in Part I of Schedule 1 in paragraphs B1(b), B4(b), B7 and B8A, that disease shall, unless the contrary is proved, be presumed to be due to the nature of that person's employed earner's employment if—

(a) that employment was in any occupation set against that disease in the second column of that Part; and

(b) that person was so employed—

(i) on the date on which, under these Regulations, that person is treated as having developed the disease; or

(ii) on a date at any time within—

(aa) in the case of B1(b) or B8A, two months;

(bb) in the case of B7, six months; or

(cc) in the case of B4(b), twelve months

immediately preceding the date on which, under these Regulations, that person is treated as having developed the disease.

(5) Where a person in relation to whom carpal tunnel syndrome is prescribed in paragraph A12 of Part I of Schedule 1 in respect of the occupation set out in sub-paragraph (b) in the second column of the entry relating to that disease, develops that disease, it shall, unless the contrary is proved, be presumed to be due to the nature of that person's employed earner's employment if that person was employed in that occupation on the date, or at any time within one month immediately preceding the date, on which under these Regulations that person is treated as having developed the disease.

(6) Where a person in relation to whom primary neoplasm of the epithelial lining of the urinary tract is prescribed in paragraph C23 of Part I of Schedule 1 in respect of the occupation set out in sub-paragraph (a), (b) or (e) in the second column of the entry relating to that disease, develops that disease, it shall, unless the contrary is proved, be presumed to be due to the nature of that person's employed earner's employment.

(7) Where a person in relation to whom pneumoconiosis is prescribed in regulation 2(b)(i) develops pneumoconiosis, the disease shall, unless the contrary is proved, be presumed to be due to the nature of that person's employed earner's employment if that person has been employed in either of the occupations set out in Part II of Schedule 1 for a period or periods amounting in aggregate to not less than 2 years in employment which either was employed earner's employment or would have been employed earner's employment if it had taken place on or after 5th July 1948.]

AMENDMENTS

1. Social Security (Industrial Injuries) (Prescribed Diseases) Amendment Regulations 2015 (SI 2015/87) reg.2 (March 16, 2015).
2. Social Security (Industrial Injuries) (Prescribed Diseases) Amendment Regulations 2017 (SI 2017/232) reg.2 (March 30, 2017).
3. Social Security (Industrial Injuries) (Prescribed Diseases) Amendment Regulations 2019 (SI 2019/1241) reg.2(2) (December 9, 2019).

GENERAL NOTE

Each paragraph of this important regulation establishes a presumption that a prescribed disease specified in the particular paragraph is due to the nature of a scheduled occupation provided that the conditions set out in the particular paragraph applicable are met. In each case, the presumption applies "unless the contrary is proved" on the balance of probabilities (*R(I) 38/52*). If a prescribed disease in Part I of Sch.1 is not listed in any of these paragraphs of this regulation no such presumption applies. **10.65**

The operation of reg.4 was the subject of detailed analysis by IIAC in its report *Presumption that a disease is due to the nature of employment: the role of rebuttal in claims assessment* (Cm 9030, March 2015). IIAC identified a number of problems posed by the existing formulation of the rule and canvassed various possibilities for reform, including the notion of in effect operating two schedules of prescribed diseases. In one schedule the presumption that the disease is due to the nature of the employment would follow directly from its prescription. In the other decision-makers would be able to gather further information and evidence as necessary. In the end, having weighed the various advantages and drawbacks of competing models for reform, the Council made no actual recommendation for any amendment to the legislative scheme, but expressed the firm view that "rebuttal is, and should only be, used sparingly" (para. 93).

PART III

DATE OF ONSET AND RECRUDESCENCE

Development of disease

5.—[1(1)] If on a claim for benefit under [sections 108 to 110] in respect of a prescribed disease a person is found to be or to have been suffering from the disease, or to have died as the result thereof, the disease shall, for the purposes of such claim, be treated as having developed on a date (hereafter in these regulations referred to as "the date of onset") determined in accordance with the provisions of the next two following regulations. **10.66**

[1 (2) Where a person claims benefit under Part V of the Contributions and Benefits Act and it is decided that he is not entitled on the basis of a finding that he was not suffering from a prescribed disease, the finding shall be conclusive for the purpose of a decision on a subsequent claim of that kind in respect of the same disease and the same person.]

AMENDMENT

1. Social Security, Child Support and Tax Credits (Miscellaneous Amendments) Regulations 2005 (SI 2005/337) reg.5 (March 18, 2005).

General Note

10.67 In *R(I) 5/04* (at para.20) Commissioner Howell had decided that neither reg.5 nor reg.6 had any operation where the claimant was *not* found to be suffering from a prescribed disease. There was not what he called a "negative date of onset" where a person was found not to be suffering from the disease on the first claim made. The effect of *R(I) 5/04* was reversed by the Social Security, Child Support and Tax Credits (Miscellaneous Amendments) Regulations 2005 (SI 2005/337), which introduced the new reg.5(2). The amended version of reg.5(2) was considered by Judge Ovey in *PH v SSWP (II)* [2016] UKUT 94 (AAC). The issue raised there was whether the words "a finding that he was not suffering from a prescribed disease" mean only a finding that the person did not have a particular disease or whether they extend to a finding that a person has the disease but is not a person in relation to whom it is prescribed (e.g. because some time limit in the terms of prescription has not been satisfied). Judge Ovey concludes that reg.5 (and reg.6) "only need to be applied once it has been determined that the disease in respect of which the claim has been made is prescribed in relation to the claimant's occupation" (at para.22). See further regs.6 and 7 below.

Date of onset

10.68 **6.**—(1) For the purposes of the first claim in respect of a prescribed disease suffered by a person, the date of onset shall be determined in accordance with the following provisions of this regulation, and, save as provided in regulation 7, that date shall be treated as the date of onset for the purposes of any subsequent claim in respect of the same disease suffered by the same person, so however that—

(a) [1 . . .] any date of onset determined for the purposes of that claim shall not preclude fresh consideration of the question whether the same person is suffering from the same disease on any subsequent claim for or award of benefit; and

(b) if, on the consideration of a claim, [2 the degree of disablement is assessed at less than one per cent.], any date of onset determined for the purposes of that claim shall be disregarded for the purposes of any subsequent claim.

(2) Where the claim for the purposes of which the date of onset is to be determined is—

(a) a claim for sickness benefit made by virtue of section [102] of the Act by a person to whom regulation 8(1) applies (except in respect of pneumoconiosis, byssinosis, diffuse mesothelioma, occupational deafness, occupational asthma, [3 primary carcinoma of the lung] [4, bilateral diffuse pleural thickening or [5chronic obstructive pulmonary disease]]) the date of onset shall be the first day on which the claimant was incapable of work as the result of the disease on or after 5th July 1948;

(b) a claim for disablement benefit (except in respect of occupational deafness), the date of onset shall be the day on which the claimant first suffered from the relevant loss of faculty on or after 5th July 1948; and the date of onset so determined shall be the date of onset for the purposes of a claim for sickness benefit made by virtue of section [102] of the Act in respect of pneumoconiosis, byssinosis, diffuse mesothelioma, occupational asthma, [3 primary carcinoma of the lung] [3, bilateral diffuse pleural thickening or [5chronic obstructive pulmonary disease]];

(c) a claim for disablement benefit in respect of occupational deafness, the date of onset shall be the day on which the claimant first suffered from the relevant loss of faculty on or after 3rd February 1975; or, if later—
   (i) 3rd September 1979 in the case of a claim made before that date which results in the payment of benefit commencing on that date, and
   (ii) in any other case, the date on which such claim is made as results in the payment of benefit; or

(d) a claim for death benefit, the date of onset shall be the date of death.

AMENDMENTS

1. Social Security Act 1998 (Commencement No.8, and Savings and Consequential and Transitional Provisions) Order 1999 (SI 1999/1958) Sch.8 para.2 (July 5, 1999).
2. Social Security (Industrial Injuries) (Prescribed Diseases) Amendment Regulations 1989 (SI 1989/1207) reg.2 (August 9, 1989).
3. Social Security (Industrial Injuries) (Prescribed Diseases) Amendment Regulations 1993 (SI 1993/862) reg.4 (April 19, 1993).
4. Social Security (Industrial Injuries) (Prescribed Diseases) Amendment (No. 2) Regulations 1993 (SI 1993/1985) reg.4 (September 13, 1993).
5. Social Security (Industrial Injuries) (Prescribed Diseases) Amendment Regulations 2015 (SI 2015/87) reg.5 (March 16, 2015).

GENERAL NOTE

This is an important provision because, under Sch.2, references in the Act to the date of the relevant accident must, in disease cases, be construed as references to the date of onset. It is also important when reduced earnings allowance is being claimed because the claimant's "regular employment" is the employment he had at that date (*CI/285/49*). Under para.(1), once there has been a claim for benefit, the date of onset established for the purposes of that claim applies for any future claim in respect of the same disease unless disablement is assessed at less than 1 per cent. Reg.7 deals with the distinction between fresh attacks of a disease and recrudescence of an earlier attack. 10.69

In *R(I) 4/96*, Commissioner Goodman makes the important point that the date of onset of a prescribed disease for a particular claimant and the date from which payment of disablement benefit can be paid on or after the disease has been prescribed (added to the Schedule) are not necessarily coincidental. So where prescribed disease D12 (miners' bronchitis etc.) was added from September 13, 1993, disablement benefit was only payable from that date, despite the fact that the date of onset (the date from which the claimant suffered from it) was much earlier. Unless the contrary is clearly indicated in the particular prescription (and it was not here), the insertion into the Schedule of a new prescribed disease is not retrospective so as to enable the payment of disablement benefit (subject to showing good cause for delay in claiming) from the date of onset.

Paragraph (2)(b)

In *CI/17220/1996*, as regards a case where the claimant first began to suffer from a disease in 1945, Commissioner Levenson held that the "obvious way" to read para. (2)(b) of reg.6 10.70

> "is that the date of onset is the 5 July 1948 or any later date on which the claimant first suffers from the relevant loss of faculty if the claimant is not suffering from the relevant loss of faculty on 5 July 1948. In other words, if a claimant begins to suffer from the relevant loss of faculty before 5 July 1948, this provision deems the date of onset to be 5 July 1948. In the present case, this interpretation avoids a potentially unfair result and is also in keeping with the notion in regulation 5 of the disease being treated as having developed on the date of onset. In the present case the date of onset is 5 July 1948. The disease is treated as having developed on that date. This is also the date on which, for the purposes of section 108(1) of

the Social Security Contributions and Benefits Act 1992 the disease developed. Accordingly since it developed after 4 July 1948, industrial injuries benefit is payable in an appropriate case. The adjudication officer and the tribunal, without spelling it out, assumed in effect that regulation 6(2)(b) meant that the claimant had to have first suffered from the disease on a date later than 4 July 1948. That was the principal error of law by the tribunal" (para.12).

The matter of the date of onset in respect of PD A11 (vibration white finger) was considered by Commissioner Williams in *CI/6027/1999*. On a first claim, the relevant provision is reg.6(2)(b), so that the date of onset is the date when there first is a "relevant loss of faculty". Citing *CSI/382/2000* in support, as well as the agreement of the parties on the point, he agreed that the date of onset is the date when the disease reached the extent necessary to meet the prescribed amount of disablement set down in the schedule of prescription. That prescription contains an "annual test"—it reads "episodic blanching, occurring throughout the year". Commissioner Williams asked:

"How is that test to be applied? In cases of doubt, the question is from what date it is more probable than not that the disease has reached the necessary extent, applying the 'annual test' prospectively (that is, it will from that date meet the test), not retrospectively. There may be doubt at a particular date whether there is blanching *episodically throughout the year,* as there appears to have been in this case in 1991. It might be argued that it cannot be finally decided that someone has the prescribed disease until at least a year of episodic blanching to the minimum physical extent has occurred, so that in one sense you can only prescribe the disease some months after the date of onset. In my view, the law does not require this because it is looking to certainty rather than probability. PD A11 is well known to be a disease that does not improve. Onset should be judged on the balance of probabilities without waiting a year. The 'date of onset' is the date that the disease probably first reaches the relevant levels and causes disablement. This part of the test for PD A11 is to be stated as 'this probably will be episodic throughout the year'. It is not a test that 'this definitely has been episodic throughout the past year'. But once it is clear that the proper test is applied, determining the date of onset is a question of fact, not of law, and is not for appeal to a Commissioner. It is of the nature of probability decisions that some will be shown by later events to be wrong. There are mechanisms for dealing with that elsewhere in social security legislation." (para.13).

10.71 The Secretary of State appealed against this decision. In *Whalley v Secretary of State for Work and Pensions* [2003] EWCA Civ 166 (reported as *R(I) 2/03*), the Court of Appeal allowed the appeal, but on grounds that do not concern the principles stated above. The appeal was successful on other grounds: that one cannot claim REA without claiming disablement benefit; and that a decision by a tribunal determining the date of onset for a PD, whether given in respect of disablement benefit or REA, as the case may be, binds a later tribunal considering the issue for either benefit. Where there was a refusal by a tribunal of a claim for disablement benefit on the ground that the claimant did not have PD A11 at the date of the decision, a later decision maker, faced with a new claim for that benefit or for REA, cannot specify a date of onset for the disease which is prior to the refusal of the first claim. See also *CI/2531/2001*, para.15:

"if a person makes a claim or successive claims for disablement benefit (and, by the same token, reduced earnings allowance, which depend on establishing the same loss of faculty) in respect of occupational deafness, the 'date of onset' can never be earlier than that of the *first* such claim which results in the actual payment of benefit; and the date so determined is also, by regulation 6(1), to be treated as the date of onset for the purposes of each subsequent claim" (*per* Commissioner Howell).

Whalley has also been applied in *R(I) 2/04* (Commissioner Rowland), *CI/226/2001, R(I) 5/04*). With the support of the Secretary of State's representative, Commissioner Howell applied in *CI/3463/2003*, his decision in *CI/5270 & 5271/2002* (now reported as *R(I) 5/04*) that *Whalley* reasoning does not apply to decisions made under the Social Security Act 1998 processes. He could not better the summary of the position as stated in his submission by that representative: 10.72

> "The effects of finality for the purposes of section 17 of the SS Act 1998 was considered by the Commissioner in *CI/5270/02*. In that case it was held that following the introduction of DMA, decisions on diagnosis were not freestanding but were a question of fact embodied in a decision of the Secretary of State under section 8(1) of the Act on entitlement to benefit. In paragraph 17 the Commissioner stated *'In the absence of such express provision, an earlier finding made under the 1998 Act machinery on such a question cannot fall within the modified statutory form of the principle of* res judicata *which now applies to social security decisions under section 17'*.
>
> The Secretary of State accepts the reasoning in decision *CI 5270/02* and submits that provided no claim had been made under the previous legislation where section 60 of the SS Admin Act [*1992*] did provide for finality on the question of the date of onset, then that question [*sc. the previous negative diagnosis*] is a matter of fact and not final for the purposes of section 17 of the SS Act 1998."

Commissioner Rowland in *R(I) 2/04* considered the remarks in *Whalley* to have been obiter. Moreover, the reasoning applied on the basis of the decision-making processes prior to the SSA 1998, so that the demise of the earlier provisions on finality of an MAT's decision, means that the binding nature of a decision on a date of onset of a PD for disablement benefit purposes flows from the terms of reg.6, now under consideration (para.14), a view endorsed by Commissioner Howell in *CI/5270 & 5271/2002* (paras16–18). On that basis the proper way to seek to challenge the earlier decision on date of onset, where the earlier decision found that the claimant was suffering from the prescribed disease, would be by way of seeking a supersession of that decision under SSA 1998, s.10, and appealing against the supersession decision or a refusal to supersede (*R(I) 2/04*, para.19). However, where the earlier decision on a first claim for disablement benefit was a negative one—the claimant was found not to be suffering from the claimed PD, there is nothing in the new decision-making and adjudication scheme or in reg.6 to make a diagnosis decision binding for any subsequent claim (*R(I) 5/04*, paras 18–22), so that the appeals tribunal had erred, having found that the claimant was, contrary to an earlier decision of the Secretary of State, suffering from carpal tunnel syndrome (PDA12), in setting the date of onset as the limited by the date of that earlier decision.

In the Northern Ireland decision *C1/04–05 (REA)*, applying *Whalley*, Commissioner Brown held that where a tribunal had in 2002 determined the date of onset for a prescribed disease, that decision bound a later tribunal in respect of any subsequent claim in respect of the same disease.

Judge Ovey in *PH v SSWP (II)* [2016] UKUT 94 (AAC) confirms that para.(2)(b) clearly requires the identification of a particular day as the date of onset; thus a tribunal's finding that a claimant developed a condition "in 2006" was insufficiently precise to be a date of onset. In effect, such a finding simply meant the tribunal had decided that the claimant fell at the first hurdle because on its finding, whatever the exact date on which the symptoms of carpal tunnel syndrome had first developed, it was long after the claimant had ceased to be employed. In those circumstances no purpose would be served by determining the date of onset for the purposes of regs. 5 and 6 and on the facts of the case the tribunal had not purported to do so.

Paragraph (2)(c)

It was clear from *McKiernon v Secretary of State for Social Services* (*The Times*, November 1, 1989), that reg.6(2)(c) was originally ultra vires. As a result, s.77(2) of the SSA 1975 (now s.109 of the SSCBA 1992) was amended by para.4(2) of Sch.6 to 10.73

the SSA 1990. Para.4(3) of Sch.6 to the 1990 Act provided that reg.6(2)(c) should be taken always to have been validly made. An argument that the 1990 Act failed to have the desired effect was rejected in *Chatterton v Chief Adjudication Officer* CA, *R(I) 1/94*).

Recrudescence

10.74 7.—(1) [1 Where in respect of a prescribed disease other than pneumoconiosis, byssinosis, diffuse mesothelioma, occupational deafness, occupational asthma, [2 primary carcinoma of the lung] [3, bilateral diffuse pleural thickening or [6chronic obstructive pulmonary disease]], a person's disablement has been assessed at not less than one per cent. and he] suffers from another attack of the same disease, or dies as a result thereof, then—

(a) if the further attack commences or the death occurs during a period taken into account by [1 that assessment] (which period is in this regulation referred to as a "relevant period") the disease shall be treated as a recrudescence of the attack to which the relevant period relates, unless it is otherwise determined in the manner referred to in the following sub-paragraph;

(b) if the further attack commences or the death occurs otherwise than during a relevant period, or if it is determined [4. . .] that the disease was in fact contracted afresh, it shall be treated as having been so contracted.

(2) For the purposes of paragraph (1), a further attack of a prescribed disease shall be deemed to have commenced on the date on which the person concerned was first incapable of work or first suffered from the relevant loss of faculty, whichever is earlier, as a result of that further attack.

(3) Where, under the foregoing provisions of this regulation, a disease is treated as having been contracted afresh, the date of onset of the disease in relation to the fresh contraction shall be the date on which the person concerned was first incapable of work or first suffered from the relevant loss of faculty, whichever is earlier as a result of the further attack, or in the event of his death, the date of death.

(4) Where, under the provisions aforesaid, a disease is treated as a recrudescence, any assessment of disablement in respect of the recrudescence during a period taken into account by a previous assessment of disablement shall be by way of [5 a supersession of the assessment relating to the relevant period].

(5) This regulation shall not apply in relation to a claim for sickness benefit made by virtue of section [102] of the Act except where such a claim is made by a person to whom regulation 8(1) applies.

AMENDMENTS

1. Social Security (Industrial Injuries) (Prescribed Diseases) Amendment Regulations 1989 (SI 1989/1207) reg.3 (August 9, 1989).

2. Social Security (Industrial Injuries) (Prescribed Diseases) Amendment Regulations 1993 (SI 1993/862) reg.5 (April 19, 1993).

3. Social Security (Industrial Injuries) (Prescribed Diseases) Amendment (No. 2) Regulations 1993 (SI 1993/1985) reg.4 (September 13, 1993).

4. Social Security (Industrial Injuries) (Prescribed Diseases) Amendment Regulations 2003 (SI 2003/270) reg.3 (March 17, 2003).

5. Social Security and Child Support (Miscellaneous Amendments) Regulations 2000 (SI 2000/1596) reg.2 (June 19, 2000).

6. Social Security (Industrial Injuries) (Prescribed Diseases) Amendment Regulations 2015 (SI 2015/87) reg.5 (March 16, 2015).

Workmen's compensation cases

8.—(1) If under the foregoing provisions of this Part of these regulations a date of onset has to be determined for the purposes of a claim for benefit in respect of a prescribed disease, other than pneumoconiosis or byssinosis, suffered by a person to whom compensation under the Workmen's Compensation Acts has been awarded or paid in respect of the same disease and, at the date of such claim for benefit, or, if it is a claim for death benefit, at the date of death— 10.75

(a) that person was in receipt of weekly payments in respect of such compensation; or

(b) any liability or alleged liability for such compensation had been redeemed by the payment of a lump sum, or had been the subject of a composition agreement under the provisions of the said Acts;

the disease in respect of which the claim is made shall be treated for the purposes of these regulations as a recrudescence of the disease in respect of which such compensation was awarded or paid and not as having developed on or after 5th July 1948 unless it is determined [2 . . .] that the disease was in fact contracted afresh.

(2) If it is determined as provided in the foregoing paragraph that the disease was contracted afresh, or if compensation is not being or has not been paid as provided in sub-paragraph (a) or (b) thereof, the date of onset shall be determined in accordance with regulations 5 to 7 as if no compensation under the Workmen's Compensation Acts has been paid in respect of that disease.

(3) If the date of onset has to be determined as aforesaid in respect of pneumoconiosis or byssinosis suffered by a person to whom compensation has been awarded or paid in respect of the same disease or in respect of whose death compensation has been awarded or paid under the provisions of any scheme made under the provisions of the Workmen's Compensation Acts relating to compensation for silicosis, asbestosis, pneumoconiosis or byssinosis, the disease in respect of which the claim is made shall (subject to the provisions of regulation 9(2)(b)) be treated for the purposes of these regulations as not having developed on or after 5th July 1948.

(4) If, after the date of a claim for benefit in respect of a prescribed disease, the claimant receives a weekly payment of compensation in respect of that disease under the Workmen's Compensation Acts which he was not receiving at the date of such claim, or if the amount of any such weekly payment which he was receiving at that date is increased, then any decision on any [1 issue] arising in connection with that claim, if given before the date of, or in ignorance of the fact of, the receipt of such weekly payment or increased weekly payment, may be [1 revised or superseded] as if it had been given in ignorance of a material fact, and on such [1 revision or supercession] the [1 issue] may be decided as if the claimant had been in receipt of such weekly payment or increased weekly payment at the date of the claim, and the foregoing provisions of this regulation shall apply accordingly.

(5) For the purposes of this regulation, a person shall be deemed to be, or to have been, in receipt of a weekly payment of compensation if—

(a) he is or was in fact receiving such payment; or

(b) he is or was entitled thereto under an award or agreement made under the Workmen's Compensation Acts.

(6) This regulation shall apply to compensation under any contracting out scheme duly certified under the Workmen's Compensation Acts as it applies to compensation under those Acts.

AMENDMENTS

1. Social Security Act 1998 (Commencement No. 8, and Savings and Consequential and Transitional Provisions) Order 1999 (SI 1999/1958) Sch.8 para.3 (July 5, 1999).
2. Social Security (Industrial Injuries) (Prescribed Diseases) Amendment Regulations 2003 (SI 2003/270) reg.4 (March 17, 2003).

Re-employment of pneumoconiotics and special provisions for benefit (workmen's compensation cases)

10.76 **9.**—(1) Where a person—

(a) has been certified by a medical board under the provisions of any scheme made under the provisions of the Workmen's Compensation Acts to be suffering from silicosis or pneumoconiosis not accompanied in either case by tuberculosis and has been awarded or paid compensation under the provisions of any such scheme, and by reason of such certification has been suspended from employment in any industry or process or in any particular operation or work in any industry, and

(b) wishes to start work in employed earner's employment in any occupation involving work underground in any coal mine, or the working or handling above ground at any coal mine of any minerals extracted therefrom, or any operation incidental thereto, being an occupation in which he is allowed by certificate of the medical board under the provisions of the scheme to engage,

he shall, before starting any such work, submit himself under arrangements made or approved by the Secretary of State for medical examination by a [1 medical practitioner].

(2) Where a person submits himself for medical examination in accordance with the provisions of the foregoing paragraph, the provisions of the Act and the regulations made thereunder shall apply to him subject to the following modifications:—

[1 (a) A medical practitioner shall provide a report to the Secretary of State to enable him to determine at what degree the extent of disablement resulting from pneumoconiosis should be assessed in his case.]

(b) Where the extent of disablement has been determined in his case in accordance with the provisions of the foregoing sub-paragraph by [1 the Secretory of State or an appeal tribunal], and he starts any such work as is mentioned in the foregoing paragraph, the provisions of regulation 38(a) (periodical examinations) shall apply to him as if he were making a claim for benefit in respect of pneumoconiosis, and the provisions of regulation 8(3) (pneumoconiosis shall in certain cases be treated as not having developed on or after 5th July 1948) shall cease to apply to him as from the date of starting such work.

(c) If, after having started work as aforesaid, he makes a claim at any time for disablement benefit in respect of pneumoconiosis, the extent of disablement in his case shall be assessed as if, [1 to the extent decided by the Secretary of State or an appeal tribunal] given under sub-paragraph (a) of this paragraph, his disabilities resulting from pneumoconiosis were contracted before the date of onset and were not incurred as the result of the relevant loss of faculty.

(d) A person to whom a disablement pension is payable in respect of an assessment made in accordance with the provisions of the last foregoing sub-paragraph and who requires constant attendance shall, if the sum of that assessment and the assessment made in his case in accordance with the provisions of sub-paragraph (a) of this paragraph is not less than 100 per cent., have the like right to payments in respect of the need of such constant attendance as if the disablement pension were payable in respect of an assessment of 100 per cent.

(3) Where a person to whom sub-paragraph (a) of paragraph (1) applies has started any such work as is mentioned in sub-paragraph (b) thereof without having submitted himself for medical examination in accordance with the provisions of that paragraph, he may nevertheless, at any time whilst he is engaged in any such work, so submit himself for medical examination, and the provisions of the foregoing paragraph shall, if he continues thereafter to be engaged in any such work, apply to him as if he had started that work immediately after the medical examination.

(4) The Secretary of State, in making or approving any such arrangements for medical examination of any person as are mentioned in paragraph (1) shall, as far as possible, co-ordinate those arrangements with any arrangements for medical examination of that person made or approved under Part V of these regulations or under the Workmen's Compensation Acts.

AMENDMENT

1. Social Security Act 1988 (Commencement No. 8, and Savings and Consequential and Transitional Provisions Order 1999 (SI 1999/1958) Sch.8 para.4 (July 5, 1999).

PART IV

APPLICATION OF [SECTIONS 94 TO 107 OF THE SOCIAL SECURITY CONTRIBUTIONS AND BENEFITS ACT 1992 AND SECTIONS 8 TO 10 OF THE SOCIAL SECURITY ADMINISTRATION ACT 1992] AND OF REGULATIONS MADE THEREUNDER

Definition of "relevant disease"

10.—In this Part of these regulations, unless the context otherwise requires, the expression "relevant disease" means, in relation to any claim for benefit in respect of a prescribed disease, the prescribed disease in respect of which benefit is claimed, but does not include any previous or subsequent attack of that disease, suffered by the same person, which, under the provisions of Part III of these regulations, is or has been treated— 10.77

(a) as having developed on a date other than the date which, under the said provisions, is treated as the date of onset for the purposes of the claim under consideration;

(b) as a recrudescence of a disease for which compensation has been paid or awarded under the Workmen's Compensation Acts.

Application of [sections 94 to 107 of the Social Security Contributions and Benefits Act 1992 and sections 8 to 10 of the Social Security Administration Act 1992]

10.78 **11.**—The provisions of [sections 94 to 107 of the Social Security Contributions and Benefits Act 1992 and sections 8 to 10 of the Social Security Administration Act 1992] which relates to industrial injuries benefit and sickness benefit made by virtue of section 50A of the Act shall, in relation to prescribed diseases, be subject to the following provisions of this Part of these regulations, and, subject as aforesaid, to the additions and modifications set out in Schedule 2 hereto.

GENERAL NOTE

10.79 Section 50A of the Social Security Act 1975 has been replaced by s.102 of the Social Security Contributions and Benefits Act 1992.

Application of Claims and Payments Regulations and Benefit Regulations

10.80 **12.**—(1) Save in so far as they are expressly varied or excluded by, or are inconsistent with, the provisions of this Part of these regulations or of regulation 25 or 36, the Claims and Payments Regulations and the Benefit Regulations shall apply in relation to prescribed diseases as they apply in relation to accidents.

(2) Save as provided in this Part of these regulations or where the context otherwise requires, references in the aforesaid regulations to accidents shall be construed as references to prescribed diseases, references to the relevant accident shall be construed as references to the relevant disease, references to the date of the relevant accident shall be construed as references to the date of onset of the relevant disease, and in regulation 17 of the Benefit Regulations (increase of disablement pension in cases of special hardship), the reference to the effects of the relevant injury shall be construed as a reference to the effects of the relevant disease.

Benefit not payable in cases covered by the Industrial Injuries and Diseases (Old Cases) Act 1975

10.81 **13.**—Benefit shall not be payable by virtue of the provisions of these regulations in respect of the incapacity, disablement or death of any person as a result of any disease, if an award of benefit under the provisions of any Scheme made under the Industrial Injuries and Diseases (Old Cases) Act 1975 (not being an award which is subsequently [[1] revised or superseded so as to terminate entitlement]) has at any time been made in respect of any attack of the disease suffered by him, or in respect of his death.

AMENDMENT

1. Social Security Act 1998 (Commencement No.8 and Savings and Consequential and Transitional Provisions) Order 1999 (SI 1999/1958) Sch.8 para.5 (July 5, 1999).

Diseases contracted outside Great Britain

10.82 **14.**—For section 50(5) (accidents happening outside Great Britain) there shall be substituted the provision that, subject to the provisions of sections 129, 131 and 132, for the purpose of determining whether a prescribed disease is, or, under the provisions of Part II of these regulations is to be presumed to be, due to the nature of the person's employed earner's employment, that person shall be regarded as not being or as not having been in employed earner's employment during any period for which he is or was outside Great Britain, and accordingly benefit shall not be payable in respect of a prescribed disease which is due to the nature of employment in an occupation in which the person has only been engaged outside Great Britain.

General Note

Sections 50(5), 129, 131 and 132 of the Social Security Act 1975 have been replaced by ss.94(5), 117, 119 and 120 of the Social Security Contributions Act 1992. 10.83

[1 Modification of paragraph 11(1) of Schedule 7 to the Social Security Contributions and Benefits Act 1992

14A.—The provisions of paragraph 11(1) of Schedule 7 to the Social Security Contributions and Benefits Act 1992 shall be modified by adding after the words "(the day on which section 3 of the Social Security Act 1990 came into force)" the words 10.84

"and a person shall not be entitled to reduced earnings allowance—

(i) in relation to a disease prescribed on or after 10th October 1994 under section 108(2) above; or

(ii) in relation to a disease prescribed before 10th October 1994 whose prescription is extended on or after that date under section 108(2) above but only in so far as the prescription has been so extended".]

Amendment

1. Social Security (Industrial Injuries) (Prescribed Diseases) Amendment Regulations 1994 (SI 1994/2343) reg.3 (October 10, 1994).

Assessment of extent of disablement

15.—For the purposes of paragraph 1(b) of Schedule 8 (disabilities to be taken into account in assessing the extent of the claimant's disablement) and of regulation 11 of the Benefit Regulations (which further defines the principles of assessment of disablement), an injury or disease other than the relevant disease shall be treated as having been received or contracted before the relevant disease if it was received or contracted on or before the date of onset, and as having been received or contracted after the relevant disease if it was received or contracted after that date. 10.85

General Note

Sch.8 to the Social Security Act 1975 has been replaced by Sch.6 to the Social Security Contributions and Benefits Act 1992. 10.86

Aggregation of percentages of disablement

[1 **15A.**—(1) After the extent of an employed earner's disablement resulting from the relevant disease has been determined, the [2 Secretary of State] 10.87

shall add to the percentage of that disablement the assessed percentage of any present disablement of his resulting from—

(a) any accident after 4th July 1948 arising out of and in the course of his employment, being employed earner's employment, or

(b) any other relevant disease due to the nature of that employment and developed after 4th July 1948,

and in respect of which a disablement gratuity was not paid to him under the Act after a final assessment of disablement.

(2) In determining the extent of an employed earner's disablement for the purposes of section 57 of the Act there shall be added to the percentage of disablement resulting from any relevant accident the assessed percentage of any present disablement of his resulting from any disease or injury prescribed for the purposes of Chapter V of Part II of the Act, which was both due to the nature of the employment and developed after 4th July 1948, and in respect of which a disablement gratuity was not paid to him under the Act after a final assessment of his disablement.

(3) This regulation is subject to the provisions of regulation 15B(3).]

AMENDMENTS

1. Social Security (Industrial Injuries and Diseases) Miscellaneous Provisions Regulations 1986 (SI 1986/1561) reg.3(2) (October 1, 1986).

2. Social Security Act 1998 (Commencement No.8, and Savings and Consequential and Transitional Provisions) Order 1999 (SI 1999/1958) Sch.8, para.6 (July 5, 1999).

GENERAL NOTE

10.88 Section 57 of the SSA 1975 has been replaced by s.103 of the SSCBA 1992.

Rounding

10.89 [1 **15B.**—(1) Subject to the provisions of this regulation, where the assessment of disablement is a percentage between 20 and 100 which is not a multiple of 10, it shall be treated—

(a) if it is a multiple of 5, as being the next higher percentage which is a multiple of 10; and

(b) if it is not a multiple of 5 as being the nearest percentage which is a multiple of 10,

and where it is 14 per cent, or more but less than 20 per cent. it shall be treated as 20 per cent.

(2) In a case to which regulation 15A (aggregation of percentages of disablement) applies, paragraph (1) shall have effect in relation to the aggregate percentage and not in relation to any percentage forming part of the aggregate.

(3) [2 Where an assessment or a reassessment] states the degree of disablement due to occupational deafness as less than 20 per cent. that percentage shall be disregarded for the purposes of regulation 15A and this regulation.]

AMENDMENTS

1. Social Security (Industrial Injuries and Diseases) Miscellaneous Provisions Regulations 1986 (SI 1986/1561) reg.3(2) (October 1, 1986).

2. Social Security (Industrial Injuries) (Prescribed Diseases) Amendment Regulations 1990 (SI 1990/2269) reg.2(3) (December 13, 1990).

Regulation 16 omitted. **10.90**

[1 Special provisions as to determination of regular occupation in relation to persons claiming reduced earnings allowance

17.—Where a person who has been assessed as at least one per cent. disabled in respect of a prescribed disease establishes that he has abandoned any occupation as a result of the relevant disease at any time after having been employed in employed earner's employment in any occupation prescribed for that disease but before the first day in respect of which he was so assessed, then for the purpose of determining his right to, or the rate of, reduced earnings allowance under section 59A, any occupation he has so abandoned may be treated as his regular occupation for the purposes of that section.] **10.91**

AMENDMENT

1. Social Security (Industrial Injuries and Diseases) Miscellaneous Provisions Regulations 1986 (SI 1986/1561) (October 1, 1986).

GENERAL NOTE

This regulation simply permits the claimant's regular occupation (see SSCBA 1992 Sch.7 para.11 (formerly SSA 1975 s.59A), above, and note thereto) to include a job he may have been forced to give up because of the effects of the relevant prescribed disease. In other circumstances, an occupation abandoned by the claimant may be disregarded for the purposes of determining his regular occupation (*R(I) 5/52*). **10.92**

Exception from requirements as to notice

18.—Regulation 24 of the Claims and Payments Regulations (giving of notice of accidents in respect of which benefit may be payable) shall not apply in relation to prescribed diseases. **10.93**

Provisions as to medical examination

19.—Those provisions of section 89(1) and (2) which relate to the obligation of claimants to submit themselves to medical examination for the purpose of determining the effect of the relevant accident shall apply also to medical examinations for the purpose of determining whether a claimant or beneficiary is suffering or has suffered from a prescribed disease, and regulation 26 of the Claims and Payments Regulations shall be construed accordingly. **10.94**

GENERAL NOTE

Section 89(1) and (2) of the SSA 1975 have been replaced by s.9(1) and (2) of the SSAA 1992. **10.95**

PART V

SPECIAL PROVISIONS AS TO PNEUMOCONIOSIS, BYSSINOSIS, OCCUPATIONAL DEAFNESS AND CERTAIN OTHER DISEASES

Section A—Benefit

Special conditions for disablement benefit for pneumoconiosis, byssinosis and diffuse mesothelioma

10.96 **20.**—[1 (1) On a claim for disablement pension in respect of pneumoconiosis, [4 or] byssinosis [4 . . .], section 57(1) shall apply as if for "14 per cent." there was substituted "1 per cent.".

(1A) Where on a claim for disablement pension in respect of pneumoconiosis [4 or] byssinosis [4 . . .] the extent of the disablement is assessed at one per cent. or more, but less than 20 per cent., disablement pension shall be payable at the 20 per cent. rate if the resulting degree of disablement is greater than 10 per cent. and if it is not at one-tenth of the 100 per cent. rate, with any fraction of a penny being for this purpose treated as a penny.

(1B) Where immediately before 1st October 1986 a person is entitled to a disablement pension on account of pneumoconiosis [4 or] byssinosis [4 . . .] and in determining the extent of his disablement other disabilities were taken into account in accordance with regulation 11 of the Social Security (General Benefit) Regulations 1982, disablement pension shall continue to be payable on or after 1st October 1986 at the weekly rate applicable to the degree of disablement determined on the last assessment made before 14th October 1986 until—

(a) [3 on a reassessment of the extent of disablement or in consequence of an application for revision or supersession the degree of disablement is assessed either as less than 1 per cent. or as equal to or more than that determined on that last assessment, or

(b) the other disability ceases to exist.]

(2) Section 78(4)(b), in so far as it provides that disablement benefit shall not be payable in respect of byssinosis unless the claimant is found to be suffering from loss of faculty which is likely to be permanent, shall not apply.

(3) Notwithstanding paragraph 4(a) of Schedule 8 (period to be taken into account by an assessment of the extent of the claimant's disablement), the period to be taken into account by an assessment of the extent of the claimant's disablement in respect of byssinosis, if not limited by reference to the claimant's life, shall not be less than one year.

[2 (4) On a claim for disablement pension in respect of diffuse mesothelioma—

(a) section 103(6) of the Social Security Contributions and Benefits Act 1992 shall apply as if for the words "after the expiry of the period of 90 days (disregarding Sundays) beginning with the day of the relevant accident" there were substituted the words, "the day on which he first suffers from a loss of faculty due to diffuse mesothelioma";

(b) paragraph 6(1) of Schedule 6 to the Social Security Contributions and Benefits Act 1992 shall apply as if the words "beginning not earlier than the end of the period of 90 days referred to in section 103(6) above and in paragraph 9(3) of that Schedule and" were omitted.]

AMENDMENTS

1. Social Security (Industrial Injuries and Diseases) Miscellaneous Provisions Regulations 1986 (SI 1986/1561) reg.3(3) (October 1, 1986).
2. Social Security (Industrial Injuries) (Miscellaneous Amendments) Regulations 1997 (SI 1997/810) reg.5 (April 9, 1997).
3. Social Security Act 1998 (Commencement No.8, and Savings and Consequential and Transitional Provisions) Order 1999 (SI 1999/1958) Sch.8 para.7 (July 5, 1999).
4. Social Security (Industrial Injuries) (Prescribed Diseases) Amendment Regulations 2002 (SI 2002/1717) reg.2(2) (July 29, 2002).

GENERAL NOTE

Sections 57(1) and 78(4)(b) of the SSA 1975 have been replaced by ss.103(1) and 110(4) of the SSCBA 1992. Sch.8 para.4(a) has been replaced by Sch.6 para.6(2)(a). **10.97**

Disablement benefit is still payable in respect of pneumoconiosis or byssinosis even if the extent of disablement is less than 1 per cent. The amount of disablement benefit payable is calculated under para.(1A) or (1B). An assessment of disablement in respect of byssinosis must be for at least one year. Para.(4) removes the usual 90-day waiting period for disablement benefit in cases where the claim is in respect of diffuse mesothelioma but makes it clear that there can be no entitlement until the disease results in a loss of faculty. Repeated assessments are seldom to be expected once the condition produces symptoms and so assessments should take into account anticipated deterioration in the claimant's condition. Thirty per cent of sufferers die within six months of the onset of symptoms. With effect from July 29, 2002, impaired function of the pleura, pericardium or peritoneum function caused by diffuse mesothelioma constitutes a loss of faculty for which the resultant degree of disablement is to be taken as 100 per cent (reg.20A, below).

[1 Diffuse mesothelioma—prescribed loss of faculty

20A.—(1) For the purposes of paragraph 1 of Schedule 6 to the Social Security Contributions and Benefits Act 1992 (which provides for the assessment of the extent of disablement for the purposes of industrial injuries disablement benefit), the loss of faculty set out in paragraph (2) below is prescribed under sub-paragraph (d) of that paragraph 1 (loss of faculty from which the resulting disabilities are to be taken as amounting to 100 per cent. disablement). **10.98**

(2) The loss of faculty referred to in paragraph (1) above is impaired function of the pleura, pericardium or peritoneum function caused by diffuse mesothelioma.]

AMENDMENT

1. This reg. was inserted by Social Security (Industrial Injuries) (Prescribed Diseases) Amendment Regulations 2002 (SI 2002/1717) reg.2(3) (July 29, 2002).

GENERAL NOTE

The effect of this new regulation is that impaired function of the pleura, pericardium or peritoneum caused by diffuse mesothelioma is a loss of faculty from which **10.99** the resulting disabilities are to be taken as amounting to 100 per cent disablement for purposes of assessment of disablement under SSCBA 1992 Sch.6.

[1Primary carcinoma of the lung and angiosarcoma of the liver–special conditions and prescribed loss of faculty

10.100 **20B.**—(1) This regulation applies to a claim for disablement pension made in respect of the diseases prescribed in paragraphs C4, C22(b), C24(a), D8, D8A, D10 and D11 of Part 1 of Schedule 1.

(2) On a claim to which this regulation applies—

(a) section 103(6) of the Social Security Contributions and Benefits Act 1992 (entitlement after expiry of 90 days) shall apply as if for the words "after the expiry of the period of 90 days (disregarding Sundays) beginning with the day of the relevant accident" there were substituted the words "the day on which that person first suffers from a loss of faculty due to primary carcinoma of the lung or bronchus or angiosarcoma of the liver"; and

(b) paragraph 6(1) of Schedule 6 to the Social Security Contributions and Benefits Act 1992 (period to be taken into account by an assessment) shall apply as if the words "beginning not earlier than the end of the period of 90 days referred to in section 103(6) above and in paragraph 9(3) of that Schedule and" were omitted.

(3) On a claim to which this regulation applies, the loss of faculty prescribed for the purposes of sub-paragraph (d) of paragraph 1 of Schedule 6 to the Social Security Contributions and Benefits Act 1992 (assessment of the extent of disablement) is lung impairment caused by primary carcinoma of the lung or bronchus, or impairment caused by angiosarcoma of the liver.]

AMENDMENT

1. This regulation was inserted by Social Security (Industrial Injuries) (Prescribed Diseases) Amendment Regulations 2015 (SI 2015/87) reg.3 (March 16, 2015).

GENERAL NOTE

10.101 The effect of this regulation, on a claim for disablement pension in respect of the diseases set out in para.(1), is twofold.

Firstly, entitlement in respect of such a claim may arise from the first day a person suffers from a loss of faculty due to one of those diseases.

Secondly lung impairment caused by primary carcinoma of the lung or bronchus, or impairment caused by angiosarcoma of the liver, rank as loss of faculty from which the resulting disabilities are to be taken as amounting to 100 per cent disablement.

Pneumoconiosis—effects of tuberculosis

10.102 **21.**—Where any person is found to be suffering from pneumoconiosis accompanied by tuberculosis, the effects of the tuberculosis shall be treated for the purposes of Chapter V of Part II of the Act and of these regulations as if they were effects of the pneumoconiosis.

GENERAL NOTE

10.103 Chapter V of Part II of the SSA 1975 has been replaced by ss.108-110 of the SSCBA 1992.

Pneumoconiosis—effects of [3chronic obstructive pulmonary disease]

22.—(1) [1 Except] in the circumstances specified in paragraph (1A),] where any person is disabled by pneumoconiosis or pneumoconiosis accompanied by tuberculosis to an extent which would, if his physical condition were otherwise normal, be assessed at not less than 50 per cent., the effects of [3any chronic obstructive pulmonary disease] from which that person is found to be suffering shall be treated for the purposes of Chapter V of Part II of the Act and of these regulations as if they were effects of the pneumoconiosis. **10.104**

[1 (1A) The circumstances referred to in paragraph (1) are that the person is entitled to industrial injuries disablement benefit on account of the disease set out in paragraph D12 of Part I of Schedule 1.]

(2) Where, on a claim for death benefit, the question arises whether the extent of a person's disablement resulting from pneumoconiosis or from pneumoconiosis accompanied by tuberculosis would, if his physical condition were otherwise normal, have been assessed at not less than 50 per cent.—

(a) if there has been no assessment of disablement resulting from pneumoconiosis or from pneumoconiosis accompanied by tuberculosis made during the person's life, or if there is no such assessment current at the time of death, [2 that issue shall be determined by the Secretary of State];

(b) if there is an assessment of disablement resulting from pneumoconiosis or from pneumoconiosis accompanied by tuberculosis current at the time of the person's death, that [2 issue] shall be treated as having been determined by the decision of the [2 Secretary of State or, as the case may be, appeal tribunal] as the case may be, which made such assessment.

AMENDMENTS

1. Social Security (Industrial Injuries) (Prescribed Diseases) Amendment (No. 2) Regulations 1993 (SI 1993/1985) reg.5 (September 13, 1993).

2. Social Security Act 1998 (Commencement No. 8, and Savings and Consequential and Transitional Provisions) Order 1999 (SI 1999/1958) Sch.8 para.8 (July 5, 1999).

3. Social Security (Industrial Injuries) (Prescribed Diseases) Amendment Regulations 2015 (SI 2015/87) reg.5 (March 16, 2015).

GENERAL NOTE

Chapter V of Part II of the SSA 1975 has been replaced by ss.108-110 of the SSCBA 1992. **10.105**

Reduced earnings allowance—special provision for pneumoconiosis cases

[1 **23.**—Where a beneficiary in receipt of a disablement pension in respect of pneumoconiosis receives advice from [2 the Secretary of State] that in consequence of the disease he should not follow his regular occupation unless he complies with certain special restrictions as to the place, duration or circumstances of his work, or otherwise, then for the purpose of determining whether he fulfils the conditions laid down in [Schedule 7 of the 1992 Act] (reduced earnings allowance) and for that purpose only— **10.106**

(a) the beneficiary shall be deemed, unless the contrary is proved by evidence other than the aforesaid advice—
   (i) to be incapable of following his regular occupation and likely to remain permanently so incapable, and
   (ii) to be incapable of following employment of an equivalent standard which is suitable in his case;

(b) where the beneficiary has ceased to follow any occupation to which the aforesaid special restrictions were applicable, the fact that he had followed such an occupation in the period between the date of onset of the disease and the date of the current assessment of his disablement, or for a reasonable period of trial thereafter, shall be disregarded.]

AMENDMENTS

1. Social Security (Industrial Injuries and Diseases) Miscellaneous Provisions Regulations 1986 (SI 1986/1561) reg.6 (October 1, 1986).

2. Social Security Act 1998 (Commencement No.8, and Savings and Consequential and Transitional Provisions) Order 1999 (SI 1999/1958) Sch.8 para.9 (July 5, 1999).

[1 Special requirement for pneumoconiosis claimants in unscheduled occupation cases

10.107 **24.**—(1) A claim for disablement benefit in respect of pneumoconiosis by a person in relation to whom the disease is prescribed by virtue of regulation 2(b)(ii) shall be referred by the Secretary of State to a medical practitioner for a report, unless the Secretary of State is satisfied on reasonable grounds that the claimant is not suffering or has not suffered from pneumoconiosis, in which case he may decide the claim without such a report.

(2) The provisions of paragraph (1) of this regulation shall apply to an appeal tribunal and a Commissioner as they apply to the Secretary of State.]

AMENDMENT

1. Social Security Act 1998 (Commencement No.8, and Savings and Consequential and Transitional Provisions) Order 1999 (SI 1999/1958) Sch.8 para.10 (July 5, 1999).

Time for claiming benefit in respect of occupational deafness

10.108 **25.**—(1) Regulation 14 of the Claims and Payments Regulations (time for claiming benefit) shall not apply in relation to occupational deafness except in relation to a claim for sickness benefit payable by virtue of section [102].

(2) Subject to regulation 27(1)(c), disablement benefit, or sickness benefit payable by virtue of section [102] of the Act, shall not be paid in pursuance of a claim in respect of occupational deafness which is made later than 5 years after the latest date, before the date of the claim, on which the claimant worked [1 in employed earner's employment] in an occupation prescribed in relation to occupational deafness [3 . . .]

AMENDMENTS

1. Social Security (Industrial Injuries) (Prescribed Diseases) Amendment Regulations 2000 (SI 2000/1588) reg.3 (July 10, 2000).

2. Social Security Act 1998 (Commencement No.8, and Savings and Consequential and Transitional Provisions) Order 1999 (SI 1999/1958) Sch.8 para.11 (July 5, 1999).

3. Social Security (Industrial Injuries) (Prescribed Diseases) Amendment Regulations 2005 (SI 2005/324) reg.2(2) (March 14, 2005).

General Note

Note that para.4(3) of Sch.6 of the SSA 1990 (effective from July 13, 1990) provides that reg.25, and any former regulations which it directly or indirectly re-enacts with or without amendment, shall be taken to be, and always to have been, validly made. *R(I) 1/92* applied in *CI/276/1988* and *CSI/22/91*, and *CSI/84/89* and *R(I) 1/94* (affirmed by the Court of Appeal in *Chatterton v Chief Adjudication Officer*, July 8, 1993) (reported as *R(I) 1/94*), all hold that the validation effected by para.4(3) of Sch.6 of the SSA 1990 (which entered into force on July 13, 1990) operates retrospectively, thus transforming initially invalid decisions (the Court of Appeal had held reg.25 ultra vires in *McKiernon v Secretary of State for Social Security*) into valid determinations. Furthermore, in *Chief Adjudication Officer v McKiernon*, also decided on July 8, 1993, the Court of Appeal upheld the CAO's appeal against Commisioner Goodman's decision in *R(I) 2/94*. The entry into force of para.4(3), notwithstanding its retrospective operation, was a change of circumstances enabling the AO to review an SSAT's decision that Mr McKiernon had good cause for his late claim so that his claim was timeous. **10.109**

The regulation prevents disablement benefit or sickness benefit (payable only because of industrial disease) being paid in pursuance of a claim in respect of occupational deafness which is made later than five years after the latest date on which the claimant *worked in* a prescribed occupation, unless further conditions are met including a condition of *employment in* the occupation for a period or aggregate of periods amounting to not less than 10 years. The exemption afforded by those further conditions was revoked with effect from March 14, 2005 by reg.2 of the Social Security (Industrial Injuries) (Prescribed Diseases) Amendment Regulations 2005 (SI 2005/324). *CI/16/91* follows *R(I) 2/79* (see above, notes to reg.2) in holding that in dealing with both time periods one looks to "the work actually done rather than the contractual obligation to do it, so that, for example, time off work through ill-health was not time spent working in the occupation for the purposes of the relevant legislation" (*CI/16/91*, para.5). So, in *CI/16/91*, although the claimant's employment had been terminated on May 11, 1985, he had been on the sick from April 25, 1984. His claim was made in June 1989. Because the focus for the five-year period had to be on when he last *worked*, the Commissioner held that he ceased work in the prescribed occupation on April 25, 1984, and his claim was time-barred by reg.25.

In *CI/286/95*, Commissioner Howell held that "worked in an occupation" in lines four and five of reg.25(2) was *not* to be construed as if it read "worked *in employment earner's employment* in an occupation". He saw no absurdity in a claimant

> "being able to claim more than 5 years after ceasing to be an employed earner but within 5 years of stopping his actual work [albeit in self-employment] in a listed occupation which gives rise to exposure to noise. Before he can get the benefit, the question whether his disease is due to the nature of his employment as an employee still has to be determined."

He therefore saw nothing inconsistent with the purpose of the legislation or rendering reg.25(2) ultra vires, in reading it in the way he and the SSAT had done (*ibid.*) Commissioner Howell's approach was followed by Commissioner Walker in *CSI/89/96*. The amendments numbered 2 to para.(2), requiring work in employed earner's employment, reverse the effect of *CI/286/95* and *CSI/89/96*, noted immediately above. The amendment is the subject of a transitional provision in reg.7(1) of the amending instrument such that it "shall not apply in relation to a claim made within 3 months after the commencement date and the amendments made by regulations 2(3), 5 and 6 shall not apply where the date of onset of the relevant disease is prior to the commencement date and the claim is made within 3 months after that date".

Claims in respect of occupational deafness

10.110 **26.**—Where it appears that a person who has made a claim for sickness benefit by virtue of section [102] of the Act in respect of occupational deafness—

(a) may be entitled to disablement benefit, and

(b) has not previously made a claim for disablement benefit in respect of occupational deafness or such a previous claim has been disallowed,

such a claim for sickness benefit may also be treated as a claim for disablement benefit.

General Note

10.111 A claim for sickness benefit on the ground of occupational deafness may be treated as a claim for disablement benefit if the claimant has not already made an unsuccessful claim. This paragraph would seem to apply even if the claimant would have satisfied the contribution conditions.

Further claims in respect of occupational deafness

10.112 **27.**—(1) In the event of disallowance of a claim for disablement benefit or sickness benefit made by virtue of section [102] of the Act in respect of occupational deafness because the claimant has failed to satisfy the minimum hearing loss requirement prescribed in column 1 of paragraph A10 of Part I of Schedule 1 hereto, disablement benefit or sickness benefit made by virtue of section [102] of the Act shall not be paid in pursuance of a further claim in respect of occupational deafness made by or on behalf of that claimant unless—

(a) it is a claim made after the expiration of three years from the date of a claim which was disallowed because the claimant was not suffering from occupational deafness; or

(b) it is a claim made after the expiration of three years from the date of a reassessment by [1 the Secretary of State or an appeal tribunal] of the extent of the claimant's disablement at less than 20 per cent; or

(c) if the claimant would otherwise be precluded by regulation 25(2) from making a further claim after the expiration of three years from the date of the disallowed claim or from the date of a reassessment by the Secretary of State or an appeal tribunal of the extent of his disablement at less than 20 per cent., as the case may be, it is the first claim made since that date and within five years from the latest date, before the date of the claim, on which he worked [2 in employed earner's employment] in any occupation specified in column 2 of paragraph A10 of Part I of Schedule I hereto.

[1 (2) A claim to be paid benefit by virtue of paragraph (1)(c) may be disallowed by the Secretary of State, an appeal tribunal or a Commissioner ("the determining authority") without reference to a medical practitioner where the determining authority is satisfied by medical evidence that the claimant is not suffering from occupational deafness.]

AMENDMENTS

1. Social Security Act 1998 (Commencement No.8, and Savings and Consequential and Transitional Provisions) Order 1999 (SI 1999/1958) Sch.8 para.12 (July 5, 1999).
2. Social Security (Industrial Injuries) (Prescribed Diseases) Amendment Regulations 2000 (SI 2000/1588) reg.4 (July 10, 2000).

GENERAL NOTE

The amendment, numbered 2 in the list above, requiring work in employed earner's employment, reverses the effect of *CI 286/95* and *CSI 89/96*, noted in the annotation to reg.25, above. The amendment is the subject of a transitional provision in regulation 7(1) of the amending instrument, reproduced later in this volume. 10.113

Availability of disablement benefit in respect of occupational deafness

28.—Where a person is awarded disablement benefit in respect of occupational deafness, section 57(4) (period for which disablement benefit is not available) shall not apply. 10.114

GENERAL NOTE

In occupational deafness cases, the date of onset of the disease is deemed to be no earlier than the date of claim (see reg.6(2)(c)) and so the usual 90-day qualifying period does not apply. Section 57(4) of the SSA 1975 has been replaced by s.103(6) of the SSCBA 1992. 10.115

Period to be covered by assessment of disablement in respect of occupational deafness

[1**29.**—Paragraph 6(1) and (2) of Schedule 6 to the Social Security Contributions and Benefits Act 1992 shall be modified so that in respect of occupational deafness, the period to be taken into account by an assessment of the extent of a claimant's disablement shall be the remainder of the claimant's life.] 10.116

AMENDMENT

1. Social Security (Industrial Injuries) (Prescribed Diseases) Amendment (No.2) Regulations 2003 (SI 2003/2190) reg.2(2) (September 22, 2003).

Supersession of a decision in respect of occupational deafness

30.—[1 . . .]. 10.117

REVOCATION

1. Social Security (Industrial Injuries) (Prescribed Diseases) Amendment (No.2) Regulations 2003 (SI 2003/2190) reg.2(3) (September 22, 2003).

Requirement for leave of appeal tribunal

31.—[1 . . .]. 10.118

REVOCATION

1. Social Security (Industrial Injuries) (Prescribed Diseases) Amendment (No.2) Regulations 2003 (SI 2003/2190) reg.2(3) (September 22, 2003).

No appeal against a decision of disablement in respect of occupational deafness

10.119 **32.**—[[1] . . .].

REVOCATION

1. Social Security (Industrial Injuries) (Prescribed Diseases) Amendment (No.2) Regulations 2003 (SI 2003/2190) reg.2(3) (September 22, 2003).

Cases in which reassessment of disablement in respect of occupational deafness is final

10.120 **33.**—[[1] . . .].

REVOCATION

1. Social Security (Industrial Injuries) (Prescribed Diseases) Amendment (No.2) Regulations 2003 (SI 2003/2190) reg.2(3) (September 22, 2003).

Assessment of extent of disablement and rate of disablement benefit payable in respect of occupational deafness

10.121 **34.**—(1) Subject to the provisions of Schedule [6] and regulations made thereunder and the following provisions of this regulation, the first assessment of the extent of disablement in respect of occupational deafness made in pursuance of a claim made before 3rd September 1979 by a person to whom disablement benefit in respect of occupational deafness is payable for a period before 3rd September 1979 [[1] shall be the percentage calculated by—

(a) determining the average total hearing loss due to all causes for each ear at 1, 2 and 3 kHz frequencies; and then by
(b) determining the percentage degree of disablement for each ear in accordance with Part I of Schedule 3; and then by
(c) determining the average percentage degree of binaural disablement in accordance with the formula set out in Part III of Schedule 3.]

(2) Except in any case to which paragraph (1) applies and subject to the provisions of Schedule [6] and regulations made thereunder and the following provisions of this regulation, the extent of disablement in respect of occupational deafness [[1] shall be the percentage calculated by—

(a) determining the average total hearing loss due to all causes for each ear at 1, 2 and 3 kHz frequencies; and then by
(b) determining the percentage degree of disablement for each ear in accordance with Part II of Schedule 3; and then by
(c) determining the average percentage degree of binaural disablement in accordance with the formula set out in Part III of Schedule 3.]

(3) In [[1] . . .] Schedule 3 hereto "better ear" means that ear in which the claimant's hearing loss due to all causes is the less and "worse ear" means that ear in which the claimant's hearing loss due to all causes is the more.

[[1] (3A) For the purposes of determining the percentage degree of disablement in Parts I and II of Schedule 3 to these Regulations, any fraction of an average hearing loss shall, where the average hearing loss is over 50 dB, be rounded down to the next whole figure.]

(4) The extent of disablement in respect of occupational deafness may be subject to such increase or reduction of the degree of disablement as may

be reasonable in the circumstances of the case where, having regard to the provisions of Schedule 8 and to regulations made thereunder, that degree of disablement does not provide a reasonable assessment of the extent of disability resulting from the relevant loss of faculty.

[[2] (5) Where on re-assessment of the extent of disability in respect of occupational deafness the average sensorineural hearing loss over 1, 2 and 3 kHz frequencies is not 50 dB or more in each ear, or where there is such a loss but the loss in one or each ear is not 50 dB or more due to occupational noise, the extent of disablement shall be assessed at less than 20 per cent.]

(6) Where the extent of disablement is reassessed at less than 20 per cent. disablement benefit [[3] or reduced earnings allowance] shall not be payable.

(7) In the case of a person to whom disablement benefit by reason of occupational deafness was payable in respect of a period before 3rd September 1979—

(a) if no assessment of the extent of his disability has been made, [[4] revised or superseded] on or after that date, the rate of any disablement benefit payable to him shall be the rate payable for the degree of disablement assessed in accordance with paragraph (1), but

(b) if such an assessment has been made, [[4] revised or superseded] in respect of a period commencing on or after that date and before 3rd October 1983, the rate of any disablement benefit payable to him shall be either—

(i) the rate which would be payable if an assessment were made in accordance with paragraph (2), or

(ii) the rate which was payable immediately before the first occasion on which such [[4] revision or supercession] took place,

whichever is the more favourable to him.

(8) Where in the case of a person to whom disablement benefit by reason of occupational deafness was payable in respect of a period before 3rd September 1979 the extent of his disability is reassessed and the period taken into account on reassessment begins on or after 3rd October 1983 and—

(a) immediately before that date, by virtue of paragraph (7) the rate at which disablement benefit was payable to him was higher than the rate which would otherwise have been payable, or,

(b) the reassessment is the first reassessment for a period commencing after 3rd September 1979,

the rate of disablement benefit payable to him shall be whichever of the rates specified in paragraph (9) is applicable.

(9) The rate of disablement benefit payable in the case of a person to whom paragraph (8) applies shall be—

(a) if the current rate appropriate to the extent of his disability as reassessed is the same as or more than the rate at which disablement benefit was payable immediately before the beginning of the period taken into account on reassessment, the current rate, or

(b) if the current rate is less than the rate at which disablement benefit was payable immediately before the beginning of the period taken into account on reassessment, the lower of the following rates—

(i) the rate at which benefit would have been payable if the reassessment of the extent of his disability had been made in accordance with paragraph (1), or

(ii) the rate at which benefit was payable immediately before the beginning of the period taken into account on reassessment.

AMENDMENTS

1. Social Security (Industrial Injuries) (Prescribed Diseases) Amendment Regulations 1989 (SI 1989/1207) reg.4 (October 16, 1989).
2. Social Security (Industrial Injuries and Adjudication) Miscellaneous Amendment Regulations 1986 (SI 1986/1374) reg.3 (September 1, 1986).
3. Social Security (Industrial Injuries and Diseases) Miscellaneous Provisions 1986 (SI 1986/1561) reg.6 (October 1, 1986).
4. Social Security Act 1998 (Commencement No.8, and Savings and Consequential and Transitional Provisions) Order 1999 (SI 1999/1958) Sch.8 para.16 (July 5, 1999).

GENERAL NOTE

10.122 This regulation and Sch.3 govern the assessment of disablement in occupational deafness cases. Note, however, that paras (1) and (2) are expressed to be subject to Sch.6 to the Social Security Contributions and Benefits Act 1992 and regulations made thereunder, including reg.11 of the Social Security (General Benefit) Regulations 1982.

Paragraph (1) of this regulation and Pt 1 of Sch.3 only apply to the first assessment of disablement in respect of claims made before September 3, 1979. Therefore, virtually all assessments are now made under para.(2) of this regulation and Pt 2 of Sch.3 which is less generous. The percentage degree of disablement for each ear is calculated separately and the formula in Pt 3 of Sch.3 is then applied to give an overall percentage of disablement. However, note that para.(4) of this regulation enables an adjudicating medical authority to depart from the Schedule if the result of applying the Schedule is to give an unreasonable assessment. A tribunal should first assess according to the Schedule and then give a reason for departing from that assessment (*R(I) 1/89*). Para.(5) applies only on a reassessment.

Paras (7)–(9) are transitional and apply to a person who was in receipt of disablement benefit before September 3, 1979. If there has been no assessment since that date, entitlement to disablement benefit is calculated under the more favourable provisions of para.(1). If there was an assessment between that date and October 3,1983, disablement benefit is payable either at the rate which would be payable on an assessment calculated under para.(2) or at the rate payable immediately before the review or variation took place, whichever is the more favourable. In view of inflation, the latter option is unlikely to be more favourable. If there has been an assessment on or after October 3, 1983, it will be usual for the claimant to receive the rate appropriate to an assessment under para.(2). However, if that rate is lower than the rate payable immediately before the beginning of the period taken into account on the reassessment, the lower of the two rates mentioned in para.(9)(b) is payable instead. The greater the lapse of time since the review or variation, the less favourable will be the latter option.

The 1989 amendments removed the requirement that hearing loss should be measured by pure tone audiometry as opposed to evoked response audiometry or any other test. In *R(I) 2/98*, it was held that those amendments (in particular, the introduction of para.(3A)) are procedural and so operate retrospectively in respect of periods before October 16, 1989.

Commencement date of period of assessment in respect of occupational deafness

10.123 **35.**—Notwithstanding Schedule [[1] . . .] [8], the period to be taken into account by an assessment of the extent of disablement in respect of occupational deafness shall not commence before 3rd February 1975.

AMENDMENT

1. Social Security Act 1998 (Commencement No.8, and Savings and Consequential and Transitional Provisions) Order 1999 (SI 1999/1958) Sch.8 para.17 (July 5, 1999).

GENERAL NOTE

Note that Sch.8 of the SSA 1975 has been replaced by Sch.6 of the SSCA 1992. 10.124

Time for claiming benefit in respect of occupational asthma

36.—(1) Subject to paragraphs (2) and (3), disablement benefit and sickness benefit payable by virtue of section 50A shall not be paid in pursuance of a claim in respect of occupational asthma which is made later than 10 years after the latest date, before the date of the claim, on which the claimant or, as the case may be, the person in respect of whom the claim is made worked [1 in employed earner's employment] in an occupation prescribed in relation to occupational asthma. 10.125

(2) Paragraph (1) shall not apply to any claim made before 29th March 1983 by or in respect of a person who ceased on or after 29th March 1972 to [1 work in employed earner's] employment in an occupation prescribed in relation to occupational asthma.

(3) Paragraph (1) shall not apply to any claim made by or in respect of a person who has at any time been found to be suffering from asthma as a result of an industrial accident and by virtue of that finding has been awarded disablement benefit either for life or for a period which includes the date on which the aforesaid claim is made.

(4) Subject to paragraphs (5) and (6), industrial death benefit shall not be paid in pursuance of a claim in respect of occupational asthma where the person in respect of whose death the benefit is being claimed died more than 10 years after the latest day on which he worked [1 in employed earner's employment] in an occupation prescribed in relation to occupational asthma.

(5) Paragraph (4) shall not apply to any claim made in respect of the death of a person who died before 29th March 1983 and who on or after 29th March 1972 had not worked [1 in employed earner's employment] in an occupation in relation to occupational asthma.

(6) Paragraph (4) shall not apply to any claim made in respect of the death of a person who had at any time been found to be suffering either from asthma as a result of an industrial accident or from occupational asthma and by virtue of that finding had been awarded disablement benefit either for life or for a period which included the date of his death.

(7) Regulation 14 of the Claims and Payments Regulations (time for claiming benefit) shall not apply to a claim in respect of occupational asthma made before 29th March 1983.

AMENDMENT

1. Social Security (Industrial Injuries) (Prescribed Diseases) Amendment Regulations 2000 (SI 2000/1588) reg.5 (July 10, 2000).

GENERAL NOTE

10.126 Note that s.50A of the SSA 1975 has been replaced by s.102 of the SSCA 1992.

It was clear from *McKiernon v Secretary of State for Social Services* (*The Times*, November 1, 1989), that reg.36 was originally ultra vires. As a result, s.77(2) of the Social Security Act 1975 (now s.109(2) of the Social Security Contributions and Benefits Act 1992) was amended by para.4(2) of Sch.6 to the Social Security Act 1990. Para.4(3) of Sch.6 to the 1990 Act provided that reg.36 should be taken always to have been validly made. See the note to reg.25.

In *CSI/89/96* Commissioner Walker followed the approach of Commissioner Howell in *CI/286/95* (see annotations to reg.25, above) in holding that "worked in an occupation" in para.(1) is not limited to employed earner's employment but can embrace self-employment so that "so long as within 10 years of the date of claim the claimant has been exposed to a sensitizing agent by his self-employment his claim may be sound in law" (para.7). The amendments, requiring work in employed earner's employment in a prescribed occupation, reverse the effect of *CI/286/95* and *CSI/89/96*. The amendment is the subject of a transitional provision in reg.7(1) of the amending instrument reproduced later in this volume.

See also *NP v SSWP (II)* [2022] UKUT 279 (AAC), discussed further in relation to Sch.1, PD D7, in which Judge Wikeley dismissed an appeal from a tribunal which had found that the claimant's workplace exposure to various agents had exacerbated his pre-existing constitutional asthma rather than triggered occupational asthma. The Judge further ruled that even if coal dust was "any other sensitising agent" within the terms of D7(x) the claim would in any event have failed as it was time barred under reg.36: "The Appellant was employed by the National Coal Board between 1964 and 1977. His claim for industrial disablement benefit was not made until January 2017. It follows that, even if coal dust was indeed 'any other sensitising agent', and so working underground at a colliery was a prescribed occupation for the purposes of PD D7, the claim on that basis was necessarily way out of time and in effect statute-barred" (para.43).

Initial examinations

10.127 **37.**—[1 . . .].

REVOCATION

1. Social Security (Industrial Injuries) (Prescribed Diseases) Amendment Regulations 1994 (SI 1994/2343) reg.5 (October 10, 1994).

Periodical examinations

10.128 **38.**—[1 . . .]

REVOCATION

1. Social Security (Industrial Injuries) (Prescribed Diseases) Amendment Regulations 1994 (SI 1994/2343) reg.5 (October 10, 1994).

Suspension from employment

10.129 **39.**—A certificate of suspension issued under the provisions of either regulation 43 or regulation 44 of the National Insurance (Industrial Injuries) (Prescribed Diseases) Regulations 1959 (regulations revoked with effect from 27th November 1974 by regulation 7(1) of the National Insurance (Industrial Injuries) (Prescribed Diseases) Amendment (No. 2) Regulations 1974) and in force immediately before 27th November 1974 shall continue in force subject to and in accordance with the provisions of regulation 40 of these regulations.

Conditions of suspension

40.—(1) A certificate of suspension issued under the provisions of either regulation 43 or regulation 44 of the National Insurance (Industrial Injuries) (Prescribed Diseases) Regulations 1959, and remaining in force by virtue of the last preceding regulation, shall suspend the person to whom it relates from further employment in any occupation in relation to which pneumoconiosis is prescribed, with such exceptions and subject to such conditions (if any) as may be specified in the certificate. 10.130

(2) [1 The Secretary of State] may at any time revoke or vary a certificate of suspension on the application of the person to whom it relates, but unless so revoked or varied such certificate shall remain in force throughout the life of such person.

(3) No person who has been suspended from employment may engage or continue in employment, and no employer may employ or continue to employ any such person, in any occupation in relation to which pneumoconiosis is prescribed, except in accordance with the terms of the certificate of suspension in his case.

AMENDMENT

1. Social Security Act 1998 (Commencement No.8, and Savings and Consequential and Transitional Provisions) Order 1999 (SI 1999/1958) Sch.8 para.18 (July 5, 1999).

Duties of employers

41.—[1 . . .]. 10.131

REVOCATION

1. Social Security (Industrial Injuries) (Prescribed Diseases) Amendment Regulations 1994 (SI 1994/2343) reg.5 (October 10, 1994).

Fees for initial and periodical examination

42.—[1 . . .]. 10.132

REVOCATION

1. Social Security (Industrial Injuries) (Prescribed Diseases) Amendment Regulations 1994 (SI 1994/2343) reg.5 (October 10, 1994).

PART VI

TRANSITIONAL PROVISIONS AND REVOCATION

Transitional provisions regarding relevant dates

43.—(1) Subject to paragraph (2) the "relevant date", in relation to each disease set out in the first column of Schedule 4 hereto, is the date set against the disease in the second column of that Schedule. 10.133

(2) Where a disease set out in the first column of Schedule 4 hereto was prescribed in relation to any person by regulations which came into operation on a date earlier than the date set against that disease in the second column of that Sch., the "relevant date" in relation to such disease is such earlier date on which the disease was prescribed in relation to the person in question.

(3) It shall be a condition of a person's right to benefit in respect of any disease set out in Schedule 4 that he was—

(a) incapable of work, or

(b) suffering from a loss of faculty,

as a result of that disease on or after the relevant date.

(4) The "relevant date" in relation to byssinosis—

(a) in the case of a person employed in an occupation involving work in any room in which the weaving of cotton or flax or any other process which takes place between, or at the same time as, the winding or beaming and weaving of cotton or flax is carried on in a factory in which any or all of those processes are carried on is 3rd October 1983;

(b) in any other case, is 6th April 1979 except that where the disease was prescribed in relation to any person by regulations which came into operation on a date earlier that 6th April 1979 the relevant date is that earlier date.

(5) Byssinosis is not prescribed in relation to any person if neither of the following conditions is satisfied, namely:—

(a) that he was suffering from a loss of faculty as a result of bysinnosis on or after the relevant date;

(b) that he has been employed in employed earner's employment in any occupation mentioned in regulation 2(c) of the old regulation for a period or periods (whether before or after 5th July 1948) amounting in the aggregate to five years.

(6) Notwithstanding that a person does not satisfy paragraph (3) infection by leptospira is prescribed in relation to any person if he is or has been either incapable of work or suffering from a loss of faculty as a result of infection by—

(a) leptospira icterohaemorrhagiae in the case of a person employed in employed earner's employment before 7th January 1980 in any occupation involving work in places which are or are liable to be, infested by rats, or

(b) leptospira canicola in the case of a person so employed in any occupation involving work at dog kennels or the care or handling of dogs.

(7) A person who, immediately before 3rd October 1983, was in receipt of benefit in respect of a disease or injury which was prescribed by virtue of the old regulations, or who makes a claim for benefit in respect of a prescribed disease after 2nd October 1983 where the date of onset of the disease or injury was before 3rd October 1983, shall be treated for the purpose only of determining whether the disease or injury is in relation to him a prescribed disease by virtue of the occupation in which he is or was engaged as if the old regulations were still in force and these regulations had not come into operation, if that would be more favourable to him.

Transitional provisions regarding dates of development and dates of onset

10.134 **44.**—Where a claim for benefit has been made before 6th April 1983 or a date of onset is determined which is before 6th April 1983 or a claim for injury benefit is made after 5th April 1983 for a day falling or a period beginning before 6th April 1983, these regulations shall take effect subject to the provisions of Schedule 5.

10.135 *Regulation 45 omitted.*

SCHEDULES

SCHEDULE 1 **Regulations 2 and 4**

PART I

LIST OF PRESCRIBED DISEASES AND THE OCCUPATIONS FOR WHICH THEY ARE PRESCRIBED

10.136

Prescribed disease or injury	*Occupation*
A. Conditions due to physical agents	*Any occupation involving:*
[1 [28 A1 Leukaemia (other than chronic lymphocytic leukaemia) or primary cancer of the bone, bladder, breast, colon, liver, lung, ovary, stomach, testis or thyroid.]	[28 Exposure to ionising radiation where the dose is sufficient to double the risk of the occurrence of the condition.]
A2. [2 . . .] cataract.	[2 Frequent or prolonged exposure to radiation from red-hot or white-hot material.].
	Any occupation involving:
[27A3 (a) Dysbarism, including decompression sickness and barotrauma; (b) Osteonecrosis.]	Subjection to compressed or rarefied air or other respirable gases or gaseous mixtures.
[25A4. Task-specific focal dystonia of the hand or forearm.	Prolonged periods of handwriting, typing or other repetitive movements of the fingers, hand or arm.]
A5. Subcutaneous cellulitis of the hand [19 . . .]	Manual labour causing severe or prolonged friction or pressure on the hand.
A6. Bursitis or subcutaneous cellulitis arising at or about the knee due to severe or prolonged external friction or pressure at or about the knee [19 . . .]	Manual labour causing severe or prolonged external friction or pressure at or about the knee.
A7. Bursitis or subcutaneous cellulitis arising at or about the elbow due to severe or prolonged external friction or pressure at or about the elbow [19 . . .]	Manual labour causing severe or prolonged external friction or pressure at or about the elbow.
A8. Traumatic inflammation of the tendons of the hand or forearm, or of the associated tendon sheaths.	Manual labour, or frequent or repeated movements of the hand or wrist.
[19 A9. *Omitted.*]	*Omitted.*]
[3 A10. Sensorineural hearing loss amounting to at least 50 dB in each ear, being the average of hearing losses at 1, 2 and 3 kHz frequencies, and being due in the case of at least one ear to occupational noise (occupational deafness).]	[16 The use of, or work wholly or mainly in the immediate vicinity of the use of, a— (a) band saw, circular saw or cutting disc to cut metal in the metal founding or forging industries, circular saw to cut products in the manufacture of steel, powered (other than hand powered) grinding tool on metal (other than sheet metal or plate metal), pneumatic percussive tool on metal, pressurised air arc tool to gouge metal, burner or torch to cut or dress steel based products, skid transfer bank, knock out and shake out grid in a foundry, machine (other than a power press machine) to forge metal including a machine used to drop stamp

Prescribed disease or injury	*Occupation*
	metal by means of closed or open dies or drop hammers, machine to cut or shape or clean metal nails, or plasma spray gun to spray molten metal; (b) pneumatic percussive tool:—to drill rock in a quarry, on stone in a quarry works, underground, for mining coal, for sinking a shaft, or for tunnelling in civil engineering works; (c) vibrating metal moulding box in the concrete products industry, or circular saw to cut concrete masonry blocks; (d) machine in the manufacture of textiles for:—weaving man-made or natural fibres (including mineral fibres), high speed false twisting of fibres, or the mechanical cleaning of bobbins; (e) multi-cutter moulding machine on wood, planing machine on wood, automatic or semi-automatic lathe on wood, multiple cross-cut machine on wood, automatic shaping machine on wood, double-end tenoning machine on wood, vertical spindle moulding machine (including a high speed routing machine) on wood, edge banding machine on wood, bandsawing machine (with a blade width of not less than 75 millimetres) on wood, circular sawing machine on wood including one operated by moving the blade towards the material being cut, or chain saw on wood; (f) jet of water (or a mixture of water and abrasive material) at a pressure above 680 bar, or jet channelling process to burn stone in a quarry; (g) machine in a ship's engine room, or gas turbine for:—performance testing on a test bed, installation testing of a replacement engine in an aircraft, or acceptance testing of an Armed Service fixed wing combat aircraft; (h) machine in the manufacture of glass containers or hollow ware for:—automatic moulding, automatic blow moulding, or automatic glass pressing and forming; *Any occupation involving:* (i) spinning machine using compressed air to produce glass wool or mineral wool; (j) continuous glass toughening furnace; (k) firearm by a police firearms training officer; or (l) shot-blaster to carry abrasives in air for cleaning.]
A11. [[20](a) Intense blanching of the skin, with a sharp demarcation line between affected and non-affected skin, where the blanching is cold-induced,	(a) the use of hand-held chain saws [[21] on wood] (b) the use of hand-held rotary tools in grinding or in the sanding or polishing of

Prescribed disease or injury	*Occupation*
episodic, occurs throughout the year and affects the skin of the distal with the middle and proximal phalanges, or distal with the middle phalanx (or in the case of a thumb the distal with the proximal phalanx), of— (i) in the case of a person with 5 fingers (including thumb) on one hand, any 3 of those fingers, or (ii) in the case of a person with only 4 such fingers, any 2 of those fingers, or (iii) in the case of a person with less than 4 such fingers, any one of them or, as the case may be, the one remaining finger, where none of the person's fingers was subject to any degree of cold-induced, episodic blanching of the skin prior to the person's employment in an occupation described in the second column in relation to this paragraph, or (b) significant, demonstrable reduction in both sensory perception and manipulative dexterity with continuous numbness or continuous tingling all present at the same time in the distal phalanx of any finger (including thumb) where none of the person's fingers was subject to any degree of reduction in sensory perception, manipulative dexterity, numbness or tingling prior to the person's employment in an occupation described in the second column in relation to this paragraph, where the symptoms in paragraph (a) or paragraph (b) were caused by vibration.]	metal, or the holding of material being ground, or metal being sanded or polished, by rotary tools; or (c) the use of hand-held percussive metal-working tools, or the holding of metal being worked upon by percussive tools, in riveting, caulking, chipping, hammering, fettling, or swaging; or (d) the use of hand-held powered percussive drills or hand-held powered percussive hammers in mining, quarrying, demolition, or on roads or footpaths, including road construction; or (e) the holding of material being worked upon by pounding machines in shoe manufacture.
	Any occupation involving:
[7A12. Carpal tunnel syndrome.]	[19 (a) The use, at the time the symptoms first develop, of hand-held powered tools whose internal parts vibrate so as to transmit that vibration to the hand, but excluding those tools which are solely powered by hand; or (b) repeated palmar flexion and dorsiflexion of the wrist for at least 20 hours per week for a period or periods amounting in aggregate to least 12 months in the 24 months prior to the onset of symptoms, where "repeated" means once or more often in every 30 seconds.]
[17 A13. Osteoarthritis of the hip.	Work in agriculture as a farmer or farm worker for a period of, or periods which amount in aggregate to, 10 years or more.]
[23A14. Osteoarthritis of the knee.	Work underground in a coal mine for a period of, or periods which amount in aggregate to, at least 10 years in any one or more of the following occupations:

Prescribed disease or injury	*Occupation*
	(a) before 1st January 1986 as a coal miner; or (b) on or after 1st January 1986 as a— (i) face worker working on a non-mechanised coal face; (ii) development worker; (iii) face-salvage worker; (iv) conveyor belt cleaner; or (v) conveyor belt attendant. "A non-mechanised coal face" means a coal face without either powered roof supports or a power loader machine which simultaneously cuts and loads the coal or without both.] [25Work wholly or mainly fitting or laying carpets or floors (other than concrete floors) for a period of, or periods which amount in aggregate to, 20 years or more.]
[30 A15 Dupuytren's contracture of the hand [31involving— (i) fixed flexion deformity of one or more metacarpophalangeal joints greater than 45 degrees that developed during the period or periods set out in the second column in relation to this paragraph; or (ii) fixed flexion deformity of one or more interphalangeal joints that developed during the period or periods set out in the second column in relation to this paragraph; or (iii) fixed flexion deformity of one or more metacarpophalangeal joints greater than 45 degrees that developed after the period or periods in the second column in relation to this paragraph if there is evidence of the onset of metacarpophalangeal joint involvement or palmar changes (nodules or thickening) during that period or periods; or (iv) fixed flexion deformity of one or more interphalangeal joints that developed after the period or periods set out in the second column in relation to this paragraph if there is evidence of the onset of metacarpophalangeal joint involvement or palmar changes (nodules or thickening) during that period or periods.]	Any occupation involving the use of hand-held powered tools whose internal parts vibrate so as to transmit that vibration to the hand (but excluding those tools which are solely powered by hand) where - (a) the use of those tools amounts to a period or periods in aggregate of at least 10 years; [31and] (b) within that period or those periods, the use of those tools amounts to at least 2 hours per day for 3 or more days per week; [31.] [(c) 31...]
B. Conditions due to biological agents	*Any occupation involving:*
[27B1 (a) Cutaneous anthrax; (b) Pulmonary anthrax.]	(a) Contact with anthrax spores, including contact with animals infected by anthrax; or (b) handling, loading, unloading or transport of animals of a type susceptible to infection with anthrax or of the products or residues of such animals.]
B2. Glanders.	Contact with equine animals or their carcases.

Prescribed disease or injury	*Occupation*
B3. Infection by leptospira.	(a) Work in places which are, or are liable to be, infested by rats, field mice or voles, or other small mammals; or (b) work at dog kennels or the care or handling of dogs; or (c) contact with bovine animals or their meat products or pigs or their meat products.
[27B4 (a) Cutaneous larva migrans; (b) Iron deficiency anaemia caused by gastrointestinal infection by hookworm.]	[17Contact with a source of ankylostomiasis.]
B5. Tuberculosis.	[27B5 Contact with a source of tuberculosis while undertaking— (a) work in a hospital, mortuary in which post mortems are conducted, or laboratory; or (b) work in any other workplace.]
B6. Extrinsic allergic alveolitis [28. . .]	Exposure to moulds or fungal spores or heterologous proteins [28 or any other biological substance that causes extrinsic allergic alveolitis] by reason of employment in: (a) agriculture, horticulture, forestry, cultivation of edible fungi or malt-working; or (b) loading or unloading or handling in storage mouldy vegetable matter or edible fungi; or (c) caring for or handling birds; or (d) handling bagasse; [19 or (e) work involving exposure to metalworking fluid mists.] [28; or (f) any other workplace]
B7. Infection by organisms of the genus brucella.	Contact with— (a) animals infected by brucella, or their carcases or parts thereof, or their untreated products; or (b) laboratory specimens or vaccines of, or containing brucella.
[17 B8A. Infection by hepatitis A virus.	Contact with raw sewage.
B8B. Infection by hepatitis B or C virus.	Contact with— (a) human blood or human blood products; or (b) any other source of hepatitis B or C virus.]
B9. Infection by Streptococcus suis.	Contact with pigs infected by Streptococcus suis, or with the carcases, products or residues of pigs so infected.
[8 B10. (a) Avian chlamydiosis.	Contact with birds infected with chlamydia psittaci, or with the remains or untreated products of such birds.
B10. (b) Ovine chlamydiosis.	Contact with sheep infected with chlamydia psittaci, or with the remains or untreated products of such sheep.
B11. Q fever.	Contact with animals, their remains or their untreated products.] *Any occupation involving:*
[9 12. Orf.	Contact with sheep, goats or with the carcasses of sheep or goats.
B13. Hydatidosis.	Contact with dogs.]
[17 B14. Lyme disease.	Exposure to deer or other mammals of a type liable to harbour ticks harbouring Borrelia bacteria.

Prescribed disease or injury	*Occupation*
B15. Anaphylaxis.	[29 Contact] with products made with natural rubber latex.]
C. Conditions due to chemical agents	
[10 C1. (a) Anaemia with a haemoglobin concentration of 9g/dL or less, and a blood film showing punctate basophilia; (b) peripheral neuropathy; (c) central nervous system toxicity.]	The use or handling of, or exposure to the fumes, dust or vapour of, lead or a compound of lead, or a substance containing lead.
[10 C2. Central nervous system toxicity characterised by parkinsonism.]	The use or handling of, or exposure to the fumes, dust or vapour of, manganese or a compound of manganese, or a substance containing manganese.
[25C3.(a) Phossy Jaw.	Work involving the use or handling of, or exposure to, white phosphorus.
C3. (b) Peripheral polyneuropathy or peripheral polyneuropathy with pyramidal involvement of the central nervous system, caused by organic compounds of phosphorus which inhibit the enzyme neuropathy target esterase.	Work involving the use or handling of, or exposure to, organic compounds of phosphorus.]
[10C4. Primary carcinoma of the bronchus lung.	Exposure to the fumes, dust or vapour of or arsenic, a compound of arsenic or a substance containing arsenic.
C5A. Central nervous system toxicity characterised by tremor and neuropsychiatric disease.	Exposure to mercury or inorganic compounds of mercury for a period of, or periods which amount in aggregate to, 10 years or more.
C5B. Central nervous system toxicity characterised by combined cerebellar and cortical degeneration.	Exposure to methylmercury.
C6. Peripheral neuropathy.	The use or handling of, or exposure to, carbon disulphide (also called carbon disulfide).
C7. Acute non-lymphatic leukaemia.	Exposure to benzene.]
C8. [10 . . .]	[10 . . .]
C9. [10 . . .]	[10 . . .]
C10. [10 . . .]	[10 . . .]
C11. [10 . . .]	[10 . . .]
[10 C12. (a) Peripheral neuropathy; (b) central nervous system toxicity.	Exposure to methyl bromide (also called bromomethane).]
[10 C13. Cirrhosis of the liver.	Exposure to chlorinated naphthalenes.]
C14. [10 . . .]	[10 . . .]
C15. [10 . . .]	[10 . . .]
[10 C16. (a) Neurotoxicity; (b) cardiotoxicity.	Exposure to the dust of gonioma kamassi.
	Any occupation involving:
C17. Chronic beryllium disease.	Inhalation of beryllium or a beryllium compound.
C18. Emphysema.	Inhalation of cadmium fumes for a period of, or periods which amount in aggregate to, 20 years or more.
C19. (a) Peripheral neuropathy; (b) central nervous system toxicity.	Exposure to acrylamide.

Prescribed disease or injury	*Occupation*
C20. Dystrophy of the cornea (including ulceration of the corneal surface) of the. eye.	Exposure to quinone or hydroquinone.
C21. Primary carcinoma of the skin.	Exposure to arsenic or arsenic compounds, tar, pitch, bitumen, mineral oil (including paraffin) or soot.
C22. (a) Primary carcinoma of the mucous membrane of the nose or paranasal sinuses; (b) primary carcinoma of the bronchus or lung.	Work before 1950 in the refining of nickel involving exposure to oxides, sulphides or water-soluble compounds of nickel.
C23. Primary neoplasm of the epithelial lining of the urinary tract.	(a) The manufacture of 1-naphthylamine, 2-naphthylamine, benzidine, auramine, magenta or 4-aminobiphenyl (also called biphenyl-4-ylamine); (b) work in the process of manufacturing methylene-bis-orthochloroaniline (also called MbOCA) for a period of, or periods which amount in aggregate to, 12 months or more; (c) exposure to 2-naphthylamine, benzidine, 4-aminobiphenyl (also called biphenyl-4-ylamine) or salts of those compounds otherwise than in the manufacture of those compounds; (d) exposure to orthotoluidine, 4-chloro-2-methylaniline or salts of those compounds; or (e) exposure for a period of, or periods which amount in aggregate to, 5 years or more, to coal tar pitch volatiles produced in aluminium smelting involving the Soderberg process (that is to say, the method of producing aluminium by electrolysis in which the anode consists of a paste of petroleum coke and mineral oil which is baked in situ).]
[[18]C24. (a) Angiosarcoma of the liver; or (b) osteolysis of the terminal phalanges of the fingers; or (c) sclerodermatous thickening of the skin of the hand; or (d) liver fibrosis, due to exposure to vinyl chloride monomer.	Exposure to vinyl chloride monomer in the manufacture of polyvinyl chloride.
C24A. Raynaud's phenomenon due to exposure to vinyl chloride monomer.	Exposure to vinyl chloride monomer in the manufacture of polyvinyl chloride before 1st January 1984.]
	Any occupation involving:
[[10]C25. Vitiligo.	The use or handling of, or exposure to, paratertiary-butylphenol (also called 4-tert-butylphenol), paratertiary-butylcatechol (also called 4-tert-butylcatechol), para-amylphenol (also called p-pentyl phenol isomers), hydroquinone, monobenzyl ether of hydroquinone (also called 4-benzyloxyphenol) or mono-butyl ether of hydroquinone (also called 4-butoxyphenol).

Prescribed disease or injury	*Occupation*
C26. (a) Liver toxicity; (b) kidney toxicity.	The use or handling of, or exposure to, carbon tetrachloride (also called tetrachloromethane).
C27. Liver toxicity.	The use or handling of, or exposure to, trichloromethane (also called chloroform).]
C28. [10 . . .]	[10 . . .]
[10 C29. Peripheral neuropathy.	The use or handling of, or exposure to, n-hexane or n-butyl methyl ketone.
C30. (a) Dermatitis; (b) ulceration of the mucous membrane or the epidermis.	The use or handling of, or exposure to, chromic acid, chromates or dichromates.]
[24C31. Bronchiolitis obliterans.	The use or handling of, or exposure to, diacetyl (also called butanedione or 2,3-butanedione) in the manufacture of— (a) diacetyl; or (b) food flavouring containing diacetyl; or (c) food to which food flavouring containing diacetyl is added.
C32. Carcinoma of the nasal cavity or associated air sinuses (nasal carcinoma).	(a) The manufacture of inorganic chromates; or (b) work in hexavalent chrome plating]
[27C33 Chloracne.	Exposure to a substance causing chloracne.]
[28 C34 Extrinsic allergic alveolitis.	Exposure to airborne isocyanates; or to any other chemical substance that causes extrinsic allergic alveolitis.]
D. Miscellaneous Conditions	
D1. Pneumoconiosis.	*Any occupation—* (a) set out in Part II of this Schedule; (b) specified in regulation 2(b)(ii).
D2. Byssinosis.	Work in any room where any process up to and including the weaving process is performed in a factory in which the spinning or manipulation of raw or waste cotton or of flax, or the weaving of cotton or flax, is carried on.
D3. Diffuse mesothelioma (primary neoplasm of the mesothelium of the pleura or of the pericardium or of the peritoneum).	[11 Exposure to asbestos, asbestos dust or any admixture of asbestos at a level above that commonly found in the environment at large.]
[7 D4. Allergic rhinitis which is due to exposure to any of the following agents— (a) isocyanates; (b) platinum salts; (c) fumes or dusts arising from the manufacture, transport or use of hardening agents (including epoxy resin curing agents) based on phthalic	Exposure to any of the agents set out in column 1 of this paragraph.]
anhydride, tetrachlorophthalic anhydride, trimelliticanhydride or triethylene-tetramine; (d) fumes arising from the use of rosin as a soldering flux; (e) proteolyticenzymes; (f) animals including insects and other arthropods used for the purposes of research or education or in laboratories;	*Any occupation involving:*

Prescribed disease or injury	*Occupation*
(g) dusts arising from the sowing, cultivation, harvesting, drying, handling, milling, transport or storage of barley, oats, rye, wheat or maize, or the handling, milling, transport or storage of meal or flour made therefrom; (h) antibiotics; (i) cimetidine; (j) wood dust; (k) ispaghula; (l) castor bean dust; (m) ipecacuanha; (n) azodicarbonamide; (o) animals including insects and other arthropods or their larval forms, used for the purposes of pest control or fruit cultivation, or the larval forms of animals used for the purposes of research, education or in laboratories; (p) glutaraldehyde; (q) persulphate slats or henna; (r) crustaceans or fish or products arising from these in the food processing industry; (s) reactive dyes; (t) soya bean; (u) tea dust; (v) green coffee bean dust; (w) fumes from stainless steel welding.] [17 (x) products made with natural rubber latex.]	
D5. Non-infective dermatitis of external origin [7 . . .] (excluding dermatitis due to ionising particles or electro-magnetic radiations other than radiant heat).	Exposure to dust, liquid or vapour or any other external agent capable of irritating the skin (including friction or heat but excluding ionising particles or electro-magnetic radiations other than radiant heat).
D6. Carcinoma of the nasal cavity or associated air sinuses (nasal carcinoma).	(a) Attendance for work [29 at a workplace] where wooden goods [29 or products made wholly or partially of wood] are manufactured or repaired; or (b) attendance for work in a building used for the manufacture of footwear or components of footwear made wholly or partly of leather or fibre board; or (c) attendance for work at a place used wholly or mainly for the repair of footwear made wholly or partly of leather or fibre board, [29; or (d) exposure to wood dust in the course of the machine processing of wood.]
	Any occupation involving:
D7. Asthma which is due to exposure to any of the following agents: (a) isocyanates; (b) platinum salts; (c) fumes or dusts arising from the manufacture, transport or use of hardening agents (including epoxy	Exposure to any of the agents set out in column 1 of this paragraph.

Prescribed disease or injury	*Occupation*
resin curing agents) based on phthalic anhydride, tetrachlorophthalic anhydride, trimelliticanhydride or triethylenetetramine; (d) fumes arising from the use of rosin as a soldering flux; (e) proteolyticenzymes; [[12](f) animals including insects and other arthropods used for the purposes of research or education or in laboratories]; (g) dusts arising from the sowing, cultivation, harvesting, drying, handling, milling, transport or storage or barley, oats, rye, wheat or maize, or the handling, milling, transport or storage of meal or flour made therefrom; [[12](h) antibiotics; (i) cimetidine; (j) wood dust; (k) ispaghula; (l) castor bean dust; (m) ipecacuanha; (n) azodicarbonamide]; [[9](o) animals including insects and other arthropods or their larval forms, used for the purposes of pest control or fruit cultivation, or the larval forms of animals used for the purposes of research, education or in laboratories; (p) glutaraldehyde; (q) persulphate slats or henna; (r) crustaceans or fish or products arising from these in the food processing industry; (s) reactive dyes; (t) soya bean; (u) tea dust; (v) green coffee bean dust; (w) fumes from stainless steel welding; [[17](wa) products made with natural rubber latex;] (x) any other sensitising agent] (occupational asthma).	
[[18]D8. Primary carcinoma of the lung where there is accompanying evidence of asbestosis.	(a) The working or handling of asbestos or any admixture of asbestos; or (b) the manufacture or repair of asbestos *Any occupation involving:* textiles or other articles containing or composed of asbestos; or (c) the cleaning of any machinery or plant used in any of the foregoing operations and of any chambers, fixtures and appliances for the collection of asbestos dust; or (d) substantial exposure to the dust arising from any of the foregoing operations.

Prescribed disease or injury	*Occupation*
D8A. Primary carcinoma of the lung.	Exposure to asbestos in the course of— (a) the manufacture of asbestos textiles; or (b) spraying asbestos; or (c) asbestos insulation work; or (d) applying or removing materials containing asbestos in the course of shipbuilding, where all or any of the exposure occurs before 1st January 1975, for a period of, or periods which amount in aggregate to, five years or more, or otherwise, for a period of, or periods which amount in aggregate to, ten years or more.]
[[18]D9. Unilateral or bilateral diffuse pleural thickening [[28]. . .] .]	(a) The working or handling of asbestos or any admixture of asbestos; or (b) the manufacture or repair of asbestos textiles or other articles containing or composed of asbestos; or (c) the cleaning of any machinery or plant used in any of the foregoing operations and of any chambers, fixtures and appliances for the collection of asbestos dust; or (d) substantial exposure to the dust arising from any of the foregoing operations.
[[15]D10. [[13] Primary carcinoma of the lung.]	(a) Work underground in a tin mine; or (b) exposure to bis (chloromethyl) ether produced during the manufacture of chloromethyl methyl ether; or (c) exposure to zinc chromate, calcium chromate or stronium chromate in their pure forms [[26]; or (d) employment wholly or mainly as a coke oven worker: (i) for a period of, or periods which amount in aggregate to, 15 years or more; or (ii) in top oven work, for a period of, or periods which amount in aggregate to, 5 years or more; or (iii) in a combination of top oven work and other coke oven work for a total aggregate period of 15 years or more where one year working in top oven work is treated as equivalent to 3 years in other coke oven work.]
	Any occupation involving:
[[13] D11. Primary carcinoma of the lung where there is accompanying evidence of silicosis.	Exposure to silica dust in the course of— (a) the manufacture of glass or pottery; tunnelling in or quarrying (b) sandstone or granite; (c) mining metal ores; (d) slate quarrying or the manufacture of artefacts from slate; (e) mining clay; (f) using siliceous materials as abrasives; (g) cutting stone; (h) stonemasonry; or (i) work in a foundry.]

Prescribed disease or injury	*Occupation*
[[11]D12. Except in the circumstances specified in regulation 2(d)— [[27]chronic obstructive pulmonary disease.] where there is [[23] . . .] evidence of a forced expiratory volume in one second (measured from the position of maximum inspiration with the claimant making maximum effort) which is— [[14](i) at least one litre below the Appropriate mean value predicted, obtained from the following prediction formulae which give the mean values predicted in litres— ii. For a man, where the measurement is made without back-extrapolation, (3.62 x Height in metres)– (0.031 x Age in years)—1.41; or, where the measurement is made with back-extrapolation,(3.71 x Height in metres)—(0.032 x Age in years)—1.44; ii. For a woman, where the measurement is made without back-extrapolation, (3.29 x Height in metres)-(0.029 x Age in years)-1.42; or, where the measurement is made with back-extrapolation, (3.37 x Height in metres)—(0.030 x Age in years)—1.46; or]] (ii) less than one litre. [[27]The value of one litre in (i) and (ii) shall be construed as fixed and shall not vary by virtue of any treatment or treatments.]	[[23] Exposure to coal dust (whether before or after 5th July 1948) by reason of working— (a) underground in a coal mine for a period or periods amounting in aggregate to at least 20 years; (b) on the surface of a coal mine as a screen worker for a period or periods amounting in aggregate to at least 40 years before 1st January 1983; or (c) both underground in a coal mine, and on the surface as a screen worker before 1st January 1983, where 2 years working as a surface screen worker is equivalent to 1 year working underground, amounting in aggregate to at least the equivalent of 20 years underground. Any such period or periods shall include a period or periods of incapacity while engaged in such an occupation.]
[[22] D13. Primary carcinoma of the nasopharynx.	Exposure to wood dust in the course of the processing of wood or the manufacture or repair of wood products, for a period or periods which amount in aggregate to at least 10 years.]

PART II **Regulations 2, 4, 38 and 40**

OCCUPATIONS FOR WHICH PNEUMOCONIOSIS IS PRESCRIBED

10.137 **1.**—Any occupation involving—

(a) the mining, quarrying or working of silica rock or the working of dried quartzose sand or any dry deposit or dry residue of silica or any dry admixture containing such materials (including any occupation in which any of the aforesaid operations are carried out incidentally to the mining or quarrying of other minerals or to the manufacture of articles containing crushed or ground silica rock);

(b) the handling of any of the materials specified in the foregoing sub-paragraph in or incidental to any of the operations mentioned therein, or substantial exposure to the dust arising from such operations.

2.—Any occupation involving the breaking, crushing or grinding of flint or the working or handling of broken, crushed or ground flint or materials containing such flint, or substantial exposure to the dust arising from any such operations.

3.—Any occupation involving sand blasting by means of compressed air with the use of quartzose sand or crushed silica rock or flint, or substantial exposure to the dust arising from sand and blasting.

4.—Any occupation involving work in a foundry or the performance of, or substantial exposure to the dust arising from, any of the following operations:—

(a) the freeing of steel castings from adherent siliceous substance;

(b) the freeing of metal castings from adherent siliceous substance—

(i) by blasting with an abrasive propelled by compressed air, by steam or by a wheel; or

(ii) by the use of power-driven tools.

5.—Any occupation in or incidental to the manufacture of china or earthenware (including sanitary earthenware, electrical earthenware and earthenware tiles), and any occupation involving substantial exposure to the dust arising therefrom.

6.—Any occupation involving the grinding of mineral graphite, or substantial exposure to the dust arising from such grinding.

7.—Any occupation involving the dressing of granite or any igneous rock by masons or the crushing of such materials, or substantial exposure to the dust arising from such operations.

8.—Any occupation involving the use, or preparation for use, of a grindstone, or substantial exposure to the dust arising therefrom.

9.—Any occupation involving—

(a) the working or handling of asbestos or any admixture of asbestos;

(b) the manufacture or repair of asbestos textiles or other articles containing or composed of asbestos;

(c) the cleaning of any machinery or plant used in any foregoing operations and of any chambers, fixtures and appliances for the collection of asbestos dust;

(d) substantial exposure to the dust arising from any of the foregoing operations.

10.—Any occupation involving—

(a) work underground in any mine in which one of the objects of the mining operations is the getting of any mineral;

(b) the working or handling above ground at any coal or tin mine of any minerals extracted therefrom, or any operation incidental thereto;

(c) the trimming of coal in any ship, barge, or lighter, or in any dock or harbour or at any wharf or quay;

(d) the sawing, splitting or dressing of slate, or any operation incidental thereto.

11.—Any occupation in or incidental to the manufacture of carbon electrodes by an industrial undertaking for use in the electrolytic extraction of aluminium from aluminium oxide, and any occupation involving substantial exposure to the dust arising therefrom.

12.—Any occupation involving boiler scaling or substantial exposure to the dust arising therefrom.

AMENDMENTS

1. Social Security (Industrial Injuries) (Prescribed Diseases) Amendment Regulations 2000 (SI 2000/1588) reg.6(1) and (2) (July 10, 2000).

2. Social Security (Industrial Injuries) (Prescribed Diseases) Amendment Regulations 2000 (SI 2000/1588) reg.6(1) and (3) (July 10, 2000).

3. Social Security (Industrial Injuries) (Prescribed Diseases) Amendment Regulations 1989 (SI 1989/1207) reg.4 (October 16, 1989).

4. Social Security (Industrial Injuries) (Prescribed Diseases) Amendment (No.2) Regulations 1987 (SI 1987/2112) reg.2 (January 4, 1988).

5. Social Security (Industrial Injuries) (Prescribed Diseases) Amendment Regulations 1994 (SI 1994/2343) reg.4 (October 10, 1994).

6. Social Security (Industrial Injuries and Diseases) (Miscellaneous Amendments) Regulations 1996 (SI 1996/425) reg.5(4) (March 24, 1996).

7. Social Security (Industrial Injuries and Diseases) (Miscellaneous Amendments) Regulations 1996 (SI 1996/425) reg.5 (March 24, 1996 with savings, see reg.7 below).

8. Social Security (Industrial Injuries) (Prescribed Diseases) Amendment Regulations 1989 (SI 1989/1207) reg.6 (August 9, 1989).

9. Social Security (Industrial Injuries) (Prescribed Diseases) Amendment Regulations 1991 (SI 1991/1938) reg.2 (September 26, 1991).

10. Social Security (Industrial Injuries) (Prescribed Diseases) Amendment Regulations 2003 (SI 2003/270) reg.5 (March 17, 2003).

11. Social Security (Industrial Injuries) (Miscellaneous Amendments) Regulations 1997 (SI 1997/810) reg.6 (April 9, 1997).

12. Social Security (Industrial Injuries and Adjudication) Miscellaneous Amendment Regulations 1986 (SI 1986/1374) reg.3 (September 1, 1986).

13. Social Security (Industrial Injuries) (Prescribed Diseases) Amendment Regulations 1993 (SI 1993/862) reg.6 (April 19, 1993).

14. Social Security (Industrial Injuries) (Prescribed Diseases) Amendment Regulations 2000 (SI 2000/1588) reg.6(1) and (4) (July 10, 2000).

15. Social Security (Industrial Injuries) (Prescribed Diseases) Amendment Regulations 1987 (SI 1987/335) reg.2 (April 1, 1987).

16. Social Security (Industrial Injuries) (Prescribed Diseases) Amendment (No.2) Regulations 2003 (SI 2003/2190) reg.3 (September 22, 2003).

17. Social Security (Industrial Injuries) (Prescribed Diseases) Amendment Regulations 2005 (SI 2005/324) reg.3 (March 14, 2005).

18. Social Security (Industrial Injuries) (Prescribed Diseases) Amendment Regulations 2006 (SI 2006/586) reg.3 (April 6, 2006).

19. Social Security (Industrial Injuries) (Prescribed Diseases) Amendment Regulations 2007 (SI 2007/811) reg.2 (April 6, 2007).

20. Social Security (Industrial Injuries) (Prescribed Diseases) Amendment (No. 2) Regulations 2007 (SI 2007/1753) reg.2(1), (2) (October 1, 2007).

21. Social Security (Industrial Injuries) (Prescribed Diseases) Amendment (No. 2) Regulations 2007 (SI 2007/1753) reg.2(1), (3) (October 1, 2007).

22. Social Security (Industrial Injuries) (Prescribed Diseases) Amendment Regulations 2008 (SI 2008/14) reg.2 (April 7, 2008).

23. Social Security (Industrial Injuries) (Prescribed Diseases) Amendment Regulations 2009 (SI 2009/1396) reg.2 (July 13, 2009).

24. Social Security (Industrial Injuries) (Prescribed Diseases) Amendment Regulations 2011 (SI 2011/1497) reg.2 (July 18, 2011).

25. Social Security (Industrial Injuries) (Prescribed Diseases) Amendment Regulations 2012 (SI 2012/647) reg.2 (March 30, 2012).

26. Social Security (Industrial Injuries) (Prescribed Diseases) Amendment (No.2) Regulations 2012 (SI 2012/1634) reg.2 (August 1, 2012).

27. Social Security (Industrial Injuries) (Prescribed Diseases) Amendment Regulations 2015 (SI 2015/87) reg. 4(2) (March 16, 2015).

28. Social Security (Industrial Injuries) (Prescribed Diseases) Amendment Regulations 2017 (SI 2017/232) reg.3 (March 30, 2017).

29. Social Security (Industrial Injuries) (Prescribed Diseases) Amendment Regulations 2018 (SI 2018/769) reg.2(2) (September 28, 2018).

30. Social Security (Industrial Injuries) (Prescribed Diseases) Amendment Regulations 2019 (SI 2019/1241) reg.2(3) (December 9, 2019).

31. Social Security (Industrial Injuries) (Prescribed Diseases) Amendment Regulations 2022 (SI 2022/214) reg.2 and Social Security (Industrial Injuries) (Prescribed Diseases) Amendment (No.2) Regulations 2022 (SI 2022/229) reg.2 (March 28, 2022). Parallel amendments which have effect in Scotland only were made by the Social Security (Industrial Injuries) (Prescribed Diseases) Amendment (Scotland) Regulations 2022 (SSI 2022/42).

GENERAL NOTE

10.138 *I. The structure of this annotation*

This annotation examines first some general matters pertaining to the whole of this Sch., dealing with prescribed industrial diseases. It then examines the prescribed diseases by category. The diseases in the Schedule are divided into four categories according to cause and are given letters and numbers for identification:

A1–14 Conditions due to physical agents;

B1–15 Conditions due to biological agents;

C1–33 Conditions due to chemical agents;

D1–13 Miscellaneous conditions.

Within each category, particular diseases will be treated in a depth consistent with the case law on that disease.

II. General matters

The diseases listed in the Schedule are there because there is some discernible link between the disease and the occupation for which it is prescribed. The power to prescribe diseases is exercised by the Secretary of State, normally upon the advice of the Industrial Injuries Advisory Council which investigates occupational diseases and reports upon them, as well as keeping the Industrial Injuries scheme generally under review. The Secretary of State exercises his power under the SSCBA 1992, s.108(2) (formerly SSA 1975, s.76(2)) and must be satisfied that the disease is a risk of the occupation and not a common risk, and also that the attribution of particular cases to the nature of the employment can be established or presumed with reasonable certainty. **10.139**

The system for decision-making and appeals for claims to industrial injuries benefits has undergone several reforms over the years. However, one constant throughout this period of change is that the question of whether a claimant is an employed or self-employed earner, and whether a specific employment is, or is not, employed earner's employment, is to be decided not by the Secretary of State, but by officers of HMRC (Social Security Contributions (Transfer of Functions, etc.) Act 1999 s.8(1)). Accordingly, such decisions are not matters of appeal for the FTT Social Entitlement Chamber but rather for appeal to the FTT Tax Chamber. Such decisions and appeals are regulated by the Social Security Contributions (Decisions and Appeals) Regs 1999 (SI 1999/1027).

Historically, for all other industrial injuries matters, there was a distinction between medical issues (the disablement questions), decided by the medical adjudicating authorities, including on appeal the former MAT, and non-medical issues, decided by insurance officers (and later adjudication officers), with appeals to the former SSAT (or its predecessor). However, on July 5, 1999, the functions of adjudication officers with respect to industrial injuries benefits and the making of industrial accident declarations were transferred to the Secretary of State (SSA 1998, ss.1, 8 and Commencement Order No. 8). He or she may, however, refer certain issues for report to a medical practitioner (now a health care professional) who has experience of the issues. The issues so referable are: (a) the extent of a personal injury for the purposes of s.94; (b) whether the claimant has a prescribed industrial disease and the extent of the resulting disablement; and (c) whether, for disablement benefit purposes, the claimant has a disablement and its extent (Decisions and Appeals Regs 1999 reg.12(1)).

After 1999 decisions by the Secretary of State on industrial injuries benefits, including those on prescribed industrial diseases, and on the matter of an industrial accident declaration, were appealable to the so-called "unified" appeal tribunal, composed of a legally qualified member and up to two medically qualified members (SSA 1998 ss.4, 12, Schs 2 and 3). Like the Secretary of State, that tribunal was competent to deal with the both the medical and non-medical aspect of industrial injuries matters. Since November 3, 2008, and as a result of the Tribunals, Courts and Enforcement Act 2007, the FTT Social Entitlement Chamber has assumed these appellate functions.

The key point from all this for industrial injuries matters is that the historic distinction between medical issues and non-medical issues – previously crucial as demarcating the respective jurisdictions of MATs (col.1 of the Schedule) and SSATs (col.2 of the Schedule) – is no longer relevant. Consequently, issues relating to the interpretation and application of any of the words in the Schedule, whether in col.1 or 2, are now within the remit of the FTT. Both the FTT and the Upper Tribunal now have jurisdiction over both medical and non-medical matters. So, an Upper Tribunal judge, allowing an appeal on a point of law, can now take his or her own decision on the facts rather than remitting it to another tribunal. Commissioner Williams did so in *CI/1307/1999* giving a staged assessment of disablement in respect of post traumatic stress disorder. The decision considers the medical aspects of the claimant's case found to be an industrial accident in *CI/15589/1996*, noted in the annotation to "accident" to SSCBA 1992, s.94(1). In paras 15–17, Commissioner Williams distinguished "diagnosis" and "disablement" decisions. The former is essentially "a question of medical expertise". A "disablement" decision in contrast is not dissimilar to the tasks performed by judges in assessing common law damages or in applying the tariff of the Criminal Injuries Compensation Authority. In assessing disablement for industrial injuries benefits, however, that Criminal Injuries tariff is not an appropriate yardstick. Instead, supplementing SSCBA 1992 s.103 and Sch.6, regard should be had also to reg.11 and Sch.2 to the General Benefit Regulations, above. Nonetheless, the import of para.37 of the decision is that exercise of the Commissioner's (and now the Upper Tribunal's) power to decide on the facts, rather than remitting to another tribunal, may well be rare. Even so, the decision contrasts markedly with the traditional view of such matters as ones for medical rather than legal judgment (see, for example, Commissioner Howell in *CI/636/93*). Note that the suitability of cross-reference to Sch.2 was also advocated in *R(I) 5/95*, where Commissioner Rowland stated that "assessment of disablement should be brought into line with those prescribed in the Schedule", with assessment also reflecting any intermittent or episodic character of the disablement (para.16).

In *R(I) 4/96*, Commissioner Goodman makes the important point that the date of onset of a prescribed disease for a particular claimant and the date from which payment of disablement benefit can be paid on or after the disease has been prescribed (added to the Schedule), are not necessarily coincidental. So where prescribed disease D12 (miner's bronchitis etc.) was added from September 13, 1993, disablement benefit was only payable from that date, despite the fact that the date of onset (the date from which the claimant suffered from it) was much earlier. Unless the contrary is clearly indicated in the particular prescription (and it was not here), the insertion into the Schedule of a new prescribed disease is not retrospective so as to enable the payment of disablement benefit (subject to showing good cause for delay in claiming) from the date of onset.

It is worth noting that the significance of some of the less serious prescribed diseases has been diminished by the abolition of injury benefit and the subsequent restrictions placed upon disablement benefit by the raising of the qualifying level to 14 per cent. Now, unless the disease is serious enough to bring an assessment of 14 per cent or more or, if the assessment is 1 per cent or more, lasts more than the ninety days which is the waiting period for reduced earnings allowance (see SSCBA 1992, Sch.7, para.11, above), the claimant will rely on incapacity benefits rather than an industrial benefit. (Different provision is made for claimants suffering from pneumoconiosis, byssinosis, or diffuse mesothelioma, where title to disablement benefit is established on an assessment of 1 per cent or more, Prescribed Diseases Regulations, reg.20, above.)

The occupations in respect of which the diseases are prescribed are commonly defined by prefacing the cause of the disease with the words "Any occupation involving". The occupations in the Schedule will be considered separately, as appropriate, but the general phrase is applicable to most of the diseases and occupations and is dealt with first.

10.140 *Any occupation involving:* The word "occupation" is not a term of art, it merely connotes the activities of an employed earner under his contract of employment (*R(I) 3/78*). Once some involvement with the prescribed cause of the disease, as a result of employment, has been established, the employment is likely to be accepted as giving rise to entitlement (*R(I) 4/53*) unless the involvement is so trivial or negligible that it can be discounted (*R(I) 8/57*). It is still important for the decision-maker or tribunal to consider carefully whether the occupation is prescribed for the disease—the fact that there is an outbreak of a prescribed disease in one factory is irrelevant to the question of whether the disease is prescribed for a particular employee or group of employees in the factory (*R(I) 2/77*). It is not the frequency of the disease which is significant, but the description of the occupation for which it is prescribed.

Although a claim for disablement benefit may be described as being in respect of a particular disease, there is nothing in the legislation to suggest that a separate claim has to be made in respect of each disease. Accordingly, if a tribunal find that a claimant is not suffering from the prescribed disease in respect of which he claimed but may be suffering from another prescribed disease, they should make a finding in respect of that other disease (*R(I) 6/94*). That may require an adjournment unless the parties are content for the new issue to be considered straightaway. It does not matter whether the diagnosis question is determined before or after the Secretary of State has decided whether the disease is prescribed in relation to the claimant (*CI/13664/96*). The more convenient course should be followed.

The proper approach to interpretation of the definitions of the prescribed occupations: In *Secretary of State for Social Security v Davies* (reported as part of *R(I) 2/01*, and noted further in the commentary on PD A11 [vibration white finger]), the Court of Appeal thought that, given the purpose of this compensation scheme, it would be wrong to give the words too narrow a definition (per Rix L.J. [para.23], Mummery L.J. expressly concurring [para. 36]). In para.35 of that case, Mummery L.J. quoted with approval from Commissioner Levenson in the decision under appeal: **10.141**

> "The Industrial Injuries Disablement Benefits Scheme was designed to compensate workers for industrial injuries and for contracting prescribed diseases, and the definitions of prescribed occupation should not be artificially narrowed. I do not see why a person doing essentially the same job in a city as is being done by a person in a forest should be denied that compensation" (*CI/729/1998*, para.15).

This approach is not to be confined to its specific context (*CI/2668/2002*, per Commissioner Williams).

Many cases make it clear that one can look for guidance to the relevant report of the IIAC recommending prescription (*Davies*; *R(I) 2/01*; *R(I) 4/99*; *R(I) 3/97*; *R(I) 3/95; R(I) 2/85; R(I) 5/83; R(I) 11/81(T); R(I) 15/75(T); CI/1884/2004; CI/2668/2002; CI/3261/2000; CI/808/95; CI/22/91)*. The reports can be used to help resolve ambiguity or problems with the drafting of regulations, but, naturally, what each decision takes from the exercise varies.

The focus should be on the work the claimant does (did) rather than on the contractual obligation to do it (*R(I) 2/79(T)*); on the activity of the employee, rather than the generic description of the employer's activity(ies) (*CI/2668/2002*, para.16); on what the claimant does rather than on how the job is labelled (*CI/2668/2002*, para.18).

As Judge Wikeley stressed in *DM v SSWP (II)* [2010] UKUT 318 (AAC), while the statutory words of prescription are always the starting point, a purposive approach had to be taken to them. "Any occupation involving" is not "a term of art" but requires a focus on the work activities performed rather than on the precise terms of the contract of employment ("the actual working test"), a proposition supported by *Davies*, above: *R(I) 2/79(T)* and *R(I) 3/78*.

III. Prescribed Diseases: Category A: Conditions due to physical agents

A1 (Leukaemia (other than chronic lymphatic leukaemia) or cancer of the bone, female breast, testis or thyroid)

PD A1 was first reformulated in 2000, subject to transitional provisions in reg.7(2) and (3) of the Social Security (Industrial Injuries) (Prescribed Diseases) Amendment Regulations 2000 (SI 2000/1588). In that formulation PD A1 only covered leukaemia or female breast cancer and cancer of the bone, testis or thyroid. **10.142**

However, the terms of prescription were extended with effect from March 30, 2017, so as to cover leukaemia or primary cancer of the bone, bladder, breast, colon, liver, lung, ovary, stomach, testis or thyroid (Social Security (Industrial Injuries) (Prescribed Diseases) Amendment Regulations 2017 (SI 2017/232) reg.3). The addition of the six further cancers for which benefit should be payable under PD A1 follows the recommendation by IIAC (see IIAC, *Cancers due to ionising radiation*, Cm 9208, February 2016). IIAC's other proposals were also accepted, namely that the prescription of breast cancer be extended to men, and that the terms of prescription be simplified to read "Any occupation involving: Exposure to ionising radiation where the dose is sufficient to double the risk of the occurrence of the condition".

A2 (Cataract)

10.143 The revision of PD A2 is subject to the same transitional provision noted under PD A1, above.

A4 (Task-specific focal dystonia)

10.144 Until April 6, 2007, the terms of prescription referred to "Hand or forearm cramp—writer's cramp". From that date, it referred to "Task-specific focal dystonia". This was recommended as valuable updating and clarification by the IIAC in its report *Completion of the review of the scheduled list of prescribed diseases*, Cm 7003 (January 2007), para.28, referring back to its 2006 report on *Work Related Upper Limb Disorders*, Cm. 6868 (July 2006), para.78.

In *SSWP v CS (II)* [2010] UKUT 198 (AAC); [2011] AACR 5, Judge Howell held that "task-specific focal dystonia" was limited to conditions affecting the hard and forearm, as those Reports indicated, and so did not cover the work-related cervical dystonia from which the claimant suffered. The wording of the current terms of prescription (effective March 30, 2012) makes that clear beyond doubt.

The occupation must involve *prolonged* periods of handwriting, etc. What amounts to prolonged periods must be a matter of fact for the Secretary of State/ tribunal, but remember to look at the nature of the job in assessing whether it displays the requisite characteristics. In *R(I) 3/97*, Commissioner Rice held that the words "other repetitive movements of the hand or arm" in A4 are to be read *ejusdem generis* (as of the same kind or nature) with "handwriting" and "typing", not at large to include repetitive movements of whatever kind and not so as to "be available at large to all those engaged in repetitive work" (para.10). So that in that case the tribunal did not err in law in finding that it did not cover the appellant analytical chemist whose laboratory bench work primarily involved the filtration and titration of chemicals. The tribunal had found that while the finger, hand and wrist movements were repetitive and carried out over a prolonged period they did not have the intensity or frequency comparable to handwriting or typing.

In *CI/349/2001*, Commissioner Angus considered the case of a cleaner who spent

> "a significant part of her working day in prolonged periods of handling the large Swiffer and the floor buffer, each involving repetitive movements of her wrists, and in prolonged periods of cleaning tables involving repetitive movements of the wrists and hands. There is also other cleaning and maintenance work such as cleaning glue off the sinks and repairs to the fabric of the school buildings which involve her in repetitive movements of the arm, wrist or hand. The A4 prescription does not mention movements of the wrist but, as the wrist is the joint between the arm and the hand, movement of the wrist involves the movement of either the hand or the arm in relation to the other. The question is whether the movements of her fingers, hands or arms which the claimant makes in the course of those prolonged periods of activity amount to 'other repetitive movements of the fingers, hand or arm' within the meaning of the prescription in the Schedule to the Regulations" (para.24).

The Commissioner decided that her occupation was not one prescribed under A4, but reached his conclusion

> "for slightly different reasons from those given by the tribunal and by the author of *R(I) 3/97*. I respectfully agree with the Commissioner who decided that the *ejusdem generis* rule is an aid to the interpretation of the Schedule 1 prescription of the occupation relevant to A4. However, apart from their involving repetitive movements of the fingers, hand or arm, there is little in common between the activities of handwriting and typing which is apparent from the face of the prescription. Because they are interpreting a regulation based code of law Commissioners and, I think tribunals, have always been entitled to go behind the text of the regulations and examine the background papers to ascertain what is the purpose of any particular provision which is under consideration. The Commissioner who decided *R(I) 3/97* looked at the report by the Industrial Injuries Advisory Council which considered the need to replace the prescriptions of telegraphist's cramp, writer's cramp and twister's cramp, which were prescribed in paragraphs 28, 29 and 30 of Schedule 1 to the 1947 Industrial Injuries and Prescribed Diseases Regulations, and the relevant occupations with one prescribed disease and relevant occupation which would cover all those who suffered from hand and arm cramps as a result of working in employments involving the use of the fingers, hands or arms. The Commissioner quoted most of paragraph 32 and all of paragraph 33 of the Committee's report in which two paragraphs the need for a new prescription which would embrace the three cramps and relevant occupations which were then prescribed as well as the cramps experienced by those engaged in the occupations involving the use of keyboards which were then proliferating. He did not quote the first sentence of paragraph 32 which identifies the characteristic which is common to all the occupations which the Committee had in mind. That sentence is as follows:—
>
> > 'These diseases are characterised by spasm or other disordered action of muscles used in the performance of duties involving rapid and finely controlled movements of the hand of a repetitive nature.'
>
> Therefore, the activity which the Committee had in mind when it devised the current prescription of the occupation relevant to A4 is movement of the hands and arms which are approximately as rapid, as finely controlled and as repetitive as the movements employed by somebody operating a typewriter or writing by hand. I do not think that there is any likelihood of the hand and wrist movements described by the claimant having the degree of rapidity, fineness of control and repetitiveness of the hand movements of a typist or somebody writing with a pen or a pencil. I take Mr Crawford's point that the twister in the textile industry would not be repairing broken yarns with the degree of repetitiveness with which a typist would be striking the keys of a typewriter but on a machine which could have as many as 70 pairs of bobbins the breaks in the yarn would be fairly frequent and I have no doubt that as the twister would be constrained to keep the pauses in the winding to a minimum the hand movements employed to repair the breaks, in particular the movements of the thumb and forefinger, would be very rapid and, to make effective joins, would be very finely controlled". (para.25).

A5 (subcutaneous cellulitis of the hand), A6 (bursitis or subcutaneous cellulitis (knee)), A7 (bursitis or subcutaneous cellulitis (elbow))

Until April 6, 2007, the terms of prescription for these referred in brackets respectively to "Beat hand", "Beat knee" and "Beat elbow". From that date, those terms were deleted on the recommendation of the IIAC as "outdated"; the term "used to denote repeated trauma at work, is not widely used or understood in modern clinical practice, being a historical description confined to the field of occupational **10.145** medicine" (see *Completion of the review of the scheduled list of prescribed diseases*, Cm 7003 (January 2007), para.28, referring back to its 2006 report on *Work Related Upper Limb Disorders*, Cm. 6868 (July 2006), para.78).

Refer back to the definition of "an occupation involving" and note that manual labour of the type described need only be one of the incidents of the prescribed occupation. Hence, the category of jobs in which manual labour is incidental includes not only those which require "muscle", but also those where some physical or bodily work is required. Note also that the pressure on the hand, knee or elbow need only be prolonged *or* severe. These three diseases are good examples of the scheme taking account of the development of an injury by process over a period which would prevent the claimant from showing that it had been caused by accident, but compare *R(I) 11/74*. See also *R(I) 78/54* and *R(I) 60/51*. In *R(I) 5/98*, dealing with A6 (Beat knee), Commissioner Rice held that the prescribed occupation is to be interpreted in the context of the disease covered. Thus it covers not any kind of friction or pressure, but only the type of friction or pressure that causes beat knee. A medical report before him identified the key feature of beat knee as

> "direct pressure and/or friction to the knee and immediate vicinity, for example just above or below the knee. This pressure or friction must be applied directly to the skin to cause cellulitis, or directly to the skin overlying the bursa" (para.7).

The anatomical parts affected are superficial, not within the knee joint itself (para.8). In this case, the damage to the claimant's knee through the consistent use of the brake pedal when operating his crane did not result in that sort of friction or pressure; the process involved repeated flexing and extending of the knee, with most of the action taking place at the ankle joint (*ibid*). Similarly in *CI/268/95* (noted in (1997) 4 J.S.S.L. D88). Commissioner Hoolahan held the tribunal decision erroneous in law: in looking at whether the claimant had been involved in any occupation within the A7 prescription (Beat elbow), it had failed to consider whether her work (as a cleaner in a social club) involved severe or prolonged "external" friction or pressure (para.6).

A8 (tenosynovitis)

10.146 For useful evidence from the medical adviser to the DWP (Dr Reed) on PD A8 (tenosynovitis), see the Sch. to *CI/3745/2006*.

A10 (Occupational deafness)

10.147 The revision from September 22, 2003 of the occupations in respect of which occupational deafness is prescribed, based largely on the IIAC Report on the prescription of occupational deafness (Cm 5672, November 2002), means that this commentary is now relevant only to those whose claim for disablement based on occupational deafness was made, or treated as made, on or after that date. See further IIAC's Position Paper no.38, *Noise, occupational deafness and Industrial Injuries Disablement Benefit* (September 2017).

For claims made, or treated as made, before September 22, 2003, please see the commentary in the 2003 edition of this volume, as updated by the relevant pages of the Supplement 2003/2004.

In PD A10 occupational deafness is defined as

> "Sensorineural hearing loss amounting to at least 50dB in each ear, being the average of hearing losses at 1, 2 and 3 kHz frequencies, and being due in the case of at least one ear to occupational noise."

CI/4567/1999 (now reported as *R(I)6/02*) contains useful material on a variety of tests measuring hearing loss.

In *CI/2012/2000*, Commissioner Jacobs said, rightly, that *CI/4567/1999* (now reported as *R(I)6/02*) neither is, nor purports to be, authority that ERA (evoked response audiometry), a form of assessment of hearing loss, is always to be preferred to PTA (pure tone audiometry), another form of assessment of hearing loss (para.16).

ERA "is a record of a person's brain activity in response to sound" (para.12), which is not dependent on the claimant to acknowledge that sound has been heard (and therefore not contingent on his honesty). However, the claimant's behaviour can affect other brain activity and render it more difficult to interpret the results (para.14). Adults are usually tested by cortical or slow vertex ERA. Young children are usually tested by another type, brainstem ERA so that the results are not affected by the anaesthetic or sedative administered to keep the child quiet and still during the test process (para.15).

PTA is cheap and fairly easy to administer. It is the starting point for all assessments by tribunals and the Secretary of State, but depends upon the claimant acknowledging when a sound (produced at different levels by the PTA equipment) has been heard (para.10).

The Commissioner advances the following approach for tribunals: 10.148

> "a tribunal . . . has to weigh the evidence as a whole in order to determine the level of the claimant's sensorineural hearing loss. There is no rule that one type of evidence is always to be preferred to another. The evidence must be considered as a whole. The tribunal may conclude that one type of evidence is preferable to another, but that must be a judgment reached after considering the merits of all the evidence" (para.16).

There was in this case no error of law in the tribunal refusing to order, at public expense, brainstem ERA.

In *CI/1/2002*, without citing Commissioner Jacobs's decision in *CI/2012/2000*, like him Commissioner Williams also concludes that *CI/4567/1999* (now reported as *R(I)6/02*) is not authority that CERA (cortical evoked response audiogram) is always to be preferred to PTA (pure tone audiometry). Noting that Prescribed Diseases Regulations, reg.34 gives precise details about testing and assessment but not the method of testing, Commissioner Williams stated that the matter is one for the experts on the tribunal using their expertise to decide. In the decision under appeal before him, the tribunal had relied on that expertise to conclude that in that case CERA would not be more reliable than PTA. However, the Commissioner noted that declining to order a CERA test on the basis of cost might be a denial of a fair hearing under the HRA 1998/ECHR.

Useful information and guidance—which cannot be binding on decision makers, tribunals or the Upper Tribunal—on both PTA and CERA can be found in the IIAC Report on the prescription of occupational deafness (Cm 5672, November 2002). See para.117 (audiometric testing) and App.6 (guidance on obtaining cortical evoked response audiometry). The IIAC recommended that PTA should be retained as the most appropriate routine assessment method for use in the benefit scheme. Where testing is not repeatable, or response to conversational voice seems better or worse than the audiogram would suggest, use of CERA should be considered. In any event, the IIAC recommended that methods of testing should be kept under review.

Tribunals can have regard to the Department's guidelines and its rather rough and ready conversational voice testing in its *Industrial Injuries Handbook for Adjudicating Medical Authorities*, so long as it was remembered that this was guidance and not statutorily prescribed. The Tables in the Handbook could be taken on board but only as part of a proper disablement assessment (*CI/5029/2002*, per Commissioner Fellner). 10.149

The wide range of occupations for which this disease is prescribed led to a significant number of Commissioners' decisions on the interpretation of the various parts of the Schedule relating to the disease. All, however, can only be authoritative today insofar as they deal with equivalent wording.

The expression which prefaces the reformulated occupations in column (2), *"wholly or mainly in the immediate vicinity of,"* was considered in *R(I)2/85*. That decision held that it was not necessary that the claimant should spend the majority of his time near the specified tools whilst they are in use, and that it was sufficient that the tools were in use more than a negligible amount whilst he was in the vicinity. But the formulation now requires work wholly or mainly in the immediate vicinity *of the use of* a specified tool or piece of equipment, removing the authority of that statement. Note also *CI/226/91* (para.7), citing *Fawcett Properties v Buckingham CC* [1961] A.C. 636 at 669 where Lord Morton said that mainly "probably means more than half". In *R(I)7/76* it was held that whether the claimant was in the vicinity should be determined by the distance from him to the specified tools, taking into account walls, screens etc., but not measuring the level of residual noise at the claimant's workplace. An employee working in an exceptionally noisy factory may, therefore, be exposed to far greater noise than is acceptable but not entitled to benefit because he is not working near enough to the machines making the noise—

> "Whether an occupation involves work in the immediate vicinity of the designated plant is a question of fact in each case. I think it is to be answered first by ascertaining the locations, that is to say the area within which the designated plants (which from their nature cover considerable areas) are situated, and the area of the claimant's activities. The question whether the area of work is in the immediate vicinity of the plant then depends in my opinion on the weight to be given to the particular circumstances. The distance at which one area lies from the other may itself be decisive of the question. A second factor may be the physical separation of one area from the other because of intervening buildings . . . A further factor, as here . . . may be the presence of walls and screening, substantially dividing, enclosing or demarking the two areas lying at a distance apart, though under the same factory roof."

See also *R(I)8/85* where the distance factor was held to be significant. In *CI/245/1991*, Commissioner Goodman stated that the notion of "working in the immediate vicinity" of percussive tools involved consideration of the physical proximity to the use of such tools and not just the noise level, so that the claimant's non-use of ear muffs or protectors supplied by his employer was legally irrelevant to the issue. The Commissioner concluded that the percussive tools were in constant and daily use and that the claimant worked in the immediate vicinity in his job as storeman, his store being separated from that work area only by a wire mesh (paras 10–13).

10.150 The original (see above) specified occupations were, broadly speaking, foundries, shipyards and mines and quarries. Whilst the occupations have been changed and widened, the Schedule still refers in paras A10(a) and (b) to the use of, or work wholly or mainly in the immediate vicinity of the use of, a pneumatic percussive tool. The nature of such a tool has been considered in *R(I)5/76* (an "impact wrench" or "screwing up machine"); *R(I)8/76* (a computer-controlled burning and marking machine); *R(I)1/80* (a rivet gun); *R(I)3/80* (upright pedestal grinder); *R(I)/13/80* (machine mounted vertical spindle surface grinder); *R(I)6/83* (press set into the ground and operating on compressed air). Whether a particular tool is pneumatic is a question of fact, and it is necessary to look at the essential nature of the tool and determine its driving force (*R(I)6/83*). But what constitutes a "tool"? The general trend of decisions has been to give the word "tool" a more technical meaning and, as a result, include some machines in the category of tools. A printing press, though pneumatic and percussive was held not to be a "tool" in *CI/17/93*. The test for "tool" was there said to be whether the machine now alleged to be a "tool" is now used to carry out a task traditionally carried out by what everyone would recognise as a hand-held tool. If there is no "recognisable previous identity as a hand-held tool" it is a machine and not a "tool" (*CI/17/93*, para.3. citing *R(I)6/83*, para.6). In *Appleby v CAO* (reported as *R(I)5/99*, judgment of June 29, 1999), the Court of Appeal stated that while the test propounded by Commissioner Sanders in *CI/17/93* was "useful", it was not "an exclusive test", particularly as regards new processes where the existence of a sufficiently manual input may enable the alleged tool to qualify. A useful starting point is whether the implement in question is classified in the trade or industry as a machine tool.

In *Appleby*, the Court held the electrodes on the spot welding machine qualified as pneumatic, percussive tools; they banged the metal to be welded to ensure a tight fit before emitting the necessary electrical charge, and were, therefore, the mechanical equivalent of the hand held hammer used in the past when welding was effected by hammering together two pieces of preheated metal. The Court, obiter, was provisionally of the opinion that the spot welding machine had sufficient manual input to qualify as a "tool".

The number of paras has been reduced from 23 to 11, and occupations once in separate paras have been regrouped and reworded to simplify matters to aid understanding and administration (IIAC Report, para.105, and App.4). The revision, however, has added occupations but not removed any previously prescribed, since the IIAC "had no evidence that any of the occupations and processes already prescribed have disappeared, ceased to be a hazard to hearing, or fundamentally altered to the extent that their removal from the list would be appropriate" (para.95).

Paragraph (a): "metal founding or forging industries": the IIAC saw no need to clarify "forging", considering it an understandable term with a definite meaning in industry (para. 101). The prescription covers the use of powered grinding tools on metal, but not hand-powered ones. On "tool" and "pneumatic percussive tool", see the discussion preceding coverage of this particular para. As regards "metal", note that despite common parlance referring to a metalled road, reg.1(2) provides that "metal" for the purposes of disease A10, does not include stone, concrete, aggregate or similar substances for use in road or railway construction. However in *CI/37/1988* the Commissioner accepted that "on metal" could include the use of pneumatic drills to break up reinforced concrete where the drill would from time to time strike the metal reinforcing rods. But in *CI/540/1994*, where the momentary or occasional contact with a metal reinforcing rod was minimal, the claim was unsuccessful. The ruling in *CI/540/1994* was held in *CI/13238/1996* to apply in respect of noise from drills striking metal reinforcing rods in concrete road structures in a claim by a foreman asphalter. 10.151

Note that the terms "foundry", "skid transfer bank" and "knock out and shake out grid" are each specifically defined in reg.1(2), above.

The term "metal nails" has a wider meaning than ordinary nails driven with a hammer; it can include any piece of wire or metal used for holding things together (*R(I)5/83*). In *CI/808/95*, Commissioner Mesher agreed

> "with the view expressed by the Commissioner in para.9 of *R(I)5/83*, supported by reference in that case to the report of the Industrial Injuries Advisory Council, that the prescription in paragraph A10(f) [the equivalent of A10(a) formulation 'machine to cut or shape or clean metal nails'] relates to the process of making nails. Thus the crucial question is whether what results from the operation of the claimant's machine can be called a nail in the extended sense described by the Commissioner in *R(I)5/83* [a piece of wire or metal used for holding things together]. One must ask what the product is used for. I conclude that its use in the manufacture of tyres is such that it cannot be called a nail. It does not hold things together in the way in which a nail or rivet holds things together. It does not hold one part of the tyre to another part of the tyre by connecting the two together." (para.9, words in square brackets added.)

The rubber-coated wire cut by the claimant's machine was used to reinforce the rubber moulding of the tyre.

There was brief consideration in *CI/246/1988* of the features of plasma spray gun to spray molten metal, but unfortunately the matter was not pursued very far since the materials deposited by the gun in the case were silica and quartz, neither of which is a metal.

Paragraph (b): On "pneumatic percussive tool", see the discussion preceding commentary on para (a). 10.152

"Underground" means properly underground, with an earth ceiling, and does not include a deep trench which is open to the air, even though the drilling operation is going on below ground level (*R(I)4/84*). It means "underneath the natural surface of the earth". It did not therefore embrace the claimant who was not but may have been working on the floor or below floor level in a prepared building, not under a natural roof (*CI/550/89*, para.6). A tunnel like the Mersey Tunnel is properly encompassed by the term "underground", although the inclusion in para.(b) of "for tunnelling in civil engineering works" in any event provides protection (*CI/13238/1996*).

In *CI/550/89*, Commissioner Heald decided, referring indirectly to *CI/308/1989* (reported as *R(I)2/92*, noted below) on the meaning of "wood", that "rock" in sub-para. (c) means "rock in its natural state . . . and not in the form of a cement aggregate, at which stage the material which was originally rock, no doubt, had changed its nature and formed part of the cement mix." (para.5). Whether the same is true of "stone", so as to not to cover solid products (e.g. paving slabs, bricks or blocks) made from reconstituted crushed or powdered stone is unclear. The inclusion of new para.(c) will help some of those who work cutting concrete masonry blocks (e.g. builders).

10.153 *Paragraph (c)*: none of the terms in this prescription is defined. Nor does there appear to be any case law on its previous partial manifestation as PD A10(q). Its expansion will help some of those who work cutting concrete masonry blocks (e.g. builders).

10.154 *Paragraph (d)*: This covers the use of machines in the manufacture of textiles. This includes "weaving", but the para is not confined to "weaving".

On "weaving", *CSI/65/94* applying *R(I)13/81* was authority that deafness from working with noisy knitting machines does not come within A10(d) because "knitting" is not "weaving". Commissioner Mitchell reached his decision "with regret" and like the Commissioner in *R(I)13/81* expressed the hope that an anomaly might be rectified by amending the paragraph, since the evidence in the case showed that the knitting machines at the claimant's place of work were just as noisy as weaving machines. This has now been done as regards the process of "high speed false twisting of fibres" after the IIAC recommending it in its 2002 Report which largely formed the basis for these revised prescriptions. The IIAC accepted that there was enough evidence that high speed false twisting is a process that can take place prior to both knitting and weaving, and one which produces yarn for both of these areas of fabric manufacture.

In *CI/2879/1995*, Commissioner Goodman gave some consideration to the phrase "the high speed false twisting of fibres". He set aside the tribunal decision as erroneous in law on the basis that they had failed to consider whether the claimant's occupation from May 6, 1987 to August 12, 1988 (one bringing her within a five-year period prior to the 1994 claim) met the description. But, approving an argument founded on para.12 of *R(I)13/81*, he held that the tribunal was entitled to rely on a definition from a research fellow in a University Department of Textile Industries in conjunction with factual information supplied by the employer on the basis that where words are used in legislation with reference to particular trades or businesses and have a particular meaning within that trade or business, the words in the legislation should be construed in the light of that meaning (para.17). The material before the tribunal and letters before the Commissioner from an officer in the Health and Safety Executive and from another expert in the same University Department all confirmed that "false twisting", a technique rather than a process, involved machines operating at speeds in revolutions per minute varying according to whether dealing with staple yarns (a few tens of thousands per minute) or filament yarns (850,000 per minute in 1968, up to 7 million per minute today). Some suggested "false twisting" was limited to synthetic yarns. But, in setting out that material and in remitting the matter back to the tribunal because factual "loose ends" precluded him giving the decision, Commissioner Goodman stressed that the prescription "high speed" is not expressed as being a minimum of revolutions a minute, nor is the word "fibres in any way qualified to limit it to artificial fibres" (para.18). The prescription now explicitly covers man-made and natural fibres, and includes mineral fibres.

The prescription also covers the "mechanical cleaning of bobbins". It was reworded from the former prescription in the old PD A10(e), "mechanical bobbin cleaning" to clarify that what is prescribed is the mechanical cleaning of bobbins, rather than the cleaning of mechanical bobbins (IIAC, Cm 5672, 2002, para. 103)

Paragraph (e): This covers various machines and saws used to work with wood—In *R(I)2/92* Commissioner Rice considered the meaning of "wood" in a previous occupational prescription in respect of occupational deafness. The claimant had worked in the newspaper print industry near machines cutting newsprint. The Commissioner supported the view of the dissenting chairman in the tribunal that this particular prescribed occupation "refers to wood in [the] accepted sense of the word, not to a material of which wood may be a constituent part. The prescribed occupation . . . clearly refers to working of wood or similar material such as chipboard, and not to the newsprint industry." Commissioner Rice stated that although "newsprint is derived from wood, it is not the same as wood. It has undergone a metamorphosis, and in its changed form as newsprint it has become an entirely different material. It follows that the claimant cannot satisfy the relevant statutory requirements," (para.7). *R(I)2/92* (then *CI/309/1989*) was approved and applied in *CI/175/90* (noted below, notes to D7). It was also followed in *CI/43/92*, where Commissioner Rice held that "logs of toilet paper and kitchen paper" had, like newsprint, undergone a metamorphosis and could not be regarded as "wood," (para.6). **10.155**

The rewording of the prescription to cover the use of specific machines or saws on wood removes the need to argue over issues such as the meaning of "forestry", which the IIAC Report saw as in need of clarification (paras.99, 100). It recommended that prescription cover the *regular* use of chainsaws. Note that this was not carried into the prescription.

The prescription has been reworded on HSE advice to cover all circular sawing machines, including those operated by moving the blade towards the material to be cut (para.104).

Paragraph (f): Removal of references to "water-jetting industry" (see *CI/2286/2002* and *CI/5331/2002*) helps clarify the scope of the prescription which is now confined (i) to the use of a jet of water (or a mixture of water and abrasive) above a specified pressure of 680 bar (10,000 psi)(much higher than the "at least 3000 psi" formulation used by the Secretary of State to denote "high pressure" in the previous prescription (see *CI/5331/2002*, paras 2 and 18), and (ii) to jet channelling process to burn stone in a quarry. The IIAC was concerned in its proposed revision to clarify that it intended to include only those water-jetting processes in which high pressure was used on a commercial basis, and where an employee would be put at regular and frequent risk of exposure to high levels of noise likely to damage hearing (para.97). In setting the 10,000 psi level evidence was taken from HSE experts on the level of pressure likely to be hazardous to hearing and produce disablement (para.98). **10.156**

Paragraph (g): this covers a machine in a ship's engine room or gas turbine, provided that it use covers the specified testing. The meaning of "ship's engine room" was considered in *R(I)2/97* where the Commissioner saw it as "clearly limited to engine rooms on ships, and does not extend to engine rooms on land, regardless of the nature of the engines located there". So, in that case, the fact that the claimant worked in an engine room providing power to a building and the engines in the room were of a type that could be used to power ships, was immaterial. So was the fact that had he been on a ship and rendered deaf by working with the self-same engines, his claim would have succeeded; the occupation has to be a prescribed one (*ibid.*, paragraph11). **10.157**

The Commissioner in so deciding on the appropriate interpretation, made use of a report on Occupational Deafness by the Industrial Injuries Advisory Council. In *CSI/248/2003*, Commissioner Parker considered the meaning of "ship". After reviewing a number of statutory definitions and case law from a variety of legal subject areas, she accepted:

> "for the present purpose the value of generally applying the Merchant Shipping Act [1995] definition of a ship (' "ship" includes every description of vessel used in navigation') and how that definition was interpreted in *Perks* [a tax case, a decision of the Court of Appeal found at [2001] EWCA Civ 1228]
>
> The fact finding tribunal must therefore ask itself what is the design and capability of any particular structure and whether 'navigation' in the sense of 'movement across water' (and not requiring 'conveying persons and cargo from place to place') *is a significant part of the function of the structure in question*. The significance of the navigation is an issue of degree on the facts of a particular case and can be overturned by an appellate court only if the conclusions are perverse.
>
> As Carnwath J. noted in *Perks*, the test has enabled the courts to include structures of very specialised kinds within the scope of the definition of 'ship', and to exclude cases where it was considered that the function of 'moving across the seas' was minimal or non-existent" (paras 57—59).

The tribunal to which the case was remitted

> "having first found on what type of structures, and when, the claimant worked during the relevant period, must then consider with respect to each whether 'movement across water' was a significant part of its particular function. If the claimant worked only on the North Alwyn, and it is, as the Secretary of State suggests, a huge, fixed platform once set up in its location, it must be doubtful if this would constitute a ship. However, as always, everything depends on the facts found having regard to the evidence" (para.65).

See also *CSI/524/1999*, where the rig had propellers to enable it to move and to turn in bad weather. But, even if the rig at issue in *CSI/248/2003* were a "ship", the question remained whether the claimant, who drove a crane on the rig, worked in the ship's engine room. The Commissioner thought that:

> "as a ship is not inevitably self-propelled, then, having regard to the underlying purpose for prescribing the occupation set out in paragraph A(10), it seems inevitable that to constitute a ship's engine room rather than *any* engine room, the engine room in question must provide power *for the ship*. It is insufficient that a claimant works in an engine room, even if integrated with the ship, where the engine of the structure on which he works provides power to that particular structure only, rather than to the ship.
>
> So the question here is whether the claimant works in an engine room of a crane, such a crane being located on a ship, which in no substantial way differs from the engine room of a land crane; alternatively, does his engine room on the crane provide power beyond the crane and for the ship?" (paras 74, 75).

The remainder of the prescription gives aid and comfort to others who work with gas turbines for various specified forms of engine testing.

10.158 *Paragraph (h)*: This applies to machines used for certain specified matters in the manufacure of glass containers and hollow war. *R(I)4/99* remains authority for the proposition that the whole of the prescription is confined to glass manufacture. In that case, considering similar wording in para.(w) of the then prescription, the claimant was a clay worker in the pottery industry. He operated a "forming machine, used in the manufacture of ceramic (pottery) hollow ware, but not glass hollow ware" (para.4). The Commissioner rejected the argument of the claimant's representative that "hollow ware" was not confined to glass, but included metal and ceramics. Taking account of the Industrial Injuries Advisory Council Report [Cm.

817 (1994)], which had led to the introduction of para.(w)) in order to interpret ambiguous wording in the legislative prescription, Commissioner Goodman came to the conclusion that the:

> "prescription is . . . confined to glass manufacture. The words, '. . . forming machines used in the manufacture of glass containers or hollow ware' do in my view read in such a way that the adjective 'glass' applies not only to 'containers' but also to 'hollow ware'. That is the natural meaning of the sentence and it also coincides with the fact that the rest of sub-paragraphs (i) and (ii) and (iii) of paragraph (w) are all clearly confined to the manufacture of various kinds of glass (save 'mineral wool' in sub-paragraph (ii)). The report of the Advisory Council leads to the same conclusion and I am entitled to look at its contents in view of the ambiguity introduced in [sub-] paragraph (i) of paragraph (w) by the use of the word 'or' between 'glass containers' and 'hollow ware'. Overall, therefore, I am satisfied that the tribunal arrived at the correct decision and that the prescribed occupation in paragraph (w) of Paragraph A10 is not intended to apply to any kind of hollow ware except that made of glass. I must therefore dismiss the claimant's appeal accordingly" (para.13).

Paragraph (k): this was recommended for prescription since evidence from the HSE supported the view that the level of exposure to noise in this situation was at least as high as in the occupations already prescribed (IIAC Report, Cm 5672, 2002, para. 94) Note that cases might also fit (as single incidents or small series of incidents producing deafness) as accidents within SSCBA 1992, s. 94(1). See further *CI/5029/2002* on assessment of disablement in respect of deafness arising from accident in connection with police firearms training. **10.159**

Paragraph (l): this was recommended for prescription since evidence from the HSE supported the view that the level of exposure to noise in this situation was at least as high as in the occupations already prescribed (IIAC Report, Cm 5672, 2002, para.94) **10.160**

A11 (Vibration white finger)

In *R(I) 2/95*, the form of prescription of prescribed disease A11 was upheld as *intra vires*. **10.161**

In *R(I) 3/02*, Commissioner Jacobs noted that the legal definition of vibration white finger in referring only to "blanching" is narrower than the medical one, which also takes on board sensory effects. He held that the legal definition only restricted those cases of vibration white finger that are to be subject to an assessment of disablement for purposes of disablement benefit. However, once a case thus comes within that definition because of blanching, when it comes to the loss of faculty causing the claimant's disabilities it is proper then to look to the broader medical concept and include the sensory effects (see paras 17, 22).

Despite suggestions from the Industrial Injuries Advisory Council in Cm.2844 (May 1995) that this should be represcribed as hand-arm vibration syndrome, vibration white finger remains prescribed only in respect of its vascular effect (blanching) and not its neurological effect. But in stressing that in *R(I) 1/02*, Commissioner Williams endorsed the approach in *R(I) 3/02* that

> "once there is episodic blanching of the relevant extent, the neurological effect of the disease will be relevant to compensation as well as the vascular effects" (para.10).

The Tribunal of Commissioners in *R(I) 2/06* approved the principle in *R(I) 3/02* as "correct, and now well-settled" (para.53). It also stressed that assessment of disablement is ultimately a matter of judgment for the tribunal which hears and sees the evidence. That Tribunal decision also elaborates on the nature of an error **10.162** of law, and on the difference between that and a disputed judgment of degree on a question of fact. It also proffers guidance on reference to Sch.2 in non-prescribed cases, on consideration of the judicial guidelines on the assessment of damages in civil personal injury cases, on cross-reference to other schemes such as that for criminal injuries, and on the status of official departmental guidance such as the Medical Assessment Framework (MAF). See further the annotation to SSCBA 1992, Sch.6.

The terms of prescription of the prescribed disease or injury PD A11 were altered, subject to a transitional provision (Social Security (Industrial Injuries) (Prescribed Diseases) Amendment (No.2) Regulations 2007 (SI 2007/1753) reg.3), with effect from October 1, 2007 so as to add sensorineural symptoms to the description of the disease and a proviso that both sets of symptoms are caused by vibration. It also provides that the prescription shall not cover blanching of the skin or sensorineural symptoms prior to employment in a prescribed occupation. Without renaming PD A11 as "hand-arm vibration syndrome" (HAVS) as there recommended, the changes in some degree reflect ones put forward by the Industrial Injuries Advisory Council in reports in Cm. 2844 (May 1995) and Cm. 6098 (July 2004), and reiterated in its review of the list of prescribed diseases in Cm. 7003 (January 2007) (see paras 38, 39), although the Explanatory Note to the amending regulations makes no mention of any of these reports. The change may also reflect the impact of *R(I) 3/02* as regards taking on board sensory effects in ascertaining loss of faculty, and *R(I) 1/02* in seeing them as relevant to compensation as well as the vascular effects. On limitations on the scope of the preclusive transitional provision, see *DG v SSWP* [2009] UKUT 41 (AAC), noted further in the commentary to the provision. On the need carefully to consider whether the tribunal is applying the "old" or the "new" blanching provision, see *SR v SSWP* [2009] UKUT 39 (AAC).

Thus, as Judge Poole QC observed in *AD v SSWP (II)* [2019] UKUT 198 (AAC) (at para.10), "A person with HAVS may or may not meet the particular criteria within PD A11 ... depending on the nature and severity of the symptoms". The judge also stressed the importance, where there is conflicting medical evidence, of tribunals making sufficient findings and providing adequate reasons to explain why a claimant falls within PD A11 or not.

In *CI/4874/2001*, Deputy Commissioner McLachlan stressed the need to keep separate the issues, on the one hand, whether the claimant has the disease [the col.1 matter] (and the consequent degree of disablement) and, on the other, the question of causation [the col.2 matter]. He stated

> "It is misleading to say that 'the question of blanching . . . has to be considered in the context of vibration induced damage . . .'. The blanching must be considered first, and if the required degree of blanching is established attention should then be turned to causation" (para.10).

In *R(I) 3/04*, Commissioner Mesher ruled the matter of occupational cause to be irrelevant to the diagnosis question. He accepted that "blanching" means more than the normal paleness in the extremities experience on exposure to cold, where there is a reduction of the blood supply to the peripheral arteries in order to protect the system as a whole. He was not, however, prepared to limit "blanching" to intense whiteness, the profound deathly white referred to in the medical paper by Dr Reed, The Blood and Nerve Supply to the Hand, which the Commissioner embodied in an appendix to his decision. That was characteristic but the meaning of "blanching" was not restricted to that, and was rather a matter to be decided in particular cases by tribunals and medical decision makers. Nor was circumferential blanching a requisite, preferring here Commissioner Rowland in *CI/3596/2001* to Commissioner Henty in *CI/1807/2002*. Indeed Commissioner Mesher rejected Commissioner Henty's view that Commissioner Rowland's decision had been given *per incuriam*. He noted that the matter of the Cold Water Provocation Test in the Department's Notes on the Diagnosis of Prescribed Diseases (NDPD) had successfully been challenged in *R. (on the application of the National Association of Colliery Overmen, Deputies and Shotfirers) v Secretary of State for Work and Pensions* [2003] EWHC 607 (Admin). There Pitchford J. found irrational the Secretary of State's refusal to revise the NDPD guidance and required him to amend it to reflect the correct intention behind the words used, namely that a positive result could have diagnostic value but a negative one should be treated as having none (paras 107–109).

In *CI/1720/2001*, Commissioner Rowland gives some guidance to tribunals on the manner of questioning those who claim to suffer from vibration white finger, suggesting that they avoid closed questioning and too technical language (paras 12–14). 10.163

In *CI/1763/2002*, having consulted Commissioner Jacobs who gave the decision in *CI/14532/1996* (now *R(I) 3/02*), Commissioner Mesher stressed that they were both agreed that

> "there cannot be an automatic and mechanical rule, without examination of the particular circumstances of each case, that Stage 2 on the Taylor Pelmear Scale means that PD A11 cannot be diagnosed. Stage 2 covers blanching during winter. But it is possible for someone to in addition experience blanching during the summer (thus going towards throughout the year as the prescription requires) without quite reaching Stage 3 on the Scale which requires 'extensive blanching with frequent episodes in summer as well as in winter'" (see paras 11–13 of *CI/1763/2002*).

Although not mentioned in the Tribunal of Commissioners' decision *CI/535/2005*, that approach is consistent with the tenor of that Tribunal decision and in particular its rejection of the view that there can be produced a ready template for decisions on the assessment of disablement. See further commentary to SSCBA 1992, Sch.6.

In *CI/421/2006*, Commissioner Turnbull held that a claimant refused permission to stand outside the tribunal for a short while in cold weather the better to support his claim that he suffered from vibration white finger was denied natural justice. The Commissioner also suggested that since this claimant had also requested that the last tribunal conduct a Cold Water Provocation Test, it might be wise to offer one at the new hearing. Although a negative result from such a test did not disprove vibration white finger, a positive result could assist a claimant whose history or symptoms were inconclusive (citing *R. (on the application of NACODS) v Secretary of State for Work and Pensions* [2003] EWHC 607, paras 41, 43). The result of any diagnostic test, however, had to be considered in the light of the history and clinical findings in the case.

In *CI/3596/2001*, Commissioner Rowland accepted that the prescription of PD A11 does not require circumferential blanching. While blanching only of the palmar side of the fingers might be atypical, it suffices to meet the terms of the prescription, the relevant question when determining whether the claimant is suffering from a prescribed disease (para.4). Its atypical nature might, however, in some cases be a basis for doubting the history given by the claimant or for deciding that it was not due to the nature of his/her employment, and might give some indication as to the degree of disablement (para.5). 10.164

The words "in forestry" in **sub-para.(a)** were replaced with the broader term "on wood" with effect (subject to a transitional provision) from October 1, 2007, thus giving effect to recommendations of the Industrial Injuries Advisory Council on the confusion generated by "in forestry" (see Cm. 6098 (July 2004), paras. 67, 78 and Cm. 7003 (January 2007), para.38). Happily, the case law on the meaning and scope of "in forestry", which had itself effected a broadening of the term (see below), is thus now only relevant to claims in respect of a period of assessment which relates to a claim made, or having effect, before the date these 2007 Regulations came into force or to a renewed break-out of a condition for which a claim was made before their entry into force. The change brings PD A11 into line with PD A10 where the broader term "on wood" has been applied since September 22, 2003. For the meaning of "wood", see the annotation to PD A10 (e). For the text of the transitional provision see the Social Security (Industrial Injuries) (Prescribed Diseases) Amendment (No. 2) Regulations 2007 (SI 2007/1753).

As indicated above, the meaning of "forestry" (now relevant to claims linked to periods prior to October 1, 2007), has been the subject of dispute, but case law gradually broadened the concept. In *CI/3924/1997*, Commissioner Rice considered it. The term "forestry" is also used in prescribed disease A10(i) and decisions *R(I) 5/96* (formerly *CI/362/94*) and *CI/319/94* on it in that context were cited in argument. Commissioner Rice used the same Shorter Oxford English Dictionary definition as in those cases: "the science and art of forming and cultivating forests, management of growing timber", the latter part of the definition being applicable to the case before Commissioner Rice. Here the claimant was employed by an urban local authority as an "arborist–tree surgeon". The Commissioner, deploying dictionary definitions, took "arborist" as someone who studies trees and, in the absence of a dictionary definition, took "tree-surgeon" as someone who cuts, trims or otherwise prunes trees. But an "arborist–tree surgeon" is not necessarily a forester and a restrictive meaning was given to the prescription:

> "He may be concerned . . . with trees which form no part of a forest and do not qualify as growing timber. They may, for example, simply be ornamental trees designed to improve the appearance of a city such as Liverpool. Where they are grown merely to enhance the scenery e.g. along the roadways or in strategic parts of the city or in parks, they clearly do not form part of a forest, nor are they normally 'growing timber' cultivated as a crop for eventual sale for commercial use. Of course when an ornamental tree reaches maturity, it may well be sold off for such a use, but that is not the primary purpose for which it was cultivated. It was merely an incidental consequence of the decorative purpose for which it was initially planted and nurtured" (para.6).

10.165 The matter was remitted to a new tribunal to consider the matter again in line with that interpretation in the light of the evidence, old and new, before them. The label attached to the claimant's department "Forestry Department" was not conclusive of its activities nor, if an accurate description of them, would it necessarily apply to all employees in the Department (para.7). Recently in *R(I) 2/01*, Commissioner Levenson took the view that "forestry" should be given a broader, ordinary non-technical meaning. He doubted that the approach in the decisions above, which followed those noted in respect of prescribed disease A10(i), accorded with the approach of the IIAC in its report on the prescription of vibration white finger (Cmnd.8350 (1981)). He declined to follow *R(I) 5/96* and the other cases (see paras 8–15). He considered that prescribed occupations should not be "artificially narrowed" (para.15). Accordingly, he held that the tribunal did not err in law in holding that the claimant who had pruned and felled trees in parks, schools and on highways for a city council had used chain saws in "forestry".

Commissioner Levenson's comments and broader approach were endorsed by the Court of Appeal in *Davis v Secretary of State for Social Security* (January 12, 2001) reported as *R(I) 2/01*. Rix L.J. stated:

> "It seems to me that while the words 'in forestry' in the statutory phrase are plainly intended as some form of limitation, it would be wrong to give to those words too narrow a definition when one considers the purpose of the statute, which was to provide compensation for those who suffered the prescribed disease as result of their occupation. There is great danger that, if too narrow a definition is adopted, then the very persons who fall within the purpose of the statutory protection would fall outside the definition. If, for instance, the requirement was that the work had to be done within a forest properly so-called, which was one part of Miss Lieven's definition of forestry, then someone who spent all his time in the use of chain saws, pruning or cutting down trees in large ornamental estates, or other amenity areas of the countryside which contained extensive woods, but which perhaps may not

have been 'forest', would find themselves outside the statutory protection. Again, if the requirement was that the trees concerned, whether in a forest or not, had to be grown for some commercial or industrial purpose, as distinct from some amenity or leisure purpose, or simply the beauty or health of the environment, a similar result would follow.

In the present case, Miss Lieven was ultimately prepared to adopt the dictionary definition, including the words 'management of growing timber', but nevertheless she submitted that to fall within the words 'in forestry' a claimant would either have to work in a forest, or in the commercial production of growing timber.

In my judgment, that is to narrow the meaning of 'in forestry' both by going beyond the dictionary definition which has been adopted in all the previous decisions as well as in the current one, and by doing so in a way which is neither justified by that definition nor justified by the purpose of the statute. Various examples were canvassed in the course of argument. It is not necessary to make a decision in respect of any of them. Decisions of this kind are ultimately always for the tribunal, provided it founds itself on a proper understanding of the statute. But, for instance, the case of an employee of Railtrack who was involved constantly in the management of growing timber beside the railway, by means of pruning or felling it, is an example where, speaking for myself, I could well understand a tribunal deciding, on the particular facts before it, that his work fell within the phrase 'in forestry'.

In my judgment the words 'in forestry' are perfectly adequately defined by the expression 'the management of growing timber', and there is no need to cut down those words any further by requiring that growing timber should be in any particular kind of area, whether described as a forest or parkland or whatever, or should be grown for any particular purpose. Moreover, I would accept that the work of clearing away growing timber is part of its management.

The fact that the statutory phrase has to be taken as a whole, namely 'any occupation involving . . . the use of hand-held chain saws in forestry' suggests that the words 'in forestry' mean no more than 'in or in connection with forestry', and are intended to express a sense of scale about the occupation involved. The words 'occupation involving' are very wide words indeed and raise, of course, the possibility that the occupation may involve the use of hand-held chain saws in only an incidental way. By putting in the words 'in forestry', in my judgment the legislators intended to exclude the use of handheld chain saws in only an incidental way, as might occur in occupations which had nothing to do with forestry (as for instance, might very frequently occur in the case of those who are in occupation merely as gardeners and make some occasional use of a hand-held chain saw)."

The clear implication is disapproval of the approach and result in *CI/3284/97* and *R(I) 5/96*.

In *CI/373/89* Commissioner Mitchell stated with respect to **sub-para. (b)**: **10.166**

"The most obvious application of the words of prescription in issue in this case is to occupations involving the holding of material in the form of a work-piece which is being ground by rotary tools. Transmission of vibration to the operator in such a process is as direct and obvious as the immediate application of the words used. The question is whether those words also cover the operation spoken to by the claimant and Mr. Alford [a consulting engineer familiar with the Churchill type machine at issue] and carried out several times daily between operations on workpieces. On the evidence before me I have no doubt that the dressing or resurfacing of the side of the grinding wheel by the manual use of the carborundum stone against it involves appreciable grinding away of the carborundum stone itself progressively from the corners at the end until it becomes too small and is discarded after about one to two weeks. That process of course also involves the transmission of substantial vibration as found by the tribunal. The stone therefore imparts a measure of grinding but also suffers grinding in its

> own turn and that to a marked extent. I have come to the conclusion that this operation comes within the prescription of an occupation involving 'the holding of material being ground . . . by rotary tools.' (para.14 words in square brackets added by annotator)
>
> 'Grinding' in para.(b) is not limited to grinding of 'metal'. In *CSI 987/00*, Deputy Commissioner Sir Crispin Agnew of Lochnaw Bt Q.C. considered the case of a claimant who had worked as a labourer to electricians. His work had involved cutting raggles in concrete walls with a grinder and then hammering and chiselling them out so that the electricians could insert conduits. Occasionally this would involve him striking the metal reinforcing rods in the concrete walls. The Deputy Commissioner rejected "the Secretary of State's submission that grinding relates to metal and that the only metal ground was the occasional action of cutting metal rods with a grinder" (para.15). Instead the Deputy Commissioner considered
>
> "that 'grinding' can be on any 'material', whereas 'sanding or polishing' can only be on 'metal'. I reach this construction of the provision having regard to (i) the use of the word 'in' before 'grinding' and again before 'the sanding or polishing of metal' which suggests that the task of grinding is separate from the task of sanding or polishing of metal and (ii) the fact that the later part of the provision refers to the 'holding of material being ground' and 'the metal being sanded or polished'. Had the intention been that prescription (b) should only apply to the grinding, sanding or polishing of metal, I would have expected the word 'metal' to be used rather than 'material'. 'Material' is a word that can be applied to any substance and not just to metal" (para.16).

Grinding concrete was the grinding of material and was therefore within PD A11(b).

In *CI/22/91* Commissioner Johnson considered whether the claimant's employment fell within the description in **sub-para.(c)**:

> "the use of hand-held percussive metal-working tools, or the holding of metal being worked on by percussive tools in riveting, caulking, chipping, hammering, fettling or swaging".

He considered that the 57lb hammer used by the claimant was a hand-held percussive tool used to hammer metal, and continued:

> "However, I have to consider whether the words 'metal-working' have any special significance, and also whether 'hammering' should be given its ordinary or has some special meaning in the context of paragraph (c). Certainly the [Industrial Injuries] Advisory Committee recommended that 'prescription should be in terms of the use of certain specified tools in certain specified occupations' . . .; broadly speaking that would appear to be the scheme of Schedule 1, although a number of occupations are very widely defined, for example A5–A8 inclusive, which specify 'manual labour' involving certain movements, and the conditions prescribed under B, C and to a great extent D, depend more on contact with biological or chemical agents than work in any particular industry.
>
> 10. So far as prescribed disease A11 is concerned, (a) is restricted to forestry and (e) to shoe manufacture, (d) covers mining, quarrying, demolition and road construction, which is a much wider category, as is (b), specifying the grinding, sanding or polishing of metal, which must take place in a variety of different trades. Looking at it as a whole it cannot be said that any very clear pattern emerges. In my view the 57Lb hammers used by Mr D were 'metal-working tools' as they were used for the purpose of working upon metal objects, whether ships' propellers, crane buckets or friction bands, or on the superstructure of the crane itself. I have also considered whether the word 'hammering' (in the description 'riveting, caulking, chipping, hammering, fettling or swaging') should be given some specialised meaning such as, for example, in the sense of producing a 'hammered' finish to a

piece of metal, but I can see no justification for giving 'hammering' anything other than its normal everyday meaning. In my judgment, although the words denote particular processes, the one thing they have in common is not some particular trade or industry, but the fact that they all involve striking metal with metal, with consequent vibration." (paras 9, 10).

"Fettling" means "to remove excess moulding material and casting irregularites from a cast component" (a dictionary definition adopted in *CI/141/93*).

In *CI/207/2004*, Commissioner Williams considered the particular tasks involved in a bedding industry process involving using an automatic staple gun (what the claimant knew as a "rammer") to fix the metal of the bed springs to the bounding metal strip that holds the bed springs together and thus to the wooden base of the bed (known as a Bonnell base). He held that the rammer was a metal-working tool. In *Secretary of State v Westgate* [2006] EWCA Civ 725 (reported as *R(I) 1/06*) the Court of Appeal rejected this view and allowed the Secretary of State's appeal. The Court held that his interpretation was not within the range of reasonable interpretations of that statutorily undefined term. For the Court of Appeal, a metal-working tool is one that "works metal" (para.5). The process involved in the rammer for fixing the metal of the bed springs to the wooden frame was no more working metal than was the act of banging a nail into a wal or driving a bolt through a hole—such processes involve "working with metal" rather than "working metal" (para.6).

A12 (Carpal tunnel syndrome)

For useful evidence from the medical adviser to the DWP (Dr Reed) on PD A12 (carpal tunnel syndrome), see the Schedule to *CI/3745/2006*. Dr Reed's evidence was cited by Judge Poynter in *SM v SSWP (IIDB)* [2020] UKUT 287 (AAC) where the FTT had wrongly directed itself that "the ulnar nerve not the median nerve serves the ring finger. Carpal tunnel syndrome does not cause symptoms in the ring finger." In fact, as Judge Poynter observed, "the Median nerve also serves the lateral half of the ring finger (i.e., the side nearest the thumb)" (at para.7). Thus by "basing its decision in this appeal on the mistaken premise that the Median nerve does not supply the ring finger, the First-tier Tribunal failed to exercise its enabling role correctly. On the contrary, it hindered the proper presentation of the claimant's case by setting up an obstacle of which she was unaware and which had no basis in fact" (at para.47). Allowing the claimant's appeal and remitting the case for re-hearing, Judge Poynter summarised the position as follows: **10.167**

"4. The fact that only the Median nerve --and not the Ulnar or Radial nerves, the other two nerves that supply the hand --pass through the carpal tunnel is important. It means that if a claimant's neurological symptoms in the hand do not follow the distribution of the Median nerve then, at least --and subject to what is said in paragraph 14 below --any loss of function in the hand is not caused solely by PD A12 and, at most, that the claimant does not suffer from that condition."

Paragraph 14 of the decision noted that there is some evidence that carpal tunnel syndrome can also produce symptoms in the hand as a whole.

In *R(I) 3/95* Commissioner Heggs considered the meaning of "hand-held vibrating tool" for the purposes of the prescription of occupation in respect of prescribed disease A12 (carpal tunnel syndrome) as worded prior to March 24, 1996 "the use of hand-held vibrating tools"). The Commissioner said:

"There is no statutory definition of the expression and the words can be given an extremely wide or narrow interpretation. Mrs Cleave [the claimant's representative] submitted that any vibrating tool falls within the terms of prescribed disease A12 if it can be shown that any part of it is supported or held by the hand of the operator. That is an attractive argument which would afford benefit to a wide category of claimants who could establish that they had sustained carpal tunnel syndrome from the use of vibrating equipment. The expression is however susceptible to the narrower interpretation that the expression 'hand-held' is descriptive

> of the actual tool in function and not the use made of the tool by the claimant. On this construction as submitted by Mr Jones [the AO's representative] it therefore applies only to the particular kind of vibrating tool which is portable and held manually. It does not extend to the use of tools of any kind in which some part of the operation may involve hand steadying or control. I am entitled to have regard to the Report of the Industrial Injuries Advisory Council (see paragraph 15 of the Tribunal of Commissioners decision *R(I) 11/81* where *Black–Clawson International Ltd v Papierweke–Walhof–Ascheffenburg AG* [1975] A.C. 591 was applied). In my view the Report supports the narrower interpretation because it refers to 'grip required to use such tools—many of which are cumbersome' and that 'other forceful and repetitive movement of the wrist is not sufficient to prescribe carpal tunnel syndrome in any other occupational category'. Accordingly I conclude that the narrower interpretation is that which must apply." (para.14).

That approach was followed by Commissioner May in *CSI/82/94*. This concept of "hand-held" as denoting portability does not necessarily mean that it covers only lightweight tools; as *R(I) 2/96* makes clear, provided the element of portability is there it can cover heavier tools. In *R(I) 2/96*, the claimant worked for a bus company and had to clean the garage floor and inspection pit with a heavy rotary scrubbing or buffing machine which had to be gripped tightly to steer it and to hold in the clutch. Pressure also had to be applied to it in order to remove stubborn patches of oil from the garage floor. As Commissioner Goodman noted:

> "There is no doubt that these machines vibrate considerably, that they have to [be] tightly held, gripped and steered about and that the kind of machine that the claimant was using was heavy in nature, though it could be lifted about by two people and to that extent was portable" (para.6).

10.168 In a decision supplementing rather than dissenting from the emphasis in *R(I) 3/95*, he held that the machine came within the prescription as a "hand-held vibrating tool", but cautioned that "there being a substantial factural element in [his] decision, that it is not necessarily a precedent for other types of machine or tool" (para.11). In the original *CI/15408/1995*, in March 1996, Commissioner Rice followed *CI/160/94*, and decided the appeal against the claimant, holding that the buffing machine operated by her was not a hand-held vibrating tool within the meaning of the legislative prescription. But his decision was given in ignorance of two of Commissioner Goodman's decisions on ostensibly similar machines: *R(I) 2/96* (a concrete floor scrubber) and *CI/514/94* (a floor buffer). When he became aware of those decisions, Commissioner Rice set aside his decision and the appeal was reheard before Commissioner Henty. The product is a new decision *R(I) 6/98*. Commissioner Henty's decision reviews all the pertinent authorities. The decision is in favour of the claimant and follows the *ratio* of Commissioner Goodman's decisions. Its effect is that the approach to "hand-held" in the quotation from *CI/160/94* is seen as correct in so far as it prevents static, fixed machines of the type at issue in that case (on which hands merely rested) being within the prescription. The requirement of "portability" in that approach was seen as *obiter* (not necessary for that decision). Having reviewed the relevant cases and the relevant report of the Industrial Injuries Advisory Council on the prescription of carpal tunnel syndrome (March 1992). Commissioner Henty gave his reasoned opinion on what he found a very difficult question:

> "All the previous decisions I have referred to are in agreement that a fixed machine, which requires the application of the hand to operate it, is not 'a hand-held tool'. However, it does not seem to me that there is much difference in fact between (i) a tool which vibrates and requires, during its operation, to be carried by hand either continuously or intermittently; and (ii) a tool which vibrates and, in its operation, requires to be moved either continuously or intermittently and that motion is provided by the energy of the operator. I exclude self-propelled machines. As I have pointed out, a buffing machine is self-supporting and is not mounted on some support. It is therefore clearly different from the fixed tools in

> *CI/160/94* and *CI/156/94* [both of which concerned fixed sewing machines]. For instance, a portable electric drill vibrates and, when in use, it has to be moved and firmly grasped by hand, and the operator, when drilling, is required to exert considerable pressure. In the same way, an industrial buffing machines vibrates, and, when in use, it has to be moved by the operator backwards and forwards, manoeuvred and guided, requiring a firm grasp, and the firmer the grasp, the more keenly will any vibration be transmitted. I have, therefore, come to the conclusion that an industrial buffing machine is within the definition of a hand-held vibrating tool . . ." (para.14).

He was assisted in so concluding by the fact that when the opportunity was taken to effect a legislative modification to the prescription to vitiate the effect of *CI/227/94* (below), no step was taken to remedy any dissatisfaction with Commissioner Goodman's decisions on hand-held, thus indicating acceptance of the effect of those decisions (*ibid.*). The previous form of prescription was wider covering use of "hand-held vibrating tools". "Vibrating tool" was held to mean nothing more than a tool which vibrates, so that any hand-held tool (powered or not) fell within the description (*CI/227/94*, para.4). So in *CI/227/94*, it covered a hammer and punch used for making marks on metal. There was no need for an independent vibration source within the tool (*CI/227/94; CI/136/95*). On the prescription as then worded, as the Court of Appeal put it in *Janicki v Secretary of State for Social Security* [2001] I.C.R.1220 (reported in *R(I) 1/01*), if the tool vibrates because of necessary contact with something else (in that case the sewing machine on which the heavy cutters held by the claimant had to rest to be used), the source of the vibration was immaterial. The occupational description was, however, altered to its current wording—"hand-held powered tools whose internal parts vibrate so as to transmit that vibration to the hand, but excluding those that are solely powered by hand—with effect from March 24, 1996. That new wording does not affect the cases on "hand-held". But it precludes the application of *CI/227/94, CI/136/95* and *Janicki* if the period under consideration falls after that date, unless the claimant's case is covered by the transitional provision noted at the end of this note, preserving for certain cases the old wording of the prescription. Similarly precluded by the new wording is the approach taken by Commissioner Howell in *CI/474/95* that the requirements are satisfied even when the source of the vibration is the force applied by the operator rather than the mechanism of the tool. Under the former wording, Commissioner Hoolahan held in *R(I) 8/98* that a bus steering wheel, which transmitted vibrations to the driver was not within the prescription: the wheel did not contain within itself "a source of vibration—it merely transmits vibration from something else" (para.16). The change in wording (from merely "hand-held vibrating tools" to "hand-held powered tools whose internal parts vibrate so as to transmit that vibration to the hand") further prevents such a claim succeeding.

A challenge to the validity of the prescription of disease A12 (carpal tunnel syndrome), because it is prescribed only for those whose occupations involved the use of certain tools, was rejected in *CI/5009/97*. **10.169**

Paragraph (b) was added to the list of occupations with effect from April 6, 2007 on the recommendation of the IIAC, because its review found evidence "that flexing and extending of the wrist, when repeated over much of the work time, was associated with a more than doubling of risk of CTS" (see *Work Related Upper Limb Disorders*, Cm. 6868 (July 2006), para.46). Appendix 2 to that report contains a useful diagram of the action involved. That Appendix is reproduced in *FR v SSWP* [2008] UKUT 12 (AAC); *R(I) 2/09*. In that decision, Judge Jacobs stressed that it is the nature and direction of the movement involved in dorsiflexion and palmar flexion, rather than the degree of movement, which are important. In that case and in *CI/1961/2008*, it was stressed that the IIAC Report is an appropriate aid to applying C23(b), even though the terms of prescription in it are not exactly the same as that recommended by the IIAC.

A13 (Osteoarthritis of the hip)

10.170 The prescription of osteoarthritis of the hip in relation to work in agriculture as a farmer or farm worker for a period of, or periods which amount in aggregate to, 10 years or more, was added to the Schedule with effect from March 14, 2005. Its prescription is subject to a transitional provision in reg.3 of the inserting regulations—Social Security (Industrial Injuries) (Prescribed Diseases) Amendment Regulations 2005 (SI 2005/324)—set out at the end of this section of the book: the prescription does not apply to a period of assessment relating to a claim made before March 14, 2005. The prescription implements the recommendations of IIAC as set out in their report on *Osteoarthritis of the Hip* (Cm 5977). The disease is common in the population at large, but the IIAC considered that the evidence now made it clear that in farmers and farmworkers there is a raised incidence of the disease sufficiently high that a clear association can be made between that occupation and the condition, even though there is still some uncertainty about exactly what aspect of farming is responsible. The Council thought that it would be most appropriate to prescribe for farmers whose work can be classified according to the Office of National Statistics Standard Occupational Classification 2000, "5111 farmers", "9111 farm workers" or "1211 farm managers", and who have been employed as employed earners in this capacity for 10 years or longer in aggregate. This definition was more restrictive than ones used in the field research, but the Council believed that it provided a workable definition of a level exposure for which the epidemiological evidence of a doubling (or greater) of risk is robust.

On accepted authority in prescribed diseases requiring work for particular periods, the focus should be on the work done rather than the contractual obligation to do it (*R(I) 2/79* and *CI/16/91*—see commentary to regs. 2 and 25, above).

On "agriculture", see *CI/56/95*, noted in the commentary to B6, below.

A14 (Osteoarthritis of the knee) (coal miners and related occupations)

10.171 This prescribed disease was inserted with effect from July 13, 2009. It is not subject to any transitional provision. This new prescription essentially implements, with one change (the inclusion of "face-salvage worker" which IIAC had subsumed within "faceworker"), the recommendations of the Industrial Injuries Advisory Council in its report, *Osteoarthritis of the knee in coal miners* (Cm 7440) (August 2008). The IIAC recommended that:

> "The diagnosis of OA knee for the purposes of the IIDB Scheme should be based on knee pain, swelling, stiffness and restricted movement and if possible x-ray evidence of Stage 3 to 4 on the Kellgren-Lawrence scale; but should also be accepted in those who are on a surgical waiting list for knee replacement or have had a knee replacement previously" (para.71).

The IIAC had:

> "identified direct research evidence of a greater than doubled risk of osteoarthritis of the knee in miners and indirect evidence of an excess risk of the disorder associated with occupational kneeling and squatting while undertaking heavy manual tasks (such as lifting or shovelling), activities traditionally undertaken by miners. The evidence suggests that the qualifying excess risk would arise after 10 or more years in aggregate of everyday occupational kneeling or squatting while undertaking heavy physical manual work.
>
> The coal mining industry has undergone many changes which have decreased the extent to which miners have been exposed to such employment conditions, notably the closure of many mines by 1986. However, we have received evidence that the relevant exposure circumstances will still have occurred after 1986 in certain categories of miner, such as faceworkers working non-mechanised coal faces" (p.4, Chairman's letter to Secretary of State)

See further paras 27–68 (the evidence and its evaluation).The two figures on p.10 show the contrast between a normal knee-joint and one affected by osteoarthritis.

Extrapolating from a wide range of case authorities, Judge Wikeley in *DM v SSWP (II)* [2010] UKUT 207 (AAC) has provided "some initial guidance on the interpretation and application of the relevant rules" in a context in which, while it was clear that the claimant (described by himself and the Coalboard Enquiry Service as an underground face electrician) had worked underground for at least 10 years, the question was whether he had done so in any of the relevant prescribed occupations. It was important to do so because there had been some 40,000 claims in the past year in respect of PD A14, many of which would generate appeals, and a significant number of which would turn on the issue now before him (para.4).

The statutory words of prescription are the starting point, but a purposive approach has to be taken to them. "Any occupation" is not "a term of art" but requires a focus on the work activities performed rather than on the precise terms of the contract of employment ("the actual working test") (paras 19–30).

PD A14 provides two sets of relevant occupations dealing with the coal industry. **10.172** The first deals with periods before January 1, 1986. The second deals with periods on or after that date. The qualifying period might be all before that date, all after, or one spanning a period either side of that date. It need not have been in a single occupation (the words used are "at least 10 years in one or more of the following occupations"). The requisite occupation for periods before January 1, 1986 is working underground as a "coal miner", this term not being defined in social security legislation. Judge Wikeley, stressing the need to avoid an unduly restrictive construction, thought the new tribunal (whose decision it would be) might well have little difficulty in concluding that this claimant was a "coal miner" (para.34). Drawing by analogy on the definition in the now-repealed Stannaries Act 1887, as giving a flavour of what "coal miner" covered, he thought a tribunal might reasonably take the view that the term covered:

> "anyone working in or about a coal mine, in a skilled, semi-skilled or unskilled 'blue collar' capacity, but not, for example, a 'white collar' colliery manager, mining engineer or mining surveyor" (para.35).

But he also considered it impossible and unwise to attempt an exhaustive or comprehensive definition, referring here to the "elephant test"—difficult to describe but knowing it when you see it (para.36). "Underground" might usefully if colloquially be summed up as "down the pit" (paras 37–38).

The second set of relevant occupations cover the period on or after January 1, 1986 as a: (i) face worker on a non-mechanised coal face; (ii) development worker; (iii) face-salvage worker; (iv) conveyor belt cleaner; or (v) conveyor belt attendant. Again, the focus must be on what the claimant was actually doing in the periods relied on, and not on the contract of employment. Nor can simple reliance be placed on the claimant's pay grade or the label on his wage packet. The matter is ultimately one of fact for the tribunal (paras 61–63). But the question is whether in the period 1986 onwards the claimant:

> "actually worked *in* one of the relevant occupations, and not whether he worked *in conditions similar to or indeed even identical to* those experienced by the listed occupations" (para.65).

PD A14 (dealing with the coal industry) requires working underground in the relevant occupation(s) for a period, or aggregate periods, of ten years. As Judge Wikeley **10.173** noted, this could pose problems where the claimant has moved from pit to pit or work underground is interspersed with work above ground or where, indeed, there was no work done at all because of a prolonged industrial dispute. He referred the new tribunal to which the appeal was remitted to the helpful guidance in *R(I) 3/78* and *R(I) 2/79(T)* on computing periods of work in scheduled occupations, remembering that the focus is to be "on what the claimant actually did" (paras 39–40).

Although PD A14 was inserted because the risk of osteoarthritis because of kneeling and squatting, there was, however, no requirement in the terms of prescription (which he saw as clear and unambiguous) that the claimant's work underground involved periods of kneeling and squatting, prolonged or otherwise (paras 41–48, 54).

In *MD v SSWP (II)* [2011] UKUT 137 (AAC), Judge Wikeley held that, where a tribunal found that the osteoarthritis was due to degenerative causes, the correct wording of the decision should be to indicate that the claimant has PD A14 but is not entitled to benefit because the causation test is not met (see paras 20–21).

In *JL and DO v SSWP (II)* [2011] UKUT 294 (AAC); [2012] AACR 15, Judge Ward considered whether it made any difference where a claimant's osteoarthritis resulted in knee replacement surgery. He held that, where the original loss of faculty was osteoarthritis of the knee, the knee replacement surgery did not break the chain of causation so as to substitute a new cause of ongoing loss of faculty. The relevance of the knee replacement surgery went rather to the stage of assessment of the degree of disablement.

In *GV v SSWP (II)* [2012] UKUT 208 (AAC); [2013] AACR 3 Judge Wikeley considered whether "patella-femoral osteoarthritis" fell within "osteoarthritis of the knee". He concluded that its did, following the broader definition of "the knee" supported by medical dictionaries, even though the IIAC Report suggested a narrower approach excluding the patella. He did so because case authorities (e.g. *R(I) 15/75* and *R(I) 4/99*) show that "if the statutory meaning is clear and unambiguous then IIAC's reports cannot be mined for material to qualify or alter the legislative language" (para.36). Moreover, the patella femoral joint was used more for walking on inclined terrain, kneeling and squatting, functions associated with underground mining and, although the Judge made no mention of them since the claimant had been a coal miner, carpet fitters and other layers of non-concrete floors. Accordingly, Judge Wikeley, regarded the statutory expression "osteoarthritis of the knee" to be unambiguous, noting that if the legislative intention had been only to cover more limited parts of the knee joint, those responsible for drafting the legislation could have said so, but had not (para.37).

A14 (Osteoarthritis of the knee) (carpet fitters and other layers of non-concrete floors)

10.174 This occupation was added from March 30, 2012. It is not subject to any transitional provision. This new prescription implements the recommendations of the Industrial Injuries Advisory Council (IIAC) in its report *Osteoarthritis (OA) of the knee in carpet fitters and carpet and floor layers* (Cm. 7964) (November 2010), but puts the Council's intention that layers of concrete floors were not included into specific statutory wording. The IIAC:

> "concluded that the evidence in carpet fitters or carpet and floor layers is sufficient to recommend that OA of the knee be added to the list of prescribed diseases for those who have worked in these occupations for at least 20 years in aggregate.
>
> There is insufficient evidence (direct or indirect), however, to support prescription of OA of the knee in other groups of construction workers." (p.4, Chairman's letter to the Secretary of State)."

The Council thus intended:

> "the work activities of qualifying claimants to include some or all of the following: installing linoleum, carpet or vinyl floorings; removal of old flooring; installing of underlay; installing of skirting board; and the associated preparatory work. Having taken additional ergonomic advice from the HSE, the Council considers that workers who lay parquet floors and wooden floors should also be covered by the terms of prescription, but not workers whose main activity is to lay concrete floors" (para.68, referring back to para.38).

The exclusion with respect to laying of concrete floors doubtless reflects that most are laid largely by standing and spreading poured concrete rather than bending or kneeling. The IIAC is to keep under review the matter of OA of the knee in other construction workers.

As with OA and the coal industry, the IIAC thought that for the purposes of the scheme:

> "a diagnosis of OA of the knee should be based on knee pain, swelling, stiffness and restricted movement and, if possible, X-ray evidence of Stage 3-4 on the Kellgren-Lawrence scale, but should also be accepted in those who are on a surgical waiting list for knee replacement or have had a knee replacement previously" (para.6).

The two figures on p.10 of the Report show the contrast between a normal knee-joint and one affected by osteoarthritis.

On constructing the requisite 20-year period, see *R (I) 3/78*, *R (I) 2/79 (T)* and *DM v SSWP (II)* [2010] UKUT 198 (AAC).

On the relevance of knee replacement surgery, see *JL and DO v SSWP (II)* [2011] UKUT 294 (AAC), noted in the commentary to PD A14 *(Osteoarthritis of the knee) (coal miners and related occupations)*, above.

"Patella-femoral osteoarthritis" falls within "osteoarthritis of the knee" (*GV v SSWP* [2012] UKUT 208 (AAC) noted in the commentary to PD A14 *(Osteoarthritis of the knee) (coal miners and related occupations)*, above.

Note that in April 2020 IIAC published a position paper on *Osteoarthritis of the knee in professional football players* (Position Paper No.44). The Council did not find enough consistent evidence that the risk of knee OA is doubled amongst football players in the absence of a traumatic knee injury. IIAC therefore decided against recommending prescription for OA of the knee in footballers, but indicated it remained open to the possibility of reviewing its position as the research evidence base continues to grow. The Council encouraged ex-professional footballers who had a documented knee injury during their playing career, and later developed osteoarthritis in that knee, to consider making a claim under the accident provisions of the scheme.

A15: Dupuytren's contracture of the hand

This prescription of Dupuytren's contracture has not been straightforward. **10.175** Dupuytren's disease involves the thickening of fibrous tissue in the palm and tendons of the finger and leads, in more advanced cases, to the digits becoming permanently bent, a stage of the disease known as Dupuytren's contracture. IIAC originally recommended that Dupuytren's contracture should be added to the list of prescribed diseases for which industrial disablement benefit may be payable in its 2014 report, *Dupuytren's contracture due to hand-transmitted vibration* (Cm 8860). The Council reviewed the link between work involving the use of hand-held vibratory tools and concluded there was sufficient evidence for this disease to be prescribed. It recommended that Dupuytren's contracture be added to the list of prescribed diseases for which benefit is payable following work for ten or more years in aggregate which involves use of hand-held powered tools whose internal parts vibrate so as to transmit vibration to the hand for at least two hours per day on three or more days per week. However, IIAC recognised that Dupuytren's disease exists across a wide spectrum of severity, with the majority of cases causing little or no functional loss. Accordingly, the Council proposed that cases affecting only the palm and with no involvement of the fingers should be excluded from consideration; for the purposes of prescription, the disease should involve fixed flexion deformity (contracture) of one or more of the digits. This was designed to encourage claims only in circumstances where the assessed level of disablement was likely to contribute meaningfully to the award of benefit. To the same end the report outlined a 'table top' test, under which the person places their hand on a table. If the hand lies completely flat on the table, the test is considered negative. If the hand cannot be placed completely flat on the table, leaving a space between the table and a part of the hand as big as the diameter of a ballpoint pen, the test is considered positive. This was intended to be used in clinical practice as an aid to define disease of the requisite severity and so act as a filter for discouraging claims that would not attract benefit.

IIAC's recommendation was initially rejected by the DWP Minister for Disabled People Health & Work, but (according to the minutes of the Council's April 2019 meeting at paragraph 3.1) "following engagement of IIAC members with the Minister, it was announced in the 2018 Budget Statement that Dupuytren's would be added to the list of IIDB prescribed diseases." Subsequently the Council reviewed the terms of its proposed prescription to ensure it reflected its recommendations regarding the severity of an individual's symptoms. In the 2014 report, the prescribed disease was given as "Dupuytren's contracture resulting in fixed flexion deformity of one or more digits". In 2019 the Council considered clarification of the prescription recommendations was needed and that the table top test should not be used as an initial filter for claims (as this would lead to a large number of claims that did would not attract any benefit). IIAC's Research Working Group (RWG) therefore suggested using the term "fixed flexion deformity of the interphalangeal joints of the digit". At its April 2019 meeting IIAC felt the terminology needed to be strengthened further and agreed on "fixed flexion deformity of one or more inter-phalangeal joints of one or more of the digits". The prescription set out in the amendment reflects those changes agreed by the Council in April 2019 (see IIAC, *Dupuytren's contracture: clarification of intention and amendment of the prescription*, December 2019). The Department's analysis estimates that there will be 30,000 additional new claims in total, between the introduction of Dupuytren's contracture as a prescribed disease and the end of financial year 2025/26. However, it is anticipated this change will mean only around 4,000 awards in total, over the same period, to both new and existing claimants. This is in the context of a total disablement benefit caseload of 235,000 as of December 2018.

The onset of the disease occurs not when the claimant first experiences Dupuytren's disease but only when the signs of the contracture stage, as contained in the statutory definition, manifest themselves: *DR v SSWP (II)* [2021] UKUT 191 (AAC).

It should be noted that the prescribed occupations involve the use of hand-held powered tools. IIAC debated whether occupations where workers were subjected to vibration without using powered hand tools e.g. fettlers, should be covered by the prescription, but decided to review this at a later date.

Note that the conditions for prescription have now been further "clarified" by regulation 2 of the Social Security (Industrial Injuries) (Prescribed Diseases) Amendment Regulations 2022 (SI 2022/214) (this SI lacked a commencement date, hence the need for the Social Security (Industrial Injuries) (Prescribed Diseases) Amendment (No.2) Regulations 2022 (SI 2022/229), giving effect to the changes as from March 28, 2022). At the request of the DWP, IIAC had produced an information note in May 2020 to clarify the assessment process and assist healthcare practitioners carrying out assessments for A15. However, the revised IIAC guidance went wider than the prescription as set out in the regulations. The DWP therefore brought forward secondary legislation to change the prescription for the disease. The previous guidance from IIAC only included reference to changes to finger joints (Interphalangeal joints (IPJ)). The clarification from IIAC included further detail in relation to IPJ involvement and also included changes to knuckle joints (Metacarpophalangeal joints (MCPJ)). According to the DWP, the new prescription as revised will be satisfied where the occupational requirements are met and there is reliable evidence of changes during or after the period of occupation.

IV. Prescribed Diseases Category: B. Conditions due to biological agents

The IIAC in their report on Conditions due to Biological Agents (Cm 5997) in November 1993 updated the references for each prescribed disease, and reviewed the prescribed occupations in each case. 10.176

B1 (cutaneous anthrax; pulmonary anthrax)

These occupational terms of prescription were added to the Schedule with effect from March 14, 2005, subject to a transitional provision in reg.3 of the inserting regulations—Social Security (Industrial Injuries) (Prescribed Diseases) Amendment Regulations 2005 (SI 2005/324)—set out at the end of this section of the book: the prescription does not apply to a period of assessment relating to a claim made before March 14, 2005. The prescription implements the recommendations of IIAC as set out in their report on Conditions due to Biological Agents (Cm 5997). The IIAC stated 10.177

> "Anthrax is a zoonotic disease (i.e. a disease passed from animals to humans) caused by the bacterium *Bacillus anthracis*. Generally, humans contract anthrax by exposure to infected herbivorous animals or their products. Bacterial spores enter the human body via the skin (cutaneous anthrax), the lungs (pulmonary anthrax) or the gut (intestinal anthrax). Cutaneous anthrax is the most common type of infection in humans, accounting for approximately 95% of all cases. It is characterised by an itchy skin lesion (or papule) which becomes a vesicle. This vesicle bursts forming a characteristic eschar (sloughed off dead tissue), with surrounding oedema and lymphangitis. This form of anthrax is readily treatable with antibiotics, but if left untreated can lead to death in a small proportion of cases. Pulmonary anthrax accounts for around 5% of human infections and has a high fatality rate. It is characterised by flu-like symptoms, which may lead to respiratory failure and death in a few days. Intestinal anthrax is rare, and is usually found outside the UK where infected meat may be eaten. Septicaemia and meningitis are possible complications of all forms of anthrax infection. Anthrax is common in livestock from parts of Turkey, Sudan and Pakistan" (para.44).

The IIAC recommended clarification of the prescription to go beyond exposure to infected herbivorous animals or their products (the previous prescription). The report acknowledged the potential for infection in other circumstances therefore the prescription has been widened to include any work involving contact with anthrax spores (see paras 45–48).

Originally the disease prescribed was "anthrax". With effect from March 16, 2015 only cutaneous anthrax and pulmonary anthrax are prescribed, reflecting the rarity of intestinal anthrax.

B3 (infection by leptospira)

This is prescribed in respect of rather wider occupations than may at first appear, with successful claims both by a building site labourer (*R(I) 20/52*) and by a surface worker at a mine (*R(I)531/92*) based on the fact that their work environment was "infested" with rats. 10.178

B4 ((a) Cutaneous larva migrans; (b) Iron deficiency anaemia caused by gastrointestinal infection by hookworm.)

The disease was originally prescribed as "ankylostomiasis" in the workmen's compensation legislation. Wider terms of occupational prescription were added to the Schedule with effect from March 14, 2005, subject to a transitional provision in reg.3 of the inserting regulations—Social Security (Industrial Injuries) (Prescribed Diseases) Amendment Regulations 2005 (SI 2005/324)—set out at the end of this section of the book: the prescription does not apply to a period of assessment relating to a claim made before March 14, 2005. Those terms of occupational prescription remain unchanged. They implement the recommendations of the IIAC as set 10.179

out in their report on *Conditions due to Biological Agents (Cm 5997)*.The IIAC recommended alteration of the occupational prescription to reflect the fact that contact with sources of ankylostomiasis is not restricted to work in mines (paras 62–67). The change in wording of the disease prescription merely makes the prescription more specific since, as described by the IIAC, ankylostomiasis is

> "a zoonotic disease caused by nematodes called hookworms, with the commonest types to infect humans being *Ancylostoma duodenale* and *Necator americanus*. The adult hookworms live, and lay eggs, in the intestines of humans and animals (in particular, dogs and cats). Infected humans or animals excrete the eggs in their faeces. In conditions of poor hygiene, the eggs develop into larvae which contaminate the soil. The larvae can enter the body via cuts in the skin or, if food is grown in the soil, may be swallowed and then penetrate the stomach wall. The larvae then make their way through the blood vessels to the lung. They are coughed up and swallowed, so completing their life cycle as adult hookworms in the intestine.
>
> Individuals infected with hookworms may exhibit acute ankylostomiasis, characterised by skin eruptions that occur at the site of larval entry. Chronic ankylostomiasis is characterised by fatigue caused by anaemia from iron deficiency due to loss of blood into the tissues and gut. Other symptoms of chronic ankylostomiasis include vague abdominal pains and, occasionally, a cough and sore throat. In severe cases, cardiac complications from larval migration can occur, such as endomyocardial fibrosis" (paras 63–64).

B5 (tuberculosis)

10.180 This is prescribed for a very wide range of occupations in which contact with a source of infection is involved. It was considered recently by Commissioner Williams in *CI/3625/2003*. There would seem to have been no other cases since 1960 and the pre-1960 cases were of limited assistance given changes in the terms of prescription. In *CI/3625/2003*, Commissioner Williams found that

> "Mr W fails to make out the case that his employment is prescribed in relation to bovine tuberculosis, prescribed disease B5. I do so without looking too closely at the details of the school and its catchment area, or his job as a senior teacher at that school. I do so because he puts the risk down to contact not with infected children or their families or home settings, but with a professional colleague who was not known to be infected, and not to contact with infected cows or badgers or individuals but with a tick on that colleague's clothing. The tribunal found that Mr W had not satisfied it that the infection from which he was suffering was tick-borne. In other words, he failed to establish a source of infection. There is sound evidence for that and I accept that finding. That answers the question. But even if—hypothetically—I found that Mr W was right and X did carry an infectious tick, and that tick had bitten Mr W and caused bovine tuberculosis, what was it about his *employment* that put him at this risk? Why was he at risk as a teacher from that tick, in a different way to any member of X's family, friends or any other contacts or, in the words of section 108, otherwise than 'as a risk common to all persons'. I find no such additional risk. On either analysis, Mr W fails to establish that his occupation was prescribed for prescribed disease B5 in the bovine form." (para.22).

B6 (extrinsic allergic alveolitis)

10.181 This was considered by Commissioner Angus in *CI/56/95*. There the claimant was an electrician by trade, whose work was said to have brought him into contact with the agents which cause the disease (e.g. he had had to clean mouldy material out of machinery in the food processing industry before repairing it and had spent some considerable time working on the wiring and cabling of a chicken farm among feathers and chicken muck and had had to handle the birds). The Commissioner, remitting the matter to another SSAT, stated that the new tribunal should first find as a fact whether the claimant had been exposed to "moulds or fungal spores or heterologous proteins". If he had, the SSAT should consider whether such exposure was by reason of his employed earner's employment in any of the activities set out in heads (a)–(d) of the prescription. These are not a list of particular trades. Rather the decision on whether the claimant's occupation (here electrician) comes within those specified is decided by reference to the work done bringing him into contact with the relevant agents. One looks to

> "whether he has been exposed to the specified agents by reason of his participation in one of the specified activities . . . in so far as that activity or those activities fell within the scope of his employed earner's employment as indicated for him by his employer" (para.12).

As to the meaning of "agriculture" in head (a), the Commissioner deployed a dictionary definition: "the science or occupation of cultivating land and rearing crops and livestock; farming" (Collins English Dictionary, cited in para.15). Where the claimant's employer was not a farmer then:

> "in order to establish whether or not the [claimant] is employed in agriculture it would be necessary to enquire into the nature and organisation of the employer's business and the nature and pattern of the duties assigned to the claimant. Just as an electrician could be regarded as employed in agriculture because he was employed full-time by a farmer, a company of electrical engineers who specialised in servicing agricultural customers might be said to be engaged in agriculture. Alternatively a firm which had no particular tendency to specialise in agricultural customers might have assigned an employee to duties so involved with farming that the employee could be said to be engaged in agriculture" (para.15).

As to (b), the tribunal would have to be satisfied that as regards any handling of mouldy vegetable matter when cleaning out machines, the matter in question was "in storage". As to (c), the question would be did his employers expect him to "handle" birds (paras 18, 19).

Paragraph (e) was added with effect from April 6, 2007, subject to a transitional provision set out in the amending regulations at the end of this part of the book. The IIAC recommended this. It considered there was little doubt that exposure to aerosolised mists of metal working fluid has been the cause of occupational occurrences of EAA (see *Extrinsic Allergic Alveolitis*, Cm 6867 (July 2006), para.39).

The new open occupational category of "(f) any other workplace" was added with effect from March 30, 2017 (see Social Security (Industrial Injuries) (Prescribed Diseases) Amendment Regulations 2017 (SI 2017/232) reg.3). This amendment, which enables exposure to other biological agents that can cause extrinsic allergic alveolitis (EEA), was part of a package of recommendations made by IIAC in its report *Extrinsic allergic alveolitis: isocyanates and other occupational causes*, Cm 9247 (April 2016). IIAC's report has also resulted in the addition of the expression "or another biological substance that causes extrinsic allergic alveolitis" in the terms of prescription. In the same vein the reference to "including farmer's lung" has been dropped from the nomenclature of B6. Furthermore, IIAC's report has resulted in the creation of a new PD C34, designed to recognise that exposure to the chemical vapour of isocyanates can cause EAA, a prescription which includes a new open category of exposure to other chemical agents that can cause EAA.

B8A Infection by hepatitis A virus and B8B (infection by hepatitis B or C virus)

Prescription of viral hepatitis was originally rather restricted but, after modifica- **10.182**
tions to the Schedule in 1983, is now prescribed for occupations involving any contact with human blood or a source of the disease. The current terms of prescription were substituted with effect from March 14, 2005, subject to a transitional provision in reg.3 of the inserting regulations—Social Security (Industrial Injuries) (Prescribed Diseases) Amendment Regulations 2005 (SI 2005/324)—set out at the end of this section of the book: the prescription does not apply to a period of assessment relating to a claim made before March 14, 2005. The prescription implements the recommendations of IIAC as set out in their report on Conditions

due to Biological Agents (Cm 5997) (see paras 88–120). In particular, the Council reviewed hepatitis A infection in sewage workers and found evidence that the risk is more than doubled in those working with raw sewage, although overall sewage workers do not have a significantly increased risk of disease. In relation to hepatitis C, the Council thought some subgroups of health workers to be at elevated risk. Furthermore, HCV infection is the most commonly reported occupationally acquired blood-borne disease in England and Wales. In view of the uncertainty about the risk in some subgroups of health workers and the similar mode of transmission to hepatitis B, the Council thought that prescription of both hepatitis B and C should continue, with wording similar to the present prescription, for all those in contact with blood or body fluids.

B14 (Lyme disease)

10.183 This was prescribed from March 14, 2005, subject to a transitional provision in reg.3 of the inserting regulations—Social Security (Industrial Injuries) (Prescribed Diseases) Amendment Regulations 2005 (SI 2005/324)—set out at the end of this section of the book: the prescription does not apply to a period of assessment relating to a claim made before March 14, 2005. The prescription implements the recommendations of IIAC as set out in their report on Conditions due to Biological Agents (Cm 5997) (see paras 195–201). Since Lyme disease (a tick borne disease with musculo-skeletal, cardiac and neurological effects) was first considered by IIAC in 1990, enough evidence of occupational risk had accumulated to warrant prescription. The high incidence of the disease in deer hunters and forestry workers suggested a clear occupational risk in respect of exposure to *Borrelia.*

B15 (Anaphylaxis)

10.184 This was prescribed from March 14, 2005, subject to a transitional provision in reg.3 of the inserting regulations—Social Security (Industrial Injuries) (Prescribed Diseases) Amendment Regulations 2005 (SI 2005/324)—set out at the end of this section of the book: the prescription does not apply to a period of assessment relating to a claim made before March 14, 2005. The prescription implements the recommendations of IIAC as set out in their report on Conditions due to Biological Agents (Cm 5997) (see paras 261–271). "Anaphylaxis is a life-threatening IgE-mediated allergic Type I hypersensitivity reaction due to contact of a sensitised individual with an allergenic protein. Common allergens which can provoke anaphylactic shock include drugs, insect stings, latex and certain food ingredients, such as nuts. Initial exposure to the allergen induces specific IgE antibody. Subsequent contact can provoke an anaphylactic reaction. An anaphylactic-like (anaphylactoid) reaction can occur during first exposure to certain drugs; but these are a manifestation of a toxic, rather than an allergic, reaction to the drug. Anaphylactic shock is due to a sudden massive release of histamine and other mediators from basophils into the bloodstream. These trigger constriction of the airways and swelling of tissue (angioedema), resulting indifficulty breathing, and dilatation of blood vessels, leading to shock and pulmonary oedema. Other symptoms of anaphylaxis include urticarial skin rash and gastrointestinal reactions, such as vomiting, abdominal cramps and diarrhoea. The onset of anaphylaxis can be very rapid, with symptoms occurring within minutes of contact with the allergen" (*ibid.*, para.261). A precipitating exposure at work could ground a claim through the accident route where loss of faculty lasting beyond 90 days, rather than death, ensued. The Committee recommended prescription of anaphylaxis and its sequelae that result from allergy to natural rubber latex in healthcare workers.

The prescription criteria for PD B15 were originally limited to "employment as a healthcare worker having contact with products made with natural rubber latex". However, many occupations outside the healthcare sector can also involve regular exposure to latex products. IIAC found a similar causal connection in other occupational roles with latex allergy only rarely acquired outside the workplace.

IIAC therefore recommended that the prescription for this disease be expanded to include any occupation involving contact with products made with natural rubber latex (see IIAC, *Extending the terms of prescription for latex anaphylaxis*, Cm 9498 (September 2017) p.11). The expansion of this prescription will extend coverage to e.g. police officers, vehicle mechanics, hairdressers, and workers from the food industry amongst others. It also provides parity with other similar diseases within the scheme, such as occupational asthma and rhinitis, which both prescribe any occupation that involves exposure to the listed agents.

V. Prescribed Diseases: Category C: Conditions due to chemical agents

The prescriptions underwent very substantial revision from March 17, 2003, subject to a transitional provision in reg.6 of the amending regulations: the Social Security (Industrial injuries) (Prescribed Diseases) Amendment Regulations 2003 (SI 2003/270). The text of the transitional provision is reproduced later in this volume. For the text of the prescriptions prior to March 17, 2003, and annotations thereto, see the 2002 edition of this volume. **10.185**

Prescribed Diseases C8, C9, C10, C11, C14, C15 and C28 were removed. New formulations were substituted for all or part of Diseases C1, C2, C4, C5A and 5B, C6, C7, C12, C13, C16–27, C29 and C30. The changes largely follow the recommendations of the IIAC in its report reviewing the prescription of conditions due to chemical agents (*Cm. 5395* (*February 2002*)). These changes were recommended reflecting the fact that many of the "C" diseases were prescribed in the early days of the scheme and there was need to reflect advances in scientific knowledge as well as to bring the wording and terminology used up to date. The removals from the list were based on the view that the very few claims that have been made for these diseases in the past could have been dealt with more appropriately under the accident provisions of the industrial injuries scheme.

Although the chemical agents in C23(c) are primarily encountered in the manufacture of dyes, that does not mean that they cannot be encountered elsewhere. In *SSWP v JS* [2008] UKUT 35 (AAC), Judge Williams upheld a tribunal decision that a claimant who had worked in a coke works was entitled on the evidence to conclude that he had probably suffered relevant exposure.

A new C24 was substituted, and C24A added, with effect from April 6, 2006 (see Social Security (Industrial Injuries) (Prescribed Diseases) Amendment Regulations 2006 (SI 2006/586), reg.3). They cannot, however be applied to a period of assessment prior to that date (*ibid.*, reg.4)). These changes implement the recommendations of the IIAC as set out in their report *Vinyl Chloride Monomer-Related Diseases* (Cm 6645). As regards C24A, the totality of the evidence led the IIAC to "conclude that an association exists between VCM exposure and Raynaud's phenomenon in the absence of osteolysis in the digits, and also between VCM exposure and scleroderma in the absence of osteolysis in the digits". That evidence indicated that the increased frequency of these conditions enabled attribution to exposure to VCM in the individual case. Consistent evidence showed that the inhalation of VCM in PVC production workers causes a characteristic clinical triad of osteolysis of the terminal phalanges, scleroderma and Raynaud's phenomenon, but that not all three are invariably present together (see para.16). As regards reformulating C24, the IIAC considered the term acro-osteolysis too confusing in that it refers both to a specific condition and to a syndrome the features of which may vary from one person to another. The term should be dropped. Osteolysis of the finger-tips, Raynaud's phenomenon and scleroderma should each be prescribed independently. The IIAC were not prepared to extend coverage to liver tumours other than angiosarcoma. Nor could exposure to PVC itself warrant prescription (para.17).

Prior to April 6, 2006, C 24 prescribed separately: angiosarcoma of the liver; liver fibrosis; and acro-osteolysis. The prescription of acrosteloysis, however, required that it be characterised by (i) lytic destruction of the terminal phalanges, (ii) in Raynaud's phenomenon, the exaggerated vasomotor response to cold causing intense blanching of the digits, and (iii) sclerodermatous thickening of the skin. It was thus open to a strict, literal interpretation that all three aspects (i)–(iii) had to be present. In *CI/1884/2004*, taking on board the IIAC report that had led to that 2003 prescription, Commissioner Williams specifically rejected this interpretation, holding instead that it "must be read disjunctively. The test is met if an individual can show that he (or she) has worked in a prescribed occupation and has thereafter evidenced any one of the three physical conditions listed" (para.38).

The prescription of bronchiolitis obliterans (PD C31) was recommended by the Industrial Injuries Advisory Council (IIAC) in its report *Bronchiolitis Obliterans and Food Flavouring Agents*, Cm. 7439 (July 2008).This is an uncommon but disabling respiratory disease characterised by fixed airway obstruction, whereby fibrous tissue narrows or blocks the bronchioles in the lung. It can be potentially severe, resulting in lung transplantation in some patients. The IIAC concluded that a causal relationship between bronchiolitis obliterans and exposure to food flavouring agents was likely, and was supported by: (a) evidence of the clustering of cases of this rare disease in several factories where exposures to diacetyl were shared in common; (b) the development of fixed airways obstruction in the absence of other explanations (e.g. emphysema); (c) a demonstrated dose response relationship between exposure to food flavouring agents and the onset of symptoms and declining lung function; and (d) experiments demonstrating pulmonary damage in animals exposed to diacetyl. The IIAC considered there to be "strong evidence of an association between work in diacetyl production or use of diacetyl as a food flavouring agent and the development of bronchiolitis obliterans" (*Summary*, para.3). Diagnosis of the disease is relatively complicated, based on clinical features, lung function tests, chest radiographs and computed tomography scans. A distinguishing feature from bronchitis and emphysema is a relatively rapid onset of symptoms (within weeks or months) following diacetyl exposure, as compared to the much slower progression of symptoms associated with the development of chronic airways disease. Cases in which benefit is sought are likely to have had extensive clinical investigations to confirm diagnosis. Diagnosis should normally be based upon prior hospital investigations, with confirmatory evidence of diagnosis being sought from the appropriate source(s).

10.186 Prescription of nasal carcinoma (PD C32) was recommended by the Industrial Injuries Advisory Council (IIAC) in its report, *Chromium and Sino-Nasal Cancer*, Cm. 7740 (December 2009). Sino-nasal cancer, a rare disease in the United Kingdom encompassing cancers of the inside of the nose and of the paranasal sinuses has for some time been prescribed in relation to exposure to wood dust and leather working (PD D6), in respect of which there is strong evidence of an increased risk. Following processing, chromium as metal exists in several forms, principally metallic chromium (chromium 0), trivalent chromium (chromium III), and hexavalent chromium (chromium VI). Evidence was considered relating to a number of industries in which exposure to these different forms of chromium occurred, namely chromate production, chrome plating, chromium pigment production, stainless steel welding and the leather and tanning industries. Positive associations, where the risk was more than doubled, were most clearly evident in workers involved in chromate production and chrome plating.

The form of prescription of C3(a) and C3(b) became effective on March 30, 2012. It is not subject to any transitional provision. It flows from the Secretary of State implementing, in narrower terms after considering further research, recommendations of the IIAC made in its 2002 Report on Category C diseases (*Conditions due to chemical agents* Cm. 5395, paras 47–58), the progress in research on which had been regularly checked by the IIAC (see *Completion of the review of the scheduled list of prescribed diseases*, Cm.7003 (January 2007), para.51).

C33 (Chloracne) was prescribed with effect from March 16, 2015. Its prescription is not subject to any transitional provision and implements recommendations made by the IIAC in its report, *Occupational Chloracne* (Cm 8670, July 2013). Chloracne is a rare but systemic disease caused by systemic exposure to certain halogenated aromatic hydrocarbons called 'chloracnegens'. Its most prominent clinical manifestation is skin involvement and leads to disfigurement of the face. It can be severely disabling and can have enduring effects, sometimes over several years or decades after exposure has ceased. The IIAC intended "prescription to relate to the skin manifestations of chloracne" but it also recognised "that psychological sequelae may accompany skin disfigurement and may comprise an important component of the resulting disablement" (para.30).

C34 (extrinsic allergic alveolitis or EEA) was prescribed with effect from March 30, 2017 (see Social Security (Industrial Injuries) (Prescribed Diseases) Amendment Regulations 2017 (SI 2017/232) reg.3). EEA has been a longstanding 'B' prescribed disease (see B6) in respect of biological agents (commonly referred to as farmer's lung). The addition of EEA as C34 in the 'C' list reflects IIAC's recommendation that the vapour of isocyanates, i.e. chemical exposure, be added to the qualifying terms of exposure for EEA. The prescribed employments are also expressed by way of an open category, a measure designed to facilitate more rapid recognition of new chemical causes of EEA: see IIAC, *Extrinsic allergic alveolitis: isocyanates and other occupational causes* (Cm 9247, April 2016).

VI. Prescribed Diseases: Category D: Miscellaneous conditions

D1 (pneumoconiosis)

D1 (pneumoconiosis) has already been considered in the note to reg.2, above, in respect of its prescription for all occupations involving exposure to dust. There is also a separate section of the Schedule which lists specific occupations for which the disease is prescribed. The diagnosis of pneumoconiosis (prescribed disease D1) was considered in *R(I) 1/96* where the Commissioner held that to say that minimal coalworker's pneumoconiosis "is insufficient radiologically for him to be eligible for industrial injuries benefit" is wrong in law. Pneumoconiosis is defined in s.122(1) of the SSCBA 1992 as "fibrosis of the lungs due to silica dust, asbestos dust or other dust, and includes the condition of the lungs known as dust-reticulation". Either the claimant has fibrosis due to dust or he does not. The International Labour Organisation's "International Classification of Radiographs of Pneumoconiosis" is a diagnostic aid but the radiological category does not determine the diagnosis. **10.187**

In *R(I) 7/98*, the Commissioner held that the definition of pneumoconiosis in s.122 of the SSCBA 1992, "fibrosis of the lungs due to silica dust, asbestos dust, or other dust, and includes the condition of the lungs known as dust-reticulation", carried the implication that dust-reticulation was to be regarded as a form of fibrosis of the lungs whether or not it would otherwise always be medically described as constituting such fibrosis. The statutory definition dates back to 1943. In *R(I) 3/03*, a Tribunal of Commissioners considered its interpretation and application in the light of developments in medical understanding and terminology, especially as they affect post mortem evidence of the effects of coal dust. Those changes meant that the medical evidence often does not reflect this statutory language. The key issue, however, was not changes in terminology, but whether the evidence showed that the statutory definition was met. As regards coal dust, tribunals cannot simply rely on "coal workers pneumoconiosis" in post mortem reports or death certificates as conclusive of the question: is the statutory definition met? This is because experts differ in their use of the term and whether it necessarily includes fibrosis. Moreover, such a statement represents only one doctor's opinion, which has to be assessed in the light of the evidence as a whole. In particular, where the phrase is found in a post mortem report, it represents only a provisional conclusion that might well be changed if microscopic examination reveals contrary findings.

The question as to what constitutes "dust reticulation" was addressed in *S (in the name of S, deceased) v SSWP* [2016] UKUT 485 (AAC), where Judge Mitchell concluded as follows (at para.96):

> "dust reticulation involves structural changes to lung tissue due to the accumulation of dust in widely distributed foci throughout the lungs. Nodularities need not be present nor is a medical diagnosis of fibrosis required and, it follows, scarring need not be present either. In the living, it is difficult to see how dust reticulation

may be found in the absence of X-ray or scanning evidence but, for the deceased, post-mortem evidence may also demonstrate the existence of dust reticulation."

Judge Mitchell also made the following observation about the way in which the earlier decision of a Tribunal of Commissioners in *R(I) 3/03* had been reported:

> "41. I think it is clear that, here, the Commissioners were simply describing the agreed medical evidence put before them. The Commissioners did not express disagreement with the evidence but that was not to be expected. They had to deal with the appeal as presented to them. Despite that, the headnote to the reported decision states that the Tribunal of Commissioners held "the term "dust reticulation" is no longer used and is unlikely to be of practical significance in pneumoconiosis cases". My respectful view is that this was potentially misleading. The Tribunal of Commissioners did not hold that the "dust reticulation" element of the statutory definition could be ignored, as the Secretary of State's first submission on this appeal seemed to assert. Such an interpretation would be contrary to the language used by the Tribunal of Commissioners elsewhere in its reasons as well as the decision of Commissioner Mitchell Q.C. which the Tribunal itself referred to and relied on."

On the level of reasoning required to explain a negative diagnosis of D1, see *KH (deceased) (by his appointee AMH) v SSWP (II)* [2021] UKUT 189 (AAC) paras 15-18.

D2 (byssinosis)

10.188 D2 (byssinosis) is prescribed for cotton and flax workers. It is neither necessary that the claimant should be employed exclusively in the room within the scheduled description (*R(I) 17/56*), nor that fine distinctions should be drawn in determining the meaning of "room" (*R(I) 26/58*).

D3 (diffuse mesothelioma)

10.189 D3 (diffuse mesothelioma) and D4 (inflammation or ulceration of nose etc.) are both prescribed, in part, in respect of occupations involving exposure to dust. The meaning of "dust" was considered by the Commissioner in *R(I) 1/85* where he defined it as earth or other solid matter in minute particles so as to be easily raised and carried by the wind. The occupational prescription in D3 was altered to its present wording with effect from April 9, 1997. In *CI/13232/1996*, Commissioner Rowland considered the meaning of the earlier wording (see p.938 of Bonner, Hooker and White, *Non-Means Tested Benefits: The Legislation* (1996)) and in particular the prescription "any occupation involving . . . (d) substantial exposure to the dust arising from any of the foregoing operations". The case concerned a claimant employed as a cooper on premises adjacent to those of another firm which handled asbestos whose extraction/ventilation equipment spewed out asbestos dust over his workplace. The Commissioner held that the Prescribed Diseases Regulations focus on the nature of the claimant's employment rather than on the nature of the employer's business, so that here the claimant had only to show that he was employed in an occupation involving something listed in col.2 of the Schedule. Commissioner Rowland stated:

> "It is true that paragraph (a), (b) and (c) are unlikely to be satisfied in the case of any claimant who is not working for an employer whose business necessarily involves work with asbestos and the overwhelming majority of cases to which paragraph (d) applies will also arise where the nature of the employer's business involves working with asbestos. However there is nothing in the language of the Regulations so to restrict it. I can see no reason for distinguishing between the present claimant and, say, a clerical worker employed in the neighbouring firm of asbestos processors. Neither was engaged in a type of work which could normally involve exposure to asbestos dust but in both cases the particular location of their employment caused them to be exposed to dust. It is difficult to see any practical

reason or any reason of principle why the clerical worker should be entitled to disablement benefit and the present claimant should not." (para.8)

The revision of the prescription's wording to the broader formulation in the current text essentially endorses the validity of that approach, but clearly a claimant whose employment exposes him to asbestos, asbestos dust or any admixture of asbestos must show that such exposure was at a level above that commonly found in the environment at large.

D4 (allergic rhinitis)

D4 (allergic rhinitis), has, since March 24, 1996, attracted the presumption that a prescribed disease is due to the nature of a scheduled occupation, provided that the claimant was employed in that occupation at the date of onset of the disease, or at any time within one month preceding the date of onset. See, on the consequences of this, *R(I) 7/02*, noted in the commentary to reg.3, above. **10.190**

D4(x)—allergic rhinitis due to exposure to products made with natural rubber latex- was added from March 14, 2005, subject to a transitional provision in reg.3 of the inserting regulations—Social Security (Industrial Injuries) (Prescribed Diseases) Amendment Regulations 2005 (SI 2005/324)—set out at the end of this section of the book: the prescription does not apply to a period of assessment relating to a claim made before March 14, 2005. The prescription implements the recommendations of IIAC as set out in their report on Conditions due to Biological Agents (Cm 5997) (see paras 252–260 on latex allergy). It is prevalent in health-care workers, especially laboratory workers, nurses and physicians, but it should be noted that the terms of the prescription are in no way confined to those groups. Indeed the IIAC noted that individuals may encounter latex in many circumstances, including as part of their work: medical and surgical procedures; dentistry; laboratory work; latex processing and product manufacture; food preparation; dish-washing and cleaning; use and manufacture of condoms; use and manufacture of actors' masks; use and manufacture of sports equipment; use and manufacture of balloons and rubber bands, such as during teaching and nursery school work; and scene of the crime work (para.253). **10.191**

D5 (non-infective dermatitis)

D5 (non-infective dermatitis) was a very common source of claims for injury benefit but it is, perhaps, less likely to give rise to claims for disablement benefit. No presumption is made in favour of the claimant. It is for him to prove that the disease was due to the nature of his employment, and that his occupation falls within the terms of the Schedule (see note to reg.4, above). **10.192**

D6 (nasal carcinoma)

D6(a) was considered by Commissioner Goodman in *R(I) 4/98*. He concluded that **10.193**

> "it is not legitimate to extend to the claimant (who in the course of his work as a painter came into contact for many years with quantities of respirable dust) the protection of sub-paragraph (a) of paragraph D6 because the wording of it does not justify it. I accept as correct in law Miss Lieven's submission that subparagraph (a) covers only buildings where, as part of the nature of the building, the manufacture or repair [of wooden goods] is carried out e.g. a factory or warehouse. It could not be said that the dwelling-houses and Royal Ordnance Factory buildings in or near which the claimant worked came within such a description . . . The intention of sub-paragraph (a), as is evidenced by the above cited Industrial Injuries Advisory Council's Report, was merely to extend the existing prescription for work on the manufacture or repair of wooden furniture to wooden goods generally. No further extension to all those who have in their work inhaled wood dust was intended nor is, in my view, shown by sub-paragraph (a)." (para.13).

In September 2017 IIAC recommended that the prescription for PD D6 (nasal carcinoma) be extended to include a new para.(d), namely "exposure to wood dust in the course of the machine processing of wood" (see IIAC, *Nasal carcinoma and occupational exposure to wood dust*, Cm 9499), p.39). This recommendation was implemented with effect from September 28, 2018, along with amendments to para.(a). The original occupational prescription under para.(a) was any occupation involving "attendance for work in or about a building where wooden goods are manufactured or repaired". However, according to the Department some tribunals have placed a narrow interpretation on the meaning of "building", effectively restricting coverage to claimants working in premises which exist to manufacture or repair wooden goods. This had the effect of placing outside the scope of benefit e.g. the carpenter who is exposed to wood dust during the fitting out of shops or on a construction site. The terms of prescription were therefore amended by replacing the words "in or about a building" with "at a workplace" and for completeness, included the manufacture or repair of "products made wholly or partially of wood".

D7 (occupational asthma)

10.194 D7 prescribes asthma in relation to a number of occupations. In D7(f) the words "used for the purpose of research or education or in laboratories" set the environment for the whole of the sub-para., so the claimant's appeal in *CI/383/92* (which is not to be reported) was disallowed because he had only worked with prawns (regarded as animals, being anthropods) in the food processing industry (see para.7).

Sub-paragraphs (o)–(x) of D7 (occupational asthma) were added with effect from September 26, 1991 (see SI 1991/1938). In *CI/175/90*. Commissioner Hallett considered whether the claimant could bring himself within sub-para.(j) because of his exposure to paper dust in the printing industry. Applying *CI/308/1989* (reported as *R(I) 2/92*), he concluded that the term "wood dust" had to be construed as an ordinary expression in the English language, that paper, while derived from wood was a different substance, so that the majority of the SSAT had been correct in regarding paper dust as different from wood dust. Nor did the claimant's exposure to printing mist help him, since the evidence showed that the inks forming the mist did not contain isocyanates, so that he did not fall within sub-para.(a) either. His claim failed. Cigarette smoke, while an irritant for those with asthma, appears not to be regarded by medical opinion as a sensitising agent within para.(x), any other "sensitising agent" (*CI/73/94*). One view is that sensitising agent has to read *ejusdem generis* (of a kind or nature) with the agents listed in paras (a)–(w) (*CI/73/94*). Another is that there is no such restriction on the term: para.(x) catches any agent so long as it is sensitising (*CI/4987/1995*). In any case the first question should be whether the identified agent relied on by the claimant is a "sensitising agent" (*CI/2543/2002*). He set out a "triage" approach to help cope with the difficulties of deciding whether something is a "sensitising agent", an approach agreed with and adopted by Commissioner Williams in *CI/564/2005*: there are agents known to be sensitising agents, agents known not to be sensitising agents, and cases where it is not known whether the agent is a sensitising agent. In *CI/3729/2005* Deputy Commissioner White found this a helpful approach. He decided that cardboard dust was not a sensitising agent. He also held (applying *R(I)2/92*) that it was not the same as wood dust and could not fall within D7(j).

In *R(I) 8/02*, Commissioner Howell considered the case of a bus driver claiming that the diesel fumes, dust and particulates he had inhaled during his work constituted "any other sensitising agent". The Commissioner stated:

> "Taking into account the terms of the report of the Industrial Injuries Advisory Council dated August 28, 1990 which led to these extra provisions being introduced (Cm 1244, October 1990) from which it is quite clear that the expression 'sensitising agent' when used medically in this context means a chemical agent which actually *causes* a person to develop an asthmatic condition when inhaled at work, the tribunal were in my judgment quite

> correct in directing themselves that the question they had to consider on the evidence in the claimant's case was whether it had been shown that the diesel fumes, particulates, dust and so forth he inhaled while driving his bus had been the actual cause of his asthmatic condition, rather than merely irritating his chest and making it worse.
>
> As the tribunal correctly recorded, the evidence before them on this issue consisted first of medical advice obtained by the department that diesel exhaust and other vehicle fumes and dust of the kind to which a person is exposed in heavy traffic, while they would certainly act as irritants, would not operate as 'sensitisors' or causative agents for occupational asthma in the way required by the regulations making this a prescribed disease. In addition there were medical reports by three separate doctors on behalf of the claimant himself at pages 35 to 41 which as the tribunal correctly recorded in their statement of reasons at page 46 did not at any point report or state that his asthma had actually been *caused* by exposure to diesel fumes, though they all agreed that it was made much worse by his continuing to work as a bus driver and that it would be a great deal better for him to move to another job" (paras 4, 5).

It would appear that asbestos is not a sensitising agent for purposes of D7 (*CI/2393/02*, paras 7, 8).

There is expert evidence that the chromium element in cement is a sensitising agent (*CI/564/2005*). **10.195**

Latex constitutes "any other sensitising agent" and falls within D7(x) (*CI/3565/2004*). This is important as regards cases occurring before the specific prescription of occupational asthma due to exposure to products made with natural rubber latex in D7(wa).

D7(wa)—occupational asthma due to exposure to products made with natural rubber latex—was added from March 14, 2005, subject to a transitional provision in reg.3 of the inserting regulations—Social Security (Industrial Injuries) (Prescribed Diseases) Amendment Regulations 2005 (SI 2005/324)—set out at the end of this section of the book: the prescription does not apply to a period of assessment relating to a claim made before March 14, 2005. The prescription implements the recommendations of IIAC as set out in their report on Conditions due to Biological Agents (Cm 5997) (see paras 252–260 on latex allergy). It is prevalent in healthcare workers, especially laboratory workers, nurses and physicians, but it should be noted that the terms of the prescription are in no way confined to those groups. Indeed the IIAC noted that Individuals may encounter latex in many circumstances, including as part of their work: medical and surgical procedures; dentistry; laboratory work; latex processing and product manufacture; food preparation; dishwashing and cleaning; use and manufacture of condoms; use and manufacture of actors' masks; use and manufacture of sports equipment; use and manufacture of balloons and rubber bands, such as during teaching and nursery school work; and scene of the crime work (para.253).

See further *NP v SSWP (II)* [2022] UKUT 279 (AAC), in which Judge Wikeley dismissed an appeal from a tribunal which had found that the claimant's workplace exposure to various agents had exacerbated his pre-existing constitutional asthma rather than triggered occupational asthma. Judge Wikeley explained as follows:

> "Work-related asthma in general means asthma where there is some association between increased symptoms and workplace exposure. There are generally accepted to be two types of work-related asthma. The first is work-aggravated asthma, meaning (as the label implies) asthma that is aggravated, but not caused, by exposure to an inhaled agent at work. This type of asthma is not compensated under the industrial injuries scheme. The second is occupational asthma, being asthma that is caused by exposure to an inhaled agent at work. Occupational asthma may be one of two types. The first is occupational asthma with sensitisation, typically where a worker has developed an allergy or sensitisation to an inhaled agent at work. Depending on the circumstances, this may be covered by the prescribed disease provisions for PD D7 in the industrial injuries scheme.

The second is acute irritant induced asthma, where asthma develops after a single very high dose exposure (or perhaps multiple symptomatic high doses) to inhaled irritants. This type of asthma may be covered by the accident provisions in the industrial injuries scheme (rather than under the prescribed disease rules)" (para.15).

Judge Wikeley held that the tribunal had provided an adequately reasoned conclusion for its finding that the claimant experienced work-*aggravated* asthma rather than work-*caused* occupational asthma. In addition, the udge ruled that "... in stating that coal dust is not a sensitising agent [within D7(x)] the FTT was simply reflecting and stating the prevailing view in medical science. It certainly had no persuasive evidence before it that coal dust was recognised as a sensitising agent for the purposes of PD D7" (para.40). Indeed, the Secretary of State's representative had relied on the fact that the UK Occupational Asthma Sensitising Information Service (OASIS) specifically lists coal dust as a <u>non</u>-sensitising agent for the purposes of PD D7. Given that OASIS is the in-house system operated by the Centre for Health and Disability Assessment, which conducts medical assessments on behalf of the DWP, and its listings are not available online, Judge Wikeley observed that "if DWP decision-makers are routinely relying on OASIS listings when deciding prescribed disease claims it would seem only fair that such material is made publicly available" (para.41).

D8 and D8A (primary carcinoma of the lung: asbestos)

10.196 A new D8 was substituted, and D8A added, with effect from April 6, 2006 (see Social Security (Industrial Injuries) (Prescribed Diseases) Amendment Regulations 2006 (SI 2006/586), reg.3). This implements IIAC recommendations in their report *Asbestos-Related Diseases* (Cm 6553). The Council recommended removing from D8 the requirement for the presence of diffuse pleural thickening because recent evidence indicates its unreliability as a marker of asbestos exposure (para.65). D8A (Primary carcinoma of the lung—with no requisite element of asbestosis) was added because the IIAC's literature review found evidence of a greater than doubled risk for lung cancer in the following groups of workers who have experienced substantial occupational asbestos exposure: workers in asbestos textile manufacture; asbestos sprayers; asbestos insulation workers, including those applying and removing asbestos-containing materials in shipbuilding and gas mask manufacturers (para.62). The requirement of exposure for the requisite number of years prior to 1975 reflects the IIAC view that the risk fell after the introduction of the 1969 Asbestos Regulations (para.63). The reformulation cannot apply to any period of assessment prior to April 6, 2006 (reg.4 of the Amendment Regs as further amended by SI 2006/769, reg.2).

In *SSWP v ER (II)* [2012] UKUT 204 (AAC), Judge May considered the position of a claimant suffering from the prescribed disease, who had as a scaffolder worked in close proximity to others working with asbestos to insulate pipes, but who was not directly himself employed in using asbestos to insulate pipes. The issue was whether his medical condition fell within the terms of the prescription in PD 8A. While Commissioner May agreed that the wording of the prescription could arguably be read as covering those who, like the claimant, had worked in close proximity to asbestos insulation workers for the required periods of time, he nonetheless considered that he was entitled to read the terms of prescription more narrowly in light of the recommendations in the IIAC Report which indicated that there was no intention to widen the range of occupations covered. He stated that this was

"not a case where the label of what the claimant did was different from what he actually did. It is accepted that his job did not involve participating in the activities referred to in the regulation. The report in my view is concerned with active involvement and in interpreting the regulation in that way this is fatal to the assertion that a claimant satisfied that he was in an occupation to which the prescribed disease applied. To determine otherwise would be to artificially widen the statutory language. The Secretary of State's appeal accordingly succeeds" (para.14).

SSWP v ER (II) [2012] UKUT 204 (AAC) was followed in *SSWP v EK (deceased) (II)* [2016] UKUT 458 (AAC), also involving a stager who had erected scaffolding in shipyards and contracted lung cancer but who was found to fall outside the terms of the prescription. For a further example of the fine lines that may have to be drawn in applying the terms of PD D8a, see *PC v SSWP (II)* [2017] UKUT 409 (AAC), in which Judge Jacobs held that an engineer installing fire alarm systems, whose work involved some cutting, drilling and disturbance of asbestos lagging, was not working in a prescribed occupation: "The work of cutting and drilling does not come within the prescription, as it is not lagging work. It is work related to the preparation for installing the cables. It was not lagging or preparatory to lagging" (at para.10). In so finding, Judge Jacobs followed *SSWP v ER (II)* [2012] UKUT 204 (AAC) and *SSWP v EK (II) (deceased)* [2016] UKUT 458 (AAC).

D9 (pleural thickening)

The reformulation of disease D9 from the same date as the amendments to D8 and D8A noted immediately above (i.e. as from April 6, 2006) implemented the IIAC recommendation that the requirement for measurements of pleural thickening be replaced by one involving costophrenic angle on plain chest radiographs (paras 70, 72(a)). However, following a further IIAC report, the definition of diffuse pleural thickening (DPT) for the purpose of D9 has now been modernised by removing the requirement for "obliteration of the costophrenic angle" from the terms of prescription (with effect from March 30, 2017: see Social Security (Industrial Injuries) (Prescribed Diseases) Amendment Regulations 2017 (SI 2017/232) reg.3). This change was made because the radiographic criterion in the former definition was potentially restrictive, since it implied to medical specialists diagnostic assessment by means of a chest radiograph. In practice, however, advances in medical imaging mean that most claimants are now investigated using a computerised tomography (CT) scan. The difficulty identified by IIAC was that some claimants who are disabled with demonstrable DPT on CT scanning fail to meet the criteria for prescription based on a traditional chest X-ray. In addition, many more claimants nowadays are likely to present medical evidence to support their claim in the form of evidence from CT imaging rather than conventional X-rays. See IIAC, *Diffuse pleural thickening*, Cm 9346 (April 2016). **10.197**

See also *KH (deceased) (by his appointee AMH) v SSWP (II)* [2021] UKUT 189 (AAC) at para 13, where Judge Poynter, giving permission to appeal, observed that "The claimant must be suffering from thickening of the "pleura" (i.e., the membrane that forms the lining of the lungs). That thickening need only affect one lung ("unilateral")—although it may affect both ("bilateral")—but it must be "diffuse", which is another word for "widespread". Pleural thickening that is localised (which is often called "pleural plaques") does not meet the definition."

D10 (primary carcinoma of the lung: tin, etc)

The insertion of para.(d) into PD D10 (primary carcinoma of the lung)to include employment wholly or mainly as a coke oven worker implements the recommendations of the IIAC in its report *Lung cancer in coke oven workers* Cm 8163 (September 2011). The IIAC identified evidence of a greater than double the risk of lung cancer associated with work involving coke ovens. For top oven workers, this occurred after only five years of employment (see para.(d)(ii) of the new entry), and for other oven workers, the after 15 years of employment (see para.(d)(i) of the new entry). Since the IIAC realised that workers could in the course of their employment move between top oven work and other oven tasks, yet fail separately to meet either of the five year or 15-year thresholds, it recommended that both periods could combined with each year of top oven work equating to three years of other oven work (see para.(d)(iii) of the new entry). **10.198**

The DWP anticipates that the amendment will result in successful claims from some 65 people a year who have worked as coke oven workers for the specified number of years.

D12 (chronic obstructive pulmonary disease)

10.199 As regards PD D12 (chronic obstructive pulmonary disease), the disease was originally prescribed for certain categories of coal miners in terms of the discrete conditions of chronic bronchitis, emphysema or both (see further N. Wikeley, (1994) *Journal of Social Security Law* 23 and (1997) 26 *Industrial Law Journal* 283). The terms of the PD were recast in 2015, on the recommendation of IIAC, with the aim of better reflecting current medical practice, which is to use the umbrella term chronic obstructive pulmonary disease (COPD) rather than the specific underlying disorder (IIAC, *Effects of treatment and the medical assessment of Chronic Bronchitis ad Emphysema (PD D12, Chronic Obstructive Pulmonary Disease,* Cm 8906, July 2014, at para.48).

An ongoing matter of controversy has been the measurement of lung function for the purposes of PD D12. In *CI/126/2002* Commissioner Angus noted that in some circumstances a spirometric test can be inaccurate. He stated:

> "In assessing the evidential value of the subsequent spirometry it would have been necessary to take into account whether or not the claimant's lung function might have been enhanced by medication. In assessing disablement it is legitimate to base the assessment on what the claimant can do when he has taken medication but for the purposes of diagnosis it is the unassisted function which is relevant" (para.16).

10.200 Commissioner Williams followed this in *CI/2683/2004*. He stressed that the regulations did not require a spirometry test—the diagnosis question must be considered in the light of all relevant evidence, including any such test—and that the focus must be on the claimant's condition as at the date of the original decision. He considered that

> "tribunals should have in mind that individuals may or may not have been given guidance and may or may not have acted on it. They should therefore, to ensure fairness, directly check any necessary facts about pre-test medication if they conduct a test. They may also need to check that the medical adviser took appropriate note and account of any relevant medicaments when performing the original test. They should, at least in marginal cases, consider the possible effects of medication when forming a view about the conclusions to be drawn from the "accompanying evidence" (para.29).

The implications of the Commissioner's decision in *CI/2683/2004* were considered by IIAC, at the request of the DWP, in its 2014 report on *Effects of treatment and the medical assessment of Chronic Bronchitis and Emphysema (PD D12, Chronic Obstructive Pulmonary Disease* (Cm 8906, July 2014). In particular, the Council addressed the issue of how, and to what extent, an allowance should be made in the interpretation of spirometry for claimants for PD D12 who use bronchodilator treatments (i.e. drugs aimed at dilating the airways and relieving airflow obstruction). There was concern that *CI/2683/2004* in practice led to arbitrary and sometimes variable offsets being applied by medical advisors in respect of PD D12 claimants taking such treatments.

IIAC furthermore noted that responses to treatments are variable and unpredictable between individuals, and that any effects in cases of COPD (in contrast to cases of asthma) are likely to be small. The Council accordingly concluded that it was not possible to recommend a scientifically valid adjustment factor that would encompass the very wide variety of different treatments now used in the management of COPD while still remaining equitable to individual claimants. In addition, when PD D12 had originally been prescribed, the Council had highlighted that it would be impractical to take account of factors such as work location, job title, actual exposures to coal dust and lifetime smoking habits. In the same way, the Council concluded that it would be impractical to apply an offset to the one litre loss of FEV_1 threshold according to an individual claimant's medical treatment; it was both "beyond the science and beyond the resources of the Scheme to be this exact" (at para.6).

Consequently IIAC recommended that the effects of treatments should be disregarded when interpreting spirometric evidence during medical assessments for PD

D12. This accounts for the amendment in force from March 16, 2015 to the effect that the value of 1 litre in the statutory test "shall be construed as fixed and shall not vary by virtue of any treatment or treatments" (see Social Security (Industrial Injuries) (Prescribed Diseases) Amendment Regulations 2015 (SI 2015/87)).

Disease D12 is subject to a transitional provision in reg.9 of the Social Security (Industrial Injuries) (Prescribed Diseases) Amendment (No.2) Regulations (SI 1993/1985) below. Furthermore, the amendment numbered "15" on the appropriate mean value and the prediction formula is subject to a transitional provision in reg.7(2) of the Social Security (Industrial Injuries) (Prescribed Diseases) Amendment Regulations 2000 (SI 2000/1588), reproduced later in this volume.

The prescription of D12 with effect from September 13, 1993 is not retrospective so as to enable payment of disablement benefit, for a period prior to prescription, to a claimant whose date of onset of the disease precedes that date and continues to suffer from it (see *R(I) 4/96*, noted in the notes to reg.6, above).

In *CI/1160/2004*, Commissioner Angus held **10.201**

> "that paragraph D12 of Schedule 1 to the Regulations is not irrational. On the matter of its application to smokers, as Mr Heath said, the fact that smokers who suffer from coal dust retention might be compensated for having contracted a coal dust related disease which they might have contracted in any case does not exclude any non-smoker with coal dust related emphysema or bronchitis from compensation under the legislation. As regards the use of the 1 litre drop in lung function as the prescribed decisive indicator of PD D12, Dr. A's opinion that it can result in the disease not being diagnosed in short men who have a disabling reduction in lung function due to the retention of coal dust has to be respected. It is an opinion which may well be shared by other chest physicians: but the D12 prescription is based on the equally respectable opinions of the members of the Industrial Injuries Advisory Council and the Secretary of State cannot be accused of irrationality in relying upon their opinion to devise the prescription" (para.26).

He also rejected the view that it was legally challengeable as discriminatory against short men.

The amendments effected from March 24, 1996 to prescribed diseases A12 (an alteration of terms), D4 (ability to benefit from the reg.4 presumption) and D5 (an alteration of its terms to reflect the newly prescribed disease C30) are subject to a transitional provision in reg.7 of the Social Security (Industrial Injuries and Diseases) (Miscellaneous Amendments) Regulations 1996 (SI 1996/425), below.

In April 2020 IIAC published a position paper (No.45) on the possible prescription of COPD in coke oven workers. The Council noted a body of evidence showing an association between coke oven exposures and non-malignant pulmonary disease but considered there was lack of detail in some studies and inconsistency in the nature and magnitude of the effects in others. IIAC concluded the published evidence was insufficient to recommend prescription.

D13 (primary carcinoma of the nasopharynx)

A new prescribed disease D13 (primary carcinoma of the nasopharynx) (nasopharyngeal cancer) was added with effect from April 7, 2008 by reg.2 of the Social Security (Industrial Injuries) (Prescribed Diseases) Amendment Regulations 2008 (SI 2008/14). The prescription, in respect of a number of occupations involving working with wood or wood products, reflects the recommendations of the Industrial Injuries Advisory Council in its report *Nasopharyngeal cancer due to exposure to wood dust* Cm 7162 (July 2007). Those suffering from this rare disease must have worked in the relevant occupations for a period or periods of at least 10 years in the aggregate. A list (not necessarily exhaustive) of the occupations at risk can be found in App.2 of the report. **10.202**

SCHEDULE 2 — **Regulation 11**

MODIFICATIONS OF [SECTIONS 94 TO 107 OF THE SOCIAL SECURITY CONTRIBUTIONS AND BENEFITS ACT 1992 AND SECTIONS 8 TO 10 OF THE SOCIAL SECURITY ADMINISTRATION ACT 1992] IN THEIR APPLICATION TO BENEFIT AND CLAIMS TO WHICH THESE REGULATIONS APPLY

10.203 In [sections 94 to 107 of the Social Security Contributions and Benefits Act 1992 and sections 8 to 10 of the Social Security Administration Act 1992] references to accidents shall be construed as references to prescribed diseases and references to the relevant accident shall be construed as references to the relevant disease and references to the date of the relevant accident shall be construed as references to the date of onset of the relevant disease.

SCHEDULE 3 — **Regulation 34**

ASSESSMENT OF THE EXTENT OF OCCUPATIONAL DEAFNESS

PART I

CLAIMS TO WHICH REGULATION 34(1) APPLIES

10.204

[[1]*Average of hearing losses (dB) due to all causes at 1, 2 and 3 kHz frequencies*]	*Degree of disablement per cent.*
50–52 dB	20
53–57 dB	30
58–62 dB	40
63–67 dB	50
68–72 dB	60
73–77 dB	70
78–82 dB	80
83–87 dB	90
88 dB or more	100

PART II

CLAIMS TO WHICH REGULATION 34(2) APPLIES

10.205

[[1]*Average of hearing losses (dB) due to all causes at 1, 2 and 3 kHz frequencies*]	*Degree of disablement per cent.*
50–53 dB	20
54–60 dB	30
61–66 dB	40
67–72 dB	50
73–79 dB	60
80–86 dB	70
87–95 dB	80
96–105 dB	90
106 dB or more	100

PART III

FORMULA FOR CALCULATING BINAURAL DISABLEMENT

10.206

$$\frac{(\text{Degree of disablement of better ear} \times 4) + \text{degree of disablement of worse ear}}{5}$$

AMENDMENT

1. Social Security (Industrial Injuries) (Prescribed Diseases) Amendment Regulations 1989 (SI 1989/1207) reg.4 (October 16, 1989).

SCHEDULE 4 **Regulation 43**

PRESCRIBED DISEASES AND RELEVANT DATES FOR THE PURPOSES OF REGULATION 43

Description of disease or injury	*Relevant date*	
A3. Dysbarism, including decompression sickness, barotrauma and osteonecrosis.	Except in the case of a person suffering from decompression sickness employed in any occupation involving subjection to compressed or rarefied air, 3rd October 1983.	10.207
A11. Episodic blanching, occurring throughout the year, affecting the middle or proximal phalanges or in the case of a thumb the proximal phalanx, of— (a) in the case of a person with 5 fingers (including thumb) on one hand, any 3 of those fingers, or (b) in the case of person with only 4 such fingers, any 2 of those fingers, or (c) in the case of a person with less than 4 such fingers, any one of those fingers or, as the case may be, the one remaining finger (vibration white finger).	1st April 1985.	
B1. Anthrax	In the case of a person employed in an occupation involving the loading and unloading or transport of animal products or residues, 3rd October 1983.	
B3. Infection by leptospira.	(a) In the case of a person employed in an occupation in places which are or are liable to be infested by small mammals other than rats, field mice or voles, 3rd October 1983; (b) in the case of a person employed in an occupation in any other place mentioned in the second column of paragraph B3 of Part I of Schedule 1 above, 7th January 1980.	
B5. Tuberculosis.	In the case of a person employed in an occupation involving contact with a source of tuberculosis infection, not being an employment set out in the second column of paragraph 38 of Part I of Schedule 1 to the old regulations, 3rd October 1983.	
B6. Extrinsic allergic alveolitis (including farmer's lung).	In the case of a person suffering from extrinsic allergic alveolitis, not being farmer's lung, employed in any occupation set out in the second column of paragraph B6 of Part I of Schedule 1 above, or in the case of a person suffering from farmer's lung, employed in any occupation involving exposure to moulds or fungal spores or heterologous proteins by	

Description of disease or injury	*Relevant date*
	reason of employment in cultivation of edible fungi or maltworking, or loading or unloading or handling in storage edible fungi or caring for or handling birds, 3rd October 1983.
B7. Infection by organisms of the genus brucella.	In the case of a person suffering from infection by organisms of the genus brucella, not being infection by Brucella abortus, or employed in an occupation set out in the second column of paragraph B7 of Part I of Schedule 1 above, not being an occupation set out in the second column of paragraph 46 of Part I of Schedule 1 to the old regulations, 3rd October 1983.
B8. Viral hepatitis.	In the case of a person employed in any occupation involving contact with human blood or human blood products, or contact with a source of viral hepatitis, 3rd December 1984.
B9. Infection by Streptococcus suis.	3rd October 1983.
[[1] B10. (a) Avian chlamydiosis.	9th August 1989.
B10. (b) Ovine chlamydiosis.	9th August 1989.
B11. Q fever.	9th August 1989.]
C3. Poisoning by phosphorus or an inorganic compound of phosphorus or poisoning due to the anti-cholinesterase or pseudo anti-cholinesterase action of organic phosphorus compounds.	In the case of a person suffering from poisoning by an inorganic compound of phosphorus or poisoning due to the pseudo anti-cholinesterase action or organic phosphorus compounds, 3rd October 1983.
C18. Poisoning by cadmium.	In the case of a person employed in an occupation involving exposure to cadmium dust, 3rd October 1983.
C23. Primary neoplasm (including papiloma, carcinoma-in-situ and invasive carcinoma) of the epithelial lining of the urinary tract (renal pelvis, ureter, bladder and urethra).	In the case of a person employed in an occupation involving work in a building in which methylene-bis-orthochloroaniline is produced for commercial purposes, 3rd October 1983.
C24. (a) Angiosarcoma of the liver; (b) osteolysis of the terminal phalanges of the finger; (c) non-cirrhotic portal fibrosis.	(a) In the case of a person suffering from angiosarcoma of the liver or osteolysis of the terminal phalanges of the fingers, 21st March 1977; (b) in the case of a person suffering from non-cirrhotic portal fibrosis, 3rd October 1983.
C25. Occupational vitiligo.	15th December 1980.
[[2]C26. Damage to the liver or kidneys due to exposure to Carbon Tetrachloride.	4th January 1988.
C27. Damage to the liver or kidneys due to exposure to Trichloromethane (Chloroform).	4th January 1988.
C28. Central nervous system dysfunction and associated gastro-intestinal disorders due to exposure to chloromethane (Methyl Chloride).	4th January 1988.
C29. Peripheral neuropathy due to exposure to n-hexane or methyl-p-butyl ketone.	4th January 1988.

Description of disease or injury	*Relevant date*
D3. Diffuse mesothelioma.	In the case of a person suffering from primary neoplasm of the pericardium, 3rd October 1983.
D6. Carcinoma of the nasal cavity or associated air sinuses (nasal carcinoma).	In the case of a person employed in an occupation involving attendance for work in or about a building where wooden goods (other than wooden furniture) are manufactured or where wooden goods are repaired, 3rd October 1983.
D7. Occupational asthma.	[3 (a) In the case of a person suffering from asthma due to exposure to any of the following agents: (i)isocyanates; (ii) platinum salts; (iii) fumes or dusts arising from the manufacture, transport or use of hardening agents (including epoxy resin curing agents) based on phthalic anhydride, tetrachlorophthalic anhydride, trimellitic anhydride or triethylenetetramine; (iv) fumes arising from the use of rosin as a soldering flux; (v) proteolytic enzymes; (vi) animals or insects used for the purposes of research or education or in laboratories; (vii) dusts arising from the sowing, cultivation, harvesting, drying, handling, milling, transport or storage of barley, oats, rye, wheat or maize, or the handling, milling, transport or storage of meal or flour made therefrom, 29th March 1982; (b) In the case of a person suffering from asthma due to exposure to any of the following agents: (i) animals including insects and other anthropods used for the purposes of research or education or in laboratories; (ii) antibiotics; (iii) cimetidine; (iv) wood dust; (v) ispaghula; (vi) castor bean dust; (vii) ipecacuanha; (viii) azodicarbonamide, 1st September 1986.]
D8. Primary carcinoma of the lung where there is accompanying evidence of one or both of the following— (a) asbestosis; (b) bilateral diffuse pleural thickening.	1st April 1985.
D9. Bilateral diffuse pleural thickening.	1st April 1985.
[4 D10. Lung cancer.	1st April 1987.]

AMENDMENTS

1. Social Security (Industrial Injuries) (Prescribed Diseases) Amendment Regulations 1989 (SI 1989/1207), reg.6 (August 9, 1989).
2. Social Security (Industrial Injuries) (Prescribed Diseases) Amendment (No. 2) Regulations 1987 (SI 1987/2112), reg.3 (January 4, 1988).
3. Social Security (Industrial Injuries and Adjudication) Miscellaneous Amendment Regulations 1986 (SI 1986/1374), reg.3 (September 1, 1986).
4. Social Security (Industrial Injuries) (Prescribed Diseases) Amendment Regulations 1987 (SI 1987/335), reg.2 (April 1, 1987).

SCHEDULE 5 **Regulation 44**

TRANSITIONAL PROVISIONS REGARDING DATES OF DEVELOPMENT AND DATES OF ONSET

10.208 **1.**—In this Schedule the "date of development" has the meaning attributed to it by regulations 5, 6, 7 and 56 of the old regulations.

2.—Where a claim for benefit has been made before 6th April 1983, a date of development shall be determined and regulation 16 of the old regulations shall apply as if the old regulations were still in force.

3.—Where a claim for benefit is made after 5th April 1983 and a date of onset is determined which is before 6th April 1983, regulation 16 of the old regulations shall apply as if the old regulations were still in force.

4.—Where in pursuance of a claim made before 6th April 1983 a date of development has been determined and an award of benefit has been made these regulations shall have effect in relation to that claim and any subsequent claim made by or on behalf of the same person in respect of the same disease (except where under regulation 7 the disease is treated as having been contracted afresh) as if references to the date of onset were references to that date of development.

5.—Subject to paragraph 6, where a claim for injury benefit for a day falling or a period beginning before 5th April 1983 is made after 6th April 1983 and no date of development or date of onset which can be treated as such for the purposes of that claim has already been determined, for the purposes only of determining the date on which the injury benefit period (if any) is to begin, a date of development shall be determined, so however that if it is later than 5th April 1983 no injury benefit period shall begin and injury benefit shall not be payable.

6.—There shall be no entitlement, in the following cases, to benefit for any day which is earlier than the date specified:—

(a)	in the case of a person who is or has been suffering from	
(i)	viral hepatitis	: 2nd February 1976
(ii)	angiosarcoma of the liver	: 21st March 1977
(iii)	osteolysis of the terminal phalanges of the fingers	: 21st March 1977
(iv)	carcinoma of the nasal cavity or associated air sinuses (nasal carcinoma)	: 8th August 1979
(v)	occupational vitiligo	: 15th December 1980
[1 (vi)	occupational asthma arising otherwise than as described at (vii) below	: 29th March 1982;
(vii)	occupational asthma which is due to exposure to antibiotics, cimetidine, wood dust, ispaghula, castor bean dust, ipecacuanha or azodicarbonamide	: 1st September 1986;]
(b)	in the case of a person who is or has been suffering from byssinosis but who has not been employed in employed earner's employment in any occupation mentioned in regulation 2(c) of the old regulations for a period or periods (whether before or after 5th July 1948) amounting in the aggregate to 5 years	: 6th April 1979;
(c)	in the case of a person who is or has been suffering from infection by leptospira but neither is nor has been either incapable of work or suffering from a loss of faculty as a result of infection by—	

(i) leptospira icterohaemorrhagiae in the case of a person employed in employed earner's employment in any occupation involving work in places which are, or are liable to be, infested byrats, or
(ii) leptospira canicola in the case of a person employed in employed earner's employment in any occupation involving work at dog kennels or the care or handling of dogs : 7th January 1980.

AMENDMENT

1. Social Security (Industrial Injuries and Adjudication) Miscellaneous Amendment Regulations 1986 (SI 1986/1374), reg.2 (September 1, 1986).

Schedule 6 omitted. **10.209**

The Social Security (Industrial Injuries and Diseases) Miscellaneous Provisions Regulations 1986

(SI 1986/1561) (*as amended*)

ARRANGEMENT OF REGULATIONS

PART II

PART IV

The Secretary of State for Social Services, in exercise of the powers set out in the Schedule below, and of all other powers enabling him in that behalf, by this instrument, which contains only provisions consequential upon section 39 of the Social Security Act 1986, makes the following regulations:

PART II

MISCELLANEOUS PROVISIONS RELATING TO INDUSTRIAL INJURIES AND DISEASES

Regular occupation for the purposes of Reduced Earnings Allowance

2.—(1) Employed earner's employment in which a claimant was engaged when the relevant accident took place but which was not his regular occupation shall be treated for the purposes of section 59A of the 1975 Act (reduced earnings allowance) as if it had been his regular occupation where the claimant, at the time the relevant accident took place, had no regular **10.211**

occupation but was pursuing a course of full-time education, either by attendance at a recognised educational establishment or, if the education is recognised by the Secretary of State in accordance with section 2(1A) of the Child Benefit Act 1975, elsewhere.

(2) In determining for the purpose of paragraph (1) whether a person was pursuing a course of full-time education, any temporary interruption of that education not exceeding a period of 6 months, or such longer period as the Secretary of State may in any particular case determine, shall be disregarded.

GENERAL NOTE

10.212 This provision permits students and others in full-time education to establish a regular occupation for the purposes of Reduced Earnings Allowance. Formerly, a vacation job would not have been regarded as a regular occupation. For commentary on SSCBA 1992 s.142(2), see above. Section 59A of the SSA 1975 has been replaced by para.11 of Sch.7 to the SSCBA 1992 while s.2(1A) of the CBA 1975 has been replaced by s.142(2) of the SSCBA 1992.

10.213 *Regulations 3–7 omitted.*

PART IV

TRANSITIONAL PROVISIONS

10.214 *Regulations 8–10 omitted.*

Unemployability Supplement and Reduced Earnings Allowance

10.215 **11.**—A reduced earnings allowance under section 59A of the 1975 Act and an unemployability supplement shall not be payable for the same period.

GENERAL NOTE

10.216 Section 59A of the SSA 1975 has been replaced by para.11 of Sch.7 to the SSCBA 1992.

10.217 *Regulation 12 omitted.*

10.218 *Regulation 13 revoked.*

Claims for disablement benefit made before 1st October 1986

10.219 **14.**—Where a claim for disablement benefit is made before 1st October 1986, that claim shall be determined as though—

(a) paragraph 3(1) of Schedule 3 to the 1986 Act had not been enacted,

(b) paragraph 3(2) had been enacted to the extent only of inserting subsection (1B) of section 57 of the 1975 Act but omitting the words "Subject to paragraph (1C)" and the words from "and where it is" to the end of the subsection.

General Note

This still has some effect because a claim is not finally determined until there is a final assessment of disablement. Where there has been a series of provisional assessments following a claim made before October 1, 1986, further awards of disablement benefit are made as though s.57 of the 1975 Act (now s.103 of the SSCBA 1992) had not been significantly amended. This means that a weekly disablement pension is awarded only if disablement is assessed as at least 20 per cent but that a disablement gratuity is payable if disablement is assessed at anything from 1 per cent to 19 per cent (see SSCBA 1992 Sch.7 para.9). **10.220**

The Social Security (Industrial Injuries) (Reduced Earnings Allowance and Transitional) Regulations 1987

(SI 1987/415) (*as amended*)

Arrangement of Regulations

Part I

General

Part II

Reduced Earnings Allowance

Part III

Transitional

The Secretary of State for Social Services, in exercise of the powers conferred by section 59A(10) of and Schedule 20 to the Social Security Act 1975 and sections 84(1) and 89(1) of the Social Security Act 1986, and of all other powers enabling him in that behalf, by this instrument, which is made before the end of the period of 12 months from the commencement of the enactments under which it is made, makes the following Regulations:

PART I

GENERAL

Citation, commencement and interpretation

10.222 **1.**—(1) These regulations may be cited as the Social Security (Industrial Injuries) (Reduced Earnings Allowance and Transitional) Regulations 1987 and shall come into force on 6th April 1987.

(2) In these regulations—

"the Act" means the [Social Security Contributions and Benefits Act 1992];

"the 1986 Act" means the Social Security Act 1986.

(3) Unless the context otherwise requires, any reference in these regulations to a numbered regulation is a reference to the regulation bearing that number in these regulations and any reference in a regulation to a numbered paragraph is a reference to the paragraph of that regulation bearing that number.

GENERAL NOTE

10.223 The reference in square brackets was added by the annotator to make the regulations more "user friendly" in the light of the consolidating legislation.

PART II

REDUCED EARNINGS ALLOWANCE

Determination of the probable standard of remuneration

10.224 **2.**—(1) On any award of reduced earnings allowance except the first award made in respect of a relevant accident or a disease prescribed in accordance with [sections 108 to 110] of the Act, a person's probable standard of remuneration shall be determined in accordance with the following provisions of this regulation or, if applicable, of regulation 3.

(2) On the second award made in respect of an accident or disease, a person's probable standard of remuneration in any employment shall be determined in the same manner as on the first award.

(3) On a third or subsequent award made in respect of an accident or disease, a person's probable standard of remuneration in an employment shall be determined—

(a) if applicable, in accordance with paragraphs (4)–(8) of this regulation or with regulation 3, or

(b) otherwise in the same manner as on the first award.

(4) Where at the time of the award a person's regular occupation has ceased to exist, his probable standard of remuneration in the regular occupation shall be determined in accordance with paragraph (6).

(5) Where at the time of the award either—

(a) a person is not employed, or

(b) he is employed but the employment is not suitable in his case, and

(c) there has been no relevant change of circumstances since the last previous award, the probable standard of remuneration in any employed earner's employment which is suitable in his case and which he is likely to be capable of following shall be determined in accordance with paragraph (6).

(6) For the purposes of paragraphs (4) and (5) a person's probable standard of remuneration shall be determined by reference to the standard determined for the purposes of the last previous award of reduced earnings allowance [1 adjusted by a percentage equal to any percentage change] in the level of relevant occupational groups.

(7) For the purposes of paragraph (6) and regulation 3(1)—

(a) the relevant occupational group is the number specified in data relating to earnings published from time to time by the Department of Employment which is the nearest to, respectively,

(i) the person's regular occupation,

(ii) any employed earner's employments which are suitable in his case and which he is likely to be capable of following; and

(b) the [1 percentage change] in the level of earnings shall be determined by reference to the movement in average gross weekly earnings of full-time employees on adult rates in the relevant occupational group where pay was not affected by absence; and

(c) a [1 percentage change] for any year shall be applied to a determination of the probable standard of remuneration on an award made for a period commencing on or after the first Wednesday in the February of the year following the year to [1 which the change relates].

(8) For the purposes of paragraph (4), a person's regular occupation has ceased to exist where—

(a) his former employer has ceased to trade in the locality, or

(b) the work the person did at his former place of employment no longer exists or has changed to such a degree that the work amounts to a different occupation,

and there is in the person's locality no employer providing work similar to that in which he was engaged.

Amendment

1. Social Security (Industrial Injuries) (Miscellaneous Amendments) Regulations 1988 (SI 1988/553) reg 4 (April 11, 1988).

General Note

This regulation provides a mechanism for the determination of the probable standard of remuneration as required by SSCBA 1992, Sch.7, para.11(10) and (13), formerly SSA 1975, s.59A(8) and (10). Formerly, the tribunal would have to make a calculation based on information supplied to it on wage rates in individual jobs. This necessitated a great deal of research and information-gathering and this new provision provides a standard method of calculation by reference to published data relating to the earnings of relevant occupational groups. **10.225**

The first award of reduced earnings allowance

The regulation does not apply to the first award when the calculation is made by reference to actual earnings in employments which would be suitable for the claimant and which he would be capable of following. **10.226**

The second award

The same procedure is adopted as for the first award.

The third and subsequent awards

10.227 On the third and later awards the tribunal should first establish whether paras (4) to (8) of the regulation apply to the claimant. If not, the same procedure is adopted as for the first and second awards. Paras (4) and (5) apply the standardised calculation to the following claimants—

(a) those whose regular occupation has ceased to exist; or

(b) those who are unemployed at the time of the award, or employed in an unsuitable employment,

and in respect of whom there has been no relevant charge of circumstances since the last award.

The workings of the regulation have been briefly considered in unreported decision *CI/203/1989*. Take care to look also at regs 3 and 4, below, before applying the standard calculation set out in para.(6).

The standard calculation

10.228 Paragraph 6 requires that the standard of remuneration be determined by reference to the percentage change in the level of remuneration in relevant occupational groups, a phrase defined in para.7. That para. also directs the precise calculation of the percentage and fixes the date from which the annual standard change shall be applicable.

Awards at the maximum rate

10.229 **3.**—(1) Where on the second or subsequent award of reduced earnings allowance in respect of an accident or disease the award—

(a) is made at the maximum rate payable under [paragraph 11(10) of Schedule 7] of the Act, or

(b) would have been made at that rate but for paragraph 5(3) of Schedule 3 to the 1986 Act or regulation 8,

then, but subject to paragraph (2), on any award thereafter the probable standard of a person's remuneration in any employment shall be determined as being the same standard as that determined for the purpose of the last previous award of reduced earnings allowance increase by a percentage equal to any percentage increase in the level of earnings for the relevant occupational groups.

(2) This regulation does not apply where—

(a) on an award, reduced earnings allowance would be payable at a rate below the maximum rate payable under [paragraph 11(10) of Schedule 7] of the Act otherwise than by virtue of paragraph 5(3) of Schedule 3 to the 1986 Act or regulation 8; or

(b) there has been a relevant change in the person's circumstances since the last previous award.

Awards following relevant change of circumstances

10.230 **4.**—An award of reduced earnings allowance following a relevant change of circumstances shall be treated for the purpose of Part II of these regulations as the first such award.

General Note

What constitutes a relevant change of circumstances was discussed by Commissioner Walker in *CI/203/1989*. He was considering the case of a person who had been made redundant and concluded that redundancy did constitute a relevant change of circumstances. The Commissioner said, 10.231

> ". . . the phrase means no more than that if at the time of making an award there are circumstances different from those obtaining at the time of the making of the previous award, and which differences may have some bearing upon the calculation then there is a relevant change for the purposes of the regulation."

The significance of a change of circumstances is, of course, that it takes the calculation outside the ambit of reg.2 since the award will then be treated as the first award.

Part III

Transitional

Claims before 6th April 1987

5.—Regulations 2 and 3 shall not apply to any award of reduced earnings allowance where the claim which resulted in that award was made before 6th April 1987. 10.232

Awards for special hardship made before 1st October 1986

6.—Any award made before 1st October 1986 of an increase in disablement pension under section 60 of the [Social Security Act 1975] (increase of disablement benefit for special hardship) shall be treated for the purposes of regulations 2 and 3 as an award of reduced earnings allowance. 10.233

Abatement of Reduced Earnings Allowance

7.—(1) For the purposes of paragraph 5(3) of Schedule 3 to the 1986 Act paragraph 5 of that Schedule shall be treated as having come into force on 6th April 1987. 10.234

(2) Paragraph 5(3) of Schedule 3 to the 1986 Act shall be modified by the substitution, in head (c), of the words "a reduced earnings allowance under section 59A" for the words "an increase under section 60" and by the substitution of the words "allowance was payable" for the words "increase was payable."

Regulation 8 omitted. 10.235

Offsetting prior payment of gratuity against subsequent award

9.—For the purpose of offsetting any amount paid by way of gratuity under an award which is subsequently varied on appeal or revised on review, regulation 85 of the Social Security (Adjudication) Regulations 1984 shall 10.236

have effect after 5th April 1987 as if made under section 53(5)(b) of the 1986 Act.

General Note

10.237 Amendments effected by the following regulations have been incorporated in the text above.

Regulations

Social Security (Industrial Injuries) (Miscellaneous Amendments) Regulations 1988 (SI 1988/553).

The Social Security (Industrial Injuries) (Regular Employment) Regulations 1990

(SI 1990/256) (*as amended*)

Arrangement of Regulations

Whereas a draft of this instrument was laid before Parliament in accordance with the provisions of section 29(2)(e) of the Social Security Act 1989 and approved by a resolution of each House of Parliament:

Now, therefore, the Secretary of State for Social Security, in exercise of the power conferred by section 59B(7) and (8) of and Schedule 20 to the Social Security Act 1975, and of all other powers enabling him in that behalf, by this instrument, which is made before the end of the period of 6 months beginning with the coming into force of the aforesaid section 59B(7) and (8), makes the following Regulations:

Citation, commencement and interpretation

10.239 **1.**—(1) These Regulations may be cited as the Social Security (Industry Injuries) (Regular Employment) Regulations 1990 and shall come into force on 1st April 1990.

(2) [1. . .]

Amendment

1. Social Security (Industrial Injuries and Diseases) (Miscellaneous Amendments) Regulations 1996/425 reg.6(2) (March 24, 1996).

[1Meaning of "regular employment"

10.240 **2.**—For the purposes of paragraph 13 of Schedule 7 to the Social Security Contributions and Benefits Act 1992, "regular employment" means gainful employment—

(a) under a contract of service which requires a person to work for an average of 10 hours or more per week in any period of five consecutive weeks, there being disregarded for this purpose any week when the contract subsists during which he is absent from that employment in circumstances where such absence is permitted under the contract (for example in the case of sickness or taking leave); or

(b) which a person undertakes for an average of 10 hours or more per week in any period of five consecutive weeks.]

AMENDMENT

1. Social Security (Industrial Injuries and Diseases) (Miscellaneous Amendments) Regulations 1996 (SI 1996/425) reg.6(3) (March 24, 1996).

GENERAL NOTE

In *R(I) 2/93*, Commissioner Hoolahan noted in passing that this provision does *not* require a person to return to regular employment within five weeks of leaving his previous employment; the five weeks can begin any time in the future (para.10). **10.241**

As regards "average", see *CI/3225/2004*. There Commissioner Levenson, deploying para.(b), used "rolling five week averages" as a convenient way of assessing continuing entitlement and determined that this claimant had not given up regular employment. The Commissioner stated:

"It has never been doubted that the word 'average' refers to the arithmetic mean. The use of the phrase 'any period of five consecutive weeks' means that weeks after a particular job comes to an end can be included, and that weeks in which no work is done or expected to be done can also be included. In so deciding, I agree with the conclusions of the Commissioner in paragraphs 20 to 22 of *CI/2517/2001*. Further, I see no reason why a five week period under consideration cannot include some weeks calculated with reference to regulation 2(a) and some calculated with reference to regulation 2(b). Although 2(b) can only be assessed or calculated retrospectively, because it must be established for those purposes whether gainful employment has in fact been undertaken, future weeks can be considered from any particular vantage point (para.12)."

The appeal in *AR v SSWP (II)* [2021] UKUT 279 (AAC) was concerned with how the reduced earnings allowance legislation drafted in 1990 applies today to zero hours contracts. The DWP decided that, as the claimant had not worked at least an average of 10 hours p.w. over a nine-week period since reaching pensionable age, his REA had to be converted to retirement allowance. The claimant appealed on the ground that he had worked under a zero-hours contract and his average hours should be calculated over a period of more than five (or indeed nine) weeks, as this would show that he had worked an average of around 24 hours p.w. (and without entitlement to sick leave or paid holiday) in the last year. The FTT dismissed his appeal, as did Judge Jacobs in the Upper Tribunal:

"12. Paragraph 13 of Schedule 7 to the 1992 Act provides that a claimant shall cease to be entitled 'as from the day on which he gives up regular employment.' Regulation 2 defines the expression 'regular employment'. The regulation provides what 'regular employment' means. That word conveys that the regulation contains an exhaustive definition of the expression. There is no scope for arguing that the claimant actually remained in regular employment as that expression might normally be understood. As Mr Commissioner Howell wrote in *CI/16202/96* at [5], regulation 2 contains: … an artificial test of when a person is to be regarded as having 'given up regular employment' and if the facts of his case are caught by the regulations it is no answer to say that he always intended to go on working regularly, or had in fact done so, in ways that for some reason or another failed to meet the prescribed conditions.

13. Regulation 2(a) does not apply to the claimant's circumstances. It only applies if a claimant is party to a contract of service (employment) that requires them to work. This applies to the traditional contract of employment in which a

claimant contracts to work for a particular number of hours a week, barring periods of holiday or sickness. It does not apply to a zero hours contract under which: (a) the employer is not obliged to make any work available for the employee; and (b) the employee is not obliged to take up any work offered.

14. Regulation 2(b) does apply to the claimant's circumstances. It was almost certainly not drafted with zero hours contracts in mind. It was probably designed for claimants who were self-employed or working on a casual basis. But that does not matter. What matters is what it says. By its terms, it applies to work actually undertaken rather than work that the claimant is required to do under a contract. That is apt to cover zero hours contracts and exactly captures the claimant's circumstances. There is no equivalent provision to the qualification in regulation 2(a) for absences allowed by the contract. The reason is that, unlike regulation 2(a), regulation 2(b) is based on actual work outside the framework of a contract."

[1 Circumstances in which a person over pensionable age is to be regarded as having given up regular employment

10.242 **3.**—Unless he is entitled to reduced earnings allowance for life by virtue of paragraph 12(1) of Schedule 7 to the Social Security Contributions and Benefits Act 1992, a person who has attained pensionable age shall be regarded as having given up regular employment at the start of the first week in which he is not in regular employment after the later of—

(a) the week during which this regulation comes into force; or
(b) the week during which he attains pensionable age.]

AMENDMENT

1. Social Security (Industrial Injuries and Diseases) (Miscellaneous Amendments) Regulations 1996 (SI 1996/425) reg.6(3) (March 24, 1996).

GENERAL NOTE

10.243 This regulation came into force on March 24, 1996, the date on which it was inserted by the Social Security (Industrial Injuries and Diseases) (Miscellaneous Amendment) Regulations 1996. In decisions reported as *R(I) 2/99* and affirmed in *Plummer v Hammond*, Commissioner Howell held that it removed entitlement to REA and replaced it with retirement allowance for life with effect from March 31, 1996 (the beginning of the week after March 24, 1996) even in the case of two ladies who had attained pensionable age prior to March 24 and had in normal parlance given up (but not retired from) regular employment because of incapacity long before either April 10, 1989 (the date in SSCBA 1992 Sch.7 para.13(1)) or March 24, 1996 (the date reg.3 came into force). The two ladies would not otherwise have been deprived of REA by para.13(1) because of the fact that they had as at October 1, 1989 been long out of work so that they could not be said to have "given up" regular employment on any day on or after that date as para.13(10)(b) as supplemented by the original 1990 regulations required, "gives up" bearing its ordinary natural meaning (*R(I) 2/93, R(I) 3/93*). Reg.3 did, however, deprive them of it and transfer them to retirement allowance by, albeit artificially, regarding them as having given it up. See in particular paras 37, 38 and 40–49.

The case is very useful in charting the bumpy and twisting path of attempts to make entitlements to REA cease on retirement, and makes clear that reg.3 is *intra vires* the rule making power in SSCBA 1992 Sch.7 13(8).

Since both ladies had attained the age of 65 before the regulation deprived them of REA, "the condition linked to pensionable age in paragraph 13(1) has no discriminatory effect", rendering it unnecessary in their case to consider any possible application of Council Dir. 79/7: see *Vol.III: Administration Appeals and the European Dimension.*

That this can work harshly in respect of persons whose work is seasonal is shown in *SSWP v NH (II)* [2010] UKUT 84 (AAC). Here the claimant did seasonal work in a museum from March to October 2007, when the contract ended. In August 2007 he became 65. He next worked from March 11, 2008 at the museum. Judge Paines, agreeing in part with Judge Howell in *CI/16202/96* (applied in *CI/2517/01*) and partly with Judge Levenson in *CI/3224/04*, took the following approach to reg.3 read with reg.2: **10.244**

> "the question becomes, for the purposes of regulation 3 when read with regulation 2(a), whether the claimant was in employment under a contract (with, to put it loosely, average contractual hours of ten or more); for the purposes of regulation 2(b) the question is whether the claimant was in fact in gainful employment which he undertook for an average of ten hours measured over five consecutive weeks.
>
> Viewing the questions in that way, it seems to me to be impossible to hold that a person is 'in' employment under a contract for the purposes of regulation 2(a) at a point in time at which the contract has ceased. In that regard I find Judge Howell's reasoning . . . compelling.
>
> As far as regulation 2(b) is concerned, I agree with Judge Howell that it embraces both casual employment and self-employment. It is in addition self-evident that the employment or self-employment does not need to be full-time. The Regulations regard a person as being 'in employment' in a week provided at least that he performs enough hours of casual or self-employed work to maintain the required ten-hour average; that is so despite the fact that, if the work is casual, the claimant will probably not be in an employment relationship except during the hours that he performs it. It is against that background that I address the question whether for the purposes of regulation 2(b) there is (as Judge Howell suggested) an implicit requirement that the claimant must perform *some* work in each week.
>
> I do not consider that there is such an implicit requirement. The question to be answered is whether, in the week under examination, the claimant is 'in' employment undertaken for an average of ten hours per week measured over five consecutive weeks. Where a claimant remains in the habit of taking employment, and moreover the five-week rolling average of ten hours' work per week is maintained, I do not find it necessary to hold that he is no longer in employment in a particular week merely because he performs no hours of work in that week.
>
> If it were otherwise, a self-employed person could not take a week off without being regarded as giving up employment for the purposes of the Regular Employment Regulations. I find it impossible to conclude that, despite specifically providing for employees' holiday and other permitted absences to be disregarded for the purposes of the contractual hours calculation under regulation 2(a), the Regulations require self-employed persons to forego time off in order to avoid deemed giving up of employment. As a matter of language I have no difficulty in regarding a self-employed person taking time off as remaining 'in' self-employment. Similarly, I would regard a person as remaining 'in' self-employment even if no customers come his way in a particular week. Likewise I would regard a person who remains in the habit of taking casual employment as remaining 'in' casual employment during a week in which (whether because of a wish to take time off or because of the unavailability of work) he does not actually perform any work. This seems to me to be consistent with Judge Rowland's approach in R(JSA) 1/03 to the concept of 'gainful employment' when used in the JSA Regulations; the same term is used in regulation 2 of the Regular Employment Regulations).
>
> It seems to me to be a matter of giving the concept of being 'in' (for example) casual employment or self-employment its natural meaning. Following this approach, a casual employee or self-employed person will be regarded as giving up regular employment if he decides no longer to take work, or if his average

hours fall below ten. The approach seems to me to be consistent with Judge Powell's approach in CI/2517/01, where the nurse's single week without agency work was not regarded as triggering regulation 3" (paras 21–26).

Consequently, Judge Paines held that reg.2(a) could not apply once the contract had ended in October 2007. Nor could he avail himself of reg.2(b) because there was no suggestion that he undertook or planned to undertake any employment in the weeks immediately following October 30. Whereas, if his job at the museum had been all year round, rather than seasonal, he would have retained entitlement to REA while he continued working. Judge Lane, who had given the Secretary of State permission to appeal, had previously noted the more flexible treatment of seasonal workers under JSA. See also *AR v SSWP (II)* [2021] UKUT 279 (AAC), discussed in the note to reg.2, on zero hours contracts.

The Social Security (Industrial Injuries) (Prescribed Diseases) Amendment (No. 2) Regulations 1993

(SI 1993/1985) (*as amended*)

ARRANGEMENT OF REGULATIONS

The Secretary of State for Social Security, in exercise of the powers conferred by sections 108(2) and (4), 109(2) and (3), 110(1) and (2), 122(1) and 175(1) and (3) of and paragraph 2 of Schedule 6 to the Social Security Contributions and Benefits Act 1992 and sections 5(1)(a) and (b), 58(1)(b) and 189(1) and (4) of the Social Security Administration Act 1992, and of all other powers enabling him in that behalf, after reference to the Industrial Injuries Advisory Council hereby makes the following Regulations:

Citation, commencement and interpretation

10.246 **1.**—(1) These Regulations may be cited as the Social Security (Industrial Injuries) (Prescribed Diseases) Amendment (No. 2) Regulations 1993 and shall come into force on 13th September 1993.

(2) In these Regulations "the principal Regulations" means the Social Security (Industrial Injuries) (Prescribed Diseases) Regulations 1985.

10.247 *Sections 2–8 omitted.*

Transitional provision with respect to claims for prescribed disease D12

10.248 **9.**—(1) In this regulation—

"prescribed disease D12" means the disease bearing that number and listed in Part I of Schedule 1 to the principal Regulations (chronic bronchitis and emphysema);

"relevant claim" means a claim for benefit in respect of prescribed disease D12; and "relevant date" means 13th September 1993 or the date upon which the claimant in question first satisfies the conditions specified in Schedule 1 to the principal Regulations in respect of prescribed disease D12, whichever is the later.

(2) The provisions of the Social Security (Claims and Payments) Regulations 1987 shall apply in relation to a relevant claim subject to the following provisions of this regulation.

(3) A person who is aged not less than 70 on 13th September 1993 may make a relevant claim at any time in the period beginning with 13th September 1993 and ending with 28th February 1994, and if so made the claim shall be treated as having been made on the relevant date.

(4) A person who is aged less than 70 on 13th September 1993 and who, on the date the claim is made, has an award of attendance allowance at the higher rate under section 65(3) of the Social Security Contributions and Benefits Act 1992 or of the care component of disability living allowance at the highest rate under section 72(4) of that Act, may make a relevant claim at any time in the period beginning with 13th September 1993 and ending with 28th February 1994, and if so made the claim shall be treated as having been made on the relevant date.

(5) A person who does not fall within either of paragraphs (3) and (4) above may not make a relevant claim before 1st March 1994, but if such a person, or a person falling within paragraph (4) above who has not previously made a relevant claim, makes a relevant claim in the period beginning with that day and ending with 31st August 1994 that claim shall be treated as having been made on the relevant date.

The Social Security (Industrial Injuries and Diseases) (Miscellaneous Amendments) Regulations 1996

(SI 1996/425)

ARRANGEMENT OF REGULATIONS

The Secretary of State for Social Security, in exercise of the powers conferred by sections 108(2), 109(2) and (3), 113(1)(b), 122(1) and 175(1), (3) and (4) of, and sub-paragraphs (8) and (9) of paragraph 13 of Schedule 7 to, the Social Security Contributions and Benefits Act 1992 and sections 5(1)(k), 27(1)(b) and 189(1) and (4)(b) of the Social Security Administration Act 1992, and of all other powers enabling him in that behalf, after reference to the Industrial Injuries Advisory Council, hereby makes the following Regulations:

Citation and commencement

1. These Regulations may be cited as the Social Security (Industrial Injuries and Diseases) (Miscellaneous Amendments) Regulations 1996 and shall come into force on 24th March 1996. **10.250**

10.251 *Sections 2–6. omitted.*

Transitional provisions

10.252 7.—(1) The amendments made by regulation 5 of these Regulations ("the relevant amendments") to the terms in which each of the prescribed diseases A12, D4 and D5 ("the relevant disease") is prescribed shall not apply in the cases specified in the following provisions of this regulation, and in this regulation "commencement date" means the date on which these Regulations come into force.

(2) The relevant amendments shall not apply in the case of a person—

(a) who had an assessment of disablement in respect of the relevant disease for period which includes commencement date; or

(b) in respect of whom a decision in relation to a relevant disease on a claim for disablement benefit made before commencement date is reviewed on or after that date under section 47 of the Social Security Administration Act 1992 (reviews of medical decisions) which results in an assessment for a period which includes commencement date;

during any period where there is in respect of him a continuous assessment of disablement in respect of that disease which began before commencement date, and for this purpose two or more assessments one of which begins on the day following the end of a preceding assessment shall be treated as continuous.

(3) The relevant amendments shall not apply in the case of a person who makes a claim for disablement benefit in respect of the relevant disease before commencement date which results in an assessment of disablement, where the date of onset of that disease is earlier than commencement date, during any period when there is in respect of him a continuous assessment of disablement in respect of that disease which began not later than 91 days (excluding Sundays) after commencement date, and for this purpose two or more assessments one of which begins on the day following the end of a preceding assessment shall be treated as continuous.

(4) The relevant amendments shall not apply in the case of a person—

(a) who had an assessment of disablement in respect of the relevant disease for a period which ended before commencement date;

(b) who suffers a further attack of that relevant disease before commencement date;

(c) who makes a claim for disablement benefit in respect of that disease after commencement date; and

(d) in respect of whom it is decided, under regulation 7 of the Social Security (Industrial Injuries) (Prescribed Diseases) Regulations 1985 (recrudescence) that the further attack is a recrudescence of that disease.

The Social Security (Industrial Injuries) (Prescribed Diseases) Amendment Regulations 2000

(SI 2000/1588)

ARRANGEMENT OF REGULATIONS

The Secretary of State for Social Security, in exercise of the powers conferred by sections 108(2) and (4), 109(2) and (3), 122(1) and 175(1) to (4) of the Social Security Contributions and Benefits Act 1992 and of all other powers enabling him in that behalf, after reference to the Industrial Injuries Advisory Council, hereby makes the following Regulations:

Citation, commencement and interpretation

1.—(1) These Regulations may be cited as the Social Security (Industrial Injuries) (Prescribed Diseases) Amendment Regulations 2000 and shall come into force on 10th July 2000. 10.254

(2) In these Regulations, "the principal Regulations" means the Social Security (Industrial Injuries) (Prescribed Diseases) Regulations1985.

Amendment of regulation 2 of the principal Regulations

2.—*Incorporated in text of principal Regulations.* 10.255

Amendment of regulation 25 of the principal Regulations

3.—*Incorporated in text of principal Regulations.* 10.256

Amendment of regulation 27 of the principal Regulations

4.—*Incorporated in text of principal Regulations.* 10.257

Amendment of regulation 36 of the principal Regulations

5.—*Incorporated in text of principal Regulations.* 10.258

Amendment of Schedule 1 to the principal Regulations

6.—*Incorporated in text of principal Regulations.* 10.259

Transitional provision

7.—(1) The amendments made by regulations 3 and 4 shall not apply in relation to a claim made within 3 months after the commencement date and the amendments made by regulations 2(3), 5 and 6 shall not 10.260

apply where the date of onset of the relevant disease is prior to the commencement date and the claim is made within 3 months after that date.

(2) The amendments made by regulations 2(3) and 6 shall not apply in the case of a person—

(a) who had an assessment of disablement in respect of the relevant disease for a period up to the date 3 months after the commencement date; or

(b) in respect of whom a decision in relation to a relevant disease on a claim for disablement benefit made before or within 3 months after the commencement date is revised or superseded after that date under section 9 or 10 of the Social Security Act 1998 resulting in an assessment;

during any period when there is in respect of him a continuous assessment of disablement in respect of that disease, and for this purpose two or more assessments, one of which begins on the day following the end of a preceding assessment, shall be treated as continuous.

(3) The amendments made by regulations 2(3) and 6(2) and (3) shall not apply in the case of a person—

(a) who had an assessment of disablement in respect of the relevant disease for a period which ended before or within 3 months after the commencement date;

(b) who suffers a further attack of that relevant disease before or within 3 months after the commencement date;

(c) who makes a claim for disablement benefit in respect of that disease after the commencement date; and

(d) in respect of whom it is decided under regulation 7 of the principal Regulations (recrudescence) that the further attack is a recrudescence of that disease.

(4) In this regulation—

"commencement date" means the date on which these Regulations come into force; and

"relevant disease" means the disease referred to in the amendment, or the regulation of the principal Regulations which is amended by the amendment.

The Social Security (Industrial Injuries) (Prescribed Diseases) Amendment Regulations 2003

(SI 2003/270)

ARRANGEMENT OF REGULATIONS

The Secretary of State for Work and Pensions, in exercise of the powers conferred on him by sections 108(2) and (4), 109(2) and (3), 122(1) and 175(1) to (4) of the Social Security Contributions and Benefits Act 1992 and of all other powers enabling him in that behalf, after reference to the Industrial Injuries Advisory Council, hereby makes the following Regulations:

Citation, commencement and interpretation

1.—(1) These Regulations may be cited as the Social Security (Industrial Injuries) (Prescribed Diseases) Amendment Regulations 2003 and shall come into force on 17th March 2003. 10.262

(2) In these Regulations "the principal Regulations" means the Social Security (Industrial Injuries) (Prescribed Diseases) Regulations 1985.

Amendment of regulation 4 of the principal Regulations

2.—*Incorporated in text of principal Regulations.* 10.263

Amendment of regulation 7 of the principal Regulations

3.—*Incorporated in text of principal Regulations.* 10.264

Amendment of regulation 8 of the principal Regulations

4.—*Incorporated in text of principal Regulations.* 10.265

Amendment of Schedule 1 to the principal Regulations

5.—*Incorporated in text of principal Regulations.* 10.266

Transitional provision

6.—(1) Regulations 2 and 5 shall not apply— 10.267

(a) to a period of assessment which relates to a claim which is made before the commencement date;

(b) to a period of assessment which relates to a claim which is made within 3 months after the commencement date in respect of a period which began before the commencement date; or

(c) where a person suffers from an attack of a disease and under regulation 7 of the principal Regulations (recrudescence) the attack is a recrudescence of a disease for which a claim was made before the commencement date (or within 3 months after the commencement date in respect of a period which began before the commencement date).

(2) For the purposes of this regulation—

(a) "commencement date" means the date on which these Regulations come into force;

(b) the date on which a claim is made is the date on which the claim is made or treated as made in accordance with the Social Security (Claims and Payments) Regulations 1987; and

(c) a period of assessment which begins on the day following the end of a preceding period of assessment, shall be treated as a continuation of the preceding period of assessment.

The Social Security (Industrial Injuries) (Prescribed Diseases) Amendment (No. 2) Regulations 2003

(SI 2003/2190)

ARRANGEMENT OF REGULATIONS

The Secretary of State for Work and Pensions, in exercise of the powers conferred on him by sections 108(2), 109(2), 122(1) and 175(1) to (4) of the Social Security Contributions and Benefits Act 1992 and sections 9(1), 10(3) and 79(1), (3) and (4) of the Social Security Act 1998 and of all other powers enabling him in that behalf, being satisfied of the matters referred to in section 108(2)(a) and (b) of that Act of 1992 and after reference to the Industrial Injuries Advisory Council, hereby makes the following Regulations:

Citation, commencement and interpretation

10.269 **1.**—(1) These Regulations may be cited as the Social Security (Industrial Injuries) (Prescribed Diseases) Amendment (No.2) Regulations 2003 and shall come into force on 22nd September 2003.

(2) In these Regulations "the principal Regulations" means the Social Security (Industrial Injuries) (Prescribed Diseases) Regulations 1985.

Amendment of the principal Regulations

10.270 **2.**—*Incorporated in text of principal Regulations.*

Amendment of Schedule 1 to the principal Regulations

10.271 **3.**—*Incorporated in text of Schedule 1 to the principal Regulations.*

Transitional provision

10.272 **4.**—(1) Regulation 3 shall not apply to a period of assessment which relates to a claim which is made before the commencement date.

(2) A provisional assessment of the extent of a claimant's disablement due to occupational deafness, which is in force immediately before the commencement date, shall, from the commencement date, have effect for the remainder of the claimant's life.

(3) For the purposes of this regulation—

(a) "commencement date" means the date on which these Regulations come into force;

(b) the date on which a claim is made is the date on which the claim is made or treated as made in accordance with the Social Security (Claims and Payments) Regulations 1987.

GENERAL NOTE

10.273 This principally protects those whose claims in respect of hearing loss were made, or treated as made, before the date of the change [September 22, 2003] (para.(1)

read with (3)(b). But note also the provision in para.(2), which turns a provisional assessment of disablement due to occupational deafness, in force on September 21, 2003, into one for life as from September 22, 2003 ("commencement date"—see para.(3)(a)).

The Social Security (Industrial Injuries) (Prescribed Diseases) Amendment Regulations 2005

(SI 2005/324)

The Secretary of State for Work and Pensions, in exercise of the powers conferred upon him by sections 108(2), 122(1) and 175(1) to (4) of the Social Security Contributions and Benefits Act 1992 and section 5(1)(a) of the Social Security Administration Act 1992 and of all other powers enabling him in that behalf, being satisfied of the matters referred to in section 108(2) (a) and (b) of the Social Security Contributions and Benefits Act and after reference to the Industrial Injuries Advisory Council, hereby makes the following Regulations: 10.274

Citation, commencement and interpretation

1.—(1) These Regulations may be cited as the Social Security (Industrial Injuries) (Prescribed Diseases) Amendment Regulations 2005 and shall come into force on 14th March 2005. 10.275

(2) In these Regulations "the principal Regulations" means the Social Security (Industrial Injuries) (Prescribed Diseases) Regulations 1985.

Amendment of regulations 2 and 25 of the principal Regulations

2.—*Incorporated in text of the principal Regulations.* 10.276

Amendment of Schedule 1 to the principal Regulations

3.– *Incorporated in text of Schedule 1 to the principal Regulations* 10.277

Transitional provision

4.—Regulation 3 shall not apply to a period of assessment which relates to a claim which is made before the date on which these Regulations come into force. 10.278

The Social Security (Industrial Injuries) (Prescribed Diseases) Amendment Regulations 2007

(SI 2007/811)

The Secretary of State for Work and Pensions makes the following Regulations in exercise of the powers conferred by sections 108(2), 122(1) and 175(1) to (4) of the Social Security Contributions and Benefits Act 1992. 10.279

The Secretary of State is satisfied of the matters referred to in section 108(2)(a) and (b) of that Act.

In accordance with section 172(2) of the Social Security Administration Act 1992, reference has been made to the Industrial Injuries Advisory Council.

Citation and commencement

10.280 **1.** These Regulations may be cited as the Social Security (Industrial Injuries) (Prescribed Diseases) Amendment Regulations 2007 and shall come into force on the 6th April 2007.

Amendment of Schedule 1 to the Social Security (Industrial Injuries) (Prescribed Diseases) Regulations 1985

10.281 **2.** — *Incorporated in text of Schedule 1 to the principal Regulations.*

Transitional provision

10.282 **3.** Regulation 2 shall not apply to a period of assessment which relates to a claim made before the date on which these Regulations come into force.

The Social Security (Industrial Injuries) (Prescribed Diseases) Amendment (No.2) Regulations 2007

(SI 2007/1753)

ARRANGEMENT OF REGULATIONS

The Secretary of State for Work and Pensions makes the following Regulations in exercise of the powers conferred by sections 108(2), 122(1) and 175(1), (3) and (4) of the Social Security Contributions and Benefits Act 1992.

He is satisfied of the matters referred to in section 108(2)(a) and (b) of that Act.

In accordance with section 172(2) of the Social Security Administration Act 1992 he has referred proposals to make these Regulations to the Industrial Injuries Advisory Council.

Citation, commencement and interpretation

10.284 **1.** —(1) These Regulations may be cited as the Social Security (Industrial Injuries) (Prescribed Diseases) Amendment (No. 2) Regulations 2007 and shall come into force on 1st October 2007.

(2) In these Regulations "the principal Regulations" means the Social Security (Industrial Injuries) (Prescribed Diseases) Regulations 1985.

Amendment of Schedule 1 to the principal Regulations

10.285 **2.** *Incorporated into the text of Schedule 1 to the principal Regulations.*

Transitional provision

10.286 **3.** —(1) Regulation 2 shall not apply to a question relating to the blanching of a claimant's fingers where—

(a) the question arises in connection with a period of assessment which relates to a claim which is made—

(i) before the commencement date, or
(ii) within 3 months after the commencement date in respect of a period which began before the commencement date, or

(b) a person suffers from an attack of a disease and under regulation 7 of the principal Regulations (recrudescence) the attack is a recrudescence of a disease for which a claim was made before the commencement date or within 3 months after the commencement date in respect of a period which began before the commencement date.

(2) For the purposes of this regulation—

(a) "commencement date" means the date on which these Regulations come into force; and
(b) a period of assessment which begins on the day following the end of a preceding period of assessment, shall be treated as a continuation of the preceding period of assessment.

GENERAL NOTE

Regulation 2 added sensorineural symptoms to the description of PD A11 with effect from October 1, 2007. There can clearly be no claim on the basis of such symptoms for any period prior to that date. This transitional provision, preventing claims within a three month period after that date, only prevents claims being made which raise a question of the blanching of a claimant's fingers, so that a claimant whose case is based on the new sensory condition does not have to wait until that three month period is over but can claim in respect of it for periods on or after October 1, 2007 (*DG v SSWP* [2009] UKUT 41 (AAC), paras 5-8). 10.287

The Industrial Injuries Benefit (Injuries arising before 5th July 1948) Regulations 2012

(SI 2012/2743) (AS AMENDED)

ARRANGEMENT OF REGULATIONS

The Secretary of State for Work and Pensions makes the following Regulations in exercise of the powers conferred by section 64(3) of the Welfare Reform Act 2012

Citation, commencement and interpretation

1.—(1) These Regulations may be cited as the Industrial Injuries Benefit (Injuries arising before [[1]5th July] 1948) Regulations 2012 and come into force on December 5, 2012. 10.289

(2) In these Regulations "the Contributions and Benefits Act" means the Social Security Contributions and Benefits Act 1992

Payment of industrial injuries benefit where compensation or benefits were previously payable under Schedule 8 to the Contributions and Benefits Act

10.290 **2.** Where, before the commencement of section 64 of the Welfare Reform Act 2012 (injuries arising before 5th July 1948), compensation or benefits were payable to any person under a provision of Schedule 8 to the Contributions and Benefits Act (industrial injuries and diseases (old cases)) mentioned in column (1) of the table in the Schedule to these Regulations, the rate or amount of industrial injuries benefit payable to that person is the corresponding rate or amount set out in column (2) of that table.

Claims made but not determined before 5th December 2012

10.291 **3.** Any claim for compensation or benefits that was made in accordance with section 111 of, and Schedule 8 to, the Contributions and Benefits Act but which was not determined before the coming into force of these Regulations, is to be treated as a claim for industrial injuries benefit.

SCHEDULE

10.292 RATES OF INDUSTRIAL INJURIES BENEFIT CORRESPONDING TO COMPENSATION OR BENEFIT PREVIOUSLY PAYABLE UNDER SCHEDULE 8 TO THE CONTRIBUTIONS AND BENEFITS ACT

(1) Compensation or benefit payable before 5th December 2012 under Schedule 8 to the Contributions and Benefits Act	*(2) Corresponding rate or amount of industrial injuries benefit payable under the Contributions and Benefits Act from 5th December 2012*
Incapacity allowance Major incapacity allowance under paragraph 2(6)(b) of Schedule 8	The rate applicable for 100% degree of disablement as specified in column (2) of the table in Part 5 of Schedule 4
Lesser incapacity allowance under paragraph 2(6)(c) of Schedule 8 payable at the weekly rate of £4.85, £13.15 or £22.05	The rate applicable for 20% degree of disablement as specified in column (2) of the table in Part 5 of Schedule 4
Lesser incapacity allowance under paragraph 2(6)(c) of Schedule 8 payable at the weekly rate of £31.95 or £45.90	The rate applicable for 30% degree of disablement as specified in column (2) of the table in Part 5 of Schedule 4
Lesser incapacity allowance under paragraph 2(6)(c) of Schedule 8 payable at the weekly rate of £58.45	The rate applicable for 40% degree of disablement as specified in column (2) of the table in Part 5 of Schedule 4
Total disablement benefit Allowance in respect of total disablement under paragraph 6(2)(a) of Schedule 8	The rate applicable for 100% degree of disablement as specified in column (2) of the table in Part 5 of Schedule 4
Partial disablement allowance Allowance in respect of disablement which is not total under paragraph 6(2)(b) of Schedule 8	The rate applicable for 40% degree of disablement as specified in column (2) of the table in Part 5 of Schedule 4

Unemployability supplement Unemployability supplement in accordance with paragraph 6(4)(a) or 7(2)(c)(i) of Schedule 8	Unemployability supplement at the rate specified in paragraphs 5 and 6 of Part 5 of Schedule 4
Exceptionally severe disablement allowance Exceptionally severe disablement allowance in accordance with paragraph 6(4)(b) or paragraph 7(2)(c)(iii) of Schedule 8	Exceptionally severe disablement allowance at the rate specified in paragraph 3 of Part 5 of Schedule 4
Constant attendance allowance Increase of allowance in respect of constant attendance in accordance with paragraph 6(4)(b) or of disablement pension under paragraph 7(2)(c)(iii) of Schedule 8	Constant attendance allowance at the rate specified in paragraph 2 of Part 5 of Schedule 4
Increase of benefit or disablement pension for a child dependant Increase of benefit for a child dependant in accordance with paragraph 6(4)(c) or of disablement pension for a child dependant in accordance with [1paragraph 7(2)(c)(ii)] of Schedule 8	Child dependency increase at the rate specified in paragraph 7 of Part 5 of Schedule 4
Increase of benefit or disablement pension for an adult dependant Increase of benefit for an adult dependant in accordance with paragraph 6(5) or of disablement pension for an adult dependant in accordance with [1paragraph 7(2)(c)(ii)] of Schedule 8	Adult dependency increase at the rate specified in [1paragraph 8] of Part 5 of Schedule 4
Payment of a capital sum Payment of a capital sum or sums in accordance with paragraph 6(6) of Schedule 8	A sum or sums of an amount or aggregate amount not exceeding £300

Amendment

1. Industrial Injuries Benefit (Injuries arising before July 5, 1948) (Amendment) Regulations 2012 (SI 2012/2812) reg.2 (December 4, 2012).

The Industrial Injuries Benefit (Employment Training Schemes and Courses) Regulations 2013

(SI 2013/2540)

Arrangement Of Regulations

10.294 The Secretary of State for Work and Pensions makes the following Regulations in exercise of the powers conferred by sections 95A, 122(1) and 175(1), (3), (4) and (5) of the Social Security Contributions and Benefits Act 1992 and section 66(3) of the Welfare Reform Act 2012.

In accordance with section 172(2) of the Social Security Administration Act 1992 reference has been made to the Industrial Injuries Advisory Council.

Citation, commencement and interpretation

10.295 **1.**—(1) These Regulations may be cited as the Industrial Injuries Benefit (Employment Training Schemes and Courses) Regulations 2013.

(2) They come into force on 31st October 2013.

(3) In these Regulations—

"the Employment and Training Act" means the Employment and Training Act 1973;

"the Contributions and Benefits Act" means the Social Security Contributions and Benefits Act 1992;

"the Jobseekers Act" means the Jobseekers Act 1995.

Employment training scheme and employment training course

10.296 **2.** The following descriptions of employment training scheme and employment training course are prescribed for the purposes of section 95A(1) of the Contributions and Benefits Act—

(a) an employment training scheme or employment training course provided pursuant to arrangements made by or on behalf of the Secretary of State or the Scottish or Welsh Ministers under section 2 of the Employment and Training Act (arrangements for the purpose of assisting persons to select, train for, obtain and retain employment);

(b) an employment training scheme or employment training course which constitutes, or participation in which forms part of, a scheme of a description prescribed under section 17A of the Jobseekers Act (schemes for assisting persons to obtain employment: "work for your benefit" schemes etc.);

(c) an employment training scheme or employment training course in which a person participates pursuant to—

(i) a requirement to undertake work-related activity imposed under regulations under section 13 of the Welfare Reform Act 2007; or

(ii) a work preparation requirement within the meaning of section 6C of the Jobseekers Act, section 11C of the Welfare Reform Act 2007 or section 16 of the Welfare Reform Act 2012.

Employer

10.297 **3.** The persons prescribed for the purposes of section 95A(2) of the Contributions and Benefits Act are any persons providing an employment training scheme or employment training course of a description prescribed under regulation 2 above.

Payment of industrial injuries benefit where payments were previously payable under section 11(3) of the Employment and Training Act

4. Where, before section 66 of the Welfare Reform Act 2012 (trainees) came into force for all purposes, payments were payable to a person in consequence of an injury or disease under section 11(3) of the Employment and Training Act (power to make payments in respect of trainees equivalent to social security benefits in respect of employees), that person is entitled to equivalent payments of industrial injuries benefit. **10.298**

Outstanding claims

5. Any claim for payments in consequence of an injury or disease under section 11(3) of the Employment and Training Act, which was made but not determined before section 66 of the Welfare Reform Act 2012 came into force for all purposes, is to be treated as a claim for industrial injuries benefit. **10.299**

PART XI

MESOTHELIOMA LUMP SUM PAYMENTS

The Mesothelioma Lump Sum Payments (Claims and Reconsiderations) Regulations 2008

(SI 2008/1595)

ARRANGEMENT OF REGULATIONS

The Secretary of State for Work and Pensions in exercise of the powers conferred by section 48(1) to (3), 49(2), 50(4) and 53(2) of the Child Maintenance and Other Payments Act 2008 makes the following Regulations.

GENERAL NOTE

See generally the annotations to ss.48–51 of the Child Maintenance and Other Payments Act 2008 above. 11.2

Citation, commencement and interpretation

1.—(1) These Regulations may be cited as the Mesothelioma Lump Sum Payments (Claims and Reconsiderations) Regulations 2008 and shall come into force on 1st October 2008. 11.3

(2) In these Regulations—

"claim" means a claim under section 46(1) of the Child Maintenance and Other Payments Act 2008;

"mesothelioma" means diffuse mesothelioma.

Making a claim

2.—(1) Subject to paragraph (2), a claim must be made in writing, signed by or on behalf of the person making the claim, on a form approved by the Secretary of State and accompanied by the documents specified in the form. 11.4

(2) A claim may be made in such other manner, being in writing, as the Secretary of State may accept as sufficient in the circumstances of any particular case.

Time for making a claim

3.—(1) A claim by a person who has been diagnosed with mesothelioma before the coming into force of these Regulations must be made within 12 months from the date on which these Regulations come into force. 11.5

(2) A claim by any other person with mesothelioma must be made within 12 months from the date on which that person was first diagnosed with mesothelioma.

(3) A claim by a dependant must be made within 12 months from the date of death of the person who, immediately before death, had mesothelioma.

(4) Where the Secretary of State considers there was good cause for the claim not being made within the 12 month time limit referred to in paragraphs (1) to (3), he may extend the time limit for such period as he considers appropriate in the circumstances, provided that the time limit is not extended for a death or diagnosis which occurred more than 12 months before the date these Regulations come into force.

Reconsideration

11.6 **4.**—(1) An application made to the Secretary of State for reconsideration of a determination that a payment should or should not be made must—

(a) be made within one month of the date of notification of the determination, [1 . . .]

[1 (aa) where a written statement is requested under regulation 4B(3) (reconsideration before appeal) and is provided within the period specified in sub-paragraph (a) above, be made within 14 days of the expiry of that period,

(ab) where a written statement is requested under regulation 4B(3) (reconsideration before appeal) and is provided after the period specified in sub-paragraph (a) above, be made within 14 days of the date on which the statement is provided, or

(ac) be made within such longer period as may be allowed under regulation 4A (late application for reconsideration), and].

(b) specify the ground for the request and give such other relevant information as the Secretary of State may require in order to deal adequately with the reconsideration.

(2) The Secretary of State may, at any time, in writing, institute a reconsideration of a determination that a payment should or should not be made.

AMENDMENT

1. Social Security, Child Support, Vaccine Damage and Other Payments (Decisions and Appeals) (Amendment) Regulations 2013 (SI 2013/2380) reg.5(2) and (3) (October 28, 2013).

[1 Late application for reconsideration

11.7 **4A.** —Where, in a case to which regulation 4B (reconsideration before appeal) applies, the Secretary of State considers there was good cause for not applying for reconsideration of a determination within the time limit specified in regulation 4(1) (reconsideration), he may extend the time limit for such period as he considers appropriate in the circumstances.]

AMENDMENT

1. Social Security, Child Support, Vaccine Damage and Other Payments (Decisions and Appeals) (Amendment) Regulations 2013 (SI 2013/2380) reg.5(4) (October 28, 2013).

[1 Reconsideration before appeal

4B. —(1) This regulation applies in a case where— 11.8

(a) the Secretary of State gives a person written notice of a determination made on a claim; and

(b) that notice includes a statement to the effect that there is a right of appeal to the First-tier Tribunal in relation to the determination only if the Secretary of State has, on an application, decided whether to reconsider the determination.

(2) In a case to which this regulation applies, a person may appeal against the determination only if the Secretary of State has decided on an application whether to reconsider the determination under section 49 of the Child Maintenance and Other Payments Act 2008 ("the 2008 Act").

(3) The notice referred to in paragraph (1) must inform the person—

(a) of the time limit specified in regulation 4(1) for making an application for reconsideration of the determination; and

(b) that, where the notice does not include a statement of the reasons for the determination ("written reasons"), he may, within one month of the date of notification of the determination, request that the Secretary of State provide him with written reasons.

(4) Where written reasons are requested under paragraph (3)(b), the Secretary of State must provide them within 14 days of receipt of the request or as soon as practicable afterwards.

(5) Where, as the result of paragraph (2), there is no right of appeal against a determination made on a claim, the Secretary of State may treat any purported appeal as an application for reconsideration of the determination under section 49 of the 2008 Act.]

AMENDMENT

1. Social Security, Child Support, Vaccine Damage and Other Payments (Decisions and Appeals) (Amendment) Regulations 2013 (SI 2013/2380) reg.5(4) (October 28, 2013).

Appeal treated as reconsideration

5.—(1) Where a person appeals against a determination made by the Secretary of State on a claim, the Secretary of State may treat the appeal as an application for reconsideration under section 49 of the Child Maintenance and Other Payments Act 2008. 11.9

(2) [1 . . .]

(3) [1 . . .]

AMENDMENT

1. Social Security, Child Support, Vaccine Damage and Other Payments (Decisions and Appeals) (Amendment) Regulations 2013 (SI 2013/2380) reg.5(5) (October 28, 2013).

GENERAL NOTE

The repeals of paras (2) and (3) are subject to the transitional and savings provisions in Social Security, Child Support, Vaccine Damage and Other Payments (Decisions and Appeals) (Amendment) Regulations 2013 (SI 2013/2380) reg.8(1), such that the amendments do not apply in any case where the notice of the decision to which the appeal relates was posted to the appellant's last known address before October 28, 2013. 11.10

[1 Appeals

11.11 **6.** [2 . . .]

Amendments

1. Mesothelioma Lump Sum Payments (Claims and Reconsiderations) (Amendment) Regulations 2008 (SI 2008/2706) reg.4 (November 3, 2008).
2. Social Security, Child Support, Vaccine Damage and Other Payments (Decisions and Appeals) (Amendment) Regulations 2013 (SI 2013/2380) reg.5(5) (October 28, 2013).

General Note

11.12 The repeals of reg.6 is subject to the transitional and savings provisions in Social Security, Child Support, Vaccine Damage and Other Payments (Decisions and Appeals) (Amendment) Regulations 2013 (SI 2013/2380) reg.8(1), such that the repeal does not apply in any case where the notice of the decision to which the appeal relates was posted to the appellant's last known address before October 28, 2013.

The Mesothelioma Lump Sum Payments (Conditions and Amounts) Regulations 2008

(SI 2008/1963)

Arrangement Of Regulations

11.13

The Secretary of State for Work and Pensions in exercise of the powers conferred by section 1(1) of the Pneumoconiosis etc. (Workers' Compensation) Act 1979 and sections 46(3) and 47 of the Child Maintenance and Other Payments Act 2008 makes the following Regulations.

Citation, commencement and interpretation

11.14 **1.**—(1) These Regulations may be cited as the Mesothelioma Lump Sum Payments (Conditions and Amounts) Regulations 2008.

(2) These Regulations shall come into force on 1st October 2008.

(3) In these Regulations—

"the Act" means the Child Maintenance and Other Payments Act 2008;

"claim" means a claim under section 46(1) of the Act;

"deceased" means a person who, immediately before death, had diffuse mesothelioma;

"mesothelioma" means diffuse mesothelioma;

"payment" includes a payment in money or money's worth or in kind.

Disqualifying payments

2.—(1) The following payments are prescribed for the purposes of section 47(1)(a), (2)(a) and (3)(e) of the Act (payments which, if made in consequence of diffuse mesothelioma, prevent the conditions provided for in section 47(1)(a) and (2)(a) from being fulfilled)— 11.15

(a) payment under the Naval, Military and Air Forces Etc. (Disablement and Death) Service Pensions Order 2006;

(b) payment under the Armed Forces and Reserve Forces (Compensation Scheme) Order 2005;

[1 (c) payment from any government department, authority, body corporate or employer exempted from insurance by or under section 3 of the Employers' Liability (Compulsory Insurance) Act 1969 or Article 7 of the Employers' Liability (Defective Equipment and Compulsory Insurance) (Northern Ireland) Order 1972];

(d) payment under the UK Asbestos Trust established on 10th October 2006, for the benefit of certain persons suffering from asbestos-related diseases;

(e) payment under the EL Scheme Trust established on 23rd November 2006, for the benefit of certain persons suffering from asbestos-related diseases.

(2) The following payments are prescribed for the purposes of section 47(1)(b) and (2)(b) of the Act (payments eligibility for which prevents the conditions provided for in section 47(1)(b) or (2)(b) from being fulfilled)—

(a) payment under the Naval, Military and Air Forces Etc. (Disablement and Death) Service Pensions Order 2006;

(b) payment under the Armed Forces and Reserve Forces (Compensation Scheme) Order 2005.

AMENDMENT

1. Social Security (Miscellaneous Amendments) (No.3) Regulations 2008 (SI 2008/2365) reg.5 (October 1, 2008).

Disregarded payments

3. A payment made in error and which in consequence is liable to be repaid in accordance with a statutory provision or rule of law, is to be disregarded for the purpose of section 47(1)(a) or (2)(a) of the Act (conditions of entitlement). 11.16

Presence in the United Kingdom

4.—(1) In the case of a person with mesothelioma it is a condition of entitlement that the person was in the United Kingdom at a time when and place where that person was exposed to asbestos. 11.17

(2) In the case of a dependant it is a condition of entitlement that the deceased was in the United Kingdom at a time when and place where the deceased was exposed to asbestos.

GENERAL NOTE

See the commentary to s.47 of the Child Maintenance and Other Payments Act 2008 for discussion as to the possibly ultra vires nature of this provision. 11.18

Amount of lump sum payment

11.19 **5.**—(1) The amount of a payment made under section 46(2) of the Act to a person with mesothelioma shall be determined in accordance with Table 1 of the Schedule.

(2) In Table 1 of the Schedule, the reference to the age of the person is a reference to—

(a) the age at which the person was first diagnosed with mesothelioma; or
(b) where the age at which the person was first diagnosed with mesothelioma is unknown, the age at which the person made the claim.

(3) The amount of a payment made under section 46(2) of the Act to a dependant shall be determined in accordance with Table 2 of the Schedule.

(4) In Table 2 of the Schedule, the reference to the age of the person with mesothelioma is a reference to the age of that person at death.

Amendment of Pneumoconiosis etc. (Workers' Compensation) (Payment of Claims) Regulations 1988

11.20 **6.** At the end of regulation 3 of the Pneumoconiosis etc. (Workers' Compensation) (Payment of Claims) Regulations 1988 (payments to persons disabled by disease), add—

"(5) Where—

(a) a payment is made to a person under section 46 of the Child Maintenance and Other Payments Act 2008 (the mesothelioma payment) in respect of diffuse mesothelioma,
(b) subsequently it is determined that the same person is entitled to a payment under section 1(1) of the Act in respect of the same diffuse mesothelioma,

the amount payable under paragraph (1) shall be reduced by the amount of the mesothelioma payment.".

SCHEDULE **Regulation 5**

11.21 **[[1] Table 1**
Amount of lump sum payment to person with mesothelioma

Age of person with mesothelioma at first diagnosis or, if unknown, date of claim	*Payment* £
37 or under	114,210
38	111,989
39	109,774
40	107,558
41	105,337
42	103,120
43	102,015
44	100,899
45	99,794

Age of person with mesothelioma at first diagnosis or, if unknown, date of claim	***Payment £***
46	98,684
47	97,575
48	94,476
49	91,373
50	88,262
51	85,162
52	82,048
53	79,833
54	77,619
55	75,406
56	73,177
57	70,960
58	65,197
59	59,428
60	53,670
61	47,902
62	42,137
63	38,588
64	35,035
65	31,493
66	27,943
67	24,395
68	23,672
69	22,947
70	22,234
71	21,513
72	20,795
73	20,181
74	19,556
75	18,957
76	18,356
77 or over	17,745

Table 2
Amount of lump sum payment to dependant

Age of person with mesothelioma at death	*Payment* £
37 or under	59,436
38	58,159
39	56,884
40	55,609
41	54,334
42	53,060
43	51,839
44	50,608
45	49,396
46	48,177
47	46,960
48	45,464
49	43,963
50	42,468
51	40,976
52	39,479
53	38,253
54	37,038
55	35,818
56	34,590
57	33,374
58	29,999
59	26,611
60	23,233
61	19,850
62	16,463
63	15,497
64	14,538
65	13,554
66	12,586
67 or over	9,840]

(SI 2008/1963 Sch.)

AMENDMENT

1. Mesothelioma Lump Sum Payments (Conditions and Amounts) (Amendment) Regulations 2024 (SI 2024/237) reg.2 (April 1, 2024).

GENERAL NOTE

Table 1 applies only in relation to a person first diagnosed with diffuse mesothelioma on or after April 1, 2024, or, where the date of the first diagnosis with diffuse mesothelioma is unknown, if a claim under s.46(1) of the Child Maintenance and Other Payments Act 2008 is made by that person on or after April 1, 2024 (see reg.1(2)). Table 2 applies only in relation to the dependant of a person who dies on or after April 1, 2024 and who, immediately before their death, had diffuse mesothelioma (see reg.1(3)). 11.22

The Diffuse Mesothelioma Payment Scheme Regulations 2014

(SI 2014/916)

ARRANGEMENT OF REGULATIONS

Introductory

1. Citation 11.23
2. Commencement and ceasing to have effect
3. Interpretation
4. Establishment of the scheme

Scheme administrator

5. General duties of the scheme administrator

Eligibility

6. First diagnosis of diffuse mesothelioma and specified payments
7. Circumstances in which a person is to be treated as unable to bring an action

Applications and procedure

8. The application
9. Time limit for making an application
10. Power of scheme administrator to obtain additional documents or evidence
11. Request to applicants to provide additional documents or evidence
12. Duty of applicants
13. Request to third parties to provide documents
14. Withdrawal of an application by person with diffuse mesothelioma
15. Notice for a person to cease to be an eligible dependant

Determination of applications

16. Determination of applications
17. Imposing conditions on the making of a payment
18. Notice of a determination

Payments

19. Payment
20. Circumstances in which a person may be required to repay

Reviews and appeals

21. Review at the request of an applicant
22. Review initiated by the scheme administrator
23. Other circumstances in which a review may be held
24. Conduct of the review
25. Appeal

Scheme administrator's functions to help people bring proceedings

26. Circumstances in which scheme administrator may help people to bring proceedings

Review of these Regulations

27. Review of these Regulations by the Secretary of State

SCHEDULE 1 First diagnosis of diffuse mesothelioma
SCHEDULE 2 Specified Payments
SCHEDULE 3 Information and other material in support of an application
SCHEDULE 4 Amount of Scheme Payments

The Secretary of State makes the following Regulations in exercise of the powers conferred by section 1 and section 17(4) of the Mesothelioma Act 2014.

In accordance with section 17(2)(a) of that Act, as these are the first regulations under section 1, a draft has been laid before Parliament and approved by a resolution of each House of Parliament.

General Note

11.24 The Diffuse Mesothelioma Payment Scheme Regulations 2014, which came into force on April 6, 2014, provide the detail which is largely absent from the Mesothelioma Act 2014. Their purpose is defined by reg.4, namely to "establish the Diffuse Mesothelioma Payment Scheme for making payments to eligible people with diffuse mesothelioma and eligible dependants under sections 2 and 3 of the Act." Although applications were accepted from April 2014, the first payments were expected to be made from July 2014, once the new compensation rates set out in the amended Sch.4 to the Regulations are in force. The Department for Work and Pensions estimates that there will be around 28,500 deaths from diffuse mesothelioma in the United Kingdom between July 2012 and March 2024. The Department's best estimate is that in the absence of the new scheme about 10 per cent (2,900) of these cases will be unable to trace either their employer or their employer's insurer. With the new scheme in place, and once behavioural changes have been factored in, the estimate is that there will be approximately 3,900 claimants and 3,500 awards made over a 10-year period (DWP, *Mesothelioma Payment Scheme: Impact Assessment*, March 2014). The DWP estimates that around 90 per cent of claims will be successful, in line with civil compensation claims for mesothelioma. However, where awards are refused, there is the possibility of review and then appeal to the First-tier Tribunal (see regs 21–25).

Note that HMRC may disclose information held by them to a person who applies for a payment under the Diffuse Mesothelioma Payment Scheme, on the basis that he or she is eligible for such a payment under s.3, for use in connection with the application (Deregulation Act 2015 s.85(1)(c)). Note also that in addition, and with effect from July 31, 2017, s.77 of the Digital Economy Act 2017 enables HMRC to share the name and address of an employer and associated reference numbers with the Employer Liability Tracing Office (ELTO) for the purpose of assisting with such claims. ELTO is a non-profit making company that maintains a database of insurance policies to enable employees to trace former or current employers and their insurers in order to obtain compensation for workplace injuries. It is anticipated that access to this information will help to improve the quality of the ELTO databases.

Citation

1.—These Regulations may be cited as the Diffuse Mesothelioma Payment Scheme Regulations 2014. **11.25**

Commencement and ceasing to have effect

2.—(1) These Regulations, apart from regulation 7(2)(c), come into force on the day after the day on which they are made. **11.26**

(2) Regulation 7(2)(c) comes into force when sections 4 to 7 (relevant persons) of the Third Parties (Rights against Insurers) Act 2010 come into force.

(3) Regulation 7(2)(a) and (b) cease to have effect when regulation 7(2)(c) comes into force.

Interpretation

3.—In these Regulations— **11.27**

"the Act" means the Mesothelioma Act 2014;

"applicant" unless the context requires otherwise, means a person who makes an application(1) on the basis that they are eligible under sections 2 or 3 of the Act;

"relevant deduction" means a deduction of—

(a) the amount of the recoverable benefit which is deducted by virtue of—
  (i) section 8A of the Social Security (Recovery of Benefits) Act 1997, or
  (ii) article 10A of the Social Security (Recovery of Benefits) (Northern Ireland) Order 1997; or

(b) the amount of a lump sum payment which is recovered under regulations made under—
  (i) section 1A of the Social Security (Recovery of Benefits) Act 1997, or
  (ii) article 3A of the Social Security (Recovery of Benefits) (Northern Ireland) Order 1997.

Establishment of the scheme

4.—These Regulations establish the Diffuse Mesothelioma Payment Scheme for making payments to eligible people with diffuse mesothelioma and eligible dependants under sections 2 and 3 of the Act. **11.28**

Scheme administrator

General duties of the scheme administrator

11.29 **5.**—(1) The scheme administrator must provide such information in connection with the operation of the scheme as the scheme administrator considers appropriate.

(2) Information provided under paragraph (1) may, in particular, relate to—

(a) the procedure for making an application;

(b) the medical evidence likely to be required to support a diagnosis of diffuse mesothelioma;

(c) any other evidence likely to be required to establish that a person is eligible under section 2 or 3 of the Act for a payment under the scheme;

(d) the determination of an application;

(e) reviews and appeals.

(3) The scheme administrator must—

(a) in considering an application, apply the normal civil standard of proof (the balance of probability) when deciding all matters of fact which require evidence to establish them;

(b) make the application forms available on request free of charge; and

(c) take all steps it considers reasonable to publicise the scheme.

(4) The scheme administrator must ensure that a sufficient number of persons with appropriate training and qualifications are available to decide the matters likely to arise in determining an application.

General Note

11.30 Gallagher Bassett, the claims-handling company which originally won the Government contract to administer the scheme, has been replaced with effect from April 1, 2018 by TopMark Claims Management Ltd (see its dedicated website at *http://www.mesoscheme.org.uk*).

Eligibility

First diagnosis of diffuse mesothelioma and specified payments

11.31 **6.**—(1) For the purposes of sections 2 and 3 of the Act (eligible people with diffuse mesothelioma and eligible dependants) and of these Regulations—

(a) the meaning of "first diagnosed" is to be determined in accordance with Schedule 1 to these Regulations; and

(b) "specified payment" means a payment specified in Schedule 2 to these Regulations.

General Note

11.32 The claimant must have been first diagnosed with the disease on or after July 25, 2012 (Mesothelioma Act 2014, s.2(1)(b)). The meaning of "first diagnosed" must be determined in accordance with Schedule 1 to the Regulations. In summary, this means that a health care professional must have made a diagnosis of diffuse mesothelioma and either the victim or a "connected person" has been officially advised of that diagnosis. There are detailed provisions in Schedule 1 defining precisely how the date of such diagnosis is to be determined, depending on whether it is communicated orally, by letter or by e-mail.

Circumstances in which a person is to be treated as unable to bring an action

7.—(1) For the purposes of section 18(3) of the Act, the circumstances in which a person is not to be treated as able to bring an action are that an employer against whom the person is able to bring an action in respect of diffuse mesothelioma can be found or does exist, but— 11.33

(a) that employer is a person whose circumstances are such that they fall within any of the relevant provisions; and

(b) no other employer or insurer can be found or exists against whom the person can maintain an action for damages.

(2) In this regulation "relevant provisions" means—

(a) section 1 of the Third Parties (Rights against Insurers) Act 1930;

(b) section 1 of the Third Parties (Rights Against Insurers) Act (Northern Ireland) 1930;

(c) sections 4 to 7 of the Third Parties (Rights against Insurers) Act 2010;

(d) section 130 of the Health and Social Care Act 2012 and any regulations made under that section;

(e) articles 41 to 43 of the Water and Sewerage Services (Northern Ireland) Order 2006; or

(f) section 17 of the Energy Act (Northern Ireland) 2011.

General Note

In *DP v Topmark Claims Management Ltd* [2020] UKUT 106 (AAC) Judge Markus QC rejected the appellant's submission that once the limitation period for a civil claim had expired, the appellant was not "able to bring an action for damages ... for any other reason" within s.3(1)(c) of the 2014 Act. The Judge found that reg.7 of the 2014 Scheme prescribes circumstances which constitute "any other reason" within s.3(1)(c) and that s.18(3) of the Act does not add a further category to those in s.3(1)(c) (at para.34). Moreover, consistent with the policy intent "the circumstances actually specified in regulation 7 are all ones in which a tortfeasor or insurer can be found but cannot satisfy a judgment as a result of insolvency, dissolution or similar circumstances" (at para.27). It followed that the expiry of the limitation period for a civil claim was not "any other reason" for the purposes of s.3(1)(c). 11.34

Applications and procedure

The application

8.—(1) Any application must be made in writing to the scheme administrator in such format as the scheme administrator may approve. 11.35

(2) An application must contain or be accompanied by such information or other material as the scheme administrator may reasonably require for the purposes of enabling the scheme administrator to determine whether the applicant is eligible under section 2 or 3 of the Act for a payment under the scheme.

(3) The scheme administrator may, in particular, require an applicant to provide the information or other material which is specified in Part 1 of Schedule 3 to these Regulations.

(4) Part 2 of Schedule 3 sets out the key issues that must be addressed by the information and other material required under Part 1 of that Schedule.

(5) The scheme administrator may require the applicant to provide evidence in support of the application, including in particular evidence dealing with matters specified in Part 3 of Schedule 3.

(6) Unless paragraph (7) applies, the application must also contain a statement signed by the applicant that the applicant believes the matters stated as facts in the application to be true.

(7) Where the applicant is unable to sign the statement on account of the applicant's physical or mental condition, a person other than the applicant may sign the statement on the application stating that the person who signs it believes the matters stated as facts in the application to be true.

Time limit for making an application

11.36 **9.**—(1) The application by a person applying on the basis that they are eligible under section 2 of the Act (eligible people with diffuse mesothelioma) must be sent so that it is received by the scheme administrator—

(a) before the end of the day that is 3 years after the date on which the applicant was first diagnosed with diffuse mesothelioma; or

(b) if the applicant was diagnosed with diffuse mesothelioma on or after 25th July 2012 but before these Regulations came into force, before the end of the day that is 3 years after the day on which these Regulations came into force.

(2) The application by a person applying on the basis that they are eligible under section 3 of the Act (eligible dependants) must be sent so that it is received by the scheme administrator—

(a) before the end of the day that is 3 years after the date on which the person with diffuse mesothelioma was first diagnosed with the disease; or

(b) if the person with diffuse mesothelioma died on or after 25th July 2012 but before these Regulations came into force, before the end of the day that is 3 years after the day on which these Regulations came into force.

(3) The scheme administrator may extend the time limits in paragraph (1) or (2) by a further period where the scheme administrator considers that there was good reason for the failure to make the application before the end of the periods mentioned in those paragraphs and for any delay since then in making the application.

Power of scheme administrator to obtain additional documents or evidence

11.37 **10.**—Before making a determination of an application, the scheme administrator may—

(a) in accordance with regulation 11, request an applicant to provide such additional documents or evidence in support of the application as the scheme administrator may reasonably require for the purposes of determining the application;

(b) in accordance with regulation 13, request a person other than the applicant to provide specified documents where it appears to the scheme administrator that the document is reasonably required for the purposes of determining the application.

Request to applicants to provide additional documents or evidence

11.—(1) A request for any additional documents or evidence ("requested material") which is made under regulation 10(a) must— **11.38**

(a) be made in writing; and

(b) specify such period, which must not be less than 14 days from the date of the written request, as is reasonable in all the circumstances within which the requested material is to be provided.

(2) Where any requested material is not provided within the specified period, the scheme administrator must—

(a) send a written notice to the applicant reminding the applicant of the request; and

(b) specify a further reasonable period, which must not be less than 7 days from the date of the written notice, within which the requested material is to be provided.

(3) On the expiry of that further period, the scheme administrator must determine the application on the basis of all the information relating to the application which is then before the scheme administrator whether or not the requested material has been provided.

(4) Any material which the scheme administrator receives after the application is determined is to be treated as a request made by the applicant for a review of the determination under regulation 21.

(5) If, in all the circumstances, the scheme administrator is satisfied that it is appropriate to do so, the scheme administrator may meet the reasonable costs of the applicant which are incurred in obtaining any requested material.

Duty of applicants

12.—(1) As soon as reasonably practicable, an applicant must inform the scheme administrator of— **11.39**

(a) any matter that comes to the applicant's attention which may be relevant to the question whether the applicant is eligible under section 2 or 3 of the Act for a payment under the scheme; and

(b) any change in the applicant's address for correspondence.

(2) An applicant must, so far as reasonably practicable, provide any other assistance to the scheme administrator which the scheme administrator requests in connection with the consideration of the application.

Request to third parties to provide documents

13.—(1) A request which is made under regulation 10(b) for a person other than the applicant to provide any document may be made following a request made by an applicant to the scheme administrator or on the scheme administrator's own initiative. **11.40**

(2) The request must be made in writing and must specify—

(a) the document or documents to be produced; and

(b) such period, which must not be less than 14 days from the date of the written request, as is reasonable in all the circumstances within which any specified document is to be produced.

(3) Where any requested document is not produced within the specified period, the scheme administrator must—

(a) send a written notice to the person reminding the person of the request; and
(b) specify a further reasonable period, which must not be less than 7 days from the date of the notice, within which the requested document is to be produced.

(4) The scheme administrator may apply to the court for an order under paragraph (5) where the person has failed to produce a requested document within the further period referred to in paragraph (3).

(5) A court may make an order requiring a person to produce any document requested if it considers it appropriate to do so.

(6) "Court" means—
(a) in England and Wales or Northern Ireland a county court or the High
(b) in Scotland the sheriff or the Court of Session.

Withdrawal of an application by person with diffuse mesothelioma

11.41 **14.**—An application which is made by a person with diffuse mesothelioma may be withdrawn by the applicant at any time before a payment under the scheme is made to the applicant.

Notice for a person to cease to be an eligible dependant

11.42 **15.**—(1) For the purposes of section 3(3) of the Act (which makes provision for a person who does not want a payment under the scheme to cease to be an eligible dependant), notice is given by a person in accordance with the scheme if it is given in writing to the scheme administrator at any time before a payment under the scheme is made to that person.

(2) On receipt of a notice sent by a person in accordance with paragraph (1), the scheme administrator must send a written acknowledgement to the person confirming receipt of the notice.

Determination of applications

Determination of applications

11.43 **16.**—(1) In making a determination the scheme administrator must—
(a) refuse to make a payment in a case where the scheme administrator determines that the applicant does not meet the conditions in sections 2 or 3 of the Act;
(b) decide to make a payment of an amount set out in the second column of the table in Schedule 4 to these Regulations (Amount of Scheme Payment) which corresponds with the age of the person with diffuse mesothelioma in the first column of that Schedule.

(2) Where the scheme administrator makes a determination under paragraph (1)(b) it must—
(i) take account of any conditions imposed under regulation 17;
(ii) take account of any relevant deduction; and
(iii) ensure that where there are two or more eligible dependants, the amount for each of them is the amount for a single eligible dependant divided by the number of eligible dependants.

(3) In this regulation and Schedule 4, the age of the person with diffuse mesothelioma means—
(a) their age at the date of first diagnosis; or

(b) where the application is made by their dependant under the circumstances mentioned in section 3(2) of the Act (where a person has been diagnosed with diffuse mesothelioma following his or her death), the date of death of the person.

Imposing conditions on the making of a payment

17.—(1) Where the scheme administrator decides to make a payment under the scheme the scheme administrator— **11.44**

(a) may impose one or more conditions on the making of the payment for the purpose of ensuring that the payment is used for the applicant's benefit; and

(b) if it considers that it would be in the interests of the applicant to do so, may impose such conditions as the scheme administrator considers are appropriate for that purpose.

(2) Conditions which may be imposed include—

(a) requiring that a trust be established on such terms or in accordance with such arrangements as the scheme administrator may direct for the purpose of administering the amount to be paid to it under the scheme;

(b) before any payment is made, requiring an application to be made for the appointment of a deputy, guardian or controller.

(3) The conditions imposed must not be such that they result in the payment being made in a form other than that of the lump sum provided for in regulation 19(2).

(4) If, in all the circumstances, the scheme administrator considers it appropriate to do so, the scheme administrator may—

(a) meet the whole or part of any reasonable costs incurred in complying with any condition imposed under this regulation;

(b) provide such advice or other assistance as the scheme administrator considers necessary in order to ensure that the payment under the scheme is used for the benefit of the applicant.

(5) The scheme administrator may vary or remove a condition imposed under paragraph (1) where the scheme administrator considers the circumstances so require.

(6) In this regulation—

(a) "deputy" has the meaning given in section 16(2)(b) of the Mental Capacity Act 2005;

(b) "guardian" has the meaning given in section 57 of the Adults with Incapacity (Scotland) Act 2000;

(c) "controller" has the meaning given by Article 101 of the Mental Health (Northern Ireland) Order 1986.

Notice of a determination

18.—(1) The scheme administrator must send a written notice which states the determination which has been made in the applicant's case— **11.45**

(a) to each applicant; or

(b) if the applicant has died, to the personal representatives of the applicant.

(2) Where a payment is refused under regulation 16(1)(a), the notice must state—

(a) the reasons for the determination;

(b) that the applicant may request a review of the decision; and
(c) the period within which such a request is to be made and the procedure for making it.

(3) Where a payment is to be made under the scheme to an applicant, the notice must state—

(a) the amount awarded to the applicant;
(b) where an amount is to be paid to more than one person, the name of the other persons and the amount awarded to each of them;
(c) whether any relevant deduction has been made from the amount awarded to the applicant and, if so—
    (i) the total amount of all relevant deductions made, and
    (ii) in relation to each relevant deduction, the nature of the deduction and its amount;
(d) whether any conditions are to be imposed (see regulation 17), the nature of the conditions and the reasons for imposing them;
(e) that the applicant may, by a written notice sent to the scheme administrator, request a review of the decision; and
(f) the period within which such a request is to be made and the procedure for making it.

Payments

Payment

11.46 **19.**—(1) This regulation applies where a determination has been made to make a payment under the scheme to an applicant.

(2) The payment must be made in a lump sum.

(3) Subject to any conditions imposed under regulation 17, the payment—

(a) may be made to the applicant by such means as the scheme administrator may determine; and
(b) must be made either at the same time as the sending of the notice under regulation 18 or as soon afterwards as is reasonably practicable.

(4) Where an applicant dies before a payment is made under the scheme (including an applicant who dies before a determination to make the payment is made), any payment which is to be made under the scheme must, where the condition in paragraph (5) is met, be made to the applicant's personal representatives.

(5) The condition is that any document that is by law sufficient evidence of the grant of—

(a) probate of the will of a deceased applicant,
(b) letters of administration of the estate of a deceased applicant, or
(c) confirmation as executor of the deceased applicant, has been provided to the scheme administrator.

General Note

11.47 Payments must be made by way of a lump sum, and be paid to the applicant, subject to any conditions under reg.17. The award must be the appropriate age-related payment for the individual concerned according to the tariff set out in Sch.4 to the Regulations. This sets out a sliding scale, with the youngest victims being eligible for the highest level of award. A victim's age is determined by reference to their age at the date of first diagnosis or, where the application is made post-mortem by an eligible dependant, the date that the victim died (reg.16(3)). The sliding scale is intended to reflect the fact that the average amount awarded in a personal injuries claim through the courts reduces as the victim's age increases. This in turn recognises that older mesothelioma victims would in any event have a shorter life expectancy, relative to their younger peers, had they not contracted the disease. In addition, older mesothelioma victims are more likely to be retired and so be on lower incomes (with claims for loss of earnings being minimal or non-existent). The simple age-based tariff, modelled on the 1979 Act, has the further advantage of facilitating the speedy and efficient handling of claims.

When the Bill was first published, the Government's proposal was that awards under Sch.4 to the Regulations would be set at 70 per cent of average civil awards. This feature of the new scheme was bitterly attacked by victims' support groups, who argued that sufferers should receive full 100 per cent compensation. Insurers argued that the 70 per cent cap was needed as that would limit the total cost of the scheme to an amount equal to 3 per cent of EL gross written premiums, a figure which was considered to be affordable without passing on the costs to current employers. Following further negotiations with the insurance industry, the Government announced, during the Bill's progress through the House of Lords, an increase in the compensation rate from 70 per cent to 75 per cent. Amendments to require compensation payments to be set at 100, 90 or even 80 per cent of civil awards of damages were pressed to the vote but were all defeated during the Bill's progress.

In the Lords, the Opposition argued that as a matter of principle nothing less than 100 per cent would suffice: "One hundred per cent of the tariff is justice; anything less is not" (Lord McKenzie, HL Debs Vol 747, c.821 (July 17, 2013)). Similar sentiments were voiced in the Commons: "Sufferers feel 100% of the injury, and the industry took 100% of the premiums" (Right Hon Mr N. Brown MP, HC Debs Vol 577, c.598 (March 17, 2014)). The Government's argument, on the other hand, supported by the insurance lobby, was that setting the tariff below that of civil damages provided an incentive for all other avenues for redress to be explored first and helped ensure the long-term sustainability of the scheme.

In the event, and shortly before the new scheme went live, the Government announced that the levels of payments under Schedule 4 were to be increased, as a result of savings made through running a competitive open tender process for the appointment of the scheme administrator. Thus two days after the original Regulations were published in April 2014, amending regulations were issued which substituted an entirely new Sch.4, providing for somewhat higher levels of payments (on average by about £8,000 in each case), to take effect from July 2014. As a result the highest award was then set at a ceiling of £216,896 (£203,788 under the original Regulations), where the victim was aged 40 or under. The rates for awards then reduced by about £3,000 a year until the sufferer was aged 90 or over, at which point awards were fixed at £69,649 (originally £65,734). This meant that in practice the tariff payment rates were set at 80 per cent of average civil compensation awards, whilst still keeping within the 3 per cent target for the levy on insurers.

The levels of awards were then increased again for all those who were first diagnosed with diffuse mesothelioma on or after February 10, 2015, or their eligible dependants. The effect of the 2015 changes was to increase the amount of payment to 100% of average civil damages. This increase was apparently made possible because the numbers of people applying to the Scheme were lower than estimated. One of the reasons for that may be ELTO's increasing ability to trace historic employers' liability insurance policies. That in turn has led to savings in the administration costs of the Scheme and this has allowed for payment levels for successful applicants to be increased. To date there has been no further uplift since 2015.

Circumstances in which a person may be required to repay

20.—(1) The scheme administrator may require a person who received a 11.48
payment under the scheme to repay the whole of the amount of a payment

under the scheme which has been received in any case where the scheme administrator is satisfied that relevant evidence shows that—

(a) the payment was made in error; or

(b) whether fraudulently or otherwise, any person has misrepresented or failed to disclose a material fact and the determination to make the payment was made in consequence of the misrepresentation or failure; or

(c) the applicant was for any other reason not eligible under section 2 or 3 of the Act to receive a payment under the scheme.

(2) The scheme administrator may require a person who received a payment to repay a specified part of the amount of a payment under the scheme in any case where the scheme administrator is satisfied that relevant evidence shows that—

(a) the amount paid exceeds the amount payable in accordance with Schedule 4; or

(b) the amount payable to each of a number of persons who are eligible under section 3 of the Act was calculated on the basis of an error (either as to the number of such persons or otherwise).

(3) The scheme administrator must send a written notice to the person required to make the repayment which states—

(a) the amount required to be repaid;

(b) the reasons why the payment was not properly made; and

(c) that an applicant, or if the applicant has died, the personal representatives of the applicant, may request a review of the decision.

(4) In paragraph (2), "specified" means specified by the scheme administrator in the notice under paragraph (3).

(5) In paragraphs (1) and (2), references to "relevant evidence" are to evidence which—

(a) is relevant to the question whether an applicant was eligible under section 2 or 3 of the Act for a payment under the scheme; and

(b) is received by the scheme administrator only after a determination to make a payment in accordance with regulation 19 has been made.

Reviews and appeals

Review at the request of an applicant

11.49 **21.**—(1) An applicant may request a review of a determination—

(a) notified to the applicant in accordance with regulation 18(1); or

(b) notified in accordance with regulation 20(4).

(2) No review may be sought on grounds that relate to any matter referred to in regulation 18(3)(c).

(3) A request for a review of a determination must—

(a) be in writing;

(b) specify the grounds on which a review is sought; and

(c) be received by the scheme administrator not later than one month after the date of the written notice of the determination.

(4) The scheme administrator may extend the time limit in paragraph (3)(c) by a further period where the scheme administrator considers that there was good reason for the failure to request the review before the end of that initial period and for any delay since then in requesting a review under this regulation.

(5) In a case where a person makes an application and then dies, the reference in this regulation or in any of regulations 22 to 25 to an applicant is to be read as if it were a reference to the applicant's personal representatives.

Review initiated by the scheme administrator

22.—(1) Where the scheme administrator receives information after a determination is made which calls the determination into question, the scheme administrator— 11.50

(a) may decide on its own initiative to conduct a review of any determination referred to in regulation 21(1); and

(b) must notify the applicant in writing of the review and the reasons for it.

(2) The grounds on which a review under this regulation may be held include that—

(a) whether fraudulently or otherwise, any person has misrepresented or failed to disclose a material fact and the determination to make a payment under the scheme or to require a repayment was made in consequence of the misrepresentation or failure;

(b) the determination to make any such payment or require any such repayment was based on a mistake as to a material fact;

(c) there was an error or omission which affected the substance of the determination whether to make a payment under the scheme or the amount of any payment made; or

(d) there was an error or omission which affected the substance of the determination whether to require a repayment or the amount of any repayment required.

(3) The applicant may submit written representations to the scheme administrator about the scheme administrator's decision to conduct a review and about any information on which the decision to conduct a review was based.

(4) Any representation which is made under paragraph (3) must be sent so that it is received by the scheme administrator not later than one month after the date of the scheme administrator's notice of the review under paragraph (1)(b).

(5) The scheme administrator may extend the time limit in paragraph (4) by a further period where the scheme administrator considers that there was good reason for the failure to submit written representations before the end of that initial period and for any delay since then in submitting written representations.

Other circumstances in which a review may be held

23.—(1) Where a notice of an appeal which is made by an applicant to the First-tier Tribunal is received by the scheme administrator before a request for a review under regulation 21 is received— 11.51

(a) that notice is to be treated for all purposes as if it were a request for a review; and

(b) the scheme administrator must delay referring the case to the First-tier Tribunal until the review has been completed.

(2) The scheme administrator must notify the applicant in writing of the matters specified in paragraph (1)(a) and (b).

(3) The applicant may submit written representations to the scheme administrator about the grounds on which the applicant is dissatisfied with the determination which is appealed against.

(4) Any representation which is made under paragraph (3) must be sent so that it is received by the scheme administrator not later than one month after the date of the scheme administrator's notice under paragraph (2).

(5) The scheme administrator may extend the time limit in paragraph (4) by a further period where the scheme administrator considers that there was good reason for the failure to submit written representations before the end of that initial period and for any delay since then in submitting written representations.

(6) Where the determination made on review is that a payment under the scheme is to be made to the applicant, the case is not to be referred to the First-tier Tribunal unless, on being notified of the determination in accordance with regulation 24(4)(b), the applicant sends a notice in writing to the scheme administrator to indicate that the applicant does not accept the determination made on review.

Conduct of the review

11.52 **24.**—(1) The scheme administrator must ensure that, in conducting a review, no member of the scheme administrator's staff who had any involvement in the determination that is subject to review under any of regulations 21 to 23 is be involved in making the determination of the review.

(2) Regulations 10 to 13 apply in relation to a review of a determination as they apply in relation to the original determination.

(3) The determinations that may be made on a review are—

(a) to confirm the original determination; or

(b) to make any other determination which the scheme administrator has power to make under regulation 16.

(4) The scheme administrator must—

(a) ensure that the review is carried out as soon as reasonably practicable; and

(b) send the applicant written notice of the result of the review.

(5) The notice under paragraph (4)(b) must—

(a) state that the original determination has been confirmed or state the terms of any new determination which has been made in the applicant's case;

(b) give reasons for the determination made on the review;

(c) in the case of a new determination that a payment under the scheme is to be made to the applicant, specify the details required by regulation 18(3)(a) to (f);

(d) state that the applicant may appeal to the First-tier Tribunal against the determination made on review; and

(e) state the period within which such an appeal is to be made and provide information as to how to make such an appeal.

(6) Nothing in this regulation prevents a determination notified to an applicant in accordance with regulation 18(1) or 20(3) from being

confirmed on review for reasons that differ in any respect from the reasons given in relation to that determination.

Appeal

25.—(1) An applicant may appeal to the First-tier Tribunal from a determination which has been reviewed under regulation 24(3). 11.53

(2) An appeal under this regulation is to be conducted in accordance with the Tribunal Procedure (First-tier Tribunal) (Social Entitlement Chamber) Rules 2008.

Circumstances in which scheme administrator may help people to bring proceedings

26.—(1) The circumstances in which the scheme administrator may help a person to bring relevant proceedings under section 10 of the Act (power of scheme administrator to help people bring proceedings) are that— 11.54

(a) a payment under the scheme was made to a person who, on the basis of the information then available, was eligible under section 2 or 3 of the Act;

(b) since the payment was made, further information has become available which indicates that there is a reasonable prospect of bringing an action for damages in relevant proceedings; and

(c) the scheme administrator considers that it would in all the circumstances be appropriate to provide help to any person in bringing such proceedings.

(2) In considering whether it is appropriate to provide help to any person to bring relevant proceedings, the scheme administrator must have regard, in particular, to—

(a) the person's prospects of success in bringing the proceedings;

(b) the level of compensation likely to be awarded in those proceedings;

(c) the aggregate amount of the payments specified in paragraph (3) that is likely to be payable to the Secretary of State in the event that any damages were to be awarded in such proceedings; and

(d) the overall balance between—

(i) the amount of the payment referred to in paragraph (1)(a); and

(ii) the costs of providing help to the person to bring relevant proceedings added to the amount referred to in sub-paragraph (c).

(3) The payments are—

(a) a payment under section 6 of the Social Security (Recovery of Benefits) Act 1997 (payment in respect of recoverable benefit) in respect of the period since the payment referred to in paragraph (1)(a) was made;

(b) a payment under article 8 of the Social Security (Recovery of Benefits) (Northern Ireland) Order 1997 (payment in respect of recoverable benefit) in respect of that period;

(c) a payment under regulation 10 of the Social Security (Recovery of Benefits) (Lump sum Payments) Regulations 2008 (payment in respect of recoverable lump sum payments) which was not recovered from the payment referred to in paragraph (1)(a);

(d) a payment under regulation 10 of the Social Security (Recovery of Benefits) (Lump sum Payments) Regulations (Northern Ireland)

2008 (payment in respect of recoverable lump sum payments) which was not recovered from the payment referred to in paragraph (1)(a).

Review of these Regulations by the Secretary of State

11.55 **27.**—(1) The Secretary of State must—

(a) carry out an annual review of these Regulations;

(b) set out the conclusions of that review in a report; and

(c) publish the report.

(2) The report must in particular—

(a) set out the objectives intended to be achieved by the scheme; and

(b) assess the extent to which those objectives have been achieved over the reporting period.

(3) The first report under this regulation must be published on or before 30th November 2015.

(4) Reports under this regulation are afterwards to be published at intervals not exceeding 13 months.

(5) In this regulation "reporting period" in any year means a period beginning with 6th April in one year and ending with 5th April in the next.

SCHEDULE 1 REGULATION 6

First diagnosis of diffuse mesothelioma

11.56 1. In this Schedule—

"P" means a person with diffuse mesothelioma;

"connected person", in relation to P, means—

(a) any person who, with P's agreement, is acting on P's behalf; or

(b) any personal representative of P;

"health care professional" means—

(a) a registered medical practitioner;

(b) a registered nurse working in a clinical nurse specialist role in relation to patients with cancer;

(c) a member of a multi-disciplinary team for the diagnosis and treatment of patients with cancer which includes one or more persons mentioned in paragraph (a) or (b) of this definition.

Application by a person with diffuse mesothelioma

11.57 2. For the purposes of section 2 of the Act—

(a) a person ("P") is to be taken as having been "first diagnosed" with diffuse mesothelioma where both of the conditions set out in paragraph 3 are met; and

(b) the date of first diagnosis is to be determined in accordance with paragraphs 4 and 5.

3. The conditions referred to in paragraph 2(a) are—

(a) that a diagnosis of diffuse mesothelioma in relation to P is made by a health care professional; and

(b) that either P or a connected person is advised of the diagnosis by a health care professional (whether by the health care professional who made the diagnosis or by a different one).

4. (1) The date of P's first diagnosis is to be determined as follows.

(2) Where the advice that P has diffuse mesothelioma is given orally, the date of first diagnosis is the date shown in P's clinical notes as being the date on which P or a connected person was advised of the diagnosis.

(3) Where the advice that P has diffuse mesothelioma is given in writing, the date of first diagnosis is—

(a) if the advice is contained in a letter, the date shown on the letter;

(b) if the advice is sent by electronic communication, the date on which the communication was sent.

(4) Where no date can be determined in accordance with sub-paragraph (2) or (3), or there is reason to doubt the accuracy of the date so determined, the date of first diagnosis is to be determined by such other evidence as the scheme administrator considers appropriate.

5. (1) In determining whether the conditions set out in paragraph 3 have been met, the scheme administrator may make further enquiries to determine whether the disease that has been diagnosed is in fact diffuse mesothelioma in any case where—

(a) the scheme administrator considers that there is reason to doubt whether the disease that has been diagnosed is diffuse mesothelioma; or

(b) P or a connected person was advised by a healthcare professional that P's diagnosis is of anything other than diffuse mesothelioma (including a diagnosis of mesothelioma without explanation of its extent).

(2) Where, as a result of the further enquiries, the scheme administrator is satisfied that the diagnosis was one of diffuse mesothelioma, the date of first diagnosis is to be determined in accordance with the provisions of paragraph 4.

(3) Where, as a result of the further enquiries, a substituted diagnosis is made in relation to P which is one of diffuse mesothelioma, the date of first diagnosis is whichever of the following occurs first—

(a) the date on which P is advised of the substituted diagnosis;

(b) the date on which a connected person is advised of the substituted diagnosis;

(c) the date on which the scheme administrator is advised of the substituted diagnosis.

Application by a dependant of a person with diffuse mesothelioma

6. For the purposes of section 3 of the Act, P who has died is to be taken as having been "first diagnosed" with diffuse mesothelioma as follows. **11.58**

7. If the conditions set out in paragraph 3 were met before P's death, the date of first diagnosis is to be determined in accordance with the provisions of paragraph 4.

8. (1) In any other case, P is to be taken as having been "first diagnosed" with diffuse mesothelioma where either of the conditions set out in sub-paragraph (2)(a) or (b) is met and the date of first diagnosis is to be determined in accordance with sub-paragraph (3).

(2) The conditions referred to in sub-paragraph (1) are—

(a) that a diagnosis of diffuse mesothelioma in relation to P is made following a post-mortem examination; or

(b) that, following P's death, a diagnosis of diffuse mesothelioma in relation to P is confirmed in writing by a health care professional without carrying out a post-mortem examination.

(3) The date of P's first diagnosis is the date shown on the report of the post-mortem examination or the date shown on the health care professional's written confirmation of the diagnosis (as the case may be).

SCHEDULE 2 REGULATION 6

SPECIFIED PAYMENTS

Payment under the Naval, Military and Air Forces Etc. (Disablement and Death) Service Pensions Order 2006. **11.59**

Payment under the Armed Forces and Reserve Forces (Compensation Scheme) Order 2011.

A compensation payment from any government department.

A compensation payment from an authority, body corporate or employer exempted from insurance by or under the compulsory insurance legislation.

Payment under the UK Asbestos Trust established on 10th October 2006, for the benefit of certain persons suffering from asbestos-related diseases.

Payment under the EL Scheme Trust established on 23rd November 2006, for the benefit of certain persons suffering from asbestos-related diseases.

Payment under a scheme established under section 213 of the Financial Services and Markets Act 2000 (the Financial Services Compensation Scheme).

SCHEDULE 3 REGULATION 8

INFORMATION AND OTHER MATERIAL IN SUPPORT OF AN APPLICATION

PART 1

THE APPLICATION

11.60 1. An applicant may be required to state whether the applicant is—

(a) the person with diffuse mesothelioma;
(b) a person who is a dependant of a person who has died with diffuse mesothelioma.

2. An applicant within paragraph 1(a) or (b) may be required to provide, in relation to the person with diffuse mesothelioma—

(a) the person's name and national insurance number;
(b) the person's date of birth;
(c) the date the person was first diagnosed with diffuse mesothelioma;
(d) the name of all employers of the person;
(e) a description of the arrangements under which the person was engaged by each employer;
(f) a statement of the kind of activities carried on by the person whilst working for each employer and the place where those activities were carried on;
(g) an indication as to whether the application relies on the person with diffuse mesothelioma having been exposed to asbestos as a result of the relevant employer's negligence or breach of statutory duty (or both);
(h) an explanation of why the application relies on the relevant employer's negligence or breach of statutory duty (or both);
(i) a statement that no action for damages has been brought against the relevant employer or any insurer with whom the relevant employer maintained employers liability insurance at the time of the person's exposure to asbestos, in respect of the disease;
(j) an explanation of why it is alleged the applicant is unable to bring an action against any employer or any insurer with whom such an employer maintained employers' liability insurance;
(k) a statement that the person has not received damages or a specified payment in respect of the disease;
(l) a statement that the person is not eligible to receive a specified payment.

11.61 3. An applicant within paragraph 1(b) may also be required to provide—

(a) the name of the applicant;
(b) their date of birth;
(c) a statement of the applicant's relationship to the deceased;
(d) where relevant, a statement of the name of each person who is in the same degree of relationship to the deceased as the applicant;
(e) a statement that no one has brought an action for damages under the fatal accidents legislation, or on behalf of the deceased's estate, against the relevant employer or any insurer with whom the relevant employer maintained employers' liability insurance at the time of the person's exposure to asbestos;
(f) an explanation of why it is alleged that no one is able to bring an action under the fatal accidents legislation, or on behalf of the deceased's estate, against any employer of the deceased or any insurer with whom such an employer maintained employers' liability insurance;
(g) a statement that no one has received damages or a specified payment in respect of the disease;
(h) a statement that no one is eligible to receive a specified payment.

PART 2

KEY ISSUES

11.62 4. The key issues to be addressed by the information and other material required under Part 1 of this Schedule, are—

(a) establishing that the person with diffuse mesothelioma was employed by a relevant employer;

(b) establishing that the person with diffuse mesothelioma was exposed to asbestos during the period of the person's employment;
(c) establishing that the exposure to asbestos resulted from a relevant employer's negligence or breach of statutory duty (or both);
(d) explaining why no action for damages in respect of the disease can be brought against any employer or any insurer with whom such an employer maintained employers' liability insurance;
(e) where the application is made by a person who is a dependant of a person who has died with diffuse mesothelioma—
  (i) establishing that the person qualifies as a dependant of the deceased for the purposes of section 3(1) of Pneumoconiosis etc. (Workers' Compensation) Act 1979;
  (ii) explaining why no one is able to bring an action for damages under the fatal accidents legislation, or on behalf of the deceased's estate, against any employer or any insurer of such an employer.

PART 3

SUPPORTING EVIDENCE

5. Supporting evidence that may be required in relation to an application includes— **11.63**
(a) medical evidence which confirms the person has been diagnosed with diffuse mesothelioma (see Schedule 1);
(b) witness statements (whether made by the person with diffuse mesothelioma or by others);
(c) the details of any investigation in contemplation of litigation which has been carried out on behalf of the applicant (including any report made by a relevant expert);
(d) the details of all steps taken to find any relevant insurer and the results of any search for a relevant insurer that has been carried out;
(e) a copy of any decision published by the Technical Committee which relates to a person named in the application as a relevant employer or an insurer of that employer.

6. (1) Any witness statement that is provided must be signed by the person making the statement and verified by a statement of truth.

(2) "Statement of truth" means a statement that the person making the witness statement believes the matters stated as facts in the witness statement to be true.

SCHEDULE 4 REGULATION 16

AMOUNT OF SCHEME PAYMENTS

[1 Table 1

Age of the person with diffuse mesothelioma (see regulation16(3))	*Scheme Payment*
40 and under	£271,120
41	£267,439
42	£263,758
43	£260,078
44	£256,396
45	£252,715
46	£249,034
47	£245,353
48	£241,671
49	£237,990
50	£234,309
51	£230,628
52	£226,946
53	£223,265
54	£219,584
55	£215,903
56	£212,221

11.64

Age of the person with diffuse mesothelioma (see regulation16(3))	***Scheme Payment***
57	£208,540
58	£204,859
59	£201,179
60	£197,498
61	£193,816
62	£190,135
63	£186,454
64	£182,773
65	£179,091
66	£175,410
67	£171,729
68	£168,048
69	£164,366
70	£160,685
71	£157,004
72	£153,323
73	£149,641
74	£145,960
75	£142,279
76	£138,599
77	£134,918
78	£131,236
79	£127,555
80	£123,874
81	£120,193
82	£116,511
83	£112,830
84	£109,149
85	£105,468
86	£101,786
87	£98,105
88	£94,424
89	£90,743
90 and over	£87,061]

AMENDMENT

1. Diffuse Mesothelioma Payment Scheme (Amendment) Regulations 2015 (SI 2015/367), reg.2 (March 31, 2015).

The Diffuse Mesothelioma Payment Scheme (Levy) Regulations 2014

SI 2014/2904

ARRANGEMENT OF REGULATIONS

Citation, commencement and interpretation

1. (1) These Regulations may be cited as the Diffuse Mesothelioma Payment Scheme (Levy) Regulations 2014. 11.66

(2) These Regulations come into force on 28th November 2014.

(3) In these Regulations—

"a financial year" means the 12 month period ending with the 31st March in any year;

"individual gross written premium" means the sum, before commission and the cost of reinsurance are taken out, of all employers' liability insurance premiums written in a calendar year by an individual active insurer;

"reference period" has the meaning given in regulation 3;

"the payment amount" means the share of the total amount of the levy that an active insurer is required to pay;

"the scheme" means the Diffuse Mesothelioma Payment Scheme established by the Diffuse Mesothelioma Payment Scheme Regulations 2014;

"total amount of the levy" means an annual sum decided by the Secretary of State under section 13 of the Mesothelioma Act 2014 in each financial year with a view to meeting the costs of the scheme;

"total gross written premium" means the sum, before commission and the cost of reinsurance are taken out, of all employers' liability insurance premiums written in a calendar year by all active insurers.

The requirement to pay a share of the total amount of the levy

2. (1) An active insurer is required to pay a share of the total amount of the levy based on that insurer's relative market share in the reference period as determined in accordance with regulation 4. 11.67

(2) The requirement in paragraph (1) is a requirement—

(a) to pay the Secretary of State the payment amount specified in the notice under regulation 5(1) in accordance with the notice under regulation 5(2); and

(b) subject to details given in a notice under regulation 5(2)(a), to pay the payment amount by the end of a financial year in respect of which the Secretary of State decides the total amount of the levy.

DEFINITIONS

"a financial year"—see reg.1(3).
"reference period"—see reg.1(3).
"the payment amount"—see reg.1(3).
"total amount of the levy"—see reg.1(3).

The reference period

11.68 **3.** (1) The reference period is a 12 month period ending on 31st December falling in a financial year.

(2) The reference period for the payment amount for the first financial year ends on 31st December 2014.

(3) In this regulation the "first financial year" means the year ending 31st March 2015.

DEFINITIONS

"a financial year"—see reg.1(3).
"reference period"—see reg.1(3).
"the payment amount"—see reg.1(3).

Determination of relative market share and amounts

11.69 **4.** (1) An active insurer's relative market share in the reference period is determined in accordance with paragraph (2) and the payment amount an active insurer must pay is determined in accordance with paragraphs (3) to (5).

(2) For the purpose of these Regulations, relative market share in the reference period is to be treated as if it were the same as the relative market share for the calendar year two years before the reference period.

(3) The payment amount an active insurer must pay in a financial year is to be determined by multiplying the total amount of the levy for that financial year by the figure for their relative market share for the calendar year two years before the reference period.

(4) In this regulation "relative market share for the calendar year two years before the reference period" means A divided by B where—

(a) "A" equals the individual gross written premium for that calendar year;
(b) "B" equals the total gross written premium attributable to the active insurer whose individual gross written premium has been ascertained for the purpose of "A".

(5) In paragraph (4) where "A" cannot be ascertained, an active insurer's relative market share for the calendar year two years before the reference period is nil.

DEFINITIONS

"a financial year"–see reg.1(3).
"individual gross written premium"–see reg.1(3).
"reference period"–see reg.1(3).
"the payment amount"–see reg.1(3).
"total amount of the levy"–see reg.1(3).
"total gross written premium"–see reg.1(3).

Information and publication

5. (1) The Secretary of State must notify active insurers in writing of the payment amount due from them. 11.70

(2) The Secretary of State must also notify active insurers in writing of—

(a) the date or dates in the financial year by which the payment amount is required; and

(b) details of how the payment amount can be made.

(3) The Secretary of State must give active insurers sufficient information to enable them to determine how the payment amount in their case was calculated.

(4) In particular the Secretary of State may give each active insurer information concerning—

(a) the basis on which they are considered to be an active insurer;

(b) the action the Secretary of State may take if the payment amount is not made in accordance with the notice under paragraphs (1) and (2).

(5) The Secretary of State must publish annually the costs of the scheme and must in particular publish information on—

(a) the costs of payments made under the scheme;

(b) the costs of administering the scheme; and

(c) any costs incurred by the Secretary of State in establishing a body to administer the scheme.

DEFINITIONS

"a financial year"–see reg.1(3).
"the payment amount"–see reg.1(3).
"the scheme"–see reg.1(3).

Recovery of the payment amount

6. If the payment amount notified to an active insurer is not paid in accordance with the notices under regulation 5(1) and (2), the payment amount, or any part of it, which has not been paid, is recoverable as a debt due to the Secretary of State. 11.71

DEFINITION

"the payment amount"–see reg.1(3).

PART XII

VACCINE DAMAGE PAYMENTS

The Vaccine Damage Payments Regulations 1979

(SI 1979/432) (*as amended*)

ARRANGEMENT OF REGULATIONS

PART I

GENERAL

1. Citation, commencement and interpretation. **12.1**

PART II

CLAIMS

2. Claims to be made to the Secretary of State in writing.
3. Information to be given when making a claim.
4. Obligations of disabled person.
5. Vaccinations to be treated as carried out in England.
5A. Circumstances prescribed in relation to cases of damage through contact.
6. Claims made prior to the passing of the Act.

PART III

REVIEW BY TRIBUNALS

7–10. *Revoked.*

PART IV

DECISIONS REVERSING EARLIER DECISIONS

11. Decisions reversing earlier decisions made by the Secretary of State or appeal tribunals.
12. Procedure by which a decision may be made under section 31A of the Act on the Secretary of State's own initiative.

The Secretary of State for Social Services in exercise of powers conferred on him by sections 2(5), 3(1)(b), 4(1), 5(2), 7(5) and 8(3) of the Vaccine Damage Payments Act 1979 and of all other powers enabling him in that behalf, hereby makes the following regulations:

PART I

GENERAL

12.2 **Citation, commencement and interpretation**

1.—(1) These regulations may be cited as the Vaccine Damage Payments Regulations 1979 and shall come into operation on 6th April 1979.

(2) In these regulations, unless the context otherwise requires—

"the Act" means the Vaccine Damage Payments Act 1979;

"hearing" means oral hearing;

"medical practitioner" means registered medical practitioner;

"payment" means a payment under section 1(1) of the Act;

[1 . . .].

(3) Any notice required to be given to any person under the provisions of these regulations may be given by being sent by post to that person at his ordinary or last known address.

AMENDMENT

1. Social Security and Child Support (Decisions and Appeals), Vaccine Damage Payments and Jobseeker's Allowance (Amendment) Regulations 1999 (SI 1999/2677) reg.2 (October 18, 1999).

PART II

CLAIMS

Claims to be made to the Secretary of State in writing

12.3 **2.**—(1) Every claim for payment shall be made in writing to the Secretary of State on the form approved by him, or in such other manner, being in writing, as he may accept as sufficient in the circumstances of any particular case or class of cases.

(2) Any person who has made a claim in accordance with the provisions of this regulation may amend his claim, at any time before a decision has been given thereon, by notice in writing delivered or sent to the Secretary of State, and any claim so amended may be treated as if it had been so amended in the first instance.

Information to be given when making a claim

12.4 **3.**—Every person who makes a claim shall furnish such certificates, documents, information and evidence for the purpose of determining the claim as may be required by the Secretary of State.

Obligations of disabled person

12.5 **4.**—(1) Subject to the following provisions of this regulation, every disabled person in respect of whom a claim has been made under section 3 of the Act shall comply with every notice given to him or, where he is not the claimant, to the claimant by the Secretary of State which requires such disabled person to submit himself to a medical examination either by a medical practitioner appointed by the Secretary of State or by [1 an appeal] tribunal for the purposes of determining whether he is severely disabled as a result of vaccination against any of the diseases to which the Act applies.

(2) Every notice given under the preceding paragraph shall be given in writing and shall specify the time and place of examination and shall not require the disabled person to submit himself to examination before the expiration of the period of fourteen days beginning with the date of the notice or such shorter period as may be reasonable in the circumstances.

AMENDMENT

1. Social Security and Child Support (Decisions and Appeals), Vaccine Damage Payments and Jobseeker's Allowance (Amendment) Regulations 1999 (SI 1999/2677) reg.3 (October 18, 1999).

Vaccinations to be treated as carried out in England

5.—(1) Vaccinations given outside the United Kingdom and the Isle of Man to serving members of Her Majesty's forces or members of their families shall be treated for the purposes of the Act as carried out in England where the vaccination in question has been given as part of medical facilities provided under arrangements made by or on behalf of the service authorities. 12.6

(2) For the purposes of section 2(5) of the Act—

(a) "serving members of Her Majesty's forces" means a member of the naval, military or air forces of the Crown or of any women's service administered by the Defence Council;

[1 (b) a person is a member of the family of a serving member of Her Majesty's forces if—

(i) he is the spouse or civil partner of that serving member,

(ii) he and that serving member live together [2as if they were a married couple or] civil partners, or

(iii) he is a child whose requirements are provided by that serving member.]

AMENDMENT

1. Vaccine Damage Payments (Amendment) Regulations 2005 (SI 2005/3070) reg.2 (December 5, 2005).

2. Civil Partnership (Opposite-sex Couples) Regulations 2019 (SI 2019/1458) reg.41(b) and Sch.3 Part 2 para.39 (December 2, 2019).

Circumstances prescribed in relation to cases of damage through contact

[1 **5A.**—The circumstances prescribed for the purposes of section 1(3) of the Vaccine Damage Payments Act 1979 (Act to have effect with respect to a person severely disabled as a result of contracting a disease through contact with a third person who was vaccinated against it) are that:— 12.7

(1) the disabled person has been in close physical contact with a person who has been vaccinated against poliomyelitis with orally administered vaccine;

(2) that contact occurred within a period of sixty days beginning with the fourth day immediately following such vaccination; and

(3) the disabled person was, within the period referred to in paragraph (2) of this regulation, either—

(a) looking after the person who has been vaccinated, or

(b) himself being looked after together with the person who has been vaccinated.]

AMENDMENT

1. Vaccine Damage Payments (Amendment) Regulations 1979 (SI 1979/1441) reg.2 (December 13, 1979).

Claims made prior to the passing of the Act

12.8 **6.**—(1) A claim made before the passing of the Act in connection with the non-statutory scheme of payments for severe vaccine damage established by the Secretary of State for Social Services in anticipation of the passing of the Act and which has not been disposed of at the commencement of the Act shall be treated as a claim falling within section 3(1) of the Act.

(2) Any information and other evidence furnished and other things done before the commencement of the Act in connection with any such claim made before the passing of the Act shall be treated as furnished or done in connection with a claim falling within section 3(1) of the Act.

PART III

REVIEW BY TRIBUNALS

12.9 *Regulations 7–10 were revoked by the Social Security and Child Support (Decisions and Appeals) Regulations 1999 (SI 1999/991) reg.59 and Sch.4 (October 18, 1999). For previous text, see Rowland, Medical and Disability Appeals Tribunal: The Legislation 1998.*

[1 PART IV

DECISIONS REVERSING EARLIER DECISIONS

Decisions reversing earlier decisions made by the Secretary of State or appeal tribunals

12.10 **11.**—(1) The Secretary of State may make a decision under 3A(1) of the Act which reverses a decision of his, made under section 3 of the Act, or of an appeal tribunal, made under section 4 of the Act—

(a) pursuant to an application in the circumstances described in paragraph (2) below; or

(b) except where paragraph (3) applies, on his own initiative.

(2) The circumstances referred to in paragraph (1)(a) above are—
(a) the application is made in writing and contains an explanation as to why the applicant believes the decision in respect of which the application is made to be wrong; and
(b) where the application is in respect of a decision of the Secretary of State, the application is made [2at any time after notification of that decision was given but before a decision of an appeal tribunal has been made]; or
(c) where the application is in respect of a decision of an appeal tribunal, the application is made before whichever is the later of—
(i) the date two years after the date on which notification of that decision was given; or
(ii) the date six years after the date on which notification of the decision of the Secretary of State which was appealed was given.
(3) This paragraph applies where—
(a) less than 21 days have elapsed since notice under regulation 12 below was given; or
(b) more than six years have elapsed since the date on which notification of that decision was given except where it appears to the Secretary of State that a payment was made in consequence of a misrepresentation or failure to disclose any material fact.
(4) Where the Secretary of State has made a decision under section 3A(1) of the Act, he shall notify—
(a) the disabled person (if he is alive) to whom the decision relates; and
(b) if the disabled person is not a claimant, the claimant who made the claim in respect of that disabled person,
of that decision and the reasons for it.

AMENDMENTS

1. Social Security and Child Support (Decisions and Appeals), Vaccine Damage Payments and Jobseeker's Allowance (Amendment) Regulations 1999 (SI 1999/2677) reg.4 (October 18, 1999).
2. Social Security, Child Support, Vaccine Damage and Other Payments (Decisions and Appeals) (Amendment) Regulations 2013 (SI 2013/2380) reg.2(1), (2) (October 28, 2013).

[1Consideration of reversal before appeal

11A.— (1) This regulation applies in a case where— 12.11
(a) the claimant's address is not in Northern Ireland;
(b) the Secretary of State gives a person written notice of a decision; and
(c) that notice includes a statement to the effect that there is a right of appeal to the First-tier Tribunal in relation to the decision only if the Secretary of State has considered an application for a reversal of the decision.
(2) In a case to which this regulation applies, a person has a right of appeal under section 4 of the Act in relation to the decision only if the Secretary of State has considered whether to reverse the decision under section 3A of the Act.
(3) The notice referred to in paragraph (1) must inform the person that, where the notice does not include a statement of the reasons for the decision, he may, within one month of the date of the notice, request that the Secretary of State provide him with written reasons.

(4) Where written reasons are requested under paragraph (3), the Secretary of State must provide them within 14 days of receipt of the request or as soon as practicable afterwards.

(5) Where, as the result of paragraph (2), there is no right of appeal against a decision, the Secretary of State may treat any purported appeal as an application for a reversal of the decision under section 3A of the Act.]

AMENDMENT

1. Social Security, Child Support, Vaccine Damage and Other Payments (Decisions and Appeals) (Amendment) Regulations 2013 (SI 2013/2380) reg.2(1), (3) (October 28, 2013).

[[1]Procedure by which a decision may be made under section 3A of the Act on the Secretary of State's own initiative

12.12 **12.**—Where the Secretary of State on his own initiative proposes to make a decision under section 3A of the Act reversing a decision ("the original decision") of his or of an appeal tribunal he shall give notice in writing of his proposal to—

(a) the disabled person (if he is alive) to whom the original decision relates; and

(b) the claimant in relation to the original decision where he is not the disabled person.]

AMENDMENT

1. Social Security and Child Support (Decisions and Appeals), Vaccine Damage Payments and Jobseeker's Allowance (Amendment) Regulations 1999 (SI 1999/2677) reg.4 (October 18, 1999).

The Vaccine Damage Payments (Specified Disease) Order 1990

(SI 1990/623)

ARRANGEMENT OF ORDER

The Secretary of State for Social Security, in exercise of the powers conferred by section 1(2)(i) of the Vaccine Damage Payments Act 1979 and of all other powers enabling him in that behalf, hereby makes the following Order:

Citation and commencement

12.14 **1.**—This Order may be cited as the Vaccine Damage Payments (Specified Disease) Order 1990 and shall come into force on 9th April 1990.

(SI 1990/623 reg.2)

Addition to the diseases to which the Vaccine Damage Payments Act applies

2.—Mumps is specified as a disease to which the Vaccine Damage Payments Act 1979 applies. 12.15

The Vaccine Damage Payments (Specified Disease) Order 1995

(SI 1995/1164)

ARRANGEMENT OF ORDER

The Secretary of State for Social Security, in exercise of powers conferred by section 1(2)(i) of the Vaccine Damage Payments Act 1979(a) and of all other powers enabling him in that behalf, hereby makes the following Order:

Citation and commencement

1.—This Order may be cited as the Vaccine Damage Payments (Specified Disease) Order 1995 and shall come into force on 31st May 1995. 12.17

Addition to the diseases to which the Vaccine Damage Payments Act applies

2.—Haemophilus influenza type b infection is specified as a disease to which the Vaccine Damage Payments Act 1979 applies. 12.18

The Vaccine Damage Payments (Specified Disease) Order 2001

(SI 2001/1652)

ARRANGEMENT OF ORDER

The Secretary of State for Social Security, in exercise of the powers conferred upon him by sections 1(2)(i) and 2(2) of the Vaccine Damage Payments Act 1979 and of all other powers enabling him in that behalf, hereby makes the following Order:

Citation, commencement and interpretation

1.—(1) This Order may be cited as the Vaccine Damage Payments (Specified Disease) Order 2001 and shall come into force on 30th May 2001. 12.20

(2) In this Order, "the Act" means the Vaccine Damage Payments Act 1979.

Addition to the diseases to which the Act applies

12.21 **2.**—Meningococcal Group C is specified as a disease to which the Act applies.

Modification of conditions of entitlement

12.22 **3.**—The condition of entitlement in section 2(1)(b) of the Act (age or time at which vaccination was carried out) shall be omitted in relation to vaccination against Meningococcal Group C.

The Vaccine Damage Payments (Specified Disease) Order 2006

(SI 2006/2066)

ARRANGEMENT OF ORDER

The Secretary of State for Work and Pensions makes the following Order in exercise of the power conferred by section 1(2)(i) of the Vaccine Damage Payments Act 1979.

Citation and commencement

12.24 **1.** This Order may be cited as the Vaccine Damage Payments (Specified Disease) Order 2006 and shall come into force on 4th September 2006.

Addition to the diseases to which the Vaccine Damage Payments Act 1979 applies

12.25 **2.** Pneumococcal infection is specified as a disease to which the Vaccine Damage Payments Act 1979 applies.

The Vaccine Damage Payments (Specified Disease) Order 2008

(SI 2008/2103)

ARRANGEMENT OF ORDER

The Secretary of State for Work and Pensions makes the following Order in exercise of the powers conferred by sections 1(2)(i) and 2(2) of the Vaccine Damage Payments Act 1979.

Citation, commencement and interpretation

1.—(1) This Order may be cited as the Vaccine Damage Payments (Specified Disease) Order 2008 and shall come into force on 1st September 2008. 12.27

(2) In this Order, "the Act" means the Vaccine Damage Payments Act 1979.

Addition to the diseases to which the Act applies

2. Human papillomavirus is specified as a disease to which the Act applies. 12.28

Modification of conditions of entitlement

3. The condition of entitlement in section 2(1)(b) of the Act (age or time at which vaccination was carried out) shall be omitted in relation to vaccination against human papillomavirus. 12.29

The Vaccine Damage Payments (Specified Disease) Order 2009

(SI 2009/2516)

ARRANGEMENT OF ORDER

The Secretary of State for Work and Pensions makes the following Order in exercise of the power conferred by sections 1(2)(i) and 2(2) of the Vaccine Damage Payments Act 1979(1).

Citation, commencement and interpretation

1.—(1) This Order may be cited as the Vaccine Damage Payments (Specified Disease) Order 2009 and comes into force on 10th October 2009. 12.31
(2) In this Order, "the Act" means the Vaccine Damage Payments Act 1979.

Addition to the diseases to which the Act applies

2. Influenza caused by the pandemic influenza A (H1N1) 2009 virus is specified as a disease to which the Act applies. 12.32

Modification of conditions of entitlement

3. The condition of entitlement in section 2(1)(b) of the Act (age or time at which vaccination was carried out) shall be omitted in relation to vaccination against influenza caused by the pandemic influenza A (H1N1) 2009 virus. 12.33

GENERAL NOTE

This Order was revoked with effect from September 1, 2010 by the Vaccine Damage Payments (Specified Disease) (Revocation and Savings) Order 2010 12.34

(SI 2010/1988), below. Influenza caused by the pandemic influenza A (H1N1) 2009 virus ("swine flu") thus ceases from that date to be one of the specified diseases to which the Act applies. Article 4 of that Revocation and Savings Order ensures, however, that protection under the Act remains applicable to anyone who received the vaccination against "swine flu" prior to September 1, 2010.

The Vaccine Damage Payments (Specified Disease) (Revocation and Savings) Order 2010

(SI 2010/1988)

ARRANGEMENT OF ORDER

The Secretary of State for Work and Pensions makes the following Order in exercise of the power conferred by sections 1(2)(i) and 2(2) of the Vaccine Damage Payments Act 1979.

Citation, commencement and interpretation

12.36 **1.** This Order may be cited as the Vaccine Damage Payments (Specified Disease) (Revocation and Savings) Order 2010 and comes into force on 1st September 2010.

12.37 **2.** The "2009 Order" means the Vaccine Damage Payments (Specified Disease) Order 2009.

Revocation

12.38 **3.** Subject to article (4), the 2009 Order is revoked.

Savings

12.39 **4.** The 2009 Order shall continue to apply to any vaccination administered prior to the date this Order comes into force.

The Vaccine Damage Payments (Specified Disease) Order 2015

(SI 2015/47)

ARRANGEMENT OF ORDER

The Secretary of State for Health, in exercise of the powers conferred by sections 1(2)(i) and 2(2) of the Vaccine Damage Payments Act 1979, makes the following Order.

Citation, commencement and interpretation

1.—(1) This Order may be cited as the Vaccine Damage Payments (Specified Disease) Order 2015 and comes into force on 28th February 2015. **12.41**

(2) In this Order, "the Act" means the Vaccine Damage Payments Act 1979.

Additions to the list of diseases to which the Act applies

2.—(1) Subject to paragraph (2), the following are specified as diseases to which the Act applies— **12.42**

(a) rotavirus; and

(b) influenza, other than influenza caused by a pandemic influenza virus.

(2) Paragraph (1)(b) does not affect any entitlement which arises under the Vaccine Damage Payments (Specified Disease) Order 2009 (addition of influenza caused by the pandemic influenza A (H1N1) 2009 virus) and references in this Order to pandemic influenza are to be interpreted accordingly.

Modification of conditions of entitlement

3. The conditions of entitlement in section 2(1) of the Act have effect subject to the following modifications— **12.43**

(a) in relation to vaccination against rotavirus, in sub-paragraph (ii) of section 2(1)(a), for "5th July 1948" substitute "1st July 2013";

[1(b) in relation to vaccination against influenza, other than influenza caused by a pandemic influenza virus, in sub-paragraph (ii) of section 2(1)(a)—

(i) in relation to a vaccination carried out at a time when the person to whom it was given was under the age of eighteen, for "5th July 1948" substitute "1st September 2013"; and

(ii) in relation to a vaccination carried out at a time when the person to whom it was given was aged eighteen or over, for "5th July 1948" substitute "24th May 2015"];

(c) in relation to vaccination against rotavirus [1 ...], for paragraph (b) of section 2(1) substitute—

"(b) that the vaccination was carried out at a time when the person to whom it was given was under the age of eighteen; and".

[1 (d) The condition of entitlement in section 2(1)(b) of the Act (age or time at which vaccination was carried out) is omitted in relation to vaccination against influenza, other than influenza caused by a pandemic influenza virus.]

AMENDMENTS

1. Vaccine Damage Payments (Specified Disease) (Amendment) Order 2021 (SI 2021/508) art.2 (May 25, 2021).

GENERAL NOTE

The Vaccine Damage Payments Act 1979 is primarily focused on diseases preventable through vaccination offered as part of the routine childhood immunisation programmes. As such, eligibility is subject to conditions in the 1979 Act which include making a claim after a vaccinated person's second birthday, but before **12.44** their twenty first birthday, or within six years of the date on which the vaccination was given, whichever is later. The effect of the amendments made in 2021 is that the protection of the 1979 Act now extends to persons vaccinated against influenza (other than influenza caused by a pandemic influenza virus) ("seasonal influenza") at a time when they were 18 years or older.

The Vaccine Damage Payments (Specified Disease) Order 2016

(SI 2016/454)

ARRANGEMENT OF ORDER

The Secretary of State for Health, in exercise of the powers conferred by sections 1(2)(i) and 2(2) of the Vaccine Damage Payments Act 1979, makes the following Order:

Citation, commencement and interpretation

12.46 **1.**—(1) This Order may be cited as the Vaccine Damage Payments (Specified Disease) Order 2016 and comes into force on 29th April 2016.

(2) In this Order, "the Act" means the Vaccine Damage Payments Act 1979.

Additions to the list of diseases to which the Act applies

12.47 **2.**— The following are specified as diseases to which the Act applies—

(a) Meningococcal Group W; and

(b) Meningococcal Group B.

Modification of conditions of entitlement

12.48 **3.**— The conditions of entitlement in section 2(1) of the Act have effect subject to the following modifications—

(a) in relation to vaccination against Meningococcal Group W, in sub-paragraph (ii) of section 2(1)(a), for "5th July 1948" substitute "1st August 2015";

(b) in relation to vaccination against Meningococcal Group B, in sub-paragraph (ii) of section 2(1)(a), for "5th July 1948" substitute "1st September 2015";

(c) in relation to vaccination against Meningococcal Group W, in paragraph (b) of section 2(1), for "eighteen" substitute "twenty-six".

GENERAL NOTE

12.49 Note that in relation to Meningococcal Group W, the condition of entitlement in s.2(1)(b) of the 1979 Act that the vaccination was carried out when the person to whom it was given was under the age of 18 is modified. For this vaccine the maximum age is raised such that the person to whom this vaccination was given was under the age of 26 at the time the vaccination was carried out. The reason for this change is that vaccination against Meningococcal Group W is also recommended for first time university and college entrants who have missed the adolescent booster. There is no change to the alternative condition of entitlement that the vaccination was carried out at the time of an outbreak within the United Kingdom or on the Isle of Man.

The Vaccine Damage Payments (Specified Disease) Order 2020

(SI 2020/1411)

ARRANGEMENT OF ORDER

The Secretary of State makes this Order in exercise of the powers conferred by sections 1(2)(i) and 2(2) of the Vaccine Damage Payments Act 1979

Citation, commencement and interpretation

1.—(1) This Order may be cited as the Vaccine Damage Payments (Specified Disease) Order 2020 and comes into force on 31st December 2020. 12.50

(2) In this Order "the Act" means the Vaccine Damage Payments Act 1979.

Addition to the list of diseases to which the Act applies

2. COVID-19 is specified as a disease to which the Act applies. 12.51

Modification of condition of entitlement

3. The condition of entitlement in section 2(1)(b) of the Act (age or time at which vaccination was carried out) is omitted in relation to vaccination against COVID-19. 12.52

GENERAL NOTE

Article 2 of this Order adds COVID-19 to the diseases to which the Vaccine Damage Payments Act 1979 applies. Article 3 modifies the condition of entitlement in s.2(1)(b) of the 1979 Act so that it is not a condition in relation to COVID-19 that the vaccinated person was under 18 at the time the vaccination was given nor that there was an outbreak of the disease within the United Kingdom (or the Isle of Man) at that time. For the cost-benefit analysis that was undertaken, see Expansion of the Vaccine Damage Payment Scheme (VDPS) for COVID-19 (Impact Assessment 9564, DHSC). 12.53

The Vaccine Damage Payments Act 1979 Statutory Sum Order 2007

(SI 2007/1931)

ARRANGEMENT OF ORDER

A draft of the following Order was laid before Parliament in accordance with section 1(4A) of the Vaccine Damage Payments Act 1979 and approved by resolution of each House of Parliament:

The Secretary of State for Work and Pensions with the consent of the Treasury, in exercise of the powers conferred by section 1(1A) of the Vaccine Damage Payments Act 1979, makes the following Order:

Citation and commencement

12.55 **1.** This Order may be cited as the Vaccine Damage Payments Act 1979 Statutory Sum Order 2007 and shall come into force on 12th July 2007.

Statutory sum for the purposes of the Vaccine Damage Payments Act 1979

12.56 **2.** For the purposes of the Vaccine Damage Payments Act 1979 the statutory sum is £120,000.

Revocation

12.57 **3.** The Vaccine Damage Payments Act 1979 Statutory Sum Order 2000 is hereby revoked.

GENERAL NOTE

12.58 This Order entered into force on July 12, 2007. It raised the statutory sum from £100,000 to £120,000.

The Transfer of Functions (Vaccine Damage Payments) Order 2021

(SI 2021/1469)

ARRANGEMENT OF ORDER

Her Majesty, in exercise of the powers conferred by section 2 of the Ministers of the Crown Act 1975, is pleased, by and with the advice of Her Privy Council, to order as follows:

Citation, commencement and interpretation

1.—(1) This Order may be cited as the Transfer of Functions (Vaccine Damage Payments) Order 2021. 12.59

(2) This Order comes into force on 18th January 2022.

(3) In this Order—

"vaccine damage payments function" means any function relating to the Vaccine Damage Payments Act 1979 so far as it was entrusted to the Secretary of State for Work and Pensions immediately before 1st November 2021 and has before the making of this Order been entrusted to the Secretary of State for Health and Social Care;

"instrument" includes Royal Charters, Royal Warrants, Orders in Council, Letters Patent, judgments, decrees, orders, rules, regulations, schemes, bye-laws, awards, licences, authorisations, consents, approvals, contracts and other agreements, memoranda and articles of association, certificates, deeds and other documents.

Transfer of property, rights and liabilities to the Secretary of State for Health and Social Care

2. There are transferred to the Secretary of State for Health and Social Care all property, rights and liabilities to which the Secretary of State for Work and Pensions is entitled or subject at the coming into force of this Order in connection with any vaccine damage payments function. 12.60

Transfer to the Secretary of State for Health and Social Care: supplementary

3.—(1) Anything (including legal proceedings) which, at the coming into force of this Order, is in the process of being done by or in relation to the Secretary of State for Work and Pensions may, so far as it relates to a vaccine damage payments function or anything transferred by article 2, be continued by or in relation to the Secretary of State for Health and Social Care. 12.61

(2) Anything done (or having effect as if done) by or in relation to the Secretary of State for Work and Pensions in connection with a vaccine damage payments function or anything transferred by article 2 has effect, so far as necessary for continuing its effect after the coming into force of this Order, as if done by or in relation to the Secretary of State for Health and Social Care.

(3) Any instrument made before the coming into force of this Order has effect, so far as necessary for the purposes of or in consequence of—

(a) the entrusting to the Secretary of State for Health and Social Care of a vaccine damage payments function, or

(b) the transfer of anything by article 2,

as if references to (and references which are to be read as references to) the Secretary of State for Work and Pensions were or included references to the Secretary of State for Health and Social Care.

(4) Documents or forms printed for use in connection with a vaccine damage payments function may be used in connection with that function even though they contain (or are to be read as containing) references to the Secretary of State for Work and Pensions.

(5) For the purposes of the use of any such documents or forms after the coming into force of this Order, those references are to be read as references to the Secretary of State for Health and Social Care.

(6) In paragraphs (1) to (5)—

(a) references to the Secretary of State for Work and Pensions include references to the department or an officer of the Secretary of State for Work and Pensions, and

(b) references to the Secretary of State for Health and Social Care include references to the department or an officer of the Secretary of State for Health and Social Care accordingly.

Validity of things done before coming into force of Order

12.62 **4.**—(1) This Order does not affect the validity of anything done (or having effect as if done) by or in relation to the Secretary of State for Work and Pensions before the coming into force of this Order.

(2) In paragraph (1) the reference to the Secretary of State for Work and Pensions includes a reference to the department or an officer of the Secretary of State for Work and Pensions.

INDEX

LEGAL TAXONOMY
FROM SWEET & MAXWELL

This index has been prepared using Sweet and Maxwell's Legal Taxonomy. Main index entries conform to keywords provided by the Legal Taxonomy except where references to specific documents or non-standard terms (denoted by quotation marks) have been included. These keywords provide a means of identifying similar concepts in other Sweet & Maxwell publications and online services to which keywords from the Legal Taxonomy have been applied. Readers may find some minor differences between terms used in the text and those which appear in the index. Suggestions to *sweetandmaxwell.taxonomy@thomson.com*.

(All references are to paragraph number)

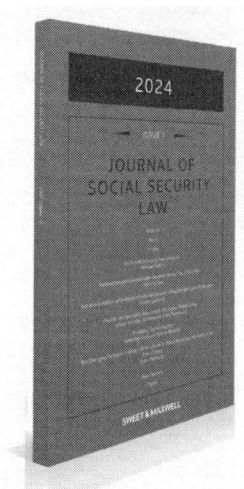

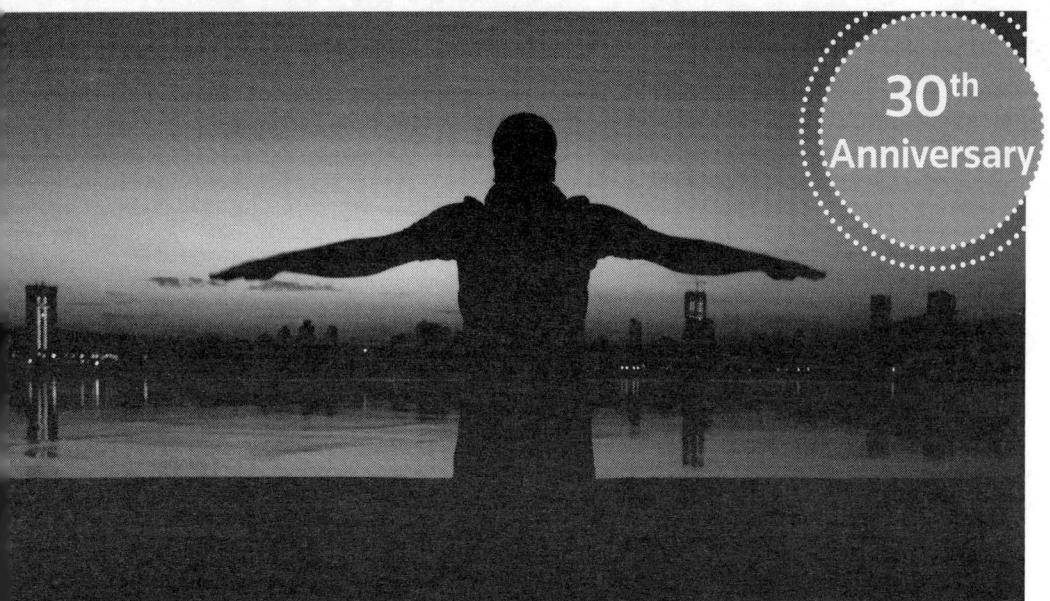